Compact Oxford Russian Dictionary

Compact Oxford Russian Dictionary

Edited by
Della Thompson

OXFORD
UNIVERSITY PRESS

OXFORD
UNIVERSITY PRESS

Great Clarendon Street, Oxford, OX2 6DP,
United Kingdom

Oxford University Press is a department of the University of Oxford.
It furthers the University's objective of excellence in research, scholarship,
and education by publishing worldwide. Oxford is a registered trade mark of
Oxford University Press in the UK and in certain other countries

© Oxford University Press 2013

Database right Oxford University Press (makers)

First Edition published in 2013

Impression: 2

British Library Cataloguing in Publication Data

Data available

ISBN 978–0–19–957617–3
ISBN 978–0–19–966628–7 (special edition)
ISBN 978–0–19–968549–3 (special edition)

Printed in Great Britain by Clays Ltd, St Ives plc

Contents

Editors and contributors

Managing Editor
Della Thompson

Editors/Proofreaders
Alison Curr
Oksana King
Anne McConnell
Viktor Pekar

Supplementary material
Alexander Levtov
Albina Ozieva
Mikhaïl Pirozhok
Lucy Popova
Terence Wade

Preface

This first edition of the *Compact Oxford Russian Dictionary* is based on the larger *Oxford Russian Dictionary*. It provides comprehensive coverage of the core vocabulary of Russian and English, and reflects the most recent changes to both languages.

Essential information on grammar, style, and pronunciation is provided in a convenient and accessible format, making the dictionary an ideal reference tool. Clear indicators and examples guide you to the appropriate translation, and British and American spelling and usage are differentiated.

All grammatical terms used are explained in a glossary at the back of the dictionary, and there are guides to Russian and English grammar and pronunciation.

This dictionary also includes an A–Z of Russian and British/US life and culture, providing information on contemporary society, traditions, festivals, and holidays, and a practical guide to writing letters and emails. A *Phrasefinder* section enables you to communicate in everyday situations such as travel, shopping, eating out, and organizing leisure activities.

Designed to meet the needs of a wide range of users, from the student at intermediate level and above to the enthusiastic traveller or business professional, the *Compact Oxford Russian Dictionary* is an invaluable practical resource for learners of contemporary, idiomatic Russian or English.

Visit the Oxford Dictionaries site (www.oxforddictionaries.com) today to find free current English definitions and translations in French, German, Spanish, and Italian, as well as grammar guidance, puzzles and games, and our popular blog about words and language.

Oxford Language Dictionaries Online is our subscription site, which you can access for one year with the purchase of this book (details on the back cover).

Предисловие

Настоящее первое издание *Compact Oxford Russian Dictionary* было разработано на основе более крупного *Oxford Russian Dictionary*. Оно посвящено базисной, наиболее употребимой части лексики русского и английского языков и отражает самые последние изменения в обоих языках.

Ключевая информация по грамматике, стилистике и произношению изложена в удобной и доступной форме, благодаря чему этот словарь является отличным инструментом поиска лексикографической информации. Он позволяет пользователю выбрать наиболее подходящий перевод с помощью чётких указателей и иллюстративных примеров употребления слов. В словаре даются отметки о словоупотреблениях, характерных для британского и американского вариантов английского языка.

Все грамматические термины поясняются в глоссарии, приводимом в конце словаря, словарь также снабжён объяснительными статьями по грамматике и произношению русского и английского языков.

Кроме того, словарь содержит краткие заметки о культурных реалиях как России, так и Великобритании и США, включая информацию о современной общественной жизни, традициях, праздниках, а также рекомендации по написанию писем и электронных сообщений. Раздел «Разговорник» поможет пользователю вести общение в стандартных коммуникативных ситуациях, таких как поездка на транспорте, покупки в магазине, посещение ресторана, проведение досуга.

Будучи предназначенным для широкого круга пользователей – от изучающих язык на среднем или продвинутом уровне до посещающих страну во время туристических или деловых поездок, *Compact Oxford Russian Dictionary* является ценным практическим ресурсом для желающих изучить современный русский или английский язык.

Предлагаем Вам посетить наш сайт *Oxford Dictionaries* (www.oxforddictionaries.com), на котором в бесплатном доступе находятся статьи из английских толковых словарей, переводные статьи на французском, немецком, испанском и итальянском языках, а также краткие пособия по грамматике, игры и головоломки, и наш популярный блог о словах и языке.

Доступ на сайт **Oxford Language Dictionaries Online** открыт по платной подписке. Приобретя это издание, Вы получите годовую подписку на этот сайт. С подробностями можно познакомиться на задней обложке.

Guide to the use of the Dictionary

Russian–English Section

Presentation

1 The following devices are used to save space:

(i) The first letter of the headword, followed by a full point, represents the whole headword, e.g.

> **автомоби́л|ь ... води́ть а.** (= **води́ть автомоби́ль**)

(ii) The swung dash, in conjunction with a vertical stroke, represents that part of the headword which is to the left of the vertical stroke, e.g.

> **ава́ри|я ... потерпе́ть ∿ю** (= **потерпе́ть ава́рию**)

Exceptions: the swung dash is not used in indicating the genitive singular of nouns or the 1st and 2nd persons singular of the present tense of verbs with unchanged stress (for examples, see below: *Grammatical Information: Nouns* and *Verbs*).

Pronunciation

2 With the general exception of monosyllables, stress is indicated for every Russian word. A stress mark above the swung dash, where this sign represents two or more syllables, indicates shift of stress to the syllables immediately preceding the vertical stroke dividing the headword, e.g.

> **запи|са́ть, шу́, ∿́шешь ...** (= **запишу́, запи́шешь**)

3 Conversely, a stress mark above a syllable to the right of the swung dash indicates shift of stress away from the syllables(s) represented by the swung dash, e.g.

> **а́дрес, а,** *pl.* **∿а́ ...** (= **адреса́**)

4 Where a variant stress is permissible, both variants are shown, e.g.

> **зап|ере́ться ... ∿́ерся́ ...** (= **за́перся** *or* **заперся́**)

Meaning

5 Separate meanings of a word are indicated by means of Arabic numerals. Shades of meaning, represented by translations not considered strictly synonymous, are indicated by the means of a semicolon, whereas translations considered synonymous are indicated by a comma, e.g.

> **ава́нс ...1** (*деньги*) advance
> **2** (*pl. only*; fig.) advances, overtures
> **авантю́ра ...1** (*приключение*) adventure; escapade
> **2** (infml) shady enterprise

6 Homonyms are indicated by repetition of the headword as a separate entry, followed by a superscript Arabic numeral, e.g.

> **блок[1] ...** (tech.) block, pulley
> **блок[2] ...** (pol.) bloc

Explanation

7 Where necessary for the avoidance of ambiguity, explanatory glosses are given in brackets in italic type. This device is used in particular in the case of words denoting specifically Russian or Soviet concepts (e.g. **ка́ша, микрорайо́н**) and makes it possible to use one-word transliterations rather than clumsy paraphrases as a substitute for translation.

8 Indications of style or usage are given, where appropriate, in brackets, e.g.

(infml), (fig.), (joc.), (agric.), (pol.), etc.

Grammatical Information

9 The following grammatical information is given:

Nouns

The genitive singular ending and gender of all nouns are shown, e.g.

мо́лот, а *m.* hammer
мо́лни|я, и *f.* lightning
блю́д|о, а *nt.* dish
пья́ниц|а, ы *c.g.* drunkard

Other case endings are shown where declension or stress is, in relation to generally accepted systems of classification, irregular, e.g.

англича́н|ин, ина, *pl.* ~е, ~ *m.* Englishman
бор|ода́, оды́, *a.* ~о́ду, *pl.* ~о́ды, ~о́д, ~ода́м *f.* beard

(But the inserted vowel in the genitive plural ending of numerous feminine nouns with nominative singular ending **-ка** is *not* regarded as irregular, e.g. **англича́нка**, *g. pl.* **англича́нок**.)

Adjectives

Only the masculine nominative singular of the full form of the adjective is shown. Endings of the short forms, where these are found, are shown in brackets in most cases, e.g.

глу́|пый, ~, ~á, ~о, ~ы́

The neuter and plural short form endings are omitted where stress is as for the feminine, e.g.

нау́ч|ный, ~ен, ~на

Verbs

Endings are shown of the 1st and 2nd persons singular of the present tense (or of the 1st person only of verbs with infinitive ending **-ать, -овать, -ять, -еть** which retain stem and stress unchanged throughout the present tense), e.g.

говор|и́ть, ю́, и́шь ...
чита́|ть, ю ...

Other endings of the present tense and endings of the past tense are shown where formation or stress is irregular, e.g.

ид|ти́, у́, ёшь, *past* шёл, шла ...
бер|е́чь, егу́, ежёшь, егу́т, *past* ~ёг, ~егла́ ...

Participles and gerunds, and forms of the passive voice, are not shown unless they have special semantic or syntactical features.

If a past participle passive has an adjectival homonym with the same or similar meaning (as a rule, a participle has a word or words syntactically related to it, whereas an adjective does not), these homonyms are given as a single entry. In such cases, if the endings of the short forms of the participle and adjective differ, this is shown, e.g.

> запу́тан|ный (∼, ∼a) *p.p.p. of* запу́тать *and* (∼, ∼на) *adj.* ...

Verbal aspects: the imperfective aspect is normally treated as the basic form of the simple verb, a cross reference to the relevant form being shown in brackets, e.g.

> чита́|ть, ю *impf.* (*of* прочита́ть, проче́сть) ...

The corresponding entries are:

> прочита́|ть, ю *pf. of* чита́ть
> про|че́сть, чту́, чтёшь, *past* ∼чёл, ∼чла́ = прочита́ть

In the case, however, of compound verbs formed by means of a prefix, the perfective aspect is treated as the basic form, e.g.

> заш|и́ть, ью́, ьёшь *pf.* (*of* ∼ива́ть) ...

Prefixes and Combining Forms

A number of prefixes and combining forms are shown as separate entries, e.g.

> без... *pref.* in-, un-, -less
> гидро... *comb. form* hydro-

English–Russian Section

Orthography

1 English spelling follows British usage, with American variations also noted, e.g. **honour**... (AmE **honor**).

Pronunciation

2 For the convenience of readers whose native language is not English, the pronunciation of headwords is given, using the International Phonetic Alphabet. A key to the phonetic symbols used is given on p. xxiii.

Presentation

3 Headwords are printed in **bold roman** type.

Alternative spellings (including American variants) are presented alongside the preferred spelling; these variants appear again in alphabetical sequence (unless adjacent to the main entry), as cross references, e.g.

> **cosy** (AmE **cozy**)   **cozy** (AmE) = **cosy**
> **curtsy, curtsey**

Similar treatment is applied to words in which an alternative termination can be used without affecting the sense, e.g.

> **cyclic, cyclical**

4 Separate headword entries with superscript numerals are created for words which, though identical in spelling, differ in basic meaning and origin (**fine** as noun and verb; **fine** as adjective and adverb), or in pronunciation and/or stress (**house** and **supplement** as nouns and as verbs), or both (**tear** meaning 'teardrop' and **tear** meaning 'rip').

5 Separate entries for adverbs in '-ly' are made only when they have meanings or usage (idiom, compounds, etc.) which cannot conveniently be treated under the corresponding adjective. Examples are **hardly**, **really**, and **surely**. When there is no separate entry, and no instance of the adverb in the adjectival entry, it can be assumed that the corresponding Russian adverb is also formed regularly from the adjective. Thus, **clumsy** неуклюжий, неловкий implies that the Russian for 'clumsily' is неуклюже and неловко; **critical** критический implies that 'critically' can be translated критически, and so on.

6 Gerundial and participial forms of English verbs, used as nouns or adjectives, are often accommodated within the verb entry (transitive or intransitive as appropriate), e.g.

> **revolving doors** is found under **revolve** *v.i.*
> **become accustomed** is found under **accustom** *v.t.*

but in certain cases, for the sake of clarity, such forms have been treated as independent headwords, e.g.

> **barbed** *adj.*; **flying** *n.* and *adj.*

7 Some headwords are divided by a vertical stroke in order that the unchanging letters preceding the stroke may subsequently be replaced, in inflected forms, by a swung dash. Where there is no divider, the swung dash represents the whole headword, e.g.

> **house** ... ~**boat**

8 The vertical divider is also used in both English and Russian to separate the main part of a word from its termination when it is necessary to show modifications or alternative forms of the latter: e.g. paragraphs 22(c) and 23.

9 Within the headword entry each grammatical function has its own paragraph, introduced by a part-of-speech indicator: *n.*, *pron.*, *adj.*, *adv.*, *v.t.*, *v.i.*, *prep.*, *conj.*, *int.* A combined heading, e.g. **adagio** *n.*, *adj.*, & *adv.*, may sometimes be used for convenience; the most common instance is *v.t. & i.* when the two uses are not clearly distinguishable, or when the Russian intransitive is expressed by means of the suffix -ся.

10 Verb-adverb combinations forming phrasal verbs normally appear in a separate paragraph headed '*with advs.*', immediately following simple verb usage; they are given in alphabetical order of the adverb.

11 There are also a few verbs (e.g. **go**) where idiomatic usage with prepositions is extensive and complex enough to call for a separate paragraph headed '*with preps.*'.

12 Compounds in which the headword forms the first element (including those that are written as two words rather than being hyphenated or written as one word), are mostly brought together or 'nested' under the headword in a final paragraph.

13 Adjective-noun expressions generally appear under the adjective unless this has relatively little weight, as in '**good riddance**'.

14 Within an entry, differences of meaning or application are defined by a synonym, context, or other means. Major differences may be distinguished by numerals in bold type, e.g.

> **gag** *n.* **1** (to prevent speech etc.) ... **2** (joke) ...

15 A second type of label indicates status or level of usage, e.g.: *archaic*, *sl*(ang), *vulg*(ar). It may apply to the headword as a whole or to one of its functions or meanings, e.g.

> **advert** *n.* (infml) ...
> **bung** ... *v.t.* ... **2** (BrE, sl., throw) ...

16 Russian expressions, especially idioms or proverbs, which parallel rather than translate their English equivalents are preceded by the symbol ≈.

17 The use of the comma or the semicolon to separate Russian words offered as translations of the same English word reflects a greater or lesser degree of equivalence; in the latter case an auxiliary English gloss is often used to express the nuance of difference, e.g.

    ineligible *adj.* (for office) ...; (for a benefit) ...

18 To avoid ambiguity the semicolon is used when the alternatives are complete phrases or sentences, and also in most cases between synonymous verbs, e.g.

    what is he getting at? что он хо́чет сказа́ть?; куда́ он кло́нит?
    allow *v.t.* ... позв|оля́ть, -о́лить; разреш|а́ть, -и́ть ...

Idiom and Illustration

19 In both English and Russian there are many instances when one word in a phrase or sentence may be replaced by a synonymous alternative. This is shown by means of a comma or oblique stroke in English, and an oblique stroke in Russian, e.g.

    I'll knock a pound off the price   я сбро́шу/ски́ну/сба́влю фунт с цены́.

20 Non-synonymous alternatives are linked by the oblique stroke in both languages, e.g.

    carry on a conversation/business   вести́ разгово́р/де́ло.

21 In most cases the oblique stroke expresses an alternative regarding only one word on either side of it. Other alternatives are generally shown in the form (*or* ...), e.g.

    I could do with a drink   я охо́тно (*or* с удово́льствием) вы́пил бы.

Grammatical Information

22 The following grammatical information is given in respect of words offered as translations of headwords:

a) the gender of *masculine* nouns ending in -ь, except when this is made clear by an accompanying adjective (e.g. **polar bear** ·бе́лый медве́дь) or by the existence of a corresponding female form (see (*d*) below).

b) the gender of nouns (e.g. neuters in -мя, masculines in -а and -я, foreign borrowings in -и and -у) whose final letter does not serve as an indicator of gender. Nouns of common gender are designated (*c.g.*). Indeclinable nouns are designated (*indecl.*), preceded by a gender indicator if required. The many adjectives used as nouns (e.g. портно́й) are not specially marked.

c) the gender (or, for *pluralia tantum*, the genitive plural termination) and number (*pl.*) of all plural nouns which translate a headword or compound, e.g.

    timpani, tympani *n.* лита́вры (*f. pl.*)
    pliers *n.* кле́щ|и (*pl., g.* -е́й)

This information, however, is not given if the singular form has already appeared in the same entry, nor in the case of neuter plurals with an accompanying adjective, where the number and gender are self-evident from the terminations. Plurals of adjectives used substantively are shown as (*pl.*).

d) the forms of nouns used where Russian differs from English in making a verbal distinction between male and female, e.g.

    teacher учи́тель (-ница)

e) aspectual information: see paragraphs 23–25 below.

f) case usage with prepositions, e.g. **before** до + *g.*

g) the case, with or without preposition, required to provide an equivalent to an English transitive verb, e.g.

    attack *v.t.* нап|ада́ть, -а́сть на + *a.*

    If no case is indicated, it is to be taken that the Russian verb is transitive.

h) Use is also made of oblique cases of the Russian pronouns кто and что (in brackets and italics) to indicate case/preposition usage after a verb, e.g.

    agree *v.t.* согласо́в|ывать, -а́ть (*что с кем*)

Aspects

23 Aspectual information is given on all verbs (except быть) offered as renderings in infinitive form (except when they are subordinate to the finite verb in a sentence). If the verb is mono-aspectual, or used in a phrase to which only one aspect applies, it is designated either imperfective (*impf.*) or perfective (*pf.*) as the case may be.

With verbs of motion a distinction is made between determinate (*det.*) and indeterminate (*indet.*) forms, the imperfective aspect being assumed unless otherwise stated. Bi-aspectual infinitives are shown as (*impf., pf.*). In all other cases both aspects are indicated (the imperfective always preceding the perfective) as in the following examples:

    (i) получ|а́ть, -и́ть; возра|жа́ть, -зи́ть; сн|оси́ть, -ести́.

    (ii) позв|оля́ть, -о́лить; встр|еча́ть, -е́тить.

    (iii) пока́з|ывать, -а́ть (i.e. *pf.* показа́ть); очаро́в|ывать, -а́ть.

    (iv) гоня́ть, гнать; брать, взять; вынужда́ть, вы́нудить.

    (v) смотре́ть, по-; звать, по- (i.e. *pf.* позва́ть); мости́ть, вы́- (i.e. *pf.* вы́мостить); жа́рить, за-/из-/по-.

    (vi) и|мити́ровать, сы-.

24 It will be seen from the above that

i) when the first two or more letters of both aspects are identical, a vertical divider in the imperfective separates these letters from those which undergo change in the perfective. The perfective is then represented by the changed letters, preceded by a hyphen.

ii) a 'change' includes change of stress only if the stress shifts *back* in the perfective to the previous vowel: the divider then precedes this vowel in the imperfective.

iii) if it shifts *forward*, only the stressed syllable of the perfective is shown.

iv) when the two aspects have only their first letter in common, or are in fact different verbs, or both begin with вы- (which is always accented in the perfective), both are given in full.

v) perfectives of the type prefix + imperfective are shown by giving the prefix only, followed by a hyphen. Prefixes are unstressed except for вы́-.

    Alternative prefixes are separated by an oblique stroke.

25 When two or three verbs separated by an oblique stroke are followed by the indication (*pf.*) or (*impf.*) this applies to both or all of them.

26 The following grammatical information is given in respect of English headwords.

a) Irregular or difficult plural forms of nouns, e.g.

    child ... (*pl.* **children**) ...

    leaf ... (*pl.* **leaves**) ...

    monkey ... (*pl.* ∼s) ...

    referend|um ... (*pl.* ∼ums *or* ∼a) ...

b) Irregular or difficult comparative and superlative forms of adjectives which take **-er, -est**, e.g.

> **chic** ... (**chicer, chicest**) ...
> **glib** ... (**glibber, glibbest**) ...
> **tatty** ... (**tattier, tattiest**) ...

c) Irregular or difficult forms of verbs, e.g.

> **eat** ... (*past* **ate;** *p.p.* **eaten**) ...
> **go** ... (*3rd pers. sg. pres.* **goes;** *past* **went;** *p.p.* **gone**) ...
> **hold** ... (*past and p.p.* **held**) ...
> **run** ... (**running;** *past* **ran;** *p.p.* **run**) ...
> **tattoo** ... (**tattoos, tattooed**) ...
> **taxi** ... (**taxis, taxied, taxiing**) ...
> **tip** ... (**tipped, tipping**) ...

In the case of compound verbs, e.g. **undo**, irregular or difficult forms follow those of the base verb, in this case **do**.

О пользовании словарём

Русско-английская часть

Заглавное слово

1 В целях экономии места в отношении заглавного слова, повторяющегося в тексте словарной статьи, используются следующие приёмы:

1) начальная буква заглавного слова с последующей точкой заменяет всё слово целиком в его неизменной форме. Например:

автомоби́л|ь ... води́ть а. (= води́ть автомоби́ль)

2) т. н. тильда (знак ∼) заменяет часть заглавного слова, расположенную до сплошной вертикальной черты. Например:

ава́ри|я ... потерпе́ть ∼ю (= потерпе́ть ава́рию)

Исключения. Тильда не применяется для обозначения форм родительного падежа единственного числа существительных и форм 1-го и 2-го лица единственного числа глаголов настоящего времени с неподвижным ударением (см. об этом ниже: *Грамматический комментарий: Существительные* и *Глаголы*).

Ударение

2 Ударение последовательно отмечается во всех русских словах за исключением односложных. Знак ударения над тильдой (если та обозначает часть слова, состоящую из двух или более слогов) показывает перенос ударения на слог, ближайший к сплошной вертикальной черте в заглавном слове. Например:

запи|са́ть, шу́, ∼́шешь ... (= запишу́, запи́шешь)

3 Напротив, знак ударения над слогом правее тильды показывает перенос ударения на этот слог со слога или слогов, заменяемых этим знаком. Например:

а́дрес, а, *pl.* ∼á ... (= адреса́)

4 Допустимые вариантные (в отношении постановки ударения) формы приводятся. Например:

зап|ере́ться ... ∼́ерся́ ... (= за́перся *или* заперся́)

Значения слова

5 Самостоятельные значения слова обозначаются арабскими цифрами. Оттенки значения, представленные переводами, которые не являются близкими синонимами, отделяются точкой с запятой, в то время как тождественные или близкие по значению переводы отделяются запятой. Например:

ава́нс ...**1** (*деньги*) advance
2 (*pl. only*; fig.) advances, overtures
авантю́ра ...**1** (*приключение*) adventure; escapade
2 (infml) shady enterprise

6 Каждый омоним выделяется в отдельную статью и нумеруется при помощи надстрочной цифры, которая помещается сразу после заглавного слова. Например:

блок[1] ... (tech.) block, pulley
блок[2] ... (pol.) bloc

Пометы и пояснения

7 Во избежание неясности, в скобках приводятся пояснения, набранные курсивом. В особенности этот приём применяется в отношении слов, обозначающих типично русские или советские понятия (как, например, **ка́ша**, **микрорайо́н**), что позволяет использовать транслитерацию в качестве замены неудачным описательным переводам.

8 В необходимых случаях в скобках приводятся стилистические, а также отраслевые и некоторые другие пометы, которые могут относиться как ко всему слову, так и к отдельным его значениям. Примеры таких помет: (infml), (fig.), (joc.), (agric.), (pol.) и т. п.

Грамматический комментарий

9 Грамматический комментарий включает в себя следующее:

Существительные

У всех существительных отмечается форма родительного падежа единственного числа, например:

> **мо́лот, а** *m.* hammer
> **мо́лни|я, и** *f.* lightning
> **блю́д|о, а** *nt.* dish
> **пья́ниц|а, ы** *c.g.* drunkard

Окончания других падежей приводятся только у существительных, которые имеют особенности в склонении или постановке ударения, и эти особенности не определяются общими правилами. Например:

> **англича́н|ин, ина,** *pl.* ∼е, ∼ *m.* Englishman
> **бор|ода́, оды́,** *a.* ∼óду, *pl.* ∼оды, ∼óд, ∼ода́м *f.* beard

Прилагательные

Прилагательные даются в форме именительного падежа единственного числа мужского рода. Окончания большинства кратких форм, если такие имеются, приводятся в скобках. Например:

> **глу́|пый,** ∼, ∼á, ∼о, ∼ы́

Окончания кратких прилагательных среднего рода и множественного числа не указываются, если постановка ударения в этих формах не отличается от формы женского рода. Например:

> **нау́ч|ный,** ∼ен, ∼на

Глаголы

У глаголов приводятся формы 1-го и 2-го лица единственного числа настоящего времени (исключение составляют глаголы, оканчивающиеся в инфинитиве на **-ать**, **-ова́ть**, **-ять**, **-еть**, у которых приводится только форма 1-го лица единственного числа настоящего времени, так как основа этих глаголов и место постановки ударения не меняются во всех формах настоящего времени). Например:

> **говор|и́ть, ю́, и́шь** ...
> **чита́|ть, ю** ...

Другие формы настоящего времени, а также формы прошедшего времени даются только у глаголов, имеющих особенности в спряжении или постановке ударения. Например:

> ид|ти́, у́, ёшь, *past* шёл, шла ...
>
> бер|е́чь, егу́, ежёшь, егу́т, *past* ~ёг, ~егла́ ...

Формы причастий (в т. ч. страдательных) и деепричастий опускаются, если они не обладают особыми семантическими или морфологическими чертами.

Если страдательное причастие прошедшего времени совпадает в полной форме с близким или тождественным по значению прилагательным, оба омонима даются в одной словарной статье, причём, если их краткие формы отличаются, это отмечается в статье. Например:

> запу́тан|ный (~, ~а) *p.p.p. of* запу́тать (~, ~на) *and adj.* ...

При подаче глаголов, образующих пары глагол несовершенного вида – глагол совершенного вида, используются следующие принципы:

1) если в названной паре глагол несовершенного вида — бесприставочный, то основной *словарной* формой глагола признаётся форма инфинитива несовершенного вида, возле которой и помещается перевод, а в скобках помещается ссылка на соответствующий глагол совершенного вида. При этом словарные статьи глаголов совершенного вида, в случае тождественности значений/переводов глаголов в видовой паре, представляют собой перекрёстные ссылки на статьи о соответствующих глаголах несовершенного вида. Например:

> чита́|ть, ю *impf.* (*of* прочита́ть, проче́сть) ...
>
> прочита́|ть, ю *pf. of* чита́ть
>
> про|че́сть, чту́, чтёшь, *past* ~чёл, ~чла́ = прочита́ть

2) если же в видовой паре глагол несовершенного вида – приставочный глагол, то основной *словарной* формой считается форма инфинитива совершенного вида, и перевод следует искать в статье о глаголе совершенного вида. Например:

> заш|и́ть, ью́, ьёшь *pf.* (*of* ~ива́ть) ...

Приставки и составные части сложных слов

Ряд приставок и составных частей сложных слов выделяется в отдельные статьи, например:

> без ... *pref.* in-, un-, -less
>
> гидро ... *comb. form* hydro-

Англо-русская часть

Орфография

1 Слова английского языка даются в соответствии с британскими правилами орфографии. Американский вариант правописания, в случае расхождения с британским, указывается в скобках, например **honour**... (AmE **honor**).

Произношение

2 В Словаре рассматривается произношение, характерное для жителей южной Англии и известное как *Received Pronunciation* или *RP* (буквально «общепринятое/нормативное произношение»). Для удобства русскоязычной читательской аудитории все заглавные слова приводятся в фонетической транскрипции. Исключение составляют аббревиатуры типа **BBC**, которые произносятся по буквам: отдельно каждая буква в соответствии с её названием.

Названия букв английского алфавита см. на с. 880. У сложных слов, у которых вторая составная часть слова представлена в Словаре в качестве отдельной статьи, приводится транскрипция только первой части.

Перечень используемых транскрипционных символов с примерами слов, содержащих тот или иной звук, см. на с. xxiii.

Заглавное слово и подача информации в словарной статье

3 Заглавные слова печатаются **полужирным** шрифтом.

Вариантные орфографические формы (включая те, которые свойственны американскому английскому) фиксируются наряду с нормативным/ преобладающим правописанием слова. Такие формы даются повторно, согласно их положению в алфавитном порядке, с обязательной отсылкой к основному варианту (кроме тех случаев, когда альтернативный вариант примыкает по алфавиту непосредственно к основному). Например:

> **cosy** (AmE **cozy**)   **cozy = cosy**
> **curtsy, curtsey**

4 В отдельные словарные статьи, нумерующиеся надстрочными цифрами после заглавного слова, выделяются слова, которые, хотя и имеют одинаковое написание, но отличаются:

1) значением и происхождением (например, **fine** существительное и глагол и **fine** прилагательное и наречие);

2) произношением и/или ударением (например, **house** существительное и **house** глагол);

3) всем вышеперечисленным (например, **tear** в значении «слеза» и **tear** в значении «разрывать, рвать»).

5 Отдельные словарные статьи о наречиях на -ly приводятся только для слов, значение которых не может быть безошибочно определено исходя из значения соответствующего прилагательного. Примеры: **hardly**, **really** и **surely**.

6 Формы герундия и причастий английских глаголов, перешедшие в разряд существительных или прилагательных, нередко помещаются внутри статьи о глаголе (переходном или непереходном, в зависимости от значения). Например:

> **revolving doors** следует искать в статье **revolve** *v.i.*
> **become accustomed** следует искать в статье **accustom** *v.t.*

Но в некоторых случаях, во избежание неясности, подобные существительные и прилагательные выделяются в самостоятельные статьи. Например:

> **barbed** *adj.*; **flying** *n.* и *adj.*

7 Некоторые заглавные слова делит сплошная вертикальная черта. Это указывает на то, что неизменяемая часть слова, находящаяся до вертикальной черты, в изменяемых формах этого слова может заменяться тильдой. При отсутствии разделительной вертикальной линии в заглавном слове, тильда обозначает всё заглавное слово целиком, например:

> **house** ... **~boat**

8 Сплошная вертикальная черта, отделяющая неизменяемую часть слова от изменяемой, используется также в английских и русских словах, когда необходимо отобразить словоизменение или привести вариантные формы. См. примеры в пункте 24.

9 Внутри словарной статьи, для каждого лексико-грамматического разряда (части речи) отводится отдельный параграф, начинающийся с указателя части речи:

n., *pron.*, *adj.*, *adv.*, *v.t.*, *v.i.*, *prep.*, *conj.*, *int.* При необходимости такие указатели объединяются в одну запись, например: **adagio** *n.*, *adj.*, *& adv.* Наиболее часто встречается объединение указателей переходного и непереходного глаголов: *v.t. & i.* Последнее наблюдается, когда отличие переходного глагола от непереходного не усматривается явно и когда в переводе русский непереходный глагол образуется при помощи постфикса -ся.

10 Сочетания типа «глагол-наречие», образующие фразовые глаголы, обыкновенно даются отдельным параграфом под заголовком *with advs.*, непосредственно вслед за примерами простого употребления глагола, и размещаются внутри параграфа в алфавитном порядке входящих в эти сочетания наречий.

11 У некоторых глаголов (например **go**), образующих многочисленные идиоматические выражения с предлогами, устойчивые сочетания «глагол-предлог» выделяются в отдельный параграф под заголовком *with preps.*

12 Сложные слова, первая составная часть которых образует заглавное слово словарной статьи, объединяются в заключительном параграфе этой статьи (включая те, которые по правилам английского языка пишутся раздельно).

13 Сочетания типа «прилагательное-существительное» приводятся преимущественно в статье о прилагательном, за исключением случаев, когда прилагательное не оказывает определяющего влияния на значение всего выражения, как например в идиоме **good riddance**.

14 Различия в значении или употреблении слова помечаются пояснительными комментариями в виде синонимов или контекстного окружения слова. Такие пояснения даются в скобках. Для обозначения существенных различий в значении или употреблении слова используются набранные полужирным шрифтом цифры, которые нумеруют самостоятельные значения слова. Например:

    gag *n.* **1** (to prevent speech etc.) ... **2** (joke) ...

15 Другой тип пояснений в скобках — стилистические пометы, а также пометы, определяющие или ограничивающие область (географический ареал, профессиональную сферу и пр.) употребления слова. Такие пометы, в зависимости от их местоположения в статье, могут относиться как ко всему слову, так и к отдельным его значениям и случаям употребления в конкретном словосочетании или предложении. Например:

    advert *n.* (infml) ...
    bung ... *v.t.* ... **2** (BrE, sl., throw) ...

16 Выражения русского языка, в особенности идиомы и пословицы, которые являются скорее переводными аналогами, нежели точными эквивалентами, помечаются предшествующим знаком приблизительного равенства $\approx$.

17 Употребление запятой либо точки с запятой для разграничения переводов одного и того же слова указывает на степень тождественности/синонимичности этих переводов: большую для переводов, разделяемых запятой, и меньшую для разделяемых точкой с запятой. В последнем случае для уточнения оттенка значения нередко используется вспомогательный комментарий на английском языке, например:

    ineligible *adj.* (for office) ...; (for a benefit) ...

18 Во избежание неясности, точка с запятой применяется для разграничения альтернативных переводов словосочетаний или предложений и большинства видовых пар синонимичных глаголов. Например:

    what is he getting at? что он хо́чет сказа́ть?; куда́ он кло́нит?
    allow *v.t.* ... позв|оля́ть, -о́лить; разреш|а́ть, -и́ть ...

Устойчивые выражения и примеры употребления слова

19 И в английском, и в русском языках существует немало примеров того, как то или иное слово в словосочетании или предложении может быть заменено синонимом без ущерба для смысла высказывания. Такие синонимы отделяются друг от друга при помощи запятой или косой черты в английских примерах, и посредством косой черты в примерах на русском языке. Например:

I'll knock a pound off the price   я сброшу/скину/сбавлю фунт с цены.

20 Переводные варианты, не являющиеся синонимами, отделяются косой чертой в примерах на обоих языках, например:

carry on a conversation/business   вести разговор/дело.

21 Косая черта, как правило, не применяется, если один из переводов, примыкающий непосредственно к косой черте, состоит из двух и более слов. В таком случае вариант(ы) перевода даются в скобках после слова *or* («или»), например:

I could do with a drink   я охотно (*or* с удовольствием) выпил бы.

Грамматический комментарий

22 В грамматическом комментарии к заглавным словам содержится следующая информация:

а) образуемые не по общим правилам либо вызывающие затруднения в образовании формы множественного числа существительных, например:

> **child** ... (*pl.* **children**) ...
> **leaf** ... (*pl.* **leaves**) ...
> **monkey** ... (*pl.* ∼**s**) ...
> **referend|um** ... (*pl.* ∼**ums** *or* ∼**a**) ...

б) сравнительная и превосходная степень прилагательных, образующих указанные формы путём прибавления -er, -est и вызывающие затруднения в образовании, например:

> **chic** ... (**chicer, chicest**) ...
> **glib** ... (**glibber, glibbest**) ...
> **tatty** ... (**tattier, tattiest**) ...

в) формы неправильных глаголов и сложные случаи образования основных форм у прочих глаголов, например:

> **eat** ... (*past* **ate**; *p.p.* **eaten**) ...
> **go** ... (*3rd pers. sg. pres.* **goes**; *past* **went**; *p.p.* **gone**) ...
> **hold** ... (*past and p.p.* **held**) ...
> **run** ... (**running**; *past* **ran**; *p.p.* **run**) ...
> **tattoo** ... (**tattoos, tattooed**) ...
> **taxi** ... (**taxis, taxied, taxiing**) ...
> **tip** ... (**tipped, tipping**) ...

Неправильные и трудные формы сложных глаголов, таких как **undo**, образуются по модели основного в смысловом отношении глагола, в нашем случае **do**. Иными словами, если известно, что глагол **do** образует неправильные формы **did, done**, то формами простого прошедшего времени и причастия прошедшего времени глагола **undo** будут **undid, undone**.

23 Русскоязычным пользователям следует обратить внимание на следующие основные моменты в грамматическом комментарии к русским переводам заглавных слов:

а) у предлогов приводится управление, например **before** до + *g.*

б) для более точного перевода английских переходных глаголов, в необходимых случаях, у русских глаголов даётся предложное (или беспредложное) управление, например:

> **attack** *v.t.* нап|ада́ть, -а́сть на + *a.*

Если русский глагол не имеет при себе уточнения в виде падежа с предлогом или без, то этот глагол — переходный.

г) управление также может объясняться при помощи местоимений «кто» и «что», приводимых в скобках в соответствующих падежных формах с предлогами или без и выделяемых курсивом, например:

> **agree** *v.t.* извин|я́ться, -и́ться согласо́в|ывать, -а́ть (*что с кем*)

Вид глагола

24 Информация о виде даётся последовательно у всех глаголов в форме инфинитива (за исключением глагола «быть»). У одновидовых глаголов (глаголов, не имеющих соотносительной пары другого вида) категория вида отмечается соответствующей пометой: (*impf.*) или (*pf.*).

Т. н. глаголы движения, подразделяющиеся на глаголы *определённого* (однонаправленного) движения и глаголы *неопределённого* (разнонаправленного) движения, снабжаются пометами, соответственно, (*det.*) и (*indet.*). При этом, если категория вида этих глаголов не указывается, предполагается, что они несовершенного вида.

Инфинитивы двувидовых глаголов помечаются (*impf., pf.*). Во всех остальных случаях указываются оба вида (форма несовершенного вида всегда предшествует форме совершенного вида), что можно проследить на следующих примерах:

(1) получ|а́ть, -и́ть; возра|жа́ть, -зи́ть; сн|оси́ть, -ести́.

(2) позв|оля́ть, -о́лить; встр|еча́ть, -е́тить.

(3) пока́з|ывать, -а́ть (т. е. *pf.* показа́ть); очаро́в|ывать, -а́ть.

(4) гоня́ть, гнать; брать, взять; вынужда́ть, вы́нудить.

(5) смотре́ть, по-; звать, по-; (т. е. *pf.* позва́ть); мости́ть, вы́- (т. е. *pf.* вы́мостить); жа́рить, за-/из-/по-.

(6) и|мити́ровать, сы-.

Символы фонетической транскрипции, используемые в Словаре

Согласные

b	*b*ut	s	*s*it
d	*d*og	t	*t*op
f	*f*ew	v	*v*oice
g	*g*et	w	*w*e
h	*h*e	z	*z*oo
j	*y*es	ʃ	*sh*e
k	*c*at	ʒ	deci*s*ion
l	*l*eg	θ	*th*in
m	*m*an	ð	*th*is
n	*n*o	ŋ	ri*ng*
p	*p*en	tʃ	*ch*ip
r	*r*ed	dʒ	*j*ar

Гласные

æ	*c*a*t*	aɪ	m*y*
ɑ:	*ar*m	aʊ	h*ow*
e	b*e*d	eɪ	d*ay*
ə:	h*er*	əʊ	n*o*
ɪ	s*i*t	eə	h*air*
i:	s*ee*	ɪə	n*ear*
ɒ	h*o*t	ɔɪ	b*oy*
ɔ:	s*aw*	ʊə	p*oor*
ʌ	r*u*n	aɪə	f*ire*
ʊ	p*u*t	aʊə	s*our*
u:	t*oo*		
ə	*a*go		

(ə) обозначает безударный беглый гласный, который слышится в таких словах, как garde*n*, car*n*al и rhyth*m*.

(r) в конце слова обозначает согласный r, который произносится в случае, если следующее слово начинается с гласного звука, как, например, в *clutter up* и *an acre of land*.

Тильда ˜ обозначает носовой гласный звук, как в некоторых заимствованиях из французского языка, например ã (*en* masse).

Основное ударение в слове отмечается знаком ' перед ударным слогом.

О произношении звуков английского языка

Произношение английских слов, приводимое в Словаре в транскрипции, соответствует британской норме. Именно о звуках британского английского и пойдёт речь ниже.

Гласные звуки

Среди *гласных звуков* современного английского языка выделяют три основные группы: **монофтонги** (гласные, состоящие из одного звука), **дифтонги** (гласные, состоящие из двух звуков, которые произносятся в пределах одного слога) и **трифтонги** (гласные, состоящие из трёх звуков, произносимых в пределах одного слога).

В современном английском языке 12 монофтонгов, 8 дифтонгов и 2 трифтонга. Особенности их произношения (артикуляции) будут рассмотрены по группам: в отдельности для каждого звука.

Монофтонги

Исторически английские *монофтонги* подразделяются на **краткие** (ɪ, e, æ, ʌ, ɒ, ʊ, ə) и **долгие** (iː, ɑː, ɔː, uː, ɜː). Долгота последних обозначается в транскрипции двоеточием (ː) после символа соответствующего гласного.

/ɪ/   Краткий гласный звук, произносится без напряжения. Качественно (по месту и способу артикуляции) и количественно (по долготе) противопоставляется долгому /iː/ (см. ниже). Английский /ɪ/ слегка напоминает безударный русский /и/ в слове *игра* и ударный русский /и/ после шипящих. Для правильной артикуляции /ɪ/ язык следует располагать во рту ниже, чем при произношении русского /и/. Согласные перед /ɪ/ не смягчаются, на что нужно обращать особое внимание. В то же время английский /ɪ/ не должен походить на русский /ы/.

Примеры: s*i*t, h*i*s, *i*n.

/e/   Краткий гласный звук, произносится без напряжения. Английский /e/ отчасти напоминает русский звук /э/ в словах *свет* и *эти*, если его произносить очень кратко. Следует, однако, помнить о том, что согласные перед английским /e/ не смягчаются. При произнесении английского /e/ средняя часть языка поднята к нёбу выше, чем при произнесении русского /э/, а расстояние между челюстями уже.

Примеры: dr*e*ss, b*e*d, m*e*n.

/æ/   Краткий гласный звук, произносится с ощутимым напряжением. Качественно противопоставляется звуку /æ/. Во избежание ошибочного произношения русского /э/ вместо /æ/ язык следует располагать низко во рту, как при произнесении русского /а/. Нижняя челюсть должна быть заметно опущена. При этом основная масса языка должна оставаться в передней части рта, а его кончик должен быть прижат к нижним зубам.

Примеры: c*a*t, b*a*d, m*a*n.

/ʌ/   Краткий гласный звук, произносится напряжённо. Положение языка во рту, как при молчании. Английский /ʌ/ похож на русский /а/, произносимый в первом предударном слоге после твёрдых согласных на месте русских букв *а* и *о*, как, например, в словах *скала* и *кора*. По сравнению с русским ударным /а/ при произнесении английского /ʌ/ язык отодвинут назад, а задняя его часть приподнята. Чрезмерно отодвинутый назад язык приведёт к образованию звука, близкого к английскому /ɑː/, что будет являться грубой фонематической ошибкой, так как данные звуки нередко выполняют смыслоразличительную функцию (d*u*ck и d*ar*k, l*u*st и l*a*st).

Примеры: b*u*t, c*u*p, r*u*n.

/ɒ/   Краткий гласный звук, произносится без напряжения. Английский /ɒ/ отчасти похож на русский /о/ в слове *конь*, если его произносить не округляя и не выпячивая губы. При произнесении /ɒ/ необходимо максимально отодвинуть назад язык, как при произнесении /ɑː/ (см. ниже), и, широко раскрывая рот, попытаться добиться минимального округления губ.

Примеры: h*o*t, wh*a*t, w*a*nt.

/ʊ/   Краткий гласный звук, произносится без напряжения. Качественно и количественно противопоставляется долгому /uː/ (см. ниже). Основное отличие от русского /у/ в том, что при произнесении /ʊ/ губы почти не округляются и не выпячиваются.

Примеры: p*u*t, g*oo*d, b*oo*k.

/ə/   Краткий нейтральный (образуемый языком в нейтральном положении) гласный звук, произносится без напряжения. Как и русский язык, английский язык характеризуется сильной качественной редукцией (ослабленным произношением гласных в безударных слогах). Так, звук, близкий английскому /ə/, можно встретить во втором предударном и в двух заударных слогах в русских словах на месте гласных букв *о*, *а* и *е* после твёрдых согласных, например: *садовод*, *даром*, *целиком*.

Ошибка при артикуляции английского /ə/ возникает вследствие смешения парадигм редукции в английском и русском языках. Нейтральный гласный звук /ə/ в английском встречается преимущественно в первом предударном и первом заударном слогах. Носители русского языка в первом и втором предударных слогах и втором заударном нередко произносят гласные, по степени качественной редукции близкие к русским. Частой ошибкой является произношение в первом предударном слоге английских слов русского /э/ вместо /ə/. Для устранения этой ошибки необходимо не смещать язык в переднюю часть рта, сохраняя его в нейтральном срединном положении.

Примеры: *a*go, f*a*ther, comm*o*n.

/iː/   Долгий гласный звук, произносится напряжённо. Качественно и количественно противопоставляется краткому /ɪ/ (см. выше). Английский /iː/ несколько напоминает русский /и/ в слове *ива*, если произнести его напряжённо и протяжно. Согласные перед /iː/ не смягчаются. Помимо долготы английский /iː/ отличается неоднородностью звучания на всем протяжении. При произнесении /iː/ язык движется в полости рта вперёд и вверх.

Примеры: s*ee*, ch*ee*se, m*ea*t.

/ɑː/   Долгий гласный звук, произносится напряжённо. Своей протяжностью, характерной придавленностью корня языка во рту и низким тембром английский /ɑː/ напоминает звук, издаваемый при показе горла врачу. Для того чтобы правильно произносить английский /ɑː/, не делая его похожим на русский /a/, следует как можно дальше отводить корень языка назад и вниз.

Примеры: *arm*, *car*, *park*.

/ɔ:/   Долгий гласный звук. Английский /ɔ:/ произносится напряжённо, при оттянутом назад языке и сильно округлённых губах. Следует избегать характерного для артикуляции русского /о/ выпячивания губ, которое приводит к образованию несвойственного английскому /ɔ:/ призвука /у/.

      Примеры: *saw*, *all*, *sort*.

/u:/   Долгий гласный звук, произносится напряжённо. Качественно и количественно противопоставляется краткому /ʊ/ (см. выше). Помимо долготы, английский /u:/, как и /i:/, отличается неоднородностью звучания на всём протяжении. При произнесении /u:/ язык движется в полости рта назад и вверх. Губы в начальный момент заметно округлены и, по мере движения языка, округляются ещё сильнее. Во избежание замены английского /u:/ русским /у/ при округлении губ не следует их выпячивать.

      Примеры: *too*, *food*, *blue*.

/ə:/   Долгий гласный звук, произносится напряжённо. Губы при произнесении /ə:/ растянуты, зубы слегка обнажены. Согласные перед /ə:/ не смягчаются. Английский /ə:/ не должен напоминать русские /о/ и /э/. Именно звук /ə:/, как правило, произносится носителями английского языка при обдумывании ответа или подборе нужного слова.

      Примеры: *her*, *first*, *work*.

Дифтонги

Дифтонги — это особые гласные звуки, произносимые без паузы в пределах одного слога. У английских дифтонгов основным, ударным элементом — **ядром** — всегда является первый из двух его составляющих. Второй элемент — **скольжение** или **глайд** — всегда безударный, произносится без напряжения.

Интонационно все английские дифтонги — нисходящие, т. е. их произношение сопровождается понижением интонации к конечному элементу.

/eɪ/   Сочетание сильного первого элемента /е/ и ослабленного второго /ɪ/ (см. выше). Следует избегать превращения глайда дифтонга /ɪ/ в английский согласный /j/ или русский /й/.

      Примеры: *day*, *they*, *break*.

/aɪ/   Сочетание сильного первого элемента /a/ и ослабленного второго /ɪ/. Английский звук /a/ — ядро дифтонга /aɪ/ — отличается от русского /a/ передним положением языка при его артикуляции. К тому же в начальной стадии звучания английского /a/ язык располагается ниже. Глайд дифтонга /ɪ/ не должен заменяться английским согласным /j/ или русский /й/.

      Примеры: *my*, *side*, *high*.

/ɔɪ/   Сочетание сильного первого элемента /ɔ/ и ослабленного второго /ɪ/. Английский звук /ɔ/ — ядро дифтонга /ɔɪ/ — представляет собой нечто среднее между английскими звуками /ɔ:/ и /ɒ/ (см. выше). Превращение глайда дифтонга /ɪ/ в английский согласный /j/ или русский /й/ является ошибкой.

      Примеры: *boy*, *soil*, *noise*.

/əʊ/   Сочетание сильного первого элемента /ə/ и незначительно ослабленного второго /ʊ/. Ядро дифтонга /əʊ/ — звук /ə/ — произносится как английский /ə:/ (см. выше), но с раскрытым шире, чем для /ə:/, ртом, и с округлёнными (но не выпяченными) губами. Дифтонг /əʊ/— единственный английский дифтонг, второй элемент которого произносится отчётливо, без заметного расслабления органов речи.

Примеры: no, show, home.

/aʊ/   Сочетание сильного первого элемента /a/ и ослабленного второго /ʊ/. При произнесении ядра дифтонга /aʊ/ — звука /a/ — язык не настолько продвигается вперёд, как при произнесении ядра /aɪ/, и первый элемент /aʊ/ во многом схож с русским /а/. В отличие от глайда /əʊ/ второй элемент дифтонга /aʊ/ звучит неясно. Следует помнить об этом и не превращать неясный глайд /ʊ/ в самостоятельный гласный /ʊ/ или /u:/, а также русский /у/, который произносится с характерным выпячиванием губ, не свойственным гласным звукам английского языка в целом.

Примеры: how, town, mouth.

/ɪə/   Сочетание сильного первого элемента /ɪ/ и ослабленного второго /ə/ (см. выше). В открытом конечном положении (на конце слова) глайд /ə/ может переходить в звук, близкий к английскому /ʌ/ (см. выше).

Примеры: beer, near, here.

/eə/   Сочетание сильного первого элемента /e/ и ослабленного второго /ə/. Рот при произнесении ядра дифтонга /eə/ — звука /e/ — раскрыт намного шире, чем при произнесении самостоятельного английского гласного /e/, что делает похожим ядро дифтонга /eə/ на русский /э/ в слове *этот* (но не *эти*).

Примеры: hair, care, there.

/ʊə/   Сочетание сильного первого элемента /ʊ/ и ослабленного второго /ə/ (см. выше).

Примеры: poor, sure, tour.

Трифтонги

В английском языке сочетания дифтонгов /aɪ/ и /aʊ/ с безударным нейтральным неслоговым гласным /ə/ называются *трифтонгами*. Как и дифтонги, английские трифтонги имеют в своём составе **ядро** — сильный ударный элемент — и **глайд** или **скольжение**, которое включает в себя два безударных элемента.

/aɪə/   Сочетание дифтонга /aɪ/ и нейтрального гласного /ə/. Элемент /ɪ/ не должен превращаться в согласный /j/.

Примеры: fire, liar, iron.

/aʊə/   Сочетание дифтонга /aʊ/ и нейтрального гласного /ə/. Элемент /ʊ/ не должен превращаться в согласный /w/.

Примеры: sour, flower, towel.

Согласные звуки

Английские *согласные* имеют следующие характерные отличительные черты по сравнению с согласными русского языка:

1) «звонкость-глухость» не является основным различительным признаком английских согласных, напротив, применительно к английскому согласному важно знать: является ли он **сильным** или **слабым**, а не звонким или глухим. В русском языке глухие согласные, как правило, слабые, а звонкие — сильные. В английском языке, наоборот, звонкие /b/, /d/, /g/, /j/, /l/, /m/, /n/, /r/, /v/, /w/, /z/, /ʒ/, /ð/, /ŋ/ и /dʒ/ — в большинстве случаев слабые, а глухие /f/, /h/, /k/, /p/, /s/, /t/, /ʃ/, /θ/ и /tʃ/ — сильные;

2) сильные глухие /k/, /p/ и /t/ отличаются от соответствующих русских согласных тем, что они произносятся с сильным **придыханием**, — промежуток между одним из этих согласных и следующим за ним гласным заполняется порцией резко выдыхаемого воздуха, причём воздух этот выходит не из ротовой полости, как в случае с русскими /к/, /п/ и /т/, а непосредственно из лёгких;

3) отличительной чертой системы русских согласных является наличие палатализации (смягчения). За исключением всегда мягких /ч/ и /щ/ и всегда твёрдых /ц/, /ш/ и /ж/ (не путать с двойным «долгим» мягким /жʲжʲ/, как в слове *вожжи*), остальные русские согласные встречаются как в мягкой, так и в твёрдой разновидностях. Согласные английского языка полностью лишены такой артикуляционной особенности, поэтому следует уделять особое внимание тому, чтобы английские согласные не смягчались перед гласными /e/, /ɪ/, /iː/;

4) английские звонкие согласные на конце слов не оглушаются, как русские;

5) удвоенные английские согласные читаются как один звук.

В современном английском языке 24 согласных звука. Особенности их произношения (артикуляции) будут рассмотрены отдельно для каждого звука.

/b/   Произносится как ослабленный русский /б/. Перед гласными /e/, /ɪ/, /iː/, /ə:/ и согласным /j/ не смягчается.

       Примеры: *b*ut, *b*ig, *b*est.

/d/   Произносится как ослабленный русский /д/. Перед гласными /e/, /ɪ/, /iː/, /ə:/ и согласным /j/ не смягчается. Следует избегать призвука /ə/ перед сочетаниями с /n/ и /l/, для чего образующейся между /d/ и /n/ мгновенной паузе надлежит придавать носовую артикуляцию, а мгновенной паузе между /d/ и /l/ соответственно боковую (по месту образования — между опущенным в одну сторону боковым краем языка и щекой).

       Примеры: *d*og, *d*ay, *d*oor.

/f/   Произносится как русский /ф/, но энергичнее и без участия верхней губы. Перед гласными /e/, /ɪ/, /iː/, /ə:/ и согласным /j/ не смягчается.

       Примеры: *f*ew, *f*it, *f*eel.

/g/   Произносится как ослабленный русский /г/. Перед гласными /e/, /ɪ/, /iː/, /ə:/ и согласным /j/ не смягчается.

       Примеры: *g*et, *g*o, *g*ive.

/h/   Аналогов этому звуку в русском языке нет. Согласный /h/ представляет собой простой выдох без участия языка и округления губ — как при дуновении на стекло с целью почистить его. Звук /h/ не является шумным и ни в коем случае не должен напоминать русский /х/.

       Примеры: *h*e, *h*ill, *h*air.

/j/   Произносится как заметно ослабленный русский /й/.

       Примеры: *y*es, *y*ou, *y*ear.

/k/   Произносится как русский /к/, но энергичнее и с придыханием перед гласными. Перед гласными /e/, /ɪ/, /i:/, /ə:/ и согласным /j/ не смягчается.

Примеры: *c*at, *k*ind, *q*uick.

/l/   В отличие от русского /л/ английский /l/ произносится с участием кончика языка, который касается тканей непосредственно за передними верхними зубами. Перед гласными звучит несколько мягче, но не так, как русский мягкий /л'/. В то же время в положении не перед гласными английский /l/ никогда не звучит так твёрдо, как русский /л/.

Примеры: *l*eg, *l*ike, *l*ook.

/m/   Произносится как ослабленный русский /м/. Перед гласными /e/, /ɪ/, /i:/, /ə:/ и согласным /j/ не смягчается.

Примеры: *m*an, *m*e, *m*ilk.

/n/   В отличие от русского /н/, который произносится при помощи языка, упирающегося в передние верхние зубы, английский /n/ произносится с участием кончика языка, который касается тканей за передними верхними зубами, но не самих зубов. Английский /n/ звучит менее энергично, чем русский /н/. Перед гласными /e/, /ɪ/, /i:/, /ə:/ и согласным /j/ не смягчается.

Примеры: *n*o, *n*ew, *n*iece.

/p/   Произносится как русский /п/, но энергичнее и с придыханием перед гласными. Перед гласными /e/, /ɪ/, /i:/, /ə:/ и согласным /j/ не смягчается.

Примеры: *p*en, *p*ut, *p*lease.

/r/   Очень слабый согласный звук, лишь условно сравниваемый с русским /р/. Произносится он с положением органов речи, как для русского /ж/, но щель, образуемая между поднятым кончиком языка и передней частью твёрдого нёба, несколько шире, чем для /ж/. Кончик языка загнут назад и не должен вибрировать. Вибрируют при произнесении английского /r/ только голосовые связки. Средняя и задняя части языка остаются плоскими. Во избежание замены английского /r/ русским /р/ следует помнить о том, что при образовании английского /r/ язык не ударяется ни о зубы, ни о верхние ткани полости рта, оставаясь неподвижным.

Примеры: *r*ed, *r*eal, *r*oot.

/s/   Напоминает русский /с/, но произносится энергичнее. Язык, по сравнению с русским /с/, при произнесении английского /s/ поднят кверху, и струя воздуха проходит между кончиком языка и тканями позади передних верхних зубов, а не между языком и самими зубами. Перед гласными /e/, /ɪ/, /i:/, /ə:/ и согласным /j/ не смягчается.

Примеры: *s*it, *s*ame, *s*o.

/t/   Напоминает русский /т/, но произносится энергичнее и с придыханием перед гласными. По сравнению с русским /т/ при произнесении английского /t/ кончик языка приподнят к тканям, расположенным позади передних верхних зубов. Перед гласными /e/, /ɪ/, /i:/, /ə:/ и согласным /j/ не смягчается. Следует избегать призвука /ə/ перед сочетаниями с /n/ и /l/, для чего образующейся между /t/ и /n/ мгновенной паузе надлежит придавать носовую артикуляцию, а мгновенной паузе между /t/ и /l/ соответственно боковую (по месту образования — между опущенным в одну сторону боковым краем языка и щекой).

Примеры: *t*op, *t*ea, *t*ime.

/v/   Произносится как ослабленный русский /в/, но без участия верхней губы. Перед гласными /e/, /ɪ/, /iː/, /əː/ и согласным /j/ не смягчается.

Примеры: *v*oice, *v*ery, *v*iew.

/w/   Аналогов этому звуку в русском языке нет. Английский /w/ получается мгновенным пропусканием струи воздуха через щель, образуемую сильно округлёнными и слегка выпяченными губами. Зубы не касаются нижней губы. Звук /w/ произносится очень кратко и слабо, губы совершают движение, как при задувании свечи.

Примеры: *w*e, *w*hat, *w*ill.

/z/   Произносится как ослабленный русский /з/. Отличается от русского /з/ тем же, чем английский /s/ от русского /c/ (см. выше). Перед гласными /e/, /ɪ/, /iː/, /əː/ и согласным /j/ не смягчается.

Примеры: *z*oo, ea*s*y, ro*s*e.

/ʃ/   Произносится как смягчённый русский /ш/, но не настолько мягкий, как /щ/. Положение кончика языка, как при произнесении английского /s/ (см. выше), но щель, в которую пропускается воздух, более широкая, а органы речи напряжены меньше.

Примеры: *sh*e, *sh*all, *sh*op.

/ʒ/   Произносится как смягчённый русский /ж/, но не настолько мягкий, как в слове *вожжи*. Отличается от /ʃ/ только использованием голоса при его произнесении.

Примеры: deci*s*ion, plea*s*ure, u*s*ual.

/θ/   Аналогов этому звуку в русском языке нет. При произнесении сильного английского согласного /θ/ язык лежит плоско во рту, и его кончик находится между передними верхними и нижними зубами. В образуемую таким образом между краем верхних зубов и кончиком языка щель выдыхается воздух. Во избежание образования звука /f/ зубы должны быть обнажены так, чтобы нижняя губа не касалась верхних зубов. Во избежание образования звука /s/ кончик языка должен находиться между зубами, а сам язык оставаться плоским, особенно его передняя часть.

Примеры: *th*in, *th*ree, *th*rough.

/ð/   Аналогов этому звуку в русском языке нет. Произносится так же, как /θ/, но с голосом и менее энергично. Во избежание образования звука /v/ зубы должны быть обнажены так, чтобы нижняя губа не касалась верхних зубов. Во избежание образования звука /z/ кончик языка должен находиться между зубами, а сам язык оставаться плоским, особенно его передняя часть.

Примеры: *th*is, *th*ere, *th*at.

/ŋ/   Аналогов этому звуку в русском языке нет. Упрощённо, английский /ŋ/ представляет собой /g/, если произносить его через нос при полностью опущенном мягком нёбе. Так же, как и для /g/, для произношения /ŋ/ задняя часть языка смыкается с мягким нёбом, но последнее при артикуляции /ŋ/ полностью опущено, и воздух проходит не через рот, а через нос. Кончик языка при произнесении /ŋ/ обязательно должен находиться у нижних зубов, а передняя и средняя части языка не касаться нёба. Следует избегать призвука /g/ после /ŋ/ и не подменять /ŋ/ звуком /n/.

Примеры: ri*ng*, so*ng*, wro*ng*.

/tʃ/   Произносится как русский /ч/, но энергично и твёрдо, без какого бы то ни было смягчения. Для правильной артикуляции английского /tʃ/ второй элемент /ʃ/ следует произносить так же твёрдо, как русский /ш/.

Примеры: *ch*ip, *ch*eese, *ch*ild.

/dʒ/   Произносится так же, как /tʃ/, но с голосом, менее энергично и всегда со вторым мягким элементом /ʒ/.

Примеры: *j*ar, *j*am, *g*in.

Russian pronunciation guide

The pronunciation of Russian headwords is not given in the dictionary because, with the help of the additional information given below, it can be worked out from the spelling.

Russian letter	Approximate English sound and phonetic transcription	
а	like the English *a* in calm, but slightly shorter, as in French *la* or German *Mann*, e.g. **ра́дио**, **мать**; transcribed /a/	❶ See Note 5 below
б	like an English *b*, but with the expulsion of less breath, e.g. **ба́бушка**, **буты́лка**; transcribed /b/	❶ See Note 4 below
в	like an English *v*, e.g. **вино́**, **вот**; transcribed /v/	❶ See Note 4 below
г	like the English *g* in go, but with the expulsion of less breath, e.g. **газе́та**, **гара́ж**; transcribed /g/	❶ See Notes 4, 6 below
д	like an English *d*, but with the expulsion of less breath, e.g. **да**, **дом**; transcribed /d/	❶ See Note 4 below
е	like the English *ye* in yes, e.g. **е́сли**, **обе́д**; transcribed /je/	❶ See Notes 2, 3 below
ё	like the English *yo* in yonder, e.g. **её**, **ёлка**; transcribed /jo/	❶ See Note 2 below
ж	like the English *s* in measure, e.g. **ждать**, **жена́**; transcribed /zh/	❶ See Notes 3, 4 below
з	like an English *z*, e.g. **за́пад**, **зо́нтик**; transcribed /z/	❶ See Note 4 below
и	like the English *ee* in see, e.g. **игра́ть**, **и́ли**; transcribed /i/	❶ See Notes 2, 3 below
й	like the English *y* in boy, e.g. **мой**, **трамва́й**; transcribed /j/	
к	like an English *k*, but with the expulsion of less breath, e.g. **кто**, **ма́рка**; transcribed /k/	❶ See Note 4 below
л	like an English *l*, but harder, pronounced with the tongue behind the front teeth, e.g. **ла́мпа**, **луна́**; transcribed /l/	
м	like an English *m*, e.g. **ма́ма**, **молоко́**; transcribed /m/	
н	like an English *n*, but harder, pronounced with the tongue behind the front teeth, e.g. **на́до**, **нога́**; transcribed /n/	
о	like the English *o* in for, but pronounced with more rounded lips, e.g. **о́чень**, **мо́ре**; transcribed /o/	❶ See Note 5 below
п	like an English *p*, but with the expulsion of less breath, e.g. **па́па**, **по́сле**; transcribed /p/	❶ See Note 4 below

Russian letter	Approximate English sound and phonetic transcription	
р	like an English *r*, but rolled at the front of the mouth, e.g. **рыба, пора́**; transcribed /r/	
с	like an English *s*, e.g. **сала́т, соба́ка**; transcribed /s/	❶ See Note 4 below
т	like an English *t*, but with the expulsion of less breath, e.g. **таре́лка, то́лько**; transcribed /t/	❶ See Note 4 below
у	like the English *oo* in p**oo**l, but pronounced with more rounded lips, e.g. **муж, у́лица**; transcribed /u/	
ф	like an English *f*, e.g. **футбо́л, фле́йта**; transcribed /f/	❶ See Note 4 below
х	like the Scottish *ch* in lo**ch**, e.g. **хлеб, хо́лодно**; transcribed /kh/	
ц	like the English *ts* in nu**ts**, e.g. **центр, цирк**; transcribed /ts/	❶ See Note 3 below
ч	like the English *ch* in **ch**urch, e.g. **чай, час**; transcribed /ch/	❶ See Notes 3, 7 below
ш	like the English *sh* in **sh**op, but harder, pronounced with the tongue lower, e.g. **шко́ла, наш**; transcribed /sh/	❶ See Notes 3, 4 below
щ	either like a long soft English *sh*, similar to the *sh* in **sh**ould, or like an English *shch*, as in fre**sh ch**eese, e.g. **щи, ещё**; transcribed /shch/	❶ See Note 3 below
ъ	hard sign (hardens the preceding consonant), e.g. **объясня́ть**; transcribed /"/	
ы	like the English *i* in b**i**t, but with the tongue further back in the mouth, e.g. **вы, ты**; transcribed /y/	
ь	soft sign (softens the preceding consonant), e.g. **мать, говори́ть**; transcribed /'/	
э	like the English *e* in th**e**re, e.g. **э́то, эта́ж**; transcribed /e/	
ю	like the English *u* in **u**nit, but pronounced with more rounded lips, e.g. **ю́бка, юг**; transcribed /ju:/	❶ See Note 2 below
я	like the English *ya* in **ya**rd, but slightly shorter, e.g. **я́блоко, моя́**; transcribed /ja/	❶ See Notes 2, 5 below

Notes

1. Stress

Russian words have one main stress. In this dictionary this is indicated by an acute accent placed over the vowel of the stressed syllable. The vowel ё is never marked as it is almost always stressed.

2. Hard and soft consonants

An important feature of Russian consonants is that they may be hard or soft. At the end of a word or before a consonant, the soft sign (ь) indicates that the preceding consonant is soft, e.g. день, брать, де́ньги. In addition, the vowels e, ё, и, ю, and я coming after a consonant indicate that the consonant is soft, e.g. нет, нёс, лить, тюрьма́, ряд. A soft consonant is pronounced by placing the tongue closer to the roof of the mouth than in the pronunciation of the equivalent hard consonant. Soft consonants are particularly discernible in the case of the sounds /d, t, n, l/. In British English they can be heard in the words due, tune, new, and illuminate.

In the transcriptions below, a soft consonant is indicated by a /j/ immediately after the consonant, e.g. нет /njet/, except when represented by a soft sign which is transcribed /'/, e.g. лить /ljit'/.

3. Consonants that are always hard or always soft

The consonants ж, ш, and ц are always hard.

If the letter и follows one of these consonants, it is pronounced as if it were ы, e.g. жир /zhyr/, маши́на /mashýnə/, цирк /tsyrk/.

If a stressed e follows one of these consonants, it is pronounced as if it were э, e.g. жечь /zhech'/, шесть /shest'/, це́лый /tsélyj/.

If ё follows ж or ш, it is pronounced /o/, e.g. жёлтый /zhóltyj/, шёл /shol/.

The consonants ч and щ are always soft.

This means that following these consonants the vowels a, o, and y are pronounced /ja/, /jo/, and /ju/, e.g. ча́сто /chjástə/, чуло́к /chjulók/.

4. Unvoicing of voiced consonants and voicing of unvoiced consonants

Voiced consonant sounds (/b, v, g, d, zh, z/) become unvoiced (/p, f, k, t, sh, s/) when they occur

a) at the end of a word, e.g.

хлеб	/khljep/
рука́в	/rukáf/
снег	/snjek/
муж	/mush/
моро́з	/marós/

or

b) before an unvoiced consonant, e.g.

во́дка	/vótkə/
авто́бус	/aftóbus/

Conversely, unvoiced consonant sounds (/p, f, k, t, sh, s/) become voiced (/b, v, g, d, zh, z/) when they occur before another voiced consonant, except before в, e.g.

| сдать | /zdat'/ |
| отдáть | /addát'/ |

but

| отвéт | /atvjét/ (no voicing before в) |

5. Unstressed vowels

The Russian vowels o, e, a, and я change their pronunciation when they are not stressed:

o is pronounced like the stressed Russian a, transcribed /a/, when it appears in the syllable before the stressed syllable, and like the indeterminate vowel in the first syllable of *amaze*, transcribed as /ə/, when it appears after the stressed syllable or more than one syllable before the stressed syllable, e.g.

окнó	/aknó/
ногá	/nagá/
мнóго	/mnógə/
хорошó	/khərashó/

e is pronounced like the Russian и, transcribed /i/, when it is unstressed, unless it follows a hard consonant (ж, ц, ш) when it is pronounced like ы, e.g.

пéрец	/pjérjits/
стенá	/stjiná/
женá	/zhyná/
на ýлице	/na úljitsy/

a is pronounced like a stressed Russian a, transcribed /a/, when it appears in the syllable before the stressed syllable, but like the indeterminate vowel in the first syllable of *amaze*, transcribed /ə/, when it appears after the stressed syllable or more than one syllable before the stressed syllable, e.g.

машúна	/mashýnə/
кассéта	/kasjétə/
магнитофóн	/məgnjitafón/

я is pronounced like the Russian и, transcribed /i/, when it occurs in the syllable before the stressed syllable, and like the indeterminate vowel in the first syllable of *amaze*, transcribed /ə/, when it appears after the stressed syllable or more than one syllable before the stressed syllable, e.g.

пятú	/pjitjí/
язы́к	/jizýk/
языкá	/jəzyká/
тётя	/tjótjə/

6.

г is pronounced as if it were в in the words егó, сегóдня, and other words with the genitive ending -ого, -его, e.g. мáленького, сúнего, ,всегó, ничегó.

7.

ч is pronounced as if it were ш in the words что, чтóбы, and конéчно.

Abbreviations used in the Dictionary
Список условных сокращений

a.	accusative (case)	винительный падеж
abbr.	abbreviat|ion, -ed (to)	сокращение, сокращённо
act.	active (voice)	действительный (залог)
adj., adjs.	adjectiv|e, -al, -es	имя прилагательное, адъективное, имена прилагательные
adv., advs.	adverb, -ial, -s	наречие, наречное, наречия
aeron.	aeronautics	авиация
agric.	agriculture	сельское хозяйство
AmE	American usage	употребительно в Америке
anat.	anatomy	анатомия
archaeol.	archaeology	археология
archit.	architecture	архитектура
astrol.	astrology	астрология
astron.	astronomy	астрономия
attr.	attributive	определительное, атрибутивное
aux.	auxiliary	вспомогательный глагол
bibl.	biblical	библейский термин
biol.	biology	биология
bot.	botany	ботаника
BrE	British usage	употребительно в Великобритании
c.g.	common gender	общий род
chem.	chemistry	химия
cin.	cinema(tography)	кинематография
collect.	collective	собирательное (существительное)
comb.	combin|ation, -ing	сочетание
comm.	commerc|e, -ial	коммерческий термин
comp.	comparative	сравнительная степень
comput.	computing	вычислительная техника
concr.	concrete	конкретный
conj., conjs.	conjunction, -s	союз, -ы
cul.	culinary	кулинария
d.	dative (case)	дательный падеж
det.	determinate	определённый
dim.	diminutive	уменьшительное
eccl.	ecclesiastical	церковный термин
econ.	economics	экономика
elec.	electric|al, -ity	электротехника

emph.	empha|size(s), -sizing; -tic	подчёркива|ть, -ет, -ющее; усилительное
esp.	especially	особенно
euph.	euphemis|m, -tic	эвфеми|зм, -стическое
expr.	express|ed, -es, -ing; -ion	выраж|енный, -ает, -ающее; выражение
f.	feminine	женский род
fem.	female	форма женского рода
fig.	figurative(ly)	в переносном смысле
fin.	financ|e, -ial	финансы, финансовый термин
fut.	future (tense)	будущее время
g.	genitive (case)	родительный падеж
geog.	geography	география
geol.	geology	геология
geom.	geometry	геометрия
gram.	grammar	грамматика
hist.	histor|y, -ical	история
hort.	horticulture	садоводство
i.	instrumental (case); intransitive in *v.i.*	творительный падеж; непереходный глагол
imper.	imperative	повелительное наклонение
impers.	impersonal	безличное
impf.	imperfective	несовершенный вид
indecl.	indeclinable	несклоняемое
indet.	indeterminate	неопределённый
inf.	infinitive	инфинитив
infml	informal	разговорное
inst.	instantaneous	однократный (глагол)
int.	interjection	междометие
interrog.	interrogative	вопросительный
intrans.	intransitive	непереходный глагол
iron.	ironical	ироническое
joc.	jocular	шутливое
ling.	linguistics	лингвистика
lit.	literal(ly)	буквально
liter.	literary	книжное
m.	masculine	мужской род
math.	mathematics	математика
med.	medic|ine, -al	медицин|а, -ский термин
meteor.	meteorology	метеорология
mil.	military	военное дело
min.	mineralogy	минералогия
mus.	music(al)	музыка, -льный термин
myth.	mythology	мифология

n.	noun	имя существительное
naut.	nautical	морское дело
neg.	negative	отрицательный
nn.	nouns	имена существительные
nom.	nominative (case)	именительный падеж
nt.	neuter	средний род
num., nums.	numeral(s)	числительное, числовой, числительные
obj.	object	дополнение
obs.	obsolete	устаревшее слово/выражение
offens.	offensive	оскорбительное
opp.	opposite (to); as opposed to	противоположное
p.	prepositional (case). *See also p.p. and p.p.p.*	предложный падеж
part.	participle	причастие
pass.	passive (voice)	страдательный (залог)
pej.	pejorative	пренебрежительное
pers.	person(s); personal	лиц|о, -а; личный
pert.	pertaining	относительно
pf.	perfective	совершенный вид
phil.	philosophy	философия
philol.	philology	языкознание
phot.	photography	фотография
phr., phrr.	phrase, -s	фраз|а, -ы
physiol.	physiology	физиология
pl.	plural	множественное число
poet.	poet|ical, -ry	поэтическое, поэзия
pol.	political	политический термин
poss.	possessive	притяжательное
p.p.	past participle	причастие второе, причастие прошедшего времени
p.p.p.	past participle passive	страдательное причастие прошедшего времени
pred.	predicate; predicative	сказуемое; предикативный
pref.	prefix	префикс
prep., preps.	preposition, -s	предлог, -и
pres.	present (tense)	настоящее время
pres. part.	present participle	причастие первое, действительное причастие настоящего времени
pron., prons.	pronoun, -s	местоимени|е, -я
pronunc.	pronunciation	произношение
propr.	proprietary term	фирменное название
prov.	proverb	пословица
psych.	psychology	психология
rail.	railway	железнодорожный термин
refl.	reflexive (verb)	возвратный (глагол)
rel.	relative (pronoun)	относительное (местоимение)

relig.	religion	религия
rhet.	rhetorical	высокого стиля
sb	somebody	кто-нибудь
Sc.	Scottish	шотландский (английский) язык
sc.	scilicet	а именно
sg.	singular	единственное число
sl.	slang	сленг
sth	something	что-нибудь
subj.	subject	подлежащее
suff.	suffix	суффикс
superl.	superlative	превосходная степень
t.	transitive in *v.t.*	переходный (глагол)
tech.	technical	техника
teleph.	telephony	телефония
text.	textiles	текстильный термин
theatr.	theatr|e, -ical	театр, театральный термин
trans.	transitive	переходный глагол
TV	television	телевидение
typ.	typography	типографский термин
univ.	university	университетский жаргон
usu.	usually	обычно
v.	verb	глагол
var.	various	разные
v. aux.	auxiliary verb	вспомогательный глагол
vbl.	verbal	отглагольное
v.i.	intransitive verb	непереходный глагол
voc.	vocative (case)	звательный падеж
v.t.	transitive verb	переходный глагол
vulg.	vulgar(ism)	грубое
vv.	verbs	глаголы
zool.	zoology	зоология

The Russian -н. or -л. in illustrative phrases within entries stands for -нибудь or -либо (in the words кто-нибудь, что-нибудь, что-либо, etc.).

This dictionary includes some words which are, or are asserted to be, proprietary names or trademarks. These words are labelled ® or (*propr.*). The presence or absence of this label should not be regarded as affecting the legal status of any proprietary name or trademark.

Aa

⚔ **а¹** *conj.* **1** (*и*) and; **вот ма́рки, а вот три рубля́ сда́чи** here are the stamps and here's three roubles change **2** (*но*) but (*or not translated*); **я иду́ не в кино́, а в теа́тр** I am not going to the cinema, but to the theatre (BrE), theater (AmE); **пиши́ карандашо́м, а не ру́чкой** write in pencil, not pen **3**: **а как же!** (infml) of course!; **а то** or (else), otherwise; **дава́й быстре́е, а то мы опозда́ем!** hurry up or (else) we'll be late!

а² *interrog. particle* (infml) eh?; what('s that)?; huh?

а³ *int.* (infml) ah, oh

абажу́р, а *m.* lampshade

абба́тств|о, а *nt.* abbey

аббревиату́р|а, ы *f.* abbreviation

абза́ц, а *m.* **1** (typ.) indention; **сде́лать а.** to indent; **нача́ть с но́вого ~а** to begin a new line, new paragraph **2** (*часть текста*) paragraph

абитурие́нт, а *m.* (university/college) entrant

абитурие́нт|ка, ки *f. of* ▸ **абитурие́нт**

абонеме́нт, а *m.* (*право пользования чем-н.*) subscription; (*многоразовый билет*) season ticket

абоне́нт, а *m.* (*телефона*) subscriber; (*библиотеки*) borrower, reader; (*театра*) season-ticket holder

абоне́нтск|ий *adj.* subscription; **~ая пла́та** subscription fee

абориге́н, а *m.* aboriginal

або́рт, а *m.* abortion; **сде́лать а.** (*о пациентке*) to have an abortion

абрико́с, а *m.* apricot

⚔ **абсолю́тно** *adv.* absolutely

абсолю́т|ный, ~ен, ~на *adj.* absolute

абстра́кт|ный, ~ен, ~на *adj.* abstract

абстра́кци|я, и *f.* abstraction

абсу́рд, а *m.* absurdity; **довести́ до ~а** to carry to the point of absurdity

абсу́рд|ный, ~ен, ~на *adj.* absurd

абха́з, а *m.* Abkhaz(ian)

абха́з|ка, ки *f. of* ▸ **абха́з**

абха́зский *adj.* Abkhazian

аванга́рд, а *m.* the avant-garde

аванга́рдный *adj. of* ▸ **аванга́рд**

ава́нс, а *m.* **1** (*деньги*) advance **2** (*in pl.*) (fig.) advances, overtures

ава́нсом *adv.* in advance, on account

авантю́р|а, ы *f.* **1** (*приключение*) adventure; escapade **2** (infml) shady enterprise

авантю́р|ный, ~ен, ~на *adj.* adventurous; **а. рома́н** adventure story

авари́йно-спаса́тельный *adj.* (emergency-)rescue, life-saving

авари́йн|ый *adj.* **1** *adj. of* ▸ **ава́рия**; **~ая поса́дка** crash landing; **а. сигна́л** distress signal **2** (*запасной*) emergency, spare

ава́ри|я, и *f.* **1** (*несчастный случай*) crash, accident **2** (*поломка*) breakdown; **потерпе́ть ~ю** to crash, have an accident

⚔ **а́вгуст, а** *m.* August

а́вгустовский *adj. of* ▸ **а́вгуст**

а́виа (*abbr. of* **авиапо́чтой**) '(by) airmail'

авиа... *comb. form, abbr. of* ▸ **авиацио́нный**

авиаба́з|а, ы *f.* air base

авиабиле́т, а *m.* airline ticket

авиадиспе́тчер, а *m.* air traffic controller

авиака́сс|а, ы *f.* air tickets booking office

авиакатастро́ф|а, ы *f.* air crash

авиакомпа́ни|я, и *f.* airline

авиаконстру́ктор, а *m.* aircraft designer

авиала́йнер, а *m.* airliner

авиали́ни|я, и *f.* airway, air route

авиано́с|ец, ца *m.* aircraft carrier

авиапо́чт|а, ы *f.* airmail

авиасало́н, а *m.* air show

авиацио́нно-косми́ческий *adj.* aerospace; **~ая промы́шленность** the aerospace industry

авиацио́нный *adj. of* ▸ **авиа́ция**

авиа́ци|я, и *f.* **1** aviation **2** (collect.) aircraft

ави́зо *nt. indecl.* (fin.) advice note

аво́сь *particle*: **на а.** on the off chance

аво́ськ|а, и *f.* (infml) string bag

австрали́|ец, йца *m.* Australian

австрали́й|ка, ки *f. of* ▸ **австрали́ец**

австрали́йский *adj.* Australian

Австра́ли|я, и *f.* Australia

австри́|ец, йца *m.* Austrian

австри́й|ка, ки *f. of* ▸ **австри́ец**

австри́йский *adj.* Austrian

А́встри|я, и *f.* Austria

а́вто... *comb. form* **1** self-, auto- **2** *abbr. of* ▸ **автомати́ческий**, ▸ **автомоби́льный**

автоба́з|а, ы *f.* motor-transport depot

автобиографи́ческий *adj.* autobiographical

автобиогра́фи|я, и *f.* **1** (*описание своей жизни*) autobiography **2** (*описание своей карьеры*) curriculum vitae, CV

⚔ **авто́бус, а** *m.* bus; (*междугородный*) coach (BrE), bus (AmE)

авто́бусн|ый *adj.* bus; **~ая остано́вка** bus stop; **~ая ста́нция** bus station

автовокза́л, а *m.* bus terminal; coach station (BrE)

a

автого́л, а *m.* (sport) own goal

автого́нк|а, и *f.* car race; (*in pl.*) motor racing (BrE), automobile racing (AmE)

автого́нщик, а *m.* racing driver

авто́граф, а *m.* autograph

автодоро́г|а, и *f.* road; highway

автозаво́д, а *m.* car factory

автозапра́вочн|ый *adj.* filling, refuelling; ∼ая ста́нция petrol *or* filling station

автоинспе́ктор, а *m.* traffic inspector

автоинспе́кци|я, и *f.* traffic inspectorate

автокатастро́ф|а, ы *f.* road accident

автоколо́нн|а, ы *f.* motorcade; (mil.) convoy

автолюби́тель, я *m.* (private) motorist

автомагистра́л|ь, и *f.* motorway (BrE), interstate (highway) (AmE)

автомастерск|а́я, о́й *f.* car repair garage

автома́т, а *m.* **1** automatic machine, slot machine; **биле́тный а.** ticket machine; **игрово́й а.** fruit machine, slot machine; **телефо́н-а.** payphone; (fig.) automaton, robot **2** (mil.) submachine gun

автоматиза́ци|я, и *f.* automation

автоматизи́рованн|ый *adj.* computer-aided; ∼ое проекти́рование CAD, computer-aided design

автоматизи́р|овать, ую *impf. and pf.* to automate

автома́тик|а, и *f.* **1** (*отрасль науки*) automation **2** (*автоматические механизмы*) automatic equipment

✎ **автомати́ческий** *adj.* **1** (tech.) automatic **2** (fig.) automatic, involuntary

автома́тчик, а *m.* (mil.) soldier armed with a submachine gun

автомаши́н|а, ы *f.* motor vehicle

автомеха́ник, а *m.* car mechanic

автомобили́ст, а *m.* motorist

✎ **автомоби́л|ь, я** *m.* motor vehicle; (motor)car; **легково́й а.** car; **грузово́й а.** lorry; **води́ть а.** to drive a car

✎ **автомоби́льный** *adj. of* ▶ **автомоби́ль**

автоно́ми|я, и *f.* autonomy

автоно́м|ный, ∼ен, ∼на *adj.* autonomous; (comput.) stand-alone

автоотве́тчик, а *m.* answering machine

автопило́т, а *m.* autopilot

автопортре́т, а *m.* self-portrait

автоприце́п, а *m.* trailer; **жило́й а.** caravan (BrE), mobile home; **тури́стский а.** caravan (BrE), camper (AmE)

✎ **а́втор, а** *m.* author

авторизо́ванный *adj.* (*издание, перевод*) authorized

авторита́р|ный, ∼ен, ∼на *adj.* authoritarian

авторите́т, а *m.* authority; **по́льзоваться ∼ом** to enjoy authority, command respect

авторите́т|ный, ∼ен, ∼на *adj.* authoritative

а́втор|ский *adj. of* ▶ **а́втор; а. гонора́р** royalty, royalties; ∼ское пра́во copyright

а́вторств|о, а *nt.* authorship

авторучк|а, и *f.* fountain pen

автосало́н, а *m.* **1** (*магазин*) car showroom **2** (*выставка*) motor show

автосе́рвис, а *m.* garage (*usu. one that repairs cars, but sometimes one that sells petrol, etc.*)

автосто́п, а *m.* (*способ путешествия*) hitch-hiking; **путеше́ствовать** (*impf.*) ∼ом to hitch-hike

автостоя́нк|а, и *f.* car park

автостра́д|а, ы *f.* motorway (BrE), interstate (highway) (AmE)

автотра́нспорт, а *m.* motor transport

автошко́л|а, ы *f.* driving school; **преподава́тель** (*m.*) ∼ы driving instructor

ага́ *int.* (infml) (*выражает злорадство*) aha!; (*выражает согласие*) uh-huh

аге́нт, а *m.* agent (*in var. senses*)

✎ **аге́нтств|о, а** *nt.* agency; **а. печа́ти** news agency, press agency; **информацио́нное/ телегра́фное а.** news agency

агенту́р|а, ы *f.* **1** (*служба*) secret service **2** (collect.) agents

агита́тор, а *m.* (pol.) agitator; campaigner

агитацио́нн|ый *adj.* (pol.) agitation; ∼ая речь campaign speech

агита́ци|я, и *f.* (pol.) agitation; campaign; **вести́ ∼ю** to campaign; **предвы́борная а.** electioneering

агити́р|овать, ую *impf.* (pol.) (**за** + *a.*) to agitate, campaign (for)

аго́ни|я, и *f.* (med., also fig.) death throes

агорафо́бия, и *f.* agoraphobia

агра́рный *adj.* agrarian

агрега́т, а *m.* **1** (*часть машины*) unit **2** (*соединение нескольких машин*) assembly

агресси́в|ный, ∼ен, ∼на *adj.* aggressive

агре́сси|я, и *f.* (pol.) aggression

агре́ссор, а *m.* aggressor

агро... *comb. form* agro-, agricultural, farm

агроно́м, а *m.* agronomist

агроно́ми|я, и *f.* agronomy; agricultural science

агропромы́шленный *adj.* agro-industrial

ад, а *m.* hell

адапта́ци|я, и *f.* adaptation (*in var. senses*)

ада́птер, а *m.* (tech.) adapter

адапти́р|овать, ую *impf. and pf.* to adapt

адапти́р|оваться, уюсь *impf. and pf.* to adapt; to get used to sth

адвока́т, а *m.* (*поверенный*) solicitor, lawyer; (*выступающий в суде*) barrister (BrE), attorney (AmE); (fig.) advocate

адвокату́р|а, ы *f.* **1** (*деятельность адвоката*) the legal profession; practising law **2** (collect.) lawyers; the Bar (BrE)

адеква́т|ный, ∼ен, ∼на *adj.* appropriate

✎ **администрати́в|ный** *adj.* administrative; **в ∼ом поря́дке** by administrative order

администра́тор, а *m.* administrator; manager (*of hotel, theatre, etc.*)

◦ **администра́ци|я, и** *f.* administration; management

адмира́л, а *m.* admiral

адренали́н, а *m.* adrenalin

◦ **а́дрес, а,** *pl.* ~**а́,** ~**о́в** *m.* address; **в а.** (+ *g.*) addressed to; (fig.) directed at; **не по** ~**у** (fig.) to the wrong quarter

адреса́т, а *m.* addressee; **в слу́чае ненахожде́ния** ~**а** 'if undelivered'; **за ненахожде́нием** ~**а** 'not known' (*on letters*)

а́дрес|ный *adj.* of ▶ **а́дрес;** ~**ная кни́га** directory; **а. стол** address bureau

адресова́ть, у́ю *impf. and pf.* (*письмо*) to address; (*критику, вопрос*) to direct

Адриати́ческ|ое мо́ре, ~**ого мо́ря** *nt.* the Adriatic (Sea)

а́дский *adj.* infernal, diabolical; (fig.) hellish, intolerable

адъюта́нт, а *m.* (mil.) aide-de-camp

аза́рт|ный, ~**ен,** ~**на** *adj.* excited, ardent; ~**ная игра́** game of chance

а́збук|а, и *f.* alphabet; the ABC (also fig.)

Азербайджа́н, а *m.* Azerbaijan

азербайджа́н|ец, ца *m.* Azerbaijani

азербайджа́н|ка, ки *f. of* ▶ **азербайджа́нец**

азербайджа́нский *adj.* Azerbaijani

азиа́т, а *m.* Asian

азиа́т|ка, ки *f. of* ▶ **азиа́т**

азиа́тский *adj.* Asian

А́зи|я, и *f.* Asia

Азо́вск|ое мо́ре, ~**ого мо́ря** *nt.* the Sea of Azov

азо́т, а *m.* (chem.) nitrogen

а́ист, а *m.* (zool.) stork

ай *int.* (*выражает страх, испуг*) oh!; (*выражает боль*) ow!, ouch!; **ай, бо́льно!** ow, that hurts!; **ай да ...!** (*выражает одобрение*) what a ...!; **ай да молоде́ц!** well done!

а́йсберг, а *m.* iceberg

акаде́мик, а *m.* academician (*member of a specific academy*)

академи́ческий *adj.* academic; **а. о́тпуск** sabbatical (leave) (*for undergraduates or postgraduates*)

академи́ч|ный, ~**ен,** ~**на** *adj.* academic, theoretical

◦ **акаде́ми|я, и** *f.* academy

аквала́нг, а *m.* aqualung

акваланги́ст, а *m.* (skin *or* scuba) diver

акваланги́ст|ка, ки *f. of* ▶ **акваланги́ст**

акваре́л|ь, и *f.* (*краски*) watercolours (BrE), watercolors (AmE); **писа́ть** ~**ью** to paint in watercolours; (*картина*) watercolour (BrE), watercolor (AmE)

аква́риум, а *m.* fish tank, aquarium

акклиматиза́ци|я, и *f.* acclimatization

акклиматизи́р|овать, ую *impf. and pf.* to acclimatize

акклиматизи́р|оваться, уюсь *impf. and pf.* to become acclimatized, acclimatize

аккомпанеме́нт, а *m.* (mus.) accompaniment (also fig.); **под а.** (+ *g.*) to the accompaniment of

аккомпани́р|овать, ую *impf.* (+ *d.*) (mus.) to accompany; **а. певцу́ на роя́ле** to accompany a singer on the piano

акко́рд, а *m.* (mus.) chord

аккордео́н, а *m.* accordion

аккордеони́ст, а *m.* accordionist

аккордеони́ст|ка, ки *f. of* ▶ **аккордеони́ст**

аккумули́р|овать, ую *impf. and pf.* to accumulate

аккумуля́тор, а *m.* (tech.) accumulator; (elec.) accumulator (BrE), storage battery (AmE)

аккура́тност|ь, и *f.* ◼ (*тщательность*) exactness, thoroughness ◼ (*опрятность*) tidiness, neatness

аккура́т|ный, ~**ен,** ~**на** *adj.* ◼ (*тщательный*) exact, thorough ◼ (*опрятный*) tidy, neat ◼ (*регулярный*) regular, punctual

акри́л, а *m.* acrylic

акри́ловый *adj.* of ▶ **акри́л**

акроба́т, а *m.* acrobat

акселера́тор, а *m.* accelerator

аксессуа́р, а *m.* ◼ accessory ◼ (*in pl.*) (theatr.) props

аксио́м|а, ы *f.* axiom

◦ **акт, а** *m.* ◼ act; **полово́й а.** sexual intercourse ◼ (theatr.) act ◼ (law) deed, document; **обвини́тельный а.** indictment

◦ **актёр, а** *m.* actor

актёрский *adj.* of ▶ **актёр**

акти́в, а *m.* (fin.) assets

активизи́р|овать, ую *impf. and pf.* (*приводить в действие*) to activate; (*оживлять*) to stimulate, enliven

активи́ст, а *m.* (pol.) activist

активи́ст|ка, ки *f. of* ▶ **активи́ст**

◦ **акти́вность|, и** *f.* activity (*being active*)

◦ **акти́в|ный,** ~**ен,** ~**на** *adj.* active, energetic

актри́с|а, ы *f.* actress

◦ **актуа́л|ьный,** ~**ен,** ~**ьна** *adj.* topical, current

аку́л|а, ы *f.* (zool.) shark (also fig.)

аку́стик|а, и *f.* acoustics

акусти́ческий *adj.* acoustic

акуше́р, а *m.* obstetrician

акуше́рк|а, и *f.* midwife

акуше́рск|ий *adj.* obstetric(al)

акце́нт, а *m.* accent

акценти́р|овать, ую *impf. and pf.* to accentuate

акционе́р, а *m.* shareholder, stockholder

акционе́р|ный *adj.* of ▶ **акционе́р;** ~**ное о́бщество** joint-stock company

◦ **а́кци|я¹, и** *f.* (fin.) share

а́кци|я², и *f.* action

алба́н|ец, ца *m.* Albanian

Алба́ни|я, и *f.* Albania

алба́н|ка, ки *f. of* ▶ **алба́нец**

алба́нский *adj.* Albanian

а́лгебр|а, ы *f.* algebra

a

алгори́тм, a *m.* algorithm
алеба́стр, a *m.* alabaster
Алжи́р, a *m.* **1** (*страна́*) Algeria **2** (*столи́ца*) Algiers
алжи́р|ец, ца *m.* Algerian
алжи́р|ка, ки *f. of* ▶ **алжи́рец**
алжи́рский *adj.* Algerian
а́либи *nt. indecl.* (law) alibi
алиме́нт|ы, ов (*no sg.*) (law) alimony
алкоголи́зм, a *m.* alcoholism
алкого́лик, a *m.* alcoholic; (infml) drunkard
алкого́л|ь, я *m.* alcohol; **прове́рить на а.** to breathalyse (BrE), breathalyze (AmE)
алкого́льный *adj.* alcoholic
Алла́х, a *m.* Allah
аллего́ри|я, и *f.* allegory
аллерги́ческий *adj.* allergic
аллерги́|я, и *f.* allergy; **а. на клубни́ку** an allergy to strawberries
алле́|я, и *f.* tree-lined path, avenue
аллига́тор, a *m.* alligator
алло́ *int.* hello!
алма́з, a *m.* (uncut) diamond
алта́р|ь, я́ *m.* **1** (*же́ртвенник*) altar **2** (*восто́чная часть це́ркви*) chancel
алфави́т, a *m.* alphabet; (comput., typ.) character set
алфави́тный *adj.* alphabetical; **а. указа́тель** index
алхи́мик, a *m.* alchemist
алхи́ми|я, и *f.* alchemy
а́лч|ный, ~ен, ~на *adj.* greedy, grasping
а́л|ый, ~, ~а *adj.* scarlet
альбо́м, a *m.* (*кни́га; пласти́нка, диск*) album
альмана́х, a *m.* anthology
альпи́йский *adj.* alpine
альпини́зм, a *m.* mountaineering
альпини́ст, a *m.* mountain-climber, mountaineer
альпини́ст|ка, ки *f. of* ▶ **альпини́ст**
А́льп|ы, ~ (*no sg.*) the Alps
альт, а́ *m.* (mus.) **1** (*певе́ц, го́лос*) alto **2** (*инструме́нт*) viola
альтернати́в|а, ы *f.* alternative
альтернати́в|ный, ~ен, ~на *adj.* alternative
альти́ст, a *m.* viola player
альти́ст|ка, ки *f. of* ▶ **альти́ст**
альт|о́вый *adj. of* ▶ **альт**; **~о́вая па́ртия** alto part; **а. конце́рт** viola concerto
альтруи́зм, a *m.* altruism
альтруисти́ческий *adj.* altruistic
алья́нс, a *m.* alliance
алюми́ниевый *adj.* aluminium (BrE), aluminum (AmE)
алюми́ни|й, я *m.* aluminium (BrE), aluminum (AmE)
Аля́ск|а, и *f.* Alaska

амбицио́з|ный, ~ен, ~на *adj.* arrogant, conceited
амби́ци|я, и *f.* **1** arrogance **2** (*in pl.*) (**на** + *a.*) claims (to)
амбулато́ри|я, и *f.* (med.) (*в больни́це*) outpatient department; (*кабине́т врача́*) doctor's surgery (BrE), doctor's office (AmE)
амбулато́рный *adj. of* ▶ **амбулато́рия**; **а. больно́й** outpatient; **а. приём** outpatient reception hours; surgery hours
Аме́рик|а, и *f.* America
америка́н|ец, ца *m.* American
америка́н|ка, ки *f. of* ▶ **америка́нец**
⚥ **америка́нский** *adj.* American
аммиа́к, a *m.* (chem.) ammonia
амнисти́р|овать, ую *impf. and pf.* to amnesty
амни́сти|я, и *f.* amnesty
амора́л|ьный, ~ен, ~ьна *adj.* (*нейтра́льный в отноше́нии мора́ли*) amoral; (*безнра́вственный*) immoral
амортиза́тор, a *m.* (tech.) shock absorber
амортиза́ци|я, и *f.* (econ.) amortization, depreciation
амортизи́р|овать, ую *impf. and pf.* (econ.) to amortize
амо́рф|ный, ~ен, ~на *adj.* amorphous
ампе́р, a, *g. pl.* **a.** *m.* (phys.) ampere
ампи́р, a *m.* Empire style (*of furniture, etc.*)
амплиту́д|а, ы *f.* amplitude
амплуа́ *nt. indecl.* (theatr.) type; (fig.) role
а́мпул|а, ы *f.* ampoule (BrE), ampule (AmE)
ампута́ци|я, и *f.* amputation
ампути́р|овать, ую *impf. and pf.* to amputate
Амстерда́м, a *m.* Amsterdam
амуле́т, a *m.* amulet
амуни́ци|я, и *f.* (collect.) (mil., hist.) accoutrements (BrE), accouterments (AmE)
амфи́би|я, и *f.* amphibian
амфитеа́тр, a *m.* (hist.) amphitheatre (BrE), amphitheater (AmE); (theatr.) circle
⚥ **ана́лиз**, a *m.* analysis; **а. кро́ви** blood test
анализи́р|овать, ую *impf. and pf.* (*pf. also* ▶ **проанализи́ровать**) to analyse (BrE), analyze (AmE)
анали́тик, a *m.* analyst
аналити́ческий *adj.* analytic(al)
ана́лог, a *m.* analogue
⚥ **аналоги́ч|ный, ~ен, ~на** *adj.* analogous
анало́ги|я, и *f.* analogy; **по ~и** (**с** + *i.*) by analogy (with), on the analogy (of); **проводи́ть ~ю** to draw an analogy
анана́с, a *m.* pineapple
анархи́ст, a *m.* anarchist
анархи́ческий *adj.* anarchic(al)
ана́рхи|я, и *f.* anarchy
анатоми́ческий *adj.* anatomical
анато́ми|я, и *f.* anatomy
анахрони́зм, a *m.* anachronism
анаша́, й *f.* (sl.) pot, hash
анга́р, a *m.* (aeron.) hangar

а́нгел, а *m.* angel; **а.-храни́тель** guardian angel; **день** ∼**а** name day

а́нгельский *adj.* angelic

анги́н|а, ы *f.* (med.) quinsy; tonsillitis

⚲ **англи́йск|ий** *adj.* English; ∼**ая була́вка** safety pin

англика́н|ец, ца *m.* Anglican

англика́н|ка, ки *f. of* ▶ **англика́нец**

англика́нский *adj.* (eccl.) Anglican

англича́н|ин, ина, *pl.* ∼**е,** ∼ *m.* Englishman

англича́нк|а, и *f.* Englishwoman

А́нгли|я, и *f.* England

англоса́кс, а *m.* Anglo-Saxon

англосаксо́нский *adj.* Anglo-Saxon

англоязы́чный *adj.* 🔳 (*англоговорящий*) English-speaking, anglophone 🔳 (*на англи́йском языке́*) English-language

Анго́л|а, ы *f.* Angola

анго́л|ец, ьца *m.* Angolan

анго́л|ка, ки *f. of* ▶ **анго́лец**

анго́льский *adj.* Angolan

андегра́унд, а *m.* (sl.) underground

А́нд|ы, ∼ (*no sg.*) the Andes

анекдо́т, а *m.* 🔳 (*рассказ*) anecdote, story 🔳 (*шутка*) joke

анеми́|я, и *f.* anaemia (BrE), anemia (AmE)

анестезио́лог, а *m.* anaesthetist (BrE), anesthetist (AmE)

анестези́р|овать, ую *impf. and pf.* to anaesthetize (BrE), anesthetize (AmE)

анестези́|я, и *f.* (med.) anaesthesia (BrE), anesthesia (AmE)

ани́с, а *m.* 🔳 (*растение*) anise 🔳 (*семя*) aniseed

Анкар|а́, ы́ *m.* Ankara

анке́т|а, ы *f.* (*опросный лист*) questionnaire; (*бланк*) form

анке́т|ный *adj. of* ▶ **анке́та;** ∼**ные да́нные** biographical details

аннекси́р|овать, ую *impf. and pf.* (pol.) to annex

аннота́ци|я, и *f.* abstract, precis

аннули́р|овать, ую *impf. and pf.* (*договор*) to annul, nullify; (*долг*) to cancel; (*закон*) to abrogate

анома́ли|я, и *f.* anomaly

анони́мк|а, и *f.* (infml, *письмо*) poison pen letter

анони́м|ный, ∼**ен,** ∼**на** *adj.* anonymous

ано́нс, а *m.* announcement, notice; (cin.) trailer

анса́мбл|ь, я *m.* ensemble

Антаркти́д|а, ы *f.* Antarctica

Анта́рктик|а, и *f.* the Antarctic

антаркти́ческий *adj.* Antarctic

анте́нн|а, ы *f.* aerial, antenna

анти... *pref.* anti-

антиалкого́льный *adj.* anti-alcohol

антибио́тик, а *m.* (med.) antibiotic

антивое́нный *adj.* anti-war

антидепресса́нт, а *m.* (med.) antidepressant

антикапиталисти́ческий *adj.* anticapitalist

антиква́р, а *m.* (*любитель антикварных предметов*) antiquary; (*дилер*) antique dealer

антиквариа́т, а *m.* (collect.) antiques

антиква́рный *adj.* (*книга*) antiquarian; (*ваза; магазин*) antique

антило́п|а, ы *f.* (zool.) antelope

антипа́ти|я, и *f.* antipathy

антисеми́т, а *m.* anti-Semite

антисемити́зм, а *m.* anti-Semitism

антисеми́т|ка, ки *f. of* ▶ **антисеми́т**

антисеми́тский *adj.* anti-Semitic

антисе́птик, а *m.* antiseptic

антитеррористи́ческий *adj.* antiterrorist

антицикло́н, а *m.* (meteor.) anticyclone

анти́чный *adj.* ancient; classical

антра́кт, а *m.* (theatr.) interval

антраци́т, а *m.* (min.) anthracite

антреко́т, а *m.* entrecôte, steak

антрепри́з|а, ы *f.* (theatr.) private theatrical company

антресо́л|ь, и *f.* (*usu. in pl.*) 🔳 (*полуэтаж*) mezzanine 🔳 (*полка*) shelf

антропо́лог, а *m.* anthropologist

антропологи́ческий *adj.* anthropological

антрополо́ги|я, и *f.* anthropology

антура́ж, а *m.* environment; (collect.) entourage, associates

анчо́ус, а *m.* anchovy

аншла́г, а *m.* (theatr.) sell-out notice; **спекта́кль идёт с** ∼**ом** the show is sold out

АО (*abbr. of* **акционе́рное о́бщество**) joint-stock company

апартаме́нт|ы, ов *m. pl.* (*sg.* ∼, ∼**а**) large apartment

апарте́йд, а *m.* apartheid

апа́ти|я, и *f.* apathy

апгре́йд, а *m.* (comput., infml) upgrade

апелли́р|овать, ую *impf. and pf.* (**к** + *d.*) to appeal (to)

апелляцио́нный *adj. of* ▶ **апелля́ция; а. суд** Court of Appeal (*in England and Wales*); court of appeals (AmE)

апелля́ци|я, и *f.* 🔳 (*обращение*) (**к** + *d.*) appeal (to) 🔳 (*обжалование*) (**на** + *a.*) appeal (against)

апельси́н, а *m.* orange

апельси́новый *adj.* orange

Апенни́н|ы, ∼ (*no sg.*) the Apennines

аперити́в, а *m.* aperitif

аплоди́р|овать, ую *impf.* (+ *d.*) to applaud

аплодисме́нт|ы, ов *m. pl.* applause

апоге́|й, я *m.* (astron.) apogee; (fig.) climax

апока́липсис, а *m.* apocalypse

апокалипти́ческий *adj.* apocalyptic

аполити́ч|ный, ∼**ен,** ∼**на** *adj.* apolitical; politically indifferent

апо́стол, а *m.* apostle (also fig.)

апостро́ф, а *m.* apostrophe

a

апофеóз, *a m.* apotheosis

Аппала́ч|и, ей (*no sg.*) the Appalachians

✍ **аппара́т**, **а** *m.* **1** (*прибор*) apparatus; appliance; **копирова́льный а.** photocopier; **косми́ческий аппара́т** spacecraft; **ка́ссовый а.** cash register; **слуховóй а.** hearing aid; **телефóнный а.** telephone **2** (*учреждения*): **госуда́рственный а.** machinery of state **3** (*штат*) staff, personnel

аппара́тн|ый *adj.* (comput.) hardware; **~ые сре́дства** hardware

аппарату́р|а, ы *f.* (tech.) (*collect.*) apparatus, equipment; (comput.) hardware

аппéндикс, а *m.* appendix

аппендици́т, а *m.* appendicitis

аппети́т, а *m.* appetite; **прия́тного ~а!** bon appétit!

аппети́т|ный, ~ен, ~на *adj.* appetizing, mouth-watering

аппликáци|я, и *f.* appliqué

✍ **апрéл|ь, я** *m.* April

апрéльский *adj. of* ▶ **апрéль**

аптéк|а, и *f.* chemist's (shop) (BrE), pharmacy

аптéкар|ь, я *m.* chemist (BrE); pharmacist

аптéчк|а, и *f.* (*первой помощи*) first-aid kit; (*коробка*) medicine chest

ара́б, а *m.* Arab

ара́б|ка, ки *f. of* ▶ **ара́б**

ара́бск|ий *adj.* Arab; Arabian; Arabic; **А~ая весна́** Arab spring; **~ие ци́фры** Arabic numerals; **а. язы́к** Arabic

арави́йский *adj.* Arabian

аранжирóвк|а, и *f.* arrangement

ара́хис, а *m.* peanut, groundnut

арбалéт, а *m.* crossbow

арби́тр, а *m.* (*в споре*) arbiter, arbitrator; (*в спорте*) umpire, referee

арбитра́ж, а *m.* arbitration

арбитра́жный *adj.*: **а. суд** court of arbitration

арбу́з, а *m.* watermelon

Аргенти́н|а, ы *f.* Argentina

аргенти́н|ец, ца *m.* Argentinian

аргенти́н|ка, ки *f. of* ▶ **аргенти́нец**

аргенти́нский *adj.* Argentinian, Argentine

аргумéнт, а *m.* argument

аргумента́ци|я, и *f.* reasoning, argumentation

аргументи́р|овать, ую *impf. and pf.* to argue; (*pf. only*) to prove

арéал, а *m.* (bot. and zool.) natural habitat; (fig.) region

арéн|а, ы *f.* arena, ring; (fig.) arena

✍ **арéнд|а, ы** *f.* lease; **сдать в ~у** to rent, lease (*of owner, landlord*); **взять в ~у** to rent, lease (*of tenant*)

аренда́тор, а *m.* tenant, lessee

арéнд|ный *adj. of* ▶ **арéнда**; **~ная пла́та** rent; **а. подря́д** contract for lease (*of land*)

арéнд|овать, ую *impf. and pf.* to rent, lease (*of tenant*)

✍ key word

арéст, а *m.* (*человека*) arrest; (*имущества*) seizure, sequestration; **взять под а.** to place under arrest; **сидéть, находи́ться под ~ом** to be under arrest, in custody; **наложи́ть а. на** (+ *a.*) to sequestrate

ареста́нт, а *m.* prisoner

арест|ова́ть, у́ю *pf.* (*of* ▶ **аресто́вывать**) (*человека*) to arrest; (*имущество*) to sequestrate

аресто́выва|ть, ю *impf. of* ▶ **арестова́ть**

аристокра́т, а *m.* aristocrat

аристократи́ческий *adj.* aristocratic

аристокра́ти|я, и *f.* aristocracy

арифмéтик|а, и *f.* arithmetic

арифмети́ческий *adj.* arithmetical

а́ри|я, и *f.* aria

а́рк|а, и *f.* arch

арка́н, а *m.* lasso

А́рктик|а, и *f.* the Arctic

аркти́ческий *adj.* arctic

армéйский *adj. of* ▶ **а́рмия**

Армéни|я, и *f.* Armenia

✍ **а́рми|я, и** *f.* army; **А. спасéния** Salvation Army; **дéйствующая а.** front-line forces

армя́н|ин, и́на, *pl.* **~е, ~** *m.* Armenian

армя́н|ка, ки *f. of* ▶ **армяни́н**

армя́нский *adj.* Armenian

аромáт, а *m.* (*цветов*) scent, fragrance; (*пищи*) aroma

ароматиза́тор, а *m.* (cul.) flavouring (BrE), flavoring (AmE)

аромáт|ный, ~ен, ~на *adj.* aromatic, fragrant

арсена́л, а *m.* arsenal

арт… ** *comb. form* **1 (*abbr. of* **артиллери́йский**) artillery **2** (*искусство*) art

артéри|я, и *f.* artery

арти́кл|ь, я *m.* (gram.) article

артиллери́йский *adj.* (mil.) artillery; **а. обстрéл** bombardment, shelling; **а. склад** ordnance depot

артиллéри|я, и *f.* artillery

арти́ст, а *m.* artist(e); **а. балéта** ballet dancer; **а. кинó** film actor

артисти́ческ|ий *adj.* artistic; (*as f. n.* **~ая, ~ой**) (theatr.) dressing room

арти́ст|ка, ки *f. of* ▶ **арти́ст**

артри́т, а *m.* arthritis

а́рф|а, ы *f.* harp

арфи́ст, а *m.* harpist

арфи́ст|ка, ки *f. of* ▶ **арфи́ст**

архаи́ч|ный, ~ен, ~на *adj.* archaic

археóлог, а *m.* archaeologist (BrE), archeologist (AmE)

археологи́ческий *adj.* archaeological (BrE), archeological (AmE)

археолóги|я, и *f.* archaeology (BrE), archeology (AmE)

✍ **архи́в, а** *m.* archive; (*collect.*) archives; **сдать в а.** (infml, fig.) to shelve, leave out of account

архи́вный *adj. of* ▶ **архи́в**

архиепи́скоп, а *m.* archbishop

архиере́|й, я *m.* member of higher orders of clergy (*bishop, archbishop, or metropolitan*)

архипела́г, а *m.* archipelago

архите́ктор, а *m.* architect

архитекту́р|а, ы *f.* architecture

архитекту́рный *adj.* architectural

арьерга́рд, а *m.* (mil.) rearguard

асбе́ст, а *m.* asbestos

асоциа́льный *adj.* antisocial

аспе́кт, а *m.* (*сторона*) aspect; (*точка зрения*) viewpoint, perspective

аспира́нт, а *m.* postgraduate student

аспира́нт|ка, ки *f. of* ▸ аспира́нт

аспиранту́р|а, ы *f.* postgraduate study

аспири́н, а *m.* (med.) aspirin; табле́тка ∼а an aspirin

ассамбле́|я, и *f.* assembly

ассениза́тор, а *m.* sewage worker

ассигн|ова́ть, у́ю *impf. and pf.* (fin.) to assign, allocate

ассимиля́ци|я, и *f.* assimilation

ассисте́нт, а *m.* **1** (*помощник*) assistant **2** (*в вузе*) junior member of teaching or research staff

ассисти́р|овать, ую *impf.* (med.) (+ *d.*) to assist

ассортиме́нт, а *m.* assortment; range (*of goods*)

⚡ **ассоциа́ци|я**, и *f.* association

ассоции́р|овать, ую *impf. and pf.* (с + *i.*) to associate (with)

астеро́ид, а *m.* asteroid

а́стм|а, ы *f.* asthma

астма́тик, а *m.* asthmatic

а́стр|а, ы *f.* aster

астро́лог, а *m.* astrologer

астрологи́ческий *f.* astrological

астроло́ги|я, и *f.* astrology

астрона́вт, а *m.* astronaut

астроно́м, а *m.* astronomer

астрономи́ческий *adj.* astronomic(al) (also fig.)

астроно́ми|я, и *f.* astronomy

астрофи́зик|а, и *f.* astrophysics

асфа́льт, а *m.* asphalt

ата́к|а, и *f.* attack

атак|ова́ть, у́ю *impf. and pf.* (mil., sport) to attack

атама́н, а *m.* ataman (*Cossack chieftain*)

атеи́зм, а *m.* atheism

атеи́ст, а *m.* atheist

атеи́ст|ка, ки *f. of* ▸ атеи́ст

ателье́ *nt. indecl.* studio; а. мод tailor's shop

Атланти́ческий океа́н, ∼ого океа́на *m.* the Atlantic Ocean; the Atlantic

а́тлас, а *m.* atlas

атла́с, а *m.* satin

атле́т, а *m.* (*спортсмен*) athlete; (*в цирке*) strongman

атле́тик|а, и *f.* athletics; лёгкая а. (track and field) athletics; тяжёлая а. weightlifting

атлети́ческ|ий *adj.* athletic; ∼ое телосложе́ние athletic build

⚡ **атмосфе́р|а**, ы *f.* atmosphere

атмосфе́рн|ый *adj.* atmospheric; ∼ые оса́дки atmospheric precipitation, rainfall

а́том, а *m.* atom

а́томн|ый *adj.* atomic; nuclear; ∼ая бо́мба atomic bomb; ∼ая электроста́нция nuclear power station

атрибу́т, а *m.* attribute

атрибу́тик|а, и *f.* **1** (collect.) (*атрибуты*) attributes **2** merchandise (*e.g. of a football club*)

АТС *f. indecl.* (*abbr. of* автомати́ческая телефо́нная ста́нция) automatic telephone exchange

атташе́ *m. indecl.* (pol.) attaché

аттеста́т, а *m.* certificate

аттестацио́нн|ый *adj.*: ∼ая коми́ссия examination board

аттеста́ци|я, и *f.* (*действие*) certification; (*отзыв*) reference

аттест|ова́ть, у́ю *impf. and pf.* (*присвоить звание*) to certify; (*оценить знания*) to grade, give a mark

аттракцио́н, а *m.* (theatr.) attraction; sideshow, ride (*at fairground*); парк ∼ов amusement park

аудие́нци|я, и *f.* audience (*official interview*)

ауди́т, а *m.* audit

ауди́тор, а *m.* auditor

аудито́ри|я, и *f.* **1** auditorium; lecture hall **2** (collect.) audience

аукцио́н, а *m.* auction, auction sale; продава́ть с ∼а to auction

а́ут, а *m.* (sport) out (*also as int.*)

аутенти́чн|ый, ∼ен, ∼на *adj.* authentic

аути́зм, а *m.* autism

афга́н|ец, ца *m.* Afghan; «а.» Afghan war vet(eran)

Афганиста́н, а *m.* Afghanistan

афга́н|ка, ки *f. of* ▸ афга́нец

афе́р|а, ы *f.* swindle, trickery

афери́ст, а *m.* swindler, trickster

афери́ст|ка, ки *f. of* ▸ афери́ст

Афи́н|ы, ∼ (*no sg.*) Athens

афи́ш|а, и *f.* poster, placard; театра́льная а. playbill

афори́зм, а *m.* aphorism

А́фрик|а, и *f.* Africa

африка́н|ец, ца *m.* African

африка́н|ка, ки *f. of* ▸ африка́нец

африка́нский *adj.* African

афроамерика́н|ец, ца *m.* African American

афроамерика́н|ка, ки *f. of* ▸ афроамерика́нец

афроамерика́нский *adj.* African-American

ах *int.* ah! oh!

аэро... *comb. form* aero-; air-, aerial

а

б

аэро́бик|а, и *f.* aerobics
аэровокза́л, а *m.* air terminal
аэродина́мик|а, и *f.* aerodynamics
аэродинами́ческий *adj.* aerodynamic
аэродро́м, а *m.* aerodrome
аэрозо́л|ь, я *m.* aerosol, spray

аэрона́втик|а, и *f.* aeronautics
⚓ аэропо́рт, а, об ~е, в ~у́ *m.* airport
АЭС *f. indecl.* (*abbr. of* а́томная
  электроста́нция) atomic power station
а/я *m. indecl.* (*abbr. of* абоне́нтский я́щик)
  PO (*abbr. of post office*) Box

Бб

⚓ **б** *particle* = бы (*after words ending in vowel*)
ба́б|а, ы *f.* (infml, also pej.) woman; сне́жная б.
  snowman
ба́бк|а, и *f.* = ба́бушка
ба́б|ки, ок *pl.* (infml) money
ба́бочк|а, и *f.* 1 butterfly; ночна́я б. moth;
  (*проститутка*) prostitute 2 (*галстук*)
  bow tie
ба́бушк|а, и *f.* grandmother; (infml) old
  woman; gran(ny) (*as mode of address*)
бага́ж, а́ *m.* luggage; сдать свои́ ве́щи в б.
  to register one's luggage, to check in one's
  luggage
бага́жник, а *m.* (*в автомобиле*) boot
  (BrE), trunk (AmE); (*на крыше*) roof rack;
  (*велосипеда*) carrier
бага́жный *adj. of* ▶ бага́ж; б. ваго́н luggage
  van (BrE), baggage car (AmE)
Багда́д, а *m.* Baghdad
багро́в|ый, ~, ~а *adj.* crimson, purple
бадминто́н, а *m.* badminton
бадминтони́ст, а *m.* badminton player
бадминтони́ст|ка, ки *f. of* ▶ бадминтони́ст
бад|ья́, ьи́, *g. pl.* ~е́й *f.* tub
⚓ ба́з|а, ы *f.* 1 (mil., archit.) base; (*склад*) depot;
  (*туристов*) centre (BrE), center (AmE); б.
  да́нных database 2 (*основание*) basis; на
  ~е (+ *g.*) on the basis (of)
база́р, а *m.* (infml) market
база́рный *adj. of* ▶ база́р; (infml) of the
  marketplace, rough, crude
бази́р|оваться, уюсь *impf.* (на + *p.*) 1 to
  be based (on) 2 (mil.) to be based (at)
ба́зис, а *m.* (archit.) base; (*основание*) basis
⚓ ба́зов|ый *adj.* 1 basic; б. курс foundation
  course 2 : б. ла́герь base camp
базу́к|а, и *f.* bazooka
байда́рк|а, и *f.* kayak; canoe
ба́йт, а *m.* (comput.) byte
бак, а *m.* cistern; tank; му́сорный б. dustbin
  (BrE), garbage can (AmE)
бакала́вр, а *m.* bachelor (*holder of degree*)

бакале́йный *adj.* grocery; б. магази́н
  grocer's shop (BrE), grocery store (AmE)
бакале́|я, и *f.* 1 (collect.) dry goods, groceries
  2 (*в магазине*) grocery section; (*магазин*)
  grocer's (shop)
ба́кен, а *m.* (*буй*) buoy
бакенба́рд|ы, ~ *f. pl.* (*sg.* ~а, ~ы) side
  whiskers
баклажа́н, а *m.* aubergine (BrE), eggplant
  (AmE)
бакла́н, а *m.* cormorant
ба́кс|ы, ов *m. pl.* (sl.) bucks, American dollars
бактериологи́ческ|ий *adj.* bacteriological;
  ~ая война́ germ warfare
бактериоло́ги|я, и *f.* bacteriology
бакте́ри|я, и *f.* bacterium
Баку́ *m. indecl.* Baku
бал, а, о ~е, на ~у́, *pl.* ~ы́ *m.* ball, dance
балала́йк|а, и *f.* balalaika
бала́нс, а *m.* (econ., tech.) balance; платёжный
  б. balance of payments
баланси́р|овать, ую *impf.* (*сохранять
  равновесие*) to balance
балери́н|а, ы *f.* ballerina
бале́т, а *m.* ballet; б. на льду́ ice show
бале́тный *adj. of* ▶ бале́т
ба́лк|а, и *f.* (*брус*) beam, girder
балка́нский *adj.* Balkan
Балка́н|ы, ~ (*no sg.*) the Balkans
балко́н, а *m.* balcony
балл, а *m.* 1 (meteor.) number; ве́тер в
  пять ~ов wind force 5 2 (*в школе*) mark;
  вы́сший б. an 'A'; проходно́й б. pass mark
  3 (sport) point; score
балла́д|а, ы *f.* ballad
балли́стик|а, и *f.* ballistics
баллисти́ческий *adj.* ballistic
балло́н, а *m.* 1 (*сосуд*) container (*of glass,
  metal, or rubber*); carboy; аэрозо́льный б.
  spray can; кислоро́дный б. oxygen cylinder
  2 (*шина*) balloon tyre (BrE), balloon tire
  (AmE)
баллоти́р|оваться, уюсь *impf.* (в + *a. or*
  на + *a.*) to stand (BrE), run (AmE) (for), be a

⚓ key word

candidate (for)

бал|ова́ть, у́ю *impf.* (*of* ▶ избалова́ть) to spoil; to pamper

бал|ова́ться, у́юсь *impf.* (infml) **1** (*шали́ть*) to get up to mischief **2** (*с + i.*) (*со спи́чками*) to play, fool about (with) **3** (*позволя́ть себе́ что-л.*) to indulge (in)

баловство́|о́, а́ *nt.* **1** (*ша́лости*) mischief **2** (*причу́да*) folly, extravagance

балти́йский *adj.* Baltic; **Балти́йское мо́ре** the Baltic Sea

Ба́лтик|а, и *f.* (*мо́ре*) the Baltic (Sea); (*райо́н*) the Baltic coast

бальза́м, а *m.* balsam; (fig.) balm; **б. для воло́с** hair conditioner

ба́л|ьный *adj. of* ▶ бал; **~ьные та́нцы** ballroom dancing

бамбу́к, а *m.* bamboo

ба́мпер, а *m.* bumper

бана́льность|ь, и *f.* **1** (*сво́йство*) banality **2** (*замеча́ние*) banal remark; platitude

бана́л|ьный, ~ен, ~ьна *adj.* banal, trite

бана́н, а *m.* banana

Бангко́к, а *m.* Bangkok

Бангладе́ш, а *m.* Bangladesh

бангладе́ш|ец, ца *m.* Bangladeshi

бангладе́ш|ка, ки *f. of* ▶ бангладе́шец

бангладе́шский *adj.* Bangladeshi

ба́нд|а, ы *f.* band, gang

бандеро́л|ь, и *f.* (*почто́вое отправле́ние*) small package

банди́т, а *m.* bandit; thug; armed robber

бандити́зм, а *m.* banditry; thuggery

банди́тский *adj. of* ▶ банди́т

⚡ **банк, а** *m.* bank (also fig.); **б. да́нных** databank

ба́нк|а, и *f.* (*стекля́нная*) jar; (*жестяна́я*) tin (BrE), can (AmE)

банке́т, а *m.* banquet

банки́р, а *m.* banker

банкно́т|а, ы *f.* banknote

⚡ **ба́нк|овский** *adj. of* ▶ банк; **б. биле́т** banknote; **~овская кни́жка** passbook, bank book

банкома́т, а *m.* cash machine

банкро́т, а *m.* bankrupt; **объявля́ть кого́-л. ~ом** to declare sb bankrupt

банкро́тств|о, а *nt.* bankruptcy

бант, а *m.* bow

ба́н|я, и *f.* (Russian) baths; bathhouse; **фи́нская б.** sauna

бапти́ст, а *m.* Baptist

бапти́ст|ка, ки *f. of* ▶ бапти́ст

бар, а *m.* bar; **пивно́й б.** pub

бараба́н, а *m.* drum

бараба́н|ить, ю, ишь *impf.* to drum

бараба́н|ный *adj. of* ▶ бараба́н; **~ная дробь** drum roll; **~ная перепо́нка** (anat.) ear drum, tympanum

бараба́нщик, а *m.* drummer

бараба́нщи|ца, цы *f. of* ▶ бараба́нщик

бара́к, а *m.* hut

бара́н, а *m.* ram; (wild) sheep

бара́н|ий *adj.* **1** sheep's; ram's **2** (*из ко́жи бара́на*) sheepskin **3** (*о еде́*) mutton; **~ья котле́та** mutton chop

бара́нин|а, ы *f.* mutton; (*молода́я*) lamb

барахл|о́, а́ *nt.* (collect.) (infml) trash, junk

барда́к, а́ *m.* (infml) chaos

бардач|о́к, ка́ *m.* (infml) glove compartment (*in car*)

Ба́ренцев|о мо́ре, ~а мо́ря *nt.* the Barents Sea

ба́рж|а, и *f.* barge

барито́н, а *m.* baritone

ба́рмен, а *m.* barman, bartender

баро́кко *nt. indecl.* baroque

баро́метр, а *m.* barometer

баро́н, а *m.* baron

бароне́сс|а, ы *f.* baroness

баррика́д|а, ы *f.* barricade

барс, а *m.* (zool.) snow leopard (*Uncia uncia*)

барсу́к, а́ *m.* badger

ба́ртер, а *m.* barter

ба́рхат, а *m.* velvet

ба́рхатный *adj.* **1** velvet; **б. сезо́н** autumn season, autumn months (*in the south of Russia*) **2** (fig.) velvety

ба́рхат|цы, цев *m. pl.* (*sg.* **~ец, ~ца**) (French/African) marigold (*genus Tagetes*)

барье́р, а *m.* **1** barrier (also fig.); **звуково́й б.** sound barrier; **языково́й б.** language barrier **2** (sport) hurdle; **взять б.** to clear a hurdle

бас, а *pl.* **~ы́** *m.* (mus.) bass

бас-гита́р|а, ы *f.* bass guitar

баск, а *m.* Basque

баскетбо́л, а *m.* basketball (*the sport*)

баскетболи́ст, а *m.* basketball player

баскетболи́ст|ка, ки *f. of* ▶ баскетболи́ст

баско́н|ка, ки *f. of* ▶ баск

ба́скский *adj.* Basque

басносло́в|ный, ~ен, ~на *adj.* (fig., infml) fabulous

ба́с|ня, ни, *g. pl.* **~ен** *f.* **1** fable **2** (fig., infml) fable, fabrication

⚡ **бассе́йн, а** *m.* **1** (man-made) pool; **пла́вательный б.** swimming pool **2** (geog.) basin; **каменноу́гольный б.** coalfield

бастио́н, а *m.* (mil., also fig.) bastion

баст|ова́ть, у́ю *impf.* to strike, go on strike; to be on strike

батальо́н, а *m.* battalion

батаре́йк|а, и *f.* (elec.) battery

батаре́|я, и *f.* (mil. and tech.) battery; (*отопи́тельная*) radiator

бато́н, а *m.* French loaf

бату́т, а *m.* trampoline; **прыжки́ на ~е** trampolining

ба́тюшк|а, и *m.* (*свяще́нник*) father

бахром|а́, ы́ *f.* fringe

башк|а́, и́ (*no g. pl.*) *f.* (infml) head

башма́к, а́ *m.* (*боти́нок*) boot; (*ту́фля*) shoe

ба́ш|ня, ни, *g. pl.* **~ен** *f.* tower; turret

бая́н, а *m.* (mus.) bayan (*a kind of accordion*)

б

бди́тельност|ь, и *f.* vigilance, watchfulness

бди́тел|ьный, ~ен, ~ьна *adj.* vigilant, watchful

бег, а, о ~е, на ~у́, pl. ~а́, ~о́в *m.* **1** run, running; jogging; **~о́м, на ~у́** running; at the double; **на всём ~у́** at full speed; **б. на ме́сте** running on the spot; marking time (also fig.) **2** (sport, *состяза́ние*) race **3** (*in pl.*) (*го́нки упря́жных лошаде́й*) harness races; trotting races **4**: **быть в ~а́х** to be on the run

бе́га|ть, ю *impf.* (*indet. of* ▶ **бежа́ть**) **1** to run (about); (**за** + *i.*) (infml) to run (after), chase (after) **2** (*о глаза́х*) to rove, roam

бегемо́т, а *m.* hippopotamus

бегле́ц, а́ *m.* fugitive

бе́глый *adj.* **1** (*убежа́вший*) fugitive, runaway **2** (*свобо́дный*) fluent, quick

бегля́нк|а, и *f. of* ▶ **бегле́ц**

бег|ово́й *adj. of* ▶ **бег**; **~ова́я доро́жка** racetrack, running track; (*in gym*) treadmill; **~ова́я ло́шадь** racehorse

беготн|я́, и́ *f.* (infml) running about; bustle

бе́гств|о, а *nt.* flight; escape; **обрати́ть в б.** to put to flight; **обрати́ться в б., спаса́ться ~ом** to take to flight

бе|гу́, ~жи́шь *see* ▶ **бежа́ть**

бегу́н, а́ *m.* runner

бед|а́, ы́, pl. ~ы *f.* **1** (*несча́стье*) misfortune; calamity; **на свою́ ~у́** to one's cost **2** (*as pred.*) it is awful!; **б. в том, что** the trouble is (that); **не б.!** it doesn't matter!

бе́дност|ь, и *f.* poverty (also fig.)

бе́д|ный, ~ен, ~на́, ~но, ~ны́ *adj.* poor; meagre (BrE), meager (AmE); (fig.) barren

бедня́г|а, и *m.* (infml) poor devil, poor thing

бедня́к, а́ *m.* pauper

бедр|о́, а́, pl. ~ра, ~ер, ~рам *nt.* (*ве́рхняя часть ноги́*) thigh; (*таз*) hip

бе́дстви|е, я *nt.* calamity, disaster; **райо́н ~я** disaster area; **сигна́л ~я** distress signal

бе́дств|овать, ую *impf.* to live in poverty

бе|жа́ть, гу́, жи́шь, гу́т *impf.* (*det. of* ▶ **бе́гать**) **1** to run; (fig., *о воде́*) to run; (*о кро́ви*) to flow **2** (*impf. and pf.*) (*спаса́ться*) to escape

бе́жевый *adj.* beige

бе́жен|ец, ца *m.* refugee

бе́жен|ка, ки *f. of* ▶ **бе́женец**

⚲ **без** *prep.* + *g.* without; in the absence of; minus, less; **не б.** not without; **б. вас** in your absence; **б. пяти́ (мину́т) три** five (minutes) to three; **б. че́тверти час** a quarter to one; **б. ма́лого** (infml) almost, all but; **быть б. ума́** (**от** + *g.*) to be crazy (about)

без... *pref.* in-, un-, -less

безалкого́льный *adj.* non-alcoholic; **б. напи́ток** non-alcoholic drink, soft drink

безапелляцио́н|ный, ~ен, ~на *adj.* peremptory, categorical

безбиле́тный *adj.* ticketless; **б. пассажи́р** fare dodger; (*на су́дне, самолёте*) stowaway

безбо́жный *adj.* **1** irreligious, anti-religious **2** (infml, *бессо́вестный*) outrageous

безболе́знен|ный, ~, ~на *adj.* painless

безбра́чный *adj.* celibate

безбре́ж|ный, ~ен, ~на *adj.* boundless

безве́трен|ный, ~, ~на *adj.* calm, windless

безве́три|е, я *nt.* calm

безвку́с|ный, ~ен, ~на *adj.* tasteless

безво́д|ный, ~ен, ~на *adj.* arid

безвозвра́т|ный, ~ен, ~на *adj.* irrevocable; irretrievable; **~ная ссу́да** permanent loan

безво́зме́здный *adj.* free (of charge); **б. труд** unpaid work

безво́ли|е, я *nt.* lack of will; weak will

безво́л|ьный, ~ен, ~ьна *adj.* weak-willed

безвре́д|ный, ~ен, ~на *adj.* harmless

безвре́мен|ный *adj.* untimely, premature; **~ая кончи́на** untimely end, untimely death

безвы́ездно *adv.* uninterruptedly, without a break

безвы́езд|ный *adj.* uninterrupted; **~ое пребыва́ние** continuous residence

безвы́ход|ный, ~ен, ~на *adj.* hopeless, desperate

безгра́мот|ный, ~ен, ~на *adj.* illiterate (also fig.); ignorant

безграни́ч|ный, ~ен, ~на *adj.* infinite, limitless, boundless

безгре́ш|ный, ~ен, ~на *adj.* innocent, without sin

безда́рност|ь, и *f.* **1** (*сво́йство*) lack of talent **2** (*челове́к*) person without talent

безда́р|ный, ~ен, ~на *adj.* (*челове́к*) talentless, undistinguished; (*произведе́ние*) third-rate

безде́йстви|е, я *nt.* inaction, idleness; (law) (criminal) negligence

безделу́шк|а, и *f.* knick-knack

безде́ль|е, я *nt.* idleness

безде́льник, а *m.* idler, loafer

безде́льнича|ть, ю *impf.* to idle, loaf about

безде́т|ный, ~ен, ~на *adj.* childless

бе́здн|а, ы *f.* abyss, chasm

бездоказа́тел|ьный, ~ен, ~ьна *adj.* unsubstantiated

бездо́м|ный, ~ен, ~на *adj.* homeless; (*о ко́шке, соба́ке*) stray

бездоро́жь|е, я *nt.* **1** (*отсу́тствие доро́г*) absence of roads **2** (*распу́тица*) bad condition of roads; season when roads are impassable

безду́м|ный, ~ен, ~на *adj.* unthinking; feckless

безе́ *nt. indecl.* meringue

безжа́лост|ный, ~ен, ~на *adj.* ruthless, pitiless

безжи́знен|ный, ~, ~на *adj.* lifeless, inanimate; (fig.) spiritless

безабо́т|ный, ~ен, ~на *adj.* carefree, light-hearted; (*безду́мный*) careless

беззако́ни|е, я *nt.* **1** (*отсу́тствие зако́нности*) lawlessness **2** (*посту́пок*) unlawful act

беззащи́т|ный, ~ен, ~на *adj.* defenceless (BrE), defenseless (AmE), unprotected

беззву́ч|ный, ~ен, ~на *adj.* soundless, noiseless

беззло́б|ный, ~ен, ~на *adj.* good-natured

беззу́б|ый, ~, ~а *adj.* toothless; (fig.) weak, feeble

безли́кий *adj.* featureless; faceless, impersonal

безли́ч|ный, ~ен, ~на *adj.* **1** without personality, characterless, impersonal **2** (gram.) impersonal

безлю́д|ный, ~ен, ~на *adj.* (*малонаселённый*) uninhabited; sparsely populated; (*улица*) empty, deserted

безмо́згл|ый, ~, ~а *adj.* (infml) brainless

безмо́лви|е, я *nt.* silence; **цари́т б.** silence reigns

безмо́лв|ный, ~ен, ~на *adj.* silent, mute; ~ное согла́сие tacit consent

безмяте́ж|ный, ~ен, ~на *adj.* serene, placid

безнадёж|ный, ~ен, ~на *adj.* hopeless; despairing

безнака́занно *adv.* with impunity; **э́то ему́ не пройдёт б.** he won't get away with this

безнака́занност|ь, и *f.* impunity

безнали́чный *adj.* (fin.) cashless

безно́г|ий, ~, ~а *adj.* (*без ног*) legless; (*без ноги*) one-legged

безнра́вственност|ь, и *f.* immorality

безнра́вствен|ный, ~, ~на *adj.* immoral

безоби́д|ный, ~ен, ~на *adj.* inoffensive

безо́блач|ный, ~ен, ~на *adj.* cloudless; (fig.) serene, unclouded

безобра́зи|е, я *nt.* **1** (*уродство*) ugliness **2** (*поступок*) outrage **3** (*as pred.*) (infml) it is disgraceful!

безобра́знича|ть, ю *impf.* (infml) to behave disgracefully; to make a nuisance of oneself

безобра́з|ный, ~ен, ~на *adj.* **1** (*уродливый*) ugly **2** (*поступок*) disgraceful, outrageous

безогово́роч|ный, ~ен, ~на *adj.* unconditional, unreserved, absolute

безопа́сност|ь, и *f.* safety, security; **поя́с/ре́мень ~и** seat belt; **Сове́т Б~и** Security Council

безопа́с|ный, ~ен, ~на *adj.* safe, secure; **б. секс** safe sex

безору́ж|ный, ~ен, ~на *adj.* unarmed; (fig.) defenceless (BrE), defenseless (AmE)

безоснова́тел|ьный, ~ен, ~ьна *adj.* groundless

безотве́тствен|ный, ~, ~на *adj.* irresponsible

безотка́з|ный, ~ен, ~на *adj.* **1** (*человек*) dependable, reliable **2** (*прибор, машина*) trouble-free, reliable

безотноси́тельно *adv.* (к + *d.*) irrespective (of)

безотчёт|ный, ~ен, ~на *adj.* **1** (*бесконтрольный*) not subject to control

2 (*бессознательный*) unconscious, instinctive

безоши́боч|ный, ~ен, ~на *adj.* correct

безрабо́тиц|а, ы *f.* unemployment

безрабо́т|ный *adj.* unemployed; (*as n. pl.* ~ые, ~ых) the unemployed

безра́дост|ный, ~ен, ~на *adj.* joyless; dismal

безразде́л|ьный, ~ен, ~ьна *adj.* (*внимание*) undivided; ~ьная власть complete sway

безразли́чи|е, я *nt.* indifference

безразли́чно *adv.* indifferently; **относи́ться б.** (к + *d.*) to be indifferent (to)

безразли́ч|ный, ~ен, ~на *adj.* indifferent; **мне ~но** it's all the same to me

безрассу́д|ный, ~ен, ~на *adj.* reckless; foolhardy

безрезульта́т|ный, ~ен, ~на *adj.* futile; unsuccessful

безру́к|ий, ~, ~а *adj.* **1** (*без рук*) armless **2** (*без руки*) one-armed **3** (fig.) clumsy

безуда́р|ный, ~ен, ~на *adj.* (ling.) unstressed

безукори́знен|ный, ~, ~на *adj.* irreproachable; impeccable

безу́м|ец, ца *m.* madman

безу́ми|е, я *nt.* madness; **довести́ до ~я** to drive crazy; **люби́ть до ~я** to love to distraction

безу́м|ный, ~ен, ~на *adj.* **1** (*план*) mad, crazy **2** (fig., infml, *страсть*) wild; ~ные це́ны absurd, crazy prices

безупре́ч|ный, ~ен, ~на *adj.* (*человек*) irreproachable; (*работа*) flawless

безусло́вно *adv.* **1** (*повиноваться, доверять*) unconditionally, absolutely **2** (infml, *несомненно*) of course, it goes without saying, undoubtedly

безусло́в|ный, ~ен, ~на *adj.* **1** (*повиновение, доверие*) unconditional, absolute **2** (*успех*) undoubted, indisputable

безуспе́ш|ный, ~ен, ~на *adj.* unsuccessful

безуте́ш|ный, ~ен, ~на *adj.* inconsolable

безуча́ст|ный, ~ен, ~на *adj.* apathetic, indifferent

безъя́дерный *adj.* nuclear-free

безымя́нный *adj.* (*не имеющий названия*) nameless; (*анонимный*) anonymous; **б. па́лец** third finger, ring finger

бей and **бе́йте** *imper. of* ▶ **бить**

Бейру́т, а *m.* Beirut

бейсбо́л, а *m.* baseball

бейсболи́ст, а *m.* baseball player

бейсболи́ст|ка, ки *f. of* ▶ **бейсболи́ст**

беко́н, а *m.* bacon

Беларус|ь, и *f.* Belarus

Белгра́д, а *m.* Belgrade

беле́|ть, ю *impf.* (*of* ▶ **побеле́ть**) **1** (*становиться белым*) to grow white **2** (*no pf.*) (*виднеться*) to show up white

белизн|а́, ы́ *f.* whiteness

бели́л|а, ~ (*no sg.*) whitewash

б

бел|и́ть, ю́, ~и́шь *impf.* (*pf.* по~) to whitewash

бе́лк|а, и *f.* squirrel; **верте́ться, крути́ться как б. в колесе́** to run round in circles

беллетри́ст, а *m.* fiction writer

беллетри́стик|а, и *f.* (liter.) fiction

бело… *comb. form* white-

белогварде́|ец, йца *m.* (pol.) White Guard

бел|о́к¹, ка́ *m.* (chem.) protein

бел|о́к², ка́ *m.* (*яйца́*) white (of egg)

бел|о́к³, ка́ *m.* (*глаза*) white (of the eye)

белоку́р|ый, ~, ~а *adj.* blond(e), fair(-haired)

белору́с, а *m.* Belarusian, Belorussian

белору́с|ка, ки *f. of* ▶ белору́с

белору́сский *adj.* Belarusian, Belorussian

белосне́ж|ный, ~ен, ~на *adj.* snow-white

белу́г|а, и *f.* beluga, white sturgeon (*Huso huso*)

⚹ **бе́л|ый**, ~, ~а́ *adj.* **1** white; ~ая берёза silver birch; **Б. дом** White House (*in Washington and Moscow*); **б. медве́дь** polar bear **2** (*светлый*) white; fair; **б. биле́т** 'white chit' (*certificate of exemption from military service*); ~ое вино́ white wine; **б. хлеб** white bread; **на ~ом све́те** in all the world; **средь ~а дня** in broad daylight; (*as n. pl.* ~ые, ~ых) white(-skinned) people **3** (*чистый*) clean; blank; **б. лист** clean sheet (*of paper*) **4**: **б. гриб** cep (*wild mushroom, Boletus edulis*)

бельги́|ец, йца *m.* Belgian

бельги́й|ка, ки *f. of* ▶ бельги́ец

бельги́йский *adj.* Belgian

Бе́льги|я, и *f.* Belgium

бель|ё, я́ *nt.* (*collect.*) linen; **да́мское б.** lingerie; **ни́жнее б.** underwear; **посте́льное б.** bedlinen

бемо́л|ь, я *m.* (*also as indecl. adj.*) (mus.) flat

бензи́н, а *m.* (*для автомоби́ля*) petrol (BrE), gas(oline) (AmE)

бензи́новый *adj. of* ▶ бензи́н; petrol (BrE), gas (AmE)

бензо… *comb. form, abbr. of* ▶ бензи́новый

бензоба́к, а *m.* petrol tank (BrE), gas tank (AmE)

бензово́з, а *m.* petrol tanker (BrE), gasoline truck (AmE)

бензоколо́нк|а, и *f.* petrol pump (BrE), gas(oline) pump (AmE)

⚹ **бе́рег**, а, о ~е, на ~у́, *pl.* ~а́ *m.* (*реки́*) bank; (*мо́ря, о́зера*) shore; (*су́ша*) land (*opp.* sea); **на ~у́ мо́ря** at the seaside; **вы́броситься на б.** to run aground; **вы́йти из ~о́в** to burst its banks; **сойти́ на б.** to go ashore

бер|ёг, ~егла́ *see* ▶ бере́чь

берегово́й *adj.* coastal; waterside; ~ая оборо́на coastal defence (BrE), defense (AmE)

бере|гу́, ~жёшь, ~гу́т *see* ▶ бере́чь

бережли́в|ый, ~, ~а *adj.* thrifty, economical

бе́реж|ный, ~ен, ~на *adj.* (*осторо́жный*) careful; cautious; (*забо́тливый*) solicitous

берёз|а, ы *f.* birch

бере́мене|ть, ю, ешь *impf.* (*of* ▶ забере́менеть) to become pregnant

бере́менн|ая, ~ая *adj.* (+ i.) pregnant (with)

⚹ **бере́менност|ь**, и *f.* (*состоя́ние*) pregnancy; (*проце́сс*) gestation

бере́т, а *m.* beret

бер|е́чь, егу́, ежёшь, егу́т, *past* ~ёг, ~егла́ *impf.* **1** (*челове́ка, здоро́вье, предме́т*) to take care (of), look after **2** (*не тра́тить*) to be careful with; **б. ка́ждую копе́йку** to count every penny

бер|е́чься, егу́сь, ежёшься, егу́тся, *past* ~ёгся, ~егла́сь *impf.* **1** (*быть осторо́жным*) to be careful, take care **2** (+ g. *or* + inf.) (*остерега́ться*) to beware (of)

Бе́рингов|о мо́ре, ~а мо́ря *nt.* the Bering Sea

Берли́н, а *m.* Berlin

берло́г|а, и *f.* den, lair

Берму́дск|ие острова́, ~их острово́в (*no sg.*) the Bermudas (*islands*), Bermuda

бер|у́, ёшь *see* ▶ брать

бес, а *m.* demon, devil, evil spirit

бесе́д|а, ы *f.* **1** talk, conversation **2** (*диску́ссия*) discussion; **провести́ ~у** to give a talk

бесе́дк|а, и *f.* summer house

бесе́д|овать, ую *impf.* (с + i.) to talk, converse (with)

бе|си́ть, шу́, ~сишь *impf.* (*of* ▶ взбеси́ть) (infml) to enrage, madden, infuriate

бе|си́ться, шу́сь, ~сишься *impf.* (*of* ▶ взбеси́ться) **1** to go mad (*of animals*) **2** (fig.) to rage, be furious; **с жи́ру б.** (infml) to grow fastidious, fussy; to be too well off

бескомпроми́сс|ный, ~ен, ~на *adj.* uncompromising

бесконе́чно *adv.* infinitely, endlessly; (infml) extremely

бесконе́чност|ь, и *f.* endlessness; infinity; **до ~и** endlessly

бесконе́ч|ный, ~ен, ~на *adj.* (*доро́га*) endless; (*вре́мя, удово́льствие*) infinite; (*сли́шком дли́нный*) interminable

бескоры́ст|ный, ~ен, ~на *adj.* disinterested, impartial; (*альтруисти́ческий*) unselfish

бескра́йний *adj.* boundless

бескро́в|ный, ~ен, ~на *adj.* (*без кровопроли́тия*) bloodless

бесперебо́й|ный, ~ен, ~на *adj.* uninterrupted; (*регуля́рный*) regular

беспереса́дочный *adj.* direct; **б. по́езд** through train

бесперспекти́в|ный, ~ен, ~на *adj.* having no prospects; (*безнадёжный*) hopeless

беспе́чност|ь, и *f.* carelessness, unconcern

беспе́ч|ный, ~ен, ~на *adj.* carefree

беспило́тный *adj.* unmanned

⚹ **беспла́тно** *adv.* free of charge, gratis

⚹ **беспла́т|ный**, ~ен, ~на *adj.* free, gratuitous

беспло́ди|е, я *nt.* (*по́чвы*) barrenness; (*же́нщины*) infertility

беспло́д|ный, ~ен, ~на *adj.* **1** (*почва*) barren; (*женщина*) infertile; (*брак*) childless **2** (fig.) fruitless, futile

беспод́об|ный, ~ен, ~на *adj.* matchless; incomparable

беспозвоно́чно|е, го *nt.* (zool.) invertebrate

беспоко́|ить, ю, ишь *impf.* **1** (*волновать*) to concern, worry **2** (*pf.* по~) (*мешать*) to disturb, worry

беспоко́|иться, юсь, ишься *impf.* **1** (о + *p.*) to worry, be worried *or* anxious (about) **2** (*pf.* по~) to trouble oneself, put oneself out; **не** ~**йтесь!** don't worry!

беспоко́|йный, ~ен, ~йна *adj.* **1** (*человек, вид, состояние*) agitated, disturbed; anxious; uneasy; (*ребёнок*) fidgety **2** (*сон*) restless, disturbed; (*поездка*) uncomfortable

беспоко́йств|о, а *nt.* **1** (*волнение*) agitation; anxiety; unrest; **с** ~**ом** anxiously **2** (*нарушение покоя*) disturbance

беспол́ез|ный, ~ен, ~на *adj.* useless

беспо́мощ|ный, ~ен, ~на *adj.* helpless, powerless; (fig.) feeble

беспоря́д|ок, ка *m.* disorder, confusion; (*pl. only*) (pol.) disturbances, riots

беспоря́доч|ный, ~ен, ~на *adj.* disorderly; untidy

беспоса́дочный *adj.*: **б. перелёт** non-stop flight

беспо́чвен|ный, ~, ~на *adj.* groundless; unfounded

беспо́шлинн|ый *adj.* (econ.) duty-free; ~**ая торго́вля** free trade

беспоща́д|ный, ~ен, ~на *adj.* merciless, relentless

бесправи|е, я *nt.* **1** (*отсутствие законности*) lawlessness; arbitrariness **2** (*отсутствие прав*) lack of rights

беспра́в|ный, ~ен, ~на *adj.* without rights

беспреде́л, а *m.* (infml) lawlessness, scandalous practices; chaos, mayhem

беспреде́л|ьный, ~ен, ~ьна *adj.* boundless, infinite

беспрепя́тствен|ный, ~, ~на *adj.* free, clear, unimpeded

беспрецеде́нт|ный, ~ен, ~на *adj.* unprecedented

беспризо́рн|ый *adj.* (*бездомный*) homeless; (*as m. n.* **б.**, ~**ого**) waif, street urchin

беспринци́п|ный, ~ен, ~на *adj.* unscrupulous, unprincipled

беспристра́сти|е, я *nt.* impartiality

беспристра́ст|ный, ~ен, ~на *adj.* impartial, unbias(s)ed

беспроводно́й *adj.*: **б. телефо́н** cordless telephone; **б. (до́ступ в) Интерне́т** wireless Internet (access), Wi-Fi®

беспро́игрыш|ный, ~ен, ~на *adj.* safe; risk-free

беспросве́т|ный, ~ен, ~на *adj.* **1** pitch-dark; ~**ная тьма** thick darkness **2** (fig.) hopeless; unrelieved

беспроце́нтный *adj.* (fin.) interest-free

бессерде́ч|ный, ~ен, ~на *adj.* heartless; callous

бесси́ли|е, я *nt.* (*слабость*) weakness; debility; (fig.) impotence

бесси́л|ьный, ~ен, ~ьна *adj.* (*слабый*) weak; (fig.) impotent, powerless

бессисте́м|ный, ~ен, ~на *adj.* unsystematic

бессла́в|ный, ~ен, ~на *adj.* ignominious; inglorious

бессле́дно *adv.* without leaving a trace; completely

бессле́д|ный, ~ен, ~на *adj.* without leaving a trace; ~**ное исчезнове́ние** complete disappearance

бесслове́с|ный, ~ен, ~на *adj.* dumb, speechless; (fig.) silent

бессме́н|ный, ~ен, ~на *adj.* permanent; continuous

бессме́рти|е, я *nt.* immortality

бессме́рт|ный, ~ен, ~на *adj.* immortal; undying

бессмы́слен|ный, ~, ~на *adj.* (*поступок*) senseless; foolish; (*слова*) meaningless, nonsensical; (*взгляд*) vacant, inane

бессо́вест|ный, ~ен, ~на *adj.* **1** (*нечестный*) unscrupulous, dishonest **2** (*бесстыдный*) shameless, brazen

бессодержа́тел|ьный, ~ен, ~ьна *adj.* (*жизнь*) empty; (*слова*) tame; dull

бессозна́тел|ьный, ~ен, ~ьна *adj.* **1** unconscious **2** (*непроизвольный*) involuntary

бессо́нниц|а, ы *f.* insomnia, sleeplessness

бессо́нный *adj.* sleepless

бесспо́рно *adv.* indisputably; undoubtedly

бесспо́р|ный, ~ен, ~на *adj.* indisputable, incontrovertible

бессро́чный *adj.* without time limit; **б. о́тпуск** indefinite leave

бесстра́ст|ный, ~ен, ~на *adj.* impassive

бесстра́ш|ный, ~ен, ~на *adj.* fearless, intrepid

бессты́д|ный, ~ен, ~на *adj.* shameless

бессчёт|ный, ~ен, ~на *adj.* innumerable

беста́ктност|ь, и *f.* **1** (*свойство*) tactlessness **2** (*поступок*) tactless action, faux pas

беста́кт|ный, ~ен, ~на *adj.* tactless

бестолко́в|ый, ~, ~а *adj.* **1** (*человек*) slow-witted, muddle-headed **2** (*объяснение*) disconnected, incoherent

бестсе́ллер, а *m.* bestseller (*book*)

бесфо́рмен|ный, ~, ~на *adj.* shapeless, formless

бесхара́ктер|ный, ~ен, ~на *adj.* weak-willed; spineless

бесхи́трост|ный, ~ен, ~на *adj.* (*человек*) artless; (*слова*) ingenuous

бесцве́т|ный, ~ен, ~на *adj.* colourless (BrE), colorless (AmE)

бесце́л|ьный, ~ен, ~ьна *adj.* aimless; idle

бесце́н|ный, ~ен, ~на *adj.* **1** (*сокровища*) priceless **2** (*опыт, совет*) invaluable

б

бесцеремо́н|ный, ∼ен, ∼на *adj.* unceremonious; familiar; cavalier

бесчелове́ч|ный, ∼ен, ∼на *adj.* inhuman

бесче́ст|ный, ∼ен, ∼на *adj.* dishonourable (BrE), dishonorable (AmE); disgraceful

бесче́сть|е, я *nt.* dishonour (BrE), dishonor (AmE); disgrace

бесчи́слен|ный, ∼, ∼на *adj.* innumerable

бесчу́вствен|ный, ∼, ∼на *adj.* **1** (*лишённый сознания*) insensible **2** (*равнодушный*) insensitive, unfeeling

бесшу́м|ный, ∼ен, ∼на *adj.* noiseless

бето́н, а *m.* concrete

бето́нный *adj.* concrete

бе́шенств|о, а *nt.* **1** (med.) hydrophobia; rabies; **коро́вье б.** mad cow disease **2** (fig.) fury, rage; **довести́ до ∼а** to enrage

бе́шен|ый **1** (med.) rabid, mad; **∼ая соба́ка** mad dog **2** (fig.) furious; violent; **∼ая ско́рость** furious pace; **∼ые це́ны** (infml) exorbitant prices

биатло́н, а *m.* biathlon

библе́йский *adj.* biblical

библио́граф, а *m.* bibliographer

библиографи́ческий *adj.* bibliographical

библиогра́фи|я, и *f.* bibliography

⚷ **библиоте́к|а, и** *f.* library

библиоте́кар|ь, я *m.* librarian

би́бли|я, и *f.* bible; (**Б.**) the Bible

бигуд|и́, е́й (*no sg.*) (*also indecl.*) (hair) curlers

биде́ *nt. indecl.* bidet

бидо́н, а *m.* can; **б. для молока́** milk can, milk churn (BrE)

бие́ни|е, я *nt.* beating; throb; **б. се́рдца** heartbeat; **б. пу́льса** pulse

бижуте́ри|я, и *f.* costume jewellery

⚷ **би́знес, а** *m.* business; **рекла́мный б.** advertising

бизнесме́н, а *m.* businessman

бики́ни *nt. indecl.* bikini

⚷ **биле́т, а** *m.* ticket; (*удостовере́ние*) card; **входно́й б.** entrance ticket, permit; **еди́ный б.** rover ticket; **обра́тный б.** return ticket; **экзаменацио́нный б.** examination question(-paper) (*at oral examination*)

биллио́н, а *m.* (10^{12}) trillion (*one million million*)

билья́рд, а *m.* **1** (*стол*) billiard table **2** (*игра*) billiards

бино́кл|ь, я *m.* binoculars; **полево́й б.** field glasses

бинт, а́ *m.* bandage

бинт|ова́ть, у́ю *impf.* to bandage

био... *comb. form* bio-

био́граф, а *m.* biographer

биографи́ческий *adj.* biographical

биогра́фи|я, и *f.* biography; (*жизнь*) life story

био́лог, а *m.* biologist

биологи́ческий *adj.* biological

биоло́ги|я, и *f.* biology

биометри́ческий *adj.* biometric

биосфе́р|а, ы *f.* biosphere

биохи́мик, а *m.* biochemist

биохи́ми|я, и *f.* biochemistry

би́рж|а, и *f.* exchange; **фо́ндовая б.** stock exchange; **б. труда́** jobcentre

биржеви́к, а́ *m.* (fin., infml) stockbroker

биржево́й *adj.* of ▶ **би́ржа**; **б. ма́клер** stockbroker

би́рк|а, и *f.* tag, label

Би́рм|а, ы *f.* Burma

бирюз|а́, ы́ (*no pl.*) *f.* turquoise

бирюзо́вый *adj.* turquoise

бисексуа́льный *adj.* bisexual

бискви́т, а *m.* sponge cake

бит, а *m.* (comput.) bit

би́т|а, ы *f.* (sport) bat

би́тв|а, ы *f.* battle

бить, бью, бьёшь *impf.* **1** (*pf.* **по∼**) (*избива́ть*) to beat (*a person, an animal, etc.*) **2** (*for pf. use* **уда́рить**) (*ударя́ть*) to strike, hit; **б. в лицо́** to strike, hit in the face (also fig.) **3** (*impf. only*) (*убива́ть*) to kill, slaughter (*animals*) **4** (*pf.* **раз∼**) (*лома́ть*) to break, smash (*crockery, etc.*) **5** (*pf.* **про∼**) (*издава́ть звуки*) to strike, sound; **б. отбо́й** to beat a retreat (also fig.); **часы́ бьют пять** the clock is striking five **6** (*impf. only*) (*вытека́ть*) to spurt, gush; **б. ключо́м** to gush out, well up; (fig.) to be in full swing **7** (*impf. only*) (*стреля́ть*) to shoot, fire; (*достига́ть на како́е-л. расстоя́ние*, also fig.) to hit; (*to have a range (of*): **б. в цель** to hit the target (also fig.); **б. наверняка́** (fig.) to take no chances

би́ться, бьюсь, бьёшься *impf.* **1** (с + *i.*) (*дра́ться*) to fight (with, against) **2** (*о се́рдце*) to beat; **се́рдце его́ переста́ло б.** his heart stopped beating **3** (о + *a.*) (*ударя́ться*) to knock (against), hit (against), strike; **б. голово́й об сте́ну** to bang one's head against a brick wall **4** (*мета́ться*) to writhe, struggle; **б. в исте́рике** to writhe in hysterics **5** (над + *i.*) (fig., *стара́ться изо всех сил*) to struggle (with); **б. над зада́чей** to rack one's brains over a problem **6** (*о стекле*) to break, smash; **легко́ б.** to be very fragile **7**: **б. об закла́д** to bet, wager

бифште́кс, а *m.* beefsteak

би́цепс, а *m.* (anat.) biceps

бич, а́ *m.* whip; (fig.) scourge

бла́г|о¹, а *nt.* good, the good; blessing; **о́бщее б.** the common weal; **всех благ!** (infml) all the best!

бла́го² *conj.* (infml) since; seeing that; **скажи́те ему́ сейча́с, б. он здесь** tell him now since he is here

благови́д|ный, ∼ен, ∼на *adj.* plausible

благодар|и́ть, ю́, и́шь *impf.* (*of* ▶ **поблагодари́ть**) to thank; **∼ю́ вас (за** + *a.*) thank you (for)

благода́рност|ь, и *f.* **1** gratitude; **не сто́ит ~и** don't mention it **2** (*usu. in pl.*) (*выраже́ние благода́рности*) thanks

благода́р|ный, ~ен, ~на *adj.* **1** grateful **2** (*стоя́щий*) rewarding; worthwhile

благода́рственн|ый *adj.* expressing thanks; ~ое письмо́ letter of thanks

🖋 **благодаря́** *prep. + d.* thanks to, owing to, because of; **б. тому́, что** owing to the fact that

благоде́тел|ь, я *m.* benefactor

благоде́тельниц|а, ы *f.* benefactress

благоду́ш|ный, ~ен, ~на *adj.* (*споко́йный*) placid, equable; (*доброду́шный*) good-humoured (BrE), -humored (AmE)

благожела́тельност|ь, и *f.* goodwill; benevolence

благожела́тел|ьный, ~ен, ~ьна *adj.* (*челове́к*) kind; well disposed; (*приём, улы́бка*) friendly, cordial; (*реце́нзия*) favourable (BrE), favorable (AmE)

благозву́ч|ный, ~ен, ~на *adj.* euphonious; (*го́лос*) melodious

благ|о́й *adj.* good; ~и́е наме́рения good intentions

благонадёжност|ь, и *f.* reliability, trustworthiness

благонадёж|ный, ~ен, ~на *adj.* reliable, trustworthy

благополу́чи|е, я *nt.* well-being; prosperity

благополу́чно *adv.* well, all right; happily; (*в це́лости и сохра́нности*) safely

благополу́ч|ный, ~ен, ~на *adj.* (*уда́чный*) successful; (*прибы́тие*) safe; **б. коне́ц** happy ending

благоприя́т|ный, ~ен, ~на *adj.* favourable (BrE), favorable (AmE); ~ные ве́сти good news

благоприя́тств|овать, ую *impf.* (+ *d.*) to favour (BrE), favor (AmE)

благоразу́ми|е, я *nt.* prudence; sense

благоразу́м|ный, ~ен, ~на *adj.* prudent; sensible

благоро́д|ный, ~ен, ~на *adj.* noble; **б. мета́лл** precious metal

благоро́дств|о, а *nt.* nobleness; nobility

благоскло́нност|ь, и *f.* favour (BrE), favor (AmE); **по́льзоваться чьей-н. ~ью** to be in sb's good graces

благоскло́н|ный, ~ен, ~на *adj.* favourable (BrE), favorable (AmE); gracious

благослове́ни|е, я *nt.* (*eccl.*, *fig.*) blessing; **с ~я** (+ *g.*) with the blessing (of)

благослов|и́ть, лю́, и́шь *pf.* (*of* ▸ **благословля́ть**) **1** (*перекрести́ть*) to bless; (*вы́разить одобре́ние*) to give one's blessing (to) **2** (*возда́ть благода́рность*) to be grateful to; **б. свою́ судьбу́** to thank one's stars

благослов|ля́ть, ля́ю *impf. of* ▸ **благослови́ть**

благосостоя́ни|е, я *nt.* well-being, welfare

благотвори́тел|ь, я *m.* (*лицо́*) philanthropist; (*организа́ция*) charity

благотвори́тельниц|а, ы *f. of* ▸ **благотвори́тель**

благотвори́тельност|ь, и *f.* charity, philanthropy

благотвори́тельный *adj.* charitable, philanthropic; **б. спекта́кль** charity performance

благотво́р|ный, ~ен, ~на *adj.* beneficial; wholesome, salutary

благоустра́ива|ть, ю *impf. of* ▸ **благоустро́ить**

благоустро́ен|ный, ~, ~а *p.p.p. of* ▸ **благоустро́ить** *and* (~, ~на) *adj.* well equipped; comfortable; **б. дом** house with all modern conveniences

благоустро́|ить, ю, ишь *pf.* (*of* ▸ **благоустра́ивать**) to equip with services and utilities

благоустро́йств|о, а *nt.* equipping with services and utilities

благочести́в|ый, ~, ~а *adj.* pious, devout

благоче́сти|е, я *nt.* piety

блаже́нств|о, а *nt.* bliss

бланк, а *m.* form; **анке́тный б.** questionnaire; **фи́рменный б.** sheet of headed notepaper; **запо́лнить б.** to fill in a form

блат, а *m.* (infml) pull, string-pulling; **получи́ть по ~у** to obtain through connections

блатн|о́й *adj.* (infml) (*достаю́щийся по бла́ту*) obtained through string-pulling; (*челове́к*) string-pulling; (*язы́к, му́зыка*) criminal, thieves'; (*as n.* **б.**, ~о́го) (*по́льзующийся бла́том*) string-puller; (*свя́занный с престу́пным ми́ром*) criminal

бл|ева́ть, юю́, юёшь *impf.* (sl.) to puke, spew (both infml)

бледне́|ть, ю, ешь *impf.* (*of* ▸ **побледне́ть**) to grow pale; to pale

бле́дност|ь, и *f.* paleness, pallor; (*fig.*) dullness

бле́д|ный, ~ен, ~на́, ~но *adj.* pale, pallid; **б. как полотно́** white as a sheet; (*fig.*) colourless (BrE), colorless (AmE), insipid, dull

блеск, а *m.* brightness, brilliance, shine; (*fig.*) splendour (BrE), splendor (AmE), magnificence; (*as int.*) (sl.): **б.!** brilliant!; great!; super!; **во всём ~е** in all (one's) glory

блесн|у́ть, у́, ёшь *pf.* to flash; **в мое́й голове́ ~у́ла мысль** a thought flashed across my mind

бле|сте́ть, щу́, сти́шь *and* ~щешь *impf.* to shine; to glitter; to sparkle; **её глаза́ ~сте́ли ра́достью** her eyes shone with joy; **он не ~щет умо́м** he's no genius

блестя́щ|ий, ~, ~а, ~е *pres. part. of* ▸ **блесте́ть** *and adj.* shining, bright; (*fig.*) brilliant

бле|щу́, ~щешь *see* ▸ **блесте́ть**

бле́|ять, ю, ешь *impf.* to bleat

ближа́йш|ий *superl. of* ▸ **бли́зкий**; (*го́род, по́чта*) nearest; (*день, год*) next; (*зада́ча*) immediate; **в ~ем бу́дущем** in the near future; **б. друг** closest friend; **б. ро́дственник** next of kin; **при ~ем**

б

рассмотре́нии on closer examination

бли́же *comp. of* ▸ **бли́зкий**; nearer; (fig.) closer

ближневосто́чный *adj.* Middle East; Middle Eastern

бли́жн|ий *adj.* **1** (*близкий*) near; (*сосе́дний*) neighbouring (BrE), neighboring (AmE); **Б. Восто́к** Middle East **2** (mil.) short range, close range **3** (*родственник*) close; (*as m. n.* **б.**, **~его**) (fig.) one's neighbour (BrE), neighbor (AmE) **4** (*путь*) shortest

бли́з|иться, ится *impf.* to approach, draw near

✔ **бли́з|кий, ~ок, ~ка́, ~ко, ~кий** *adj.* **1** (*место*) nearby, close; **на ~ком расстоя́нии** a short way off; at close range **2** (*конец*) near; imminent **3** (*в те́сных отноше́ниях*) intimate, close; **б. друг** close friend; **быть ~ким с кем-н.** to be on intimate terms with sb; **быть ~ким** (+ *d.*) to be dear (to); (*as n.* **~кие, ~ких**) one's nearest and dearest **4** (*похо́жий*) (к + *d.*) like; similar (to); close (to); **б. нам по ду́ху челове́к** kindred spirit

бли́зко *adv.* **1** (от + *g.*) near, close (to) **2** (*as pred.*) it is not far

близлежа́щий *adj.* neighbouring (BrE), neighboring (AmE), nearby

близне́ц, а́ *m.* twin (*also triplet, etc.*); **Б~ы́** (*созве́здие*) Gemini

близору́к|ий, ~, ~а *adj.* short-sighted (BrE), nearsighted (AmE) (*also fig.*)

бли́зост|ь, и *f.* nearness, proximity; (*близкие отношения*) intimacy

блик, а *m.* spot/speck/patch of light; **со́лнечный б.** patch of sunlight

блин, а́ *m.* pancake; **пе́рвый б. ко́мом** (*proverb*) practice makes perfect; (*as int.*) (sl.) damn!; shit! (vulg.)

блиста́тел|ьный, ~ен, ~ьна *adj.* brilliant, splendid

блиста́|ть, ю *impf.* to shine

блог, а *m.* (comput.) blog, weblog

бло́ггер and **бло́гер а** *m.* (comput.) blogger, weblogger

бло́гер, а *m.* = **бло́ггер**

блогосфе́р|а, ы *f.* (comput.) blogosphere

блок¹, а *m.* (tech.) block, pulley

блок², а *m.* (pol.) bloc

блок³, а *m.* carton (of cigarettes); unit; **б. пита́ния** power supply (unit)

блока́д|а, ы *f.* blockade; **снять ~у** to raise the blockade

блоки́р|овать, ую *impf. and pf.* **1** to blockade **2** (sport) to block

блокно́т, а *m.* notebook, notepad

блокпо́ст, á, о ~é, на ~ý *m.* checkpoint

блонди́н, а *m.* fair-haired man

блонди́нк|а, и *f.* blonde (woman)

блох|á, и́, pl. ~и, d. ~áм and ~ам *f.* flea; **иска́ть ~** to nitpick (fig.)

бло́чный *adj.* modular

✔ key word

блужда́|ть, ю *impf.* to roam, wander; to rove; **б. по у́лицам** to roam the streets

блужда́ющий *pres. part. of* ▸ **блужда́ть**; **б. огонёк** will-o'-the-wisp

блу́зк|а, и *f.* blouse

✔ **блю́д|о, а** *nt.* dish; **обе́д из трёх ~** three-course dinner; **вку́сное б.** a tasty dish

блю́д|це, ца, *g. pl.* **~ец** *nt.* saucer

блюз, а *m.* (mus.) the blues

блю|сти́, ду́, дёшь, *past* **~л, ~ла́** *impf.* to guard, watch over; **б. поря́док** to keep order

блюсти́тел|ь, я *m.* keeper, guardian; **б. поря́дка** (infml, iron.) arm of the law

бляд|ь, и, *g. pl.* **~е́й** *n.* (vulg.) (*женщина*) whore; (*мужчина*) bastard; (*as int.*) fuck!

боб, á *m.* bean

боб|ёр, pá *m.* (*мех*) beaver (fur)

бобр, á *m.* beaver

✔ **Бог, а,** *voc. sg.* **Бо́же** *m.* God; god; **Бо́же мой!** good God!, my God!; **Б. зна́ет!, Б. весть!** God knows!; **Б. его́ зна́ет!** who knows!; **не дай Б.!** God forbid!; **ра́ди ~a!** for God's sake!; **Б. с ним!** blow it; **сла́ва ~y!** thank God!

богате́|ть, ю, ешь *impf.* (*of* ▸ **разбогате́ть**) to grow rich

бога́тств|о, а *nt.* **1** riches, wealth; **есте́ственные ~а** natural resources **2** (fig.) richness, wealth

✔ **бога́т|ый, ~, ~а** *adj.* (+ *i.*) rich (in), wealthy; **~ая расти́тельность** luxuriant vegetation; **б. о́пыт** wide experience; (*as m. n.* **б.**, **~ого**) rich man

богаты́р|ь, я́ *m.* **1** bogatyr (*hero in Russian folklore*) **2** (fig.) Hercules; hero

бога́ч, á *m.* rich man; **~и́** (collect.) the rich

боге́м|а, ы *f.* (collect.) Bohemians; (*образ жи́зни*) Bohemianism

боге́мный *adj.* Bohemian

боги́н|я, и *f.* goddess (*also fig.*)

Богоро́диц|а, ы *f.* the Virgin, Our Lady

богосло́ви|е, я *nt.* theology

богосло́вский *adj.* theological

богослуже́ни|е, я *nt.* divine service, worship; liturgy

боготвор|и́ть, ю́, и́шь *impf.* to worship, idolize

богоху́льств|о, а *nt.* blasphemy

бо́дрост|ь, и *f.* cheerfulness; good spirits; (*мужество*) courage

бо́дрствовани|е, я *nt.* keeping awake; vigilance

бо́дрств|овать, ую *impf.* to stay awake; to keep vigil

бо́др|ый, ~, ~á, ~о, ~ы́ *adj.* cheerful, bright; (*старик*) hale and hearty

боеви́к, á *m.* **1** (*солдат*) fighter; militant **2** (infml, *остросюжетный фильм*) action movie, thriller

✔ **боев|о́й** *adj.* **1** military, fighting, battle; **~ы́е де́йствия** operations; **б. дух** fighting spirit; **~о́е креще́ние** baptism of fire; **б. патро́н** live cartridge **2** (infml, *воинственный*)

militant; energetic

боеголо́вк|а, и *f.* (mil.) warhead

боеприпа́с|ы, ов (*no sg.*) ammunition

боеспосо́б|ный, ∼ен, ∼на *adj.* (mil.) battle-worthy

бо|е́ц, йца́ *m.* (*участник боя*) fighter; (*солдат*) private soldier

Бо́же *see* ▶ **Бог**

боже́ствен|ный, ∼, ∼на *adj.* divine (also fig.)

божество́, а́ *nt.* deity, divine being

бож|ий, ья, ье *adj.* God's; **я́сно как б. день** it is as clear as could be; **∼ья коро́вка** (zool.) ladybird

☞ **бо|й, я, *pl.* ∼и́, ∼ёв** *m.* **1** (*сражение*) battle, fight, action, combat; **∼и́** fighting; **в ∼ю́** in action **2** (*часов*) striking, strike; **бараба́нный б.** drumbeat **3** (*убой*) killing, slaughtering; **б. кито́в** whaling

бо́|йкий, ∼ек, ∼йка́, ∼йко *adj.* **1** (*дерзкий*) bold, spry, smart; **б. ум** ready wit; **б. язы́к** glib tongue **2** (*живой*) lively, animated; **∼йкая торго́вля** brisk trade; **∼йкая у́лица** busy street

бойко́т, а *m.* boycott; **объяви́ть б.** (+ *d.*) to declare a boycott (of)

бойкоти́р|овать, ую *impf.* to boycott

бойн|я, и, *g. pl.* бо́ен *f.* slaughterhouse, abattoir; (fig.) slaughter, butchery, carnage

бо́йче *comp. of* ▶ **бо́йкий**

бойче́е = **бо́йче**

бок, а, о ∼е, на ∼у́, *pl.* ∼а́ *m.* side; flank; **в б.** sideways; **схвати́ться за ∼а́ (от сме́ха)** to split one's sides (with laughter); **на́ б.** sideways, to the side; **на ∼у́** on one side; **б. о́ б.** side by side; **под ∼ом** nearby, close at hand; **с ∼у** from the side, from the flank

бока́л, а *m.* (wine)glass, goblet; **подня́ть б.** (**за** + *a.*) to drink the health (of), raise one's glass (to)

боков|о́й *adj.* side, flank, lateral, sidelong; **∼а́я у́лица** side street

бо́ком *adv.* sideways; **ходи́ть б.** to sidle

бокс[1]**, а** *m.* (sport) boxing

бокс[2]**, а** *m.* (*в больнице*) cubicle

боксёр, а *m.* (*спортсмен; собака*) boxer

болва́нк|а, и *f.* **1** (tech.) pig (*of iron, etc.*) **2** (*компактный диск*) blank CD, DVD

болга́р|ин, ина, *pl.* ∼ы, ∼ *m.* Bulgarian

Болга́ри|я, и *f.* Bulgaria

болга́р|ка, ки *f. of* ▶ **болга́рин**

болга́рский *adj.* Bulgarian

болев|о́й *adj. of* ▶ **боль**; **∼о́е ощуще́ние** sensation of pain

☞ **бо́лее** *adv.* more; **б. то́лстый** thicker; **б. того́** and what is more; **б. и́ли ме́нее** more or less; **не б. и не ме́нее, как** neither more nor less than; **б. всего́** most of all; **тем б., что** especially as

боле́знен|ный, ∼, ∼на *adj.* **1** (*нездоровый*) sickly; unhealthy; (fig.) abnormal, morbid; **∼ное любопы́тство** morbid curiosity **2** (*вызывающий боль*) painful

☞ **боле́зн|ь, и** *f.* illness; disease; (fig.) abnormality; **б. Да́уна** Down's syndrome; **б. Паркинсо́на** Parkinson's disease; **морска́я б.** seasickness

боле́льщик, а *m.* (infml) fan, supporter

боле́льщи|ца, цы *f. of* ▶ **боле́льщик**

боле́|ть[1]**, ю, ешь** *impf.* **1** (+ *i.*) to be ill, be down (with); to ail (*intrans.*); **она́ с де́тства ∼ет а́стмой** she has suffered from asthma since childhood; **б. душо́й** (**за** + *a.*) to be worried (about) **2** (**за** + *a.*) (infml) to be a fan (of), support

бол|е́ть[2]**, и́т, я́т** *impf.* to ache, hurt; **у меня́ зу́бы ∼я́т** I have toothache

болеутоля́ющ|ий *adj.* soothing, analgesic; **∼ее сре́дство** (med.) painkiller, analgesic

боливи́|ец, йца *m.* Bolivian

боливи́й|ка, ки *f. of* ▶ **боливи́ец**

боливи́йский *adj.* Bolivian

Боли́ви|я, и *f.* Bolivia

боло́тист|ый, ∼, ∼а *adj.* marshy, boggy, swampy

боло́тн|ый *adj.* marsh; **∼ая лихора́дка** marsh fever, malaria

боло́т|о, а *nt.* marsh, bog, swamp; **торфяно́е б.** peat bog; (fig.) mire, slough

болт, а́ *m.* (tech.) bolt

болта́|ть[1]**, ю** *impf.* **1** (*мешать*) to stir; (*взбалтывать*) to shake **2** (+ *i.*) (*ногами*) to dangle

болта́|ть[2]**, ю** *impf.* (infml) to chatter, jabber (away); **б. глу́пости** to talk nonsense; **б. по-францу́зски** to jabber away in French

болта́|ться, юсь *impf.* (infml) **1** (*качаться*) to dangle, swing; to hang loosely **2** (*слоняться*) to hang about, loaf

болтли́в|ый, ∼, ∼а *adj.* garrulous, talkative; (*бестактный*) indiscreet

болтовн|я́, и́ *f.* (infml) chatter; (*сплетня*) gossip

болту́н, а́ *m.* (infml) **1** (*пустослов*) chatterbox; gasbag **2** (*сплетник*) gossip

☞ **бол|ь, и** *f.* pain; ache; **б. в боку́** stitch; **зубна́я б.** toothache; **душе́вная б.** mental anguish

☞ **больни́ц|а, ы** *f.* hospital; **лечь в ∼у** to go to hospital; **лежа́ть в ∼е** to be in hospital

больни́чный *adj. of* ▶ **больни́ца**; **б. лист** medical certificate

бо́льно *adv.* **1** painfully, badly; **б. уши́бться** to be badly bruised **2** (*as pred.*) it is painful (also fig.); **мне б. дыша́ть** it hurts me to breathe **3** (infml) very, too; **э́то б. далеко́** it's too far

☞ **бол|ьно́й, ∼ен, ∼ьна́** *adj.* (*человек*) ill, sick; (*орган*) diseased; (*часть тела*) sore (also fig.); **∼ьны́е дёсны** sore gums; **б. зуб** bad tooth; **он тяжело́ ∼ен** he is seriously ill; **б. вопро́с** sore subject; **∼ьно́е ме́сто** sore spot; **он б.** (*as n.*), **∼ьно́го, *f.* ∼ьна́я, ∼ьно́й**) patient, invalid; **амбулато́рный б.** outpatient; **стациона́рный б.** inpatient

☞ **бо́льше** **1** (*comp. of* ▶ **большо́й**, ▶ **вели́кий**)

б

bigger, larger; (*об отвлечённых понятиях*) greater; Ло́ндон б. Пари́жа London is larger than Paris **2** (*comp. of* ▶ мно́го) more; чем б. ..., тем б. the more ... the more; б. не no more, no longer; он б. не живёт на той у́лице he does not live in that street any longer, he no longer lives in that street; б. не бу́ду! I won't do it again!; б. нет вопро́сов? any more questions?; б. у (+ *g.*) (tennis) advantage

большеви́к, а́ *m.* Bolshevik

✎ **бо́льш|ий** *comp. of* ▶ большо́й, ▶ вели́кий; greater, larger; по ~ей ча́сти for the most part; са́мое ~ее at most

✎ **большинств|о́**, а́ *nt.* majority; most (of); в ~е́ слу́чаев in most cases; б. голосо́в а majority vote

✎ **больш|о́й** *adj.* (*по величине́*) big, large; (*значи́тельный; ва́жный*) great; (*infml, взро́слый*) grown-up; ~а́я бу́ква capital (letter); ~а́я доро́га high road; б. па́лец thumb; б. па́лец ноги́ big toe; б. свет haut monde, society; когда́ я бу́ду б. when I grow up

боля́чк|а, и *f.* sore; scab; (*fig.*) defect

бо́мб|а, ы *f.* bomb; кассе́тная б. cluster bomb

бомбардиро́вк|а, и *f.* bombardment; bombing; ковро́вая б. carpet bombing

бомбардиро́в|щик, а *m.* **1** (*самолёт*) bomber; пики́рующий б. dive-bomber **2** (*infml, лётчик*) bomber pilot

бомб|и́ть, лю́, и́шь *impf.* to bomb

бомбоубе́жищ|е, а *nt.* air-raid shelter, bomb shelter

бомж, а *m.* (*abbr. of* без определённого ме́ста жи́тельства) homeless person, vagrant

бор, а, о ~е, в ~у́, *pl.* ~ы́, ~о́в *m.* coniferous forest (*usu. pine*)

борде́л|ь, я *m.* (infml) brothel

бордо́вый *adj.* claret-coloured (BrE), -colored (AmE)

бордю́р, а *m.* border; (*тротуа́ра*) kerb (BrE), curb (AmE)

бор|е́ц, ца́ *m.* **1** (*за* + *a.*) fighter (for); campaigner; activist; б. за права́ же́нщин women's liberationist **2** (sport) wrestler

борз|а́я, о́й *f.*: англи́йская б. greyhound; ру́сская б. borzoi, Russian wolfhound

бормаши́н|а, ы *f.* (dentist's) drill

бормота́ни|е, я *nt.* muttering

бормо|та́ть, чу́, ~чешь *impf.* (*of* ▶ пробормота́ть) to mutter

Борне́о *nt. indecl.* Borneo

бо́ров, а *m.* hog

бор|ода́, оды́, *a.* ~оду, *pl.* ~оды, ~о́д, ~ода́м *f.* beard

борода́вк|а, и *f.* wart

борода́т|ый, ~, ~а *adj.* bearded

бор|озда́, озды́, *a.* ~озду́ *and* ~озду́, *pl.* ~озды, ~о́зд, ~озда́м *f.* furrow

✎ key word

бороз|ди́ть, жу́, ди́шь *impf.* (*of* ▶ изборозди́ть) to furrow

✎ **бор|о́ться**, ю́сь, ~ешься *impf.* (с + *i.*) to wrestle (with) (also fig.); (fig.) (*за* + *a. or* про́тив + *g.*) to struggle, fight (for; against)

борт, а, о ~е, на ~у́, *pl.* ~а́, ~о́в *m.* (*су́дна, грузовика́*) side; на ~у́ on board (*ship or aircraft*); вы́бросить за́ б. to throw overboard (also fig.)

бортово́й *adj. of* ▶ борт; б. журна́л (ship's) logbook

бортпроводни́к, а́ *m.* air steward

бортпроводни́ц|а, ы *f.* stewardess; air hostess (BrE)

борщ, а́ *m.* (cul.) bor(t)sch

✎ **борьб|а́**, ы́ *f.* **1** (sport) wrestling **2** (fig.) (с + *i. or* про́тив + *g.*) struggle, fight (with, against); (*за* + *a.*) struggle, fight (for); душе́вная б. mental strife; кампа́ния по ~е́ с престу́пностью crime-prevention campaign

босано́в|а, ы *f.* (*та́нец, му́зыка*) bossa nova

босико́м *adv.* barefoot; ходи́ть б. to go barefoot

Бо́сния и Герцегови́на, Бо́снии и Герцегови́ны *f.* Bosnia-Herzegovina, Bosnia and Herzegovina

бос|о́й, ~, ~а́, ~о *adj.* barefooted; на ~у́ но́гу with bare feet, barefoot

босоно́ж|ки, ек *f. pl.* (*sg.* ~а, ~и) sandals

босс, а *m.* boss

Босфо́р, а *m.* the Bosporus

бота́ник, а *m.* botanist

бота́ник|а, и *f.* botany

ботани́ческий *adj.* botanical; б. сад botanical gardens

боти́н|ок, ка, *g. pl.* б. *m.* boot (*ankle-high*)

бо́цман, а *m.* (naut.) boatswain

бо́чк|а, и *f.* barrel, cask

бочо́н|ок, ка *m.* small barrel, keg

боязли́в|ый, ~, ~а *adj.* timid, timorous

боя́зн|ь, и *f.* (+ *g.*) fear (of), dread of; б. темноты́ fear of the dark; из ~и for fear of, lest

боя́рышник, а *m.* (bot.) hawthorn

✎ **бо|я́ться**, ю́сь, и́шься *impf.* (+ *g.*) **1** (*испы́тывать страх*) to fear, be afraid (of); она́ ~и́тся темноты́ she is afraid of the dark; он ~и́тся пойти́ к врачу́ he is afraid to go to the doctor; ~ю́сь, что он (не) прие́дет I am afraid that he will (not) come; ~ю́сь, как бы он не прие́хал I am afraid that he may come **2** (*не переноси́ть*) to be afraid of, suffer from; э́ти расте́ния ~я́тся хо́лода these plants do not like the cold

бра́вый *adj.* gallant; manly

брази́л|ец, ьца *m.* Brazilian

Брази́ли|я, и *f.* Brazil

брази́льский *adj.* Brazilian

бразилья́нк|а, и *f. of* ▶ брази́лец

✎ **брак**[1], а *m.* (*супру́жество*) marriage; matrimony; свиде́тельство о ~е certificate of marriage

брак², а *m.* (*проду́кция*) rejects; (*изъя́н*) defect

брако́ван|ный, ~, ~а *p.p.p.* of ▶ бракова́ть *and adj.* rejected; defective

брак|ова́ть, у́ю *impf.* (*of* ▶ забракова́ть) to reject

браконье́р, а *m.* poacher

браконье́рств|о, а *nt.* poaching

бракоразво́дный *adj.* divorce; **б. проце́сс** divorce suit

бракосочета́ни|е, я *nt.* wedding, wedding ceremony

бра́нн|ый *adj.* abusive; ~ое сло́во swear word

бран|ь, и *f.* swearing; abuse; bad language

брасле́т, а *m.* bracelet

брасс, а *m.* (sport) breast stroke

✍ **брат, а**, *pl.* ~ья, ~ьев *m.* **1** brother; сво́дный б. stepbrother; единокро́вный б. half-brother (*by father*); единоутро́бный б. half-brother (*by mother*); двою́родный б. cousin **2** (fig.) brother; comrade; ~ья-писа́тели fellow-writers

бра́тск|ий *adj.* brotherly, fraternal; ~ая моги́ла communal grave (*esp. of war dead*)

бра́тств|о, а *nt.* brotherhood, fraternity

✍ **бра|ть, беру́, берёшь**, *past* ~л, ~ла́, ~ло *impf.* (*of* ▶ взять) **1** to take (*in var. senses*); б. наза́д to take back; б. курс (на + *a.*) to make (for), head (for); б. нача́ло (в + *p.*) to originate (in); б. но́ту to sing, play a note; б. приме́р (с + *g.*) to follow the example (of); б. сло́во (*выступа́ть*) to take the floor; б. в плен to take prisoner; б. на себя́ to take upon oneself; б. под аре́ст to put under arrest **2** (*получи́ть*) to get, obtain; (*принима́ть*) to take on; б. верх to get the upper hand; б. такси́ to take a taxi; б. своё to get one's way; to make itself felt; го́ды беру́т своё age tells; б. взаймы́ to borrow; б. в аре́нду to rent; б. напрока́т to hire **3** (в + *nom.-a.*) to take (as); б. в жёны to marry **4** (*захвати́ть*) to seize; to grip; б. власть to seize power **5** (*тре́бовать*) to exact; to take (= *to demand, require*); б. штраф to exact a fine **6** (*преодолева́ть*) to take; to surmount; б. барье́р to clear a hurdle **7** (+ *adv. of place*) (infml) to bear; б. вле́во to bear left

бра́|ться, беру́сь, берёшься, *past* ~лся, ~ла́сь, ~ло́сь *impf.* (*of* ▶ взя́ться) **1** *pass.* of ▶ брать **2** (за + *a.*) (*тро́гать*) to touch, lay hands (upon); б. за́ руки to link arms **3** (за + *a.*) (*принима́ться*) to take up; to get down (to); б. за де́ло to get down to business **4** (за + *a. or* + *inf.*) (*принима́ть на себя́*) to undertake; to take upon oneself; б. за поруче́ние to undertake a commission; б. вы́полнить рабо́ту to undertake a job; не беру́сь суди́ть I do not presume to judge **5** (*3rd person only*) (infml, *появля́ться*) to appear, arise; не зна́ю, отку́да у них де́ньги беру́тся I don't know where they get their money from **6**: б. за ум (infml) to come to one's senses

бра́тья *see* ▶ брат

бра́узер, а *m.* (comput.) browser

бра́чн|ый *adj.* marriage; conjugal; б. во́зраст marriageable age; ~ая конто́ра marriage bureau; ~ое свиде́тельство marriage certificate

брев|но́, на́, *pl.* ~на, ~ен, ~нам *nt.* log, beam; (sport) caber; (fig., *тупо́й челове́к*) dullard, insensitive person

бред, а, о ~е, в ~у́ *m.* delirium; ravings; (fig.) gibberish; быть в ~у́ to be delirious

бре́|дить, жу, дишь *impf.* to be delirious, rave

бредо́вый *adj.* crackpot, crazy

бре́|жу, дишь *see* ▶ бре́дить

брезгли́в|ый, ~, ~а *adj.* squeamish, fastidious; ~ое чу́вство feeling of disgust

брезе́нт, а *m.* tarpaulin

брело́к, а *m.* charm (*on bracelet*); б. для ключе́й key ring

бре́м|я, ~ени, i. ~енем, о ~ени *nt.* burden; load

бренд, а *m.* (comm.) brand

бре́ндинг, а *m.* (comm.) branding

бренча́|ть, у́, и́шь *impf.* **1** (+ *i.*) to jingle **2** (infml, *игра́ть*) to strum

бре́|ю, ешь *see* ▶ брить

брига́д|а, ы *f.* **1** (mil.) brigade; (naut.) subdivision **2** (*гру́ппа рабо́чих*) brigade, (work) team

бригади́р, а *m.* team leader; foreman

брига́дный *adj.* of ▶ брига́да

бридж, а *m.* bridge (*card game*)

брике́т, а *m.* briquette

бриллиа́нт, а *m.* (cut) diamond

бриллиа́нтовый *adj.* of ▶ бриллиа́нт

брита́н|ец, ца *m.* Briton; ~цы the British

Брита́ни|я, и *f.* Britain

брита́н|ка, ки *f.* of ▶ брита́нец

Брита́нск|ие острова́, ~их острово́в (*no sg.*) the British Isles

брита́нский *adj.* British

бри́тв|а, ы *f.* razor

бри́твенн|ый *adj.* shaving; ~ые принадле́жности shaving things

бритоголо́в|ый *adj.* shaven-headed; (*as m. n.* б., ~ого) skinhead

бри́т|ый, ~, ~а *p.p.p.* of ▶ брить *and adj.* clean-shaven

бр|ить, е́ю, е́ешь *impf.* (*of* ▶ побри́ть) to shave

брить|ё, я́ *nt.* shave; (*проце́сс*) shaving; лосьо́н по́сле ~я́ aftershave

бри́ться, е́юсь, е́ешься *impf.* (*of* ▶ побри́ться) to shave, have a shave

бров|ь, и, *pl.* ~и, ~е́й *f.* eyebrow; brow; хму́рить ~и to knit one's brows, frown

брод, а *m.* ford

бро|ди́ть¹, жу́, ~дишь *impf.* (*гуля́ть*) to wander, roam

бро|ди́ть², ~дит *impf.* (*о пи́ве*) to ferment

бродя́г|а, и *c.g.* tramp, vagrant; down-and-out

б

б

бродя́ч|ий *adj.* vagrant; wandering, roving; (fig.) restless; ∼ая соба́ка stray dog

броже́ни|е, я *nt.* fermentation

бро|жу́, ∼дишь *see* ▶ броди́ть[1]

бро́кер, а *m.* broker; **биржево́й б.** stockbroker

бро́кколи *f. indecl.* broccoli

броне... *comb. form* (mil.) armoured (BrE), armored (AmE)

броневи́к, а́ *m.* armoured car (BrE), armored car (AmE)

бронев|о́й *adj.* armoured (BrE), armored (AmE); ∼ы́е пли́ты (mil.) armour plating (BrE), armor plating (AmE)

бронежиле́т, а *m.* bulletproof vest

бронено́с|ец, ца *m.* (naut.) battleship

бронетранспортёр, а *m.* armoured (BrE), armored (AmE) personnel carrier

бро́нз|а, ы *f.* bronze

бро́нзовый *adj.* bronze; (загоре́лый) tanned; **б. век** the Bronze Age; **б. зага́р** sunburn, suntan

брони́рованный *p.p.p. of* ▶ брони́ровать *and adj.* reserved

брониро́ванный *p.p.p. of* ▶ брони́ровать *and adj.* armoured (BrE), armored (AmE)

брони́р|овать, ую *impf.* (of ▶ заброни́ровать) to reserve, book

бронир|ова́ть, у́ю *impf. and pf.* to armour (BrE), armor (AmE)

бронхи́т, а *m.* bronchitis

брон|ь, и *f.* (infml) reservation

брон|я́, и́ *f.* armour (BrE), armor (AmE); (танка, судна) armour plate (BrE), armor plate (AmE)

броса́|ть, ю *impf.* (of ▶ бро́сить) **1** (мета́ть) to throw, cast, fling; **б. взгляд** to dart a glance; **б. обвине́ния** to hurl accusations; **б. тень** to cast a shadow; **б. на ве́тер** to throw away, waste **2** (поки́нуть) to leave, abandon, desert; **б. му́жа** to desert one's husband; **б. рабо́ту** to give up, chuck in one's job **3** (+ *inf.*) (перестава́ть) to give up, leave off; **он бро́сил кури́ть** he gave up smoking

броса́|ться, а́юсь *impf.* **1** (*impf. only*) (+ *i.*) to throw at one another, pelt one another (with) **2** (*impf. only*) (+ *i.*) to throw away; **б. деньга́ми** to throw away, squander one's money **3** (*pf.* ∼иться) (на, в + *a.*) to throw oneself (on, upon), rush (to); **б. на коле́ни** to fall on one's knees; **б. в объя́тия** (+ *d.*) to fall into the arms (of); **б. на по́мощь** to rush to assistance **4** (*pf.* ∼иться) **б. в глаза́** to be striking, arrest attention **5** (*pf.* ∼иться) (+ *inf.*) to begin, start

бро́|сить, шу, сишь *pf.* (of ▶ броса́ть): ∼сь(те)! stop it!

бро́|ситься, шусь, сишься *pf. of* ▶ броса́ться

брос|о́к, ка́ *m.* **1** (взмах руки) throw; **штрафно́й б.** (sport) free throw **2** (скачо́к) bound; spurt

бро́|шу, сишь *see* ▶ бро́сить

брош|ь, и *f.* brooch

брошю́р|а, ы *f.* pamphlet; (реклáмная) brochure

брус, а, *pl.* ∼ья, ∼ьев *m.* beam; **паралле́льные б.** (sport) parallel bars

брусни́к|а, и *f.* cowberry (*Vaccinium vitis-idaea*)

брус|о́к, ка́ *m.* bar; ingot; **точи́льный б.** whetstone

бру́тто *adj. indecl.* gross; **вес б.** gross weight

бры́з|гать, жу, жешь *impf.* (of ▶ бры́знуть) (чем) **1** to splash, spatter; (заби́ть струёй) to gush, spurt **2** (*pres.* ∼жу *or* ∼гаю) (окропля́ть) to sprinkle

бры́зга|ться, юсь *impf.* (infml) to splash; to splash oneself, one another

бры́зг|и, ∼ (no sg.) spray, splashes

бры́з|жу, жешь *see* ▶ бры́згать

бры́з|нуть, ну, нешь *inst. pf. of* ▶ бры́згать

брыка́|ться, юсь *impf.* (ребёнок) to kick; (ло́шадь) to buck; (fig.) to kick, rebel

брюзж|а́ть, у́, и́шь *impf.* to grumble

брюк|и, ∼ (no sg.) trousers; **б.-ю́бка** culottes

брюне́т, а *m.* dark-haired man

брюне́тк|а, и *f.* brunette

Брюссе́л|ь, я *m.* Brussels

брюссе́льск|ий *adj.* Brussels; ∼ая капу́ста Brussels sprouts

брю́х|о, а, *pl.* ∼и *nt.* (infml) belly; (большо́й живо́т) paunch

брюшн|о́й *adj.* abdominal; **б. тиф** typhoid (fever)

БТР *m. indecl.* (abbr. of **бронетранспортёр**) APC (armoured personnel carrier)

бу́б|ен, на *m.* tambourine

бу́бны[1] *pl. of* ▶ бу́бен

бу́б|ны[2], ен *f. pl.* (sg. infml ∼на, ∼ны) (в ка́ртах) **1** diamonds; **дво́йка ∼ен** the two of diamonds **2** (sg.) a diamond

бу́ги-ву́ги *nt. indecl.* boogie-woogie

Будапе́шт, а *m.* Budapest

будди́зм, а *m.* Buddhism

будди́йский *adj.* Buddhist

будди́ст, а *m.* Buddhist

будди́ст|ка, ки *f. of* ▶ будди́ст

бу́дет 1 *3rd person sg. fut. of* ▶ быть; **б. ему́ за э́то!** he'll catch it! **2** (*as pred.*) (infml) that's enough!; that'll do!; **б. вам писа́ть!** it's time you stopped writing!

буди́льник, а *m.* alarm clock

бу|ди́ть, жу́, ∼дишь *impf.* **1** (*pf.* раз∼) to wake, awaken, call **2** (*pf.* про∼) (fig., возбужда́ть) to rouse, arouse; to stir up; **б. мысль** to set (one) thinking

бу́дк|а, и *f.* (сторожа́) box, booth; (ларёк) stall; **карау́льная б.** sentry box; **соба́чья б.** dog kennel; **телефо́нная б.** telephone booth

бу́дн|и, ей *pl.* **1** weekdays; working days, workdays; **по ∼ям** on weekdays **2** (однообра́зная жизнь) humdrum life; colourless existence

бу́дний *adj.:* **б. день** weekday

⚹ key word

будто 1 *conj.* as if, as though **2** *conj.* that (*implying doubt as to the truth of a statement*); **он утверждает, б. свободно говорит на десяти языках** he claims that he speaks ten languages fluently **3** (*also* **б. бы, как б.**) *particle* (infml, *кажется*) apparently

буд\|у, ешь *fut. of* ▶ **быть**

будучи *pres. gerund of* ▶ **быть**; being

будущ\|ий *adj.* future; next; ... to be; ~**ее время** (gram.) future tense; **в ~ем году** next year; ~**ая мать** expectant mother; (*as nt. n.* ~**ее,** ~**его**) (gram.) future tense; **в ближайшем ~ем** in the near future

будь and **будьте** *imper. of* ▶ **быть**; **будьте добры, будьте любезны** (+ *inf. or imper.*) please; would you be good enough (to), kind enough (to); **будь, что будет** come what may; **будь он богат, будь он беден, мне всё равно** be he rich or be he poor, it is all one to me; (*sg. also used in place of 'if' clause in conditional sentences*) **не будь вас, всё бы пропало** but for you, all would have been lost

буженин\|а, ы *f.* boiled salted pork

бу\|жу, ~**дишь** *see* ▶ **будить**

бузин\|а, ы *f.* (bot., *красная; чёрная*) elder

буй\|ный, ~**ен,** ~**йна,** ~**йно** *adj.* **1** (*непокорный*) wild; tempestuous; **б. сумасшедший** violent, dangerous lunatic **2** (*обильный*) luxuriant, lush; **б. рост** luxuriant growth

буйств\|о, а *nt.* unruly conduct

бук, а *m.* beech

букв\|а, ы, *g. pl.* ~ *f.* letter (*of the alphabet*); **б. закона** the letter of the law

буквально *adv.* literally; (*дословно*) word for word

буквальн\|ый *adj.* literal; ~**ое значение** literal meaning; **б. перевод** literal translation

букварь, я *m.* ABC; primer

букет, а *m.* **1** bouquet; bunch of flowers **2** (*аромат*) bouquet; aroma

букинистический *adj.*: **б. магазин** second-hand bookshop

буклет, а *m.* (fold-out) leaflet

букмекер, а *m.* bookmaker, bookie (infml)

буксир, а *m.* **1** (*судно*) tug, tugboat **2** (*канат*) tow rope; **взять на б.** to take in tow; (fig.) to give a helping hand

буксир\|овать, ую *impf.* to tow, have in tow

букс\|овать, ую *impf.* to skid

булавк\|а, и *f.* pin; **английская б.** safety pin

булк\|а, и *f.* (*булочка*) roll; (*белый хлеб*) white bread; **сдобная б.** bun

булочн\|ая, ой *f.* bakery; baker's shop

булыжник, а *m.* cobblestone (*also collect.*)

бульвар, а *m.* avenue; boulevard

бульвар\|ный *adj. of* ▶ **бульвар;** ~**ная литература** pulp fiction; ~**ная пресса** the tabloids; the gutter press

бульдог, а *m.* bulldog

бульдозер, а *m.* bulldozer

бульон, а *m.* broth; stock

бум, а *m.* (econ.) boom

бумаг\|а, и *f.* **1** (*материал*) paper; **газетная б.** newsprint **2** (*документ*) document; (*in pl.*) (official) papers; **ценные ~и** (fin.) securities

бумажк\|а, и *f.* piece of paper

бумажник, а *m.* wallet

бума\|жный *adj. of* ▶ **бумага;** (fig.) (existing only on) paper; ~**жная волокита** red tape; ~**жные деньги** paper money; **б. змей** kite; ~**жная фабрика** paper mill

бумеранг, а *m.* boomerang

бунгало *nt. indecl.* bungalow (*in tropical countries*)

бункер, а *m.* bunker

бунт, а *m.* revolt; riot

бунтарский *adj.* **1** seditious; mutinous **2** (fig.) rebellious; turbulent; **б. дух** rebellious spirit

бунтарь, я *m.* rebel (also fig.); insurgent; mutineer; rioter

бунт\|овать, ую *impf.* (*pf.* **взбунтоваться**) to revolt, rebel; to mutiny; to riot; (fig.) to rage, go berserk

бунтовщик, а *m.* rebel, insurgent; mutineer; rioter

буревестник, а *m.* stormy petrel

бурени\|е, я *nt.* (tech.) boring, drilling

буржуази\|я, и *f.* bourgeoisie; **мелкая б.** petty bourgeoisie

буржуаз\|ный, ~**ен,** ~**на** *adj.* bourgeois

бур\|ить, ю, ишь *impf.* (*of* ▶ **пробурить**) (tech.) to bore; to drill

бурл\|ить, ю, ишь *impf.* to seethe, boil up (*also fig.*)

бур\|ный, ~**ен,** ~**на,** ~**но** *adj.* **1** (*погода, море*) stormy, rough; (*спор*) heated; (*жизнь, восторг, аплодисменты*) wild **2** (*рост*) rapid

буров\|ой *adj.* boring; ~**ая вышка** derrick; ~**ая скважина** bore, borehole, well

бур\|ый, ~**,** ~**á,** ~**о** *adj.* brown; **б. медведь** brown bear

бур\|я, и *f.* storm (also fig.); **б. в стакане воды** storm in a teacup

бурят, а, *g. pl.* **б. м.** Buryat

бурят\|ка, ки *f. of* ▶ **бурят**

бурятский *adj.* Buryat

бус\|ы, ~ (*no sg.*) beads

бутерброд, а *m.* slice of bread and butter; sandwich; **закон ~а** Sod's Law, Murphy's Law

бутик, а *m.* boutique

бутон, а *m.* bud

бутс\|ы, ~ *pl.* (*sg.* ~**а,** ~**ы**) football boots

бутылк\|а, и *f.* bottle

буфер, а, *pl.* ~**á м.** (rail., comput.) (also fig.) buffer

буфет, а *m.* **1** (*шкаф*) sideboard **2** (*закусочная*) buffet, snack bar; (*стойка*) (refreshment) bar, counter

буханк\|а, и *f.* loaf

Бухарест, а *m.* Bucharest

б

бу́х|ать, аю *impf.* (*of* ▸ **бу́хнуть¹**) **1** (*ударять*) to thump, bang **2** (*о выстреле*) to thud, thunder

бух|а́ть, а́ю *impf.* (*of* ▸ **бу́хнуть²**) (infml, *пить*) to drink heavily, binge-drink

бухга́лтер, а *m.* bookkeeper, accountant

бухгалте́ри|я, и *f.* **1** bookkeeping, accountancy **2** (*отдел*) counting house

бухга́лтерск|ий *adj.* bookkeeping, account; ~ая кни́га account book

бу́х|нуть¹, ну, нешь, *past* ~нул *pf. of* ▸ **бу́хать**

бу́х|нуть², ну, нешь, *past* ~нул *pf. of* ▸ **буха́ть**

бу́хт|а, ы *f.* (geog.) bay

буш|ева́ть, у́ю *impf.* to rage; (fig.) to rage, storm

Буэ́нос-А́йрес, а *m.* Buenos Aires

⚘ **бы** (*abbr.* **б**) *particle* **1** (*выражает предположительную возможность*) (*see also* ▸ **е́сли**) я мог бы об э́том догада́ться I might have guessed it; **бы́ло бы о́чень прия́тно вас ви́деть** it would be very nice to see you **2**: (**+ ни**) (*forms indefinite prons.*) **кто бы ни** whoever; **что бы ни** whatever; **как бы ни** however; **кто бы ни пришёл** whoever comes; **что бы ни случи́лось** whatever happens; **как бы то ни́ было** however that may be, be that as it may **3** (*выражает пожелание*): **я бы вы́пил пи́ва** I should like a drink of beer **4** (*выражает предложение*): **вы бы отдохну́ли** you should take a rest

быва́ло *see* ▸ **быва́ть**

быва́лый *adj.* experienced; worldly-wise

⚘ **быва́|ть, ю** *impf.* **1** (*случаться*) to happen; (*происходить*) to take place; ~ет, что **поезда́ с се́вера опа́здывают** trains from the north are sometimes late **2** (*быть*) to be; (*находиться*) to be present; (*посещать*) to frequent; **они́ ре́дко ~ют в теа́тре** they seldom go to the theatre **3** (*быть склонным*) to be inclined to be, tend to be; **он ~ет раздражи́тельным** he is inclined to be irritable **4**: **как ни в чём не ~ло** (infml) as if nothing had happened; **как не ~ло** (+ g.) to have completely disappeared; **головно́й бо́ли у меня́ как не ~ло** my headache has completely gone

⚘ **бы́вший** *p.p. of* ▸ **быть** *and adj.* former, ex-; one-time; **б. президе́нт** former president, ex-president

бык, а́ *m.* bull; ox; **здоро́в как б.** as strong as an ox

бы́ло *particle* (*indicates that an action was impending or had just begun, but was not completed*): **он отпра́вился б. с ни́ми, но верну́лся** he started out with them but turned back; **чуть б.** very nearly; **они́ чуть б. не уби́ли его́** they all but killed him

был|ь, и *f.* fact, true story

быстроде́йстви|е, я *nt.* (tech.) speed, response time

быстрот|а́, ы́ *f.* rapidity, quickness; (*скорость*) speed

быстрохо́д|ный, ~ен, ~на *adj.* fast, high-speed

⚘ **бы́стр|ый, ~, ~а́, ~о** *adj.* rapid, fast, quick; (*немедленный*) prompt

быт, а, о ~е, в ~у́ (*no pl.*) *m.* way of life; life; **солда́тский б.** army life

быти|é, я́ *nt.* (phil.) being, existence, objective reality; **кни́га Б~я** (bibl.) Genesis

быт|ово́й *adj. of* ▸ **быт**; social; ~овы́е прибо́ры domestic appliances; ~ово́е обслу́живание населе́ния consumer services; ~ово́е явле́ние everyday occurrence

⚘ **быть,** *pres. only used in 3rd person sg.* **есть,** *fut.* **бу́ду, бу́дешь,** *past* **был, была́, бы́ло,** *neg.* **не́ был, не была́, не́ было,** *imper.* **будь(те)** (*see also* ▸ **бу́дет,** ▸ **будь,** ▸ **бы́ло,** ▸ **есть²**) *impf.* **1** (*существовать*) to be; **есть таки́е лю́ди** there are such people, such people do exist **2**: **б. у** (*see also* ▸ **есть¹**) (*иметь*) to be in the possession (of); **у них была́ прекра́сная да́ча** they had a lovely dacha **3** (*находиться*) to be; **где вы бы́ли вчера́?** where were you yesterday?; **он тут был не при чём** he had nothing to do with it; **на ней была́ ро́зовая ко́фточка** she had on a pink blouse **4** (*случаться*) to be, happen, take place; **э́того не мо́жет б.!** it cannot be!; **так и б.** so be it, all right, very well, have it your own way
  ● (*as v. aux.*) to be

быч|о́к¹, ка́ *m.* (*бык*) steer

быч|о́к², ка́ *m.* (*рыба*) goby

бью, бьёшь *see* ▸ **бить**

⚘ **бюдже́т, а** *m.* budget

бюдже́тник, а *m.* (infml) person who is paid from the state budget (*e.g. a teacher*)

⚘ **бюдже́тный** *adj.* budgetary; **б. год** fiscal year

бюллете́н|ь, я *m.* **1** bulletin; **информацио́нный б.** newsletter **2**: (*избира́тельный*) **б.** ballot paper **3**: (*больни́чный*) **б.** medical certificate

бюро́ *nt. indecl.* **1** (*конто́ра*) bureau, office; **б. нахо́док** lost property office; **б. по трудоустро́йству** employment agency; **спра́вочное б.** inquiry office, information office; **туристи́ческое б.** travel agency **2** (*стол*) bureau, writing desk

бюрокра́т, а *m.* bureaucrat

бюрократи́ческий *adj.* bureaucratic

бюрокра́ти|я, и *f.* bureaucracy (*also collect.*)

бюст, а *m.* (*скульпту́ра*) bust; (*же́нский*) bust, bosom

бюстга́льтер, а *m.* bra(ssiere)

Вв

◦ **в** *prep.*

● **I.** (+ *a.* and *p.*) **1** (+ *a.*) (*указывает на направление*) into, to; (+ *p.*) (*указывает на место*) in, at; **пое́хать в Москву́** to go to Moscow; **роди́ться в Москве́** to be born in Moscow; **сесть в ваго́н** to get into the carriage; **сиде́ть в ваго́не** to be in the carriage; **смотре́ть в окно́** to look out of the window **2** (*указывает на вид*): **руба́шка в кле́тку** check(ed) shirt; **ходи́ть в шу́бе** to wear a fur coat **3** (+ *nom.-a. pl. and p. pl.*) (*указывает на профессию*): **пойти́ в учителя́** to become a teacher **4** (*обозначает время*): **в понеде́льник** on Monday; **в январе́** in January; **в 1899 году́** in 1899; **в двадца́том ве́ке** in the twentieth century; **в четы́ре часа́** at four o'clock; **в четвёртом часу́** between three and four; **в на́ши дни** in our day; **в тече́ние** (+ *g.*) during, in the course (of)

● **II.** (+ *a.*) **1** (*указывает на сходство*): **быть в кого́-н.** to take after sb; to be like sb; **она́ вся в тётю** she is just like her aunt **2** (*указывает на цель*) for, as; **сказа́ть в шу́тку** to say for a joke **3** (+ *раз and comp. adv.*) (*указывает на сравнение*): **в два ра́за бо́льше** twice as big, twice the size; **в два ра́за ме́ньше** half as big, half the size **4** (*указывает на игру, спорт*): **игра́ть в ка́рты, ша́хматы, футбо́л** to play cards, chess, football

● **III.** (+ *p.*) **1** at a distance of; **в трёх киломе́трах от го́рода** three kilometres from the town; **они́ живу́т в десяти́ мину́тах ходьбы́ отсю́да** they live ten minutes' walk from here **2** in; of (= *consisting of, amounting to*); **пье́са в трёх де́йствиях** play in three acts

◦ **в.** (*abbr. of* **век**) c., century

ваго́н, а *m.* **1** carriage (BrE), coach (BrE), car (AmE); **мя́гкий, жёсткий в.** soft-seated, hard-seated carriage (BrE), car (AmE); **бага́жный в.** luggage van; **в.-рестора́н** dining car, restaurant car; **спа́льный в.** sleeping car **2** (*груз*) wagonload; (fig., infml) loads, lots

вагоне́тк|а, и *f.* truck; trolley

ва́жность|ь, и *f.* **1** importance; significance **2** (*надменность*) pomposity, pretentiousness

◦ **ва́ж|ный, ~ен, ~на́, ~но, ~ны́** *adj.* **1** (*short form pl.* **~ны́**) important; weighty, consequential; **са́мое ~ное** the (important) thing (is); **~ная пти́ца/ши́шка** (infml) bigwig **2** (*short form pl.* **~ны́**) (*гордый*) pompous, pretentious

ва́з|а, ы *f.* vase, bowl

вай-фа́й *m. indecl.* (*in full* **техноло́гия в.**) (comput.) Wi-Fi (technology)®

вака́нси|я, и *f.* vacancy; **я́рмарка ~й** jobs fair

вака́нт|ный, ~ен, ~на *adj.* vacant, unfilled; **~ная до́лжность** vacancy

ва́кс|а, ы *f.* black (shoe) polish

ва́куум, а *m.* vacuum

вакци́н|а, ы *f.* vaccine

вал¹, а, *pl.* **~ы́** *m.* (*волна́*) billow, roller

вал², а, *pl.* **~ы́** *m.* (*на́сыпь*) bank, earthen wall; (mil.) rampart

вал³, а, *pl.* **~ы́** *m.* (tech.) shaft

вале́жник, а (*no pl.*) *m.* (collect.) brushwood

ва́лен|ки, ок *m. pl.* (*sg.* **~ок, ~ка**) valenki (*felt boots*)

вале́т, а *m.* (cards) jack

вал|и́ть¹, ю́, ~ишь *impf.* **1** (*pf.* **по~** and **с~**) (*заставля́ть па́дать*) to throw down, bring down; to overthrow; **в. кого́-н. с ног** to knock sb off his feet; **в. дере́вья** to fell trees **2** (*pf.* **с~**) (*в ку́чу*) to heap up, pile up **3** (*pf.* **с~**) (infml): **в. вину́** (**на** + *a.*) to lump the blame (on)

вал|и́ть², и́т *impf.* (infml, *дви́гаться ма́ссой*) to flock, throng, pour; **снег ~и́т кру́пными хло́пьями** the snow is coming down in large flakes

вал|и́ться, ю́сь, ~ишься *impf.* (*of* ▸ **повали́ться**, ▸ **свали́ться**) to fall, collapse; to topple over; **в. от уста́лости** to drop from tiredness

валли́|ец, йца *m.* Welshman

валли́йк|а, и *f.* Welshwoman

валли́йский *adj.* Welsh

валово́й *adj.* (econ.) gross; wholesale; **в. вну́тренний проду́кт** gross domestic product; **в. национа́льный проду́кт** gross national product

валто́рн|а, ы *f.* (mus.) French horn

валторни́ст, а *m.* hornist, (French) horn player

валторни́ст|ка, ки *f. of* ▸ **валторни́ст**

валу́н, а́ *m.* boulder

вальс, а *m.* waltz

валю́т|а, ы *f.* (fin., econ.) **1** (*де́нежная систе́ма*) currency; **курс ~ы** rate of exchange **2** (collect.) (*иностра́нные де́ньги*) foreign currency; **твёрдая/свобо́дно конверти́руемая в.** hard currency

валю́тно-фина́нсов|ый *adj.*: **~ая би́ржа** foreign exchange market

валю́тный *adj. of* ▸ **валю́та**; currency; **в. фонд** monetary fund

валя́|ть, ю *impf.* **1** (*pf.* **вы́~**) (*валя́я, покры́ть чем-н.*) to roll, drag; **в. в грязи́** to drag in the mire **2**: **в. дурака́** (infml) to play the fool

B

валя́|ться, юсь *impf.* **1** (*кататься*) to roll **2** (infml, *бездельничать*) to lie about

вам *d. of* ▸ **вы**

ва́ми *i. of* ▸ **вы**

вампи́р, а *m.* vampire

ванда́л, а *m.* vandal

вандали́зм, а *m.* vandalism

вани́л|ь, и *f.* vanilla

вани́льный *adj. of* ▸ **вани́ль**

ва́нн|а, ы *f.* bath; **приня́ть** ∼**у** to take a bath

ва́нн|ая, ой *f.* bathroom

ва́рварский *adj.* barbaric

ва́рварств|о, а *nt.* barbarity

ва́режк|а, и *f.* mitten

варе́ник, а *m.* varenik (*curd or fruit dumpling*)

варёный *adj.* boiled

варе́нь|е, я *nt.* preserve(s) (*containing whole fruit*); jam (BrE)

⚜ **вариа́нт, а** *m.* (*разновидность*) variant; version; (*возможность*) option; (*сценарий*) scenario; model

вар|и́ть, ю́, ∼ишь *impf.* (*of* ▸ **свари́ть 1**) **1** to boil; to cook; **в. карто́фель** to boil potatoes; **в. обе́д** to cook dinner; **в. пи́во** to brew beer **2** (*о голове*): **голова́/башка́ у него́ ва́рит** (infml) he's quick on the uptake

вар|и́ться, ∼ится *impf.* (*of* ▸ **свари́ться**) **1** (*в кипятке*) to boil; (*приготовляться на огне*) to cook **2** *pass. of* ▸ **вари́ть**

Варша́в|а, ы *f.* Warsaw

варьи́р|овать, ую *impf.* to vary, modify

вас *g., a., and p. of* ▸ **вы**

васил|ёк, ька́ *m.* (bot.) cornflower

ва́т|а, ы *f.* cotton wool (BrE), absorbent cotton (AmE); (*для подкладки*) wadding

Ватика́н, а *m.* the Vatican

ва́тник, а *m.* quilted jacket

ва́тн|ый *adj.* wadded, quilted; ∼**ое одея́ло** quilt

ватру́шк|а, и *f.* curd tart

ватт, а, g. pl. в. *m.* watt

ва́учер, а *m.* voucher

ва́ф|ля, ли, g. pl. ∼**ель** *f.* waffle; wafer

ва́хт|а, ы *f.* (*сменная работа*) shift; **нести́** ∼**у** to be on duty; (naut.) watch; **стоя́ть на** ∼**е** to keep watch

вахтёр, а *m.* janitor, porter

ва́хтовый *adj.* shift-based

⚜ **ваш,** ∼**его,** *f.* ∼**а,** ∼**ей,** *nt.* ∼**е,** ∼**его,** *pl.* ∼**и,** ∼**их** *poss. pron.* (*при существительном*) your; (*без существительного*) yours; **э́то** ∼ **каранда́ш** this is your pencil; **э́тот каранда́ш в.** this pencil is yours; (*as pl. n.* ∼**и,** ∼**их**) your people, your folk

Вашингто́н, а *m.* Washington

вая́|ть, ю *impf.* (*of* ▸ **изва́ять**) to sculpt; (*из камня, дерева*) to carve, chisel

вбега́|ть, ю *impf.* (**в** + *a.*) to run (into)

вбе|жа́ть, гу́, жи́шь, гу́т *pf. of* ▸ **вбега́ть**

вбива́|ть, ю *impf. of* ▸ **вбить**

вбить, вобью́, вобьёшь *pf.* (*of* ▸ **вбива́ть**) to drive in, hammer in

вблизи́ *adv.* (**от** + *g.*) close by; not far (from); **рассма́тривать в.** to examine closely

вбок *adv.* sideways, to one side

вбра́сывани|е, я *nt.*: **в.** (**мяча́**) throw-in (*in football*); **в.** (**ша́йбы**) face-off (*in ice hockey*)

вбра́сыва|ть, ю *impf. of* ▸ **вбро́сить**

вбро́|сить, шу, сишь *pf.* (*of* ▸ **вбра́сывать**) to throw in(to)

вва́лива|ться, юсь *impf. of* ▸ **ввали́ться**

ввал|и́ться, ю́сь, ∼**ишься** *pf.* **1** (fig., infml, *входить*) to burst into **2** (*стать впалым*) to become hollow, sunken; **с** ∼**и́вшимися щека́ми** hollow-cheeked

⚜ **введе́ни|е, я** *nt.* introduction

вве|ду́, дёшь *see* ▸ **ввести́**

вве|зти́, у́, ёшь, *past* ∼**,** ∼**ла́** *pf.* (*of* ▸ **ввози́ть**) to import

вверх *adv.* up, upward(s); **идти́ в. по ле́стнице** to go upstairs; **в. по тече́нию** upstream; **в. дном** upside down; **в. нога́ми** head over heels

вверху́ *adv. and prep.* + *g.* above, overhead; **в. страни́цы** at the top of the page

вве|сти́, ду́, дёшь, *past* ∼**л,** ∼**ла́** *pf.* (*of* ▸ **вводи́ть**) (*человека, животное*) to lead in, bring in, take in; (*закон, пошлины*) to introduce, bring in; (*поместить внутрь*) to introduce, put into; (*данные*) to enter, key in; **в. в заблужде́ние** to mislead; **в. в курс чего́-н.** to acquaint with (the facts of) sth

ввиду́ *prep.* + *g.* in view (of); **в. того́, что** as

ввин|ти́ть, чу́, ти́шь *pf.* (*of* ▸ **ввинчивать**) (**в** + *a.*) to screw (in)

вви́нчива|ть, ю *impf. of* ▸ **ввинти́ть**

⚜ **вво|ди́ть, жу́,** ∼**дишь** *impf. of* ▸ **ввести́**

вво́дный *adj.* introductory; (gram.): ∼**ое сло́во** parenthetic word, parenthesis

вво|жу́[1], ∼**дишь** *see* ▸ **вводи́ть**

вво|жу́[2], ∼**зишь** *see* ▸ **ввози́ть**

ввоз, а (*no pl.*) *m.* **1** (*действие*) importation **2** (*импорт*) import

вво|зи́ть, жу́, ∼**зишь** *impf. of* ▸ **ввезти́**

ввозн|о́й *adj.* (*товар*) imported; (*attr.*) import; ∼**ая по́шлина** import duty

ВВП *m. indecl.* (*abbr. of* **валово́й вну́тренний проду́кт**) GDP (*gross domestic product*)

ВВС *pl. indecl.* (*abbr. of* **вое́нно-возду́шные си́лы**) Air Force

вvя|за́ться, жу́сь, ∼**жешься** *pf.* (*of* ▸ **ввя́зываться**) (infml) (**в** + *a.*) (*вмешаться*) to meddle (in); (*впутаться*) to get involved (in), mixed up (in)

ввя́зыва|ться, юсь *impf. of* ▸ **ввяза́ться**

вглубь *adv. and prep.* + *g.* deep down; deep into, into the depths

вдалеке́ *adv.* in the distance; **в. от** (+ *g.*) a long way from

вдали́ *adv.* in the distance, far off; **в. от го́рода** a long way from the city; **исчеза́ть в.** to vanish into the distance

⚜ key word

вдаль *adv.* afar, at a distance; **гляде́ть в.** to look into the distance

вдво́е *adv.* twice; double; **в. лу́чше** twice as good; **сложи́ть в.** to fold double

вдвоём *adv.* the two together; **они́ написа́ли статью́ в.** the two of them together wrote the article

вдвойне́ *adv.* twice, double; doubly (also fig.); **плати́ть в.** to pay double; **он в. винова́т** he is doubly to blame

вдева́|ть, ю *impf. of* ▶ вдеть

вде|ть, ́ну, ́нешь *pf.* (*of* ▶ вдева́ть) (**в** + *a.*) to put in(to); **в. ни́тку в иго́лку** to thread a needle

вдоба́вок *adv.* (infml) in addition; moreover; into the bargain; **в. к** (+ *d.*) in addition to

вдов|а́, ы́, *pl.* **́ы** *f.* widow

вдов|е́ц, ца́ *m.* widower

вдо́воль *adv.* **1** (*в изоби́лии*) in abundance **2** (*вполне́ доста́точно*) enough; **он нае́лся в.** he ate his fill

вдого́нку *adv.* (infml) after, in pursuit of; **бро́ситься в.** (**за** + *i.*) to rush (after)

вдоль 1 *prep.* (+ *g. or* по + *d.*) along; **в. бе́рега** along the bank **2** *adv.* lengthwise, longways; **в. и поперёк** (*повсю́ду*) in all directions, far and wide

вдох, а *m.* breath; **сде́лать глубо́кий в.** to take a deep breath

вдохнове́ни|е, я *nt.* inspiration

вдохнов|и́ть, лю́, и́шь *pf.* (*of* ▶ вдохновля́ть) (+ *a. or* на + *a.*) to inspire (to)

вдохновля́|ть, ю *impf. of* ▶ вдохнови́ть

вдохн|у́ть, у́, ёшь *pf.* (*of* ▶ вдыха́ть) **1** (*во́здух*) to breathe in; (*дым*) inhale **2** (*настрое́ние*) (**в** + *a.*) to instil (into); **в. му́жество в кого́-н.** to instil courage into sb

вдре́безги *adv.* (*на ме́лкие ча́сти*) to pieces, to smithereens

✎ вдруг *adv.* **1** (*неожи́данно*) suddenly, all of a sudden **2** (*as interrog. particle*) (infml, *а что е́сли*) what if, suppose; **(а) в. они́ узна́ют?** but suppose they find out?

вду́м|аться, аюсь *pf.* (*of* ▶ вду́мываться) (**в** + *a.*) to think over, ponder, meditate (on)

вду́мыва|ться, юсь *impf. of* ▶ вду́маться

вдыха́ни|е, я *nt.* inhalation

вдыха́|ть, ю *impf. of* ▶ вдохну́ть

веб-са́йт, а *m.* (comput.) website

веб-страни́ц|а, ы *f.* (comput.) web page

вегетариа́н|ец, ца *m.* vegetarian; **стро́гий в.** vegan

вегетариа́н|ка, ки *f. of* ▶ вегетариа́нец

вегетариа́нский *adj.* vegetarian

ве́да|ть, ю *impf.* **1** (*знать*) to know **2** (+ *i.*) (*заве́довать*) to manage, be in charge of

✎ ве́дени|е, я *nt.* authority; jurisdiction; **э́ти дела́ в моём ́ ∼и** I am in charge of these things

✎ веде́ни|е, я *nt.* conducting, conduct; **в. хозя́йства** the running of a household

ве́дома (*only in phrr.*): **без в., с в.; без моего́ в.** unknown to me; **с моего́ в.** with my knowledge, with my consent

ве́домост|ь, и *f.* list, register; **платёжная в.** payroll

ве́домственный *adj.* departmental

ве́домств|о, а *nt.* department

вед|ро́, ра́, *pl.* **∼ра, ∼ер** *nt.* bucket, pail

веду́, ёшь *see* ▶ вести́

✎ веду́щ|ий *pres. part. act. of* ▶ вести́ *and adj.* leading; (tech.): **∼ее колесо́** driving wheel; (*as m. n.* **в., ∼его**) presenter; compère

✎ ведь *conj.* **1** (*де́ло в том, что*) you see, you know (*but often requires no translation*); **она́ всё вре́мя покупа́ет но́вые пла́тья: в. она́ о́чень бога́та** she is always buying new dresses — she is very rich, you know **2** (*particle*) (*не пра́вда ли?*) is it not?; is it?; **в. э́то пра́вда?** it's the truth, isn't it?

ве́дьм|а, ы *f.* witch

ве́ер, а, *pl.* **∼а́** *m.* fan

ве́жливост|ь, и *f.* politeness, courtesy

ве́жлив|ый, ∼, ∼а *adj.* polite, courteous

везде́ *adv.* everywhere; **в. и всю́ду** here, there, and everywhere

вездесу́щ|ий, ∼, ∼а *adj.* (*челове́к*) ubiquitous; (*Бог*) omnipresent

вездехо́д, а *m.* four-wheel drive (vehicle)

везе́ни|е, я *nt.* luck

вез|ти́, у́, ёшь, *past* **∼, ∼ла́** *impf.* (*of* ▶ повезти́, *det. of* ▶ вози́ть) **1** (*перемеща́ть*) to take, convey, carry (*of beasts of burden, mechanical transport, or people when on transport*) **2** (*impers.*) (*impers.* + *d.*) (*об уда́че*) to have luck; **ему́ не ∼ёт в ка́рты** he has no luck at cards

везу́чий *adj.* (infml) lucky

✎ век, а, о ∼е, на ∼у́, *pl.* **∼а́** (obs. **∼и**) *m.* **1** (*столе́тие*) century **2** (*эпо́ха*) age; **ка́менный в.** Stone Age; **Сре́дние ∼а́** the Middle Ages; **испоко́н ∼о́в** from time immemorial; **в ко́и-то ∼и** once in a blue moon **3** (*жизнь*) life, lifetime; **на моём ∼у́** in my lifetime

ве́к|о, а, *pl.* **∼и, ∼** *nt.* eyelid

вwith **вил**

вечно́й *adj.* ancient, age-old

вёл, вела́ *see* ▶ вести́

вел|е́ть, ю́, и́шь *impf. and pf.* (+ *d. and inf. or* что́бы) to order; **я ∼е́л ему́ сде́лать э́то** *or* **что́бы он сде́лал э́то** I ordered him to do this

велика́н, а *m.* giant

✎ велик|ий, ∼, ∼а́ *adj.* **1** (*short form* ∼а, ∼о, *pl.* ∼и) (*выдаю́щийся*) great; **∼ие держа́вы** the Great Powers **2** (*short form* ∼а́, ∼о́, *pl.* ∼и́) (*большо́й*) big, large; **∼ое мно́жество** a lot, a great deal **3** (*short form only* ∼а́, ∼о́, *pl.* ∼и́) (+ *d. or* для + *g.*) (*сли́шком большо́й*) too big; **э́ти брю́ки мне ∼и́** these trousers are too big for me

Великобрита́ни|я, и *f.* Great Britain

великоду́ши|е, я *nt.* magnanimity, generosity

великоду́ш|ный, ∼ен, ∼на *adj.* magnanimous, generous

великоле́пи|е, я *nt.* magnificence

B

великоле́п|ный, ~ен, ~на *adj.*
1 (*роскошный*) splendid, magnificent
2 (*отличный*) excellent; **~но!** (*int.*)
splendid!; excellent!

великосве́тский *adj.* high-society (*attr.*)

велича́йший *adj.* (*superl. of* ▶ **вели́кий**)
greatest, extreme, supreme

вели́чественност|ь, и *f.* majesty, grandeur

вели́чествен|ный, ~, ~на *adj.* majestic,
grand

вели́честв|о, а *nt.* majesty; **Ва́ше В.** Your
Majesty

вели́чи|е, я *nt.* greatness; grandeur; **ма́ния
~я** megalomania

ᵏ **велич|ина́, ины́,** *pl.* **~и́ны, ~и́н, ~и́нам** *f.*
1 size **2** (*math.*) quantity, magnitude;
(*значение*) value

вело... *comb. form* bicycle-, cycle-

велого́нк|а, и *f.* cycle race

велого́нщик, а *m.* racing cyclist

велосипе́д, а *m.* bicycle

велосипеди́ст, а *m.* cyclist

велоспо́рт, а *m.* cycling

велотренажёр, а *m.* exercise bicycle

вельве́т, а *m.* corduroy

вельве́товый *adj.* corduroy

велю́р, а *m.* velour

Ве́н|а, ы *f.* Vienna

ве́н|а, ы *f.* (*anat.*) vein

венге́р|ка, ки *f. of* ▶ **венгр**

венге́рский *adj.* Hungarian

венгр, а *m.* Hungarian

Ве́нгри|я, и *f.* Hungary

венери́ческий *adj.* (*med.*) venereal

Венесуэ́л|а, ы *f.* Venezuela

венесуэ́л|ец, ца *m.* Venezuelan

венесуэ́л|ка, ки *f. of* ▶ **венесуэ́лец**

венесуэ́льский *adj.* Venezuelan

вен|е́ц, ца́ *m.* (*корона*) crown

венециа́нский *adj.* Venetian

Вене́ци|я, и *f.* Venice

ве́ник, а *m.* **1** (*из прутьев*) besom, broom
2 (*в бане*) birch twigs (*used in Russian baths*)

вен|о́к, ка́ *m.* wreath

ве́нский *adj.* Viennese

ве́нтил|ь, я *m.* valve

вентиля́тор, а *m.* extractor (fan)

вентиля́ци|я, и *f.* ventilation

венча́ни|е, я *nt.* (*бракосочетание*) wedding
ceremony

венча́|ть, ю *impf.* **1** (*pf.* **в.** *and* **у~**)
(*находиться наверху*) to crown **2** (*pf.*
у~) (fig.) to crown **3** (*pf.* **об~** *and* **по~**)
(*соединять браком*) to marry (*of officiating
priest*)

венча́|ться, юсь *impf.* (*pf.* **об~** *and* **по~**)
to be married, marry

ве́нчурный *adj.* (fin.) venture; **в. капита́л**
venture capital

ᵏ **ве́р|а, ы** *f.* (**в** + *a.*) faith, belief (in);
(*уверенность*) trust, confidence; **приня́ть
на ~у** to take on trust

вера́нд|а, ы *f.* veranda

ве́рб|а, ы *f.* willow

верблю́д, а *m.* camel

ве́рб|ный *adj. of* ▶ **ве́рба**; (eccl.): **В~ное
воскресе́нье** Palm Sunday; **В~ная неде́ля**
Holy Week

верб|ова́ть, у́ю *impf.* (*of* ▶ **завербова́ть**)
to recruit, enlist

верди́кт, а *m.* verdict

верёвк|а, и *f.* cord, rope; string

верени́ц|а, ы *f.* file, line

ве́реск, а *m.* (bot.) heather

веретен|о́, а́, *pl.* **веретёна, веретён** *nt.*
spindle

ᵏ **ве́р|ить, ю, ишь** *impf.* (*of* ▶ **пове́рить**) (+ *d.*
or **в** + *a.*) to believe, have faith (in); (+ *d.*)
(*доверять*) to trust (in), rely (upon); **в. в
Бо́га** to believe in God; **в. на́ слово** to take
on trust; **я не ~ил свои́м уша́м, свои́м
глаза́м** I could not believe my ears, eyes

ве́р|иться, ится *impf.* (*impers.* + *d.*): (**мне**)
~ится с трудо́м I find it hard to believe

вермише́л|ь, и *f.* vermicelli

верне́е *adv.* (*comp. of* ▶ **ве́рно**) rather; **в.
(сказа́ть)** to be more exact

верниса́ж, а *m.* (art) **1** (*закрытый просмотр*)
private viewing, preview **2** (*день открытия*)
opening day (*of an exhibition*)

ве́рно *adv. of* ▶ **ве́рный**

ве́рност|ь, и *f.* **1** (*преданность*) faithfulness,
loyalty **2** (*правильность*) truth, correctness

верн|у́ть, у́, ёшь *pf.* (*of* ▶ **возвраща́ть**)
1 (*отдать обратно*) to give back, return
2 (*получить обратно*) to get back, recover,
retrieve

ᵏ **верн|у́ться, у́сь, ёшься** *pf.* (*of*
▶ **возвраща́ть**) to return (also fig.);
в. домо́й to return home

ᵏ **ве́р|ный, ~ен, ~на́, ~но, ~́ны́** *adj.*
1 (*правильный*) true, correct **2** (*преданный*)
faithful, loyal, true; **в. свои́м убежде́ниям**
true to one's convictions **3** (*надёжный*)
sure, reliable; **в. при́знак** sure sign
4 (*несомненный*) certain, sure; **~ная
смерть** certain death

ве́ровани|е, я *nt.* belief, creed

ве́р|овать, ую *impf.* (**в** + *a.*) to believe (in)

вероиспове́дани|е, я *nt.* creed,
denomination; **свобо́да ~я** freedom of
religion

вероло́м|ный, ~ен, ~на *adj.* treacherous,
perfidious

вероуче́ни|е, я *nt.* (relig.) dogma, teachings

вероя́тно *adv.* probably

вероя́тност|ь, и *f.* probability; **по всей ~и**
in all probability

вероя́т|ный, ~ен, ~на *adj.* probable, likely;
~нее всего́ most probably

ᵏ key word

ꚱ **ве́рси|я, и** *f.* version
верста́к, а́ *m.* (tech.) (work)bench
ве́ртел, а, pl. ～á *m.* spit; skewer
вер|те́ть, чу́, ～тишь *impf.* (+ *a. or i.*)
(*рукоятку, колесо́*) to turn; (*быстро*) to
twirl; **в. голово́й** to shake one's head; **в.**
что-н. в рука́х to fiddle with sth
вер|те́ться, чу́сь, ～тишься *impf.*
1 (*враща́ться*) to rotate, turn (round),
revolve (also fig.); **его́ фами́лия весь день**
～те́лась у меня́ на языке́ his name was on
the tip of my tongue all day; **в. под нога́ми,**
пе́ред глаза́ми (infml) to be under one's feet,
in the way **2** (infml *ёрзать*) to fidget
вертика́л|ь, и *f.* (*ли́ния*) vertical line;
(*в кроссво́рде*) down
вертика́л|ьный, ～ен, ～ьна *adj.* vertical
вертолёт, а *m.* helicopter
вертолётчик, а *m.* helicopter pilot
ве́рующ|ий *adj.* religious; (*as m. n.* **в., ～его**)
believer
верф|ь, и *f.* dockyard; shipyard
верх, а, pl. ～и́ *m.* **1** (*ве́рхняя часть*) top;
(*горы́*) summit (also fig.); **встре́ча в ～а́х** (pol.)
summit conference; (*кра́йняя сте́пень*)
height; **в. глу́пости** the height of folly
2 (*автомаши́ны*) hood (BrE), folding top
(AmE); **«верх!»** 'this side up!' (*sign on package,*
etc.); **взять в. (над + i.)** to gain the upper
hand (over) **3** (*лицева́я сторона́*) outside,
top; right side (*of material*)
ꚱ **ве́рхн|ий** *adj.* upper; **～яя оде́жда** outer
clothing; **～яя пала́та** (pol.) upper chamber
верхо́вн|ый *adj.* supreme; **～ое**
кома́ндование high command; **В. Сове́т**
(hist.) Supreme Soviet; **В. суд** Supreme Court
верх|ово́й *adj.*: **～ова́я езда́** riding (BrE),
horseback riding (AmE); **～ова́я ло́шадь**
mount; (*as m. n.* **в., ～ово́го**) rider
верхо́вье, я, g. pl. ～ев *nt.* upper reaches
верхо́м *adv.* astride; on horseback; **е́здить**
в. to ride
верху́шк|а, и *f.* **1** top; **в. а́йсберга** (fig.) tip
of the iceberg **2** (fig., infml, *организа́ции*)
elite, top
вер|чу́, ～тишь *see* ▸ **верте́ть**
верши́н|а, ы *f.* **1** (*де́рева, холма́*) top; (*горы́*)
summit, peak; (fig.) peak, acme **2** (math.)
vertex; apex
ꚱ **вес, а** (*pl., specialist use only,* **～á**) *m.* weight;
ли́шний в. excess weight; (*бага́ж*) excess
baggage; (fig., *значе́ние*) weight, authority;
на в. by weight; **на ～у́** balanced, hanging,
suspended; **приба́вить, уба́вить в ～е** to put
on, lose weight
весел|и́ть, ю́, и́шь *impf.* (*of* ▸ **развесели́ть**)
to amuse
весел|и́ться, ю́сь, и́шься *impf.* to enjoy
oneself; to have fun
ве́село *adv.* gaily, merrily; (*as pred.*) (+ *d.*) to
enjoy oneself; **бы́ло в.** it was fun
вес|ёлый, ～ел, ～ела́, ～ело *adj.* **1** cheerful,
merry **2** (*no short forms*) (*фильм, расска́з*)

cheerful, feel-good; (*кра́ски, обо́и*) bright,
cheerful
весе́нний *adj.* of ▸ **весна́**
ве́|сить, шу, сишь *impf.* (*име́ть тот и́ли*
ино́й вес) to weigh; **груз ～сит три то́нны** the
cargo weighs three tons
ве́с|кий, ～ок, ～ка *adj.* weighty
весл|о́, á, pl. ～ла, ～ел, ～лам *nt.* oar
ꚱ **вес|на́, ны́, pl. ～ны, ～ен, ～нам** *f.* spring
(*season*)
весно́й *adv.* in the spring
весну́ш|ки, ек *f. pl.* (*sg.* **～ка, ～ки**) freckles
весну́шчатый *adj.* freckled
вес|ово́й *adj.* **1** *of* ▸ **вес**; **～ова́я катего́рия**
(sport) weight category **2** (*продава́емый на*
вес) sold by weight
весо́м|ый, ～, ～а *adj.* (fig.) weighty; substantial
ве́стерн, а *m.* western (*film*)
ꚱ **ве|сти́, ду́, дёшь, past ～л, ～ла́** *impf.* (*det.*
of ▸ **води́ть**) **1** (*pf.* **по～**) (*сопровожда́ть*)
to lead; to take; (*войска́*) to lead **2** (*pf.*
про～) (+ *i. and* **по** + *d.*) to run (over), pass
(over, across) **3** (*pf.* **про～**) (*осуществля́ть,*
де́лать) to conduct; to carry on; **в. войну́**
to wage war; **в. ого́нь** (**по** + *d.*) (impf. only)
to fire (on); **в. перегово́ры** to carry on
negotiations; **в. перепи́ску** (**с** + *i.*) (impf.
only) to correspond (with); **в. проце́сс** to
carry on a lawsuit **4** (impf. only) (*маши́ну*)
to drive; **в. кора́бль** to navigate a ship;
в. самолёт to pilot an aircraft **5** (impf.
only) (*руководи́ть*) to conduct, direct, run;
(*переда́чу*) to present; (*собра́ние*) to chair;
в. де́ло to run a business; **в. хозя́йство** to
keep house **6** (impf. only) (*учёт*) to keep;
в. дневни́к to keep a diary; **в. протоко́л** to
keep minutes **7** (impf. only): **в. себя́** to
behave **8** (*pf.* **при～**) (*служи́ть путём*
куда́-нибудь) to lead (also fig.); **куда́ ～дёт э́та**
доро́га? where does this road lead (to)?
вестибю́л|ь, я *m.* entrance hall, lobby
Вест-И́нди|я, и *f.* the West Indies
ве́стник, а *m.* messenger, herald
ве́стни|ца, цы *f. of* ▸ **ве́стник**
вест|ь, и, pl. ～и, ～е́й *f.* news; piece of news;
пропа́сть бе́з ～и (mil.) to be missing
вес|ы́, о́в (*no sg.*) **1** scales, balance **2** (**В.**)
(astron., astrol.) the Scales, Libra
ꚱ **весь, вся, всё, g. всего́, всей, всего́, pl.**
все, всех *pron.* all; **весь день** all day; **вся**
страна́ the whole country; **вся Фра́нция** the
whole of France; **по всему́ го́роду** all over
the town; **он весь в отца́** he is the (very)
image of his father; **во весь го́лос** at the
top of one's voice; **от всего́ се́рдца** from the
bottom of one's heart; **пре́жде всего́** before
all, first and foremost; **вот и всё** that's all;
there's nothing more to it; **всего́ хоро́шего!**
goodbye!, all the best!; (*as nt. n.* **всё, всего́**)
everything; **все, всех** (*no sg.*) all, everyone
ꚱ **весьма́** *adv.* very, highly
ветви́ст|ый, ～, ～а *adj.* branchy, spreading
ветв|ь, и, pl. ～и, ～е́й *f.* branch; (fig.) branch

B

✍ **ве́т|ер, ра** *m.* wind; (fig.): **у него́ в. в голове́** he is a thoughtless fellow

ветера́н, а *m.* veteran

ветерина́р, а *m.* veterinary surgeon (BrE), veterinarian (AmE)

ветерина́рный *adj.* veterinary

ве́тк|а, и *f.* branch; (*мелкая*) twig; **железнодоро́жная в.** branch line

вет|ла́, лы́, *pl.* **~лы, ~ел** *f.* (bot., *белая/серебристая ива*) white willow

ве́то *nt. indecl.* veto; **наложи́ть в. (на** + *a.*) to veto

ве́тошь, и *f.* old clothes, rags

ве́трен|ый, ~, ~а *adj.* 1 windy 2 (fig., *человек*) empty-headed

ветров|о́й *adj. of* ► **ве́тер**; **~о́е стекло́** windscreen (BrE), windshield (AmE)

ветря́нк|а, и *f.* (med.) chickenpox

ветрян|о́й *adj.* wind(-powered); **~а́я ме́льница** windmill

ве́тх|ий, ~, ~а́, ~о *adj.* (*очень старый*) old, ancient; (*здание*) dilapidated, tumbledown, decrepit; **В. Заве́т** the Old Testament

ветчин|а́, ы́ (*no pl.*) *f.* ham

ветша́|ть, ю *impf.* (*of* ► **обветша́ть**) to decay; to become dilapidated

ве́х|а, и *f.* landmark (also fig.); milestone

✍ **ве́чер, а,** *pl.* **~а́** *m.* 1 (*время*) evening; **по ~а́м** in the evenings; **под в., к ~у** towards evening 2 (*собрание*) party; evening, soirée

вечере́|ть, ет *impf.* (*impers.*) to grow dark; **~ет** night is falling

вечери́нк|а, и *f.* party

вече́рн|ий *adj. of* ► **ве́чер**; **~яя заря́** twilight, dusk; **~ие ку́рсы** evening classes; **~ее пла́тье** evening dress

ве́чером *adv.* in the evening

ве́чно *adv.* (*всегда*) for ever, eternally; (infml, *постоянно*) always; **они́ в. ссо́рятся** they are always quarrelling

вечнозелёный *adj.* (bot.) evergreen

ве́чность, и *f.* eternity; **це́лую в.** (infml) for ages

ве́ч|ный, ~ен, ~на *adj.* 1 (*льды, слава*) eternal, everlasting; **~ная мерзлота́** permafrost 2 (*бессрочный*) indefinite, perpetual 3 (infml, *постоянный*) perpetual, continual

ве́шалк|а, и *f.* 1 (*крючок*) peg; (*планка*) rack; (*стойка*) stand 2 (*петля*) tab (*on clothes for hanging on pegs*) 3 (*плечики*) (coat) hanger

ве́ша|ть¹, ю *impf.* (*of* ► **пове́сить**) to hang; **в. бельё на верёвку** to hang washing on a line; **в. уби́йцу** to hang a murderer

ве́ша|ть², ю *impf.* (*of* ► **взве́сить**) to weigh, weigh out

ве́ша|ться, юсь *impf.* (*of* ► **пове́ситься**) 1 *pass. of* ► **ве́шать¹** (*картина*) to be hung 2 (*кончать свою жизнь*) to hang oneself

ве́|шу, сишь *see* ► **ве́сить**

✍ key word

веща́ни|е, я *nt.* broadcasting

веща́|ть, ю *impf.* 1 (*по радио, телевидению*) to broadcast 2 (*говорить высокопарно*) to pontificate, lay down the law

вещев|о́й *adj. of* ► **вещь**; **в. мешо́к** holdall; kitbag; **в. ры́нок** merchandise market; **в. склад** storage warehouse, store; (mil.) stores

веще́ственн|ый *adj.* substantial, material; **~ые доказа́тельства** material evidence

✍ **вещество́, а́** *nt.* substance

✍ **вещ|ь, и,** *pl.* **~и, ~е́й** *f.* 1 thing (*in var. senses*) 2 (*in pl.*) things (= *belongings; baggage; clothes*); **э́то ва́ши ~и?** are these things yours? 3 (*произведение*) work; piece, thing

ве́яни|е, я *nt.* (fig., *тенденция*) current, tendency, trend; **в. вре́мени** spirit of the times

ве́|ять, ю, ешь *impf.* (*о ветре*) to blow; **~ял прохла́дный ветеро́к** a cool breeze was blowing; (*impers.* + *i.*) **~ет весно́й** spring is in the air

взаи́мность, и *f.* reciprocity; return (*of affection*); **отвеча́ть кому́-н. ~ью** to reciprocate sb's feelings, return sb's love; **любо́вь без ~и** unrequited love

взаи́м|ный, ~ен, ~на *adj.* mutual, reciprocal

взаимовы́год|ный, ~ен, ~на *adj.* mutually beneficial

✍ **взаимоде́йстви|е, я** *nt.* (*связь*) interaction; (mil.) cooperation, coordination

взаимоде́йств|овать, ую *impf.* to interact; (mil.) to cooperate

взаимозачёт, а *m.* (fin.) offsetting of debts

взаимоотноше́ни|е, я *nt.* (*usu. in pl.*) relationship(s), relation(s)

взаимопо́мощ|ь, и *f.* mutual aid; mutual assistance

взаиморасчёт|ы, ов *m. pl.* (fin.) mutual settlement of accounts

взаимосвя́з|ь, и *f.* interrelationship

взаймы́ *adv.*: **взять в.** to borrow; **дать в.** to lend, loan

взаме́н *prep.* + *g.* (*вместо*) instead (of); (*в обмен на что-н.*) in return (for), in exchange (for)

взаперти́ *adv.* 1 (*под замком*) under lock and key 2 (infml, *в уединении*) in seclusion

взба́лтыва|ть, ю *impf. of* ► **взболта́ть**

взбега́|ть, ю *impf.* (*of* ► **взбежа́ть**) to run up; **в. на́ гору** to run up a hill; **в. по ле́стнице** to run upstairs

взбе|жа́ть, гу́, жи́шь, гу́т *pf. of* ► **взбега́ть**

взбе|си́ть, шу́, ~сишь *pf. of* ► **беси́ть**

взбе|си́ться, шу́сь, ~сишься *pf. of* ► **беси́ться**

взбива́|ть, ю *impf. of* ► **взбить**

взбира́|ться, юсь *impf. of* ► **взобра́ться**

взб|ить, обью́, обьёшь *pf.* (*of* ► **взбива́ть**) 1 (*яйца*) to beat (up); **в. сли́вки** to whip cream 2 (*подушку*) to fluff up

взболта́|ть, ю *pf.* (*of* ► **взба́лтывать**) to shake (up) (*liquids*)

взбунт|ова́ться, у́юсь *pf. of* ▶ бунтова́ть
взбу́чк|а, и *f.* (infml) **1** (*побои*) thrashing, beating **2** (*выговор*) dressing-down
взва́лива|ть, ю *impf. of* ▶ взвали́ть
взвал|и́ть, ю́, ∼ишь. (*of* ▶ взва́ливать) to load, lift (onto); в. мешо́к на́ спину to hoist a pack onto one's back; всю вину́ ∼и́ли на него́ he was made to shoulder all the blame
взве́|сить, шу, сишь *pf.* (*of* ▶ взве́шивать, ▶ ве́шать²) (*груз*) to weigh; (fig., *варианты*) to weigh, consider
взве́шен|ный, ∼, ∼на *adj.* (*решение, ответ*) carefully thought out, balanced
взве́шива|ть, ю *impf. of* ▶ взве́сить
взвива́|ться, юсь *impf. of* ▶ взви́ться
взви́згива|ть, ю *impf. of* ▶ взви́згнуть
взви́згн|уть, у, ешь *pf.* to scream, cry out; (*собака*) to yelp
взви́|ться, взовью́сь, взовьёшься *pf.* (*of* ▶ взвива́ться) to fly up, soar; (*о флагах*) to be raised, go up
взвод, а *m.* (mil.) platoon
взволно́ван|ный, ∼, ∼на *adj.* anxious, worried; (*от счастья*) excited
взволн|ова́ть, у́ю *pf. of* ▶ волнова́ть
◆ взгляд, а *m.* **1** (*выражение глаз*) look; (*быстрый*) glance; (*пристальный*) gaze, stare; бро́сить в. (на + *a.*) to glance (at); на пе́рвый в., с пе́рвого ∼а at first sight **2** (*мнение*) view; opinion; на мой в. in my opinion, as I see it
взгля́н|уть, у́, ∼ешь *pf.* (на + *a.*) to look (at); (*быстро*) to cast a glance (at)
вздор, а (*no pl.*) *m.* (infml) nonsense; говори́ть, нести́ в. to talk nonsense
вздо́р|ный, ∼ен, ∼на *adj.* **1** (*нелепый*) foolish, stupid **2** (infml, *сварливый*) cantankerous, quarrelsome
вздох, а *m.* sigh; deep breath; испусти́ть после́дний в. to breathe one's last
вздохн|у́ть, у́, ёшь *pf. of* ▶ вздыха́ть) **1** to sigh **2**: в. свобо́дно to breathe freely; to relax (*after having been frightened or after exertion*)
вздра́гива|ть, ю *impf. of* ▶ вздро́гнуть
вздремн|у́ть, у́, ёшь *pf.* (infml) to have a nap, doze
вздро́гн|уть, у, ешь *pf.* (*of* ▶ вздра́гивать) (*от неожиданности*) to start; (*от боли*) to wince, flinch; (*дрожать*) to tremble, shudder
вздыха́|ть, ю *impf.* (*of* ▶ вздохну́ть) **1** to breathe; to sigh **2** (*московать*) (о + *p. or* по + *d.*) to pine, yearn (for); (*по девушке*) to be in love (with)
взима́|ть, ю *impf.* (*налог, штраф*) to levy, collect, raise
взла́мыва|ть, ю *impf. of* ▶ взлома́ть
взлёт, а *m.* (*самолёта*) take-off
взлета́|ть, ю *impf. of* ▶ взлете́ть
взле|те́ть, чу́, ти́шь *pf.* (*of* ▶ взлета́ть) (*птица*) to fly up; (*самолёт*) to take off; в. на во́здух to explode, blow up

взлёт|ный *adj. of* ▶ взлёт; (aeron.): ∼ная доро́жка runway; ∼но-поса́дочная полоса́ landing strip
взлом, а *m.* (*сейфа*) breaking (into); (*двери*) forcing; кра́жа со ∼ом housebreaking; (*в ночное время*) burglary
взлома́|ть, ю *pf.* (*of* ▶ взла́мывать) to break open, force; (*разворотить*) to smash; в. замо́к to force a lock; (comput.) to hack into
взло́мщик, а *m.* burglar; компью́терный в. hacker
взмах, а *m.* (*руки*) wave; (*крыльев*) flap, flapping; (*весла*) stroke; одни́м ∼ом at one stroke
взма́хива|ть, ю *impf. of* ▶ взмахну́ть
взмахн|у́ть, у́, ёшь *pf.* (+ *i.*) (*рукой*) to wave; (*крылом*) flap
взметн|у́ть, у́, ёшь *pf.* (+ *i.*) to throw up, fling up; в. рука́ми to throw up one's hands
взметн|у́ться, у́сь, ёшься *pf.* to leap up, fly up
взмо́рь|е, я *nt.* seashore; seaside
взмыва́|ть, ю *impf. of* ▶ взмыть
взм|ыть, о́ю, о́ешь *pf.* (*of* ▶ взмыва́ть) to soar (up)
взнос, а *m.* (*платёж*) payment; (*членский*) fee, dues; вступи́тельный в. membership fee; очередно́й в. instalment
взобра́|ться, взберу́сь, взберёшься, *past* ∼лся, ∼ла́сь *pf.* (*of* ▶ взбира́ться) (на + *a.*) to climb (up)
взобью́|ю, ёшь *see* ▶ взбить
взо|йти́, йду́, йдёшь, *past* ∼шёл, ∼шла́, *p.p.* ∼ше́дший *pf.* (*of* ▶ всходи́ть, ▶ восходи́ть 1) **1** (на + *a.*) to ascend, mount **2** (*солнце; тесто*) to rise **3** (*семена*) to come up
взор, а *m.* look; glance
взорв|а́ть, у́, ёшь *pf.* (*of* ▶ взрыва́ть) (*здание*) to blow up; (*бомбу*) to detonate
взорв|а́ться, у́сь, ёшься, *past* ∼а́лся, ∼ала́сь *pf.* (*of* ▶ взрыва́ться) (*о бомбе, газе*) to explode; (*о здании*) to blow up; (fig., *о человеке*) to blow up, explode
взо|шёл, шла́ *see* ▶ взойти́
взрев|е́ть, у́, ёшь *pf.* to let out a roar
◆ взро́сл|ый *adj.* grown-up, adult; (*also as n.* в., ∼ого, *f.* ∼ая, ∼ой) grown-up (person), adult
взрыв, а *m.* explosion; (fig.) burst, outburst; «Большо́й в.» the Big Bang
взрыва́тел|ь, я *m.* detonator
взрыва́|ть, ю *impf. of* ▶ взорва́ть
взрыва́|ться, юсь *impf. of* ▶ взорва́ться
взрывни́к, а́ *m.* explosives expert; shot-firer
взрывн|о́й *adj.* explosive; ∼а́я волна́ blast
взрывоопа́с|ный, ∼ен, ∼на *adj.* explosive (also fig.)
взрывча́тк|а, и *f.* (infml) explosive
взры́вчат|ый *adj.* explosive; ∼ое вещество́ explosive
взыска́ни|е, я *nt.* **1** (*выговор*) reprimand; (*наказание*) penalty; punishment

B

2 (*штрафа*) exaction; (*долга*) recovery

взы|ска́ть, щу́, ~щешь *pf.* (*of* ▶ **взы́скивать**)
1 (*штраф*) to exact; (*долг*) to recover
2 (*c + g.*) to call to account

взы́скива|ть, ю *impf. of* ▶ **взыска́ть**

взы́щу́, ~щешь *see* ▶ **взыска́ть**

взя́ти|е, я *nt.* taking; (*крепости*) capture;
(*власти*) seizure

взя́тк|а, и *f.* **1** bribe; backhander **2** (*cards*)
trick; **с него́ ~и гла́дки** (infml) he isn't going
to take responsibility

взя́точник, а *m.* bribe-taker

взя́точни|ца, цы *f. of* ▶ **взя́точник**

взя́точничеств|о, а *nt.* bribery, bribe-taking

✐ **взя|ть, возьму́, возьмёшь**, *past* **~л, ~ла́,
~ло** *pf.* (*of* ▶ **брать**) **1** *see* ▶ **брать 2** (infml,
думать): **с чего́ ты взял?** what makes you
think so? **3**: **в. да, в. и, в. да и…** (infml) to
do sth suddenly; **он ~л да убежа́л** he upped
and ran off **4**: **чёрт возьми́!** (infml) damn it!

взя|ться, возьму́сь, возьмёшься, *past*
~лся, ~ла́сь *pf.* (*of* ▶ **бра́ться**): **отку́да
ни возьми́сь** (infml) from nowhere, out of
the blue

вибрафо́н, а *m.* (mus.) vibraphone

вибра́ци|я, и *f.* vibration

вибри́р|овать, ую *impf.* to vibrate

вигва́м, а *m.* wigwam

✐ **вид**[1], **а** *m.* **1** (*внешность*) air, look; appearance;
aspect; **у него́ был мра́чный в.** he looked
gloomy; **сде́лать в., бу́дто** to make it appear
that, pretend that; **для ~а** for the sake of
appearances; **под ~ом** (*+ g.*) under the guise
(of) **2** (*состояние*) shape, form; condition
3 (*панорама*) view; **ко́мната с ~ом на го́ры**
room with a view of the mountains **4** (*in pl.*)
(*перспективы*) prospect; **~ы на бу́дущее**
prospects for the future; **име́ть ~ы на** (*+ a.*)
to have designs on **5** (*поле зрения*) sight;
упусти́ть из ~у to lose sight (of); **на ~у у**
(*+ g.*) within sight of; **быть на ~у** to be in
the public eye; **при ~е** (*+ g.*) at the sight (of);
име́ть в ~у (*намереваться*) to plan, intend;
(*подразумевать*) to mean; (*не забывать*)
to bear in mind; **что вы име́ли в ~у, говоря́
э́то?** what did you mean when you said that?;
име́й(те) в ~у bear in mind, don't forget;
име́ться в ~у to be intended, be envisaged;
to be meant

✐ **вид**[2], **а** *m.* **1** (biol.) species; **исчеза́ющий в.**
endangered *or* threatened species **2** (*тип*)
type, kind **3** (gram.) aspect; **соверше́нный,
несоверше́нный в.** perfective, imperfective
aspect

ви́дени|е, я *nt.* (*способность видеть*) vision;
(*восприятие, подход*) vision, outlook

виде́ни|е, я *nt.* (*призрак*) vision, apparition

✐ **ви́део** *nt. indecl.* video (recorder, film,
cassette)

ви́део… comb. form video-

видеоза́пис|ь, и *f.* video recording

видеоигр|а́, ы́, *pl.* **~ы** *f.* video game

видеока́мер|а, ы *f.* video camera, camcorder

видеокассе́т|а, ы *f.* video cassette

видеокли́п, а *m.* video clip, music video

видеомагнитофо́н, а *m.* video recorder

видеонаблюде́ни|е, я *nt.* (*оборудование*)
CCTV

видеофи́льм, а *m.* video (film)

✐ **ви́|деть, жу, дишь** *impf.* (*of* ▶ **уви́деть 1**) to
see; **в. кого́-н. наскво́зь** to see through sb;
в. во сне to dream (of); **~дишь (ли)** you see;
вот уви́дишь (infml) you'll see

ви́|деться, жусь, дишься *impf.*
1 (*встречаться*) to see one another; (*c + i.*)
to meet with **2** (*pf.* **при~**) to appear; **ему́
~делся стра́шный сон** he had a terrifying
dream

ви́димо *adv.* evidently, apparently

ви́димост|ь, и *f.* **1** (*различаемость*) visibility
2 (*внешность*) outward appearance; **для
~и** (infml) for show **3**: **по всей ~и** to all
appearances

ви́дим|ый, ~, ~а *adj.* **1** visible **2** (*очевидный*)
apparent, evident; **без ~ой причи́ны** for no
apparent reason **3** (*кажущийся*) apparent,
seeming

видне́|ться, ется, ются *impf.* to be visible

✐ **ви́дно** *adv.* **1** obviously, evidently; (*as pred.*)
it is obvious, it is apparent; **в. бы́ло, как
она́ расстро́илась** you could see how upset
she was; **там в. бу́дет** (infml) we'll see **2** (*as
pred.*) visible; in sight; **берега́ ещё не́ было
в.** the coast was not yet visible

ви́дн|ый *adj.* **1** (**~ен, ~на́, ~но, ~ны́**)
(*заметный*) visible; conspicuous
2 (*важный*) distinguished, prominent

видово́й *adj.* (*of* ▶ **вид**[2]) **1** (biol.) species
2 (gram.) aspectual

видоизмен|и́ть, ю́, и́шь *pf.* (*of*
▶ **видоизменя́ть**) to modify, alter

видоизмен|и́ться, ю́сь, и́шься *pf.* (*of*
▶ **видоизменя́ться**) to alter

видоизмен|я́ть, я́ю *impf. of* ▶ **видоизмени́ть**

видоизмен|я́ться, я́юсь *impf. of*
▶ **видоизмени́ться**

ви́з|а, ы *f.* **1** visa **2** (*пометка*) official
signature

визажи́ст, а *m.* make-up artist

Виза́нти|й, я *m.* (hist.) Byzantium

византи́йский *adj.* Byzantine

Византи́|я, и *f.* (hist.) Byzantine Empire

визг, а *m.* (*человека*) scream; (*поросёнка*)
squeal; (*собаки*) yelp; (*тормозов*) screech

визгли́в|ый, ~, ~а *adj.* **1** (*голос*) shrill
2 (*крикливый*) given to screaming,
squealing, yelping

визж|а́ть, у́, и́шь *impf.* to scream; to squeal;
to yelp

визи́т, а *m.* visit; call; **нанести́ в.** to make an
(official) visit; **прийти́ с ~ом к кому́-н.** to
visit sb, pay sb a call

визи́тк|а, и *f.* (*карточка*) (business) card

визи́т|ный *adj. of* ▶ **визи́т**; **~ная ка́рточка**
(business) card

✐ key word

визуа́л|ьный, ~ен, ~ьна *adj.* visual
вика́ри|й, я *m.* (eccl.) vicar
ви́ки *f. indecl.* (comput.) wiki; **техноло́гия в.** wiki technology
викторин|а, ы *f.* quiz
ви́лк|а, и *f.* **1** fork **2** (elec.) plug
ви́лл|а, ы *f.* villa
вильн|у́ть, у́, ёшь *pf. of* ▶ виля́ть
Ви́льнюс, а *m.* Vilnius
виля́|ть, ю *impf. of* ▶ вильну́ть **1**: **в. хвосто́м** to wag one's tail **2** (infml, *доро́га*) to wind, turn sharply
вин|а́, ы́, *pl.* ~ы *f.* fault, guilt; (*причи́на*) blame; **моя́ в.** it is my fault; **не по их ~é** through no fault of theirs; **поста́вить кому́-н. в ~у́** to accuse sb of, blame sb for; **свали́ть ~у́ (на + *a.*)** to lay the blame (on); **по ~é (+ *g.*)** because of
виндсёрф, а and **виндсёрфер**, а *m.* (infml) sailboard
виндсёрфинг, а *m.* windsurfing
винегре́т, а *m.* ≈ beetroot salad (*of diced cooked beetroot, potato, and carrot, pickled cucumber, and vegetable oil dressing*); (fig., *смесь*) mishmash
вини́л, а *m.* vinyl
вини́тельный *adj.* (gram.): **в. паде́ж** accusative case
вин|и́ть, ю́, и́шь *impf.* (**в** + *p.*) (*обвиня́ть*) to accuse (of); (*счита́ть винова́тым*) to blame; **я ~ю́ его́ за наш прова́л** I blame him for our failure
ви́нный *adj.* wine; winey; **в. спирт** alcohol
◆ **вин|о́**, а́, *pl.* ~а *nt.* wine
винова́т|ый, ~, ~а *adj.* **1** (*взгляд*) guilty; (*челове́к*) guilty; to blame; **мы все ~ы в э́том** we are all to blame for this **2**: **~!** sorry!, my fault!
вино́вник, а *m.* culprit; (*торжества́, пра́здника*) cause, reason
вино́вност|ь, и *f.* guilt
вино́в|ный, ~ен, ~на *adj.* (**в** + *p.*) guilty (of); **призна́ть себя́ ~ным** to plead guilty
виногра́д, а *m.* **1** (*расте́ние*) vine **2** (collect.) (*я́годы*) grapes
виногра́дник, а *m.* vineyard
винт, а́ *m.* **1** (*сте́ржень*) screw **2** (*самолёта*) propeller **3** (*спира́ль*) spiral
винто́вк|а, и *f.* rifle
винт|ово́й *adj. of* ▶ винт; spiral; **~ова́я ле́стница** spiral staircase
виолончели́ст, а *m.* cellist
виолончели́ст|ка, ки *f. of* ▶ виолончели́ст
виолонче́л|ь, и *f.* cello
вира́ж, а́ *m.* (*поворо́т*) turn; **круто́й в.** steep turn
виртуа́л|ьный, ~ен, ~ьна *adj.* virtual; **~ьная реа́льность** (comput.) virtual reality
виртуо́з, а *m.* virtuoso
виртуо́з|ный, ~ен, ~на *adj.* masterly, virtuosic

ви́рус, а *m.* (med.) virus, bug (infml); (comput.) virus
ви́русный *adj. of* ▶ ви́рус
виселиц|а, ы *f.* gallows, gibbet
вис|е́ть, шу́, си́шь *impf.* to hang; to be suspended; **в. над (+ *i.*)** (fig.) to hang over; **в. на телефо́не** (infml) to talk a lot on the phone
ви́ски *nt. indecl.* whisky (BrE), whiskey (AmE)
ви́сн|уть, ет *impf.* (comput.) to crash
вис|о́к, ка́ *m.* (anat.) temple
високо́сный *adj.*: **в. год** leap year
вися́чий *adj.* hanging; **в. замо́к** padlock; **в. мост** suspension bridge
◆ **витами́н**, а *m.* vitamin
витами́н|ный *adj.* **1** *adj. of* ▶ витами́н; **~ная недоста́точность** vitamin deficiency **2** vitamin-rich *or* -packed
вит|о́к, ка́ *m.* **1** (*спира́ли*) turn, twist **2** (*про́волоки*) coil **3** (*при полёте*) orbit **4** (fig., *цикл*) round
витра́ж, а́ *m.* stained-glass window
витри́н|а, ы *f.* **1** (*в магази́не*) (shop) window **2** (*в музе́е*) showcase
ви|ть, вью, вьёшь, *past* ~л, ~ла́, ~ло *impf.* (*of* ▶ свить) to weave
ви|ться, вьётся, *past* ~лся, ~ла́сь *impf.* (*of* ▶ сви́ться) **1** (*расте́ние*) to wind, twine **2** (*во́лосы*) to curl, wave **3** (*пти́ца*) to hover, circle **4** (*змея́*) to writhe, twist **5** (*пыль, дым*) to spiral up
вихр|ь, я *m.* whirlwind; **сне́жный в.** blizzard; (fig.) whirlwind, maelstrom
ви́це-... *comb. form* vice-
ви́це-президе́нт, а *m.* vice-president
ВИЧ *m. indecl.* (*abbr. of* ви́рус иммунодефици́та челове́ка) (med.) HIV (*human immunodeficiency virus*); **ВИЧ-инфици́рованный** HIV-positive
вишнёвый *adj.* **1** cherry; **в. сад** cherry orchard **2** (*о цве́те*) cherry-coloured; burgundy
ви́ш|ня, ни, *g. pl.* ~ен *f.* **1** (*де́рево*) cherry tree **2** (*плод*) cherry; (collect.) cherries
вка́лыва|ть, ю *impf. of* ▶ вколо́ть
вка́пыва|ть, ю *impf. of* ▶ вкопа́ть
вка|ти́ть, чу́, ~тишь *pf.* (*of* ▶ вка́тывать) to roll into, onto; (*на колёсах*) to wheel in, into
вка́тыва|ть, ю *impf. of* ▶ вкати́ть
вклад, а *m.* **1** (*в ба́нке*) deposit **2** (*де́йствие*) investment **3** (fig.) contribution
вкла́дк|а, и *f.* supplementary sheet, insert
вкла́дчик, а *m.* depositor, investor
вкла́дчи|ца, цы *f. of* ▶ вкла́дчик
вкла́дыва|ть, ю *impf. of* ▶ вложи́ть
вкла́дыш, а *m.* = вкла́дка
◆ **вклю|чи́ть**, а́ю *impf. of* ▶ включи́ть
включ|а́ться, а́юсь *impf. of* ▶ включи́ться
◆ **включа́я** *pres. gerund of* ▶ включа́ть; (*as prep.* + *a.*) including
включе́ни|е, я *nt.* **1** (**в** + *a.*) inclusion (in) **2** (*ла́мпы, станка́*) switching on, turning on

включи́тельно *adv.* inclusive; **с пя́того по девя́тое в.** from the 5th to the 9th inclusive

включ|и́ть, у́, и́шь *pf.* (*of* ▶ **включа́ть**)
■ (**в** + *a.*) to include (in); **в. себя́** to include, comprise, take in; **в. в спи́сок** to include on a list ② (tech.) to switch on, turn on; (*в розетку*) to plug in; **в. ра́дио** to switch on the radio; **в. ско́рость** to engage a gear

включ|и́ться, у́сь, и́шься *pf.* (*of* ▶ **включа́ться**) ■ (**в** + *a.*) to join (in), enter (into) ② (*о свете, радио*) to come on

вкола́чива|ть, ю *impf. of* ▶ **вколоти́ть**

вкол|оти́ть, очу́, о́тишь *pf.* (*of* ▶ **вкола́чивать**) to knock in, hammer in (*also fig.*)

вкол|о́ть, ю́, ~ешь *pf.* (*of* ▶ **вка́лывать**) (**в** + *a.*) to stick (in, into)

вкопа́|ть, ю *pf.* (*of* ▶ **вка́пывать**) to dig in

вкра́дчив|ый, ~, ~а *adj.* insinuating, ingratiating

вкра́тце *adv.* briefly; succinctly

вкру|ти́ть, чу́, ~тишь *pf.* (*of* ▶ **вкру́чивать**) to screw in

вкру́чива|ть, ю *impf. of* ▶ **вкрути́ть**

вкру|чу́, ~тишь *see* ▶ **вкрути́ть**

ᵒ⁄ **вкус, а** *m.* taste (*also fig.*); **в чьём-н. ~е** to sb's taste; **э́то де́ло ~а** it is a matter of taste; **челове́к со ~ом** a man of taste; **одева́ться со ~ом** to dress tastefully

вку́с|ный, ~ен, ~на́, ~но *adj.* tasty, delicious, good

вла́г|а, и (*no pl.*) *f.* moisture

влага́лище, а *nt.* vagina

ᵒ⁄ **владе́л|ец, ьца** *m.* owner

владе́л|ица, ицы *f. of* ▶ **владе́лец**

владе́ни|е, я *nt.* ■ ownership; possession ② (*территория в собственности*) estate

владе́|ть, ю, ешь *impf.* (+ *i.*) ■ (*иметь*) to own, possess ② (*подчинять себе*) to control; to be in possession (of); **в. собо́й** to control oneself ③ (fig., *уметь пользоваться*) to have (a) command (of); to have the use (of); **она́ ~ет шестью́ языка́ми** she has a command of six languages

вла́жност|ь, и *f.* (*воздуха*) humidity; (*почвы*) dampness

вла́ж|ный, ~ен, ~на́, ~но *adj.* (*воздух, климат*) humid, damp; (*простыня*) damp; (*глаза, лоб*) moist

вла́мыва|ться, юсь *impf. of* ▶ **вломи́ться**

вла́ст|ный, ~ен, ~на *adj.* ■ (*характер, жест*) imperious, commanding; **~ные структу́ры** authorities ② (*над* + *i., or inf.*) authoritative, competent; **он не ~ен над собо́й** he can't control himself; **он не ~ен изменить что́-нибудь** he is powerless to change anything

ᵒ⁄ **власт|ь, и, *pl.* ~и, ~е́й** *f.* ■ (*политическая*) power; (*in pl.*) authorities; **прийти́ к ~и** to come to power; **у ~и** in power ② (*родительская*) power, authority; **во ~и** (+ *g.*) at the mercy (of), in the power (of);

(*над чувствами*) control

вле́во *adv.* to the left (*also fig., pol.*)

влеза́|ть, ю *impf. of* ▶ **влезть**

влез|ть, у, ешь, *past* ~, **~ла** *pf.* (*of* ▶ **влеза́ть**) ■ (*в окно*) to climb in(to); (*на дерево*) to climb (up); (*на крышу*) to climb onto; **в. в долги́** (fig.) to get into debt ② (infml, *уместиться*) to fit in, go in, go on; **все э́ти ве́щи не ~ут в мою́ су́мку** these things will not all go into my bag

влет|а́ть, а́ю *impf. of* ▶ **влете́ть**

вле|те́ть, чу́, ти́шь *pf.* (*of* ▶ **влета́ть**) to fly in, into; (fig., infml) to rush in, into; (*impers.*) **ему́ опя́ть ~те́ло** he is in trouble again

влече́ни|е, я *nt.* (**к** + *d.*) attraction (to)

вле|чь, ку́, чёшь, ку́т, *past* **влёк, ~кла́** *impf.* (*тащить*) to draw, drag; (*привлекать*) to attract; **в. за собо́й** to involve, entail

влива́ни|я, й *nt. pl.* (econ.) investment, (financial) aid

влива́|ть, ю *impf. of* ▶ **влить**

вли|ть, волью́, вольёшь, *past* ~**л**, **~ла́**, **~ло** *pf.* (*of* ▶ **влива́ть**) to pour in; (med.) to infuse

ᵒ⁄ **влия́ни|е, я** *nt.* influence; **под ~ем** (+ *g.*) under the influence of; **оказа́ть в. на** (+ *a.*) to influence; **по́льзоваться ~ем** to have influence, be influential

ᵒ⁄ **влия́тел|ьный, ~ен, ~ьна** *adj.* influential

ᵒ⁄ **влия́|ть, ю** *impf.* (*of* ▶ **повлия́ть**) (**на** + *a.*) to influence, have an influence on; (*действовать*) to affect

вложе́ни|е, я *nt.* ■ enclosure ② (fin.) investment

влож|и́ть, у́, ~ишь *pf.* (*of* ▶ **вкла́дывать**) ■ to put in, insert; (*в письмо*) to enclose (*with a letter*) ② (fin.) to invest

вломи́ться, люсь, ~ишься *pf.* (*of* ▶ **вла́мываться**) to break in, into

влюб|и́ться, лю́сь, ~ишься *pf.* (*of* ▶ **влюбля́ться**) (**в** + *a.*) to fall in love (with)

влюбл|ённый, ~ён, ~ена́ *adj.* (*человек*) in love; (*no short forms*) (*взгляд*) loving; tender

влюбля́|ться, юсь *impf. of* ▶ **влюби́ться**

вмен|и́ть, ю́, и́шь *pf.* (*of* ▶ **вменя́ть**): **в. (что́-н.) в вину́** (+ *d.*) to blame (sth) on (sb); **в. в обя́занность кому́-н.** to impose as a duty on (sb)

вменя́ем|ый, ~, ~а *adj.* (law) sane, of sound mind

вменя́|ть, ю *impf. of* ▶ **вмени́ть**

ᵒ⁄ **вме́сте** *adv.* together; at the same time; **в. с** (+ *i.*) together with; **в. с тем** at the same time, also; **но в. с тем** but; **а в. с тем** and also

вмести́мост|ь, и *f.* capacity

вмести́тел|ьный, ~ен, ~ьна *adj.* capacious; roomy

вме|сти́ть, щу́, сти́шь *pf. of* ▶ **вмеща́ть**

вме|сти́ться, щу́сь, сти́шься *pf. of* ▶ **вмеща́ться**

ᵒ⁄ **вме́сто** *prep.* + *g.* instead of; in place of

вмеша́тельств|о, а *nt.* interference; (pol., mil., med.) intervention

---

ᵒ⁄ key word

вмеш|а́ться, **а́юсь** *pf.* (*of* ▶ вме́шиваться) (в + *a.*) (*вторгнуться*) to interfere (in), meddle (with); (*для пресечения нежелательных последствий*) to intervene (in)

вме́шива|ться, юсь *impf. of* ▶ вмеша́ться

вмеща́|ть, ю *impf.* (*of* ▶ вмести́ть)
1 (*контейнер*) to contain; to hold; (*дом, зал*) to accommodate; **э́та бо́чка ~ет пятьдеся́т ли́тров** this barrel holds fifty litres **2** (в + *a.*) to put, place (in, into)

вмеща́|ться, юсь *impf.* (*of* ▶ вмести́ться)
1 to fit, go in **2** *pass. of* ▶ вмеща́ть 2

вмиг *adv.* in an instant; in a flash

ВМФ *m. indecl.* (*abbr. of* вое́нно-морско́й флот) Navy

вмя́тин|а, ы *f.* dent

внаём, внаймы́ *adv.*: **отда́ть в.** to let, hire out, rent; **взять в.** to hire, rent; **сдаётся в.** 'to let'

внача́ле *adv.* at first, in the beginning

✓ **вне** *prep.* + *g.* outside; out of; **объяви́ть в. зако́на** to outlaw; **в. о́череди** out of turn; **в. себя́** beside oneself; **в. вся́ких сомне́ний** beyond any doubt

вне... *comb. form* extra-

внебра́чный *adj.* extramarital; **в. ребёнок** illegitimate child

внедоро́жник, а *m.* four-wheel drive (vehicle)

✓ **внедре́ни|е**, я *nt.* (*методов*) introduction; (*идей*) inculcation

внедр|и́ть, ю́, и́шь *pf.* (*of* ▶ внедря́ть)
1 (*методы*) to introduce **2** (*идеи*) to inculcate, instil (BrE), instill (AmE)

внедр|и́ться, ю́сь, и́шься *pf.* (*of* ▶ внедря́ться) to take root

внедря́|ть, ю *impf. of* ▶ внедри́ть

внедря́|ться, юсь *impf. of* ▶ внедри́ться

внеза́пно *adv.* suddenly, all of a sudden

внеза́пный *adj.* sudden

внеочередно́й *adj.* **1** out of turn; **зада́ть в. вопро́с** to ask a question out of turn **2** (*заседание*) extraordinary; (*рейс*) extra

внепла́новый *adj.* (econ.) not provided for by the plan; extraordinary

внесе́ни|е, я *nt.* **1** (*денег*) paying in, deposit **2** (*предложения*) moving, submission

внес|ти́, у́, ёшь, *past* ~, ~ла́ *pf.* (*of* ▶ вноси́ть)
1 (*принести внутрь*) to bring in, carry in **2** (fig.) to introduce, put in; **в. я́сность в де́ло** to clarify a matter; **в. свой вклад в де́ло** to do one's bit; to make one's contribution **3** (*деньги*) to pay in, deposit **4** (*предложение*) to make, move, table **5** (*вписать*) to insert, enter

вне́шне *adv.* outwardly

внешнеторго́вый *adj.* foreign-trade (*attr.*)

✓ **вне́шн|ий** *adj.* **1** outer, exterior; outward, external; outside; **в. вид** appearance **2** (*иностранный*) foreign; **~яя поли́тика** foreign policy

вне́шност|ь, и *f.* appearance; exterior

внешта́тный *adj.* freelance; casual

вниз *adv.* down, downwards; **в. голово́й** head first; **идти́ в. по ле́стнице** to go downstairs; **в. по тече́нию** downstream; **в. по Во́лге** down the Volga

внизу́ *adv.* below; downstairs; *prep.* + *g.* **в. страни́цы** at the foot of the page

вник|а́ть, а́ю *impf. of* ▶ вни́кнуть

вни́к|нуть, ну, нешь, *past* ~, ~ла *pf.* (*of* ▶ вника́ть) (в + *a.*) (*изучить*) to go carefully (into), investigate thoroughly; (*понять*) to understand, penetrate

✓ **внима́ни|е**, я *nt.* **1** (*сосредоточенность*) attention; heed; notice, note; **обраща́ть в.** (на + *a.*) to pay attention (to); to draw attention (to); **удели́ть в. кому́-н.** to give sb attention; **принима́я во в.** taking into account **2** (*забота*) kindness, consideration **3** (*int.*): **в.!** attention!

внима́тельност|ь, и *f.* attentiveness

внима́тел|ьный, ~ен, ~ьна *adj.*
1 attentive **2** (к + *d.*) (*заботливый*) thoughtful, considerate (towards)

вничью́ *adv.* (sport): **па́ртия око́нчилась в.** the game ended in a draw; **на́ша кома́нда сыгра́ла сего́дня в.** our team drew today

✓ **вновь** *adv.* **1** (*опять*) afresh, anew; again **2** (*недавно*) newly; **в. при́бывший** newcomer

✓ **вно|си́ть, шу́, ~сишь** *impf. of* ▶ внести́

ВНП *m. indecl.* (*abbr. of* валово́й национа́льный проду́кт) GNP (*gross national product*)

внук, а *m.* grandson; grandchild

✓ **вну́тренн|ий** *adj.* **1** inner, interior; internal; intrinsic; **в. мир** inner life, inner world **2** (*в государстве*) domestic, inland; **~ие дохо́ды** inland revenue; **~яя поли́тика** internal politics; **Министе́рство ~их дел** Ministry of Internal Affairs

вну́тренност|ь, и *f.* interior; (*pl. only*) entrails, intestines; internal organs

✓ **внутри́** *adv. and prep.* + *g.* inside, within; **в. до́ма** inside the house

внутри... *comb. form* intra-

внутриве́нный *adj.* (med.) intravenous

внутрь *adv. and prep.* + *g.* within, inside; inwards; **открыва́ться в.** to open inwards; **войти́ в. до́ма** to go inside the house

вну́чк|а, и *f.* granddaughter

внуша́|ть, а́ю *impf. of* ▶ внуши́ть

внуше́ни|е, я *nt.* **1** (*выговор*) reprimand **2** (psych.) suggestion

внуши́тел|ьный, ~ен, ~ьна *adj.* imposing, impressive

внуш|и́ть, у́, и́шь *pf.* (*of* ▶ внуша́ть) (+ *a. and d.*) to inspire (with); to instil (BrE), instill (AmE); to suggest; **его́ вид ~и́л мне страх** the sight of him inspired me with fear

вня́т|ный, ~ен, ~на *adj.* distinct

✓ **во** *prep.* = **в**

вовлека́|ть, ю *impf. of* ▶ вовле́чь

вовл|е́чь, еку́, ечёшь, еку́т, *past* ~ёк, ~екла́ *pf.* to draw in, involve

вовну́трь *adv. and prep.* + *g.* (infml) inside

B

во́время *adv.* in time, on time; **не в.** at the wrong time

✓ **во́все** *adv.* (infml) completely; (+ *neg.*) at all; **он в. не бога́тый челове́к** he is not at all a rich man

во-вторы́х *adv.* secondly, in the second place

во́гнут|ый, ~, ~а *adj.* concave

✓ **вод|а́**, ы́, *a.* ~у, *pl.* ~ы, ~, ~ам *f.* **1** water; **выводи́ть на чи́стую** ~у to show up, unmask; **похо́жи как две ка́пли** ~ы as like as two peas **2** (*in pl.*) (*минеральные*) the waters; (*курорт*) spa

✓ **води́тел|ь**, я *m.* driver

води́тельск|ий *adj.*: ~ие права́ driving licence (BrE), driver's license (AmE)

во|ди́ть, жу́, ~дишь *impf.* (*indet. of* ▸ вести́) **1** (*see also* ▸ вести́) (*сопровождать*) to take; to lead; to conduct; (*машину*) to drive **2** (infml) (*see also* ▸ вести́): **в. дру́жбу** (**с** + *i.*) to be friends with; **в. знако́мство** (**с** + *i.*) to keep up an acquaintance (with) **3** (+ *i.*; *see also* ▸ вести́) to pass (**по** + *d.* over, across)

во|ди́ться, жу́сь, ~дишься *impf.* **1** (**с** + *i.*) to associate (with); (*о детях*) to play (with) **2** (*обитать*) to be, be found; **льв́ы не** ~дятся в Евро́пе lions are not found in Europe **3** (*быть принятым*) to be the custom; to happen; **как** ~дится as usually happens **4** (infml, *быть в наличии, иметься*) be abundant; **де́ньги у него́** ~дятся he's always in the money

во́дк|а, и *f.* vodka

во́дн|ый *adj.* water; ~ые лы́жи (*вид спорта*) waterskiing; (*экипировка*) waterskis

водоворо́т, а *m.* whirlpool; (fig.) maelstrom

водоём, а *m.* reservoir

водола́з, а *m.* diver; (*ныряльщик с аквалангом*) frogman

водола́зк|а, и *f.* thin polo-necked sweater

водола́зный *adj. of* ▸ водола́з; **в. костю́м** diving suit

Водоле́|й, я *m.* (*созвездие*) Aquarius

водонепроница́ем|ый, ~, ~а *adj.* watertight; waterproof

водопа́д, а *m.* waterfall

водопрово́д, а *m.* water supply system; plumbing

водопрово́дчик, а *m.* plumber

водоро́д, а *m.* (chem.) hydrogen

во́дорос|ль, и *f.* (bot.) water plant; **морска́я в.** seaweed

водосто́к, а *m.* drain; (*на улице, крыше*) gutter

водосто́|чный *adj. of* ▸ водосто́к; ~чная труба́ drainpipe

водохрани́лищ|е, а *nt.* reservoir

во́дочный *adj. of* ▸ во́дка

водяно́й *adj.* **1** *adj. of* ▸ вода́ **2** (*живущий, растущий в воде*) water, aquatic **3** (*приводимый в движение водой*) water-driven

✓ **key word**

во|ева́ть, ю́ю, ю́ешь *impf.* (**с** + *i.*) to wage war (with), make war (upon); to be at war

воен... *comb. form, abbr. of* ▸ вое́нный

военача́льник, а *m.* commander

военкома́т, а *m.* (*abbr. of* вое́нный комиссариа́т) military recruitment office

вое́нно-... *comb. form, abbr. of* ▸ вое́нный

вое́нно-возду́шн|ый *adj.*: ~ые си́лы Air Force(s)

вое́нно-морско́й *adj.* naval; **в. флот** the Navy

военнообя́занн|ый, ого *m.* man liable for call-up (*including reservists*)

военноплённ|ый, ого *m.* prisoner of war

вое́нно-полево́й *adj.* (mil.) field; **в. суд** court martial

вое́нно-промы́шленный *adj.* military-industrial

военнослу́жащ|ий, его *m.* serviceman

✓ **вое́нн|ый** *adj.* military; war; (*форма*) army; **в. врач** (army) medical officer; ~ое вре́мя wartime; ~ое положе́ние martial law; ~ое учи́лище military college; (*as m. n.* **в.**, ~ого) soldier, serviceman; ~ые (*collect.*) the military

вожделе́ни|е, я *nt.* desire, lust (also fig.)

вожд|ь, я́ *m.* (*организации*) leader; (*племени*) chief

во́жж|и, е́й *f. pl.* (*sg.* ~а́, ~и́) reins

во|жу́¹, ~дишь *see* ▸ води́ть

во|жу́², ~зишь *see* ▸ вози́ть

воз, а *o* ~е, на ~у́, *pl.* ~ы́ *m.* cart, wagon

возбуди́м|ый, ~, ~а *adj.* excitable

возбу|ди́ть, жу́, ди́шь *pf.* (*of* ▸ возбужда́ть) **1** to excite, rouse, arouse; **в. аппети́т** to whet the appetite **2** (law) to institute; **в. де́ло** (**про́тив** + *g.*) to institute proceedings (against), bring an action (against); **в. иск** (**про́тив** + *g.*) to bring a suit (against)

возбу|ди́ться, жу́сь, ди́шься *pf.* (*of* ▸ возбужда́ться) (*о человеке*) to get excited

возбужда́|ть, ю *impf. of* ▸ возбуди́ть

возбужда́|ться, юсь *impf. of* ▸ возбуди́ться

возбужде́ни|е, я *nt.* excitement

возбуждённый *p.p.p. of* ▸ возбуди́ть *and adj.* excited

возбу|жу́, ди́шь *see* ▸ возбуди́ть

возбу|жу́сь, ди́шься *see* ▸ возбуди́ться

возве|сти́, ду́, дёшь, *past* ~л, ~ла́ *pf.* (*of* ▸ возводи́ть) **1** (*возвысить*) to elevate; **в. в сан патриа́рха** to elect to the patriarchate **2** (*строить*) to erect, put up **3** (math.) to raise; **в. в куб** to cube

возво|ди́ть, жу́, ~дишь *impf. of* ▸ возвести́

возвра́т, а *m.* return; repayment, reimbursement; **без** ~а irrevocably

возвра|ти́ть, щу́, ти́шь *pf.* (*of* ▸ возвраща́ть) **1** (*отдать обратно*) to return, give back; (*деньги*) to pay back **2** (*получить обратно*) to recover, retrieve; **в. де́ньги, о́тданные взаймы́** to recover a loan

возвра|ти́ться, щу́сь, ти́шься *pf.* (*of* ▸ возвраща́ться) to return; (fig.) to revert

возвраща́|ть, ю *impf. of* ▶ **возврати́ть,** ▶ **верну́ть**

возвраща́|ться, юсь *impf. of* ▶ **возврати́ться,** ▶ **верну́ться**

возвраще́ни|е, я *nt.* return; **в. домо́й** homecoming

возвра|щу́, ти́шь *see* ▶ **возврати́ть**

возвы́|ситься, шусь, сишься *pf.* (*of* ▶ **возвыша́ться**) to rise, go up

возвыша́|ться, юсь *impf. of* **1** *impf. of* ▶ **возвы́ситься 2** (*impf. only*) (**над** + *i.*) to tower (above) (also fig.)

возвыше́ни|е, я *nt.* **1** (*де́йствие*) rise; raising **2** (*ме́сто*) elevation; raised place

возвы́шенность|ь, и *f.* (geog.) height; elevation

возвы́шен|ный, ~, ~на *adj.* **1** (*высо́кий*) high; elevated **2** (*благоро́дный*) lofty, sublime, elevated; ~ные идеа́лы lofty ideals

возгла́в|ить, лю, ишь *pf.* (*of* ▶ **возглавля́ть**) to head, be at the head of

возглавля́|ть, ю *impf. of* ▶ **возгла́вить**

во́згласх, а *m.* cry, exclamation

воздвига́|ть, ю *impf. of* (*of* ▶ **воздви́гнуть**) to raise, erect

воздви́г|нуть, ну, нешь, *past* ~, ~ла *pf. of* ▶ **воздвига́ть**

✎ **возде́йстви|е, я** *nt.* influence; **он э́то сде́лал под физи́ческим ~ем** he did it under coercion

возде́йств|овать, ую *impf. and pf.* (**на** + *a.*) to influence, affect; to exert influence

возде́л|ать, аю *pf.* (*of* ▶ **возде́лывать**) to cultivate, till

возде́лыва|ть, ю *impf. of* ▶ **возде́лать**

воздержа́вш|ийся *p.p. of* ▶ **воздержа́ться**; (*as n.* **в.,** ~**егося**) *m.* abstainer; **предложе́ние бы́ло при́нято при трёх ~ихся** the motion was carried with three abstentions

воздержа́ни|е, я *nt.* **1** abstinence **2** (**от** + *g.*) abstention (from)

воз|держа́ться, держу́сь, де́ржишься *pf.* (*of* ▶ **возде́рживаться**) (**от** + *g.*) **1** (*от замеча́ния, куре́ния*) to refrain (from); (*от алкого́ля, куре́ния, мя́са*) to abstain (from) **2** (*от голосова́ния*) to abstain

возде́ржива|ться, юсь *impf. of* ▶ **возде́рживаться**

✎ **во́здух, а** (*no pl.*) *m.* **1** air; **на** (**откры́том**) ~**е** out of doors; **вы́йти на в.** to go out of doors; **в** ~**е** (fig.) in the air **2** (*атмосфе́ра*) atmosphere

возду́ш|ный *adj.* **1** air, aerial; **в. змей** kite; ~**ная трево́га** air-raid warning; **в. шар** balloon **2** (*приводи́мый в движе́ние во́здухом*) air-driven **3** (~**ен,** ~**на**) (*о́чень лёгкий*) airy, light; flimsy

воззва́ни|е, я *nt.* appeal

во|зи́ть, жу́, ~зишь *impf.* (*indet. of* ▶ **везти́**) to take, convey; to carry; (*тяну́ть*) to draw

во|зи́ться, жу́сь, ~зишься *impf.* (**с** + *i.*) (*с чем-н. тру́дным*) to take trouble (over); (*с детьми́*) to spend time, busy oneself

---

(with); (infml, *копа́ться*) to potter; **он лю́бит в. в саду́** he likes pottering about in the garden

возлага́|ть, ю *impf. of* ▶ **возложи́ть**

во́зле *prep.* + *g.* by, near; *adv.* nearby

возлож|и́ть, у́, ~ишь *pf.* (*of* ▶ **возлага́ть**) **1** (*положи́ть*) to lay; **в. вено́к на моги́лу** to lay a wreath on a grave **2** (*поручи́ть*) (**на** + *a.*) to entrust (to); **в. вину́/отве́тственность на** (+ *a.*) to lay the blame/responsibility on

возлю́бленн|ый, ого *m.* (*n. declined as an adj.; f.* ~**ая,** ~**ой**) beloved, sweetheart; (*любо́вник*) lover; (*любо́вница*) mistress

возме́зди|е, я *nt.* retribution

возме|сти́ть, щу́, сти́шь *pf.* (*of* ▶ **возмеща́ть**) to compensate (for), make up (for); **в. расхо́ды** to refund expenses

возмеща́|ть, ю *impf. of* ▶ **возмести́ть**

возмеще́ни|е, я *nt.* **1** (*су́мма*) compensation; (law) damages **2** (*расхо́дов*) reimbursement

возме|щу́, сти́шь *see* ▶ **возмести́ть**

✎ **возмо́жно** *adv.* **1** possibly **2** (*as pred.*) it is possible; **в., что мы за́втра уе́дем** we may possibly go away tomorrow

✎ **возмо́жность|ь, и** *f.* **1** possibility; **по (ме́ре)** ~**и** as far as possible **2** (*удо́бный слу́чай*) opportunity; **при пе́рвой** ~**и** at the first opportunity **3** (*in pl.*) (*сре́дства*) means, resources

✎ **возмо́ж|ный, ~ен, ~на** *adj.* **1** possible; **врач сде́лал для неё всё** ~**ное** the doctor did all in his power for her **2** (*наибо́льший*) the greatest possible

возмути́тел|ьный, ~ен, ~ьна *adj.* disgraceful, outrageous, scandalous

возму|ти́ть, щу́, ти́шь *pf.* to anger, outrage

возму|ти́ться, щу́сь, ти́шься *pf.* (+ *i.*) to be indignant (at); to be outraged (at)

возмуща́|ть, ю *impf. of* ▶ **возмути́ть**

возмуща́|ться, юсь *impf. of* ▶ **возмути́ться**

возмуще́ни|е, я *nt.* indignation, outrage

возму|щу́, ти́шь *see* ▶ **возмути́ть**

вознагражде́ни|е, я *nt.* **1** (*за труд, за по́двиг*) reward, recompense; (*компенса́ция*) compensation **2** (*опла́та*) fee, remuneration

✎ **возника́|ть, а́ю** *impf.* (*of* ▶ **возни́кнуть**) **1** (*тру́дности, подозре́ние*) to arise, spring up; **у меня́** ~**ла мысль** the thought occurred to me **2** (infml, *появля́ться*) to appear, pop up **3** (*начина́ться*) to begin

✎ **возникнове́ни|е, я** *nt.* rise, beginning, origin

✎ **возни́к|нуть, ну, нешь,** *past* ~, ~ла *pf. of* ▶ **возника́ть**

возн|я́, и́ (*no pl.*) *f.* (infml) **1** (*шум*) row, noise **2** (*хло́поты*) bother, trouble

возоблада́|ть, ю *pf.* (**над** + *i.*) to prevail (over)

возобнов|и́ть, лю́, и́шь *pf.* (*of* ▶ **возобновля́ть**) (*перегово́ры, отноше́ния*) to resume; (*абонеме́нт, контра́кт*) to renew

возобновле́ни|е, я *nt.* resumption, renewal

возобновля́|ть, ю *impf. of* ▶ **возобнови́ть**

B

возража́|ть, ю *impf.* (*of* ▸ возрази́ть): не ~ю I have no objection

возраже́ни|е, я *nt.* objection; (*резкий ответ*) retort

возра|зи́ть, жу́, зи́шь *pf.* (*of* ▸ возража́ть) **1** (про́тив + *g. or* на + *a.*) to object (to); to take exception (to); про́тив э́того не́чего в. nothing can be said against it **2** (*pf. only*) (*ответить резко*) to retort

✐ **во́зраст**, а *m.* age; в ~е двадцати́ лет at the age of twenty; ребёнок в ~е двена́дцати лет a twelve-year-old child

возраста́ни|е, я *nt.* growth, increase

возраст|а́ть, а́ю *impf. of* ▸ возрасти́

возраст|и́, у́, ёшь, *past* возро́с, возросла́ *pf.* (*of* ▸ возраста́ть) to grow, increase

возраст|но́й *adj. of* ▸ во́зраст; ~на́я гру́ппа age group

возро|ди́ть, жу́, ди́шь *pf.* (*of* ▸ возрожда́ть) (*хозяйство, город*) to regenerate; (*надежду, культуру*) to revive

возро|ди́ться, жу́сь, ди́шься *pf.* (*of* ▸ возрожда́ться) to revive

возрожда́|ть, ю *impf. of* ▸ возроди́ть

возрожда́|ться, юсь *impf. of* ▸ возроди́ться

возрожде́ни|е, я *nt.* regeneration; revival; эпо́ха В~я Renaissance

возьм|у́, ёшь *see* ▸ взять

возьм|у́сь, ёшься *see* ▸ взя́ться

во́ин, а *m.* warrior; fighter

во́инск|ий *adj.* **1** military; ~ая пови́нность conscription **2** (*свойственный военному*) martial, warlike

во́инствен|ный, ~, ~на *adj.* **1** (*народ*) warlike **2** (*вид, тон*) bellicose

во́|й, я (*no pl.*) *m.* howl, howling; wail, wailing

во́й|ду́, дёшь *see* ▸ войти́

во́йлок, а *m.* felt

✐ **войн|а́**, ы́, *pl.* ~ы f. war; (*ведение войны*) warfare; вести́ ~у́ to wage war; объяви́ть ~у́ to declare war

✐ **войск|а́**, ~ *nt. pl.* (*sg.* ~о, ~а) troops; forces; наёмные в. mercenaries

войсково́й *adj.* military

✐ **во|йти́**, йду́, йдёшь, *past* ~шёл, ~шла́ *pf.* (*of* ▸ входи́ть) (в. + *a.*) (*вступить*) to enter; (*из данного места внутрь*) to go in(to); (*извне в данное место*) to come in(to); (*уместиться*) to go in, fit in; (*в состав чего-н.*) to enter; в. в исто́рию to go down in history; в. в мо́ду to become fashionable; в. в систе́му (comput.) to log on

вокали́ст, а *m.* (mus.) vocalist

вокали́ст|ка, ки *f. of* ▸ вокали́ст

вока́льный *adj.* vocal

вокза́л, а *m.* (large) station; железнодоро́жный в. railway (esp. main or terminus) station; морско́й в. port arrival and departure building

✐ **вокру́г** *adv. and prep.* + *g.* round, around; (*по поводу*) about; в. све́та round the world;

✐ *key word*

ходи́ть в. да о́коло (infml) to beat about the bush

вол, а́ *m.* ox, bullock

Во́лг|а, и *f.* the Volga (*river*)

волды́р|ь, я́ *m.* (*пузырь*) blister

волево́й *adj.* (*человек, натура*) strong-willed; (*лицо, голос*) determined

волейбо́л, а *m.* volleyball

волейболи́ст, а *m.* volleyball player

волейболи́ст|ка, ки *f. of* ▸ волейболи́ст

волк, а, *pl.* ~и, ~о́в *m.* wolf

волкода́в, а *m.* wolfhound

✐ **волн|а́**, ы́, *pl.* ~ы, ~, ~а́м *f.* wave

волне́ни|е, я *nt.* **1** (*на воде*) choppiness **2** (fig.) (*нервное*) agitation; (*радостное*) excitement; (*душевное*) emotion; прийти́ в в. to become agitated, excited **3** (*usu. in pl.*) (pol.) disturbance(s); unrest

волни́ст|ый, ~, ~а *adj.* wavy

волн|ова́ть, у́ю *impf.* (*of* ▸ взволнова́ть) (*возбуждать*) to excite; (*беспокоить*) to worry; (*воду*) to disturb, agitate (also fig.)

волн|ова́ться, у́юсь *impf.* **1** (*нервно*) to worry, be nervous; (*радостно*) to be excited; она́ ~у́ется о де́тях/за дете́й she worries about her children **2** (*вода*) to be agitated, choppy

волноре́з, а *m.* breakwater

волну́ющий *pres. part. act. of* ▸ волнова́ть *and adj.* (*беспокоящий*) disturbing, worrying; (*захватывающий*) exciting, thrilling

волоки́т|а¹, ы *f.* (infml, *бюрократизм*) red tape

волоки́т|а², ы *m.* (infml, *мужчина*) philanderer

волок|но́, на́, *pl.* ~на, ~он, ~нам *nt.* fibre (BrE), fiber (AmE)

волонтёр, а *m.* volunteer

✐ **во́лос**, а, *pl.* ~ы, воло́с, ~а́м *m.* hair; (*in pl.*) hair (*of the head*); рвать на себе́ ~ы to tear one's hair

волоса́т|ый, ~, ~а *adj.* hairy

волос|о́к, ка́ *m. dim. of* ▸ во́лос; на в. (от + *g.*) within a hair's breadth (of); висе́ть, держа́ться на ~ке́ to hang by a thread

волоч|и́ть, у́, ~ишь *impf.* to drag; в. но́ги to shuffle one's feet

вол|о́чь, оку́, очёшь, оку́т, *past* ~о́к, ~окла́ *impf.* (infml) to drag

волше́бник, а *m.* magician; wizard

волше́бниц|а, ы *f.* enchantress

волше́б|ный, ~ен, ~на *adj.* **1** magic (*attr.*); magical; ~ная па́лочка magic wand **2** (fig.) magical, bewitching; enchanting

волшебств|о́, а́ *nt.* magic

волы́нк|а, и *f.* bagpipes

вольер, а *m.* cage; enclosure

вольер|а, ы *f.* = вольер

вольнонаёмный *adj.* (*рабочий, труд*) hired; freelance

во́льность, и *f.* freedom; liberty; поэти́ческая в. poetic licence (BrE), poetic license (AmE)

во́л|ьный *adj.* **1** free **2** (sport) free, freestyle; ~ьная борьба́ freestyle wrestling **3** (~ен,

⁓ьна́, ⁓ьно, pl. ⁓ьны́) (short forms only) free, at liberty; вы ⁓ьны́ де́лать, что хоти́те you are at liberty to do as you wish

ВОЛЬТ, а, g. pl. в. m. (elec.) volt

ВОЛЬ|Ю́, ю́ ёшь see ▸ влить

⁓ **ВО́Л|Я**, и (no pl.) f. **1** will; после́дняя в. last will; си́ла ⁓и willpower; по до́брой ⁓е of one's own free will; не по свое́й ⁓е against one's will **2** (свобо́да) freedom, liberty; на ⁓е at liberty; дать ⁓ю (+ d.) to give free rein (to)

ВОН¹ adv. out; off, away; вы́йти в. to go away; в. отсю́да! get out!

ВОН² particle (на отдале́нии) there, over there; в. он идёт there he goes

ВОН|ЖУ́, зи́шь see ▸ вонзи́ть

ВОНЗА́|ТЬ, ю impf. of ▸ вонзи́ть

ВОНЗА́|ТЬСЯ, юсь **1** impf. of ▸ вонзи́ться **2** pass. of ▸ вонза́ть

ВОН|ЗИ́ТЬ, жу́, зи́шь pf. (of ▸ вонза́ть) (в + a.) to plunge, thrust (into)

ВОН|ЗИ́ТЬСЯ, жу́сь, зи́шься pf. (of ▸ вонза́ться 1) to pierce, penetrate; стрела́ ⁓зи́лась ему́ в се́рдце the arrow pierced his heart

ВОН|Ь, и (no pl.) f. stink, stench

ВОНЯ́|ТЬ, ю impf. (infml) (+ i.) to stink, reek (of)

ВООБРАЖА́|ЕМЫЙ pres. part. pass. of ▸ воображáть and adj. imaginary; fictitious

ВООБРАЖА́|ТЬ, ю (of ▸ вообрази́ть) to imagine

ВООБРАЖЕ́НИ|Е, я nt. imagination

ВООБРА|ЗИ́ТЬ, жу́, зи́шь pf. (of ▸ вообража́ть): ⁓зи́(те)! (just) imagine!

⁓ **ВООБЩЕ́** adv. **1** (в о́бщем) in general; on the whole; в. говоря́ generally speaking **2** (всегда́) always **3** (with neg.) at all

ВООДУШЕВ|И́ТЬ, лю́, и́шь pf. (of ▸ воодушевля́ть) (кого́-н. на + a.) to inspire (to), rouse (to)

ВООДУШЕВЛЕ́НИ|Е, я nt. **1** (де́йствие) rousing **2** (увлече́ние) enthusiasm, fervour (BrE), fervor (AmE)

ВООДУШЕВЛЯ́|ТЬ, ю impf. of ▸ воодушеви́ть

ВООРУЖ|А́ТЬ, а́ю impf. of ▸ вооружи́ть

ВООРУЖ|А́ТЬСЯ, а́юсь impf. of ▸ вооружи́ться

ВООРУЖЕ́НИ|Е, я nt. **1** (де́йствие) arming **2** (ору́жие) arms, armament; быть на ⁓и to be deployed **3** (принадле́жности) equipment

ВООРУЖ|ЁННЫЙ, ⁓ён, ⁓ена́ p.p.p. of ▸ вооружи́ть and adj. armed; ⁓ённые си́лы armed forces

ВООРУЖ|И́ТЬ, у́, и́шь pf. (of ▸ вооружа́ть) (+ i.) to arm; to equip (with) (also fig.)

ВООРУЖ|И́ТЬСЯ, у́сь, и́шься pf. (of ▸ вооружа́ться) to arm oneself; (fig.) to equip oneself

⁓ **ВО-ПЕ́РВЫХ** adv. first, first of all, in the first place

ВОПЛО|ТИ́ТЬ, щу́, ти́шь pf. (of ▸ воплоща́ть) to embody, personify; в. в себе́ to be the embodiment (of); в. в жизнь (пла́ны) to realize

ВОПЛО|ТИ́ТЬСЯ, щу́сь, ти́шься pf. (of ▸ воплоща́ться) to be realized; to be fulfilled

ВОПЛОЩА́|ТЬ, ю impf. of ▸ воплоти́ть

ВОПЛОЩА́|ТЬСЯ, юсь impf. of ▸ воплоти́ться

ВОПЛОЩЕ́НИ|Е, я nt. embodiment

ВОПЛ|Ь, я m. cry, wail; wailing, howling

ВОПРЕКИ́ prep. + d. (несмотря́ на) despite, in spite of; (напереко́р) against, contrary to

⁓ **ВОПРО́С**, а m. **1** question; зада́ть в. to ask, put a question; отве́тить на в. to answer a question **2** (пробле́ма) question, problem; (де́ло) matter; подня́ть, поста́вить в. (о + p.) to raise the question (of); в. жи́зни и сме́рти matter of life and death; спо́рный в. moot point

ВОПРОСИ́ТЕЛЬНЫЙ adj. interrogative; в. знак question mark; в. взгляд inquiring look

ВОР, а, pl. ⁓ы, ⁓о́в m. thief

ВОРВ|А́ТЬСЯ, у́сь, ёшься, past ⁓а́лся, ⁓ала́сь pf. (of ▸ врыва́ться) to burst (into)

ВОРОБ|Е́Й, ья́ m. sparrow

ВОРО́ВАННЫЙ adj. stolen

ВОР|ОВА́ТЬ, у́ю impf. (infml pf. с⁓) to steal; в. де́ньги у кого́-н. to steal money from sb

ВОРО́ВК|А, и f. of ▸ вор

ВОРОВСТВ|О́, а́ nt. stealing; theft

ВО́РОН, а m. raven

ВОРО́Н|А, ы f. crow

ВОРО́НК|А, и f. **1** (для перелива́ния) funnel (for pouring liquids) **2** (mil.) (я́ма) crater

ВОРО́Т|А, ⁓ (no sg.) **1** gate, gates; (вход) gateway **2** (sport) goal

ВОРОТИ́Л|А, ы m. (infml) big shot

ВОРОТНИ́К, а́ m. collar

ВО́РОХ, а, pl. ⁓а́ m. heap, pile

ВОРОЧА́|ТЬСЯ, юсь impf. (infml) to turn, move; в. с бо́ку на́ бок to toss and turn

ВОРЧ|А́ТЬ, у́, и́шь impf. (на + a.) to grumble (at); (о соба́ке) to growl (at)

ВОРЧЛИ́В|ЫЙ, ⁓, ⁓а adj. querulous

ВОСЕМНА́ДЦАТЫЙ adj. eighteenth

ВОСЕМНА́ДЦАТ|Ь, и num. eighteen

ВО́С|ЕМЬ, ьми́, i. емью́ and ьмью́ num. eight

ВО́С|ЕМЬДЕСЯТ, ьми́десяти num. eighty

ВОС|ЕМЬСО́Т, ьмисо́т, i. емьюста́ми and ьмьюста́ми num. eight hundred

ВОСК, а m. wax

ВОСКЛИ́К|НУТЬ, у, ешь pf. of ▸ восклица́ть

ВОСКЛИЦА́НИ|Е, я nt. exclamation

ВОСКЛИЦА́ТЕЛЬНЫЙ adj. exclamatory; в. знак exclamation mark

ВОСКЛИЦА́|ТЬ, ю impf. (of ▸ воскли́кнуть) to exclaim

ВОСКОВО́Й adj. wax; (цвет) waxen

ВОСКРЕС|А́ТЬ, а́ю impf. (of ▸ воскре́снуть) to rise again, rise from the dead; (fig.) to revive

ВОСКРЕСЕ́НИ|Е, я nt. resurrection

ВОСКРЕСЕ́НЬ|Е, я nt. Sunday

ВОСКРЕ|СИ́ТЬ, шу́, си́шь pf. (of ▸ воскреша́ть) to raise from the dead, resurrect; (fig.) to revive

В

B

воскре́с|нуть, ну, нешь, *past* ~, ~ла *pf. of*
▶ воскреса́ть

воскре́сный *adj.* Sunday

воскреша́|ть, ю *impf. of* ▶ воскреси́ть

воскреше́ни|е, я *nt.* resurrection; (fig.)
revival

воспале́ни|е, я *nt.* (med.) inflammation;
в. лёгких pneumonia

воспал|ённый, ~ён, ~ена́ *adj.* sore;
inflamed

воспал|и́ться, ю́сь, и́шься *pf.* (*of*
▶ воспаля́ться) to become inflamed

воспал|я́ться, я́юсь *impf. of* ▶ воспали́ться

✓ **воспита́ни|е, я** *nt.* ❶ upbringing; (*образование*)
education ❷ (*воспитанность*) (good)
breeding

воспи́танник, а *m.* ❶ (*школьник*) pupil
❷ (*приёмыш*) ward

воспи́танный *p.p.p. of* ▶ воспита́ть *and adj.*
well brought up

воспита́тел|ь, я *m.* teacher; (*приёмыша*)
guardian

воспита́тель|ница, ницы *f. of*
▶ воспита́тель

воспит|а́ть, а́ю *pf.* (*of* ▶ воспи́тывать)
(*вырастить*) to bring up; (*дать*
образование) to educate

воспи́тыва|ть, ю *impf. of* ▶ воспита́ть

воспламен|и́ть, ю́, и́шь *pf.* (*of*
▶ воспламеня́ть) to kindle, ignite; (fig.)
to inflame

воспламен|и́ться, ю́сь, и́шься *pf.* (*of*
▶ воспламеня́ться) to catch fire, ignite; (fig.)
to flare up

воспламеня́|ть, ю *impf. of* ▶ воспламени́ть

воспламеня́|ться, юсь *impf. of*
▶ воспламени́ться

воспо́лн|ить, ю, ишь *pf.* to fill in

восполня́|ть, ю *impf. of* ▶ воспо́лнить

✓ **воспо́льз|оваться, уюсь** *pf. of*
▶ по́льзоваться 2

воспомина́ни|е, я *nt.* ❶ recollection,
memory ❷ (*in pl.*) (*мемуары*) memoirs;
reminiscences

воспрепя́тств|овать, ую *pf. of*
▶ препя́тствовать

воспреща́|ться, ется *impf.* to be prohibited

восприи́мчив|ый, ~, ~а *adj.* ❶ (*ум,*
натура) receptive; impressionable
❷ (*подверженный*) susceptible

восприм|у́, ~ешь *see* ▶ восприня́ть

воспринима́|ть, ю *impf. of* ▶ восприня́ть

воспри|ня́ть, му́, ~мешь, *past* ~ня́л,
~няла́, ~няло **pf.** (*of* ▶ воспринима́ть)
❶ (*ощутить*) to perceive, apprehend;
(*понять*) to grasp, take in ❷ (*понять как*)
to take (for), interpret

восприя́ти|е, я *nt.* (phil., psych.) perception

воспроизведе́ни|е, я *nt.* ❶ reproduction;
в. челове́ческого ро́да reproduction of
the human species; ве́рное в. карти́ны

Ру́бенса faithful reproduction of a painting
by Rubens ❷ (electronics) playback, replay;
заме́дленное/уско́ренное в. slow-motion/
high-speed playback

воспроизве|сти́, ду́, дёшь, *past* ~л, ~ла́
pf. (*of* ▶ воспроизводи́ть) to reproduce; в. в
па́мяти to recall

воспроизво|ди́ть, жу́, ~дишь *impf. of*
▶ воспроизвести́

воссоедине́ни|е, я *nt.* reunification

воссоедин|и́ть, ю́, и́шь *pf.* (*of*
▶ воссоединя́ть) to reunite

воссоединя́|ть, ю *impf. of* ▶ воссоедини́ть

воссозда|ва́ть, ю́, ёшь *impf. of* ▶ воссозда́ть

воссозда́ни|е, я *nt.* reconstruction

**воссоз|да́ть, да́м, да́шь, да́ст, дади́м,
дади́те, даду́т,** *past* ~да́л, ~дала́, ~да́ло
pf. (*of* ▶ воссоздава́ть) to reconstruct,
reconstitute

восста|ва́ть, ю́, ёшь *impf. of* ▶ восста́ть

восстана́влива|ть, ю *impf. of*
▶ восстанови́ть

восста́ни|е, я *nt.* uprising, insurrection

восстанови́тельн|ый *adj.* restorative;
в. пери́од period of reconstruction; ~ые
рабо́ты restoration work

восстанов|и́ть, лю́, ~ишь *pf.* (*of*
▶ восстана́вливать) ❶ to restore; в. в
па́мяти to recall, recollect ❷ (про́тив + g.)
to set (against), antagonize

✓ **восстановле́ни|е, я** *nt.* restoration,
renewal; в. в до́лжности reinstatement

восста́|ть, ну, нешь, *imper.* ~нь **pf.**
(*of* ▶ восстава́ть) (про́тив + g.) to rise
(against); (fig.) to be up in arms (against),
revolt (against)

✓ **восто́к, а** *m.* ❶ east; на в., с ~а to, from the
east ❷ (В.) the East; the Orient; Бли́жний
В~ the Middle East; Да́льний В. the Far
East

восто́рг, а *m.* delight; rapture; быть в ~е (от
+ g.) to be delighted (with); приходи́ть в в.
от (+ g.) to go into raptures (over)

восто́ржен|ный, ~, ~на *adj.* (*поклонник*)
enthusiastic; (*приём, отзыв*) rapturous

восторжеств|ова́ть, у́ю *pf. of*
▶ торжествова́ть

✓ **восто́чный** *adj.* east, eastern; (*направление,*
ветер) easterly; (*культура*) oriental

востре́бовани|е, я *nt.* claiming, demand; до
~я poste restante

восхити́тельн|ый, ~ен, ~ьна *adj.*
(*женщина, красота*) ravishing; (*вечер,*
музыка) delightful; (*вкус, запах*) delicious

восхи|ти́ть, щу́, ти́шь *pf.* to delight, captivate

восхи|ти́ться, щу́сь, ти́шься *pf.* (+ *i.*) to
be delighted (by); to be carried away (by);
to admire

восхища́|ть, ю *impf. of* ▶ восхити́ть

восхища́|ться, юсь *impf. of* ▶ восхити́ться

восхище́ни|е, я *nt.* admiration; (*восторг*)
delight, rapture; прийти́ в в. от (+ g.) to be
delighted with

восхи|щу́, ти́шь *see* ▸ **восхити́ть**

восхи|щу́сь, ти́шься *see* ▸ **восхити́ться**

восхо́д, а *m.* rising; **в. со́лнца** sunrise

восхо|ди́ть, жу́, ∼дишь *impf. of* **1** *impf. of* ▸ **взойти́ 2** (*impf. only*) (**к +** *d.*) to go back (to), date (from); **в. к дре́вности** to go back to antiquity

восходя́щий *pres. part. of* ▸ **восходи́ть** *and adj.*: ∼**ящая звезда́** (fig.) rising star

восхожде́ни|е, я *nt.* ascent; **в. на Монбла́н** the ascent of Mont Blanc

восьма́я *see* ▸ **восьмо́й**

восьмёрк|а, и *f.* **1** (*цифра, игральная карта*) eight **2** (*infml, автобус, трамвай*) No. 8 (*bus, tram, etc.*) **3** (*группа из восьмерых*) (group of) eight **4** (*фигура*) (figure of) eight

восьми́... *comb. form* eight-, octo-

восьмиуго́льный *adj.* octagonal

восьмичасово́й *adj.* eight-hour; **в. рабо́чий день** eight-hour (working) day

восьм|о́й *adj.* eighth; (*as f. n.* ∼**а́я,** ∼**о́й**) an eighth

◦ **ВОТ** *particle* **1** (*здесь*) here (is); (*там*) there (is); (*это*) this is; **в. мой дом** here is my house, this is my house; **в. идёт авто́бус** here comes the bus; **в. мы пришли́** here we are; **в. где я живу́** this is where I live **2** (*emphasizing prons.; unstressed*): **в. э́ти ту́фли ей нра́вились** *these* are the shoes she liked **3** (*in int.*) here's a ..., there's a ... (for you); **вот так исто́рия!** here's a pretty kettle of fish!; **в. и всё** I've said it all, that's that; (*expr. surprise*) **вот как!, вот (оно́) что!** really? you don't mean to say so!; **в. тебе́ на́!** well!; well, I never!; (*expr. surprise and disapproval*) **в. ещё!** no way!; what(ever) next!; (*expr. approval and/or encouragement*) **в. так!, в.-в.!** that's right!; that's it!; **в. так** and that's that; **вот тебе́ и...** so much for ...; **вот тебе́ и пое́здка в Пари́ж!** so much for the trip to Paris!; **в. и** (*указывает на завершение чего-н.*): **в. и пришли́** here we are

вот-во́т *adv.* (infml) just, on the point of, any minute; **по́езд в.-в. придёт** the train is just coming

воткн|у́ть, у́, ёшь *pf.* (*of* ▸ **втыка́ть**) (**в +** *a.*) to stick (into); (*с больши́м уси́лием*) to drive (into)

вотр|у́, ёшь *see* ▸ **втере́ть**

во́тум, а (*no pl.*) *m.* vote; **в. (не)дове́рия** (**+** *d.*) vote of (no) confidence (in)

воцар|и́ться, ю́сь, и́шься *pf.* (*of* ▸ **воцаря́ться**) **1** to come to power **2** (fig.) to set in; to be established

воцаря́|ться, юсь *impf. of* ▸ **воцари́ться**

вош|ёл, ла́ *see* ▸ **войти́**

вошь, вши, *i.* ∼**ю,** *pl.* **вши, вшей** *f.* louse

во́|ю, ешь *see* ▸ **выть**

вою́|ю, ешь *see* ▸ **воева́ть**

впада́|ть, ю *impf.* **1** *impf. of* ▸ **впасть** **2** (*impf. only*) (*о реке́*) (**в +** *a.*) flow (into)

впа́дин|а, ы *f.* cavity, hollow

впад|у́, ёшь *see* ▸ **впасть**

впа|сть, ду́, дёшь, *past* ∼**л,** ∼**ла** *pf.* (*of* ▸ **впада́ть 1**) (**в +** *a.*) to fall (into), lapse (into), sink (into)

◦ **впервы́е** *adv.* for the first time, first; **в. слы́шу об э́том** it's the first I've heard of it

◦ **вперёд** *adv.* **1** forward(s), ahead; **взад и в.** (infml) back and forth **2** (*ава́нсом*) in advance

впереди́ **1** *adv.* in front, ahead **2** *adv.* (*в бу́дущем*) in (the) future; ahead; **у него́ всё в.** he has his whole life in front of him **3** *prep.* **+** *g.* in front of, before

◦ **впечатле́ни|е, я** *nt.* impression; **произвести́ в.** (**на +** *a.*) to make an impression (upon)

впечатли́тел|ьный, ∼**ен,** ∼**ьна** *adj.* impressionable

впечатля́|ть, ю *impf.* to impress

впечатля́ющий *adj.* impressive

впива́|ться, юсь *impf. of* ▸ **впи́ться**

впи|са́ть, шу́, ∼**шешь** *pf.* (*of* ▸ **впи́сывать**) to enter; to insert; **в. своё и́мя в спи́сок** to enter one's name on a list

впи|са́ться, шу́сь, ∼**шешься** *pf.* (*of* ▸ **впи́сываться**) (*гармони́ровать*) to fit in, blend in

впи́сыва|ть, ю *impf. of* ▸ **вписа́ть**

впи́сыва|ться, юсь *impf. of* ▸ **вписа́ться**

впит|а́ть, а́ю *pf.* (*of* ▸ **впи́тывать**) to absorb; (fig.) to absorb, take in

впит|а́ться, а́юсь *pf.* (*of* ▸ **впи́тываться**) (**в +** *a.*) to soak (into)

впи́тыва|ть, ю *impf. of* ▸ **впита́ть**

впи́тыва|ться, юсь *impf. of* ▸ **впита́ться**

впи́|ться, вопью́сь, вопьёшься, *past* ∼**лся,** ∼**ла́сь** *pf.* (*of* ▸ **впива́ться**) (**в +** *a.*) (*вонзи́ться*) to stick (into); (*укуси́ть*) to bite; (*ужа́лить*) to sting; **гвоздь** ∼**лся мне в но́гу** a nail stuck into my foot

ВПК *m. indecl.* (*abbr. of* **вое́нно-промы́шленный ко́мплекс**) military-industrial complex

вплавь *adv.* by swimming

вплотну́ю *adv.* close; (fig.) in earnest; **в. к стене́** right up against the wall

вплоть *adv.*: **в. до** (**+** *g.*) (*до преде́ла*) (right) up to; until; (*включа́я*) including

вплыва́|ть, ю *impf. of* ▸ **вплыть**

вплы|ть, ву́, вёшь, *past* ∼**л,** ∼**ла́,** ∼**ло** *pf.* (*of* ▸ **вплыва́ть**) (*о челове́ке*) to swim in; (*о корабле́*) to sail in

вполго́лоса *adv.* in an undertone, under one's breath

вполз|а́ть, а́ю *impf. of* ▸ **вползти́**

вполз|ти́, у́, ёшь, *past* ∼**, ∼ла́** *pf.* (*of* ▸ **вполза́ть**) to creep in, crawl in; (*подня́ться вверх*) to creep up, crawl up

◦ **вполне́** *adv.* fully, entirely; quite

впосле́дствии *adv.* subsequently; afterwards

впра́ве *as pred.*: **быть в.** (**+** *inf.*) to have a right (to)

впра́в|ить, лю, ишь *pf.* (*of* ▸ **вправля́ть**) (*med., кость*) to set

В

B

вправля́|ть, ю impf. of ▶ **впра́вить**
впра́во adv. (от + g.) to the right (of)
впредь adv. in future, henceforth; **в. до** until
впрок adv. **1** (про запас) for future use; **заготовить в.** to stock up on **2** (as pred.) (на пользу) to advantage; **э́то не пойдёт ему́ в.** it will do him no good
✓ **впро́чем** adv. and conj. **1** (однако, но) however, but **2** (выражает нерешимость) or rather; but then again; **приезжа́йте за́втра, в., лу́чше да́же послеза́втра** come tomorrow, or, even better, the day after
впряга́|ть, ю impf. of ▶ **впрячь**
впряга́|ться, юсь impf. of ▶ **впря́чься**
впря|чь, гу́, жёшь, гу́т, past **впряг, ~гла́** pf. (of ▶ **впряга́ть**) (в + a.) to harness (to)
впря́|чься, гу́сь, жёшься, гу́тся, past **впря́гся, ~гла́сь** pf. (of ▶ **впряга́ться**) (в + a.) to harness oneself (to)
впуска́|ть, ю impf. of ▶ **впусти́ть**
впу|сти́ть, щу́, ~стишь pf. (of ▶ **впуска́ть**) to admit, let in
впусту́ю adv. (infml) for nothing, to no purpose
впу|щу́, ~стишь see ▶ **впусти́ть**
впятеро́м adv. five (together)
✓ **враг, а́** m. enemy; (collect.) the enemy
вражд|а́, ы́ f. enmity, hostility
враждеб|ный, ~ен, ~на adj. hostile
вражд|ова́ть, у́ю impf. (с + i.) to be at enmity (with), at odds (with)
вра́жеский adj. (mil.) enemy; hostile
вран|ьё, я́ nt. (infml) (ложь) lies; (вздор) nonsense
врасплóх adv. (infml): **заста́ть, захвати́ть, засти́гнуть в.** to take unawares; to catch off guard
враст|а́ть, а́ю impf. (of ▶ **врасти́**) to grow in(to); **~а́ющий но́готь** ingrowing nail
враст|и́, у́, ёшь, past **врос, вросла́** pf. of ▶ **враста́ть**
врата́р|ь, я́ m. (sport) goalkeeper
вр|ать, у, ёшь, past **~ал, ~ала́, ~а́ло** impf. (of ▶ **навра́ть, ▶ совра́ть**) (infml) **1** (лгать) to lie, tell lies **2** (говорить вздор) to talk nonsense **3** (быть неточным) to be wrong (of inanimate objects only)
✓ **врач, а́** m. doctor, physician; **де́тский в.** paediatrician (BrE), pediatrician (AmE); **зубно́й в.** dentist
враче́бный adj. medical
враща́|ть, ю impf. to revolve, rotate; **в. глаза́ми** to roll one's eyes
враща́|ться, юсь impf. to revolve, rotate; **он ~ется в худо́жественных круга́х** he moves in artistic circles
враще́ни|е, я nt. rotation; revolution
вред, а́ (no pl.) m. (челове́ку) harm, injury; (здоро́вью, зда́нию) damage; **без ~а́** (для + g.) without detriment (to); **во ~** (+ d.) to the detriment of

вреди́тел|ь, я m. (agric.) pest
вре|ди́ть, жу́, ди́шь impf. (of ▶ **навреди́ть, ▶ повреди́ть** 1) (+ d.) (челове́ку) to injure, harm, hurt; (здоро́вью, зда́нию) to damage
вре́дно adv. as pred. it is harmful; **в. для здоро́вья** it is bad for one's health
вре́д|ный, ~ен, ~на́, ~но, ~ны́ adj. harmful, unhealthy; (произво́дство) hazardous; (no short forms) (infml, челове́к) nasty
вре́|жу, жешь see ▶ **вреза́ть**
вре|жу́, жешь see ▶ **вреди́ть**
вре́|жусь, жешься see ▶ **вреза́ться**
вре́|зать, жу, жешь pf. (of ▶ **вреза́ть**) **1** to cut in; (вста́вить) to set in **2** (pf. only) (infml) (+ d.) (уда́рить) to whack (sb)
вреза́|ть, а́ю impf. of ▶ **вре́зать** 1
вре́|заться, жусь, жешься pf. (of ▶ **вреза́ться**) (уда́риться) (в + a.) to smash (into)
вреза́|ться, а́юсь impf. of ▶ **вре́заться**
времена́ми adv. at times, now and then, now and again
вре́менный adj. temporary; provisional
✓ **вре́м|я, ени,** i. **~енем,** o. **~ени,** pl. **~ена́, ~ён, ~ена́м** nt. **1** time; **в. от ~ени** from time to time; **в да́нное в.** at present, at the present moment; **(в) пе́рвое в.** at first; **(в) после́днее в.** lately, of late; **в своё в.** (о про́шлом) in one's time, once, at one time; (о бу́дущем) in due course; in one's own time; **за после́днее в.** lately; **на в.** for a while; **на пе́рвое в.** for the time being; **одно́ в.** once (in the past); **с тече́нием ~ени** in the course of time; **всё в.** all the time, continually; **ско́лько ~ени?** what is the time?; **тем ~енем** meanwhile **2**: **в. го́да** season **3** (gram.) tense **4**: **в то в. как** while, whereas **5**: **во в.** (+ g.) during, in
времяпрепровожде́ни|е, я and **времяпровожде́ни|е, я** nt. pastime; way of spending one's time
вро́вень adv. (с + i.) level (with); **в. с края́ми** to the brim
✓ **вро́де 1** prep. + g. like; **не́что в.** (infml) a sort of, a kind of **2** particle (infml, ка́жется) it looks as if
врождён|ный, ~, ~на adj. (спосо́бность) innate; (недоста́ток) congenital
врозь adv. separately, apart
врун, а́ m. (infml) liar
вруча́|ть, а́ю impf. of ▶ **вручи́ть**
вручи́ть, у́, и́шь pf. (of ▶ **вруча́ть**) (письмо́, посы́лку) to hand, deliver; (меда́ль) to present
вручну́ю adv. by hand
врыва́|ться, юсь impf. of ▶ **ворва́ться**
✓ **вряд, ли** adv. (infml) hardly, it is unlikely; **в. ли сто́ит** it is hardly worth it; **они́ в. ли приду́т** they are unlikely to come
вса́дник, а m. rider, horseman
вса́дниц|а, ы f. rider, horsewoman
✓ **все** see ▶ **весь**

✓ **всё 1** *pron. see* ▶ **весь 2** *adv.* (infml) always; all the time **3**: в. (ещё) still; дождь в. (ещё) идёт it is still raining; в. же after all, nevertheless **4** (infml) only, all; в. из-за тебя́! it is all because of you! **5** (*as conj.*) (*всё равно*) however, nevertheless **6** (*as particle, strengthening comp.*): в. бо́лее и бо́лее more and more; он в. толсте́ет he is getting fatter and fatter **7** (*pred.*) (infml, *кончено*) that's it!

все... *comb. form* all-, omni-, pan-; most (*gracious, etc.*)

всевозмо́жн|ый *adj.* all kinds of; every possible; ~ые това́ры goods of all kinds

Всевы́шн|ий, ~его *n.* (relig.) the Almighty

✓ **всегда́** *adv.* always

всего́ 1 *pron. see* ▶ **весь**; бо́льше в. (the) most; лу́чше в. (the) best; ча́ще в. most often **2** *adv.* (*итого́*) in all, all told; (*лишь*) only; в. лишь (infml) only; в.-на́всего only, all in all; то́лько и в. (infml) that's all

вседозво́ленност|ь, и *f.* permissiveness

Вселе́нн|ая, ой (*no pl.*) *f.* (*ко́смос*) the universe

вселе́нский *adj.* universal; (eccl.) ecumenical; в. собо́р ecumenical council

всел|и́ть, ю́, и́шь *pf.* (*of* ▶ **вселя́ть**) **1** (*жильца́*) to move (sb) in; to install **2** (fig., rhet.) to instil (BrE), instill (AmE) (in); в. страх (в + *a.*) to strike fear (into)

всел|и́ться, ю́сь, и́шься *pf.* (*of* ▶ **вселя́ться**) (в + *a.*) **1** (*в дом*) to move in(to) **2** (fig.) to be implanted (in)

вселя́|ть, ю *impf. of* ▶ **всели́ть**

вселя́|ться, юсь *impf. of* ▶ **всели́ться**

всем *see* ▶ **весь**

всеме́рный *adj.* all possible

всеми́рный *adj.* world (*attr.*); worldwide

всемогу́щ|ий, ~, ~а *adj.* omnipotent, all-powerful; В. (*о Бо́ге*) Almighty

всенаро́дно *adv.* publicly

всенаро́дный *adj.* national; nationwide

все́нощн|ая, ой *f.* (eccl.) vespers

всео́бщ|ий *adj.* universal; general; ~ая во́инская пови́нность universal military service; ~ая забасто́вка general strike; ~ие вы́боры general election

всеобъе́млющ|ий, ~, ~а *adj.* all-embracing, comprehensive

всеросси́йский *adj.* all-Russian

всерьёз *adv.* seriously, in earnest

всеси́л|ьный, ~ен, ~ьна *adj.* all-powerful

всесторо́нний *adj.* (*образова́ние*) all-round; (*ана́лиз*) thorough, detailed

✓ **всё-таки** *conj. and particle* still, all the same

всех *see* ▶ **весь**

всеце́ло *adv.* completely

всея́дный *adj.* omnivorous

вска́кива|ть, ю *impf. of* ▶ **вскочи́ть**

вска́пыва|ть, ю *impf. of* ▶ **вскопа́ть**

вскара́бк|аться, аюсь *pf. of* ▶ **кара́бкаться**

вски́дыва|ть, ю *impf. of* ▶ **вски́нуть**

вски́|нуть, ну, нешь *pf.* (*of* ▶ **вски́дывать**) (*ки́нуть*) to throw up; в. на пле́чи to shoulder; (*подня́ть*) to raise (*suddenly*); в. глаза́ to look up suddenly

вскипа́|ть, ю *impf. of* ▶ **вскипе́ть**

вскип|е́ть, лю́, и́шь *pf.* (*of* ▶ **вскипа́ть**) **1** (*вода́*) to boil up **2** (fig.) to flare up, fly into a rage

вскипя́|ти́ть, чу́, ти́шь *pf. of* ▶ **кипяти́ть**

вскользь *adv.* slightly; in passing; упомяну́ть в. to mention in passing

вскопа́|ть, ю *pf.* (*of* ▶ **вска́пывать**, ▶ **копа́ть 1**) to dig over

✓ **вско́ре** *adv.* soon, shortly after

вскоч|и́ть, у́, ~ишь *pf.* (*of* ▶ **вска́кивать**) **1** (в/на + *a.* or с + *g.*) to leap up (into/on to; from) **2** (infml, *ши́шка*) to come up (*of bumps, boils, etc.*)

вскро́|ю, ешь *see* ▶ **вскрыть**

вскрыва́|ть, ю *impf. of* ▶ **вскрыть**

вскрыва́|ться, юсь *impf. of* ▶ **вскры́ться**

вскры́ти|е, я *nt.* **1** (*письма́*) opening, unsealing; (*сейфа́*) unlocking **2** (med., *нары́ва*) lancing **3** (med., *тру́па*) autopsy, post-mortem

вскры́|ть, о́ю, о́ешь *pf.* (*of* ▶ **вскрыва́ть**) **1** (*письмо́*) to open, unseal; (*сейф*) to unlock **2** (med., *нары́в*) to lance

вскры́|ться, о́юсь, о́ешься *pf.* (*of* ▶ **вскрыва́ться**) **1** (*река́*) to become clear (of ice); to become open **2** (med.) to break, burst

вслед 1 *adv.* (за + *i.*) after **2** *prep. + d.* after; смотре́ть в. to follow with one's eyes

всле́дствие *prep. + g.* in consequence of, owing to, due to

вслух *adv.* aloud, out loud

вслу́ш|аться, аюсь *pf.* (*of* ▶ **вслу́шиваться**) (в + *a.*) to listen attentively (to)

вслу́шива|ться, юсь *impf. of* ▶ **вслу́шаться**

всмя́тку *adv.*: яйцо́ в. soft-boiled, lightly-boiled egg

вспа|ха́ть, шу́, ~шешь *pf.* (*of* ▶ **вспа́хивать**, ▶ **паха́ть 1**) to plough up (BrE), plow up (AmE)

вспа́хива|ть, ю *impf. of* ▶ **вспаха́ть**

вспле́ск, а *m.* splash

всплыва́|ть, ю *impf. of* ▶ **всплыть**): всплыва́ющее окно́ (comput.) pop-up (window)

всплы́|ть, ву́, вёшь, *past* ~л, ~ла́, ~ло *pf.* (*of* ▶ **всплыва́ть**) to rise to the surface, surface; (fig., *факт*) to come to light; (*вопро́с*) to arise

✓ **вспомина́|ть**, ю *impf. of* ▶ **вспо́мнить**

вспо́м|нить, ню, нишь *pf.* (*of* ▶ **вспомина́ть**) (*де́тство*) to remember, recall, recollect; (о + *p.*, *что*) to remember

вспомога́тельный *adj.* auxiliary; subsidiary; (gram.) auxiliary

вспоте́|ть, ю *pf.* (*of* ▶ **потеть**) to come out in a sweat

вспу́гива|ть, ю *impf. of* ▶ **вспугну́ть**

В

В

вспуг|ну́ть, ну́, нёшь pf. (of ▸ вспу́гивать) to scare away; (дичь) to put up

вспыл|и́ть, ю́, и́шь pf. to flare up; **в. (на** + a.) to fly into a rage (with)

вспы́льчив|ый, ~, ~а adj. hot-tempered; irascible

вспы́хива|ть, ю impf. of ▸ вспы́хнуть

вспы́х|нуть, ну, нешь pf. (of ▸ вспы́хивать) (огонь, свет) to flash; (бумага) to burst into flames, blaze up; (пожар) to break out; (fig., ссора, конфликт) to flare up; (паника, война) to break out

вспы́шк|а, и f. flash; (phot.) flash (attachment); (гнева) outburst; (энергии) burst; (болезни) outbreak

встава́|ть, ю́, ёшь impf. of ▸ встать

вста́в|ить, лю, ишь pf. (of ▸ вставля́ть) to put in, insert; **в. в ра́му** to frame; **в. себе́ зу́бы** to have false teeth, dentures made

вста́вк|а, и f. 1 (действие) fixing, insertion 2 (в одежде) inset 3 (в тексте) insertion

вставля́|ть, ю impf. of ▸ вста́вить

вставн|о́й adj. inserted; **~ы́е зу́бы** false teeth, dentures; **~ы́е ра́мы** removable window frames

вста|ть, ну, нешь pf. (of ▸ встава́ть) 1 (с постели) to get up, rise; (на ноги) to stand up, rise, get up; (солнце) to rise 2 (в + a.) (infml) to go (into), fit (into); **большо́й шкаф не ~нет в э́ту ко́мнату** the large cupboard will not go into this room 3 (вопрос, образ) to appear, arise 4 (impf. only) (infml, часы) to stop (working)

встрево́жен|ный adj. (выражающий тревогу) (~, ~на) anxious; (испытывающий тревогу) (~, ~а) anxious

встре́|тить, чу, тишь pf. (of ▸ встреча́ть) 1 (запланированно) to meet; (случайно) to meet, come across; (сопротивление) to meet with, encounter; (обнаружить) to come across 2 (оказать приём) to receive, greet; (Новый год, Пасху) to celebrate

встре́|титься, чусь, тишься pf. (of ▸ встреча́ться 1) 1 (с + i.) to meet (with), encounter, come across; **в. с затрудне́ниями** to encounter difficulties 2 (на пути) to be found, occur 3 (собраться) to gather, congregate

✿ **встре́ч|а, и** f. 1 meeting; (приём) reception; **в. в верха́х** (pol.) summit; **в. Но́вого го́да** New Year's Eve party 2 (sport) match, meeting

✿ **встреча́|ть, ю** impf. of ▸ встре́тить

✿ **встреча́|ться, юсь** impf. 1 impf. of ▸ встре́титься 2 (impf. only) (ареал распространения) to be found; **в Шотла́ндии ещё ~ются ди́кие ко́шки** wild cats are still found in Scotland

встре́чный adj. 1 (поезд, машина) proceeding from opposite direction; oncoming; (as n. **пе́рвый в.**) the first person you meet, anyone 2 (предложение) counter; **в. иск** (law) counterclaim

встро́енный adj. built-in

встря́хива|ть, ю impf. of ▸ встряхну́ть

встря́х|нуть, ну́, нёшь pf. (of ▸ встря́хивать) to shake; (fig.) to shake up, rouse

вступа́|ть, ю impf. of ▸ вступи́ть

вступа́|ться, юсь impf. of ▸ вступи́ться

вступи́тельный adj. introductory; **в. взнос** entrance fee; **в. экза́мен** entrance exam

вступ|и́ть, лю́, ~ишь pf. (of ▸ вступа́ть) 1 (в + a.) (войти, въехать) to enter; (стать членом) to join; (в спор, переговоры) to enter into; **в. в бой** to join battle; **в. в де́йствие** (договор, закон) to come into force; **в. в брак** to marry 2 (на + a.) to mount, go up; **в. на престо́л** to ascend the throne

вступ|и́ться, лю́сь, ~ишься pf. (of ▸ вступа́ться) (за + a.) to stand up (for)

вступле́ни|е, я nt. 1 (в клуб) joining; (в должность) assumption (of) 2 (в музыке) prelude; (в книге) introduction

всхли́п|нуть, ну, нешь pf. (of ▸ всхли́пывать) to sob

всхли́пывани|е, я nt. (действие) sobbing; (звуки) sobs

всхли́пыва|ть, ю impf. of ▸ всхли́пнуть

всхо́д|и́ть, жу́, ~дишь impf. of ▸ взойти́

всхо́д|ы, ов (no sg.) shoots

всю́ду adv. everywhere

вся see ▸ весь

✿ **вся́к|ий** pron. 1 any; **во ~ом слу́чае** in any case, at any rate; (as n.) anyone 2 (разнообразный) all sorts of; every; **на в. слу́чай** just in case

Вт (abbr. of ватт) W, watt

вта́йне adv. secretly, in secret

вта́лкива|ть, ю impf. of ▸ втолкну́ть

втека́|ть, ет, ют impf. of ▸ втечь

втер|е́ть, вотру́, вотрёшь, past ~, ~ла pf. (of ▸ втира́ть) (в + a.) to rub in(to)

вте|чь, чёт, ку́т, past ~к, ~кла́ pf. (of ▸ втека́ть) to flow in(to)

втира́|ть, ю impf. of ▸ втере́ть

втолкн|у́ть, у́, ёшь pf. (of ▸ вта́лкивать) (в + a.) to push in(to), shove in(to)

вторга́|ться, а́юсь impf. of ▸ вто́ргнуться

вто́рг|нуться, нусь, нешься, past ~ся, ~лась pf. (of ▸ вторга́ться) (в + a.) (в страну) to invade; (в чужие дела) to interfere (in)

вторже́ни|е, я nt. invasion; interference

втори́чн|ый adj. 1 (второй) second 2 (второстепенный) secondary 3: **~ое сырьё** recyclable material

вто́рник, а m. Tuesday; **во в.** on Tuesday; **на в.** for Tuesday; **в сле́дующий/про́шлый в.** next/last Tuesday

✿ **втор|о́й** adj. 1 second; **в. час** (it is) past one; (не главный) secondary; **на ~о́м пла́не** (fig.) in the background 2 (as nt. n. **~о́е, ~о́го**) main course (of meal)

второсо́ртный adj. of the second-best quality; second-rate

второстепе́н|ный, ~ен, ~на *adj.* secondary; minor

в-тре́тьих *adv.* thirdly, in the third place

втро́е *adv.* three times; **в. бо́льше** three times as big; **увели́чить в.** to triple

втроём *adv.* three (together); **мы в.** the three of us

втройне́ *adv.* three times as much, treble

втыка́|ть, ю *impf. of* ▶ воткну́ть

втя́гива|ть, ю *impf. of* ▶ втяну́ть

втя́гива|ться, юсь *impf. of* ▶ втяну́ться

втя|ну́ть, ну́, ~нешь *pf.* (*of* ▶ втя́гивать) **1** (*лодку; щёки, живот*) to draw (in, into, up), pull (in, into, up); (*воздух, жидкость*) to absorb, take in **2** (fig.) (**в** + *a.*) to draw (into), involve (in); **в. в спор** to draw into an argument

втя|ну́ться, ну́сь, ~нешься *pf.* (*of* ▶ втя́гиваться) (**в** + *a.*) **1** (*постепенно войти*) to draw (into), enter **2** (*щёки*) to sag, fall in **3** (infml, *привыкнуть*) to get accustomed (to), used (to)

вуа́л|ь, и *f.* veil

вуз, а *m.* (abbr. of **вы́сшее уче́бное заведе́ние**) institution of higher education

вулка́н, а *m.* volcano

вульга́р|ный, ~ен, ~на *adj.* vulgar

вход, а *m.* **1** (*действие*) entry **2** (*место*) entrance

вхо|ди́ть, жу́, ~дишь *impf. of* ▶ войти́

входн|о́й *adj. of* ▶ вход; **в. биле́т** entrance ticket; ~а́я пла́та entrance fee

входя́щий *pres. part. of* ▶ входи́ть *and adj.* (*почта, звонок*) incoming

вцеп|и́ться, лю́сь, ~ишься *impf.* (*of* ▶ вцепля́ться) (**в** + *a.*) to seize hold of

вцепля́|ться, юсь *impf. of* ▶ вцепи́ться

вчера́ *adv.* yesterday

вчера́шн|ий *adj.* (*дождь, суп*) yesterday's; **в. день** yesterday; (fig.) yesterday, the past; **жить ~им днём** to live in the past

вче́тверо *adv.* four times

въезд, а *m.* **1** (*действие*) entry; «**В. запрещён**» 'No entry' (*official notice and road sign*) **2** (*место*) entrance

въездн|о́й *adj. of* ▶ въезд; ~а́я ви́за entry visa

въезжа́|ть, ю *impf. of* ▶ въе́хать

въе́|хать, ду, дешь *pf.* (*of* ▶ въезжа́ть) **1** (**в** + *a.*) to enter, ride in(to), drive in(to); (**на** + *a.*) (*наверх*) to ride up, drive up **2** (*в дом*) to move in **3** (sl.) to understand

вы, вас, вам, ва́ми, вас *pers. pron.* (*pl. and formal or respectful mode of address to one person*) you; **быть на в.** (**с** + *i.*) to be on formal terms (with)

вы... *pref. indicating* **1** motion outwards **2** action directed outwards **3** acquisition (*as outcome of a series of actions*) **4** completion of a process

выбега́|ть, ю *impf. of* ▶ вы́бежать

вы́бе|жать, гу, жишь, гут *pf.* (*of* ▶ выбега́ть) to run out

вы́бер|у, ешь *see* ▶ вы́брать

выбива́|ть, ю *impf. of* ▶ вы́бить

выбива́|ться, юсь *impf. of* ▶ вы́биться

выбира́|ть, ю *impf. of* ▶ вы́брать

выбира́|ться, юсь *impf. of* ▶ вы́браться

вы́б|ить, ью, ьешь *pf.* (*of* ▶ выбива́ть) **1** (*заставить выпасть*) to knock out; (*врага*) to drive out; to dislodge **2** (*очистить*) to beat (clean); **в. ковёр** to beat a carpet

вы́б|иться, ьюсь, ьешься *pf.* (*of* ▶ выбива́ться): **в. в лю́ди** to make one's way in the world; **в. из сил** to wear oneself out; to be exhausted

вы́бор, а *m.* **1** choice; option **2** (*ассортимент*) selection; assortment; **по своему́** ~у of one's choice **3** (*pl. only*) election(s); **дополни́тельные** ~ы by-election

вы́борк|а, и *f.* **1** (*статистическая*) selection; sample **2** (*usu. in pl.*) (*цитата*) excerpt

вы́борный *adj.* **1** (*кампания*) election (*attr.*); **в. бюллете́нь** ballot paper **2** (*орган, должность*) elective

вы́борочный *adj.* selective

вы́борщик, а *m.* (pol.) elector (*in indirect elections*); **колле́гия** ~ов electoral college

вы́бор|ы, ов *see* ▶ вы́бор 3

выбра́сыва|ть, ю *impf. of* ▶ вы́бросить

вы́б|рать, еру, ерешь *pf.* (*of* ▶ выбира́ть) **1** to choose, select, pick out **2** (*голосованием*) to elect

вы́б|раться, ерусь, ерешься *pf.* (*of* ▶ выбира́ться) **1** (*из* + *g.*) to get out (of) **2** (infml, *найти возможность*) to get to; (to find time to) to get to; **в. в о́перу** to manage to get to the opera

вы́брос, а *m.* discharge, emission; spillage; (*in pl.*) emissions

вы́бро|сить, шу, сишь *pf.* (*of* ▶ выбра́сывать) **1** (*за пределы чего-н., наружу*) to throw out **2** (*старые вещи*) to discard, throw away; (*отходы*) to discharge

выбыва́|ть, ю *impf. of* ▶ вы́быть

вы́б|ыть, уду, удешь *pf.* (*of* ▶ выбыва́ть) (*из* + *g.*) (*из города*) to leave; (*из соревнования*) to be eliminated

выва́лива|ть, ю *impf. of* ▶ вы́валить

выва́лива|ться, юсь *impf. of* ▶ вы́валиться

вы́вал|ить, ю, ишь *pf.* (*of* ▶ выва́ливать) (*из* + *g.*) **1** to empty out (of) **2** (infml, *толпа*) to pour out (of)

вы́вал|иться, юсь, ишься *pf.* (*of* ▶ выва́ливаться) (*из* + *g.*) to fall out (of), tumble out (of)

вы́валя|ть, ю *pf. of* ▶ валя́ть 1

выведе́ни|е, я *nt.* **1** leading out, bringing out **2** (*формулы*) deduction, conclusion **3** (*цыплят*) hatching (out); (*растений*) growing; (*животных*) breeding, raising **4** (*пятен*) removal (*of stains*); (*вредителей*) extermination (*of pests*)

В

вы́вез|ти, у, ешь, *past* ~, ~ла *pf.* (*of*
▶ **вывози́ть**) **1** (*везя, удалить*) to take
out, remove; (*везя, отправить*) to take;
(*привезти с собой*) to bring **2** (econ., *за
границу*) to export

вы́вер|нуть, ну, нешь *pf.* (*of*
▶ **вывора́чивать**) **1** (*винт*) to unscrew;
(*пробку*) to pull out **2** (infml, *ногу*) to twist,
wrench **3** (*карман*) to turn (inside) out

вы́ве|сить, шу, сишь *pf.* (*of* ▶ **выве́шивать**)
1 (*объявление*) to put up; to post up
2 (*бельё, флаг*) to hang out

вы́веск|а, и *f.* **1** sign, signboard **2** (fig.)
screen, pretext; **под** ~**ой** (+ *g.*) under the
guise of

вы́ве|сти, ду, дешь, *past* ~л, ~ла *pf.* (*of*
▶ **выводи́ть**) **1** to lead out, bring out;
(*войска*) to withdraw; **в. кого́-н. в лю́ди** to
help sb on in life; **в. кого́-н. из себя́** to drive
sb out of his wits; **в. из стро́я** to disable,
put out of action; (also fig.): **в. из терпе́ния**
to exasperate **2** (*исключить*) to force out,
expel **3** (*пятна*) to remove; (*вредителей*)
to exterminate **4** (*заключить*) to deduce,
conclude **5** (*птенцов*) to hatch (out);
(*растения*) to grow; (*животных*) to breed,
raise

вы́ве|стись, дется, *past* ~лся, ~лась *pf.*
(*of* ▶ **выводи́ться**) (*цыплята*) to hatch out

выве́шива|ть, ю *impf. of* ▶ **вы́весить**

вы́вин|тить, чу, тишь *pf.* (*of* ▶ **выви́нчивать**)
to unscrew

выви́нчива|ть, ю *impf. of* ▶ **вы́винтить**

вы́вих, а *m.* dislocation

выви́хива|ть, ю *impf. of* ▶ **вы́вихнуть**

вы́вих|нуть, ну, нешь *pf.* (*of* ▶ **выви́хивать**)
to dislocate, put out (of joint)

⚜ **вы́вод, а** *m.* **1** (*заключение*) deduction,
conclusion **2** (*выведение*) leading out,
bringing out; **в. войск** withdrawal of troops;
в. да́нных (comput.) output

выво|ди́ть, жу́, ~**дит** *impf. of* ▶ **вы́вести**

выво|ди́ться, ~**дится** *impf. of* ▶ **вы́вестись**

выво|жу́[1], ~**дишь** *see* ▶ **выводи́ть**

выво|жу́[2], ~**зишь** *see* ▶ **вывози́ть**

вы́воз, а *m.* **1** (*отправление*) sending,
dispatch **2** (*экспорт*) export

выво|зи́ть, жу́, ~**зишь** *impf. of* ▶ **вы́везти**

вывозн|о́й *adj.* (*товар*) exported; (*attr.*)
export; ~**ая по́шлина** export duty

вывора́чива|ть, ю *impf. of* ▶ **вы́вернуть**

выгиба́|ть, ю *impf. of* ▶ **вы́гнуть**

выгиба́|ться, юсь *impf. of* ▶ **вы́гнуться**

вы́гла|дить, жу, дишь *pf. of* ▶ **гла́дить 1**

⚜ **вы́гля|деть, жу, дишь** *impf.* (*человек*) to
look (like); **он** ~**дит о́чень мо́лодо** he looks
very young; **она́ пло́хо** ~**дит** she does not
look well; (*показания*) to appear (to be)

выгля́дыва|ть, ю *impf. of* ▶ **вы́глянуть**

вы́гля|нуть, ну, нешь *pf.* (*of* ▶ **выгля́дывать**)
1 (*из окна*) to look out **2** (*показаться*) to
peep out, emerge

вы́г|нать, оню, онишь *pf.* (*of* ▶ **выгоня́ть**)
1 (*удалить*) to drive out; to expel; **в. с
рабо́ты** (infml) to sack (BrE), fire (AmE)
2 (*скот*) to send out to pasture

вы́гнут|ый, ~, ~**а** *adj.* curved; convex

вы́гн|уть, у, ешь *pf.* (*of* ▶ **выгиба́ть**) to bend

вы́гн|уться, усь, ешься *pf.* (*of*
▶ **выгиба́ться**) to bend

выгова́рива|ть, ю *impf. of* ▶ **вы́говорить**

вы́говор, а *m.* **1** (*произношение*) accent;
pronunciation **2** (*порицание*) reprimand;
rebuke

вы́говор|ить, ю, ишь *pf.* (*of* ▶ **выгова́ривать**)
to articulate, speak

вы́год|а, ы *f.* (*польза*) advantage, benefit;
(*прибыль*) profit, gain

вы́годно *adv.* **1** advantageously **2** (*as pred.*)
it is profitable, it pays

вы́годн|ый, ~**ен,** ~**на** *adj.* (*дающий пользу*)
advantageous, beneficial; (*прибыльный*)
profitable

выгоня́|ть, ю *impf. of* ▶ **вы́гнать**

вы́гравир|овать, ую *pf. of* ▶ **гравирова́ть**

выгружа́|ть, ю *impf. of* ▶ **вы́грузить**

выгружа́|ться, юсь *impf. of* ▶ **вы́грузиться**

вы́гру|зить, жу, зишь *pf.* (*of* ▶ **выгружа́ть**)
to unload

вы́гру|зиться, жусь, зишься *pf.* (*of*
▶ **выгружа́ться**) (*люди*) to disembark;
(*корабль*) to unload

вы́грузк|а, и *f.* unloading; (*людей*)
disembarkation

выгу́лива|ть, аю *impf. of* ▶ **вы́гулять**

выгуля́|ть, ю *pf.* (*of* ▶ **выгу́ливать**) to walk
(*a dog, etc.*)

⚜ **выда|ва́ть, ю́, ёшь** *impf. of* ▶ **вы́дать**

выда|ва́ться, ю́сь, ёшься *impf. of*
▶ **вы́даться**

вы́дав|ить, лю, ишь *pf.* (*of* ▶ **выда́вливать**)
1 (*выжать*) to press out, squeeze out (also
fig.); **в. улы́бку** to force a smile **2** (*выломать*)
to break, knock out

выда́влива|ть, ю *impf. of* ▶ **вы́давить**

вы́да|ть, м, шь, ст, дим, дите, дут *pf.* (*of*
▶ **выдава́ть**) **1** (*дать*) to give (out), issue;
(*изготовить*) to produce; **в. зарпла́ту** to
pay out wages; **в. про́пуск** to issue a pass; **в.
кого́-н. за́муж** (за + *a.*) to give sb in marriage
(to) **2** (*предать*) to give away, betray;
(*в чужую страну*) to extradite **3** (*за + a.*)
to pass off (as), give out to be; **в. (себя́)** to
pose as)

**вы́да|ться, мся, шься, стся, димся,
дитесь, дутся** *pf.* (*of* ▶ **выдава́ться**)
1 to protrude, project, jut out **2** (infml,
случиться) to happen

вы́дач|а, и *f.* **1** (*предоставление*) giving,
issuing; (*изготовление*) production
2 (*преступника*) extradition

выдаю́щийся *pres. part. of* ▶ **выдава́ться** *and*
adj. prominent, salient; (fig., *замечательный*)
outstanding, eminent; prominent

выдвига́|ть, ю *impf. of* ▶ **вы́двинуть**

выдвига́|ться, юсь *impf. of* ▶ **вы́двинуться**

вы́дви|нуть, ну, нешь *pf. (of* ▶ **выдвига́ть)**
1 (*стол, шкаф*) to move out, pull out; (*ящик*) to pull open **2** (fig., *предложить*) to put forward, advance; **в. обвине́ние** to bring an accusation **3** (*по рабо́те*) to promote **4** (*кандида́та*) to nominate, propose

вы́дви|нуться, нусь, нешься *pf. (of* ▶ **выдвига́ться) 1** (*вперёд*) to move forward; (*нару́жу*) to move, move out; (*ящик*) to slide in and out **2** (*рабо́тник*) to rise, get on (in the world)

выделе́ни|е, я *nt.* **1** (*сре́дств*) allocation, assignment **2** (physiol.) secretion; (*обрабо́танных веще́ств*) excretion

вы́дел|ить, ю, ишь *pf. (of* ▶ **выделя́ть) 1** (*сре́дства*) to allocate, assign, earmark; (*вре́мя*) to allot **2** (*отобра́ть*) to pick out, single out; (mil.) to detach, detail; (comput.) to highlight; (typ.): **в. курси́вом** to italicize

вы́дел|иться, юсь, ишься *pf. (of* ▶ **выделя́ться) 1** (*отдели́ться от це́лого*) to split off, separate **2** (*+ i.*) to stand out (on account of) **3** (*пот*) to ooze out, exude; (*газ*) to be emitted

вы́делк|а, и *f.* **1** (*ка́чество*) workmanship **2** (*ко́жи*) dressing, currying

✎ **выделя́|ть, ю** *impf. of* ▶ **вы́делить**

выделя́|ться, юсь *impf. of* ▶ **вы́делиться**

выдёргива|ть, ю *impf. of* ▶ **вы́дернуть**

вы́держа|нный, ~н, ~на *p.p.p. of* ▶ **вы́держать** *and* (*~н, ~нна*) *adj.*
1 (*после́довательный*) consistent **2** (*владе́ющий собо́й*) self-possessed; (*сто́йкий*) firm **3** (*сыр, вино́*) mature; (*де́рево*) seasoned

вы́держ|ать, у, ишь *pf. (of* ▶ **выде́рживать) 1** (*под тя́жестью, давле́нием*) to bear, hold; (*э́тот*) **лёд вас не ~ит** the ice will not hold you **2** (fig., *вы́терпеть*) to bear, stand (up to), endure; **не в.** to give in, break down; **я не мог э́того бо́льше в.** I could stand it no longer **3**: **в. не́сколько изда́ний** to run into several editions **4** (*сыр, вино́*) to mature; (*де́рево*) to season **5** (*соблюсти́*) to maintain, sustain; **в. па́узу** to pause

выде́ржива|ть, ю *impf. of* ▶ **вы́держать**

вы́держк|а¹, и *f.* **1** (*самооблада́ние*) self-possession; (*терпе́ние*) endurance **2** (phot.) exposure **3** (*вина́, сы́ра*) maturation; **вино́ 8-ле́тней ~и** eight-year-old wine

вы́держк|а², и *f.* (*цита́та*) excerpt, quotation

вы́дер|нуть, ну, нешь *pf. (of* ▶ **выдёргивать)** to pull out

вы́дох, а *m.* exhalation

вы́дохн|уть, у, ешь *pf. (of* ▶ **выдыха́ть)** to breathe out

вы́дрессиро́|вать, ую *pf. of* ▶ **дрессирова́ть**

вы́дума|нный, ~, ~а *p.p.p. of* ▶ **вы́думать** *and* (*~, ~на*) *adj.* made-up, fabricated; **~ная исто́рия** fabrication, fiction

вы́дума|ть, аю *pf. (of* ▶ **выду́мывать)** to invent; to make up, fabricate

вы́думк|а, и *f.* **1** invention **2** (*изобрета́тельность*) inventiveness **3** (*вы́мысел*) invention, fabrication (*lie*)

выду́мыва|ть, ю *impf. of* ▶ **вы́думать**

выдыха́|ть, ю *impf. of* ▶ **вы́дохнуть**

вы́еб|ать, у, ешь *pf. of* ▶ **еба́ть**

вы́езд, а *m.* **1** (*отъе́зд*) departure **2** (*ме́сто*) exit

выезжа́|ть, ю *impf. of* ▶ **вы́ехать**

вы́е|хать, ду, дешь *pf. (of* ▶ **выезжа́ть) 1** (*уе́хать*) to depart, leave (*in or on a vehicle or on an animal*); (*из го́рода, из воро́т*) (*на маши́не*) to drive out; (*на ло́шади*) to ride out **2** (*из кварти́ры*) to leave, move (out)

вы́ж|ать, му, мешь *pf. (of* ▶ **выжима́ть)** (*бельё*) to wring (out); (*лимо́н*) to squeeze; (*сок*) to squeeze out; **~атый лимо́н** a has-been; **как ~атый лимо́н** absolutely exhausted; (fig., *извле́чь*) to wring (out), squeeze (out)

вы́жд|ать, у, ешь *pf. (of* ▶ **выжида́ть)** to wait (for); to bide one's time

вы́ж|ечь, гу, жешь *pf. (of* ▶ **выжига́ть) 1** (*сжечь целико́м*) to burn down; to burn out; (*со́лнце*) to scorch **2** (*сде́лать знак*) to make a mark *etc.*, by burning; **в. клеймо́** (**на** *+ p.*) to brand

выжива́ни|е, я *nt.* survival

выжива́|ть, ю *impf. of* ▶ **вы́жить**

выжига́|ть, ю *impf. of* ▶ **вы́жечь**

выжида́|ть, ю *impf. of* ▶ **вы́ждать**

выжима́|ть, ю *impf. of* ▶ **вы́жать**

вы́жи|ть, ву, вешь *pf. (of* ▶ **выжива́ть) 1** (*оста́ться в живы́х*) to survive **2**: **в. из ума́** to lose possession of one's faculties

вы́з|вать, ову, овешь *pf. (of* ▶ **вызыва́ть) 1** (*пригласи́ть*) to call (out); to send for; (*потре́бовать яви́ться*) to summon; **в. врача́** to send for a doctor **2** (*гнев, любопы́тство*) to provoke, arouse; (*пожа́р, боле́знь*) to cause; (*интере́с*) to stimulate; (*спор*) to provoke

выздора́влива|ть, ю *impf. of* ▶ **вы́здороветь**

вы́здорове|ть, ю, ешь *pf. (of* ▶ **выздора́вливать)** to recover, get better

выздоровле́ни|е, я *nt.* recovery; convalescence

вы́зов, а *m.* **1** (*приглаше́ние*) call **2** (*тре́бование яви́ться*) summons **3** (*предложе́ние вступи́ть в борьбу́*) challenge; **бро́сить в. кому́-н.** to throw down a challenge to sb

✎ **вызыва́|ть, ю** *impf. of* ▶ **вы́звать**

вызыва́ющий *pres. part. act. of* ▶ **вызыва́ть** *and adj.* defiant; provocative

вы́игр|ать, аю *pf. (of* ▶ **вы́игрывать)** (*войну́, па́ртию; мно́го де́нег*) to win; (*получи́ть по́льзу*) to gain; **в. вре́мя** to gain time

выи́грыва|ть, ю *impf. of* ▶ **вы́играть**

вы́игрыш, а *m.* **1** (*побе́да*) win; winning **2** (*де́ньги*) winnings; (*пре́мия*) prize; (*вы́года*) gain; **быть в ~е** (*в игре́*) to be the winner; (fig.) to stand to gain

вы́игрышный *adj.* **1** winning; **в. ход** winning move **2** (*вы́годный*) advantageous

✍ **вы́|йти, йду, йдешь,** *past* ~шел, ~шла *pf.* (*of* ▶ **выходи́ть** 1) **1** to go out; to come out; **она́** ~шла **из ко́мнаты** she went out of/ left the room; **в. в отста́вку** to retire; **в. в фина́л** (sport) to reach the final; **в. из грани́ц/ преде́лов** (+ *g.*) (fig.) to exceed the bounds (of); **в. из себя́** to lose one's temper; **в. из систе́мы** (comput.) to log off; **в. из терпе́ния** to lose patience; **в. на прогу́лку** to go out for a walk **2**: **в. (в свет)** (*быть и́зданным*) to come out, appear **3**: **в. (за́муж)** (за + *a.*) (*о же́нщине*) to marry **4** (*получа́ться*) to come (out); to turn out (*also impers.*); to ensue; (*произойти́*) to happen, occur; **в. победи́телем** to come out victor; **из э́того ничего́ не** ~йдет nothing will come of it; ~шло, **что он винова́т** it turned out that he was to blame **5** (*быть ро́дом*) to be by origin; **она́** ~шла **из крестья́н** she is of peasant stock **6** (*израсхо́доваться*) to be used up; (*о сро́ке*) to have expired; **срок уже́** ~шел time is up

вы́ка́лыва|ть, ю *impf. of* ▶ **вы́колоть**

вы́ка́пыва|ть, ю *impf. of* ▶ **вы́копать**

вы́ки́дыва|ть, ю *impf. of* ▶ **вы́кинуть**

вы́кидыш, а *m.* (med.) miscarriage

вы́ки|нуть, ну, нешь *pf.* (*of* ▶ **вы́кидывать**) **1** (*вы́бросить*) to throw out **2** (*вы́весить*) to put out; **в. флаг** to hoist a flag **3** (infml, pej.): **в. фо́кус** to play a trick

вы́кипа́|ть, ет *impf. of* ▶ **вы́кипеть**

вы́кип|еть, ит *pf.* (*of* ▶ **выкипа́ть**) to boil away

вы́кла́дыва|ть, ю *impf. of* ▶ **вы́ложить**

выключа́тел|ь, я *m.* switch

выключа́|ть, ю *impf. of* ▶ **вы́ключить**

выключа́|ться, юсь *impf. of* ▶ **вы́ключиться**

вы́ключ|ить, у, ишь *pf.* (*of* ▶ **выключа́ть**) **1** (*свет, ра́дио*) to turn off, switch off **2** (*исключи́ть*) to remove, exclude

вы́ключ|иться, усь, ишься *pf.* (*of* ▶ **выключа́ться**) **1** (*о све́те*) to go out **2** (*о челове́ке*) to switch off

вы́к|овать, ую, уешь *pf.* (*of* ▶ **кова́ть** 1

вы́кол|оть, ю, ешь *pf.* (*of* ▶ **выка́лывать**) to poke out

вы́копа|ть, ю *pf.* (*of* ▶ **выка́пывать**, ▶ **копа́ть** 2) (*я́му*) to dig; (*карто́фель*) to dig up; (*труп*) to exhume

выкра́ива|ть, ю *impf. of* ▶ **вы́кроить**

вы́кра́|сить, шу, сишь *pf.* (*of* ▶ **выкра́шивать**) (*сте́ну*) to paint; (*ткань, во́лосы*) to dye

выкра́шива|ть, ю *impf. of* ▶ **вы́красить**

вы́кро|ить, ю, ишь *pf.* (*of* ▶ **выкра́ивать**) **1** (*вы́резать*) to cut out **2** (fig., *удели́ть*) to find; **в. вре́мя** to find time

вы́кройк|а, и *f.* pattern

вы́кру|тить, чу, тишь *pf.* (*of* ▶ **выкру́чивать**) **1** (*ла́мпочку, винт*) to unscrew **2** (*ру́ку*) to

---

twist, wrench

вы́кру|титься, чусь, тишься *pf.* (*of* ▶ **выкру́чиваться**) **1** (*винт*) to come unscrewed **2** (fig., infml, *вы́путаться*) to extricate oneself, get oneself out (of)

выкру́чива|ть, ю *impf. of* ▶ **вы́крутить**

выкру́чива|ться, юсь *impf. of* ▶ **вы́крутиться**

вы́куп, а *m.* **1** (law) redemption **2** (*пла́та*) ransom

выкупа́|ть, ю *pf. of* ▶ **купа́ть**

выкупа́|ть, аю *impf. of* ▶ **вы́купить**

выкупа́|ться, юсь *pf. of* ▶ **купа́ться**

вы́куп|ить, лю, ишь *pf.* (*of* ▶ **выкупа́ть**) **1** (*зало́жника*) to ransom **2** (*ве́щи*) to redeem

вы́лазк|а, и *f.* (mil.) sortie (also fig.)

вы́ла́мыва|ть, ю *impf. of* ▶ **вы́ломать**

вылеза́|ть, ю *impf. of* ▶ **вы́лезти**

вы́лез|ти, у, ешь, *past* ~, ~ла *pf.* (*of* ▶ **вылеза́ть**) **1** (*по́лзком*) to crawl out; (*караба́ясь*) to climb out; (infml, *вы́йти*) to get out, alight **2** (infml, *вы́пасть*) to fall out, come out

вы́лет, а *m.* (*самолёта*) take-off; **зал** ~**а** departure lounge

вылета́|ть, ю *impf. of* ▶ **вы́лететь**

вы́ле|теть, чу, тишь *pf.* (*of* ▶ **вылета́ть**) (*пти́ца*) to fly out; (*самолёт*) to take off; (fig., infml) to rush out; **в. из головы́** to slip one's mind

вылéчива|ть, ю *impf. of* ▶ **вы́лечить**

вылéчива|ться, юсь *impf. of* ▶ **вы́лечиться**

вы́леч|ить, у, ишь *pf.* (*of* ▶ **вылéчивать**) (от + *g.*) to cure (of) (also fig.)

вы́леч|иться, усь, ишься *pf.* (*of* ▶ **вылéчиваться**) (от + *g.*) to be cured (of); to get over (also fig.)

вы́лечу[1]**, ишь** *see* ▶ **вы́лечить**

вы́ле|чу[2]**, тишь** *see* ▶ **вы́лететь**

вылива́|ть, ю, ет *impf. of* ▶ **вы́лить**

вылива́|ться, ется *impf. of* ▶ **вы́литься**

вы́л|ить, ью, ешь *pf.* (*of* ▶ **вылива́ть**) to pour out; (*ведро́*) to empty (out)

вы́л|иться, ьется *pf.* (*of* ▶ **вылива́ться**) (*жи́дкость*) to run out, flow out; (fig.) to flow (from), spring (from)

вы́лож|ить, у, ишь *pf.* (*of* ▶ **выкла́дывать**) **1** (*това́р, ве́щи*) to lay out, spread out; (fig., infml, *сказа́ть*) to tell; to reveal **2** (+ *i.*) (*покры́ть*) to cover, lay (with); **в. дёрном** to turf; **в. ка́мнем** to face with masonry

вы́лома|ть, ю *pf.* (*of* ▶ **выла́мывать**) (*замо́к*) to break open; (*дверь*) to break down

вы́луп|иться, ится *pf.* (*of* ▶ **вылупля́ться**) to hatch (out)

вылупля́|ться, ется *impf. of* ▶ **вы́лупиться**

вы́л|ью, ьешь *see* ▶ **вы́лить**

выма́нива|ть, ю *impf. of* ▶ **вы́манить**

вы́ман|ить, ю, ишь *pf.* (*of* ▶ **выма́нивать**) **1** (*что-н. у кого́-н.*) (*получи́ть обма́ном*) to cheat sb out of sth; (*получи́ть ле́стью*) to wheedle (out of) **2** (из + *g.*) to lure (out of, from)

вы́м|ереть, рет, рут, *past* ~ер, ~ерла *pf.* (*of* ▶ **вымира́ть**) **1** (*исчезнуть*) to die out, become extinct **2** (*опусте́ть*) to become desolate, deserted

вы́мерший *p.p. act. of* ▶ **вы́мереть** *and adj.* extinct

вымира́ни|е, я *nt.* dying out, extinction

вымира́|ть, ю *impf. of* ▶ **вы́мереть**

вымога́тел|ь, я *m.* extortionist

вымога́тельств|о, а *nt.* extortion

вымога́|ть, ю *impf.* to extort; **в. де́ньги у кого́-н.** to extort money from sb

вымока́|ть, ю *impf. of* ▶ **вы́мокнуть**

вы́мок|нуть, ну, нешь, *past* ~, ~ла *pf.* (*of* ▶ **вымока́ть**) to be drenched, be soaked; **мы** ~**ли до ни́тки** we are soaked to the skin

вы́м|ою, оешь *see* ▶ **вы́мыть**

вы́мпел, а *m.* pennant

вы́мр|ет, ут *see* ▶ **вы́мереть**

вымыва́|ть, ю *impf. of* ▶ **вы́мыть**

вы́мысел, ла *m.* **1** (*ложь*) invention, fabrication **2** (*фанта́зия*) fantasy

вы́м|ыть, ою, оешь *pf.* (*of* ▶ **мыть,** ▶ **вымыва́ть**) **1** (*сделать чистым*) to wash; **в. посу́ду** to wash up **2** (*размыть*) to wash away

вы́м|ыться, оюсь, оешься *pf.* (*of* ▶ **мы́ться**) to wash oneself

вы́мышлен|ный, ~, ~а *adj.* fictitious, imaginary, invented

вына́шива|ть, ю *impf. of* ▶ **выноси́ть**

вынесе́ни|е, я *nt.* **1** (*решения*) taking **2** (*благода́рности*) giving, expressing **3** (*на рассмотре́ние*) submitting **4** (*приговора*) pronouncement

вы́нес|ти, у, ешь, *past* ~, ~ла *pf.* (*of* ▶ **выноси́ть** 1) **1** (*удали́ть за преде́лы*) to carry out, take out; to take away (*убра́ть*) to carry away; (*доста́вить*) to bring; **в. на бе́рег** to wash ashore **2** (fig., *получи́ть*) to take away, receive, derive; **в. прия́тное впечатле́ние** to be favourably impressed **3**: **в. вопро́с (на собра́ние, на обсужде́ние)** to put, submit a question to a meeting, for discussion) **4** (*вы́терпеть*) to bear, stand, endure; **в. на свои́х плеча́х** (fig.) to shoulder, take the full weight (of), bear the full brunt (of) **5**: **в. благода́рность** to express gratitude; **в. пригово́р** (+ *d.*) to pass sentence (on), pronounce sentence (on); **в. реше́ние** to decide; (law) to pronounce judgement

вынима́|ть, ю *impf. of* ▶ **вы́нуть**

вы́нос, а *m.* (*поко́йника*) bearing-out; **на в.** (*о еде́*) to take away (BrE), to take out (AmE)

вы́но|сить, шу, сишь *pf.* (*of* ▶ **вына́шивать**) (*ребёнка*) to bear, bring forth (*a child at full term*); (*план, мысль*) to nurture

выно|си́ть, шу́, ~**сишь** *impf.* **1** *impf. of* ▶ **вы́нести 2** (*impf. only*) (+ *neg.*) to be unable to bear/stand; **я его́ не** ~**шу́** I can't

stand him

выно́сливост|ь, и *f.* (power of) endurance; staying power

выно́слив|ый, ~, ~а *adj.* (*челове́к, расте́ние*) hardy

вы́но|шу, сишь *see* ▶ **выноси́ть**

выно|шу́, ~**сишь** *see* ▶ **выноси́ть**

вы́ну|дить, жу, дишь *pf.* (*of* ▶ **вынужда́ть**) (+ *inf.*) to force, compel

вынужда́|ть, ю *impf. of* ▶ **вы́нудить**

вы́нужден|ный, ~, ~а *p.p.p. of* ▶ **вы́нудить** *and* (~, ~на) *adj.* forced; ~**ная поса́дка** (aeron.) forced landing

вы́н|уть, у, ешь *pf.* (*of* ▶ **вынима́ть**) to take out; to pull out, extract

вы́пад, а *m.* (*вражде́бное выступле́ние*) attack

выпада́|ть, ю *impf. of* ▶ **вы́пасть**

вы́па|сть, ду, дешь, *past* ~л *pf.* (*of* ▶ **выпада́ть**) **1** (*упа́сть нару́жу*) to fall out **2** (*дождь, снег*) to fall **3** (+ *d.*) (*зада́ча*) to befall, fall (to); **мне** ~**ло сча́стье** (+ *inf.*) I had the luck (to) **4** (*случи́ться*) to occur, turn out; **ночь** ~**ла звёздная** it turned out a starry night

вы́пек *see* ▶ **вы́печь**

выпека́|ть, ю *impf. of* ▶ **вы́печь**

вы́печк|а, и *f.* baking

вы́пе|чь, ку, чешь, кут, *past* ~к, ~кла *pf.* (*of* ▶ **выпека́ть**) to bake

выпива́|ть, ю *impf.* **1** *impf. of* ▶ **вы́пить 2** (*impf. only*) (infml) to be fond of the bottle

вы́пивк|а, и *f.* (infml, collect.) drinks

выпи|са́ть, шу, шешь *pf.* (*of* ▶ **выпи́сывать**) **1** (*переписа́ть*) to copy out; to excerpt **2** (*докуме́нт*) to write out; **в. квита́нцию** to write out a receipt **3** (*сде́лать зака́з*) to send for (*in writing*) **4** (*из больни́цы*) to discharge **5** (*газе́ту, журна́л*) to subscribe to

вы́пи|саться, шусь, шешься *pf.* (*of* ▶ **выпи́сываться**) (*из больни́цы*) to be discharged; **он уже́** ~**сался из больни́цы** he is already out of hospital; (*из кварти́ры*) to officially change one's place of residence

вы́писк|а, и *f.* **1** (*спи́сывание*) copying, excerpting **2** (*цита́та*) extract, excerpt **3** (*книг, газе́т*) subscription **4** (*из больни́цы*) discharge

выпи́сыва|ть, ю *impf. of* ▶ **вы́писать**

выпи́сыва|ться, юсь *impf. of* ▶ **вы́писаться**

вы́п|ить, ью, ьешь *pf.* (*of* ▶ **выпива́ть** 1, ▶ **пить**) to drink

вы́пи|шу, шешь *see* ▶ **вы́писать**

вы́плат|а, ы *f.* payment

вы́пла|тить, чу, тишь *pf.* (*of* ▶ **выпла́чивать**) **1** to pay (out) **2** (*долг*) to pay off

выпла́чива|ть, ю *impf. of* ▶ **вы́платить**

вы́пла|чу, тишь *see* ▶ **вы́платить**

выплёвыва|ть, ю *impf. of* ▶ **вы́плюнуть**

выплёскива|ть, ю *impf. of* ▶ **вы́плеснуть**

вы́плес|нуть, ну, нешь *pf.* (*of* ▶ **выплёскивать**) to pour out

вы́плюн|уть, у, ешь *pf. (of* ▶ **выплёвывать)**
to spit out

выполза́|ть, ю *impf. of* ▶ **вы́ползти**

вы́ползти, у, ешь, *past* ∼, ∼ла *pf. (of*
▶ **выполза́ть) (из** + *g.)* to crawl out, creep
out (from); *(змея)* to slither out

✒ **выполне́ни|е, я** *nt. (работы, приказа)*
execution, carrying-out; *(желания)*
fulfilment; *(обязанность, желание, план)* fulfillment (AmE)

вы́полним|ый, ∼, ∼а *adj.* practicable,
feasible

вы́полн|ить, ю, ишь *pf. (of* ▶ **выполня́ть)**
(приказание, работу) to carry out;
(обязанность, желание, план) to fulfil (BrE),
fulfill (AmE); *(рисунок)* to execute

✒ **выполня́|ть, ю** *impf. of* ▶ **вы́полнить**

вы́прав|ить, лю, ишь *pf. (of* ▶ **выправля́ть)**
1 *(сделать прямым)* to straighten (out)
2 *(исправить)* to correct; *(улучшить)* to
improve

вы́прав|иться, люсь, ишься *pf. (of*
▶ **выправля́ться) 1** *(выпрямиться)* to
become straight **2** *(стать лучше)* to
improve

выправля́|ть, ю *impf. of* ▶ **вы́править**

выправля́|ться, юсь *impf. of* ▶ **вы́правиться**

выпра́шива|ть, ю *impf.* **1** *impf. of*
▶ **вы́просить 2** *(impf. only)* to try to get,
beg for

вы́про|сить, шу, сишь *pf. (of* ▶ **выпра́шивать)**
1) **(y** + *g.)* to get (out of sb), obtain, elicit (by
begging sb)

вы́про|шу, сишь *see* ▶ **вы́просить**

выпры́гива|ть, ю *impf. of* ▶ **вы́прыгнуть**

вы́прыг|нуть, ну, нешь *pf. (of*
▶ **выпры́гивать)** to jump out, spring out

вы́прям|ить, лю, ишь *pf. (of* ▶ **выпрямля́ть)**
to straighten (out)

вы́прям|иться, люсь, ишься *pf. (of*
▶ **выпрямля́ться)** to become straight; **в. во
весь рост** to draw oneself up to one's full
height

выпрямля́|ть, ю *impf. of* ▶ **вы́прямить**

выпрямля́|ться, юсь *impf. of*
▶ **вы́прямиться**

вы́пуклост|ь, и *f. (неровность)*
protuberance; bulge

вы́пукл|ый, ∼, ∼а *adj. (неровный)*
protuberant; prominent, bulging

✒ **вы́пуск, а** *m.* **1** *(товаров)* output; *(денег,
акций)* issue; **в. новостей** newscast;
сро́чный в. новостей newsflash **2** *(романа)*
part, instalment (BrE), installment (AmE)
3 *(в школе, институте)* leavers; graduates

✒ **выпуска́|ть, ю** *impf. of* ▶ **вы́пустить**

выпускни́к, а́ *m.* **1** *(окончивший учебное
заведение)* graduate; **бы́вший в.** old boy
2 *(на последнем курсе)* final-year student

выпускни́|ца, цы *f. of* ▶ **выпускни́к**

выпускн|о́й *adj.* **1** *of* ▶ **вы́пуск; в. экза́мен**
final examination, finals **2** *(as m. n.* **в.,**

∼**о́го)** school leaving party, prom (AmE)

вы́пу|стить, щу, стишь *pf. (of* ▶ **выпуска́ть)**
1 *(дать выйти)* to let out; *(заключённого,
фильм)* to release; *(из учебного заведения)*
to turn out; **в. из рук** to let go of; **в. из
тюрьмы́** to release from prison **2** *(деньги,
акции)* to issue; *(продукцию)* to turn out,
produce; **в. в прода́жу** to put on the market;
в. (в свет) to publish

вы́пя|тить, чу, тишь *pf. (of* ▶ **выпя́чивать)**
(infml) to stick out; **в. грудь** to stick out one's
chest

выпя́чива|ть, ю *impf. of* ▶ **вы́пятить**

выраба́тыва|ть, ю *impf. of* ▶ **вы́работать**

вы́работа|ть, ю *pf. (of* ▶ **выраба́тывать)**
1 *(произвести)* to manufacture; to produce,
make **2** *(план)* to work out, draw up;
(привычку) to develop

вы́работк|а, и *f. (производство)* manufacture;
production, making

выра́внива|ть, ю *impf. of* ▶ **вы́ровнять**

выра́внива|ться, юсь *impf. of*
▶ **вы́ровняться**

✒ **выража́|ть, ю** *impf. of* ▶ **вы́разить**

выража́|ться, юсь *impf. (of* ▶ **вы́разиться):
мя́гко** ∼**ясь** to put it mildly

✒ **выраже́ни|е, я** *nt.* expression

вы́ражен|ный, ∼, ∼а *p.p.p. of* ▶ **вы́разить**
and (∼, ∼**на**) *adj.* pronounced, marked

вырази́тел|ьный, ∼**ен,** ∼**ьна** *adj.*
expressive

вы́ра|зить, жу, зишь *pf. (of* ▶ **выража́ть)**
to express

вы́ра|зиться, жусь, зишься *pf. (of*
▶ **выража́ться) 1** *(сказать словами)* to
express oneself **2** *(обнаружиться)* **(в** + *p.)*
to manifest itself (in) **3** *(произносить
неприличные слова)* to swear, use swear
words

выраста́|ть, ю *impf. of* ▶ **вы́расти**

✒ **вы́ра|сти, асту, астешь,** *past* ∼**ос,** ∼**осла**
pf. (of ▶ **выраста́ть,** ▶ **расти́) 1** to grow (up)
2 **(в** + *a.* or *i.) (стать)* to grow (into),
develop (into), become **3** **(из** + *g.)* to grow
(out of) *(clothing)* **4** *(увеличиться)* to
increase **5** *(появиться)* to appear, rise up

вы́ра|стить, щу, стишь *pf. (of* ▶ **выра́щивать)**
(детей) to bring up; *(животных)* to rear,
breed; *(растения)* to grow, cultivate

выра́щива|ть, ю *impf. of* ▶ **вы́растить**

вы́рв|ать¹, у, ешь *pf. (of* ▶ **вырыва́ть¹) 1** to
pull out, tear out; **в. зуб** to pull out a tooth;
(отнять) to snatch **2** (fig., *добиться)* to
extort, wring; **в. призна́ние у кого́-н.** to
wring a confession out of sb

вы́рв|ать², у, ешь *pf. of* ▶ **рвать²**

вы́рв|аться, усь, ешься *pf. (of*
▶ **вырыва́ться) 1** **(из** + *g.) (освободиться)*
to tear oneself away (from); to break out
(from), break loose (from), break free
(from); **в. из чьих-н. объя́тий** to tear
oneself away from sb's embrace; *(уехать)*
to get away (from) **2** *(стон, замечание)*
to burst (from), escape **3** *(3rd pers. only)*

✒ **key word**

(*стремительно устремиться наружу*) to shoot up, shoot out

вы́рез, а *m.* (*выемка*) cut; notch; (*в одежде*) neck; **пла́тье с больши́м** ~ом low-necked dress

вы́ре|зать, жу, жешь *pf.* (*of* ▶ вырезáть) **1** (*опухоль; заметку из газеты*) to cut out; (comput.) to cut **2** (*из дерева*) to cut, carve; (*на металле, на камне*) to engrave **3** (fig., infml, *убить*) to slaughter, butcher

вырезá|ть, ю *impf. of* ▶ вы́резать

вы́рез|ка, и *f.* **1**: газéтная в. press cutting **2** (*говя́жья*) sirloin steak; (*свиная, баранья и т. д.*) fillet steak

вы́рис|оваться, уется *pf.* (*of* ▶ вырисóвываться) to appear (in outline); to stand out; (fig., *ситуация*) to emerge

вырисóвыва|ться, ется *impf. of* ▶ вы́рисоваться

вы́ровня|ть, ю *pf.* (*of* ▶ выра́внивать) **1** (*шероховатое*) to smooth (out), level; (*шаг, дыхание*) to regulate **2** (*по прямой линии*) to align

вы́ровня|ться, юсь *pf.* (*of* ▶ выра́вниваться) to become level; to become even

вы́род|иться, ится *pf.* (*of* ▶ вырожда́ться) to degenerate

вырожда́|ться, ется *impf. of* ▶ вы́родиться

вырожде́ни|е, я *nt.* degeneration

вы́рон|ить, ю, ишь *pf.* to drop

вы́р|ою, оешь *see* ▶ вы́рыть

вы́руб|ка, и *f.* **1** cutting down, felling; **в. ле́са** (*or* лесóв) deforestation **2** (*вырубленное место*) clearing

вы́руга|ть, ю *pf. of* ▶ руга́ть

вы́руга|ться, юсь *pf. of* ▶ руга́ться

выруча́|ть, ю *impf. of* ▶ вы́ручить

вы́руч|ить, у, ишь *pf.* (*of* ▶ выруча́ть) (*помочь*) to help out; to come to the help, aid (of)

вы́руч|ка, и *f.* **1** help, assistance; прийти́ на ~у to come to the rescue **2** (*деньги*) takings; earnings

вырыва́|ть¹, ю *impf. of* ▶ вы́рвать¹

вырыва́|ть², ю *impf. of* ▶ вы́рыть

вырыва́|ться, юсь *impf. of* ▶ вы́рваться

вы́р|ыть, ою, оешь *pf.* (*of* ▶ вырыва́ть²) (*землю, яму*) to dig; (*предмет*) to dig up, dig out

вы́са|дить, жу, дишь *pf.* (*of* ▶ выса́живать) **1** (*пассажира*) to drop off, set down; **в. на бéрег** to put ashore; (*заставить выйти*) to throw off, out **2** (*растение*) to plant out

вы́са|диться, жусь, дишься *pf.* (*of* ▶ выса́живаться) (из, с + *g.*) to alight (from), get off; (*с судна, самолёта*) to disembark

вы́сад|ка, и *f.* **1** (*с судна*) debarkation, disembarkation; (*из автобуса*) alighting, getting off **2** (*растения*) planting out

выса́жива|ть, ю *impf. of* ▶ вы́садить

выса́жива|ться, юсь *impf. of* ▶ вы́садиться

вы́са|жу, дишь *see* ▶ вы́садить

вы́свобо|дить, жу, дишь *pf.* (*of* ▶ высвобожда́ть) **1** (*вынуть, освободить*) to free **2** (*средства, рабочих*) to free up, release

высвобожда́|ть, ю *impf. of* ▶ вы́свободить

выселе́ни|е, я *nt.* eviction

вы́сел|ить, ю, ишь *pf.* (*of* ▶ выселя́ть) **1** (*из квартиры*) to evict **2** (*переселить*) to evacuate, move

вы́сел|иться, юсь, ишься *pf.* (*of* ▶ выселя́ться) to move

выселя́|ть, ю *impf. of* ▶ вы́селить

выселя́|ться, юсь, ишься *impf. of* ▶ вы́селиться

вы́с|иться, ится *impf.* to tower (up), rise

вы́ска|зать, жу, жешь *pf.* (*of* ▶ выска́зывать) to express; to state; **в. предположе́ние** to come out with a suggestion

вы́ска|заться, жусь, жешься *pf.* (*of* ▶ выска́зываться) **1** to speak out; to speak one's mind; to have one's say **2** (за + *a.* or про́тив + *g.*) to speak (for or against)

выска́зывани|е, я *nt.* (*суждение*) pronouncement; (*мнение*) opinion

выска́зыва|ть, ю *impf. of* ▶ вы́сказать

выска́зыва|ться, юсь *impf. of* ▶ вы́сказаться

выска́кива|ть, ю *impf. of* ▶ вы́скочить

выска́льзыва|ть, ю *impf. of* ▶ вы́скользнуть

вы́скользн|уть, у, ешь *pf.* (*of* ▶ выска́льзывать) to slip out (also fig.)

вы́скоч|ить, у, ишь *pf.* (*of* ▶ выска́кивать) (*выпрыгнуть*) to jump out; to leap out, spring out; (*выбежать*) to run out

вы́слать, шлю, шлешь *pf.* (*of* ▶ высыла́ть) **1** (*посылку, помощь*) to send, send out; dispatch **2** (pol.) to exile; (*иностранца*) to deport

вы́сле|дить, жу, дишь *pf.* (*of* ▶ высле́живать 1) to trace; to track down

высле́жива|ть, ю *impf.* **1** *impf. of* ▶ вы́следить **2** (*impf. only*) to be on the track of; to shadow

вы́слежу, дишь *see* ▶ вы́следить

вы́слуша|ть, ю *pf.* (*of* ▶ выслу́шивать) to hear out

выслу́шива|ть, ю *impf. of* ▶ вы́слушать

высма́трива|ть, ю *impf. of* ▶ вы́смотреть

высме́ива|ть, ю *impf. of* ▶ вы́смеять

вы́сме|ять, ю, ешь *pf.* (*of* ▶ высме́ивать) to ridicule

вы́сморка|ть, ю *pf. of* ▶ сморка́ть

вы́сморка|ться, юсь *pf. of* ▶ сморка́ться

вы́смотр|еть, ю, ишь *pf.* (*of* ▶ высма́тривать) (*найти*) to spy out; to locate (*by eye*)

высо́выва|ть, ю *impf. of* ▶ вы́сунуть

высо́выва|ться, юсь *impf. of* ▶ вы́сунуться

✍ **высо́к|ий, ~, ~á** *adj.* (*дом, гора; цена, температура; качество, мнение*) high; (*человек*) tall; (*мысль, стиль*) lofty; (*гость*) distinguished; (*честь*) great; **в ~ой сте́пени** highly

высоко́ *adv.* **1** (*располагаться*) high (up) **2** (*as pred.*) it is high (up); it is a long way

В

up; окно́ бы́ло в. от земли́ the window was high up off the ground **3**: оцени́ть в. to value highly

высоко́… *comb. form* high-, highly-

высокого́рный *adj.* alpine, mountain

высокока́чественный *adj.* high-quality

высококвалифици́рованный *adj.* highly qualified

высокоме́ри|е, я *nt.* haughtiness, arrogance

высокоме́р|ный, ~ен, ~на *adj.* haughty, arrogant

высокоопла́чиваемый *adj.* highly-paid

высокопоста́вленный *adj.* high-ranking

✍ **высот|а́, ы́,** *pl.* **~ы, ~** *f.* **1** (*здания, столба*) height; (*над земной поверхностью*) altitude; (*температуры, давления*) level; (*mus.*) pitch; набра́ть ~у́ (aeron.) to gain altitude **2** (*возвышенность*) height; кома́ндные ~ы commanding heights (also fig.) **3** (*искусства, мастерства*) high level; дости́гнуть но́вых высо́т to reach new heights **4** (fig.): оказа́ться на ~е́ положе́ния to rise to the occasion

высо́тк|а, и *f.* (infml) tower block

высо́тн|ый *adj.* **1** high-altitude **2**: ~ое зда́ние high-rise building, tower block

вы́сох|нуть, ну, нешь, *past* ~, ~ла *pf.* (of ► высыха́ть) **1** (*бельё*) to dry (out); (*река*) to dry up **2** (*растение*) to wither, fade; (fig., *исхудать*) to waste away, fade away

вы́сохший *p.p. act. of* ► вы́сохнуть *and adj.* dried-up; shrivelled; wizened

Высо́честв|о, а *nt.*: (Ва́ше) В. (Your) Highness

вы́сп|аться, люсь, ишься *pf.* (of ► высыпа́ться²) to have a good sleep

вы́став|ить, лю, ишь *pf.* (of ► выставля́ть) **1** (*поставить наружу*) to put out, move out; (*картины, товары*) to exhibit, display; в. на прода́жу to put on sale; в. напока́з to show off, parade **2** (*часовых*) to post **3** (+ *i.*) (*представить*) to represent (as), make out (as); в. в плохо́м све́те to represent in an unfavourable light; его́ ~или тру́сом he was made out to be a coward **4** (*предложить*) to put forward; в. свою́ кандидату́ру to come forward as a candidate

вы́став|иться, люсь, ишься *pf.* (of ► выставля́ться) (*о художнике*) to exhibit

✍ **вы́ставк|а, и** *f.* exhibition, show

выставля́|ть, ю *impf. of* ► вы́ставить

выставля́|ться, юсь *impf. of* ► вы́ставиться

вы́ставочный *adj. of* ► вы́ставка

выста́ива|ть, ю, ешь *impf. of* ► вы́стоять 1

вы́ст|елю, елешь *see* ► вы́стлать

выстила́|ть, ю *impf. of* ► вы́стлать

вы́стира|ть, ю *pf. of* ► стира́ть²

вы́ст|лать, елю, елешь *pf.* (*покрыть*) to cover; (*вымостить*) to pave

вы́сто|ять, ю, ишь *pf.* (of ► выста́ивать) **1** (*долго простоять*) to stand **2** (*pf. only*)

✍ key word

(*не сдаться*) to stand one's ground

вы́страда|ть, ю *pf.* **1** (*пережить много страданий*) to suffer; to go through **2** (*достигнуть страданиями*) to gain, achieve through suffering

выстра́ива|ть, ю *impf. of* ► вы́строить

выстра́ива|ться, юсь *impf. of* ► вы́строиться

вы́стрел, а *m.* shot; произвести́ в. to fire a shot; разда́лся в. a shot rang out

вы́стрел|ить, ю, ишь *pf.* to shoot, fire; я ~ил в него́ три ра́за I fired three shots at him

вы́стро|ить, ю, ишь *pf.* (of ► выстра́ивать) **1** to build **2** (mil.) to draw up, form up

вы́стро|иться, юсь, ишься *pf.* (of ► выстра́иваться) **1** (mil.) to form up **2** (*стоять рядами*) to stand in rows

вы́ступ, а *m.* projection, ledge

✍ **выступа́|ть, ю** *impf. of* ► вы́ступить **2** (*impf. only*) to project, jut out, stick out

✍ **вы́ступ|ить, лю, ишь** *pf.* (of ► выступа́ть 1) **1** (*выйти вперёд*) to come forward; to come out **2** (*публично*) to appear (*publicly*); в. за + *a.* to come out in favour of; в. про́тив + *g.* to come out against; в. в печа́ти to appear in print; в. с ре́чью to make a speech; в. по телеви́дению to appear on television

✍ **выступле́ни|е, я** *nt.* (*публичное*) appearance; (*речь*) speech; (*актёра*) performance

вы́сун|уть, у, ешь *pf.* (of ► высо́вывать) to put out, thrust out, stick out; в. язы́к to put/stick one's tongue out

вы́сун|уться, усь, ешься *pf.* (of ► высо́вываться) **1** (*о человеке*) to show oneself, thrust oneself forward; в. из окна́ to lean out of the window **2** (*о ноге, руке*) to stick out

высу́шива|ть, ю *impf. of* ► вы́сушить

вы́суш|ить, у, ишь *pf. of* ► суши́ть

вы́суш|иться, усь, ишься *pf. of* ► суши́ться

вы́счита|ть, ю *pf.* (of ► высчи́тывать) to calculate

высчи́тыва|ть, ю *impf. of* ► вы́считать

вы́с|ший *adj.* (*comp. and superl. of* ► высо́кий) (*самый высокий*) highest; (*самый главный*) supreme; (*более высокий*) higher; ~шего ка́чества of the highest quality; ~шая ме́ра наказа́ния capital punishment; ~шее образова́ние higher education; ~шее уче́бное заведе́ние *see* ► вуз; в ~шей сте́пени in the highest degree

высыла́|ть, ю *impf. of* ► вы́слать

вы́сып|ать, лю, лешь *pf.* (of ► высыпа́ть) **1** to pour out (*trans.*); (*нечаянно*) to spill **2** (infml) to pour out (*intrans.*)

высыпа́|ть, ю *impf. of* ► вы́сыпать

вы́сып|аться, люсь, лешься *pf.* (of ► высыпа́ться¹) to pour out (*intrans.*); (*нечаянно*) to spill (*intrans.*)

высыпа́|ться¹, ется *impf. of* ► вы́сыпаться

высыпа́|ться², юсь *impf. of* ► вы́спаться

высыха́|ть, ю *impf. of* ► вы́сохнуть

вытáлкива|ть, ю *impf. of* ▸ **вы́толкнуть**
вытáскива|ть, ю *impf. of* ▸ **вы́тащить**
вы́тащ|ить, у, ишь *pf.* (*of* ▸ **вытáскивать**) (*из кармана, из сумки*) to pull out, extract
вытека́|ть, ю *impf.* **1** *impf. of* ▸ **вы́течь** **2** (*impf. only*) (*река*) to flow (from, out of) **3** (*impf. only*) (fig., *вывод*) to result, follow (from)
вы́текут *see* ▸ **вы́течь**
вы́т|ереть, ру, решь, *past* ~ер, ~ерла *pf.* (*of* ▸ **вытира́ть**) (*руки, глаза, посуду, стол*) to wipe; (*грязь*) to wipe up; **в. пыль** to dust
вы́терп|еть, лю, ишь *pf.* to bear, endure
вытеснéни|е, я *nt.* ousting; (*замена собой*) displacing, supplanting
вы́тесн|ить, ю, ишь *pf.* (*of* ▸ **вытеснять**) (*врага*) to force out; to oust; (*заменить собой*) to displace, supplant
вытесня́|ть, ю *impf. of* ▸ **вы́теснить**
вы́те|чь, чет, кут, *past* ~к, ~кла *pf.* (*of* ▸ **вытека́ть** 1) to flow out, run out
вытира́|ть, ю *impf. of* ▸ **вы́тереть**
вы́толкн|уть, у, ешь *pf.* (*of* ▸ **вытáлкивать**) **1** to throw out **2** (*пробку*) to push out, force out
вы́торг|овать, ую *pf.* (▸ **выторгóвывать**) (infml) (*получить уступку*) to get a reduction (of); (fig.) to manage to get
выторгóвыва|ть, ю *impf.* (infml) **1** *impf. of* ▸ **вы́торговать 2** to try to get (*by bargaining*); to haggle over
вы́трав|ить, лю, ишь *pf. of* ▸ **трави́ть**
вы́т|ру, решь *see* ▸ **вы́тереть**
вытряса́|ть, ю *impf. of* ▸ **вы́трясти**
вы́тряс|ти, у, ешь, *past* ~, ~ла *pf.* (*песок, мусор*) to shake out
вытря́хива|ть, ю *impf. of* ▸ **вы́тряхнуть**
вы́тряхн|уть, у, ешь *pf.* (*of* ▸ **вытря́хивать**) (*песок, мусор; скатерть*) to shake out
выть, вóю, вóешь *impf.* (*собака, волк, ветер*) to howl; (*сирена*) to wail
вытя́гива|ть, ю *impf. of* ▸ **вы́тянуть**
вытя́гива|ться, юсь *impf. of* ▸ **вы́тянуться**
вы́тян|уть, у, ешь *pf.* (*of* ▸ **вытя́гивать**) **1** (*вытащить*) to pull out **2** (*ноги, руки*) to stretch (out); (*сделать длиннее*) to extend **3** (*дым, гной*) to draw out, extract (also fig.); (*impers.*) **газ** ~**уло в окнó** the gas had escaped through the window
вы́тян|уться, усь, ешься *pf.* (*of* ▸ **вытя́гиваться**) **1** (*растянуться*) to stretch (*intrans.*); (*вдоль реки; на полу*) to stretch out; **лицó у неё** ~**улось** (infml) her face fell **2** (*выпрямиться*) to stand erect
выу́чива|ть, ю *impf. of* ▸ **вы́учить**
вы́уч|ить, у, ишь *pf.* (*of* ▸ **учи́ть 4,** ▸ **выу́чивать**) **1** to learn **2** (*+ a. and d. or + inf.*) to teach; **он** ~**ил нас испáнскому языкý** he taught us Spanish
вы́уч|иться, усь, ишься *pf.* (*of* ▸ **учи́ться 3**) (*+ d. or inf.*) to learn; (infml, *на кого-н.*) to learn (to be)

вы́хва|тить, чу, тишь *pf.* **1** (*отнять*) to snatch out; to grab **2** (*вытащить*) to pull out, draw; **в. нож** to draw a knife
выхва́тыва|ть, ю *impf. of* ▸ **вы́хватить**
вы́хва|чу, тишь *see* ▸ **вы́хватить**
выхлопн|óй *adj.* (tech.) exhaust; ~**áя трубá** exhaust pipe; ~**ые гáзы** exhaust (fumes)
✍ **вы́ход, а** *m.* **1** (*на улицу*) going out; (*с целью уйти*) leaving, departure; (*из партии*) leaving; (*поезда, корабля*) departure; **в. в отстáвку** retirement **2** (*место выхода*) way out, exit; (*трубки*) outlet; (*способ*) way out; **дать в.** (*+ d.*) to give vent (to) **3** (*издания*) appearance; (*фильма*) release; (theatr.) entrance **4** (comput.) exit; logoff
вы́ход|ец, ца *m.* **1** (*из другой страны*) immigrant **2** (*из другой социальной среды*) person moving from one social group to another; **он — в. из крестья́н** he is of peasant origin
✍ **выхо|ди́ть, жý,** ~**дишь** *impf.* **1** *impf. of* ▸ **вы́йти 2** (*impf. only*) to look out (on), give (on); face; **егó кóмната** ~**дит óкнами на ýлицу** his room looks onto the street **3:** **не в. из головы́, из умá** to be unforgettable, stick in one's mind **4** (*as pred.*) ~**дит(, что)** (infml) it turns out that
вы́ходк|а, и *f.* (pej.) trick; escapade
выходн|óй *adj.* **1** exit; ~**áя дверь** street door **2: в. день** day off; ~**áя одéжда** 'best' clothes
• *n.* **1** (**в.,** ~**óго**) (*день*) day off **2** (**в.,** ~**óго,** *f.* ~**áя,** ~**óй**) (infml, *человек*) person having day off; **он сегóдня в.** it is his day off today **3** (*in pl.*) (~**ые,** ~**ых**) severance pay
выхо|жý, ~**дишь** *see* ▸ **выходи́ть**
вы́ч|ел, ла *see* ▸ **вы́честь**
вычёркива|ть, ю *impf. of* ▸ **вы́черкнуть**
вы́черкн|уть, у, ешь *pf.* (*слова*) to cross out; (*из списка*) to cross off; **в. из пáмяти** to erase from one's memory
вы́черпа|ть, ю *pf.* (*of* ▸ **вычéрпывать**) (*из + g.*) (*содержимое*) to take out; (*из лодки*) to bail (out); **в. вóду из лóдки** to bail out a boat
вычéрпыва|ть, ю *impf. of* ▸ **вы́черпать**
вы́ч|есть, ту, тешь, *past* ~ел, ~ла, *pres. gerund* ~тя *pf.* (*of* ▸ **вычитáть**) **1** (math.) to subtract **2** (*удержать*) to deduct, keep back
вычислéни|е, я *nt.* calculation
вычисли́тельн|ый *adj.* calculating, computing; ~**ая тéхника** computers
вы́числ|ить, ю, ишь *pf.* (*of* ▸ **вычисля́ть**) to calculate, compute
вычисля́|ть, ю *impf. of* ▸ **вы́числить**
вы́чи|стить, щу, стишь *pf.* (*of* ▸ **чи́стить 2,** ▸ **вычищáть**) to clean (up, out)
вычитáни|е, я *nt.* (math.) subtraction
вычитá|ть, ю *impf. of* ▸ **вы́честь**
вычищá|ть, ю *impf. of* ▸ **вы́чистить**
вы́чи|щу, стишь *see* ▸ **вы́чистить**
вы́ч|ту, тешь *see* ▸ **вы́честь**

B

Г

вы́ше **1** *comp. of* ▶ высо́кий, ▶ высоко́; higher, taller **2** *prep. + g.* (*вверх от*) above, beyond; (*больше*) over; в. нуля́ above zero; (*за пределами*) beyond; э́то в. моего́ понима́ния it is beyond my comprehension **3** *adv.* (liter.) above; смотри́ в. see above

вы́ше... *comb. form* above-, afore-

вы́|шел, шла *see* ▶ вы́йти

вышеска́занный *adj.* aforesaid

вышестоя́щий *adj.* higher

вышеука́занный *adj.* foregoing

вышеупомя́нутый *adj.* aforementioned

вышива́ни|е, я *nt.* embroidery, needlework

вышива́|ть, ю *impf. of* ▶ вы́шить

вы́шивк|а, и *f.* embroidery, needlework

вы́ш|ить, ью, ьешь, *imper.* ~ей *pf.* (*of* ▶ вышива́ть) to embroider

вы́шк|а, и *f.* (*башня*) (watch)tower; сторожева́я в. watchtower; бурова́я в. derrick

вы́|шлю, шлешь *see* ▶ вы́слать

выщип|а́ть, лю, лешь *pf.* (*of* ▶ выщи́пывать) to pull out, pluck; в. пе́рья у ку́рицы to pluck a chicken

выщи́пыва|ть, ю *impf. of* ▶ вы́щипать

вы́яв|ить, лю, ишь *pf.* (*of* ▶ выявля́ть) **1** (*предать гласности*) to bring out; to make known **2** (*недостатки*) to expose

вы́яв|иться, люсь, ишься *pf.* (*of* ▶ выявля́ться) (*недостатки*) to come to light, be revealed, be exposed

☞ **выявля́|ть, ю** *impf. of* ▶ вы́явить

выявля́|ться, юсь *impf. of* ▶ вы́явиться

выясне́ни|е, я *nt.* clarification; explanation

вы́ясн|ить, ю, ишь *pf.* (*of* ▶ выясня́ть) (*сделать понятным*) to clarify, clear up, explain; (*установить*) to find out, ascertain

вы́ясн|иться, ится *pf.* (*of* ▶ выясня́ться) (*объясниться*) to become clear; (*стать явным*) to turn out, prove

выясня́|ть, я́ю, я́ет *impf. of* ▶ вы́яснить

выясня́|ться, я́ется *impf. of* ▶ вы́ясниться

Вьетна́м, а *m.* Vietnam

вьетна́м|ец, ца *m.* Vietnamese

вьетна́м|ка, ки *f.* **1** *of* ▶ вьетна́мец **2** (*usu. in pl.*) (infml, *обувь*) flip-flop

вьетна́мский *adj.* Vietnamese

вью, вьёшь *see* ▶ вить

вью́г|а, и *f.* snowstorm, blizzard

вью́щ|ийся *pres. part. of* ▶ ви́ться *and adj.:* ~иеся во́лосы curly hair; ~ееся расте́ние (bot.) creeper, climber

вя́ж|у, ~жешь *see* ▶ вяза́ть

вяз, а *m.* elm (tree)

вяза́ни|е, я *nt.* knitting, crocheting

вяза́нк|а, и *f.* bundle

вя́заный *adj.* knitted

вя|за́ть, жу́, ~жешь *impf.* **1** (*pf.* с~) to tie, bind **2** (*pf.* с~) (*спицами*) to knit; (*крючком*) to crochet **3** (*impf. only*) to be astringent; (*impers.*) у меня́ ~жет во рту my mouth feels constricted

вя|за́ться, жу́сь, ~жешься *impf.* (infml) (с + *i.*) to agree, tally (with)

вя́з|кий, ~ок, ~ка́, ~ко *adj.* **1** (*клейкий*) viscous, sticky **2** (*топкий*) boggy

вя́з|нуть, ну, нешь, *past* ~, ~ла *impf.* (в + *p.*) to get stuck (in)

вя́лост|ь, и *f.* (*кожи, мышц*) flabbiness; limpness; (fig.) sluggishness; inertia; slackness

вя́л|ый *adj.* **1** (*растение*) faded **2** (~, ~а) (*кожа, тело*) flabby; limp; (fig.) sluggish, inert; slack

вя́|нуть, у, ешь, *past* вял/вя́нул, вя́ла, вя́ло, вя́ли *impf.* (*of* ▶ завя́нуть) (*растение*) to fade, wither; (fig., *красота, способности*) to fade

---

Гг

☞ **г.** *abbr. of* **1** (**год**) yr (year) **2** (**го́род**) city, town **3** (**гора́**) Mt (Mount)

габари́т, а *m.* (*usu. in pl.*) (tech.) size, dimensions

габари́т|ный *adj. of* ▶ габари́т; ~ные огни́ sidelights (BrE), sidemarker lights (AmE)

Гава́й|и, ев *m. pl.* Hawaii

га́ван|ь, и *f.* harbour (BrE), harbor (AmE)

га́вка|ть, ю *impf.* (infml) to bark

☞ key word

гага́р|а, ы *f.* (zool.) diver (BrE), loon (AmE)

гад, а *m.* (fig., infml) louse, rat, skunk

гада́лк|а, и *f.* fortune teller

гада́ни|е, я *nt.* (*догадка*) guesswork

гада́|ть, ю *impf.* **1** (*pf.* по~) (на + *p. or* по + *d.*) (*предсказывать*) to tell fortunes (by) **2** (*impf. only*) (о + *p.*) (*предполагать*) to guess

га́дин|а, ы *f.* = гад

га́|дить, жу, дишь *impf.* (*of* ▶ нага́дить) (infml) **1** (*о животных*) to defecate **2** (+ *d.*)

(*вредить*) to play dirty tricks (on)

га́д|кий, ∼ок, ∼ка́, ∼ко *adj.* nasty, vile, repulsive; **г. утёнок** ugly duckling

га́дост|ь, и *f.* **1** (*infml*, *дрянь*) filth, muck **2** (*поступок*) dirty trick; **говори́ть** ∼и to say foul things

гадю́к|а, и *f.* adder, viper

га́ечный *adj. of* ▶ **га́йка**; **г. ключ** spanner, wrench

га́же *comp. of* ▶ **га́дкий**

⚥ **газ**, а *m.* **1** gas **2** (*infml*): **педа́ль** ∼а accelerator, gas pedal; **дать** ∼у to step on the gas; **сба́вить г.** to reduce speed **3** (*in pl.*) (*в кишечнике*) wind

⚥ **газе́т|а**, ы *f.* newspaper

газиро́ванный *adj.* carbonated

газиро́вк|а, и *f.* (*infml*) carbonated water, soda (water)

газовщи́к, а́ *m.* gasman

га́зов|ый *adj. of* ▶ **газ**; ∼ая плита́ gas cooker, gas stove; **г. счётчик** gas meter; ∼ая ка́мера gas chamber

газо́н, а *m.* grassed area, lawn

газонокоси́лк|а, и *f.* lawnmower

газопрово́д, а *m.* gas pipeline; gas main

ГАИ *f. indecl.* (*abbr. of* **Госуда́рственная автомоби́льная инспе́кция**) State Motor Vehicle Inspectorate; traffic police

Гаи́ти *indecl.* (*госуда́рство*) Haiti; (*m.*) (*остров*) Hispaniola

гаитя́н|ин, ина, *pl.* ∼е, ∼ *m.* Haitian

гаитя́н|ка, ки *f. of* ▶ **гаитя́нин**

гаитя́нский *adj.* Haitian

га́ишник, а *m.* (*infml*) traffic cop

Гайа́н|а, ы *f.* Guyana

гайа́н|ец, ца *m.* Guyanese

гайа́н|ка, ки *f. of* ▶ **гайа́нец**

гайа́нский *adj.* Guyanese

га́йк|а, и *f.* nut; **закрути́ть** ∼и (*fig.*) to put the screws on

гаймори́т, а *m.* (*med.*) sinusitis

гала́ктик|а, и *f.* (*astron.*) galaxy

галантере́йный *adj. of* ▶ **галантере́я**; **г. магази́н** haberdashery, fancy goods shop

галантере́|я, и *f.* haberdashery, fancy goods

гала́нт|ный, ∼ен, ∼на *adj.* chivalrous

галер|а, ы *f.* galley

⚥ **галере́|я**, и *f.* gallery

га́лк|а, и *f.* jackdaw

галло́н, а *m.* gallon

галлюцина́ци|я, и *f.* hallucination

галлюциноге́н, а *m.* hallucinogen

га́лочк|а, и *f.* tick, check (*AmE*)

га́лстук, а *m.* tie; **г.-ба́бочка** bow tie

га́л|ька, ьки *f.* (*g. pl.* ∼ек) pebble; (*collect.*) pebbles, shingle

гам, а *m.* (*infml*) din, uproar

гама́к, а́ *m.* hammock

Га́мби|я, и *f.* Gambia

га́мбургер, а *m.* (ham)burger

га́мм|а, ы *f.* (*mus.*) scale; (*fig.*) gamut

Га́н|а, ы *f.* Ghana

га́нгстер, а *m.* gangster

гандбо́л, а *m.* handball

гандболи́ст, а *m.* handball player

гандболи́ст|ка, ки *f. of* ▶ **гандболи́ст**

га́н|ец, ца *m.* Ghanaian

га́нк|а, и *f. of* ▶ **га́нец**

га́нский *adj.* Ghanaian

гара́ж, а́ *m.* garage

гара́нт, а *m.* guarantor

гаранти́йный *adj.* guarantee

гаранти́р|овать, ую *impf. and pf.* to guarantee, vouch for

⚥ **гара́нти|я**, и *f.* guarantee; (*охрана*) safeguard

гардеро́б, а *m.* **1** (*шкаф*) wardrobe **2** (*помещение*) cloakroom **3** (*collect.*) (*одежда*) wardrobe

гардеро́бщик, а *m.* cloakroom attendant

гардеро́бщи|ца, цы *f. of* ▶ **гардеро́бщик**

гаре́м, а *m.* harem

гармони́р|овать, ую *impf.* (**с** + *i.*) to be in harmony (with); (*о красках*) to tone (with), go (with)

гармони́ст, а *m.* accordion player

гармони́ч|ный, ∼ен, ∼на *adj.* harmonious

гармо́ни|я, и *f.* **1** (*mus.*) harmony **2** (*fig.*) harmony, concord

гармо́н|ь, и *f.* accordion, concertina

гарнизо́н, а *m.* garrison

гарни́р, а *m.* (*cul.*) garnish; (*из овощей*) vegetables; **на г.** as a side dish

гарниту́р, а *m.* set; (*мебели*) suite

гарпу́н, а́ *m.* harpoon

га|си́ть, шу́, ∼сишь *impf.* (*of* ▶ **погаси́ть**) **1** (*pf. also* **за**∼) (*пожар, свет*) to put out, extinguish; **г. свет** to put out the light **2** (*погашать*) to cancel; **г. задо́лженность** to liquidate a debt

га́с|нуть, ну, нешь, *past* ∼, ∼ла *impf.* (*of* ▶ **пога́снуть**) (*переставать гореть*) to be extinguished, go out; (*слабеть*) to grow feeble; (*о чувствах*) to fade, weaken

гастри́т, а *m.* gastritis

гастроли́р|овать, ую *impf.* to tour, be on tour (*of an artiste*)

гастро́л|ь, и *f.* (*usu. in pl.*) tour; engagement (*of touring artiste*)

гастроно́м, а *m.* grocer's (shop) (*BrE*), grocery store (*AmE*)

гастроно́ми|я, и *f.* **1** (*продукты*) high-quality cooked meats, fish, cheeses, *etc.* **2** (*гастрономический отдел*) delicatessen counter

гаши́ш, а *m.* hashish

ГБ (*abbr. of* **о́рганы госуда́рственной безопа́сности**) (organs of) state security

гвалт, а *m.* (*infml*) row, uproar, rumpus

гварде́|ец, йца *m.* (*mil.*) guardsman

гва́рди|я, и *f.* (*mil.*) Guards (*pl.*); ∼и капита́н *и т. п.* (*в званиях*) Captain, *etc.*, of the Guards

Гватема́л|а, ы *f.* Guatemala

гватема́л|ец, ьца *m.* Guatemalan

гватема́л|ка, ки *f. of* ▶ **гватема́лец**

гватема́льский *adj.* Guatemalan

гвине́|ец, йца *m.* Guinean

гвине́й|ка, ки *f. of* ▶ **гвине́ец**

гвине́йский *adj.* Guinean

Гвине́|я, и *f.* Guinea

гвозди́к|а¹, и *f.* (bot.) pink(s); carnation(s)

гвозди́к|а², и *f.* (collect.) (*пряность*) cloves

гвозд|ь, я́, pl. ~и, ~е́й *m.* **1** nail **2** (+ *g.*) (fig., infml) (*программы*) highlight, main attraction

◆ **гг.** *abbr. of* **1** (*го́ды*) yrs (years) **2** (*города́*) cities, towns

◆ **где** *adv.* **1** (interrog. and rel.) where; **г. бы ни** wherever; **г. бы то ни́ было** no matter where **2** (infml, *где-нибудь*) somewhere; anywhere

где́-либо *adv.* anywhere

где́-нибудь *adv.* somewhere; anywhere

◆ **где́-то** *adv.* somewhere

ге́|й, я *m.* (sl.) gay (*homosexual*); **г.-клуб** gay club

гекта́р, а *m.* hectare (*10,000 square metres*)

гел|ь, я *m.* gel

геморро́|й, я *m.* (med.) haemorrhoids (BrE), hemorrhoids (AmE), piles

гемофи́лик, а *m.* (med.) haemophiliac (BrE), hemophiliac (AmE)

гемофили́|я, и *f.* (med.) haemophilia (BrE), hemophilia (AmE)

ген, а *m.* (physiol.) gene

ген... *comb. form, abbr. of* ▶ **генера́льный**

генеалоги́ческий *adj.* genealogical

генеало́ги|я, и *f.* genealogy

генера́л, а *m.* general; **г.-майо́р** major general; **г.-губерна́тор** governor general

◆ **генера́льн|ый** *adv.* general; **г. констру́ктор** chief designer; **~ая репети́ция** dress rehearsal; **г. секрета́рь** general secretary; **~ая убо́рка** spring-clean; **г. штаб** general staff

генера́льский *adj.* general's; **г. чин** rank of general

генера́тор, а *m.* (tech.) generator

гене́тик|а, и *f.* genetics

генети́ческий *adj.* genetic

гениа́л|ьный, ~ен, ~ьна *adj.* (*поэт, произведе́ние*) brilliant; (*реше́ние*) ingenious

ге́ни|й, я *m.* (*тала́нт, спосо́бность*) genius; (*челове́к*) a genius

генита́ли|и, й (*no sg.*) (med.) genitalia, genitals

ге́н|ный *adj. of* ▶ **ген; ~ная инжене́рия** genetic engineering

гено́м, а *m.* genome; **~ челове́ка** human genome

генофо́нд, а *m.* gene pool

геноци́д, а *m.* genocide

◆ *key word*

генсе́к, а *m.* (*abbr. of* **генера́льный секрета́рь**) (infml) general secretary

гео... *comb. form, abbr. of* ▶ **географи́ческий**

гео́граф, а *m.* geographer

географи́ческий *adj.* geographical

геогра́фи|я, и *f.* geography

геодези́ст, а *m.* land surveyor

геоде́зи|я, и *f.* geodesy, (land) surveying

гео́лог, а *m.* geologist

геологи́ческий *adj.* geological

геоло́ги|я, и *f.* geology

геометри́ческий *adj.* geometric(al)

геоме́три|я, и *f.* geometry

геополити́ческий *adj.* geopolitical

георги́н, а *m.* dahlia

гепати́т, а *m.* hepatitis

гера́н|ь, и *f.* geranium

герб, á *m.* arms, coat of arms

геркуле́с, а *m.* (sg. only) (*крупа́*) rolled oats; porridge

Герма́ни|я, и *f.* Germany

герма́нский *adj.* Germanic

геро́йзм, а *m.* heroism

герои́н, а *m.* heroin

герои́н|я, и *f.* heroine

герои́ческий *adj.* heroic

◆ **геро́|й, я** *m.* hero; (liter., *де́йствующее лицо́*) character; **гла́вный г.** protagonist

геро́йский *adj.* heroic

ге́рпес, а *m.* herpes

герц, а, g. pl. г. *m.* (phys.) hertz

ге́рцог, а *m.* duke; **г. Эдинбу́ргский** the Duke of Edinburgh

герцоги́н|я, и *f.* duchess

гетеросексуа́льный *adj.* heterosexual

ге́тр|ы, ретр *f. pl.* (sg. ~a, ~ы) **1** gaiters **2** (sport) football socks **3** (*балетные*) leg warmers

ге́тто *nt. indecl.* ghetto

г-жа (*abbr. of* **госпожа́**) (*за́мужняя*) Mrs; (*незамужняя*) Miss; (*без указа́ния на семе́йное положе́ние*) Ms

гиаци́нт, а *m.* hyacinth

ГИБДД (*abbr. of* **Госуда́рственная инспе́кция безопа́сности доро́жного движе́ния**) State Road Safety Inspectorate

ги́бел|ь, и *f.* (*смерть*) death; (*уничтоже́ние*) destruction, ruin; (*поте́ря*) loss; (*госуда́рства*) downfall

ги́б|кий, ~ок, ~ка́, ~ко *adj.* **1** flexible; (*те́ло*) supple; **г. диск** (comput.) floppy (disk) **2** (*ум*) adaptable, versatile

ги́бкост|ь, и *f.* **1** flexibility; (*те́ла*) suppleness **2** (*ума́*) versatility, resourcefulness

ги́блый *adj.* (infml) (*ме́сто*) godforsaken; (*безнадёжный*) hopeless

ги́б|нуть, ну, нешь, *past* ~ *and* ~нул, ~ла *impf.* (*of* ▶ **поги́бнуть**) to perish

Гибралта́р, а *m.* Gibraltar

гибри́д, а *m.* hybrid

ги́га... *comb. form* giga-

гигаба́йт, а *m.* (comput.) gigabyte

гига́нт, а *m.* giant

гига́нтский *adj.* gigantic

гигие́н|а, ы *f.* hygiene

гигиени́ческ|ий *adj.* hygienic, sanitary; ∼ая
проклáдка sanitary towel (BrE), napkin (AmE)

гид, а *m.* guide

гидро... *comb. form* hydro-

гидроста́нци|я, и *f.* hydroelectric (power)
station

гидроэлектроста́нци|я, и *f.* hydroelectric
power station

ги́льз|а, ы *f.* cartridge case

Гимала́|и, ев (*no sg.*) the Himalayas

гимн, а *m.* hymn; госуда́рственный г.
national anthem

гимна́зи|я, и *f.* grammar school (BrE), high
school

гимна́ст, а *m.* gymnast

гимна́стик|а, и *f.* gymnastics; спорти́вная
г. artistic gymnastics; худо́жественная г.
rhythmic gymnastics

гимнасти́ческий *adj.* gymnastic; г. зал
gymnasium

гимна́ст|ка, ки *f. of* ▶ гимна́ст

гинеко́лог, а *m.* gynaecologist (BrE),
gynecologist (AmE)

гинекологи́ческий *adj.* gynaecological
(BrE), gynecological (AmE)

гинеколо́ги|я, и *f.* gynaecology (BrE),
gynecology (AmE)

гиперма́ркет, а *m.* hypermarket (BrE)

гиперссы́лк|а, и *f.* (comput.) hyperlink

гипертони́я, и *f.* (med.) hypertension, high
blood pressure

гипно́з, а *m.* hypnosis

гипнотизёр, а *m.* hypnotist

гипнотизи́р|овать, ую *impf.* (*of*
▶ загипнотизи́ровать) to hypnotize

гипноти́ческий *adj.* hypnotic

гипо́тез|а, ы *f.* hypothesis

гипотети́ческий *adj.* hypothetical

гипс, а *m.* **1** (min.) gypsum **2** (art, *материал*)
plaster of Paris **3** (*хирургическая повязка*)
plaster cast, plaster

гирля́нд|а, ы *f.* garland

ги́р|я, и *f.* (*для весов*) weight; (sport) weight,
dumb-bell

гита́р|а, ы *f.* guitar

гитари́ст, а *m.* guitarist

гитари́ст|ка, ки *f. of* ▶ гитари́ст

глав... *comb. form, abbr. of* ▶ гла́вный

✓ **глав|á¹**, ы́, *pl.* ∼ы *c.g.* (*начальник*) head,
chief; г. делега́ции head of a delegation;
быть/стоя́ть во ∼é (+ *g.*) to be at the
head (of), lead; во ∼é (с + *i.*) under the
leadership (of), led (by)

✓ **глав|á²**, ы́, *pl.* ∼ы *f.* (*раздел книги*) chapter

главнокома́ндующий, его *m.*
commander-in-chief; Верхо́вный г. Supreme
Commander

✓ **гла́вн|ый** *adj.* (*самый важный*) chief, main,
principal; (*старший*) head, senior; г. врач
head physician; г. инжене́р chief engineer;
∼ое управле́ние central directorate; ∼ым
о́бразом chiefly, mainly, for the most part;
(*as nt. n.* ∼ое, ∼ого) the chief thing, the
main thing; the essentials

глаго́л, а *m.* verb

гла́дильн|ый *adj.* ironing; ∼ая доска́
ironing board

гладио́лус, а *m.* gladiolus

гла́|дить, жу, дишь *impf.* (*of* ▶ погла́дить)
1 (*pf. also* вы́∼) (*выравнивать утюгом*) to
iron, press **2** (*ласково проводить рукой по
чему-н.*) to stroke

гла́д|кий, ∼ок, ∼ка́, ∼ко *adj.* (*дорога*)
smooth; (*волосы*) straight; (*ткань*) plain

гла́дко *adv. of* ▶ гла́дкий; smoothly

гла́же *comp. of* ▶ гла́дкий

гла́жены|е, я *nt.* ironing

✓ **глаз**, а, о ∼е, в ∼у́, *pl.* ∼á, ∼, ∼а́м *m.*
(*орган зрения*) eye; (*зрение*) eyesight; в
∼á to one's face; в ∼áх (+ *g.*) in the eyes
(of); я его́ в ∼á не ви́дел I have never
seen him; руга́ть кого́-н. за ∼á to abuse sb
behind his back; на ∼áх before one's eyes;
не попада́йся мне на ∼á! keep out of my
sight!; на г. approximately, by eye; с ∼у на
г. tête-à-tête, cheek by jowl; с г. доло́й out
of sight; смотре́ть во все ∼á to be all eyes;
закрыва́ть ∼á (на + *a.*) to close one's eyes
(to); открыва́ть кому́-н. ∼á (на + *a.*) to open
sb's eyes (to); идти́ куда́ ∼á гляд́ят to follow
one's nose

глазн|о́й *adj. of* ▶ глаз; г. врач ophthalmologist;
∼о́е я́блоко eyeball

глаз|о́к, ка́, *pl.* ∼ки, ∼ок *and* ∼ки́, ∼ко́в *m.*
1 (*pl.* ∼ки) *dim. of* ▶ глаз; стро́ить ∼ки
кому́-н. to make eyes at sb **2** (*pl.* ∼ки) (infml)
peephole

глазу́нь|я, ьи, *g. pl.* ∼ий *f.* fried eggs (*with
yolk and white unmixed*)

глазу́р|ь, и *f.* **1** (*на посуде*) glaze **2** (cul.)
icing

гламу́р|ный, ∼ен, ∼на *adj.* (infml)
glamorous, glitzy

гла́нд|а, ы *f.* (anat.) tonsil; удали́ть ∼ы
to take out tonsils; воспале́ние гланд
glandular fever

гла|си́ть, шу́, си́шь *impf.* to say, run;
докуме́нт ∼си́т сле́дующее the paper runs
as follows; как ∼си́т погово́рка as the saying
goes

гла́сно *adv.* openly, publicly

гла́сность, и *f.* **1** (*известность*) publicity;
преда́ть ∼и to make public, make known,
publish **2** (pol.) openness, glasnost

гла́сный¹ *adj.* (*открытый*) open, public; г.
суд public trial

гла́сный² *adj.* (ling.) vowel, vocalic; (*as m. n.*
г., ∼ого) vowel

глауко́м|а, ы *f.* glaucoma

гли́н|а, ы *f.* clay

глиноби́тный *adj.* adobe; mud

глинтве́йн, а *m.* mulled wine

гли́нян|ый *adj.* (*сделанный из глины*) clay; earthenware; ~ая посу́да earthenware crockery

глобализа́ци|я, и *f.* globalization

глоба́льный *adj.* global; (fig.) extensive

гло́бус, а *m.* globe

гло|да́ть, жу́, ~жешь *impf.* to gnaw (at) (also fig.)

глота́|ть, ю *impf.* (*of* ▸ проглоти́ть) to swallow

гло́тк|а, и *f.* **1** (anat.) gullet **2** (infml, *горло*) throat

глото́к, ка́ *m.* gulp, mouthful; (*небольшое количество*) drop

гло́х|нуть, ну, нешь, *past* ~нул *and* ~, ~ла *impf.* **1** (*pf.* о~) (*становиться глухим*) to become deaf **2** (*pf.* за~) (*о звуках*) to die away, subside; (*о моторе*) to stall

глу́бже *comp. of* ▸ глубо́кий, ▸ глубоко́[1]

◆ **глубин|а́, ы́,** *pl.* ~ы *f.* **1** depth; на ~е́ трёхсо́т ме́тров at a depth of 300 metres **2** (*in pl.*) (the) depths **3** (+ *g.*) heart, interior (also fig.); в ~е́ ле́са in the heart of the forest; в ~е́ души́ at heart, in one's heart of hearts

глуби́нный *adj.* deep

◆ **глубо́к|ий, ~, ~а́** *adj.* **1** deep; г. сон deep sleep; ~ая таре́лка soup plate **2** (*основательный*) profound; thorough; (*серьёзный*) serious **3** (*время, возраст*) late; advanced; extreme; до ~ой но́чи (until) far into the night; ~ая ста́рость extreme old age **4** (*очень сильный*) deep, profound, intense; с ~им приско́рбием with deep regret (*in obituary formula*)

глубоко́[1] *adv.* deep; (fig.) deeply, profoundly

глубоко́[2] *as pred.* it is deep

глубоково́д|ный, ~ен, ~на *adj.* deepwater

глубокоуважа́емый *adj.* (*в письмах*) dear

глубоча́йший *superl. of* ▸ глубо́кий

глум|и́ться, лю́сь, и́шься *impf.* (над + *i.*) to mock (at)

глу́пост|ь, и *f.* **1** (*свойство*) foolishness, stupidity **2** (*поступок*) foolish, stupid action; foolish, stupid thing **3** (*usu. in pl.*) (*вздор*) nonsense; ~и! nonsense!

глу́п|ый, ~, ~а́, ~о, ~ы́ *adj.* foolish, stupid; silly

глуха́р|ь, я́ *m.* (zool.) capercaillie, woodgrouse

глух|о́й, ~, ~а́, ~о *adj.* **1** (*лишенный слуха*) deaf (also fig.); (*as m. n. г.,* ~о́го) deaf person **2** (*звук*) muffled, indistinct **3** (*густо заросший*) thick, dense; г. лес dense forest **4** (*отдалённый*) remote; godforsaken **5** (*затаённый, скрытый*) concealed, hidden **6** (*закрытый*) sealed; blank, blind; ~а́я стена́ blind wall **7** (*время, сезон*) quiet, dead; ~а́я ночь dead of night

глухонем|о́й *adj.* deaf and mute (often offens.), profoundly deaf; (*as m. n. г.,* ~о́го) deaf mute (often offens.), profoundly deaf person

глухот|а́, ы́ *f.* deafness

глу́ше *comp. of* ▸ глухо́й

глуши́тел|ь, я *m.* (tech.) silencer, muffler (AmE)

глуш|и́ть, у́, ~и́шь *impf.* **1** (*pf.* о~) (*рыбу*) to stun, stupefy **2** (*pf.* за~) (*звуки*) to muffle; г. боль to dull pain; г. мото́р to stop the engine **3** (*pf.* за~) (*растения*) to choke, stifle

глуш|ь, и́ *f.* (*заросшая часть*) overgrown part; (*пустынное место*) backwoods (also fig.); жить в ~и́ to live in the back of beyond

глюк, а *m.* (sl.) **1** (*often in pl.*) (*галлюцинация*) trip (*effect of drugs*) (infml) **2** (comput.) glitch, bug (infml)

глюко́з|а, ы *f.* glucose

гля|де́ть, жу́, ди́шь *impf.* (*of* ▸ погляде́ть 1) (на + *a.*) to look (at); to peer (at); to gaze (upon)

гля́н|ец, ца *m.* gloss, lustre (BrE), luster (AmE)

гля́н|уть, ну, нешь *pf.* (на + *a.*) glance (at)

гля́нцев|ый *adj.* glossy, lustrous; ~ая кра́ска gloss paint; г. журна́л glossy magazine, glossy (infml)

г-н (*abbr. of* господи́н) Mr

гна|ть, гоню́, го́нишь, *past* ~л, ~ла́, ~ло *impf.* (*det. of* ▸ гоня́ть) **1** (*стадо*) to drive **2** (*торопить*) to urge (on); (infml, *автомобиль*) to drive hard **3** (infml, *быстро ехать*) to dash, tear **4** (*преследовать*) to hunt, chase **5** (*выгонять*) to throw out, turf out **6** (*водку*) to distil (BrE), distill (AmE)

гна́|ться, гоню́сь, го́нишься, *past* ~лся, ~ла́сь *impf.* (*det. of* ▸ гоня́ться) (за + *i.*) (*преследовать*) to pursue; (*стремиться*) to strive (for, after); (fig., *стараться быть не хуже*) to (try to) keep up with

гнев, а *m.* anger, rage, wrath

гне́в|ный, ~ен, ~на́, ~но *adj.* angry, irate

гнез|ди́ться, ди́тся *impf.* to nest

гнезд|о́, а́, *pl.* гнёзда *nt.* **1** (*птицы*) nest; оси́ное г. wasps' nest (fig.), hornets' nest **2** (*животного*) den, lair (also fig.) **3** (tech.) socket; seat; housing

гнёт, а *m.* oppression, yoke; г. ра́бства the yoke of slavery

гние́ни|е, я *nt.* decay, putrefaction, rot

гнил|о́й, ~, ~а́, ~о *adj.* rotten (also fig.)

гнил|ь, и *f.* **1** (*что-н. гнилое*) rotten stuff **2** (*плесень*) mould

гни|ть, ю́, ёшь *impf.* (*of* ▸ сгнить) to rot, decay

гно|и́ться, ю́сь, и́шься *impf.* to suppurate, fester

гно|й, я, в ~е *or* в ~ю́ *m.* pus

гнойни́к, а́ *m.* (*нарыв*) abscess; (*язва*) ulcer

гно́йный *adj.* purulent

гну́с|ный, ~ен, ~на́, ~но *adj.* vile, foul

гнуть, гну, гнёшь *impf.* (*of* ▸ согну́ть) (*проволоку*) to bend; (*деревья*) to bow;

◆ key word

г. спи́ну, ше́ю (**пе́ред** + *i.*) (*infml*) to cringe (before), kowtow (to)

гну́ться, гнусь, гнёшься *impf.* (*of* ▶ **согну́ться**) (*о материале, палке*) to bend; (*о деревьях*) to be bowed

гобеле́н, а *m.* tapestry

гобо́ист, а *m.* oboist

гобо́ист|ка, ки *f. of* ▶ **гобо́ист**

гобо́|й, я *m.* oboe

говн|о́, а *nt.* (*vulg.*) shit

⚔ **говор|и́ть, ю́, и́шь** *impf.* **1** (*impf. only*) (*владеть устной речью*) to speak, talk; **он ещё не ∼и́т** he can't speak yet; **по-францу́зски** to speak French **2** (*pf.* ▶ **сказа́ть**) (*выражать, сообщать*) to say; to tell; to speak, talk; **г. пра́вду** to tell the truth; **∼я́т** they say, it is said; **стро́го ∼я́** strictly speaking; **не ∼я́ уже́** (о + *p.*) not to mention **3** (*pf.* ▶ **поговори́ть 1**) (о + *p.*) (*беседовать*) to talk (about), discuss **4** (*impf. only*) (*значить*) to mean, convey, signify; **э́то и́мя мне ничего́ не ∼и́т** this name means nothing to me **5** (*impf. only*) (о + *p.*) (*свидетельствовать*) to point (to), indicate, testify (to); **всё ∼и́т о том, что он поко́нчил с собо́й** everything points to his having committed suicide

⚔ **говор|и́ться, и́тся** *impf.* (*pass. of* ▶ **говори́ть**): **как ∼и́тся** as they say, as the saying goes

говя́дин|а, ы *f.* beef

говя́жий *adj.* beef

го́гот, а *m.* (*крик гусей*) cackle; (*infml, хохот*) loud laughter

гого|та́ть, чу́, ∼чешь *impf.* to cackle

⚔ **год, а, о ∼е, в ∼у́, pl. ∼ы́ and ∼а́, g. ∼о́в and лет** *m.* **1** (*g. pl.* **лет**) year; **високо́сный г.** leap year; **кру́глый г.** (*as adv.*) the whole year round; **в бу́дущем, про́шлом ∼у́** next, last year; **в г. а** year, per annum; **спустя́ три ∼а** three years later; **че́рез три ∼а** in three years' time; **ей пошёл пятна́дцатый г.** she is in her fifteenth year **2**: **двадца́тые, тридца́тые** *и т. п.* **∼ы** (*g.* **∼о́в**) (*pl. only*) the twenties, the thirties, *etc.* **3** (**∼á and ∼ы, ∼о́в**) (*pl. only*) years, age, time; **в ∼ы** (+ *g.*) in the days (of); during; **в те ∼ы** in those days; **не по ∼а́м** beyond one's years, precocious(ly)

года́ми *adv.* for years (on end)

го|ди́ться, жу́сь, ди́шься *impf.* **1** (**на** + *a.* or **для** + *g.*, or + *d.*) (*быть полезным*) to be fit (for), be suited (for), do (for), serve (for) **2** (**в** + *nom.-a.*) (*быть впору*) to serve (as), be suited to be **3** (**в** + *nom.-a.*) (*подходить по возрасту*) to be old enough to be; **она́ ∼ди́тся тебе́ в ма́тери** she is old enough to be your mother **4**: **не ∼ди́тся** (+ *inf.*) it does not do (to), one should not

го́дность|ь, и *f.* fitness, suitability; (*билета*) validity; **срок ∼** expiry date

го́д|ный, ∼ен, ∼на́, ∼но, ∼ны́ *adj.* fit, suitable; (*о билете*) valid; **г. к вое́нной слу́жбе** fit for military service

годова́лый *adj.* one-year-old, yearling

годово́й *adj.* annual, yearly

годовщи́н|а, ы *f.* anniversary

гол, а *m.* (*sport*) goal; **заби́ть г.** to score a goal

голени́щ|е, а *nt.* top (*of a boot*)

го́лен|ь, и *f.* shin

голки́пер, а *m.* (*sport*) goalkeeper

голла́нд|ец, ца *m.* Dutchman

Голла́нди|я, и *f.* Holland

голла́ндк|а, и *f.* Dutchwoman

голла́ндский *adj.* Dutch

⚔ **голов|а́, ы́, a. го́лову, pl. го́ловы, голо́в, ∼а́м** *f.* **1** head (also fig.); **на све́жую го́лову** while one is fresh; **быть на́ голову вы́ше кого́-н.** (fig.) to be head and shoulders above sb; **с ∼ы́ до ног** from head to foot; **у неё г. шла кру́гом** her head was going round and round; **у меня́ г. кру́жится** I feel giddy **2** (*единица счёта скота*) head (*of cattle*) **3** (*fig., ум*) head; brain, mind; wits; **ей пришла́ в го́лову мысль** it occurred to her, it struck her **4** (fig., *человек, как носитель каких-либо свойств*) head (= *person*); **горя́чая г.** hothead **5** (*fig., жизнь*) head, life; **на свою́ го́лову** to one's cost; **отвеча́ть ∼о́й за что-н.** to stake one's life on sth

голова́стик, а *m.* tadpole

голо́вк|а, и *f.* (*булавки, спички, цветка*) head; **г. лу́ка** an onion, onion bulb; **г. чеснока́** head of garlic

головн|о́й *adj.* **1** *adj. of* ▶ **голова́**; **∼а́я боль** headache; **г. платок** headscarf; **г. убо́р** headgear, headdress **2** (*anat.*): **г. мозг** brain, cerebrum **3** (fig.) head, leading

головокруже́ни|е, я *nt.* giddiness

головокружи́тельн|ый *adj.* dizzy, giddy (also fig.); **∼ая высота́** dizzy height

головоло́мк|а, и *f.* puzzle, conundrum

го́лод, а (у) *m.* **1** hunger; (*длительное недоедание*) starvation; **умира́ть с ∼у** to die of starvation; **мори́ть ∼ом** to starve (*trans.*) **2** (*народное бедствие*) famine **3** (*недостаток продуктов питания*) dearth, acute shortage

голода́ни|е, я *nt.* **1** (*недоедание*) starvation **2** (*воздержание*) fasting

голод|а́ть, а́ю *impf.* **1** (*скудно питаться*) to starve **2** (*воздерживаться от пищи*) to fast, go without food **3** (*быть на диете*) to diet

голода́ющ|ий *pres. part. act. of* ▶ **голода́ть** *and adj.* starving, hungry; (*as n.* **г., ∼его**, *f.* **∼ая, ∼ей**) starving person

гол|о́дный, ∼оден, ∼одна́, ∼одно, ∼одны́ *adj.* **1** (*желающий есть*) hungry **2** (*вызванный голодом*) hunger, starvation **3** (*скудный*) meagre, scanty, poor; **г. год** lean year

голодо́вк|а, и *f.* (*в знак протеста*) hunger strike

гололёд, а *m.* = гололе́дица

гололе́диц|а, ы *f.* black ice

⚔ **го́лос, а, pl. ∼а́** *m.* **1** voice; **во весь г.** at the top of one's voice **2** (mus.) voice, part

3 (fig., *мне́ние*) voice, word, opinion **4** (pol.) vote; **пра́во** ~a the vote, suffrage; **пода́ть г.** to answer; (**за** + *a.*) to vote (for)

голосло́в|ный, ~**ен,** ~**на** *adj.* unsubstantiated

голосова́ни|е, я *nt.* voting; poll

голос|ова́ть, у́ю *impf.* (*of* ▸ **проголосова́ть**) **1** (**за** + *a. or* **про́тив** + *g.*) to vote (for; against) **2** (*ста́вить на голосова́ние*) to put to the vote, vote on

голосов|о́й *adj.* vocal, (anat.): ~**ы́е свя́зки** vocal chords; ~**а́я по́чта** voice mail

голуби́к|а, и *f.* great bilberry, bog whortleberry (*Vaccinium uliginosum*)

голу́бк|а, и *f.* (*са́мка го́лубя*) female pigeon, dove

голуб|о́й *adj.* pale blue, sky blue; ~**а́я кровь** (fig.) blue blood; (*as m. n.* **голуб|о́й, о́го**) (sl.) gay (= *homosexual*)

го́луб|ь, я, *g. pl.* ~**е́й** *m.* pigeon, dove

голубя́т|ня, ни, *g. pl.* ~**ен** *f.* dovecot(e), pigeon loft

го́л|ый, ~, ~**а́,** ~**о** *adj.* naked, bare (also fig.); ~**ыми рука́ми** with one's bare hands

гольф, а *m.* golf; **игро́к в г.** golfer

го́льф|ы, ов (*sg.* ~, ~**а**) *m. pl.* (infml) knee-length socks

гомеопа́т, а *f.* homeopath(ist)

гомеопати́ческий *adj.* homeopathic

гомеопа́ти|я, и *f.* homeopathy

го́мик, а *m.* (infml, pej.) queer, poof(ter) (infml, pej.), gay

гомосексуали́зм, а *m.* homosexuality

гомосексуали́ст, а *m.* homosexual; gay

гомосексуа́льный *adj.* homosexual; gay

гонг, а *m.* gong

гондо́л|а, ы *f.* **1** (*ло́дка*) gondola **2** (aeron.) car (*of balloon*)

Гондура́с, а *m.* Honduras

гондура́с|ец, ца *m.* Honduran

гондура́с|ка, ки *f. of* ▸ **гондура́сец**

гондура́сский *adj.* Honduran

гоне́ни|е, я *nt.* persecution

го́нк|а, и *f.* (sport) (*usu. in pl.*) race; **г. вооруже́ний** arms race

Гонко́нг, а *m.* Hong Kong

гонора́р, а *m.* fee; **а́вторский г.** royalties

гоноре́|я, и *f.* gonorrhoea (BrE), gonorrhea (AmE)

го́ночный *adj. of* ▸ **го́нка; г. автомоби́ль** racing car

гонча́р, а́ *m.* potter

го́нщик, а *m.* racing driver

гоню́, го́нишь *see* ▸ **гнать**

гоню́сь, го́нишься *see* ▸ **гна́ться**

гоня́|ть, ю *impf.* (indet. of ▸ **гнать**) (*стада́*) to drive; (*птиц*) to chase off

гоня́|ться, юсь *impf.* (indet. of ▸ **гна́ться**) (**за** + *i.*) to chase, pursue; (*на охо́те*) to hunt

---
ᵠ key word

гор... *comb. form, abbr. of* **1** ▸ **городско́й** **2** ▸ **го́рный**

ᵠ **гор|а́, ы́,** *a.* ~**у́,** *pl.* ~**ы,** *d.* ~**а́м** *f.* mountain; hill; **г. Эвере́ст** Mount Everest; **в** ~**у** uphill (also fig.); **под** ~**у** downhill (also fig.)

ᵠ **гора́здо** *adv.* (+ *comp. adjs. and advs.*) much, far, by far; **г. лу́чше** far better

горб, а́, о ~**е́, на** ~**у́** *m.* hump

горба́т|ый, ~, ~**а** *adj.* hunchbacked; **г. нос** hooked nose

горб|и́ться, лю́сь, ишься *impf.* (*of* ▸ **сго́рбиться**) (*о челове́ке*) to stoop; (*о спине́*) to become bent

горбу́ш|а, и *f.* humpback salmon

горд|и́ться, жу́сь, ди́шься *impf.* (+ *i.*) to be proud (of), pride oneself (on)

го́рдост|ь, и *f.* pride

го́рд|ый, ~, ~**а́,** ~**о,** ~**ы́** *adj.* proud

го́р|е, я *nt.* **1** (*печа́ль*) grief, sorrow, woe; **на своё г.** to one's sorrow **2** (*беда́*) misfortune, trouble **3** (*as pred.*) (+ *d.*) (infml) woe (unto); woe betide

гор|ева́ть, ю́ю, ю́ешь *impf.* (**о** + *p.*) to grieve (for)

горе́лк|а, и *f.* burner; **при́мусная г.** Primus stove®

горе́ни|е, я *nt.* burning, combustion; (fig.) enthusiasm

гор|е́ть, ю́, и́шь *impf.* **1** (*о до́ме*) to burn, be on fire **2** (*о дрова́х, све́те*) to burn, be alight; **в ку́хне у них** ~**е́л свет** the lights were on in their kitchen **3** (+ *i.*) (fig.) to burn (with); **г. жела́нием** (+ *inf.*) to be itching (to), be impatient (to)

го́р|ец, ца *m.* mountain-dweller

го́реч|ь, и *f.* **1** (*вкус*) bitter taste **2** (*го́рькое чу́вство*) bitterness

горизо́нт, а *m.* horizon (also fig.); skyline

горизонта́л|ь, и *f.* **1** horizontal; **по** ~**и** across (*in crossword*) **2** (geog.) contour line

горизонта́л|ьный, ~**ен,** ~**ьна** *adj.* horizontal

гори́лл|а, ы *f.* gorilla

гори́ст|ый, ~, ~**а** *adj.* mountainous, hilly

го́рк|а, и *f.* **1** hill, hillock **2** (*для дете́й*) slide

го́рлиц|а, ы *f.* turtle dove

го́рл|о, а *nt.* **1** throat; **дыха́тельное г.** windpipe; **во всё г.** at the top of one's voice; **сыт по г.** full up; (fig.) fed up **2** (*сосу́да*) neck

горлови́н|а, ы *f.* mouth, orifice; **г. вулка́на** crater

гормо́н, а *m.* hormone

гормона́льный *adj.* hormone, hormonal

горн, а *m.* (*печь*) furnace, forge

го́рничн|ая, ой *f.* (*в гости́нице*) chambermaid; (*в до́ме*) maid

горнолы́жник, а *m.* Alpine skier

горнолы́жный *adj.*: **г. спорт** Alpine skiing; ~**ая тра́сса** piste

горноста́|й, я *m.* ermine

го́рн|ый *adj.* **1** *adj. of* ▸ **гора́;** mountain; (*гори́стый*) mountainous; ~**ые лы́жи**

downhill skis; ∼ая цепь mountain range **2** (*минеральный*) mineral; ∼ая поро́да rock; г. хруста́ль rock crystal **3** (*относящийся к разработке недр*) mining; ∼ое де́ло mining

⚹ **го́род, а,** *pl.* ∼á *m.* town; city; вы́ехать зá г. to go out of town; жить зá ∼ом to live out of town

город|о́к, ка́ *m.* small town; университе́тский г. campus

⚹ **городск|о́й** *adj.* urban; city; municipal; (*as m. n.* г., ∼о́го) city-dweller, town-dweller

горожа́н|ин, ина, *pl.* ∼е, ∼ *m.* city-dweller, town-dweller; townsman

горожа́н|ка, ки *f. of* ▶ горожа́нин; townswoman

гороско́п, а *m.* horoscope

горо́х, а (*no pl.*) *m.* **1** pea **2** (*collect.*) peas

горо́ш|ек, ка *m.* **1** *dim. of* ▶ горо́х; души́стый г. (bot.) sweet peas **2** (*collect.*) polka dots; пла́тье в г. polka-dot dress

горо́шин|а, ы *f.* a pea

горст|ь, и, *g. pl.* ∼е́й *f.* **1** (*ладонь с согнутыми пальцами*) cupped hand **2** (*находящееся на/в ладони*) handful (also fig.)

го́рче *comp. of* ▶ го́рький 1

горч|и́ть, и́т *impf.* (*impers.*) to have a bitter taste

горчи́ц|а, ы *f.* mustard

го́рше *comp. of* ▶ го́рький 2

горш|о́к, ка́ *m.* pot; ночно́й г. chamber pot; (*ребёнка*) potty

го́р|ький, ∼ек, ∼ка́, ∼ько, ∼ький *adj.* **1** (*comp.* ∼че) bitter **2** (*comp.* ∼ше) (fig.) bitter; hard; ∼ькие слёзы bitter tears

го́рько¹ *adv.* bitterly

го́рько² *as pred.* **1**: у меня́ г. во рту I have a bitter taste in my mouth **2** it is bitter; мне г. I am very disappointed **3**: г.! ≈ kiss the bride! (*shouted by wedding guests, asking the bride and groom to kiss*)

горю́ч|ее, его *nt.* fuel

горю́чий *adj.* combustible, inflammable

⚹ **горя́ч|ий, ∼, ∼á** *adj.* **1** hot (also fig.); ∼ая ли́ния hotline **2** (*любовь, желание*) passionate **3** (*человек*) hot-tempered **4** (*спор*) heated; (*речь*) impassioned **5** (*время*) busy, hectic

горячо́¹ *adv.* hot

горячо́² *as pred.* it is hot

гос... *comb. form, abbr. of* ▶ госуда́рственный

Госду́м|а, ы *f.* State Duma (*lower house of the Russian parliament*)

го́спел, а *m.* (*жанр музыки*) gospel music

госпитализи́р|овать, ую *impf. and pf.* to hospitalize

го́спитал|ь, я *m.* hospital (esp. mil.)

госпита́льный *adj. of* ▶ го́спиталь

Го́споди *int.* good heavens!; good Lord!

⚹ **господ|и́н, и́на,** *pl.* ∼á, ∼, ∼áм *m.* (*при фамилии*) Mr; ∼á (*при обращении*) gentlemen; (*мужчины и женщины*) ladies and gentlemen

госпо́дств|о, а *nt.* **1** (*власть*) supremacy **2** (*преобладание*) predominance

госпо́дств|овать, ую *impf.* **1** (*обладать властью*) to hold sway **2** (*преобладать*) to predominate, prevail **3** (над + *i.*) (*возвышаться*) to command, dominate; to tower (above)

госпо́дствующий *pres. part. act. of* ▶ госпо́дствовать *and adj.* **1** (*властвующий*) ruling **2** (*преобладающий*) predominant, prevailing **3** (*возвышающийся*) commanding

Госпо́дь, Го́спода, *voc.* **Го́споди** *m.* God, the Lord

госпож|á, и́ *f.* (*при фамилии; замужняя*) Mrs, Ms; (*незамужняя*) Miss, Ms

гостеприи́м|ный, ∼ен, ∼на *adj.* hospitable

гостеприи́мств|о, а *nt.* hospitality

гости́н|ая, ой *f.* living room, sitting room

гости́н|ец, ца *m.* (infml) present

⚹ **гости́ниц|а, ы** *f.* hotel

гост|и́ть, гощу́, гости́шь *impf.* (у + *g.*) to stay (with), be on a visit (to)

⚹ **гост|ь, я,** *g. pl.* ∼е́й *m.* guest, visitor; пойти́ в ∼и (к + *d.*) to visit; быть в гостя́х (у + *g.*) to be a guest (at, of); to be visiting

го́ст|ья, ьи, *g. pl.* ∼ий *f. of* ▶ гость

госуда́рственник, а *m.* supporter of a powerful state

⚹ **госуда́рственн|ый** *adj.* state, public; г. переворо́т coup d'état; ∼ая изме́на high treason; ∼ая слу́жба public service; г. служащий civil servant

⚹ **госуда́рств|о, а** *nt.* state

госуда́р|ь, я *m.* sovereign; (**Г.**) Your Majesty, Sire (*as form of address*)

го́тик|а, и *f.* Gothic (style)

готи́ческий *adj.* Gothic

⚹ **гото́в|ить, лю, ишь** *impf.* **1** to prepare, make ready; (*обучать*) to train **2** (*пищу*) to cook

гото́в|иться, люсь, ишься *impf.* **1** (к + *d.* or + *inf.*) to get ready (for, to); to prepare (oneself) (for) **2** (*предстоять*) to be at hand, in the offing

гото́вност|ь, и *f.* **1** readiness, preparedness; в боево́й ∼и ready for action **2** (*согласие*) readiness, willingness

⚹ **гото́в|ый, ∼, ∼а** *adj.* **1** (к + *d.*) ready (for), prepared (for) **2** (на + *a.* or + *inf.*) (*согласный*) ready (for, to), prepared (for, to); willing (to); мы ∼ы на всё we are prepared for anything; она́ не ∼а идти́ she is not willing to go **3** (+ *inf.*) (*находящийся в состоянии близком к чему-либо*) on the point (of), on the verge (of), ready (to) **4** (*окончательно сделанный*) ready-made, finished; ready-to-wear; ∼ые изде́лия finished articles, the finished product

граб, а *m.* (bot.) hornbeam

грабёж, á *m.* robbery (also fig., infml)

граби́тел|ь, я *m.* robber; (*дома*) burglar

гра́б|ить, лю, ишь *impf.* **1** (*pf.* о∼) (*человека*) to rob; (*дом*) to burgle; (fig.) to rob

г

2 (*pf.* **раз**~) (*город*) to loot, pillage

гра́б|ли, лей *or* **~ель** (*no sg.*) rake

гра́ви|й, я *m.* gravel

гравир|ова́ть, у́ю, у́ешь *impf.* (*of* ▶ **вы́гравировать**) to engrave

гравиро́вк|а, и *f.* engraving

гравита́ци|я, и *f.* (phys.) gravitation

гравю́р|а, ы *f.* engraving, print; (*офорт*) etching

град, а *m.* **1** hail **2** (fig., *поток*) hail, shower, torrent

града́ци|я, и *f.* gradation, scale

гра́дус, а *m.* degree; **у́гол в 40** ~**ов** angle of 40 degrees; **сего́дня 20** ~**ов тепла́, моро́за** it is twenty degrees above, below zero today

гра́дусник, а *m.* thermometer

⚜ **граждани́н, а,** *pl.* **гра́ждане, гра́ждан** *m.* citizen

гражда́н|ка, ки *f. of* ▶ **граждани́н**

⚜ **гражда́нск|ий** *adj.* **1** (law, etc.) civil; citizen's; civic; **г. иск** civil suit; ~**ое пра́во** civil law **2** (*нецерковный, светский*) civil, secular; **г. брак** civil marriage **3** (*невоенный*) civilian; ~**ое пла́тье** civilian clothes **4** (*подобающий гражданину*) civic, befitting a citizen **5**: ~**ая война́** civil war

гражда́нств|о, а *nt.* citizenship, nationality; **права́** ~**a** civic rights

грамм, а *m.* gramme, gram

грамма́тик|а, и *f.* **1** (*раздел языкознания*) grammar **2** (*учебник*) grammar (book)

граммати́ческий *adj.* grammatical

граммофо́н, а *m.* gramophone

гра́мотност|ь, и *f.* **1** (*умение читать и писать*) literacy (also fig.) **2** (*отсутствие грамматических ошибок*) grammatical correctness **3** (*умелость*) competence

гра́мот|ный, ~ен, ~на *adj.* **1** (*умеющий читать и писать*) literate; able to read and write **2** (*без ошибок*) grammatically correct **3** (*умелый*) competent

грампласти́нк|а, и *f.* gramophone record (BrE), phonograph record (AmE)

грана́т, а *m.* pomegranate

грана́т|а, ы *f.* (mil.) shell, grenade; **ручна́я г.** hand grenade

гранатомёт, а *m.* (mil.) grenade launcher

грандио́з|ный, ~ен, ~на *adj.* grandiose; mighty; vast

гранён|ый *adj.* (*алмаз*) cut, faceted; (*стакан*) cut-glass; ~**ое стекло́** cut glass

грани́т, а *m.* granite

грани́тный *adj.* granite

⚜ **грани́ц|а, ы** *f.* **1** frontier, border; **за** ~**ей** abroad; **éхать за** ~**y** to go abroad **2** (fig.) boundary, limit

грани́ч|ить, у, ишь *impf.* (**с** + *i.*) **1** to border (on) **2** (fig.) to border (on), verge (on)

грант, а *m.* grant

⚜ *key word*

гран|ь, и *f.* **1** border, verge, brink; **на** ~**и безу́мия** on the verge of insanity **2** (geom.) face; (*алмаза*) facet

граф, а *m.* count

граф|а́, ы́ *f.* (*столбец*) column; (*раздел*) section

⚜ **гра́фик, а** *m.* **1** (*диаграмма*) graph, chart **2** (*расписание*) schedule; **пло́тный г.** packed schedule; **скользя́щий г.** flexible working hours; flexitime

гра́фик|а, и *f.* (art) graphic art; (comput.) graphics

графи́н, а *m.* carafe; (*с пробкой*) decanter

графи́н|я, и *f.* countess

графи́т, а *m.* **1** (min.) graphite **2** (*карандаша*) pencil lead

графи́ческий *adj.* graphic; **г. паке́т** (comput.) graphics package

гра́фств|о, а *nt.* county

грацио́з|ный, ~ен, ~на *adj.* graceful

гра́ци|я, и *f.* grace, gracefulness

грач, а́ *m.* (zool.) rook

гре́б|ень, ня *m.* **1** (*для расчёсывания волос*) comb **2** (*птицы*) comb, crest **3** (*волны, горы*) crest

гре́бл|я, и *f.* rowing

грейпфру́т, а *m.* grapefruit

грек, а *m.* Greek

гре́лк|а, и *f.* hot-water bottle

грем|е́ть, лю́, и́шь *impf.* (*of* ▶ **прогреме́ть**) to thunder, roar; (*о колоколах*) to peal; (*посудой*) to clatter; (*ключами*) to jangle; (fig.) to resound, ring out

гре́нк|а, и *f.* toast; (*для супа, салата*) crouton

Гренла́нди|я, и *f.* Greenland

гре|сти́, бу́, бёшь, *past* ~**б,** ~**бла́** *impf.* **1** to row; (*веслом, руками*) to paddle **2** (*граблями*) to rake

греть, гре́ю, гре́ешь *impf.* **1** (*intrans.*) to give out warmth **2** (*trans.*) to warm, heat (up); (*предохранять от холода*) to keep warm

гре́|ться, юсь, ешься *impf.* (*о человеке*) to warm oneself; (*о воде*) to warm, heat (up)

грех, а́ *m.* **1** (relig.) (also fig.) sin **2** (*as pred.* + *inf.*) (infml) it is a sin, it is sinful; **не г.** (+ *inf.*) there is no harm (in) **3**: **с** ~**óм попола́м** (only) just

Гре́ци|я, и *f.* Greece

гре́цкий *adj.*: **г. оре́х** walnut

греча́нк|а, и *f. of* ▶ **грек**

гре́ческий *adj.* Greek

гречи́х|а, и *f.* buckwheat

гре́чк|а, и *f.* (infml) buckwheat

гре́чнев|ый *adj.* buckwheat; ~**ая ка́ша** buckwheat porridge

греш|и́ть, у́, и́шь *impf.* **1** (*pf.* **со**~) to sin **2** (*pf.* **по**~) (*против* + *g.*) (*допуская ошибку*) to sin (against)

гре́шник, а *m.* sinner

гре́шни|ца, цы *f. of* ▶ **гре́шник**

гре́ш|ный, ~ен, ~на́, ~но, ~ны́ *adj.* sinful

гриб, á *m.* fungus; (*съедобный*) mushroom; (*поганка*) toadstool

грибно́й *adj. of* ▶ **гриб**; mushroom; **г. дождь** rain while the sun is shining

гриб|о́к, ка́ *m.* **1** *dim. of* ▶ **гриб 2** (biol.) fungus, microorganism

гри́в|а, ы *f.* mane

гри́зли *m. indecl.* grizzly (bear)

грил|ь, я *m.* grill (BrE), broiler (AmE)

грим, а *m.* (theatr.) make-up; greasepaint

грима́с|а, ы *f.* grimace; **стро́ить ~ы** to make *or* pull faces

гримёр, а *m.* (theatr.) make-up artist

гримёрн|ая, ой *f.* (theatr.) make-up (room)

гримир|ова́ть, у́ю *impf.* (*of* ▶ **загримирова́ть**) (theatr.) to make up

гримир|ова́ться, у́юсь *impf.* (*of* ▶ **загримирова́ться**) (theatr.) to make up (*intrans.*); (+ *i. or* **под** + *a.*) (fig.) to make oneself out

грипп, а *m.* influenza; flu

гриф¹, а *m.* (zool.) vulture

гриф², а *m.* (mus.) fingerboard

гриф³, а *m.* (*штемпель*) seal, stamp

гри́фел|ь, я *m.* (*карандаша*) lead

гроб, а, о/на ~е, в ~у́, *pl.* ~ы́ *m.* **1** coffin **2** (fig.) the grave; **вогна́ть в г.** to drive to the grave; **до ~а, по г. жи́зни** (infml) until the end of one's days

гробни́ц|а, ы *f.* tomb

гробов|о́й *adj. of* ▶ **гроб**; ~**áя доска́** (fig.) the grave; **ве́рный до ~о́й доски́** faithful unto death **2** (*мрачный*) sepulchral, deathly; ~**áя тишина́** deathly silence

гроз|á, ы́, *pl.* ~ы́ *f.* **1** (thunder)storm **2** (fig.) (+ *g.*) threat (to)

грозд|ь, и, *pl.* ~и, ~е́й *and* ~ья, ~ьев *f.* cluster, bunch (*of fruit or flowers*)

гро|зи́ть, жу́, зи́шь *impf.* (*pf.* при~) (+ *d. and i. or* + *inf.*) (*предупреждать с угрозой*) to threaten **2** (*pf.* по~) (*делать угрожающий жест*) to make threatening gestures **3** (*no pf.*) (*предстоять*) to threaten; **ему́ ~зи́т банкро́тство** he is threatened with bankruptcy

гро́з|ный, ~ен, ~на́, ~но *adj.* **1** (*угрожающий*) menacing, threatening **2** (*ужасный*) terrible; formidable

гроз|ово́й *adj. of* ▶ **гроза́**; ~**овáя ту́ча** storm cloud, thundercloud

гром, а, *pl.* ~ы́, ~о́в *m.* thunder (also fig.); **уда́р ~a** thunderclap

громá́д|ный, ~ен, ~на *adj.* huge, vast, enormous

гром|и́ть, лю́, и́шь *impf.* (*of* ▶ **разгроми́ть**) to destroy; (mil.) to smash, rout

гро́м|кий, ~ок, ~ка́, ~ко *adj.* **1** loud **2** (*известный*) famous; (*пресловутый*) notorious **3** (*напыщенный*) fine-sounding; ~**кие словá** (iron.) big words

гро́мко *adv.* loud(ly); (*вслух*) aloud

громкоговори́тел|ь, я *m.* loudspeaker

гро́мкост|ь, и *f.* (*звука*) loudness, volume

громов|о́й *adj.* **1** *adj. of* ▶ **гром**; ~**ые раскáты** peals of thunder **2** (*громкий*) thunderous, deafening

громоглáс|ный, ~ен, ~на *adj.* **1** (*громкий*) loud; (*о человеке*) loud-voiced **2** (*открытый*) public, open

громóзд|кий, ~ок, ~ка *adj.* cumbersome, unwieldy

гро́мче *compr. of* ▶ **гро́мкий**, ▶ **гро́мко**

гроссме́йстер, а *m.* grandmaster (*at chess*)

гроте́ск, а *m.* (art) grotesque

гро́хот, а *m.* crash, din

грох|отáть, очу́, о́чешь *impf.* to crash; roll, rumble; roar

грош, á, *pl.* ~и́, ~е́й *m.* (fig., infml) penny, cent; **рабо́тать за ~и** to work for peanuts

груб|и́ть, лю́, и́шь *impf.* (*of* ▶ **нагруби́ть**) (+ *d.*) to be rude (to)

гру́бо *adv.* **1** (*неискусно*) crudely **2** (*невежливо*) rudely **3** (*приблизительно*) roughly; **г. говоря́** roughly speaking

гру́бост|ь, и *f.* **1** (*невежливость*) rudeness **2** (*замечание*) rude remark; **говори́ть ~и** to be rude

гру́б|ый, ~, ~á, ~о, ~ы́ *adj.* **1** (*без изящества*) coarse, rough **2** (*недопустимый*) gross, flagrant; **г. обмáн** gross deception **3** (*человек, слово*) rude; coarse, crude **4** (*приблизительный*) rough

грудн|о́й *adj. of* ▶ **грудь**; ~**áя кле́тка** (anat.) thorax; **г. ребёнок** baby

✓ **груд|ь**, и́, *i.* ~ью, в/на/о ~и́, *pl.* ~и, ~е́й *f.* **1** (anat.) chest **2** (*женщины*) breast; bosom, bust; **корми́ть ~ью** to breastfeed

✓ **груз**, а *m.* **1** (*тяжесть*) weight; (*кладь*) load, cargo, freight **2** (fig.) weight, burden

грузи́н, а, *g. pl.* **г. ~** Georgian

грузи́н|ка, ки *f. of* ▶ **грузи́н**

грузи́нский *adj.* Georgian

гру|зи́ть, жу́, ~зишь *impf.* **1** (*pf.* за~ *and* на~) (*судно*) to load **2** (*pf.* по~) (*товар*) to load

гру|зи́ться, жу́сь, ~зишься *impf.* (*of* ▶ **погрузи́ться 2**) (*о судне*) to load (*intrans.*), take on cargo; (*о людях*) to board

Гру́зи|я, и *f.* Georgia

грузови́к, á *m.* lorry (BrE), truck

грузов|о́й *adj.* goods, cargo, freight; ~**о́е су́дно** cargo boat, freighter

грузоподъёмност|ь, и *f.* payload capacity; freight-carrying capacity

гру́зчик, а *m.* loader; (*в порту*) docker (BrE), stevedore

грунт, а *m.* (*почва*) soil, earth; (*дно*) bottom

грунтов|о́й *adj. of* ▶ **грунт**; ~**ые во́ды** subsoil waters; ~**áя доро́га** dirt road

✓ **гру́пп|а**, ы *f.* group; **г. кро́ви** (med.) blood group; **операти́вная г.** task force; **рабо́чая г.** working party

группир|ова́ть, у́ю *impf.* (*of* ▶ **сгруппирова́ть**) to group;

(*классифицировать*) to classify

группиро́вк|а, и *f.* **1** grouping; (*классификация*) classification; **г. сил** (mil.) distribution of forces **2** (*совокупность лиц*) group, grouping **3** (*бандитская*) (criminal) gang

группов|о́й *adj.* group; **~ые заня́тия** group study, group work

гру|сти́ть, щу́, сти́шь *impf.* to grieve, mourn; (**о** + *p. or* **по** + *d.*) to pine (for)

гру́стно[1] *adv.* sadly, sorrowfully

гру́стно[2] *as pred.* it is sad; **ей г.** she feels sad

гру́ст|ный, ~ен, ~на́, ~но *adj.* sad, melancholy

грусть, и *f.* sadness, melancholy

гру́ш|а, и *f.* **1** pear **2**: **боксёрская г.** punchball

гры́ж|а, и *f.* (med.) hernia

гры́з|ть, у́, ёшь, *past* **~, ~ла** *impf.* to gnaw; to nibble; **г. но́гти** to bite one's nails

грызу́н, а́ *m.* rodent

гряд|а́, ы́, *pl.* **~ы, ~, ~а́м** *f.* **1** (*pl.* **~ы, ~, ~а́м**) (*гор*) ridge **2** (*pl.* **~ы, ~, ~а́м**) (*в огоро́де*) bed **3** (*pl.* **~ы, ~, ~а́м**) (*ряд*) row, series

гря́дк|а, и *f. dim. of* ▶ **гряда́** 2

гряду́щ|ий *adj.* coming, future; **~ие го́ды** years to come; (*as nt. n.* **~ее, ~его**) the future

гря́зно[1] *adv. of* ▶ **гря́зный**

гря́зно[2] *as pred.* it is dirty

гря́з|ный, ~ен, ~на́, ~но, ~ны́ *adj.* **1** (*покрытый грязью*) muddy **2** (*нечистый*) dirty; **~ное бельё** dirty washing (also fig.) **3** (*неопрятный*) untidy **4** (fig., *непристойный*) dirty, filthy; **~ное де́ло** dirty business

грязь, и, о ~и, в ~и́ *f.* **1** mud (also fig.) **2** (*in pl.*) (*лечебное средство*) mud baths **3** (*отсутствие чистоты*) dirt, filth (also fig.)

губ|а́, ы́, *pl.* **~ы, ~, ~а́м** *f.* lip; **наду́ть ~ы** to pout

⚲ **губерна́тор, а** *m.* governor

губ|и́ть, лю́, ~ишь *impf.* (*of* ▶ **погуби́ть**) (*разрушать*) to destroy; (*портить*) to ruin, spoil

гу́бк|а, и *f.* sponge; **мыть ~ой** to sponge

губн|о́й *adj.* lip; **~а́я пома́да** lipstick

гуверна́нтк|а, и *f.* governess

гувернёр, а *m.* tutor

гуде́ни|е, я *nt.* drone; hum; (*об автомобильном гудке*) honk

гу|де́ть, жу́, ди́шь *impf.* **1** to drone; to hum; (*impers.*) **у меня́ ~де́ло в уша́х** there was a buzzing in my ears **2** (*о гудке*) to hoot; to honk

гуд|о́к, ка́ *m.* **1** (*устройство*) (*автомобиля*) horn; (*фабрики*) siren **2** (*звук*) hoot(ing); honk; toot **3** (teleph.) tone

гул, а *m.* (*машин, голосов*) drone, hum; (*орудий*) rumble

гуля́нь|е, ья, *g. pl.* **~ий** *nt.* (*празднество*) outdoor party

гуля́|ть, ю *impf.* (*of* ▶ **погуля́ть**) **1** to walk, stroll; to go for a walk **2** (infml, *веселиться*) to make merry, have a good time

гуля́ш, а́ *m.* (cul.) goulash

гумани́зм, а *m.* humanism

гуманита́р|ный *adj.* **1** pertaining to the humanities; **~ые нау́ки** the humanities, the liberal arts; **~ое образова́ние** liberal education **2** (*гуманный*) humane; **~ая по́мощь** humanitarian aid

гума́нность|, и *f.* humanity, humaneness

гума́н|ный, ~ен, ~на *adj.* humane

гурма́н, а *m.* gourmet

гу́ру *m. indecl.* guru

гуса́р, а *m.* hussar

гу́сениц|а, ы *f.* **1** (zool.) caterpillar **2** (*трактора*) (caterpillar) track

гус|ёнок, ёнка, *pl.* **~я́та** *m.* gosling

гу́сто *adv.* thickly, densely

густ|о́й, ~, ~а́, ~о, ~ы́ *adj.* **1** thick, dense; **~ые бро́ви** bushy eyebrows **2** (*о цвете*) deep, rich

густонаселённый *adj.* densely populated

густот|а́, ы́ *f.* **1** thickness, density **2** (*цвета*) deepness, richness

гусь, я, *pl.* **~и, ~ей** *m.* goose

гу́щ|а, и *f.* **1** (*осадок*) sediment; **кофе́йная г.** coffee grounds **2** (*чаща*) thicket; (fig.) thick, centre; **в са́мой ~е собы́тий** in the thick of things

гу́ще *comp. of* ▶ **густо́й**

Гц (*abbr. of* **герц**) Hz (= hertz)

гэ́льский *adj.* Gaelic

ГЭС *f. indecl.* (*abbr. of* **гидроэлектроста́нция**) hydroelectric power station

да¹ *particle* **1** yes **2** (*interrog.*) yes?, is that so?, really? **3** (*emph.*) why; well; **да нет!** of course not!; not likely! **4** (*emph. pred.*): **когдá-н. э́то да кóнчится** it must end some time **5**: **вот э́то да!** (*infml*) splendid!

да² *particle* (+ *3rd pers. pres. or fut. of v.*) (*пусть*) may, let; **да здрáвствует Россия!** long live Russia!

да³ *conj.* **1** *mainly in conventional phrr.* (*и*) and; **кóжа да кóсти** skin and bone **2**: **да ещё** (*к тому же*) and (besides); and what is more **3**: **да и тóлько** and that's all **4** but; **я охóтно проводил бы тебя, да врéмени нéт** I would gladly come with you, but I haven't the time

давáй and **давáйте** *imper.* **1** (+ *inf. or 1st pers. pl. of fut.*) let's **2** (+ *imper.*) (*infml*) come on; **давáй, расскажи что-н.!** come on, tell us a story!

да|вáть, ю, ёшь *impf. of* ▶ **дать**

да|вáться, юсь, ёшься *impf.* (*of* ▶ **дáться**) **1** *pass. of* ▶ **давáть 2**: **легкó д.** to come easily, naturally; **рýсский язык емý даётся легкó** Russian comes easily to him

дав|и́ть, лю́, ~ишь *impf.* **1** (+ *a. or* на + *a.*) to press (upon); (*о сапоге*) to pinch; (fig., *угнетать*) to oppress, weigh (upon) **2** (*насекомых*) to crush; to trample; (*о машине*) to run over **3** (*лимон, сок*) to squeeze

дав|и́ться, лю́сь, ~ишься *impf.* (*of* ▶ **подави́ться**) (+ *i. or* от + *g.*) to choke (with)

дáвк|а, и *f.* throng, crush

давлéни|е, я *nt.* pressure

дáвн|ий *adj.* **1** ancient **2** (*существующий издавна*) of long standing; **с ~их пор, времён** for a long time

давнó *adv.* **1** (*много времени тому назад*) long ago; **2** (*в течение долгого времени*) for a long time

давны́м-давнó *adv.* (*infml*) ages ago

Дагестáн, а *m.* Dagestan

дагестáн|ец, ца *m.* Dagestani

дагестáн|ка, ки *f. of* ▶ **дагестáнец**

дагестáнский *adj.* Dagestani

дáже *particle* even; **éсли д.** even if; **óчень д. плóхо** extremely bad

дактилоскопи́|я, и *f.* identification by means of fingerprints; **гéнная д.** genetic fingerprinting

далáй-лáм|а, ы *m.* Dalai Lama

дáлее *adv.* further; **и так д.** (*abbr.* **и т. д.**) and so on, et cetera

дал|ёкий, ~ёк, ~екá, ~екó and ~ёко *adj.* (*страна, выстрел*) distant; **д. путь** long journey; **~ёкое прóшлое** distant past

далекó¹ *adv.* **1** (*о расстоянии*) far, far off; (**от** + *g.*) far (from) **2** (fig.) far, by a long way, by much; (*of time*): **бы́ло д. за пóлночь** it was long after midnight; **д. не** far from

далекó² *as pred.* it is far, it is a long way; (+ *d. and* до + *g.*) (fig.) to be far (from), much inferior (to); **емý д. до совершéнства** he is far from perfect

дал|ь, и, о ~и, в ~й *f.* **1** (*далёкое пространство*) distance; distant prospect **2** (*infml, далёкое место*) distant spot

дальневостóчный *adj.* Far Eastern

дальнéйш|ий *adj.* further, furthest; **в ~ем** (*в будущем*) in future, henceforth

дáльн|ий *adj.* **1** (*далёкий*) distant, remote; **Д. Востóк** the Far East; **~ее плáвание** long voyage; **~его дéйствия** long-range; **~его слéдования** (*о поезде*) long-distance **2** (*о родстве*) distant

дальнови́д|ный, ~ен, ~на *adj.* far-sighted

дальнозóр|кий, ~ок, ~ка *adj.* long-sighted (BrE), far-sighted (AmE); (fig.) far-sighted

дáльност|ь, и *f.* distance; range

дальтóник, а *m.* colour-blind (BrE), color-blind (AmE) person

дáльше 1 *comp. of* ▶ **далёкий 2** *adv.* further; **д. нéкуда** (*infml*) that's the limit; **ти́ше éдешь, д. бýдешь** (*proverb*) more haste, less speed **3** *adv.* (*продолжая начатое*) further; **д.!** go on! **4** *adv.* (*затем*) then, next **5** *adv.* (*далее*) longer

дáм|а, ы *f.* **1** (*женщина*) lady **2** (*игральная карта*) queen

дáмб|а, ы *f.* dike

дáм|ский *adj. of* ▶ **дáма**; **~ская сýмка** ladies' handbag

Дáни|я, и *f.* Denmark

дáнн|ые, ых (*no sg.*) **1** (also comput.) data; (*факты*) facts, information **2** (*свойства*) qualities, gifts

дáнн|ый *p.p.p. of* ▶ **дать** *and adj.* given; present; in question; **в д. момéнт** at present; **в ~ом слýчае** in this case

дан|ь, и *f.* (fig., *моде, традиции*) tribute; debt; **отдáть д.** (+ *d.*) to pay tribute to, recognize

дар, а, *pl.* **~ы́** *m.* **1** (*подарок*) gift, donation **2** (+ *g.*) (*талант, способность*) gift (of)

дари́тел|ь, я *m.* donor

дар|и́ть, ю́, ~ишь *impf.* (*of* ▶ **подари́ть**) (+ *d. and a.*) (*давать*) to give

дарови́ни|е, я *nt.* gift, talent

даровóй *adj.* free (of charge), gratuitous

да́ром *adv.* **1** (*бесплатно*) free (of charge), gratis **2** (*напрасно*) in vain, to no purpose; **пропа́сть д.** to be wasted

✓ **да́т|а, ы** *f.* date

да́тельный *adj.* (gram.) dative

дати́р|овать, ую *impf. and pf.* to date

да́тский *adj.* Danish

да́тчик, а *m.* sensor

✓ **дать, дам, дашь, даст, дади́м, дади́те, даду́т,** *past* **дал, дала́, да́ло, да́ли** *pf.* (*of* ▶ **дава́ть**) **1** to give; **д. взаймы́** to lend (*money*); **на чай** to tip; **д. конце́рт** to give a concert **2** to give, administer; **д. лека́рство** to give medicine **3** (**по** + *d. or* **в** + *a.*) (infml, *уда́рить*) to give (it); to hit (on; in) **4** (fig.) to give; **д. сло́во** to give one's word **5** (fig.) to give, grant; **д. во́лю** (+ *d.*) to give (free) rein (to), give vent (to); **д. доро́гу** (+ *d.*) to make way (for) **6** (*with certain nn. expr. action related to meaning of n.*): **д. звоно́к** to ring (*a bell*); **д. тре́щину** to crack **7** (+ *inf.*) (*позволить*) to let; **д. поня́ть** to give to understand; **да́йте ему́ сказа́ть** let him speak

да́ться, да́мся, да́шься *etc.*, *past* **да́лся, дала́сь** *pf. of* ▶ **дава́ться**

да́ч|а, и *f.* **1** (*загородный дом*) dacha **2**: **быть на ∼е** to be in the country; **пое́хать на ∼у** to go to the country

да́чник, а *m.* (holiday) visitor (*in the country*)

дБ (*abbr. of* **дециб́ел**) dB, decibel(s)

✓ **два,** *f.* **две,** *m., f., nt.* **двух, двум, двумя́, о двух** *пит.* two; **в двух слова́х** briefly, in short; **в д. счёта** in no time; **в двух шага́х** a short step away; **ка́ждые д. дня** every other day

двадцати́... *comb. form* twenty-

двадцатиле́тний *adj.* **1** (*срок*) twenty-year, of twenty years **2** (*человек*) twenty-year-old

двадца́т|ый *adj.* twentieth; **одна́ ∼ая** a twentieth; **∼ое января́** the twentieth of January; **∼ые го́ды** the twenties

два́дцат|ь, и, *i.* **ью** *пит.* twenty; **д. оди́н** *и т. п.* twenty-one, *etc.*

два́жды *adv.* twice; **д. два — четы́ре** twice two is four

двена́дцатый *adj.* twelfth

двена́дцат|ь, и *пит.* twelve

дверно́й *adj. of* ▶ **дверь**

две́р|ца, ы, *g. pl.* **∼ец** *f.* door (*of car, cupboard, etc.*)

✓ **двер|ь, и, о ∼и, в ∼и,** *pl.* **∼и, ∼е́й,** *i.* **∼я́ми** *and* **∼ьми́** *f.* door; **в ∼я́х** in the doorway

две́сти, двухсо́т, двумста́м, двумяста́ми, о двухста́х *пит.* two hundred

✓ **дви́гател|ь, я** *m.* motor, engine; (fig.) motive force

дви́га|ть, ю *and* **дви́жу** *impf.* (*of* ▶ **дви́нуть**) **1** (∼**ю**) to move **2** (∼**ю**) (+ *i.*) (*шевелить*) to move (*part of the body*); to make a movement (of) **3** (**дви́жу**) (*приводить в*

✓ *key word*

движе́ние) to set in motion, get going (also fig.)

дви́га|ться, юсь *and* **дви́жусь** *impf.* (*of* ▶ **дви́нуться**) **1** to move; **д. вперёд** to advance (also fig.) **2** (*отправляться*) to start, get going **3** *pass. of* ▶ **дви́гать**

✓ **движе́ни|е, я** *nt.* **1** movement; motion; **привести́ в д.** to set in motion; **д. «зелёных»** the green movement **2** (*физическое*) movement, exercise **3** (*дорожное*) traffic; **односторо́ннее д.** one-way traffic

дви́|нуть, ну, нешь *pf. of* ▶ **дви́гать**

дви́|нуться, нусь, нешься *pf. of* ▶ **дви́гаться**

дво́е, двои́х *пит.* **1** (collect.) two; **нас бы́ло д.** there were two of us; **д. су́ток** forty-eight hours **2** (+ *nn. denoting objects usu. found in pairs*) two pairs; **д. чуло́к** two pairs of stockings

двоето́чи|е, я *nt.* (gram.) colon

дво́|иться, ю́сь, и́шься *impf.* (*казаться двойным*) to appear double; **у него́ ∼и́лось в глаза́х** he saw (objects) double

дво́ичный *adj.* (math.) binary

дво́йк|а, и *f.* **1** (*цифра, игральная карта*) two **2** (*отметка*) 'two' (out of five) **3** (infml, *автобус, трамвай*) No. 2 (*bus, tram, etc.*)

двойни́к, а́ *m.* (*кого-н.*) double

двойн́|о́й *adj.* double; **∼а́я фами́лия** double-barrelled (BrE), double-barreled (AmE) surname

дво́|йня, йни, *g. pl.* **∼ен** *f.* twins

✓ **двор, а́** *m.* **1** (*при одном доме*) yard; (*между домами*) courtyard **2**: **ско́тный д.** farmyard **3**: **на ∼е́** out of doors, outside **4** (*королевский*) court; **при ∼е́** at court

дворе́|ц, ца́ *m.* palace

дворе́цк|ий, ого *m.* butler

дво́рник, а *m.* **1** (*работник*) caretaker **2** (infml, *в машине*) windscreen wiper (BrE), windshield wiper (AmE)

дворяни́|н, и́на, *pl.* **∼е, ∼** *m.* nobleman

дворя́н|ка, ки *f. of* ▶ **дворяни́н**

дворя́нский *adj.* of the nobility

дворя́нств|о, а *nt.* (collect.) nobility

двою́родный *adj.* related through grandparent; **д. брат** (first) cousin (*male*); **д. дя́дя** (first) cousin once removed

дву..., двух... *comb. form* bi-, di-, two-, double-

двузна́чный *adj.* two-digit

двули́ч|ный, ∼ен, ∼на *adj.* (fig.) two-faced

двуро́г|ий *adj.* two-horned; **∼ая луна́** crescent moon

двуру́чный *adj.* two-handled

двусмы́слен|ный, ∼, ∼на *adj.* ambiguous

двуспа́льный *adj.* double (*of beds*)

двуство́лк|а, и *f.* double-barrelled (BrE), double-barreled gun (AmE)

двусторо́н|ний, ∼ен, ∼ня *adj.* **1** double-sided; **∼нее воспале́ние лёгких** double pneumonia **2** (*движение*) two-way **3** (*соглашение*) bilateral

двухдне́вный *adj.* two-day

двухколёсный *adj.* two-wheeled
двухме́стный *adj.* two-seater; **д. но́мер** double room
двухмото́рный *adj.* twin-engined
двухсо́тый *adj.* two-hundredth
двухчасово́й *adj.* **1** (*фильм*) two-hour **2** (*поезд*) two o'clock
двухэта́жный *adj.* two-storey (BrE), two-story (AmE); (*автобус*) double-decker
двуязы́чный *adj.*, ~ен, ~на *adj.* bilingual
деба́т|ы, ов (*no sg.*) debate
де́бет, а *m.* debit
дебет|ова́ть, у́ю *impf. and pf.* to debit
дебето́в|ый *adj. of* ▶ де́бет; ~ая ка́рточка debit card
дебил, а *m.* **1** learning-disabled person **2** (infml, pej.) moron
де́бр|и, ей (*no sg.*) **1** jungle; thickets **2** (fig.) maze, labyrinth
дебю́т, а *m.* debut
дебюта́нт, а *m.* debutant
дебюта́нтк|а, и *f.* debutante
дебюти́р|овать, ую *impf. and pf.* to make one's debut
де́в|а, ы *f.* **1** (obs.) girl, maiden; **ста́рая д.** (infml) old maid **2** (**Д.**) (*созвездие*) Virgo
девальва́ци|я, и *f.* devaluation
дева́|ть, ю *impf. of* ▶ деть
дева́|ться, юсь *impf. of* ▶ деться
де́вер|ь, я, *pl.* ~ья́, ~е́й *m.* brother-in-law (*husband's brother*)
деви́з, а *m.* motto
деви́ц|а, ы *f.* girl, maiden
деви́честв|о, а *nt.* girlhood; **в ~е Ивано́ва** née Ivanova
де́вич|ий *adj.* girlish; ~ья фами́лия maiden name
де́вочк|а, и *f.* (little) girl
де́вственник, а *m.* virgin
де́вственниц|а, ы *f.* virgin
де́вственност|ь, и *f.* virginity; chastity
де́вствен|ный, ~, ~на *adj.* **1** (*целомудренный*) virgin **2** (*невинный*) virginal; innocent **3** (fig.) virgin; **д. лес** virgin forest
де́вушк|а, и *f.* **1** (unmarried) girl **2** (infml, *обращение*) miss
девчо́нк|а, и *f.* (infml) (little) girl
девяно́ст|о, *g., d., i., and p.* а *num.* ninety
девяно́стый *adj.* ninetieth
де́вятер|о, ы́х *num.* (*collect.*) nine; **нас д.** there are nine of us
девятисо́тый *adj.* nine-hundredth
девя́тк|а, и *f.* **1** (*цифра, игральная карта*) nine **2** (infml, *автобус, трамвай*) No. 9 (*bus, tram, etc.*) **3** (*группа из девятерых*) (group of) nine
девятна́дцатый *adj.* nineteenth
девятна́дцат|ь, и *num.* nineteen
девя́тый *adj.* ninth
де́вят|ь, й, *i.* ью *num.* nine

девятьсо́т, девятисо́т, девятиста́м, девятьюста́ми, о девятиста́х *num.* nine hundred
дёг|оть, тя (*no pl.*) *m.* tar
деграда́ци|я, и *f.* degradation
дегради́р|овать, ую *impf. and pf.* to become degraded
дегуста́ци|я, и *f.* tasting; **д. вин** wine tasting
дед, а *m.* **1** grandfather; (*in pl.*) (fig.) grandfathers, forefathers **2** (infml, *старик*) grandad, grandpa **3**: **Д. Моро́з** Father Christmas, Santa Claus
дедовщи́н|а, ы *f.* (mil., sl.) bullying, harassment (*of subordinates*)
деду́кци|я, и *f.* deduction
де́душк|а, и *m.* grandfather, grandpa
дееприча́сти|е, я *nt.* (gram.) gerund (*e.g.* **читая, прочита́в**)
дееспосо́б|ный, ~ен, ~на *adj.* **1** able to function, active **2** (law) capable
дежу́р|ить, ю, ишь *impf.* **1** (*быть дежурным*) to be on duty **2** (*неотлучно находиться*) to be in constant attendance
дежу́рн|ый *adj.* **1** duty; on duty; **д. офице́р** (mil.) orderly officer; ~ая апте́ка chemist's shop open outside normal opening hours **2** (*as m. n.* **д.**, ~ого, *f.* ~ая, ~ой) man, woman on duty; **кто д.?** who is on duty?
дежу́рств|о, а *nt.* (being on) duty; **гра́фик ~** rota; (mil.) roster
дезерти́р, а *m.* deserter
дезерти́р|овать, ую *impf. and pf.* to desert
дезинфе́кци|я, и *f.* disinfection
дезинфици́р|овать, ую *impf. and pf.* to disinfect
дезинформа́ци|я, и *f.* misinformation; (*намеренная*) disinformation
дезинформи́р|овать, ую *impf. and pf.* to misinform
дезодора́нт, а *m.* deodorant
дезорганиз|ова́ть, у́ю *impf. and pf.* to disrupt
дезориенти́р|овать, ую *impf. and pf.* to disorient
де́йстви|е, я *nt.* **1** (*деятельность*) action, operation; activity; **ввести́ в д.** to bring into operation, bring into force **2** (*функционирование*) functioning (*of a machine, etc.*) **3** (*влияние*) effect; action; **под ~ем** (+ *g.*) under the influence (of) **4** (*события, о которых идёт речь*) action (*of a story, etc.*) **5** (*часть пьесы*) act **6** (*in pl.*) (*поступки*) actions; (mil.) operations
действи́тельно *adv.* really; indeed
действи́тельност|ь, и *f.* reality; **в ~и** in reality, in fact
действи́тель|ный, ~ен, ~на *adj.* **1** (*настоящий*) real, actual; true, authentic; ~ное положе́ние веще́й the true state of affairs; ~ная слу́жба (mil.) active service **2** (*имеющий силу*) valid
де́йств|овать, ую *impf.* **1** (*impf. only*)

д

(*совершать действия*) to act; (*функционировать*) to work, function; to operate **2** (*pf.* **по~**) (**на** + *a.*) (*влиять*) to affect, have an effect (upon), act (upon); **лека́рство ~ует** the medicine is taking effect

де́йствующ|ий *pres. part. act. of* ▶ **де́йствовать** *and adj.*: **~ая а́рмия** army in the field; **д. вулка́н** active volcano; **~ие ли́ца** (*theatr.*) characters

дека́бр|ь, я́ *m.* December

дека́брьский *adj. of* ▶ **дека́брь**

дека́д|а, ы *f.* (*срок*) ten-day period

деклара́ци|я, и *f.* declaration; **нало́говая д.** tax return

деклари́р|овать, ую *impf. and pf.* to declare, proclaim

декоди́р|овать, ую *impf. and pf.* to decode

декольте́ *nt. indecl.* décolleté (*also as adj.*); décolletage

декорати́в|ный, ~ен, ~на *adj.* decorative, ornamental

декора́тор, а *m.* (*помещения*) interior decorator; (*theatr.*) scene painter

декора́ци|я, и *f.* (*theatr.*) set, scenery

декре́тный *adj.*: **д. о́тпуск** maternity leave

де́ланный *adj.* artificial, forced, affected

де́ла|ть, ю *impf.* (*of* ▶ **сде́лать**)
  1 (*производить*) to make **2** (*приводить в какое-н. состояние*) to make; **д. кого́-н. несча́стным** to make sb unhappy **3** (*поступать*) to do; **д. не́чего** it can't be helped **4** (+ *var. nn.*) to make, do, give; **д. вид** to pretend, feign; **д. вы́воды** to draw conclusions

де́ла|ться, юсь *impf.* (*of* ▶ **сде́латься**)
  1 (*становиться*) to become, get, grow **2** (*происходить*) to happen; **что там ~ется?** what is going on?

делега́т, а *m.* delegate

делега́ци|я, и *f.* delegation; group

делеги́р|овать, ую *impf. and pf.* to delegate

деле́ни|е, я *nt.* **1** division **2** (*на шкале*) point, degree, unit

Де́ли *m. indecl.* Delhi

деликате́с, а *m.* delicacy; **магази́н ~ов** delicatessen

делика́тност|ь, и *f.* delicacy

делика́т|ный, ~ен, ~на *adj.* delicate

дел|и́ть, ю́, ~ишь *impf.* **1** (*pf.* **раз~**) to divide; **д. шесть на́ три** to divide six by three **2** (*pf.* **по~**) (**с** + *i.*) to share (with); **д. с кем-н. го́ре и ра́дость** to share sb's sorrows and joys

дел|и́ться, ю́сь, ~ишься *impf.* **1** (*pf.* **раз~**) (**на** + *a.*) to divide (into) **2** (*pf.* **по~**) (+ *i. and* **с** + *i.*) to share (with); to communicate (to); **д. куско́м хле́ба с кем-н.** to share a crust of bread with sb **3** (*impf. only*) (**на** + *a.*) to be divisible (by); **число́ со́рок де́вять ~ится на семь** forty-nine is divisible by seven

де́л|о, а, *pl.* **~а́, ~, ~а́м** *nt.* **1** (*работа, занятие*) business, affair(s); **по ~у, по ~а́м** on business; **э́то моё д.** that is my affair; **име́ть д.** (**с** + *i.*) to have to do (with), deal (with); **не вме́шивайтесь не в своё д.** mind your own business; **как (ва́ши) ~а́?** how are things going (with you)?, how are you getting on?; **привести́ свои́ ~а́ в поря́док** to put one's affairs in order; **како́е мне до э́того д.?** what has this to do with me?; **пе́рвым ~ом** in the first instance, first of all **2** (*идеи*) cause; **д. ми́ра** the cause of peace **3** (+ *adj.*) (*специальность*) occupation; (*предприятие*) business, concern; **го́рное д.** mining **4** matter, point; **д. вку́са** matter of taste; **д. че́сти** point of honour; **д. в том, что...** the point is that ...; **в то́м-то и д.** that's (just) the point; **не в э́том д.** that's not the point **5** (*факт*) fact, deed; thing; **на са́мом ~е** in actual fact, as a matter of fact; **в са́мом ~е** really, indeed **6** (*поступок*) act, deed **7** (*law, судебное*) case; cause; **вести́ д.** to plead a cause; **возбуди́ть д.** (**про́тив** + *g.*) to bring an action (against), institute proceedings (against) **8** (*досье*) file, dossier; **ли́чное д.** personal file

делови́т|ый, ~, ~а *adj.* businesslike, efficient

делов|о́й *adj.* **1** business; work; **~о́е письмо́** business letter; **~а́я пое́здка** business trip **2** (*человек, тон*) businesslike

де́льт|а, ы *f.* delta

дельтапла́н, а *m.* hang-glider (*craft*)

дельтапланери́ст, а *m.* hang-glider (*person*)

дельтапланери́ст|ка, ки *f. of* ▶ **дельтапланери́ст**

дельфи́н, а *m.* dolphin

демаго́г, а *m.* demagogue

демаго́ги|я, и *f.* demagogy

демилитариз|ова́ть, у́ю *impf. and pf.* to demilitarize

демисезо́н|ный *adj.*: **~ое пальто́** light coat (*for spring and autumn wear*)

демобилиз|ова́ть, у́ю *impf. and pf.* to demobilize

демобилиз|ова́ться, у́юсь *impf. and pf.* to be demobilized

демографи́ческий *adj.* demographic; **д. взрыв** population explosion

демокра́т, а *m.* democrat

демократи́ческий *adj.* democratic

демокра́ти|я, и *f.* democracy

де́мон, а *m.* demon

демонстра́нт, а *m.* (*pol.*) demonstrator

демонстра́нт|ка, ки *f. of* ▶ **демонстра́нт**

демонстрати́в|ный, ~ен, ~на *adj.* (*вызывающий*) demonstrative, done for effect

демонстра́ци|я, и *f.* **1** demonstration **2** (*публичный показ*) showing (*of a film, etc.*)

демонстри́р|овать, ую *impf. and pf.* (*pf. also* **про~**) to show, display; to give a demonstration (of)

демонти́р|овать, ую *impf. and pf.* (tech.) to dismantle

деморализ|ова́ть, у́ю *impf. and pf.* to demoralize

⚬ **де́нежный** *adj.* **1** monetary; money; **д. автома́т** cash dispenser; **д. знак** banknote; **д. перево́д** money order **2** (infml, *богатый*) rich; **д. мешо́к** moneybags

⚬ **день, дня** *m.* **1** day; afternoon; **в 4 ч дня** at 4 p.m.; **днём** in the afternoon; **д. рожде́ния** birthday; **д. ото дня** with every passing day, day by day; **день день** one fine day; **изо дня в д.** day after day; **на друго́й, сле́дующий д.** next day; **на днях** (*недавно*) the other day; (*скоро*) one of these days, any day now; **со дня на д.** daily, from day to day; **че́рез д.** every other day **2** (*in pl.*) (*время; жизнь*) days; **его́ дни сочтены́** his days are numbered

⚬ **де́н|ьги, ег, ьга́м** *pl.* money; **ме́лкие д.** small change; **нали́чные д.** cash, ready money

⚬ **департа́мент, а** *m.* department

депе́ш|а, и *f.* dispatch

депо́ *nt. indecl.* (rail.) depot

депози́т, а *m.* (fin.) deposit

депорта́ци|я, и *f.* deportation

депорти́р|овать, ую *impf. and pf.* to deport

депресси́вный *adj. of* ▸ **депре́ссия**

депре́сси|я, и *f.* (econ., psych.) depression

⚬ **депута́т, а** *m.* deputy; delegate

депута́тский *adj. of* ▸ **депута́т**

дёрга|ть, ю *impf.* (*of* ▸ **дёрнуть**) (*тянуть*) to pull, tug

дёрга|ться, юсь *impf.* (*of* ▸ **дёрнуться**) **1** *pass. of* ▸ **дёргать** **2** to twitch

дереве́нский *adj.* **1** (*магазин*) village **2** (*тишина, пейзаж*) rural; (*житель, воздух*) country

⚬ **дере́в|ня, ни, g. pl. ~éнь** *f.* **1** (*селение*) village **2** (*местность*) (the) country (*opp. the town*)

⚬ **де́рев|о, а, pl. ~ья, ~ьев** *nt.* **1** (*растение*) tree **2** (*sg. only*) (*древесина*) wood (*as material*)

деревообрабо́тк|а, и *f.* woodworking

дереву́шк|а, и *f.* hamlet

⚬ **деревя́нный** *adj.* wood; wooden

держа́в|а, ы *f.* (pol.) power

держа́тел|ь, я *m.* **1** (fin.) holder **2** (*приспособление*) holder

⚬ **держа́|ть, у́, ~ишь** *impf.* **1** (*в руках*) to hold; (*не отпускать*) to hold on to; **~и́те во́ра!** stop thief! **2** (*поддерживать*) to hold up, support **3** (*заставлять находиться в каком-н. состоянии*) to keep, hold; **д. путь** (**к** + *d.* or **на** + *a.*) to head (for), make (for); **д. пари́** to bet; **д. чью-н. сто́рону** to take sb's side **4** (*животных*) to keep; **д. лошаде́й** to keep horses **5** (+ *certain nouns*) to carry out; **д. речь** to make a speech

держа́|ться, у́сь, ~ишься *impf.* **1** (**за** + *a.*) to hold (on to); **~и́тесь за пери́ла** hold on to the banister **2** (**на** + *p.*) to be held up (by),

be supported (by) **3** (*находиться где-либо*) to keep, stay, be; **д. вме́сте** to stick together; **д. в стороне́** to hold aloof **4** (*стоять*) to hold oneself; (fig., *вести себя*) to behave **5** (*сохраняться*) to last **6** (*не сдаваться*) to hold out, stand firm **7** (+ *g.*) (*придерживаться определённого направления*) to keep (to); **д. ле́вой стороны́** to keep to the left **8** (+ *g.*) (*следовать чему-либо*) to adhere (to), stick (to)

де́рз|кий, ~ок, ~ка́, ~ко *adj.* **1** (*грубый*) impertinent, cheeky **2** (*смелый*) audacious

де́рзост|ь, и *f.* **1** (*грубость*) impertinence; cheek; **говори́ть ~и** to be impertinent **2** (*смелость*) audacity

дермати́н, а *m.* leatherette

дермати́т, а *m.* dermatitis

дермато́лог, а *m.* dermatologist

дерматоло́ги|я, и *f.* dermatology

дёрн, а *m.* turf

дёрн|уть, у, ешь *pf. of* ▸ **дёргать**

дёрн|уться, усь, ешься *pf.* (*of* ▸ **дёргаться**) to start up (with a jerk); to dart

дер|у́, ёшь *see* ▸ **драть**

дерьм|о́, а́ *nt.* (vulg.) (*животных*) dung; (*человека*) crap; (fig.) crap

деса́нт, а *m.* (mil.) **1** (*высадка войск*) landing **2** (*войска*) landing force; **вы́садить, выбросить д.** to make a landing

деса́нтник, а *m.* paratrooper

десе́рт, а *m.* dessert

десн|а́, ы́, pl. ~ы, дёсен *f.* (anat.) gum

деся́тер|о, ы́х *num.* (collect.) ten

десятибо́рь|е, я *nt.* (sport) decathlon

десятикра́тный *adj.* tenfold

десятиле́ти|е, я *nt.* **1** (*срок*) decade **2** (*годовщина*) tenth anniversary

деся́ти́чн|ый *adj.* decimal; **~ая дробь** decimal fraction

деся́тк|а, и *f.* **1** (*цифра, игральная карта*) ten **2** (infml, *автобус, трамвай*) No. 10 (*bus, tram, etc.*) **3** (*группа из десятерых*) (group of) ten **4** (infml, *десять рублей*) ten-rouble note, tenner

⚬ **деся́т|ок, ка** *m.* **1** (*десять*) ten **2** (*десять лет*) ten years, decade (*of life*) **3** (*in pl.*) (math.) tens **4** (*in pl.*) (*множество*) dozens, scores; **~ки люде́й** scores of people

деся́тый *num.* tenth

⚬ **де́сят|ь, и, i. ью** *num.* ten

⚬ **дета́л|ь, и** *f.* **1** (*подробность*) detail **2** (*часть машины*) part, component

детдо́м, а *m.* children's home

детекти́в, а *m.* **1** (*человек*) detective **2** (*роман*) detective story **3** (*фильм*) detective film

детекти́вный *adj.* detective (*attr.*)

детёныш, а *m.* young (*of animals*)

де́т|и, ~е́й, ~ям, ~ьми, о ~ях *nt. pl.* (*sg.* **дитя́**, *oblique cases in sg. not used*) children

детса́д, а *m.* kindergarten, nursery school

де́тск|ая, ой *f.* playroom; nursery

д

дéтский *adj.* **1** child's, children's; **д. дом** children's home; **д. сад** kindergarten, nursery school; **д. церебрáльный парали́ч** (med.) cerebral palsy **2** (*ребя́ческий*) childish; **д. язы́к** baby talk

дéтств|о, а *nt.* childhood

деть, дéну, дéнешь *pf.* (*of* ▸ **девáть**) (infml) to put, do (with); **кудá ты дел мою́ ру́чку?** what have you done with my pen?

дé|ться, нусь, нешься *pf.* (*of* ▸ **девáться**) to get to, disappear; **кудá ~лись мои́ часы́?** where has my watch got to?

дефéкт, а *m.* defect

дефи́с, а *m.* hyphen

дефици́т, а *m.* **1** (econ.) deficit **2** (*нехвáтка*) shortage, deficiency

дефици́т|ный, ~ен, ~на *adj.* in short supply; scarce

дефóлт, а *m.* (fin.) default (in payment)

деформáци|я, и *f.* deformation

деформи́р|овать, ую *impf. and pf.* (*исказить*) to deform; (*изменить форму чего-н.*) to change the form of

деформи́р|оваться, уюсь *impf. and pf.* to change shape; to become deformed

деци... *comb. form* deci-

децибéл, а, *g. pl.* **д. м.** decibel

дециме́тр, а *m.* decimetre (BrE), decimeter (AmE)

дешевé|ть, ю *impf.* (*of* ▸ **подешевéть**) to fall in price, become cheaper

дешеви́зн|а, ы *f.* cheapness; low price

дешéвле *comp. of* ▸ **дешёвый,** ▸ **дёшево**

дёшево *adv.* cheap, cheaply; (fig.) cheaply, lightly

дешёвый, дёшев, дешевá, дёшево *adj.* cheap; (fig.) cheap; empty, worthless

дешифр|овáть, у́ю *impf. and pf.* to decipher, decode

дéятел|ь, я *m.* agent; **госудáрственный д.** statesman; **общéственный д.** public figure

дéятельност|ь, и *f.* **1** activity, activities; work; **общéственная д.** public work **2** (physiol., psych., etc.) activity, operation

дéятельн|ый, ~ен, ~ьна *adj.* active, energetic

джаз, а *m.* jazz

джаз-бáнд, а *m.* jazz band

джази́ст, а *m.* jazzman, jazz musician

джазмéн, а *m.* = **джази́ст**

джем, а *m.* jam (BrE), jelly (AmE)

джéмпер, а *m.* jumper

джентльмéн, а *m.* gentleman

джентльмéнский *adj.* gentlemanly

джин, а *m.* gin (*liquor*); **д.-тóник** gin and tonic

джинсóвый *adj.* denim

джи́нс|ы, ов (*no sg.*) jeans

джип, а *m.* jeep®

джихáд, а *m.* (relig.) jihad

джóйстик, а *m.* (comput.) joystick

джóкер, а *m.* (cards) joker

джу́нгл|и, ей (*no sg.*) jungle

джут, а *m.* (bot.) jute

дзюдó *nt. indecl.* judo

дзюдои́ст, а *m.* judoist, judoka

дзюдои́ст|ка, ки *f. of* ▸ **дзюдои́ст**

диабéт, а *m.* diabetes

диабéтик, а *m.* diabetic

диáгноз, а *m.* diagnosis

диагности́р|овать, ую *impf. and pf.* to diagnose; (tech.) to check

диагонáл|ь, и *f.* diagonal; **по ~и** diagonally

диагрáмм|а, ы *f.* diagram; chart

диадéм|а, ы *f.* diadem, tiara

диалéкт, а *m.* dialect

диалóг, а *m.* dialogue (BrE), dialog (AmE)

диалóгов|ый *adj.* (comput.) interactive; **~ое окнó** dialog box

диáметр, а *m.* diameter

диапазóн, а *m.* **1** (mus.) diapason, range **2** (fig.) range, compass **3** (tech., fig.) range; **д. волн** (radio) waveband

диáспор|а, ы *f.* diaspora

дивáн, а *m.* divan (*couch*); sofa; **д.-кровáть** sofa bed

диверсáнт, а *m.* saboteur

диверсификáци|я, и *f.* diversification

диве́рси|я, и *f.* **1** (mil.) diversion **2** sabotage

дивидéнд, а *m.* dividend

Ди-ви-ди́ (*usu. spelt* **DVD**) *m. indecl.* DVD

диви́зи|я, и *f.* (mil.) division

диéз, а *m.* (*also as indecl. adj.*) (mus.) sharp

диéт|а, ы *f.* diet; **сидéть на ~е** to be on a diet; **соблюдáть ~у** to keep to a diet

диети́ческий *adj.* dietetic

дизáйн, а *m.* design

дизáйнер, а *m.* designer

ди́зел|ь, я *m.* diesel engine

ди́зельный *adj.* diesel

дизентери́|я, и *f.* dysentery

дикáр|ь, я́ *m.* savage; (*некультурный человек*) barbarian

ди́к|ий, ~, ~á, ~о *adj.* **1** (*животное, растение*) wild; **~ая кóшка** wild cat **2** (*племя*) savage **3** (*необузданный*) wild; **~ие кри́ки** wild cries; **д. востóрг** wild delight **4** (*абсурдный*) ridiculous **5** (*застенчивый*) shy; unsociable **6** (*страшный*) terrible, awful

ди́ко¹ *adv.* **1** *adv. of* ▸ **ди́кий 2** (*в испуге*) in fright; startled; **д. озирáться** to look around wildly

ди́ко² *as pred.* it is ridiculous

дикобрáз, а *m.* porcupine

дикорасту́щий *adj.* wild

ди́кост|ь, и *f.* absurdity; **э́то совершéнная д.** it is quite absurd

диктáнт, а *m.* dictation

дикта́тор, а *m.* dictator

диктату́р|а, ы *f.* dictatorship

дикт|овáть, у́ю, у́ешь *impf.* (*of* ▸ **продиктовáть**) to dictate

ди́ктор, а *m.* announcer; (*программы новостей*) newscaster

диктофо́н, а *m.* Dictaphone®

ди́кци|я, и *f.* diction; enunciation

ди́лер, а *m.* dealer

дилета́нт, а *m.* amateur, dilettante, dabbler

дина́мик, а *m.* loudspeaker

дина́мик|а, и *f.* dynamics

динами́т, а *m.* dynamite

динами́ческий *adj.* dynamic

динами́чный *adj.* dynamic

дина́сти|я, и *f.* dynasty

ди́нго *m. indecl.* (zool.) dingo

диноза́вр, а *m.* dinosaur

дио́д, а *m.*: **светоизлуча́ющий д.** light-emitting diode, LED

дипло́м, а *m.* **1** (*документ*) diploma, certificate; degree **2** (infml, *работа*) degree work, research

диплома́т, а *m.* **1** diplomat **2** (infml) attaché case, (rigid) briefcase

дипломати́ческий *adj.* diplomatic

дипломати́ч|ный, ~ен, ~на *adj.* (fig.) diplomatic

дипломати́|я, и *f.* diplomacy

дипло́м|ный *adj. of* ▸ **дипло́м**; **~ная рабо́та** degree work, degree thesis

директи́в|а, ы *f.* directive

⚹ **дире́ктор, а,** *pl.* **~á** *m.* director, manager; **д. шко́лы** head (master, mistress); principal

дире́кци|я, и *f.* management; board (of directors)

дирижа́бл|ь, я *m.* airship, dirigible

дирижёр, а *m.* (mus.) conductor

дирижи́р|овать, ую *impf.* (+ *i.*) (mus.) to conduct

⚹ **диск, а** *m.* **1** disk; (*телефонный*) telephone dial **2** (sport) discus **3** (*грампластинка*) disc, record **4** (*компьютерный, музыкальный*) disk, CD, DVD

дисквалифика́ци|я, и *f.* disqualification

дискéт|а, ы *f.* (comput.) diskette

ди́ско *nt. indecl.* disco music

дисково́д, а *m.* (comput.) disk drive

дискомфо́рт, а *m.* discomfort

диско́нт|ный *adj.*: **~ая ка́рта** discount card

дискотéк|а, и *f.* disco(theque)

дискредити́р|овать, ую *impf. and pf.* to discredit

дискримина́ци|я, и *f.* discrimination; **д. же́нщин** sexism; **д. по во́зрасту** ageism

дискримини́р|овать, ую *impf. and pf.* to discriminate against

диску́сси|я, и *f.* discussion

дискути́р|овать, ую *impf. and pf.* (+ *a. or* о + *p.*) to discuss

дислока́ци|я, и *f.* (mil.) deployment, distribution (*of troops*)

диспансéр, а *m.* (med.) clinic, (health) centre

диспéтчер, а *m.* controller (*of movement of transport, etc.*); (comput.) manager

диспéтчер|ский *adj. of* ▸ **диспéтчер**; (aeron.): **~ская слу́жба** flying control organization; (*as f. n.* **~ская, ~ской**) controller's office; (aeron.) control tower

дисплé|й, я *m.* (comput.) display, VDU (*visual display unit*)

диспропо́рци|я, и *f.* disproportion

ди́спут, а *m.* (public) debate

диссерта́ци|я, и *f.* dissertation, thesis

диссидéнт, а *m.* dissident

диссона́нс, а *m.* (mus., also fig.) dissonance, discord

дистанцио́нн|ый *adj.*: **~ое управлéние** remote control

диста́нци|я, и *f.* **1** distance; **на большо́й, ма́лой ~и** at a great, short distance **2** (sport) distance; **сойти́ с ~и** to withdraw **3** (mil.) range

дистрибью́тор, а *m.* distributor, supplier

дисципли́н|а, ы *f.* discipline

дисциплини́рованный *adj.* disciplined

дитя́, ди. **дéти** (*oblique cases not used in sg.*) *nt.* child; baby

дифтери́|я, и *f.* diphtheria

дифференциа́л, а *m.* **1** (math.) differential **2** (tech.) differential gear

дифференциа́льн|ый *adj.* differential; **~ое исчислéние** (math.) differential calculus

дича́|ть, ю *impf.* (*of* ▸ **одича́ть**) to run wild, become wild; (fig.) to become unsociable

дич|ь, и *f.* (*collect.*) game; wildfowl

⚹ **длин|а́, ы́** *f.* length; **в ~у́** longways, lengthwise; **во всю ~у́** at full length; **~о́й (в) шесть мéтров** six metres long (BrE), six meters long (AmE)

длинно… *comb. form* long-

⚹ **дли́н|ный, ~ен, ~á, ~о** *adj.* long; lengthy

⚹ **дли́тельност|ь, и** *f.* duration

⚹ **дли́тельн|ый, ~ен, ~ьна** *adj.* long, protracted

⚹ **дли́|ться, ится** *impf.* (*of* ▸ **продли́ться**) to last

⚹ **для** *prep.* + *g.* **1** (*в пользу кого, чего*) for (the sake of); **э́то д. тебя́** this is for you **2** (*выражает цель*) for; **д. того́, что́бы…** in order to … **3** (*по отношению к*) for, to; **врéдно д. детéй** bad for children **4** (*по отношению к норме*) for, of; **он о́чень высо́к д. свои́х лет** he is very tall for his age

дневни́к, á *m.* diary, journal; **вести́ д.** to keep a diary

дневн|о́й *adj.* **1** day; **в ~о́е врéмя** during daylight hours; **д. свет** daylight **2** (*одного дня*) day's, daily

днём *adv.* **1** in the daytime, by day **2** (*после обеда*) in the afternoon; **сего́дня д.** this afternoon

дни́щ|е, а *nt.* bottom (*of vessel or barrel*)

ДНК *f. indecl.* (*abbr. of* **дезоксирибонуклеи́новая кислота́**) (chem.) DNA (*deoxyribonucleic acid*)

дно, дна, *pl.* **до́нья, до́ньев** *nt.* **1** (*сосуда*) bottom; **вверх дном** upside down; (пей)

до дна! bottoms up! **2** (*no pl.*) (*моря, реки*) bottom, bed

✧ **до¹** *prep. + g.* **1** (*о пределе, границе*) to, up to; as far as; **от Лóндона до Москвы** from London to Moscow **2** (*о временном пределе*) to, up to; until, till; **до сих пор** up to now, till now, hitherto; **до тех пор** till then, before; **до тех пор, пока** until; **до свидáния!** goodbye! **3** (*перед*) before; **до войны** before the war; **до нáшей эры (до н. э.)** before Christ (*abbr.* BC); **до тогó как** before **4** (*о пределе состояния*) to, up to, to the point of; **до бóли** until it hurt(s); **до тогó..., что** to the point where **5** (*о количественном пределе*) under, up to (= *not over, not more than*); **дéти до пяти лет** children under five; **до тысячи рублéй** up to a thousand roubles **6** (*приблизительно*) about, approximately **7** (*относительно*) with regard to, concerning; **что до меня** as far as I am concerned; **мне** *и т. п.* **не до** (*infml*) I don't *etc.* feel like, am not in the mood for; **мне не до разговóра** I don't feel like talking

до² *nt. indecl.* (mus.) C

до...¹ *vbl. pref.* **1** (*expr. completion of action*): **дочитáть книгу** to finish (reading) a book **2** (*indicates that action is carried to a certain point*): **дочитáть до страницы 270** to read as far as page 270 **3** (*expr. supplementary action*): **докупить** to buy in addition **4** (+ *refl. vv., expr. eventual attainment of goal*): **дозвониться** to ring until one gets an answer

до...² *pref.* (*of nn. and adjs., used to indicate priority in chronological sequence*) pre-

✧ **добáв|ить, лю, ишь** *pf.* (*of* ▶ добавлять) (+ *a. or g.*) to add

добáвк|а, и *f.* **1** (*пищевая*) additive **2** (*дополнительная порция*) second helping

✧ **добавлéни|е, я** *nt.* addition

✧ **добавля́|ть, ю** *impf. of* ▶ добáвить

добáвочн|ый *adj.* **1** additional, extra; **~ое врéмя** (sport) extra time **2** (teleph.) extension; **д. тридцать** extension 30

✧ **добегá|ть, ю** *impf. of* ▶ добежáть

добе|жáть, гу, жишь, гут *pf.* (*of* ▶ добегáть) (**до** + *g.*) to run (to, as far as); (*достигнуть*) to reach (also fig.)

добермáн, а and добермáн-пинчер, добермáна-пинчера *m.* Dobermann (pinscher)

добивá|ть, ю *impf. of* ▶ добить

✧ **добивá|ться, юсь** *impf.* **1** *impf. of* ▶ добиться **2** (+ *g.*) to try to get, strive (for), aim (at)

добирá|ться, юсь *impf. of* ▶ добрáться

до|бить, бью, бьёшь *pf.* (*of* ▶ добивáть) to finish off, do for

до|биться, бьюсь, бьёшься *pf.* (*of* ▶ добивáться) (+ *g.*) to get, obtain, secure; **д. своегó** to get one's own way

дóблест|ь, и *f.* valour (BrE), valor (AmE), gallantry

✧ key word

до|брáться, берусь, берёшься, *past* **~брáлся, ~бралáсь** *pf.* (*of* ▶ добирáться) **1** (**до** + *g.*) to get (to), reach **2** (infml) to get (one's hands on); **я до тебя ~берусь!** I'll get you!

добр|ó, á *nt.* **1** good; (*поступок*) good deed; **не к ~у́ это** it is a bad omen **2** (*collect.*) (infml, *имущество*) goods, property **3**: **д. пожáловать!** welcome!

добровóл|ец, ьца *m.* volunteer

добровóльно *adv.* voluntarily

добровóл|ьный, ~ен, ~ьна *adj.* voluntary

добродéтел|ь, и *f.* virtue

добродуш|ный, ~ен, ~на *adj.* good-natured

доброжелáтел|ьный, ~ен, ~ьна *adj.* benevolent

доброкáчествен|ный, ~, ~на *adj.* **1** of good quality **2** (med.) benign

добросóвест|ный, ~ен, ~на *adj.* conscientious

добрóт|а, ы́ *f.* goodness, kindness

добрóт|ный, ~ен, ~на *adj.* of good, high quality; durable

✧ **добр|ый, ~, ~á, ~о, ~ы** *adj.* **1** (*хороший*) good; **~ое имя** good name; **~ое утро!** good morning!; **всегó ~ого!** goodbye!; all the best!; **по ~ой вóле** of one's own free will **2** (*отзывчивый*) kind, good; **бу́дьте ~ы** (+ *imper.*) please, would you be so kind as to **3** (infml, *не меньше чем*) a good; **д. час** a good hour

добывá|ть, ю *impf. of* ▶ добыть

до|быть, бу́ду, бу́дешь, *past* **~был, ~была́, ~было** *pf.* (*of* ▶ добывáть) **1** (*достать*) to get, obtain, procure **2** (*из земли*) to extract, mine, quarry

добыч|а, и *f.* **1** (*действие*) extraction (*of minerals*); mining, quarrying **2** (*захваченное*) booty, spoils, loot **3** (*охотника*) bag; (*рыболова*) catch **4** (*добытое из недр земли*) mineral products; output

довез|ти, у́, ёшь, *past* **~, ~ла́** *pf.* (*of* ▶ довозить) to take (to)

довéренност|ь, и *f.* warrant, power of attorney; **по ~и** by proxy

довéр|енный *p.p.p. of* ▶ довéрить *and adj.* trusted; **~енное лицó** (*as m. n.* **д., ~енного**) agent, proxy

довéри|е, я *nt.* trust, confidence; **служба/телефóн ~я** helpline

доверительный *adj.* confiding, trusting

довéр|ить, ю, ишь *pf.* (*of* ▶ доверять 1) (+ *d.*) to entrust (to)

довéр|иться, юсь, ишься *pf.* (*of* ▶ доверяться) (+ *d.*) to trust (in), confide (in)

дóверху *adv.* to the top; to the brim

довéрчив|ый, ~, ~а *adj.* trustful, credulous

довер|я́ть, я́ю *impf.* **1** *impf. of* ▶ довéрить **2** (*impf. only*) (+ *d.*) to trust, confide (in)

довер|я́ться, я́юсь *impf. of* ▶ довériться

довéс|ок, ка *m.* makeweight

дове|сти́, ду́, дёшь, *past* ~л, ~ла́ *pf.* (*of* ▶ **доводи́ть**) **1** (*до какого-то места*) to lead (to), take (to), accompany (to) **2** (*до какого-то состояния*) to bring (to); to drive (to), reduce (to); **д. до соверше́нства** to perfect; **д. до све́дения** (+ *g.*) to inform, let know

до́вод, а *m.* argument

дово|ди́ть, жу́, ~дишь *impf. of* ▶ **довести́**

довое́нный *adj.* pre-war

дово|зи́ть, жу́, ~зишь *impf. of* ▶ **довезти́**

✐ **дово́льно¹** *adv.* (*достаточно*) quite, fairly; rather, pretty; **д. хоро́ший фильм** quite a good film

✐ **дово́льно²** *adv.* (*с удовлетворением*) contentedly

дово́л|ьный, ~ен, ~ьна *adj.* **1** contented, satisfied; **д. вид** contented expression **2** (+ *i.*) contented (with), satisfied (with), pleased (with); **д. собо́й** pleased with oneself, self-satisfied

дово́льств|оваться, уюсь *impf.* (+ *i.*) to be content (with), be satisfied (with)

дог, а *m.* mastiff; **далма́тский д.** Dalmatian

догад|а́ться, а́юсь *pf.* (*of* ▶ **дога́дываться 1**) to guess

дога́дк|а, и *f.* surmise, conjecture; (*in pl.*) guesswork; **теря́ться в ~ах** to be lost in conjecture

дога́длив|ый, ~, ~а *adj.* quick-witted, bright

дога́дыва|ться, юсь *impf.* **1** *impf. of* ▶ **догада́ться 2** (*impf. only*) to suspect

до́гм|а, ы *f.* dogma

до́гмат, а *m.* **1** (*relig.*) doctrine, dogma **2** (*принцип*) tenet, foundation

до|гна́ть, гоню́, го́нишь, *past* ~гна́л, ~гнала́, ~гна́ло *pf.* (*of* ▶ **догоня́ть**) to catch up (with) (also fig.)

догова́рива|ть, ю *impf. of* ▶ **договори́ть**

догова́рива|ться, юсь *impf.* **1** *impf. of* ▶ **договори́ться 2** (*impf. only*) (о + *p.*) to negotiate (about)

✐ **догово́р, а** *m.* agreement; (*pol.*) treaty, pact

договорённост|ь, и *f.* agreement, understanding; (*pol.*) accord

договор|и́ть, ю́, и́шь *pf.* (*of* ▶ **догова́ривать**) to finish saying; to finish telling

договор|и́ться, ю́сь, и́шься *pf.* (*of* ▶ **догова́риваться 1**) **1** (о + *p.*) to come to an agreement, understanding (about); to arrange; ~и́лись! agreed!; it's a deal! **2** (**до** + *g.*) to come (to); to talk (to the point of)

догово́рн|ый *adj.* agreed; contractual; ~ая цена́ agreed price

догола́ *adv.* stark naked; **разде́ться д.** to strip naked

догоня́|ть, ю *impf. of* ▶ **догна́ть**

догоря́|ть, а́ю *impf. of* ▶ **догоре́ть**

догор|е́ть, ю́, и́шь *pf.* (*of* ▶ **догора́ть**) (*сгореть до какого-либо предела*) to burn down; (*сгореть до конца*) to burn out

дода|ва́ть, ю́, ёшь *impf. of* ▶ **дода́ть**

дода́|ть, м, шь, ст, ди́м, ди́те, ду́т, *past* до́дал, ~ла́, до́дало *pf.* (*of* ▶ **додава́ть**) to make up (the rest of); to pay up

доде́л|ать, аю *pf.* (*of* ▶ **доде́лывать**) to finish

доде́лыва|ть, ю *impf. of* ▶ **доде́лать**

доду́м|аться, аюсь *pf.* (*of* ▶ **доду́мываться**) (**до** + *g.*) to hit (upon) (*afterthought*)

доду́мыва|ться, юсь *impf. of* ▶ **доду́маться**

доеда́|ть, ю *impf. of* ▶ **дое́сть**

доезжа́|ть, ю *impf. of* ▶ **дое́хать**

до|е́сть, е́м, е́шь, е́ст, еди́м, еди́те, едя́т *pf.* (*of* ▶ **доеда́ть**) to eat up, finish eating

до|е́хать, е́ду, е́дешь *pf.* (*of* ▶ **доезжа́ть**) (**до** + *g.*) to reach, arrive (at)

дожд|а́ться, у́сь, ёшься, *past* ~а́лся, ~ала́сь *pf.* **1** (+ *g.*) to wait (for); **д. конца́ спекта́кля** to wait until the end of the show **2**: **д. того́, что** to end up (by); **он ~а́лся того́, что ему́ указа́ли на дверь** he ended up by being shown the door

дождеви́к, а́ *m.* (infml) raincoat

дождево́й *adj. of* ▶ **дождь**

до́ждик, а *m.* shower

дождли́в|ый, ~, ~а *adj.* rainy

дожд|ь, я́ *m.* **1** rain (also fig.); **под ~ём** in the rain; **ме́лкий д.** drizzle; **проливно́й д.** downpour; **идёт д.** it is raining **2** (fig.) cascade

дожива́|ть, ю *impf.* **1** *impf. of* ▶ **дожи́ть 2** (*impf. only*) to live out; **д. свой век** to live out one's days

дожида́|ться, юсь *impf.* (*of* ▶ **дожда́ться**) (+ *g.*) to wait (for)

до|жи́ть, живу́, живёшь, *past* ~жи́л, ~жила́, ~жи́ло *pf.* (*of* ▶ **дожива́ть 1**) **1** (**до** + *g.*) (*прожить*) to live (until); **она́ ~жила́ до конца́ войны́** she lived to see the end of the war **2** (**до** + *g.*) (*дойти до какого-л. состояния*) to come (to), be reduced (to); **до чего́ мы ~жили!** what have we come to!

до́з|а, ы *f.* dose

дозапра́вк|а, и *f.* refuelling (BrE), refueling (AmE)

дозвон|и́ться, ю́сь, и́шься *pf.* (**до** + *g. or* к + *d. or* в + *a.*) to ring until one gets an answer; to get through (to) (*on telephone*); **я не мог д. к тебе́/до тебя́** I could not get through (to you); **в институ́т не дозвони́ться** it's impossible to get through to the institute

дозиро́вк|а, и *f.* dosage

дозна́ни|е, я *nt.* (law) inquiry; inquest

дозо́р, а *m.* patrol

дозо́р|ный *adj. of* ▶ **дозо́р**; (*as m. n.* **д., ~ного**) (mil.) scout

дозрева́|ть, ю *impf. of* ▶ **дозре́ть**

дозр|е́ть, е́ю *pf.* (*of* ▶ **дозрева́ть**) to ripen

доигра́|ть, а́ю *pf.* (*of* ▶ **дои́грывать**) to finish (playing)

дои́грыва|ть, ю *impf. of* ▶ **доигра́ть**

Д

д

доистори́ческий *adj.* prehistoric

до|йть, ю́, ~йшь *impf.* (*of* ▸ подои́ть) to milk

до|йти́, йду́, йдёшь, *past* ~шёл, ~шла́ *pf.*
(*of* ▸ доходи́ть) **1** (до + *g.*) to reach; д. до
того́, что... to reach a point where ...; ру́ки
не ~шли́ (до + *g.*) I, *etc.*, had no time (for)
2 (infml) (до + *g.*) (*произвести впечатление*)
to make an impression (upon); (*стать
понятным в ходе объяснения*) to get
through (to) **3** (*impers.; also* де́ло ~йдёт,
~шло́ до + *g.*) to come (to); (де́ло) чуть не
~шло́ до дра́ки it nearly came to blows

док, а *m.* dock

доказа́тельств|о, а *nt.* proof, evidence

док|аза́ть, ажу́, а́жешь *pf.* (*of* ▸ дока́зывать 1)
to demonstrate, prove; счита́ть ~а́занным
to take for granted

доказыва|ть, ю *impf.* **1** *impf. of* ▸ доказа́ть
2 (*impf. only*) to argue, try to prove

дока́пыва|ться, юсь *impf. of* ▸ докопа́ться

док|ати́ться, ачу́сь, а́тишься *pf.* (*of*
▸ дока́тываться) **1** (до + *g.*) to roll (to)
2 (*о звуках*) to roll, thunder, boom

дока́тыва|ться, юсь *impf. of* ▸ докати́ться

до́кер, а *m.* docker

докла́д, а *m.* report; lecture; paper; talk;
чита́ть д. to give a report; to read a paper

докла́дчик, а *m.* speaker

докла́дчи|ца, цы *f. of* ▸ докла́дчик

докла́дыва|ть, ю *impf. of* ▸ доложи́ть¹

докопа́|ться, юсь *pf.* (*of* ▸ дока́пываться)
(до + *g.*) **1** to dig down (to) **2** (fig.) to get to
the bottom (of); to find out, discover

до́ктор, а, *pl.* ~а́ *m.* doctor

до́ктор|ский *adj. of* ▸ до́ктор; ~ская
диссерта́ция doctoral thesis

доктри́н|а, ы *f.* doctrine

докуме́нт, а *m.* document

документа́льный *adj.* documentary; д.
фильм documentary (film)

документа́ци|я, и *f.* (*collect.*)
documentation

долб|и́ть, лю́, и́шь *impf.* to hollow out; to
gouge

долг, а, о ~е, в ~у́, *pl.* ~и́ *m.* **1** (*обязанность*)
duty **2** (*одолженное*) debt; в д. on credit;
быть у кого́-н. в ~у́ to be indebted to sb

до́л|гий, ~ог, ~га́, ~го *adj.* long

до́лго *adv.* long, (for) a long time

долгове́ч|ный, ~ен, ~на *adj.* lasting;
durable

долгов|о́й *adj. of* ▸ долг 2; ~о́е
обяза́тельство promissory note

долговре́мен|ный, ~, ~на *adj.* of long
duration, prolonged

долговя́з|ый, ~, ~а *adj.* (infml) lanky

долгожда́нный *adj.* long-awaited

долгожи́тел|ь, я *m.* long-lived person

долгожи́тель|ница, ницы *f. of*
▸ долгожи́тель

долголе́ти|е, я *nt.* longevity

долголе́тний *adj.* of many years; longstanding

долгосро́чн|ый, ~ен, ~а *adj.* (*кредит*)
long-term; (*отпуск*) of long duration

долгот|а́, ы́, *pl.* ~ы f. **1** (*sg. only*) (*дня*)
duration **2** (geog.) longitude

долет|а́ть, а́ю *impf. of* ▸ долете́ть

долет|е́ть, чу́, ти́шь *pf.* (*of* ▸ долета́ть) (до
+ *g.*) to fly (to, as far as); to reach

до́лж|ен, ~на́, ~но́ *pred. adj.* **1** owing; он д.
мне три рубля́ he owes me three roubles
2 (+ *inf.*) (*обязан, вынужден*): я д. идти́
I must go, I have to go **3** (+ *inf.*) (*вероятно*):
она́ ~на́ ско́ро прийти́ she should be here
soon; ~но́ быть probably

должни́к, а́ *m.* debtor

должностн|о́й *adj.* official; ~о́е лицо́
official, functionary, public servant

до́лжност|ь, и, *g. pl.* ~е́й *f.* post, office

до́лжн|ый *adj.* due, fitting, proper; ~ым
о́бразом properly; (*as n.* ~ое, ~ого) due

долива́|ть, ю *impf. of* ▸ доли́ть

доли́н|а, ы *f.* valley

дол|и́ть, ью́, ьёшь, *past* ~и́л, ~ила́, ~и́ло
pf. (*of* ▸ долива́ть) **1** (*жидкость*) to add;
to pour in addition (*сосуд*) to fill (up);
to refill

до́ллар, а *m.* dollar

долож|и́ть¹, у́, ~ишь *pf.* (*of* ▸ докла́дывать)
1 (+ *a.* or *o* + *p.*) (*сделать доклад*) to report;
to give a report (on) **2** (*o* + *p.*) (*сообщить
о приходе посетителя*) to announce (*a
guest, etc.*)

долож|и́ть², у́, ~ишь *pf.* (*of* ▸ докла́дывать)
(*добавить*) to add

доло́й *adv.* (+ *a.*) (infml) down (with), away
(with); д. изме́нников! down with the traitors!

долот|о́, а́, *pl.* ~а́, ~ *nt.* chisel

до́льше *adv.* longer

до́л|я, и, *g. pl.* ~е́й *f.* **1** (*часть*) part, portion;
share; quota; войти́ в ~ю (с + *i.*) to go
shares (with) **2** (*судьба*) lot, fate; вы́пасть
на чью-н. ~ю to fall to sb's lot

дом, а (у), *pl.* ~а́ *m.* **1** (*жилое здание*)
house; (*многоквартирный*) block (of
flats) (BrE), apartment block (AmE); (*здание
учреждения*) building; д. культу́ры palace
of culture; ≈ arts (and leisure) centre; д.
о́тдыха holiday home; д.-музе́й... ... House;
Д.-музе́й Пу́шкина Pushkin House **2** (*своё
жильё*) home; (*семья*) household

дом... *comb. form, abbr. of* ▸ дома́шний

до́ма *adv.* at home, in; быть как д. to feel at
home; бу́дьте как д. make yourself at home;
у него́ не все д. he's not all there

дома́шн|ий *adj.* **1** house; home; domestic; д.
а́дрес home address; ~яя страни́ца (comput.)
home page; под ~им аре́стом under house
arrest **2** (*самодельный*) home-made **3** (*не
дикий*) domestic; ~ие живо́тные domestic
animals; ~яя пти́ца (collect.) poultry

доме́н *m.* (comput.) domain

до́мик, a *m. dim. of* ▸ **дом**

Доминика́нск|ая Респу́блика, ∼ой **Респу́блики** *f.* the Dominican Republic

домини́р|овать, ую *impf.* to dominate, prevail (fig.)

домино́ *nt. indecl.* (*игра*) dominoes

домкра́т, a *m.* (tech.) jack

домо... *comb. form* **1** home- **2** *abbr. of* ▸ **дома́шний**

домовладе́л|ец, ьца *m.* house-owner; (*по отношению к нанимателю*) landlord

домога́тельств|о, a *nt.* solicitation, demand, bid; **сексуа́льное д.** sexual harassment

⚡ **домо́й** *adv.* home, homewards; **нам пора́ д.** it's time for us to go home

домофо́н, a *m.* electronic security system (*at entrance to building*); entryphone® (BrE)

домохозя́йк|а, и *f.* housewife

домрабо́тниц|а, ы *f.* domestic (servant), maid; **приходя́щая д.** home help

до́мысел|ел, ла *m.* conjecture

дона́шива|ть, ю *impf. of* ▸ **доноси́ть¹**

донесе́ни|е, я *nt.* report, message

донес|ти́¹, у́, ёшь, *past* ∼́, ∼ла́ *pf.* (*of* ▸ **доноси́ть²**) (*до + g.*) to carry (to, as far as); (*звук, запах*) to carry, bear

донес|ти́², у́, ёшь, *past* ∼́, ∼ла́ *pf.* (*of* ▸ **доноси́ть³**) **1** to report, announce; (+ *d.*) to inform **2** (**на** + *a.*) (*сделать донос*) to inform (on, against), denounce

донес|ти́сь, у́сь, ёшься, *past* ∼ся, ∼ла́сь *pf.* (*of* ▸ **доноси́ться²**) **1** (*о звуках, запахах, новостях*) to reach **2** (infml, *быстро доехать, добежать*) to reach quickly

до́низу *adv.* to the bottom

до́нор, a *m.* donor

доно́с, a *m.* denunciation

дон|оси́ть¹, ошу́, ∼о́сишь *pf.* (*of* ▸ **дона́шивать**) **1** to wear out **2** to wear sth handed down **3** (*usu. with neg.*): **д. ребёнка** to carry a child to full term

дон|оси́ть², ошу́, ∼о́сишь *impf. of* ▸ **донести́¹**

дон|оси́ть³, ошу́, ∼о́сишь *impf. of* ▸ **донести́²**

дон|оси́ться¹, ∼о́сится *pf.* to wear out, be worn out

дон|оси́ться², ∼о́сится *impf. of* ▸ **донести́сь**

доно́счик, a *m.* informer

доно́счиц|а, цы *f. of* ▸ **доно́счик**

допива́|ть, ю *impf. of* ▸ **допи́ть**

до́пинг, a *m.* drugs, dope

допи|са́ть, шу́, ∼шешь *pf.* (*of* ▸ **допи́сывать**) **1** (*письмо*) to finish writing; (*картину*) to finish painting **2** (*приписать*) to add

допи́сыва|ть, ю *impf. of* ▸ **дописа́ть**

доп|и́ть, ью́, ьёшь, *past* ∼и́л, ∼ила́, ∼и́ло *pf.* (*of* ▸ **допива́ть**) to drink (up)

допла́т|а, ы *f.* additional payment; surcharge

допла|ти́ть, чу́, ∼́тишь *pf.* (*of* ▸ **допла́чивать**) to pay in addition, pay

the remainder

допла́чива|ть, ю *impf. of* ▸ **доплати́ть**

доплыва́|ть, ю *impf. of* ▸ **доплы́ть**

доплы́|ть, ву́, вёшь, *past* ∼л, ∼ла́, ∼ло *pf.* (*of* ▸ **доплыва́ть**) (*до + g.*) (*вплавь*) to swim (to, as far as); (*на корабле*) to sail (to, as far as); (fig.) to reach

допоздна́ *adv.* (infml) till late

дополне́ни|е, я *nt.* supplement, addition; addendum

дополни́тельно *adv.* in addition

⚡ **дополни́тельн|ый** *adj.* supplementary, additional, extra; ∼ое вре́мя (sport) extra time

допо́лн|ить, ю, ишь *pf.* (*of* ▸ **дополня́ть**) to supplement, add to

дополн|я́ть, я́ю *impf. of* ▸ **допо́лнить**

допото́пный *adj.* antediluvian

допра́шива|ть, ю *impf. of* ▸ **допроси́ть**

допро́с, a *m.* (law) interrogation

допр|оси́ть, ошу́, о́сишь *pf.* (*of* ▸ **допра́шивать**) (law) to interrogate, question

до́пуск, a *m.* (к + *d.*) access (to); (в + *a.*) right of entry, admittance

⚡ **допуска́|ть**, ю *impf. of* ▸ **допусти́ть**

допусти́м|ый, ∼, ∼а *adj.* permissible, admissible

допу|сти́ть, щу́, ∼́стишь *pf.* (*of* ▸ **допуска́ть**) **1** (*до + g. or* к + *d.*) to admit, to give access (to); **д. к ко́нкурсу** to allow to compete **2** (*позволить*) to allow, permit **3** (*предположить*) to grant, assume; ∼́стим let us assume **4** (*сделать*): **д. оши́бку** to make a mistake

допуще́ни|е, я *nt.* (*предположение*) assumption

допыт|а́ться, а́юсь *pf.* (*of* ▸ **допы́тываться**) to find out

допы́тыва|ться, юсь *impf.* (*of* ▸ **допыта́ться**) (*impf. only*) to try to find out, to try to elicit

дораба́тыва|ть, ю *impf. of* ▸ **дорабо́тать**

дорабо́та|ть, ю *pf.* (*of* ▸ **дораба́тывать**) **1** (*усовершенствовать*) to refine **2** (*до + g.*) to work (until)

дораст|а́ть, а́ю *impf. of* ▸ **дорасти́**

дораст|и́, у́, ёшь, *past* **доро́с, доросла́** *pf.* (*of* ▸ **дораста́ть**) (*до + g.*) to grow (to); (fig.) to attain (to), come up (to)

дорв|а́ться, у́сь, ёшься, *past* ∼а́лся, ∼ала́сь, ∼а́лось *pf.* (*до + g.*) (infml) to fall upon, seize upon

дореволюцио́нный *adj.* pre-revolutionary

⚡ **доро́г|а**, и *f.* **1** (*путь сообщения*) road; (*путь следования*) way (also fig.); **желе́зная д.** railway (BrE), railroad (AmE); **дать, уступи́ть кому́-н.** ∼у to make way for sb (also fig.) **2** (*путешествие*) journey; **отпра́виться в** ∼у to set out; **в** ∼е on the journey, en route **3** (*направление пути, маршрут*) (the) way, route; **показа́ть** ∼у to show the way; **сби́ться** с ~и to lose one's way

до́рого adv. dear, dearly; **д. обойти́сь** (+ d.) to cost one dear

дорогови́зн|а, ы f. high prices

доро́гой adv. on the way, en route

◌ **дорог|о́й, до́рог, дорога́, до́рого** adj. **1** dear, expensive **2** (*близкий сердцу*) dear; precious; (*as n.* **д., ~о́го,** f. **~а́я, ~о́й**) (my) dear

дорожа́|ть, ет impf. (of ▶ **подорожа́ть**) to rise (in price), go up

доро́же comp. of ▶ **дорого́й,** ▶ **до́рого**

дорож|и́ть, у́, и́шь impf. (+ i.) to value

доро́жк|а, и f. **1** path **2** (sport) track; lane **3** (*коврик*) runner **4** (*магнитофона*) track

◌ **доро́жн|ый** adj. **1** adj. of ▶ **доро́га**; **д. знак** road sign; **~ая поли́ция** traffic police **2** (*для путешествия*) travel, travelling (BrE), traveling (AmE); **д. чек** traveller's cheque (BrE), traveler's check (AmE)

доса́д|а, ы f. annoyance; **кака́я д.!** what a nuisance!

досади́|ть, жу́, ди́шь pf. (of ▶ **досажда́ть**) (+ d.) (*раздражить*) to annoy, vex

доса́д|ный, ~ен, ~на adj. annoying

досажда́|ть, ю impf. of ▶ **досади́ть**

доск|а́, и́, a. **~у,** pl. **~и, досо́к, ~а́м** f. **1** board, plank; **д. объявле́ний** noticeboard **2** (*мраморная*) slab; (*металлическая*) plaque, plate **3** (для сёрфинга, скейтбординга и т. n.) board

доскона́л|ьный, ~ен, ~ьна adj. thorough

до|сла́ть, шлю́, шлёшь pf. (of ▶ **досыла́ть**) to send in addition; to send the remainder

досло́вно adv. verbatim, word for word

досло́вный adj. literal, verbatim; **д. перево́д** literal translation

дослу́ша|ть, ю pf. (of ▶ **дослу́шивать**) to listen to (sth) till the end

дослу́шива|ть, ю impf. of ▶ **дослу́шать**

досма́трива|ть, ю impf. of ▶ **досмотре́ть**

досмо́тр, а m. examination; inspection

досмотр|е́ть, ю́, ~ишь pf. (of ▶ **досма́тривать**) (до + g.) to watch, look at (to, as far as); **мы ~е́ли пье́су до тре́тьего а́кта** we saw the play as far as the third act

доспе́х|и, ов m. pl. (sg. **~, ~а**) armour (BrE), armor (AmE)

досро́ч|ный, ~ен, ~на adj. ahead of schedule, early

доста|ва́ть, ю́, ёшь impf. of ▶ **доста́ть**

доста|ва́ться, ю́сь, ёшься impf. of ▶ **доста́ться**

доста́в|ить, лю, ишь pf. (of ▶ **доставля́ть**) **1** (*груз, посылку*) to deliver; (*пассажиров*) to transport, convey **2** (*удовольствие*) to give; (*трудности*) to cause

◌ **доста́вк|а, и** f. delivery

доставля́|ть, ю impf. of ▶ **доста́вить**

доста́т|ок, ка m. prosperity

◌ **key word**

◌ **доста́точно¹** adv. sufficiently, enough; (*значительно*) considerably

доста́точно² as pred. it is enough; **д. сказа́ть** suffice it to say

доста́точ|ный, ~ен, ~на adj. sufficient

доста́|ть, ну, нешь pf. (of ▶ **достава́ть**) **1** (*взять*) to fetch; to take out; **д. плато́к из карма́на** to take a handkerchief out of one's pocket **2** (+ g. or до + g.) (*коснуться*) to touch; to reach **3** (*получить*) to get, obtain

доста́|ться, нусь, нешься pf. (of ▶ **достава́ться**) (+ d.) **1** (*перейти в собственность*) to pass (to) (by inheritance) **2** (*выпасть на долю*) to fall to one's lot

◌ **достига́|ть, ю** impf. of ▶ **дости́гнуть,** ▶ **дости́чь**

◌ **дости́г|нуть, ну, нешь,** past **~, ~ла** pf. (of ▶ **достига́ть**) (+ g.) **1** (*дойти, доехать*) to reach **2** (*добиться*) to attain, achieve

◌ **достиже́ни|е, я** nt. achievement, attainment

достижи́м|ый, ~, ~а adj. achievable, attainable

дости́чь = **дости́гнуть**

достове́рност|ь, и f. (*правдивость*) trustworthiness, reliability; (*о документе*) authenticity

достове́р|ный, ~ен, ~на adj. (*правдивый*) reliable, trustworthy; (*о документе*) authentic

◌ **досто́инств|о, а** nt. **1** (*хорошее качество*) merit, virtue **2** (sg. only) (*уважение*) dignity; **чу́вство со́бственного ~а** self-respect **3** (*стоимость*) value; **моне́та ~ом в пять рубле́й, моне́та пятирублёвого ~а** a five-rouble coin

досто́йно adv. suitably, fittingly

◌ **досто́|йный, ~ин, ~йна** adj. **1** (+ g.) (*стоящий*) worthy (of), deserving; **д. внима́ния** worthy of note **2** (*заслуженный*) deserved; fitting, adequate **3** (*соответствующий*) suitable, fit

достопримеча́тельност|ь, и f. sight; place, object of note; **осма́тривать ~и** to see the sights

◌ **до́ступ, а** m. access, admittance

◌ **досту́п|ный, ~ен, ~на** adj. **1** (*место*) accessible **2** (для + g.) open (to); available (to) **3** (*книга*) easily understood; intelligible **4** (*цены*) moderate, reasonable

досу́г, а m. leisure, leisure time; **на ~е** at leisure, in one's spare time

до́суха adv. (until) dry; **вы́тереть д.** to rub dry

досчита́|ть, ю pf. (of ▶ **досчи́тывать**) **1** to finish counting **2** (до + g.) to count (up to); **д. до ста** to count up to a hundred

досчи́тыва|ть, ю impf. of ▶ **досчита́ть**

досыла́|ть, ю impf. of ▶ **досла́ть**

досье́ nt. indecl. dossier, file

досяга́емост|ь, и f. reach; (mil.) range; **вне преде́лов ~и** beyond reach

дота́скива|ть, ю impf. of ▶ **дотащи́ть**

дота́ци|я, и *f.* grant, subsidy

дотащ|и́ть, у́, ∼ишь *pf.* (*of* ▶ **дота́скивать**) (infml) (**до** + *g.*) to carry, drag (to)

дотла́ *adv.* utterly, completely; **сгоре́ть д.** to burn to the ground

дотра́гива|ться, юсь *impf. of* ▶ **дотро́нуться**

дотро́н|уться, усь, ешься *pf.* (*of* ▶ **дотра́гиваться**) (**до** + *g.*) to touch

дотя́гива|ть, ю, ешь *impf. of* ▶ **дотяну́ть**

дотя́гива|ться, юсь, ешься *impf. of* ▶ **дотяну́ться**

дотян|у́ть, у́, ∼ешь *pf.* (*of* ▶ **дотя́гивать**) (**до** + *g.*) ■ to draw, drag (to, as far as) ■ (infml, *дойти, доехать*) to reach, make ■ (infml, *выдержать*) to hold out (till); (*дожить*) to live (till)

дотян|у́ться, у́сь, ∼ешься *pf.* (*of* ▶ **дотя́гиваться**) (**до** + *g.*) to reach; to touch

до́хл|ый, ∼а́, ∼о *adj.* (*мёртвый*) dead (*of animals*)

до́х|нуть, ну, нешь, *past* ∼, ∼**ла** *impf.* (*of* ▶ **издо́хнуть,** ▶ **подо́хнуть,** ▶ **сдо́хнуть**) ■ (*о животных*) to die ■ (infml, pej., *о людях*) to peg out, kick the bucket

⚬ **дохо́д, а** *m.* income; receipts; revenue

дохо|ди́ть, жу́, ∼дишь *impf. of* ▶ **дойти́**

дохо́д|ный, ∼ен, ∼на *adj.* ■ profitable, lucrative, paying ■ *adj. of* ▶ **дохо́д**

дохо́дчив|ый, ∼, ∼а *adj.* intelligible, easy to understand

доце́нт, а *m.* reader (BrE), associate professor (AmE)

до́чери, до́черью *see* ▶ **дочь**

дочéрний *adj.* (*о компании, предприятии*) daughter; branch

дочит|а́ть, а́ю *pf.* (*of* ▶ **дочи́тывать**) ■ (*окончить чтение чего-н.*) to finish reading ■ (**до** + *g.*) to read (to, as far as)

дочи́тыва|ть, ю *impf. of* ▶ **дочита́ть**

до́чк|а, и *f.* (infml) = **дочь**

⚬ **дочь, ∼ери,** *i.* ∼**ерью,** *pl.* ∼**ери,** ∼**ерéй,** ∼**еря́м,** ∼**ерьми́, о** ∼**еря́х** *f.* daughter

дошко́льник, а *m.* preschooler

дошко́льни|ца, цы *f. of* ▶ **дошко́льник**

дошко́льный *adj.* preschool

доща́тый *adj.* made of planks, boards; **д. насти́л** duckboards

доя́рк|а, и *f.* milkmaid

⚬ **др.** (*abbr. of* **други́е**) **и** ∼ & co.; (*при опускании фамилий авторов в научных изданиях*) et al.

д-р (*abbr. of* **до́ктор**) Dr, Doctor

драгоце́нност|ь, и *f.* jewel; gem; (*in pl.*) jewellery

драгоце́н|ный, ∼ен, ∼на *adj.* precious

дразн|и́ть, ю́, ∼ишь *impf.* ■ (*собаку*) to tease ■ (*аппетит, любопытство*) to stimulate

дра́йвер, а *m.* (comput.) driver

дра́к|а, и *f.* fight

драко́н, а *m.* dragon

дра́м|а, ы *f.* ■ drama ■ (fig.) crisis, calamity

драматизи́р|овать, ую *impf. and pf.* to dramatize

драмати́ческий *adj.* ■ dramatic; drama; **д. теа́тр** theatre (BrE), theater (AmE) ■ (*напыщенный*) dramatic, theatrical

драмати́ч|ный, ∼ен, ∼на *adj.* (fig.) dramatic

драмату́рг, а *m.* playwright, dramatist

драп, а *m.* thick woollen cloth

дра|ть, деру́, дерёшь, *past* ∼**л,** ∼**ла́,** ∼**ло** *impf.* ■ (*impf. only*) (*рвать*) to tear (up, to pieces) ■ (*pf.* **со**∼) (*снимать*) to tear off

дра́|ться, деру́сь, дерёшься, *past* ∼**лся,** ∼**ла́сь,** ∼**ло́сь** *impf.* ■ (*pf.* **по**∼) (**с** + *i.*) to fight (with) ■ (fig.) (**за** + *a.*) to fight, struggle (for)

дребезж|а́ть, и́т *impf.* to jingle, tinkle

древеси́н|а, ы *f.* ■ (*плотная часть дерева*) wood ■ (*лесоматериалы*) timber

древнегре́ческий *adj.* ancient, classical Greek

древнееврéйский *adj.* ancient, classical Hebrew

древнеру́сский *adj.* Old Russian

⚬ **дре́в|ний, ∼ен, ∼ня** *adj.* ancient; ∼**няя исто́рия** ancient history

дре́вност|ь, и *f.* ■ (*sg. only*) (*далёкое прошлое*) antiquity ■ (*in pl.*) antiquities

дрези́н|а, ы *f.* (rail.) trolley (BrE), handcar (AmE)

дрейф|ова́ть, у́ю *impf.* (naut.) to drift

дре́л|ь, и *f.* (tech.) drill

дрем|а́ть, лю́, ∼лешь *impf.* to doze; **не д.** (also fig.) to be watchful; to be wide awake

дрена́ж, а и á *m.* drainage

дрена́ж|ный *adj. of* ▶ **дрена́ж;** ∼**ная труба́** drainpipe

дрессиро́ванн|ый *p.p.p. of* ▶ **дрессирова́ть** *and adj.*: ∼**ые живо́тные** performing animals

дрессир|ова́ть, у́ю *impf.* (*of* ▶ **вы́дрессировать**) to train

дрессиро́вщик, а *m.* trainer

дресс-ко́д, а *m.* dress code

⚬ **дро́б|ный, ∼ен, ∼на** *adj.* ■ (math.) fractional ■ (*частый и мелкий*) staccato, abrupt; **д. стук** staccato knocking; **д. дождь** pattering rain

дробови́к, á *m.* shotgun

дроб|ь, и, *pl.* ∼**и,** ∼**éй** *f.* ■ (collect.) (*для стрельбы*) small shot ■ (*звуки*) drumming; tapping; patter; **бараба́нная** ∼ drum roll ■ (math.) fraction ■ (*черта*) slash

дров|á, ∼, ∼áм (*no sg.*) firewood

дровосéк, а *m.* woodcutter

дро́гн|уть, у, ешь, *past* ∼**ул,** ∼**ула** *pf.* ■ to shake, move; (*о свете*) to flicker ■ (*о человеке*) to waver, falter

дрож|а́ть, у́, и́шь *impf.* ■ to tremble; to shiver, shake; to quiver; to vibrate; (*о свете*) to flicker ■ (**за** + *a.* or **пéред** + *i.*) (fig.) to tremble (for; before) ■ (**над** + *i.*) to grudge; **д. над ка́ждой копéйкой** to count every penny

дро́жж|и, éй (*no sg.*) yeast, leaven

дрож|ь, и *f.* shivering, trembling; (*в го́лосе*) tremor, quaver

дрозд, а́ *m.* thrush; **чёрный д.** blackbird

дро́тик, а *m.* **1** (*ору́жие*) spear, javelin **2** (*в игре́*) dart

✍ **друг¹, а, *pl.* друзья́, друзе́й** *m.* friend

друг² (*short form of* ▸ **друго́й**) **д. ~а** each other, one another; **д. за ~ом** one after another; **д. с ~ом** with each other

✍ **друг|о́й** *adj.* **1** other, another; different; **и тот и д.** both; **ни тот ни д.** neither; (*э́то*) **совсе́м ~о́е де́ло** (that is) quite another matter; **~и́ми слова́ми** in other words; **с ~о́й стороны́** on the other hand; **на д. день** the next day; (*as n. pl.* **~и́е, ~и́х**) others **2** (*второ́й*) second

дру́жб|а, ы *f.* friendship

дружелю́б|ный, ~ен, ~на *adj.* friendly, amicable

дру́жеский *adj.* friendly

дру́жественный *adj.* friendly, amicable; (comput.) user-friendly

дружи́|ть, у́, ~ишь *impf.* (*c + i.*) to be friends (with)

дру́жно *adv.* **1** harmoniously, in concord **2** (*вме́сте*) (all) together, in concert

дру́ж|ный, ~ен, ~на́, ~но, ~ны́ *adj.* **1** (*единоду́шный*) amicable; harmonious **2** (*одновреме́нный*) simultaneous, concerted

друзья́ *see* ▸ **друг¹**

дря́бл|ый, ~, ~а́, ~о *adj.* flabby

дрян|но́й, ~ен, ~на́, ~но, ~ны́ *adj.* (infml) worthless, rotten; good-for-nothing

дрян|ь, и *f.* (infml) trash, rubbish

дря́хл|ый, ~, ~а́, ~о *adj.* decrepit, senile

ДТП *nt. indecl.* (*abbr. of* **доро́жно-тра́нспортное происше́ствие**) road accident

дуб, а, *pl.* **~ы́** *m.* oak

дуби́нк|а, и *f.* cudgel, truncheon

дублёнк|а, и *f.* (infml) sheepskin coat

дублёр, а *m.* (theatr.) understudy; (cin.) stand-in

Ду́блин, а *m.* Dublin

дубли́р|овать, ую *impf.* to duplicate; **д. роль** (theatr.) to understudy a part

дубо́вый *adj.* **1** oak **2** (fig., infml, *глу́пый*) thick

дуг|а́, и́, *pl.* **~и** *f.* arc

ду́дк|а, и *f.* pipe, fife; **пляса́ть под чью-н. ~у** (fig.) to dance to sb's tune

ду́л|о, а *nt.* (*отве́рстие ствола́*) muzzle; (*ствол*) barrel

✍ **Ду́м|а, ы** *f.* Duma (*lower house of the Russian parliament*)

✍ **ду́ма|ть, ю** *impf.* (*of* ▸ **поду́мать 1**) **1** (o + *p. or* над + *i.*) to think (about); to be concerned (about) **2** (*impf. only*) **д. что...** to think, suppose that ... **3** (+ *inf.*) to think of, plan to; **он ~ет пое́хать в Ло́ндон** he is thinking of

going to London

ду́ма|ться, ется *impf.* (impers., + *d.*) to seem; **мне ~ется** I think, I fancy; **~ется** it seems

ду́м|ец, ца *m.* (infml) member of Duma

ду́мский *adj. of* ▸ **Ду́ма**

ду́н|уть, у, ешь *pf.* to blow

дупл|о́, а́, *pl.* **~а́, ду́пел** *nt.* **1** (*в стволе́ де́рева*) hollow **2** (*в зу́бе*) cavity

ду́р|а, ы *f. of* ▸ **дура́к**

дура́к, а́ *m.* fool, ass; **оста́вить в ~а́х** to make a fool of

дура́цкий *adj.* (infml) stupid, foolish, idiotic

дура́ч|ить, у, ишь *impf.* (*of* ▸ **одура́чить**) to fool, dupe

дура́ч|иться, усь, ишься *impf.* to play the fool

дурдо́м, а *m.* (infml) madhouse

ду́рно *as pred.* (impers.+ *d.*): **мне** *и т. п.* **д.** I feel, *etc.*, faint, bad

дур|но́й, ~ён, ~на́, ~но, ~ны́ *adj.* **1** (*плохо́й*) bad, evil; nasty; **д. вкус** nasty taste; **~ны́е мы́сли** evil thoughts; **~ны́е привы́чки** bad habits **2**: **д.** (*собо́ю*) (*некраси́вый*) ugly

дуршла́г, а *m.* (cul.) colander

дуть, ду́ю, ду́ешь *impf.* (*of* ▸ **поду́ть 1**) to blow; **сего́дня ду́ет за́падный ве́тер** there is a west wind today

✍ **дух, а** *m.* **1** (relig., phil., fig. also) spirit; **Свято́й Д.** the Holy Spirit **2** (*мора́льное состоя́ние*) spirit(s); heart; mind; **быть в ~е** to be in good (high) spirits; **не в ~е** in low spirits **3** (*дыха́ние*) breath; (infml) air; **перевести́ д.** to take breath **4** (*при́зрак*) spectre (BrE), specter (AmE), ghost

дух|и́, о́в (*no sg.*) perfume, scent

духове́нств|о, а *nt.* (*collect.*) clergy, priesthood

духо́вк|а, и *f.* oven

духовни́к, а́ *m.* (eccl.) confessor

духо́вност|ь, и *f.* spirituality

✍ **духо́вный** *adj.* **1** spiritual; inner; **д. мир** inner world **2** (*церко́вный*) ecclesiastical, church; religious; **д. сан** holy orders

духово́й *adj.* (mus.) wind; **д. инструме́нт** wind instrument; **д. орке́стр** brass band

духот|а́, ы́ *f.* stuffiness, closeness

душ, а *m.* shower; **приня́ть д.** to take a shower

✍ **душ|а́, и́, а. ~у,** *pl.* **~и** *f.* **1** soul; (fig.) heart; **д. в ~у** at one, in harmony; **в ~е́** inwardly, secretly; at heart **2** (*чу́вства*) feelings, spirit **3** (fig., *челове́к, при указа́нии коли́чества*) soul; **на ~у** per head

душев|а́я, о́й *f.* shower room

душевнобольн|о́й *adj.* insane; mentally ill; (*as n.* **д.,** **~о́го,** *f.* **~а́я,** **~о́й**) insane person; psychiatric patient

душе́вн|ый *adj.* **1** mental; **~ая боле́знь** mental illness **2** (*и́скренний*) sincere, heartfelt; **д. челове́к** understanding person

души́ст|ый, ~, ~а *adj.* fragrant, sweet-scented

✍ key word

души́ть¹, у́, ∼ишь *impf.* (*of* ▶ **задуши́ть**)
1 (*убивать*) to strangle; to stifle, smother, suffocate; (fig., *угнетать*) to stifle, suppress **2** (*impf. only*) (*лишать возможности дышать*) to choke; **его́** ∼**и́л гнев** he choked with rage

души́ть², у́, ∼ишь *impf.* (*of* ▶ **надуши́ть**) to scent, perfume

души́ться¹, у́сь, ∼ишься *impf., pass. of* ▶ **души́ть¹**

души́ться², у́сь, ∼ишься *impf.* (*of* ▶ **надуши́ться**) (+ *i.*) to perfume oneself (with)

ду́шно *as pred.* it is stuffy; it is stifling, suffocating; **мне ста́ло д.** I felt suffocated

ду́ш|ный, ∼ен, ∼на́, ∼но *adj.* stuffy, close, sultry; stifling

дуэ́л|ь, **и** *f.* duel

дуэ́т, **а** *m.* duet

ДЦП *m. indecl.* (*abbr. of* **де́тский церебра́льный парали́ч**) (med.) cerebral palsy

ды́бом *adv.* on end; **во́лосы у него́ вста́ли д.** his hair stood on end

дым, **а** (**у**), **о** ∼**е**, **в** ∼**у́**, *pl.* ∼**ы́** *m.* smoke

дым|и́ться, **и́тся** *impf.* to smoke; (*о тумане*) to billow

ды́мк|а, **и** *f.* haze (also fig.)

дымово́й *adj. of* ▶ **дым**

дымохо́д, **а** *m.* flue

ды́мчат|ый, ∼, ∼**а** *adj.* smoke-coloured (BrE), smoke-colored (AmE); (*очки*) tinted

ды́н|я, **и** *f.* melon

дыр|а́, **ы́**, *pl.* ∼**ы** *f.* hole (also fig., infml)

ды́рк|а, **и** *f.* hole

дыроко́л, **а** *m.* hole puncher, hole punch

дыря́в|ый, ∼, ∼**а** *adj.* full of holes, holey

дыха́ни|е, **я** *nt.* breathing; breath; **иску́сственное д.** artificial respiration

дыха́тельн|ый *adj.* respiratory; ∼**ые пути́** respiratory tract

дыш|а́ть, **у́**, ∼**ишь** *impf.* (+ *i.*) to breathe; (*быть проникнутым чем-либо*) to exude

дья́вол, **а** *m.* devil

дья́вольский *adj.* devilish, diabolical

дья́кон, **а** *m.* (eccl.) deacon

дю́жин|а, **ы** *f.* dozen

дюйм, **а** *m.* inch

дю́н|а, **ы** *f.* dune

дюра́л|ь, **я** *m.* = **дюралюми́ний**

дюралюми́ни|й, **я** *m.* (tech.) Duralumin®

дя́д|я, **и**, *g. pl.* ∼**ей** *m.* **1** (*родственник*) uncle **2** (infml, *обращение*) mister (*as term of address*) **3** (infml, *мужчина*) guy

дя́т|ел, **ла** *m.* woodpecker

Ee

ёбаный *adj.* (vulg.) fucking

еб|а́ть, **у́**, **ёшь** *impf.* (*of* ▶ **вы́ебать**) (vulg.) to fuck; (*as int.*) (*чёрт возьми!*) fuck!; fucking hell!; **ёб твою́ мать!** fuck you!

Ева́нгели|е, **я** *nt.* (collect.) the Gospels; gospel (also fig.)

евразийский *adj.* Eurasian

Евра́зи|я, **и** *f.* Eurasia

евре́|й, **я** *m.* Jew; (*древний*) Hebrew

евре́йк|а, **и** *f.* Jewish woman, girl

евре́йский *adj.* Jewish; ∼ **язы́к** (*иврит*) Hebrew

⚔ **е́вро** *m. indecl.* euro (*currency unit*)

евро... *comb. form* Euro-

еврозо́н|а, **ы** *f.* eurozone

Евро́п|а, **ы** *f.* Europe

Европарла́мент, **а** *m.* European Parliament

европе́|ец, **йца** *m.* European

европе́йк|а, **ки** *f. of* ▶ **европе́ец**

⚔ **европе́йский** *adj.* European

евроремо́нт, **а** *m.* restoration carried out to Western standards

Евросою́з, **а** *m.* European Union

Еги́п|ет, **та** *m.* Egypt

еги́петский *adj.* Egyptian

египтя́н|ин, **ина**, *pl.* ∼**е**, ∼ *m.* Egyptian

египтя́н|ка, **ки** *f. of* ▶ **египтя́нин**

его́ 1 *g. and a. sg. of* ▶ **он 2** *poss. pron.* (*относящийся к человеку*) his; (*относящийся к предмету*) its

⚔ **ед|а́**, **ы́** *f.* **1** (*пища*) food **2** (*трапеза*) meal; **во вре́мя** ∼**ы́** at mealtimes, while eating

едва́ *adv. and conj.* **1** *adv.* (*с трудом*) hardly, barely **2** *adv.* (*чуть*) hardly, scarcely **3**: **е. ли** *adv.* hardly, scarcely (*in judgements of probability*) **4**: **е. (ли) не** *adv.* nearly, almost, all but; **я е. не по́мер со́ смеху** I nearly died laughing **5** *conj.* hardly, scarcely, barely; **е. ..., как** scarcely ... when; no sooner ... than; **е. самолёт взлете́л, как отказа́л оди́н из дви́гателей** no sooner had the plane taken off than one of the engines seized up

еди́м *see* ▶ **есть¹**

⚔ **едини́ц|а**, **ы** *f.* **1** (*цифра*) one; figure 1; (math.) unity **2** unit; **е. мо́щности** unit of

power; **боевы́е ~ы фло́та** naval units;
15 ~ боево́й те́хники 15 military vehicles
3 (*отме́тка*) 'one' (*lowest mark in Russian school marking system*)

едини́чный *adj.* single; **е. слу́чай** isolated case

единобо́жи|е, я *nt.* monotheism

единобо́рств|о, а *nt.* single combat

единовла́сти|е, я *nt.* autocracy, absolute rule

единовре́мен|ный, ~ен, ~на *adj.* extraordinary, unique; **~ное посо́бие** extraordinary grant

единогла́сно *adv.* unanimously

единогла́с|ный, ~ен, ~на *adj.* unanimous

единоду́ши|е, я *nt.* unanimity

единоду́ш|ный, ~ен, ~на *adj.* unanimous

единомы́шленник, а *m.* person who holds the same views; like-minded person

единообра́з|ный, ~ен, ~на *adj.* uniform

единоро́г, а *m.* (myth.) unicorn

еди́нственно *adv.* only, solely; **е. возмо́жный ход** the only possible move

✐ **еди́нствен|ный, ~ and ~ен, ~на** *adj.* only, sole; **е. сын** only son; **он е. оста́лся в живы́х** he was the sole survivor; **~ное число́** (gram.) singular (number)

еди́нств|о, а *nt.* unity

✐ **еди́н|ый, ~, ~а** *adj.* **1** (*еди́нственный*) one; single, sole; **там не́ было ни ~ой души́** there was not a soul there; **все до ~ого** to a man **2** (*оди́н*) united, unified **3** (*о́бщий*) common, single; **~ая во́ля** single will/purpose

еди́те *see* ▸ **есть¹**

е́д|кий, ~ок, ~ка, ~ко *adj.* **1** caustic; acrid, pungent **2** (fig.) caustic, sarcastic

е́д|у, ешь *see* ▸ **е́хать**

едя́т *see* ▸ **есть¹**

✐ **её 1** *g. and a. of* ▸ **она́ 2** *poss. pron.* (*относя́щийся к челове́ку*) (*при существи́тельном*) her; (*без существи́тельного*) hers; (*относя́щийся к предме́ту*) its

ёж, ежа́ *m.* hedgehog

ежеви́к|а, и *f.* **1** (collect.) blackberries **2** (*куста́рник*) bramble, blackberry bush

ежего́дный *adj.* annual, yearly

ежедне́в|ный, ~ен, ~на *adj.* daily; everyday

ежеме́сячный *adj.* monthly

ежемину́т|ный, ~ен, ~на *adj.* **1** occurring every minute, at intervals of a minute **2** (*непреры́вный*) incessant, continual

еженеде́льный *adj.* weekly

ежеча́сный *adj.* hourly

езд|а́, ы́ *f.* **1** ride, riding; (*на маши́не*) drive **2** (*in phrr.* indicating distance from one point to another) journey, drive; **отсю́да до о́зера — до́брых три часа́ ~ы́** from here to the lake is a good three hours' journey

е́з|дить, жу, дишь *impf.* (indet. of ▸ **е́хать**) **1** to go (*in or on a vehicle or on an animal*); to

ride, drive; **е. верхо́м** to ride (on horseback) **2** (*уме́ть е́здить*) to (be able to) ride, drive **3** (к + *d.*) (*посеща́ть*) to visit

езжа́|ть (infml): **~й(те)!** (*as imper. of* ▸ **е́хать**) go!; get going!

ей *d. and i. of* ▸ **она́**

ел, е́ла *see* ▸ **есть¹**

е́ле *adv.* **1** (*с трудо́м*) hardly, barely, only just **2** (*почти́ не*) hardly, scarcely, barely, only just; **по́езд е. дви́гался** the train was scarcely moving

ёлк|а, и *f.* **1** fir (tree), spruce; **нового́дняя ё.** Christmas tree **2** (infml, *пра́здник*) Christmas, New Year's party

ёлоч|ный *adj. of* ▸ **ёлка**; **~ые украше́ния** Christmas tree decorations

ел|ь, и *f.* spruce (*Picea*); fir (tree)

ем *see* ▸ **есть¹**

ём|кий, ~ок, ~ка *adj.* capacious

ёмкост|ь, и *f.* (*вмести́мость*) capacity, cubic content; (*вмести́лище*) container

ему́ *d. of* ▸ **он**

ено́т *m.* raccoon

епа́рхи|я, и *f.* (eccl.) diocese

епи́скоп, а *m.* bishop

ерала́ш, а *m.* (infml) jumble, muddle

е́рес|ь, и, *pl.* **~и, ~ей** *f.* heresy

ёрза|ть, ю *impf.* (infml) to fidget

ерунд|а́, ы́ *f.* (infml) **1** (*чепуха́*) nonsense, rubbish; **говори́ть ~у́** to talk nonsense **2** (*пустя́к*) trifle, trifling matter; child's play

ЕС *m. indecl.* (*abbr. of* **Европе́йский сою́з**) EU (*European Union*)

✐ **е́сли** *conj.* if; **е. не** unless; **е. то́лько** provided; **е. бы не** but for, if it were not for; **е. бы** (*в восклица́ниях*) if only; **что е. ...?** what if ...?

ест *see* ▸ **есть¹**

есте́ственно¹ *adv.* **1** naturally **2** (*as particle*) naturally, of course

есте́ственно² *as pred.* it is natural

✐ **есте́ствен|ный, ~, ~на** *adj.* natural; **~ные нау́ки** natural sciences; **е. отбо́р** (biol.) natural selection

естествозна́ни|е, я *nt.* (natural) science

есть¹, ем, ешь, ест, еди́м, еди́те, едя́т, *past* **ел, е́ла**, *imper.* **ешь**, *impf.* (of ▸ **съесть**) **1** (*принима́ть пи́щу*) to eat **2** (impf. only) (*мета́лл*) to corrode, eat away **3** (impf. only) (*о ды́ме*) to sting, cause to smart

есть² **1** *3rd pers. sg.* (*also, rarely, substituted for all persons*) *pres. of* ▸ **быть 2** there is; there are; **у меня́, него́** *и т. п. е.* I have, he has, *etc.*

✐ **е́хать, е́ду, е́дешь** *impf.* (of ▸ **пое́хать**, *det. of* ▸ **е́здить**) to go (*in or on a vehicle or on an animal*); to ride, drive; **е. верхо́м** to ride (*on horseback*); **е. по́ездом, на по́езде** to go by train

ехи́д|ный, ~ен, ~на *adj.* (infml) malicious, spiteful; **~ные замеча́ния** snide remarks, taunts

ешь *see* ▸ **есть¹**

✐ key word

✔ **ещё** *adv.* **1** (*по-прежнему*) still; yet; **е. не, нет е.** not yet; **всё е.** still **2** (*больше*) some more; any more; yet, further; again; **вам нали́ть е. (вина́ и т. п.)?** may I pour you some more (wine, *etc.*)?; **е. оди́н** one more, yet another; **е. раз** once more, again **3** (*уже*) already; as long ago as, as far back as; **е. в 1900 году́** in 1900 already; as long ago as 1900 **4** (*дополнительно*) else; **кто е. хо́чет ко́фе?** who else wants coffee?; **вы хоти́те е. что-нибудь?** do you want anything else? **5** (+ *comp.*) still, yet, even; **е. гро́мче** even louder; **е. и е.** more and more **6** (+ *prons. and advs., as emph. particle*): **ты не ви́дел кота́? — како́го е. кота́?** have you seen the cat? — what cat, for heaven's sake? **7**: **е. бы!** (infml, *конечно, безусловно*) yes, rather!; you bet!, of course!

ЕЭС *nt. indecl.* (*abbr. of* **Европе́йское экономи́ческое соо́бщество**) EEC (*European Economic Community*)

е́ю *i. of* ▶ **она́**

e

ж

Жж

✔ **Ж = же¹, же²**

жа́б|а, ы *f.* (zool.) toad

жа́воро́н|ок, ка *m.* (zool.) lark; (fig.) early riser

жа́дност|ь, и *f.* **1** (*к деньга́м, еде, де́йствию*) greed (for); greediness **2** (*скупость*) avarice, meanness

жа́д|ный, ~ен, ~на́, ~но *adj.* **1** (к + *d.*) greedy (for); avid (for) **2** (*скупой*) avaricious, mean

жа́жд|а, ы (*no pl.*) *f.* thirst; (+ *g.*) (fig.) thirst, craving (for); **ж. зна́ний** thirst for knowledge

жа́жд|ать, у *impf.* (+ *g. or inf.*) (fig.) to thirst (for, after), crave

жаке́т, а *m.* jacket (*ladies'*)

жале́|ть, ю *impf.* (*of* ▶ **пожале́ть**) **1** (*чу́вствовать жа́лость*) to pity, feel sorry (for) **2** (**о** + *p. or* + *g. or* **что**) (*сожале́ть*) to regret, be sorry (for, about) **3** (+ *d. or g.*) (*скупи́ться*) to spare; to grudge; **не ~я сил** not sparing oneself, unsparingly

жа́л|ить, ю, ишь *impf.* (*of* ▶ **ужа́лить**) to sting; to bite

жа́л|кий, ~ок, ~ка́, ~ко *adj.* pitiful, pathetic, wretched; **име́ть ж. вид** to be a sorry sight

жа́лко¹ *adv. of* ▶ **жа́лкий**

жа́лко² *as pred.* (*impers.*) **1** (+ *d. and a.*) (*о чу́встве сострада́ния*) to pity, feel sorry (for); **мне ж. бра́та** I feel sorry for my brother **2** (*о чу́встве гру́сти*) (it is) a pity, a shame; (+ *d. and g. or a.*) it grieves me, *etc.*; to regret **3** (+ *g. or* + *inf.*) (*скупи́ться*) to grudge

жа́л|о, а *nt.* (*пчелы́*) sting (also fig.)

жа́лоб|а, ы *f.* complaint; **пода́ть ~у (на** + *a.*) to make, lodge a complaint (about)

жа́лоб|ный, ~ен, ~на *adj.* plaintive; mournful

жа́лованье, я *nt.* salary

жа́л|оваться, уюсь *impf.* (*of* ▶ **пожа́ловаться**) (**на** + *a.*) to complain (of, about)

жа́лост|ь, и *f.* pity, compassion; **из ~и (к** + *d.*) out of pity (for); **кака́я ж.!** what a pity!

жаль *as pred.* (*impers.*) **1** (+ *d. and a.*) (*о чу́встве сострада́ния*) to pity, feel sorry (for); **мне ж. тебя́** I pity you **2** (*о чу́встве гру́сти*) (it is) a pity, a shame; (+ *d.*) it grieves (*me, etc.*); to regret, feel sorry **3** (+ *g. or* + *inf.*) (*скупи́ться*) to grudge; **(мне) ж. де́нег** I begrudge the money

жалюзи́ *pl. indecl.* Venetian blind

жанда́рм, а *m.* gendarme

жанр, а *m.* genre

жар, а (у), о ~е, в ~у́ (*no pl.*) *m.* **1** heat; heat of the day; hot place **2** (*лихора́дка*) fever; (high) temperature

жар|а́, ы́ *f.* heat; hot weather; **в са́мую ~у́** in the heat of the day

жарго́н, а *m.* jargon; slang

жа́реный *adj.* (*на сковороде́*) fried; (*в духо́вке*) roast; (*на решётке*) grilled (BrE), broiled (AmE)

жа́р|ить, ю, ишь *impf.* (*pf.* **за~** *or* **из~** *or* **по~**) (*на сковороде́*) to fry; (*в духо́вке*) to roast; (*на решётке*) to grill (BrE), broil (AmE)

жа́р|иться, юсь, ишься *impf.* **1** (*pf.* **за~** *or* **из~**) to roast, fry **2**: **ж. на со́лнце** (infml) to bask in the sun, sun oneself **3** *pass. of* ▶ **жа́рить**

жа́р|кий, ~ок, ~ка́, ~ко *adj.* **1** hot; (*тропи́ческий*) tropical **2** (fig.) hot, heated; ardent; passionate; **ж. спор** heated argument

жа́рко¹ *adv. of* ▶ **жа́ркий**

жа́рко² *as pred.* it is hot; **мне** *и т. п.* **ж.** I am, *etc.*, hot

жарк|о́е, о́го *nt.* (fried) meat

жаропро́ч|ный, ~ен, ~на *adj.* ovenproof; **~ная кастрю́ля** casserole (dish)

жар-пти́ц|а, ы *f.* the Firebird (*in folklore*)

жа́рче *comp. of* ▶ **жа́ркий**, ▶ **жа́рко**[1]

жасми́н, а *m.* jasmine

жа́тв|а, ы (*no pl.*) *f.* reaping, harvesting; harvest (also fig.)

жа́тк|а, и *f.* harvester, reaping machine

жать[1], жму, жмёшь *impf.* (*no pf.*) **1** (*руку*) to press, squeeze; **ж. ру́ку** to shake (sb) by the hand **2** (*о платье, обуви*) to pinch, be tight; (*impers.*) **в плеча́х жмёт** it is tight on the shoulders

жать[2], жну, жнёшь *impf.* (*of* ▶ **сжать**[2]) to reap, cut, mow

жва́чк|а, и *f.* (infml) chewing gum

жва́чн|ый *adj.* (zool.) ruminant; (*as nt. n.* ~ое, ~ого) ruminant

жгу, жжёшь, жгут *see* ▶ **жечь**

жгут, а́ *m.* **1** plait (BrE); braid **2** (med.) tourniquet

жгу́ч|ий, ~, ~а, ~е *adj.* burning hot (also fig.); ~ая боль smart, smarting pain; **ж. брюне́т** person with jet-black hair and eyes

ж. д. (*abbr. of* **желе́зная доро́га**) railway (BrE), railroad (AmE)

⚹ **ждать, жду, ждёшь,** *past* ждал, ждала́, жда́ло *impf.* (+ *g.*) to wait (for); to await; **заста́вить себя́ ж.** to keep waiting; **не заста́вить себя́ ж.** to come quickly; **что нас ждёт?** what is in store for us? **2** (*надеяться на, предполагать*) to expect

⚹ **же**[1] *conj.* **1** (*при противопоставлении*) but; **иди́, е́сли тебе́ охо́та, я же оста́нусь здесь** go, if you feel like it, but I shall stay here **2** (*для присоединения*) and; **Ока́ впада́ет в Во́лгу, Во́лга же в Каспи́йское мо́ре** the Oka flows into the Volga, and the Volga flows into the Caspian Sea **3** (*ведь*) after all; **расскажи́ ей: она́ же твоя́ мать** tell her — she's your mother, after all

⚹ **же**[2] *emph. particle:* **что же ты де́лаешь?** whatever are you doing, what *are* you doing?

⚹ **же**[3] *particle* (*подчёркивает значение слова, после которого ставится*): **тот же, тако́й же** the same; **тогда́ же** at the same time

жева́тельн|ый *adj.:* ~ая рези́нка chewing gum

жева́ть, жую́, жуёшь *impf.* to chew

жёг, жгла *see* ▶ **жечь**

жезл, а́ *m.* (*символ власти*) rod, staff (of office); (*милиционера*) baton

⚹ **жела́ни|е**, я *nt.* **1** (+ *g.*) wish (for), desire (for); **при всём** ~и with the best will in the world **2** (*просьба*) request **3** (*вожделение*) desire, lust

жела́нный *p.p.p. of* ▶ **жела́ть** *and adj.* wished for, longed for, desired, beloved; **ж. гость** welcome visitor

жела́тельно[1] *adv.* preferably

жела́тельно[2] *as pred.* it is desirable; it is advisable, preferable

жела́тел|ьный, ~ен, ~ьна *adj.* desirable; advisable

⚹ **жела́|ть**, ю *impf.* (*of* ▶ **пожела́ть**) **1** (+ *g.*) to wish (for), desire **2** (**что́бы** *or* + *inf.*) to wish, want **3** (+ *d. and g. or inf.*) to wish (*sb sth*); ~ю вам успе́ха/уда́чи! good luck!; **э́то оставля́ет ж. лу́чшего** it leaves much to be desired

жела́|ющий *pres. part. act. of* ▶ **жела́ть**; ~ющие persons interested, those who so desire

желе́ *nt. indecl.* jelly

желез|а́, ы́, *pl.* же́лезы, желёз, ~а́м *f.* (anat.) gland; *pl.* tonsils

железнодоро́жник, а *m.* railway worker

железнодоро́жный *adj.* rail, railway, railroad (AmE); **ж. путь** (railway) track; **ж. у́зел** (railway) junction

⚹ **желе́зн|ый** *adj.* **1** iron (also fig.); (chem.) ferric, ferrous; **ж. век** the Iron Age; **ж. за́навес** the 'Iron Curtain' **2**: ~ая доро́га railway (BrE), railroad (AmE); **по** ~ой доро́ге by rail

желе́з|о, а *nt.* iron

железобето́н, а *m.* (tech.) reinforced concrete, ferroconcrete

жёлоб, а, *pl.* желеба́, желебо́в *m.* (*водосточный*) gutter; (*для ссыпания чего-л.*) chute

желте́|ть, ю *impf.* (*pf.* ▶ **пожелте́ть**) (*становиться жёлтым*) to turn yellow

желт|о́к, ка́ *m.* yolk

желту́х|а, и *f.* (med.) jaundice

жёлт|ый, жёлт, желта́, жёлто *and* жёлто *adj.* yellow; **жёлтая пре́сса** the yellow press, the tabloids; **Жёлтые страни́цы** Yellow Pages®

желу́д|ок, ка *m.* stomach; **несваре́ние** ~ка indigestion

желу́дочный *adj.* stomach; gastric; **ж. сок** gastric juice

жёлуд|ь, я, *g. pl.* желуде́й *m.* acorn

жёлч|ь, и *and* (infml) **желч|ь**, и (*no pl.*) *f.* bile, gall (also fig.)

жема́н|ный, ~ен, ~на *adj.* affected

же́мчуг, а, *pl.* ~а́ *m.* (collect.) pearl(s)

жемчу́жин|а, ы *f.* pearl (also fig.)

жемчу́жн|ый *adj. of* ▶ **же́мчуг**; (fig.) pearly(-white); ~ое ожере́лье pearl necklace

⚹ **жен|а́**, ы́, *pl.* ~ы, ~, ~а́м *f.* wife; **быть у** ~ы́ **под каблуко́м** to be henpecked

жена́т|ый, ~ *adj.* married; **ж.** (**на** + *p.*) (*о мужчине*) married (to)

жени́тьб|а, ы *f.* marriage

жени́|ться, юсь, ~ишься *impf. and pf.* (**на** + *p.*) (*о мужчине*) to marry, get married (to)

жени́х, а́ *m.* **1** fiancé **2** (*на свадьбе*) bridegroom

женоподо́б|ный, ~ен, ~на *adj.* effeminate

⚹ **же́нский** *adj.* woman's; female; feminine

⚹ **же́нствен|ный**, ~ *and* ~ен, ~на *adj.* feminine, womanly

⚹ **же́нщин|а**, ы *f.* woman

женьше́н|ь, я *m.* (bot., med.) ginseng

⚹ key word

жереб|ёнок, ёнка, pl. ~я́та, ~я́т m. foal, colt

жереб|е́ц, ца́ m. stallion

жеребьёвк|а, и f. casting of lots; (sport) draw (for play-off)

жёрнов, а, pl. жернова́, жерново́в m. millstone

жёртв|а, ы f. **1** sacrifice (also fig.); принести́ ~у (+ d.) to make a sacrifice (to); принести́ в ~у to sacrifice **2** (пострада́вший) victim; пасть ~ой (+ g.) to fall victim (to)

же́ртв|овать, ую impf. (of ▶ поже́ртвовать) **1** (да́рить) to make a donation (of), present **2** (+ i.) (подверга́ть опа́сности) to sacrifice, give up

жертвоприноше́ни|е, я nt. sacrifice

жест, а m. gesture (also fig.)

жестикули́р|овать, ую impf. to gesticulate

жестикуля́ци|я, и f. gesticulation

жёсткий, жёсток, жестка́, жёстко adj. hard; tough; (fig.) rigid, strict; ж. диск (comput.) hard disk

жёстко[1] adv. of ▶ жёсткий

жёстко[2] as pred. it is hard

жесто́к|ий, ~, ~а adj. cruel; brutal; (fig.) severe, sharp

жесто́кост|ь, и f. cruelty, brutality

жёстче comp. of ▶ жёсткий, ▶ жёстко[1]

жест|ь, и f. tinplate

жест|яно́й adj. of ▶ жесть; ~яна́я посу́да tinware

жестя́нщик, а m. tinsmith

жето́н, а m. **1** (награ́да) medal; (опознава́тельный знак) badge (of police officer, porter, etc.) **2** (сре́дство опла́ты) token

жечь, жгу, жжёшь, жгут, past жёг, жгла impf. **1** (pf. с~) to burn; (до́тла) to burn down **2** (impf. only) to burn, sting; (impers.) от э́того ликёра жжёт в го́рле this liqueur burns one's throat

же́чься, жгусь, жжёшься, жгу́тся, past жёгся, жгла́сь impf. to burn, sting

жжёшь see ▶ жечь

жи́во adv. **1** (я́рко) vividly **2** (оживлённо) with animation **3** (о́стро) keenly **4** (infml, бы́стро) quickly, promptly

жив|о́й, ~, ~а́, ~о adj. **1** (облада́ющий жи́знью) living, live, alive; оста́ться в ~ых to survive **2** (энерги́чный) lively; keen; active **3** (вырази́тельный) lively, vivacious; bright; ~ы́е глаза́ bright eyes **4** (без предвари́тельной за́писи) live; ~а́я му́зыка live music

живопи́с|ец, ца m. painter

живопи́с|ный, ~ен, ~на adj. **1** (относя́щийся к жи́вописи) pictorial **2** (краси́вый) picturesque (also fig.); ~ное ме́сто beauty spot

жи́вопис|ь, и f. **1** painting **2** (collect.) paintings

жи́вост|ь, и f. liveliness, vivacity; animation

жив|о́т, а́ m. abdomen, belly; stomach; (infml) tummy

животново́дств|о, а nt. stockbreeding, animal husbandry

живо́тно|е, го nt. animal; дома́шнее ж. pet

живо́тный adj. **1** animal **2** (гру́бый) bestial, brute

живу́ч|ий, ~, ~а adj. **1** tenacious of life; (bot.) hardy; он ~ как ко́шка he has nine lives like a cat **2** (fig., обы́чай) deep-rooted, enduring

живьём adv. (infml) alive; петь ж. to sing live; постара́йтесь взять его́ ж. try to catch him alive

жи́голо m. indecl. gigolo

жи́д|кий, ~ок, ~ка́, ~ко adj. **1** (име́ющий сво́йство течь) liquid; fluid **2** (водяни́стый) watery; weak, thin; ж. суп thin soup **3** (о волоса́х) sparse, scanty; ~кая борода́ straggly beard

жидкокристалли́ческий adj.: ж. диспле́й liquid crystal display (abbr. LCD)

жи́дкост|ь, и f. liquid; fluid

жи́ж|а, и (no pl.) f. liquid; swill; slush

жи́же comp. of ▶ жи́дкий

жизнеде́ятельност|ь, и f. (biol.) vital activity

жи́зненный, ~, ~на adj. **1** (of) life; (biol.) vital; ж. у́ровень standard of living **2** (бли́зкий к жи́зни, реа́льный) close to life; lifelike **3** (fig.) vital, vitally important

жизнеобеспе́чени|е, я nt.: систе́ма ~я life-support system

жизнеописа́ни|е, я nt. biography

жизнера́дост|ный, ~ен, ~на adj. cheerful; vivacious

жизнеспосо́б|ный, ~ен, ~на adj. capable of living; (biol.) viable; (fig.) vigorous, flourishing

жизн|ь, и f. life; (существова́ние) existence; зараба́тывать на ж. to earn one's living; как ж.? (infml) how is life?; лиши́ть себя́ ~и to take one's life; о́браз ~и way of life; lifestyle

жи́л|а, ы f. **1** (сухожи́лие) tendon, sinew; (infml, кровено́сный сосу́д) vein **2** (min.) vein

жиле́т, а m. waistcoat (BrE), vest (AmE); спаса́тельный ж. life jacket

жил|е́ц, ьца́ m. tenant

жи́лист|ый, ~, ~а adj. **1** (ру́ки) having prominent veins **2** (те́ло) sinewy; (стари́к) wiry; ~ое мя́со stringy meat

жили́щ|е, а nt. dwelling, abode, (living) quarters

жили́щ|ный adj. of ▶ жили́ще; ~ные усло́вия housing conditions

жил|о́й adj. **1** dwelling; residential; ж. дом dwelling house, block of flats; ж. кварта́л residential area; ~а́я пло́щадь = жилпло́щадь **2** (обита́емый) inhabited

жилпло́щад|ь, и f. housing, accommodation

жил|ьё, я́ nt. **1** (селе́ние) habitation; dwelling **2** (жили́ще) lodging; (living) accommodation

жи́молост|ь, и f. (bot.) honeysuckle

ж

з

жир, а (у), о ~е, в ~у́, pl. ~ы́ m. fat; grease

жира́ф, а m. giraffe

жи́р|ный, ~ен, ~на́, ~но adj. **1** (*пища, мясо*) fatty; (*руки, волосы*) greasy **2** (*человек*) fat, plump **3** (*земля*) rich **4** (*тип.*) bold

жиров|о́й adj. fatty, aliphatic; (anat.) adipose; ~а́я ткань adipose tissue

жите́йск|ий adj. **1** worldly; of life; ~ая му́дрость worldly wisdom **2** (*обыденный*) everyday

⚜ жи́тел|ь, я m. inhabitant; dweller; ми́рные ~и civilians

жи́тель|ница, ницы f. of ▶ жи́тель

жи́тельств|о, а nt. residence; вид на ж. residence permit

⚜ жить, живу́, живёшь, past жил, жила́, жи́ло, neg. не́ жил, не жила́, не́ жило impf. **1** to live; ж. в Москве́ to live in Moscow **2** (+ i. or на + a.) to live (on); (+ i.) (fig.) to live (in, for); нам не́ на что ж. we have nothing to live on

жи́ться, живётся, past жило́сь impf. (impers., + d.) (infml) to live, get on; ей ве́село живётся she enjoys her life

ЖК-диспле́|й, я m. (abbr. of жидкокристалли́ческий диспле́й) liquid crystal display

жму, жмёшь see ▶ жать¹

жму́р|ки, ок (no sg.) blind man's buff

жнец, а́ m. reaper

жни́ц|а, ы f. of ▶ жнец

жну, жнёшь see ▶ жать²

жоке́|й, я m. jockey

жонгли́р|овать, ую impf. (+ i.) to juggle (with) (also fig.)

жо́п|а, ы f. (vulg.) arse (BrE), ass (AmE); иди́/ пошёл (ты) в ~у! piss off!; пья́ный в ~у very drunk

жр|ать, у́, ёшь, past ~а́л, ~ала́, ~а́ло impf. (of ▶ сожра́ть) **1** (*о животных*) to eat

2 (sl., *о человеке*) to guzzle, gobble

жре́би|й, я m. **1** lot; броса́ть ж. to cast lots; тяну́ть ж. to draw lots **2** (fig.) lot, fate, destiny; ж. бро́шен the die is cast

жрец, а́ m. (pagan) priest; (fig.) devotee

жри́ц|а, ы f. priestess

жу́желиц|а, ы f. (zool.) ground beetle

жужжа́ни|е, я nt. hum, buzz, drone; humming, buzzing, droning

жужж|а́ть, у́, и́шь impf. to hum, buzz, drone; (*о пулях*) to whizz

жук, а́ m. **1** beetle; ма́йский ж. May bug, cockchafer **2** (infml, *плут*) rogue, swindler

жу́лик, а m. petty thief; cheat, swindler

жура́вл|ь, я́ m. (zool.) crane

⚜ журна́л, а m. **1** (*периодическое издание*) magazine; periodical; journal **2** (*книга для записи*) journal, diary; (*классный*) register

⚜ журнали́ст, а m. journalist

журнали́стик|а, и f. journalism

журч|а́ть, и́т impf. to babble, murmur (*of water*) (also fig., poet.)

жу́т|кий, ~ок, ~ка́, ~ко adj. terrible, terrifying; awe-inspiring, eerie

жу́тко¹ adv. terrifyingly; (infml) terribly, awfully

жу́тко² as pred.: ж. поду́мать об э́том it's terrible to think about it; (impers. + d.) мне и т. п. ж. I am, etc., terrified, feel awestruck

жут|ь, и f. (infml) **1** (*страх*) terror; awe **2** (as pred.): ж.! it is terrible!

жучо́к, ка́ m. **1** dim. of ▶ жук **1 2** (infml, *пробка*) makeshift fuse **3** (infml, *подслушивающее устройство*) bug

жу|ю́, ёшь see ▶ жева́ть

ЖЭК, а and жэк, а m. (abbr. of жили́щно-эксплуатацио́нная конто́ра) housing office

жюри́ nt. indecl. (collect.) judges (*of competition, etc.*)

Зз

⚜ за prep. I. (+ a. and i.; + a.: indicates motion or action; + i.: indicates rest or state) **1** (*позади*) behind; за крова́ть, за крова́тью behind the bed **2** (*вне*) beyond; across, the other side of; за́ борт, за бо́ртом overboard; за́ угол, за угло́м round the corner; за́ городом out of town **3** (у) at; сесть за роя́ль to sit down at the piano **4** (*занимаясь данным предметом*) at, to (*or translated by part.*);

приня́ться за рабо́ту to get down to work; заста́ть кого́-н. за рабо́той to find sb at work, working; проводи́ть всё своё вре́мя за чте́нием to spend all one's time reading **5**: вы́йти за́муж за (+ a.) to marry (*of a woman*); (быть) за́мужем за (+ i.) (to be) married (to)

● II. (+ a.) **1** (*свыше*) after (*of time*); over (*of age*); далеко́ за́ полночь long after midnight; ему́ уже́ за со́рок he is already over forty **2** (*на расстоянии*): самолёт разби́лся за ми́лю от дере́вни the aeroplane crashed a mile from the village; **за час** an hour before, an hour early **3** (*в течение*) during, in the space of; **за́ ночь** during the night, overnight; **за су́тки** in (the space of) twenty-four hours **4** (*указывает на предмет, который охватывается*) by; **вести́ за́ руку** to lead by the hand **5** for (*in var. senses*); **плати́ть за биле́т** to pay for a ticket; **подписа́ть за дире́ктора** to sign for the director; **боя́ться, ра́доваться за кого́-н.** to fear, be glad for sb

•III. (+ *i.*) **1** (*после*) after; **друг за дру́гом** one after another; **год за го́дом** year after year; **следовать за кем-н.** to follow sb **2** (*заботясь*) after; **следи́ть за детьми́** to look after children **3** (*чтобы достать, получить*) for; **идти́ за молоко́м** to go for milk; **зайти́ за кем-н.** to call for sb **4** (*во время*) at, during; **за за́втраком** at breakfast **5** (*по причине*) for, on account of, because of; **за неиме́нием** (+ *g.*) for want of **6** (+ *prons.*) (*указывает на ответственного должника*): **за тобо́й пять рубле́й** you are owing five roubles

•IV. (*as pred.*) (*согласен*) for, in favour (BrE), favor (AmE)

за… *pref.* I. (*of vv.*) **1** (*indicates commencement of action*): **зала́ять** to start barking **2** (*indicates direction of action beyond given point*): **заверну́ть за́ угол** to turn a corner **3** (*indicates continuation of action to excess*): **закорми́ть** to overfeed **4** *forms pf. aspect of some vv.*

•II. (*of nn. and adjs.*) trans-; **Закавка́зье** Transcaucasia

заба́в|а, ы *f.* **1** (*игра*) game; (*развлечение*) pastime **2** (*потеха*) amusement, fun; **он э́то сде́лал для ∼ы** he did it for fun

заба́вно¹ *adv. of* ▸ **заба́вный**

заба́вно² *as pred.* it is amusing, funny; (**мне**) **з.** I find it amusing, funny; **з.!** how funny!

заба́в|ный, ∼ен, ∼на *adj.* amusing; funny

забасто́вк|а, и *f.* strike; **всео́бщая з.** general strike; **голо́дная з.** hunger strike

забасто́вщик, а *m.* striker

забасто́вщи|ца, цы *f. of* ▸ **забасто́вщик**

забве́ни|е, я *nt.* oblivion; **преда́ть ∼ю** to consign to oblivion

забе́г, а *m.* (sport) race

забега́ловк|а, и *f.* (infml) snack bar

забе́га|ть, ю *pf.* **1** (*начать бегать*) to start running **2** (*о глазах*) to become shifty

забега́|ть, ю *impf. of* ▸ **забежа́ть**

забе|жа́ть, гу́, жи́шь, гу́т *pf.* (*of* ▸ **забега́ть**) **1** (**в** + *a.*) to run (in(to)) **2** (**к** + *d.*) (infml) to drop in (to see) **3** (*далеко*) to run off; (*неизвестно куда*) to stray **4**: **з. вперёд** to run ahead; (fig., infml) to rush ahead

забеле́|ть, ет *pf.* **1** (*начать белеть*) to begin to turn white **2** (*показаться*) to appear white (in the distance)

забере́мене|ть, ю *pf.* (*of* ▸ **бере́менеть**) to become pregnant

забеспоко́|иться, юсь, ишься *pf.* to begin to worry

забива́|ть, ю *impf. of* ▸ **заби́ть¹**

забива́|ться, юсь *impf. of* ▸ **заби́ться**

забинт|ова́ть, у́ю *pf.* (*of* ▸ **забинто́вывать**) to bandage

забинто́выва|ть, ю *impf. of* ▸ **забинтова́ть**

забира́|ть, ю *impf. of* ▸ **забра́ть**

забира́|ться, юсь *impf. of* ▸ **забра́ться**

заб|и́ть¹, ью́, ьёшь *pf.* (*of* ▸ **забива́ть**) **1** (*вбить*) to drive in, hammer in, ram in **2** (sport) to score; **з. мяч** to kick the ball into the goal **3** (*заделать*) to seal, block up **4** (*закрыть проход*) to obstruct **5** (+ *i.*) (infml, *наполнить*) to cram, stuff (with) **6** (*избить*) to beat up; **з. до́ смерти** to beat to death; (fig.) to render defenceless (BrE), defenseless (AmE) **7** (*убить*) to slaughter (*cattle*)

заб|и́ть², ью́, ьёшь *pf.* to begin to beat (trans. and intrans.) (*in some cases forms pf. aspect of* ▸ **бить**)

заб|и́ться, ью́сь, ьёшься *pf.* (*of* ▸ **забива́ться**) **1** (**в** + *a.*) (*спрятаться*) to hide (in), take refuge (in) **2** (**в** + *a.*) (*проникнуть*) to get (into), penetrate **3** (+ *i.*) (*засоряться*) to become cluttered (with), clogged (with)

заблаговре́менно *adv.* in good time; well in advance

забле|сте́ть, щу́, сти́шь *pf.* to begin to shine, glitter, glow

заблу|ди́ться, жу́сь, ∼дишься *pf.* to lose one's way, get lost

заблужда́|ться, юсь *impf.* to be mistaken

заблужде́ни|е, я *nt.* error; delusion; **ввести́ в з.** to delude, mislead

забо́|й, я *m.* (*убой*) slaughter

⚘ **заболева́ни|е, я** *nt.* sickness, illness

заболева́|ть¹, ю *impf. of* ▸ **заболе́ть¹**

заболева́|ть², ет *impf. of* ▸ **заболе́ть²**

заболе́|ть¹, ю, ешь *pf.* (*of* ▸ **заболева́ть¹**) (*заразиться*) to fall ill, fall sick; (+ *i.*) to be taken ill (with), go down (with)

заболе́|ть², и́т *pf.* (*of* ▸ **заболева́ть²**) (*о появившейся боли*) to (begin to) ache, hurt; **у меня́ ∼е́л зуб** my tooth has started to ache

забо́р, а *m.* fence

забо́т|а, ы *f.* **1** (*беспокойство*) care(s), trouble(s); **без ∼** carefree **2** (*уход*) care, attention(s); concern

забо́|титься, чусь, тишься *impf.* (*of* ▸ **позабо́титься**) (**о** + *p.*) **1** (*беспокоиться*) to worry, be troubled (about) **2** (*ухаживать*) to take care (of); to take trouble (about); to care (about)

забо́тлив|ый, ∼, ∼а *adj.* solicitous, thoughtful; caring

забрако́ванный *p.p.p. of* ▸ **забракова́ть**; **з. това́р** rejects

забрак|ова́ть, у́ю *pf. of* ▸ **бракова́ть**

забра́л|о, а *nt.* visor

забрáсыва|ть, ю *impf. of* ▶ **забросáть,**
▶ **забрóсить**

забрá|ть, заберý, заберёшь, *past* ∼**л,**
∼**лá,** ∼**ло** *pf.* (*of* ▶ **забирáть**) **1** (*взять*)
to take (*in one's hands*); (*человека*) to take
(with one); **з. с собóй вéщи** to take one's
things with one **2** (*арестовáть*) to arrest;
(*отнять*) to take away; to seize, appropriate

забрá|ться, заберýсь, заберёшься, *past*
∼**лся,** ∼**лáсь,** ∼**лóсь** *pf.* (*of* ▶ **забирáться**)
1 (**в** + *a.*) to get (into); (**в, на** + *a.*) to climb
(into, on to) **2** (*уйти, уехать*) to get to;
(*спрятаться*) to hide out, go into hiding

заброни́р|овать, ую *pf.* (*of* ▶ **брони́ровать**)
to reserve

заброса́|ть, ю *pf.* (*of* ▶ **забрáсывать**) (+ *a.*
and i.) (*заполнить*) to fill (up) (with)

забрó|сить, шу, сишь *pf.* (*of* ▶ **забрáсывать**)
1 (*метнуть*) to throw (*with force or to a*
distance) **2** (*оставить*) to throw up, give
up, abandon; to neglect, let go; **з. детéй**
to neglect children **3** (*доставить в*
определённое место) to take, bring

забрóшенный *p.p.p. of* ▶ **забрóсить** *and adj.*
1 (*сад, человек*) neglected **2** (*место*)
deserted, desolate

забры́зг|ать, аю *pf.* (+ *i.*) to splash (with)

забýд|у, ýдешь *see* ▶ **забы́ть**

☞ **забыва́|ть, ю** *impf. of* ▶ **забы́ть**

забыва́|ться, юсь *impf. of* ▶ **забы́ться**

забы́вчив|ый, ∼**,** ∼**а** *adj.* forgetful; absent-
minded

☞ **забы́|ть, ýду, ýдешь** *pf.* (*of* ▶ **забыва́ть**)
1 (+ *a. or* **о** + *p. or inf.*) to forget **2** (*случайно*
оставить) to leave behind, forget (to bring)

забы́|ться, ýдусь, ýдешься *pf.* (*of*
▶ **забыва́ться**) **1** (*задремать*) to doze off,
drop off **2** (*замечтаться*) to sink into a
reverie **3** (infml, *выйти из границ приличия*)
to forget oneself

зава́л, а *m.* obstruction, blockage

зава́лива|ть, ю *impf. of* ▶ **завали́ть**

зава́лива|ться, юсь *impf. of* ▶ **завали́ться**

завал|и́ть, ю, ∼**ишь** *pf.* (*of* ▶ **зава́ливать**)
1 (*загромоздить*) to block up, obstruct;
to fill (*so as to block up*); **з. вход мешкáми**
с песко́м to block up the entrance with
sandbags **2** (+ *i.*) (infml, *заполнить*) to
pile (with); to fill cram-full (with); (fig.,
переобременить) to overload with work;
редáкция ∼**ена рабóтой** the editors are
snowed under with work

завал|и́ться, ю́сь, ∼**ишься** *pf.* (*of*
▶ **зава́ливаться**) **1** (*упасть*) to fall; to
collapse; **нож** ∼**и́лся за шкаф** the knife has
fallen behind the cupboard **2** (infml, *лечь*)
to lie down; **з. спать** to fall into bed **3** (infml,
опрокинуться) to overturn, tip up

зава́рива|ть, ет *impf. of* ▶ **завари́ть**

зава́рива|ться, ется *impf. of* ▶ **завари́ться**

завар|и́ть, ю, ∼**ишь** *pf.* (*of* ▶ **зава́ривать**)
to make (*drinks, etc., by pouring on boiling*

water); **з. чай** to brew tea

завар|и́ться, ю, ∼**ится** *pf.* (*of*
▶ **зава́риваться**) (*о напитках*) to brew

завáр|ка, и *f.* (*действие*) brewing (*of tea,*
etc.) **2** (infml) (*сухой чай*) enough tea for one
brew; (*заваренный чай*) brew

☞ **заведéни|е, я** *nt.* establishment, institution

завéд|овать, ую *impf.* (+ *i.*) to manage,
superintend; to be in charge (of)

завéдомо *adv.* wittingly; (+ *adj.*) known to
be; **з. зная** being fully aware

заве|дý, дёшь *see* ▶ **завести́**

завéдующ|ий, его *m.* (+ *i.*) manager (of);
head (of); person in charge (of); **з. отдéлом**
head of a department

завез|ти́, ý, ёшь, *past* ∼**,** ∼**лá** *pf.* (*of*
▶ **завози́ть**) **1** (*привезти*) to deliver, drop
off; **з. запи́ску по доро́ге домо́й** to deliver
a note on the way home **2** (*увезти*) to take
(*to a distance or out of one's way*); **з. далеко́**
в лес to take deep into the forest

заверб|ова́ть, у́ю *pf. of* ▶ **вербова́ть**

завéр|ить, ю, ишь *pf.* (*of* ▶ **заверя́ть**)
1 (**в** + *p.*) (*убедить*) to assure (of)
2 (*удостоверить*) to certify; **з. по́дпись**
to witness a signature

заверн|у́ть, у́, ёшь *pf.* (*of* ▶ **завора́чивать**)
1 (**в** + *a.*) (*обернуть*) to wrap (in)
2 (*загнуть*) to tuck up, roll up (*sleeve,*
etc.) **3** (*свернуть в сторону*) to turn; **з.**
напра́во to turn to the right **4** (*завинтить*)
to screw tight; (*закрыть*) to turn off (*by*
screwing); **з. кран** to turn off a tap

заверн|у́ться, у́сь, ёшься *pf.* (*of*
▶ **завора́чиваться**) **1** (**в** + *a.*) to wrap
oneself up (in), muffle oneself (in) **2** *pass.*
of ▶ **заверну́ть**

заверш|а́ть, а́ю *impf. of* ▶ **заверши́ть**

заверше́ни|е, я *nt.* completion; end; **в з.** in
conclusion

заверш|и́ть, у́, и́шь *pf.* (*of* ▶ **заверша́ть**) to
complete, conclude, crown

заверя́ть, я́ю *impf. of* ▶ **завéрить**

завéс|а, ы *f.* (fig.) veil, screen; **дымова́я з.**
(mil.) smokescreen

завé|сить, шу, сишь *pf.* (*of* ▶ **завéшивать**)
to curtain (off)

заве|сти́, ду́, дёшь, *past* ∼**л,** ∼**ла́** *pf.* (*of*
▶ **заводи́ть**) **1** (*привести*) to take, bring
(*to a place*); to leave, drop off (*at a place*)
2 (*увести*) to take (to a distance *or* out of
one's way) **3** (*основать*) to set up; to start;
з. семью́ to start a family **4** (*приобрести*)
to acquire **5** (*ввести*) to institute, introduce (*as*
a custom); **з. привы́чку** (+ *inf.*) to get into the
habit (of) **6** (*часы*) to wind (up); (*машину*)
to start; **з. мото́р** to start an engine

заве|сти́сь, ду́сь, дёшься, *past* ∼**лся,**
∼**ла́сь** *pf.* (*of* ▶ **заводи́ться**) **1** (*появиться*)
to be; to appear; **в по́гребе** ∼**ли́сь кры́сы**
there are rats in the cellar **2** (*о механизме*)
to start

Завéт, а *m.*: **Вéтхий, Но́вый З.** the Old, the
New Testament

☞ key word

заве́тный *adj.* (*мечты*) cherished

заве́шива|ть, ю *impf. of* ▶ заве́сить

завеща́ни|е, я *nt.* will, testament

завеща́|ть, ю *impf. and pf.* (+ *a. and d.*) to leave (to), bequeath (to); (+ *d.* + *inf.*) (*поручить*) to instruct

завива́|ть, ю *impf. of* ▶ зави́ть

завива́|ться, юсь *impf. of* ▶ зави́ться

зави́дно *as pred.* (*impers.* + *d.*) to feel envious; **мне з.** I feel envious

зави́д|ный, ~ен, ~на *adj.* enviable

зави́д|овать, ую *impf.* (*of* ▶ позави́довать) (+ *d.*) to envy; to be jealous of

завизж|а́ть, у́, и́шь *pf.* to begin to scream, squeal

завин|ти́ть, чу́, ти́шь *pf.* (*of* ▶ зави́нчивать) to screw up

зави́нчива|ть, ю *impf. of* ▶ завинти́ть

зависа́|ть, ю *impf. of* ▶ зави́снуть

зави|са́ть, иса́ет *impf. of* ▶ зави́снуть

⚲ **зави́|сеть, шу, сишь** *impf.* (**от** + *g.*) to depend (on)

⚲ **зави́симост|ь, и** *f.* dependence; **з. от нарко́тиков** dependence on drugs, drug dependence; **в ~и** (**от** + *g.*) depending (on), subject (to)

зави́сим|ый, ~, ~а *adj.* (**от** + *g.*) dependent (on)

зави́с|нуть, ну, нешь, *past* **~, ~ла** *pf.* (*of* ▶ зависа́ть) **1** (*о вертолёте и т. д.*) to hover, hang (in the air) **2** (comput.) to crash **3** (infml, *о вопросе, ситуации*) to be in limbo, unresolved, up in the air

зави́сн|уть, ет *pf.* (*of* ▶ зависа́ть) (comput.) to crash

зави́стлив|ый, ~, ~а *adj.* envious

за́вист|ь, и *f.* envy; jealousy

завит|о́к, ка́ *m.* **1** (*локон*) curl, lock **2** (*почерка*) flourish

зав|и́ть, ью́, ьёшь, *past* **~и́л, ~ила́, ~и́ло** *pf.* (*of* ▶ завива́ть) to curl, wave, twist, wind

зав|и́ться, ью́сь, ьёшься, *past* **~и́лся, ~ила́сь, ~и́ло́сь** *pf.* (*of* ▶ завива́ться) **1** (*виться*) to curl, wave, twine **2** (*завить себе волосы*) to curl, wave one's hair; (*у парикмахера*) to have one's hair curled, waved

завладева́|ть, ю *impf. of* ▶ завладе́ть

завладе́|ть, ю *pf.* (*of* ▶ завладева́ть) (+ *i.*) to take possession (of); to seize, capture (also fig.); **он ~л внима́нием слу́шателей** he captured the audience's attention

завлека́|ть, ю *impf. of* ▶ завле́чь

завле́|чь, ку́, чёшь, ку́т, *past* **~к, ~кла́** *pf.* (*of* ▶ завлека́ть) **1** (*заманить*) to lure, entice **2** (*соблазнить*) to fascinate, captivate

⚲ **заво́д¹, а** *m.* **1** factory, mill; works **2**: (**ко́нный**) **з.** stud (farm)

заво́д², а *m.* (*у часов*) winding mechanism; **игру́шка с ~ом** clockwork toy

заво|ди́ть, жу́, ~дишь *impf. of* ▶ завести́

заводи́ться, ~ится *impf. of* ▶ завести́сь

заводско́й *adj. of* ▶ заво́д¹

завоева́ни|е, я *nt.* **1** (*действие*) conquest; winning **2** (*захваченная территория*) conquest; (fig., *достижение*) achievement

завоева́тел|ь, я *m.* conqueror

заво|ева́ть, ю́ю, ю́ешь *pf.* (*of* ▶ завоёвывать) to conquer; (fig.) to win, gain; **з. симпа́тии** to gain sympathy

завоёвыва|ть, ю *impf.* (*of* ▶ завоева́ть) to try to get

заво|зи́ть, жу́, ~зишь *impf. of* ▶ завезти́

завола́кива|ть, ю, ет *impf. of* ▶ заволо́чь

завола́кива|ться, ется *impf. of* ▶ заволо́чься

заволн|ова́ться, у́юсь *pf.* to become agitated

заволо́|чь, ку́, чёшь, ку́т, *past* **~к, ~кла́** *pf.* (*of* ▶ завола́кивать) to cloud; to obscure; **тума́н ~к со́лнце** the sun was obscured by fog; **её глаза́ ~кло́ слеза́ми** her eyes were clouded with tears

заволо́|чься, чётся, ку́тся, *past* **~кся, ~кла́сь** *pf.* (*of* ▶ завола́киваться) to cloud over, become clouded

завоп|и́ть, лю́, и́шь *pf.* (infml) to cry out, yell; to give a cry

завора́чива|ть, ю *impf. of* ▶ заверну́ть

завора́чива|ться, юсь *impf. of* ▶ заверну́ться

за́втра *adv.* tomorrow; **до з.!** see you tomorrow!

за́втрак, а *m.* breakfast; **второ́й з.** elevenses, mid-morning snack

за́втрака|ть, ю *impf.* (*of* ▶ поза́втракать) to (have) breakfast; (*среди дня*) to (have) lunch

за́втрашний *adj.* tomorrow's; **з. день** tomorrow

за́вуч, а *m.* (*abbr. of* **заве́дующий/ заве́дующая уче́бной ча́стью**) director of studies

завхо́з, а *m.* (*abbr. of* **заве́дующий/ заве́дующая хозя́йством**) bursar, steward

завыва́|ть, ю *impf.* to howl

завы́|сить, шу, сишь *pf.* (*of* ▶ завыша́ть) to raise too high; **з. отме́тку на экза́мене** to give too high a mark in an examination

завы́|ть, о́ю, о́ешь *pf.* to begin to howl

завыша́|ть, ю *impf. of* ▶ завы́сить

завя|за́ть¹, жу́, ~жешь *pf.* (*of* ▶ завя́зывать) **1** (*узел, шнурки*) to tie; (*пакет*) to tie up; (*галстук*) to knot **2** (*палец*) to bind (up) **3** (fig., *начать*) to start; **з. разгово́р** to strike up a conversation

завя|за́ть², ю *impf. of* ▶ завя́знуть

завя|за́ться, ~жется *pf.* (*of* ▶ завя́зываться) **1** pass. of ▶ завяза́ть¹ **2** (*начаться*) to start; to arise

завя́з|нуть, ну, нешь, *past* **~, ~ла** *pf.* (*of* ▶ завя́знуть) to stick, get stuck

завя́зыва|ть, ет *impf. of* ▶ завяза́ть¹

3

завя́зыва|ться, ется *impf. of* ▶ **завяза́ться**

завя́|нуть, ну, нешь, *past* ~**л** *pf. of* ▶ **вя́нуть**

загада́|ть, а́ю *pf.* (*of* ▶ **зага́дывать**) **1**: з. зага́дки to ask riddles **2** (*заду́мать*) to think of; ~**а́йте число́** think of a number

зага́дк|а, и *f.* riddle; (fig.) enigma; mystery

зага́доч|ный, ~ен, ~на *adj.* enigmatic; mysterious

зага́дыва|ть, ю *impf. of* ▶ **загада́ть**

загазо́ванность, и *f.* pollution (*with gases*)

загазо́ван|ный, ~, ~а *adj.* polluted (*with gases*)

зага́р, а *m.* sunburn, (sun)tan

зага́|сить, шу́, ~сишь *pf. of* ▶ **гаси́ть 1**

загиба́|ть, ю *impf. of* ▶ **загну́ть**

загиба́|ться, юсь *impf. of* ▶ **загну́ться**

загипнотизи́р|овать, ую *pf. of* ▶ **гипнотизи́ровать**

загла́ви|е, я *nt.* title; heading; **под** ~**ем** entitled, headed

загла́в|ный *adj. of* ▶ **загла́вие;** ~**ная бу́ква** capital letter

загла́|дить, жу, дишь *pf.* (*of* ▶ **загла́живать**) **1** (*сде́лать гла́дким*) to iron (out), press **2** (fig., *смягчи́ть*) to make up (for), make amends (for)

загла́жива|ть, ю *impf. of* ▶ **загла́дить**

загла́тыва|ть, ю *impf. of* ▶ **заглота́ть**

заглота́|ть, ю *pf.* (*of* ▶ **загла́тывать**) to swallow

загло́хн|уть, у, ешь *pf. of* ▶ **гло́хнуть 2**

заглуш|а́ть, а́ю *impf. of* ▶ **заглуши́ть**

заглуш|и́ть, у́, и́шь *pf.* (*of* ▶ **глуши́ть 3,** ▶ **заглуша́ть**) **1** (*зву́ки*) to drown, deaden, muffle **2** (*переда́чи*) to jam **3** (*расте́ния*) to choke

загля|де́ться, жу́сь, ди́шься *pf.* (*of* ▶ **загля́дываться**) (**на** + *a.*) (infml) to stare (at); to stare (at); to be lost in admiration (of)

загля́дыва|ть, ю *impf. of* ▶ **загляну́ть**

загля́дыва|ться, юсь *impf. of* ▶ **загляде́ться**

загля́н|уть, у́, ~ешь *pf.* (*of* ▶ **загля́дывать**) **1** (*взгляну́ть*) to peep; to glance **2** (infml, *зайти́*) to look in, drop in

загна́ива|ться, ется *impf. of* ▶ **загнои́ться**

загна́|ть, загоню́, заго́нишь, *past* ~**л,** ~**ла́,** ~**ло** *pf.* (*of* ▶ **загоня́ть**) **1** to drive in; **з. коро́в в хлев** to drive the cows into the shed, get the cows in **2** (infml, *вбить*) to drive home **3** (infml, *прода́ть*) to sell, flog (BrE)

загнива́|ть, ю *impf. of* ▶ **загни́ть**

загни́|ть, ю́, ёшь, *past* ~**л,** ~**ла́,** ~**ло** *pf.* (*of* ▶ **загнива́ть**) to begin to rot; to rot, decay (also fig.)

загно|и́ться, и́тся *pf.* (*of* ▶ **загна́иваться**) to fester

загн|у́ть, у́, ёшь *pf.* (*of* ▶ **загиба́ть**) (*вверх*) to turn up; (*вниз*) to turn down; (*сгиба́ть*) to

---

bend, fold; to crease

загн|у́ться, у́сь, ёшься *pf.* (*of* ▶ **загиба́ться**) **1** (*вверх*) to turn up, stick up; (*вниз*) to turn down **2** (sl., *умере́ть*) to turn up one's toes

загова́рива|ться, юсь *impf.* (*of* ▶ **заговори́ться**) **1** (*увле́чься разгово́ром*) to be carried away by a conversation **2** (*impf. only*) (*говори́ть бессмы́слицу*) to rave; to ramble (*in speech*)

за́говор¹, а *m.* plot, conspiracy

за́гово́р², а *m.* (*заклина́ние*) charm, spell

заговор|и́ть, ю́, и́шь *pf.* (*нача́ть говори́ть*) to begin to speak

заговор|и́ться, ю́сь, и́шься *pf. of* ▶ **загова́риваться**

заго́ворщик, а *m.* conspirator, plotter

заго́ворщи|ца, цы *f. of* ▶ **заго́ворщик**

заголо́в|ок, ка *m.* **1** (*загла́вие*) title; heading **2** (*газе́тный*) headline

заго́н, а *m.* (*для скота́*) enclosure; (*для ове́ц*) pen

за|гоню́, го́нишь *see* ▶ **загна́ть**

загоня́|ть, ю *impf. of* ▶ **загна́ть**

загора́жива|ть, ю *impf. of* ▶ **загороди́ть**

загора́|ть, ю *impf. of* ▶ **загоре́ть**

загора́|ться, юсь *impf. of* ▶ **загоре́ться**

загоре́лый *adj.* sunburnt; brown, bronzed

загор|е́ть, ю́, и́шь *pf.* (*of* ▶ **загора́ть**) to become sunburnt; to acquire a tan

загор|е́ться, ю́сь, и́шься *pf.* (*of* ▶ **загора́ться**) (*нача́ть горе́ть*) to catch fire; to begin to burn

загоро|ди́ть, жу́, ~дишь *pf.* (*of* ▶ **загора́живать**) **1** (*огороди́ть*) to enclose, fence in **2** (*прегради́ть*) to barricade; to obstruct; **з. кому́-н. свет** to stand in sb's light

загоро́дк|а, и *f.* (infml) fence

за́городный *adj.* out-of-town; country

загота́влива|ть, ю *impf. of* ▶ **загото́вить**

загото́в|ить, лю, ишь *pf.* (*of* ▶ **загота́вливать,** ▶ **заготовля́ть**) (*созда́ть запа́с чего́-либо*) to lay in; to stockpile

загото́вк|а, и *f.* **1** (*зерна́, ко́рма*) laying in; stockpiling **2** (*заку́пка госуда́рством*) procurement

заготовля́|ть, ю *impf. of* ▶ **загото́вить**

загражде́ни|е, я *nt.* obstacle, barrier, obstruction

заграни́ц|а, ы *f.* (infml) foreign countries (*see also* ▶ **грани́ца**)

заграни́чный *adj.* foreign

За́греб, а *n.* Zagreb

загреба́|ть, ю *impf. of* ▶ **загрести́**

загре|сти́, бу́, бёшь, *past* ~́**б,** ~**бла́** *pf.* (*of* ▶ **загреба́ть**) (infml) to rake up; (fig.) to rake in

загримир|ова́ть, у́ю *pf. of* ▶ **гримирова́ть**

загримир|ова́ться, у́юсь *pf. of* ▶ **гримирова́ться**

загро́б|ный *adj.* beyond the grave; ~**ая жизнь** life after death

загружа́|ть, ю *impf. of* ▶ **загрузи́ть 3**

загр|узи́ть, ужу́, у́зишь *pf.* **1** (*impf.* **грузи́ть**) to load **2** (*impf.* **~ужа́ть**) (tech.) to feed, charge, prime; (comput., *компью́тер*) to boot; (*програ́мму, да́нные*) to load; (*скопи́ровать, откуда*) to download; (*куда*) to upload **3** (*impf.* **~ужа́ть**) (infml, *заня́ть рабо́той*) to keep fully occupied

загру́зк|а, и *f.* **1** (*де́йствие*) loading **2** (*объём рабо́ты*) capacity, workload

загру|сти́ть, щу́, сти́шь *pf.* to grow sad

загрыза́|ть, ю *impf. of* ▶ **загры́зть**

загры́з|ть, у́, ёшь, *past* **~, ~ла** *pf.* (*of* ▶ **загрыза́ть**) (*уби́ть*) to kill

загрязне́ни|е, я *nt.* soiling; (*приро́ды*) pollution

загрязн|и́ть, ю́, и́шь *pf.* (*of* ▶ **загрязня́ть**) to soil, make dirty; (*приро́ду*) to pollute

загрязня́|ть, ю *impf. of* ▶ **загрязни́ть**

ЗАГС, а and **загс, а** *m.* (*abbr. of* (**отде́л**) за́писи а́ктов гражда́нского состоя́ния) registry office

загуб|и́ть, лю́, ~ишь *pf.* (*погуби́ть*) to ruin; **з. чью-н. жизнь** to make sb's life a misery

зад, а, о ~е, на/в ~у́, *pl.* **~ы́** *m.* **1** (*маши́ны, до́ма*) back; **~ом наперёд** back to front **2** (*живо́тного*) hind quarters; rump; (*челове́ка*) behind, buttocks

⚔ **зада|ва́ть, ю́, ёшь** *impf. of* ▶ **зада́ть**

задав|и́ть, лю́, ~ишь *pf.* to crush; (*о маши́не*) to run over, knock down

⚔ **зада́ни|е, я** *nt.* task, job

зада́ром *adv.* (infml, *беспла́тно*) for nothing; very cheaply; **купи́ть з.** to buy for a song

зада́т|ок, ка *m.* deposit

за|да́ть, да́м, да́шь, да́ст, дади́м, дади́те, даду́т, *past* **~да́л, ~дала́, ~да́ло** *pf.* (*of* ▶ **задава́ть**) to set; to give; **з. вопро́с** to put a question

⚔ **зада́ч|а, и** *f.* **1** (math., etc.) problem **2** (*цель*) task; mission

зада́чник, а *m.* book of (mathematical) problems

задви́га|ть, ю *pf.* to begin to move

задвига́|ть, ю *impf. of* ▶ **задви́нуть**

задви́н|уть, у, ешь *pf.* (*of* ▶ **задви́гать**) **1** (*перемести́ть*) to push **2**: **з. за́навески** to draw the curtains

задво́р|ки, ок (*no sg.*) backyard; (fig.) out-of-the-way place, backwoods

задева́|ть, ю *impf. of* ▶ **заде́ть**

заде́л|ать, аю *pf.* (*of* ▶ **заде́лывать**) (*ды́ру, щель*) to block up, close up; **з. течь** to stop up a leak

заде́лыва|ть, ю *impf. of* ▶ **заде́лать**

задёргива|ть, ю *impf. of* ▶ **задёрнуть**

задержа́ни|е, я *nt.* (*престу́пника*) detention, arrest

задержа́нн|ый, ого *m.* detainee

задерж|а́ть, у́, ~ишь *pf.* (*of* ▶ **заде́рживать**) **1** (*останови́ть*) to stop, hold back, delay, detain; (*отсро́чить*) to delay **2** (*удержа́ть*) to withhold, keep back; **з. зарпла́ту** to stop wages; **з. дыха́ние** to hold one's breath

3 (*арестова́ть*) to detain, arrest

задерж|а́ться, у́сь, ~ишься *pf.* (*of* ▶ **заде́рживаться**) **1** (*на рабо́те, в гостя́х*) to be held up, delayed; to stay too long **2** (*у вхо́да, перед магази́ном*) to linger **3** (*не сде́лать во́время*) to be late

заде́ржива|ть, ю *impf. of* ▶ **задержа́ть**

заде́ржива|ться, юсь *impf. of* ▶ **задержа́ться**

заде́ржк|а, и *f.* delay; hold-up

задёрн|уть, у, ешь *pf.* (*of* ▶ **задёргивать**) to pull; to draw; **з. занаве́ски** to draw the curtains

заде́|ть, ну, нешь *pf.* (*of* ▶ **задева́ть**) (*косну́ться*) to touch, brush (against); (fig., *оби́деть*) to offend, wound; **его́ ~ло за живо́е** he was stung to the quick

задира́|ть, ю, ет *impf. of* ▶ **задра́ть**

задира́|ться, ется *impf. of* ▶ **задра́ться**

⚔ **за́дн|ий** *adj.* (*сиде́нье*) back, rear; (*но́ги*) hind; **~яя мысль** ulterior motive; **прохо́д** (anat.) anus; **дать з. ход** to go into reverse; to back up; **~им число́м** later, with hindsight

за́дник, а *m.* **1** back, counter (*of shoe*) **2** (theatr.) backdrop

за́дниц|а, ы *f.* (infml) backside, butt (AmE)

задо́лго *adv.* long before

задо́лженност|ь, и *f.* debts; **погаси́ть з.** to pay off one's debts

за́дом *adv.* backwards

задо́р, а *m.* fervour (BrE), fervor (AmE), ardour (BrE), ardor (AmE); passion

задо́р|ный, ~ен, ~на *adj.* fervent, ardent; impassioned

задох|ну́ться, ну́сь, нёшься *pf.* (*of* ▶ **задыха́ться**) **1** (*умере́ть*) to suffocate; to choke **2** (*тяжело́ дыша́ть*) to pant; to gasp for breath

зад|ра́ть, еру́, ерёшь, *past* **~ра́л, ~рала́, ~ра́ло** *pf.* (*of* ▶ **задира́ть**) (infml, *подня́ть кве́рху*) to lift up; to pull up; **з. го́лову** to crane one's neck; **з. нос** (fig.) to cock one's nose

зад|ра́ться, ерётся, *past* **~ра́лся, ~рала́сь** *pf.* (*of* ▶ **задира́ться**) (infml, *о пла́тье*) to ride up

задрем|а́ть, лю́, ~лешь *pf.* to doze off, begin to nod

задрож|а́ть, у́, и́шь *pf.* to begin to tremble; (*от хо́лода*) to begin to shiver

задува́|ть, ю *impf. of* ▶ **заду́ть**

заду́ма|ть, ю *pf.* (*of* ▶ **заду́мывать**) **1** (+ *a.* or *inf.*) (*реши́ть*) to plan; to intend; to conceive the idea (of) **2** (*число́*) to think of

заду́ма|ться, юсь *pf.* to become thoughtful, pensive; to fall to thinking

заду́мчив|ый, ~, ~а *adj.* thoughtful, pensive

заду́мыва|ть, ю *impf. of* ▶ **заду́мать**

заду́мыва|ться, юсь *impf.* (*погружа́ться в свои́ мы́сли*) to be thoughtful, be pensive; (*размышля́ть*) to meditate; to ponder; **з. о** (+ *p.*) to think about

заду́|ть, ю, ешь *pf.* (*of* ▶ задува́ть)
1 (*погаси́ть*) to blow out **2** (*нача́ть дуть*) to begin to blow

задуши́|ть, у́, ~ишь *pf. of* ▶ души́ть¹

задыха́|ться, юсь *impf. of* ▶ задохну́ться

заеда́|ть, ю *impf. of* ▶ зае́сть¹, ▶ зае́сть²

заезжа́|ть, ю *impf. of* ▶ зае́хать

заём, за́йма *m.* loan

заёмщик, а *m.* borrower, debtor

зае́|сть¹, м, шь, ст, ди́м, ди́те, дя́т, *past*
~**л** *pf.* (*of* ▶ заеда́ть) **1** (*уку́сами*) to bite
to death; (*загры́зть*) to kill; (fig., infml,
изму́чить) to torment, oppress; **его́** ~**ла**
тоска́ he fell prey to melancholy **2** (*impers.*)
(tech.) to jam; (naut.) to foul; **кана́т** ~**ло** the
cable has fouled

зае́|сть², м, шь, ст, ди́м, ди́те, дя́т, *past* ~**л**
pf. (*of* ▶ заеда́ть) (+ *a. and i.*) to take (with);
он ~**л лека́рство са́харом** he took the
medicine with sugar

зае́|хать, ду, дешь *pf.* (*of* ▶ заезжа́ть)
1 (к + *d.*) to call in (at); to drop in (on);
(в + *a.*) to enter, ride into, drive into; (за +
a.) to go beyond; past; (за + *i.*) to call for;
to fetch, pick up **2** (*уе́хать или попа́сть*
куда́-н. далеко́ или куда́ не сле́дует) to get
(to), go; **он** ~**хал в кана́ву** he landed in the
ditch

зажа́р|ить, ю, ит *pf. of* ▶ жа́рить

зажа́р|иться, ится *pf. of* ▶ жа́риться

зажа́т|ый, ~, ~а *p.p.p. of* ▶ зажа́ть *and adj.*
(infml, *о челове́ке*) tense, uptight

зажа́|ть, му́, мёшь *pf.* (*of* ▶ зажима́ть)
(*сти́снуть*) to squeeze; to press; to clutch;
(*заткну́ть*) to stop up; **з. в руке́** to grip; **з.**
рот кому́-н. (fig.) to stop sb's mouth

зажж|гу́, жёшь, гу́т *see* ▶ заже́чь

зажж|е́чь, гу́, жёшь, гу́т, *past* ~**ёг, ~гла́** *pf.*
(*of* ▶ зажига́ть) (*ого́нь, ла́мпу*) to light;
(*свет*) to turn on; **з. спи́чку** to strike a match

зажж|е́чься, гу́сь, жёшься, гу́тся, *past*
зажёгся, зажгла́сь *pf.* (*of* ▶ зажига́ться)
(*об огне́*) to begin to burn; (*о фонаря́х*) to go
on, light up

зажива́|ть, ю *impf. of* ▶ зажи́ть

зажига́лк|а, и *f.* (cigarette) lighter

зажига́ни|е, я *nt.* (*в маши́не*) ignition

зажига́|ть, ю *impf. of* ▶ заже́чь

зажига́|ться, юсь *impf. of* ▶ заже́чься

зажи́м, а *m.* **1** (tech.) clamp; clip **2** (elec.)
terminal

зажима́|ть, ю *impf. of* ▶ зажа́ть

зажи́точ|ный, ~ен, ~на *adj.* well-to-do;
prosperous; affluent

зажи́|ть, ву́, вёшь, *past* **за́жил, ~ла́,**
за́жило *pf.* (*of* ▶ зажива́ть) **1** (*о ра́не*) to
heal; to close up **2** (*нача́ть жить*) to begin
to live; **з. по-но́вому** to begin a new life

зазвене́|ть, ю, и́шь *pf.* to begin to ring

зазвон|и́ть, ю́, и́шь *pf.* to begin to ring

зазвуч|а́ть, у́, и́шь *pf.* to begin to sound; to
begin to resound

заземле́ни|е, я *nt.* (elec.) **1** (*де́йствие*)
earthing (BrE), grounding (AmE)
2 (*устро́йство*) earth (BrE), ground (AmE)

заземл|и́ть, ю́, и́шь *pf.* (elec.) to earth

зазим|ова́ть, у́ю *pf.* to winter; to pass the
winter

зазна|ва́ться, ю́сь, ёшься *impf. of*
▶ зазна́ться

зазна́|ться, юсь *pf.* (*of* ▶ зазнава́ться)
(infml) to give oneself airs, become conceited

зазо́р, а *m.* gap

зазо́р|ный, ~ен, ~на *adj.* (infml) shameful,
disgraceful

заигра́|ть, ю *pf.* (*нача́ть игра́ть*) to begin
to play

заигра́|ться, юсь *pf.* (*of* ▶ заи́грываться) to
become absorbed in playing

заи́грыва|ть, ю *impf.* (с + *i.*) (infml) to flirt
(with); to make advances (to) (also fig.)

заи́грыва|ться, юсь *impf. of* ▶ заигра́ться

заика́ни|е, я *nt.* stammer(ing), stutter(ing)

заика́|ться, юсь *impf.* to stammer, stutter;
(*нереши́тельно говори́ть*) to falter (*in
speech*)

заимств|овать, ую *impf.* (*of*
▶ позаи́мствовать) to borrow

заинтересо́ван|ный, ~, ~а *p.p.p. of*
▶ заинтересова́ть *and* (~, ~на) *adj.* (в + *p.*)
interested (in); ~**ная сторона́** interested
party

заинтерес|ова́ть, у́ю *pf.* to interest; to
excite the curiosity (of)

заинтерес|ова́ться, у́юсь *pf.* (+ *i.*) to
become interested; to take an interest (in)

заи́скива|ть, ю *impf.* (*пе́ред* + *i.*) to try to
ingratiate oneself (with)

зай|ду́, дёшь *see* ▶ зайти́

за́йма *see* ▶ заём

займ|у́, ёшь *see* ▶ заня́ть

зай|ти́, ду́, дёшь, *past* ~**шёл, ~шла́**
pf. (*of* ▶ заходи́ть) **1** (к + *d.* or в + *a.*)
(*посети́ть*) to call (on); to look in; to drop
in (at) **2** (за + *i.*) (*что́бы взять*) to call for,
fetch **3** (в + *a.*) (*войти́*) to go into, get into;
(*попа́сть*) to get (*to a place*); to find oneself
(*in a place*) **4** (*о разгово́ре*) to turn to **5** (за
+ *a.*) (*скры́ться за чем-н.*) to go behind;
(*продолжа́ться*) to go on, continue (after);
(*закати́ться*) to set (*of sun, etc.*); **з. за́ угол**
to turn a corner; **з. сли́шком далеко́** (fig.) to
go too far

Закавка́зь|е, я *nt.* Transcaucasia

зака́дровый *adj.*: **з. коммента́рий** (TV, cin.)
voice-over

⚔ **зака́з, а** *m.* order; (*биле́тов, стола́*)
reservation; (*портре́та*) commission; **на з.**
to order; **как по** ~**у** as if to order

зака|за́ть, жу́, ~жешь *pf.* (*of* ▶ зака́зывать)
to order; (*биле́ты, стол*) to reserve;
(*портре́т*) to commission

зака́зник, а *m.* (game) reserve

заказн|ой *adj.* **1** done or made to order; ~ая статья article written to order; ~ая журналистика chequebook journalism; ~ое убийство contract killing **2**: ~ое письмо registered letter

☞ **заказчик, а** *m.* customer, client

☞ **заказыва|ть, ю** *impf. of* ▶ заказать

закал|ённый, ~ён, ~ена *p.p.p. of* ▶ закалить *and* (~ён, ~ённа) *adj.* hardened, hard

закал|ить, ю, ишь *pf.* (*of* ▶ закалять) (tech.) to temper; to case-harden; (fig.) to temper, harden; to make hard, hardy

закалк|а, и *f.* tempering; hardening; (sport) conditioning

закалыва|ть, ю *impf. of* ▶ заколоть

закаля|ть, ю *impf. of* ▶ закалить

☞ **заканчива|ть, ю, ет** *impf. of* ▶ закончить

заканчива|ться, ется *impf. of* ▶ закончиться

закап|ать, аю *pf.* (*impf.* ~ывать) to spot, stain

закапыва|ть, ю *impf. of* ▶ закопать, ▶ закапать

закармлива|ть, ю *impf. of* ▶ закормить

закат, а *m.* setting; з. (солнца) sunset; (fig.) decline

заката|ть, ю *pf.* (*of* ▶ закатывать) **1** (infml, рукава) to roll up **2** (банку, крышку) to close, hermetically seal

зака|тить, чу, ~тишь *pf.* (*of* ▶ закатывать) (мяч) to roll; з. истерику (infml) to go off into hysterics; з. глаза to roll one's eyes

зака|титься, чусь, ~тишься *pf.* (*of* ▶ закатываться) **1** (о мяче) to roll **2** (о солнце) to set (of heavenly bodies); (fig., о славе) to wane; to vanish

закатыва|ть, ю *impf. of* ▶ закатать, ▶ закатить

закатыва|ться, юсь *impf. of* ▶ закатиться

закашля|ться, юсь *pf.* to have a fit of coughing

закваск|а, и *f.* (для теста) leaven; (для кефира) culture

закида|ть, ю *pf.* (*of* ▶ закидывать) (+ *a. and i.*) **1** (осыпать) to bespatter (with); to shower (with); з. камнями to stone **2** (заполнить) to fill up (with); (сверху) to cover (with)

закидыва|ть, ю *impf. of* ▶ закидать, ▶ закинуть

закин|уть, у, ешь *pf.* (мяч в сетку, майку под кровать) to throw; (невод, удочку) to cast

закипа|ть, ет *impf. of* ▶ закипеть

закип|еть, ит *pf.* (*of* ▶ закипать) (начать кипеть) to begin to boil; (кипеть) to be on the boil; (fig., о работе) to be in full swing

заклад, а *m.* (залог) pawning; (недвижимости) mortgaging

закладк|а, и *f.* (в книге) bookmark (also comput.)

закладыва|ть, ю *impf. of* ▶ заложить

заклеива|ть, ю, ет *impf. of* ▶ заклеить

закле|ить, ю, ишь *pf.* (*of* ▶ заклеивать) to glue up; to stick up; з. конверт to seal an envelope

заклина́ни|е, я *nt.* **1** (магические слова) incantation; spell **2** (мольба) entreaty

заклина́тел|ь, я *m.* exorcist; з. змей snake charmer

заклина́тель|ница, ницы *f. of* ▶ заклинатель

закли́нива|ть, ю *impf. of* ▶ заклинить

закли́н|ить, ю, ишь *pf.* (*of* ▶ заклинивать) **1** (закрепить) to wedge, fasten with a wedge **2** (лишить возможности вращаться) to jam; (also. impers.) дверь ~ило the door jammed

☞ **заключа́|ть, ю** *impf. of* ▶ заключить

☞ **заключа́|ться, а́ется** *impf.* **1** *pass. of* ▶ заключа́ть **2** (*impf. only*) (в + *p.*) to consist (of); to lie (in)

☞ **заключе́ни|е, я** *nt.* **1** (конец) conclusion, end; (завершение) conclusion, ending; в з. in conclusion **2** (вывод) conclusion, inference **3** (договора, сделки) conclusion, signing **4** (лишение свободы) confinement, detention; тюре́мное з. imprisonment

заключ|ённый, ~ён, ~ена́ *p.p.p. of* ▶ заключи́ть; (*as n.* з., ~ённого, *f.* ~ённая, ~ённой) (law) prisoner, convict

заключи́тельный *adj.* final, concluding

заключ|и́ть, у́, и́шь *pf.* (*of* ▶ заключа́ть) **1** (сделать вывод) to conclude, infer **2** (принять) to conclude, enter into; з. брак to contract marriage; з. догово́р to conclude a treaty; з. сде́лку to strike a bargain **3**: з. в себе́ to contain, enclose; to comprise; з. в ско́бки to enclose in brackets **4** (лишить свободы) to confine; з. в тюрьму́ to imprison

зак|ова́ть, у́ю, уёшь *pf.* (*of* ▶ зако́вывать) to chain; з. в канда́лы to shackle, put in irons

зако́выва|ть, ю *impf. of* ▶ закова́ть

закола́чива|ть, ю *impf. of* ▶ заколоти́ть

заколдо́ванный *p.p.p. of* ▶ заколдова́ть *and adj.* enchanted; spellbound; (fig.): з. круг vicious circle

заколд|ова́ть, у́ю *pf.* (*of* ▶ заколдо́вывать) to bewitch, enchant; to lay a spell (on)

заколдо́выва|ть, ю *impf. of* ▶ заколдова́ть

заколеб|а́ться, ~лю́сь, ~лешься *pf.* to begin to shake; (fig.) to begin to waver, begin to vacillate

зако́лк|а, и *f.* hairgrip (BrE), bobby pin (AmE)

заколо|ти́ть, чу́, ~тишь *pf.* (*of* ▶ закола́чивать) (досками) to board up; (гвоздями) to nail up

зако́л|оть, ю́, ~ешь *pf.* (*of* ▶ зака́лывать, ▶ коло́ть² 2, ▶ коло́ть² 3) **1** (убить) to stab (to death); (животное) to slaughter **2** (прикрепить) to pin (up) **3** (*impers.*): у меня́ *и т. п.* ~о́ло в боку́ I have, *etc.*, a stitch in my side

☞ **зако́н, а** *m.* law; свод ~ов code, statute book; объяви́ть вне ~а to outlaw

зако́нност|ь, и *f.* **1** (документа, постановления) lawfulness, legality **2** (соблюдение законов) law and order

зако́н|ный, ~ен, ~на *adj.* **1** (*действия*) lawful, legal; (*документ, договор*) legal; **з. брак** lawful wedlock; **з. владе́лец** rightful owner **2** (fig., *возмуще́ние*) legitimate, understandable, natural

законода́тел|ь, я *m.* legislator; lawgiver; **з. мод/мо́ды** trendsetter

законода́тельный *adj.* legislative

✧ **законода́тельств|о**, а *nt.* legislation

закономе́рност|ь, и *f.* regularity; conformity with a law; normality

закономе́р|ный, ~ен, ~на *adj.* **1** (*развитие, успех*) natural, logical **2** (fig., *поня́тный*) legitimate, understandable, natural

законопослу́ш|ный, ~ен, ~на *adj.* law-abiding

законопрое́кт, а *m.* (pol., law) bill

законсерви́р|овать, ую *pf. of* ▸ консерви́ровать

зако́нчен|ный, ~, ~а *p.p.p. of* ▸ зако́нчить *and* (~, ~на) *adj.* (*де́ло*) finished; (*мысль, фра́за*) complete; (*него́дяй*) consummate; **з. лгун** consummate liar

зако́нч|ить, у, ишь *pf.* (*of* ▸ зака́нчивать) to end, finish

зако́нч|иться, у, ится *pf.* (*of* ▸ зака́нчиваться) to end, finish

закопа́|ть, ю *pf.* (*of* ▸ зака́пывать) (*спря́тать в земле́*) to bury

закоп|ти́ть, чу́, ти́шь *pf.* (*of* ▸ копти́ть) **1** (*ры́бу, о́корок*) to smoke **2** (*покры́ть ко́потью*) to blacken with smoke

закоп|ти́ться, чу́сь, ти́шься *pf.* (*покры́ться ко́потью*) to become covered with soot

закорм|и́ть, лю́, ~ишь *pf.* (*of* ▸ зака́рмливать) to overfeed; to stuff

закра́|сить, шу, сишь *pf.* (*of* ▸ закра́шивать) to paint over, paint out

закра́шива|ть, ю *impf. of* ▸ закра́сить

закреп|и́ть, лю́, и́шь *pf.* (*of* ▸ закрепля́ть) **1** to fasten, secure; (naut.) to make fast; (phot.) to fix **2** (fig.) to consolidate **3** (+ *a. and* за + *i.*) (*помеще́ние*) to allot, assign (to); (*челове́ка*) to appoint, attach (to); **з. за собо́й** to secure

закреп|и́ться, лю́сь, и́шься *pf.* (*of* ▸ закрепля́ться) **1** (*о войска́х*) (на + *a.*) to consolidate one's hold (on) **2** (*о сло́ве, привы́чке*) to establish itself

закрепля́|ть, ю *impf. of* ▸ закрепи́ть

закрепля́|ться, юсь *impf. of* ▸ закрепи́ться

закрича́|ть, у́, и́шь *pf.* **1** (*нача́ть крича́ть*) to begin to shout **2** (*однокра́тно*) to give a shout, cry out

закро́йщик, а *m.* cutter

закро́йщи|ца, цы *f. of* ▸ закро́йщик

закругл|и́ть, ю́, и́шь *pf.* (*of* ▸ закругля́ть) to make round; to round off

закругл|и́ться, ю́сь, и́шься *pf.* (*of* ▸ закругля́ться) (infml) to round off, conclude

закругля́|ть, ю *impf. of* ▸ закругли́ть

закругля́|ться, юсь *impf. of* ▸ закругли́ться

закруж|и́ться, у́сь, ~и́шься *pf. of* ▸ кружи́ться

закру|ти́ть, чу́, ~тишь *pf.* (*of* ▸ закру́чивать) **1** (*верёвку*) to twist; (*усы́*) to twirl; (*вокру́г*) to wind round **2** (*кран*) to turn; (*га́йку*) to screw in

закру|ти́ться, чу́сь, ~тишься *pf.* (*of* ▸ закру́чиваться) to twist; to twirl; to wind round

закру́чива|ть, ю *impf. of* ▸ закрути́ть

закру́чива|ться, юсь *impf. of* ▸ закрути́ться

✧ **закрыва́|ть**, ю *impf. of* ▸ закры́ть

закрыва́|ться, юсь *impf. of* ▸ закры́ться

закры́ти|е, я *nt.* closing; shutting; (*коне́ц*) close

закры́т|ый, ~, ~а *p.p.p. of* ▸ закры́ть *and adj.* closed, shut; (*не для всех*) private; **с ~ыми глаза́ми** (fig.) blindly; **в ~ом помеще́нии** indoors

закро́|ть, о́ю, о́ешь *pf.* (*of* ▸ закрыва́ть) **1** (*сде́лать недосту́пным*) to close, shut; **з. глаза́ (на** + *a.*) to shut one's eyes (to); **з. счёт** to close an account **2** (*вы́ключить*) to shut off, turn off **3** (*ликвиди́ровать*) to close down, shut down **4** (*покры́ть*) to cover

закро́|ться, о́юсь, о́ешься *pf.* (*of* ▸ закрыва́ться) **1** (*стать недосту́пным*) to close, shut; (*око́нчиться*) to end; (*переста́ть существова́ть*) to close down **2** (*покры́ть себя́*) to cover oneself; to take cover

закули́сный *adj.* (fig.) secret; underhand, undercover

закупа́|ть, ю *impf. of* ▸ закупи́ть

закуп|и́ть, лю́, ~ишь *pf.* (*of* ▸ закупа́ть) **1** (*скупи́ть*) to buy up (wholesale) **2** (*запасти́сь*) to lay in; to stock up with

заку́порива|ть, ю *impf. of* ▸ заку́порить

заку́пор|ить, ю, ишь *pf.* (*of* ▸ заку́поривать) to cork; to stop up

заку́рива|ть, ю *impf. of* ▸ закури́ть

закур|и́ть, ю́, ~ишь *pf.* (*of* ▸ заку́ривать) **1** (*сигаре́ту*) to light up **2** (*стать кури́льщиком*) to begin to smoke

заку|си́ть, шу́, ~сишь *pf.* (*of* ▸ заку́сывать) **1** (*пое́сть*) to have a snack, have a bite **2** (+ *a. and i.*) to take (with); **з. во́дку ры́бой** to drink vodka with fish hors d'oeuvres

заку́ск|а, и *f.* (*usu. in pl.*) hors d'oeuvre; snack; **на ~у** for a titbit; (fig., infml) as a special treat

заку́сыва|ть, ю *impf. of* ▸ закуси́ть

заку́та|ть, ю *pf.* (*of* ▸ заку́тывать) to wrap up, muffle; **з. в одея́ло** to tuck up (in bed)

заку́та|ться, юсь *pf.* (*of* ▸ заку́тываться) to wrap oneself up, muffle oneself

заку́тыва|ть, ю *impf. of* ▸ заку́тать

заку́тыва|ться, юсь *impf. of* ▸ заку́таться

✧ **зал**, а *m.* hall; **з. ожида́ния** waiting room; **з. вы́лета** departure lounge (*in airport*)

залега́|ть, ю *impf. of* ▸ зале́чь

залеза́|ть, ю *impf. of* ▸ зале́зть

3

залéз|ть, у, ешь, *past* ∼, ∼ла *pf.* **1** (на + *a.*) (*на дéрево, крышу*) to climb (up, on to) **2** (в + *a.*) (infml, *в комнату*) to get (into); to break into

залета́|ть, ю *impf. of* ▶ залетéть

зале|тéть, чý, ти́шь *pf.* **1** (в + *a.*) to fly (into); (за + *a.*) to fly (over, beyond) **2** (в + *a.*) to make a stopover (at), call in (at)

зал|éчь, я́гу, я́жешь, я́гут, *past* ∼ёг, ∼егла́ *pf.* (*of* ▶ залега́ть) **1** (*лечь*) to lie down; (*притаи́ться*) to lie low **2** (geol.) to lie, be deposited

зали́в, а *m.* bay; (*длинный*) gulf; (*маленький*) cove

залива́|ть, ю *impf. of* ▶ зали́ть

залива́|ться, юсь *impf. of* ▶ зали́ться

зaливн|óе, óго *nt.* fish or meat in aspic

зал|и́ть, ью́, ьёшь, *past* ∼и́л, ∼ила́, ∼и́ло *pf.* (*of* ▶ залива́ть) **1** (*покрыть жидкостью*) to flood, inundate **2** (*испачкать жидким*) (+ *a. and i.*) to pour (over); to spill (on) **3** (*потушить водóй*) to quench, extinguish (*with water*); з. пожáр to put out a fire **4** (*наполнить, покрыть жидким*) to fill, cover with **5** (*налить, наполнив что-н.*): з. бензи́н в бак to fill up with petrol (BrE), gas (AmE)

зал|и́ться, ью́сь, ьёшься, *past* ∼и́лся, ∼ила́сь *pf.* (*of* ▶ залива́ться) **1** (*попасть*) to pour; to spill; водá ∼ила́сь мне за воротни́к water has gone down my neck **2** (+ *i.*) (*зазвучать*) to break into, burst out (into); собáка ∼ила́сь лáем the dog began to bark furiously

зало́г, а *m.* **1** deposit; pledge; security; (law) bail; под з. (+ *g.*) on the security of; отда́ть в з. (*в ломбáрде*) to pawn; (*дом*) to mortgage; вы́купить из ∼а to redeem; to pay off mortgage (on); з. успéха guarantee of success **2** (fig., *доказáтельство*) pledge, token

залож|и́ть, у́, ∼ишь *pf.* (*of* ▶ закла́дывать) **1** (*положить за*) to put (behind); он ∼и́л рýки зá спину he put his hands behind his back **2** (*положить основáние чему-л.*) to lay (the foundation of) **3** (+ *i.*) (*загромозди́ть*) to pile up, heap up (with); to block up (with); (*impers. + d.*) мне ∼и́ло нос my nose is blocked up **4** (*сдéлать в книге*) to mark, put a marker in **5** (*для хранéния*) to lay in, store, put by **6** (*часы*) to pawn; (*дом*) to mortgage

зало́жник, а *m.* hostage

зало́жни|ца, цы *f.* ▶ зало́жник

залп, а *m.* volley; salvo; ∼ом (fig., infml) without pausing for breath; вы́пить ∼ом to drain at one draught

зама́|зать, жу, жешь *pf.* (*of* ▶ ма́зать 3, ▶ зама́зывать) **1** (*покрыть краской*) to paint over; (*зачеркнуть*) to efface; (fig.) to slur over **2** (*залепить*) to putty **3** (*запачкать*) to daub, smear, to soil

зама́|заться, жусь, жешься *pf.* (*of* ▶ ма́заться 1, ▶ зама́зываться) to smear oneself; to get dirty

зама́зк|а, и *f.* **1** (*вещество*) putty **2** (*дéйствие*) puttying

зама́зыва|ть, ю *impf. of* ▶ зама́зать

зама́зыва|ться, юсь *impf. of* ▶ зама́заться

зама́нива|ть, ю *impf. of* ▶ замани́ть

заман|и́ть, ю́, ∼ишь *pf.* (*of* ▶ зама́нивать) to entice, lure; (*обмáном*) to decoy

зама́нчив|ый, ∼, ∼а *adj.* tempting, alluring

замарин|ова́ть, у́ю *pf. of* ▶ маринова́ть

замаскир|ова́ть, у́ю *pf. of* ▶ маскирова́ть

замаскир|ова́ться, у́юсь *pf. of* ▶ маскирова́ться

зама́тыва|ть, ю *impf. of* ▶ замота́ть

зама|ха́ть, шý, ∼шешь *pf.* to begin to wave

зама́хива|ться, юсь *impf. of* ▶ замахну́ться

замахн|у́ться, у́сь, ёшься *pf.* **1** (+ *i. and* на + *a.*) to raise (sth) threateningly (at sb) **2** (*поднять руку*) (на + *a.*) to raise a hand against **3** (на + *a.*) (fig., infml) to set one's sights on

зама́чива|ть, ю *impf. of* ▶ замочи́ть 1

замби́|ец, йца *m.* Zambian

замби́йк|а, и *f.* Zambian

замби́йский *adj.* Zambian

За́мби|я, и *f.* Zambia

заме́дленн|ый *p.p.p. of* ▶ заме́длить *and* *adj.* delayed; бóмба ∼ого дéйствия delayed-action bomb, time bomb; (fig.) time bomb; ∼ое воспроизведéние slow-motion replay

заме́дл|ить, ю, ишь *pf.* (*of* ▶ замедля́ть) to slow down, delay; з. шаг to slacken one's pace; з. ход to reduce speed

заме́дл|иться, юсь, ишься *pf.* (*of* ▶ замедля́ться) to slow down; to slacken, become slower

замедля́|ть, ю *impf. of* ▶ заме́длить

замедля́|ться, юсь *impf. of* ▶ заме́длиться

✓ заме́н|а, ы *f.* **1** (*дéйствие*) substitution; replacement **2** (*тот, кто (или то, что) заменяет*) substitute

замени́тел|ь, я *m.* (+ *g.*) substitute; з. са́хара sweetener

замен|и́ть, ю́, ∼ишь *pf.* (*of* ▶ заменя́ть) **1** (+ *a. and i.*) to replace (by), substitute (for); з. ма́сло маргари́ном to use margarine instead of butter **2** (*занять место кого-то, чего-то*) to take the place of; трýдно бýдет з. его́ it will be hard to replace him

✓ заменя́|ть, я́ю *impf. of* ▶ замени́ть

зам|ерéть, рý, рёшь, *past* ∼ер, ∼ерла́, ∼ерло́ *pf.* (*of* ▶ замира́ть) **1** (*стать неподвижным*) to stand still; to freeze, be rooted to the spot; to die (fig.) **2** (*о звуках*) to die down, die away

замерза́|ть, ю *impf. of* ▶ замёрзнуть

замёрз|нуть, ну, нешь, *past* ∼, ∼ла *pf.* (*of* ▶ замерза́ть) (*о реке, окне*) to freeze (up); (*умереть от морóза*) to freeze to death; (*о растениях*) to be killed by frost; я ∼ I'm frozen

за́мертво *adv.* like one dead; онá упáла з. she collapsed in a dead faint

заме́|си́ть, ешу́, е́сишь *pf. of* ► меси́ть
заме|сти́, ту́, тёшь, *past* ~л, ~ла́ *pf.* (*of* ► замета́ть) **1** (*подмести*) to sweep up **2** (*покрыть*) to cover (up); (*impers.*) доро́гу ~ло́ сне́гом the road is covered with snow
 замести́тел|ь, я *m.* substitute; deputy; з. дире́ктора deputy director
заме|сти́ть, щу́, сти́шь *pf.* (*of* ► замеща́ть) **1** (+ *a. and i.*) (*заменить*) to replace (by); to substitute (for) **2** (*должность*) to fill **3** (*заменить собой*) to deputize for, act for
замета́|ть, ю *impf. of* ► замести́
заме|та́ться, чу́сь, ~чешься *pf.* to begin to rush about; (*в постели*) to begin to toss
 заме́|тить, чу, тишь *pf.* (*of* ► замеча́ть) **1** (*увидеть*) to notice **2** (*обратить внимание (на)*) to take notice (of); (*пометить*) to make a note (of) **3** (*сказать*) to remark, observe
заме́тк|а, и *f.* **1** (*запись*) note **2** (*краткое сообщение*) notice; paragraph
заме́т|ный, ~ен, ~на *adj.* (*видимый*) noticeable; (*ощутимый*) appreciable; ~но (*as pred.*) it is noticeable
замеча́ни|е, я *nt.* **1** remark, observation **2** (*упрёк*) reprimand; reproof
замеча́тельно *adv.* **1** (*with verbs*) splendidly, brilliantly, wonderfully **2** (*with adjectives, adverbs*) remarkably **3** (*pred.*): з.! (it's) splendid!, wonderful!
 замеча́тельн|ый, ~ен, ~ьна *adj.* remarkable; splendid, wonderful
 замеча́|ть, ю *impf. of* ► заме́тить
замеша́тельств|о, а *nt.* confusion; embarrassment; привести́ в з. to throw into confusion; прийти́ в з. to be confused, be embarrassed
заме́шка|ться, юсь *pf.* (infml) to linger, dawdle
замеща́|ть, ю *impf. of* ► замести́ть
замини́р|овать, ую *pf. of* ► мини́ровать
замира́|ть, ю *impf. of* ► замере́ть
за́мкнут|ый, ~, ~а *adj.* **1** (*no short forms*) (*среда, жизнь*) isolated, secluded **2** (*человек*) reserved, withdrawn
замкн|у́ть, у́, ёшь *pf.* (*of* ► замыка́ть) to lock; to close; з. ше́ствие, з. коло́нну to bring up the rear
замкн|у́ться, у́сь, ёшься *pf.* (*of* ► замыка́ться) **1** (*цепь*) to be joined at the ends; круг ~у́лся (fig.) everything fell into place **2** to shut oneself up; (fig.): з. в себе́ to become reserved, retire into oneself
 за́м|ок, ка *m.* castle
 зам|о́к, ка́ *m.* **1** lock; вися́чий з. padlock **2** (*браслета*) clasp; (*серьги*) clip
замолча́|ть, у́, и́шь *pf.* to fall silent; (fig.) to cease corresponding
замора́жива|ть, ю *impf. of* ► заморо́зить
заморо́|женный *p.p.p. of* ► заморо́зить *and adj.* frozen; iced; ~женное мя́со frozen meat

заморо́|зить, жу, зишь *pf.* (*of* ► замора́живать) to freeze
за́мороз|ок, ка *m.* (*usu. in pl.*) (light) frost
заморо́ч|ить, у, ишь *pf. of* ► моро́чить
замо́тан|ный, ~, ~а *adj.* (infml) worn out, shattered
замота́|ть, ю *pf.* (*of* ► зама́тывать) **1** to wind, twist; (+ *i.*) (*обмотать*) to wrap (in, with) **2** (fig., infml, *утомить*) to tire out
замоч|и́ть, у́, ~ишь **1** *pf.* (*of* ► зама́чивать) (*слегка*) to wet; (*погрузить в воду*) to soak **2** *pf. of* ► мочи́ть 2
за́муж *adv.*: вы́йти з. за кого́-н. to marry sb (*of woman*); вы́дать кого́-н. з. (за + *a.*) to give sb in marriage (to); to marry off (to)
за́мужем *adv.*: быть з. (за + *i.*) to be married (to) (*of woman*)
замур|ова́ть, у́ю *pf.* to brick up; (*человека*) to immure
замуро́выва|ть, ю *impf. of* ► замурова́ть
заму́ч|ить, у, ишь *pf.* (*of* ► му́чить) to torment; (*утомить*) to wear out; (*разговорами*) to bore to tears; (*убить*) to torture to death
заму́ч|иться, усь, ишься *pf.* (*of* ► му́читься) to be worn out
за́мш|а, и *f.* chamois (leather); suede
замыка́ни|е, я *nt.* locking; коро́ткое з. (elec.) short circuit
замыка́|ть, ю *impf. of* ► замкну́ть
замыка́|ться, юсь *impf. of* ► замкну́ться
за́мыс|ел, ла *m.* (*план*) project, plan; design, scheme; (*смысл*) idea
замы́сл|ить, ю, ишь *pf.* (*of* ► замышля́ть) (+ *a. or inf.*) to plan; to contemplate; он ~ил самоуби́йство he contemplated suicide
замылова́т|ый, ~, ~а *adj.* intricate, complicated
замышля́|ть, ю *impf. of* ► замы́слить
за́навес, а *m.* curtain
занаве́|сить, шу, сишь *pf.* (*of* ► занаве́шивать) to curtain; to cover
занаве́ск|а, и *f.* curtain
занаве́шива|ть, ю *impf. of* ► занаве́сить
занес|ти́, у́, ёшь, *past* ~, ~ла́ *pf.* (*of* ► заноси́ть) **1** (*принести*) to bring; (*доставить мимоходом*) to drop off **2** (*поднять*) to raise, lift **3** (*записать*) to note down; з. в протоко́л/спи́сок to enter in the minutes/list **4** (*impers.*): з. сне́гом to cover with snow; доро́гу ~ло́ сне́гом the road is snowed up
занима́тел|ьный, ~ен, ~ьна *adj.* entertaining, diverting; absorbing
 занима́|ть¹, ю *impf.* (*of* ► заня́ть) **1** (*город, квартиру*) to occupy; кро́вать ~ет мно́го ме́ста the bed takes up a lot of room; он ~ет высо́кое положе́ние (fig.) he occupies a high post **2** (*увлекать*) to occupy; to interest; бо́льше всего́ его́ ~ют вопро́сы филосо́фии his chief interest is in philosophy **3** (*время*) to take; э́то ~ет мно́го вре́мени this takes a lot of time

4 (*пост, должность*) to take up **5**: з. ме́сто кому́-н./для кого́-н. to reserve a seat for sb; з. пе́рвое ме́сто to take first place

⚲ занима́|ть², ю *impf.* (*of* ▸ заня́ть) (*деньги*) to borrow

⚲ занима́|ться, юсь *impf.* (*of* ▸ заня́ться) (+ *i.*) **1** to be occupied (with), be engaged (in); (*рабо́тать*) to work (at, on); (*учи́ться*) to study; to practise; чем он ~ется? what does he do? (*for a living*) **2** (*посвяща́ть себя́*) to devote oneself (to); з. есте́ственными нау́ками to devote oneself to the natural sciences; з. собо́й to devote time to oneself **3** (с + *i.*) (*помога́ть в уче́нии*) to assist with (*study*)

за́ново *adv.* anew

зано́з|а, ы *f.* splinter

зано|зи́ть, жу́, зи́шь *pf.* to get a splinter into

зано́с, а *m.* drift; сне́жные ~ы snowdrifts; песча́ный з. sand drift

зано|си́ть, шу́, ~сишь *impf. of* ▸ занести́

зано́счив|ый, ~, ~а *adj.* arrogant, haughty

зану́д|а, ы *c.g.* (infml) tiresome person, pain in the neck

зану́д|ный, ~ен, ~на *adj.* (infml) tiresome

⚲ заня́ти|е, я *nt.* **1** (*де́ло*) occupation; pursuit **2** (*in pl.*) studies; (*usu. in pl.*) (*уро́к*) lesson, class

заня́т|ный, ~ен, ~на *adj.* (infml) entertaining, amusing

занято́й *adj.* busy

за́нятост|ь, и *f.* **1** busyness, lack of time **2** (econ.) employment; по́лная з. full employment; центр ~и jobcentre (BrE), employment agency

за́нят|ый, ~, ~а́, ~о *p.p.p. of* ▸ заня́ть *and adj.* **1** occupied; ~о (*телефо́н, туале́т*) engaged **2** (*only short forms*) (*челове́к*) busy; он сейча́с ~ he is busy at the moment

⚲ зан|я́ть, займу́, за́ймёшь, *past* ~я́л, ~яла́, ~я́ло *pf. of* ▸ занима́ть¹

зан|я́ться, займу́сь, за́ймёшься, *past* ~я́лся, ~яла́сь *pf. of* ▸ занима́ться

заодно́ *adv.* in concert, at one; де́йствовать з. to act in concert

заокеа́нский *adj.* transoceanic

заор|а́ть, у́, ёшь *pf.* (infml) to begin to bawl, begin to yell

заострённый *adj.* pointed, sharp

зао́чно *adv.* **1** (*в отсу́тствие кого́-н.*) in one's absence **2** (*об обуче́нии*) by correspondence course, externally

зао́чн|ый *adj.*: з. курс correspondence course; ~ое обуче́ние distance learning

⚲ за́пад, а *m.* **1** west **2** (3.) (pol.) the West

⚲ за́падн|ый *adj.* west, western; (*направле́ние, ве́тер*) westerly

западн|я́, и́, *g. pl.* ~е́й *f.* trap, snare; попа́сть в ~ю́ to fall into a trap (also fig.)

запак|ова́ть, у́ю *pf.* (*of* ▸ запако́вывать) to pack (up); to wrap up, do up

запако́выва|ть, ю *impf. of* ▸ запакова́ть

запа́л, а *m.* fuse

⚲ запа́с, а *m.* **1** supply, stock; reserve; про з. for an emergency; отложи́ть про з. to put by; слова́рный з. vocabulary; у меня́ день в ~е I have one day in reserve, to spare **2** (mil.) reserve; его́ уво́лили в з. he has been transferred to the reserve

запаса́|ть, ю *impf. of* ▸ запасти́

запаса́|ться, юсь *impf. of* ▸ запасти́сь

запасно́й *adj.* spare; (*игро́к*) reserve; з. вы́ход emergency exit; (*as m. n.* з., ~о́го) (mil.) reservist; (sport) reserve

запас|ти́, у́, ёшь, *past* ~́, ~ла́ *pf.* (*of* ▸ запаса́ть) (+ *a. or g.*) to stock, store; to lay in a stock of

запас|ти́сь, у́сь, ёшься, *past* ~ся, ~ла́сь *pf.* (*of* ▸ запаса́ться) (+ *i.*) to provide oneself (with); to stock up (on, with); з. терпе́нием (fig.) to arm oneself with patience

запатентова́ть *pf. of* ▸ патентова́ть

за́пах, а *m.* smell

запа́чка|ть, ю *pf. of* ▸ па́чкать

запа́чка|ться, юсь *pf. of* ▸ па́чкаться

запева́|ть, ю *impf. of* ▸ запе́ть

запека́|ть, ю *impf. of* ▸ запе́чь

зап|ере́ть, ру́, рёшь, *past* ~ер, ерла́, ~ерло́ *pf.* (*of* ▸ запира́ть) **1** (*дверь*) to lock; з. на засо́в to bolt **2** (*челове́ка*) to lock in; to shut up **3** (*прегради́ть до́ступ*) to bar; to block up

зап|ере́ться, ру́сь, рёшься, *past* ~ерся́, ~ерла́сь, ~ерло́сь *pf.* (*of* ▸ запира́ться) **1** to lock oneself in **2** (*дверь*) to lock

зап|е́ть, ою́, оёшь *pf.* (*of* ▸ запева́ть) (*нача́ть петь*) to begin to sing; з. пе́сню to break into a song

запеча́т|ать, аю *pf.* (*of* ▸ запеча́тывать) to seal

запеча́тыва|ть, ю *impf. of* ▸ запеча́тать

запе́|чь, ку́, чёшь, ку́т, *past* ~к, ~кла́ *pf.* (*of* ▸ запека́ть) to bake

запива́|ть, ю *impf. of* ▸ запи́ть

запина́|ться, юсь *impf.* (*of* ▸ запну́ться) to stumble

запира́|ть, ю *impf. of* ▸ запере́ть

запира́|ться, юсь *impf. of* ▸ запере́ться

запи|са́ть, шу́, ~шешь *pf.* (*of* ▸ запи́сывать) **1** (*занести́ на бума́гу*) to note, make a note (of); to take down (in writing); (*конце́рт, фильм*) to record (*with apparatus*); з. (на плёнку) to tape; з. (на ви́део) to video **2** (*включи́ть в соста́в чего́-либо*) to enter, register, enrol

запи|са́ться, шу́сь, ~шешься *pf.* (*of* ▸ запи́сываться) to register, enter one's name, enrol; з. в клуб to join a club; з. к врачу́ to make an appointment with the doctor

запи́ск|а, и *f.* note; делова́я з. memorandum, minute

записн|о́й *adj.*: ~а́я кни́жка notebook

запи́сыва|ть, ю *impf. of* ▸ записа́ть

запи́сыва|ться, юсь *impf. of* ▸ записа́ться

⚲ за́пис|ь, и *f.* **1** (*де́йствие*) writing down;

recording; registration **2** (*в дневнике*) entry; (comput.) record; (*заметка*) note; (*на плёнку*) recording; (law) deed

зап|и́ть, ью́, ьёшь *pf.* (*of* ▸ **запива́ть**) **1** (*past* **∼и́л, ∼ила́, ∼и́ло**) (+ *a. and i.*) to wash down (with); to take (with, after); **з. табле́тку водо́й** to take a tablet with water **2** (*past* **∼́ил, ∼ила́, ∼́ило**) to begin to drink heavily

запи|шу́, ∼́шешь *see* ▸ **записа́ть**

запла́кан|ный, ∼, ∼а *adj.* tear-stained; in tears

запла́|кать, чу, чешь *pf.* to begin to cry

заплани́р|овать, ую *pf. of* ▸ **плани́ровать**

запла́т|а, ы *f.* patch (*in garments*); **наложи́ть ∼у** (**на** + *a.*) to patch

запла|ти́ть, чу́, ∼́тишь *pf. of* ▸ **плати́ть**

запла́|чу, чешь *see* ▸ **запла́кать**

запла|чу́, ∼́тишь *see* ▸ **заплати́ть**

запле|сти́, ту́, тёшь, *past* **∼́л, ∼ла́** *pf.* (*of* ▸ **заплета́ть**) (*волосы*) to braid, plait

заплета́|ть, ю *impf. of* ▸ **заплести́**

запломбир|ова́ть, у́ю *pf.* (*of* ▸ **пломбирова́ть**) **1** (*зуб*) to fill **2** (*вагон, избирательную урну*) to seal

заплыва́|ть, ю *impf. of* ▸ **заплы́ть**[1], ▸ **заплы́ть**[2]

заплы́|ть[1]**, ву́, вёшь,** *past* **∼л, ∼ла́, ∼ло** *pf.* (*of* ▸ **заплыва́ть**) (*о пловце*) to swim far out; (*о судне*) to sail away

заплы́|ть[2]**, ву́, вёшь,** *past* **∼л, ∼ла́, ∼ло** *pf.* (*of* ▸ **заплыва́ть**) to be swollen; to be bloated; **∼вшие жи́ром глаза́** bloated eyes

запн|у́ться, у́сь, ёшься *pf. of* ▸ **запина́ться**

запове́дник, а *m.* reserve; preserve; sanctuary; **госуда́рственный з.** national park

за́поведь, и *f.* precept; (relig., fig. also) commandment; **де́сять ∼ей** the Ten Commandments

подозр

запода́рива|ть, ю *impf. of* ▸ **заподо́зрить**

заподо́зр|ить, ю, ишь *pf.* (*of* ▸ **запода́ривать**) (+ *a. and* **в** + *p.*) to suspect (of)

запозда́лый *adj.* belated

заполза́|ть, ю *impf. of* ▸ **заползти́**

заполз|ти́, у́, ёшь, *past* **∼́, ∼ла́** *pf.* (*of* ▸ **заполза́ть**) (**в, под** + *a.*) to creep, crawl (into, under)

запо́лн|ить, ю, ишь *pf.* (*of* ▸ **заполня́ть**) to fill in, fill up; **з. бланк** to fill in (BrE), fill out (AmE) a form

запо́лн|иться, ится *pf.* (*of* ▸ **заполня́ться**) to fill up

заполня́|ть, ю, ет *impf. of* ▸ **запо́лнить**

заполня́|ться, ется *impf. of* ▸ **запо́лниться**

заполя́рь|е, я *nt.* (geog.) polar regions

запомина́|ть, ю *impf. of* ▸ **запо́мнить**

запомина́|ться, юсь *impf. of* ▸ **запо́мниться**

запо́мн|ить, ю, ишь *pf.* (*of* ▸ **запомина́ть**) **1** (*текст, номер*) to memorize **2** (*человека, картину, событие*) to remember

запо́мн|иться, юсь, ишься *pf.* (*of* ▸ **запомина́ться**) to stick, remain in one's memory

за́понк|а, и *f.* cufflink; stud

запо́р, а *m.* (med.) constipation

запотева́|ть, ю *impf. of* ▸ **запоте́ть**

запоте́|ть, ю *pf.* (*of* ▸ **поте́ть,** ▸ **запотева́ть**) to mist over

зап|ою́, оёшь *see* ▸ **запе́ть**

запра́в|ить, лю, ишь *pf.* (*of* ▸ **заправля́ть**) **1** (*вставить*) to insert; **з. брю́ки в сапоги́** to tuck one's trousers into one's boots **2** (*приготовить*) to prepare; **з. автомоби́ль бензи́ном** to fill a car up with petrol **3** (+ *i.*) (*добавить*) to mix in; (*сдобрить*) to season (with)

запра́в|иться, люсь, ишься *pf.* (*of* ▸ **заправля́ться**) (*горючим*) to refuel

запра́вк|а, и *f.* **1** (*приправа*) seasoning; **з. для сала́та** salad dressing **2** (*машины*) refuelling (BrE), refueling (AmE) **3** (infml, *заправочная станция*) filling station

заправля́|ть, ю *impf.* (*of* ▸ **запра́вить**) (+ *i.*) (infml) to be in charge (of)

заправля́|ться, юсь *impf. of* ▸ **запра́виться**

запра́вочн|ый *adj.*: **∼ая ста́нция** filling station

запра́шива|ть, ю *impf. of* ▸ **запроси́ть**

запре́т, а *m.* prohibition, ban; **быть под ∼ом** to be banned; **наложи́ть з.** (**на** + *a.*) to place a ban (on)

запре|ти́ть, щу́, ти́шь *pf.* (*of* ▸ **запреща́ть**) (*не позволять*) to prohibit, forbid; **«въезд запрещён»** 'No Entry'; (*книгу, наркотики, оружие*) to ban

запре́тн|ый *adj.* forbidden; **∼ая те́ма** taboo subject

🔑 **запреща́|ть, ю** *impf. of* ▸ **запрети́ть**

запреща́|ться, ется *impf.* to be forbidden, to be prohibited

запрограмми́р|овать, ую *pf. of* ▸ **программи́ровать**

запроки́дыва|ть, ю *impf. of* ▸ **запроки́нуть**

запроки́н|уть, у, ешь *pf.* to throw back

🔑 **запро́с, а** *m.* **1** inquiry; (pol.) question **2** (*pl. only*) (*потребности*) needs, requirements

запро|си́ть, шу́, ∼́сишь *pf.* (*of* ▸ **запра́шивать**) **1** (**о** + *p.*) to inquire (about); (+ *a.*) (*попросить*) to request **2**: **з. сли́шком высо́кую це́ну** (infml) to ask an exorbitant price

за́просто *adv.* (infml) (*без формальностей*) without ceremony, without formality; (*легко*) without any problem, easily

зап|ру́, рёшь *see* ▸ **запере́ть**

запры́гива|ть, ю *impf. of* ▸ **запры́гнуть**

запры́гн|уть, у, ешь *pf.* (*of* ▸ **запры́гивать**) (**за** + *a.*) to leap (over); (**на** + *a.*) to jump (onto)

запряга́|ть, ю *impf. of* ▸ **запря́чь**

запря́|чь, гу́, жёшь, гу́т, *past* **∼г, ∼гла́** *pf.* (*of* ▸ **запряга́ть**) to harness (also fig.)

🔑 key word

запу́ганный *p.p.p. of* ▶ запуга́ть *and adj.* broken-spirited; frightened

запуга́|ть, ю *pf.* (*of* ▶ запу́гивать) to intimidate, cow; to frighten

запу́гива|ть, ю *impf. of* ▶ запуга́ть

за́пуск, а *m.* (*мотора*) starting; (*ракеты*) launch, launching; (comput.) running

запус|ка́ть, ка́ю *impf. of* ▶ запусти́ть¹, ▶ запусти́ть²

запусте́ни|е, я *nt.* neglect; desolation

запу|сти́ть¹, щу́, ~стишь *pf.* (*of* ▶ запуска́ть) **1** (+ *i. and* в + *a.*) (infml, *бросить*) to throw (at), fling (at) **2** (в + *a.*) (*засунуть*) to thrust (hands, *etc.*) (into); з. ко́гти, ла́пы, ру́ки (в + *a.*) (fig.) to get one's hands on **3** (*привести в действие*) to start (up); (comput.) to run; з. мото́р to start up the engine; з. раке́ту to launch a rocket

запу|сти́ть², щу́, ~стишь *pf.* (*of* ▶ запуска́ть) **1** (*оставить без ухода*) to neglect, allow to fall into neglect; з. дела́ to neglect one's affairs; з. сад to neglect a garden **2** (*дать развиться*) to allow to develop unchecked

запу́тан|ный, ~, ~а *p.p.p. of* ▶ запу́тать *and* (~, ~на) *adj.* tangled; (fig.) intricate, involved; з. вопро́с knotty question

запу́та|ть, ю *pf.* (*of* ▶ запу́тывать, ▶ пу́тать) **1** (*нитки, волосы*) to tangle (up) **2** (fig.) (*человека*) to confuse; (*дело*) to complicate; to muddle

запу́та|ться, юсь *pf.* (*of* ▶ запу́тываться, ▶ пу́таться) **1** (*нитки, волосы*) to become entangled; to foul; (в + *p.*) (*в сетях*) to entangle oneself (in), be caught (in) **2** (в + *p.*) (fig., *в деле*) to become entangled (in); become involved (in); (*дело, речь*) to become confused, complicated; (*сбиться с толку*) to get into a muddle

запу́тыва|ть, ю *impf. of* ▶ запу́тать

запу́тыва|ться, юсь *impf. of* ▶ запу́таться

запу́щен|ный, ~, ~а *p.p.p. of* ▶ запусти́ть² *and* (~, ~на) *adj.* neglected

запча́ст|и, е́й *f. pl.* (sg. ~ь, ~и) (abbr. of запасна́я ча́сть) (spare parts); spares

запыха́|ться, юсь *pf.* (infml) to be out of breath

запя́сть|е, я *nt.* wrist

запят|а́я, о́й *f.* comma

⚡ **зараба́тыва|ть, ю** *impf. of* ▶ зарабо́тать 1

зарабо́та|ть, ю *pf.* (*of* ▶ зараба́тывать) **1** (*приобрести работой*) to earn **2** (*по impf.*) (*начать работать*) to begin to work; to start (up)

за́работн|ый *adj.*: ~ая пла́та wages, pay, salary

за́работ|ок, ка *m.* earnings; лёгкий з. easy money

зара́внива|ть, ю *impf. of* ▶ заровня́ть

заража́|ть, ю *impf. of* ▶ зарази́ть

заража́|ться, юсь *impf. of* ▶ зарази́ться

зараже́ни|е, я *nt.* infection; (*местности*) contamination

зара|жу́, зи́шь *see* ▶ зарази́ть

зара́з|а, ы **1** infection, contagion **2** (fig., infml, *негодяй*) pest

зарази́тел|ьный, ~ен, ~ьна *adj.* infectious; catching; з. смех infectious laughter

зара|зи́ть, жу́, зи́шь *pf.* (*of* ▶ заража́ть) (+ *i.*) to infect (with) (also fig.); (*местность*) to contaminate

зара|зи́ться, жу́сь, зи́шься *pf.* (*of* ▶ заража́ться) (+ *i.*) to be infected (with); catch (also fig.)

зара́з|ный, ~ен, ~на *adj.* infectious; contagious; з. больно́й infectious case; (*as n.* з., ~ного, *f.* ~ная, ~ной) infectious case

⚡ **зара́нее** *adv.* beforehand; in good time; заплати́ть з. to pay in advance

зараста́|ть, ю *impf. of* ▶ зарасти́

зараст|и́, у́, ёшь, *past* заро́с, заросла́ *pf.* (*of* ▶ зараста́ть) **1** (+ *i.*) to be overgrown (with); тропа́ заросла́ мхом the path was overgrown with moss **2** (*о ране*) to heal

⚡ **зарегистри́р|овать, ую** *pf.* (*of* ▶ регистри́ровать) to register

зарегистри́р|оваться, уюсь *pf.* (*of* ▶ регистри́роваться) to register oneself

заре́|зать, жу, жешь *pf.* (*of* ▶ ре́зать 3) (*человека*) to murder; to knife; (*животное*) to slaughter; (infml, *о волке*) to devour, kill

зарезерви́р|овать, ую *pf. of* ▶ резерви́ровать

зарекоменд|ова́ть, у́ю *pf.*: з. себя́ (+ *i.*) to prove oneself, show oneself (to be); хорошо́ з. себя́ to show oneself to advantage

заржаве́|ть, ет *pf.* (*of* ▶ ржаве́ть) to rust; to have got rusty

зарис|ова́ть, у́ю *pf.* (*of* ▶ зарисо́вывать) to sketch

зарисо́вк|а, и *f.* sketch

зарисо́выва|ть, ю *impf. of* ▶ зарисова́ть

заровня́|ть, ю *pf.* (*of* ▶ зара́внивать) to level, even up; з. я́му to fill up a hole

заро|ди́ться, жу́сь, ди́шься *pf.* (*of* ▶ зарожда́ться) (*возникнуть*) to arise, come into being; у него́ ~ди́лось сомне́ние a doubt arose in his mind

заро́дыш, а *m.* (biol.) embryo; (fig.) embryo, germ; подави́ть в ~е to nip in the bud

заро́дышевый *adj.* embryonic

зарожда́|ться, юсь *impf. of* ▶ зароди́ться

за́росл|ь, и *f.* (*usu. in pl.*) thicket

зар|о́ю, о́ешь *see* ▶ зары́ть

⚡ **зарпла́т|а, ы** *f.* (abbr. of за́работная пла́та) wages, pay, salary; сего́дня з. today is pay day

заруба́|ть, ю *impf. of* ▶ заруби́ть

⚡ **зарубе́жный** *adj.* foreign

зарубе́жь|е, я *nt.* foreign countries; бли́жнее з. the countries of the former Soviet Union; да́льнее з. abroad (*excluding the countries of the former Soviet Union*)

заруб|и́ть, лю́, ~ишь *pf.* (*of* ▶ заруба́ть) **1** (*убить*) to hack to death **2** (*сделать зарубку*) to notch, make an incision (on)

зарыва́|ть, ю *impf. of* ▶ зары́ть

3

зарыва́|ться, юсь *impf. of* ▶ зары́ться

зар|ы́ть, о́ю, о́ешь *pf.* (*of* ▶ зарыва́ть) to bury

зар|ы́ться, о́юсь, о́ешься *pf.* (*of* ▶ зарыва́ться) to bury oneself

зар|я́, и́, *pl.* **зо́ри, зорь, зо́рям** *f.* daybreak, dawn (also fig.)

заря|ди́ть, жу́, ~ди́шь *pf.* (*of* ▶ заряжа́ть) **1** (*орудие, фотоаппарат*) to load **2** (elec., *батарею*) to charge

заря́дк|а, и *f.* **1** (*ружья*) loading; (elec.) charging **2** (*упражнения*) exercises; drill

заря́дн|ый *adj.:* ~ое устро́йство charger, charging unit (*for battery*)

заряжа́|ть, ю *impf. of* ▶ заряди́ть

заря|жу́, ~ди́шь *see* ▶ заряди́ть

заса́д|а, ы *f.* ambush

заса́лива|ть, ю *impf. of* ▶ засоли́ть

заса́сыва|ть, ю *impf. of* ▶ засоса́ть

засверка́|ть, ю *pf.* to begin to sparkle, begin to twinkle

засве|ти́ться, ~тится *pf.* to light up (also fig.)

⚜ **заседа́ни|е, я** *nt.* (*собрание*) meeting; (*совещание*) conference; (*суда*) session, sitting

заседа́|ть, ю *impf.* to sit; to meet

засе́ива|ть, ю *impf. of* ▶ засе́ять

засекре́|тить, чу, тишь *pf.* (*of* ▶ засекре́чивать) to place on secret list; to classify as secret, restrict

засекре́ченный *p.p.p. of* ▶ засекре́тить *and adj.* secret; (*документы, сведения*) classified

засекре́чива|ть, ю *impf. of* ▶ засекре́тить

засел|и́ть, ю́, и́шь *pf.* (*of* ▶ заселя́ть) (*землю*) to settle; to colonize; з. но́вый дом to occupy a new house

заселя́|ть, я́ю *impf. of* ▶ засели́ть

засе́|ять, ю, ешь *pf.* (*of* ▶ засе́ивать) to sow

заска́кива|ть, ю *impf. of* ▶ заскочи́ть

заскоч|и́ть, у́, ~ишь *pf.* (*of* ▶ заска́кивать) **1** (за + *a.* ог на + *a.*) to jump, spring (behind, onto) **2** (в + *a.*) (fig.) to drop in (to, at)

заскуча́|ть, ю *pf.* **1** to get bored **2** (по + *d.*) to begin to miss

за|сла́ть, шлю́, шлёшь *pf.* (*of* ▶ засыла́ть) to send, dispatch; з. шпио́на to send out a spy

заслон|и́ть, ю́, и́шь *pf.* (*of* ▶ заслоня́ть) (*закрыть*) to hide, cover; (*защитить*) to shield, screen

заслон|и́ться, ю́сь, и́шься *pf.* (*of* ▶ заслоня́ться) (от + *g.*) to shield oneself, screen oneself (from)

засло́нк|а, и *f.* oven door; (*регулятор тяги*) damper

заслон|я́ть, я́ю *impf. of* ▶ заслони́ть

заслон|я́ться, я́юсь *impf. of* ▶ заслони́ться

заслу́г|а, и *f.* service; contribution; они́ получи́ли по ~ам they got what they deserved

заслу́жива|ть, ю *impf. of* ▶ заслужи́ть (+ *g.*) to deserve, merit

заслуж|и́ть, у́, ~ишь *pf.* (*of* ▶ заслу́живать) (+ *a.*) to deserve, merit; (*выслужить*) to win, earn

засме|я́ться, ю́сь, ёшься *pf.* to begin to laugh

засне́жен|ный, ~, ~а *adj.* snow-covered

засн|у́ть, у́, ёшь *pf.* (*of* ▶ засыпа́ть¹) to go to sleep, fall asleep

засо́в, а *m.* bolt, bar

засо́выва|ть, ю *impf. of* ▶ засу́нуть

засол|и́ть, ю́, ~и́шь *pf.* (*of* ▶ заса́ливать) to salt; to pickle

засор|и́ть, ю́, и́шь *pf.* (*of* ▶ засоря́ть) **1** (*трубу*) to clog, block up, stop **2** (*глаза*) to get dirt into

засор|и́ться, и́тся *pf.* (*of* ▶ засоря́ться) to become obstructed, blocked up

засоря́|ть, ю, ет *impf. of* ▶ засори́ть

засоря́|ться, ется *impf. of* ▶ засори́ться

засос|а́ть, у́, ёшь *pf.* (*of* ▶ заса́сывать) to suck in, engulf, swallow up (also fig.)

засо́х|нуть, ну, нешь, *past* ~, ~ла *pf.* (*of* ▶ засыха́ть) **1** (*о булке, красках*) to dry (up) **2** (*о траве*) to wither

заста́в|а, ы *f.* **1** (*пограничная застава*) border post **2** (mil.) picket; outpost

заста|ва́ть, ю́, ёшь *impf. of* ▶ заста́ть

заста́в|ить¹, лю, ишь *pf.* (*of* ▶ заставля́ть¹) **1** (*загромоздить*) to cram, fill; з. ко́мнату ме́белью to cram a room with furniture **2** (*загородить*) to block up, obstruct

заста́в|ить², лю, ишь *pf.* (*of* ▶ заставля́ть²) (+ *a. and inf.*) (*принудить*) to compel, force, make

заста́вк|а, и *f.* (TV) repeated image at the start of TV programme; logo; музыка́льная з. signature tune

заставля́|ть¹, ю *impf. of* ▶ заста́вить¹

⚜ **заставля́|ть², ю** *impf. of* ▶ заста́вить²

заста́|ну, нешь *see* ▶ заста́ть

заста́|ть, ну, нешь *pf.* (*of* ▶ застава́ть) to find; вы ~ли его́ до́ма? did you find him in?; з. враспло́х to catch napping; з. на ме́сте преступле́ния to catch red-handed

заста|ю́, ёшь *see* ▶ застава́ть

застёгива|ть, ю *impf. of* ▶ застегну́ть

застёгива|ться, юсь *impf.* (*of* ▶ застегну́ться) **1** to fasten, do up; воротни́к ~ется на пу́говицу the collar does up with a button **2** to button oneself up; з. на все пу́говицы to do up all one's buttons

застег|ну́ть, ну́, нёшь *pf.* (*of* ▶ застёгивать) to fasten, do up; з. (на пу́говицы) to button up

застег|ну́ться, ну́сь, нёшься *pf. of* ▶ застёгиваться

застёжк|а, и *f.* fastening; clasp

застекл|и́ть, ю́, и́шь *pf.* (*of* ▶ застекля́ть, ▶ стекли́ть) to glaze, fit with glass; з. портре́т to frame a portrait

застекл|я́ть, я́ю *impf. of* ▶ застекли́ть

застел|и́ть, ю́, ~ешь *pf.* = застла́ть 1

засте́нчив|ый, ~, ~а *adj.* shy; bashful

3

засти́|г, гла *see* ▶ засти́чь

застига́ть, га́ю *impf. of* ▶ засти́гнуть,
▶ засти́чь

засти́гнуть = засти́чь

застила́|ть, ю *impf. of* ▶ застла́ть

засти́|чь, гну, гнешь, *past* ~г, ~гла *past* (*of*
▶ застига́ть) to catch; to take unawares; **нас**
~гла гроза́ we were caught by the storm

заст|ла́ть, елю́, е́лешь *pf.* (*of* ▶ застила́ть)
1 (+ *i.*) to cover (with); **з. ковро́м** to carpet,
lay a carpet (over) **2** (fig.) to hide from
view; to cloud; **слёзы ~ла́ли её глаза́** tears
dimmed her eyes **3** (*кровать*) to make

засто́|й, я *m.* stagnation (fig.); **в ~е** at a
standstill; (econ.) depression

засто́ль|е, я *nt.* (infml) celebratory meal

засто́льн|ый *adj.* table-, occurring at table;
~ая бесе́да table talk; ~ая пе́сня drinking
song

застра́ива|ть, ю *impf. of* ▶ застро́ить

застрахо́ван|ный *p.p.p. of* ▶ застрахова́ть
and adj. insured; (*as m. n.* з., ~ного) insured
person

застрах|ова́ть, у́ю *pf.* (*of*
▶ страхова́ть)
(от + *g.*) to insure (against)

застрах|ова́ться, у́юсь *pf.* (*of*
▶ страхова́ться) to insure oneself

застрева́|ть, ю *impf. of* ▶ застря́ть

застре́лива|ть, ю *impf. of* ▶ застрели́ть

застре́лива|ться, юсь *impf. of*
▶ застрели́ться

застрел|и́ть, ю́, ~ишь *pf.* (*of* ▶ застре́ливать)
to shoot (dead)

застрел|и́ться, ю́сь, ~ишься *pf.* (*of*
▶ застре́ливаться) to shoot oneself; to blow
one's brains out

застро́енный *p.p.p. of* ▶ застро́ить *and adj.*
built-up

застро́|ить, ю, ишь *pf.* (*of* ▶ застра́ивать) to
build on, develop

застро́йк|а, и *f.* building; development;
пра́во ~и building permit

застря́|ну, нешь *see* ▶ застря́ть

застря́|ть, ну, нешь *pf.* (*of* ▶ застрева́ть)
1 to stick; **з. в грязи́** to get stuck in the mud;
слова́ ~ли у него́ в го́рле the words stuck
in his throat **2** (fig., infml, *задержаться*) to
be held up; to become bogged down

за́ступ, а *m.* spade

заступа́|ться, юсь *impf. of* ▶ заступи́ться

заступ|и́ться, лю́сь, ~ишься *pf.* (за + *a.*)
to stand up for; to plead (for)

застыва́|ть, ю *impf. of* ▶ засты́ть

засты́|ну, нешь *see* ▶ засты́ть

засты́ть *pf.* (*of* ▶ застыва́ть) **1** (*о желе,
цементе*) to set; (*о лаве*) to harden **2** (infml,
о руках) to become stiff; (fig.): **з. от у́жаса** to
be paralysed with fright **3** (infml, *о воде*) to
freeze (also fig.)

засу́н|уть, у, ешь *pf.* (*of* ▶ засо́вывать)
to stick in, thrust in; **з. ру́ки в карма́ны** to
thrust one's hands into one's pockets

за́сух|а, и *f.* drought

засу́чива|ть, ю *impf. of* ▶ засучи́ть

засуч|и́ть, у́, ~ишь *pf.* (*of* ▶ засу́чивать): ~
рукава́ *и m. n.* to roll up sleeves, *etc.*

засу́шива|ть, ю, ет *impf. of* ▶ засуши́ть

засу́шива|ться, ется *impf. of* ▶ засуши́ться

засуш|и́ть, у́, ~ишь *pf.* (*of* ▶ засу́шивать) to
dry up (*plants*) (also fig.)

засуш|и́ться, ~ится *pf.* (*of* ▶ засу́шиваться)
to dry up (*intrans.*), shrivel

засу́шлив|ый, ~, ~а *adj.* dry, droughty

засчит|а́ть, а́ю *pf.* (*of* ▶ засчи́тывать) to
take into consideration; **з. в упла́ту до́лга** to
reckon towards payment of a debt

засчи́тыва|ть, ю *impf. of* ▶ засчита́ть

засыла́|ть, ю *impf. of* ▶ засла́ть

засы́п|ать, лю, лешь *pf.* (*of* ▶ засыпа́ть²)
1 (*яму*) to fill up **2** (+ *i.*) (*покрыть*) to
cover (with), strew (with) **3** (+ *i.*) (fig., infml):
з. вопро́сами to bombard with questions
4 (в + *a.*) (infml) to put (into)

засыпа́|ть¹, ю *impf. of* ▶ засну́ть

засыпа́|ть², ю *impf. of* ▶ засы́пать

засыха́|ть, ю *impf. of* ▶ засо́хнуть

зата́ива|ть, ю *impf. of* ▶ затаи́ть

зата́ива|ться, юсь *impf. of* ▶ затаи́ться

зата|и́ть, ю́, и́шь *pf.* (*of* ▶ зата́ивать)
(*мечту, злобу*) to harbour (BrE), harbor
(AmE), cherish; **з. оби́ду** (на + *a.*) to nurse
a grievance (against); **з. дыха́ние** to hold
one's breath

зата|и́ться, ю́сь, и́шься *pf.* (*of*
▶ зата́иваться) (infml) to hide

зата́лкива|ть, ю *impf. of* ▶ затолка́ть,
▶ затолкну́ть

зата́плива|ть, ю *impf. of* ▶ затопи́ть¹

зата́птыва|ть, ю *impf. of* ▶ затопта́ть

зата́скива|ть, ю *impf. of* ▶ затащи́ть

зата́чива|ть, ю *impf. of* ▶ заточи́ть

затащ|и́ть, у́, ~ишь *pf.* (*of* ▶ зата́скивать)
(infml) to drag off, drag away (also fig.)

затвердева́|ть, ет *impf. of* ▶ затверде́ть

затверде́|ть, ет *pf.* (*of* ▶ затвердева́ть,
▶ тверде́ть) (*о земле, цеме́нте*) to harden,
become hard; (*о жи́дкости*) to set

затво́р, а *m.* **1** (*винто́вки*) bolt; breechblock;
(*плоти́ны*) floodgate **2** (phot.) shutter

затева́|ть, ю *impf. of* ▶ зате́ять

затека́|ть, ю *impf. of* ▶ зате́чь

✎ зате́м *adv.* **1** (*после этого*) after that, then,
next **2** (*для этого*) for that reason; **з. что**
because, since, as; **она́ прие́хала з., чтобы
уха́живать за тобо́й** she has come (in order)
to look after you

зате́|чь, чёт, ку́т, *past* ~к, ~кла́ *pf.* (*of*
▶ затека́ть) (*онеме́ть*) to become numb;
у меня́ нога́ ~кла́ my foot's gone numb

зате́|я, и *f.* undertaking, enterprise, venture

зате́|ять, ю *pf.* (*of* ▶ затева́ть) (infml)
(*путеше́ствие*) to undertake; (*игру*) to
organize; (*разгово́р, дра́ку, спор*) to start

затих|а́ть, а́ю *impf. of* ▶ зати́хнуть

3

зати́х|нуть, ну, нешь, *past* ∼, ∼**ла** *pf.* (*of* ▶ **затиха́ть**) (*о звуке, ветре, буре*) to die down, abate; (*о человеке*) to quieten down (BrE), quiet down (AmE)

зати́шь|е, я *nt.* calm; lull

заткн|у́ть, у́, ёшь *pf.* (*of* ▶ **затыка́ть**) **1** (+ *a. and i.*) to stop up; to plug; **з. буты́лку про́бкой** to cork a bottle; **з. рот, гло́тку кому́-н.** (infml) to shut sb up **2** (*засунуть*) to stick, thrust; **з. кого́-н. за по́яс** (fig., infml) to outdo sb

заткн|у́ться, у́сь, ёшься *pf.* (infml) to shut up; ∼**и́сь!** shut up!

затмева́|ть, ю *impf. of* ▶ **затми́ть**

затме́ни|е, я *nt.* **1** (astron.) eclipse **2** (fig., infml) blackout

затм|и́ть, и́шь *pf.* (*of* ▶ **затмева́ть**) **1** to obscure **2** (fig.) to eclipse; to overshadow

⚬ **зато́** *conj.* (infml) but then, but on the other hand; but to make up for it; **до́рого, з. хоро́шая вещь** it is expensive, but then it is good stuff

затолка́|ть, ю *pf.* (*of* ▶ **зата́лкивать**) to jostle

затолкн|у́ть, у́, ёшь *pf.* (*of* ▶ **зата́лкивать**) (infml) to shove in

затон|у́ть, у́, ∼**ешь** *pf. of* ▶ **тону́ть 1**

затоп|и́ть¹, лю́, ∼**ишь** *pf.* (*of* ▶ **зата́пливать**) (*печь*) to light; (*включить отопление*) to turn on the heating

затоп|и́ть², лю́, ∼**ишь** *pf.* (*of* ▶ **затопля́ть**) **1** (*остров, окрестности*) to flood; to submerge **2** (*судно*) to sink; **з. кора́бль** to scuttle a ship

затопля́|ть, ю *impf. of* ▶ **затопи́ть²**

затоп|та́ть, чу́, ∼**чешь** *pf.* (*of* ▶ **зата́птывать**) (*траву, цветы*) to trample down; (*костёр, папиросу*) to stamp out

затоп|чу́, ∼**чешь** *see* ▶ **затопта́ть**

зато́р, а *m.* blocking, obstruction; **з. у́личного движе́ния** traffic jam, congestion

затормо|зи́ть, жу́, зи́шь *pf. of* ▶ **тормози́ть**

заточ|и́ть, у́, ∼**ишь** *pf.* (*of* ▶ **зата́чивать**) to sharpen

затра́гива|ть, ю *impf. of* ▶ **затро́нуть**

⚬ **затра́т|а, ы** *f.* **1** (*действие*) expenditure **2** (*usu. in pl.*) (*расходы*) expenses, outlay

затра́|тить, чу, тишь *pf.* (*of* ▶ **затра́чивать**) to expend, spend

затра́чива|ть, ю *impf. of* ▶ **затра́тить**

затре́щин|а, ы *f.* (infml) box on the ears

затро́н|уть, у, ешь *pf.* (*of* ▶ **затра́гивать**) **1** to affect **2** (fig.) to touch (on); **з. вопро́с** to broach a question

затрудне́ни|е, я *nt.* difficulty

затруднённый *p.p.p. of* ▶ **затрудни́ть** *and adj.* laboured (BrE), labored (AmE)

затрудни́тел|ьный, ∼**ен,** ∼**ьна** *adj.* difficult; embarrassing

затрудн|и́ть, ю́, и́шь *pf.* (*of* ▶ **затрудня́ть**) **1** (*кого-н.*) to trouble; to cause trouble (to); to embarrass **2** (*что-н.*) to make difficult; to hamper

затрудн|я́ть, я́ю *impf. of* ▶ **затрудни́ть**

затуп|и́ть, лю́, ∼**ишь** *pf.* (*of* ▶ **затупля́ть**) to blunt; to dull

затуп|и́ться, ∼**ится** *pf.* (*of* ▶ **затупля́ться**) to become blunt(ed)

затупля́|ть, ю, ет *impf. of* ▶ **затупи́ть**

затупля́|ться, ется *impf. of* ▶ **затупи́ться**

затуха́|ть, а́ет *impf. of* ▶ **затухнуть**

затух|нуть, нет, *past* ∼, ∼**ла** *pf.* (*of* ▶ **затуха́ть**) **1** (*перестать гореть*) to go out, be extinguished **2** (fig., infml, *о звуке*) to die away

затуш|и́ть, у́, ∼**ишь** *pf.* to put out, extinguish; (fig.) to suppress

за́тхл|ый, ∼**а** *adj.* (*запах*) musty; (*воздух*) stale, stuffy; (fig.) stagnant

затыка́|ть, ю *impf. of* ▶ **заткну́ть**

заты́л|ок, ка *m.* **1** back of the head **2**: **в з.** in single file

заты́чк|а, и *f.* (infml) stopper; plug; **з. для уше́й** earplug

затя́гива|ть, ю *impf. of* ▶ **затяну́ть**

затя́гива|ться, юсь *impf. of* ▶ **затяну́ться**

затяжн|о́й *adj.* long drawn-out, protracted; ∼**ая боле́знь** protracted, lingering illness; ∼**ые дожди́** long periods of rain

затя|ну́ть, ну́, ∼**нешь** *pf.* (*of* ▶ **затя́гивать**) **1** (*узел, пояс*) to tighten; (naut.) to haul taut **2** (*покрыть*) to cover; to close; (*impers.*) **не́бо** ∼**ну́ло ту́чами** it has clouded over **3** (*засосать*) to drag down, drag in; (fig., infml, *вовлечь*) to inveigle **4** (infml, *продлить*) to drag out, spin out

затя|ну́ться, ну́сь, ∼**нешься** *pf.* (*of* ▶ **затя́гиваться**) **1** (*затянуть на себе*) to lace oneself up; (*туго завязаться*) to tighten; **у́зел** ∼**ну́лся** the knot tightened **2** (*покрыться*) to be covered; (*of a wound*) to close, heal over **3** (infml, *продлиться*) to drag on **4** (*при курении*) to inhale

зау́м|ный, ∼**ен,** ∼**на** *adj.* abstruse, esoteric, unintelligible

зауны́в|ный, ∼**ен,** ∼**на** *adj.* doleful, plaintive

заупоко́й|ный *adj.* for the repose of the soul; ∼**ая слу́жба** requiem

заура́д|ный, ∼**ен,** ∼**на** *adj.* (*обыкновенный*) ordinary, commonplace; (*посредственный*) mediocre

зау́ченный *p.p.p. of* ▶ **заучи́ть** *and adj.* studied

зау́чива|ть, ю *impf. of* ▶ **заучи́ть**

зау|чи́ть, чу́, ∼**чишь** *pf.* (*of* ▶ **зау́чивать**) (*твёрдо выучить*) to learn by heart

зафарширова́|ть, у́ю *pf. of* ▶ **фарширова́ть**

зафикси́р|овать, ую *pf. of* ▶ **фикси́ровать**

зафрахт|ова́ть, у́ю *pf. of* ▶ **фрахтова́ть**

захва́т, а *m.* seizure, capture; (*власти*) seizure; **з. зало́жников** hostage-taking

захва|ти́ть, чу́, ∼**тишь** *pf.* (*of* ▶ **захва́тывать**) **1** (*взять*) to take; **они́** ∼**ти́ли с собо́й дете́й** they have taken the children with

them **2** (*завладеть*) to seize; to capture;
з. власть to seize power; мы ~ти́ли три́ста
пле́нных we took three hundred prisoners
3 (fig., *увлечь*) to carry away; to thrill, excite

захва́тчик, а *m.* invader; aggressor

захва́тыва|ть, ю *impf. of* ▶ захвати́ть

захва́тывающий *pres. part. act. of*
▶ захва́тывать *and adj.* (fig.) gripping

захлеб|ну́ть, ну́, нёшь *pf.* (*of*
▶ захлёбываться) **1** to choke; to swallow
the wrong way **2** (fig., infml): з. от восто́рга to
be breathless with delight; ата́ка ~ну́лась
(mil.) the attack misfired

захлёбыва|ться, юсь *impf.* (*of*
▶ захлебну́ться) to choke

захло́п|нуть, ну, нешь *pf.* (*of* ▶ захло́пывать)
(*дверь*) to slam

захло́п|нуться, нется *pf.* (*of*
▶ захло́пываться) to slam to; to close with
a bang

захло́пыва|ть, ю, ет *impf. of* ▶ захло́пнуть

захло́пыва|ться, ется *impf. of*
▶ захло́пнуться

захо́д, а *m.* **1** (*also* з. со́лнца) sunset
2 (*куда-н.*) stopping, putting in (at);
без ~а в Ло́ндон without calling at London

захо|ди́ть, жу́, ~дишь *impf. of* ▶ зайти́

захороне́ни|е, я *nt.* burial

захорон|и́ть, ю́, ~ишь *pf. of* ▶ хорони́ть

захо|те́ть, чу́, ~чешь, ~чет, ти́м, ти́те, тя́т
pf. of ▶ хоте́ть

захо|те́ться, ~чется *pf. of* ▶ хоте́ться

зацве|сти́, ту́, тёшь, *past* ~л, ~ла́ *pf.* (*of*
▶ зацвета́ть) to break into blossom

зацвета́|ть, ю *impf. of* ▶ зацвести́

зацве|ту́, тёшь *see* ▶ зацвести́

зацеп|и́ть, лю́, ~ишь *pf.* (*of* ▶ зацепля́ть)
to hook

зацеп|и́ться, лю́сь, ~ишься *pf.* (*of*
▶ зацепля́ться) (за + *a.*) **1** to catch (on);
чуло́к у неё ~и́лся за гвоздь her stocking
caught on a nail **2** (infml, *ухвати́ться*) to
catch hold (of)

зацепля́|ть, ю *impf. of* ▶ зацепи́ть

зацепля́|ться, юсь *impf. of* ▶ зацепи́ться

заци́клива|ться, юсь *impf. of* ▶ заци́клиться

заци́кл|иться, юсь, ишься *pf.* (*of*
▶ заци́кливаться) (на + *p.*) (infml) to become
obsessed (with)

зачаро́ванный *p.p.p. of* ▶ зачарова́ть *and*
adj. spellbound

зачар|ова́ть, у́ю *pf.* (*of* ▶ зачаро́вывать) to
bewitch, enchant, captivate

зачаро́выва|ть, ю *impf. of* ▶ зачарова́ть

зачасту́ю *adv.* (infml) often, frequently

зача́ти|е, я *nt.* (physiol.) conception

зача́|ть, ну́, нёшь, *past* ~а́л, ~ала́, ~а́ло
pf. (*of* ▶ зачина́ть) to conceive (*trans. and*
intrans.)

зача́х|нуть, ну, нешь, *past* ~, ~ла *pf. of*
▶ ча́хнуть

зача́ч|нуть ... [see above]

зачем *interrog. and rel. adv.* why; what for;
з. ты пришла́? why did you come?; так *вот*
ты з. пришла́ so that's why you came

зачем-то *adv.* for some reason or other

зачёркива|ть, ю *impf. of* ▶ зачеркну́ть

зачерк|ну́ть, ну́, нёшь *pf.* (*of* ▶ зачёркивать)
to cross out, strike out

зачерп|ну́ть, ну́, нёшь *pf.* (*of* ▶ заче́рпывать)
to scoop up; (*ложкой*) to ladle out

заче́рпыва|ть, ю *impf. of* ▶ зачерпну́ть

зачёт, а *m.* **1** reckoning; в з. пла́ты in
payment **2** (*экзамен*) test; получи́ть
з., сдать з. (по + *d.*) to pass a test (in);
поста́вить (*кому*) з. по (+ *d.*) to pass
(a person) (in); мне поста́вили з. по
исто́рии they have passed me in history

зачина́|ть, ю *impf. of* ▶ зача́ть

зачи́нщик, а *m.* (pej.) instigator, ringleader

зачисле́ни|е, я *nt.* enrolment

зачи́сл|ить, ю, ишь *pf.* (*of* ▶ зачисля́ть)
1 (*записать*) to include; з. на счёт to enter
in an account **2** (*включить в состав*) to
enrol, enlist; з. в штат to take on

зачи́сл|иться, юсь, ишься *pf.* (*of*
▶ зачисля́ться) (в + *a.*) to join, enter

зачисля́|ть, я́ю *impf. of* ▶ зачи́слить

зачисля́|ться, я́юсь *impf. of* ▶ зачи́слиться

зашива́|ть, ю *impf. of* ▶ заши́ть

заши́|ть, ью́, ьёшь *pf.* (*of* ▶ зашива́ть)
1 (*дыру, пальто*) to mend **2** (med.) to stitch
(up)

зашифр|ова́ть, у́ю *pf.* (*of* ▶ шифрова́ть,
▶ зашифро́вывать) to encipher, put into
code

зашифро́выва|ть, ю *impf. of*
▶ зашифрова́ть

за|шлю́, шлёшь *see* ▶ засла́ть

зашнур|ова́ть, у́ю *pf. of* ▶ шнурова́ть

зашто́па|ть, ю *pf. of* ▶ што́пать) to darn

защёлк|а, и *f.* (в *двери*) latch; (в *механизме*)
catch

защёлкива|ть, ю *impf. of* ▶ защёлкнуть

защёлк|нуть, ну, нешь *pf.* (*of*
▶ защёлкивать) (infml) to latch

защи́т|а, ы (*no pl.*) *f.* defence (BrE), defense
(AmE); (от, про́тив + *g.*) protection (from,
against); (*collect.*) the defence (BrE), defense
(AmE) (law and sport); в ~у (+ *g.*) in defence
(BrE), defense (AmE) (of); под ~ой (+ *g.*) under
the protection (of); з. окружа́ющей среды́ *or*
приро́ды environmentalism, conservation

защи|ти́ть, щу́, ти́шь *pf. of* ▶ защища́ть

защи|ти́ться, щу́сь, ти́шься *pf. of*
▶ защища́ться

защи́тник, а *m.* **1** defender, protector;
(law) counsel for the defence (BrE), defense
attorney (AmE) **2** (sport) (full)back; ле́вый,
пра́вый з. left, right back

защи́тн|ый *adj.* protective; ~ые очки́
goggles; з. цвет khaki

защища́|ть, ю *impf.* (*impf. of* ▶ защити́ть)
1 to defend, protect **2** (law) to defend;

3

з. диссерта́цию to defend a thesis (*before examiners*)

защища́|ться, юсь *impf.* (*of* ▶ защити́ться) **1** to defend oneself, protect oneself **2** *pass. of* ▶ защища́ть

защищённост|ь, и *f.* protection

✐ **заяв|и́ть, лю́, ~ишь** *pf.* (*of* ▶ заявля́ть) (+ *a. or о* + *p. or* что) to announce, declare; **з. свои́ права́** (**на** + *a.*) to claim one's rights (to); **з. об ухо́де со слу́жбы** to announce one's resignation

✐ **зая́вк|а, и** (**на** + *a.*) (*просьба*) application (for); (*о своих правах*) claim (for); demand (for); (*заказ*) order (for); **з. на изобрете́ние** patent application; **бланк ~и** application form

✐ **заявле́ни|е, я** *nt.* **1** (*сообщение*) statement, declaration **2** (*просьба*) application; **пода́ть з.** to put in an application

✐ **заявля́|ть, ю** *impf. of* ▶ заяви́ть

за́|яц, йца *m.* **1** hare; **одни́м уда́ром уби́ть двух ~йцев** (*proverb*) to kill two birds with one stone **2** (*infml, пассажир*) stowaway; fare-dodger; **е́хать ~йцем** to travel without paying for a ticket

зва́ни|е, я *nt.* rank; title; **ры́царское з.** knighthood

зва|ть, зову́, зовёшь, *past* ~л, ~ла́, ~ло *impf.* (*of* ▶ позва́ть) **1** to call; **з. на по́мощь** to call for help **2** (*приглашать*) to ask, invite **3** (*impf. only*) (*называть*) to call; **как вас зову́т?** what is your name?; **меня́ зову́т Влади́мир** my name is Vladimir

✐ **звезд|а́, ы́,** *pl.* **~ы, ~, ~ам** *f.* **1** star; **но́вая з.** (astron.) nova; (fig.): **з. экра́на** film star **2** (zool.): **морска́я з.** starfish

звёздн|ый *adj. of* ▶ звезда́; **з. дождь** meteor shower; shooting stars; **~ая ночь** starlit night; **з. час** finest hour

звёздочк|а, и *f.* **1** *dim. of* ▶ звезда́ **2** (typ.) asterisk

звен|е́ть, ю́, и́шь *impf.* **1** to ring; **у неё ~е́ло в уша́х** there was a ringing in her ears **2** (+ *i.*): **з. моне́тами** to jingle coins

звен|о́, а́, *pl.* **~ья, ~ьев** *nt.* **1** (*цепи*) link (also fig.) **2** (fig.) (*на предприятии*) team, section; (aeron.) flight

звере́|ть, ю, ешь *impf.* (*of* ▶ озвере́ть) to become brutalized

звери́н|ец, ца *m.* menagerie

звери́ный *adj. of* ▶ зверь; animal; savage

зве́рски *adv.* **1** brutally, bestially **2** (infml) terribly, awfully

зве́рский *adj.* **1** brutal, bestial **2** (infml, *чрезвычайный*) terrific, tremendous; **у него́ з. аппети́т** he has a tremendous appetite

зве́рств|о, а *nt.* brutality; atrocity; **~а** atrocities (*in war, etc.*)

звер|ь, я, *pl.* **~и, ~е́й** *m.* **1** wild animal, wild beast; **пушно́й з.** fur-bearing animal **2** (fig., *человек*) brute, beast

звон, а *m.* (ringing) sound, peal

звон|и́ть, ю́, и́шь *impf.* (*pf. of* ▶ позвони́ть) (**в** + *a.*) to ring; **з. кому́-н.** (**по телефо́ну**) to phone sb, call sb; **вы не туда́ ~и́те** you've got the wrong number; **~я́т** sb is ringing

зво́н|кий, ~ок, ~ка́, ~ко *adj.* ringing, clear; **~кая моне́та** hard cash, coin

звон|о́к, ка́ *m.* bell; **дать з.** to ring; **з.** (**по телефо́ну**) (phone) call

зво́нче *comp. of* ▶ зво́нкий

✐ **звук, а** *m.* sound; **пусто́й звук** (fig.) (mere) name, empty phrase; (ling.): **гла́сный з.** vowel; **согла́сный з.** consonant

звук|ово́й *adj. of* ▶ звук; **з. барье́р** sound barrier; **~ова́я ка́рта** (comput.) sound card

звукоза́пис|ь, и *f.* sound recording

звукоизоля́ци|я, и *f.* soundproofing

звуконепроница́ем|ый, ~, ~а *adj.* soundproof

звукорежиссёр, а *m.* sound engineer

звуч|а́ть, у́, и́шь *impf.* (*of* ▶ прозвуча́ть) **1** (*раздаваться*) to be heard; to sound; **вдали́ ~а́ли голоса́** voices could be heard in the distance **2** (+ *adv. or i.*) (fig., *выражаться*) to sound; to express, convey; **з. и́скренно** to ring true

зву́ч|ный, ~ен, ~на́, ~но *adj.* sonorous

звя́к|ать, аю *impf. of* ▶ звя́кнуть 1

звя́к|нуть, ну, нешь *pf.* (*of* ▶ звя́кать) **1** (+ *i.*) to jingle; to tinkle **2** (*pf. only*) **з.** (**по телефо́ну**) (infml) to ring up; to give sb a buzz

✐ **зда́ни|е, я** *nt.* building

✐ **здесь** *adv.* **1** here **2** (infml) here, at this point (*of time*); in this; **з. мы засме́ялись** here we burst out laughing; **з. нет ничего́ смешно́го** there is nothing funny in this

зде́шний *adj.* local; of this place; **вы з.? — нет, я не з.** are you a local? — no, I am a stranger here

здоро́ва|ться, юсь *impf.* (*of* ▶ поздоро́ваться) (**с** + *i.*) to greet; to say hello (to); **з. за́ руку** to shake hands (*in greeting*)

здо́рово (infml) *adv.* **1** (*отлично*) splendidly, magnificently; **ты з. порабо́тал** you have worked splendidly **2** (*очень сильно*) very, very much; **вчера́ они́ з. вы́пили** they had a great deal to drink yesterday **3** (*as int.*) great!; well done!

здоро́во *int.* (infml) hello!, hi!

✐ **здоро́в|ый¹, ~, ~а** *adj.* **1** healthy; **бу́дь(те) ~(ы)!** take care! (*said on parting*); (*to sb sneezing*) bless you! **2** (*полезный*) health-giving, wholesome; (fig.) sound, healthy; **з. кли́мат** healthy climate

✐ **здоро́в|ый², ~, ~а́, ~о** *adj.* (infml) **1** (*большой, сильный: о человеке*) robust, sturdy **2** (*большой, сильный: о предметах, явлениях*) strong, powerful; sound

✐ **здоро́вь|е, я** (*no pl.*) *nt.* health; **пить за чьё-н. з.** to drink sb's health; (**за**) **ва́ше з.!** your health!; **как ва́ше з.?** how are you?; **на з.** to your heart's content, as you please

здравоохране́ни|е, я *nt.* health care; public health; **Министе́рство ~я** Ministry of Health

здра́вств|овать, ую *impf.* to be healthy; (*процвета́ть*) to thrive, prosper; ~уй(те)! how do you do?; how are you?; да ~ует Росси́я! long live Russia!

здра́в|ый, ~, ~а *adj.* sensible; з. смысл common sense; быть в ~ом уме́ to be in one's right mind

зе́бр|а, ы *f.* **1** (zool.) zebra **2** (*ме́сто перехо́да*) zebra crossing (BrE)

зева́|ть, а́ю *impf.* **1** (*pf.* ~ну́ть) to yawn **2** (*no pf.*) (infml) to gape, stand gaping; не ~а́й! keep your wits about you! **3** (*pf.* про~) (infml) to miss opportunities

зев|ну́ть, ну́, нёшь *pf. of* ▶ зева́ть 1

зелене́|ть, ю *impf.* **1** (*pf.* по~) (*станови́ться зелёным*) to turn green, come out green **2** (*видне́ться*) to show green

зелено́гла́з|ый, ~, ~а *adj.* green-eyed

зелё|ный, зе́лен, зелена́, зе́лено, зе́лены *and* зелены́ *adj.* green (also fig.); з. горо́шек green peas; з. лук spring onions (BrE), green onions (AmE)

зе́лен|ь, и (*no pl.*) *f.* **1** (*зелёный цвет*) green colour (BrE), color (AmE) **2** (*collect.*) (*расти́тельность*) greenery **3** (*collect.*) (*о́вощи*) greens

земе́ль|ный *adj.* land; з. наде́л plot of land; ~ая ре́нта ground rent

землевладе́л|ец, ьца *m.* landowner

земледе́л|ец, ьца *m.* arable farmer

земледе́ли|е, я *nt.* arable farming

земледе́льческий *adj.* agricultural

землеко́п, а *m.* navvy

землеме́р, а *m.* land surveyor

землеро́йк|а, и *f.* (zool.) shrew

землетрясе́ни|е, я *nt.* earthquake

землечерпа́лк|а, и *f.* (tech.) dredger, excavator

земл|я́, и́, *a.* ~лю, *pl.* ~ли, ~е́ль, ~лям *f.* **1** (З.) (*плане́та*) Earth **2** (*су́ша*) (dry) land; уви́деть ~лю to sight land; упа́сть на ~лю to fall to the ground **3** (*владе́ние*) land; soil (fig.) **4** (*по́чва*) earth, soil

земля́к, а́ *m.* fellow countryman, compatriot

земляни́к|а, и (*no pl.*) *f.* (collect.) wild strawberries

земля́н|ин, ина, *pl.* ~е, ~ *m.* earth-dweller, earthling

земля́нк|а, и *f.* dugout

земля́н|о́й *adj.* **1** earthen, of earth; ~ые рабо́ты excavations **2** earth-; з. оре́х peanut

земля́чк|а, и *f.* fellow countrywoman, compatriot

земново́дн|ый *adj.* amphibious; (zool.) (*as pl. n.* ~ые, ~ых) amphibia; (*as nt. sg. n.* ~ое, ~ого) amphibian

земн|о́й *adj.* **1** earthly; terrestrial; ~а́я кора́ (earth's) crust; з. шар the globe **2** (*мирско́й*) mundane

зени́т, а *m.* zenith (also fig.)

зе́ркал|о, а, *pl.* ~а́, зерка́л, ~а́м *nt.* mirror (also fig.); криво́е з. distorting mirror

зерка́льн|ый *adj. of* ▶ зе́ркало; (fig.) smooth; ~ое стекло́ plate glass; ~ое окно́ plate-glass window; ~ая пове́рхность smooth surface

зер|но́, на́, *pl.* ~на, ~ен, ~нам *nt.* **1** (*пшени́цы*) (*ма́ка*) seed; (fig.) grain; (*ядро́*) kernel, core; ко́фе в ~нах coffee beans **2** (*collect., sg. only*) grain, cereal

зернов|о́й *adj.* grain, cereal; ~ы́е зла́ки cereals

зернохрани́лищ|е, а *nt.* granary

зигза́г, а *m.* zigzag

зи́м|а́, ы́, *a.* ~у, *pl.* ~ы, *d.* ~ам *f.* winter; на ~у for the winter; всю ~у all winter

зи́мний *adj. of* ▶ зима́; winter; (*пого́да*) wintry

зим|ова́ть, у́ю *impf.* (*of* ▶ перезимова́ть) to winter, pass the winter

зимо́й *adv.* in winter

злак, а *m.* (bot.) grass; хле́бные ~и cereals

злейший *superl. of* ▶ злой

зл|ить, ю, ишь *impf.* (*of* ▶ разозли́ть) to anger; to vex; to irritate

зл|и́ться, юсь, и́шься *impf.* (*of* ▶ разозли́ться) (на + *a.*) to be in a bad temper; to be angry (with)

зло¹, зла, *no pl. except g.* зол *nt.* **1** (*не́что ду́рное*) evil; harm; отплати́ть ~м за добро́ to repay good with evil **2** (*беда́*) evil, misfortune, disaster; жела́ть кому́-н. зла to bear sb malice **3** (*sg. only*) (*доса́да*) malice, spite; vexation; меня́ з. берёт it annoys me, I feel annoyed

зло² *adv. of* ▶ злой

зло́б|а, ы *f.* malice; spite; anger; по ~е out of spite; со ~ой maliciously

зло́б|ный, ~ен, ~на *adj.* malicious, spiteful; bad-tempered

злове́щий, ~, ~а *adj.* ominous, ill-omened; sinister

злово́н|ный, ~ен, ~на *adj.* fetid, stinking

зловре́д|ный, ~ен, ~на *adj.* harmful, pernicious

злоде́|й, я *m.* villain, scoundrel (also joc.)

злоде́йк|а, ки *f. of* ▶ злоде́й

злодея́ни|е, я *nt.* crime, evil deed

злой, зол, зла, зло *adj.* **1** (*о челове́ке*) evil; bad; з. ге́ний evil genius **2** (*выража́ющий зло́бу*) wicked; malicious; malevolent; vicious; зла́я улы́бка malevolent smile; со злым у́мыслом with malicious intent; (law) of malice prepense **3** (*short form only*) (на + *a.*) (*серди́т*) angry; она́ зла на всех she is angry with everybody **4** (*о живо́тных*) fierce, savage; «осторо́жно, зла́я соба́ка!» 'beware of the dog!'

злока́чествен|ный, ~, ~на *adj.* (med.) malignant; ~ная о́пухоль malignant tumour (BrE), tumor (AmE)

злопа́мят|ный, ~ен, ~на *adj.* rancorous, unforgiving

злора́д|ный, ~ен, ~на *adj.* gloating

зло́ст|ный, ~ен, ~на *adj.* **1** (*созна́тельно недобросо́вестный*) conscious, intentional; ~ное банкро́тство fraudulent bankruptcy;

з. неплате́льщик persistent defaulter (*in payment of debt*) **2** (*закоренелый*) inveterate, hardened

злост|ь, и *f.* malice, fury

злоумы́шленник, а *m.* plotter; criminal

злоупотреб|и́ть, лю́, и́шь *pf.* (*of* ▶ **злоупотребля́ть**) (+ *i.*) to abuse; (*сладким*) to indulge in to excess; **з. вла́стью** to abuse power; **з. чьим-н. внима́нием** to take up too much of sb's time

злоупотребле́ни|е, я *nt.* (+ *i.*) abuse (of); **з. дове́рием** breach of confidence

злоупотреб|ля́ть, ля́ю *impf. of* ▶ **злоупотреби́ть**

змей, зме́я *m.*: **(бума́жный) з.** kite; **запусти́ть зме́я** to fly a kite

зме|я́, и́, й, *pl.* **~и, ~й** *f.* snake (also fig.)

♂ **знак, а** *m.* **1** sign; (*след*) mark; (*символ*) token, symbol; (comput.) character; **номерно́й з.** number plate (BrE); license plate (AmE); **~и препина́ния** punctuation marks; **~и отли́чия** decorations (and medals); **в з.** (+ *g.*) as a mark (of), as a token (of), to show **2** (*предзнаменование*) omen **3** (*сигнал*) signal; **пода́ть з.** to give a signal

знако́м|ить, лю, ишь *impf.* (*of* ▶ **познако́мить**) (+ *a.* and *c* + *i.*) to acquaint sb (with); to introduce sb

знако́м|иться, люсь, ишься *impf.* (*of* ▶ **познако́миться**) (*c* + *i.*) **1** (*с человеком*) to meet, make the acquaintance (*of a person*) **2** (*представляться*) to introduce oneself; **~ьтесь!** (informal mode of introduction) may I introduce you? **3** (*с вещью*) to become acquainted (with), familiarize oneself (with); to study, investigate

♂ **знако́мств|о, а** *nt.* **1** (*c* + *i.*) (*между людьми*) acquaintance (with); **слу́жба ~** dating service **2** (*collect.*) (circle of) acquaintances; **по ~у** by exploiting one's personal connections, by pulling strings **3** (*c* + *i.*) (*знание*) familiarity (with), knowledge (of)

♂ **знако́м|ый, ~, ~а** *adj.* **1** familiar; **его́ лицо́ мне ~о** his face is familiar (to me) **2** (*c* + *i.*) familiar (with); **быть ~ым** (*c* + *i.*) to be acquainted (with), know **3** (*as n.* **з.**, **~ого,** *f.* **~ая, ~ой**) acquaintance, friend

зна́м|ени, енем *etc., see* ▶ **зна́мя**

знамени́тост|ь, и *f.* celebrity

♂ **знамени́т|ый, ~, ~а** *adj.* celebrated, famous, renowned; **печа́льно з.** infamous, notorious

знамено́с|ец, ца *m.* standard-bearer (also fig.)

зна́м|я, *g., d., and p.* **~ени,** *i.* **~енем,** *pl.* **~ёна, ~ён** *nt.* banner; standard; **под ~енем** (+ *g.*) (fig., rhet.) in the name of

♂ **зна́ни|е, я** *nt.* **1** knowledge; **со ~ем де́ла** capably, competently **2** (*in pl.*) learning; accomplishments

зна́т|ный, ~ен, ~на́, ~но *adj.* (*аристократический*) noble

знато́к, а́ *m.* expert; connoisseur

♂ **key word**

♂ **зна|ть¹, ~ю** *impf.* to know, have a knowledge of; **вы ~ете Алекса́ндрова?** do you know Alexandrov?; **з. в лицо́** to know by sight; **з. ме́ру** to know when to stop; **не з. поко́я** to know no peace; **дать кому́-н. з.** to let sb know; **кто/Бог/чёрт его́ ~ет!** (infml) goodness knows!; God knows!; the devil (only) knows!; **вам лу́чше з.** you know best; **~ешь (ли), ~ете (ли)** (infml) you know, do you know what

знат|ь², и (*no pl.*) *f.* (*collect.*) the nobility, the aristocracy

♂ **значе́ни|е, я** *nt.* **1** (*смысл*) meaning, significance **2** (*важность*) importance, significance; **придава́ть большо́е з.** (+ *d.*) to attach great importance (to); **э́то не име́ет ~я** it is of no importance **3** (math.) value

зна́чимост|ь, и *f.* significance

зна́чит (infml) so, then; well then; **он у́мер до войны́? з., вы не́ были с ним знако́мы** he died before the war? then you didn't know him

♂ **значи́тельно** *adv.* considerably, significantly

♂ **значи́тел|ьный, ~ен, ~ьна** *adj.* **1** (*большой*) considerable, sizeable; **в ~ьной сте́пени** to a considerable extent **2** (*важный*) important **3** (*выразительный*) significant, meaningful

♂ **зна́ч|ить, у, ишь** *impf.* (*иметь смысл*) to mean, signify **2** (*иметь значение*) to mean, have significance, be of importance; **ничего́ не ~ит** it is of no importance; **э́то о́чень мно́го ~ит для неё** it means a great deal to her

значо́к, ка́ *m.* **1** badge **2** (*пометка*) mark

зна́ющий *pres. part. act. of* ▶ **знать¹** *and adj.* expert; learned, erudite

зно|й, я *m.* intense heat; sultriness

зно́|йный, ~ен, ~йна *adj.* hot, sultry; torrid; burning (also fig.)

зоб, а, *pl.* **~ы́, ~о́в** *m.* **1** (*птицы*) crop, craw **2** (med.) goitre (BrE), goiter (AmE)

зов, а *m.* call, summons

зов|у́, ёшь *see* ▶ **звать**

зодиа́к, а *m.* (astron.) zodiac; **зна́ки ~а** signs of the zodiac

зол¹ *see* ▶ **злой**

зол² *g. pl. of* ▶ **зло¹**

зол|а́, ы́ (*no pl.*) *f.* ashes, cinders

золо́вк|а, и *f.* sister-in-law (*husband's sister*)

золоти́ст|ый, ~, ~а *adj.* golden (of colour)

зо́лот|о, а (*no pl.*) *nt.* gold; (*collect.*) gold (*coins, ware*) (fig.); **она́ — настоя́щее з.** she is pure gold, a treasure; **на вес ~а** worth its weight in gold

♂ **золот|о́й** *adj.* gold; golden (also fig.); **~ы́х дел ма́стер** goldsmith; **з. песо́к** gold dust; **з. запа́с** (econ.) gold reserves; **~а́я ры́бка** goldfish; **з. век** the Golden Age; **~а́я молодёжь** gilded youth; **~а́я середи́на** golden mean

золочёный *adj.* gilded, gilt

♂ **зо́н|а, ы** *f.* **1** zone; area **2** (geol.) stratum, layer **3** (sl.) (*тюрьма*) prison; (*лагерь*) prison camp

зонд, а *m.* **1** (med.) probe **2** (meteor.) weather balloon

зонт, а́ *m.* **1** umbrella **2** (*навес*) awning

зо́нтик, а *m.* umbrella; (*от со́лнца*) sunshade, parasol

зоо... *comb. form, abbr. of* ▶ **зоологи́ческий**

зоо́лог, а *m.* zoologist

зоологи́ческий *adj.* zoological; **з. парк**, **з. сад** zoological garden(s)

зооло́ги|я, и *f.* zoology

зоомагази́н, а *m.* pet shop

зоопа́рк, а *m.* zoo

зо́ри *see* ▶ **заря́**

зо́р|кий, ~ок, ~ка́, ~ко *adj.* **1** sharp-sighted **2** (fig.) (*проница́тельный*) perspicacious, penetrating; (*бди́тельный*) vigilant

зрач|о́к, ка́ *m.* pupil (*of the eye*)

зре́лищ|е, а *nt.* **1** (*предме́т наблюде́ния*) sight **2** (*представле́ние*) spectacle; show; pageant

зре́лость, и *f.* (*виногра́да*) ripeness; (*челове́ка*) maturity (also fig.); **полова́я з.** puberty

зре́л|ый, ~, ~а́, ~о *adj.* (*виногра́д*) ripe; (*челове́к*) mature (also fig.); **дости́гнуть ~ого во́зраста** to reach maturity; **з. ум** mature mind

⚥ **зре́ни|е**, я *nt.* (eye)sight; **по́ле ~я** (phys.) field of vision; **обма́н ~я** optical illusion; **то́чка ~я** point of view

зре|ть, ю, ешь *impf. of* ▶ **созре́ть**

⚥ **зри́тел|ь**, я *m.* spectator, observer; **быть ~ем** to look on

зри́тельный *adj.* **1** visual; optic; **з. нерв** optic nerve **2**: **з. зал** hall, auditorium

зря *adv.* (infml) to no purpose, for nothing; **болта́ть з.** to chatter idly; **рабо́тать з.** to work in vain

⚥ **зуб**, а *m.* **1** (*pl.* ~ы, ~о́в) (*во рту*) tooth; **з. му́дрости** wisdom tooth; **вооружённый до ~о́в** armed to the teeth; **не по ~а́м** beyond one's capacity **2** (*pl.* ~ья, ~ьев) (*зубе́ц*) tooth, cog

зуба́ст|ый, ~, ~а *adj.* (infml) sharp-toothed; (fig.) sharp-tongued

зуб|е́ц, ца́ *m.* tooth, cog

зуби́л|о, а *nt.* (tech.) chisel

зубн|о́й *adj.* dental; **~а́я боль** toothache; **з. врач** dentist; **~а́я па́ста** toothpaste; **~а́я щётка** toothbrush

зубочи́стк|а, и *f.* toothpick

зубр, а *m.* (zool.) (European) bison

зуд, а *m.* itch; (fig.) itch, urge

зы́б|кий, ~ок, ~ка́, ~ко *adj.* (*пове́рхность*) rippling; (*по́чва*) unsteady, shaky; (fig.) unstable, vacillating

зэк, а *m.* (sl.) prisoner, convict

зя́блик, а *m.* chaffinch

зят|ь, я, *pl.* ~ья́, ~ьёв *m.* (*муж до́чери*) son-in-law; (*муж сестры́, муж сестры́ му́жа*) brother-in-law

Ии

и *conj.* **1** and **2**: **и... и** both ... and; **и тот и друго́й** both **3** (*то́же*) too; (*with neg.*) either; **она́ сказа́ла, что и муж придёт** she said that her husband would come too **4** (*да́же*) even; **и знатоки́ ошиба́ются** even experts may be mistaken

⚥ **и́бо** *conj.* for

и́в|а, ы *f.* willow

иври́т, а *m.* (modern) Hebrew

игл|а́, ы́, *pl.* ~ы, ~ *f.* **1** (*для шитья́*) needle **2** (bot.) (*у хво́йных дере́вьев*) needle; (*у расте́ния*) thorn, prickle **3** (*ежа́*) quill, spine **4** (*проигрыва́теля*) needle, stylus

иглоука́лывани|е, я *nt.* acupuncture

игнори́р|овать, ую *impf. and pf.* to ignore; to disregard

иго́лк|а, и *f.* needle; **сиде́ть как на ~ах** to be on tenterhooks

иго́рный *adj.* gambling, gaming; **и. дом** casino

⚥ **игр|а́**, ы́, *pl.* ~ы *f.* **1** (*де́йствие*) play, playing; **и. слов** play on words **2** (*заня́тие*) game

игра́льн|ый *adj.* playing; **~ые ка́рты** playing cards

⚥ **игра́|ть**, ю *impf.* (*of* ▶ **сыгра́ть**) **1** to play; **и. пье́су** to put on a play; **и. роль** to play a part; **э́то не ~ет ро́ли** it is of no importance; **и. в ка́рты, те́ннис, футбо́л, ша́хматы** to play cards, tennis, football, chess; **и. на роя́ле, скри́пке** to play the piano, the violin **2** (*impf. only*) (+ *i.* or *c* + *i.*) (*относи́ться несерьёзно*) to play with, toy with, trifle with (also fig.); **и. с огнём** (fig.) to play with fire **3** (*impf. only*) (*сверка́ть*) to play; to sparkle (*of wine, jewellery, etc.*); **улы́бка ~ла на её лице́** a smile played on her face

игри́в|ый, ~, ~а *adj.* playful; (infml) naughty, ribald

игри́ст|ый, ~, ~а *adj.* sparkling (*of wine*)

⚥ **игр|ово́й** *adj. of* ▶ **игра́**; **и. автома́т** one-armed bandit, fruit machine (BrE); **~ова́я приста́вка** (comput.) game(s) console

⚥ **игро́к**, а́ *m.* **1** (в + *a.* or на + *p.*) player (of)

2 (*в азартные игры*) gambler

игру́шечный *adj.* toy; **и. парово́з** toy engine

игру́шк|а, и *f.* toy; (fig.) plaything; **ёлочные ~и** Christmas tree decorations

идеа́л, а *m.* ideal

идеализи́р|овать, ую *impf. and pf.* to idealize

идеали́зм, а *m.* idealism

идеали́ст, а *m.* idealist

идеалисти́ческий *adj.* idealistic

⚘ **идеа́л|ьный, ~ен, ~ьна** *adj.* ideal (*also phil.*); perfect; **~ьное состоя́ние** perfect condition

иде́|йный, ~ен, ~йна *adj.* **1** (*идеологический*) ideological **2** (*преданный какой-н. идее*) expressing an idea *or* ideas; committed, engagé **3** (*принципиальный*) high-principled, acting on principle

идентифика́ци|я, и *f.* identification

идентифици́р|овать, ую *impf. and pf.* to identify

иденти́чность|ь, и *f.* identity

иденти́ч|ный, ~ен, ~на *adj.* identical

идео́лог, а *m.* ideologist

идеологи́ческий *adj.* ideological

идеоло́ги|я, и *f.* ideology

⚘ **иде́|я, и** *f.* **1** idea (*also* infml); notion, concept **2** (*главная мысль*) point, purport (*of a work of art*); **по ~е** (infml) in principle

идио́м|а, ы *f.* idiom

идиосинкрази́|я, и *f.* (med.) allergy

идио́т, а *m.* idiot, imbecile

идио́тский *adj.* idiotic, imbecile

идио́тств|о, а *nt.* idiocy, stupidity

йдиш *m. indecl.* Yiddish (*language*)

йдол, а *m.* idol (also fig.)

⚘ **ид|ти́, у́, ёшь,** *past* **шёл, шла** *impf.* (*of* ▸ **пойти́ 1,** *det. of* ▸ **ходи́ть**) **1** to go; (*impf. only*) (*приближаться*) to come; **и. в го́ру** to go uphill; **авто́бус ~ёт** the bus is coming **2** (**на** + *a.*) (*поступать*) to enter; (**в** + *nom.-a.*) to become; **и. на госуда́рственную слу́жбу** to enter government service (**в** + *a.*) (*использоваться*) to be used (for); (**на** + *a.*) to go to make; **и. в корм** to be used for fodder; **и. в лом** to go for scrap; **и. на ю́бку** to go to make a skirt **4** (**из, от** + *g.*) (*о дыме, воде*) to come (from), proceed (from); **из трубы́ шёл чёрный дым** black smoke was coming from the chimney **5** (infml, *находить сбыт*) to sell, be sold; **хорошо́ и.** to be selling well **6** (*о механизме*) to go, run, work **7** (*о дожде, снеге*) to fall; **дождь, снег ~ёт** it is raining, snowing **8** (*о времени*) to pass; **шли го́ды** years passed; **ей пошёл тридца́тый год** she is in her thirtieth year **9** (*происходить*) to go on, be in progress; (*о спектакле*) to be on, be showing; **перегово́ры ~у́т** talks are in progress; **сего́дня ~ёт «Дя́дя Ва́ня»** 'Uncle Vanya' is on today **10** (+ *d. or* **к** + *d.*) (*быть к лицу*) to suit, become; **э́та шля́па ей**

не ~ёт this hat does not suit her **11** (**о** + *p.*) (*о разговоре*) to be (about); **речь ~ёт о том, что…** the point is that …, it is a matter of …

иезуи́т, а *m.* (eccl.) Jesuit

ие́н|а, ы *f.* yen (*Japanese currency*)

иерархи́ческий *adj.* hierarchical

иера́рхи|я, и *f.* hierarchy

иеро́глиф, а *m.* (*египетский*) hieroglyph; (*китайский, японский*) character

Иерусали́м, а *m.* Jerusalem

иждиве́н|ец, ца *m.* dependant; (*нахлебник*) sponger

иждиве́ни|е, я *nt.* maintenance; **на чьём-н. ~и** at sb's expense

иждиве́н|ка, ки *f.* ▸ **иждиве́нец**

⚘ **из, изо** *prep.* + *g.* **1** (*обозначает источник действия*) from, out of; of; **прие́хать из Ло́ндона** to come from London; **пить из ча́шки** to drink out of a cup **2** (*обозначает часть целого*): **оди́н из её покло́нников** one of her admirers; (**ни**) **оди́н из ста** (not) one in a hundred **3** (*обозначает состав, компоненты*): **из чего́ э́то сде́лано?** what is it made of?; **варе́нье из абрико́сов** apricot jam; **обе́д из трёх блюд** a three-course dinner **4** (*обозначает средство*): **изо всех сил** with all one's might **5** (*обозначает причину*): **из благода́рности** in/out of gratitude

из…, *also* **изо…, изъ…, ис…** *vbl. pref. indicating* **1** motion outwards **2** action over entire surface of object, in all directions **3** expenditure of instrument *or* object in course of action; continuation *or* repetition of action to extreme point; exhaustiveness of action

изб|а́, ы́, *pl.* **~ы** *f.* izba (*peasant's hut or cottage*)

изба́в|ить, лю, ишь *pf.* (*of* ▸ **избавля́ть**) (**от** + *g.*) to save, deliver (from); **~ьте меня́ от ва́ших замеча́ний** spare me your remarks

изба́в|иться, люсь, ишься *pf.* (*of* ▸ **избавля́ться**) (**от** + *g.*) to be saved (from), escape; to get out (of); to get rid (of); **и. от привы́чки** to get out of a habit

избавля́|ть, ю *impf. of* ▸ **изба́вить**

избавля́|ться, юсь *impf. of* ▸ **изба́виться**

избало́ванный *p.p.p. of* ▸ **избалова́ть** *and adj.* spoilt

избал|ова́ть, у́ю *pf.* (*of* ▸ **балова́ть,** ▸ **избало́вывать**) to spoil (*a child, etc.*)

избало́выва|ть, ю *impf. of* ▸ **избалова́ть**

⚘ **избег|а́ть, а́ю** *impf.* (*of* ▸ **избе́гнуть,** ▸ **избежа́ть**) (+ *g. or inf.*) (*сторониться*) to avoid; (*избавиться*) to escape, evade

избе́г|нуть, ну, нешь, *past* **~нул** *and* **~, ~ла** *pf. of* ▸ **избега́ть**

избе|жа́ть, гу́, жи́шь, гу́т *pf. of* ▸ **избега́ть**

избива́|ть, ю *impf. of* ▸ **изби́ть**

избие́ни|е, я *nt.* (*убийство*) slaughter, massacre

избира́тел|ь, я *m.* elector, voter

избира́тельн|ый *adj.* **1** electoral; **и. бюллете́нь** voting paper; **~ая кампа́ния**

⚘ key word

election campaign **2** (tech.) selective

избира́|ть, ю *impf. of* ▸ **избра́ть**

изби́тый *p.p.p. of* ▸ **изби́ть** *and adj.* (fig.) hackneyed, trite

из|би́ть, обью́, обьёшь *pf. (of* ▸ **избива́ть)** (*человека*) to beat up

изборозди́ть, жу́, ди́шь *pf. of* ▸ **борозди́ть**

избра́ни|е, я *nt.* election

и́збран|ный *p.p.p. of* ▸ **избра́ть** *and adj.* **1** (*отобранный*) selected; **∼ные сочине́ния Пу́шкина** selected works of Pushkin **2** (*лучший*) select; (*as pl. n.* **∼ные, ∼ных**) elite

из|бра́ть, беру́, берёшь, *past* **∼бра́л, ∼брала́, ∼бра́ло** *pf. (of* ▸ **избира́ть)** (*+ a. and i.*) to elect (as, for); to choose; **его́ ∼бра́ли чле́ном парла́мента** he has been elected a Member of Parliament

избы́т|ок, ка *m.* (*излишек*) surplus, excess; (*обилие*) abundance, plenty; **в ∼ке** in plenty; **от ∼ка чувств** from a fullness of heart

избы́точ|ный, ∼ен, ∼на *adj.* surplus

изва́я́ни|е, я *nt.* statue, sculpture; graven image

изва́я́|ть, ю *pf. of* ▸ **вая́ть**

и́зверг, а *m.* monster, fiend

изверг|а́ться, а́ется *impf.* to erupt (*of volcanoes*)

изверже́ни|е, я *nt.* **1** (*вулкана*) eruption **2** (fig.) ejection, expulsion

изверн|у́ться, у́сь, ёшься *pf. (of* ▸ **изворачиваться)** (infml) to dodge, take evasive action (also fig.)

изве́сти|е, я *nt.* (о + *p.*) news (of); **после́дние ∼я** the latest news

изве|сти́ть, щу́, сти́шь *pf. (of* ▸ **извеща́ть)** to inform, notify

извёстк|а, и *f.* (slaked) lime

⚡ **изве́стно** *as pred.* it is (well) known; **как и.** as is well known; **наско́лько мне и.** as far as I know

изве́стност|ь, и *f.* (*слава*) fame, reputation; (*лгуна, преступника*) notoriety; **приноси́ть и.** (+ *d.*) to bring fame (to); **поста́вить кого́-н. в и.** to inform, notify

⚡ **изве́ст|ный, ∼ен, ∼на** *adj.* **1** (+ *d.*) well known (to); (+ *i.*) (well) known (for); (**за** + *a.*) (well) known (as) **2** (*лгун, преступник*) infamous, notorious **3** (*некоторый*) (a) certain; **до ∼ной сте́пени, в ∼ной ме́ре** to a certain extent

известня́к, а́ *m.* limestone

и́звест|ь, и *f.* lime

извеща́|ть, ю *impf. of* ▸ **извести́ть**

извеще́ни|е, я *nt.* notification, notice; (comm.) advice

извива́|ться, юсь *impf.* **1** (*о змее, канате*) to coil; (*о черве*) to wriggle **2** (*impf. only*) (*о дороге, реке*) to twist, wind; to meander

извили́ст|ый, ∼, ∼а *adj.* winding, twisting, tortuous

извине́ни|е, я *nt.* **1** (*оправдание*) excuse **2** (*просьба о прощении*) apology; **приня́ть**

∼**я** to accept an apology **3** (*прощение*) pardon

извин|и́ть, ю́, и́шь *pf. (of* ▸ **извиня́ть)** **1** (*простить*) to excuse; **∼и́те (меня́)!** I beg your pardon; excuse me!; (I'm) sorry!; **∼и́те, что я опозда́л** sorry I'm late; **прошу́ и. меня́ за беста́ктное замеча́ние** I apologize for my tactless remark **2** (*оправдать*) to excuse; **э́то ниче́м нельзя́ и.** this is inexcusable

извин|и́ться, ю́сь, и́шься *pf. (of* ▸ **извиня́ться)** **1** (*пе́ред* + *i.*) (*попросить прощения*) to apologize (to); (**∼и́тесь за меня́** present my apologies, make my excuses **2** (+ *i.*) (*оправдаться*) to excuse oneself (on account of, on the ground of); to make excuses

извиня́|ть, яю *impf. of* ▸ **извини́ть**

извиня́|ться, яюсь *impf. (of* ▸ **извини́ться):** **∼я́юсь!** (infml) I apologize!; (I'm) sorry!

извлека́|ть, ю *impf. of* ▸ **извле́чь**

извле́|чь, ку́, чёшь, ку́т, *past* **∼к, ∼кла́** *pf. (of* ▸ **извлека́ть)** to extract; (fig.) to derive, elicit; **и. уро́к** (из + *g.*) to learn a lesson (from); **и. по́льзу** (из + *g.*) to derive benefit (from); **и. ко́рень** (math.) to find the root

извне́ *adv.* from without

изворачива|ться, юсь *impf. of* ▸ **изверну́ться**

изворо́тлив|ый, ∼, ∼а *adj.* (*спорщик, ум*) versatile, resourceful; (*человек*) wily, shrewd

извра|ти́ть, щу́, ти́шь *pf. (of* ▸ **извраща́ть)** **1** (*испортить*) to pervert **2** (*ложно истолкова́ть*) to misinterpret, misconstrue; **и. и́стину** to distort the truth; **и. чью-н. мысль** to misinterpret sb

извраща́|ть, ю *impf. of* ▸ **изврати́ть**

извраще́н|ец, ца *m.* pervert

извраще́ни|е, я *nt.* **1** (*ненормальность*) perversion **2** (*искажение*) misinterpretation, distortion (fig.)

изги́б, а *m.* bend, twist

изгиба́|ть, ю *impf. of* ▸ **изогну́ть**

изгиба́|ться, юсь *impf. of* ▸ **изогну́ться**

изгна́ни|е, я *nt.* **1** (*действие*) banishment; expulsion **2** (*ссылка*) exile

изгна́нник, а *m.* exile (*person*)

из|гна́ть, гоню́, го́нишь, *past* **∼гна́л, ∼гнала́, ∼гна́ло** *pf. (of* ▸ **изгоня́ть)** to banish, expel; (*сослать*) to exile

из|гоню́, го́нишь *see* ▸ **изгна́ть**

изгоня́|ть, ю *impf. of* ▸ **изгна́ть**

и́згород|ь, и *f.* fence; **жива́я и.** hedge

изгота́влива|ть, ю *impf.* = **изготовля́ть**

изготови́тел|ь, я *m.* manufacturer, producer

изгото́в|ить, лю, ишь *pf. (of* ▸ **изготовля́ть)** to manufacture

⚡ **изготовле́ни|е, я** *nt.* manufacture

изготовля́|ть, ю *impf. of* ▸ **изгото́вить**

изда|ва́ть, ю́, ёшь *impf. of* ▸ **изда́ть**

изда|ва́ться, ю́сь, ёшься *impf. of* ▸ **изда́ться**

и́здавна *adv.* for a long time; from time immemorial

издалека́ *adv.* from afar; from a distance; **го́род ви́ден и.** the town is visible from afar; **прие́хать и.** to come from a distance

и́здали *adv.* = издалека́

⚐ **изда́ни|е, я** *nt.* **1** (*книг*) publication; (*закона*) promulgation **2** (*то, что издано*) edition

изда́тел|ь, я *m.* publisher

изда́тель|ский *adj. of* ▶ изда́тель, ▶ изда́тельство; **~ское де́ло** publishing

изда́тельств|о, а *nt.* publishing house, publisher

изда́|ть, м, шь, ст, ди́м, ди́те, ду́т, *past* **~л, ~ла́, ~ло** *pf.* (*of* ▶ издава́ть) **1** (*опубликовать*) to publish; **и. ука́з** to issue an edict **2** (*запах*) to produce, emit; (*звук*) to let out; **и. крик** to let out a cry

изда́|ться, мся, шься, стся, ди́мся, ди́тесь, ду́тся, *past* **~лся, ~ла́сь, ~лось** *pf.* to be published

издева́тельский *adj.* mocking

издева́тельств|о, а *nt.* (*действие*) mockery; (*насмешка*) taunt, insult; (*оскорбительное поведение*) ill-treatment

издева́|ться, юсь *impf.* (над + *i.*) to mock (at), scoff (at)

⚐ **изде́ли|е, я** *nt.* (manufactured) article; (*in pl.*) wares

изде́рж|ки, ек *f. pl.* (*sg.* **~ка, ~ки**) expenses; costs; **суде́бные и.** (law) costs; **и. произво́дства** production costs

издо́х|нуть, ну, нешь, *past* **~, ~ла** *pf.* (*of* ▶ до́хнуть, ▶ издыха́ть) to die (*of animals*)

издыха́|ть, ю *impf. of* ▶ издо́хнуть

изжа́р|ить, ю, ишь *pf. of* ▶ жа́рить

изжа́р|иться, юсь, ишься *pf. of* ▶ жа́риться

изжива́|ть, ю *impf. of* ▶ изжи́ть

изжи́|ть, ву́, вёшь, *past* **~л, ~ла́, ~ло** *pf.* (*of* ▶ изжива́ть) **1** (*искоренить*) to eliminate **2**: **и. себя́** to become obsolete

⚐ **из-за** *prep. + g.* **1** from behind; **из-за две́ри** from behind the door; **встать из-за стола́** to rise from the table **2** (*по причине*) because of, through **3** (*ради*) for; **жени́ться из-за де́нег** to marry for money

излага́|ть, ю *impf. of* ▶ изложи́ть

излече́ни|е, я *nt.* **1** (*лечение*) medical treatment **2** (*выздоровление*) recovery

изле́чива|ть, ю *impf. of* ▶ излечи́ть

изле́чива|ться, юсь *impf. of* ▶ излечи́ться

излечи́м|ый, ~, ~а *adj.* curable

излечи́|ть, у́, ~ишь *pf.* (*of* ▶ изле́чивать) to cure

излечи́|ться, у́сь, ~ишься *pf.* (*of* ▶ изле́чиваться) (от + *g.*) to make a complete recovery (from); to be cured (of); (fig.) to rid oneself (of), shake off

изли́ш|ек, ка *m.* surplus; remainder

изли́шеств|о, а *nt.* excess; overindulgence

изли́шний, ~ен, ~ня, ~не *adj.* (*чрезмерный*) excessive; (*ненужный*) unnecessary, superfluous

изложе́ни|е, я *nt.* exposition, account; **кра́ткое и.** synopsis, outline

изло́ж|ить, у́, ~ишь *pf.* (*of* ▶ излага́ть) to expound, state; to set forth; **и. на бума́ге** to commit to paper

изло́м, а *m.* **1** (*место перелома*) break, fracture **2** (*изгиб*) sharp bend

излуча́|ть, а́ю *impf.* to radiate (also fig.); **её глаза́ ~а́ли не́жность** her eyes radiated tenderness

излуча́|ться, а́ется *impf.* **1** (из + *g.*) to emanate (from) **2** *pass. of* ▶ излуча́ть

излуче́ни|е, я *nt.* radiation; emanation

излю́бленный *adj.* favourite (BrE), favorite (AmE)

изма́|зать, жу, жешь *pf.* (*of* ▶ ма́зать 3, ▶ изма́зывать) (infml) to make dirty, smear; **и. пальто́ кра́ской** to get paint all over one's coat

изма́|заться, жусь, жешься *pf.* (*of* ▶ ма́заться 1, ▶ изма́зываться) (infml) to get dirty; **он весь ~зался в кра́ске** he has got paint all over himself

изма́зыва|ть, ю *impf. of* ▶ изма́зать

изма́зыва|ться, юсь *impf. of* ▶ изма́заться

изма́тыва|ть, ю *impf. of* ▶ измота́ть

измена́, ы *f.* betrayal; treachery; **госуда́рственная и.** high treason; **супру́жеская и.** unfaithfulness, (conjugal) infidelity

⚐ **измене́ни|е, я** *nt.* change, alteration

измени́ть[1], ю́, ~ишь *pf.* (*of* ▶ изменя́ть) to change, alter; (pol.): **и. законопрое́кт** to amend a bill

измени́ть[2], ю́, ~ишь *pf.* (*of* ▶ изменя́ть) (+ *d.*) (*родине, другу*) to betray; (*мужу*) to be unfaithful (to); (fig.): **зре́ние ~и́ло ему́** his eyesight had failed him

⚐ **измени́|ться, ю́сь, ~ишься** *pf.* (*of* ▶ изменя́ться) to change, alter; **и. к лу́чшему, к ху́дшему** to change for the better, for the worse

изме́нник, а *m.* traitor

изме́нни|ца, цы *f. of* ▶ изме́нник

изме́нчивост|ь, и *f.* changeableness; (*непостоянство*) inconstancy, fickleness

⚐ **изменя́|ть, я́ю** *impf. of* ▶ измени́ть[1], ▶ измени́ть[2]

изменя́|ться, я́юсь *impf. of* ▶ измени́ться

⚐ **измере́ни|е, я** *nt.* **1** measurement, measuring; (*глубины моря*) sounding, fathoming; (*температуры*) taking **2** (math.) dimension

измери́тельный *adj.* (for) measuring

изме́р|ить, ю, ишь *pf.* (*of* ▶ измеря́ть) to measure; **и. кому́-н. температу́ру** to take sb's temperature

измеря́|ть, я́ю *impf. of* ▶ изме́рить

и́зморо|зь, и *f.* hoar frost

и́зморо|сь, и *f.* drizzle

⚐ key word

измота́|ть, ю *pf.* (*of* ▶ изма́тывать) (*infml*) to exhaust, wear out

измуч|аться, аюсь *pf.* = измучиться

изму́ченный *adj.* worn out, tired out

изму́чива|ть, ю *impf. of* ▶ измучить

изму́чива|ться, юсь *impf. of* ▶ измучиться

изму́ч|ить, у, ишь *pf.* (*of* ▶ измучивать) to torment; to tire out, exhaust

изму́ч|иться, усь, ишься *pf.* (*of* ▶ измучиваться) to be tired out, be exhausted

измышле́ни|е, я *nt.* fabrication, invention

из|мя́ть, омну́, омнёт *pf. of* ▶ мять 2

из|мя́ться, омнётся *pf. of* ▶ мя́ться

изна́нк|а, и *f.* the wrong side (*of material, clothing*); **с ~и** on the inner side; **и. жи́зни** the seamy side of life

изнаси́ловани|е, я *nt.* rape

изнаси́л|овать, ую *pf.* (*of* ▶ наси́ловать 2) to rape

изна́шива|ть, ю *impf. of* ▶ износи́ть

изна́шива|ться, юсь *impf. of* ▶ износи́ться

изне́женный *adj.* pampered; soft, effete

изнеможе́ни|е, я *nt.* exhaustion; **рабо́тать до ~я** to work to the point of exhaustion

изно́с, а (у) *m.* (*infml*) wear; wear and tear

изно|си́ть, шу́, ~сишь *pf.* (*of* ▶ изна́шивать) to wear out

изно|си́ться, шу́сь, ~сишься *pf.* (*of* ▶ изна́шиваться) to wear out; (*fig., infml*) to be used up, be played out

изно́шенный *p.p.p. of* ▶ износи́ть *and adj.* worn out

изнури́тел|ьный, ~ен, ~ьна *adj.* exhausting; gruelling; **~ьная боле́знь** wasting disease

изнутри́ *adv.* from within; **дверь запира́ется и.** the door fastens on the inside

изо *prep.* = из

изо...[1] *pref.* = из...

изо...[2] *comb. form* **1** iso- **2** *abbr. of* ▶ изобрази́тельный

изоби́ли|е, я *nt.* abundance, plenty

изоби́л|овать, ует *impf.* (*+ i.*) to abound (in), be rich (in)

изоблича́|ть, а́ю *impf.* **1** *impf. of* ▶ изобличи́ть **2** (*no pf.*) (**в** + *p. and a.*) to show (to be), point to (as being); **все его́ посту́пки ~а́ли в нём моше́нника** his every action pointed to his being a swindler

изоблич|и́ть, у́, и́шь *pf.* (*of* ▶ изоблича́ть 1) (*+ a. and* **в** *+ p.*) to expose (as); to unmask; **его́ ~и́ли во лжи** he stands exposed as a liar

изобража́|ть, ю *impf. of* ▶ изобрази́ть

⚹ **изображе́ни|е, я** *nt.* representation, portrayal; image

изобрази́тельный *adj.* graphic; decorative

изобра|зи́ть, жу́, зи́шь *pf.* (*of* ▶ изобража́ть) **1** (*+ i.*) to depict, portray, represent (as); **и. из себя́** to make oneself out (to be), represent oneself (as) **2** (*имити́ровать*) to imitate, take off **3** (*вы́разить*) to express, show

изобре|сти́, ту́, тёшь, *past* **~л, ~ла́** *pf.* (*of* ▶ изобрета́ть) (*созда́ть что-либо но́вое*) to invent; (*приду́мать*) to devise, contrive

изобрета́тел|ь, я *m.* inventor

изобрета́тел|ьный, ~ен, ~ьна *adj.* inventive; resourceful

изобрета́|ть, ю *impf. of* ▶ изобрести́

изобрете́ни|е, я *nt.* invention

изо́гнутый *p.p.p. of* ▶ изогну́ть *and adj.* bent, curved, winding

изогн|у́ть, у́, ёшь *pf.* (*of* ▶ изгиба́ть) to bend, curve

изогн|у́ться, у́сь, ёшься *pf.* (*of* ▶ изгиба́ться) to bend, curve

изо|йти́, йду́, йдёшь, *past* **~шёл, ~шла́** *pf. of* ▶ исходи́ть 3

изоли́рованный *p.p.p. of* ▶ изоли́ровать *and adj.* isolated; separate

изоли́р|овать, ую *impf. and pf.* to isolate

изоля́тор, а *m.* **1** (*med.*) isolation ward **2** (*в тюрьме́*) solitary confinement cell

изорв|а́ть, у́, ёшь, *past* **~а́л, ~ала́, ~а́ло** *pf.* (*of* ▶ изрыва́ть¹) to tear (to shreds)

изощрённый *adj.* (*ум, вкус*) refined; (*слух*) keen, acute

из-под *prep. + g.* **1** from under **2** (*го́рода*) from near **3** (*о вмести́лище*) for (*or not translated*); **ба́нка из-под варе́нья** jam jar

Изра́ил|ь, я *m.* Israel

изра́ильский *adj.* Israeli

израильтя́н|ин, ина, *pl.* **~е, ~** *m.* Israeli

израильтя́н|ка, ки *f. of* ▶ израильтя́нин

изра́н|ить, ю, ишь *pf.* to cover with wounds

израсхо́д|овать, ую *pf. of* ▶ расхо́довать

и́зредка *adv.* now and then; from time to time

изре́|зать, жу, жешь *pf.* (*of* ▶ изре́зывать, ▶ изреза́ть) **1** (*на мно́го часте́й*) to cut into pieces; to cut up; (*сде́лать на чём-н. мно́го надре́зов*) to make cuts in **2** (*geog.*) to cut across

изреза́|ть, а́ю *impf.* (*infml*) *of* ▶ изре́зать

изре́зыва|ть, ю *impf. of* ▶ изре́зать

изрис|ова́ть, у́ю *pf.* (*of* ▶ изрисо́вывать) to cover with drawings

изрисо́выва|ть, ю *impf. of* ▶ изрисова́ть

изрыва́|ть¹, ю *impf. of* ▶ изорва́ть

изрыва́|ть², ю *impf. of* ▶ изры́ть

изр|ы́ть, о́ю, о́ешь *pf.* (*of* ▶ изрыва́ть²) to dig up; to dig through

изря́д|ный, ~ен, ~на *adj.* (*infml*) fair, handsome; fairly large, tolerable; **~ное коли́чество** a fair amount

изуве́чива|ть, ю *impf. of* ▶ изуве́чить

изуве́ч|ить, у, ишь *pf.* (*of* ▶ изуве́чивать) to maim, mutilate

изуми́тел|ьный, ~ен, ~ьна *adj.* amazing, astounding

изум|и́ть, лю́, и́шь *pf.* (*of* ▶ изумля́ть) to amaze, astound

изум|и́ться, лю́сь, и́шься *pf.* (*of* ▶ изумля́ться) to be amazed, astounded

И

изумле́ни|е, я *nt.* amazement

изумлённый *p.p.p. of* ▸ изуми́ть *and adj.* amazed, astounded; dumbfounded

изумля́|ть, ю *impf. of* ▸ изуми́ть

изумля́|ться, юсь *impf. of* ▸ изуми́ться

изумру́д, а *m.* emerald

изумру́дный *adj.* **1** emerald **2** (*цвет*) emerald(-green)

изуро́д|овать, ую *pf. of* ▸ уро́довать

✐ **изуч|а́ть, а́ю** *impf.* (*of* ▸ изучи́ть) to learn; (*impf. only*) to study

✐ **изуче́ни|е, я** *nt.* study, studying

изуч|и́ть, у́, ~ишь *pf.* (*of* ▸ изуча́ть) **1** to learn **2** (*понять*) to come to know (very well), come to understand

изъ... *pref.* = из...

изъе́з|дить, жу, дишь *pf.* (*of* ▸ изъе́зживать) to travel all over, round; **мы ~дили весь свет** we have been all round the world

изъе́зжива|ть, ю *impf. of* ▸ изъе́здить

изъяв|и́ть, лю́, ~ишь *pf.* (*of* ▸ изъявля́ть) to indicate, express; **и. своё согла́сие** to give one's consent

изъявля́|ть, ю *impf. of* ▸ изъяви́ть

изъя́н, а *m.* defect, flaw

изъя́ти|е, я *nt.* withdrawal; removal

изъя́|ть, изыму́, и́мешь *pf.* (*of* ▸ изыма́ть) to withdraw; to remove; **и. из обраще́ния** to withdraw from circulation; **и. в по́льзу госуда́рства** to confiscate

изыма́|ть, ю *impf. of* ▸ изъя́ть

изыму́, и́мешь *see* ▸ изъя́ть

изы́скан|ный, ~, ~на *adj.* refined

изыск|а́ть, щу́, ~щешь *pf.* (*of* ▸ изы́скивать) to find; to search out; **и. сре́дства на постро́йку домо́в** to find funds for house-building

изы́скива|ть, ю *impf.* (*of* ▸ изыска́ть) to search out; to try to find

изю́м, а (у) (*no pl.*) *m.* raisins

изя́щество, а *nt.* elegance, grace

изя́щ|ный, ~ен, ~на *adj.* elegant, graceful

Иису́с, а *m.* (*bibl.*): **И. (Христо́с)** Jesus Christ

ик|а́ть, а́ю *impf.* (*of* ▸ икну́ть) to hiccup

ик|ну́ть, ну́, нёшь *pf. of* ▸ ика́ть

ико́н|а, ы *f.* (*relig., comput.*) icon

ико́нк|а, и *f.* (*comput.*) icon

ико́т|а, ы *f.* hiccups

икр|а́[1], ы́ (*no pl.*) *f.* **1** (hard) roe; spawn; **мета́ть ~у́** to spawn; (*fig., infml*) to rage **2** (*рыбный деликатес*) caviar; (*из овощей*) pâté; **баклажа́нная и.** aubergine pâté

икр|а́[2], ы́, *pl.* **~ы** *f.* (*anat.*) calf

икри́нк|а, и *f.* grain of caviar

ил, а *m.* silt

✐ **и́ли** *conj.* or; **и. ... и.** either ... or

иллю́зи|я, и *f.* illusion

иллюзо́р|ный, ~ен, ~на *adj.* illusory

иллюмина́тор, а *m.* (*naut., aeron.*) porthole

иллюмина́ци|я, и *f.* illuminations

иллюстра́тор, а *m.* illustrator

иллюстра́ци|я, и *f.* illustration

иллюстри́рованный *p.p.p. of* ▸ иллюстри́ровать *and adj.* illustrated

иллюстри́р|овать, ую *impf. and pf.* (*pf. also* ▸ проиллюстри́ровать) to illustrate (also fig.)

им 1 *i. of prons.* ▸ он, ▸ оно́ **2** *d. of pron.* ▸ они́

им. (*abbr. of* и́мени) named after; **музе́й им. Пу́шкина** Pushkin Museum

има́м, а *nt.* imam (*Muslim priest or leader*)

имби́р|ь, я́ *m.* ginger

и́м|ени, енем *see* ▸ и́мя

име́ни|е, я *nt.* estate

имени́нник, а *m.* person whose birthday it is; birthday boy; (*relig.*) person whose name day it is

имени́нни|ца, цы *f. of* ▸ имени́нник

имени́т|ый, ~, ~а *adj.* distinguished

✐ **и́менно** *adv.* **1**: (a) **и.** (*перед перечислением*) namely; to wit **2** (*как раз, точно*) just, exactly; to be exact; **где и. она́ живёт?** where exactly does she live?; **вот и.!** exactly!; precisely!

имен|ова́ть, у́ю *impf.* (*of* ▸ наименова́ть) to name

имен|ова́ться, у́юсь *impf.* (+ *i.*) to be called; to be termed

✐ **име́|ть, ю, ешь** *impf.* to have (*of abstract possession*); **и. возмо́жность** (+ *inf.*) to have an opportunity (to), be in a position (to); **и. де́ло** (**с** + *i.*) to have dealings (with), have to do (with); **и. значе́ние** (**для** + *g.*) to be important (to); **и. ме́сто** to take place; **и. в виду́** (*не забыва́ть*) to bear in mind, think of; (*подразумева́ть*) mean

✐ **име́|ться, ется** *impf.* **1** to be; to be present, be available; **в на́шем го́роде ~ется два кинотеа́тра** there are two cinemas in our town **2**: **~ется у, ~ются у = есть[2] 2**

име́ющий *pres. part. of* ▸ име́ться *and adj.* available; present

и́ми *i. of* ▸ они́

и́мидж, а *m.* image

имиджме́йкер, а *m.* image-maker

имита́ци|я, и *f.* mimicry; mimicking; imitation

имити́р|овать, ую *impf.* (*of* ▸ сымити́ровать) to mimic, imitate

иммигра́нт, а *m.* immigrant

иммигра́нт|ка, ки *f. of* ▸ иммигра́нт

иммигра́ци|я, и *f.* **1** immigration **2** (*collect.*) (*иммигра́нты*) immigrants

иммигри́р|овать, ую *impf. and pf.* to immigrate

иммуните́т, а *m.* (*med., law*) immunity

импера́тор, а *m.* emperor

императри́ц|а, ы *f.* empress

империали́зм, а *m.* imperialism

импе́ри|я, и *f.* empire

импе́рский *adj.* imperial

импи́чмент *m.* (*pol.*) impeachment

и́мпорт, а *m.* **1** (*ввоз товаров*) import **2** (*collect.*) (*infml, товары*) foreign goods

импорти́р|овать, ую *impf. and pf.* (*econ.*) to import

и́мпорт|ный *adj. of* ▸ **и́мпорт**; ∼**ные по́шлины** import duties

импрессиони́зм, а *m.* (*art*) impressionism

импрессиони́ст, а *m.* (*art*) impressionist

импровиза́ци|я, и *f.* improvisation

импровизи́р|овать, ую *impf.* (*of* ▸ **сымпровизи́ровать**) to improvise; to extemporize

и́мпульс, а *m.* (к + *d.*) impulse, impetus (for)

◊ иму́щество, а *nt.* property, belongings; **дви́жимое и.** (*law*) personalty, personal estate; **недви́жимое и.** (*law*) realty, real estate

◊ и́м|я, *g., d., and p.* ∼**ени**, *i.* ∼**енем**, *pl.* ∼**ена́**, ∼**ён**, ∼**ена́м** *nt.* **1** name; (*личное название*) first, Christian name; **вы́мышленное и.** alias, false name; **во и.** (+ *g.*) in the name of; **от** ∼**ени** (+ *g.*) on behalf of **2** (*fig., репутация*) name, reputation **3** (*gram.*): **и. прилага́тельное** adjective; **и. существи́тельное** noun, substantive; **и. числи́тельное** numeral

ин… and ино… *comb. form, abbr. of* ▸ **иностра́нный**

инакомы́сли|е, я *nt.* dissidence; nonconformism

инакомы́слящ|ий *adj.* dissident; nonconformist; (*as m. n.* **и.**, ∼**его**) dissident

◊ ина́че **1** *adv.* differently, otherwise; **так и́ли и.** in either event, at all events **2** *conj.* otherwise, or (else); **поторопи́тесь, и. вы опозда́ете** hurry up, or you will be late

инвали́д, а *m.* invalid; disabled person

инвали́дность, и *f.* disablement; disability; invalidity (BrE); **посо́бие по** ∼**и** disability/ invalidity benefit

инвентариза́ци|я, и *f.* inventory making, stocktaking

инвента́р|ь, я *m.* stock; equipment, appliances; **сельскохозя́йственный и.** agricultural implements

инвести́р|овать, ую *impf. and pf.* to invest

◊ инвестицио́нный *adj.* investment

◊ инвести́ци|я, и *f.* investment

◊ инве́стор, а *m.* (*fin.*) investor

ингаля́ци|я, и *f.* (*med.*) inhaling

ингредие́нт, а *m.* ingredient

ингу́ш, á, *g. pl.* ∼**е́й** *m.* Ingush

Ингуше́ти|я, и *f.* Ingushetia

ингу́ш|ка, ки *f. of* ▸ **ингу́ш**

ингу́шский *adj.* Ingush

инде́|ец, йца, *pl.* ∼**йцы**, ∼**йцев** *m.* American Indian, Native American

инде́йк|а, и *f.* turkey (hen)

инде́йский *adj. of* ▸ **инде́ец**

и́ндекс, а *m.* index; **и. цен** (*econ.*) price index; **почто́вый и.** postcode (BrE), zip code (AmE)

индекса́ци|я, и *f.* (*econ.*) indexation

индиа́н|ка, ки *f. of* ▸ **инде́ец**, ▸ **инди́ец**

индивидуа́льность, и *f.* individuality

◊ индивидуа́л|ьный, ∼**ен**, ∼**ьна** *adj.* individual

индиви́дуум, а *m.* individual

инди́го *nt. indecl.* indigo; **пла́тье цве́та и.** indigo dress

инди́|ец, йца, *pl.* ∼**йцы**, ∼**йцев** *m.* Indian

инди́йский *adj.* Indian

Инди́йский океа́н, ∼**ого океа́на** *m.* the Indian Ocean

индика́тор, а *m.* (*tech.*) indicator

И́нди|я, и *f.* India

индонези́|ец, йца, *pl.* ∼**йцы**, ∼**йцев** *m.* Indonesian

индонези́й|ка, ки *f. of* ▸ **индонези́ец**

индонези́йский *adj.* Indonesian

Индоне́зи|я, и *f.* Indonesia

индуи́зм, а *m.* Hinduism

инду́кци|я, и *f.* (*phil., phys.*) induction

инду́с, а *m.* Hindu

инду́с|ка, ки *f. of* ▸ **инду́с**

инду́сский *adj.* Hindu

индустриализа́ци|я, и *f.* industrialization

индустриа́льный *adj.* industrial

индустри́|я, и *f.* industry

индю́к, á *m.* turkey (cock)

и́не|й, я (*no pl.*) *m.* hoar frost

ине́рт|ный, ∼**ен**, ∼**на** *adj.* (*phys.*) inert; (*fig.*) sluggish, inactive

ине́рци|я, и *f.* (*phys., also fig.*) inertia; momentum; **дви́гаться по** ∼**и** to move under its own momentum; (*fig.*): **де́лать что-н. по** ∼**и** to do sth from force of inertia, mechanically

инжене́р, а *m.* engineer; **и.-меха́ник** mechanical engineer

инжене́р|ный *adj.* engineering; ∼**ое де́ло** engineering

инжи́р, а (*no pl.*) *m.* (*дерево; плод*) fig

инициа́л|ы, ов *m. pl.* (*sg.* ∼, ∼**а**) initials

◊ инициати́в|а, ы *f.* initiative; **по со́бственной** ∼**е** on one's own initiative

инициати́в|ный, ∼**ен**, ∼**на** *adj.* full of initiative, enterprising; dynamic, go-getting

инициа́тор, а *m.* initiator

инкасса́тор, а *m.* (*fin.*) security guard (*delivering money to a bank*)

инквизи́ци|я, и *f.* inquisition

инко́гнито **1** *adv.* incognito **2** *n.; c.g. indecl.* incognito (*person*)

инкримини́р|овать, ую *impf. and pf.* (+ *d. and a.*) to charge (with); **ему́** ∼**уют поджо́г** he is being charged with arson

инкруста́ци|я, и *f.* inlaid work, inlay

инкуба́тор, а *m.* incubator

инкубацио́нный *adj.* incubative, incubatory; **и. пери́од** (*med.*) incubation

ино… *see* ▸ **ин…**

инове́р|ец, ца *m.* (*relig.*) adherent of different faith, creed

и

иногда́ *adv.* sometimes
иногоро́дний *adj.* of, from another town
иноземный *adj.* foreign
ин|о́й *adj.* **1** (*друго́й*) different; other; ~ы́ми слова́ми in other words; не кто и., как; не что ~о́е, как none other than **2** (*не́который*) some; и. раз sometimes
иноми́рк|а, и *f.* foreign car, foreign make of car
инопланетный *adj.* alien, extraterrestrial
инопланетя́н|ин, ина, *pl.* ~е, ~ *m.* alien, extraterrestrial
иноро́д|ный, ~ен, ~на *adj.* alien; ~ное те́ло (*med., also fig.*) foreign body
иностра́н|ец, ца *m.* foreigner
иностра́н|ка, ки *f.* of ▸ **иностра́нец**
иностра́нный *adj.* foreign
иноязы́чный *adj.* **1** (*населе́ние*) speaking another language **2** (*сло́во*) belonging to another language
инсектици́д, а *m.* insecticide
инсину́а́ция, и *f.* insinuation
инспе́ктор, а *m.* inspector; (*mil.*) inspecting officer
инспе́кци|я, и *f.* **1** (*де́йствие*) inspection; и. на ме́сте (*mil.*) on-site inspection **2** (*организа́ция*) inspectorate
инсти́нкт, а *m.* instinct
инстинкти́в|ный, ~ен, ~на *adj.* instinctive
институ́т, а *m.* **1** (*обще́ственное установле́ние*) institution; и. бра́ка the institution of marriage **2** (*уче́бное или нау́чное заведе́ние*) institute; school; медици́нский и. medical school
инструкта́ж, а *m.* instructing; (*mil., aeron.*) briefing
инструкти́р|овать, ую *impf. and pf.* (*pf. also* ▸ **проинструкти́ровать**) to instruct, brief
инстру́ктор, а *m.* instructor
инстру́кци|я, и *f.* instructions, directions; (instructions) manual
инструме́нт, а *m.* (*mus.; tech.*) instrument; (*tech.*) tool, implement; (*sg.; collect.*) tools
инсули́н, а *m.* insulin
инсу́льт, а *m.* (*med.*) stroke
инсцени́р|овать, ую *impf. and pf.* **1** (*рома́н*) to dramatize, adapt (for stage *or* screen) **2** (*fig.*) to feign, stage; и. о́бморок to stage a faint
интегра́ци|я, и *f.* integration
интелле́кт, а *m.* intellect; иску́сственный и. (*comput.*) artificial intelligence
интеллектуа́л, а *m.* intellectual
интеллектуа́л|ьный, ~ен, ~ьна *adj.* intellectual
интеллиге́нт, а *m.* member of the intelligentsia, intellectual
интеллиге́нт|ный, ~ен, ~на *adj.* cultured, educated

интеллиге́нци|я, и *f.* (*collect.*) intelligentsia
интенси́в|ный, ~ен, ~на *adj.* intensive
интеракти́вный *adj.* interactive
интерва́л, а *m.* interval
интерве́нци|я, и *f.* (*pol.*) intervention
интервью́ *nt. indecl.* interview; взять ~ у (+ *g.*) to interview (a person)
интере́с, а *m.* **1** interest; представля́ть и. to be of interest; прояви́ть и. (к + *d.*) to show interest (in) **2** (*вы́года*) interest; (*in pl.*) interests; в ва́ших ~ах пое́хать it is in your interest to go
интере́сно *as pred.* it is, would be interesting; и., что из него́ вы́йдет I wonder how he will turn out
интере́с|ный, ~ен, ~на *adj.* interesting
интерес|ова́ть, у́ю *impf.* to interest
интерес|ова́ться, у́юсь *impf.* (+ *i.*) to be interested (in); (*infml, осведомля́ться*) to enquire
интерна́т, а *m.* **1** (*шко́ла*) boarding school **2** (*общежи́тие*) boarding house (*at private school*)
интернациона́льный *adj.* international
Интерне́т, а *m.* the Internet; путеше́ствовать по ~у to surf the Internet
Интерне́т-са́йт, а *m.* website
интерпрета́ци|я, и *f.* interpretation
интерпрети́р|овать, ую *impf. and pf.* to interpret
интерфе́йс, а *m.* (*comput.*) interface
интерфере́нци|я, и *f.* (*phys.*) interference
интерье́р, а *m.* (*art*) interior
инти́м|ный, ~ен, ~на *adj.* intimate; ~ные места́ private parts
интоксика́ци|я, и *f.* (*med.*) intoxication; алкого́льная и. alcoholic poisoning
интона́ци|я, и *f.* intonation
интри́г|а, и *f.* intrigue
интрове́рт, а *m.* introvert
интуити́в|ный, ~ен, ~на *adj.* intuitive
интуи́ци|я, и *f.* intuition
инфанти́л|ьный, ~ен, ~ьна *adj.* infantile
инфа́ркт, а *m.* (*med.*) heart attack; infarction
инфекцио́н|ный *adj.* infectious; ~ая больни́ца isolation hospital
инфе́кци|я, и *f.* infection
инфля́ци|я, и *f.* (*econ.*) inflation
информати́в|ный, ~ен, ~на *adj.* informative
информа́тик|а, а *f.* information science, information technology
информа́тор, а *m.* informant
информацио́нный *adj.* of ▸ **информа́ция**
информа́ци|я, и *f.* information
информи́р|овать, ую *impf. and pf.* (*pf. also* ▸ **проинформи́ровать**) to inform
инфраструкту́р|а, ы *f.* infrastructure
инциде́нт, а *m.* incident; пограни́чный и. frontier incident
инъе́кци|я, и *f.* injection

и. о. (*abbr. of* **исполня́ющий обя́занности**) (+ *g.*) acting ...

Иорда́н, а *m.* Jordan (*river*)

иорда́н|ец, ца *m.* Jordanian

Иорда́ни|я, и *f.* Jordan (*country*)

иорда́н|ка, ки *f. of* ▶ **иорда́нец**

иорда́нский *adj.* Jordanian

ипоте́к|а, и *f.* mortgage

ипоте́чный *adj. of* ▶ **ипоте́ка; и. банк** mortgage bank; ≈ building society

ипподро́м, а *m.* racecourse

Ира́к, а *m.* Iraq

ира́к|ец, ца *m.* Iraqi

ира́кский *adj.* Iraqi

Ира́н, а *m.* Iran

ира́н|ец, ца *m.* Iranian

ира́н|ка, ки *f. of* ▶ **ира́нец**

ира́нский *adj.* Iranian

и́рис, а *m.* (bot.) iris

ири́с, а *m.* toffee

ирла́нд|ец, ца *m.* Irishman

Ирла́нди|я, и *f.* Ireland

ирла́нд|ка, ки *f.* Irishwoman

ирла́ндский *adj.* Irish

иронизи́р|овать, ую *impf.* (**над** + *i.*) to speak ironically (about)

ирони́ческий *adj.* ironic(al)

ирони́ч|ный, ~ен, ~на *adj.* = **ирони́ческий**

иро́ни|я, и *f.* irony

иррациона́л|ьный, ~ен, ~ьна *adj.* irrational

иррига́ци|я, и *f.* (agric. and med.) irrigation

ис... *pref.* = **из...**

иск, а *m.* (law) suit, action; **предъяви́ть и. (к) кому́-н.** to sue, prosecute sb, bring an action against sb

искажа́|ть, ю *impf. of* ▶ **искази́ть**

искаже́ни|е, я *nt.* distortion, perversion

искажённый *p.p.p. of* ▶ **искази́ть** *and adj.* distorted, perverted

иска|зи́ть, жу́, зи́шь *pf.* (*of* ▶ **искажа́ть**) to distort, pervert, twist; to misrepresent; **и. чьи-н. слова́** to twist sb's words; **и. фа́кты** to misrepresent the facts

искале́ченный *p.p.p. of* ▶ **искале́чить** *and adj.* (*человек, животное*) maimed, disabled; (*машина, стол*) damaged; (fig.) perverted, corrupt

искале́ч|ить, у, ишь *pf.* (*человека, животного*) to maim, disable; (*машину, стол*) to damage; (fig.) to pervert, corrupt

иска́тел|ь, я *m.* seeker, searcher; **и. жёмчуга** pearl diver

☞ **иска́ть, ищу́, и́щешь** *impf.* **1** (+ *a.*) to look for, search for; to seek (*sth concrete*) **2** (+ *g.*) to seek, look for, try to obtain (*sth abstract*); **и. слу́чая, сове́та** to seek an opportunity, seek advice

☞ **исключа́|ть, а́ю** *impf. of* ▶ **исключи́ть**

исключа́я *pres. gerund of* ▶ **исключа́ть**; (*as prep.* + *g.*) excepting, with the exception

of; **и. прису́тствующих** present company excepted

☞ **исключе́ни|е, я** *nt.* **1** (*отклонение от нормы*) exception; **за ~ем** (+ *g.*) with the exception (of) **2** (*из списка*) exclusion; (*из организации*) expulsion; **ме́тодом ~я** by process of elimination

☞ **исключи́тельно** *adv.* **1** (*необыкновенно*) exceptionally **2** (*только*) exclusively, solely

исключи́тел|ьный, ~ен, ~ьна *adj.* **1** (*необыкновенный*) exceptional **2** (*не для всех*) exclusive; **~ьное пра́во** exclusive right, sole right

исключ|и́ть, у́, и́шь *pf.* (*of* ▶ **исключа́ть**) **1** (*удалить*) to exclude; to eliminate; **и. из спи́ска** to strike off a list **2** (*из организации*) to expel; to dismiss **3** (*не допустить*) to rule out; **не ~ено́, что на́ши проигра́ют** our side could conceivably lose

иско́нный *adj.* (*права*) immemorial, age-old; (*население*) native, indigenous

ископа́ем|ое, ого *nt.* **1** fossil (also fig., iron.) **2** (*also* **поле́зное ~**) (*usu. in pl.*) mineral

искорен|и́ть, ю́, и́шь *pf.* (*of* ▶ **искореня́ть**) to eradicate

искорен|я́ть, я́ю *impf. of* ▶ **искорени́ть**

и́скр|а, ы *f.* spark; (fig.) flash

и́скренне *adv.* sincerely, candidly; **и. Ваш** Yours sincerely; Yours faithfully (*in letters, etc.*)

и́скрен|ний, ~ен, ~на, ~не and ~но, pl. ~ни and ~ны *adj.* sincere, candid

и́скренност|ь, и *f.* sincerity, candour

искрив|и́ть, лю́, и́шь *pf.* (*of* ▶ **искривля́ть**) to bend; (fig.) to distort

искривля́|ть, ю *impf. of* ▶ **искриви́ть**

и́скр|и́ться, ~и́тся *impf.* to sparkle; to scintillate (also fig.)

искупа́|ть¹, ю *pf.* to bath

искуп|а́ть², а́ю *impf. of* ▶ **искупи́ть**

искупа́|ться, юсь *pf.* (*of* ▶ **купа́ться**) to bathe; to take a bath

искуп|и́ть, лю́, ~ишь *pf.* (*of* ▶ **искупа́ть²**) (relig., also fig., *вину, грех*) to expiate, atone for

искупле́ни|е, я *nt.* redemption, expiation, atonement

искус|а́ть, а́ю *pf.* (*of* ▶ **иску́сывать**) (*о комарах*) to bite badly, all over; (*о пчёлах*) to sting badly, all over

иску|си́ть, шу́, си́шь *pf. of* ▶ **искуша́ть**

иску́с|ный, ~ен, ~на *adj.* skilful (BrE), skillful (AmE); expert

иску́сствен|ный *adj.* **1** artificial; (*ткань, волокно*) synthetic, man-made; **~ное дыха́ние** artificial respiration **2** (~, ~на) (fig., *смех*) artificial, feigned

☞ **иску́сств|о, а** *nt.* **1** art; **изобрази́тельные, изя́щные ~а** fine arts **2** (*умение*) craftsmanship, skill; **и. верховой езды́** horsemanship

искусствове́д, а *m.* art historian

искусствове́дени|е, я *nt.* history of art, art history

искусыва|ть, ю *impf. of* ▶ искусать

искуша|ть, ю *impf.* (*of* ▶ искусить) to tempt; to seduce; **и. судьбу** to tempt fate

искуше́ни|е, я *nt.* temptation; seduction; **поддаться ~ю, впасть в и.** to yield to temptation

искушённый *p.p.p. of* ▶ искусить *and adj.* (*политик*) experienced; (*публика*) sophisticated

исла́м, а *m.* Islam

исла́мский *adj.* Islamic

Исла́нди|я, и *f.* Iceland

испа́н|ец, ца *m.* Spaniard, Spanish man

Испа́ни|я, и *f.* Spain

испа́нк|а, и *f.* Spaniard, Spanish woman

испа́нский *adj.* Spanish

испаре́ни|е, я *nt.* **1** (*действие*) evaporation **2** (*usu. in pl.*) (*пар*) fumes

испар|и́ться, ю́сь, и́шься *pf.* (*of* ▶ испаря́ться) to evaporate; (fig., joc., *исчезнуть*) to vanish into thin air

испар|я́ться, я́юсь *impf. of* ▶ испари́ться

испа́чка|ть, ю *pf. of* ▶ па́чкать

испа́чка|ться, юсь *pf. of* ▶ па́чкаться

испепел|и́ть, ю́, и́шь *pf.* (*of* ▶ испепеля́ть) to reduce to ashes, incinerate

испепел|я́ть, я́ю *impf. of* ▶ испепели́ть

испе́|чь, ку́, чёшь, ку́т, *past* ~к, ~кла́ *pf. of* ▶ печь¹

испе́|чься, чётся, ку́тся, *past* ~кся, ~кла́сь *pf. of* ▶ пе́чься

испещр|и́ть, ю́, и́шь *pf.* (*of* ▶ испещря́ть) (+ *a. and i.*) to spot (with); to mark all over (with)

испещр|я́ть, я́ю *impf. of* ▶ испещри́ть

испи|са́ть, шу́, ~шешь *pf.* (*of* ▶ испи́сывать) **1** (*тетрадь*) to cover with writing; **он уже́ ~са́л два́дцать тетра́дей** he has already filled up twenty exercise books **2** (*карандаш, бумагу*) to use up (in writing)

испи́сыва|ть, ю *impf. of* ▶ исписа́ть

испове́д|ать, аю *pf.* (infml) = исповедовать¹

испове́д|аться, аюсь *pf.* (infml) = исповедоваться

испове́д|овать¹, ую *impf. and pf.* (eccl.) to hear the confession (of)

испове́д|овать², ую *impf.* (*веру*) to profess

испове́д|оваться, уюсь *impf. and pf.* **1** (+ *d. or* y + *g.*) (eccl.) to confess, make one's confession (to) **2** (+ *d. or* пе́ред + *i.*) (fig., infml) to confess; to unburden oneself of; **он ~овался мне в свои́х сомне́ниях** he confessed his doubts to me

и́споведь, и *f.* (eccl.) confession

исподло́бья *adv.* from under the brows (*distrustfully, sullenly*)

исподтишка́ *adv.* (infml) in an underhand way; on the quiet, on the sly; **смея́ться и.** to laugh in one's sleeve

✎ **исполне́ни|е, я** *nt.* **1** (*желания*) fulfilment

✎ key word

(BrE), fulfillment (AmE); (*приказа*) execution; (*долгов*) discharge; **привести́ в и.** to carry out, execute **2** (*роли, музыки*) performance; (theatr., mus.): **в ~и** (+ *g.*) (as) played (by), (as) performed (by)

исполни́тел|ь, я *m.* **1** executor; **суде́бный и.** bailiff **2** (theatr., mus., etc.) performer; **соста́в ~ей** cast

исполни́тель|ница, ницы *f. of* ▶ исполни́тель

✎ **исполни́тель|ный** *adj.* **1** (*власть, директор, комитет*) executive **2** (~ен, ~ьна) (*человек*) efficient and dependable

испо́лн|ить, ю, ишь *pf.* (*of* ▶ исполня́ть) **1** (*заказ*) to carry out, execute; (*желание*) to fulfil (BrE), fulfill (AmE); **и. обеща́ние** to keep a promise; **и. про́сьбу** to grant a request **2** (*роль, танец*) to perform; **и. роль** (+ *g.*) to take the part (of)

испо́лн|иться, юсь, ишься *pf.* (*of* ▶ исполня́ться) **1** (*осуществиться*) to be fulfilled **2** (impers. + *d.*) (*о возрасте, сроке*): **ему́ ~илось семь лет** he is seven, he was seven last birthday

✎ **исполн|я́ть, я́ю** *impf.* (*of* ▶ испо́лнить): **~я́ющий обя́занности** (+ *g.*) acting

исполн|я́ться, я́юсь *impf. of* ▶ исполни́ться

✎ **использова́ни|е, я** *nt.* use; (*сырья*) utilization

✎ **испо́льз|овать, ую** *impf. and pf.* to use, make use of, utilize

испо́р|тить, чу, тишь *pf. of* ▶ по́ртить

испо́р|титься, чусь, тишься *pf. of* ▶ по́ртиться

испо́рченн|ый *p.p.p. of* ▶ испо́ртить *and adj.* **1** (*человек*) depraved; corrupted **2** (*настроение, день*) ruined; (*товары*) spoiled; bad, rotten; **~ое мя́со** tainted meat **3** (infml, *ребёнок*) spoiled **4** (comput.) corrupt

исправ|ить, лю, ишь *pf.* (*of* ▶ исправля́ть) **1** (*ошибку*) to rectify, correct, emend **2** (*починить*) to repair, mend

исправ|иться, люсь, ишься *pf.* (*of* ▶ исправля́ться) to improve; to reform

исправле́ни|е, я *nt.* correcting; repairing; correction

исправл|я́ть, я́ю *impf. of* ▶ испра́вить

исправл|я́ться, я́юсь *impf. of* ▶ испра́виться

испра́в|ный, ~ен, ~на *adj.* (*механизм*) in good order

испражне́ни|е, я *nt.* **1** (*действие*) defecation **2** (in pl.) (*экскременты*) faeces

испражн|и́ться, ю́сь, и́шься *pf. of* ▶ испражня́ться

испражн|я́ться, я́юсь *impf.* (*of* ▶ испражни́ться) to defecate

испу́г, а (y) *m.* fright; alarm; **с ~у/~а** from fright

испу́ганный *p.p.p. of* ▶ испуга́ть *and adj.* frightened, scared, startled

испуга́|ть, ю *pf. of* ▶ пуга́ть

испуга́|ться, юсь *pf. of* ▶ пуга́ться

испуска́|ть, ю *impf. of* ▶ испусти́ть

испу|сти́ть, щу́, ~стишь *pf.* (*of* ▶ испуска́ть) (*свет, лучи́*) to emit; (*стон*) to let out; **и. дух** to breathe one's last

ⱷ испыта́ни|е, я *nt.* test, trial; (fig.) ordeal

испы́танный *p.p.p. of* ▶ испыта́ть *and adj.* tried, well tried

испыта́тел|ь, я *m.* tester; **лётчик-и.** test pilot

испыт|а́ть, а́ю *pf.* (*of* ▶ испы́тывать) **1** (*прове́рить*) to test, put to the test **2** (*ощути́ть*) to feel, experience

ⱷ испы́тыва|ть, ю *impf. of* ▶ испыта́ть

ⱷ иссле́довани|е, я *nt.* **1** (*те́мы*) research; (*ме́стности*) exploration; (*пробле́мы*) examination; (*кро́ви, соста́ва*) analysis **2** (*нау́чный труд*) paper; study

иссле́дователь|, я *m.* researcher; (*страны́*) explorer

иссле́дователь|ница, ницы *f. of* ▶ иссле́дователь

иссле́довательский *adj.* research

иссле́д|овать, ую *impf. and pf.* (*ситуа́цию, пробле́му*) to investigate; (*те́му*) to research into; (*страну́*) to explore; (*кровь*) to analyse (BrE), analyze (AmE)

иссяк|а́ть, а́ю *impf. of* ▶ исся́кнуть

исся́к|нуть, ну, нешь, *past* ~, ~ла *pf.* (*of* ▶ иссяка́ть) to run dry, dry up; (fig., *терпе́ние, си́лы*) to run out

истека́|ть, ю *impf. of* ▶ исте́чь

исте́|кший *p.p. of* ▶ исте́чь 1 *and adj.* past, preceding; **в тече́ние ~кшего го́да** during the past year

истерза́|ть, ю *pf.* **1** (*разорва́ть на ча́сти*) to tear in pieces; to mutilate **2** (*измучить*) to torment

исте́рик|а, и *f.* hysterics

истери́ческий *adj.* hysterical; **и. припа́док** fit of hysterics

истери́|я, и *f.* (med.) hysteria; (fig.): **ма́ссовая и.** mass hysteria

ист|е́ц, ца́ *m.* (law) plaintiff

истече́ни|е, я *nt.* **1** outflow; **и. кро́ви** haemorrhage (BrE), hemorrhage (AmE) **2** (*оконча́ние*) expiry, expiration; **по ~и сро́ка гара́нтии** on the expiry of the guarantee period

исте́|чь, ку́, чёшь, ку́т, *past* ~к, ~кла́ *pf.* (*of* ▶ истека́ть) **1**: **и. кро́вью** to bleed profusely **2** (*оконча́ться*) to expire, elapse; **вре́мя ~кло́** time is up

и́стин|а, ы *f.* truth; **изби́тая и.** truism

и́стин|ный, ~ен, ~на *adj.* true, veritable

исти́|ца, йцы *f. of* ▶ исте́ц

исто́к, а *m.* source (also fig.)

истолк|ова́ть, у́ю *pf.* (*of* ▶ истолко́вывать) (*смысл, сло́во*) to interpret; (*пи́сьменный па́мятник*) to comment upon; **и. замеча́ние в дурну́ю сто́рону** to put a nasty construction on a remark

истолко́выва|ть, ю *impf. of* ▶ истолкова́ть

исто́м|а, ы *f.* languor

истопни́к, а́ *m.* stoker; (*котло́в*) boilerman

исто́рик, а *m.* historian

ⱷ истори́ческ|ий *adj.* **1** historical; **~ое лицо́** historical figure **2** (*ва́жный*) historic; **~ое реше́ние** historic decision

ⱷ исто́ри|я, и *f.* **1** history; **и. боле́зни** case history **2** (infml, *расска́з*) story **3** (infml, *собы́тие*) incident, event; scene; **вчера́ со мной произошла́ заба́вная и.** a funny thing happened to me yesterday

ⱷ исто́чник, а *m.* **1** spring **2** (fig.) source; **и. информа́ции** source of information; **и. све́та** source of light; **служи́ть ~ом** (+ *g.*) to be a source (of)

истоще́ни|е, я *nt.* exhaustion

истощённый *adj.* exhausted; (*исхуда́лый*) emaciated

истра́|тить, чу, тишь *pf. of* ▶ тра́тить

истреби́тел|ь, я *m.* **1** (*челове́к*) destroyer **2** (*самолёт*) fighter **3** (*лётчик*) fighter pilot

истреб|и́ть, лю́, и́шь *pf.* (*of* ▶ истребля́ть) (*посе́вы*) to destroy; (*крыс*) to exterminate

истребле́ни|е, я *nt.* (*посе́вов*) destruction; (*крыс*) extermination

истребля́|ть, ю *impf. of* ▶ истреби́ть

истука́н, а *m.* idol, statue

истяза́ни|е, я *nt.* torture

истяза́|ть, ю *impf.* to torture

исхо́д, а *m.* (*ито́г*) outcome; (*коне́ц*) end; **быть на ~е** to be nearing the end, be coming to an end; **на ~е дня** towards evening

ⱷ исхо|ди́ть, жу́, ~дишь *impf.* (*of* ▶ изойти́) **1** (*impf. only*) (*из* + *g.*) (*происходи́ть*) to come (from); to emanate (from); **отку́да исхо́дит э́тот слух?** where does this rumour (BrE), rumor (AmE) come from? **2** (*impf. only*) (*из* + *g.*) (*осно́вываться*) to proceed (from), base oneself (on) **3**: **и. кро́вью** to become weak through loss of blood

исхо́дный *adj.* initial; **~ое положе́ние** point of departure

исходя́щий *adj.* outgoing

исхуда́|ть, ю *pf.* to become emaciated, become wasted

исцеле́ни|е, я *nt.* **1** (*де́йствие*) healing, cure **2** (*выздоровле́ние*) recovery

исцел|и́ть, ю́, и́шь *pf.* (*of* ▶ исцеля́ть) to heal, cure

исцел|я́ть, я́ю *impf. of* ▶ исцели́ть

исчез|а́ть, а́ю *impf.* (*of* ▶ исче́знуть) to disappear, vanish

исчезнове́ни|е, я *nt.* disappearance

исче́з|нуть, ну, нешь, *past* ~, ~ла *pf. of* ▶ исчеза́ть

исче́рп|ать, аю *pf.* (*of* ▶ исче́рпывать) **1** to exhaust, drain **2** (*довести́ до конца́*) to settle, conclude; **и. вопро́с** to settle a question

исче́рпыва|ть, ю *impf. of* ▶ исче́рпать

исче́рпывающий *pres. part. act. of* ▶ исче́рпывать *and adj.* exhaustive

И

исчисле́ни|е, я *nt.* calculation; (math.)
  calculus

✧ **ита́к** *conj.* thus; so then

Ита́ли|я, и *f.* Italy

италья́н|ец, ца *nt.* Italian

италья́н|ка, ки *f. of* ▶ италья́нец

италья́нский *adj.* Italian

✧ **и т. д.** (*abbr. of* **и так да́лее**) etc., et cetera,
  and so on

✧ **ито́г, а** *m.* **1** (*общая сумма*) sum, total;
  о́бщий и. grand total **2** (fig., *результат*)
  result; **подвести́ и.** to sum up; **в ~е** (*в конце
  концов*) in the end; (*в результате*) as a
  result

итого́ *adv.* in all, altogether; (sub)total

ито́говый *adj.* (*сумма*) total;
  (*завершающий*) final, concluding

✧ **и т. п.** (*abbr. of* **и тому́ подо́бное**) etc., et
  cetera, and so on

иудаи́зм, а *m.* Judaism

иуде́|й, я *m.* (liter.) Jew

иуде́й|ка, ки *f. of* ▶ иуде́й

иуде́йский *adj.* (hist., relig.) Judaic

их[1] *a. and g. of* ▶ они́

их[2] *poss. pron.* (*при существительном*) their;
  (*без существительного*) theirs; **их маши́на
  ме́ньше, чем на́ша** their car is smaller than
  ours

иша́к, á *m.* donkey, ass; (fig., infml) dogsbody
  (BrE), gofer

ишь *int.* (infml, *выражает удивление,
  отвращение, возражение*) look!; just look!;
  well I never!; **и. ты!** fancy that!

ище́йк|а, и *f.* bloodhound

и́щущий *pres. part. act. of* ▶ иска́ть *and adj.*:
  и. взгляд searching look

✧ **ию́л|ь, я** *m.* July

ию́льский *adj. of* ▶ ию́ль

✧ **ию́н|ь, я** *m.* June

ию́ньский *adj. of* ▶ ию́нь

Йе́мен, а *m.* Yemen

йе́мен|ец, ца *m.* Yemeni

йе́мен|ка, ки *f. of* ▶ йе́менец

йе́менский *adj.* Yemeni

йо́г|а, и *f.* yoga

йо́гурт, а *m.* yog(h)urt

йод, а *m.* iodine

Кк

✧ **к, ко** *prep. + d.* **1** (*при обозначении места*) to,
  towards; **мы подъезжа́ли к Москве́** we were
  nearing Moscow; **прислони́те ле́стницу к
  стене́** place the ladder against the wall; (fig.):
  лицо́м к лицу́ face to face; **к лу́чшему** for
  the better; **к (не)сча́стью** (un)fortunately;
  к тому́ же besides, moreover **2** (*при
  обозначении предельного срока*) to,
  towards; by; **зима́ подходи́ла к концу́** winter
  was drawing to a close; **к пе́рвому января́**
  by the first of January; **к тому́ вре́мени** by
  then, by that time; **к сро́ку** on time **3** (*при
  указании назначения*) for; **к чему́?** what for?;

э́то ни к чему́ it is no use

-ка *particle* (infml) **1** (*modifying force of imper.*):
  скажи́-ка мне come on now, tell me; **да́й-ка
  мне посмотре́ть** come on, let me take a look;
  ну́-ка well; **ну́-ка, спо́йте что-н.!** come on,
  give us a song! **2** (*with 1st pers. sg. of fut.*)
  (*выражает неуверенное решение*): **напишу́-
  ка ей письмо́** I think I'll write to her; **куплю́-
  ка тот га́лстук** maybe I'll buy that tie

каба́к, á *m.* tavern; (infml, fig.) noisy place

кабал|á, ы́ *f.* servitude, bondage

каба́н, á *m.* (wild) boar

кабаре́ *nt. indecl.* cabaret

кабачо́к, ка́ *m.* (*растение*) (vegetable)
  marrow (BrE), squash (AmE)

✧ key word

ка́бел|ь, я *m.* cable; **óптико-волокóнный к.** (*or* **волокóнно-опти́ческий к.**) fibre-optic cable (BrE), fiber-optic cable (AmE)

ка́бель|ный *adj. of* ▶ **ка́бель**; **~ное телеви́дение** cable television

каби́н|а, ы *f.* (*в самолёте, для пассажиров*) cabin; (*в самолёте, для лётчика*) cockpit; (*грузовика*) cab; (*в туалете*) cubicle; (*телефонная; для голосования*) booth; (*для купальщиков*) bathing hut; (*лифта*) cage

⚹ **кабине́т¹, а** *m.* **1** (*в доме*) study; (*на рабо́те*) office; (*врача*) surgery (BrE), office (AmE) **2** (*комплект мебели*) suite

⚹ **кабине́т², а** *m.* (*also* **к. мини́стров**, *often* **К.**) (pol.) cabinet

каблу́к, á *m.* heel (*of footwear*)

кабриоле́т, а *m.* cabriolet

Кабу́л, а *m.* Kabul

кавале́р¹, а *m.* **1** (*в танце*) partner; (*мужчина*) (gentle)man **2** (infml, *поклонник*) admirer, suitor

кавале́р², а *m.*: **к. (órдена)** knight, holder (of an order)

кавалери́ст, а *m.* cavalryman

кавале́ри|я, и *f.* cavalry

ка́вер-ве́рси|я, и *f.* cover version (*of a song*)

Кавка́з, а *m.* the Caucasus

кавка́з|ец, ца *m.* Caucasian

кавка́з|ка, ки *f. of* ▶ **кавка́зец**

кавка́зский *adj.* Caucasian

кавы́ч|ки, ек *f. pl.* (*sg.* **~ка, ~ки**) inverted commas, quotation marks; **в ~ках** in inverted commas, in quotes; (fig., iron.) so-called

каде́т, а *m.* cadet

ка́дк|а, и *f.* tub, vat

⚹ **кадр, а** *m.* (cin.) (*снимок*) frame; (*эпизод*) shot; **гóлос за ~ом** voice-over

кадри́л|ь, и *f.* quadrille (*dance*)

ка́дровый *adj.* **1** (mil., *офицер*) regular **2** (*рабочий*) skilled; best

ка́др|ы, ов *pl.* (*collect.*) **1** (mil.) (regular, peacetime) establishment **2** (*работники*) personnel; **~ов ~ов** HR department **3** (pol.) cadres

кады́к, á *m.* (infml) Adam's apple

каждодне́вный *adj.* daily

⚹ **ка́ждый** *adj.* **1** every, each; **к. день** every day; **к. из них получи́л по пять фу́нтов** they received five pounds each **2** (*as n.*) everyone

ка́жущийся *adj.* apparent

каза́к, á, *pl.* **~и** *m.* Cossack

каза́рм|а, ы *f.* barracks

⚹ **ка|за́ться, жу́сь, ~жешься** *impf.* (*of* ▶ **показа́ться 1**) **1** to seem, appear; **онá ~жется стáрше свои́х лет** she looks older than she is **2** (*impers.*): **мне** *и т. п.* **~жется,** **~зáлось** it seems, seemed (to me, *etc.*); apparently; **мне ~жется, что он был прав** I think he was right; **вы, ~жется, из Москвы́?** you are from Moscow, I believe?; **~зáлось бы** it would seem, one would think

каза́х, а *m.* Kazakh

каза́хский *adj.* Kazakh

Казахстáн, а *m.* Kazakhstan

каза́честв|о, а *nt.* (*collect.*) the Cossacks

каза́чий *adj.* Cossack

каза́ч|ка, ки *f. of* ▶ **каза́к**

каза́ш|ка, ки *f. of* ▶ **каза́х**

каземáт, а *m.* casemate; (*камера*) (prison) cell (*for one person*)

казённ|ый *adj.* **1** (*государственный*) state, public; **~ое иму́щество** state property; **на к. счёт** at public cost **2** (fig., *бюрократи́ческий*) bureaucratic, formal; **к. язы́к** language of officialdom, official jargon

казинó *nt. indecl.* casino

казн|á, ы́ (*no pl.*) *f.* (*государственное иму́щество*) Exchequer, Treasury

казначе́|й, я *m.* **1** (*кассир*) treasurer, bursar (BrE) **2** (mil.) paymaster; (naut.) purser

казначе́йств|о, а *nt.* Treasury, Exchequer

казн|и́ть, ю́, и́шь *impf. and pf.* to execute, put to death

казнокра́дств|о, а *nt.* embezzlement of public funds

казн|ь, и *f.* execution, capital punishment; **смéртная к.** death penalty

Каи́р, а *m.* Cairo

ка|ймá, ймы́, *pl.* **~ймы́, ~ём, ~ймáм** *f.* edging, border

каймáн, а *m.* (zool.) cayman

кайф, а *m.* (infml) kicks, 'high'; turn-on; buzz; **быть под ~ом** to be high *or* spaced out

⚹ **как¹** *adv. and particle* **1** how; **к. вам нрáвится Москвá?** how do you like Moscow?; **к. (вáши) делá?** how are you getting on?; **забы́л, к. э́то дéлается** I have forgotten how to do this; **к. вам не сты́дно!** you ought to be ashamed!; **к. егó фами́лия?, к. егó зову́т?** what is his name?, what is he called?; **к. назывáется э́тот цветóк?** what is this flower called?; **к. вы ду́маете?** what do you think?; (*выражает удивление, неудовольствие*): **к.! ты опя́ть здесь?** what! are you here again?; **к. же так?** how is that?; (infml): **к. сказáть** it all depends; **кому́ к.** it depends on the person **2** (infml, *о внезапном действии*): **онá к. закричи́т!** she suddenly cried out **3**: **к. ни, к. ... ни** however; **к. ни старáйтесь** however hard you may try, try as you may

⚹ **как²** *conj.* **1** (*выражает сравнение*) as; like; **бéлый к. снег** white as snow; **бу́дьте к. дóма** make yourself at home; **к. мóжно, к. нельзя́** as ... as possible; **к. мóжно скорéе** as soon as possible **2**: **к. ..., так и** both ... and; **к. мáльчики, так и дéвочки** both the boys and the girls **3** (*что*) (*following vv. of perceiving, not translated*): **я ви́дел, к. онá ушлá** I saw her go out **4** (*когда*) when; (*с тех пор, как*) since; **прошлó два гóда, к. мы встрéтились** it is two years since we met; **к. тóлько** as soon as, when **5** (+ *neg.*) but, except, than; **кому́ ему́ остáвалось дéлать, к. не сознáться?** what could he do but confess?; **кому́, к. не мне знать э́то!** if anyone knows, I do! **6**: **в то врéмя к.;**

К

до того́ к.; ме́жду тем к.; тогда́ к. *see* ▶ вре́мя

какаду́ *m. indecl.* (zool.) cockatoo

кака́о *nt. indecl.* cocoa

ка́к|ать, аю *impf.* (baby talk) to (do a) poo

как бу́дто, бы 1 *conj.* as if, as though; **к. б. вы не зна́ете!** as if you didn't know! **2** *particle* (infml, *ка́жется*) it would seem

как бы 1 (+ *inf.*) how; **к. б. э́то сде́лать?** how is it to be done, I wonder **2**: **к. б. ни** however; **к. б. то ни́ было** however that may be, be that as it may **3** as if, as though **4**: **к. б. не** (*выража́ет опасе́ние*) what if, supposing; (*following v.*) that, lest; **к. б. он не опозда́л!** what if he is late!

ка́к-либо *adv.* somehow

ка́к-нибудь *adv.* **1** (*так или ина́че*) somehow (or other) **2** (infml, *когда́-нибудь*) some time; **загляни́те к.-н.** look in some time

как-ника́к *adv.* (infml) nevertheless, for all that

како́в, ~á, ~ó, ~ы́ *pron.* (*interrog., and in exclamations expr. strong feeling*) what; of what sort?; **к. результа́т?** what is the result?; **к. он?** what is he like?; **к. он собо́й?** what does he look like?; **а пого́да-то ~а́!** what (*splendid, filthy*) weather!

☞ **как|о́й** *pron.* **1** (*interrog. and rel.; and in exclamations*) what; **~о́е сего́дня число́?** what is today's date?; **~и́м о́бразом?** how? **2**: (*тако́й*) **к.** such as; **гнев, ~о́го он никогда́ не испы́тывал** anger such as he had never felt **3**: **к. ни** whatever, whichever

☞ **како́й-либо** *pron.* = **како́й-нибудь**

☞ **како́й-нибудь** *pron.* some; any

☞ **как|о́й-то** *pron.* **1** (*неизве́стно како́й*) some, a **2** (*напомина́ющий*) a kind of; **э́то ~а́я-то боле́знь** it is a kind of disease

как ра́з *adv.* just, exactly; **к. р. то, что мне ну́жно** just what I need; (*as pred.*) **э́ти ту́фли мне к. р.** these shoes are just right

☞ **ка́к-то** *adv.* **1** somehow; **он к.-то ухитри́лся сде́лать э́то** he managed to do it somehow **2** (infml): **к.-то (раз)** once

ка́ктус, а *m.* (bot.) cactus

кал, а *m.* faeces, excrement

каламбу́р, а *m.* pun

каланч|а́, и́, *g. pl.* **~е́й** *f.* watchtower; **пожа́рная к.** fire observation tower; (infml, pej., *о челове́ке*) beanpole

калейдоско́п, а *m.* kaleidoscope

кале́к|а, и *c.g.* disabled person (*who has difficulty walking*)

календа́р|ь, я́ *m.* calendar

кале́ч|ить, у, ишь *impf.* to maim, mutilate; (fig.) to twist, pervert; to ruin

кали́бр, а *m.* **1** calibre (BrE), caliber (AmE) **2** (tech.) gauge

ка́ли|й, я *m.* (chem.) potassium

кали́н|а, ы (*no pl.*) *f.* (bot.) guelder rose, viburnum

кали́тк|а, и *f.* (wicket) gate

☞ key word

кали́ф, а *m.* caliph; **к. на час** (iron.) king for a day

Калифо́рни|я, и *f.* California

ка́лл|а, ы *f.* (bot.) arum lily (BrE), calla lily (AmE)

каллигра́фи|я, и *f.* calligraphy

калмы́к, а *m.* Kalmyk

калмы́цкий *adj.* Kalmyk

калмы́ч|ка, ки *f. of* ▶ **калмы́к**

калори́йност|ь, и *f.* **1** (*пи́щи*) calorie content **2** (phys.) calorific value

калори́|йный, ~ен, ~йна *adj.* high-calorie; fattening

кало́ри|я, и *f.* calorie

ка́л|ька, ьки, *g. pl.* **~ек** *f.* **1** (*бума́га*) tracing paper **2** (*ко́пия*) (tracing paper) copy **3** (ling.) loan translation, calque

калькуля́тор, а *m.* calculator

Калькутт|а, ы *f.* Calcutta, Kolkata

кальма́р, а *m.* (zool.) squid

кальсо́н|ы, ~ (*no sg.*) long johns

ка́льци|й, я *m.* (chem.) calcium

калья́н, а *m.* hookah, shisha

ка́мбал|а, ы *f.* plaice; flounder

Камбо́дж|а, и *f.* Cambodia

камбоджи́|ец, йца *m.* Cambodian

камбоджи́й|ка, ки *f. of* ▶ **камбоджи́ец**

камбоджи́йский *adj.* Cambodian

каме́ли|я, и *f.* (bot.) camellia

камене́|ть, ю *impf.* (*of* ▶ **окамене́ть**) (*станови́ться твёрдым*) to become petrified, turn to stone; (fig., *о се́рдце*) to harden; (*от стра́ха*) to be petrified

камени́ст|ый, ~, ~а *adj.* stony

ка́менн|ый *adj.* **1** stone-; stony; **к. век** the Stone Age; **~ая кла́дка** stonework **2** (fig.) stony; **~ое се́рдце** stony heart

каменоло́м|ня, ни, *g. pl.* **~ен** *f.* quarry

ка́менщик, а *m.* bricklayer

☞ **ка́м|ень, ня,** *pl.* **~ни, ~не́й** *m.* stone; (*зубно́й*) tartar; **драгоце́нный к.** precious stone, gem

☞ **ка́мер|а, ы** *f.* **1** chamber (*in var. senses*); (*в тюрьме́*) cell; **морози́льная к.** freezer compartment (*of refrigerator*); **к. хране́ния** (*багажа́*) left-luggage office (BrE), baggage room (AmE) **2** (*фо́то*) camera; (*ви́део*) camcorder **3** (*ши́ны*) inner tube; (*мяча́*) bladder

ка́мерн|ый *adj.* (mus.): **~ая му́зыка** chamber music

камерто́н, а *m.* tuning fork

каме́|я, и *f.* cameo

камика́дзе *m. indecl.* kamikaze pilot

ками́н, а *m.* fireplace

камнепа́д, а *m.* rockfall

камо́рк|а, и *f.* (infml) closet, tiny room; box room

кампа́ни|я, и *f.* campaign

камуфля́ж, а (*no pl.*) *m.* camouflage

Камча́тк|а, и *f.* Kamchatka

камы́ш, á *m.* reed, rush (*also collect.*)

кана́в|а, ы *f.* ditch; сто́чная к. gutter

Кана́д|а, ы *f.* Canada

кана́д|ец, ца, *g. pl.* ~цев *m.* Canadian

кана́д|ка, ки *f. of* ▸ кана́дец

кана́дский *adj.* Canadian

⚓ кана́л, а *m.* ❶ (*искусственное русло*) canal; (*морской*) channel ❷ (*fig., путь*) channel; дипломати́ческие ~ы diplomatic channels ❸ (anat.) duct, canal ❹ (*телевизионный*) channel

канализа|цио́нный *adj. of* ▸ канализа́ция; ~цио́нная труба́ sewer (pipe)

канализа́ци|я, и *f.* sewerage system

канаре́йк|а, и *f.* canary

Кана́рск|ие острова́, ~их острово́в (*no sg.*) Canary Islands

кана́т, а *m.* rope; cable

кандал|ы́, о́в (*no sg.*) shackles, fetters; ручны́е к. manacles; закова́ть в к. to put into irons

⚓ кандида́т, а *m.* candidate; ~ нау́к (*учёная степень*) Doctor

кандидату́р|а, ы *f.* candidature; вы́ставить чью-н. ~у to nominate sb for election; (*кандидат*) candidate

кани́кул|ы, ~ (*no sg.*) (*школьные*) holidays (BrE), vacation (AmE); (*университетские*) vacation

кани́стр|а, ы *f.* jerrycan

канифо́л|ь, и *f.* rosin

ка́нн|а, ы *f.* (bot.) canna (lily)

каннибал, а *m.* cannibal

каннибали́зм, а *m.* cannibalism

кано́н, а *m.* canon

канона́д|а, ы *f.* cannonade

канониза́ци|я, и *f.* (eccl.) canonization

канонизи́р|овать, ую *impf. and pf.* (eccl., also fig.) to canonize

кано́э *nt. indecl.* canoe

кану́н, а *m.* eve; к. Но́вого го́да New Year's Eve; к. Рождества́ Christmas Eve

канцеля́ри|я, и *f.* clerical office

канцеля́р|ский *adj. of* ▸ канцеля́рия; ~ские принадле́жности/това́ры stationery, office supplies

канцероге́нный *adj.* carcinogenic

ка́нцлер, а *m.* chancellor

каньо́н, а *m.* (geog.) canyon

ка́п|ать, аю *impf.* (*of* ▸ нака́пать) ❶ (*no pf., 3rd pers. only*) (*падать каплями*) to drip, drop; to trickle; to dribble; (in drops); слёзы ~али у неё из глаз teardrops were falling from her eyes ❷ (*наливать каплями*) to pour out (*in drops*); к. лека́рство в рю́мку to pour medicine into a glass ❸ (+ *i.*) (*проливать*) to spill; ты ~аешь водо́й на ска́терть you are spilling water on the cloth

капе́лл|а, ы *f.* ❶ (*хор*) choir ❷ (*часовня*) chapel

капелла́н, а *m.* chaplain

ка́пельниц|а, ы *f.* (med.) drip

ка́перс|ы, ов *m. pl.* (cul.) capers

⚓ капита́л, а *m.* (fin.) capital; (fig.): полити́ческий к. political capital

капитали́зм, а *m.* capitalism

капитали́ст, а *m.* capitalist

капиталисти́ческий *adj.* capitalist

капиталовложе́ни|е, я *nt.* capital investment

капита́льный *adj.* (fin.) capital; (*основной*) main, fundamental; (*самый важный*) most important; к. ремо́нт major repairs, refurbishment

капита́н, а *m.* captain

капитуля́ци|я, и *f.* capitulation

капка́н, а *m.* trap; попа́сться в к. to fall into a trap (also fig.)

ка́п|ля, ли, *g. pl.* ~ель *f.* ❶ drop; похо́жи как две ~ли воды́ as like as two peas; (fig.): к. в мо́ре a drop in the ocean (BrE), bucket (AmE) ❷ (*in pl.*) (med.) drops ❸ (fig., infml) drop, bit; в нём (нет) ни ~ли благоразу́мия he hasn't a drop of sense

ка́п|нуть, ну, нешь *pf.* to drop, let fall a drop

капо́т, а *m.* (*машины*) bonnet (BrE), hood (AmE)

капри́з, а *m.* caprice, whim; к. судьбы́ twist of fate

капри́знича|ть, ю *impf.* to behave capriciously; (*о ребёнке*) to play up

капри́з|ный, ~ен, ~на *adj.* capricious

капро́н, а *m.* kapron (*synthetic fibre, similar to nylon*)

ка́псул|а, ы *f.* capsule

капу́ст|а, ы *f.* cabbage; брюссе́льская к. Brussels sprouts; цветна́я к. cauliflower

капу́стный *adj. of* ▸ капу́ста

капюшо́н, а *m.* hood

ка́р|а, ы *f.* (rhet.) punishment, retribution

караби́н, а *m.* (*винтовка*) carbine

кара́бка|ться, юсь *impf.* (*of* ▸ вскара́бкаться) to clamber

карава́|й, я *m.* cottage loaf

карава́н, а *m.* ❶ (*верблюдов*) caravan ❷ (*судов*) convoy

каракати́ц|а, ы *f.* (zool.) cuttlefish

кара́кул|ь, я (*no pl.*) *m.* Persian lamb; astrakhan

кара́кул|я, и, *g. pl.* ~ей *and* ~ь *f.* scrawl, scribble

караме́л|ь, и (*no pl.*) *f.* ❶ (collect.) (*конфеты*) caramels ❷ (*жжёный сахар*) caramel

каранда́ш, á *m.* pencil

каранти́н, а *m.* quarantine

карао́ке *nt. indecl.* karaoke

кара́т, а *m.* carat

карате́ *nt. indecl.* karate

кара́тельный *adj.* punitive; к. отря́д death squad

кара́|ть, ю *impf.* (*of* ▸ покара́ть) to punish

карау́л, а *m.* guard; watch; нести́ к. to be on guard duty; смени́ть к. to relieve the guard

карау́л|ить, ю, ишь *impf.* to guard

карбюра́тор, а *m.* (tech., chem.) carburettor (BrE), carburetor (AmE)

К

кардина́л, а *m.* (eccl.) cardinal

кардина́л|ьный, ~ен, ~ьна *adj.* cardinal; fundamental

кардиогра́мм|а, ы *f.* cardiogram

кардио́лог, а *m.* cardiologist

кардиоло́ги|я, и *f.* cardiology

кардиохиру́рг, а *m.* heart surgeon

каре́т|а, ы *f.* carriage, coach

кари́бский *adj.* Caribbean

Кари́бск|ое мо́ре, ~ого мо́ря *nt.* the Caribbean Sea; the Caribbean

ка́риес, а *m.* (med.) caries

ка́рий *adj.* (*глаза*) brown, hazel

карикату́р|а, ы *f.* caricature, cartoon; (fig.) caricature

карка́с, а *m.* (tech.) frame; (fig.) framework

ка́рк|ать, аю *impf.* to caw

ка́рк|нуть, ну, нешь *pf.* to give a caw

ка́рлик, а *m.* dwarf (offens.), abnormally small person

ка́рликовый *adj.* dwarf

ка́рли|ца, цы *f. of* ▶ **ка́рлик**

карма́н, а *m.* pocket; (fig., infml): э́то мне не по ~у I can't afford it

карма́нник, а *m.* pickpocket

карма́н|ный *adj. of* ▶ **карма́н**; к. вор pickpocket; ~ные де́ньги pocket money

карнава́л, а *m.* carnival

карни́з, а *m.* (archit., mountaineering) cornice

карп, а *m.* carp (*fish*)

ка́рри *nt. indecl.* curry

◆ **ка́рт|а**, ы *f.* **1** (geog.) map **2** (*игра́льная*) (playing) card; игра́ть в ~ы to play cards; поста́вить на ~у to stake, risk **3** (*бланк*) form **4** = **ка́рточка 1**; магни́тная к. swipe card

карт-бла́нш *m. indecl.* carte blanche

◆ **карти́н|а**, ы *f.* **1** picture **2** (theatr.) scene

◆ **карти́нк|а**, и *f.* (small) picture

карти́н|ный, ~ен, ~на *adj.* **1** *adj. of* ▶ **карти́на**; ~ная галере́я art gallery, picture gallery **2** (*жест, поза*) theatrical, mannered

карто́граф, а *m.* cartographer

картогра́фи|я, и *f.* cartography

карто́н, а *m.* card, cardboard

картоте́к|а, и *f.* card index

карто́фелин|а, ы *f.* (infml) potato

карто́фел|ь, я (*no pl.*) *m.* **1** (collect.) potatoes; жа́реный к. fried potatoes; молодо́й к. new potatoes **2** (*растение*) potato plant

карто́фель|ный *adj. of* ▶ **карто́фель**; ~ное пюре́ mashed potatoes

ка́рточк|а, и *f.* **1** card; визи́тная к. visiting card, business card; креди́тная к. credit card **2** (*проездно́й биле́т*) season ticket

ка́рточ|ный *adj. of* ▶ **ка́рта**; к. долг gambling debt; (infml): к. до́мик house of

◆ key word

cards (also fig.); к. фо́кус card trick **2** *adj. of* ▶ **ка́рточка**; ~ная систе́ма rationing system

карто́шк|а, и *f.* (infml) **1** (collect.) (*карто́фель*) potatoes **2** (*картофе́лина*) potato

ка́ртридж, а *m.* cartridge

карусе́л|ь, и *f.* merry-go-round, carousel

ка́рцер, а *m.* isolation cell

карье́р[1], а *m.* (*гало́п*) career, full gallop; (fig.): с ме́ста в к. straight away, without more ado

карье́р[2], а *m.* (*каменоло́мня*) quarry; (*песо́чный*) sandpit; у́гольный к. open-cast mine

карье́р|а, ы *f.* career; сде́лать ~у to make good, get on

карьери́ст, а *m.* careerist

каса́ни|е, я *nt.* contact

каса́тельно *prep. + g.* touching, concerning

◆ **каса́|ться, юсь** *impf.* (of ▶ **косну́ться**) **1** (+ g.) to touch **2** (+ g.) (fig., *вопроса, темы*) to touch (on, upon) **3** (+ g.) (fig., *име́ть отноше́ние*) to concern, relate (to); э́то тебя́ не ~ется it is no concern of yours; что ~ется as to, as regards, with regard to

ка́ск|а, и *f.* helmet

каска́д, а *m.* cascade

каскадёр, а *m.* stunt man

Каспи́йск|ое мо́ре, ~ого мо́ря *nt.* the Caspian Sea

ка́сс|а, ы *f.* **1** (*я́щик*) cash box; (*аппара́т в магази́не*) till, cash register; (*ме́сто в магази́не*) cash desk **2** (*де́ньги*) cash **3** (*железнодоро́жная*) booking office; (*театра́льная*) box office; сберега́тельная к. savings bank

касса|цио́нный *adj.*: ~цио́нная жа́лоба appeal; к. суд Court of Appeal

кассе́т|а, ы *f.* cassette

кассе́тный *adj. of* ▶ **кассе́та**; к. магнитофо́н cassette recorder

касси́р, а *m.* cashier

ка́сс|овый *adj.* **1** *adj. of* ▶ **ка́сса**; ~овая кни́га cash book **2**: к. спекта́кль, фильм a box office success

кастет, а *m.* knuckleduster

кастри́р|овать, ую *impf. and pf.* to castrate

кастрю́л|я, и *f.* saucepan

◆ **катало́г**, а *m.* catalogue (BrE), catalog (AmE)

катамара́н, а *m.* catamaran

ката́ни|е, я *nt.* **1** (*мяча́*) rolling **2**: к. в экипа́же driving; к. верхо́м riding; к. на ло́дке boating; к. на конька́х skating; к. на ро́ликах roller skating

катапу́льт|а, ы *f.* catapult

катапульти́р|оваться, уюсь *impf. and pf.* (*о лётчике*) to eject

Ка́тар, а *m.* Qatar

ката́р, а *m.* (med.) catarrh

катара́кт|а, ы *f.* (med.) cataract

катастро́ф|а, ы *f.* catastrophe, disaster; (*ава́рия*) accident

катастрофи́ческий *adj.* catastrophic

кат|а́ть, а́ю *impf.* (*indet. of* ▶ кати́ть) **1** (мяч) to roll; (велосипед, тачку) to wheel, trundle **2** (человека) to drive, take for a drive; (на санках) to take for a ride **3** (*pf.* с∼) (из глины, теста) to roll

кат|а́ться, а́юсь *impf.* (*indet. of* ▶ кати́ться) **1** (о мяче) to roll; к. с горы́ to slide down a hill **2** (на машине) to go for a drive; к. верхо́м to ride, go riding; к. на велосипе́де to cycle, go cycling; к. на конька́х to skate, go skating; к. на ло́дке to go boating

катафа́лк, а *m.* hearse

категори́чески *adv.* categorically; к. отказа́ться to flatly refuse

◦ катего́ри|я, и *f.* category

ка́тер, а, *pl.* ∼а́ *m.* (naut.) boat; сторожево́й к. patrol boat

кате́тер, а *m.* (med.) catheter

ка|ти́ть, чу́, ∼тишь *impf.* (*of* ▶ покати́ть 1) **1** *det. of* ▶ ката́ть **2** (infml, быстро ехать) to bowl along, tear

ка|ти́ться, чу́сь, ∼тишься *impf.* (*of* ▶ покати́ться 1) **1** *det. of* ▶ ката́ться; к. под го́ру (fig.) to go downhill **2** (течь) to flow, stream; (fig.) to roll; слёзы ∼ти́лись по её щека́м tears were rolling down her cheeks **3** (infml): ∼ти́сь; ∼ти́сь отсю́да! get out!; clear off!

кат|о́к¹, ка́ *m.* (ледяная площадка) skating rink

кат|о́к², ка́ *m.* (машина) roller

като́лик, а *m.* (Roman) Catholic

католици́зм, а *m.* (Roman) Catholicism

католи́ческий *adj.* (Roman) Catholic

католи́честв|о, а *nt.* (Roman) Catholicism

католи́чк|а, и *f. of* ▶ като́лик

ка́торг|а, и (*no pl.*) *f.* penal servitude, hard labour (BrE), labor (AmE)

ка́торжник, а *m.* convict

кату́шк|а, и *f.* **1** reel, spool **2** (elec.) coil

каучу́к, а *m.* (India) rubber, caoutchouc

каучу́ковый *adj. of* ▶ каучу́к; rubber

кафе́ *nt. indecl.* cafe; к.-моро́женое ice-cream parlour (BrE), parlor (AmE)

◦ ка́федр|а, ы *f.* **1** (в церкви) pulpit; (для оратора) rostrum, platform **2** (профессорство) chair; получи́ть ∼у to obtain a chair **3** (в университете) department

кафедра́льный *adj.*: к. собо́р cathedral

ка́фел|ь, я *m.* (collect.) Dutch tiles

ка́фель|ный *adj. of* ▶ ка́фель; ∼ная печь tiled stove; ∼ная пли́тка Dutch tile

кафете́ри|й, я *m.* cafeteria

кача́ть, а́ю *impf.* (*of* ▶ качну́ть) **1** (+ *a.*) (ребёнка, колыбель) to rock; (+ *i.*) (головой, ногой) to shake; (impers.) ло́дку ∼а́ет the boat is rolling **2** (подбрасывать вверх) (infml) to lift up, chair (as mark of esteem or congratulation) **3** (*pf.* накача́ть) (насосом) to pump **4** (*pf.* накача́ть) (infml): к. му́скулы to do bodybuilding exercises; to work out; to pump iron

кача́|ться, а́юсь *impf.* (*of* ▶ качну́ться) **1** to rock, swing; (о лодке) to roll, pitch **2** (при ходьбе) to reel, stagger **3** (*pf.* ▶ накача́ться) (infml) to practise bodybuilding; to work out; to pump iron

каче́л|и, ей (*no sg.*) swing (child's); (доска-качели) see-saw

◦ ка́чествен|ный, ∼, ∼на *adj.* **1** (различие, изменение) qualitative **2** (товар) quality

◦ ка́честв|о, а *nt.* quality; ни́зкого ∼а poor quality; low-grade; в ∼е (+ *g.*) in the capacity (of); в ∼е исключе́ния as a special concession

кач|ну́ть, ну́, нёшь *pf. of* ▶ кача́ть

кач|ну́ться, ну́сь, нёшься *pf. of* ▶ кача́ться

кач|у́, ∼тишь *see* ▶ кати́ть

ка́ш|а, и *f.* **1** kasha (dish of cooked grain or groats); porridge; ма́нная к. semolina; ри́совая к. boiled rice **2** (fig., infml) (месиво) jumble; (путаница) muddle; расхлёбывать ∼у to put things right

кашало́т, а *m.* (zool.) sperm whale

ка́ш|ель, ля *m.* cough

ка́шлян|уть, у, ешь *pf.* to give a cough

ка́шля|ть, ю *impf.* **1** to cough **2** (как болезнь) to have a cough

кашне́ *nt. indecl.* scarf, muffler

кашпо́ *nt. indecl.* decorative flowerpot holder

кашта́н, а *m.* **1** (орех) chestnut **2** (дерево) chestnut tree; ко́нский к. horse chestnut

кашта́новый *adj.* **1** *adj. of* ▶ кашта́н **2** (цвет) chestnut(-coloured)

каю́т|а, ы *f.* cabin

кая́к, а *m.* kayak

ка́|яться, юсь, ешься *impf.* (*of* ▶ пока́яться) (в + *p.*) **1** (сожалеть) to repent (of); он сам тепе́рь ∼ется he is sorry himself now **2** (признаться) to confess

КБ (*abbr of* констру́кторское бюро́) construction office

◦ кв. (*abbr. of* кварти́ра) flat (BrE), apartment (AmE)

квадра́т, а *m.* (math.) square; возвести́ в к. to square; в ∼е squared

квадра́тный *adj.* square; к. ко́рень square root; к. метр square metre (BrE), meter (AmE)

ква́ка|ть, ю *impf.* to croak

ква́кн|уть, у, ешь *pf.* to give a croak

квалифика́ци|я, и *f.* qualification; (профессия) profession

квалифици́ро|ванный, ∼н, ∼на *p.p.p. of* ▶ квалифици́ровать *and* (∼н, ∼нна) *adj.* **1** (работник) qualified, skilled **2** (труд) skilled

квалифици́р|овать, ую *impf. and pf.* **1** (специалиста, спортсмена) to rank, test **2** (оценить) to categorize; как к. тако́е поведе́ние? how should one describe such conduct?

квант, а *m.* (phys.) quantum

ква́нт|овый *adj. of* ▶ квант; (phys.): ∼овая меха́ника quantum theory; ∼овая тео́рия quantum theory

⚥ **кварта́л**, а *m.* **1** (*домов*) block **2** (*часть города*) quarter; **кита́йский к.** Chinatown **3** (*года*) quarter

кварте́т, а *m.* (*mus.*) quartet

⚥ **кварти́р|а**, ы *f.* **1** flat (BrE), apartment (AmE) **2** (*снимаемое жильё*) lodgings; **жить на ~е** to live in lodgings

квартира́нт, а *m.* lodger, tenant

квартира́нт|ка, ки *f. of* ▸ **квартира́нт**

кварти́р|ный *adj. of* ▸ **кварти́ра**; **~ная пла́та** rent

квартпла́т|а, ы *f.* (*abbr. of* **кварти́рная пла́та**) rent

кварц, а *m.* (*min.*) quartz

ква́рцевый *adj. of* ▸ **кварц**

квас, а, *pl.* **~ы́** *m.* kvass (*drink made from fermented rye bread*)

кве́рху *adv.* up, upwards

квита́нци|я, и *f.* receipt; **бага́жная к.** luggage ticket (BrE), baggage check (AmE)

кво́т|а, ы *f.* quota

кВт (*abbr. of* **килова́тт**) kW, kilowatt(s)

⚥ **кг** (*abbr of* **килогра́мм**) k, kg, kilo(s), kilogram(s)

КГБ *m. indecl.* (*abbr. of* **Комите́т госуда́рственной безопа́сности**) (hist.) KGB, State Security Committee

ке́гл|и, ей *f. pl.* (*sg* **~я**, **~и**) **1** skittles, ninepins; **спорти́вные к.** bowls **2** (*in sg.*) skittle; pin

кедр, а *m.* cedar; **сиби́рский к.** Siberian pine

кедро́вый *adj. of* ▸ **кедр**

ке́д|ы, ов *or* **~** *m. pl.* (*sg.* **кед**, а) trainers (BrE), sneakers (AmE)

кекс, а *m.* fruit cake

кельт, а *m.* Celt

ке́льтский *adj.* Celtic

кем *i. of* ▸ **кто**

Ке́мбридж, а *m.* Cambridge

ке́мпинг, а *m.* campsite

кенгуру́ *m. indecl.* kangaroo

кени́|ец, йца *m.* Kenyan

кени́йк|а, и *f.* Kenyan

кени́йский *adj.* Kenyan

Ке́ни|я, и *f.* Kenya

ке́пк|а, и *f.* cloth cap

кера́мик|а, и *f.* ceramics

керами́ческий *adj.* ceramic

кероси́н, а *m.* paraffin (BrE), kerosene (AmE)

ке́тчуп, а *m.* ketchup

кефа́л|ь, и *f.* grey mullet

кефи́р, а *m.* kefir (*thin yoghurt drink*)

кибератáк|а, и *f.* (*comput.*) cyberattack

кибернéтик|а, и *f.* cybernetics

киберпреступлéни|е, я *nt.* (*comput.*) cybercrime (*single offence*)

киберпрестýпность, и *f.* (*comput.*) cybercrime (*collect.*)

кив|áть, áю *impf.* (*of* ▸ **кивнýть**): **к. (головóй)** to nod (one's head); (*в знак согласия*) to

⚥ key word

nod assent

ки́ви *m. & nt. indecl.* **1** *m.* (zool.) kiwi **2** *m. & nt.* kiwi fruit

кив|ну́ть, ну́, нёшь *pf. of* ▸ **кива́ть**

киво́к, ка́ *m.* nod

ки|да́ть, да́ю *impf.* (*of* ▸ **ки́нуть**) **1** to throw, fling, cast (*usage as for броса́ть*); **куда́ ни кинь** whichever way you turn **2** (sl., *обма́нывать*) to cheat, con

ки|да́ться, да́юсь *impf.* (*of* ▸ **ки́нуться**) **1** to throw oneself, fling oneself; (*устреми́ться куда́-н.*) to rush **2** (+ *i.*) to throw, fling **3** *pass. of* ▸ **кида́ть**

Ки́ев, а *m.* Kiev

киевля́н|ин, ина, *pl.* **~е**, **~** *m.* Kievan

киевля́н|ка, ки *f. of* ▸ **киевля́нин**

ки|й, я́, *pl.* **~й**, **~ёв** *m.* (sport) cue

ки́ллер, а *m.* contract killer, hit man

килоба́йт, а *m.* (comput.) kilobyte

килова́тт, а, *g. pl.* **к. ~** (elec.) kilowatt

килогра́мм, а *m.* kilogram

киломе́тр, а *m.* kilometre (BrE), kilometer (AmE)

кил|ь, я *m.* (naut.) keel

ки́льк|а, и *f.* sprat

кимоно́ *nt. indecl.* kimono

кинемато́граф, а *m.* cinematography

кинематографи́ст, а *m.* cinematographer, film-maker

кинематогра́фи|я, и *f.* cinematography

кинжа́л, а *m.* dagger

кино́ *nt. indecl.* **1** (*как искусство*) the cinema **2** (infml, *здание*) cinema (BrE), movie theater (AmE) **3** (infml, *фильм*) film, movie

кино... *comb. form* cinema, film

киноактёр, а *m.* film actor (BrE), movie actor (AmE)

киноактри́с|а, ы *f.* film actress (BrE), movie actress (AmE)

киноза́л, а *m.* **1** (*здание*) cinema (BrE), movie theater (AmE) **2** (*зал*) auditorium

кинозвезд|á, ы́, *pl.* **~ы**, **~**, **~ам** *f.* film star (BrE), movie star (AmE)

кинозри́тел|ь, я *m.* filmgoer, moviegoer

кинока́мер|а, ы *f.* cine camera (BrE), movie camera

кинокоме́ди|я, и *f.* comedy film, movie

кинокри́тик, а *m.* film critic

кинооперáтор, а *m.* cameraman

киноплёнк|а, и *f.* cine film (BrE), movie film (AmE)

кинорежиссёр, а *m.* film director

киносеáнс, а *m.* (cinema) performance, showing

киностýди|я, и *f.* film studio (BrE), movie studio (AmE)

киносценáри|й, я *m.* screenplay

киносъёмк|а, и *f.* filming, shooting

кинотеáтр, а *m.* cinema (BrE), movie theater (AmE)

кинофи́льм, а *m.* film, movie

кинохро́ник|а, и *f.* newsreel

ки́|нуть, ну, нешь *pf. of* ▶ **кида́ть**

ки́|нуться, нусь, нешься *pf. of* ▶ **кида́ться**

кио́ск, а *m.* kiosk, stall; **газе́тный к.** news stand

ки́п|а, ы *f.* pile, stack

кипари́с, а *m.* (bot.) cypress

кипе́ни|е, я *nt.* boiling; **то́чка ∼я** boiling point

кип|е́ть, лю́, и́шь *impf.* to boil, seethe; **рабо́та ∼е́ла** work was in full swing

Кипр, а *m.* Cyprus

киприо́т, а *m.* Cypriot

киприо́т|ка, ки *f. of* ▶ **киприо́т**

ки́прский *adj.* Cypriot

кипяти́льник, а *m.* kettle, boiler

кипя|ти́ть, чу́, ти́шь *impf.* (*of* ▶ **вскипяти́ть**) to boil

кипят|о́к, ка́ *m.* boiling water

кипячёный *adj.* boiled

кирги́з, а *m.* Kyrgyz

Кирги́зи|я, и *f.* Kyrgyzstan

кирги́з|ка, ки *f. of* ▶ **кирги́з**

кирги́зский *adj.* Kyrgyz

кири́ллиц|а, ы *f.* Cyrillic alphabet

кирилли́ческий *adj.* Cyrillic

кирк|а́, и́ *f.* pick(axe)

кирпи́ч, а́ *m.* **1** brick **2** (*collect.*) bricks **3** (infml, *дорожный знак*) no-entry sign

кисе́л|ь, я́ *m.* kissel (*a kind of blancmange*)

кислоро́д, а *m.* oxygen

ки́сло-сла́д|кий, ∼ок, ∼ка *adj.* sweet-and-sour

кислот|а́, ы́, pl. ∼ы *f.* **1** sourness; acidity **2** (chem.) acid

кисло́тный *adj.* (chem.) acid; **к. дождь** acid rain

ки́с|лый, ∼ел, ∼ла́, ∼ло *adj.* **1** (*яблоко*) sour; (fig.): **∼лое настрое́ние** sour mood **2** (*закисший*) sour, fermented; **∼лая капу́ста** sauerkraut **3** (chem.) acid

кист|ь¹, и, pl. ∼и, ∼е́й *f.* **1** (bot.) cluster, bunch; **к. виногра́да** bunch of grapes **2** (*для рисования*) brush; **маля́рная к.** paintbrush **3** (*на скатерти*) tassel

кист|ь², и, pl. ∼и, ∼е́й *f.* hand

кит, а́ *m.* whale

кита́|ец, йца, pl. ∼йцы, ∼йцев *m.* Chinese

Кита́|й, я *m.* China

кита́й|ский *adj.* Chinese; **∼ая гра́мота** double Dutch

китая́нк|а, и *f. of* ▶ **кита́ец**

китч, а *m.* kitsch

киш|е́ть, и́т *impf.* (+ *i.*) to swarm (with), teem (with)

кише́чник, а *m.* (anat.) bowels, intestines

киш|ка́, ки́, g. pl. ∼о́к *f.* (anat.) gut, intestine

клавеси́н, а *m.* (mus.) harpsichord

клавиату́р|а, ы *f.* keyboard

кла́виш|а, и *f.* key (*of piano, computer, etc.*)

кла́вишны|е, х *m. pl.* keyboard(s) (*musical instrument*)

клад, а *m.* treasure; (fig., infml) treasure

кла́дбищ|е, а *nt.* cemetery, graveyard; (*при церкви*) churchyard

кладов|а́я, о́й *f.* (*для провизии*) pantry, larder; (*для товаров*) storeroom

кла|ду́, дёшь *see* ▶ **класть**

клад|ь, и *f.* (*sg. only*) load; **ручна́я к.** hand luggage (BrE), baggage (AmE)

клан, а *m.* clan

кла́ня|ться, юсь *impf.* (*of* ▶ **поклони́ться**) **1** (+ *d. or* с + *i.*) to bow (to); (*приветствовать*) to greet **2** (*передавать привет*) to send, convey greetings; **∼йтесь ему́ от меня́** give him my regards **3** (+ *d. or* пе́ред + *i.*) (infml, *униженно просить*) to cringe (before); to humiliate oneself (before)

кла́пан, а *m.* valve

кларне́т, а *m.* clarinet

кларнети́ст, а *m.* clarinettist

кларнети́ст|ка, ки *f. of* ▶ **кларнети́ст**

☞ **класс, а** *m.* **1** class **2** (*комната*) classroom

кла́ссик|а, и *f.* the classics

классифика́ци|я, и *f.* classification

классифици́р|овать, ую *impf. and pf.* to classify

классици́зм, а *m.* classicism

☞ **класси́ческий** *adj.* (*музыка, образование, язык*) classical; (*работа, пример, одежда*) classic

кла́сс|ный *adj.* (*of* ▶ **класс**) **1**: **∼ная рабо́та** class work **2** (infml, *отличный*) excellent, great

кла́ссов|ый *adj.* (pol.) class; **∼ая борьба́** class struggle

кла|сть, ду́, дёшь, past ∼л, ∼ла *impf.* **1** (*pf.* **положи́ть**) (*помещать*) to lay; to put; to place **2** (*pf.* **сложи́ть**) (*строить*) to build

клаустрофо́би|я, и *f.* claustrophobia

клёв, а *m.* biting, bite; **сего́дня хоро́ший к.** the fish are biting well today

кл|ева́ть, юю́, юёшь *impf.* (*of* ▶ **клю́нуть**) **1** (*о птице*) to peck (*о рыбе*) to bite

кле́вер, а *m.* (bot.) clover

клевет|а́, ы́ *f.* slander; (*в печати*) libel

клевет|а́ть, щу́, ∼щешь *impf.* (*of* ▶ **оклевета́ть** (*кого*), ▶ **наклевета́ть** (*на кого* + *d.*)) to slander, malign; (*в печати*) to libel; **он оклевета́л меня́/он наклевета́л на меня́** he slandered me; **он клевета́л начáльнику на всех сотру́дников в тече́ние двух лет** he made slanderous remarks/complained to the boss about all the staff over a period of two years; **он наклевета́л мне на вас** he made slanderous remarks/complained to me about you

клеве|щу́, ∼щешь *see* ▶ **клевета́ть**

клёвый *adj.* (sl.) brill, knockout, fantastic

клеёнк|а, и *f.* oilcloth

кле́|ить, ю, ишь *impf.* (*of* ▶ **скле́ить**) to glue; to gum; to paste

кле́|й, я, о ~е, в ~е́/~ю, на ~ю *m.* glue

кле́йк|ий *adj.* sticky; **~ая ле́нта** adhesive tape

клейм|о́, а́, *pl.* **~а** *nt.* brand, stamp

кле́йстер, а *m.* paste

клён, а *m.* maple

клено́вый *adj. of* ▶ **клён**

♂ **кле́тк|а, и** *f.* **1** cage; (*для кур*) coop; (*для кроликов*) hutch **2** (*на бумаге*) square; (*на ткани*) check **3** (anat.): **грудна́я к.** thorax **4** (biol.) cell

кле́тчатый *adj.* checked; **к. плато́к** checked headscarf

клёш, а *m. and indecl. adj.* flare; **брю́ки к.** flared trousers

клещ, а́ *m.* (zool.) tick

клещ|и́, е́й (*no sg.*) pincers, pliers, tongs

♂ **клие́нт, а** *m.* client

клие́нт|ка, ки *f. of* ▶ **клие́нт**

клиенту́р|а, ы *f.* (collect.) clientele

кли́зм|а, ы *f.* (med.) enema

кли́макс, а *m.* menopause

кли́мат, а *m.* climate

климати́ческий *adj.* climatic

клин, а, *pl.* **~ья, ~ьев** *m.* wedge

кли́ник|а, и *f.* clinic

клини́ческий *adj.* clinical

клин|о́к, ка́ *m.* blade

клип, а *m.* video clip

кли́пс|ы, ~ *f. pl.* (*sg.* **~а, ~ы**) clip-on earrings; clip-ons

клич, а *m.* (rhet.) call; **боево́й к.** war cry

кли́чк|а, и *f.* **1** (*животного*) name **2** (*человека*) nickname

клише́ *nt. indecl.* (fig., also fig.) cliché

клозе́т, а *m.* (infml) water closet, W.C.

клок, а́, *pl.* **кло́чья, кло́чьев** *and* **~и́, ~о́в** *m.* rag, shred; **разорва́ть в кло́чья** to tear to shreds

клоко|та́ть, чу́, ~чешь *impf.* to bubble; to gurgle; (*кипеть*) to boil up (also fig.)

клон, а *m.* (biol., etc.) clone

клони́р|овать, ую *impf. and pf.* (biol., etc.) to clone

клон|и́ть, ю́, ~ишь *impf.* **1** to bend; to incline; (*impers.*) **старика́ уже́ ~и́ло ко сну́** the old man was already nodding off **2** (fig., infml) to lead (*conversation*); **куда́ ты ~ишь?** what are you driving at?

клон|и́ться, ю́сь, ~ишься *impf.* **1** to bow, bend **2** (**к** + *d.*) (fig.) to be nearing; to be leading up (to)

клоп, а́ *m.* bedbug

кло́ун, а *m.* clown

♂ **клуб¹, а** *m.* **1** (*общество*) club **2** (*здание*) clubhouse

клуб², а, *pl.* **~ы́, ~о́в** *m.* (*дыма*) puff; **~ы́ пы́ли** clouds of dust

клуб|и́ться, и́тся *impf.* to swirl; to curl, wreathe

клубни́к|а, и *f.* (cultivated) strawberry

клуб|о́к, ка́ *m.* **1** ball; **сверну́ться ~ко́м, в к.** to roll oneself up into a ball **2** (fig., *запутанное сцепление чего-н.*) tangle, mass; **к. противоре́чий** a mass of contradictions

клу́мб|а, ы *f.* (flower) bed

клык, а́ *m.* **1** (*у человека*) canine (tooth) **2** (*у животного*) fang; (*бивень*) tusk

клюв, а *m.* beak; bill

клю́кв|а, ы *f.* cranberry

клю́н|уть, у, ешь *pf. of* ▶ **клева́ть**

♂ **ключ¹, а́** *m.* key; **запере́ть на к.** to lock; **га́ечный к.** spanner, wrench

♂ **ключ², а́** *m.* (*источник*) spring; source; **бить ~о́м** to spout; jet; (fig.) to be in full swing

♂ **ключ|ево́й** *adj. of* ▶ **ключ¹**; **~евы́е о́трасли промы́шленности** key industries

ключи́ц|а, ы *f.* (anat.) collarbone

клю́шк|а, и *f.* (*гольф*) (golf) club; (*хоккей*) (hockey) stick

кл|юю́, юёшь *see* ▶ **клева́ть**

кля́кс|а, ы *f.* blot, smudge

кля́нч|ить, у, ишь *impf.* (infml) (**у** + *g.*) to pester, nag (*sb for*); **к. де́ньги у кого́-н.** to pester sb for money

кляп, а *m.* gag; **засу́нуть к. в рот** (+ *d.*) to gag

кля|́сться, ну́сь, нёшься, *past* **~лся, ~ла́сь** *impf.* (*of* ▶ **покля́сться**) (**в** + *p. or* + *inf. or* + **что**) to swear, vow; **к. отомсти́ть** to vow vengeance; **к. че́стью** to swear on one's honour (BrE), honor (AmE)

кля́тв|а, ы *f.* oath, vow; **дать ~у** to take an oath

кля́уз|а, ы *f.* (infml) petty slander, malicious gossip

♂ **км** (*abbr. of* **киломе́тр**) km, kilometre(s) (BrE), kilometer(s) (AmE)

КНДР *f. indecl.* (*abbr. of* **Коре́йская Наро́дно-Демократи́ческая Респу́блика**) Democratic People's Republic of Korea

♂ **кни́г|а, и** *f.* book

книгоизда́тел|ь, я *m.* publisher

книготорго́в|ец, ца *m.* bookseller

книготорго́вл|я, и *f.* book trade

кни́жк|а, и *f.* **1** *dim. of* ▶ **кни́га**; **записна́я к.** notebook **2** (*документ*) book, card; **че́ковая к.** chequebook (BrE), checkbook (AmE)

кни́жн|ый *adj.* **1** *adj. of* ▶ **кни́га**; **~ая по́лка** bookshelf; **к. шкаф** bookcase **2** (*отвлечённый*) bookish; **к. червь** bookworm

кни́зу *adv.* downwards

♂ **кно́пк|а, и** *f.* **1** (*гвоздик*) drawing pin (BrE), thumbtack (AmE); **прикрепи́ть ~ой** to pin **2** (*застёжка*) press stud, popper (BrE), snap (AmE) **3** (elec.) button; knob

КНР *f. indecl.* (*abbr. of* **Кита́йская Наро́дная Респу́блика**) PRC (People's Republic of China)

кнут, а́ *m.* whip

княги́н|я, и *f.* princess (*wife of prince*)

княз|ь, я, *pl.* **~ья́, ~е́й** *m.* prince; **вели́кий к.** grand duke

---

⚔ **ко** *see* ▶ **к**

коали́ци|я, и *f.* (pol.) coalition

ко́бр|а, ы *f.* cobra

кобур|а́, ы́ *f.* holster

кобы́л|а, ы *f.* (*лошадь*) mare

ко́ваный *adj.* **1** forged; hammered **2** (fig.) terse

кова́р|ный, ~ен, ~на *adj.* crafty; treacherous

кова́ть, кую́, куёшь *impf.* **1** (*pf.* вы́~) to forge (also fig.); (*железо*) to hammer **2** (*pf.* под~) to shoe (*horses*)

ковбо́|й, я *m.* cowboy

ков|ёр, ра́ *m.* carpet; (*маленький*) rug; mat

ко́врик, а *m.* rug; mat; **к. для мы́ши** mouse mat (BrE), mouse pad (AmE)

ковче́г, а *m.* ark; **Но́ев к.** Noah's ark

ковш, а́ *m.* **1** scoop, ladle **2** (tech.) bucket

ковыля́|ть, ю *impf.* (infml) to hobble

ковыр|ну́ть, ну́, нёшь *pf. of* ▶ **ковыря́ть**

ковыр|я́ть, я́ю *impf.* (*of* ▶ **ковырну́ть**) to dig into; (**в** + *p.*) to pick (at); **к. в зуба́х/носу́** to pick one's teeth/nose

когда́[1] *adv.* **1** interrog. *and* rel. when **2**: **к. (бы) ни** whenever; **к. бы вы ни пришли́** whenever you come **3** (infml): **к. ..., к.** sometimes ..., sometimes; **я занима́юсь к. у́тром, к. ве́чером** sometimes I work in the morning, sometimes in the evening **4** (infml): **к. как** it depends

⚔ **когда́[2]** *conj.* when; while; as; **я встре́тил её, к. шёл домо́й** I met her as I was going home

когда́-либо *adv.* = **когда́-нибудь**

когда́-нибудь *adv.* **1** (*в будущем*) some time, some day **2** (*в вопросах*) ever; **вы бы́ли к-н. в Кита́е?** have you ever been to China?

когда́-то *adv.* once; some time; formerly

кого́ *a. and g. of* ▶ **кто**

ко́г|оть, тя, *pl.* **~ти, ~те́й** *m.* claw

⚔ **код, а** *m.* code

⚔ **ко́декс, а** *m.* (law, also fig.) code; **гражда́нский к.** civil code; **уголо́вный к.** criminal code

ко́дов|ый *adj. of* ▶ **код**; **~ое назва́ние** code name

ко́е-где́ *adv.* here and there, in places

ко́е-ка́к *adv.* **1** (*плохо, небрежно*) anyhow **2** (*с трудом*) somehow (or other), just; **к.-к. мы доплы́ли до того́ бе́рега** somehow we managed to swim to the other side

ко́е-како́й, ко́е-како́го *pron.* some

ко́е-кто́, ко́е-кого́ *pron.* somebody; some people

ко́е-что́, ко́е-чего́ *pron.* something; (*немного*) a little

⚔ **ко́ж|а, и** *f.* **1** (*у человека и животных*) skin; (*у крупных животных*) hide **2** (*материал*) leather

ко́жаный *adj.* leather

кожур|а́, ы́ *f.* rind, peel, skin

коз|а́, ы́, *pl.* **~ы** *f.* **1** (*вид*) goat **2** (*самка козла*) nanny goat

коз|ёл, ла́ *m.* (*животное*) billy goat

Козеро́г, а *m.* (*созвездие*) Capricorn; **тро́пик ~a** (geog.) Tropic of Capricorn

ко́з|ий *adj. of* ▶ **коза́**; **~ье молоко́** goat's milk

козл|ёнок, ёнка, *pl.* **~я́та, ~я́т** *m.* kid

козл|и́ный *adj. of* ▶ **козёл**; **~и́ная боро́дка** goatee

козл|я́та, я́т *see* ▶ **козлёнок**

козыр|ёк, ька́ *m.* (cap) peak; **взять под к.** (+ *d.*) to salute

ко́зыр|ь, я, *pl.* **~и, ~е́й** *m.* (cards, also fig.) trump

ко́йк|а, и *f.* **1** (*на судне*) berth, bunk **2** (*в больнице*) bed

койо́т, а *m.* coyote

кока́ин, а *m.* cocaine

кока́рд|а, ы *f.* cockade

ко́кер-спание́л|ь, я, м. cocker spaniel

коке́тк|а, и *f.* coquette, flirt

коке́тлив|ый, ~, ~а *adj.* coquettish, flirtatious

коклю́ш, а *m.* whooping cough

ко́кон, а *m.* cocoon

коко́с, а *m.* **1** (*дерево*) coconut palm **2** (*плод*) coconut

кокте́йл|ь, я, м. cocktail; (*встреча*) cocktail party; **моло́чный к.** milk shake

кол, а́ *m.* **1** (*pl.* **~ья, ~ьев**) stake, picket **2** (*pl.* **~ы́, ~о́в**) (infml, *низшая школьная отметка*) a 'very poor' (*mark*)

ко́лб|а, ы *f.* (chem.) flask

колбас|а́, ы́, *pl.* **~ы** *f.* sausage

колго́т|ки, ок (*no sg.*) tights

колд|ова́ть, у́ю *impf.* to practise witchcraft

колдовств|о́, а́ *nt.* witchcraft, sorcery, magic

колду́н, а́ *m.* sorcerer, magician, wizard

колду́н|ья, ьи, *g. pl.* **~ий** *f.* witch, sorceress

колеба́ни|е, я *nt.* **1** (phys.) oscillation, vibration; **к. ма́ятника** swing of the pendulum **2** (*изменение*) fluctuation, variation **3** (fig., *сомнение*) hesitation, wavering, vacillation

колеб|а́ть, ~лю, ~лешь *impf.* (*of* ▶ **поколеба́ть**) to shake

колеб|а́ться, ~люсь, ~лешься *impf.* (*of* ▶ **поколеба́ться 1**) **1** to shake to and fro, sway; (phys.) to oscillate **2** (*изменяться*) to fluctuate, vary **3** (fig., *не решаться*) to hesitate; to waver, vacillate

коле́н|о, а *nt.* **1** (*pl.* **~и, ~ей, ~ям**) knee; **стать на ~и (пе́ред)** to kneel (to); **по к., по ~и** knee-deep, up to one's knees **2** (*pl. only:* **~и, ~ей, ~ям**) lap; **сиде́ть у кого́-н. на ~ях** to sit on sb's lap **3** (*pl.* **~ья, ~ьев**) (tech.) knee, joint

колесни́ц|а, ы *f.* chariot

⚔ **колес|о́, а́,** *pl.* **~а** *nt.* wheel; **запасно́е к.** spare wheel; **рулево́е к.** driving wheel

коле|я́, и́ *f.* **1** rut; (fig.): **войти́ в ~ю́** to settle down (again); **вы́битый из ~и́** unsettled **2** (rail.) track; gauge

коли́бри *f. and m. indecl.* (zool.) hummingbird

коли́т, а *m.* (med.) colitis

К

коли́чественн|ый adj. quantitative; ~ое числи́тельное cardinal number; ~ое смягче́ние (econ.) quantitative easing

◆ **коли́честв|о**, а nt. quantity, amount; number

коллаборациони́ст, а m. (pol., pej.) collaborator

колла́ж, а m. collage

колла́пс, а m. collapse

◆ **коллє́г|а**, и c.g. colleague

коллє́ги|я, и f. board; к. адвока́тов the Bar; к. вы́борщиков electoral college

ко́лледж, а m. college

◆ **коллекти́в**, а m. collective, team; (in many phrr. does not require separate translation) нау́чный к. (the) scientists

коллекти́вн|ый, ~ен, ~на adj. collective; joint; ~ное владе́ние joint ownership

коллекционе́р, а m. collector

коллекциони́р|овать, ую impf. to collect

◆ **колле́кци|я**, и f. collection

ко́лли f. indecl. collie (dog)

коло́д|а¹, ы f. block, log

коло́д|а², ы f. (карт) pack (of cards)

коло́д|ец, ца m. **1** well **2** (tech.) shaft

ко́локол, а, pl. ~а́, ~о́в m. bell

колоко́л|ьня, ьни, g. pl. ~ен f. bell tower

колоко́льчик, а m. **1** small bell **2** (bot.) campanula

колониа́льный adj. colonial

колониза́ци|я, и f. colonization

колонизи́р|овать, ую impf. and pf. to colonize

коло́ни|я, и f. colony; settlement

коло́нк|а, и f. **1** dim. of ▶ коло́нна **2** (для нагре́ва воды́) geyser (BrE), water heater **3** (на у́лице) standpipe; water pump **4**: бензи́новая к. petrol pump (BrE), gas pump (AmE) **5** (столбе́ц) column (in a table, in a newspaper) **6** (infml, громкоговори́тель) (loud)speaker

коло́нн|а, ы f. column; (mil.): та́нковая к. tank column

колори́т, а m. colouring, colour (BrE); coloring, color (AmE); (fig.): ме́стный к. local colour (BrE), color (AmE)

колори́тн|ый, ~ен, ~на adj. colourful (BrE), colorful (AmE); graphic (also fig.)

ко́лос, а, pl. ~ья, ~ьев m. (agric.) ear, spike

коло́сс, а m. colossus

колосса́льн|ый, ~ен, ~ьна adj. colossal; (infml) terrific, great

коло|ти́ть, чу́, ~тишь impf. (of ▶ поколоти́ть) **1** (impf. only) (по + d. or в + a.) to strike (on); to batter (on), pound (on); к. в дверь to bang on the door **2** (infml, бить) to thrash, beat

коло́|ть¹, ю́, ~ешь impf. (of ▶ расколо́ть 1) to break, chop, split; к. дрова́ to chop wood; к. оре́хи to crack nuts

◆ key word

коло́|ть², ю́, ~ешь impf. **1** (pf. y~) (була́вкой) to prick **2** (pf. за~) (ра́нить, убива́ть чем-нибудь о́стрым) to stab; (impers.) у меня́ ~ет в боку́ I've got a stitch in my side **3** (pf. за~) (живо́тных) to slaughter

коло́|ться¹, ю́сь, ~ешься impf., pass. of ▶ коло́ть¹

коло́|ться², ю́сь, ~ешься impf. **1** (причиня́ть уко́л) to be prickly **2** (pf. y~) (infml, о наркома́не) to inject oneself; to be on drugs

колпа́к, á m. **1** cap **2** (ла́мпы) lampshade; (tech.) cowl

колумби́|ец, йца m. Colombian

колумби́й|ка, ки f. of ▶ колумби́ец

колумби́йский adj. Colombian

Колу́мби|я, и f. Colombia

колу́н, á m. chopper, hatchet

колхо́з, а m. (abbr. of коллекти́вное хозя́йство) collective farm

колхо́зник, а m. member of collective farm

колхо́зн|ица, ицы f. of ▶ колхо́зник

колыбе́л|ь, и f. cradle; (fig.): с ~и from the cradle

колыбе́льн|ый adj. of ▶ колыбе́ль; ~ная (пе́сня) lullaby

колы́|хаться, ~шется impf. (of ▶ колыхну́ться) (о ве́тках) to sway; (о мо́ре) to heave; (о фла́гах) to flutter

колых|ну́ться, ну́сь, нёшься pf. of ▶ колыха́ться

колье́ m. indecl. necklace

коль|ну́ть, ну́, нёшь inst. pf. of ▶ коло́ть²

кольра́би f. indecl. (bot.) kohlrabi

кольцев|о́й adj. annular; circular; ~а́я доро́га ring road; ~а́я развя́зка roundabout

коль|цо́, ~ца́, pl. ~ца, ~е́ц, ~цам nt. ring; обруча́льное к. wedding ring

колю́ч|ий, ~, ~а adj. prickly; thorny; (fig.) sharp, biting; ~ая про́волока barbed wire

колю́чк|а, и f. (infml) prickle; thorn; (у ежа́) quill

коля́ск|а, и f. **1** (экипа́ж) carriage **2**: (де́тская) к. pram (BrE), baby carriage (AmE); (раскладна́я) pushchair (BrE), stroller (AmE); инвали́дная к. wheelchair **3** (у мотоцикла) sidecar

ком¹, а, pl. ~ья, ~ьев m. lump; ball; (fig.): к. в го́рле lump in the throat

ком² p. of ▶ кто

ком... comb. form, abbr. of **1** ▶ коммунисти́ческий **2** ▶ команди́р

ко́м|а, ы f. (med.) coma

◆ **кома́нд|а**, ы f. **1** (прика́з) command, order; дать ~у to give a command **2** (mil., отря́д) party, detachment, crew; (naut.) crew; пожа́рная к. fire brigade **3** (sport) team

команди́р, а m. (mil.) commander, commanding officer

командиро́вк|а, и f. business trip; е́хать в ~у to go on a business trip; он в ~е he is away on business

кома́нд|ный adj.: ∼ная игра́ team game
кома́ндовани|е, я nt. **1** commanding, command; приня́ть к. (над + i.) to take command (of, over) **2** (collect.) command
кома́нд|овать, ую impf. (pf. ▶ скома́ндовать) **1** to give orders **2** (no pf.) (+ i.) (быть команди́ром) to command, be in command (of)
кома́ндующ|ий, его m. commander
кома́р, а́ m. mosquito
комба́йн, а m. (tech.) combine; **зерново́й к.** combine harvester; **ку́хонный к.** food processor
комбина́т, а m. industrial complex; plant
комбина́ци|я¹, и f. **1** combination **2** (fig.) scheme, system; (pol., sport) manoeuvre (BrE), maneuver (AmE)
комбина́ци|я², и f. (же́нское бельё) slip
комбинезо́н, а m. overalls; dungarees
комбини́р|овать, ую impf. (of ▶ скомбини́ровать) to combine, arrange
коме́ди|я, и f. **1** comedy **2** (fig.) farce; лома́ть ∼ю to put on an act
коменда́нт, а m. **1** (mil.) commandant **2** (обще́ственного зда́ния) manager; warden; **к. общежи́тия** warden of a hostel
коменда́нтский adj. of ▶ комендант; **к. час** (mil.) curfew
коме́т|а, ы f. comet
ко́мик, а m. **1** comic actor **2** (fig.) comedian
ко́микс, а m. (кни́жка) comic (book); (се́рия рису́нков) comic strip
комисса́р, а m. commissar, commissioner; **верхо́вный к.** high commissioner
комиссариа́т, а m. commissariat
комисс|ио́нный adj.: **к. магази́н** second-hand shop (where goods are sold on commission); (as pl. n. ∼ио́нные, ∼ио́нных) (comm.) commission
✍ **коми́сси|я, и** f. commission, committee
✍ **комите́т, а** m. committee
коми́ческий adj. **1** comic **2** (смешно́й) comical, funny
ко́мка|ть, ю impf. (of ▶ ско́мкать) to crumple
✍ **коммента́ри|й, я** m. **1** (разъясни́тельные замеча́ния) commentary **2** (in pl.) (рассужде́ния) comment; ∼и изли́шни comment is superfluous; без ∼ев! no comment!
коммента́тор, а m. commentator
коммента́р|овать, ую impf. and pf. to comment (upon)
коммерса́нт, а m. businessman
комме́рци|я, и f. commerce, trade
✍ **комме́рческий** adj. **1** commercial; **к. флот** merchant navy **2** (негосуда́рственный) private
коммивояжёр, а m. commercial traveller (BrE), travelling salesman (BrE), traveling salesman (AmE)
комму́н|а, ы f. commune

коммуна́лк|а, и f. (infml) 'communal' flat (BrE), apartment (AmE)
коммуна́льн|ый adj. **1** communal; municipal; ∼ая кварти́ра 'communal' flat (in which kitchen, bathroom, and toilet are shared by several tenants); ∼ые услу́ги public utilities **2** adj. of ▶ комму́на
коммуни́зм, а m. communism
коммуника́бел|ьный, ∼ен, ∼ьна adj. sociable, communicative
коммуника́ци|я, и f. communication; (mil.) line of communication
коммуни́ст, а m. communist
коммунисти́ческий adj. communist
коммуни́ст|ка, ки f. of ▶ коммуни́ст
коммута́тор, а m. **1** (elec.) commutator **2** (teleph.) switchboard
коммюнике́ nt. indecl. communiqué
✍ **ко́мнат|а, ы** f. room
ко́мнатн|ый adj. **1** adj. of ▶ ко́мната **2** (дома́шний) indoor; ∼ые расте́ния house plants; ∼ая температу́ра room temperature
компа́кт-ди́ск, а m. compact disc, CD; **про́игрыватель** (m.) ∼ов compact disc or CD player
компа́ктн|ый, ∼ен, ∼на adj. compact; (fig.) concise
✍ **компа́ни|я, и** f. company; соста́вить кому́-н. ∼ю to keep sb company; за ∼ю for company
компаньо́н, а m. **1** (comm.) partner **2** (това́рищ) companion
компаньо́н|ка, ки f. **1** f. of ▶ компаньон **2** (lady's) companion; chaperone
компа́рти|я, и f. Communist Party
компенса́ци|я, и f. compensation
компенси́р|овать, ую impf. and pf. to compensate
компете́нтн|ый, ∼ен, ∼на adj. competent; **к. исто́чник** reliable source
компете́нци|я, и f. (о́бласть зна́ния) competence; (круг полномо́чий) jurisdiction; **э́то не в мое́й ∼и** it is beyond my scope
✍ **ко́мплекс, а** m. complex; (набо́р) set; **к. неполноце́нности** inferiority complex; **к. мероприя́тий** package of measures
✍ **ко́мплексный** adj. all-embracing, all-in; **к. обе́д** table d'hôte dinner
комплекс|ова́ть, у́ю impf. (infml) to suffer from complexes; to feel inadequate, insecure
✍ **компле́кт, а** m. set; kit; **к. белья́** bedding, bedclothes
компле́кци|я, и f. build
комплиме́нт, а m. compliment; **сде́лать к.** (+ d.) to pay a compliment (to)
компози́тор, а m. (mus.) composer
компози́ци|я, и f. composition
✍ **компоне́нт, а** m. component
компо́т, а m. compote, stewed fruit
компре́сс, а m. (med.) compress; **поста́вить к.** to apply a compress
компре́ссор, а m. (tech., med.) compressor

компрома́т, а *m.* (*abbr. of* **компромети́рующий материа́л**) compromising material

компромети́р|овать, ую *impf.* (*of* ▶ **скомпромети́ровать**) to compromise

компроми́сс, а *m.* compromise; **идти́ на к.** to make a compromise, meet halfway

◆ **компью́тер, а** *m.* computer; **порта́тивный к.** laptop (computer); **со зна́нием ~а** computer literate

◆ **компью́тер|ный** *adj. of* ▶ **компью́тер**; **~ная игра́** computer game

компью́терщик, а *m.* (*infml*) computer specialist; computer buff

кому́ *d. of* ▶ **кто**

комфо́рт, а *m.* comfort

комфорта́бел|ьный, ~ен, ~ьна *adj.* comfortable

конве́йер, а *m.* (tech.) conveyor (*belt*); **сбо́рочный к.** assembly line

конве́рси|я, и *f.* (econ., fin.) conversion

конве́рт, а *m.* **❶** (*для пи́сем*) envelope **❷** (*для грампласти́нки*) sleeve

конверти́р|овать, ую *impf. and pf.* (fin.) to convert

конверти́руемый *adj.* (fin.) convertible

конво́й, я *m.* escort

конво́|й, я *m.* escort

конву́льси|я, и *f.* (med.) convulsion

Ко́нго *nt. indecl.* Congo; **Демократи́ческая Респу́блика Ко́нго** Democratic Republic of the Congo (*formerly Zaire*)

конголе́з|ец, ца *m.* Congolese

конголе́з|ка, ки *f. of* ▶ **конголе́зец**

конголе́зский *adj.* Congolese

конгре́сс, а *m.* congress; (*в США*) Congress

конгрессме́н, а *m.* congressman

конденса́т, а *m.* condensation

конденса́ци|я, и *f.* condensation

конди́тер, а *m.* confectioner, pastry cook

конди́терск|ая, ой *f.* (*продаю́щая конфе́ты*) confectioner's, sweet shop (BrE), candy store (AmE); (*продаю́щая то́рты*) cake shop, pastry shop

кондиционе́р, а *m.* air conditioner

ко́ндор, а *m.* (zool.) condor

конду́ктор, а, *pl.* **~а́, ~о́в** *m.* (*челове́к*) conductor (*of bus, tram*); (rail.) guard

кон|ёк, ька́ *m.* **❶** *dim. of* ▶ **конь**; **морско́й к.** (zool.) sea horse **❷** (fig., infml) hobby horse; hobby; **сесть на своего́ ~ька́** to mount one's hobby horse **❸** *see* ▶ **конько́й**

◆ **кон|е́ц, ца́** *m.* **❶** end; **в ~це́ ~цо́в** in the end, after all; **положи́ть к.** (+ *d.*) to put an end to; **своди́ть ~цы́ с ~ца́ми** (infml) to make both ends meet **❷** (infml, *расстоя́ние, путь*) distance, way; **в оди́н к.** one way; **в о́ба ~ца́** there and back, return; **биле́т в о́ба ~ца́** return ticket

◆ **коне́чно** *adv.* of course, certainly

◆ **коне́чност|ь, и** *f.* (anat.) extremity

◆ **коне́ч|ный, ~ен, ~на** *adj.* **❶** final, last; ultimate; **~ная ста́нция** terminus; **~ная цель** ultimate aim; **в ~ном ито́ге, счёте** ultimately, in the last analysis **❷** (*име́ющий коне́ц*) finite

кони́н|а, ы (*no pl.*) *f.* horseflesh

◆ **конкре́т|ный, ~ен, ~на** *adj.* concrete; specific

конкуре́нт, а *m.* competitor; rival

конкуре́нт|ка, ки *f. of* ▶ **конкуре́нт**

конкурентоспосо́бност|ь, и *f.* competitiveness

конкурентоспосо́б|ный, ~ен, ~на *adj.* competitive

конкуре́нци|я, и *f.* competition; **вне ~и** unrivalled

конкури́р|овать, ую *impf.* (**с** + *i.*) to compete (with)

◆ **ко́нкурс, а** *m.* competition; contest

конкурса́нт, а *m.* competitor; contestant

конкурса́нт|ка, ки *f. of* ▶ **конкурса́нт**

ко́нкурсный *adj. of* ▶ **ко́нкурс**; **к. экза́мен** competitive examination

ко́нник, а *m.* cavalryman

ко́нниц|а, ы *f.* cavalry

ко́нный *adj. of* ▶ **конь**; horse; mounted; equestrian; **к. спорт** equestrianism

конопл|я́, и́ *f.* (bot.) hemp; (*нарко́тик*) cannabis

консерва́нт, а *m.* preservative

консервати́в|ный, ~ен, ~на *adj.* conservative

консервати́зм, а *m.* conservatism

консерва́тор, а *m.* (esp. pol.) conservative

консервато́ри|я, и *f.* conservatoire, music college

консерви́рован|ный, ~, ~а *p.p.p. of* ▶ **консерви́ровать** *and adj.*: **~ные фру́кты** bottled fruit, canned fruit

консерви́р|овать, ую *impf. and pf.* (*pf. also* **за~**) to preserve; to can; to bottle

консе́рв|ный *adj. of* ▶ **консе́рвы**; **~ная ба́нка** tin can; **к. нож** can opener

консе́рв|ы, ов (*no sg.*) canned food

консолида́ци|я, и *f.* consolidation

консо́л|ь, и *f.* (comput.) console

конспе́кт, а *m.* outline, summary

конспирати́в|ный, ~ен, ~на *adj.* secret, clandestine

конспира́тор, а *m.* conspirator

констати́р|овать, ую *impf. and pf.* to ascertain; to establish; **к. смерть** to certify death; **к. факт** to establish a fact

конституцио́нный *adj.* (pol.) constitutional

конститу́ци|я, и *f.* (pol., med.) constitution

констру́и́р|овать, ую *impf. and pf.* (*pf. also* **с~**) (*стро́ить*) to construct; (*проекти́ровать*) to design

конструктиви́зм, а *m.* (art) constructivism

конструкти́в|ный, ~ен, ~на *adj.*
1 structural; construction **2** (*критика*) constructive

констру́ктор, а *m.* designer

констру́ктор|ский *adj. of* ▸ констру́ктор; ~ское бюро́ design office

🖉 **констру́кци|я**, и *f.* **1** (*состав*) construction; design **2** (*сооружение*) structure

ко́нсул, а *m.* consul

ко́нсульств|о, а *nt.* consulate

консульта́нт, а *m.* consultant, adviser; (*в вузе*) tutor

🖉 **консульта́ци|я**, и *f.* **1** consultation; specialist advice **2** (*учреждение*) advice bureau; же́нская к. antenatal (BrE), prenatal (AmE) clinic; gynaecological (BrE), gynecological (AmE) clinic; юриди́ческая к. legal advice office

консульти́р|овать, ую *impf.* (*pf.* **про~**) to advise; (*в вузе*) to act as tutor (to)

консульти́роваться, уюсь *impf.* (*of* ▸ проконсульти́роваться) (с + *i.*) to consult

🖉 **конта́кт**, а *m.* contact; вступи́ть в к. с кем-н. to come into contact, get in touch with sb

конта́кт|ный, ~ен, ~на *adj.* **1** contact; к. телефо́н contact number; ~ные ли́нзы (med.) contact lenses **2** (infml, *о человеке*) sociable

конте́йнер, а *m.* container

конте́кст, а *m.* context

континге́нт, а *m.* contingent; batch; к. войск a military force; к. новобра́нцев batch, squad of recruits

контине́нт, а *m.* continent

континента́льный *adj.* continental

конто́р|а, ы *f.* office, bureau

контраба́нд|а, ы *f.* **1** (*действие*) contraband, smuggling; занима́ться ~ой to smuggle **2** (*товары*) contraband

контрабанди́ст, а *m.* smuggler

контрабанди́ст|ка, ки *f. of* ▸ контрабанди́ст

контраба́с, а *m.* (mus.) double bass

контрабаси́ст, а *m.* double bass player

контрабаси́ст|ка, ки *f. of* ▸ контрабаси́ст

🖉 **контра́кт**, а *m.* contract

контра́ктник, а *m.* (infml) contract worker

контра́льто *nt. indecl.* (mus.) (*голос*) contralto; (*f. indecl.*) (infml, *певица*) contralto

контра́ст, а *m.* contrast; по ~у (с + *i.*) by contrast (with)

контра́ст|ный, ~ен, ~на *adj.* contrasting

контрата́к|а, и *f.* (mil., sport) counter-attack

контрацепти́в, а *m.* contraceptive

контролёр, а *m.* inspector; (*билетов*) ticket collector

контроли́р|овать, ую *impf.* (*of* ▸ проконтроли́ровать) (*проверять*) to check; (*держать под своим контролем*) to control

🖉 **контро́л|ь**, я *m.* **1** control **2** (*проверка*) check(ing); inspection; (tech., mil.)

monitoring; (mil.) verification

контро́льно-пропускно́й *adj.*: к. пункт checkpoint

контро́ль|ный *adj. of* ▸ контро́ль; ~ная рабо́та test

контрразве́дк|а, и *f.* counter-espionage; counter-intelligence

контрреволю́ци|я, и *f.* counter-revolution

конту́зи|я, и *f.* contusion, bruising; (*при разрыве снаряда*) shell shock

ко́нтур, а *m.* **1** contour **2** (elec.) circuit

конур|а́, ы́ *f.* kennel; (fig.) hovel, dump

ко́нус, а *m.* cone

конфедера́ци|я, и *f.* confederation

конферансье́ *m. indecl.* (theatr.) compère, master of ceremonies (*abbr.* MC)

конфере́нц-за́л, а *m.* conference hall

🖉 **конфере́нци|я**, и *f.* conference

конфе́сси|я, и *f.* confession, faith

конфе́т|а, ы *f.* sweet; шокола́дная к. chocolate

конфигура́ци|я, и *f.* configuration

конфиденциа́льность, и *f.* confidentiality

конфиденциа́л|ьный, ~ен, ~ьна *adj.* confidential

конфиска́ци|я, и *f.* confiscation, seizure

конфиск|ова́ть, у́ю *impf. and pf.* to confiscate

🖉 **конфли́кт**, а *m.* conflict

конфликт|ова́ть, у́ю *impf.* (с + *i.*) (infml) to clash (with), come up (against)

конфо́рк|а, и *f.* ring (*on cooker*)

конфронта́ци|я, и *f.* confrontation, showdown

конфу́з, а *m.* (infml) discomfiture, embarrassment

концентра́т, а *m.* concentrate

концентрацио́нный *adj.*: к. ла́герь concentration camp

концентра́ци|я, и *f.* concentration

концентри́рованный *p.p.p. of* ▸ концентри́ровать *and adj.* concentrated

концентри́р|овать, ую *impf.* (*of* ▸ сконцентри́ровать) to concentrate; (mil.) to mass

концентри́р|оваться, уюсь *impf.* (*of* ▸ сконцентри́роваться) **1** to mass, collect **2** (fig.) (на + *p.*) to concentrate

концептуа́л|ьный, ~ен, ~ьна *adj.* conceptual

🖉 **конце́пци|я**, и *f.* conception, idea

конце́рн, а *m.* (econ.) concern

🖉 **конце́рт**, а *m.* (mus.) **1** concert; recital; симфони́ческий к. symphony concert; быть на ~е to be at a concert **2** (*произведение*) concerto

конце́сси|я, и *f.* (econ.) concession

концла́гер|ь, я *m.* (*abbr. of* концентрацио́нный ла́герь) concentration camp

концо́вк|а, и *f.* ending

конч|а́ть, а́ю *impf. of* ▸ ко́нчить

К

конч|а́ться, а́юсь *impf. of* ▶ **ко́нчиться**

ко́нч|енный *p.p.p. of* ▶ **ко́нчить**; (*as int.*) ~**ено!** enough!; всё ~**ено!** it's all over!

ко́нчик, а *m.* tip; point; на ~**е** языка́ on the tip of one's tongue

кончи́н|а, ы *f.* (rhet.) decease, demise

ко́нч|ить, у, ишь *pf.* (*of* ▶ **конча́ть**) **1** to finish, end; на э́том он ~**ил** here he stopped; к. шко́лу to finish/leave school; к. университе́т to graduate; к. (жизнь) самоуби́йством to commit suicide; пло́хо к. to come to a bad end **2** (c + *i.*) to be finished (with), give up **3** (+ *inf.*) to stop **4** (infml) to come (= have an orgasm)

ко́нч|иться, усь, ишься *pf.* (*of* ▶ **конча́ться**) (+ *i.*) to end (in), finish (by); to come to an end; де́ло ~**илось** ниче́м it came to nothing

конъюнкту́р|а, ы *f.* **1** state of affairs, juncture; междунаро́дная к. international situation **2** (econ.) state of the market

конъюнкту́р|ный 1 *adj. of* ▶ **конъюнкту́ра** 2; ~**ные це́ны** (free) market prices **2** (pej., *поведение, человек*) ready to compromise; opportunistic

кон|ь, я́, *pl.* ~**и,** ~**е́й** *m.* **1** horse **2** (*шахматы*) knight

конь|ки́, ько́в *m. pl.* (*sg.* ~**ёк,** ~**ька́**) skates; ро́ликовые к. roller skates; ката́ться на ~**ька́х** to skate

конькобе́ж|ец, ца *m.* skater

конькобе́жный *adj.* skating; к. спорт skating

конья́к, á ý *m.* brandy

ко́нюх, а *m.* groom, stableman

конюш|ня, ни, *g. pl.* ~**ен** *f.* stable

кооперати́в, а *m.* **1** (*организация*) cooperative society **2** (infml) (*магазин*) cooperative store; (*квартира*) flat in housing cooperative

кооперати́вный *adj.* cooperative

координа́т|а, ы *f.* (math.) coordinate; (*in pl.*) (infml) contact details (*address, telephone number, etc.*)

координа́ци|я, и *f.* coordination

коп|а́ть, а́ю *impf.* **1** (*pf.* вс~) to dig **2** (*pf.* вы́~) to dig up, dig out

копа́|ться, юсь *impf.* **1** (в + *p.*) (*в сундуке*) to rummage (in); (*в песке*) to root around (in); (fig.): к. в душе́ to be given to soul-searching **2** (infml) (c + *i.*) (*канителиться*) to dawdle (over) **3** *pass. of* ▶ **копа́ть**

копе́йк|а, и, *g. pl.* **копе́ек** *f.* kopek

Копенга́ген, а *m.* Copenhagen

ко́п|и, ей *f. pl.* (*sg.* ~**ь,** ~**и**) mines

копи́лк|а, и *f.* money box

копира́йт, а *m.* copyright

копи́р|овать, ую *impf.* (*of* ▶ **скопи́ровать**) to copy; to imitate, mimic

коп|и́ть, лю́, ~**ишь** *impf.* (*of* ▶ **накопи́ть**) to accumulate, amass; to store up; к. де́ньги to save up; (fig.): к. си́лы to save one's strength

коп|и́ться, ~**ится** *impf.* (*of* ▶ **накопи́ться**) to accumulate

ко́пи|я, и *f.* copy; печа́тная к. (comput.) hard copy; резе́рвная к. (comput.) backup; снять ~**ю** (c + *g.*) to copy, make a copy (of)

коп|на́, ны́, *pl.* ~**ны,** ~**ён,** ~**на́м** *f.* shock, stook (*of corn*); к. се́на haycock; к. воло́с shock of hair

ко́пот|ь, и *f.* soot; lampblack

копош|и́ться, у́сь, и́шься *impf.* **1** (*о насекомых*) to swarm **2** (fig., infml, *о мыслях*) to stir, creep in **3** (infml, *возиться*) to potter about

коп|ти́ть, чу́, ти́шь *impf. of* ▶ **закопти́ть**

копчёный *adj.* smoked

коп|чу́, ти́шь *see* ▶ **копти́ть**

копы́тн|ый *adj.* (zool.) hoofed, ungulate; (*as pl. n.* ~**ые,** ~**ых**) ungulates

копы́т|о, а *nt.* hoof

копь *see* ▶ **ко́пи**

копь|ё, я́, *pl.* ~**я,** ~**ий,** ~**ьям** *nt.* spear, lance

кор|а́, ы́ *f.* **1** (bot.) bark **2** (anat.): к. головно́го мо́зга cerebral cortex **3** (*Земли*) crust; земна́я к. the earth's crust

кораблекруше́ни|е, я *nt.* shipwreck; потерпе́ть к. to be shipwrecked

кораблестрое́ни|е, я *nt.* shipbuilding

⚓ **кора́бл|ь, я́** *m.* ship, vessel; лине́йный к. battleship; косми́ческий к. spaceship; сади́ться на к. to go on board (ship), to embark

кора́лл, а *m.* coral

Кора́н, а *m.* the Koran

коре́|ец, йца *m.* Korean

коре́йк|а, и *f.* smoked back bacon

коре́йский *adj.* Korean

корена́ст|ый, ~**,** ~**а** *adj.* thickset, stocky

коренн|о́й *adj.* radical, fundamental; к. зуб molar (tooth); к. жи́тель native; ~**о́е** населе́ние indigenous population

⚓ **ко́р|ень, ня,** *pl.* ~**ни,** ~**не́й** *m.* (*in var. senses*) root; вы́рвать с ~**нем** to uproot (also fig.)

Коре́|я, и *f.* Korea

коре́я́н|ка, ки *f. of* ▶ **коре́ец**

корзи́н|а, ы *f.* basket

кориа́ндр, а *m.* coriander

коридо́р, а *m.* corridor, passage

кори́ц|а, ы *f.* cinnamon

кори́чневый *adj.* brown

ко́рк|а, и *f.* **1** (*хлеба*) crust **2** (*апельсина*) peel, rind

корм, а, о ~**е,** на ~**е** *and* на ~**ý,** *pl.* ~**á,** ~**о́в** *m.* **1** (*пища*) food, fodder; пти́чий к. birdseed **2** (*действие*) feeding

корм|á, ы́ *f.* (naut.) stern

корм|и́ть, лю́, ~**ишь** *impf.* **1** (*pf.* на~ *and* по~) (*давать корм*) to feed; к. гру́дью to nurse, (breast)feed **2** (*pf.* про~) (*содержать*) to keep, maintain

корм|и́ться, лю́сь, ~ишься *impf.* (*of*
▶ прокорми́ться) (+ *i.*) (*содержа́ть себя́*)
to live (on); к. уро́ками to make a living by
giving tuition

кормле́ни|е, я *nt.* feeding

корму́шк|а, и *f.* (agric.) (feeding) trough; (*для
пти́ц*) bird table, bird feeder

корнепло́д, а *m.* root vegetable

корнишо́н, а *m.* (cul.) gherkin

коро́бк|а, и *f.* box, case; к. скоросте́й (tech.)
gearbox; черепна́я к. (anat.) cranium

короб|о́к, ка́ *m.* (small) box

коро́в|а, ы *f.* cow

коро́в|ий *adj. of* ▶ коро́ва; ~ье ма́сло butter

коро́в|ка, ки *f.* affectionate dim. of ▶ коро́ва;
бо́жья к. ladybird

коро́вник, а *m.* cowshed

короле́в|а, ы *f.* queen

короле́вский *adj.* royal

короле́вств|о, а *nt.* kingdom

коро́л|ь, я́ *m.* king; (fig.) baron

коро́н|а, ы *f.* crown (also fig.)

корона́ци|я, и *f.* coronation

коро́нк|а, и *f.* crown (*of tooth*)

корон|ова́ть, у́ю *impf. and pf.* to crown

коро́ст|а, ы *f.* scab

♂ **коро́т|кий**, ко́роток, коротка́, ко́ротко, pl.
ко́ротки́ *adj.* short; э́то пальто́ тебе́ ко́ротко
this coat is too short for you

ко́ротко¹ *see* ▶ коро́ткий

ко́ротко² *adv.* briefly

короткометра́жный *adj.*: к. фильм short
(film)

коро́че *comp. of* ▶ коро́ткий, ▶ ко́ротко¹;
shorter; к. говоря́ in short, to cut a long
story short

♂ **корпорати́в|ный**, ~ен, ~на *adj.* corporate

корпора́ци|я, и *f.* corporation

ко́рпус¹, а, pl. ~ы *m.* **1** (*ту́ловище*) body
2 (*ме́ра*) length (*of animal, as unit of
measurement*)

♂ **ко́рпус²**, а, pl. ~а́, ~о́в *m.* **1** (mil.) corps;
каде́тский, морско́й к. military school, naval
college; дипломати́ческий к. diplomatic corps
2 (*зда́ние*) building; block **3** (*корабля́*) hull;
(tech.) frame, body, case

корректи́р|овать, ую *impf.* (*of*
▶ скорректи́ровать) to correct

корре́кт|ный, ~ен, ~на *adj.* correct, proper

корре́ктор, а *m.* proofreader

корре́кци|я, и *f.* correction

корреспонде́нт, а *m.* correspondent

корреспонде́нтк|а, ки *f. of* ▶ корреспонде́нт

корреспонде́нци|я, и *f.* **1** (*перепи́ска;
пи́сьма*) correspondence **2** (*сообще́ние*)
dispatch, report

корри́д|а, ы *f.* bullfight

корро́зи|я, и *f.* (chem.) corrosion

коррумпи́рован|ный, ~, ~а *adj.* corrupt

корру́пци|я, и *f.* (pol.) corruption

корса́ж, а *m.* bodice

корсе́т, а *m.* corset

корт, а *m.* (tennis) court

корте́ж, а *m.* procession, cortège;
(*автомоби́лей*) motorcade

ко́ртик, а *m.* dagger

ко́рточ|ки, ек (*no sg.*) сиде́ть на ~ках, сесть
на к. to squat

корч|ева́ть, у́ю *impf.* to uproot, root out

ко́ршун, а *m.* (zool.) kite

коры́ст|ный, ~ен, ~на *adj.* mercenary,
selfish

коры́т|о, а *nt.* tub; trough

кор|ь, и *f.* measles

коря́в|ый, ~, ~а *adj.* (infml) **1** (*дуб, па́льцы*)
gnarled **2** (*по́черк, речь, стиль*) clumsy

коря́г|а, и *f.* (*ве́твь*) dead branch; (*пень*) dead
tree stump (*often submerged under water*)

кос|а́¹, ы́, a. ~у́, pl. ~ы *f.* (*во́лосы*) plait,
pigtail, braid

кос|а́², ы́, pl. ~ы *f.* (*ору́дие*) scythe

коса́тк|а, и *f.* killer whale

ко́свенн|ый *adj.* indirect, oblique; ~ые
ули́ки circumstantial evidence; (gram.): ~ая
речь indirect speech

коси́лк|а, и *f.* mowing machine, mower;
газо́нная к. lawn mower

ко|си́ть¹, шу́, ~сишь *impf.* (*of* ▶ скоси́ть¹)
(*тра́ву*) to mow; to cut

ко|си́ть², шу́, си́шь *impf.* (*of* ▶ скоси́ть²)
1 (*глаза́ при косогла́зии*) to squint **2** (*рот,
глаза́*) to twist, slant **3** (*no pf.*) (*быть
косогла́зым*) to have a squint

ко|си́ться, шу́сь, си́шься *impf.* (*of*
▶ покоси́ться) **1** (*о до́ме*) to slant **2** (infml)
(на + *a.*) to cast a sidelong look (at); (fig.) to
look askance (at)

коси́чк|а, и *f. dim. of* ▶ коса́¹

косма́т|ый, ~, ~а *adj.* shaggy

косме́тик|а, и *f.* cosmetics, make-up

космети́ческ|ий *adj.* cosmetic; к. кабине́т
beauty salon; ~ая ма́ска face pack; к.
ремо́нт redecoration

космети́чк|а, и *f.* (infml) make-up bag

космето́лог, а *m.* **1** (*врач в кли́нике*)
cosmetic surgeon **2** (*специали́ст в сало́не*)
beautician

косми́ческий *adj.* **1** space (*attr.*) **2** (*пыль,
радиа́ция*) cosmic; к. кора́бль spaceship

космодро́м, а *m.* cosmodrome, space centre
(BrE), center (AmE)

космона́вт, а *m.* astronaut, cosmonaut,
spaceman

космона́втик|а, и *f.* astronautics, space
exploration

космополи́т, а *m.* cosmopolitan

космополити́ческий *adj.* cosmopolitan

ко́смос, а *m.* cosmos; outer space

косноязы́ч|ный, ~ен, ~на *adj.* speaking
thickly

косн|у́ться, у́сь, ёшься *pf. of* ▶ каса́ться

ко́с|ный, ~ен, ~на *adj.* (*ум*) inert, sluggish;
(*о́браз жи́зни, о́бщество*) stagnant

К

ко́со *adv.* slantwise, askew; obliquely; **смотре́ть к.** to look askance, scowl

Ко́сово, а *nt.* Kosovo

косогла́зи|е, я *nt.* squint, cast in the eye

косогла́з|ый, ~, ~а *adj.* cross-eyed, squint-eyed

кос|о́й, ~, ~а́, ~о *adj.* **1** slanting; oblique **2** (*косогла́зый*) squinting; cross-eyed

косола́п|ый, ~, ~а *adj.* pigeon-toed; (*fig.*) clumsy

косте́л, а *m.* (Roman Catholic) church

кост|ёр, ра́ *m.* bonfire; (*похо́дный*) campfire; **заже́чь/развести́ к.** to make a fire

костля́в|ый, ~, ~а *adj.* bony

ко́стный *adj.* osseous; (*anat.*): **к. мозг** marrow

ко́сточк|а, и *f.* **1** *dim. of* ▸ **кость 2** (*сли́вы, абрико́са*) stone; (*лимо́на, виногра́да*) pip

кост|ы́ль, я́ *m.* crutch; **ходи́ть на ~я́х** to walk on crutches

кост|ь, и, *pl.* **~и, ~е́й** *f.* **1** bone; **слоно́вая к.** ivory **2** (*in pl.*) (*в игре́*) dice

костю́м, а *m.* **1** (*оде́жда*) dress, clothes; **маскара́дный к.** fancy dress **2** (*пиджа́к и брю́ки; жаке́т и ю́бка*) suit; **вече́рний к.** dress suit; **купа́льный к.** swimsuit **3** (*theatr.*) costume

костюме́р, а *m.* (*theatr.*) wardrobe master

костя́к, а́ *m.* (*fig.*) (+ *g.*) backbone (of)

косу́л|я, и *f.* roe deer

косы́нк|а, и *f.* (triangular) kerchief, scarf

кося́к[1], а́ *m.* (*дверно́й*) (door)post; jamb

кося́к[2], а́ *m.* **1** (*лошаде́й*) herd **2** (*рыб*) shoal, school; (*птиц*) flock

кося́к[3], а́ *m.* (sl., *с марихуа́ной*) joint

кот, а́ *m.* tomcat

Кот-д'Ивуа́р, а *m.* the Ivory Coast

кот|ёл, ла́ *m.* **1** pot, cauldron; **о́бщий к.** communal pot **2** (*tech.*) boiler

котел|о́к, ка́ *m.* **1** pot **2** (*mil.*) mess tin **3** (*шля́па*) bowler (hat)

коте́льн|ая, ой *f.* boiler house

кот|ёнок, ёнка, *pl.* **~я́та, ~я́т** *m.* kitten

ко́тик, а *m.* **1** (*тюле́нь*) fur seal **2** (*мех*) sealskin

коти́р|овать, ую *impf. and pf.* (fin.) to quote

коти́р|оваться, уюсь *impf. and pf.* **1** (fin.) to be quoted **2** (fig.) to be rated

котле́т|а, ы *f.* burger; rissole; (**отбивна́я**) **к.** chop

котлова́н, а *m.* (tech.) foundation pit

кото́мк|а, и *f.* knapsack

✎ **кото́рый** *pron.* **1** *interrog. and rel.* (*о предме́тах*) which; **к. час?** what time is it? **2** (infml, *не оди́н*) some, quite a few; **к. год он не пи́шет** he hasn't been writing for some years **3** *rel.* (*о лю́дях*) who

котте́дж, а *m.* cottage

кот|я́та, я́т *see* ▸ **котёнок**

ко́фе *m. indecl.* coffee; **раствори́мый к.** instant coffee; **к. в зёрнах** coffee beans

✎ *key word*

кофева́рк|а, и *f.* coffee maker

кофеи́н, а *m.* caffeine

кофе́йник, а *m.* coffee pot

кофе́йный *adj. of* ▸ **ко́фе**

кофе́|йня, йни, *g. pl.* **~ен** *f.* coffee house

кофемо́лк|а, и *f.* coffee grinder

ко́фт|а, ы *f.* jacket, cardigan (*woman's*)

ко́фточк|а, и *f.* blouse

коч|а́н, а́ *m.*: **к. капу́сты** head of cabbage

коч|ева́ть, у́ю *impf.* **1** (*о племена́х*) to be a nomad, to roam from place to place; (fig., *передвига́ться*) to wander **2** (*о живо́тных*) to migrate

коче́вник, а *m.* nomad

кочево́й *adj.* **1** (*лю́ди*) nomadic **2** (*живо́тные*) migratory

кочега́р, а *m.* stoker, fireman

кочер|га́, ги́, *g. pl.* **~ёг** *f.* poker

ко́чк|а, и *f.* hummock; tussock

кошел|ёк, ька́ *m.* purse

кошёлк|а, и *f.* (infml) small basket

ко́шк|а, и *f.* cat; (fig., infml): **игра́ть в ~и-мы́шки** to play cat-and-mouse; **жить как к. с соба́кой** to lead a cat-and-dog life

кошма́р, а *m.* **1** nightmare (also fig.) **2** (*as pred.*) (infml) it is a nightmare

кошма́р|ный, ~ен, ~на *adj.* nightmarish; (fig.) horrible, awful

ко|шу́, ~си́шь *see* ▸ **коси́ть[1]**, ▸ **коси́ть[2]**

кощу́нств|о, а *nt.* blasphemy

коэффицие́нт, а *m.* (math.) coefficient; (tech.): **к. поле́зного де́йствия** efficiency (also fig.); **к. у́мственных спосо́бностей** intelligence quotient, IQ

КПП *m. indecl.* (*abbr. of* **контро́льно-пропускно́й пункт**) checkpoint

краб, а *m.* (zool.) crab

кра́ден|ый *adj.* stolen; **~ое** (collect.) stolen goods

кра|ду́, дёшь *see* ▸ **красть**

кра́ж|а, и *f.* theft; **к. со взло́мом** burglary; **магази́нная к.** shoplifting

✎ **кра|й, я, о ~е, в ~ю́,** *pl.* **~я́, ~ёв** *m.* **1** (*по́ля, оде́жды*) edge; (*сосу́да*) brim; (*про́пасти*) brink (also fig.); **на ~ю́ све́та** at the world's end **2** (*страна́, о́бласть*) land, country; **в на́ших ~я́х** in our part of the world; **в чужи́х ~я́х** in foreign parts

✎ **кра́йне** *adv.* extremely

✎ **кра́йн|ий** *adj.* **1** extreme; (*после́дний*) last; **К. Се́вер** the Far North; **в ~ем слу́чае** in the last resort; **к. срок** deadline; **по ~ей ме́ре** at least **2** (sport) outside, wing

кра́йност|ь, и *f.* (*кра́йняя сте́пень*) extreme; (*тяжёлое положе́ние*) (*no pl.*) extremity

крал, а *see* ▸ **красть**

кран[1], а *m.* (*водопрово́дный*) tap, faucet (AmE); (*на трубопрово́дах*) valve

кран[2], а *m.* (*маши́на*) crane

крапи́в|а, ы *f.* (stinging) nettle; (collect.) nettles

краса́в|ец, ца *m.* handsome man; good-looker (*male*)

краса́виц|а, ы *f.* beauty; good-looker (*female*)

ᵈ **краси́в|ый, ~, ~а** *adj.* beautiful; (*мужчина*) handsome; (*поступок, слова*) fine

краси́тел|ь, я *m.* dye(-stuff); **пищево́й к.** food colouring

кра́|сить, шу, сишь *impf.* (*of* ▶ **покра́сить**) **1** (*стену, губы*) to paint **2** (*ткань, волосы*) to dye; (*дерево, стекло*) to stain

кра́|ситься, шусь, сишься *impf.* **1** (*pf.* **на~**) to make up one's face **2** (*pf.* **по~**) to dye one's hair **3** (*no pf.*) (*пачкать собой*) to run **4** *pass. of* ▶ **кра́сить**

ᵈ **кра́ск|а, и** *f.* **1** (*материал*) paint; (*для ткани*) dye; **акваре́льная к.** watercolour (BrE), watercolor (AmE); **ма́сляная к.** oil paint **2** (*in pl.*) (fig., *колорит*) colours (BrE), colors (AmE); **сгуща́ть ~и** (infml) to lay it on thick

красне́|ть, ю *impf.* (*of* ▶ **покрасне́ть**) **1** (*становиться красным*) to redden, become red **2** (*от стыда*) to blush; (fig.): **к. за** (+ *a.*) to blush for

красноречи́в|ый, ~, ~а *adj.* eloquent

красноре́чи|е, я *nt.* eloquence

красну́х|а, и *f.* (med.) German measles

ᵈ **кра́с|ный, ~ен, ~на́, ~но** *adj.* red (also fig., pol.); **~ное де́рево** mahogany; **К. Крест** Red Cross; **~ная строка́** (first line of) new paragraph

ᵈ **красот|а́, ы́,** *pl.* **~ы** *f.* beauty

красо́тк|а, и *f.* (infml) good-looking girl; beauty

кра́с|очный *adj.* **1** *adj. of* ▶ **кра́ска 2** (**~очен, ~очна**) colourful (BrE), colorful (AmE)

кра|сть, ду́, дёшь, *past* **~л, ~ла** *impf.* (*of* ▶ **укра́сть**) to steal

кра́|сться, ду́сь, дёшься, *past* **~лся, ~лась** *impf.* to steal, creep, sneak

кра́тер, а *m.* crater

кра́т|кий, ~ок, ~ка́, ~ко *adj.* short; brief; **я бу́ду ~ок** I'll be brief; (*сжатый*) concise; **«и» ~кое** the Russian letter «й»

кра́тко *adv.* briefly

кратковре́мен|ный, ~ and ~ен, ~на *adj.* of short duration, brief; **к. дождь** shower

краткосро́ч|ный, ~ен, ~на *adj.* (*ссуда*) short-term; (*отпуск*) short

кратча́йший *superl. of* ▶ **кра́ткий**

краудсо́рсинг, а *m.* crowdsourcing (*carrying out a piece of work by recruiting a number of people, esp. via the Internet*)

крах, а *m.* (fin., also fig.) crash, collapse; (fig., *провал*) failure; **потерпе́ть к.** to fail

крахма́л, а *m.* starch

кра́шен|ый *adj.* **1** (*стена*) painted; **~ое яйцо́** (decorated) Easter egg **2** (*ткань*) dyed

креве́тк|а, и *f.* (zool.) (*мелкая*) shrimp; (*крупная*) prawn

ᵈ **креди́т, а** *m.* credit; **в к.** on credit

креди́тк|а, и *f.* (infml) credit card

ᵈ **креди́т|ный** *adj. of* ▶ **креди́т; к. биле́т** banknote; **~ная ка́рточка/ка́рта** credit card; **~ный кри́зис** credit crisis

кредито́р, а *m.* creditor

кредитоспосо́бность, и *f.* creditworthiness, credit rating

кредитоспосо́б|ный, ~ен, ~на *adj.* creditworthy

кре́йсер, а, *pl.* **~ы and ~а́** (mil.) *m.* cruiser; **лине́йный к.** battle cruiser

кре́кер, а *m.* cracker

крем, а *m.* cream; **к. для о́буви** shoe polish

кремато́ри|й, я *m.* crematorium

крема́ци|я, и *f.* cremation

кре́м|ень, ня́ *m.* flint

кремлёвский *adj. of* ▶ **кремль**

кремл|ь, я́ *m.* citadel; **(моско́вский) К.** the Kremlin

кре́мни|й, я *m.* (chem.) silicon

кре́мовый *adj.* cream(-coloured)

креп|и́ть, лю́, и́шь *impf.* **1** (*прочно прикреплять*) to fasten **2** (*усиливать*) to strengthen

креп|и́ться, лю́сь, и́шься *impf.* **1** to hold out **2** *pass. of* ▶ **крепи́ть**

кре́п|кий, ~ок, ~ка́, ~ко, ~ки́ *adj.* (*чай, кофе; запах; ветер; организм; ткань*) strong; (*сон*) sound; (*забор*) sturdy, robust; (*мороз, удар*) hard; (fig., *стойкий*) firm; **~кие напи́тки** spirits; **~кое словцо́** (infml) swear word, strong language

кре́пко *adv.* (*держать; завяза́ть*) tight; (*построенный*) strongly; (*спать*) soundly

крепле́ни|е, я *nt.* **1** (naut.) lashing; furling **2** (*лыжное*) binding

крепн|уть, у, ешь *impf.* (*of* ▶ **окре́пнуть**) to get stronger

кре́пост|ь¹, и *f.* (*свойство*) strength

кре́пост|ь², и *f.* (mil.) fortress

кре́пче *comp. of* ▶ **кре́пкий,** ▶ **кре́пко**

кре́с|ло, ла, *g. pl.* **~ел** *nt.* armchair, easy chair; (fig., *должность*) post, office; **инвали́дное к.** wheelchair; **к.-кача́лка** rocking chair; **к.-крова́ть** sofa bed; (theatr.) seat

крест, а́ *m.* **1** cross; **поста́вить к.** (**на** + *p.*) to give up for lost **2** (*жест*) the sign of the cross

кре|сти́ть, щу́, ~стишь *impf.* **1** (*pf.* **к.** or **о~**) to baptize, christen **2** (+ *a.* and **y** + *gen.*) to be godfather, godmother (*to the child of*); **я у них ~сти́ла дочь** I was godmother to their daughter **3** (*pf.* **пере~**) to make the sign of the cross over

кре|сти́ться, щу́сь, ~стишься *impf.* **1** (*pf.* **к.**) to be baptized, be christened **2** (*pf.* **пере~**) to cross oneself

крест-на́крест *adv.* crosswise

кре́стник, а *m.* godson, godchild

кре́стниц|а, ы *f.* goddaughter, godchild

крёстн|ый *adj.*: **к. оте́ц** (*also as m. n.* **к., ~ого**) godfather; **~ая мать** (*also as f. n.* **~ая, ~ой**) godmother; **~ые де́ти** godchildren

крестоно́с|ец, ца *m.* crusader

крестья́н|ин, ина, *pl.* **~е, ~** *m.* peasant

крестья́нк|а, и *f.* peasant (woman)

крестья́нский *adj.* peasant

крестья́нств|о, а *nt.* (*collect.*) the peasants, peasantry

крети́н, а *m.* (*med.*) cretin (*person with learning difficulties and physical deformities because of congenital thyroid deficiency*); (*fig.*, *infml*) idiot, imbecile

креще́ни|е, я *nt.* baptism, christening; **боево́е к.** (*fig.*) baptism of fire

кре|щу́, ~сти́шь *see* ▸ **крести́ть**

крив|а́я, о́й *f.* (*math.*, *econ.*, *etc.*) curve

кривля́|ться, юсь *impf.* to behave affectedly; to show off

крив|о́й, ~, ~а́, ~о adj. crooked; **~о́е зе́ркало** (*also fig.*) distorting mirror

кривоно́г|ий, ~, ~а *adj.* bandy-legged, bow-legged

ꞔ **кри́зис, а** *m.* crisis

кри́зис|ный *adj. of* ▸ **кри́зис**; **~ная ситуа́ция** crisis situation, crisis

крик, а *m.* cry, shout; (*in pl.*) clamour (BrE), clamor (AmE), outcry; **к. души́** emotional outpouring

кри́кет, а *m.* cricket; **игро́к в к.** cricketer

крикли́в|ый, ~, ~а *adj.* **1** (*ребёнок*) clamorous, bawling **2** (*голос*) loud, penetrating

кри́кн|уть, у, ешь *inst. pf. of* ▸ **крича́ть**

кримина́л, а *m.* (*infml*) **1** (*плохое поведение*) foul play **2** (*преступление*) crime

криминали́ст, а *m.* (*law*) specialist in crime detection

криминали́стик|а, и *f.* (science of) crime detection

кримина́л|ьный, ~ен, ~ьна *adj.* criminal

криминоге́н|ный, ~ен, ~на *adj.* criminogenic, conducive to crime

криста́лл, а *m.* crystal

ꞔ **крите́ри|й, я** *m.* criterion

кри́тик, а *m.* critic

кри́тик|а, и *f.* **1** criticism **2** (*отрицательное суждение*) critique

критик|ова́ть, у́ю *impf.* to criticize

крити́ческий *adj.* critical; **к. моме́нт** (*fig.*) crucial moment

кри|ча́ть, чу́, чи́шь *impf.* (*of* ▸ **кри́кнуть**) **1** to cry, shout; to yell, scream; **к. (на + *a.*)** to shout (at); **к. о по́мощи** to call for help **2** (**о** + *p.*) (*infml*) to make a song and dance (about), talk a lot (about)

крича́щий *pres. part. act. of* ▸ **крича́ть** *and adj.* (*fig.*) loud; blatant

крова́вый *adj.* (*режим, события*) bloody

крова́тк|а, и *f.*: **де́тская к.** cot (BrE), crib (AmE)

крова́т|ь, и *f.* bed; **двухъя́русная к.** bunk bed

кро́в|ля, ли, *g. pl.* **~ель** *f.* roof

кро́в|ный *adj.* blood; **~ая месть** blood feud

кровожа́д|ный, ~ен, ~на *adj.* bloodthirsty

кровоизлия́ни|е, я *nt.* (*med.*) haemorrhage (BrE), hemorrhage (AmE)

кровообраще́ни|е, я *nt.* circulation of the blood

кровопроли́ти|е, я *nt.* bloodshed

кровотече́ни|е, я *nt.* bleeding; (*сильное*) haemorrhage (BrE), hemorrhage (AmE)

кровоточ|и́ть, ~и́т *impf.* to bleed

ꞔ **кров|ь, и, о ~и, в ~и́,** *g. pl.* **~е́й** *f.* blood (*also fig.*); **в к., до ~и** till it bleeds; **пусти́ть к.** (+ *d.*) to bleed; (*fig.*): **по ~и** by birth

кровяно́й *adj. of* ▸ **кровь**

кро|и́ть, ю́, и́шь *impf.* (*of* ▸ **скрои́ть**) to cut (out)

кро́|й, я *m.* **1** cutting (out) **2** (*фасон*) cut (*of dress, etc.*)

кро́йк|а, и *f.* cutting (out)

кроке́т, а *m.* (*игра*) croquet

крокоди́л, а *m.* crocodile

кро́кус, а *m.* (*bot.*) crocus

кро́лик, а *m.* **1** (*животное*) rabbit **2** (*мех*) rabbit fur

ꞔ **кро́ме** *prep.* + *g.* **1** (*за исключением*) except **2** (*в добавление*) besides, in addition to; **к. того́** besides, moreover, furthermore; (*infml*): **к. шу́ток** joking apart

кро́мк|а, и *f.* edge; (*ткани*) selvage; **к. тротуа́ра** kerb (BrE), curb (AmE)

кро́н|а, ы *f.* (*дерева*) crown

кронште́йн, а *m.* (*tech.*) (*полки*) bracket; (*балкона*) corbel

кропотли́в|ый, ~, ~а *adj.* painstaking, precise

кроссво́рд, а *m.* crossword

кроссо́вк|и, ок *f. pl.* (*sg.* **~ка, ~ки**) trainers (BrE), sneakers (AmE)

крот, á *m.* mole

кро́т|кий, ~ок, ~ка́, ~ко *adj.* meek, mild

кро́хотный *adj.* (*infml*) tiny, minute

кро́шеч|ный, ~ен, ~на *adj.* (*infml*) tiny, minute

крош|и́ть, у́, ~и́шь *impf.* **1** (*pf.* **на~** *or* **рас~**) (*хлеб*) to crumb, crumble; (*нарезать*) to dice; (*fig.*) to hack to pieces **2** (*pf.* **на~**) (+ *i.*) (*сорить*) to drop, spill crumbs (of)

крош|и́ться, ~и́тся *impf.* (*of* ▸ **раскроши́ться**) to crumble

кро́шк|а, и *f.* (*хлеба*) crumb

круасса́н, а *m.* (*cul.*) croissant

ꞔ **круг, а,** *pl.* **~и́** *m.* **1** (= *circular area, p. sg.* **в, на ~у́,** = *circumference, p. sg.* **в, на ~е**) circle; **движе́ние по ~у** movement in a circle **2** (*круглый предмет*) ring; **спаса́тельный к.** lifebelt; **~и́ под глаза́ми** rings round the eyes **3** (*sport*) (*p. sg.* **на ~е**) беговой к. racecourse, ring; **к. почёта** lap of honour (BrE), honor (AmE) **4** (*fig.*) (*p. sg.* **в ~у́**) (*сфера, область*) sphere, range; compass; **к. вопро́сов** range of questions **5** (*fig.*) (*p. sg.* **в ~у́**) (*группа людей*) circle (*of persons*); **официа́льные**

~й official quarters; **в семе́йном** ~ý in the family circle

круглогоди́чный adj. year-round

круглоли́ц|ый, ~, ~а adj. round-faced

круглосу́точный adj. round-the-clock, twenty-four-hour

⚥ **кру́гл|ый**, ~, ~а́, ~о, ~ы́ adj. **1** round; **к. год** all the year round; ~**ая да́та** 10th, 20th, 30th, etc. anniversary; ~**ые ско́бки** round brackets; ~**ые су́тки** day and night; ~**ая су́мма** round sum **2** (no short forms) (infml) complete, utter, perfect; **к. дура́к** utter fool; **к.**, ~**ая сирота́** orphan (having neither father nor mother)

круговоро́т, а m. (цикличность) cycle; (событий) flow

кругозо́р, а m. **1** prospect **2** (fig.) horizon, range of interests

круго́м¹ adv. **1** round, around **2** (вокруг) (all) round, round about; **к. всё бы́ло ти́хо** all around was still **3** (infml, совершенно) completely, entirely; **вы к. винова́ты** you are entirely to blame

круго́м² prep. + g. round, around

круглообра́з|ный, ~ен, ~на adj. circular

кругосве́тный adj. round-the-world

круже́в|а́, ~е́в, ~ева́м = **кру́жево**

кружевно́й adj. of ▶ кружева́, ▶ кру́жево

кру́жев|о, а nt. lace

кружи́|ть, ý, ~йшь impf. **1** (заставлять двигаться по кругу) to whirl, spin round **2** (кружиться) to circle

кружи́|ться, у́сь, ~йшься impf. (of ▶ закружи́ться) to whirl, spin round; (о птицах) to circle; **у меня́ ~ится голова́** my head is going round, I feel giddy

кру́жк|а, и f. mug

кружо́к, ка́ m. **1** dim. of ▶ круг **2** (группа) circle, club; (учебный) study group

круи́з, а m. cruise

круп|а́, ы́, pl. ~ы f. (collect.) groats; **гре́чневая к.** buckwheat; **ма́нная к.** semolina; **овся́ная к.** oatmeal

крупномасшта́б|ный, ~ен, ~на adj. large-scale; (fig.) ambitious

⚥ **кру́п|ный**, ~ен, ~на́, ~но, ~ны́ adj. **1** (большой) large, big; (крупномасштабный) large-scale; (fig., значительный) prominent, outstanding; **к. рога́тый скот** cattle; ~**ный план** (cin.) close-up **2** (песок) coarse **3** (важный) important; (серьёзный) serious; ~**ная неприя́тность** serious trouble

крупье́ m. indecl. croupier

кру|ти́ть, чу́, ~тишь impf. **1** (pf. с~) to twist; to twirl **2** (pf. за~) (кран, ручку) to turn, wind

кру|ти́ться, чу́сь, ~тишься impf. **1** (вращаться) to turn, spin, revolve **2** (кружиться) to whirl **3** (fig., infml, быть в хлопотах) to be in a whirl

кру́то adv. **1** (вверх, вниз) steeply **2** (внезапно) suddenly; abruptly, sharply; **к. поверну́ть** to turn round sharply **3** (infml) harshly; **к.**

распра́виться с кем-н. to give sb short shrift **4** (туго) tightly

крут|о́й, ~, ~а́, ~о adj. **1** (подъём) steep **2** (внезапный) sudden; abrupt, sharp **3** (infml) (характер) severe; (меры) drastic **4** (cul., каша) thick; ~**о́е яйцо́** hard-boiled egg **5** (sl.) (отличный) cool; ~о! cool!; (сильный и властный) (влиятельный) influential; (богатый) well off

кру́че comp. of ▶ круто́й, ▶ кру́то

кру|чу́, ~тишь see ▶ крути́ть

круше́ни|е, я nt. **1** (авария) crash; (судна) wreck; **потерпе́ть к.** (поезд, самолёт) to crash; (корабль) to be wrecked **2** (fig., надежд; коммунизма) collapse

круш|и́ть, ý, и́шь impf. to destroy (also fig.)

крыжо́вник, а m. gooseberry

крыла́т|ый adj. winged (also fig.); ~**ые слова́** pithy saying(s); ~**ая раке́та** cruise missile

крыл|о́, á, pl. ~ья, ~ьев nt. (птицы, самолёта, дома) wing; (мельницы) sail, vane; (автомобиля) wing, mudguard (BrE), fender (AmE)

крыл|ьцо́, ьца́, pl. ~ьца, ~е́ц, ~ьца́м nt. porch

Крым, а, о ~е, в ~ý m. the Crimea

кры́с|а, ы f. rat

кры́тый adj. covered; sheltered; **к. ры́нок** covered market

кры́ш|а, и f. roof; (infml, преступная группировка, охранное предприятие и т. п., обеспечивающие защиту или покровительство) protection, front

кры́шк|а, и f. **1** (кастрюли, банки, чемодана) lid; (люка) cover **2** (infml) death, end; **ему́ к.** he's done for; he's finished

крю́к, ка́ m. (pl. ~ки́, ~ко́в) hook

крючо́к, ка́ m. hook; **спусково́й к.** trigger

кря́ду adv. (infml) running; in a row

кряж, а m. **1** (горный) (mountain) ridge **2** (дубовый) block, log

кря́к|ать, аю impf. to quack

кря́к|нуть, ну, нешь pf. to give a quack

кряхт|е́ть, чу́, ти́шь impf. to groan

ксенофо́би|я, и f. xenophobia

ксероко́пи|я, и f. Xerox®, photocopy

ксе́рокс, а m. **1** (ксерография) xerography **2** (устройство) Xerox (machine)®, photocopier **3** (infml, копия) Xerox®, photocopy

ксилофо́н, а m. (mus.) xylophone

⚥ **кста́ти** adv. **1** (уместно) to the point, apropos **2** (своевременно) opportunely; **э́тот пода́рок оказа́лся о́чень к.** the present has proved most welcome **3** (infml, заодно) at the same time, incidentally; **к., зайди́те, пожа́луйста, в апте́ку** will you please call at the chemist's at the same time **4**; **к. (сказа́ть)** by the way

к/т (abbr. of **кинотеа́тр**) cinema

⚥ **кто**, кого́, кому́, кем, о ком pron. **1** (interrog.) (какой человек?) who; **к. э́то тако́й?** who is that? **2** (rel.) (в придаточных) who (normally after pron. antecedent); **тот, к.**

К

he who; **те, к.** those who **3** (*indefinite*): **к. (бы) ни** who(so)ever; **к. бы то ни́ был** whoever it may be **4** (*indefinite*): **к. ... к.** some ... others; (+ *adv.*) **разбежа́лись к. куда́** they scattered in all directions; **как они́ устро́ились? — к. как** how did they settle in? — in all sorts of ways

кто́-либо, кого́-либо *pron.* = **кто́-нибудь**

кто́-нибудь, кого́-нибудь *pron.* (*в вопросах*) anyone, anybody; (*в утверждениях*) someone, somebody

⚹ **кто́-то, кого́-то** *pron.* someone, somebody

куб, а, *pl.* **~ы́** *m.* **1** (math.) cube; **два в ~е** two cubed **2** (infml, *кубический метр*) cubic metre (BrE), meter (AmE)

Ку́б|а, ы *f.* Cuba

куби́зм, а *m.* (art) cubism

ку́бик, а *m.* (*in pl.*) (*игрушка*) blocks, bricks

куби́н|ец, ца *m.* Cuban

куби́н|ка, ки *f. of* ▶ **куби́нец**

куби́нский *adj.*

ку́б|ок, ка *m.* **1** (*бокал*) goblet **2** (sport) cup

кубоме́тр, а *m.* cubic metre (BrE), meter (AmE)

кува́лд|а, ы *f.* sledgehammer

Куве́йт, а *m.* Kuwait

куве́йт|ец, ца *m.* Kuwaiti

куве́йт|ка, ки *f. of* ▶ **куве́йтец**

куве́йтский *adj.* Kuwaiti

кувши́н, а *m.* jug; pitcher

кувши́нк|а, и *f.* (bot.) water lily

кувырк|а́ться, а́юсь *impf.* (*of* ▶ **кувыркну́ться**) to turn somersaults, go head over heels

кувырк|ну́ться, ну́сь, нёшься *inst. pf. of* ▶ **кувырка́ться**

кувырко́м *adv.* (infml) head over heels; topsy-turvy; **полете́ть к.** to go head over heels; **всё пошло́ к.** everything went haywire

кугуа́р, а *m.* (zool.) puma, cougar

⚹ **куда́** *adv.* **1** (*interrog. and rel.*) where, whither; **к. ты идёшь?** where are you going? **2**: **к. (бы)** wherever **3** (infml, *для чего*) what for; **к. вам сто́лько багажа́?** what do you want so much luggage for? **4** (+ *comp.*) (infml, *гораздо*) much, far; **сего́дня мне к. лу́чше** I am much better today

куда́-либо *adv.* = **куда́-нибудь**

куда́-нибудь *adv.* anywhere; somewhere

куда́-то *adv.* somewhere

куда́х|тать, чу, чешь *impf.* to cackle, cluck

ку́др|и, ей (*no sg.*) curls

кудря́в|ый, ~, ~а *adj.* (*волосы*) curly; (*человек*) curly-headed

кузе́н, а *m.* cousin

кузи́н|а, ы *f.* cousin

кузне́ц, а́ *m.* (black)smith; farrier

кузне́чик, а *m.* grasshopper

ку́зниц|а, ы *f.* forge, smithy

ку́зов, а, *pl.* **~а́** *and* **~ы** *m.* (*автомобиля*) body

кукаре́ка|ть, ю *impf.* to crow

ку́киш, а *m.* (infml) fig (*gesture of derision or contempt, consisting of thumb placed between index and middle fingers*); **показа́ть кому́-н. к.** to make this gesture, ≈ to cock a snook, give the V-sign

ку́к|ла, лы, *g. pl.* **~ол** *f.* doll; (*в театре*) puppet

ку́колк|а, и *f.* (zool.) chrysalis, pupa

ку́кольный *adj.* doll's; **к. теа́тр** puppet theatre (BrE), theater (AmE)

кукуру́з|а, ы *f.* maize, (sweet)corn; **возду́шная к.** popcorn

кукуру́зный *adj. of* ▶ **кукуру́за**

куку́шк|а, и *f.* cuckoo; **часы́ с ~ой** cuckoo clock

кула́к, а́ *m.* fist

кул|ёк, ька́ *m.* (paper) bag

кули́к, а́ *m.* (zool.) stint; sandpiper (*Calidris*)

кулинари́|я, и *f.* **1** (*искусство*) cookery **2** (*магазин*) delicatessen

кулина́рн|ый *adj.* culinary; **~ая кни́га** cookery book (BrE), cookbook (AmE); **к. отде́л** delicatessen counter

кули́с|ы, ~ *f. pl.* (*sg.* **~а, ~ы**) (theatr.) wings; **за ~ами** behind the scenes (also fig.)

кули́ч, а́ *m.* Easter cake

куло́н, а *m.* pendant

кульби́т, а *m.* somersault

ку́льман, а *m.* drawing board

кульмина́ци|я, и *f.* culmination

культ, а *m.* cult; **к. ли́чности** personality cult; cult of personality

культ... *comb. form, abbr. of* ▶ **культу́рный**

культиви́р|овать, ую *impf.* to cultivate (also fig.)

ку́льт|овый *adj. of* ▶ **культ**; **~овый режиссёр** cult filmmaker

⚹ **культу́р|а, ы** *f.* **1** culture; **Министе́рство ~ы** Ministry of Culture **2** (*уровень*) standard, level; **к. ре́чи** standard of speech **3** (*usu. in pl.*) (agric., *растение*) crop; **зерновы́е ~ы** cereals; **кормовы́е ~ы** forage crops **4**: **физи́ческая к.** physical education

культури́зм, а *m.* bodybuilding

⚹ **культу́р|ный, ~ен, ~на** *adj.* **1** (*человек, общество*) cultured, cultivated **2** (*уровень, связи, обмен*) cultural **3** (agric., hort., *не дикий*) cultivated

кум, а, *pl.* **~овья́, ~овьёв** *m.* godfather of one's child; father of one's godchild

кум|а́, ы́ *f.* godmother of one's child; mother of one's godchild

куми́р, а *m.* idol (also fig.)

кунжу́т, а *m.* (bot.) sesame

куни́ц|а, ы *f.* (zool.) marten

купа́льник, а *m.* bathing costume (BrE), bathing suit (AmE), swimsuit

купа́льный *adj.* bathing, swimming; **к. костю́м** bathing costume (BrE), bathing suit (AmE), swimsuit

купа́|ть, ю *impf.* (*of* ▶ **вы́купать**, ▶ **искупа́ть¹**) to bathe; to bath

купа́|ться, юсь *impf.* (*of* ▶ **вы́купаться**, ▶ **искупа́ться**) (*плавать*) to swim, bathe;

⚹ key word

(*в ва́нне*) to have, take a bath; **к. в луча́х сла́вы** to bask in glory

купе́ *nt. indecl.* compartment (*of railway carriage*)

куп|е́ц, ца́ *m.* merchant

✎ **куп|и́ть, лю́, ∼ишь** *pf.* (*of* ▸ покупа́ть) to buy, purchase

купле́т, а *m.* **1** (*строфа*) stanza, strophe, verse **2** (*in pl.*) (*сатири́ческие песе́нки*) satirical ballad(s), song(s)

ку́пол, а, *pl.* ∼а́ *m.* cupola, dome

купо́н, а *m.* coupon

купю́р|а, ы *f.* **1** (*сокраще́ние*) cut **2** (fin.) (*де́ньги*) banknote, bill (AmE); (*облига́ция*) bond

кураг|а́, и́ *f.* (*collect.*) dried apricots

кура́нт|ы, ов *m.* chiming clock; chimes

кура́тор, а *m.* **1** (*попечи́тель*) curator **2** (*студе́нта*) (academic) supervisor

курга́н, а *m.* burial mound

курд, а *m.* Kurd

ку́рдский *adj.* Kurdish

курдя́нк|а, и *f. of* ▸ курд

куре́ни|е, я *nt.* **1** (*де́йствие*) smoking **2** (*ла́дан*) incense

кури́льщик, а *m.* smoker

кури́льщи|ца, цы *f. of* ▸ кури́льщик

кури́ный *adj.* (*яйцо́*) hen's; (*бульо́н*) chicken

кури́р|овать, ую *impf.* to supervise

кури́тельн|ый *adj.* smoking; ∼ая (ко́мната) smoking room

кур|и́ть, ю́, ∼ишь *impf.* (*of* ▸ покури́ть 1) **1** to smoke; **к. тру́бку** to smoke a pipe **2** (+ *a. or i.*) to burn

ку́р|ица, ицы, *pl.* ∼ы, ∼ *f.* hen

курно́с|ый, ∼, ∼а *adj.* snub-nosed

кур|о́к, ка́ *m.* hammer; **взвести́ к.** to cock; **спусти́ть к.** to pull the trigger

куропа́тк|а, и *f.* (zool.): (се́рая) к. partridge; **бе́лая к.** willow grouse

куро́рт, а *m.* holiday resort; **водолече́бный к.** spa

куро́ртный *adj. of* ▸ куро́рт

✎ **курс, а** *m.* **1** course; **взять к. на се́вер** to steer northwards; (pol.) policy; **к. ле́кций/ обуче́ния** course of lectures/instruction; **быть на тре́тьем** ∼е to be to be in the third year (*of a course of studies*); **держа́ть к.** (**на** + *a.*) to head (for); **быть в** ∼е (**де́ла**) to be au courant, be in the know **2** (fin.) exchange rate; **ра́зница** ∼ов (валю́т) difference in exchange rates

курса́нт, а *m.* (mil.) cadet

курси́в, а *m.* italic type, italics; ∼ом in italics

курс|ово́й *adj. of* ▸ курс; ∼ова́я рабо́та project; short dissertation

курсо́р, а *m.* (comput.) cursor

ку́ртк|а, и *f.* jacket; anorak

курча́в|ый, ∼, ∼а *adj.* (*во́лосы*) curly; (*челове́к*) curly-haired

ку́ры *see* ▸ ку́рица

курьёз|ный, ∼ен, ∼на *adj.* curious; funny

курье́р, а *m.* (*в учрежде́нии*) messenger; (*дипломати́ческий*) courier

курье́рский *adj.* **1** *adj. of* ▸ курье́р **2** fast; **к. по́езд** express

куря́тин|а, ы *f.* (infml) chicken (*as meat*)

куря́тник, а *m.* henhouse

кур|я́щий *pres. part. act. of* ▸ кури́ть; (*as n.* **к.**, ∼я́щего) smoker

куса́|ть, ю *impf.* (*о соба́ке, о челове́ке*) to bite; (*о пчеле́*) to sting

куса́|ться, юсь *impf.* **1** (*о соба́ке*) to bite; (*о крапи́ве, о пчеле́*) to sting **2** (*куса́ть друг дру́га*) to bite one another

куса́ч|ки, ек (*no sg.*) pliers; wire cutters

кус|о́к, ка́ *m.* piece, bit; (*хле́ба*) slice; (*са́хара*) lump; (*мы́ла*) cake

кусо́ч|ек, ка *m.* bit

куст, а́ *m.* bush, shrub; **спря́таться в** ∼ы́ (fig.) to scarper, make oneself scarce

куста́рник, а *m.* (*collect.*) bushes, shrubs; shrubbery

куста́рн|ый *adj.* **1** handicraft; ∼ые изде́лия craftwork **2** (fig., pej.) amateurish, primitive

куста́р|ь, я́ *m.* craftsman

ку|ти́ть, чу́, ∼тишь *impf.* (*of* ▸ кутну́ть) to carouse; to go on the booze

кут|ну́ть, ну́, нёшь *inst. pf. of* ▸ кути́ть

куха́рк|а, и *f.* cook

✎ **ку́хн|я, ни,** *g. pl.* ∼онь *f.* **1** (*помеще́ние*) kitchen **2** (*ку́шанья*) cooking, cuisine

ку́хонн|ый *adj.* kitchen; ∼ая плита́ kitchen range

ку́ц|ый, ∼, ∼а, ∼е *adj.* **1** (*живо́тное*) tailless; bobtailed **2** (*оде́жда*) skimpy; (fig.) limited, abbreviated

ку́ч|а, и *f.* **1** heap, pile; (*люде́й*) group; (infml): **вали́ть всё в одну́** ∼у to lump everything together **2** (infml) (+ *g.*) heaps (of), piles (of); **у него́ к. де́нег** he has heaps of money

ку́чер, а, *pl.* ∼а́, ∼о́в *m.* coachman

ку́ша|ть, ю *impf.* (*of* ▸ поку́шать, ▸ ску́шать) to eat (*esp. in polite invitation*); **ку́шайте, пожа́луйста** please help yourself/yourselves

куше́тк|а, и *f.* couch

ку|ю́, ёшь *see* ▸ кова́ть

к/ф (*abbr. of* кинофи́льм) (cinema) film, movie

Кыргызста́н, а *m.* Kyrgyzstan

кюве́т, а *m.* ditch (*at side of road*)

Лл

☞ **л** (*abbr. of* **литр**) l, litre(s) (BrE), liter(s) (AmE)

лабири́нт, а *m.* labyrinth, maze

лабора́нт, а *m.* laboratory assistant

лабора́нт|ка, ки *f. of* ▶ **лабора́нт**

лаборато́ри|я, и *f.* laboratory

лабрадо́р, а *m.* labrador (*dog*)

ла́в|а, ы *f.* (*вулканическая*) lava

лава́нд|а, ы *f.* (bot.) lavender

лава́ш, а *m.* lavash (*flat white loaf*)

лави́н|а, ы *f.* avalanche (also fig.)

лави́р|овать, ую *impf.* **1** (naut.) to tack **2** (fig.¹) to manoeuvre (BrE), maneuver (AmE)

ла́вк|а¹, и *f.* (*скамья*) bench

ла́вк|а², и *f.* (*магазин*) small shop

лавр, а *m.* **1** (bot.) laurel; bay (tree) **2** (*in pl.*) (fig.) laurels

ла́вр|овый *adj. of* ▶ **лавр**; ~о́вый вено́к laurel wreath; (fig.) laurels; ~о́вый лист bay leaf

ла́герный *adj. of* ▶ **ла́герь**

☞ **ла́гер|ь**, я *m.* **1** (*pl.* ~я́, ~е́й) camp; (mil.): **располага́ться, стоя́ть** ~ем to camp, be encamped **2** (*pl.* ~и, ~е́й) (fig.) camp

лагу́н|а, ы *f.* lagoon

лад, а, о ~е, в ~у́, *pl.* ~ы́, ~о́в *m.* **1** (mus., also fig.) (*согласие*) harmony, concord; **жить в ~у́** (с + *i.*) to live in harmony (with); **быть не в ~а́х** (с + *i.*) to be at odds (with); (infml): **идти́, пойти́ на л.** to go well, be successful **2** (*способ*) manner, way; **на свой л.** in one's own way

ла́дан, а *m.* incense; **дыша́ть на л.** (fig., infml) to have one foot in the grave

ла́|дить, жу, дишь *impf.* (с + *i.*) to get on (with), be on good terms (with); **они́ не ~дят** they don't get on

ла́дно *particle* (infml) all right!, OK!

ладо́н|ь, и *f.* palm (*of hand*); **быть (ви́дным) как на ~и** to be clearly visible

лазаре́т, а *m.* (mil.) field hospital; (naut.) sickbay

ла́з|ать, аю *impf.* (infml) = **ла́зить**

лазе́йк|а, и *f.* hole, gap; (fig., infml) loophole

ла́зер, а *m.* (phys., tech.) laser

ла́зерный *adj. of* ▶ **ла́зер**; **л. при́нтер** laser printer

ла́|зить, жу, зишь *impf.* (indet. of ▶ **лезть**) **1** (на + *a.* or по + *d.*) to climb, clamber (on to, up); **л. по дере́вьям** to climb trees **2** (в + *a.*) to climb (into), get (into)

лазу́рный, ~ен, ~на *adj.* sky blue, azure; **Л. Бе́рег** French Riviera

───────────

☞ key word

ла́|й, я *m.* bark(ing)

ла́йк|а¹, и *f.* (*собака*) husky

ла́йк|а², и *f.* (*кожа*) kidskin

ла́йнер, а *m.* (naut., aeron.) liner

лак, а *m.* varnish, lacquer; **л. для воло́с** hair spray

лаке́|й, я *m.* footman; lackey, flunkey (also fig., pej.)

лакиро́в|анный *p.p.p. of* ▶ **лакирова́ть** *and adj.* varnished, lacquered; ~анная ко́жа patent leather

лакир|ова́ть, у́ю *impf.* (*of* ▶ **отлакирова́ть**) to varnish, lacquer; (fig., pej.) to varnish

ла́к|овый *adj. of* ▶ **лак**; varnished, lacquered; ~овые ту́фли patent leather shoes

ла́ком|ый, ~, ~а *adj.* tasty, delicious; **л. кусо́(че)к** tasty morsel (also fig.)

лакони́чный, ~ен, ~на *adj.* laconic

лакри́ц|а, ы *f.* (bot.) liquorice (BrE), licorice (AmE)

ла́м|а, ы *m.* llama

Ла-Ма́нш, а *m.* the (English) Channel

ла́мп|а, ы *f.* **1** lamp; **л. дневно́го све́та** fluorescent lamp **2** (radio) valve; tube

лампа́д|а, ы *f.* icon lamp

лампа́с, а *m.* stripe (*down side of trousers*)

ла́мпочк|а, и *f.* **1** *dim. of* ▶ **ла́мпа** **2** (electric light) bulb; **стова́ттная л.** 100-watt bulb **3**: **мне э́то до ~и** (sl.) I couldn't care less about it

лангу́ст, а *m.* spiny lobster, langouste

ландша́фт, а *m.* landscape

ла́ндыш, а *m.* lily of the valley

ланце́т, а *m.* (med.) lancet; **вскрыть ~ом** to lance

ланч, а *m.* lunch

Лао́с, а *m.* Laos

лао́с|ец, ца *m.* Laotian

лао́с|ка, ки *f. of* ▶ **лао́сец**

лао́сский *adj.* Laotian

ла́п|а, ы *f.* (*животного*) paw; (*птицы*) foot; (fig., infml, *нога*) big foot; (fig., infml, *рука*) big hand; **попа́сть в ~ы к кому́-н.** to fall into sb's clutches

ла́п|оть, тя, *pl.* ~ти, ~те́й *m.* **1** (*обувь*) bast shoe **2** (infml, *о человеке*) oaf, bumpkin

лапш|а́, и́ *f.* **1** noodles (*pl.*) **2** (*syn*) noodle soup **3**: **ве́шать кому́-н. ~у́ на у́ши** (infml) to deceive sb

лар|ёк, ька́ *m.* stall

лар|е́ц, ца́ *m.* casket

ларинги́т, а *m.* laryngitis

ла́ск|а, и *f.* **1** caress, endearment; (*in pl.*) petting **2** (*доброе отношение*) kindness

ласка́|ть, ю *impf.* to caress, fondle, pet; (*о ветре, о воде*) to caress

ласка́|ться, юсь *impf.* (**к** + *d.*) to show affection (towards); (*о собаке*) to fawn (on)

ла́сков|ый, ∼, ∼а *adj.* affectionate, tender; (fig.) gentle; **л. ве́тер** gentle wind

лассо́ *nt. indecl.* lasso

ласт, а *m.* flipper

ла́стик, а *m.* (infml, *для стирания написанного*) rubber (BrE), eraser

ла́сточк|а, и *f.* swallow; **берегова́я л.** sand martin; **городска́я л.** (house) martin

латви́|ец, йца *m.* Latvian

латви́й|ка, ки *f. of* ▶ **латви́ец**

латви́йский *adj.* Latvian

Ла́тви|я, и *f.* Latvia

ла́текс, а *m.* latex

лати́ниц|а, ы *f.* Roman alphabet, Roman letters

латиноамерика́н|ец, ца *m.* Latin American

латиноамерика́н|ка, ки *f. of* ▶ **латиноамерика́нец**

латиноамерика́нский *adj.* Latin American

лати́нск|ий *adj.* Latin; **Л∼ая Аме́рика** Latin America

лату́к, а *m.* (bot.) lettuce

лату́н|ь, и *f.* brass

латы́н|ь, и *f.* Latin (*language*)

латы́ш, á, *pl.* **∼й, ∼éй** *m.* Latvian

латы́ш|ка, ки *f. of* ▶ **латы́ш**

латы́шский *adj.* Latvian

лауреа́т, а *m.* prizewinner; laureate; **л. Но́белевской пре́мии** Nobel prizewinner

ла́цкан, а, *pl.* **∼ы, ∼ов** *m.* lapel

лачу́г|а, и *f.* (infml) hovel, shack

ла́|ять, ю, ешь *impf.* to bark; (*о гончих*) to bay

лба, лбу *etc., see* ▶ **лоб**

лгать, лгу, лжёшь, лгут, *past* **лгал, лгала́, лга́ло** *impf.* (*of* ▶ **солга́ть**) to lie; to tell lies

лгун, á *m.* liar

лгу́н|ья, ьи, *g. pl.* **∼ий** *f. of* ▶ **лгун**

лебёдк|а, и *f.* (tech.) winch, windlass

ле́бед|ь, я, *pl.* **∼и, ∼éй** *m.* swan

лев, льва *m.* **1** (*животное*) lion; **морско́й л.** sea lion **2** (**Л.**) (astron., astrol.) Leo

левита́ци|я, и *f.* levitation

левобере́жный *adj.* left-bank

левш|á, и́, *i.* **∼о́й,** *g. pl.* **∼éй** *c.g.* left-hander

✧ **ле́в|ый** *adj.* **1** left; (*со стороны левой руки*) left-hand; (naut.) port; **л. борт** port side; **∼ая сторона́** left-hand side **2** (infml, *незаконный*) illegal, unofficial; **∼ая рабо́та** work on the side **3** (pol.) left-wing; (*as m. n. pl.* **л., ∼ого**) left-winger; (*pl.; collect.*) the left

лега́в|ая, ой *f.* (*in full* **длинношёрстная л.**) setter; (*in full* **коротношёрстная л.**) pointer

легализа́ци|я, и *f.* legalization

легализ|ова́ть, у́ю *impf. and pf.* to legalize

лега́л|ьный, ∼ен, ∼ьна *adj.* legal

леге́нд|а, ы *f.* legend; (*на карте*) key, legend

легенда́р|ный, ∼ен, ∼на *adj.* legendary

легио́н, а *m.* legion; (fig., *очень много*) plethora

легионе́р, а *m.* **1** (hist.) legionary **2** (sport, *игрок-иностранец*) foreign player

легити́м|ный, ∼ен, ∼на *adj.* (*власть*) legitimate

✧ **лёг|кий, ∼ок, легка́** *adj.* **1** (*на вес*) light; **л. за́втрак** light breakfast; **∼ая промы́шленность** light industry **2** (*нетрудный*) easy; **у него́ л. хара́ктер** he is easy to get on with; **∼кая атле́тика** (sport) athletics (BrE), track and field (AmE) **3** (*незначительный*) light; slight; **∼кая просту́да** slight cold

✧ **легко́** *adv.* (*несильно*) lightly; (*без труда*) easily; (*слегка*) slightly; **это ему́ л. даётся** it comes easily to him; (*as pred.*) it is easy; **л. сказа́ть!** easier said than done!

легкоатле́т, а *m.* (track and field) athlete

легкове́р|ный, ∼ен, ∼на *adj.* credulous, gullible

легково́й *adj.* passenger (*conveyance*); **л. автомоби́ль** (motor) car

лёгк|ое, ого *nt.* (anat.) lung; **односторо́ннее, двусторо́ннее воспале́ние ∼их** single, double pneumonia

легкомы́слен|ный, ∼, ∼на *adj.* thoughtless; flippant, frivolous

лёгкост|ь, и *f.* **1** (*веса*) lightness **2** (*нетрудность*) easiness **3** (*свобода*) ease; **с ∼ью** with ease

ле́гче *comp. of* ▶ **лёгкий,** ▶ **легко́**; (*as pred.*) **больно́му л.** the patient is feeling better; **мне от э́того не л.** I am none the better for it

лёд, льда, о льде́, во/на льду́ *m.* ice; **л. сло́ман** (fig.) the ice is broken

ледене́|ть, ю *impf.* (*of* ▶ **оледене́ть**) to freeze

леден|е́ц, ца́ *m.* fruit drop

ледни́к, á *m.* glacier

леднико́вый *adj.* glacial; **л. пери́од** ice age

ледо́в|ый *adj.* ice; **∼ое пла́вание** Arctic voyage

ледоко́л, а *m.* ice-breaker

ледору́б, а *m.* ice axe

ледохо́д, а *m.* drifting of ice

лед|яно́й *adj.* **1** *adj. of* ▶ **лёд**; **∼яная гора́/го́рка** ice slope (*for tobogganing*) **2** (*ветер; взгляд*) icy; ice-cold

лёжа *adv.* lying down, in lying position

✧ **леж|а́ть, у́, и́шь** *impf.* to lie; (*о предметах*) to be (situated); **л. в больни́це** to be in hospital; **на нём ∼и́т отве́тственность за э́то** it is his responsibility

лежа́чий *adj.* lying, recumbent; **л. больно́й** bed patient

ле́звие, я *nt.* blade

лез|ть, у, ешь, *past* **∼, ∼ла** *impf.* (*of* ▶ **поле́зть 1,** *det. of* ▶ **ла́зить**) **1** (**на** + *a.* or **по** + *d.*) (*взбираться вверх*) to climb (up, on to); **л. на де́рево** to climb a tree **2** (**в** + *a.* or **под** + *a.*) (*проникать*) to climb, clamber, crawl (through, into, under) **3** (*тайком*) to sneak **4** (в + *a.*) (*проникать рукой*) to thrust the hand (into) **5** (infml, *вмешиваться*) to interfere; **л. не в своё дело** to poke one's nose into sb else's affairs

лейбл, а *m.* (comm., mus.) label

лейбори́ст, а *m.* (pol.) Labourite (BrE), Laborite (AmE); labour supporter (BrE), labor supporter (AmE)

лейбори́стск|ий adj. (pol.) Labour (BrE), Labor (AmE); ~ая па́ртия Labour Party (BrE), Labor Party (AmE)

ле́йк|а, и *f.* **1** (*для поливки*) watering can **2** (infml, *воронка*) funnel

лейкеми́|я, и *f.* (med.) leukaemia (BrE), leukemia (AmE)

лейкопла́стыр|ь, я *m.* sticking plaster (BrE), adhesive tape (AmE), Band-Aid® (AmE)

лейкоци́т, а *m.* (physiol.) leucocyte

лейтена́нт, а *m.* lieutenant

лека́рственный adj. (*растение, настой*) medicinal; **л. препара́т** medicine, drug

лека́рств|о, а *nt.* medicine; **л. от ка́шля** cough medicine

ле́ксик|а, и *f.* vocabulary; (*всего языка*) lexis

ле́ктор, а *m.* (*в учебном заведении*) lecturer; (*выступающий*) speaker

ле́кци|я, и *f.* lecture; **чита́ть ~ю** to lecture, deliver a lecture

леле́|ять, ю *impf.* **1** to coddle, pamper **2** (fig.) to cherish, foster; **л. мечту́** to cherish a hope

ле́мминг, а *m.* (zool.) lemming

лён, льна *m.* (bot.) flax; (*ткань*) linen

лени́в|ец, ца *m.* (zool.) sloth

лени́в|ый, ~, ~а adj. lazy, idle; (*походка, вид*) sluggish

Ленингра́д, а *m.* (hist.) Leningrad

лен|и́ться, ю́сь, ~ишься *impf.* **1** to be lazy, idle **2** (+ *inf.*) to be too lazy (to)

ле́нт|а, ы *f.* (*украшение; орденская*) ribbon; (*магнитная*) tape; (*фильм*) film

лентя́|й, я *m.* lazybones

лен|ь, и *f.* **1** laziness **2** (as pred.) (+ *d. and inf.*) (infml) to feel too lazy (to), to not feel like; **ему́ бы́ло л. вы́ключить ра́дио** he was too lazy to turn the radio off

леопа́рд, а *m.* leopard

лепест|о́к, ка́ *m.* petal

лепе|та́ть, чу́, ~чешь *impf.* to babble

лепёшк|а, и *f.* flat cake, unleavened bread, flatbread

леп|и́ть, лю́, ~ишь *impf.* **1** (*pf.* с~) to model, fashion; to mould **2** (*pf.* на~) (infml, *наклеить*) to stick (on)

ле́пк|а, и *f.* modelling (BrE), modeling (AmE)

лепни́н|а, ы *f.* (collect.) moulding(s) (BrE), molding(s) (AmE)

✒ **лес**, а (у), *pl.* ~а́ *m.* **1** (в ~у́) (*большой*) forest; (*небольшой*) wood(s); **вы́йти из**

~а (из ~у) to come out of the wood; **тропи́ческий л.** rainforest **2** (в ~е) (*sg. only; collect.*) timber (BrE), lumber (AmE)

леса́¹ *pl. of* ▶ **лес**

лес|а́², о́в *m. pl.* (*строительные*) scaffolding

лесбия́нк|а, и *f.* lesbian

ле́ск|а, и *f.* fishing line

лесни́ч|ий, его *m.* forestry officer; forest warden

лес|но́й adj. of ▶ **лес**; **л. двор, склад** timber yard; **~но́е хозя́йство** forestry

лесопа́рк, а *m.* wooded park

лесопи́лк|а, и *f.* sawmill

лесопова́л, а *m.* tree felling

лесору́б, а *m.* lumberjack

ле́стниц|а, ы *f.* stairs, staircase; (*приставная*) ladder; **пожа́рная л.** fire escape; **складна́я л.** steps, stepladder; **служе́бная л.** career ladder

ле́стни|чный adj. of ▶ **ле́стница**; **~чная кле́тка** stairwell; **~чная площа́дка** landing

лест|ный, ~ен, ~на adj. flattering

лест|ь, и *f.* flattery

лет|а́, ~ *pl.* **1** years; age; **с де́тских ~** from childhood; **сре́дних ~** middle-aged **2** (*in g.*) (*as g. pl. of* ▶ **год**) (of age) years; **ско́лько вам ~?** how old are you?; **ему́ бо́льше, ме́ньше сорока́ ~** he is over, under forty

лет|а́ть, а́ю indet. of ▶ **лете́ть**

лета́ющ|ий adj.: **~ая таре́лка** (infml) flying saucer

ле|те́ть, чу́, ти́шь *impf.* of ▶ **полете́ть** 1, det. of ▶ **лета́ть** **1** to fly **2** (fig., *мчаться*) to fly; to rush, tear **3** (fig., infml, *падать*) to fall, drop

✒ **ле́тний** adj. summer; **л. сад** pleasure garden(s)

-ле́тний comb. form -year-old; **пятиле́тняя де́вочка** five-year-old girl

✒ **ле́т|о**, а *nt.* summer; **ба́бье л.** Indian summer; **ско́лько ~, ско́лько зим!** it's been ages!

летоисчисле́ни|е, я *nt.* chronology

ле́том adv. in summer

ле́топис|ь, и *f.* chronicle, annals

лету́ч|ий adj. **1** flying; **~ая мышь** bat **2** (chem.) volatile

лётчик, а *m.* pilot; **л.-испыта́тель** test pilot; **л.-истреби́тель** fighter pilot

лече́бниц|а, ы *f.* clinic (*usu. psychiatric or veterinary*)

лече́бный adj. **1** (*учреждение; средства*) medical **2** (*свойства; мазь*) medicinal; **л. препара́т** medicine, drug

✒ **лече́ни|е**, я *nt.* (medical) treatment; **амбулато́рное л.** outpatient treatment

леч|и́ть, у́, ~ишь *impf.* to treat (*medically*)

леч|и́ться, у́сь, ~ишься *impf.* **1** (от + *g.*) to receive, undergo (medical) treatment (for) **2** (у + *g.*) to be sb's patient

ле|чу́¹, ти́шь see ▶ **лете́ть**

леч|у́², ~ишь see ▶ **лечи́ть**

лечь, ля́гу, ля́жешь, ля́гут, past лёг, легла́, imper. ляг, ля́гте pf. (of ▶ **ложи́ться**) to lie (down); **л. в постéль**, **л. спать** to go to bed; **л. в больни́цу** to go into hospital

лéш|ий, **его** *m.* wood goblin

лещ, **á** *m.* bream (*fish*)

лжец, **á** *m.* liar

лжёшь *see* ▶ **лгать**

лжи́в|ый, **∼**, **∼а** *adj.* **1** (*человек*) lying; mendacious **2** (*улыбка*) false, deceitful

✓ **ли**, **ль** **1** (*interrog. particle*): **возмóжно ли?** is it possible? **2** (*conj.*) whether, if; **не знáю, придёт ли он** I don't know whether he is coming **3**: **ли... ли** whether ... or; **сегóдня ли, зáвтра ли** whether today or tomorrow

либерáл, **а** *m.* liberal; **л.-демокрáт** Liberal Democrat

либерализáци|я, **и** *n.* liberalization

либерали́зм, **а** *m.* liberalism

либерализ|овáть, **ýю** *impf. and pf.* to liberalize

либерáл|ьный, **∼ен**, **∼ьна** *adj.* liberal

либери́|ец, **йца** *m.* Liberian

либери́й|ка, **ки** *f. of* ▶ **либери́ец**

либери́йский *adj.* Liberian

Либéри|я, **и** *f.* Liberia

✓ **ли́бо** *conj.* or; **л. ... л.** (either) ... or

либрéтто *nt. indecl.* libretto

Ливáн, **а** *m.* (the) Lebanon

ливáн|ец, **ца** *m.* Lebanese

ливáн|ка, **ки** *f. of* ▶ **ливáнец**

ливáнский *adj.* Lebanese

ли́в|ень, **ня** *m.* heavy shower, downpour

ли́вер, **а** *m.* (cul.) offal

ли́вер|ный *adj. of* ▶ **ли́вер**; **∼ная колбасá** offal sausage

ливи́|ец, **йца** *m.* Libyan

ливи́й|ка, **ки** *f. of* ▶ **ливи́ец**

ливи́йский *adj.* Libyan

Ли́ви|я, **и** *f.* Libya

ли́г|а, **и** *f.* league

✓ **ли́дер**, **а** *m.* leader

лиди́р|овать, **ую** *impf.* to lead, be in the lead

ли|зáть, **жу́**, **∼жешь** *impf.* (*of* ▶ **лизну́ть**) to lick

ли́зинг, **а** *m.* (econ.) leasing

лиз|ну́ть, **ну́**, **нёшь** *inst. pf. of* ▶ **лизáть**

лизоблю́д, **а** *m.* (infml, pej.) lickspittle, bootlicker

ликвидáци|я, **и** *f.* **1** (comm.) liquidation **2** (pol., etc., *отмена*) liquidation; elimination, abolition

ликвиди́р|овать, **ую** *impf. and pf.* **1** (comm.) to liquidate, wind up **2** (*отменять*) to liquidate; to eliminate, abolish

ликви́д|ный, **∼ен**, **∼на** *adj.* (fin.) liquid; **∼ные акти́вы**, **срéдства** liquid assets

ликёр, **а** *m.* liqueur

ликёроводóчный *adj.*: **∼ завóд** distillery

лик|овáть, **ýю** *impf.* to rejoice, exult

лилипýт, **а** *m.* (*человек*) dwarf (offens.) (*person affected by dwarfism*)

ли́ли|я, **и** *f.* lily

лилóв|ый *adj.* purple

лимáн, **а** *m.* estuary; (*солёное озеро*) salt marshes

лими́т, **а** *m.* (*норма*) quota; (**на** + *a.*) (*ограничение*) limit (on)

лимóн, **а** *m.* lemon

лимонáд, **а** *m.* **1** lemonade; lemon squash **2** (*любой газированный напиток*) fizzy drink

лимузи́н, **а** *m.* limousine

ли́мф|а, **ы** *f.* (physiol.) lymph

лингви́ст, **а** *m.* linguist

лингви́стик|а, **и** *f.* linguistics

лингвисти́ческий *adj.* linguistic

линéйк|а, **и** *f.* **1** (*на бумаге*) (ruled) line **2** (*инструмент*) ruler **3** (*строй в шеренгу*) line; parade

ли́нз|а, **ы** *f.* lens

✓ **ли́ни|я**, **и** *f.* line; (fig.) policy

линóлеум, **а** *m.* linoleum

линя́|ть, **ет** *impf.* (*of* ▶ **полиня́ть**) **1** (*о материи*) to fade; (*о краске*) to run **2** (*о животных*) to moult (BrE), molt (AmE)

ли́п|а, **ы** *f.* lime (tree)

ли́п|кий, **∼ок**, **∼кá**, **∼ко** *adj.* sticky, adhesive

ли́р|а, **ы** *f.* lyre

ли́рик|а, **и** *f.* lyric poetry

лири́ческий *adj.* **1** (*поэзия, сопрано*) lyric **2** (*настроение*) lyrical

лис|á, **ы́**, *pl.* **∼ы** *f.* fox; **чернобýрая л.** silver fox

лис|ёнок, **ёнка**, *pl.* **∼я́та**, **∼я́т** *m.* fox cub

ли́сий *adj. of* ▶ **лисá**

лиси́ц|а, **ы** *f.* fox; vixen

Лиссабóн, **а** *m.* Lisbon

✓ **лист¹**, **á**, *pl.* **∼ья**, **∼ьев** *m.* (*растения*) leaf

✓ **лист²**, **á**, *pl.* **∼ы́**, **∼óв** *m.* **1** (*бумаги*) sheet **2**: **опрóсный л.** questionnaire; **охрáнный л.** safe conduct

листá|ть, **ю** *impf.* (infml) to leaf through

листв|á, **ы́** *f.* (collect.) leaves, foliage

ли́ственниц|а, **ы** *f.* (bot.) larch

ли́ственный *adj.* (bot.) deciduous

листóвк|а, **и** *f.* leaflet

лист|óк, **кá** *m.* **1** *dim. of* ▶ **лист¹**, ▶ **лист²** **2** (*листовка*) leaflet **3** (*бланк*) form

листопáд, **а** *m.* fall of the leaves

литáвр|ы, **∼** *f. pl.* (*sg.* **∼а**, **∼ы**) kettledrum

Литв|á, **ы́** *f.* Lithuania

литéйный *adj.* founding, casting

литерáтор, **а** *m.* man of letters

✓ **литератýр|а**, **ы** *f.* literature; **худóжественная л.** fiction

литератýр|ный, **∼ен**, **∼на** *adj.* literary

литературовéд, **а** *m.* literary critic

литóв|ец, **ца** *m.* Lithuanian

литóв|ка, **ки** *f. of* ▶ **литóвец**

литóвский *adj.* Lithuanian

литогрáфи|я, **и** *f.* **1** (*оттиск*) lithograph **2** (*искусство*) lithography

лит|о́й *adj.* cast; ~**а́я сталь** cast steel
литр, а *m.* litre (BrE), liter (AmE)
литурги́|я, и *f.* liturgy
лить, лью, льёшь, *past* **лил, лила́, ли́ло,** *imper.* **лей** *impf.* **1** to pour (*trans. and intrans.*); **л. слёзы** to shed tears; **дождь льёт как из ведра́** it is raining cats and dogs **2** (tech.) to found, cast, mould (BrE), mold (AmE)
ли́|ться, льётся, *past* ~**лся,** ~**ла́сь** *impf.* **1** to flow; to stream, pour **2** *pass. of* ▶ **лить**
лифт, а *m.* lift, elevator
лифтёр, а *m.* lift operator
ли́фчик, а *m.* bra
лих|о́й, ~, ~**а́,** ~**о,** ~**и́** *adj.* (infml) dashing, spirited; jaunty
лихора́дк|а, и *f.* **1** fever (also fig.); **сенна́я л.** hay fever **2** (*на губа́х*) cold sore
лицев|о́й *adj.* **1** (anat.) facial **2** exterior; ~**а́я сторона́** (*зда́ния*) facade, front; (*мате́рии*) right side; (*моне́ты*) obverse **3** (bookkeeping): **л. счёт** personal account
лице́|й, я *m.* lycée
лицеме́р, а *m.* hypocrite
лицеме́ри|е, я *nt.* hypocrisy
лицеме́р|ный, ~**ен,** ~**на** *adj.* hypocritical
лицензио́нный *adj.* (econ.) (*сде́лка*) licensing; (*произведённый по лице́нзии*) licensed
лицензи́р|овать, ую *impf. and pf.* (econ.) to license
лице́нзи|я, и *f.* (econ.) licence (BrE), license (AmE)
✎ **лиц|о́, а́,** *pl.* ~**а** *nt.* **1** face; **черты́** ~**а** features; **сказа́ть в л. кому́-н.** to say to sb's face; **знать кого́-н. в л.** to know sb by sight; **быть к** ~**у́** (+ *d.*) to suit, become; (fig.) to become, befit; ~**о́м к** ~**у́** face to face; **пе́ред** ~**о́м** (+ *g.*) in the face (of) **2** (*нару́жная сторона́*) exterior; (*мате́рии*) right side; (fig.): **показа́ть това́р** ~**о́м** to show sth to advantage; to make the best of sth **3** (*челове́к*) person; **гражда́нское л.** civilian; **должностно́е л.** official; **духо́вное л.** clergyman; **в** ~**е́** (+ *g.*) in the person (of); **от** ~**а́** (+ *g.*) in the name (of), on behalf (of) **4** (*индивидуа́льный о́блик*) identity
личи́нк|а, и *f.* larva, grub; maggot
✎ **ли́чно** *adv.* personally, in person
✎ **ли́чност|ь, и** *f.* **1** (*индивидуа́льность*) personality **2** (*челове́к*) person, individual; **удостовере́ние** ~**и** identity card; **установи́ть чью-н. л.** to establish sb's identity
✎ **ли́чн|ый** *adj.* personal; (*ча́стный*) private; ~**ая охра́на** bodyguard; ~**ая со́бственность** personal property; **л. соста́в** staff
лиша́йник, а *m.* (bot.) lichen
лиша́|ть, а́ю *impf. of* ▶ **лиши́ть**
лиша́|ться, а́юсь *impf. of* ▶ **лиши́ться**
лише́ни|е, я *nt.* **1** (*де́йствие*) deprivation; **л. гражда́нских прав** (law) disenfranchisement

✎ key word

2 (*usu. in pl.*) (*недоста́ток*) privation, hardship
лиш|ённый, ~**ён,** ~**ена́,** ~**ено́** *p.p.p. of* ▶ **лиши́ть** *and adj.* (+ *g.*) lacking (in), devoid (of)
лиш|и́ть, у́, и́шь *pf.* (*of* ▶ **лиша́ть**) (+ *g.*) to deprive (of); **л. кого́-н. насле́дства** to disinherit sb; **л. себя́ жи́зни** to take one's life
лиш|и́ться, у́сь, и́шься *pf.* (*of* ▶ **лиша́ться**) (+ *g.*) to lose, be deprived (of); **л. зре́ния** to lose one's sight
✎ **ли́шн|ий** *adj.* **1** (*избы́точный*) superfluous; unnecessary; (*unwanted*) **2** (*запасно́й*) spare, odd; **л. раз** once more; **с** ~**им** (infml) and more, odd
✎ **лишь** *adv. and conj.* only; **не хвата́ет л. одного́** one thing only is lacking; **л. то́лько** as soon as; **л. бы** if only, provided that; **л. бы он мог прие́хать** provided that he can come
лоб, лба, о лбе, во на лбу́, *pl.* **лбы, лбов** *m.* forehead, brow
ло́бби *nt. indecl.* (pol.) lobby
лобби́р|овать, ую *impf. and pf.* (pol.) **1** (*кого́*) to lobby (*sb*) **2** (*что*) to lobby for (*sth*)
ло́бзик, а *m.* fretsaw
лобов|о́й *adj.* frontal; ~**а́я ата́ка** (mil.) frontal attack; ~**о́е стекло́** windscreen (BrE), windshield (AmE)
лов|и́ть, лю́, ~**ишь** *impf.* (*of* ▶ **пойма́ть**) to (try to) catch; (fig.): **л. (удо́бный) моме́нт** to (try to) seize an opportunity; to look for an opportunity; **л. себя́ на чём-н.** to catch oneself at sth; **л. ста́нцию** (radio) to try to pick up a station
ло́в|кий, ~**ок,** ~**ка́,** ~**ко** *adj.* **1** (*иску́сный*) adroit, dexterous, deft; **л. ход** master stroke **2** (*хи́трый*) cunning, smart
ло́вко *adv.* (*иску́сно*) adroitly; **он л. устро́ился** he fixed himself up with a good job
ло́вкост|ь, и *f.* **1** (*иску́сность*) adroitness, dexterity, deftness; **л. рук** sleight of hand **2** (*хи́трость*) cunning, smartness
ло́в|ля, ли, *g. pl.* ~**ель** *f.* catching, hunting; **ры́бная л.** fishing
лову́шк|а, и *f.* snare, trap (also fig.)
ло́в|че *and* ~**че́е** *comp. of* ▶ **ло́вкий,** ▶ **ло́вко**
логари́фм, а *m.* (math.) logarithm
ло́гик|а, и *f.* logic
логи́ческий *adj.* logical
логи́ч|ный, ~**ен,** ~**на** *adj.* = **логи́ческий**
ло́гов|о, а *nt.* den, lair
логопе́д, а *m.* speech therapist
логоти́п, а *m.* (*эмбле́ма*) logo
ло́дк|а, и *f.* boat; **подво́дная л.** submarine; **спаса́тельная л.** lifeboat; **ката́ться на** ~**е** to go boating
ло́дочник, а *m.* boatman
лоды́жк|а, и *f.* (anat.) ankle bone
ло́ж|а, и *f.* **1** (theatr.) box **2** (*масо́нская*) lodge
ложби́н|а, ы *f.* (geog.) hollow, dip
лож|и́ться, у́сь, и́шься *impf. of* ▶ **лечь**

ло́жк|а, и *f.* **1** spoon; **столо́вая л.** tablespoon; **ча́йная л.** teaspoon **2** (*количество*) spoonful

ло́ж|ный, ~ен, ~на *adj.* false; **~ная трево́га** false alarm

ложь, лжи *f.* lie

лоз|а́, ы́, *pl.* **~ы** *f.* vine

ло́зунг, а *m.* **1** (*призыв*) slogan **2** (*плакат*) banner

лока́л|ьный, ~ен, ~ьна *adj.* local; **~ьная сеть** (comput.) local area network

лока́тор, а *m.* locator

локомоти́в, а *m.* locomotive

ло́кон, а *m.* lock, curl, ringlet

ло́к|оть, тя, *pl.* **~ти, ~те́й** *m.* elbow

лом, а, *pl.* **~ы́, ~о́в** *m.* **1** (*инструмент*) crowbar **2** (*sg. only; collect.*) (*ломаные предметы*) scrap, waste; **желе́зный л.** scrap iron

ло́маный *adj.* broken; **л. англи́йский язы́к** broken English

лома́|ть, ю *impf.* (*of* ▶ **слома́ть**) **1** to break **2** (*no pf.*) (fig.): **л. себе́ го́лову** (**над** + *i.*) to rack one's brains (over); **л. ру́ки** to wring one's hands

лома́|ться, юсь *impf.* **1** (*pf.* **с~**) to break **2** (*pf.* **с~**) (*о голосе*) to crack, break **3** (*pf.* **по~**) (infml, *кривляться*) to pose, put on airs

ломба́рд, а *m.* pawnshop; **заложи́ть в л.** to pawn

лом|и́ть, лю́, ~ишь *impf.* **1** (*impers.*) to cause to ache; **у меня́ ~ит спи́ну** my back aches **2** (infml, *пробиваться*) to break through, rush

лом|и́ться, лю́сь, ~ишься *impf.* **1** (*быть переполненным*) to be (near to) breaking; (**от** + *g.*) to burst (with), be crammed (with); **ве́тви ~я́тся от плодо́в** the boughs are groaning with fruit **2** (infml) (*стремиться проникнуть*) to force one's way; (*идти толпами*) (**на** + *a.*) to flock (to)

ло́м|кий, ~ок, ~ка́, ~ко *adj.* fragile, brittle

ло́мтик, а *m.* slice; **ре́зать ~ами** to slice

Ло́ндон, а *m.* London

лондо́н|ец, ца *m.* Londoner

лондо́н|ка, ки *f. of* ▶ **лондо́нец**

лондо́нский *adj.* London

лопа́т|а, ы *f.* spade, shovel

лопа́тк|а, и *f.* **1** (*лопата*) shovel; (*садовника*) trowel; (cul.) spatula; blade (*of turbine*) **2** (anat.) shoulder blade; (*часть туши*) shoulder

ло́п|аться, аюсь *impf. of* ▶ **ло́пнуть**

ло́п|нуть, ну, нешь *pf.* (*of* ▶ **ло́паться**) **1** (*о пузыре, шине, почке*) burst; (*о стекле*) to break, crack; (*о верёвке, струне*) to snap, break; (fig., infml): **чуть не л. от сме́ха** to split one's sides with laughter, burst with laughter; **моё терпе́ние ~нуло** my patience is exhausted **2** (fig., infml) (*потерпеть неудачу*) to fail, be a failure; (fin.) to go bankrupt, crash

лопу́х, а́ *m.* **1** (bot.) burdock **2** (sl.) fool

лорд, а *m.* lord; **пала́та ~ов** House of Lords

Лос-А́нджелес, а *m.* Los Angeles

лоск, а *m.* lustre (BrE), luster (AmE), gloss, shine (also fig.)

лоску́т, а́, *pl.* **~ы́, ~о́в** *and* **~ья, ~ьев** *m.* rag, shred, scrap

лосн|и́ться, ю́сь, и́шься *impf.* to be glossy, shine

лосо́с|ь, я, *pl.* **~и, ~ей** *m.* salmon

лос|ь, я, *pl.* **~и, ~е́й** *m.* elk (BrE), moose (AmE)

лосьо́н, а *m.* lotion; (*после бритья*) aftershave

лот, а *m.* (*на аукционе*) lot

лотере́йный *adj. of* ▶ **лотере́я**; **л. биле́т** lottery ticket

лотере́|я, и *f.* lottery, raffle

лот|о́к, ка́ *m.* **1** (*прилавок*) hawker's stand; (*ящик для торговли*) hawker's tray **2** (*для ссыпания*) chute; (*для стока*) gutter

ло́тос, а *m.* (bot.) lotus

лото́чник, а *m.* hawker

лох, а *m.* (sl.) simpleton, halfwit

лохма́т|ый, ~, ~а *adj.* **1** (*животное*) shaggy(-haired) **2** (*человек, волосы*) dishevelled (BrE), disheveled (AmE), tousled

лохмо́ть|я, ев (*no sg.*) rags; **в ~ях** in rags, ragged

лошади́н|ый *adj.* of horses; equine; **~ая си́ла** horsepower

ло́шад|ь, и, *pl.* **~и, ~е́й, ~я́м, ~ьми́, о ~я́х** *f.* horse; **бегова́я, скакова́я л.** racehorse; **чистокро́вная л.** thoroughbred; **сади́ться на л.** to mount

лоя́льност|ь, и *f.* loyalty

лоя́л|ьный, ~ен, ~ьна *adj.* loyal (*to the State authorities*)

ЛСД *m. indecl.* (*abbr. of* **диэтиламид лизерги́новой кислоты́**) LSD

луг, а, о ~е, на ~у́, *pl.* **~а́, ~о́в** *m.* meadow; **заливно́й л.** water meadow

лу́ж|а, и *f.* puddle, pool; **сесть в ~у** (fig., infml) to get into a mess; to slip up

лужа́йк|а, и *f.* (*полянка*) (forest) glade; (*газон*) lawn

лу́з|а, ы *f.* (billiard) pocket

лук¹, а *m.* (*collect.*) (*растение*) onions; **голо́вка ~а** (a single) onion; **зелёный л.** spring onion(s) (BrE), scallion(s); **л.-поре́й** leek(s)

лук², а *m.* (*оружие*) bow

лука́в|ый, ~, ~а *adj.* **1** (*хитрый*) crafty, sly, cunning **2** (*игривый*) arch

лу́ковиц|а, ы *f.* **1** (*головка лука*) onion **2** (bot.) bulb

лун|а́, ы́, *pl.* **~ы** *f.* moon; **Л.** the Moon

луна́тик, а *m.* sleepwalker, somnambulist

лу́нк|а, и *f.* hole

лу́н|ный *adj.* of ▶ **луна́**; (astron.) lunar; **~ное затме́ние** lunar eclipse; **~ная ночь** moonlit night; **л. свет** moonlight

лу́п|а, ы *f.* magnifying glass

луч, а́ *m.* ray; beam; **рентге́новские ~и** X-rays

луч|ево́й *adj.* **1** *adj. of* ▶ **луч** **2** radial **3** (med.): **~ева́я боле́знь** radiation sickness

лу́чник, а *m.* archer

л

лу́чше ◼1 (*comp. of* ▸ **хоро́ший**, ▸ **хорошо́**[1]) better; **тем л.** so much the better; **л. всего́, л. всех** best of all; **как мо́жно л.** as well as possible; **нам л. верну́ться** we had better go back ◼2 (*as particle*) (*предпочти́тельнее*) rather, instead; **дава́йте л. поговори́м об э́том** let's talk it over instead

лу́чш|ий *adj.* (*comp. and superl. of* ▸ **хоро́ший**) better; best; **к ~ему** for the better; **в ~ем слу́чае** at best

лы́ж|а, и *f.* ski; **го́рные ~и** alpine skis; **бе́гать, ходи́ть на ~ах** to ski

лы́жник, а *m.* skier

лы́жни|ца, цы *f. of* ▸ **лы́жник**

лыжн|я́, и́ *f.* ski track

лысе́|ть, ю *impf.* (*of* ▸ **облысе́ть**, ▸ **полысе́ть**) to go bald

лы́син|а, ы *f.* bald patch

лы́с|ый, ~, ~а́, ~о *adj.* bald; (*гора́*) bare

ль = **ли**

льв|ёнок, ёнка, *pl.* **~я́та, ~я́т** *m.* lion cub

льви́н|ый *adj. of* ▸ **лев**; **~ая до́ля** (fig.) the lion's share

льви́ц|а, ы *f.* lioness

львя́та *see* ▸ **львёнок**

льго́т|а, ы *f.* (*блока́дникам, инвали́дам*) privilege; advantage; benefit; (*при опла́те*) discount

льго́тный *adj.* privileged; favourable (BrE), favorable (AmE); **л. биле́т** concessionary ticket

льда *g. sg. of* ▸ **лёд**

льди́н|а, ы *f.* block of ice, ice floe

льна, льну *see* ▸ **лён**

льнян|о́й *adj.* ◼1 of flax; **~о́го цве́та** flaxen ◼2 (*пла́тье*) linen

льстец, а́ *m.* flatterer

льсти́в|ый, ~, ~а *adj.* (*слова́*) flattering; (*челове́к*) smooth-tongued

льстить, льщу, льстишь *impf.* (*of* ▸ **польсти́ть**) ◼1 (+ *d.*) to flatter; to gratify; **э́то льстит его́ самолю́бию** it flatters his self-esteem ◼2 (+ *a., with refl. pron. only*) to delude; **л. себя́ наде́ждой** to flatter oneself with the hope

лью, льёшь *see* ▸ **лить**

лэпто́п, а *m.* laptop (computer)

любе́зность|ь, и *f.* ◼1 (*сво́йство*) courtesy; politeness; civility ◼2 (*услуга*) kindness; **оказа́ть, сде́лать кому́-н. л.** to do sb a kindness

любе́зн|ый, ~ен, ~на *adj.* ◼1 (*ве́жливый*) courteous; polite; obliging ◼2 (*ми́лый*) kind, amiable; **бу́дьте ~ны...** (polite form of request) be so kind as ...

люби́м|ец, ца *m.* favourite (BrE), favorite (AmE), darling

люби́м|ица, ицы *f. of* ▸ **люби́мец**

люби́мчик, а *m.* (pej.) pet, blue-eyed boy

◆ **люби́м|ый, ~, ~а** *adj.* ◼1 (*дорого́й*) beloved, loved; (*as n.* **л., ~ого, f. ~ая, ~ой**) (my)

beloved ◼2 (*предпочита́емый*) favourite (BrE), favorite (AmE)

люби́тел|ь, я *m.* ◼1 (+ *g. or* + *inf.*) lover; **л. му́зыки** music lover; **л. соба́к** dog lover; **он л. спле́тничать** he loves gossiping ◼2 (*непрофессиона́л*) amateur

люби́тель|ница, ницы *f. of* ▸ **люби́тель**

люби́тельский *adj.* ◼1 amateur; **л. спекта́кль** amateur performance ◼2 (pej.) amateurish

◆ **люб|и́ть, лю, ~ишь** *impf.* ◼1 (*мать, ро́дину*) to love ◼2 (*чита́ть, му́зыку*) to like, be fond (of) ◼3 (infml, *о растениях*) to like; **фиа́лки ~ят тень** violets like shade

люб|ова́ться, у́юсь *impf.* (*of* ▸ **полюбова́ться**) (+ *i. or* на + *a.*) to admire

любо́вник, а *m.* lover

любо́вниц|а, ы *f.* lover, mistress

любо́вн|ый *adj.* ◼1 love-; **~ая исто́рия** love affair ◼2 (*отноше́ние*) loving

◆ **люб|о́вь, ви,** *i.* **~о́вью** *f.* (к + *d.*) love (for, of); **занима́ться ~о́вью** to make love

любозна́тель|ный, ~ен, ~ьна *adj.* inquisitive

◆ **любо́й** ◼1 *adj.* any; (*из двои́х*) either; **л. цено́й** at any price ◼2 (*as n.*) anyone; (*из двои́х*) either

любопы́т|ный, ~ен, ~на *adj.* curious; interesting; (*impers. as pred. and inf.*) **~но, придёт ли она́** I wonder if she will come

любопы́тств|о, а *nt.* curiosity

лю́д|и, е́й, ~ям, ~ьми́, о ~ях (*no sg.*) ◼1 (*pl. of* ▸ **челове́к**) people ◼2 (mil.) men ◼3 (*ка́дры*) staff, people

людое́д, а *m.* ◼1 (*челове́к*) cannibal; (*живо́тное*) maneater; **тигр-л.** man-eating tiger ◼2 (*в ска́зках*) ogre

люк, а *m.* ◼1 (naut., aeron.) hatch, hatchway ◼2 (theatr.) trap ◼3: **светово́й л.** skylight

люкс *adj. indecl.* de luxe, luxury

Люксембу́рг, а *m.* Luxembourg

люксембу́ргский *m.* Luxembourg

люксембу́рж|енка and **люксембу́рж|ка, (ен)ки** *f. of* ▸ **люксембу́ржец**

люксембу́рж|ец, ца *m.* Luxembourger

лю́тик, а *m.* (bot.) buttercup

лю́т|ня, ни, *g. pl.* **~ен** and **~ней** *f.* (mus.) lute

лю́т|ый, ~, ~а́, ~о *adj.* ferocious, fierce, cruel; (*моро́з*) sharp; (*не́нависть*) intense

ля *nt. indecl.* (mus.) А; **л. бемо́ль** A flat

ляг and **ля́гте** *imper. of* ▸ **лечь**

ляга́|ть, а́ю *impf.* (*of* ▸ **лягну́ть**) to kick

ляга́|ться, юсь *impf.* to kick (*intrans*); (*друг дру́га*) to kick one another

ляг|ну́ть, ну́, нёшь *inst. pf. of* ▸ **ляга́ть**

ля́|гу, жешь, гут *see* ▸ **лечь**

лягу́шк|а, и *f.* frog

ля́жк|а, и *f.* (infml) thigh, haunch

лязг, а (*no pl.*) *m.* clank, clang

ля́зга|ть, ю *impf.* (+ *i.*) to clank, clang; **он ~л зуба́ми** his teeth were chattering

ля́мк|а, и *f.* strap

ля́п|нуть, ну, нешь *pf.* (infml) to blurt out

◆ key word

Л

Мм

♂ **м** (*abbr. of* **метр**) m, metre(s) (BrE), meter(s) (AmE)

мавзоле́|й, я *m.* mausoleum

Маврита́ни|я, и *f.* Mauritania

маг, а *m.* magician, wizard

♂ **магази́н, а** *m.* **1** shop; **гастрономи́ческий/ продово́льственный м.** grocer's (shop) (BrE), grocery store (AmE); **универса́льный м.** department store **2** (*у стрелкового оружия*) magazine

МАГАТЭ *nt. indecl.* (*abbr. of* **Междунаро́дное аге́нтство по а́томной эне́ргии**) IAEA (*International Atomic Energy Agency*)

маги́стр, а *m.* **1** (*лицо*) holder of a master's degree **2** (*учёная степень*) master's degree

магистра́л|ь, и *f.* **1** (*водная, газовая*) main; (*железнодорожная*) main line **2** (*улица*) arterial road, main road

маги́ческий *adj.* magic(al)

ма́ги|я, и *f.* magic

магна́т, а *m.* magnate, tycoon

магнети́зм, а *m.* magnetism

магнети́ческий *adj.* magnetic

ма́гни|й, я *m.* (chem.) magnesium

магни́т, а *m.* magnet

магни́тн|ый *adj.* magnetic; **~ая ка́рточка** smart card, swipe card

магнито́л|а, ы *f.* radio cassette player

магнитофо́н, а *m.* tape recorder; **ви́део~** video (cassette) recorder, VCR

магно́ли|я, и *f.* (bot.) magnolia

маде́р|а, ы *f.* Madeira (wine)

мадо́нн|а, ы *f.* madonna

Мадри́д, а *m.* Madrid

мажо́р, а *m.* (mus.) major key

ма́|зать, жу, жешь *impf.* **1** (*pf.* **на~, по~**) (*смазывать*) to oil, grease, lubricate **2** (*pf.* **на~, по~**) (*намазывать*) to smear (with); **м. хлеб ма́слом** to spread butter on bread, butter bread **3** (*pf.* **из~, за~**) (infml, *пачкать*) to soil, stain **4** (*pf.* **про~**) (*не попадать*, infml) to miss

ма́|заться, жусь, жешься *impf.* **1** (*pf.* **из~, за~**) (*пачкаться*) to soil oneself, stain oneself **2** (*pf.* **на~**) to make up **3** (*pf.* **на~**) (+ *i.*) (*ointment, cream, etc.*)

мазохи́ст, а *m.* masochist

мазохи́ст|ка, ки *f. of* ▸ **мазохи́ст**

мазу́т, а *m.* (tech.) fuel oil

маз|ь, и *f.* **1** (*лекарство*) ointment **2** (*для смазки*) grease

♂ **ма́|й, я** *m.* May

ма́йк|а, и *f.* sleeveless top; (*нижняя*) vest (BrE), undershirt (AmE)

майоне́з, а *m.* (cul.) mayonnaise

майо́р, а *m.* major (*military rank*)

майора́н, а *m.* (bot.) marjoram

ма́йский *adj. of* ▸ **май**; **м. жук** cockchafer

мак, а *m.* (*растение*) poppy; (*семена*) poppy seed(s)

мака́к|а, и *f.* (zool.) macaque

макаро́н|ы, ~ *pl.* pasta

мак|а́ть, а́ю *impf.* (*of* ▸ **макну́ть**) to dip

македо́н|ец, ца *m.* Macedonian

Македо́ни|я, и *f.* Macedonia

македо́н|ка, ки *f. of* ▸ **македо́нец**

македо́нский *adj.* Macedonian; **Алекса́ндр М.** Alexander the Great

маке́т, а *m.* model; (*книги*) dummy

макия́ж, а *m.* make-up

ма́клер, а *m.* (comm.) broker

мак|ну́ть, ну́, нёшь *inst. pf. of* ▸ **мака́ть**

максимали́зм, а *m.* uncompromisingness

максимали́ст, а *m.* uncompromising person

♂ **максима́л|ьный, ~ен, ~ьна** *adj.* maximum

ма́ксимум, а *m.* **1** maximum **2** (*as adv.*) at most; **м. сто рубле́й** a hundred roubles at most

макулату́р|а, ы *f.* paper for recycling

маку́шк|а, и *f.* **1** (*дерева*) top **2** (*головы*) crown

мала́|ец, йца *m.* Malay

Мала́йзи|я, и *f.* Malaysia

мала́й|ка, ки *f. of* ▸ **мала́ец**

мала́йский *adj.* Malay, Malayan

Мала́й|я, и *f.* Malaya

малахи́т, а *m.* (min.) malachite

мале́йший *adj.* (*superl. of* ▸ **ма́лый**) least, slightest

мал|ёк, ька́ *m.* young fish; (*collect.*) fry

♂ **ма́леньк|ий** *adj.* **1** little, small **2** (*незначительный*) slight **3** (*малолетний*) young; (*as n.* **м.**, **~ого**, *f.* **~ая**, **~ой**) the baby, the child; **~ие** the young

мали́н|а, ы *f.* (*no pl.*) (*кустарник*) raspberry bush; (*ягоды*) raspberries

мали́новый *adj.* **1** (*варенье*) raspberry **2** (*цвет*) crimson

♂ **ма́ло** *adv.* (*времени, денег*) little, not much; (*книг, людей*) few; (*недостаточно*) not enough; (*читать*) not enough; **э́того ма́ло** this is not enough; **я м. где быва́л** I have hardly been anywhere; **м. того́** moreover; **м. того́, что...** not only ..., it is not enough that ...; **м. того́, что он сам прие́хал, он привёз всех това́рищей** it was not enough that he came himself, but he had to bring all his friends

малова́ж|ный, ~ен, ~на *adj.* of little importance, insignificant

малова́т, ~а, ~о *adj.* (infml) on the small side

малоду́ш|ный, ~ен, ~на *adj.* faint-hearted

маложи́рный *adj.* low-fat

малоиму́щ|ий, ~, ~а *adj.* needy, indigent

малокалори́|йный, ~ен, ~йна *adj.* low-calorie

малокро́ви|е, я *nt.* anaemia (BrE), anemia (AmE)

малоле́тн|ий *adj.* **1** young; juvenile **2** (*as n. м.*, ~его, *f.* ~яя, ~ей) (*ребёнок*) infant; (*подросток*) juvenile, minor

малолитра́жк|а, и *f.* (infml) compact (car); mini

маломо́щ|ный, ~ен, ~на *adj.* low-powered; weak

малоподви́ж|ный, ~ен, ~на *adj.* not mobile, slow-moving

малоро́сл|ый, ~, ~а *adj.* undersized, stunted

малоупотреби́тел|ьный, ~ен, ~ьна *adj.* infrequent, rarely used

малочи́слен|ный, ~, ~на *adj.* small (in numbers); scanty

М ✎ **ма́л|ый**, ~, ~а́, ~о́ *adj.* little, (too) small; э́ти сапоги́ мне ~ы́ these boots are too small for me; (*as nt. n.* ~ое, ~ого) little; са́мое ~ое (infml) at the least; без ~ого almost, all but

✎ **малы́ш**, а́ *m.* (infml) child, kid; little boy

ма́льв|а, ы *f.* (bot.) mallow

Мальо́рк|а, и *f.* Majorca

Ма́льт|а, ы *f.* Malta

мальти́|ец, йца *m.* Maltese

мальти́й|ка, ки *f. of* ▶ мальти́ец

мальти́йский *adj.* Maltese

✎ **ма́льчик**, а *m.* boy

мальчи́шеский *adj.* boyish

мальчи́шк|а, и *m.* (infml) (little) boy

маля́р, а́ *m.* (house) painter, decorator

маляри́|я, и *f.* (med.) malaria

маля́р|ный *adj. of* ▶ маля́р; ~ная кисть paintbrush

✎ **ма́м|а**, ы *f.* mum, mummy (BrE), mom, mommy (AmE)

ма́мин *adj.* mother's

ма́монт, а *m.* mammoth

ма́нго *nt. indecl.* (bot.) mango

мангу́ст, а *m.* (zool.) mongoose

мандари́н, а *m.* (*дерево, плод*) mandarin, tangerine

манда́т, а *m.* mandate

мандоли́н|а, ы *f.* (mus.) mandolin

манёвр, а *m.* **1** manoeuvre (BrE), maneuver (AmE); manoeuvres (BrE), maneuvers (AmE) **2** (*in pl.*) (rail.) shunting

маневри́р|овать, ую *impf.* (*of* ▶ сманеври́ровать) to manoeuvre (BrE),

maneuver (AmE)

мане́ж, а *m.* **1** riding school, manège **2** (*цирка*) ring **3**: спорти́вный м. sports hall **4**: (де́тский) м. playpen

манеке́н, а *m.* mannequin; dummy

манеке́нщик, а *m.* male model

манеке́нщиц|а, ы *f.* model

мане́р|а, ы *f.* **1** manner, style; м. вести́ себя́ way of behaving; м. держа́ть себя́ bearing, carriage; петь в ~е Кару́зо to sing in the style of Caruso **2** (*in pl.*) manners; у него́ плохи́е ~ы he has no manners

мане́р|ный, ~ен, ~на *adj.* affected

манже́т|а, ы *f.* cuff

маникю́р, а *m.* manicure

маникю́рш|а, и *f.* manicurist

манипули́р|овать, ую *impf.* (+ *i.*) to manipulate

манипуля́ци|я, и *f.* **1** manipulation **2** (fig.) machination, intrigue

ман|и́ть, ю́, ~ишь *impf.* (*of* ▶ помани́ть) to beckon

манифе́ст, а *m.* manifesto; proclamation

манифеста́ци|я, и *f.* (street) demonstration

мани́шк|а, и *f.* (false) shirt front, dicky

ма́ни|я, и *f.* **1** mania; м. вели́чия megalomania **2** (fig.) passion, craze

ма́нк|а, и *f.* (infml) semolina

манса́рд|а, ы *f.* attic, garret

ма́нти|я, и *f.* cloak, mantle; robe, gown

манто́ *nt. indecl.* fur coat (lady's)

манускри́пт, а *m.* manuscript

манья́к, а *m.* maniac

мара́зм, а *m.* (med.) marasmus; ста́рческий м. senility; (fig.) decay

марафо́н, а *m.* marathon

маргари́н, а *m.* margarine

маргари́тк|а, и *f.* (bot.) daisy

маргина́л, а *m.* person living on the fringes of society

маргина́л|ьный, ~ен, ~ьна *adj.* marginal

марина́д, а *m.* marinade

марини́ст, а *m.* painter of seascapes

марино́ванный *p.p.p. of* ▶ маринова́ть *and adj.* (cul.) pickled

марин|ова́ть, у́ю *impf.* (*pf.* за~) to pickle

марионе́т|ка, ки *f.* marionette; puppet (also fig.)

марионе́т|очный *adj. of* ▶ марионе́тка; ~очное госуда́рство puppet state

марихуа́н|а, ы *f.* marijuana

✎ **ма́рк|а**, и *f.* **1** (*почтовая*) (postage) stamp **2** (*сорт*) brand, make; фабри́чная м. trademark

ма́ркер, а *m.* (*фломастер*) marker (pen)

ма́рке́тинг, а *m.* marketing

марки́з|а, ы *f.* marchioness

маркси́зм, а *m.* Marxism

ма́рл|я, и *f.* gauze

мармела́д, а *m.* (*конфеты*) fruit jellies

мароде́р, а *m.* marauder, pillager

мародёрств|о, а *nt.* pillage, looting

марокка́н|ец, ца *m.* Moroccan

марокка́н|ка, ки *f. of* ▶ **марокка́нец**

марокка́нский *adj.* Moroccan

Маро́кко *nt. indecl.* Morocco

Марс, а *m.* (astron., myth.) Mars

марсиа́н|ин, ина, *pl.* ∼**е,** ∼ *m.* Martian

☞ **март, а** *m.* March

ма́ртовский *adj. of* ▶ **март**

марты́шк|а, и *f.* marmoset; (fig., infml) monkey

марципа́н, а *m.* (кондитерское изделие) (из теста) marzipan cake; (не из теста) marzipan sweet; (начинка, глазурь) marzipan

марш, а *m.* march; **м. проте́ста** protest march

ма́ршал, а *m.* marshal

маршир|ова́ть, у́ю *impf.* (of ▶ **промарширова́ть**) to march

☞ **маршру́т, а** *m.* route

ма́ск|а, и *f.* mask; (fig.): **сбро́сить с себя́** ∼**у** to throw off the mask

маскара́д, а *m.* masked ball; (fig.) masquerade

маскара́дный *adj. of* ▶ **маскара́д; м. костю́м** fancy dress

маскир|ова́ть, у́ю *impf.* (of ▶ **замаскирова́ть**) to mask, disguise; (mil.) to camouflage

маскир|ова́ться, у́юсь *impf.* (of ▶ **замаскирова́ться**) to disguise oneself; (mil.) to camouflage oneself

Ма́слениц|а, ы *f.* Shrovetide; carnival

маслёнк|а, и *f.* 1 (посуда для сливочного масла) butter dish 2 (tech.) oilcan

масли́н|а, ы *f.* 1 (дерево) olive tree 2 (плод) olive

☞ **ма́с|ло, ла,** *pl.* ∼**ла́,** ∼**ел,** ∼**ла́м** *nt.* 1 (in full **сли́вочное м.**) butter 2 (растительное) oil; **как по** ∼**лу** (fig., infml) swimmingly 3 (краски) oil (paints); **писа́ть** ∼**лом** to paint in oils

масляни́ст|ый, ∼, ∼**а** *adj.* oily

масо́н, а *m.* Freemason, Mason

масо́нский *adj.* Masonic

☞ **ма́сс|а, ы** *f.* 1 mass; (in pl.) (pol.) the masses; **в (о́бщей)** ∼**е** on the whole 2 (infml, множество) a lot, lots

масса́ж, а *m.* massage; **то́чечный м.** shiatsu, acupressure

массажи́ст, а *m.* masseur

массажи́стк|а, и *f.* masseuse

масси́в, а *m.* (geog.) massif; (fig.) expanse; **жило́й м.** housing development

масси́в|ный, ∼**ен,** ∼**на** *adj.* massive

масси́рование, я *nt.* massing, concentration

масси́рованный *adj.* intensive

масс-ме́диа *pl. indecl.* mass media

☞ **ма́ссов|ый** *adj.* mass; ∼**ое произво́дство** mass production; **м. чита́тель** general reader

☞ **ма́стер, а,** *pl.* ∼**а́ м.** 1 (цеха) foreman 2 (ремесленник) craftsman, skilled workman 3 (на + a. or + inf.) (знаток) expert, master (at, of); (sport) vet(eran); **м. (по ремо́нту)** repairman; **телевизио́нный м.**

TV repairman; **м. на все ру́ки** person able to turn his hand to anything, jack of all trades

ма́стер-кла́сс, а *m.* masterclass

мастерск|а́я, о́й *f.* (столяра) workshop; (художника) studio; (на заводе) shop; **авторемо́нтная м.** car repair garage

ма́стерски *adv.* skilfully; in masterly fashion

мастерств|о́, а́ *nt.* 1 (ремесло) trade, craft 2 (умение) skill, craftsmanship

масти́к|а, и *f.* 1 (смола) mastic 2 (замазка) putty 3 (для натирания полов) floor polish

мастурба́ци|я, и *f.* masturbation

мастурби́р|овать, ую *impf.* to masturbate

маст|ь, и, и, *pl.* ∼**и,** ∼**е́й** *f.* 1 (цвет шерсти) colour (BrE), color (AmE) 2 (cards) suit; **ходи́ть в м.** to follow suit

масшта́б, а *m.* scale; **конфли́кт большо́го** ∼**а** large-scale conflict

масшта́б|ный, ∼**ен,** ∼**на** *adj.* 1 scale; ∼**ная моде́ль** scale model 2 (большой) large-scale

мат¹, а *m.* (chess) checkmate, mate; **объяви́ть м.** (+ d.) to mate

мат², а *m.* (половик, тюфяк) mat

мат³, а *m.* (брань) foul language, abuse; **руга́ться** ∼**ом** to use foul language

матема́тик, а *m.* mathematician

матема́тик|а, и *f.* mathematics

математи́ческий *adj.* mathematical

☞ **материа́л, а** *m.* material; (для публикации в прессе) copy

материали́зм, а *m.* materialism

материализ|ова́ться, у́юсь *impf. and pf.* to materialize

материали́ст, а *m.* materialist

☞ **материа́л|ьный,** ∼**ен,** ∼**ьна** *adj.* material; ∼**ьные затрудне́ния** financial difficulties; ∼**ьное положе́ние** economic conditions

матери́к, а́ м. 1 (континент) continent 2 (суша) mainland

материко́вый *adj.* continental

матери́нск|ий *adj.* maternal, motherly; ∼**ая пла́та** (comput.) motherboard

матер|и́ться, ю́сь, и́шься *impf.* (infml) to swear

мате́ри|я¹, и *f.* (phil.) matter

мате́ри|я², и *f.* (text.) material, cloth

мате́рчатый *adj.* made of cloth, cloth

мате́р|ый, ∼, ∼**а** *adj.* 1 (достигший полной зрелости) full-grown, mature (of animal) 2 (опытный) experienced, practised 3 (неисправимый) inveterate, out-and-out

ма́тк|а, и *f.* 1 (anat.) uterus, womb 2 (самка) female; (пчелиная) queen (bee)

ма́тов|ый *adj.* matt; ∼**ое стекло́** frosted glass

матра́с, а *m.* mattress; **надувно́й м.** air bed, inflatable mattress

матра́|ц, ца = **матра́с**

матрёшк|а, и *f.* matryoshka, (set of) nested Russian dolls

ма́триц|а, ы *f.* 1 (typ.) matrix 2 (tech.) die, mould (BrE), mold (AmE)

M

матро́с, а *m.* sailor, seaman

✓ **матч**, а *m.* (sport) match; **междунаро́дный м.** Test (match)

✓ **мат|ь**, *g., d., p.* ~ери, ~ерью, *pl.* ~ери, ~ере́й *f.* **1** mother; **бу́дущая м.** expectant mother, mother-to-be; **м.-одино́чка** single mother **2** (infml) *familiar form of address to a woman*

мафио́зи *m. indecl.* Mafioso

мафио́зный *adj. of* ▶ **ма́фия**

ма́фи|я, и *f.* Mafia

мах, а (у) *m.* (*рукой*) swing, stroke; (*крыла*) flap; **одни́м ~ом** at one stroke, in a trice; **с ~у** (infml) rashly, without thinking

ма|ха́ть, шу́, ~шешь *impf.* (*of* ▶ **махну́ть 1**) (+ *i.*) (*рукой*) to wave; (*веткой*) to brandish; (*хвостом*) to wag; (*крыльями*) to flap

махи́н|а, ы *f.* (infml) bulky and cumbersome object

махина́ци|я, и *f.* machination, intrigue

мах|ну́ть, ну́, нёшь *pf.* **1** *pf. of* ▶ **маха́ть; м. руко́й** (на + *a.*) (fig., infml) to give up as a bad job **2** (infml, *поехать*) to go, travel

махови́к, а́ *m.* flywheel

махро́вый *adj.* (*ткань*) terry

мац|а́, ы́ (*no pl.*) *f.* matzos (*Jewish biscuits for Passover*)

маче́те *nt. indecl.* machete

ма́чех|а, и *f.* stepmother

ма́чт|а, ы *f.* mast

✓ **маши́н|а**, ы *f.* **1** (*механическое устройство*) machine (also fig.); **посудомо́ечная м.** dishwasher **2** (*автомобиль*) car; vehicle; **м. «ско́рой по́мощи»** ambulance

машина́л|ьный, ~ен, ~ьна *adj.* automatic (fig.); **м. отве́т** an automatic response

машини́ст, а *m.* **1** (*комбайна*) driver, operator (*workman in charge of machinery*) **2** (*локомотива*) engine driver (BrE), engineer (AmE)

машини́стк|а, и *f.* typist

маши́н|ка, ки *f. dim. of* ▶ **маши́на; (пи́шущая) м.** typewriter

машинопи́сный *adj.* typewritten; **м. текст** typescript

машинострое́ни|е, я *nt.* mechanical engineering, machinery construction

машинострои́тельный *adj. of* ▶ **машинострое́ние**

мая́к, а́ *m.* lighthouse; beacon (also fig.)

ма́ятник, а *m.* pendulum

ма́|яться, юсь, ешься *impf.* (infml) **1** (с + *i.*) (*трудиться*) to toil (with, over) **2** (*томиться*) to pine, suffer

мая́ч|ить, у, ишь *impf.* (infml) to loom (up), appear indistinctly

МВД *nt. indecl.* (*abbr. of* **Министе́рство вну́тренних дел**) Ministry of Internal Affairs; ≈ Home Office

МВФ *m. indecl.* (*abbr. of* **Междунаро́дный валю́тный фонд**) IMF (*International Monetary Fund*)

мг (*abbr of* **миллигра́мм**) mg, milligram(s)

мгл|а́, ы́ *f.* **1** (*туман*) haze; mist **2** (*темнота*) gloom, darkness

мгнове́ни|е, я *nt.* instant, moment; **в м. о́ка** in the twinkling of an eye

мгнове́нно *adv.* instantly, in a flash

мгнове́н|ный, ~ен, ~на *adj.* **1** (*сразу возника́ющий*) instantaneous **2** (*быстро проходящий*) momentary

МГУ *m. indecl.* (*abbr. of* **Моско́вский госуда́рственный университе́т**) Moscow State University

✓ **ме́бел|ь**, и *f.* furniture

ме́бельщик, а *m.* furniture maker

меблир|ова́ть, у́ю *impf. and pf.* to furnish

мегаба́йт, а *m.* (comput.) megabyte

мегафо́н, а *m.* megaphone

мёд, а, о ~е, в меду́/~е, на меду́, *pl.* меды́, медо́в *m.* **1** honey **2** (*стари́нный напи́ток*) mead

мед... *comb. form, abbr. of* ▶ **медици́нский**

медали́ст, а *m.* medallist (BrE), medalist (AmE); medal winner

медали́стк|а, и *f. of* ▶ **медали́ст**

меда́л|ь, и *f.* medal

медальо́н, а *m.* medallion, locket

медве́диц|а, ы *f.* she-bear; (astron.): **Больша́я М.** the Great Bear (Ursa Major)

медве́д|ь, я *m.* bear (also fig.); **бе́лый м.** polar bear

медвежа́та *pl. of* ▶ **медвежо́нок**

медве́|жий *adj. of* ▶ **медве́дь; ~жья услу́га** well-meant action having opposite effect

медвеж|о́нок, о́нка, *pl.* ~а́та, ~а́т *m.* bear cub

меди́йный *adj.* media

ме́дик, а *m.* **1** (*врач*) physician, doctor **2** (*студент*) medical student

медикаме́нт, а *m.* (usu. in pl.) medicine

медита́ци|я, и *f.* meditation

медити́р|овать, ую *impf.* to meditate

ме́диум, а *m.* medium, spiritualist

медици́н|а, ы *f.* medicine

✓ **медици́нский** *adj.* medical

ме́дленно *adv.* slowly

ме́длен|ный, ~/~ен, ~на *adj.* slow

медли́тел|ьный, ~ен, ~ьна *adj.* sluggish; slow

ме́дл|ить, ю, ишь *impf.* to linger; to tarry; (с + *i.*) to be slow (in); **он ~ит с отве́том** he takes a long time to reply, he is slow in replying

ме́дный *adj.* **1** copper **2** (chem.) cupric, cuprous; **м. купоро́с** copper sulphate, bluestone **3** (mus.) brass

медо́вый *adj. of* ▶ **мёд; м. ме́сяц** honeymoon

медосмо́тр, а *m.* medical (examination), checkup; **пройти́ м.** to have a checkup

медпу́нкт, а *m.* first-aid station

медсестр|а́, ы́ *f.* (med.) nurse

✓ key word

меду́з|а, ы *f.* (zool.) jellyfish

мед|ь, и *f.* **1** copper; **жёлтая м.** brass **2** (*collect.*) (*моне́ты*) coppers

меж (infml) = **ме́жду**

**меж... ** *comb. form* inter-

межгосуда́рственный *adj.* interstate

междоме́ти|е, я *nt.* (gram.) interjection

междоусо́бный *adj.* internecine

ме́жду *prep.* (+ *i.*) or (obs.) (+ *g. pl.*) **1** between; **м. про́чим** incidentally; **м. тем** meanwhile; **м. тем как** while, whereas **2** (*среди́*) among, amongst

междугоро́дний *adj.* = **междугоро́дный**

междугоро́дный *adj.* intercity; long-distance

междунаро́дный *adj.* international; **М. валю́тный фонд** International Monetary Fund

межконтинента́льн|ый *adj.* intercontinental; **~ая баллисти́ческая раке́та** intercontinental ballistic missile

межправи́тельственный *adj.* intergovernmental

межрегиона́льный *adj.* inter-regional

межэтни́ческий *adj.* interethnic

мейнстри́м, а *m.* (infml) the mainstream (*of culture, music*)

Ме́кк|а, и *f.* Mecca

Ме́ксик|а, и *f.* Mexico

мексика́н|ец, ца *m.* Mexican

мексика́н|ка, ки *f. of ►* **мексика́нец**

мексика́нский *adj.* Mexican

мел, а, о ~е, в ~у́ *m.* chalk

меланхо́ли|я, и *f.* melancholy

мелиора́ци|я, и *f.* (agric.) land improvement, reclamation

ме́л|кий, ~ок, ~ка́, ~ко *adj.* **1** (*небольшо́й*) small **2** (*неглубо́кий*) shallow **3** (*дождь; песо́к*) fine **4** (fig., *челове́к*) petty, small-minded; **~кая со́шка** small fry

ме́лко *adv.* **1** (*некру́пно*) fine, into small particles **2** (*неглубо́ко*) not deep

мелково́д|ный, ~ен, ~на *adj.* shallow

мелоди́ч|ный, ~ен, ~на *adj.* melodious, melodic

мело́ди|я, и *f.* melody, tune

мелодра́м|а, ы *f.* melodrama

мелома́н, а *m.* music lover

ме́лоч|ный, ~ен, ~на *adj.* **1** petty, trifling **2** (pej., *челове́к*) petty, small-minded

ме́лоч|ь, и, *pl.* **~и, ~е́й** *f.* **1** (*collect.*) (*ме́лкие предме́ты*) small items; small fry **2** (*collect.*) (*моне́ты*) (small) change **3** (*in pl.*) (*пустяки́*) trifles, trivialities

мел|ь, и, о ~и, на ~и́ *f.* shoal; bank; **песча́ная м.** sandbank; **на ~и́** aground; (fig.) on the rocks, high and dry; **сесть на м.** to run aground

мельк|а́ть, а́ю *impf.* (*of ►* **мелькну́ть**) **1** (*явля́ться и исчеза́ть*) to flash (past) **2** (*мерца́ть*) to twinkle **3** (*о мы́слях*) to flash

мельк|ну́ть, ну́, нёшь *inst. pf.* (*of ►* **мелька́ть**): **у меня́ ~ну́ла мысль** I had a sudden idea

ме́льком *adv.* in passing, cursorily

ме́льник, а *m.* miller

ме́льниц|а, ы *f.* mill

мельхио́р, а *m.* cupro-nickel

мельча́йший *superl. of ►* **ме́лкий**

ме́льче *comp. of ►* **ме́лкий**, *►* **ме́лко**

мелю́, ме́лешь *see ►* **моло́ть**

мембра́н|а, ы *f.* (tech.) diaphragm; (biol.) membrane

мемора́ндум, а *m.* memorandum

мемориа́л, а *m.* memorial

мемориа́льный *adj.* memorial

мемуа́р|ы, ов (*no sg.*) memoirs

ме́неджер, а *m.* manager; **м. по сбы́ту** sales manager

ме́неджмент, а *m.* management

ме́нее *adv.* (*comp. of ►* **ма́ло**) less; **тем не м.** none the less

менестре́л|ь, я *m.* (hist.) minstrel

мензу́рк|а, и *f.* (chem.) measuring glass

менинги́т, а *m.* (med.) meningitis

менструа́льный *adj.* menstrual

менструа́ци|я, и *f.* menstruation

мент, а́ *m.* (sl.) police officer, cop

менталите́т, а *m.* mentality

менто́л, а *m.* (chem.) menthol

менуэ́т, а *m.* minuet

ме́ньше *comp. of ►* **ма́ленький**, *►* **ма́ло**; smaller; less

ме́ньш|ий *adj.* (*comp. of ►* **ма́ленький**) lesser, smaller; younger; **по ~ей ме́ре** at least; **са́мое ~ee** at the least

меньшинств|о́, а́ *nt.* minority

меню́ *nt. indecl.* menu

меня́ *a. and g. of ►* **я**

меня́|ть, ю *impf.* **1** (*no pf.*) to change **2** (*pf.* **об~, по~**) (+ *a. and* **на** + *a.*) to exchange (for)

меня́|ться, юсь *impf.* **1** (*no pf.*) to change; **м. в лице́** to change countenance **2** (+ *i.*) (*pf.* **об~, по~**) to exchange; **м. с кем-н. ко́мнатами** to exchange rooms with sb

ме́р|а, ы *f.* measure; **вы́сшая м. наказа́ния** capital punishment; **по ~е возмо́жности, по ~е сил** as far as possible; **по ~е того́, как** as, (in proportion) as; **по кра́йней, ме́ньшей ~е** at least; **в ~у** fairly; **сверх ~ы** excessively, immoderately; **знать ~у** *see ►* **знать**[1]

мерза́в|ец, ца *m.* (infml) swine, bastard

ме́рз|кий, ~ок, ~ка́, ~ко *adj.* disgusting, loathsome; abominable, foul

мерзлот|а́, ы́ *f.* frozen condition of ground; **ве́чная м.** permafrost

мёрз|нуть, ну, нешь, *past* **~, ~ла** *impf.* (*of ►* **замёрзнуть**) to freeze

ме́рзост|ь, и *f.* **1** (*сво́йство*) vileness, loathsomeness **2** (*ме́рзкая вещь*) abomination

меридиа́н, а *m.* meridian; **Гри́нвичский м.** Greenwich meridian

M

мéрин, а *m.* gelding

мéр|ить, ю, ишь *impf.* **1** (*pf.* **с~**) to measure; **м. взгля́дом** to look up and down **2** (*pf.* **по~, при~**) (*примерять*) to try on (*clothing, footwear*)

мéр|иться, юсь, ишься *impf.* (*of* ▶ **помéриться**) (+ *i.*) to measure (against); **м. рóстом с кем-н.** to compare heights with sb

мéрк|а, и *f.* **1** (*определённый размер*) measurements **2** (*предмет для измерения*) measure; (*fig.*) yardstick

меркантѝл|ьный, ~ен, ~ьна *adj.* (*fig., pej.*) mercenary

мéрк|нуть, нет, *past* **~нул** *and* **~, ~ла** *impf.* (*of* ▶ **помéркнуть**) to grow dark, grow dim; (*fig.*) to fade

Меркýри|й, я *m.* (*myth., astron.*) Mercury

✓ **мероприя́ти|е, я** *nt.* **1** (*мера*) measure **2** (*событие*) event, function

мертвéц, á *m.* corpse, dead person

мёртв|ый, ~, мертвá, ~о *and* **мертвó** *adj.* dead; **спать ~ым сном** (*infml*) to sleep like the dead; **~ая хвáтка** mortal grip

мерцá|ть, ю *impf.* to twinkle, glimmer, flicker

мéсив|о, а *nt.* (*мешанина*) medley, jumble, mishmash; (*корм*) mash; (*на дороге*) slush

ме|сѝть, шý, ~сишь *impf.* (*of* ▶ **замесѝть**) to knead

мéсс|а, ы *f.* (*relig., mus.*) Mass

месси́|я, и *m.* Messiah

местáми *adv.* here and there, in places

ме|стѝ, тý, тёшь, *past* **мёл, ~лá** *impf.* **1** (*пол, двор*) to sweep; (*сор*) to sweep up **2** (*развевать*) to whirl; (*impers.*) **~тёт** there is a snowstorm

мéстност|ь, и *f.* **1** (*дачная, сельская*) locality, district; area **2** (*mil., гористая, открытая*) ground, country, terrain

✓ **мéстный** *adj.* local

-мéстный *comb. form* -seated, -seater

✓ **мéст|о, а,** *pl.* **~á, ~, ~áм** *nt.* **1** place; site; **больнóе м.** (*fig.*) tender spot, sensitive point; **имéть м.** to take place; **не с ~у** (*fig.*) out of place; **ни с ~а!** don't move!; stay put! **2** (*в театре*) seat; (*на пароходе, поезде*) berth, seat **3** (*свободное пространство*) space; room; **нет ~а** there is no room **4** (*должность*) post, situation; job **5** (*часть текста*) passage **6** (*о багаже*) piece (*of luggage*)

местоимéни|е, я *nt.* (*gram.*) pronoun

местонахождéни|е, я *nt.* location, the whereabouts

месторождéни|е, я *nt.* (*geol.*) deposit

мест|ь, и *f.* vengeance, revenge

✓ **мéсяц, а** *m.* **1** month; **медóвый м.** honeymoon **2** (*луна*) moon; **молодóй м.** new moon

мéсячн|ый *adj.* monthly; (*as pl. n.* **~ые, ~ых**) (*infml*) (menstrual) period

метаболѝзм, а *m.* metabolism

✓ **метáлл, а** *m.* metal

✓ key word

✓ **металлѝческий** *adj.* metal; (*звук, привкус*) metallic

металлоискáтел|ь, я *m.* metal detector

металлýрг, а *m.* metallurgist

металлургѝческий *adj.* metallurgical; **м. завóд** metal works, iron and steel works

металлургѝ|я, и *f.* metallurgy

метáн, а *m.* (*chem.*) methane

ме|тáть, чý, ~чешь *impf.* (*of* ▶ **метнýть**) (*бросать*) to throw, cast, fling

ме|тáться, чýсь, ~чешься *impf.* (*по комнате*) to rush about; (*в постели*) to toss

метафѝзик|а, и *f.* metaphysics

метáфор|а, ы *f.* metaphor

метéл|ь, и *f.* snowstorm; blizzard

метеорѝт, а *m.* (*astron.*) meteorite

метеорóлог, а *m.* meteorologist; weather forecaster; (*infml*) weatherman

метеорологѝческ|ий *adj.* meteorological; **~ая стáнция** weather station

метеорологѝ|я, и *f.* meteorology

метеосвóдк|а, и *f.* weather report

мé|тить¹, чу, тишь *impf.* (*of* ▶ **помéтить**) (*ставить знак на*) to mark

мé|тить², чу, тишь (**в** + *a.*) (*стараться попасть*) to aim at; (*fig., infml*) (**в** + *nom.-a. pl.*) to aim (at), aspire (to)

мéтк|а, и *f.* mark

мéт|кий, ~ок, ~ká, ~ко *adj.* well aimed, accurate; **м. стрелóк** a good shot; (*fig.*): **~кое замечáние** apt remark

мéткост|ь, и *f.* marksmanship; accuracy; (*fig.*) aptness

мет|лá, лы́, *pl.* **~лы, ~ел, ~лам** *f.* broom

мет|нýть, нý, нёшь *inst. pf. of* ▶ **метáть**

✓ **мéтод, а** *m.* method

✓ **метóдик|а, и** *f.* method(s), system; principles; **м. преподавáния рýсского языкá** methods of teaching Russian

метѝдѝч|ный, ~ен, ~на *adj.* methodical, orderly

✓ **метр, а** *m.* **1** (*единица длины; в стихе*) metre (BrE), meter (AmE) **2** (*линейка такой длины*) metre (BrE), meter (AmE), rule

метрáж, á *m.* (*квартиры*) metric area; (*ткани*) length in metres (BrE), meters (AmE)

метрдотéл|ь, я *m.* head waiter

мéтрик|а, и *f.* birth certificate

метрѝческий *adj.* metric

метрó *nt. indecl.* (*abbr. of* **метрополитéн**) **1** (*железная дорога*) underground (railway system) (BrE); the tube (BrE), subway (AmE) **2** (*infml, станция*) metro station; tube station (BrE), subway station (AmE)

метрополитéн, а *m.* underground (railway) (BrE), subway (AmE)

метрополѝ|я, и *f.* mother country, centre (*of empire*)

ме|тý, тёшь *see* ▶ **мести́**

мéтче *comp. of* ▶ **мéткий**

мех, а, о ~е, в ~ý/~е, на ~ý, *pl.* **~á, ~óв** *m.* fur; **на ~ý** fur-lined

⚡ **механи́зм, а** *m.* mechanism, gear(ing); (*pl.; collect.*) machinery (also fig.)

меха́ник, а *m.* mechanic

меха́ник|а, и *f.* mechanics

механи́ческий *adj.* mechanical; **м. цех** machine shop

мехи́, ~о́в *m. pl.* bellows

Ме́хико *m. indecl.* Mexico City

меховой *adj. of* ▶ **мех; м. магази́н** furrier's

мецена́т, а *m.* patron

ме́ццо-сопра́но *nt. indecl.* (*mus.*) (*голос*) mezzo-soprano; (*f. indecl.*) (*infml, певица*) mezzo-soprano

меч, а́ *m.* sword

мече́т|ь, и *f.* mosque

меч-ры́б|а, ы *f.* swordfish

мечт|а́, ы́ (*g. pl. not used*) *f.* **1** dream, daydream **2** (*предмет желаний*) dream, ambition

мечта́тел|ь, я *m.* dreamer; daydreamer

мечта́тель|ница, ницы *f. of* ▶ **мечта́тель**

мечта́тельный, ~ен, ~ьна *adj.* dreamy

мечта́|ть, ю *impf.* (о + *p.*) to dream (of, about)

ме́|чу, тишь *see* ▶ **мети́ть¹**, ▶ **ме́тить²**

ме|чу́, ~чешь *see* ▶ **мета́ть**

⚡ **меша́|ть¹, ю** *impf.* (*of* ▶ **помеша́ть¹**) **1** (+ *d.* + *inf.*) (*препятствовать*) to prevent (from); to hinder, impede, hamper; **что ~ет вам прие́хать в Москву?** what prevents you from coming to Moscow? **2** (+ *d.*) (*беспокоить*) to disturb; **не ~ло бы** (+ *inf.*) (*infml*) it would not hurt (to)

⚡ **меша́|ть², ю** *impf.* **1** (*pf.* **по~**) (*чай, кашу*) to stir; **м. в котле́** to stir the pot **2** (*pf.* **с~**) (с + *i.*) (*вино с водой*) to mix (with), blend (with) **3** (*pf.* **с~**) (*путать*) to confuse, mix up

ме́шка|ть, ю *impf.* (*infml*) (с + *i.*) to linger, dawdle, be slow (with)

мешкови́н|а, ы *f.* sacking, hessian

меш|о́к, ка́ *m.* bag; sack

мещан|и́н, и́на, *pl.* **~е, ~** *m.* **1** (*hist.*) petty bourgeois **2** (*fig.*) Philistine

меща́нский *adj. of* ▶ **мещани́н;** (*fig.*) Philistine; bourgeois, narrow-minded

ми *nt. indecl.* (*mus.*) E

миг, а *m.* moment, instant

миг|а́ть, а́ю *impf.* (*of* ▶ **мигну́ть**) **1** (*непроизвольно*) to blink **2** (+ *d.*) (*подавать знак*) to wink (at); (fig., *мерцать*) to wink, twinkle

миг|ну́ть, ну́, нёшь *inst. pf. of* ▶ **мига́ть**

мигра́нт, а *m.* migrant

миграцио́нный *adj. of* ▶ **мигра́ция**

мигра́ци|я, и *f.* migration

мигре́н|ь, и *f.* migraine

мигри́р|овать, ую *impf.* to migrate

МИД, а *m.* (*abbr. of* **Министе́рство иностра́нных дел**) Ministry of Foreign Affairs; Foreign Office (BrE), State Department (AmE)

ми́ди|я, и *f.* mussel

мизантро́п, а *m.* misanthrope

мизи́н|ец, ца *m.* (*на руке*) little finger; (*на ноге*) little toe

микро... *comb. form* micro-

микроавто́бус, а *m.* minibus

микро́б, а *m.* microbe

микробио́лог, а *m.* microbiologist

микробиоло́ги|я, и *f.* microbiology

микробло́г, а *m.* (*comput.*) microblog

микроволно́в|ый *adj.*: **~ая пе́чь** microwave (oven)

микрокли́мат, а *m.* microclimate

микро́н, а *m.* (*phys.*) micron

микрооргани́зм, а *m.* (*biol.*) micro-organism; **разлага́емый ~ами** biodegradable

микроплён|ка, и *f.* microfilm

микропроце́ссор, а *m.* microprocessor

микрорайо́н, а *m.* neighbourhood (*administrative subdivision of urban area*)

микроско́п, а *m.* microscope

микросхе́м|а, ы *f.* microcircuit, microchip

микрофо́н, а *m.* microphone

микрохирурги́|я, и *f.* microsurgery

микрочи́п, а *m.* microchip

ми́ксер, а *m.* (*cul.*) mixer, blender, liquidizer

миксту́р|а, ы *f.* (*liquid*) medicine, mixture

милитари́зм, а *m.* militarism

милице́йский *adj. of* ▶ **мили́ция**

милиционе́р, а *m.* policeman (*in Russia*)

мили́ци|я, и *f.* police (*in Russia*)

миллиа́рд, а *m.* (*10⁹*) billion (= *thousand million*)

миллиарде́р, а *m.* billionaire

миллиа́рдный *adj.* billionth

миллигра́мм, а *m.* milligram(me)

миллили́тр, а *m.* millilitre (BrE), milliliter (AmE)

миллиме́тр, а *m.* millimetre (BrE), millimeter (AmE)

⚡ **миллио́н, а** *m.* million

миллионе́р, а *m.* millionaire

миллио́нный *adj.* millionth

ми́л|овать, ую *impf.* (*of* ▶ **поми́ловать**) to pardon, spare

милови́д|ный, ~ен, ~на *adj.* pretty, nice-looking

милосе́рди|е, я *nt.* mercy, charity

милосе́рд|ный, ~ен, ~на *adj.* merciful, charitable

ми́лостын|я, и *f.* alms

ми́лост|ь, и *f.* **1** (*благодеяние*) favour (BrE), favor (AmE) **2** (*доброта*) kindness; charity; **из ~и** out of charity

ми́л|ый, ~, ~а́, ~о, ~лы́ *adj.* **1** nice, sweet; lovable; **э́то о́чень ~о с ва́шей стороны́** it is very nice of you **2** dear; (*as n.* **м., ~ого**, *f.* **~ая, ~ой**) dear, darling

ми́л|я, и *f.* mile

ми́мик|а, и *f.* facial expressions

ми́мо *adv. and prep.* + *g.* by, past; **пройти́, прое́хать м.** to pass by, pass; **м.!** miss(ed)!

мимо́з|а, ы *f.* (*bot.*) mimosa

мимолёт|ный, ∼ен, ∼на *adj.* fleeting, transient

мимохо́дом *adv.* in passing; **м. упомяну́ть** (*fig., infml*) to mention in passing

мин. (*abbr of* **мину́та**) min., minute(s)

✍ **ми́н|а¹, ы** *f.* **1** (*mil., naut.*) mine **2** (*mil., сна́ряд миноме́та*) mortar shell, mortar bomb

ми́н|а², ы *f.* (*выражение лица*) expression, mien

минаре́т, а *m.* minaret

минда́л|ь, я́ *m.* **1** (*дерево*) almond tree **2** (*collect.*) (*орехи*) almonds

минера́л, а *m.* mineral

минера́лк|а, и *f.* (*infml*) mineral water

Минздра́в, а *m.* (*abbr. of* **Министе́рство здравоохране́ния**) Ministry of Health

ми́ни *nt. indecl.* mini (*garment*)

миниатю́р|а, ы *f.* (*art, mus.*) miniature; (*theatr.*) short piece, play

миниатю́р|ный, ∼ен, ∼на *adj.* **1** *adj. of* ▶ **миниатю́ра 2** (*fig.*) diminutive, tiny, dainty

ми́ни-ди́ск, а *m.* minidisc

✍ **минима́л|ьный**, ∼ен, ∼ьна *adj.* minimum

✍ **ми́нимум, а** *m.* **1** minimum; **прожи́точный м.** living wage **2** (*as adv.*) at the least, at the minimum

мини́р|овать, ую *impf. and pf.* (*pf. also* **за∼**) (*mil., naut.*) to mine

министе́рский *adj.* ministerial

✍ **министе́рств|о, а** *nt.* (*pol.*) ministry

✍ **мини́стр, а** *m.* (*pol.*) minister; **премье́р-м.** Prime Minister, premier

мин|ова́ть, у́ю *impf. and pf.* **1** (*пройти/ проехать мимо*) to pass (by); **∼у́я подро́бности** omitting details **2** (*pf. only*) (*окончиться*) to be over, be past; **опа́сность ∼ова́ла** the danger is past **3** (*only with* **не** + *g.*) (*избежать*) to escape, avoid; **не м. тебе́ тюрьмы́** you cannot escape being sent to prison

миномёт, а *m.* (*mil.*) mortar

миноно́с|ец, ца *m.* (*naut.*) torpedo boat; **эска́дренный м.** destroyer

мино́р, а *m.* (*mus.*) minor key

Минск, а *m.* Minsk

мину́вш|ий *adj.* past; (*as nt. n.* ∼ее, ∼его) the past

ми́нус, а *m.* **1** (*math.*) minus **2** (*fig., infml, недостаток*) shortcoming, drawback

✍ **мину́т|а, ы** *f.* minute

мину́т|ный *adj.* **1** *adj. of* ▶ **мину́та**; ∼ная стре́лка minute hand **2** momentary; ∼ная встре́ча brief encounter

✍ **мир¹, а** *m.* (*согласие*) peace; **заключи́ть м. to** make peace

✍ **мир², а**, *pl.* ∼ы́ *m.* (*вселенная*) world; universe; **живо́тный м.** fauna; **расти́тельный м.** flora

мира́ж, а́ *m.* mirage; optical illusion

мир|и́ть, ю́, и́шь *impf.* **1** (*pf.* **по∼**) (*враждующих*) to reconcile **2** (*pf.* **при∼**)

(*с* + *i.*) (*заставлять терпимо относиться*) to reconcile (to)

мир|и́ться, ю́сь, и́шься *impf.* (*с* + *i.*) **1** (*pf.* **по∼**) (*прекращать вражду*) to be reconciled (with), make it up (with) **2** (*pf.* **при∼**) (*терпимо относиться*) to reconcile oneself (to); **м. со свои́м положе́нием** to accept the situation

ми́р|ный, ∼ен, ∼на *adj.* **1** *adj. of* ▶ **мир¹ 2** peaceful; peaceable

мировоззре́ни|е, я *nt.* (world) outlook, Weltanschauung; (one's) philosophy (of life)

✍ **мир|ово́й** *adj. of* ▶ **мир²**; ∼ова́я война́ world war

мирозда́ни|е, я *nt.* the universe

миролюби́в|ый, ∼, ∼а *adj.* peaceable

миротво́р|ец, ца *m.* peacemaker

мирско́й *adj.* secular, lay; mundane, worldly

мирт, а *m.* (*bot.*) myrtle

ми́ск|а, и *f.* basin, bowl

ми́сс *f. indecl.* Miss

миссионе́р, а *m.* missionary

ми́ссис *nt. indecl.* Mrs

ми́сси|я, и *f.* mission

ми́стер, а *m.* mister, Mr

ми́стик|а, и *f.* mysticism; (*infml*) mystery

мистифика́ци|я, и *f.* hoax, leg-pull

мистифици́р|овать, ую *impf. and pf.* to hoax, mystify

мисти́ческий *adj.* mystic(al)

ми́тинг, а *m.* (political) mass meeting; rally

митрополи́т, а *m.* (*eccl.*) metropolitan

миф, а *m.* myth (also *fig.*)

мифи́ческий *adj.* mythical

мифологи́ческий *adj.* mythological

мифоло́ги|я, и *f.* mythology

мише́н|ь, и *f.* target

ми́шк|а, и *m.*: **плю́шевый м.** teddy (bear)

мл (*abbr. of* **миллили́тр**) ml, millilitre(s)

младе́н|ец, ца *m.* baby, infant

младе́нческий *adj.* infantile

мла́дший *adj.* (*comp. and superl. of* ▶ **молодо́й**) **1** (*более молодо́й*) younger **2** (*самый молодо́й*) the youngest **3** (*по служебному положе́нию*) junior; **м. лейтена́нт** second lieutenant

млекопита́ющее, его *nt.* (*zool.*) mammal

мле|ть, ю *impf.* (*от* + *g.*) to be overcome (*with delight, fright, etc.*)

✍ **млн.** (*abbr. of* **миллио́н**) m, million(s)

✍ **млрд.** (*abbr. of* **миллиа́рд**) b., billion(s) (= *thousand million*)

✍ **мм** (*abbr. of* **миллиме́тр**) mm, millimetre(s) (BrE), millimeter(s) (AmE)

мне *d. and p. of* ▶ **я**

✍ **мне́ни|е, я** *nt.* opinion

мни́мый *adj.* **1** (*воображаемый*) imaginary **2** (*притворный*) sham, pretended; **м. больно́й** hypochondriac

мни́тел|ьный, ∼ен, ∼ьна *adj.* **1** (*ипохондрический*) hypochondriac

М

2 (*подозри́тельный*) mistrustful, suspicious

⚡ **мно́г|ие, их** *adj. and n.* many; **во ~их отноше́ниях** in many respects

⚡ **мно́го** *adv.* (+ *g.*) much; many; a lot (of); **м. вре́мени** much time; **м. лет** many years

мно́го... *comb. form* many-, poly-, multi-

многобо́р|ец, ца *m.* all-round athlete, multieventer

многобо́рь|е, я *nt.* multi-discipline event *or* competition

многогра́н|ный, ~ен, ~на *adj.* (math.) polyhedral; (fig.) many-sided; multi-faceted

многоде́т|ный, ~ен, ~на *adj.* having many children

многодне́вный *adj.*: **м. путь** a journey lasting several days

⚡ **мно́г|ое, ого** *nt.* much, a great deal; **во ~ом** in many respects

многожёнств|о, а *nt.* polygamy

многозначи́тел|ьный, ~ен, ~ьна *adj.* significant

многозна́ч|ный, ~ен, ~на *adj.* **1** (math.) multi-digit **2** (ling.) polysemantic

многокра́т|ный, ~ен, ~на *adj.* repeated; frequent

многоле́тний *adj.* **1** lasting *or* living many years; of many years' standing **2** (bot.) perennial

многоли́к|ий, ~, ~а *adj.* many-sided

многолю́д|ный, ~ен, ~на *adj.* (*райо́н*) populous; (*у́лица*) crowded

многонациона́л|ьный, ~ен, ~ьна *adj.* multinational

многообеща́ющий *adj.* **1** (*учени́к*) promising, hopeful **2** (*взгляд*) significant

многообра́зи|е, я *nt.* variety, diversity

многопарти́йный *adj.* multiparty

многосери́йный *adj.* serial

многосло́в|ный, ~ен, ~на *adj.* verbose

многосторо́н|ний, ~ен, ~ня *adj.* **1** (*no short forms*) (math.) polygonal **2** (*догово́р*) multilateral **3** (*челове́к*) many-sided, versatile

многострада́л|ьный, ~ен, ~ьна *adj.* long-suffering

многоуго́льник, а *m.* (math.) polygon

многоцелево́й *adj.* multipurpose

⚡ **многочи́слен|ный, ~, ~на** *adj.* numerous

многоэта́жный *adj.* multistorey (BrE), multistory (AmE), high-rise

мно́жественн|ый *adj.* plural; **~ое число́** (gram.) plural (number)

⚡ **мно́жеств|о, а** *nt.* a great number, a quantity; multitude; (math.) set

мно́ж|ить, у, ишь *impf.* (*of* ▶ **помно́жить,** ▶ **умно́жить**) (math.) to multiply

мной, мно́ю *i. of* ▶ **я**

мобилиза́ци|я, и *f.* mobilization

мобилизова́ть, у́ю *impf. and pf.* (**на** + *a.*) to mobilize (for)

моби́л|ьник, а *m.* (infml) mobile (phone) (BrE), cellphone

⚡ **моби́л|ьный, ~ен, ~ьна** *adj.* mobile; (*as n.* infml **м., ~ьного**) (phone) (BrE), cellphone

моги́л|а, ы *f.* grave

моги́льщик, а *m.* gravedigger

мо|гу́, ~́гут *see* ▶ **мочь**

могу́ч|ий, ~, ~а *adj.* mighty, powerful

могу́ществен|ный, ~, ~на *adj.* powerful; potent

могу́ществ|о, а *nt.* power, might

мо́д|а, ы *f.* fashion, vogue; **выходи́ть из ~ы** to go out of fashion

⚡ **моде́л|ь, и** *f.* model; (*пла́тья*) design; (*для отли́вки*) pattern

модель|е́р, а *m.* fashion designer; couturier

моде́м, а *m.* (comput.) modem

моде́рн, а *m.* modernist style, art nouveau

модерниза́ци|я, и *f.* modernization; updating; (comput., *of hardware*) upgrade

модернизи́р|овать, ую *impf. and pf.* to modernize; to update; (comput., *hardware*) to upgrade

модерни́зм, а *m.* (art) modernism

модифика́ци|я, и *f.* modification

модифици́р|овать, ую *impf. and pf.* to modify

мо́д|ный, ~ен, ~на́, ~но *adj.* **1** fashionable, stylish **2** *adj. of* ▶ **мо́да; м. журна́л** fashion magazine

⚡ **мо́дул|ь, я** *m.* (math.) modulus; (tech.) module

мо́жет *see* ▶ **мочь**

можжеве́льник, а *m.* (bot.) juniper

⚡ **мо́жно** *pred.* (*impers.* + *inf.*) **1** (*возмо́жно*) it is possible; **м. бы́ло э́то предви́деть** it could have been foreseen; **как м.** (+ *comp.*) as ... as possible; **как м. скоре́е** as soon as possible **2** (*разреша́ется*) it is permissible, one may; **м.** (**мне/нам**) **идти́?** may I/we go?

моза́ик|а, и *f.* mosaic; (*иску́сство*) mosaic work

Мозамби́к, а *m.* Mozambique

мозамби́к|ец, ца *m.* Mozambican

мозамби́кский *adj.* Mozambican

⚡ **мозг|а, в ~у́, pl. ~и́, ~о́в** *m.* **1** brain (also fig.); (fig.) nerve centre (BrE), center (AmE); **головно́й м.** brain, cerebrum; **спинно́й м.** spinal cord **2** (anat.) marrow; **до ~а косте́й** (fig., infml) to the core

мозо́л|ь, и *f.* corn; callus; **ру́ки в ~ях** calloused hands

⚡ **мой** *poss. pron.* (*при существи́тельном*) my; (*без существи́тельного*) mine; (*as pl. n.* **мои́, мои́х**) my people; **по-мо́ему** (*по моему́ мне́нию*) in my opinion; (*так, как я счита́ю пра́вильным*) as I think right

мо́йк|а, и *f.* **1** (*де́йствие*) washing **2** (*маши́на*) washer **3** (*ра́ковина*) sink

мо́йщик, а *m.* washer; cleaner

мокри́ц|а, ы *f.* **1** (zool.) woodlouse **2** (bot.) chickweed (*Stellaria media*)

мо́кр|ый, ~, ~а́, ~о *adj.* wet; **м. снег** sleet; (*impers., pred.*) **~о** it is wet

M

мол[1], **а** *m.* mole, pier

мол[2] *abbr.* (*of obs.* **мо́лвить**) (infml) he says (said), they say (said), *etc.*; (*indicating reported speech*): **он, м., никогда́ там не́ был** he said he had never been there

молдава́н|**ин, ина,** *pl.* **~е, ~** *m.* Moldovan

молдава́н|**ка, ки** *f. of* ▶ **молдава́нин**

молда́вский *adj.* Moldovan; (*язы́к*) Moldavian

Молдо́в|**а, ы** *f.* Moldova

моле́кул|**а, ы** *f.* (phys.) molecule

моли́тв|**а, ы** *f.* prayer

мол|**и́ть, ю́, ~ишь** *impf.* (*a. and* o + *p.*) to pray (for), implore (for), beseech; **~ю́ вас о по́мощи** I beg you to help me

мол|**и́ться, ю́сь, ~ишься** *impf.* **1** (*pf.* **по~**) (+ *d.*) to pray (to) **2** (fig.) (**на** + *a.*) to idolize

моллю́ск, а *m.* mollusc; shellfish

молниено́с|**ный, ~ен, ~на** *adj.* (quick as) lightning; **~ная война́** blitzkrieg

мо́лни|**я, и** *f.* **1** lightning **2**: (**застёжка-**)**м.** zip (BrE), zipper (AmE)

молодёжный *adj. of* ▶ **молодёжь**

✓ **молодёж**|**ь, и** *f.* (collect.) youth; young people

молод|**е́ц, ца́** *m.* fine fellow; (*о же́нщине*) fine girl; (*as int.*) **м.!** well done!

молодожён|**ы, ов** *m. pl.* (*sg.* **~, ~а**) newly married couple, newly-weds

✓ **молод**|**о́й, мо́лод, ~а́, мо́лодо** *adj.* **1** young; (*свойственный молодости*) youthful **2** (*as n.*) (infml) (**м., ~о́го**) bridegroom; (**~а́я, ~о́й**) bride; (**~ы́е, ~ы́х**) newly married couple, newly-weds

мо́лодост|**ь, и** *f.* youth; youthfulness

моложа́в|**ый, ~, ~а** *adj.* (*челове́к*) young-looking; (*вид*) youthful

моло́же *comp. of* ▶ **молодо́й**

✓ **молок**|**о́, а́** (*no pl.*) *nt.* milk

мо́лот, а *m.* hammer; **кузне́чный м.** sledgehammer

молот|**о́к, ка́** *m.* hammer; **отбо́йный м.** pneumatic drill; **прода́ть с ~ка́** to sell by auction, auction

мо́лот|**ый, ~, ~а** *p.p.p. of* ▶ **моло́ть** *and adj.* ground

моло́ть, мелю́, ме́лешь *impf.* (*of* ▶ **смоло́ть**) to grind; **м. вздор** (*no pf.*) (fig., infml) to talk nonsense

моло́чн|**ый** *adj.* **1** *adj. of* ▶ **молоко́**; **м. брат** foster-brother; **~ые проду́кты** dairy products; **~ое хозя́йство** dairy farm(ing) **2** milky; lactic

мо́лча *adv.* silently, in silence

молчали́в|**ый, ~, ~а** *adj.* **1** (*челове́к*) taciturn, silent **2** (*одобре́ние*) tacit, unspoken

молча́ни|**е, я** *nt.* silence

молч|**а́ть, у́, и́шь** *impf.* to be silent; (o + *p.*) to keep silent (about)

мол|**ь, и** *f.* (clothes) moth

мольб|**а́, ы́** *f.* entreaty, supplication

мольбе́рт, а *m.* easel

✓ **моме́нт, а** *m.* **1** (*миг*) moment; instant; **в да́нный м.** at the present time; at the moment **2** (*черта́*) feature, element, factor

момента́льно *adv.* in a moment, instantly

момента́л|**ьный, ~ен, ~ьна** *adj.* instantaneous; **м. сни́мок** snapshot

мона́рх, а *m.* monarch

монархи́зм, а *m.* monarchism

мона́рхи|**я, и** *f.* monarchy

монасты́р|**ь, я́** *m.* monastery; (*же́нский*) **м.** convent, nunnery

мона́х, а *m.* monk

мона́хин|**я, и** *f.* nun

монго́л, а *m.* Mongol, Mongolian

Монго́ли|**я, и** *f.* Mongolia

монго́л|**ка, ки** *f. of* ▶ **монго́л**

монго́льский *adj.* Mongolian

моне́т|**а, ы** *f.* coin; **разме́нная м.** change; **приня́ть за чи́стую ~у** (fig., infml) to take at face value, take in good faith

монито́р, а *m.* (TV, comput.) monitor

мо́но *nt. indecl.* mono

моногра́фи|**я, и** *f.* monograph

моноли́т, а *m.* monolith

моноли́т|**ный, ~ен, ~на** *adj.* (pol., also fig.) monolithic; (fig.) solid

моноло́г, а *m.* monologue, soliloquy

монопо́ли|**я, и** *f.* (econ., also fig.) monopoly

монотеи́зм, а *m.* monotheism

моното́н|**ный, ~ен, ~на** *adj.* monotonous

монстр, а *m.* monster

✓ **монта́ж, а́** *m.* **1** (tech., *де́йствие*) assembling, mounting, installation **2** (cin.) editing, montage; (art, mus., liter.) arrangement

монта́жник, а *m.* (*на стро́йке*) rigger; (*на заво́де*) fitter

монтёр, а *m.* **1** fitter **2** (*электромонтёр*) electrician

монти́р|**овать, ую** *impf.* (*of* ▶ **смонти́ровать**) **1** (tech.) to assemble, mount, fit **2** (cin.) to edit; (art, mus., liter.) to arrange

монуме́нт, а *m.* monument

монумента́л|**ьный, ~ен, ~ьна** *adj.* monumental (also fig.)

мопе́д, а *m.* moped

мора́л|**ь, и** *f.* **1** (*но́рмы поведе́ния*) (code of) morals, ethics **2** (infml, *нравоуче́ние*) moralizing; **чита́ть м.** to moralize, preach

мора́л|**ьный, ~ен, ~ьна** *adj.* moral; ethical

морато́ри|**й, я** *m.* (law, comm.) moratorium

морг, а *m.* morgue, mortuary

морг|**а́ть, а́ю** *impf.* (*of* ▶ **моргну́ть**) to blink; to wink

морг|**ну́ть, ну́, нёшь** *pf.* (*of* ▶ **морга́ть**): **гла́зом не ~ну́в** (infml) without batting an eyelid

мо́рд|**а, ы** *f.* **1** snout, muzzle **2** (infml, *лицо́*) mug

мордв|**а́, ы́** *f.* (collect.) the Mordva, the Mordvins

✓ key word

мордви́н, а *m.* Mordvin

мордви́н|ка, ки *f. of* ▶ мордви́н

Мордо́ви|я, и *f.* Mordvinia

мордо́вский *adj.* Mordvinian

мо́р|е, я, *pl.* ∼я́, ∼е́й *nt.* sea; у ∼я by the sea; на́ м./на ∼е at sea; за́ ∼ем overseas; из-за ∼я from overseas; **пое́хать на м.** to go to the seaside

морепла́вани|е, я *nt.* navigation, seafaring

морж, а́ *m.* walrus; (infml) (open-air) winter bather

морко́вк|а, и *f.* (infml) a carrot

морко́в|ь, и *f.* carrot; (collect.) carrot(s)

моро́жен|ое, ого *nt.* ice (cream)

моро́женый *adj.* frozen; (карто́фель) frost-damaged

моро́з, а *m.* **1** frost; **у меня́ м. по ко́же** (*or* **пошёл**) it makes (made) my flesh creep **2** (*usu. in pl.*) intensely cold weather

морози́лк|а, и *f.* (infml) freezer compartment; freezer

морози́льник, а *m.* freezer

моро́зн|ый *adj.* frosty; (impers., pred.) ∼о it is freezing

морозосто́|йкий, ∼ек, ∼йка *adj.* (bot.) frost-resistant

морос|и́ть, и́т *impf.* to drizzle

моро́ч|ить, у, ишь *impf.* (*of* ▶ заморо́чить) (infml) to fool; **м. го́лову кому́-н.** to take sb in

морс, а *m.* fruit drink

морск|о́й *adj.* **1** sea; maritime; marine, nautical; **м. волк** (infml) old salt; ∼а́я звезда́ starfish; **м. конёк** (zool.) sea horse; ∼а́я сви́нка guinea pig **2** naval; ∼а́я пехо́та marines; **м. флот** navy, fleet

мо́рфи|й, я *m.* (chem.) morphine

морфоло́ги|я, и *f.* morphology

морщи́н|а, ы *f.* wrinkle

морщи́нист|ый, ∼, ∼а *adj.* wrinkled

мо́рщ|иться, усь, ишься *impf.* (*of* ▶ смо́рщиться) **1** (*де́лать грима́сы*) to make a wry face, wince **2** (*об оде́жде*) to crease, wrinkle

моря́к, а́ *m.* sailor

Москв|а́, ы́ *f.* **1** (*го́род*) Moscow **2** (*река́*) the Moskva

москви́ч, а́ *m.* Muscovite

москви́ч|ка, ки *f. of* ▶ москви́ч

моски́т, а *m.* mosquito

моски́тн|ый *adj. of* ▶ моски́т; ∼ая се́тка mosquito net

моско́вский *adj.* (of) Moscow

мост, ∼а́, о ∼е́, на ∼у́, *pl.* ∼ы́ *m.* **1** (*че́рез ре́ку*) bridge **2** (*автомоби́ля*) axle

мо́стик, а *m.* **1** *dim. of* ▶ мост **2**: **капита́нский м.** (naut.) bridge (*on a ship*)

мостк|и́, о́в (*no sg.*) **1** (*для перехо́да*) planked walkway **2** (*площа́дка*) wooden platform

мостов|а́я, о́й *f.* road(way), carriageway

мот|а́ть, а́ю *impf.* **1** (*pf.* на∼) (*ни́тки, шерсть*) to wind, reel **2** (*pf.* ∼ну́ть) (+ *i.*)

(infml, *голово́й*) to shake (*head, etc.*)

мота́|ться[1], ется *impf.* (infml) to dangle

мота́|ться[2], юсь *impf.* (infml) to rush about

моте́л|ь, я *m.* motel

моти́в[1], а *m.* **1** (*по́вод*) motive **2** (*до́вод*) reason

моти́в[2], а *m.* **1** (mus.) tune, motif **2** (fig.) motif

мотиви́р|овать, ую *impf. and pf.* to give reasons (for), justify

мот|ну́ть, ну́, нёшь *inst. pf. of* ▶ мота́ть

мотого́н|ки, ок (*no sg.*) motorcycle races

мотого́нщик, а *m.* motorcycle racer

мотого́нщи|ца, цы *f. of* ▶ мотого́нщик

мот|о́к, ка́ *m.* skein, hank

мото́р, а *m.* motor; (*автомоби́ля, самолёта*) engine

моторо́ллер, а *m.* (motor) scooter

мотоспо́рт, а *m.* motorcycle racing

мотоци́кл, а *m.* motorcycle

мотоцикли́ст, а *m.* motorcyclist; biker

мотоцикли́ст|ка, ки *f. of* ▶ мотоцикли́ст

моты́г|а, и *f.* hoe

мотыл|ёк, ька́ *m.* moth

мох, мха *and* мо́ха, о мхе *and* о мо́хе, во (на) мху́, *pl.* мхи, мхов *m.* moss

мохе́р, а *m.* mohair

мохна́т|ый, ∼, ∼а *adj.* hairy, shaggy

моч|а́, и́ *f.* urine

моча́лк|а, и *f.* bath sponge, loofah

мочев|о́й *adj.* urinary, uric; **м. пузы́рь** (anat.) bladder

моч|и́ть, у́, ∼ишь *impf.* **1** *impf. of* ▶ намочи́ть 1 **2** (*pf.* за∼) (sl., *убива́ть*) to kill

мочь, могу́, мо́жешь, мо́гут, *past* мог, могла́ *impf.* (*of* ▶ смочь) to be able; **мо́жет быть, быть мо́жет** perhaps, maybe; **мо́жет** (infml): **= мо́жет быть; не мо́жет быть!** impossible!

моше́нник, а *m.* swindler, crook

моше́нничá|ть, ю *impf.* (*of* ▶ смоше́нничать) to swindle

моше́нничеств|о, а *nt.* swindling; cheating

мо́шк|а, и *f.* midge

мощён|ый *adj.* paved

мо́щ|и, е́й (*no sg.*) (relig.) relics

мо́щност|ь, и *f.* power; (tech.) capacity, rating; output; **дви́гатель ∼ью в сто лошади́ных сил** hundred horsepower engine

мо́щ|ный, ∼ен, ∼на́, ∼но *adj.* powerful, mighty; (*рост*) vigorous

мощ|ь, и *f.* power, might

мо́|ю, ешь *see* ▶ мыть

мо́ющий *pres. part. act. of* ▶ мыть *and adj.* detergent; ∼ие сре́дства detergents

мо́ющийся *adj.* washable; ∼иеся обо́и washable wallpaper

мраз|ь, и (*no pl.*) *f.* (infml) dregs, scum

мрак, а *m.* darkness, gloom (also fig., rhet.)

мра́мор, а *m.* marble

мра́морный adj. marble; (fig.) (white as) marble; (бума́га) marbled

мра́ч|ный, ~ен, ~на́, ~но, ~ны́ adj. **1** dark, sombre (BrE), somber (AmE) **2** (fig.) gloomy, dismal

мсти́ть, мщу, мсти́шь impf. (of ▶ **отомсти́ть**) **1** (+ d.) to take revenge/vengeance (on sb) **2** (за + a.) to avenge; **м. за дру́га** to avenge one's friend **3** (+ d. and за + a.) to take revenge on sb for sth; to avenge oneself on sb for sth

мудре́ц, а́ m. (rhet.) sage, wise man

му́дрост|ь, и f. wisdom

му́др|ый, ~, ~а́, ~о, ~ы́ adj. wise

✐ **муж, а** m. **1** (pl. ~ья́, ~е́й, ~ья́м) husband **2** (pl. ~и́, ~е́й, ~а́м) (rhet., мужчи́на) man; **госуда́рственный м.** statesman; **учёный м.** scholar

мужа́|ться, юсь impf. to take heart, take courage; **~йтесь!** courage!

му́жествен|ный, ~, ~на adj. manly, steadfast

му́жеств|о, а nt. courage, fortitude

мужи́к, а́ m. **1** (крестья́нин) muzhik (Russian peasant) **2** (infml, мужчи́на) bloke, guy

✐ **мужско́й** adj. (го́лос, рукопожа́тие) masculine; (пол, кле́тка) male; (туале́т, пла́тье) men's; **м. род** (gram.) masculine gender

✐ **мужчи́н|а, ы** m. man

му́з|а, ы f. muse

✐ **музе́|й, я** m. museum

✐ **му́зык|а, и** f. music

✐ **музыка́л|ьный, ~ен, ~ьна** adj. music (attr.); musical

музыка́нт, а m. musician

музыкове́д, а m. musicologist

му́к|а, и f. torment; torture; (in pl.) pangs, throes; **родовы́е ~и** labour (BrE), labor (AmE) pains

мук|а́, и́ f. (пшени́чная, кукуру́зная) flour; (костяна́я, ры́бная) meal

мулл|а́, ы́ m. mullah

мультиме́диа pl. indecl. multimedia

мультимеди́йный adj. multimedia

мультиплика́ци|я, и f. (film) animation

мультфи́льм, а m. cartoon, animation

му́ми|я, и f. mummy (corpse)

мунди́р, а m. full dress uniform

мундшту́к, а́ m. **1** (сигаре́ты, тру́бки) mouthpiece; (тру́бочка, в кото́рую вставля́ют сигаре́ту) cigarette holder **2** (mus.) mouthpiece

муниципалите́т, а m. municipality; town council; **зда́ние ~а** town hall

✐ **муниципа́л|ьный** adj. municipal; **~ая кварти́ра** council flat

мурав|е́й, ья́ m. ant

мураве́йник, а m. anthill

муравье́д, а m. (zool.) anteater

мурлы́|кать, чу, чешь impf. **1** (о ко́шке) to purr **2** (infml, о челове́ке) to hum

муска́т, а m. **1** (оре́х) nutmeg **2** (виногра́д) muscadine, muscat **3** (вино́) muscatel, muscat

му́скул, а m. muscle

мускулату́р|а, ы f. (collect.) muscular system, musculature

мускули́ст|ый, ~, ~а adj. muscular, brawny

му́сор, а m. rubbish (BrE), garbage (AmE)

му́сорный adj. of ▶ **му́сор; м. я́щик** dustbin (BrE), garbage can (AmE)

мусорово́з, а m. dustcart (BrE), garbage truck (AmE)

мусоропрово́д, а m. refuse chute

му́сорщик, а m. dustman (BrE), garbage collector (AmE)

мусульма́н|ин, ина, pl. **~е, ~** m. Muslim

мусульма́н|ка, ки f. of ▶ **мусульма́нин**

мусульма́нский adj. Muslim

мусульма́нств|о, а nt. Islam

мута́нт, а m. (biol.) mutant

мута́ци|я, и f. (biol.) mutation

мути́р|овать, ую impf. and pf. (biol.) to mutate

му́т|ный, ~ен, ~на́, ~но, ~ны́ adj. **1** cloudy, turbid **2** (fig.) dull(ed); confused

му́фт|а, ы f. **1** (для рук) muff **2** (tech.) coupling; (elec.) connecting box; **м. сцепле́ния** clutch

му́фти|й, я m. (relig.) mufti

му́х|а, и f. fly; **де́лать из ~и слона́** (fig.) to make a mountain out of a molehill

мухомо́р, а m. (гриб) fly agaric (mushroom)

муче́ни|е, я nt. torment, torture

му́ченик, а m. martyr

му́чени|ца, цы f. of ▶ **му́ченик**

мучи́тел|ьный, ~ен, ~ьна adj. excruciating; agonizing

му́ч|ить, у, ишь impf. (of ▶ **заму́чить**) to torment; to worry, harass

му́ч|иться, усь, ишься impf. (of ▶ **заму́читься**) **1** (от + g. or + i.) passive of ▶ **му́чить; м. от бо́ли** to be racked with pain; **м. сомне́ниями** to be tormented by doubts **2** (из-за + g.) to worry (about), feel unhappy **3** (над + i.) to torment oneself (over, about)

мха, мху see ▶ **мох**

мч|а́ться, усь, и́шься impf. to rush, race, tear along; **м. во весь опо́р** to go at full speed; **вре́мя ~и́тся** time flies

МЧС m. (abbr. of **Министе́рство по чрезвыча́йным ситуа́циям**) Ministry of Emergency Situations

✐ **мы, a., g., p. нас,** d. **нам,** i. **на́ми** pers. pron. we; **мы с ва́ми** you and I

мы́л|о, а nt. **1** soap **2** (у ло́шади) foam, lather

мы́льница, ы f. soap dish

мы́л|ьный adj. of ▶ **мы́ло; ~ьная о́пера** soap opera

мыс, а m. (geog.) cape, promontory

✐ key word

мы́сленный *adj.* mental; **м. о́браз** mental image

мысли́м|ый, ~, ~а *adj.* conceivable, thinkable

мысли́тел|ь, я *m.* thinker

мысли́тельный *adj.* intellectual, of thought; **м. проце́сс** thought process

мы́сл|ить, ю, ишь *impf.* **1** (*ду́мать*) to think; to reason **2** (*представля́ть себе́*) to conceive, imagine

☛ **мысл|ь**, и *f.* (o + *p.*) thought (of, about); (*иде́я*) idea; **о́браз ~ей** way of thinking, views; **собира́ться с ~ями** to collect one's thoughts

мыть, мо́ю, мо́ешь *impf.* (*of* ▶ **вы́мыть**) to wash

мы́ться, мо́юсь, мо́ешься *impf.* (*of* ▶ **вы́мыться**) **1** to wash (oneself) **2** *pass.* *of* ▶ **мыть**

мыч|а́ть, у́, и́шь *impf.* **1** (*о коро́ве*) to moo; (*о быке́*) to bellow **2** (fig., infml, *о челове́ке*) to mumble

мышело́вк|а, и *f.* mousetrap

мыши́ный *adj. of* ▶ **мышь**; **~йная возня́** pointless fussing over trifles

мы́шк|а¹, и *f. dim. of* ▶ **мышь**

мы́шк|а², и *f.* armpit; **под ~у, под ~ой** under one's arm; **нести́ под ~ой** to carry under one's arm

мышле́ни|е, я *nt.* thinking, thought

мы́шц|а, ы *f.* muscle

мыш|ь, и, *pl.* ~и, ~е́й *f.* **1** (also comput.) mouse **2** **летучая м.** bat

мышья́к, á *m.* (chem.) arsenic

Мья́нм|а, ы *f.* Myanmar

мэр, а *m.* mayor

мэ́ри|я, и *f.* **1** (*управле́ние*) town council **2** (*зда́ние*) town hall

мю́зикл, а *m.* musical

мю́зик-хо́лл, а *m.* music hall

мю́сли *pl. and nt. indecl.* muesli

☛ **мя́г|кий**, ~ок, ~ка́, ~ко *adj.* soft; (fig.) mild, gentle; (*о пригово́ре*) lenient; **м. ваго́н** (rail.) soft(-seated) carriage (BrE), sleeping car; **м. знак** (ling.) soft sign (*name of Russian letter* «ь»); **~кое кре́сло** easy chair

мя́гко *adv.* softly; (fig.) mildly, gently

мя́гче *comp. of* ▶ **мя́гкий**, ▶ **мя́гко**

мя́кот|ь, и *f.* **1** (*мя́са*) flesh **2** (*плода́*) pulp (*of fruit*)

мяси́ст|ый, ~, ~а *adj.* fleshy; meaty

мясни́к, á *m.* butcher

мяс|но́й *adj. of* ▶ **мя́со**; **~ны́е консе́рвы** tinned meat

☛ **мя́с|о**, а *nt.* meat; **пу́шечное м.** (fig.) cannon fodder

мясору́бк|а, и *f.* mincer

мя́т|а, ы *f.* (bot.) mint; **пе́речная м.** peppermint

мяте́ж, á *m.* mutiny, revolt

мяте́жник, а *m.* mutineer, rebel

мяте́ж|ный, ~ен, ~на *adj.* **1** rebellious, mutinous **2** (fig.) restless; stormy

мя́тый *p.p.p. of* ▶ **мять** *and adj.* creased

мять, мну, мнёшь *impf.* **1** (*pf.* **раз~**) (*гли́ну*) to work up, knead **2** (*pf.* **из~** *and* **с~**) (*бума́гу, пла́тье*) to crumple; **м. траву́** to trample grass

мя́ться, мнётся *impf.* (*of* ▶ **измя́ться**, ▶ **смя́ться**) to become crumpled; to crease easily

мяу́ка|ть, ю *impf.* to mew, miaow

мяч, á *m.* ball

М

Н

Нн

☛ **на** *prep.* I. (+ *a.*) **1** on (to); to; into; over, through; **положи́те кни́гу на стол** put the book on the table; **сесть на авто́бус, по́езд** to board a bus, a train; **на се́вер** to the north; **на заво́д** to the factory; **перевести́ на англи́йский** to translate into English **2** (*при обозначе́нии вре́мени де́ятельности*) at; on; until, to (*or untranslated*); **на друго́й день, на сле́дующий день** (the) next day; **на э́тот раз** this time, for this once **3** (*при обозначе́нии сро́ка*) for; **на два дня** for two days; **собра́ние назна́чено на понеде́льник** the meeting is fixed for Monday; (*при обозначе́нии це́ли, назначе́ния*) for; **на зиму** for the winter; **ко́мната на двои́х** a room for two **4** (*при обозначе́нии ме́ры*) by (*or untranslated*); **коро́че на дюйм** shorter by an inch; **опозда́ть на час** to be an hour late; **ста́рше на три го́да** three years older; **четы́ре ме́тра (в длину́) на два (в ширину́)** four metres (long) by two (broad); (*при умноже́нии, деле́нии*): **помно́жить пять на́ три** to multiply five by three; **дели́ть на́ два** to divide into two **5** (*при обозначе́нии сто́имости*) worth (*of sth*); **ма́рок на рубль** a rouble's worth of stamps

● II. (+ *p.*) **1** on, upon; in; at; **на столе́** on the table; **на бума́ге** on paper; (also fig.):

на се́вере in the north; **на заво́де** at the factory; **на со́лнце** in the sun; **на во́здухе** in the open air; **на дворе́, на у́лице** out of doors; **на рабо́те** at work; **игра́ть на рои́ле** to play the piano; **писа́ть на неме́цком языке́** to write in German **2** (*во время чего-н.*) in (*or untranslated*); during; **на э́той неде́ле** this week **3** (*при помощи чего-н.*) on (*or untranslated*); **на ва́те** padded; **э́тот дви́гатель рабо́тает на не́фти** this engine runs on oil (*о транспорте*) by; **е́хать на по́езде/авто́бусе** to go by train/bus

на́ *int.* (infml) here; here you are; here, take it; **на кни́гу!** here, take the book!

на... *vbl. pref.* **1** forms pf. aspect **2** indicates action continued to sufficiency, to point of satisfaction or exhaustion **3** indicates action relating to determinate quantity or number of objects

набалда́шник, а *m.* knob

набе́г, а *m.* raid; foray

набега́|ть, ю *impf. of* ▶ **набежа́ть**

набе́|гу, жи́шь, гу́т *see* ▶ **набежа́ть**

набе|жа́ть, гу́, жи́шь, гу́т *pf.* (*of* ▶ **набега́ть**) **1** (*натолкну́ться*) (**на** + *a.*) to run into, smash into; (*о волна́х*) to lap against **2** (*сбежа́ться*) to come running (*together*)

на́бережн|ая, ой *f.* embankment

набива́|ть, ю *impf. of* ▶ **наби́ть**

набира́|ть, ю *impf. of* ▶ **набра́ть**

набира́|ться, юсь *impf. of* ▶ **набра́ться**

наб|и́ть, ью, ьёшь *pf.* (*of* ▶ **набива́ть**) (+ *a. and i.*) to stuff (with), pack (with), fill (with); **н. трубку** to fill one's pipe

наблюда́тел|ь, я *m.* observer

наблюда́тел|ьный *adj.* **1** (**~ен, ~ьна**) (*внима́тельный*) observant **2** (*для наблюде́ния*) observation (*attr.*); **н. пункт** (mil.) observation post

⚯ **наблюда́|ть, ю** *impf.* **1** (*следи́ть глаза́ми; изуча́ть*) to observe; to watch **2** (**за** + *i.*) (*за детьми́*) to take care (of), look after **3** (**за** + *i.*) to supervise, superintend; **н. за у́личным движе́нием** to control traffic

⚯ **наблюде́ни|е, я** *nt.* **1** observation **2** (*надзо́р*) supervision, superintendence

на́бок *adv.* on one side, awry

⚯ **набо́р, а** *m.* **1** (*рабо́чих*) recruitment; (*ско́рости, высоты́*) gaining, gathering **2** (typ.) composition, typesetting **3** (*компле́кт*) set, collection

набра́сыва|ть, ю *impf. of* ▶ **наброса́ть¹**, ▶ **набро́сить**

набра́сыва|ться, юсь *impf. of* ▶ **набро́ситься**

набра́|ть, наберу́, наберёшь, *past* **~л, ~ла́, ~ло** *pf.* (*of* ▶ **набира́ть**) **1** (+ *g. or a.*) (*собра́ть*) to collect, gather, assemble; **н. угля́** to take on coal; **н. но́мер** to dial a (*telephone*) number; **н. ско́рость** to pick up, gather speed; **н. высоту́** (aeron.) to gain height; to climb **2** (*рабо́чих*) to recruit,

enrol, engage **3** (typ.) to compose, set up

набра́|ться, наберу́сь, наберёшься, *past* **~лся, ~ла́сь, ~ло́сь** *pf.* (*of* ▶ **набира́ться**) **1** (*usu. impers.*) (*скопи́ться*) (*о лю́дях*) to assemble, gather, collect; (*о пыли, деньга́х, рабо́те*) to accumulate **2** (+ *g.*) (*хра́брости, сил*) to find, muster; (*зна́ний*) to acquire

наброса́|ть¹, ю *pf.* (▶ **набра́сывать**) (*рису́нок и т. п.*) to sketch, outline

наброса́|ть², ю *pf.* (*накида́ть*) to throw about; to throw (*in successive instalments*)

набро́|сить, шу, сишь *pf.* (*of* ▶ **набра́сывать**) to throw (on, over)

набро́|ситься, шусь, сишься *pf.* (*of* ▶ **набра́сываться**) (**на** + *a.*) to fall upon; to go for; **соба́ка ~силась на меня́** the dog went for me; (infml, *на рабо́ту, на еду́*) to attack, get stuck into

набро́с|ок, ка *m.* (*рису́нок*) sketch; (*статьи́*) draft

набух|а́ть, а́ю *impf. of* ▶ **набу́хнуть**

набу́х|нуть, ну, нешь, *past* **~, ~ла** *pf.* (*of* ▶ **набуха́ть**) to swell

наб|ью́, ьёшь *see* ▶ **наби́ть**

наважде́ни|е, я *nt.* delusion; (*при́зрак*) hallucination

нава́лива|ть, ю *impf. of* ▶ **навали́ть**

нава́лива|ться, юсь *impf. of* ▶ **навали́ться**

навал|и́ть, ю́, ~ишь *pf.* (*of* ▶ **нава́ливать**) (*наложи́ть наве́рх*) to heap, pile; (*возложи́ть*) to load (also fig.); (*impers.*) **сне́гу ~и́ло по коле́но** the snow had piled up knee deep

навал|и́ться, ю́сь, ~ишься *pf.* (*of* ▶ **нава́ливаться**) (**на** + *a.*) **1** (infml, *на еду́, на рабо́ту*) to attack, get stuck into **2** (*на дверь, на челове́ка*) to lean (on, upon); to bring all one's weight to bear (on) **3** (*насы́паться*) to pile up (on)

наве|ду́, дёшь *see* ▶ **навести́**

наве́к *adv.* for ever

наве́ки = **наве́к**

⚯ **наве́рно** and **наве́рное** *adv.* (*вво́дное сло́во*) probably, most likely; **он, н., не позвони́т** he probably won't phone

наверняка́ *adv.* (infml) **1** (*несомне́нно*) for sure, certainly **2** (*безоши́бочно*) safely, without taking risks; **бить н.** to take no chances

наверста́|ть, ю *pf.* (*of* ▶ **навёрстывать**) to make up (for); **н. поте́рянное вре́мя** to make up for lost time; **н. упу́щенное** to repair an omission; to catch up

навёрстыва|ть, ю *impf. of* ▶ **наверста́ть**

наве́рх *adv.* (*вверх*) up, upward; (*по ле́стнице*) upstairs; (*на пове́рхность*) to the top

наверху́ *adv.* above; (*в ве́рхнем этаже́*) upstairs; (fig., *в руково́дстве*) at the top

наве́с, а *m.* **1** (*кры́ша*) roof; (*тент*) awning **2** (*скалы́*) overhang **3** (sport) lob

наве́|сить, шу, сишь *pf.* (*of* ▶ **наве́шивать¹**) **1** (+ *a. or g.*) (*дверь, замо́к*) to hang; (*пове́сить мно́го*) to hang (*a number of*)

⚯ key word

pictures **2** (sport) to lob

наве|сти́, ду́, дёшь, *past* ~л, ~ла́ *pf.*
(*of* ▶ **наводи́ть**) **1** (на + *a.*) (*указать
направление*) to direct (at); (*орудие,
прожектор*) to aim (at); **н. кого́-н. на
мысль** to suggest an idea to sb; **н. на след**
to put on the track **2** (*устроить, сделать*)
to lay, put, make; **н. поря́док** to introduce
order, establish order; **н. спра́вку** to make
an inquiry

наве|сти́ть, щу́, сти́шь *pf.* (*of* ▶ **навеща́ть**)
to visit, call on

наве́тренный *adj.* windward

наве́чно *adv.* for ever

наве́ш|ать, аю *pf.* (*of* ▶ **наве́шивать²**) (+ *a.
or g.*) to hang (up), suspend

наве́шива|ть¹, ю *impf. of* ▶ **наве́сить**

наве́шива|ть², ю *impf. of* ▶ **наве́шать**

навеща́|ть, ю *impf. of* ▶ **навести́ть**

на́взничь *adv.* backwards, on one's back

навига́ци|я, и *f.* navigation

навис|а́ть, а́ю *impf.* (*of* ▶ **нави́снуть**) (на
+ *a. or* над + *i.*) to hang (over), overhang;
(fig.) to impend, threaten; **над на́ми** ~ла
опа́сность danger threatened us

нави́с|нуть, ну, нешь, *past* ~, ~ла *pf. of*
▶ **нависа́ть**

навлека́|ть, ю *impf. of* ▶ **навле́чь**

навле|ку́, чёшь, ку́т *see* ▶ **навле́чь**

навле́|чь, ку́, чёшь, ку́т, *past* ~к, ~кла́ *pf.*
(*of* ▶ **навлека́ть**) (на + *a.*) to bring (on); **н. на
себя́ гнев** to incur anger

наво|ди́ть, жу́, ~дишь *impf. of* ▶ **навести́**

наводне́ни|е, я *nt.* flood, flooding;
(*товарами*) flooding, inundation

наводн|и́ть, ю́, и́шь *pf.* (*of* ▶ **наводня́ть**)
(+ *a. and i.*) to flood (with), inundate (with);
(fig.): **н. ры́нок дешёвыми това́рами** to flood
the market with cheap goods

наводн|я́ть, я́ю *impf. of* ▶ **наводни́ть**

наво|жу́, ~дишь *see* ▶ **наводи́ть**

наво́з, а *m.* manure

на́волочк|а, и *f.* pillowcase, pillowslip

навор|ова́ть, у́ю *pf.* (infml) to steal (*a
quantity of*)

наворо́чен|ный, ~, ~а *adj.* (infml) fancy

навр|а́ть, у́, ёшь, *past* ~а́л, ~ала́, ~а́ло *pf.*
(*of* ▶ **врать**) (infml) **1** to tell lies **2** (в + *p.*) to
make mistakes (in); **н. в расска́зе** to get the
story wrong

навре|ди́ть, жу́, ди́шь *pf. of* ▶ **вреди́ть**

навря́д ли *adv.* scarcely, hardly

навсегда́ *adv.* for ever, for good; **раз и н.**
once (and) for all

навстре́чу *adv. and prep.* (+ *d.*) to meet;
towards; **он вы́шел н. гостя́м** he went
out to meet the guests; (fig.) to help,
show sympathy to sb; **идти́ н. чьим-н.
пожела́ниям** to meet sb's wishes

⚒ **на́вык, а** *m.* skill

навы́нос *adv.* to take away (BrE), to go (AmE);
for consumption off the premises

навя́|за́ть, жу́, ~жешь *pf.* (*of* ▶ **навя́зывать**)
1 (на + *a.*) (*привязать*) to tie on (to),
fasten (to) **2** (fig.) (+ *d. and a.*) (*заставить
принять*) to foist (on); **н. кому́-н. сове́т** to thrust advice on sb

навя|за́ться, жу́сь, ~жешься *pf.* (*of*
▶ **навя́зываться**) (infml) (+ *d.*) to thrust
oneself (upon), intrude (upon)

навя́зчив|ый, ~, ~а *adj.* **1** (*человек*)
importunate; annoying **2** (*мысль*)
persistent; ~ая иде́я idée fixe, obsession

навя́зыва|ть, ю *impf. of* ▶ **навяза́ть**

навя́зыва|ться, юсь *impf. of* ▶ **навяза́ться**

нага́|дить, жу, дишь *pf. of* ▶ **га́дить**

нагиба́|ть, ю *impf. of* ▶ **нагну́ть**

нагиба́|ться, юсь *impf. of* ▶ **нагну́ться**

нагишо́м *adv.* (infml) stark naked

нагле́ц, а́ *m.* impudent fellow, insolent fellow

на́глост|ь, и *f.* impudence, insolence,
impertinence

на́гл|ый, ~, ~а́, ~о *adj.* impudent, insolent,
impertinent

нагля́д|ный, ~ен, ~на *adj.* **1** (*очевидный*)
clear; graphic, obvious **2** (*no short forms*)
(*в обучении*) visual

наг|на́ть, оню́, о́нишь, *past* ~на́л, ~нала́,
~на́ло *pf.* (*of* ▶ **нагоня́ть**) **1** (*догнать*) to
overtake, catch up (with) **2** (*наверстать*)
to make up (for) **3** (+ *a. or g.*) to herd
together (*a number of*) **4** (fig., infml,
внушить) to inspire, arouse, occasion

нагн|у́ть, у́, ёшь *pf.* (*of* ▶ **нагиба́ть**) to bend

нагн|у́ться, у́сь, ёшься *pf.* (*of*
▶ **нагиба́ться**) to bend (down), stoop

нагова́рива|ть, ю *impf. of* ▶ **наговори́ть¹**

наговор|и́ть¹, ю́, и́шь *pf.* (*of* ▶ **нагова́ривать**)
(infml) (на + *a.*) to slander, calumniate

наговор|и́ть², ю́, и́шь *pf.* (+ *a. or g.*) to
talk, say a lot (of); **н. чепухи́** to talk a lot of
nonsense

наг|о́й, ~, ~а́, ~о *adj.* (*о человеке*) naked,
nude; (*о части тела*) bare

нагоня́|ть, ю *impf. of* ▶ **нагна́ть**

наго́рь|е, я *nt.* tableland, plateau

нагот|а́, ы́ *f.* nakedness, nudity

нагото́ве *adv.* in readiness; ready to hand;
быть н. to hold oneself in readiness, be on
call

награ́б|ить, лю, ишь *pf.* (+ *a. or g.*) to amass
by robbery

награ́д|а, ы *f.* **1** reward, recompense; **в** ~**у**
as a reward **2** (*почётный знак, орден*)
award; decoration; (*в школе*) prize

награ|ди́ть, жу́, ди́шь *pf.* (*of* ▶ **награжда́ть**)
(+ *a. and i.*) **1** to reward (with) **2** (*орденом,
медалью*) to decorate (with); to award,
confer; (fig.) to endow (with)

награжда́|ть, ю *impf. of* ▶ **награди́ть**

награждён|ный *p.p.p. of* ▶ **награди́ть**; (*as n.*
н., ~**ого**) *m.* recipient (*of an award*)

нагрева́ни|е, я *nt.* heating

нагрева́тел|ь, я *m.* (tech.) heater

нагрева́|ть, ю *impf. of* ▶ **нагре́ть**

нагрева́|ться, юсь *impf. of* ▶ **нагре́ться**

нагре́|ть, ю *pf.* (*of* ▶ **нагрева́ть**) to warm, heat

нагре́|ться, юсь *pf.* (*of* ▶ **нагрева́ться**) (*стать тёплым*) to become warm; (*стать горячим*) to become hot; to warm up, heat up

нагроможде́ни|е, я *nt.* pile, heap

нагруб|и́ть, лю́, и́шь *pf. of* ▶ **груби́ть**

нагру́дник, а *m.* (*детский*) bib

нагружа́|ть, ю *impf. of* ▶ **нагрузи́ть**

нагру|зи́ть, жу́, ~зишь *pf.* (*of* ▶ **грузи́ть** 1, ▶ **нагружа́ть**) (+ *a. and i.*) to load (with)

◆ **нагру́зк|а, и** *f.* **1** (*груз*) load **2** (*fig.*) work; commitments

нагря́н|уть, у, ешь *pf.* (*вдруг появиться*) to appear unexpectedly; (**на** + *a.*) to descend (on)

◆ **над** *prep.* + *i.* **1** (*выше*) over, above **2** (*при обозначении предмета труда*) on; at; **рабо́тать над диссерта́цией** to be working on a dissertation; **смея́ться над** to laugh at

**над... ** *comb. form* super-, over-

нада|ва́ть, ю́, ёшь *pf.* (*infml*) **1** (+ *d., and a. or g.*) to give (*a large quantity of*) **2** (*побить*) (+ *d.*) to thrash

надав|и́ть, лю́, ~ишь *pf.* (*of* ▶ **нада́вливать**) (**на** + *a.*) (*кнопку*) to press (on)

нада́влива|ть, ю *impf. of* ▶ **надави́ть**

надба́вк|а, и *f.* **1** (*повышение*) addition, increase; (*о цене*) extra charge; **н. к зарпла́те** rise (BrE), raise (AmE) (*in wages*)

надвига́|ть, ю *impf. of* ▶ **надви́нуть**

надвига́|ться, юсь *impf. of* ▶ **надви́нуться**

надви́н|уть, у, ешь *pf.* (*of* ▶ **надвига́ть**) to move, pull (up to, over)

надви́н|уться, усь, ешься *pf.* (*of* ▶ **надвига́ться**) to approach, draw near

на́двое *adv.* in two

надева́|ть, ю *impf. of* ▶ **наде́ть**

◆ **наде́жд|а, ы** *f.* hope; **в ~е на** (+ *a.*) in the hope of; **подава́ть ~ы** to promise well

◆ **надёж|ный, ~ен, ~на** *adj.* (*человек*) reliable, trustworthy; (*замок, фунда́мент*) solid, secure; (*средство*) safe

наде́ла|ть, ю *pf.* (+ *a. or g.*) **1** (*пельменей*) to make (*a quantity of*) **2** (*infml*) (+ *g.*) (*неприятностей*) to cause (*a lot of*); (*ошибок*) to make (*a lot of*) **3** (*infml, сделать что-то плохое*) to do (*sth wrong*); **что ты ~л?** what have you done?

надел|и́ть, ю́, и́шь *pf.* (*of* ▶ **наделя́ть**) (+ *a. and i.*) to provide (with); (*fig.*) to endow (with)

наделя́|ть, ю *impf. of* ▶ **надели́ть**

наде́|ну, нешь *see* ▶ **наде́ть**

наде́|ть, ну, нешь *pf.* (*of* ▶ **надева́ть**) to put on (*clothes, etc.*)

◆ **наде́|яться, юсь, ешься** *impf.* (*of* ▶ **понаде́яться**) **1** (**на** + *a.*) (*успех*) to hope (for); **н. на лу́чшее** to hope for the best **2** (**на** + *a.*) (*друга, помощь*) to rely (on),

count on **3** (+ *inf.*) to hope to

надзе́мный *adj.* (*над пове́рхностью*) overground; (*на пове́рхности*) surface

надзира́тел|ь, я *m.* overseer, supervisor; **тюре́мный н.** prison guard

надзира́|ть, ю *impf.* (**за** + *i.*) to oversee, supervise

надзо́р, а *m.* **1** supervision; (*за подозрева́емым*) surveillance **2** (*collect.*) (*орган*) inspectorate

надлежа́щий *adj.* appropriate; fitting, proper

надме́н|ный, ~ен, ~на *adj.* haughty, arrogant

◆ **на́до**[1] = **над**

◆ **на́до**[2] (+ *d. and inf.*) it is necessary; one must, one ought; (+ *a. or g.*) there is need of; **не н.** (*не нужно*) one need not; (*нельзя*) one must not; **мне н. идти́** I must go, I ought to go; **так ему́ и н.!** serves him right!; **н. же!** well, I never!

надоеда́|ть, ю *impf. of* ▶ **надое́сть**

надое́дливый, ~, ~а *adj.* annoying, boring, tiresome

надое́|сть, м, шь, ст, ди́м, ди́те, дя́т *pf.* (*of* ▶ **надоеда́ть**) **1** (+ *d. and i.*) to get on the nerves (of); (*про́сьбами*) to pester (with), plague (with) **2** (*impers.*) (*inf.*): **мне** *и т. п.* **~ло** I am, *etc.*, tired (of), sick (of); **нам ~ло гуля́ть** we are tired of walking

надо́лго *adv.* for a long time

надорва́|ться, у́сь, ёшься, ** *past* **~а́лся, ~ала́сь, ~ало́сь *pf.* (*of* ▶ **надрыва́ться** 1) to (over)strain oneself; (*переутоми́ться*) to tire oneself out

надпи|са́ть, шу́, ~шешь *pf.* (*of* ▶ **надпи́сывать**) (*кни́гу*) to inscribe

надпи́сыва|ть, ю *impf. of* ▶ **надписа́ть**

на́дпис|ь, и *f.* inscription

надре́з, а *m.* cut, incision; (*зару́бка*) notch

надре́|зать, жу, жешь *pf.* (*of* ▶ **надреза́ть**) to make an incision (in)

надреза́|ть, а́ю *impf. of* ▶ **надре́з**

надруга́|ться, юсь *pf.* (**над** + *i.*) to commit an outrage (against)

надры́в, а *m.* **1** (*надо́рванное ме́сто*) slight tear, rent **2** (*физи́ческий*) strain **3** (*fig., не́рвный*) breakdown **4** (*возбуждённость*) hysteria

надрыва́|ться, юсь *impf.* **1** *impf. of* ▶ **надорва́ться** **2** (*no pf.*) (*стара́ться*) to exert oneself; to break one's neck **3** (*no pf.*) (*крича́ть*) to yell, bellow

надсмо́трщик, а *m.* overseer, supervisor; (*тюре́мный*) jailer

надстра́ива|ть, ю *impf. of* ▶ **надстро́ить**

надстро́|ить, ю, ишь *pf.* (*of* ▶ **надстра́ивать**) **1** (*эта́ж*) to build on **2** (*зда́ние*) to raise the height (of)

надстро́йк|а, и *f.* **1** (*де́йствие*) building on; raising **2** (*надстро́енная часть*) superstructure (*also phil.*)

надува́|ть, ю *impf. of* ▶ **наду́ть**

надува́|ться, юсь *impf. of* ▶ **наду́ться**

надувн|о́й *adj.* pneumatic; **н. матра́с** air bed; **~а́я/рези́новая ло́дка** inflatable/rubber dinghy

наду́ман|ный, **~**, **~на** *adj.* far-fetched, forced

наду́|ть, ю, ешь *pf.* (*of* ▸ надува́ть) **1** (*шар, мяч, колесо*) to inflate, blow up; (*паруса*) to puff out; **н. велосипе́дную ка́меру** to inflate, blow up a bicycle tyre (BrE), tire (AmE); **н. гу́бы** (infml) to pout one's lips **2** (infml, *обмануть*) to dupe; to swindle

наду́|ться, юсь, ешься *pf.* (*of* ▸ надува́ться) (*шар, мяч, колесо*) to fill out, swell out; (*вена, почка*) to swell

надуш|и́ть, у́, ~ишь *pf. of* ▸ души́ть²

надуш|и́ться, у́сь, ~ишься *pf. of* ▸ души́ться²

наеда́|ться, юсь *impf. of* ▸ нае́сться

наедине́ *adv.* privately, in private; **н. с** (+ *i.*) alone (with); **н. с собо́й** alone, by oneself

нае́|ду, дешь *see* ▸ нае́хать

нае́зд, а *m.* **1** (*столкновение*) collision; **маши́на соверши́ла н. на пешехо́да** the car hit a pedestrian **2** (*визит*) flying visit; **быва́ть ~ом/~ами** to pay short, infrequent visits

нае́здник, а *m.* horseman, rider

нае́здни|ца, цы *f. of* ▸ нае́здник

наезжа́|ть, ю *impf. of* ▸ нае́хать

на|ём, ~йма *m.* (*на короткий период, рабочих*) hire; (*в длительное пользование, квартиры*) renting; **взять в н.** to rent; **сдать в н.** to let

наёмник, а *m.* **1** (mil.) mercenary **2** (*наёмный работник*) hireling; (fig.) mercenary

наёмный *adj.* hired; rented; **н. уби́йца** hit man

нае́|сться, мся, шься, стся, ди́мся, ди́тесь, дя́тся, *past* **~лся, ~лась** *pf.* (*of* ▸ наеда́ться) **1** to eat one's fill **2** (+ *g. or i.*) to eat (a large quantity of), stuff oneself (with)

нае́|хать, ду, дешь *pf.* (*of* ▸ наезжа́ть) **1** (на + *a.*) to run (into, over), collide (with); **на нас ~хал авто́бус** a bus ran into us, hit us **2** (infml, *приехать*) to come, arrive (*unexpectedly or in numbers*) **3** (sl.) (на + *a.*) (*придраться; выругать*) to go on (at), give (sb) a hard time; (*о рэкете*) to try to blackmail (sb)

наж|а́ть, му́, мёшь *pf.* (*of* ▸ нажима́ть) **1** (+ *a. or* на + *a.*) to press (on); **н. (на) кно́пку** to press the button **2** (fig., infml) (на + *a.*) (*понудить*) to put pressure (upon)

нажи́в|а, ы *f.* gain, profit

нажива́|ть, ю *impf. of* ▸ нажи́ть

нажива́|ться, юсь *impf. of* ▸ нажи́ться

нажи́вк|а, и *f.* bait

нажи|ву́, вёшь *see* ▸ нажи́ть

нажи́м, а *m.* pressure (also fig.); **сде́лать что-н. под ~ом** to do sth under pressure

нажима́|ть, ю *impf. of* ▸ нажа́ть

наж|и́ть, иву́, ивёшь, *past* **~ил, ~ила́, ~ило** *pf.* (*of* ▸ нажива́ть) (*богатство*) to acquire, gain; (fig., infml, *болезнь*) to contract, get

наж|и́ться, иву́сь, ивёшься, *past* **~и́лся, ~ила́сь** *pf.* (*of* ▸ нажива́ться) (на + *p.*) to become rich (from), make a fortune (from)

наж|му́, мёшь *see* ▸ нажа́ть

наза́д *adv.* **1** (*оглянуться*) back; (*катиться*) backwards; (*на прежнее место*) back; **н.!** back!; stand back! **2**: **(тому) н.** ago

назва́ни|е, я *nt.* name; **под ~ем** named

наз|ва́ть, ову́, овёшь, *past* **~ва́л, ~вала́, ~ва́ло** *pf.* (*of* ▸ называ́ть) (+ *a. and i.*) to call; to name

наз|ва́ться, ову́сь, овёшься, *past* **~ва́лся, ~вала́сь** *pf.* (*of* ▸ называ́ться) (+ *i.*) **1** (*получить какое-н. имя*) to call oneself; to be named **2** (*представиться*) to give one's name **3** (*журналистом*) to claim to be

назе́мн|ый *adj.* ground, surface; **~ые войска́** (mil.) ground troops; **~ая по́чта** surface mail

назида́тел|ьный, **~ен**, **~ьна** *adj.* edifying

назло́ 1 *adv.* (*сделать*) out of spite **2** *prep.* (+ *d.*) (*родителям*) to spite

назнач|а́ть, а́ю *impf. of* ▸ назна́чить

назначе́ни|е, я *nt.* **1** (*на работу*) appointment **2** (med.) prescription **3** (*цель*) purpose; **испо́льзовать что́-н. по ~ю** to use sth properly, appropriately; **отря́д осо́бого ~я** special task force **4**: **ме́сто ~я** destination

назна́ч|ить, у, ишь *pf.* (*of* ▸ назнача́ть) **1** (*дату, место, размер*) to fix, set, appoint; **н. день встре́чи** to fix, appoint a day for a meeting; **н. кому́-н. свида́ние** to make a date with sb **2** (+ *a. and i.*) to appoint, nominate; **его́ ~или дире́ктором** he has been appointed director **3** (med.) to prescribe

назо́йлив|ый, **~**, **~а** *adj.* importunate, troublesome

назрева́|ть, ю *impf.* (*of* ▸ назре́ть) to become imminent; **кри́зис ~л** a crisis was brewing

назре́|ть, ю, ешь *pf. of* ▸ назрева́ть

называ́емый *pres. part. pass. of* ▸ называ́ть; **так н.** so-called

называ́|ть, ю *impf.* (*of* ▸ назва́ть): **н. ве́щи свои́ми имена́ми** to call a spade a spade

называ́|ться, юсь *impf.* (*of* ▸ назва́ться) (*носить какое-н. наименование, имя*) to be called; **как ~ется э́то село́?** what is this village called?

наибо́лее *adv.* (the) most

наибо́льший *adj.* the greatest; (*по величине*) the largest

найвност|ь, и *f.* naivety

найв|ный, **~ен, ~на** *adj.* naive; (*простой*) artless

наивы́сш|ий *adj.* the highest; **в ~ей сте́пени** to the utmost

наизна́нку *adv.* inside out; **вы́вернуть н.** to turn inside out

наизу́сть *adv.* by heart; from memory

Н

наилу́чший *adj.* (the) best

наиме́нее *adv.* (the) least

наимен|ова́ть, у́ю *pf. of* ▸ именова́ть

наиме́ньший *adj.* (the) least; (*по величине́*) the smallest

наискосо́к *adv.* = на́искось

на́искось *adv.* obliquely, slantwise

наиху́дший *adj.* (the) worst

⚹ **на|йти́**[1]**, йду́, йдёшь,** *past* ~шёл, ~шла́ *pf.* (*of* ▸ находи́ть) to find; **н. иде́ю интере́сной** to find the idea interesting

на|йти́[2]**, йду́, йдёшь,** *past* ~шёл, ~шла́ *pf.* (*of* ▸ находи́ть) (**на** + *a.*) (*натолкну́ться*) to come (across, upon); (*о чувствах*) to come over; **что э́то на неё ~шло́?** what has come over her?; (*закры́ть собо́й*) to cover

на|йти́сь, йду́сь, йдёшься, *past* ~шёлся, ~шла́сь *pf.* (*of* ▸ находи́ться[1]) **1** (*обнаружи́ться*) (*по́сле по́исков*) to be found; to turn up; (*вы́зваться*) to volunteer **2** (*не растеря́ться*) to not be at a loss; **я не ~шёлся, что сказа́ть** I was at a loss for what to say

наказа́ни|е, я *nt.* punishment

нака|за́ть, жу́, ~жешь *pf.* (*of* ▸ нака́зывать) to punish

нака́зыва|ть, ю *impf. of* ▸ наказа́ть

нака́лива|ть, ю *impf. of* ▸ накали́ть

нака́лива|ться, юсь *impf. of* ▸ накали́ться

накал|и́ть, ю́, и́шь *pf.* (*of* ▸ нака́ливать) to heat, incandesce; (fig., *ситуа́цию*) to inflame

накал|и́ться, ю́сь, и́шься *pf.* (*of* ▸ нака́ливаться, ▸ накаля́ться) to glow, incandesce; (fig., *обстано́вка*) to become inflamed; **стра́сти ~и́лись** passions were running high

накаля́|ть, ю *impf. of* ▸ накали́ть

накаля́|ться, юсь *impf. of* ▸ накали́ться

накану́не 1 *adv.* the day before **2** (*prep.*) (+ *g.*) on the eve (of); **н. Рождества́** on Christmas Eve

нака́п|ать, аю *pf. of* ▸ ка́пать

нака́пливать *impf. of* ▸ накопи́ть

нака́пливаться *impf. of* ▸ накопи́ться

накач|а́ть[1]**, а́ю** *pf.* (*of* ▸ нака́чивать) (*ши́ну, ка́меру*) to pump up, pump full

накач|а́ть[2]**, а́ю** *pf.* (*of* ▸ нака́чивать, ▸ кача́ть 3) (*воды́*) to pump (*a quantity of*)

накач|а́ть[3]**, а́ю** *pf.* (*of* ▸ кача́ть 4, ▸ нака́чивать) (infml) to be muscly from pumping iron

накача́|ться, юсь *pf. of* ▸ кача́ться 3

нака́чива|ть, ю *impf. of* ▸ накача́ть[1], ▸ кача́ть[3], ▸ накача́ть[3]

наки́дк|а, и *f.* cloak, mantle; wrap

наки́дыва|ться, юсь *impf. of* ▸ наки́нуться

наки́|нуться, нусь, нешься *pf.* (*of* ▸ наки́дываться) (**на** + *a.*) to fall (on, upon); (*на еду́, на рабо́ту*) to attack, get stuck into

накладн|а́я, о́й *f.* invoice, waybill

⚹ key word

накладн|о́й *adj.* **1** (*прикреплённый пове́рх чего́-н.*) superimposed; **н. карма́н** patch pocket; **~ые расхо́ды** overheads **2** (*иску́сственный*) false; **~а́я борода́** false beard

накла́дыва|ть, ю *impf. of* ▸ наложи́ть[1], ▸ наложи́ть[2]

наклеве|та́ть, щу́, ~щешь *pf. of* ▸ клевета́ть

накле́ива|ть, ю *impf. of* ▸ накле́ить

накле́|ить, ю, ишь *pf.* (*of* ▸ накле́ивать) to stick on, paste on

накле́йк|а, и *f.* sticker

накло́н, а *m.* (*головы́*) inclination; (*по́черка*) slope, slant; (*пока́тая пове́рхность*) slope, incline

наклон|и́ть, ю́, ~ишь *pf.* (*of* ▸ наклоня́ть) to incline, bend

наклон|и́ться, ю́сь, ~ишься *pf.* (*of* ▸ наклоня́ться) to stoop, bend

накло́нност|ь, и *f.* (**к** + *d.*) inclination (towards), tendency (towards), propensity (for)

накло́нн|ый *adj.* inclined, sloping; **~ая пло́скость** inclined plane

наклоня́|ть, яю *impf. of* ▸ наклони́ть

наклоня́|ться, яюсь *impf. of* ▸ наклони́ться

накова́льн|я, ьни, *g. pl.* ~ен *f.* anvil

⚹ **наконе́ц** *adv.* at last, finally, in the end; **н.-то!** at last!; about time too!; (*ещё, кро́ме всего́*) after all; (*выража́ет недово́льство*) ever; **переста́ньте, н., спо́рить!** will you ever stop arguing!

наконе́чник, а *m.* tip, point

накоп|и́ть, лю́, ~ишь *pf.* (*of* ▸ копи́ть, ▸ нака́пливать) (+ *a. or g.*) to accumulate, amass

накоп|и́ться, ~ится *pf.* (*of* ▸ нака́пливаться, ▸ копи́ться) to accumulate

накопле́ни|е, я *nt.* **1** accumulation **2** (*in pl.*) (*сбереже́ния*) savings

накорм|и́ть, лю́, ~ишь *pf. of* ▸ корми́ть 1

накра́|сить, шу, сишь *pf.* (*of* ▸ накра́шивать) **1** (*но́гти, гу́бы*) to paint **2** (*лицо́*) to make up

накра́|ситься, шусь, сишься *pf. of* ▸ кра́ситься 1

накра́шива|ть, ю *impf. of* ▸ накра́сить

накрош|и́ть, у́, ~ишь *pf.* (*of* ▸ кроши́ть) **1** to crumble, shred (*a quantity of*) **2** (*насори́ть кро́шками*) to spill crumbs

накро́|ю, ёшь *see* ▸ накры́ть

накру|ти́ть, чу́, ~тишь *pf.* (*of* ▸ накру́чивать) **1** (*намота́ть*) (**на** + *a.*) to wind (around, on to) **2** (*верёвок*) to twist (*a quantity of*)

накру́чива|ть, ю *impf. of* ▸ накрути́ть

накрыва́|ть, ю *impf. of* ▸ накры́ть

накрыва́|ться, юсь *impf. of* ▸ накры́ться

накры́|ть, о́ю, о́ешь *pf.* (*of* ▸ накрыва́ть) to cover; **н. (на) стол** to lay the table; **н. к у́жину** to lay supper

накры́|ться, о́юсь, о́ешься *pf.* (*of* ▸ накрыва́ться) (+ *i.*) to cover oneself (with)

накуп|а́ть, а́ю *impf. of* ▸ накупи́ть

накуп|и́ть, лю́, ~ишь *pf.* (*of* ▶ **накупа́ть**)
(+ *a. or g.*) to buy up (*a number or quantity of*)

нал, а *m.* (infml) cash

налага́|ть, ю *impf. of* ▶ **наложи́ть**[1] 2,
▶ **наложи́ть**[1] 4

нала́|дить, жу, дишь *pf.* (*of* ▶ **нала́живать**)
[1] (*отрегули́ровать*) to regulate, adjust;
(*испра́вить*) to repair, put right
[2] (*организова́ть*) to set going, arrange; **н.
де́ла** to get things going

нала́|диться, дится *pf.* (*of* ▶ **нала́живаться**)
to go right; **рабо́та ~дилась** the work is
well in hand

нала́жива|ть, ю, ет *impf. of* ▶ **нала́дить**

нала́жива|ться, ется *impf. of* ▶ **нала́диться**

нале́во *adv.* [1] (от + *g.*) to the left (of); **н.!**
(mil.) left turn! [2] (infml, *продава́ть*) on the
side (= *illicitly*); **рабо́тать н.** to moonlight

налеп|и́ть[1]**, лю́, ~ишь** *pf.* (*of* ▶ **лепи́ть** 2)
to stick on

налеп|и́ть[2]**, лю́, ~ишь** *pf.* (+ *a. or g.*) to
model (*a number of*)

налёт[1]**, а** *m.* (*нападе́ние*) raid; (*на кварти́ру,
на магази́н*) robbery, burglary; **возду́шный
н.** air raid

налёт[2]**, а** *m.* (*то́нкий слой*) deposit; thin
coating; (*на бро́нзе*) patina; **зубно́й н.** dental
plaque; (fig.) touch, soupçon; **с ~ом иро́нии**
with a touch of irony

налет|а́ть, а́ю *impf. of* ▶ **налете́ть**[1]**,
▶ налете́ть**[2]

нале|те́ть[1]**, чу́, ти́шь** *pf.* (*of* ▶ **налета́ть**)
[1] (на + *a.*) (*набро́ситься*) to fall (upon);
(*о пти́це*) to swoop down (on); to fly (upon,
against); (*натолкну́ться*) to run (into)
[2] (*о ве́тре, буре*) to spring up

нале|те́ть[2]**, чу́, ти́шь** *pf.* (*of* ▶ **налета́ть**)
(*прилете́ть*) to fly in, drift in (*in quantities,
in large numbers*)

налива́|ть, ю *impf. of* ▶ **нали́ть**

нал|и́ть, ью́, ьёшь, *past* **~и́л, ~ила́, ~и́ло**
pf. (*of* ▶ **налива́ть**) [1] (*вли́ть*) to pour out;
(*напо́лнить*) (+ *i.*) to fill (with) [2] (*проли́ть*)
to spill

налицо́ *adv.* present, available, on hand

⚔ **нали́чи|е, я** *nt.* presence; **быть, оказа́ться в
~и** to be present, be available

нали́чник, а *m.* (*две́ри, окна́*) casing

нали́чн|ый *adj.* on hand, available; **~ые
(де́ньги)** ready money, cash; **плати́ть ~ыми**
to pay in cash

налов|и́ть, лю́, ~ишь *pf.* (+ *a or g.*) to catch
(*a number of*)

⚔ **нало́г, а** *m.* tax; **подохо́дный н.** income tax;
н. на доба́вленную сто́имость value added
tax, VAT; **н. на при́быль** profits tax

⚔ **нало́г|овый** *adj. of* ▶ **нало́г**; **~овая
деклара́ция** tax return; **н. инспе́ктор** tax
inspector

налогообложе́ни|е, я *nt.* taxation

налогоплате́льщик, а *m.* taxpayer

налож|и́ть[1]**, у́, ~ишь** *pf.* [1] (*impf.*
накла́дывать) (*повя́зку; лак*) to apply;
(*положи́ть све́рху*) to put on, over [2] (*impf.*
накла́дывать, налага́ть) (*печать, ви́зу*)
to affix; **н. отпеча́ток на** (+ *a.*) (fig.) to have a
great influence (on) [3] (*impf.* **накла́дывать**)
(*навали́ть*) to load, pack [4] (*impf.* **налага́ть**)
(на + *a.*) (*подве́ргнуть*) to lay (on), impose;
н. штраф to impose a fine; **н. аре́ст на чьё-н.
иму́щество** (law) to seize sb's property

нало́ж|ить[2]**, у́, ~ишь** *pf.* (*of* ▶ **накла́дывать**)
(+ *a. or g.*) to put, lay (*a quantity of*)

нал|ью́, ьёшь *see* ▶ **нали́ть**

нам *d. of* ▶ **мы**

нама́з, а *m.* Muslim prayer

нама́|зать, жу, жешь *pf. of* ▶ **ма́зать** 2,
▶ **нама́зывать**

нама́|заться, жусь, жешься *pf.* [1] (*impf.*
~зываться) (+ *i.*) to rub oneself (with)
[2] *pf. of* ▶ **ма́заться** 2, ▶ **ма́заться** 3

нама́зыва|ть, ю *impf. of* ▶ **нама́зать**

нама́зыва|ться, юсь *impf. of* ▶ **нама́заться**

нама́тыва|ть, ю *impf.* (*of* ▶ **намота́ть**) to
wind, reel

нама́чива|ть, ю *impf. of* ▶ **намочи́ть** 1

намёк, а *m.* hint; **сде́лать н.** to drop a hint

намек|а́ть, а́ю *impf.* (*of* ▶ **намекну́ть**) (на +
a. or о + *p.*) to hint (at), allude (to)

намек|ну́ть, ну́, нёшь *pf. of* ▶ **намека́ть**

намерева́|ться, юсь *impf.* (+ *inf.*) to intend
(to), mean (to)

наме́рен, ~а, ~о *adj. as pred.* (+ *inf.*)
intending; **я н. за́втра е́хать** I intend to go
tomorrow; **что вы ~ы де́лать?** what do you
intend to do?

наме́рени|е, я *nt.* intention; purpose; **без
вся́кого ~я** unintentionally

наме́ренно *adv.* intentionally, deliberately

наме́рен|ный, ~, ~на *adj.* intentional,
deliberate

наме́|тить[1]**, чу, тишь** *pf.* (*of* ▶ **намеча́ть**[1])
(*изобрази́ть*) to sketch, outline

наме́|тить[2]**, чу, тишь** *pf.* (*of* ▶ **намеча́ть**[2])
[1] (*плани́ровать*) to plan, project; to have
in view; **н. пое́здку в Росси́ю** to plan a
visit to Russia [2] (*предположи́ть*) to
nominate; (*назна́чить*) to select; **н. зда́ние
к разруше́нию** to designate a building for
demolition

наме́|титься, тится *pf.* (*of* ▶ **намеча́ться**) to
begin to appear; to take shape

намеча́|ть[1]**, ю** *impf. of* ▶ **наме́тить**[1]

намеча́|ть[2]**, ю** *impf. of* ▶ **наме́тить**[2]

намеча́|ться, ется *impf. of* ▶ **наме́титься**

на́ми *i. of* ▶ **мы**

намиби|ец, йца *m.* Namibian

намиби́й|ка, ки *f. of* ▶ **намиби́ец**

намиби́йский *adj.* Namibian

Нами́би|я, и *f.* Namibia

намно́го *adv.* much, far (*with comparatives*);
н. лу́чше much, far better; greatly,
considerably (*with verbs*)

намок|а́ть, а́ю *impf.* (*of* ▶ **намо́кнуть**) to
become wet, get wet

Н

намо́к|нуть, ну, нешь, past ∼, ∼ла pf. of
▶ намока́ть

намо́рдник, а m. muzzle

намота́|ть, ю pf. of ▶ мота́ть 1, ▶ нама́тывать

намочи́|ть, у́, ∼ишь pf. **1** (of ▶ нама́чивать,
▶ мочи́ть 2) (де́лать мокрым) to wet,
moisten; (бельё) to soak **2** (пол) to splash,
spill water on

нанес|ти́, у́, ёшь, past ∼, ∼ла́ pf. (of
▶ наноси́ть) **1** (+ a. or g.) to bring (a
quantity of); to pile up (a quantity of);
(о снеге, песке) (usu. impers.) to drift
2 (начертить) (на + a.) to draw, plot (on a
map, etc.) **3** (причинить) to cause; to inflict;
н. оскорбле́ние to insult; н. ущёрб to inflict
damage **4** (лак, краску) to apply

нани|за́ть, жу́, ∼жешь pf. of ▶ нани́зывать

нани́зыва|ть, ю impf. to string, thread

нанима́тел|ь, я m. **1** (квартиры) tenant
2 (рабочей силы) employer

нанима́тель|ница, ницы f. of ▶ нанима́тель

нанима́|ть, ю impf. of ▶ наня́ть

нанима́|ться, юсь impf. of ▶ наня́ться

нано|си́ть, шу́, ∼сишь impf. of ▶ нанести́

нан|я́ть, найму́, наймёшь, past ∼я́л, ∼яла́,
∼я́ло pf. (of ▶ нанима́ть) (квартиру)
to rent; (машину, рабочих) to hire; н. на
рабо́ту to engage, take on

нан|я́ться, найму́сь, наймёшься, past
∼я́лся, ∼яла́сь pf. (of ▶ нанима́ться) to
get a job

⚷ **наоборо́т** adv. **1** (обратной стороной)
back to front; прочёсть сло́во н. to read
a word backwards **2** (не так) the other
way round; the wrong way (round) **3** (при
противопоставлении) on the contrary; как
раз н. quite the contrary; и н. and vice versa

наобу́м adv. (не подумав) without thinking;
(наудачу) at random

наор|а́ть, у́, ёшь pf. (на + a.) (infml) to shout
(at)

наотре́з adv. flatly, point-blank

напада́|ть, ю impf. of ▶ напа́сть

напада́ющ|ий, его m. (sport) forward

нападе́ни|е, я nt. attack, assault; (sport)
(collect.) forwards, forward line

напа|ду́, дёшь see ▶ напа́сть

напа́рник, а m. fellow worker, mate

напа́|сть, ду́, дёшь, past ∼л pf. (of
▶ напада́ть) (на + a.) **1** to attack; to descend
(on) **2** (о чувстве) to come (over); to grip,
seize; на нас ∼л страх fear seized us

напева́|ть, ю 1 impf. of ▶ напе́ть
2 (тихо, вполголоса) to hum; to croon

наперере́з adv. and prep. (+ d.) so as to cross
one's path; бежа́ть кому́-н. н. to run to head
sb off

напёрст|ок, ка m. thimble

напе́|ть, ою́, оёшь pf. (of ▶ напева́ть 1) to
hum, sing sketchily

напеча́та|ть, ю pf. of ▶ печа́тать

напеча́та|ться, юсь pf. of ▶ печа́таться

напива́|ться, юсь impf. of ▶ напи́ться

напи́льник, а m. (tech.) file

⚷ **напи|са́ть, шу́, ∼шешь** pf. of ▶ писа́ть

напи́т|ок, ка m. drink, beverage

нап|и́ться, ью́сь, ьёшься, past ∼и́лся,
∼ила́сь, ∼и́ло́сь pf. (of ▶ напива́ться)
1 (+ g.) (утолить жажду) to slake one's
thirst (with, on); (выпить) to have a drink
(of) **2** (infml, стать пьяным) to get drunk

напих|а́ть, а́ю pf. (of ▶ напи́хивать) (в + a.)
to cram (into), stuff (into)

напи́хива|ть, ю impf. of ▶ напиха́ть

напишу́, ∼шешь see ▶ написа́ть

напл|ева́ть, юю́, юёшь pf. **1** (+ g.) to spit
(out) **2** (fig., infml) (на + a.) to wash one's
hands (of); н.! to hell with it!, who cares!;
мне н.! I couldn't care less!

нап|ои́ть, ою́, ои́шь pf. (of ▶ пои́ть)
1 (дать попить) to give to drink; to water
(an animal) **2** (довести до опьянения) to
make drunk

напока́з adv. for show; вы́ставить н. to show
off (also fig.)

напо́лн|ить, ю, ишь pf. (of ▶ наполня́ть)
(+ i.) to fill (with)

напо́лн|иться, юсь, ишься pf. (of
▶ наполня́ться) (+ i.) to fill (with)

наполня́|ть, я́ю impf. of ▶ напо́лнить

наполня́|ться, я́юсь impf. of ▶ напо́лниться

наполови́ну adv. half; зал ещё н. пуст the
hall is still half empty

напомина́ни|е, я nt. **1** (действие) reminding
2 (что-н. напоминающее) reminder

напомина́|ть, ю impf. of ▶ напо́мнить

⚷ **напо́мн|ить, ю, ишь** pf. (of ▶ напомина́ть)
1 (+ d. and o + p., or + d. and a.) (заставить
вспомнить) to remind (of); портре́т ∼ил
мне о про́шлом the portrait reminded
me of the past **2** (иметь сходство) to
remind (of), recall (= to resemble); он ∼ил
мне моего́ де́да he reminded me of my
grandfather

напо́р, а m. (воздуха, воды) pressure (also
fig.); под ∼ом under pressure

напо́рист|ый, ∼, ∼а adj. energetic; pushy

напосле́док adv. (infml) in the end, finally,
after all

нап|ою́[1], оёшь see ▶ напе́ть

нап|ою́[2], ишь see ▶ напои́ть

⚷ **напра́в|ить, лю, ишь** pf. (of ▶ направля́ть)
1 (на + a.) (устремить) to direct (to,
at); н. внима́ние (на + a.) to direct one's
attention (to) **2** (отправить) to send; н. уда́р to aim a blow (at)
2 (отправить) to send; н. заявле́ние to
send in an application; (к врачу, к юристу)
to refer

напра́в|иться, люсь, ишься pf. (of
▶ направля́ться) (к + d. or в + a. or на +
a.) (двинуться куда-н.) to make (for);
(двинуться куда-н.) to make (for)

⚷ **направле́ни|е, я** nt. **1** (линия, путь)
direction; по ∼ю (к + d.) in the direction (of),
towards **2** (fig., в экономике, в политике)

⚷ key word

trend, tendency; **либера́льное н.** liberal tendency; (*группиро́вка*) movement **3** (*докуме́нт*) order, warrant

напра́вленност|ь, и *f.* direction, focus, purposefulness

⚥ **направля́|ть, ю** *impf. of* ▶ напра́вить

направля́|ться, юсь *impf.* (*of* ▶ напра́виться): **~емся в Му́рманск** we are bound for Murmansk

направля́ющ|ая, ей *f.* (tech.) guide

напра́во *adv.* (**от** + *g.*) to the right (of)

напра́сно *adv.* **1** (*беспол́езно*) vainly, in vain; **to no purpose 2** (*несправедли́во*) wrong, unjustly, mistakenly

напра́с|ный, ~ен, ~на *adj.* **1** (*беспол́езный*) vain, idle; **~ная наде́жда** vain hope **2** (*нену́жный*) needless

напра́шива|ться, юсь *impf.* (*of* ▶ напроси́ться) (*impf. only*) to arise, suggest itself; **~ется вопро́с** the question arises

⚥ **наприме́р** for example, for instance

напрока́т *adv.* for hire, on hire; **взять н.** to hire, rent; **дать н.** to hire out, let

напроло́м *adv.* straight, regardless of obstacles (also fig.)

напроро́ч|ить, у, ишь *pf. of* ▶ проро́чить

напро|си́ться, шу́сь, ~си́шься *pf.* (*of* ▶ напра́шиваться) (infml) to thrust oneself upon; (**на** + *a.*) to provoke; **н. на комплиме́нты** to fish for compliments

напро́тив *adv. and prep.* + *g.* **1** opposite; **он живёт н. (на́шего до́ма)** he lives opposite (our house) **2** (*при противопоставле́нии*) on the contrary

на́прочь *adv.* (infml) completely

напря́г, а *m.* (sl.) pressure, difficulties; **у меня́ сейча́с ~ деньга́ми** I don't have much money at the moment

напряга́|ть, ю *impf. of* ▶ напря́чь

напряга́|ться, юсь *impf. of* ▶ напря́чься

напря|гу́, жёшь *see* ▶ напря́чь

⚥ **напряже́ни|е, я** *nt.* **1** (*затра́та уси́лий*) effort, exertion; **рабо́тать с ~ем** to exert oneself; (*тру́дное положе́ние*) strain, tension **2** (phys., tech.) strain; stress; (elec.) voltage

напряжённост|ь, и *f.* tension, strain

напряжён|ный, ~, ~на *adj.* tense, strained; **~ные отноше́ния** strained relations; **~ная рабо́та** intensive work

напрями́к *adv.* **1** (*пойти́*) straight **2** (fig., *сказа́ть*) straight out, bluntly

напря́|чь, гу́, жёшь, гу́т, *past* **~г, ~гла́** *pf.* (*of* ▶ напряга́ть) (*му́скулы*) to tense; (*го́лос, слух, внима́ние*) to strain (also fig.)

напря́|чься, гу́сь, жёшься, гу́тся, *past* **~гся, ~гла́сь** *pf.* (*of* ▶ напряга́ться) **1** (*о му́скулах*) to become tense **2** (*о челове́ке*) to exert oneself, strain oneself **3** (*о взгля́де, си́лах*) to be concentrated

напуга́|ть, ю *pf. of* ▶ пуга́ть

напу́др|ить, ю, ишь *pf. of* ▶ пу́дрить

напу́др|иться, юсь, ишься *pf. of* ▶ пу́дриться

напуска́|ть, ю *impf. of* ▶ напусти́ть

напускно́й *adj.* assumed, put on

напу|сти́ть, щу́, ~сти́шь *pf.* (*of* ▶ напуска́ть) **1** (+ *g.*) (*ды́ма, мух*) to let in; **н. воды́ в ва́нну** to fill a bath **2** (*напра́вить для нападе́ния*) (**на** + *a.*) to let loose on, set on **3** (**на себя́** + *a.*) to affect, put on; **н. на себя́ ва́жность** to assume an air of importance

напу́та|ть, ю *pf.* (infml) (**в** + *p.*) to make a mess (of), make a hash (of); (*ошиби́ться*) to confuse, get wrong

напу|щу́, ~сти́шь *see* ▶ напусти́ть

наравне́ *adv.* (**с** + *i.*) equally (with); on an equal footing (with); together (with)

нараст|а́ть, а́ю *impf. of* ▶ нарасти́

нараст|и́, ту́, тёшь, *past* **наро́с, наросла́** *pf.* (*of* ▶ нараста́ть) **1** (**на** + *p.*) to grow (on), form (on); **мох наро́с на камня́х** moss has grown on the stones **2** (*увели́читься*) to increase; (*о зву́ке*) to swell **3** (*накопи́ться*) to accumulate

нара|сти́ть, щу́, сти́шь *pf.* (*of* ▶ нара́щивать) **1** (*му́скулы*) to develop **2** (*удлини́ть*) to lengthen; (fig., *увели́чить*) to increase, augment

нара́щивани|е, я *nt.* increase; build-up; **н. вооруже́ний** arms build-up; **н. воло́с** hair extension

нара́щива|ть, ю *impf. of* ▶ нарасти́ть

на́рд|ы, ов *pl.* backgammon

наре́|жу, жешь *see* ▶ наре́зать

наре́|зать, жу, жешь *pf.* (*of* ▶ нареза́ть) **1** (+ *a. or g.*) (*хле́ба, сыр*) to cut; to slice **2** (tech.) to thread

нареза́|ть, а́ю *impf. of* ▶ наре́зать

нарека́ни|е, я *nt.* censure; reprimand

наре́чи|е, я *nt.* (gram.) adverb

нарис|ова́ть, у́ю *pf. of* ▶ рисова́ть

наркоби́знес, а *m.* drug trafficking

нарко́з, а *m.* anaesthetic (BrE), anesthetic (AmE); **ме́стный н.** local anaesthetic; **о́бщий н.** general anaesthetic

нарко́лог, а *m.* expert in drug and alcohol abuse

наркома́н, а *m.* drug addict

наркома́ни|я, и *f.* drug addiction

наркома́н|ка, ки *f. of* ▶ наркома́н

нарко́тик, а *m.* narcotic; drug; **торго́вля ~ами** drug trafficking

наркоти́ческ|ий *adj.* narcotic; **~ие сре́дства** narcotics, drugs

наркоторго́в|ец, ца *m.* drug dealer

⚥ **наро́д, а (у)** *m.* (*все жи́тели*) people; (*на́ция*) nation; **~ы ми́ра** nations of the world; **англи́йский н.** the English people, the people of England; **челове́к из ~а** a man of the people; **на ми́тинге бы́ло ма́ло ~у** there were not many people at the meeting

наро́дност|ь, и *f.* **1** (*наро́д*) nationality **2** (*sg. only*) (*иску́сства*) national character; national traits

⚥ **наро́дн|ый** *adj.* **1** (*национа́льный*) national; **~ое хозя́йство** national economy **2** (*пе́сня,*

искусство) folk **3** (*восстание, движение*)
of the (*sc. common, working*) people, popular
4 (*в составе почётных званий, названий
некоторых учреждений, коммунистических
штатов и т. п.*): **Н. арти́ст Росси́и** National
Artist of Russia; **Н. суд** the People's Court;
Кита́йская Н~ая Респу́блика the People's
Republic of China

наро́ст, а *m.* **1** (*грязи*) layer **2** (*на растении*)
excrescence, growth

наро́чно *adv.* **1** (*намеренно*) on purpose,
purposely; **как н.** (infml) to make things worse;
н. не приду́маешь it is quite something
2 (infml, *в шутку*) for fun, pretending

наруб|и́ть, лю́, ~ишь *pf.* (+ *a.* or *g.*) to chop
(*a quantity of*)

нару́жност|ь, и *f.* exterior; (outward)
appearance; **н. обма́нчива** appearances are
deceptive

нару́жн|ый *adj.* (*стена, дверь*) external,
exterior; (*изменение*) external; (*спокойствие*)
outward; (tech.) male (*of screw thread*); **~ое
(лека́рство)** medicine for external application

нару́жу *adv.* outside, on the outside; **вы́йти н.**
to come out; (fig.) to come to light, transpire

нарука́вник, а *m.* oversleeve; armlet

нарука́вн|ый *adj.* (worn on the) sleeve; **~ая
повя́зка** armband

нару́чник, а *m.* (*usu. in pl.*) handcuff, manacle

нару́чн|ый *adj.* worn on the arm; **~ые часы́**
wristwatch

наруша́|ть, ю, ет *impf. of* ▸ **нару́шить**

наруша́|ться, ется *impf. of* ▸ **нару́шиться**

⚡ **наруше́ни|е, я** *nt.* **1** (*закона, дисциплины*)
breach; violation; (*обещания*) breaking
2 (*покоя*) disturbance

наруши́тел|ь, я *m.* (*правила, закона*)
transgressor, infringer

наруши́тель|ница, ницы *f. of* ▸ **наруши́тель**

нару́ш|ить, у, ишь *pf.* (*of* ▸ **наруша́ть**)
1 (*сон, покой*) to break, disturb **2** (*закон,
обещание*) to break; **н. грани́цу** to cross a
border illegally

нару́ш|иться, ится *pf.* (*of* ▸ **наруша́ться**)
(*сон, покой, связь*) to be broken

нарци́сс, а *m.* narcissus; (*жёлтый*) daffodil

на́р|ы, ~ (*no sg.*) plank bed; bunk

нары́в, а *m.* abscess; boil

наря́д, а *m.* (*одежда*) attire, apparel, costume

наряди́|ть, жу́, ~дишь *pf.* (*of* ▸ **наряжа́ть**)
1 (*в* + *a.*) to dress (in), array (in); **н. ёлку** to
decorate a Christmas tree **2** (+ *i.*) to dress
up (as)

наряди́|ться, жу́сь, ~дишься *pf.* (*of*
▸ **наряжа́ться**) **1** (*в* + *a.*) to array oneself
(in) **2** (+ *i.*) to dress up (as)

наря́д|ный, ~ен, ~на *adj.* (*человек*)
well dressed; elegant; (*одежда*) smart;
(*комната*) well decorated

наряду́ *adv.* (*с* + *i.*) side by side (with),
equally (with); together (with); **н. с э́тим**

⚡ key word

at the same time

наряжа́|ть, ю *impf. of* ▸ **наряди́ть**

наряжа́|ться, юсь *impf. of* ▸ **наряди́ться**

нас *a., g., and p. of* ▸ **мы**

наса|ди́ть¹, жу́, ~дишь *pf.* (*of* ▸ **наса́живать**)
(*надеть*) to put; to stick, pin; **н. червяка́ на
крючо́к** to fix a worm on to a hook

наса|ди́ть², жу́, ~дишь *pf.* (*of* ▸ **насажда́ть**)
(fig.) to inculcate; to propagate

насажда́|ть, ю *impf. of* ▸ **насади́ть²**

насажде́ни|е, я *nt.* **1** (*действие*) planting;
(fig.) propagation, dissemination **2** (*деревья*)
plantation

наса́жива|ть, ю *impf. of* ▸ **насади́ть¹**

наса́лива|ть, ю *impf. of* ▸ **насоли́ть**

насви́стыва|ть, ю *impf.* to whistle (*a tune*)

наседа́|ть, ю *impf.* (*of* ▸ **насе́сть**) (**на** + *a.*)
to press

насе́дк|а, и *f.* sitting hen

насеко́м|ое, ого *nt.* insect

⚡ **населе́ни|е, я** *nt.* population; (*города,
деревни*) inhabitants

населённый *p.p.p. of* ▸ **насели́ть** *and adj.*
(*район*) densely populated; **н. пункт** (official
designation) locality, place

насел|и́ть, ю́, и́шь *pf.* (*of* ▸ **населя́ть**) to
people, settle

населя́|ть, ю, ешь *impf. of* ▸ **насели́ть**

нас|е́сть, я́ду, я́дешь, *past* **~е́л** *pf. of*
▸ **наседа́ть**

наси́ли|е, я *nt.* (*физическое*) violence;
(*принуждение*) force

наси́л|овать, ую *impf.* **1** (*принуждать*) to
coerce, constrain **2** (*pf.* **из~**) (*принуждать
к половому акту*) to rape

наси́льник, а *m.* **1** tyrant; aggressor
2 (*сексуальный*) rapist

наси́льно *adv.* by force, forcibly

наси́льственн|ый *adj.* (*меры*) violent;
(*выселение*) forcible; **~ая смерть** murder

наска́кива|ть, ю *impf. of* ▸ **наскочи́ть**

наскво́зь *adv.* (*полностью*) through (and
through); throughout; **промо́кнуть н.** to
get wet through; (*пробить, прострелить*)
through

⚡ **наско́лько** *adv.* **1** (*interrog.*) how?; **н. э́то
серьёзно?** how serious is it?; (*in clauses*)
я не зна́ю, н. э́то сро́чно I don't know how
urgent it is **2** (*rel.*) (*помню, знаю*) as far as;
н. мне изве́стно as far as I know **3** (*в тако́й
сте́пени*) so; **н. э́то трудне́е!** it is so much
more difficult!

наскоч|и́ть, у́, ~ишь *pf.* (*of* ▸ **наска́кивать**)
(**на** + *a.*) **1** (*столкнуться*) to run (against),
collide (with) **2** (fig., infml, *с упрёками*) to
fly (at)

наску́ч|ить, у, ишь *pf.* (+ *d.*) to bore; **мне э́то
~ило** I am sick of it

насла|ди́ться, жу́сь, ди́шься *pf.* (*of*
▸ **наслажда́ться**) (+ *i.*) to enjoy; to take
pleasure (in), delight (in)

наслажда́|ться, юсь *impf. of* ▸ **наслади́ться**

наслажде́ни|е, я *nt.* enjoyment, delight

насле́ди|е, я *nt.* legacy; (*культурное*) heritage

насле́дник, а *m.* heir; (*fig.*) successor, inheritor

насле́дниц|а, ы *f.* heiress

насле́д|овать, ую *impf. and pf.* **1** (*pf. also* **у~**) to inherit **2** (+ *d.*) to succeed (to)

насле́дственност|ь, и *f.* heredity

насле́дств|о, а *nt.* **1** inheritance, legacy; **получи́ть в н., по ~у** to inherit **2** (*fig.*) heritage

наслу́ша|ться, юсь *pf.* (+ *g.*) **1** (*услышать много*) to hear (a lot of) **2** (*вдоволь послушать*) to hear enough, listen to long enough

на́смерть *adv.* to death; **испуга́ть н.** (*fig.*) to frighten to death

насмеха́|ться, юсь *impf.* (**над** + *i.*) to mock, ridicule

насмеш|и́ть, у́, и́шь *pf. of* ▶ смеши́ть

насме́шк|а, и *f.* jibe, taunt; (*in pl.*) mockery; **сказа́ть что-н. в ~у** to say sth to hurt sb

насме́шлив|ый, ~, ~а *adj.* mocking

на́сморк, а *m.* cold (*in the head*); **схвати́ть, получи́ть н.** to catch a cold

насмотр|е́ться, ю́сь, ~ишься *pf.* **1** (+ *g.*) (*увидеть много*) to see a lot (of) **2** (**на** + *a.*) to have looked enough (at), to see enough (of); **не н.** to not tire of looking (at)

насол|и́ть, ю́, ~и́шь *pf.* (*of* ▶ наса́ливать) **1** (*usu.* ~ишь) (+ *a. or g.*) (*огурцо́в, грибо́в*) to salt, pickle (*a quantity of*) **2** (*usu.* ~йшь) (*fig.*) (+ *d.*) (*сделать неприятность*) to spite; to do a bad turn (to)

насор|и́ть, ю́, и́шь *pf. of* ▶ сори́ть

насо́с, а *m.* pump

на́спех *adv.* hastily; carelessly

насра́|ть, у́, ёшь *pf. of* ▶ срать

наста|ва́ть, ёт, ю́т *impf. of* ▶ наста́ть

наста́в|ить¹, лю, ишь *pf.* (*of* ▶ наставля́ть) **1** (*платье*) to lengthen; (*кусок ткани*) to put on, add on **2** (**на** + *a.*) (*нацелить*) to aim (at), point (at); **н. револьве́р на кого́-н.** to point a revolver at sb

наста́в|ить², лю, ишь *pf.* (*of* ▶ наставля́ть) (*научить*) to edify; to exhort, admonish; **н. на путь и́стинный** to set on the right path

наста́в|ить³, лю, ишь *pf.* (+ *a. or g.*) (*стульев*) to set up, place (*a quantity of*); (*синяков*) to cause

наставля́|ть, ю *impf. of* ▶ наста́вить¹, ▶ наста́вить²

наста́вник, а *m.* (*воспитатель*) mentor; (*преподаватель*) teacher, instructor

настаёт *see* ▶ настава́ть

наста́ива|ть, ю *impf. of* ▶ настоя́ть

наста́ива|ться, ется *impf. of* ▶ настоя́ться

наста́|ть, нет, нут *pf.* (*of* ▶ настава́ть) (*наступить*) to come, begin

на́стежь *adv.* wide open; **откры́ть н.** to open wide

насте́нный *adj.* wall (*attr.*)

настига́|ть, а́ю *impf. of* ▶ насти́гнуть, ▶ насти́чь

насти́г|нуть, у, ешь *pf.* = насти́чь

насти́л, а *m.* flooring; planking

насти́|чь, гну, гнешь, *past.* ~г, ~гла *pf.* (*of* ▶ настига́ть) to overtake (also fig.)

насто́йк|а, и *f.* **1** (*спиртной напиток*) liqueur **2** (*med.*) tincture

насто́йчив|ый, ~, ~а *adj.* **1** (*человек*) persistent **2** (*просьба, тон*) urgent, insistent

⚘ **насто́лько** *adv.* so; so much; **н., наско́лько** as much as

насто́льн|ый *adj.* **1** table, desk; desktop; **~ая игра́** board game; **~ая изда́тельская систе́ма** desktop publishing system; **н. те́ннис** table tennis **2** (*fig.*) for constant reference, in constant use; **~ая кни́га** bible

настора́жива|ть, юсь *impf. of* ▶ насторожи́ться

насторож|и́ться, у́сь, и́шься *pf.* (*of* ▶ настора́живаться) to prick up one's ears

настоя́тел|ь, я *m.* (*eccl.*) **1** (*монастыря*) prior, superior **2** (*церкви*) senior priest

настоя́тельниц|а, ы *f.* (*eccl.*) prioress, mother superior

настоя́тел|ьный, ~ен, ~ьна *adj.* **1** (*требование*) persistent; insistent; **~ьная про́сьба** urgent request **2** (*необходимость*) urgent, pressing

насто|я́ть, ю́, и́шь *pf.* (*of* ▶ наста́ивать) (**на** + *p.*) to insist (on); **н. на своём** to insist on having it one's own way; **он ~я́л на том, что́бы пойти́ самому́** he insisted on going himself

насто|я́ться, и́тся, я́тся *pf.* (*of* ▶ наста́иваться) (*о чае, травах*) to infuse, draw, brew

⚘ **настоя́щ|ий** *adj.* **1** (*теперешний*) present; this; **в ~ее вре́мя** at present, now; (*as nt. n.* ~ее, ~его) the present (time); **жить ~им** to live in the present **2** (*подлинный*) real, genuine; **н. друг** real friend **3** (*infml, совершенный*) complete, utter, absolute; **он н. дура́к** he is an absolute fool

настрада́|ться, юсь *pf.* (*infml*) to suffer much

настра́ива|ть, ю *impf. of* ▶ настро́ить

⚘ **настрое́ни|е, я** *nt.* **1** (*душевное состояние*) mood, temper, humour (BrE), humor (AmE); **припо́днятое/пода́вленное н.** high/low spirits; **быть в плохо́м** *и т. п.* **~и** to be in a bad, *etc.*, mood; **не в ~и** in a bad mood **2** (+ *inf.*) mood (for); **у меня́ нет ~я танцева́ть** I don't feel like dancing

настро́|ить, ю, ишь *pf.* (*of* ▶ настра́ивать) **1** (*mus.*) (*пианино, рояль*) to tune; (*скрипку, флейту*) to tune up, tune **2** (*приёмник*) to tune **3** (*механизм*) to tune, adjust **4** (*fig.*) (**на** + *a.*) to dispose (to), incline (to); to incite; **н. кого́-н. (про́тив** + *g.*) to incite sb (against)

⚘ **настро́йк|а, и** *f.* (*mus., radio*) tuning

настро́йщик, а *m.* tuner

наступ|а́ть¹, а́ю *impf. of* ▸ **наступи́ть¹**,
▸ **наступи́ть²**

наступа́|ть², ю *impf.* (*mil.*) to advance, be on
the offensive

наступа́ющ|ий *pres. part. act. of* ▸ **наступа́ть¹**
and adj. coming; **с ~им днём рожде́ния!** have
a great birthday!

наступ|и́ть¹, лю́, ~ишь *pf.* (*of* ▸ **наступа́ть¹**)
(**на** + *a.*) to tread (on)

наступ|и́ть², ~ит *pf.* (*of* ▸ **наступа́ть¹**)
(*о вре́мени, состоя́нии*) to come, begin;
(*о молча́нии, тишине́*) to ensue; to set in;
~ит вре́мя, когда́… there will come a time,
when …

наступле́ни|е¹, я *nt.* (*mil.*) offensive; attack;
перейти́ в н. to assume the offensive

наступле́ни|е², я *nt.* (*зимы́*) coming,
approach; onset

насту́ч|а́ть, у́, и́шь *pf. of* ▸ **стуча́ть 3**

насу́щ|ный, ~ен, ~на *adj.* vital, urgent;
хлеб н. daily bread (*also fig.*)

насчёт *prep. + g.* about; as regards,
concerning

насы́п|ать, лю, лешь *pf.* (*of* ▸ **насыпа́ть**)
1 (+ *a. or g.*) to pour (in, into); to fill (with);
н. муки́ в мешо́к to pour flour into a bag
2 (+ *a. or g. and* **на** + *a.*) (*посыпа́ть*) to
spread (on) **3** (*холм*) to raise (*a heap or pile
of sand, etc.*)

насып|а́ть, а́ю *impf. of* ▸ **насы́пать**

на́сып|ь, и *f.* embankment

насы́|титься, щусь, тишься *pf.* (*of*
▸ **насыща́ться**) **1** (*нае́сться*) to be full; to
be sated **2** (*chem.*) to become saturated

насыща́|ться, юсь *impf. of* ▸ **насы́титься**

насы́щен|ный *adj.* **1** (~, ~а) saturated
2 (~, ~на) (*fig., содержа́тельный*) rich

ната́лкива|ться, юсь *impf. of*
▸ **натолкну́ться**

ната́плива|ть, ю *impf. of* ▸ **натопи́ть**

натвор|и́ть, ю́, и́шь *pf.* (+ *g.*) (*infml, pej.*) to
do, get up to; **н. вся́ких глу́постей** to get up
to every sort of stupid trick; **что ты ~и́л!**
whatever have you done now?

на|тере́ть, тру́, трёшь, *past* **~тёр, ~тёрла**
pf. (*of* ▸ **натира́ть**) **1** (*нама́зать*) to rub
(in, on) **2** (*пол*) to polish **3** (*повреди́ть*)
to rub sore; to chafe; **н. себе́ мозо́ль** to get
a corn **4** (+ *a. or g.*) (*сыр(у)*) to grate (*a
quantity of*)

на|тере́ться, тру́сь, трёшься, *past*
~тёрся, ~тёрлась *pf.* (*of* ▸ **натира́ться**)
(+ *i.*) to rub oneself (with)

натира́|ть, ю *impf. of* ▸ **натере́ть**

натира́|ться, юсь *impf. of* ▸ **натере́ться**

наткн|у́ться, у́сь, ёшься *pf.* (*of*
▸ **натыка́ться**) (**на** + *a.*) **1** to run (against),
strike; to stumble (upon); **н. на гвоздь** to
run against a nail **2** (*fig.*) to stumble (upon,
across), come (across); **н. на интере́сную
мысль** to stumble across an interesting idea

НА́ТО *nt. indecl.* NATO (*abbr. of North
Atlantic Treaty Organization — Организа́ция
Североатланти́ческого догово́ра*)

на́товский *adj. of* ▸ **НА́ТО**

натолкн|у́ться, у́сь, ёшься *pf.* (*of*
▸ **ната́лкиваться**) (**на** + *a.*) to run (against);
(*fig.*) to run across

натоп|и́ть, лю́, ~ишь *pf.* (*of* ▸ **ната́пливать**)
to heat well, heat up

наточ|и́ть, у́, ~ишь *pf. of* ▸ **точи́ть 1**

натрав|и́ть, лю́, ~ишь *pf.* (*of*
▸ **натра́вливать**) (**на** + *a.*) (*соба́ку*) to set
(on); (*fig.*) to set (against)

натра́влива|ть, ю *impf. of* ▸ **натрави́ть**

на́три|й, я *m.* (*chem.*) sodium

на́трое *adv.* in three

нат|ру́, рёшь *see* ▸ **натере́ть**

нату́р|а, ы *f.* **1** (*хара́ктер*) nature
2 (*нату́рщик*) (artist's) model, sitter
3 (*econ.*) kind; **плати́ть ~ой** to pay in kind
4 (*есте́ственная обстано́вка*) natural
setting; **рисова́ть с ~ы** to paint from life

натурализа́ци|я, и *f.* naturalization

натурализ|ова́ть, у́ю *impf. and pf.* to
naturalize

натурализ|ова́ться, у́юсь *impf. and pf.* to
become naturalized

натурали́ст, а *m.* naturalist

натура́л|ьный, ~ен, ~ьна *adj.* **1** natural;
в ~ьную величину́ life-size **2** (*настоя́щий*)
(*мех, ко́жа, ко́фе*) real; (*смех*) genuine
3 (*econ.*) in kind; **н. обме́н** barter

нату́рщик, а *m.* (artist's) model, sitter

нату́рщи|ца, цы *f. of* ▸ **нату́рщик**

натыка́|ться, юсь *impf. of* ▸ **наткну́ться**

натюрмо́рт, а *m.* (*art*) still life

натя́гива|ть, ю, ет *impf. of* ▸ **натяну́ть**

натя́гива|ться, ется *impf. of* ▸ **натяну́ться**

натя́жк|а, и *f.* strained interpretation; **с ~ой**
(*fig.*) at a stretch

натя́н|утый *p.p.p. of* ▸ **натяну́ть** *and adj.*
1 tight **2** (*fig.*) strained; forced; **~утые
отноше́ния** strained relations

натя|ну́ть, ну́, ~нешь *pf.* (*of* ▸ **натя́гивать**)
1 (*сде́лать туги́м*) to stretch; to draw
(tight); **н. лук** to draw a bow **2** (*наде́ть*) to
pull on; **н. ша́пку на́ уши** to pull a cap over
one's ears

натя|ну́ться, ~нется, ~нутся *pf.* (*of*
▸ **натя́гиваться**) to stretch

науга́д *adv.* at random, by guesswork

науда́чу *adv.* at random, by guesswork

⚡ **нау́к|а, и** *f.* (*систе́ма зна́ний*) science;
(*уче́ние*) learning; scholarship;
есте́ственные ~и science

наукоёмк|ий, ~ок, ~ка *adj.* high-
technology, high-tech

нау́тро *adv.* next morning

научи́ть, у́, ~ишь *pf.* (*of* ▸ **учи́ть 1**) (+ *a.
and d. or* + *inf.*) to teach; **н. кого́-н. ру́сскому
языку́** to teach sb Russian; **н. кого́-н. води́ть
маши́ну** to teach sb to drive (a car)

научи́ться, у́сь, ∼ишься pf. (of ▸ учи́ться 1) (+ d. or inf.) to learn

нау́чно-иссле́довательск|ий adj. scientific research; ∼ая рабо́та (scientific) research work

нау́чно-фантасти́ческий adj. science fiction

♂ **нау́чн|ый, ∼ен, ∼на** adj. scientific; **н. рабо́тник** researcher; ∼ная фанта́стика science fiction

нау́шник, а m. (in pl.) headphones

наха́л, а m. (infml) impudent fellow, cheeky fellow

наха́лк|а, и f. (infml) impudent woman, cheeky woman

наха́л|ьный, ∼ен, ∼ьна adj. impudent, cheeky

нахам|и́ть, лю́, и́шь pf. of ▸ хами́ть

нахват|а́ть, а́ю pf. (of ▸ нахва́тывать) (infml) (+ a. or g.) to pick up, get hold (of); (fig., зна́ний) to pick up, come by

нахват|а́ться, а́юсь pf. (of ▸ нахва́тываться) (infml, fig.) (+ g.) (слов, привы́чек, зна́ний) to pick up

нахва́тыва|ть, ю impf. of ▸ нахвата́ть

нахва́тыва|ться, юсь impf. of ▸ нахвата́ться

нахле́бник, а m. parasite, hanger-on

нахлобу́чива|ть, ю impf. of ▸ нахлобу́чить

нахлобу́ч|ить, у, ишь pf. (of ▸ нахлобу́чивать) (infml) to pull down (over one's head or eyes)

нахму́р|ить, ю, ишь pf. of ▸ хму́рить

нахму́р|иться, юсь, ишься pf. of ▸ хму́риться

♂ **нахо|ди́ть, жу́, ∼дишь** impf. of ▸ найти́¹, ▸ найти́²

нахо|ди́ться¹, жу́сь, ∼дишься impf. of ▸ найти́сь

♂ **нахо|ди́ться², жу́сь, ∼дишься** impf. to be (situated); где ∼дится ста́нция? where is the station?; (под наблюде́нием, стре́ссом) to be

нахо́дк|а, и f. **1** find **2** (fig.) (подходя́щее) godsend; (приём) device

нахо́дчив|ый, ∼, ∼а adj. **1** (челове́к) resourceful **2** (отве́т) quick-witted

наце|ди́ть, жу́, ∼дишь pf. (+ a. or g.) to strain

наце́лива|ть, ю impf. of ▸ наце́лить

наце́лива|ться, юсь impf. of ▸ наце́литься

наце́л|ить, ю, ишь pf. **1** (impf. це́лить and ∼ивать) (ору́жие) to aim, level **2** (impf. ∼ивать) (fig.) (на + a.) (на выполне́ние) to aim, direct

наце́л|иться, юсь, ишься pf. (of ▸ наце́ливаться) **1** (в + a.) to aim (at), take aim (at) **2** (fig.) (на + a.) to aim (at, for), strive (for) **3** (fig.) (+ inf.) to aim, strive (to do)

наце́нк|а, и f. markup

нацеп|и́ть, лю́, ∼ишь pf. (of ▸ нацепля́ть) **1** to fasten on; to attach (by means of hook or pin) **2** (infml, наде́ть) to put on

нацеп|ля́ть, ля́ю impf. of ▸ нацепи́ть

наци́зм, а m. Nazism

национализа́ци|я, и f. nationalization

национализи́р|овать, ую impf. and pf. to nationalize

национали́зм, а m. nationalism

национали́ст, а m. nationalist

националисти́ческий adj. nationalist(ic)

национали́ст|ка, ки f. of ▸ национали́ст

национа́льност|ь, и f. **1** (принадле́жность к на́ции) nationality **2** (на́ция) nation

♂ **национа́льн|ый** adj. national; ∼ое меньшинство́ national minority

наци́ст, а m. Nazi

наци́ст|ка, ки f. of ▸ наци́ст

наци́стский adj. Nazi

на́ци|я, и f. nation

♂ **нача́л|о, а** nt. **1** beginning; start; в ∼е четвёртого soon after three (o'clock); по ∼у at first; положи́ть, дать н. (+ d.) to begin, commence; (тради́ции, па́ртии) to establish **2** (исто́чник) origin, source; брать н. (в + p.) to originate (from, in)

♂ **нача́льник, а** m. head, chief; superior; **н. отде́ла** head of a department, section

♂ **нача́льн|ый** adj. **1** (находя́щийся в нача́ле) initial, first **2** (первонача́льный) primary, elementary; ∼ая шко́ла primary school (BrE), elementary school (AmE)

нача́льств|о, а nt. **1** (collect.) (the) authorities, management **2** (infml, нача́льник) chief, boss

♂ **нач|а́ть, ну́, нёшь,** past ∼ал, ∼ала́, ∼ало pf. (of ▸ начина́ть) **1** to begin, start, commence; **н. с нача́ла** to begin at the beginning; **н. всё снача́ла** to start all over again, start afresh **2** (но́вую па́чку, тетра́дь) to start

♂ **нач|а́ться, нётся,** past ∼а́лся, ∼ала́сь pf. (of ▸ начина́ться) to begin, start

начеку́ adv. on the alert, on one's guard

начер|ти́ть, чу́, ∼тишь pf. of ▸ черти́ть

начина́ни|е, я nt. undertaking, initiative

♂ **начина́|ть, ю, ет** impf. of ▸ нача́ть

♂ **начина́|ться, ется** impf. of ▸ нача́ться

начина́|ющий pres. part. act. of ▸ начина́ть and adj. (писа́тель) fledgling; (as m. & n., ∼ющего) beginner

начина́я as prep. **1** (с + g.) (о вре́мени) as from, starting from; (в том числе́) starting with, including **2** (от + g.) starting with, including

начи́нк|а, и f. (cul.) (ку́рицы, у́тки) stuffing; (пирожка́) filling

начи́|стить, щу, стишь pf. (of ▸ начища́ть) (сапоги́, кастрю́лю) to polish, shine

на́чисто adv. **1** clean, fair; **переписа́ть н.** to make a fair copy (of) **2** (infml, совсе́м) completely, thoroughly

начи́тан|ный, ∼, ∼на adj. well read, widely read

начита́|ться, юсь pf. **1** (+ g.) (прочита́ть мно́го) to have read (a lot of) **2** (почита́ть *вдово́ль*) to have read one's fill

начища́|ть, ю *impf. of* ▶ **начи́стить**

начн|у́, нёшь *see* ▶ **нача́ть**

◆ **наш**, ~его, *f.* ~а, ~ей, *nt.* ~е, ~его, *pl.* ~и, ~их *poss. pron. & adj.* (*при существи́тельном*) our; (*без существи́тельного*) ours; (*as pl. n.* ~и, ~их) our people, people on our side; **eró счита́ют одни́м из ~их** they regard him as one of us

наше́стви|е, я *nt.* (also fig.) invasion, descent

наши́вк|а, и *f.* stripe, chevron

нашинк|ова́ть, у́ю *pf. of* ▶ **шинкова́ть**

нащу́п|ать, аю *pf.* (*of* ▶ **нащу́пывать**) to find, discover (*by groping*)

нащу́пыва|ть, ю *impf.* (*of* ▶ **нащу́пать**) to grope (for, after); to fumble (for, after); to feel about (for) (also fig.)

наяву́ *adv.* waking; in reality

НДС *m. indecl.* (*abbr. of* **нало́г на доба́вленную сто́имость**) VAT (*Value Added Tax*)

◆ **не¹** *not*; **я не зна́ю** I do not know; **я не могу́ не сказа́ть** I can't but say; I must say; **не без волне́ния** with some excitement; **не до** (+ *g.*) not time for; **мне не до шу́ток** I have no time for jokes; **не..., не** neither ... nor; **не то** otherwise, or else

◆ **не²** *separable component of prons.* ▶ **не́кого**, ▶ **не́чего; о чём бы́ло говори́ть** there was nothing to talk about

не... *pref.* un-, in-, non-, mis-, dis-

неаккура́т|ный, ~ен, ~на *adj.*
1 (*небре́жный*) careless; inaccurate
2 (*неопря́тный*) untidy

неаппети́т|ный, ~ен, ~на *adj.* unappetizing (also fig.)

небезопа́с|ный, ~ен, ~на *adj.* unsafe, insecure

небезоснова́тел|ьный, ~ен, ~ьна *adj.* not unfounded

небезразли́ч|ный, ~ен, ~на *adj.* not indifferent

небезуспе́ш|ный, ~ен, ~на *adj.* not unsuccessful

небезызве́ст|ный, ~ен, ~на *adj.* not unknown; (iron.) notorious; ~но, что... it is no secret that ...

небезынтере́с|ный, ~ен, ~на *adj.* not without interest

небеса́ *pl. of* ▶ **не́бо**

небе́сн|ый *adj.* heavenly, celestial; ~ые свети́ла heavenly bodies; Ца́рство Н~ое the Kingdom of Heaven; ~ого цве́та sky blue

неблагови́д|ный, ~ен, ~на *adj.* unseemly, improper

неблагода́рност|ь, и *f.* ingratitude

неблагода́р|ный, ~ен, ~на *adj.* **1** (*челове́к*) ungrateful **2** (*зада́ча*) thankless

неблагозву́ч|ный, ~ен, ~на *adj.* disharmonious

◆ **key word**

неблагополу́ч|ный, ~ен, ~на *adj.* unfavourable (BrE), unfavorable (AmE), bad; unsuccessful

неблагоприя́т|ный, ~ен, ~на *adj.* unfavourable (BrE), unfavorable (AmE), inauspicious

неблагоскло́н|ный, ~ен, ~на *adj.* unfavourable (BrE), unfavorable (AmE); (к + *d.*) ill-disposed (towards)

◆ **не́б|о**, а, *pl.* ~еса́, ~е́с, ~еса́м *nt.* sky; (relig.) heaven; **под откры́тым ~ом** in the open (air)

нёб|о, а *nt.* (anat.) palate

◆ **небольш|о́й** *adj.* small; not great; **о́чень ~о́е расстоя́ние** a very short distance; **ты́сяча с ~и́м** a thousand odd

небосво́д, а *m.* firmament; the vault of heaven

небоскло́н, а *m.* horizon (*strictly, sky immediately over the horizon*)

небоскрёб, а *m.* skyscraper

небре́жност|ь, и *f.* carelessness, negligence

небре́ж|ный, ~ен, ~на *adj.* (*челове́к, рабо́та*) careless; (*оде́жда, по́черк*) untidy; (*тон, мане́ра*) offhand

небри́т|ый, ~, ~а *adj.* unshaven

небыва́л|ый, ~, ~а *adj.* unprecedented

небыли́ц|а, ы *f.* (*ска́зка*) fable; (*вы́думка*) cock-and-bull story

небытие́, я́ *nt.* non-existence

небью́щийся *adj.* unbreakable

Нев|а́, ы́ *f.* the Neva (*river*)

нева́жно *adv.* not too well, indifferently; **дела́ иду́т н.** things are not going too well

нева́ж|ный, ~ен, ~на́, ~но *adj.*
1 (*незначи́тельный*) unimportant **2** (infml, *посре́дственный*) poor, indifferent

невдалеке́ *adv.* not far away, not far off

неве́дени|е, я *nt.* ignorance; **пребыва́ть в блаже́нном ~и** (iron.) to be in a state of blissful ignorance

неве́домо *adv.* (infml) + что, как, когда́, куда́ и т. п. God knows, no one knows; **он так и появи́лся, н. отку́да** he just turned up, God knows where from

неве́дом|ый, ~, ~а *adj.* **1** unknown **2** (fig., *таи́нственный*) mysterious

неве́ж|а, и *c.g.* boor, lout

неве́жд|а, ы *c.g.* ignoramus

неве́жествен|ный, ~, ~на *adj.* ignorant

неве́жеств|о, а *nt.* ignorance

неве́жлив|ый, ~, ~а *adj.* rude, impolite

невезе́ни|е, я *nt.* (infml) bad luck

неве́ри|е, я *nt.* unbelief; lack of faith

неве́рност|ь, и *f.* **1** (*непра́вильность*) incorrectness **2** (*дру́га*) disloyalty; (*супру́га*) infidelity, unfaithfulness

неве́р|ный, ~ен, ~на́, ~но *adj.*
1 (*оши́бочный*) incorrect; ~ная но́та false note **2** (*друг*) faithless, disloyal; (*муж, жена́*) unfaithful

невероя́тно *adv.* incredibly, unbelievably

Н

невероя́т|ный, ~ен, ~на *adj.*
1 (*неправдоподобный*) improbable,
unlikely **2** (*чрезвычайный*) incredible,
unbelievable (also fig.); (*impers., as pred.*)
~но it is incredible, it is unbelievable; it is
beyond belief

неве́рующ|ий *adj.* (relig.) unbelieving; (*as n.
н., ~его, f. ~ая, ~ей*) unbeliever

невес|ёлый, ~ел, ~ела́, ~ело *adj.* sad,
gloomy, melancholy

невесо́мост|ь, и *f.* weightlessness

невест|а́, ы *f.* fiancée; (*в день свадьбы*) bride

неве́стк|а, и *f.* **1** (*жена сына*) daughter-in-
law **2** (*жена брата*) sister-in-law

невзира́я *prep.* (**на** + *a.*) in spite of,
regardless of

невзра́ч|ный, ~ен, ~на *adj.*
unprepossessing, unattractive; plain

неви́дан|ный, ~, ~на *adj.* unprecedented

неви́дим|ый, ~, ~а *adj.* invisible

неви́нност|ь, и *f.* innocence; (*девственность*)
virginity

неви́н|ный, ~ен, ~на *adj.* innocent;
(*девственный*) virgin(al); ~ная же́ртва
innocent victim

невино́в|ный, ~ен, ~на *adj.* (**в** + *p.*)
innocent (of); (law) not guilty; призна́ть
~ным to acquit

невку́с|ный, ~ен, ~на́, ~но *adj.*
unpalatable

невменя́ем|ый, ~, ~а *adj.* **1** (law)
irresponsible **2** (infml) beside oneself

невмеша́тельств|о, а *nt.* (pol.) non-
intervention, non-interference

невнима́ни|е, я *nt.* **1** (*рассеянность*)
inattention, carelessness **2** (**к** + *d.*)
(*пренебрежение*) lack of consideration (for)

невнима́тельност|ь, и *f.* inattention;
(*небрежность*) thoughtlessness

невнима́тель|ный, ~ен, ~ьна *adj.*
(*рассеянный*) inattentive; (*незаботливый*)
thoughtless

невня́т|ный, ~ен, ~на *adj.* indistinct,
incomprehensible

не́вод, а, *pl.* **~а́, ~о́в** *m.* seine, sweep net

невозмо́ж|ный, ~ен, ~на *adj.* impossible;
(*impers., pred.*) ~но it is impossible; (*as nt.
n.* ~ное, ~ного) the impossible

невозмути́м|ый, ~, ~а *adj.* **1** (*человек*)
imperturbable **2** (*тон*) calm, unruffled

невозобновля́емый *adj.* non-renewable

нево́льно *adv.* involuntarily;
unintentionally, unwittingly

нево́льный *adj.* **1** (*вздох, трепет*)
involuntary; (*ложь, обида*) unintentional
2 (*вынужденный*) forced

нево́л|я, и *f.* bondage; captivity

невообрази́м|ый, ~, ~а *adj.* unimaginable,
inconceivable; **н. шум** (fig.) unimaginable din

невооружён|ный, ~, ~на *adj.* unarmed; ~ым
гла́зом with the naked eye

невоспи́тан|ный, ~, ~на *adj.* ill-bred;
bad-mannered

невосполни́м|ый, ~, ~а *adj.* irreplaceable

невосприи́мчив|ый, ~, ~а *adj.* **1** (**к**
знаниям) unreceptive **2** (med.) (**к** + *d.*)
immune (to)

невразуми́тель|ный, ~ен, ~ьна *adj.*
unintelligible, incomprehensible

невралги́|я, и *f.* neuralgia

неврасте́ник, а *m.* neurasthenic

неврастени́|я, и *f.* neurasthenia

невреди́м|ый, ~, ~а *adj.* unharmed, intact;
цел и ~ safe and sound

невро́з, а *m.* neurosis

невропато́лог, а *m.* neuropathologist

невы́год|ный, ~ен, ~на *adj.* **1** (*положение*)
disadvantageous, unfavourable (BrE),
unfavorable (AmE); показа́ть себя́ с ~ной
стороны́ to show oneself at a disadvantage
2 (*сделка*) unprofitable, unremunerative;
(*impers., pred.*) ~но it does not pay

невыноси́м|ый, ~, ~а *adj.* unbearable,
insufferable, intolerable

невыполни́м|ый, ~, ~а *adj.* impracticable;
unrealizable

невырази́м|ый, ~, ~а *adj.* inexpressible,
beyond expression

невырази́тель|ный, ~ен, ~ьна *adj.*
inexpressive, expressionless

**невысо́к|ий, ~, ~а́, ~о and ~о́, ~и and
~и́** *adj.* (*забор, потолок, голос*) rather low;
(*человек*) rather short; ~ого ка́чества of
poor quality; быть ~ого мне́ния (о + *p.*) to
have a low opinion (of)

негати́в, а *m.* (phot.) negative

негати́в|ный, ~ен, ~на *adj.* negative

не́где *adv.* (+ *inf.*) there is nowhere; **н. доста́ть
э́ту кни́гу** this book is nowhere to be had

негла́с|ный, ~ен, ~на *adj.* secret

неглу́п|ый, ~, ~а́, ~о *adj.* quite intelligent;
он о́чень ~ he is no fool

него́ *a. and g.* of ▸ **он** *after preps.*

него́д|ный, ~ен, ~на *adj.* unfit, unsuitable

негодова́ни|е, я *nt.* indignation

негод|ова́ть, у́ю *impf.* (**на** + *a. or* про́тив + *g.*)
to be indignant (with)

негра́мотност|ь, и *f.* illiteracy (also fig.)

негра́мот|ный, ~ен, ~на *adj.* illiterate
(also fig.); (*as n. н., ~ного, f. ~ная, ~ной*)
illiterate (*person*)

негро́м|кий, ~ок, ~ка́, ~ко *adj.* quiet, low

негума́н|ный, ~ен, ~на *adj.* inhumane

неда́вний *adj.* recent

неда́вно *adv.* recently

недал|ёкий *adj.* **1** (~ёк, ~ека́, ~ёко *and*
~еко́) (*место*) nearby, not far off, near;
(*путешествие, прогулка, расстояние*) short
2 (~ёк, ~ёка) (fig., *глуповатый*) not bright,
dull-witted

недалеко́ *adv.* not far, near

недальнови́д|ный, ~ен, ~на *adj.* short-
sighted (fig.)

неда́ром *adv.* not for nothing; for good
reason

⚹ **недви́жимост|ь, и** *f.* (law) (immovable) property, real estate

недви́жим|ый *adj.*: ~ое иму́щество = недви́жимость

недееспосо́бност|ь, и *f.* (law) incapacity

недееспосо́б|ный, ~ен, ~на *adj.* (law, *человек*) incapacitated

недействи́тел|ьный, ~ен, ~ьна *adj.* (law) invalid

недели́м|ый, ~, ~а *adj.* indivisible

неде́льный *adj.* of a week's duration

⚹ **неде́л|я, и** *f.* week; на э́той ~e this week

недоброжела́тел|ь, я *m.* ill-wisher

недоброжела́тел|ьный, ~ен, ~ьна *adj.* malevolent, ill-disposed

недобросо́вест|ный, ~ен, ~на *adj.* **1** (*нечестный*) unscrupulous **2** (*небрежный*) lacking in conscientiousness; careless

недо́бр|ый *adj.* **1** (*человек, взгляд*) unkind; unfriendly **2** (*намерение, чувство*) evil; ~ая весть bad news

недове́ри|е, я *nt.* distrust; mistrust; во́тум ~я vote of no confidence

недове́рчив|ый, ~, ~а *adj.* distrustful; mistrustful

недово́л|ьный, ~ен, ~ьна *adj.* (+ *i.*) dissatisfied, discontented, displeased (with); (*as n. n.*, ~ьного, *f.* ~ьная, ~ьной) malcontent

недово́льств|о, а *nt.* dissatisfaction, discontent, displeasure

недога́длив|ый, ~, ~а *adj.* slow(-witted)

недогля|де́ть, жу́, ди́шь *pf.* to overlook, miss

недода|ва́ть, ю́, ёшь *impf. of* ▶ недода́ть

недо|да́ть, да́м, да́шь, да́ст, дади́м, дади́те, даду́т, *past* ~да́л, ~дала́, ~да́ло *pf.* (*of* ▶ недодава́ть) to give short; to deliver short; он мне ~да́л пятьдеся́т рубле́й he gave me fifty roubles short

недоеда́|ть, ю *impf.* to be undernourished, be underfed

недозво́лен|ный, ~, ~а *adj.* illicit, unlawful

недозре́лый *adj.* (*яблоко*) unripe; (fig., *человек*) immature

недо́лг|ий, ~ог, ~га́, ~го *adj.* short, brief

недо́лго *adv.* **1** not long; н. ду́мая without hesitation **2** (infml, *легко*): н. и (+ *inf.*) one can easily; it is easy (to)

недолгове́ч|ный, ~ен, ~на *adj.* short-lived, ephemeral

недолю́блива|ть, ю *impf.* (+ *a.* or *g.*) (infml) to be not overfond of; они́ ~ли друг дру́га there was no love lost between them

недомога́ни|е, я *nt.* indisposition

недоно́шен|ный, ~, ~а *adj.* (med.) premature

недооце́нива|ть, ю *impf. of* ▶ недооцени́ть

недооцен|и́ть, ю́, ~ишь *pf.* (*of* ▶ недооце́нивать) to underestimate,

⚹ *key word*

underrate

недополуч|а́ть, а́ю *impf. of* ▶ недополучи́ть

недополуч|и́ть, у́, ~ишь *pf.* (*of* ▶ недополуча́ть) to receive less (than one's due)

недопусти́м|ый, ~, ~а *adj.* inadmissible, intolerable

недора́звит|ый, ~, ~а *adj.* underdeveloped, backward

недоразуме́ни|е, я *nt.* misunderstanding

недо́рого *adv.* not dear, cheaply

недор|ого́й, ~ог, ~ога́, ~ого *adj.* inexpensive; reasonable (*of price*)

недоса́лива|ть, ю *impf. of* ▶ недосоли́ть

недосмотр|е́ть, ю́, ~ишь *pf.* **1** (+ *g.*) to overlook, miss **2** (за + *i.*) not to look after properly

недосол|и́ть, ю́, ~ишь *pf.* (*of* ▶ недоса́ливать) to put too little salt in

недос|па́ть, плю́, пи́шь *pf.* (*of* ▶ недосыпа́ть) to not get enough sleep

недоста|ва́ть, ёт *impf.* (*of* ▶ недоста́ть) (*impers.* + *g.*) to be missing, be lacking, be wanting; ему́ ~ёт о́пыта he lacks experience

⚹ **недоста́т|ок, ка** *m.* **1** (+ *g.* or в + *p.*) shortage (of), lack (of); име́ть н. в рабо́чей си́ле to be short-handed **2** (*несовершенство*) shortcoming, imperfection; defect; н. зре́ния defective eyesight

недоста́точно *adv.* **1** insufficiently **2** (*pred.* + *g.*) (*не хватает*) not enough

недоста́точ|ный, ~ен, ~на *adj.* insufficient; inadequate

недоста́|ть, нет *pf. of* ▶ недостава́ть

недостижи́м|ый, ~, ~а *adj.* unattainable

недостове́р|ный, ~ен, ~на *adj.* unreliable, apocryphal

недосто́йн|ый, ~ин, ~йна *adj.* unworthy

недосту́п|ный, ~ен, ~на *adj.* inaccessible (also fig.); э́то ~но моему́ понима́нию it is beyond my comprehension

недосчит|а́ться, а́юсь *pf.* (*of* ▶ недосчи́тываться) (+ *g.*) to find missing, miss; to be out (in one's accounts); он ~а́лся десяти́ рубле́й he found he was ten roubles short

недосчи́тыва|ться, юсь *impf. of* ▶ недосчита́ться

недосыпа́|ть, ю *impf. of* ▶ недоспа́ть

недосяга́ем|ый, ~, ~а *adj.* unattainable

недоумева́|ть, ю *impf.* to be perplexed, be at a loss

недоуме́ни|е, я *nt.* perplexity, bewilderment; быть в ~и to be in a quandary

недочёт, а *m.* (*usu. in pl.*) defect, shortcoming

не́др|а, ~ (*no sg.*) **1** depths (*of the earth*); н. земли́ bowels of the earth; разве́дка ~ prospecting of mineral wealth **2** (fig.) depths, heart

не́друг, а *m.* enemy, foe

недружелю́б|ный, ~ен, ~на *adj.* unfriendly

неду́г, а *m.* ailment, disease

неё *a. and g. of* ▶ **она́** *after preps.*

неесте́ствен|ный, ∼, ∼на *adj.* unnatural

нежда́нный *adj.* unexpected

нежела́тел|ьный, ∼ен, ∼ьна *adj.* undesirable

нежена́т|ый, ∼ *adj.* unmarried (*of a man*)

неживо́й *adj.* **1** (*мёртвый*) lifeless, dead **2** (*неорганический*) inanimate, inorganic **3** (fig., *вялый*) dull, lifeless

нежило́й *adj.* **1** (*необитаемый*) uninhabited **2** (*негодный для жилья*) not fit for habitation; uninhabitable

не́ж|иться, усь, ишься *impf.* to luxuriate; **н. на со́лнце** to bask in the sun

не́жность, и *f.* **1** (*ласковость*) tenderness **2** (*тонкость*) delicacy

не́ж|ный, ∼ен, ∼на́, ∼но *adj.* **1** tender; affectionate; ∼ный во́зраст tender age **2** (*тонкий*) delicate (= *soft, fine; of colours, taste, skin, etc.*) **3** (*хрупкий*) delicate

незабу́дк|а, и *f.* (bot.) forget-me-not

незабыва́ем|ый, ∼, ∼а *adj.* unforgettable

незави́симо *adv.* independently; **н. от** irrespective of

незави́симость, и *f.* independence

незави́сим|ый, ∼, ∼а *adj.* independent

незадо́лго *adv.* (до + g. or пе́ред + i.) shortly (before), not long (before)

незако́н|ный, ∼ен, ∼на *adj.* illegal, unlawful

незако́нчен|ный, ∼, ∼на *adj.* incomplete, unfinished

незамедли́тельно *adv.* without delay

незамени́м|ый, ∼, ∼а *adj.* **1** irreplaceable **2** (*очень нужный*) indispensable

незаме́тно *adv.* imperceptibly; **н., что́бы ...** you cannot tell that ...

незаме́т|ный, ∼ен, ∼на *adj.* **1** (*следы*) imperceptible **2** (*человек*) unremarkable

незаму́жняя *adj.* unmarried, single

незаслу́жен|ный, ∼, ∼на *adj.* undeserved, unmerited

незауря́д|ный, ∼ен, ∼на *adj.* outstanding, exceptional

не́зачем *adv.* (+ *inf.*) there is no point (in), it is pointless; there is no need (to)

незде́шний *adj.* (infml) not of these parts; **я н.** I am a stranger here

нездоро́вит|ься, ∼ся *impf.* (impers. + d.) to feel unwell

нездоро́в|ый, ∼, ∼а *adj.* **1** unhealthy (also fig.) **2** (*as pred.*) unwell, poorly

неземно́й *adj.* unearthly

незнако́м|ец, ца *m.* stranger

незнако́м|ка, ки *f. of* ▶ **незнако́мец**

незнако́м|ый, ∼, ∼а *adj.* **1** unknown, unfamiliar **2** (c + *i.*) unacquainted (with)

незна́ни|е, я *nt.* ignorance

незначи́тел|ьный, ∼ен, ∼ьна *adj.* insignificant, negligible, trivial

незре́лость, и *f.* unripeness; (fig.) immaturity

незре́л|ый, ∼, ∼а *adj.* unripe (also fig.); (fig.) immature

незри́м|ый, ∼, ∼а *adj.* invisible

незы́блем|ый, ∼, ∼а *adj.* unshakeable, stable

неизбе́ж|ный, ∼ен, ∼на *adj.* inevitable, unavoidable; inescapable

неизве́стность, и *f.* **1** (*отсутствие сведений*) uncertainty; **быть в ∼и** (о + *p.*) to be uncertain (about), be in the dark (about) **2** (*незаметное существование*) obscurity; **жить в ∼и** to live in obscurity

неизве́ст|ный, ∼ен, ∼на *adj.* unknown; ∼но где, когда́ *и т. п.* no one knows where, when, *etc.* (= somewhere, at some time, etc.); (*as n.* н., ∼ного, *f.* ∼ная, ∼ной) unknown person; (*as nt.* н. ∼ное, ∼ного) (math.) unknown (quantity)

неизлечи́м|ый, ∼, ∼а *adj.* incurable

неизме́н|ный, ∼ен, ∼на *adj.* (*постоянный*) invariable, immutable

неиме́ни|е, я *nt.* lack, want; **за ∼ем лу́чшего** for want of sth better

неимове́р|ный, ∼ен, ∼на *adj.* incredible, unbelievable

неиму́щий *adj.* indigent, poor

неинтере́с|ный, ∼ен, ∼на *adj.* uninteresting

нейскрен|ний, ∼ен, ∼на *adj.* insincere

неисправи́м|ый, ∼, ∼а *adj.* **1** (*человек*) incorrigible **2** (*недостаток, ошибка*) irremediable, irreparable

неиспра́вность, и *f.* (*машины*) disrepair; fault, defect

неиспра́в|ный, ∼ен, ∼на *adj.* (*машина*) out of order; faulty, defective

неиссяка́ем|ый, ∼, ∼а *adj.* inexhaustible

неи́стов|ый, ∼, ∼а *adj.* furious, frenzied

неистощи́м|ый, ∼, ∼а *adj.* inexhaustible

неистреби́м|ый, ∼, ∼а *adj.* ineradicable; undying

неисчерпа́ем|ый, ∼, ∼а *adj.* inexhaustible

неисчисли́м|ый, ∼, ∼а *adj.* innumerable; incalculable

ней *d., i., and p. of* ▶ **она́** *after preps.*

нейло́н, а *m.* nylon

нейло́новый *adj.* nylon, made of nylon

нейрохиру́рг, а *m.* neurosurgeon

нейтрализа́ци|я, и *f.* neutralization

нейтрализ|ова́ть, у́ю *impf. and pf.* to neutralize

нейтралите́т, а *m.* (pol.) neutrality

нейтра́л|ьный, ∼ен, ∼ьна *adj.* neutral

нейтро́н, а *m.* (phys.) neutron

нека́чествен|ный, ∼, ∼на *adj.* poor-quality

неквалифици́рован|ный, ∼, ∼на *adj.* unqualified; **н. рабо́чий** unskilled labourer (BrE), laborer (AmE)

⚭ **не́кий** *pron.* a certain; a kind of; **вас спра́шивал н. господи́н Па́влов** a (certain) Mr Pavlov was asking for you

не́когда¹ *adv.* once, formerly; in the old days

Н

не́когда² *adv.* there is no time; **мне сего́дня н. разгова́ривать** I have no time to chat today

не́кого, не́кому, не́кем, не́ о ком *pron.* (+ *inf.*) there is nobody (to); **н. вини́ть** nobody is to blame; **ей не́ с кем пойти́** she has nobody to go with (her)

некомпете́нт|ный, ~ен, ~на *adj.* incompetent, unqualified

неконкурентоспосо́б|ный, ~ен, ~на *adj.* uncompetitive

неконституцио́н|ный, ~ен, ~на *adj.* unconstitutional

некорре́ктный, ~ен, ~на *adj.* discourteous, impolite

⚔ **не́котор|ый** *pron.* some; **мы с ~ых пор живём здесь** we have been living here for some time; **~ым о́бразом** somehow, in some way; **в, до ~ой сте́пени** to some extent, to a certain extent; (*as pl. n.* **~ые, ~ых**) (*infml*) some; some people

некраси́в|ый, ~, ~а *adj.* **1** ugly, unattractive **2** (*infml, поведение*) unseemly, not nice

некредитоспосо́б|ный, ~ен, ~на *adj.* insolvent

некроло́г, а *m.* obituary (notice)

некста́ти *adv.* (*прийти, сказать*) at the wrong moment, inopportunely; (*о замечании*) inopportune, inappropriate

некта́р, а *m.* nectar

не́кто *pron.* someone; **н. Петро́в** one Petrov, a certain Petrov

не́куда *adv.* (+ *inf.*) there is nowhere (to); **мне н. пойти́** I have nowhere to go

некульту́р|ный, ~ен, ~на *adj.* **1** (*нецивилизованный*) uncivilized; backward **2** (*грубый*) rough(-mannered), boorish

некуря́щ|ий *adj.* non-smoking; (*as m. n.* **~его**) non-smoker; **ваго́н для ~их** non-smoking carriage

нелега́л, а *m.* (*infml*) illegal person (*person living somewhere illegally or doing sth illegally*)

нелега́л|ьный, ~ен, ~ьна *adj.* illegal

нелёг|кий, ~ок, нелегка́ *adj.* **1** (*трудный*) difficult, not easy **2** (*тяжёлый*) heavy, not light (also fig.)

неле́п|ый, ~, ~а *adj.* absurd, ridiculous

нело́в|кий, ~ок, ~ка́, ~ко *adj.* **1** (*неуклюжий*) awkward; clumsy **2** (fig.) awkward; embarrassing; **~кое молча́ние** awkward silence

нело́вко *adv.* awkwardly; uncomfortably; **чу́вствовать себя́ н.** to feel ill at ease, feel awkward, feel uncomfortable

нело́вкост|ь, и *f.* **1** (*свойство*) awkwardness, clumsiness (also fig.) **2** (*поступок*) blunder, gaffe

нелоги́ч|ный, ~ен, ~на *adj.* illogical

⚔ **нельзя́** *adv.* (+ *inf.*) **1** (*нет возможности*)

⚔ key word

it is impossible; **н. не призна́ть** it is impossible not to admit, one cannot but admit **2** (*запрещается*) it is not allowed; **здесь н. кури́ть** smoking is not allowed here **3** (*нехорошо*) one ought not, one should not; **н. ложи́ться (спать) так по́здно** you ought not to go to bed so late

нём *p. of* ▶ **он** after preps.

нема́ло *adv.* **1** (+ *g.*) (*времени, денег*) not a little; a good deal of; (*людей*) quite a few **2** (*читать, гордиться*) a good deal, quite a lot

немалова́ж|ный, ~ен, ~на *adj.* of no small importance

нема́л|ый, ~, ~а́ *adj.* considerable

неме́дленно *adv.* immediately

неме́|ть, ю *impf.* (*of* ▶ **онеме́ть**) **1** (*становиться немым*) to become dumb, grow dumb **2** (*цепенеть*) to become numb, grow numb

не́м|ец, ца *m.* German

⚔ **неме́цк|ий** *adj.* German; **~ая овча́рка** Alsatian (dog) (BrE), German shepherd

неминуе́м|ый, ~, ~а *adj.* inevitable, unavoidable

не́м|ка, ки *f. of* ▶ **немец**

немно́г|ие *adj.* few, a few; (*as pl. n.* **н., ~их**) few

⚔ **немно́го** *adv.* **1** (+ *g.*) (*времени, денег*) a little, some, not much; (*людей*) a few, not many **2** (*слегка*) a little, somewhat, slightly; **я н. уста́л** I am a little tired

немно́г|ое, ого *nt.* few things, little

немно́жко *adv.* (*infml*) a little; a bit

нем|о́й, ~, ~á, ~о *adj.* **1** mute (often offens.), profoundly deaf; (*as m. n.* **н., ~о́го**) mute (often offens.), profoundly deaf person **2** (fig.) silent; **н. фильм** silent film

не|молодо́й, ~мо́лод, ~молода́, ~мо́лодо *adj.* not young, elderly

немот|а́, ы́ *f.* muteness (often offens.), profound deafness

нему́ *d. of* ▶ **он** after preps.

немы́слим|ый, ~, ~а *adj.* unthinkable, inconceivable

ненави́|деть, жу, дишь *impf.* to hate, detest, loathe

ненави́ст|ный, ~ен, ~на *adj.* hated; hateful

не́нави́ст|ь, и *f.* hatred, detestation

ненавя́зчив|ый, ~, ~а *adj.* unobtrusive

ненадёж|ный, ~ен, ~на *adj.* (*человек; сведение*) unreliable, untrustworthy; (*защита; лёд*) insecure

ненадо́лго *adv.* for a short while, not for long

ненаме́ренно *adv.* unintentionally, unwittingly, accidentally

ненаме́рен|ный, ~, ~на *adj.* unintentional, accidental

ненаст|ный, ~ен, ~на *adj.* (*погода*) bad, foul

ненастоя́щий *adj.* (*мех*) artificial; (*деньги*) counterfeit

нена́сть|е, я *nt.* bad, foul weather

ненорма́л|ьный, ~ен, ~ьна *adj.*
　1 abnormal **2** (*сумасшедший*) mad
нену́ж|ный, ~ен, ~на́, ~но. (*мягкость*)
　unnecessary; (*книга, человек*) superfluous
необду́ман|ный, ~, ~на *adj.* thoughtless,
　precipitate
необита́ем|ый, ~, ~а *adj.* uninhabited; **н.**
　о́стров desert island
необозри́м|ый, ~, ~а *adj.* boundless,
　immense
необосно́ван|ный, ~, ~на *adj.* unfounded,
　groundless
необрабо́тан|ный, ~, ~а *adj.* **1** (*земля́*)
　uncultivated, untilled **2** (*минера́л*) raw, crude
необразо́ван|ный, ~, ~на *adj.* uneducated
необрати́м|ый, ~, ~а *adj.* irreversible
необу́здан|ный, ~, ~на *adj.* (*фанта́зия*)
　unbridled; (*нрав*) ungovernable
♂ **необходи́мост|ь**, и *f.* necessity; **по ~и** out
　of necessity; **при ~и** if necessary
♂ **необходи́м|ый**, ~, ~а *adj.* necessary,
　essential; (*impers., as pred.*) ~о it is
　necessary *or* imperative
необщи́тел|ьный, ~ен, ~ьна *adj.*
　unsociable
необъекти́в|ный, ~ен, ~на *adj.* not
　objective; biased
необъясни́м|ый, ~, ~а *adj.* inexplicable,
　unaccountable
необъя́т|ный, ~ен, ~на *adj.* immense,
　unbounded
необыкнове́н|ный, ~ен, ~на *adj.* unusual,
　uncommon
необыча́й|ный, ~ен, ~йна *adj.*
　extraordinary, exceptional
необы́ч|ный, ~ен, ~на *adj.* unusual
необяза́тел|ьный, ~ен, ~ьна *adj.*
　1 (*предмет, курс*) not obligatory, optional
　2 (*челове́к*) unreliable
неограни́чен|ный, ~, ~на *adj.* unlimited,
　unbounded
неоднозна́ч|ный, ~ен, ~на *adj.*
　1 ambiguous, equivocal **2** (*сло́жный*)
　complex, complicated
неоднокра́тно *adv.* repeatedly
неоднокра́т|ный, ~ен, ~на *adj.* repeated
неоднор́од|ный, ~ен, ~на *adj.*
　heterogeneous; dissimilar
неодобре́ни|е, я *nt.* disapproval
неодоли́м|ый, ~, ~а *adj.* insuperable
неодушевлённый *adj.* inanimate
неожи́данност|ь, и *f.* **1** unexpectedness,
　suddenness **2** (*собы́тие*) surprise
неожи́дан|ный, ~, ~на *adj.* unexpected,
　sudden
неоко́нченный *adj.* unfinished
нео́н, а *m.* (chem.) neon
неонаци́ст, а *m.* neo-Nazi
неонаци́ст|ка, ки *f. of ▶* **неонаци́ст**
нео́новый *adj.*: ~ **свет** neon light
неопа́с|ный, ~ен, ~на *adj.* (*ме́сто,
　путеше́ствие*) safe; (*боле́знь, соба́ка*)

harmless
неопису́ем|ый, ~, ~а *adj.* indescribable
неопо́знан|ный, ~, ~а *adj.* unidentified
неопра́вдан|ный, ~, ~на *adj.* unjustified,
　unwarranted
неопределённост|ь, и *f.* vagueness,
　uncertainty
неопределён|ный, ~ен, ~на *adj.*
　1 indefinite; ~**ная фо́рма глаго́ла** (gram.)
　infinitive **2** indeterminate; vague, uncertain
неопроверж́им|ый, ~, ~а *adj.* irrefutable
неопря́т|ный, ~ен, ~на *adj.* slovenly;
　untidy, sloppy
нео́пыт|ный, ~ен, ~на *adj.* inexperienced
неосмотри́тел|ьный, ~ен, ~ьна *adj.*
　imprudent, incautious
неоспори́м|ый, ~, ~а *adj.* unquestionable,
　incontestable, indisputable
неосторо́жност|ь, и *f.* carelessness;
　imprudence
неосторо́ж|ный, ~ен, ~на *adj.* careless;
　imprudent, incautious
неотврати́м|ый, ~, ~а *adj.* inevitable
не́откуда *adv.* there is nowhere; **мне н. э́то
　получи́ть** there is nowhere I can get it from
неотло́ж|ный, ~ен, ~на *adj.* urgent,
　pressing; ~**ная медици́нская по́мощь**
　emergency medical service
неотрази́м|ый, ~, ~а *adj.* irresistible (also fig.)
неотъе́млем|ый, ~, ~а *adj.* inalienable;
　~**ое пра́во** inalienable right; ~**ая часть**
　integral part
неофаши́зм, а *m.* neo-fascism
неофаши́ст, а *m.* neo-fascist
неофаши́ст|ка, ки *f. of ▶* **неофаши́ст**
неофаши́стский *adj.* neo-fascist
неофициа́л|ьный, ~ен, ~ьна *adj.* unofficial
неохо́т|а, ы *f.* **1** reluctance **2** (+ *d., as pred.*)
　(infml): **мне** *и т. п.* **н. идти́ н.** I have, *etc.*, no
　wish to go, don't feel like going
неохо́тно *adv.* reluctantly; unwillingly
неоцени́м|ый, ~, ~а *adj.* inestimable,
　priceless, invaluable
Непа́л, а *m.* Nepal
непа́л|ец, ьца *m.* Nepalese
непа́л|ка, ки *fem. of ▶* **непа́лец**
непа́льский *adj.* Nepalese
непереводи́м|ый, ~, ~а *adj.* untranslatable
непередава́ем|ый, ~, ~а *adj.* inexpressible,
　indescribable
непереход́ный *adj.* (gram.) intransitive
неплатёжеспосо́б|ный, ~ен, ~на *adj.*
　(fin.) insolvent
неплате́льщик, а *m.* defaulter; person in
　arrears with payment (*of taxes, etc.*)
непло́хо *adv.* not badly, quite well
непло́х|ой, ~́, ~а́, ~о *adj.* not bad, quite good
непобеди́м|ый, ~, ~а *adj.* invincible
неповоро́тлив|ый, ~, ~а *adj.* (*неуклю́жий*)
　clumsy, awkward; (*медли́тельный*) sluggish,
　slow

Н

неповтори́м|ый, ~, ~а *adj.* unique

непого́д|а, ы *f.* bad weather

неподалёку *adv.* not far off

неподви́жность|ь, и *f.* immobility

неподви́ж|ный, ~ен, ~на *adj.* motionless, immobile, immovable (also fig.); fixed, stationary

неподде́л|ьный, ~ен, ~ьна *adj.* genuine; unfeigned, sincere

неподку́п|ный, ~ен, ~на *adj.* incorruptible

неподража́ем|ый, ~, ~а *adj.* inimitable

непозволи́тел|ьный, ~ен, ~ьна *adj.* inadmissible, impermissible

непоколеби́м|ый, ~, ~а *adj.* steadfast, unshakeable

непоко́р|ный, ~ен, ~на *adj.* recalcitrant; unruly

непола́дк|а, и *f.* defect, fault

неполноце́нность|ь, и *f.* inferiority; ко́мплекс ~и inferiority complex

неполноце́н|ный, ~ен, ~на *adj.* inferior; substandard; у́мственно н. learning-disabled; физи́чески н. disabled

непо́л|ный, ~он, ~на́, ~но, ~ны́ *adj.* (*ведро́, корзи́на*) not full; (*зна́ния, пере́чень*) incomplete; ~ная семья́ single-parent family; рабо́тать ~ную неде́лю to work part-time

непонима́ни|е, я *nt.* incomprehension

непоня́тлив|ый, ~, ~а *adj.* slow (to grasp things), dim

непоня́т|ный, ~ен, ~на *adj.* unintelligible, incomprehensible; (*impers., as pred.*) ~но it is incomprehensible; мне ~но, как он мог э́то сде́лать I cannot understand how he could do it

непоправи́м|ый, ~, ~а *adj.* irreparable, irremediable; irretrievable

непоря́доч|ный, ~ен, ~на *adj.* dishonourable (BrE), dishonorable (AmE)

непосе́длив|ый, ~, ~а *adj.* fidgety, restless

непосле́довательность|ь, и *f.* inconsistency; inconsequence

непосле́довател|ьный, ~ен, ~ьна *adj.* inconsistent; inconsequent

непослу́ш|ный, ~ен, ~на *adj.* disobedient, naughty

непосре́дственность|ь, и *f.* spontaneity, ingenuousness

⚹ **непосре́дствен|ный**, ~, ~на *adj.* **1** (*результа́т*) immediate, direct; в ~ной бли́зости (от + *g.*) in the immediate vicinity (of) **2** (fig., *нату́ра*) direct; spontaneous, ingenuous

непостижи́м|ый, ~, ~а *adj.* incomprehensible, inscrutable; уму́ ~о it passes understanding

непостоя́н|ный, ~ен, ~на *adj.* inconstant, changeable

непостоя́нств|о, а *nt.* inconstancy

непра́вд|а, ы *f.* untruth, lie

⚹ key word

неправдоподо́б|ный, ~ен, ~на *adj.* improbable, unlikely; implausible

непра́вильно *adv.* incorrectly, erroneously; (*in conjunction with vv. frequently*) mis-; н. истолкова́ть to misinterpret

непра́вил|ьный, ~ен, ~ьна *adj.* **1** (*разви́тие, черты́, фо́рма*) irregular; н. глаго́л irregular verb **2** (*расчёт, сужде́ние*) incorrect, erroneous, wrong, mistaken

неправоме́р|ный, ~ен, ~на *adj.* illegal

непра́в|ый, ~, ~а́, ~о *adj.* **1** (*заблужда́ющийся*) wrong, mistaken **2** (*несправедли́вый*) unjust

непредвзя́т|ый, ~, ~а *adj.* unbiased

непредви́денный *adj.* unforeseen

непреднаме́рен|ный, ~, ~на *adj.* unpremeditated

непредсказу́ем|ый, ~, ~а *adj.* unpredictable

непредумы́шленн|ый *adj.* unpremeditated; ~ое уби́йство manslaughter

непрекло́н|ный, ~ен, ~на *adj.* inflexible, unbending; inexorable, adamant

непреме́нно *adv.* **1** (*обяза́тельно*) without fail; certainly; они́ н. приду́т за́втра they are sure to come tomorrow **2** (*о́чень*) absolutely; мне н. ну́жно поговори́ть с ним it is absolutely essential that I speak to him

непреме́н|ный, ~ен, ~на *adj.* (*усло́вие*) necessary; (*сле́дствие*) unavoidable; (*черта́*) indispensable

непреодоли́м|ый, ~, ~а *adj.* insuperable, insurmountable; (*жела́ние*) irresistible; ~ая си́ла (law) force majeure

непреры́вно *adv.* uninterruptedly, continuously

непреры́вность|ь, и *f.* continuity

непреры́в|ный, ~ен, ~на *adj.* uninterrupted, unbroken; continuous

непреста́нно *adv.* incessantly, continually

неприве́тлив|ый, ~, ~а *adj.* (*челове́к, взгляд*) unfriendly, ungracious; (*ме́стность*) bleak, forbidding

непривлека́тел|ьный, ~ен, ~ьна *adj.* unattractive

непривы́ч|ный, ~ен, ~на *adj.* unaccustomed, unwonted; unusual

непригля́д|ный, ~ен, ~на *adj.* unattractive, unsightly

неприго́д|ный, ~ен, ~на *adj.* unfit, useless; unserviceable; (*для вое́нной слу́жбы*) ineligible

неприе́млем|ый, ~, ~а *adj.* unacceptable

непри́знан|ный, ~, ~а *adj.* unrecognized, unacknowledged

неприкоснове́нность|ь, и *f.* inviolability; дипломати́ческая н. diplomatic immunity

неприкоснове́н|ный, ~ен, ~на *adj.* inviolable; н. запа́с (mil.) emergency ration, iron ration

неприли́ч|ный, ~ен, ~на *adj.* indecent, improper; unseemly, unbecoming

неприме́т|ный, ~ен, ~на *adj.* **1** (*ра́зница*) imperceptible **2** (fig., *челове́к*) unremarkable, undistinguished

непримири́м|ый, ~, ~а *adj.* (*противоречия*) irreconcilable; (*характер*) intransigent, uncompromising

непринуждён|ный, ~, ~на *adj.* natural, relaxed; laid-back

непристо́йность|, и *f.* obscenity; indecency

непристо́|йный, ~ен, ~йна *adj.* obscene; indecent

непристу́п|ный, ~ен, ~на *adj.* **1** (*скала*) inaccessible; (*крепость*) unassailable, impregnable **2** (fig., *начальник*) inaccessible, unapproachable

неприхотли́в|ый, ~, ~а *adj.* **1** (*человек*) unpretentious; modest; (*растение, животное*) undemanding **2** (*рисунок*) simple, plain; ~ая пи́ща frugal meal

неприча́ст|ный, ~ен, ~на *adj.* (к + *d.*) not implicated (in), not involved (in)

неприя́тел|ь, я *m.* enemy; (mil.) the enemy

неприя́тность|, и *f.* unpleasantness; trouble

неприя́т|ный, ~ен, ~на *adj.* unpleasant, disagreeable

непродолжи́тел|ьный, ~ен, ~ьна *adj.* of short duration, short-lived

непроду́ман|ный, ~, ~на *adj.* ill-considered

непрозра́ч|ный, ~ен, ~на *adj.* opaque

непроизво́л|ьный, ~ен, ~ьна *adj.* involuntary

непромока́ем|ый, ~, ~а *adj.* waterproof; **н. плащ** waterproof (coat), raincoat

непроница́ем|ый, ~, ~а *adj.* (*мрак, ночь; тайна*) impenetrable; (*для жидкостей, газов*) impermeable; **н. для зву́ка** soundproof

непрости́тел|ьный, ~ен, ~ьна *adj.* unforgivable, unpardonable, inexcusable

непроходи́м|ый, ~, ~а *adj.* impassable

непро́ч|ный, ~ен, ~на́, ~но *adj.* fragile, flimsy; (fig.) precarious, unstable

неработоспосо́б|ный, ~ен, ~на *adj.* unable to work, disabled

нерабо́ч|ий *adj.* non-working; ~ее вре́мя time off, free time

нера́венств|о, а *nt.* inequality, disparity

неравноду́ш|ный, ~ен, ~на *adj.* (к + *d.*) not indifferent (to)

неравноме́р|ный, ~ен, ~на *adj.* uneven, irregular

нера́в|ный, ~ен, ~на́ *adj.* unequal

неради́в|ый, ~, ~а *adj.* negligent, careless

неразбо́рчив|ый, ~, ~а *adj.* **1** (*почерк*) illegible, indecipherable **2** (fig., *читатель, вкус*) undiscriminating; not fastidious; **н. в сре́дствах** unscrupulous; **сексуа́льно н.** promiscuous

неразгово́рчив|ый, ~, ~а *adj.* taciturn, not talkative

неразличи́м|ый, ~, ~а *adj.* indistinguishable; indiscernible

неразлу́ч|ный, ~ен, ~на *adj.* inseparable

неразреши́м|ый, ~, ~а *adj.* insoluble

неразу́м|ный, ~ен, ~на *adj.* unreasonable; unwise; foolish

нерасторо́п|ный, ~ен, ~на *adj.* sluggish, slow

нерв, а *m.* nerve; **де́йствовать кому́-н. на ~ы** to get on sb's nerves

не́рвнича|ть, ю *impf.* to be *or* become fidgety; to fret; to be *or* become irritable

не́рв|ный, ~ен, ~на́, ~но *adj.* **1** (*болезнь, тик; похо́дка, жест; состоя́ние*) nervous; ~ная систе́ма the nervous system; **н. центр** (fig.) nerve centre (BrE), center (AmE) **2** (*человек*) nervous, highly strung **3** (*работа*) nerve-racking

нерво́з|ный, ~ен, ~на *adj.* nervy, irritable

нереа́л|ьный, ~ен, ~ьна *adj.* **1** (*местность*) unreal **2** (*предложение*) impracticable

нере́дко *adv.* not infrequently, quite often

нерезиде́нт, а *m.* non-resident

нерента́бел|ьный, ~ен, ~ьна *adj.* unprofitable

нере́ст, а *m.* (zool.) spawning

нереши́тельность|, и *f.* indecision; indecisiveness; **быть в ~и** to be undecided

нереши́тел|ьный, ~ен, ~ьна *adj.* indecisive, irresolute

нержаве́ющ|ий *adj.* non-rusting; ~ая сталь stainless steel

неро́в|ный, ~ен, ~на́, ~но *adj.* **1** (*пове́рхность*) uneven, rough **2** (*пульс, дыха́ние*) irregular **3** (*ли́ния*) crooked

не́рп|а, ы *f.* (zool.) ringed seal

несве́дущ|ий, ~, ~а *adj.* (в + *p.*) ignorant (about), not well informed (about)

несве́ж|ий, ~, ~а́, ~е *adj.* **1** (*еда*) not fresh, stale **2** (*бельё; во́здух*) dirty

несвоевре́мен|ный, ~, ~на *adj.* inopportune, untimely, unseasonable

несгиба́ем|ый, ~, ~а *adj.* unbending, inflexible

несгово́рчив|ый, ~, ~а *adj.* intractable

несде́ржан|ный, ~, ~на *adj.* unrestrained

несерьёз|ный, ~ен, ~на, ~но *adj.* **1** (*человек*) frivolous **2** (*замеча́ние*) flippant **3** (*де́ло, ра́на*) trivial

несклáд|ный, ~ен, ~на *adj.* ungainly, awkward; absurd

несклоня́ем|ый, ~, ~а *adj.* (gram.) indeclinable

✒ **не́скольк|о¹, их** *пит.* some, several; a few; **в ~их слова́х** in a few words; **н. челове́к** several people

✒ **не́сколько²** *adv.* somewhat, rather, slightly; **они́ н. разочаро́ваны** they are rather disillusioned

нескро́м|ный, ~ен, ~на́, ~но *adj.* **1** (*человек*) immodest; vain **2** (*вопро́с*) indiscreet **3** (*жест*) indecent

нескрыва́ем|ый, ~, ~а *adj.* undisguised

несло́ж|ный, ~ен, ~на́, ~но *adj.* simple, uncomplicated

неслы́хан|ный, ~, ~на *adj.* unheard-of, unprecedented

неслы́ш|ный, ~ен, ~на *adj.* inaudible

несмолка́ем|ый, ~, ~а *adj.* ceaseless, unremitting

🖋 **несмотря́** *prep.* (на + *a.*) in spite of, despite; **н. ни на что** in spite of everything

несовершенноле́тн|ий *adj.* under-age; (*as n.* **н.**, ~его, *f.* ~яя, ~ей) minor

несоверше́н|ный, ~ен, ~на *adj.* imperfect, incomplete

несовмести́м|ый, ~, ~а *adj.* incompatible

несогла́си|е, я *nt.* **1** disagreement **2** (*разлад*) discord **3** (*sg. only*) (*отказ*) refusal

несоизмери́м|ый, ~, ~а *adj.* incommensurable, incommensurate

несокруши́м|ый, ~, ~а *adj.* unshakeable

несомне́нно *adv.* undoubtedly, doubtless

несомне́н|ный, ~ен, ~на *adj.* undoubted, indubitable, unquestionable

несостоя́тел|ьный, ~ен, ~ьна *adj.* **1** (*обанкротившийся*) insolvent, bankrupt; (*бедный*) poor **2** (*необоснованный*) groundless, unsupported

неспе́л|ый, ~, ~а́, ~о *adj.* unripe

неспе́ш|ный, ~ен, ~на *adj.* unhurried

неспоко́й|ный, ~ен, ~йна *adj.* (*сон, характер*) restless; (*жизнь*) troubled; (*море, погода*) rough

неспосо́бност|ь, и *f.* incapacity, inability

неспосо́б|ный, ~ен, ~на *adj.* dull, not able; (к + *d. or* на + *a.*) incapable (of); **она́** ~на к языка́м she has no aptitude for languages; **н. на ложь** incapable of a lie

несправедли́вост|ь, и *f.* injustice, unfairness

несправедли́в|ый, ~, ~а *adj.* **1** (*человек, суд*) unjust, unfair **2** (*мнение*) incorrect, unfounded

неспроста́ *adv.* (infml) not without purpose; with an ulterior motive

несравне́нно *adv.* **1** incomparably **2** (+ *comp.*) far, by far; **н. лу́чше** far better

несравне́н|ный, ~ен, ~на *adj.* incomparable

нестаби́льност|ь, и *f.* instability

нестаби́л|ьный, ~ен, ~ьна *adj.* unstable

нестерпи́м|ый, ~, ~а *adj.* unbearable, intolerable

🖋 **нес|ти́**[1], **у́, ёшь**, *past* ~, ~ла́ *impf.* (*of* ▶ **понести́** 1, *det. of* ▶ **носи́ть** 1) **1** (*перемещать на себе*) to carry **2** (*поддерживать*) to bear; to support **3** (fig., *терпеть*) to bear; to suffer; to incur; **н. убы́тки** (fin.) to incur losses **4** (*выполнять*) to perform; **н. дежу́рство** to be on duty **5** (fig., *причинять*) to bear, bring; **н. ги́бель** to bring destruction **6** (infml): ~**ти вздор, чепуху́** *и т. п.* to talk (nonsense)

🖋 **нес|ти́**[2], **ёт**, *past* ~, ~ла́ *impf.* (*of* ▶ **снести́**[2])

🖋 key word

(*яйца*) to lay

нес|ти́сь, у́сь, ёшься, *past* нёсся, ~ла́сь *impf.* (*of* ▶ **понести́сь** 1) (*det.*) **1** (*о человеке, машине*) to rush, tear, fly; (*по воздуху, воде*) to float, drift; (по + *d. or* вдоль + *g. or* над + *i.*) to skim (along, over) **2** (*о звуке, запахе*) to spread, be diffused

несура́з|ный, ~ен, ~на *adj.* **1** (*глупый*) absurd, senseless **2** (*неуклюжий*) awkward

несуще́ствен|ный, ~, ~на *adj.* inessential, immaterial

несча́ст|ный, ~ен, ~на *adj.* **1** unhappy; unfortunate, unlucky; **н. слу́чай** accident **2** (*as m. n. н.*, ~ного) wretch; an unfortunate

несча́сть|е, я *nt.* **1** (*беда*) misfortune; **к** ~**ю** unfortunately **2** (*несчастный случай*) accident

несъедо́б|ный, ~ен, ~на *adj.* inedible

🖋 **нет**[1] **1** (*при отрицании*) no; not; **вы его́ ви́дели? — н.** You saw him? — No; **вы не ви́дели его́? — н.** You didn't see him? — Yes, I did **2** nothing, naught; **свести́ на н.** to bring to naught; **свести́сь (сойти́) на н.** to come to naught

🖋 **нет**[2] (+ *g.*) (*не имеется*) (there) is no, (there) are no; **у меня́ н. вре́мени** I have no time

нетакти́ч|ный, ~ен, ~на *adj.* tactless

нетвёрдо *adv.* **1** (*ходить*) unsteadily, not firmly **2** (fig.) not definitely; **знать н.** to have a shaky knowledge of

нетерпели́в|ый, ~, ~а *adj.* impatient

нетерпе́ни|е, я *nt.* impatience

нетерпи́мост|ь, и *f.* intolerance

нетерпи́м|ый, ~, ~а *adj.* **1** (*поступок*) intolerable **2** (*человек*) intolerant

неторопл́ив|ый, ~, ~а *adj.* leisurely, unhurried

нето́чност|ь, и *f.* **1** (*свойство*) inaccuracy, inexactitude **2** (*ошибка*) error, slip

нето́ч|ный, ~ен, ~на́, ~но, ~:ны́ *adj.* inaccurate, inexact

нетрадицио́н|ный, ~ен, ~на *adj.* unconventional

нетре́зв|ый, ~, ~а́, ~о *adj.* not sober, drunk; **в** ~**ом ви́де** in a state of intoxication

нетривиа́л|ьный, ~ен, ~ьна *adj.* not trivial; outstanding, exceptional

нетро́нут|ый, ~, ~а *adj.* (*почва, снег*) virgin; (*обед*) untouched; (fig., *целомудренный*) unsullied, virginal

нетрудоспосо́б|ный, ~ен, ~на *adj.* disabled; invalid

не́ту (infml) = **нет**[2]

неубеди́тел|ьный, ~ен, ~ьна *adj.* unconvincing

неуваже́ни|е, я *nt.* disrespect, lack of respect; (law): **н. к суду́** contempt of court

неуважи́тел|ьный, ~ен, ~ьна *adj.* **1** (*причина*) inadequate; not acceptable **2** (infml, *непочтительный*) disrespectful

неуве́ренност|ь, и *f.* uncertainty; **н. в себе́** lack of self-confidence неуве́рен|ный, ~, ~на and (with syntactically related word(s)) ~a adj. **1** (человек) lacking confidence, unsure; **н. в себе́** lacking self-confidence, unsure of oneself **2** (походка, движение) uncertain

неувя́зк|а, и f. (infml) (в расчётах) discrepancy; (недоразумение) misunderstanding

неуда́ч|а, и f. failure

неуда́чник, а m. unlucky person, failure, loser

неуда́чни|ца, цы f. of ▶ неуда́чник

неуда́ч|ный, ~ен, ~на adj. unsuccessful; (несчастливый) unfortunate; (плохой) bad; ~ное нача́ло bad start

неудержи́м|ый, ~, ~a adj. irrepressible

неудо́б|ный, ~ен, ~на adj. **1** (одежда, постель) uncomfortable **2** (fig.) (время) inconvenient; (положение) awkward; embarrassing

неудо́бств|о, а nt. **1** (постели) discomfort **2** (положения) awkwardness; embarrassment

неудовлетвори́тел|ьный, ~ен, ~ьна adj. unsatisfactory

неудово́льстви|е, я nt. dissatisfaction, displeasure

неуже́ли interrog. particle really? is it possible?; **н. он так ду́мает?** does he really think that?; **н. ты не знал, что мы здесь?** did you really not know that we were here?; surely you knew that we were here!

неузнава́ем|ый, ~, ~a adj. unrecognizable

неуклю́ж|ий, ~, ~a, ~e adj. clumsy, awkward

неулови́м|ый, ~, ~a adj. **1** (человек) elusive, difficult to catch **2** (fig., звук) imperceptible

неуме́л|ый, ~, ~a adj. clumsy; unskilful (BrE), unskillful (AmE)

неуме́рен|ный, ~, ~на adj. (аппетит, восторг) immoderate; excessive

неуме́ст|ный, ~ен, ~на adj. **1** (шутка) inappropriate **2** (факт, информация) irrelevant

неу́м|ный, ~ён, ~на́ adj. foolish; (решение) unwise

неумоли́м|ый, ~, ~a adj. implacable; inexorable

неуравнове́шен|ный, ~, ~на adj. (psych.) unbalanced

неурожа́|й, я m. bad harvest, crop failure

неусто́йчив|ый, ~, ~a adj. unstable, unsteady

неустраши́м|ый, ~, ~a adj. fearless, intrepid

неутеши́тел|ьный, ~ен, ~ьна adj. not comforting, depressing; ~ьные ве́сти distressing news

неутоми́м|ый, ~, ~a adj. tireless, indefatigable

неучти́в|ый, ~, ~a adj. discourteous, impolite, uncivil

неую́т|ный, ~ен, ~на adj. bleak, comfortless

неуязви́м|ый, ~, ~a adj. **1** (позиция, человек, подводная лодка) invulnerable **2** (доказательство) unassailable

неформа́л, а m. (infml) member of an unofficial organization

неформа́л|ьный, ~ен, ~ьна adj. unofficial; informal

нефтедо́ллар, а m. petrodollar

нефтеперераба́тывающий adj. oil-refining; **н. заво́д** oil refinery

нефтепрово́д, а m. oil pipeline

нефт|ь, и f. oil, petroleum; **сыра́я н.** crude oil

нефтя́ник, а m. oil (industry) worker

нефтян|о́й adj. oil; ~а́я вы́шка derrick

нехва́тк|а, и f. (infml) shortage

нехоро́ш|ий, ~, ~а́ adj. bad

не́хотя adv. reluctantly, unwillingly

нецелесообра́з|ный, ~ен, ~на adj. inexpedient; pointless

нецензу́р|ный, ~ен, ~на adj. unprintable; ~ные слова́ swear words, obscenities

неча́янный adj. accidental; unintentional

не́чего, не́чему, не́чем, не́ о чем **1** pron. (+ inf) there is nothing (to); **мне н. чита́ть** I have nothing to read; **не́ о чем бы́ло говори́ть** there was nothing to talk about; **от н. де́лать** for want of sth better to do, to while away the time **2** (as pred.) (impers. + inf.) (незачем) it's no good, it's no use; there is no need; **н. жа́ловаться** it's no use complaining

нечелове́ческий adj. **1** (усилия) superhuman **2** (отношения) inhuman

нече́стност|ь, и f. dishonesty

нече́ст|ный, ~ен, ~на́, ~но, ~ны́ adj. **1** (человек) dishonest **2** (поступок) dishonourable (BrE), dishonorable (AmE); ~ная игра́ (sport) foul play

нечёт|кий, ~ок, ~ка adj. (почерк) illegible; (рисунок) indistinct; (изложение) unclear

нечётный adj. odd

нечистопло́т|ный, ~ен, ~на adj. **1** (грязный) dirty; (неопрятный) untidy, slovenly **2** (fig., нечестный) unscrupulous

нечистот|а́, ы́, pl. ~ы, ~ f. **1** (sg. only) dirtiness **2** (pl. only) (отбросы) sewage, garbage

нечи́ст|ый, ~, ~а́, ~о, ~ы́ adj. **1** (грязный) unclean, dirty (also fig.); ~ое де́ло suspicious affair **2** (с примесью чего-л.) impure, adulterated **3** (неаккуратный) careless, inaccurate **4** (нечестный) dishonourable (BrE), dishonorable (AmE); dishonest; **быть ~ым на́ руку** to be light-fingered **5**: ~ая си́ла evil spirits

не́что pron. (nom. and a. cases only) something

нечувстви́тел|ьный, ~ен, ~ьна adj. (к + d.) insensitive (to)

нешу́точ|ный, ~ен, ~на adj. grave, serious; **де́ло ~ное** it is no joke; it is no laughing matter

неэффекти́в|ный, ~ен, ~на adj. ineffective; inefficient

нея́с|ный, ∼ен, ∼на́, ∼но *adj.* vague, obscure

☞ **ни 1** (*correlative conj.*): ни... ни neither ... nor; ни тот ни друго́й neither (the one nor the other) **2** (*particle*) not a; ни оди́н, ни одна́, ни одно́ not a, not one, not a single; на у́лице не́ было ни души́ there was not a soul about **3** (*separable component of prons.* никако́й, никто́, ничто́, *following preps.*): ни в како́м (ни в ко́ем) слу́чае on no account; ни за что (на све́те!) in no circumstances; not for the world! **4** (*particle, in comb. with* как, кто, куда́, *etc.*) -ever; как бы мы ни стара́лись however hard we tried; что бы он ни говори́л whatever he might say

нигде́ *adv.* nowhere

Ни́гер, а *m.* **1** (*страна*) Niger **2** (*река*) the Niger

нигери́|ец, йца *m.* Nigerian

нигери́й|ка, ки *f. of* ▸ нигери́ец

нигери́йский *adj.* Nigerian

Ниге́ри|я, и *f.* Nigeria

нидерла́ндский *adj.* Dutch, Netherlands; (*язык*) Dutch

Нидерла́нд|ы, ов (*no sg.*) the Netherlands

ни́же 1 *comp. of* ▸ ни́зкий **2** *prep.* (+ *g.*) *and adv.* below, beneath

☞ **ни́жн|ий** *adj.* lower; ∼ее бельё underclothes, underwear; ∼яя пала́та Lower Chamber, Lower House; ∼яя ю́бка slip

низ, а, *pl.* ∼ы́ *m.* **1** bottom **2** (*in pl.*) (*общества*) lower classes

низи́н|а, ы *f.* low-lying area

☞ **ни́з|кий**, ∼ок, ∼ка́, ∼ко *adj.* **1** low; ∼кого происхожде́ния of humble origin; быть ∼кого мне́ния о (+ *p.*) to have a low opinion of **2** (*подлый*) base, mean; н. посту́пок shabby act

низкока́чествен|ный, ∼, ∼на *adj.* low-quality

низкоопла́чиваем|ый, ∼, ∼а *adj.* poorly-paid

низкоро́сл|ый, ∼, ∼а *adj.* (*человек*) short; (*дерево*) undersized, stunted

низкоуглево́д|ный, ∼ен, ∼на *adj.* low-carb

низкоуглеро́дистый *adj.* low-carbon

ни́зменность, и *f.* (geog.) lowland (*not exceeding 200 m above sea level*)

ни́змен|ный, ∼, ∼на *adj.* **1** low-lying **2** (*подлый*) low; base, vile; ∼ные инсти́нкты basic instincts

низо́в|ье, ья, *g. pl.* ∼ьев *nt.* the lower reaches (*of a river*)

ни́зость, и *f.* lowness; (*подлость*) baseness, meanness

ни́зший *superl. of* ▸ ни́зкий; lowest

НИИ *m. indecl.* (*abbr. of* нау́чно-иссле́довательский институ́т) research institute

☞ key word

☞ **ника́к** *adv.* (*никаким образом*) by no means, in no way; он н. не мог узна́ть её а́дрес in no way could he discover her address

☞ **никак|о́й** *pron.* no; не... ∼о́го, ∼о́й, ∼и́х no ... whatever; я не име́ю ∼о́го представле́ния (поня́тия) I have no idea, no conception; ∼и́х возраже́ний! no objections!

Никара́гуа *nt. & f. indecl.* Nicaragua

никарагуа́н|ец, ца *m.* Nicaraguan

никарагуа́н|ка, ки *f. of* ▸ никарагуа́нец

никарагуа́нский *adj.* Nicaraguan

ни́кел|ь, я *m.* nickel

☞ **никогда́** *adv.* never; как н. as never before

никой *pron.*: ∼им о́бразом by no means, in no way; ни в ко́ем слу́чае on no account, in no circumstances

никоти́н, а *m.* nicotine

никоти́новый *adj. of* ▸ никоти́н

☞ **никто́, никого́, никому́, нике́м, ни о ком** *pron.* nobody, no one; ни у кого́ нет э́того no one has it

никуда́ *adv.* nowhere; э́то н. не годи́тся (fig.) this won't do; it is no good at all

никчём|ный, ∼ен, ∼на *adj.* (infml) useless, good-for-nothing

Нил, а *m.* the Nile (*river*)

ним *i. of* ▸ он, *d. of* ▸ они́ *after preps.*

нима́ло *adv.* not in the least, not at all

ни́ми *i. of* ▸ они́ *after preps.*

ни́мф|а, ы *f.* nymph

ниотку́да *adv.* from nowhere; н. не сле́дует, что... it in no way follows that ...

нирва́н|а, ы *f.* nirvana

ниско́лько *adv.* not at all, not in the least; ей от э́того бы́ло н. не лу́чше she was none the better for it

ни́тк|а, и *f.* thread; н. же́мчуга string of pearls; промо́кнуть до ∼и (fig.) to get soaked to the skin

нитра́т, а *m.* (chem.) nitrate

нитроглицери́н, а *m.* (chem.) nitroglycerine

нит|ь, и *f.* **1** thread **2** (bot., elec.) filament **3** (med.) suture

них *a., g., and p. of* ▸ они́ *after preps.*

ничего́[1] *g. of* ▸ ничто́

ничего́[2] *adv.* (infml) **1** (*also* н. себе́) so-so; passably, not (too) badly; all right; как вы чу́вствуете себя́? — н. how do you feel? — all right **2** (*as indecl. adj.*) not (too) bad, passable, tolerable; па́рень он н. he is not a bad chap

ниче́|й, ∼ья́, ∼ье́ *pron.* nobody's, no one's; ∼ья́ земля́ no man's land; (*as f. n.* ∼ья́, *g., d., i., p.* ∼ье́й) (sport) draw, drawn game

ничко́м *adv.* prone, face downwards

☞ **ничто́, ничего́, ничему́, ниче́м, ни о чём** *pron.* nothing; э́то ничего́ не зна́чит it means nothing; ничего́ подо́бного! nothing of the kind!; ничего́! (infml) that's all right!; never mind!

ничто́жеств|о, а *nt.* **1** (*убожество*) poverty **2** (*человек*) a nonentity, a nobody

ничто́ж|ный, ~ен, ~на *adj.* (*незначительный*) insignificant; (*человек*) paltry, worthless

ничу́ть *adv.* (*infml*) not at all, not in the least, not a bit; **н. не быва́ло** not at all

ничь|я́, е́й *f.* *see* ▶ **ниче́й**

ни́ш|а, и *f.* niche, recess; (*archit.*) alcove, bay

ни́щенский *adj.* beggarly

ни́щенств|овать, ую *impf.* **1** (*заниматься нищенством*) to beg, go begging **2** (*жить в нищете*) to be destitute

нищет|а́, ы́ *f.* poverty (*also fig.*)

ни́щ|ий *adj.* **1** destitute; poverty-stricken **2** (*as m. n. н., ~его*) beggar; pauper

НЛО *m. indecl.* (*abbr. of* **неопо́знанный лета́ющий объе́кт**) UFO (*unidentified flying object*)

✓ но *conj.* but; (*after concessive clause not translated or*) still, nevertheless; **хотя́ он и бо́лен, но наме́рен прийти́** although he is ill, he (still) intends to come

Но́в|ая Зела́ндия, ~ой Зела́ндии *f.* New Zealand

нове́йший *superl. of* ▶ **но́вый**; newest; (*последний*) latest

нове́лл|а, ы *f.* novella

новизн|а́, ы́ *f.* novelty; newness

нови́нк|а, и *f.* new thing, novelty; **кни́жные ~и** new books

новичо́к, ка́ m. **1** (**в** + *p.*) novice (at), beginner (at) **2** (*в школе*) new boy; new girl

новобра́н|ец, ца m. recruit

новобра́чн|ые, ых *pl.* newly-weds

нововведе́ни|е, я *nt.* innovation

нового́дн|ий *adj.* New Year's; **~яя ночь** New Year's Eve

новозела́нд|ец, ца m. New Zealander

новозела́нд|ка, ки *f. of* ▶ **новозела́ндец**

новозела́ндский *adj.* New Zealand

новолу́ни|е, я *nt.* new moon

новорождённ|ый *adj.* newborn; (*as n. н., ~ого, f. ~ая, ~ой*) the baby; (*med.*) neonate

новосе́ль|е, я *nt.* house-warming; **справля́ть ~** to give a house-warming party

новостно́й *adj.* news (*attr.*)

✓ но́вост|ь, и, g. pl. ~е́й *f.* news

но́вшеств|о, а *nt.* innovation, novelty

✓ но́в|ый, ~, ~а́, ~о, ~ы́ *adj.* **1** new; **соверше́нно н.** brand new; **Н. год** New Year's Day; **Н. Заве́т** the New Testament; **что ~ого?** what's the news?; what's new? **2** (*современный*) modern; recent; **~ая исто́рия** modern history

✓ ног|а́, и́, a. ~у, pl. ~и, ~, ~а́м *f.* (*ступня*) foot; (*до ступни*) leg; **вверх ~а́ми** head over heels; **положи́ть ~у на́ ~у** to cross one's legs

ноготк|и́, о́в m. pl. (common *or* pot) marigold (*genus Calendula*)

но́г|оть, тя, pl. ~ти, ~те́й m. (finger/toe)nail

нож, а́ m. knife; **перочи́нный н.** penknife; **садо́вый н.** pruning knife; **н. в спи́ну** (*fig.*)

stab in the back

но́жик, а m. (small) knife

но́жк|а, и *f.* **1** *dim. of* ▶ **нога́**; **подста́вить ~у** (+ *d.*) to trip up **2** (*мебели, утвари*) leg; (*рюмки*) stem **3** (*bot.*) stalk; (*гриба*) stem

но́жниц|ы, ~ pl. **1** scissors, pair of scissors; (*большие*) shears **2** (*econ., расхожде́ние*) discrepancy

ножно́й *adj. of* ▶ **нога́**; **н. то́рмоз** foot brake

но́ж|ны, ~ен, ~нам *pl.* sheath; scabbard

ножо́вк|а, и *f.* hacksaw

ноздр|я́, и́, pl. ~и, ~е́й *f.* nostril

ноль|ь, я́ m. = **нуль**

✓ но́мер, а, g. ~а m. **1** (*телефона, машины, дома*) number; (*газеты, журнала*) number, issue **2** (*размер*) size **3** (*в гости́нице*) room **4** (*конце́рта*) item on the programme (BrE); program (AmE); number, turn; **со́льный н.** solo (number)

номеро́к, ка́ m. (*в гардеробе*) ticket

номина́льн|ый *adj.* nominal; **~ая цена́** face value

номина́нт, а m. nominee

номина́нт|ка, ки *f. of* ▶ **номина́нт**

номина́ци|я, и *f.* nomination

номини́р|овать, ую *impf. and pf.* to nominate

нор|а́, ы́, pl. ~ы, ~, ~а́м *f.* (*зайца*) burrow, hole; (*лисы*) lair

Норве́ги|я, и *f.* Norway

норве́ж|ец, ца m. Norwegian

норве́ж|ка, ки *f. of* ▶ **норве́жец**

норве́жский *adj.* Norwegian

но́рк|а, и *f.* mink

✓ но́рм|а, ы *f.* **1** (*поведения*) standard, norm **2** (*величина*) rate; **н. вы́работки** rate of output

норма́льно *as pred.* (*infml*) it is all right, fine, OK

✓ норма́льн|ый, ~ен, ~ьна *adj.* normal

норма́тивн|ый, ~ен, ~на *adj.* standard

нос, а, o ~e, в/на ~у́, pl. ~ы́ m. **1** nose; **оста́ться с ~ом** (*infml*) to be duped, be left looking a fool; **сова́ть н. не в своё де́ло** (*infml*) to poke one's nose into other people's affairs **2** (*птицы*) beak **3** (*naut.*) bow, head; prow

носа́т|ый, ~, ~а *adj.* big-nosed

но́сик, а m. (*чайника*) spout

носи́л|ки, ок (*no sg.*) stretcher

носи́льщик, а m. porter

носи́тел|ь, я m. **1** (*fig., идей*) bearer; repository **2** (*инфекции, гриппа*) carrier

✓ но|си́ть, шу́, ~сишь *impf.* **1** *indet. of* ▶ **нести́**[1] **2** (*indet. only*) (*вещи; ребёнка*) to carry; (*большу́ю тя́жесть*) to bear (*also fig.*); **н. свою́ де́вичью фами́лию** to use one's maiden name **3** (*indet. only*) (*одежду, украшения*) to wear **4** (*indet. only*) (*характер*) to have (*a certain character*); to be of (*a certain nature*)

но|си́ться, шу́сь, ~сишься *impf.* **1** *indet. of* ▶ **нести́сь**; **э́то ~сится в во́здухе** (*fig.*)

it is in the air, it is rumoured (BrE), rumored (AmE) **2** (*c + i.*) (*с человеком*) to make a fuss (of); **н. с мы́слью** to be obsessed with an idea **3** *intr.* (*одежда*) to wear; **э́та матéрия хорошó ~сится** this material wears well

носовóй *adj. of ▶* **нос**; **н. платóк** (pocket) handkerchief

нос|óк¹, кá *m.* (*ботинка, чулка*) toe

нос|óк², кá, *pl.* **~ки́, ~кóв** *or* **~óк** *m.* (*чулок*) sock

носорóг, а *m.* rhinoceros

ностальги́|я, и *f.* homesickness; (*о прошлом*) nostalgia

нóт|а¹, ы *f.* (mus.) **1** note **2** (*in pl.*) (*текст*) (sheet) music; **игра́ть по ~ам (без нот)** to play from music (without music)

нóт|а², ы *f.* (diplomatic) note

нота́риус, а *m.* notary

ноутбу́к, а *m.* notebook (computer)

нóу-ха́у *nt. indecl.* know-how

ноч|ева́ть, у́ю *impf.* (*of ▶* **переночева́ть**) to spend, pass the night

ночни́к, а́ *m.* night light

ночн|óй *adj.* night; **н. пóезд** overnight train; **~а́я руба́шка** (*мужская*) nightshirt; (*женская*) nightdress

✎ **ночь, и, о ~и, в ~й,** *pl.* **~и, ~éй** *f.* night; **споко́йной ~и!** goodnight!; **по ~а́м** by night, at night

нóчью *adv.* by night

нóш|а, и *f.* burden

нóшеный *adj.* second-hand

нó|ю, ешь *see ▶* **ныть**

✎ **ноя́бр|ь, я́** *m.* November

ноя́брьский *adj. of ▶* **ноя́брь**

нрав, а *m.* **1** (*характер*) disposition, temper; **быть (+ d.) по ~у** to please **2** (*in pl.*) (*обычаи*) customs, ways

✎ **нра́в|иться, люсь, ишься** *impf.* (*of ▶* **понра́виться**) (*+ d.*) to please; **мне, ему́** *и m. п.* **~ится** I like, he likes, *etc.*; **мне óчень ~ится э́та пьéса** I like this play very much; (*impers.*) **ей не ~ится ката́ться на лóдке** she does not like going in boats

нра́вственность, и *f.* morality; morals

нра́вствен|ный, ~, ~на *adj.* moral

✎ **ну** *int. and particle* (infml) **1** well!; well ... then!; come on!; **ну, ну!** come, come!; come now! **2**: **да ну!** really?; you don't say (so)! **3** (*выражает удивление, восхищение, негодование, иронию*) well; what; why; **ну и...!** what (a) ...!; here's ... (for you)!; there's ... (for you)!; **ну вот и..!** there you are,

you see ...! **4** (*выражает согласие, уступку, примирение, облегчение*) well; **ну вот** (*в повествовании*) well, well then; **ну что ж, ну так** well then; **ну хорошó** all right then

нуди́ст, а *m.* nudist, naturist

нуди́ст|ка, ки *f. of ▶* **нуди́ст**

ну́д|ный, ~ен, ~на́, ~но, ~ны́ *adj.* (infml) tedious

нужд|а́, ы́, *pl.* **~ы** *f.* **1** (*sg. only*) (*бедность*) want, poverty **2** (*необходимость*) need; necessity

✎ **нужда́|ться, юсь** *impf.* **1** (*жить в бедности*) to be in want; to be needy, hard up **2** (*в + p.*) to need, require; to be in need (of)

✎ **ну́жно** (*+ d.*) **1** (*impers.; + inf. or + чтобы*) it is necessary; (one) ought; (one) should, (one) must, (one) need(s); **н. бы́ло (бы) взять такси́** you should have taken a taxi; **н., чтóбы она́ реши́лась** she ought to make up her mind **2** (*impers., + a. or g.*) (infml) I need, *etc.*; **мне н. пять рублéй** I need five roubles **3** *see ▶* **ну́жный**

✎ **ну́ж|ный, ~ен, ~на́, ~но, ~ны́** *adj.* necessary; requisite; (*pred. forms + d.*) I need, *etc.*; **что вам ~но?** what do you need?, what do you want?

ну́-ка *int.* (infml) now then!; come on!

нулевóй *adj. of ▶* **нуль**; (math.) zero; **н. вариа́нт** (pol.) zero option

нул|ь, я́ *m.* nought; (*о температуре*) zero; (*в играх*) nil

ны́не *adv.* now, currently, at present

✎ **ны́нешний** *adj.* (infml) present; present-day; **н. президéнт** the incumbent president

ны́нче *adv.* (infml) **1** (*сегодня*) today **2** (*теперь*) nowadays

нырн|у́ть, у́, нёшь *pf. of ▶* **ныря́ть**

ныря́льщик, а *m.* diver

ныря́льщи|ца, цы *f. of ▶* **ныря́льщик**

ныр|я́ть, я́ю *impf.* (*of ▶* **нырну́ть**) to dive

ныть, нóю, нóешь *impf.* **1** (*болеть*) to ache **2** (infml, *жаловаться*) to moan

Нью-Йóрк, а *m.* New York

н. э. (*abbr. of* **на́шей э́ры**) AD; **до н. э.** (*abbr. of* **до на́шей э́ры**) BC

нюа́нс, а *m.* nuance

нюх, а *m.* scent; (fig.) (*на + a.*) a nose (for)

ню́ха|ть, ю *impf.* (*of ▶* **поню́хать**) (*цветок*) to smell; (*воздух; наркотик*) to sniff

ня́нч|ить, у, ишь *impf.* to look after, mind

ня́н|я, и *f.* **1** nanny; childminder; **приходя́щая н.** babysitter **2** (infml, *в больнице*) auxiliary nurse

Oo

о, об, обо *prep.* **1** (+ *p.*) (*указывает на предмет речи, мысли*) of, about, concerning; on; **о чём вы ду́маете?** what are you thinking about? **2** (+ *a.*) (*указывает на соприкосновение, столкновение*) against; on, upon; over; **опере́ться о сте́ну** to lean against the wall; **споткну́ться о ка́мень** to stumble on, over a stone; **бок о бок** side by side; **рука́ об руку** hand in hand

оа́зис, а *m.* oasis (also fig.)

об *prep. see* ▶ о

о́ба, *m. and nt.* обо́их, *f.* о́бе, обе́их *num.* both; **обе́ими рука́ми** (fig., infml) zealously; very willingly, readily

обанкро́|титься, чусь, тишься *pf.* to go bankrupt

обая́ни|е, я *nt.* fascination, charm

обая́тел|ьный, ~ен, ~ьна *adj.* fascinating, charming

обва́л, а *m.* (*стены*) collapse; caving-in; (*камней*) rockfall; (*снежный*) avalanche; (econ.) collapse, dive

обва́лива|ться, ется *impf. of* ▶ обвали́ться

обвал|и́ться, ~ится *pf.* (*of* ▶ обва́ливаться) to fall, collapse, cave in

обве|ду́, дёшь *see* ▶ обвести́

обвенча́|ть, ю *pf. of* ▶ венча́ть

обвенча́|ться, юсь *pf. of* ▶ венча́ться

обве|сти́, ду́, дёшь, *past* ~л, ~ла́ *pf.* (*of* ▶ обводи́ть) **1** (*провести вокруг*) to lead round, take round; **о. вокру́г па́льца** (fig., infml) to twist round one's little finger **2** (*очертить*) to outline; **о. чертёж ту́шью** to outline a sketch in ink

обве́тренный *adj.* (*скалы, лицо*) weather-beaten; (*губы*) chapped

обветша́|ть, ю *pf. of* ▶ ветша́ть

обвива́|ть, ю *impf. of* ▶ обви́ть

обвива́|ться, юсь *impf. of* ▶ обви́ться

обвине́ни|е, я *nt.* **1** charge, accusation; **по ~ю** (в + *p.*) on a charge (of) **2** (law) (collect.) the prosecution

обвини́тел|ь, я *m.* accuser; (law) prosecutor

обвини́тельный *adj.*: **о. пригово́р** verdict of 'guilty'

обвин|и́ть, ю́, и́шь *pf.* (*of* ▶ обвиня́ть) **1** (в + *p.*) to accuse (of), charge (with) **2** (law) to prosecute, indict

обвиня́ем|ый, ого *m.* (law) the accused; defendant

обвин|я́ть, я́ю *impf. of* ▶ обвини́ть

обви́|ть, обовью́, обовьёшь, *past* ~л, ~ла́, ~ло *pf.* (*of* ▶ обвива́ть) to wind (round), entwine; **о. ше́ю рука́ми** to throw one's arms round sb's neck

обви́|ться, обовью́сь, обовьёшься, *past* ~лся, ~ла́сь *pf.* (*of* ▶ обвива́ться) to wind round, twine round

обво|ди́ть, жу́, ~дишь *impf. of* ▶ обвести́

обволакива|ть, ю *impf. of* ▶ обволо́чь

обволо́|чь, ку́, чёшь, ку́т, ~к, ~кла́ *pf.* (*of* ▶ обволакивать) to cover; to envelop (also fig.)

обвор|ова́ть, у́ю *pf.* (*of* ▶ обворо́вывать) (infml) to rob

обворо́выва|ть, ю *impf. of* ▶ обворова́ть

обворожи́тел|ьный, ~ен, ~ьна *adj.* fascinating, charming, enchanting

обвя|за́ться, жу́сь, ~жешься *pf.* (*of* ▶ обвя́зываться) (+ *i.*) to tie round oneself; **о. верёвкой** to tie a rope round oneself

обвя́зыва|ться, юсь *impf. of* ▶ обвяза́ться

обгла́дыва|ть, ю *impf. of* ▶ обглода́ть

обгло|да́ть, жу́, ~жешь *pf.* (*of* ▶ обгла́дывать) to pick, gnaw round

обгова́рива|ть, ю *impf. of* ▶ обговори́ть

обговор|и́ть, ю́, и́шь *pf.* (*of* ▶ обгова́ривать) (infml) to discuss

обго́н, а *m.* passing, overtaking

обгон|ю́, ~ишь *see* ▶ обогна́ть

обгоня́|ть, ю *impf. of* ▶ обогна́ть

обгора́|ть, а́ю *impf. of* ▶ обгоре́ть

обгор|е́ть, ю́, и́шь *pf.* (*of* ▶ обгора́ть) to be burnt; (*на со́лнце*) to get burnt

обда|ва́ть, ю́, ёшь *impf. of* ▶ обда́ть

обда́|ть, а́м, а́шь, а́ст, ади́м, ади́те, аду́т, *past* ~ал, ~ала́, ~ало *pf.* (*of* ▶ обдава́ть) (+ *i.*) **1** to pour over; **о. кого́-н. кипятко́м** to pour boiling water over sb **2** (fig.) to seize, cover; **меня́ ~ало хо́лодом** (*impers.*) I came over cold

обде́л|ать, аю *pf.* (*of* ▶ обде́лывать) (infml) **1** to finish; to dress (*leather, stone, etc.*); **о. драгоце́нные ка́мни** to set precious stones **2** (fig.) to manage, arrange; **о. свои́ дели́шки** to manage one's affairs with profit

обдел|и́ть, ю́, ~ишь *pf.* (*of* ▶ обделя́ть) (+ *a. and i.*) to do out of one's (fair) share (of); **он ~и́л сестёр насле́дством** he did his sisters out of their share of the legacy

обде́лыва|ть, ю *impf. of* ▶ обде́лать

обдел|я́ть, я́ю *impf. of* ▶ обдели́ть

обдер|у́, ёшь *see* ▶ ободра́ть

обдира́|ть, ю *impf. of* ▶ ободра́ть

обду́ман|ный **1** (~, ~а) *p.p.p. of* ▶ обду́мать **2** (~, ~на) *adj.* well considered, carefully thought out

о

обду́м|ать, аю *pf.* (*of* ▶ **обду́мывать**) to consider, think over

обду́мыва|ть, ю *impf. of* ▶ **обду́мать**

о́бе *see* ▶ **о́ба**

обега́|ть, ю *impf. of* ▶ **обежа́ть**

обе́|д, а *m.* **1** lunch, dinner **2** (*время*) lunchtime, dinner time (= *midday*); **пе́ред ~ом** before lunch, dinner; in the morning; **по́сле ~а** after lunch, dinner; in the afternoon

обе́да|ть, ю *impf.* (*of* ▶ **пообе́дать**) to have lunch, dinner

обе́д|енный *adj. of* ▶ **обе́д**; **~енное вре́мя** lunch, dinner time; **о. переры́в** lunch hour, lunch break; **о. стол** dinner table

обе|жа́ть, гу́, жи́шь, гу́т *pf.* (*of* ▶ **обега́ть**) to run round

обезбо́ливани|е, я *nt.* anaesthetization (BrE), anesthetization (AmE)

обезбо́лива|ть, ю *impf. of* ▶ **обезбо́лить**

обезбо́лива|ющий *pres. part. act. of* ▶ **обезбо́ливать**; **~ющее сре́дство** anaesthetic (BrE), anesthetic (AmE)

обезбо́л|ить, ю, ишь *pf.* (*of* ▶ **обезбо́ливать**) to anaesthetize (BrE), anesthetize (AmE)

обезво́жен|ный, ~, ~а *adj.* dehydrated

обезвре́|дить, жу, дишь *pf.* (*of* ▶ **обезвре́живать**) (*человека*) to render harmless; (*бомбу*) to defuse; (*мину*) to deactivate

обезвре́жива|ть, ю *impf. of* ▶ **обезвре́дить**

обезгла́в|ить, лю, ишь *pf.* (*of* ▶ **обезгла́вливать**) **1** to behead, decapitate **2** (fig., *лишить главы*) to deprive of a head, of a leader

обезгла́влива|ть, ю *impf. of* ▶ **обезгла́вить**

обездо́лен|ный, ~, ~а *adj.* unfortunate, hapless

обезжи́ренный *adj.* fat-free; skimmed

обезопа́|сить, шу, сишь *pf.* (**от** + *g.*) to protect (against)

обезопа́|ситься, шусь, сишься *pf.* (**от** + *g.*) to secure oneself, protect oneself (against)

обезору́жива|ть, ю *impf. of* ▶ **обезору́жить**

обезору́ж|ить, у, ишь *pf.* (*of* ▶ **обезору́живать**) to disarm (also fig.)

обезу́ме|ть, ю *pf.* to lose one's senses, lose one's head; **о. от испу́га** to become panic-stricken

обезья́н|а, ы *f.* monkey; (*бесхвостая*) ape

обели́ск, а *m.* obelisk

оберега́|ться, юсь *impf. of* ▶ **обере́чься**

обере́|чься, гу́сь, жёшься, гу́тся, *past* **~гся, ~гла́сь** *pf.* (*of* ▶ **обере́чься**) (**от** + *g.*) to guard oneself (from, against), protect oneself (from)

оберн|у́ть, у́, ёшь *pf.* (*of* ▶ **обора́чивать**) **1** (*шарф вокруг шеи*) to wind (round), twist (round) **2** (*посылку*) to wrap up

оберн|у́ться, у́сь, ёшься *pf.* (*of* ▶ **обора́чиваться**) **1** (*повернуться*) to turn; **о. лицо́м** to turn one's head **2** (*о делах*) to turn out; **собы́тия ~у́лись ина́че, чем мы ожида́ли** events turned out otherwise than we expected **3** (infml, *сходить, съездить туда и обратно*) to (go and) come back; **я ~у́сь за два часа́** I shall be back in two hours

обёртк|а, и *f.* wrapper; (*книги*) dust jacket, dust cover

⚘ **обеспе́чени|е, я** *nt.* **1** (*мира, успеха*) securing, guaranteeing; ensuring **2** (+ *i.*) (*углём*) providing (with), provision (of, with), supplying (of, with) **3** (*гарантия*) guarantee; security (= *pledge*) **4** (*материальные средства к жизни*) security; safeguard(s); **социа́льное о.** social security **5** (comput.): **аппара́тное о.** hardware; **програ́ммное о.** software

обеспе́ч|енный, ~ен, ~ена *p.p.p. of* ▶ **обеспе́чить** *and* (**~, ~на**) *adj.* well-to-do; well provided for

⚘ **обеспе́чива|ть, ю** *impf. of* ▶ **обеспе́чить**

обеспе́ч|ить, у, ишь *pf.* (*of* ▶ **обеспе́чивать**) **1** (*семью; старость*) to provide for **2** (+ *i.*) (*снабдить чем-н.*) to provide (with), guarantee supply (of) **3** (*успех*) to secure, guarantee; to ensure

обеспоко́енный *adj.* worried, concerned

обесси́ле|ть, ю *pf.* to grow weak, lose one's strength

обесси́лива|ть, ю *impf. of* ▶ **обесси́лить**

обесси́л|ить, ю, ишь *pf.* (*of* ▶ **обесси́ливать**) to weaken

обесце́ненный *p.p.p. of* ▶ **обесце́нить** *and adj.* depreciated

обесце́нива|ть, ю, ет *impf. of* ▶ **обесце́нить**

обесце́нива|ться, ется *impf. of* ▶ **обесце́ниться**

обесце́н|ить, ю, ишь *pf.* (*of* ▶ **обесце́нивать**) to depreciate, cheapen

обесце́н|иться, ится *pf.* (*of* ▶ **обесце́ниваться**) to depreciate

обеща́ни|е, я *nt.* promise; **дать, сдержа́ть, нару́шить о.** to give, keep, break a promise (*or* one's word)

⚘ **обеща́|ть, ю** *impf. and pf.* (*pf. also* ▶ **пообеща́ть**) to promise

обжа́л|овать, ую (law) to appeal (against)

обжа́рива|ть, ю *impf. of* ▶ **обжа́рить**

обжа́р|ить, ю, ишь *pf.* (*of* ▶ **обжа́ривать**) (cul.) to fry on both sides, to brown all over

обже́чь, обожгу́, обожжёшь, обожгу́т, *past* **обжёг, обожгла́** *pf.* (*of* ▶ **обжига́ть**) **1** to burn, scorch; **о. себе́ па́льцы** to burn one's fingers (also fig.) **2** (*кирпич*) to fire, bake **3** (*о крапиве*) to sting

обже́чься, обожгу́сь, обожжёшься, обожгу́тся, *past* **обжёгся, обожгла́сь** *pf.* (*of* ▶ **обжига́ться**) (+ *i.* *or* **на** + *p.*) to burn oneself (on, with); **о. горя́чим ча́ем** to scald oneself with hot tea

обжига́|ть, ю *impf. of* ▶ **обже́чь**

⚘ key word

обжига́|ться, юсь *impf. of* ▶ обже́чься

обжо́р|а, ы *c.g.* (infml) glutton

обжо́рств|о, а *nt.* gluttony

обзаве|сти́сь, ду́сь, дёшься, *past* ~лся, ~ла́сь *pf.* (*of* ▶ обзаводи́ться) (+ *i.*) (infml) to get oneself; to set up; **о. семьёй** to start a family; **о. хозя́йством** to set up home

обзаво|ди́ться, жу́сь, ~дишься *impf. of* ▶ обзавести́сь

обзо́р, а *m.* **1** (*сжатое сообщение*) survey, review, overview **2** (mil.) field of view

обзо́р|ный *adj.* giving an overall view; ~ная ле́кция, ~ная статья́ survey

обзыва́|ть, ю *impf. of* ▶ обозва́ть

обива́|ть, ю *impf. of* ▶ оби́ть

оби́вк|а, и *f.* upholstery

оби́д|а, ы *f.* insult; (*чувство*) offence, (sense of) grievance, resentment; **зата́ить** ~у to nurse a grievance; **не дава́ть себя́ в** ~у to (be able to) stick up for oneself

оби́|деть, жу, дишь *pf.* (*of* ▶ обижа́ть) **1** to offend; to hurt (the feelings of), wound **2** (*причинить ущерб*) to hurt; to do damage (to); **му́хи не** ~дит (fig.) he would not harm a fly **3** (+ *i.*) (*наделить чем-л. недостаточно*) to stint, begrudge; **приро́да не** ~дела его́ тала́нтом he has plenty of natural ability

оби́|деться, жусь, дишься *pf.* (*of* ▶ обижа́ться) (на + *a.*) to take offence (at); to feel hurt (by), resent

оби́д|ный, ~ен, ~на *adj.* **1** offensive; **мне** ~но I feel hurt, it pains me **2** (*досадный*) annoying; ~но (*impers.*) it is a pity, it is a nuisance; ~но, что мы опозда́ли it is a pity that we are late

оби́дчив|ый, ~, ~а *adj.* touchy, sensitive

оби́дчик, а *m.* offender

обижа́|ть, ю *impf. of* ▶ оби́деть

обижа́|ться, юсь *impf.* (*of* ▶ оби́деться): **не** ~йтесь don't be offended

оби́|женный *p.p.p of* ▶ оби́деть *and adj.* offended, aggrieved; **быть** ~женным (на + *a.*) to have a grudge (against); **о. Бо́гом, о. приро́дой** (joc.) not over-blessed (with talents); ill-starred

оби́ли|е, я *nt.* abundance, plenty

оби́л|ьный, ~ен, ~ьна *adj.* abundant, plentiful; (+ *i.*) rich (in); ~ьное угоще́ние lavish entertainment

обира́|ть, ю *impf. of* ▶ обобра́ть

обита́ем|ый, ~, ~а *adj.* inhabited

обита́тел|ь, я *m.* inhabitant

обита́|ть, ю *impf.* (в + *p.*) to live (in)

оби́|ть, обобью́, обобьёшь *pf.* (*of* ▶ обива́ть) (+ *i.*) to cover (with); **о. гвоздя́ми** to stud; **о. желе́зом** to bind with iron

обихо́д, а *m.* (*употребление*) use; **войти́ в о.** to come into (general) use; **вы́йти из** ~а to go out of use, fall into disuse

обихо́д|ный, ~ен, ~на *adj.* everyday; ~ное выраже́ние colloquial expression

обкла́дыва|ть, ю *impf. of* ▶ обложи́ть 1, ▶ обложи́ть 2, ▶ обложи́ть 3

обкра́дыва|ть, ю *impf. of* ▶ обокра́сть

обку́рен|ный, ~, ~ная *adj.* (sl.) stoned (*from smoking marijuana, etc.*)

обла́в|а, ы *f.* (*на преступников*) raid; round-up

облага́|ть, ю *impf. of* ▶ обложи́ть 4

облада́тел|ь, я *m.* possessor

⚡ **облада́|ть, ю** *impf.* (+ *i.*) to possess, have; **о. пра́вом** to have the right

о́блак|о, а, *pl.* ~а́, ~о́в *nt.* cloud; **вита́ть в** ~а́х (fig.) to live in the clouds

обла́мыва|ть, ю *impf. of* ▶ обломи́ть

обла́мыва|ться, юсь *impf. of* ▶ обломи́ться

⚡ **областно́й** *adj.* regional

⚡ **о́бласт|ь, и,** *g. pl.* ~е́й *f.* **1** (*административная единица*) oblast; province **2** (*часть страны*) region, district; belt **3** (fig., *отрасль*) field, sphere, realm, domain

о́блачность, и *nf.* cloudiness; **переме́нная о.** overcast with sunny periods

о́блач|ный, ~ен, ~на *adj.* cloudy

облега́|ть, ю *impf.* (*об одежде*) to fit tightly; to cling to

облега́ющий *adj.* tight-fitting

облегч|а́ть, а́ю *impf. of* ▶ облегчи́ть

облегч|а́ться, а́юсь *impf. of* ▶ облегчи́ться

облегче́ни|е, я *nt.* **1** (*действие*) facilitation, lightening, easing **2** (*чувство успокоения*) relief; **вздохну́ть с** ~ем to heave a sigh of relief

облегч|и́ть, у́, и́шь *pf.* (*of* ▶ облегча́ть) **1** (*груз, вес*) to lighten **2** (*сделать менее трудным*) to make easier **3** (*упростить*) to simplify

облегч|и́ться, у́сь, и́шься *pf.* (*of* ▶ облегча́ться) (*стать более лёгким*) to become easier; (*impers.*) to become lighter

обледене́|ть, ю *pf.* to ice over, become covered with ice

обле́зл|ый, ~, ~а *adj.* (infml) shabby, bare; ~ая ко́шка mangy cat

обле́нива|ться, юсь *impf. of* ▶ облени́ться

облен|и́ться, ю́сь, ~ишься *pf.* (*of* ▶ обле́ниваться) to grow lazy

облеп|и́ть, лю́, ~ишь *pf.* (*of* ▶ облепля́ть) **1** (*прилипнуть*) to stick (to); (fig.) to cling (to); (*окружить*) to surround, throng; **нас** ~и́ла ку́ча мальчи́шек we were surrounded by a swarm of small boys **2** (+ *a. and i.*) (*заклеить*) to paste all over (with), plaster (with)

облепля́|ть, ю *impf. of* ▶ облепи́ть

облет|а́ть, а́ю *impf. of* ▶ облете́ть

обле|те́ть, чу́, ти́шь *pf.* (*of* ▶ облета́ть) **1** (+ *a. or* вокру́г + *g.*) to fly (round) **2** (*о новостях*) to spread (round, all over); **за полчаса́ весть о побе́де** ~те́ла весь го́род in half an hour the news of the victory had spread round the town **3** (*о листьях*) to fall

облива́|ть, ю *impf. of* ▶ обли́ть

облива́|ться, юсь *impf.* (*of* ▶ обли́ться): **се́рдце у меня́ кро́вью** ~ется my heart bleeds

облига́ци|я, и *f.* (fin.) bond, debenture

обли|за́ть, жу́, ~жешь *pf.* (*of* ► **обли́зывать**) to lick (all over); to lick clean

обли|за́ться, жу́сь, ~жешься *pf.* (*of* ► **обли́зываться**) **1** (*о челове́ке*) to smack one's lips (also fig.) **2** (*о живо́тном*) to lick itself

обли́зыва|ть, ю *impf.* (*of* ► **облиза́ть**): **о. гу́бы** (*fig.*, *infml*) to smack one's lips

обли́зыва|ться, юсь *impf. of* ► **облиза́ться**

о́блик, а *m.* look, appearance

обл|и́ть, оболью́, обольёшь, *past* **~ил, ~ила́, ~ило** *and* **~йл, ~ила́, ~йло** *pf.* (*of* ► **облива́ть**) (*наме́ренно*) to pour (over); (*случа́йно*) to spill (over); **о. гря́зью** (*fig.*, *infml*) to vilify

обли́|ться, оболью́сь, обольёшься, *past* **~лся, ~ла́сь, ~ло́сь** *pf.* (*of* ► **облива́ться**) (+ *i.*) **1** to have a shower; to sponge down; **о. холо́дной водо́й** to have a cold shower **2** (*случа́йно*) to spill over oneself

облицо́вк|а, и *f.* facing, cladding

облич|а́ть, а́ю *impf.* (*of* ► **обличи́ть**) **1** (*разобла́чать*) to expose, unmask, denounce **2** (*impf. only*) (*пока́зывать*) to reveal, display, manifest; to point (to)

облич|и́ть, у́, и́шь *pf. of* ► **облича́ть**

обло|жи́ть, у́, ~жишь *pf.* **1** (*impf.* **обкла́дывать**) (*положи́ть вокру́г*) to put (round); to edge; **о. больно́го поду́шками** to surround a patient with pillows **2** (*impf.* **обкла́дывать**) (*покры́ть*) to cover **3** (*impf.* **обкла́дывать**) (*окружи́ть*) to surround **4** (*impf.* **облага́ть**) to assess; **о. нало́гом** to tax

обло́жк|а, и *f.* (dust) cover; (*для бума́г*) folder

облока́чива|ться, юсь *impf. of* ► **облокоти́ться**

облоко|ти́ться, чу́сь, ти́шься *pf.* (*of* ► **облока́чиваться**) (на + *a.*) to lean one's elbow(s) (on, against)

обло́м, а *m.* **1** (*де́йствие*) breaking off **2** (*ме́сто*) break **3** (*sl.*, *неуда́ча*) failure, misfortune

облома́|ть, ю *pf.* (*of* ► **обла́мывать**) to break off, snap

облома́|ться, юсь *pf.* (*of* ► **обла́мываться**) **1** (*ве́тка*) to break off, snap **2** (*sl.*) to fail

облом|и́ть, лю́, ~ишь *pf.* to break off

облом|и́ться, лю́сь, ~ишься *pf.* = **облома́ться**

обло́м|ок, ка *m.* **1** fragment **2** (*in pl.*) debris, wreckage

облуче́ни|е, я *nt.* (med.) irradiation

облысе́|ть, ю, ешь *pf. of* ► **лысе́ть**

облюб|ова́ть, у́ю *pf.* (*of* ► **облюбо́вывать**) to pick, choose

облюбо́выва|ть, ю *impf. of* ► **облюбова́ть**

обма́|зать, жу, жешь *pf.* (*of* ► **обма́зывать**) to coat (with)

обма́зыва|ть, ю *impf. of* ► **обма́зать**

обма́кива|ть, ю *impf. of* ► **обмакну́ть**

обмак|ну́ть, ну́, нёшь, *past* **~ну́л** *pf.* (*of* ► **обма́кивать**) to dip

обма́н, а *m.* fraud, deception; **о. зре́ния** optical illusion

обман|у́ть, у́, ~ешь *pf.* (*of* ► **обма́нывать**) to deceive; (*моше́ннически*) to cheat, swindle; (*нару́шить обеща́ние*) to fail; to let sb down; **о. чьи-н. наде́жды** to disappoint sb's hopes

обман|у́ться, у́сь, ~ешься *pf.* (*of* ► **обма́нываться**) to be deceived; **о. в свои́х ожида́ниях** to be disappointed in one's expectations

обма́нчив|ый, ~, ~а *adj.* deceptive, delusive; **вне́шность ~а** appearances are deceptive

обма́нщик, а *m.* deceiver; cheat, fraud

обма́нщи|ца, цы *f. of* ► **обма́нщик**

обма́ныва|ть, ю *impf. of* ► **обману́ть**

обма́ныва|ться, юсь *impf. of* ► **обману́ться**

обма́тыва|ть, ю *impf. of* ► **обмота́ть**

обма́тыва|ться, юсь *impf. of* ► **обмота́ться**

⚲ обме́н, а *m.* (+ *i.*) exchange (of); **о. мне́ниями** exchange of opinions; **о. веще́ств** (biol.) metabolism; **в о.** (**на** + *a.*) in exchange (for)

обме́нива|ть, ю *impf. of* ► **обменя́ть**

обме́нива|ться, юсь *impf. of* ► **обменя́ться**

обме́нный *adj. of* ► **обме́н**

обмен|я́ть, я́ю *pf.* (*of* ► **меня́ть 2,** ► **обме́нивать**) (+ *a. and* **на** + *a.*) to exchange (sth for sth)

обмен|я́ться, я́юсь *pf.* (*of* ► **меня́ться 2,** ► **обме́ниваться**) (+ *i.*) to exchange; to swap; **о. впечатле́ниями** to compare notes

обме́рива|ть, ю *impf. of* ► **обме́рить**

обме́р|ить, ю, ишь *pf.* (*of* ► **обме́ривать**) (*изме́рить*) to measure

обмо́лв|иться, люсь, ишься *pf.* (infml) **1** (*оговори́ться*) to make a slip in speaking **2** (+ *i.*) (*сказа́ть*) to say; to utter; **не о. ни сло́вом** (**о** + *p.*) to say not a word (about)

обмороже́ни|е, я *nt.* frostbite

обморо́|зить, жу, зишь *pf.*: **я ~зил себе́ нос, ру́ки** my nose is, hands are, frostbitten

о́бморок, а *m.* fainting fit; **упа́сть в о.** to faint

обмота́|ть, ю *pf.* (*of* ► **обма́тывать**) (+ *a. and i.*, *or* + *a.* **вокру́г** + *g.*) to wind (round); **о. ше́ю ша́рфом** to wind a scarf round one's neck

обмота́|ться, юсь *pf.* (*of* ► **обма́тываться**) **1** (+ *i.*) to wrap oneself (in) **2** *pass. of* ► **обмота́ть**

обмундирова́ни|е, я *nt.* uniform

обнадёжива|ть, ю *impf. of* ► **обнадёжить**

обнадёж|ить, у, ишь *pf.* (*of* ► **обнадёживать**) to reassure

обнаж|а́ть, а́ю *impf. of* ► **обнажи́ть**

обнаж|а́ться, а́юсь *impf. of* ► **обнажи́ться**

обнажённый *p.p.p. of* ► **обнажи́ть** *and adj.* naked, bare; nude

обнаж|и́ть, у́, и́шь *pf.* (*of* ► **обнажа́ть**) **1** to bare, uncover; **о. го́лову** to bare one's head; **о. шпа́гу** to draw the sword **2** (*fig.,* *раскры́ть*) to lay bare, reveal

обнаж|и́ться, у́сь, и́шься *pf.* (*of* ▶ **обнажа́ться**) **1** to bare oneself, uncover oneself **2** (fig., *стать я́вным*) to be revealed

обнаро́д|овать, ую *impf. and pf.* (liter.) to publish, promulgate (*esp. official documents*)

обнаруже́ни|е, я *nt.* **1** displaying, revealing **2** discovery; detection

⌖ **обнару́жива|ть, ю** *impf. of* ▶ **обнару́жить**

обнару́жива|ться, юсь *impf. of* ▶ **обнару́житься**

обнару́ж|ить, у, ишь *pf.* (*of* ▶ **обнару́живать**) **1** (*показа́ть*) to display, reveal; **о. свою́ ра́дость** to betray one's joy **2** (*найти́*) to discover; to detect

обнару́ж|иться, усь, ишься *pf.* (*of* ▶ **обнару́живаться**) **1** (*оказа́ться*) to be revealed; to come to light **2** (*найти́сь*) to turn up, be found

обнес|ти́, у́, ёшь, *past* **~, ~ла́** *pf.* (*of* ▶ **обноси́ть**) (+ *i.*) to enclose (with); **о. и́згородью** to fence (in)

обнима́|ть, ю *impf. of* ▶ **обня́ть**

обнима́|ться, юсь *impf. of* ▶ **обня́ться**

обнов|и́ть, лю́, и́шь *pf.* (*of* ▶ **обновля́ть**) **1** (*па́мятник*) to renovate; (*жизнь, ду́шу*) to revitalize; (*го́речь*) to renew; (*гардеро́б, репертуа́р*, also comput.) to update; to replenish **2**: **о. свои́ зна́ния** (fig.) to refresh one's knowledge

обнов|и́ться, лю́сь, и́шься *pf.* (*of* ▶ **обновля́ться**) to revive, be restored

обновле́ни|е, я *nt.* renovation; revitalization; renewal; replenishment; (comput., *of software*) upgrade, update; (*вне́шнее о.*) facelift

обновля́|ть, ю *impf. of* ▶ **обнови́ть**

обновля́|ться, юсь *impf. of* ▶ **обнови́ться**

обно|си́ть, шу́, ~сишь *impf. of* ▶ **обнести́**

обню́х|ать, аю *pf.* (*of* ▶ **обню́хивать**) to sniff (around)

обню́хива|ть, ю *impf. of* ▶ **обню́хать**

обн|я́ть, иму́, и́мешь, *past* **~я́л, ~яла́, ~я́ло** *pf.* (*of* ▶ **обнима́ть**) to embrace; to clasp in one's arms; (fig.) to envelop; **он шёл, ~я́в её за та́лию** he was walking with his arm round her waist

обн|я́ться, иму́сь, и́мешься, *past* **~я́лся, ~яла́сь, ~яло́сь** *pf.* (*of* ▶ **обнима́ться**) to embrace; to hug (one another)

обо *prep.* = **о**

обобра́|ть, оберу́, оберёшь, *past* **~л, ~ла́, ~ло** *pf.* (*of* ▶ **обира́ть**) (infml) to rob, clean out (infml)

обобщ|а́ть, а́ю *impf. of* ▶ **обобщи́ть**

обобще́ни|е, я *nt.* generalization

обобщ|и́ть, у́, и́шь *pf.* (*of* ▶ **обобща́ть**) to generalize (from)

обога|ти́ть, щу́, ти́шь *pf.* (*of* ▶ **обогаща́ть**) to enrich

обога|ти́ться, щу́сь, ти́шься *pf.* (*of* ▶ **обогаща́ться**) to become rich; (+ *i.*) to enrich oneself (with)

обогаща́|ть, ю *impf. of* ▶ **обогати́ть**

обогаща́|ться, юсь *impf. of* ▶ **обогати́ться**

обогаще́ни|е, я *nt.* enrichment

обогна́|ть, обгоню́, обго́нишь, *past* **~л, ~ла́, ~ло** *pf.* (*of* ▶ **обгоня́ть**) to pass, overtake; (fig.) to outstrip, outdistance

обогн|у́ть, у́, ёшь *pf.* (*of* ▶ **огиба́ть**) to round; to skirt

обогрева́тел|ь, я *m.* (tech.) heater

обогрева́|ть, ю *impf. of* ▶ **обогре́ть**

обогрева́|ться, юсь *impf. of* ▶ **обогре́ться**

обогре́|ть, ю, ешь *pf.* (*of* ▶ **обогрева́ть**) (*помеще́ние*) to heat; (*челове́ка*) to warm

обогре́|ться, юсь, ешься *pf.* (*of* ▶ **обогрева́ться**) to warm oneself; (*о помеще́нии*) to warm up

о́бод, а, *pl.* **~ья, ~ьев** *m.* (*колеса́*) rim; (*бо́чки*) hoop

ободра́|ть, обдеру́, обдерёшь, *past* **ободра́л, ободрала́, ободра́ло** *pf.* (*of* ▶ **обдира́ть**) **1** (*сте́ну, пру́тик*) to strip; (*уби́того зве́ря*) to skin; (infml, *лицо́, ру́ку*) to scratch; **о. кору́ с де́рева** to bark a tree **2** (fig., infml) to fleece

ободр|и́ть, ю́, и́шь *pf.* (*of* ▶ **ободря́ть**) to cheer up; to encourage, reassure

ободр|я́ть, я́ю *impf. of* ▶ **ободри́ть**

обожа́|ть, ю *impf.* to adore, worship

обож|гу́, жёшь, гу́т *see* ▶ **обже́чь**

обожжённый *p.p.p. of* ▶ **обже́чь**

обо́з, а *m.* convoy

обозва́|ть, обзову́, обзовёшь, *past* **~л, ~ла́, ~ло** *pf.* (*of* ▶ **обзыва́ть**) (+ *a.* and *i.*) to call; **о. кого́-н. дурако́м** to call sb a fool

обозна|ва́ться, ю́сь, ёшься *impf. of* ▶ **обозна́ться**

обозна́|ться, юсь, ешься *pf.* (*of* ▶ **обознава́ться**) (infml) to take sb for sb else; to be mistaken

обознач|а́ть, а́ю *impf.* **1** (*no pf.*) (*зна́чить*) to mean **2** (*pf.* **~ить**) (*отмеча́ть*) to mark **3** (*pf.* **~ить**) (*де́лать заме́тным*) to reveal; to emphasize

обозначе́ни|е, я *nt.* **1** (*де́йствие*) marking **2** (*знак*) sign, symbol; **усло́вные ~я** conventional signs, legend (*on maps, etc.*)

обозна́ч|ить, у, ишь *pf. of* ▶ **обознача́ть** 3

обозрева́тел|ь, я *m.* commentator; columnist

обозре́ни|е, я *nt.* **1** (*де́йствие*) surveying, viewing; looking round **2** (*обзо́р*) survey; overview

обо́|и, ев (*no sg.*) (also comput.) wallpaper; **окле́ить ~ями** to paper

обо́йм|а, ы, *g. pl.* **~** *f.* (mil.) cartridge clip

обо|йти́, йду́, йдёшь, *past* **~шёл, ~шла́** *pf.* (*of* ▶ **обходи́ть¹**) **1** (*пройти́, окружа́я, минуя́*) to go round **2** (*пройти́ по всему́ простра́нству чего́-л.*) to make the round (of), go (all) round; (*о враче́*) to make one's round(s); **слух ~шёл весь го́род** the rumour spread all over the town **3** (*избежа́ть*) to avoid; to leave out; to pass over; **о. зако́н** to get round (evade) a law

обо|йти́сь, йду́сь, йдёшься, *past* ~шёлся, ~шла́сь *pf.* (*of* ▶ обходи́ться) **1** (с + *i.*) to treat; пло́хо о. с кем-н. to treat sb badly **2** (*infml*) to cost, come to **3** (+ *i.*) to manage (with, on), make do (with, on) **4** (*закончиться*) to turn out, end; всё ~шло́сь everything worked out; всё ~шло́сь благополу́чно everything turned out all right

обокра́|сть, обкраду́, обкрадёшь, *past* ~л, ~ла *pf.* (*of* ▶ обкра́дывать) to rob

обо|лга́ть, лгу́, лжёшь, *past* ~лга́л, ~лгала́, ~лга́ло *pf.* to slander

оболо́чк|а, и *f.* **1** (*скорлупа*) shell; (tech.) casing **2** (anat.) membrane; ра́дужная о. iris

обольсти́|ться, щу́сь, сти́шься *pf.* (*of* ▶ обольща́ться) to be *or* labour (BrE), labor (AmE) under a delusion; (+ *i.*) to flatter oneself (with)

обольща́|ться, юсь *impf. of* ▶ обольсти́ться

обольщ|ю́, ёшь *see* ▶ обли́ть

обоня́ни|е, я *nt.* sense of smell; име́ть то́нкое о. to have a fine sense of smell

обора́чива|ть, ю *impf. of* ▶ оберну́ть

обора́чива|ться, юсь *impf. of* ▶ оберну́ться

оборв|а́ть, у́, ёшь, *past* ~а́л, ~ала́, ~а́ло *pf.* (*of* ▶ обрыва́ть) **1** (*цветы, яблоки*) to tear off, pluck **2** (*нитку*) to break; to snap **3** (fig., *разговор; человека*) to cut short, interrupt

оборв|а́ться, у́сь, ёшься, *past* ~а́лся, ~ала́сь, ~а́лось *pf.* (*of* ▶ обрыва́ться) **1** (*о верёвке*) to break; to snap **2** (*о человеке*) to fall; (*о вещах*) to come away **3** (*о жизни, песне*) to be cut short, come abruptly to an end

обо́рк|а, и *f.* frill, flounce

оборо́н|а, ы (*no pl.*) *f.* defence (BrE), defense (AmE)

оборони́тельный *adj.* defensive

оборон|и́ть, ю́, и́шь *pf.* (*of* ▶ обороня́ть) to defend

оборон|и́ться, ю́сь, и́шься *pf.* (*of* ▶ обороня́ться) (от + *g.*) to defend oneself (from)

оборон|я́ть, я́ю *impf. of* ▶ оборони́ть

оборон|я́ться, я́юсь *impf. of* ▶ оборони́ться

✍ оборо́т, а *m.* **1** turn **2** (*употребление*) circulation; (fin., comm.) turnover; ввести́ в о. to put into circulation **3** (*обратная сторона*) back; смотри́ на ~е please turn over

оборо́т|ень, ня *m.* werewolf

оборо́т|ный *adj. of* ▶ оборо́т; о. капита́л (fin., comm.) working capital; ~ная сторона́ verso; reverse side (also fig.)

✍ обору́довани|е, я *nt.* **1** (*действие*) equipping **2** (*приборы*) equipment

обору́д|овать, ую *impf. and pf.* to equip, fit out

обоснова́ни|е, я *nt.* **1** (*действие*) substantiation **2** (*довод*) basis, ground

обосно́ванный *p.p.p. of* ▶ обоснова́ть *and adj.* well founded, well grounded

обосн|ова́ть, у́ю, у́ешь *pf.* (*of* ▶ обосно́вывать) to substantiate

обосн|ова́ться, у́юсь, у́ешься *pf.* (*of* ▶ обосно́вываться) to settle

обосно́выва|ть, ю *impf. of* ▶ обоснова́ть

обосно́выва|ться, юсь *impf. of* ▶ обоснова́ться

обосо́бленный *adj.* isolated, solitary

обостре́ни|е, я *nt.* **1** (*чувств*) sharpening, intensification **2** (*боли*) aggravation, exacerbation; (*отношений*) straining; (*кризиса, конфликта*) worsening, deepening

обостр|и́ться, ю́сь, и́шься *pf.* (*of* ▶ обостря́ться) **1** (*об ощущениях*) to become more sensitive, become keener **2** (*о боли*) to become aggravated, become exacerbated; (*об отношениях*) to become strained; (*о кризисе, конфликте*) to worsen, deepen

обостр|я́ться, я́юсь *impf. of* ▶ обостри́ться

обо́чин|а, ы *f.* (*дороги*) edge, side; (*тротуара*) kerb (BrE), curb (AmE)

обою́д|ный, ~ен, ~на *adj.* mutual, reciprocal; по ~ному согла́сию by mutual consent

обраба́тыва|ть, ю *impf. of* ▶ обрабо́тать

обрабо́та|ть, ю *pf.* (*of* ▶ обраба́тывать) **1** (*кожу*) to treat, process; о. зе́млю to work the land; о. ра́ну to dress a wound **2** (*статью; голос*) to polish, perfect

✍ обрабо́тк|а, и *f.* **1** (*кожи*) treatment, processing; о. земли́ cultivation of land **2** (*статьи*) polishing

обра́д|овать, ую *pf. of* ▶ ра́довать

обра́д|оваться, уюсь *pf. of* ▶ ра́доваться

✍ о́браз, а *m.* **1** (*вид*) shape, form; appearance **2** (*представление*) image; мы́слить ~ами to think in images **3** (liter., *тип*) type; figure; о. Га́млета the Hamlet type **4** (*порядок*) mode, manner; way; о. жи́зни way of life, lifestyle; каки́м ~ом? how?; таки́м ~ом thus; гла́вным ~ом mainly, chiefly, largely

✍ образе́ц, ца́ *nt.* **1** model, pattern **2** (*товарный*) specimen, sample; (*материи*) pattern

о́браз|ный, ~ен, ~на *adj.* picturesque, vivid; (liter.) figurative; employing images

✍ образова́ни|е¹, я *nt.* (*действие*) formation

✍ образова́ни|е², я *nt.* (*обучение*) education

образо́ванный *p.p.p. of* ▶ образова́ть *and adj.*: о. челове́к educated person

✍ образова́тельный *adj.* educational

образ|ова́ть, у́ю *impf. (in pres. tense), and pf.* (*of* ▶ образо́вывать) to form; to make up

образ|ова́ться, у́ется *pf.* (*of* ▶ образо́вываться) to form; to arise

образо́выва|ть, ю, ет *impf. of* ▶ образова́ть

образо́выва|ться, ется *impf. of* ▶ образова́ться

образцо́вый *adj.* model; exemplary

обраст|а́ть, а́ю *impf. of* ▶ обрасти́

обраст|и́, у́, ёшь, *past* **обро́с, обросла́** *pf. (of* ▸ **обраста́ть)** (+ *i.*) **1** (*покры́ться растительностью*) to become/be overgrown (with) **2** (fig., *созда́ть вокру́г себя́*) to become/be surrounded (by); to acquire, accumulate

обрати́м|ый, ~, ~а *adj.* reversible

обра|ти́ть, щу́, ти́шь *pf. (of* ▸ **обраща́ть)** to turn; **(в** + *a.*) to turn (into); **о. внима́ние (на** + *a.*) to pay attention (to), take notice (of); **о. чьё-н. внима́ние (на** + *a.*) to call, draw sb's attention (to); **о. на себя́ внима́ние** to attract attention (to oneself)

✵ **обра|ти́ться, щу́сь, ти́шься** *pf. (of* ▸ **обраща́ться** 1) **1** (*кого́*) to turn; **о. в бе́гство** to take to flight **2** (**к** + *d.*) to turn (to), appeal (to); to apply (to); to accost; **она́ не зна́ла, к кому́ о. за по́мощью** she did not know to whom to turn for help

обра́тно *adv.* **1** back; **туда́ и о.** there and back; **пое́здка туда́ и о.** round trip **2** (*наоборо́т*) conversely; inversely

✵ **обра́тн|ый** *adj.* **1** reverse; **о. а́дрес** sender's address; **о. биле́т** return (BrE), round trip (AmE) ticket; **о. путь** return journey; **на ~ом пути́** on the way back **2** (*противополо́жный*) opposite; **в ~ую сто́рону** in the opposite direction **3** (math.) inverse; **~ое отноше́ние** inverse ratio

✵ **обраща́|ть, ю** *impf. of* ▸ **обрати́ть**

✵ **обраща́|ться, юсь** *impf.* **1** *impf. of* ▸ **обрати́ться 2** (physiol., econ., etc.) to circulate **3** (**с** + *i.*) to treat; **пло́хо о. с кем-н.** to treat sb badly, maltreat sb **4** (**с** + *i.*) (*по́льзоваться*) to handle, manage (*an inanimate object*)

✵ **обраще́ни|е, я** *nt.* **1** (**к** + *d.*) appeal (to), address (to) **2** (**в** + *a.*) conversion (into) **3** (econ.) circulation **4** (**с** + *i.*) treatment (of); **плохо́е о.** ill-treatment **5** (**с** + *i.*) (*по́льзование*) handling (of), use (of)

обреза́ни|е, я *nt.* (relig.) circumcision

обре́|зать, жу, жешь *pf. (of* ▸ **обреза́ть)** to clip, trim; to cut

обрез|а́ть, а́ю *impf. of* ▸ **обре́зать**

обре́|заться, жусь, жешься *pf. (of* ▸ **обре́заться)** (*порани́ть себя́*) to cut oneself

обрез|а́ться, а́юсь *impf. of* ▸ **обре́заться**

обрека́|ть, ю *impf. of* ▸ **обре́чь**

обре|ку́, чёшь, ку́т *see* ▸ **обре́чь**

обремени́тел|ьный, ~ен, ~ьна *adj.* burdensome, onerous

обречённый *adj.* doomed

обре́|чь, ку́, чёшь, ку́т, *past* **~к, ~кла́** *pf. (of* ▸ **обрека́ть)** (**на** + *a.*) to condemn, doom (to)

обрис|ова́ть, у́ю *pf. (of* ▸ **обрисо́вывать)** to outline, delineate, depict (also fig.)

обрисо́выва|ть, ю *impf. of* ▸ **обрисова́ть**

обр|и́ть, е́ю, е́ешь *pf.* (*го́лову*) to shave; (*усы́*) to shave off

обр|и́ться, е́юсь, е́ешься *pf.* to shave one's head

обруга́|ть, ю *pf. of* ▸ **руга́ть 2,** ▸ **руга́ть 3**

обрусе́|ть, ю *pf.* to become Russified, become Russianized

о́бруч, а, *pl.* **~и, ~е́й** *m.* (*на бо́чке; гимнасти́ческий*) hoop; (*для воло́с*) hairband

обруча́льн|ый *adj.:* **~ое кольцо́** wedding ring

обруч|а́ться, а́юсь *impf. of* ▸ **обручи́ться**

обруч|и́ться, у́сь, и́шься *pf. (of* ▸ **обруча́ться)** (**с** + *i.*) to become engaged (to)

обру́шива|ть, ю *impf. of* ▸ **обру́шить**

обру́шива|ться, юсь *impf. of* ▸ **обру́шиться**

обру́ш|ить, у, ишь *pf. (of* ▸ **обру́шивать)** to bring down, rain down

обру́ш|иться, усь, ишься *pf. (of* ▸ **обру́шиваться)** **1** (*о зда́нии, кры́ше*) to come down, collapse, cave in **2** (fig.) (**на** + *a.*) to come down (upon), fall (upon)

обры́в, а *m.* **1** precipice **2** (tech.) break, rupture

обрыва́|ть, ю *impf. of* ▸ **оборва́ть**

обрыва́|ться, юсь *impf. of* ▸ **оборва́ться**

обры́в|ок, ка *m.* (*бума́ги; разгово́ра*) scrap; (*верёвки*) piece; (*пе́сни, мело́дии*) snatch

обры́зг|ать, аю *pf. (of* ▸ **обры́згивать)** (+ *i.*) (*водо́й*) to besprinkle (with); (*гря́зью*) to splash; to bespatter (with)

обры́згива|ть, ю *impf. of* ▸ **обры́згать**

обря́д, а *m.* rite, ceremony

обса|ди́ть, жу́, ~дишь *pf. (of* ▸ **обса́живать)** to plant round

обса́жива|ть, ю *impf. of* ▸ **обсади́ть**

обсервато́ри|я, и *f.* observatory

обсле́дование, я *nt.* (+ *g.*) (*осмо́тр*) inspection (of); (*в больни́це*) observation, tests

обсле́д|овать, ую *impf. and pf.* (*произвести́ осмо́тр*) to inspect; (*иссле́довать*) to investigate; **о. больно́го** to examine a patient

✵ **обслу́живани|е, я** *nt.* service; (tech.) servicing, maintenance; **медици́нское о.** health service

обслу́жива|ть, ю *impf. of* ▸ **обслужи́ть**

обслуж|и́ть, у́, ~ишь *pf. (of* ▸ **обслу́живать)** to serve; **о. потреби́теля** to serve a customer

обсо́х|нуть, ну, нешь, *past* **~, ~ла** *pf. (of* ▸ **обсыха́ть)** to dry (off)

✵ **обстано́вк|а, и** *f.* **1** (*кварти́ры*) furniture; decor **2** (theatr.) set **3** (*положе́ние*) situation **4** (*атмосфе́ра*) atmosphere, environment

обстоя́тел|ьный, ~ен, ~ьна *adj.* thorough, detailed

✵ **обстоя́тельств|о, а** *nt.* circumstance; **по незави́сящим от меня́ ~ам** for reasons beyond my control; **ни при каки́х ~ах** in no circumstances

обсто|я́ть, и́т *impf.* to be; to get on; **как ~и́т де́ло?** how is it going?; **вот как ~и́т дела́** that is the way it is; that's how matters stand

обстре́л, а *m.* firing, fire; **артиллери́йский о.** bombardment, shelling; **попа́сть под о.** to come under fire

о

обстре́лива|ть, ю *impf. of* ▶ обстреля́ть

обстрел|я́ть, я́ю *pf.* (*of* ▶ обстре́ливать) to fire (at, on); to bombard

обступ|а́ть, а́ю *impf. of* ▶ обступи́ть

обступ|и́ть, лю́, ~ишь *pf.* (*of* ▶ обступа́ть) to surround; to cluster (round)

обсу|ди́ть, жу́, ~дишь *pf.* (*of* ▶ обсужда́ть) to discuss; to consider

✎ **обсужда́|ть**, ю *impf. of* ▶ обсуди́ть

✎ **обсужде́ни|е**, я *nt.* discussion

обсу́шива|ть, ю *impf. of* ▶ обсуши́ть

обсу́шива|ться, юсь *impf. of* ▶ обсуши́ться

обсуш|и́ть, у́, ~ишь *pf.* (*of* ▶ обсу́шивать) to dry (out)

обсуш|и́ться, у́сь, ~ишься *pf.* (*of* ▶ обсу́шиваться) to dry oneself, get dry

обсчит|а́ть, а́ю *pf.* (*of* ▶ обсчи́тывать) to shortchange

обсчит|а́ться, а́юсь *pf.* (*of* ▶ обсчи́тываться) to make a mistake (*in counting*)

обсчи́тыва|ть, ю *impf. of* ▶ обсчита́ть

обсчи́тыва|ться, юсь *impf. of* ▶ обсчита́ться

обсыха́|ть, ю *impf. of* ▶ обсо́хнуть

обта́чива|ть, ю *impf. of* ▶ обточи́ть

обтека́ем|ый, ~, ~а *adj.* **1** (tech.) streamlined **2** (fig., infml) evasive

обтека́|ть, ю *impf. of* ▶ обте́чь

обтер|е́ть, оботру́, оботрёшь, *past* ~, ~ла *pf.* (*of* ▶ обтира́ть) **1** (*высушить*) to wipe; to wipe dry **2** (+ *i.*) (*натереть*) to rub all over (with)

обтер|е́ться, оботру́сь, оботрёшься, *past* ~ся, ~лась *pf.* (*of* ▶ обтира́ться) **1** (*обтереть себя*) to wipe oneself dry, dry oneself **2** (*водой*) to sponge down

обте́|чь, ку́, чёшь, ку́т, *past* ~к, ~кла́ *pf.* (*of* ▶ обтека́ть) **1** to flow round **2** (mil.) to bypass

обтира́ни|е, я *nt.* **1** sponge-down **2** (infml, *жидкость*) lotion

обтира́|ть, ю *impf. of* ▶ обтере́ть

обтира́|ться, юсь *impf. of* ▶ обтере́ться

обточ|и́ть, у́, ~ишь *pf.* (*of* ▶ обта́чивать) to grind smooth; (*на станке*) to turn

обтя́гивающий *adj.* skin-tight, figure-hugging

обува́|ть, ю *impf. of* ▶ обу́ть

обува́|ться, юсь *impf. of* ▶ обу́ться

обувно́й *adj. of* ▶ о́бувь; **о. магази́н** shoe shop

о́бувь, и (*no pl.*) *f.* footwear; shoes

обу́глива|ться, юсь *impf. of* ▶ обу́глиться

обу́гл|иться, юсь, ишься *pf.* (*of* ▶ обу́гливаться) to become charred, char

обусло́влива|ться, ется *impf.* (+ *i.*) to be conditional (upon); to depend (on); **разме́р ~ется тре́бованиями** the size is conditioned by the requirements

обу́|ть, ю, ешь *pf.* (*of* ▶ обува́ть) **1**: **о. кого́-н.** to put sb's boots/shoes on for him/her

2 (infml, *снабдить обувью*) to provide with boots/shoes **3** (*сапоги*) to put on

обу́|ться, юсь, ешься *pf.* (*of* ▶ обува́ться) **1** (*надеть обувь*) to put on one's boots/shoes **2** (infml, *снабдить себя обувью*) to provide oneself with boots/shoes

обуча́|ть, а́ю *impf. of* ▶ обучи́ть

обуча́|ться, а́юсь *impf. of* ▶ обучи́ться

✎ **обуче́ни|е**, я *nt.* teaching; instruction, training

обуч|и́ть, у́, ~ишь *pf.* (*of* ▶ учи́ть 1, ▶ обуча́ть) (*кого-н. чему́-н.*) to teach (sb sth); to instruct, train (sb in)

обуч|и́ться, у́сь, ~ишься *pf.* (*of* ▶ учи́ться 1, ▶ обуча́ться) (+ *d.* or *inf.*) to learn

обхо́д, а *m.* **1** (*врача, почтальона*) round **2** (*кружной путь*) roundabout way; bypass **3** (*уклонение*) evasion, circumvention (*of law, etc.*); **в о.** (+ *g.*) round, bypassing; (*минуя*) evading

обхо|ди́ть¹, жу́, ~дишь *impf. of* ▶ обойти́

обхо|ди́ть², жу́, ~дишь *pf.* (*город, друзей*) to go all round

обхо|ди́ться, жу́сь, ~дишься *impf. of* ▶ обойти́сь

обша́рива|ть, ю *impf. of* ▶ обша́рить

обша́р|ить, ю, ишь *pf.* (*of* ▶ обша́ривать) (infml) to ransack

обшива́|ть, ю *impf. of* ▶ обши́ть

обши́вк|а, и *f.* **1** (*воротника*) trim **2** (*корабля*) plating **3** (*дома*) cladding; (*стен*) panelling (BrE), paneling (AmE)

обши́р|ный, ~ен, ~на *adj.* extensive (also fig.); (*комната*) spacious; (*пространство*) vast

об|ши́ть, ошью, ошьёшь *pf.* (*of* ▶ обшива́ть) **1** (*одежду*) to edge, trim **2** (*корабль*) to plate; (*дом*) to clad; (*стены*) to panel

обща́|ться, юсь *impf.* (с + *i.*) to associate (with), mix (with)

общедосту́п|ный, ~ен, ~на *adj.* **1** available to all **2** (*цены*) moderate **3** (*книга, лекция*) accessible, popular

общежи́ти|е, я *nt.* (*рабочее*) hostel; (*студенческое*) hall of residence (BrE), dormitory (AmE)

общеизве́ст|ный, ~ен, ~на *adj.* well known, generally known; (*преступник*) notorious

общенаро́д|ный, ~ен, ~на *adj.* national; public; **о. пра́здник** public holiday

✎ **обще́ни|е**, я *nt.* relations, links; **ли́чное о.** personal contact

общеобразова́тельный *adj.* of general education

общепри́знан|ный, ~, ~а *adj.* universally recognized

общепри́нят|ый, ~, ~а *adj.* generally accepted

обще́ственност|ь, и *f.* (collect.) (the) public, the community; **англи́йская о.** the British public; **нау́чная о.** the scientific community

обще́ственн|ый *adj.* **1** social, public; ~**ая жизнь** public life; ~**ое мне́ние** public opinion **2** (*доброво́льный*) voluntary, unpaid; ~**ые организа́ции** voluntary organizations

о́бществ|о, а *nt.* **1** society **2** (*компа́ния*) company; **в** ~**е кого́-н.** in sb's company; **попа́сть в дурно́е о.** to fall into bad company

обществове́дени|е, я *nt.* social science

общеупотреби́тел|ьный, ~ен, ~ьна *adj.* in general use

общечелове́ческий *adj.* common to all mankind

о́бщ|ий *adj.* general; common; **о. знако́мый** mutual acquaintance; ~**ее собра́ние** general meeting; ~**ая су́мма** sum total

общи́н|а, ы *f.* (*о́бщество*) community; (*комму́на*) commune

общи́тел|ьный, ~ен, ~ьна *adj.* sociable

объеда́|ться, юсь *impf. of* ▸ **объе́сться**

объедине́ни|е, я *nt.* **1** (*де́йствие*) unification; amalgamation **2** (*сою́з*) union, association

объединённый *p.p.p. of* ▸ **объедини́ть** *and adj.* united; **Организа́ция Объединённых На́ций** United Nations (Organization)

объедин|и́ть, ю́, и́шь *pf.* (*of* ▸ **объединя́ть**) (*люде́й*) to unite; (*организа́ции*) to amalgamate; **о. уси́лия** to combine efforts

объедин|и́ться, ю́сь, и́шься *pf.* (*of* ▸ **объединя́ться**) (**с** + *i.*) to unite (with); to amalgamate (with)

объедин|я́ть, я́ю *impf. of* ▸ **объедини́ть**

объедин|я́ться, я́юсь *impf. of* ▸ **объедини́ться**

объе́д|ки, ков *m. pl.* (*sg.* ~**ок,** ~**ка**) (*infml*) leftovers, scraps

объе́зд, а *m.* **1** (*де́йствие*) travelling (BrE), traveling (AmE) round, riding round, going round **2** (*ме́сто*) detour, diversion (BrE); **пое́хать в о.** to make a detour

объе́з|дить¹, жу, дишь *pf.* (*of* ▸ **объезжа́ть¹**) (*страну́*) to travel all over; (*друзе́й*) to go round visiting

объе́з|дить², жу, дишь *pf.* (*of* ▸ **объезжа́ть²**) (*лошаде́й*) to break in

объезжа́|ть¹, ю *impf. of* ▸ **объе́здить¹,** ▸ **объе́хать**

объезжа́|ть², ю *impf. of* ▸ **объе́здить²**

объе́кт, а *m.* **1** object **2** (mil.) objective **3** (*предприя́тие*) establishment; **строи́тельный о.** building site

объекти́в, а *m.* (optics) lens

объекти́вност|ь, и *f.* objectivity

объекти́в|ный, ~ен, ~на *adj.* objective

объём, а *m.* volume (also fig.); (*величина́*) size

объём|ный, ~, ~а *adj.* **1** by volume, volumetric; (*изображе́ние*) three-dimensional **2** (*большо́й по объёму*) voluminous, bulky

объе́|сться, мся, шься, стся, ди́мся, ди́тесь, дя́тся, *past* ~**лся** *pf.* (*of* ▸ **объеда́ться**) to overeat

объе́|хать, ду, дешь *pf.* (*of* ▸ **объезжа́ть¹**) **1** (*боло́то*) to go round, skirt **2** (*всю*

страну́) to travel over

объяв|и́ть, лю́, ~ишь *pf.* (*of* ▸ **объявля́ть**) to declare, announce; **о. войну́** to declare war

объявле́ни|е, я *nt.* **1** declaration, announcement **2** (*выве́ска*) notice **3** (*рекла́мное*) advertisement; **дать о. в газе́ту, помести́ть о. в газе́те** to put an advertisement in a paper

объявл|я́ть, я́ю *impf. of* ▸ **объяви́ть**

объясне́ни|е, я *nt.* explanation

объясн|и́ть, ю́, и́шь *pf.* (*of* ▸ **объясня́ть**) to explain

объясн|и́ться, ю́сь, и́шься *pf.* (*of* ▸ **объясня́ться**) **1** to explain oneself; (**с** + *i.*) to have a talk (with); to have it out (with); **о. в любви́** (+ *d.*) to make a declaration of love (to) **2** (*найти́ себе́ объясне́ние*) to become clear, be explained

объясн|я́ть, я́ю *impf. of* ▸ **объясни́ть**

объясн|я́ться, я́юсь *impf.* **1** *impf. of* ▸ **объясни́ться 2** to speak; to make oneself understood; **о. же́стами и зна́ками** to use sign language **3** (+ *i.*) to be explained (by), be accounted for (by); **э́тим** ~**я́ется его́ стра́нное поведе́ние** that accounts for his strange behaviour

объя́ти|е, я *nt.* embrace; **с распростёртыми** ~**ями** with open arms

обыва́тел|ь, я *m.* philistine

обыва́тельский *adj.* philistine; narrow-minded

обыгр|а́ть, а́ю *pf.* (*of* ▸ **обы́грывать**) **1** (*сопе́рника*) to beat (*at a game*) **2** (theatr.) to use with (good) effect, play up; (fig., *оши́бку*) to turn to advantage, turn to account

обы́грыва|ть, ю *impf. of* ▸ **обыгра́ть**

обы́ден|ный, ~, ~на *adj.* ordinary; commonplace, everyday

обыкнове́нно *adv.* usually, as a rule

обыкнове́н|ный, ~ен, ~на *adj.* usual; ordinary; commonplace; ~**ная исто́рия** everyday occurrence

о́быск, а *m.* search; **о́рдер на о.** search warrant

обы|ска́ть, щу́, ~щешь *pf.* (*of* ▸ **обы́скивать**) to search

обы́скива|ть, ю *impf. of* ▸ **обыска́ть**

обы́ча|й, я *m.* custom

обы́чно *adv.* usually; as a rule; **как о.** as usual

обы́ч|ный, ~ен, ~на *adj.* usual; ordinary

обя́занност|ь, и *f.* duty; responsibility; **во́инская о.** military service; **исполня́ть** ~**и дире́ктора** to act as director; **исполня́ющий** ~**и дире́ктора** acting director

обя́зан|ный, ~, ~а *adj.* **1** (+ *inf.*) obliged, bound; **он** ~ **верну́ться** he is obliged to go back; it is his duty to go back **2** (+ *d.*) obliged, indebted (to); **она́ вам** ~**а свое́й жи́знью** she owes her life to you

обяза́тельно *adv.* without fail; definitely; **он о. там бу́дет** he is sure to be there, he is bound to be there; **не о.** not necessarily

⚲ **обяза́тел|ьный**, ~ен, ~ьна *adj.*
1 obligatory; compulsory; binding; ~ьное обуче́ние compulsory education **2** (*челове́к*) reliable

⚲ **обяза́тельств|о**, а *nt.* **1** obligation; взять на себя́ о. (+ *inf.*) to commit oneself (to), undertake (to) **2** (*in pl.*) (*law*) liabilities

обя|за́ться, жу́сь, ~жешься *pf.* (*of* ▸ обя́зываться) to bind oneself, pledge oneself, undertake

обя́зыва|ться, юсь *impf. of* ▸ обяза́ться

ова́л, а *m.* oval

ова́л|ьный, ~ен, ~ьна *adj.* oval

ова́ци|я, и *f.* ovation

Óве́н, Овна́ *m.* (astron., astrol.) Aries

ов|ёс, са́ *m.* oats

овладе́|ть, ю *impf. of* ▸ овладе́ть

овладе́|ть, ю *pf.* (*of* ▸ овладева́ть) (+ *i.*)
1 (*взять*) to seize; to take possession (of); о. собо́й to get control of oneself, regain self-control **2** (*fig., усвои́ть*) master

óвод, а, *pl.* ~ы, ~ов (*and* ~á, ~óв) *m.* gadfly

óвощ|и, е́й *m. pl.* (*sg.* ~, ~а) vegetables

овощно́й *adj.* vegetable; о. магази́н greengrocer's (shop)

овра́г, а *m.* ravine, gully

овся́нк|а, и *f.* (infml) **1** (*крупа́*) oatmeal **2** (*ка́ша*) porridge (BrE), oatmeal (AmE)

овся́н|ый *adj.* made of oats; oatmeal; ~ая ка́ша (oatmeal) porridge (BrE), oatmeal (AmE); ~ая крупа́ oatmeal

овц|á, ы́, *pl.* ~ы, ове́ц, ~ам *f.* sheep; (*са́мка*) ewe

овча́рк|а, и *f.* sheepdog; неме́цкая о. Alsatian (BrE), German shepherd (*dog*)

огиба́|ть, ю *impf. of* ▸ обогну́ть

оглавле́ни|е, я *nt.* table of contents

огла|си́ть, шу́, си́шь *pf.* (*of* ▸ оглаша́ть) (*объяви́ть*) to proclaim, announce; о. резолю́цию to read out a resolution

огла́ск|а, и *f.* publicity; избега́ть ~и to shun publicity; преда́ть ~е to make public, make known

оглаша́|ть, ю *impf. of* ▸ огласи́ть

огло́х|нуть, ну, нешь, *past* ~, ~ла *pf. of* ▸ гло́хнуть 1

оглуш|а́ть, а́ю *impf. of* ▸ оглуши́ть 2

оглуши́тел|ьный, ~ен, ~ьна *adj.* deafening

оглуш|и́ть, у́, и́шь *pf.* **1** *pf. of* ▸ глуши́ть 1 **2** (*impf.* ~а́ть) to deafen; (*уда́ром*) to stun (also fig.)

огля́дыва|ться, юсь *impf. of* ▸ огляну́ться

огля|ну́ться, ну́сь, ~нешься *pf.* (*of* ▸ огля́дываться) to turn (back) to look at sth; to glance back

óгнен|ный, ~, ~на *adj.* fiery (also fig.)

огнеопа́с|ный, ~ен, ~на *adj.* inflammable

огнетуши́тел|ь, я *m.* fire extinguisher

огнеупо́р|ный, ~ен, ~на *adj.* fire-resistant, fireproof

⚲ key word

огова́рива|ть, ю *impf. of* ▸ оговори́ть¹

огова́рива|ться, юсь *impf. of* ▸ оговори́ться

оговор|и́ть¹, ю́, и́шь *pf.* (*of* ▸ огова́ривать) (*оклевета́ть*) to slander

оговор|и́ть², ю́, и́шь *pf.* (*of* ▸ огова́ривать)
1 (*зара́нее усло́виться о чём-л.*) to stipulate (for); to fix, agree (on); мы ~и́ли усло́вия рабо́ты we have fixed the conditions of work **2** (*сде́лать огово́рку*) to spell out; to specify

оговор|и́ться, ю́сь, и́шься *pf.* (*of* ▸ огова́риваться) **1** (*сде́лать огово́рку*) to make a reservation, make a proviso **2** (*в ре́чи*) to make a slip in speaking

огово́р|ка, ки *f.* **1** reservation, proviso; он согласи́лся, но с не́которыми ~ками he agreed but made certain reservations **2** (*в ре́чи*) slip of the tongue

огол|и́ть, ю́, и́шь *pf.* (*of* ▸ оголя́ть) to bare; (*про́вод*) to strip; (*ша́шку*) to draw; о. фланг (mil.) to expose one's flank

огол|и́ться, ю́сь, и́шься *pf.* (*of* ▸ оголя́ться) **1** to strip (oneself) **2** (*о про́воде*) to become exposed; (*о де́реве*) to become bare

оголя́|ть, я́ю *impf. of* ▸ оголи́ть

оголя́|ться, я́юсь *impf. of* ▸ оголи́ться

⚲ **ог|о́нь, ня́** *m.* **1** (*пла́мя*) fire (also fig.) **2** (*свет*) light

огора́жива|ть, ю *impf. of* ▸ огороди́ть

огоро́д, а *m.* kitchen garden, vegetable garden

огоро|ди́ть, жу́, ~ди́шь *pf.* (*of* ▸ огора́живать) to fence in, enclose

огорч|а́ть, а́ю *impf. of* ▸ огорчи́ть

огорч|а́ться, а́юсь *impf. of* ▸ огорчи́ться

огорче́ни|е, я *nt.* distress; chagrin

огорч|и́ть, у́, и́шь *pf.* (*of* ▸ огорча́ть) to distress, upset

огорч|и́ться, у́сь, и́шься *pf.* (*of* ▸ огорча́ться) to be distressed; не ~а́йтесь! cheer up!

огра́б|ить, лю, ишь *pf. of* ▸ гра́бить

ограбле́ни|е, я *nt.* robbery; (*до́ма*) burglary

огра́д|а, ы *f.* (*забо́р*) fence; (*решётка*) railings

огра|ди́ть, жу́, ди́шь *pf.* (*of* ▸ огражда́ть) (от + *g.*) to guard (against, from), protect (against)

огра|ди́ться, жу́сь, ди́шься *pf.* (*of* ▸ огражда́ться) (от + *g.*) to defend oneself (against); to protect oneself (against)

огражда́|ть, ю *impf. of* ▸ огради́ть

огражда́|ться, юсь *impf. of* ▸ огради́ться

огражде́ни|е, я *nt.* barrier

⚲ **ограниче́ни|е**, я *nt.* limitation, restriction

ограни́ченный *p.p.p. of* ▸ ограни́чить *and adj.* limited; о. челове́к (fig.) narrow(-minded) person

ограни́чива|ть, ю *impf. of* ▸ ограни́чить

ограни́чива|ться, юсь *impf. of* ▸ ограни́читься

ограничи́тельный *adj.* restrictive, limiting

ограни́ч|ить, у, ишь *pf.* (*of* ▸ ограни́чивать) to limit, restrict, cut down; о. себя́ в расхо́дах to cut down one's expenditure

ограни́ч|иться, усь, ишься *pf.* (*of* ▶ ограни́чиваться) (+ *i.*) **1** (*удовлетвори́ться*) to limit oneself (to), confine oneself (to) **2** (*оста́ться в каки́х-л. преде́лах*) to be limited (to), be confined (to)

♂ **огро́м|ный, ~ен, ~на** *adj.* huge; vast; enormous

огрыз|а́ться, а́юсь *impf.* (*of* ▶ огрызну́ться) (infml) (**на** + *a.*) to snap (at)

огрыз|ну́ться, ну́сь, нёшься *pf. of* ▶ огрыза́ться

огры́з|ок, ка *m.* (infml) (*я́блока, соси́ски*) leftover bit; (*каранда́ша*) stub

огур|е́ц, ца́ *m.* cucumber

о́д|а, ы *f.* ode

ода́лжива|ть, ю *impf. of* ▶ одолжи́ть

одарённый *adj.* gifted, talented

одева́|ть, ю *impf. of* ▶ оде́ть

одева́|ться, юсь *impf. of* ▶ оде́ться

♂ **оде́жд|а, ы** *f.* clothes; clothing; **ве́рхняя о.** outer clothing, overcoat; **мужска́я о.** menswear; **фо́рменная о.** uniform

одеколо́н, а *m.* eau de cologne

одёргива|ть, ю *impf. of* ▶ одёрнуть

одержи́м|ый, ~, ~а *adj.* (+ *i.*) possessed (by); afflicted (by); **о. стра́хом** consumed with fear

одёр|нуть, ну, нешь *pf.* (*of* ▶ одёргивать) **1** (*руба́шку, ю́бку*) to pull down, straighten **2** (fig., infml, *челове́ка*) to call to order; to silence; to snub

оде́тый *p.p.p. of* ▶ оде́ть *and adj.* (+ *i. or* в + *a.*) dressed (in), clothed (in); with one's clothes on; **хорошо́ о.** well dressed

оде́|ть, ну, нешь *pf.* (*of* ▶ одева́ть) **1** (в + *a.*) to dress (in), clothe (in); **о. ребёнка в брю́ки** to dress a child in trousers; (+ *i.*) (*покры́ть*) to cover (with), wrap (in) **2** (*снабди́ть оде́ждой*) to clothe

оде́|ться, нусь, нешься *pf.* (*of* ▶ одева́ться) **1** to dress (oneself); to clothe oneself; **о. в вече́рнее пла́тье** to put on an evening dress **2** (*покры́ться*) (+ *i.*) to be covered with

одея́л|о, а *nt.* blanket

♂ **оди́н, одного́,** *f.* **одна́, одно́й,** *nt.* **одно́, одного́,** *pl.* **одни́, одни́х** *num. and pron.* **1** (*число́*) one; **одно́** one thing; **о. за други́м** one after the other, one by one; **одни́... други́е** some ..., (while) others; **с одно́й стороны́... с друго́й (стороны́)** on the one hand ... on the other hand; **одно́ вре́мя** at one time; **о. раз** once; **одни́м сло́вом** in a word **2** (*не́кий*) a, an; a certain; **я встре́тил одного́ моего́ бы́вшего колле́гу** I met an old colleague of mine **3** (*без други́х*) alone; by oneself; **я живу́ о.** I live alone **4** (*без супру́ги*) single **5** (infml, *то́лько*) only; **она́ чита́ет одни́ детекти́вные рома́ны** she reads nothing but detective stories **6**: **о., о. и тот же** the same, one and the same; **мы с ней одного́ во́зраста** she and I are the same age

одина́ково *adv.* equally, alike

одина́ков|ый, ~, ~а *adj.* (с + *i.*) identical (with), the same (as)

оди́ннадцатый *adj.* eleventh

оди́ннадцат|ь, и *num.* eleven

одино́к|ий, ~, ~а *adj.* **1** solitary; lonely; lone **2** (*as n. о., ~ого*) single man, bachelor; (**~ая, ~ой**) single woman

одино́ко *adv.* lonely; **чу́вствовать себя́ о.** to feel lonely

одино́честв|о, а *nt.* solitude; loneliness

одино́чк|а, и *c.g.* lone person; **мать-о.** single mother; **оте́ц-о.** single father

одино́чн|ый *adj.* **1** (*одного́ челове́ка*) individual; one-man; **~ое заключе́ние** solitary confinement **2** (*отде́льный*) solitary; single

одича́|ть, ю *pf. of* ▶ дича́ть

одна́жды *adv.* once; one day; **о. у́тром (ве́чером, но́чью)** one morning (evening, night)

♂ **одна́ко** *adv. and conj.* however; but; though

♂ **одновре́ме́нно** *adv.* simultaneously, at the same time

одновр|е́ме́нный, ~е́менен, ~е́менна *adj.* simultaneous

одногла́зый *adj.* one-eyed

однодне́вный *adj.* one-day

однозна́ч|ный, ~ен, ~на *adj.* **1** (*тожде́ственный*) synonymous **2** (fig., *недвусмы́сленный*) unambiguous; simple, straightforward

одноимён|ный, ~ен, ~на *adj.* of the same name

однокла́ссник, а *m.* classmate

однокла́ссни|ца, цы *f. of* ▶ однокла́ссник

одноку́рсник, а *m.* person in the same year of study

одноку́рсни|ца, цы *f. of* ▶ одноку́рсник

одноме́стный *adj.* single-seated, single-seater

одноно́гий *adj.* one-legged

однообра́з|ный, ~ен, ~на *adj.* monotonous

однопо́л|ый *adj.* of the same sex; **о. брак** same-sex marriage, gay marriage

однора́зовый *adj.* (*шприц*) disposable; (*про́пуск*) temporary, valid only once

однор́од|ный, ~ен, ~на *adj.* (*одина́ковый во всех частя́х*) homogeneous

однору́кий *adj.* one-armed

односельча́н|ин, ина, *pl.* **~е, ~** *m.* fellow villager

односельча́н|ка, ки *f. of* ▶ односельча́нин

односло́ж|ный *adj.* **1** monosyllabic **2** (**~ен, ~на**) (fig.) terse, abrupt

односторо́нн|ий *adj.* **1** (*ткань*) one-sided (also fig.); (*разоруже́ние, до́говор*) unilateral **2** (*ток*) one-way; **~ее движе́ние** one-way traffic; **о. ум** (fig.) one-track mind

одноти́п|ный, ~ен, ~на *adj.* of the same type, of the same kind; **о. кора́бль** sister ship

однофами́л|ец, ьца *m.* (с + *i.*) person having the same surname (as), namesake

однофами́л|ица, ицы *f. of* ▶ однофами́лец

о

одноцве́т|ный, ~ен, ~на *adj.* (*ткань*) plain; (fig.) monochrome

одноэта́жный *adj.* single-storey (BrE), single-story (AmE)

одобре́ни|е, я *nt.* approval

одобри́тель|ный, ~ен, ~ьна *adj.* approving; (*отзыв*) favourable (BrE), favorable (AmE)

одо́бр|ить, ю, ишь *pf.* (*of* ▸ одобря́ть) to approve (of); **не о.** to disapprove (of)

одобр|я́ть, я́ю *impf. of* ▸ одо́брить

одолева́|ть, ю *impf. of* ▸ одоле́ть

одоле́|ть, ю *pf.* (*of* ▸ одолева́ть) **1** to overcome, conquer; **его́** ~**л сон** he was overcome by sleepiness **2** (fig.) to master; to cope (with); to get through

одолже́ни|е, я *nt.* favour (BrE), favor (AmE), service; **сде́лайте мне о.** do me a favour (BrE), favor (AmE)

одолж|и́ть, у́, и́шь *pf.* (*of* ▸ ода́лживать) **1** (+ *d.*) to lend **2** (infml) (**у** + *g.*) to borrow (from)

одува́нчик, а *m.* (bot.) dandelion

оду́м|аться, аюсь *pf.* (*of* ▸ оду́мываться) to change one's mind; to think better of it

оду́мыва|ться, юсь *impf. of* ▸ оду́маться

одура́чива|ть, ю *impf. of* ▸ одура́чить

одура́ч|ить, у, ишь *pf.* (*of* ▸ дура́чить, ▸ одура́чивать) (infml) to make a fool (of), fool

одухотворённый *adj.* inspired; (*лицо*) spiritual

оды́шк|а, и *f.* short breath; **страда́ть** ~**ой** to be short-winded

ожере́ль|е, я *nt.* necklace

ожесточа́|ть, а́ю *impf. of* ▸ ожесточи́ть

ожесточа́|ться, а́юсь *impf. of* ▸ ожесточи́ться

ожесточе́ни|е, я *nt.* bitterness

ожесточённый *p.p.p. of* ▸ ожесточи́ть *and adj.* (*бой, спор*) bitter; (*человек*) embittered; hardened

ожесточ|и́ть, у́, и́шь *pf.* (*of* ▸ ожесточа́ть) to embitter; to harden

ожесточ|и́ться, у́сь, и́шься *pf.* (*of* ▸ ожесточа́ться) to become embittered; to become hardened

ожива́|ть, ю *impf. of* ▸ ожи́ть

ожив|и́ть, лю́, и́шь *pf.* (*of* ▸ оживля́ть) **1** (*человека; воспоминание*) to revive **2** (fig.) (*общество, вечер*) to liven up, enliven; (*торговлю*) to revitalize; (*лицо, картину*) to brighten up

ожив|и́ться, лю́сь, и́шься *pf.* (*of* ▸ оживля́ться) **1** (*человек, разговор*) to become animated, liven (up); (*взгляд*) to brighten up **2** (*улица*) to come to life

оживле́ни|е, я *nt.* **1** (*состояние*) animation, gusto **2** (*действие*) reviving; enlivening

оживлённый *p.p.p. of* ▸ оживи́ть *and adj.* animated; lively

оживля́|ть, ю *impf. of* ▸ оживи́ть

оживля́|ться, юсь *impf. of* ▸ оживи́ться

ожида́ни|е, я *nt.* expectation; waiting; **обману́ть** ~**я** to disappoint; **в** ~**и** (+ *g.*) pending; **сверх** ~**я** beyond expectation

ожида́|ть, ю *impf.* (+ *g.*) to wait (for); (*предвидеть*) to expect, anticipate; **как я и** ~**л** just as I expected

ожире́ни|е, я *nt.* obesity

ож|и́ть, иву́, ивёшь, *past* ~́ил, ~ила́, ~́ило *pf.* (*of* ▸ ожива́ть) to come to life, revive (also fig.)

ожо́г, а *m.* burn; (*жидкостью, паром*) scald

озабо́|тить, чу, тишь *pf.* to trouble, worry

озабо́ченность, и *f.* anxiety

озабо́чен|ный, ~, ~а *p.p.p. of* ▸ озабо́тить *and* (~, ~на) *adj.* anxious, worried

озагла́в|ить, лю, ишь *pf.* (*of* ▸ озагла́вливать) to entitle; (*главу, раздел*) to head

озагла́влива|ть, ю *impf. of* ▸ озагла́вить

озада́ч|енный, ~, ~ена *p.p.p. of* ▸ озада́чить *and* (~ен, ~енна) *adj.* perplexed, puzzled

озада́чива|ть, ю *impf. of* ▸ озада́чить

озада́ч|ить, у, ишь *pf.* (*of* ▸ озада́чивать) to perplex, puzzle, take aback

озвере́|ть, ю *pf. of* ▸ звере́ть

озву́чива|ть, ю *impf. of* ▸ озву́чить

озву́ч|ить, у, ишь *pf.* (*of* ▸ озву́чивать) **1** (cin.) to add a soundtrack to **2** (infml, *высказать*) to state, formulate

о́зер|о, а, *pl.* озёра, озёр *nt.* lake

ози́м|ый *adj.* winter; (*as pl. n.* ~ые, ~ых) winter crops

означа́|ть, ет *impf.* to mean, signify, stand for; **что** ~**ют э́ти бу́квы?** what do these letters stand for?

озно́б, а *m.* shivering; chill; **почу́вствовать о.** to feel shivery

озо́н, а *m.* ozone

озо́н|овый *adj. of* ▸ озо́н; ~**овая дыра́** ozone hole; **о. слой** ozone layer

озорно́й *adj.* (infml) mischievous

озорств|о́, а́ *nt.* (infml) mischief

ози́б|нуть, ну, нешь, *past* ~, ~ла *pf.* (infml) to be cold; **я** ~**!** I am frozen!

ой and **ой-ой-о́й** *int* (*выражает удивление, удовольствие*) oh; (*выражает боль*) ow, ouch!; (*выражает удивление собственной ошибки*) oops!

оказа́ни|е, я *nt.* rendering (*of first aid, etc.*)

ока|за́ть, жу́, ~́жешь *pf.* (*of* ▸ ока́зывать) to render, show; **о. влия́ние** (**на** + *a.*) to influence, exert influence (upon); **о. де́йствие** (**на** + *a.*) to have an effect (upon); to take effect; **о. по́мощь** (+ *d.*) to help, give (sb) help; **о. услу́гу** (+ *d.*) to do, render (sb) a service; to do (sb) a good turn

ока|за́ться, жу́сь, ~́жешься *pf.* (*of* ▸ ока́зываться) **1** to turn out (to be), prove (to be) **2** (*очути́ться*) to find oneself; to be found; **я ~зался в больни́це** I found myself in hospital

♂ **ока́зыва|ть, ю** *impf. of* ▶ **оказа́ть**

♂ **ока́зыва|ться, юсь** *impf. of* ▶ **оказа́ться**

окайм|и́ть, лю́, и́шь *pf.* (*of* ▶ **окаймля́ть**) (+ *i.*) to border (with), edge (with)

окаймля́|ть, ю *impf. of* ▶ **окайми́ть**

окамене́|ть, ю *pf. of* ▶ **камене́ть**

ока́нчива|ть, ю, ет *impf. of* ▶ **око́нчить**

ока́нчива|ться, ется *impf. of* ▶ **око́нчиться**

ока|ти́ть, чу́, ~тишь *pf.* (*of* ▶ **ока́чивать**) to pour (over); **о. холо́дной водо́й** to pour cold water (over) (*also fig.*)

ока|ти́ться, чу́сь, ~тишься *pf.* (*of* ▶ **ока́чиваться**) to pour over oneself

ока́чива|ть, ю *impf. of* ▶ **окати́ть**

ока́чива|ться, юсь *impf. of* ▶ **окати́ться**

окая́нный *adj.* damned, cursed

океа́н, а *m.* ocean

Океа́ни|я, и *f.* Oceania (*the islands of the Pacific and adjacent seas*)

океа́нский *adj.* ocean; oceanic; **о. парохо́д** ocean(-going) liner

о́кис|ь, и *f.* (chem.) oxide

оккупа́ци|я, и *f.* (mil.) occupation

оккупи́р|овать, ую *impf. and pf.* (mil.) to occupy

окла́д, а *m.* salary

оклеве|та́ть, щу́, ~щешь *pf. of* ▶ **клевета́ть**

окле́ива|ть, ю *impf. of* ▶ **окле́ить**

окле́|ить, ю, ишь *pf.* (*of* ▶ **окле́ивать**) (+ *i.*) to cover (with); to paste over (with); **о. ко́мнату обо́ями** to paper a room

оклик|а́ть, а́ю *impf. of* ▶ **окли́кнуть**

окли́к|нуть, ну, нешь *pf.* (*of* ▶ **оклика́ть**) to hail, call (to)

♂ **окн|о́, а́, *pl.* ~а, о́кон, ~ам** *nt.* **1** (*also comput.*) window; **диало́говое о.** (comput.) dialog box **2** (fig., *отве́рстие*) gap, break

око́в|ы, ~ (*no sg.*) fetters (*also fig.*)

♂ **о́коло** *prep. + g. and adv.* **1** (*ря́дом, во́зле*) by; (*вблизи́*) close (to), near; (*вокру́г*) around; **о.** (*приблизи́тельно*) about; **о. полу́ночи** about midnight

око́нн|ый *adj. of* ▶ **окно́**; **~ая ра́ма** window frame; **~ое стекло́** windowpane

♂ **оконча́ни|е, я** *nt.* (*заверше́ние*) completion, conclusion; (*коне́ц*) end; **о. сро́ка** expiration; **по ~и университе́та** on graduating; (gram.) ending

оконча́тельно *adv.* (*бесповоро́тно*) finally, definitively; (*соверше́нно*) completely

оконча́тел|ьный, ~ен, ~ьна *adj.* (*бесповоро́тный*) final, definitive; (*соверше́нный*) complete

око́нч|ить, у, ишь *pf.* (*of* ▶ **ока́нчивать**) to finish, end; **о. шко́лу** to leave school (BrE), to graduate from high school (AmE); **о. университе́т** to graduate

око́нч|иться, ится *pf.* (*of* ▶ **ока́нчиваться**) to finish, end; to be over

око́п, а *m.* (mil.) trench; entrenchment

о́коро|к, ка, *pl.* ~ка́ *m.* ham; (*бара́нины, теля́тины*) leg

око́ш|ко, ка, *pl.* ~ки, ~ек, ~кам *nt.* window

ОКР (*abbr. of* **обсесси́вно-компульси́вное расстро́йство**) (med.) OCD (*obsessive-compulsive disorder*)

окра́ин|а, ы *f.* **1** (*го́рода*) outskirts; outlying districts; (*леса, дере́вни*) edge **2** (*in pl.*) (*страны*) border areas

окра́|сить, шу, сишь *pf.* (*of* ▶ **окра́шивать**) (*сте́ну, кры́шу*) to paint; (*ткань, во́лосы*) to dye; (*жизнь*) to colour (BrE), color (AmE); **слегка́ о.** to tinge, tint

окра́ск|а, и *f.* **1** (*де́йствие*) painting; dyeing **2** (*цвет*) colouring (BrE), coloring (AmE), coloration; **защи́тная о.** (zool.) protective coloration **3** (fig.) tinge, tint; (pol.) slant

окра́шива|ть, ю *impf. of* ▶ **окра́сить**

окре́п|нуть, ну, нешь, *past* **~, ~ла** *pf. of* ▶ **кре́пнуть**

окре|сти́ть, щу́, ~стишь *pf. of* ▶ **крести́ть 1**

окре́стност|ь, и *f.* (*usu. in pl.*) **1** (*столи́цы, дере́вни*) environs **2** (*окружа́ющее простра́нство*) neighbourhood (BrE), neighborhood (AmE), vicinity

о́крик, а *m.* shout, cry

окрова́влен|ный, ~, ~а *adj.* bloodstained; bloody

♂ **о́круг, а, *pl.* ~а́** *m.* region, district; circuit; **избира́тельный о.** electoral district

окру́г|а, и *f.* (infml) neighbourhood (BrE), neighborhood (AmE)

округл|и́ть, ю́, и́шь *pf.* (*of* ▶ **округля́ть**) (*счёт, ци́фры*) to express in round numbers

окру́гл|ый, ~, ~а *adj.* rounded; (*лицо́*) round

округл|я́ть, я́ю *impf. of* ▶ **округли́ть**

окруж|а́ть, а́ю *impf. of* ▶ **окружи́ть**

♂ **окружа́|ющий** *pres. part. act. of* ▶ **окружа́ть** *and adj.* surrounding; (*as nt. n.* **~ющее, ~ющего**) environment; (*as pl. n.* **~ющие, ~ющих**) the people around/surrounding one

окруже́ни|е, я *nt.* **1** (*де́йствие*) encirclement **2** (*среда́*) surroundings; environment; milieu; **в ~и** (+ *g.*) surrounded (by), in the midst (of); (*лю́ди*) the people around/surrounding one

окруж|и́ть, у́, и́шь *pf.* (*of* ▶ **окружа́ть**) to surround; to encircle; **о. кого́-н. забо́тами** to lavish attentions on sb

окружн|о́й *adj.* **1** *adj. of* ▶ **о́круг**; **о. суд** circuit court **2** operating (situated) about a circle; **~а́я желе́зная доро́га** circle line

окру́жност|ь, и *f.* circumference; (*за́мкнутая крива́я*) circle

О́ксфорд, а *m.* Oxford

окта́в|а, ы *f.* (mus.) octave

♂ **октя́бр|ь, я́** *m.* October (fig.) (= *Russian revolution of October 1917*)

октя́брьский *adj. of* ▶ **октя́брь**

окули́ст, а *m.* ophthalmic optician

окуля́р, а *m.* eyepiece

окун|а́ть, а́ю *impf. of* ▶ **окуну́ть**

о

окуна́|ться, а́юсь *impf. of* ▶ **окуну́ться**

окуну́|ть, у́, ёшь *pf.* (*of* ▶ **окуна́ть**) to dip

окуну́|ться, у́сь, ёшься *pf.* (*of* ▶ **окуна́ться**) **1** to dip (oneself) **2** (fig.) (**в** + *a.*) to plunge (into); to become (utterly) absorbed (in), engrossed (in)

о́кун|ь, я, *pl.* **~и, ~е́й** *m.* (zool.) perch; **морско́й о.** redfish, North Atlantic rockfish

окупа́|ть, а́ю *impf. of* ▶ **окупи́ть**

окупа́|ться, а́юсь *impf. of* ▶ **окупи́ться**

окуп|и́ть, лю́, ~ишь *pf.* (*of* ▶ **окупа́ть**) to compensate, repay, make up (for); **о. расхо́ды** to cover one's outlay

окуп|и́ться, лю́сь, ~ишься *pf.* (*of* ▶ **окупа́ться**) to be compensated, be repaid; (fig.) to pay; to be justified, be requited, be rewarded; **затра́ченные на́ми уси́лия ~и́лись** our efforts were rewarded

оку́р|ок, ка *m.* (*сигареты*) butt

оку́т|ать, аю *pf.* (*of* ▶ **оку́тывать**) (+ *i.*) **1** to wrap up (in) **2** (fig.) to shroud, cloak (in)

оку́т|аться, аюсь *pf.* (*of* ▶ **оку́тываться**) (+ *i.*) **1** to wrap oneself up (in) **2** (fig.) to shroud, cloak oneself (in); **о. та́йной** to shroud oneself in mystery

оку́тыва|ю, ю *impf. of* ▶ **оку́тать**

оку́тыва|ться, юсь *impf. of* ▶ **оку́таться**

ола́д|ья, ьи, *pl.* **~ьи, ~ий** *f.* fritter; **карто́фельная о.** potato cake

оледене́|ть, ю *pf. of* ▶ **ледене́ть**

олени́н|а, ы *f.* venison

оле́н|ь, я *m.* deer; **благоро́дный о.** stag, red deer; **се́верный о.** reindeer

оли́вк|а, и *f.* olive

оли́вков|ый *adj.* **1** olive; **~ое ма́сло** olive oil **2** (*цвет*) olive-green

олига́рх, а *m.* oligarch

олимпиа́д|а, ы *f.* **1** (**О.**) (*олимпийские игры*) Olympics **2** (*соревнования*) Olympiad

олимпи́йск|ий *adj.* Olympic; **О~е и́гры** Olympic Games, Olympics

олицетворе́ни|е, я *nt.* personification

олицетвор|и́ть, ю́, и́шь *pf.* (*of* ▶ **олицетворя́ть**) to personify

олицетвор|я́ть, я́ю *impf. of* ▶ **олицетвори́ть**

о́лов|о, а *nt.* tin

оловя́нн|ый *adj.* tin; **~ая фо́льга** tin foil

О́льстер, а *m.* Ulster

ольх|а́, и́, *pl.* **~и** *f.* alder (tree)

ома́р, а *m.* lobster

омерзи́тельн|ый, ~ен, ~ьна *adj.* loathsome, disgusting

омле́т, а *m.* omelette (BrE), omelet (AmE)

ОМО́Н *m. indecl.* (*abbr. of* **отря́д мили́ции осо́бого назначе́ния**) special forces unit; riot squad

омо́нов|ец, ца *m.* member of the special force

ОМП (*abbr. of* **ору́жие ма́ссового пораже́ния**) WMD (*weapons of mass destruction*)

омрач|а́ть, а́ю *impf. of* ▶ **омрачи́ть**

омрач|а́ться, а́юсь *impf. of* ▶ **омрачи́ться**

омрач|и́ть, у́, и́шь *pf.* (*of* ▶ **омрача́ть**) to darken, cloud

омрач|и́ться, у́сь, и́шься *pf.* (*of* ▶ **омрача́ться**) to darken, become clouded (also fig.)

о́мут, а *m.* **1** (*водоворот*) whirlpool; (fig.) maelstrom **2** (*глубокое место*) deep place (*in river or lake*)

⚔ **он, его́, ему́, им, о нём** *pers. pron.* he

⚔ **она́, её, ей, ей (éю), о ней** *pers. pron.* she

онани́зм, а *m.* masturbation

онда́тр|а, ы *f.* muskrat, musquash

онеме́|ть, ю *pf. of* ▶ **неме́ть**

⚔ **они́, их, им, и́ми, о них** *pers. pron.* they

о́никс, а *m.* (min.) onyx

онко́лог, а *m.* oncologist

онкологи́ческий *adj.* oncological

онколо́ги|я, и *f.* oncology

⚔ **онла́йн, а** *m., adv., adj. indecl.* (comput.): **в ~е** (*or* **в режи́ме**) **о.**) online; **ба́нковские опера́ции в режи́ме о.** online banking; **о.-кинотеа́тр** online cinema

онла́йновый *adj.* (comput.) online

⚔ **оно́, его́, ему́, им, о нём** *pers. pron.* **1** it **2** (*это*) this, that; **о. и ви́дно** that is evident **3** (*as emph. particle*): **вот о. что!** oh, I see!

ООН *f. indecl.* (*abbr. of* **Организа́ция Объединённых На́ций**) UN (*United Nations Organization*)

⚔ **ООО** (*abbr. of* **о́бщество с ограни́ченной отве́тственностью**) Ltd

опада́|ть, ет *impf. of* ▶ **опа́сть**

опа́здыва|ть, ю *impf.* **1** *impf. of* ▶ **опозда́ть** **2** (*impf. only*) (infml, *о часах*) to be slow

опа́л, а *m.* opal

опа́лива|ть, ю *impf. of* ▶ **опали́ть**

опал|и́ть, ю́, и́шь *pf.* (*of* ▶ **опа́ливать**) to singe

опаса́|ться, юсь *impf.* **1** (+ *g.*) (*бояться*) to fear, be afraid (of) **2** (+ *g. or inf.*) (*избегать*) to beware (of); to avoid, keep off

опасе́ни|е, я *nt.* fear; apprehension

⚔ **опа́сност|ь, и** *f.* danger; peril; **вне ~и** out of danger

⚔ **опа́с|ный, ~ен, ~на** *adj.* dangerous, perilous

опа́|сть, дёт *pf.* (*of* ▶ **опада́ть**) **1** (*о листьях*) to fall (off) **2** (*об опухоли*) to go down; (*о суфле*) to sink

ОПЕ́К *f. indecl.* OPEC (*abbr. of Organization of Petroleum Exporting Countries —* **Организа́ция стран - экспортёров не́фти**)

опе́к|а, и *f.* guardianship (also fig.); (*над имуществом*) trusteeship; **взять под ~у** to take into one's care; (fig.) to take charge (of)

опека́|ть, ю *impf.* **1** (*сирот*) to be guardian (to) **2** (fig., *младших*) to take care (of)

опеку́н, а́ *m.* (law) guardian; (*над имуществом*) trustee

опеку́н|ша, ши *f.* (infml) *of* ▶ **опеку́н**

о́пер|а, ы *f.* opera; «**мы́льная о.**» soap (opera)

операти́вник, а *m.* detective

операти́в|ный *adj.* **1** (~ен, ~на)
(*руково́дство*) efficient **2** (*штаб, рабо́та*)
executive **3** (med.) surgical **4** (comput.): ~ная
па́мять random-access memory

◇ **опера́тор, а** *m.* **1** (*обору́дования*) operator
2 (*кинооперáтор*) cameraman **3** (comput.)
computer operator

опера|цио́нный *adj. of* ▸ **опера́ция**;
~цио́нная систе́ма (comput.) operating
system; **о. стол** operating table; **о. зал**
(**на би́рже**) (fin.) trading floor; (*as f. n.*
~цио́нная, ~цио́нной) operating theatre
(BrE), operating room (AmE)

◇ **опера́ци|я, и** *f.* (med., mil., etc.) operation;
перенести́ ~ю to have an operation; to be
operated (upon); **сде́лать** ~ю to perform
an operation

опере|ди́ть, жу́, ди́шь *pf.* (*of* ▸ **опережа́ть**)
1 (*в бе́ге, в разви́тии*) to outstrip, leave
behind **2** (*успе́ть ра́ньше*) to forestall

опережа́|ть, ю *impf. of* ▸ **опереди́ть**

опере́ни|е, я *nt.* plumage

опере́тт|а, ы *f.* musical comedy, operetta

опере́ться, обопру́сь, обопрёшься, *past*
опёрся, оперла́сь *pf.* (*of* ▸ **опира́ться**)
1 (**на** + *a. or* **о** + *a.*) to lean (on; against); **о.**
о подоко́нник to lean against the window
sill **2** (fig.) to rely on; to depend on

опери́р|овать, ую *impf. and pf.* **1** (med.) to
operate (upon) **2** (mil.) to operate, act
3 (+ *i.*) (fin.) to deal (in); (fig.) to use, handle;
о. недоста́точными да́нными to operate
with inadequate data

опеча́т|ка, ки *f.* misprint; **спи́сок** ~ок (list
of) errata

опира́|ться, юсь *impf. of* ▸ **опере́ться**

◇ **описа́ни|е, я** *nt.* description; account; **э́то не**
поддаётся ~ю it is beyond description

опи|са́ть, шу́, ~шешь *pf.* (*of* ▸ **опи́сывать**)
1 to describe **2** (*сде́лать опись*) to list,
inventory

опи́ск|а, и *f.* slip of the pen

◇ **опи́сыва|ть, ю** *impf. of* ▸ **описа́ть**

о́пис|ь, и *f.* list; inventory; **о. иму́щества** (law)
distraint

о́пиум, а *m.* opium

опла́|кать, чу, чешь *pf.* (*of* ▸ **опла́кивать**) to
mourn (over); to bewail, bemoan

опла́кива|ть, ю *impf. of* ▸ **опла́кать**

◇ **опла́т|а, ы** *f.* pay, payment

опла|ти́ть, чу́, ~тишь *pf.* to pay (for); **о.**
счёт to settle the account, pay the bill; **о.**
убы́тки to pay damages

опла́чива|ть, ю *impf. of* ▸ **оплати́ть**

опла́|чу, чешь *see* ▸ **опла́кать**

опла́|чу, ~тишь *see* ▸ **оплати́ть**

оплеу́х|а, и *f.* (infml) slap in the face

оплодотворе́ни|е, я *nt.* fertilization

оплодотвор|и́ть, ю́, и́шь *pf.* (*of*
▸ **оплодотворя́ть**) to fertilize

оплодотвор|я́ть, я́ю *impf. of*
▸ **оплодотвори́ть**

опломбир|ова́ть, у́ю *pf. of*
▸ **пломбирова́ть 1**

опло́шност|ь, и *f.* blunder

опове|сти́ть, щу́, сти́шь *pf.* (*of* ▸ **оповеща́ть**)
to notify, inform

оповеща́|ть, ю *impf. of* ▸ **оповести́ть**

опозда́ни|е, я *nt.* lateness; delay; **без** ~я on
time; **с** ~ем **на де́сять мину́т** ten minutes
late

опозда́|ть, ю *pf.* (*of* ▸ **опа́здывать 1**) to be
late; **о. на ле́кцию** to be late for the lecture;
о. на полчаса́ to be half an hour late

опозна|ва́ть, ю́, ёшь *impf. of* ▸ **опозна́ть**

опозна́ни|е, я *nt.* (law) identification

опозна́|ть, ю *pf.* (*of* ▸ **опознава́ть**) to identify

опозо́р|ить, ю, ишь *pf. of* ▸ **позо́рить**

опозо́р|иться, юсь, ишься *pf. of*
▸ **позо́риться**

ополо́скива|ть, ю *impf. of* ▸ **ополосну́ть**

о́полз|ень, ня *m.* landslide, landslip

ополосн|у́ть, у́, ёшь *pf.* (*of* ▸ **ополо́скивать**)
to rinse

ополче́н|ец, ца *m.* militiaman; home guard

ополче́ни|е, я *nt.* **1** militia; home guard
2 (collect.) (hist.) irregulars; levies

опо́мн|иться, юсь, ишься *pf.* (*прийти́ в*
созна́ние) to come round; (*оду́маться*) to
come to one's senses

опо́р|а, ы *f.* support (also fig.); (*моста́*) pier

опоро́жн|ить, ю́, и́шь *pf.* (*of* ▸ **опорожня́ть**)
to empty

опорожн|я́ть, ю *impf. of* ▸ **опорожни́ть**

оппози́ци|я, и *f.* opposition

оппоне́нт, а *m.* opponent

опра́в|а, ы *f.* frame; (*очко́в*) frames

оправда́ни|е, я *nt.* **1** justification
2 (*извине́ние*) excuse **3** (law) acquittal,
discharge

оправда́тельный *adj.*: **о. пригово́р** verdict
of 'not guilty'

оправд|а́ть, а́ю *pf.* (*of* ▸ **опра́вдывать**)
1 (*показа́ть себя́ досто́йным*) to justify,
warrant; **о. ожида́ния** to come up to
expectations **2** (*извини́ть*) to excuse
3 (law) to acquit, discharge

оправд|а́ться, а́юсь *pf.* (*of* ▸ **опра́вдываться**
1) **1** to justify oneself **2** to be justified;
на́ши опасе́ния ~а́лись our fears have been
confirmed

опра́вдыва|ть, ю *impf.* (*of* ▸ **оправда́ть**):
о. незна́нием (law) to plead ignorance

опра́вдыва|ться, юсь *impf.* **1** *impf.*
of ▸ **оправда́ться 2** to try to justify *or*
vindicate oneself

опра́шива|ть, ю *impf. of* ▸ **опроси́ть**

◇ **определе́ни|е, я** *nt.* (*поня́тия*) definition;
(chem., phys., etc.) determination

◇ **определённ|ый, ~ен, ~на** *adj.* **1** (*то́чно*
устано́вленный) definite; fixed **2** (*не́который*)

certain; в ~ных случаях in certain cases

определ|и́ть, ю́, и́шь *pf.* (*of* ▸ определя́ть) (*понятие*) to define; (*установить*) to determine; (*назначить*) to fix, appoint

определ|и́ться, ю́сь, и́шься *pf.* (*of* ▸ определя́ться) to be formed; to take shape; to be determined

◆ **определ|я́ть, я́ю** *impf. of* ▸ определи́ть

◆ **определ|я́ться, я́юсь** *impf. of* ▸ определи́ться

опро́б|овать, ую *pf.* to test

опроверга́|ть, а́ю *impf. of* ▸ опрове́ргнуть

опрове́рг|нуть, ну, нешь, *past* ~ *and* ~нул, ~ла *pf.* (*of* ▸ опроверга́ть) to refute, disprove

опроверже́ни|е, я *nt.* refutation; disproof; denial

опроки́дыва|ть, ю *impf. of* ▸ опроки́нуть

опроки́дыва|ться, юсь *impf. of* ▸ опроки́нуться

опроки́|нуть, ну, нешь *pf.* (*of* ▸ опроки́дывать) (*чашку*) to knock over; (*лодку*) to overturn

опроки́|нуться, нусь, нешься *pf.* (*of* ▸ опроки́дываться) (*о стакане*) to fall over, topple over; (*о лодке*) to capsize

опроме́тчив|ый, ~, ~а *adj.* precipitate, hasty

опро́с, а *m.* (*свидетелей*) questioning; **о. обще́ственного мне́ния** opinion poll

опро|си́ть, шу́, ~сишь *pf.* (*of* ▸ опра́шивать) (*свидетелей*) to question; (*общественное мнение*) to canvass, survey

опроти́ве|ть, ю *pf.* to become loathsome, become repulsive

опры́ск|ать, ю *pf.* (*of* ▸ опры́скивать) (+ *i.*) to sprinkle (with); to spray (with)

опры́ск|аться, аюсь *pf.* (*of* ▸ опры́скиваться) (+ *i.*) to sprinkle oneself (with); to spray oneself (with)

опры́скива|ть, ю *impf. of* ▸ опры́скать

опры́скива|ться, юсь *impf. of* ▸ опры́скаться

опря́т|ный, ~ен, ~на *adj.* neat, tidy

о́птик|а, и *f.* **1** (*раздел физики*) optics **2** (*collect.*) optical instruments

◆ **оптима́л|ьный, ~ен, ~ьна** *adj.* optimum, optimal

оптими́зм, а *m.* optimism

оптими́ст, а *m.* optimist

оптимисти́ч|ный, ~ен, ~на *adj.* optimistic

оптими́ст|ка, ки *f. of* ▸ оптими́ст

опти́ческ|ий *adj.* optic, optical; ~ое волокно́ optical fibre (BrE), fiber (AmE); **о. обма́н** optical illusion

оптови́к, á *m.* wholesaler

опто́вый *adj.* wholesale

о́птом *adv.* wholesale; **о. и в ро́зницу** wholesale and retail

опублик|ова́ть, у́ю *pf.* (*of* ▸ публикова́ть, ▸ опублико́вывать) to publish; **о. зако́н** to

◆ **key word**

promulgate a law

◆ **опублико́выва|ть, ю** *impf. of* ▸ опубликова́ть

опуска́|ть, ю *impf. of* ▸ опусти́ть

опуска́|ться, юсь *impf. of* ▸ опусти́ться

опусте́|ть, ет *pf. of* ▸ пусте́ть

опу|сти́ть, щу́, ~стишь *pf.* (*of* ▸ опуска́ть) **1** (*шторы*) to lower; to let down; **о. глаза́** to look down; **о. ру́ки** (fig.) to lose heart **2** (*воротник*) to turn down

опу|сти́ться, щу́сь, ~стишься *pf.* (*of* ▸ опуска́ться) **1** to lower oneself; **о. в кре́сло** to sink into a chair; **о. на коле́ни** to go down on one's knees **2** (*о солнце*) to sink, go down **3** (fig., *внешне, морально*) to let oneself go; to go to pieces

опустош|а́ть, а́ю *impf. of* ▸ опустоши́ть

опустош|и́ть, у́, и́шь *pf.* (*of* ▸ опустоша́ть) to devastate, lay waste, ravage

опу́т|ать, аю *pf.* (*of* ▸ опу́тывать) to enmesh, entangle (also fig.); (fig.) to ensnare

опу́тыва|ть, ю *impf. of* ▸ опу́тать

опуха́|ть, а́ю *impf. of* ▸ опу́хнуть

опу́х|нуть, ну, нешь, *past* ~, ~ла *pf.* (*of* ▸ опуха́ть) to swell (up)

о́пухол|ь, и *f.* swelling; (med.) tumour (BrE), tumor (AmE); **о. мо́зга** brain tumour (BrE), tumor (AmE)

◆ **о́пыт, а** *m.* **1** experience; **на ~е, по ~у** by experience **2** (*эксперимент*) experiment; test, trial; (*попытка*) attempt

о́пытност|ь, и *f.* experience

о́пыт|ный *adj.* **1** (~ен, ~на) (*человек*) experienced **2** (*экспериментальный*) experimental; **узна́ть ~ным путём** to learn by means of experiment

опьяне́ни|е, я *nt.* intoxication

опьяне́|ть, ю *pf. of* ▸ пьяне́ть

◆ **опя́ть** *adv.* again

ора́кул, а *m.* oracle

орангута́н, а and орангута́нг, а *m.* orang-utan

ора́нжевый *adj.* orange (*colour*)

оранжере́|я, и *f.* hothouse, greenhouse, conservatory

ора́тор, а *m.* orator, (public) speaker

ор|а́ть, у́, ёшь *impf.* (infml) to bawl, yell

орби́т|а, ы *f.* (astron., also fig.) orbit; **вы́вести на ~у** to put into orbit

орга́зм, а *m.* orgasm, climax

◆ **о́рган, а** *m.* (biol., pol., etc.) organ; **~ы вла́сти** organs of government; **половы́е ~ы** genitals

орга́н, а *m.* (mus.) organ

◆ **организа́тор, а** *m.* organizer

◆ **организа́ци|я, и** *f.* organization; **О. Объединённых На́ций** United Nations Organization

◆ **органи́зм, а** *m.* organism

организо́ван|ный, ~, ~а *p.p.p. of* ▸ организова́ть *and* (~, ~на) *adj.* organized; **~ная престу́пность** organized crime

организ|ова́ть, у́ю *impf. and pf.* to organize

организо́выва|ть, ю *impf. of* ▸ организова́ть

органи́ст, а *m.* organist

органи́ст|ка, ки *f. of* ▸ органи́ст

органи́чный, ~ен, ~на *adj.* organic

о́рги|я, и *f.* orgy

оргте́хник|а, и *f.* (*abbr. of* организацио́нная те́хника) office equipment

о́рден[1], а, *pl.* ~а́, ~о́в *m.* (*знак отли́чия*) order; decoration

о́рден[2], а, *pl.* ~ы, ~ов *m.* (*организа́ция*) order; иезуи́тский о. Society of Jesus

о́рдер, а, *pl.* ~а́, ~о́в *m.* order, warrant; (law) writ; о. на о́быск search warrant

ор|ёл, ла́ *m.* eagle; о. и́ли ре́шка? heads or tails?

орео́л, а *m.* halo, aureole

оре́х, а *m.* **1** (*плод*) nut; гре́цкий о. walnut; коко́совый о. coconut; лесно́й о. hazelnut **2** (*де́рево*) nut tree **3** (*древеси́на*) walnut

оригина́льность, и *f.* originality

оригина́л|ьный, ~ен, ~ьна *adj.* original

ориента́ци|я, и *f.* (на + *a.*) orientation (towards)

ориенти́р, а *m.* reference point; guiding line; (есте́ственный) о. landmark

ориенти́р|овать, ую *impf. and pf.* (*pf. also* ▸ сориенти́ровать) to orient, orientate

ориенти́р|оваться, уюсь *impf. and pf.* (*pf. also* ▸ сориенти́роваться) to orient oneself; to find one's bearings (also fig.)

ориенти́ровочно *adv.* tentatively; approximately

орке́стр, а *m.* orchestra; (духово́й, джа́зовый) band

оркестро́вк|а, и *f.* orchestration

оркестро́вый *adj.* orchestral

орна́мент, а *m.* ornament

орнито́лог, а *m.* ornithologist

орнитоло́ги|я, и *f.* ornithology

ороше́ни|е, я *nt.* irrigation; поля́ ~я sewage farm (BrE), sewage plant (AmE)

ортодокса́л|ьный, ~ен, ~ьна *adj.* orthodox

ортопе́д, а *m.* orthopaedist (BrE), orthopedist (AmE)

ортопеди́ческий *adj.* orthopaedic (BrE), orthopedic (AmE)

ору́ди|е, я *nt.* **1** instrument; implement; tool (also fig.) **2** (артиллери́йское) gun

оружено́с|ец, ца *m.* armour-bearer, sword-bearer; (fig.) henchman

ору́жи|е, я *nt.* weapon; (*collect.*) arms, weapons

орфогра́фи|я, и *f.* orthography, spelling

орхиде́|я, и *f.* (bot.) orchid

ос|а́, ы́, *pl.* ~ы *f.* wasp

оса́д|а, ы *f.* siege; снять ~у to raise a siege

осади́ть, жу́, ди́шь *pf.* (*of* ▸ осажда́ть) to besiege, lay siege to; to beleaguer; о. про́сьбами to bombard with requests

оса́д|ок, ка *m.* **1** (in pl.) (атмосфе́рные) precipitation **2** (части́цы) sediment, deposit

осажда́|ть, ю *impf. of* ▸ осади́ть

оса́нк|а, и *f.* carriage, bearing

осва́ива|ть, ю *impf. of* ▸ осво́ить

осва́ива|ться, юсь *impf. of* ▸ осво́иться

осве́дом|ить, лю, ишь *pf.* (*of* ▸ осведомля́ть) to inform

осве́дом|иться, люсь, ишься *pf.* (*of* ▸ осведомля́ться) (о + *p.*) to inquire (about)

осведом|ля́ть, ля́ю *impf. of* ▸ осве́домить

осведом|ля́ться, ля́юсь *impf. of* ▸ осве́домиться

освежа́|ть, а́ю *impf. of* ▸ освежи́ть

освежи́тел|ьный, ~ен, ~ьна *adj.* refreshing

освеж|и́ть, у́, и́шь *pf.* (*of* ▸ освежа́ть) to refresh, revive

освети́тел|ь, я *m.* lighting technician

освети́тельный *adj.* lighting, illuminating; о. прибо́р light

осве|ти́ть, щу́, ти́шь *pf.* (*of* ▸ освеща́ть) to light up; to illuminate; (fig.) to throw light on; (в пре́ссе) to cover, report

осве|ти́ться, щу́сь, ти́шься *pf.* (*of* ▸ освеща́ться) to light up; to brighten

освеща́|ть, ю *impf. of* ▸ освети́ть

освеща́|ться, юсь *impf. of* ▸ освети́ться

освеще́ни|е, я *nt.* light, lighting, illumination; (в пре́ссе) coverage; электри́ческое о. electric light

освещённый *p.p.p. of* ▸ освети́ть; о. луно́й moonlit

освободи́тел|ь, я *m.* liberator

освобо|ди́ть, жу́, ди́шь *pf.* (*of* ▸ освобожда́ть) **1** (го́род, страну́, челове́ка) to free, liberate; (заключённого; живо́тное) to release, set free **2** (от до́лжности) to dismiss **3** (кварти́ру) to vacate; (ме́сто; по́лку от книг) to clear, empty

освобо|ди́ться, жу́сь, ди́шься *pf.* (*of* ▸ освобожда́ться) **1** (от + *g.*) to free oneself (of, from); to become free **2** *pass. of* ▸ освободи́ть

освобожда́|ть, ю *impf. of* ▸ освободи́ть

освобожда́|ться, юсь *impf. of* ▸ освободи́ться

освобожде́ни|е, я *nt.* (го́рода) liberation; (заключённого) release

освобождённый *p.p.p. of* ▸ освободи́ть; о. от нало́га tax-free, exempt from tax

осво́|ить, ю, ишь *pf.* (*of* ▸ осва́ивать) to assimilate, master; to cope (with); to become familiar (with)

осво́|иться, юсь, ишься *pf.* (*of* ▸ осва́иваться) **1** (с + *i.*) to familiarize oneself (with) **2** to feel at home; о. в но́вой среде́ to get the feel of new surroundings

освя|ти́ть, щу́, ти́шь *pf.* (*of* ▸ освяща́ть) (eccl.) to bless

освяща́|ть, ю *impf. of* ▸ освяти́ть

оседа́|ть, ю *impf. of* ▸ осе́сть

ос|ёл, ла́ *m.* donkey; ass (also fig.)

осе́нний *adj. of* ▸ о́сень; autumnal

о́сен|ь, и f. autumn

о́сенью adv. in autumn

ос|е́сть, я́ду, я́дешь, past **~е́л, ~е́ла** pf. (of ▸ оседа́ть) **1** (о зда́нии) to subside; (о пыли, осадке) to settle **2** (о лю́дях) to settle

осети́н, а, g. pl. o. m. Ossetian

осети́н|ка, ки f. of ▸ осети́н

осети́нский adj. Ossetian

осётр, а́ m. sturgeon

осетри́н|а, ы f. (flesh of) sturgeon

осе́чк|а, и f. misfire; **дать ~у** to misfire (also fig.)

оси́н|а, ы f. aspen

оска́лива|ть, ю impf. of ▸ оска́лить

оска́лива|ться, юсь impf. of ▸ оска́литься

оска́л|ить, ю, ишь pf. (of ▸ оска́ливать): **о. зу́бы** to bare one's teeth

оска́л|иться, юсь, ишься pf. (of ▸ оска́ливаться) to bare one's teeth

оскверн|и́ть, ю́, и́шь pf. (of ▸ оскверня́ть) to defile; to profane

оскверн|я́ть, я́ю impf. of ▸ оскверни́ть

оско́л|ок, ка m. splinter; fragment

оскорби́тел|ьный, ~ен, ~ьна adj. insulting, abusive

оскорб|и́ть, лю́, и́шь pf. (of ▸ оскорбля́ть) to insult, offend

оскорбле́ни|е, я nt. insult

оскорбл|я́ть, ю impf. of ▸ оскорби́ть

ослабева́|ть, ю impf. of ▸ ослабе́ть

ослабе́|ть, ю pf. (of ▸ слабе́ть, ▸ ослабева́ть) (о челове́ке, стране́, реши́тельности) to weaken, grow weaker, become weak; (о внима́нии, кана́те, напряже́нии) to slacken; (о шу́ме, ве́тре) to abate

осла́б|ить, лю, ишь pf. (of ▸ ослабля́ть) **1** to weaken **2** (сде́лать ме́нее натя́нутым) to slacken, relax; to loosen; о. внима́ние to relax one's attention; **о. по́яс** to loosen a belt

ослабл|я́ть, ю impf. of ▸ осла́бить

осла́б|нуть, ну, нешь, past **~, ~ла** pf. = ослабе́ть

ослепи́тел|ьный, ~ен, ~ьна adj. blinding, dazzling

ослеп|и́ть, лю́, и́шь pf. (of ▸ ослепля́ть) to blind, dazzle (also fig.)

ослепле́ни|е, я nt. **1** blinding, dazzling **2** (fig.) blindness

ослепл|я́ть, ю impf. of ▸ ослепи́ть

осле́п|нуть, ну, нешь, past **~, ~ла** pf. of ▸ сле́пнуть

О́сло m. indecl. Oslo

осложне́ни|е, я nt. complication

осложн|и́ть, ю́, и́шь pf. (of ▸ осложня́ть) to complicate

осложн|и́ться, и́тся pf. (of ▸ осложня́ться) to become complicated; (о боле́зни) to develop complications

осложн|я́ть, я́ю impf. of ▸ осложни́ть

осложн|я́ться, я́ется impf. of ▸ осложни́ться

ослу́ш|аться, аюсь pf. (of ▸ ослу́шиваться) to disobey

ослу́шива|ться, юсь impf. of ▸ ослу́шаться

ослы́ш|аться, усь, ишься pf. to mishear

осма́трива|ть, ю impf. of ▸ осмотре́ть

осма́трива|ться, юсь impf. of ▸ осмотре́ться

осме́ива|ть, ю impf. of ▸ осмея́ть

осме́лива|ться, юсь impf. of ▸ осме́литься

осме́л|иться, юсь, ишься pf. (of ▸ осме́ливаться) (+ inf.) to dare; to take the liberty (of)

осме|я́ть, ю́, ёшь pf. (of ▸ осме́ивать) to mock, ridicule

осмо́тр, а m. (багажа́) examination, inspection; (шко́лы) inspection; **медици́нский о.** medical (examination); check-up

осмотр|е́ть, ю́, ~ишь pf. (of ▸ осма́тривать) (бага́ж, больно́го) to examine; (шко́лу) to inspect; (вы́ставку) to look round, look over

осмотр|е́ться, ю́сь, ~ишься pf. (of ▸ осма́триваться) **1** to look round **2** (fig.) to take one's bearings, see how the land lies

осмотри́тел|ьный, ~ен, ~ьна adj. circumspect, cautious

осмы́слен|ный, ~, ~, ~на p.p.p. of ▸ осмы́слить and (~, ~на) adj. intelligent, sensible

осмы́слива|ть, ю impf. of ▸ осмы́слить

осмы́сл|ить, ю, ишь pf. (of ▸ осмы́сливать, ▸ осмысля́ть) (истолкова́ть) to interpret; (поня́ть) to comprehend

осмысл|я́ть, я́ю impf. = осмы́сливать

осна|сти́ть, щу́, сти́шь pf. (of ▸ оснаща́ть) (naut.) to rig; (fig.) to fit out, equip

оснаща́|ть, ю impf. of ▸ оснасти́ть

оснаще́ни|е, я nt. **1** (де́йствие) rigging; fitting out **2** (обору́дование) equipment

осно́в|а, ы f. (зда́ния) foundation; (fig.) basis, foundation; (in pl.) fundamentals; **лежа́ть в ~е** (+ g.) to be the basis (of)

основа́ни|е, я nt. **1** (де́йствие) founding, foundation **2** (chem., math., etc.) base; (зда́ния) foundation; **о. горы́** foot of a mountain; **разру́шить до ~я** to raze to the ground **3** (fig.) foundation, basis; ground, reason; **на како́м ~и вы э́то утвержда́ете?** on what grounds do you assert this?; **име́ть о. предполага́ть** to have reason to suppose

основа́тел|ь, я m. founder

основа́тель|ница, ницы f. of ▸ основа́тель

основа́тел|ьный, ~ен, ~ьна adj. **1** (сове́т, причи́на) well founded; just **2** (постро́йка) solid, sound; (челове́к) solid; (осмо́тр) thorough; **~ьные до́воды** sound arguments

осн|ова́ть, ую́, уёшь pf. (of ▸ осно́вывать) **1** (учреди́ть) to found **2** (на + p.) to base (on)

основн|о́й adj. (причи́на, цель) main; (при́нцип) fundamental, basic; **~а́я мысль** keynote; **~ы́е цвета́** primary colours; **в ~о́м** on the whole; basically

основополо́жник, а m. founder, initiator

осно́выва|ть, ю *impf. of* ▶ **основа́ть**

осно́выва|ться, юсь, юсь *impf.* (**на** + *p.*) to base oneself (on); to be based, founded (on)

осо́б|а, ы *f.* person, individual, personage; **ва́жная о.** (iron.) bigwig

осо́бенно *adv.* especially; particularly; unusually; **не о.** not very, not particularly

осо́бенност|ь, и *f.* peculiarity; **в ~и** especially, in particular, (more) particularly

осо́бенн|ый *adj.* (e)special, particular, peculiar; **ничего́ ~ого** nothing in particular; nothing much

особня́к, а́ *m.* private residence; mansion, manor house

осо́бо *adv.* especially, particularly

осо́б|ый *adj.* special; particular; peculiar; **удели́ть ~ое внима́ние** (+ *d.*) to give special attention (to)

осозна|ва́ть, ю́, ёшь *impf. of* ▶ **осозна́ть**

осо́знанный *adj.* deliberate; conscious

осозна́|ть, ю *pf.* (*of* ▶ **осознава́ть**) to realize

осо́к|а, и *f.* (bot.) sedge

о́сп|а, ы *f.* smallpox; **ве́тряная о.** chicken pox

оспа́рива|ть, ю *impf.* **1** *impf. of* ▶ **оспо́рить** **2** (*impf. only*) to contend (for)

оспо́р|ить, ю, ишь *pf.* (*of* ▶ **оспа́ривать** 1) to dispute, question; **о. завеща́ние** to dispute a will

оста|ва́ться, ю́сь, ёшься *impf. of* ▶ **оста́ться**

оста́в|ить, лю, ишь *pf.* (*of* ▶ **оставля́ть**) **1** to leave; (*покинуть*) to abandon; (*надежду*) to give up; (*перестать, бросить*) to stop, give up; **о. в поко́е** to leave alone, let alone; **о. госте́й ночева́ть/обе́дать** to ask guests to stay the night/stay to dinner **2** (*сохранить*) to reserve; to keep; **о. за собо́й пра́во** to reserve the right

оставля́|ть, ю *impf.* (*of* ▶ **оста́вить**) **~ет жела́ть лу́чшего** it leaves much to be desired

остальн|о́й *adj.* the rest of; **в ~о́м** in other respects; (*as pl. n.* **~ы́е**) the others; (*as nt. n.* **~о́е**) the rest; **всё ~о́е** everything else

остана́влива|ть, ю *impf. of* ▶ **останови́ть**

остана́влива|ться, юсь *impf. of* ▶ **останови́ться**

оста́нк|и, ов (*no sg.*) remains

останов|и́ть, лю́, ~ишь *pf.* (*of* ▶ **остана́вливать**) **1** to stop **2** (*сдержать*) to stop short, restrain **3** (**на** + *p.*) (*направить*) to direct (to), concentrate (on); **о. взгляд** to rest one's gaze (on)

останов|и́ться, лю́сь, ~ишься *pf.* (*of* ▶ **остана́вливаться**) **1** to stop; to come to a stop, come to a halt **2** (*переночевать*) to stay, put up; stop (infml); **о. у знако́мых** to stay with friends **3** (**на** + *p.*) (fig., *в речи, докладе*) to dwell (on); (*о взгляде*) to settle (on), rest (on)

остано́вк|а, и *f.* **1** (*в пути, работе*) stop; (*задержка*) stoppage **2** (*автобусная*) stop; **коне́чная о.** terminus; **мне на́до прое́хать ещё одну́ ~у** I have to go one stop further

оста́т|ок, ка *m.* **1** remainder; rest; (*ткани*) remnant; (*in pl.*) remains; (*еды*) leftovers **2** (fin., comm.) rest, balance

оста́|ться, нусь, нешься *pf.* (*of* ▶ **остава́ться**) to remain; to stay; to be left (over); **о. в живы́х** to survive, come through; **о. на́ ночь** to stay the night; **от обе́да ничего́ не ~лось** there is nothing left over from dinner; (*impers.*) **~ётся, ~лось** (+ *d.*) it remains (remained), it is (was) necessary; **~лось то́лько заплати́ть** it remained only to pay

остекл|и́ть, ю́, и́шь *pf.* (*of* ▶ **остекля́ть**) to glaze

остекл|я́ть, я́ю *impf. of* ▶ **остекли́ть**

остерега́|ться, юсь *impf.* (*of* ▶ **остере́чься**) (+ *g. or inf.*) to beware (of); to be careful (of); **~йтесь соба́ки!** beware of the dog!

остере́|чься, гу́сь, жёшься, гу́тся, *past* **~гся, ~гла́сь** *pf.* (*of* ▶ **остерега́ться**

о́стов, а *m.* frame, framework (also fig.)

осторо́жно *adv.* carefully; cautiously; **о.!** look out!

осторо́жност|ь, и *f.* care; caution

осторо́ж|ный, ~ен, ~на *adj.* careful; cautious; **бу́дьте ~ны!** take care!

остри|ё, я́ *nt.* **1** (*иголки, штыка*) point **2** (*ножа, бритвы*) (cutting) edge

остр|и́ть, ю́, и́шь *impf.* (*of* ▶ **состри́ть**) (*говорить остроты*) to be witty; to make witticisms, crack jokes

остри́|чь, гу́, жёшь, гу́т, *past* **~г, ~гла** *pf. of* ▶ **стричь 1,** ▶ **стричь 2**

о́стров, а, *pl.* **~а́** *m.* island; isle

островитя́н|ин, ина, *pl.* **~е, ~** *m.* islander

островитя́н|ка, ки *f.* (*of* ▶ **островитя́нин**

остроконе́ч|ный, ~ен, ~на *adj.* pointed

острот|а, ы *f.* witticism, joke; **пло́ская о.** stupid joke; **то́нкая о.** subtle crack

острот|а́, ы́ *f.* (*ножа, ума*) sharpness; (*зрения, слуха*) keenness; (*ситуации; боли*) acuteness; (*запаха*) pungency; (*чувства*) poignancy

остроу́ми|е, я *nt.* **1** wit; wittiness **2** (*изобретательность*) ingenuity

остроу́м|ный, ~ен, ~на *adj.* **1** witty **2** (*изобретательный*) ingenious

о́стр|ый, остёр *and* **~, ~а́, ~о,** (*in fig. sense*) **~о́, ~ы,** (*in fig. sense*) **~ы́** *adj.* (*нож, ум*) sharp; (*нос*) pointed (also fig.); (*ситуация; боль*) acute; (*зрение, слух*) keen; **~ое зре́ние** keen eyesight; **о. интере́с** (**к** + *d.*) keen interest (in); **о. у́гол** (math.) acute angle

остря́к, а́ *m.* wit

осту|ди́ть, жу́, ~дишь *pf.* (*of* ▶ **остужа́ть**) to cool

остужа́|ть, ю *impf. of* ▶ **остуди́ть**

оступ|а́ться, а́юсь *impf. of* ▶ **оступи́ться**

оступ|и́ться, лю́сь, ~ишься *pf.* (*of* ▶ **оступа́ться**) to stumble

остыва́|ть, ю *impf. of* ▶ **осты́ть**

осты́|ть, ну, нешь *pf.* (*of* ▶ **остыва́ть**) to get cold; (fig.) to cool (down); **у вас чай ~л** your tea is cold

о

осуди́ть, жу́, ~дишь *pf.* (*of* ▶ **осужда́ть**) **1** (*порицать*) to censure, condemn **2** (law) (*на смерть*) to condemn, sentence; (*за* + *a.*) to convict (of) **3** (**на** + *a.*) (fig., *обречь*) to condemn

осужда́|ть, ю *impf. of* ▶ **осуди́ть**

осужде́ни|е, я *nt.* **1** censure, condemnation **2** (law) conviction

осуждённ|ый *p.p.p. of* ▶ **осуди́ть** *and adj.* condemned; convicted; (*as n.* **о.**, ~**ого**, *f.* ~**ая**, ~**ой**) convict

осу́н|уться, усь, ешься *pf.* (*о лице*) to grow thin, get pinched(-looking)

осуш|а́ть, а́ю *impf. of* ▶ **осуши́ть**

осуш|и́ть, у́, ~ишь *pf.* (*of* ▶ **осуша́ть**) (*болото, луга; стакан*) to drain; (*помещение*) to dry

осуществи́м|ый, ~, ~а *adj.* practicable, feasible

осуществ|и́ть, лю́, и́шь *pf.* (*of* ▶ **осуществля́ть**) (*мечту*) to realize, bring about; (*намерение*) to carry out; (*решение*) to implement; (*контроль, руководство*) to exercise

осуществ|и́ться, и́тся *pf.* (*of* ▶ **осуществля́ться**) to be fulfilled, come true

⚟ **осуществле́ни|е, я** *nt.* realization; accomplishment; implementation

⚟ **осуществля́|ть, ю, ет** *impf. of* ▶ **осуществи́ть**

⚟ **осуществля́|ться, ется** *impf. of* ▶ **осуществи́ться**

осчастли́в|ить, лю, ишь *pf.* (*of* ▶ **осчастли́вливать**) to make happy

осчастли́влива|ть, ю *impf. of* ▶ **осчастли́вить**

осы́п|ать, лю, лешь *pf.* (*of* ▶ **осыпа́ть**) (+ *a. and i.*) (*покрыть*) to strew (with); to shower (on); (fig.) to heap (on); **о. поцелу́ями** to smother with kisses

осып|а́ть, а́ю *impf. of* ▶ **осы́пать**

осы́п|аться, люсь, лешься *pf.* (*of* ▶ **осыпа́ться**) (*о насыпи*) to crumble; (*о листьях*) to fall

осып|а́ться, а́юсь *impf. of* ▶ **осы́паться**

ос|ь, и, *pl.* ~**и,** ~**е́й** *f.* **1** (geom.) axis; **земна́я о.** axis of the equator **2** (*колеса*) axle

осьмино́г, а *m.* (zool.) octopus

осяза́ем|ый, ~, ~а *adj.* tangible; ~**ые результа́ты** tangible results

осяза́ни|е, я *nt.* touch; **чу́вство** ~**я** a sense of touch

⚟ **от, ото** *prep.* + *g.* **1** from; of; for; (*указывает на исходную точку, источник чего-н.*): **от це́нтра го́рода** from the centre of the town; **от нача́ла до конца́** from beginning to end; **де́ти от пяти́ до десяти́ лет** children from five to ten (years); **бли́зко от го́рода** near the town; **на се́вер от Москвы́** to the north of Moscow; **от всей души́** with all one's heart; **от и́мени** (+ *g.*) on behalf

(of); **я получи́л письмо́ от до́чери** I have received a letter from my daughter; **сын от пре́жнего бра́ка** a son by a previous marriage **2** (*указывает на причину чего-н.*): **вскри́кнуть от ра́дости** to cry out for joy; **дрожа́ть от стра́ха** to tremble with fear; **умере́ть от го́лода** to die of hunger; **глаза́, кра́сные от слёз** eyes red with weeping **3** (*указывает на дату документа*): **ва́ше письмо́ от пе́рвого а́вгуста** your letter of the first of August **4** (*указывает на целое, которому принадлежит часть*): **ключ от две́ри** door key; **пу́говица от пиджака́** coat button **5** (*против*) for; against; **миксту́ра от ка́шля** cough mixture; **защища́ть глаза́ от со́лнца** to shield one's eyes from the sun; **застрахова́ть от огня́** to insure against fire

ота́плива|ть, ю *impf. of* ▶ **отопи́ть**

ота́р|а, ы *f.* large flock (*of sheep*)

отбега́|ть, ю *impf. of* ▶ **отбежа́ть**

отбе|жа́ть, гу́, жи́шь, гу́т *pf.* (*of* ▶ **отбега́ть**) to run off

отбе́ливател|ь, я *m.* bleach

отбе́лива|ть, ю *impf. of* ▶ **отбели́ть**

отбел|и́ть, ю́, ~ишь *pf.* (*of* ▶ **отбе́ливать**) to bleach

отбива́|ть, ю *impf. of* ▶ **отби́ть**

отбива́|ться, юсь *impf. of* ▶ **отби́ться**

отбивн|о́й *adj.*: ~**а́я котле́та** (cul.) chop

отбира́|ть, ю *impf. of* ▶ **отобра́ть**

отб|и́ть, отобью́, отобьёшь *pf.* (*of* ▶ **отбива́ть**) **1** to beat off, repel; **о. ата́ку** to beat off an attack; **о. уда́р** to parry a blow **2** (*вернуть себе силой*) to retake, recapture; (*привлечь к себе*) to win over; (infml) **о.** *кого/что* **у кого́-н.** to take *sb/sth* off sb, do sb out of *sb/sth* **3** (*удалить*) to remove, dispel; **о. у кого́-н. охо́ту к чему́-н.** to discourage sb from sth, take away sb's inclination for sth **4** (*отколоть*) to break off, knock off; **о. но́сик у ча́йника** to knock the spout off a teapot **5**: **о. такт** to beat (out) time **6** (*повредить ударами*) to damage by blows, by knocks; **о. ру́ку нело́вким уда́ром** to hurt one's hand with a clumsy blow

отб|и́ться, отобью́сь, отобьёшься *pf.* (*of* ▶ **отбива́ться**) **1** (**от** + *g.*) to defend oneself (against); to repel, beat off **2** (*отстать*) to drop behind, straggle; **о. от ста́да** to stray from the herd

отблагодар|и́ть, ю́, и́шь *pf.* to show one's gratitude (to)

отбо́р, а *m.* selection; **есте́ственный о.** (biol.) natural selection

отбо́рный *adj.* choice, select(ed)

отбра́сыва|ть, ю *impf. of* ▶ **отбро́сить**

отбро́|сить, шу, сишь *pf.* (*of* ▶ **отбра́сывать**) **1** to throw off; to cast away; **о. тень** to cast a shadow **2** (mil.) to repel **3** (*отвергнуть*) to give up, reject, discard; **о. мысль** to give up an idea

отбро́с|ы, ов *m. pl.* (*sg.* ~, ~**а**) garbage, refuse; **о. произво́дства** industrial waste;

O

о. о́бщества (fig.) dregs of society

отва́г|а, и f. courage, bravery

отва́ж|ный, ~ен, ~на adj. courageous, brave

отва́лива|ться, юсь impf. of ▶ отвали́ться

отвали́|ться, ю́сь, ~ишься pf. (of ▶ отва́ливаться) to fall off

отва́рива|ть, ю impf. of ▶ отвари́ть

отвар|и́ть, ю́, ~ишь pf. (of ▶ отва́ривать) to boil

отвез|ти́, у́, ёшь, past ~, ~ла́ pf. (of ▶ отвози́ть) (везя, доставить) to take; (везя, убрать) to take away

отверг|а́ть, а́ю impf. of ▶ отве́ргнуть

отве́рг|нуть, ну, нешь, past ~/~нул, ~ла pf. (of ▶ отверга́ть) to reject, turn down

отвер|ну́ться, ну́сь, нёшься pf. (of ▶ отвора́чиваться) to turn away, turn aside; о. от кого́-н. (fig.) to turn one's back upon sb

отве́рсти|е, я nt. opening; (дыра) hole; (в торговом/игровом автомате) slot

отвёртк|а, и f. screwdriver

отве́с|ный, ~ен, ~на adj. (линия) perpendicular; (скала) steep

отве|сти́, ду́, дёшь, past ~л, ~ла́ pf. (of ▶ отводи́ть) **1** (ведя, доставить) to lead, take, conduct **2** (ведя, направить в сторону) to draw aside, take aside **3** (изменить направление движения чего-либо) to deflect; он не мог о. от неё глаз he could not take his eyes off her **4** (выделить) to allot, assign

⚔ **отве́т, а** m. **1** answer, reply, response; в о. (на + a.) in reply (to), in response (to) **2**: быть в ~е (за + a.) to be answerable (for); призва́ть к ~у to call to account

ответвле́ни|е, я nt. branch, offshoot (also fig.)

⚔ **отве́|тить, чу, тишь** pf. (of ▶ отвеча́ть 1) **1** (на + a.) to answer, reply (to); о. на письмо́ to answer a letter; о. уро́к to repeat one's lesson **2** (на + a. and i.) to answer (with), return; о. на чьё-н. чу́вство to return sb's feelings **3** (за + a.) to answer (for), pay (for); вы ~тите за э́ти слова́! you will pay for these words!

отве́тный adj. given in reply; (визит) return; (меры) retaliatory

⚔ **отве́тственност|ь, и** f. responsibility; привле́чь к ~и (за + a.) to call to account, bring to book

отве́тствен|ный, ~, ~на adj. **1** (человек; работа) responsible **2** (решающий) crucial; о. моме́нт crucial point

отве́тчик, а m. (law) defendant

отве́тчи|ца, цы f. of ▶ отве́тчик

⚔ **отвеча́|ть, ю** impf. **1** impf. of ▶ отве́тить **2** (за + a.) to answer (for), be answerable (for) **3** (+ d.) to answer (to), meet, be up (to); о. тре́бованиям to meet requirements

отвинти́|ть, чу́, ти́шь pf. (of ▶ отви́нчивать) to unscrew

отвин|ти́ться, ти́тся pf. (of ▶ отви́нчиваться) to unscrew, come unscrewed

отви́нчива|ть, ю, ет impf. of ▶ отвинти́ть

отви́нчива|ться, ется impf. of ▶ отвинти́ться

отвлека́|ть, ю impf. of ▶ отвле́чь

отвлека́|ться, юсь impf. of ▶ отвле́чься

отвлечён|ный, ~, ~на adj. abstract

отвле́|чь, ку́, чёшь, ку́т, past ~к, ~кла́ pf. (of ▶ отвлека́ть) to distract, divert; о. чьё-н. внима́ние to divert sb's attention

отвле́|чься, ку́сь, чёшься, ку́тся, past ~кся, ~кла́сь pf. (of ▶ отвлека́ться) **1** to be distracted; о. от те́мы to digress **2** (от + g.) (абстрагироваться) to abstract oneself (from)

отво|ди́ть, жу́, ~дишь impf. of ▶ отвести́

отвоева́ть¹, юю, юешь pf. (of ▶ отвоёвывать) (у + g.) (вернуть войной) to win back (from), retake (from)

отвоева́ть², юю, юешь pf. (infml) **1** (какое-н. время) to fight, spend in fighting; мы де́сять лет ~ева́ли we have fought for ten years **2** (кончить воевать) to finish fighting

отвоёвыва|ть, ю impf. of ▶ отвоева́ть¹

отво|зи́ть, жу́, ~зишь impf. of ▶ отвезти́

отвора́чива|ться, юсь impf. of ▶ отверну́ться

отвор|и́ть, ю́, ~ишь pf. (of ▶ отворя́ть) to open

отвор|и́ться, ~ится pf. (of ▶ отворя́ться) to open

отворо́т, а m. (на пиджаке) lapel; (на брюках) turn-up (BrE), cuff (AmE); (сапога, рукава) cuff

отворя́|ть, я́ю, я́ет impf. of ▶ отвори́ть

отворя́|ться, я́ется impf. of ▶ отвори́ться

отврати́тел|ьный, ~ен, ~ьна adj. repulsive, disgusting

отвраще́ни|е, я nt. disgust, repugnance; пита́ть о. (к + d.) to have an aversion (for), loathe

отвык|а́ть, а́ю impf. of ▶ отвы́кнуть

отвы́к|нуть, ну, нешь, past ~, ~ла pf. (of ▶ отвыка́ть) (от + g. or inf.) (от плохой привычки) to break oneself (of the habit of), give up; (от работы, ходьбы) to get out of the habit of, become unaccustomed to; (от друзей, своей страны) to become estranged from

отвя|за́ть, жу́, ~жешь pf. (of ▶ отвя́зывать) to untie, unfasten

отвя|за́ться, жу́сь, ~жешься pf. (of ▶ отвя́зываться) **1** (освободиться от привязи) to come untied, come loose **2** (fig., infml) (от + g.) (отделаться) to get rid of, shake off, get shot (of) **3** (fig., infml) (от + g.) (перестать надоедать) to leave alone, leave in peace; to stop nagging; ~жи́сь от меня́! leave me alone!

отвя́зыва|ть, ю impf. of ▶ отвяза́ть

отвя́зыва|ться, юсь impf. of ▶ отвяза́ться

отгад|а́ть, а́ю pf. (of ▶ отга́дывать) to guess

отга́дк|а, и f. answer, solution (to a riddle)

отга́дыва|ть, ю impf. of ▶ отгада́ть

отгиба́|ть, ю, ет impf. of ▶ отогну́ть

отгиба́|ться, ется impf. of ▶ отогну́ться

о

отговáрива|ть, ю *impf. of* ▶ отговори́ть
отговор|и́ть, ю́, и́шь *pf.* (*of* ▶ отговáривать) (от + *g. or* + *inf.*) to dissuade (from); я ~и́л его́ éхать I have talked him out of going
отговóрк|а, и *f.* excuse
отгоня́|ть, ю *impf. of* ▶ отогнáть
отгорáжива|ть, ю *impf. of* ▶ отгороди́ть
отгорáжива|ться, юсь *impf. of* ▶ отгороди́ться
отгоро|ди́ть, жу́, ~ди́шь *pf.* (*of* ▶ отгорáживать) to fence off, partition off
отгоро|ди́ться, жу́сь, ~ди́шься *pf.* (*of* ▶ отгорáживаться) to fence oneself off; (fig., infml) (от + *g.*) to shut *or* cut oneself off (from)
отгрыз|áть, áю *impf. of* ▶ отгры́зть
отгры́з|ть, у́, ёшь, *past* ~, ~ла *pf.* (*of* ▶ отгрызáть) to bite off, gnaw off
ⱷ **отда|вáть**, ю́, ёшь *impf. of* ▶ отдáть
отда|вáться, ю́сь, ёшься *impf. of* ▶ отдáться
отдав|и́ть, лю́, ~ишь *pf.* to crush; о. комý-н. нóгу to tread on sb's foot
отдалён|ный, ~, ~на *adj.* distant, remote
отд|áть, áм, áшь, áст, ади́м, ади́те, адýт, *past* ~áл, ~алá, ~áло *pf.* (*of* ▶ отдавáть) **1** (*дать обрáтно*) to give back, return; о. себé отчёт (в + *p.*) to be aware (of), realize **2** (*посвяти́ть*) to devote; о. жизнь наýке to devote one's life to scholarship **3** (+ *a. and d., or* + *a. and* за + *a.*) (*вы́дать зáмуж*) to give in marriage (to); to give away **4** (в + *a. or* под + *a.*) (*вручи́ть*) to give, put, place (= *hand over for certain purpose*); о. кни́гу в переплёт to send a book to be bound; о. под суд to prosecute **5** (*in comb. with certain nn.*) to give; to make (*or not requiring separate translation*); о. прикáз (+ *d.*) to issue an order (to)
отд|áться, áмся, áшься, áстся, ади́мся, ади́тесь, адýтся, *past* ~áлся, ~алáсь *pf.* (*of* ▶ отдавáться) **1** (+ *d.*) (*победи́телю*) to give oneself up (to); (*наýке*) to devote oneself (to); (*о жéнщине*) to give oneself (to) **2** (*о гóлосе, об эхе*) to resound; to reverberate; to ring
отдáч|а, и *f.* **1** (*от влóженного*) return **2** (*эффекти́вность*) efficiency, performance **3** (*при вы́стреле*) recoil
ⱷ **отдéл, а** *m.* department; о. кáдров personnel department
отдéл|ать, аю *pf.* (*of* ▶ отдéлывать) to finish, put the finishing touches (to); to decorate
отдéл|аться, аюсь *pf.* (*of* ▶ отдéлываться) (infml) **1** (от + *g.*) to get rid (of), get shot (of) **2** (+ *i.*) to escape (with); легко́ о. to have a lucky escape
ⱷ **отделéни|е, я** *nt.* **1** (*дéйствие*) separation; о. цéркви от госудáрства separation of church and state, secularization; (*с обретéнием незави́симости*) secession **2** (*учреждéние*) department, branch; о.

мили́ции local police station **3** (*вмести́лище*) compartment, section; (*представлéния*) part **4** (mil.) section
отдел|и́ть, ю́, ~ишь *pf.* (*of* ▶ отделя́ть) **1** (*отня́ть*) to separate off; о. перегорóдкой to partition off
отдел|и́ться, ю́сь, ~ишься *pf.* (*of* ▶ отделя́ться) (*отодви́нуться*) to move away, separate; (*оторвáться*) to get detached; to come off; (*быть отграни́ченным от чего́-л.*) to be separated
отдéлк|а, и *f.* **1** (*дéйствие*) finishing; trimming **2** (*украшéние*) finish, decoration; (*в кóмнате*) decor
отдéлыва|ть, ю *impf. of* ▶ отдéлать
отдéлыва|ться, юсь *impf. of* ▶ отдéлаться
отдéльно *adv.* separately
ⱷ **отдéльный** *adj.* **1** separate; (*нéкоторый*) individual; (*еди́ничный*) isolated **2** (mil.) independent
отделя́|ть, я́ю *impf. of* ▶ отдели́ть
отделя́|ться, я́юсь *impf. of* ▶ отдели́ться
отдёргива|ть, ю *impf. of* ▶ отдёрнуть
отдёр|нуть, ну, нешь *pf.* (*of* ▶ отдёргивать) **1** (*в стóрону*) to draw aside, pull aside **2** (*рýку*) to pull back, withdraw
отдирá|ть, ю *impf. of* ▶ отодрáть
отдохн|у́ть, у́, ёшь *pf.* (*of* ▶ отдыхáть) to rest; to have a rest
отдýшин|а, ы *f.* air hole, (air) vent; (fig.) outlet
ⱷ **óтдых, а** *m.* rest; relaxation; (*óтпуск*) holiday (BrE), vacation (AmE)
ⱷ **отдыхá|ть**, ю *impf.* (*of* ▶ отдохну́ть) to be resting; (*быть в óтпуске*) to be on holiday (BrE), vacation (AmE); (*проводи́ть óтпуск*) to holiday (BrE), vacation (AmE)
отдыхá|ющий *pres. part. of* ▶ отдыхáть; (*as n.* о., ~ющего, *f.* ~ющая, ~ющей) holidaymaker (BrE), vacationer (AmE)
отдыш|áться, ýсь, ~ишься *pf.* to recover one's breath
отёк, а *m.* (med.) oedema (BrE), edema (AmE); о. лёгких emphysema
ⱷ **отéл|ь, я** *m.* hotel
ⱷ **отéц, цá** *m.* father (also fig.); О. Небéсный (relig.) the heavenly Father
ⱷ **отéчественн|ый** *adj. of* ▶ отéчество; Вели́кая О~ая войнá the Great Patriotic War (1941-45)
отéчеств|о, а *nt.* native land, fatherland, homeland
отжá|ть, отожмý, отожмёшь *pf.* (*of* ▶ отжимáть) to wring out
отжимá|ть, ю *impf. of* ▶ отжáть
óтзвук, а *m.* echo (also fig.)
ⱷ **óтзыв, а** *m.* **1** (*мнéние*) opinion, judgement **2** (*рекомендáция*) reference; testimonial; дать хорóший о. о ком-н. to give sb a good reference **3** (*рецéнзия*) review
отзывá|ться, юсь *impf. of* ▶ отозвáться
отзы́вчив|ый, ~, ~а *adj.* responsive

О

отит, а *m.* (med.) otitis (*inflammation of the ear*)

отказ, а *m.* **1** refusal; получить о. to be refused, be turned down; до ∼a to the maximum; стакан наполнен до ∼a the glass is full to overflowing; поверните ручку до ∼a turn the handle to the maximum **2** (от + *g.*) renunciation (of), giving up (of) **3** (*механизма*) failure

отка|зать, жу, ∼жешь pf. (of ▶ отказывать) **1** (+ *d. and* в + *p.*) to refuse, deny; она ∼зала ему в просьбе she refused his request; ему нельзя о. в таланте there is no denying that he has talent **2** (*о механизме*) to fail, break down

отка|заться, жусь, ∼жешься pf. (of ▶ отказываться) **1** (от + *g. or* + *inf.*) to refuse, decline; о. от предложения to turn down a proposal; о. от своих слов to retract one's words **2** (*отречься*) to renounce, give up; (*от права*) to relinquish; (*от власти*) to abdicate; о. от борьбы to give up the struggle

отказыва|ть, ю impf. of ▶ отказать

отказыва|ться, юсь impf. of ▶ отказаться

откалыва|ть, ю impf. of ▶ отколоть

откалыва|ться, юсь impf. of ▶ отколоться

откапыва|ть, ю impf. of ▶ откопать

откармлива|ть, ю impf. of ▶ откормить

отка|тить, чу, ∼тишь pf. (of ▶ откатывать) (*бревно*) to roll away

отка|титься, чусь, ∼тишься pf. (of ▶ откатываться) to roll away

откатыва|ть, ю impf. of ▶ откатить

откатыва|ться, юсь impf. of ▶ откатиться

откач|ать, аю pf. (of ▶ откачивать) **1** (*воздух, воду*) to pump out **2** (*человека*) to resuscitate

откачива|ть, ю impf. of ▶ откачать

откашл|иваться, иваюсь impf. of ▶ откашляться

откашл|яться, яюсь pf. (of ▶ откашливаться) to clear one's throat

откидыва|ться, юсь impf. of ▶ откинуться

отки|нуться, нусь, нешься pf. (of ▶ откидываться) to lean back; to recline, settle back

откладыва|ть, ю impf. of ▶ отложить

отклеива|ть, ю, ет impf. of ▶ отклеить

отклеива|ться, ется impf. of ▶ отклеиться

отклe|ить, ю, ишь pf. (of ▶ отклеивать) to peel off

отклe|иться, ится pf. (of ▶ отклеиваться) to come unstuck

отклик, а *m.* (*ответ на зов*) response; (fig., *в печати*) comment

отклик|аться, аюсь impf. (of ▶ откликнуться) (на + *a.*) to answer, respond (to) (also fig.)

отклик|нуться, нусь, нешься pf. (of ▶ откликаться

отклонени|е, я *nt.* **1** (*отход в сторону; от нормы*) deviation; divergence **2** (*отказ*) declining, refusal

отклон|ить, ю, ∼ишь pf. (of ▶ отклонять) **1** (*в сторону*) to deflect **2** (*отказать*) to decline; о. предложение to decline an offer

отклон|иться, юсь, ∼ишься pf. (of ▶ отклоняться) (*от курса*) to deviate; (*от удара*) to dodge; (*отодвинуться*) to move aside; о. от темы to digress

отклоня|ть, ю impf. of ▶ отклонить

отклоня|ться, юсь impf. of ▶ отклониться

отключа|ть, аю impf. of ▶ отключить

отключа|ться, аюсь impf. of ▶ отключиться

отключ|ить, у, ишь pf. (of ▶ отключать) (elec.) to cut off, disconnect

отключ|иться, усь, ишься pf. (of ▶ отключаться) **1** to become disconnected **2** (infml, *о человеке*) to switch off

откол|оть, ю, ∼ешь pf. (of ▶ откалывать) **1** (*отломать*) to break off; (*отбить*) to chop off; (*от семьи*) to cut off **2** (*булавку, чепец*) to unpin

откол|оться, юсь, ∼ешься pf. (of ▶ откалываться) **1** (*отломаться*) to break off **2** (*о булавке, чепце*) to come unpinned *or* undone **3** (fig., *от семьи*) to break away; to cut oneself off

откопа|ть, ю pf. (of ▶ откапывать) **1** to dig out; (*труп*) to exhume, disinter **2** (fig., infml, *найти*) to dig up, unearth

откорм|ить, лю, ∼ишь pf. (of ▶ откармливать) to fatten (up)

откос, а *m.* **1** (*покатый спуск*) slope, side (of *embankment, etc.*); о. холма hillside **2** (rail.) embankment; пустить поезд под о. to derail a train

откровени|е, я *nt.* revelation

откровенност|ь, и *f.* candour (BrE), candor (AmE), frankness; (*in pl.*) (infml) candid revelations

откровен|ный, ∼ен, ∼на adj. **1** (*искренний*) candid, frank **2** (*нескрываемый*) open, unconcealed; ∼ная неприязнь unconcealed hostility **3** (infml, *о платье*) revealing

откру|тить, чу, ∼тишь pf. (of ▶ откручивать) to untwist; о. кран to turn off a tap

откручива|ть, ю impf. of ▶ открутить

открывалк|а, и *f.* (infml) **1** (*для банок*) can opener **2** (*для бутылок*) bottle opener

открыва|ть, ю impf. of ▶ открыть

открыва|ться, юсь impf. of ▶ открыться

открыти|е, я *nt.* **1** (*действие*) opening **2** (*научное*) discovery

открытк|а, и *f.* postcard

открыто *adv.* openly

открыт|ый p.p.p. of ▶ открыть *and adj.* open; на ∼ом воздухе, под ∼ым небом out of doors, in the open (air); ∼ое море the open sea; ∼ое платье low-necked dress

откр|ыть, ою, оешь pf. (of ▶ открывать) **1** to open; о. кому-н. глаза на что-н. (fig.) to open sb's eyes to sth; о. огонь (mil.) to open fire; о. счёт to open an account **2** (*обнажить*) to uncover, reveal (also fig.); о. секрет to reveal a secret **3** (*обнаружить*) to discover; о.

Аме́рику (fig., iron.) to retail stale news **4** (*во́ду, газ*) to turn on

откр|ь́ться, о́юсь, о́ешься pf. (of ▸ **открыва́ться**) **1** (*дверь, глаза́*) to open **2** (*обнаружиться*) to come to light, be revealed; **пе́ред на́ми ∼ы́лся великоле́пный вид** a magnificent view unfolded before us

⚹ **отку́да** adv. interrog. where from; *rel.* whence, from which; **о. вы?** where are you from?; **о. вы об э́том зна́ете?** how come you know about it?

отку́да-нибудь adv. from somewhere or other

отку́да-то adv. from somewhere

откуп|а́ться, а́юсь impf. of ▸ **откупи́ться**

откуп|и́ться, лю́сь, ∼ишься pf. (of ▸ **откупа́ться**) (от + g.) to pay off

отку́порива|ть, ю impf. of ▸ **отку́порить**

отку́пор|ить, ю, ишь pf. (of ▸ **отку́поривать**) (*буты́лку*) to uncork; (*ба́нку*) to open

отку|си́ть, шу́, ∼сишь pf. (of ▸ **отку́сывать**) to bite off; (*щипца́ми*) to cut off

отку́сыва|ть, ю impf. of ▸ **откуси́ть**

отла́дчик, а m. (comput., *програ́мма*) debugger

отлакир|ова́ть, у́ю pf. of ▸ **лакирова́ть**

отла́мыва|ть, ю, ет impf. of ▸ **отлома́ть**, ▸ **отломи́ть**

отла́мыва|ться, ется impf. of ▸ **отлома́ться**, ▸ **отломи́ться**

отлет|а́ть, а́ю impf. of ▸ **отлете́ть**

отле|те́ть, чу́, ти́шь pf. (of ▸ **отлета́ть**) **1** (*улете́ть*) to fly (away, off); (fig., *исче́знуть*) to fly, vanish **2** (*о мяче́*) to rebound, bounce back **3** (infml, *о пу́говице*) to come off

отли́в, а m. ebb, ebb tide

отлива́|ть, ю impf. of ▸ **отли́ть**

отли́ть, отолью́, отольёшь, past **о́тлил, отлила́, о́тлило** pf. (of ▸ **отлива́ть**) **1** (+ a. or g.) (*молока́*) to pour off; (*отхлы́нуть*) to flood back **2** (tech.) to cast, found

отлич|а́ть, а́ю impf. of ▸ **отличи́ть**

⚹ **отлич|а́ться, а́юсь** impf. **1** (pf. ∼**и́ться**) to distinguish oneself, excel (also joc., iron.) **2** (impf. only) (от + g.) to differ (from) **3** (impf. only) (+ i.) to be notable (for)

⚹ **отли́чи|е, я** nt. **1** difference, distinction; **в о. от** (+ g.) unlike, in contrast to **2** (*оце́нка*) distinction; (*заслу́га*) distinguished services

отличи́тельный adj. distinctive; distinguishing; **о. при́знак** distinguishing feature

отлич|и́ть, у́, и́шь pf. (of ▸ **отлича́ть**) **1** to distinguish; **о. одно́ от друго́го** to tell one thing from another **2** (*вы́делить из числа́ други́х*) to single out

отлич|и́ться, у́сь, и́шься pf. of ▸ **отлича́ться 1**

отли́чно 1 adv. excellently; perfectly; extremely well; **о. знать** to know perfectly

well **2** n., nt. indecl. 'excellent' mark (*in school, etc.*)

⚹ **отли́ч|ный, ∼ен, ∼на** adj. **1** (от + g.) (*ино́й*) different (from) **2** (*превосхо́дный*) excellent; perfect; extremely good; **∼но!** excellent!

отло́г|ий, ∼, ∼а adj. sloping

отлож|и́ть, у́, ∼ишь pf. (of ▸ **откла́дывать**) **1** (*положи́ть в сто́рону*) to put aside, set aside; (*сохрани́ть*) to put away, put by; **о. на чёрный день** to put by for a rainy day **2** (*отсро́чить*) to put off, postpone **3** (*о пти́цах*) to lay

отлома́|ть, ю pf. (of ▸ **отла́мывать**) to break off

отлома́|ться, ю, ет, ется pf. (of ▸ **отла́мываться**) to break off

отлом|и́ть, лю́, ∼ит pf. = **отлома́ть**

отлом|и́ться, ∼ится pf. = **отлома́ться**

отлуч|а́ться, а́юсь impf. of ▸ **отлучи́ться**

отлуч|и́ться, у́сь, и́шься pf. (of ▸ **отлуча́ться**) to absent oneself

отма́хива|ть, ю impf. of ▸ **отмахну́ть**

отма́хива|ться, юсь impf. of ▸ **отмахну́ться**

отмах|ну́ть, ну́, нёшь pf. (of ▸ **отма́хивать**) to wave away, brush off (*with one's hand*)

отмах|ну́ться, ну́сь, нёшься pf. (of ▸ **отма́хиваться**) (от + g.) **1** = **отмахну́ть**; **о. от комаро́в** to brush mosquitoes off **2** (fig.) to brush aside

о́тмел|ь, и f. sandbank

отме́н|а, ы f. abolition; repeal; cancellation

отмен|и́ть, ю́, ∼ишь pf. (of ▸ **отменя́ть**) (*нало́г*) to abolish; (*зако́н*) to repeal; (*реше́ние, приказа́ние*) to revoke; (*заседа́ние*) to cancel

отме́н|ный, ∼ен, ∼на adj. excellent

отмен|я́ть, я́ю impf. of ▸ **отмени́ть**

отмер|е́ть, отомрёт, past **о́тмер, ∼ла́, о́тмерло** pf. (of ▸ **отмира́ть**) to die off; (fig.) to die out, die away

отмерз|а́ть, а́ет impf. of ▸ **отмёрзнуть**

отмёрз|нуть, нет, past **∼, ∼ла** pf. (of ▸ **отмерза́ть**) (infml) to freeze; **ру́ки у меня́ ∼ли** my hands are frozen

отме́рива|ть, ю impf. of ▸ **отме́рить**

отме́р|ить, ю, ишь pf. (of ▸ **отме́ривать**, ▸ **отмеря́ть**) to measure off

отмер|я́ть, я́ю impf. = **отме́ривать**

отме|сти́, ту́, тёшь, past **∼л, ∼ла́** pf. (of ▸ **отмета́ть**) to sweep aside (also fig.)

отмета́|ть, ю impf. of ▸ **отмести́**

⚹ **отме́|тить, чу, тишь** pf. (of ▸ **отмеча́ть**) **1** (*ме́сто в кни́ге*) to mark, note; (*прису́тствующих; высоту́*) to make a note (of); **о. га́лочкой** to tick off **2** (*досто́инства*) to point to, mention, record; **о. чьи-н. по́двиги** to point to sb's feats **3** (*день рожде́ния*) to celebrate

отме́тк|а, и f. **1** (*знак*) mark; (*за́пись*) note **2** (*оце́нка*) mark

⚹ **отмеча́|ть, ю** impf. of ▸ **отме́тить**

отмира́|ть, ет impf. of ▸ **отмере́ть**

отмора́жива|ть, ю *impf. of* ▶ **отморо́зить**

отморо́|зить, жу, зишь *pf.* (*of*
▶ **отмора́живать**) to injure by frostbite;
я ~зил у́ши my ears are frostbitten

отмыва́ни|е, я *nt.*: **о. де́нег** money
laundering

отмыва́|ть, ю *impf. of* ▶ **отмы́ть**

отмыва́|ться, юсь *impf. of* ▶ **отмы́ться**

отмы́|ть, о́ю, о́ешь *pf.* (*of* ▶ **отмыва́ть**)
1 (*руки*) to wash clean **2** (*грязь*) to wash
off, wash away **3** (fig., infml): **о. де́ньги** to
launder money

отмы́|ться, о́юсь, о́ешься *pf.* (*of*
▶ **отмыва́ться**) **1** (*о человеке*) to wash
oneself clean **2** (*о руках*) to become/get
clean **3** (*о грязи*) to come out, come off

отнес|ти́, у́, ёшь, *past* **~, ~ла́** *pf.* (*of*
▶ **относи́ть**) **1** (**в** + *a. or* **к** + *d.*) (*доставить*)
to take (to) **2** to carry away, carry off;
(*impers.*) **ло́дку ~ло́ тече́нием** the
boat was carried away by the current;
(*переместить*) to move **3** (**к** + *d.*) to ascribe
(to), attribute (to), refer (to); **мы ~ли́ его́
раздражи́тельность на счёт глухоты́** we put
his irritability down to his deafness

отнес|ти́сь, у́сь, ёшься, *past* **~ся, ~ла́сь**
pf. (*of* ▶ **относи́ться 1**) (**к** + *d.*) to treat; to
regard; **хорошо́ о. к кому́-н.** to treat sb well,
be nice to sb; **как вы ~ли́сь к его́ слова́м?**
what did you think of what he said?

отнима́|ть, ю *impf. of* ▶ **отня́ть**

⚹ **относи́тельно 1** *adv.* relatively **2** *prep.*
(+ *g.*) concerning, about, with regard to

относи́тельност|ь, и *f.* relativity; **тео́рия
~и Эйнште́йна** Einstein's Theory of
Relativity

относи́тель|ный, ~ен, ~ьна *adj.* relative

⚹ **отно́|си́ть, шу́, ~сишь** *impf. of* ▶ **отнести́**

⚹ **отно́|си́ться, шу́сь, ~сишься** *impf.*
1 *impf. of* ▶ **отнести́сь 2** (*impf. only*)
(**к** + *d.*) to concern, have to do (with), relate
(to); **э́то к де́лу не ~сится** that's beside
the point, that is irrelevant **3** (*impf. only*)
(**к** + *d.*) to date (from); **э́тот храм ~сится к
двена́дцатому ве́ку** this church dates from
the twelfth century

⚹ **отноше́ни|е, я** *nt.* **1** (**к** + *d.*) attitude (to);
treatment (of) **2** (*связь*) relation; respect;
име́ть о. к чему́-н. to bear a relation to sth,
have a bearing on sth; **не име́ть ~я** (**к** + *d.*)
to bear no relation (to), have nothing to do
(with); **в ~и** (+ *g.*) *or* **по ~ю** (**к** + *d.*) with
respect (to), with regard (to) **3** (*in pl.*) (*связи
между людьми*) relations; terms; **быть в
дру́жеских ~ях** (**с** + *i.*) to be on friendly
terms (with); **вы́яснить ~я** (**с** + *i.*) to have
it out (with) **4** (math.) ratio; **в прямо́м
(обра́тном) ~и** in direct (inverse) ratio

отны́не *adv.* (rhet.) henceforth

отню́дь *adv.* by no means, not at all

от|ня́ть, ниму́, ни́мешь, *past* **~ня́л, ~няла́,
~ня́ло** *pf.* (*of* ▶ **отнима́ть**) to take (away);
о. жизнь у кого́-н. to take sb's life; **от шести́
о. три** to take away three from six

ото *prep.* = **от**

отобража́|ть, ю *impf. of* ▶ **отобрази́ть**

отобра|зи́ть, жу́, зи́шь (*of* ▶ **отобража́ть**)
to reflect; to represent

от|обра́ть, беру́, берёшь, *past* **~обра́л,
~обрала́, ~обра́ло** *pf.* (*of* ▶ **отбира́ть**)
1 (*отнять*) to take (away) **2** (*выбрать*) to
select, pick out

отовсю́ду *adv.* from everywhere, from every
quarter

от|огна́ть, гоню́, го́нишь, *past* **~огна́л,
~огнала́, ~огна́ло** *pf.* (*of* ▶ **отгоня́ть**) to
drive away, chase away

отогн|у́ть, у́, ёшь *pf.* (*of* ▶ **отгиба́ть**) to bend
back

отогн|у́ться, ётся *pf.* (*of* ▶ **отгиба́ться**) to
bend back

отогрева́|ть, ю *impf. of* ▶ **отогре́ть**

отогрева́|ться, юсь *impf. of* ▶ **отогре́ться**

отогре́|ть, ю *pf.* (*of* ▶ **отогрева́ть**) to warm

отогре́|ться, юсь *pf.* (*of* ▶ **отогрева́ться**) to
warm oneself

отодвига́|ть, ю *impf. of* ▶ **отодви́нуть**

отодвига́|ться, юсь *impf. of* ▶ **отодви́нуться**

отодви́|нуть, ну, нешь *pf.* (*of* ▶ **отодвига́ть**)
1 to move aside **2** (fig., infml, *отсрочить*) to
put back, put back

отодви́|нуться, нусь, нешься *pf.* (*of*
▶ **отодвига́ться**) **1** to move aside **2** (infml,
о сроке) to be postponed

от|одра́ть, деру́, дерёшь, *past* **~одра́л,
~одрала́, ~одра́ло** *pf.* (*of* ▶ **отдира́ть**) to
tear off, rip off

от|озва́ться, зову́сь, зовёшься,
past **~озва́лся, ~озвала́сь** *pf.* (*of*
▶ **отзыва́ться**) **1** (**на** + *a.*) to answer; to
respond (to) **2** (**о** + *p.*) to speak (of)
3 (*сказаться*) (**на** + *a.*) to tell (on, upon)

от|ойти́, йду́, йдёшь, *past* **~шёл, ~шла́** *pf.*
(*of* ▶ **отходи́ть**) **1** to move away; to move
off; (*о поезде*) to leave, depart **2** (*оставить
свою́ пре́жнюю пози́цию*) to withdraw; to
recede; (mil.) to withdraw, fall back; (fig.) (**от**
+ *g.*) to move away (from); to digress (from),
diverge (from) **3** (*о пятнах*) to come out;
(**от** + *g.*) to come away (from), come off; **обо́и
~шли́ от стены́** the paper has come off (the
wall) **4** (*прийти́ в обы́чное состоя́ние*) to
recover (normal state) **5** (**к** + *d.*) (*перейти́ в
чью-л. со́бственность*) to pass (to), go (to)

отом|сти́ть, щу́, сти́шь *pf. of* ▶ **мсти́ть**

отоп|и́ть, лю́, ~ишь *pf.* (*of* ▶ **ота́пливать**)
to heat

отопле́ни|е, я *nt.* heating

оторв|а́ть, у́, ёшь, *past* **~а́л, ~ала́, ~а́ло**
pf. (*of* ▶ **отрыва́ть**) (*пу́говицу*) to tear off;
(*отвле́чь*) to tear away (fig.); **о. кого́-н. от
рабо́ты** to tear sb away from his work

оторв|а́ться, у́сь, ёшься, *past* **~а́лся,
~ала́сь** *pf.* (*of* ▶ **отрыва́ться**) **1** (*о пу́говице*)
to come off, be torn off **2** (aeron.): **о. от
земли́** to take off **3** (fig.) (**от** + *g.*) (*от
друзе́й*) to be cut off (from), lose touch

о

(with); (*от соперников; от отряда*) to
break away (from) **4** (fig.) (**от** + *g.*) to tear
oneself away (from); **я не мог о. от э́той
кни́ги** I could not tear myself away from
this book

ото|слáть, шлю́, шлёшь *pf.* (*of* ▶ отсылáть)
1 to send off, dispatch **2** (**к** + *d.*) to refer (to)

ото|шёл, шлá *see* ▶ отойти́

ото|шлю́, шлёшь *see* ▶ отослáть

отпадá|ть, ю *impf. of* ▶ отпáсть

отпáрыва|ть, ю *impf. of* ▶ отпоро́ть

отпá|сть, дý, дёшь, *past* ∼л *pf.* (*of*
▶ отпадáть) **1** (*отделиться*) to fall off,
drop off **2** (fig.) (**от** + *g.*) to drop out (of)
3 (fig., *утратить силу*) to pass, fade; **вопро́с
об э́том** ∼л the question no longer arises

отпере́ть, отопру́, отопрёшь, *past* **о́тпер,
отперлá, о́тперло** *pf.* (*of* ▶ отпирáть) to
unlock; to open

отпере́ться, отопрётся, *past* **отперся́,
отперлáсь** *pf.* (*of* ▶ отпирáться) to open

отпечáт|ать, аю *pf.* **1** (*impf.* печáтать) to
print (off) **2** (*impf.* ∼ывать) to imprint
3 (*impf.* ∼ывать) (*помещение*) to open
(up)

отпечáт|аться, ается *pf.* to leave an imprint;
to be imprinted

отпечáт|ок, ка *m.* imprint (also fig.); **о. пáльца**
fingerprint

отпечáтыва|ть, ю, ет *impf. of* ▶ отпечáтать

отпечáтыва|ться, ется *impf. of*
▶ отпечáтаться

отпивá|ть, ю *impf. of* ▶ отпи́ть

отпи́лива|ть, ю *impf. of* ▶ отпили́ть

отпили́|ть, ю́, ∼ишь *pf.* (*of* ▶ отпи́ливать)
to saw off

отпирá|ть, ю, ет *impf. of* ▶ отпере́ть

отпирá|ться, ется *impf. of* ▶ отпере́ться

от|пи́ть, опью́, опьёшь, *past* ∼пи́л, ∼пилá,
∼пи́ло *pf.* (*of* ▶ отпивáть) (+ *a.* or *g.*) to take
a sip (of)

отплатú|ть, чý, ∼тишь *pf.* (*of* ▶ отплáчивать)
(+ *d.*) to pay back (to); to repay; **о. кому́-н. то́й
же моне́той** to pay sb in his own coin

отплáчива|ть, ю *impf. of* ▶ отплати́ть

отплывá|ть, ю *impf. of* ▶ отплы́ть

отплы́ти|е, я *nt.* sailing, departure

отплы́|ть, вý, вёшь, *past* ∼л, ∼лá, ∼ло *pf.*
(*of* ▶ отплывáть) (*о корабле*) to sail, set sail;
(*о плывущих людях*) to swim off

отползá|ть, áю *impf. of* ▶ отползти́

отполз|ти́, ý, ёшь, *past* ∼, ∼лá *pf.* (*of*
▶ отползáть) to crawl away

отполиро́в|ать, ýю *pf. of* ▶ полирова́ть

отпо́р, а *m.* repulse; rebuff; **дать о.** (+ *d.*) to
repulse; **встре́тить о.** to be repulsed; to meet
with a rebuff

отпор|о́ть, ю́, ∼ешь *pf.* (*of* ▶ отпáрывать)
to rip off

отпрáв|ить, лю, ишь *pf.* (*of* ▶ отправля́ть)
to send; (*по почте*) to post (BrE), mail

(AmE); to send off; **о. на тот свет** to send to
kingdom come

отпрáв|иться, люсь, ишься *pf.* (*of*
▶ отправля́ться) to set out, set off, start;
(*о поезде*) to leave, depart

отправле́ни|е, я *nt.* **1** (*действие*) sending
2 (*почтовое, заказное*) item **3** (*поезда*)
departure

  отправля́|ть, ю *impf. of* ▶ отпрáвить

отправля́|ться, юсь *impf. of* ▶ отпрáвиться

отпрáздн|овать, ую *pf. of* ▶ прáздновать

отпрáшива|ться, юсь *impf.* (*of*
▶ отпроси́ться) (*просить разрешения*) to
ask (for) leave

отпро|си́ться, шýсь, ∼сишься *pf.* (*of*
▶ отпрáшиваться) (*получить разрешение*)
to obtain leave

отпры́гива|ть, ю *impf. of* ▶ отпры́гнуть

отпры́г|нуть, ну, нешь *pf.* (*of* ▶ отпры́гивать)
(*назад*) to jump back; (*в сторону*) to jump
aside

отпу́гива|ть, ю *impf. of* ▶ отпугну́ть

отпуг|ну́ть, ну́, нёшь *pf.* (*of* ▶ отпу́гивать)
to frighten off, scare away

о́тпуск, а, в ∼е, *pl.* ∼á, ∼о́в *m.* leave,
holiday(s) (BrE), vacation (AmE); (mil.) leave,
furlough(s); **в ∼е** on leave

отпускá|ть, ю *impf. of* ▶ отпусти́ть

отпу|сти́ть, щу́, ∼стишь *pf.* (*of* ▶ отпускáть)
1 (*позволить кому-н. уйти; перестать
держать*) to let go; (*в сад, во двор*) to let
out; (*освободить*) to set free; to release;
(*дать отпуск*) to give leave (of absence)
2 (*ослабить*) to relax, slacken **3** (*бороду*) to
(let) grow; (*платье*) to let down **4** (*выдать*)
to issue, give out; (*продать*) to sell

отрабáтыва|ть, ю *impf. of* ▶ отрабо́тать

отрабо́танный *p.p.p. of* ▶ отрабо́тать *and*
adj. (tech.) worked out; spent; **о. газ** waste gas

отрабо́та|ть, ю *pf.* (*of* ▶ отрабáтывать)
1 (*долг*) to work off **2** (*какое-н. время*) to
work **3** (*придать окончательный вид*) to
put the finishing touches to **4** (*упражнение,
приём*) to work through, give a workout to

отрáв|а, ы *f.* poison

отрав|и́ть, лю́, ∼ишь *pf.* (*of* ▶ отравля́ть)
to poison (also fig.)

отрав|и́ться, лю́сь, ∼ишься *pf.* (*of*
▶ отравля́ться) to poison oneself

отравле́ни|е, я *nt.* poisoning

отравля́|ть, ю *impf. of* ▶ отрави́ть

отравля́|ться, юсь *impf. of* ▶ отрави́ться

отрáд|ный, ∼ен, ∼на *adj.* gratifying,
pleasing; comforting

  отражá|ть, ю *impf. of* ▶ отрази́ть

отражá|ться, юсь *impf. of* ▶ отрази́ться

отраже́ни|е, я *nt.* **1** reflection **2** (*нападения*)
repelling; warding off

отраз|и́ть, жý, зи́шь *pf.* (*of* ▶ отражáть) **1** to
reflect (also fig.) **2** (*нападение*) to repel; to
ward off

отра|зи́ться, жу́сь, зи́шься *pf.* (*of*
▶ отражáться) **1** to be reflected **2** (fig.)

(на + *p.*) to affect; to tell (on); **поéздка в гóры благоприя́тно ~зи́лась на егó рабóте** the mountain trip had a beneficial effect on his work

⚡ **óтрасл|ь, и** *f.* branch; **о. промы́шленности** branch of industry

отраст|áть, áю *impf. of* ▸ **отрасти́**

отраст|и́, ý, ёшь, *past* **отрóс, отрослá** *pf.* (*of* ▸ **отрастáть**) to grow

отра|сти́ть, щý, сти́шь *pf.* (*of* ▸ **отрáщивать**) to (let) grow; **о. вóлосы** to grow one's hair long

отрáщива|ть, ю *impf. of* ▸ **отрасти́ть**

отреаги́р|овать, ую *pf.* (infml) *of* ▸ **реаги́ровать 2**

отрегули́р|овать, ую *pf. of* ▸ **регули́ровать 3**

отредакти́р|овать, ую *pf. of* ▸ **редакти́ровать 1**

отре́|зать, жу, жешь *pf.* (*of* ▸ **отрезáть**) **1** to cut off (also fig.) **2** (infml, *резко отве́тить*) to snap back

отрез|áть, áю *impf. of* ▸ **отрéзать**

отрéз|ок, ка *m.* (*ткани*) piece, cut; (*пути*) section; (math.) segment; **о. врéмени** stretch of time

отрекá|ться, юсь *impf. of* ▸ **отрéчься**

отремонти́р|овать, ую *pf. of* ▸ **ремонти́ровать**

отрепети́р|овать, ую *pf. of* ▸ **репети́ровать**

отрестáври́р|овать, ую *pf. of* ▸ **реставри́ровать**

отрé|чься, кýсь, чёшься, кýтся, *past* **~кся, ~клáсь** *pf.* (*of* ▸ **отрекáться**) (от + *g.*) to renounce, disavow, give up; **о. от престóла** to abdicate

отрицáни|е, я *nt.* denial; negation

отрицáтел|ьный, ~ен, ~ьна *adj.* negative

отрицá|ть, ю *impf.* to deny; to disclaim; **о. винóвность** (law) to plead not guilty

отруб|áть, áю *impf. of* ▸ **отруби́ть**

отруб|и́ть, лю́, ~ишь *pf.* (*of* ▸ **отрубáть**) (*сук*) to chop off

отругá|ть, ю *pf. of* ▸ **ругáть 1,** ▸ **ругáть 2**

отры́|в, а *m.* **1** tearing off **2** (fig.) alienation, isolation; loss of contact; **в ~е** (от + *g.*) out of touch (with)

отрывá|ть, ю *impf. of* ▸ **оторвáть**

отрывá|ться, юсь *impf. of* ▸ **оторвáться**

отры́вист|ый, ~, ~а *adj.* jerky, abrupt; (*речь*) curt

отры́в|ок, ка *m.* (*разговора*) fragment; (*книги*) excerpt; passage; **о. из фи́льма** film clip

отры́жк|а, и *f.* belch

отря́|д, а *m.* (mil.) detachment; (*группа*) group, party, brigade; **передовóй о.** (fig.) vanguard

отря́хива|ть, ю *impf. of* ▸ **отряхнýть**

отря́хива|ться, юсь *impf. of* ▸ **отряхнýться**

отря́х|нýть, нý, нёшь *pf.* (*of* ▸ **отря́хивать**) to shake down, shake off

отря́х|нýться, нýсь, нёшься *pf.* (*of* ▸ **отря́хиваться**) to shake oneself down

óтсвет, а *m.* reflection; reflected light

отсéива|ть, ю *impf. of* ▸ **отсéять**

отсéива|ться, юсь *impf. of* ▸ **отсéяться**

отсéк, а *m.* **1** (naut., etc.) compartment **2** (astronautics) module

отсекá|ть, ю *impf. of* ▸ **отсéчь**

отсé|чь, кý, чёшь, кýт, *past* **~к, ~клá** *pf.* (*of* ▸ **отсекáть**) to cut off, chop off

отсé|ять, ю, ешь *pf.* (*of* ▸ **отсéивать**) **1** to sift, screen **2** (fig.) to eliminate, screen out

отсé|яться, юсь, ешься *pf.* (*of* ▸ **отсéиваться**) **1** to be separated **2** (fig.) to fall off, fall away

отси|дéть, жý, ди́шь *pf.* (*of* ▸ **отси́живать**) **1** (*просидеть*) to stay (for); to sit out; **он ~дéл дéсять лет в тюрьмé** he has done ten years (in prison) **2** (*вызвать онемение части тела*) to make numb by sitting; **я ~дéл себé нóгу** I have pins and needles in my leg

отси|дéться, жýсь, ди́шься *pf.* (*of* ▸ **отси́живаться**) (infml) to sit tight

отси́жива|ть, ю *impf. of* ▸ **отсидéть**

отси́жива|ться, юсь *impf. of* ▸ **отсидéться**

отскáкива|ть, ю *impf. of* ▸ **отскочи́ть**

отскоч|и́ть, ý, ~ишь *pf.* (*of* ▸ **отскáкивать**) **1** (*отпрыгнуть*) to jump (aside, away); (*о мяче*) to rebound, bounce back **2** (infml, *отделиться*) to come off, break off

отскреб|áть, ю *impf. of* ▸ **отскрести́**

отскре|сти́, бý, бёшь, *past* **~б, ~блá** *pf.* (*of* ▸ **отскребáть**) to scrape off

отслуж|и́ть, ý, ~ишь *pf. of* ▸ **служи́ть 5**

отсоедин|и́ть, ю́, и́шь *pf.* ▸ **отсоединя́ть** to disconnect

отсоединя́|ть, ю *impf. of* ▸ **отсоедини́ть**

отсортир|овáть, ýю *pf.* (*of* ▸ **отсортирóвывать**) to sort (out)

отсортирóвыва|ть, ю *impf. of* ▸ **отсортировáть**

отсрóчива|ть, ю *impf. of* ▸ **отсрóчить**

отсрóч|ить, у, ишь *pf.* (*of* ▸ **отсрóчивать**) to postpone, defer

отсрóчк|а, и *f.* postponement, deferment

отставáни|е, я *nt.* lag

отста|вáть, ю́, ёшь *impf. of* ▸ **отстáть**

отстáвк|а, и *f.* (mil.) retirement; (hist., *с государственной службы*) resignation; **вы́йти в ~у** to retire; to resign

отстáвн|ой *adj.* (mil.) retired

отстáива|ть, ю *impf. of* ▸ **отстоя́ть**

отстáл|ый *adj.* (fig.) backward; **ýмственно о.** learning-disabled

отстá|ть, ну, нешь *pf.* (*of* ▸ **отставáть**) **1** (от + *g.*) (*оказаться позади*) to fall behind; to lag behind; (*умственно*) to be learning-disabled **2** (от + *g.*) (*отделиться*) to become detached (from); **о. от пóезда** to be left behind by the train (*sc., at a station en route*); **обóи ~ли от стены́** the wallpaper came off **3** (*о часах*) to be slow; **о. на полчасá** to be half an hour slow **4** (infml) (от + *g.*)

(*перестать надоедать*) to leave alone; ~нь от меня! leave me alone!

отстёгива|ть, ю *impf. of* ▶ отстегнуть

отстег|нуть, ну, нёшь *pf.* (*of* ▶ отстёгивать) (*крючок*) to unfasten, undo; (*пуговицы*) to unbutton

отстир|ать, аю *pf.* (*of* ▶ отстирывать) to wash off

отстир|аться, ается *pf.* (*of* ▶ отстирываться) to wash off, come out in the wash

отстиры|ва|ть, ю, ет *impf. of* ▶ отстирать

отстиры|ва|ться, ется *impf. of* ▶ отстираться

отсто|ять, ю, ишь *pf.* (*of* ▶ отстаивать) to defend

отстраива|ть, ю *impf. of* ▶ отстроить

отстран|ить, ю, ишь *pf.* (*of* ▶ отстранять) **1** (*отодвинуть*) to push aside **2** (*уволить*) to dismiss, discharge

отстран|ять, яю *impf. of* ▶ отстранить

отстрелива|ться, юсь *impf. of* ▶ отстреляться

отстрел|яться, яюсь *pf.* (*of* ▶ отстреливаться) **1** (от + *g.*) to defend oneself (by shooting) (against) **2** (*ответить стрельбой на стрельбу*) to return fire, fire back

отстрига|ть, ю *impf. of* ▶ отстричь

отстри|чь, гу, жёшь, гут, *past* ~г, ~гла *pf.* (*of* ▶ отстригать) to cut off, clip

отстро|ить, ою, оишь *pf.* (*of* ▶ отстраивать) to complete the construction of, finish building

отступ, а *m.* (*тур.*) indentation

отступ|ать, аю *impf. of* ▶ отступить

отступ|аться, аюсь *impf. of* ▶ отступиться

отступ|ить, лю, ~ишь *pf.* (*of* ▶ отступать) **1** (*отойти назад*) to step back; to recede **2** (mil.) to retreat, fall back **3** (fig.) (от + *g.*) (*от чего-н. установленного*) to deviate (from); о. от темы to digress

отступ|иться, люсь, ~ишься *pf.* (*of* ▶ отступаться) (infml) (от + *g.*) to give up, renounce; о. от своего слова to go back on one's word

отступлени|е, я *nt.* **1** (mil., also fig.) retreat **2** (*от темы*) deviation; digression

⚲ отсутстви|е, я *nt.* absence; (+ *g.*) lack (of); в его о. in his absence; за ~ем (+ *g.*) (*кого-н.*) in the absence (of); (*чего-н.*) for lack (of), for want (of)

⚲ отсутств|овать, ую *impf.* (*о человеке*) to be absent; (*о доказательстве*) to be lacking

отсутств|ующий *pres. part. of* ▶ отсутствовать *and adj.* absent (also fig.); о. вид blank expression; (*as m. n.* о., ~ующего) absentee

отсчит|ать, аю *pf.* (*of* ▶ отсчитывать) to count out, count off; о. кому-н. пятьсот рублей to count out five hundred roubles to sb

отсчиты|ва|ть, ю *impf. of* ▶ отсчитать

отсыла|ть, ю *impf. of* ▶ отослать

отсы́п|ать, лю, лешь *pf.* (*of* ▶ отсыпать) (+ *a.* or *g.*) to pour off; to measure off

отсып|ать, аю *impf. of* ▶ отсыпать

отсыре|ть, ю *pf. of* ▶ сыреть

отсюда *adv.* from here; hence (also fig.); (fig.) from this; о. следует, что... from this it follows that ...

Оттав|а, ы *f.* Ottawa

оттаива|ть, ю *impf. of* ▶ оттаять

отталкива|ть, ю *impf. of* ▶ оттолкнуть

отталкива|ться, юсь *impf. of* ▶ оттолкнуться

оттаскива|ть, ю *impf. of* ▶ оттащить

оттащ|ить, у, ~ишь *pf.* (*of* ▶ оттаскивать) to drag aside (away), pull aside (away)

отта|ять, ю, ешь *pf.* (*of* ▶ оттаивать) to thaw out (*trans. and intrans.*)

оттен|ок, ка *m.* (*цвета*) shade, hue; (fig.) shade, nuance; он говорил с ~ком иронии there was a note of irony in his voice

оттепел|ь, и *f.* thaw

оттер|еть, ототру, ототрёшь, *past* ~, ~ла *pf.* (*of* ▶ оттирать) (*грязь*) to rub off, rub out

оттесн|ить, ю, ишь *pf.* (*of* ▶ оттеснять) to drive back; to press back; to push aside, shove aside (also fig.); о. противника (mil.) to force the enemy back

оттесн|ять, яю *impf. of* ▶ оттеснить

оттира|ть, ю *impf. of* ▶ оттереть

оттого *adv.* = потому

отток, а *m.* mass departure, haemorrhage (BrE), hemorrhage (AmE) (*of specialists, sportsmen, etc.*)

оттолкн|уть, у, ёшь *pf.* (*of* ▶ отталкивать) **1** (*стул*) to push away, push aside **2** (fig., *друзей*) to antagonize, alienate

оттолкн|уться, усь, ёшься *pf.* (*of* ▶ отталкиваться) **1** (от + *g.*) to push off (from) **2** (fig.) (от + *g.*) to take as a starting point

оттопы́рен|ный, ~, ~а *adj.* (infml) protruding, sticking out; (*карманы*) bulging

отторжени|е, я *nt.* tearing away, seizure; (med.) rejection (*of a transplanted organ*)

оттуда *adv.* from there

оттягива|ть, ю *impf. of* ▶ оттянуть

оття|нуть, ну, ~нешь *pf.* (*of* ▶ оттягивать) **1** to pull, drag (away) **2** (mil., *отряд*) to draw off **3** (*карман*) to stretch, weigh down

отупени|е, я *nt.* stupefaction, dullness, torpor

отуч|ать, аю *impf. of* ▶ отучить

отуч|аться, аюсь *impf. of* ▶ отучить, ▶ отучиться¹

отучива|ться, юсь *impf. of* ▶ отучиться²

отуч|ить, у, ~ишь *pf.* (*of* ▶ отучать) (от + *g.* or + *inf.*) to break (of); о. от груди to wean

отуч|иться¹, усь, ~ишься *pf.* (*of* ▶ отучаться) (от + *g.* or + *inf.*) (*отвыкнуть*) to break oneself (of)

отуч|иться², усь, ~ишься *pf.* (*of* ▶ отучаться) (*кончить учиться*) to have

---

finished one's lessons; to finish learning

отфильтр|ова́ть, у́ю *pf.* (*of* ▶ фильтрова́ть)

отформати́р|овать, ую *pf.* (*of* ▶ формати́ровать)

отхва|ти́ть, чу́, ~тишь *pf.* (*of* ▶ отхва́тывать) (infml) **1** (*отрезать*) to snip off; (*отрубить*) to chop off **2** (*достать*) to get hold of

отхва́тыва|ть, ю *impf. of* ▶ отхвати́ть

отхлеб|ну́ть, ну́, нёшь *pf.* (*of* ▶ отхлёбывать) (infml) (+ *a. or g.*) to take a sip (of); to take a mouthful (of)

отхлёбыва|ть, ю *impf. of* ▶ отхлебну́ть

отхлы́н|уть, у, ешь *pf.* to rush back, flood back (also fig.)

отхо́д, а *m.* **1** departure **2** (mil.) withdrawal **3** (от + *g.*) (*отклонение*) deviation (from); (*разрыв*) break (with) **4** *see* ▶ отхо́ды

отхо|ди́ть, жу́, ~дишь *impf. of* ▶ отойти́

отхо́д|ы, ов (tech.) waste (products)

отцеп|и́ть, лю́, ~ишь *pf.* (*of* ▶ отцепля́ть) to unhook; to uncouple

отцеп|и́ться, лю́сь, ~ишься *pf.* (*of* ▶ отцепля́ться) to come unhooked; to come uncoupled

отцепля́|ть, ю *impf. of* ▶ отцепи́ть

отцепля́|ться, юсь *impf. of* ▶ отцепи́ться

отцо́вский *adj.* one's father's; paternal

отча́ива|ться, юсь *impf. of* ▶ отча́яться

отча́сти *adv.* partly

отча́яни|е, я *nt.* despair

отча́ян|ный, ~, ~на *adj.* (*положение, взор, крик*) desperate; (*смелый до безрассудности*) daring, reckless; (infml, *ужасный*) terrible, awful

отча́|яться, юсь, ешься *pf.* (*of* ▶ отча́иваться) (в + *p. or* + *inf.*) to despair (of)

отчего́ *adv.* why; **вот о.** that's why

отчего́-нибудь *adv.* for some reason or other

отчего́-то *adv.* for some reason

о́тчеств|о, а *nt.* patronymic; **как его́ по ~у?** what is his patronymic?

⚹ **отчёт**, а *m.* account; **дать о.** (в + *p.*) to give an account (of), report (on); **отдава́ть себе́ о.** (в + *p.*) to be aware (of), realize

отчётлив|ый, ~, ~а *adj.* intelligible, clear, distinct

отчётный *adj. of* ▶ отчёт; **о. год** financial year, current year; **о. докла́д** report

о́тчим, а *m.* stepfather

отчи́|стить, щу, стишь *pf.* (*of* ▶ отчища́ть) **1** (*пятно*) to clean off; to brush off **2** (*одежду*) to clean

отчи́|ститься, щусь, стишься *pf.* (*of* ▶ отчища́ться) **1** (*о грязи*) to come off, come out **2** (*об одежде*) to become clean

отчит|а́ться, а́юсь *pf.* (*of* ▶ отчи́тываться) (в + *p.*) to give an account (of), report (on); **о. пе́ред избира́телями** to report back to the electors

отчи́тыва|ться, юсь *impf. of* ▶ отчита́ться

отчища́|ть, ю *impf. of* ▶ отчи́стить

отчища́|ться, юсь *impf. of* ▶ отчи́ститься

отшатну́|ться, у́сь, ёшься *pf.* (*of* ▶ отша́тываться) (от + *g.*) **1** (*от удара*) to start back (from); to recoil (from) **2** (fig., *прекратить общение*) to give up; to break (with)

отша́тыва|ться, юсь *impf. of* ▶ отшатну́ться

отшвы́рива|ть, ю *impf. of* ▶ отшвырну́ть

отшвыр|ну́ть, ну́, нёшь *pf.* (*of* ▶ отшвы́ривать) to fling away; to throw off

отше́льник, а *m.* hermit; recluse

отшлёпа|ть, ю *pf. of* ▶ шлёпать

отшлиф|ова́ть, у́ю *pf.* (*of* ▶ отшлифо́вывать, ▶ шлифова́ть) **1** (tech.) to polish; to grind **2** (fig., *совершенствовать*) to polish, perfect

отшлифо́выва|ть, ю *impf. of* ▶ отшлифова́ть

отъеда́|ть, ю *impf. of* ▶ отъе́сть

отъеда́|ться, юсь *impf. of* ▶ отъе́сться

отъе́зд, а *m.* departure; **быть в ~е** to be away

отъезжа́|ть, ю *impf. of* ▶ отъе́хать

отъе́|сть, м, шь, ст, ди́м, ди́те, дя́т, *past* ~л, ~ла *pf.* (*of* ▶ отъеда́ть) to bite off and eat

отъе́|сться, мся, шься, стся, ди́мся, ди́тесь, дя́тся, *past* ~лся, ~лась *pf.* (*of* ▶ отъеда́ться) to put on weight; to feed well

отъе́|хать, ду, дешь *pf.* (*of* ▶ отъезжа́ть) to depart

отъя́вленный *adj.* (infml, pej.) thorough, inveterate, out-and-out

отыгр|а́ться, а́юсь *pf.* (*of* ▶ оты́грываться) to win (having lost); to get back what one has lost

оты́грыва|ться, юсь *impf. of* ▶ отыгра́ться

оты́|скать, щу́, ~щешь *pf.* (*of* ▶ оты́скивать 1) to find; to track down, run to earth

оты́|скаться, щу́сь, ~щешься *pf.* (*of* ▶ оты́скиваться) to turn up, appear

оты́скива|ть, ю *impf.* **1** *impf. of* ▶ отыска́ть **2** (*impf. only*) to look for, try to find

оты́скива|ться, юсь *impf. of* ▶ отыска́ться

отяжеле́|ть, ю *pf.* to become heavy

⚹ **о́фис**, а *m.* office

о́фисный *adj.* office (*attr.*)

офице́р, а *m.* officer

офице́р|ский *adj. of* ▶ офице́р; **~ское собра́ние** officers' mess

⚹ **официа́льн|ый** *adj.* official; **~ое лицо́** an official

официа́нт, а *m.* waiter

официа́нтк|а, и *f.* waitress

офла́йновый *adj.* (comput.) offline

оформи́тел|ь, я *m.* designer; **о. спекта́кля** set designer

оформи́тель|ница, ницы *f. of* ▶ оформи́тель

офо́рм|ить, лю, ишь *pf.* (*of* ▶ оформля́ть) **1** to design; **о. витри́ну** to dress a window **2** (*узаконить*) to register officially, legalize; **о. догово́р** to draw up an agreement **3** (*на работу*) to enrol, take on

О

офо́рм|иться, люсь, ишься *pf.* (*of*
▸ **оформля́ться**) **1** (*об идеях*) to take shape
2 (*узакониться*) to be registered; to legalize
one's position **3** (*на рабо́ту*) to be taken on,
join the staff

◢ **оформле́ни|е, я** *nt.* **1** design; **сцени́ческое**
о. staging **2** (*узаконение*) registration,
legalization

◢ **оформля́|ть, ю** *impf. of* ▸ **офо́рмить**

оформля́|ться, юсь *impf. of* ▸ **офо́рмиться**

офо́рт, а *m.* (*вид гравю́ры на мета́лле*) etching

офтальмо́лог, а *m.* ophthalmologist

офтальмоло́ги|я, и *f.* ophthalmology

офшо́рный *adj.* (fin.) offshore

о́х|ать, аю *impf.* (*of* ▸ **о́хнуть**) (*от бо́ли*) to
moan, groan; (*от печа́ли*) to sigh

охва|ти́ть, чу́, ~тишь *pf.* (*of* ▸ **охва́тывать**)
1 (*обхвати́ть*) to envelop; to enclose; **дом**
~ти́ло пла́менем the house was enveloped
in flames **2** (*о чу́встве*) to grip, seize; **их**
~ти́л у́жас they were seized with panic

охва́тыва|ть, ю *impf. of* ▸ **охвати́ть**

охва́ченный *p.p.p. of* ▸ **охвати́ть**; **о. у́жасом**
terror-stricken

охла|ди́ть, жу́, ди́шь *pf.* (*of* ▸ **охлажда́ть**) to
cool, cool off (also fig.)

охла|ди́ться, жу́сь, ди́шься *pf.* (*of*
▸ **охлажда́ться**) to become cool, cool down
(also fig.)

охлажда́|ть, ю *impf. of* ▸ **охлади́ть**

охлажда́|ться, юсь *impf. of* ▸ **охлади́ться**

охлажда́|ющий *pres. part. act. of* ▸ **охлажда́ть**
and adj. cooling, refrigerating; **~ющая**
жи́дкость coolant

охлажде́ни|е, я *nt.* **1** cooling (off); **с**
возду́шным ~ем air-cooled **2** (fig.) coolness

о́х|нуть, ну, нешь *pf. of* ▸ **о́хать**

охо́т|а¹, ы *f.* hunt, hunting; chase

охо́т|а², ы *f.* (**к** + *d.* or + *inf.*) desire, wish,
inclination; **о. тебе́ спо́рить с ним!** (infml)
what makes you argue with him!

охо́|титься, чусь, тишься *impf.* to hunt;
(fig.) (**за** + *i.*) to hunt for

охо́тник, а *m.* hunter

охо́тничий *adj.* hunting

охо́тно *adv.* willingly, gladly, readily

о́хр|а, ы *f.* ochre (BrE), ocher (AmE)

◢ **охра́н|а, ы** *f.* **1** (*помеще́ния*) guarding;
(*приро́ды*) protection; **о. труда́** health and
safety measures **2** (*гру́ппа люде́й*) guard;
ли́чная о. bodyguard; **пограни́чная о.**
frontier guard

охран|и́ть, ю́, и́шь *pf.* (*of* ▸ **охраня́ть**)
(*грани́цу, помеще́ние*) to guard; (*приро́ду;*
интере́сы) to protect

охра́нник, а *m.* guard

охран|я́ть, я́ю *impf. of* ▸ **охрани́ть**

охри́п|нуть, ну, нешь, *past* **~, ~ла** *pf.* (*of*
▸ **хри́пнуть**) to become hoarse

оцара́па|ть, ю *pf.* (*of* ▸ **цара́пать**) to scratch

◢ **оце́нива|ть, ю** *impf. of* ▸ **оцени́ть**

оцен|и́ть, ю́, ~ишь *pf.* (*of* ▸ **оце́нивать**)
1 (*определи́ть це́ну чего́-н.*) to estimate
the value of, value; (*назна́чить це́ну*
чему́-н.) to price; (*определи́ть це́нность,*
значи́тельность чего́-н.) to evaluate,
appraise **2** (*призна́ть досто́инства*
чего́-н.) to appreciate; **о. что-н. по**
досто́инству to appreciate sth at its true
value

◢ **оце́нк|а, и** *f.* **1** (*иму́щества*) valuation;
(*рабо́ты*) evaluation, appraisal **2** (*мне́ние*
о це́нности) appreciation **3** (*отме́тка*)
mark, grade

оцепене́ни|е, я *nt.* stupor

оцеп|и́ть, лю́, ~ишь *pf.* (*of* ▸ **оцепля́ть**) to
surround; to cordon off

оцепле́ни|е, я *nt.* **1** (*де́йствие*) surrounding;
cordoning off **2** (*лю́ди*) cordon

оцепля́|ть, ю *impf. of* ▸ **оцепи́ть**

оча́г, а́ *m.* **1** hearth (also fig.); **дома́шний о.**
(fig.) hearth, home **2** (fig.) centre, seat

очарова́тел|ьный, ~ен, ~ьна *adj.*
charming, fascinating

очар|ова́ть, у́ю *pf.* (*of* ▸ **очаро́вывать**) to
charm, fascinate

очаро́выва|ть, ю *impf. of* ▸ **очарова́ть**

очеви́д|ец, ца *m.* eyewitness

◢ **очеви́дно** *adv.* obviously, evidently; **вы, о.,**
не согла́сны you obviously do not agree

◢ **очеви́д|ный, ~ен, ~на** *adj.* obvious, evident

◢ **о́чень** *adv.* (*при прилага́тельных и наре́чиях*)
very; (*при глаго́лах*) very much

◢ **очередно́й** *adj.* **1** next; next in turn; **о.**
вопро́с the next question; **о. вы́пуск** latest
issue (*of a journal, etc.*) **2** usual; regular; **о.**
о́тпуск regular holidays

◢ **о́черед|ь, и**, *pl.* **~и, ~е́й** *f.* **1** turn; **о. за**
ва́ми it is your turn; **в свою́ о.** in one's turn;
по ~и in turn, in order; **в пе́рвую о.** in the
first place/instance **2** (*ряд*) queue (BrE),
line (AmE); **стоя́ть в ~и (за** + *i.*) to queue
(for) (BrE), stand in line (for) (AmE); **стать**
в о́чередь to queue (up) (BrE), stand in line
(AmE) **3** (mil.): (*пулемётная*) **о.** burst

о́черк, а *m.* essay, sketch, study; (*ко́нтур*)
outline; **~и ру́сской исто́рии** studies in
Russian history

очерта́ни|е, я *nt.* (*usu. in pl.*) outline

очи́|стить, щу, стишь *pf.* (*of* ▸ **очища́ть**,
▸ **чи́стить 3**) **1** (*таре́лку, о́бувь*) to clean;
(*во́ду, спирт*) to purify; (*со́весть*) to salve,
clear; (*ду́шу*) to cleanse, purify **2** (**от** + *g.*)
(*стол*) to clear (of); **о. кише́чник** to open
bowels **3** (*карто́фелину, я́блоко*) to peel

очи́|ститься, щусь, стишься *pf.* (*of*
▸ **очища́ться**) (**от** + *g.*) to become clear (of)

очи́стк|а, и *f.* **1** (*о́буви*) cleaning; (*души́*)
cleansing, purification; (*воды́*) purification;
(*овоще́й*) peeling **2** (**от** + *g.*) clearing,
clearance (of); freeing (of)

очи́стк|и, ов (*no sg.*) peelings

◢ **очища́|ть, ю** *impf. of* ▸ **очи́стить**

о

очища́|ться, юсь *impf. of* ▶ **очи́ститься**

очк|и́, о́в (*no sg.*) glasses, spectacles (BrE), eyeglasses (AmE); (*защитные*) goggles

✧ **очк|о́, а́,** *pl.* ∼**и́,** ∼**о́в** *nt.* (sport) point

очну́|ться, у́сь, ёшься *pf.* **1** (*после сна*) to wake **2** (*после обморока*) to come to, regain consciousness

о́чн|ый *adj.* **1** (*opp.* **зао́чный**) internal (*instruction, student, etc., as opposed to external, extra-mural*) **2**: ∼**ая ста́вка** (law) confrontation

очути́|ться, ∼**ишься** *pf.* to find oneself; to come to be; **как вы здесь** ∼**и́лись?** how did you come to be here?

оше́йник, а *m.* collar (*animal's*)

ошеломи́|ть, лю́, йшь *pf.* (*of* ▶ **ошеломля́ть**) to stun

ошеломля́|ть, ю *impf. of* ▶ **ошеломи́ть**

ошиб|а́ться, а́юсь *impf. of* ▶ **ошиби́ться**

ошиб|и́ться, у́сь, ёшься, *past* ∼́**ся,** ∼́**лась** *pf.* (*of* ▶ **ошиба́ться**) to be mistaken, make a mistake, make mistakes

✧ **оши́бк|а, и** *f.* mistake; error; **по** ∼**е** by mistake

оши́боч|ный, ∼**ен,** ∼**на** *adj.* erroneous, mistaken

ошпа́рива|ть, ю *impf. of* ▶ **ошпа́рить**

ошпа́р|ить, ю, ишь *pf.* (*of* ▶ **ошпа́ривать,** ▶ **шпа́рить** 1) (infml) to scald

оштраф|ова́ть, у́ю *pf. of* ▶ **штрафова́ть**

оштукату́р|ить, ю, ишь *pf. of* ▶ **штукату́рить**

ощети́нива|ться, юсь *impf. of* ▶ **ощети́ниться**

ощети́н|иться, юсь, ишься *pf.* (*of* ▶ **ощети́ниваться,** ▶ **щети́ниться**) to bristle (also fig.)

ощип|а́ть, лю́, ∼́**лешь** *pf.* (*of* ▶ **щипа́ть** 3, ▶ **ощи́пывать**) to pluck

ощи́пыва|ть, ю *impf. of* ▶ **ощипа́ть**

ощу́п|ать, аю *pf.* (*of* ▶ **ощу́пывать**) to feel

ощу́пыва|ть, ю *impf. of* ▶ **ощу́пать**

о́щуп|ь, и *f.*: **на о.** to the touch; by touch; **идти́ на о.** to grope one's way

ощути́м|ый, ∼, ∼**а** *adj.* **1** (*запах, похолодание*) perceptible, noticeable **2** (fig., *недостатки, расходы*) appreciable

ощу|ти́ть, щу́, ти́шь *pf.* (*of* ▶ **ощуща́ть**) to feel, sense; **о. го́лод** to feel hunger

ощуща́|ть, ю *impf. of* ▶ **ощути́ть**

✧ **ощуще́ни|е, я** *nt.* **1** (physiol.) sensation **2** (*страха, радости*) feeling, sense

Пп

павильо́н, а *m.* **1** pavilion **2** (cin.) film studio

павли́н, а *m.* peacock

па́вод|ок, ка *m.* flood (*esp. resulting from melting of snow*)

па́год|а, ы *f.* pagoda

па́дал|ь, и *f.* (*usu. collect.*) carrion

па́да|ть, ю *impf.* **1** (*pf.* **пасть** *and* **упа́сть**) to fall; (*о настроении*) to sink; (*о нравах*) to decline; **п. в о́бморок** to faint **2** (*pf.* **пасть**) (fig.) **1** (**на** + *a.*) to fall (on, to); **отве́тственность** ∼**ет на вас** the responsibility falls on you

паде́ж, а́ *m.* (gram.) case

паде́ни|е, я *nt.* fall; (*нравов*) decline

па́дчериц|а, ы *f.* stepdaughter

па́ёк, йка́ *m.* ration

пазл, а *m.* jigsaw puzzle

па́зух|а, и *f.* bosom; **за** ∼**ой** in one's bosom

✧ **паке́т, а** *m.* **1** (*свёрток*) parcel, package **2** (*письмо*) (official) letter **3** (*мешок*) (paper) bag **4** (comput.) package

Пакиста́н, а *m.* Pakistan

пакиста́н|ец, ца *m.* Pakistani

пакиста́н|ка, ки *f. of* ▶ **пакиста́нец**

пакиста́нский *adj.* Pakistani

пак|ова́ть, у́ю *impf.* (*of* ▶ **упакова́ть**) to pack

па́кост|ь, и *f.* **1** (*о поступке*) dirty trick; **де́лать** ∼**и** (+ *d.*) to play dirty tricks (on) **2** (*дрянь*) filth

пакт, а *m.* pact; **п. о ненападе́нии** non-aggression pact

✧ **пала́т|а, ы** *f.* **1** (*в больнице*) ward **2** (pol.) chamber, house; **ве́рхняя, ни́жняя п.** Upper, Lower Chamber; **п. ло́рдов** House of Lords; **п. о́бщин** House of Commons **3** (*название некоторых государственных учреждений*): **Торго́вая п.** Chamber of Commerce

пала́тк|а, и *f.* **1** tent; (*большая*) marquee **2** (*ларёк*) stall, booth

пала́ч, а́ *m.* executioner; (fig.) butcher

палеонто́лог, а *m.* palaeontologist (BrE), paleontologist (AmE)

палеонтоло́ги|я, и *f.* palaeontology (BrE), paleontology (AmE)

Палести́н|а, ы *f.* Palestine

палести́н|ец, ца *m.* Palestinian

палести́н|ка, ки *f. of* ▶ **палести́нец**

палести́нский *adj.* Palestinian

✧ **па́л|ец, ьца** *m.* finger; **п. ноги́** toe; **большо́й п.** thumb; **смотре́ть сквозь** ∼**ьцы на что-н.**

(infml) to shut one's eyes to sth

палиса́дник, а *m.* small front garden

пали́тр|а, ы *f.* palette

пал|и́ть, ю́, и́шь *impf.* (infml, *стреля́ть*) to fire (*from gun*)

па́лк|а, и *f.* stick; **вставля́ть кому́-н. ~и в колёса** to put a spoke in sb's wheel

пало́мник, а *m.* pilgrim (also fig.)

па́лочк|а, и *f. dim. of* ▸ **па́лка**; **бараба́нная п.** drumstick; **волше́бная п.** magic wand; **дирижёрская п.** conductor's baton

па́лтус, а *m.* halibut; (*также в рыболо́встве*) turbot

па́луб|а, ы *f.* deck

па́льм|а, ы *f.* palm (tree)

пал|ьну́ть, ьну́, ьнёшь *inst. pf.* (*of* ▸ **пали́ть**) (infml) to fire a shot

пальто́ *nt. indecl.* (over)coat

пампа́с|ы, ов (*no sg.*) (geog.) pampas

памфле́т, а *m.* lampoon

па́мятк|а, и *f.* (list of) instructions, guidelines

✎ **па́мятник**, а *m.* monument; (*на моги́ле*) tombstone; (*ста́туя*) statue; (*археологи́ческий*) relic

па́мят|ный, ~ен, ~на *adj.* memorable

✎ **па́мят|ь**, и *f.* **1** (also comput.) memory; **на мое́й ~и** within my memory; **по ~и** from memory **2** (*воспомина́ние*) memory, recollection, remembrance; **в п.** (+ *g.*) in memory (of); **подари́ть на п.** to give as a keepsake **3** (*созна́ние*) mind, consciousness; **быть без ~и** to be unconscious; **быть от кого́-н. без ~и** (infml) be crazy about sb

Пана́м|а, ы *f.* Panama

пана́м|а, ы *f.* panama (hat)

па́нд|а, ы *f.* panda

✎ **пане́л|ь**, и *f.* **1** (*тротуа́р*) pavement (BrE), sidewalk (AmE) **2** (*обши́вка*) panel, panelling (BrE), paneling (AmE) **3**: **прибо́рная п.** instrument panel; dashboard

па́ник|а, и *f.* panic

паник|ова́ть, у́ю *impf.* (*no pf.*) (infml) to panic

панихи́д|а, ы *f.* funeral service; requiem; **гражда́нская п.** civil funeral

пани́ческий *adj.* panic-stricken; **п. страх** utter terror

панк, а *m.* (also as indecl. adj.) punk

панно́ *nt. indecl.* panel

панора́м|а, ы *f.* panorama

панора́мный *adj.* panoramic

пансио́н, а *m.*: **по́лный ~** (full) board and lodging

пансиона́т, а *m.* boarding house, guest house

пантеи́зм, а *m.* pantheism

пантео́н, а *m.* pantheon

панте́р|а, ы *f.* panther

пантоми́м|а, ы *f.* mime

па́нцир|ь, я *m.* (zool.) shell

па́п|а¹, ы *m.* (infml) dad, daddy, papa (AmE)

па́п|а², ы *m.*: **П. Ри́мский** pope; the Pope

папа́й|я, и *f.* papaya, pawpaw

папара́цци *c.g. indecl.* paparazzo

па́перт|ь, и *f.* church porch, parvis

папиро́с|а, ы *f.* cigarette (*of Russian type, with cardboard mouthpiece*)

папи́рус, а *m.* papyrus

па́пк|а, и *f.* folder, file; (comput.) folder

па́поротник, а *m.* fern

па́прик|а, и *f.* paprika

Па́пуа — Но́вая Гвине́я, Па́пуа — Но́вой Гвине́и *f.* Papua New Guinea

папуа́с, а *m.* Papuan

папуа́с|ка, ки *f. of* ▸ **папуа́с**

папуа́сский *adj.* Papuan

папье́-маше́ *nt. indecl.* papier mâché

пар, а, о ~е, в ~у́, *pl.* ~ы́ *m.* **1** steam **2** (*ви́димое испаре́ние*) vapour (BrE), vapor (AmE)

✎ **па́р|а**, ы *f.* (*сапо́г, чуло́к, но́жниц*) pair; (*два предме́та, дво́е люде́й*) couple; **супру́жеская п.** married couple; **она́ ему́ не п.** she is no match for him

Парагва́|й, я *m.* Paraguay

пара́граф, а *m.* paragraph

пара́д, а *m.* (*ше́ствие*) parade; (mil.) review

паради́гм|а, ы *f.* paradigm

пара́д|ный, ~ен, ~на *adj.* **1** (*торже́ственный*) ceremonial; ~ная фо́рма full dress (uniform) **2** (*пы́шный*) gala **3** (*гла́вный*) main, front; **п. подъе́зд** main entrance; (*as f. n.* ~ная, ~ной) front door

парадо́кс, а *m.* paradox

парази́т, а *m.* (biol., also fig.) parasite

парализо́ванный *p.p.p. of* ▸ **парализова́ть** and *adj.* paralysed (also fig.)

парализ|ова́ть, у́ю *impf. and pf.* to paralyse (also fig.)

парали́ч, а́ *m.* paralysis; **он разби́т ~о́м** he is completely paralysed

паралле́л|ь, и *f.* parallel; **провести́ п.** (ме́жду + *i.*) to draw a parallel (between)

паралле́льно *adv.* **1** (+ *d.* or *c* + *i.*) parallel (to, with) **2** (*одновреме́нно*) simultaneously (with), at the same time (as)

паралле́л|ьный, ~ен, ~ьна *adj.* parallel

✎ **пара́метр**, а *m.* parameter

парано́ик, а *m.* (med.) paranoid

парано́й|я, и *f.* (med.) paranoia

паранорма́льный *adj.* paranormal

параолимпи́йск|ий *adj.* Paralympic; **П~е и́гры** Paralympics

парапе́т, а *m.* parapet

парафи́н, а *m.* paraffin (wax)

парашю́т, а *m.* parachute

парашюти́ст, а *m.* parachutist; skydiver

✎ **па́р|ень**, ня, *pl.* ~ни, ~не́й *m.* **1** (*ю́ноша*) boy, lad **2** (infml, *мужчи́на*) chap (BrE), fellow, guy; **свой п.** a good guy

пари́ *nt. indecl.* bet; **держа́ть п.** to bet, lay a bet; **держу́ п., что...** I bet that ...

п

Пари́ж, а *m.* Paris

парижа́н|ин, ина, *pl.* ∼е, ∼ *m.* Parisian

парижа́н|ка, ки *f. of* ▶ парижа́нин Parisienne

пари́жский *adj.* Parisian

пари́к, á *m.* wig

парикма́хер, а *m.* hairdresser; (*мужско́й*) barber

парикма́херск|ая, ой *f.* hairdresser's; hairdressing salon; (*мужска́я*) barber's (shop)

парите́т, а *m.* parity

пар|и́ть, ю́, и́шь *impf.* (*no pf.*) to soar, swoop, hover; **п. в облака́х** (fig.) to live in the clouds

па́р|иться, юсь, ишься *impf. of* ▶ попа́риться

парк, а *m.* **1** (*сад*) park; **разби́ть п.** to lay out a park **2** (*ме́сто стоя́нки*) yard, depot **3** (*подвижно́й соста́в*) fleet; stock; pool

парке́т, а *m.* parquet; parquetry

парк|ова́ть, у́ю *impf. of* ▶ припаркова́ть

парк|ова́ться, у́юсь *impf. of* ▶ припаркова́ться

парко́вк|а, и *f.* parking

парла́мент, а *m.* parliament

парламента́ри|й, я *m.* parliamentarian

парла́ментский *adj.* parliamentary; **п. запро́с** interpellation

парни́к, á *m.* hotbed, polytunnel; (*из стекла́*) greenhouse

парн|о́й *adj.* fresh; ∼о́е мя́со fresh meat

па́рн|ый *adj.* pair; forming a pair; twin; **н. носо́к, п. сапо́г** *и т. п.* pair, fellow (*other one of pair of socks, boots, etc.*); ∼ое ката́ние (*на конька́х*) pair skating

парово́з, а *m.* (steam) engine, locomotive

паров|о́й *adj.* **1** *adj. of* ▶ пар; ∼а́я маши́на steam engine **2** (cul.) steamed

пароди́ст, а *m.* impressionist, mimic

паро́ди|я, и *f.* **1** (*произведе́ние*) parody **2** (**на** + *a.*) (*на справедли́вость*) travesty, caricature

паро́л|ь, я *m.* password

паро́м, а *m.* ferry (boat); **перепра́вить на ∼е** to ferry

парохо́д, а *m.* steamship

па́рт|а, ы *f.* (school) desk

парте́р, а *m.* (theatr.) the stalls

партиза́н, а, *g. pl.* ∼ *m.* (*на войне́*) partisan; (*про́тив ре́жима*) guerrilla

парти́йн|ый *adj.* (pol.) party; **п. биле́т** party-membership card

партиту́р|а, ы *f.* (mus.) score

⚔ **па́рти|я¹, и** *f.* (pol.) party

⚔ **па́рти|я², и** *f.* **1** (*гру́ппа лиц*) party, group **2** (*в произво́дстве*) batch; lot; (*гру́за*) consignment; (*отпра́вленных това́ров*) shipment **3** (sport) game; set **4** (mus.) part

⚔ **партнёр, а** *m.* partner

па́рус, а, *pl.* ∼á *m.* sail; **на всех ∼а́х** in full sail (also fig.)

паруси́н|а, ы *f.* canvas, sailcloth

па́русник, а *m.* sailing vessel

па́русный *adj. of* ▶ па́рус; **п. спорт** sailing

парфюме́р, а *m.* perfumer

парфюме́ри|я, и *f.* (*промы́шленность*) perfumery; (*духи́*) perfumes; (*косме́тика*) cosmetics; (*отде́л духо́в*) perfume department; (*отде́л косме́тики*) cosmetics department

парфюме́рный *adj. of* ▶ парфюме́рия; **п. магази́н** (*то́лько духи́*) perfumery, perfumer's shop; (*косме́тика*) cosmetics shop

парч|á, и́, *g. pl.* ∼е́й *f.* brocade

парши́в|ый, ∼, ∼а *adj.* (infml, fig.) rotten, lousy

пас, а, *m.* (sport) pass

па́смур|ный, ∼ен, ∼на *adj.* **1** (*день*) dull, cloudy; overcast **2** (fig., *лицо́*) gloomy, sullen

пас|ова́ть, у́ю *impf. and pf.* (sport) to pass

па́спорт, а, *pl.* ∼á *m.* **1** passport **2** (*маши́ны, аппара́та*) registration certificate

пасса́ж, а *m.* **1** (*галере́я*) arcade **2** (mus.) passage

пассажи́р, а *m.* passenger

пассажи́р|ка, ки *f. of* ▶ пассажи́р

пассажи́рский *adj. of* ▶ пассажи́р

пасса́т, а *m.* (meteor.) trade wind

пасси́в|ный, ∼ен, ∼на *adj.* passive

па́ст|а, ы *f.* paste; **зубна́я п.** toothpaste; **тома́тная п.** tomato purée

па́стбищ|е, а *nt.* pasture

па́ств|а, ы *f.* (eccl.) flock, congregation

пасте́л|ь, и *f.* **1** (collect.) (*карандаши́*) pastel(s) **2** (*in full* рису́нок ∼ью) pastel (drawing)

пастериз|ова́ть, у́ю *impf. and pf.* to pasteurize

пастерна́к, а *m.* parsnip

пас|ти́, у́, ёшь, *past* ∼, ∼ла́ *impf.* (*no pf.*) (*скот*) to graze, pasture; (*гусе́й*) to tend

пас|ти́сь, ётся, *past* ∼ся, ∼ла́сь *impf.* (*no pf.*) to graze; to browse; (infml, fig.) to hang about

па́стор, а *m.* (Protestant) minister, pastor

пасту́х, á *m.* (*коро́в*) herdsman; (*ове́ц*) shepherd

пасту́шк|а, и *f.* shepherdess

па́стыр|ь, я *m.* (eccl.) pastor

па|сть¹, ду́, дёшь, *past* ∼л, ∼ла́ **1** *pf. of* ▶ па́дать **2** (*pf. only*) (*поги́бнуть*) to die, fall; **п. же́ртвой чего́-н.** to fall victim to **3** (*pf. only*) (*о кре́пости, о го́роде*) to fall, surrender **4**: **п. ду́хом** to despair

па́ст|ь², и *f.* (*зве́ря*) mouth; jaws

Па́сх|а, и *f.* **1** (*в иудаи́зме*) Passover **2** (*в христиа́нстве*) Easter **3**: **п.** (cul.) paskha (*sweet cream cheese dish eaten at Easter*)

па́сын|ок, ка *m.* stepson, stepchild

пате́нт, а *m.* (**на** + *a.*) (*на изобрете́ние*) patent (for); (*торго́вый*) licence (BrE), license (AmE) (for)

патент|ова́ть, у́ю *impf.* (*of* ▶ запатентова́ть) to patent; to take out a patent for

патети́ческий *adj.* passionate; emotional

п

пато́лог, а *m.* pathologist

патологи́ческ|ий *adj.* pathological; ~ая анато́мия (anatomical) pathology

патоло́ги|я, и *f.* pathology

патологоанато́м, а *m.* (anatomical) pathologist

патриа́рх, а *m.* patriarch

патриарха́л|ьный, ~ен, ~ьна *adj.* patriarchal

патриархи́|я, и *f.* (eccl.) patriarchate

патрио́т, а *m.* patriot

патриоти́зм, а *m.* patriotism

патриоти́ческий *adj.* patriotic

патрио́т|ка, ки *f. of ▸* **патрио́т**

патро́н¹, а *m.* **1** (*покровитель*) patron **2** (*хозяин*, infml) boss

патро́н², а *m.* **1** (mil.) cartridge **2** (tech.) chuck (*of drill, lathe*), holder **3** (*лампочки*) socket

патрули́р|овать, ую *impf.* (*no pf.*) (mil.) to patrol

патру́л|ь, я́ *m.* patrol

патч, а *m.* (comput.) patch

па́уз|а, ы *f.* pause; interval; (mus.) rest

пау́к, а́ *m.* spider

паути́н|а, ы *f.* cobweb, spider's web; (fig.) web; Всеми́рная п. (comput.) the Web

па́фос, а *m.* **1** (+ *g.*) enthusiasm (for), zeal (for) **2** (*сущность*) spirit; emotional content

пах, а, о ~е, в ~у́ *m.* (anat.) groin

па́хар|ь, я *m.* ploughman (BrE), plowman (AmE)

па|ха́ть, шу́, ~шешь *impf.* **1** (*pf.* вс~) to plough (BrE), plow (AmE), till **2** (infml, *работать*) to slave (away)

па́х|нуть, ну, нешь, *past* ~ *or* ~нул, ~ла *impf.* (*no pf.*) (+ *i.*) to smell (of); ~нет лу́ком there is a smell of onions; (fig.) (*usu. impers.*) to savour (BrE), savor (AmE) (of), smack (of); ~ло ссо́рой a quarrel was in the air

пахӱ́ч|ий, ~, ~а *adj.* strong-smelling

паца́н, а́ *m.* (infml) boy, lad

⚔ **пацие́нт**, а *m.* patient

пацие́нт|ка, ки *f. of ▸* **пацие́нт**

пацифи́зм, а *m.* pacifism

пацифи́ст, а *m.* pacifist

па́чк|а, и *f.* **1** (*писем, газет*) bundle; (*сигарет, чая, печенья*) packet (BrE), pack **2** (*балерины*) tutu

па́чка|ть, ю *impf.* (*of ▸* запа́чкать, ▸ испа́чкать) to dirty, soil, stain, sully (also fig.); п. ру́ки (fig.) to soil one's hands

па́чка|ться, юсь *impf.* (*of ▸* запа́чкаться, ▸ испа́чкаться) **1** (*человек*) to make oneself dirty; to soil oneself **2** (*вещь*) to become dirty

па́ш|ня, ни, *g. pl.* ~ен *f.* arable land; ploughland (BrE), plowland (AmE)

паште́т, а *m.* pâté

пая́льник, а *m.* soldering iron

пая́снича|ть, ю *impf.* (*no pf.*) (infml) to clown, play the fool

пая́|ть, ю *impf.* (*no pf.*) to solder

⚔ key word

пая́ц, а *m.* (fig., pej.) clown

пев|е́ц, ца́ *m.* singer

певи́ц|а, ы *f. of ▸* **певе́ц**

пе́вч|ий **1** *adj.* singing; ~ая пти́ца songbird **2** (*as m. n. п.*, ~его) chorister

педаго́г, а *m.* teacher

педагоги́ческий *adj.* pedagogic(al); educational; п. институ́т college of education (BrE), teachers' college (AmE)

педа́л|ь, и *f.* pedal

педа́нт, а *m.* pedant

педанти́ч|ный, ~ен, ~на *adj.* pedantic

педиа́тр, а *m.* paediatrician (BrE), pediatrician (AmE)

педиатри́ческий *adj.* paediatric (BrE), pediatric (AmE)

педиатри́|я, и *f.* paediatrics (BrE), pediatrics (AmE)

пе́дик, а *m.* (infml, pej.) queer, poof (BrE)

педикю́р, а *m.* pedicure

педофи́л, а *m.* paedophile (BrE), pedophile (AmE)

педофили́|я, и *f.* paedophilia (BrE), pedophilia (AmE)

пе́йджер, а *m.* pager

пейза́ж, а *m.* **1** landscape; scenery **2** (*картина*) landscape

пёк, пекла́ *see ▸* **печь¹**

пека́р|ня, ни, *g. pl.* ~ен *f.* bakery, bakehouse

пе́кар|ь, я, *pl.* ~и, ~ей *m.* baker

Пеки́н, а *m.* Beijing

пе́кл|о, а *nt.* **1** (*сильный жар*) scorching heat **2** (*ад*) hell, hellfire

пеку́, пеку́т *see ▸* **печь¹**

пелена́, ы́, *pl.* ~ы́, ~, ~а́м *f.* shroud; у него́ сло́вно п. с глаз упа́ла the scales fell from his eyes

пелён|ка, ки *f.* (*usu. in pl.*) swaddling clothes; с пелёнок (fig.) from the cradle

пелика́н, а *m.* pelican

пельме́н|и, ей *m. pl.* (*sg.* ~ь, ~я) (cul.) pelmeni (*a kind of ravioli*)

пе́н|а, ы *f.* (*на море*) foam; (*на бульоне*) scum; (*на пиве*) froth

пена́л, а *m.* pencil case

пе́ни|е, я *nt.* singing

пе́нист|ый, ~, ~а *adj.* foamy; frothy

пе́н|иться, ится *impf.* to foam; to froth (up)

пеницилли́н, а *m.* penicillin

пе́нный *adj.* = **пе́нистый**

пенопла́ст, а *m.* foam plastic

пенс, а *m.* penny

пенсионе́р, а *m.* pensioner

пенсионе́р|ка, ки *f. of ▸* **пенсионе́р**

пенсио́нный *adj. of ▸* **пе́нсия**; п. во́зраст retirement age; п. фонд pension fund

пе́нси|я, и *f.* pension; он на ~ю he is retired; вы́йти на ~ю to retire

пенсне́ *nt. indecl.* pince-nez

пентха́ус, а *m.* penthouse

пень, пня *m.* stump

пеньк|а́, и́ *f.* hemp

пенько́вый *adj.* hempen

пеньюа́р, а *m.* peignoir, negligee

пе́н|я, и *f.* fine

пе́п|ел, ла *m.* ash(es)

пе́пельниц|а, ы *f.* ashtray

пе́пельн|ый *adj.* ashy; ~ого цве́та ash-grey

пе́рвенств|о, а *nt.* first place; (sport) championship

перви́чный *adj.* (*гла́вный*) primary; (*первонача́льный*) initial

первобы́т|ный, ~ен, ~на *adj.* primitive; primordial; primeval (also fig.)

✧ **пе́рв|ое, ого** *nt.* first course (*of a meal*)

первозда́нный *adj.* primordial; (geol.) primitive, primary; **п. ха́ос** primordial chaos (also fig., iron.)

первоисто́чник, а *m.* (*све́дений*) primary source; (*осно́ва*) origin

первокла́сс|ный, ~ен, ~на *adj.* first-class, first-rate

первонача́л|ьный, ~ен, ~ьна *adj.* **1** (*са́мый пе́рвый*) original **2** (*явля́ющийся нача́лом*) initial

первооткрыва́тел|ь, я *m.* discoverer

первоочередн|о́й *adj.* immediate; ~а́я зада́ча immediate task

первопрохо́д|ец, ца *m.* (also fig., rhet.) pioneer; trailblazer

первосо́рт|ный, ~ен, ~на *adj.* **1** top-quality **2** (infml, *превосхо́дный*) first-class, first-rate

✧ **пе́рв|ый** *adj.* **1** first; (*по вре́мени*) earliest; first; ~ого января́ on the first of January; **быть ~ым, идти́ ~ым** to come first, lead; ~ое вре́мя at first; ~ая скри́пка first violin; **п. эта́ж** ground floor (BrE), first floor (AmE); **в** ~ую о́чередь in the first place; **на п. взгля́д, с** ~ого взгля́да at first sight **2** (*лу́чший*) best

перга́мент, а *m.* parchment

пер|де́ть, ди́шь *impf.* (vulg.) to fart

пере... *vbl. pref. indicating* **1** (*action across or through sth*) trans- **2** (*repetition of action*) re- **3** (*superiority, excess, etc.*) over-, out- **4** (*extension of action to encompass many or all objects or cases of a given kind*) **5** (*division into two or more parts*) **6** (*reflexives*) reciprocity of action

переадрес|ова́ть, у́ю *pf.* (*of* ▶ переадресо́вывать) to re-address; to forward

переадресо́выва|ть, ю *impf. of* ▶ переадресова́ть

перебази́р|оваться, уюсь *pf.* to relocate

перебарщива|ть, ю *impf. of* ▶ переборщи́ть

перебега́|ть, ю *impf. of* ▶ перебежа́ть

перебе|жа́ть, гу́, жи́шь, гу́т *pf.* (*of* ▶ перебега́ть) **1** (*че́рез + a.*) to cross (running); **п. (че́рез) у́лицу** to run across the street **2** (fig., infml) (**к** + *d.*) (*к проти́внику*) to go over (to), desert (to)

перебе́жчик, а *m.* deserter; (fig.) turncoat

перебе́жчи|ца, цы *f. of* ▶ перебе́жчик

перебива́|ть, ю *impf. of* ▶ переби́ть

перебинт|ова́ть, у́ю *pf.* (*of* ▶ перебинто́вывать) (*поменя́ть повя́зку*) to change the dressing (on), put a new dressing (on)

перебинто́выва|ть, ю *impf. of* ▶ перебинтова́ть

перебира́|ть¹, ю *impf. of* ▶ перебра́ть

перебира́|ть², ю *impf.* **1** (*каса́ться па́льцами*) to finger; **п. стру́ны** to run one's fingers over the strings **2** (+ *i.*) (*нога́ми, па́льцами*) to move (*in turn or in a regular manner*)

перебира́|ться, ~юсь *impf. of* ▶ перебра́ться

переб|и́ть, ью́, ьёшь *pf.* (*of* ▶ перебива́ть) (*говоря́щего*) to interrupt

перебо́|й, я *m.* (*переры́в*) interruption; (*заде́ржка*) hold-up; (*дви́гателя*) misfire; (*се́рдца*) irregularity; **пульс с** ~ями irregular pulse

переболе́|ть, ю *pf.* (+ *i.*) to have had, have been down (*with an illness*); **де́ти все** ~ли ветря́нкой the children have all been down with chickenpox

перебо́рк|а, и *f.* (*перегоро́дка*) partition; (naut.) bulkhead

перебор|о́ть, ю́, ~ешь *pf.* (*no impf.*) to overcome

переборщ|и́ть, у́, и́шь *pf.* (*of* ▶ переба́рщивать) (**в** + *p.*) (infml) to go too far; to overdo it; to go over the top

перебра́сыва|ть, ю *impf. of* ▶ перебро́сить

пере|бра́ть, беру́, берёшь, *past* ~бра́л, ~бра́ла, ~бра́ло *pf.* (*of* ▶ перебира́ть¹) **1** (*сортирова́ть*) to sort; (*пересмотре́ть*) to look through **2** (fig., *в уме́*) to turn over (in one's mind) **3** (*взять сли́шком мно́го*) to take too much

пере|бра́ться, беру́сь, берёшься, *past* ~бра́лся, ~брала́сь, ~брало́сь *pf.* (*of* ▶ перебира́ться) (infml) (*перейти́*) to get over, cross (*пересели́ться*) to move

перебро́|сить, шу, сишь *pf.* (*of* ▶ перебра́сывать) **1** (*мяч*) to throw over **2** (*перемести́ть*) to transfer (*troops, etc.*)

перева́л, а *m.* (geog.) pass

перева́лива|ть, ю *impf. of* ▶ перевали́ть

перева́лива|ться¹, юсь *impf. of* ▶ перевали́ться

перева́лива|ться², юсь *impf.* (*no pf.*) to waddle

перевал|и́ть, ю́, ~ишь *pf.* (*of* ▶ перева́ливать) **1** (*перемести́ть*) to transfer, shift **2** (*перейти́*) to cross; (*impers.*) (infml, *о преде́ле*) to be past; ~и́ло за́ полночь it is past midnight

перевал|и́ться, ю́сь, ~ишься *pf.* (*of* ▶ перева́ливаться¹) to roll over

перева́рива|ть, ю *impf. of* ▶ перевари́ть

перевар|и́ть, ю́, ~ишь *pf.* (*of* ▶ перева́ривать) to digest

перевез|ти́, у́, ёшь, *past* ~, **~ла́** *pf.* (*of* ▶ **перевози́ть**) **1** (*переместить, людей через реку*) to take across, transport across **2** (*везя, доставить, детей на дачу*) to transport, take (*from A to B*)

переверн|у́ть, у́, ёшь *pf.* (*of* ▶ **перевора́чивать**) **1** (*с одной стороны на другую*) to turn over; (*вверх дном*) to turn upside down **2** (*изменить*) to change radically, transform **3** (*потрясти*) to shake, stun

переверну́ться, у́сь, ёшься *pf.* (*of* ▶ **перевора́чиваться**) to turn over

переве́|сить¹, шу, сишь *pf.* (*of* ▶ **переве́шивать**) (*пальто*) to hang somewhere else; **п. карти́ну с одно́й стены́ на другу́ю** to move a picture from one wall to another

переве́|сить², шу, сишь *pf.* (*of* ▶ **переве́шивать**) to outweigh, outbalance (also fig.); (fig., *оказаться более весомым*) to tip the scales

переве|сти́, ду́, дёшь, *past* ~л, **~ла́** *pf.* (*of* ▶ **переводи́ть**) **1** (*ведя, переместить*) to take across; **п. дете́й че́рез у́лицу** to take children across the road **2** (*в другое место*) to transfer, move, switch, shift; **п. на другу́ю рабо́ту** to transfer to another post; **п. де́ньги** to transfer money **3** (*c + g. and* **на** *+ a.*) to translate (from, into); (**в, на** *+ a.*) (*в другие единицы*) to convert (to), express (as, in); **п. с ру́сского языка́ на англи́йский** to translate from Russian into English; **п. в метри́ческие ме́ры** to convert to metric units **4** (*взгляд, разговор*) to shift; **п. разгово́р на другу́ю те́му** to change the subject

переве́шива|ть, ю *impf. of* ▶ **переве́сить¹**, ▶ **переве́сить²**

перевива́|ть, ю *impf. of* ▶ **переви́ть**

перевира́|ть, ю *impf. of* ▶ **перевра́ть**

перев|и́ть, ью́, ьёшь, *past* ~и́л, **~ила́**, **~и́ло** *pf.* (*of* ▶ **перевива́ть**) (*+ i.*) to interweave (with), intertwine (with)

◆ **перево́д, а** *m.* **1** (*в другое место*) transfer, move, switch, shift; **де́нежный п.** remittance; **почто́вый п.** postal order **2** (*с одного языка на другой*) translation; (*в другие единицы*) conversion

перево|ди́ть, жу́, ~дишь *impf. of* ▶ **перевести́**

перево́дчик, а *m.* translator; (*устный*) interpreter

перево́дчи|ца, цы *f. of* ▶ **перево́дчик**

перево|зи́ть, жу́, ~зишь *impf. of* ▶ **перевезти́**

перево́зк|а, и *f.* transportation, conveyance

перевоплоще́ни|е, я *nt.* reincarnation; (fig.) transformation

перевора́чива|ть, ю *impf. of* ▶ **переверну́ть**

перевора́чива|ться, юсь *impf. of* ▶ **переверну́ться**

переворо́т, а *m.* revolution; **госуда́рственный п.** coup d'état

◆ key word

перевоспита́ни|е, я *nt.* re-education; rehabilitation

перевр|а́ть, у́, ёшь, *past* ~а́л, **~ала́**, **~а́ло** *pf.* (*of* ▶ **перевира́ть**) (infml) to garble, confuse; to misinterpret; **п. цита́ту** to misquote

перевы́бор|ы, ов (*no sg.*) re-election

перевя́|за́ть, жу́, ~жешь *pf.* (*of* ▶ **перевя́зывать**) **1** (*рану*) to dress, bandage **2** (*коробку*) to tie up, cord

перевя́зк|а, и *f.* dressing, bandage

перевя́зочный *adj. of* ▶ **перевя́зка**; **п. материа́л** dressing; **п. пункт** dressing station

перевя́зыва|ть, ю *impf. of* ▶ **перевяза́ть**

переги́б, а *m.* **1** bend, twist; (*линия*) fold **2** (fig., *преувеличение*) exaggeration; (*в политике, в руководстве*): **допусти́ть п. в чём-н.** to carry sth too far

перегиба́|ть, ю *impf. of* ▶ **перегну́ть**

перегиба́|ться, юсь *impf. of* ▶ **перегну́ться**

перегля́дыва|ться, юсь *impf. of* ▶ **перегляну́ться**

перегля|ну́ться, ну́сь, ~нешься *pf.* (*of* ▶ **перегля́дываться**) (*с + i.*) to exchange glances (with)

переп|гна́ть, гоню́, го́нишь, *past* ~гна́л, **~гнала́**, **~гна́ло** *pf.* (*of* ▶ **перегоня́ть**) **1** (*обогнать*) to outdistance, leave behind; (fig.) to overtake, surpass **2** (*скот*) to drive (*somewhere else; from A to B*) **3** (chem.) to distil (BrE), distill (AmE)

перегно́|й, я *m.* humus

переп|гну́ть, ну́, нёшь *pf.* (*of* ▶ **перегиба́ть**) to bend; (fig., infml) to go too far; **п. па́лку** (fig.) to go too far

переп|гну́ться, ну́сь, нёшься *pf.* (*of* ▶ **перегиба́ться**) **1** (*о человеке*) to lean over, bend over **2** (*о ветви*) to bend

перегова́рива|ться, юсь *impf.* (*с + i.*) to exchange remarks (with)

◆ **перегово́р|ы, ов** (*no sg.*) negotiations, talks; **вести́ п.** (*с + i.*) to negotiate, hold talks (with)

перегоня́|ть, ю *impf. of* ▶ **перегна́ть**

перегора́жива|ть, ю *impf. of* ▶ **перегороди́ть**

перегор|а́ть, а́ю *impf. of* ▶ **перегоре́ть**

перегор|е́ть, и́т *pf.* (*of* ▶ **перегора́ть**) **1** (*о лампочке*) to burn out **2** (*о балке*) to burn through

перегоро|ди́ть, жу́, ~ди́шь *pf.* (*of* ▶ **перегора́живать**) to partition off

перегоро́дк|а, и *f.* **1** partition **2** (fig.) barrier

перегре́в, а *m.* overheating

перегрева́|ть, ю *impf. of* ▶ **перегре́ть**

перегрева́|ться, юсь *impf. of* ▶ **перегре́ться**

перегре́|ть, ю *pf.* (*of* ▶ **перегрева́ть**) to overheat

перегре́|ться, юсь *pf.* (*of* ▶ **перегрева́ться**) to overheat; (*на солнце*) to spend too long in the sun

перегружа́|ть, ю *impf. of* ▶ **перегрузи́ть¹**

перегру|зи́ть¹, жу́, ~зишь *pf.* (*of* ▶ **перегружа́ть**) to overload; **п. рабо́той** to overwork

перегру|зи́ть², жу́, ~зишь *pf.* (*of*
▶ **перегружа́ть**) to load (*somewhere else; from A to B*); to trans-ship; **п. с по́езда на парохо́д** to load from a train on to a ship
перегру́зк|а, и *f.* overloading; (*usu. in pl.*) strain, stress
перегрыза́|ть, ю *impf. of* ▶ **перегры́зть**
перегры́з|ть, у́, ёшь, *past* ~, ~ла *pf.* (*of* ▶ **перегрыза́ть**) to gnaw through, bite through
перегры́з|ться, усь, ёшься, *past* ~ся, ~лась *pf.* (*no impf.*) (из-за + *g.*) (infml, *о собаках*) to fight (over); (fig.) to quarrel (over), wrangle (about)
ⱷ **пе́ред** and **пе́редо** *prep.* + *i.* **1** (*при обозначении места*) in front of; before; **п. до́мом** in front of the house; (*also fig.*): **п. опа́сностью/тру́дностями** in the face of danger/difficulties **2** (*раньше*) before; **п. обе́дом** before dinner; **п. тем, как** (*conj.*) before **3** (*в присутствии*) in the presence of, in front of; **п. учи́телем** in front of the teacher **4** (*в отношении; по сравнению*) to; **извини́ться п. кем-н.** to apologize to sb
ⱷ **переда|ва́ть**, ю́, ёшь *impf. of* ▶ **переда́ть**
переда|ва́ться, ю́сь, ёшься *impf. of* ▶ **переда́ться**
переда́тчик, а *m.* transmitter
переда́|ть, м, шь, ст, ди́м, ди́те, ду́т, *past* пе́редал, ~ла́, пе́редало *pf.* (*of* ▶ **передава́ть**) **1** (*отдать через кого-н.*) to pass; (*вручить*) to hand; (*свои права, коллекцию*) to hand over; to transfer **2** (*сообщить*) to tell; to communicate; **переда́йте ему́, что я приезжа́ю за́втра** tell him I shall be arriving tomorrow; (*распространить*) to transmit, convey; **п. по ра́дио/телеви́дению** to broadcast (on the radio/television); **п. приве́т** to send one's regards **3** (*воспроизвести*) to reproduce (*a sound, a thought, etc.*)
переда́|ться, стся, ду́тся, *past* ~лся, ~ла́сь *pf.* (*of* ▶ **передава́ться**) to pass; (*о тревоге, болезни*) to be transmitted, be communicated; (*по наследству*) to be inherited; **корь ~ла́сь ему́ от сосе́дских дете́й** he picked up measles from the children next door
ⱷ **переда́ч|а**, и *f.* **1** (*действие*) passing; transmission; communication; transfer, transference **2** (*больному, заключённому*) parcel **3** (*по телевидению, по радио*) broadcast; **пряма́я п.** live broadcast; (*программа*) programme (BrE), program (AmE) **4** (tech.) drive; gear(ing); transmission; **ремённая п.** belt drive
передвига́|ть, ю *impf. of* ▶ **передви́нуть**
передвига́|ться, юсь *impf. of* ▶ **передви́нуться**
передвижно́й *adj.* **1** (*перегородка*) movable **2** (*библиотека*) mobile, travelling (BrE), traveling (AmE)
передви́|нуть, ну, нешь *pf.* (*of* ▶ **передвига́ть**) to move, shift (also fig.); **п. сро́ки экза́менов** to alter the date of

examinations
передви́|нуться, нусь, нешься *pf.* (*of* ▶ **передвига́ться**) to move, shift
переде́л|ать, аю *pf.* (*of* ▶ **переде́лывать**) (*сделать заново*) to redo; (*сделать по-иному*) to alter; (fig.) to refashion, recast; **п. пла́тье** to alter a dress
переде́лыва|ть, ю *impf. of* ▶ **переде́лать**
передерж|а́ть, у́, ~ишь *pf.* (*of* ▶ **переде́рживать**) **1** (*кушанье*) to overdo; to overcook **2** (phot.) to overexpose
переде́ржива|ть, ю *impf. of* ▶ **передержа́ть**
ⱷ **пере́дн|ий** *adj.* front; ~ие коне́чности forelegs; **п. план** foreground
пере́дник, а *m.* apron
пере́дн|яя, ей *f.* (entrance) hall, lobby
пе́редо = **пе́ред**
передово́й *adj.* (*отряд*) forward; (*технология*) advanced; (*взгляды*) progressive
передозиро́вк|а, и *f.* (med.) overdose
передохн|у́ть, у́, ёшь *pf.* (*of* ▶ **передыха́ть**) (infml) to pause for breath, take a short rest
передра́знива|ть, ю *impf. of* ▶ **передразни́ть**
передразн|и́ть, ю́, ~ишь *pf.* (*of* ▶ **передра́знивать**) to take off, mimic
пере|дра́ться, деру́сь, дерёшься, *past* ~дра́лся, ~драла́сь, ~дра́лось *pf.* (*no impf.*) (infml) to fight, brawl (*of many people, etc.*)
переду́м|ать, аю *pf.* (*of* ▶ **переду́мывать**) to change one's mind
переду́мыва|ть, ю *impf. of* ▶ **переду́мать**
передыха́|ть, ю *impf. of* ▶ **передохну́ть**
перееда́|ть, ю *impf. of* ▶ **перее́сть**
перее́зд¹, а *m.* (*место*) crossing
перее́зд², а *m.* (*переселение*) move
переезжа́|ть, ю *impf. of* ▶ **перее́хать**
перее́|сть, м, шь, ст, ди́м, ди́те, дя́т, *past* ~л *pf.* (*of* ▶ **перееда́ть**) to overeat
перее́|хать, ду, дешь *pf.* (*of* ▶ **переезжа́ть**) **1** (+ *a.* ог че́рез + *a.*) (*дорогу*) to cross **2** (*задавить*) to run over, knock down **3** (*переселиться*) to move
пережда́|ть, у́, ёшь, *past* ~а́л, ~ала́, ~а́ло *pf.* (*of* ▶ **пережида́ть**) to wait through; **мы ~а́ли грозу́** we waited till the storm was over
переж|ева́ть, ую́, уёшь *pf.* (*of* ▶ **пережёвывать**) to masticate, chew
пережёвыва|ть, ю *impf. of* ▶ **пережева́ть**
пережива́ни|е, я *nt.* (*события*) experience; (*душевное состояние*) feeling
пережива́|ть, ю **1** *impf. of* ▶ **пережи́ть** **2** (*impf. only*) (за + *a.*) (infml) to be upset, worry (for, on behalf of)
пережида́|ть, ю *impf. of* ▶ **пережда́ть**
пережи́т|ок, ка *m.* relic, vestige, survival
пережи́|ть, ву́, вёшь, *past* пе́режи́л, ~ла́, пе́режи́ло *pf.* (*of* ▶ **пережива́ть 1**) **1** (*испытать*) to experience; to go/live through; (*выдержать*) to endure, suffer;

п (margin tab)

тяжело́ п. что-н. to take sth hard; (*оста́ться в живы́х*) to survive **2** (*прожи́ть до́льше*) to outlive, survive

перезагру|жа́ть, жа́ю *impf. of*
▶ **перезагрузи́ть**

перезагру|зи́ть, ужу́, у́зишь *pf.* (*of*
▶ **перезагружа́ть**) (comput.) to reboot

перезаря|ди́ть, жу́, ∼ди́шь *pf.* (*of*
▶ **перезаряжа́ть**) **1** (*аккумуля́тор*) to recharge **2** (*револьве́р, фотоаппара́т*) to reload

перезаряжа́|ть, ю *impf. of* ▶ **перезаряди́ть**

перезва́нива|ть, ю *impf. of* ▶ **перезвони́ть**

перезвон|и́ть, ю́, и́шь *pf.* (*of*
▶ **перезва́нивать**) to ring back (BrE), call back (AmE)

перезим|ова́ть, у́ю *pf.* (*of* ▶ **зимова́ть**) to winter, pass the winter

перезрева́|ть, ю *impf. of* ▶ **перезре́ть**

перезре́лый *adj.* overripe; (fig.) passé, past one's prime

перезре́|ть, ю *pf.* (*of* ▶ **перезрева́ть**) **1** to become overripe **2** (fig.) to be past one's prime

переигр|а́ть, а́ю *pf.* (*of* ▶ **переи́грывать**) **1** (*па́ртию*) to play again **2** (*сыгра́ть мно́гое и мно́гократно или повто́рно*); to play (*a lot, or many times, or repeatedly*); to play (*all, a number of*) **3** (infml, sport) to outplay; to beat **4** (theatr., infml) to overact, overdo

переи́грыва|ть, ю *impf. of* ▶ **переигра́ть**

переизбира́|ть, ю *impf. of* ▶ **переизбра́ть**

переиз|бра́ть, беру́, берёшь, *past* ∼бра́л, ∼брала́, ∼бра́ло *pf.* (*of* ▶ **переизбира́ть**) to re-elect

переизда|ва́ть, ю́, ёшь *impf. of* ▶ **переизда́ть**

переизда́|ть, м, шь, ст, ди́м, ди́те, ду́т, *past* ∼л, ∼ла́, ∼ло *pf.* (*of* ▶ **переиздава́ть**) to republish, reprint

переимен|ова́ть, у́ю *pf.* (*of*
▶ **переимено́вывать**) (*в* + *a.*) to rename

переимено́выва|ть, ю *impf. of*
▶ **переименова́ть**

пере|йти́, йду́, йдёшь, *past* ∼шёл, ∼шла́ *pf.* (*of* ▶ **переходи́ть**) **1** (+ *a.* or *че́рез* + *a.*) (*перепра́виться*) to cross; to get across, get over, go over; п. грани́цу to cross the frontier; п. че́рез мо́ст to go across a bridge **2** (*в, на* + *a.* or *к* + *d.*) (*в друго́е ме́сто*) to pass (to); п. в сосе́днюю ко́мнату to go into the next room; п. на другу́ю рабо́ту to change one's job **3** (*в* + *a.*) (*преврати́ться*) to turn (into); их ссо́ра ∼шла́ в дра́ку their quarrel turned into a fight

перека́пыва|ть, ю *impf. of* ▶ **перекопа́ть**

перека́рмлива|ть, ю *impf. of* ▶ **перекорми́ть**

перека|ти́ть, чу́, ∼тишь *pf.* (*of*
▶ **перека́тывать**) (*бо́чку*) to roll; (*велосипе́д*) to wheel

перека|ти́ться, чу́сь, ∼тишься *pf.* (*of*
▶ **перека́тываться**) to roll

перека́тыва|ть, ю *impf. of* ▶ **перекати́ть**

перека́тыва|ться, юсь *impf. of*
▶ **перекати́ться**

перекач|а́ть, а́ю *pf.* (*of* ▶ **перека́чивать**) to pump over, pump across

перека́чива|ть, ю *impf. of* ▶ **перекача́ть**

перекид|а́ть, а́ю *pf.* (*of* ▶ **переки́дывать**) to throw (one after another)

переки́дыва|ть, ю *impf. of* ▶ **перекида́ть,**
▶ **переки́нуть**

переки́дыва|ться, юсь *impf. of*
▶ **переки́нуться**

переки́|нуть, ну *pf.* (*of*
▶ **переки́дывать**) to throw (over)

переки́|нуться, нусь, нешься *pf.*
(*of* ▶ **переки́дываться**) **1** (*бы́стро перемести́ться*) to leap (over) **2** (*огонь*) to spread **3** (+ *i.*) (*мячо́м*) to throw (one to another); (*слова́ми*) to bandy, exchange

перекла́дин|а, ы *f.* **1** (*брус*) cross-beam, crosspiece, transom **2** (sport) horizontal bar

перекла́дыва|ть, ю *impf. of* ▶ **переложи́ть**

переклик|а́ться, а́юсь *impf.* (*с* + *i.*) **1** (*pf.* ∼**нуться**) to call to one another **2** (*no pf.*) (fig., *быть подо́бным*) to have sth in common (with)

перекли́к|нуться, нусь, нешься *pf. of*
▶ **перекли́каться 1**

перекли́чк|а, и *f.* roll-call; де́лать ∼у to call the roll

переключа́тел|ь, я *m.* (tech.) switch

переключ|а́ть, а́ю *impf. of* ▶ **переключи́ть**

переключ|а́ться, а́юсь *impf. of*
▶ **переключи́ться**

переключ|и́ть, у́, и́шь *pf.* (*of* ▶ **переключа́ть**) (tech., also fig.) (*на* + *a.*) to switch (over to); п. ско́рость to change gear (BrE), shift gears (AmE); п. телеви́зор/ра́дио на другу́ю програ́мму to switch over, change channels (*on the TV/radio*)

переключ|и́ться, у́сь, и́шься *pf.* (*of*
▶ **переключа́ться**) (tech, also fig.) (*на* + *a.*) to switch (over to); внима́ние пу́блики ∼и́лось на говоря́щего attention switched to the speaker

перекоп|а́ть, ю *pf.* (*of* ▶ **перека́пывать**) **1** (*карто́фель; огоро́д*) to dig up **2** (*чемода́н*) to rummage through **3** (*доро́гу*) to dig a ditch across

перекорм|и́ть, лю́, ∼ишь *pf.* (*of*
▶ **перека́рмливать**) to overfeed

переко́с, а *m.* **1** (*искривле́ние*) warping **2** (fig., *тенденцио́зность*) slant

переко́шен|ный, ∼, ∼а *adj.* distorted, twisted

перекра́ива|ть, ю *impf. of* ▶ **перекрои́ть**

перекра́|сить, шу, сишь *pf.* (*of*
▶ **перекра́шивать**) (*сте́ну*) to repaint; (*в друго́й цвет*) to paint another colour (BrE), color (AmE); (*во́лосы*) to re-dye

перекра́шива|ть, ю *impf. of* ▶ **перекра́сить**

перекре|сти́ть, щу́, ∼сти́шь *pf.* (*of*
▶ **крести́ть 3**) to make the sign of the

П

cross over

перекре|сти́ться, щу́сь, ∼сти́шься *pf.*
(*of* ▶ крести́ться 2) (*о человеке*) to cross
oneself

перекрёстн|ый *adj.* cross; **п. ого́нь** (mil.)
crossfire; ∼**ая ссы́лка** cross reference

перекрёст|ок, ка *m.* crossroads, crossing

перекри́кива|ть, ю *impf. of* ▶ перекрича́ть

перекри|ча́ть, чу́, чи́шь *pf.* (*of*
▶ перекри́кивать) (*шум*) to shout above;
(*человека*) to shout down

перекро|и́ть, ю́, и́шь *pf.* (*of*
▶ перекра́ивать) to cut out again; (fig.,
статью, план) to rehash; to re-shape

перекрыва́|ть, ю *impf. of* ▶ перекры́ть¹,
▶ перекры́ть²

перекры́|ть¹, о́ю, о́ешь *pf.* (*of*
▶ перекрыва́ть) (*покрыть заново*) to
re-cover

перекры́|ть², о́ю, о́ешь *pf.* (*of*
▶ перекрыва́ть) (*дорогу*) to close; (*воду,
доступ*) to cut off; (*реку*) to dam

перекувы́ркива|ться, юсь *impf. of*
▶ перекувырну́ться

перекувыр|ну́ться, ну́сь, нёшься *pf.* (*of*
▶ перекувы́ркиваться) (infml) **1** (*упасть*)
to topple over **2** (*перевернуться кувырком*)
to turn a somersault

переку́р, а *m.* (infml) smoking break; (*перерыв
вообще*) break; **пойдём на п.** let's take five

переку|си́ть, шу́, ∼сишь *pf.* (*of*
▶ переку́сывать) (infml, *поесть*) to have a
bite, have a snack

переку́сыва|ть, ю *impf. of* ▶ перекуси́ть

перела́мыва|ть, ю, ет *impf. of* ▶ переломи́ть

перела́мыва|ться, ется *impf. of*
▶ переломи́ться

перелеза́|ть, а́ю *impf. of* ▶ переле́зть

переле́з|ть, у, ешь, *past* ∼, ∼ла *pf.* (*of*
▶ перелеза́ть) to climb over, get over

перелес|ок, ка *m.* copse, coppice

перелёт, а *m.* **1** (*самолёта*) flight **2** (*птиц*)
migration

перелет|а́ть, а́ю *impf. of* ▶ перелете́ть

переле|те́ть, чу́, ти́шь (*of* ▶ перелета́ть)
1 (+ *a. or* че́рез + *a.*) to fly over **2** (*дальше
нужного*) to fly too far; to overshoot (the
mark)

перелётн|ый *adj.*: ∼**ая пти́ца** bird of
passage (also fig.); migratory bird

пере|ле́чь, ля́гу, ля́жешь, ля́гут, *past*
∼лёг, ∼легла́ *pf.* (*no impf.*) to lie
somewhere else; to move; **п. с дива́на на
крова́ть** to move from the sofa to the bed

перели́в, а *m.* (*цвета*) tint, tinge; (*цветов*)
play (of colours (BrE), colors (AmE)); (*голоса*)
modulation

перелива́ни|е, я *nt.* **1** decanting, pouring
2 (med.) transfusion

перелива́|ть, ю *impf. of* ▶ перели́ть

перелива́|ться, ется *impf. of* ▶ перели́ться

перелист|а́ть, а́ю *pf.* (*of* ▶ перели́стывать)
1 to leaf through **2** (*бегло просмотреть*)

to look through, flick through

перели́стыва|ть, ю *impf. of* ▶ перелиста́ть

перел|и́ть, ью́, ьёшь, *past* ∼и́л, ∼ила́,
∼и́ло *pf.* (*of* ▶ перелива́ть) **1** to pour
(*somewhere else; from A into B*); to decant;
п. молоко́ из кастрю́ли в кувши́н to pour
milk from a saucepan into a jug **2** (med.) to
transfuse; **п. кровь** (+ *d.*) to administer a
blood transfusion (to) **3** (*через край*) to let
overflow

перел|и́ться, ьётся, *past* ∼и́лся, ∼ила́сь
pf. (*of* ▶ перелива́ться) **1** (*литься в другое
место*) to flow **2** (*вылиться*) to overflow,
run over

перелож|и́ть, у́, ∼ишь *pf.* (*of*
▶ перекла́дывать) **1** to put somewhere
else; to shift, move; (fig.) to shift, transfer;
п. отве́тственность на кого́-н. to shift
the responsibility on to sb **2** (+ *a. and i.*)
to interlay (with); **п. посу́ду соло́мой** to
interlay crockery with straw

перело́м, а *m.* break, breaking; (*кости*)
fracture

перелом|и́ть, лю́, ∼ишь *pf.* (*of*
▶ перела́мывать) **1** to break in two **2** (fig.)
to break, master; **п. ход собы́тий** to turn
events around

перелом|и́ться, ∼ится *pf.* (*of*
▶ перела́мываться) to break in two; to be
fractured

перело́мный *adj. of* ▶ перело́м; **п. моме́нт**
critical moment, crucial moment

перема́лыва|ть, ю, ет *impf. of* ▶ перемоло́ть

перема́лыва|ться, ется *impf. of*
▶ перемоло́ться

перема́нива|ть, ю *impf. of* ▶ перемани́ть

переман|и́ть, ю́, ∼ишь *pf.* (*of*
▶ перема́нивать) (infml) to entice; **п. на свою́
сто́рону** to win over

перема́тыва|ть, ю *impf. of* ▶ перемота́ть

перемежа́|ть, ю *impf.* (*no pf.*) (+ *a. and
i. or* с + *i.*) to alternate; **он** ∼**л угро́зы (с)
обеща́ниями** he alternated threats and
promises

перемежа́|ться, ется *impf.* (*no pf.*) (+ *i. or*
с + *i.*) to alternate; **снег** ∼**лся (с) дождём**
snow alternated with rain, it snowed and
rained by turns

переме́н|а, ы *f.* **1** change **2** (*в школе*) break
(BrE), recess (AmE)

перемен|и́ть, ю́, ∼ишь *pf.* (*of* ▶ переменя́ть)
to change; **п. пози́цию** to shift one's ground
(also fig.); **п. тон** (fig.) to change one's tune

перемен|и́ться, ю́сь, ∼ишься *pf.* (*of*
▶ переменя́ться) to change; **п. в лице́** to
change countenance; **п. к кому́-н.** to change
(one's attitude) towards sb

переме́нн|ый *adj.* variable; ∼**ая величина́**
(math.) variable (quantity); **п. ток** (elec.)
alternating current; **с** ∼**ым успе́хом** with
varying success

переменя́|ть, я́ю *impf. of* ▶ перемени́ть

переменя́|ться, я́юсь *impf. of*
▶ перемени́ться

п

переме|сти́ть, щу́, сти́шь *pf.* (of
▸ **перемеща́ть**) to move (*somewhere else*);
(*на другую работу*) to transfer

переме|сти́ться, щу́сь, сти́шься *pf.* (of
▸ **перемеща́ться**) to move

перемеш|а́ть, а́ю *pf.* (of ▸ **переме́шивать**)
to (inter)mix, intermingle; **п. у́гли в пе́чке**
to poke the fire

перемеш|а́ться, а́юсь *pf.* (of
▸ **переме́шиваться**) to get mixed (up); **всё у
него́ в голове́ ∼а́лось** he has got everything
mixed up

переме́шива|ть, ю *impf. of* ▸ **перемеша́ть**

переме́шива|ться, юсь *impf. of*
▸ **перемеша́ться**

перемеща́|ть, ю *impf. of* ▸ **перемести́ть**

перемеща́|ться, юсь *impf. of*
▸ **перемести́ться**

перемеще́ни|е, я *nt.* (*изменение положения*)
transference, shift; (*движение*) movement;
(*по службе*) transfer

переми́ри|е, я *nt.* armistice, truce

перемнож|а́ть, а́ю *impf. of* ▸ **перемно́жить**

перемно́ж|ить, у, ишь *pf.* (of
▸ **перемножа́ть**) to multiply

перем|оло́ть, елю́, е́лешь *pf.* (of
▸ **перема́лывать**) (*кофе, зерно*) to grind,
mill; (fig., *разрушить*) to pulverize

перем|оло́ться, е́лется *pf.* (of
▸ **перема́лываться**): **∼е́лется — мука́ бу́дет**
(*proverb*) it will all come right in the end

перемота́|ть, ю *pf.* (of ▸ **перема́тывать**)
1 (*на что-н. другое*) to wind; to reel; **п.
наза́д** to rewind; **п. вперёд** to fast forward
2 (*намотать заново*) to rewind

перемыва́|ть, ю *impf. of* ▸ **перемы́ть**

перем|ы́ть, о́ю, о́ешь *pf.* (of ▸ **перемыва́ть**)
1 (*вымыть заново*) to wash up again
2 (*вымыть многое*) to wash (up) (*all or a
quantity of*)

перемы́чк|а, и *f.* (tech.) **1** (*соединение*)
crosspiece **2** (*заграждение*) cofferdam

перенапряга́|ться, юсь *impf. of*
▸ **перенапря́чься**

перенапря́|чься, гу́сь, жёшься, *past*
∼гся, ∼гла́сь *pf.* (of ▸ **перенапряга́ться**)
to overstrain oneself

перенес|ти́[1]**, у́, ёшь,** *past* **∼, ∼ла́** *pf.* (of
▸ **переноси́ть**) **1** (*через пространство*)
to carry (*somewhere else*); (*поместить в
другое место*) to move, transfer **2**: **п. сло́во**
(typ.) to carry over (*part of word*) to the
next line **3** (*отсрочить*) to put off, postpone; to
carry over

перенес|ти́[2]**, у́, ёшь,** *past* **∼, ∼ла́** *pf.* (of
▸ **переноси́ть**) (*выдержать*) to endure,
bear, stand; **п. боле́знь** to have an illness;
я э́того не мог п. I couldn't stand that

перенес|ти́сь, у́сь, ёшься, *past* **∼ся,
∼ла́сь** *pf.* (of ▸ **переноси́ться**) to be
carried, be borne

♂ key word

перено́с, а *m.* **1** transfer; moving **2** (typ.)
hyphenation at the end of a line; word
division; (*знак*) hyphen (*at the end of
a line*); **знак ∼а** hyphen **3** (*заседания*)
postponement

перено|си́ть, шу́, ∼сишь *impf. of*
▸ **перенести́**[1]

перено|си́ться, шу́сь, ∼сишься *impf. of*
▸ **перенести́сь**

перено́сиц|а, ы *f.* bridge of the nose

переносно́й *adj.* (*приёмник*) portable

перено́сный *adj.* (ling.) figurative

переноч|ева́ть, у́ю *pf.* (of ▸ **ночева́ть**) to
spend the night

переобува́|ть, ю *impf. of* ▸ **переобу́ть**

переобува́|ться, юсь *impf. of* ▸ **переобу́ться**

переобу́|ть, ю, ешь *pf.* (of ▸ **переобува́ть**)
to change sb's shoes; **п. ту́фли** to change
one's shoes

переобу́|ться, юсь, ешься *pf.* (of
▸ **переобува́ться**) to change one's shoes,
boots, *etc.*

переобуча́|ть, ю *impf. of* ▸ **переобучи́ть**

переобуче́ни|е, я *nt.* retraining

переобу́|чить, чу́, ∼чишь *pf.* (of
▸ **переобуча́ть**) to retrain

переодева́|ть, ю *impf. of* ▸ **переоде́ть**

переодева́|ться, юсь *impf. of* ▸ **переоде́ться**

переоде́тый *adj.* disguised

переоде́|ть, ну, нешь *pf.* (of ▸ **переодева́ть**)
1 (*платье, свитер*) to change; (*ребёнка,
больного*) to change sb's clothes; **п. пла́тье**
to change one's dress **2** (+ *i.* or в + *a.*) to
dress up, disguise (as, in)

переоде́|ться, нусь, нешься *pf.* (of
▸ **переодева́ться**) **1** to change (one's
clothes) **2** (+ *i.* or в + *a.*) to disguise oneself
or dress up (as, in); **она́ ∼лась в ма́льчика**
she disguised herself as a boy

переосмы́сл|ить, ю, ишь *pf.* (of
▸ **переосмысля́ть**) to re-examine

переосмысля́|ть, ю *impf. of*
▸ **переосмы́слить**

переоце́нива|ть, ю *impf. of* ▸ **переоцени́ть**

переоце́н|ить, ю́, ∼ишь *pf.* (of
▸ **переоце́нивать**) to overestimate, overrate

перепа́д, а *m.* (*температур, давления*)
differential, difference

перепа́чка|ть, ю *pf.* to make all dirty

перепа́чка|ться, юсь *pf.* to make oneself
dirty (all over)

пе́репел, а, *pl.* **∼á** *m.* (zool.) quail

перепелен|а́ть, а́ю *pf.* (of
▸ **перепелёнывать**) **п. ребёнка** to change
a baby

перепелёныва|ть, ю *impf. of*
▸ **перепелена́ть**

перепи́лива|ть, ю *impf. of* ▸ **перепили́ть**

перепил|и́ть, ю́, ∼ишь *pf.* (of
▸ **перепи́ливать**) to saw in two

перепи|са́ть[1]**, шу́, ∼шешь** *pf.* (of
▸ **перепи́сывать**) **1** (*заново*) to rewrite; **п.**

на́бело to make a fair copy (of) **2** (*списать*) to copy

перепи|са́ть², шу́, ~шешь *pf.* (*of* ▶ перепи́сывать) (*сделать список*) to make a list (of), list; **п. всех прису́тствующих** to take the names of all those present

перепи́ск|а, и *f.* **1** (*действие*) copying **2** (*корреспонденция*) correspondence; **быть в ~е** (**с** + *i.*) to be in correspondence (with) **3** (*collect.*) (*все пи́сьма*) correspondence, letters

перепи́сыва|ть, ю *impf. of* ▶ переписа́ть¹

перепи́сыва|ться, юсь *impf.* (**с** + *i.*) to correspond (with)

пе́репис|ь, и *f.* census

переплав|ить, лю, ишь *pf.* (*of* ▶ переплавля́ть) (*руду́*) to smelt

переплавля́|ть, ю *impf. of* ▶ переплавить

перепланиро́вк|а, и *f.* replanning

переплат|а, ы *f.* overpayment

перепле|сти́, ту́, тёшь, *past* ~л, ~ла́ *pf.* (*of* ▶ переплета́ть) **1** (*книгу*) to bind **2** (+ *i.*) (*ни́ти, верёвки*) to interlace (with), interknit (with)

перепле|сти́сь, тётся, *past* ~лся, ~ла́сь *pf.* (*of* ▶ переплета́ться) **1** (*стебли́, верёвки*) to interlace, interweave **2** (fig., *собы́тия*) to be interwoven

переплёт, а *m.* **1** (*действие*) binding; **отда́ть кни́гу в п.** to have a book bound **2** (*обло́жка*) binding, book cover

переплета́|ть, ю, ет *impf. of* ▶ переплести́сь

переплета́|ться, ется *impf. of* ▶ переплести́сь

переплете́ни|е, я *nt.* **1** (*ните́й*) weave **2** (*собы́тий*) interweaving

переплыва́|ть, ю *impf. of* ▶ переплы́ть

переплы́|ть, ву́, вёшь, *past* ~л, ~ла́, ~ло *pf.* (*of* ▶ переплыва́ть) (*вплавь*) to swim (across); (*на парохо́де*) to sail (across)

переподгото́вк|а, и *f.* retraining

переполз|а́ть, а́ю *impf. of* ▶ переползти́

переполз|ти́, у́, ёшь, *past* ~, ~ла́ *pf.* (*of* ▶ переполза́ть) to crawl across

перепо́лн|ить, ю, ишь *pf.* (*of* ▶ переполня́ть) (*сосу́д*) to overfill; (*авто́бус*) to overcrowd

перепо́лн|иться, юсь *pf.* (*of* ▶ переполня́ться) (*о сосу́де*) to be overfilled; (*о се́рдце, душе́*) to overflow; (*об авто́бусе*) to be overcrowded; **её се́рдце ~илось ра́достью** her heart overflowed with joy

переполн|я́ть, я́ю *impf. of* ▶ перепо́лнить

переполн|я́ться, я́юсь *impf. of* ▶ перепо́лниться

перепо́нк|а, и *f.* membrane; **бараба́нная п.** (anat.) eardrum, tympanum

перепоруч|а́ть, а́ю *impf. of* ▶ перепоручи́ть

перепоруч|и́ть, у́, ~ишь *pf.* (*of* ▶ перепоруча́ть) (+ *d.*) to turn over (to), reassign (to)

перепра́в|а, ы *f.* (*действие*) crossing; (*ме́сто*) crossing (place); (*брод*) ford

перепра́в|ить¹, лю, ишь *pf.* (*of* ▶ переправля́ть) **1** (*перевезти́*) to convey, transport; to take across **2** (*письмо́*) to forward (*mail*)

перепра́в|ить², лю, ишь *pf.* (*of* ▶ переправля́ть) (*испра́вить*) to correct

перепра́в|иться, люсь, ишься *pf.* (*of* ▶ переправля́ться) to cross, get across; (*вплавь*) to swim across; (*на парохо́де*) to sail across

переправля́|ть, ю *impf. of* ▶ перепра́вить¹, ▶ перепра́вить²

переправля́|ться, юсь *impf. of* ▶ перепра́виться

перепро́б|овать, ую *pf.* (*еду́*) to taste (*all or a quantity of*); (fig., *сре́дства*) to try

перепрода|ва́ть, ю́, ёшь *impf. of* ▶ перепрода́ть

перепрода́|ть, м, шь, ст, ди́м, ди́те, ду́т, *past* перепро́дал, ~ла́, перепро́дало *pf.* (*of* ▶ перепродава́ть) to resell

перепроизво́дств|о, а *nt.* overproduction

перепры́гива|ть, ю *impf. of* ▶ перепры́гнуть

перепры́г|нуть, ну, нешь *pf.* (*of* ▶ перепры́гивать) (+ *a.* or **че́рез** + *a.*) to jump (over)

перепуга́|ть, ю *pf.* (*no impf.*) to frighten, give a fright

перепуга́|ться, юсь *pf.* (*no impf.*) to get a fright

перепу́т|ать, аю *pf.* (*of* ▶ перепу́тывать) **1** (*ни́ти*) to entangle **2** (fig., *имена́, фа́кты*) to confuse, mix up, muddle up

перепу́т|аться, ается *pf.* (*of* ▶ перепу́тываться) **1** (*ни́ти*) to get entangled **2** (fig., *мы́сли*) to get confused, get mixed up

перепу́тыва|ть, ю, ет *impf. of* ▶ перепу́тать

перепу́тыва|ться, ется *impf. of* ▶ перепу́таться

перераба́тыва|ть, ю *impf. of* ▶ перерабо́тать¹

перерабо́та|ть¹, ю *pf.* (*of* ▶ перераба́тывать) **1** (*сырьё*) to process; (*преобразова́ть*) to convert (to); (*переде́лать*) to treat; **п. свёклу в са́хар** to convert beet to sugar **2** (*переде́лать*) to remake; (fig., *статью́*) to revise, recast, reshape

перерабо́та|ть², ю *pf.* (*of* ▶ перераба́тывать) to exceed fixed hours of work, work overtime; (infml, *переутоми́ться*) to overwork

перерабо́тк|а¹, и *f.* **1** (*сырья́*) processing, treatment **2** (*переде́лка*) remaking; (*втори́чное использование*) recycling

перерабо́тк|а², и *f.* (*вре́мя*) overtime work

перераспределе́ни|е, я *nt.* redistribution

перераспредел|и́ть, ю́, ишь *pf.* (*of* ▶ перераспределя́ть) to redistribute

перераспредел|я́ть, я́ю *impf. of* ▶ перераспредели́ть

перераст|а́ть, а́ю *impf. of* ▶ перерасти́

п

перераст|и́, у́, ёшь, *past* переро́с, переросла́ *pf.* (*of* ▶ перераста́ть) **1** (*стать выше*) to outgrow, (over)top; (*превзойти́*) to outstrip (*in height, also fig.*); п. своего́ учи́теля to outstrip one's teacher **2** (fig.) (в + *a.*) (*превратиться*) to grow (into), develop (into), turn (into) **3** (*оказаться по возрасту старше, чем нужно*) to be too old (for)

перерасхо́д, а *m.* **1** (*денег, энергии*) overspending, over-expenditure **2** (fin., *в банковском счёте*) overdraft

перерасхо́д|овать, ую *pf.* (*no impf.*) **1** (*деньги, энергию*) to overspend, spend to excess **2** (fin., *в банковском счёте*) to overdraw

перерасчёт, а *m.* recalculation; (*в другие единицы*) conversion

перере́|зать, жу, жешь *pf.* (*of* ▶ перереза́ть) **1** (*верёвку*) to cut (in two) **2** (fig., *путь*) to cut off

перерез|а́ть, а́ю *impf. of* ▶ перере́зать

переруб|а́ть, а́ю *impf. of* ▶ переруби́ть

переруб|и́ть, лю́, ~ишь *pf.* (*of* ▶ переруба́ть) to chop in two

переры́в, а *m.* break; обе́денный п. lunch break; без ~а without a break; с ~ами off and on

перерыва́|ть, ю *impf. of* ▶ переры́ть

перер|ы́ть, о́ю, о́ешь *pf.* (*of* ▶ перерыва́ть) (fig., infml) to rummage (*through*)

пересад|и́ть, жу́, ~дишь *pf.* (*of* ▶ переса́живать) **1** (*заставить пересесть*) to move, make sb change his seat; (*на другой поезд*) to transfer **2** (bot.) to transplant **3** (med.) (*сердце*) to transplant; (*кожу*) to graft

переса́дк|а, и *f.* **1** (bot.) transplantation **2** (med.) transplant; grafting; опера́ция по ~е се́рдца heart transplant operation **3** (*переход на другой поезд, автобус*) change; сде́лать ~у to change (*trains, buses, etc.*)

переса́жива|ть, ю *impf. of* ▶ пересади́ть

переса́жива|ться, юсь *impf. of* ▶ пересе́сть

переса́лива|ть, ю *impf. of* ▶ пересоли́ть

пересда|ва́ть, ю́, ёшь *impf. of* ▶ пересда́ть

пересда|ть, м, шь, ст, ди́м, ди́те, ду́т, *past* ~л, ~ла́, ~ло *pf.* (*of* ▶ пересдава́ть) **1** (*помещение*) to relet; to sublet **2** (cards) to redeal **3** (*экзамен*) to resit (BrE), retake

пересека́|ть, ю, ет *impf. of* ▶ пересе́чь

пересека́|ться, ется *impf. of* ▶ пересе́чься

переселе́н|ец, ца *m.* settler

переселе́ни|е, я *nt.* migration; resettlement

пересел|и́ть, ю́, и́шь *pf.* (*of* ▶ переселя́ть) to move; (*на новую территорию*) to resettle

пересел|и́ться, ю́сь, и́шься *pf.* (*of* ▶ переселя́ться) to move; (*на новую территорию*) to migrate

пересел|я́ть, я́ю *impf. of* ▶ пересели́ть

пересел|я́ться, я́юсь *impf. of* ▶ пересели́ться

перес|е́сть, я́ду, я́дешь *pf.* (*of* ▶ переса́живаться) **1** (*на другое место*) to change one's seat **2** (*сделать пересадку*) to change (trains, etc.)

пересече́ни|е, я *nt.* crossing, intersection

пересе́|чь, ку́, чёшь, ку́т, *past* ~к, ~кла́ *pf.* (*of* ▶ пересека́ть) **1** (*перейти*) to cross; to traverse; п. у́лицу to cross the road **2** (*город, местность*) to cross, cut across

пересе́|чься, чётся, ку́тся, *past* ~кся, ~кла́сь *pf.* (*of* ▶ пересека́ться) to cross, intersect

переси́лива|ть, ю *impf. of* ▶ переси́лить

переси́л|ить, ю, ишь *pf.* (*of* ▶ переси́ливать) to overcome, master

переска́з, а *m.* **1** (*содержания романа*) retelling, narration **2** (*изложение*) exposition

переска|за́ть, жу́, ~жешь *pf.* (*of* ▶ переска́зывать) **1** to retell, narrate **2** (*рассказать подробно*) to retail, relate; п. слу́хи to retail rumours (BrE), rumors (AmE)

переска́зыва|ть, ю *impf. of* ▶ пересказа́ть

переска́кива|ть, ю *impf. of* ▶ перескочи́ть

перескоч|и́ть, у́, ~ишь *pf.* (*of* ▶ переска́кивать) **1** (+ *a.* or че́рез + *a.*) to jump (over); (fig., *пропустить*) to skip (over) **2** (fig.) to skip; п. с одно́й те́мы на другу́ю to skip from one topic to another

пере|сла́ть, шлю́, шлёшь *pf.* (*of* ▶ пересыла́ть) (*отправить*) to send; (*деньги*) to remit; (*по другому адресу*) to forward

пересма́трива|ть, ю *impf. of* ▶ пересмотре́ть

пересмотр|е́ть, ю́, ~ишь *pf.* (*of* ▶ пересма́тривать) **1** (*книгу, документ*) to look through; to go over again **2** (*решение*) to reconsider; (law) to review **3** (*ища что-л.*) to go through (*in search of sth*)

переснима́|ть, ю *impf. of* ▶ пересня́ть

пересн|я́ть, иму́, и́мешь, *past* ~я́л, ~яла́, ~я́ло *pf.* (*of* ▶ переснима́ть) **1** (*фотографировать заново*) to photograph/film again **2** (*копировать*, infml) to make a copy of

пересол|и́ть, ю́, ~ишь *pf.* (*of* ▶ переса́ливать) to put too much salt (into)

пересо́х|нуть, нет, нет, *past* ~, ~ла *pf.* (*of* ▶ пересыха́ть) (*о белье*) to dry out; (*о земле, речке*) to dry up, become parched

пересп|а́ть, лю́, и́шь, *past* ~а́л, ~ала́, ~а́ло *pf.* (infml) **1** (*проспать слишком долго*) to oversleep **2** (с + *i.*) (euph.) to sleep (with)

переспо́р|ить, ю, ишь *pf.* to defeat in argument

переспра́шива|ть, ю *impf. of* ▶ переспроси́ть

переспро|си́ть, шу́, ~сишь *pf.* (*of* ▶ переспра́шивать) (*повторить вопрос*) to ask again; (*просить повторить*) to ask to repeat

переста|ва́ть, ю́, ёшь *impf. of* ▶ переста́ть

переста́в|ить, лю, ишь *pf.* (*of* ▶ переставля́ть) to move, shift; п. ме́бель

◆ key word

to rearrange the furniture

переставля́|ть, ю *impf. of* ▸ **переста́вить**

перестано́вк|а, и *f.* **1** rearrangement, transposition **2** (math.) permutation

переста́|ть, ну, нешь *pf. (of* (+ *inf.*) to stop, cease; **они́ ∼ли разгова́ривать** they stopped talking; **∼ньте!** stop it!

перестел|и́ть, ю́, ∼ешь *pf. (of* ▸ **перестила́ть**) to relay; **п. посте́ль** to remake a bed

перестила́|ть, ю *impf. of* ▸ **перестели́ть**

перестра́ива|ть, ю *impf. of* ▸ **перестро́ить**

перестра́ива|ться, юсь *impf. of* ▸ **перестро́иться**

перестрах|ова́ться, у́юсь *pf. (of* ▸ **перестрахо́вываться**) **1** to reinsure oneself **2** (fig., pej.) to play safe

перестрахо́выва|ться, юсь *impf. of* ▸ **перестрахова́ться**

перестре́лк|а, и *f.* exchange of fire, shoot-out

перестро́|ить, ю, ишь *pf. (of* ▸ **перестра́ивать**) **1** (*дом*) to rebuild, reconstruct **2** (*план, рабо́ту*) to redesign, refashion, reshape; to reorganize; **п. фра́зу** to reshape a sentence

перестро́|иться, юсь, ишься *pf. (of* ▸ **перестра́иваться**) to re-form; to reorganize oneself; to restructure

перестро́йк|а, и *f.* **1** (*зда́ния*) rebuilding, reconstruction; (pol., econ.) perestroika **2** (*реорганиза́ция*) reorganization

переступ|а́ть, а́ю *impf. of* ▸ **переступи́ть**

переступ|и́ть, лю́, ∼ишь *pf. (of* ▸ **переступа́ть**) (+ *a. or* **че́рез** + *a.*) to step over; (fig.) to overstep; **п. поро́г** to cross the threshold; **п. зако́н** to break the law

пересу́шива|ть, ю *impf. of* ▸ **пересуши́ть**

пересуш|и́ть, у́, ∼ишь *pf. (of* ▸ **пересу́шивать**) to overdry

пересчит|а́ть¹, а́ю *pf. (of* ▸ **пересчи́тывать**) **1** to recount **2** (**в** + *p.*) to convert (to), express (in terms of)

пересчит|а́ть², а́ю *pf. (no impf.)* (*мно́гое*) to count

пересчи́тыва|ть, ю *impf. of* ▸ **пересчита́ть¹**

пересыла́|ть, ю *impf. of* ▸ **пересла́ть**

пересы́п|ать, лю, лешь *pf. (of* ▸ **пересыпа́ть**) to pour (*dry substance*) into another container; **п. зерно́ в мешки́** to pour off grain into bags

пересып|а́ть, а́ю *impf. of* ▸ **пересы́пать**

пересыха́|ть, ет *impf. of* ▸ **пересо́хнуть**

перета́скива|ть, ю *impf. of* ▸ **перетащи́ть**

перетас|ова́ть, у́ю *pf. of* ▸ **тасова́ть**

перетащ|и́ть, у́, ∼ишь *pf. (of* ▸ **перета́скивать**) (*волоча́*) to drag over; (*неся́*) to carry over; (*перемести́ть*) to move, shift; **п. сунду́к на чорда́к** to move a trunk into the attic

перетека́|ть, ю *impf. of* ▸ **перете́чь**

перете́|чь, ку́, чёшь, ку́т, *past* **∼к, ∼кла́** *pf. (of* ▸ **перетека́ть**) to overflow

перетя́гива|ть, ю *impf. of* ▸ **перетяну́ть**

перетя|ну́ть, ну́, ∼нешь *pf. (of* ▸ **перетя́гивать**) **1** to pull, draw (*somewhere else; from A to B*); **п. ло́дку от одного́ бе́рега к друго́му** to pull the boat from one bank to the other **2** (fig., infml) to pull over, attract; **п. на свою́ сто́рону** to win over, gain support of **3** (*кре́пко стяну́ть*) to tighten

переубе|ди́ть, ди́шь *pf. (of* ▸ **переубежда́ть**) to make *sb* change his, her, *etc.* mind

переубежда́|ть, ю *impf. of* ▸ **переубеди́ть**

переу́л|ок, ка *m.* lane, side street

переутом|и́ть, лю́, и́шь *pf. (of* ▸ **переутомля́ть**) to tire out; to overwork

переутом|и́ться, лю́сь, и́шься *pf. (of* ▸ **переутомля́ться**) to tire oneself out; to overwork; (*pf. only*) to be run down

переутомле́ни|е, я *nt.* exhaustion; overwork

переутомля́|ть, ю *impf. of* ▸ **переутоми́ть**

переутомля́|ться, юсь *impf. of* ▸ **переутоми́ться**

перефрази́р|овать, ую *impf. and pf.* to paraphrase

перехва|ти́ть, чу́, ∼тишь *pf. (of* ▸ **перехва́тывать**) to intercept, catch; **я ∼ти́л его́ по доро́ге на рабо́ту** I caught him on the way to work

перехва́тыва|ть, ю *impf. of* ▸ **перехвати́ть**

перехитр|и́ть, ю́, и́шь *pf.* to outwit

⚡ **перехо́д, а** *m.* **1** (*де́йствие; ме́сто*) crossing; (*к друго́му состоя́нию, к друго́й систе́ме*) transition, switch(-over); **подзе́мный п.** underpass, subway **2** (mil.) (day's) march

⚡ **перехо|ди́ть, жу́, ∼дишь** *impf. of* ▸ **перейти́**

переходни́к, а́ *m.* adaptor

перехо́дный *adj.* **1** (*пери́од*) transitional **2** (gram.) transitive

пе́р|ец, ца *m.* pepper

пе́реч|ень, ня *m.* (*спи́сок*) list; (*перечисле́ние*) enumeration

перечёркива|ть, ю *impf. of* ▸ **перечеркну́ть**

перечерк|ну́ть, ну́, нёшь *pf. (of* ▸ **перечёркивать**) to cross (out); (fig., *уничто́жить*) to cancel

перечи́сл|ить, ю, ишь *pf. (of* ▸ **перечисля́ть**) **1** to enumerate **2** (*перевести́*) to transfer; **п. на теку́щий счёт** (fin.) to transfer to one's current account

перечисл|я́ть, я́ю *impf. of* ▸ **перечи́слить**

перечит|а́ть¹, а́ю *pf. (of* ▸ **перечи́тывать**) (*за́ново*) to reread

перечит|а́ть², а́ю *pf. (всё или мно́гое*) to read (*all or a quantity of*); **он ∼а́л все кни́ги в библиоте́ке** he has read all the books in the library

перечи́тыва|ть, ю *impf. of* ▸ **перечита́ть¹**

пе́речниц|а, ы *f.* (*для моло́того пе́рца*) pepper pot

переша́гива|ть, ю *impf. of* ▸ **перешагну́ть**

перешаг|ну́ть, ну́, нёшь *pf. (of* ▸ **переша́гивать**) to step over; **п. (че́рез) поро́г** to cross the threshold

перешé|ек, йка *m.* isthmus

перешивá|ть, ю *impf. of* ▶ **перешúть**

перешú|ть, ью, ьёшь *pf.* (*of* ▶ **перешивáть**) to alter; to have altered

перúл|а, ~ (*no sg.*) rail(ing); handrail; (*лестницы*) banisters

перúметр, а *m.* (math.) perimeter

перúн|а, ы *f.* feather bed

⚬ **перú|од, а** *m.* period; **ледникóвый п.** (geol.) ice age

перúодик|а, и *f.* (*collect.*) periodicals

периодúческ|ий *adj.* periodic(al); recurring; **п. журнáл** periodical, magazine; **~ое явлéние** recurrent phenomenon

перископ, а *m.* periscope

периферú|я, и *f.* **1** periphery **2** (*collect.*) (*местность, удалённая от центра*) the provinces; the outlying districts **3** (comput.) peripherals, peripheral devices

перламýтр, а *m.* mother-of-pearl

перламýтровый *adj. of* ▶ **перламýтр**

перманéнт|ный, ~ен, ~на *adj.* permanent

пернá|тый, ~, ~а *adj.* feathered; (*as n. pl.* **~ые, ~ых**) birds

пёр|нуть, ну, нешь *inst. pf. of* ▶ **пердéть** (vulg.) to fart

пер|ó, á, *pl.* **~ья, ~ьев** *nt.* **1** (*птицы*) feather **2** (hist.) quill; (*стальное*) nib

перочú|нный *adj.*: **п. нож** penknife

перпендикуля|рный, ~ен, ~на *adj.* perpendicular

перрóн, а *m.* platform (*at railway station*)

персúдский *adj.*: **П. залúв** the Persian Gulf

пéрсик, а *m.* **1** (*плод*) peach **2** (*дерево*) peach tree

персóн|а, ы *f.* person; **обéд нá шесть ~** dinner for six

персонáж, а *m.* (liter.) character; (fig.) personage

⚬ **персонáл, а** *m.* personnel, staff

персонáльный *adj.* personal; individual; **п. компьютер** personal computer

⚬ **перспектú|в|а, ы** *f.* **1** (art) perspective **2** (fig.) prospect, outlook; **имéть ~у** to have prospects, have a future (before one)

перспектú|вный *adj.* **1** (art) perspective **2** (*план*) long-term **3** (**~ен, ~на**) (*многообещающий*) having prospects; promising

пéрст|ень, ня *m.* ring

Перý *nt. & f. indecl.* Peru

перуáн|ец, ца *m.* Peruvian

перуáн|ка, ки *f. of* ▶ **перуáнец**

перуáнский *adj.* Peruvian

перфéкт, а *m.* (gram.) perfect (tense)

пéрхот|ь, и *f.* dandruff

перчáтк|а, и *f.* glove; **брóсить ~у** (fig.) to throw down the gauntlet

пéрч|úть, ~ý, ~úшь *impf.* (*of* ▶ **попéрчить**) to pepper

⚬ *key word*

пёс, псá *m.* dog

пес|éц, цá *m.* Arctic fox

⚬ **пéс|ня, ни,** *g. pl.* **~ен** *f.* song

пес|óк, кá *m.* **1** sand; **сáхарный п.** granulated sugar **2** (*in pl.*) sands

песóчн|ый *adj.* **1** *adj. of* ▶ **песóк**; sandy; **~ые часы́** sandglass, hourglass **2** (cul.) short; **~ое печéнье** shortbread

пессимúзм, а *m.* pessimism

пессимúст, а *m.* pessimist

пессимистúческий *adj.* pessimistic

пессимистú|чный, ~ен, ~на *adj.* = **пессимистúческий**

пессимúст|ка, ки *f. of* ▶ **пессимúст**

пёстр|ый, ~, пестрá, ~о and пестрó *adj.* **1** variegated, multicoloured (BrE), -colored (AmE) **2** (fig., infml) mixed; **п. состáв населéния** mixed population

песчáн|ый *adj.* sandy; **~ая косá** sandbar; **~ холм** dune

песчúнк|а, и *f.* grain of sand

петáрд|а, ы *f.* banger (BrE), firecracker

петербýргский *adj.* St Petersburg

петербýрж|ец, ца *m.* St Petersburger

петúци|я, и *f.* petition

петлú|ца, ы *f.* buttonhole; tab

пет|ля, лú, *pl.* **~ли, ~ель** *f.* **1** loop **2** (fig.) noose **3** (*для пуговицы*) buttonhole **4** (*в вязании*) stitch **5** (*двери*) hinge

петля|ть, ю *impf.* (infml) to dodge

петрýшк|а, и *f.* parsley

петýх, á *m.* cock; **вставáть с ~áми** to rise with the lark

петь, пою, поёшь *impf.* (*of* ▶ **спеть²**) to sing; **п. бáсом** to have a bass voice; **п. вполгóлоса** to hum

пехóт|а, ы *f.* infantry; **морскáя п.** (the) marines

пехотú|нец, ца *m.* infantryman

печáл|ь, и *f.* grief, sorrow

печáл|ьный, ~ен, ~ьна *adj.* **1** sad, doleful **2** (*прискорбный*) bad, regrettable; **п. конéц** bad end

печáта|ть, ю *impf.* (*of* ▶ **напечáтать,** ▶ **отпечáтать 1**) to print; (*на машинке*) to type

печáта|ться, юсь *impf.* (*of* ▶ **напечáтаться**) **1** to have (*literary compositions, etc.*) published; **в трúдцать лет он ещё нигдé не ~лся** at thirty he had not yet had anything published **2** (*находиться в печати*) to be at the printer's

печáтн|ый *adj.* **1** printing; **п. лист** quire, printer's sheet **2** (*напечатанный*) printed; in the press; **~ая кнúга** printed book (*opp. manuscript*) **3**: **писáть ~ыми бýквами** to (write in) print; to write in block capitals

⚬ **печáт|ь¹, и** *f.* (*для получения оттиска*) seal, stamp (also fig.); **на моúх устáх п. молчáния** my lips are sealed

⚬ **печáт|ь², и** *f.* **1** (*печатание*) print(ing); **вы́йти из ~и** to come out, be published **2** (*вид напечатанного*) print, type; **мéлкая**

п. small print; **кру́пная п.** large print
3 (*пресса*) (the) press; **свобо́да** ~**и** freedom of the press

печёнк|а, и *f.* liver (*of animal, as food*)

печёный *adj.* (cul.) baked

пе́чен|ь, и *f.* liver

пече́нь|е, я *nt.* biscuit (BrE), cookie (AmE)

пе́чк|а, и *f.* stove

печь¹, пеку́, печёшь, пеку́т, *past* **пёк, пекла́** *impf.* (*of* ▶ **испе́чь**) to bake; **со́лнце пекло́** there was a scorching sun

печ|ь², и, о ~**и, в** ~**й,** *pl.* ~**и,** ~**е́й** *f.*
1 stove; (*духовка*) oven **2** (tech.) furnace; (*обжиговая*) kiln

пе́чься, печётся, пеку́тся, *past* **пёкся, пекла́сь** *impf.* (*of* ▶ **испе́чься**) to bake

пешехо́д, а *m.* pedestrian

пешехо́дный *adj.* pedestrian; **п. мост** footbridge

пе́ший *adj.* **1** pedestrian **2** (mil.) unmounted, foot

пе́шк|а, и *f.* (chess, also fig.) pawn

пешко́м *adv.* on foot

пеще́р|а, ы *f.* cave

пиани́но *nt. indecl.* (upright) piano

пиани́ст, а *m.* pianist

пиани́ст|ка, ки *f. of* ▶ **пиани́ст**

пиа́р, а *m.* PR (*public relations*)

пивн|а́я, о́й *f.* pub

пи́в|о, а *nt.* beer

пивова́р, а *m.* brewer

пивова́рени|е, я *nt.* brewing

пивова́ренн|ый *adj.*: **п. заво́д** brewery; ~**ая промы́шленность** brewing

пигме́нт, а *m.* pigment

пиджа́к, á *m.* jacket, coat

пижа́м|а, ы *f.* pyjamas (BrE), pajamas (AmE)

пижо́н, а *m.* (infml) fop

пизд|а́, ы́ (*pl. not generally used*) *f.* (vulg.) cunt

пик¹, а *m.* (geog.) peak; (fig.) pinnacle

пик², а *m.* **1** peak (*of work, traffic, etc.*); **п. нагру́зки** (elec.) peak load **2** (*adj. indecl.*): **часы́ пик** rush hour

пи́к|а¹, и *f.* (*оружие*) pike, lance

пи́к|а², и *f.* (cards) spade

пика́п, а *m.* pickup (truck)

пике́т, а *m.* (*группа бастующих*) picket

пикети́р|овать, ую *impf.* to picket

пи́кколо *nt. indecl.* piccolo

пикни́к, á *m.* picnic

пи́ксел|ь, я *m.* (comput.) pixel

пиктогра́мм|а, ы *f.* pictogram; (comput.) icon

пил|а́, ы́, *pl.* ~**ы,** ~ *f.* saw

пила́-ры́ба, пилы́-ры́бы *f.* sawfish

пилигри́м, а *m.* pilgrim

пил|и́ть, ю́, ~**ишь** *impf.* to saw

пило́т, а *m.* pilot

пило́тк|а, и *f.* (mil.) forage cap

пилю́л|я, и *f.* pill (also fig.)

пина́|ть, ю *impf. of* ▶ **пнуть**

пингви́н, а *m.* penguin

пинг-по́нг, а *m.* ping-pong

пинце́т, а *m.* (tech.) pincers; (med.) tweezers

пи́нчер, а *m.* (*собака*) pinscher

пио́н, а *m.* (bot.) peony

пионе́р, а *m.* pioneer

пипе́тк|а, и *f.* pipette; medicine dropper

пир, а, о ~**е, на** ~**у́,** *pl.* ~**ы́** *m.* feast, banquet

пирами́д|а, ы *f.* (also fin.) pyramid

пира́т, а *m.* pirate

пира́тский *adj.* (*судно*) pirate; (*обычаи*) piratical; (*издание*) pirated

пира́тств|о, а *nt.* piracy

Пирене́|и, ев (*no sg.*) the Pyrenees

пиро́г, á *m.* pie; **п. с мя́сом** meat pie

пиро́г|а, и *f.* pirogue, canoe

пиро́жн|ое, ого *nt.* (fancy) cake, pastry

пирож|о́к, ка́ *m.* pasty (BrE), patty, pie

пи́рсинг, а *m.* body piercing

пи́ршеств|о, а *nt.* feast, banquet

✓ **писа́тел|ь, я** *m.* writer, author

писа́тель|ница, ницы *f. of* ▶ **писа́тель**

писа́|ть, ю *impf.* (*of* ▶ **попи́сать**) (infml) to pee, have a pee

✓ **пи|са́ть, шу́,** ~**шешь** *impf.* (*of* ▶ **написа́ть**)
1 to write; (*на машинке*) to type **2** (+ *i.*) (*красками*) to paint (in)

писк, а *m.* (*ребёнка, мыши*) squeak; (*цыплят*) cheep

пи́скн|уть, у, ешь *inst. pf.* (*of* ▶ **пища́ть**) (infml) to give a squeak, cheep

пистоле́т, а *m.* pistol

пи́сьменност|ь, и *f.* **1** (*литературные памятники*) literature; (*collect.*) literary texts **2** (*средства письменного общения*) the written language

пи́сьменн|ый *adj.* **1** (*для письма*) writing; **п. стол** writing table, bureau **2** (*написанный*) written; **в** ~**ом ви́де, в** ~**ой фо́рме** in writing, in written form; **п. экза́мен** written examination

✓ **письм|о́, á,** *pl.* ~**а, пи́сем,** ~**ам** *nt.* **1** letter; **заказно́е п.** registered letter **2** (*система графических знаков*) script; **ара́бское п.** Arabic script

✓ **пита́ни|е, я** *nt.* **1** (*действие*) feeding, nutrition; (*характер пищи*) diet; **недоста́точное п.** malnutrition; (*пища*) food **2** (tech.) feed, supply **3** (elec.) power supply

пита́тел|ьный, ~**ен,** ~**ьна** *adj.* nourishing, nutritious; ~**ьная среда́** (biol.) culture medium; (fig.) breeding ground

пита́|ться, юсь *impf.* (+ *i.*) to feed (on), live (on); **хорошо́ п.** to be well fed, eat well

Пи́тер, а *m.* (infml) St Petersburg

пи́терский *adj. of* ▶ **Пи́тер**

пито́мник, а *m.* nursery (*for plants or animals*) (also fig.)

пито́н, а *m.* python

✓ **пить, пью, пьёшь,** *past* **пил, пила́, пи́ло** *impf.* (*of* ▶ **вы́пить**) to drink; **мне хо́чется п.**

I am thirsty; **п. за** (+ *a.*), **за здоро́вье** (+ *g.*) to drink to, to the health (of)

пить|ё, я́ *nt.* drink

пих|а́ть, а́ю *impf.* (*of* ▸ **пихну́ть**) (*infml*) **1** (*толка́ть*) to push; shove, jostle **2** (*запи́хивать*) to shove, cram

пих|ну́ть, ну́, нёшь *pf. of* ▸ **пиха́ть**

пи́хт|а, ы *f.* fir (tree)

пи́цц|а, ы *f.* pizza

✎ **пи́щ|а, и** (*no pl.*) *f.* food

пищ|а́ть, у́, и́шь *impf.* (*of* ▸ **пи́скнуть**) (*о мы́ши, о две́ри*) to squeak; (*о цыпля́тах*) to cheep

пищеваре́ни|е, я *nt.* digestion; **расстро́йство ~я** indigestion

пищ|ево́й *adj. of* ▸ **пи́ща**; **~евы́е проду́кты** foodstuffs

пия́вк|а, и *f.* leech

ПК *m. indecl.* (*abbr. of* **персона́льный компью́тер**) PC (*personal computer*)

пла́вани|е, я *nt.* **1** swimming **2** (*на судне́*) sailing; navigation; **отпра́виться в п.** to put out to sea

пла́вательный *adj.* swimming; **п. бассе́йн** swimming pool

пла́ва|ть, ю *impf.* **1** *indet. of* ▸ **плыть** **2** (*держа́ться на воде́*) to float

пла́в|ить, лю, ишь *impf.* to smelt

пла́в|иться, ится *impf.* to melt

пла́вк|а, и *f.* fusing; fusion

пла́в|ки, ок (*no sg.*) swimming trunks

плавни́к, а́ *m.* (*рыбы*) fin; (*дельфина, тюленя*) flipper

пла́в|ный, ~ен, ~на *adj.* smooth; **~ная речь** flowing speech

плаву́чий *adj.* floating

плагиа́т, а *m.* plagiarism

пла́зм|а, ы *f.* (*biol., phys.*) plasma

пла́зменный *adj.*: **~ экра́н** (TV, comput.) plasma screen

плака́т, а *m.* poster

пла́|кать, чу, чешь *impf.* to cry, weep; **п. навзры́д** to sob

плакси́в|ый, ~, ~а *adj.* (*infml*) (*ребёнок*) given to crying; whining; (*голос, лицо́, улы́бка*) pathetic

пла́мен|ный, ~ен, ~на *adj.* ardent, burning

пла́м|я, ени *nt.* flame; (*я́ркое*) blaze

✎ **план, а** *m.* **1** (*наме́рение; чертёж, ка́рта*) plan; **по ~y** according to plan **2** (*ме́сто*): **пере́дний п.** foreground; **за́дний п.** background; **кру́пный п.** close-up (*in filming*)

пла́нер, а *m.* (*aeron.*) glider

✎ **плане́т|а, ы** *f.* **1** planet **2** (*Земля́*) (the) planet (= *Earth*)

плани́ровани|е, я *nt.* planning

✎ **плани́р|овать, ую** *impf.* (*of* ▸ **заплани́ровать**) to plan

плани́ровк|а, и *f.* layout

✎ key word

пла́нк|а, и *f.* lath, slat

планкто́н, а *m.* (*biol.*) plankton

пла́нов|ый *adj.* planned, systematic; **~ое хозя́йство** planned economy

планоме́р|ный, ~ен, ~на *adj.* systematic, planned

планта́ци|я, и *f.* plantation

планше́т, а *m.* (*comput.*) tablet (computer)

планше́тный *adj.*: **п. компью́тер** tablet (computer); **п. ска́нер** flatbed scanner

пласт, а́ *m.* layer; sheet; (*archit.*) course; (*geol.*) stratum, bed

пла́стик, а *m.* plastic (*material*)

пла́стиковый *adj.* plastic

пластили́н, а *m.* plasticine®

пласти́н|а, ы *f.* plate (*thin flat sheet*)

пласти́нк|а, и *f.* **1** plate; (**вини́ловая**) **п.** (vinyl) record **2** (*infml, зубно́й проте́з*) plate

пласти́ческ|ий *adj.* plastic; **~ая хирурги́я** plastic surgery

пласти́чный, ~ен, ~на *adj.* **1** (*материа́л, вещество́*) plastic; pliant **2** (*пла́вный*) rhythmical; fluent, flowing; (*изя́щный*) graceful; (*гармони́чный*) harmonious

пластма́сс|а, ы *f.* plastic

пластма́ссовый *adj. of* ▸ **пластма́сса**

пла́стыр|ь, я *m.* (*med.*) plaster

✎ **пла́т|а¹, ы** *f.* **1** (*за труд*) pay; salary; **за́работная п.** wages **2** (*за получе́ние, испо́льзование чего́-н.*) payment, charge; fee; **входна́я п.** entrance fee; **кварти́рная п.** rent; **п. за прое́зд** fare

пла́т|а², ы *f.* (*comput.*) card, board; **монта́жная п.** circuit board

плата́н, а *m.* plane (tree)

✎ **плат|ёж, ежа́** *m.* payment

платёжеспосо́б|ный, ~ен, ~на *adj.* solvent

платёж|ный *adj. of* ▸ **платёж**; **~ная ве́домость** payroll; **~ное поруче́ние** payment order

пла́тин|а, ы *f.* (*min.*) platinum

✎ **пла|ти́ть, чу́, ~тишь** *impf.* (*of* ▸ **заплати́ть**) **1** to pay; **п. нали́чными** to pay in cash, pay in ready money **2** (*fig.*) (+ *i. and* **за** + *a.*) to pay back, return; **п. кому́-н. услу́гой за услу́гу** to make it up to sb, return a favour (BrE), favor (AmE)

пла́тн|ый *adj.* **1** paid; requiring payment, chargeable; **~ая доро́га** toll road **2** paying; (*шко́ла*) fee-paying; (*больни́ца*) private

плато́ *nt. indecl.* (*geog.*) plateau

плат|о́к, ка́ *m.* (*на пле́чи*) shawl; (*на го́лову*) headscarf; **носово́й п.** (pocket) handkerchief

платфо́рм|а, ы *f.* **1** (*перро́н*) platform **2** (*ваго́н*) (open) goods truck (BrE), flatcar (AmE) **3** (*fig., pol.*) platform

пла́ть|е, я, *g. pl.* **~ев** *nt.* **1** (*же́нское*) dress; (*дли́нное*) gown; **вече́рнее п.** evening dress **2** (*оде́жда*) clothes, clothing

плач, а *m.* weeping, crying

плаче́в|ный, ~ен, ~на *adj.* lamentable, deplorable, sorry; **в ~ном состоя́нии** in a sorry state

плашмя́ *adv.* flat; flatways; prone

плащ, á *m.* **1** (*непромокаемое пальто*) raincoat **2** (*накидка*) cloak

плева́ть, плюю́, плюёшь *impf.* (*of* ▶ **плю́нуть**) **1** to spit **2** (**на** + *a.*) (infml) to spit (upon); **им п. на всё** they don't give a damn about anything

плев|о́к, ка́ *m.* spit(tle)

плед, а *m.* travelling rug (BrE), lap robe (AmE)

пле́ер, а *m.* (*аудиокассет, аудиодисков*) personal stereo, Walkman®; MP3, DVD, *etc.*, player

пле́м|я, ени, *pl.* **∼ená, ∼ён, ∼енáм** *nt.* tribe

племя́нник, а *m.* nephew

племя́нниц|а, ы *f.* niece

плен, а, о ∼е, в ∼у́ *m.* captivity; **попа́сть в п.** (**к** + *d.*) to be taken prisoner (by)

плени́тел|ьный, ∼ен, ∼ьна *adj.* captivating, charming

плёнк|а, и *f.* (*тонкий слой*) film (also phot.); (*магнитофонная*) tape

пле́нник, а *m.* prisoner, captive

пле́нни|ца, цы *f. of* ▶ **пле́нник**

пле́нн|ый *adj.* captive; (*as m. n.* **п.**, **∼ого**) captive, prisoner

пле́нум, а *m.* plenum, plenary session

пле́сен|ь, и *f.* mould (BrE), mold (AmE)

плеск, а *m.* splash; **п. волн** lapping of waves

пле|ска́ть, щу́, ∼щешь *impf.* (*of* ▶ **плесну́ть**) to splash; **п. на кого́-н. водо́й** to splash sb (with water)

пле|ска́ться, щу́сь, ∼щешься *impf.* to splash; (*о волнах*) to lap

плес|ну́ть, ну́, нёшь *inst. pf. of* ▶ **плеска́ть**

пле|сти́, ту́, тёшь, *past* **∼л, ∼лá 1** *impf. of* ▶ **сплести́ 2** (*pf.* ▶ **заплести́**) (*волосы*) to braid, plait

пле|сти́сь, ту́сь, тёшься, *past* **∼лся, ∼лась** *impf.* (infml) to trudge, plod (along)

плет|ь, и, *pl.* **∼и, ∼ей** *f.* lash

плечи́ст|ый, ∼, ∼а *adj.* broad-shouldered

⚢ **плеч|о́, á, о ∼е, на ∼áм** *nt.* shoulder; **име́ть го́лову на ∼áх** to have a good head on one's shoulders; **э́то ему́ не по ∼у́** he is not up to it; **пожа́ть ∼а́ми** to shrug one's shoulders

плеши́в|ый, ∼, ∼а *adj.* bald

плешь, и *f.* bald patch

пли́нтус, а *m.* **1** (archit.) plinth **2** (*между стеной и полом*) skirting board (BrE), baseboard (AmE)

плит|á, ы́, *pl.* **∼ы́ 1** (*металлическая*) plate; (*каменная*) slab; (*для настилки полов*) flag(stone); **моги́льная п.** gravestone, tombstone; **мра́морная п.** marble slab **2** (*печь*) stove; cooker

пли́тк|а, и *f.* **1** *dim. of* ▶ **плита́**; (*облицовочная*) tile, (thin) slab; **п. шокола́да** bar of chocolate **2** (*печь*) small stove

плов, а *m.* (cul.) pilaf

плов|е́ц, ца́ *m.* swimmer

пло́в|чи́ха, чи́хи *f. of* ▶ **пловец**

плод, á *m.* **1** fruit (also fig.); **приноси́ть ∼ы́** to bear fruit; **запре́тный п.** (fig.) forbidden fruit **2** (biol.) fetus

плодо́в|ый *adj. of* ▶ **плод;** **∼ое де́рево** fruit tree

плодоро́ди|е, я *nt.* fertility

плодоро́д|ный, ∼ен, ∼на *adj.* fertile

плодотво́р|ный, ∼ен, ∼на *adj.* fruitful

пло́мб|а, ы *f.* **1** (*на вагоне*) seal **2** (*в зубе*) filling; **ста́вить ∼у** to fill a tooth

пломбир|ова́ть, у́ю *impf.* **1** (*pf.* **о∼, за∼**) (*вагон, избирательную урну*) to seal **2** (*pf.* **за∼**) (*зуб*) to fill

пло́с|кий, ∼ок, ∼ка́, ∼ко *adj.* **1** flat; plane; **∼кая пове́рхность** plane surface; **∼кий экра́н** flat screen **2** (fig., *пошлый*) trivial; tame; **∼кая шу́тка** feeble joke

плоского́р|ье, я *nt.* plateau; tableland

плоскогу́бц|ы, ев (*no sg.*) pliers

пло́скост|ь, и, *pl.* **∼и, ∼е́й** *f.* (*поверхность*) plane (also fig.); **накло́нная п.** inclined plane

плот, á, о ∼é, на ∼у́ *m.* raft

плотв|á, ы́ *f.* roach (*fish*)

плоти́н|а, ы *f.* dam

пло́тник, а *m.* carpenter

пло́тно *adv.* **1** close(ly), tightly; **п. заколоти́ть дверь** to board up a door **2**: **п. поéсть** to eat heartily

пло́тност|ь, и *f.* **1** (*тумана, населения*) density (also phys.) **2** (*человека*) solidity

пло́т|ный, ∼ен, ∼á, ∼но, ∼ны́ *adj.* **1** (*туман, население*) dense (also phys.) **2** (*бумага*) thick, solid, strong; (*человек*) thickset, solidly built **3** (*папка*) tightly-filled **4** (infml, *завтрак*) hearty

плотоя́д|ный, ∼ен, ∼на *adj.* **1** carnivorous **2** (fig., *сладострастный*) lustful; voluptuous

плот|ь, и *f.* flesh; **во ∼и** in the flesh

⚢ **пло́хо** *adv.* bad(ly); ill; **чу́вствовать себя́ п.** to feel unwell; **п. па́хнуть** to smell bad

⚢ **плох|о́й, ∼, ∼á,** *as pred.* bad; poor; **∼о́е настрое́ние** bad mood; (*as pred.*) **ему́ о́чень ∼о** he is in a very bad way

⚢ **площа́дк|а, и** *f.* **1** ground, area; **де́тская п.** children's playground; **спорти́вная п.** sports ground; **строи́тельная п.** building site; **те́ннисная п.** tennis court; **киносъёмочная п.** (film) set; **п. для игры́ в го́льф** golf course **2** (*лестничная*) landing (*on staircase*) **3** (*в вагоне*) platform; **пускова́я п.** launch pad (*of rocket*)

⚢ **пло́щад|ь, и,** *pl.* **∼и, ∼е́й** *f.* **1** (*в городе*) square **2** (*пространство*) area; space; **жила́я п.** living space **3** (math.) area

плуг, а, *pl.* **∼и́** *m.* plough (BrE), plow (AmE)

плут, á *m.* cheat; rogue

плы|ть, ву́, вёшь, *past* **∼л, ∼лá, ∼ло** *impf.* (*det. of* ▶ **пла́вать** 1) **1** (*о человеке, о животном*) to swim; (*об облаках, о звуках*) to float **2** (*ехать на судне*) to sail; **п. на вёслах** to row; **п. под паруса́ми** to sail

плю́н|уть, у, ешь *pf. of* ▶ **плева́ть**

плюрали́зм, а *m.* (phil. & pol.) pluralism

п

ϭ **плюс, а** *m.* **1** plus; (math.): **два п. два равно́ четырём** two plus two equals four **2** (fig., infml, *преиму́щество*) advantage

плю́х|аться, аюсь *impf. of* ▸ **плю́хнуться**

плю́х|нуться, нусь, нешься *pf.* (*of* ▸ **плю́хаться**) (infml) to flop (down)

плюш, а *m.* plush

плю́шевый *adj. of* ▸ **плюш**

плющ, á *m.* ivy

пляж, а *m.* beach

пля|са́ть, шу́, ~шешь *impf.* (*of* ▸ **спляса́ть**) to dance

пля́ск|а, и *f.* (*де́йствие*) dancing; (*та́нец*) dance (*esp. folk dance*)

пневмати́ческий *adj.* pneumatic

пневмони́|я, и *f.* pneumonia; **атипи́чная п.** SARS (*severe acute respiratory syndrome*)

пнуть, пну, пнёшь *inst. pf.* (*of* ▸ **пина́ть**) (infml) to kick

ϭ **по** *prep.* I. (+ *d.*) **1** (*на пове́рхности*) on; (*вдоль*) along; **идти́ по траве́** to walk on the grass; **е́хать по у́лице** to go along the street; **идти́ по следа́м** (+ *g.*) to follow in the tracks (of); **по всему́, по всей** all over **2** (*в ра́зные места́*) round, about; **ходи́ть по магази́нам** to go round the shops **3** (*посре́дством*) by, on, over; **по желе́зной доро́ге** by rail; **по по́чте** by post; **по ра́дио** on/over the radio; **по телефо́ну** on/over the telephone **4** (*в соотве́тствии, согла́сно*) according to; by; in accordance with; **по пра́ву** by right(s); **по расписа́нию** according to schedule; **звать по и́мени** to call by first name **5** (*в отноше́нии*) by, in (= *in respect of*); **по профе́ссии** by profession; **по происхожде́нию он армяни́н** he is of Armenian origin; **лу́чший по ка́честву** better in quality; **това́рищ по шко́ле** schoolmate **6** (*в о́бласти*) at, on, in (= *in the field of*); **ле́кции по европе́йской исто́рии** lectures on European history; **специали́ст по я́дерной фи́зике** specialist in nuclear physics **7** (*из-за*) by (reason of); on account of; from; **по боле́зни** on account of sickness; **по рассе́янности** from absent-mindedness **8** (*ука́зывает на предме́т де́йствия*) at, for (*or not translated*); **скуча́ть по де́тям** to miss one's children **9** (*ука́зывает вре́мя*) on; in; **по пра́здникам** on holidays

• II. (*в распредели́тельном значе́нии*): **по одному́(одно́й)/по ты́сяче/по миллио́ну/ по миллиа́рду** one/a thousand/a million/a billion each; (*with other numerals* + *a.*) **по́ два (две)/по́ три/по четы́ре/по две́сти/по три́ста/по четы́реста** two/three/four/two hundred/three hundred/four hundred each; **да́йте им по** (*sc. одному́*) **я́блоку** give them an apple each; **мы получи́ли по три фу́нта** we received three pounds each; **по рублю́ штýка** one rouble each

• III. (+ *a.*) (*до*) to, up to; **по по́яс в воде́** up to the waist in water

• IV. (+ *p.*) (*по́сле*) on, after; **по прибы́тии** on arrival

по...[1] *vbl. pref.* **1** forms pf. aspect **2** (*indicates action of short duration or of incomplete character*): **порабо́тать** to do a little work; **поспа́ть** to have a sleep **3** (*with* **...ыва...**, **...ива...**) (*indicates action repeated at intervals or of indet. duration*): **позва́нивать** to keep ringing

по...[2] *pref. modifying comp. adj. or adv., as*: **погро́мче** a little louder

по- + *d.* of adj. or in names of languages, forms adv. indicating **1** (*manner of action, conduct, etc.*): **жить по-ста́рому** to live in the old manner **2** (*use of given language*): **говори́ть по-ру́сски** to speak Russian **3** (*accordance with opinion or wish*): **по-мо́ему** in my opinion

поба́ива|ться, юсь *impf.* (+ *g. or inf.*) (infml) to be rather afraid

поба́лива|ть, ю *impf.* (infml) (*немно́го*) to ache a little; (*иногда́*) to ache on and off

побе́г, а *m.* flight; escape

ϭ **побе́д|а, ы** *f.* victory; **одержа́ть ~у** to gain a victory

ϭ **победи́тел|ь, я** *m.* victor; (sport) winner

победи́тель|ница, ницы *f. of* ▸ **победи́тель**

победи́|ть, и́шь *pf.* (*of* ▸ **побежда́ть**) (*врага́*) to conquer; (*сопе́рника*) to defeat, beat; **на́ша кома́нда победи́ла** our team won; (fig.) to master, overcome

побе́дный *adj.* victorious, triumphant; **п. гол** winning goal

побе|жа́ть, гу́, жи́шь, гу́т *pf.* **1** *pf. of* ▸ **бежа́ть 1 2** to break into a run

побежда́|ть, ю *impf. of* ▸ **победи́ть**

побеле́|ть, ю *pf. of* ▸ **беле́ть 1**

побел|и́ть, ю́, ~и́шь *pf. of* ▸ **бели́ть**

побе́лк|а, и *f.* whitewashing

побере́жь|е, я *nt.* coast, seaboard

побесе́д|овать, ую *pf.* to have a (little) talk, have a chat

побеспоко́|ить, ю, ишь *pf.* (*of* ▸ **беспоко́ить 2**): **позво́льте вас п.!** may I trouble you?

побеспоко́|иться, юсь, ишься *pf. of* ▸ **беспоко́иться 2**

побива́|ть, ю *impf.* (*of* ▸ **поби́ть 2**) (*проти́вника*) to beat; (*реко́рд*) to break

поби́|ть, ью́, ёшь *pf.* **1** *pf. of* ▸ **бить 1 2** *pf. of* ▸ **побива́ть 3** (*pf. only*) (*расте́ния*) to beat down, damage; (*о моро́зе*) to nip **4** (*pf. only*) (*посу́ду*) to break, smash

поби́|ться, ью́сь, ёшься *pf.* (infml) **1** (*used only in 3rd pers.*) (*получи́ть поврежде́ния*) to get damaged; (*о фру́ктах и овоща́х*) to bruise; (*о посу́де, яйца́х*) to break, smash **2** (*над* + *i.*) (fig.) to struggle (with) (for some time)

поблагодар|и́ть, ю́, и́шь *pf. of* ▸ **благодари́ть**

поблед|не́ть, ю *pf. of* ▸ **бледне́ть**

поблёскива|ть, ю *impf.* to gleam

побли́зости *adv.* nearby; **п.** (*от* + *g.*) near (to)

поболта́|ть, ю *pf.* (infml) to have a chat

побор|о́ть, ю́, ~ешь *pf.* to overcome

побо́чный *adj.* secondary; **п. эффе́кт** side effect; **п. проду́кт** by-product

побоя́|ться, ю́сь, и́шься *pf.* (+ *g.* or *inf.*) to be afraid

побре́|ить, е́ю *pf. of* ▶ **брить**

побре́|иться, е́юсь *pf. of* ▶ **бри́ться**

поброса́|ть, ю *pf.* **1** (*бросить как попало*) to throw **2** (*покинуть*) to desert, abandon

побыва́|ть, ю *pf.* **1** (*посетить*) to have been, have visited; **в про́шлом году́ мы ∼ли в Норве́гии и Шве́ции** last year we were in Norway and Sweden **2** (*зайти*) to drop in, call in; **он ∼л у друзе́й** he dropped in to see some friends

по|бы́ть, бу́ду, бу́дешь, *past* ∼**был,** ∼**была́,** ∼**было** *pf.* to stay (*for a short time*); **мы ∼были в Ло́ндоне два дня** we stayed in London for two days

пова́дк|а, и *f.* (infml) habit

повали́|ть¹, ю́, ∼ишь *pf. of* ▶ **вали́ть¹ 1**

повали́|ть², ю́, ∼ишь *pf.* to begin to throng, begin to pour; **дым ∼и́л из трубы́** smoke began to pour from the chimney

повали́|ться, ю́сь, ∼ишься *pf. of* ▶ **вали́ться**

пова́льный *adj.* general, mass

по́вар, а, *pl.* ∼**а́** *m.* cook

по-ва́шему *adv.* **1** (*по вашему мнению*) in your opinion **2** (*как вы хотите*) as you wish

поведе́ни|е, я *nt.* behaviour (BrE), behavior (AmE)

повез|ти́, у́, ёшь, *past* ∼**, ∼ла́** *pf. of* ▶ **везти́**

повели́тельн|ый *adj.*: ∼**ое наклоне́ние** (gram.) imperative mood, the imperative

повенча́|ть, ю *pf. of* ▶ **венча́ть**

повенча́|ться, юсь *pf. of* ▶ **венча́ться**

поверг|а́ть, а́ю *impf. of* ▶ **пове́ргнуть**

пове́рг|нуть, ну, нешь, *past* ∼ **and ∼нул,** ∼**ла** *pf.* (*of* ▶ **поверга́ть**) (**в** + *a.*) to plunge (into); **п. в отча́яние** to plunge into despair

пове́р|ить, ю, ишь *pf. of* ▶ **ве́рить**

повер|ну́ть, ну́, нёшь *pf.* (*of* ▶ **повора́чивать**) to turn; (fig.) to change

повер|ну́ться, ну́сь, нёшься *pf.* (*of* ▶ **повора́чиваться**) to turn; **п. круго́м** to turn round, turn about; **п. спино́й** (**к** + *d.*) to turn one's back (upon)

пове́рх *prep.* + *g.* over, above; on top of; **смотре́ть п. очко́в** to look over the top of one's spectacles

пове́рхностн|ый *adj.* **1** surface, superficial; ∼**ое натяже́ние** (tech.) surface tension **2** (∼**ен,** ∼**на**) (fig.) superficial

пове́рхност|ь, и *f.* surface

по́верху *adv.* on the surface, on top

повеселе́|ть, ю *pf.* to cheer up, become cheerful

по-весе́ннему *adv.* as in spring

пове́|сить, шу, сишь *pf. of* ▶ **ве́шать¹**

пове́|ситься, шусь, сишься *pf. of* ▶ **ве́шаться 2**

повествова́ни|е, я *nt.* narrative, narration

повеств|ова́ть, у́ю *impf.* (**о** + *p.*) to narrate, recount, relate

пове|сти́, ду́, дёшь, *past* ∼**л, ∼ла́** *pf. of* ▶ **вести́ 1**

пове́стк|а, и *f.* notice, notification; **п. в суд** summons, writ, subpoena; **на ∼е дня** on the agenda (also fig.)

по́вест|ь, и, *pl.* ∼**и, ∼е́й** *f.* story, tale

повзросле́|ть, ю *pf.* to grow up

повида́|ть, ю *pf.* (infml) to see

повида́|ться, юсь *pf.* (infml) (**с** + *i.*) to meet; to see one another

по-ви́димому *adv.* apparently, seemingly

пови́дл|о, а *nt.* jam

пови́нност|ь, и *f.* duty, obligation; **во́инская п.** compulsory military service, conscription

повин|ова́ть, у́юсь *impf.* (*in past tense also pf.*) (+ *d.*) to obey

повинове́ни|е, я *nt.* obedience

повис|а́ть, а́ю *impf. of* ▶ **пови́снуть**

пови́с|нуть, ну, нешь, *past* ∼**, ∼ла** *pf.* (*of* ▶ **повиса́ть**) **1** (**на** + *i.*) to hang (by) **2** (*склониться*) to hang down, droop; **п. в во́здухе** (fig.) to hang in mid-air; (*о шутке*) to fall flat

повле́|чь, ку́, чёшь, ку́т, *past* ∼**к, ∼кла́** *pf.*: (**за собо́й**) to entail, bring in one's train; **п. за собо́й неприя́тные после́дствия** to have unpleasant consequences

повлия́|ть, ю *pf. of* ▶ **влия́ть**

по́вод, а, *pl.* ∼**ы** *m.* (**к** + *d.*) occasion, cause, ground (for, of); **дать п.** (+ *d.*) to give occasion (to), give cause (for); **без вся́кого ∼а** without cause; **по ∼у** (+ *g.*) apropos (of), as regards, concerning

пово́д|о́к, ка́ *m.* lead (BrE), leash (AmE)

пово́зк|а, и *f.* cart

повора́чива|ть, ю *impf.* (*of* ▶ **поверну́ть**)

повора́чива|ться, юсь *impf.* (*of* ▶ **поверну́ться**): ∼**йся!, ∼йтесь!** (infml) get a move on!, look sharp!

поворо́т, а *m.* turn(ing); **указа́тели ∼а** (direction) indicator lamps/lights (*of car*); (fig.) turning point; **на ∼е доро́ги** at the turn of the road

повре|ди́ть, жу́, ди́шь *pf.* **1** *pf. of* ▶ **вреди́ть 2** (*pf. of* ▶ **поврежда́ть**) (*испортить*) to damage; (*поранить*) to injure, hurt

повре|ди́ться, жу́сь, ди́шься *pf.* (*of* ▶ **поврежда́ться**) (*испортиться*) to be damaged

поврежда́|ть, ю *impf. of* ▶ **повреди́ть**

поврежда́|ться, юсь *impf. of* ▶ **повреди́ться**

поврежде́ни|е, я *nt.* damage; injury

повседне́вный *adj.* daily; everyday

повсеме́стно *adv.* everywhere

повста́н|ец, ца *m.* rebel, insurgent

повстреча́|ть, ю *pf.* (infml) to meet, run into

повстреча́|ться, юсь *pf.* (infml) (+ *d.* or **с** + *i.*) to meet, run into; **я ∼лся со знако́мым**

п

I met an acquaintance

повсю́ду *adv.* everywhere

повто́р, а *m.* replay

повторе́ни|е, я *nt.* **1** (*действия*) repetition **2** (*события*) recurrence **3** (*урока*) revision

повтор|и́ть, ю́, и́шь *pf.* (of ▶ повторя́ть) **1** to repeat **2** (*уроки*) to revise

повтор|и́ться, ю́сь, и́шься *pf.* (of ▶ повторя́ться) **1** (*повторить сказанное*) to repeat oneself **2** (*о событиях*) to reoccur; (*о болезни*) to recur

повто́р|ный, ∼ен, ∼на *adj.* (*визит*) second, repeated; (*заболевание*) recurring

♂ **повтор|я́ть, я́ю** *impf. of* ▶ повтори́ть

повтор|я́ться, я́юсь *impf. of* ▶ повтори́ться

повы́|сить, шу, сишь *pf.* (of ▶ повыша́ть) **1** to raise, heighten; п. вдво́е, втро́е to double, treble; п. в пять раз *и т. п.* to raise fivefold, *etc.*; п. давле́ние to increase pressure; п. го́лос to raise one's voice; (*улучшить*) to improve **2** (*работника*) to promote, advance; п. кого́-н. по слу́жбе to give sb promotion

повы́|ситься, шусь, сишься *pf.* (of ▶ повыша́ться) to rise; (*увеличиться*) to increase; (*улучшиться*) to improve; на́ши а́кции ∼сились our shares have gone up; (*fig.*) our stock has risen

♂ **повыша́|ть, ю** *impf. of* ▶ повы́сить

повыша́|ться, юсь *impf. of* ▶ повы́ситься

повы́ше *comp. adj. and adv.* a little higher (up); (*о росте человека*) a little taller

♂ **повыше́ни|е, я** *nt.* rise, increase; п. по слу́жбе advancement, promotion

♂ **повы́шенный** *p.p.p. of* ▶ повы́сить *and adj.* increased, heightened

повя|за́ть, жу́, ∼жешь *pf.* (of ▶ повя́зывать) to tie; п. га́лстук to tie a tie

повя́зк|а, и *f.* **1** (*лента*) band **2** (*бинт*) bandage

повя́зыва|ть, ю *impf. of* ▶ повяза́ть

погада́|ть, ю *pf. of* ▶ гада́ть 1

пога́нк|а, и *f.* (*гриб*) toadstool

пога|си́ть, шу́, ∼сишь *pf.* (of ▶ гаси́ть, ▶ погаша́ть) to liquidate, cancel; п. долг to clear a debt

пога́с|нуть, ну, нешь *past* ∼, ∼ла *pf. of* ▶ га́снуть

погаша́|ть, ю *impf. of* ▶ погаси́ть

погиба́|ть, а́ю *impf. of* ▶ погибнуть

погиб|нуть, ну, нешь *past* ∼, ∼ла *pf.* (▶ ги́бнуть, ▶ погиба́ть) to perish; (*naut., also fig.*) to be lost; кора́бль ∼ со всей кома́ндой the ship was lost with all hands

погибший *p.p. of* ▶ поги́бнуть *and adj.* lost, ruined

погла́|дить, жу, дишь *pf. of* ▶ гла́дить

погла́жива|ть, ю *impf.* to stroke (*every so often*)

поглоти́ть, щу́, ∼тишь *pf.* (of ▶ поглоща́ть) to soak up, absorb (*also fig.*); п. во́ду to absorb water

поглоща́|ть, ю *impf. of* ▶ поглоти́ть

погля|де́ть, жу́, ди́шь *pf.* **1** *pf. of* ▶ гляде́ть **2** (*взглянуть*) to have a look **3** (*некоторое время*) to look for a while

погля́дыва|ть, ю *impf.* **1** (на + *a.*) to glance from time to time (at) **2** (за + *i.*) (*infml*) to keep an eye (on)

по|гна́ть, гоню́, го́нишь, *past* ∼гна́л, ∼гнала́, ∼гна́ло *pf.* to drive; (*начать гнать*) to begin to drive

по|гна́ться, гоню́сь, го́нишься, *past* ∼гна́лся, ∼гнала́сь, ∼гна́ло́сь *pf.* (за + *i.*) to run (after); to give chase; (*fig.*) to strive (after, for)

погн|у́ть, у́, ёшь *pf.* to bend

погн|у́ться, ётся *pf.* to bend

погова́рива|ть, ю *impf.* (о + *p.*) to talk (of); ∼ют there is talk (of)

поговор|и́ть, ю́, и́шь **1** *pf. of* ▶ говори́ть 3 **2** (*pf. only*) to have a talk

погово́рк|а, и *f.* saying

пого́д|а, ы *f.* weather

поголо́вный *adj.* general, universal

пого́н, а, *g. pl.* ∼ *m.* (mil.) shoulder strap

пого́н|я, и *f.* pursuit, chase

погоня́|ть, ю *impf.* (*торопить*) to urge on, drive (*also fig.*)

пого|сти́ть, щу́, сти́шь *pf.*: (у + *g.*) to stay for a while (at, with)

пограни́чник, а *m.* border guard, frontier guard

пограни́чн|ый *adj.* (*страны*) border, frontier; (*участки*) boundary; ∼ая стра́жа border guards

по́греб, а, *pl.* ∼а́ *m.* cellar (*also fig.*); ви́нный п. wine cellar

погребе́ни|е, я *nt.* burial, interment

погрему́шк|а, и *f.* rattle

погре́|ть, ю *pf.* to warm

погре́|ться, юсь *pf.* to warm oneself

погреш|и́ть, у́, и́шь *pf. of* ▶ греши́ть 2

погре́шност|ь, и *f.* error, mistake

погро|зи́ть, жу́, зи́шь *pf. of* ▶ грози́ть 2

погро́м, а *m.* pogrom; (*infml*) chaos

погружа́|ть, ю *impf. of* ▶ погрузи́ть

погружа́|ться, юсь *impf. of* ▶ погрузи́ться

погруже́ни|е, я *nt.* submergence; immersion; (*подводной лодки*) dive, diving

погру|зи́ть, жу́, ∼зи́шь *pf.* **1** (∼зи́шь) (*pf. of* ▶ погружа́ть) (в + *a.*) to immerse; (*в темноту*) to plunge **2** (∼зишь) *pf. of* ▶ грузи́ть 2

погру|зи́ться, жу́сь, ∼зи́шься *pf.* **1** (∼зи́шься) (*pf. of* ▶ погружа́ться) (в + *a.*) to sink (into), plunge (into); (*о подводной лодке*) to submerge, dive; (*fig.*) to be plunged (in); to be absorbed (in), be buried (in), be lost (in); п. в темноту́ to be plunged into darkness; п. в размышле́ния to be deep in thought **2** (∼зишься) *pf. of* ▶ грузи́ться

♂ key word

погру́зк|а, и *f.* loading

погряз|а́ть, а́ю *impf. of* ▶ **погря́знуть**

погря́з|нуть, ну, нешь, *past* ~, ~**ла** *pf.* (*of* ▶ **погрязать**) (**в** + *p.*) to be stuck (in); to be bogged down (in); (*в разврате*) to wallow (in); **п. в долга́х** to be up to one's eyes in debt

погуб|и́ть, лю́, ~ишь *pf. of* ▶ **губи́ть**

погуля́|ть, ю *pf. of* ▶ **гуля́ть**

⚹ **под,** *also* **подо** *prep.* **1** (+ *a.* and *i.*) (*ниже*) under; **поста́вить п. стол** to put under the table; **п. ви́дом** (+ *g.*) in the guise (of); **п. влия́нием** (+ *g.*) under the influence (of); **п. вопро́сом** open to question; **п. землёй** underground; **взять кого́-н. по́д руку** to take sb's arm; **п. руко́й** (close) at hand, to hand; **отда́ть п. суд** to prosecute **2** (+ *a.* and *i.*) (*около*) in the environs of, near; **жить п. Москво́й** to live near Moscow **3** (+ *a.*) (*для*) for; (to serve) as; **отвести́ помеще́ние п. шко́лу** to earmark premises for a school **4** (+ *a.*) (*о времени*) towards; on the eve of; **п. ве́чер** towards evening; **п. Но́вый год** on New Year's Eve; **ему́ п. пятьдеся́т (лет)** he is getting on for fifty **5** (+ *a.*) (*в сопровождении*) to (the accompaniment of); **танцева́ть п. му́зыку** to dance to music **6** (+ *i.*) (*при обозначении понятия*) by; **что на́до понима́ть п. э́тим выраже́нием?** what is meant by this expression?; **что п. э́тим подразумева́ется?** what is implied by this? **7** (+ *a.*) (*в обмен*) on (= *in exchange for*); **п. зало́г** (+ *g.*) on security (of); **п. распи́ску** on receipt

под...[1] **and подо..., подъ...** *vbl. pref.* **1** (*action from beneath or affecting lower part of sth*): **подчеркну́ть** to underline **2** (*motion upwards*): **подня́ть** to raise **3** (*motion towards*): **подъе́хать** to approach

под...[2] **and подо..., подъ...** *as pref. of nn. and adjs.* under-, sub-

⚹ **пода|ва́ть, ю́, ёшь** *impf. of* ▶ **пода́ть**

подав|и́ть, лю́, ~ишь *pf.* (*of* ▶ **подавля́ть**) **1** (*восстание; стон*) to suppress; to repress **2** (fig., *ослабить, угнетать*) to depress; to crush, overwhelm

пода|ви́ться, авлю́сь, а́вишься *pf. of* ▶ **дави́ться**

пода́вленный *p.p.p. of* ▶ **подави́ть** *and adj.* **1** (*стон, смех*) suppressed, stifled **2** (*человек, настроение*) depressed, dispirited

подавля́|ть, ю *impf. of* ▶ **подави́ть**

подавля́ющий *pres. part. act. of* ▶ **подавля́ть** *and adj.* overwhelming

пода́гр|а, ы *f.* gout

пода́льше *adv.* (infml) a little further

подар|и́ть, ю́, ~ишь *pf. of* ▶ **дари́ть**

⚹ **пода́р|ок, ка** *m.* present, gift; **получи́ть в п.** to receive as a present

пода́тлив|ый, ~, ~а *adj.* **1** pliant, pliable **2** (fig., *уступчивый*) complaisant

по|да́ть, да́м, да́шь, да́ст, дади́м, дади́те, даду́т, *past* ~**дал,** ~**дала́,** ~**дало** *pf.* (*of* ▶ **подава́ть**) **1** to give; **п. приме́р** to set an example; **п. ру́ку** (+ *d.*) to offer one's hand;

п. сигна́л to give the signal **2** (*еду*) to serve; **обе́д** ~**дан** dinner is served **3** (sport): **п. мяч** to serve **4** (*заявление, жалобу*) to serve, present, hand in; **п. заявле́ние** to hand in an application; **п. в отста́вку** to tender one's resignation; **п. в суд** (**на** + *a.*) to bring an action (against)

пода́ч|а, и *f.* **1** giving, presenting; **п. заявле́ния** sending in of application **2** (*в теннисе, волейболе*) service, serve; (*в футболе*) pass

подбега́|ть, ю *impf. of* ▶ **подбежа́ть**

подбе|жа́ть, гу́, жи́шь, гу́т *pf.* (*of* ▶ **подбега́ть**) (**к** + *d.*) to run up (to), come running up (to)

подбива́|ть, ю *impf. of* ▶ **подби́ть**

⚹ **подбира́|ть, ю** *impf. of* ▶ **подобра́ть**

подбира́|ться, юсь *impf. of* ▶ **подобра́ться**

под|би́ть, обью́, обьёшь *pf.* (*of* ▶ **подбива́ть**) **1** (+ *i.*) (*пальто*) to line (with) **2** (*обувь*) to resole **3** (*ушибить*) to injure; **п. кому́-н. глаз** to give sb a black eye **4** (*самолёт, утку*) to shoot down **5** (+ *a.* or + *inf.*) (infml, *подстрекать*) to incite (to)

подбодр|и́ть, ю́, и́шь *pf.* (*of* ▶ **подбодря́ть**) to cheer up

подбодр|я́ть, я́ю *impf. of* ▶ **подбодри́ть**

подбо́р, а *m.* selection, assortment

подбо́рк|а, и *f.* set, selection

подборо́д|ок, ка *m.* chin

подбра́сыва|ть, ю *impf. of* ▶ **подбро́сить**

подбро́|сить, шу, сишь *pf.* (*of* ▶ **подбра́сывать**) **1** to throw up, toss up; (**под** + *a.*) to throw (under); **п. моне́ту** to toss up **2** (+ *a.* or *g.*) to throw in, throw on; **п. дров в печь** to throw more wood on the fire **3** (*положить скрытно*) to place surreptitiously

подва́л, а *m.* cellar; basement

подвез|ти́, у́, ёшь, *past* ~, ~**ла́** *pf.* (*of* ▶ **подвози́ть**) **1** (*довезти*) to bring, take (with one); to give a lift (*on the road*) **2** (+ *a.* or *g.*) (*доставить*) to bring up, transport

подверг|а́ть, а́ю *impf. of* ▶ **подве́ргнуть**

подверг|а́ться, а́юсь *impf. of* ▶ **подве́ргнуться**

подве́рг|нуть, ну, нешь, *past* ~ *and* ~**нул,** ~**ла** *pf.* (*of* ▶ **подверга́ть**) (+ *d.*) to subject (to); to expose (to); **п. испыта́нию** to put to the test; **п. опа́сности** to expose to danger, endanger

подве́рг|нуться, нусь, нешься, *past* ~**ся** *and* ~**нулся,** ~**лась** *pf.* (*of* ▶ **подверга́ться**) (+ *d.*) to undergo, be subjected to

подве́ржен|ный, ~, ~а *adj.* (+ *d.*) (*влиянию ветров*) subject (to); (*простуде*) prone (to), susceptible (to)

подверн|у́ть, у́, нёшь *pf.* (*of* ▶ **подвёртывать**) **1** (*подвинтить*) to screw up a little **2** (*подоткнуть*) to tuck in, tuck up; **п. брю́ки** to tuck up one's trousers **3** (*повредить*) to twist; to sprain; **п. но́гу** to sprain one's ankle

подверн|у́ться, у́сь, нёшься *pf.* (*of* ▶ **подвёртываться**) **1** to be twisted,

п

sprained **2** (fig., infml, *попа́сться*) to turn up, show up; **он кста́ти ~ну́лся** he turned up just at the right moment

подвёртыва|ть, ю *impf. of* ▶ **подверну́ть**

подвёртыва|ться, юсь *impf. of* ▶ **подверну́ться**

подве́|сить, шу, сишь *pf.* (*of* ▶ **подве́шивать**) to hang up, suspend

подве́ск|а, и *f.* **1** (*де́йствие*) hanging up, suspension **2** (*украше́ние*) pendant

подве|сти́, ду́, дёшь, *past* **~л, ~ла́** *pf.* (*of* ▶ **подводи́ть**) **1** (к + *d.*) (*челове́ка*) to lead up (to); (*по́езд*) to bring up (to); (*доро́гу*) to extend (to) **2** (под + *a.*) to place (under) **3** (infml, *поста́вить в тру́дное положе́ние*) to let down; to put in a spot

подве́тренный *adj.* leeward

подве́шива|ть, ю *impf. of* ▶ **подве́сить**

по́двиг, а *m.* exploit, feat; heroic deed

подвига́|ть, ю *impf. of* ▶ **подви́нуть**

подвига́|ться, юсь *impf. of* ▶ **подви́нуться**

подви́д, а (biol.) subspecies

подви́ж|ный, ~ен, ~на *adj.* **1** (*гру́ппа войск*) mobile **2** (*ребёнок*) lively; **~ное лицо́** mobile features

подви́|нуть, ну, нешь *pf.* (*of* ▶ **подвига́ть**) to move; to push; **~ньте стул!** pull up a chair!

подви́|нуться, нусь, нешься *pf.* (*of* ▶ **подвига́ться**) to move; **~ньтесь и да́йте мне сесть!** move up and let me sit down!

подвла́ст|ный, ~ен, ~на *adj.* (+ *d.*) subject to, under the control of

подво|ди́ть, жу́, ~дишь *impf. of* ▶ **подвести́**

подво́дный *adj.* submarine; underwater; **~ая ло́дка** submarine

подво|зи́ть, жу́, ~зишь *impf. of* ▶ **подвезти́**

подгиба́|ть, ю *impf. of* ▶ **подогну́ть**

подгля|де́ть, жу́, ди́шь *pf.* (*of* ▶ **подгля́дывать**) (за + *i.*) (infml) to peep (at); to spy (on), watch furtively

подгля́дыва|ть, ю *impf. of* ▶ **подгляде́ть**

подгова́рива|ть, ю *impf. of* ▶ **подговори́ть**

подговор|и́ть, ю́, и́шь *pf.* (*of* ▶ **подгова́ривать**) (на + *a.* or *inf.*) to put up (to), incite (to)

подголо́вник, а *m.* headrest

подгоня́|ть, ю *impf. of* ▶ **подогна́ть**

подгор|а́ть, а́ет *impf. of* ▶ **подгоре́ть**

подгор|е́ть, и́т *pf.* (*of* ▶ **подгора́ть**) to burn slightly

✍ **подгота́влива|ть, ю** *impf. of* ▶ **подгото́вить**

подгота́влива|ться, юсь *impf. of* ▶ **подгото́виться**

подготови́тельный *adj.* preparatory

подгото́в|ить, лю, ишь *pf.* (*of* ▶ **подгота́вливать**) (для + *g.* or к + *d.*) to prepare (for); **п. по́чву** (fig.) to pave the way

подгото́в|иться, люсь, ишься *pf.* (*of* ▶ **подгота́вливаться**) (к + *d.*) to prepare (for), get ready (for)

✍ key word

✍ **подгото́вк|а, и** *f.* **1** (к + *d.*) preparation (for), training (for) **2** (в + *p.* or по + *d.*) grounding (in), schooling (in)

подгру́пп|а, ы *f.* subgroup

подгу́зник, а *m.* nappy (BrE), diaper (AmE)

подда|ва́ться, ю́сь, ёшься *impf. of* ▶ **подда́ться**

по́дданн|ый, ~ого, *f.* **~ая, ~ой** *n.* subject, national

по́дданств|о, а *nt.* citizenship, nationality

под|да́ться, да́мся, да́шься, да́стся, дади́мся, дади́тесь, даду́тся, *past* **~да́лся, ~дала́сь** *pf.* (*of* ▶ **поддава́ться**) (+ *d.*) to yield (to), give way (to), give in (to); **дверь не ~дала́сь** the door would not give; **п. искуше́нию** to yield to temptation; **не ~дава́ться описа́нию** to beggar description

поддева́|ть, ю *impf. of* ▶ **подде́ть**

подде́л|ать, аю *pf.* (*of* ▶ **подде́лывать**) to forge; to counterfeit

подде́лк|а, и *f.* forgery; counterfeit, fake; **п. под же́мчуг** imitation pearls

подде́лыва|ть, ю *impf. of* ▶ **подде́лать**

подде́льный *adj.* forged, counterfeit; (*неи́скренний*) sham; **п. па́спорт** forged passport

поддерж|а́ть, у́, ~ишь *pf.* (*of* ▶ **подде́рживать** 1) **1** to support (also fig.); to back, second; **п. резолю́цию** to second a resolution **2** (*не дать прекрати́ться*) to keep up, maintain; **п. разгово́р** to keep up a conversation

✍ **подде́ржива|ть, ю** *impf.* **1** *impf. of* ▶ **поддержа́ть**; **подде́рживать отноше́ния** (с + *i.*) to keep in touch (with) **2** (*impf. only*) to bear, support

✍ **подде́ржк|а, и** *f.* support; backing; seconding

подде́|ть, ну, нешь *pf.* (*of* ▶ **поддева́ть**) **1** (под + *a.*) (infml) to put on under, wear under; **~нь(те) сви́тер под ку́ртку** put a sweater on under your jacket **2** (*зацепи́ть*) to hook; to catch up **3** (fig., infml, *челове́ка*) to catch out; to have a dig at sb

поддо́н, а *m.* (*для кирпиче́й*) pallet; (*подста́вка*) stand, tray

поде́йств|овать, ую *pf. of* ▶ **де́йствовать 2**

поде́ла|ть, ю *pf.* (*no impf.*) (infml) to do; **ничего́ не ~ешь** it can't be helped

подел|и́ть, ю́, ~ишь *pf. of* ▶ **дели́ть 2**

подел|и́ться, ю́сь, ~ишься *pf. of* ▶ **дели́ться 2**

поде́лк|а, и *f.* handmade article; **~и из де́рева** handmade wooden articles

поде́ржанный *adj.* second-hand

подерж|а́ть, у́, ~ишь *pf.* (*в рука́х*) to hold for some time; (*у себя́*) to keep for some time

подерж|а́ться, ержу́сь, е́ржишься *pf.* **1** (за + *a.*) to hold (on to) for some time **2** (*сохрани́ться*) to hold (out), last

подешеве́|ть, ет *pf. of* ▶ **дешеве́ть**

поджа́рива|ть, ю *impf. of* ▶ **поджа́рить**

п

поджа́р|ить, ю, ишь *pf.* (*of* ▸ поджа́ривать) (*на сковороде*) to fry; (*в духо́вке*) to roast; **п. хлеб** to toast bread

под|жа́ть, ожму́, ожмёшь *pf.* (*of* ▸ поджима́ть) to draw in; **п. гу́бы** to purse one's lips

под|же́чь, ожгу́, ожжёшь, ожгу́т, *past* ∼жёг, ∼ожгла́ *pf.* (*of* ▸ поджига́ть) to set fire (to), set on fire

поджига́|ть, ю *impf. of* ▸ подже́чь

поджида́|ть, ю *impf.* to wait (for)

поджима́|ть, ю *impf. of* ▸ поджа́ть

поджо́г, а *m.* arson; arson attack

подзаголо́в|ок, ка *m.* subtitle, subheading

подзаты́льник, а *m.* (infml) clip round the ear

подзащи́тн|ый, ого *m.* (law) client

подземе́л|ье, ья, *g. pl.* ∼ий *nt.* cave; (*тюрьма́*) dungeon

подзе́мк|а, и *f.* (infml) underground (railway), tube

подзе́мный *adj.* underground, subterranean

подзыва́|ть, ю *impf. of* ▸ подозва́ть

подка́лыва|ть, ю *impf. of* ▸ подколо́ть

подка́пыва|ться, юсь *impf. of* ▸ подкопа́ться

подка́рмлива|ть, ю *impf. of* ▸ подкорми́ть

подка|ти́ть, чу́, ∼тишь *pf.* (*of* ▸ подка́тывать) **1** (*мяч*) to roll; (*велосипе́д*) to wheel **2** (infml, *об автомоби́ле, экипа́же*) to roll up, drive up

подка|ти́ться, чу́сь, ∼тишься *pf.* (*of* ▸ подка́тываться) (**под** + *a.*) to roll (under)

подка́тыва|ть, ю *impf. of* ▸ подкати́ть

подка́тыва|ться, юсь *impf. of* ▸ подкати́ться

подки́дыва|ть, ю *impf. of* ▸ подки́нуть

подки́|нуть, ну, нешь *pf.* (*of* ▸ подки́дывать) = подбро́сить

подкла́дк|а, и *f.* lining

подкла́дыва|ть, ю *impf. of* ▸ подложи́ть

подкле́ива|ть, ю *impf. of* ▸ подкле́ить

подкле́|ить, ю, ишь *pf.* (*of* ▸ подкле́ивать) to glue up, paste up

подключа́|ть, а́ю *impf. of* ▸ подключи́ть

подключа́|ться, а́юсь *impf. of* ▸ подключи́ться

подключ|и́ть, у́, и́шь *pf.* (*of* ▸ подключа́ть) (**к** + *d.*) **1** (tech.) to link up (to), connect up (to) **2** (fig.) to attach (to); to involve; **к рабо́те ∼и́ли специали́стов** specialists were involved in the work

подключ|и́ться, у́сь, и́шься *pf.* (*of* ▸ подключа́ться) **1** (tech.) to be connected up **2** (fig.) to get involved, become a participant

подко́в|а, ы *f.* (horse)shoe

подк|ова́ть, ую́, уёшь *pf.* (*of* ▸ подко́вывать) to shoe

подко́выва|ть, ю *impf. of* ▸ подкова́ть

подкол|о́ть, ю́, ∼ешь *pf.* (*of* ▸ подка́лывать) **1** (*во́лосы*) to pin up **2** (*докуме́нт к де́лу*)

to attach, append

подкопа́|ться, юсь *pf.* (*of* ▸ подка́пываться) (**под** + *a.*) **1** (*о живо́тных*) to burrow (under) **2** (fig., infml) to undermine

подкорм|и́ть, лю́, ∼ишь *pf.* (*of* ▸ подка́рмливать) to feed up; to fatten (up)

подкра́дыва|ться, юсь *impf. of* ▸ подкра́сться

подкра́|сить, шу, сишь *pf.* (*of* ▸ подкра́шивать) (*сте́ну*) to tint, colour (BrE), color (AmE); (*гу́бы*) to touch up

подкра́|сться, ду́сь, дёшься *pf.* (*of* ▸ подкра́дываться) (**к** + *d.*) to steal up (to), sneak up (to)

подкра́шива|ть, ю *impf. of* ▸ подкра́сить

подкреп|и́ться, лю́сь, и́шься *pf.* (*of* ▸ подкрепля́ться) to fortify oneself (*with food and/or drink*)

подкрепля́|ться, ю́сь *impf. of* ▸ подкрепи́ться

по́дкуп, а *m.* bribery; corruption

подкуп|а́ть, а́ю *impf. of* ▸ подкупи́ть

подкуп|и́ть, лю́, ∼ишь *pf.* (*of* ▸ подкупа́ть) **1** (*деньга́ми*) to bribe **2** (fig., *добро́той*) to win over

подла́мыва|ться, ется *impf. of* ▸ подломи́ться

по́дле *prep.* + *g.* by the side of, beside

подлежа́|ть, у́, и́шь *impf.* (+ *d.*) to be liable (to), be subject (to); **э́тот дом ∼и́т сно́су** this house is to be pulled down

подлежа́щее, его *nt.* (gram.) subject

подлеза́|ть, а́ю *impf. of* ▸ подле́зть

подле́з|ть, у, ешь *pf.* (*of* ▸ подлеза́ть) (**под** + *a.*) to crawl (under), creep (under)

подлет|а́ть, а́ю *impf. of* ▸ подлете́ть

подле|те́ть, чу́, ти́шь *pf.* (*of* ▸ подлета́ть) (**к** + *d.*) to fly up (to); (fig.) to rush up (to)

подле́ц, а́ *m.* scoundrel, villain, rascal

подле́чива|ть, ю *impf. of* ▸ подлечи́ть

подле́чива|ться, юсь *impf. of* ▸ подлечи́ться

подлеч|и́ть, у́, ∼ишь *pf.* (*of* ▸ подле́чивать) (infml) to treat

подлеч|и́ться, у́сь, ∼ишься *pf.* (*of* ▸ подле́чиваться) (infml) to take medical treatment

подлива́|ть, ю *impf. of* ▸ подли́ть

подли́вк|а, и *f.* sauce; (*сала́тная*) dressing; (*мясна́я*) gravy

по́длинник, а *m.* original (opp. ко́пи)

по́длинн|ый, ∼ен, ∼на *adj.* **1** (*не подде́льный*) genuine; authentic; (*не ко́пия*) original **2** (*и́стинный*) true, real; **п. учёный** a true scholar

под|ли́ть, олью́, ольёшь, *past* ∼ли́л, ∼лила́, ∼ли́ло *pf.* (*of* ▸ подлива́ть) (+ *a. or g. and* **в** + *a.*) to add (to); **п. ма́сла в ого́нь** (fig.) to add fuel to the fire

подлож|и́ть, у́, ∼ишь *pf.* (*of* ▸ подкла́дывать) **1** (**под** + *a.*) to lay under **2** (+ *a. or g.*) (*доба́вить*) to add; **∼и́те дров** put some more wood on **3** (*скры́тно*) to put furtively;

п. кому́-н. свинью́ to play a dirty trick on sb

подлоко́тник, а *m.* elbow rest; arm (*of chair*)

подлом|и́ться, ~ится *pf.* (*of ▶ подла́мываться*) (под + *i.*) to break (under)

по́длост|ь, и *f.* **1** (*свойство*) meanness, baseness **2** (*поступок*) mean trick, low-down trick

по́дл|ый, ~, ~а́, ~о *adj.* mean, base, despicable

подма́нива|ть, ю *impf. of ▶ подмани́ть*

подман|и́ть, ю́, ~ишь *pf.* (*of ▶ подма́нивать*) to call (to); to beckon

подме́н|а, ы *f.* substitution (*of sth false for sth real*)

подмен|и́ть, ю́, ~ишь *pf.* (*of ▶ подменя́ть*) (+ *a. and i.*) to substitute (for) (*intentionally*); кто́-то на вече́ринке ~и́л мне шля́пу sb at the party took my hat (and left his instead)

подмен|я́ть, я́ю *impf. of ▶ подмени́ть*

подме|сти́, ту́, тёшь, *past* ~л, ~ла́ *pf.* (*of ▶ подмета́ть*) **1** (*место*) to sweep **2** (*мусор*) to sweep up

подмета́|ть, ю *impf. of ▶ подмести́*

подмётк|а, и *f.* sole

подмеш|а́ть, а́ю *pf.* (*of ▶ подме́шивать*) to stir in, mix in

подме́шива|ть, ю *impf. of ▶ подмеша́ть*

подми́гива|ть, ю *impf. of ▶ подмигну́ть*

подмиг|ну́ть, ну́, нёшь *pf.* (*of ▶ подми́гивать*) (+ *d.*) to wink (at)

подмина́|ть, ю *impf. of ▶ подмя́ть*

подмоско́вный *adj.* (situated) near Moscow

подмыва́|ть, ю *impf. of ▶ подмы́ть*

подм|ы́ть, о́ю, о́ешь *pf.* (*of ▶ подмыва́ть*) **1** (*ребёнка*) to wash sb's bottom **2** (*берег*) to wash away, undermine

подмы́шк|а, и *f.* armpit

под|мя́ть, омну́, омнёшь *pf.* (*of ▶ подмина́ть*) to crush

поднес|ти́, у́, ёшь, *past* ~, ~ла́ *pf.* (*of ▶ подноси́ть*) **1** (*нести*) (к + *d.*) to take (to), bring (to) **2** (+ *d. and a.*) (*подарить*) to present (with); to take (as a present); (*угостить*) to treat (to); п. кому́-н. буке́т цвето́в to present sb with a bouquet

⚜ **поднима́|ть**, ю *impf. of ▶ подня́ть*

поднима́|ться, юсь *impf. of ▶ подня́ться*

поднов|и́ть, лю́, и́шь *pf.* (*of ▶ подновля́ть*) (*краску*) to freshen up, touch up; (*мебель*) to renovate

подновля́|ть, ю *impf. of ▶ поднови́ть*

подно́жи|е, я *nt.* **1** (*горы, башни*) foot **2** (*пьедестал*) pedestal

подно́жк|а¹, и *f.* (*автобуса*) step, footboard

подно́жк|а², и *f.* (*в борьбе*) backheel; дать кому́-н. ~у to trip sb up

подно́с, а *m.* tray

подно|си́ть, шу́, ~сишь *impf. of ▶ поднести́**

под|ня́ть, ниму́, ни́мешь, *past* ~ня́л, ~няла́, ~няло́ *pf.* (*of ▶ поднима́ть*) **1** to raise; to lift; п. настрое́ние (+ *g. or d.*) to cheer up, raise the spirits (of); п. паруса́ to set sail; п. флаг to hoist a flag **2** (*подобрать*) to pick up **3** (*возбудить*) to rouse, stir up; п. восста́ние to rouse to rebellion; п. ссо́ру to pick a quarrel; п. на́ ноги to rouse

под|ня́ться, ниму́сь, ни́мешься, *past* ~ня́лся, ~няла́сь *pf.* (*of ▶ подниматься*) **1** (*о температуре, ценах, солнце*) to rise; (*по лестнице*) to go up; (*встать*) to get up; п. на́ ноги to rise to one's feet **2** (на + *a.*) (*гору*) to climb, ascend, go up **3** (*возникнуть*) to arise; to break out, develop; ~ня́лся ве́тер a wind got up **4** (econ., fig., *улучшиться*) to improve; to recover

подо *prep.* = под

подо...¹ *vbl. pref.* = под...¹

подо...² *as pref. of nn. and adjs.* = под...²

подо́би|е, я *nt.* **1** likeness; по своему́ о́бразу и ~ю in one's own image **2** (math.) similarity

подо́бно *adv.* + *d.* like; п. тому́, как just as

⚜ **подо́б|ный**, ~ен, ~на *adj.* like; similar; ~ное поведе́ние such behaviour (BrE), behavior (AmE); ничего́ ~ного! (infml) nothing of the kind!; и тому́ ~ное (*abbr* и т. п.) and so on, and such like

под|обра́ть, беру́, берёшь, *past* ~обра́л, ~обрала́, ~обра́ло *pf.* (*of ▶ подбира́ть*) **1** (*поднять*) to pick up **2** (*ноги*) to tuck up; (*вожжи*) to take up **3** (*выбрать*) to select, pick; п. дже́мпер под цвет костю́ма to choose a jumper to match a suit

под|обра́ться, беру́сь, берёшься, *past* ~обра́лся, ~обрала́сь, ~обрало́сь *pf.* (*of ▶ подбира́ться*) **1** (*составиться, образоваться*) to get together, be formed **2** (к + *d.*) (*незаметно подойти*) to steal up (to), approach stealthily

под|огна́ть, гоню́, го́нишь, *past* ~огна́л, ~огнала́, ~огна́ло *pf.* (*of ▶ подгоня́ть*) **1** (к + *d.*) (*приблизить*) to drive (to) **2** (infml, *заставить идти быстрее*) to drive on, urge on, hurry **3** (к + *d.*) (*приспособить*) to adjust (to), fit (to)

под|огну́ть, огну́, огнёшь *pf.* (*of ▶ подгиба́ть*) to tuck in; to bend under

подогрева́|ть, ю *impf. of ▶ подогре́ть*

подогре́|ть, ю *pf.* (*of ▶ подогрева́ть*) to warm up, heat up

пододвига́|ть, ю *impf. of ▶ пододви́нуть*

пододви́|нуть, ну, нешь *pf.* (*of ▶ пододвига́ть*) (к + *d.*) to move up (to), push up (to)

пододея́льник, а *m.* blanket cover, duvet cover

подожд|а́ть, у́, ёшь, *past* ~а́л, ~ала́, ~а́ло *pf.* (+ *a. or g.*) to wait (for)

под|озва́ть, зову́, зовёшь, *past* ~озва́л, ~озвала́, ~озва́ло *pf.* (*of ▶ подзыва́ть*) to call over; (*жестом*) to beckon

подозрева́|ть, ю *impf.* (*no pf.*) to suspect (*sb or that sth is the case*); **я ~ю его́ в преступле́нии** I suspect him of a crime

подозре́ни|е, я *nt.* suspicion; **по ~ю** (в + *p.*) on suspicion (of); **быть под ~ем, на ~и** to be under suspicion

подозри́тел|ьный, ~ен, ~ьна *adj.* suspicious

подо|йти́, ю́, ~й́шь *pf. of* ▸ **дойти́**

⚡ **подо|йти́, йду́, йдёшь,** *past* ~шёл, ~шла́ *pf.* (*of* ▸ **подходи́ть**) **1** (к + *d.*) (*приблизиться*) to approach (also fig.); to come up (to), go up (to); **по́езд ~шёл к ста́нции** the train pulled in to the station **2** (*годиться*) (+ *d.*) to do (for); to suit; (*по размеру*) to fit

подоко́нник, а *m.* window sill

подо́лгу *adv.* for a long time; for ages; for long periods of time; **они́ п. не разгова́ривали друг с дру́гом** they had long periods of not speaking to each other

подо́н|ки *m. pl.* (*sg.* ~ок, ~ка) dregs (also fig.); (fig.) scum; riff-raff

подорв|а́ть, у́, ёшь, *past* ~а́л, ~ала́, ~а́ло *pf.* (*of* ▸ **подрыва́ть**) **1** to blow up **2** (fig.) to undermine; to damage severely; **п. здоро́вье** to damage one's health

подорожа́|ть, ю *pf. of* ▸ **дорожа́ть**

подо|сла́ть, шлю, шлёшь *pf.* (*of* ▸ **подсыла́ть**) to send, dispatch (*secretly*)

под|остла́ть, стелю́, сте́лешь *pf.* (*of* ▸ **подстила́ть**) (**под** + *a.*) to lay (under), stretch (under)

подоткн|у́ть, у́, ёшь *pf.* (*of* ▸ **подтыка́ть**) (infml) to tuck in, tuck up; **п. ю́бку** to tuck up one's skirt

подо́х|нуть, ну, нешь, *past* ~, ~ла *pf.* (*of* ▸ **до́хнуть**) **1** (*о живо́тных*) to die **2** (sl., pej., *о лю́дях*) to peg out, kick the bucket

подохо́дный *adj.*: **п. нало́г** income tax

подо́шв|а, ы *f.* sole

подпада́|ть, ю *impf. of* ▸ **подпа́сть**

подпа́|сть, ду́, дёшь, *past* ~л *pf.* (*of* ▸ **подпада́ть**) (**под** + *a.*) to fall (under); **п. под чьё-н. влия́ние** to fall under sb's influence

подпева́|ть, ю *impf. of* (+ *d.*) to join (in singing); (fig.) to echo

под|пере́ть, опру́, опрёшь, *past* ~пёр, ~пёрла *pf.* (*of* ▸ **подпира́ть**) to prop up

подпи́лива|ть, ю *impf. of* ▸ **подпили́ть**

подпил|и́ть, ю́, ~ишь *pf.* (*of* ▸ **подпи́ливать**) **1** (*подрезать пилой*) to saw; (*напильником*) to file **2** (*укоротить пилой*) to saw a little off; (*напильником*) to file down

подпира́|ть, ю *impf. of* ▸ **подпере́ть**

подпи|са́ть, шу́, ~шешь *pf.* (*of* ▸ **подпи́сывать**) **1** (*поставить подпись* (*на*)) to sign **2** (*включить в число подписчиков*) to subscribe

подпи|са́ться, шу́сь, ~шешься *pf.* (*of* ▸ **подпи́сываться**) **1** (**под** + *i.*) to sign; (fig., *согласиться*) to subscribe (to) **2** (**на** + *a.*)

subscribe (to, for); **п. на журна́л** to subscribe to a magazine

подпи́ск|а, и *f.* **1** (*на журнал*) subscription **2** (*письменное обязательство*) written undertaking; signed statement

подпи́счик, а *m.* (+ *g.*) subscriber (to)

подпи́сыва|ть, ю *impf. of* ▸ **подписа́ть**

подпи́сыва|ться, юсь *impf. of* ▸ **подписа́ться**

по́дпис|ь, и *f.* **1** signature; **поста́вить свою́ п.** (**под** + *i.*) to put one's signature (to) **2** (*надпись*) caption; inscription

подплыва́|ть, ю *impf. of* ▸ **подплы́ть**

подплы|ть, ву́, вёшь, *past* ~л, ~ла́, ~ло *pf.* (*of* ▸ **подплыва́ть**) **1** (к + *d.*) (*вплавь*) to swim up (to); (*на лодке*) to sail up (to) **2** (**под** + *a.*) to swim under

подполз|а́ть, а́ю *impf. of* ▸ **подползти́**

подполз|ти́, у́, ёшь, *past* ~, ~ла́ *pf.* (*of* ▸ **подполза́ть**) (к + *d.*) to creep up (to); to crawl up (to); (**под** + *a.*) to creep (under); to crawl (under)

подполко́вник, а *m.* lieutenant colonel

подпо́ль|е, я *nt.* (fig.) underground (*organization, activities*); **уйти́ в п.** to go underground

подпо́льный *adj.* underground (also fig.)

подпо́рк|а, и *f.* prop, support

подпо́р|тить, чу, тишь *pf.* (infml) to spoil slightly

подпоя́|саться, шусь, шешься *pf.* (*of* ▸ **подпоя́сываться**) to belt oneself; to put on a belt

подпоя́сыва|ться, юсь *impf. of* ▸ **подпоя́саться**

подпра́в|ить, лю, ишь *pf.* (*of* ▸ **подправля́ть**) to touch up

подправля́|ть, ю *impf. of* ▸ **подпра́вить**

подпры́гива|ть, ю *impf. of* ▸ **подпры́гнуть**

подпры́г|нуть, ну, нешь *pf.* (*of* ▸ **подпры́гивать**) to leap up, jump up

подпуска́|ть, ю *impf. of* ▸ **подпусти́ть**

подпу|сти́ть, щу́, ~стишь *pf.* (*of* ▸ **подпуска́ть**) to allow to approach; **п. на расстоя́ние вы́стрела** to allow to come within range

подраба́тыва|ть, ю *impf. of* ▸ **подрабо́тать**

подрабо́та|ть, ю *pf.* (*of* ▸ **подраба́тывать**) (infml, *ради дополнительного заработка*) to earn additionally

подра́внива|ть, ю *impf. of* ▸ **подровня́ть**

подража́|ть, ю *impf.* (*no pf.*) (+ *d.*) to imitate

подразде́л, а *m.* subsection

⚡ **подразделе́ни|е, я** *nt.* **1** subdivision **2** (mil.) subunit

подраздел|и́ть, ю́, и́шь *pf.* (*of* ▸ **подразделя́ть**) to subdivide

подразделя́|ть, яю *impf. of* ▸ **подраздели́ть**

подразумева́|ть, ю *impf.* to mean

подразумева́|ться, ется *impf.* to be implied, be meant

подраст|а́ть, а́ю *impf.* (*of* ▶ подрасти́):
~а́ющее поколе́ние the rising generation

подраст|и́, у́, ёшь, *past* **подро́с, подросла́**
pf. to grow (a little)

по|дра́ться, деру́сь, дерёшься, *past*
~дра́лся, ~драла́сь, ~драло́сь *pf. of*
▶ дра́ться 1

подре́|зать, жу, жешь *pf.* (*of* ▶ подреза́ть)
(*волосы*) to cut; (*ногти, куст*) to clip, trim;
(*деревья*) to prune, lop

подреза́|ть, ю *impf. of* ▶ подре́зать

подрис|ова́ть, у́ю *pf.* (*of* ▶ подрисо́вывать)
1 (*подправить*) to touch up **2** (*добавить*)
to add, put in (*on a painting, etc.*)

подрисо́выва|ть, ю *impf. of* ▶ подрисова́ть

подро́бно *adv.* minutely, in detail; at (great)
length

подро́бност|ь, и *f.* detail; вдава́ться в ~и
to go into detail; во всех ~ях in every detail

подро́б|ный, ~ен, ~на *adj.* detailed, minute

подровня́|ть, ю *pf.* (*of* ▶ подра́внивать)
(*сделать более ровным*) to level; (*бороду,
волосы*) to trim

подро́ст|ок, ка *m.* adolescent, teenager

подру́г|а, и *f.* (female) friend, girlfriend;
п. по шко́ле school friend

по-дру́жески *adv.* in a friendly way; as a
friend

подр|ужи́ться, ужу́сь, у́жишься *pf.* (с + *i.*)
to make friends (with)

подру́жк|а, и *f. affectionate dim. of*
▶ подру́га; п. неве́сты bridesmaid

подру́чн|ый *adj.* **1** (*инструмент*) at hand,
to hand; (*средства*) improvised, makeshift
2 (*as m. n.* п., ~ого) assistant, mate

подрыва́|ть, ю *impf. of* ▶ подорва́ть

подря́д¹ *adv.* in succession; running; on end;
три го́да п. three years running; не́сколько
дней п. шёл дождь it rained for days on end

подря́д², а *m.* contract; взять п. на постро́йку
плоти́ны to contract to build a dam

подря́дчик, а *m.* contractor

подса|ди́ть, жу́, ~дишь *pf.* (*of*
▶ подса́живать) **1** (в, на + *a.*) to help (into,
on to); п. кого́-н. на ло́шадь to help sb on to
a horse **2** (к + *d.*) to place next (to)

подса́жива|ть, ю *impf. of* ▶ подсади́ть

подса́жива|ться, юсь *impf. of* ▶ подсе́сть

подсве́чник, а *m.* candlestick

под|се́сть, ся́ду, ся́дешь, *past* ~се́л *pf.* (*of*
▶ подса́живаться) (к + *d.*) to sit down (near,
next to), take a seat (near, next to)

подска|за́ть, жу́, ~жешь *pf.* (*of*
▶ подска́зывать) (+ *d. and a.*) **1** (*напомнить*)
to prompt (sb with sth) (also fig.) **2** (*решение*)
to suggest

подска́зк|а, и *f.* prompt(ing)

подска́зыва|ть, ю *impf. of* ▶ подсказа́ть

подска́кива|ть, ю *impf. of* ▶ подскочи́ть

подскоч|и́ть, у́, ~ишь *pf.* (*of* ▶ подска́кивать)
1 (к + *d.*) to run up (to), come running (to)

2 to jump up, leap up; п. от ра́дости to jump
with joy; це́ны ~или (infml) prices soared

подслу́ш|ать, аю *pf.* (*of* ▶ подслу́шивать)
to overhear; to eavesdrop (on)

подслу́шива|ть, ю *impf. of* ▶ подслу́шать

подсма́трива|ть, ю *impf. of* ▶ подсмотре́ть

подсме́ива|ться, юсь *impf.* (над + *i.*) to
laugh (at), make fun (of)

подсмотр|е́ть, ю́, ~ишь *pf.* (*of*
▶ подсма́тривать) to spy

подсне́жник, а *m.* (bot.) snowdrop

подсо́выва|ть, ю *impf. of* ▶ подсу́нуть

подсоедин|и́ть, ю́, и́шь *pf.* (*of*
▶ подсоединя́ть) (*телефон*) to connect up;
(*стиральную машину*) to plumb in

подсоедин|я́ть, я́ю *impf. of* ▶ подсоедини́ть

подсозна́ни|е, я *nt.* the subconscious

подсозна́тельн|ый, ~ен, ~ьна *adj.*
subconscious

подсо́лнечник, а *m.* sunflower

подсо́лнечн|ый *adj. of* ▶ подсо́лнечник;
~ое ма́сло sunflower oil

подсо́лнух, а *m.* (infml) **1** (*цветок*)
sunflower **2** (*семена*) sunflower seeds

подста́в|ить, лю, ишь *pf.* (*of* ▶ подставля́ть)
1 (под + *a.*) to put (under); place (under);
п. го́лову под струю́ воды́ из кра́на to put
one's head under a tap **2** (fig.) to expose;
(infml, *поставить кого-л. в неприятное
положение*) to leave sb holding the baby
(BrE), bag (AmE)

подста́вк|а, и *f.* stand; (*для бутылки,
стакана*) coaster

подставля́|ть, ю *impf. of* ▶ подста́вить

подстерега́|ть, ю *impf. of* ▶ подстере́чь

подстере́|чь, гу́, жёшь, гу́т, *past* ~г, ~гла́
pf. (*of* ▶ подстерега́ть) to be on the watch
(for), lie in wait (for)

подстила́|ть, ю *impf. of* ▶ подостла́ть

подсти́лк|а, и *f.* bedding

подстра́ива|ть, ю *impf. of* ▶ подстро́ить

подстрах|ова́ть, у́ю *pf.* (*of*
▶ подстрахо́вывать) **1** (*гимнаста*) to stand
by ready to help **2** (fig.) to (take measures
to) protect; to provide with additional
insurance

подстрахо́выва|ть, ю *impf. of*
▶ подстрахова́ть

подстрек|а́ть, а́ю *impf.* (к + *d. or* на + *a.*) to
incite (to)

подстре́лива|ть, ю *impf. of* ▶ подстрели́ть

подстрел|и́ть, ю́, ~ишь *pf.* (*of*
▶ подстре́ливать) to wound (*by a shot*); to
wing

подстрига́|ть, ю *impf. of* ▶ подстри́чь

подстрига́|ться, юсь *impf. of* ▶ подстри́чься

подстри́|чь, гу́, жёшь, гу́т, *past* ~г, ~гла
pf. (*of* ▶ подстрига́ть) (*волосы, ногти,
газон*) to cut, trim; (*дерево*) to prune

подстри́|чься, гу́сь, жёшься, гу́тся, *past*
~гся, ~глась *pf.* (*of* ▶ подстрига́ться) to
trim one's hair; to have a haircut

подстро́|ить, ю, ишь *pf.* (*of* ▶ **подстра́ивать**) (infml) to contrive; (pej.) to arrange; **э́то де́ло** ∼**ено** it's a put-up job

подступ|а́ть, а́ю *impf. of* ▶ **подступи́ть**

подступ|а́ться, а́юсь *impf. of* ▶ **подступи́ться**

подступ|и́ть, лю́, ∼ишь *pf.* (*of* ▶ **подступа́ть**) (к + *d.*) to approach, come up (to), come near; **слёзы** ∼**и́ли к её глаза́м** tears came to her eyes

подступ|и́ться, лю́сь, ∼ишься *pf.* (*of* ▶ **подступа́ться**) (к + *d.*) to approach

подсуди́м|ый, ого *m.* (law) defendant; the accused

подсу́н|уть, у, ешь *pf.* (*of* ▶ **подсо́вывать**) **1** (под + *a.*) to shove (under) **2** (+ *d. and a.*) (infml) to slip (into); to palm off (on, upon); **они́ мне** ∼**ули не ту кни́гу** they palmed off the wrong book on me

подсу́шива|ть, ю *impf. of* ▶ **подсуши́ть**

подсуш|и́ть, у́, ∼ишь *pf.* (*of* ▶ **подсу́шивать**) to dry a little

подсчёт, а *m.* calculation; count

подсыла́|ть, ю *impf. of* ▶ **подосла́ть**

подсы́п|ать, лю, лешь *pf.* (*of* ▶ **подсыпа́ть**) (+ *a. or g.*) to add, pour in

подсыпа́|ть, а́ю *impf. of* ▶ **подсы́пать**

подта́скива|ть, ю *impf. of* ▶ **подтащи́ть**

подтащ|и́ть, у́, ∼ишь *pf.* (*of* ▶ **подта́скивать**) (к + *d.*) to drag up (to)

подтвер|ди́ть, жу́, ди́шь *pf.* (*of* ▶ **подтвержда́ть**) to confirm; to corroborate, bear out; **п. получе́ние чего́-н.** to acknowledge receipt of sth

подтвер|ди́ться, ди́тся *pf.* (*of* ▶ **подтвержда́ться**) to be confirmed

✍ **подтвержда́|ть, ю, ет** *impf. of* ▶ **подтверди́ть**

подтвержда́|ться, ется *impf. of* ▶ **подтверди́ться**

подтвержде́ни|е, я *nt.* confirmation; corroboration

подтыка́|ть, ю *impf. of* ▶ **подоткну́ть**

подтя́гива|ть, ю *impf. of* ▶ **подтяну́ть**

подтя́гива|ться, юсь *impf. of* ▶ **подтяну́ться**

подтя́ж|ки, ек (*no sg.*) braces (BrE); suspenders (AmE)

подтя́н|уть, у́, ∼нешь *pf.* (*of* ▶ **подтя́гивать**) **1** (*пояс*) to tighten **2** (к + *d.*) (*подтащи́ть*) to pull up (to), haul up (to); **п. ло́дку к бе́регу** to haul up a boat on shore **3** (mil.) to bring up, move up **4** (fig., infml, *ученика*) to take in hand, pull up, chase up

подтя́н|уться, у́сь, ∼нешься *pf.* (*of* ▶ **подтя́гиваться**) **1** to gird oneself more tightly; **п. по́ясом** to tighten one's belt **2** (*на перекла́дине*) to pull oneself up (*on gymnastic apparatus, etc.*) **3** (mil.) to move up, move in **4** (fig., infml, *об ученике*) to pull oneself together, take oneself in hand

✍ **поду́ма|ть, ю** *pf.* **1** *pf. of* ▶ **ду́мать**; **п. (то́лько)!** just think!; ∼**ешь!** (*as int.*) (infml, iron.) I say!; what do you know?; **мо́жно п.** one might think **2** (*немно́го*) to think a little,

for a while

по-дура́цки *adv.* (infml) foolishly, like a fool

поду́|ть, ю, ешь *pf.* **1** *pf. of* ▶ **дуть 2** (*нача́ть ду́ть*) to begin to blow

подуш|и́ться, у́сь, ∼ишься *pf.* to put some perfume on

поду́шк|а, и *f.* (*в посте́ли*) pillow; (*дива́нная*) cushion

подхали́м, а *m.* toady

подхва|ти́ть, чу́, ∼тишь *pf.* (*of* ▶ **подхва́тывать**) to catch (up); to pick up; to take up; **п. на́сморк** to catch, pick up a cold; **п. пе́сню** to catch up a melody, join in a song

подхва́тыва|ть, ю *impf. of* ▶ **подхвати́ть**

подхлест|ну́ть, ну́, нёшь *pf.* (*of* ▶ **подхлёстывать**) to whip up (also fig., infml)

подхлёстыва|ть, ю *impf. of* ▶ **подхлестну́ть**

✍ **подхо́д, а** *m.* approach

✍ **подхо|ди́ть, жу́, ∼дишь** *impf. of* ▶ **подойти́**

подходя́щий *pres. part. of* ▶ **подходи́ть** *and adj.* suitable, appropriate; **п. моме́нт** the right moment

подцеп|и́ть, лю́, ∼ишь *pf.* (*of* ▶ **подцепля́ть**) (infml) to hook on, couple on; (fig., joc., *де́вушку*) to pick up; **п. на́сморк** to pick up a cold

подцепля́|ть, ю *impf. of* ▶ **подцепи́ть**

подча́с *adv.* sometimes, at times

✍ **подчёркива|ть, ю** *impf. of* ▶ **подчеркну́ть**

подчерк|ну́ть, ну́, нёшь *pf.* (*of* ▶ **подчёркивать**) **1** to underline **2** (fig.) to emphasize, stress

подчине́ни|е, я *nt.* subordination; submission; subjection; **быть в** ∼**и** (у + *g.*) to be subordinate (to)

подчин|ённый 1 *p.p.p. of* ▶ **подчини́ть**; (+ *d.*) under, under the command (of) **2** *adj.* subordinate; (*as m. n.* **п.**, ∼**ённого**) subordinate

подчин|и́ть, ю́, и́шь *pf.* (*of* ▶ **подчиня́ть**) (+ *d.*) to subordinate (to), subject (to); to place under the command (of); **п. свое́й во́ле** to bend to one's will

подчин|и́ться, ю́сь, и́шься *pf.* (*of* ▶ **подчиня́ться**) (+ *d.*) to submit (to); **п. прика́зу** to obey an order

подчин|я́ть, я́ю *impf. of* ▶ **подчини́ть**

подчин|я́ться, я́юсь *impf. of* ▶ **подчини́ться**

подшива́|ть, ю *impf. of* ▶ **подши́ть**

подши́пник, а *m.* (tech.) bearing

под|ши́ть, ошью́, ошьёшь *pf.* (*of* ▶ **подшива́ть**) **1** (*приши́ть*) to sew on, in; (*пла́тье, плато́к*) to hem; (*с изна́нки*) to line; (*о́бувь*) to sole **2** (*бума́ги*) to file

подшу|ти́ть, чу́, ∼тишь *pf.* (*of* ▶ **подшу́чивать**) (над + *i.*) to make fun of; to mock; to play a trick (on)

подшу́чива|ть, ю *impf. of* ▶ **подшути́ть**

подъ...[1] *vbl. pref.* = **под...**[1]

подъ...[2] *as pref. of nn. and adjs.* = **под...**[2]

подъе́зд, а *m.* **1** (*вход*) entrance, doorway **2** (*к реке́*) approach(es)

п

подъезжа́|ть, ю *impf. of* ▶ подъе́хать
подъём, а *m.* **1** (*груза*) lifting; (*флага*) raising **2** (*в гору*) ascent **3** (aeron.) climb **4** (fig., *рост, развитие*) development; rise; **промы́шленный п.** boom, upsurge **5** (fig.) elan; enthusiasm, animation; **говори́ть с больши́м ~ом** to speak with great animation
подъёмник, а *m.* lift (BrE), elevator (AmE); hoist
подъёмн|ый *adj.* **1** lifting; **п. кран** crane; **~ое окно́** sash window **2**: **п. мост** drawbridge
подъе́|хать, ду, дешь *pf.* (*of* ▶ подъезжа́ть) (**к** + *d.*) to drive up (to), draw up (to)
подыгр|а́ть, а́ю *pf.* (*of* ▶ поды́грывать) (+ *d.*) (infml) **1** (mus.) to accompany **2** (theatr.) to play up (to)
поды́грыва|ть, ю *impf. of* ▶ подыгра́ть
поды|ска́ть, щу́, ~щешь *pf.* (*of* ▶ поды́скивать) to find
поды́скива|ть, ю *impf.* (*of* ▶ подыска́ть) to seek, try to find
подыха́|ть, ю *impf. of* ▶ подо́хнуть
подыш|а́ть, у́, ~ишь *pf.* to breathe; **вы́йти п. све́жим во́здухом** to go out for a breath of fresh air
поеда́|ть, ю *impf. of* ▶ пое́сть 3
поеди́н|ок, ка *m.* duel
по́езд, а, *pl.* ~а́ *m.* train; **~ом** by train; **п. да́льнего сле́дования** long-distance train
⚹ **пое́здк|а**, и *f.* trip, excursion, outing, tour
по|е́сть, е́м, е́шь, е́ст, еди́м, еди́те, едя́т, *past* ~е́л *pf.* **1** (*pf. only*) to eat (up) **2** (*pf. only*) (*немно́го*) to eat a little; to take some food, have a bite **3** (impf. ~еда́ть) (*о кро́ликах, насеко́мых*) to eat, devour
пое́|хать, ду, дешь *pf.* (*of* ▶ е́хать) to go (*in or on a vehicle or on an animal*); (*отпра́виться*) to set off, depart; **~хали!** (infml) let's go!
пожале́|ть, ю *pf. of* ▶ жале́ть
пожа́л|оваться, уюсь *pf. of* ▶ жа́ловаться
пожа́луй *adv.* perhaps; very likely; it may be
⚹ **пожа́луйста** *particle* **1** (*при про́сьбе*) please; **сади́тесь, п.!** please sit down! **2** (*при согла́сии*) certainly!, by all means!, with pleasure! (*or not translated*) **переда́йте мне, п., кни́гу!** — **п.** would you mind passing me the book? — there you are **3** (*в ответ на «спаси́бо»*) don't mention it; not at all
пожа́р, а *m.* fire
пожа́рить *pf. of* ▶ жа́рить
пожа́рник, а *m.* (infml) fireman, firefighter
пожа́р|ный *adj. of* ▶ пожа́р; **~ная кома́нда** fire brigade; **~ная ле́стница** fire escape; **~ная маши́на** fire engine; (*as m. n.* **п.**, **~ного**) fireman, firefighter
по|жа́ть, жму, жмёшь *pf.* (*of* ▶ пожима́ть) to press, squeeze; **п. ру́ку** (+ *d.*) to shake hands (with); **п. плеча́ми** to shrug one's shoulders

пожела́ни|е, я *nt.* wish, desire
пожела́|ть, ю *pf. of* ▶ жела́ть
пожелте́|ть, ю *pf. of* ▶ желте́ть
пожен|и́ться, ~имся *pf.* (*pl. used only*) to get married (*of two people*)
поже́ртвовани|е, я *nt.* donation
поже́ртв|овать, ую *pf. of* ▶ же́ртвовать
пожива́|ть, ю *impf.*: **как (вы) ~ете?** how are you (getting on)?
пожи́зненн|ый, ~, ~на *adj.* life(long); for life; **~ное заключе́ние** life imprisonment
пожило́й *adj.* elderly
пожима́|ть, ю *impf. of* ▶ пожа́ть
пожира́|ть, ю *impf. of* ▶ пожра́ть
пожи́тк|и, ов (*no sg.*) (infml) belongings; (one's) things
по|жи́ть, живу́, живёшь, *past* ~жил, ~жила́, ~жило *pf.* to live (*for a time*); to stay; **мы ~жили три го́да в Ки́еве** we lived for three years in Kiev
пожм|у́, ёшь *see* ▶ пожа́ть
пожр|а́ть, у́, ёшь, *past* ~а́л, ~ала́, ~а́ло *pf.* (*of* ▶ пожира́ть) to devour
по́з|а, ы *f.* pose, attitude, posture; (fig.) pose; **приня́ть каку́ю-н. ~у** to strike an attitude, adopt a pose
позаба́в|ить, лю, ишь *pf.* to amuse a little
позаба́в|иться, люсь, ишься *pf.* to amuse oneself a little
позабо́|титься, чусь, тишься *pf. of* ▶ забо́титься
позабыва́|ть, ю *impf. of* ▶ позабы́ть
позаб|ы́ть, у́ду, у́дешь *pf.* (*of* ▶ позабыва́ть) (+ *a.* or о + *p.*) (infml) to forget (about)
позави́д|овать, ую *pf. of* ▶ зави́довать
поза́втрака|ть, ю *pf. of* ▶ за́втракать
позавчера́ *adv.* the day before yesterday
позади́[1] *adv.* behind; **оста́вить п.** to leave behind; **все пробле́мы п.** all our/your problems are in the past; all our/your problems are behind us/you
позади́[2] *prep.* + *g.* behind
позаи́мств|овать, ую *pf. of* ▶ заи́мствовать
позапро́шлый *adj.* before last; **п. год** the year before last
по|зва́ть, зову́, зовёшь, *past* ~зва́л, ~звала́, ~зва́ло *pf. of* ▶ звать 2
⚹ **позво́л|ить**, ю, ишь *pf.* (*of* ▶ позволя́ть) (+ *d.* of person and inf., + *a.* of inanimate object) to allow, permit; **п. себе́** (+ *inf.*) to venture, take the liberty (of); (+ *a.*) to be able to afford; **п. себе́ сде́лать замеча́ние** to venture a remark; **~ь(те)** (*ве́жливая фо́рма обраще́ния с про́сьбой*): **~ьте предста́вить до́ктора X.** allow me to introduce Doctor X.; (*выраже́ния несогла́сия, возраже́ния*): **~ьте, что э́то зна́чит?** excuse me, what does that mean?
⚹ **позвол|я́ть**, я́ю *impf. of* ▶ позво́лить
позвон|и́ть, ю́, и́шь *pf. of* ▶ звони́ть
позвоно́чник, а *m.* (anat.) spine, backbone
позвоно́чно|е, го *nt.* (zool.) vertebrate

⚹ key word

поздне́е *comp. of* ▸ по́здний, ▸ по́здно; later

поздне́йший *adj.* (*бо́лее по́здний*) later; (*са́мый по́здний*) latest

ꝏ **по́здн|ий** *adj.* late; **до ~ей но́чи** until late at night, late into the night; **~о it is late**

по́здно *adv.* late

поздоро́ва|ться, юсь *pf. of* ▸ здоро́ваться

поздра́в|ить, лю, ишь *pf.* (*of* ▸ поздравля́ть) (**c** + *i.*) to congratulate (on, upon); **п. кого́-н. с Но́вым го́дом** to wish sb a happy New Year

поздравле́ни|е, я *nt.* congratulation, greeting(s)

поздравля́|ть, ю *impf. of* ▸ поздра́вить

позелене́|ть, ю *pf. of* ▸ зелене́ть 1

по́зже *comp. of* ▸ по́здний, ▸ по́здно; later (on)

пози́р|овать, ую *impf.* (+ *d.*) to pose (for)

позити́в|ный, ~ен, ~на *adj.* positive

ꝏ **пози́ци|я, и** *f.* position

познако́м|ить, лю, ишь *pf. of* ▸ знако́мить

познако́м|иться, люсь, ишься *pf. of* ▸ знако́миться

позна́ни|е, я *nt.* (*phil.*) cognition; **тео́рия ~я** epistemology 2 (*in pl.*) knowledge

позоло́т|а, ы *f.* gilding, gilt

позо́р, а *m.* shame, disgrace

позо́р|ить, ю, ишь *impf.* (*of* ▸ опозо́рить) to disgrace

позо́р|иться, юсь, ишься *impf.* (*of* ▸ опозо́риться) to disgrace oneself

позо́р|ный, ~ен, ~на *adj.* shameful, disgraceful; ignominious

поигра́|ть, ю *pf.* to have a game, play a little

пойм́к|а, и *f.* capture

по-ино́му *adv.* differently, in a different way

поинтерес|ова́ться, у́юсь *pf.* (+ *i.*) to be curious (about); to display interest (in); **он ~ова́лся узна́ть, кто вы** he was curious to find out who you are

ꝏ **по́иск, а** *m.* (*comput.*) search; (*in pl.*) search; **в ~ах** (+ *g.*) in search (of), in quest (of)

пои|ска́ть, щу́, ~щешь *pf.* to look for, search for; **~щи́те хороше́нько** have a good look

поиско́в|ый *adj.*: **~ая систе́ма/маши́на** (*comput.*) search engine

пои́стине *adv.* indeed, in truth

по|и́ть, ю́, ~и́шь *impf.* (*of* ▸ напои́ть) to give to drink; (*скот*) to water; **п. вино́м** to treat to wine

по|ищу́, и́щешь *see* ▸ поиска́ть

пой|ду́, дёшь *see* ▸ пойти́

пойма́|ть, ю *pf. of* ▸ лови́ть

пойм|у́, ёшь *see* ▸ поня́ть

ꝏ **пой|ти́, ду́, дёшь,** *past* **пошёл, пошла́** *pf.* 1 *pf. of* ▸ идти́, ▸ ходи́ть; **пошёл вон!** be off!; off with you! 2 (*нача́ть ходи́ть*) to begin to (be able to) walk 3 (**в** + *a.*) to take after; **он пошёл в отца́** he takes after his father

ꝏ **пока́**[1] *adv.* for the present, for the time being; **п. что** (infml) in the meanwhile; **п.!** (infml) bye!

ꝏ **пока́**[2] *conj.* 1 while; **нам на́до попроси́ть его́, п. он тут** we must ask him while he is here

2: **п. не** until, till, before; **п. (ещё) не по́здно** before it's too late

ꝏ **показа́тел|ь, я** *m.* 1 indicator; index 2 (*math.*) exponent, index

показа́тел|ьный, ~ен, ~ьна *adj.* 1 (*характе́рный*) significant; instructive, revealing 2 (*образцо́вый*) model; demonstration; **п. проце́сс** show trial; **п. уро́к** object lesson 3 (*math.*) exponential

ꝏ **пока|за́ть, жу́, ~жешь** *pf.* (*of* ▸ пока́зывать) 1 to show; to display, reveal; **п. свои́ зна́ния** to display one's knowledge 2 (*о прибо́ре*) to show, register, read 3 (**на** + *a.*) to point (at, to)

пока|за́ться, жу́сь, ~жешься *pf.* 1 *pf. of* ▸ каза́ться 2 (*pf. of* ▸ пока́зываться) to show oneself; to appear; to come in sight; **из-за облако́в ~за́лась луна́** the moon appeared from behind the clouds; **п. врачу́** to see a doctor 3 *pass. of* ▸ показа́ть

показно́й *adj.* (*сочу́вствие*) affected; (*ро́скошь*) ostentatious

ꝏ **пока́зыва|ть, ю** *impf. of* ▸ показа́ть

пока́зыва|ться, юсь, ешься *impf. of* ▸ показа́ться

покара́|ть, ю *pf. of* ▸ кара́ть

поката́|ть[1]**, ю** *pf.* to roll

поката́|ть[2]**, ю** *pf.* to take for a drive; **п. дете́й на са́нках** to take children tobogganing

поката́|ться, юсь *pf.* to go for a drive; **п. на ло́дке** to go out boating

пока|ти́ть, чу́, ~тишь *pf.* 1 *pf. of* ▸ кати́ть 2 (*мяч*) to start (rolling), set rolling

пока|ти́ться, чу́сь, ~тишься *pf.* 1 *pf. of* ▸ кати́ться 2 (*нача́ть кати́ться*) to start rolling

пока́чива|ться, юсь *impf.* to rock slightly; **идти́ ~ясь** to walk unsteadily

пока́шлива|ть, ю *impf.* to have a slight cough; to cough intermittently

покая́ни|е, я *nt.* 1 (*eccl., испо́ведь*) confession 2 (*раска́яние*) penitence, repentance; **принести́ п.** (**в** + *p.*) to repent (of)

пока́|яться, юсь, ешься *pf. of* ▸ ка́яться

по́кер, а *m.* poker (*card game*)

покида́|ть, ю *impf. of* ▸ поки́нуть

поки́нутый *p.p.p. of* ▸ поки́нуть *and adj.* deserted, abandoned

поки́|нуть, ну, нешь *pf.* (*of* ▸ покида́ть) to leave; to desert, abandon, forsake

покла́дист|ый, ~, ~а *adj.* complaisant, obliging

покло́н, а *m.* bow

поклон|и́ться, ю́сь, ~ишься *pf. of* ▸ кла́няться

покло́нник, а *m.* admirer; fan

покло́нни|ца, цы *f. of* ▸ покло́нник

поклоня́|ться, юсь *impf.* (+ *d.*) to worship

покля́|сться, ну́сь, нёшься *pf. of* ▸ кля́сться

поко́|й, я *m.* rest, peace; **оста́вить в ~e** to leave in peace; **уйти́ на п., удали́ться на п.** to retire

поко́йник, а *m.* the deceased

П

покойни|ца, цы *f. of* ▸ покойник

покойн|ый *adj. (умерший)* (the) late; (*as n.* **п., ~ого,** *f.* **~ая, ~ой**) the deceased

поколеб|а́ть, ~лю, ~лешь *pf. of* ▸ колебать

поколеб|а́ться, ~лю́сь, ~лешься *pf.* **1** *pf. of* ▸ колеба́ться **2** to waver (for a time), hesitate (for a time)

⚘ **поколе́ни|е, я** *nt.* generation

поколо|ти́ть, чу́, ~тишь *pf. of* ▸ колоти́ть 2

поко́нч|ить, у, ишь *pf.* (с + *i.*) **1** *(завершить)* to finish off; to finish (with), be through (with), have done (with); **с э́тим ~ено** that's done with **2** *(уничтожить)* to put an end (to); to do away (with); **п. жизнь самоубийством** to commit suicide

покоре́ни|е, я *nt.* conquest

покори́тел|ь, я *m.* conqueror

покор|и́ть, ю́, и́шь *pf.* (*of* ▸ покоря́ть) to conquer, subdue

покор|и́ться, ю́сь, и́шься *pf.* (*of* ▸ покоря́ться) (+ *d.*) to submit (to); to resign oneself (to); **п. свое́й у́части** to resign oneself to one's lot

покорм|и́ть, лю́, ~ишь *pf. of* ▸ корми́ть 1

поко́р|ный, ~ен, ~на *adj.* (+ *d.*) submissive (to), obedient; **п. судьбе́** resigned to one's fate

покор|я́ть, я́ю *impf. of* ▸ покори́ть

покор|я́ться, я́юсь *impf. of* ▸ покори́ться

поко|си́ться, шу́сь, си́шься *pf. of* ▸ коси́ться

покра́|сить, шу, сишь *pf. of* ▸ кра́сить

покра́|ситься, шусь, сишься *pf. of* ▸ кра́ситься

покрасне́|ть, ю *pf. of* ▸ красне́ть

покрови́тел|ь, я *m.* patron, protector

покрови́тельниц|а, ы *f.* patroness, protectress

покрови́тельствен|ный, ~, ~на *adj.* **1** protective; **~ная окра́ска** (zool.) protective colouring **2** *(снисходительный)* condescending, patronizing

покрови́тельств|о, а *nt.* protection, patronage; **под ~ом** (+ *g.*) under the patronage (of), under the auspices (of)

покрыва́л|о, а *nt.* **1** *(кусок ткани)* cover; *(на кровать)* bedspread, counterpane **2** shawl; *(вуаль)* veil

покрыва́|ть, ю *impf. of* ▸ покры́ть

покрыва́|ться, юсь *impf. of* ▸ покры́ться

⚘ **покры́ти|е, я** *nt.* **1** covering; **п. доро́ги** road surfacing; **п. кры́ши** roofing **2** *(возмещение)* covering, discharge, payment; **п. расхо́дов** defrayment of expenses

покр|ы́ть, о́ю, о́ешь *pf.* (*of* ▸ покрыва́ть) **1** to cover; **п. кра́ской** to coat with paint; **п. ла́ком** to varnish, lacquer; **п. позо́ром** to cover with shame **2** *(возместить)* to meet, pay off; **п. расхо́ды** to cover expenses, defray expenses **3** *(расстояние)* to cover

покр|ы́ться, о́юсь, о́ешься *pf.* (*of* ▸ покрыва́ться) (+ *i.*) **1** *(накрыть себя)* to cover sb (with) **2** *(заполниться, усеяться)* to be, get covered (with)

покры́шк|а, и *f.* tyre (BrE), tire (AmE)

⚘ **покупа́тел|ь, я** *m. (дома, машины)* buyer, purchaser; *(в магазине)* customer

покупа́тель|ница, ницы *f. of* ▸ покупа́тель

⚘ **покупа́|ть, ю** *impf. of* ▸ купи́ть

⚘ **поку́пк|а, и** *f.* **1** *(действие)* buying; purchasing, purchase **2** *(вещь)* purchase; **вы́годная п.** bargain; **де́лать ~и** to go shopping

покур|и́ть, ю́, ~ишь *pf.* **1** *pf. of* ▸ кури́ть **2** to have a smoke; **дава́й ~им** let's have a smoke

покуса́|ть, ю *pf.* to bite; *(о пчёлах)* to sting

поку|си́ться, шу́сь, си́шься *pf.* (*of* ▸ покуша́ться) (на + *a.*) **1** *(попытаться сделать что-н.)* to attempt, make an attempt (upon) **2** *(попытаться завладеть чем-н.)* to encroach (on, upon)

поку́ша|ть, ю *pf. of* ▸ ку́шать

покуша́|ться, юсь *impf. of* ▸ покуси́ться

покуше́ни|е, я *nt.* attempt; **п. на жизнь** (+ *g.*) *or* **п. на** (+ *a.*) attempt upon the life (of)

⚘ **пол¹, а, о ~е, на/в ~у́,** *pl.* **~ы́** *m.* floor

⚘ **пол², а,** *pl.* **~ы́, ~о́в** *m.* sex; **обо́его ~а** of both sexes

пол... *comb. form, abbr. of* ▸ полови́на; half; **полчаса́** half an hour; **полдеся́того** half past nine

⚘ **полага́|ть, ю** *impf.* to suppose, think; **на́до п.** it is to be supposed; one must suppose

полага́|ться, юсь *impf.* **1** *impf. of* ▸ положи́ться **2** *(impers.):* **~ется** one is supposed (to) **3:** **~ется** (+ *d.*) to be due (to)

пола́|дить, жу, дишь *pf.* (с + *i.*) to come to an understanding (with); to get on (with)

полве́ка, полуве́ка *m.* half a century

полго́да, полуго́да *m.* half a year, six months

по́лдень, полу́дня *and* **по́лдня** *m.* noon, midday; **за́ полдень** past noon; **к полу́дню** towards noon

по́лдник, а *m.* (afternoon) snack

полдоро́г|и *f.* halfway; **останови́ться на ~е** to stop halfway (also fig.)

⚘ **по́л|е, я,** *pl.* **~я́, ~е́й** *nt.* **1** field; **п. би́твы, п. сраже́ния** battlefield; **п. зре́ния** field of vision **2** (art) ground; (heraldry) field **3** (*in pl.*) *(чистая полоса)* margin **4** (*in pl.*) *(шляпы)* brim

полев|о́й *adj.* (bot., mil.) field; **п. команди́р** warlord; **~ы́е усло́вия** field conditions; **~ы́е цветы́** wild flowers

⚘ **поле́з|ный, ~ен, ~на** *adj.* useful; helpful; *(пища)* wholesome, health-giving; **чем могу́ быть ~ен?** can I help you?

поле́з|ть, у, ешь, *past* **~, ~ла** *pf.* **1** *pf. of* ▸ лезть **2** *(начать лезть)* to start to climb

поле́мик|а, и *f.* polemic(s); dispute, controversy

⚘ key word

полени́|ться, ю́сь, ∼ишься *pf.* (+ *inf.*) to be too lazy to

поле́н|о, а, *pl.* ∼ья, ∼ьев *nt.* log

полёт, а *m.* flight; flying; **вид с высоты́ пти́чьего** ∼а bird's-eye view; **п. фанта́зии** flight of fancy

поле|те́ть, чу́, ти́шь *pf.* **1** *pf. of* ▸ **лете́ть 2** (*нача́ть лете́ть*) to start to fly; to fly off

по-ле́тнему *adv.* as in summer, as for summer; **оде́т п.** (dressed) in summer clothes

полеч|и́ть, у́, ∼ишь *pf.* to treat (*for a while*)

полеч|и́ться, у́сь, ∼ишься *pf.* to undergo treatment (*for a while*)

пол|е́чь, я́гу, я́жешь, я́гут, *past* ∼ёг, ∼егла́ *pf.* **1** to lie down (*in numbers*) **2** (fig., *поги́бнуть*) to fall, be killed (*in numbers*)

по́лз|ать, аю *impf., indet. of* ▸ **ползти́**

ползт|и́, у́, ёшь, *past* ∼, ∼ла́ *impf.* **1** to crawl, creep (along); **по́езд** ∼ the train was crawling **2** (*о жи́дкости*) to ooze (out)

полиартри́т, а *m.* (med.) polyarthritis

полива́|ть, ю *impf. of* ▸ **поли́ть**

полива́|ться, юсь *impf. of* ▸ **поли́ться**

поли́вк|а, и *f.* watering

полигло́т, а *m.* polyglot

полиго́н, а *m.* (mil.) (artillery *or* bombing) range; **испыта́тельный п.** proving ground, testing area

полигра́фи|я, и *f.* printing

поликли́ник|а, и *f.* clinic; health centre (BrE), center (AmE)

полинези́|ец, йца *m.* Polynesian

полинези́й|ка, ки *f.* ▸ **полинези́ец**

полинези́йский *adj.* Polynesian

Полине́зи|я, и *f.* Polynesia

полиня́|ть, ет *pf. of* ▸ **линя́ть**

поли́п, а *m.* (zool., med.) polyp

полир|ова́ть, у́ю *impf.* (*of* ▸ **отполирова́ть**) to polish

по́лис, а *m.* policy; **страхово́й п.** insurance policy

полистиро́л, а *m.* polystyrene

политехни́ческий *adj.*: **п. институ́т** polytechnic

политзаключённ|ый, ого *m.* political prisoner

поли́тик, а *m.* politician

⚬ **поли́тик|а, и** *f.* **1** policy; **проводи́ть** ∼у to carry out a policy **2** (*нау́ка*) politics; **п. си́лы** power politics

⚬ **полити́ческ|ий** *adj.* political; **п. де́ятель** political figure, politician; ∼ая корре́ктность political correctness; ∼ое убе́жище political asylum

полито́лог, а *m.* political scientist

политоло́ги|я, и *f.* political science

политтехно́лог, а *m.* spin doctor

пол|и́ть, ью́, ьёшь, *past* ∼и́л, ∼ила́, ∼и́ло *pf.* (*impf.* ▸ **полива́ть**) **1** (+ *a. and i.*) (*смочи́ть*) to pour (on, upon); **п. цветы́** to water the flowers **2** (*no impf.*) (*нача́ть*

лить) to begin to pour

пол|и́ться, ью́сь, ьёшься, *past* ∼и́лся, ∼ила́сь *pf.* (*of* ▸ **полива́ться**) **1** (+ *i.*) (*поли́ть себя́*) to pour over oneself **2** (*нача́ть ли́ться*) to begin to flow

полице́йск|ий *adj.* police; **п. уча́сток** police station; (*as m. n.* **п.,** ∼**ого**) policeman, police officer

поли́ци|я, и *f.* police

полиэтиле́н, а *m.* polythene

полк, á, о ∼**é, в** ∼**ý** *m.* regiment

по́лк|а, и *f.* **1** shelf; **кни́жная п.** bookshelf **2** (*в по́езде*) berth

полко́вник, а *m.* colonel

полково́д|ец, ца *m.* commander; military leader

поллино́з, а *m.* hay fever

пол-ли́тра, полули́тра *m.* half a litre (BrE), liter (AmE)

полне́йший *adj.* sheer, utter(most)

полне́|ть, ю *impf.* (*of* ▸ **пополне́ть**) to grow stout, put on weight

полно́ *adv.* (+ *g.*) (infml) lots; **в ко́мнате полно́ наро́ду** the room is packed with people

полнолу́ни|е, я *nt.* full moon

полномо́чи|е, я *nt.* authority, power; (law) proxy; **превыше́ние** ∼**й** exceeding one's commission; **дать** ∼**я** (+ *d.*) to empower

полнопра́в|ный, ∼ен, ∼на *adj.* enjoying full rights; **п. член** full member

⚬ **по́лностью** *adv.* fully, in full; completely

полнот|á, ы́ (*no pl.*) *f.* **1** fullness, completeness; **п. вла́сти** absolute power **2** (*ту́чность*) stoutness, corpulence

полноце́н|ный, ∼ен, ∼на *adj.* proper; fully fledged (BrE), full fledged (AmE)

по́лночь, полу́ночи *and* **по́лночи** *f.* midnight; **за́ п.** after midnight

⚬ **по́л|ный, ∼он, ∼на́, ∼но́** *adj.* **1** (+ *g. or i.*) (*напо́лненный*) full (of); (*соверше́нный*) complete, entire, total; absolute; **п. карма́н** (+ *g.*) a pocketful (of); ∼**ное собра́ние сочине́ний** complete works; **в** ∼**ной ме́ре** fully, in full measure; **на** ∼**ном ходу́** at full speed **2** (*то́лстый*) stout, portly; plump

по́ло *nt. indecl.* (sport) polo; **во́дное п.** water polo

полови́к, á *m.* mat; long narrow carpet, runner

⚬ **полови́н|а, ы** *f.* half; **два с** ∼**ой** two and a half; **п. шесто́го** half past five; **во второ́й** ∼**е дня** in the afternoon

полови́к, а *m.* ladle

полово́дь|е, я *nt.* flood, high water (*at time of spring thaw*)

полов|о́й *adj.* sexual; ∼**ая зре́лость** puberty; ∼**ые о́рганы** genitals, sexual organs; ∼**ая связь** sexual intercourse

поло́г|ий, ∼, ∼а *adj.* gently sloping

⚬ **положе́ни|е, я** *nt.* **1** (*местонахожде́ние*) position; whereabouts **2** (*те́ла*) position; posture; attitude; **в сидя́чем** ∼**и** in a sitting position **3** (*состоя́ние*) position; condition, state; situation; (*социа́льное*) status;

п

(обстоя́тельство) circumstances; семе́йное п. marital status; вое́нное п. martial law; чрезвыча́йное п. state of emergency; п. веще́й state of affairs; вы́ходить из ~я to find a way out

поло́женный adj. agreed, appointed; в п. час at the appointed hour

поло́жено pred. (impers.) one is supposed to, it is customary; э́того де́лать не п. one is not supposed to do that

поло́жим let us assume; п., что вы пра́вы let us assume that you are right

ⳠⳠ положи́тел|ьный, ~ен, ~ьна adj. **1** positive **2** (утверди́тельный) affirmative; п. отве́т affirmative reply **3** (благоприя́тный) favourable (BrE), favorable (AmE)

полож|и́ть, у́, ~ишь pf. of ▶ класть 1

полож|и́ться, у́сь, ~ишься pf. (of ▶ полага́ться 1) (на + a.) to rely (upon), count (upon)

полома́|ть, ю pf. (infml) to break, put out of action

полома́|ться, юсь pf. of ▶ лома́ться 3

поло́мк|а, и f. **1** (маши́ны) breakdown **2** (ме́сто) damaged part; damage

полоне́з, а m. polonaise

полос|а́, ы́, a. по́лосу, pl. по́лосы, поло́с, ~а́м f. **1** (како́го-н. цве́та) stripe; streak **2** (воды́, бума́ги) strip **3** (пери́од) period; phase **4** (газе́ты) page

полоса́т|ый, ~, ~а adj. striped

поло́ск|а, и f. dim. of ▶ полоса́; в ~у striped

поло|ска́ть, щу́, ~щешь impf. of ▶ прополоска́ть

полоте́н|це, ца, g. pl. ~ец nt. towel

полоте́р, а m. floor polisher

полот|но́, на́, pl. ~на, поло́тен, ~нам nt. **1** (ткань) linen; бле́дный как п. white as a sheet **2** (карти́на) canvas **3** (доро́ги) roadbed **4** (tech., пилы́) blade

полотня́ный adj. linen

полоу́м|ный, ~ен, ~на adj. (infml) crazy

полпути́ m. indecl.: на п. halfway; останови́ться на п. (fig.) to stop halfway

полста́вки pl. indecl.: на п. part-time

полтора́, полу́тора (used with m. and nt. nouns) one and a half; в п. ра́за бо́льше half as much again

полтора́ста, полу́тораста num. a hundred and fifty

полторы́ num. (used with f. nouns) = полтора́; п. ты́сячи one and a half thousand

полу... comb. form half-, semi-, demi-

полуго́ди|е, я nt. half-year, six months

полугодова́лый adj. six-month-old

полужив|о́й, ~, ~а́, ~о adj. half dead; more dead than alive

полузащи́тник, а m. (sport) halfback, midfield player; центра́льный п. centre half (BrE), center half (AmE)

полукру́г, а m. semicircle

полукру́глый adj. semicircular

полулеж|а́ть, у́, и́шь impf. to recline

полуме́сяц, а m. half moon; crescent

полумра́к, а m. semi-darkness

полуоде́т|ый, ~, ~а adj. half-dressed, half-clothed

полуо́стров, а m. peninsula

полуоткры́т|ый, ~, ~а adj. half-open; (дверь, окно́) ajar (pred.)

полупроводни́к, а́ m. (phys.) semiconductor

полуразру́шен|ный, ~, ~а tumbledown, dilapidated

полуфабрика́т, а m. (изде́лие) semi-finished product; (пищево́й) semi-prepared foodstuff, convenience food

полуфина́л, а m. semi-final

ⳠⳠ получ|а́ть, а́ю, ет impf. of ▶ получи́ть

ⳠⳠ получ|а́ться, ется impf. of ▶ получи́ться

ⳠⳠ получе́ни|е, я nt. receipt; obtaining; распи́ска в ~и receipt

ⳠⳠ получ|и́ть, у́, ~ишь pf. (of ▶ получа́ть) to get, receive, obtain; п. на́сморк to catch a cold; п. удово́льствие to derive pleasure

ⳠⳠ получ|и́ться, ~ится pf. (of ▶ получа́ться) **1** (оказа́ться) to turn out, prove, be; ~и́лось, что он был прав it turned out that he was right, he proved right **2** (infml) (оказа́ться уда́чным) to work out; (о сни́мке) to come out

полу́чше adv. (infml) a little better

полуша́ри|е, я nt. hemisphere

полушу́б|ок, ка m. (knee-length) sheepskin coat

полцены́ f. indecl.: за п. at half price; for half its value

полчаса́, получа́са pl. half an hour; ка́ждые п. every half-hour

по́лый adj. hollow

полы́н|ь, и f. wormwood

полысе́|ть, ю pf. of ▶ лысе́ть

ⳠⳠ по́льз|а, ы f. use; advantage, benefit, profit; извлека́ть из чего́-н. ~у to benefit from sth; to profit by sth; принести́ ~у (+ d.) to be of benefit (to); в ~у (+ g.) in favour (BrE), favor (AmE) (of), on behalf (of); два-ноль в ~у Дина́мо (sport) 2-0 to Dynamo; пойти́ на ~у кому́-н. to be of benefit to sb

по́льзовани|е, я nt. (+ i.) use (of)

ⳠⳠ по́льзовател|ь, я m. user

ⳠⳠ по́льз|оваться, уюсь impf. (+ i.) **1** (pf. вос~) to make use (of), use, utilize **2** (pf. вос~) (извлека́ть вы́году) to profit (by); п. слу́чаем to take an opportunity **3** (облада́ть) to enjoy; п. успе́хом to enjoy success, be a success

по́льк|а¹, и f. (же́нщина) Pole, Polish woman

по́льк|а², и f. (та́нец) polka

по́льский adj. Polish

польсти́ть, щу́, сти́шь pf. of ▶ льстить

По́льш|а, и f. Poland

п

полюби́|ть, лю́, ~ишь *pf.* to come to like, grow fond (of); (*влюбиться*) to fall in love (with)

полюб|ова́ться, у́юсь *pf.* (*of* ▶ любова́ться): **~у́йся, ~у́йтесь (на** + *a.*) (infml, iron.) just look; **~у́йся на э́того дурака́!** just look at that fool!

по́люс, а *m.* (geog., phys., also fig.) pole; **Се́верный п.** North Pole

поля́к, а *m.* Pole

поля́н|а, ы *f.* glade, clearing

поля́рн|ый *adj.* **1** polar, arctic; **П~ая звезда́** Pole star, North Star; **Се́верный п. круг** Arctic Circle **2** (fig.) polar, diametrically opposed

пома́д|а, ы *f.* pomade; **губна́я п.** lipstick

пома́|зать, жу, жешь *pf. of* ▶ ма́зать 1, ▶ ма́зать 2

помаз|о́к, ка́ *m.* (small) brush

пома́лкива|ть, ю *impf.* (infml) to hold one's tongue, keep quiet

поман|и́ть, ю́, ~ишь *pf. of* ▶ мани́ть

пома́рк|а, и *f.* (*исправление*) correction (*by hand*); (*вычеркнутое место*) crossing-out

пома|ха́ть, шу́, ~шешь *pf.* (+ *i.*) to wave (*for a while, a few times*)

пома́хива|ть, ю *impf.* (+ *i.*) to wave, brandish, swing (*from time to time*); **соба́ка ~ла хвосто́м** the dog would wag his tail

поме́ньше *comp. of* ▶ ма́ленький, ▶ ма́ло (infml) (*по размеру*) somewhat smaller, a little smaller; (*по количеству*) somewhat less, a little less

поменя́|ть, ю *pf. of* ▶ меня́ть 2

поменя́|ться, юсь *pf. of* ▶ меня́ться 2

по|мере́ть, мру́, мрёшь, *past* ~́мер, ~мерла́, ~́мерло *pf. of* ▶ помира́ть) (infml) to die; **п. со́ смеху** to split one's sides (with laughing)

поме́р|ить, ю, ишь *pf. of* ▶ ме́рить

поме́р|иться, юсь, ишься *pf. of* ▶ ме́риться

поме́рк|нуть, ну, нешь, *past* ~, ~ла *pf. of* ▶ ме́ркнуть

поме|сти́ть, щу́, сти́шь *pf.* (*of* ▶ помеща́ть) **1** (*поселить*) to lodge, accommodate; to put up **2** (*поставить*) to put, place; (fin.) to invest; **п. объявле́ние в газе́те** to put an advertisement in a paper

поме|сти́ться, щу́сь, сти́шься *pf.* (*of* ▶ помеща́ться 3) **1** (*ожить*) to find room; to put up; (*о вещах*) to go in; **в э́тот я́щик мои́ ве́щи не ~стя́тся** my things will not go into this drawer **2** *pass. of* ▶ помести́ть

поме́ст|ье, ья, *g. pl.* ~ий *nt.* estate

по́мес|ь, и *f.* **1** hybrid; cross; **п. терье́ра и овча́рки, п. терье́ра с овча́ркой** a cross between a terrier and a sheepdog **2** (fig.) mixture, hotchpotch

поме́|тить, чу, тишь *pf.* (▶ помеча́ть, ▶ ме́тить¹) to mark; to date; **п. га́лочкой** to tick

поме́х|а, и *f.* **1** hindrance; obstacle; **быть ~ой** (+ *d.*) to hinder, impede **2** (*usu. in pl.*)

(radio, TV) interference

помеча́|ть, ю *impf. of* ▶ поме́тить

поме́шан|ный, ~, ~а *adj.* **1** mad, crazy; insane; (*as n.* **п., ~ного**) madman; (**~ная, ~ной**) madwoman **2** (**на** + *p.*) (fig., infml) mad (on, about), crazy (about)

помеша́|ть¹, ю *pf. of* ▶ меша́ть¹

помеша́|ть², ю *pf. of* ▶ меша́ть² 1

помеща́|ть, ю *impf. of* ▶ помести́ть

помеща́|ться, юсь *impf.* **1** (*impf. only*) (*находиться*) to be; to be located, be situated; (*храниться*) to be housed **2** (*impf. only*): **на э́том стадио́не ~ется се́мьдесят ты́сяч челове́к** this stadium holds seventy thousand people **3** *impf. of* ▶ помести́ться

ℰ **помеще́ни|е, я** *nt.* **1** (*действие*) placing, location; (*капитала*) investment **2** (*жильё*) room, lodging, apartment; (*для учреждения*) premises; **жило́е п.** housing

поме́щик, а *m.* landowner

помидо́р, а, *g. pl.* ~ов *m.* tomato

помилова́ни|е, я *nt.* (law) pardon, forgiveness; **про́сьба/проше́ние о ~и** appeal (for pardon)

поми́л|овать, ую *pf.* (*of* ▶ ми́ловать) to pardon, forgive

ℰ **поми́мо** *prep.* + *g.* **1** (*кроме*) apart from; besides; **п. всего́ про́чего** apart from anything else **2** (*минуя*) without the knowledge (of), unbeknown (to); **всё э́то реши́лось п. меня́** all this was decided without my knowledge

поми́н|ки, ок (*no sg.*) funeral repast, wake

помину́т|ный, ~ен, ~на *adj.* **1** occurring every minute; (fig., infml, *очень частый*) continual, constant **2** (*оплата*) by the minute

помира́|ть, ю *impf. of* ▶ помере́ть

помир|и́ть, ю́, и́шь *pf. of* ▶ мири́ть 1

помир|и́ться, ю́сь, и́шься *pf. of* ▶ мири́ться 1

ℰ **по́мн|ить, ю, ишь** *impf.* (+ *a.* or *о* + *p.*) to remember

по́мн|иться, ится *impf.* (*impers.* + *d.*) I remember, *etc.*; **наско́лько мне ~ится** as far as I can remember

помно́гу *adv.* (infml) in plenty, in large quantities; in large numbers

помно́ж|ить, у, ишь *pf. of* ▶ мно́жить

ℰ **помога́|ть, ю** *impf. of* ▶ помо́чь

пом|огу́, о́жешь, о́гут *see* ▶ помо́чь

по-мо́ему *adv.* **1** (*по моему мнению*) in my opinion **2** (*как я хочу*) as I wish

помо́|и, ев (*no sg.*) slops; **обли́ть кого́-н. ~ями** (fig., infml) to fling mud at sb

помо́й|ка, ки, *g. pl.* помо́ек *f.* rubbish dump (BrE), garbage dump (AmE); (*яма*) cesspit

помо́йный *adj.*: **~йное ведро́** slop bucket; **~йная я́ма** cesspit

помо́лвк|а, и *f.* betrothal, engagement

помол|и́ться, ю́сь, ~ишься *pf. of* ▶ моли́ться 1

помолч|а́ть, у́, и́шь *pf.* to be silent for a while

помо́ст, а *m.* platform, rostrum

✧ **помо́|чь, гу́, жешь, гут,** *past* ~г, ~гла́ *pf.* (*of* ▶ помога́ть) **1** (+ *d.*) to help, aid, assist; ~ги́(те) ей наде́ть пальто́ help her on with her coat **2** (*о лекарстве*) to relieve, bring relief; уко́лы ~гли́ от бо́ли the injections relieved the pain

помо́щник, а *m.* **1** helper **2** (*заместитель*) assistant; **п. дире́ктора** assistant director; **п. капита́на** (naut.) mate

помо́щни|ца, цы *f. of* ▶ помо́щник 1

✧ **по́мощ|ь, и** *f.* help, assistance; **оказа́ть п.** to help, assist; **позва́ть на п.** to call for help; **прийти́ на п.** (+ *d.*) to come to the aid (of); **на п.!** help!; **с ~ью** (+ *g.*) *or* **при ~и** (+ *g.*) with the help (of), by means (of); **ско́рая п.** ambulance; **пе́рвая п.** first aid

по́мп|а, ы *f.* pump

помпе́з|ный, ~ен, ~на *adj.* pompous

помуч|ить, у, ишь *pf.* to make suffer, torment (*for a time*)

помуч|иться, усь, ишься *pf.* to suffer (*for a while*)

помча́|ться, у́сь, и́шься *pf.* to begin to rush, begin to tear along

помы́|ть, о́ю, о́ешь *pf. of* ▶ мыть

помы́|ться, о́юсь, о́ешься *pf. of* ▶ мы́ться

пом|я́ть, ну́, нёшь *pf.* to rumple slightly; to crumple slightly

пом|я́ться, нётся *pf. of* ▶ мя́ться

понаде́|яться, юсь, ешься *pf. of* ▶ наде́яться

понадо́б|иться, люсь, ишься *pf.* to be, become necessary; **е́сли ~ится** if necessary

по-настоя́щему *adv.* properly

понача́лу *adv.* (infml) at first

по-на́шему *adv.* **1** (*по нашему мнению*) in our opinion **2** (*как мы хотим*) as we wish

понево́ле *adv.* against one's will

понеде́льник, а *m.* Monday

понемно́гу *adv.* **1** (*немного*) little, a little at a time **2** (*постепенно*) little by little

понес|ти́, у́, ёшь, *past* ~, ~ла́ *pf.* **1** *pf. of* ▶ нести́[1] **2** (*о лошадях*) to bolt

понес|ти́сь, у́сь, ёшься, *past* ~ся, ~ла́сь *pf.* **1** *pf. of* ▶ нести́сь **2** to rush off, tear off, dash off

по́ни *m. indecl.* pony

понижа́|ть, ю, ет *impf. of* ▶ пони́зить

понижа́|ться, ется *impf. of* ▶ пони́зиться

пониже́ни|е, я *nt.* fall, drop; lowering; reduction; **п. цен** reduction, fall in prices; **п. по слу́жбе** demotion

пони́|зить, жу, зишь *pf.* (*of* ▶ понижа́ть) (*голос*) to lower; (*цены*) to reduce; **п. по слу́жбе** to demote

пони́|зиться, зится *pf.* (*of* ▶ понижа́ться) to fall, drop, go down, be reduced

по́низу *adv.* (infml) low; along the ground

поника́|ть, ю *impf. of* ▶ пони́кнуть

пони́к|нуть, ну, нешь, *past* ~, ~ла *pf.* (*of* ▶ поника́ть) to droop, wilt; **п. голово́й** to hang one's head

✧ **понима́ни|е, я** *nt.* **1** understanding, comprehension; **э́то вы́ше моего́ ~я** it is beyond me **2** (*толкование*) interpretation, conception

✧ **понима́|ть, ю** *impf.* (*of* ▶ поня́ть) **1** to understand; to comprehend; to realize; **~ю!** I see! **2** (*толковать*) to interpret; **непра́вильно п.** to misunderstand; **как вы ~ете э́тот посту́пок?** what do you make of this action? **3** (*impf. only*) (+ *a. or* в + *p.*) (*знать толк*) to be a (good) judge of, know (about); **я ничего́ не ~ю в му́зыке** I know nothing about music

по-но́вому *adv.* in a new fashion; **нача́ть жить п.** to start life afresh, turn over a new leaf

поно́с, а *m.* diarrhoea (BrE), diarrhea (AmE)

поно́|сить, шу́, ~сишь *pf.* **1** (*ребёнка*) to carry (*for a while*) **2** (*свитер*) to wear (*for a while*)

поно́шенный *p.p.p. of* ▶ поноси́ть *and adj.* worn, shabby, threadbare

✧ **понра́в|иться, люсь, ишься** *pf. of* ▶ нра́виться

понто́н, а *m.* pontoon

пону́р|ый, ~, ~а *adj.* downcast

по́нчик, а *m.* doughnut (BrE), donut (AmE)

по́нчо *nt. indecl.* poncho

поню́ха|ть, ю *pf. of* ▶ ню́хать

✧ **поня́ти|е, я** *nt.* **1** (*общая мысль*) conception **2** (*представление*) notion, idea; **~я не име́ю!** (infml) I've no idea!; I haven't a clue! **3** (*usu. in pl.*) (*понимание*) notions; level (of understanding)

поня́тлив|ый, ~, ~а *adj.* sharp, quick (on the uptake)

✧ **поня́т|ный, ~ен, ~на** *adj.* **1** (*обоснованный*) understandable; **~но, что...** it is understandable that ...; it is natural that ...; **~ное де́ло** (infml) of course, naturally **2** (*ясный*) clear, intelligible; **~но?** (infml) (do you) see?; is that clear?; **~но!** (infml) I see!; I understand!

✧ **пон|я́ть, пойму́, поймёшь,** *past* ~я́л, ~яла́, ~я́ло *pf.* (*of* ▶ понима́ть 2) to understand; to comprehend; (*осознать*) to realize; **дать п.** to give to understand

пообе́да|ть, ю *pf. of* ▶ обе́дать

пообеща́|ть, ю *pf.* (*of* ▶ обеща́ть) to promise

поочерёдно *adv.* in turn, by turns

поощр|и́ть, ю́, и́шь *pf.* (*of* ▶ поощря́ть) to encourage

поощря́|ть, я́ю *impf. of* ▶ поощри́ть

попада́ни|е, я *nt.* hit (*on target*); **прямо́е п.** direct hit

✧ **попада́|ть, ю** *impf. of* ▶ попа́сть

попада́|ться, юсь *impf. of* ▶ попа́сться

попа́р|иться, юсь, ишься *pf.* (impf. па́риться) (*в бане*) to steam, sweat

---
✧ key word

поп-а́рт, а *m.* pop art

⚥ **попа́|сть, ду́, дёшь,** *past* ~л *pf. (of*
▶ попада́ть) **1** (в + *a.*) to hit; **п. в цель**
to hit the target; **не п. в цель** to miss
2 (в + *a.*) (*оказаться*) to get (to), find
oneself (in); (**на** + *a.*) to hit (upon), come
(upon); **п. домо́й** to get home; **п. в плен** to
be taken prisoner; **п. кому́-н. в ру́ки** to fall
into sb's hands; **не туда́ п.** to get the wrong
number (*on telephone*); **п. в беду́** to get into
trouble, come to grief

попа́|сться, ду́сь, дёшься, *past* ~лся *pf.*
(*of* ▶ попада́ться) **1** (+ *d.*) to come across;
он мне ~лся навстре́чу на у́лице I ran into
him in the street; **п. кому́-н. на глаза́** to catch
sb's eye; **пе́рвый** ~вшийся the first person
one happens to meet **2** (*быть по́йманным*)
to be caught; (в + *a.*) to get (into); **п. с
поли́чным** to be taken red-handed

попа́хива|ть, ет *impf.* (infml) (+ *i.*) to smell
slightly (of)

поперёк *adv. and prep.* + *g.* across; **де́рево
упа́ло п. доро́ги** the tree fell across the road;
стоя́ть у кого́-н. п. доро́ги to be in sb's way;
знать что-н. вдоль и п. to know sth inside out

попере́чн|ый *adj.* transverse, cross-; ~ая
ба́лка cross-beam; **п. разре́з,** ~ое сече́ние
cross section

поперхн|у́ться, у́сь, ёшься *pf.* (+ *i.*) to
choke (over)

поп|е́рчить, е́рчу, е́рчишь *pf. of* ▶ пе́рчить

попи́са|ть, ю *pf. of* ▶ писа́ть

по|пи́ть, пью, пьёшь, *past* ~пи́л, ~пила́,
~пи́ло *pf.* to have a drink

попко́рн, а *m.* popcorn

попла́ва|ть, ю *pf.* to have, take a swim

поплав|о́к, ка́ *m.* float

попла́|кать, чу, чешь *pf.* to cry (*a little, for a
while*); to shed a few tears

попла|ти́ться, чу́сь, ~тишься *pf.* (+ *i.
and* за + *a.*) to pay (with, for); **она́** ~ти́лась
жи́знью за свою́ неосторо́жность she paid
for her carelessness with her life

поплы́|ть, ву́, вёшь, *past* ~л, ~ла́, ~ло *pf.*
(*о челове́ке*) to strike out, start swimming;
(*о су́дне*) to set sail

поп-му́зык|а, и *f.* pop music

попола́м *adv.* in two, in half; half-and-half;
раздели́ть п. to divide in two, divide in half,
halve; **ви́ски п. с водо́й** whisky and water
half-and-half

пополне́|ть, ю *pf. of* ▶ полне́ть

попо́лн|ить, ю, ишь *pf. (of* ▶ пополня́ть)
to replenish, fill up; to restock; (*колле́кцию*)
to enlarge; (mil.) to reinforce; **п. горю́чим** to
refuel; **п. свои́ зна́ния** to supplement one's
knowledge

попо́лн|иться, ится *pf. (of* ▶ пополня́ться)
1 to increase **2** *pass. of* ▶ попо́лнить

пополня́|ть, яю, яет *impf. of* ▶ попо́лнить

пополня́|ться, яется *impf. of* ▶ попо́лниться

пополу́дни *adv.* in the afternoon, p.m.; **в два
часа́ п.** at 2 p.m.

пополу́ночи *adv.* after midnight, a.m.; **в два
часа́ п.** at 2 a.m.

попо́н|а, ы *f.* horse blanket/cloth

попра́в|ить, лю, ишь *pf. (of* ▶ поправля́ть)
1 (*починить*) to mend, repair **2** (*оши́бку,
ученика́*) to correct, set right, put right
3 (*шля́пу*) to adjust, set straight; **п. причёску**
to tidy one's hair **4** (*улу́чшить*) to improve,
better

попра́в|иться, люсь, ишься *pf. (of*
▶ поправля́ться) **1** (*испра́вить свою́
оши́бку*) to correct oneself **2** (*вы́здороветь*)
to get better, recover; **я совсе́м** ~ился I am
completely recovered **3** (*пополне́ть*) to put
on weight; to look better; **он о́чень** ~ился
he has put on a lot of weight; he looks much
better **4** (*о дела́х*) to improve

попра́вк|а, и *f.* **1** (*почи́нка*) mending,
repairing **2** (*оши́бки*) correction;
amendment; **внести́** ~и в законопрое́кт to
amend a bill

поправля́|ть, ю *impf. of* ▶ попра́вить

поправля́|ться, юсь *impf. of*
▶ попра́виться

по-пре́жнему *adv.* as before; as usual

⚥ **попро́б|овать, ую** *pf. of* ▶ про́бовать

⚥ **попро|си́ть, шу́,** ~сишь *pf. of* ▶ проси́ть

попро|си́ться, шу́сь, ~сишься *pf. of*
▶ проси́ться

по́просту *adv.* (infml) simply; **п. говоря́** to put
it bluntly

попроща́|ться, юсь *pf.* (с + *i.*) to take leave
(of), say goodbye (to)

попря́|тать, чу, чешь *pf.* (infml) to hide
(*many objects*)

попря́|таться, чемся, чутся *pf.* (infml,
о мно́гих) to hide (oneself)

попс|а́, ы́ *f.* (infml) **1** popular culture; sth
trendy **2** (mus.) pop music

попсо́в|ый *adj.* (infml) pop

попуга́|й, я *m.* parrot; **волни́стый** ~й(чик)
budgie, budgerigar

попу́др|ить, ю, ишь *pf.* to powder

попу́др|иться, юсь, ишься *pf.* to powder
one's face

попули́ст, а *m.* populist

популяризи́р|овать, ую *impf. and pf.* to
popularize

популяриз|ова́ть, у́ю *impf. and pf.*
= популяризи́ровать

популя́рност|ь, и *f.* popularity

⚥ **популя́р|ный,** ~ен, ~на *adj.* popular

попу́тн|ый *adj.* **1** accompanying; (*маши́на*)
passing; **п. ве́тер** fair wind, favourable (BrE),
favorable (AmE) wind; ~ая струя́ backwash
2 (fig.) passing, incidental; ~ое замеча́ние
passing remark

попу́тчик, а *m.* fellow-traveller (BrE),
-traveler (AmE) (also fig., pol.)

попу́тчиц|а, цы *f.* = попу́тчик (lit. only)

попыта́|ться, юсь *pf. of* ▶ пыта́ться

⚥ **попы́тк|а, и** *f.* attempt, try; **предприня́ть** ~у
to make an attempt; **со второ́й** ~и at the

second attempt

попя́|титься, чусь, тишься *pf. of* ▶ **пя́титься**

по́р|а, ы *f.* pore

♂ **пор|а́, ы́,** *a.* **~у** *f.* **1** time, season; **весе́нняя п.** springtime; **осе́нняя п.** autumn; **до каки́х ~?** till when?, till what time?; **до каки́х ~ вы пробу́дете здесь?** how long will you be here?; **до сих ~** till now, up to now; **с да́вних ~** long, for a long time, for ages; **с тех ~, как...** (ever) since ...; **с э́тих ~** since then, since that time **2** (*as pred.*) it is time; **давно́ п.** it is high time; **п. спать!** (it is) bedtime!

порабо́та|ть, ю *pf.* to do some work

поравня́|ться, юсь *pf.* (**с** + *i.*) to pull alongside (of)

пора́д|овать, ую *pf. of* ▶ **ра́довать**

пора́д|оваться, уюсь *pf. of* ▶ **ра́доваться**

поража́|ть, ю *impf. of* ▶ **порази́ть**

поража́|ться, юсь *impf. of* ▶ **порази́ться**

пораже́ни|е, я *nt.* defeat

порази́тел|ьный, ~ен, ~ьна *adj.* striking; staggering, startling

пора|зи́ть, жу́, зи́шь *pf.* (*of* ▶ **поража́ть**) **1** to hit, strike; (**в. кинжа́лом**) to stab with a dagger **2** (fig., *удиви́ть*) to strike; to stagger; **меня́ ~зи́л её мра́чный вид** I was struck by her gloomy appearance

пора|зи́ться, жу́сь, зи́шься *pf.* (*of* ▶ **поража́ться**) to be staggered, be astounded

по-ра́зному *adv.* differently, in different ways

пора́н|ить, ю, ишь *pf.* to wound, injure, hurt (*slightly*)

пора́н|иться, юсь, ишься *pf.* to injure, hurt oneself (*slightly*)

порв|а́ть, у́, ёшь, *past* **~а́л, ~ала́, ~а́ло** *pf.* **1** to tear slightly **2** (*impf.* **порыва́ть**) (**с** + *i.*) (fig.) to break (with); to break off (with); **она́ давно́ ~ала́ с ним** she broke with him long ago

порв|а́ться, ётся, *past* **~а́лся, ~ала́сь, ~а́лось** *pf.* **1** (*о верёвке*) to break (off), snap **2** (*об оде́жде*) to tear

пореде́|ть, ет *pf. of* ▶ **реде́ть**

поре́з, а *m.* cut

поре́|зать, жу, жешь *pf.* **1** (*пора́нить*) to cut; **п. себе́ па́лец** to cut one's finger **2** (+ *a.* or *g.*) (*наре́зать*) to cut (*a quantity of*)

поре́|заться, жусь, жешься *pf.* to cut oneself

порекоменд|ова́ть, у́ю *pf. of* ▶ **рекомендова́ть**

порица́|ть, ю *impf.* to censure; to reprimand

по́рно *nt. indecl.* (infml) porn

порнографи́ческий *adj.* pornographic

порногра́фи|я, и *f.* pornography

порнофи́льм, а *m.* porno film, blue movie

по́ровну *adv.* equally, in equal parts; **раздели́ть п.** to divide equally, into equal parts

♂ **key word**

поро́г, а *m.* **1** threshold (also fig.); **переступи́ть п.** to cross the threshold **2** (geog.) (*usu. in pl.*) rapids

поро́д|а, ы *f.* **1** (*живо́тных*) breed; (*дере́вьев*) species; (fig., *люде́й*) kind, sort, type **2** (geol.) rock; **го́рная п.** rock; (*пласт*) layer, stratum

породи́ст|ый, ~, ~а *adj.* thoroughbred, pedigree

поро|ди́ть, жу́, ди́шь *pf.* (*of* ▶ **порожда́ть**) to give rise (to), spawn, engender

порожда́|ть, ю *impf. of* ▶ **породи́ть**

поро́й and **поро́ю** *adv.* at times, now and then

поро́к, а *m.* **1** (*челове́ка*) vice **2** (*ве́щи*) defect; flaw, blemish; **п. се́рдца** heart disease

пороло́н, а *m.* foam rubber

порос|ёнок, ёнка, *pl.* **~я́та, ~я́т** *m.* piglet

по́росл|ь, и *f.* verdure, shoots

по́рох, а (у), *pl.* **~а́, ~о́в** *m.* gunpowder; powder

поро́ч|ный, ~ен, ~на *adj.* **1** (*безнра́вственный*) depraved; wanton **2** (*непра́вильный*) faulty; fallacious; **п. круг** vicious circle

порош|о́к, ка́ *m.* powder

порт, а, о ~е, в ~ý, *pl.* **~ы́, ~о́в** *m.* port; (*га́вань*) harbour; (comput.) port; **возду́шный п.** airport; **морско́й п.** seaport

порта́л, а *m.* (comput.) portal

портати́в|ный, ~ен, ~на *adj.* portable

портве́йн, а *m.* port (*wine*)

по́ртик, а *m.* portico

по́р|тить, чу, тишь *impf.* (*of* ▶ **испо́ртить**) **1** (*аппети́т, ве́чер, настрое́ние, ребёнка*) to spoil; (*маши́ну, здоро́вье, зре́ние*) to damage **2** (*развраща́ть*) to corrupt

по́р|титься, чусь, тишься *impf.* (*of* ▶ **испо́ртиться**) **1** (*о здоро́вье, пого́де, отноше́ниях*) to deteriorate; (*о проду́ктах*) to go off; (*о зуба́х*) to decay; to rot; **отноше́ния ста́ли п.** relations have begun to deteriorate **2** (*о механи́зме*) to get out of order **3** (*нра́вственно*) to become corrupt

портни́х|а, и *f.* dressmaker

портн|о́й, о́го *m.* tailor

портре́т, а *m.* portrait

портсига́р, а *m.* cigarette case

португа́л|ец, ьца *m.* Portuguese

Португа́ли|я, и *f.* Portugal

португа́л|ка, ки *f. of* ▶ **португа́лец**

португа́льский *adj.* Portuguese

портфе́л|ь, я *m.* **1** briefcase **2** (pol., comm.) portfolio

портье́ *m. indecl.* (*in hotel*) porter, doorman

портье́р|а, ы *f.* portière; (*heavy*) curtain

портя́нк|а, и *f.* foot binding; puttee

поруб|и́ть, лю́, ~ишь *pf.* to chop down (*all or a large number of*)

поруга́|ться, юсь *pf.* **1** to swear, curse **2** (**с** + *i.*) (infml) to fall out (with)

по-ру́сски *adv.* (in) Russian; **говори́ть п.** to speak Russian

поруч|а́ть, а́ю *impf. of* ▶ поручи́ть
поруче́ни|е, я *nt.* (*зада́ние*) errand; (*ве́сомое*) mission, assignment; по ~ю (+ *g.*) on the instructions (of); (*от и́мени*) per procurationem (p.p.)
по́руч|ень, ня *m.* handrail
поруч|и́ть, у́, ~ишь *pf.* (*of* ▶ поруча́ть)
1 (*возложи́ть на кого́-н. исполне́ние чего́-н.*) to charge, commission; to instruct; он ~и́л мне переда́ть вам де́ньги he charged me to hand you the money **2** (*вве́рить кого́-, что́-н. забо́те кого́-н.*) to entrust
поруч|и́ться, у́сь, ~ишься *pf. of* ▶ руча́ться
порх|а́ть, а́ю *impf.* (*of* ▶ порхну́ть) to flutter, fly about
порх|ну́ть, ну́, нёшь *pf. of* ▶ порха́ть
по́рци|я, и *f.* portion
по́рш|ень, ня *m.* (tech.) (*дви́гателя*) piston; (*насо́са*) plunger
поры́в, а *m.* **1** (*ве́тра*) gust; rush **2** (fig., *чу́вства*) fit; upsurge; п. гне́ва fit of temper
порыва́|ть, ю *impf. of* ▶ порва́ть 2
поры́в|истый, ~, ~а *adj.* **1** (*ве́тер*) gusty **2** (*движе́ние*) jerky **3** (fig., *хара́ктер*) impetuous, violent
пор|ы́ться, о́юсь, о́ешься *pf.* (в + *p.*) (infml) to rummage (in, among); п. в па́мяти to give one's memory a jog
поря́дков|ый *adj.* ordinal; ~ое числи́тельное ordinal numeral
поря́д|ок, ка *m.* **1** order; (*пра́вильное состоя́ние, расположе́ние*): привести́ в п. to put in order; привести́ себя́ в п. to tidy oneself up; всё в ~ке! everything is all right!; не в ~ке out of order, not right **2** (*после́довательность*) алфави́тный п. alphabetical order; по ~ку in order, in succession **3** (*спо́соб*) manner, way; procedure; в обяза́тельном ~ке without fail **4** (mil., *построе́ние*): боево́й п. battle order **5** (*in pl.*) (*обы́чаи*) customs, usages, observances
поря́доч|ный, ~ен, ~на *adj.* **1** (*че́стный*) decent; honest; ~ные лю́ди decent folk **2** (infml, *значи́тельный*) fair, considerable; он п. плут he is pretty much of a rogue
поса|ди́ть, жу́, ~дишь *pf. of* ▶ сажа́ть
поса́дк|а, и *f.* **1** (*семя́н*) planting **2** (*на судно́*) embarkation; (*на по́езд, авто́бус*) boarding **3** (aeron.) landing; вы́нужденная п. forced landing
поса́дочный *adj.* (aeron.) landing; п. биле́т/тало́н boarding pass
поса́хар|ить, ю, ишь *pf. of* ▶ са́харить
посве|ти́ть, чу́, ~тишь *pf.* **1** to shine for a while **2** (+ *d.*) to hold a light (for)
посви|сте́ть, щу́, сти́шь *pf.* to whistle, give a whistle
посви́стыва|ть, ю *impf.* to whistle (*softly, from time to time*)
по-сво́ему *adv.* in one's own way; де́лайте п., поступа́йте п. have it your own way

посвя|ти́ть, щу́, ти́шь *pf.* (*of* ▶ посвяща́ть)
1 (+ *a.* and в + *a.*) to let (into); мы вас ~ти́м в на́шу та́йну we will let you into our secret **2** (+ *a.* and *d.*) (*жизнь*) to devote (to), give up (to); (*кни́гу*) to dedicate (to); п. себя́ нау́ке to devote oneself to (the cause of) learning; он ~ти́л пе́рвую кни́гу свое́й ма́тери he dedicated his first book to his mother **3** (+ *a.* and в + *nom.-a.*) (*в сан*) to ordain, consecrate; п. в ры́цари to knight, confer a knighthood (upon)
посвяща́|ть, ю *impf. of* ▶ посвяти́ть
посе́в, а *m.* **1** (*де́йствие*) sowing **2** (*то, что посе́яно*) crops; пло́щадь ~ов sown area, area under crops
посе́де|ть, ю *pf. of* ▶ седе́ть
посе́лен|ец, ца *m.* **1** settler **2** (*со́сланный*) deportee
посе́лени|е, я *nt.* settlement
посе́лен|ка, ки *f. of* ▶ посе́ленец
посел|и́ть, ю́, и́шь *pf.* (*of* ▶ поселя́ть, ▶ сели́ть) to settle; to lodge
посел|и́ться, ю́сь, и́шься *pf.* (*of* ▶ поселя́ться, ▶ сели́ться) to settle, take up residence
посёл|ок, ка *m.* village; settlement
посел|я́ть, я́ю *impf. of* ▶ посели́ть
посел|я́ться, я́юсь *impf. of* ▶ посели́ться
посереди́не *adv. and prep.* (+ *g.*) in the middle (of)
посети́тел|ь, я *m.* visitor
посети́тель|ница, ницы *f. of* ▶ посети́тель
посе|ти́ть, щу́, ти́шь *pf.* (*of* ▶ посеща́ть) to visit; п. ле́кции to attend lectures
посеща́|ть, ю *impf. of* ▶ посети́ть
посеще́ни|е, я *nt.* visit; (*ле́кций*) attendance
посе́|ять, ю *pf. of* ▶ се́ять
посиде́ть, жу́, ди́шь *pf.* to sit (*for a while*)
поска|ка́ть, чу́, ~чешь *pf. of* ▶ скака́ть 1, ▶ скака́ть 2
поскользн|у́ться, у́сь, ёшься *pf.* to slip
поско́льку *conj.* **1** as far as; мы путеше́ствуем посто́льку, п. позволя́ют сре́дства we travel (just) as much as we can afford **2** (*так как*) in so far as, since; so long as
поскоре́е *adv.* (infml) somewhat quicker; (*int.*) п.! quick!
посла́ни|е, я *nt.* **1** (*официа́льное*) dispatch; (*дру́жеское*) message **2** (liter.) epistle; П~я (bibl.) the Epistles
посла́нник, а *m.* envoy, minister
по|сла́ть, шлю́, шлёшь *pf.* (*of* ▶ посыла́ть) to send; п. по по́чте to post; п. приве́т to send one's regards; п. кого́-н. к чёрту (fig., infml) to tell sb to go to hell
по́сле *adv. and prep.* (+ *g.*) after; afterwards, later (on); (*after a neg.*) since; п. войны́ after the war; п. чего́ whereupon; п. того́, как after
послевое́нный *adj.* post-war
после́дн|ий *adj.* **1** last; (*реше́ние, сло́во*) final; (в) ~ее вре́мя, за ~ее вре́мя lately, of

late, recently; **(в) п. раз** for the last time **2** (*самый новый*) (the) latest; **~ие изве́стия** the latest news **3** (*из упомянутых*) the latter **4** (infml, *самый плохой*) worst, lowest; **~яя ка́пля** the last straw

после́довател|ь, я *m.* follower

после́довательност|ь, и *f.* succession, sequence

после́довател|ьный, ~ен, ~ьна *adj.* **1** (*следующий один за другим*) successive, consecutive **2** (*логичный*) consistent, logical

после́д|овать, ую *pf. of* ▶ **сле́довать¹** 1, ▶ **сле́довать¹** 2

♂ **после́дстви|е, я** *nt.* consequence

♂ **после́дующий** *adj.* subsequent

послеза́втра *adv.* the day after tomorrow

послеобе́денный *adj.* after-dinner

послеоперацио́нный *adj.* post-operative

послеродово́й *adj.* post-natal

послесло́ви|е, я *nt.* afterword, postface; concluding remarks

посло́виц|а, ы *f.* proverb

послуж|и́ть, у́, ~ишь *pf. of* ▶ **служи́ть** 4

послу́ша|ть, ю *pf. of* ▶ **слу́шать**

послу́ша|ться, юсь *pf. of* ▶ **слу́шаться**

послу́ш|ный, ~ен, ~на *adj.* obedient

послы́ш|аться, ится *pf. of* ▶ **слы́шаться**

посма́трива|ть, ю *impf.* (**на** + *a.*) to look (at) from time to time

посме́ива|ться, юсь *impf.* to chuckle, laugh softly; **п. в кула́к** to laugh up one's sleeve

посме́ртный *adj.* posthumous

посме́|ть, ю *pf. of* ▶ **сметь**

♂ **посмотр|е́ть, ю́, ~ишь** *pf. of* ▶ **смотре́ть**

посмотр|е́ться, ю́сь, ~ишься *pf. of* ▶ **смотре́ться** 1

посо́би|е, я *nt.* **1** (*денежная помощь*) allowance, benefit; **п. по безрабо́тице** unemployment benefit; **п. на дете́й** child benefit **2** (*учебник*) textbook; (*учебный предмет*) (educational) aid; **уче́бные ~я** educational supplies; school textbooks

посове́т|овать, ую *pf. of* ▶ **сове́товать**

посове́т|оваться, уюсь *pf. of* ▶ **сове́товаться**

пос|о́л, ла́ *m.* (*дипломатический представитель*) ambassador

посол|и́ть, ю́, ~ишь *pf. of* ▶ **соли́ть**

посо́льств|о, а *nt.* embassy

по́сох, а *m.* **1** (*пастуха*) staff, crook **2** (*епископа, монарха*) crozier

посп|а́ть, лю́, и́шь, *past* **~а́л, ~ала́, ~а́ло** *pf.* to have a sleep, have a nap

поспева́|ть, ет *impf. of* ▶ **поспе́ть**

поспе́|ть, ет *pf.* (*of* ▶ **поспева́ть**) (infml) to ripen

поспеш|и́ть, у́, и́шь *pf. of* ▶ **спеши́ть** 1

поспе́ш|ный, ~ен, ~на *adj.* hasty, hurried

поспо́р|ить, ю, ишь *pf.* **1** *pf. of* ▶ **спо́рить** **2** (*заключить пари*) to bet, have a bet

посреди́ *adv. and prep.* + *g.* in the middle (of), in the midst (of)

посре́дник, а *m.* **1** mediator, intermediary; go-between **2** (comm.) middleman

посре́дственно *adv.* so-so, mediocrely, not particularly well; **он игра́ет в те́ннис п.** he is not particularly good at tennis

посре́дственност|ь, и *f.* (*свойство, о человеке*) mediocrity

посре́дствен|ный, ~, ~на *adj.* **1** mediocre, middling **2** (*отметка*) fair, satisfactory

посре́дством *prep.* + *g.* by means of; with the aid of

поссо́р|ить, ю, ишь *pf. of* ▶ **ссо́рить**

поссо́р|иться, юсь, ишься *pf. of* ▶ **ссо́риться**

♂ **пост¹, а́, о ~é, на ~у́,** *pl.* **~ы́** *m.* post; **наблюда́тельный п.** observation post; **занима́ть высо́кий п.** to hold a high post

пост², а́, о ~é и ~é **1** (**в ~é**) (*воздержание от пищи*) fasting; (fig., infml) abstinence **2** (**в ~у́**) (eccl.) fast; **Вели́кий п.** Lent

♂ **поста́в|ить¹, лю, ишь** *pf. of* ▶ **ста́вить**

поста́в|ить², лю, ишь *pf.* (*of* ▶ **поставля́ть**) (*снабдить*) to supply

♂ **поста́вк|а, и** *f.* supply; delivery; **ма́ссовая п.** bulk delivery

♂ **поставля́|ть, ю** *impf. of* ▶ **поста́вить²**

поставщи́к, а́ *m.* supplier

постаме́нт, а *m.* pedestal, base

постанов|и́ть, лю́, ~ишь *pf.* to decide, resolve; to decree

постано́вк|а, и *f.* **1** (*дела, работы*) arrangement, organization **2** (theatr.) staging, production

♂ **постановле́ни|е, я** *nt.* **1** (*решение*) decision, resolution; **вы́нести п.** to pass a resolution **2** (*распоряжение*) decree; **изда́ть п.** to issue a decree

постара́|ться, юсь *pf. of* ▶ **стара́ться**

постаре́|ть, ю *pf. of* ▶ **старе́ть** 1

по-ста́рому *adv.* **1** (*как раньше*) as before **2** (*как в старые времена*) as of old

постел|и́ть, ю́, ~ешь *pf. of* ▶ **стели́ть**

посте́л|ь, и *f.* bed; **лечь в п.** to get into bed; **встать с ~и** to get out of bed

♂ **постепе́нно** *adv.* gradually, little by little

постепе́н|ный, ~ен, ~на *adj.* gradual

постесня́|ться, юсь *pf. of* ▶ **стесня́ться**

постига́|ть, а́ю *impf. of* ▶ **пости́гнуть**, ▶ **пости́чь**

пости́гнуть = **пости́чь**

постила́|ть, ю *impf. of* ▶ **постла́ть**

постимпрессиони́зм, а *m.* post-impressionism

постира́|ть, ю *pf.* to wash

по|сти́ться, щу́сь, сти́шься *impf.* to fast

пости́|чь, гну, гнешь, *past* **~г** *pf.* (*of* ▶ **постига́ть**) **1** (*понять*) to comprehend, grasp **2** (*о горе, о несчастье*) to befall, strike; их ~гло ещё одно́ несча́стье yet another misfortune has befallen them

постл|а́ть, елю́, е́лешь *pf.* (*of* ▸ **стлать**, ▸ **постила́ть**) to spread, lay; **п. ковёр** to lay a carpet; **п. посте́ль** to make one's bed

постмодерни́зм, а *m.* postmodernism

постмодерни́стский *adj.* postmodern

по́ст|ный, ~ен, ~на́, ~но *adj.* **1** Lenten; **п. день** (eccl.) fast day; **п. обе́д** meatless dinner **2** (infml, *о мясе*) lean

посто́льку *conj.*: **п., поско́льку** in so far as ...

посторо́нн|ий *adj.* **1** (*побочный*) extraneous, outside; **без ~ей по́мощи** unaided **2** (*чужой*) strange; (*as m. n.* **п., ~его**) stranger; outsider; «~им вход воспрещён» 'unauthorized persons not admitted'

⚘ **постоя́нно** *adv.* constantly, continually

⚘ **постоя́н|ный** *adj.* **1** constant, continual; **п. посети́тель** constant visitor **2** (*не временный*) constant; permanent, invariable; **п. а́дрес** permanent address; **~ная рабо́та** a permanent job; **п. ток** (elec.) direct current **3** (**~ен, ~на**) (*не изменчивый*) constant, unchanging

посто|я́ть¹, ю́, и́шь *pf.* (*некоторое время*) to stand (*for a while*)

посто|я́ть², ю́, и́шь *pf.* (**за** + *a.*) (*защитить*) to stand up (for)

постра́да|вший *p.p. of* ▸ **пострада́ть**; (*as m. n.* **п., ~вшего**) victim

пострада́|ть, ю *pf. of* ▸ **страда́ть 3**

постре́лива|ть, ю *impf.* to fire intermittently

постреля́|ть, ю *pf.* **1** (*некоторое время*) to do some shooting **2** (+ *a. or g.*) (infml, *застрелить многих*) to shoot, bag (*a number of*)

постри́|чь, гу́, жёшь, гу́т, *past* ~г, ~гла́ *pf. of* ▸ **стричь**

постри́|чься, гу́сь, жёшься, гу́тся, *past* ~гся, ~гла́сь *pf. of* ▸ **стри́чься 1**

построе́ни|е, я *nt.* construction

⚘ **постро́|ить, ю, ишь** *pf. of* ▸ **стро́ить**

постро́|иться, юсь, ишься *pf. of* ▸ **стро́иться**

постро́йк|а, и *f.* **1** (*действие*) building, erection, construction **2** (*здание*) building

постскри́птум, а *m.* postscript

⚘ **поступ|а́ть, а́ю** *impf. of* ▸ **поступи́ть**

поступ|а́ться, а́юсь *impf. of* ▸ **поступи́ться**

⚘ **поступ|и́ть, лю́, ~ишь** *pf.* (*of* ▸ **поступа́ть**) **1** to act; **они́ с ним пло́хо ~и́ли** they have treated him badly **2** (**в, на** + *a.*) (*зачислиться*) to enter, join; **п. в университе́т** to enter the university; **п. на рабо́ту** to start work **3** (*о посланном, дойти*) to come through; to be received; **~и́ла жа́лоба** a complaint has been received, has come in; **п. в прода́жу** to go on sale, come on the market

поступ|и́ться, лю́сь, ~ишься *pf.* (*of* ▸ **поступа́ться**) (+ *i.*) to waive, forgo; to give up

поступле́ни|е, я *nt.* **1** (*в университет*) entering; (*в партию, клуб*) joining; **п. на вое́нную слу́жбу** enlisting, joining up **2** (*денежное*) receipt; (*в библиотеке*) acquisition

посту́п|ок, ка *m.* action; deed; (*pl., collect.*) behaviour (BrE), behavior (AmE)

постуч|а́ть, у́, и́шь *pf. of* ▸ **стуча́ть**

постуч|а́ться, у́сь, и́шься *pf. of* ▸ **стуча́ться**

постыди́ться, жу́сь, ди́шься *pf. of* ▸ **стыди́ться**

посты́д|ный, ~ен, ~на *adj.* shameful

посу́д|а, ы *f.* (collect.) crockery; **гли́няная п., фая́нсовая п.** earthenware; **ку́хонная п.** kitchen utensils

посудомо́ечн|ый *adj.*: **~ая маши́на** dishwasher, dishwashing machine

посчастли́в|иться, ится *pf.* (*impers.* + *d.*) to have the luck (to); to be lucky enough (to)

посчита́|ть, ю *pf. of* ▸ **счита́ть**

посыла́|ть, ю *impf. of* ▸ **посла́ть**

посы́лк|а, и *f.* parcel

посы́п|ать, лю, лешь *pf.* (*of* ▸ **посыпа́ть**) (+ *i.*) to sprinkle (with)

посып|а́ть, а́ю *impf. of* ▸ **посы́пать**

посы́п|аться, лется *pf.* to begin to fall; (fig.) to rain down

посяг|а́ть, а́ю *impf. of* ▸ **посягну́ть**

посяг|ну́ть, ну́, нёшь *pf.* (*of* ▸ **посяга́ть**) (**на** + *a.*) to encroach (on, upon), infringe (on, upon)

пот, а, о ~е, в ~у́, *pl.* ~ы́, ~о́в *m.* sweat, perspiration; **весь в ~у́** all of a sweat, bathed in sweat

по-тво́ему *adv.* **1** (*по твоему мнению*) in your opinion **2** (*как ты хочешь*) as you wish

потемне́|ть, ю *pf. of* ▸ **темне́ть 1**

потенциа́л, а *m.* potential

потенциа́л|ьный, ~ен, ~ьна *adj.* potential

потепле́ни|е, я *nt.* warm(er) spell

потепле́|ть, ет *pf. of* ▸ **тепле́ть**

потерп|е́ть, лю́, ~ишь *pf. of* ▸ **терпе́ть 1**

потёрт|ый, ~, ~а *adj.* shabby, threadbare

⚘ **поте́р|я, и** *f.* loss; (*in pl.*) (mil.) losses

⚘ **потеря́|ть, ю** *pf. of* ▸ **теря́ть**

потеря́|ться, юсь *pf. of* ▸ **теря́ться**

поте́|ть, ю *impf.* **1** to sweat, perspire **2** *impf. of* ▸ **запоте́ть**

поте́|чь, ку́, чёшь, ку́т, *past* ~к, ~кла́ *pf.* to begin to flow

потихо́ньку *adv.* (infml) **1** (*медленно*) slowly **2** (*тихо*) softly, noiselessly **3** (*тайно*) on the sly, secretly

по́т|ный, ~ен, ~на́, ~но *adj.* sweaty, damp with perspiration

⚘ **пото́к, а** *m.* stream; flow; **п. слов** flow of words

пото́ков|ый *adj.* streaming; **~ое ви́део** streaming video

потол|о́к, ка́ *m.* ceiling

П

потолсте́|ть, ю *pf. of* ▶ толсте́ть

✍ **пото́м** *adv.* (*после*) afterwards; (*позже*) later (on); (*затем*) then, after that; **мы п. придём** we shall come later

пото́м|ок, ка *m.* descendant; (*in pl.*) offspring, progeny

пото́мств|о, а *nt.* (*collect.*) posterity, descendants

✍ **потому́** **1** (*adv.*) that is why **2** (*conj.*): **п. что;** **п. ...,** что because, as; **я не знал об э́том, п. что был в о́тпуске** I did not know about it because I was on leave

пото́п, а *m.* flood, deluge; **Всеми́рный п.** (bibl.) the Flood

потоп|и́ть, лю́, ∼ишь *pf.* (*of* ▶ потопля́ть, ▶ топи́ть³ 1) to sink

потопля́|ть, ю *impf. of* ▶ потопи́ть

потороп|и́ть, лю́, ∼ишь *pf. of* ▶ торопи́ть

потороп|и́ться, лю́сь, ∼ишься *pf. of* ▶ торопи́ться

потра́|тить, чу, тишь *pf. of* ▶ тра́тить

✍ **потреби́тель|ь**, я *m.* consumer, user

потреб|и́ть, лю́, и́шь *pf.* (*of* ▶ потребля́ть) to consume, use

потребле́ни|е, я *nt.* consumption

потребля́|ть, ю *impf. of* ▶ потреби́ть

✍ **потре́бность|ь**, и *f.* need, requirement; **испы́тывать п. в чём-н.** to feel a need for sth

потре́б|овать, ую *pf. of* ▶ тре́бовать

потре́б|оваться, уюсь *pf. of* ▶ тре́боваться

потрево́ж|ить, у, ишь *pf. of* ▶ трево́жить

потрево́ж|иться, усь, ишься *pf. of* ▶ трево́житься

потрёпанный *p.p.p. of* ▶ потрепа́ть *and adj.* **1** (*руба́ха*, *кни́га*) shabby; tattered **2** (fig., *вид*) worn, seedy

потреп|а́ть, лю́, ∼лешь *pf. of* ▶ трепа́ть

потреп|а́ться, лю́сь, ∼лешься *pf. of* ▶ трепа́ться

потре́ска|ться, ется *pf. of* ▶ тре́скаться

потро́га|ть, ю *pf.* to touch, run one's hand over; **п. па́льцем** to finger

потроха́|, о́в (*no sg.*) giblets

потру|ди́ться, жу́сь, ∼дишься *pf.* to take pains; to do some work

потряса́|ть, а́ю *impf. of* ▶ потрясти́¹

потряса́ющий *pres. part. act. of* ▶ потряса́ть *and adj.* (infml) staggering, stupendous, tremendous

потрясе́ни|е, я *nt.* shock; (*социа́льное*) upheaval

потряс|ти́¹, у́, ёшь, *past* ∼, ∼ла́ *pf.* (*of* ▶ потряса́ть) **1** to shake; to rock; **п. до основа́ния** to rock to its foundations **2** (+ *i.*) (*взмахну́ть*) to brandish, shake; **п. кулако́м** to shake one's fist **3** (fig., *удиви́ть*) to shake; to stagger, stun

потряс|ти́², у́, ёшь, *past* ∼, ∼ла́ *pf.* to shake (*a little, a few times*)

потускне́|ть, ет *pf. of* ▶ тускне́ть

потух|а́ть, а́ю *impf. of* ▶ поту́хнуть

поту́х|нуть, ну, нешь, *past* ∼, ∼ла *pf.* (*of* ▶ ту́хнуть¹, ▶ потуха́ть) to go out; (fig.) to be extinguished, die out

потуш|и́ть¹, у́, ∼ишь *pf. of* ▶ туши́ть¹

потуш|и́ть², у́, ∼ишь *pf.* (*мя́со*) to stew (*for a while*)

потя́гива|ться, юсь *impf. of* ▶ потяну́ться

потян|у́ть, у́, ∼ешь *pf.* to begin to pull

потян|у́ться, у́сь, ∼ешься *pf.* (*of* ▶ потя́гиваться) to stretch oneself; (*растяну́ться*) to stretch out

поу́жина|ть, ю *pf. of* ▶ у́жинать

поумне́|ть, ю *pf. of* ▶ умне́ть

поуча́|ть, ю *impf.* (infml, iron.) to preach (at), lecture

поучи́тел|ьный, ∼ен, ∼ьна *adj.* instructive

поучи́|ться, у́сь, ∼ишься *pf.* to study (*for a while*); to do a bit of studying

похвал|а́, ы́ *f.* praise; **отозва́ться с ∼о́й** (*o* + *p.*) to praise, speak favourably (BrE), favorably (AmE) (of)

похвал|и́ть, ю́, ∼ишь *pf. of* ▶ хвали́ть

похва́л|ьный, ∼ен, ∼ьна *adj.* **1** (*заслу́живающий похвалы́*) praiseworthy, commendable **2** (*содержа́щий похвалу́*) laudatory; **∼ьная гра́мота** certificate of merit

похва́ста|ть, ю *pf. of* ▶ хва́стать

похва́ста|ться, юсь *pf. of* ▶ хва́статься

похити́тел|ь, я *m.* thief; kidnapper; abductor; hijacker

похити́тель|ница, ницы *f. of* ▶ похити́тель

похи́|тить, щу, тишь *pf.* (*of* ▶ похища́ть) (*вещь*) to steal; (*челове́ка*) to kidnap; to abduct; (*самолёт*) to hijack

похища́|ть, ю *impf. of* ▶ похи́тить

похище́ни|е, я *nt.* theft; kidnapping; abduction; hijacking

похлёбк|а, и *f.* soup, broth

похло́па|ть, ю *pf.* to slap, clap (a few times)

похме́ль|е, я *nt.* hangover; **быть с ∼я** to have a hangover

похо́д, а *m.* **1** (mil.) march; (naut.) cruise **2** (mil., fig.) campaign; **кресто́вый п.** (also fig.) crusade **3** (*прогу́лка*) walking tour, hike

похо|ди́ть, жу́, ∼дишь *impf.* (на + *a.*) to resemble, look like

похо|ди́ть², жу́, ∼дишь *pf.* to walk (*for a while*)

похо́дк|а, и *f.* gait, walk, step

похожде́ни|е, я *nt.* adventure, escapade

✍ **похо́ж|ий**, ∼, ∼а *adj.* **1** resembling, alike; (на + *a.*) like; **он ∼ на де́да** he is like his grandfather; **они́ о́чень ∼и друг на дру́га** they are very much alike **2** (infml): **∼е на то** it appears, it would appear; **∼е на то, что...** it looks as if ...; **он, ∼е, бо́лен** it would appear he is ill

похолода́ни|е, я *nt.* fall of temperature, cold spell

похолода́|ть, ет *pf. of* ▶ холода́ть

похолоде́|ть, ю *pf. of* ▶ холоде́ть

✍ key word

П

похорон|и́ть, ю́, ~ишь *pf. of* ▶ **хорони́ть**

похоро́нн|ый *adj.* funeral; **~ое бюро́** undertaker's

по́хор|оны, о́н, она́м (*no sg.*) funeral; burial

по-хоро́шему *adv.* in an amicable way

похотли́в|ый, ~, ~а *adj.* lustful, lewd, lascivious

ℰ **похуде́|ть, ю** *pf. of* ▶ **худе́ть**

поцара́па|ть, ю *pf.* to scratch (slightly)

поцара́па|ться, юсь *pf.* to get slightly scratched

поцел|ова́ть, у́ю *pf. of* ▶ **целова́ть**

поцел|ова́ться, у́юсь *pf. of* ▶ **целова́ться**

поцелу́|й, я *m.* kiss

по́чв|а, ы *f.* **1** soil, ground, earth **2** (fig., *основа*) foundation, basis; **на ~е** (+ *g.*) owing (to), because (of)

почём *interrog. and rel. adv.* (infml) how much; **п. сего́дня я́блоки?** how much are apples today?

ℰ **почему́ 1** *interrog. and rel. adv.* why; **п. вы так ду́маете?** why do you think that? **2** *as conj.* (and) so; which is why; **она́ простуди́лась, п. и оста́лась до́ма** she has caught a cold, which is why she has stayed at home

почему́-либо = **почему́-нибудь**

почему́-нибудь *adv.* for some reason or other

почему́-то *adv.* for some reason

по́черк, а *m.* handwriting; (fig.) hallmark

почерне́|ть, ю *pf. of* ▶ **черне́ть 1**

поче|са́ть, шу́, ~шешь *pf. of* ▶ **чеса́ть**

поче|са́ться, шу́сь, ~шешься *pf. of* ▶ **чеса́ться**

почёт, а *m.* honour (BrE), honor (AmE); respect, esteem; **быть в ~е у кого́-н.** to stand high in sb's esteem

почёт|ный *adj.* **1** (*пользующийся почётом*) honoured (BrE), honored (AmE); **п. гость** guest of honour (BrE), honor (AmE) **2** (*избираемый в знак почёта*) honorary; **п. член** honorary member **3** (~ен, ~на) (*являющийся проявлением почёта; доставляющий почёт*) honourable (BrE), honorable (AmE)

почин|и́ть, ю́, ~ишь *pf.* (*of* ▶ **чини́ть**) to repair, mend

почи́нк|а, и *f.* repairing, mending; **отда́ть что́-н. в ~у** to have sth repaired, mended

почи́|стить, щу, стишь *pf. of* ▶ **чи́стить**

почита́|ть, ю *pf.* to read (*a little, for a while*)

по́чк|а¹, и *f.* (bot.) bud

по́чк|а², и *f.* (anat.) kidney; **иску́сственная п.** (med.) kidney machine

ℰ **по́чт|а, ы** *f.* **1** (*система*) post; **возду́шная п.** airmail; **электро́нная п.** email; **посла́ть по ~е, ~ой** to send by post, post **2** (*письма*) (the) post, (the) mail; **пришла́ ли п.?** has the post come? **3** (*учреждение*) post office

почтальо́н, а *m.* postman, postwoman (BrE), letter carrier (AmE)

почтальо́нк|а, и *f.* (infml) postwoman (BrE), letter carrier (AmE)

почта́мт, а *m.* main post office (*of city or town*)

почте́ни|е, я *nt.* respect, esteem; deference

ℰ **почти́** *adv.* almost, nearly; **п. ничего́** next to nothing; **п. что** (infml) almost, nearly

почти́тел|ьный, ~ен, ~ьна *adj.* respectful, deferential

почт|о́вый *adj. of* ▶ **по́чта**; **п. и́ндекс** postcode (BrE), zip code (AmE); **~овая ка́рточка** postcard; **~овая ма́рка** (postage) stamp; **~о́вое отделе́ние** post office; **п. я́щик** letter box, postbox (BrE), mailbox (AmE); (comput.) mailbox

ℰ **почу́вств|овать, ую** *pf. of* ▶ **чу́вствовать**

пошатн|у́ться, у́сь, ёшься *pf.* **1** to sway, totter, stagger **2** (fig.) to be shaken; **её здоро́вье ~у́лось** her health has suffered

пошевел|и́ть, ю́, ~и́шь *pf. of* ▶ **шевели́ть**

пошевел|и́ться, ю́сь, ~и́шься *pf. of* ▶ **шевели́ться**

пошевельн|у́ть, у́, ёшь *pf.* (infml) = **пошевели́ть**

пошевельн|у́ться, у́сь, ёшься *pf.* (infml) = **пошевели́ться**

пошёл, ла́ *see* ▶ **пойти́**

по́шлин|а, ы *f.* duty; **и́мпортная п.** import duty; **э́кспортная п.** export duty

по́шлост|ь, и *f.* **1** (*свойство*) vulgarity, commonness **2** (*замечание*) trite remark, banality; **говори́ть ~и** to utter banalities

по́шл|ый, ~, ~а, ~о *adj.* **1** (*ни́зкий*) vulgar; **у него́ о́чень ~ые вку́сы** he has very vulgar tastes **2** (*бана́льный*) trite, banal; **~ая по́весть** banal story

пошум|е́ть, лю́, и́шь *pf.* to make a bit of a noise

пошу|ти́ть, чу́, ~тишь *pf. of* ▶ **шути́ть**

поща|ди́ть, жу́, ди́шь *pf. of* ▶ **щади́ть**

пощеко|та́ть, чу́, ~чешь *pf. of* ▶ **щекота́ть**

пощёчин|а, ы *f.* slap in the face (also fig.); **дать ~у** (+ *d.*) to slap in the face

пощу́па|ть, ю *pf. of* ▶ **щу́пать**

поэ́зи|я, и *f.* poetry

поэ́м|а, ы *f.* (narrative) poem (*usu. of epic proportions*)

поэ́т, а *m.* poet

поэте́сс|а, ы *f.* poetess

поэти́ческий *adj.* poetic(al)

ℰ **поэ́тому** *adv.* therefore, and so

по|ю́¹, ёшь *see* ▶ **петь**

по|ю́², ~йшь *see* ▶ **пойти́**

ℰ **появ|и́ться, лю́сь, ~ишься** *pf.* (*of* ▶ **появля́ться**) to appear

ℰ **появле́ни|е, я** *nt.* appearance

ℰ **появля́|ться, юсь** *impf. of* ▶ **появи́ться**

по́яс, а, pl. ~á, ~о́в *m.* **1** belt; **спаса́тельный п.** lifebelt **2** (*та́лия*) waist; **по п.** up to the waist, waist-deep, waist-high **3** (geog., econ.) zone, belt

поясне́ни|е, я *nt.* explanation

п

поясн|и́ть, ю́, и́шь *pf.* (*of* ▶ поясня́ть) to explain, elucidate

поясни́ц|а, ы *f.* small of the back; **боль в ~е** lumbago

поясн|я́ть, я́ю *impf. of* ▶ поясни́ть

прабабушк|а, и *f.* great-grandmother

✎ **пра́вд|а, ы** *f.* **1** truth; the truth; **су́щая п.** the honest truth; **э́то п.** it is true; it is the truth; **по ~е сказа́ть, говоря́** to tell the truth **2** (*справедливость*) justice; **иска́ть ~ы** to seek justice **3**: **п.?** is that so?; really?; **п. (ли), что он умира́ет?** is it true that he is dying?; **не п. ли?** *in interrog. sentences indicates that affirmative answer is expected;* **вы погаси́ли свет, не п. ли?** you (did) put out the light, didn't you? **4** (*as concessive conj.*) true; **п., я ему́ не написа́л, но я вот-во́т собира́лся позвони́ть** true I had not written to him, but I was on the point of phoning

правди́в|ый, ~, ~а *adj.* **1** true; veracious; **п. расска́з** true story **2** (*человек*) truthful; upright; **п. отве́т** honest answer

правдоподо́б|ный, ~ен, ~на *adj.* probable, likely; plausible

пра́вед|ный, ~ен, ~на *adj.* **1** (*благочестивый*) righteous; upright **2** (*справедливый*) just

✎ **пра́вил|о, а** *nt.* **1** rule; regulation; **~а у́личного движе́ния** traffic regulations; **как п.** as a rule **2** (*принцип*) rule, principle; **взять за п.** to make it a rule; **взять себе́ за п.** (+ *inf.*) to make a point (of)

✎ **пра́вильно** *adv.* **1** (*верно*) rightly; correctly; **п. ли иду́т ва́ши часы́?** is your watch right? **2** (*регулярно*) regularly

✎ **пра́вил|ьный, ~ен, ~ьна** *adj.* **1** (*верный*) right, correct; **п. отве́т** the right answer; **~ьно** (*as pred.*) it is correct; **~ьно!** that's right! **2** (*регулярный*) regular; **~ьные черты́ лица́** regular features

прави́тел|ь, я *m.* ruler

прави́тельственн|ый *adj.* governmental; government; **~ое учрежде́ние** government establishment

✎ **прави́тельств|о, а** *nt.* government

пра́в|ить¹, лю, ишь *impf.* (+ *i.*) to rule (over), govern

пра́в|ить², лю, ишь *impf.* to correct; **п. корректу́ру** (*typ.*) to read, correct proofs

пра́вк|а, и *f.* correcting; **п. корректу́ры** (*typ.*) proofreading

правле́ни|е, я *nt.* **1** (*действие*) government; **фо́рма ~я** form of government **2** (*орган*) board, governing body

пра́внук, а *m.* great-grandson

пра́внучк|а, и *f.* great-granddaughter

✎ **пра́в|о, а,** *pl.* **~á** *nt.* **1** (*наука*) law; **гражда́нское п.** civil law; **уголо́вное п.** criminal law **2** (*свобода*) right; **(води́тельские) ~á** driving licence (BrE), driver's license (AmE); **п. го́лоса,**

избира́тельное п. the vote, suffrage; **~á челове́ка** human rights; **по ~у** by rights; **име́ть п. (на** + *a.*) to have the right (to), be entitled (to)

правове́р|ный, ~ен, ~на *adj.* (relig.) orthodox

✎ **правово́|й** *adj.* legal; lawful; **~о́е госуда́рство** (pol.) state based on the rule of law

правозащи́тник, а *m.* human rights activist

правозащи́тни|ца, цы *f. of* ▶ правозащи́тник

правоме́р|ный, ~ен, ~на *adj.* (*действие, поступок*) lawful, rightful; (*вопрос, сомнение*) legitimate

правомо́ч|ный, ~ен, ~на *adj.* competent, authorized

правонаруше́ни|е, я *nt.* infringement of the law, offence

правонаруши́тел|ь, я *m.* offender

правоохрани́тельн|ый *adj.* law enforcement; **~ые о́рганы** law enforcement agencies

правописа́ни|е, я *nt.* spelling, orthography

правопоря́д|ок, ка *m.* law and order

правосла́ви|е, я *nt.* (relig.) Orthodoxy

✎ **правосла́вн|ый** *adj.* (relig.) orthodox; **~ая це́рковь** Orthodox Church; (*as in п.,* **~ого,** *f.* **~ая, ~ой**) member of the Orthodox Church

правосу́ди|е, я *nt.* justice

правот|а́, ы́ *f.* rightness; (law) innocence

✎ **пра́в|ый¹** *adj.* **1** (*по направлению*) right; right-hand; (naut.) starboard; **~ая рука́** (fig.) right-hand man **2** (pol.) right-wing, right; **~ая па́ртия** party of the right

✎ **пра́в|ый², ~, ~á, ~о** *adj.* right, correct; **вы не совсе́м ~ы** you are not quite right

Пра́г|а, и *f.* Prague

прагмати́зм, а *m.* pragmatism

прагмати́ческий *adj.* pragmatic

пра́дед, а *m.* **1** great-grandfather **2** (*in pl.*) ancestors, forefathers

праде́душк|а, и *m. dim. of* ▶ пра́дед 1

✎ **пра́здник, а** *m.* **1** (public) holiday; (*религиозный*) (religious) feast, festival; **по ~ам** on high days and holidays **2** (*день радости, торжества*) festive occasion; **по слу́чаю ~а** to celebrate the occasion

пра́здничн|ый *adj.* holiday; festive; **п. день** holiday; **~ое настрое́ние** festive mood

пра́здн|овать, ую *impf.* (*of* ▶ отпра́здновать) to celebrate

пра́зд|ный, ~ен, ~на *adj.* idle, inactive; empty; **~ное любопы́тство** idle curiosity

✎ **пра́ктик|а, и** *f.* **1** practice; **на ~е** in practice; **вам не хвата́ет разгово́рной ~и** you need more conversational practice **2** (*форма обучения*) practical work **3** (*работа врача, юриста*) practice

практика́нт, а *m.* trainee

практика́нт|ка, ки *f. of* ▶ практика́нт

практик|ова́ть, у́ю *impf.* **1** to practise (BrE), practice (AmE) **2** (*о враче, юристе*) to practise (BrE), practice (AmE)

п

практик|ова́ться, у́юсь *impf.* **1** (в + *p.*) to practise (BrE), practice (AmE); **п. в игре́ на скри́пке** to practise the violin **2** *pass. of* ▶ **практикова́ть**; э́тот приём бо́льше не ~у́ется this method is no longer used

◆ **практи́ческ|ий** *adj.* practical; ~ие заня́тия practical training

практи́ч|ный *adj.*, ~ен, ~на *adj.* practical

прах, а (*no pl.*) *m.* **1** (liter., *пыль*) dust, earth; **обрати́ть в п., пове́ргнуть в п.** to reduce to dust/ashes **2** (rhet., *уме́ршего*) ashes, remains; **мир ~у его́** may he rest in peace

пра́чечн|ая, ой *f.* laundry; **п. самообслу́живания** (*автомати́ческая*) launderette

пра́чк|а, и *f.* laundress

пращ|а́, и́, *g. pl.* ~е́й *f.* sling (*weapon*)

пре...[1] *adj. pref.* (*indicating superl. degree*) very, most, exceedingly

пре...[2] *vbl. pref.* (*indicating action in extreme degree or superior measure*) sur-, over-, out- (*cf.* ▶ **пере...**)

пребыва́ни|е, я *nt.* stay; **ме́сто постоя́нного** ~я permanent residence; **п. в до́лжности, п. на посту́** tenure/period of office

превали́р|овать, ую *impf.* (**над** + *i.*) to prevail (over)

превзо|йти́, йду́, йдёшь, *past* ~шёл, ~шла́ *pf.* (*of* ▶ **превосходи́ть**) (в + *p.* or + *i.*) to surpass (in); to excel (in); **п. все ожида́ния** to exceed all expectations

превозмога́|ть, ю *impf. of* ▶ **превозмо́чь**

превозмо́|чь, гу́, ~жешь, ~гут, *past* ~г, ~гла́ *pf.* (*of* ▶ **превозмога́ть**) to overcome, surmount

превознес|ти́, у́, ёшь, *past* ~, ~ла́ *pf.* (*of* ▶ **превозноси́ть**) to extol

превозно|си́ть, шу́, ~сишь *impf. of* ▶ **превознести́**

превосхо|ди́ть, жу́, ~дишь *impf. of* ▶ **превзойти́**

превосхо́д|ный, ~ен, ~на *adj.* **1** superb, outstanding **2** ~ная сте́пень (gram.) superlative degree

превосхо́дств|о, а *nt.* superiority

превра|ти́ть, щу́, ти́шь *pf.* (*of* ▶ **превраща́ть**) (в + *a.*) to turn (to, into), convert (into); **п. в ка́мень** to turn to stone

превра|ти́ться, щу́сь, ти́шься *pf.* (*of* ▶ **превраща́ться**) (в + *a.*) to turn (into), change (into)

превра́т|ный, ~ен, ~на *adj.* wrong, false

превраща́|ть, ю *impf. of* ▶ **преврати́ть**

превраща́|ться, юсь *impf. of* ▶ **преврати́ться**

превраще́ни|е, я *nt.* transformation, conversion

превы́|сить, шу, сишь *pf.* (*of* ▶ **превыша́ть**) to exceed; **п. полномо́чия** to exceed one's authority

◆ **превыша́|ть, ю** *impf. of* ▶ **превы́сить**

превы́ше *adv.* far above; **п. всего́** above all

прегра́д|а, ы *f.* barrier; obstacle

прегра|ди́ть, жу́, ди́шь *pf.* (*of* ▶ **прегражда́ть**) to bar, obstruct, block; **п. путь кому́-н.** to bar sb's way

прегражда́|ть, ю *impf. of* ▶ **прегради́ть**

преда|ва́ть, ю́, ёшь *impf. of* ▶ **преда́ть**

преда|ва́ться, ю́сь, ёшься *impf. of* ▶ **преда́ться**

пре́данност|ь, и *f.* devotion

пре́дан|ный, ~, а *p.p.p. of* ▶ **преда́ть** *and* (~, ~на) *adj.* (+ *d.*) devoted (to); (*делу*) dedicated (to); **п. друг** staunch friend

преда́тел|ь, я *m.* traitor

преда́тель|ница, ницы *f. of* ▶ **преда́тель**

преда́тельск|ий *adj.* treacherous (also fig.)

преда́тельств|о, а *nt.* treachery, betrayal

пре|да́ть, да́м, да́шь, да́ст, дади́м, дади́те, даду́т, *past* ~дал, ~дала́, ~дало *pf.* (*of* ▶ **предава́ть**) **1** (+ *d.*) (*отда́ть*) to hand over (to), commit (to); **п. забве́нию** to consign to oblivion; **п. земле́** to commit to the earth **2** (*измени́ть*) to betray

пре|да́ться, да́мся, да́шься, да́стся, дади́мся, дади́тесь, даду́тся, *past* ~да́лся, ~дала́сь *pf.* (*of* ▶ **предава́ться**) (+ *d.*) to give oneself up (to); **п. отча́янию** to give way to despair

предвари́тельно *adv.* in advance, beforehand

◆ **предвари́тельн|ый,** ~ен, ~ьна *adj.* (*замеча́ния, рабо́та*) preliminary; (*прода́жа, зака́з*) advance; **п. пока́з** preview; ~ьное усло́вие precondition

предвеща́|ть, ю *impf.* (*no pf.*) herald, presage, portend; **ту́чи** ~ли грозу́ the clouds heralded a storm

предвзя́т|ый, ~, ~а *adj.* prejudiced, biased

предви́дени|е, я *nt.* foresight; (*предсказа́ние*) prediction

предви́|деть, жу, дишь *impf.* (*no pf.*) to foresee; (*предсказа́ть*) to predict

предвкуша́|ть, ю *impf.* to look forward (to)

предвкуше́ни|е, я *nt.* anticipation (*of something pleasant*); **в** ~и (+ *g.*) in anticipation (of)

предводи́тел|ь, я *m.* leader

предвое́нный *adj.* pre-war

предвосхи́|тить, щу, тишь *pf.* (*of* ▶ **предвосхища́ть**) to anticipate

предвосхища́|ть, ю *impf. of* ▶ **предвосхи́тить**

предвы́борн|ый *adj.* (pre-)election; ~ая кампа́ния election campaign

предго́р|ье, ья, *g. pl.* ~ий *nt.* (*often in pl.*) foothills

◆ **преде́л, а** *m.* limit; bound; **в** ~ах (+ *g.*) within, within the limits (of), within the bounds (of); **за** ~ами (+ *g.*) outside, beyond; **в** ~ах досяга́емости within reach

преде́л|ьный *adj.* **1** *adj. of* ▶ **преде́л**; **п. во́зраст** age limit; **п. срок** time limit, deadline **2** (*кра́йний*) maximum; utmost; **с** ~ьной я́сностью with the utmost clarity

предзнаменова́ни|е, я nt. omen, augury

предисло́ви|е, я nt. preface, foreword

⚔ **предлага́|ть, ю** impf. of ▶ **предложи́ть**

предло́г¹, а m. pretext; **под ~ом** (+ g.) on the pretext (of)

предло́г², а m. (gram.) preposition

⚔ **предложе́ни|е¹, я** nt. **1** (помощи) offer; (идея) suggestion, proposition; (брака) proposal (of marriage); **сде́лать п. кому́-н.** to propose (marriage) to sb **2** (на заседании) proposal, motion; **внести́ п.** to introduce a motion; **отклони́ть п.** to turn down a proposal **3** (econ.) supply; **зако́н спро́са и ~я** law of supply and demand

предложе́ни|е², я nt. (gram.) sentence

⚔ **предлож|и́ть, у́, ~ишь** pf. (of ▶ **предлага́ть**) **1** (помощь, услуги) to offer **2** (решение, проект) to propose; to suggest; **мы ~и́ли ей обрати́ться к врачу́** we suggested that she should see a doctor **3** (задать) to put, set; **п. зада́чу** to set a problem **4** (потребовать) to order, require; **им ~и́ли освободи́ть кварти́ру** they have been ordered to vacate their apartment

предме́ст|ье, ья, g. pl. **~ий** nt. suburb

⚔ **предме́т, а** m. **1** object; (вещь) article, item; (in pl.) goods; **~ы пе́рвой необходи́мости** necessities **2** (тема) subject, topic, theme; (+ g.) object (of); **п. спо́ра** point at issue **3** (в школе) subject **4** (цель) object; **на п.** (+ g.) with the object (of)

⚔ **предназнача́|ть, а́ю** impf. of ▶ **предназна́чить**

предназна́ч|ить, у, ишь pf. (of ▶ **предназнача́ть**) (для + g. or на + a.) to intend (for); **мы ~или э́ти де́ньги для поку́пки автомоби́ля** we set aside this money to buy a car

преднаме́рен|ный, ~, ~на adj. premeditated; deliberate

пре́д|ок, ка m. forefather, ancestor; (in pl.) forbears

предопределе́ни|е, я nt. predestination

предоста́в|ить, лю, ишь pf. (of ▶ **предоставля́ть**) **1** (+ d. and inf.) (дать право) to let; to leave; **нам ~или сами́м реши́ть де́ло** we were left to decide the matter for ourselves **2** (дать) to give, grant; **п. креди́т** to give credit; **п. пра́во** to concede a right; **п. возмо́жность** to afford an opportunity, give a chance

⚔ **предоставле́ни|е, я** nt. granting

⚔ **предоставля́|ть, ю** impf. of ▶ **предоста́вить**

предостерега́|ть, ю impf. of ▶ **предостере́чь**

предостереже́ни|е, я nt. warning, caution

предостере́|чь, гу́, жёшь, гу́т, past **~г, ~гла́** pf. (of ▶ **предостерега́ть**) (от + g.) to warn (against), caution (against)

предосторо́жност|ь, и f. **1** (осторожное поведение) caution; **ме́ры ~и** precautionary measures, precautions **2** (мера) precaution

⚔ key word

предотвра|ти́ть, щу́, ти́шь pf. (of ▶ **предотвраща́ть**) to prevent, avert; to stave off; **п. войну́** to avert a war; **п. опа́сность** to stave off, avert danger

предвраща́|ть, ю impf. of ▶ **предотврати́ть**

предохрани́тел|ь, я m. guard, safety device; (elec.) fuse

предохрани́тельный adj. (tech.) safety; protective; **п. кла́пан** safety valve

предохран|и́ть, ю́, и́шь pf. (of ▶ **предохраня́ть**) (от + g.) to protect (from, against)

предохран|и́ться, ю́сь, и́шься pf. (of ▶ **предохраня́ться**) (от + g.) to protect oneself (from, against)

предохраня́|ть, я́ю impf. of ▶ **предохрани́ть**

предохраня́|ться, я́юсь impf. of ▶ **предохрани́ться**

предписа́ни|е, я nt. order, injunction; (in pl.) directions, instructions; (med.) prescription; **по ~ю врача́** on doctor's orders

предпле́ч|ье, ья, g. pl. **~ий** nt. (anat.) forearm

предполага́емый pres. part. pass. of ▶ **предполага́ть** and adj. proposed

⚔ **предполага́|ть, ю** impf. **1** impf. of ▶ **предположи́ть 2** (impf. only) (намереваться) to intend, propose **3** (impf. only) (иметь своим условием) to presuppose

предполага́|ться, ется impf. **1** to be planned; **сва́дьба ~лась ле́том** the wedding was planned for the summer **2** (impers.): **~ется, что** it is proposed, it is intended

предположе́ни|е, я nt. supposition, assumption

предположи́тельно adv. **1** hypothetically; supposedly, presumably **2** (in parenthesis) (вероятно) probably

предположи́тельный adj. (дата, результат) hypothetical; (доход) estimated, anticipated

предполож|и́ть, у́, ~ишь pf. (of ▶ **предполага́ть 1**) to suppose, assume; **~им, что он опозда́л на по́езд** (let us) suppose he missed the train

предпосле́дний adj. penultimate, last but one, next to last; one from the bottom (on list)

предпосы́лк|а, и f. **1** prerequisite, precondition **2** (phil.) premise

предпоч|е́сть, ту́, тёшь, past **~ёл, ~ла́** pf. (of ▶ **предпочита́ть**) (+ a. and d.) to prefer; **п. говя́дину бара́нине** to prefer beef to lamb; **я ~ёл бы идти́ пешко́м** I would rather walk; (+ inf.) to choose to; **он ~ёл уйти́** he chose to leave

предпочита́|ть, ю impf. of ▶ **предпоче́сть**

предпочте́ни|е, я nt. preference; **отда́ть п.** (+ d.) to show a preference (for), give preference (to)

предпочти́тельный, ~ен, ~ьна adj. preferable

предприи́мчивост|ь, и *f.* enterprise

предприи́мчив|ый, ~, ~а *adj.* enterprising

♂ **предпринима́тел|ь, я** *m.* entrepreneur; businessman

предпринима́тельств|о, а (*no pl.*) *nt.* enterprise; **сво́бодное п.** free enterprise

предпринима́|ть, ю *impf. of* ▸ **предприня́ть**

предпри|ня́ть, му́, ~мешь, *past* ~ня́л, ~няла́, ~ня́ло *pf.* (*of* ▸ **предпринима́ть**) to undertake; (*mil.,* etc.) to launch; **п. шаги́** to take steps

♂ **предприя́ти|е, я** *nt.* **1** (*предпринятое дело*) undertaking, enterprise; (*инициатива*) venture; **риско́ванное п.** risky undertaking, venture **2** (econ.) enterprise, concern, business; (*завод, фабрика*) works; **совме́стное п.** joint venture

предрасполо́женност|ь, и *f.* (**к** + *d.*) predisposition (to)

предрассу́д|ок, ка *m.* prejudice

предрека́|ть, ю *impf. of* ▸ **предре́чь**

предре́|чь, ку́, чёшь, ку́т, *past* ~к, ~кла́ *pf.* (*of* ▸ **предрека́ть**) to foretell

предреш|а́ть, а́ю *impf. of* ▸ **предреши́ть**

предреш|и́ть, у́, и́шь *pf.* (*of* ▸ **предреша́ть**) to predetermine

♂ **председа́тел|ь, я** *m.* (*собрания, правления*) chairman; (*общества*) president

предсказа́ни|е, я *nt.* prediction

предска|за́ть, жу́, ~жешь *pf.* (*of* ▸ **предска́зывать**) to foretell, predict

предска́зыва|ть, ю *impf. of* ▸ **предсказа́ть**

♂ **представи́тел|ь, я** *m.* **1** representative; (*должностное лицо*) (+ *g.*) spokesman (for); **полномо́чный п.** plenipotentiary **2** (bot., etc.) specimen

представи́тель|ница, ницы *f. of* ▸ **представи́тель 1**

представи́тельств|о, а *nt.* **1** representation, representing **2** (*collect.*) representation, representatives; **торго́вое п.** trade mission

♂ **предста́в|ить, лю, ишь** *pf.* (*of* ▸ **представля́ть 1**) **1** (*причинить*) to present; **п. интере́с** to be of interest **2** (*предъявить*) to produce, submit; **п. доказа́тельства** to produce evidence **3** (+ *a. and d.*) (*познакомить*) to introduce (to), present (to) **4**: **п. (себе́)** to imagine **5** (*изобразить*) to represent, display

предста́в|иться, люсь, ишься *pf.* (*of* ▸ **представля́ться**) **1** (*возникнуть*) to present itself, arise; **~ился слу́чай пое́хать в Москву́** a chance arose to go to Moscow **2** (+ *d.*) (*познакомиться*) to introduce oneself (to)

♂ **представле́ни|е, я** *nt.* **1** introduction; **п. но́вого сотру́дника** introduction of a new colleague **2** (theatr.) performance **3** (psych., math.) representation **4** (*понимание*) idea, notion, conception; **дать п.** (**о** + *p.*) to give an idea (of); **я не име́ю ни мале́йшего ~я** I have not the faintest idea

♂ **представля́|ть, ю** *impf.* **1** *impf. of*

▸ **предста́вить 2** (*impf. only*) (*страну, интересы*) to represent **3** (*являться*) to represent, be, constitute; **п. угро́зу** to represent a threat **4**: **п. собо́й** (*являться*) to represent, be; to constitute; **э́то ~ет собо́й исключе́ние** this constitutes an exception

представля́|ться, юсь *impf. of*

▸ **предста́виться**

предсто|я́ть, и́т *impf.* (+ *d.*) to be in prospect (for), lie ahead (of), be at hand; to be in store (for); **~я́ла суро́вая зима́** a hard winter lay ahead; **нам ~и́т столкну́ться со мно́гими неприя́тностями** we are in for a lot of trouble

предстоя́|щий *pres. part. of* ▸ **предстоя́ть** *and adj.* forthcoming; impending; **~щие вы́боры** the forthcoming elections

предубежде́ни|е, я *nt.* prejudice, bias

предубеждённый, ~ён, ~ена́ *adj.* (**про́тив** + *g.*) prejudiced, biased (against)

предупреди́тельный *adj.* (*меры*) preventive, precautionary

предупре|ди́ть, жу́, ди́шь *pf.* (*of* ▸ **предупрежда́ть**) **1** (**о** + *p.*) to let know beforehand (about), notify in advance (about), warn (about); to give notice (of, about); **п. об увольне́нии за неде́лю** to give a week's notice (*of dismissal*) **2** (*предотвратить*) to prevent, avert; **п. ава́рию** to prevent an accident

предупрежда́|ть, ю *impf. of* ▸ **предупреди́ть**

предупрежде́ни|е, я *nt.* **1** (*извещение*) notice; notification **2** (*предотвращение*) prevention **3** (*предостережение*) warning; (*взыскание*) caution

♂ **предусма́трива|ть, ю** *impf. of*

▸ **предусмотре́ть**

предусмотр|е́ть, ю́, ~ишь *pf.* (*of* ▸ **предусма́тривать**) (*предвидеть*) to envisage, foresee; (*обеспечить*) to provide (for), make provision (for)

предусмотри́тельный, ~ен, ~на *adj.* prudent; far-sighted

предчу́встви|е, я *nt.* presentiment; (*дурного*) foreboding, premonition

предчу́вств|овать, ую *impf.* to have a presentiment (of, about), have a premonition (of, about)

предше́ственник, а *m.* predecessor; forerunner, precursor

предше́ственни|ца, цы *f. of* ▸ **предше́ственник**

предше́ств|овать, ую *impf.* (+ *d.*) to go in front (of); to precede; **её сме́рти ~овала дли́тельная боле́знь** her death was preceded by a long illness

предъяв|и́ть, лю́, ~ишь *pf.* (*of* ▸ **предъявля́ть**) to show, produce, present; **п. биле́т** to show one's ticket; **п. доказа́тельства** to produce evidence, present proofs **2** (law, etc.) to bring (forward); **ему́ ~или обвине́ние в поджо́ге** he is charged with arson

предъявля́|ть, ю *impf. of* ▸ **предъяви́ть**

П

✓ **предыду́щ|ий** *adj.* previous, preceding; (*as nt. n.* ~ee, ~ero) the foregoing

прее́мник, а *m.* successor

прее́мственност|ь, и *f.* succession; (*тради́ции, культу́ры*) continuity

✓ **пре́жде 1** (*adv.*) (*opp.* ▸ **пото́м**) (*снача́ла*) before; first; **п. чем** (*as conj.*) before **2** (*adv.*) (*opp.* ▸ **тепе́рь**) (*ра́ньше*) formerly, in former times; before **3** (*prep. + g.*) before; **они́ пришли́ п. нас** they arrived before us; **п. всего́** first of all, to begin with; (*са́мое ва́жное*) first and foremost

преждевре́менно *adv.* prematurely; (*умере́ть*) before one's time

преждевре́мен|ный, ~ and ~ен, ~на *adj.* premature, untimely; ~**ные ро́ды** (med.) premature birth

✓ **пре́жний** *adj.* previous, former

презента́ци|я, и *f.* presentation; launch; **п. кни́ги** book launch

презервати́в, а *m.* condom

✓ **президе́нт, а** *m.* president

президе́нт|ский *adj.* of ▸ **президе́нт**; ~**ские вы́боры** presidential elections

президе́нтств|о, а *nt.* presidency

прези́диум, а *m.* presidium

презира́|ть, ю *impf.* to despise, hold in contempt

презре́ни|е, я *nt.* contempt, scorn

презри́тел|ьный, ~ен, ~ьна *adj.* contemptuous, scornful

преиму́щественно *adv.* mainly, chiefly, predominantly

✓ **преиму́ществ|о, а** *nt.* advantage; **получи́ть п.** (**пе́ред** + *i.*) to gain an advantage (over)

прейскура́нт, а *m.* price list

преклон|и́ться, ю́сь, и́шься *pf.* (*of* ▸ **преклоня́ться**) (**пе́ред** + *i.*) to admire, worship

преклон|я́ться, я́юсь *impf. of* ▸ **преклони́ться**

✓ **прекра́сно** *adv.* **1** excellently; (*знать, понима́ть*) perfectly well; **они́ п. зна́ют, что э́то запрещено́** they know perfectly well that it is forbidden **2** (*as int.*) excellent!; splendid!

✓ **прекра́с|ный, ~ен, ~на** *adj.* **1** (*краси́вый*) beautiful, fine; **в оди́н п. день** one fine day, once upon a time; (*as nt. n.* ~**ное**, ~**ного**) the beautiful **2** (*отли́чный*) excellent, capital, first-rate

прекра|ти́ть, щу́, ти́шь *pf.* (*of* ▸ **прекраща́ть**) to stop; (*положи́ть коне́ц*) to put a stop (to), put an end (to); (*отноше́ния*) to break off; **п. войну́** to end the war

прекра|ти́ться, ти́тся *pf.* (*of* ▸ **прекраща́ться**) to cease, end

прекраща́|ть, ю, ет *impf. of* ▸ **прекрати́ть**

прекраща́|ться, ется *impf. of* ▸ **прекрати́ться**

прекраще́ни|е, я *nt.* stopping, cessation; **п. вое́нных де́йствий** cessation of hostilities;

✓ **key word**

п. огня́ ceasefire

преле́ст|ный, ~ен, ~на *adj.* charming, delightful, lovely

пре́лест|ь, и *f.* charm, delight; **кака́я п.!** how lovely!

преломле́ни|е, я *nt.* **1** (phys.) refraction **2** (fig.) interpretation, construction

пре́л|ый, ~, ~а *adj.* rotten, fusty

прель|сти́ться, щу́сь, сти́шься *pf.* (*of* ▸ **прельща́ться**) (+ *i.*) to be attracted (by); to be tempted (by), fall (for)

прельща́|ться, юсь *impf. of* ▸ **прельсти́ться**

прелюбодея́ни|е, я *nt.* adultery

прелю́ди|я, и *f.* (mus., also fig.) prelude

✓ **пре́ми|я, и** *f.* **1** (*победи́телю*) prize; (*рабо́тнику*) bonus; **Но́белевская п.** Nobel Prize; **п. О́скар** Oscar **2** (fin., *в страхова́нии*) premium; **страхова́я п.** insurance premium

премье́р|а, ы *f.* (theatr.) premiere, opening night

премье́р-мини́стр, а *m.* prime minister, premier

пренебрега́|ть, ю *impf. of* ▸ **пренебре́чь**

пренебреже́ни|е, я *nt.* **1** (*презре́ние*) scorn, contempt, disdain **2** (*невнима́ние*) neglect, disregard; **п. свои́ми обя́занностями** neglect of one's duties, dereliction of duty

пренебрежи́тел|ьный, ~ен, ~ьна *adj.* scornful, disdainful

пренебре́|чь, гу́, жёшь, гу́т, *past* ~г, ~гла́ *pf.* (*of* ▸ **пренебрега́ть**) (+ *i.*) **1** (*презре́ть*) to scorn, despise; **п. сове́том** to scorn advice **2** (*обя́занностями*) to neglect, disregard

преоблада́|ть, ет *impf.* to predominate; to prevail

преобража́|ть, ю *impf. of* ▸ **преобрази́ть**

преобража́|ться, юсь *impf. of* ▸ **преобрази́ться**

преобра|зи́ть, жу́, зи́шь *pf.* (*of* ▸ **преображать**) to transform

преобра|зи́ться, жу́сь, зи́шься *pf.* (*of* ▸ **преображаться**) to be transformed

преобразова́ни|е, я *nt.* **1** (*в что-н. друго́е*) transformation **2** (*рефо́рма*) reform; reorganization

преобраз|ова́ть, у́ю *pf.* (*of* ▸ **преобразо́вывать**) **1** to transform (also phys., tech.) **2** (*реформи́ровать*) to reform; (*реорганизова́ть*) to reorganize

преобразо́выва|ть, ю *impf. of* ▸ **преобразова́ть**

преодолева́|ть, ю *impf. of* ▸ **преодоле́ть**

преодоле́|ть, ю *pf.* (*of* ▸ **преодолева́ть**) to overcome, get over; **п. препя́тствия** to surmount obstacles; **п. тру́дности** to overcome difficulties

✓ **препара́т, а** *m.* (chem., med.) preparation

препина́ни|е, я *nt.*: **зна́ки** ~**я** (gram.) punctuation marks

препира́|ться, юсь *impf.* (**с** + *i.*) to wrangle (with), squabble (with)

✓ **преподава́тел|ь, я** *m.* teacher; (*ву́за*)

lecturer, instructor

преподава́тель|ница, ницы *f.* (infml) *of*
▶ преподава́тель

препода|ва́ть, ю́, ёшь *impf.* to teach

преподнес|ти́, у́, ёшь, *past* ~, ~ла́ *pf.* (*of*
▶ преподноси́ть) (+ *a. and d.*) to present
(with); (*све́дения*) to convey; (*сюрприз*)
to give

преподно|си́ть, шу́, ~сишь *impf. of*
▶ преподнести́

препя́тстви|е, я *nt.* **1** obstacle, impediment,
hindrance **2** (sport) obstacle; бег с ~ями,
ска́чки с ~ями steeplechase; взять п. to
clear an obstacle; (fig.) to clear a hurdle

препя́тств|овать, ую *impf.* (*of*
▶ воспрепя́тствовать) (+ *d.*) to hinder,
impede; to stand in the way (of)

прерв|а́ть, у́, ёшь, *past* ~а́л, ~ала́, ~а́ло
pf. (*of* ▶ прерыва́ть) (*прекрати́ть*) to
break off, sever; (*переби́ть*) to interrupt,
cut short; п. ора́тора to interrupt a speaker; нас
~а́ли we have been cut off (*while on the
telephone*)

прерв|а́ться, ётся, *past* ~а́лся, ~ала́сь,
~а́ло́сь *pf.* (*of* ▶ прерыва́ться)
1 (*приостанови́ться*) to be interrupted;
(*оборва́ться*) to be broken off **2** (*о го́лосе,
от волне́ния*) to break

пререка́|ться, юсь *impf.* (с + *i.*) to argue
(with)

прерогати́в|а, ы *f.* prerogative

прерыва́|ть, ю, ет *impf. of* ▶ прерва́ть

прерыва́|ться, ется *impf. of* ▶ прерва́ться

преры́вист|ый, ~, ~а *adj.* (*дыха́ние, звук*)
intermittent; (*ли́ния*) broken, dotted

пресека́|ть, ю, ешь *impf. of* ▶ пресе́чь

пресе́|чь, ку́, чёшь, ку́т, *past* ~к, ~кла́
pf. (*of* ▶ пресека́ть) to cut short, stop; п. в
ко́рне to nip in the bud

пресле́довани|е, я *nt.* **1** (*пого́ня*) pursuit
2 (*притесне́ние*) persecution, victimization;
ма́ния ~я persecution complex **3** (law):
суде́бное п. prosecution

пресле́дователь, я *m.* **1** (*тот, кто
го́нится за кем-н.*) pursuer **2** (*тот, кто
притесня́ет кого́-н.*) persecutor

пресле́д|овать, ую *impf.* **1** (*врага́, зве́ря*)
to pursue; (fig., *о мы́слях, чу́вствах*) to haunt
2 (fig., *интере́сы, за́мысел, же́нщину*)
to pursue; п. цель to pursue an end
3 (*притесни́ть*) to persecute **4** (law) to
prosecute

пресмыка́ющ|ееся, егося *nt.* reptile

пресново́дный *adj.* freshwater

пре́с|ный, ~, ~на́, ~но *adj.* **1** (*вода́*)
fresh, sweet **2** (*хлеб*) unleavened **3** (*пи́ща*)
flavourless (BrE), flavorless (AmE), tasteless;
(fig.) insipid, vapid

пресс, а *m.* press

пре́сс|а, ы *f.* (collect.) the press; ло́жа ~ы
press gallery

пресс-конфере́нци|я, и *f.* press conference

пресс|ова́ть, у́ю *impf.* (*of* ▶ спрессова́ть)
to press, compress

пресс-рели́з, а *m.* press release

пресс-секрета́р|ь, я́ *m.* press secretary

пресс-це́нтр, а *m.* press office

престаре́л|ый *adj.* aged, old; дом ~ых old
people's home

прести́ж, а *m.* prestige

прести́ж|ный, ~ен, ~на *adj.* prestigious

престо́л, а *m.* **1** throne; взойти́ на п. to
come to the throne; отре́чься от ~а to
abdicate **2** (eccl.) altar

✒ **преступле́ни|е, я** *nt.* crime, offence

престу́пник, а *m.* criminal; вое́нный п. war
criminal

престу́пни|ца, цы *f. of* ▶ престу́пник

престу́пност|ь, и *f.* (collect.) crime;
организо́ванная п. organized crime

престу́п|ный, ~ен, ~на *adj.* criminal

претенде́нт, а *m.* (на + *a.*) (*на престо́л*)
pretender, claimant (to); (*на насле́дство*)
claimant (to); (*на до́лжность*) candidate
(for); (sport) contender

претенде́нт|ка, ки *f. of* ▶ претенде́нт

претенд|ова́ть, у́ю *impf.* (на + *a.*) (*на
престо́л, на остроу́мие*) to have pretensions
(to); (*на насле́дство*) to lay claim (to); (*на
до́лжность*) to aspire (to); он ~у́ет на
пост мини́стра he aspires to the position of
minister

прете́нзи|я, и *f.* **1** (*заявле́ние прав*) claim;
заявля́ть ~ю (на + *a.*) to claim, lay claim
(to), make claims (on) **2** (*на остроу́мие*)
pretension; быть в ~и на кого́-н. to have a
grievance against sb **3** (*жа́лоба*) complaint

претенцио́з|ный, ~ен, ~на *adj.*
pretentious, affected

претерпева́|ть, ю *impf. of* ▶ претерпе́ть

претерп|е́ть, лю́, ~ишь *pf.* (*of*
▶ претерпева́ть) (*подве́ргнуться*) to
undergo; (*вы́терпеть*) to suffer, endure;
план ~е́л измене́ния the plan has
undergone changes

преувеличе́ни|е, я *nt.* exaggeration;
overstatement

преувели́чива|ть, ю *impf. of* ▶ преувели́чить

преувели́ч|ить, у, ишь *pf.* (*of*
▶ преувели́чивать) to exaggerate; to
overstate

преуменьш|а́ть, а́ю *impf. of* ▶ преуме́ньшить

преуме́ньш|ить, у, ишь *pf.* (*of*
▶ преуменьша́ть) (*предста́вить ме́ньшим*)
to underestimate, minimize; (*предста́вить
ме́нее ва́жным*) to belittle; to understate;
п. опа́сность to underestimate the danger

преуспева́|ть, ю *impf.* **1** *impf. of* ▶ преуспе́ть
2 (*impf. only*) to thrive, prosper, flourish

преуспева́ющий *pres. part. act. of*
▶ преуспева́ть *and adj.* successful,
prosperous

преуспе́|ть, ю *pf.* (*of* ▶ преуспева́ть 1)
(в + *p.*) to succeed (in), be successful (in);
п. в жи́зни to get on in life

прецеде́нт, а *m.* precedent

⚜ при *prep. + p.* **1** (*около*) by, at; (*в прису́тствии*) in the presence of; би́тва при Ватерло́о the Battle of Waterloo; письмо́ бы́ло подпи́сано при мне the letter was signed in my presence **2** (*под эги́дой*) attached to, affiliated to, under the auspices of (*usu. not translated*); при магази́не есть кафе́ there is a cafe attached to the shop **3** (*с собо́й*) by, with; about, on; у него́ не́ было при себе́ де́нег he had no money on him **4** (*при нали́чии*) with; (*несмотря́ на*) for, notwithstanding; при таки́х тала́нтах он далеко́ пойдёт with such talent he will go far; при уча́стии (+ *g.*) with the participation (of); при всём том with it all, moreover, for all that; при чём тут я? what has it to do with me? **5** (*во вре́мя, в эпо́ху*) in the time of, in the days of; under (*sc. the rule of*); during; при Ива́не Гро́зном during the reign of, in the time of Ivan the Terrible **6** (*ука́зывает на обстоя́тельства*) by; при све́те ла́мпы by lamplight **7** (*когда́*) when; on; in case of; при перехо́де че́рез у́лицу when crossing the street; при усло́вии(, что) under the condition (that)

при...¹ *vbl. pref. indicating* **1** *completion of action or motion up to given terminal point*: прие́хать to arrive **2** *action of attaching*: пристро́ить to build on **3** *direction of action towards speaker*: пригласи́ть to invite **4** *direction of action from above downward*: придави́ть to press down **5** *incompleteness or tentativeness of action*: приоткры́ть to open slightly **6** *exhaustiveness of action*: приучи́ть to train

при...² *as pref. of nn. and adjs.* (*esp. geog.*) *indicates juxtaposition or proximity*: приозе́рье lakeside; прибре́жный, примо́рский coastal

приба́в|ить, лю, ишь *pf.* (*of* ▸ прибавля́ть) **1** (+ *a. or g.*) to add; к пяти́ п. три to add three to five; п. (в ве́се) to put on (weight) **2** (+ *g.*) (*увели́чить*) to increase; п. ша́гу to hasten one's steps

приба́в|иться, ится *pf.* (*of* ▸ прибавля́ться) to increase; (*о воде́*) to rise; (*о луне́*) to wax

прибавле́ни|е, я *nt.* addition; п. семе́йства addition to the family; сказа́ть в п. to say in addition, add

прибавля́|ть, ю, ет *impf. of* ▸ приба́вить

прибавля́|ться, ется *impf. of* ▸ приба́виться

прибалти́йский *adj.* Baltic (= adjacent to the Baltic Sea, esp. of former Soviet republics)

Приба́лтик|а, и *f.* the Baltic States (*esp. the former Soviet republics*)

прибега́|ть¹, ю, *impf. of* ▸ прибе́гнуть

прибега́|ть², ю, *impf. of* ▸ прибежа́ть

прибе́г|нуть, ну, нешь, *past* ~(нул), ~ла *pf.* (*of* ▸ прибега́ть¹) (к + *d.*) to resort (to), have resort (to); п. к си́ле to resort to force

прибе|жа́ть, гу́, жи́шь, гу́т *pf.* (*of* ▸ прибега́ть²) (*бего́м или в спе́шке*) to come running

прибе́жищ|е, а *nt.* refuge; после́днее п. (fig.) last resort; найти́ п. (в + *p.*) to take refuge (in)

приберега́|ть, ю *impf. of* ▸ прибере́чь

прибере|чь, гу́, жёшь, гу́т, *past* ~̃г, ~гла́ *pf.* (*of* ▸ приберега́ть) to save up

прибива́|ть, ю *impf. of* ▸ приби́ть

прибира́|ть, ю *impf. of* ▸ прибра́ть

прибира́|ться, юсь *impf. of* ▸ прибра́ться

приб|и́ть, ью́, ьёшь *pf.* (*of* ▸ прибива́ть) **1** (*гвоздя́ми*) to nail; п. до́ску к стене́ to nail a board to a wall **2** (*usu. impers.*) (*волно́й, тече́нием*) to wash up; труп ~и́ло к бе́регу a body was washed ashore

приближа́|ть, ю *impf. of* ▸ прибли́зить

приближа́|ться, юсь *impf. of* ▸ прибли́зиться

приближе́ни|е, я *nt.* approach; approaching, drawing near

приблизи́тельно *adv.* approximately, roughly

приблизи́тел|ьный, ~ен, ~ьна *adj.* approximate, rough

прибли́|зить, жу, зишь *pf.* (*of* ▸ приближа́ть) **1** (*придви́нуть бли́же*) to bring nearer, move nearer; (*сде́лать бли́зким*) to bring closer **2** (*уско́рить*) to hasten, advance

прибли́|зиться, жусь, зишься *pf.* (*of* ▸ приближа́ться) (к + *d.*) to approach, draw near; to draw nearer (to), come nearer (to)

прибо́|й, я *m.* surf, breakers

⚜ прибо́р, а *m.* **1** instrument, device, apparatus, appliance **2** (*компле́кт*) set; бри́твенный п. shaving things

при|бра́ть, беру́, берёшь, *past* ~бра́л, ~брала́, ~бра́ло *pf.* (*of* ▸ прибира́ть) (infml) **1** (*привести́ в поря́док*) to clear up, clean up, tidy (up); п. ко́мнату, п. в ко́мнате to do a room; п. что-н. к рука́м to lay one's hands on sth **2** (*убра́ть*) to put away

при|бра́ться, беру́сь, берёшься, *past* ~бра́лся, ~брала́сь, ~бра́ло́сь *pf.* (*of* ▸ прибира́ться) (infml) (*произвести́ убо́рку*) to tidy/clear/clean up; (*привести́ себя́ в поря́док*) to tidy oneself up; to get dressed up

прибре́жн|ый *adj.* **1** (*у бе́рега мо́ря*) coastal; ~ая полоса́ coastal strip **2** (*у бе́рега реки́*) riverside

прибыва́|ть, ю *impf. of* ▸ прибы́ть

⚜ при́был|ь, и *f.* profit; чи́стая п. net profit

при́был|ьный, ~ен, ~ьна *adj.* profitable, lucrative

прибы́ти|е, я *nt.* arrival

при|бы́ть, бу́ду, бу́дешь, *past* ~бы́л, ~была́, ~бы́ло *pf.* (*of* ▸ прибыва́ть) (*прийти́, прие́хать*) to arrive

прива́л, а *m.* **1** (*остано́вка*) halt, stop **2** (*ме́сто остано́вки*) stopping place

прива́рива|ть, ю *impf. of* ▸ привари́ть

привар|и́ть, ю́, ~ишь *pf.* (*of* ▸ прива́ривать) (к + *d.*) to weld on (to)

приватиза́ци|я, и *f.* privatization

приватизи́р|овать, ую *impf. and pf.* to privatize

п

привез|ти́, у́, ёшь, *past* ~, ~ла́ *pf.* (*of* ▶ **привози́ть**) to bring (*not on foot*); (*товар, почту*) to deliver

привере́длив|ый, ~, ~a *adj.* fussy, finicky

приве́ржен|ный, ~, ~a *adj.* (+ *d.*) attached (to), devoted (to)

◦ **приве|сти́, ду́, дёшь**, *past* ~л, ~ла́ *pf.* (*of* ▶ **приводи́ть**, ▶ **вести́ 8**) **1** to bring; (*о дороге*) to lead, take; **он ~л с собо́й неве́сту** he has brought his fiancée (with him) **2** (**к** + *d.*) (fig.) to lead (to), bring (to), result (in); **это к добру́ не ~дёт** no good will come of it **3** (**в** + *a.*) to put, set (*or translated by v. corresponding to n. governed by* **в**); **п. в бе́шенство** to throw into a rage, drive mad, madden; **п. в движе́ние, в де́йствие** to set in motion, set going; **п. в отча́яние** to reduce to despair; **п. в поря́док** to put in order, tidy (up); to arrange, fix **4** (*слова, доказа́тельства*) to adduce, cite; **п. приме́р** to give an example

приве́т, a *m.* greeting(s); regards; **п.!** (infml) hi!; **переда́ть п.** to send one's regards

приве́тлив|ый, ~, ~a *adj.* friendly; affable; cordial

приве́тстви|е, я *nt.* **1** greeting, salutation **2** (*речь*) speech of welcome

приве́тств|овать, ую *impf.* **1** (*in past tense also pf.*) to greet; to welcome **2** (fig.) to welcome

привива́|ть, ю, ет *impf. of* ▶ **приви́ть**

привива́|ться, ется *impf. of* ▶ **приви́ться**

приви́вк|а, и *f.* (**от, про́тив** + *g.*) (med.) inoculation (against); vaccination

привиде́ни|е, я *nt.* ghost, spectre (BrE), specter (AmE); apparition

приви́|деться, дится *pf. of* ▶ **ви́деться 2**

привилегиро́ванный *adj.* privileged

привиле́ги|я, и *f.* privilege; (*для ветера́нов, инвали́дов*) benefit

привин|ти́ть, чу́, ти́шь *pf.* (*of* ▶ **приви́нчивать**) to screw on

приви́нчива|ть, ю *impf. of* ▶ **привинти́ть**

приви́|ть, ью́, ёшь, *past* ~йл, ~ила́, ~йло *pf.* (*of* ▶ **привива́ть**) (+ *a. and d.*) (med.) to inoculate (with); **п. кому́-н. о́спу** to vaccinate sb against smallpox

приви́|ться, ьётся, *past* ~йлся, ~ила́сь *pf.* (*of* ▶ **привива́ться**) **1** (*о вакци́не, черенке́*) to take **2** (fig.) (*иде́и, тео́рия*) to find acceptance; (*мо́да, интере́с*) to catch on

при́вкус, a *m.* (*посторо́нний вкус*) aftertaste; (*характе́рный вкус*) flavour (BrE), flavor (AmE)

привлека́тел|ьный, ~ен, ~ьна *adj.* attractive

◦ **привлека́|ть, ю** *impf. of* ▶ **привле́чь**

привле́|чь, ку́, чёшь, ку́т, *past* ~к, ~кла́ *pf.* (*of* ▶ **привлека́ть**) **1** to attract; **п. внима́ние** to attract attention **2** (*сде́лать уча́стником*) to draw in, involve; **п. на свою́ сто́рону** to win over (*to one's side*) **3** (law) to have up; **п. к суду́** to take to court; to put on trial; **п. к отве́тственности/отве́ту** (**за** + *a.*)

to make answer (for), call to account (for)

при́вод, a *m.* (comput., tech.) drive

◦ **приво|ди́ть, жу́, ~дишь** *impf. of* ▶ **привести́**

приво|жу́[1], **~дишь** *see* ▶ **приводи́ть**

приво|жу́[2], **~зишь** *see* ▶ **привози́ть**

приво|зи́ть, жу́, ~зишь *impf. of* ▶ **привезти́**

привра́тник, a *m.* doorman, porter

привста|ва́ть, ю́, ёшь *impf. of* ▶ **привста́ть**

привста́|ть, ну, нешь *pf.* (*of* ▶ **привстава́ть**) to half-rise

привыка́|ть, а́ю *impf. of* ▶ **привы́кнуть**

◦ **привы́к|нуть, ну, нешь**, *past* ~, ~ла *pf.* (*of* ▶ **привыка́ть**) (**к** + *d.* or + *inf.*) **1** (*осво́иться*) to get accustomed (to), get used (to) **2** (*получи́ть привы́чку*) to get into the habit (of); **он ~ руга́ться** he has got into the habit of swearing

привы́чк|а, и *f.* habit; **войти́ в ~y** to become a habit; **име́ть ~y** (**к** + *d.*) to be accustomed (to); to be in the habit (of); **приобрести́ ~y** (+ *inf.*) to get into the habit (of); **сде́лать что-н. по ~e** to do sth out of habit

привы́ч|ный, ~ен, ~на *adj.* habitual, usual, customary

привя́занност|ь, и *f.* (**к** + *d.*) attachment (to); affection (for, towards)

привя|за́ть, жу́, ~жешь *pf.* (*of* ▶ **привя́зывать**) (**к** + *d.*) to tie (to), fasten (to), attach (to); **п. верёвку/соба́ку к забо́ру** to tie a rope/the dog to the fence

привя|за́ться, жу́сь, ~жешься *pf.* (*of* ▶ **привя́зываться**) (**к** + *d.*) **1** to become attached (to); **она́ о́чень к вам ~за́лась** she has become very attached to you **2** to attach oneself (to); **на доро́ге к нам ~за́лся како́й-то ни́щий** a beggar attached himself to us on the road

привя́зыва|ть, ю *impf. of* ▶ **привяза́ть**

привя́зыва|ться, юсь *impf. of* ▶ **привяза́ться**

пригла́|дить, жу, дишь *pf.* (*of* ▶ **пригла́живать**) to smooth

пригла́жива|ть, ю *impf. of* ▶ **пригла́дить**

пригла|си́ть, шу́, си́шь *pf.* (*of* ▶ **приглаша́ть**) **1** to invite, ask; **п. кого́-н. на та́нец** to ask sb to dance, ask for a dance; **п. в го́сти** to invite, ask round **2** (*врача́*) to call

◦ **приглаша́|ть, ю** *impf. of* ▶ **пригласи́ть**

приглаше́ни|е, я *nt.* **1** invitation; **по ~ю** by invitation; **разосла́ть ~я** to send out invitations **2** (*на рабо́ту*) offer (*of employment*)

приглуш|а́, а́ю *impf. of* ▶ **приглуши́ть**

приглуш|и́ть, у́, и́шь *pf.* (*of* ▶ **приглуша́ть**) (*звук*) to muffle, deaden; (*го́лос, речь*) to mute; (*свет, ра́дио*) to turn down; (*ого́нь*) to choke, damp; (*то́ску*) to relieve

пригля|де́ть, жу́, ди́шь *pf.* (*of* ▶ **пригля́дывать**) (infml) (*подыска́ть*) to find, look out (BrE) **2** (**за** + *i.*) to look after; **п. за детьми́** to look after children

пригля|де́ться, жу́сь, ди́шься *pf.* (*of* ▶ **пригля́дываться**) (infml) (**к** + *d.*)

п

1 (*внимательно посмотреть*) to look closely (at), scrutinize **2** (*привыкнуть*) to get accustomed (to), get used (to); **п. к темноте́** to get accustomed to darkness

пригля́дыва|ть, ю *impf. of* ▶ пригляде́ть

пригля́дыва|ться, юсь *impf. of*
▶ пригляде́ться

пригля́ну|ться, усь, ~ешься *pf.* (+ *d.*) (*infml*) to take one's fancy, attract; **она́ сра́зу ~у́лась ему́** he was attracted to her instantly

при|гна́ть¹, гоню́, го́нишь, *past* ~гна́л, ~гнала́, ~гна́ло *pf.* (*of* ▶ пригоня́ть) (*гоня, доставить*) to drive

при|гна́ть², гоню́, го́нишь, *past* ~гна́л, ~гнала́, ~гна́ло *pf.* (*of* ▶ пригоня́ть) (*приладить*) to fit, adjust

пригова́рива|ть, ю *impf. of* ▶ приговори́ть

пригово́р, а *m.* (*судьи*) sentence; **вы́нести п.** to pass sentence; **отмени́ть п.** to quash a sentence; (*присяжных*) verdict

приговор|и́ть, ю́, и́шь *pf.* (*of*
▶ пригова́ривать) (**к** + *d.*) to sentence (to), condemn (to)

приго|ди́ться, жу́сь, ди́шься *pf.* (+ *d.*) to prove useful (to), come in handy; to stand in good stead

приго́д|ный, ~ен, ~на *adj.* (**к** + *d.*) fit (for), suitable (for), good (for)

пригоня́|ть, ю *impf. of* ▶ пригна́ть¹,
▶ пригна́ть²

пригор|а́ть, а́ет *impf. of* ▶ пригоре́ть

пригор|е́ть, и́т (*of* ▶ пригора́ть) to be burnt

при́город, а *m.* suburb

при́городный *adj.* suburban; **п. по́езд** local train

пригота́влива|ть, ю *impf.* = приготовля́ть

пригота́влива|ться, юсь *impf.*
= приготовля́ться

пригото́в|ить, лю, ишь *pf.* (*of*
▶ пригота́вливать, ▶ приготовля́ть) to prepare; **п. обе́д** to cook, prepare a dinner

пригото́в|иться, люсь, ишься *pf.* (*of*
▶ пригота́вливаться, ▶ приготовля́ться)
(+ *inf.*) to prepare (to); (**к** + *d.*) to prepare (oneself) (for)

✐ **приготовле́ни|е, я** *nt.* preparation

приготовля́|ть, ю *impf. of* ▶ пригото́вить

приготовля́|ться, юсь *impf. of*
▶ пригото́виться

пригро|зи́ть, жу́, зи́шь *pf. of* ▶ грози́ть 1

прида|ва́ть, ю́, ёшь *impf. of* ▶ прида́ть

прида́|ть, м, шь, ст, ди́м, ди́те, ду́т, *past*
~л, ~ла́, ~ло *pf.* (*of* ▶ придава́ть) **1** to add **2** (*усилить*) to increase, strengthen;
п. бо́дрости (+ *d.*) to hearten, put heart (into) **3** (+ *a. and d.*) (*свойство, состояние*) to give (to), impart (to); (fig.) to attach (to);
п. значе́ние to attach importance (to); **п. фо́рму** to shape (to)

придвига́|ть, ю *impf. of* ▶ придви́нуть

придвига́|ться, юсь *impf. of* ▶ придви́нуться

придви́|нуть, ну, нешь *pf.* (*of* ▶ придвига́ть) to move (up), draw (up); **~нь(те) кре́сло к пе́чке** draw your chair up to the stove

придви́|нуться, нусь, нешься *pf.* (*of*
▶ придвига́ться) (**к** + *d.*) to move

придво́рн|ый *adj.* court; **п. шут** court jester;
(*as m. n.* **п., ~ого**) courtier

приде́ла|ть, ю *pf.* (*of* ▶ приде́лывать)
(**к** + *d.*) to fix (to), attach (to)

приде́лыва|ть, ю *impf. of* ▶ приде́лать

приде́ржива|ться, юсь *impf.* **1** (**за** + *a.*)
to hold on (to) **2** (+ *g.*) to hold (to), keep (to) (also fig.); (fig.) to stick (to), adhere (to); (*моды, советов*) to follow; **п. пра́вой стороны́** to keep to the right; **п. догово́ра** to adhere to an agreement; **п. мне́ния** to hold the opinion, be of the opinion; **п. пра́вил** to stick to, follow the rules

придира́|ться, юсь *impf. of* ▶ придра́ться

при|дра́ться, деру́сь, дерёшься, *past*
~дра́лся, ~драла́сь, ~дра́ло́сь *pf.* (*of*
▶ придира́ться) (**к** + *d.*) to find fault (with), carp (at); to nag (at), pick (on); **п. к кому́-н. из-за пустяко́в/по пустяка́м** to find fault with sb over trifles

приду́ *see* ▶ прийти́

приду́ма|ть, аю *pf.* (*of* ▶ приду́мывать)
1 (*отговорку, выход*) to think of, think up;
(*приспособление*) to devise, invent; (*сказку, песню*) to make up; (*музыку*) to compose, make up; **наконе́ц я ~ал, что де́лать** at last I have thought of what to do **2** (*вообразить*) to imagine

приду́мыва|ть, ю *impf. of* ▶ приду́мать

придур|ок, ка *m.* (infml) idiot, fool

прие́зд, а *m.* arrival, coming; **с ~ом!** welcome!

✐ **приезжа́|ть, ю** *impf. of* ▶ прие́хать

прие́зж|ий *adj.* newly arrived; visiting; (*as n. п., ~его, f. ~ая, ~ей*) newcomer; (*гость*) visitor

✐ **приём, а** *m.* **1** (*действие*) receiving; reception; **часы́ ~а** (reception) hours, calling hours; (*врача*) surgery (hours) (BrE), office hours (AmE) **2** (*гостей*) reception, welcome; **оказа́ть кому́-н. ра́душный п.** to accord sb a hearty welcome **3** (*в па́ртию, клуб*) admittance **4** (*собрание приглашённых*) reception **5** (*лека́рства*) dose **6** (*отдельное действие*) go; motion, movement; **в оди́н п.** at one go; **испо́лнить кома́нду в три ~а** to execute a command in three movements **7** (*способ*) method, way, mode; (*уловка*) device, trick (also pej.);
(sport) hold, grip; **лече́бный п.** method of treatment **8** (radio, TV) reception

прие́млем|ый, ~, ~а *adj.* acceptable; admissible

приёмн|ая, ой *f.* **1** (*для ожидания*) waiting room **2** (*где принимают гостей*) reception room

приёмник, а *m.* (*радиоприёмник*) radio (set); (*для приёма сигналов*) receiver

---

✐ key word

приёмн|ый *adj.* **1** receiving; reception; **п. день** visiting day; **~ые часы́** (reception) hours; (*врача́*) surgery (hours) (BrE), office hours (AmE); **п. поко́й** casualty ward **2** selection; entrance; **~ая коми́ссия** selection committee **3** foster, adoptive; **п. оте́ц** foster-father; **п. сын** adopted son, foster-son

♂ **прие́|хать, ду, дешь** *pf.* (*of* ▶ приезжа́ть) to arrive, come (*not on foot*)

прижа́|ть, му́, мёшь *pf.* (*of* ▶ прижима́ть) (**к** + *d.*) to press (to), clasp (to); **п. к груди́** to clasp to one's bosom; **п. к стене́** (fig.) to drive into a corner

прижа́|ться, му́сь, мёшься *pf.* (*of* ▶ прижима́ться) (**к** + *d.*) (*прислони́ться*) to press oneself (to, against); (*к ма́тери*) to cuddle up (to), snuggle up (to), nestle up (to); **п. к стене́** to flatten oneself against the wall

прижжё́чь, жгу́, жжёшь, жгу́т, *past* **~жёг, ~жгла́** *pf.* (*of* ▶ прижига́ть) to cauterize, sear

прижива́|ться, юсь *impf. of* ▶ прижи́ться

прижига́|ть, ю *impf. of* ▶ прижже́чь

прижима́|ть, ю *impf. of* ▶ прижа́ть

прижима́|ться, юсь *impf. of* ▶ прижа́ться

прижи́|ться, иву́сь, ивёшься, *past* **~и́лся, ~ила́сь** *pf.* (*of* ▶ прижива́ться) **1** (*прожив, привы́кнуть*) to settle down, get acclimatized (BrE), acclimated (AmE) **2** (*о расте́ниях*) to take root

приз, а, *pl.* **~ы́** *m.* prize; **получи́ть п.** to win a prize; **присуди́ть п.** (+ *d.*) to award a prize (to)

призва́ни|е, я *nt.* (*назначе́ние*) vocation, calling; **сле́довать своему́ ~ю** to follow one's vocation; (*скло́нность*) aptitude; (*му́зыки, теа́тра*) mission, purpose

при|зва́ть, зову́, зовёшь, *past* **~зва́л, ~звала́, ~зва́ло** *pf.* (*of* ▶ призыва́ть) (*позва́ть яви́ться*) to call, summon; (*позва́ть де́лать что-н.*) to call upon, appeal; **п. на вое́нную слу́жбу** to call up (*for military service*); **п. к поря́дку** to call to order

призе́мист|ый, ~, ~а *adj.* stocky, squat; thickset

приземле́ни|е, я *nt.* (aeron.) landing, touchdown

приземл|и́ться, ю́сь, и́шься *pf.* (*of* ▶ приземля́ться) (aeron.) to land, touch down

приземля́|ться, юсь *impf. of* ▶ приземли́ться

призёр, а *m.* prizewinner

при́зм|а, ы *f.* prism

♂ **призна|ва́ть, ю́, ёшь** *impf. of* ▶ призна́ть

призна|ва́ться, ю́сь, ёшься *impf. of* ▶ призна́ться

♂ **при́знак, а** *m.* sign; indication; **служи́ть ~ом** (+ *g.*) to be a sign (of); **обнару́живать ~и** (+ *g.*) to show signs (of); **не подава́ть ~ов**

жи́зни to show no sign of life

призна́ни|е, я *nt.* **1** (*заявле́ние*) confession, declaration; admission, acknowledgement; **п. вины́** (*обвиня́емым*) admission of guilt; **п. вино́вным** (*судо́м*) guilty verdict; **п. в любви́** declaration of love **2** (*оце́нка по досто́инству*) recognition; **получи́ть п.** to obtain, win recognition

при́знанный *p.p.p. of* ▶ призна́ть *and adj.* acknowledged, recognized

призна́тел|ьный, ~ен, ~ьна *adj.* grateful

призна́|ть, ю *pf.* (*of* ▶ признава́ть) **1** (law, pol.) to recognize; **п. прави́тельство** to recognize a government **2** (*созна́ть*) to admit, acknowledge; **п. себя́ вино́вным** (law) to plead guilty; **п. свою́ оши́бку** to admit one's mistake **3** (*счита́ть*) to deem; **п. недействи́тельным** to declare invalid; **п. (не)вино́вным** to find (not) guilty

призна́|ться, юсь *pf.* (*of* ▶ признава́ться) (**в** + *p.*) to confess (to)

при́зрак, а *m.* spectre (BrE), specter (AmE), ghost, apparition

призы́в, а *m.* **1** (*про́сьба*) call, appeal; **откли́кнуться на чей-н. п.** to respond to sb's call **2** (mil.) call-up, conscription

призыва́|ть, ю *impf. of* ▶ призва́ть

призывни́к, а́ *m.* conscript

при́иск, а *m.* mine; **золоты́е ~и** gold field(s)

♂ **при|йти́, ду́, дёшь,** *past* **~шёл, ~шла́** *pf.* (*of* ▶ приходи́ть) to come; to arrive; **п. пе́рвым** to come first; **п. в восто́рг** (**от** + *g.*) to go into raptures (over); **п. в у́жас** to be horrified; **п. в я́рость** to fly into a rage; **п. в го́лову кому́-н.** to occur to sb, strike sb, cross sb's mind; **п. в себя́, п. в чу́вство** to come round, regain consciousness; (fig.) to come to one's senses; **п. к соглаше́нию** to come to an agreement

♂ **при|йти́сь, ду́сь, дёшься,** *past* **~шёлся, ~шла́сь** *pf.* (*of* ▶ приходи́ться) **1** (**по** + *d.*) to fit; **п. кому́-н. по вку́су, по нра́ву** to be to sb's taste, liking **2** (**на** + *a.*) (*о да́тах, собы́тиях*) to fall (on); **Па́сха ~шла́сь на 28-е ма́рта** Easter fell on the 28th of March **3** (*impers.* + *d.*) (*оказа́ться ну́жным*) to have (to); **ей ~дётся неме́дленно верну́ться в Москву́** she will have to return to Moscow immediately **4** (*impers.* + *d.*) (*вы́пасть на до́лю*) to happen (to), fall to the lot (of); **мне ~шло́сь быть ря́дом в тот моме́нт, когда́ он упа́л в о́бморок** I happened to be standing by when he fainted; **ему́ ~шло́сь тяжело́** he had a hard time; **как ~дётся** (infml) anyhow; **что ~дётся** anything; whatever comes along

♂ **прика́з, а** *m.* order, command; **вы́полнить п.** to carry out an order; **отда́ть п.** to give an order; **по ~у** by order

прика|за́ть, жу́, ~жешь *pf.* (*of* ▶ прика́зывать) (+ *d.*) to order; to give orders; **дире́ктор ~за́л соста́вить но́вый гра́фик** the director ordered that a new schedule should be worked out

прика́зыва|ть, ю *impf. of* ▶ приказа́ть

прика́лыва|ть, ю *impf. of* ▶ **приколо́ть**

прика́нчива|ть, ю *impf. of* ▶ **прико́нчить**

прикаса́|ться, юсь *impf. of* ▶ **прикосну́ться**

прики́дыва|ться, юсь *impf. of*
▶ **прики́нуться**

прики́|нуться, нусь, нешься *pf. (of*
▶ **прики́дываться**) (+ *i.*) (infml) to pretend
(to be), feign; **п. больны́м** to pretend to be
ill; to feign illness

прикла́д, а *m.* (*ружья́*) butt

прикладн|о́й *adj.* applied; **~о́е иску́сство**
applied arts; **~а́я програ́мма** (comput.)
application (program)

прикла́дыва|ть, ю *impf. of* ▶ **приложи́ть 1,**
▶ **приложи́ть 2**

прикле́ива|ть, ю, ет *impf. of* ▶ **прикле́ить**

прикле́ива|ться, ется *impf. of*
▶ **прикле́иться**

прикле́|ить, ю, ишь *pf.* (*of* ▶ **прикле́ивать**)
to stick; to glue; **п. ма́рку** to stick on a stamp;
п. афи́шу к стене́ to stick a bill (up) on a wall

прикле́|иться, ится *pf.* (*of* ▶ **прикле́иваться**)
(**к** + *d.*) to stick (to), adhere (to)

приключа́|ться, а́ется *impf. of*
▶ **приключи́ться**

приключе́ни|е, я *nt.* adventure

приключи́|ться, и́тся *pf.* (*of*
▶ **приключа́ться**) (infml) to happen, occur

прик|ова́ть, ую́, уёшь *pf.* (*of* ▶ **прико́вывать**)
(**к** + *d.*) **1** to chain (to) **2** (fig.) (*взгляд*) to fix;
(*внима́ние*) to rivet; **боле́знь ~ова́ла его́ к
посте́ли** illness confined him to his bed

прико́выва|ть, ю *impf. of* ▶ **прикова́ть**

прикола́чива|ть, ю *impf. of* ▶ **приколоти́ть**

приколо|ти́ть, чу́, ~тишь *pf.* (*of*
▶ **прикола́чивать**) to nail, fasten with nails

прикол|о́ть, ю́, ~ешь *pf.* (*of*
▶ **прика́лывать**) to pin, fasten with a pin

прико́нч|ить, у, ишь *pf.* (*of* ▶ **прика́нчивать**)
(infml) **1** (*израсхо́довать*) to use up **2** (fig.,
умертви́ть) to finish off

прикоснове́ни|е, я *nt.* touch

прикосну́|ться, у́сь, ёшься *pf.* (*of*
▶ **прикаса́ться**) (**к** + *d.*) to touch (lightly)

прикреп|и́ть, лю́, и́шь *pf.* (*of*
▶ **прикрепля́ть**) (**к** + *d.*) to fasten (to)

прикрепля́|ть, ю *impf. of* ▶ **прикрепи́ть**

прикру|ти́ть, чу́, ~тишь *pf.* (*of*
▶ **прикру́чивать**) (**к** + *d.*) to tie (to), bind
(to), fasten (to)

прикру́чива|ть, ю *impf. of* ▶ **прикрути́ть**

прикрыва́|ть, ю *impf. of* ▶ **прикры́ть**

прикрыва́|ться, юсь *impf. of* ▶ **прикры́ться**

прикр|ы́ть, о́ю, о́ешь *pf.* (*of* ▶ **прикрыва́ть**)
1 (+ *i.*) (*покры́ть*) to cover (with); to screen
2 (*защити́ть*) to protect, shield; **п. глаза́
руко́й** to shade, shield one's eyes (with
one's hand); (*о войска́х*) to cover **3** (infml,
ликвиди́ровать) to close down, wind up

4 (infml, *закры́ть непло́тно*) to close (*a door,
etc.*) to

прикр|ы́ться, о́юсь, о́ешься *pf.* (*of*
▶ **прикрыва́ться**) **1** (+ *i.*) to cover oneself
(with); (fig.) to use as a cover, take refuge
(in), shelter (behind); **он ~ы́лся боле́знью**
he took refuge in being ill **2** (infml,
ликвиди́роваться) to close down, go out
of business **3** (infml, *закры́ться непло́тно*)
to close to

прикури́ва|ть, ю *impf. of* ▶ **прикури́ть**

прикур|и́ть, ю́, ~ишь *pf.* (*of*
▶ **прику́ривать**): **п. у кого́-н.** to get a light
(*from sb's cigarette*)

прила́в|ок, ка *m.* counter; (*на ры́нке*) stall

прилага́тельн|ое *adj.*: **и́мя ~ое** (*or as nt. n.*
~ое, ~ого) adjective

прилага́|ть, ю *impf. of* ▶ **приложи́ть 3**

прилата́|ть, ю *pf.* to caress, pet;
(*отнести́сь хорошо́*) to show kindness to

прилата́|ться, юсь *pf.* (**к** + *d.*) to snuggle
up (to)

приле́ж|ный, ~ен, ~на *adj.* diligent,
assiduous

прилеп|и́ть, лю́, ~ишь *pf.* (*of*
▶ **прилепля́ть**) (**к** + *d.*) to stick (to, on)

прилеп|и́ться, лю́сь, ~ишься *pf.* (*of*
▶ **прилепля́ться**) (**к** + *d.*) to stick (to, on)

прилепля́|ть, ю *impf. of* ▶ **прилепи́ть**

прилепля́|ться, юсь *impf. of*
▶ **прилепи́ться**

прилёт, а *m.* arrival (*by air*)

прилета́|ть, а́ю *impf. of* ▶ **прилете́ть**

приле|те́ть, чу́, ти́шь *pf.* (*of* ▶ **прилета́ть**)
1 to arrive (*by air*), fly in **2** (fig., infml,
бы́стро прибы́ть) to fly, come flying

при|ле́чь, ля́гу, ля́жешь, ля́гут, *past* **~лёг,
~легла́** *pf.* to lie down, have a lie-down (BrE)

прили́в, а *m.* **1** rising tide; (fig., *люде́й,
де́нег*) influx; **п. и отли́в** ebb and flow
2 (med.) congestion; (fig.): **п. эне́ргии,
негодова́ния** surge of energy, indignation

прилип|а́ть, а́ет *impf. of* ▶ **прили́пнуть**

прили́п|нуть, нет, *past* **~, ~ла** *pf.* (*of*
▶ **прилипа́ть**) (**к** + *d.*) to stick (to), adhere
(to)

прили́ч|ный, ~ен, ~на *adj.* **1** decent,
proper; decorous, seemly **2** (infml,
доста́точно хоро́ший) decent, fair; **~ная
зарпла́та** a decent wage; (*доста́точно
большо́й*) sizeable

✍ **приложе́ни|е, я** *nt.* **1** (*докуме́нтов к
письму́*) enclosure; (comput., *к электро́нному
письму́*) attachment **2** (*к журна́лу,
газе́те*) supplement **3** (*к кни́ге*) appendix;
(*к докуме́нту*) addendum **4** (comput.)
(*прикладна́я програ́мма*) application;
(*небольшо́е*) applet

прилож|и́ть, у́, ~ишь *pf.* **1** (*impf.*
прикла́дывать) (**к** + *d.*) (*положи́ть*)
to put (to), hold (to); **п. ру́ку ко лбу** to
put one's hand to one's head **2** (*impf.*
прикла́дывать *and* **прилага́ть**)

(*прибавить*) to add; (*к письму*) to enclose; (*печать*) to affix **5** (*impf.* **прилагáть**) (*использовать*) to apply; **п. все усúлия** to make every effort

примáнива|ть, ю *impf. of* ▶ **приманúть**

приман|úть, ю, ~ишь *pf.* (*of* ▶ **примáнивать**) (infml) to lure; to entice

примáнк|а, и *f.* bait; (fig.) enticement, allurement

примáт, а *m.* (zool.) primate

⚘ **применéни|е, я** *nt.* application; (*употребление*) use, employment; **нáши мéтоды получúли широ́кое п.** our methods have been widely adopted; **непрáвильное п.** misuse; **в ~и** (*к + d.*) in application (to)

примен|úть, ю, ~ишь *pf.* (*of* ▶ **применя́ть**) to apply; to employ, use; **п. свои́ знáния** to apply one's knowledge; **п. на прáктике** to put into practice

примен|úться, ю́сь, ~ишься *pf.* (*of* ▶ **применя́ться**) (*к + d.*) to be used; to be applied

⚘ **применя́|ть, ю** *impf. of* ▶ **применúть**

⚘ **применя́|ться, юсь** *impf. of* ▶ **применúться**

⚘ **примéр, а** *m.* **1** example, instance; **привестú п.** to give an example; **к ~у** for example **2** (*образец*) example; model; **брать п. с кого́-н., слéдовать чьему́-н. ~у** to follow sb's example; **показáть п.** to give an example, give the lead; **по ~у** (*+ g.*) after the example (of), on the pattern (of)

примéр|ить, ю, ишь *pf.* (*of* ▶ **мéрить 2,** ▶ **примеря́ть**) to try on

⚘ **примéрно** *adv.* approximately, roughly

примéр|ный, ~ен, ~на *adj.* **1** (*отличный*) exemplary, model **2** (*приблизительный*) approximate, rough

примéрочн|ая, ой *f.* fitting room

примеря́|ть, я́ю *impf. of* ▶ **примéрить**

при́мес|ь, и *f.* admixture; dash; (fig.) touch; **без ~ей** unadulterated

примéт|а, ы *f.* (*признак*) sign, token; mark; (*суеверие*) omen; **осо́бые ~ы** distinguishing marks

примéт|ный, ~ен, ~на *adj.* **1** (*след, волнение*) perceptible, noticeable **2** (*человек, внешность*) conspicuous, prominent

примечáни|е, я *nt.* note, comment; (*сноска*) footnote

примечáтел|ьный, ~ен, ~ьна *adj.* noteworthy, notable, remarkable

примина́|ть, ю *impf. of* ▶ **примя́ть**

примирéни|е, я *nt.* reconciliation

примир|úть, ю́, úшь *pf.* (*of* ▶ **примиря́ть,** ▶ **мирúть 2**) to reconcile; **п. супру́гов** to reconcile a husband and wife

примир|úться, ю́сь, úшься *pf.* (*of* ▶ **примиря́ться,** ▶ **мирúться 2**) (*с чем-н.*) to reconcile oneself (to); **п. с неудо́бствами** to reconcile oneself to discomforts

примиря́|ть, я́ю *impf. of* ▶ **примирúть**

примиря́|ться, я́юсь *impf. of* ▶ **примирúться**

примитúв|ный, ~ен, ~на *adj.* primitive

примкн|у́ть, у́, ёшь *pf.* (*of* ▶ **примыкáть 1**) (*к + d.*) (*плотно придвинуть, присоединить*) to fix (to), attach (to) **2** (fig., *присоединиться*) to join, attach oneself (to); to side (with)

примо́рский *adj.* seaside; (*растение, климат*) maritime

примо́чк|а, и *f.* wash, lotion

при́мус, а *m.* Primus (stove)®

примч|áться, у́сь, úшься *pf.* to come tearing along

примыкá|ть, ю *impf.* **1** *impf. of* ▶ **примкну́ть** **2** (*impf. only*) (*к + d.*) to adjoin, abut (upon)

при|мя́ть, мну́, мнёшь *pf.* (*of* ▶ **примина́ть**) to crush, flatten; (*ногами*) to trample down, tread down

⚘ **принадлеж|áть, у́, úшь** *impf.* **1** (*+ d.*) to belong (to) **2** (*к + d.*) (*быть членом*) to belong (to), be a member (of); (*входить в состав*) to be among; to be one/some of **3**: **Герма́нии ~úт веду́щая роль в химúческой промышленности** Germany plays a leading role in the chemical industry **4**: **п. ки́сти/перу́** (*+ g.*) to be the work of

⚘ **принадлéжность, и** *f.* **1** (*к + d.*) belonging (to), membership (of) **2** (*in pl.*) accessories; equipment; gear; **канцеля́рские ~и** stationery

⚘ **принес|тú, у́, ёшь,** *past* **~, ~лá** *pf.* (*of* ▶ **приносúть**) **1** (*неся, доставить*) to bring (also fig.); to fetch; **п. обрáтно** to bring back; **п. в жéртву** to sacrifice; **п. извинéния** to apologize **2** (*приплод, урожай*) to bear, yield; to result; **п. результáт** to yield/give results; (*причинить*) to bring in; **п. большо́й дохо́д** to bring in big revenues, show a large return; **п. по́льзу** to be of use, be of benefit; (*о чём-л. нежелательном*) **отку́да тебя́ ~ло́ в тако́й час?** where have you come from at this hour?

приник|áть, áю *impf. of* ▶ **приникнуть**

прини́к|нуть, ну, нешь, *past* **~, ~ла** *pf.* (*of* ▶ **приникáть**) (*к + d.*) to press oneself (against, to); (*прильнуть*) to nestle up (against, to); **мы ~ли к землé** we pressed ourselves to the ground

⚘ **принимá|ть, ю** *impf. of* ▶ **приня́ть**

принимá|ться, юсь *impf. of* ▶ **приня́ться**

принорáвлива|ться, юсь *impf. of* ▶ **приноровúться**

приноров|úться, лю́сь, úшься *pf.* (*of* ▶ **принорáвливаться**) (*к + d.*) to adapt oneself (to), accommodate oneself (to)

⚘ **прино|сúть, шу́, ~сишь** *impf. of* ▶ **принестú**

при́нтер, а *m.* (comput.) printer

принудúтел|ьный, ~ен, ~ьна *adj.* compulsory, forced; **~ьные рабо́ты** forced labour (BrE), labor (AmE)

прину|дúть, жу́, ди́шь *pf.* (*of* ▶ **принуждáть**) to force, compel, coerce

принуждá|ть, ю *impf. of* ▶ **принудúть**

принуждéни|е, я *nt.* compulsion, coercion; **по ~ю** under duress

принц, а *m.* prince

принцéсс|а, ы *f.* princess

✔ **при́нцип, а** *m.* principle; **в ~е** in principle
принципиа́льно *adv.* **1** (*из принципа*) on principle; **п.** отказа́ться to refuse on principle **2** (*в принципе*) in principle **3**: **п.** отлича́ться to differ fundamentally
принципиа́л|ьный, ~ен, ~ьна *adj.* **1** of principle; based on, guided by principle; **п.** челове́к man of principle; **име́ть ~ное** значе́ние to be a matter of principle **2** (*в основном*) in principle; general; **они́** да́ли **~ное** согла́сие they consented in principle **3** (*коренной*): **~ное** разли́чие fundamental difference
принюх|аться, аюсь *pf.* (*of* ▶ **принюхиваться**) (infml) to sniff
принюхива|ться, юсь *impf. of* ▶ **принюхаться**
✔ **приня́ти|е, я** *nt.* **1** (*пищи, лекарства, решения, присяги*) taking; (*поста, позы*) taking up **2** (*приглашения, предложения*) acceptance **3** (*гостей, пациентов*) receiving **4** (*в партию*) admission, admittance; **п.** гражда́нства naturalization
при́нят|ый *p.p.p. of* ▶ **приня́ть**; **~о** (+ *inf.*) it is accepted, it is usual (*to do sth*); **не ~о** it is not done, it is not accepted
✔ **при|ня́ть, му́, ~мешь,** *past* **~ня́л, ~няла́, ~няло** *pf.* (*of* ▶ **принима́ть**) **1** to take; (*взять как дар; согласиться*) to accept; **п.** ва́нну/душ to take, have a bath/shower; **п.** лека́рство to take medicine; **п. ме́ры** to take measures; **п.** пода́рок to accept a present; **п.** реше́ние to take, reach a decision; **п.** уча́стие (**в** + *p.*) to take part (in); to participate (in); **п.** во внима́ние to take into consideration; **не п.** во внима́ние to disregard **2** (*пост*) to take up; **п. дела́** (**от** + *g.*) to take over duties (from) **3** (*через голосование*) to accept; **п.** резолю́цию to pass, adopt, carry a resolution **4** (**в, на** + *a.*) (*зачислить*) to admit (to); to accept (for); **п. на** слу́жбу to accept for a job **5** (*посетителей, пациентов, заказ*) to receive; **они́ ~ня́ли** нас раду́шно they gave us a warm welcome, a cordial reception **6** (*приобрести*) to assume, take (on); **перегово́ры ~ня́ли** благоприя́тный оборо́т the talks took a favourable (BrE), favorable (AmE) turn **7** (+ *a. and* **за** + *a.*) (*счесть по ошибке*) to take (for); **я ~нял** вас **за** шотла́ндца I took you for a Scotsman
при|ня́ться, му́сь, ~мешься, *past* **~ня́лся, ~няла́сь** *pf.* (*of* ▶ **принима́ться**) **1** (+ *inf.*) (*начать*) to begin; to start **2** (**за** + *a.*) to set (to), get down (to); **п. за** рабо́ту to set to work
приободр|и́ть, ю́, и́шь *pf.* (*of* ▶ **приободря́ть**) to cheer up, encourage, hearten
приободр|я́ть, я́ю *impf. of* ▶ **приободри́ть**
приобре|сти́, ту́, тёшь, *past* **~л, ~ла́** *pf.* (*of* ▶ **приобрета́ть**) **1** (*дом, друзей, маши́ну*) to acquire; (*авторитет, репутацию*) to gain; **п. о́пыт** to gain experience **2** (*свойство*) to take on, assume; **пробле́ма ~ла́** осо́бое

значе́ние the problem took on a special significance
✔ **приобрета́|ть, ю** *impf. of* ▶ **приобрести́**
✔ **приобрете́ни|е, я** *nt.* acquisition
приобща́|ть, а́ю *impf. of* ▶ **приобщи́ть**
приобща́|ться, а́юсь *impf. of* ▶ **приобщи́ться**
приобщ|и́ть, у́, и́шь *pf.* (*of* ▶ **приобща́ть**) **1** (**к** + *d.*) (*познакомить*) to introduce (to); **п.** ребёнка **к** иску́сству to introduce a child to art **2** (*присоединить*) to join, attach; **п. к** де́лу to file
приобщ|и́ться, у́сь, и́шься *pf.* (*of* ▶ **приобща́ться**) (**к** + *d.*) to join (in), become involved (in)
приоде́|ть, ну, нешь *pf.* (infml) to dress up, smarten up
приоде́|ться, нусь, нешься *pf.* (infml) to dress up; to get dressed up; to smarten oneself up
приорите́т, а *m.* priority
приоса́нива|ться, юсь *impf. of* ▶ **приоса́ниться**
приоса́н|иться, юсь, ишься *pf.* (infml) to assume a dignified air
приостана́влива|ть, ю *impf. of* ▶ **приостанови́ть**
приостана́влива|ться, юсь *impf. of* ▶ **приостанови́ться**
приостанов|и́ть, лю́, ~ишь *pf.* (*of* ▶ **приостана́вливать**) to halt, suspend
приостанов|и́ться, лю́сь, ~ишься *pf.* (*of* ▶ **приостана́вливаться**) to halt, come to a halt; (*о человеке*) to pause
приоткрыва́|ть, ю *impf. of* ▶ **приоткры́ть**
приоткрыва́|ться, юсь *impf. of* ▶ **приоткры́ться**
приоткр|ы́ть, о́ю, о́ешь *pf.* (*of* ▶ **приоткрыва́ть**) to open slightly, half-open; **п.** дверь to half-open the door, set the door ajar
приоткр|ы́ться, о́юсь, о́ешься *pf.* (*of* ▶ **приоткрыва́ться**) to open slightly, half-open
припада́|ть, ю *impf. of* ▶ **припа́сть**
припа́д|ок, ка *m.* fit; attack; не́рвный **п.** attack of nerves
припа́ива|ть, ю *impf. of* ▶ **припая́ть**
припарк|ова́ть, у́ю *pf.* (*of* ▶ **паркова́ть**) to park
припарк|ова́ться, у́юсь *pf.* (*of* ▶ **паркова́ться**) to park
припа́|сть, ду́, дёшь, *past* **~л** *pf.* (*of* ▶ **припада́ть**) (**к** + *d.*) (*к земле, к груди*) to press oneself (to); (*склониться*) to fall down (before); **п.** у́хом to press one's ear (to)
припая́|ть, ю *pf.* (*of* ▶ **припа́ивать**) (**к** + *d.*) to solder (to)
припи|са́ть, шу́, ~шешь *pf.* (*of* ▶ **припи́сывать**) **1** (*написать в добавление*) to add **2** (**к** + *d.*) (*причислить, записать*) to register (at) **3** (+ *d.*) to attribute (to); to ascribe (to); to put down

п

(to); **п. стихотворе́ние Пу́шкину** to attribute a poem to Pushkin; **п. неуда́чу ле́ни** to put a failure down to laziness

припи́сыва|ть, ю *impf. of* ▶ **приписа́ть**

приплыва́|ть, ю *impf. of* ▶ **приплы́ть**

приплы́|ть, ву́, вёшь, *past* **∼л, ∼ла́, ∼ло** *pf.* (*of* ▶ **приплыва́ть**) (*вплавь*) to swim up; (*на ло́дке*) to sail up

приплю́снут|ый, ∼, ∼а *adj.* flattened; **п. нос** flat nose

приподнима́|ть, ю *impf. of* ▶ **приподня́ть**

приподнима́|ться, юсь *impf. of* ▶ **приподня́ться**

припо́днятый *p.p.p. of* ▶ **приподня́ть** *and adj.* (*оживлённый*) elated; animated; (*торже́ственный*) elevated

приподня́|ть, иму́, и́мешь, *past* **∼́ял, ∼яла́, ∼́яло** *pf.* (*of* ▶ **приподнима́ть**) to raise slightly; to lift slightly

приподня́|ться, иму́сь, и́мешься, *past* **∼́ялся, ∼яла́сь** *pf.* (*of* ▶ **приподнима́ться**) to raise oneself (a little); **п. на носка́х** to rise on one's toes

приполза́|ть, а́ю *impf. of* ▶ **приползти́**

приполз|ти́, у́, ёшь, *past* **∼, ∼ла́** *pf.* (*of* ▶ **приполза́ть**) to creep up, crawl up

припомина́|ть, ю *impf. of* ▶ **припо́мнить**

припо́м|нить, ню, нишь *pf.* (*of* ▶ **припомина́ть**) **1** to remember, recollect, recall **2** (+ *d.*) to remind; **я э́то тебе́ ∼ню!** (infml) you won't forget this!; I'll get even with you for this!

припра́в|а, ы *f.* flavouring (BrE), flavoring (AmE), seasoning; (*соус*) dressing; **п. к сала́ту** salad dressing

припра́в|ить, лю, ишь *pf.* (*of* ▶ **приправля́ть**) (+ *i.*) to season (with), flavour (BrE), flavor (AmE) (with); (*со́усом*) to dress (with)

приправля́|ть, ю *impf. of* ▶ **припра́вить**

припря́|тать, чу, чешь *pf.* (*of* ▶ **припря́тывать**) (infml) to put by, store up (*for future use*)

припря́тыва|ть, ю *impf. of* ▶ **припря́тать**

припу́гива|ть, ю *impf. of* ▶ **припугну́ть**

припуг|ну́ть, ну́, нёшь *pf.* (*of* ▶ **припу́гивать**) (infml) to intimidate, scare

прира́внива|ть, ю *impf. of* ▶ **приравня́ть**

приравн|я́ть, я́ю *pf.* (*of* ▶ **прира́внивать**) (к + *d.*) to equate (with)

прираст|а́ть, а́ю *impf. of* ▶ **прирасти́**

прираст|и́, у́, ёшь, *past* **прирос, приросла́** *pf.* (*of* ▶ **прираста́ть**) **1** (к + *d.*) to adhere (to); (*о переса́женной тка́ни, о черенке*) to take **2** (*увели́читься*) to increase; (*проце́нты*) to accrue

✧ **приро́д|а, ы** *f.* **1** nature **2** (*хара́ктер*) nature, character; **от ∼ы** by nature, congenitally; **по ∼е** by nature, naturally

✧ **приро́дн|ый** *adj.* **1** (*со́зданный приро́дой*) natural; **∼ые бога́тства** natural resources; **п. газ** natural gas **2** (*врождённый*) inborn, innate; **п. ум** native wit

природове́дени|е, я *nt.* natural history

прирождённый *adj.* **1** (*о спосо́бностях*) inborn, innate **2** (*о челове́ке*) a born; **п. лгун** a born liar

прирост, а *m.* increase, growth

прируч|а́ть, а́ю *impf. of* ▶ **приручи́ть**

прируче́ни|е, я *nt.* taming; domestication

приру́ч|ить, у́, и́шь *pf.* (*of* ▶ **прируча́ть**) to tame (also fig.); to domesticate

приса́жива|ться, юсь *impf. of* ▶ **присе́сть 1**

приса́сыва|ться, юсь *impf. of* ▶ **присоса́ться**

присва́ива|ть, ю *impf. of* ▶ **присво́ить**

присво́|ить, ю, ишь *pf.* (*of* ▶ **присва́ивать**) **1** (*завладе́ть*) to appropriate; **незако́нно п. сре́дства** to misappropriate funds **2** (+ *a. and d.*) (*дать*) to give, award, confer; **ему́ ∼или сте́пень до́ктора нау́к** he has been given the degree of Doctor

приседа́|ть, ю *impf. of* ▶ **присе́сть 2**

при|се́сть, ся́ду, ся́дешь, *past* **∼сел** *pf.* **1** (*impf.* **∼са́живаться**) (*сесть*) to sit down, take a seat **2** (*impf.* **∼седа́ть**) (*на ко́рточки*) to squat; (*от стра́ха*) to cower

приска|ка́ть, чу́, ∼чешь *pf.* to come galloping, arrive at a gallop; (fig., infml) to rush, tear

приско́рб|ный, ∼ен, ∼на *adj.* regrettable, deplorable

при|сла́ть, шлю, шлёшь *pf.* (*of* ▶ **присыла́ть**) to send

прислон|и́ть, ю́, ∼и́шь *pf.* (*of* ▶ **прислоня́ть**) (к + *d.*) to lean (against), rest (against)

прислон|и́ться, ю́сь, ∼и́шься *pf.* (*of* ▶ **прислоня́ться**) (к + *d.*) to lean (against), rest (against)

прислон|я́ть, я́ю *impf. of* ▶ **прислони́ть**

прислон|я́ться, я́юсь *impf. of* ▶ **прислони́ться**

прислу́г|а, и *f.* **1** maid, servant **2** (*collect.*) servants, domestics

прислу́ш|аться, аюсь *pf.* (*of* ▶ **прислу́шиваться**) (к + *d.*) **1** to listen (to) **2** (fig., *приня́ть во внима́ние*) to listen (to); to heed; **п. к чьему́-н. сове́ту** to listen to sb's advice

прислу́шива|ться, юсь *impf. of* ▶ **прислу́шаться**

присма́трива|ть, ю *impf.* **1** *impf. of* ▶ **присмотре́ть 1 2** (*impf. only*) to seek, try to find

присма́трива|ться, юсь *impf. of* ▶ **присмотре́ться**

присмире́|ть, ю *pf.* to grow quiet, calm down

присмир|и́ть, ю́, и́шь *pf.* (*of* ▶ **присмиря́ть**) to quieten (BrE), quiet (AmE)

присмир|я́ть, я́ю *impf. of* ▶ **присмири́ть**

присмотр|е́ть, ю́, ∼ишь *pf.* (*of* ▶ **присма́тривать**) **1** (*за* + *i.*) to look after, keep an eye (on); **п. за ребёнком** to mind the baby **2** (*pf. only*) (infml, *подыска́ть*) to find; **п. себе́ рабо́ту** to find a job

присмотр|е́ться, ю́сь, ∼ишься *pf.* (*of* ▶ **присма́триваться**) (к + *d.*) to look closely (at); **п. к кому́-н.** to size sb up

присн|и́ться, ю́сь, и́шься *pf. of* ▶ **сни́ться**

присоедине́ни|е, я *nt.* **1** addition **2** (pol.) annexation

присоедин|и́ть, ю́, и́шь *pf.* (*of* ▶ **присоединя́ть**) **1** to add; to join **2** (pol.) to annex **3** (elec.) to connect

присоедин|и́ться, ю́сь, и́шься *pf.* (*of* ▶ **присоединя́ться**) (**к** + *d.*) **1** to join; **пора́ нам п. к остальны́м** it is time we joined the others **2** (*согласи́ться*) to endorse, associate oneself (with); **п. к мне́нию** to subscribe to an opinion

присоединя́|ть, я́ю *impf. of* ▶ **присоедини́ть**

присоединя́|ться, я́юсь *impf. of* ▶ **присоедини́ться**

присос|а́ться, у́сь, ёшься *pf.* (*of* ▶ **приса́сываться**) (**к** + *d.*) to stick (to), adhere to (*by suction*)

приспоса́блива|ть, ю *impf. of* ▶ **приспосо́бить**

приспоса́блива|ться, юсь *impf. of* ▶ **приспосо́биться**

приспосо́б|ить, лю, ишь *pf.* (*of* ▶ **приспоса́бливать**) to adapt, convert; **п. шко́лу под больни́цу** to convert a school into a hospital

приспосо́б|иться, люсь, ишься *pf.* (*of* ▶ **приспоса́бливаться**) (**к** + *d.*) to adapt oneself (to)

приспособле́ни|е, я *nt.* device; appliance

приспуска́|ть, ю *impf. of* ▶ **приспусти́ть**

приспу|сти́ть, щу́, ∼сти́шь *pf.* (*of* ▶ **приспуска́ть**) to lower a little; **п. флаг** to lower a flag to half mast

приста|ва́ть, ю́, ёшь *impf. of* ▶ **приста́ть**

приста́в|ить, лю, ишь *pf.* (*of* ▶ **приставля́ть**) (**к** + *d.*) to put (to, against), lean (against); **п. ле́стницу к стене́** to put a ladder against the wall

приста́вк|а, и *f.* attachment; (gram.) prefix

приставля́|ть, ю *impf. of* ▶ **приста́вить**

при́стально *adv.* intently; **п. смотре́ть (на** + *a.*) to look intently (at); to stare (at), gaze (at)

при́стал|ьный, ∼ен, ∼ьна *adj.* fixed, intent; **п. взгляд** intent look; stare, gaze

при́стан|ь, и, *pl.* ∼и, ∼е́й *f.* landing stage, jetty; pier; wharf

приста́|ть, ну, нешь *pf.* (*of* ▶ **приставать́ь**) (**к** + *d.*) **1** (*прилипнуть*) to stick (to), adhere (to) **2** (*присоедини́ться*) to join; to attach oneself (to); **п. к гру́ппе экскурса́нтов** to join a party of tourists **3** (*надое́сть*) to pester, bother; **п. с предложе́ниями** to pester with suggestions **4** (naut.) to put in (to), come alongside

пристёгива|ть, ю *impf. of* ▶ **пристегну́ть**

пристег|ну́ть, ну́, нёшь *pf.* (*of* ▶ **пристёгивать**) to fasten; to button up

пристра́ива|ть, ю *impf. of* ▶ **пристро́ить**

пристра|сти́ться, щу́сь, сти́шься *pf.* (**к** + *d.*) to develop a passion (for)

пристра́ст|ный, ∼ен, ∼на *adj.* partial, biased

пристре́лива|ть, ю *impf. of* ▶ **пристрели́ть**

пристрел|и́ть, ю́, ∼ишь *pf.* (*of* ▶ **пристре́ливать**) to shoot (down)

пристро́|ить, ю, ишь *pf.* (*of* ▶ **пристра́ивать**) (**к** + *d.*) to add (to a building), build on (to)

пристро́йк|а, и *f.* annex, extension

при́ступ, а *m.* **1** (mil.) assault, storm; **пойти́ на п.** to go in to the assault **2** (*припа́док*) fit, attack; **п. гне́ва/ка́шля** fit of temper/coughing; **серде́чный п.** heart attack

приступа́|ть, а́ю *impf. of* ▶ **приступи́ть**

приступ|и́ть, лю́, ∼ишь *pf.* (*of* ▶ **приступа́ть**) (**к** + *d.*) to set about, get down (to), start; **п. к де́лу** to set to work, get down to business

пристыди́ть, жу́, ди́шь *pf. of* ▶ **стыди́ть**

присуд|и́ть, жу́, ∼дишь *pf.* (*of* ▶ **присужда́ть**) **1** (+ *a.* and **к** + *d.*, or + *a.* and *d.*) to sentence (to), condemn (to); **п. к штра́фу, п. штраф** (+ *d.*) to fine, impose a fine (on) **2** (+ *d.*) to award; to confer (on); **ему́ ∼ди́ли сте́пень до́ктора** a doctorate has been conferred on him

присужда́|ть, ю *impf. of* ▶ **присуди́ть**

прису́тстви|е, я *nt.* presence; **в ∼и дете́й** in the presence of the children, in front of the children

✎ **прису́тств|овать, ую** *impf.* (**на** + *p.*) to be present (at), attend

прису́тств|ующий *pres. part. act. of* ▶ **прису́тствовать** *and adj.* present; (*as pl. n.* ∼**ующие, ∼ующих**) those present

прису́щ|ий, ∼, ∼а *adj.* (+ *d.*) inherent (in); characteristic; **∼ая ей ще́дрость** her characteristic generosity

присыла́|ть, ю *impf. of* ▶ **присла́ть**

прися́г|а, и *f.* oath; **под ∼ой** on oath, under oath

прися́жн|ый *adj.*: **п. заседа́тель** juror; (*as m. n. n.* ∼**ый**) juror; **суд ∼ых** jury

прита́скива|ть, ю *impf. of* ▶ **притащи́ть**

притащ|и́ть, у́, ∼ишь *pf.* (*of* ▶ **прита́скивать**) to bring, drag, haul

притвор|и́ться, ю́сь, и́шься *pf.* (*of* ▶ **притворя́ться**) (+ *i.*) to pretend (to be); to feign; **п. больны́м** to pretend to be ill, feign illness

притвор|я́ться, я́юсь *impf. of* ▶ **притвори́ться**

притесне́ни|е, я *nt.* oppression

притесн|и́ть, ю́, и́шь *pf.* (*of* ▶ **притесня́ть**) to oppress, keep down

притесн|я́ть, я́ю *impf. of* ▶ **притесни́ть**

притиха́|ть, а́ю *impf. of* ▶ **притихну́ть**

прити́х|нуть, ну, нешь, *past* ∼, ∼**ла** *pf.* (*of* ▶ **притиха́ть**) to quieten (BrE), quiet (AmE) down; to grow quiet

прито́к, а *m.* **1** (geog.) tributary **2** (*воздуха, воды, денег*) inflow; (*людей*) influx

п

притóм *conj.* (and) besides; and what's more

притóн, а *m.* den; **воровскóй п.** den of thieves

при́тор|ный, ~ен, ~на *adj.* sickly sweet, cloying (also fig.); **~ная улы́бка** unctuous smile

притрáгива|ться, юсь *impf. of* ▶ притрóнуться

притрóн|уться, усь, ешься *pf.* (*of* ▶ притрáгиваться) (к + *d.*) to touch; **они́ не ~ули́сь к ýжину** they have not touched their supper

притуп|и́ть, лю́, ~ишь *pf.* (*of* ▶ притупля́ть) to blunt; (fig.) to dull, deaden

притуп|и́ться, лю́, ~ится *pf.* (*of* ▶ притупля́ться) to become blunt; (fig., *о па́мяти, зре́нии*) to fail

притупля́|ть, ю, ет *impf. of* ▶ притупи́ть

притупля́|ться, ется *impf. of* ▶ притупи́ться

притуш|и́ть, ý, ~ишь *pf.* (infml, *огонь*) to damp; **п. фáры** to dip lights

при́тч|а, и *f.* parable

притя́гива|ть, ю *impf. of* ▶ притяну́ть

притяжáтельный *adj.* (gram.) possessive

притяжéни|е, я *nt.* (phys.) attraction; **закóн земнóго ~я** law of gravity

притязáни|е, я *nt.* claim, pretension; **имéть ~я** (**на** + *a.*) to have claims (to, on)

притя́|ну́ть, ну́, ~нешь *pf.* (*of* ▶ притя́гивать) **1** to drag (up), pull (up) **2** (fig., *привле́чь*) to draw, attract; **п. как магни́т** to attract like a magnet

приукрá|сить, шу, сишь *pf.* (*of* ▶ приукрáшивать) (infml) (*успе́хи*) to exaggerate; (*расска́з*) to embellish, embroider

приукрáшива|ть, ю *impf. of* ▶ приукрáсить

приуменьшáть, áю *impf. of* ▶ приумéньшить

приумéньш|ить, у, ишь *pf.* (*of* ▶ приуменьшáть) to diminish, lessen, reduce

приуч|áть, áю *impf. of* ▶ приучи́ть

приуч|áться, áюсь *impf. of* ▶ приучи́ться

приуч|и́ть, ý, ~ишь *pf.* (*of* ▶ приучáть) (к + *d. or* + *inf.*) to train (to), school (to, in); **п. когó-н. к дисципли́не** to inculcate discipline in sb

приуч|и́ться, ýсь, ~ишься *pf.* (*of* ▶ приучáться) (+ *inf.*) to train oneself (to); to accustom oneself (to)

прихва|ти́ть, чý, ~тишь *pf.* (*of* ▶ прихвáтывать) (infml) to catch up, seize up

прихвáтыва|ть, ю *impf. of* ▶ прихвати́ть

прихóд[1]**, а** *m.* (*прибы́тие*) coming, arrival

прихóд[2]**, а** *m.* (eccl.) parish

  ▱ **прихо|ди́ть, жý, ~дишь** *impf. of* ▶ прийти́

  ▱ **прихо|ди́ться, жýсь, ~дишься** *impf.* **1** *impf. of* ▶ прийти́сь **2** (*impf. only*) (+ *d. and i.*) to be (in *a given degree of relationship to*); **я ей ~жýсь дя́дей** I am her uncle

прихожáн|ин, ина, *pl.* **~е** *m.* parishioner

прихожáн|ка, ки *f. of* ▶ прихожáнин

прихóж|ая, ей *f.* (entrance) hall, lobby

прихотли́в|ый, ~, ~а *adj.* intricate

при́хот|ь, и *f.* whim, caprice, fancy

прицéл, а *m.* (back)sight; **взять на п.** to take aim (at), aim (at); (fig.) to keep a watch on

прицéлива|ться, юсь *impf. of* ▶ прицéлиться

прицéл|иться, юсь, ишься *pf.* (*of* ▶ прицéливаться) to take aim

прицéп, а *m.* trailer

прицеп|и́ть, лю́, ~ишь *pf.* (*of* ▶ прицепля́ть) (к + *d.*) **1** to hitch (to), hook on (to); (*ваго́ны*) to couple (to) **2** (infml, *бро́шку, бант*) to pin on (to), fasten (to)

прицеп|и́ться, лю́сь, ~ишься *pf.* (*of* ▶ прицепля́ться) (к + *d.*) **1** to stick (to), cling (to) **2** (fig., infml) (*приста́ть*) to pester; to nag (at)

прицепля́|ть, ю *impf. of* ▶ прицепи́ть

прицепля́|ться, юсь *impf. of* ▶ прицепи́ться

причáл, а *m.* berth, moorage

причáлива|ть, ю *impf. of* ▶ причáлить

причáл|ить, ю, ишь *pf.* (*of* ▶ причáливать) **1** (к + *d.*) to moor (to) **2** to moor up

причáсти|е[1]**, я** *nt.* (gram.) participle

причáсти|е[2]**, я** *nt.* (eccl.) **1** communion; the Eucharist **2** (*причаще́ние*) making one's communion, communicating

прича|сти́ться, щýсь, сти́шься *pf.* (*of* ▶ причащáться) (eccl.) to receive communion

причáст|ный, ~ен, ~на *adj.* (к + *d.*) connected (with), involved (in); **быть ~ным** (к + *d.*) to be connected (with), be involved (in)

причащá|ться, юсь *impf. of* ▶ причасти́ться

  ▱ **причём** *conj.* moreover, and; **бы́ло óчень темнó, п. я плóхо ориенти́ровалась на мéстности** it was very dark and I didn't know the area well

приче|сáть, шý, ~шешь *pf.* (*of* ▶ причёсывать) to comb; **п. когó-н.** to brush, comb sb's hair

приче|сáться, шýсь, ~шешься *pf.* (*of* ▶ причёсываться) to brush, comb one's hair

причёск|а, и *f.* hair style, hairdo; **сдéлать причёску** to style one's hair; (*у парикма́хера*) to have one's hair done

причёсыва|ть, ю *impf. of* ▶ причесáть

причёсыва|ться, юсь *impf. of* ▶ причесáться

  ▱ **причи́н|а, ы** *f.* (*пожа́ра, боле́зни*) cause; (*основа́ние*) reason; **по той простóй ~е, что** for the simple reason that; **по ~е** (+ *g.*) by reason (of), on account (of), owing (to), because (of)

причин|и́ть, ю́, и́шь *pf.* (*of* ▶ причиня́ть) to cause

причиня́|ть, я́ю *impf. of* ▶ причини́ть

причитá|ть, ю *impf.* (по + *p.*) to lament (for); to bewail

пришварт|овáть, ýю *pf. of* ▶ швартовáть

пришварт|ова́ться, у́юсь *pf. of*
▶ швартова́ться

пришéл|ец, ьца *m.* alien

пришива́|ть, ю *impf. of* ▶ приши́ть

приш|и́ть, ью, ьёшь *pf.* (*of* ▶ пришива́ть)
to sew on

прищем|и́ть, лю́, и́шь *pf.* (*of* ▶ прищемля́ть)
to pinch, catch; **п. себе́ па́лец две́рью** to
pinch one's finger in the door

прищемля́|ть, ю *impf. of* ▶ прищеми́ть

прищёпк|а, и *f.* (clothes) peg (BrE),
clothespin (AmE)

прищу́рива|ться, юсь *impf. of*
▶ прищу́риться

прищу́р|иться, юсь, ишься *pf.* (*of*
▶ прищу́риваться) to screw up one's eyes,
squint

прию́т, а *m.* **1** shelter, refuge **2**: **дéтский п.**
orphanage

прия́тел|ь, я *m.* friend

прия́тельниц|а, ы *f.* (female) friend

⚹ **прия́т|ный, ∼ен, ∼на** *adj.* nice, pleasant,
pleasing; (*impers., predic.*) ∼но it is pleasant;
it is nice; **о́чень ∼но!** pleased to meet you!;
how do you do?

⚹ **про** *prep.* (+ *a.*) **1** (*o*) about **2**: **про себя́** to
oneself; **чита́ть про себя́** to read to oneself

про...[1] *vbl. pref. indicating* **1** *action through,
across or past object:* **простре́ли́ть** to shoot
through; **прое́хать** to pass (by) **2** *overall
or exhaustive action:* **прогре́ть** to warm
thoroughly **3** *duration of action throughout
given period of time:* **просиде́ть всю ночь** to
sit up all night **4** *loss or failure:* **проигра́ть**
to lose (*a game*)

про...[2] *as pref. of nn. and adjs.* pro-

проанализи́р|овать, ую *pf. of*
▶ анализи́ровать

про́б|а, ы *f.* **1** (*маши́ны*) trial, test; try-
out; (*металла*) assay; (*theatr.*) audition;
п. сил trial of strength **2** (*для ана́лиза*)
sample **3** (*драгоце́нного мета́лла*) standard
(*measure of purity of gold*); **зо́лото 96-й
∼ы** pure gold, 24-carat gold **4** (*клеймо́*)
hallmark

проба́лтыва|ться, юсь *impf. of*
▶ проболта́ться

пробега́|ть, ю *impf. of* ▶ пробежа́ть

пробе|жа́ть, гу́, жи́шь, гу́т *pf.* (*of* ▶ пробега́ть)
1 (*ми́мо*) to run past; (*че́рез*) to run
through; (*по*) to run along; **п. па́льцами по
клавиату́ре** to run one's fingers over the
keyboard **2** (fig., *пронести́сь*) to run, flit
(over, down, across); **хо́лод ∼жа́л по её
спине́** a chill ran down her spine

пробе́жк|а, и *f.* run, jog

пробе́л, а *m.* **1** blank, gap; **запо́лнить
∼ы** to fill in the blanks **2** (*недоста́ток*)
deficiency, gap; **∼ы в зна́ниях** gaps in one's
knowledge

⚹ key word

пробива́|ть, ю *impf. of* ▶ проби́ть[1]

пробива́|ться, юсь *impf. of* ▶ проби́ться

пробира́|ться, юсь *impf. of* ▶ пробра́ться

проби́рк|а, и *f.* test tube

про|би́ть[1]**, бью, бьёшь,** *past* ∼би́л,
∼би́ла, ∼би́ло *pf. of* ▶ бить 5

про|би́ть[2]**, бью, бьёшь** *pf.* (*of* ▶ пробива́ть)
to make a hole (in); to pierce; to punch; **п.
сте́ну** to breach a wall

про|би́ться, бью́сь, бьёшься *pf.* (*of*
▶ пробива́ться) **1** to fight one's way
through; to break, strike through; **п. сквозь
толпу́** to fight one's way through the crowd
2 (*о расте́ниях*) to appear, push up

про́бк|а, и *f.* **1** (*материа́л*) cork (*substance*)
2 (*для буты́лок*) cork; stopper; (*в ра́ковину*)
plug; **глуп как п.** (infml) daft as a brush
3 (elec.) fuse **4** (fig., *на у́лице*) traffic jam;
congestion

⚹ **пробле́м|а, ы** *f.* problem

проблемати́чный *adj.* problematic(al)

про́блеск, а *m.* flash; ray, gleam (also fig.);
п. наде́жды ray of hope

про́бный *adj.* trial, test; **п. ка́мень**
touchstone; **п. полёт** test flight

про́б|овать, ую *impf.* (*of* ▶ попро́бовать)
1 (*проверя́ть*) to test; **п. пи́щу** to taste,
try food **2** (+ *inf.*) (*стара́ться*) to try (to),
attempt (to)

проболта́|ться, юсь *pf.* (*of*
▶ проба́лтываться) (infml) to shoot one's
mouth off, let the cat out of the bag

пробо́р, а *m.* parting (BrE), part (AmE) (*of the
hair*); **прямо́й п.** middle part(ing); **косо́й п.**
side part(ing)

пробормо|та́ть, чу́, ∼чешь *pf. of*
▶ бормота́ть

про|бра́ться, беру́сь, берёшься, *past*
∼бра́лся, ∼брала́сь, ∼брало́сь *pf.* (*of*
▶ пробира́ться) **1** (*с трудо́м*) to fight, force
one's way **2** (*ти́хо*) to steal (through, past);
п. о́щупью to feel one's way; **п. на цы́почках**
to tiptoe (through)

пробу|ди́ть, жу́, ∼дишь *pf.* (*of* ▶ буди́ть 2,
▶ пробужда́ть) to wake; to awaken, rouse,
arouse (also fig.)

пробу|ди́ться, жу́сь, ∼дишься *pf.* (*of*
▶ пробужда́ться) to wake up, awake (also fig.)

пробужда́|ть, ю *impf. of* ▶ пробуди́ть

пробужда́|ться, юсь *impf. of* ▶ пробуди́ться

пробужде́ни|е, я *nt.* waking up, awakening

пробур|и́ть, ю́, и́шь *pf. of* ▶ бури́ть

проб|ы́ть, у́ду, у́дешь, *past* ∼ы́л, ∼ыла́,
∼ы́ло *pf.* to stay, remain; to be (*for a certain
time*); **он ∼ы́л у нас три неде́ли** he stayed
with us for three weeks

прова́йдер, а *m.* Internet service provider
(*abbr.* ISP)

прова́л, а *m.* **1** (*де́йствие*) collapse **2** (geog.)
gap; hole **3** (*неуда́ча*) failure; **по́лный п.** a
complete flop

прова́лива|ться, юсь *impf. of*
▶ провали́ться

провал|и́ться, ю́сь, ~ишься *pf.* (*of*
▸ прова́ливаться) **1** to collapse, fall
through; **пото́лок ~и́лся** the ceiling has come
down **2** (*fig., infml*) (*потерпеть неудачу*) to
fail, fall through; (*на экзамене*) (*на экзамене*) to fail

проведе́ни|е, я *nt.* **1** (*человека*) leading,
taking; (*судна*) piloting **2** (*дороги*)
construction; (*электричества*) installation
3 (*операции*) carrying out, carrying
through; (*заседания*) conducting; **п.
кампа́нии** (mil., pol.) conduct of a campaign; **п.
в жизнь** putting into effect, implementation

провез|ти́, у́, ёшь, *past* ~, ~ла́ *pf.* (*of
▸ провози́ть*) **1** (*везя, доставить*) to
convey, transport; **п. контраба́ндой** to
smuggle **2** (*перевезти с собой*) to bring
(with one)

прове́р|ить, ю, ишь *pf.* (*of ▸ проверя́ть*)
1 to check; to verify; **п. биле́ты** to examine
tickets **2** (*на практике*) to test; **п. свои́
си́лы** to try one's strength

прове́рк|а, и *f.* **1** checking; examination;
verification; check-up **2** (*на практике*)
testing

проверя́|ть, я́ю *impf. of ▸ прове́рить*

прове|сти́, ду́, дёшь, *past* ~л, ~ла́ *pf.* (*of
▸ проводи́ть*[1] 1, ▸ вести́ 2, ▸ вести́ 3)
1 (*человека*) to lead, take; (*машину*) to
take; (*судно*) to pilot **2** (*дорогу*) to build;
(*электричество*) to install **3** (*реформы,
опыты*) to carry out; (*кампанию*) to carry
on; (*урок, заседание*) to conduct, hold;
п. бесе́ду to give a talk **4** (*черту*) to draw;
п. грани́цу to draw a boundary line **5** (*+ i.*)
(*рукой*) to pass over, run over; **она́ ~ла́
руко́й по лбу** she passed her hand over her
forehead **6** (*время*) to spend, pass; **чтобы п.
вре́мя** to pass the time **7** (infml, *обмануть*)
to take in, trick, fool

прове́трива|ть, ю *impf. of ▸ прове́трить*

прове́тр|ить, ю, ишь *pf.* (*of ▸ прове́тривать*)
to air; to ventilate

прови́зи|я, и (*no pl.*) *f.* provisions

провин|и́ться, ю́сь, и́шься *pf.* (**в** + *p.*) to be
guilty (of); to commit an offence; **п. пе́ред
кем-н.** to wrong sb; **в чём мы ~и́лись?** what
have we done wrong?

провинциа́льный, ~ен, ~ьна *adj.*
provincial (*also fig.*)

прови́нци|я, и *f.* **1** (*область*) province
2 (*удалённая местность*) the provinces;
жить в глухо́й ~и to live in the depths of
the country

про́вод, а, *pl.* ~а́ *m.* wire, lead; **п. под
напряже́нием** live wire

прово|ди́ть[1], жу́, ~дишь *impf.* **1** *impf.
of ▸ провести́* **2** (*impf. only*) (phys., elec.) to
conduct

прово|ди́ть[2], жу́, ~дишь *pf.* (*of
▸ провожа́ть*) to accompany; to see off; **п.
кого́-н. домо́й** to take, see sb home; **п. кого́-н.
до двере́й** to see sb to the door; **п. глаза́ми**
to follow with one's eyes

прово́дк|а, и *f.* (*collect.*) (elec.) wiring, wires

проводни́к[1], а́ *m.* **1** (*провожатый*) guide
2 (*в поезде*) conductor; guard (BrE)

проводни́к[2], а́ *m.* (phys., elec.) conductor

проводни́|ца, цы *f. of ▸ проводни́к*[1]

про́вод|ы, ов (*no sg.*) seeing-off; send-off

провожа́|ть, ю *impf. of ▸ проводи́ть*[2]

провоз, а *m.* carriage, conveyance, transport;
пла́та за п. payment for carriage

провозгла|си́ть, шу́, си́шь *pf.* (*of
▸ провозглаша́ть*) to proclaim; **его́ ~си́ли
королём** he was proclaimed king

провозглаша́|ть, ю *impf. of
▸ провозгласи́ть*

прово|зи́ть, жу́, ~зишь *impf. of ▸ провезти́*

провока́тор, а *m.* **1** agent provocateur
2 (fig.) instigator, provoker

провока́ци|я, и *f.* provocation

про́волок|а, и *f.* wire; **колю́чая п.** barbed wire

прово́р|ный, ~ен, ~на *adj.* **1** (*быстрый*)
quick, swift, expeditious **2** (*ловкий*) agile,
nimble, adroit, dexterous

провоци́р|овать, ую *impf. and pf.* (*pf. also
с~*) to provoke

прогиба́|ться, юсь *impf. of ▸ прогну́ться*

прогла́тыва|ть, ю *impf.* (*of ▸ проглоти́ть*):
говори́ть, ~я слова́ to swallow one's words

прогло|ти́ть, чу́, ~тишь *pf.* (*of
▸ прогла́тывать, ▸ глота́ть*) to swallow (also
fig.); **п. язы́к** to lose one's tongue; **п. кни́гу** to
devour a book

прогля|де́ть, жу́, ди́шь *pf.* (*of
▸ прогля́дывать*) **1** (*просмотреть*) to
look through, skim through **2** (*pf. only*) (*не
заметить*) to overlook

прогля́дыва|ть, ю *impf. of ▸ прогляде́ть*

про|гна́ть, гоню́, го́нишь, *past* ~гна́л,
~гнала́, ~гна́ло *pf.* (*of ▸ прогоня́ть*)
(*заставить уйти*) to drive away (also fig.);
(fig.) to banish

прогнива́|ть, ет *impf. of ▸ прогни́ть*

прогн|и́ть, иёт, *past* ~и́л, ~ила́, ~и́ло *pf.*
(*of ▸ прогнива́ть*) to rot through

прогно́з, а *m.* prognosis; forecast; **п. пого́ды**
weather forecast

прогн|у́ться, у́сь, ёшься *pf.* (*of
▸ прогиба́ться*) to cave in, sag

прогова́рива|ть, ю *impf. of ▸ проговори́ть*

прогова́рива|ться, юсь *impf. of
▸ проговори́ться*

проговор|и́ть, ю́, и́шь *pf.* (*of
▸ прогова́ривать*) **1** (*сказать*) to say, utter;
п. сквозь зу́бы to mutter **2** (*некоторое
время*) to speak, talk

проговор|и́ться, ю́сь, и́шься *pf.* (*of
▸ прогова́риваться*) to shoot one's mouth
off, let the cat out of the bag

прогол|ода́ться, ю́сь *pf.* to get hungry,
grow hungry

проголос|ова́ть, у́ю *pf. of ▸ голосова́ть*

прогоня́|ть, ю *impf. of ▸ прогна́ть*

прогор|а́ть, а́ю *impf. of ▸ прогоре́ть*

п

прогор|е́ть, ю́, и́шь *pf.* (*of* ▶ **прогора́ть**) **1** (*сгоре́ть совсе́м*) to burn through; to burn to a cinder **2** (*infml, разори́ться*) to go bankrupt, go bust

◌̄ **програ́мм|а, ы** *f.* programme (BrE), program (AmE); (*comput.*) program, application

программи́р|овать, ую *impf.* (*of* ▶ **запрограмми́ровать**) to programme (BrE), program (AmE); (*comput.*) to program

программи́ст, а *m.* (computer) programmer

программи́ст|ка, ки *f. of* ▶ **программи́ст**

◌̄ **програ́мм|ный** *adj. of* ▶ **програ́мма**; **~ное обеспе́чение** (*comput.*) software

прогрева́|ть, ю *impf. of* ▶ **прогре́ть**

прогрева́|ться, юсь *impf. of* ▶ **прогре́ться**

прогрем|е́ть, лю́, и́шь *pf. of* ▶ **греме́ть**

прогре́сс, а *m.* progress

прогресси́в|ный, ~ен, ~на *adj.* progressive

прогре́|ть, ю *pf.* (*of* ▶ **прогрева́ть**) to heat, warm up

прогре́|ться, юсь *pf.* (*of* ▶ **прогрева́ться**) to warm up

прогу́л, а *m.* (*на рабо́те*) absence; (*в шко́ле*) truancy

прогу́лива|ть, ю *impf. of* ▶ **прогуля́ть**

прогу́лива|ться, юсь *impf.* **1** *impf. of* ▶ **прогуля́ться** **2** (*impf. only*) to stroll, saunter

прогу́лк|а, и *f.* **1** (*хожде́ние*) walk; stroll **2** (*пое́здка*) outing; (*в автомоби́ле*) drive; (*верхо́м*) ride

прогуля́|ть, ю *pf.* (*of* ▶ **прогу́ливать**) (*на рабо́те*) to be absent from work; (*шко́лу*) to play truant

прогуля́|ться, юсь *pf.* (*of* ▶ **прогу́ливаться 1**) to take a walk, stroll

◌̄ **прода|ва́ть, ю́, ёшь** *impf. of* ▶ **прода́ть**

прода|ва́ться, ю́сь, ёшься *impf.* **1** (*impf. only*) to be on sale, be for sale; **дом ~ётся** the house is for sale; «**~ётся мотоци́кл**» 'motorcycle for sale' (*formula of advertisement of sale*) **2** (*impf. only*) to sell; **дёшево п.** to sell cheap, go cheap; **его́ но́вый рома́н хорошо́ ~ётся** his new novel is selling well **3** *impf. of* ▶ **прода́ться**

продав|е́ц, ца́ *m.* **1** seller; vendor **2** (*в магази́не*) salesman, shop assistant

продавщи́ц|а, ы *f.* **1** seller; vendor **2** (*в магази́не*) saleswoman, shop assistant

◌̄ **прода́ж|а, и** *f.* sale; **опто́вая п.** wholesale; **п. в ро́зницу/ро́зничная п.** retail; **нет в ~е** out of stock; sold out

прода́ж|ный *adj.* **1** sale; selling; **~ная цена́** selling price **2** (**~ен, ~на**) (*fig.*) corrupt; **~ная же́нщина** prostitute

прода́лблива|ть, ю *impf. of* ▶ **продолби́ть**

прода́|ть, м, шь, ст, ди́м, ди́те, ду́т, *past* **про́дал, ~ла́, про́дало** *pf.* (*of* ▶ **продава́ть**) to sell; **п. о́птом** to sell wholesale; **п. в ро́зницу** to sell retail

прода́|ться, мся, шься, стся, ди́мся, ди́тесь, ду́тся, *past* **~лся, ~ла́сь** *pf.* (*of* ▶ **продава́ться 3**) (*о челове́ке*) to sell oneself

продвига́|ться, юсь *impf. of* ▶ **продви́нуться**

продвиже́ни|е, я *nt.* **1** advancement **2** (*mil., fig.*) progress, advance

продви́нут|ый, ~, ~а (*infml*) *adj.* advanced

продви́|нуться, нусь, нешься *pf.* (*of* ▶ **продвига́ться**) **1** to advance (*also fig.*); to move on, move forward; to push on **2** (*по слу́жбе*) to be promoted

продева́|ть, ю *impf. of* ▶ **проде́ть**

проде́л|ать, аю *pf.* (*of* ▶ **проде́лывать**) **1** (*отве́рстие, прохо́д*) to make **2** (*рабо́ту, упражне́ния*) to do, perform, accomplish

проде́лыва|ть, ю *impf. of* ▶ **проде́лать**

продемократи́ческий *adj.* pro-democracy

продемонстри́р|овать, ую *pf. of* ▶ **демонстри́ровать**

продерж|а́ть, у́, ~ишь *pf.* (*чемода́н*) to hold (*for a certain time*); (*челове́ка*) to keep (*for a certain time*); **его́ ~а́ли два ме́сяца в больни́це** he was kept in hospital for two months

продерж|а́ться, у́сь, ~ишься *pf.* to hold out

проде́|ть, ну, нешь *pf.* (*of* ▶ **продева́ть**) to pass, run; **п. ни́тку в иго́лку** to thread a needle

продикт|ова́ть, у́ю *pf. of* ▶ **диктова́ть**

продира́|ться, юсь *impf. of* ▶ **продра́ться**

продлева́|ть, ю *impf. of* ▶ **продли́ть**

продле́ни|е, я *nt.* extension, prolongation

продл|и́ть, ю́, и́шь *pf.* (*of* ▶ **продлева́ть**) to extend, prolong; **п. срок де́йствия ви́зы** to extend a visa

продл|и́ться, и́тся *pf. of* ▶ **дли́ться**

продово́льств|енный *adj. of* ▶ **продово́льствие**; **п. магази́н** grocery (store); **п. склад** food store; (*mil.*) ration store, ration dump; **~енные това́ры** foodstuffs

продово́льстви|е, я *nt.* foodstuffs, provisions; (*mil.*) rations

продолб|и́ть, лю́, и́шь *pf.* (*of* ▶ **прода́лбливать**) to make a hole (in), chisel through

продолгова́т|ый, ~, ~а *adj.* oblong

◌̄ **продолж|а́ть, а́ю** *impf.* **1** to continue, go on; **п. рабо́тать** to continue to work, go on working **2** *impf. of* ▶ **продо́лжить**

продолж|а́ться, а́ется *impf.* (*of* ▶ **продо́лжиться**) to continue, last, go on; **восста́ние ~а́ется уже́ второ́й год** the insurrection is now in its second year

продолже́ни|е, я *nt.* **1** continuation **2** (*расска́за*) continuation; sequel; **п. сле́дует** to be continued **3**: **в п.** (+ *g.*) in the course (of), during, for, throughout; **в п. почти́ двух лет я ни ра́зу её не ви́дел** for almost two years I did not see her once

продолжи́тельност|ь, и *f.* duration, length

◌̄ key word

продолжи́тел|ьный, ~ен, ~ьна *adj.* long; prolonged, protracted

продо́лж|ить, у, ишь *pf.* (*of* ▸ продолжа́ть) to extend, prolong

продо́лж|иться, ится *pf.* *of* ▸ продолжа́ться

продо́льн|ый *adj.* longitudinal; ~ая ось longitudinal axis

про|дра́ться, деру́сь, дерёшься, *past* ~дра́лся, ~драла́сь, ~дра́ло́сь *pf.* (*of* ▸ продира́ться) (infml) to squeeze through, force one's way through

продрема́|ть, лю́, ~́лешь *pf.* to doze (*for a certain time*)

продро́г|нуть, ну, нешь, *past* ~, ~ла *pf.* to be chilled to the marrow

продува́|ть, ю *impf. of* ▸ проду́ть

☛ **проду́кт, а** *m.* **1** product; побо́чный п. by-product **2** (*in pl.*) produce; provisions, foodstuffs; моло́чные ~ы dairy produce

продукти́в|ный, ~ен, ~на *adj.* productive; (fig.) fruitful

продукто́вый *adj.* food; п. магази́н grocery (store)

☛ **проду́кци|я, и** *f.* production, output

проду́м|ать, аю *pf.* (*of* ▸ проду́мывать) (*вопрос*) to think over; (*план*) to think out

проду́мыва|ть, ю *impf. of* ▸ проду́мать

проду́|ть, ю, ешь *pf.* (*of* ▸ продува́ть) **1** (*прочистить*) to blow through; to clean by blowing **2** (*impers.* + *a.*) to be in a draught (BrE), draft (AmE); меня́ *и т. п.* ~ло I have, *etc.*, caught a cold from being in a draught (BrE), draft (AmE) **3** (infml, *проиграть*) to lose (*at games*)

продыря́в|ить, лю, ишь *pf.* (*of* ▸ продыря́вливать) to make a hole (in), pierce

продыря́влива|ть, ю *impf. of* ▸ продыря́вить

продю́сер, а *m.* producer

прое́зд, а *m.* **1** (*место*) passage, thoroughfare; «~а нет!» 'no thoroughfare!' **2** (*в транспорте*) trip, journey

проездно́й *adj.* travelling (BrE), traveling (AmE); п. биле́т ticket

проезжа́|ть, ю *impf. of* ▸ прое́хать

☛ **прое́кт, а** *m.* **1** (*здания*) design **2** (*предварительный текст*) draft; п. догово́ра draft treaty **3** (*замысел*) plan, project

проекти́рование, я *nt.* designing; автоматизи́рованное п. CAD, computer-aided design

проекти́р|овать, ую *impf.* (*of* ▸ спроекти́ровать) to design; п. теа́тр to design a theatre (BrE), theater (AmE)

проектиро́вщик, а *m.* designer

прое́ктн|ый *adj.* **1** planning, designing; ~ое бюро́ planning office **2** (*предусмотренный*) planned; ~ая мо́щность (tech.) rated capacity

прое́ктор, а *m.* projector

прое́кци|я, и *f.* projection

проём, а *m.* (archit.) aperture; embrasure; дверно́й п. doorway

прое́|хать, ду, дешь *pf.* (*of* ▸ проезжа́ть) **1** (*на транспорте*) to pass (by, through); to drive (by, through), ride (by, through) **2** (*по ошибке*) to pass, go past **3** (*расстояние*) to go, do, make, cover

проеци́р|овать, ую *impf. and pf.* (*изображение*) to project

прожа́рива|ть, ю, ет *impf. of* ▸ прожа́рить

прожа́рива|ться, ется *impf. of* ▸ прожа́риться

прожа́р|ить, ю, ишь *pf.* (*of* ▸ прожа́ривать) to fry, roast thoroughly

прожа́р|иться, ится *pf.* (*of* ▸ прожа́риваться) to fry, roast thoroughly

прожда́|ть, у́, ёшь, *past* ~а́л, ~ала́, ~а́ло *pf.* (+ *a. or g.*) to wait (for), spend (*a certain time*) waiting (for)

прож|ева́ть, ую́, уёшь *pf.* (*of* ▸ прожёвывать) to chew well

прожёвыва|ть, ю *impf. of* ▸ прожева́ть

прожёктор, а, *pl.* ~ы and ~а́ *m.* searchlight, floodlight

про|же́чь, жгу, жжёшь, жгу́т, *past* ~жёг, ~жгла́ *pf.* (*of* ▸ прожига́ть) to burn a hole in

☛ **прожива́|ть, ю** *impf.* **1** (*иметь жилище*) to live, reside **2** *impf. of* ▸ прожи́ть

прожига́|ть, ю *impf. of* ▸ проже́чь

про|жи́ть, живу́, живёшь, *past* ~жи́л, ~жила́, ~жи́ло *pf.* (*of* ▸ прожива́ть 2) **1** (*пробыть живым*) to live; он ~жи́л сто лет he lived to be a hundred **2** (*провести*) to spend; мы ~жи́ли ме́сяц а́вгуст на берегу́ мо́ря we spent the month of August at the seaside

прожо́рлив|ый, ~, ~а *adj.* voracious, gluttonous

про́з|а, ы *f.* prose

проза́ик, а *m.* prose writer

про|зва́ть, зову́, зовёшь, *past* ~зва́л, ~звала́, ~зва́ло *pf.* (*of* ▸ прозыва́ть) (+ *a. and i.*) to nickname (sb sth)

про́звищ|е, а *nt.* nickname

прозвуч|а́ть, и́т *pf. of* ▸ звуча́ть

прозева́|ть, ю *pf.* (*of* ▸ зева́ть 3) (infml) to miss

прозорли́в|ый, ~, ~а *adj.* sagacious, perspicacious

прозра́чность|, и *f.* transparency

прозра́ч|ный, ~ен, ~на *adj.* transparent (also fig.); (*вода, воздух*) clear, pellucid; (*ткань, одежда*) see-through, transparent; п. намёк transparent hint

прозрева́|ть, ю *impf. of* ▸ прозре́ть

прозре́ни|е, я *nt.* **1** recovery of sight **2** (fig.) insight

прозре́|ть, ю, ешь *pf.* (*of* ▸ прозрева́ть) **1** to recover one's sight **2** (fig.) to see the light

прозыва́|ть, ю *impf. of* ▸ прозва́ть

П

проигнори́р|овать, ую pf. to ignore

проигра́|ть, а́ю pf. (of ▶ про́игрывать)
1 (потерпе́ть неуда́чу) to lose; п. суде́бный
проце́сс to lose a case **2** (сыгра́ть) to play
(through, over); п. конце́рт to play through
a concerto **3** (pf. only) (не́которое вре́мя)
to play

про́игрыватель|ь, я m. record player;
п. компа́кт-ди́сков CD player

про́игрыва|ть, ю impf. of ▶ проигра́ть 2

про́игрыш, а m. loss; оста́ться в ~е to be
the loser, come off loser

◆ произведе́ни|е, я nt. **1** (иску́сства,
литерату́ры) work; и́збранные ~я Л. Н.
Толсто́го selected works of L. N. Tolstoy
2 (math.) product

произве|сти́, ду́, дёшь, past ~л, ~ла́
pf. (of ▶ производи́ть 1) **1** (сде́лать) to
make; (ремо́нт, о́пыты) to carry out; п.
вы́стрел to fire a shot **2** (вы́звать) to cause,
produce; п. впечатле́ние (на + a.) to create
an impression (on, upon); п. сенса́цию to
cause a sensation

◆ производи́тель|ь, я m. producer; ме́лкие ~и
small producers

производи́тельност|ь, и f. productivity

◆ произво|ди́ть, жу́, ~дишь impf. **1** impf. of
▶ произвести́ **2** (impf. only) (изготовля́ть)
to produce

◆ произво|ди́ться, ~дится impf. to be
produced

произво́дн|ый adj. derivative, derived;
(as f. n. ~ая, ~ой) (math.) derivative

◆ производ́ственный adj. of ▶ произво́дство;
production; industrial

◆ произво́дств|о, а nt. **1** (това́ров)
production, manufacture; япо́нского ~а
Japanese-made **2** (заво́д) factory, works

произво́л, а m. **1** (необосно́ванность)
arbitrariness **2** (своево́лие) arbitrary rule

произво́льно adv. **1** (необосно́ванно)
arbitrarily **2** (по жела́нию) at will

произво́льн|ый, ~ен, ~ьна adj. arbitrary

произне|сти́, су́, ёшь, past ~с, ~ла́ pf.
(of ▶ произноси́ть) **1** (вы́говорить) to
pronounce; to articulate **2** (сказа́ть) to
pronounce, say, utter; п. речь to deliver a
speech

произно|си́ть, шу́, ~сишь impf. of
▶ произнести́

произноше́ни|е, я nt. pronunciation

◆ произо|йти́, йду́, йдёшь, past ~шёл, ~шла́
pf. (of ▶ происходи́ть 1) **1** (случи́ться) to
happen, occur, take place **2** (от, из-за + g.)
(по причи́не) to arise (from), result (from)
3 (из, от + g.) (роди́ться) to come (from,
of), be descended (from)

произраст|а́ть, а́ет impf. of ▶ произрасти́

произраст|и́, ёт, past произро́с,
произросла́ pf. (of ▶ произраста́ть) to
grow, spring up

проиллюстри́р|овать, ую pf. (of
▶ иллюстри́ровать) to illustrate

проинструкти́р|овать, ую pf. (of
▶ инструкти́ровать) to instruct, give
instructions (to)

проинформи́р|овать, ую pf. (of
▶ информи́ровать) to inform

про́иск|и, ов (no sg.) intrigues; machinations

◆ происхо|ди́ть, жу́, ~дишь impf. **1** impf.
of ▶ произойти́ **2** (impf. only) to go on, be
going on; что тут ~дит? what is going on
here?

происхожде́ни|е, я nt. origin; (по
рожде́нию) birth; по ~ю он армяни́н he is
(an) Armenian by birth

происше́стви|е, я nt. event, incident,
happening, occurrence; (ава́рия) accident

◆ про|йти́, йду́, йдёшь, past ~шёл, ~шла́
pf. (of ▶ проходи́ть¹ 1) **1** (передви́нуться)
to pass (by, through); to go (by, through);
п. ми́мо to pass by, go by, go past **2** (по
оши́бке) to pass, go past **3** (расстоя́ние)
to go, do, cover; п. две ты́сячи миль за
неде́лю to do two thousand miles in a week
4 (о новостя́х, слу́хах) to travel, spread
5 (о дожде́, сне́ге) to fall **6** (о вре́мени)
to pass, elapse, go, go by; ~шёл це́лый год
a whole year had passed **7** (минова́ть)
to be over; (прекрати́ться) to pass (off),
stop, let up; ~шло́ ле́то summer was over;
дождь ~шёл the rain stopped **8** (+ a. or
че́рез + a.) to pass, go through, get through
9 (заверши́ться) to go, go off; заседа́ние
~шло́ уда́чно the meeting went off
successfully **10** (ку́рсы) to do, take; п. курс
лече́ния to take a course of treatment

про|йти́сь, йду́сь, йдёшься, past ~шёлся,
~шла́сь pf. (of ▶ проха́живаться) to walk,
stroll; (прогуля́ться) to take a stroll; п. по
ко́мнате to pace up and down the room

прока́з|а¹, ы f. (боле́знь) leprosy

прока́з|а², ы f. (ша́лость) mischief, prank,
trick

прока́зник, а m. mischief-maker; prankster

прока́зни|ца, цы f. of ▶ прока́зник

прока́лыва|ть, ю impf. of ▶ проколо́ть

прока́т, а m. (аре́нда) hire

прока|ти́ться, чу́сь, ~тишься pf. (of
▶ прока́тываться) **1** (о мяче́) to roll;
(о гро́ме) to roll **2** (для развлече́ния) to go
for a drive, go for a spin

прока́тыва|ться, юсь impf. of ▶ прокати́ться

прока́шлива|ться, юсь impf. of
▶ прока́шляться

прока́шл|яться, яюсь pf. (of
▶ прока́шливаться) to clear one's throat

прокипя|ти́ть, чу́, ти́шь pf. to boil
thoroughly

прокис|а́ть, а́ет impf. of ▶ проки́снуть

проки́с|нуть, нет pf. (of ▶ прокиса́ть) to
turn (sour)

прокла́дк|а, и f. **1** (де́йствие) laying;
building, construction; п. трубопрово́да
pipe laying **2** (tech., дета́ль) washer, gasket;

packing, padding **3** (infml, *гигиеническая*) sanitary towel

проклáдыва|ть, ю *impf. of* ▸ проложи́ть

проклина́|ть, ю *impf. of* ▸ прокля́сть

прокля́|сть, ну́, нёшь, *past* ~я́л, ~яла́, ~я́ло *pf.* (*of* ▸ проклина́ть) to curse, damn

прокля́ти|е, я *nt.* **1** (*осуждение*) damnation **2** (*слово, выражение*) curse

прокля́тый *adj.* damned; cursed

прокóл, а *m.* **1** (*в шине*) puncture **2** (*на билете; на ухе*) hole **3** (infml) (*неудача*) failure; (*оплошность*) blunder

прокол|óть, ю́, ~ешь *pf.* (*of* ▸ прокáлывать) **1** (*шину*) to puncture **2** (*уши*) to pierce **3** (*дыру*) to pierce, prick

проконсульти́р|овать, ую *pf. of* ▸ консульти́ровать

проконсульти́р|оваться, уюсь *pf. of* ▸ консульти́роваться

проконтроли́р|овать, ую *pf. of* ▸ контроли́ровать

прокорм|и́ть, лю́, ~ишь *pf. of* ▸ корми́ть

прокорм|и́ться, лю́сь, ~ишься *pf. of* ▸ корми́ться

прокрáдыва|ться, юсь *impf. of* ▸ прокрáсться

прокрá|сться, ду́сь, дёшься *pf.* (*of* ▸ прокрáдываться) to steal; п. ми́мо to steal by, past

прокрич|áть, ý, и́шь *pf.* **1** to shout, cry; to give a shout, raise a cry **2** (о + *p.*) (infml) to trumpet

прокурату́р|а, ы *f.* office of public prosecutor

прокурóр, а *m.* public prosecutor

проку|си́ть, шý, ~сишь *pf.* (*of* ▸ прокýсывать) to bite through

прокýсыва|ть, ю *impf. of* ▸ прокуси́ть

пролáмыва|ть, ю, ет *impf. of* ▸ проломи́ть

пролáмыва|ться, ется *impf. of* ▸ проломи́ться

пролегá|ть, ет *impf.* to lie, run; дорóга ~ла вдоль бéрега канáла the path lay by the canal

пролез|áть, áю *impf. of* ▸ пролéзть

пролéз|ть, у, ешь, *past* ~, ~ла *pf.* (*of* ▸ пролезáть) **1** (*проникнуть куда-н.*) to get through, climb through **2** (в + *a.*) (fig., infml, pej., *хитростью*) to worm oneself (into, on to); он ~ в члéны комитéта he has wormed his way on to the committee

пролетариáт, а *m.* proletariat

пролет|áть¹, áю *impf. of* ▸ пролетéть

пролет|áть², áю *pf.* to fly (*for a certain time*)

проле|тéть, чý, ти́шь *pf.* (*of* ▸ пролетáть¹) **1** (*какое-н. расстояние*) to fly, cover **2** (*мимо*) to fly (by, through, past) (also fig.); кани́кулы ~тéли the holidays flew by **3** (fig., *мелькнуть*) to flash, flit

проли́в, а *m.* (geog.) strait, sound

пролива́|ть, ю *impf. of* ▸ проли́ть

проливнóй *adj.*: п. дождь pouring rain; шёл п. дождь it was pouring

прол|и́ть, ью́, ьёшь, *past* ~и́л, ~ила́, ~и́ло *pf.* (*of* ▸ пролива́ть) to spill, shed; п. чью-н. кровь to shed sb's blood; п. свет (на + *a.*) (fig.) to shed light (on)

прологь, а *m.* prologue (BrE), prolog (AmE)

пролож|и́ть, ý, ~ишь *pf.* (*of* ▸ проклáдывать) **1** to lay; to build, construct; п. путь (fig.) to pave the way **2** (мéжду + *i.* or + *a.* and *i.*) to interlay; to insert (between)

пролóм, а *m.* break; gap

пролом|и́ть, лю́, ~ишь *pf.* (*of* ▸ пролáмывать) to break (through); п. чéреп to fracture one's skull

пролом|и́ться, ~ится *pf.* (*of* ▸ пролáмываться) to break, give way

промá|зать, жу, жешь *pf. of* ▸ мáзать 4

промарширов|áть, ýю *pf. of* ▸ марширова́ть

прóмах, а *m.* miss; (fig.) slip, blunder

промáхива|ться, юсь *impf. of* ▸ промахну́ться

промах|ну́ться, ну́сь, нёшься *pf.* (*of* ▸ промáхиваться) to miss

промáчива|ть, ю *impf. of* ▸ промочи́ть

промедлéни|е, я *nt.* delay; procrastination

промежу́т|ок, ка *m.* (*между событий*) interval; (*между предметами*) space; п. врéмени period, stretch of time

промежу́точный *adj.* (*положение*) intermediate; (*период*) intervening

промельк|ну́ть, ну́ *pf.* **1** to flash; (*о времени*) to fly by **2** (*появиться*) to be faintly perceptible; в его́ словáх ~у́ло разочарова́ние there was a shade of disappointment in his words

променива|ть, ю *impf. of* ▸ променя́ть

промен|я́ть, я́ю *pf.* (*of* ▸ променива́ть) (на + *a.*) to exchange, swap (for); to trade (for), barter (for)

промерз|а́ть, а́ю *impf. of* ▸ промёрзнуть

промёрз|нуть, ну, нешь, *past* ~, ~ла *pf.* (*of* ▸ промерза́ть) to freeze through

промóзглый *adj.* dank

промок|а́ть, а́ю *impf.* **1** *impf. of* ▸ промóкнуть **2** (impf. only) to let water through, not be waterproof; э́ти боти́нки ~а́ют these boots are not waterproof

промóк|нуть, ну, нешь *pf.* (*of* ▸ промока́ть 1) to get soaked, get drenched

промолч|а́ть, ý, и́шь *pf.* to keep silent, say nothing

промóутер, а *m.* promoter

промóушен, а *m.* promotion

промоч|и́ть, ý, ~ишь *pf.* (*of* ▸ промáчивать) to get wet (through); to soak, drench; п. нóги to get one's feet wet

промч|а́ться, у́сь, и́шься *pf.* **1** to tear (by, past, through); to dart (by, past), flash (by, past) **2** (*о времени*) to fly (by)

промыва́|ть, ю *impf. of* ▸ промы́ть

прóмыс|ел, ла *m.* **1** (*охота*) hunting, catching; пушнóй п. trapping **2** (*занятие*)

п

trade, business; **го́рный п.** mining **3** (*in pl.*) (*предприятие*) fields, mines; **нефтяны́е ∼лы** oilfields

промы́|ть, о́ю, о́ешь *pf.* (*of* ▶ промыва́ть) **1** to wash well, thoroughly (fig.) to brainwash **2** (med.) to bathe

промы́шленник, а *m.* manufacturer, industrialist

◌ **промы́шленност|ь, и** *f.* industry

◌ **промы́шленный** *adj.* industrial

пронес|ти́, у́, ёшь, *past ∼, ∼ла́ pf.* (*of* ▶ проноси́ть) **1** to carry (by, past, through) **2**: **∼ло́!** (infml) the danger is over!

пронес|ти́сь, у́сь, ёшься, *past ∼ся, ∼ла́сь pf.* (*of* ▶ проноси́ться) **1** to rush (by, past, through); (*об облаках*) to scud (past) **2** (*о времени*) to fly by

пронз|а́ть, а́ю *impf. of* ▶ пронзи́ть

пронзи́тел|ьный, ∼ен, ∼ьна *adj.* piercing

прон|зи́ть, жу́, зи́шь (*of* ▶ пронза́ть) to pierce

прони|за́ть, жу́, ∼жешь *pf.* (*of* ▶ прони́зывать) to pierce; to permeate, penetrate; (fig.) to run through; **свет ∼за́л темноту́** the light pierced the darkness; **одна́ иде́я ∼за́ла все его́ произведе́ния** one idea ran through all his works

прони́зыва|ть, ю *impf. of* ▶ пронизать

прони́зывающий *pres. part. act. of* ▶ прони́зывать *and adj.* piercing

проник|а́ть, а́ю *impf. of* ▶ прони́кнуть

прони́к|нуть, ну, нешь, *past ∼, ∼ла pf.* (*of* ▶ проника́ть) (**в** + *a.*) to penetrate (also fig.); (**че́рез** + *a.*) to percolate (through)

проница́тел|ьный, ∼ен, ∼ьна *adj.* perspicacious; shrewd; penetrating, piercing

проно|си́ть, шу́, ∼сишь *impf. of* ▶ пронести́

проно|си́ться, шу́сь, ∼сишься *impf. of* ▶ пронести́сь

проо́браз, а *m.* prototype

пропага́нд|а, ы *f.* propaganda; promotion, advocacy

пропаганди́р|овать, ую *impf.* to propagandize; to advocate

пропада́|ть, ю *impf. of* ▶ пропа́сть

пропа́ж|а, и *f.* loss

пропа́лыва|ть, ю *impf. of* ▶ прополо́ть

пропа́н, а *m.* propane

про́паст|ь, и *f.* precipice (also fig.); abyss; **на краю́ ∼и** (fig.) on the brink of disaster

пропа́|сть, ду́, дёшь, *past ∼л pf.* (*of* ▶ пропада́ть) **1** (*потеряться*) to be missing; to be lost; **п. бе́з вести** (mil.) to be missing **2** (*исчезнуть*) to disappear, vanish; **куда́ вы ∼ли?** where did you vanish to? **3** (*погибнуть*) to be lost, be done for; (*о цветах*) to die; **тепе́рь мы ∼ли!** now we're done for!

пропа́х|нуть, ну, нешь, *past ∼, ∼ла pf.* to become permeated with the smell (of)

пропека́|ть, ю, ет *impf. of* ▶ пропе́чь

пропека́|ться, ется *impf. of* ▶ пропе́чься

пропе́ллер, а *m.* propeller

пропе́|чь, ку́, чёшь, ку́т, *past ∼к, ∼кла́ pf.* (*of* ▶ пропека́ть) to bake well, thoroughly

пропе́|чься, чётся, ку́тся, *past ∼кся, ∼кла́сь pf.* (*of* ▶ пропека́ться) to bake well, get baked through

пропива́|ть, ю *impf. of* ▶ пропи́ть

пропи́лива|ть, ю *impf. of* ▶ пропили́ть

пропил|и́ть, ю́, ∼ишь *pf.* (*of* ▶ пропи́ливать) to saw through

пропи|са́ть, шу́, ∼шешь *pf.* (*of* ▶ пропи́сывать) **1** (*лекарство*) to prescribe **2** (*жильца*) to register

пропи|са́ться, шу́сь, ∼шешься *pf.* (*of* ▶ пропи́сываться) to register

пропи́ск|а, и *f.* **1** (*регистрация*) registration **2** (*отметка в паспорте*) residence permit

пропи́сыва|ть, ю *impf. of* ▶ прописа́ть

пропи́сыва|ться, юсь *impf. of* ▶ прописа́ться

прописно́й *adj.* (*буква*) capital; **писа́ться с п. бу́квы** to be written with a capital letter

пропит|а́ть, а́ю *pf.* (*of* ▶ пропи́тывать) (+ *i.*) to impregnate (with), steep (in); **п. ма́слом** to oil

пропит|а́ться, а́юсь *pf.* (*of* ▶ пропи́тываться) (+ *i.*) to become saturated (with)

пропи́тыва|ть, ю *impf. of* ▶ пропита́ть

пропи́тыва|ться, юсь *impf. of* ▶ пропита́ться

про|пи́ть, пью́, пьёшь, *past ∼пи́л, ∼пила́, ∼пи́ло pf.* (*of* ▶ пропива́ть) **1** (*деньги*) to spend on drink, squander on drink **2** (infml, *талант*) to ruin (*through excessive drinking*)

проплава́|ть, ю *pf.* (*вплавь*) to swim (*for a certain time*); (*на судне*) to sail (*for a certain time*)

проплá|кать, чу, чешь *pf.* to cry, weep (*for a certain time*)

проплыва́|ть, ю *impf. of* ▶ проплы́ть

проплы́|ть, ву́, вёшь, *past ∼л, ∼ла́, ∼ло pf.* (*of* ▶ проплыва́ть) **1** (*вплавь*) to swim (by, past, through); (*на судне*) to sail (by, past, through); (*о предмете*) to float, drift (by, past, through) **2** (*расстояние*) to cover (*a certain distance*)

пропове́дник, а *m.* **1** preacher **2** (+ *g.*) (fig.) advocate (of)

пропове́д|овать, ую *impf.* **1** to preach **2** (fig.) to advocate, propagate

про́повед|ь, и *f.* sermon; homily

прополз|а́ть, а́ю *impf. of* ▶ проползти́

пропол|зти́, у́, ёшь, *past ∼, ∼ла́ pf.* (*of* ▶ проползать) to creep, crawl (by, past, through)

прополо|ска́ть, щу́, ∼щешь *pf.* (*of* ▶ полоска́ть) to rinse, swill; **п. го́рло** to gargle

прополо́|ть, ю́, ∼ешь *pf.* (*of* ▶ пропа́лывать) to weed

◌ key word

пропорциона́л|ьный, ~ен, ~ьна *adj.*
1 proportional; proportionate
2 (*обладающий правильными пропорциями*) well proportioned

пропо́рци|я, и *f.* proportion

про́пуск, а *m.* **1** (*no pl.*) (*действие*) admission **2** (*pl.* ~á) (*документ*) pass, permit **3** (*pl.* ~á) (mil.) password **4** (*pl.* ~и) (+ *g.*) (*непосещение*) non-attendance (at), absence (from) **5** (*pl.* ~и) (*пустое место*) blank, gap

пропуска́|ть, ю *impf.* **1** *impf. of* ▶ пропусти́ть **2** (*impf. only*) to let pass; **п. во́ду** to leak; **не п. воды́** to be waterproof

пропускн|о́й *adj.*: **п. пункт** checkpoint; ~а́я спосо́бность capacity; (*comput.*) bandwidth

пропу|сти́ть, щу́, ~стишь *pf.* (*of* ▶ пропуска́ть 1) **1** (*дать пройти*) to let pass, let through; to make way (for); (*впустить*) to let in, admit; (*обслужить*) to put through, deal with; **п. на перро́н** to let on to the platform **2** (*через* + *a.*) to run (through), pass (through); **п. через фильтр** to filter **3** (*при чтении, письме*) to omit, leave out; to skip **4** (*не явиться*) to miss; **п. ле́кцию** to miss a lecture

пропылесо́с|ить, ишь *pf. of* ▶ пылесо́сить

прораба́тыва|ть, ю *impf. of* ▶ прорабо́тать¹

прорабо́та|ть¹, ю *pf.* (*of* ▶ прораба́тывать) (infml) **1** (*изучить*) to work (at), study **2** (*критиковать*) to pick holes (in)

прорабо́та|ть², ю *pf.* (*некоторое время*) to work (*for a while*)

прораст|а́ть, а́ет *impf. of* ▶ прорасти́

прораст|и́, ёт, *past* проро́с, проросла́ *pf.* (*of* ▶ прораста́ть) to germinate, sprout, shoot (*of plant*)

прорв|а́ть, у́, ёшь, *past* ~а́л, ~ала́, ~а́ло *pf.* (*of* ▶ прорыва́ть¹) **1** to break through; to tear, make a hole (in); **п. ли́нию оборо́ны проти́вника** to break through the enemy's defence line; (*impers.*) плоти́ну ~а́ло the dam has burst **2** (*impers.*) (infml) to lose patience

прорв|а́ться, у́сь, ёшься, *past* ~а́лся, ~ала́сь, ~а́ло́сь *pf.* (*of* ▶ прорыва́ться) **1** (*сломаться*) to break, burst (open) **2** (*разорваться*) to tear **3** (*силой проложить себе путь*) to break (out, through); to force one's way (through)

прореаги́р|овать, ую *pf. of* ▶ реаги́ровать 2

проре́|зать, жу, жешь *pf.* (*of* ▶ проре́зывать, ▶ проре́зать) to cut through (*also fig.*)

проре́за|ть, ю *impf. of* ▶ проре́зать

проре́зыва|ть, ю *impf. of* ▶ проре́зать

про́рез|ь, и *f.* opening, aperture

проржаве́|ть, ет *pf.* to rust through

проро́к, а *m.* prophet

проро́ч|ить, у, ишь *impf.* (*of* ▶ напроро́чить) to prophesy, predict

проруб|а́ть, а́ю *impf. of* ▶ проруби́ть

проруб|и́ть, лю́, ~ишь *pf.* (*of* ▶ прорубать) to hack through, cut through

про́руб|ь, и *f.* ice hole

проры́в, а *m.* break; (mil.) breakthrough, breach

прорыва́|ть¹, ю *impf. of* ▶ прорва́ть

прорыва́|ть², ю *impf. of* ▶ проры́ть

прорыва́|ться, юсь *impf. of* ▶ прорва́ться

прор|ы́ть, о́ю, о́ешь *pf.* (*of* ▶ прорыва́ть²) to dig through

проса́чива|ться, ется *impf. of* ▶ просочи́ться

просверл|и́ть, ю́, и́шь *pf. of* ▶ сверли́ть

просве́т, а *m.* shaft of light; (fig.) ray of hope

просве|ти́ть¹, щу́, ти́шь *pf.* (*of* ▶ просвеща́ть) to educate; to enlighten

просве|ти́ть², чу́, ~тишь *pf.* (*of* ▶ просве́чивать¹) (med.) to X-ray

просве́чива|ть¹, ю *impf. of* ▶ просвети́ть²

просве́чива|ть², ю *impf.* **1** (*быть прозрачным*) to be translucent; (*одежда, занавески*) to be see-through **2** (*через, сквозь* + *a.*) (*быть видным*) to be visible (through), show (through), appear (through); (*о солнце*) to shine (through)

просвеща́|ть, ю *impf. of* ▶ просвети́ть¹

просвеще́ни|е, я *nt.* **1** (*образование*) education; наро́дное п. public education **2** enlightenment; эпо́ха П~я (hist.) the Age of the Enlightenment

просве|щённый *p.p.p. of* ▶ просвети́ть¹ *and adj.* enlightened; educated, cultured; ~щённое мне́ние expert opinion; п. челове́к educated person

про́сек|а, и *f.* cutting (*in a forest*)

проси|де́ть, жу́, ди́шь *pf.* (*of* ▶ проси́живать) to sit (*for a certain time*); п. ночь у посте́ли больно́го to sit up all night with a patient

проси́жива|ть, ю *impf. of* ▶ просиде́ть

☞ про|си́ть, шу́, ~сишь *impf.* (*of* ▶ попроси́ть) **1** (+ *a.* of person asked; + *a.* or *g.* of thing sought or о + *p.*) to ask (for), beg; ~шу́ (вас) please; п. кого́-н. о по́мощи to ask sb for help, ask sb's assistance; п. разреше́ния to ask permission; п. сове́та to ask (for) advice; п. извине́ния у кого́-н. to apologize to sb **2** (за + *a.*) (*вступаться*) to intercede (for) **3** (*приглашать*) to invite; вас ~сят к столу́ please take your places at the table

про|си́ться, шу́сь, ~сишься *impf.* (*of* ▶ попроси́ться) (+ *inf.* or в + *a.* or на + *a.*) to ask (for); п. в о́тпуск to apply for leave

проска́кива|ть, ю *impf. of* ▶ проскочи́ть

проска́льзыва|ть, ю *impf. of* ▶ проскользну́ть

проскользн|у́ть, у́, ёшь *pf.* (*of* ▶ проска́льзывать) (infml) to slip in, creep in (also fig.); ~у́ло мно́го оши́бок many errors have crept in

проскоч|и́ть, у́, ~ишь *pf.* (*of* ▶ проска́кивать) **1** (*пробежать*) to rush by, tear by **2** (*через* + *a.*) to slip (through) **3** (*сквозь* + *a.* or *между* + *i.*) to fall (through, between); п. ме́жду па́льцами to fall through one's fingers **4** (*не остановиться, где нужно*) to overshoot

прослав|иться, люсь, ишься pf. (of
▶ прославля́ться) (+ i.) to become famous
(for)

прославля́|ться, юсь impf. of
▶ просла́виться

просле|ди́ть, жу́, ди́шь pf. (of
▶ просле́живать) **1** (выследить) to track
(down) **2** (исследовать) to trace (through);
to trace back, retrace

просле́жива|ть, ю impf. of ▶ проследи́ть

просло́йк|а, и f. layer, stratum (also fig.)

прослужи́ть, у́, ~ишь pf. **1** to work,
serve (for a certain time) **2** (пробыть в
употреблении) to last (for a certain time);
э́то пальто́ ~ит мне ещё оди́н год this coat
will last me another year

прослу́ш|ать, аю pf. **1** (impf. слу́шать) to
hear (through); п. курс ле́кций to attend a
course of lectures **2** (impf. ~ивать) (med.)
to listen to; п. чьё-н. се́рдце to listen to sb's
heart **3** (impf. ~ивать) (infml) to miss, not
catch; прости́те, я ~ал, что вы сказа́ли I am
sorry, I did not catch what you said

прослу́шивани|е, я nt. audition

прослу́шива|ть, ю impf. of ▶ прослу́шать 2,
▶ прослу́шать 3

просма́трива|ть, ю impf. of ▶ просмотре́ть

☞ просмо́тр, а m. survey; view, viewing;
предвари́тельный п. preview

просмотр|е́ть, ю́, ~ишь pf. (of
▶ просма́тривать) **1** to survey; to view
2 (читая) to look over, look through;
(бегло) to glance over, glance through; п.
ру́копись to glance through a manuscript
3 (пропустить) to overlook, miss

прос|ну́ться, ну́сь, нёшься pf. (of
▶ просыпа́ться¹) to wake up, awake

просо́выва|ть, ю impf. of ▶ просу́нуть

просо́выва|ться, юсь impf. of
▶ просу́нуться

просо́х|нуть, ну, нешь, past ~, ~ла pf. (of
▶ просыха́ть) to get dry, dry out

просочи́|ться, и́тся pf. (of ▶ проса́чиваться)
1 to percolate; to filter; to leak; to seep
out **2** (fig.) to filter through; to leak out

просп|а́ть¹, лю́, и́шь, past ~а́л, ~ала́, ~а́ло
pf. (of ▶ просыпа́ть²) **1** (не проснуться
вовремя) to oversleep **2** (пропустить) to
miss, pass (due to being asleep)

просп|а́ть², лю́, и́шь, past ~а́л, ~ала́,
~а́ло pf. (некоторое время) to sleep (for a
certain time)

проспе́кт¹, а m. (улица) avenue

проспе́кт², а m. **1** (справочное издание)
brochure, prospectus **2** (план) outline,
résumé

проспо́рива|ть, ю impf. of ▶ проспо́рить

проспо́р|ить, ю, ишь pf. (of ▶ проспо́ривать)
(деньги) to lose (in a bet)

проспряга́|ть, ю pf. of ▶ спряга́ть

просро́ченный p.p.p. of ▶ просро́чить and
adj. overdue

просро́чива|ть, ю impf. of ▶ просро́чить

просро́ч|ить, у, ишь pf. (of ▶ просро́чивать)
to exceed the time limit; п. платёж to fail to
pay in time

проста́ива|ть, ю impf. of ▶ простоя́ть

проста́к, а́ m. simpleton

проста́т|а, ы f. (anat.) prostate (gland)

проститу́тк|а, и f. prostitute

проститу́ци|я, и f. prostitution

про|сти́ть, щу́, сти́шь pf. (of ▶ проща́ть)
1 to forgive, pardon; ~сти́те (меня́)! excuse
me!; I beg your pardon! **2** (долг) to remit; п.
долг кому́-н. to remit sb's debt

про|сти́ться, щу́сь, сти́шься pf. (of
▶ проща́ться) (с + i.) to say goodbye (to),
bid farewell (to)

☞ про́сто adv. simply; п. так for no particular
reason; э́то п. невероя́тно it is simply
incredible

простоду́ш|ный, ~ен, ~на adj. simple-
hearted; ingenuous, artless

☞ прост|о́й, ~, ~а́, ~о, ~ы́ adj. **1** (нетрудный)
simple; easy; вам ~о критикова́ть it is easy
(or all very well) for you to criticize
2 (однородный) simple (= unitary);
~о́е число́ (math.) prime number
3 (обыкновенный) simple; ordinary;
п. наро́д the common people **4** (без
претензий) simple, plain; unaffected,
unpretentious; ~ые лю́ди ordinary people;
homely people **5** (не более как) mere;
п. сме́ртный a mere mortal; по той ~о́й
причи́не, что for the simple reason that

простон|а́ть, у́, ~ешь pf. to groan

просто́р, а m. **1** (пространство)
spaciousness; space, expanse **2** (свобода)
freedom, scope

просто́р|ный, ~ен, ~на adj. spacious,
roomy; (об одежде) loose-fitting

простот|а́, ы́ f. simplicity

просто|я́ть, ю́, и́шь pf. (of ▶ проста́ивать)
1 (некоторое время) to stay, stand; по́езд
~я́л на запасно́м пути́ всю ночь the train
stood in a siding all night **2** (бездействовать)
to stand idle, lie idle **3** (о здании) to stand,
last

простра́н|ный, ~ен, ~на adj. verbose

простра́нственный adj. spatial

☞ простра́нств|о, а nt. space; (неограниченная
протяжённость) expanse; возду́шное п. air
space; пусто́е п. void

простра́ци|я, и f. prostration

простре́лива|ть, ю impf. of ▶ прострели́ть

простре́л|ить, ю, ~ишь pf. (of
▶ простре́ливать) **1** (выстрелом пробить
насквозь) to shoot through **2** (sport) to cross
low

просту́д|а, ы f. (chest) cold; схвати́ть/
подхвати́ть ~у (infml) to catch (a) cold

просту|ди́ть, жу́, ～ди́шь *pf.* (*of*
▶ **простужа́ть**) to let catch cold; **п. себе́
го́рло** to get a sore throat

просту|ди́ться, жу́сь, ～ди́шься *pf.* (*of*
▶ **простужа́ться**) to catch (a) cold

простужа́|ть, ю *impf. of* ▶ **простуди́ть**

простужа́|ться, юсь *impf. of* ▶ **простуди́ться**

проступ|а́ть, а́ет *impf. of* ▶ **проступи́ть**

проступ|и́ть, ～ит *pf.* (*of* ▶ **проступа́ть**)
to appear, show through, come through;
сыры́е пя́тна ～и́ли на сте́на́х damp patches
have appeared on the walls

просту́п|ок, ка *m.* misdeed; (law)
misdemeanour (BrE), misdemeanor (AmE)

простыва́|ть, ю *impf. of* ▶ **просты́ть**

простын|я́, и́, pl. ～и, ～е́й/～ь, ～я́м *f.* sheet

просты́|ть, ну, нешь *pf.* (*of* ▶ **простыва́ть**)
(infml) to catch cold

просу́н|уть, у, ешь *pf.* (*of* ▶ **просо́вывать**)
(**в** + *a.*) to push (through, in), shove
(through, in), thrust (through, in)

просу́н|уться, усь, ешься *pf.* (*of*
▶ **просо́вываться**) to push through, force
one's way through

просу́шива|ть, ю *impf. of* ▶ **просуши́ть**

просу́шива|ться, юсь *impf. of*
▶ **просуши́ться**

просуш|и́ть, у́, ～ишь *pf.* (*of* ▶ **просу́шивать**)
to dry thoroughly, properly

просуш|и́ться, у́сь, ～ишься *pf.* (*of*
▶ **просу́шиваться**) to (get) dry

просуществ|ова́ть, у́ю *pf.* (*прожи́ть*) to
exist; (*продли́ться*) to last, endure

просчёт, а *m.* ① (*де́йствие*) counting (up),
reckoning (up) ② (*оши́бка*) error (*in
counting, reckoning*)

просчит|а́ться, а́юсь *pf.* (*of*
▶ **просчи́тываться**) to miscalculate

просчи́тыва|ться, юсь *impf. of*
▶ **просчита́ться**

просы́п|ать, лю, лешь *pf.* (*of* ▶ **просыпа́ть**[1])
to spill

просыпа́|ть[1]**, а́ю** *impf. of* ▶ **просы́пать**

просыпа́|ть[2]**, а́ю** *impf. of* ▶ **проспа́ть**[1]

просы́п|аться, лется *pf.* (*of* ▶ **просыпа́ться**[2])
to spill, get spilled

просыпа́|ться[1]**, а́юсь** *impf. of* ▶ **просну́ться**

просыпа́|ться[2]**, а́ется** *impf. of*
▶ **просыпа́ться**

просыха́|ть, ю *impf. of* ▶ **просо́хнуть**

✧ **про́сьб|а, ы** *f.* request; **обраща́ться с ～ой**
to make a request; **у меня́ к вам п.** I have
a favour (BrE), favor (AmE) to ask you; **по
мое́й ～е** at my request; **«п. не кури́ть!»** 'no
smoking, please!'

прота́лкива|ть, ю *impf. of* ▶ **протолкну́ть**

прота́птыва|ть, ю *impf. of* ▶ **протопта́ть**

прота́скива|ть, ю *impf. of* ▶ **протащи́ть**

протащ|и́ть, у́, ～ишь *pf.* (*of*
▶ **прота́скивать**) to pull (through, along),
drag (through, along), trail

протеже́ *c.g. indecl.* protégé (*fem.* protégée)

проте́з, а *m.* prosthesis; artificial limb;
зубно́й п. false tooth, denture

протеи́н, а *m.* (chem.) protein

протека́|ть, ю *impf.* ① *impf. of* ▶ **проте́чь**
② (*impf. only*) (*о реке́, струе́*) to flow, run
③ (*impf. only*) (*о кры́ше*) to leak, be leaky

про|тере́ть, тру́, трёшь, *past* **～тёр,
～тёрла** *pf.* (*of* ▶ **протира́ть**) ① (*о́кна*) to
rub over, wipe over ② **п. глаза́** (infml) to rub
one's eyes

проте́ст, а *m.* ① protest; **заяви́ть п.** to make
a protest ② (law) objection

протеста́нт, а *m.* (relig.) Protestant

протеста́нт|ка, ки *f. of* ▶ **протеста́нт**

протеста́нтский *adj.* (relig.) Protestant

протест|ова́ть, у́ю *impf.* (*про́тив* + *g.*) to
protest (against)

проте́|чь, чёт, ку́т, *past* **～к, ～кла́** *pf.* (*of*
▶ **протека́ть**) ① to ooze, seep ② (*о вре́мени*)
to elapse, pass ③ (*о боле́зни*) to take its course

✧ **про́тив** *prep.* + *g.* ① against; **п. тече́ния**
against the current; **за и п.** for and against,
pro and con; **име́ть что-н. п.** to have
sth against; to mind, object; **вы ничего́
не име́ете п. того́, что я курю́?** do you
mind my smoking? ② (*пря́мо перед*)
opposite; facing; **друг п. дру́га** facing one
another ③ (*вопреки́*) contrary to; **п. на́ших
ожида́ний** contrary to our expectations

про́тив|ень, ня *m.* (*неглубо́кий*) baking
sheet, baking tray; (*глубо́кий*) roasting pan

✧ **проти́вник, а** *m.* ① opponent, adversary
② (collect.) (mil.) the enemy

проти́вн|ый[1] *adj.* opposite; contrary; **в ～ом
слу́чае** otherwise; **доказа́тельство от ～ого**
the rule of contraries

проти́вный[2]**, ～ен, ～на** *adj.*
(*отврати́тельный*) nasty, disgusting;
п. за́пах nasty smell; **он мне ～ен** I find
him offensive

противове́с, а *m.* (tech., also fig.)
counterbalance, counterpoise

противога́з, а *m.* gas mask

противоде́йстви|е, я *nt.* opposition,
counteraction

противоде́йств|овать, ую *impf.* (+ *d.*)
to oppose, counteract

противоесте́ствен|ный, ～, ～на *adj.*
unnatural

противозако́н|ный, ～ен, ～на *adj.*
unlawful; (law) illegal

противозача́точн|ый *adj.* contraceptive;
～ое сре́дство contraceptive

противопожа́рн|ый *adj.* fire-prevention;
～ая дверь fire door

противополо́жность, и *f.* ① (*несхо́дство*)
opposition; contrast; **в п.** (+ *d.*) as opposed
(to), by contrast (with) ② (*что-н.
противополо́жное*) opposite, antithesis;
пряма́я п. exact opposite

противополо́ж|ный, ～ен, ～на *adj.*
① (*бе́рег*) opposite ② (*мне́ние*) opposed,
contrary

противопоста́в|ить, лю, ишь pf. (of
  ▶ **противопоставля́ть**) (+ d.) **1** (*направить
  против*) to oppose (with), counter (with);
  си́ле п. си́лу to oppose force with force
  2 (*сравни́ть*) to contrast (with), set off
  (against)

противопоставля́|ть, ю impf. of
  ▶ **противопоста́вить**

противопра́в|ный, ∼ен, ∼на adj.
  unlawful, illegal

противоречи́в|ый, ∼, ∼а adj.
  contradictory; conflicting; ∼ые сообще́ния
  conflicting reports

противоре́чи|е, я nt. **1** (*несоответствие*)
  contradiction; inconsistency **2** (*возражение*)
  contrariness; defiance **3** (*конфликт*)
  conflict, clash; **находи́ться в ∼и** (**с** + i.) to be
  at variance (with), conflict (with)

противоре́ч|ить, у, ишь impf. (+ d.)
  1 (*возражать*) to contradict
  2 (*несоответствовать*) to be at variance
  (with), conflict (with), be contrary (to); **их
  показа́ния ∼ат друг дру́гу** their evidence is
  conflicting

противостоя́ни|е, я nt. **1** (astron.)
  opposition **2** (pol.) confrontation

противоя́ди|е, я nt. antidote

протира́|ть, ю impf. of ▶ **протере́ть**

проткн|у́ть, у́, ёшь pf. (of ▶ **протыка́ть**)
  to pierce

прото́к, а m. **1** channel **2** (anat.) duct

протоко́л, а m. **1** (*заседания*) minutes;
  report; **вести́ п.** to take the minutes **2** (law)
  statement; charge sheet; **соста́вить п.** to
  draw up a report **3** (pol., comput.) protocol

протолкн|у́ть, у́, ёшь pf. (of
  ▶ **прота́лкивать**) to push through, press
  through

прото́н, а m. (phys.) proton

протоп|та́ть, чу́, ∼чешь pf. (of
  ▶ **прота́птывать**) to beat, make (*by
  walking*); **п. тропи́нку** to make a path

прототи́п, а m. prototype

прото́чн|ый adj. flowing, running; ∼ая вода́
  running water; **п. пруд** pond fed by springs

протрезве́|ть, ю pf. of ▶ **трезве́ть**

протрезв|и́ться, лю́сь, и́шься pf. (of
  ▶ **протрезвля́ться**) to sober up

протрезвля́|ться, юсь impf. of
  ▶ **протрезви́ться**

протух|а́ть, а́ет impf. of ▶ **проту́хнуть**

проту́х|нуть, нет, past ∼, ∼ла pf. (of
  ▶ **протуха́ть**) (*мясо, рыба*) to go bad

проту́хший p.p. act. of ▶ **проту́хнуть** and adj.
  rotten; bad

протыка́|ть, ю impf. of ▶ **проткну́ть**

протя́гива|ть, ю impf. of ▶ **протяну́ть**

протя́гива|ться, юсь impf. of ▶ **протяну́ться**

✓ **протяже́ни|е, я** nt. **1** extent; (*пространство*)
  expanse, area; **на всём ∼и** (+ g.) along the

whole length (of), all along **2**: **на ∼и** (+ g.)
  during, for the duration (of)

протя́ж|ный, ∼ен, ∼на adj. long drawn-out

прот|яну́ть, яну́, ∼я́нешь pf. (of
  ▶ **протя́гивать**) **1** (*верёвку*) to stretch;
  (*линию связи*) to extend **2** (*руки, ноги*) to
  stretch out; (*газету, книгу*) to hold out;
  п. ру́ку по́мощи to extend a helping hand

прот|яну́ться, яну́сь, ∼я́нешься pf.
  (of ▶ **протя́гиваться**) **1** (*о дороге, о
  пространстве*) to extend, stretch, reach
  2 (pf. only) (*продлиться*) to last, go on

проу́чива|ть, ю impf. of ▶ **проучи́ть**

проуч|и́ть, у́, ∼ишь pf. (of ▶ **проу́чивать**)
  (infml, *наказать*) to teach (a lesson)

профа́н, а m. ignoramus; (*неспециалист*)
  layman

профессиона́л, а m. professional

профессионали́зм, а m. professionalism

✓ **профессиона́льный** adj. **1** professional,
  occupational; **п. диплома́т** career diplomat;
  п. секре́т trade secret; **п. сою́з** trade union
  2 (*компетентный*) professional (*opp.
  amateur*)

профе́сси|я, и f. profession, occupation,
  trade; **по ∼и** by profession, by trade

✓ **профе́ссор, а,** pl. ∼а́ m. professor

про́фи c.g. indecl. (infml) professional; pro
  (infml)

профила́ктик|а, и f. **1** (med.) prophylaxis
  2 (*collect.*) preventive measures, precautions

профилакто́ри|й, я m. sanatorium, health
  farm

про́фил|ь, я m. **1** (*вид сбоку*) profile; side
  view; **в п.** in profile **2** (*специфический
  характер*) type; **шко́лы ра́зного ∼я** schools
  of various types

профильтр|ова́ть, у́ю pf. (of
  ▶ **фильтрова́ть**)

профсою́з, а m. trade union

проха́жива|ться, юсь impf. of ▶ **пройти́сь**

прохла́д|а, ы f. coolness

прохла́д|ный, ∼ен, ∼на adj. **1** cool;
  (*impers., pred.*) ∼но it is cool **2** (fig.) cool

прохо́д, а m. **1** (*действие*) passage; **не
  дава́ть ∼а** (+ d.) to give no peace, pester
  2 (*место*) passageway; (*между рядами*)
  gangway, aisle

проходи́м|ец, ца m. (infml) rogue, rascal

проходи́м|ый, ∼, ∼а adj. passable

✓ **прохо|ди́ть¹, жу́, ∼дишь** impf. **1** impf. of
  ▶ **пройти́ 2** (impf. only) (**че́рез** + a.) to lie
  (through), go (through), pass (through)

прохо|ди́ть², жу́, ∼дишь pf. (*некоторое
  время*) to walk; **мы ∼ди́ли весь день** we
  have spent the whole day walking

прохо́ж|ий adj. passing, in transit; (*as n.* **п.**,
  ∼его, f. ∼ая, ∼ей) passer-by

процвета́ни|е, я nt. prosperity, well-being;
  flourishing

процвета́|ть, ю impf. to prosper, flourish,
  thrive

✓ key word

проце|ди́ть, жу́, ∼дишь *pf.* (*of* ▶ **проце́живать**) **1** to filter, strain **2**: **п. сквозь зу́бы** to say through clenched teeth

⚥ **процеду́р|а, ы** *f.* **1** procedure **2** (*usu. in pl.*) (med.) treatment

проце́жива|ть, ю *impf. of* ▶ **процеди́ть**

⚥ **проце́нт, а** *m.* **1** percentage; per cent; **сто ∼ов** one hundred per cent **2** (*доход с капитала*) interest

⚥ **проце́сс, а** *m.* **1** process **2** (law) trial; legal proceedings; lawsuit

проце́сси|я, и *f.* procession

проце́ссор, а *m.* (comput.) processor; **центра́льный п.** central processing unit

процессуа́льн|ый *adj.* procedural; **∼ые но́рмы** legal procedure

процити́р|овать, ую *pf. of* ▶ **цити́ровать**

про́черк, а *m.* dash, line

про|че́сть, чту́, чтёшь, *past* **∼чёл, ∼чла́** *pf.* = **прочита́ть**

⚥ **про́ч|ий** *adj.* other; **и ∼ее** (*abbr.* **и пр., и проч.**) et cetera, and so on; **∼ие** (the) others; **ме́жду ∼им** by the way; **поми́мо (всего́) ∼его** in addition

прочи́|стить, щу, стишь *pf.* (*of* ▶ **прочища́ть**) to clean out

прочита́|ть, ю *pf. of* ▶ **чита́ть**

прочища́|ть, ю *impf. of* ▶ **прочи́стить**

про́чно *adv.* firmly, soundly, solidly, well

про́чность, и *f.* firmness, soundness, stability, solidity; durability; strength; **запа́с ∼и, коэффицие́нт ∼и** safety factor, safety margin

про́ч|ный, ∼ен, ∼на́, ∼но, ∼ны́ *adj.* firm, sound, stable, solid; durable, lasting; **∼ные зна́ния** sound knowledge; **∼ная ткань** durable fabric

прочь *adv.* **1** away, off; **(поди́) п.!** go away!; be off!; **п. с доро́ги!** (get) out of the way!, make way!; **ру́ки п.!** hands off! **2** (*as pred.*) averse (to); **не п.** (+ *inf.*) (infml) to have no objection (to); **то be not averse (to)

проше́дш|ий *p.p. act. of* ▶ **пройти́** *and adj.* past; last; **∼ее вре́мя** (gram.) past tense; (*as nt. n.* **∼ее**) the past

прошеп|та́ть, чу́, ∼чешь *pf. of* ▶ **шепта́ть**

прошива́|ть, ю *impf. of* ▶ **проши́ть**

прош|и́ть, ью́, ьёшь *pf.* (*of* ▶ **прошива́ть**) to sew, stitch (on)

прошлого́дний *adj.* last year's; of last year

⚥ **про́шл|ый** *adj.* **1** (*происходивший ранее*) past; former; (*as nt. n.* **∼ое, ∼ого**) the past; **далёкое ∼ое** the distant past **2** (*предшествовавший настоящему*) last; **в ∼ом году́** last year; **на ∼ой неде́ле** last week

прошмы́гива|ть, ю *impf. of* ▶ **прошмыгну́ть**

прошмыг|ну́ть, ну́, нёшь *pf.* (*of* ▶ **прошмы́гивать**) (infml) (*человек*) to slip (by, past, through); (*животное*) to scurry past

проща́й and **проща́йте** goodbye!; farewell!

проща́ни|е, я *nt.* farewell; parting, leave-taking; **на п.** at parting

проща́|ть, ю *impf. of* ▶ **прости́ть**

проща́|ться, юсь *impf. of* ▶ **прости́ться**

про́ще *comp. of* ▶ **просто́й**, ▶ **про́сто**; simpler; plainer; easier

проще́ни|е, я *nt.* forgiveness; (*преступника*) pardon; (*греха*) absolution; **проси́ть ∼я у кого́-н.** to ask sb's pardon; **прошу́ ∼я!** I beg your pardon!; (I am) sorry!

проэкзамен|ова́ть, у́ю *pf. of* ▶ **экзаменова́ть**

прояв|и́ть, лю́, ∼ишь *pf.* (*of* ▶ **проявля́ть**) **1** to show, display; **п. интере́с (к** + *d.*) to show interest (in); **п. себя́** (+ *i.*) to show oneself, prove (to be) **2** (phot.) to develop

прояв|и́ться, ∼ится *pf.* (*of* ▶ **проявля́ться**) to show (itself), reveal itself, manifest itself

проявле́ни|е, я *nt.* display, manifestation

⚥ **проявля́|ть, ю, ет** *impf. of* ▶ **прояви́ть**

проявля́|ться, ется *impf. of* ▶ **прояви́ться**

проясн|и́ть, ю́, и́шь *pf.* (*of* ▶ **проясня́ть**) to clarify

проясн|и́ться, и́тся *pf.* (*of* ▶ **проясня́ться**) **1** (*о погоде*) to clear (up); **днём ∼и́лось** in the afternoon it cleared up **2** (*о мыслях, о положении*) to become clear

проясня́|ть, я́ю *impf. of* ▶ **проясни́ть**

проясня́|ться, я́ется *impf. of* ▶ **проясни́ться**

пруд, а́, в ∼у́, *pl.* **∼ы́** *m.* pond

пружи́н|а, ы *f.* spring

Пру́сси|я, и *f.* Prussia

прут, а́ *m.* (*pl.* **∼ья, ∼ьев**) twig; switch; **и́вовый п.** withe, withy

прыга́л|ка, и *f.* (infml) skipping rope (BrE), jump rope (AmE)

пры́га|ть, аю *impf.* (*of* ▶ **пры́гнуть**) **1** to jump, leap, spring; to bound; **п. на одно́й ноге́** to hop on one leg; **п. со скака́лкой** to skip **2** (*о мяче*) to bounce

пры́г|нуть, ну, нешь *pf.* *inst. of* ▶ **пры́гать**

прыгу́н, а́ *m.* (sport) jumper; **п. в во́ду** diver; **п. в длину́** long jumper

прыгу́н|ья, ьи, *g. pl.* **∼ий** *f. of* ▶ **прыгу́н**

прыж|о́к, ка́ *m.* **1** jump, leap, spring **2** (sport) jump; **∼ки́** jumping; **∼ки́ в во́ду** diving; **п. в высоту́** high jump; **п. в длину́** long jump

пры́ска|ть, ю *impf. of* ▶ **пры́снуть**

пры́с|нуть, ну, нешь *pf.* (*of* ▶ **пры́скать**) (infml) **1** (+ *i.*) to sprinkle (with); to spray (with) **2** (*политься струёй*) to spurt, gush

пры́т|кий, ∼ок, ∼ка *adj.* quick, lively, sharp (*often disapproving*)

прыщ, а́ *m.* pimple, spot

прядь, и *f.* lock (*of hair*)

пря́ж|а, и (*no pl.*) *f.* yarn

пря́жк|а, и *f.* buckle

пря́лк|а, и *f.* spinning wheel

прям|а́я, о́й *f.* straight line; **провести́ ∼у́ю** to draw a straight line; **расстоя́ние по ∼о́й** distance as the crow flies

прямико́м *adv.* (infml) straight

⚥ **пря́мо** *adv.* **1** straight (on); **иди́те п.!** (go) straight on!; **держа́ться п.** to hold oneself straight *or* erect **2** (*непосредственно*) straight, directly; смотре́ть п. в глаза́ кому́-н. to look sb straight in the face **3** (fig., *откровенно*) straight; frankly, openly; сказа́ть что-н. кому́-н. п. в лицо́ to say sth to sb's face **4** (infml, *точно*) just, exactly; он вы́глядит п. как оте́ц he looks just like his father

✓ прям|о́й, ~, ~á, ~о, ~ы́ adj. **1** (*без изги́бов*) straight; (*вертика́льный*) upright, erect; п. у́гол (math.) right angle **2** (*без промежу́точных пу́нктов*) through; direct; ~ая ли́ния direct (*telephone*) line **3** (*непосре́дственный*) direct; ~ые вы́боры direct elections; ~ая противополо́жность direct opposite **4** (*открове́нный*) straightforward, frank

прямолине́й|ный, ~ен, ~йна adj. **1** rectilinear **2** (fig.) straightforward; direct

прямоуго́льник, a m. (math.) rectangle

пря́ник, a m. spice cake; gingerbread; ме́довый п. honey cake

пря́ность, и f. spice

пря|сть, ду́, дёшь, past ~л, ~ла́, ~ло impf. (of ▸ спрясть) to spin

пря́|тать, чу, чешь impf. (of ▸ спря́тать) to hide, conceal

пря́|таться, чусь, чешься impf. (of ▸ спря́таться) to hide; to conceal oneself; to take refuge

пря́т|ки, ок (no sg.) hide-and-seek; игра́ть в п. to play hide-and-seek

пря́х|а, и f. spinner

псал|о́м, ма́ m. psalm

псевдони́м, a m. pseudonym; (comput.) alias

псих, a m. (infml) loony, nutcase

психиа́тр, a m. psychiatrist

психиатри́ческий adj. psychiatric

психиатри́|я, и f. psychiatry

пси́хик|а, и f. state of mind; psyche; вре́дно де́йствовать на ~у to have a harmful effect on the psyche

психи́чески adv. mentally, psychically, psychologically; п. больно́й mentally ill; (*as m. n.* п. больно́й, п. больно́го) mental patient

психи́ческ|ий adj. mental; ~ая боле́знь mental illness

психоана́лиз, a m. psychoanalysis

психоанали́тик, a m. psychoanalyst

психо́з, a m. mental illness; (med.) psychosis

психо́лог, a m. psychologist

✓ психологи́ческий adj. psychological

психоло́ги|я, и f. psychology

психопа́т, a m. psychopath; (infml) lunatic

психотерапе́вт, a m. psychotherapist

психотерапи́|я, и f. psychotherapy

псориа́з, a m. (med.) psoriasis

птен|е́ц, ца́ m. chick; fledgling (also fig.)

✓ пти́ц|а, ы f. bird; дома́шняя п. (*collect.*) poultry; хи́щные ~ы birds of prey; ва́жная п.

(fig., infml) big noise

птицефе́рм|а, ы f. poultry farm

ПТУ nt. indecl. (abbr. of профессиона́льно-техни́ческое учи́лище) vocational technical school

пу́блик|а, и f. (*collect.*) (the) public; (*зри́тели, слу́шатели*) (the) audience

✓ публика́ци|я, и f. **1** (*де́йствие*) publication **2** (*объявле́ние*) advertisement, notice

публик|ова́ть, у́ю impf. (of ▸ опубликова́ть) to publish

публици́стик|а, и f. sociopolitical journalism

публи́чно adv. publicly; in public; openly

публи́чн|ый adj. public; ~ая библиоте́ка public library; п. дом brothel

пу́гал|о, а nt. scarecrow

пуга́|ть, ю impf. (of ▸ испуга́ть, ▸ напуга́ть) **1** to frighten, scare **2** (+ i.) to threaten (with)

пуга́|ться, юсь impf. (of ▸ испуга́ться) (+ g.) to be frightened (of), be scared (of); to take fright (at); (*о ло́шади*) to shy (at)

пугли́в|ый, ~, ~а adj. fearful, timid

пу́говиц|а, ы f. button

пу́дел|ь, я, pl. ~и, ~ей or ~я, ~е́й m. poodle

пу́динг, a m. pudding

пу́др|а, ы f. powder

пу́др|ить, ю, ишь impf. (of ▸ напу́дрить) to powder

пу́др|иться, юсь, ишься impf. (of ▸ напу́дриться) to use powder, powder one's face

пуза́т|ый, ~, ~а adj. (infml) pot-bellied

пу́з|о, а nt. (infml) belly, paunch

пузы́р|ь, я́ m. **1** (*ша́рик*) bubble; мы́льный п. soap bubble **2** (anat.): мочево́й п. (urinary) bladder

пулемёт, a m. machine gun

пулемётчик, a m. machine-gunner

пуленепробива́емый adj. bulletproof

пуло́вер, a m. pullover

пульвериза́тор, a m. atomizer, sprayer

пульс, a m. pulse

пульси́р|овать, ую impf. to pulsate; (*о бо́ли*) to throb

пульт, a m. **1** (*пюпи́тр*) desk, stand **2** (*диспе́тчерский*) control panel; п. ДУ, п. дистанцио́нного управле́ния (TV etc.) remote control

пу́л|я, и f. bullet

✓ пункт, a m. **1** point; spot; населённый п. inhabited area **2** (*организацио́нный центр*) station, centre (BrE), center (AmE); post, point; медици́нский п. first-aid station; наблюда́тельный п. observation post, point **3** (*докуме́нта*) point; paragraph, item; соглаше́ние из трёх ~ов a three-point agreement

пункти́р, a m. dotted line

пунктуа́л|ьный, ~ен, ~ьна adj. punctual

пунктуа́ци|я, и f. punctuation

пунцо́в|ый, ~, ~а adj. crimson

✓ key word

пунш, а *m.* punch (*drink*)

пупови́н|а, ы *f.* (anat.) umbilical cord

пуп|о́к, ка́ *m.* navel

пурпу́рный *adj.* purple

пуск, а *m.* starting (up); setting in motion

пуска́й *particle, conj.* (infml) = **пусть**

пуска́|ть, ю *impf. of* ▶ **пусти́ть**

пуска́|ться, юсь *impf. of* ▶ **пусти́ться**

пусте́|ть, ет *impf.* (*of* ▶ **опусте́ть**) to (become) empty; to become deserted

пу|сти́ть, щу́, ~сти́шь *pf.* (*of* ▶ **пуска́ть**) **1** (*дать свобо́ду*) to let go **2** (*разреши́ть идти́*) to let; to allow, permit; **нас не ~сти́ли в пала́ту** they would not let us into the ward **3** (*разреши́ть войти́*) to let in, allow to enter; **не п.** to keep out **4** (*привести́ в движе́ние*) to start, set in motion, set going; to set working; **п. во́ду** to turn on water; **п. слух** to start a rumour (BrE), rumor (AmE) **5** (*заста́вить и́ли дать возмо́жность дви́гаться*) to set, put; to send; **п. в ход** to start, launch, set going, set in train; **п. кора́бль ко дну** to send a ship to the bottom

пу|сти́ться, щу́сь, ~сти́шься *pf.* (*of* ▶ **пуска́ться**) (**в** + *a. or* + *inf.*) (infml) **1** (*отпра́виться*) to set out, start; **п. в путь** to set out, get on the way **2** (*нача́ть*) to begin, start; to set to; **п. в пляс** to break into a dance

пуст|ова́ть, у́ю *impf.* to be empty, stand empty; (*о земле́*) to lie fallow

пуст|о́й, ~, ~а́, ~о, ~ы́ *adj.* **1** empty; **п. взгляд** vacant look; **~о́е ме́сто** blank space **2** (fig., *несерьёзный*) idle; shallow; frivolous; **п. челове́к** shallow person **3** (fig., *напра́сный*) vain, ungrounded; **~ые слова́** mere words; **~ые угро́зы** empty threats, bluster

пустот|а́, ы́, *pl.* **~ы** *f.* **1** emptiness; void; (phys.) vacuum **2** (fig.) emptiness, shallowness **3** (*по́лое ме́сто*) cavity

пу́стош|ь, и *f.* waste (plot of) land, waste ground

пусты́н|ный, ~ен, ~на *adj.* **1** (*необита́емый*) uninhabited; **п. о́стров** desert island **2** (*безлю́дный*) deserted

пусты́н|я, и *f.* desert, wilderness

пусты́р|ь, я́ *m.* wasteland, vacant plot (of land)

пусты́шк|а, и *f.* (infml, *у младе́нца*) dummy (BrE), pacifier (AmE)

⚔ **пусть 1** (*particle*) let; **п. она́ сама́ реши́т** let her decide herself **2** (*as conj.*) though, even if; **п. им бу́дет проти́вно, но я до́лжен вы́сказать своё мне́ние** even if they hate it, I must express my opinion **3** (*particle*) (infml, *ла́дно*) all right, very well

пустя́к, а́ *m.* (infml) trifle; **~и́!** (*ничего́*) it's nothing!; never mind!; (*вздор*) nonsense!; rubbish!

пу́таниц|а, ы *f.* muddle, confusion; mess, tangle

пу́та|ть, ю *impf.* (*of* ▶ **спу́тать**, ▶ **запу́тать**) **1** (*ни́тки*) to tangle **2** (*сбива́ть с то́лку*) to confuse, muddle **3** (*сме́шивать*) to confuse,

mix up; **ты (всё) ещё ~ешь на́ши имена́** you are still mixing our names up

пу́та|ться, юсь *impf.* (*of* ▶ **спу́таться**, ▶ **запу́таться**) **1** (*о ни́тках*) to get tangled **2** (*о мы́слях*) to get confused **3** (*сбива́ться с то́лку*) to get mixed up, get muddled; **п. в расска́зе** to give a muddled account

путёвк|а, и *f.* **1** (*удостовере́ние*) pass, authorization; **пода́ть зая́вку на ~у в санато́рий** to apply for a place in a sanatorium **2** place on a tour, package holiday; **я купи́л ~у в Ита́лию** I have booked a package holiday to Italy **3** (*води́теля тра́нспорта*) schedule of duties

путеводи́тел|ь, я *m.* guide, guidebook

путём¹ *prep.* (+ *g.*) by means of, by dint of

путём² *adv.* (infml, *как сле́дует*) properly; **он ничего́ п. не уме́ет объясни́ть** he cannot explain anything properly

путепрово́д, а *m.* (*над доро́гой*) overpass, flyover; (*под доро́гой*) underpass

путеше́ственник, а *m.* traveller (BrE), traveler (AmE)

путеше́ственни|ца, цы *f. of* ▶ **путеше́ственник**

⚔ **путеше́стви|е, я** *nt.* **1** journey; trip; (*морско́й*) voyage; cruise **2** (*also in pl.*) (*as literary genre*) travels

путеше́ств|овать, ую *impf.* to travel, go on travels; (*по мо́рю*) to voyage

путч, а *m.* (pol.) putsch

⚔ **пут|ь, и́, i. ём, о ~и́, pl. ~и́, ~е́й, ~я́м** *m.* **1** (*доро́га*) way, track, path; (aeron.) track; (astron.) race; (fig.) road, course; **~и́ сообще́ния** communications; **на пра́вильном ~и́** on the right track **2** (rail.) track **3** (*путеше́ствие*) journey; voyage; **в ~и́** on one's way, en route; **в четырёх днях ~и́ (от** + *g.*) four days' journey (from); **на обра́тном ~и́** on the way back; **по ~и́** on the way **4** (fig., *сре́дство*) way, means; **ми́рным ~ём** amicably, peaceably; **пойти́ по ~и́** (+ *g.*) to take the path (of)

пух, а, о ~е, в ~у́ *m.* down; fluff; **ни ~а ни пера́!** (infml) good luck!

пу́хл|ый, ~, ~а́, ~о *adj.* (*челове́к*) chubby, plump; (*кни́га, досье́*) fat

пу́х|нуть, ну, нешь, *past* ~ *and* ~нул, ~ла *impf.* to swell

пучегла́з|ый, ~, ~а *adj.* (infml) goggle-eyed

пучи́н|а, ы *f.* gulf, abyss (also fig.); (*морска́я бе́здна*) the deep

пуши́ст|ый, ~, ~а *adj.* fluffy, downy

пу́шк|а, и *f.* gun, cannon

пуэрторика́н|ец, ца *m.* Puerto Rican

пуэрторика́н|ка, ки *f. of* ▶ **пуэрторика́нец**

пуэрторика́нский *adj.* Puerto Rican

Пуэ́рто-Ри́ко *nt. indecl.* Puerto Rico

пчел|а́, ы́, *pl.* **~ы** *f.* bee

пшени́ц|а, ы *f.* wheat

пшени́чный *adj.* wheat(en)

пшённый *adj. of* ▶ **пшено́**

пшен|о́, а́ *nt.* millet

пыла́|ть, ю *impf.* **1** to blaze, flame **2** (*о лице*) to glow **3** (*fig.*) to burn (with); **п. стра́стью** to be burning with passion
пылесо́с, а *m.* vacuum cleaner, Hoover®
пылесо́с|ить, ишь *impf.* (*of*
▶ **пропылесо́сить**) to vacuum(-clean), hoover
пыли́нк|а, и *f.* speck of dust
пы́л|кий, ~ок, ~ка́, ~ко *adj.* (*желание, речь*) ardent, passionate; (*воображение*) fervid
пыл|ь, и, о ~и, в ~и́ *f.* dust
пы́л|ьный, ~ен, ~ьна́, ~ьно *adj.* dusty
пыльца́|, ы́ *f.* (*bot.*) pollen
пыта́|ть, ю *impf.* to torture (also fig.); (fig.) to torment
пыта́|ться, юсь *impf.* (*of* ▶ **попыта́ться**) to try, attempt
пы́тк|а, и *f.* torture, torment (also fig.); **ору́дие ~и** instrument of torture
пытли́в|ый, ~, ~а *adj.* inquisitive
пых|те́ть, чу́, ти́шь *impf.* to puff, pant
пы́ш|ный, ~ен, ~на́, ~но *adj.*
1 (*великолепный*) splendid, magnificent
2 (*пушистый*) fluffy; light; luxuriant; ~ные во́лосы fluffy hair
пьедеста́л, а *m.* pedestal (also fig.)
пье́с|а, ы *f.* **1** (*theatr.*) play **2** (*mus.*) piece
пьяне́|ть, ю, ешь *impf.* (*of* ▶ **опьяне́ть**) to get drunk, get intoxicated
пья́ница, ы *c.g.* drunkard
пья́нк|а, и *f.* (*infml*) drinking bout, binge, booze-up
пья́нств|о, а *nt.* drunkenness
пья́н|ый, ~, ~а́, ~о, ~ы́ *adj.* drunk; drunken; intoxicated; (*as m. n.* **п.**, ~ого) (a) drunk

пюре́ *nt. indecl.* (*cul.*) purée; **карто́фельное п.** mashed potatoes
пятёрк|а, и *f.* **1** (*цифра, игральная карта*) five **2** (*отметка*) five (*highest mark in Russian educational marking system*) **3** (*infml, автобус, трамвай*) No. 5 (*bus, tram, etc.*) **4** (*группа из пятерых*) (group of) five **5** (*infml, пять рублей*) five-rouble note, fiver
пя́тер|о, ы́х *num.* (*collect.*) five
пятидеся́т|ый *adj.* fiftieth; ~ые го́ды the fifties
пятизвёздочный *adj.* five-star
пятикра́тный *adj.* fivefold
пятисо́тый *adj.* five-hundredth
пя́|титься, чусь, тишься *impf.* (*of* ▶ **попя́титься**) to back, move backward(s); (*о лошади*) to jib
пя́тк|а, и *f.* heel (*also of sock or stocking*)
пятна́дцатый *adj.* fifteenth
пятна́дцат|ь, и *num.* fifteen
пятни́ст|ый, ~, ~а *adj.* spotted, dappled; **п. оле́нь** spotted deer
пя́тниц|а, ы *f.* Friday
пятн|о́, а́, *pl.* ~а, ~ен, ~ам *nt.*
1 (*место иной окраски*) spot; patch; (*запачканное место*) stain; **роди́мое п.** birthmark **2** (*fig.*) blot, stain; blemish
пя́т|ый *adj.* fifth; **глава́ ~ая** chapter five; **в ~ом часу́** after four (o'clock)
пят|ь, и́, *i.* ью́ *num.* five
пятьдеся́т, пяти́десяти, *i.* пятью́десятью *num.* fifty
пятьсо́т, пятисо́т, пятиста́м, пятьюста́ми *num.* five hundred
пя́тью *adv.* five times; **п. шесть** five times six

Рр

раб, а́ *m.* slave
рабо́т|а, ы *f.* **1** (*действие*) work, working; (*функционирование*) functioning, running **2** (*занятие, труд*) work; labour (BrE), labor (AmE); **дома́шняя р.** homework; **сельскохозя́йственные ~ы** agricultural work **3** (*как источник заработка*) work, job; **постоя́нная р.** regular work; **случа́йная р.** casual work, odd job(s); **иска́ть ~у** to look for a job
рабо́та|ть, ю *impf.* **1** (**над** + *i.*) to work (on); **он ~ет над но́вым рома́ном** he is working on a new novel; (**на** + *a.*) to work (for, on

behalf of); **она́ ~ет на поли́цию** she works for the police **2** (*функционировать*) to work, run, function; **не р.** to not work, to be out of order **3** (*быть открытым*) to be open; **галере́я не ~ет по воскресе́ньям** the gallery is not open on Sundays **4** (+ *i.*) (*управлять*) to work, operate; **р. вёслами** to ply the oars
рабо́тник, а *m.* worker; (*учреждения*) employee
рабо́тниц|а, ы *f.* (female) worker; (*учреждения*) (female) employee
работода́тел|ь, я *m.* employer
работоспосо́б|ный, ~ен, ~на *adj.*
1 (*могущий работать*) able to work,

able-bodied **2** (*спосо́бный мно́го*
рабо́тать) able to work hard, hardworking
работя́щий *adj.* (infml) hard-working,
industrious
◢ **рабо́ч|ий¹**, **его** *m.* worker; workman; ∼ие
(*collect.*) the workers (*as a social class*)
◢ **рабо́ч|ий²** *adj.* **1** (*относя́щийся к рабо́чим*)
workers', working-class; **р. класс** the
working class **2** (*выполня́ющий рабо́ту*)
work, working; ∼ая си́ла manpower
3 (*предназна́ченный для рабо́ты*) working;
∼ее вре́мя working time, working hours;
р. день working day (BrE), workday (AmE);
∼ее ме́сто (*помеще́ние*) working place,
workplace; (*пост*) job **4**: **в** ∼ем поря́дке
while working, without breaking off from
work
ра́бский *adj.* **1** *adj. of* ▸ **раб**; **р. труд** slave
labour (BrE), labor (AmE) **2** (*fig., рабо́лепный*)
servile
ра́бств|о, **а** *nt.* slavery, servitude
рабы́н|я, **и**, *g. pl.* ∼ь *f.* (female) slave
равви́н, **а** *m.* rabbi
ра́венств|о, **а** *nt.* equality; parity; **знак** ∼а
(math.) equals sign
равио́л|и, **ей** *m. pl.* ravioli
равни́н|а, **ы** *f.* plain
равно́ *nt. pred. form of* ▸ **ра́вный** **1** (math.)
make(s), equals, is; **три плюс три р. шести́**
three plus three equals six **2**: **всё р.** it is all
the same, it makes no difference; (*as adv.*)
all the same; **всё р., что** it is just the same
as, it is equivalent to; **мне всё р.** I don't care;
it's all the same, all one to me; **я всё р. вам**
позвоню́ I will ring you all the same
равнове́си|е, **я** *nt.* equilibrium (also fig.);
balance; **душе́вное р.** mental equilibrium;
сохраня́ть р. to keep one's balance
равноде́нстви|е, **я** *nt.*: **весе́ннее**, **осе́ннее**
р. spring, autumn equinox
равноду́ши|е, **я** *nt.* indifference
равноду́ш|ный, ∼ен, ∼на *adj.* (**к** + *d.*)
indifferent (to)
равнозна́ч|ный, ∼ен, ∼на *adj.* equivalent
равноме́р|ный, ∼ен, ∼на *adj.* even;
uniform
равнопра́ви|е, **я** *nt.* (possession of) equal
rights; equality
равноси́л|ьный, ∼ен, ∼ьна *adj.* (+ *d.*)
equal (to), equivalent (to), tantamount
(to); **э́то** ∼ьно изме́не it is tantamount to
treachery; it amounts to treachery
равноце́н|ный, ∼ен, ∼на *adj.* of equal
value, of equal worth; equivalent
◢ **ра́в|ный**, ∼ен, ∼на́, ∼но́ *adj.* equal; **ему́ нет**
∼ных he has no equal
равня́|ться, **юсь** *impf.* **1** (**по** + *d.*) (mil.) to
dress; ∼йсь! eyes right! (*word of command*)
2 (*impf. only*) (+ *d.*) to equal, be equal (to);
(fig.) to be equivalent (to); **два́жды пять**
∼ется десяти́ twice five is ten
рагу́ *nt. indecl.* (cul.) stew
◢ **рад**, ∼а, ∼о *pred. adj.* (+ *d. or* + *inf. or* что)

glad (of; to; that); (о́чень) р. познако́миться
с ва́ми! pleased to meet you!
рада́р, **а** *m.* radar
◢ **ра́ди** *prep.* (+ *g.*) for the sake of; **чего́ р.?** what
for?; **р. бо́га** (infml) for God's sake
радиа́тор, **а** *m.* radiator
радиа́ци|я, **и** *f.* radiation
ра́ди|й, **я** *m.* (chem.) radium
радика́л, **а** *m.* (pol., chem.) radical
радикализа́ци|я, **и** *f.* radicalization
радикализи́р|овать, **ую** *impf. and pf.* to
radicalize
радика́л|ьный, ∼ен, ∼ьна *adj.* **1** (pol.)
radical **2** (*реши́тельный*) radical, drastic;
∼ьное сре́дство drastic remedy
радикули́т, **а** *m.* radiculitis; sciatica
ра́дио *nt. indecl.* **1** (*сре́дство свя́зи*) radio;
по р. by radio, over the air; **переда́ть по р.**
to broadcast; **слу́шать р.** to listen in
2 (*радиоприёмник*) radio
радиоакти́вность, **и** *f.* radioactivity
радиоакти́в|ный, ∼ен, ∼на *adj.*
radioactive
радиовеща́ни|е, **я** *nt.* (radio) broadcasting
радиолока́тор, **а** *m.* radar set
радиоприёмник, **а** *m.* radio (set)
радиоста́нци|я, **и** *f.* radio station
радиотелефо́н, **а** *m.* cordless (tele)phone
радиотерапи́|я, **и** *f.* radiotherapy
ради́ст, **а** *m.* radio operator
ради́ст|ка, **ки** *f. of* ▸ **ради́ст**
ра́диус, **а** *m.* radius; **р. де́йствия** range
ра́д|овать, **ую** *impf.* (*of* ▸ обра́довать,
▸ пора́довать) to gladden, make happy
ра́д|оваться, **уюсь** *impf.* (*of* ▸ обра́доваться,
▸ пора́доваться) (+ *d.*) to be glad (at), rejoice
(in)
ра́дост|ный, ∼ен, ∼на *adj.* glad, joyous,
joyful; ∼ное изве́стие glad tidings, good
news
◢ **ра́дост|ь**, **и** *f.* gladness, joy; **к всео́бщей** ∼и
to everybody's delight; **с** ∼ью with pleasure,
gladly
ра́дуг|а, **и** *f.* rainbow
ра́дужн|ый *adj.* **1** (*переливчатый*)
iridescent, opalescent; ∼ая оболо́чка (гла́за)
(anat.) iris **2** (*све́тлый, ра́достный*) cheerful;
optimistic; ∼ые наде́жды high hopes
раду́ш|ный, ∼ен, ∼на *adj.* cordial
◢ **раз¹**, **а**, *pl.* ∼ы́, ∼, ∼а́м *m.* **1** time; occasion;
оди́н р., **ка́к-то р.** once; **два** ∼а twice; **мно́го**
р. many times; **ещё р.** once again, once more;
не р. more than once; time and again; **ни** ∼у
not once, never; **р. (и) навсегда́** once (and)
for all; **р. в день** once a day; **вся́кий р.** every
time, each time; **вся́кий р., когда́** whenever;
в друго́й р. another time, some other time;
на э́тот р. this time, on this occasion, for
(this) once; **с пе́рвого** ∼а from the very first;
как р. just, exactly **2** (*при счёте, оди́н*) one
раз² *conj.* if; since; **р. вы бу́дете во Фра́нции,**
не смо́жете ли вы прие́хать и сюда́? if you

р

are going to be in France, can't you come here too?

раз…[1] and **разо…, разъ…, рас…** *vbl. pref. indicating* **1** *division into parts* (dis-, un-) **2** *distribution, direction of action in different directions* (dis-) **3** *action in reverse* (un-) **4** *termination of action or state* **5** *intensification of action*

раз…[2] and **разо…, разъ…, рас…** (infml) *adjectival pref. indicating high degree of a quality*

разба́в|ить, лю, ишь *pf.* (*of* ▶ разбавля́ть) to dilute

разбавля́|ть, ю *impf. of* ▶ разба́вить

разба́лива|ться, юсь *impf. of* ▶ разболе́ться[1], ▶ разболе́ться[2]

разба́лтыва|ть, ю *impf. of* ▶ разболта́ть[1], ▶ разболта́ть[2]

разба́лтыва|ться, юсь *impf. of* ▶ разболта́ться

разбе́г, а *m.* run, running start; **пры́гнуть с ∼а** to take a running jump; **р. при взлёте** (aeron.) take-off run

разбега́|ться, юсь *impf. of* ▶ разбежа́ться

разбе|жа́ться, гу́сь, жи́шься, гу́тся *pf.* (*of* ▶ разбега́ться) **1** (*взять разбег*) to take a run, run up **2** (*в разные стороны*) to scatter, disperse **3** (*о мыслях*) to be scattered; **глаза́ у меня́ ∼жа́лись** I was dazzled

разбива́|ть, ю *impf. of* ▶ разби́ть

разбива́|ться, юсь *impf. of* ▶ разби́ться

разбинт|ова́ть, у́ю *pf.* (*of* ▶ разбинто́вывать) to remove a bandage (from)

разбинто́выва|ть, ю *impf. of* ▶ разбинтова́ть

разбира́тельств|о, а *nt.* (law) examination, investigation; **суде́бное р.** court examination

разбира́|ть, ю *impf. of* ▶ разобра́ть

разбира́|ться, юсь *impf. of* ▶ разобра́ться

раз|би́ть, обью́, обьёшь *pf.* (*of* ▶ разбива́ть) **1** (*impf. also* бить 4) (*окно, чашку*) to break, smash **2** (*разделить*) to divide (up); to break up; **р. на гру́ппы** to divide up into groups **3** (*расположить*) to lay out, mark out; **р. ла́герь** to pitch a camp **4** (*повредить*) to damage severely, hurt badly; to fracture; **р. кому́-н. нос в кровь** to make sb's nose bleed **5** (*победить*) to beat, defeat, smash (also fig.)

раз|би́ться, обью́сь, обьёшься *pf.* (*of* ▶ разбива́ться) **1** (*расколоться*) to break, get broken, get smashed **2** (*разделиться*) to divide; to break up **3** (*пораниться*) to hurt oneself badly; to smash oneself up

разбогате́|ть, ю, ешь *pf. of* ▶ богате́ть

разбо́|й, я *m.* robbery; **морско́й р.** piracy

разбо́йник, а *m.* robber; **морско́й р.** pirate

разболе́|ться[1], юсь, ешься *pf.* (*of* ▶ разба́ливаться) (infml) to become ill; **он**

совсе́м ∼лся his health has completely cracked

разболе́|ться[2], и́тся *pf.* (*of* ▶ разба́ливаться) to begin to ache badly

разболта́|ть[1], ю *pf.* (*of* ▶ разба́лтывать) (*размешать*) to mix in

разболта́|ть[2], ю *pf.* (*of* ▶ разба́лтывать) (infml, *секрет*) to blab out, give away

разболта́|ться, юсь *pf.* (*of* ▶ разба́лтываться) **1** (*о муке*) to mix in (*as result of stirring*) **2** (*о гайке*) to come loose, work loose **3** (fig., *об ученике*) to get out of hand; to come unstuck

разбомб|и́ть, лю́, и́шь *pf.* (*no impf.*) to destroy by bombing

разбо́рк|а, и *f.* **1** (*бумаг*) sorting out **2** (*механизма*) stripping, dismantling **3** (infml, *ссора*) quarrel, fight, argument

разбо́рчив|ый, ∼, ∼а *adj.* **1** (*требовательный*) fastidious, exacting; discriminating; scrupulous **2** (*чёткий*) legible

разбра́сыва|ть, ю *impf. of* ▶ разброса́ть

разбреда́|ться, юсь *impf. of* ▶ разбрести́сь

разбре|сти́сь, ду́сь, дёшься, *past* ∼лся, ∼ла́сь *pf.* (*of* ▶ разбреда́ться) to disperse; **р. по дома́м** to disperse and go home

разбро́д, а *m.* disorder

разброса́|ть, ю *pf.* (*of* ▶ разбра́сывать) to scatter, spread

разбры́зг|ать, аю *pf.* (*of* ▶ разбры́згивать) to splash; to spray

разбры́згиватель, я *m.* sprinkler

разбры́згива|ть, ю *impf. of* ▶ разбры́згать

разбу|ди́ть, жу́, ∼дишь *pf. of* ▶ буди́ть 1

разбуха́|ть, а́ет *impf. of* ▶ разбу́хнуть

разбу́х|нуть, нет, *past* ∼, ∼ла *pf.* (*of* ▶ разбуха́ть) to swell (also fig.)

разбуш|ева́ться, у́юсь *pf.* (*о буре*) to rage; to blow up; (*о море*) to run high

разва́л, а *m.* **1** (*распад*) breakdown, disintegration; (*беспорядок*) disorder **2** (*рынок*) flea market

разва́лива|ть, ю *impf. of* ▶ развали́ть

разва́лива|ться, юсь *impf. of* ▶ развали́ться

разва́лин|а, ы *f.* (*in pl.*) ruins; **лежа́ть в ∼ах** to be in ruins; **преврати́ть в ∼ы** to reduce to ruins

развал|и́ть, ю́, ∼ишь *pf.* (*of* ▶ разва́ливать) **1** to pull down (*a building, etc.*) **2** (fig., *хозяйство*) to ruin

развал|и́ться, ю́сь, ∼ишься *pf.* (*of* ▶ разва́ливаться) **1** (*распасться*) to fall down, collapse **2** (fig., *прийти в упадок*) to go to pieces, fall to pieces, break down **3** (infml, *сидеть, раскинувшись*) to lounge, sprawl

⚔ **ра́зве 1** (*interrog. particle, neutral or indicating that neg. answer is expected; + neg. indicates that affirmative answer is expected*): **р. они́ все поместя́тся в э́той маши́не?** will they (really) all get in this car?; **р. ты не знал, что он ру́сский?** didn't you know that he is Russian?; surely you knew that he is Russian! **2**: **р. (что), р. (то́лько)** (*as adv.*) only; perhaps; (*as conj.*) except that, only; **он вы́глядит так же как всегда́, р. что похуде́л** he looks the same as ever, except that he has lost weight

развева́|ться, ется *impf.* (*фла́га*) to flutter; (*во́лосы, плащ*) to blow about

разве́д|ать, аю *pf.* (*of* ▸ **разве́дывать**) **1** (infml) to find out (about) **2** (mil.) to reconnoitre (BrE), reconnoiter (AmE) **3** (geol.) to prospect (for); (*pf. only*) to locate; **р. нефть** to prospect for oil

разведе́ни|е, я *nt.* (*ско́та*) breeding, rearing; (*са́да*) cultivation; (*костра́*) making

разведённ|ый *p.p.p. of* ▸ **развести́¹**, ▸ **развести́²** *and adj.* divorced; (*as n.* **р.**, ∼ого, *f.* ∼ая, ∼ой) divorcee

разве́дк|а, и *f.* **1** (geol., etc.) prospecting **2** (mil., *для получе́ния све́дений*) reconnaissance **3** (pol.) intelligence service

разве́дчик, а *m.* **1** (mil.) scout **2** (pol.) intelligence officer

разве́дывательный *adj.* **1** (mil.) reconnaissance; **р. бой** probing attack; **р. отря́д** reconnaissance detachment **2** (pol.) intelligence; **р. отде́л** intelligence section

разве́дыва|ть, ю *impf. of* ▸ **разве́дать**

развез|ти́, у́, ёшь, *past* ∼, ∼ла́ *pf.* (*of* ▸ **развози́ть**) (*доста́вить*) to deliver

разве́ива|ть, ю *impf. of* ▸ **разве́ять**

разве́ива|ться, юсь *impf. of* ▸ **разве́яться**

развёрнутый *p.p.p. of* ▸ **разверну́ть** *and adj.* **1** (*предпри́нятый в широ́ких масшта́бах*) extensive **2** (*подро́бный*) detailed

разверну́ть, ну́, нёшь *pf.* (*of* ▸ **развора́чивать**) **1** (*бума́гу*) to unfold; (*ковёр*) to unroll; (*свёрток*) to unwrap; (*зна́мя*) to unfurl **2** (mil., *перестро́ить*) to deploy **3** (fig., *прояви́ть*) to show, display **4** (fig., *стро́йку, торго́влю, рабо́ту*) to develop; to expand **5** (*маши́ну*) to turn (around)

развер|ну́ться, ну́сь, нёшься *pf.* (*of* ▸ **развора́чиваться**) **1** (*о бума́ге*) to come unfolded; (*о ковре́*) to come unrolled; (*о свёртке*) to come undone **2** (mil., *перестро́иться*) to deploy **3** (fig., *прояви́ться*) to show or display oneself **4** (fig., *о стро́йке, торго́вле, рабо́те*) to develop; to expand **5** (*о маши́не*) to turn (around)

развесел|и́ть, ю́, и́шь *pf. of* ▸ **весели́ть**

развесел|и́ться, ю́сь, и́шься *pf.* to cheer up

разве́|сить¹, шу, сишь *pf.* (*of* ▸ **разве́шивать**) **1** (*карти́ны*) to hang **2** (*ве́тви*) to spread

разве́|сить², шу, сишь *pf.* (*of* ▸ **разве́шивать**) (*бельё*) to hang out

разве|сти́¹, ду́, дёшь, *past* ∼л, ∼ла́ *pf.* (*of* ▸ **разводи́ть**) **1** (*ведя́, доставля́я*) to take, conduct; **р. дете́й по дома́м** to take the children to their homes **2** (*в ра́зные сто́роны*) to part, separate; **р. мост** to raise

a bridge; **р. рука́ми** to shrug one's shoulders **3** (*сок*) to dilute; (*порошо́к*) to dissolve

разве|сти́², ду́, дёшь, *past* ∼л, ∼ла́ *pf.* (*of* ▸ **разводи́ть**) **1** (*живо́тных*) to breed, rear; (*сад*) to cultivate; **р. парк** to lay out a park **2** (*разже́чь*) to start; **р. костёр** to make a campfire

разве|сти́сь¹, ду́сь, дёшься, *past* ∼лся, ∼ла́сь *pf.* (*of* ▸ **разводи́ться**) (с + *i.*) to divorce, get divorced (from)

разве|сти́сь², дётся, *past* ∼лся, ∼ла́сь *pf.* (*of* ▸ **разводи́ться**) (*о живо́тных*) to breed, multiply

разветвле́ни|е, я *nt.* **1** (*де́йствие*) branching; forking **2** (*ме́сто*) branch; fork (*of road, etc.*)

разве́ш|ать, аю *pf.* (*of* ▸ **разве́шивать**) to hang

разве́шива|ть, ю *impf. of* ▸ **разве́сить¹**, ▸ **разве́сить²**, ▸ **разве́шать**

разве́|ять, ю, ешь *pf.* (*of* ▸ **разве́ивать**) to scatter, disperse; (fig., *грусть, сомне́ния*) to dispel; **р. миф** to shatter a myth

разве́|яться, юсь, ешься *pf.* (*of* ▸ **разве́иваться**) **1** (*о тума́не*) to disperse; (fig., *о тоске́*) to be dispelled **2** (infml, *о челове́ке*) to relax

✓ **развива́|ть, ю** *impf. of* ▸ **разви́ть**

✓ **развива́|ться, юсь** *impf. of* ▸ **разви́ться**

развин|ти́ть, чу́, ти́шь *pf.* (*of* ▸ **разви́нчивать**) to unscrew

развин|ти́ться, чу́сь, ти́шься *pf.* (*of* ▸ **разви́нчиваться**) to come unscrewed

разви́нчива|ть, ю *impf. of* ▸ **развинти́ть**

разви́нчива|ться, юсь *impf. of* ▸ **развинти́ться**

✓ **разви́ти|е, я** *nt.* development; evolution

разви́т|ой, ра́звит, ∼а́, ра́звито *adj.* **1** developed **2** (*у́мственно*) (intellectually) mature; adult

раз|ви́ть, овью́, овьёшь, *past* ∼ви́л, ∼вила́, ∼ви́ло *pf.* (*of* ▸ **развива́ть**) to develop; **р. мускулату́ру** to develop one's muscles; **р. ско́рость** to gather speed

раз|ви́ться, овью́сь, овьёшься, *past* ∼ви́лся, ∼вила́сь *pf.* (*of* ▸ **развива́ться**) (*о му́скулах, о тала́нте*) to develop

развлека́тельный, ∼ен, ∼ьна *adj.* entertaining; ∼ьное чте́ние light reading

развлека́|ть, ю *impf. of* ▸ **развле́чь**

развлека́|ться, юсь *impf. of* ▸ **развле́чься**

развлече́ни|е, я *nt.* entertainment; amusement

развле́|чь, ку́, чёшь, ку́т, *past* ∼к, ∼кла́ *pf.* (*of* ▸ **развлека́ть**) **1** (*повесели́ть*) to entertain, amuse **2** (*отвле́чь*) to divert

развле́|чься, ку́сь, чёшься, ку́тся, *past* ∼кся, ∼кла́сь *pf.* (*of* ▸ **развлека́ться**) **1** (*повесели́ться*) to have a good time; to amuse oneself **2** (*отвле́чься*) to be distracted

разво́д, а *m.* divorce; **они́ в ∼е** they are divorced

р

разво|ди́ть, жу́, ∼дишь *impf. of* ▶ развести́¹,
▶ развести́²

разво|ди́ться, жу́сь, ∼дишься *impf. of*
▶ развести́сь¹, ▶ развести́сь²

разво|зи́ть, жу́, ∼зишь *impf. of* ▶ развезти́

разволн|ова́ться, у́юсь *pf.* to get excited,
get agitated

развора́чива|ть, ю *impf. of* ▶ разверну́ть

развора́чива|ться, юсь *impf. of*
▶ разверну́ться

разворо́ва|ть, у́ю *pf.* (*of* ▶ разворо́вывать)
to loot, clean out

разворо́выва|ть, ю *impf. of* ▶ разворова́ть

разворо́т, а *m.* **1** (*машины*) U-turn
2 (*в книге*) double page

разворош|и́ть, у́, и́шь *pf.* to turn upside
down, scatter

развра́т, а *m.* (*половой*) debauchery;
(*духовный*) depravity

разврати́|ть, щу́, ти́шь *pf.* (*of* ▶ развраща́ть)
to corrupt

развра́т|ный, ∼ен, ∼на *adj.* debauched;
corrupt

развраща́|ть, ю *impf. of* ▶ разврати́ть

развя|за́ть, жу́, ∼жешь *pf.* (*of* ▶ развя́зывать)
to untie, undo; to unleash; **р. кому́-н. ру́ки**
to untie sb's hands; (*also fig.*): **р. войну́** to
unleash war

развя|за́ться, жу́сь, ∼жешься *pf.* (*of*
▶ развя́зываться) to come untied, come
undone

развя́зк|а, и *f.* **1** (liter.) denouement
2 (*завершение*) outcome, upshot; **де́ло
идёт к ∼е** things are coming to a head
3: (**тра́нспортная**) **р.** (traffic) roundabout

развя́з|ный, ∼ен, ∼на *adj.* (unduly)
familiar; free and easy

развя́зыва|ть, ю *impf. of* ▶ развяза́ть

развя́зыва|ться, юсь *impf. of*
▶ развяза́ться

разгада́|ть, а́ю *pf.* (*of* ▶ разга́дывать)
(*тайну, замысел*) to guess; (*загадку*) to
solve; (*сны*) to interpret; (*шифр*) to break;
(*человека*) to figure out

разга́дк|а, и *f.* solution (*of a riddle, etc.*)

разга́дыва|ть, ю *impf. of* ▶ разгада́ть

разга́р, а *m.*: **в ∼е** (+ *g.*) at the height (of);
в по́лном ∼е in full swing; **в ∼е бо́я** in the
heat of the battle; **р. сезо́на** peak season

разгиба́|ть, ю *impf. of* ▶ разогну́ть

разгиба́|ться, юсь *impf. of* ▶ разогну́ться

разглаго́льств|овать, ую *impf.* (infml) to
hold forth; to talk big

разгла́|дить, жу, дишь *pf.* (*of*
▶ разгла́живать) to smooth out; to iron out,
press

разгла́|диться, дится *pf.* (*of*
▶ разгла́живаться) (*платье*) to become
smoothed out; (*морщины*) to drop out

разгла́жива|ть, ю, ет *impf. of* ▶ разгла́дить

разгла́жива|ться, ется *impf. of*
▶ разгла́диться

разгла|си́ть, шу́, си́шь *pf.* (*of* ▶ разглаша́ть)
to divulge, give away, let out

разглаша́|ть, ю *impf. of* ▶ разгласи́ть

разгля|де́ть, жу́, ди́шь *pf.* to make out,
discern

разгля́дыва|ть, ю *impf.* to examine closely,
scrutinize

разгова́рива|ть, ю *impf.* (c + *i.*) to talk (to,
with), speak (to, with); **переста́ньте р.!** stop
talking!; **они́ друг с дру́гом не ∼ют** they are
not on speaking terms

⚷ **разгово́р, а** *m.* **1** talk, conversation; **без
∼ов!** and no argument! **2** (*in pl.*) (infml,
толки) gossip

разговор|и́ть, ю́, и́шь *pf.* (infml) to get (sb)
to talk

разговор|и́ться, ю́сь, и́шься *pf.* **1** (c + *i.*)
to get into conversation (with) **2** (*увлечься
разговором*) to warm to one's theme

разгово́рник, а *m.* phrase book

разгово́рный *adj.* colloquial

разгово́рчив|ый, ∼, ∼а *adj.* talkative

разго́н, а *m.* **1** (*толпы*) dispersal; **р.
собра́ния** breaking up of a meeting **2** (sport)
running start **3** (*машины*) acceleration

разгоня́|ть, ю *impf. of* ▶ разогна́ть

разгоня́|ться, юсь *impf. of* ▶ разогна́ться

разгор|а́ться, а́ется *impf. of* ▶ разгоре́ться

разгор|е́ться, и́тся *pf.* (*of* ▶ разгора́ться)
1 (*об огне*) to flare up **2** (fig., *о битве, о
споре*) to flare up

разгра́б|ить, лю, ишь *pf.* to plunder, loot

разграниче́ни|е, я *nt.* **1** (*размежевание*)
demarcation, delimitation **2** (*определение*)
differentiation

разграни́чива|ть, ю *impf. of*
▶ разграни́чить

разграни́ч|ить, у, ишь *pf.* (*of*
▶ разграни́чивать) **1** (*размежевать*) to
delimit, demarcate **2** (*точно определить*)
to differentiate, distinguish

разгреба́|ть, ю *impf. of* ▶ разгрести́

разгре|сти́, бу́, бёшь, *past* ∼б, ∼бла́ *pf.*
(*of* ▶ разгреба́ть) to rake (aside); to shovel
(aside)

разгро́м, а *m.* (*неприятеля*) crushing defeat,
rout

разгром|и́ть, лю́, и́шь *pf. of* ▶ громи́ть

разгружа́|ть, ю *impf. of* ▶ разгрузи́ть

разгружа́|ться, юсь *impf. of*
▶ разгрузи́ться

разгру|зи́ть, жу́, ∼зишь *pf.* (*of* ▶ разгружа́ть)
1 to unload **2** (от + *g.*) (fig., infml) to relieve
(of)

разгру|зи́ться, жу́сь, ∼зишься *pf.* (*of*
▶ разгружа́ться) to unload

разгру́зк|а, и *f.* unloading

разгрыза́|ть, ю *impf. of* ▶ разгры́зть

разгры́з|ть, у́, ёшь, *past* ∼, ∼ла *pf.* (*of*
▶ разгрыза́ть) to crack (*with one's teeth*)

р

разгу́л, а *m.* **1** (*веселье*) revelry **2** (+ *g.*) (fig.) wave (of); outburst (of); **р. антисемити́зма** a wave of anti-Semitism

разгу́лива|ть, ю *impf.* to stroll about, walk about

разда|ва́ть, ю́, ёшь *impf. of* ▶ **разда́ть**

разда|ва́ться, ёшься *impf. of* ▶ **разда́ться**

раздав|и́ть, лю́, ~ишь *pf.* (*of* ▶ **разда́вливать**) (*насекомых*) to crush, squash; (*о машине*) to run over

разда́влива|ть, ю *impf. of* ▶ **раздави́ть**

разда́|ть, м, шь, ст, ди́м, ди́те, ду́т, *past* ~л, ~ла́, ~ло *pf.* (*of* ▶ **раздава́ть**) to distribute, give out, serve out, dispense; **р. кни́ги** to give out books

разда́|ться, стся, ду́тся, *past* ~лся, ~ла́сь, ~ло́сь *pf.* (*of* ▶ **раздава́ться**) to be heard; to resound; to ring (out); ~лся вы́стрел a shot rang out; ~лся стук (в дверь) a knock at the door was heard

разда́ч|а, и *f.* distribution

раздва́ива|ть, я *impf. of* ▶ **раздвои́ть**

раздвига́|ть, ю, ет *impf. of* ▶ **раздви́нуть**

раздвига́|ться, ется *impf. of* ▶ **раздви́нуться**

раздви́|нуть, ну, нешь *pf.* (*of* ▶ **раздвига́ть**) to move apart, slide apart; **р. занаве́ски** to draw back the curtains; **р. стол** to extend a table

раздви́|нуться, нется *pf.* (*of* ▶ **раздвига́ться**) to move apart; **за́навес** ~нулся the curtain was drawn back; (*в теа́тре*) the curtain rose; **толпа́** ~нулась the crowd made way

раздвое́ни|е, я *nt.* division into two; bifurcation; **р. ли́чности** (med.) split personality

раздво|и́ться, ю́сь, и́шься *pf.* (*of* ▶ **раздва́иваться**) to bifurcate, fork, split, become double

раздева́лк|а, и *f.* (infml) **1** (*гардероб*) cloakroom **2** (*в баня́х*) changing room

раздева́ни|е, я *nt.* undressing

раздева́|ть, ю *impf. of* ▶ **разде́ть**

раздева́|ться, юсь *impf. of* ▶ **разде́ться**

⚥ **разде́л**, а *m.* **1** (*иму́щества*) division; (*земли́*) allotment **2** (*часть*) section, part (*of book, etc.*)

разде́л|ать, аю *pf.* (*of* ▶ **разде́лывать**) (*ту́шу*) to dress, prepare

разде́л|аться, аюсь *pf.* (*of* ▶ **разде́лываться**) (**с** + *i.*) **1** (*с поруче́ниями*) to be through (with); (*с кредито́рами*) to settle (accounts) (with); **р. с долга́ми** to pay off debts **2** (fig., *расправи́ться*) to settle accounts (with), get even (with), make short work of

разделе́ни|е, я *nt.* division; **р. труда́** division of labour

раздел|и́ть, ю́, ~ишь *pf.* (*of* ▶ **разделя́ть**, ▶ **дели́ть** 1) **1** (*де́ньги*) to divide **2** (*разъедини́ть*) to separate, part **3** (*мне́ние, убежде́ние*) to share

раздел|и́ться, ю́сь, ~ишься *pf.* (*of* ▶ **разделя́ться**, ▶ **дели́ться** 1) (**на** + *a.*) to divide (into); to be divided; **мне́ния** ~йлись

opinions were divided

разде́лыва|ть, ю *impf. of* ▶ **разде́лать**

разде́лыва|ться, юсь *impf. of* ▶ **разде́латься**

разде́льн|ый *adj.* separate; ~ое обуче́ние separate education for boys and girls

раздел|я́ть, я́ю *impf. of* ▶ **раздели́ть**

раздел|я́ться, я́юсь *impf. of* ▶ **раздели́ться**

разде́|ть, ну, нешь *pf.* (*of* ▶ **раздева́ть**) to undress

разде́|ться, нусь, нешься *pf.* (*of* ▶ **раздева́ться**) to undress, get undressed; (*снять пальто́, ша́пку*) to take off one's things

раздира́|ть, ю *impf.* **1** *impf. of* ▶ **разодра́ть** **2** (*impf. only*) (fig.) to rend, tear, lacerate, harrow

раздобыва́|ть, ю *impf. of* ▶ **раздобы́ть**

раздо|бы́ть, бу́ду, бу́дешь, *past* ~бы́л *pf.* (*of* ▶ **раздобыва́ть**) (infml) get, procure, get hold of

раздраж|а́ть, а́ю *impf. of* ▶ **раздражи́ть**

раздраж|а́ться, а́юсь *impf. of* ▶ **раздражи́ться**

раздража́ющий *pres. part. act. of* ▶ **раздража́ть** *and adj.* irritating, annoying

раздраже́ни|е, я *nt.* irritation

раздражи́тел|ьный, ~ен, ~ьна *adj.* irritable; short-tempered

раздраж|и́ть, у́, и́шь *pf.* (*of* ▶ **раздража́ть**) **1** to irritate, annoy **2** (med.) to irritate

раздраж|и́ться, у́сь, и́шься *pf.* (*of* ▶ **раздража́ться**) **1** to get irritated, get annoyed **2** (med.) to become inflamed

раздува́|ть, ю *impf. of* ▶ **разду́ть**

раздува́|ться, юсь *impf. of* ▶ **разду́ться**

разду́м|ать, аю *pf.* (*of* ▶ **разду́мывать** 1) to change one's mind; (+ *inf.*) to decide not (to); **я** ~**ал подава́ть заявле́ние на э́то ме́сто** I decided not to apply for that job; I changed my mind about applying for that job

разду́мыва|ть, ю *impf.* **1** *impf. of* ▶ **разду́мать** **2** (*impf. only*) (**о** + *p.*) to ponder (on, over), consider; **не** ~**я** without a moment's thought

разду́|ть, ю, ешь *pf.* (*of* ▶ **раздува́ть**) **1** (*разже́чь*) to blow; to fan; **р. пла́мя** (fig.) to fan the flames **2** (*наду́ть*) to blow (out); **р. щёки** to blow out one's cheeks **3** (fig., infml, *преувели́чить*) to exaggerate; to inflate, swell; **р. поте́ри** to exaggerate losses **4** (*разве́ять*) to blow about; (*impers.*) **бума́ги** ~**ло по́ полу** the papers had blown all over the floor

разду́|ться, юсь, ешься *pf.* (*of* ▶ **раздува́ться**) to swell

разева́|ть, ю *impf. of* ▶ **рази́нуть**

разжа́лоб|ить, лю, ишь *pf.* to move (to pity)

разжа́л|овать, ую *pf.* (mil.) to demote; **р. в солда́ты** to reduce to the ranks

раз|жа́ть, ожму́, ожмёшь *pf.* (*of* ▶ **разжима́ть**) (*ру́ки*) to unclasp; (*пружи́ну*) to release; (*кула́к, зу́бы*) to unclench

р

раз|жа́ться, ожмётся *pf.* (*of* ▶ разжима́ться) (*о пружине*) to come loose; (*о кулаке, губах*) to relax

разж|ева́ть, ую́, уёшь *pf.* (*of* ▶ разжёвывать) **1** to chew **2** (fig., infml, *разъяснить*) to spell out

разжёвыва|ть, ю *impf. of* ▶ разжева́ть

раз|же́чь, ожгу́, ожжёшь, ожгу́т, *past* ~жёг, ~ожгла́ *pf.* (*of* ▶ разжига́ть) **1** (*заставить гореть*) to kindle, rouse, stir up; р. стра́сти to arouse passion

разжига́|ть, ю *impf. of* ▶ разже́чь

разжима́|ть, ю, ет *impf. of* ▶ разжа́ть

разжима́|ться, ется *impf. of* ▶ разжа́ться

рази́|нуть, у, ешь *pf.* (*of* ▶ разева́ть) (infml) to open wide (*the mouth*); to gape; слу́шать, ~ув рот to listen open-mouthed

разлага́|ть, ю *impf. of* ▶ разложи́ть²

разлага́|ться, ю, ет *impf. of* ▶ разложи́ться²

разла́д, а *m.* discord, dissension

разла́мыва|ть, ю, ет *impf. of* ▶ разлома́ть, ▶ разломи́ть

разла́мыва|ться, ется *impf. of* ▶ разлома́ться, ▶ разломи́ться

разле́нива|ться, юсь *impf. of* ▶ разлени́ться

разлен|и́ться, ю́сь, ~ишься *pf.* (*of* ▶ разле́ниваться) (infml) to become sunk in sloth

разлет|а́ться, а́юсь *impf. of* ▶ разлете́ться

разле|те́ться, чу́сь, ти́шься *pf.* (*of* ▶ разлета́ться) **1** (*о птицах*) to fly away; to scatter (*in the air*); (*о людях*) to scatter **2** (infml, *разбиться*) to smash, shatter **3** (fig., infml, *о мечтах*) to vanish, be shattered **4** (*о новостях*) to spread

разл|е́чься, я́гусь, я́жешься, *past* ~ёгся, ~егла́сь *pf.* (infml) to sprawl; to stretch oneself out

разли́в, а *m.* **1** (*вина*) bottling **2** (*реки*) flood; overflow

разлива́|ть, ю, ет *impf. of* ▶ разли́ть

разлива́|ться, ется *impf. of* ▶ разли́ться

разливно́й *adj.* (*пиво*) on tap; draught (BrE), draft (AmE)

раз|ли́ть, олью́, ольёшь, *past* ~ли́л, ~лила́, ~ли́ло *pf.* (*of* ▶ разлива́ть) to pour out; р. по буты́лкам to bottle; р. чай to pour out tea

раз|ли́ться, ольётся, *past* ~ли́лся, ~лила́сь *pf.* (*of* ▶ разлива́ться) **1** (*пролиться*) to spill; суп ~ли́лся по ска́терти the soup has spilled over the tablecloth **2** (*о реке*) to overflow **3** (fig., *распространиться*) to spread; по её лицу́ ~лила́сь улы́бка a smile spread across her face

различ|а́ть, а́ю *impf. of* ▶ различи́ть

различа́|ться, юсь *impf.* to differ

разли́чи|е, я *nt.* distinction; difference; де́лать р. (ме́жду + *i.*) to make distinctions

(between); без ~я without distinction

различ|и́ть, у́, и́шь *pf.* (*of* ▶ различа́ть) **1** (*установить различие*) to distinguish; to tell the difference (between) **2** (*воспринять*) to discern, make out

ⱷ разли́ч|ный, ~ен, ~на *adj.* **1** (*несходный*) different; у нас бы́ли ~ные мне́ния our opinions differed **2** (*разнообразный*) various, diverse; по ~ным соображе́ниям for various reasons

разложе́ни|е, я *nt.* **1** (*на составные части*) breaking down **2** (*гниение*) decomposition, decay **3** (fig., *демора́лизация*) demoralization; disintegration

разлож|и́ть¹, у́, ~ишь *pf.* (*of* ▶ раскла́дывать) **1** (*положить по разным местам*) to put; р. свои́ ве́щи по я́щикам to put one's things in their respective drawers **2** (*в определённом порядке*) to lay out, spread (out)

разлож|и́ть², у́, ~ишь *pf.* (*of* ▶ разлага́ть) **1** (*на составные части*) to break down; р. вещество́ на составны́е ча́сти to break a substance down into its component parts **2** (fig., *демора́лизовать*) to break down, demoralize

разлож|и́ться¹, у́сь, ~ишься *pf.* (*of* ▶ раскла́дываться) (infml, *разместить свои ве́щи*) to lay one's things out

разлож|и́ться², у́сь, ~ишься *pf.* (*of* ▶ разлага́ться) **1** (*сгнить*) to decompose, rot; труп уже́ ~и́лся the body has already decomposed **2** (fig., *демора́лизоваться*) to become demoralized; to go to pieces

разло́м, а *m.* (*место*) break

разлома́|ть, ю *pf.* (*of* ▶ разла́мывать) to break (in pieces)

разлома́|ться, ется *pf.* (*of* ▶ разла́мываться) to break (in pieces); to break up

разлом|и́ть, лю́, ~ишь *pf.* (*of* ▶ разла́мывать) to break (in pieces)

разлом|и́ться, ~ится *pf.* (*of* ▶ разла́мываться) to break in pieces

разлу́к|а, и *f.* **1** separation; жить в ~е (с + *i.*) to live apart (from), be separated (from) **2** (*расставание*) parting; час ~и hour of parting

разлуч|а́ть, а́ю *impf. of* ▶ разлучи́ть

разлуч|а́ться, а́юсь *impf. of* ▶ разлучи́ться

разлуч|и́ть, у́, и́шь *pf.* (*of* ▶ разлуча́ть) (+ *a. and* с + *i.*) to separate (from), part (from)

разлуч|и́ться, у́сь, и́шься *pf.* (*of* ▶ разлуча́ться) (с + *i.*) to separate, part (from)

разлюб|и́ть, лю́, ~ишь *pf.* (*человека*) to cease to love, stop loving; (*гулять; Москву*) to cease to like

разма́|зать, жу, жешь *pf.* (*of* ▶ разма́зывать) to spread, smear; р. варе́нье по всему́ лицу́ to get jam all over one's face

разма́|заться, жется *pf.* (*of* ▶ разма́зываться) to spread; to get smeared

разма́зыва|ть, ю, ет *impf. of* ▶ разма́зать

ⱷ key word

размáзыва|ться, ется *impf. of* ▸ размáзаться

размáлыва|ть, ю *impf. of* ▸ размолóть

размáтыва|ть, ю, ет *impf. of* ▸ размотáть

размáтыва|ться, ется *impf. of* ▸ размотáться

размáх, а *m.* (*рук, крыльев*) span; (fig.) scope, range

размáхива|ть, ю *impf.* (+ *i.*) to swing; to brandish; **р. рукáми** to gesticulate

размáхива|ться, юсь *impf. of* ▸ размахнýться

размах|нýться, нýсь, нёшься *pf.* (*of* ▸ размáхиваться) to swing one's arm (*to strike or as if to strike*)

размáчива|ть, ю *impf. of* ▸ размочи́ть

размельч|áть, áю *impf. of* ▸ размельчи́ть

размельч|и́ть, ý, и́шь *pf.* (*of* ▸ размельчáть) to divide into particles; to pulverize

размéн, а *m.* exchange; **р. дéнег** changing of money

размéнива|ть, ю *impf. of* ▸ разменя́ть

размéнн|ый *adj.:* ∼ая монéта small change

размен|я́ть, я́ю *pf.* (*of* ▸ размéнивать) to change; **р. сторублёвку** to change a hundred-rouble note

⚲ **размéр, а** *m.* **1** (*масштаб*) dimensions; **ворóнка** ∼**ом в дéсять квадрáтных мéтров** a crater measuring ten square metres **2** (*одежды, обуви*) size (in); (*in pl.*) measurements; **какóй у вас р.?** what size do you take? **3** (*зарплаты, процентов*) rate, amount; **получáть зарплáту в** ∼**е ты́сячи рублéй в день** to be paid at the rate of a thousand roubles per day **4** (*степень*) scale, extent; (*in pl.*) proportions; **увели́читься до огрóмных** ∼**ов** to assume enormous proportions **5** (*ритм стиха, музыки*) rhythm

размéренн|ый *adj.* measured; ∼ая похóдка measured tread

разме|сти́, тý, тёшь, past ∼́**л,** ∼**лá** *pf.* (*of* ▸ разметáть¹) **1** (*дорóжку*) to sweep clean **2** (*снег*) to shovel, sweep away

разме|сти́ть, щý, сти́шь *pf.* (*of* ▸ размещáть) (*поместить по местам*) to place, accommodate; **р. делегáтов по гости́ницам** to accommodate the delegates in hotels

разме|сти́ться, щýсь, сти́шься *pf.* (*of* ▸ размещáться) **1** (*занять места*) to take one's seat **2** (*поместиться*) to be housed, located

разметá|ть¹, ю *impf. of* ▸ размести́

разме|тáть², чý, ∼́**чешь** *pf.* (*of* ▸ размётывать) to scatter, disperse

разме|тить, чу, тишь *pf.* (*of* ▸ размечáть) to mark

размётыва|ть, ю *impf. of* ▸ разметáть²

размечá|ть, ю *impf. of* ▸ размéтить

размеш|áть, áю *pf.* (*of* ▸ размéшивать) to stir

размéшива|ть, ю *impf. of* ▸ размешáть

⚲ **размещá|ть, ю** *impf. of* ▸ размести́ть

размещá|ться, юсь *impf. of* ▸ размести́ться

⚲ **размещéни|е, я** *nt.* **1** (*по местам*) placing, accommodation; **р. промы́шленности** location of industry **2** (fin., *капитáла*) placing, investment

размина́|ть, ю *impf. of* ▸ размя́ть

размина́|ться, юсь *impf. of* ▸ размя́ться

размини́р|овать, ую *pf.* to clear of mines

размни́нк|а, и *f.* (sport) limbering-up; warm-up

размин|ýться, ýсь, ёшься *pf.* (infml) **1** (с + *i.*) to pass (*without meeting*); to miss; **мы, должнó быть,** ∼**ýлись с ним на дорóге** we must have passed one another on the road **2** (*о письмах*) to cross

размнож|áть, áю, áет *impf. of* ▸ размнóжить

размнож|áться, áется *impf. of* ▸ размнóжиться

размножéни|е, я *nt.* **1** duplicating; photocopying **2** (biol.) reproduction, propagation

размнóж|ить, у, ишь *pf.* (*of* ▸ размножáть) to duplicate; to photocopy

размнóж|иться, ится *pf.* (*of* ▸ размножáться) (biol.) to reproduce; to breed

размок|áть, áет *impf. of* ▸ размóкнуть

размóк|нуть, нет, past ∼, ∼**ла** *pf.* (*of* ▸ размокáть) to get soaked; to get sodden

размóлвк|а, и *f.* tiff, disagreement

раз|молóть, мелю́, мéлешь *pf.* (*of* ▸ размáлывать) to grind

разморáжива|ть, ю, ет *impf. of* ▸ разморóзить

разморáжива|ться, ется *impf. of* ▸ разморóзиться

разморó|зить, жу, зишь *pf.* (*of* ▸ разморáживать) to defrost

разморó|зиться, зится *pf.* (*of* ▸ разморáживаться) to defrost

размотá|ть, ю *pf.* (*of* ▸ размáтывать) to unwind, uncoil, unreel

размотá|ться, ется *pf.* (*of* ▸ размáтываться) to unwind, uncoil, unreel; to come unwound

размоч|и́ть, ý, ∼́**ишь** *pf.* (*of* ▸ размáчивать) to soak, steep

размывá|ть, ю *impf. of* ▸ размы́ть

размыкá|ть, ю *impf. of* ▸ разомкнýть

разм|ы́ть, óю, óешь *pf.* (*of* ▸ размывáть) to wash away; (geol.) to erode

размышлéни|е, я *nt.* reflection, meditation, thought; **быть погружённым в** ∼**я** to be lost in thought

размышля́|ть, ю *impf.* (о + *p.*) to reflect (on, upon), meditate (on, upon), ponder (over)

размягч|áть, áю *impf. of* ▸ размягчи́ть

размягч|и́ть, ý, и́шь *pf.* (*of* ▸ размягчáть) to soften

раз|мя́ть, омнý, омнёшь *pf.* (*of* ▸ мять 1, ▸ размина́ть) (*глину*) to knead; (*картóшку*) to mash

раз|мя́ться, омнýсь, омнёшься *pf.* (*of* ▸ размина́ться) **1** to grow soft (*as result*

p

of kneading) **2** (infml) to stretch one's legs; (sport) to limber up, loosen up

разне́рвнича|ться, юсь *pf.* (infml) to become very nervous

разнес|ти́, у́, ёшь, *past* ~, ~ла́ *pf.* (*of* ▸ **разноси́ть**) **1** to carry, convey; to take round; **р. газе́ты** to deliver newspapers; (*слух*) to spread **2** (infml, *разбить*) to smash, break up **3** (*рассеять*) to scatter, disperse

разнес|ти́сь, ётся, *past* ~ся, ~ла́сь *pf.* (*of* ▸ **разноси́ться**) **1** (*о слухах*) to spread **2** (*о звуках*) to resound

разнима́|ть, ю *impf. of* ▸ **разня́ть**

ơ **ра́зниц|а, ы** *f.* difference; disparity; **кака́я р.?** (infml) what difference does it make?

разнови́дность|, и *f.* variety

разногла́си|е, я *nt.* **1** (*во мнениях*) difference, disagreement; ~я во взгля́дах difference of opinion **2** (*противоречие*) discrepancy; **р. в показа́ниях** conflicting evidence

разнообра́зи|е, я *nt.* variety, diversity; **для** ~я for a change

ơ **разнообра́з|ный, ~ен, ~на** *adj.* various, varied, diverse

разноро́д|ный, ~ен, ~на *adj.* heterogeneous

разно|си́ть, шу́, ~сишь *impf. of* ▸ **разнести́**

разно|си́ться, ~сится *impf. of* ▸ **разнести́сь**

разносторо́н|ний, ~ен, ~ня *adj.* many-sided; versatile

ра́зност|ь, и *f.* difference

разно́счик, а *m.* (*газет, телеграмм*) delivery man; (*новостей*) bearer; (*инфекции*) carrier

разноцве́т|ный, ~ен, ~на *adj.* of different colours, colors (AmE); multicoloured (BrE), multicolored (AmE)

ơ **ра́зн|ый** *adj.* **1** (*взгляды*) different, differing **2** (*разнообразный*) various, diverse; ~ого ро́да of various kinds; (*as nt. n.* ~ое, ~ого) (*на повестке дня*) miscellaneous

раз|ня́ть, ниму́, ни́мешь, *past* ~ня́л, ~няла́, ~ня́ло *pf.* (*of* ▸ **разнима́ть**) to part, separate

разо... *vbl. pref.* = **раз...**[1], **раз...**[2]

разоблача́|ть, а́ю *impf. of* ▸ **разоблачи́ть**

разоблаче́ни|е, я *nt.* exposure, unmasking

разоблач|и́ть, у́, и́шь *pf.* (*of* ▸ **разоблача́ть**) to expose, unmask

раз|обра́ть, беру́, берёшь, *past* ~обра́л, ~обрала́, ~обра́ло *pf.* (*of* ▸ **разбира́ть**) **1** (*механизм*) to take to pieces, dismantle **2** (*раскупить*) to buy up; (*взять*) to take **3** (*привести в порядок*) to sort out **4** (*ссору, дело*) to investigate, look into **5** (*понять*) to make out, understand

раз|обра́ться, беру́сь, берёшься, *past* ~обра́лся, ~обрала́сь *pf.* (*of* ▸ **разбира́ться**) (**в** + *p.*) (*понимать*) to understand, know about; (infml, *разложить свои вещи*) to unpack, sort out one's things

ơ key word

разобщённо *adv.* apart, separately; **де́йствовать р.** to act independently

ра́зов|ый *adj.* valid for one occasion (only); ~ого по́льзования disposable

раз|огна́ть, гоню́, го́нишь, *past* ~огна́л, ~огнала́, ~огна́ло *pf.* (*of* ▸ **разгоня́ть**) **1** to drive away; to disperse; (fig.) to dispel; **р. демонстра́цию** to break up a demonstration **2** (infml, *автомобиль*) to drive at high speed, race

раз|огна́ться, гоню́сь, го́нишься, *past* ~огна́лся, ~огнала́сь, ~огна́ло́сь *pf.* (*of* ▸ **разгоня́ться**) to gather speed; to gather momentum

разогн|у́ть, у́, ёшь *pf.* (*of* ▸ **разгиба́ть**) to unbend, straighten; **р. спи́ну** to straighten one's back

разогн|у́ться, у́сь, ёшься *pf.* (*of* ▸ **разгиба́ться**) to straighten oneself up

разогрева́|ть, ю *impf. of* ▸ **разогре́ть**

разогрева́|ться, юсь *impf. of* ▸ **разогре́ться**

разогре́|ть, ю *pf.* (*of* ▸ **разогрева́ть**) to warm up

разогре́|ться, юсь *pf.* (*of* ▸ **разогрева́ться**) to warm up, grow warm

разоде́|ть, ну, нешь *pf.* (infml) to dress up

разоде́|ться, нусь, нешься *pf.* (infml) to dress up

раз|одра́ть, деру́, дерёшь, *past* ~одра́л, ~одрала́, ~одра́ло *pf.* (*of* ▸ **раздира́ть** 1) to tear up

разозл|и́ть, ю́, и́шь *pf.* (*of* ▸ **злить**) to make angry, enrage

разозл|и́ться, ю́сь, и́шься *pf.* (*of* ▸ **зли́ться**) to get angry, get in a rage

раз|ойти́сь, ойду́сь, ойдёшься, *past* ~ошёлся, ~ошла́сь *pf.* (*of* ▸ **расходи́ться**) **1** (*уйти*) to go away; (*рассеяться*) to disperse; **толпа́** ~ошла́сь the crowd broke up **2** (**с** + *i.*) (*расстаться*) to part (from); (*о супругах*) to separate (from); **он** ~ошёлся **с жено́й** he has separated from his wife **3** (*о линиях, о дорогах*) to branch off, diverge; (*о лучах*) to radiate **4** (*разминуться*) to pass (*without meeting*) **5** (**с** + *i.*) (*обнаружить разногласие*) to conflict (with); **р. во мне́нии с кем-н.** to disagree with sb **6** (*раствориться*) to dissolve; (*растаять*) to melt **7** (infml, *дать волю себе*) to get going; **бу́ря** ~ошла́сь the storm raged

разомкн|у́ть, у́, ёшь *pf.* (*of* ▸ **размыка́ть**) to open, unfasten; (tech.) to break, disconnect

разонра́в|иться, люсь, ишься *pf.* (infml) (+ *d.*) to cease to please, lose its attraction (for)

разор|а́ться, у́сь, ёшься *pf.* (infml) to start shouting

разорв|а́ть, у́, ёшь, *past* ~а́л, ~ала́, ~а́ло *pf.* (*of* ▸ **разрыва́ть**[1]) **1** (*письмо*) to tear up; (*пакет, конверт*) to tear open; (*одежду*) to tear **2** (impers.) (*взорвать*) to blow up, burst; **котёл** ~а́ло the boiler has blown up

3 (fig., *прекрати́ть*) to break (off), sever;
р. дипломати́ческие отноше́ния to break off
diplomatic relations

разорв|а́ться, у́сь, ёшься, *past* ~а́лся,
~ала́сь, ~ало́сь *pf.* (*of* ▶ разрыва́ться)
1 (*о верёвке*) to break, snap; (*об оде́жде*)
to tear, become torn **2** (*взорва́ться*) to blow
up; to explode **3** (*об отноше́ниях*) to be
broken off, severed

разоре́ни|е, я *nt.* (*го́рода*) destruction,
ravage; (*наро́да*) ruin

разор|и́ть, ю́, и́шь *pf.* (*of* ▶ разоря́ть)
1 (*опустоши́ть*) to destroy, ravage
2 (*довести́ до нищеты́*) to ruin, bring to
ruin

разор|и́ться, ю́сь, и́шься *pf.* (*of*
▶ разоря́ться) **1** (*прийти́ в упа́док*) to be
ruined **2** (*впасть в нищету́*) to go broke,
ruin oneself

разоруж|а́ть, а́ю *impf. of* ▶ разоружи́ть

разоруж|а́ться, а́юсь *impf. of*
▶ разоружи́ться

разоруже́ни|е, я *nt.* (*де́йствие*) disarming;
(*поли́тика*) disarmament

разоруж|и́ть, у́, и́шь *pf.* (*of* ▶ разоружа́ть)
to disarm

разоруж|и́ться, у́сь, и́шься *pf.* (*of*
▶ разоружа́ться) to disarm

разоря́|ть, я́ю *impf. of* ▶ разори́ть

разоря́|ться, я́юсь *impf. of* ▶ разори́ться

разо|сла́ть, шлю́, шлёшь *pf.* (*of*
▶ рассыла́ть) to send out

разостла́ть, расстелю́, рассте́лешь *pf.*
= расстели́ть

разостла́ться, рассте́лется *pf.*
= расстели́ться

разочарова́ни|е, я *nt.* disappointment

разочар|ова́ть, у́ю *pf.* (*of*
▶ разочаро́вывать) to disappoint

разочар|ова́ться, у́юсь *pf.* (*of*
▶ разочаро́вываться) (в + *p.*) to be
disappointed (in sb, with sth)

разочаро́выва|ть, ю *impf. of*
▶ разочарова́ть

разочаро́выва|ться, юсь *impf. of*
▶ разочарова́ться

✍ **разраба́тыва|ть, ю** *impf. of* ▶ разрабо́тать

разрабо́та|ть, ю *pf.* (*of* ▶ разраба́тывать)
1 (*подгото́вить*) to develop; to elaborate;
р. пла́н to work out a plan **2** (mining) to
work, exploit

✍ **разрабо́тк|а, и** *f.* **1** (*прое́кта*) working
out; development; elaboration **2** (mining)
working, exploitation; **откры́тая р.** opencast
mining **3: нефтяна́я р.** oilfield

разра́внива|ть, ю *impf. of* ▶ разровня́ть

разража́|ться, юсь *impf. of* ▶ разрази́ться

разра|зи́ться, жу́сь, зи́шься *pf.* (*of*
▶ разража́ться) (*о грозе́, о катастро́фе*)
to break out, burst out; **р. слеза́ми** to burst
into tears; **р. сме́хом** to burst out laughing

разраст|а́ться, а́ется *impf. of* ▶ разрасти́сь

разраст|и́сь, ётся, *past* разро́сся,
разросла́сь *pf.* (*of* ▶ разраста́ться) to
grow; to spread; **де́ло разросло́сь** the
business has grown; **сире́нь разросла́сь** the
lilac has spread

разре́з, а *m.* **1** (*отве́рстие*) cut; slit;
ю́бка с ~ом slit skirt **2** (*сече́ние*) section;
попере́чный р. cross section; **р. глаз** shape
of one's eyes

разре́|зать, жу, жешь *pf.* (*of* ▶ разреза́ть)
to cut; to slit

разреза́|ть, а́ю *impf. of* ▶ разре́зать

разреша́|ть, а́ю *impf. of* ▶ разреши́ть

разреша́|ться, а́ется *impf.* **1** *impf. of*
▶ разреши́ться **2** (*impf. only*) to be allowed;
здесь кури́ть не ~а́ется smoking is not
allowed here

✍ **разреше́ни|е, я** *nt.* **1** (*пра́во*) permission;
с ва́шего ~я with your permission, by your
leave **2** (*докуме́нт*) permit, authorization;
р. на въезд entry permit **3** (*пробле́мы*)
solution **4** (*спо́ра*) settlement **5** (tech.,
сте́пень детализа́ции) resolution

разреши́м|ый, ~, ~а *adj.* solvable

разреш|и́ть, у́, и́шь *pf.* (*of* ▶ разреша́ть)
1 (+ *d.*) to allow, permit; ~и́те пройти́! do
you mind letting me pass? **2** (*кни́гу, фильм*)
to authorize; **р. кни́гу к печа́ти** to authorize
the printing of a book **3** (*пробле́му*) to solve
4 (*конфли́кт*) to settle; **р. сомне́ния** to
resolve doubts

разреш|и́ться, и́тся *pf.* (*of* ▶ разреша́ться 1)
1 (*о пробле́ме*) to be solved **2** (*о конфли́кте*)
to be settled

разрис|ова́ть, у́ю *pf.* (*of* ▶ разрисо́вывать)
to cover with drawings

разрисо́выва|ть, ю *impf. of* ▶ разрисова́ть

разровня́|ть, ю *pf.* (*of* ▶ разра́внивать) to
level

разро́знен|ный, ~, ~на *adj.* **1** (*лишённый
еди́нства*) uncoordinated **2: р. компле́кт**
incomplete set; ~ные тома́ odd volumes

разруб|а́ть, а́ю *impf. of* ▶ разруби́ть

разруб|и́ть, лю́, ~ишь *pf.* (*of* ▶ разруба́ть)
to cut, cleave

разру́х|а, и *f.* ruin, collapse

разруш|а́ть, а́ю, а́ет *impf. of* ▶ разру́шить

разруш|а́ться, а́ется *impf. of* ▶ разру́шиться

разруше́ни|е, я *nt.* destruction; (*in pl.*) havoc

разруши́тел|ьный, ~ен, ~ьна *adj.*
destructive

разру́ш|ить, у, ишь *pf.* (*of* ▶ разруша́ть)
1 to destroy; to ruin **2** (fig.) to ruin; **р.
чьи-н. наде́жды** to ruin sb's hopes

разру́ш|иться, ится *pf.* (*of* ▶ разруша́ться)
to go to ruin, be destroyed, collapse

разры́в, а *m.* **1** (*простра́нство*) break;
gap; (*проре́ха*) tear; (*отноше́ний*)
breaking, severance; (*с кем-н.*) break-
up; (*несоотве́тствие*) gap; **р. ме́жду
поколе́ниями** generation gap **2** (*снаря́да*)
burst, explosion

разрыва́|ть¹, ю *impf. of* ▶ разорва́ть

разрыва́|ть², ю *impf. of* ▸ разры́ть

разрыва́|ться, юсь *impf. of* ▸ разорва́ться

разры́|ть, о́ю, о́ешь *pf.* (*of* ▸ разрыва́ть²)
1 to dig up **2** (fig., infml, *раскидать*) to turn upside-down, rummage through

разря́д¹, а *m.* (*электричества*) discharge

разря́д², а *m.* (*категория*) category, sort; (*в профессии, в спорте*) rank, class; **пе́рвого** ~а first class

разря|ди́ть, жу́, ди́шь *pf.* (*of* ▸ разряжа́ть)
1 (elec.) to discharge; **р. атмосфе́ру** (fig.) to clear the air **2** (*ружьё*) to unload; (*стреляя*) to discharge

разря|ди́ться, ди́тся *pf.* (*of* ▸ разряжа́ться)
1 (elec.) to run down; (fig.) to clear, ease **2** (*об оружии*) to be unloaded; (*стреляя*) to be discharged

разряжа́|ть, ю, ет *impf. of* ▸ разряди́ть

разряжа́|ться, ется *impf. of* ▸ разряди́ться

разубе|ди́ть, жу́, ди́шь *pf.* (*of* ▸ разубежда́ть) (*в + p.*) to dissuade (from)

разубе|ди́ться, жу́сь, ди́шься *pf.* (*of* ▸ разубежда́ться) (*в + p.*) to change one's mind (about)

разубежда́|ть, ю *impf. of* ▸ разубеди́ть

разубежда́|ться, юсь *impf. of* ▸ разубеди́ться

разува́|ть, ю *impf. of* ▸ разу́ть

разува́|ться, юсь *impf. of* ▸ разу́ться

разуве́р|ить, ю, ишь *pf.* (*of* ▸ разуверя́ть) (*в + p.*) to cause sb to lose faith, stop believing (in); to persuade to the contrary; **он меня́ ~ил в том, что э́того мо́жно доби́ться** he persuaded me that it could not be achieved

разуве́р|иться, юсь, ишься *pf.* (*of* ▸ разуверя́ться) (*в + p.*) to lose faith (in)

разуверя́|ть, ю *impf. of* ▸ разуве́рить

разуверя́|ться, юсь *impf. of* ▸ разуве́риться

разузна|ва́ть, ю́, ёшь *impf.* **1** *impf. of* ▸ разузна́ть **2** (*impf. only*) to make inquiries (about)

разузна́|ть, ю *pf.* (*of* ▸ разузнава́ть 1) to find out

разукра́|сить, шу, сишь *pf.* (*of* ▸ разукра́шивать) to adorn; to decorate; to embellish

разукра́шива|ть, ю *impf. of* ▸ разукра́сить

ра́зум, а *m.* reason; (*интеллект*) intellect

⚬ **разуме́|ться**, ется *impf.* (**под** + *i.*) to be understood (by), be meant (by); **под э́тим ~ется...** by this is meant ...; (**само́ собо́й**) ~ется it goes without saying, of course; **он, ~ется, не знал, что вы уже́ пришли́** he, of course, did not know that you were already here

разу́м|ный, ~ен, ~на *adj.* **1** (*существо*) rational, intelligent **2** (*парень*) intelligent, clever **3** (*поступок*) reasonable; **э́то** (**вполне́**) ~но it is (perfectly) reasonable

разу́|ть, ю, ешь *pf.* (*of* ▸ разува́ть): **р. кого́-н.** to take sb's shoes off

разу́|ться, юсь, ешься *pf.* (*of* ▸ разува́ться) to take one's shoes off

разучива|ть, ю *impf. of* ▸ разучи́ть

разучива|ться, юсь *impf. of* ▸ разучи́ться

разучи́|ть, у́, ~ишь *pf.* (*of* ▸ разу́чивать) to learn (up); **р. роль** to learn, study one's part

разучи́|ться, у́сь, ~ишься *pf.* (*of* ▸ разу́чиваться) (+ *inf.*) to forget (how to); **я ~и́лся ходи́ть на лы́жах** I have forgotten how to ski

разъ... *vbl. pref.* = раз...¹, раз...²

разъеда́|ть, ю *impf. of* ▸ разъе́сть

разъедине́ни|е, я *nt.* **1** separation **2** (elec.) disconnection, breaking

разъедин|и́ть, ю́, и́шь *pf.* (*of* ▸ разъединя́ть)
1 (*друзей*) to separate **2** (elec.) to disconnect; **нас ~и́ли** we were cut off (*on telephone*)

разъедин|и́ться, и́тся *pf.* (*of* ▸ разъединя́ться) to separate, part; (*о проводах*) to come apart, be disconnected

разъедин|я́ть, я́ет *impf. of* ▸ разъедини́ть

разъедин|я́ться, я́ется *impf. of* ▸ разъедини́ться

разъе́зд, а *m.* **1** (*людей*) departure **2** (*in pl.*) (*поездки*) travels **3** (mil.) mounted patrol **4** (rail.) siding

разъезжа́|ть, ю *impf.* to drive (about, around), ride (about, around); to travel; **р. по дела́м** to travel about on business

разъезжа́|ться, юсь *impf. of* ▸ разъе́хаться

разъе́|сть, ст, дя́т, *past* ~л *pf.* (*of* ▸ разъеда́ть) to eat away; to corrode (also fig.)

разъе́|хаться, дусь, дешься *pf.* (*of* ▸ разъезжа́ться) **1** (*уехать*) to depart; to disperse **2** (*о супругах*) to separate, stop living together **3** (*о машинах*) to (be able to) pass **4** (*разминуться*) to pass one another (*without meeting*); to miss one another

разъяр|и́ться, ю́сь, и́шься *pf.* (*of* ▸ разъяря́ться) to fly into a rage

разъяр|я́ться, я́юсь *impf. of* ▸ разъяри́ться

разъясне́ни|е, я *nt.* explanation

разъясн|и́ть, ю́, и́шь *pf.* (*of* ▸ разъясня́ть) to explain

разъясн|и́ться, и́тся *pf.* (*of* ▸ разъясня́ться) to become clear, be cleared up

разъясн|я́ть, я́ю, я́ет *impf. of* ▸ разъясни́ть

разъясн|я́ться, я́ется *impf. of* ▸ разъясни́ться

разыгр|а́ть, а́ю *pf.* (*of* ▸ разы́грывать)
1 (*исполнить*) to play (through); to perform; **р. дурака́** to play the fool **2** (*игру, карту*) to play **3** (*в лотерее*) to raffle **4** (infml, *одурачить*) to play a trick (on)

разыгр|а́ться, а́юсь *pf.* (*of* ▸ разы́грываться)
1 (*увлечься игрой*) to be carried away by a game, by play **2** (*о музыканте, об актёре*) to warm up **3** (*о ветре, буре*) to get up; (*о чувствах*) to run high

⚬ key word

разы́грыва|ть, ю *impf. of* ▶ разыгра́ть

разы́грыва|ться, юсь *impf. of*
▶ разыгра́ться

разы|ска́ть, щу́, ~щешь *pf.* to find (*after searching*)

разы́скива|ть, ю *impf.* to hunt, search for

разы́скива|ться, юсь *impf.* to be searched, hunted for; **р. поли́цией** to be wanted by the police

ра|й, я, о ~е, в ~ю́ *m.* paradise

⚬ **райо́н, а** *m.* **1** region **2** (*административная едини́ца*) district

райо́нный *adj. of* ▶ райо́н

рак, а *m.* **1** (zool.) (*речно́й*) crayfish (BrE), crawfish (AmE); (*морско́й*) spiny lobster **2** (med.) cancer **3** (**Р.**) (astrol., astron.) Crab, Cancer

раке́т|а, ы *f.* **1** (*для сигна́лов; фейерве́рк; косми́ческая*) rocket; **пусти́ть ~у** to let off a rocket **2** (mil.) rocket, ballistic missile; **крыла́тая р.** cruise missile

раке́т|ка, ки *f.* (sport) racket

раке́тчик, а *m.* missile specialist

ра́ковин|а, ы *f.* **1** (*моллю́ска*) shell **2** (*для умыва́ния*) sink; washbasin

раку́шк|а, и *f.* shell; seashell

ра́лли *nt. indecl.* rally

ра́м|а, ы *f.* **1** frame; **вста́вить в ~у** to frame **2** (*маши́ны*) chassis

Рамада́н, а *m.* = Рамаза́н

Рамаза́н, а *m.* (relig.) Ramadan

⚬ **ра́мк|а, и** *f.* frame; (*те́кста*) border

ра́м|ки, ок (*pl. only*) framework; limits; **в ~ках** (+ *g.*) within the framework (of), within the limits (of); **вы́йти за р.** (+ *g.*) to exceed the limits (of)

ра́мп|а, ы *f.* (theatr.) footlights

ра́н|а, ы *f.* wound

ранг, а *m.* class, rank

⚬ **ра́нее** *adv.* = ра́ньше

ране́ни|е, я *nt.* **1** (*де́йствие*) wounding; injuring **2** (*ра́на*) wound; injury

ра́нен|ый *adj.* wounded; injured; (*as m. n. p.*, **~ого**) injured man; wounded man; casualty; (*in pl.*) the injured; the wounded

ра́н|ец, ца *m.* (*похо́дный, солда́тский*) knapsack, pack; (*учени́ческий*) satchel

рани́м|ый, ~, а *adj.* vulnerable

ра́н|ить, ю, ишь *impf. and pf.* to wound; to injure

⚬ **ра́нн|ий** *adj.* early; **~им у́тром** early in the morning; **с ~его де́тства** from early childhood

ра́но¹ *pred.* it is early; **ещё р. ложи́ться спать** it is too early for bed

ра́но² *adv.* early; **р. и́ли по́здно** sooner or later

рантье́ *m. indecl.* rentier

ра́нчо *nt. indecl.* ranch

ра́ньше *adv.* **1** earlier; **как мо́жно р.** as early as possible; as soon as possible **2** (+ *g.*)

(*пре́жде*) before; **до Ло́ндона он р. ве́чера не дое́дет** he will not reach London before evening **3** (*пре́жде*) before, formerly; **р. мы жи́ли в дере́вне** we used to live in the country

ра́порт, а *m.* report

рапорт|ова́ть, у́ю *impf. and pf.* to report

рапс, а *m.* (bot.) rape

рарите́т, а *m.* rarity, curiosity

рас... *vbl. pref.* = раз...¹, раз...²

ра́с|а, ы *f.* race

раси́зм, а *m.* racism

раси́ст, а *m.* racist

раси́ст|ка, ки *f. of* ▶ раси́ст

раси́стский *adj.* racist

раска́ива|ться, юсь *impf. of* ▶ раска́яться

раскалённый *p.p.p. of* ▶ раскали́ть *and adj.* scorching, burning hot

раскал|и́ть, ю́, и́шь *pf.* (*of* ▶ раскаля́ть) to bring to a great heat

раскал|и́ться, ю́сь, и́шься *pf.* (*of* ▶ раскаля́ться) to glow, become hot

раска́лыва|ть, ю *impf. of* ▶ расколо́ть

раска́лыва|ться, юсь *impf. of*
▶ расколо́ться

раскал|я́ть, я́ю *impf. of* ▶ раскали́ть

раскал|я́ться, я́юсь *impf. of* ▶ раскали́ться

раска́пыва|ть, ю *impf. of* ▶ раскопа́ть

раска́т, а *m.* roll, peal; **р. гро́ма** peal of thunder

раскат|а́ть, а́ю *pf.* (*of* ▶ раска́тывать)
1 (*ковёр*) to unroll **2** (*те́сто*) to roll (out); (*доро́гу*) to level

раска́тыва|ть, ю *impf. of* ▶ раската́ть

раскач|а́ть, а́ю *pf.* (*of* ▶ раска́чивать)
1 (*каче́ли*) to swing; to rock **2** (*расшата́ть*) to loosen, shake loose

раскач|а́ться, а́юсь *pf.* (*of* ▶ раска́чиваться)
1 (*на каче́лях*) to swing (back and forth); (*о ло́дке*) to rock **2** (*расшата́ться*) to shake loose

раска́чива|ть, ю *impf. of* ▶ раскача́ть

раска́чива|ться, юсь *impf. of* ▶ раскача́ться

раска́яни|е, я *nt.* repentance

раска́|яться, юсь *pf.* (*of* ▶ раска́иваться)
(**в** + *p.*) to repent (of)

расквартир|ова́ть, у́ю *pf.* (*of*
▶ расквартиро́вывать) to quarter, billet

расквартиро́выва|ть, ю *impf. of*
▶ расквартирова́ть

раскид|а́ть, а́ю *pf.* (*of* ▶ раски́дывать) to scatter

раски́дыва|ть, ю *impf. of* ▶ раскида́ть,
▶ раски́нуть

раски́дыва|ться, юсь *impf. of* ▶ раски́нуться

раски́|нуть, ну, нешь *pf.* (*of* ▶ раски́дывать)
1 (*ру́ки*) to stretch (out) **2** (*ковёр*) to spread (out); (*ла́герь*) to set up; (*пала́тку*) to pitch

раски́|нуться, нусь, нешься *pf.* (*of*
▶ раски́дываться) **1** to spread out, stretch out **2** (infml) to sprawl

р

раскла́д, а *m.* (*расположение*) disposition, arrangement; (*сил, средств*) apportionment; (*положение дел*) state of affairs

расклади|о́й *adj.* folding; ~а́я крова́ть camp bed (BrE), cot (AmE)

расклади́шк|а, и *f.* (infml) camp bed (BrE), cot (AmE)

раскла́дыва|ть, ю *impf. of* ▶ разложи́ть[1]

раскла́дыва|ться, юсь *impf. of* ▶ разложи́ться[1]

раскла́нива|ться, юсь *impf. of* ▶ раскла́няться

раскла́н|яться, яюсь *pf.* (*of* ▶ раскла́ниваться) [1] to exchange bows (*on meeting or leave-taking*) [2] (*об актёре*) to take a bow

раскле́ива|ть, ю *impf. of* ▶ раскле́ить

раскле́ива|ться, юсь *impf. of* ▶ раскле́иться

раскле́|ить, ю, ишь *pf.* (*of* ▶ раскле́ивать) [1] (*конверт*) to unstick [2] (*афиши*) to stick, paste (*in various places*)

раскле́|иться, юсь, ишься *pf.* (*of* ▶ раскле́иваться) [1] to come unstuck [2] (fig., infml, *о планах*) to fall through, to come unstuck [3] (fig., infml, *о человеке*) to feel unwell; **он совсе́м ~ился** he has gone to pieces

раско́ванный *adj.* relaxed, uninhibited

раско́л, а *m.* [1] (relig., hist.) schism, dissent [2] (pol., etc.) split, division

раскол|о́ть, ю́, ~ешь [1] *pf. of* ▶ коло́ть[1] [2] (*impf.* раска́лывать) (fig.) to disrupt, break up

раскол|о́ться, ю́сь, ~ешься *pf.* (*of* ▶ раска́лываться) to split (also fig.)

раскопа́|ть, ю *pf.* (*of* ▶ раска́пывать) to dig up, unearth (also fig.); (*об археологах*) to excavate

раско́пк|а, и *f.* (*действие*) digging up; (*in pl.*) (*археологические*) excavations

раскра́ива|ть, ю *impf. of* ▶ раскро́ить

раскра́|сить, шу, сишь *pf.* (*of* ▶ раскра́шивать) to paint, colour (BrE), color (AmE)

раскра́ск|а, и *f.* [1] (*действие*) painting, colouring (BrE), coloring (AmE) [2] (*расцветка*) colours (BrE), colors (AmE), colour scheme (BrE), color scheme (AmE)

раскра́шива|ть, ю *impf. of* ▶ раскра́сить

раскрепо|сти́ться, щу́сь, сти́шься *pf.* (*of* ▶ раскрепоща́ться) to free *or* liberate oneself

раскрепоща́|ться, юсь *impf. of* ▶ раскрепости́ться

раскритик|ова́ть, у́ю *pf.* to criticize severely, slam

раскрич|а́ться, у́сь, и́шься *pf.* [1] to start shouting, start crying [2] (на + *a.*) to shout (at)

раскро|и́ть, ю́, и́шь *pf.* (*of* ▶ раскра́ивать) [1] (*ткань*) to cut out [2] (fig., infml) to cut

open; **р. кому́-н. че́реп** to split sb's skull

раскрош|и́ть, у́, ~ит *pf. of* ▶ кроши́ть

раскрош|и́ться, ~ится *pf. of* ▶ кроши́ться

раскру|ти́ть, чу́, ~тишь *pf.* (*of* ▶ раскру́чивать) [1] (*развить*) to untwist, undo [2] (*колесо*) to spin, rotate [3] (infml) (*заставить развиваться*) to develop, establish; (*рекламировать*) promote, popularize

раскру|ти́ться, чу́сь, ~тишься *pf.* (*of* ▶ раскру́чиваться) [1] (*развиться*) to come untwisted, come undone [2] (*начать крутиться*) to start spinning, rotating [3] (infml) (*начать действовать*) to develop, get established; (*получить известность*) to become famous, popular

раскру́чива|ть, ю *impf. of* ▶ раскрути́ть

раскру́чива|ться, юсь *impf. of* ▶ раскрути́ться

раскрыва́|ть, ю *impf. of* ▶ раскры́ть

раскрыва́|ться, юсь *impf. of* ▶ раскры́ться

раскр|ы́ть, о́ю, о́ешь *pf.* (*of* ▶ раскрыва́ть) [1] (*открыть*) to open (wide); **р. зо́нтик** to put up an umbrella; **р. кни́гу** to open a book [2] (*сделать видным*) to expose, bare [3] (*обнаружить*) to reveal, disclose, lay bare; (*найти*) to discover; **р. секре́т** to disclose a secret

раскр|ы́ться, о́юсь, о́ешься *pf.* (*of* ▶ раскрыва́ться) [1] to open [2] (*раскрыть себя́*) to uncover oneself [3] (*обнаружиться*) to come out; to come to light

раскупа́|ть, а́ю *impf. of* ▶ раскупи́ть

раскуп|и́ть, лю́, ~ишь *pf.* (*of* ▶ раскупа́ть) to buy up

раску́рива|ть, ю, ет *impf. of* ▶ раскури́ть

раскур|и́ть, ю́, ~ишь *pf.* (*of* ▶ раску́ривать) [1] (*заставить куриться*) to puff at (*a pipe or cigarette*) [2] (*зажечь*) to light up

раску|си́ть, шу́, ~сишь *pf.* (*of* ▶ раску́сывать) [1] (*конфету*) to bite into [2] (*pf. only*) (infml, *узнать, понять*) to suss out

раску́сыва|ть, ю *impf. of* ▶ раскуси́ть

ра́совый *adj.* racial

распа́д, а *m.* [1] disintegration, break-up; (fig.) collapse [2] (chem.) decomposition

распада́|ться, ется *impf. of* ▶ распа́сться

распак|ова́ть, у́ю *pf.* (*of* ▶ распако́вывать) to unpack

распако́выва|ть, ю *impf. of* ▶ распакова́ть

распа́рыва|ть, ю *impf. of* ▶ распоро́ть

распа́|сться, де́тся, *past* ~лся *pf.* (*of* ▶ распада́ться) [1] to disintegrate; (fig.) to break up; to collapse; **коали́ция ~ла́сь** the coalition broke up [2] (chem.) to decompose

распа|ха́ть, шу́, ~шешь *pf.* (*of* ▶ распа́хивать) to plough up (BrE), plow up (AmE)

распа́хива|ть, ю *impf. of* ▶ распаха́ть, ▶ распахну́ть

распа́хива|ться, юсь *impf. of* ▶ распахну́ться

распах|ну́ть, ну́, нёшь *pf. (of*
▸ **распа́хивать**) to open wide; to throw
open; **широко́ р. две́ри** (+ *d.*) to open wide
the doors (to) (also *fig.*)

распах|ну́ться, ну́сь, нёшься *pf. (of*
▸ **распа́хиваться**) **1** (*о две́ри, об окне́*) to
fly open, swing open **2** (*распахну́ть по́лы
свое́й оде́жды*) to throw open one's coat

распере́ть, разопру́, разопрёшь, *past*
распёр, распёрла *pf. (of* ▸ **распира́ть**)
(infml) to burst open, cause to burst

распеча́т|ать, аю *pf. (of* ▸ **распеча́тывать**)
1 (*вскрыть*) to unseal; **р. письмо́** to
open a letter **2** (*напеча́тать во мно́гих
экземпля́рах*) to print off **3** (comput.) to
print (out)

распеча́тк|а, и *f.* printout; (*де́йствие*)
printing out

распеча́тыва|ть, ю *impf. of* ▸ **распеча́тать**

распи́лива|ть, ю *impf. of* ▸ **распили́ть**

распил|и́ть, ю́, ~ишь *pf. (of*
▸ **распи́ливать**) to saw up

распира́|ть, ю *impf. of* ▸ **распере́ть**

расписа́ни|е, я *nt.* timetable, schedule

распи|са́ть, шу́, ~шешь *pf. (of*
▸ **распи́сывать**) **1** (*све́дения*) to enter; to
note down; **р. счета́ по кни́гам** to enter bills
in the account book **2** (*распредели́ть*) to
assign, allot **3** (*разрисова́ть*) to paint

распи|са́ться, шу́сь, ~шешься *pf. (of*
▸ **распи́сываться**) **1** to sign (one's name);
(**в** + *p.*) to sign (for); **р. в получе́нии
заказно́го письма́** to sign for a registered
letter **2** (infml, *регистри́ровать брак*)
to register one's marriage **3** (**в** + *p.*)
(fig., *призна́ться*) to acknowledge; **р. в
со́бственном неве́жестве** to acknowledge
one's own ignorance

распи́ск|а, и *f.* receipt; **р. в получе́нии** (+ *g.*)
receipt (for)

распи́сыва|ть, ю *impf. of* ▸ **расписа́ть**

распи́сыва|ться, юсь *impf. of*
▸ **расписа́ться**

распих|а́ть, а́ю *pf. (of* ▸ **распи́хивать**) (infml)
1 (*растолка́ть*) to push aside **2** (*рассова́ть*)
to shove; **р. я́блоки по карма́нам** to stuff
apples into one's pockets

распи́хива|ть, ю *impf. of* ▸ **распиха́ть**

распла́в|ить, лю, ишь *pf. (of*
▸ **расплавля́ть**) to melt, fuse

распла́в|иться, ится *pf. (of*
▸ **расплавля́ться**) to melt, fuse

расплавля́|ть, ю, ет *impf. of* ▸ **распла́вить**

расплавля́|ться, ется *impf. of*
▸ **распла́виться**

распла́|каться, чусь, чешься *pf.* to burst
into tears

распла́т|а, ы *f.* payment; (fig.) retribution;
час ~ы day of reckoning

распла|ти́ться, чу́сь, ~тишься *pf. (of*
▸ **распла́чиваться**) **1** (**с** + *i.*) to pay off; to
settle accounts (with), get even (with) (also
fig.); **р. с долга́ми** to pay off one's debts

2 (**за** + *i.*) (fig.) to pay (for)

распла́чива|ться, юсь *impf. of*
▸ **расплати́ться**

распле|ска́ть, щу́, ~щешь *pf. (of*
▸ **расплёскивать**) to spill

распле|ска́ться, ~щется *pf. (of*
▸ **расплёскиваться**) to spill

расплёскива|ть, ю *impf. of* ▸ **расплеска́ть**

расплёскива|ться, ется *impf. of*
▸ **расплеска́ться**

распле|сти́, ту́, тёшь, *past ~л, ~ла́ pf.*
(*of* ▸ **расплета́ть**) (*верёвку*) to untwine,
untwist; (*ко́су*) to undo

распле|сти́сь, тётся, *past ~лся, ~ла́сь pf.*
(*of* ▸ **расплета́ться**) (*о верёвке*) to untwine,
untwist; (*о косе́*) to come undone

расплета́|ть, ю, ет *impf. of* ▸ **расплести́**

расплета́|ться, ется *impf. of* ▸ **расплести́сь**

расплыва́|ться, ется *impf. of*
▸ **расплы́ться**

расплы́вчат|ый, ~, ~а *adj.* (*рису́нок*)
blurred; (*отве́т*) vague

расплы́|ться, вётся, *past ~лся, ~ла́сь*
pf. (of ▸ **расплыва́ться**) **1** (*о жи́дкости*)
to run; **черни́ла ~лись** the ink has run;
(*о фигу́рах*) to become blurred; (*о ма́ссе*)
to disperse; (*уплы́ть*) to swim off **2** (infml,
потолсте́ть) to spread; to run to fat; **р. в
улы́бку** to break into a smile

расплю́щива|ть, ю, ет *impf. of*
▸ **расплю́щить**

расплю́щива|ться, ется *impf. of*
▸ **расплю́щиться**

расплю́щ|ить, у, ишь *pf. (of*
▸ **расплю́щивать**) to flatten, crush

расплю́щ|иться, ится *pf. (of*
▸ **расплю́щиваться**) to become flat

распозна|ва́ть, ю́, ёшь *impf. of* ▸ **распозна́ть**

распозна́|ть, ю, ешь *pf. (of* ▸ **распознава́ть**)
to recognize, identify; **р. боле́знь** to diagnose
an illness

располага́|ть¹, ю *impf. (+ i.*) to have at one's
disposal, have available; **р. вре́менем** to have
time available

⚥ **располага́|ть², ю** *impf. of* ▸ **расположи́ть**

располага́|ться, юсь *impf. of*
▸ **расположи́ться**

располага́ющий 1 *pres. part. act. of*
▸ **располага́ть¹ 2** *pres. part. act. of*
▸ **располага́ть² and adj.** pleasant,
prepossessing

располз|а́ться, а́юсь *impf. of*
▸ **расползти́сь**

располз|ти́сь, у́сь, ёшься, *past ~ся,
~ла́сь pf. (of* ▸ **располза́ться**) **1** to
crawl (away) **2** (infml, *об оде́жде*) to come
unravelled; to tear, give at the seams

расположе́ни|е, я *nt.* **1** (*предме́тов*)
disposition, arrangement; **р. по кварти́рам**
(mil.) billeting **2** (*местоположе́ние*)
situation, location **3** (*симпа́тия*) favour
(BrE), favor (AmE); sympathies; **по́льзоваться**

р

чьим-н. ∼ем to enjoy sb's favour (BrE),
favor (AmE), to be liked by sb **4**: **р. (ду́ха)**
disposition, mood, humour (BrE), humor
(AmE); **быть в плохо́м ∼и ду́ха** to be in a
bad mood

располо́жен|ный, ∼, ∼а *p.p.p. of*
▶ **расположи́ть** *and pred. adj.* **1** (к + *d.*)
(*питаю́щий чу́вство симпа́тии*) well
disposed (to, towards) **2** (к + *d. or* + *inf.*)
(*склонный*) disposed (to), inclined (to);
in the mood (for); **я не о́чень ∼ сего́дня
рабо́тать** I don't feel much like working
today

располож|и́ть, у́, ∼ишь *pf. (of*
▶ **располага́ть²**) **1** (*размести́ть*) to
dispose, arrange, set out **2** (*вы́звать
симпа́тию в ком-н.*) to win over, gain; **р.
кого́-н. к себе́, в свою́ по́льзу** to gain sb's
favour (BrE), favor (AmE)

располож|и́ться, у́сь, ∼ишься *pf. (of*
▶ **располага́ться**) (*размести́ться*) to take
up position; to settle *or* compose oneself;
to make oneself comfortable

распор|о́ть, ю́, ∼ешь *pf. (of* ▶ **распа́рывать**)
to unstitch, unpick

распоря|ди́ться, жу́сь, ди́шься *pf. (of*
▶ **распоряжа́ться** 1) **1** (о + *p. or* + *inf.*) to
order; to see (that); **я ∼жу́сь, что́бы вам
возмести́ли расхо́ды** I will see that you
are reimbursed for the expenses **2** (+ *i.*)
to manage; to deal (with)

распоря́д|ок, ка *m.* order; routine;
пра́вила вну́треннего ∼ка (*в учрежде́нии,
на фа́брике и т. д.*) office, factory, *etc.*,
regulations

распоряжа́|ться, юсь *impf.* **1** *impf. of*
▶ **распоряди́ться 2** (*impf. only*) to give
orders, be in charge

распоряже́ни|е, я *nt.* **1** (*прика́з*) order;
instruction, direction; **до осо́бого ∼я** until
further notice **2**: **име́ть в своём ∼и** to have
at one's disposal

распоя́|саться, шусь, шешься *pf. (of*
▶ **распоя́сываться**) **1** to take off one's belt;
to ungird oneself **2** (fig., infml, pej., *стать
распу́щенным*) to throw aside all restraint;
to let oneself go

распоя́сыва|ться, юсь *impf. of*
▶ **распоя́саться**

распра́в|а, ы *f.* harsh punishment; reprisal;
крова́вая р. massacre

распра́в|ить, лю, ишь *pf. (of* ▶ **расправля́ть**)
1 (*вы́прямить*) to straighten; to smooth
out **2** (*вы́тянуть*) to spread, stretch; **р.
кры́лья** to spread one's wings (also fig.)

распра́в|иться¹, ится *pf. (of*
▶ **расправля́ться**) (*вы́прямиться*) to get
smoothed out

распра́в|иться², люсь, ишься *pf. (of*
▶ **расправля́ться**) (с + *i.*) (*произвести́
распра́ву*) to deal (with); **р. без суда́**
to take the law into one's own hands;
(*распоряди́ться*) to deal with, dispose of

расправля́|ть, ю *impf. of* ▶ **распра́вить**

расправля́|ться, юсь *impf. of*
▶ **распра́виться¹**, ▶ **распра́виться²**

распределе́ни|е, я *nt.* distribution;
allocation, assignment; **р. нало́гов**
assessment of taxes

распредели́тел|ь, я *m.* **1** (*устро́йство*)
regulator; **р. зажига́ния** distributor
2 (*учрежде́ние*) distribution centre (BrE),
center (AmE)

распредели́тельн|ый *adj.* distributive,
distributing; (∼ая доска́, *m.*) (tech.)
switchboard; **р. щит(о́к) (с предохрани́телями/
про́бками)** (elec.) fuse box; **р. вал** (tech.)
camshaft

распредел|и́ть, ю́, и́шь *pf. (of*
▶ **распределя́ть**) to distribute; to allocate,
assign; **р. своё вре́мя** to allocate one's time

распредел|я́ть, я́ю *impf. of* ▶ **распредели́ть**

распрода|ва́ть, ю́, ёшь *impf. of*
▶ **распрода́ть**

распрода́ж|а, и *f.* sale; clearance sale

распрода́|ть, м, шь, ст, ди́м, ди́те, ду́т,
past **распро́дал, ∼ла́, распро́дало** *pf. (of*
▶ **распродава́ть**) (*зе́млю, ве́щи*) to sell off;
(*биле́ты*) to sell out of; **биле́ты распро́даны**
all the tickets are sold

распро|сти́ться, щу́сь, сти́шься *pf.*
(с + *i.*) to say goodbye to; **р. с мечто́й** to bid
farewell to one's dream(s)

⚹ **распростране́ни|е, я** *nt.* (*слу́хов, зара́зы*)
spreading; (*зна́ния, иде́й*) dissemination;
(*владе́ний*) expansion; (*ору́жия*)
proliferation; (*това́ров*) distribution; **име́ть
большо́е р.** to be widely practised (BrE),
practiced (AmE)

⚹ **распространённый** *p.p.p. of*
▶ **распространи́ть** *and adj.* (*мне́ние*)
widespread, prevalent; (*расте́ния*) common

распространи́тел|ь, я *m.* (*слу́хов, зна́ний*)
spreader, disseminator; (*книг, газе́т*)
distributor

распространи́тель|ница, ницы *f. of*
▶ **распространи́тель**

распростран|и́ть, ю́, и́шь *pf. (of*
▶ **распространя́ть**) **1** (*слу́хи, зара́зу*)
to spread; (*зна́ния, информа́цию*) to
disseminate; (*това́ры, кни́ги*) to distribute;
(*письмо́, мемора́ндум*) to circulate;
(*владе́ния*) to increase **2** (*расши́рить*)
to extend; **р. де́йствие зако́на на всех** to
extend the application of a law to all
3 (*за́пах*) to give off

распростран|и́ться, и́тся *pf. (of*
▶ **распространя́ться**) (*ого́нь, слу́хи, за́пах*)
to spread; (*стать бо́льше*) to extend;
(*о зако́не*) to apply

распростран|я́ть, я́ю, я́ет *impf. of*
▶ **распространи́ть**

распростран|я́ться, я́ется *impf. of*
▶ **распространи́ться**

распроща́|ться, юсь *pf.* (с + *i.*)
= **распрости́ться**

распряга́|ть, ю *impf. of* ▶ **распря́чь**

р

распрям|и́ть, лю́, и́шь *pf.* (*of* ▶ **распрямля́ть**) (*проволоку*) to straighten, unbend; (*спину*) to straighten

распрям|и́ться, лю́сь, и́шься *pf.* (*of* ▶ **распрямля́ться**) to straighten oneself up

распрямля́|ть, ю *impf. of* ▶ **распрями́ть**

распрямля́|ться, юсь *impf. of* ▶ **распрями́ться**

распря́|чь, гу́, жёшь, гу́т, *past* ~г, ~гла́ *pf.* (*of* ▶ **распряга́ть**) to unharness

распуга́|ть, а́ю *pf.* (*of* ▶ **распу́гивать**) (infml) to scare away, frighten away

распу́гива|ть, ю *impf. of* ▶ **распуга́ть**

распуска́|ть, ю *impf. of* ▶ **распусти́ть**

распуска́|ться, юсь *impf. of* ▶ **распусти́ться**

распу|сти́ть, щу́, ~сти́шь *pf.* (*of* ▶ **распуска́ть**) **1** (*ученико́в*) to dismiss; (*расформирова́ть*) to disband; **р. парла́мент** to dissolve parliament **2** (*ре́мень, у́зел галсту́ка*) to loosen, let out; **р. во́лосы** to let one's hair down; **р. паруса́** to set sail **3** (fig., infml, *избалова́ть*) to allow to get out of hand; to spoil **4** (infml, *слу́хи*) to spread, put out

распу|сти́ться, щу́сь, ~сти́шься *pf.* (*of* ▶ **распуска́ться**) **1** (bot.) to open, come out **2** (fig., infml, *о де́тях*) to become undisciplined, get out of hand

распу́т|ать, аю *pf.* (*of* ▶ **распу́тывать**) **1** (*у́зел*) to untangle; to unravel **2** (*живо́тное*) to untie **3** (fig., *сло́жный вопро́с*) to disentangle; to puzzle out

распу́т|аться, аюсь *pf.* (*of* ▶ **распу́тываться**) **1** to get disentangled; to come undone **2** (fig., infml) to get disentangled, be cleared up

распу́т|ный, ~ен, ~на *adj.* dissolute, dissipated, debauched

распу́тыва|ть, ю *impf. of* ▶ **распу́тать**

распу́тыва|ться, юсь *impf. of* ▶ **распу́таться**

распух|а́ть, а́ю *impf. of* ▶ **распу́хнуть**

распу́х|нуть, ну, нешь, *past* ~, ~ла *pf.* (*of* ▶ **распуха́ть**) to swell up

распу́щенный *p.p.p. of* ▶ **распусти́ть** *and adj.* **1** (*недисциплини́рованный*) undisciplined; **р. ребёнок** spoiled child **2** (*безнра́вственный*) dissolute, dissipated

распыли́тел|ь, я *m.* spray(er)

распыл|и́ть, ю́, и́шь *pf.* (*of* ▶ **распыля́ть**) **1** (*кра́ску*) to spray **2** (fig.) to scatter; **р. си́лы** to scatter one's forces

распыл|и́ться, и́тся *pf.* (*of* ▶ **распыля́ться**) to disperse; to get scattered

распыл|я́ть, я́ю, ет *impf. of* ▶ **распыли́ть**

распыл|я́ться, ется *impf. of* ▶ **распыли́ться**

распя́ти|е, я *nt.* cross, crucifix

расса́д|а, ы (*no pl.*) *f.* seedlings

расса|ди́ть, жу́, ~дишь *pf.* (*of* ▶ **расса́живать**) **1** (*госте́й*) to seat, offer seats **2** (*посади́ть по́рознь*) to separate, seat separately **3** (*расте́ния*) to plant out

расса́жива|ть, ю *impf. of* ▶ **рассади́ть**

расса́жива|ться, юсь *impf. of* ▶ **рассе́сться**

расса́сыва|ться, ется *impf. of* ▶ **рассоса́ться**

рассве|сти́, тёт, *past* ~ло́ *pf.* (*of* ▶ **рассвета́ть**) to dawn; **уже́** ~ло́ it was already light

рассве́т, а *m.* dawn, daybreak; (fig., *нача́ло*) dawn

рассвета́|ть, ет *impf.* (*of* ▶ **рассвести́**): ~ет day is breaking

рассе́ива|ть, ю, ет *impf. of* ▶ **рассе́ять**

рассе́ива|ться, ется *impf. of* ▶ **рассе́яться**

рассека́|ть, ю *impf. of* ▶ **рассе́чь**

рассекре́|тить, чу, тишь *pf.* (*of* ▶ **рассекре́чивать**) to declassify

рассекре́чива|ть, ю *impf. of* ▶ **рассекре́тить**

расселе́ни|е, я *nt.* **1** settling (*in a new place*) **2** (*по́рознь*) separation; settling apart

рассел|и́ть, ю́, и́шь *pf.* (*of* ▶ **расселя́ть**) **1** to settle (*in a new place*) **2** (*по́рознь*) to separate; to settle apart

рассел|и́ться, ю́сь, и́шься *pf.* (*of* ▶ **расселя́ться**) **1** to settle (*in a new place*) **2** (*по́рознь*) to separate, settle separately

рассел|я́ть, я́ю *impf. of* ▶ **рассели́ть**

рассел|я́ться, я́юсь *impf. of* ▶ **рассели́ться**

рассер|ди́ть, жу́, ~дишь *pf.* of ▶ **серди́ть**

рассер|ди́ться, жу́сь, ~дишься *pf.* (*of* ▶ **серди́ться**) (на + *a.*) to get, become angry (with, at, about)

рас|се́сться, ся́дусь, ся́дешься, *past* ~се́лся *pf.* (*of* ▶ **расса́живаться**) **1** to take one's seat **2** (infml, *развали́ться*) to sprawl

рассе́|чь, ку́, чёшь, ку́т, *past* ~к, ~кла́ *pf.* (*of* ▶ **рассека́ть**) **1** (*разруби́ть*) to cut through; (*во́лну, не́бо*) to cleave **2** (*порани́ть*) to cut (badly); **я** ~к себе́ па́лец I have cut my finger (badly)

рассе́янно *adv.* absent-mindedly; (*смотре́ть*) vacantly

рассе́янност|ь, и *f.* (*невнима́тельность*) absent-mindedness

рассе́янный *p.p.p. of* ▶ **рассе́ять** *and adj.* **1** (*свет*) diffused **2** (*населе́ние*) scattered, dispersed **3** (*невнима́тельный*) absent-minded; **р. взгляд** vacant look

рассе́|ять, ю, ешь *pf.* (*of* ▶ **рассе́ивать**) **1** (*населе́ние, толпу́*) to scatter, disperse **2** (*сомне́ния*) to dispel

рассе́|яться, ется *pf.* (*of* ▶ **рассе́иваться**) to disperse; (*в беспоря́дке*) to scatter; (*о неприя́тном чу́встве*) to pass; **толпа́** ~я́лась the crowd dispersed; **тума́н** ~я́лся the fog cleared

расси|де́ться, жу́сь, ди́шься *pf.* (*of* ▶ **расси́живаться**) (infml) to sit for a long time; to sit around

расси́жива|ться, юсь *impf. of* ▶ **рассиде́ться**

✔ **расска́з, а** *m.* **1** story **2** (*очеви́дца*) account

✔ **расска|за́ть, жу́, ~жешь** *pf.* (*of* ▶ **расска́зывать**) **1** (+ *a. and d.*) to tell, relate (*sth to sb*) **2** (о + *p.*) to tell of; **р. о** де́тство to tell of one's childhood **3**: p., как всё произошло́ to tell how it all happened

расска́зчик, а *m.* storyteller, narrator

расска́зчи|ца, цы *f. of* ▸ расска́зчик

♂ расска́зыва|ть, ю *impf. of* ▸ рассказа́ть

рассла́б|ить, лю, ишь *pf. (of* ▸ расслабля́ть**)** **1** *(пояс, воротничо́к)* to loosen **2** *(мы́шцы)* to relax

рассла́б|иться, люсь, ишься *pf. (of* ▸ расслабля́ться**)** to relax

расслабля́|ть, ю *impf. of* ▸ рассла́бить

расслабля́|ться, юсь *impf. of* ▸ рассла́биться

рассла́ива|ться, ется *impf. of* ▸ расслои́ться

рассле́дование, я *nt.* investigation; (law) inquiry; провести́ p. (+ *g.*) to hold an inquiry (into)

рассле́д|овать, ую *impf. and pf.* to investigate

расслои́|ться, и́тся *pf. (of* ▸ рассла́иваться**)** to become stratified (also fig.); *(отслои́ться)* to flake off

расслы́ш|ать, у, ишь *pf.* to catch; я не ~ал вас I didn't catch what you said

♂ рассма́трива|ть, ю *impf.* **1** *impf. of* ▸ рассмотре́ть **2** *(impf. only) (счита́ть)* to regard (as), consider **3** *(impf. only) (внима́тельно смотре́ть)* to scrutinize, examine

рассмеш|и́ть, у́, и́шь *pf.* to make laugh

рассме|я́ться, ю́сь, ёшься *pf.* to burst out laughing

♂ рассмотре́ни|е, я *nt.* examination, scrutiny; *(обсужде́ние)* consideration; предста́вить на p. to submit for consideration; быть на ~и to be under consideration

рассмотр|е́ть, ю́, ~ишь *pf. (of* ▸ рассма́тривать 1) *(различи́ть)* to discern, make out; мы с трудо́м ~е́ли на́дпись на па́мятнике we had difficulty in making out the inscription on the monument **2** *(обсуди́ть)* to examine, consider; p. заявле́ние to consider an application

рассо|ва́ть, ую́, уёшь *pf. (of* ▸ рассо́вывать**)** (infml) to shove, stuff; p. свои́ ве́щи по чемода́нам to stuff one's things into suitcases

рассо́выва|ть, ю *impf. of* ▸ рассова́ть

рассо́л, а *m.* brine

рассо́р|иться, юсь, ишься *pf.* (с + *i.*) to fall out (with)

рассортир|ова́ть, у́ю *pf. (of* ▸ рассортиро́вывать**)** to sort out; *(по ассорти́менту)* to classify; *(по ка́честву)* to grade, sort

рассортиро́выва|ть, ю *impf. of* ▸ рассортирова́ть

рассос|а́ться, ётся *pf. (of* ▸ расса́сываться**)** *(об о́пухоли)* to go down; (infml, *о толпе́)* to disperse

рассо́х|нуться, нется, *past* ~ся, ~лась *pf.* *(of* ▸ рассыха́ться**)** to crack

расспра́шива|ть, ю *impf. of* ▸ расспроси́ть

расспро|си́ть, шу́, ~сишь *pf. (of* ▸ расспра́шивать**)** to question; (o + *p.*) *(узна́ть, спра́шивая)* to find out

рассро́чк|а, и *f.* instalment system; в ~у by, in instalments

расстава́ни|е, я *nt.* parting; при ~и on parting

расста|ва́ться, ю́сь, ёшься *impf. of* ▸ расста́ться

расста́в|ить, лю, ишь *pf. (of* ▸ расставля́ть**)** **1** *(размести́ть) (кни́ги, ме́бель)* to place, arrange; *(ка́дры, рабо́тников)* to place, position; p. часовы́х to post sentries; *(запя́тые)* to put, add **2** *(раздви́нуть)* to move apart; p. но́ги to stand with one's legs apart

расставля́|ть, ю *impf. of* ▸ расста́вить

расстано́вк|а, и *f.* placing, arrangement

расста́|ться, нусь, нешься *pf. (of* ▸ расстава́ться**)** (c + *i.*) **1** to part (with); я ~лся с ней I parted with her; ~немся друзья́ми let us part friends **2** *(с мечто́й, с мы́слью)* to give up

расстёгива|ть, ю *impf. of* ▸ расстегну́ть

расстёгива|ться, юсь *impf. of* ▸ расстегну́ться

расстег|ну́ть, ну́, нёшь *pf. (of* ▸ расстёгивать**)** to undo, unfasten

расстег|ну́ться, ну́сь, нёшься *pf. (of* ▸ расстёгиваться**)** **1** *(об оде́жде, о предме́те)* to come undone **2** *(о челове́ке)* to undo one's coat, shirt, *etc.*; to undo one's buttons

расстел|и́ть, ю́, ~ешь *pf. (of* ▸ расстила́ть**)** to spread (out), lay (out)

расстел|и́ться, ~ется *pf. (of* ▸ расстила́ться**)** to spread

расстила́|ть, ю, ет *impf. of* ▸ расстели́ть, ▸ разостла́ть

расстила́|ться, ется *impf. of* ▸ расстели́ться, ▸ разостла́ться

♂ расстоя́ни|е, я *nt.* distance; на ~и *(ви́деть)* at a distance; *(управля́ть)* from a distance; на бли́зком ~и (от + *g.*) at a short distance (from); они́ живу́т на ~и двух миль от ближа́йшего го́рода they live two miles from the nearest town

расстра́ива|ть, ю *impf. of* ▸ расстро́ить

расстра́ива|ться, юсь *impf. of* ▸ расстро́иться

расстре́л, а *m.* **1** *(казнь)* execution *(by firing squad)*; приговори́ть к ~у to sentence to be shot **2** *(обстре́л)* (+ *g.*) shooting at; firing at, on

расстре́лива|ть, ю *impf. of* ▸ расстреля́ть

расстрел|я́ть, я́ю *pf. (of* ▸ расстре́ливать**)** **1** *(уби́ть)* to shoot, execute by shooting **2** *(та́нки)* to shoot at; *(демонстра́цию)* to open fire on **3** *(снаря́ды)* to use up *(in firing)*

расстро́енный *p.p.p. of* ▶ **расстро́ить** *and*
adj. (*здоро́вье*) damaged, weak; (*не́рвы*)
shattered; (*челове́к, вид*) upset; (*роя́ль*) out
of tune

расстро́|ить, ю, ишь *pf.* (*of* ▶ **расстра́ивать**)
1 (*здоро́вье, хозя́йство*) to damage;
(*пла́ны*) to upset **2** (*челове́ка*) to upset

расстро́|иться, юсь, ишься *pf.* (*of*
▶ **расстра́иваться**) **1** (*о здоро́вье,
хозя́йстве*) to be damaged; (*о пла́нах*) to
fall through **2** (*из-за* + *g.*) (*о челове́ке*) to
be upset (over, about) **3** (*mus.*) to become
out of tune

расстро́йств|о, а *nt.* disorder; confusion;
р. желу́дка stomach upset; р. пищеваре́ния
indigestion; не́рвное р. nervous breakdown;
р. ре́чи speech defect; дела́ пришли́ в р.
things are in disarray

расступа́|ться, а́ется *impf. of*
▶ **расступи́ться**

расступ|и́ться, ~ится *pf.* (*of*
▶ **расступа́ться**) to part, make way; толпа́
~и́лась the crowd parted

рассуди́тел|ьный, ~ен, ~ьна *adj.*
reasonable; sensible

рассу|ди́ть, жу́, ~дишь *pf.* **1** (*люде́й*)
to judge (between), arbitrate (between);
~ди́те нас be our judge; settle our dispute
2 (*реши́ть*) to decide

рассу́д|ок, ка *m.* **1** (*спосо́бность*) reason;
intellect; лиши́ться ~ка to lose one's reason
2 (*здра́вый смысл*) good sense

рассужда́|ть, ю *impf.* **1** (*мы́слить*) to
reason **2** (*о* + *p. or* на + *a.*) (*обсужда́ть*) to
debate; to argue (about); р. на каку́ю-н. те́му
to discuss a topic

рассужде́ни|е, я *nt.* **1** (*проце́сс*) reasoning
2 (*usu. in pl.*) (*обсужде́ние*) debate;
argument; без ~й without argument

рассчи́т|анный *p.p.p. of* ▶ **рассчита́ть** *and*
adj. **1** calculated, deliberate **2** (на + *a.*)
intended (for), designed (for); кни́га, ~анная
на широ́кого чита́теля a book intended for
the general public

рассчита́|ть, а́ю *pf.* (*of* ▶ **рассчи́тывать** 1)
(*сто́имость, расхо́ды*) to calculate; он не
~а́л свои́х сил he miscalculated his strength

рассчита́|ться, а́юсь *pf.* (*of*
▶ **рассчи́тываться**) (с + *i.*) to settle accounts
(with); (fig.) to settle scores (with)

⚓ **рассчи́тыва|ть, ю** *impf.* **1** *impf. of*
▶ **рассчита́ть 2** (*impf. only*) (на + *a.*)
(*предполага́ть*) to count (on, upon), reckon
(on, upon); (+ *inf.*) to expect (to), hope (to);
мы ~ли зако́нчить рабо́ту в э́том году́ we
were hoping to finish the work this year
3 (*impf. only*) (на + *a.*) (*полага́ться*) to
count (on, upon), rely (on, upon), depend
(upon)

рассчи́тыва|ться, юсь *impf. of*
▶ **рассчита́ться**

рассыла́|ть, ю *impf. of* ▶ **разосла́ть**

рассы́лк|а, и *f.* distribution, dispatch;
(*по электро́нной по́чте*) mailing

рассы́п|ать, лю, лешь *pf.* (*of* ▶ **рассыпа́ть**)
(*нево́льно*) to spill; (*разбро́сать*) to strew,
scatter

рассыпа́|ть, а́ю *impf. of* ▶ **рассы́пать**

рассы́п|аться, люсь, лешься *pf.* (*of*
▶ **рассыпа́ться**) **1** (*о муке́*) to spill; моне́ты
~а́лись по́ полу the coins spilt onto the
floor; (*о толпе́*) to scatter; (*о дома́х*) to be
scattered **2** (*о стене́, о хле́бе*) to crumble;
to disintegrate (also fig.) **3** (infml) (в + *p.*)
to be profuse (in); р. в похвала́х (+ *d.*) to
shower praises (upon)

рассыпа́|ться, а́юсь *impf. of* ▶ **рассы́паться**

рассыха́|ться, ется *impf. of* ▶ **рассо́хнуться**

растáлкива|ть, ю *impf. of* ▶ **растолка́ть**

растáплива|ть, ю *impf. of* ▶ **растопи́ть¹**

растáптыва|ть, ю *impf. of* ▶ **растопта́ть**

растаск|а́ть, а́ю *pf.* (*of* ▶ **растáскивать**)
(infml) **1** (*унести́ по частя́м*) to take away,
remove (*little by little, bit by bit*) **2** (*укра́сть*)
to pilfer, filch (infml)

растáскива|ть, ю *impf. of* ▶ **растаска́ть**,
▶ **растащи́ть**

растащ|и́ть, у́, ~ишь *pf.* (*of* ▶ **растáскивать**)
1 (*деру́щихся*) to part, separate, drag apart
2 = **растаска́ть**

растá|ять, ю, ешь *pf. of* ▶ **тáять**

раство́р, а *m.* **1** (chem.) solution **2** (tech.,
строи́тельный) mortar

раствори́м|ый, ~, ~а *adj.* soluble; р. ко́фе
instant coffee

раствори́тел|ь, я *m.* solvent

раствор|и́ть¹, ю́, ~ишь *pf.* (*of*
▶ **растворя́ть**) (*окно́*) to open

раствор|и́ть², ю́, и́шь *pf.* (*of* ▶ **растворя́ть**)
(*соль*) to dissolve

раствор|и́ться¹, ~ится *pf.* (*of*
▶ **растворя́ться**) (*об окне́*) to open

раствор|и́ться², и́тся *pf.* (*of* ▶ **растворя́ться**)
(*о со́ли*) to dissolve; (fig., *исче́знуть*) to
vanish

раствор|я́ть, я́ю, я́ет *impf. of* ▶ **раствори́ть¹**,
▶ **раствори́ть²**

раствор|я́ться, я́ется *impf. of*
▶ **раствори́ться¹**, ▶ **раствори́ться²**

растека́|ться, юсь *impf. of* ▶ **растéчься**

⚓ **растéни|е, я** *nt.* plant

растер|е́ть, разотру́, разотрёшь, *past*
растёр, растёрла *pf.* (*of* ▶ **растира́ть**)
1 to grind; р. в порошо́к to grind to powder
2 (по + *d.*) (*мазь*) to rub (over), spread
(over) **3** (*те́ло*) to rub, massage

растер|е́ться, разотру́сь, разотрёшься,
past растёрся, растёрлась *pf.* (*of*
▶ **растира́ться**) **1** (*о зёрнах*) to become
powdered, turn into powder **2** (+ *i.*)
(*обтере́ть себя́*) to rub oneself briskly
(with)

растерз|а́ть, а́ю *pf.* (*of* ▶ **растéрзывать**)
1 (*умертви́ть*) to tear to pieces **2** (fig., poet.,
изму́чить) to lacerate; to harrow

растéрзыва|ть, ю *impf. of* ▶ **растерза́ть**

растéрянност|ь, и *f.* confusion, bewilderment

р

расте́рянный *p.p.p. of* ▸ **растеря́ть** *and adj.* confused, bewildered

растер|я́ть, я́ю *pf.* to lose (*little by little*)

растер|я́ться, я́юсь *pf.* (*утратить самообладание*) to lose one's head, nerve; **он не ~я́лся пе́ред лицо́м опа́сности** he kept his head in the face of danger

расте́|чься, чётся, ку́тся, *past* **~кся, ~кла́сь** *pf.* (*of* ▸ **растека́ться**) (*о воде*) to spill; (*о краске*) to run

ꝏ **раст|и́, у́, ёшь,** *past* **рос, росла́** *impf.* (*of* ▸ **вы́расти**) **1** (biol.) to grow; (*о детях*) to grow up; **он рос на Украи́не** he grew up in Ukraine **2** (*увеличиваться*) to grow, increase **3** (*совершенствоваться*) to advance, develop

растира́|ть, ю *impf. of* ▸ **растере́ть**

растира́|ться, юсь *impf. of* ▸ **растере́ться**

расти́тельност|ь, и *f.* **1** (*растения*) vegetation **2** (*волосы*) hair (*on face or body*)

расти́тельн|ый *adj.* vegetable; **~ое ма́сло** vegetable oil

ра|сти́ть, щу́, сти́шь *impf.* **1** (*детей*) to raise, bring up; (*кадры*) to nurture **2** (*цветы*) to grow, cultivate; (*животных*) to rear; **р. бо́роду** to grow a beard

растлева́|ть, ю *impf. of* ▸ **растли́ть**

растл|и́ть, ю́, и́шь *pf.* (*of* ▸ **растлева́ть**) **1** (*малолетних*) to sexually abuse (*minors*) **2** (*морально*) to corrupt, deprave

растолка́|ть, ю *pf.* (*of* ▸ **раста́лкивать**) (infml) **1** (*толпу*) to push asunder, apart **2** (*спящего*) to shake (*in order to awaken*)

растолсте́|ть, ю *pf.* to put on weight

растоп|и́ть[1]**, лю́, ~ишь** *pf.* (*of* ▸ **раста́пливать**) (*печь*) to light

растоп|и́ть[2]**, лю́, ~ишь** *pf.* (*of* ▸ **раста́пливать**) (*сало, лёд*) to melt

растоп|та́ть, чу́, ~чешь *pf.* (*of* ▸ **раста́птывать**) to trample, stamp (on), crush (*also fig.*)

растопы́рива|ть, ю *impf. of* ▸ **растопы́рить**

растопы́р|ить, ю, ишь *pf.* (*of* ▸ **растопы́ривать**) (infml) to spread wide, open wide

расторга́|ть, а́ю *impf. of* ▸ **расто́ргнуть**

расто́рг|нуть, ну, нешь, *past* **~, ~ла** *pf.* (*of* ▸ **расторга́ть**) (*контракт, договор*) to dissolve, annul; **р. брак** to dissolve a marriage

расточи́тельн|ый, ~ен, ~ьна *adj.* extravagant, wasteful

растра́т|а, ы *f.* **1** (*денег, времени*) waste, squandering **2** (*незаконная*) embezzlement

растра́|тить, чу, тишь *pf.* (*of* ▸ **растра́чивать**) **1** to waste, squander **2** (*незаконно*) to embezzle

растра́чива|ть, ю *impf. of* ▸ **растра́тить**

растрёпанный *p.p.p. of* ▸ **растрепа́ть** *and adj.* (*волосы*) dishevelled; (*книга*) tattered

растреп|а́ть, лю́, ~лешь *pf.* **1** (*волосы*) to mess up, tousle **2** (*книгу*) to reduce to tatters, tear

растреп|а́ться, ~лется *pf.* **1** (*о волосах*) to get messed up, get dishevelled **2** (*о книге*) to get tattered, get torn

растро́га|ть, ю *pf.* to move, touch; **р. кого́-н. до слёз** to move sb to tears

растя́гива|ть, ю *impf. of* ▸ **растяну́ть**

растя́гива|ться, юсь *impf. of* ▸ **растяну́ться**

растяже́ни|е, я *nt.* (med.) strain, sprain

растя́|нуть, ну́, ~нешь *pf.* (*of* ▸ **растя́гивать**) **1** (*ковёр, скатерть*) to stretch, spread (out); (*лишить упругости*) to stretch; (*платежи*) to spread **2** (med.) to strain, sprain **3** (*сделать слишком длинным*) to stretch out; (fig.) to protract, drag out

растя́|нуться, ну́сь, ~нешься *pf.* (*of* ▸ **растя́гиваться**) **1** to stretch (out); (*стать менее упругим*) to be stretched **2** (*стать слишком длинным*) to stretch too far; (fig., *работа, собрание*) to drag on; **обсужде́ние его́ докла́да ~ну́лось на полтора́ часа́** discussion of his lecture dragged on for an hour and a half

растя́п|а, ы *c.g.* (infml) bungler

расхва́лива|ть, ю *impf. of* ▸ **расхвали́ть**

расхвал|и́ть, ю́, ~ишь *pf.* (*of* ▸ **расхва́ливать**) to lavish, shower praise (on, upon)

расхи́|тить, щу, тишь *pf.* (*of* ▸ **расхища́ть**) to embezzle, misappropriate

расхища́|ть, ю *impf. of* ▸ **расхи́тить**

ꝏ **расхо́д, а** *m.* **1** (*затрата*) expense; (*in pl.*) expenses, outlay, cost; **доро́жные ~ы** travel expenses; **накладны́е ~ы** overheads; **де́ньги на карма́нные ~ы** pocket money **2** (*энергии*) consumption; **р. горю́чего** fuel consumption **3** (*в бухгалтерии*) expenditure, outlay; **прихо́д и р.** income and expenditure

расхо|ди́ться, жу́сь, ~дишься *impf. of* ▸ **разойти́сь**

расхо́д|овать, ую *impf.* (*of* ▸ **израсхо́довать**) **1** (*деньги, время*) to spend, expend **2** (*ресурсы*) to use (up), consume; **маши́на ~ует мно́го бензи́на** the car uses a lot of petrol (BrE), gas (AmE)

расхожде́ни|е, я *nt.* (*лучей, дорог*) divergence; (*идейное*) difference; **р. во мне́ниях** difference of opinion; (*в тексте*) discrepancy

расхо|те́ть, чу́, ~чешь, ти́м, ти́те, тя́т *pf.* (+ *g. or a. or inf.*) (infml) to no longer want; **я ~те́л спать** I am no longer sleepy

расхо|те́ться, ~чется *pf.* (*impers.* + *d.*) (infml) to no longer want; **мне ~те́лось есть** I no longer want to eat

расхохо|та́ться, чу́сь, ~чешься *pf.* to burst out laughing

расцве|сти́, ту́, тёшь, *past* **~л, ~ла́** *pf.* (*of* ▸ **расцвета́ть**) (*цветок, девушка*) to blossom; (*наука, искусство*) to flourish; (*повеселеть*) to become radiant

р

расцве́т, а *m.* blossoming; (*нау́ки*) flourishing; flowering; в ~е сил in one's prime

расцвета́|ть, ю *impf. of* ▶ расцвести́

расцве́тк|а, и *f.* colour (BrE), color (AmE) scheme, colours (BrE), colors (AmE)

расцел|ова́ть, у́ю *pf.* to smother with kisses

расце́нива|ть, ю *impf. of* ▶ расцени́ть

расце́нива|ться, ется *impf.* to be regarded

расцен|и́ть, ю́, ~ишь *pf.* (*of* ▶ расце́нивать) (*посту́пок, слова́*) to regard; его́ речь ~и́ли как провока́цию his speech was regarded as provocation

расце́нк|а, и *f.* (*usu. in pl.*) (*цена́*) tariff, rates

расчер|ти́ть, чу́, ~тишь *pf.* (*of* ▶ расче́рчивать) to rule, line

расче́рчива|ть, ю *impf. of* ▶ расчерти́ть

расче|са́ть, шу́, ~шешь *pf.* (*of* ▶ расчёсывать) **1** (*во́лосы*) to comb; (*лён, шерсть*) to card **2** (*ру́ку*) to scratch

расче|са́ться, шу́сь, ~шешься *pf.* (*of* ▶ расчёсываться) (*infml, расчеса́ть во́лосы*) to comb one's hair

расчёск|а, и *f.* comb

расчёсыва|ть, ю *impf. of* ▶ расчеса́ть

расчёсыва|ться, юсь *impf. of* ▶ расчеса́ться

✍ **расчёт¹**, а *m.* **1** (*сто́имости*) calculation; (*сме́та*) statement; (*приблизи́тельный*) estimate, reckoning; из ~а on the basis (of), at a rate (of); приня́ть в р. to take into account, consideration; по мои́м ~ам by my reckoning; в ~е на (+ *a.*) hoping for, reckoning on **2** (*c + i.*) settling (with); (*опла́та*) payment; нали́чный р. cash payment; быть в ~е (*c + i.*) to be quits (with), be even (with); производи́ть ~ы (*c + i.*) to settle accounts (with)

расчёт², а *m.* (mil.) crew; ору́дийный р. gun crew

расчётлив|ый, ~, ~а *adj.* thrifty

расчётн|ый *adj.* **1** calculation; ~ая табли́ца calculation table **2** pay, accounts; р. день pay day **3** (tech.) rated; ~ая мо́щность rated capacity

расчи́|стить, щу, стишь *pf.* (*of* ▶ расчища́ть) to clear; р. путь, доро́гу (fig.) to pave the way

расчи́|ститься, стится *pf.* (*of* ▶ расчища́ться) (*о не́бе*) to clear

расчища́|ть, ю, ет *impf. of* ▶ расчи́стить

расчища́|ться, ется *impf. of* ▶ расчи́ститься

расчлен|и́ть, ю́, и́шь *pf.* (*of* ▶ расчленя́ть) to break up, divide

расчленя́|ть, я́ю *impf. of* ▶ расчлени́ть

расшат|а́ть, а́ю *pf.* (*of* ▶ расша́тывать) **1** to shake loose; to make rickety **2** (fig.) (*дисципли́ну*) to undermine, impair; (*хозя́йство*) to cripple; (*не́рвы, здоро́вье*) to damage

расшат|а́ться, а́юсь *pf.* (*of* ▶ расша́тываться) **1** to get loose; to become rickety **2** (fig.) (*дисципли́на*) to be undermined; (*хозя́йство*) to be crippled; (*не́рвы, здоро́вье*) to go to pieces, crack up

расша́тыва|ть, ю *impf. of* ▶ расшата́ть

расша́тыва|ться, юсь *impf. of* ▶ расшата́ться

расшеве́лива|ть, ю *impf. of* ▶ расшевели́ть

расшевел|и́ть, ю́, и́шь *pf.* (*of* ▶ расшеве́ливать) to stir, shake; (fig., *стимули́ровать*) to stir, rouse

расшиб|а́ть, а́ю *impf. of* ▶ расшиби́ть

расшиб|а́ться, а́юсь *impf. of* ▶ расшиби́ться

расшиб|и́ть, у́, ёшь, *past* ~, ~ла *pf.* (*of* ▶ расшиба́ть) **1** (*уши́бить*) to hurt; to knock, stub **2** (infml, *разби́ть*) to break up, smash to pieces

расшиб|и́ться, у́сь, ёшься, *past* ~ся, ~лась *pf.* (*of* ▶ расшиба́ться) to hurt oneself, knock oneself

расшива́|ть, ю *impf. of* ▶ расши́ть

✍ **расшире́ни|е**, я *nt.* **1** (*отве́рстия*) widening; (*кругозо́ра, зна́ний*) broadening **2** (*произво́дства*) expansion **3** (med.) dilation, dilatation **4** (comput., *фа́йла*) extension; пла́та ~я expansion card (*graphics card, sound card, etc.*)

расши́ренный *p.p.p. of* ▶ расши́рить *and adj.* (*отве́рстие*) widened; (*програ́мма*) broadened, more extensive; (*заседа́ние*) expanded; (*зрачки́*) dilated

расши́р|ить, ю, ишь *pf.* (*of* ▶ расширя́ть) (*отве́рстие*) to expand; (*кругозо́р, зна́ния*) to broaden; (*сфе́ру влия́ния*) to extend

расши́р|иться, ится *pf.* (*of* ▶ расширя́ться) (*об отве́рстии*) to widen; (*о произво́дстве, о зна́ниях*) to expand; (*о кругозо́ре*) to broaden; (*о зрачка́х*) to dilate

расширя́|ть, я́ю, я́ет *impf. of* ▶ расши́рить

расширя́|ться, я́ется *impf. of* ▶ расши́риться

расши́ть, разошью́, разошьёшь *pf.* (*of* ▶ расшива́ть) to embroider

расшифр|ова́ть, у́ю *pf.* (*of* ▶ расшифро́вывать) to decipher, decode; (fig., *угада́ть смысл*) to figure out

расшифро́вк|а, и *f.* deciphering, decoding; (fig.) interpretation

расшифро́выва|ть, ю *impf. of* ▶ расшифрова́ть

расшнур|ова́ть, у́ю *pf.* (*of* ▶ расшнуро́вывать) to unlace

расшнур|ова́ться, у́юсь *pf.* (*of* ▶ расшнуро́вываться) to come unlaced, come undone

расшнуро́выва|ть, ю *impf. of* ▶ расшнурова́ть

расшнуро́выва|ться, юсь *impf. of* ▶ расшнурова́ться

расшум|е́ться, лю́сь, и́шься *pf.* (infml) to get noisy, kick up a din

расще́лин|а, ы *f.* cleft, crevice

ратифика́ци|я, и *f.* ratification

ратифици́р|овать, ую *impf. and pf.* to ratify

ра́унд, а *m.* (sport) round; (*переговоров*) series, round

ра́ут, а *m.* reception

рафини́рован|ный, ~, ~а *adj.* refined

рацио́н, а *m.* ration

рационализа́ци|я, и *f.* rationalization, improvement

рационализи́р|овать, ую *impf. and pf.* to rationalize, improve

рационали́зм, а *m.* (phil.) rationalism

рациона́льно *adv.* (*мыслить, поступать*) rationally; (*вести хозяйство*) efficiently; **р. испо́льзовать** to make efficient use (of)

рациона́л|ьный, ~ен, ~ьна *adj.* (*поступок*) rational; (*использование средств*) efficient; **~ьное пита́ние** sound nutrition

ра́ци|я, и *f.* (*на корабле, в здании*) radio set; (*небольшая переносная*) walkie-talkie

рван|у́ть, у́, ёшь *pf.* **1** (*дёрнуть резко*) to jerk; to tug (at); **р. кого́-н. за рука́в** to tug sb by the sleeve **2** (*машина*) to start (with a jerk) **3** (infml, помчаться) to dash off, shoot off **4** (infml, взорвать) to explode, blow up; **в сосе́днем до́ме ~уло** there was an explosion in the next house

рван|у́ться, у́сь, ёшься *pf.* to rush, dash

рва́н|ый *adj.* torn; lacerated; **~ые башмаки́** broken shoes; **~ая ра́на** (med.) laceration

рвать¹, рву, рвёшь, *past* **рвал, рвала́, рва́ло** *impf.* **1** (*одежду*) to tear (up); to rip; **р. на ча́сти** (*предмет*) to tear to pieces; (*человека*) to overburden; **р. письмо́** to tear up a letter; **р. на себе́ во́лосы** to tear one's hair **2** (*выдёргивать*) to pull out, tear out; **р. зу́бы** to pull out teeth; **р. с ко́рнем** to uproot **3** (*брать*) to pick, pluck; **р. цветы́** to pick flowers

рвать², рвёт, *past* **рва́ло́** *impf.* (*of* ▶ **вы́рвать²**) (*impers.*) (infml) to vomit, throw up, be sick

рва́|ться¹, рвётся, *past* **~лся, ~ла́сь, ~́лось** *impf.* **1** (*об одежде*) to break; to tear; (*об отношениях*) to break up, be severed **2** (*взрываться*) to burst, explode

рва́|ться², рвусь, рвёшься, *past* **~лся, ~ла́сь, ~́лось** *impf.* (*стремиться*) to strain (to, at); to be bursting (to); **р. в бой/дра́ку** to be spoiling for a fight; **р. к вла́сти** to be hungry for power

рве́ни|е, я *nt.* zeal, enthusiasm

рво́т|а, ы *f.* **1** (*действие*) vomiting **2** (*масса*) vomit

ре *nt. indecl.* (mus.) D

реабилита́ция, и *f.* rehabilitation

реабилити́р|овать, ую *impf. and pf.* to rehabilitate

реабилити́р|оваться, уюсь *impf. and pf.* **1** to vindicate oneself **2** *pass. of* ▶ **реабилити́ровать**

реаги́р|овать, ую *impf.* (**на** + *a.*) **1** (*pf.* **от~,** **с~**) (*на свет*) to react (to) **2** (*pf.* **от~, про~,**

⚔ key word

с~) (*на критику*) to react (to), respond (to)

реакти́вный *adj.* **1** (chem., phys.) reactive **2** (tech., aeron.) jet(-propelled); **р. дви́гатель** jet engine; **р. самолёт** jet-propelled aircraft, jet

реа́ктор, а *m.* (tech.) reactor

реакцио́н|ный, ~ен, ~на *adj.* (pol.) reactionary

⚔ **реа́кци|я, и** *f.* reaction

⚔ **реализа́ци|я, и** *f.* (*планов*) realization; (*договора*) implementation; (*товаров*) sale, disposal

реали́зм, а *m.* realism

⚔ **реализ|ова́ть, у́ю** *impf. and pf.* (*pf. also* ▶ **реализо́вывать**) (*планы*) to realize; (*договор*) to implement; (*товар*) to sell, dispose of; **р. це́нные бума́ги** to realize securities

реализо́ва|ть, ю *impf. of* ▶ **реализова́ть**

реали́ст, а *m.* realist

реалисти́ческий *adj.* **1** (*искусство*) realist **2** (*взгляд*) realistic

реалисти́ч|ный, ~ен, ~на *adj.* = **реалисти́ческий 2**

⚔ **реа́льност|ь, и** *f.* **1** (*действительность*) reality **2** (*осуществимость*) practicability, feasibility

⚔ **реа́л|ьный, ~ен, ~ьна** *adj.* **1** (*действительный*) real; **~ьная действи́тельность** reality **2** (*осуществимый*) practicable, feasible, workable; **р. план** workable plan **3** (*практический*) realistic; practical

реанимацио́нн|ый *adj.*: **~ое отделе́ние** intensive care unit

реанима́ци|я, и *f.* resuscitation; **отделе́ние ~и** intensive care unit

реаними́р|овать, ую *impf. and pf.* **1** (*человека*) to resuscitate **2** (fig.) to revive

⚔ **ребён|ок, ка,** *pl.* **ребя́та, ребя́т** *and* **де́ти, дете́й** *m.* child; (*младенец*) infant; **грудно́й р.** baby

ребре́ндинг, а *m.* (comm.) rebranding

ребр|о́, а́, *pl.* **~а, рёбер, ~ам** *nt.* **1** (anat., tech.) rib **2** (*край*) edge; **поста́вить ~о́м** to place edgeways, place on its side

⚔ **ребя́т|а, ребя́т** *m. pl.* **1** *pl. of* ▶ **ребёнок**; children **2** (infml, *парни*) boys, lads

рёв, а *m.* **1** roar; bellow; howl; **р. ве́тра** the howling of the wind **2** (infml, *плач*) howl (*of a child, etc.*); **подня́ть р.** to raise a howl

рева́нш, а *m.* revenge; (sport) return match

реве́н|ь, я́ *m.* rhubarb

reveráнс, а *m.* curtsy

рев|е́ть, у́, ёшь *impf.* **1** to roar; to bellow; howl **2** (infml, *плакать*) to howl

реви́зи|я, и *f.* **1** (*учреждения*) inspection; (*бухгалтерская*) audit **2** (*взглядов*) revision

ревизо́р, а *m.* inspector; (*финансов*) auditor

ревмати́зм, а *m.* rheumatism

ревни́в|ый, ~, ~а *adj.* jealous

ревн|ова́ть, у́ю *impf.* to be jealous; **р. кого́-н. (к** + *d.*) to be jealous because of sb's

р

attachment (to), begrudge sb's attachment (to); она́ ∼ова́ла му́жа к его́ рабо́те she was jealous of her husband's work

ре́вност|ный, ∼ен, ∼на *adj.* zealous, fervent

ре́вност|ь, и *f.* jealousy

револьве́р, а *m.* revolver

революционе́р, а *m.* revolutionary

революционе́р|ка, ки *f. of* ▸ революционе́р

революцио́н|ный, ∼ен, ∼на *adj.* revolutionary

✑ **револю́ци|я, и** *f.* (pol., *also* fig.) revolution

рега́т|а, ы *f.* regatta

ре́гби *nt. indecl.* rugby (football), rugger

регби́ст, а *m.* rugby player

ре́гги *m. indecl.* reggae

ре́гент, а *m.* **1** regent **2** (mus.) conductor of church choir, precentor

✑ **регио́н, а** *m.* region, area

✑ **региона́льный** *adj.* regional

реги́стр, а *m.* register

регистра́тор, а *m.* registrar; (*в поликлинике, гостинице*) receptionist

регистрату́р|а, ы *f.* records office, registry; (*в поликлинике*) reception desk

✑ **регистра́ци|я, и** *f.* registration; (*в гостинице*) reception desk

регистри́р|овать, ую *impf. and pf.* (*pf. also* за∼) to register, record

регистри́р|оваться, уюсь *impf. and pf.* (*pf. also* за∼) **1** to register (oneself) **2** (*пожениться*) to register one's marriage **3** *pass. of* ▸ регистри́ровать

регла́мент, а *m.* **1** (*правила*) regulations; standing orders **2** (*время для речи*) time limit

регули́ровани|е, я *nt.* (*движения, цен*) regulation, control

регули́р|овать, ую *impf.* **1** (*движение, цены*) to regulate; to control **2** (*pf.* у∼) (*отношения*) to normalize **3** (*pf.* от∼) to adjust; **р. мото́р** to tune an engine

регуля́р|ный, ∼ен, ∼на *adj.* regular; ∼ные войска́ regular troops

регуля́тор, а *m.* (tech.) regulator; (*in pl.*) controls (*on TV, etc.*)

редакти́р|овать, ую *impf.* **1** (*pf.* от∼) (*рукопись*) to edit **2** (*impf. only*) (*журнал*) to be editor of; to edit

реда́ктор, а *m.* **1** editor; **гла́вный р.** editor-in-chief, chief editor **2** (comput.): **те́кстовый р.** (*программа*) word processor

редакцио́нн|ый *adj.* editorial, editing; ∼ая колле́гия editorial board; ∼ая статья́ editorial

реда́кци|я, и *f.* **1** (*работники*) editorial staff **2** (*учреждение*) editorial office **3** (*действие*) editing; **под** ∼ей (+ *g.*) edited (by) **4** (*формулировка*) wording **5** (*вариант текста*) edition

реде́|ть, ю *impf.* (*of* ▸ пореде́ть) to thin, thin out; ∼ющие во́лосы thinning hair

реди́с, а (*no pl.*) *m.* (collect.) radish(es)

реди́ск|а, и *f.* (single) radish; (collect.) radishes

✑ **ре́д|кий**, ∼ок, ∼ка́, ∼ко *adj.* **1** (*негустой*) thin, sparse; ∼кие во́лосы thin hair; **р. лес** sparse wood **2** (*необычный*) rare; uncommon, unusual; ∼кая кни́га rare book; ∼кая красота́ rare beauty **3** (*гость, письмо*) occasional

ре́дко *adv.* **1** (*не густо*) sparsely; far apart **2** (*не часто*) rarely, seldom

редколле́ги|я, и *f.* editorial board

ре́дкост|ь, и *f.* **1** (*населения*) sparseness **2** (*книги*) rarity; **на р.** uncommonly; **на р. проница́тельный челове́к** a person of rare discernment **3** (*редкая вещь*) rarity

рее́стр, а *m.* list, roll, register

ре́же *comp. of* ▸ ре́дкий, ▸ ре́дко

✑ **режи́м, а** *m.* **1** (pol.) regime **2** (*распорядок*) routine; procedure; (med.) regimen; (*станка*) mode of operation; **р. пита́ния** diet; **р. рабо́ты** mode of operation **3** (*условия*) conditions; (tech.) operating conditions

✑ **режиссёр, а** *m.* (*в театре*) producer; (*в кино*) director

режиссёрский *adj. of* ▸ режиссёр

ре́|зать, жу, жешь *impf.* **1** (*impf. only*) to cut; э́ти но́жницы бо́льше не ∼жут these scissors do not cut any longer **2** (*impf. only*) (*хлеб*) to cut; to slice **3** (*pf.* за∼) (*убивать*) to kill; to slaughter **4** (*impf. only*) (**по** + *d.*) (*делать изображения*) to carve (on), engrave (on) **5** (*impf. only*) (*причинять боль*) to cut (into); to cause sharp pain; **реме́нь** ∼зал ему́ плечо́ the strap was cutting into his shoulder; **р. слух** to grate upon the ears

резв|и́ться, лю́сь, и́шься *impf.* to gambol, romp

ре́зв|ый, ∼, ∼а́, ∼о *adj.* **1** playful, frisky **2** (*лошадь*) fast

резе́рв, а *m.* (mil., etc.) reserve(s)

резерва́ци|я, и *f.* reservation

резерви́р|овать, ую *impf. and pf.* (*pf. also* за∼) to reserve, book

резе́рвн|ый *adj.* (mil. and fin.) reserve; (comput.) backup; ∼ая ко́пия backup copy

резервуа́р, а *m.* reservoir, tank

резиде́нци|я, и *f.* residence

рези́н|а, ы *f.* (India) rubber

рези́нк|а, и *f.* **1** (*ластик*) rubber (BrE), eraser (AmE) **2** (*тесёмка*) (piece of) elastic **3** (*жвачка*) chewing gum

рези́нов|ый *adj.* rubber; ∼ая тесьма́, ле́нта rubber band, elastic band

ре́з|кий, ∼ок, ∼ка́, ∼ко *adj.* (*ветер, слова, увеличение, движение, черты лица*) sharp; (*голос, свет, критика*) harsh; (*изменение, манера*) abrupt; **р. за́пах** strong smell

резно́й *adj.* carved

резн|я́, и́ *f.* slaughter

резолю́ци|я, и *f.* **1** (*решение*) resolution; **вы́нести, приня́ть** ∼ю to pass, carry a resolution **2** (*на докуме́нте*) instructions; наложи́ть ~ю to append instructions

резона́нс, а *m.* **1** (*phys.*) resonance **2** (*fig.*) response

резонёрств|овать, ую *impf.* to moralize

резо́н|ный, ~ен, ~на *adj.* reasonable

⚡ **результа́т**, а *m.* result; outcome; дать ~ы to yield results; в ~е (*в ито́ге*) in the end; (+ *g.*) (*всле́дствие*) as a result (of)

ре́зче *comp. of* ▶ ре́зкий

ре́зчик, а *m.* engraver, carver

резьб|а́, ы́ *f.* carving

резюме́ *nt. indecl.* summary, résumé

рейд, а *m.* raid

рейс, а *m.* (*авто́буса*) trip, run; (*парохо́да*) voyage, passage; (*самолёта*) flight; но́мер ~a flight number

⚡ **ре́йтинг**, а *m.* rating

рейту́з|ы, ~ (*no sg.*) leggings

⚡ **рек|а́**, и́, а. ~у́, *pl.* ~и *f.* river (also fig.)

ре́квием, а *m.* (*eccl. and mus.*) requiem

реквизи́р|овать, ую *impf. and pf.* to requisition

реквизи́т, а *m.* (*theatr.*) props

⚡ **рекла́м|а**, ы *f.* **1** (*това́ра, собы́тия*) advertising, publicity **2** (*объявле́ние*) advertisement

реклами́ровать, ую *impf. and pf.* to advertise, publicize

⚡ **рекла́мный** *adj.* (*аге́нтство, кампа́ния*) advertising; (*оповеща́тельный*) publicity

реклимода́тел|ь, я *m.* advertiser

рекоменда́тельн|ый *adj.* recommendatory; ~ое письмо́ letter of recommendation

⚡ **рекоменда́ци|я**, и *f.* recommendation

⚡ **рекоменд|ова́ть**, у́ю *impf. and pf.* (*pf. also* ▶ порекомендова́ть*) **1** (*предложи́ть приня́ть*) to recommend **2** (+ *d. + inf.*) (*сове́товать*) to recommend, advise; я вам ~у́ю сходи́ть к врачу́ I recommend you to see a doctor

реконструи́р|овать, ую *impf. and pf.* to reconstruct

реконстру́кци|я, и *f.* reconstruction

реко́рд, а *m.* record; поби́ть р. to break a record; установи́ть р. to set up, establish a record

реко́рдный *adj.* record, record-breaking

рекордсме́н, а *m.* record holder; record breaker; р. ми́ра world record holder

рекордсме́н|ка, ки *f. of* ▶ рекордсме́н

ре́ктор, а *m.* principal

реле́ *nt. indecl.* (*tech.*) relay

⚡ **религио́з|ный**, ~ен, ~на *adj.* religious

рели́ги|я, и *f.* religion

рели́кви|я, и *f.* relic; (*семе́йная*) heirloom

релье́ф, а *m.* (*art and geol.*) relief

рельє́ф|ный, ~ен, ~на *adj.* relief, raised; (*ткань, обо́и*) embossed; ~ная ка́рта relief map; (*fig., отчётливый*) clear-cut

⚡ *key word*

рельс, а *m.* rail; сойти́ с ~ов to be derailed, go off the rails

рем|е́нь, ня́ *m.* (*по́яс*) belt; (*для багажа́*) strap; р. безопа́сности seat belt

реме́сленник, а *m.* artisan, craftsman

ремес|ло́, ла́, *pl.* ~ла, ~ел *nt.* trade

реми́сси|я, и *f.* (*med., comm.*) remission

⚡ **ремо́нт**, а *m.* repair(s); maintenance; (*зда́ния*) refurbishment; (*ме́лкий*) redecoration; капита́льный р. overhaul, refit, major refurbishment, repairs; в ~е under repair; р. о́буви shoe repair

ремонти́р|овать, ую *impf. and pf.* (*pf. also* от~) (*чини́ть*) to repair; (*кварти́ру*) to refurbish, redecorate

ремо́нт|ный *adj. of* ▶ ремо́нт; ~ная мастерска́я repair shop; ~ные рабо́ты repair/maintenance work

Ренесса́нс, а *m.* renaissance

ре́нт|а, ы *f.* **1** rent; земе́льная р. ground rent **2** (*проце́нты*) income (*from investments, etc.*); ежего́дная р. annuity

рента́бел|ьный, ~ен, ~ьна *adj.* profitable

рентге́н, а *m.* X-ray treatment, X-rays

рентгено́лог, а *m.* radiologist

рентгеноло́ги|я, и *f.* radiology

реорганиза́ци|я, и *f.* reorganization

реорганиз|ова́ть, у́ю *impf. and pf.* to reorganize

ре́п|а, ы *f.* turnip

репатриа́ци|я, и *f.* repatriation

репатрии́р|овать, ую *impf. and pf.* to repatriate

репертуа́р, а *m.* (*theatr., also* fig.) repertoire; он в своём ~е he is in his element

репети́р|овать, ую *impf.* (*pf.* от~) (*theatr.*) to rehearse

репети́тор, а *m.* tutor, coach

репети́ци|я, и *f.* rehearsal; генера́льная р. dress rehearsal

ре́плик|а, и *f.* **1** (*возраже́ние*) retort; (*отве́т*) reply; (*вражде́бная*) heckling comment **2** (*theatr.*) cue; пода́ть ~у to give the cue

репорта́ж, а *m.* (*де́ятельность*) reporting; (*сообще́ние*) report

репортёр, а *m.* reporter

репресси́р|овать, ую *impf. and pf.* to subject to repression

репре́сси|я, и *f.* (*usu. in pl.*) punitive measure

репроду́ктор, а *m.* loudspeaker

репроду́кци|я, и *f.* reproduction (*of a picture, etc.*)

репти́ли|я, и *f.* reptile

репута́ци|я, и *f.* reputation

ре́пчатый *adj.*: р. лук (common) onion

ресни́ц|а, ы *f.* eyelash

респекта́бел|ьный, ~ен, ~ьна *adj.* respectable

респира́тор, а *m.* respirator

⚡ **респу́блик|а**, и *f.* republic

республика́н|ец, ца *m.* republican

республика́н|ка, ки *f. of* ▶ **республика́нец**
республика́нский *adj.* republican
рессо́р|а, ы *f.* spring (*of vehicle*)
реставра́тор, а *m.* restorer
реставра́ци|я, и *f.* restoration
реставри́р|овать, ую *impf. and pf.* (*pf. also*
▶ **отреставри́ровать**) to restore
⚔ **рестора́н, а** *m.* restaurant; **р. бы́строго
обслу́живания** fast-food restaurant
⚔ **ресу́рс, а** *m.* (*usu. in pl.*) resource; **де́нежные
~ы** financial resources; **после́дний р.**
the last resort; **приро́дные ~ы** natural
resources
рефера́т, а *m.* **1** (*кни́ги, статьи́*) synopsis,
abstract **2** (*докла́д*) paper, essay
рефере́ндум, а *m.* referendum
ре́фери *m. indecl.* referee
рефле́кс, а *m.* reflex
рефле́кси|я, и *f.* reflection; introspection
рефлексоло́ги|я, и *f.* reflexology
рефо́рм|а, ы *f.* reform; **проводи́ть ~ы** to
implement reforms
реформа́тор, а *m.* reformer
Реформа́ци|я, и *f.* (hist.) Reformation
реформи́р|овать, ую *impf. and pf.* to
reform
рефрижера́тор, а *m.* (*грузови́к*)
refrigerated lorry (BrE), truck (AmE); (*судно*)
refrigerated ship
рецензе́нт, а *m.* reviewer
реце́нзи|я, и *f.* review; **р. на кни́гу** book
review
⚔ **реце́пт, а** *m.* **1** (med.) prescription; **вы́писать
р.** to write a prescription **2** (cul.) recipe
рециди́в, а *m.* (med., etc.) recurrence; relapse
ре́чк|а, и *f.* small river; rivulet
речн|о́й *adj.* river; **~ы́е пути́ сообще́ния**
inland waterways; **~о́е судохо́дство** river
navigation
⚔ **реч|ь, и** *f.* **1** (*спосо́бность*) speech
2 (*произноше́ние*) way of speaking;
отчётливая р. distinct enunciation **3** (*стиль
языка́*) language; **делова́я р.** business
language **4** (*разгово́р*) conversation, talk;
о чём шла р.? what were they/you talking
about?, what was it all about?; **р. идёт о том,
где/как/когда́** *и т. п.* the question is where/
how/when, *etc.*; **об э́том не мо́жет быть и ~и**
that is out of the question **5** (*выступле́ние*)
speech; address; **вы́ступить с ~ью** to make
a speech **6** (gram.) speech; **прямáя р.** direct
speech; **ко́свенная р.** indirect speech; **ча́сти
~и** parts of speech
⚔ **реш|а́ть, а́ю** *impf. of* ▶ **реши́ть**
реш|а́ться, а́юсь *impf. of* ▶ **реши́ться**
реша́ющий *pres. part. act. of* ▶ **реша́ть** *and
adj.* decisive, deciding; **р. го́лос** casting vote;
р. фа́ктор decisive factor
⚔ **реше́ни|е, я** *nt.* **1** decision; **прийти́ к ~ю**
to come to a decision; **приня́ть р.** to take
a decision, make up one's mind **2** (*суда́,
дире́кции*) judgement; decision, verdict;
вы́нести р. to deliver a judgement; to pass

a resolution **3** (*зада́чи*) solving; (*к зада́че*)
solution; answer; (*пробле́мы*) solution
решётк|а, и *f.* **1** grating; (*око́нная*) grille;
(*огра́да*) railings; (*садо́вая*) trellis; (*пе́ред
ками́ном*) fireguard; (*радиа́тора*) grille;
за ~ой (fig., infml) behind bars (= *in prison*);
посади́ть за ~у to put behind bars **2** (comput.)
(*also* **знак ~и**) hash, hash sign **3** (*в ками́не*)
(fire) grate **4** (*в духо́вке*) shelf
решет|о́, а́, *pl.* **~а** *nt.* sieve
реши́мост|ь, и *f.* resolution, resoluteness
реши́тельно *adv.* **1** (*твёрдо*) resolutely
2 (*категори́чески*) decidedly, definitely;
р. отказа́ться to flatly refuse
реши́тел|ьный, ~ен, ~ьна *adj.* resolute,
determined; **~ьные ме́ры** drastic measures
⚔ **реш|и́ть, ý, и́шь** *pf.* (*of* ▶ **реша́ть**) **1** (+ *inf.
or* + *a.*) to decide; **он ~и́л уе́хать** he decided
to go away **2** (*найти́ отве́т*) to solve;
to settle; **р. зада́чу** to solve a problem; to
accomplish a task
реш|и́ться, у́сь, и́шься *pf.* (*of* ▶ **реша́ться**)
1 (**на** + *a. or* + *inf.*) to make up one's mind
(to), decide (to) **2** (*получи́ть реше́ние*) to
be resolved
ре́|ять, ет *impf.* **1** (*о пти́це*) to soar, hover
2 (*о фла́ге*) to flutter
ржаве́|ть, ет *impf.* (*of* ▶ **заржаве́ть**) to rust
ржа́вчин|а, ы *f.* rust
ржа́вый *adj.* rusty
ржан|о́й *adj.* rye
рж|ать, у, ёшь *impf.* to neigh; (infml) to laugh
loudly
Ри́г|а, и *f.* Riga
рикоше́т, а *m.* ricochet, rebound; **~ом** on the
rebound (also fig.)
Рим, а *m.* Rome
ри́млян|ин, ина, *pl.* **~е, ~** *m.* Roman
ри́млян|ка, ки *f. of* ▶ **ри́млянин**
ри́мск|ий *adj.* Roman; **Па́па Р.** the Pope; **~ие
ци́фры** Roman numerals
ринг, а *m.* (sport) ring
ри́н|уться, усь, ешься *pf.* to dash, dart
Ри́о-де-Жане́йро *m. indecl.* Rio de Janeiro
⚔ **рис, а** *m.* rice
⚔ **риск, а** *m.* risk; **на свой (страх и) р.** at one's
own risk, at one's peril; **с ~ом (для** + *g.*) at
the risk (of); **пойти́ на р.** to run risks, take
chances
рискн|у́ть, у́, ёшь *pf.* (+ *inf.*) to take the risk
(of), venture (to)
риско́ван|ный, ~, ~на *adj.* **1** risky; **~ное
предприя́тие** risky venture **2** (*шу́тка,
те́ма*) risqué
риск|ова́ть, у́ю *impf.* **1** to run risks, take
chances **2** (+ *i.*) to risk; (+ *inf.*) to risk, take
the risk (of); **ниче́м не р.** to run no risk; **р.
опозда́ть на по́езд** to risk missing the train
рисова́ни|е, я *nt.* (*карандашо́м*) drawing;
(*кра́сками*) painting
⚔ **рис|ова́ть, у́ю** *impf.* (*of* ▶ **нарисова́ть**)
1 (*карандашо́м*) to draw; (*кра́сками*) to
paint; **р. с нату́ры** to draw, paint from life

р

2 (*fig.*, *описывать*) to depict, paint, portray

ри́сов|ый *adj.* rice; ∼ая ка́ша rice pudding

⚬ **рису́н|ок, ка** *m.* (*изображение*) drawing; (*в книге*) illustration; (*в научной статье*) figure; (*на ткани*) pattern, design; (*контур*) outline; **акваре́льный р.** watercolour (BrE), watercolor (AmE)

ритм, а *m.* (*музыки, сердца*) rhythm; (*работы, жизни*) pace

ритми́ческ|ий *adj.* rhythmic; ∼ая гимна́стика aerobics

ритми́ч|ный, ∼ен, ∼на *adj.* rhythmic; ∼ная рабо́та smooth functioning

рито́рик|а, и *f.* rhetoric

ритори́ческий *adj.* rhetorical

ритуа́л, а *m.* ritual

ритуа́льн|ый *adj.* ritual; ∼ые услу́ги funeral services

риф, а *m.* reef; **кора́лловый р.** coral reef

ри́фм|а, ы *f.* rhyme

рифм|ова́ть, у́ю *impf.* (*слова*) to make rhyme

рифм|ова́ться, у́юсь *impf.* to rhyme

ро́б|а, ы *f.* working clothes, overalls

ро́б|кий, ∼ок, ∼ка́, ∼ко *adj.* timid, shy

ро́бост|ь, и *f.* timidity, shyness

ро́бот, а *m.* robot

ров, рва, о рве, во рву *m.* ditch; **крепостно́й р.** moat

рове́сник, а *m.* person of the same age; peer; **мы с ним ∼и** we are of the same age

рове́сни|ца, цы *f. of* ▸ **рове́сник**

ро́вно *adv.* **1** (*равномерно*) regularly, evenly **2** (*точно*) exactly; **р. пять рубле́й** five roubles exactly; (*о времени*) sharp; **р. в час** at one o'clock sharp

ро́в|ный, ∼ен, ∼на́, ∼но *adj.* **1** (*дорога, поверхность*) flat, even, level; (*линия*) straight **2** (*пульс*) regular; (*шаг, голос*) even; (*характер*) stable **3** (*одинаковый*) equal; **для ∼ного счёта** to make it even; to bring to a round figure; **∼ным счётом** exactly

ровня́|ть, ю *impf.* (*of* ▸ **сровня́ть**) to even, level

рог, а, *pl.* **∼а́, ∼о́в** *m.* **1** horn; (*оленьий*) antler **2** (*музыкальный инструмент*) bugle, horn; **охо́тничий р.** hunting horn

рога́лик, а *m.* crescent-shaped roll, croissant

рога́тк|а, и *f.* catapult (BrE), slingshot (AmE)

рога́т|ый, ∼, ∼а *adj.* horned; **кру́пный р. скот** cattle

⚬ **род, а, о ∼е, в ∼у́** *m.* **1** (*pl.* **∼ы́, ∼о́в**) family, kin, clan; **челове́ческий р.** mankind, human race **2** (*pl.* **∼ы, ∼о́в**) (*происхождение*) birth, origin, stock; (*поколение*) generation; **он ∼ом из Ирла́ндии** he is an Irishman by birth **3** (*pl.* **∼ы, ∼о́в**) (biol.) genus **4** (*pl.* **∼а́, ∼о́в**) (*тип*) sort, kind; **р. войск** arm of the service; **вся́кого ∼а** of all kinds; **тако́го ∼а** of such a kind, such; **в не́котором ∼е** to

some extent; **в своём ∼е** in one's own way **5** (*pl.* **∼ы́, ∼о́в**) (gram.) gender; **же́нский р.** feminine (gender)

родо́м, а *m.* (*abbr. of* **роди́льный дом**) maternity hospital

роде́о *nt. indecl.* rodeo

роди́льн|ый *adj.*: **р. дом** maternity hospital; **∼ое отделе́ние** maternity unit

⚬ **ро́дин|а, ы** *f.* native land; home, homeland; **верну́ться на ∼у** to return home; **тоска́ по ∼е** homesickness

ро́динк|а, и *f.* birthmark

⚬ **роди́тел|и, ей** (*no sg.*) parents

роди́тельн|ый *adj.* (gram.) genitive; **в ∼ом падеже́** in the genitive (case)

роди́тельский *adj.* parental, parents'; paternal; **р. комите́т** parents' committee

⚬ **ро|ди́ть, жу́, ди́шь,** *past impf.* **∼ди́л, ∼ди́ла, ∼ди́ло,** *past pf.* **∼ди́л, ∼дила́, ∼ди́ло** *impf. and pf.* **1** (*impf. also* **рожа́ть**) to bear, give birth (to) **2** (*impf. also* **рожда́ть**) (fig.) to give birth, rise (to); (*о почве*) to yield

⚬ **ро|ди́ться, жу́сь, ди́шься,** *past* **∼ди́лся, ∼дила́сь, ∼дило́сь** *impf. and pf.* (*impf. also* **рожда́ться**) **1** to be born; **р. преподава́телем** to be a born teacher; (**у** + *g.*) to be born of; **у неё ∼дила́сь дочь** she had a daughter; **от пе́рвой жены́ у него́ ∼ди́лся сын** he had a son by his first wife **2** (fig., *мысль, план, город*) to arise, come into being

родни́к, а́ *m.* spring (*where water wells up*)

⚬ **родно́й** *adj.* **1** (*мать, брат, дядя*) related by blood; natural; **р. брат** one's brother (*opp. cousin, etc.*); (*as pl. n.* **∼ы́е, ∼ы́х**) relations, relatives **2** (*отечественный*) native; home; **р. язы́к** mother tongue

родня́, и́ *f.* (collect.) (*родственники*) relatives

родово́й¹ *adj.* **1** family, tribal, ancestral **2** (biol.) generic

родов|о́й² *adj.* birth, labour (BrE), labor (AmE); **∼ы́е схва́тки** contractions

родонача́льник, а *m.* ancestor, forefather; (fig., *литературы*) father

ро́дственник, а *m.* relation, relative; **ближа́йший р.** next of kin

ро́дственни|ца, цы *f. of* ▸ **ро́дственник**

ро́дствен|ный, ∼ *and* **∼ен, ∼на** *adj.* **1** kindred, related; **∼ные свя́зи** kinship ties **2** (*близкий*) related, allied **3** (*свойственный родственникам*) familiar, intimate

родств|о́, а́ *nt.* relationship, kinship (also fig.); **быть в ∼е́** (**с** + *i.*) to be related (to)

ро́д|ы, ов (*no sg.*) birth; childbirth; **в ∼ах** in labour (BrE), labor (AmE)

ро́ж|а, и *f.* (infml) mug (= *face*); **ко́рчить, стро́ить ∼у** to make faces

рожа́|ть, ю *impf. of* ▸ **роди́ть 1**

рожда́емост|ь, и *f.* birth rate

рожда́|ть, ю *impf. of* ▸ **роди́ть**

рожда́|ться, юсь *impf. of* ▸ **роди́ться**

⚬ key word

♂ **рожде́ни|е, я** *nt.* birth; **день** ∼**я** birthday; **ме́сто** ∼**я** birthplace; **глухо́й от** ∼**я** deaf from birth

рождённый *p.p.p. of* ▶ **роди́ть**; (+ *inf.*) born (to), destined (to)

рожде́ственск|ий *adj.* Christmas; ∼**ая ёлка** Christmas tree; ∼**ая пе́сня** carol; **р. соче́льник** Christmas Eve

Рождеств|о́, а́ *nt.* (*праздник*) Christmas; **на Р.** at Christmas (time); **под Р.** on Christmas Eve; (*само рождение*) Nativity

рож|о́к, ка́ *m.* (*mus.*) horn; bugle; **англи́йский р.** cor anglais

рожь, ржи *f.* rye

ро́з|а, ы *f.* (*цветок*) rose; (*растение*) rose tree, rose bush

розе́тк|а, и *f.* **1** (*украшение*) rosette **2** (*elec.*) socket; electric outlet **3** (*для варенья*) jam dish

розмари́н, а *m.* (*bot.*) rosemary

ро́зниц|а, ы *f.* retail; **торгова́ть в** ∼**у** to engage in retail trade; to retail

ро́зничн|ый *adj.* retail; **р. торго́вец** retailer; ∼**ая цена́** retail price

ро́зов|ый, ∼, ∼а *adj.* **1** *adj. of* ▶ **ро́за**; ∼**ое де́рево** rosewood; **р. куст** rose bush **2** (*цвет*) pink, rose-coloured (BrE), -colored (AmE) **3** (*fig.*) rosy

ро́зыгрыш, а *m.* **1** (*лотереи*) drawing **2** (*шутка*) practical joke

ро́зыск, а *m.* **1** (*разыскивание*) search **2** (*law, дознание*) inquiry; **Уголо́вный р.** Criminal Investigation Department (BrE), Federal Bureau of Investigation (AmE)

рой, ро́я, *pl.* **рои́** *m.* (*пчёл, комаров*) swarm

рок¹, а *m.* (*судьба*) fate

рок², а *m.* (*mus.*) rock; **тяжёлый р.** hard rock

рок-гру́пп|а, ы *f.* rock band

рок-му́зык|а, и *f.* rock music

рок-музыка́нт, а *m.* rock musician

рок-н-ро́лл, а *m.* rock 'n' roll

роков|о́й *adj.* **1** fateful; fated; ∼**ая же́нщина** femme fatale **2** (*имеющий тяжёлые последствия*) fatal

ро́кот, а *m.* roar, rumble

ро́лик, а *m.* **1** roller, castor **2** (*in pl.*) (*коньки*) roller skates **3**: **рекла́мный р.** (*cin.*) advertisement; (*фильма*) trailer **4** (*бумаги, плёнки*) roll

ро́лик|овый *adj. of* ▶ **ро́лик**; ∼**овые коньки́** roller skates

♂ **ро́л|ь, и,** *pl.* ∼**и,** ∼**е́й** *f.* (*theatr.*) role (also *fig.*); (*текст*) part; **в** ∼**и** (+ *g.*) in the role (of); **игра́ть р.** (+ *g.*) to take the part (of), play, act; (*fig.*) to matter, count, be of importance; **э́то не игра́ет** ∼**и** it is of no importance, it does not count

ром, а *m.* rum

♂ **рома́н, а** *m.* **1** novel **2** (infml, *любовная связь*) love affair; romance

рома́нс, а *m.* (*mus.*) romance

рома́нский *adj.* Romance; (*archit.*) Romanesque

романти́зм, а *m.* romanticism

рома́нтик, а *m.* romantic

рома́нтик|а, и *f.* romance

романти́ческий *adj.* romantic

романти́ч|ный, ∼ен, ∼на *adj.* = **романти́ческий**

рома́шк|а, и *f.* camomile

ромб, а *m.* (*math.*) rhombus

роня́|ть, ю *impf.* (*of* ▶ **урони́ть**) **1** (*из рук*) to drop; (*голову, руки*) to let fall; (*книгу с полки*) to knock off; **р. слёзы** to shed tears **2** (*impf. only*) (*лишаться*) to shed **3** (fig., *унижать*) to discredit; **р. себя́ в чьих-н. глаза́х** to discredit oneself in sb's eyes; (*авторитет*) to lose

ро́пот, а *m.* murmur, grumble

рос, ∼ла́ *see* ▶ **расти́**

рос|а́, ы́, *pl.* ∼**ы** *f.* dew

роско́ш|ный, ∼ен, ∼на *adj.* luxurious

ро́скош|ь, и *f.* **1** (*излишества*) luxury; **жить в** ∼**и** to live in luxury **2** (*великолепие*) splendour (BrE), splendor (AmE)

ро́слый *adj.* tall, strapping

ро́спис|ь, и *f.* painting; **р. стен** wall painting(s), mural(s)

♂ **росси́йский** *adj.* Russian

Росси́|я, и *f.* Russia

россия́н|ин, а, *pl.* ∼**е, ∼** *m.* (*русский*) Russian; (*житель России*) Russian citizen

россия́н|ка, ки *f.* of ▶ **россия́нин**

♂ **рост, а** *m.* **1** (*растений, городов, индустрии*) growth; (fig., *цен, преступности*) increase, rise **2** (*вышина*) height, stature; ∼**ом** in height; **он** ∼**ом с вас** he is (of) your height; **высо́кого** ∼**а** tall; **во весь р.** full length; (fig.) in all its magnitude; **встать во весь р.** to stand upright, stand up straight **3** (*одежды*) length

ростовщи́к, а́ *m.* usurer, moneylender

рост|о́к, ка́ *m.* shoot; **пусти́ть** ∼**ки́** to sprout; (*in pl.*) (+ *g.*) beginnings (of)

♂ **рот, рта, о рте́, во рту́** *m.* mouth; **не брать в р.** (+ *g.*) to not touch; **зажа́ть, заткну́ть кому́-н. р.** (infml) to shut sb up

ро́т|а, ы *f.* (mil.) company

рота́ци|я, и *f.* rotation

ротве́йлер, а *m.* Rottweiler

ро́щ|а, и *f.* small wood, grove

роя́л|ь, я *m.* piano; grand piano; **игра́ть на** ∼**е** to play the piano

ртут|ь, и *f.* mercury

руба́н|ок, ка *m.* (tech.) plane

руба́шк|а, и *f.* **1** shirt; **ночна́я р.** nightdress **2** (*игральной карты*) back

рубе́ж, а́ *m.* boundary, border(line); **жить за** ∼**о́м** to live abroad

руб|е́ц, ца́ *m.* **1** (*от ран*) scar **2** (*шов*) hem, seam

руби́н, а *m.* ruby

руби́новый *adj.* ruby

руб|и́ть, лю́, ∼ишь *impf.* **1** (*дерево*) to fell **2** (*дрова*) to chop **3** (cul.) to mince, chop up

⚲ **рубл|ь, я́** *m.* rouble; **биле́т сто́ит два ~я́** a ticket costs two roubles

ру́брик|а, и *f.* **1** (*заголовок*) rubric, heading **2** (*раздел*) column

ру́ган|ь, и *f.* (*непристойная*) bad language, swearing, abuse

руга́тельств|о, а *nt.* abuse; (*непристойное*) swear word

руга́|ть, ю *impf.* **1** (*pf.* **от~** *or* **вы~**) (*отчитывать*) to scold, tell off **2** (*pf.* **об~** *or* **от~**) (*оскорблять*) to curse, swear (at), abuse **3** (*pf.* **об~**) (*критиковать*) to tear to pieces

руга́|ться, юсь *impf.* **1** to curse, swear, use bad language **2** (**с** + *i.*) (*ссориться*) to quarrel (with), have a row (with)

руд|а́, ы́, *pl.* **~ы** *f.* ore; **желе́зная р.** iron ore

рудиме́нт, а *m.* rudiment

рудни́к, а́ *m.* mine, pit

руж|ье́, ья́, *pl.* **~ья, ~ей, ~ьям** *nt.* (hand)gun, rifle

руи́н|а, ы *f.* (*usu. in pl.*) ruin; **го́род лежа́л в ~ах** the town lay in ruins

⚲ **рук|а́, и́, а. ~у,** *pl.* **~и, ~, ~а́м** *f.* **1** (*кисть*) hand; (*от кисти до плеча*) arm; **пожа́ть ~у** (+ *d.*) to shake hands (with); **вести́ за́ ~у** to lead by the hand; **держа́ть на ~а́х** to hold in one's arms; **р. об ~у** hand in hand; **написа́ть от ~и́** to write out by hand; **взять кого́-н. под ~у** to take sb's arm **2** (*почерк*) hand, handwriting **3** (*сторона*) side; **по пра́вую ~у** on the right, to the right **4** (*fig.*) hand; **э́то бу́дет им на́ ~у** that will serve their purpose; it will be playing into their hands; **на ско́рую ~у** offhand; **под ~ой** at hand, to hand; **махну́ть ~о́й** (**на** + *a.*) to give up as lost; **наложи́ть на себя́ ~и** (*infml*) to commit suicide

рука́в, а́, *pl.* **~а́** *m.* **1** (*одежды*) sleeve **2** (tech., *шланг*) hose

рукави́ц|а, ы *f.* (*меховая*) mitten; (*рабочая*) gauntlet

⚲ **руководи́тел|ь, я** *m.* **1** (*учреждения, отдела*) head, manager; (*делегации, похода, восстания*) leader; **р. прое́кта** project manager; **кла́ссный р.** (*в школе*) class teacher **2** (*воспитатель*) instructor; guide; **нау́чный р.** supervisor of studies

руководи́тель|ница, ницы *f.* (infml of) ▶ **руководи́тель**

руково|ди́ть, жу́, ди́шь *impf.* (+ *i.*) (*учреждением, отделом*) to be in charge of; to manage; (*походом, восстанием*) to lead; (*кружком, клубом*) to run; (*аспирантами*) to supervise; (*побуждать*) to govern

⚲ **руково́дств|о, а** *nt.* **1** (*действие*) leadership; guidance; management **2** (*то, чему следуют*) guiding principle, guide; **р. к де́йствию** guide to action **3** (*книга*) handbook, guide, manual; **р. по эксплуата́ции** instructions for use; user guide **4** (*collect.*) (*руководители*) (the) leadership, leaders; governing body

руково́дств|оваться, уюсь *impf.* (+ *i.*) to follow; to be guided (by)

рукоде́ли|е, я *nt.* needlework

рукопи́сный *adj.* (*текст*) handwritten; (*фонд*) manuscript

ру́копис|ь, и *f.* manuscript

рукопожа́ти|е, я *nt.* handshake

рукоя́тк|а, и *f.* handle

рулев|о́й *adj. of* ▶ **руль**; **~о́е колесо́** steering wheel; **~а́я коло́нка** steering column; (*as m. n.* **р., ~о́го**) (sport) cox(swain); (*на судне*) helmsman

руле́т, а *m.* (cul.) **1** (*пирог*) roll; **мясно́й р.** meat loaf **2** (*окорок без кости*) boned gammon

руле́тк|а, и *f.* **1** (*для измерения*) tape measure **2** (*игра*) roulette

рул|и́ть, ю́, и́шь *impf.* (*в машине, в лодке*) to steer

руло́н, а *m.* roll

рул|ь, я́ *m.* (*судна*) rudder; helm (also fig.); (*автомобиля*) (steering) wheel; (*велосипеда*) handlebars; **стоя́ть у ~я́** (fig.) to be at the helm

румы́н, а *m.* Romanian

Румы́ни|я, и *f.* Romania

румы́н|ка, ки *f. of* ▶ **румы́н**

румы́нский *adj.* Romanian

румя́н|а, ~ (*no sg.*) *f.* rouge; blusher

румя́н|ец, ца *m.* (high) colour (BrE), color (AmE); flush; blush

румя́н|ый, ~, ~а *adj.* rosy, ruddy

ру́н|а, ы *f.* (philol.) rune

ру́пор, а *m.* megaphone; loud hailer; (fig., *партии*) mouthpiece

руса́лк|а, и *f.* mermaid

ру́сл|о, а, *g. pl.* **ру́сел** *and* **~** *nt.* **1** (river) bed, channel; **измени́ть р. реки́** to change the course of a river **2** (fig., *направление*) channel, course; **войти́ в обы́чное р.** to resume the normal course

ру́сск|ая, ой *f. of* ▶ **ру́сский** (*as n.*)

⚲ **ру́сск|ий** *adj.* Russian; (*also as m. n.* **р., ~ого**) Russian (person)

ру́с|ый, ~, ~а *adj.* light brown

рути́н|а, ы *f.* (pej.) routine; rut

ру́хляд|ь, и *f.* (collect.) (infml) junk

ру́хн|уть, у, ешь *pf.* to crash down, tumble down, collapse; (fig., *планы, мечты*) to collapse, fall through

руча́|ться, юсь *impf.* (*of* ▶ **поручи́ться**) (**за** + *a.*) to guarantee; to answer (for), vouch (for); **р. голово́й** (**за** + *a.*) to stake one's life (on)

руче́й, ья́ *m.* brook, stream

ру́чк|а, и *f.* **1** *dim. of* ▶ **рука́** **2** (*двери, чайника*) handle; (*кресла, дивана*) arm; **р. две́ри** door handle, doorknob **3** (*для письма*) pen; **ша́риковая р.** ballpoint pen

ручн|о́й *adj.* **1** hand; (*управление*) manual; **~а́я кладь** hand luggage; **~а́я рабо́та**

handwork; ~о́й рабо́ты handmade; **р. труд**
manual labour (BrE), labor (AmE) **2** (*зверь,
птица*) tame

ру́ш|ить, у, ишь *impf.* (*здание*) to pull down;
(*семью*) to wreck

ру́ш|иться, ится *impf. and pf.* to fall down,
collapse; (fig., *планы, надежды*) to collapse

РФ *f. indecl.* (*abbr. of* **Росси́йская
Федера́ция**) Russian Federation

♂ **ры́б|а, ы** *f.* fish; (*in pl.* **Р~ы**) (astron., astrol.)
Pisces; **ни р. ни мя́со** neither fish nor fowl;
чу́вствовать себя́ как р. в воде́ to feel in
one's element

рыба́к, а́ *m.* fisherman

рыба́лк|а, и *f.* fishing; fishing trip; **идти́ на
~у** to go fishing

ры́бн|ый *adj.* fish; ~ые консе́рвы tinned
fish; ~ая ло́вля fishing; **р. магази́н** fish
shop, fishmonger's

рыболо́в, а *m.* fisherman; angler

рыболо́вн|ый *adj.* fishing; ~ые
принадле́жности, ~ая снасть fishing tackle

рыв|о́к, ка́ *m.* **1** (*резкое движение*) jerk
2 (*бегуна*) dash, spurt; (*в тяжёлой
атле́тике*) snatch **3** (*в работе*) push, spurt

рыга́|ть, а́ю *impf.* (*of* ▶ **рыгну́ть**) to belch, to
burp (infml)

рыгн|у́ть, у́, нёшь *inst. pf. of* ▶ **рыга́ть**

рыда́ни|е, я *nt.* sobbing

рыда́|ть, ю *impf.* to sob

ры́ж|ий, ~, ~а́, ~е *adj.* (*волосы*) red,
ginger; (*человек*) red-haired, ginger-haired;
(*лошадь*) chestnut

ры́л|о, а *nt.* snout (*of pig, etc.*)

♂ **ры́н|ок, ка** *m.* **1** market(place) **2** (econ.)
market; **вне́шний р.** foreign market;
вну́тренний р. domestic, internal market;
на ~ке on the market

ры́но|чный *adj. of* ▶ **ры́нок**; ~чная
эконо́мика market economy; **по ~чной цене́**
at the market price

рыса́к, а́ *m.* trotter (*horse*)

ры́|скать, щу, щешь *impf.* **1** (**по** + *d.*) (*в
по́исках*) to scour, ransack; **р. по карма́нам**
to ransack one's pockets **2** (*блужда́ть*) to
rove, roam; **р. глаза́ми** to let one's eyes roam

рыс|ь¹, и, о ~и, на ~й *f.* (*бег*) trot

рыс|ь², и *f.* (*живо́тное*) lynx

ры́твин|а, ы *f.* rut, groove

рыть, ро́ю, ро́ешь *impf.* **1** (*яму, око́пы*)
to dig; (*карто́шку*) to dig up **2** (*в по́исках*)
to rummage, root about (in)

ры́ться, ро́юсь, ро́ешься *impf.* (**в** + *p.*) (*в
земле́*) to dig (in); (fig., *в му́соре, в чемода́не*)
to rummage (in); (*в кни́гах*) to root about (in)

ры́хл|ый, ~, ~а́, ~о *adj.* (*по́чва, ка́мень*)
friable, crumbly; (*снег*) loose

ры́царский *adj.* **1** *adj. of* ▶ **ры́царь; р.
поеди́нок** joust; **р. рома́н** tale of chivalry
2 (fig.) chivalrous

ры́цар|ь, я *m.* knight

рыча́г, а́ *m.* lever

рыча́ни|е, я *nt.* growl, snarl

рыч|а́ть, у́, и́шь *impf.* to growl, snarl

рья́н|ый, ~, ~а́ *adj.* zealous

рэ́кет, а *m.* racket

рэкети́р, а *m.* racketeer

рэп, а *m.* rap (music)

рэ́ппер, а *m.* rapper (*performer of rap music*)

рюкза́к, а́ *m.* rucksack; backpack

рю́мк|а, и *f.* (small) glass

ряби́н|а, ы *f.* **1** (*де́рево*) rowan tree,
mountain ash **2** (*я́года*) rowan berry

ряб|и́ть, и́т *impf.* **1** to ripple **2** (*impers.*):
у меня́ ~и́т в глаза́х I am dazzled

ряб|о́й, ~, ~а́, ~о, ~ы́ *adj.* **1** (*лицо́*)
pockmarked **2** (*ку́рица*) speckled

ря́бчик, а *m.* (zool.) hazel grouse

ряб|ь, и *f.* **1** (*на воде́*) ripple(s) **2** (*в глаза́х*)
stars

ря́вк|ать, аю *impf.* (*of* ▶ **ря́вкнуть**) (**на** + *a.*)
(infml) to bellow (at), to bark (at)

ря́вк|нуть, ну, нешь *pf. of* ▶ **ря́вкать**

♂ **ряд, а, в ~е** *and* **в ~у́, pl. ~ы́, ~о́в** *m.*
1 (*предме́тов, лиц*) row; **пе́рвый/после́дний
р.** (theatr.) front/back row; **стоя́ть в одно́м ~у́**
(с + *i.*) to rank (with) **2** (*в а́рмии, в па́ртии*)
file, rank; **в пе́рвых ~а́х** in the first ranks;
(fig.) in the forefront **3** (*се́рия*) series (*also
math.*); (*совоку́пность*) number; **в це́лом ~е
слу́чаев** in a number of cases **4** (*на ры́нке*)
stalls (*of one type of goods set out in a row*);
ры́бный ~ the fish stalls

рядов|о́й *adj.* **1** (*член, рабо́тник, слу́чай*)
ordinary, common **2** (mil.): **р. соста́в** rank
and file; men, other ranks; (*as m. n.* **р.,
~о́го**) private (soldier)

♂ **ря́дом** *adv.* **1** alongside; (*о двух лю́дях*) side
by side; (**с** + *i.*) (*о́коло*) next to; (*в сравне́нии
с*) compared with; **он сиди́т р. с премье́р-
мини́стром** he is sitting next to the prime
minister **2** (*поблизости*) near, close by, next
door; **э́то совсе́м р.** it is quite near, close

ря́с|а, ы *f.* cassock

р

Cc

⚡ **с** *prep.*
- **I.** (+ *g.*) **1** from; off; **с ю́го-восто́ка** from the south-east; **перево́д с ру́сского** translation from Russian; **верну́ться с рабо́ты** to return from work **2** (*по причи́не*) for, from, with; **со стыда́** for shame, with shame **3** on, from; **с одно́й, с друго́й стороны́** on the one, on the other hand **4** (*на основа́нии*) with; **с ва́шего согла́сия** with your consent **5** (*посре́дством*) by, with; **писа́ть с большо́й бу́квы** to write with a capital letter **6** (*о вре́мени*) from, since; as from; **с девяти́ (часо́в) до пяти́** from nine (o'clock) till five; **с де́тства** from childhood; **мы с ней не ви́делись с января́** I have not seen her since January
- **II.** (+ *a.*) (*приблизи́тельно*): **с пятиэта́жный дом** the size of a five-storey (BrE), five-story (AmE) house; **на́ша до́чка ро́стом с ва́шу** our daughter is about the same height as yours
- **III.** (+ *i.*) **1** with; and; **с удово́льствием** with pleasure; **мы с ва́ми** you and I **2** (*ука́зывает на нали́чие чего́-л.*): **хлеб с ма́слом** bread and butter; **челове́к со стра́нностями** peculiar person **3** (*посре́дством*) by, on; **получи́ть с пе́рвой по́чтой** to receive by first post **4** (*при наступле́нии чего́-л.*) with; **с года́ми** with the years; **с ка́ждым днём** every day **5** (*относи́тельно*) with (*or not translated*); **как у вас дела́ с рабо́той?** how is the work going?; **что с ва́ми?** what is the matter with you?; what's up?

с..., *also* **со...** *and* **съ...** *vbl. pref. indicating* **1** *unification, movement from various sides to a point:* **свари́ть** (*мета́лл*) to weld **2** *movement or action made in a downward direction:* **спусти́ться** to descend **3** *removal of sth from somewhere:* **сорва́ть** to tear off

са́б|ля, ли, *g. pl.* ~**ель** *f.* sabre (BrE), saber (AmE)

сабота́ж, а *m.* sabotage

сабота́жник, а *m.* saboteur

са́ван, а *m.* shroud, cerement; **сне́жный с.** blanket of snow

сава́нн|а, ы *f.* (geog.) savannah

са́г|а, и *f.* saga

⚡ **сад, а, о** ~**е, в** ~**у́,** *pl.* ~**ы́** *m.* garden; **фрукто́вый с.** orchard; **де́тский с.** kindergarten

сади́зм, а *m.* sadism

сади́ст, а *m.* sadist

сади́ст|ка, ки *f. of* ▶ **сади́ст**

сади́стский *adj.* sadistic

сади́|ться, жу́сь, ди́шься *impf.* (*of* ▶ **сесть¹**): ~**ди́(те)сь!** (polite request) take a seat!

садо́вник, а *m.* gardener

садово́дств|о, а *nt.* (*хо́бби*) gardening; (*нау́ка*) horticulture

садо́вый *adj.* **1** *adj. of* ▶ **сад 2** (*культу́рный*) garden, cultivated

сад|о́к, ка́ *m.* place for keeping live creatures; **кро́личий с.** rabbit hutch; **ры́бный с.** fish pond

са́ж|а, и *f.* soot

сажа́|ть, ю *impf.* (*of* ▶ **посади́ть**) **1** (*цветы́*) to plant **2** (*го́стя*) to seat; (*помеща́ть*) to set, put; (*предлага́ть сесть*) to offer a seat; **с. в тюрьму́** to put into prison, imprison, jail; **с. под аре́ст** to put under arrest

са́жен|ец, ца *m.* seedling; sapling

саза́н, а *m.* wild carp (*Cyprinus carpio*)

⚡ **сайт, а** *m.* (comput.) (web)site

саквоя́ж, а *m.* travelling bag (BrE), traveling bag (AmE)

саксофо́н, а *m.* saxophone

саксофони́ст, а *m.* saxophonist

саксофони́ст|ка, ки *f. of* ▶ **саксофони́ст**

саламандр|а, ы *f.* salamander

сала́т, а *m.* **1** (*расте́ние*) lettuce **2** (*куша́нье*) salad

сала́тниц|а, ы *f.* salad dish, salad bowl

сала́т|ный *adj. of* ▶ **сала́т;** ~**ного цве́та** light green

са́л|ки, ок *f. pl.* (sg. ~**ка,** ~**ки**) (*игра́*) tag, touch

са́л|о, а *nt.* fat; lard

⚡ **сало́н, а** *m.* **1** (*для вы́ставок; магази́н*) salon; **автомоби́льный с.** car showroom **2** (*самолёта, авто́буса*) passenger section **3** (*в оте́ле*) lounge; (*на парохо́де*) saloon

салфе́тк|а, и *f.* napkin, serviette (BrE)

Сальвадо́р, а *m.* El Salvador

сальвадо́р|ец, ца *m.* Salvadorean

сальвадо́р|ка, ки *f. of* ▶ **сальвадо́рец**

сальвадо́рский *adj.* Salvadorean

са́л|ьный, ~**ен,** ~**ьна** *adj.* greasy

са́льто *nt. indecl.* somersault

салю́т, а *m.* salute; (*фейерве́рк*) fireworks display

саля́ми *f. indecl.* salami

⚡ **сам, самого́,** *f.* **сама́, само́й,** *nt.* ~**о́, самого́,** *pl.* **са́ми, сами́х** *refl. pron.* (*я*) myself; (*ты, вы*) yourself; (*он*) himself, *etc.*; **с. по себе́** in itself, per se; (*без по́мощи*) by oneself, unassisted; **с. собо́й** of itself, of its own accord

са́мб|а, ы *f.* samba

сам|е́ц, ца́ *m.* male (*of species*)

сáмк|а, и *f.* female (*of species*)

сáммит, а *m.* (pol.) summit (meeting)

само... *comb. form* self-, auto-

самобичевáни|е, я *nt.* self-reproach

самобы́т|ный, ~ен, ~на *adj.* original

самовáр, а *m.* samovar

самовлюблённый *adj.* narcissistic

самовóлк|а, и *f.* (infml) absence without leave

самовóл|ьный, ~ен, ~ьна *adj.* **1** (*человек*) wilful, self-willed **2** (*отсутствие*) unauthorized; **~ьная отлу́чка** (mil.) absence without leave

самогóн, а *m.* home-made vodka, hooch, moonshine (AmE)

самодéльный *adj.* home-made

самодержáви|е, я *nt.* autocracy

самодéятельност|ь, и *f.* **1** (*художественная с.*) amateur activities (*theatricals, music, etc.*) **2** initiative, self-motivation

самодéятел|ьный, ~ен, ~ьна *adj.* **1** (*не профессиональный*) amateur **2** self-motivated

самодовóл|ьный, ~ен, ~ьна *adj.* self-satisfied, smug, complacent

самодостáточ|ный, ~ен, ~на *adj.* self-sufficient

самозабвéн|ный, ~ен, ~на *adj.* selfless

самозащи́т|а, ы *f.* self-defence (BrE), self-defense (AmE)

самозвáн|ец, ца *m.* impostor, pretender

самокáт, а *m.* (child's) scooter

самоконтрóл|ь, я *m.* self-control

самокри́тик|а, и *f.* self-criticism

самокру́тк|а, и *f.* (infml) roll-up (BrE), roll-your-own

◇ **самолёт, а** *m.* (aero)plane (BrE), (air)plane (AmE); aircraft

самолюби́в|ый, ~, ~а *adj.* proud, haughty

самолюби|е, я *nt.* pride, self-esteem; **лóжное с.** false pride

самомнéни|е, я *nt.* conceit, self-importance

самонадéян|ный, ~, ~на *adj.* conceited, arrogant

самообладáни|е, я *nt.* self-control, self-possession, composure

самообмáн, а *m.* self-deception

самооборóн|а, ы *f.* self-defence (BrE), self-defense (AmE)

самообслу́живани|е, я *nt.* self-service

самоопределéни|е, я *nt.* self-determination

самоотвéржен|ный, ~, ~на *adj.* selfless, self-sacrificing

самооцéнк|а, и *f.* self-appraisal

самопи́с|ец, ца *m.*: **бортовóй с.** (aeron.) flight recorder

самопожéртвовани|е, я *nt.* self-sacrifice

самопроизвóл|ьный, ~ен, ~ьна *adj.* spontaneous

саморóд|ок, ка *m.* (min.) nugget

самосвáл, а *m.* dump truck

самосохранéни|е, я *nt.* self-preservation

◇ **самостоя́тельно** *adv.* independently; on one's own

самостоя́тельност|ь, и *f.* independence

самостоя́тел|ьный, ~ен, ~ьна *adj.* independent

самосу́д, а *m.* lynch law, mob law

самоуби́йственный *adj.* suicidal (also fig.)

самоуби́йств|о, а *nt.* suicide; **покóнчить жизнь ~ом** to commit suicide

самоуби́йц|а, ы *c.g.* suicide (*victim*)

самоуважéни|е, я *nt.* self-esteem

самоувéрен|ный, ~, ~на *adj.* self-confident, self-assured

самоуправлéни|е, я *nt.* self-government; **мéстное с.** local government

самоупрáвств|о, а *nt.* arbitrariness

самоучи́тел|ь, я *m.* manual for self-tuition; **с. англи́йского языкá** teach-yourself English book

самоу́чк|а, и *c.g.* self-taught person

самоцвéт, а *m.* semi-precious stone, gem

самоцéл|ь, и *f.* end in itself

самочу́встви|е, я *nt.* general state; **у негó плохóе с.** he feels bad; **как вáше с.?** how are you (keeping)?

самши́т, а *m.* box (tree)

◇ **сáм|ый** *pron.* **1** (*in conjunction with nouns, esp. denoting time or place*) the very, right; **с ~ого начáла** from the very outset, right from the start; **с ~ого утрá** ever since the morning, since first thing; **в ~ом углу́** right in the corner; **до ~ого Владивостóка** right to, all the way to Vladivostok; **в ~ом дéле?** indeed?, really?; **на ~ом дéле** actually, in (actual) fact; **тот с., э́тот с.** the very, this very; **тот с. человéк, котóрый...** the very man who ...; **на э́том сáмом мéсте** in this very place **2**: **тот же с. (, котóрый/что)** the same (as); **э́тот же с.** the same **3** (*forms superl. of adjs.; also expr. superl. in conjunction with certain nn. denoting degree of quantity or quality*): **с. глу́пый** the stupidest, the most stupid

сан, а *m.* rank; office; **высóкий с.** high office; **духóвный с.** holy orders, the cloth

санатóри|й, я *m.* sanatorium

сандáл, а *m.* (bot.) sandalwood tree

сандáли|я, и *f.* sandal

сáн|и, éй (*no sg.*) sledge (BrE), sled (AmE); sleigh

санитáр, а *m.* hospital orderly; (mil.) medical orderly

санитáр|ка, ки *f. of* ▶ **санитáр**

санитáр|ный *adj.* **1** (*связанный с медицинской службой*) medical; hospital; **~ая слу́жба** health service, medical service **2** (*связанный с санитарией*) sanitary; sanitation; **с. врач** sanitary inspector; **~ые прáвила** sanitary regulations

сáн|ки, ок (*no sg.*) **1** = **сáни 2** (*детские*) toboggan

с

⚹ **Санкт-Петербу́рг, а** *m.* St Petersburg

санкт-петербу́ргский *adj.* St Petersburg

санкциони́р|овать, ую *impf. and pf.* to sanction

са́нкци|я, и *f.* **1** sanction, approval **2** (*in pl.*) (pol., econ.) sanctions

санскри́т, а *m.* Sanskrit

Са́нта-Кла́ус, Са́нта-Кла́уса *m.* Santa Claus

санте́хник, а *m.* plumber

санте́хник|а, и *f.* plumbing equipment

сантиме́тр, а *m.* **1** centimetre (BrE), centimeter (AmE) **2** (infml, *лента*) tape measure

Сан-Франци́ско *m. indecl.* San Francisco

сапёр, а *m.* (mil.) sapper

сапо́г, á, *g. pl.* **сапо́г** *m.* boot

сапо́жник, а *m.* shoemaker, cobbler

сапо́жный *adj.* boot, shoe; **с. крем** shoe polish

сапфи́р, а *m.* sapphire

сара́|й, я *m.* (*для дров, животных*) shed; (*для сена*) barn

сарафа́н, а *m.* (*платье*) pinafore dress (BrE), jumper (AmE)

сарде́льк|а, и *f.* sausage (*fat, of frankfurter type*)

сарди́н|а, ы *f.* sardine, pilchard

сарка́зм, а *m.* sarcasm

саркасти́ческий *adj.* sarcastic

сатан|а́, ы́ *m.* Satan

сатани́нский *adj.* satanic

сати́р|а, ы *f.* satire

сати́рик, а *m.* satirist

сатири́ческий *adj.* satirical

сау́дов|ец, ца *m.* Saudi

сау́дов|ка, ки *f. of* ▶ **сау́довец**

Сау́довск|ая Ара́вия, ∼ой Ара́вии *f.* Saudi Arabia

сау́довский *adj.* Saudi

сау́н|а, ы *f.* sauna

саундтре́к, а *m.* soundtrack

сафа́ри *nt. indecl.* safari; **с.-па́рк** safari park

са́хар, а (у) *m.* sugar

Саха́р|а, ы *f.* the Sahara (*desert*)

сахари́н, а *m.* saccharin

са́хар|ить, ю, ишь *impf. (of* ▶ **поса́харить**) to sugar, sweeten

са́харниц|а, ы *f.* sugar bowl

са́харный *adj. of* ▶ **са́хар**; (fig.) sugary; **с. песо́к** granulated sugar

сач|о́к, ка́ *m.* net; **с. для ба́бочек** butterfly net

сба́в|ить, лю, ишь *pf. (of* ▶ **сбавля́ть**) (с + *g.*) to reduce

сбавля́|ть, ю *impf. of* ▶ **сба́вить**

сбаланси́рован|ный, ∼, ∼а *adj.* well balanced, emotionally stable

сбега́|ть, ю *pf.* (за + *i.*) (infml) to run (for), run to fetch; **∼й за до́ктором!** run for a doctor!

сбега́|ть, ю, ет *impf. of* ▶ **сбежа́ть**

сбега́|ться, ется *impf. of* ▶ **сбежа́ться**

сбе|жа́ть, гу́, жи́шь, гу́т (*of* ▶ **сбега́ть**) **1** (с + *g.*) (*спусти́ться*) to run down (from); **с. с ле́стницы** to run downstairs **2** (*убежа́ть*) to run away

сбе|жа́ться, жи́тся, гу́тся *pf.* (*of* ▶ **сбега́ться**) to come running; to gather, collect

сберба́нк, а *m.* (infml) savings bank

сберега́тельн|ый *adj.*: **∼ый банк** savings bank; **∼ая кни́жка** passbook, bank book

сберега́|ть, ю *impf. of* ▶ **сбере́чь**

сбереже́ни|е, я *nt.* (*in pl.*) (*де́ньги*) savings

сбере́|чь, гу́, жёшь, гу́т, *past* **∼г, ∼гла́** *pf.* (*of* ▶ **сберега́ть**) (*вре́мя*) to save; (*семью́*) to protect, look after; (*здоро́вье*) to preserve

сберка́сс|а, ы *f.* (infml, hist.) savings bank

сберкни́жк|а, и *f.* (infml) savings book

сбива́|ть, ю *impf. of* ▶ **сбить**

сбива́|ться, юсь *impf.* **1** *impf. of* ▶ **сби́ться 2** (*impf. only*) (на + *a.*) to resemble; to remind one (of)

сби́вчив|ый, ∼, ∼а *adj.* inconsistent, contradictory

сбить, собью́, собьёшь *pf.* (*of* ▶ **сбива́ть**) **1** (*уда́ром*) to bring down, knock down; (с *чего́-л.*) to knock off, dislodge; (*пти́цу, самолёт*) to bring down, shoot down; (*це́ну, температу́ру*) to bring down **2** (*запу́тать*) to distract; to deflect; **с. кого́-н. с то́лку** to confuse sb **3** (*каблуки́, ту́фли*) to wear down **4** (*соста́вить*) to knock together; **с. я́щик из досо́к** to knock together a box out of planks

сби́ться, собью́сь, собьёшься *pf.* (*of* ▶ **сбива́ться** 1) **1** (*сдви́нуться с ме́ста*) to be dislodged; to slip; **у тебя́ шля́па сби́лась** на́бок your hat is crooked, skew-whiff **2** (*ошиби́ться*) to go wrong; **с. с доро́ги, с. с пути́** to lose one's way; to go astray; (*also* fig.): **с. со счёта** to lose count

сближа́|ть, ю *impf. of* ▶ **сбли́зить**

сближа́|ться, юсь *impf. of* ▶ **сбли́зиться**

сближе́ни|е, я *nt.* **1** (pol.) rapprochement **2** (*дру́жба*) intimacy

сбли́|зить, жу, зишь *pf. (of* ▶ **сближа́ть**) to bring together, draw together

сбли́|зиться, жусь, зишься *pf. (of* ▶ **сближа́ться**) **1** (*об интере́сах*) to converge **2** (с + *i.*) (*о лю́дях*) to become close friends (with)

сбо|й, я *m.* interruption; malfunction

сбо́ку *adv.* from one side; on one side; **вид с.** side view; **смотре́ть на кого́-н. с.** to look sideways at sb

сболтн|у́ть, у́, ёшь *pf.* (infml) to blurt out, let out

⚹ **сбор, а** *m.* **1** (*де́йствие*) collection; **с. урожа́я** harvest; (с. *нало́гов* tax collection **2** (*де́ньги*) dues; duty; (*вы́ручка*) takings, returns; **тамо́женный с.** customs duty; **де́лать хоро́шие ∼ы** (theatr.) to play to full houses, get good box office returns **3** (*встреча*) assembly, gathering; **быть в ~е** to be assembled, be in session **4** (*in pl.*) (*приготовления*) preparations

сбо́рк|а, и *f.* assembling, assembly, erection

сбо́рник, а *m.* collection; (*литературных произведений*) anthology

сбо́рный *adj.* **1** (*дом*) prefabricated; (*мебель*) in kit form **2** (*из разнородных частей*) mixed, combined; (*as n.*) national team **3** (mil.) assembly; **с. пункт** assembly point

сбра́сыва|ть, ю *impf. of* ▸ сбро́сить

сбрива́|ть, ю *impf. of* ▸ сбрить

сбрить, сбре́ю, сбре́ешь *pf.* (*of* ▸ сбрива́ть) to shave off

сброд, а (*no pl.*) *m.* (*collect.*) riff-raff, rabble

сбро́|сить, шу, сишь *pf.* (*of* ▸ сбра́сывать) **1** (*бросить вниз*) to throw down; to drop; **с. бо́мбы** to drop bombs **2** (*скинуть*) to throw off (also fig.); (*кожу, листья*) to shed; **с. (с себя́) одея́ло** to throw off a blanket; (*свергнуть*) to overthrow **3** (*сбавить*) to reduce

сбру́|я, и *f.* (*collect.*) harness

сбыва́|ться, юсь *impf. of* ▸ сбы́ться

сбыт, а (*no pl.*) *m.* (econ., comm.) sale; **ры́нок ~a** (seller's) market

сбы́ться, сбу́дется, *past* сбы́лся, сбыла́сь *pf.* (*of* ▸ сбыва́ться) to come true, be realized

св. (*abbr. of* свято́й) St, Saint

сва́дебный *adj.* wedding; **с. пода́рок** wedding present

сва́д|ьба, ьбы, *g. pl.* **~eб** *f.* wedding; **справля́ть ~ьбу** to celebrate a wedding

сва́лива|ть, ю *impf. of* ▸ свали́ть

сва́лива|ться, юсь *impf. of* ▸ свали́ться

свал|и́ть, ю́, ~ишь *pf.* (*of* ▸ вали́ть¹, ▸ сва́ливать) **1** (*ударом*) to throw down, bring down; (infml, *о болезни*) to lay low **2** (*дрова, уголь*) to heap up, pile up; **с. вину́** (**на** + *a.*) to lump the blame (on)

свал|и́ться, ю́сь, ~ишься *pf.* (*of* ▸ вали́ться, ▸ сва́ливаться) to fall (down), collapse; **с. как снег на́ голову** to come like a bolt from the blue

сва́лк|а, и *f.* dump; scrap heap

сваля́|ться, ется *pf.* to get tangled

сва́рива|ть, ю *impf. of* ▸ свари́ть

свар|и́ть, ю́, ~ишь *pf.* **1** *pf. of* ▸ вари́ть **2** (*impf.* ~ивать) (tech.) to weld

свар|и́ться, ~ится *pf. of* ▸ вари́ться

сва́рк|а, и *f.* (tech.) welding

сварли́в|ый, ~, ~a *adj.* quarrelsome, shrewish

сва́рщик, а *m.* welder

сва́стик|а, и *f.* swastika

сва́|я, и *f.* pile

  ♂ **сведе́ни|е, я** *nt.* **1** (*известие*) piece of information; (*in pl.*) information, intelligence **2** (*знание*) knowledge; attention, consideration, notice; **приня́ть**

к ~ю to take into consideration

све́дущ|ий, ~, ~a *adj.* (**в** + *p.*) knowledgeable (about); (well) versed (in)

све́жест|ь, и *f.* freshness; (*прохлада*) coolness

  ♂ **све́ж|ий, ~, ~á, ~ó, ~й** *adj.* fresh; **~ee бельё** clean underclothes; **с. ве́тер** fresh breeze; **на ~ем во́здухе** in the fresh air; **~ие но́вости** recent news

свёкл|а, ы *f.* beet, beetroot (BrE)

свёк|ор, ра *m.* father-in-law (*husband's father*)

свекро́в|ь, и *f.* mother-in-law (*husband's mother*)

сверг|а́ть, а́ю *impf. of* ▸ све́ргнуть

све́рг|нуть, ну, нешь, *past* ~ *and* ~нул, ~ла *pf.* (*of* ▸ сверга́ть) to throw down, overthrow; **с. с престо́ла** to dethrone

све́р|ить, ю, ишь *pf.* (*of* ▸ сверя́ть) (+ *a. and* **c** + *i.*) to check (sth against)

све́рк|а, и *f.* collation

сверка́|ть, ю *impf.* to sparkle; to glitter; to gleam; (*о молнии*) to flash

сверкн|у́ть, у́, ёшь *inst. pf.* to flash (also fig.)

сверл|и́ть, ю́, и́шь *impf.* (*of* ▸ просверли́ть) **1** (tech.) to bore, drill; **с. зуб** to drill a tooth **2** (*о насекомых*) to bore through

сверл|о́, á, *pl.* **~а, ~** *nt.* (tech.) (*инструмент*) drill; (*наконечник*) drill bit

сверн|у́ть, у́, ёшь *pf.* (*of* ▸ свора́чивать) **1** to roll (up); **с. ковёр** to roll up the carpet; **с. ше́ю кому́-н.** to wring sb's neck **2** (fig., *сократить*) to reduce, contract, cut down **3** (*повернуть*) to turn; **с. нале́во** to turn to the left; **с. с доро́ги** to turn off the road

сверн|у́ться, у́сь, ёшься *pf.* (*of* ▸ свора́чиваться) **1** to roll up, curl up; to coil up; **с. клубко́м** to roll oneself up into a ball **2** (*о молоке*) to curdle; (*о крови*) to coagulate, clot **3** (fig., *сократиться*) to contract

све́рстник, а *m.* person of the same age; contemporary, peer; **они́ ~и** they are the same age

све́рстни|ца, цы *f. of* ▸ све́рстник

сверх *prep.* + *g.* (*нормы*) above, beyond; over and above; in excess of; **с. пла́на** in excess of the plan; **с. (вся́кого) ожида́ния** beyond (all) expectation

сверх... *comb. form* super-, supra-, extra-, over-, preter-

сверхдержа́в|а, ы *f.* superpower

сверхзвуково́й *adj.* (phys., aeron.) supersonic

сверхпла́новый *adj.* over and above the plan

све́рху *adv.* **1** from above (also fig.); from the top; **с. до́низу** from top to bottom; **смотре́ть на кого́-н. с. вниз** (fig.) to look down on sb **2** (*на пове́рхности*) on the surface; on the top

сверхуро́чн|ый *adj.* overtime; **~ая рабо́та** overtime; (*as pl. n.* ~ые, ~ых) overtime pay

сверхчелове́к, а *m.* superman

сверхъесте́ствен|ный, ~, ~на adj. supernatural

сверч|о́к, ка́ m. (zool.) cricket

сверя́|ть, я́ю impf. of ▶ све́рить

све́|сить, шу, сишь pf. (of (of ▶ све́шивать) to let down, lower; сиде́ть, ~сив но́ги to sit with one's legs dangling

све́|ситься, шусь, сишься pf. (of ▶ све́шиваться) to lean over; to hang over; (о ветвях) to overhang; с. че́рез пери́ла to lean over the banisters

све|сти́, ду́, дёшь, past ~л, ~ла́ pf. (of ▶ своди́ть¹) 1 (спусти́ть све́рху вниз) to take down (from, off); с. с ума́ to drive mad 2 (соедини́ть; собра́ть) to bring together; to put together; to unite; судьба́ ~ла́ их fate threw them together; с. концы́ с конца́ми to make (both) ends meet 3 (к + d. or на + a.) (довести́) to reduce (to), bring (to); с. на нет to bring to naught 4 (о су́дороге) to cramp, convulse; у меня́ ~ло́ но́гу I have cramp in my foot

све|сти́сь, дётся, past ~лся, ~ла́сь pf. (of ▶ своди́ться) (к + d.) to come (to), reduce (to)

⚹ свет¹, а m. light (also fig.); лу́нный с. moonlight; заже́чь с. to turn the light on; в ~е (+ g.) in the light (of); на ~у́ in the light; при ~е (+ g.) by the light (of)

⚹ свет², а m. 1 (мир) world (also fig.); Ста́рый, Но́вый С. the Old, the New World; тот с. the next world; коне́ц ~а doomsday, the end of the world; появи́ться на с. to come into the world; ни за что на ~е not for the world 2 (вы́сшее о́бщество) society; вы́сший с. high society

света́|ть, ет impf. (impers.): ~ет it is dawning, it is getting light, day is breaking

свети́л|о, а nt. luminary (also fig.); небе́сные ~а heavenly bodies

свети́льник, а m. lamp

све|ти́ть, чу́, ~тишь impf. 1 (излуча́ть свет) to shine 2 (+ d.) to light the way (for); to shine a light (for)

све|ти́ться, чу́сь, ~тишься impf. to shine, gleam

све́тло-... comb. form light (with names of colours); све́тло-зелёный light green

световоло́с|ый, ~, ~а adj. light-haired

све́т|лый, ~ел, ~ла́, ~ло, ~лы and in pred. use ~ло́, ~лы adj. 1 (ко́мната, во́лосы, кра́ски) light; (день) bright; на у́лице ~ло́ it is daylight 2 (fig., ра́достный) bright, radiant, joyous; pure, unclouded; ~лое бу́дущее bright future 3 (fig., проница́тельный) lucid, clear; он — ~лая голова́ he has a lucid mind

светопреставле́ни|е, я nt. 1 the end of the world, doomsday 2 (fig., infml) chaos

светофи́льтр, а m. light filter

светофо́р, а m. traffic lights

све́тск|ий adj. 1 society, fashionable; ~ая жизнь high life; с. челове́к man of the world 2 (мане́ры) refined 3 (не церко́вный) temporal, lay, secular; worldly

светя́щийся pres. part. of ▶ свети́ться and adj. luminous, luminescent

свеч|а́, и, i. ~о́й, pl. ~и, ~е́й, ~а́м f. 1 candle 2: с. зажига́ния spark plug 3 (med.) suppository

свече́ни|е, я nt. luminescence, fluorescence; phosphorescence

све́шива|ть, ю impf. of ▶ све́сить

све́шива|ться, юсь impf. of ▶ све́ситься

свида́ни|е, я nt. meeting; (делово́е) appointment; (влюблённых) date; назна́чить с. (на + a.) to arrange a meeting (for), make an appointment (for), make a date (for); до ~я! goodbye!

свиде́тел|ь, я m. witness; с. обвине́ния, защи́ты witness for the prosecution, for the defence (BrE), defense (AmE)

свиде́тель|ница, ницы f. of ▶ свиде́тель

свиде́тельств|о, а nt. 1 evidence 2 (докуме́нт) certificate; с. о бра́ке marriage certificate

свиде́тельств|овать, ую impf. 1 to give evidence (concerning); to testify; (о + p. or + a. or + что) (law) to give evidence (concerning); to testify 2 (о + p.) (подтвержда́ть, дока́зывать) to show, attest to, be evidence (of); э́то письмо́ ~ует о его́ беста́ктности this letter is evidence of his tactlessness

свина́рник, а m. pigsty

свин|е́ц, ца́ m. lead

свини́н|а, ы f. pork

сви́н|ка¹, ки f. dim. of ▶ свинья́; морска́я с. guinea pig

сви́нк|а², и f. (med.) mumps

свин|о́й adj. of ▶ свинья́; ~а́я ко́жа pigskin; ~а́я котле́та pork chop; ~о́е са́ло lard

сви́нский adj. (infml) (по́длый) swinish; (гря́зный) filthy

сви́нств|о, а nt. (infml) (по́длость) swinishness; (посту́пок) swinish trick; (грязь) filth

свин|ти́ть, чу́, ти́шь pf. (of ▶ сви́нчивать) 1 (соедини́ть) to screw together 2 (га́йку) to unscrew

сви́нчива|ть, ю impf. of ▶ свинти́ть

свин|ья́, ьи́, pl. ~ьи, ~е́й, ~ья́м f. 1 pig; (са́мка) sow 2 (fig., pej., челове́к) swine; подложи́ть ~ью́ (+ d.) (infml) to play a dirty trick (on)

свире́л|ь, и f. (reed) pipe

свире́п|ый, ~, ~а adj. fierce, ferocious

свиса́|ть, а́ю impf. to hang down

свист, а m. whistle; whistling

сви|сте́ть, щу́, сти́шь impf. to whistle

сви́стн|уть, у, ешь pf. 1 to give a whistle 2 (infml, укра́сть) to steal, snatch

свист|о́к, ка́ m. whistle

сви́тер, а m. sweater

сви́т|ок, ка m. roll, scroll

свить, совью́, совьёшь, *past* **свил, свила́, сви́ло** *pf.* (*of* ▸ **вить**) to twist, wind

сви́ться, совьётся, *past* **сви́лся, свила́сь** *pf.* (*of* ▸ **ви́ться**) to roll up, curl up, coil

свихн|у́ться, у́сь, ёшься *pf.* (infml) to go off one's head

◌ **свобо́д|а, ы** *f.* freedom, liberty; **с. во́ли** free will; **с. сло́ва** freedom of speech; **на** ∼**е** at large

свобо́дно *adv.* **1** (*без принужде́ния*) freely; (*с лёгкостью*) with ease; **она́ с. говори́т на пяти́ языка́х** she speaks five languages fluently **2** (*просто́рно*) loose, loosely

◌ **свобо́д|ный,** ∼**ен,** ∼**на** *adj.* **1** free **2** (*без поме́х*) free; easy; **с. до́ступ** easy access **3** (*не за́нятый*) free; (*но́мер*) vacant; (*ме́сто*) spare; ∼**ное вре́мя** free time; ∼**ное ме́сто** vacant seat, spare seat; **вы** ∼**ны сего́дня ве́чером?** are you free this evening? **4** (*поведе́ние*) free (and easy) **5** (*оде́жда*) loose, loose-fitting; flowing

свободолюби́в|ый, ∼, ∼**а** *adj.* freedom-loving

свод¹, а *m.* code; (*докуме́нтов*) collection; **с. зако́нов** code of laws

свод², а *m.* (*перекры́тие*) arch, vault; **небе́сный с.** the firmament

сво|ди́ть¹, жу́, ∼**дишь** *impf. of* ▸ **свести́**

сво|ди́ть², жу́, ∼**дишь** *pf.* (*отвести́ и привести́ обра́тно*) to take (*and bring back*); **мы** ∼**ди́ли дете́й в кино́** we took the children to the cinema

сво|ди́ться, ∼**дится** *impf. of* ▸ **свести́сь**

сво́дк|а, и *f.* summary; report; **с. пого́ды** weather forecast, weather report

сво́дн|ый *adj.* **1** combined; collated; ∼**ая табли́ца** summary table, index **2** step-; **с. брат** stepbrother

сво́дчатый *adj.* arched, vaulted

своево́л|ьный, ∼**ен,** ∼**ьна** *adj.* self-willed, wilful

своевре́мен|ный, ∼ *and* ∼**ен,** ∼**на** *adj.* timely, opportune

своенра́в|ный, ∼**ен,** ∼**на** *adj.* wilful, capricious

своеобра́з|ный, ∼**ен,** ∼**на** *adj.* original; peculiar, distinctive

сво|зи́ть, жу́, ∼**зишь** *pf.* (*отвезти́ и привезти́ обра́тно*) to take (*and bring back*); **мы** ∼**зи́ли дете́й в цирк** we took the children to the circus

◌ **свой** *poss. adj.* one's (my, your, his, *etc.*, *in accordance with subject of sentence or clause*), one's own; **у них с. дом** they have a house of their own; **умере́ть свое́й сме́ртью** to die a natural death; **в своё вре́мя** at one time, in my, his, *etc.*, time; (*своевре́менно*) in due time, in due course; **он не в своём уме́** he is not right in the head; (*as pl. n.* **свои́**) one's (own) people; **свои́** one's own; **доби́ться своего́** to get one's own way

сво́йствен|ный, ∼ *and* ∼**ен,** ∼**на** *adj.* (+ *d.*) characteristic (of)

◌ **сво́йств|о, а** *nt.* characteristic

сво́лоч|ь, и, *g. pl.* ∼**е́й** *f.* (infml) scum, swine

свора́чива|ть, ю *impf. of* ▸ **сверну́ть**

свора́чива|ться, юсь *impf. of* ▸ **сверну́ться**

свор|ова́ть, у́ю (infml) *pf. of* ▸ **ворова́ть**

свояк, а́ *m.* brother-in-law (*husband of wife's sister*)

своя́чениц|а, ы *f.* sister-in-law (*wife's sister*)

свык|а́ться, а́юсь *impf. of* ▸ **свы́кнуться**

свы́к|нуться, нусь, нешься, *past* ∼**ся,** ∼**лась** *pf.* (*of* ▸ **свыка́ться**) (**с** + *i.*) to get used (to)

свысока́ *adv.* condescendingly; **обраща́ться с кем-н. с.** to talk down, patronize sb

свы́ше 1 *adv.* from above; (relig.) from on high **2** *prep.* (+ *g.*) (*бо́лее*) over, more than; (*вне*) beyond; **с. ты́сячи самолётов уча́ствовало в налёте** over a thousand planes took part in the raid

◌ **свя|за́ть, жу́,** ∼**жешь** *pf.* (*of* ▸ **вяза́ть 2,** ▸ **свя́зывать**) **1** to tie; to bind (also fig.); **с. свою́ судьбу́** (**с** + *i.*) to throw in one's lot (with) **2** (fig., *соедини́ть*) to connect, link; **быть (те́сно)** ∼**занным** (**с** + *i.*) to be (closely) connected (with), be bound up (with) **3**: **быть** ∼**занным** (**с** + *i.*) (fig., *повле́чь*) to involve, entail; **э́то предприя́тие бу́дет** ∼**зано с огро́мными расхо́дами** this undertaking will involve huge expense **4** (*установи́ть связь*) to link, associate; **не́которые** ∼**зали эпиде́мию с плохи́м водоснабже́нием** some connected the epidemic with the bad water supply

свя|за́ться, жу́сь, ∼**жешься** *pf.* (*of* ▸ **свя́зываться 1**) (**с** + *i.*) **1** to get in touch (with), communicate (with) **2** (infml, pej.) to get involved (with), get mixed up (with)

свя́зк|а, и *f.* **1** (*ключе́й*) bunch; (*книг, бума́г*) bundle **2** (anat.) cord; ligament; **голосовы́е** ∼**и** vocal cords

свя́з|ный, ∼**ен,** ∼**на** *adj.* connected, coherent

свя́зыва|ть, ю *impf. of* ▸ **связа́ть**

свя́зыва|ться, юсь *impf.* **1** *impf. of* ▸ **связа́ться 2** (*impf. only*) (**с** + *i.*) to have to do (with); **не** ∼**йся с ни́ми** don't have anything to do with them

◌ **связ|ь, и, о** ∼**и, в** ∼**и́** *f.* **1** (*отноше́ние*) connection; **в связи́ с** (+ *i.*) (*всле́дствие*) due to; owing to; (*по по́воду*) in connection with; **в связи́ с э́тим** in this connection **2** (*те́сное обще́ние*) link, tie, bond; **дру́жеские** ∼**и** friendly relations, ties of friendship **3** (*любо́вная*) liaison, relationship **4** (*in pl.*) (*бли́зкое знако́мство*) connections, contacts; **у него́ мно́го** ∼**ей в Москве́** he has many influential connections in Moscow **5** (*сообще́ние*) communication; **с. по ра́дио** radio communication **6** (*sg. only*) (*по́чта, телефо́н*) (post and tele)communications; **отделе́ние** ∼**и** (branch) post office

◌ **свят|о́й,** ∼, ∼**а́,** ∼**о** *adj.* **1** (*свяще́нный*) holy; sacred (also fig.); ∼**а́я вода́** holy water; **С. Дух**

the Holy Ghost, the Holy Spirit **2** (*человек*) saintly **3** (*preceding name, or as n.* с., ~о́го, *f.* ~а́я, ~о́й) saint; причи́слить к ли́ку ~ых (eccl.) to canonize

свя́тост|ь, и *f.* holiness; sanctity

святота́тств|о, а *nt.* sacrilege

святы́н|я, и *f.* **1** (eccl.) (*предмет*) object of worship; (*место*) sacred place **2** (fig., *предмет*) sacred object

свяще́нник, а *m.* (*православный*) priest (*of Orthodox Church*); clergyman

свяще́н|ный, ~ен, ~на *adj.* holy; sacred (also fig.); C~ное Писа́ние Holy Writ, Scripture

сгиб, а *m.* **1** bend **2** (anat.) flexion

сгиба́|ть, ю *impf. of* ▸ согну́ть

сгиба́|ться, юсь *impf. of* ▸ согну́ться

сги́н|уть, у, ешь *pf.* (infml) to disappear, vanish

сгла́|дить, жу, дишь *pf.* (*of* ▸ сгла́живать) **1** (*выровнять*) to smooth out **2** (fig., *смягчить*) to smooth over, soften

сгла́|диться, дится *pf.* (*of* ▸ сгла́живаться) **1** (*выровняться*) to become smooth **2** (fig., *смягчиться*) to be smoothed over, be softened

сгла́жива|ть, ю, ет *impf. of* ▸ сгла́дить

сгла́жива|ться, ется *impf. of* ▸ сгла́диться

сглаз, а *m.* (infml) the evil eye

сгла́|зить, жу, зишь *pf.* to put the evil eye (on, upon); (fig., infml) to jinx

сгни́|ть, ю́, ёшь *pf.* (*of* ▸ гнить) to rot, decay

сгова́рива|ться, юсь *impf. of* ▸ сговори́ться

сговор|и́ться, ю́сь, и́шься *pf.* (*of* ▸ сгова́риваться) (с + *i.*) to arrange (with)

сгово́рчив|ый, ~, ~а *adj.* compliant, tractable

сгора́ни|е, я *nt.* combustion; дви́гатель вну́треннего ~я internal-combustion engine

сгор|а́ть, а́ю *impf.* **1** *impf. of* ▸ сгоре́ть **2** (от + *g.*) (fig.) to be dying (of); с. от стыда́, любопы́тства to be dying of shame, curiosity

сго́рб|иться, люсь, ишься *pf. of* ▸ го́рбиться

сго́рблен|ный, ~, ~а *adj.* crooked, bent; hunchbacked

сгор|е́ть, ю́, и́шь *pf.* (*of* ▸ сгора́ть 1) **1** to burn down; to be burnt out, down; наш дом ~е́л our house was burnt down **2** (*о топливе*) to be consumed, be used up

сгоряча́ *adv.* in the heat of the moment; in a fit of temper

сгреба́|ть, ю *impf. of* ▸ сгрести́

сгре|сти́, бу́, бёшь, past ~б, ~бла́ *pf.* (*of* ▸ сгреба́ть) (*собрать*) to rake up, rake together

сгруд|и́ться, и́тся *pf.* (infml) to crowd, mill, bunch

сгруппир|ова́ть, у́ю *pf. of* ▸ группирова́ть

⚔ key word

сгуб|и́ть, лю́, ~ишь *pf.* (infml) to ruin

сгу|сти́ть, щу́, сти́шь *pf.* (*of* ▸ сгуща́ть) to thicken; (*конденсировать*) to condense; с. кра́ски (fig.) to lay it on thick

сгу|сти́ться, стится *pf.* (*of* ▸ сгуща́ться) to thicken; (*конденсироваться*) to condense; (*о крови*) to clot

сгу́ст|ок, ка *m.* clot

сгуща́|ть, ю, ет *impf. of* ▸ сгусти́ть

сгуща́|ться, ется *impf. of* ▸ сгусти́ться

⚔ **сда|ва́ть, ю́, ёшь** *impf.* (*of* ▸ сдать): с. экза́мен to take, sit an examination

сда|ва́ться, ю́сь, ёшься *impf. of* ▸ сда́ться

сдав|и́ть, лю́, ~ишь *pf.* (*of* ▸ сда́вливать) to squeeze

сда́влива|ть, ю *impf. of* ▸ сдави́ть

сдать, сдам, сдашь, сдаст, сдади́м, сдади́те, сдаду́т, past сдал, сдала́, сда́ло *pf.* (*of* ▸ сдава́ть) **1** (*передать*) to hand over, pass; с. бага́ж на хране́ние to deposit one's luggage **2** (*отдать внаём*) to let, let out, hire out; с. в аре́нду to lease **3** (*возвратить*) to give change **4** (*уступить*) to surrender, yield, give up **5** (*экзамен*) to pass (*an examination, a subject, etc.*); он сдал то́лько латы́нь he only passed in Latin **6** (*карты*) to deal (cards) **7** (infml) (*о моторе, сердце*) to give out; (*о старике, здоровье*) to become weaker

сда́|ться, мся, шься, стся, ди́мся, ди́тесь, ду́тся, past ~лся, ~ла́сь *pf.* (*of* ▸ сдава́ться) to surrender, yield; (chess) to resign

сда́ч|а, и *f.* **1** (*квартиры*) letting out, hiring out; с. в аре́нду leasing **2** (*города*) surrender **3** (*деньги*) change; три рубля́ ~и three roubles change; с. с рубля́ change from one rouble; дать ~и (+ *d.*) (fig., infml) to give as good as one gets

сдвиг, а *m.* **1** displacement; (geol.) fault **2** (fig., *улучшение*) change (for the better), improvement

сдвига́|ть, ю *impf. of* ▸ сдви́нуть

сдвига́|ться, юсь *impf. of* ▸ сдви́нуться

сдви́|нуть, ну, нешь *pf.* (*of* ▸ сдвига́ть) **1** to shift, move, displace; с. с ме́ста (fig.) to get moving, set in motion **2** (*соединить*) to move together, bring together

сдви́|нуться, нусь, нешься *pf.* (*of* ▸ сдвига́ться) to move, budge; с. с ме́ста (fig.) to progress; де́ло не ~нулось с ме́ста no headway has been made

⚔ **сде́ла|ть, ю** *pf. of* ▸ де́лать

⚔ **сде́ла|ться, юсь** *pf. of* ▸ де́латься

⚔ **сде́лк|а, и** *f.* transaction, deal, bargain

сде́льн|ый *adj.* piecework; ~ая опла́та payment by the piece, by the job; ~ая рабо́та piecework

сде́ржан|ный, ~, ~а *p.p.p. of* ▸ сдержа́ть *and* (~, ~на) *adj.* restrained, reserved

сдерж|а́ть, у́, ~ишь *pf.* (*of* ▸ сде́рживать) **1** to hold (back); (*неприятеля*) to hold in check, contain **2** (*fig.*, *чувства*) to keep back, restrain; **с. слёзы** to suppress tears **3** (*обещание*) to keep; **с. сло́во** to keep one's word

сдерж|а́ться, у́сь, ~ишься *pf.* (*of* ▶ **сде́рживаться**) to restrain oneself, contain oneself; to check oneself

сде́ржива|ть, ю *impf. of* ▶ **сдержа́ть**

сде́ржива|ться, юсь *impf. of* ▶ **сдержа́ться**

сдира́|ть, ю *impf. of* ▶ **содра́ть**

сдо́хн|уть, у, ешь *pf.* (*of* ▶ **сдыха́ть**) **1** (*infml*, *о животных*) to die **2** (*vulg. sl.*, *pej.*, *о людях*) to peg out, kick the bucket

сдруж|и́ться, у́сь, ~ишься *pf.* (с + *i.*) to become friends (with)

сдува́|ть, ю *impf. of* ▶ **сдуть**

сду|ть, ~ю, ~ешь *pf.* (*of* ▶ **сдува́ть**) to blow away, blow off

сдыха́|ть, ю *impf. of* ▶ **сдо́хнуть**

сеа́нс, а *m.* **1** (*представление*) performance, show **2** (*массажа*, *гипноза*) session **3** (*портретиста*) sitting **4** (*спиритический*) seance

себе́[1] *see* ▶ **себя́**

себе́[2] *particle* (infml) (*modifying v. or pron. and usu. containing hint of reproach*): **ничего́ с.** not bad; **так с.** so-so

себесто́имост|ь, и *f.* (econ.) cost (*of manufacture*); cost price; **прода́ть по ~и** to sell at cost price

⚘ **себя́, себе́, собо́й** *and* **собо́ю, о себе́** *refl. pron.* oneself; (*я*) myself; (*ты*, *вы*) yourself; (*он*) himself, *etc.*; **прийти́ в с.** (**от** + *g.*) to get over; to come to one's senses; **не в себе́** not oneself; **от с.** away from oneself, outwards; (*лично*, *от своего́ и́мени*) for oneself, on one's own behalf; **чита́ть про с.** to read to oneself; **у с.** at home, at one's (own) place

себялюби́в|ый, ~, ~а *adj.* egotistical, selfish

се́вер, а *m.* north

⚘ **се́верн|ый** *adj.* north, northern; (*направление*, *ветер*) northerly; **с. оле́нь** reindeer; **С. по́люс** North Pole; **С. Ледови́тый океа́н** Arctic Ocean; **С. поля́рный круг** Arctic Circle; **~ое сия́ние** Northern Lights, aurora borealis

североамерика́нский *adj.* North American

се́веро-восто́к, а *m.* north-east

се́веро-восто́чный *adj.* north-east, north-eastern

се́веро-за́пад, а *m.* north-west

се́веро-за́падный *adj.* north-west, north-western

североирла́ндский *adj.* Northern Irish

северя́н|ин, ина, *pl.* **~е, ~** *m.* northerner

севрю́г|а, и *f.* stellate sturgeon (*Acipenser stellatus*)

сегме́нт, а *m.* segment

⚘ **сего́дня** *adv.* today; **с. ве́чером** this evening, tonight

⚘ **сего́дня|шний** *adj. of* ▶ **сего́дня**; **с. день**

today; **~шняя газе́та** today's paper

седе́|ть, ю *impf.* (*of* ▶ **поседе́ть**) to go grey (BrE), gray (AmE)

седин|а́, ы́, *pl.* **~ы, ~** *f.* grey (BrE), gray (AmE) hair(s)

сед|ло́, ла́, *pl.* **~ла, ~ел** *nt.* saddle

сед|о́й, ~, ~а́, ~о, ~ы́ *adj.* (*волосы*) grey (BrE), gray (AmE); (*человек*) grey-haired (BrE), gray-haired (AmE)

седьм|о́й *adj.* seventh; **быть на ~о́м не́бе** to be in seventh heaven

⚘ **сезо́н, а** *m.* season

сезо́нн|ый *adj.* seasonal; **с. биле́т** season ticket; **~ые рабо́ты** seasonal work

⚘ **сей,** *f.* **сия́,** *nt.* **сие́,** *pl.* **сий** *pron.* this; **сию́ мину́ту** this (very) minute; at once, instantly; **до сих пор** up to now, till now, hitherto; **на с. раз** this time, for this once; **по с. день** to this day

сейсми́ческий *adj.* seismic

сейсмоопа́с|ный, ~ен, ~на *adj.* earthquake-prone

сейсмосто́йкий, ~ек, ~йка *adj.* earthquake-proof

сейф, а *m.* safe

⚘ **сейча́с** *adv.* **1** (*теперь*) (right) now, at present, at the (present) moment **2** (*очень скоро*) presently, soon; **с. же** at once, immediately; **с.!** in a minute!; half a minute!

секи́р|а, ы *f.* axe (BrE), ax (AmE)

⚘ **секре́т, а** *m.* secret; **по ~у** confidentially, in confidence

секрета́р|ша, ши *f.* (infml) *of* ▶ **секрета́рь**

секрета́р|ь, я́ *m.* secretary; **ли́чный с.** private secretary, personal secretary; **генера́льный с.** secretary general

секре́тно *adv.* secretly, in secret; (*надпись*) 'secret', 'confidential'; **соверше́нно с.** 'top secret'

секре́тност|ь, и *f.* secrecy

секре́т|ный, ~ен, ~на *adj.* secret; confidential

секре́ци|я, и *f.* (physiol.) secretion

⚘ **секс, а** *m.* sex

сексо́лог, а *m.* sexologist

сексоло́ги|я, и *f.* sexology

сексуа́льность|, и *f.* sexuality

сексуа́л|ьный, ~ен, ~ьна *adj.* sexual; (*эроти́чный*) sexy; **~ьное домога́тельство** sexual harassment; **~ьные отноше́ния** sexual relations

се́кт|а, ы *f.* sect

секта́нт, а *m.* sectarian; member of a sect

⚘ **се́ктор, а,** *pl.* **~ы, ~ов** *and* **~а́, ~о́в** *m.* **1** (math., mil.) sector; **с. Га́за** the Gaza Strip **2** (*отдел*) section, department; (econ.) sector

⚘ **секу́нд|а, ы** *f.* second; **одну́ ~у!** just a moment!

секундоме́р, а *m.* stopwatch

се́кци|я, и *f.* section

селёдк|а, и *f.* herring

селезёнк|а, и *f.* (physiol.) spleen

се́лез|ень, ня *m.* drake

селекционе́р, а *m.* **1** (agric.) breeder **2** (sport) scout

селе́кци|я, и *f.* **1** (agric.) selective breeding **2** (sport) selection

селе́ни|е, я *nt.* settlement

сели́тр|а, ы *f.* (chem.) saltpetre (BrE), saltpeter (AmE)

сел|и́ть, ю́, и́шь *impf.* (*of* ▶ посели́ть) to settle

сел|и́ться, ю́сь, и́шься *impf.* (*of* ▶ посели́ться) to settle

ɢ **сел|о́, а́,** *pl.* ∼а *nt.* village

сел|ь, я *m.* (seasonal) mountain torrent

сельдере́|й, я *m.* celery

сельд|ь, и, *pl.* ∼и, ∼е́й *f.* herring

ɢ **се́льск|ий** *adj.* **1** (*не городской*) country, rural; ∼ая ме́стность rural area; countryside; ∼ое хозя́йство agriculture, farming **2** (*школа, улица*) village

сельскохозя́йственный *adj.* agricultural, farming

сема́нтик|а, и *f.* **1** (*наука*) semantics **2** (*значение слова*) meanings

семафо́р, а *m.* semaphore

сёмг|а, и *f.* salmon

ɢ **семе́йн|ый** *adj.* **1** family; domestic; по ∼ым обстоя́тельствам for domestic reasons **2** (*имеющий семью*) having a family; **с. челове́к** family man

семе́йств|о, а *nt.* family

семена́ *see* ▶ се́мя

семёрк|а, и *f.* **1** (*цифра, игральная карта*) seven **2** (infml, *автобус, трамвай*) No. 7 (*bus, tram, etc.*) **3** (*группа из семерых*) (group of) seven; **Больша́я с.** the seven economically most developed nations

се́мер|о, ы́х *num.* (collect.) seven

семе́стр, а *m.* term (BrE), semester (AmE)

се́меч|ко, ка, *pl.* ∼ки, ∼ек *nt.* **1** *dim. of* ▶ се́мя **2** (*in pl.*) (*подсолнечника*) sunflower seeds; (*тыквенные*) pumpkin seeds

семибо́рь|е, я *nt.* heptathlon

семидеся́т|ый *adj.* seventieth; ∼ые го́ды the seventies

семиле́тний *adj.* **1** (*срок*) seven-year **2** (*ребёнок*) seven-year-old

ɢ **семина́р, а** *m.* seminar

семина́ри|я, и *f.* seminary, training college; **духо́вная с.** theological college

семисо́тый *adj.* seven-hundredth

семи́т, а *m.* Semite

семна́дцатый *adj.* seventeenth

семна́дцат|ь, и *num.* seventeen

ɢ **сем|ь, и́,** *i.* ∼ью́ *num.* seven

се́мьдесят, семи́десяти, *i.* **семью́десятью** *num.* seventy

семьсо́т, семисо́т, семиста́м, семьюста́ми, о семиста́х *num.* seven hundred

ɢ *key word*

се́мью *adv.* seven times

ɢ **сем|ья́, ьи́,** *pl.* ∼ьи, ∼е́й, ∼ьям *f.* family

се́м|я, ени, *pl.* ∼ена́, ∼я́н, ∼ена́м *nt.* **1** (bot., *also fig.*) seed **2** (*сперма*) semen, sperm

сена́т, а *m.* senate

сена́тор, а *m.* senator

сенберна́р, а *m.* St Bernard (*dog*)

Сенега́л, а *m.* Senegal

сенега́л|ец, ьца *m.* Senegalese

сенега́л|ка, ки *f. of* ▶ сенега́лец

сенега́льский *adj.* Senegalese

сенн|о́й *adj.* hay; ∼а́я лихора́дка hay fever

се́н|о, а *nt.* hay

сеноко́с, а *m.* haymaking; hayfield

сенсацио́н|ный, ∼ен, ∼на *adj.* sensational

сенса́ци|я, и *f.* sensation

сентимента́л|ьный, ∼ен, ∼ьна *adj.* sentimental

ɢ **сентя́бр|ь, я́** *m.* September

сентя́брьский *adj. of* ▶ сентя́брь

сепарати́зм, а *m.* (pol.) separatism

сепарати́ст, а *m.* (pol.) separatist

се́р|а, ы *f.* **1** (chem.) sulphur (BrE), sulfur (AmE) **2** (*в ушах*) earwax

серб, а *m.* Serb, Serbian

Се́рби|я, и *f.* Serbia

се́рб|ка, ки *f. of* ▶ серб

се́рбский *adj.* Serb, Serbian

серва́нт, а *m.* sideboard

ɢ **се́рвер, а** *m.* (comput.) server

серви́з, а *m.* service, set; **столо́вый с.** dinner service

сервир|ова́ть, у́ю *impf. and pf.*: **с. стол** to lay a table

ɢ **се́рвис, а** *m.* (consumer) service

серде́чно-сосу́дистый *adj.* cardiovascular

серде́ч|ный, ∼ен, ∼на *adj.* **1** of the heart (*also fig.*); (anat.) cardiac; **с. при́ступ** heart attack **2** (*приём*) cordial; (*благодарность*) heartfelt, sincere **3** (*человек*) warm, warm-hearted

серди́т|ый, ∼, ∼а *adj.* (на + *a.*) angry (with, at, about), cross (with, about); irate

серд|и́ть, жу́, ∼ишь *impf.* (*of* ▶ рассерди́ть) to anger, make angry

серд|и́ться, жу́сь, ∼ишься *impf.* (*of* ▶ рассерди́ться) (на + *a.*) to be angry (with, at, about), be cross (with, about)

ɢ **се́рд|це, ца,** *pl.* ∼ца́, ∼е́ц *nt.* heart; **приня́ть (бли́зко) к ∼цу** to take to heart; **от всего́ ∼ца** from the bottom of one's heart, wholeheartedly

сердцебие́ни|е, я *nt.* palpitation; (med.) tachycardia

сердцеви́н|а, ы *f.* (*плода, стебля*) core

серебри́ст|ый, ∼, ∼а *adj.* silvery

серебр|о́, а́ *nt.* **1** silver **2** (collect.) silver; **столо́вое с.** silver, plate

сере́бряный *adj.* silver

ɢ **середи́н|а, ы** *f.* middle, midst; **золота́я с.**

the golden mean

серёжк|а, и *f.* **1** earring **2** (bot.) catkin

сержа́нт, а *m.* sergeant

сериа́л, а *m.* (TV/radio) serial

сери́йный *adj.* serial; **сери́йный но́мер** serial number; **сери́йный уби́йца** serial killer

✧ **сери|я, и** *f.* series; (*часть фильма*) part

се́рн|а, ы *f.* (zool.) chamois

се́рн|ый *adj.* sulphuric (BrE), sulfuric (AmE); **∼ая кислота́** sulphuric acid

сероводоро́д, а *m.* (chem.) hydrogen sulphide (BrE), sulfide (AmE)

серп, á *m.* sickle

серпанти́н, а *m.* **1** (*бумажная лента*) paper streamer **2** (*дорога*) winding mountain road

сертифика́т, а *m.* certificate

сёрфинг, а *m.* surfing

сёрфинги́ст, а *m.* surfer

сёрфинги́ст|ка, ки *f. of* ▸ **сёрфинги́ст**

се́р|ый, ∼, ∼á, ∼о *adj.* **1** grey (BrE), gray (AmE) **2** (fig.) (*бесцветный*) grey (BrE), gray (AmE); dull; drab; **с. день** grey day **3** (fig., infml, *необразованный*) dull, dim

серьг|á, и́, pl. ∼и, серёг, ∼ám *f.* earring

серьёзно *adv.* seriously; **с.?** seriously?; really?

✧ **серьёз|ный, ∼ен, ∼на** *adj.* serious

се́сси|я, и *f.* session, sitting

✧ **сестр|á, ы́, pl. ∼ы, сестёр, ∼ám** *f.* **1** sister; **двою́родная с.** (first) cousin **2**: **медици́нская с.** nurse

сесть¹, ся́ду, ся́дешь, *past* **сел, се́ла** *pf.* (*of* ▸ **сади́ться**) **1** to sit down; **с. за стол** to sit down to table; **с. рабо́тать** to get down to work **2** (**в, на** + *a.*) to board, take; **с. на по́езд** to board a train; **с. на ло́шадь** to mount a horse **3** (*о птице*) to alight, settle, perch; (*о самолёте*) to land **4** (*о солнце*) to set **5**: **с. в тюрьму́** to go to prison, jail

сесть², ся́дет, *past* **сел** *pf.* (*of* ▸ **сади́ться**) (*о ткани*) to shrink

сетево́й *adj.* net, netting, mesh; (comput.) network; Internet

се́тк|а, и *f.* net; (*для багажа*) (luggage) rack

✧ **сет|ь, и, о ∼и, в ∼и and ∼й, pl. ∼и, ∼е́й** *f.* **1** net (also fig.) **2** (*система*) network; system; **лока́льная с.** (comput.) local area network, LAN **3** (**Сеть**) the Net (*Internet*)

Сеу́л, а *m.* Seoul

сече́ни|е, я *nt.* section; **ке́сарево с.** Caesarean (BrE), Cesarean (AmE) (section); **попере́чное с.** cross section

се́|ять, ю, ешь *impf.* (*of* ▸ **посе́ять**) to sow (also fig.); **с. семена́ раздо́ра** to sow the seeds of dissension

сжа́тый *p.p.p. of* ▸ **сжать¹** *and adj.* **1** compressed (*air, gas*) **2** (fig.) condensed, concise

сжать¹, сожму́, сожмёшь *pf.* (*of* ▸ **сжима́ть**) to squeeze; (*жидкость, газ; изложение*) to compress (also fig.); (*чью-н. руку*) to grip;

с. зу́бы to grit one's teeth; **с. кулаки́** to clench one's fists

сжать², сожну́, сожнёшь *pf. of* ▸ **жать²**

сжа́|ться, сожму́сь, сожмёшься *pf.* (*of* ▸ **сжима́ться**) **1** (*о пальцах, зубах*) to tighten, clench **2** (*о теле*) to contract

сжечь, сожгу́, сожжёшь, сожгу́т, *past* **сжёг, сожгла́** *pf.* (*of* ▸ **жечь 1,** ▸ **сжига́ть**) to burn (up, down); (*в крематории*) to cremate

сжива́|ться, юсь *impf. of* ▸ **сжи́ться**

сжига́|ть, ю *impf. of* ▸ **сжечь**

сжима́|ть, ю *impf. of* ▸ **сжать¹**

сжима́|ться, юсь ся *impf. of* ▸ **сжа́ться**

сжи́|ться, ву́сь, вёшься, *past* **∼лся, ∼ла́сь** *pf.* (*of* ▸ **сжива́ться**) (infml) (**с** + *i.*) to get used (to), get accustomed (to)

сза́ди *adv. and prep.* **1** *adv.* from behind; behind; from the end; from the rear; **вид с.** rear view; **тре́тий ваго́н с.** the third coach from the rear **2** *prep.* + *g.* behind

си *nt. indecl.* (mus.) B

сиби́рск|ий *adj.* Siberian; **∼ая я́зва** (med.) anthrax

Сиби́р|ь, и *f.* Siberia

сига́р|а, ы *f.* cigar

сигаре́т|а, ы *f.* cigarette

✧ **сигна́л, а** *m.* signal; **с. бе́дствия** distress signal

сигнализа́ци|я, и *f.* **1** (*действие*) signalling (BrE), signaling (AmE) **2** (*устройство*) alarm system **3** (*система*) signalling (BrE), signaling (AmE) system

сигнализи́р|овать, ую *impf. and pf.* **1** to signal **2** (+ *a. or* **о** + *p.*) (fig.) to give warning (of)

сиде́лк|а, и *f.* nurse (*looking after sick people*)

сиде́нь|е, я *nt.* seat

✧ **сид|е́ть, жу́, ди́шь** *impf.* **1** to sit; **с. на ко́рточках** to squat **2** (*находиться*) to be; **с. (в тюрьме́)** to be in prison **3** (**на** + *p.*) (*об одежде*) to fit, sit (on)

сид|е́ться, и́тся *impf.* (impers. + *d.*): **ему́** *и m. n.* **не ∼и́тся до́ма** he, *etc.*, can't bear staying at home; **ей не ∼и́тся на ме́сте** she can't keep still

Си́дне|й, я *m.* Sydney

си́з|ый, ∼, ∼á, ∼о *adj.* blue-grey (BrE), blue-gray (AmE)

си́квел, а *m.* (+ *g. or* **к** + *d.*) sequel (to)

сикх, а *m.* Sikh

си́кхский *adj.* Sikh

✧ **си́л|а, ы** *f.* **1** strength, force; **в ∼у** (+ *g.*) by virtue (of), because (of); **быть в ∼ах** (+ *inf.*) to be able to, have the strength (to); **изо всех ∼, что есть ∼ы** with all one's might; **че́рез ∼у** with the greatest of effort; **∼ой** by force; **свои́ми ∼ами** unaided; **с. во́ли** willpower **2** (phys., tech.) force, power; **лошади́ная с.** horsepower; **с. тя́жести, с. притяже́ния** force of gravity **3** (law, also fig.) force; **име́ющий в ∼е** valid; **войти́, вступи́ть в ∼у** to come into force, take effect **4** (*in pl.*) (mil.) forces; **вооружённые ∼ы** armed forces

сила́ч, á *m.* strong man

силико́н, а *m.* silicone

си́л|иться, юсь, ишься *impf.* to try very hard, make efforts

силов|о́й *adj.* power; ~**а́я устано́вка** power plant; ~**ы́е структу́ры** law enforcement agencies

си́лой *adv.* (*infml*) by force

сил|о́к, ка́ *m.* snare

силуэ́т, а *m.* silhouette

⚔ **си́льно** *adv.* **1** strongly; violently **2** (*очень*) very much, greatly; badly

⚔ **си́л|ьный, ~ён, ~ьна́, ~ьно, ~ьны́** *adj.* strong; powerful; **с. дождь** heavy rain; ~**ьное жела́ние** intense desire; **с. за́пах** strong smell

симбио́з, а *m.* (biol.) symbiosis

⚔ **си́мвол**, а *m.* symbol; **с. ве́ры** (relig.) creed

символизи́р|овать, ую *impf.* to symbolize

символи́зм, а *m.* symbolism

символи́ческий *adj.* symbolic(al)

сим-ка́рт|а, ы *f.* SIM (card)

симметри́ч|ный, ~ен, ~на *adj.* symmetrical

симме́три|я, и *f.* symmetry

симпатизи́р|овать, ую *impf.* (+ *d.*) to like, be fond of

симпати́ч|ный, ~ен, ~на (*человек*) nice, pleasant; (*лицо, голос, город*) attractive, pleasant

симпа́ти|я, и *f.* (**к** + *d.*) liking, fondness (for); **чу́вствовать** ~**ю к кому́-н.** to take a liking to sb, be drawn to sb

симпо́зиум, а *m.* symposium

симпто́м, а *m.* symptom

симули́р|овать, ую *impf. and pf.* to simulate, fake, sham

симфони́ческий *adj.* symphonic; **с. орке́стр** symphony orchestra

симфо́ни|я, и *f.* symphony

синаго́г|а, и *f.* synagogue

Сингапу́р, а *m.* Singapore

сингапу́р|ец, ца *m.* Singaporean

сингапу́р|ка, ки *f. of* ▶ **сингапу́рец**

сингапу́рский *adj.* Singaporean

синдика́т, а *m.* (econ.) syndicate

синдро́м, а *m.* (med.) syndrome

синев|а́, ы́ *f.* blue

синегла́з|ый, ~, ~а *adj.* blue-eyed

си́н|ий, ~ь, ~я, ~е *adj.* (dark) blue

сини́ц|а, ы *f.* tit (*bird*)

сино́ним, а *m.* synonym

сино́птик, а *m.* weather forecaster

си́нтаксис, а *m.* syntax

си́нтез, а *m.* synthesis

синтеза́тор, а *m.* synthesizer

синтези́р|овать, ую *impf. and pf.* to synthesize

синте́тик|а, и *f.* (*collect.*) synthetic, synthetics

синтети́ческий *adj.* synthetic

⚔ key word

синхро́нный *adj.* synchronous; (*перевод*) simultaneous

синя́к, а́ *m.* bruise; **с. под гла́зом** black eye

сиони́зм, а *m.* Zionism

сиони́ст, а *m.* Zionist

сиони́ст|ка, ки *f. of* ▶ **сиони́ст**

си́пл|ый, ~, ~а *adj.* hoarse, husky

сире́н|а, ы *f.* siren

сире́невый *adj.* lilac; lilac-coloured

сире́н|ь, и *f.* lilac

сири́|ец, йца *m.* Syrian

сири́й|ка, ки *f. of* ▶ **сири́ец**

сири́йский *adj.* Syrian

Си́ри|я, и *f.* Syria

сиро́п, а *m.* syrup

сирот|а́, ы́, *pl.* ~**ы** *c.g.* orphan

сиротли́в|ый, ~, ~а *adj.* lonely

⚔ **систе́м|а, ы** *f.* **1** system **2** (*тип*) type

систематизи́р|овать, ую *impf. and pf.* to systematize, order

системати́ческий *adj.* **1** systematic; methodical **2** (*регулярный*) regular

систе́мный *adj. of* ▶ **систе́ма; с. ана́лиз/ анали́тик** systems analysis/analyst; **с. диск** system disk

си́с|ька, ьки, *g. pl.* ~**ек** *f.* (sl.) (*сосок*) nipple; (*грудь*) tit (vulg.)

си́т|ец, ца *m.* cotton (print); chintz

си́т|о, а *nt.* sieve

⚔ **ситуа́ци|я, и** *f.* situation

си́филис, а *m.* (med.) syphilis

сифо́н, а *m.* siphon

сия́ни|е, я *nt.* radiance

сия́|ть, ю *impf.* (*о солнце*) to shine; (*о человеке, от радости*) to beam; (*о лице*) to be radiant

сказа́ни|е, я *nt.* story, tale, legend

⚔ **ска|за́ть, жу́,** ~**жешь** *pf.* (*of* ▶ говори́ть 2): **как с.!** it depends; **точне́е с.** or rather

ска|за́ться, ~**жется** *pf.* (*of* ▶ ска́зываться) (**на** + *p.*) to take its toll (on)

ска́зк|а, и *f.* **1** fairy tale **2** (infml, *ложь*) (tall) story, fib

ска́зочник, а *m.* storyteller

ска́зочн|ый *adj.* fairy-tale; (*необычайный*) fabulous, fantastic; ~**ое бога́тство** fabulous wealth

сказу́ем|ое, ого *nt.* (gram.) predicate

ска́зыва|ться, ется *impf. of* ▶ сказа́ться

скака́лк|а, и *f.* skipping rope (BrE), jump rope (AmE)

ска|ка́ть, чу́, ~**чешь** *impf.* **1** (*pf.* по~) to skip, jump; **с. на одно́й ноге́** to hop **2** (*pf.* по~) (*о лошади, о вса́днике*) to gallop **3** (infml, *резко изменяться*) to fluctuate

скаков|о́й *adj.* race, racing; **с. круг, ~а́я доро́жка** racecourse; ~**а́я ло́шадь** racehorse

скаку́н, а́ *m.* racehorse

скал|а́, ы́, *pl.* ~**ы** *f.* rock face, crag; (*отве́сная*) **с.** cliff

скали́ст|ый, ~, ~а *adj.* rocky

ска́лк|а, и *f.* (cul.) rolling pin

скалола́з, а *m.* rock climber

скальп, а *m.* scalp

ска́льпел|ь, я *m.* scalpel

скаме́йк|а, и *f.* bench

скам|ья́, ьи́, *pl.* ~ьи́, ~е́й *f.* bench;
с. подсуди́мых (law) the dock

сканда́л, а *m.* **1** scandal **2** (*ссора*) row,
(rowdy) scene

сканда́л|ьный, ~ен, ~ьна *adj.*
1 (*поведение*) scandalous **2** (infml,
человек) rowdy, quarrelsome **3** scandal;
~ьная хро́ника scandal column, page (*of
newspaper*)

скандина́в, а *m.* Scandinavian

Скандина́ви|я, и *f.* Scandinavia

скандина́в|ка, ки *f. of* ▶ **скандина́в**

скандина́вский *adj.* Scandinavian

ска́нер, а *m.* (med., comput.) scanner

скани́р|овать, ую *impf. and pf.* (med., comput.)
to scan

ска́плива|ть, ю, ет *impf. of* ▶ **скопи́ть**

ска́плива|ться, ется *impf. of* ▶ **скопи́ться**

скарлати́н|а, ы *f.* (med.) scarlet fever

ска́рмлива|ть, ю *impf. of* ▶ **скорми́ть**

скат, а *m.* (zool.) ray, skate

скат|а́ть, а́ю *pf.* (*of* ▶ **ска́тывать**, ▶ **ката́ть** 3)
to roll (up)

ска́терт|ь, и, *pl.* ~и, ~е́й *f.* tablecloth

ска|ти́ть, чу́, ~тишь *pf.* (*of* ▶ **ска́тывать**)
to roll down

ска|ти́ться, чу́сь, ~тишься *pf.* (*of*
▶ **ска́тываться**) to roll down

ска́тыва|ть, ю *impf. of* ▶ **ската́ть**, ▶ **скати́ть**

ска́тыва|ться, юсь *impf. of* ▶ **скати́ться**

скафа́ндр, а *m.* protective suit; (*водолаза*)
diving suit; (*космонавта*) spacesuit

♂ **скача́|ть**, ю *pf.* (*of* ▶ **ска́чивать**) (comput.)
to download

ска́чива|ть, ю *impf. of* ▶ **скача́ть**

ска́чк|а, и *f.* **1** gallop, galloping **2** (*in pl.*)
(*состязание*) horse race; race meeting, the
races; с. с препя́тствиями steeplechase

скач|о́к, ка́ *m.* **1** jump, leap, bound; ~ка́ми
by leaps **2** (fig., *цен, температуры*) leap

сква́жин|а, ы *f.* slit, chink; замо́чная с.
keyhole; нефтяна́я с. oil well

сквер, а *m.* small public garden

скве́р|ный, ~ен, ~на́, ~но *adj.* (*человек,
поступок*) nasty; (*погода, настроение*)
foul, awful

сквозн|о́й *adj.* **1** through; ~о́е движе́ние
through traffic **2** (*рана, отверстие*)
going right through **3** (*просвечивающий*)
transparent

сквозня́к, á *m.* draught (BrE), draft (AmE)

сквозь *prep.* (+ *a.*) through

скворе́ц, ца́ *m.* starling

сквош, а *m.* (sport) squash

скейтбо́рд, а *m.* skateboard

скейтбо́рдинг, а *m.* skateboarding

скеле́т, а *m.* skeleton

ске́птик, а *m.* sceptic (BrE), skeptic (AmE)

скепти́ческий *adj.* sceptical (BrE), skeptical
(AmE)

ски́дк|а, и *f.* **1** reduction, discount; со ~ой
(в + *a.*) with a reduction (of), at a discount
(of) **2** (на + *a.*) (fig.) allowance(s) (for);
сде́лать ~у на во́зраст to make allowances
for age

ски́дыва|ть, ю *impf. of* ▶ **ски́нуть**

ски́|нуть, ну, нешь *pf.* (*of* ▶ **ски́дывать**)
(infml) **1** (*одежду*) to throw off, cast off;
(*снег с крыши*) to throw down **2** (*с цены*)
to knock off (*from price*)

скинхе́д, а *m.* skinhead

ски́петр, а *m.* sceptre (BrE), scepter (AmE)

скипида́р, а *m.* turpentine

скиса́|ть, а́ю *impf. of* ▶ **ски́снуть**

ски́с|нуть, ну, нешь, *past* ~, ~ла *pf.* (*of*
▶ **скиса́ть**) to go sour, turn sour; (fig.) to
lose heart

склад[1], а *m.* **1** (*место*) storehouse; (mil.)
depot; това́рный с. warehouse **2** (*запас*)
store; с. боеприпа́сов (mil.) ammunition
dump

склад[2], а *m.* (*образ*) way; с. ума́ cast of mind,
mentality, mindset

скла́дк|а, и *f.* **1** pleat, tuck; crease; ю́бка в
~у pleated skirt; с. на брю́ках trouser crease
2 (*на коже*) wrinkle

складн|о́й *adj.* folding, collapsible; ~а́я
крова́ть camp bed (BrE), cot (AmE); с. нож
penknife

скла́дыва|ть, ю *impf. of* ▶ **сложи́ть**[1]

♂ **скла́дыва|ться**, юсь *impf. of* ▶ **сложи́ться**[1],
▶ **сложи́ться**[2]

скле́ива|ть, ю, ет *impf. of* ▶ **скле́ить**

скле́ива|ться, ется *impf. of* ▶ **скле́иться**

скле́|ить, ю, ишь *pf.* (*of* ▶ **скле́ивать**,
▶ **кле́ить**) to stick together; to glue together

скле́|иться, ится *pf.* (*of* ▶ **скле́иваться**) to
stick together

склеп, а *m.* burial vault, crypt

склеро́з, а *m.* (med.) sclerosis; рассе́янный с.
multiple sclerosis

скло́к|а, и *f.* squabble; row

склон, а *m.* slope

склоне́ни|е, я *nt.* (gram.) declension

склон|и́ть, ю́, ~ишь *pf.* (*of* ▶ **склоня́ть**)
1 to incline, bend, bow; с. го́лову (пе́ред + *i.*)
(fig.) to bow one's head (to, before) **2** (fig.)
(*убедить*) to talk *sb* over; to win *sb* over

склон|и́ться, ю́сь, ~ишься *pf.* (*of*
▶ **склоня́ться**) **1** to bend, bow **2** (к + *d.*)
(fig.) to give in (to), yield (to)

скло́нност|ь, и *f.* (к + *d.*) (*к музыке,
живописи*) aptitude (for); (*к полноте,
меланхолии*) susceptibility (to), tendency
(towards); (*к театру, к пиву*) liking,
penchant (for)

скло́н|ный, ~ен, ~на *adj.* (к + *d.*) (*к
болезни*) prone, susceptible (to); (+ *inf.*)
inclined (to)

склоня́|ть, я́ю *impf. of* ▶ **склони́ть**

склон|я́ться, я́юсь *impf. of* ▶ склони́ться

скоб|а́, ы́, *pl.* **∼ы, ∼а́м** *f.* (*зажим*) clamp; (*изогнутая железная полоса*) staple

скобк|а, и *f.* **1** *dim. of* ▶ скоба́ **2** (*знак*) bracket; (*in pl.*) brackets, parentheses; **в ∼ах** in brackets; (*fig.*) in parenthesis, by the way, incidentally

скобл|и́ть, ю́, ∼ишь *impf.* to scrape; (*доску*) to plane

ско́ванный 1 *p.p.p. of* ▶ скова́ть; **с. льда́ми** ice-bound **2** *adj.* (*движения, мысль*) constrained

скова́ть, скую́, скуёшь *pf.* (*of* ▶ ско́вывать) **1** (*соединить*) to weld together **2** (*заковать*) to chain; to fetter (*also fig.*)

сковород|а́, ы́, *pl.* **сковоро́ды, сковоро́д, ∼а́м** *f.* frying pan

сковоро́дк|а, и *f.* (*infml*) frying pan

ско́выва|ть, ю *impf. of* ▶ скова́ть

скола́чива|ть, ю *impf. of* ▶ сколоти́ть

сколо|ти́ть, чу́, ∼тишь *pf.* (*of* ▶ скола́чивать) **1** (*соединить*) to knock together; (*изготовить*) to knock up **2** (*fig., infml, набрать*) to get together; to scrape together

сколь *adv.* how

сколь|зи́ть, жу́, зи́шь *impf.* (*плавно двигаться*) to slide; to glide; (*терять устойчивость*) to slip

ско́льз|кий, ∼ок, ∼ка́, ∼ко *adj.* slippery (*also fig.*); (*fig.*) tricky; sensitive, delicate, treacherous

⚲ **ско́лько** *interrog. and rel. adv.* **1** (*денег, хлеба*) how much; (*книг, людей*) how many; **с. сто́ит?** how much does it cost?; **с. вам лет?** how old are you?; **с. вре́мени?** what time is it? **2** = насколько

ско́лько-нибудь *adv.* any; **у вас при себе́ есть с.-н. де́нег?** have you any money on you?

скома́нд|овать, ую *pf. of* ▶ кома́ндовать 1

скомбини́р|овать, ую *pf. of* ▶ комбини́ровать

ско́мка|ть, ю *pf. of* ▶ ко́мкать

скомпромети́р|овать, ую *pf. of* ▶ компромети́ровать

сконструи́р|овать, ую *pf. of* ▶ конструи́ровать

сконцентри́р|овать, ую *pf. of* ▶ концентри́ровать

сконцентри́р|оваться, уюсь *pf. of* ▶ концентри́роваться

сконча́|ться, юсь *pf.* to pass away (= *to die*)

скопи́р|овать, ую *pf. of* ▶ копи́ровать

скоп|и́ть, лю́, ∼ишь *pf.* (*of* ▶ ска́пливать) (+ *a. or g.*) (*накопить*) to save (up); to amass, pile up

скоп|и́ться, ∼ится *pf.* (*of* ▶ ска́пливаться) **1** to accumulate, pile up **2** (*о людях*) to gather, collect

скопле́ни|е, я *nt.* (*народа*) crowd; (*предметов*) accumulation, mass

⚲ *key word*

скорб|е́ть, лю́, и́шь *impf.* (о + *p.*) to grieve (for, over), mourn (for, over), lament

скорб|ь, и, *pl.* **∼и, ∼е́й** *f.* sorrow, grief

скоре́е and скоре́й 1 *comp. of* ▶ ско́рый, ▶ ско́ро; **как мо́жно с.** as soon as possible; **с.!** (be) quick! **2** *adv.* rather, sooner; **с. всего́** most likely, most probably

скорлуп|а́, ы́, *pl.* **∼ы** *f.* shell; **с. оре́ха** nutshell; **яи́чная с.** eggshell

скорм|и́ть, лю́, ∼ишь *pf.* (*of* ▶ ска́рмливать) (+ *d.*) to feed (to)

⚲ **ско́ро** *adv.* **1** (*быстро*) quickly, fast **2** (*вскоре*) soon

скороговор|ка, и *f.* **1** (*быстрая речь*) rapid speech, patter **2** (*придуманная фраза*) tongue-twister

скоростн|о́й *adj.* high-speed

⚲ **ско́рост|ь, и,** *pl.* **∼и, ∼е́й** *f.* **1** speed; velocity; rate; **со ∼ью три́дцать миль в час** at thirty miles per hour **2**: **перейти́ на другу́ю с.** to change gear

скоросшива́тел|ь, я *m.* binder, file; (*на кольца́х*) ring binder

скорпио́н, а *m.* scorpion; (**С.**) Scorpio (*sign of zodiac*)

корректи́р|овать, ую *pf. of* ▶ корректи́ровать

скорректи́ровать *pf. of* ▶ корректи́ровать

⚲ **ско́р|ый, ∼, ∼а́, ∼о** *adj.* **1** (*быстрый*) quick, fast; rapid; **∼ая по́мощь** ambulance (service); **на ∼ую ру́ку** in rough-and-ready fashion **2** (*близкий по времени*) near, forthcoming, impending; **в ∼ом бу́дущем** in the near future

скос, а *m.* **1** (*горы, берега*) slope **2** (*предмета*) slant, bevel

ско|си́ть¹, шу́, ∼сишь *pf. of* ▶ коси́ть¹

ско|си́ть², шу́, сишь *pf. of* ▶ коси́ть² 1, 2

скот, а́ *m.* (*collect.*) cattle; livestock

скоти́н|а, ы *f.* **1** (*collect.*) cattle; livestock **2** (*also m.*) (*fig., infml, грубый человек*) swine, beast

скотобо́|йня, йни, *g. pl.* **∼ен** *f.* slaughterhouse

скотово́дств|о, а *nt.* cattle breeding, cattle raising

ско́тский *adj.* (*infml*) brutal, brutish, bestial

скотч, а *m.* (*infml*) adhesive tape; Sellotape (BrE); Scotch tape® (AmE)

скра́|сить, шу, сишь *pf.* (*of* ▶ скра́шивать) (*fig.*) to relieve; **он мно́го чита́л, чтобы с. своё одино́чество** he read a lot to relieve his loneliness

скра́шива|ть, ю *impf. of* ▶ скра́сить

скреб|о́к, ка́ *m.* scraper

скре́жет, а *m.* (*металла*) grating, scraping; (*зубов*) gnashing

скреп|и́ть, лю́, и́шь *pf.* (*of* ▶ скрепля́ть) **1** (*соединить*) to fasten (together); (*tech.*) to clamp, brace; (*дружбу*) to cement **2** (*удостоверить*) to countersign, ratify

скре́пк|а, и *f.* paper clip

скрепля́|ть, ю *impf. of* ▶ скрепи́ть

скре|сти́, бу́, бёшь, *past* ~б, ~бла́ *impf.*
(*о кошке, ногтями*) to scratch, claw;
(*дерево*) to sand; (*кастрюлю*) to scour

скре|сти́сь, бу́сь, бёшься, *past* ~бся,
~бла́сь *impf.* to scratch, make a scratching
noise

скре|сти́ть, щу́, сти́шь *pf.* (*of* ▶ скре́щивать)
1 to cross; **с. мечи́, с. шпа́ги** (**с** + *i.*) to cross
swords (with) (*also fig.*) **2** (biol.) to cross,
interbreed

скрест|и́ться, и́тся *pf.* (*of* ▶ скре́щиваться)
1 to cross; (fig.) to clash **2** (biol.) to cross,
interbreed

скре́щива|ть, ю, ет *impf. of* ▶ скрести́ть

скре́щива|ться, ется *impf. of* ▶ скрести́ться

скринсе́йвер, а *m* (comput.) screensaver

скриншо́т, а *m* (comput.) screenshot, screen
grab

скрип, а *m.* (*двери*) squeak, creak; (*снега*)
crunch

скрипа́ч, á *m.* violinist

скрипа́ч|ка, ки *f. of* ▶ скрипа́ч

скрип|е́ть, лю́, и́шь *impf.* (*of* ▶ скри́пнуть)
(*о двери*) to squeak, creak; (*о снеге*) to
crunch

скри́пк|а, и *f.* violin; **пе́рвая с.** first violin;
(fig., infml) first fiddle

скри́пн|уть, у, ешь *inst. pf. of* ▶ скрипе́ть

скрипт, а *m.* (comput.) script

скро|и́ть, ю́, и́шь *pf. of* ▶ крои́ть

скро́мност|ь, и *f.* modesty

скро́м|ный, ~ен, ~на́, ~но *adj.* modest

скрупулёз|ный, ~ен, ~на *adj.* scrupulous

скру|ти́ть, чу́, ~тишь *pf.* (*of* ▶ крути́ть 1,
▶ скру́чивать) **1** (*верёвки*) to twist
(together); (*папиросу*) to roll **2** (*руки*) to
bind, tie up

скру́чива|ть, ю *impf. of* ▶ скрути́ть

скрыва́|ть, ю *impf. of* ▶ скрыть

скрыва́|ться, юсь *impf.* **1** *impf. of*
▶ скры́ться **2** (*impf. only*) to lie in hiding;
to lie low

скры́т|ный, ~ен, ~на *adj.* secretive

скры́тый *p.p.p. of* ▶ скрыть *and adj.* secret,
concealed; **с. смысл** hidden meaning

скр|ы́ть, о́ю, о́ешь *pf.* (*of* ▶ скрыва́ть)
(**от** + *g.*) to hide (from), conceal (from)

скр|ы́ться, о́юсь, о́ешься *pf.* (*of*
▶ скрыва́ться 1) (**от** + *g.*) **1** (*спря́таться*)
to hide (oneself) (from); (*о преступнике*) to
go into hiding **2** (*удали́ться*) to steal away
(from), escape, give the slip **3** (*исчезнуть*)
to disappear, vanish

ску́д|ный, ~ен, ~на́, ~но *adj.* (*средства,
обед*) meagre (BrE), meager (AmE);
(*урожай*) poor; (*знания, сведения*) scanty;
(*растительность*) sparse

ску́к|а, и *f.* boredom, tedium; **кака́я с.!** what
a bore!

скул|а́, ы́, *pl.* ~ы *f.* cheekbone

скул|и́ть, ю́, и́шь *impf.* to whine, whimper
(*also fig.*)

ску́льптор, а *m.* sculptor

скульпту́р|а, ы *f.* sculpture

ску́мбри|я, и *f.* mackerel

скунс, а *m.* skunk

скуп|а́ть, а́ю *impf. of* ▶ скупи́ть

скуп|и́ть, лю́, ~ишь *pf.* (*of* ▶ скупа́ть) to
buy up

скуп|о́й, ~, ~а́, ~о, ~ы́ *adj.* **1** stingy,
miserly; **с. на слова́** sparing of words
2 (fig., *недостаточный*) inadequate

ску́пост|ь, и *f.* stinginess, miserliness

ску́тер, а *m.* (*катер*) outboard motor boat;
(*мотороллер*) scooter

скуча́|ть, ю *impf.* **1** to be bored **2** (**по** + *d.*)
to miss, yearn (for)

ску́ч|ный, ~ен, ~на́, ~но *adj.* **1** (*книга*)
boring, tedious, dull **2** (*человек, взгляд*)
bored; (*as pred.*) **мне** *и т. п.* ~но I am,
etc., bored

ску́ша|ть, ю *pf. of* ▶ ку́шать

слабе́|ть, ю *impf. of* ▶ ослабе́ть

слаби́тельн|ый *adj.* (med.) laxative; (*as nt. n.*
~ое, ~ого) laxative

слабоалкого́льный *adj.* low-alcohol

слабоне́рв|ный, ~ен, ~на *adj.* having
weak nerves; nervous

сла́бост|ь, и *f.* **1** weakness, feebleness
2 (**к** + *d.*) (*наклонность*) weakness (for)

слабоу́ми|е, я *nt.* learning disability;
ста́рческое с. senile dementia

слабоу́м|ный, ~ен, ~на *adj.* learning-
disabled

✓ **сла́б|ый, ~, ~а́, ~о** *adj.* (*человек, характер,
зрение, воля*) weak; (*голос*) feeble; (*верёвка*)
slack, loose; (*ветер, боль, надежда*) slight;
(*ученик, знания*) weak, poor; (*ребёнок,
здоровье*) delicate; ~ое ме́сто weak point;
с. пол the weaker sex

✓ **сла́в|а, ы** *f.* **1** glory; fame; **во** ~**y** (+ *g.*) to the
glory (of); **на** ~**y** (infml) wonderfully well,
excellently; (*as int.*, + *d.*) hurrah (for)!; **с. бо́гу**
thank God, thank goodness **2** (*репута́ция*)
name, reputation; **до́брая с.** good name;
дурна́я с. infamy **3** (infml, *слухи*) rumour
(BrE), rumor (AmE)

слав|и́ться, лю́сь, ишься *impf.* (+ *i.*) to be
famous (for), be renowned (for); to have a
reputation (for)

сла́в|ный, ~ен, ~на́, ~но *adj.* **1** glorious;
famous, renowned **2** (infml) splendid; lovely;
с. ма́лый nice chap

славя́н|ин, ина, *pl.* ~е, ~ *m.* Slav

славя́н|ка, ки *f. of* ▶ славяни́н

славянофи́л, а *m.* Slavophil(e)

славя́нский *adj.* Slavonic; Slavic; Slav

слага́|ть, ю *impf. of* ▶ сложи́ть² 2

сла́д|кий, ~ок, ~ка́, ~ко *adj.* sweet (*also fig.*);
(*as nt. n.* ~кое, ~кого) dessert

сладкое́жк|а, и *c.g.* (infml) (person with a)
sweet tooth

сладостра́ст|ный, ~ен, ~на *adj.* sensual,
voluptuous

сла́дост|ь, и *f.* **1** sweetness **2** (*in pl.*) (*кондитерские изделия*) sweets, sweetmeats

сла́зить, жу, зишь *pf.* (infml) to go, climb; **с. в подва́л за дрова́ми** to go down to the cellar for logs

слайд, а *m.* slide, transparency

сла́лом, а *m.* (sport) slalom

сла́н|ец, ца *m.* **1** (min.) slate **2** (*usu. in pl.*) flip-flop

сласт|ь, и, *pl.* **~и, ~е́й** *f.* sweets, sweetmeats

слать, шлю, шлёшь *impf.* to send

сла́ще *comp. of* ▶ **сла́дкий**

сле́ва *adv.* (**от** + *g.*) on the left (of), to the left (of); **с. напра́во** from left to right

слегка́ *adv.* lightly, gently; (*немного*) slightly; **с. суту́литься** to stoop slightly

☞ **след, а,** *pl.* **~ы́** *m.* **1** (*отпечаток*) track; (*ноги*) footprint, footstep; **идти́ по чьим-н. ~а́м** (fig.) to follow in sb's footsteps; **напа́сть на чей-н. с.** to get on sb's trail **2** (fig., *признак*) trace, sign, vestige

☞ **сле|ди́ть, жу́, ди́шь** *impf.* (**за** + *i.*) **1** (*смотреть*) to watch; to follow; **с. (глаза́ми) за полётом мяча́** to follow (with one's eyes) the flight of a ball **2** (fig.) to follow; to keep up (with); **с. за междунаро́дными собы́тиями** to keep up with international affairs **3** (*заботиться*) to look after; to keep an eye (on); **с. за детьми́** to look after children; **с. за поря́дком** to keep order; **с. за тем, что́бы** to see to it that

сле́дователь, я *m.* investigator

сле́довательно *conj.* consequently, therefore, hence

☞ **сле́д|овать¹, ую** *impf.* (*of* ▶ **после́довать**) **1** (**за** + *i.*) to follow, go after **2** (+ *d.*) (*поступать подобно кому-н.*) to follow; (*поступать согласно чему-н.*) to follow; to comply (with); **с. пра́вилам** to conform to the rules **3** (*impf. only*) (**до** + *g.* or **в** + *a.*) (*отправляться*) to be bound (for); **э́тот по́езд ~ует в Варша́ву** this train is (bound) for Warsaw **4** (*impf. only*) (*быть следствием*) to follow; to result; **из э́того ~ует, что мы оши́блись** it follows from this that we were mistaken

☞ **сле́д|овать², ует** *impf.* (impers. + *d. and inf.*) (*нужно, должно*) ought, should; **вам ~ует обрати́ться к ре́ктору** you should approach the rector; **как и ~ова́ло ожида́ть** as was to be expected; **как ~ует** as it should be, properly, well and truly

сле́дом *adv.* (**за** + *i.*) immediately (after, behind); **идти́ с. за кем-н.** to follow sb close(ly)

следопы́т, а *m.* pathfinder, tracker

сле́дств|енный *adj. of* ▶ **сле́дствие²**; investigatory; **~енная коми́ссия** committee of inquiry

☞ **сле́дстви|е¹, я** *nt.* (*результат*) consequence, result; **причи́на и с.** cause and effect

☞ **сле́дстви|е², я** *nt.* (law, *расследование*) investigation

☞ **сле́д|ующий** *pres. part. act. of* ▶ **сле́довать¹** *and adj.* following, next; **на с. день** next day; **на ~ующей неде́ле** next week

сле́жк|а, и *f.* surveillance; shadowing

слез|а́, ы́, *pl.* **~ы, ~, ~а́м** *f.* tear; **довести́ до ~** to reduce to tears

слеза́|ть, ю *impf. of* ▶ **слезть**

слез|и́ться, и́тся *impf.* to water; **её глаза́ ~и́лись** her eyes were watering

слез|ть, у, ешь, *past* **~, ~ла** *pf.* (*of* ▶ **слеза́ть**) (**с** + *g.*) **1** (*с дерева*) to come down (from), get down (from); (*с лошади, велосипеда*) to get off; to dismount (from) **2** (infml, *с автобуса, трамвая*) to get off **3** (infml, *о краске, коже*) to come off, peel

сленг, а *m.* slang

слеп|ень, ня́ *m.* gadfly, horsefly

слеп|е́ц, ца́ *m.* blind man

слеп|и́ть¹, лю́, и́шь *impf.* to blind; to dazzle

слеп|и́ть², лю́, ~ишь *pf. of* ▶ **лепи́ть 1**

слеп|ну́ть, ну, нешь, *past* **~, ~ла** *impf.* (*of* ▶ **осле́пнуть**) to go blind

слеп|о́й, ~, ~а́, ~о *adj.* blind (also fig.); **с. на оди́н глаз** blind in one eye; (*as n.* **с., ~о́го,** *f.* **~а́я, ~о́й**) blind person; (*pl., collect.*) the blind

слепот|а́, ы́ *f.* blindness (also fig.)

слеса́р|ь, я *m.* metal worker; (*специалист по замка́м*) locksmith; (*специалист по почи́нке*) repair man

слета́|ть¹, ю *pf.* to fly (*there and back*)

слета́|ть², ю *impf. of* ▶ **слете́ть**

слета́|ться, а́юсь *impf. of* ▶ **слете́ться**

слет|е́ть, чу́, ти́шь *pf.* (*of* ▶ **слета́ть²**) (**с** + *g.*) **1** (*вниз*) to fly down (from) **2** (infml, *упасть*) to fall down, fall off; **с. с ло́шади** to fall from a horse **3** (*улететь*) to fly away

слет|е́ться, и́тся *pf.* (*of* ▶ **слета́ться**) to fly together; (*о птицах*) to congregate

слечь, сля́гу, сля́жешь, *past* **слёг, слегла́** *pf.* to take to one's bed

сли́в|а, ы *f.* **1** (*плод*) plum **2** (*дерево*) plum tree

слива́|ть, ю *impf. of* ▶ **слить**

слива́|ться, юсь *impf. of* ▶ **сли́ться**

сли́в|ки, ок (*no sg.*) cream (also fig.)

сли́вочн|ый *adj.* cream; creamy; **~ое ма́сло** butter

сли|за́ть, жу́, ~жешь *pf.* (*of* ▶ **сли́зывать**) to lick off

сли́зист|ый, ~, ~а *adj.* **1** slimy **2** (anat.) mucous

слизня́к, а́ *m.* slug

сли́зыва|ть, ю *impf. of* ▶ **слиза́ть**

слизь, и *f.* **1** slime **2** (anat.) mucus

слипа́|ться, а́ется *impf. of* ▶ **сли́пнуться**

сли́п|нуться, нется, *past* **~ся, ~лась** *pf.* (*of* ▶ **слипа́ться**) to stick together

сли́тный *adj.* united, continuous

сли́т|ок, ка *m.* ingot, bar; **зо́лото в ~ках** gold bullion

слить, солью́, сольёшь, *past* **слил, слила́, сли́ло** *pf.* (*of* ▶ **слива́ть**) **1** (*вы́лить*) to pour out; (*отли́ть*) to pour off **2** (*вме́сте*) to pour together; (fig.) to merge, amalgamate

сли́ться, солью́сь, сольёшься, *past* **сли́лся, слила́сь** *pf.* (*of* ▶ **слива́ться**) **1** (*о ручья́х*) to flow together **2** (fig.) (*о голоса́х*) to blend, mingle; (*о конце́рнах*) to merge, amalgamate

слича́|ть, а́ю *impf. of* ▶ **сличи́ть**

сличи́|ть, у́, и́шь *pf.* (*of* ▶ **слича́ть**) (**с** + *i.*) to check (with, against)

✍ **сли́шком** *adv.* too; (*перед глаго́лами*) too much; **э́то с.!** this is too much!

слия́ни|е, я *nt.* **1** (*рек*) confluence **2** (fig.) (*голосо́в*) blending; merging; (*конце́рнов*) amalgamation, merger

слова́к, а *m.* Slovak

Слова́ки|я, и *f.* Slovakia

словар|ь, я́ *m.* **1** (*кни́га*) dictionary; (*глосса́рий*) glossary, vocabulary (*to particular text*) **2** (collect.) (*запа́с слов*) vocabulary

слова́цкий *adj.* Slovak, Slovakian

слова́ч|ка, ки *f. of* ▶ **слова́к**

слове́н|ец, ца *m.* Slovene

Слове́ни|я, и *f.* Slovenia

слове́н|ка, ки *f. of* ▶ **слове́нец**

слове́нский *adj.* Slovene, Slovenian

слове́сный *adj.* verbal, oral

✍ **сло́вно** *conj.* **1** (*как бу́дто*) as if **2** (*как*) like, as

✍ **сло́в|о, а,** *pl.* **~а́** *nt.* **1** word; **други́ми ~а́ми** in other words; **одни́м ~ом** in a word; **на ~а́х** (*у́стно*) by word of mouth; (*то́лько в разгово́ре*) empty words; **сдержа́ть с.** to keep one's word **2** (*речь*) speech, speaking; **свобо́да ~а** freedom of speech **3** (*выступле́ние*) speech, address; **дать, предоста́вить с.** (+ *d.*) to give the floor, call upon to speak

словоблу́ди|е, я *nt.* (mere) verbiage, phrase-mongering

сло́вом *adv.* in a word, in short

словоохо́тлив|ый, ~, ~а *adj.* talkative, loquacious

словосочета́ни|е, я *nt.* combination of words

слог, а, *pl.* **~и, ~о́в** *m.* syllable

сло́ган, а *m.* slogan

слоёный *adj.*: **~ое те́сто** puff pastry

слож|и́ть[1], у́, ~ишь *pf.* (*of* ▶ **скла́дывать**) **1** (*положи́ть вме́сте*) to put (together); (*в ку́чу*) to pile, stack; **с. свои́ ве́щи в чемода́н** to pack one's things in a suitcase **2** (*чи́сла*) to add (up) **3** (*лист, пла́тье*) to fold (up) **4** *pf. of* ▶ **класть 2**

слож|и́ть[2], у́, ~ишь *pf.* **1** (*impf.* **скла́дывать**) (*сняв, положи́в*) to take off, put down, set down **2** (*impf.* **слага́ть**) (**с** + *g.*) (fig.) to relieve oneself (of); **с. ору́жие** to lay down one's arms; **с. с себя́ обя́занности** to resign

слож|и́ться[1], у́сь, ~ишься *pf.* (*of* ▶ **скла́дываться**) (**с** + *i.*) to club together (with); to pool one's resources

слож|и́ться[2], ~ится *pf.* (*of* ▶ **скла́дываться**) (*о хара́ктере; об убежде́нии*) to form; (*об обстоя́тельствах*) to turn out; (*о ситуа́ции*) to arise

✍ **сло́жно** *as pred.* it is difficult; **мне с.** I find it difficult

✍ **сло́жност|ь, и** *f.* complication; complexity

✍ **сло́ж|ный, ~ен, ~на́, ~но, ~ны́** *adj.* **1** (*составно́й*) compound; complex **2** (*тру́дный*) complicated, complex; (*узо́р, компози́ция*) intricate

✍ **сло|й, я,** *pl.* **~и́** *m.* layer; stratum (also fig.); **все ~и населе́ния** all sections of the population

сло́йк|а, и *f.* (*бу́лочка*) puff

слома́|ть, ю *pf. of* ▶ **лома́ть**

слома́|ться, юсь *pf. of* ▶ **лома́ться**

слом|и́ть, лю́, ~ишь *pf.* to break, smash; (fig.) to overcome; **~я́ го́лову** (infml) like mad, at breakneck speed

слон, а́ *m.* **1** elephant **2** (*в ша́хматах*) bishop (chess)

слоня́|ться, юсь *impf.* (infml) to loiter about, mooch about (BrE)

слуг|а́, и́, *pl.* **~и, ~** *m.* servant

служа́нк|а, и *f.* maid

служа́щ|ий, его *m.* office worker, white-collar worker

✍ **слу́жб|а, ы** *f.* **1** service; (*рабо́та*) work; employment; **быть на ~е у кого́-н.** to work for sb **2** (*специа́льная о́бласть рабо́ты*) (special) service **3** (eccl., *богослуже́ние*) church service

служе́бн|ый *adj.* **1** *adj. of* ▶ **слу́жба**; office; official; work; **с. автомоби́ль** company car; **~ое вре́мя** office hours; **~ая пое́здка** business trip **2** (*вспомога́тельный*) auxiliary; secondary

✍ **служ|и́ть, у́, ~ишь** *impf.* (*of* ▶ **послужи́ть**) **1** (+ *d.*) to serve, devote oneself (to) **2** (*no pf.*) (*рабо́тать*) to serve (as); to work (as), be employed (as), be; **с. в а́рмии** to serve in the army **3** (+ *i. or* **для** + *g.*) (*функциони́ровать*) to serve (for), do (for), be used (for); **гости́ная ~ит нам и спа́льней** our sitting room serves also as a bedroom; **с. доказа́тельством** (+ *g.*) to serve as evidence (of) **4** (*быть поле́зным*) to be in use, do duty, serve; **мой ста́рый плащ ещё ~ит** my old mac(k)intosh is still in use **5** (*pf.* **от~**) (eccl.) to celebrate; to conduct, officiate (at); **с. обе́дню** to celebrate mass

слух, а *m.* **1** hearing; (mus.) ear; **игра́ть на с., по ~у** to play by ear **2** (*изве́стие*) rumour (BrE), rumor (AmE); **прошёл с., что** it was rumoured (BrE), rumored (AmE) that

слухово́й *adj.* auditory, aural; **с. аппара́т** hearing aid

С

◦ **слу́ча|й, я** *m.* **1** case; **во вся́ком ~е** in any case, anyhow, anyway; **ни в ко́ем ~е** in no circumstances; **в лу́чшем, ху́дшем ~е** at best, at worst; **в проти́вном ~е** otherwise; **в тако́м ~е** in that case; **на вся́кий с.** to be on the safe side, just in case; **по ~ю** (+ *g.*) by reason (of), on account (of), on the occasion (of) **2** (*происшествие*) event, incident, occurrence; **несча́стный с.** accident **3** (*возмо́жность*) opportunity, occasion, chance; **упусти́ть удо́бный с.** to miss an opportunity; **при ~е** when an opportunity presents itself **4** (*случа́йность*) chance

случа́йно *adv.* **1** by chance, by accident, accidentally; **я с. подслу́шал их разгово́р** I happened to overhear their conversation **2** (*как вводное слово*) by any chance; **вы, с., не ви́дели моего́ зо́нтика?** have you by any chance seen my umbrella?

случа́йност|ь, и *f.* chance; **по счастли́вой ~и** by a lucky chance, by sheer luck

случа́|йный, ~ен, ~йна *adj.* **1** (*оши́бка*) accidental; (*встре́ча, разгово́р*) chance; (*гость, уда́ча*) unexpected **2** (*расхо́ды, поруче́ния*) incidental; **с. за́работок** casual earnings

◦ **случа́ться, а́ется** *impf. of* ▸ **случи́ться**

◦ **случ|и́ться, и́тся** *pf.* (*of* ▸ **случа́ться**) to happen, come about; **что бы ни ~и́лось** whatever happens, come what may

слу́шани|е, я *nt.* (law) hearing

слу́шатель|, я *m.* **1** listener; (*pl.; collect.*) audience **2** (*студе́нт*) student

слу́шательн|ица, ицы *f. of* ▸ **слу́шатель**

◦ **слу́ша|ть, ю** *impf.* (*of* ▸ **послу́шать**, ▸ **прослу́шать** 1) **1** (*му́зыку, ра́дио*) to listen (to); **с. ле́кцию** to attend a lecture; **~й(те)!** (infml) listen!, look here!; **~ю!** at your service!; very good!; (*по телефо́ну*) hello! **2** (*изуча́ть*) to attend lectures (on), go to lectures (on) **3** (*слу́шаться*) to listen (to), obey **4** (law) to hear

слу́ша|ться, юсь *impf.* (*of* ▸ **послу́шаться**) to listen (to), obey; **~юсь!** (mil.) yes, sir! (*indicating readiness to carry out order*)

◦ **слы́ш|ать, у, ишь** *impf.* (*of* ▸ **услы́шать**) **1** to hear; **~ишь?, ~ите?** (infml) do you hear? (*emph. command or direction*) **2** (*impf. only*) (*облада́ть слу́хом*) to have the sense of hearing; **не с.** to be hard of hearing

слы́ш|аться, ится *impf.* (*of* ▸ **послы́шаться**) to be heard; to be audible

слы́шно *as pred.* (*impers.*) **1** one can hear; **бы́ло с., как она́ рыда́ла** one could hear her sobbing **2** (infml) **что с.?** what news?, any news?; **о них ничего́ не с.** nothing has been heard of them

слы́ш|ный, ~ен, ~на́, ~но, ~ны́ *adj.* audible

слюд|а́, ы́ *f.* mica

слюн|а́, ы́ *f.* saliva

слю́н|и, ей (*no sg.*) (infml) slobber, spittle; **пусти́ть с.** to dribble

сля́кот|ь, и *f.* slush

◦ **см** (*abbr. of* **сантиме́тр**) cm, centimetre(s) (BrE), centimeter(s) (AmE)

см. (*abbr. of* **смотри́**) see (*vide*)

сма́|зать, жу, жешь *pf.* (*of* ▸ **сма́зывать**) **1** to lubricate; to grease; **с. йо́дом** to paint with iodine **2** (*разма́зать*) to smudge; (*стере́ть*) to rub off **3** (fig., infml, *лиши́ть чёткости*) to slur (over)

сма́зк|а, и *f.* **1** (*де́йствие*) lubrication; greasing **2** (*вещество́*) lubricant; grease

сма́зыва|ть, ю *impf. of* ▸ **сма́зать**

◦ **сма́йл** and **сма́йлик** *a m.* (*изображе́ние*) smiley

смак|ова́ть, у́ю *impf.* (infml) to savour (BrE), savor (AmE); to relish (also fig.)

сманеври́р|овать, ую *pf. of* ▸ **маневри́ровать**

смартфо́н, а *m.* smartphone

сма́тыва|ть, ю *impf. of* ▸ **смота́ть**

сма́тыва|ться, юсь *impf. of* ▸ **смота́ться**

сма́хива|ть¹, ю *impf. of* ▸ **смахну́ть**

сма́хива|ть², ю *impf.* (**на** + *a.*) (infml) to look like, resemble

смах|ну́ть, ну́, нёшь *pf.* (*of* ▸ **сма́хивать¹**) to brush (away, off), flick (away, off); **с. пыль** (**с** + *g.*) to dust

сма́чива|ть, ю *impf. of* ▸ **смочи́ть**

сме́ж|ный, ~ен, ~на *adj.* (*ко́мнаты, уча́стки*) adjacent, adjoining; (*профе́ссии, поня́тия*) related

смека́лк|а, и *f.* (infml) native wit; nous; sharpness

смека́ть, а́ю *impf.* (*of* ▸ **смекну́ть**) (infml) to see the point (of), grasp

смек|ну́ть, ну́, нёшь *pf.* (*of* ▸ **смека́ть**)

сме́ло *adv.* **1** boldly **2** (*с по́лной уве́ренностью*) confidently; **я могу́ с. сказа́ть** I can safely say

сме́лост|ь, и *f.* boldness, audacity; **взять на себя́ с.** (+ *inf.*) to take the liberty (of doing sth); to make so bold (as to do sth)

сме́л|ый, ~, ~а́, ~о, ~ы́ *adj.* bold, audacious, daring

◦ **сме́н|а, ы** *f.* **1** (*де́йствие*) changing, change; (*заме́на*) replacement; **с. карау́ла** changing of the guard **2** (*collect.*) replacements; successors; (mil.) relief **3** (*на заво́де*) shift; **у́тренняя, дневна́я, вече́рняя с.** morning, day, night shift **4** (*белья́*) change

смен|и́ть, ~и́шь *pf.* (*of* ▸ **сменя́ть**) **1** to change; (*рабо́тника*) to replace; (mil.) to relieve; **с. бельё** to change linen **2** (*замести́ть*) to replace, relieve, succeed (sb)

смен|и́ться, ю́сь, ~и́шься *pf.* (*of* ▸ **сменя́ться**) **1** to hand over; (mil.) to be relieved; **с. с дежу́рства** to go off duty **2** (+ *i.*) to give way (to); **дневно́й зно́й ~и́лся прохла́дой ве́чера** the day's heat gave way to the coolness of evening

---

◦ **key word**

сме́нн|ый *adj.* shift; ∼ая рабо́та shift work

сменя́|ть, я́ю *impf. of* ▶ смени́ть

сменя́|ться, я́юсь *impf. of* ▶ смени́ться

сме́р|ить, ю, ишь *pf. of* ▶ ме́рить 1

смерка́|ться, а́ется *impf.* (*of* ▶ сме́ркнуться) to get dark; ∼а́лось it was getting dark, twilight was falling

сме́рк|нуться, нется *pf. of* ▶ смерка́ться

смерте́льно *adv.* ❶ mortally; с. ра́ненный mortally wounded ❷ (*infml*, *очень*) extremely, terribly

смерте́л|ьный, ∼ен, ∼ьна *adj.* ❶ (*борьба́, враг*) mortal, deadly ❷ (*infml, fig., сильный, крайний*) deadly, extreme

сме́ртност|ь, и *f.* mortality, death rate

сме́рт|ный, ∼ен, ∼на *adj.* ❶ mortal; (*as m. n. с.*, ∼ного) mortal; просто́й с. ordinary mortal ❷ deadly, death; ∼ная казнь capital punishment, death penalty; с. пригово́р death sentence

смертоно́с|ный, ∼ен, ∼на *adj.* mortal, fatal, lethal

⚘ **смерт|ь, и,** *pl.* ∼и, ∼е́й *f.* death; умере́ть свое́й ∼ью to die a natural death; до́ ∼и (*fig., infml*) terribly; быть при ∼и to be dying

смерч, а *m.* tornado, whirlwind

смеси́тел|ь, я *m.* mixer; (*кран*) mixer tap (BrE), mixing faucet (AmE)

сме|сти́, ту́, тёшь, *past* ∼л, ∼ла́ *pf.* (*of* ▶ смета́ть) ❶ to sweep off, sweep away; с. кро́шки со стола́ to sweep crumbs off the table ❷ (*метя, собрать*) to sweep into, together

сме|сти́ть, щу́, сти́шь *pf.* (*of* ▶ смеща́ть) ❶ to displace, remove; to shift, move ❷ (*fig., уволить*) to remove, dismiss

сме|сти́ться, щу́сь, сти́шься *pf.* (*of* ▶ смеща́ться) to change position, become displaced

⚘ **смес|ь, и** *f.* mixture; (*продукт*) blend

смета́н|а, ы *f.* sour cream

смета́|ть, ю *pf. of* ▶ смести́

сме|ть, ю *impf.* (*of* ▶ посме́ть) to dare; to make bold; не ∼й(те)! don't you dare!

смех, а (у) *m.* laughter; laugh

смехотво́р|ный, ∼ен, ∼на *adj.* laughable, ludicrous

смеш|а́ть, а́ю *pf.* (*of* ▶ меша́ть² 2, ▶ меша́ть² 3, ▶ сме́шивать) ❶ (с + *i.*) (*соединить*) to mix (with), blend (with) ❷ (*перепутать, путать*) to mix up

смеш|а́ться, а́юсь *pf.* (*of* ▶ сме́шиваться) ❶ (*о кра́сках*) to mix, blend; to mingle; с. с толпо́й to mingle in the crowd ❷ (*прийти в беспорядок; перепутаться*) to become confused, get mixed up

сме́шива|ть, ю *impf. of* ▶ смеша́ть

сме́шива|ться, юсь *impf. of* ▶ смеша́ться

смеш|и́ть, у́, и́шь *impf.* (*of* ▶ насмеши́ть) to make (sb) laugh

смешн|о́й, ∼о́н, ∼а́ *adj.* ❶ funny; (*as pred.*) ∼но́ it is funny; вам ∼но́? do you find it funny? ❷ (*нелепый*) absurd, ridiculous,

ludicrous

смеш|о́к, ка́ *m.* (*infml*) chuckle; giggle

смеща́|ть, ю *impf. of* ▶ смести́ть

смеща́|ться, юсь *impf. of* ▶ смести́ться

смеще́ни|е, я *nt.* ❶ displacement; shift, removal ❷ (*увольнение*) dismissal

сме|я́ться, ю́сь, ёшься *impf.* ❶ to laugh; с. шу́тке to laugh at a joke ❷ (*над + i.*) to laugh (at), mock, make fun (of) ❸ (*infml, говорить в шутку*) to joke, say in jest

⚘ **СМИ** *pl. indecl.* (*abbr. of* сре́дства ма́ссовой информа́ции) mass media

смире́ни|е, я *nt.* humbleness, humility, meekness

смири́|ться, ю́сь, и́шься *pf.* (*of* ▶ смиря́ться) to submit; to resign oneself

сми́р|ный, ∼ен, ∼на́, ∼но *adj.* quiet; submissive

смиря́|ться, я́юсь *impf. of* ▶ смири́ться

смо́кинг, а *m.* dinner jacket

смол|а́, ы́, *pl.* ∼ы *f.* resin; (*дёготь*) pitch, tar

смоли́ст|ый, ∼, ∼а *adj.* resinous

смолка́|ть, а́ю *impf. of* ▶ смо́лкнуть

смо́лк|нуть, ну, нешь, *past* ∼, ∼ла *pf.* (*of* ▶ смолка́ть) (*о голосе, о человеке*) to fall silent; (*о шуме*) to cease

смоло́ть, смелю́, сме́лешь *pf. of* ▶ моло́ть

смолча́|ть, у́, и́шь *pf.* to hold one's tongue

смонти́р|овать, ую *pf. of* ▶ монти́ровать

сморка́|ть, ю *impf.* (*of* ▶ вы́сморкать) с. нос to blow one's nose

сморка́|ться, юсь *impf.* (*of* ▶ вы́сморкаться) to blow one's nose

сморо́дин|а, ы (*no pl.*) *f.* ❶ (*кустарник*) currant bush ❷ (*collect.*) (*ягоды*) currants; бе́лая, кра́сная, чёрная с. white currants, redcurrants, blackcurrants

смо́рщен|ный, ∼, ∼а *adj.* wrinkled

смо́рщ|иться, усь, ишься *pf. of* ▶ мо́рщиться

смота́|ть, ю *pf.* (*of* ▶ сма́тывать) to wind, reel; (*infml*) с. у́дочки to take to one's heels, make off

смота́|ться, юсь *pf.* (*of* ▶ сма́тываться) (*infml*) ❶ (*сходить*) to dash (there and back) ❷ (*убраться*) to take to one's heels, make off

⚘ **смотр|е́ть, ю́, ∼ишь** *impf.* (*of* ▶ посмотре́ть) ❶ (*на + a.* *or* в + *a.*) to look (at); с. в окно́ to look out of the window; с. в глаза́, в лицо́ (+ *d.*) to look in the face ❷ (*фильм, пьесу*) to see; (*фильм, телевидение*) to watch; (*книгу, журнал*) to look through ❸ (*за + i.*) to look (after); (*о работе*) to be in charge (of), supervise; с. за поря́дком to keep order ❹: ∼я́ где, как, *и т. n.* it depends (where, how, *etc.*); ∼я́ (по + *d.*) depending (on), in accordance (with)

смотр|е́ться, ю́сь, ∼ишься *impf.* (*of* ▶ посмотре́ться) ❶ to look at oneself; с. в зе́ркало to look at oneself in the mirror ❷ (*no pf.*) (*infml, хорошо выглядеть*) to look good

⚘ **смоч|и́ть, у́, ∼ишь** *pf.* (*of* ▶ сма́чивать) to damp, wet, moisten

♂ **смо|чь**, гу́, ~же́шь, *past* ~г, ~гла́ *pf. of*
▶ **мочь**

смоше́ннича|ть, ю *pf. of* ▶ **моше́нничать**

смрад, а *m.* stink, stench

сму́гл|ый, ~, ~а́, ~о, ~ы *adj.* swarthy

сму|ти́ть, щу́, ти́шь *pf.* (*of* ▶ **смуща́ть**) to
embarrass, confuse

сму|ти́ться, щу́сь, ти́шься *pf.* (*of*
▶ **смуща́ться**) to be embarrassed, be
confused

сму́т|ный, ~ен, ~на́, ~но *adj.* vague;
confused; ~ные воспомина́ния dim
recollections

смуща́|ть, ю *impf. of* ▶ **смути́ть**

смуща́|ться, юсь *impf. of* ▶ **смути́ться**

смуще́ни|е, я *nt.* embarrassment, confusion

смыва́|ть, ю *impf. of* ▶ **смыть**

смыва́|ться, юсь *impf. of* ▶ **смы́ться**

смыка́|ть, ю, ет *impf. of* ▶ **сомкну́ть**

смыка́|ться, ется *impf. of* ▶ **сомкну́ться**

♂ **смысл**, а *m.* **1** sense, meaning; прямо́й,
перено́сный с. literal, metaphorical sense;
в изве́стном ~е in a sense; в ~е (+ *g.*) as
regards **2** (*цель, разумное основание*) sense,
point; име́ть с. to make sense; нет никако́го
~а (+ *inf.*) there is no sense (in), there is no
point (in) **3** (*разум*) (good) sense; здра́вый
с. common sense

смыслов|о́й *adj. of* ▶ **смысл**; ~ые отте́нки
shades of meaning

смыть, смо́ю, смо́ешь *pf.* (*of* ▶ **смыва́ть**)
1 (*удалить*) to wash off; (fig., *позор*) to
clear, wipe out **2** (*снести*) to wash away
3 (*туалет*) to flush

смы́ться, смо́юсь, смо́ешься *pf.* (*of*
▶ **смыва́ться**) **1** to wash off, come off
2 (fig., infml, *уйти*) to slip away

смыч|о́к, ка́ *m.* (mus.) bow

смягча́|ть, а́ю *impf. of* ▶ **смягчи́ть**

смягча́|ться, а́юсь *impf. of* ▶ **смягчи́ться**

смягч|и́ть, у́, и́шь *pf.* (*of* ▶ **смягча́ть**)
1 (*кожу, тон*) to soften **2** (*боль*) to ease,
alleviate; (*наказание*) to mitigate

смягч|и́ться, у́сь, и́шься *pf.* (*of*
▶ **смягча́ться**) **1** (*о коже, тоне, взгляде*) to
soften, become softer **2** (*о человеке*) to be
mollified; (*о боли, ветре, холоде, ситуации*)
to ease (off)

смяте́ни|е, я *nt.* confusion, disarray;
commotion

смять, сомну́, сомнёшь *pf.* (*of* ▶ **мять 2**)
to crumple; to rumple; с. пла́тье to crush
a dress

смя́ться, сомнётся *pf.* (*of* ▶ **мя́ться**) to get
creased; to get crumpled

снаб|ди́ть, жу́, ди́шь *pf.* (*of* ▶ **снабжа́ть**)
(+ *i.*) to supply (with), furnish (with),
provide (with)

снабжа́|ть, ю *impf. of* ▶ **снабди́ть**

снабже́ни|е, я *nt.* supply, supplying, provision

сна́йпер, а *m.* sniper

♂ key word

снару́жи *adv.* on the outside; from (the)
outside

снаря́д, а *m.* **1** (mil.) projectile, missile; shell
2 (*прибор*) contrivance, machine, gadget;
гимнасти́ческие ~ы gymnastic apparatus

снаря|ди́ть, жу́, ди́шь *pf.* (*of* ▶ **снаряжа́ть**)
to equip, fit out

снаря|ди́ться, жу́сь, ди́шься *pf.* (*of*
▶ **снаряжа́ться**) to equip oneself, get ready

снаряжа́|ть, ю *impf. of* ▶ **снаряди́ть**

снаряжа́|ться, юсь *impf. of* ▶ **снаряди́ться**

снаряже́ни|е, я *nt.* equipment, outfit;
ко́нское с. harness

снаст|ь, и, *pl.* ~и, ~е́й *f.* **1** (collect.) tackle,
gear **2** (*usu. in pl.*) (*на судне*) rigging

♂ **снача́ла** *adv.* **1** (*прежде*) at first, at the
beginning **2** (*снова*) all over again

сна́шива|ть, ю *impf. of* ▶ **сноси́ть**[1]

СНГ *nt. indecl.* (*abbr. of* Содру́жество
Незави́симых Госуда́рств) CIS
(*Commonwealth of Independent States*)

♂ **снег**, а, о ~е, в/на ~у́, *pl.* ~а́ *m.* snow;
идёт с. it's snowing; мо́крый с. sleet

снеги́р|ь, я́ *m.* bullfinch

снегоочисти́тель|ный *adj.*: ~ая маши́на
snowplough (BrE), snowplow (AmE)

снегопа́д, а *m.* snowfall

снегохо́д, а *m.* snowmobile

снежи́нк|а, и *f.* snowflake

сне́жн|ый *adj.* snow; snowy; ~ая ба́ба
snowman; с. зано́с, с. сугро́б snowdrift;
~ая зима́ snowy winter

снеж|о́к, ка́ *m.* **1** light snow **2** (*комок*)
snowball; игра́ть в ~ки́ to have a snowball
fight

снес|ти́[1], у́, ёшь, *past* ~, ~ла́ *pf.* (*of*
▶ **сноси́ть[1]**) **1** (*вниз*) to fetch down, bring
down **2** (*usu. impers.*) (*о воде*) to carry
away; (*о ветре*) to blow off, take off
3 (*разрушить*) to demolish, pull down
4 (*срезать*) to cut off, chop off; с. го́лову
кому́-н. to chop sb's head off

снес|ти́[2], у́, ёшь *pf.* (*of* ▶ **нести́[2]**) to lay (eggs)

♂ **снижа́|ть**, ю *impf. of* ▶ **сни́зить**

снижа́|ться, юсь *impf. of* ▶ **сни́зиться**

♂ **сниже́ни|е**, я *nt.* **1** lowering, reduction;
с. зарпла́ты wage cut **2** (aeron.) descent

сни́|зить, жу, зишь *pf.* (*of* ▶ **снижа́ть**)
1 (*спустить ниже*) to bring down, lower
2 (*цены*) to bring down, lower, reduce

сни́|зиться, жусь, зишься *pf.* (*of*
▶ **снижа́ться**) **1** (*спуститься ниже*) to
descend, come down **2** (*температура*)
to fall, sink, come down

сни́зу *adv.* from below; from the bottom;
с. вверх upwards; с. до́верху from top to
bottom; (*внизу*) at, on the bottom

♂ **снима́|ть**, ю *impf. of* ▶ **снять**

снима́|ться, юсь *impf. of* ▶ **сня́ться**

сни́м|ок, ка *m.* photograph, photo

снисходи́тель|ный, ~ен, ~ьна *adj.*
(*не строгий*) indulgent, tolerant, lenient

сни́|ться, снюсь, сни́шься *impf. (of* ▶ **присни́ться)** (+ *d.*) to dream; **ей ~лось, что** she dreamed that; **мне ~лся лев** I dreamed about a lion

сноб, а *m.* snob

сноби́зм, а *m.* snobbery

✓ **сно́ва** *adv.* again, anew, afresh

сновиде́ни|е, я *nt.* dream

сноро́вк|а, и *f.* skill, knack

снос, а *m.* demolition, pulling down; **дом предназна́чен на с.** the house is to be pulled down

сно|си́ть¹, шу́, ~сишь *pf. (of* ▶ **сна́шивать)** to wear out

сно|си́ть², шу́, ~сишь *pf.* (infml, *снести и принести*) to take (*and bring back*)

сно|си́ть³, шу́, ~сишь *impf. of* ▶ **снести́¹**

сно́ск|а, и *f.* footnote

сно́с|ный, ~ен, ~на *adj.* (infml) tolerable; fair, reasonable

снотво́р|ный *adj.* soporific (also fig.); **~ное сре́дство** soporific; (*as nt. n.* **~ное, ~ного)** sleeping pill

сноубо́рд, а *m.* snowboard

сноубо́рдинг, а *m.* snowboarding

сноха́|а́, и́, *pl.* ~и *f.* daughter-in-law

сноше́ни|е, я *nt.* (*usu. in pl.*) relations, dealings; (*половой акт*) (sexual) intercourse

сня|ть, сниму́, сни́мешь, *past* **~л, ~ла́, ~ло** *pf. (of* ▶ **снима́ть)** **1** (*одежду, крышку*) to take off; (*вниз*) to take down; **с. карти́ну** to take down a picture; **с. оса́ду** to raise a siege; **с. с себя́ отве́тственность** to decline responsibility **2** (*устранить, отменить*) to remove; to withdraw, cancel; **с. запре́т** to lift a ban; **с. с рабо́ты** to discharge, sack **3** (*изготовить*) to take, make; to photograph, make a photograph (of); **с. ко́пию** (**с** + *g.*) to copy, make a copy (of); **с. фильм** to shoot a film **4** (*взять внаём*) to take, rent (*a house, etc.*) **5** (sl., *девушку*) to pick up, pull

сня|ться, сниму́сь, сни́мешься, *past* **~лся, ~ла́сь** *pf. (of* ▶ **снима́ться)** **1** (*отделиться*) to come off **2** (*отправиться*) to move off; **с. с я́коря** to weigh anchor; to get under way (also fig.) **3** (*фотографироваться*) to have one's photograph taken **4** (*сыграть роль в фильме*) to play a part in a film

✓ **со** *prep.* = **с**

со... ** *vbl. pref.* = **с...

соа́втор, а *m.* co-author

✓ **соба́к|а, и** *f.* **1** dog; **охо́тничья с.** gun dog, hound; **с.-поводы́рь** guide dog; **служе́бная с.** guard dog; **уста́ть как с.** (infml) to be dog-tired **2** (comput.) @ sign (*as used in email addresses, where it is pronounced 'at'*)

соба́|чий *adj. of* ▶ **соба́ка**; canine; **~чья жизнь** dog's life; **с. хо́лод** intense cold

собесе́дник, а *m.* interlocutor; **он — заба́вный с.** he is amusing company

собесе́дни|ца, цы *f. of* ▶ **собесе́дник**

собесе́довани|е, я *nt.* conversation, discussion, interview

✓ **собира́|ть, ю** *impf. of* ▶ **собра́ть**

✓ **собира́|ться, юсь** *impf.* **1** *impf. of* ▶ **собра́ться** **2** (+ *inf.*) to intend (to), be about (to), be going (to)

собла́зн, а *m.* temptation

соблазни́тель|ный, ~ен, ~ьна *adj.* tempting; alluring; (*женщина*) seductive

соблазн|и́ть, ю́, и́шь *pf. (of* ▶ **соблазня́ть)** **1** (*прельстить*) to tempt **2** (*обольстить*) to seduce

соблазня́|ть, я́ю *impf. of* ▶ **соблазни́ть**

соблюда́|ть, ю *impf. of* ▶ **соблюсти́**

соблю|сти́, ду́, дёшь, *past* **~л, ~ла́** *pf.* (*of* ▶ **соблюда́ть)** (*диету*) to keep (to), stick to; (*порядок*) to maintain; to observe; **с. зако́н** to observe a law; **с. сро́ки** to keep to schedule

собо́й *see* ▶ **себя́**

соболе́зновани|е, я *nt.* sympathy; (*in pl.*) condolences

соболе́зн|овать, ую *impf.* (+ *d.*) to sympathize (with), commiserate (with)

со́бол|ь, я, *pl.* (*furs*) **~я́, ~е́й** and (*animals*) **~и, ~е́й** *m.* sable

собо́р, а *m.* **1** (hist., also eccl.) (*съезд*) council, synod, assembly; **вселе́нский с.** ecumenical council **2** (*церковь*) cathedral

собо́ю = **собо́й** *see* ▶ **себя́**

✓ **собра́ни|е, я** *nt.* **1** (*заседание*) meeting, gathering; **о́бщее с.** general meeting **2** (*государственный орган*) assembly; **учреди́тельное с.** constituent assembly **3** (*коллекция*) collection; **с. сочине́ний** collected works

со́бранный *p.p.p. of* ▶ **собра́ть** *and adj.*: **с. челове́к** self-disciplined person

собр|а́ть, соберу́, соберёшь, *past* **~а́л, ~ала́, ~а́ло** *pf. (of* ▶ **собира́ть)** **1** (*сведения*) to gather; (*книги, деньги*) to collect; (*цветы*) to pick **2** (*людей*) to assemble, muster; to convene; **с. после́дние си́лы** to make a last effort **3** (tech., *радиоприёмник*) to assemble

собр|а́ться, соберу́сь, соберёшься, *past* **~а́лся, ~ала́сь, ~а́ло́сь** *pf.* (*of* ▶ **собира́ться)** **1** (*сойтись*) to gather, assemble **2** (**в** + *a.*) (*приготовиться*) to prepare (for); **с. в го́сти** to get ready to go away (*to visit sb*) **3** (+ *inf.*) (*решить*) to intend (to), to be about (to), be going (to) **4** (**с** + *i.*) (fig., *сосредоточиться*) to collect; **с. с си́лами** to summon up one's strength

со́бственник, а *m.* owner, proprietor; **земе́льный с.** landowner

со́бственни|ца, цы *f. of* ▶ **со́бственник**

✓ **со́бственно** *adv.* actually; **с. говоря́** strictly speaking, as a matter of fact

собственнору́чно *adv.* with one's own hand

✓ **со́бственност|ь, и** *f.* **1** (*имущество*) property **2** (*владение*) possession,

C

ownership; **приобрести в с.** to become the owner (of)

⚘ **со́бственн|ый** *adj.* (one's) own; **∼ыми глаза́ми** with one's own eyes; **чу́вство ∼ого досто́инства** self-respect; **∼ой персо́ной** in person; **и́мя ∼ое** (gram.) proper noun

⚘ **собы́ти|е, я** *nt.* event; **теку́щие ∼я** current affairs

сов|а́, ы́, *pl.* **∼ы** *f.* owl; (fig.) night owl

сова́ть, сую́, суёшь *impf.* (*of* ▶ **су́нуть**) to shove, thrust, poke; **с. ру́ки в карма́ны** to stick one's hands in one's pockets; **с. нос (в + a.)** (infml) to poke one's nose (into), pry (into)

сова́ться, сую́сь, суёшься *impf.* (*of* ▶ **су́нуться**) (infml) **1** to push, strain **2** (**в + a.**) (fig., *в чужие дела*) to butt (in); (*с советами*) to poke one's nose (into)

⚘ **соверш|а́ть, а́ю, а́ет** *impf. of* ▶ **соверши́ть**

⚘ **соверш|а́ться, а́ется** *impf. of* ▶ **соверши́ться**

⚘ **соверше́нно** *adv.* **1** (*превосходно*) perfectly **2** (*совсем*) absolutely, utterly, completely; **с. ве́рно!** quite right!; perfectly true!

совершенноле́ти|е, я *nt.* majority; **дости́гнуть ∼я** to come of age, attain one's majority

совершенноле́тний *adj.* of age

соверше́н|ный, ∼ен, ∼на *adj.* **1** (*превосходный*) perfect **2** (infml, *полный*) absolute, complete

соверше́нств|о, а *nt.* perfection; **в ∼е** perfectly, to perfection

соверше́нств|овать, ую *impf.* (*of* ▶ **усоверше́нствовать**) to perfect; to develop, improve

соверше́нств|оваться, уюсь *impf.* (*of* ▶ **усоверше́нствоваться**) (**в + p.**) to perfect oneself (in); to improve

⚘ **соверш|и́ть, у́, и́шь** *pf.* (*of* ▶ **соверша́ть**) **1** (*подвиг*) to accomplish, carry out; to perform; (*преступление*) to commit **2** (*заключить*) to complete, conclude; **с. сде́лку** to complete a transaction, make a deal

соверш|и́ться, и́тся *pf.* (*of* ▶ **соверша́ться**) (liter.) **1** (*о событии*) to happen **2** (*о подвиге*) to be accomplished; (*о сделке*) to be completed

со́вестлив|ый, ∼, ∼а *adj.* conscientious

со́вест|ь, и *f.* conscience; **чи́стая, нечи́стая с.** clear, guilty conscience; **на ∼и** on one's conscience; **со споко́йной ∼ю** with a clear conscience

⚘ **сове́т, а** *m.* **1** advice; **проси́ть ∼а** to ask for advice **2** (*совместное обсуждение*) discussion; **вое́нный с.** council of war **3** (hist., *орган управления в СССР*) soviet **4** (*административный орган*) council; **С. безопа́сности** Security Council

сове́тник, а *m.* adviser, counsellor

сове́т|овать, ую *impf.* (*of* ▶ **посове́товать**) (+ *d.*) to advise

сове́т|оваться, уюсь *impf.* (*of* ▶ **посове́товаться**) (**с + i.**) to consult, ask advice (of), seek advice (from)

⚘ **сове́тск|ий** *adj.* (hist.) Soviet; **∼ая власть** Soviet rule *or* power; **с. наро́д** the Soviet people

Сове́тск|ий Сою́з, ∼ого Сою́за *m.* (hist.) the Soviet Union

совеща́ни|е, я *nt.* conference, meeting

совеща́|ться, юсь *impf.* **1** (**о + p.**) to deliberate (on, about) **2** (**с + i.**) to confer (with), consult

совлада́|ть, ю *pf.* (**с + i.**) (infml) to control; **с. с собо́й** to control oneself

совладе́л|ец, ьца *m.* joint owner

совладе́л|ица, ицы *f. of* ▶ **совладе́лец**

совмести́м|ый, ∼, ∼а *adj.* compatible

совме|сти́ть, щу́, сти́шь *pf.* (*of* ▶ **совмеща́ть**) to combine

совме́стно *adv.* in common, jointly

⚘ **совме́стн|ый** *adj.* joint, combined; **∼ые де́йствия** concerted action; **∼ое предприя́тие** joint venture

совмеща́|ть, ю *impf. of* ▶ **совмести́ть**

сов|о́к, ка́ *m.* shovel, scoop; **с. для му́сора** dustpan

совокупле́ни|е, я *nt.* copulation

совоку́пност|ь, и *f.* aggregate, sum total; totality; **в ∼и** in the aggregate

совпада́|ть, ю *impf. of* ▶ **совпа́сть**

совпаде́ни|е, я *nt.* coincidence

совпа́|сть, ду́, дёшь, *past* **∼л** *pf.* (*of* ▶ **совпада́ть**) **1** (**с + i.**) (*произойти одновременно*) to coincide (with); **части́чно с.** to overlap **2** (*оказаться общим*) to agree, tally; **их показа́ния не ∼да́ли** their evidence did not tally

совра|ти́ть, щу́, ти́шь *pf.* (*of* ▶ **совраща́ть**) (*соблазнить*) to lead astray; (*женщину*) to seduce; (*ребёнка*) to (sexually) abuse

совр|а́ть, у́, ёшь, *past* **∼а́л, ∼ала́, ∼а́ло** *pf. of* ▶ **врать**

совраща́|ть, ю *impf. of* ▶ **соврати́ть**

совраще́ни|е, я *nt.* corrupting; (*женщины*) seducing, seduction; (*ребёнка*) (sexual) abuse; **с. малоле́тних** child (sexual) abuse

совреме́нник, а *m.* contemporary

совреме́нни|ца, цы *f. of* ▶ **совреме́нник**

совреме́нност|ь, и *f.* **1** (*актуальность*) contemporaneity **2** (*современная эпоха*) the present (time)

⚘ **совреме́н|ный, ∼ен, ∼на** *adj.* (*относящийся к настоящему времени*) contemporary, present-day; (*человек*) modern; (*техника*) up-to-date, state-of-the-art; **∼ная англи́йская литерату́ра** modern English literature

⚘ **совсе́м** *adv.* quite, entirely, completely; **с. не** not at all, not in the least; **с. не то** nothing of the kind

согла́си|е, я *nt.* **1** (*разрешение*) consent; **с ва́шего ∼я** with your consent **2** (*единомыслие*) agreement; **в ∼и (с + i.)**

in accordance (with); **прийти́ к ~ю** to come to an agreement **3** (*единоду́шие*) harmony

согла|си́ться, шу́сь, си́шься *pf.* (*of* ▶ **соглаша́ться**) **1** (**на** + *a.* or + *inf.*) to consent (to), agree (to) **2** (**с** + *i.*) to agree (with)

согла́сно *prep.* (+ *d.* or **с** + *i.*) in accordance (with); according (to); **с. догово́ру** in accordance with the treaty
● *adv.* (*жить, петь*) in harmony

согла́с|ный[1], **~ен, ~на** *adj.* **1** (**на** + *a.*) agreeable (to); **они́ не́ были ~ны на на́ши усло́вия** they would not agree to our conditions **2** (**с** + *i.*) in agreement (with); **быть ~ным** to agree (with); **~ен, ~на, ~ны?** do you agree?

согла́сн|ый[2] *adj.* (*gram.*) consonant(al); (*as m. n.* **с., ~ого**) consonant

соглас|ова́ть, у́ю *pf.* (*of* ▶ **согласо́вывать**) (**с** + *i.*) **1** to coordinate (with) **2**: **с. что-н. с кем-н.** to agree sth with sb, come to an agreement with sb about sth

согласо́выва|ть, ю *impf. of* ▶ **согласова́ть**

соглаша́|ться, юсь *impf. of* ▶ **согласи́ться**

соглаше́ни|е, я *nt.* agreement; **заключи́ть с.** to conclude an agreement

согн|у́ть, у́, ёшь *pf.* (*of* ▶ **гнуть,** ▶ **сгиба́ть**) to bend, curve, crook

согн|у́ться, у́сь, ёшься *pf.* (*of* ▶ **гну́ться,** ▶ **сгиба́ться**) to bend, bow (down)

согрева́|ть, ю *impf. of* ▶ **согре́ть**

согрева́|ться, юсь *impf. of* ▶ **согре́ться**

согре́|ть, ю *pf.* (*of* ▶ **согрева́ть**) to warm, heat

согре́|ться, юсь *pf.* (*of* ▶ **согрева́ться**) to get warm; to warm oneself

согреш|и́ть, у́, и́шь *pf.* (*of* ▶ **греши́ть** 1) (**про́тив** + *g.*) to sin (against), trespass (against)

со́д|а, ы *f.* soda, sodium carbonate; **питьева́я с.** baking soda

соде́йстви|е, я *nt.* assistance, help

соде́йств|овать, ую *impf. and pf.* (+ *d.*) to assist; to further; to contribute (to)

содержа́ни|е, я *nt.* **1** (*семьи*) maintenance, upkeep; (*де́нежное*) **с.** allowance, financial support; **с. под аре́стом** custody **2** (*зарпла́та*) pay **3** (*содержи́мое*) content; **с больши́м ~ем** (+ *g.*) rich (in) **4** (*су́щность*) substance; content; **фо́рма и с.** form and content **5** (*кни́ги*) content(s); (*рома́на*) plot **6** (*оглавле́ние*) table of contents

содержа́тел|ьный, ~ен, ~ьна *adj.* rich in content

содерж|а́ть, у́, ~ишь *impf.* **1** (*семью́*) to keep, maintain, support **2** (*магази́н*) to keep, have **3** (**в** + *p.*) to keep (*in a given state*); **с. в поря́дке** to keep in order **4** (*име́ть в себе́*) to contain

содерж|а́ться, у́сь, ~ишься *impf.* **1** (*обеспе́чиваться*) to be kept, be maintained **2** (*находи́ться*) to be kept, be **3** (**в** + *p.*) (*заключа́ться*) to be contained (by); **в э́той руде́ ~ится ура́н** this ore contains uranium

содержи́м|ое, ого *nt.* contents

со́дов|ый *adj.* soda; **~ая (вода́)** soda (water)

содра́|ть, сдеру́, сдерёшь, *past* **~л, ~ла́, ~ло** *pf.* (*of* ▶ **сдира́ть,** ▶ **драть** 2) to tear off, strip off; **с. ко́жу** (**с** + *g.*) to skin, flay

содрога́|ться, а́юсь *impf. of* ▶ **содрогну́ться**

содрог|ну́ться, ну́сь, нёшься *pf.* (*of* ▶ **содрога́ться**) to shudder, shake, quake

содру́жеств|о, а *nt.* community, commonwealth; **Брита́нское С. на́ций** the British Commonwealth

соедине́ни|е, я *nt.* **1** joining, combination **2** (*tech.*) joint **3** (*chem.*) compound **4** (*mil.*) formation

Соединённое Короле́вство (Великобрита́нии и Се́верной Ирла́ндии), Соединённого Короле́вства (В. и С. И.) *nt.* United Kingdom (of Great Britain and Northern Ireland)

Соединённые Шта́ты (Аме́рики), Соединённых Шта́тов (Аме́рики) (*no sg.*) United States (of America)

соединённый *p.p.p. of* ▶ **соедини́ть** *and adj.* united, joint

соедин|и́ть, ю́, и́шь *pf.* (*of* ▶ **соединя́ть**) **1** (*объедини́ть*) to join, unite **2** (*присоедини́ть*) to connect, link; **с. (по телефо́ну)** to put through

соедин|и́ться, ю́сь, и́шься *pf.* (*of* ▶ **соединя́ться**) **1** to join, unite **2** (*chem.*) to combine **3** *pass. of* ▶ **соедини́ть**

соедин|я́ть, я́ю *impf. of* ▶ **соедини́ть**

соедин|я́ться, я́юсь *impf. of* ▶ **соедини́ться**

сожале́ни|е, я *nt.* **1** (**о** + *p.*) regret (for); **к ~ю** unfortunately **2** (**к** + *d.*) pity (for)

сожале́|ть, ю *impf.* (**о** + *p.* or **что**) to regret, deplore

сожи́тел|ь, я *m.* **1** (*по кварти́ре*) flatmate (BrE), room-mate (AmE) **2** (*любо́вник*) lover

сожи́тельни|ца, цы *f. of* ▶ **сожи́тель**

сожр|а́ть, у́, ёшь, *past* **~а́л, ~ала́, ~а́ло** *pf. of* ▶ **жрать**

созва́нива|ться, юсь *impf. of* ▶ **созвони́ться**

созва́|ть, созову́, созовёшь, *past* **~л, ~ла́, ~ло** *pf.* (*of* ▶ **созыва́ть**) **1** (*госте́й*) to gather; to invite **2** (*люде́й на сове́т*) to call (together); summon; (*ми́тинг, парла́мент*) to convoke, convene

созве́зди|е, я *nt.* constellation

созвон|и́ться, ю́сь, и́шься *pf.* (*of* ▶ **созва́ниваться**) (**с** + *i.*) (*infml*) to speak on the telephone (to)

созву́ч|ный, ~ен, ~на *adj.* (+ *d.*) consonant (with), in keeping (with)

созда|ва́ть, ю́, ёт *impf. of* ▶ **созда́ть**

созда|ва́ться, ётся *impf. of* ▶ **созда́ться**

созда́ни|е, я *nt.* **1** (*де́йствие*) creation, making **2** (*произведе́ние*) creation, work

3 (*существо*) creature

созда́тел|ь, я *m.* **1** creator; (*организации*) founder; (*теории*) originator **2** (**С.**) (*Бог*) the Creator

созда́тель|ница, ницы *f. of* ▶ **созда́тель 1**

♂ **созда́|ть, м, шь, ст, ди́м, ди́те, ду́т,** *past* **со́здал, ∼ла́, со́здало** *pf.* (*of* ▶ **создава́ть**) to create; (*организацию*) to found; (*теорию*) to originate; **с. впечатле́ние** to give the impression; **с. иллю́зию** to create an illusion

созда́|ться, стся, ду́тся, *past* **∼лся, ∼ла́сь, ∼ло́сь** *and* **∼лось** *pf.* (*of* ▶ **создава́ться**) to be created; to arise; **у нас созда́ло́сь впечатле́ние, что** we gained the impression that

созерца́|ть, ю *impf.* to contemplate

созида́тельный, ∼ен, ∼ьна *adj.* creative, constructive

созна|ва́ть, ю́, ёшь *impf.* **1** *impf. of* ▶ **созна́ть** **2** to be conscious (of), realize; **я́сно с.** to be alive (to)

созна|ва́ться, ю́сь, ёшься *impf. of* ▶ **созна́ться**

♂ **созна́ни|е, я** *nt.* **1** consciousness; **потеря́ть с.** to lose consciousness; **прийти́ в с.** to regain, recover consciousness **2** (*ошибки, вины*) recognition, acknowledgement

созна́тел|ьный, ∼ен, ∼ьна *adj.* **1** conscious **2** (*отношение*) intelligent **3** (*намеренный*) deliberate

созна́|ть, ю *pf.* (*of* ▶ **сознава́ть 1**) to recognize, acknowledge

созна́|ться, ю́сь *pf.* (*of* ▶ **сознава́ться**) (**в** + *p.*) (*в ошибке*) to admit (to); (*в преступлении*) to confess (to); (*law*) to plead guilty

созрева́|ть, ю *impf. of* ▶ **созре́ть**

созре́|ть, ю *pf.* (*of* ▶ **зреть**, ▶ **созрева́ть**) (*о плоде*) to ripen; (*о человеке*) to mature; (*о плане*) to develop, mature

созыва́|ть, ю *impf. of* ▶ **созва́ть**

со|йти́, йду́, йдёшь, *past* **∼шёл, ∼шла́** *pf.* (*of* ▶ **сходи́ть¹**) **1** (*с лестницы, горы*) to go down, come down; (*с автобуса, поезда*) to get off; **с. на нет** to come to naught **2** (*покинуть, уйти*) to leave; **с. с доро́ги** to get out of the way, step aside; **с. с ре́льсов** to come off the rails; **с. с ума́** to go mad, go off one's head **3** (*о краске, о коже*) to come off

со|йти́сь, йду́сь, йдёшься, *past* **∼шёлся, ∼шла́сь** *pf.* (*of* ▶ **сходи́ться**) **1** (*встретиться*) to meet; to come together, gather **2** (**с** + *i.*) (*подружиться*) to meet, take up (with), become friends (with); (*вступить в сожительство*) to become (*sexually*) intimate (with) **3** (+ *i.* or **в** + *p.*) (*быть похожим*) to be similar; **они не ∼шли́сь хара́ктерами** they could not get on; (**в** + *p.* or **на** + *p.*) (infml, *договориться*) to agree (about); **они ∼шли́сь в цене́** they

agreed on a price **4** (*совпасть*) to agree, tally; **счета́ не ∼шли́сь** the figures did not tally

сок, а (у), о ∼е, в ∼е *and* **∼у́** *m.* juice

соковыжима́лк|а, и *f.* juicer

со́кол, а *m.* falcon

сокра|ти́ть, щу́, ти́шь *pf.* (*of* ▶ **сокраща́ть**) **1** (*статью, путь, рабочий день*) to shorten **2** (*расходы, штаты*) to reduce, cut down **3** (*уволить*) (infml) to dismiss, discharge, lay off, make redundant

сокра|ти́ться, ти́тся *pf.* (*of* ▶ **сокраща́ться**) **1** (*о днях*) to grow shorter **2** (*о расходах*) to decrease **3** (*о мышцах*) to contract

сокраща́|ть, ю, ет *impf. of* ▶ **сократи́ть**

сокраща́|ться, ется *impf. of* ▶ **сократи́ться**

сокраще́ни|е, я *nt.* **1** (*рабочего дня*) shortening **2** (*статьи*) abridgement; **с ∼ями** abridged **3** (*слова*) abbreviation **4** (*штатов, вооружений*) reduction, cutting down

сокра|щённый *p.p.p. of* ▶ **сократи́ть** *and adj.* brief; **∼щённое сло́во** abbreviation, contraction

сокрове́н|ный, ∼, ∼на *adj.* secret, concealed; **∼ные мы́сли** innermost thoughts

сокро́вищ|е, а *nt.* treasure

сокруши́тел|ьный, ∼ен, ∼ьна *adj.* shattering; **нанести́ с. уда́р** (+ *d.*) to deal a crippling blow

со|лга́ть, лгу́, лжёшь, лгу́т, *past* **∼лга́л, ∼лгала́, ∼лга́ло** *pf. of* ▶ **лгать**

солда́т, а, *g. pl.* **∼** *m.* soldier

солда́тик, а *m.* **1** *dim. of* ▶ **солда́т** **2** (*игрушка*) toy soldier; **игра́ть в ∼и** to play soldiers

солда́тский *adj. of* ▶ **солда́т**

солё|ный *adj.* **1** salt; **∼ое о́зеро** salt lake **2** (**со́лон, солона́, со́лоно**) (*суп*) salty **3** (*консервированный*) salted; pickled; **с. огуре́ц** pickled cucumber; (*as nt. n.* **∼ое, ∼ого**) salty food

соле́нь|е, я *nt.* (*usu. in pl.*) salted food(s); pickles

солида́рност|ь, и *f.* solidarity; **из ∼и** (**с** + *i.*) in sympathy (with)

солида́р|ный, ∼ен, ∼на *adj.* (**с** + *i.*) at one (with), in sympathy (with)

соли́д|ный, ∼ен, ∼на *adj.* **1** (*прочный*) solid, strong, sound; **∼ные зна́ния** sound knowledge **2** (*серьёзный*) solid, sound; (*надёжный*) reliable, respectable; **с. челове́к** a solid man; **с. журна́л** respectable magazine **3** (infml, *значительный*) respectable, sizeable; **∼ная су́мма** tidy sum

соли́ст, а *m.* soloist

соли́ст|ка, ки *f. of* ▶ **соли́ст**

со|ли́ть, ю́, ∼ишь *impf.* (*of* ▶ **посоли́ть**) **1** (*суп*) to salt **2** (*огурцы*) to pickle; **с. мя́со** to preserve meat in salt

♂ **со́лнечн|ый** *adj.* **1** sun; solar; **∼ое затме́ние** solar eclipse; **с. луч** sunbeam; **с. свет** sunlight, sunshine; **С∼ая систе́ма** solar system; **с. уда́р** (med.) sunstroke **2** (*день, пого́да*) sunny

⚬ **со́лнц|е, а** *nt.* sun; **на с.** in the sun

солнцезащи́тн|ый *adj.*: **с. крем** suncream; **∼ые очки́** sunglasses

со́ло 1 *adv.* solo **2** *n., nt. indecl.* solo

солов|е́й, ья́ *m.* nightingale

со́лод, а *m.* malt

соло́м|а, ы *f.* straw; (*для кры́ши*) thatch

соло́менн|ый *adj.* straw; **∼ая кры́ша** thatch, thatched roof; **∼ая шля́па** straw hat

соло́минк|а, и *f.* straw; **хвата́ться за ∼у** to clutch at straws

солони́н|а, ы *f.* salted beef, corned beef

соло́нк|а, и *f.* salt cellar

сол|ь¹, и, *pl.* **∼и, ∼е́й** *f.* salt

соль² *nt. indecl.* (mus.) G; **с.-дие́з** G sharp; **ключ с.** treble clef

со́л|ьный *adj. of* ▶ **со́ло**; **с. но́мер** solo; **∼ьная па́ртия** solo part

соля́нк|а, ∼и *f.* solyanka (*a sharp-tasting Russian soup of vegetables and meat or fish*)

Сомали́ *nt. indecl.* Somalia

сомали́ *m. indecl.* Somali (*language*)

сомали́|ец, йца *m.* Somali (*person*)

сомали́й|ка, ки *f. of* ▶ **сомали́ец**

сомали́йский *adj.* Somali

сомкн|у́ть, у́, ёшь *pf.* (*of* ▶ **смыка́ть**) to close; **с. глаза́** to close one's eyes

сомкн|у́ться, ётся *pf.* (*of* ▶ **смыка́ться**) to close (up)

сомнева́|ться, юсь *impf.* **1** (**в** + *p.*) to doubt; to question; **я не ∼юсь в его́ че́стности** I do not question his integrity **2** to worry; **мо́жете не с.** you need not worry

⚬ **сомне́ни|е, я** *nt.* doubt; uncertainty; **без ∼я, вне (вся́кого) ∼я** without (any) doubt, beyond doubt

сомни́тельн|ый, ∼ен, ∼ьна *adj.* **1** (*непрове́ренный*) doubtful, questionable; **∼ьно** it is doubtful, it is open to question **2** (*подозри́тельный*) dubious

⚬ **сон, сна** *m.* **1** sleep; **во сне, сквозь с.** in one's sleep; **со сна** half awake **2** (*сновиде́ние*) dream; **ви́деть во сне** to dream, have a dream (about)

сона́т|а, ы *f.* (mus.) sonata

соне́т, а *m.* sonnet

со́нный *adj.* sleepy, drowsy (also fig.)

со́н|я, и *f. and c.g.* **1** *f.* (*грызу́н*) dormouse **2** *c.g.* (infml, *челове́к*) sleepyhead

сообража́|ть, ю *impf.* **1** *impf. of* ▶ **сообрази́ть 2** (*impf. only*): **хорошо́, пло́хо с.** to be quick, slow on the uptake

соображе́ни|е, я *nt.* **1** (*причи́на*) consideration, reason; (*мысль*) notion, idea; **по фина́нсовым ∼ям** for financial reasons; **вы́сказать свои́ ∼я** to express one's views

сообрази́тельн|ый, ∼ен, ∼ьна *adj.* quick-witted, sharp, bright

сообра|зи́ть, жу́, зи́шь *pf.* (*of* ▶ **сообража́ть 1**) **1** (*взве́сить*) to consider, ponder; to weigh

(the pros and cons of) **2** (*поня́ть*) to understand, grasp

сообра́зно *adv.* (**с** + *i.*) in conformity (with)

сообща́ *adv.* together, jointly

⚬ **сообща́|ть, а́ю, а́ет** *impf. of* ▶ **сообщи́ть**

сообща́|ться, а́ется *impf. of* ▶ **сообщи́ться**

⚬ **сообще́ни|е, я** *nt.* **1** (*изве́стие*) communication, report; **сро́чное** *or* **экстренное с.** news flash **2** (*связь*) communication; **прямо́е с.** through connection; **пути́ ∼я** communications (*rail, road, canal, etc.*)

сообще́ств|о, а *nt.* (*междунаро́дное, мирово́е*) community

⚬ **сообщ|и́ть, у́, и́шь** *pf.* (*of* ▶ **сообща́ть**) (+ *a. or* **о** + *p.*) (*уве́домить*) to communicate, report, inform, announce; **с. после́дние изве́стия** to report the latest news

сообщ|и́ться, и́тся *pf.* (*of* ▶ **сообща́ться**) to be communicated

сообщник, а *m.* accomplice; partner (*in crime*); (law) accessory

сообщни|ца, цы *f. of* ▶ **сообщник**

сооруд|и́ть, жу́, ди́шь *pf.* (*of* ▶ **сооружа́ть**) to build, erect

сооружа́|ть, ю *impf. of* ▶ **сооруди́ть**

⚬ **сооруже́ни|е, я** *nt.* **1** (*де́йствие*) building, erection **2** (*постро́йка*) building, structure

⚬ **соотве́тственно** *adv.* accordingly

⚬ **соотве́тстви|е, я** *nt.* accordance, conformity, correspondence; **в ∼и (с** + *i.*) in accordance (with)

⚬ **соотве́тств|овать, ую** *impf.* (+ *d.*) to correspond (to, with), conform (to); **с. действи́тельности** to correspond to the facts; **с. тре́бованиям** to meet the requirements

⚬ **соотве́тств|ующий** *pres. part. act. of* ▶ **соотве́тствовать** *and adj.* **1** (+ *d.*) corresponding (to) **2** (*подходя́щий*) proper, appropriate; **поступа́ть ∼ующим о́бразом** to act accordingly

соотéчественник, а *m.* compatriot, fellow countryman

соотéчественни|ца, цы *f. of* ▶ **соотéчественник**

соотноше́ни|е, я *nt.* correlation, ratio; **с. сил** correlation of forces, alignment of forces

сопе́рник, а *m.* rival

сопе́рни|ца, цы *f. of* ▶ **сопе́рник**

сопе́рнича|ть, ю *impf.* to be rivals; (**с** + *i.*) to compete (with)

соп|е́ть, лю́, и́шь *impf.* to sniff (heavily and noisily)

сопли́в|ый, ∼, ∼а *adj.* (infml) snotty

сопл|о́, á, *pl.* **∼a, ∼ел** *and* **∼л** *nt.* nozzle

сопля́к, á *m.* (infml, pej.) milksop

сопоста́в|ить, лю, ишь *pf.* (*of* ▶ **сопоставля́ть**) (**с** + *i.*) to compare (with)

сопоставля́|ть, ю *impf. of* ▶ **сопоста́вить**

сопра́но *nt. indecl.* (mus.) soprano (*voice*); (*f. indecl.*) (infml) soprano (*singer*)

с

сопреде́л|ьный, ~ен, ~ьна *adj.*
neighbouring (BrE), neighboring (AmE);
contiguous

соприкаса́|ться, юсь *impf.* (*of*
▶ **соприкосну́ться**) (с + *i.*) to adjoin, be
contiguous (to)

соприкосн|у́ться, у́сь, ёшься *pf. of*
▶ **соприкаса́ться**

сопрово|ди́ть, жу́, ди́шь *pf. of*
▶ **сопровожда́ть**

сопровожда́|ть, ю *impf.* (*of*
▶ **сопроводи́ть**) to accompany

сопровожда́|ться, ется *impf.* (+ *i.*) to be
accompanied (by)

сопровожде́ни|е, я *nt.* **1** (*действие*)
accompanying, escort; **в ~и** (+ *g.*)
accompanied (by); escorted (by) **2** (mus.)
accompaniment; **звуково́е с.** soundtrack

сопротивле́ни|е, я *nt.* resistance,
opposition; (phys., tech.) strength; (elec.)
resistance, impedance; **оказа́ть с.** to put up
resistance

сопротивля́|ться, юсь *impf.* (+ *d.*) to
resist, oppose

сопу́тств|овать, ую *impf.* (+ *d.*) to
accompany; **~ующие обстоя́тельства**
attendant circumstances, concomitants

сор, а *m.* litter, rubbish

сора́тник, а *m.* comrade-in-arms

сорван|е́ц, ца́ *m.* (infml) (*ребёнок*) a terror;
(*девочка*) tomboy

сорв|а́ть, у́, ёшь, *past* **~а́л, ~ала́, ~а́ло** *pf.*
(*of* ▶ **срыва́ть**) **1** (*отдели́ть*) to tear off,
break off, tear away, tear down; (*цвето́к*)
to pick, pluck; **с. ве́тку** to break off a
branch **2** (*на* + *p.*) (*вы́местить*) to vent
(upon); **с. гнев на ком-н.** to vent one's anger
upon sb **3** (*нару́шить*) to wreck, ruin, spoil;
с. забасто́вку to break a strike

сорв|а́ться, у́сь, ёшься, *past* **~а́лся,
~ала́сь, ~а́лось** *pf.* (*of* ▶ **срыва́ться**)
1 (*освободи́ться*) to break away, break
loose; **с. с пе́тель** to come off its hinges
2 (*упа́сть*) to fall, come down; **с. с
колоко́льни** to fall from the belfry **3** (infml,
не уда́ться) to fall through

⚹ **соревнова́ни|е, я** *nt.* **1** (sport) competition,
contest; event **2** (*действие*) competition

соревн|ова́ться, у́юсь *impf.* (с + *i.*) to
compete (with, against)

сориенти́р|овать, ую *pf. of* ▶ **ориенти́ровать**

сориенти́р|оваться, у́юсь *pf. of*
▶ **ориенти́роваться**

сор|и́ть, ю́, и́шь *impf.* (*of* ▶ **насори́ть**)
(+ *a. or i.*) to drop litter; to make a mess;
с. деньга́ми to throw one's money about

сорня́к, а́ *m.* weed

со́рок, *all other cases* **а́** *num.* forty

соро́к|а, и *f.* magpie

сороков|о́й *adj.* fortieth; **~ы́е го́ды** the
forties

сороконо́жк|а, и *f.* centipede

соро́чк|а, и *f.* shirt; blouse; (*ни́жняя*)
camisole; **ночна́я с.** (*мужска́я*) nightshirt;
(*же́нская*) nightdress

сорт, а, *pl.* **~а́** *m.* **1** (*ка́чество*) grade, quality;
вы́сший с. best quality; **пе́рвого ~а** first
grade, first-rate **2** (*разнови́дность*) sort,
kind, variety

сортир|ова́ть, у́ю *impf.* (*това́р, у́голь*)
to sort, grade; (*корреспонде́нцию*) to sort;
(comput.) to sort

сортиро́вк|а, и *f.* sorting, grading

сос|а́ть, у́, ёшь *impf.* to suck

сосе́д, а, *pl.* **~и, ~ей** *m.* neighbour (BrE),
neighbor (AmE)

сосе́д|ка, ки *f. of* ▶ **сосе́д**

сосе́дн|ий *adj.* neighbouring (BrE),
neighboring (AmE); adjacent, next; **с. дом**
the house next door; **~яя ко́мната** the next
room

соси́ск|а, и *f.* sausage; (*варёная*) frankfurter

со́ск|а, и *f.* **1** (*пусты́шка*) dummy (BrE),
pacifier (AmE) **2** (*на буты́лке*) teat

соска́бл|ивать, ю *impf. of* ▶ **соскобли́ть**

соска́к|ивать, ю *impf. of* ▶ **соскочи́ть**

соска́льзыва|ть, ю *impf. of* ▶ **соскользну́ть**

соскобл|и́ть, ю́, и́шь *pf.* (*of*
▶ **соска́бливать**) to scrape off

соскольз|ну́ть, у́, ёшь *pf.* (*of*
▶ **соска́льзывать**) (*упа́сть*) to slip off, slide
off; (*с горы́*) to slide down

соскоч|и́ть, у́, ~ишь *pf.* (*of* ▶ **соска́кивать**)
1 (*с трамва́я, коня́*) to jump off, leap off;
(*с де́рева*) to jump down, leap down; **с. с
крова́ти** to jump out of bed **2** (*упа́сть*) to
come off; **с. с пе́тель** to come off its hinges

соскреба́|ть, ю *impf. of* ▶ **соскрести́**

соскре|сти́, бу́, бёшь, *past* **~б, ~бла́** *pf.*
(*of* ▶ **соскреба́ть**) to scrape away, off

соску́ч|иться, усь, ишься *pf.*
1 (*почу́вствовать ску́ку*) to become bored
2 (по + *d.*) to miss, yearn (for); **с. по
друзья́м** to miss one's friends; (*по ро́дине,
го́роду*) be homesick (for)

сослага́тельный *adj.* (gram.) subjunctive

со|сла́ть, шлю́, шлёшь *pf.* (*of* ▶ **ссыла́ть**)
to exile, banish

со|сла́ться, шлю́сь, шлёшься *pf.* (*of*
▶ **ссыла́ться**) (на + *a.*) **1** (*указа́ть*) to
refer (to), allude (to); (*процити́ровать*) to
cite, quote **2** (*оправда́ться*) to plead; **с. на
недомога́ние** to plead indisposition

сосло́ви|е, я *nt.* (social) class; **дворя́нское с.**
the nobility; **духо́вное с.** the clergy

сослужи́в|ец, ца *m.* colleague, fellow
employee

сослужи́в|ица, ицы *f. of* ▶ **сослужи́вец**

сосн|а́, ы́, *pl.* **~ы, со́сен** *f.* pine (tree)

сос|о́к, ка́ *m.* nipple

сосредото́ченност|ь, и *f.* (degree of)
concentration

сосредото́ченный *p.p.p. of* ▶ **сосредото́чить**
and adj. concentrated; **с. взгляд** fixed stare

с

сосредото́чива|ть, ю *impf. of*
▶ **сосредото́чить**

сосредото́чива|ться, юсь *impf. of*
▶ **сосредото́читься**

сосредото́ч|ить, у, ишь *pf.* (*of*
▶ **сосредото́чивать**) to concentrate; to
focus; **с. внима́ние** (**на** + *p.*) to concentrate
one's attention (on, upon)

сосредото́ч|иться, усь, ишься *pf.*
(*of* ▶ **сосредото́чиваться**) **1** (**на** + *p.*)
to concentrate (on, upon) **2** *pass. of*
▶ **сосредото́чить**

✧ **соста́в, а** *m.* **1** (*вещества*) composition,
make-up; structure; **входи́ть в с.** (+ *g.*) to
form part (of) **2** (*коллектив людей*) staff,
personnel; **ли́чный с.** personnel; **в по́лном**
~**е** at full strength; **в** ~**е** (+ *g.*) numbering,
consisting of; **делега́ция в** ~**е тридцати́**
челове́к a delegation of thirty (persons);
входи́ть в с. (+ *g.*) to be a member (of)

✧ **соста́в|ить¹, лю, ишь** *pf.* (*of* ▶ **составля́ть**)
1 (*собрать, соедини́ть*) to put together;
с. посу́ду to stack crockery **2** (*список,*
прое́кт) to make, draw up; to compile;
to form, construct; **с. мне́ние** to form an
opinion; **с. предложе́ние** to construct a
sentence; **с. слова́рь** to compile a dictionary
3 (*явля́ться*) to be, constitute, make; **э́то не**
~**ит большо́го труда́** this will not constitute
a lot of work **4** (*образова́ть*) to form, make,
amount to, total; **с. в сре́днем** to average;
расхо́ды ~**или пятьсо́т фу́нтов** expenditure
amounted to five hundred pounds

соста́в|ить², лю, ишь *pf.* (*of* ▶ **составля́ть**)
(*све́рху вниз*) to take down, put down;
с. я́щики на́ пол to put the drawers down
on the floor

соста́в|иться, ится *pf.* (*of* ▶ **составля́ться**)
to form, be formed, come into being

✧ **составля́|ть, ю, ет** *impf. of* ▶ **соста́вить¹**

составля́|ться, ется *impf. of* ▶ **соста́виться**

составн|о́й *adj.* **1** (*составленный из*
некоторых частей) compound, composite
2 (*входящий в состав чего-н.*) component;
~**а́я часть** component, constituent

соста́р|ить, ю *pf. of* ▶ **ста́рить**

соста́р|иться, юсь *pf. of* ▶ **ста́риться**

✧ **состоя́ни|е, я** *nt.* **1** state, condition;
position; **в хоро́шем, плохо́м** ~**и** in good,
bad condition; **быть в** ~**и** (+ *inf.*) to be able
(to), be in a position (to) **2** (*имущество*)
fortune; **нажи́ть с.** to make a fortune

состоя́тел|ьный¹, ~ен, ~ьна *adj.*
(*богатый*) well off

состоя́тел|ьный², ~ен, ~ьна *adj.*
(*обоснованный*) well grounded

✧ **состо|я́ть, ю́, и́шь** *impf.* **1** (**из** + *g.*) to
consist (of), comprise, be made up (of);
кварти́ра ~**и́т из трёх ко́мнат** the flat
consists of three rooms **2** (**в** + *p.*) to consist
(in), lie (in), be; **ра́зница** ~**и́т в том, что...**
the difference is that ... **3** (*быть*) to be; **с. в**
па́ртии to be a member of a party

✧ **состо|я́ться, и́тся** *pf.* to take place; **визи́т не**

~**я́лся** the visit did not take place

сострада́ни|е, я *nt.* compassion, sympathy

состр|и́ть, ю́, и́шь *pf. of* ▶ **остри́ть**

состяза́ни|е, я *nt.* competition, contest;
match; **с. по фехтова́нию** fencing match

состяза́|ться, юсь *impf.* (**с** + *i.*) to compete
(with)

сосу́д, а *m.* vessel

сосу́льк|а, и *f.* icicle

сосчита́|ть, ю *pf. of* ▶ **счита́ть 1**

сотвор|и́ть, ю́, и́шь *pf. of* ▶ **твори́ть**

со́тк|а, и *f.* (infml) 100 square metres
(= 0.01 hectare)

сотк|а́ть, у́, ёшь, *past* ~а́л, ~ала́, ~а́ло *pf.*
of ▶ **ткать**

✧ **со́т|ня, ни, *g. pl.* ~ен** *f.* (*сто*) a hundred (*esp.*
a hundred roubles)

со́товый *adj.* cellular; **с. телефо́н** cellphone,
mobile phone (BrE)

✧ **сотру́дник, а** *m.* **1** (*коллега*) colleague
2 (*служащий*) employee, worker; **нау́чный**
с. research assistant; **с. посо́льства** embassy
official **3** (*газеты, журна́ла*) contributor

сотру́дни|ца, цы *f. of* ▶ **сотру́дник**

сотру́дни|ча|ть, ю *impf.* **1** (**с** + *i.*) to work
(with) **2** (**в** + *p.*) to contribute (to); **с. в**
газе́те to contribute to a newspaper; to work
on a newspaper

✧ **сотру́дничеств|о, а** *nt.* collaboration,
cooperation

сотрясе́ни|е, я *nt.* shaking; **с. мо́зга** (med.)
concussion

со́т|ы, ~ and ~ов (*no sg.*) honeycombs

со́т|ый *adj.* hundredth; **с. год** the year one
hundred; (*as f. n.* ~**ая**, ~**ой**) (a) hundredth

со́ул, а *m.*: (*му́зыка*) м. soul music

со́ус, а *m.* sauce; (*мясно́й*) gravy; (*к сала́ту*)
dressing

со́усник, а *m.* sauce boat, gravy boat

соуча́стник, а *m.* accomplice; **с.**
преступле́ния (law) accessory to a crime

соуча́стни|ца, цы *f. of* ▶ **соуча́стник**

софи́зм, а *m.* sophism, sophistry

Софи́|я, и *f.* Sofia

со́х|нуть, ну, нёшь, *past* ~, ~ла *impf.*
1 (*о белье́*) to dry, get dry; (*о губах*) to
become parched **2** (*вя́нуть*) to wither;
(*fig., infml, от любви́*) to pine

✧ **сохране́ни|е, я** *nt.* **1** preservation;
conservation; (*попечение*) care, custody
2 (*права*) retention

сохран|и́ть, ю́, и́шь *pf.* (*of* ▶ **сохраня́ть**)
1 (*бере́чь*) to preserve, keep; to keep safe;
с. ве́рность (+ *d.*) to remain faithful, loyal
(to); **с. на па́мять** to keep as a souvenir
2 (*не теря́ть*) to keep, retain, reserve;
с. хладнокро́вие to keep cool; **с. за собо́й**
пра́во to reserve the right; (comput.) to save

сохран|и́ться, ю́сь, и́шься *pf.* (*of*
▶ **сохраня́ться**) **1** to remain (intact); to last
out, hold out; **он хорошо́** ~**и́лся** he is well

с

preserved **2** *pass. of* ► сохрани́ть

сохра́нност|ь, и *f.* safety, undamaged state; в ~и safe, intact

✓ сохран|я́ть, я́ю *impf. of* ► сохрани́ть

сохран|я́ться, я́юсь *impf. of* ► сохрани́ться

социа́л-демокра́т, а *m.* social democrat

социа́л-демократи́ческий *adj.* social democratic

социали́зм, а *m.* socialism

социали́ст, а *m.* socialist

социалисти́ческий *adj.* socialist

социали́ст|ка, ки *f. of* ► социали́ст

✓ социа́льн|ый *adj.* social; ~ое обеспе́чение social security; ~ое положе́ние social status; ~ая сеть social network

социо́лог, а *m.* sociologist

социологи́ческий *adj.* sociological

социоло́ги|я, и *f.* sociology

✓ сочета́ни|е, я *nt.* combination

сочета́|ть, ю *impf. and pf.* (с + *i.*) to combine (with)

сочета́|ться, ется *impf. and pf.* **1** to combine; в ней ~лся ум с красото́й she combined intelligence and good looks **2** (с + *i.*) (*гармони́ровать*) to harmonize (with), go (with); to match

сочине́ни|е, я *nt.* **1** (*де́йствие*) composing **2** (*произведе́ние*) work **3** (*шко́льное*) composition, essay

сочин|и́ть, ю́, и́шь *pf.* (*of* ► сочиня́ть) **1** (*созда́ть*) to compose (*a literary or musical work*); to write **2** (*вы́думать*) to make up, fabricate

сочин|я́ть, я́ю *impf. of* ► сочини́ть

соч|и́ться, и́тся *impf.* to ooze (out), exude; с. кро́вью to bleed

со́ч|ный, ~ен, ~на́, ~но *adj.* **1** juicy (also fig.); succulent **2** (fig.) (*кра́ски*) rich; (*зе́лень*) lush

сочу́вствие, я *nt.* sympathy; вы́звать с. to gain sympathy

сочу́вств|овать, ую *impf.* (+ *d.*) to sympathize (with), feel (for)

сочу́вств|ующий *pres. part. act. of* ► сочу́вствовать *and adj.* sympathetic; (*as m. n. as.*, ~ующего) sympathizer

✓ сою́з¹, а *m.* **1** (*соглаше́ние*) alliance, union; (*едине́ние*) agreement; заключи́ть с. (с + *i.*) to conclude an alliance (with) **2** (*организа́ция*) union; league; профессиона́льный с. trade union

сою́з², а *m.* (gram.) conjunction

сою́зник, а *m.* ally

сою́зни|ца, цы *f. of* ► сою́зник

сою́зн|ый *adj.* allied; ~ые держа́вы allied powers; (hist.) the Allies

со́|я, и *f.* soya bean

спаге́тти *nt. and pl. indecl.* spaghetti

спад, а *m.* (econ.) slump, recession

спада́|ть, ет *impf. of* ► спасть

✓ key word

спазм, а *m.* spasm

спа́ива|ть, ю *impf. of* ► спои́ть

спа́льн|ый *adj.* sleeping; с. ваго́н sleeping car; ~ое ме́сто berth, bunk; с. мешо́к sleeping bag

спа́л|ьня, ьни, g. pl. ~ен *f.* **1** (*ко́мната*) bedroom **2** (*ме́бель*) bedroom suite

спа́рж|а, и *f.* asparagus

спа́рива|ться, ется *impf. of* ► спа́риться

спа́р|иться, ится *pf.* (*of* ► спа́риваться) (*о живо́тных*) to mate

спа́рыва|ть, ю *impf. of* ► споро́ть

спаса́тел|ь, я *m.* lifeguard; rescuer; (*in pl.*) rescue party or team

спаса́тельн|ый *adj.* rescue, life-saving; с. круг, с. по́яс lifebelt; ~ая ло́дка lifeboat

спаса́|ть, ю *impf. of* ► спасти́

спаса́|ться, юсь *impf. of* ► спасти́сь

спасе́ни|е, я *nt.* **1** (*де́йствие*) rescuing, saving **2** (*возмо́жность спасти́сь*) rescue, escape; (relig.) salvation

✓ спаси́бо *particle* thanks; thank you; (*as n.*) thanks; большо́е вам с. thank you very much, many thanks

спаси́тел|ь, я *m.* **1** rescuer **2** (С.) (relig.) the Saviour (BrE), Savior (AmE)

спас|ти́, у́, ёшь, *past* ~, ~ла́ *pf.* (*of* ► спаса́ть) to save; to rescue; с. положе́ние to save the situation

спас|ти́сь, у́сь, ёшься, *past* ~ся, ~ла́сь *pf.* (*of* ► спаса́ться) **1** to save oneself, escape **2** (relig.) to be saved, save one's soul

спа|сть, дёт, *past* ~л *pf.* (*of* ► спада́ть) **1** (+ *i.*) (*упа́сть вниз*) to fall down (from) **2** (*о ве́тре, шу́ме, жаре́*) to abate; (*о температу́ре*) to fall

✓ спа|ть, сплю, спишь, *past* ~л, ~ла́, ~ло *impf.* to sleep, be asleep; лечь с. to go to bed; пора́ с. it is bedtime; с. с (+ *i.*) to sleep with (euph.)

спа́|ять, я́ю *pf.* to solder (together)

СПб (*abbr. of* Санкт-Петербу́рг) St Petersburg

спекта́кл|ь, я *m.* (theatr.) performance; show

спектр, а *m.* spectrum

спекули́р|овать, ую *impf.* **1** (+ *i. or* на + *p.*) to speculate (in); to profiteer (in) **2** (на + *p.*) (fig.) to exploit; to profit (by)

спекуля́нт, а *m.* speculator, profiteer

спекуляти́вный *adj.* speculative

спекуля́ци|я, и *f.* **1** (+ *i. or* на + *p.*) speculation (in); profiteering **2** (на + *p.*) (fig.) exploitation (of)

спелеоло́ги|я, и *f.* speleology; potholing

спе́л|ый, ~, ~а́, ~о *adj.* ripe

сперва́ *adv.* (infml) at first; first

спе́реди *adv. and prep.* + *g.* in front (of); at the front, from the front

спе́рм|а, ы *f.* sperm

сперматозо́ид, а *m.* (biol.) spermatozoon

спеси́в|ый, ~, ~а *adj.* arrogant, conceited, haughty

спе|ть¹, ет *impf.* to ripen

спеть², спою́, споёшь *pf. of* ▸ петь

специализа́ци|я, и *f.* specialization

специализи́р|оваться, уюсь *impf. and pf.* (в + *p.* or по + *d.*) to specialize (in)

⚹ специали́ст, а *m.* (в + *p.* or по + *d.*) specialist (in), expert (in)

специали́ст|ка, ки *f. of* ▸ специали́ст

⚹ специа́льно *adv.* specially, especially

специа́льност|ь, и *f.* **1** speciality, special interest **2** (*профессия*) profession

⚹ специа́л|ьный *adj.* **1** special; с. корреспонде́нт special correspondent **2** (∼ен, ∼ьна) specialist; ∼ьное образова́ние specialist education

специ́фик|а, и *f.* specific character

специфи́ческий *adj.* specific

спе́ци|я, и *f.* (*usu. in pl.*) spice

спецна́з, а *m.* (*abbr. of* отря́д специа́льного назначе́ния) special unit

спецоде́жд|а, ы *f.* working clothes, overalls

спецслу́жб|а, ы *f.* (*usu. in pl.*) special force

спецэффе́кт, а *m.* special effect

спеш|и́ть, у́, и́шь *impf.* (*of* ▸ поспеши́ть) **1** to hurry, be in a hurry; to make haste; (с + *i.*) to hurry up (with); с. домо́й to be in a hurry to get home; де́лать не ∼á to do in leisurely style, take one's time over **2** (*no pf.*) (*о часах*) to be fast

спе́шк|а, и *f.* (infml) hurry, rush

СПИД, а *m.* (*abbr. of* синдро́м приобретённого иммунодефици́та) (med.) Aids (*acquired immune deficiency syndrome*)

спидо́метр, а *m.* speedometer

спи́кер, а *m.* (pol.) speaker

спи́лива|ть, ю *impf. of* ▸ спили́ть

спил|и́ть, ю́, ∼ишь *pf.* (*of* ▸ спи́ливать) (*дерево*) to saw down; (*сук, верхушку*) to saw off

⚹ спин|а́, ы́, *a.* ∼у, *pl.* ∼ы *f.* back; за ∼о́й у кого́-н. (fig.) behind sb's back

спи́нк|а, и *f.* **1** *dim. of* ▸ спина́ **2** back (*of article of furniture or clothing*)

спинно́й *adj.* spinal; с. мозг spinal cord

спира́л|ь, и *f.* spiral

спиритуи́зм, а *m.* spiritualism

спирт, а *m.* alcohol, spirit(s)

спиртн|о́й *adj.* alcoholic, spirituous; ∼ы́е напи́тки alcoholic drinks, spirits; (*as nt. n.* ∼о́е, ∼о́го) alcoholic drinks, spirits

спи|са́ть, шу́, ∼шешь *pf.* (*of* ▸ спи́сывать) **1** (с + *i.*) to copy from **2** (у + *g.*) to copy (off), crib (off) **3** (*оборудование, долг*) to write off

⚹ спи́с|ок, ка *m.* **1** (*рукописная копия*) manuscript copy **2** (*письменный перечень*) list; roll **3**: послужно́й с. service record

спи́сыва|ть, ю *impf. of* ▸ списа́ть

спи́хива|ть, ю *impf. of* ▸ спихну́ть

спих|ну́ть, ну́, нёшь *pf.* (*of* ▸ спи́хивать) to push aside, shove aside; (*вниз*) to push down

спи́ц|а, ы *f.* **1** (*для вязания*) knitting needle **2** (*колеса*) spoke

спи́чк|а, и *f.* match

сплав, а *m.* (tech.) alloy

спла́чива|ть, ю, ет *impf. of* ▸ сплоти́ть

спла́чива|ться, ется *impf. of* ▸ сплоти́ться

сплёвыва|ть, ю *impf. of* ▸ сплю́нуть

спле|сти́, ту́, тёшь, *past* ∼л, ∼ла́ *pf.* (*of* ▸ плести́ 1) to weave, plait, interlace

спле́тник, а *m.* gossip, scandalmonger

спле́тниц|а, ы *f. of* ▸ спле́тник

спле́т|ня, ни, *g. pl.* ∼ен *f.* gossip; piece of scandal

спло|ти́ть, чу́, ти́шь *pf.* (*of* ▸ спла́чивать) **1** to join **2** (fig.) to unite, rally; с. ряды́ to close ranks

спло|ти́ться, ти́тся *pf.* (*of* ▸ спла́чиваться) to unite, rally; to close ranks

сплошн|о́й *adj.* **1** unbroken, continuous; ∼а́я ма́сса solid mass **2** (*всеобщий*) complete

сплошь *adv.* **1** (*по всей поверхности*) all over **2** (infml) (*целиком*) completely, entirely; (*без исключения*) without exception; (*исключительно*) only, exclusively

сплю́н|уть, у, ешь *pf.* (*of* ▸ сплёвывать) **1** (*плюнуть*) to spit **2** (infml, *косточку*) to spit out

сплю́щива|ть, ю, ет *impf. of* ▸ сплю́щить

сплю́щива|ться, ется *impf. of* ▸ сплю́щиваться

сплю́щ|ить, у, ишь *pf.* (*of* ▸ сплю́щивать) to flatten

сплю́щ|иться, ится *pf.* (*of* ▸ сплю́щиваться) to become flat

спля|са́ть, шу́, ∼шешь *pf. of* ▸ пляса́ть

спо|и́ть, ю́, и́шь *pf.* (*of* ▸ спа́ивать) (infml) to get drunk; to make a drunkard (of)

споко́|йный, ∼ен, ∼йна *adj.* **1** quiet; calm, tranquil; ∼йное мо́ре calm sea; ∼йной но́чи! good night! **2** (*человек*) quiet, composed

споко́йстви|е, я *nt.* **1** (*покой*) quiet, tranquillity; calm **2** (*порядок*) order; наруше́ние обще́ственного ∼я breach of the peace **3** (*душевное*) composure, serenity; с. ду́ха peace of mind

спола́скива|ть, ю *impf. of* ▸ сполосну́ть

сполз|а́ть, а́ю *impf. of* ▸ сползти́

сполз|ти́, у́, ёшь, *past* ∼, ∼ла́ *pf.* (*of* ▸ сполза́ть) **1** (с + *g.*) to climb down (from) **2** (*о шапке*) to slip down

сполосн|у́ть, у́, ёшь *pf.* (*of* ▸ спола́скивать) to rinse (out)

спонси́р|овать, ую *impf. and pf.* to sponsor

спо́нсор, а *m.* sponsor, backer

спо́нсорств|о, а *nt.* sponsorship

спонта́н|ный, ∼ен, ∼на *adj.* spontaneous

спор, а *m.* **1** argument; controversy; debate **2** (law) dispute

спо́р|ить, ю, ишь *impf.* (*of* ▸ поспо́рить 1) (о + *p.*) **1** to argue (about); to dispute

(about), debate **2** (law) (o + *p. or* за + *a.*)
to dispute; **с. о насле́дстве** to dispute a
legacy **3** (*держа́ть пари́*) to bet (on), have
a bet (on)

спо́р|ный, ~ен, ~на *adj.* debatable,
questionable; disputed, at issue; **с. вопро́с**
moot point

спор|о́ть, ю́, ~ешь *pf.* (*of ▶ спа́рывать*) to
unstitch, take off (*by cutting stitches*)

ꝏ **спорт, а** *m.* sport; **ко́нный с.** equestrianism

спортза́л, а *m.* sports hall

ꝏ **спорти́вн|ый** *adj.* (*инвента́рь,
комменnта́тор*) sports; (*челове́к, фигу́ра*)
sporty; (*оде́жда*) casual; **с. зал** gymnasium;
~ая площа́дка sports ground, playing field

спортко́мплекс, а *m.* sports complex

спортсме́н, а *m.* sportsman

спортсме́нк|а, и *f.* sportswoman

спо́рщик, а *m.* debater, wrangler

спо́рщи|ца, цы *f. of ▶ спо́рщик*

ꝏ **спо́соб, а** *m.* way, method; means; **таки́м
~ом** in this way

ꝏ **спосо́бност|ь, и** *f.* **1** (*usu. in pl.*) (к + *d.*)
(*тала́нт*) ability (for), talent (for), aptitude
(for); **челове́к с больши́ми ~ями** person
of great abilities; **с. к языка́м** talent for
languages, linguistic ability **2** (*возмо́жность*)
capacity; **покупа́тельная с.** purchasing power;
пропускна́я с. capacity

ꝏ **спосо́б|ный, ~ен, ~на** *adj.* **1** (*тала́нтливый*)
able, talented, clever; **с. к матема́тике** good
at mathematics **2** (**на** + *a. or* + *inf.*) capable
(of), able (to); **они́ ~ны на всё** they are
capable of anything

ꝏ **спосо́бств|овать, ую** *impf.* (+ *d.*)
1 (*помога́ть*) to assist **2** (*де́лать
возмо́жным*) to be conducive (to), further,
promote

споткн|у́ться, у́сь, ёшься *pf.* (*of
▶ спотыка́ться*) **1** (о + *a.*) to stumble
(against, over) **2** (**на** + *p. or* о + *a.*) (fig., infml)
to get stuck (on) **3** (infml, *оступи́ться*) to
slip up

спотыка́|ться, юсь *impf. of ▶ споткну́ться*

спохва|ти́ться, чу́сь, ~тишься *pf.* (*of
▶ спохва́тываться*) (infml) to remember
suddenly, think suddenly

спохва́тыва|ться, юсь *impf. of
▶ спохвати́ться*

спра́ва *adv.* (от + *g.*) on the right (of), to the
right (of)

справедли́вост|ь, и *f.* **1** justice; fairness;
поступа́ть по ~и to act fairly
2 (*пра́вильность*) truth, correctness

справедли́в|ый, ~, ~а *adj.* **1** just; fair;
с. судья́ impartial judge **2** (*пра́вильный*)
justified, true, correct; **на́ши подозре́ния
оказа́лись ~ыми** our suspicions proved to
be justified

спра́в|ить, лю, ишь *pf.* (*of ▶ справля́ть*)
(infml, *сва́дьбу, день рожде́ния*) to celebrate

ꝏ key word

спра́в|иться¹, люсь, ишься *pf.* (*of
▶ справля́ться*) (с + *i.*) **1** (*с рабо́той,
детьми́*) to cope (with), manage **2** (*с
проти́вником*) to deal (with), get the better
(of); **я с ним ~лю́сь!** I'll deal with him!
3 (*с волне́нием, со стра́хом*) to control

спра́в|иться², люсь, ишься *pf.* (*of
▶ справля́ться*) (o + *p.*) to ask (about),
inquire (about); **с. в словаре́** to consult a
dictionary

спра́вк|а, и *f.* **1** (*све́дение*) information;
навести́ ~и (o + *p.*) to inquire (about)
2 (*докуме́нт*) certificate; **с. с ме́ста рабо́ты**
document confirming that one works at a
place

справля́|ть, ю *impf. of ▶ спра́вить**

справля́|ться, юсь *impf. of ▶ спра́виться¹*

спра́вочник, а *m.* reference book,
handbook, guide; **телефо́нный с.** telephone
directory

спра́вочн|ый *adj.* inquiry, information;
~ая directory enquiries (BrE), directory
assistance (AmE); **~ое бюро́, с. стол**
inquiries/information office

ꝏ **спра́шива|ть, ю** *impf. of ▶ спроси́ть**

спресс|ова́ть, у́ю *pf. of ▶ прессова́ть**

спринт, а *m.* (sport) sprint

спри́нтер, а *m.* (sport) sprinter

спровоци́р|овать, ую *pf. of
▶ провоци́ровать**

спроекти́р|овать, ую *pf. of
▶ проекти́ровать**

ꝏ **спрос, а** *m.* (econ.) demand; (**на** + *a.*) demand
(for); **с. и предложе́ние** supply and demand;
по́льзоваться больши́м ~ом to be much
in demand

ꝏ **спро|си́ть, шу́, ~сишь** *pf.* (*of ▶ спра́шивать*)
1 (o + *p.*) (*осве́домиться*) to ask (about),
inquire (about); **с. доро́гу** to ask the way
2 (+ *a. or g.*) (*попроси́ть*) to ask (for);
(*пожела́ть ви́деть*) to ask to see, desire
to speak (to); **~си́те хозя́йку** ask to see the
landlady **3** (**с** + *g.*) (*призва́ть к отве́ту*) to
make answer (for), make responsible (for)

спрут, а *m.* octopus

спры́гива|ть, ю *impf. of ▶ спры́гнуть**

спры́г|нуть, ну, нешь *pf.* (*of ▶ спры́гивать*)
(с + *g.*) to jump off; to jump down (from)

спряга́|ть, ю *impf.* (*of ▶ проспряга́ть*) (gram.)
to conjugate

спряже́ни|е, я *nt.* (gram.) conjugation

спря|сть, ду́, дёшь, *past* ~л, ~ла́, ~ло *pf.
of ▶ прясть**

спря́|тать, чу, чешь *pf. of ▶ пря́тать**

спря́|таться, чусь, чешься *pf. of
▶ пря́таться**

спу́гива|ть, ю *impf. of ▶ спугну́ть**

спуг|ну́ть, ну́, нёшь *pf.* (*of ▶ спу́гивать*)
to frighten off, scare off

ꝏ **спуск, а** *m.* **1** (*фла́га*) lowering; **с. корабля́**
launch(ing) **2** (*с высоты́*) descent,
descending **3** (*воды́*) release; draining
4 (*отко́с*) slope, descent

спуска́|ть, ю *impf. of* ▶ спусти́ть

спуска́|ться, юсь *impf. of* ▶ спусти́ться

спу|сти́ть, щу́, ~стишь *pf.* (*of* ▶ спуска́ть)
1 (*флаг, занавеску*) to let down, lower;
с. кора́бль (на во́ду) to launch a ship
2 (*освободить*) to let go, let loose, release;
с. куро́к to pull, release the trigger; **с. соба́ку
с при́вязи** to unleash a dog **3** (*воду, воздух*)
to let out; **с. во́ду в туале́те** to flush a
lavatory **4** (*о шине*) to go down, deflate
5 (infml, *деньги*) to throw away, squander

спу|сти́ться, щу́сь, ~стишься *pf.* (*of*
▶ спуска́ться) to descend; to come down, go
down; (*вниз по течению*) to go downstream;
(*о мраке*) to fall; **с. с ле́стницы** to come
downstairs

спустя́ *prep.* (+ *a.*) after; later; **с. год** after a
year, a year later

спу́та|ть, ю *pf. of* ▶ пу́тать

спу́та|ться, юсь *pf. of* ▶ пу́таться

спу́тник, а *m.* **1** (*человек*) (travelling (BrE),
traveling (AmE)) companion; **с. жи́зни**
husband **2** (*обстоятельство*) concomitant
3 (astron.) satellite; **с. свя́зи** communications
satellite

спу́тников|ый *adj.*: ~ая связь satellite link;
~ое телеви́дение satellite television

спу́тни|ца, цы *f. of* ▶ спу́тник 1; **с. жи́зни**
wife

спя|ти́ть, чу, тишь *pf.* (infml) to go nuts, go
off one's rocker

спя́чк|а, и *f.* hibernation

сраба́тыва|ть, ю *impf. of* ▶ срабо́тать

срабо́та|ть, ю *pf.* (*of* ▶ сраба́тывать)
(*машина, сигнализация*) to work

✐ **сравне́ни|е, я** *nt.* comparison; **по ~ю, в ~и**
(с + *i.*) by, in comparison (with), compared
(with)

сра́внива|ть, ю *impf. of* ▶ сравни́ть,
▶ сравня́ть

сравни́тельно *adv.* **1** (с + *i.*) by, in
comparison (with) **2**: **с. недорого́й/
хоро́ший** comparatively cheap/good

сравни́тельн|ый *adj.* comparative; ~ая
сте́пень (gram.) comparative (degree)

сравн|и́ть, ю́, и́шь *pf.* (*of* ▶ сра́внивать)
(с + *i.*) to compare (to, with)

сравн|и́ться, ю́сь, и́шься *pf.* (с + *i.*) to
compare (with)

сравня́|ть, я́ю *pf.* (*of* ▶ сра́внивать) to make
even; **с. счёт** (sport) to equalize, bring the
score level

сравня́|ться, юсь *pf.* (с + *i.*) to become
equal (with)

сража́|ть, ю *impf. of* ▶ срази́ть

сража́|ться, юсь *impf.* (*of* ▶ срази́ться)
(с + *i.*) to fight; to join battle (with)

сраже́ни|е, я *nt.* battle, engagement

сра|зи́ть, жу́, зи́шь *pf.* (*of* ▶ сража́ть)
1 (*убить*) to slay **2** (fig.) to overwhelm,
crush; **весть о катастро́фе ~и́ла её** she
was crushed by the news of the disaster

сра|зи́ться, жу́сь, зи́шься *pf. of* ▶ сража́ться

✐ **сра́зу** *adv.* **1** (*в один приём*) (all) at once
2 (*немедленно*) straight away, immediately
3 (*рядом*) right, just; **с. за до́мом** right
behind the house

сраст|а́ться, а́ется *impf. of* ▶ срасти́сь

сраст|и́сь, ётся, *past* сро́сся, сросла́сь
pf. (*of* ▶ сраста́ться) **1** (*о корнях*) to grow
together; (*о костях*) to knit **2** (fig.) (с + *i.*)
(*соединиться*) to merge (with)

ср|ать, у, ёшь *impf.* (*of* ▶ насра́ть) (vulg.)
to shit

среаги́р|овать, ую *pf. of* ▶ реаги́ровать

✐ **сред|а́¹, ы́, *a.* ~у́,** *pl.* ~ы f. **1** (*природная*)
environment, surroundings; **окружа́ющая
с.** the environment; (*социальная*)
environment, milieu; (biol.) habitat; **в ~е́**
(+ *g.*) among **2** (phys., chem.) medium

✐ **сред|а́², ы́, *a.* ~у, pl. ~ы, *d.* ~а́м** *f.* (*день
недели*) Wednesday; **в ~у** on Wednesday

✐ **среди́** *prep.* + *g.* (*в числе*) among; amidst; **с.
них** among them, in their midst **2** (*посредине*)
in the middle (of)

Средизе́мн|ое мо́ре, ~ого мо́ря *nt.* the
Mediterranean (Sea)

средиземномо́рский *adj.* Mediterranean

среднеазиа́тский *adj.* central Asian

средневеко́вый *adj.* medieval

Средневеко́вь|е, я *nt.* the Middle Ages

✐ **сре́дн|ий** *adj.* **1** (*комната, ряд*) middle;
(*рост*) medium; **С~ие века́** the Middle
Ages; ~их лет middle-aged; ~его ро́ста
of medium height **2** (*в среднем*) mean,
average; **с. за́работок** average earnings; (*as
nt. n.* ~ее, ~его) mean, average; **в ~ем**
on average **3** (*посредственный*) middling,
average; **ни́же ~его** below average **4** (*школа,
образование*) secondary **5**: **с. род** (gram.)
neuter (gender)

средото́чи|е, я *nt.* focus, centre (BrE), center
(AmE) point

✐ **сре́дств|о, а** *nt.* **1** means; facilities; ~а
ма́ссовой информа́ции mass media;
~а передвиже́ния means of conveyance;
~а к существова́нию livelihood **2** (от + *g.*)
remedy (for); **с. от ка́шля** cough medicine,
sth for a cough **3** (*in pl.*) (*деньги, капитал*)
resources; funds **4** (*in pl.*) (*состояние*)
means; **жить не по ~ам** to live beyond one's
means

срез, а *m.* **1** (*место*) cut **2** (*слой*) section

сре́|зать, жу, жешь *pf.* (*of* ▶ среза́ть)
(*ветку*) to cut off; **с. у́гол** (fig.) to cut off
a corner

среза́|ть, ю *impf. of* ▶ сре́зать

срис|ова́ть, у́ю *pf.* (*of* ▶ срисо́вывать)
to copy

срисо́выва|ть, ю *impf. of* ▶ срисова́ть

сровня́|ть, ю *pf.* (*of* ▶ ровня́ть): **с. с землёй**
to raze to the ground

✐ **срок, а (у)** *m.* **1** (*промежуток времени*)
time, period; term; **ме́сячный с.** period of
one month; **с. де́йствия** period of validity;
с. полномо́чий term of office; **~ом на** (+ *a.*)
for a period of **2** (*дата*) date; **кра́йний с.**

С

closing date; **с. хране́ния** shelf life; **в с., к ~у** in time, to time

сро́чно *adv.* urgently; quickly

сро́чность, и *f.* urgency

сро́ч|ный, ~ен, ~на *adj.* **1** (*сообще́ние, зака́з*) urgent **2** (*ссу́да, вклад*) fixed-term; for a fixed period

сруба́|ть, а́ю *impf. of ▶* **сруби́ть**

сруб|и́ть, лю́, ~ишь *pf.* (*of ▶* **сруба́ть**) to fell, cut down

срыв, а *m.* **1** (*пла́на, рабо́ты*) disruption; **с. рабо́ты** stoppage **2** (*неуда́ча*) failure

срыва́|ть, ю *impf. of ▶* **сорва́ть**

срыва́|ться, юсь *impf. of ▶* **сорва́ться**

сса́дин|а, ы *f.* scratch, abrasion

ссад|и́ть, жу́, ~дишь *pf.* (*of ▶* **сса́живать**) **1** (*помо́чь сойти́*) to help down; **с. кого́-н. с ло́шади** to help sb down from a horse **2** (*заста́вить вы́йти*) to put off, make get off (*from public transport*)

сса́жива|ть, ю *impf. of ▶* **ссади́ть**

ссо́р|а, ы *f.* quarrel; **она́ в ~е с сестро́й** she's fallen out with her sister

ссо́р|ить, ю, ишь *impf.* (*of ▶* **поссо́рить**) to cause to quarrel, cause to fall out

ссо́р|иться, юсь, ишься *impf.* (*of ▶* **поссо́риться**) (**с** + *i.*) to quarrel (with), fall out (with)

✦ **СССР** *m. indecl.* (*abbr. of* **Сою́з Сове́тских Социалисти́ческих Респу́блик**) (hist.) USSR (*Union of Soviet Socialist Republics*)

ссу́д|а, ы *f.* loan; **ба́нковская с.** bank loan

ссуту́л|иться, юсь, ишься *pf. of ▶* **суту́литься**

ссыла́|ть, ю *impf. of ▶* **сосла́ть**

ссыла́|ться, юсь *impf. of ▶* **сосла́ться**

ссы́лк|а¹, и *f.* exile, banishment

✦ **ссы́лк|а², и** *f.* (**на** + *a.*) (*указа́ние*) reference (to); (comput.) link

ссы́п|ать, лю, лешь *pf.* (*of ▶* **ссыпа́ть**) to pour

ссып|а́ть, а́ю *impf. of ▶* **ссы́пать**

✦ **ст.** (*abbr. of* **столе́тие**) cent. (century)

стабилизи́р|овать, ую *impf. and pf.* to stabilize

стабилизи́р|оваться, уется *impf. and pf.* to become stable

стаби́льность, и *f.* stability

стаби́л|ьный, ~ен, ~ьна *adj.* stable, firm

ста́в|ень, ня, g. pl. ~ней *m.* shutter (*on window*)

✦ **ста́в|ить, лю, ишь** *impf.* (*of ▶* **поста́вить¹**) **1** (*помеща́ть*) to put, place, set; (*что-н. вертика́льное*) to stand; **цветы́ в ва́зу** to put flowers in a vase; **с. диа́гноз** to diagnose; **с. реко́рд** to set up, create a record; **с. то́чку** to put a full stop; **с. кого́-н. в нело́вкое положе́ние** to put sb in an awkward position **2** (*сооружа́ть*) to put up, erect; (*устана́вливать*) to install; **с. па́мятник** to erect a monument **3** (*назнача́ть*) to put in,

✦ *key word*

install; **с. но́вого гла́вного инжене́ра** to put in a new chief engineer **4** (*накла́дывать*) to apply, put on; **с. кому́-н. гра́дусник** to take sb's temperature **5** (*вопро́с, пробле́му*) to put, present; (*пье́су*) to put on, stage **6** (**на** + *a.*) (*в игре́*) to place, stake (*money on*); **с. на ло́шадь** to back a horse

✦ **ста́вк|а, и** *f.* **1** (fin.) rate; **проце́нтная с.** interest rate **2** (*в игра́х*) stake; **де́лать ~у** (**на** + *a.*) to stake (on); (fig.) to count (on), gamble (on)

ста́вленник, а *m.* protégé

ста́в|ня, ни, g. pl. ~ен *f.* = **ста́вень**

стадио́н, а *m.* stadium

✦ **ста́ди|я, и** *f.* stage

ста́дный *adj.* (*живо́тное*) gregarious; **с. инсти́нкт** herd instinct

ста́д|о, а, pl. ~а́ *nt.* herd; flock

стаж, а *m.* length of service

стажёр, а *m.* **1** (*проходя́щий испыта́тельный срок*) probationer **2** (*студе́нт*) student (*on special practical course*); exchange student

стака́н, а *m.* glass, tumbler

сталева́р, а *m.* steel founder

сталелите́йный *adj.*: **с. заво́д** steelmill, steel works

✦ **ста́лкива|ть, ю** *impf. of ▶* **столкну́ть**

ста́лкива|ться, юсь *impf. of ▶* **столкну́ться**

стал|ь, и *f.* steel; **нержаве́ющая с.** stainless steel

стальн|о́й *adj.* steel; **~а́я во́ля** iron will; **~ы́е не́рвы** nerves of steel

Стамбу́л, а *m.* Istanbul

стаме́ск|а, и *f.* (tech.) chisel

✦ **станда́рт, а** *m.* **1** standard **2** (fig., *шабло́н*) cliché, stereotype

✦ **станда́рт|ный, ~ен, ~на** *adj.* standard

✦ **станов|и́ться, лю́сь, ~ишься** *impf. of ▶* **стать¹**, **▶ стать²**

становле́ни|е, я *nt.* (*иде́й, хара́ктера, госуда́рства*) formation; **в проце́ссе ~я** in the making

стан|о́к, ка́ *m.* (tech.) machine tool, machine; **печа́тный с.** printing press; **тка́цкий с.** loom; **тока́рный с.** lathe

✦ **ста́нци|я, и** *f.* station; **авто́бусная с.** bus station; **железнодоро́жная с.** railway (BrE), railroad (AmE) station

ста́птыва|ть, ю *impf. of ▶* **стопта́ть**

стара́тель|ный, ~ен, ~ьна *adj.* assiduous, diligent

✦ **стара́|ться, юсь** *impf.* (*of ▶* **постара́ться**) **1** (*усе́рдствовать*) to try; to apply oneself; **с. изо всех сил** to do one's utmost **2** (+ *inf.*) (*стреми́ться*) to try, endeavour; **я ~юсь помо́чь ему́** I'm trying to help him

старе́е *comp. of ▶* **ста́рый**

старе́ни|е, я *nt.* ageing

старе́|ть, ю *impf.* **1** (*pf.* **по~**) (*челове́к*) to grow old, age **2** (*pf.* **у~**) (*иде́я, маши́на*) to become obsolete

стари́к, á *m.* old man; глубо́кий с. very old man; ∼и old people

старин|á, ы́ *f.* antiquity, olden times; в ∼ý in olden days

стари́нный *adj.* (*книга, обычай*) ancient, old; (*мебель*) antique

ста́р|ить, ю, ишь *impf.* (*of* ▶ соста́рить) to age

ста́р|иться, юсь, ишься *impf.* (*of* ▶ соста́риться) to age; to grow old

старомо́д|ный, ∼ен, ∼на *adj.* old-fashioned; out-of-date

ста́рост|а, ы *m.* head; с. кла́сса (*в шко́ле*) class prefect, monitor

ста́рост|ь, и *f.* old age

старт, а *m.* (sport, fig.) start; на с.! on your marks!

старт|ова́ть, у́ю *impf. and pf.* 1 (sport) to start 2 (aeron.) to take off 3 (*отправля́ться*) to start out; to depart 4 (*начина́ться*) to begin, commence

стару́х|а, и *f.* old woman, old lady

стару́шк|а, и *f.* (little) old lady, old woman

ста́рческий *adj.* old person's; с. во́зраст old age; с. мара́зм senility

ста́рше *comp. of* ▶ ста́рый; (*взросле́е*): она́ с. меня́ на три го́да she is three years older than me; (*по служе́бному положе́нию*): он с. меня́ по зва́нию he is senior to me in rank

старшекла́ссник, а *m.* senior (pupil)

старшекла́ссни|ца, цы *f. of* ▶ старшекла́ссник

ста́рш|ий *adj.* 1 (*бо́лее ста́рый*) elder, older; с. брат older brother; (*as pl. n.* ∼ие, ∼их) (one's) elders, grown-ups 2 (*са́мый ста́рый*) oldest, eldest 3 (*по служе́бному положе́нию*) senior, superior; (*в назва́ниях*) chief, head; ∼ая медсестра́ senior nurse, sister (BrE); (*as m. n.* с., ∼его) (mil.) man in charge; chief 4 (*вы́сший*) senior, upper, higher; с. класс (*в шко́ле*) higher form (BrE), senior grade (AmE)

старшинств|о́, á *nt.* seniority; по ∼ý by seniority

ста́р|ый, ∼, ∼á, ∼ó *adj.* old; с. стиль the Old Style (*of the Julian calendar*)

ста́скива|ть, ю *impf. of* ▶ стащи́ть 1

стати́стик|а, и *f.* statistics

статисти́ческий *adj.* statistical

стати́ческий *adj.* static

ста́тус, а *m.* status

ста́тус-кво́ *m. & nt. indecl.* status quo

ста́ту|я, и *f.* statue

стать¹, ста́ну, ста́нешь *pf.* (*of* ▶ станови́ться) 1 (*встать*) to stand; с. на коле́ни to kneel; (*поддержа́ть*) to stand up for; с. на чью-н. сто́рону to take sb's side, stand up for sb 2 (*расположи́ться*) to take up position; с. на я́корь to anchor 3 (*останови́ться*) to stop, come to a halt; мои́ часы́ ста́ли my watch has stopped

стать², ста́ну, ста́нешь *pf.* (*of* ▶ станови́ться) 1 (+ *inf.*) (*нача́ть*) to begin (to), start; она́

ста́ла говори́ть she began talking 2 (+ *i.*) (*сде́латься*) to become, get, grow; ста́ло темно́ it got dark; ей ста́ло лу́чше she was better; she had got better 3 (с + *i.*) (*случи́ться*) to become (of), happen (to); что с ни́ми ста́ло? what has become of them? 4: не с. (*impers.* + *g.*) (*умере́ть*) to die; (*исче́знуть*) to disappear, go

стат|ья́, ьи́, *g. pl.* ∼е́й *f.* 1 (*газе́тная, нау́чная*) article 2 (*зако́на, догово́ра*) clause; (*фина́нсового докуме́нта*) item; (*в словаре́*) entry; расхо́дная с. debit item

стациона́р|ный *adj.* 1 (*не изменя́ющийся*) stationary; с. объе́кт (mil.) stationary target 2 (*постоя́нный*) permanent, fixed 3 (*больни́чный*) hospital; с. больно́й in-patient; ∼ое лече́ние hospitalization

ста́чива|ть, ю *impf. of* ▶ сточи́ть

ста́чк|а, и *f.* (*забасто́вка*) strike

стащ|и́ть, ý, ∼ишь *pf.* (*of* ▶ ста́скивать) 1 (*сапоги́*) to drag off, pull off 2 (*no impf.*) (infml, *укра́сть*) to nick (BrE), pinch, swipe (infml)

ста́|я, и *f.* (*птиц*) flock; (*рыб*) school, shoal; (*волко́в*) pack

ствол, á *m.* 1 (*де́рева*) trunk 2 (*ору́жия*) barrel; (infml, *само́ ору́жие*) gun

ствол|ово́й *adj. of* ▶ ствол; ∼ова́я кле́тка (biol.) stem cell

ство́рк|а, и *f.* (*две́ри, зерка́ла*) leaf, fold; (*воро́т, ста́вней*) half, side

стéб|ель, ля, *pl.* ∼ли, ∼ле́й *m.* stem, stalk

стёган|ый *adj.* quilted; ∼ое одея́ло quilt

стеж|о́к, ка́ *m.* stitch

стека́|ть, ет *impf. of* ▶ стечь

стекл|и́ть, ю́, и́шь *impf.* (*of* ▶ застекли́ть) to glaze

стекл|о́, á, *pl.* ∼а, ∼ол *nt.* glass; (*collect.*) glassware

стекловолокн|о́, á *nt.* fibreglass (BrE), fiberglass (AmE)

стеклоочисти́тел|ь, я *m.* windscreen (BrE), windshield (AmE) wiper

стекля́нный *adj.* 1 glass; ∼ые изде́лия glassware; (*окно́, дверь*) glazed 2 (fig., *взгляд, глаза́*) glassy

стекóльщик, а *m.* glazier

стéл|а, ы *f.* obelisk

стел|и́ть, ю́, ∼ешь *impf.* (*of* ▶ постели́ть) to spread; с. посте́ль to make a bed; с. ска́терть to lay a tablecloth

стелла́ж, á *m.* shelves

стéльк|а, и *f.* insole

стемне́|ть, ет *pf. of* ▶ темне́ть 2

стен|á, ы́, *a.* ∼ý, *pl.* ∼ы, *d.* ∼а́м *f.* wall (also fig.); в ∼а́х (+ *g.*) inside, within the precincts (of)

стенд, а *m.* 1 (*на вы́ставке*) stand (BrE), booth (AmE) 2 (*для испыта́ний*) test bed 3 (*для стрельбы́*) rifle range

стéнк|а, и *f.* 1 (*стена́*) wall; гимнасти́ческая с. wall bars 2 (*я́щика, кастрю́ли*) side; (*желу́дка*) wall 3 (*ме́бель*) wall unit

стеногра́фи|я, и *f.* shorthand

стенокарди́|я, и *f.* angina (pectoris)

степе́н|ный, ~ен, ~на *adj.* staid

⚹ **сте́пен|ь**, и, *g. pl.* ~е́й *f.* **1** degree, extent; **до изве́стной ~и, до не́которой ~и** to some extent, to a certain extent **2** (math.) power; **возвести́ в тре́тью с.** to raise to the third power **3** (*зва́ние*) (academic) degree; (*разря́д*) class; **с. бакала́вра** bachelor's degree; **учёная с. до́ктора нау́к** doctorate

сте́плер, а *m.* stapler

степ|ь, и, о ~и́, в ~и́, *pl.* ~и, ~е́й *f.* steppe

сте́рв|а, ы *f.* (sl.) (*о же́нщине*) bitch

стервя́тник, а *m.* (zool.) carrion crow

стереосисте́м|а, ы *f.* stereo (system)

стереоти́п, а *m.* stereotype

стере́|ть, сотру́, сотрёшь, *past* ~, ~ла *pf.* (*of* ▸ **стира́ть¹**) **1** (*рису́нок*) to rub out, erase; (*кассе́ту, перезапи́сываемый диск*) to erase; (comput.) to delete; (*пыль, пот*) to wipe off; **с. с лица́ земли́** to wipe off the face of the earth **2** (*но́гу*) to rub sore **3** (*в порошо́к*) to grind (down)

стере́|ться, сотрётся, *past* ~ся, ~лась *pf.* (*of* ▸ **стира́ться¹**) **1** (*о на́дписи, кра́ске*) to rub off; (fig., *забы́ться*) to fade **2** (*о подо́швах, па́льцах*) to become worn down

стере́|чь, гу́, жёшь, гу́т, *past* ~г, ~гла́ *impf.* (*ве́щи, ста́до*) to guard, watch (over)

сте́рж|ень, ня *m.* **1** (tech.) pivot; shank, rod; **поршнево́й с.** piston rod **2** (fig., *осно́ва*) core

стерилиза́ци|я, и *f.* sterilization

стерилиз|ова́ть, у́ю *impf. and pf.* to sterilize

стери́л|ьный, ~ен, ~ьна *adj.* sterile

сте́рлинг, а *m.* (fin.) sterling; **фунт ~ов** pound sterling

сте́рляд|ь, и *f.* (zool.) sterlet

стеро́ид, а *m.* steroid

стерп|е́ть, лю́, ~ишь *pf.* to bear, suffer, endure

стёртый *p.p.p. of* ▸ **стере́ть** *and adj.* (*на́дпись, моне́та*) worn, faded; (fig., *очерта́ние*) faint

стесне́ни|е, я *nt.* (*ограниче́ние*) constraint; (*смуще́ние*) shyness, timidness

стесни́тел|ьный, ~ен, ~ьна *adj.* shy; awkward

стесня́|ться, юсь *impf.* (*of* ▸ **постесня́ться**) (+ *inf.*) to feel too shy (to), be ashamed (to); (+ *g.*) to feel shy (before, of); **не ~йтесь!** don't be shy!; **не с. в сре́дствах** to use any means possible

сте|чь, чёт, ку́т, *past* ~к, ~кла́ *pf.* (*of* ▸ **стека́ть**) to flow down

стилиз|ова́ть, у́ю *impf. and pf.* to stylize

стили́ст, а *m.* **1** (*ма́стер сти́ля*) stylist **2** (*гримёр*) make-up artist

стилисти́ческий *adj.* stylistic

⚹ **стил|ь**, я *m.* style

сти́л|ьный, ~ен, ~ьна *adj.* stylish

сти́мул, а *m.* incentive, stimulus

стимули́р|овать, ую *impf. and pf.* to stimulate, encourage

стимуля́ци|я, и *f.* stimulation; **с. ро́дов** (med.) induction

стипе́нди|я, и *f.* grant, scholarship

стира́льн|ый *adj.* washing; **~ая маши́на** washing machine; **с. порошо́к** washing powder

стира́|ть¹, ю *impf. of* ▸ **стере́ть**

стира́|ть², ю *impf.* (*of* ▸ **вы́стирать**) to wash, launder

стира́|ться¹, ется *impf. of* ▸ **стере́ться**

стира́|ться², ется *impf.* to wash; **хорошо́ с.** to wash well

сти́рк|а, и *f.* washing, laundering; **отда́ть в ~у** to send to the laundry

сти́с|нуть, ну, нешь *pf.* to squeeze; **с. зу́бы** to clench one's teeth

⚹ **стих¹**, а́ *m.* verse; (*in pl.*) verses; poetry

стих² *see* ▸ **сти́хнуть**

стих|а́ть, а́ю *impf. of* ▸ **сти́хнуть**

стихи́|йный, ~ен, ~йна *adj.* **1** elemental; **~йное бе́дствие** natural disaster **2** (fig., *проте́ст*) spontaneous, uncontrolled

стихи́|я, и *f.* element

сти́х|нуть, ну, нешь, *past* ~, ~ла *pf.* (*of* ▸ **стиха́ть**) (*шум, ве́тер, дождь*) to abate, subside, die down; (*челове́к*) to calm down

стихотворе́ни|е, я *nt.* poem

стла́ть, стелю́, сте́лешь *impf.* (*of* ▸ **постла́ть**) = **стели́ть**

сто, ста, *pl.* (*no nom. & a.*) сот, стам, ста́ми, стах *num.* hundred; **не́сколько сот рубле́й** several hundred roubles; **я сто раз тебе́ говори́л** (infml) I've told you a hundred times

стог, а, в/на ~у́ *and* в/на ~е, *pl.* ~а́ *m.* (agric.) stack, rick

⚹ **сто́имост|ь**, и *f.* **1** (*цена́*) cost; **с. прое́зда** fare; **с. жи́зни** cost of living; **о́бщей ~ью в** (+ *a.*) to a total value of **2** (econ., *це́нность*) value; **номина́льная ~** face/nominal value

⚹ **сто́|ить**, ю, ишь *impf.* **1** to cost (also fig.); **ско́лько ~ит э́то пла́тье?** how much is this dress?; **до́рого с.** to cost dear **2** (+ *g.*) (*заслу́живать*) to be worth; to deserve; **он её не ~ит** he doesn't deserve her; **чего́ ~ят его́ обеща́ния?** his promises are worth nothing; (*impers.*) **~ит** it is worth while; **об э́том ~ит поду́мать** it's worth thinking about **3**: **~ит то́лько** (*impers.* + *inf.*) one has only (to)

сто́йк|а, и *f.* **1** (sport) stand, stance; **с. на рука́х** handstand **2** (tech.) support, prop; (*во́рот*) bar **3** (*прила́вок*) bar, counter

сто́|йкий, ~ек, ~йка́, ~йко *adj.* **1** firm, stable; (*за́пах*) persistent **2** (fig., *хара́ктер*) stable; steadfast, staunch

сто́йл|о, а *nt.* stall

сток, а *m.* **1** (*де́йствие*) flow; drainage, outflow **2** (*ме́сто, устро́йство*) drain, gutter; sewer

Стокго́льм, а *m.* Stockholm

⚹ key word

стол, а́ m. **1** (*предмет мебели*) table; **пи́сьменный с.** desk; **сесть за с.** to sit down to table; **за ~о́м** at table **2** (*питание*) board; (*кухня*) cooking, cuisine; **ры́бный с.** fish diet; **«шве́дский» с.** smorgasbord **3** (*отделение*) department; office; **с. нахо́док** lost property office

столб, а́ m. post, pole, pillar, column; **телегра́фный с.** telegraph pole

столб|е́ц, ца́ m. (*в газете, словаре*) column

столбня́к m. **1** (med.) tetanus **2** (infml) stupor; **на неё нашёл с.** she was in a stupor

столе́ти|е, я nt. **1** (*век*) century **2** (*годовщина*) centenary

столе́тн|ий adj. **1** hundred-year; **С~яя война́** the Hundred Years' War **2** (*дуб, старец*) hundred-year-old; **~яя годовщи́на** centenary

сто́л|ик, а m. dim. of ▸ стол 1; table (*e.g. in a restaurant*); **журна́льный с.** coffee table

столи́ц|а, ы f. capital; metropolis

столи́чный adj. of ▸ столи́ца; **с. го́род** capital (city)

столкнове́ни|е, я nt. (*автомобилей*) collision; (mil., also fig.) clash; **вооружённое с.** armed conflict, hostilities; **с. интере́сов** clash of interests

столкн|у́ть, у́, ёшь pf. (of ▸ ста́лкивать) **1** (*сбросить, сдвинуть*) to push off; **с. ло́дку в во́ду** to push a boat off (into the water) **2** (*сблизить*) to cause to collide; to knock together **3** (*о случае, обстоятельствах*) to bring together

столкн|у́ться, у́сь, ёшься pf. (of ▸ ста́лкиваться) (с + i.) **1** to collide (with) (also fig.); (*вступить в конфликт*) to clash (with), conflict (with) **2** (fig.) (*встретиться*) to run (into), bump (into); (*с трудностями, равнодушием*) to encounter

столо́в|ая, ой f. (*в доме*) dining room; (*в армии*) mess; (*на работе*) canteen, cafeteria; (*общественная*) cafeteria

столо́в|ый adj. table; **~ое вино́** table wine; **с. прибо́р** cover

столп|и́ться, и́тся pf. to crowd

столь adv. so; **э́то не с. ва́жно** it's of no particular importance

сто́лько adv. (*с неисчисляемыми*) so much; (*с исчисляемыми*) so many; **с. любви́/де́нег** so much love/money; **нельзя́ с. рабо́тать** you should not work so much; **с. ..., ско́лько** as much ... as; **не с. ..., ско́лько** not so much ... as

столя́р, а́ m. joiner (BrE), cabinetmaker

стомато́лог, а m. dental surgeon

стоматологи́ческий adj. dental

стоматоло́ги|я, и f. dentistry

стон, а m. moan, groan

стон|а́ть, у́, ~ешь impf. to moan, groan (also fig.)

стоп int. stop!

стоп|а́, ы́, pl. **~ы́** f. (*ноги*) foot (also fig.)

сто́пк|а, и f. (*куча*) pile, heap

стоп-ка́др, а m. (*пауза*) freeze-frame; (*снимок*) still (picture/image), snapshot

стоп-кра́н, а m. emergency cord (*on train*)

стопроце́нтный adj. hundred per cent

стоп|та́ть, чу́, ~чешь pf. (of ▸ ста́птывать) (*обувь*) to wear down

сторг|ова́ться, у́юсь pf. of ▸ торгова́ться 1

сто́рож, а, pl. **~а́, ~е́й** m. watchman, guard

сторожев|о́й adj. watch; **~а́я соба́ка** watchdog

сторож|и́ть, у́, и́шь impf. (*дом, стадо*) to guard, watch, keep watch (over)

сторо́жк|а, и f. lodge

сторон|а́, ы́, a. **сто́рону**, pl. **сто́роны, сторо́н, ~а́м** f. **1** side; (*направление*) direction; **в сто́рону** (+ g.) in the direction of; **со ~ы́** (+ g.) from the direction of; **в сто́рону, ~е́** aside; **держа́ться в ~е́** to keep aloof; **по ту сто́рону** (+ g.) across, on the other side (of); **пра́вая/ле́вая с.** right/left hand side; **с пра́вой/ле́вой ~ы́** on the right/left side; **с мое́й ~ы́** for my part; **э́то о́чень любе́зно с ва́шей ~ы́** it is very kind of you; **наблюда́ть со ~ы́** to observe from the outside; **со ~ы́** (+ g.) on the side of (*indicating line of descent*); **дед со ~ы́ ма́тери** maternal grandfather; **с одно́й ~ы́..., с друго́й ~ы́** on the one hand ..., on the other hand **2** (*в споре*) side, party; **вы на чьей ~е́?** whose side are you on?; **тре́тья с.** third party **3** (*элемент, свойство*) aspect, side

сторо́нник, а m. supporter, advocate; **с. ми́ра** peace campaigner

сторо́нни|ца, цы f. of ▸ сторо́нник

сточ|и́ть, у́, ~ишь pf. (of ▸ ста́чивать) to grind off

сто́чн|ый adj. sewage, drainage; **~ые во́ды** sewage

стошн|и́ть, и́т pf. (impers.) to be sick, vomit; **меня́ ~и́ло** I was sick

сто́я adv. standing up

стоя́нк|а, и f. **1** (*остановка*) stop; (*автомобилей*) parking; **«с. запрещена́!»** 'no parking!' **2** (*место остановки*) stopping place; (*автомобилей*) parking area; (*судов*) moorage; **автомоби́льная с.** car park (BrE), parking lot (AmE)

сто|я́ть, ю́, и́шь impf. **1** to stand; **с. в о́череди** to stand in a queue; **с. на коле́нях** to kneel **2** (*находиться*) to be, be situated, lie; **кни́ги ~я́т на по́лке** the books are on the shelf; **ча́йник ~и́т на плите́** the kettle is on the stove **3** (*быть*) to be; to continue; **~а́ла хоро́шая пого́да** the weather continued fine **4** (*жить*) to stay, put up; (mil.) to be stationed; **с. ла́герем** to be encamped **5** (*за* + a.) (*защищать*) to stand up (for); (*на* + p.) (*настаивать*) to insist (on); **с. на своём** to refuse to give in **6** (*не двигаться*) to have stopped; to have come to a halt; standstill; **мой часы́ ~я́т** my watch has stopped; ∼й(те)! stop!; halt!

сто́ящий *pres. part. act. of* ▶ **сто́ить** *and adj.* (*человек*) deserving, worthy; (*дело, предложение*) worthwhile

стр. *abbr. of* **1** (**страни́ца**) p, page **2** (**страни́цы**) pp., pages

страда́ни|е, я *nt.* suffering

страда́тельный *adj.* (gram.) passive; **с. зало́г** passive voice

страда́|ть, ю *impf.* **1** (*impf. only*) (+ *i.*) to suffer (from); to be subject (to); **с. бессо́нницей** to suffer from insomnia **2** *impf. only* (**от** + *g.*) to suffer (from), be in pain (with); **с. от зубно́й бо́ли** to have (a) toothache **3** *pf.* **по∼**) (**за** + *a.*) to suffer (for, as a result of)

стра́ж|а, и *f.* guard, watch; **под ∼ей** under arrest, in custody; **взять, заключи́ть под ∼у** to take into custody

✓ **стран|а́, ы́,** *pl.* **∼ы** *f.* country; land

✓ **страни́ц|а, ы** *f.* (also comput., fig., rhet.) page

стра́нно *adv.* **1** strangely, in a strange way **2** (*as pred.*) (*необычно*) it is strange; (*непонятно*) funny, odd, queer; **как э́то ни с.** strangely enough; (**мне**) **с., что** I find it strange that

стра́нност|ь, и *f.* **1** strangeness **2** (*странная манера*) oddity, eccentricity; **за ним води́лись ∼и** he was an odd person

✓ **стра́н|ный, ∼ен, ∼на́, ∼но** *adj.* (*необычный*) strange; (*непонятный*) funny, odd

стра́нств|овать, ую *impf.* to wander, travel; **с. по све́ту** to wander the earth; to travel the world

Стра́сбург, а *m.* Strasbourg

страстн|о́й *adj.* of Holy Week; **С∼а́я пя́тница** Good Friday

стра́ст|ный, ∼ен, ∼на *adj.* (*речь, поцелуй, человек*) passionate; (*сторонник, поклонник*) ardent

страст|ь, и, *g. pl.* **∼е́й** *f.* (**к** + *d.*) passion (for); **со ∼ью** with passion, fervour (BrE), fervor (AmE)

стратеги́ческий *adj.* strategic

✓ **страте́ги|я, и** *f.* strategy

стратосфе́р|а, ы *f.* stratosphere

стра́ус, а *m.* ostrich

✓ **страх, а** *m.* fear; (*сильный*) terror; **со ∼у** from fear; **под ∼ом сме́рти** on pain of death

✓ **страхова́ни|е, я** *nt.* insurance; **с. жи́зни** life insurance

страх|ова́ть, у́ю *impf.* (*of* ▶ **застрахова́ть**) (**от** + *g.*) to insure (against); **с. себя́** (**от** + *g.*) (fig.) to insure (against), safeguard oneself (against)

страх|ова́ться, у́юсь *impf.* (*of* ▶ **застрахова́ться**) (**от** + *g.*) to insure oneself (against) (also fig.)

страхо́вк|а, и *f.* insurance

✓ **страхово́й** *adj.* insurance; **с. по́лис** insurance policy

страш|и́ть, у́, и́шь *impf.* to frighten, scare

страш|и́ться, у́сь, и́шься *impf.* (+ *g.*) to be afraid (of), fear

стра́шно *adv.* **1** terribly, awfully; **с. испуга́ться** to get a terrible fright; **с. обра́доваться** to be awfully glad **2** (*as pred.*) it is terrible; it is terrifying; **мне с.** I am terrified; **мне с.** (+ *inf.*) I am terrified to do sth

✓ **стра́ш|ный, ∼ен, ∼на́, ∼но** *adj.* (*очень плохой*) terrible, awful, dreadful; (*вызывающий страх*) terrifying, frightening; **с. расска́з** terrifying story; **с. сон** bad dream; **с. шум** (infml) awful din; **С. суд** the Day of Judgement, doomsday; **ничего́ ∼ного** it doesn't matter

стреко́з|а, ы́, *pl.* **∼ы** *f.* dragonfly

стреко|та́ть, чу́, ∼чешь *impf.* (*о кузнечиках*) to chirr; (*о сороках*) to chatter; (fig., infml, *болтать*) to rattle, chatter

стрел|а́, ы́, *pl.* **∼ы** *f.* arrow (also fig.)

Стреле́|ц, ьца́ *m.* Sagittarius

стре́л|ка, и *f.* **1** pointer, indicator; (*часов*) hand; (*компаса*) needle **2** (*знак*) arrow (*on diagram, etc.*) **3** (rail.) point(s) (BrE), switch (AmE); **перевести́ ∼у** to change the points; (fig., sl.): **перевести́ ∼и на** (+ *a.*) to lump the blame on

стрел|о́к, ка́ *m.* **1** shot; **отли́чный с.** good shot **2** (mil.) rifleman; (*в самолёте, в танке*) gunner

стрельб|а́, ы́, *pl.* **∼ы** *f.* shooting, firing

стрельн|у́ть, у́, ёшь *inst. pf.* **1** to fire a shot **2** (*impers.*): **у меня́ ∼у́ло в у́хе** I had a stab of pain in my ear **3** (infml, *сигарету*) to cadge (BrE), bum (AmE)

стреля́|ть, ю *impf.* **1** (**в** + *a. or* **по** + *d.*) to shoot (at), fire (at); **с. из револьве́ра, из ружья́** to fire a revolver, a gun; **с. в цель** to shoot at a target; **с. по самолёту** to fire at an aeroplane (BrE), airplane (AmE) **2** (*убивать*) to shoot; **с. куропа́ток** to go partridge shooting **3** (infml, *сигареты*) to cadge (BrE), bum (AmE) **4** (*impers.*) (*о боли*) to have a shooting pain

стреля́|ться, юсь *impf.* **1** (*самоубийца*) to shoot oneself **2** (**с** + *i.*) (*на дуэли*) to fight a duel with firearms (with)

стремгла́в *adv.* headlong

стреми́тел|ьный, ∼ен, ∼ьна *adj.* (*полёт, бег*) swift, headlong; (*рост, развитие*) rapid; (*ручей*) fast-flowing

✓ **стрем|и́ться, лю́сь, и́шься** *impf.* **1** (*устремиться*) to rush **2** (**к** + *d.*) (*добиваться*) to strive (for), seek, aspire (to); (+ *inf.*) to strive (to), try (to); **с. к соверше́нству** to strive for perfection **3** (**в, на** + *a.*) (*желать попасть*) to want to go (to)

стремле́ни|е, я *nt.* (**к** + *d.*) striving (for), aspiration (to)

стре́м|я, *g., d. and p.* **∼ени,** *i.* **∼енем,** *pl.* **∼ена́, ∼я́н, ∼ена́м** *nt.* stirrup

c

стремя́нк|а, и *f.* stepladder, steps

стресс, а *m.* (psych.) stress

стре́ссовый *adj.* (*положение*) stressful; (*состояние*) stressed

стриж, а́ *m.* (zool.) swift

стри́жк|а, и *f.* **1** (*действие*) hair cutting; shearing; clipping **2** (*причёска*) haircut, hairstyle

стрипти́з, а *m.* striptease

стриптизёр, а *m.* (male) stripper

стриптизёр|ка, ки *and* ~**ша**, ~**ши** *f.* (female) stripper

стри́|чь, гу́, жёшь, гу́т, *past* ~**г,** ~**гла** *impf.* **1** (*pf.* **остри́чь** *and* **постри́чь**) (*волосы, ногти, кусты*) to cut, clip **2** (*pf.* **остри́чь** *and* **постри́чь**) (*овец*) to shear; (*пуделя*) to clip **3** (*pf.* **постри́чь**) (*человека*) **с. кого́-н.** to cut sb's hair; to give sb a haircut

стри́|чься, гу́сь, жёшься, гу́тся, *past* ~**гся,** ~**глась** *impf.* (*pf.* ▸ **постри́чься**) **1** to cut one's hair; to have one's hair cut **2** (*no pf.*) (*носить короткие волосы*) to wear one's hair short

строга́|ть, ю *impf.* (tech.) to plane

стро́г|ий, ~, ~**á,** ~**о** *adj.* (*начальник, правила, диета*) strict; (*наказание, причёска*) severe; ~**ие ме́ры** strong measures; **с. пригово́р** severe sentence

стро́го *adv.* strictly; severely; **с. говоря́** strictly speaking

стро́гост|ь, и *f.* strictness; severity

строево́й *adj.* (mil.) **1** combatant, line; ~**áя слу́жба** (front-)line service, combatant service **2** drill; ~**áя подгото́вка** drill; **с. шаг** goose-step

строе́ни|е, я *nt.* **1** (*здание*) building, structure **2** (*структура*) structure, composition

строжа́йший *superl. of* ▸ **стро́гий**

стро́же *comp. of* ▸ **стро́гий,** ▸ **стро́го**

строи́тел|ь, я *m.* builder, constructor; (fig.) creator

⚔ **строи́тельн|ый** *adj.* building, construction; ~**ая площа́дка** building site; **с. раство́р** mortar

⚔ **строи́тельств|о, а** *nt.* building, construction (also fig.); **доро́жное с.** road-building; **жили́щное с.** house-building

стро́|ить, ю, ишь *impf.* (*of* ▸ **постро́ить**) **1** (*здание, дорогу, мост, плотину*) to build, construct; (*корабль, танк*) to build **2** (*новую жизнь, общество, счастье*) to create, build **3** (*фигуры, фразы, мысли*) to construct; to formulate; **с. фра́зу** to construct a sentence **4** (*на + p.*) (*обосновывать*) to base (on); **с. расчёт на** (+ p.) to base one's calculations on; **с. отноше́ния на дове́рии** to base relations on trust **5** (*планы, догадки*) to make; **с. гипоте́зу** to advance a hypothesis **6** (*ставить строй*) to draw up, form (up)

стро́|иться, юсь, ишься *impf.* (*of* ▸ **постро́иться**) **1** (*строить себе дом*) to build (*a house, etc.*) for oneself **2** (mil.) to draw up, form up; ~**йся!** (mil.) fall in! **3** *pass. of* ▸ **стро́ить**

стро|й¹, я, о ~**е, в** ~**е,** *pl.* ~**и,** ~**ев** *m.* system, order; structure; **обще́ственный с.** social system

стро|й², ~я, о ~**е, в** ~**ю,** *pl.* ~**й,** ~**ёв** *m.* **1** (mil., naut., aeron., *порядок*) formation; **со́мкнутый с.** close order **2** (mil., *шеренга, часть*) unit in formation; **пе́ред** ~**ем** in front of the ranks **3** (mil., also fig., *действующий состав*) service, commission; **вы́вести из** ~**я** to disable; to put out of action; **вступи́ть в с.** to come into service, come into operation; **вы́йти из** ~**я** to be disabled; to become unserviceable; (*машина*) to break down

стро́йк|а, и *f.* **1** (*действие*) building, construction **2** (*место*) building site

стройматериа́л|ы, ов (*no sg.*) building materials

стро́йн|ый, ~**ен,** ~**йна́,** ~**йно,** ~**йны́** *adj.* **1** (*фигура*) well proportioned; shapely **2** (*пение*) harmonious; (*ряды*) orderly; (*фраза, доклад*) well-constructed

⚔ **строк|а́, и́,** *pl.* ~**и,** ~, ~**áм** *f.* line; (comput.) string; **нача́ть с кра́сной/но́вой** ~**й** to begin a new paragraph; **чита́ть ме́жду** ~ to read between the lines

стропи́л|о, а *nt.* rafter, beam

стропти́в|ый, ~, ~**а** *adj.* obstinate

строф|а́, ы́, *pl.* ~**ы,** ~, ~**áм** *f.* (liter.) stanza, verse

стро́чк|а, и *f.* = **строка́**

⚔ **стру|и́ться, и́тся** *impf.* to stream, flow

⚔ **структу́р|а, ы** *f.* structure

структурали́зм, а *m.* structuralism

структу́рный *adj.* structural

струн|а́, ы́, *pl.* ~**ы** *f.* string

стру́нный *adj.* (mus.): **с. инструме́нт** stringed instrument; **с. кварте́т** string quartet

струп, а, *pl.* ~**ья,** ~**ьев** *m.* scab

стру́|сить, шу, сишь *pf. of* ▸ **тру́сить**

струч|о́к, ка́ *m.* pod

стру|я́, и́, *pl.* ~**и** *f.* **1** (*воды*) jet, spurt, stream; (*света, воздуха*) stream; **бить** ~**ёй** to spurt **2** (fig.) spirit; impetus

стряс|ти́сь, ётся, *past* ~**ся,** ~**ла́сь** *pf.* (**с** + *i.*) (infml) to befall; **беда́** ~**ла́сь с на́ми** a disaster befell us; **что с тобо́й** ~**ло́сь?** what's the matter with you?

стря́хива|ть, ю *impf. of* ▸ **стряхну́ть**

стря́х|ну́ть, ну́, нёшь *pf.* (*of* ▸ **стря́хивать**) to shake off

⚔ **студе́нт, а** *m.* student, undergraduate; **с.-ме́дик** medical student

студе́нт|ка, ки *f. of* ▸ **студе́нт**

студе́нческий *adj. of* ▸ **студе́нт; с. биле́т** student card

сту́д|ень, ня *m.* galantine; aspic

сту́ди|я, и *f.* **1** (*живописца; телестудия*) studio; **с. звукоза́писи** recording studio **2** (*школа*) (art, drama, music, etc.) school

сту́ж|а, и *f.* severe cold, hard frost

стук, а *m.* (*в дверь*) knock; (*сердца*) thump; (*пишущей машинки*) clatter; (*падающего* *предмета*) thud; **с. в дверь** knock at/on the door; **с. колёс** rumble of wheels

сту́к|ать, аю *impf. of* ▶ **сту́кнуть**

сту́к|аться, аюсь *impf. of* ▶ **сту́кнуться**

стука́ч, а́ *m.* (sl.) police informer

сту́к|нуть, ну, нешь *pf.* (*of* ▶ **сту́кать**) **1** (в + *a. or* по + *d.*) to knock; to bang; **с. в дверь** to knock, bang at/on the door **2** (*ударить*) to bang, hit, strike; **с. кого́-н. по спине́** to slap/clap sb on the back

сту́к|нуться, нусь, нешься *pf.* (*of* ▶ **сту́каться**) (о + *a.*) to bang oneself (against), bump oneself (against)

стул, а, *pl.* ~ья, ~ьев *m.* chair

сту́п|а, ы *f.* mortar

ступа́|ть, а́ю *impf. of* ▶ **ступи́ть**

ступ|е́нь, е́ни *f.* **1** (*g. pl.* ~е́ней) (*лестницы*) step; (*стремянки*) rung **2** (*g. pl.* ~ене́й) (*этап*) stage; (*разряд*) grade; (*уровень*) level

ступе́нь|ка, ки *f.* = **ступе́нь** 1

ступ|и́ть, лю́, ~ишь *pf.* (*of* ▶ **ступа́ть**) to step; to tread

ступн|я́, й, *pl.* ~и́, ~е́й *f.* **1** (*стопа*) foot **2** (*подошва*) sole

сту́пор, а *m.* stupor

стуч|а́ть, у́, и́шь *impf.* **1** (*pf.* по~) to knock; to bang; to rap; (*о зубах*) to chatter **2** (*no pf.*) (*о сердце*) to thump, pound **3** (*pf.* на~) (sl.) (*доносить*) to report (*sb*)

стуч|а́ться, у́сь, и́шься *impf.* (*of* ▶ **постуча́ться**) (в + *a.*) to knock (at/on); **с. к сосе́ду** to knock at/on a neighbour's (BrE), neighbor's (AmE) door

стыд, а́ *m.* shame; **к на́шему** ~у́ to our shame

стыд|и́ть, жу́, ди́шь *impf.* (*of* ▶ **пристыди́ть**) to shame, put to shame

стыд|и́ться, жу́сь, ди́шься *impf.* (*of* ▶ **постыди́ться**) (+ *g.*) to be ashamed (of)

стыдли́в|ый, ~, ~а *adj.* bashful

стыд|но *as pred.* it is a shame; **ему́** *и т. п.* **с.** he is, *etc.*, ashamed

стыко́вк|а, и *f.* docking

стю́ард, а *m.* steward

стюарде́сс|а, ы *f.* stewardess

стя́гива|ть, ю *impf. of* ▶ **стяну́ть** 1

стя́гива|ться, юсь *impf. of* ▶ **стяну́ться**

стя|ну́ть, ну́, ~нешь *pf.* (*of* ▶ **стя́гивать**) **1** (*сапоги*) to pull off **2** (*pf. only*) (infml, *украсть*) to pinch (infml, BrE), steal

стя|ну́ться, ну́сь, ~нешься *pf.* (*of* ▶ **стя́гиваться**) **1** to tighten **2** (infml, *туго подпоясаться*) to gird oneself tightly **3** (*о войсках, демонстрантах*) to gather, assemble

суахи́ли *m. indecl.* Swahili (*language, people*)

суббо́т|а, ы *f.* Saturday

субмари́н|а, ы *f.* submarine

субподря́д, а *m.* subcontract

субподря́дчик, а *m.* subcontractor

субсиди́р|овать, ую *impf. and pf.* to subsidize

субси́ди|я, и *f.* subsidy

субста́нци|я, и *f.* substance

субти́тр, а *m.* (*usu. in pl.*) subtitle (*in film*)

субтро́пик|и, ов (*no sg.*) subtropics

субтропи́ческий *adj.* subtropical

⚜ **субъе́кт, а** *m.* **1** (phil., gram., med., law) subject **2** (infml, *человек*) fellow, character, type

субъекти́в|ный, ~ен, ~на *adj.* subjective

сувени́р, а *m.* souvenir

суверените́т, а *m.* (pol., law) sovereignty

сувере́нный *adj.* (pol., law) sovereign

сугро́б, а *m.* snowdrift

⚜ **суд, а́** *m.* **1** court, law court; **зал** ~а́ courtroom; **заседа́ние** ~а́ sitting of the court **2** (*разбирательство*) trial, legal proceedings; **пода́ть в с. на кого́-н.** to bring an action against sb; **отда́ть под с.**, **преда́ть** ~у́ to prosecute; **с. прися́жных** jury **3** (*collect.*) (*судьи*) the judges; the bench **4** (*мнение*) judgement, verdict; **с. исто́рии** verdict of history

суда́к, а́ *m.* pikeperch (*fish*)

Суда́н, а *m.* (the) Sudan

суда́н|ец, ца *m.* Sudanese

суда́н|ка, ки *f. of* ▶ **суда́нец**

суда́нский *adj.* Sudanese

⚜ **суде́б|ный** *adj.* judicial; legal; (*медицина, психиатрия*) forensic; **с. исполни́тель** bailiff, officer of the court; ~ая оши́бка miscarriage of justice; ~ое разбира́тельство legal proceedings, hearing of a case; ~ое реше́ние court decision, court order

⚜ **су|ди́ть, жу́, ~дишь** *impf.* **1** (о + *p.*) (*составлять мнение*) to judge; to form an opinion (about, on); **наско́лько мы могли́ с.** as far as we could judge; ~дя (по + *d.*) judging (by), to judge (from); ~дя по всему́ to all appearances **2** (law) (за + *a.*) (*преступника*) to try (for) **3** (*осуждать*) to judge, pass judgement (upon); **не** ~ди́те их стро́го! don't be hard on them! **4** (sport) (*в крикете, теннисе*) to umpire

су|ди́ться, жу́сь, ~дишься *impf.* (с + *i.*) to sue

су́д|но, на, *pl.* ~а́, ~о́в *nt.* vessel

судове́рф|ь, и *f.* shipyard

судовладе́л|ец, ьца *m.* shipowner

судопроизво́дств|о, а *nt.* legal proceedings

су́дорог|а, и *f.* cramp, convulsion, spasm

судостро́ени|е, я *nt.* shipbuilding

судохо́д|ный, ~ен, ~на *adj.* **1** navigable; **с. кана́л** shipping canal **2**: ~ная компа́ния shipping company

судохо́дств|о, а *nt.* navigation, shipping

⚜ **судьб|а́, ьбы́,** *pl.* ~ьбы, ~еб, ~ьбам *f.* fate, fortune; (*будущее*) destiny; (*история существования*) story; **благодари́ть** ~ьбу́ to thank one's lucky stars; **искуша́ть** ~ьбу́

⚜ key word

to tempt fate

суд|ья́, ьи́, *pl.* ~ьи, ~éй, ~ьям *m.* (*also f.*) (infml, *о женщине*) **1** judge; **я вам не с.!** who am I to judge you? **2** (sport) referee; (*в крикете, теннисе*) umpire; **с. на ли́нии** linesman

су́дя *see* ▶ суди́ть

суеве́ри|е, я *nt.* superstition

суеве́р|ный, ~ен, ~на *adj.* superstitious

сует|а́, ы́ *f.* **1** (*тщетность*) vanity **2** (*хлопоты*) bustle, fuss

суе|ти́ться, чу́сь, ти́шься *impf.* to bustle, fuss

суетли́в|ый, ~, ~а *adj.* fussy, bustling

сужде́ни|е, я *nt.* (*мнение*) opinion; (*в логике*) judgement

су́жива|ться, ется *impf. of* ▶ су́зиться

су́|зиться, зится *pf.* (*of* ▶ су́живаться) to narrow (*intrans.*), get narrow; to taper

суици́д, а *m.* suicide

сук, á, о ~é, на ~ý, *pl.* су́чья, су́чьев *m.* bough

су́к|а, и *f.* bitch (*also as term of abuse*)

сук|нó, ná, *pl.* ~на, ~он *nt.* (heavy, coarse) cloth

сумасбро́д|ный, ~ен, ~на *adj.* wild, extravagant

сумасше́дш|ий *adj.* **1** mad; (*as m. n.* **с.**, ~его) madman, lunatic; (~ая, ~ей) madwoman, lunatic) **2** : **с. дом** (infml) madhouse **3** (fig.) mad, lunatic; ~ая ско́рость lunatic speed; **э́то бу́дет сто́ить** ~их де́нег it will cost the earth

сумасше́стви|е, я *nt.* madness, lunacy

сумато́х|а, и *f.* confusion, chaos

сумбу́р|ный, ~ен, ~на *adj.* confused, chaotic

суме́|ть, ю *pf.* (+ *inf.*) to be able (to), manage (to)

су́мк|а, и *f.* **1** bag; **хозя́йственная с.** shopping bag **2** (biol.) pouch

су́мм|а, ы *f.* sum; **о́бщая/по́лная с.** sum total; (*количество*) amount

сумма́р|ный, ~ен, ~на *adj.* **1** (*количество*) total **2** (*обзор*) summary

сумми́р|овать, ую *impf. and pf.* **1** (*складывать*) to add up **2** (*обобщить*) to summarize; to sum up

су́мочк|а, и *f.* (*дамская*) handbag

су́мрак, а *m.* dusk, twilight

су́мрач|ный, ~ен, ~на *adj.* gloomy (also fig.)

сунду́к, á *m.* trunk, box, chest

сунни́т, а *m.* Sunni (Muslim)

су́н|уть, у, ешь *pf. of* ▶ сова́ть

су́н|уться, усь, ешься *pf. of* ▶ сова́ться

суп, а, *pl.* ~ы́ *m.* soup

суперзапре́т, а *m.* superinjunction

суперзвезд|á, ы́, *pl.* ~ы, ~, ~ам *f.* superstar

суперма́ркет, а *m.* supermarket

супермоде́л|ь, и *f.* supermodel

суперобло́жк|а, и *f.* dust jacket

су́пниц|а, ы *f.* soup tureen

супру́г, а *m.* **1** husband, spouse **2** (*in pl.*) (*муж и жена*) husband and wife, married couple

супру́г|а, и *f.* wife, spouse

супру́жеский *adj.* (*чета, жизнь*) married; (*верность, счастье*) marital

супру́жеств|о, а *nt.* matrimony, wedlock

суро́в|ый, ~, ~а *adj.* **1** (*взгляд, критика*) severe, stern; (*зима, жизнь, приговор*) harsh; (*красота, воспитание*) austere **2** (*ткань*) coarse

сур|óк, ка́ *m.* marmot; **спать как с.** to sleep like a log

суррога́т, а *m.* surrogate, substitute

суррога́тн|ый *adj.* surrogate, substitute; ~ая мать surrogate mother

су́слик, а *m.* (zool.) ground squirrel, gopher (AmE)

суста́в, а *m.* (anat.) joint

сутенёр, а *m.* pimp

су́т|ки, ок (*no sg.*) twenty-four hours; twenty-four-hour period; **це́лые с.** for days and nights

суту́л|иться, юсь, ишься *impf.* (*of* ▶ ссуту́литься) to stoop

суту́л|ый, ~, ~а *adj.* round-shouldered, stooping

сут|ь, и *f.* essence; **с. де́ла** the heart, crux of the matter; **по ~и де́ла** as a matter of fact

су́ффикс, а *m.* (gram.) suffix

суха́р|ь, я́ *m.* (*хлебный*) rusk

су́хо *adv.* **1** coldly; **нас при́няли с.** we were received coldly **2** (*as pred.*) it is dry; **на у́лице с.** it is dry out of doors

сухогру́з, а *m.* bulk carrier

сухожи́ли|е, я *nt.* (anat.) tendon, sinew

сух|о́й, ~, ~á, ~o *adj.* **1** dry; ~и́е дрова́ dry firewood; ~óе ру́сло реки́ dried-up river bed **2** (*хлеб*) dry; (*фрукты*) dried; ~óе молоко́ dried milk **3** (*кожа*) dried-up; (*рука*) withered; (*худощавый*) lean **4** (*без влаги, жидкости*) dry; **с. ка́шель** dry cough **5** (fig., *холодный*) chilly, cold; **с. приём** chilly reception

сухопу́тн|ый *adj.* land (*opp. marine, air*); ~ые си́лы (mil.) ground forces

сухофру́кт|ы, ов (*no sg.*) dried fruits

суч|óк, ка́ *m.* twig

су́ш|а, и *f.* (dry) land (*opp. sea*); **по ~e** by land

су́ше *comp. of* ▶ сухо́й, ▶ су́хо

сушёный *adj.* dried

суши́лк|а, и *f.* **1** (*устройство*) drying apparatus, dryer; **напо́льная с.** clothes horse **2** (*помещение*) drying room

суш|и́ть, у́, ~ишь *impf.* (*of* ▶ вы́сушить) to dry (out)

суш|и́ться, у́сь, ~ишься *impf.* (*of* ▶ вы́сушиться) to dry (out); (*человек*) to get dry

су́шк|а, и *f.* **1** drying **2** (cul.) dry (ring-shaped) cracker

с

суще́ствен|ный, ~, ~на *adj.* (*черта, разница*) essential; (*роль, значение*) vital; (*крупный*) substantial; (*вопрос*) important

существи́тельно|е *adj.*: и́мя с. (*or as nt. n. с.*, ~ого) noun; **с. мужско́го/же́нского/сре́днего ро́да** masculine/feminine/neuter noun

существ|о́, а́ *nt.* **1** (*сущность*) essence; **по ~у́** (*говоря*) in essence, essentially; **говори́ть по ~у́** to speak to the point; **не по ~у́** off the point, beside the point **2** (*живая особь*) being, creature; **люби́мое с.** loved one

существова́ни|е, я *nt.* existence; **борьба́ за с.** struggle for survival

существ|ова́ть, у́ю *impf.* to exist

существу́ющий *pres. participle of* ▶ **существова́ть** *and adj.* existing

су́щ|ий *adj.* (infml, *правда*) absolute; utter; **с. ад** absolute hell; **~ая ерунда́** utter rubbish; **э́то/он ~ее наказа́ние** it/he is the bane of my life

су́щност|ь, и *f.* essence; **в ~и (говоря́)** in essence, essentially

сфабрик|ова́ть, у́ю *pf. of* ▶ **фабрикова́ть**

сфе́р|а, ы *f.* sphere; **с. влия́ния** (pol.) sphere of influence; **вы́сшие ~ы** highest circles

сфери́ческий *adj.* spherical

сфокуси́р|овать, ую *pf. of* ▶ **фокуси́ровать**

сфокуси́р|оваться, уюсь *pf. of* ▶ **фокуси́роваться**

сформир|ова́ть, у́ю *pf. of* ▶ **формирова́ть**

сформир|ова́ться, у́юсь *pf. of* ▶ **формирова́ться**

сформули́р|овать, ую *pf. of* ▶ **формули́ровать**

сфотографи́р|овать, ую *pf. of* ▶ **фотографи́ровать**

сфотографи́р|оваться, уюсь *pf. of* ▶ **фотографи́роваться**

схва|ти́ть, чу́, ~тишь *pf.* **1** *pf. of* ▶ **хвата́ть**[1] 1 **2** (*pf. only*, *простуду*) to catch **3** (*impf.* ~тывать) (infml, *мысль*) to grasp, comprehend; **с. смысл** to grasp the meaning, catch on

схва|ти́ться, чу́сь, ~тишься *pf.* **1** *pf. of* ▶ **хвата́ться 2** (*impf.* ~тываться) (c + i.) to grapple (with) (also fig.)

схва́тк|а, и *f.* skirmish, fight; (*в спорте*) fight; (*в споре*) clash; **рукопа́шная с.** hand-to-hand fight

схва́т|ки, ок (*no sg.*) (med.) contractions (*of muscles*); spasms; **родовы́е с.** labour (BrE), labor (AmE)

схва́тыва|ть, ю *impf. of* ▶ **схвати́ть**

схва́тыва|ться, юсь *impf. of* ▶ **схвати́ться**

схе́м|а, ы *f.* (*чертёж*) diagram, chart; **с. метро́** metro map **2** (*сочинения*) sketch, outline, plan **3** (elec., radio) circuit

схемати́ч|ный, ~ен, ~на *adj.* sketchy, (over)simplified

схитри́|ть, ю, и́шь *pf. of* ▶ **хитри́ть**

схлы́н|уть, у, ешь *pf.* **1** (*о волнах*) to break and flow back **2** (*о толпе*) to break up; to dwindle **3** (*о чувствах*) to subside

схо|ди́ть[1], жу́, ~дишь *impf. of* ▶ **сойти́**

схо|ди́ть[2], жу́, ~дишь *pf.* to go (*and come back*); (за + i.) to go to fetch; **с. посмотре́ть** to go to see; **~ди́ за врачо́м!** go and fetch a doctor!

схо|ди́ться, жу́сь, ~дишься *impf. of* ▶ **сойти́сь**

схо́дк|а, и *f.* gathering, assembly

схо́дн|и, ей *f. pl.* (*sg.* ~я, ~и) gangway, gangplank

схо́д|ный, ~ен, ~на *adj.* (c + i.) similar (to)

схо́дств|о, а *nt.* likeness, similarity, resemblance; **вне́шнее с.** similarity in appearance

схо́ж|ий, ~, ~а *adj.* (infml) (c + i.) similar (to)

сца́па|ть, ю *pf.* (infml) to grab, catch hold (of)

сце|ди́ть, жу́, ~дишь *pf.* (*of* ▶ **сце́живать**) to pour off, decant; (*через сито, марлю*) to strain off

сце́жива|ть, ю *impf. of* ▶ **сцеди́ть**

сце́н|а, ы *f.* **1** (*подмостки*) stage (also fig.) **2** (*эпизод, происшествие*) scene **3** (infml) scene; **устро́ить ~у** to make a scene

сцена́ри|й, я *m.* **1** (*фильма, передачи*) scenario, script **2** (*детальный план*) plan, programme (BrE), program (AmE) **3** (fig., *вариант*) scenario

сценари́ст, а *m.* scriptwriter

сценари́ст|ка, ки *f. of* ▶ **сценари́ст**

сцеп|и́ть, лю́, ~ишь *pf.* (*of* ▶ **сцепля́ть**) **1** (*вагоны, кузова*) to couple **2** (*пальцы*) to clasp

сцеп|и́ться, лю́сь, ~ишься *pf.* (*of* ▶ **сцепля́ться**) **1** (*вагоны, детали*) to be coupled; (*ветки*) to be intertwined; to intertwine; (*частицы*) to stick together **2** (c + i.) (infml, *начать дра́ться*) to grapple (with)

сцепле́ни|е, я *nt.* **1** (*действие*) coupling **2** (tech.) clutch; (*клеток, вещества*) cohesion; **выключе́ние ~я** clutch release

сцепля́|ть, ю *impf. of* ▶ **сцепи́ть**

сцепля́|ться, юсь *impf. of* ▶ **сцепи́ться**

сча́стливо *adv.* (*жить, улыбаться*) happily; **с. отде́латься** (от + g.) to have a lucky escape (from); **сча́стливо (остава́ться)!** good luck!

счастли́вый, ~лив, ~лива *adj.* **1** (*лицо, детство, человек*) happy; **с. коне́ц** happy end **2** (*игрок, случай, день*) lucky **3**: **~ли́вого пути́!** bon voyage!

сча́сть|е, я *nt.* **1** (*чувство*) happiness; **жела́ю вам с.** I wish you happiness **2** (*удача*) luck, good fortune; **к ~ю** luckily, fortunately; **на на́ше с.** luckily for us; **како́е с., что...** how fortunate that ...

сче́сть, сочту́, сочтёшь, *past* **счёл, сочла́** *pf. of* ▶ **счита́ть** 3

счёт, а (у), *pl.* ~ы and **счета́** *m.* **1** (*sg. only*) (*действие*) counting, calculation, reckoning; **вести́ с.** (+ d.) to keep count (of); **в два**

~a in a jiffy, in a trice **2** (*sg. only*) (*sport*) score; **со ~ом** 2:1 with a score of 2-1 **3** (*pl.* **счета́**) (*в рестора́не, за газ, за телефо́н*) bill; (*накладна́я*) invoice; **уплати́ть по ~у** to pay the bill **4** (*pl.* **счета́**) (*в ба́нке*) account; **откры́ть с.** to open an account; **за с.** (+ *g.*) at the expense (of) **5** (*sg. only*) (fig.) account, expense; **в с.** (+ *g.*) on the strength (of); **в коне́чном ~е** in the end; **за с.** (+ *g.*) at the expense (of); owing (to); **приня́ть на свой с.** to take (sth) personally; **на э́тот с.** in this respect **6** (**~ы**, *no sg.*) (fig., *прете́нзии*) accounts, score(s); **ста́рые ~ы** old scores; **свести́ ~ы** (**с** + *i.*) to settle a score (with), get even (with) **7** *see* ▶ **счёты**[1]

счётчик, **а** *m.* meter; counter; **га́зовый с.** gas meter

счёт|ы[1], **ов** (*no sg.*) abacus

счёты[2] *see* ▶ **счёт 6**

счи́|стить, **щу**, **стишь** *pf.* (*of* ▶ **счища́ть**) to clean off

счита́н|ый *adj.* a few; **остаю́тся ~ые дни** (**до** + *g.*) one can count the days (until); there are only a few days left (until); **~ое коли́чество** (*де́нег*) very little; (*предме́тов*) very few

ꝏ **счита́|ть**, **ю** *impf.* (*of* ▶ **посчита́ть**) **1** (*pf. also* **со~**) to count; **с. дни, мину́ты** to count the days, minutes; **не ~я** not counting **2** (*pf. also* **счесть**) (+ *i. or* **за** + *a.*) to count, consider, think; to regard (as); **я ~ю его́ надёжным челове́ком** I consider him a reliable person; **с. необходи́мым/ну́жным** to consider it necessary **3** (*pf. also* **счесть**): **с. (что)** to consider (that), hold (that)

ꝏ **счита́|ться**, **юсь** *impf.* (*no pf.*) **1** (+ *i.*) to be considered, be thought, be reputed; to be regarded (as); **он ~ется первокла́ссным специали́стом** he is considered a first-rate specialist; **~ется, что...** it is considered that ... **2** (**с** + *i.*) (*принима́ть в расчёт*) to consider, take into consideration; to take into account, reckon (with); **он всегда́ ~лся с мои́м мне́нием** he always took my opinion into consideration; **он ни с кем не ~ется** he has no consideration for anyone

счища́|ть, **ю** *impf. of* ▶ **счи́стить**

США *pl. indecl.* (*abbr. of* **Соединённые Шта́ты Аме́рики**) US(A) (*United States of America*)

сшиб|а́ть, **а́ю** *impf. of* ▶ **сшиби́ть**

сшиб|и́ть, **у́, ёшь**, *past* **~, ~ла** *pf.* (*of* ▶ **сшиба́ть**) (infml) to knock off; **с. с ног** to knock down, knock over

сши|ва́ть, **ю** *impf. of* ▶ **сшить 2**

сшить, **сошью́, сошьёшь** *pf.* **1** *pf. of* ▶ **шить 2** (*impf.* **сшива́ть**) to sew together; (med.) to suture

съ... *vbl. pref.* = **с...**

съеда́|ть, **ю** *impf.* (*of* ▶ **съесть**) to eat (up)

съедо́б|ный, **~ен**, **~на** *adj.* edible

съёжива|ться, **юсь** *impf. of* ▶ **съёжиться**

съёж|иться, **усь**, **ишься** *pf.* (*of* ▶ **съёживаться**) (*в комо(че)к; от хо́лода*) to huddle up; (*о ли́стьях, лице́*) to shrivel up;

(*о тка́ни*) to shrink

съезд[1], **а** *m.* (*собра́ние*) congress; conference, convention

съезд[2], **а** *m.* (*спуск*) descent

съе́з|дить, **жу, дишь** *pf.* to go (*and come back*); **как (ты) ~дила?** how was your trip?

съезжа́|ть, **ю** *impf. of* ▶ **съе́хать**

съезжа́|ться, **юсь** *impf. of* ▶ **съе́хаться**

съел *see* ▶ **съесть**

съёмк|а, **и** *f.* **1** (*ме́стности*) survey, surveying; plotting **2** (*usu. in pl.*) (*фи́льма*) shooting

съёмный *adj.* detachable, removable

съёмщик, **а** *m.* tenant

съёмщи|ца, **ы** *f. of* ▶ **съёмщик**

съестн|о́й *adj.* food; **~ы́е припа́сы** food supplies, provisions; (*as nt. n.* **~о́е**, **~о́го**) food

съе|сть, **м, шь, ст, ди́м, ди́те, дя́т**, *past* **~л, ~ла** *pf. of* ▶ **есть**[1], ▶ **съеда́ть**

съе́|хать, **ду, дешь** *pf.* (*of* ▶ **съезжа́ть**) **1** (*спусти́ться*) to go down, come down **2** (*с кварти́ры*) to move out **3** (fig., infml, *дви́нуться с ме́ста*) to come down, slip; **у тебя́ га́лстук ~хал наба́к** your tie is on one side

съе́|хаться, **дусь, дешься** *pf.* (*of* ▶ **съезжа́ться**) **1** (*встре́титься*) to meet **2** (*собра́ться*) to arrive, gather, assemble

сы́воротк|а, **и** *f.* serum

сыгра́|ть, **ю** *pf.* (*of* ▶ **игра́ть**): **с. шу́тку** (**с** + *i.*) to play a practical joke (on)

сымити́р|овать, **ую** *pf. of* ▶ **имити́ровать**

сымпровизи́р|овать, **ую** *pf. of* ▶ **импровизи́ровать**

ꝏ **сын**, **а**, *pl.* **~овья́, ~ове́й** *m.* son

сы́п|ать, **лю, лешь** *impf.* to pour

сы́п|аться, **летя** *impf.* **1** (*о чём-н. ме́лком*) to fall; (*о сыпучем*) to pour out; (*разбега́ться*) to scatter; **мука́ ~алась из мешка́** flour poured out of the bag **2** (infml, *о зву́ках*) to pour forth (*intrans.*), rain down; **уда́ры ~ались гра́дом** blows were raining down, falling thick and fast **3** (*о штукату́рке*) to flake off

сыпь, **и** *f.* (med.) rash, eruption

сыр, **а**, *pl.* **~ы́** *m.* cheese

сыре́|ть, **ю** *impf.* (*of* ▶ **отсыре́ть**) to become damp

сы́ро *as pred.* it is damp

сыроёжк|а, **и** *f.* russula (*mushroom*)

сыр|о́й, **~, ~а́, ~о** *adj.* **1** (*вла́жный*) damp; (*ле́то, день*) wet **2** (*о́вощи, те́сто*) raw, uncooked; **~ая вода́** unboiled water; **~о́е мя́со** raw meat **3** (*незре́лый*) green, unripe **4** (*необрабо́танный*) raw; (*расска́з, план*) unfinished, unrefined

сыр|о́к, ка́ *m.* (med.) (*творо́жный*) curd cheese; **пла́вленый с.** processed cheese

сы́рост|ь, **и** *f.* dampness, humidity

сырь|ё, я́ (*no pl.*) *nt.* raw material(s)

сырьев|о́й *adj. of* **сырьё**; **~а́я ба́за** raw material supply

сыск, а *m.* investigation, detection (*of criminals*)

сы́т|ный, ~ен, ~на́, ~но *adj.* (*обед*) substantial, copious; (*пирог*) filling, rich; (*питательный*) nourishing

сы́т|ый, ~, ~а́, ~о *adj.* **1** satisfied, full; спаси́бо, я ~ thank you, I am full **2** (*откормленный*) well fed **3** (fig.) (+ *i.*) (*пресыщенный*) fed up with; я ~ по го́рло I'm fed up to the back teeth (with)

сы́щик, а *m.* detective

сэконо́м|ить, лю, ишь *pf. of* ▶ эконо́мить

сэр, а *m.* sir

✧ **сюда́** *adv.* here, hither

сюже́т, а *m.* (*картины, симфонии*) subject; (*романа*) plot

сюи́т|а, ы *f.* (mus.) suite

сюрпри́з, а *m.* surprise

сюрреали́зм, а *m.* surrealism

сюрреали́ст, а *m.* surrealist

сюрреалисти́ческий *adj.* surrealist

сюрту́к, а́ *m.* frock coat

сюсю́ка|ть, ю *impf.* (infml) to lisp

Тт

т (*abbr. of* **то́нна**) t, ton(s), tonne(s)

таба́к, а́ ý *m.* tobacco

табаке́рк|а, и *f.* snuffbox

та́бел|ь, я *m.* **1** (*график*) table, chart **2** (*на заводе*) time board (*for tracking attendance*)

та́бельщик, а *m.* timekeeper

табле́тк|а, и *f.* tablet, pill; **т. аспири́на** aspirin

✧ **табли́ц|а**, ы *f.* table; **электро́нная т.** (comput.) spreadsheet

табло́ *nt. indecl.* (*на вокза́ле*) information board; (sport) scoreboard

табло́ид, а *m.* tabloid (newspaper)

та́бор, а *m.* **1** (*лагерь*) camp **2** (*группа цыган*) band of gypsies

табу́ *nt. indecl.* taboo

табу́н, а́ *m.* herd (*usu. of horses*)

табуре́т, а *m.* = табуре́тка

табуре́т|ка, ки *f.* stool

тавр|о́, а́, *pl.* ~а, ~, ~а́м *nt.* brand (*on cattle, etc.*)

тавтоло́ги|я, и *f.* tautology

тага́н, а́ *m.* trivet

таджи́к, а *m.* Tajik

Таджикиста́н, а *m.* Tajikistan

таджи́кский *adj.* Tajik

таджи́ч|ка, ки *f. of* ▶ таджи́к

таз[1], а, в ~ý, *pl.* ~ы́ *m.* bowl

таз[2], а, в ~е and в ~ý, *pl.* ~ы́ *m.* (anat.) pelvis

тазобе́дренный *adj.* (anat.) hip; **т. суста́в** hip joint

Таила́нд, а *m.* Thailand

таила́нд|ец, ца *m.* Thai

таила́нд|ка, ки *f. of* ▶ таила́ндец

таила́ндский *adj.* Thai

таи́нствен|ный, ~ and ~ен, ~на *adj.* **1** (*место, шорох, взгляд*) mysterious; (*человек*) enigmatic **2** (*цель*) secret **3** (*вид*) secretive

та́инств|о, а *nt.* (relig.) sacrament

Таи́ти *m. indecl.* Tahiti

таи́ть, ю́, и́шь *impf.* (*горе*) to hide, conceal; (*злобу*) to harbour (BrE), harbor (AmE); **т. зло́бу** (про́тив + *g.*) to harbour a grudge (against); **не́чего/что греха́ т.** it must be admitted, we must admit

таи́ться, ю́сь, и́шься *impf.* **1** (infml, *скрываться*) to be (in) hiding, lurk **2** (fig., *иметься*) to lurk, be lurking; **что за э́тим ~и́тся?** what lies behind this?

Тайва́н|ь, я *m.* Taiwan

тайг|а́, и́ *f.* (geog.) taiga

тайко́м *adv.* in secret, surreptitiously; on the quiet

тайм-а́ут, а *m.* (*перерыв в чём-л.*) time off, time out; (sport) timeout

та́йн|а, ы *f.* **1** (*то, что непонятно*) mystery **2** (*секрет*) secret; **храни́ть ~у** to keep a secret

тайни́к, а́ *m.* hiding place (*for a thing*)

та́йн|ый *adj.* secret; clandestine; **т. аге́нт** undercover agent; **~ое голосова́ние** secret ballot

та́йский *adj.* Thai

тайфу́н, а *m.* typhoon

тайцзицюа́нь *f. indecl.* t'ai chi (chu'an)

✧ **так** *adv.* **1** (*таким образом*) so; thus, in this way, like this; in such a way; **т. мно́го** so many; **мы сде́лали т.** this is what we did, we did as follows; **т. вот** (*выражает продолжение повествования после отступления*) and so, then; **т. же** in the same way; **т. и́ли ина́че** whatever happens, one way or another; **т. себе́** so-so, middling; **т. сказа́ть** so to speak; **и т. да́лее** (*usu. spelt* **и т. д.**) and so on, and so forth; **(не) т. ли?**

isn't it so? **2** (*как сле́дует*) as it should be; **не т.** amiss, wrong; **не совсе́м т.** not quite right **3** (*без специа́льных средств; без после́дствий*) just like that; **ему́ э́то т. не пройдёт** he won't get away with it like that **4**: **т. (то́лько), про́сто т.** for no special reason, for no reason in particular; just for fun **5**: **т. как** (*conj.*) as, since **6**: **т. что** (*conj.*) so; **т. что́бы** so that

такела́ж, а *m.* rigging

✓ **та́кже** *adv.* also, too, as well; (*after neg.*) or, nor

-таки *particle* (infml) however, though; **опя́ть-таки** again

тако́в, f. ～а́, *nt.* ～о́, *pl.* ～ы́ *pron.* such; ～ы́ **тре́бования зако́на** such/these are the legal requirements; **и был т.** (infml) and that was the last we saw of him

таково́й *adj.*: **как т.** as such

✓ **так|о́й** *pron.* **1** such; so; **т. же** the same; **он т. до́брый!** he is such a kind man!; ～им о́бразом** thus, in this way; **в** ～о́м слу́чае** in that case **2**: **кто он т.?** who is he?; **что э́то** ～о́е?** what is this?

тако́й-то *pron.* so-and-so; such-and-such

такси́ *nt. indecl.* taxi

такси́ст, а *m.* taxi driver

таксофо́н, а *m.* payphone

такт¹, а *m.* **1** (mus., etc., *ритм*) time; **отбива́ть т.** to beat time; (*в но́тах*) bar **2** (tech.) stroke (*of engine*)

такт², а *m.* (*такти́чность*) tact

та́ктик|а, и *f.* tactics

такти́ческий *adj.* tactical

такти́ч|ный, **～ен, ～на *adj.* tactful

тала́нт, а *m.* **1** (*дар*) talent, gift(s) **2** (*челове́к*) gifted person

тала́нтлив|ый, **～, ～а *adj.* talented, gifted

талисма́н, а *m.* talisman, charm, mascot

та́ли|я, и *f.* waist

Та́ллин, а *m.* Tallinn

тало́н, а *m.* (*на бензи́н*) coupon; **поса́дочный т.** boarding pass

тальк, а *m.* talcum powder

✓ **там** *adv.* there; **т. же** in the same place; (*при ссы́лках*) ibid

та́мбур, а *m.* (*железнодоро́жного ваго́на*) platform (*of railway carriage*)

тамбури́н, а *m.* tambourine

тами́л, а *m.* Tamil

тами́л|ка, ки *f. of* ▸ **тами́л**

тами́льский *adj.* Tamil

тамо́женник, а *m.* customs official

тамо́женный *adj.* customs

тамо́жн|я, и *f.* customs

тампо́н, а *m.* tampon

та́н|ец, ца *m.* **1** (*иску́сство*) dance; dancing; **уро́ки** ～цев** dancing lessons **2** (*in pl.*) (*ве́чер*) a dance; dancing; **пойти́ на** ～цы** to go to a dance, go dancing

танзани́|ец, йца *m.* Tanzanian

танзани́й|ка, ки *f. of* ▸ **танзани́ец**

танзани́йский *adj.* Tanzanian

Танза́ни|я, и *f.* Tanzania

танк, а *m.* (mil.) tank

та́нкер, а *m.* (naut.) tanker

танки́ст, а *m.* member of tank crew

танцева́ть, у́ю *impf.* to dance

танцо́вщик, а *m.* (professional) dancer

танцо́вщиц|а, ы *f. of* ▸ **танцо́вщик**

танцо́р, а *m.* (professional) dancer

та́почк|а, и *f.* slipper; **спорти́вная т.** sports shoe, sneaker (AmE)

та́р|а, ы *f.* packing, packaging

тарака́н, а *m.* cockroach

тара́н, а *m.* (mil.) **1** ram; ramming **2** (hist.) battering ram

таранту́л, а *m.* tarantula

тарато́р|ить, ю, ишь *impf.* (infml) to jabber; to gabble

тарах|те́ть, чу́, ти́шь *impf.* (infml) to rattle, rumble

таре́лк|а, и *f.* **1** plate; **глубо́кая т.** soup plate **2** (tech.) plate, disc; (infml, *спутнико́вая*) (satellite) dish **3** (*in pl.*) (mus.) cymbals

тари́ф, а *m.* tariff, rate

таска́|ть, ю *impf.* (indet. of ▸ **тащи́ть**)

таска́|ться, юсь *impf.* (indet. of ▸ **тащи́ться**)

тас|ова́ть, у́ю *impf.* (of ▸ **перетасова́ть**) (cards) to shuffle

тата́р|ин, ина, pl. ～ы, ～** *m.* Tatar

тата́р|ка, ки *f. of* ▸ **тата́рин**

татаромонго́л, а *n.* Tartar (hist.)

татаромонго́льский *adj.* Tartar (hist.)

тата́рский *adj.* Tatar

татуи́р|овать, ую *impf. and pf.* to tattoo

татуиро́вк|а, и *f.* tattoo

тахт|а́, ы́ *f.* ottoman

та́чк|а, и *f.* wheelbarrow; (infml, *автомоби́ль*) car

Ташке́нт, а *m.* Tashkent

тащ|и́ть, у́, ～ишь** *impf.* (det. of ▸ **таска́ть**) **1** (*тяну́ть*) to pull; (*что-н. тяжёлое*) to drag, lug; (*нести́*) to carry **2** (infml) (*вести́*) to take; (fig., *заставля́ть пойти́ куда́-н.*) to drag off **3** (*извлека́ть*) to pull out

тащ|и́ться, у́сь, ～ишься** *impf.* (det. of ▸ **таска́ться**) **1** (*идти́ с трудо́м*) to drag oneself along; (*ме́дленно е́хать*) to trundle along; (*за кем-н.*) to trail along **2** (*о подо́ле*) to drag, trail **3** (**от** + *g.*) (sl.) to be crazy about

та́яни|е, я *nt.* thaw, thawing

та́|ять, ю, ешь *impf.* (of ▸ **раста́ять**) **1** to melt; to thaw; ～ет** it is thawing **2** (fig., *исчеза́ть*) to melt away, dwindle, wane; **его́ си́лы** ～яли** his strength was ebbing **3** (**от** + *g.*) (fig., *от любви́*) to melt (with), languish (with)

Тбили́си *m. indecl.* Tbilisi

ТВ (*abbr. of* **телеви́дение**) (*abbr. of* **телеви́дение**) TV (television)

твар|ь, и *f.* creature; (also pej.) (*collect.*) creatures; all creation; (pej., *по́длый челове́к*) swine

т

твердé|ть, ет *impf.* to harden, become hard

твер|дúть, жý, дúшь *impf.* (+ *a.* or *o* + *p.*) to repeat, say over and over again

твёрдо *adv.* firmly; (*знать, выучить*) thoroughly

твердолóб|ый, ~, ~а *adj.* diehard

твёрдост|ь, и *f.* hardness; (fig.) firmness

твёрд|ый, ~, твердá, ~о, ~ы and **твёрды** *adj.* **1** (*не мягкий*) hard **2** (*крепкий*) firm; (*не жидкий*) solid; **т. переплёт** stiff binding; **~ое тéло** (phys., chem.) solid **3** (fig.) (*непоколебимый*) firm; (*установленный*) stable; (*стойкий*) steadfast; **~ое решéние** firm decision; **~ые цéны** stable, fixed prices **4** (ling.) hard; **т. знак** hard sign (*name of Russian letter «ъ»*)

твердын|я, и *f.* stronghold (also fig.)

твит, а *m.* (comput.) tweet (*a message posted using Twitter* (propr.))

твúт|ить, ю, ишь *impf.* (comput., *общаться в Интернете через сервис Твиттер*) to tweet

Твúттер, а *m.* (comput, *сервис микроблогов*) Twitter®

✦ **тво|й, егó,** *f.* **~я, ~éй,** *nt.* **~ё, ~егó,** *pl.* **~й, ~úх** *poss. pron.* (*при существительном*) your; (*без существительного*) yours

творéни|е, я *nt.* **1** (*произведение*) creation; work **2** (*существо*) creature, being

твор|éц, цá *m.* creator; (**Т.**) (*Бог*) the Creator

творúтельный *adj.*: **т. падéж** (gram.) instrumental case

твор|úть, ю, úшь *impf.* (*of* ▶ **сотворúть**) **1** (*создавать*) to create **2** (*делать*) to do; to make; **т. чудесá** to work wonders

творúться, úтся *impf.* (infml) to happen, go on

творóг, á and **твóрог, а** *m.* curd cheese

✦ **твóрческий** *adj.* creative; **т. путь Толстóго** Tolstoy's career as a writer

✦ **твóрчеств|о, а** *nt.* **1** creation; creative work **2** (*collect.*) works

✦ **т. е.** (*abbr. of* **то есть**) i.e., that is, viz.

✦ **теáтр, а** *m.* theatre (BrE), theater (AmE); **т. и кинó** stage and screen; **т. воéнных дéйствий** (mil.) theatre of operations

театрáл, а *m.* theatregoer (BrE), theatergoer (AmE)

театрá|льный, ~ен, ~ьна *adj.* **1** theatre (BrE), theater (AmE); theatrical; **~ьная кáсса** box office; **~ьная шкóла** drama school **2** (fig., *жест, поза*) theatrical

Тегерáн, а *m.* Teh(e)ran

тезáурус, а *m.* thesaurus

тéзис, а *m.* thesis, proposition

тёзк|а, и *c.g.* namesake

✦ **текст, а** *m.* **1** text **2** (*песни*) words, lyrics; (*оперы*) libretto

текстúльный *adj.* textile

текстúльщик, а *m.* textile worker

текстúльщи|ца, цы *f. of* ▶ **текстúльщик**

тéкстовый *adj. of* ▶ **текст**; **т. редáктор** (comput.) word processor

текýч|ий, ~, ~а *adj.* **1** (phys.) fluid **2** (*непостоянный*) fluctuating, unstable

✦ **текýщ|ий** *pres. part. act. of* ▶ **течь²** *and adj.* **1** current; of the present moment; **~ие событ́ия** current events, current affairs; **т. счёт** current account (BrE), checking account (AmE) **2** (*повседневный*) routine, ordinary; **т. ремóнт** routine repairs

тел. (*abbr. of* **телефóн**) tel., telephone

теле... *comb. form* tele-

телевещáни|е, я *nt.* television broadcasting

телевúдени|е, я *nt.* television, TV

телевизиóнный *adj.* television

телевúзор, а *m.* television set

телéг|а, и *f.* cart, wagon

телегрáмм|а, ы *f.* telegram

телегрáф, а *m.* **1** (*система*) telegraph **2** (*учреждение*) telegraph office

телеграфú|ровать, ую *impf. and pf.* to telegraph, wire

телеграфúст, а *m.* telegraphist

телеграфúст|ка, ки *f. of* ▶ **телеграфúст**

телегрáфн|ый *adj.* telegraph; telegraphic; **~ое агéнтство** news agency; **т. столб** telegraph pole (BrE), telephone pole (AmE)

телéжк|а, и *f.* **1** dim. of ▶ **телéга 2** (*багажная; в супермаркете*) trolley (BrE), cart (AmE)

телезрúтел|ь, я *m.* (television) viewer

телеигр|á, ы́ *f.* game show

телекáмер|а, ы *f.* television camera

телеканáл, а *m.* TV channel

телекоммуникáци|и, й *f. pl.* telecommunications

телекомпáни|я, и *f.* TV company

телеконферéнци|я, и *f.* teleconference, conference call

тéлекс, а *m.* telex

телеметри|я, и *f.* telemetry

телемóст, а and **~á, pl. ~ы́** *m.* satellite (TV) link-up

тел|ёнок, ёнка, pl. ~я́та, ~я́т *m.* calf

телеоперáтор, а *m.* TV cameraman

телепáт, а *m.* telepathic person

телепáти|я, и *f.* telepathy

телепередáч|а, и *f.* TV programme (BrE), program (AmE)

телескóп, а *m.* telescope

телескопúческий *adj.* telescopic

телéсн|ый *adj.* bodily; corporal; physical; **~ое наказáние** corporal punishment; **~ого цвéта** flesh-coloured (BrE), flesh-colored (AmE)

телестýди|я, и *f.* television studio

телесуфлёр, а *m.* teleprompter, Autocue®

телетéкст, а *m.* teletext

телефáкс, а *m.* (tele)fax (machine)

✦ **телефóн, а** *m.* **1** telephone; **позвонúть по ~у** (+ *d.*) to telephone, phone, ring up (BrE); **т.-автомáт** public telephone, call box (BrE)

✦ key word

2 (infml, *номер*) telephone number

телефони́ст, а *m.* telephone operator, telephonist

телефони́ст|ка, ки *f. of* ▶ **телефони́ст**

телефо́н|ный *adj. of* ▶ **телефо́н**; ∼ная кни́га telephone directory

Тел|е́ц, ьца́ *m.* Taurus

те́лик, а *m.* (infml) (the) telly (BrE), (the) TV

те́л|о, а, *pl.* ∼á, ∼, ∼áм *nt.* body

телогре́йк|а, и *f.* body warmer

телосложе́ни|е, я *nt.* build, frame

телохрани́тел|ь, я *m.* bodyguard

Тель-Ави́в, а *m.* Tel Aviv

теля́тин|а, ы *f.* veal

теля́ч|ий *adj. of* ▶ **телёнок**; ∼ья ко́жа calf(skin); (cul.) veal

тем 1 *i. sg. m. and nt., d. pl. of* ▶ **тот 2** *conj.* (so much) the; **чем вы́ше, т. лу́чше** the taller, the better; **т. лу́чше** so much the better; **т. бо́лее, что** especially as; **т. не ме́нее** nonetheless, nevertheless; **т. са́мым** thus, thereby

те́м|а, ы *f.* **1** subject, topic, theme; **перейти́ к друго́й** ∼е to change the subject **2** (mus.) theme

тема́тик|а, и *f.* (collect.) subject matter

тембр, а *m.* timbre

Те́мз|а, ы *f.* the Thames (*river*)

те́ми *i. pl. of* ▶ **тот**

темне́|ть, ю *impf.* **1** (*pf.* **по**∼) to grow *or* become dark; to darken **2** (*pf.* **с**∼): ∼ет (*impers.*) it gets dark; it is getting dark **3** (*impf. only*) (*виднеться*) to show up darkly

темн|и́ть, ю́, и́шь *impf.* (infml) to be deliberately obscure

темни́ц|а, ы *f.* dungeon

темно́ *as pred.* it is dark

тёмно-... *comb. form* dark (*with names of colours*); **тёмно-си́ний** dark blue, navy blue

темноволо́с|ый, ∼, ∼а *adj.* dark-haired

темноко́ж|ий, ∼, ∼а *adj.* dark-skinned, swarthy

темнот|а́, ы́ *f.* dark, darkness; **в** ∼é in the dark; **до** ∼ы́ before dark

тём|ный, ∼ен, темна́ *adj.* **1** dark; ∼ное пятно́ (fig., *что-л. позорящее*) dark stain, blemish **2** (*неясный*) obscure, vague; ∼ное пятно́ obscure place **3** (*мрачный*) gloomy, sombre (BrE), somber (AmE) **4** (*подозрительный*) shady, suspicious; ∼ное де́ло shady business **5** (*невежественный*) ignorant

темп, а *m.* **1** (mus.) tempo **2** (fig.) tempo; rate, speed, pace; **в** ∼е (infml) quickly

темпера́мент, а *m.* temperament

темпера́мент|ный, ∼ен, ∼на *adj.* energetic; spirited

температу́р|а, ы *f.* **1** temperature; **ме́рить кому́-н.** ∼у to take sb's temperature **2** (infml) (heightened) temperature; **у него́ т.** he's got a temperature

тём|я, ени (*no pl.*) *nt.* crown, top of the head

тенденцио́з|ный, ∼ен, ∼на *adj.* (pej.) tendentious, biased

тенде́нци|я, и *f.* (к + d.) tendency (to, towards)

те́ндер, а *m.* **1** (rail., *вагон*) tender **2** (naut., *корабль*) cutter **3** (comm.) tender, bid

тенев|о́й *adj.* shady (also fig.); ∼áя сторона́ shady side; (fig.) bad side, seamy side; ∼áя эконо́мика shadow economy

те́ннис, а *m.* tennis

тенниси́ст, а *m.* tennis player

тенниси́ст|ка, ки *f. of* ▶ **тенниси́ст**

те́нниск|а, и *f.* (infml) tennis shirt, polo shirt

те́ннис|ный *adj.* tennis; **т. корт**, ∼ая площа́дка tennis court

те́нор, а, *pl.* ∼á, ∼о́в *m.* (mus.) tenor

тент, а *m.* awning

тен|ь, и, в ∼и́, *pl.* ∼и, ∼е́й *f.* **1** (*тенистое место*) shade; **сиде́ть в** ∼и́ to sit in the shade; **держа́ться в** ∼и́ (fig.) to keep in the background **2** (*тёмное отражение*) shadow; **дава́ть т.** to cast a shadow **3** (*призрак*) shadow, ghost **4** (fig., *малейшая доля*) shadow, atom; **нет ни** ∼и сомне́ния there is not a shadow of doubt **5** (*подозрение*) suspicion; **бро́сить т. на кого́-н.** to cast suspicion on sb

теодоли́т, а *m.* (*инструмент*) theodolite

теокра́ти|я, и *f.* theocracy

теологи́ческий *adj.* theological

теоло́ги|я, и *f.* theology

теоре́м|а, ы *f.* theorem

теоре́тик, а *m.* theorist

теорети́ческий *adj.* theoretical

тео́ри|я, и *f.* theory

тепе́рь *adv.* now; nowadays, today

тепле́|ть, ет *impf.* (of ▶ **потепле́ть**) to get warm

тепли́ц|а, ы *f.* greenhouse, hothouse

тепло́¹ *adv.* **1** warmly **2** (*as pred.*) it is warm

тепл|о́², á *nt.* heat; warmth; **де́сять гра́дусов** ∼á ten degrees (Celsius) above zero

теплово́з, а *m.* diesel locomotive

теплов|о́й *adj.* heat; thermal; **т. уда́р** (med.) heat stroke; ∼áя эне́ргия thermal energy

теплот|а́, ы́ *f.* **1** (phys.) heat; **едини́ца** ∼ы́ thermal unit **2** warmth (also fig.); **душе́вная т.** warm-heartedness

теплохо́д, а *m.* motor ship

тёп|лый, ∼ел, тепла́ *adj.* **1** (*одежда, цвета*) warm; ∼лое месте́чко (infml) cushy job **2** (*дача*) warmed, heated **3** (*приём*) warm, cordial **4** (*слова*) heartfelt

терабáйт, а *m.* (comput.) terabyte

тера́кт, а *m.* act of terrorism, terrorist act

терапе́вт, а *m.* therapist

терапевти́ческий *adj.* therapeutic

терапи́|я, и *f.* therapy; **интенси́вная т.** intensive care

тереб|и́ть, лю́, и́шь *impf.* **1** (*дёргать*) to pull (at), tug (at) **2** (fig., infml, *вопросами*) to pester, bother

т

терéть, тру, трёшь, *past* тёр, тёрла *impf.* ◼1 (*глаза; грязное место*) to rub ◼2 (*сыр*) to grate ◼3 (*ногу, об обуви*) to rub, chafe

терéться, трусь, трёшься, *past* тёрся, тёрлась *impf.* to rub oneself; (о, об(о) + *a.*) to rub (against)

тёрк|а, и *f.* (cul.) grater

тéрмин, а *m.* term

термина́л, а *m.* terminal (*in var. senses*)

терминоло́ги|я, и *f.* terminology

терми́т, а *m.* (zool.) termite

термобель|ё, я́ *nt.* (collect.) thermal underwear

термо́метр, а *m.* thermometer

тéрмос, а *m.* Thermos (flask)®

термоста́т, а *m.* thermostat

терни́ст|ый, ~, ~а *adj.* (obs.) thorny, prickly; т. путь (fig.) difficult path

терно́вник, а *m.* (bot.) blackthorn

терпели́в|ый, ~, ~а *adj.* patient

терпéни|е, я *nt.* patience; вы́вести из ~я to exasperate

терпéть, лю́, ~ишь *impf.* ◼1 (*pf.* по~) (*испытывать*) to suffer, undergo; т. пораже́ние to suffer a defeat ◼2 (*стойко переносить*) to bear, endure, stand ◼3 (*запастись терпением*) to have patience ◼4 (*допускать*) to tolerate, suffer, put up (with); т. не могу́ I can't stand it; I hate it; дéло не ~ит отлага́тельства the matter won't wait

терпéться, ~ится *impf.* (impers.): ему́ и т. *п.* не ~ится (+ *inf.*) he is, *etc.*, impatient (to)

терпи́мост|ь, и *f.* tolerance; indulgence

терпи́м|ый, ~, ~а *adj.* ◼1 (*человек, характер*) tolerant; indulgent, forbearing ◼2 (*условия, боль, жара*) tolerable, bearable

тёрп|кий, ~ок, ~ка́, ~ко *adj.* (*вкус, запах*) astringent, sharp; (*яблоко, виноград*) tart, sharp; (*вино*) sharp, rough

террако́т|а, ы *f.* (*глина; изделие*) terracotta

терра́с|а, ы *f.* terrace

территориа́льный *adj.* territorial

террито́ри|я, и *f.* territory, confines; area

терро́р, а *m.* terror

терроризи́р|овать, ую *impf. and pf.* to terrorize

террори́зм, а *m.* terrorism

террори́ст, а *m.* terrorist

террористи́ческий *adj.* terrorist

террори́ст|ка, ки *f. of* ▸ террори́ст

терьéр, а *m.* terrier (*dog*)

теря́|ть, ю *impf.* (of ▸ потеря́ть) to lose; т. наде́жду to lose hope; т. си́лу to become invalid; т. вре́мя на что-н. to waste time on sth; т. в вéсе to lose weight; не т. из ви́ду/ви́да to keep in sight; нам нéчего т. we have nothing to lose

теря́|ться, юсь *impf.* (of ▸ потеря́ться) ◼1 to be lost; to get lost; (*исчезать*) to disappear

◼2 (*становиться слабее*) to fail, decline, weaken ◼3 (*лишаться самообладания*) to become flustered ◼4: т. в дога́дках to be lost in conjecture

те|са́ть, шу́, ~шешь *impf.* to cut, hew

тéсно *adv.* ◼1 closely (also fig.); tightly; narrowly; быть т. свя́занным (с + *i.*) to be closely linked (with) ◼2 (*as pred.*) it is crowded; it is (too) tight; в трамва́е бы́ло о́чень т. the tram was very crowded

тесно́т|а, ы́ *f.* ◼1 (*свойство*) crowded state; narrowness; tightness; closeness ◼2 (*недостаток места*) crush, squash; жить в ~é to live cooped up

тéс|ный, ~ен, ~на́, ~но, ~ны́ *adj.* ◼1 (*непросторный*) crowded, cramped; мир ~ен! it's a small world! ◼2 (*узкий*) narrow ◼3 (*пиджак*) (too) tight ◼4 (fig., *близкий*) close, tight; т. круг друзéй circle of friends

тест, а *m.* test

тести́р|овать, ую *impf. and pf.* to test

тéст|о, а *nt.* dough; pastry

тест|ь, я *m.* father-in-law (*wife's father*)

тесьм|а́, ы́ *f.* tape, ribbon

тéтерев, а, *pl.* ~а́, ~о́в *m.* (zool.) black grouse

тетив|а́, ы́ *f.* bowstring

тётк|а, и *f.* ◼1 aunt ◼2 (infml, pej., *о немолодой женщине*) woman

тетра́д|ь, и *f.* exercise book (BrE), notebook; т. для рисова́ния drawing book; sketchbook

тёт|я, и, *g. pl.* ~ей *f.* ◼1 aunt ◼2 (*знакомая немолодая женщина; в сочетании с именем собственным*) auntie ◼3 (infml, *женщина*) lady

тефтéл|и, ей *f. pl.* (*sg.* infml ~я, ~и) (cul.) meatballs

тех *g., a., p. pl. of* ▸ тот

тéхник, а *m.* technician

тéхник|а, и *f.* ◼1 technology; нау́ка и т. science and technology ◼2 (*приёмы исполнения*) technique, art ◼3 (collect.) (*машины*) machinery; technical devices

тéхникум, а *m.* technical college

техни́ческ|ий *adj.* technical; ~ие нау́ки engineering sciences; т. тéрмин technical term; ~ое обслу́живание maintenance

техно́лог, а *m.* technologist

технологи́ческий *adj.* technological

техноло́ги|я, и *f.* technology

течéни|е, я *nt.* ◼1 (*поток*) flow ◼2 (fig.) course; с ~ем врéмени in the course of time, in time ◼3 (*ток, струя*) current, stream (also fig.); по ~ю, про́тив ~я with the stream, against the stream (also fig.) ◼4 (fig., *направление*) trend, tendency ◼5: в т. (+ *g.*) during, in the course (of)

течь[1], и *f.* leak; дать т. to spring a leak; заде́лать т. to stop a leak

течь[2], течёт, теку́т, *past* тёк, текла́ *impf.* ◼1 to flow (also fig.); to stream; (fig., *о времени*) to pass; у тебя́ кровь течёт из но́са your nose is bleeding **2** (*имéть течь*) to leak, be leaky

тёщ|а, и *f.* mother-in-law (*wife's mother*)

Тибéт, а *m.* Tibet

тибéт|ец, ца *m.* Tibetan

тибéт|ка, ки *f. of* ▶ **тибéтец**

тибéтский *adj.* Tibetan

тигр, а *m.* tiger

тúкан|е, я *nt.* tick, ticking (*of a clock*)

тúка|ть, ет *impf.* to tick

тúн|а, ы (*no pl.*) *f.* slime; mire

тинéйджер, а *m.* teenager

⚘ **тип, а** *m.* **1** type; model **2** (infml, *человéк*) fellow, character; **стрáнный т.** odd character

типúч|ный, ~ен, ~на *adj.* typical

типогрáфи|я, и *f.* printing house, press

типогрáфск|ий *adj.* typographical; **~ое дéло** typography

тир, а *m.* shooting range; shooting gallery

тирáж, á *m.* **1** drawing (*of loan or lottery*); **вúйти в т.** to be drawn **2** (*колúчество экземпляров*) circulation; edition; print run

тирáн, а *m.* tyrant

тирани́|я, и *f.* tyranny

тирé *nt. indecl.* dash

тис, а *m.* yew (tree)

тúска|ть, ю *impf.* (*of* ▶ **тúснуть**) (infml) to press, squeeze

тиск|ú, óв (*no sg.*) (tech.) vice (BrE), vise (AmE); **в ~áх** (+ *g.*) in the grip (of)

тúснуть *pf. of* ▶ **тúскать**

титáн¹, а *m.* (myth., also fig.) titan

титáн², а *m.* (chem.) titanium

титанúческий *adj.* titanic

титр, а *m.* (*usu. in pl.*) (cin.) title, credit

тúтул, а *m.* title

тúтульный *adj. of* ▶ **тúтул; т. лист** title page

тиф, а *m.* typhus; **брюшнóй т.** typhoid (fever)

тúх|ий, ~, ~á, ~о *adj.* **1** quiet; (*звук*) low, soft; (*мягкий*) gentle; (*слáбый*) faint; **т. гóлос** low voice **2** (*бесшýмный*) silent, noiseless; still; **~ая ночь** still night **3** (fig., *спокóйный*) quiet, calm; gentle; still; **~ая жизнь** quiet life **4** (*мéдленный*) slow, slow-moving; **т. ход** slow speed, slow pace

Тúх|ий океáн, ~ого океáна *m.* the Pacific (Ocean)

тúхо¹ *adv.* **1** (*негрóмко*) quietly; softly, gently; **т. постучáть** to knock gently **2** (*бесшýмно*) silently, noiselessly **3** (fig., *спокóйно*) quietly, calmly; still; **сидéть т.** to sit still; **т.!** gently!, careful! **4** (*мéдленно*) slowly

тúхо² *as pred.* it is quiet, there is not a sound; **стáло т.** it became quiet

тихóнько *adv.* (infml) quietly; softly, gently

тихоокеáнский *adj.* Pacific

тúше 1 *comp. of* ▶ **тúхий,** ▶ **тúхо¹,** ▶ **тúхо² 2: т.!** (*молчáть!*) (be) quiet!, silence!; (*осторóжнее!*) gently!; careful!

тишин|á, ы́ *f.* quiet, silence; stillness; **нарýшить ~ý** to break the silence;

соблюдáть ~у to keep quiet

т. к. (*abbr. of* **так как**) as, since

ткáный *adj.* woven

⚘ **ткан|ь, и** *f.* **1** fabric, cloth; **льняны́е ~и** linen(s); **шёлковые ~и** silks **2** (anat.) tissue

ткать, тку, ткёшь, *past* **ткал, ткалá, ткáло** *impf.* (*of* ▶ **соткáть**) to weave; **т. паутúну** to spin a web

ткáцкий *adj.* weaver's, weaving; **т. станóк** loom

ткач, á *m.* weaver

ткачú́х|а, и *f. of* ▶ **ткач**

ткн|ýть, ý, ёшь *pf. of* ▶ **тúкать**

тле|ть, ет *impf.* **1** (*гнить*) to rot, decay, decompose **2** (*горéть*) to smoulder (BrE), smolder (AmE) (also fig.)

тл|я, и, *g. pl.* **~ей** *f.* aphid

тмин, а *m.* caraway

то¹ *pron.* (*nom. and a. sg. nt. of* ▶ **тот**) that; **то, что...** the fact that ...; **тó есть** that is (to say); **а то** *see* ▶ **а¹; (да)** and that, at that

⚘ **то²** *conj.* **1** (*in main clause of conditional sentence*) then (*or not translated*) **2: то..., то...** now ..., now ...; **то тут, то там** now here, now there **3: не то..., не то...** either ... or ...; whether ... or ...; half ..., half ...; **не то по глýпости, не то по злóбе** either through stupidity or through malice **4: не то, чтóбы..., но...** it is not, it was not that ... (but) ...

-то¹ *emphatic particle* (in infml Russian often merely adds familiar tone) just, precisely, exactly (*or not translated*); **в тóм-то и дéло** that's just it; **вáм-то чегó боя́ться?** what have *you* to be afraid of?

-то² *particle* (*forming indefinite prons. and advs.*): **ктó-то, какóй-то, когдá-то,** *etc.*

тобóй *i. of* ▶ **ты**

⚘ **товáр, а** *m.* (*collect. or in pl.*) goods; wares; (*sg.*) article; product, commodity; **~ы широ́кого потреблéния** consumer goods

товáрищ, а *m.* **1** comrade; (*друг*) friend; (*коллéга*) colleague; **т. по несчáстью** fellow sufferer, companion in distress; **т. по рабóте** colleague; workmate; **т. по шкóле** school friend **2** (*официáльное обращéние к граждани́ну*) comrade

товáрищеск|ий *adj.* **1** comradely; friendly **2** (sport) friendly, unofficial; **~ое состязáние, ~ая встрéча** friendly (match) (BrE)

товáр|ный *adj.* **1** goods (BrE), freight; **т. знак** trademark; **т. склад** warehouse **2** (rail.) goods (BrE), freight; **т. состáв** goods train (BrE), freight train **3** (econ.) (*цéны, продýкция*) commodity; (*вид*) marketable

⚘ **тогдá 1** *adv.* **1** (*в то врéмя*) then, at that time; (*в такóм слýчае*) in that case **2: когдá..., т. ...** *conj.* when; **когдá решýсь, т. напишý тебé** I will write to you when I have decided **3: т. как** *conj.* whereas, while

тогдáшний *adj.* (infml) of that time; the then

тогó *g. sg. m. and nt. of* ▶ **тот**

тождéствен|ный, ~, ~на *adj.* identical

то́же *adv.* also, as well, too

ток, а *m.* (elec.) current

тока́рный *adj.* (tech.) turning; **т. стано́к** lathe

то́кар|ь, я *m.* turner, lathe operator

То́кио *m. indecl.* Tokyo

токсикома́н, а *m.* glue-sniffer, solvent abuser

токсикома́ни|я, и *f.* glue-sniffing, solvent abuse

токси́н, а *m.* (med.) toxin

токси́ческий *adj.* toxic

ток-шо́у *nt. indecl.* talk show

толера́нтност|ь, и *f.* tolerance

толк, а (у) *m.* **1** (*смысл*) sense; understanding; **бе́з ~у** senselessly **2** (infml, *польза*) use, profit; **знать т. (в + *p*.)** to know what one is talking about (in)

толк|а́ть, а́ю *impf.* (*of* ▸ **толкну́ть**) **1** to push, shove; (*нечаянно*) to jog; **т. ло́ктем** to nudge **2** (sport): **т. шта́нгу** to lift weights **3** (**на** + *a*.) (*побуждать*) to push (into), incite (to)

толк|а́ться, а́юсь *impf. only* (*толкать друг друга*) to push (one another)

толк|ну́ть, ну́, нёшь *pf. of* ▸ **толка́ть**

толкова́ни|е, я *nt.* interpretation

толк|ова́ть, у́ю *impf.* to interpret; **оши́бочно, неве́рно т. чьи-н. слова́** to misinterpret, misconstrue sb's words

толко́в|ый, ~, ~а *adj.* **1** (*человек*) intelligent, sensible **2** (*объяснение*) intelligible, clear **3**: **т. слова́рь** defining dictionary

то́лком *adv.* (infml) plainly, clearly

толп|а́, ы́, *pl.* **~ы** *f.* crowd; throng; multitude

толп|и́ться, и́тся *impf.* to crowd; to throng

толсте́|ть, ю *impf.* (*of* ▸ **потолсте́ть**) to grow fat; to put on weight

толсто́вк|а, и *f.* (infml) sweatshirt

толстоко́ж|ий, ~, ~а *adj.* thick-skinned (also fig.)

то́лст|ый, ~, ~а́, ~о, ~ы́ *adj.* **1** (*человек*) fat **2** (*книга, бумага, слой*) thick

толстя́к, а́ *m.* (*мужчина*) fat man; (*мальчик*) fat boy

толч|о́к, ка́ *m.* **1** (*толкающий удар*) push, shove **2** (*при езде*) jolt, bump; (*при землетрясении*) (earthquake) shock, tremor **3** (fig., *побуждение*) push, shove; stimulus; **дать т. эконо́мике** to kick-start the economy

то́лщ|а, и *f.* thickness; **т. сне́га** depth of snow

то́лще *comp. of* ▸ **то́лстый**

толщин|а́, ы́ *f.* **1** (*человека*) fatness, corpulence **2** (*бревна, слоя*) thickness

то́лько 1 (*adv.*) only; solely; alone; just; **не т. ..., но и** not only ..., but also; **поду́май(те) т.!** just think!; **т. и всего́, да и т.** (infml) that's all **2**: **т. что** (*adv. and conj.*) just, only just; **он т. что позвони́л** he has just rung up **3** (*conj.*): **(+ как, лишь)** as soon

as; one has only to ... **4** (*conj.*) only, but; **с удово́льствием, т. не сего́дня** with pleasure, only not today **5**: **т. бы** (+ *inf.*) (*particle*) if only

том, а, *pl.* **~а́, ~о́в** *m.* volume

тома́т, а *m.* tomato

тома́тный *adj.* tomato; **т. сок** tomato juice

томи́тел|ьный, ~ен, ~ьна *adj.* (*скучный*) tedious; wearing; (*утомительный*) tiring, exhausting; (*гнетущий*) oppressive; (*мучительный*) agonizing, painful

том|и́ться, лю́сь, и́шься *impf.* (*голодом, ожиданием*) to be tormented (by); **т. в тюрьме́** to languish in prison

то́м|ный, ~ен, ~на́, ~но *adj.* languid, languorous

томогра́фи|я, и *f.* tomography, CT scanning

тон, а, *pl.* **~ы́** *and* **~а́ м. 1** (*pl.* **~ы́**) (mus., also fig.) tone; **~ом вы́ше, ни́же** a tone higher, lower; **хоро́ший, дурно́й т.** good, bad form **2** (*pl.* **~а́**) (*краски, цвета*) tone, tint

тона́льност|ь, и *f.* (mus.) key

то́нер, а *m.* toner

тонзилли́т, а *m.* tonsillitis

то́ник, а *m.* tonic (water)

то́н|кий, ~ок, ~ка́, ~ко, ~кий *adj.* **1** (*слой*) thin; (*фигура*) slim; **т. ло́мтик** thin slice **2** (*изысканный*) fine; delicate; refined; **~кое бельё** fine linen; (*не грубый*) subtle, fine; **~кое разли́чие** subtle, fine distinction **3** (*звук*) high, squeaky **4** (fig., *проницательный*) shrewd, subtle, penetrating; **т. знато́к** connoisseur **5** (*зрение, слух*) keen

то́нко *adv.* **1** (*резать*) thinly **2** (*чувствовать*) subtly, delicately, finely

то́нкост|ь, и *f.* **1** thinness; (*фигуры*) slimness **2** (*ткани, работы*) fineness **3** (*ума*) subtlety **4** (*мелкая подробность*) nice point, subtle point; **до ~ей** to a nicety

то́нн|а, ы *f.* metric ton, tonne

тонне́л|ь, я *m.* tunnel; (*пешеходный*) subway

то́нус, а *m.* (physiol., med.) tone; **жи́зненный т.** vitality

тон|у́ть, у́, ~ешь *impf.* **1** (*pf.* **за~**) (*о судне*) to sink, go down **2** (*pf.* **у~**) (*о человеке*) to drown **3** (*pf.* **у~**) (**в** + *p*.) to sink (in); to be lost (in); to be hidden (in, by); **т. в дела́х** to be up to one's eyes in work

то́ньше *comp. of* ▸ **то́нкий** *and* ▸ **то́нко**

топ, а *m.* *одежда* crop top

то́п|ать, аю *impf.* (*of* ▸ **то́пнуть**) to stamp; **т. нога́ми** to stamp one's feet

топ|и́ть¹, лю́, ~ишь *impf.* **1** (*камин*) to stoke (*a boiler, stove, etc.*) **2** (*помещение*) to heat

топ|и́ть², лю́, ~ишь *impf.* **1** (*воск*) to melt (down), render **2**: **т. молоко́** to bake milk

топ|и́ть³, лю́, ~ишь *impf.* **1** (*pf.* **по~**) (*корабль*) to sink **2** (*pf.* **у~**) (*человека*) to drown; (fig., infml) to wreck, ruin

топ|и́ться¹, ~ится *impf.* (*о камине*) to burn, be alight

т

топ|и́ться², **~ится** *impf.* **1** (*о воске*) to melt **2** *pass of* ▸ **топи́ть²**

топ|и́ться³, **люсь**, **~ишься** *impf.* (*of* ▸ **утопи́ться**) (*о человеке*) to drown oneself

то́пк|а, **и** *f.* **1** (*камина*) stoking **2** (*помещения*) heating **3** (*часть печи*) furnace; (*rail.*) firebox

✍ **то́плив|о**, **а** *nt.* fuel; **жи́дкое т.** fuel oil; **твёрдое т.** solid fuel

топ-моде́л|ь, **и** *f.* top model

то́п|нуть, **ну**, **нешь** *pf. of* ▸ **то́пать**

топографи́ческий *adj.* topographical

то́пол|ь, **я**, *pl.* **~я́** *m.* poplar

топо́р, **а́** *m.* axe (BrE), ax (AmE)

топо́рщ|иться, **ится** *impf.* (*infml*) **1** (*о волосах*) to stand on end, bristle **2** (*о еже*) to bristle; (*о птице*) to puff up its feathers **3** (*об одежде*) to stick out, pucker

то́пот, **а** *m.* tramp; **ко́нский т.** clatter of horses' hoofs

топ|та́ть, **чу́**, **~чешь** *impf.* **1** (*траву*) to trample (down) **2** (*пол*) to make dirty (*with one's feet*)

топ|та́ться, **чу́сь**, **~чешься** *impf.* to shift from one foot to the other; **т. на ме́сте** to mark time (also *fig.*)

топча́н, **а́** *m.* trestle bed

топ|ь, **и** *f.* bog, marsh, swamp

То́р|а, **ы** *f.* (*relig.*) Torah

торг, **а**, **о ~е**, **на ~у́**, *pl.* **~и́** *m.* **1** (*действие*) trading **2** (*in pl.*) (*аукцион*) auction; **прода́ть с ~о́в** to sell by auction

торг|ова́ть, **у́ю** *impf.* (+ *i.*) to trade (in), deal (in), sell

торг|ова́ться, **у́юсь** *impf.* **1** (*pf.* **с~**) (*c* + *i.*) to bargain (with), haggle (with) **2** (*infml, спорить*) to argue

торго́в|ец, **ца** *m.* merchant; dealer; tradesman; **т. нарко́тиками** drug trafficker/pusher

торго́вк|а, **и** *f.* (*infml*) (female) stallholder; (woman) street trader

✍ **торго́вл|я**, **и** *f.* trade, commerce

✍ **торго́в|ый** *adj.* trade, commercial; **т. дом** firm; **~ая то́чка** shop

тореадо́р, **а** *m.* toreador

тор|е́ц, **ца́** *m.* butt end, short side, face; (*здания*) gable end

торже́ствен|ный, **~**, **~на** *adj.* **1** ceremonial; (*праздничный*) festive; gala; **т. день** red-letter day **2** (*серьёзный*) solemn

торжеств|о́, **а́** *nt.* **1** celebration; (*in pl.*) (*празднество*) festivities, rejoicings **2** (*победа*) triumph (= *victory*) **3** (*радость*) triumph, exultation

торжеств|ова́ть, **у́ю** *impf.* **1** to celebrate; (*fig.*, *радоваться*) to rejoice **2** (*над* + *i.*) to triumph (over); to exult (over)

то́ри *m. indecl.* (*pol.*) Tory

то́рмоз, **а** *m.* (*pl.* **~а́**) brake

тормо|зи́ть, **жу́**, **зи́шь** *impf.* (*of* ▸ **затормози́ть**) **1** (*tech.*) to brake, apply the brake (to) **2** (*fig.*, *замедлить*) to hamper, impede **3** (*psych.*) to inhibit

тормош|и́ть, **у́**, **и́шь** *impf.* (*infml*) **1** (*дёргать*) to pull (at), tug (at) **2** (*fig.*, *вопросами*) to pester, plague

тороп|и́ть, **лю́**, **~ишь** *impf.* (*of* ▸ **поторопи́ть**) **1** to hurry, hasten; to press; **меня́ ~ят с оконча́нием рабо́ты** I am being pressed to finish my work **2** (*события*) to precipitate

тороп|и́ться, **лю́сь**, **~ишься** *impf.* (*of* ▸ **поторопи́ться**) to hurry, be in a hurry, hasten

торопли́в|ый, **~**, **~а** *adj.* hurried, hasty

торо́с, **а** *m.* ice hummock

торпе́д|а, **ы** *f.* torpedo

торс, **а** *m.* trunk; torso

торт, **а** *m.* cake

торф, **а** *m.* peat

торч|а́ть, **у́**, **и́шь** *impf.* **1** (*вверх*) to stick up; (*в сторону*) to stick out; (*о волосах*) to stand on end **2** (*infml*) (*в каком-л. месте*) to hang about **3** (*sl.*) (*получать удовольствие*) to feel euphoric (from), get a kick (out of); (*от наркотиков*) to get high (on)

торше́р, **а** *m.* standard lamp

тоск|а́, **и́** *f.* **1** (*уныние*) melancholy; (*тревога*) anguish **2** (*скука*) boredom, ennui; **одна́ т.**, **сплошна́я т.** a frightful bore **3** (*no* + *d.*) longing (for); yearning (for), nostalgia (for); **т. по ро́дине** homesickness

тоскли́в|ый, **~**, **~а** *adj.* **1** (*настроение*) melancholy; depressed, miserable **2** (*погода*, *город*) dull, dreary, depressing

тоск|ова́ть, **у́ю** *impf.* **1** to be melancholy, be depressed, be miserable **2** (*no* + *d.*) to long (for), yearn (for), pine (for), miss

тост¹, **а** *m.* toast; **провозгласи́ть**, **предложи́ть т.** (**за** + *a.*) to toast, drink (to); to propose a toast (to)

тост², **а** *m.* (*ломтик хлеба*) piece of toast

то́стер, **а** *m.* toaster

✍ **тот**, **та**, **то**, **те** *pron.* **1** (*opp.* **э́тот**) that; (*in pl.*) those; **в то вре́мя** then, at that time, in those days **2** (*opp.* **э́тот**) the former; *replacing 3rd pers. sg. pron.* he; she; it **3** (*opp.* **э́тот**) (*другой*) the other; the opposite; **на той стороне́** on the other side **4** (*opp.* **друго́й**, **ино́й**) the one; **и тот**, **и друго́й** both; **ни тот**, **ни друго́й** neither **5**: **тот...**, **(кото́рый)** the ... (which); **тот**, **(кто)** the one (who), the person (who); **тот факт**, **что** the fact that; *see also* ▸ **то¹** **6**: **тот (же)**, **тот (же) са́мый** the same; **одно́ и то же** one and the same thing; the same thing over again; **в то же са́мое вре́мя** at the same time, on the other hand **7** (*такой*, *какой ну́жен*) the right; **не тот** the wrong; **э́то не та дверь** that's the wrong door **8** (+ *preps.*) *forms the following conjs.*): **для того́**, **что́бы** in order that, in order to; **ме́жду тем**, **как** whereas; **несмотря́ на то**, **что** in spite of the fact that; **пе́ред тем**, **как** before; **по́сле того́**, **как** after; **с тем**, **что́бы** in order to, with a view to **9** (*forms part of var. adv. phrr. and*

particles) *see also* ▶ **то¹**; **вме́сте с тем** at
the same time; **к тому́ же** moreover; **кро́ме
того́** besides; **ме́жду тем, тем вре́менем**
meanwhile; **тем са́мым** hereby; **тому́ наза́д**
ago

тотализа́тор, а *m.* tote, totalizator

тоталита́рный *adj.* (pol.) totalitarian

то́тчас *adv.* at once; immediately (*also of
spatial relations*)

точёный *adj.* finely moulded (BrE), finely
molded (AmE); (*о чертах лица́*) chiselled
(BrE), chiseled (AmE)

точи́лк|а, и *f.* (infml) (*для ноже́й*) steel,
knife sharpener; (*для карандаше́й*) pencil
sharpener

точи́|ть, у́, ∼ишь *impf.* 1 (*pf.* на∼) (*нож,
каранда́ш*) to sharpen; **т. зу́бы на кого́-н.**
to have a grudge against sb 2 (*impf. only*)
(*на тока́рном станке́*) to turn

то́чк|а, и *f.* 1 spot, dot; **ста́вить ∼и над «и»**
to dot one's i's (and cross one's t's) 2 (gram.)
full stop; **т. с запято́й** semicolon 3 (math.,
phys., tech.) point; **т. замерза́ния, кипе́ния**
freezing, boiling point; **т. опо́ры** fulcrum,
point of support; (fig.) rallying point 4 (fig.)
point; **т. зре́ния** point of view; **горя́чая т.**
trouble spot

то́чно¹ *adv.* 1 exactly, precisely; (*пунктуа́льно*)
punctually 2 **т. так** just so, exactly, precisely;
т. тако́й (же) just the same 3 (*действи́тельно*)
indeed

то́чно² *conj.* as though, as if; like

то́чност|ь, и *f.* exactness; precision; accuracy;
punctuality; **в ∼и** exactly, precisely

то́ч|ный, ∼ен, ∼на́, ∼но, ∼ны *adj.* exact,
precise; accurate; (*пунктуа́льный*) punctual;
∼ные нау́ки exact sciences; **т. перево́д**
accurate translation; **т. прибо́р** precision
instrument

тошн|и́ть, и́т *impf.* (impers.): **меня́**, *etc.*, **∼и́т**
I feel, *etc.*, sick; **меня́ от э́того ∼и́т** (fig.) it
makes me sick, it sickens me

тошнот|а́, ы́ *f.* sickness, nausea (also fig.)

тошнотво́р|ный, ∼ен, ∼на *adj.* sickening,
nauseating (also fig.)

то́щ|ий, ∼, ∼а́, ∼е *adj.* gaunt, emaciated;
skinny

трав|а́, ы́, *pl.* **∼ы** *f.* grass; (*специя,
лека́рственная*) herb; **со́рная т.** weed

трави́нк|а, и *f.* blade of grass

трав|и́ть, лю́, ∼ишь *impf.* (*of* ▶ **вы́травить**)
(*тарака́нов, крыс*) to exterminate, destroy
(*by poisoning*)

тра́вл|я, и *f.* hunting; (fig.) persecution,
tormenting

тра́вм|а, ы *f.* (med.) (*психи́ческая*) trauma;
(*физи́ческая*) injury

травмати́ческий *adj.* (med., psych.) traumatic

травматологи́ческ|ий *adj.*: **∼ое отделе́ние**
casualty department; **т. пункт** first-aid room

травоя́дный *adj.* herbivorous

травян|о́й *adj.* 1 grass; herbaceous; **т. покро́в**
grass 2 **∼а́я насто́йка** herb tea

траге́ди|я, и *f.* tragedy

траги́ческ|ий *adj.* tragic; **т. актёр** tragic
actor; **∼ое зре́лище** tragic sight

традицио́н|ный, ∼ен, ∼на *adj.* traditional

тради́ци|я, и *f.* tradition

траекто́ри|я, и *f.* trajectory

тракта́т, а *m.* (*сочине́ние*) treatise

тракт|ова́ть, у́ю *impf.* 1 (*вопро́с*) to treat,
discuss 2 (*роль*) to interpret (*a part in a
play, etc.*)

тракто́вк|а, и *f.* treatment; interpretation

тра́ктор, а *m.* tractor; **гу́сеничный т., т. на
гу́сеничном ходу́** caterpillar tractor

тракторри́ст, а *m.* tractor driver

тракторри́ст|ка, ки *f. of* ▶ **тракторри́ст**

трамб|ова́ть, у́ю *impf.* to ram, tamp

трамва́|й, я *m.* tram (BrE), streetcar (AmE);
речно́й т. river bus

трампли́н, а *m.* (sport, *also* fig.) springboard;
(*лы́жный*) ski jump

транзи́стор, а *m.* transistor

транзи́т, а *m.* transit

транзи́т|ный *adj. of* ▶ **транзи́т**; **∼ная ви́за**
transit visa

транквилиза́тор, а *m.* tranquillizer (BrE),
tranquilizer (AmE)

транс, а *m.* trance

трансатланти́ческий *adj.* transatlantic

транскри́пци|я, и *f.* transcription

трансли́р|овать, ую *impf. and pf.* to
broadcast; to relay

транслитера́ци|я, и *f.* transliteration

трансля́ци|я, и *f.* (*де́йствие*) transmission,
broadcasting; (*переда́ча*) broadcast

трансми́сси|я, и *f.* (tech.) transmission

транснациона́льный *adj.* transnational

транспара́нт, а *m.* banner

транспланта́ци|я, и *f.* (med.) transplantation

тра́нспорт, а *m.* 1 (*систе́ма перево́зки*)
transport; **обще́ственный т.** public transport
2 (*перево́зка*) transportation, conveyance
3 (mil.) train, transport 4 (naut.) supply ship;
troopship

транспорти́р|овать, ую *impf. and pf.* to
transport

транспортиро́вк|а, и *f.* transport,
transportation

тра́нспортный *adj. of* ▶ **тра́нспорт**

транссексуа́л, а *m.* transsexual

транссиби́рск|ий *adj.* Trans-Siberian; **Т∼ая
магистра́ль** the Trans-Siberian Railway

трансформа́тор, а *m.* (elec.) transformer

трансформа́ци|я, и *f.* transformation

трансформи́р|овать, ую *impf. and pf.* to
transform

транше́|я, и *f.* (mil.) trench

трап, а *m.* (naut., aeron.) gangway

тра́пез|а, ы *f.* 1 (*о́бщий стол*) dining table
(*esp. in a monastery*) 2 (*еда́*) meal; **дели́ть**

~у (c + i.) to share a meal (with)

трапе́ци|я, и f. **1** (math.) trapezium **2** (*цирковая*) trapeze

тра́сс|а, ы f. **1** (*трубопровода, метро*) route, course; **2** (*дорога*) main road, highway (AmE)

тра́т|а, ы f. expenditure; **пуста́я т. вре́мени** waste of time

тра́|тить, чу, тишь impf. (*of* ▶ **истра́тить,** ▶ **потра́тить**) to spend, expend, use up; (*понапрасну*) to waste

тра́улер, а m. trawler

тра́ур, а m. mourning

тра́урн|ый adj. **1** mourning; funeral; **т. марш** funeral march; **~ое ше́ствие** funeral procession **2** (*скорбный*) mournful, sorrowful; funereal

трафаре́т, а m. stencil

тра́фик, а (comput.) m. traffic

тра́х|ать, аю impf. of ▶ **тра́хнуть**

тра́х|аться, аюсь impf. of ▶ **тра́хнуться**

тра́х|нуть, ну, нешь pf. (*of* ▶ **тра́хать**) **1** (infml, *стукнуть*) to bang, crash **2** (vulg., *совершить половой акт*) to screw, hump

тра́х|нуться, нусь, нешься pf. (*of* ▶ **тра́хаться**) **1** (infml, *стукнуться*) to bang, crash **2** (vulg., *совершить половой акт*) to screw, hump

⚘ **тре́бовани|е, я** nt. **1** (*действие*) demand, request; **по ~ю** on demand, by request; **остано́вка по ~ю** request stop **2** (*настоятельная просьба*) demand; (*притязание*) claim; **согласи́ться на чьи-н. ~я** to agree to sb's demands; **вы́двинуть т.** to put in a claim **3** (*usu. in pl.*) (*условие*) requirement, condition; **отвеча́ть, соотве́тствовать ~ям** to meet requirements **4** (*in pl.*) (*запросы*) aspirations; needs

тре́бовател|ьный, ~ен, ~ьна adj. demanding

⚘ **тре́б|овать, ую** impf. (*of* ▶ **потре́бовать**) **1** (+ g. *or* чтобы) to demand, require; **они́ ~уют, чтобы мы извини́лись** they demand that we apologize **2** (impf. only) (+ g. and от + g.) to expect (from), ask (of); **вы ~уете сли́шком мно́го от ва́ших ученико́в** you expect too much from your pupils **3** (+ g.) (*нуждаться*) to require, need, call (for)

⚘ **тре́б|оваться, уется** impf. (*of* ▶ **потре́боваться**) to be needed, be required; **на э́то ~уется мно́го вре́мени** it takes a lot of time; **фи́рме ~уется бухга́лтер** the company seeks an accountant

требух|а́, и́ (*no pl.*) f. entrails; (cul.) offal, tripe

трево́г|а, и f. **1** (*беспокойство*) alarm, anxiety **2** (*сигнал*) alarm; **бить ~у** to sound the alarm (also fig.); **подня́ть ~у** to raise the alarm

трево́ж|ить, у, ишь impf. (*of* ▶ **потрево́жить**) (*мешать*) to disturb, interrupt

трево́ж|иться, усь, ишься impf. (*of* ▶ **потрево́житься**) to trouble oneself,

put oneself out; **не ~ьтесь!** don't bother (yourself)!

трево́ж|ный, ~ен, ~на adj. **1** (*полный трево́ги*) anxious, uneasy, troubled **2** (*вызывающий тревогу*) alarming, disturbing

трезве́|ть, ю impf. (*of* ▶ **протрезве́ть**) to sober (up), become sober

тре́звост|ь, и f. **1** sobriety (also fig.); **т. ума́** cool-headedness **2** (*воздержание от спиртного*) abstinence; temperance

трезв|ый, ~, ~а́, ~о, ~ы́ adj. **1** sober (also fig.) **2** (*не пьющий*) teetotal, abstinent

трезу́б|ец, ца m. trident

тре́йдер, а m. trader (*in stocks and shares*)

тре́йлер, а m. (*передвижной дом-прицеп*) caravan (BrE), trailer (AmE)

трек, а m. (sport) track

трелья́ж, а m. **1** (*зеркало*) three-leaved mirror **2** (*для растений*) trellis

тренажёр, а m. training apparatus; **лётный т.** flight simulator; (sport) piece of gym equipment

тренажёрный adj.: **т. зал** gym

⚘ **тре́нер, а** m. (sport) trainer, coach

тре́ни|е, я nt. **1** friction, rubbing **2** (*in pl.*) (fig.) friction

тре́нинг, а m. training

трениро́в|ать, у́ю impf. to train, coach; (*память*) to train

трениро́в|аться, у́юсь impf. to train oneself, coach oneself; to be in training

трениро́вк|а, и f. training, coaching

трено́г|а, и f. tripod

тре́нька|ть, ю impf. (infml, *на гитаре*) to strum

трепа́|ть, лю́, ~лешь impf. (*of* ▶ **потрепа́ть**) **1** to pull about; (*о ветре*) to blow about; **т. языко́м** (infml) to prattle; **т. чьи-н. не́рвы** to get on sb's nerves **2** (*одежду*) to wear out **3** (*по плечу*) to pat

трепа́|ться, лю́сь, ~лешься impf. **1** (pf. **по~**) (*об одежде*) to wear out **2** (impf. only) (*о флагах*) to flutter; (*о волосах*) to blow about **3** (pf. **по~**) (infml) to prattle

тре́пет, а m. (*дрожь*) trembling, quivering; (*сердца*) palpitation; (*страх*) trepidation, terror; (*волнение*) agitation; (*уважительность*) awe

трепе|та́ть, щу́, ~щешь impf. **1** (*дрожать*) to tremble, quiver **2** (fig., *испытывать волнение*) to tremble; to thrill; **т. от восто́рга** to thrill with joy; **т. при мы́сли** (о + p.) to tremble at the thought (of) **3** (*перед* + i.) (fig., *испытывать страх*) to tremble (before)

треск, а m. crack; crackle, crackling; **т. огня́** crackling of a fire; **с ~ом провали́ться** (fig., infml) to be a flop

треск|а́, и́ f. cod

треска́|ться, ется impf. (*of* ▶ **потреска́ться**) to crack, to chap

тре́сн|уть, у, ешь pf. **1** (*о ветке*) to snap **2** (*о стакане, коже*) to crack; (*лопнуть*)

т

to burst **3** (+ *i. or a. and* по + *d.*) (*infml*) to bring down with a crash (on); to hit, bang

трест, а *m.* (*econ.*) trust; *строи́тельный* company

🗝 **тре́т|ий, ья, ье** *adj.* **1** third; **т. но́мер** number three; **полови́на** ∼**ьего** half past two; **стра́ны** ∼**ьего ми́ра** Third World countries **2** (*as nt. n.* ∼**ье,** ∼**ьего**) sweet, dessert

трет|ь, и, *pl.* ∼**и,** ∼**е́й** *f.* third

третьесо́ртный *adj.* third-rate

треуго́льник, а *m.* triangle

треф|ы, ∼ *f. pl.* (*sg.* ∼**а,** ∼**ы**) (cards) clubs; **да́ма** ∼ queen of clubs

трёх... *comb. form* three-, tri-

трёхзна́чный *adj.* three-digit

трёхколёсный *adj.* three-wheeled; **т. велосипе́д** tricycle

трёхле́тний *adj.* **1** (*срок*) three-year **2** (*ребёнок*) three-year-old

трёхме́рный *adj.* three-dimensional

трёхме́стный *adj.* three-seater

трёхсо́тый *adj.* three-hundredth

трёхцве́тный *adj.* three-coloured (BrE), three-colored (AmE); tricolour(ed) (BrE), tricolor(ed) (AmE)

трёхчасово́й *adj.* **1** (*экза́мен*) three-hour **2** (*по́езд*) three o'clock

трёхэта́жный *adj.* three-storey (BrE), three-story (AmE)

трещ|а́ть, у́, и́шь *impf.* **1** (*о льде́*) to crack; **у меня́ голова́** ∼**и́т** I have a splitting headache; **т. по всем швам** (fig.) to go to pieces **2** (*о дрова́х*) to crackle; (*о ме́бели*) to creak; (*о кузне́чиках*) to chirr

тре́щин|а, ы *f.* crack, split (also fig.); **дать** ∼**у** to crack, split; (fig.) to show signs of cracking

🗝 **три, трёх, трём, тремя́, о трёх** *num.* three

трибу́н|а, ы *f.* **1** platform, rostrum **2** (*на стадио́нах*) stand

трибуна́л, а *m.* tribunal

тривиа́л|ьный, ∼**ен,** ∼**ьна** *adj.* trivial, banal; (*по́шлый*) trite

тригономе́три|я, и *f.* trigonometry

тридца́т|ый *adj.* thirtieth; ∼**ые го́ды** the thirties

три́дцат|ь, и, *i.* ∼**ью** *num.* thirty

три́жды *adv.* three times, thrice

трико́ *nt. indecl.* (*колго́тки*) tights; (*костю́м*) leotard

трикота́ж, а *m.* **1** (*из ше́рсти*) jersey; (*из хло́пка*) cotton jersey **2** (*collect.*) (*изде́лия*) knitwear

трикота́жн|ый *adj.* (*шерстяно́й*) jersey; (*из хло́пка*) knitted; ∼**ые изде́лия** knitwear

три́ллер, а *m.* thriller

триллио́н, а *m.* (10^{12}) trillion

трило́ги|я, и *f.* trilogy

трина́дцатый *adj.* thirteenth

трина́дцат|ь, и *num.* thirteen

три́о *nt. indecl.* (*mus.*) trio

три́ста, трёхсо́т, трёмста́м, тремяста́ми, трёхста́х *num.* three hundred

триу́мф, а *m.* triumph; **с** ∼**ом** triumphantly, in triumph

триумфа́льн|ый *adj.* triumphal; ∼**ая а́рка** triumphal arch

тро́гател|ьный, ∼**ен,** ∼**ьна** *adj.* touching; moving, affecting

тро́га|ть, ю *impf.* (*of* ▶ **тро́нуть**) **1** (*прикаса́ться*) to touch **2** (*беспоко́ить*) to disturb, trouble; **не** ∼**й его́!** don't disturb him!; leave him alone! **3** (*волнова́ть*) to touch, move, affect; **т. до слёз** to move to tears

тро́га|ться¹, юсь *impf.* (*of* ▶ **тро́нуться¹ 1**) to be touched, be moved, be affected

тро́га|ться², юсь *impf. of* ▶ **тро́нуться²**

тро́е, трои́х *num.* (*collect.*) three; **т. су́ток** seventy-two hours, three days and three nights; **т. друзе́й** three friends

троебо́рь|е, я *nt.* triathlon

троекра́тный *adj.* threefold, treble; (*вы́зов*) thrice-repeated; (*чемпио́н*) three-times; (*штраф*) trebled

тро́ечник, а *m.* mediocre student

Тро́иц|а, ы *f.* (*relig.*) Trinity; (*пра́здник*) Whitsun

Тро́ицын *adj.*: **Т. день** Whit Sunday

тро́йк|а, и *f.* **1** (*ци́фра, игра́льная ка́рта*) three **2** (*отме́тка*) three (*out of five*) **3** (*infml, авто́бус, трамва́й*) No. 3 (bus, tram, etc.) **4** (*гру́ппа из трои́х*) (group of) three; (*три челове́ка*) threesome **5** (*упря́жка*) troika **6** (*костю́м*) three-piece suit

тройни́к, а́ *m.* (*elec.*) three-way adaptor

тройн|о́й *adj.* triple, threefold, treble; **т. кана́т** three-ply rope; **т. прыжо́к** triple jump; **в** ∼**ом разме́ре** threefold, treble

тролле́йбус, а *m.* trolleybus

тромб, а *m.* (*med.*) blood clot

тромбо́з, а *m.* (*med.*) thrombosis; **т. глубо́ких вен** deep vein thrombosis

тромбо́н, а *m.* trombone

тромбони́ст, а *m.* trombonist

трон, а *m.* throne

тро́|нуть, ну, нешь *pf. of* ▶ **тро́гать**

тро́|нуться¹, нусь, нешься *pf. of* ▶ **тро́гаться¹ 2** (*pf. only*) (fig., infml) to be touched (= *to lose one's mind*); **он немно́го** ∼**нулся** he is a bit touched, he is a bit cracked

тро́|нуться², нусь, нешься *pf.* (*of* ▶ **тро́гаться²**) (*дви́нуться с ме́ста*) to start, set out; **т. с ме́ста** to make a move, get going; **по́езд** ∼**нулся** the train started

троп|а́, ы́, *pl.* ∼**ы,** ∼, ∼**а́м** *f.* path

тро́пик, а *m.* (*geog.*) **1** tropic; **т. Ра́ка** tropic of Cancer; **т. Козеро́га** tropic of Capricorn **2** (*in pl.*) the tropics

тропи́нк|а, и *f.* path

тропи́ческ|ий *adj.* tropical; ∼**ая лихора́дка** jungle fever

трос, а *m.* rope, cable, hawser

тростни́к, а́ *m.* reed; **са́харный т.** sugar cane

трост|**ь, и**, *pl.* ~**и**, ~**е́й** *f.* cane, walking stick

тротуа́р, а *m.* pavement

трофе́|**й, я** *m.* trophy

трою́родн|**ый** *adj.*: **т. брат**, ~**ая сестра́** second cousin; **т. племя́нник** second cousin once removed (*son of second cousin*)

♂ **труб**|**а́, ы́**, *pl.* ~**ы** *f.* **1** pipe; **водопрово́дная т.** water pipe; **водосто́чная т.** drainpipe; **канализацио́нная т.** sewage pipe; **подзо́рная т.** telescope **2** (*дымовая, заводская*) chimney; (*парохода*) funnel, smokestack **3** (mus.) trumpet; **игра́ть на** ~**е́** to play the trumpet **4** (anat.) tube; duct

трубаду́р, а *m.* troubadour

труба́ч, а́ *m.* trumpeter, trumpet player

труб|**и́ть, лю́, и́шь** *impf.* **1** (**в** + *a.*) (mus.) to blow **2** (*о трубах*) to sound; to blare **3** (*давать сигнал*) to sound (*by blast of trumpet, etc.*); **т. сбор** (mil.) to sound assembly **4** (**о** + *p.*) (infml, *разглашать*) to trumpet, proclaim from the housetops

тру́бк|**а, и** *f.* **1** tube; pipe; (*свёрток*) roll; **сверну́ть** ~**ой** to roll up **2** (*курительная*) (tobacco) pipe; **наби́ть** ~**у** to fill a pipe **3** (*телефона*) receiver; **взять, подня́ть** ~**у** to answer the phone

трубопрово́д, а *m.* pipeline

трубочи́ст, а *m.* chimney sweep

♂ **труд**, а́ *m.* **1** (*работа*) labour (BrE), labor (AmE), work **2** (*трудность*) difficulty, trouble; **взять на себя́ т.** (+ *inf.*) to take the trouble (to); **с** ~**о́м** with difficulty; **без** ~**а́** without difficulty **3** (*произведение*) (scholarly) work; (*in pl.*) (*издание*) transactions

тру|**ди́ться, жу́сь**, ~**дишься** *impf.* (**над** + *i.*) to toil (over), labour (BrE), labor (AmE) (over), work (on)

♂ **тру́дно** *as pred.* it is hard, it is difficult; **т. сказа́ть** it is hard to say; **мне т.** I find it difficult; **ему́ т. прихо́дится** he has a hard time

труднодосту́п|**ный**, ~**ен**, ~**на** *adj.* difficult to gain access to

тру́дност|**ь, и** *f.* difficulty; (*препятствие*) obstacle

тру́д|**ный**, ~**ен**, ~**на́**, ~**но**, ~**ны́** *adj.* **1** difficult, hard; (*изнурительный*) arduous; **в** ~**ную мину́ту** in a time of need **2** (*человек*) difficult, awkward **3** (*случай*) serious, grave

♂ **трудов**|**о́й** *adj.* **1** labour (BrE), labor (AmE), work; ~**о́е законода́тельство** labour (BrE), labor (AmE) legislation; ~**а́я кни́жка** work record book; **т. стаж** length of service **2** (*полученный трудом*) earned; hard-earned

трудого́лик, а *m.* (infml) workaholic

трудоём|**кий**, ~**ок**, ~**ка** *adj.* labour-intensive (BrE), labor-intensive (AmE)

трудолюби́в|**ый**, ~, ~**а** *adj.* hard-working, industrious

трудоспосо́б|**ный**, ~**ен**, ~**на** *adj.* able-bodied; capable of working

трудоустро́йств|**о, а** *nt.* placement in a job

труд|**я́щийся** *pres. part. of* ▶ **труди́ться** *and adj.* working; (*as pl. n.* ~**ящиеся**, ~**ящихся**) working people, the workers

тру́женик, а *m.* (*много работающий*) toiler; (+ *g.*) worker, employee

тру́жени|**ца, цы** *f. of* ▶ **тру́женик**

труп, а *m.* dead body, corpse; (*животного*) carcass; **то́лько че́рез мой т.** over my dead body

тру́пп|**а, ы** *f.* company

трус, а *m.* coward

трусик|**и, ов** (*no sg.*) **1** (*шорты*) shorts **2** (*плавки*) swimming trunks **3** (*бельё*) (under)pants; (*женские*) knickers (BrE), panties

тру́|**сить, шу, сишь** *impf.* (*of* ▶ **стру́сить**) **1** to be a coward; to get cold feet **2** (**пе́ред** + *i.*) to be afraid (of), be frightened (of)

трусли́в|**ый**, ~, ~**а** *adj.* cowardly

тру́сост|**ь, и** *f.* cowardice

трусц|**а́, ы́** *f.* (infml) **бег** ~**о́й** (sport) jogging

трус|**ы́, о́в** (*no sg.*) = **тру́сики**

трут, а *m.* tinder

тру́т|**ень, ня** *m.* (zool.) drone; (fig.) parasite

трух|**а́, и́** *f.* dust (*of rotted wood*); (fig., *о чём-н. никчёмном*) rubbish

трущо́б|**а, ы** *f.* (*often in pl.*) (*жильё, район*) slum

трюк, а *m.* **1** (*акробатический*) feat; (*каскадёра*) stunt; **рекла́мный т.** advertising gimmick **2** (fig., pej., *проделка*) trick

трюм, а *m.* (naut.) hold

трю́фел|**ь, я** *m.* (*гриб, конфета*) truffle

тря́пк|**а, и** *f.* **1** rag; (*для пыли*) duster **2** (*in pl.*) (infml, *одежда*) finery, clothes **3** (infml, pej., *человек*) drip

тряси́н|**а, ы** *f.* quagmire

тряс|**ти́, у́, ёшь**, *past* ~, ~**ла́** *impf.* **1** to shake **2** (*ковёр; крошки*) to shake out **3** (*о дрожи*) to cause to shake, cause to shiver (*usu. impers.*); **её** ~**ло́ от стра́ха** she was trembling with fear **4** (+ *i.*) (*головой, кулаком*) to shake; ~**ти гри́вой** to toss its mane **5** (*о вагоне*) to jolt, be jolty; (*impers.*) **в авто́бусе** ~**ёт** the bus is jolting

тряс|**ти́сь, у́сь, ёшься**, *past* ~**ся**, ~**ла́сь** *impf.* **1** to shake; to tremble, shiver; **т. от хо́лода** to shiver with cold **2** (**за** + *a.*) (*опасаться*) to worry about **3** (**пе́ред** + *i.*) (*бояться*) to tremble before, dread

тряхну́ть, **у́, ёшь** *pf.* to shake; (*в машине*) to give a jolt

туале́т, а *m.* **1** (*уборная*) lavatory, toilet **2** (*наряд*) dress; attire

туале́т|**ный** *adj. of* ▶ **туале́т**; ~**ная бума́га** toilet paper; ~**ная вода́** toilet water; ~**ные принадле́жности** toiletries; **т. сто́лик** dressing table

ту́б|**а¹, ы** *f.* (mus.) tuba

ту́б|**а², ы** *f.* (*большой тюбик*) tube

туберкулёз, а *m.* tuberculosis

т

ту́го *adv.* **1** tight(ly), taut; **т. набить чемода́н** to pack a suitcase tight **2** (*с трудом*) with difficulty

туг|о́й, ~, ~а́, ~о, ~й *adj.* **1** (*узел, воротничок*) tight; (*струна, пружина*) taut **2** (*плотно набитый*) tightly filled; **т. кошелёк** tightly stuffed purse

✓ **туда́** *adv.* there; (*в ту сторону*) that way; (*куда нужно*) to the right place; **биле́т т. и обра́тно** return ticket; **не т.!** not that way!; **вы не т.** попа́ли (*по телефону*) you have got the wrong number

ту́же *comp. of* ▶ туго́й, ▶ ту́го

тужу́рк|а, и *f.* double-breasted jacket (*man's*)

туз, á *m.* (cards) ace; **ходи́ть** ~о́м to play an ace

тузе́м|ец, ца *m.* native

тузе́м|ка, ки *f. of* ▶ тузе́мец

тузе́мный *adj.* native, indigenous

ту́ловищ|е, а *nt.* trunk; torso

тулу́п, а *m.* sheepskin coat

тума́к, á *m.* (infml) cuff, punch

тума́н, а *m.* fog; mist; haze; (*в голове*) fog, haze; **как в** ~е in a daze

тума́нност|ь, и *f.* **1** (astron.) nebula **2** (*изложения, мысли*) haziness, obscurity

тума́н|ный, ~ен, ~на *adj.* **1** foggy; misty; hazy **2** (fig., *тусклый*) dull, lacklustre (BrE), lackluster (AmE) **3** (fig., *неясный*) hazy, obscure, vague

ту́мб|а, ы *f.* **1** (*столб*) bollard **2** (*подставка*) pedestal **3** (*афишная*) advertisement hoarding (*of cylindrical shape*)

ту́мблер, а *m.* toggle (switch)

ту́мбочк|а, и *f.* bedside table, night table (AmE)

ту́ндр|а, ы *f.* (geog.) tundra

тун|е́ц, ца́ *m.* tuna (fish)

тунея́д|ец, ца *m.* parasite, sponger

тунея́д|ка, ки *f. of* ▶ тунея́дец

Туни́с, а *m.* (*страна*) Tunisia

туни́с|ец, ца *m.* Tunisian

туни́с|ка, ки *f. of* ▶ туни́сец

туни́сский *adj.* Tunisian

тунне́л|ь, я *m.* = тонне́ль

тупи́к, á *m.* **1** blind alley, cul-de-sac **2** (rail.) siding **3** (fig., *безвыходное положение*) impasse, deadlock; **зайти́ в т.** to reach a deadlock **4**: **поста́вить в т.** to stump, nonplus

туп|и́ть, лю́, ~ишь *impf.* to blunt

тупи́ц|а, ы *c.g.* (infml) dimwit

туп|о́й, ~, ~а́, ~о, ~ы́ *adj.* **1** (*нож*) blunt **2**: **т. у́гол** (math.) obtuse angle **3** (fig., *боль, чувство*) dull **4** (fig., *взгляд, улыбка*) vacant, stupid **5** (fig., *человек; ум*) dim; dull

ту́пост|ь, и *f.* **1** (*ножа*) bluntness **2** (fig., *взгляда*) vacancy **3** (fig., *ума*) dullness, slowness

тупоу́м|ный, ~ен, ~на *adj.* dull, obtuse

✓ **тур, а** *m.* **1** (*турнира, выборов*) round

2 (*артиста*) tour

тураге́нт, а *m.* travel agent

тураге́нтств|о, а *nt.* travel agency

турба́з|а, ы *f.* tourist centre (BrE), center (AmE)

турби́н|а, ы *f.* (tech.) turbine

туре́цкий *adj.* Turkish

тури́зм, а *m.* (*путешествия*) tourism; (*спорт*) hiking; **во́дный т.** boating

✓ **тури́ст, а** *m.* tourist; (*в походах*) hiker

туристи́ческ|ий *adj.* tourist; ~ое аге́нтство travel agency; **т. похо́д** hiking tour

тури́ст|ка, ки *f. of* ▶ тури́ст

туркме́н, а, *g. pl.* ~ *m.* Turkmen

Туркмениста́н, а *m.* Turkmenistan

туркме́н|ка, ки *f. of* ▶ туркме́н

туркме́нский *adj.* Turkmen

турне́ *nt. indecl.* tour (*esp. of artistes or sportsmen*)

турни́к, á *m.* (sport) horizontal bar

турнике́т, а *m.* turnstile

✓ **турни́р, а** *m.* tournament

ту́р|ок, ка, *g. pl.* **т.** *m.* Turk

Ту́рци|я, и *f.* Turkey

турча́н|ка, ки *f. of* ▶ ту́рок

ту́скл|ый, ~, ~а́, ~о, ~ы́ *adj.* **1** (*свет*) dim, dull; (*стекло*) opaque; (*металл*) tarnished; (*краска, лак*) matt **2** (fig., *взгляд, глаза; стиль*) dull, lacklustre (BrE), lackluster (AmE)

тускне́|ть, ет *impf.* (*of* ▶ потускне́ть) (*о свете*) to grow dim; (*о красках, таланте*) to fade; (*о металле, зеркале*) to tarnish

тус|ова́ться, у́юсь *impf.* (infml) to get together, meet, hang out

тусо́вк|а, и *f.* (infml) get-together; (*место*) meeting place, hang-out

✓ **тут** *adv.* **1** here; **кто т.?** who's there? **2** (*о времени*) now; **т. же** there and then

ту́ф|ля, ли, *g. pl.* ~**ель** *f.* shoe

ту́хл|ый, ~, ~а́, ~о *adj.* rotten, bad

ту́х|нуть¹, нет, *past* ~, ~ла *impf.* (*of* ▶ поту́хнуть) (*огонь*) to go out; (*взгляд, глаза*) to become dull

ту́х|нуть², нет, *past* ~, ~ла *impf.* (*загнивать*) to go bad, become rotten

ту́ч|а, и *f.* **1** (rain) cloud; storm cloud (also fig.); ~и собрали́сь, нави́сли (**над** + *i.*) (fig.) the clouds are gathering (over) **2** (*пыли*) cloud; (*мух*) swarm

ту́ч|ный, ~ен, ~на́, ~но *adj.* **1** (*человек*) stout, obese, corpulent **2** (*почва*) rich, fertile

ту́ш|а, и *f.* carcass

туше́нк|а, и *f.* (infml) tinned meat (BrE), canned meat (AmE)

туше́ный *adj.* (cul.) braised, stewed

туш|и́ть¹, у́, ~ишь *impf.* (*of* ▶ потуши́ть¹) (*огонь, пожар*) to extinguish, put out

туш|и́ть², у́, ~ишь *impf.* (cul.) to braise, stew

тушка́нчик, а *m.* jerboa

тушь|, и *f.* Indian ink; **т. (для ресни́ц)** mascara

тща́тел|ьный, ~ен, ~ьна *adj.* thorough, careful; painstaking

тщеду́ш|ный, ~ен, ~на *adj.* feeble, frail, weak

тщесла́ви|е, я *nt.* vanity, vainglory

тщесла́в|ный, ~ен, ~на *adj.* vain, vainglorious

тще́тно *adv.* vainly, in vain

тще́т|ный, ~ен, ~на *adj.* vain, futile

⚥ **ты, тебя́, тебе́, тобо́й, о тебе́** *pers. pron.* (*informal mode of address to one person*) you; **быть с кем-л.**) **на «ты», говори́ть «ты» (кому́-л.)** to be on familiar terms (with); (*для обобще́ния*) one, you

ты́|кать, чу, чешь *impf.* (*of* ▶ ткну́ть) (+ *i. and* в + *a., or* в + *a.*) to stick (into) (also fig.); to poke (into); to prod; to jab (into); **т. па́лкой** to prod with a stick

ты́кв|а, ы *f.* pumpkin, gourd

тыл, а, о ~е, в ~у́, *pl.* ~ы́ *m.* **1** back, rear **2** (mil.) rear; (*вся страна́*) home front **3** (*in pl.*) (mil., *вспомога́тельные ча́сти*) rear services

ты́льн|ый *adj.* back, rear; ~ая пове́рхность руки́ back of the hand

⚥ **тыс.** (*abbr. of* ты́сяча) thousand(s)

⚥ **ты́сяч|а**, и, *i.* ~ей *and* ~ью *num. and n., f.* thousand; **в ~у раз** a thousand times (also fig.); ~и люде́й thousands of people

тысячеле́ти|е, я *nt.* **1** (*срок*) a thousand years; millennium **2** (*годовщи́на*) thousandth anniversary

тысячеле́тний *adj.* **1** (*пери́од, годовщи́на*) thousand-year; millennial **2** (*зда́ние*) thousand-year-old

ты́сячн|ый *adj.* **1** thousandth; (*as f. n.* ~ая, ~ой) thousandth **2** (*толпа́, ста́до*) of many thousands

тьм|а, ы (*no pl.*) *f.* (*мрак*) darkness

тю́бик, а *m.* tube (*of toothpaste, etc.*)

тюк, а́ *m.* bale, package

тюле́н|ь, я *m.* (zool.) seal

тюл|ь, я *m.* (text.) tulle

тюльпа́н, а *m.* tulip

тюрба́н, а *m.* turban

тюр|е́мный *adj. of* ▶ тюрьма́; ~е́мное заключе́ние imprisonment

тюр|ьма́, ьмы́, *pl.* ~ьмы, ~ем *f.* prison; jail; **заключи́ть, посади́ть в ~ьму́** to put into prison, jail; **сиде́ть в ~ьме́** to be in prison

тюфя́к, а́ *m.* mattress (*filled with straw, hay, etc.*)

тя́вк|ать, аю *impf.* (*of* ▶ тя́вкнуть) to yap, yelp

тя́вк|нуть, ну, нешь *inst. pf. of* ▶ тя́вкать

тя́г|а, и *f.* **1** (*действие*) pulling; (*назе́много транспо́рта*) traction; **на ко́нной ~е** horse-drawn **2** (*от возду́шного транспо́рта*) thrust; (*сте́ржень рычага́*) rod **3** (*в пе́чи*) draught (BrE), draft (AmE) **4** (к + *d.*) (fig., *влече́ние*) pull (towards), attraction (towards); (*стремле́ние*) thirst (for), craving (for); (*скло́нность*) inclination

(to, for); **т. к зна́ниям** thirst for knowledge

тяга́ч, а́ *m.* tractor (*for pulling train of trailers*)

тя́гост|ный, ~ен, ~на *adj.* painful, distressing; ~ное зре́лище painful spectacle

тяго|ти́ть, щу́, ти́шь *impf.* (*обременя́ть*) to burden, be a burden (on, to); (*мы́сли, обя́занности*) to lie heavy (on), oppress

тяго|ти́ться, щу́сь, ти́шься *impf.* (+ *i.*) to be weighed down, oppressed (by)

тягча́йший *superl. of* ▶ тя́жкий

тя́жб|а, ы *f.* (civil) suit, lawsuit; litigation

тяжеле́е *comp. of* ▶ тяжёлый, ▶ тяжело́[1], ▶ тяжело́[2]

тяжеле́|ть, ю *impf.* **1** (*станови́ться тяжеле́е*) to become heavier; (*толсте́ть*) to put on weight **2** (*о глаза́х*) to become heavy with sleep

тяжело́[1] *adv.* **1** heavily **2** (*серьёзно*) seriously, gravely; **т. больно́й** seriously ill **3** (*с трудо́м*) with difficulty

тяжело́[2] *as pred.* **1** (*при подня́тии*) it is heavy; (*тру́дно*) it is hard; **мне т. ходи́ть пешко́м** it's hard for me to walk; (*мучи́тельно*) it is painful, it is distressing **2**; **ему́ и т. п. т.** (*о настрое́нии*) he feels, *etc.*, miserable, wretched

тяжелоатле́т, а *m.* (*штанги́ст*) weightlifter

⚥ **тяжёл|ый**, ~, тяжела́ *adj.* **1** heavy; **т. чемода́н** heavy suitcase; ~ая атле́тика (sport) weightlifting; ~ое дыха́ние heavy breathing; ~ая промы́шленность heavy industry **2** (*доставля́ющий беспоко́йство, неприя́тность*): **т. за́пах** oppressive, strong smell; ~ая пи́ща heavy, indigestible food **3** (*тру́дный*) hard, difficult; ~ая зада́ча hard task **4** (*суро́вый*) heavy, severe; ~ые поте́ри heavy casualties; **т. уда́р** severe blow **5** (*серьёзный*) serious, grave, bad; ~ое ране́ние serious injury (*горестный*) hard, painful; ~ые времена́ hard times; **т. день** bad, hard day **7** (*хара́ктер*) difficult **8** (*стиль*) heavy, ponderous, unwieldy

тя́жест|ь, и *f.* **1** (phys.) gravity; **центр ~и** centre of gravity (also fig.) **2** (*тяжёлый предме́т*) weight, heavy object **3** (*вес*) weight, heaviness **4** (*тру́дность*) difficulty

тя́ж|кий, ~ек, ~ка́, ~ко *adj.* **1** (*суро́вый*) severe; (*серьёзный*) serious, grave; ~кое преступле́ние grave crime, felony **2** (*судьба́*) hard, difficult

тян|у́ть, у́, ~ешь *impf.* **1** (*невод*) to pull, draw; to haul; to drag; **т. на букси́ре** to tow; (*ру́ку, ше́ю*) to stretch out; **т. ру́ку к** (+ *d.*) to reach out for, towards **2** (tech., *про́волоку*) to draw **3** (*прокла́дывать*) to lay; **т. телефо́нную ли́нию** to lay a telephone cable **4**: **т. жре́бий** to draw lots **5** (fig., *влечь*) to draw, attract; **меня́** *и т. п.* ~ет I long/want, *etc.*; **его́** ~ет **домо́й** he wants to go home **6** (*произноси́ть*) to drawl, drag out; **т. но́ту** to sustain a note **7** (*ме́длить*) to drag out, protract, delay; **т. с отве́том** to delay one's answer **8** (*вса́сывать*) to draw up; to take

Т

in, suck in; т. че́рез соло́минку to suck through a straw **9** (из, с + g.) to extract (from); to extort (from) **10** (убежда́ть идти́) to drag; никто́ тебя́ си́лой не ~у́л nobody forced you to go

тяну́ться, у́сь, ~ешься impf. **1** (о резине) to stretch **2** (о равни́не) to stretch, extend; тайга́ ~ется на со́тни киломе́тров the taiga stretches for hundreds of kilometres (BrE),

kilometers (AmE) **3** (о вре́мени) to drag on; to hang heavy **4** (к + d.) (к ма́тери) to reach (for), reach out (for); (к сла́ве) to strive (after) **5** (за + i.) (fig., infml, стреми́ться сравня́ться) to try to keep up (with), try to equal **6** (дви́гаться оди́н за други́м) to move one after the other

тяну́чк|а, и f. (infml) toffee, caramel

тя́пк|а, и f. hoe

Уу

⚹ **у** prep. + g. **1** (во́зле) by; at; **у окна́** by the window; **у воро́т** at the gate; **у руля́** at the wheel; **у мо́ря** by the sea; **у вла́сти** in power **2** (обознача́ет ме́сто де́йствия) at; with (often = French 'chez'); **у нас** (в до́ме) at our place, with us; (в стране́) in our country; **у себя́** at one's (own) place, at home; **я был у парикма́хера** I was at the hairdresser's **3** (обознача́ет принадле́жность): **у меня́ боли́т зуб** my tooth aches; **я был больна́ мать** her mother is ill **4** (ука́зывает на исто́чник) from, of; **я за́нял де́сять рубле́й у сосе́да** I borrowed ten roubles from a neighbour (BrE), neighbor (AmE) **5** (обознача́ет владе́льца): **у меня́** и т. п. I have, etc.; **у вас есть радиоприёмник?** do you have a radio?; **у меня́ к вам ма́ленькая про́сьба** I have a small favour (BrE), favor (AmE) to ask of you

у... vbl. pref. indicating **1** movement away from a place: **улете́ть** to fly away **2** insertion in sth: **умести́ть** to put in **3** covering of sth all over: **усе́ять** to strew **4** reduction, curtailment, etc.: **уба́вить** to reduce **5** achievement of aim sought: **уговори́ть** to persuade; with adj. roots, forms vv. expr. comp. degree: **уско́рить** to accelerate

уба́в|ить, лю, ишь pf. (of ▸ убавля́ть) **1** (+ a. or g.) (жа́лованье, це́ну) to reduce, lower; **у. ход** to reduce speed **2**: **у. в ве́се** to lose weight

уба́в|иться, ится pf. (of ▸ убавля́ться) to diminish, decrease; **воды́ ~илось** the water (level) has fallen

убавля́|ть, ю, ет impf. of ▸ уба́вить

убавля́|ться, ется impf. of ▸ уба́виться

убаю́к|ать, аю pf. (of ▸ убаю́кивать) to lull (also fig.)

убаю́кива|ть, ю impf. of ▸ убаю́кать

убега́|ть, ю impf. of ▸ убежа́ть

убеди́тел|ьный, ~ен, ~ьна adj. **1** (доказа́тельный) convincing, persuasive; **быть ~ьным** to be convincing, carry conviction **2** (настойчивый) pressing; earnest; **~ьная про́сьба** pressing request, earnest entreaty

убе|ди́ть (1st pers. sg. not used) ди́шь pf. (of ▸ убежда́ть) **1** (в + p.) to convince (of) **2** (+ inf.) (уговори́ть) to persuade (to), prevail on (to)

убе|ди́ться (1st pers. sg. not used) ди́шься pf. (of ▸ убежда́ться) (в + p.) to satisfy oneself (of); to be convinced (of); **мы ~ди́лись в необходи́мости рефо́рм** we are convinced of the need for reform; **он ~ди́лся, что э́то тру́дно** he is convinced that it is difficult

убе|жа́ть, гу́, жи́шь, гу́т pf. (of ▸ убега́ть) **1** (удали́ться бего́м) to run away, run off **2** (спасти́сь бе́гством) to escape, flee

убежда́|ть, ю impf. of ▸ убеди́ть

убежда́|ться, юсь impf. of ▸ убеди́ться

убежде́ни|е, я nt. **1** (де́йствие) persuasion **2** (мне́ние) conviction, belief

убеждённо adv. with conviction

убеждённост|ь, и f. conviction

убежд|ённый p.p.p. of ▸ убеди́ть and adj. **1** (p.p.p.) (~ён, ~ена́) (в + p.) convinced (of) **2** (adj.) (~ён, ~ённа) (тон) assured **3** (adj., no short forms) (непоколеби́мый) convinced; staunch; **у. сторо́нник** staunch supporter

убе́жищ|е, а nt. **1** (защи́та) refuge, asylum; **полити́ческое ~е** political asylum **2** (укры́тие) shelter

убере́га|ть, ю impf. of ▸ убере́чь

убере́га|ться, юсь impf. of ▸ убере́чься

убере́|чь, гу́, жёшь, гу́т, past ~г, ~гла́ pf. (of ▸ убере́га́ть) (от or + g.) to protect (against), guard (against), keep safe (from), preserve (from)

т
у

уберечься, гусь, жёшься, гутся, *past*
~гся, ~глась *pf.* (*of* ▸ уберегаться) (от
+ *g.*) to protect oneself (against), guard
(*intrans.*) (against)

ⱷ убивать, ю *impf. of* ▸ убить

убийственный, ~, ~на *adj.* (*жара, голод*)
unbearable, killing; murderous; (*известие,
результат, взгляд, критика*) devastating

убийство, а *nt.* killing; (*с заранее
обдуманным злым умыслом*) murder;
(*политическое*) assassination; заказное у.
contract killing

убийца, ы *c.g.* killer; murderer; assassin

убирать, ю *impf.* (*of* ▸ убрать)

убираться, юсь *impf.* (*of* ▸ убраться):
~йся! clear off!, beat it!, hop it!

убитый, ~, ~а *p.p.p. of* ▸ убить *and adj.*
1 (*лишённый жизни*): неприятель потерял
две тысячи ~ыми the enemy lost two
thousand killed; (*as m. n.* у., ~ого) dead
man; (*жертва преступления*) murdered
man; (*при аварии*) fatality; спать как у.
to sleep like a log **2** (*fig., подавленный*)
crushed, broken

убить, ью, ьёшь *pf.* (*of* ▸ убивать) **1** to
kill; (*предумышленно*) to murder; (*по
политическим мотивам*) to assassinate
2 (*fig., уничтожить*) to kill, destroy; её
отказ ~ил его her refusal destroyed him
3 (*infml, потратить*) to waste; у. время to
kill time

убогий, ~, ~а *adj.* (*нищенский*) poverty-
stricken (also fig.); (*жилище*) wretched;
(*мысль, работа*) pathetic, dismal

убор, а *m.*: головной у./головные ~ы headgear

убористый, ~, ~а *adj.* close, small (*of
handwriting, etc.*)

уборка, и *f.* **1** (*урожая*) harvesting; (*хлопка,
ягод*) picking **2** (*помещения*) clearing up,
tidying up

уборная, ой *f.* (*туалет*) lavatory; toilet

уборщик, а *m.* cleaner

уборщица, цы *f. of* ▸ уборщик

убрать, уберу, уберёшь, *past* ~л, ~ла,
~ло *pf.* (*of* ▸ убирать) **1** (*унести*) to
remove, take away; у. со стола to clear the
table **2** (*привести в порядок*) to clear up,
tidy up; у. постель to make the bed
3 (*спрятать куда-н.*) to put away; to
store **4** (*урожай*) to harvest **5** (*fig., infml*)
(*выгнать*) to kick out; (*убить*) to kill, take
out

убраться, уберусь, уберёшься, *past*
~лся, ~лась, ~лось *pf.* (*of* ▸ убираться)
(infml) **1** (*навести порядок*) to clear up, tidy
up **2** (*уйти*) to clear off

убывать, ю *impf. of* ▸ убыть

убыток, ка *m.* **1** loss; терпеть, нести ~ки
to incur losses **2** (*in pl.*) (*возмещение*)
damages; взыскать ~ки to claim damages

убыточный, ~ен, ~на *adj.* unprofitable

убыть, убуду, убудешь, *past* убыл,
убыла, убыло *pf.* (*of* ▸ убывать) to
decrease; (*о воде*) to subside, go down;
(*о луне*) to wane (also fig.)

ⱷ уважаемый *pres. part. pass. of* ▸ уважать
and adj. respected; (*в письме*) dear

уважать, ю *impf.* to respect, esteem

ⱷ уважение, я *nt.* (к + *d.*) respect, esteem
(for); внушать у. to command respect;
из ~я (к + *d.*) out of respect (for); с ~ем
(*в письме*) yours sincerely

уважительный, ~ен, ~на *adj.*
1 (*достаточный для оправдания*) valid;
~ьная причина valid cause, good reason
2 (*почтительный*) respectful, deferential

увалень, ьня *m.* (infml) clumsy oaf,
clodhopper

уведомить, млю, ишь *pf.* (*of* ▸ уведомлять)
to inform, notify

уведомление, я *nt.* notification;
(*документ*) letter of advice

уведомлять, ю *impf. of* ▸ уведомить

увезти, у, ёшь, *past* ~, ~ла *pf.* (*of
*▸ увозить) to take (away); (*с собой*) to take
with one

увековечивать, ю *impf. of* ▸ увековечить

увековечить, у, ишь *pf.* (*of
*▸ увековечивать) **1** (*героев*) to
immortalize **2** (*порядок, систему*)
to perpetuate

ⱷ увеличение, я *nt.* **1** (*зарплаты*) increase;
(*температуры*) rise **2** (*изображения*)
magnification; (*phot., снимка*) enlargement

ⱷ увеличивать, ю, ет *impf. of* ▸ увеличить

увеличиваться, ется *impf. of*
▸ увеличиться

увеличительный *adj.* magnifying; ~ое
стекло magnifying glass

увеличить, у, ишь *pf.* (*of* ▸ увеличивать)
1 (*в количестве, в объёме*) to increase
2 (*изображение*) to magnify; (*phot.*) to
enlarge

увеличиться, ится *pf.* (*of* ▸ увеличиваться)
to increase, grow, rise

увенчать, аю *pf.* (*of* ▸ венчать 1, ▸ венчать
2, ▸ увенчивать) to crown

увенчаться, ается *pf.* (*of* ▸ увенчиваться)
(+ *i.*) (fig.) to be crowned (with); у. успехом
to be crowned with success

увенчивать, ю, ет *impf. of* ▸ увенчать

увенчиваться, ется *impf. of* ▸ увенчаться

уверенно *adv.* confidently, with confidence

уверенность, и *f.* **1** (*шага, голоса*)
confidence; у. в себе self-confidence
2 (*убеждённость*) (в + *p.*) confidence (in),
certainty (of); можно с ~ью сказать one
can say with confidence, it is safe to say

ⱷ уверенный, ~, ~на *adj.* **1** (*твёрдый*)
confident, sure; ~ная рука sure hand
2 (*as pred.* ~, ~а) (*убеждённый*) (в + *p.*)
confident (in), sure (of), certain (of); быть

у

~ным to be sure, be certain; **он ~ в себе́** he is self-confident; **я ~а в нём** I have confidence in him

уве́р|ить, ю, ишь *pf.* (*of* ▶ **уверя́ть**) to assure; (*убеди́ть*) to convince, persuade

уве́р|иться, юсь, ишься *pf.* (*of* ▶ **уверя́ться**) to assure oneself, satisfy oneself

увер|ну́ться, ну́сь, нёшься *pf.* (*of* ▶ **увора́чиваться**) (**от** + *g.*) to dodge; (*also fig.*): **у. от прямо́го отве́та** to avoid giving a direct answer

уве́р|овать, ую *pf.* (**в** + *a.*) to come to believe (in)

уверя́|ть, я́ю *impf. of* ▶ **уве́рить**

уверя́|ться, я́юсь *impf. of* ▶ **уве́риться**

увесели́тельн|ый *adj.* pleasure, entertainment; ~**ая пое́здка** pleasure trip, jaunt

уве́сист|ый, ~, ~а *adj.* (*том*) weighty; **у. уда́р** (infml) heavy blow

уве|сти́, ду́, дёшь, *past* ~**л,** ~**ла́** *pf.* (*of* ▶ **уводи́ть**) to take (away); (*с собо́й*) to take with one

уве́ч|ить, у, ишь *impf.* to maim, mutilate

уве́чь|е, я *nt.* (*повреждение*) (serious) injury; **нанести́ у. кому́-н.** to maim, injure sb

уве́ш|ать, аю *pf.* (*of* ▶ **уве́шивать**) to cover (*with objects suspended*); **у. сте́ну карти́нами** to cover a wall with pictures

уве́шива|ть, ю *impf. of* ▶ **уве́шать**

☛ **уви́|деть, жу, дишь** ❶ *pf. of* ▶ **ви́деть**; ~**дим** we'll see ❷ *pf.* to catch sight of

увива́|ть, ю *impf.* (**от** + *g.*) ❶ *impf. of* ▶ **увильну́ть** ❷ (*impf. only*) to try to get out (of)

увильн|у́ть, у́, ёшь *pf.* (*of* ▶ **уви́ливать** 1) (**от** + *g.*) (infml) ❶ to dodge ❷ (fig., *от ответственности, от налогов*) to evade; to get out (of); **у. от отве́та** to get out of replying

увлажн|и́ть, ю́, и́шь *pf.* (*of* ▶ **увлажня́ть**) to moisten, damp, wet

увлажн|и́ться, и́тся *pf.* (*of* ▶ **увлажня́ться**) to become moist, damp, wet

увлажня́|ть, я́ю, я́ет *impf. of* ▶ **увлажни́ть**

увлажня́|ться, я́ется *impf. of* ▶ **увлажни́ться**

увлека́тельн|ый, ~ен, ~ьна *adj.* fascinating, absorbing

увлека́|ть, ю *impf. of* ▶ **увле́чь**

увлека́|ться, юсь *impf. of* ▶ **увле́чься**

увлече́ни|е, я *nt.* ❶ (*воодушевление*) animation ❷ (+ *i.*) (*большой интерес*) passion (for); enthusiasm (for); (*влюблённость*) crush (on) ❸ (*предмет любви*) (object of) passion

увле́|чь, ку́, чёшь, ку́т, *past* ~**к,** ~**кла́** *pf.* (*of* ▶ **увлека́ть**) ❶ (*увести*) to carry along ❷ (fig., *о работе*) to carry away, distract ❸ (*восхитить*) to captivate, fascinate

увле́|чься, ку́сь, чёшься, ку́тся, *past* ~**кся,** ~**кла́сь** *pf.* (*of* ▶ **увлека́ться**) (+ *i.*)

❶ (*забыться*) to be carried away (by); (*заинтересоваться*) to become keen (on); **ора́тор ~кся** the speaker got carried away ❷ (*влюбиться*) to fall (for)

уво|ди́ть, жу́, ~дишь *impf. of* ▶ **увести́**

уво|зи́ть, жу́, ~зишь *impf. of* ▶ **увезти́**

уво́л|ить, ю, ишь *pf.* (*of* ▶ **увольня́ть**) (*с работы*) to dismiss; to sack; (mil.) to discharge

уво́л|иться, юсь, ишься *pf.* (*of* ▶ **увольня́ться**) (*уйти*) to resign; (mil.) to get one's discharge; **у. в отста́вку** to retire

увольне́ни|е, я *nt.* dismissal; (mil.) discharge; (*на пенсию*) retiring, pensioning off

увольня́|ть, ю *impf. of* ▶ **уво́лить**

увольня́|ться, юсь *impf. of* ▶ **уво́литься**

увора́чива|ться, юсь *pf. of* ▶ **увернуться**

увы́ *int.* alas!

увяда́|ть, ю *impf. of* ▶ **увя́нуть**

увя|за́ть¹, жу́, ~жешь *pf.* (*of* ▶ **увя́зывать**) to coordinate

увя|за́ть², а́ю *impf. of* ▶ **увя́знуть**

увя|за́ться, жу́сь, ~жешься *pf.* (*of* ▶ **увя́зываться**) (infml) (**за** + *i.*) to tag along (behind), follow closely

увя́з|нуть, ну, нешь, *past* ~, ~**ла** *pf.* (*of* ▶ **увяза́ть²**) (**в** + *p.*) to get stuck (in); to get bogged down (in) (also fig.)

увя́зыва|ть, ю *impf. of* ▶ **увяза́ть¹**

увя́зыва|ться, юсь *impf. of* ▶ **увяза́ться**

увя́|нуть, ну, нешь *pf.* (*of* ▶ **увяда́ть**) to fade, wither (also fig.)

угада́|ть, а́ю *pf.* (*of* ▶ **уга́дывать**) to guess (right), divine; (*желания*) to anticipate

уга́дыва|ть, ю *impf. of* ▶ **угада́ть**

Уга́нд|а, ы *f.* Uganda

уганди́|ец, йца *m.* Ugandan

уганди́|йка, йки *f. of* ▶ **уганди́ец**

уганди́йский *adj.* Ugandan

уга́рный *adj.*: **у. газ** carbon monoxide

угаса́|ть, а́ет *impf.* ❶ *impf. of* ▶ **уга́снуть** ❷ (*impf. only*) (*огонь*) to die down; **си́лы у него́ ~а́ли** his strength was fading, ebbing

уга́с|нуть, нет, *past* ~, ~**ла** *pf.* (*of* ▶ **угаса́ть** 1) (*пламя, свеча*) to go out; (*звук*) to die away; (*чувство*) to be extinguished; (*человек*) to die

углево́д, а *m.* carbohydrate

углеки́слый *adj.*: **у. газ** carbon dioxide

углеро́д, а *m.* carbon

углова́т|ый, ~, ~а *adj.* (infml) awkward

углов|о́й *adj.* ❶ angle; angular ❷ (*на углу*) corner; **у. дом** corner house; **у. уда́р** (sport) corner; (*as m. n.* **у.,** ~**о́го**) (sport) corner

углуб|и́ть, лю́, и́шь *pf.* (*of* ▶ **углубля́ть**) ❶ (*яму*) to deepen, make deeper ❷ (*поместить глубоко, глубже*) to drive in deep, sink deeper ❸ (fig.) to deepen, extend

углуб|и́ться, лю́сь, и́шься *pf.* (*of* ▶ **углубля́ться**) ❶ (*яма*) to deepen, become deeper ❷ (fig.) (*о знаниях*) to deepen, become deeper; (*о противоречиях*) to

у

become intensified **3** (в + *a.*) (*в лес*) to go deep (into); (*в воспоминания*) to become absorbed in, lose oneself in **4** (в + *a.*) (fig., *в чтение*) to become absorbed (in)

углубле́ни|е, я *nt.* **1** deepening **2** (fig.) deepening, extending; intensification **3** (geog.) hollow, depression, dip

углубл|ённый, ~ён, ~ена́ *adj.* intensive; (*интерес*) profound

углубля́|ть, ю *impf. of* ▶ углуби́ть

углубля́|ться, юсь *impf. of* ▶ углуби́ться

угна́|ть, угоню́, уго́нишь, *past* ~ла́, ~ло́ *pf.* (*of* ▶ угоня́ть) (*украсть*) to steal; (*самолёт*) to hijack

угнета́|ть, ю *impf.* **1** (*жестоко притеснять*) to oppress **2** (*удручать*) to depress, dispirit

угнете́ни|е, я *nt.* oppression

угнетённ|ый *adj.* **1** (*притесняемый*) oppressed **2** (*удручённый*) depressed; **быть в ~ом состоя́нии** to be depressed, be in low spirits

угова́рива|ть, ю *impf.* **1** *impf. of* ▶ уговори́ть **2** (*impf. only*) to try to persuade, urge

угова́рива|ться, юсь *impf. of* ▶ уговори́ться

уговор|и́ть, ю́, и́шь *pf.* (*of* ▶ угова́ривать 1) (+ *inf.*) to persuade (to); to talk (into)

уговор|и́ться, ю́сь, и́шься *pf.* (*of* ▶ угова́риваться) (infml) (+ *inf.*) to arrange (to), agree (to)

уго|ди́ть¹, жу́, ди́шь *pf.* (*of* ▶ угожда́ть) (+ *d.*) (*удовлетворить*) to please, oblige

уго|ди́ть², жу́, ди́шь *pf.* (infml) (в + *a.*) (*попасть*) to fall (into), get (into); (*при падении*) to bang (against); **у. в западню́** to fall into a trap; **у. в тюрьму́** to land up in prison

уго́длив|ый, ~, ~а *adj.* obsequious

уго́дно **1** (*as pred.*): **там есть всё что у.** there is everything one could wish for; (+ *d.*) **как вам у.** as you like; please yourself **2** (*particle forming indefinite prons. and advs.*): **кто у.** anyone (you like), whoever you like; **что у.** anything (you like); whatever you like; **ско́лько у.** as much as you like; any amount; **когда́ у.** any time

угожда́|ть, ю *impf. of* ▶ угоди́ть¹

у́г|ол, ла́, об ~ле́, в ~лу́ *m.* **1** (в ~ле́) (math., phys.) angle; **под ~лом** (в + *a.*) at an angle (of); **под прямы́м ~лом** at right angles; **у. зре́ния** (fig.) point of view **2** (*улицы, стола, комнаты*) corner; **в ~лу́** in the corner; **на ~лу́** at the corner; **за ~лом** round the corner; **из-за ~ла́** (from) round the corner; (fig.) on the sly, behind sb's back; **сре́зать у.** to cut off a corner

уголо́вник, а *m.* (infml) criminal

уголо́вн|ый *adj.* criminal; **~ое де́ло** criminal case; **у. ко́декс** criminal code; **~ое пра́во** criminal law; **~ое преступле́ние** crime, felony

угол|о́к, ка́ *m.* corner

у́голь, угля́ *m.* **1** (*pl.* у́гли, у́глей) coal; **ка́менный у.** coal; **древе́сный у.** charcoal **2** (*pl.* у́гли, у́гле́й) (*кусок обгоревшего дерева*) a (piece of) coal **3** (*pl.* у́гли, угле́й) (art) charcoal

угомон|и́ть, ю́, и́шь *pf.* (infml) to calm

угомон|и́ться, ю́сь, и́шься *pf.* (infml) to calm down

уго́н, а *m.* (*велосипеда*) stealing; (*самолёта*) hijacking; **у. маши́ны** car theft

уго́нщик, а *m.* thief; (*самолёта*) hijacker; **у. маши́ны** car thief

угоня́|ть, ю *impf. of* ▶ угна́ть

у́г|орь¹, ря́ *m.* (*рыба*) eel

у́г|орь², ря́ *m.* (*often in pl.*) (*на коже*) blackhead

уго|сти́ть, щу́, сти́шь *pf.* (*of* ▶ угоща́ть) (+ *i.*) to entertain (to), treat (to); **у. кого́-н. обе́дом** to treat sb to dinner

угоща́|ть, ю *impf. of* ▶ угости́ть

угоща́|ться, юсь *impf.*: **угоща́йтесь!** help yourself/yourselves!

угоще́ни|е, я *nt.* **1** (+ *i.*) entertaining (to, with), treating (to) **2** (*то, чем угощают*) refreshments; fare

угро́б|ить, лю, ишь *pf.* (infml) **1** (*убить*) to do in **2** (fig., *загубить*) to ruin, wreck; **у. чью-н. репута́цию** to ruin sb's reputation

угрожа́|ть, ю *impf.* (*кому чем*) to threaten (with); **он ~л ему́ тюрьмо́й** he threatened him with prison; **ему́ ~ет разоре́ние** he is in danger of bankruptcy; **ему́ ~ет опа́сность** he is in danger

угрожа́|ющий *pres. part. act. of* ▶ угрожа́ть *and adj.* threatening, menacing; **~ющее положе́ние** perilous situation

☞ **угро́з|а, ы** *f.* threat

угрызе́ни|е, я *nt.*: **~я со́вести** pangs of conscience

угрю́м|ый, ~, ~а *adj.* gloomy

уда|ва́ться, ётся *impf. of* ▶ уда́ться

удалённый **1** *p.p.p. of* ▶ удали́ть **2** *adj.* (*район, доступ к компьютеру*) remote

удал|и́ть, ю́, и́шь *pf.* (*of* ▶ удаля́ть) **1** (*отдалить*) to take away, move away **2** (*убрать, устранить*) to remove; **у. зуб** to extract a tooth **3** (*заставить уйти*) to remove, send away; (*от дел, обязанностей*) to remove; **у. с по́ля** (sport) to send off (the field)

удал|и́ться, ю́сь, и́шься *pf.* (*of* ▶ удаля́ться) **1** (*отдалиться*) to move off, move away **2** (*уйти*) to leave, withdraw, retire; **у. на поко́й** to retire to a quiet life

удал|о́й, уда́л, ~а́, уда́ло, удалы́ *adj.* daring, bold

удал|я́ть, я́ю *impf. of* ▶ удали́ть

удал|я́ться, я́юсь *impf. of* ▶ удали́ться

☞ **уда́р, а** *m.* **1** (*рукой, палкой, топором*) blow; (*ногой*) kick; (*ножом*) stab; **одни́м ~ом** at one stroke; **нанести́ у. кому́-н.** to strike sb a blow; **у. в спи́ну** (fig.) stab in the back; **у. гро́ма** thunderclap; (*неприятность*) blow;

у. судьбы́ a stroke of bad luck **2** (*колокола*) stroke **3** (mil.) blow; attack; thrust; **под ~ом** exposed (to attack) **4** (med.) (*кровоизлияние в мозг*) stroke; (*сердца, пульса*) beat; **со́лнечный у.** sunstroke

ударе́ни|е, я *nt.* **1** (ling.) stress, accent; (fig.) stress, emphasis **2** (*знак*) stress (mark)

уда́р|ить, ю, ишь *pf.* (*of* ▸ **ударя́ть**) **1** (+ *a. and* по + *d. or* в + *a.*) (*нанести удар*) to strike; to hit; (*нанести удар*): **у. кого́-н. по лицу́** to slap sb's face; **у. кулако́м по́ столу** to bang on the table with one's fist **2** (в + *a. or* + *a.*) (*дать сигнал*) to strike; to sound; to beat; **у. в бараба́н** to beat a drum; **у. трево́гу** to sound the alarm; **часы́ ~или по́лночь** the clock struck midnight **3** (*раздаться*) to sound; **~ил гром** there was a clap of thunder; (*фонтан, пар*) to gush; (*подействовать резко*): **я́ркий свет ~ил в глаза́** a bright light struck his eyes **4** (по + *d.*) (mil.) to attack **5** (по + *d.*) to strike (at); to combat; **у. по карма́ну** (infml) to hit one's pocket, set one back

уда́р|иться, юсь, ишься *pf.* (*of* ▸ **ударя́ться**) **1** (о + *a. or* в + *a.*) to strike (against), hit **2** (в + *a. or* + *inf.*) to break (into)

уда́рник, а *m.* (mus.) percussionist

уда́рн|ый *adj.* **1** (tech. and mil.) percussive; percussion; **~ая си́ла** striking power, force of impact **2** (mus.) percussion **3** (mil.) striking, shock; **~ые ча́сти** shock troops **4** (*гласный*) stressed

удар|я́ть, я́ю *impf. of* ▸ **уда́рить**

ударя́|ться, я́юсь *impf. of* ▸ **уда́риться**

⚔ **уда́|ться, стся, ду́тся**, *past* **~лся**, **~ла́сь** *pf.* (*of* ▸ **удава́ться**) **1** (*получиться*) to be successful, work (well), succeed; **опера́ция ~ла́сь** the operation was a success; **ему́ всё ~ётся** he succeeds in everything he does **2** (impers. + *d. and inf.*) to succeed, manage; **мне не ~ло́сь написа́ть статью́ во́время** I did not manage to write the article on time

уда́ч|а, и *f.* success; (*везение*) good luck, good fortune

уда́члив|ый, ~, ~а *adj.* successful, lucky

уда́ч|ный, ~ен, ~на *adj.* **1** (*успешный*) successful **2** (*хороший*) good

удва́ива|ть, ю *impf. of* ▸ **удво́ить**

удво́|ить, ю, ишь *pf.* (*of* ▸ **удва́ивать**) (*увеличить вдвое*) to double; (*усилия*) to redouble

уде́л, а *m.* lot, destiny

удел|и́ть, ю́, и́шь *pf.* (*of* ▸ **уделя́ть**) to give, spare, devote; **у. вре́мя чему́-н.** to spare the time for sth

уделя́|ть, я́ю *impf. of* ▸ **удели́ть**

удерж|а́ть, у́, ~ишь *pf.* (*of* ▸ **уде́рживать**) **1** (*не выпустить*) to hold, hold on to, not let go **2** (*сохранить*) to keep, retain; **у. в па́мяти** to retain in one's memory **3** (*не отпустить; не дать сделать*) to hold back, restrain **4** (*вычесть*) to deduct, keep back

⚔ key word

удерж|а́ться, у́сь, ~ишься *pf.* (*of* ▸ **уде́рживаться**) **1** (*не отступить*) to hold one's ground, hold out; to stand firm; **у. на нога́х** to remain on one's feet **2** (от + *g.*) to keep oneself (from), refrain (from); **у. от собла́зна** to resist a temptation; **мы не могли́ у. от сме́ха** we couldn't help laughing

уде́ржива|ть, ю *impf. of* ▸ **удержа́ть**

уде́ржива|ться, юсь *impf. of* ▸ **удержа́ться**

удешев|и́ть, лю́, и́шь *pf.* (*of* ▸ **удешевля́ть**) to reduce the price (of)

удешев|и́ться, и́тся *pf.* (*of* ▸ **удешевля́ться**) to become cheaper

удешевля́|ть, ю, ет *impf. of* ▸ **удешеви́ть**

удешевля́|ться, ется *impf. of* ▸ **удешеви́ться**

удиви́тельно *adv.* **1** amazingly, surprisingly **2** (*чудесно*) wonderfully, marvellously (BrE), marvelously (AmE) **3** (*очень*) very, extremely **4** (*as pred.*) it is amazing, it is surprising; (*странно*) it is funny

удиви́тел|ьный, ~ен, ~ьна *adj.* **1** amazing, surprising **2** (*чудесный*) wonderful, marvellous (BrE), marvelous (AmE)

удив|и́ть, лю́, и́шь *pf.* (*of* ▸ **удивля́ть**) to amaze, surprise

удив|и́ться, лю́сь, и́шься *pf.* (*of* ▸ **удивля́ться**) (+ *d.*) to be amazed (at), be surprised (at); to marvel (at)

удивле́ни|е, я *nt.* surprise, amazement; **к моему́ вели́кому ~ю** to my great surprise

удивля́|ть, ю *impf. of* ▸ **удиви́ть**

удивля́|ться, юсь *impf. of* ▸ **удиви́ться**

удира́|ть, ю *impf. of* ▸ **удра́ть**

уди́ть, ужу́, у́дишь *impf.* (*also* **у. ры́бу**) to fish, angle

удлини́тел|ь, я *m.* extension lead

удлин|и́ть, ю́, и́шь *pf.* (*of* ▸ **удлиня́ть**) to lengthen; (*срок*) to extend, prolong

удлин|и́ться, и́тся *pf.* (*of* ▸ **удлиня́ться**) (*о тенях*) to become longer; (*о сроке*) to be extended, be prolonged

удлин|я́ть, я́ю, я́ет *impf. of* ▸ **удлини́ть**

удлин|я́ться, я́ется *impf. of* ▸ **удлини́ться**

удму́рт, а *m.* Udmurt

удму́рт|ка, ки *f. of* ▸ **удму́рт**

удму́ртский *adj.* Udmurt

удо́бно[1] *adv.* **1** (*сидеть*) comfortably **2** (*расположить*) conveniently

удо́бно[2] *as pred.* (+ *d.*) **1** (*хорошо*) to feel, be comfortable; to be at one's ease; **нам здесь вполне́ у.** we are very comfortable here **2** (*подходит*) it is convenient (for), it suits; **у. ли вам прие́хать сра́зу?** is it convenient for you to come at once?

⚔ **удо́б|ный, ~ен, ~на** *adj.* **1** (*кресло, туфли*) comfortable; (*уютный*) cosy (BrE), cozy (AmE) **2** (*подходящий*) convenient, suitable; **в ~ное для вас вре́мя** at your convenience; **по́льзоваться ~ным слу́чаем** (+ *inf.*) to take an opportunity (to do sth)

удобре́ни|е, я *nt.* (agric.) fertilizer; (*навоз*) manure

удо́бр|ить, ю, ишь *pf.* (*of* ▸ удобря́ть)
to fertilize

удобр|я́ть, я́ю *impf. of* ▸ удо́брить

удо́бств|о, а *nt.* (*употребления*) convenience;
кварти́ра со все́ми ∼ами flat (BrE), apartment
(AmE) with all (modern) conveniences

удовлетворе́ни|е, я *nt.* satisfaction,
gratification

удовлетвори́тельно 1 *adv.* satisfactorily
2 *n., nt. indecl.* (*отметка*) 'satisfactory',
'fair' (*mark*)

удовлетвори́тел|ьный, ∼ен, ∼ьна *adj.*
satisfactory

удовлетвор|и́ть, ю́, и́шь *pf.* (*of*
▸ удовлетворя́ть) **1** to satisfy; to comply
(with); у. запро́сы to satisfy requirements;
у. про́сьбу to comply with a request **2** (+ *d.*)
to answer, meet; у. тре́бованиям to answer
requirements

удовлетвор|и́ться, ю́сь, и́шься *pf.* (*of*
▸ удовлетворя́ться) (+ *i.*) to content oneself
(with), be satisfied (with)

удовлетвор|я́ть, я́ю *impf. of*
▸ удовлетвори́ть

удовлетвор|я́ться, я́юсь *impf. of*
▸ удовлетвори́ться

⚔ **удово́льстви|е, я** *nt.* **1** (*sg. only*) pleasure;
доста́вить у. (+ *d.*) to give pleasure; с ∼ем!
with pleasure! **2** (*забава*) amusement; жить
в своё у. to live a life of leisure

удорож|а́ть, а́ю *impf. of* ▸ удорожи́ть

удорож|и́ть, у́, и́шь *pf.* (*of* ▸ удорожа́ть) to
raise the price (of)

удоста́ива|ть, ю *impf. of* ▸ удосто́ить

удоста́ива|ться, юсь *impf. of*
▸ удосто́иться

удостовере́ни|е, я *nt.* (*документ*)
certificate; у. ли́чности identity card, ID

удостове́р|ить, ю, ишь *pf.* (*of*
▸ удостоверя́ть) to certify, attest, witness; у.
по́дпись to witness a signature

удостове́р|иться, юсь, ишься *pf.* (*of*
▸ удостоверя́ться) (в + *p.*) to make sure
(of); to assure oneself (of)

удостовер|я́ть, я́ю *impf. of* ▸ удостове́рить

удостовер|я́ться, я́юсь *impf. of*
▸ удостове́риться

удосто́|ить, ю, ишь *pf.* (*of* ▸ удоста́ивать)
1 (+ *a. and g.*) (*звания, степени*) to award
(to), confer (on); у. кого́-н. Нобелевской
пре́мии to award sb a Nobel prize **2** (+ *i.*)
(usu. iron.) (*внима́нием*) to favour (BrE), favor
(AmE) (with); to deign to give; он не ∼ил
нас отве́том he did not deign to give us an
answer

удосто́|иться, юсь, ишься *pf.* (*of*
▸ удоста́иваться) (+ *g.*) **1** (*награды*) to
receive, be awarded **2** (usu. iron., *улыбки*)
to be favoured (BrE), favored (AmE) (with)

удосу́жива|ться, юсь *impf. of*
▸ удосу́житься

удосу́ж|иться, усь, ишься *pf.* (*of*
▸ удосу́живаться) (+ *inf.*) (infml) to find time

(to); to manage

удочере́ни|е, я *nt.* adoption (*of daughter*)

удочер|и́ть, ю́, и́шь *pf.* (*of* ▸ удочеря́ть) to
adopt (*as a daughter*)

удочер|я́ть, я́ю *impf. of* ▸ удочери́ть

у́дочк|а, и *f.* (fishing) rod; (*in fig., infml phrr.*)
заки́нуть ∼у to cast a line; to put a line out
(= *to try to discover sth*); попа́сться на ∼у to
swallow the bait

**удра́|ть, удеру́, удерёшь, past ∼л, ∼ла́,
∼ло** *pf.* (*of* ▸ удира́ть) (infml) to make off;
to do a bunk (BrE)

удруж|и́ть, у́, и́шь *pf.* (+ *d.*) (infml) to do sb a
good turn; (iron.) to do sb a bad turn

удруч|а́ть, а́ю *impf. of* ▸ удручи́ть

удруч|и́ть, у́, и́шь *pf.* (*of* ▸ удруча́ть) to
depress, dishearten

уду́шлив|ый, ∼, ∼а *adj.* suffocating; ∼ая
жара́ stifling heat

уду́ш|е, я *nt.* breathlessness; suffocation

уедине́ни|е, я *nt.* solitude; seclusion

уединён|ный, ∼, ∼на *adj.* solitary, secluded

уедин|и́ться, ю́сь, и́шься *pf.* (*of*
▸ уединя́ться) (от + *g.*) to retire (from),
withdraw (from); to go off (by oneself); у. в
свое́й ко́мнате to retire to one's room

уедин|я́ться, я́юсь *impf. of* ▸ уедини́ться

уезжа́|ть, ю *impf. of* ▸ уе́хать

УЕФА́ *m. & f. indecl.* UEFA (*Union of
European Football Associations*)

уе́хать, уе́ду, уе́дешь, imper. уезжа́й(те)
pf. (*of* ▸ уезжа́ть) to go away, leave, depart

уж¹, а́ *m.* grass snake

⚔ **уж² 1** *adv.* = у́же **2** *emph. particle* (infml,
безусловно) to be sure, indeed, certainly;
уж он узна́ет he is sure to find out; (*очень*)
very; э́то не так уж сло́жно it's not so very
complicated

ужа́л|ить, ю, ишь *pf. of* ▸ жа́лить

у́жас, а *m.* **1** (*чувство страха*) horror,
terror; прийти́ в у. to be horrified; привести́
в у. to horrify **2** (usu. *in pl.*) (*предмет
страха*) horror; ∼ы го́лода the horrors of
famine; фильм ∼ов horror film/movie
3 (*as pred.*) (infml) it is awful, it is terrible;
ти́хий у. horror of horrors; како́й у.! how
awful!

ужас|а́ть, а́ю *impf. of* ▸ ужасну́ть

ужас|а́ться, а́юсь *impf. of* ▸ ужасну́ться

ужаса́ющий *adj.* awful, terrible

ужа́сно¹ *adv.* **1** horribly, terribly; у.
себя́ чу́вствовать to feel awful **2** (infml,
чрезвыча́йно) awfully, terribly; он у. пло́хо
игра́ет he plays terribly badly

ужа́сно² *as pred.* (infml) it is awful, it is terrible

ужас|ну́ть, ну́, нёшь *pf.* (*of* ▸ ужаса́ть) to
horrify, terrify

ужас|ну́ться, ну́сь, нёшься *pf.* (*of*
▸ ужаса́ться) to be horrified, be terrified

ужа́с|ный, ∼ен, ∼на *adj.* awful, terrible

у́же *comp. of* ▸ у́зкий

⚔ **уже́ 1** *adv.* already; now; by now; у. не

no longer; **они́ у. прие́хали** they are here already; **она́ у. не ребёнок** she is no longer a child **2** *emph. particle* = **уж¹**

ужесточа́|ть, ю *impf. of* ▶ **ужесточи́ть**

ужесточи́|ть, у́, и́шь *pf.* (*of* ▶ **ужесточа́ть**) to make stricter/harsher

ужива́|ться, юсь *impf. of* ▶ **ужи́ться**

у́жин, а *m.* supper

у́жина|ть, ю *impf.* (*of* ▶ **поу́жинать**) to have supper

ужи́|ться, ву́сь, вёшься, *past* ~**лся,** ~**ла́сь** *pf.* (*of* ▶ **ужива́ться**) (**с** + *i.*) to get on (with); **мы с ней так и не** ~**ли́сь** she and I simply couldn't get on

узако́нивани|е, я *nt.* legalization

узако́нива|ть, ю *impf. of* ▶ **узако́нить**

узако́н|ить, ю, ишь *pf.* (*of* ▶ **узако́нивать**) (*придать законную силу*) to legalize

узбе́к, а *m.* Uzbek

Узбекиста́н, а *m.* Uzbekistan

узбе́кский *adj.* Uzbek

узбе́ч|ка, ки *f. of* ▶ **узбе́к**

узде́чк|а, и *f.* bridle

у́з|ел, ла́ *m.* **1** (*на верёвке*) knot (also fig.); (*мера скорости*) knot; **завяза́ть у.** to tie a knot **2** (*место пересечения*) junction; (*центр*) centre (BrE), center (AmE); **телефо́нный у.** telephone exchange

узел|о́к, ка́ *m.* **1** small knot **2** (*свёрток*) small bundle

у́з|кий, ~**ок,** ~**ка́,** ~**ко,** ~**ки** *adj.* **1** narrow; ~**кое ме́сто** (fig.) bottleneck **2** (*об одежде*) tight **3** (fig., *ограниченный*) narrow, limited; **у. круг друзе́й** narrow circle of friends

узколо́б|ый, ~, ~**а** *adj.* (fig.) narrow-minded

✍ **узна|ва́ть, ю́, ёшь** *impf. of* ▶ **узна́ть**

✍ **узна́|ть, ю** *pf.* (*of* ▶ **узнава́ть**) **1** (*старого друга, свою машину*) to recognize **2** (*новости*) to learn, hear; (*обнаружить, выяснить*) to find out **3** (*нужду, любовь*) to get to know; to become familiar with

у́зник, а *m.* (rhet.) prisoner

у́зниц|а, ы *f. of* ▶ **у́зник**

узо́р, а *m.* pattern, design

у́зост|ь, и *f.* narrowness (also fig.); (*одежды*) tightness

уике́нд, а *m.* weekend

уи́к-э́нд, а *m.* = **уике́нд**

уйду́, дёшь *see* ▶ **уйти́**

у́йм|а, ы *f.* (+ *g.*) (infml) lots (of), masses (of)

уйму́, ёшь *see* ▶ **уня́ть**

✍ **уй|ти́, ду́, дёшь,** *past* **ушёл, ушла́** *pf.* (*of* ▶ **уходи́ть** 1) **1** (*покинуть место*) to go away, go off, leave; (**из, от, с** + *g.*) to leave: **у. из ко́мнаты** to leave the room; **у. домо́й** to go (off) home; **мне на́до у.** I must leave **2** (**от, из** + *g.*) (*спастись, избавиться*) to escape (from), get away (from); to evade **3** (**от, из, с** + *g.*) (*перестать заниматься чем-н.*) to retire (from), give up; **она́ ушла́ с рабо́ты** she left her job; **у. из поли́тики** to retire

from politics; **у.** (**из жи́зни**) to pass away (= *to die*) **4** (**в** + *a.*) (*погрузиться*) to sink (into); (fig.) to bury oneself (in); **у. в себя́** to retire into one's shell **5** (**на** + *a.*) (*израсходоваться*) to be spent; **на кни́гу ушёл год** a year was spent on the book **6** (*о времени, об эпохе*) to pass away, slip away

ука́з, а *m.* decree

указа́ни|е, я *nt.* (*инструкция*) instructions, directions

✍ **ука́з|анный** *p.p.p. of* ▶ **указа́ть** *and adj.* fixed, appointed; **на** ~**анном ме́сте** at the place appointed; **как** ~**ано** according to instructions, as instructed

указа́тел|ь, я *m.* **1** (*прибор, стрелка*) indicator; (*надпись*) sign; (comput.) cursor; **доро́жный у.** road sign; **у. у́ровня воды́** water gauge **2** (*справочный список*) index; **у. имён со́бственных** index of proper names **3** (*справочная книга*) guide, directory

указа́тельн|ый *adj.* indicating; ~**ая стре́лка** pointer; **у. па́лец** index finger; **у. знак** road sign

ука|за́ть, жу́, ~**жешь** *pf.* (*of* ▶ **ука́зывать** 1) **1** (*дорогу*) to show; (*адрес, день*) to indicate **2** (**на** + *a.*) (*жестом*) to point (at, to); (fig., *на ошибку, недостаток*) to point out

ука́зк|а, и *f.* pointer

✍ **ука́зыва|ть, ю** **1** *impf. of* ▶ **указа́ть** **2** (*no pf.*) (*свидетельствовать*) (**на** + *a.*) to indicate

ука|та́ть, а́ю *pf.* (*of* ▶ **ука́тывать¹**) **1** to roll (out); **у. доро́гу** (*катком*) to roll a road; (*ездой*) to make a road smooth **2** (infml, *утомить*) to wear out, tire out

ука|та́ться, а́ется *pf.* (*of* ▶ **ука́тываться¹**) (*о дороге*) to become smooth

ука|ти́ть, чу́, ~**тишь** *pf.* (*of* ▶ **ука́тывать²**) **1** (*бочку*) to roll away; (*велосипед*) to wheel away **2** (infml, *уехать*) to go off

ука|ти́ться, ~**тится** *pf.* (*of* ▶ **ука́тываться²**) to roll away

ука́тыва|ть¹, ю *impf. of* ▶ **укатать**

ука́тыва|ть², ю *impf. of* ▶ **укати́ть**

ука́тыва|ться¹, ется *impf. of* ▶ **ука́таться**

ука́тыва|ться², ется *impf. of* ▶ **укати́ться**

укач|а́ть, а́ю *pf.* (*of* ▶ **ука́чивать**) **1** (*до сна*) to rock to sleep **2** (*о море, о езде*) to make sick; (*impers.*) **меня́** ~**а́ло на парохо́де** I was (sea)sick on the boat; **в маши́не её ука́чивает** she gets travel-sick in cars

ука́чива|ть, ю *impf. of* ▶ **укача́ть**

укла́д, а *m.* structure; **у. жи́зни** style of life; **обще́ственно-экономи́ческий у.** social and economic structure

укла́дыва|ть, ю *impf. of* ▶ **уложи́ть**

укла́дыва|ться¹, юсь *impf.* (*of* ▶ **уложи́ться**): **э́то не** ~**ется в голове́** it is hard to take it in

укла́дыва|ться², юсь *impf. of* ▶ **уле́чься** 1, ▶ **уле́чься** 2

укло́н, а *m.* **1** slope; (*градиент*) gradient; **под у.** downhill **2** (fig., *направленность*) bias; шко́ла с математи́ческим ∼ом school with a mathematical bias

уклон|и́ться, ю́сь, и́шься *pf.* (*of* ▸ **уклоня́ться**) (от + *g.*) (*избежа́ть*) to avoid; to evade; **у. от отве́тственности** to evade responsibility; **у. от уда́ра** to dodge a blow; **у. от прямо́го отве́та** to avoid giving a direct answer

укло́нчив|ый, ∼, ∼а *adj.* evasive

уклон|я́ться, я́юсь *impf. of* ▸ **уклони́ться**

уко́л, а *m.* **1** (*була́вкой*) prick **2** (med.) injection; jab (BrE, infml) **3** (fig., *замеча́ние*) jibe

укол|о́ть, ю́, ∼ешь *pf. of* ▸ **коло́ть²** 1

укол|о́ться, ю́сь, ∼ешься *pf.* **1** (*була́вкой*) to prick oneself **2** (*impf.* ∼ **коло́ться²** 2) (infml, *о наркома́не*) to inject oneself

укора́чива|ть, ю *impf. of* ▸ **укороти́ть**

укорен|и́ться, и́тся *pf.* (*of* ▸ **укореня́ться**) to take, strike root (also fig.)

укорен|я́ться, я́ется *impf. of* ▸ **укорени́ться**

укоро|ти́ть, чу́, ти́шь *pf.* (*of* ▸ **укора́чивать**) to shorten

укра́дкой *adv.* stealthily, furtively

Украи́н|а, ы *f.* Ukraine

украи́н|ец, ца *m.* Ukrainian

украи́н|ка, ки *f. of* ▸ **украи́нец**

украи́нский *adj.* Ukrainian

укра́|сить, шу, сишь *pf.* (*of* ▸ **украша́ть**) (*дом, ко́мнату*) to decorate; (*ёлку*) to decorate (BrE), trim (AmE); (*речь, стиль*) to embellish; (*жизнь*) to enrich

укра́|сть, ду́, дёшь, *past* ∼**л** *pf.* (*of* ▸ **красть**) to steal

украша́|ть, ю *impf. of* ▸ **укра́сить**

украше́ни|е, я *nt.* **1** (*де́йствие*) decorating, decoration **2** (*предме́т*) decoration, ornament; (*ювели́рное*) jewellery **3** (*го́рдость*) pride; (*вы́ставки*) centrepiece (BrE), centerpiece (AmE)

укреп|и́ть, лю́, и́шь *pf.* (*of* ▸ **укрепля́ть**) **1** (*сте́ны, огра́ду, му́скулы*) to strengthen **2** (mil.) to fortify **3** (fig., *убежде́ние, любо́вь, власть, положе́ние, семью́*) to strengthen; **у. дисципли́ну** to tighten up discipline

укреп|и́ться, лю́сь, и́шься *pf.* (*of* ▸ **укрепля́ться**) **1** to become stronger **2** (mil.) to fortify one's position **3** (fig., *дисципли́на, власть*) to become firmly established; **у. в убежде́нии** to be confirmed in one's belief

укрепле́ни|е, я *nt.* **1** strengthening **2** (mil.) fortification

укрепля́|ть, ю *impf. of* ▸ **укрепи́ть**

укрепля́|ться, юсь *impf. of* ▸ **укрепи́ться**

укро́м|ный, ∼ен, ∼на *adj.* secluded; sheltered

укро́п, а *m.* (bot.) dill

укро|ти́ть, щу́, ти́шь *pf.* (*of* ▸ **укроща́ть**) **1** (*зве́ря*) to tame **2** (*чу́вство*) to curb

укроща́|ть, ю *impf. of* ▸ **укроти́ть**

укрыва́|ть, ю *impf. of* ▸ **укры́ть**

укрыва́|ться, юсь *impf. of* ▸ **укры́ться**

укры́ти|е, я *nt.* (mil., etc.) cover, concealment; shelter

укры́|ть, о́ю, о́ешь *pf.* (*of* ▸ **укрыва́ть**) **1** (*но́ги, поля́*) to cover (up) **2** (*престу́пника*) to conceal, harbour (BrE), harbor (AmE); (*бе́женца*) to (give) shelter

укры́|ться, о́юсь, о́ешься *pf.* (*of* ▸ **укрыва́ться**) **1** (*одея́лом*) to cover oneself (up) **2** (*от дождя́*) to take cover; to seek shelter **3** (*оста́ться незаме́тным*) to escape (sb's) notice

у́ксус, а (**у**) *m.* vinegar

уку́с, а *m.* bite; (*насеко́мого*) sting

уку|си́ть, шу́, ∼сишь *pf.* to bite; (*о насеко́мом*) to sting

уку́т|ать, аю *pf.* (*of* ▸ **уку́тывать**) (+ *i.* or **в** + *a.*) to wrap up (in)

уку́т|аться, аюсь *pf.* (*of* ▸ **уку́тываться**) (+ *i.* or **в** + *a.*) to wrap oneself up (in)

уку́тыва|ть, ю *impf. of* ▸ **уку́тать**

уку́тыва|ться, юсь *impf. of* ▸ **уку́таться**

✍ **ул.** (*abbr. of* **у́лица**) St., Street; Rd, Road

ула́влива|ть, ю *impf. of* ▸ **улови́ть**

ула́|дить, жу, дишь *pf.* (*of* ▸ **ула́живать**) (*спо́рный вопро́с, де́ло, недоразуме́ние*) to settle, resolve

ула́|диться, дится *pf.* (*of* ▸ **ула́живаться**) to be settled, resolved

ула́жива|ть, ю, ет *impf. of* ▸ **ула́дить**

ула́жива|ться, ется *impf. of* ▸ **ула́диться**

ула́мыва|ть, ю *impf. of* ▸ **уломать**

Ула́н-Ба́тор, а *m.* Ulan Bator

у́л|ей, ья *m.* (bee)hive

улет|а́ть, а́ю *impf. of* ▸ **улете́ть**

уле|те́ть, чу́, ти́шь *pf.* (*of* ▸ **улета́ть**) (*о пти́це*) to fly (away); (*о самолёте, о челове́ке*) to leave (*by air*)

уле́|чься, я́гусь, я́жешься, я́гутся, *past* ∼**гся,** ∼**егла́сь** *pf.* **1** (*impf.* **укла́дываться**) (*лечь*) to lie down **2** (*impf.* **укла́дываться**) (*умести́ться*) to find room (*to lie down*) **3** (*о пы́ли*) to settle

улизн|у́ть, у́, ёшь *pf.* (infml) to slip away, steal away

ули́к|а, и *f.* (piece of) evidence; **ко́свенная у.** circumstantial evidence

ули́тк|а, и *f.* (zool.) snail

✍ **у́лиц|а, ы** *f.* street; **на ∼е** in the street; (*вне до́ма*) out (of doors), outside

улич|а́ть, а́ю *impf. of* ▸ **уличи́ть**

улич|и́ть, у́, и́шь *pf.* (*of* ▸ **улича́ть**) (+ *a. and* **в** + *p.*) to expose (as); **его́ ∼и́ли в кра́же/ моше́нничестве** he was exposed as a thief/ fraud

у́личный *adj.* street

уло́в, а *m.* catch (*of fish*)

улов|и́ть, лю́, ∼ишь *pf.* (*of* ▸ **ула́вливать**) (*заме́тить*) to detect, perceive; (*смысл, связь*) to grasp, understand

уло́вк|а, и *f.* trick, ruse

улож|и́ть, у́, ∼ишь *pf.* (*of* ▸ **укла́дывать**) **1** (*положи́ть*) to lay; (*положи́ть спать*)

у

to put to bed; **у. в посте́ль** to put to bed **2** (*чемода́н, вещи*) to pack; (*в груду*) to pile, stack **3** (+ *i.*) (*покры́ть*) to cover (with), lay (with) **4** (*рельсы*) to lay **5** (*волосы*) to style

уложи́ться, у́сь, ~ишься *pf.* (*of* ▸ укла́дываться[1]) **1** (*упакова́ть ве́щи*) to pack (up) **2** (**в** + *a.*) (*умести́ться*) to go (in), fit (in) **3** (**в** + *a.*) (*в преде́лы*) to keep (within), confine oneself (to); **у. в полчаса́** to confine oneself to half an hour **4**: **у. в голове́**, to sink in, go in

уложа́|ть, ю *pf.* (*of* ▸ ула́мывать) (infml) to talk round; (+ *inf.*) to talk into, prevail upon (to)

✓ **улучш|а́ть, а́ю, ет** *impf. of* ▸ улу́чшить

улучши́|а́ться, ется *impf. of* ▸ улу́чшиться

✓ **улучше́ни|е, я** *nt.* improvement

улу́чш|ить, у, ишь *pf.* (*of* ▸ улучша́ть) to improve

улу́чш|иться, ится *impf.* (*of* ▸ улучша́ться) to improve

улыб|а́ться, а́юсь *impf.* (*of* ▸ улыбну́ться) **1** (+ *d.*) to smile (at); **она́ мне ~ну́лась** she smiled at me **2** (+ *d.*) (fig., *о жи́зни, о судьбе́*) to smile (upon)

улы́бк|а, и *f.* smile

улыб|ну́ться, ну́сь, нёшься *pf. of* ▸ улыба́ться

улы́бчив|ый, ~, ~а *adj.* (infml) smiling; happy

ультима́тум, а *m.* ultimatum

ультразву́к, а *m.* ultrasound

ультразвуково́й *adj.* (phys.) ultrasonic

ультрамари́н, а *m.* ultramarine

ультрафиоле́товый *adj.* ultraviolet

✓ **ум, а́** *m.* mind, intellect; wits; **склад ~а́** mentality; **быть без ~а́** (**от** + *g.*) to be out of one's mind (about), be crazy (about); (**счита́ть** *и т. п.*) **в ~е́** (to count, *etc.*) in one's head; **прийти́ на ум** (+ *d.*) to occur to one, cross one's mind; **быть на ~е́** (infml) to be on one's mind; **свести́ с ~а́** to drive mad; (fig., *очарова́ть*) to send wild; **сойти́ с ~а́** to go mad

умал|и́ть, ю́, и́шь *pf.* (*of* ▸ умаля́ть) to belittle, disparage

умалишённ|ый *adj.* mad, mentally ill; (*as n.* **у.**, **~ого**, *f.* **~ая**, **~ой**) madman; madwoman; **дом ~ых** mental hospital

ума́лчива|ть, ю *impf. of* ▸ умолча́ть

умал|я́ть, я́ю *impf. of* ▸ умали́ть

уме́лый *adj.* able, skilful (BrE), skillful (AmE)

уме́ни|е, я *nt.* ability, skill

уменьш|а́ть, а́ю *impf. of* ▸ уме́ньшить

уменьш|а́ться, а́юсь *impf. of* ▸ уме́ньшиться

уменьше́ни|е, я *nt.* reduction, diminution, decrease

уменьши́тельн|ый *adj.* (gram.) diminutive; **~ое и́мя** pet name (*as Kolya for Nikolai*)

уме́ньш|ить, ~у, ~ишь *pf.* (*of* ▸ уменьша́ть) to reduce, decrease

уме́ньш|иться, ~усь, ~ишься *pf.* (*of* ▸ уменьша́ться) to diminish, decrease; to abate

уме́р|енный *adj.* **1** (**~ен**, **~енна**) moderate (pol., also fig.); **~енная поли́тика** moderate policy **2** (geog., meteor.) temperate; moderate

✓ **умере́ть, умру́, умрёшь**, *past* **у́мер, ~ла́, у́мерло** *pf.* (*of* ▸ умира́ть 1) to die; **у. есте́ственной, наси́льственной сме́ртью** to die a natural, violent death

уме́р|ить, ю, ишь *pf.* (*of* ▸ умеря́ть) (*тре́бования*) to restrain

умер|тви́ть, щвлю́, тви́шь *pf.* (*of* ▸ умерщвля́ть) to kill, destroy (also fig.)

умерщвля́|ть, ю *impf. of* ▸ умертви́ть

умер|я́ть, я́ю *impf. of* ▸ уме́рить

уме|сти́ть, щу́, сти́шь *pf.* (*of* ▸ умеща́ть) to fit, find room (for)

уме|сти́ться, щу́сь, сти́шься *pf.* (*of* ▸ умеща́ться) to go in, fit in, find room

уме́ст|ный, ~ен, ~на *adj.* appropriate; pertinent; (*сде́ланный во́время*) opportune, timely; **ва́ше предложе́ние вполне́ ~но** your suggestion is quite in order

✓ **уме́|ть, ю** *impf.* (+ *inf.*) to be able (to), know how (to); **она́ ~ет ката́ться на конька́х** she can skate; **она́ не ~ет притворя́ться** she is incapable of pretending

умеща́|ть, ю *impf. of* ▸ умести́ть

умеща́|ться, юсь *impf. of* ▸ умести́ться

умил|и́ть, ю́, и́шь *pf.* (*of* ▸ умиля́ть) to move, touch

умил|и́ться, ю́сь, и́шься *pf.* (*of* ▸ умиля́ться) to be moved, be touched

умил|я́ть, я́ю *impf. of* ▸ умили́ть

умил|я́ться, я́юсь *impf. of* ▸ умили́ться

умира́|ть, ю *impf.* **1** *impf. of* ▸ умере́ть **2** (fig., *о́чень хоте́ть*) to be dying to; **~ю, как хочу́ спать** I'm dying to have a sleep; (**от** + *g.*) to be dying of; **у. от ску́ки** to be dying of boredom; to be bored to death

умиротворён|ный, ~, ~на *adj.* tranquil; contented

умне́е *comp. of* ▸ у́мный, ▸ умно́

умне́|ть, ю *impf.* (*of* ▸ поумне́ть) to grow wiser

у́мник, а *m.* (infml, iron.) know-all, smart alec

у́мниц|а, ы *c.g.* (infml) **1** (*о де́вочке*) good girl; (*о ма́льчике*) good boy **2** (*о челове́ке*) clever person

умно́ *adv.* cleverly, wisely; (*разу́мно*) sensibly

умнож|а́ть, а́ю *impf. of* ▸ умно́жить

умноже́ни|е, я *nt.* **1** increase, rise **2** (math.) multiplication

умно́ж|ить, у, ишь *pf.* (▸ мно́жить, ▸ умножа́ть) **1** to increase **2** (math.) to multiply

у́м|ный, ~ён, ~на́ *adj.* (*челове́к*) clever, wise, intelligent; (*лицо́, глаза́, кни́га*) intelligent; (*разу́мный*) sensible; (*as pred.*) **~но́** it is wise, it is sensible

умозри́тел|ьный, ~ен, ~ьна *adj.* (phil.) speculative; (*отвлечённый*) abstract

✓ **key word**

умол|и́ть, ю́, ~ишь pf. (of ▶ **умоля́ть 1**) to prevail upon

умолк|а́ть, а́ю impf. of ▶ **умо́лкнуть**

умо́лк|нуть, ну, нешь, past ~, ~ла pf. (of ▶ **умолка́ть**) (о человеке) to fall silent; (о звуках) to cease, stop; (о славе) to fade

умолча́ни|е, я nt. (comput.): **по ~ю** (by) default; **шрифт/настро́йки по ~ю** default font/settings

умолча́|ть, ю́ pf. (of ▶ **ума́лчивать**) (о + p.) to pass over in silence, fail to mention, suppress, hush up; **нельзя́ у. о** (+ p.) one must mention

умол|я́ть, я́ю impf. **1** impf. of ▶ **умоли́ть 2** to entreat, implore

умопомрачи́тел|ьный, ~ен, ~ьна adj. stupendous, tremendous, terrific

умори́тел|ьный, ~ен, ~ьна adj. (infml) hilarious

у́мственно adv. of ▶ **у́мственный; у. отста́лый** learning-disabled

у́мственный adj. mental, intellectual

умч|а́ться, у́сь, и́шься pf. **1** to whirl, hurtle away **2** (fig., время, детство) to fly past

умыва́льник, а m. washbasin

умыва́|ть, ю impf. of ▶ **умы́ть**

умыва́|ться, юсь impf. of ▶ **умы́ться**

умы́с|ел, ла m. design, intent(ion)

умы́|ть, о́ю, о́ешь pf. (of ▶ **умыва́ть**) to wash; **у. ру́ки** to wash one's hands (also fig.)

умы́|ться, о́юсь, о́ешься pf. (of ▶ **умыва́ться**) to wash (oneself)

умы́шленно adv. purposely, intentionally

умы́шленный adj. intentional, deliberate; (убийство) premeditated

унасле́д|овать, ую pf. of ▶ **насле́довать 1**

унес|ти́, у́, ёшь, past ~, ~ла́ pf. (of ▶ **уноси́ть**) **1** (уходя, взять с собой) to take away **2** (о воде, ветре) to carry away, remove; (impers.) **ло́дку ~ло́ тече́нием** the boat was carried away by the current **3** (fig., о мыслях, мечтах) to carry (in thought) **4** (fig., жизнь, здоровье) to claim; **война́ ~ла́ мно́го жи́зней** the war claimed many lives

унес|ти́сь, у́сь, ёшься, past ~ся, ~ла́сь pf. (of ▶ **уноси́ться**) **1** (поезд, машина) to speed away; (тучи) to be whisked away **2** (fig., миновать) to fly away, fly by **3** (fig., в мыслях, мечтах) to be carried away

универма́г, а m. (abbr. of **универса́льный магази́н**) department store

универса́л, а m. (infml, машина) estate car (BrE), station wagon (AmE)

универса́л|ьный, ~ен, ~ьна adj. **1** (проблема, язык) universal **2** (разносторонний) many-sided; versatile; **~ьные зна́ния** encyclopedic, knowledge; **~ьное образова́ние** all-round education **3** (инструмент) multi-purpose, all-purpose; **у. магази́н** department store; **у. си́мвол** (comput.) wild card

универса́м, а m. (abbr. of **универса́льный магази́н самообслу́живания**) supermarket

ꞏꞏ университе́т, а m. university; **поступи́ть в у.** to enter, start university; **око́нчить у.** to graduate (from a university)

университе́тский adj. of ▶ **университе́т**

унижа́|ть, ю impf. of ▶ **уни́зить**

унижа́|ться, юсь impf. of ▶ **уни́зиться**

униже́ни|е, я nt. humiliation, degradation, abasement

унизи́тел|ьный, ~ен, ~ьна adj. humiliating, degrading

уни́|зить, жу, зишь pf. (of ▶ **унижа́ть**) to humiliate; to degrade

уни́|зиться, жусь, зишься pf. (of ▶ **унижа́ться**) to demean oneself; **у. до лжи/про́сьбы/шантажа́** to stoop to lying/asking/blackmail

ꞏꞏ уника́л|ьный, ~ен, ~ьна adj. unique

унима́|ть, ю impf. of ▶ **уня́ть**

унима́|ться, юсь impf. of ▶ **уня́ться**

унита́з, а m. toilet (bowl)

унифо́рм|а, ы f. uniform

уничтож|а́ть, а́ю impf. of ▶ **уничто́жить**

уничтоже́ни|е, я nt. **1** destruction, annihilation **2** (упразднение) abolition, elimination

уничто́ж|ить, у, ишь pf. (of ▶ **уничтожа́ть**) **1** to destroy; (врага) to annihilate; (насекомых) to exterminate **2** (упразднить) to abolish; to do away with **3** (fig., унизить) to crush

уно|си́ть, шу́, ~сишь impf. of ▶ **унести́**

уно|си́ться, шу́сь, ~сишься impf. of ▶ **унести́сь**

у́нци|я, и f. ounce (measure)

уны́л|ый, ~, ~а adj. **1** (человек) despondent **2** (мысль, взгляд) melancholy, cheerless

уны́ни|е, я nt. despondency, depression

уня́|ть, уйму́, уймёшь, past ~л, ~ла́, ~ло pf. (of ▶ **унима́ть**) **1** (успокоить) to calm, soothe, pacify **2** (боль, кровотечение, слёзы) to stop; **у. пожа́р** to stop a fire **3** (чувства) to suppress

уня́|ться, уйму́сь, уймёшься, past ~лся, ~ла́сь pf. (of ▶ **унима́ться**) **1** (успокоиться) to calm down **2** (ветер, буря) to abate, die down; (боль, обида) to die down

упа́д|ок, ка m. decline; **у. ду́ха** depression; **у. сил** breakdown

упа́доч|ный, ~ен, ~на adj. **1** (искусство) decadent **2** depressive; **~ное настрое́ние** depression

упак|ова́ть, у́ю pf. (of ▶ **пакова́ть**, ▶ **упако́вывать**) to pack (up)

упако́вк|а, и f. **1** (действие) packing, packaging **2** (материал) packaging; (пакет) package

упако́выва|ть, ю impf. of ▶ **упакова́ть**

упа́|сть, ду́, дёшь, past ~л pf. (of ▶ **па́дать 1**) to fall

у

упер|éть, упру́, упрёшь, *past* ~, ~ла *pf.* (*of* ▸ упирáть 1) (+ *a. and* в + *a.*) to rest (against), prop (against), lean (against); **у. лéстницу в стéну** to rest a ladder against the wall

упер|éться, упрусь, упрёшься, *past* ~ся, ~лась *pf.* (*of* ▸ упирáться 1) **1** (+ *i. and* в + *a.*) to rest (against), lean (against); **у. ногáми в зéмлю** to dig one's heels in the ground **2** (infml, fig., *не согласиться*) to dig one's heels in

упирá|ть, ю *impf.* **1** *impf. of* ▸ уперéть **2** (*impf. only*) (на + *a.*) (infml) to stress, insist (on)

упирá|ться, юсь *impf.* **1** *impf. of* ▸ уперéться **2** (*impf. only*) (в + *a.*) (*сопротивляться*) to come up (against), be held up (by)

упи́тан|ный, ~, ~на *adj.* well fed; (*толстый*) plump

упла|ти́ть, чу́, ~тишь *pf.* (*of* ▸ уплáчивать) to pay; **у. по счёту** to pay a bill, settle an account

уплáчива|ть, ю *impf. of* ▸ уплати́ть

уплывá|ть, ю *impf. of* ▸ уплы́ть

уплы́|ть, ву́, вёшь, *past* ~л, ~лá, ~ло *pf.* (*of* ▸ уплывáть) (*вплавь*) to swim away; (*о кораблях*) to sail away; (*о вещах*) to float away

уподóб|ить, лю, ишь *pf.* (*of* ▸ уподобля́ть) to liken

уподóб|иться, люсь, ишься *pf.* (*of* ▸ уподобля́ться) (+ *d.*) to become like

уподобля́|ть, ю *impf. of* ▸ уподóбить

уподобля́|ться, юсь *impf. of* ▸ уподóбиться

упои́тель|ный, ~ен, ~ьна *adj.* intoxicating, ravishing

уполз|áть, áю *impf. of* ▸ уползти́

уполз|ти́, у́, ёшь, *past* ~, ~лá *pf.* (*of* ▸ уползáть) to creep, crawl away

уполномóченный *p.p.p. of* ▸ уполномóчить; (*as m. n. у.*, ~енного) representative, authorized person; **у. по правáм человéка** ombudsman

уполномóчива|ть, ю *impf. of* ▸ уполномóчить

уполномóч|ить, у, ишь *pf.* (*of* ▸ уполномóчивать) (на + *a.*) to authorize

упоминáни|е, я *nt.* mentioning; (о + *p.*) mention (of)

упоминá|ть, ю *impf. of* ▸ упомяну́ть

упомяну́|ть, у́, ~ешь *pf.* (*of* ▸ упоминáть) (+ *a. or* о + *p.*) to mention, refer (to)

упóр, а *m.* **1** rest, support; (tech.) brace **2**: **в у.** (mil.) point-blank (also fig.); **сказáть комý-н. в у.** to tell sb point-blank **3**: **сдéлать у.** (на + *a. or p.*) to lay stress (on)

упóр|ный, ~ен, ~на *adj.* (*упрямый*) stubborn; (*настойчивый*) persistent

упóрств|о, а *nt.* (*упрямство*) stubbornness; (*настойчивость*) persistence

---

упорхн|у́ть, у́, ёшь *pf.* to fly, flit away

упоря́дочива|ть, ю *impf. of* ▸ упоря́дочить

упоря́доч|ить, у, ишь *pf.* (*of* ▸ упоря́дочивать) to regulate, put in (good) order

употреби́тель|ный, ~ен, ~ьна *adj.* (widely-)used; common, usual

употреб|и́ть, лю́, и́шь *pf.* (*of* ▸ употребля́ть) to use; to make use (of)

употреблéни|е, я *nt.* use; (*применение*) application; **вы́йти из ~я** to fall into disuse

употребля́|ть, ю *impf. of* ▸ употреби́ть

упрáв|иться, люсь, ишься *pf.* (*of* ▸ управля́ться) (с + *i.*) **1** (*с работой*) to cope (with), manage **2** (*с противником*) to deal (with) (= *to get the better of*)

☛ **управлéни|е**, я *nt.* **1** management, administration; direction; **оркéстр под ~ем Спивакóва** orchestra conducted by Spivakov **2** (tech.) control; (*автомобилем*) driving; (*самолётом*) piloting; (*кораблём*) steering; **дистанциóнное у.** remote control **3** (*деятельность органов власти*) government **4** (*учреждение*) office **5** (tech., *совокупность приборов*) controls

управля́|ть, ю *impf.* (+ *i.*) **1** (*учреждением*) to manage, run; (*оркестром, хором*) to conduct; (*страной*) to govern **2** (tech.) (*машиной*) to control, operate; (*автомобилем*) to drive; (*самолётом*) to pilot; (*кораблём, яхтой*) to steer, navigate

управля́|ться, юсь *impf. of* ▸ упрáвиться

управля́ющ|ий, ~его *n.* (в учреждении) manager; (в имении) steward

☛ **упражнéни|е**, я *nt.* (*гимнастическое, музыкальное*) exercise; (*действие*) (*мышц*) exercising; (*на рояле*) practice, practising (BrE), practicing (AmE); **у. пáмяти** memory training

упражня́|ть, ю *impf.* to exercise, train

упражня́|ться, юсь *impf.* (в + *p. or* на + *p. or* с + *i.*) to practise (BrE), practice (AmE), train (at)

упраздни́|ть, ю́, и́шь *pf.* (*of* ▸ упраздня́ть) to abolish

упраздня́|ть, я́ю *impf. of* ▸ упраздни́ть

упрáшива|ть, ю *impf. of* ▸ упроси́ть 1

упре|ди́ть, жу́, ди́шь *pf.* (*of* ▸ упреждáть) to forestall, anticipate

упреждá|ть, ю *impf. of* ▸ упреди́ть

упрёк, а *m.* reproach; **брóсить у. комý-н.** to reproach sb; **стáвить комý-н. что-н. в у.** to hold sth against sb

упрек|áть, áю *impf.* (*of* ▸ упрекну́ть) (в + *p.*) to reproach (for)

упрек|ну́ть, ну́, нёшь *inst. pf. of* ▸ упрекáть

упро|си́ть, шу́, ~сишь *pf.* (*of* ▸ упрáшивать) **1** (*настойчиво просить*) to beg, entreat **2** (*pf. only*) (*убедить сделать что-н.*) to prevail upon

упро|сти́ть, щу́, сти́шь *pf.* (*of* ▸ упрощáть) to simplify; (до + *g.*) to reduce (to)

☛ key word

упро|сти́ться, сти́тся *pf.* (*of* ▸ упроща́ться) to become simpler, be simplified

упро́чива|ть, ю *impf. of* ▸ упро́чить

упро́чива|ться, юсь *impf. of* ▸ упро́читься

упро́ч|ить, у, ишь *pf.* (*of* ▸ упро́чивать) to strengthen, consolidate; to establish firmly

упро́ч|иться, усь, ишься *pf.* (*of* ▸ упро́чиваться) **1** to be strengthened, consolidated; to be firmly established; **на́ше положе́ние ~илось** our position is firmly established **2** (*упрочить своё положение*) to establish oneself (firmly), settle oneself

упроща́|ть, ю, ет *impf. of* ▸ упрости́ть

упроща́|ться, ется *impf. of* ▸ упрости́ться

упроще́ни|е, я *nt.* simplification

упру́г|ий, ~, ~а *adj.* elastic, resilient; **~ая похо́дка** springy gait

упру́гост|ь, и *f.* elasticity, resilience; (*походки*) spring

у́пряж|ь, и *f.* harness, gear

упря́м|ец, ца *m.* obstinate person

упря́м|иться, люсь, ишься *impf.* to be obstinate; (**в** + *p.*) to persist (in)

упря́мств|о, а *nt.* obstinacy, stubbornness

упря́м|ый, ~, ~а *adj.* **1** (*неуступчивый*) obstinate, stubborn **2** (*настойчивый*) persistent

упря́|тать, чу, чешь *pf.* (*of* ▸ упря́тывать) **1** (*спрятать*) to hide, conceal **2** (*fig., infml*) (*убрать*) to put away; (*услать*) to banish; **у. в тюрьму́** to lock up

упря́тыва|ть, ю *impf. of* ▸ упря́тать

упуска́|ть, ю *impf. of* ▸ упусти́ть

упу|сти́ть, щу́, ~стишь *pf.* (*of* ▸ упуска́ть) **1** (*из рук*) to let go, let slip, let fall; (*отпустить*) to let go; (*не заметить*) to miss **2** (*fig., пропустить*) to let go, let slip; to miss; to lose; **у. возмо́жность, слу́чай** to miss an opportunity

ура́ *int.* hurrah!, hurray!

уравне́ни|е, я *nt.* **1** (*в правах*) equalization **2** (*math.*) equation

уравнове́|сить, шу, сишь *pf.* (*of* ▸ уравнове́шивать) **1** to balance **2** (*fig.*) to counterbalance, offset

уравнове́шенный *p.p.p. of* ▸ уравнове́сить *and adj.* (*fig.*) balanced, steady

уравнове́шива|ть, ю *impf. of* ▸ уравнове́сить

урага́н, а *m.* hurricane; (*fig., событий*) storm

Ура́л, а *m.* (*горы*) the Urals (*pl.*)

ура́н, а *m.* **1** (chem.) uranium **2** (astron.) (**У.**) Uranus

урв|а́ть, у́, ёшь, past ~а́л, ~ала́, ~а́ло *pf.* (*of* ▸ урыва́ть) (infml) to snatch (also fig.), grab; **у. мину́ту-две для бесе́ды** to snatch a minute or two for a chat

урегули́р|овать, ую *pf.* (*of* ▸ регули́ровать 2) (*отношения*) to normalize; (*вопрос, спор*) to settle

уре́|зать, жу, жешь *pf.* (*of* ▸ урезáть) **1** (infml, *края*) to cut off; to shorten

2 (*бюджет*) to cut down, reduce; (*права*) to reduce; **у. шта́ты** to cut down the staff

урезáть, áю *impf. of* ▸ уре́зать

у́рн|а, ы *f.* **1** (*для праха*) urn **2**: **избира́тельная у.** ballot box **3** (*для мусора*) refuse bin (BrE), garbage can (AmE)

✧ **у́ров|ень, ня** *m.* level; (fig.) standard; **у. мо́ря** sea level; **высота́ над ~нем мо́ря** altitude above sea level; **у. жи́зни** standard of living

уро́д, а *m.* **1** freak, monster **2** (*некрасивый человек*) ugly person **3** (*оскорбление*) bastard (*as a term of abuse, usu. of a man*)

уро́длив|ый, ~, ~а *adj.* **1** (*с уродством*) deformed, misshapen **2** (*некрасивый*) ugly **3** (fig., *плохой, ненормальный*) bad; abnormal; faulty; distorted

уро́д|овать, ую *impf.* (*of* ▸ изуро́довать) **1** (*калечить*) to deform, disfigure, mutilate **2** (*делать некрасивым*) to make ugly **3** (fig., *искажать*) to distort

уро́дств|о, а *nt.* **1** (*физический недостаток*) deformity; disfigurement **2** (*некрасивость*) ugliness **3** (fig., *ненормальность*) abnormality

урожа́|й, я *m.* **1** harvest; crop; **собра́ть у.** to gather in the harvest **2** (*хороший сбор*) bumper crop, abundance (also fig., infml)

уроже́н|ец, ца *m.* (+ *g.*) native (of)

уроже́н|ка, ки *f. of* ▸ уроже́нец

✧ **уро́к, а** *m.* **1** lesson (also fig.); **брать ~и** (+ *g.*) to have, take lessons (in); **дава́ть ~и** (+ *g.*) to give lessons (in) **2** (*задание*) homework; **зада́ть у.** to set homework; **сде́лать ~и** to do one's homework

уро́н, а (*no pl.*) *m.* (*материальный*) damages, losses; (*о людях*) casualties; **нанести́ у.** (*урожаю*) to inflict damage (on); (*врагу*) to inflict casualties (on)

уро́н|ить, ю́, ~ишь *pf. of* ▸ роня́ть 3

уругва́|ец, йца *m.* Uruguayan

Уругва́|й, я *m.* Uruguay

уругва́й|ка, ки *f. of* ▸ уругва́ец

уругва́йский *adj.* Uruguayan

урч|а́ть, у́, и́шь *impf.* to rumble; (*о собаке*) to growl

урыва́|ть, ю *impf. of* ▸ урва́ть

ус, а *m.* **1** (*see also* ▸ усы́) (*человека*) moustache hair (BrE), mustache hair (AmE) **2** (*животного*) whisker

уса|ди́ть, жу́, ~дишь *pf.* (*of* ▸ уса́живать) **1** (*помочь усесться*) to seat, help sit down; (*заставить усесться*) to make sit down **2** (**за** + *a. or* + *inf.*) to sit (*sb*) down; **у. за уро́ки** to sit *sb* down to his/her lessons

уса́дьб|а, ы, g. pl. уса́деб *f.* **1** (hist., *помещика*) country estate **2** (*ферма*) farmstead

уса́жива|ть, ю *impf. of* ▸ усади́ть

уса́жива|ться, юсь *impf. of* ▸ усе́сться

уса́т|ый, ~, ~а *adj.* **1** (*человек*) with a moustache (BrE), mustache (AmE) **2** (*животное*) whiskered

усва́ива|ть, ю *impf. of* ▸ усво́ить

усво́|ить, ю, ишь *pf.* (of ▶ усва́ивать)
1 (*привычку*) to adopt, acquire; to imitate
2 (*урок*) to master; to assimilate **3** (*пищу*)
to assimilate

усе́ива|ть, ю *impf. of* ▶ усе́ять

усе́рд|ный, ∼ен, ∼на *adj.* diligent,
painstaking

усе́|сться, уся́дусь, уся́дешься, *past*
∼лся, ∼лась *pf.* (of ▶ уса́живаться)
1 to take a seat; to settle (down) **2** (за + *a.*
or + *inf.*) to set (to), settle down (to)

усе́|ять, ю, ешь *pf.* (of ▶ усе́ивать) (+ *i.*)
1 (*засеять*) to sow (with) **2** (*покрыть*) to
cover (with), dot (with), stud (with), strew
(with); лицо́, ∼янное весну́шками face
covered with freckles

усиде́ть, жу́, ди́шь *pf.* **1** (*остаться
сидеть*) to keep one's place, remain sitting;
он так волнова́лся, что е́ле ∼де́л he was so
excited that he could hardly sit still **2** (infml,
удержаться на каком-н. месте) to stay
around in a place

у́сик, а *m.* (zool.) antenna, feeler

усиле́ни|е, я *nt.* **1** (*контроля*) strengthening;
(*охраны, прочности*) reinforcement
2 (*работы*) intensification; (*проблем*)
aggravation; (radio) amplification

уси́л|енный *p.p.p. of* ▶ уси́лить *and adj.*
1 (*охрана*) reinforced; ∼енное пита́ние
high-calorie diet **2** (*внимание, скорость*)
intensified, increased

уси́лива|ть, ю, ет *impf. of* ▶ уси́лить

уси́лива|ться, ется *impf. of* ▶ уси́литься

▶ **уси́ли|е**, я *nt.* effort; exertion; приложи́ть все
∼я to make every effort, spare no effort

усили́тел|ь, я *m.* amplifier

уси́л|ить, ю, ишь *pf.* (of
▶ уси́ливать) **1** (*войска, конструкцию*)
to strengthen, reinforce **2** (*наблюдение,
волнение*) to intensify, increase; (*звук*) to
amplify

уси́л|иться, ится *pf.* (of ▶ уси́ливаться)
(*о ветре, чувстве*) to become stronger;
(*о дожде, боли*) to intensify, increase; (*звук*)
to grow louder

уска|ка́ть, чу́, ∼чешь *pf.* **1** (*о зайце*) to
bound away; (infml, *о человеке*) to run off
2 (*о лошади; на лошади*) to gallop off

ускольза́|ть, а́ю *impf. of* ▶ ускользну́ть

ускользн|у́ть, у́, нёшь *pf.* (of ▶ ускольза́ть)
1 (*из рук*) to slip out; (*из-под ног*) to slip
away **2** (fig., infml, *о человеке*) to slip off
3 (fig.) (*от* + *g.*) to escape; у. от чьего́-л.
внима́ния to escape one's notice

ускоре́ни|е, я *nt.* acceleration; speeding up

ускори́тел|ь, я *m.* (tech.) accelerator;
у. части́ц particle accelerator

уско́р|ить, ю, ишь *pf.* (of ▶ ускоря́ть)
1 (*убыстрить*) to quicken; to speed up,
accelerate; у. шаг to quicken one's pace
2 (*приблизить*) to hasten; (*смерть, что-н.
плохое*) to precipitate

уско́р|иться, ится *pf.* (of ▶ ускоря́ться)
1 (*шаги*) to quicken; (*ход механизма*) to
accelerate **2** (*выздоровление, отъезд*) to be
speeded up

ускоря́|ть, я́ю, я́ет *impf. of* ▶ уско́рить

ускоря́|ться, я́ется *impf. of* ▶ уско́риться

уследи́ть, жу́, ди́шь *pf.* (за + *i.*) **1** (*за
ребёнком*) to keep an eye (on), mind **2** (*за
ходом разговора*) to follow

▶ **усло́ви|е**, я *nt.* **1** (*требование*) condition;
stipulation, proviso; поста́вить ∼ем to
make it a condition, stipulate; при ∼и, что;
с ∼ем, что on condition that, provided
that, providing **2** (*in pl.*) (*правила,
обстоятельства*) conditions; пого́дные ∼я
weather conditions

усло́в|ный *adj.* **1** (*принятый*) conventional;
(*знак, жест*) agreed, prearranged **2** (∼ен,
∼на) (*с условием*) conditional; у. пригово́р
(law) suspended sentence **3** (∼ен, ∼на)
(*относительный*) relative **4** (∼ен, ∼на)
(*воображаемый*) imaginary **5** (gram.)
conditional

усложне́ни|е, я *nt.* complication

усложн|и́ть, ю́, и́шь *pf.* (of ▶ усложня́ть)
to complicate

усложн|и́ться, и́тся *pf.* (of ▶ усложня́ться)
to become complicated

усложня́|ть, я́ю, я́ет *impf. of* ▶ усложни́ть

усложня́|ться, я́ется *impf. of* ▶ усложни́ться

▶ **услу́г|а**, и *f.* **1** service; favour (BrE), favor
(AmE), good turn; оказа́ть ∼у кому́-н. to do
sb a service; к ва́шим ∼ам at your service
2 (*in pl.*) service(s); коммуна́льные ∼и
public utilities

услу́жлив|ый, ∼, ∼а *adj.* obliging

▶ **услы́ш|ать**, у, ишь *pf. of* ▶ слы́шать 1

усмех|а́ться, а́юсь *impf. of* ▶ усмехну́ться

усмех|ну́ться, ну́сь, нёшься *pf.* (of
▶ усмеха́ться) to smirk; to grin

усмир|и́ть, ю́, и́шь *pf.* (of ▶ усмиря́ть)
1 (*успокоить*) to pacify; to calm, quieten;
(*укротить*) to tame (also fig.) **2** (*мятеж*)
to suppress, put down

усмиря́|ть, я́ю *impf. of* ▶ усмири́ть

усн|у́ть, у́, ёшь *pf.* to go to sleep, fall asleep
(also fig.)

усоверше́нств|овать, ую *pf. of*
▶ соверше́нствовать

усоверше́нств|оваться, уюсь *pf. of*
▶ соверше́нствоваться

усомн|и́ться, ю́сь, и́шься *pf.* (в + *p.*)
to doubt

усо́х|нуть, ну, нешь, *past* ∼, ∼ла *pf.* (of
▶ усыха́ть) to dry up, dry out; (*о человеке*)
to wither

успева́|ть, ю *impf.* **1** *impf. of* ▶ успе́ть
2 (*impf. only*) (в + *p.* or по + *d.*) to make
progress (in), get on well (in, at) (*studies*)

▶ **успе́|ть**, ю *pf.* (of ▶ успева́ть 1) **1** to have
time; to manage; у. написа́ть to have time
to write; у. к по́езду to manage to catch the
train; не ∼л я вы́йти из до́ма, как пошёл

ꙮ key word

у

дождь no sooner had I left the house than it started to rain

✧ **успе́х, а** *m.* **❶** success; **име́ть большо́й у.** to be a great success; **по́льзоваться ~ом** to be successful with sb; **с тем же ~ом** equally well, with the same result; **с ~ом** successfully **❷** (*in pl.*) success, progress; **де́лать ~и (в + р.)** to make progress (in)

✧ **успе́шно** *adv.* successfully

✧ **успе́ш|ный, ~ен, ~на** *adj.* successful

успока́ива|ть, ю *impf. of* ▶ **успоко́ить**

успока́ива|ться, юсь *impf. of* ▶ **успоко́иться**

успокойтельный, ~ен, ~ьна *adj.* calming, soothing; reassuring; (*as nt. n.* **~ьное, ~ьного**) sedative

успоко́|ить, ю, ишь *pf.* (*of* ▶ **успока́ивать**) **❶** to calm (down); (*убедить не тревожиться*) to reassure **❷** (*боль*) to assuage, deaden

успоко́|иться, юсь, ишься *pf.* (*of* ▶ **успока́иваться**) **❶** (*о человеке*) to calm down; to compose oneself **❷** (*быть довольным*) to be satisfied; **у. на дости́гнутом** to be content with what has been achieved **❸** (*о боли*) to abate; (*о море*) to become still; (*о ветре*) to drop

уста́в, а *m.* regulations, rules, statutes; (*mil.*) service regulations; (*в монастыре*) rule; **у. университе́та** university statutes; **У. ООН** UN Charter

уста|ва́ть, ю́, ёшь *impf. of* ▶ **уста́ть**

уста́лост|ь, и *f.* fatigue, tiredness

уста́лый *adj.* tired, weary

✧ **устана́влива|ть, ю, ет** *impf. of* ▶ **установи́ть**

устана́влива|ться, ется *impf. of* ▶ **установи́ться**

установ|и́ть, лю́, ~ишь *pf.* (*of* ▶ **устана́вливать**) **❶** (*поставить, поместить*) to place, put, set up; (*оборудование, механизм*) to install, rig up; (*памятник*) to put up; (*comput., программу*) to install **❷** (*показание*) to adjust, regulate, set (to, by); **у. часы́ по ра́дио** to set one's watch by the radio **❸** (*власть, контакт*) to establish; **у. связь (с + i.)** (mil.) to establish communication (with) **❹** (*назначить*) to fix, establish; **у. гра́фик** to fix the schedule **❺** (*обнаружить, выяснить*) to establish, determine; to ascertain; **у. причи́ну ава́рии** to establish the cause of a crash

установ|и́ться, ~ится *pf.* (*of* ▶ **устана́вливаться**) to be established; to set in; **~и́лся обы́чай** it has become a custom

✧ **устано́вк|а, и** *f.* **❶** (*действие*) placing, setting up, arrangement; (*оборудования, механизма*) installation, setting up; (*величины*) setting **❷** (*часов*) adjustment, setting **❸** (comput.) set-up **❹** (*цель*) aim, purpose **❺** (*директива*) directive

установле́ни|е, я *nt.* establishment; (*определение*) determination

устано́в|ленный *p.p.p. of* ▶ **установи́ть** *and adj.* established, fixed, prescribed,

regulation; **в ~ленном поря́дке** in prescribed manner

устарева́|ть, ю *impf. of* ▶ **устаре́ть**

устаре́вший *past. part. act. of* ▶ **устаре́ть** *and adj.* obsolete

устаре́|ть, ю *pf.* (*of* ▶ **устарева́ть**, ▶ **старе́ть** 2) to become obsolete; to become antiquated, out of date

уста́|ть, ну, нешь *pf.* (*of* ▶ **уставать**) to become tired; **я ~л** I am tired; **у. от** (+ *g.*) get tired of (sb, sth); **мы ~ли с доро́ги** we're tired from the journey

устила́|ть, ю *impf. of* ▶ **устла́ть**

устла́|ть, устелю́, усте́лешь *pf.* (*of* ▶ **устила́ть**) (+ *i.*) to cover (with); (*плитами, камнями*) to pave (with)

у́стн|ый *adj.* verbal, oral; **~ая речь** spoken language; **у. экза́мен** oral (examination)

усто́йчивост|ь, и *f.* (*опоры*) stability, steadiness; (*веры*) firmness

усто́йчив|ый, ~, ~ая *adj.* (*опора, плот*) stable, steady; (*вера, принцип*) firm; **~ая пого́да** settled weather

усто|я́ть, ю́, и́шь *pf.* **❶** (*не упасть*) to keep one's balance, remain standing; **у. на нога́х** to keep one's balance **❷** (fig., *в споре*) to stand one's ground **❸** (*не поддаться*) to resist, hold out; **у. пе́ред собла́зном** to resist a temptation

усто|я́ться, и́тся *pf.* (*о взглядах*) to become fixed, become permanent

✧ **устра́ива|ть, ю** *impf. of* ▶ **устро́ить**

устра́ива|ться, юсь *impf. of* ▶ **устро́иться**

устран|и́ть, ю́, и́шь *pf.* (*of* ▶ **устраня́ть**) **❶** (*убрать в сторону*) to remove; **у. прегра́ды** to remove obstacles; (*уничтожить*) to eliminate **❷** (*уволить*) to remove (*from office*); to dismiss

устран|я́ть, я́ю *impf. of* ▶ **устрани́ть**

устраша́ющий *adj.* frightening, appalling

устрем|и́ться, лю́сь, и́шься *pf.* (*of* ▶ **устремля́ться**) **❶** (**на** + *a.*) (*направиться*) to rush (upon, at); to head (for) **❷** (**на** + *a.* or **к** + *d.*) (*сосредоточиться*) to be directed (at, towards), be fixed (upon), be concentrated (on); (*о человеке*) to concentrate (on)

устремля́|ться, юсь *impf. of* ▶ **устреми́ться**

у́стриц|а, ы *f.* oyster

устро́|ить, ю, ишь *pf.* (*of* ▶ **устра́ивать**) **❶** (*изготовить, сооружить*) to make, construct **❷** (*концерт*) to arrange, organize **❸** (*вызвать*) to make, cause, create; **у. сканда́л** to make a scene **❹** (*наладить*) to settle, put in (good) order; **у. свои́ дела́** to put one's affairs in order **❺** (*поместить*) to place, fix up; **у. кого́-н. на рабо́ту** to fix sb up with work **❻** (*impers.*) (infml, *оказаться удобным*) to suit, be convenient (to, for)

устро́|иться, юсь, ишься *pf.* (*of* ▶ **устра́иваться**) **❶** (*прийти в порядок*) to work out (well) **❷** (*наладить свои дела*) to manage, get by **❸** (*расположиться*) to settle down, get settled **❹** (*на работу*) to get (*a job*); **он ~ился на желе́зную доро́гу**

у

проводнико́м he has got a job on the railway as a conductor

ꝏ **устро́йств|о, а** *nt.* **1** (*расположение, конструкция*) construction; layout; (tech.) working principle(s) **2** (*прибор*) apparatus, device **3** (*порядок, строй*) structure, system; **обще́ственное у.** social structure

усту́п, а *m.* (*в стене, скале*) shelf, ledge; (agric.) terrace

уступа́|ть, а́ю *impf. of* ▸ **уступи́ть**

уступ|и́ть, лю́, ~ишь *pf.* (*of* ▸ **уступа́ть**) (+ *d.*) **1** (*в пользу другого*) to let have, give up (to); **у. кому́-н. ме́сто** to give up one's place/seat to sb; **у. доро́гу** (+ *d.*) to make way (for), let pass **2** (*покориться*) to yield (to), give in (to); **у. кому́-н. в спо́ре** to give in to sb's argument **3** (*быть хуже кого-н., чего-н.*) to be inferior (to); **как расска́зчик он никому́ не ~ит** as a storyteller he is second to none

усту́пк|а, и *f.* **1** concession, compromise **2** (*в цене*) reduction, discount

усту́пчив|ый, ~, ~а *adj.* pliant, pliable; compliant

у́сть|е, я, *g. pl.* **~ев** *nt.* (*реки*) mouth, estuary

усугуб|и́ть, ~лю́, ~и́шь *pf.* (*of* ▸ **усугубля́ть**) to increase; to intensify; to aggravate

усугубля́|ть, ю *impf. of* ▸ **усугуби́ть**

ус|ы́, о́в *m. pl.* (*sg.* **ус, а**) (*человека*) moustache (BrE), mustache (AmE) (*see also* ▸ **ус**)

усынов|и́ть, лю́, и́шь *pf.* (*of* ▸ **усыновля́ть**) to adopt (*as a son*)

усыновле́ни|е, я *nt.* adoption (*of son*)

усыновля́|ть, ю *impf. of* ▸ **усынови́ть**

усы́п|ать, лю, лешь *pf.* (*of* ▸ **усыпа́ть**) (+ *i.*) to strew (with), scatter (with); (*покрыть*) to cover (with)

усыпа́|ть, а́ю *impf. of* ▸ **усы́пать**

усып|и́ть, лю́, и́шь *pf.* (*of* ▸ **усыпля́ть**) **1** (*перед операцией*) to put to sleep; (*пением, чтением*) to lull to sleep **2** (fig.) (*подозрения*) to lull; (*внимание*) to weaken, undermine **3** (*больную собаку*) to put to sleep

усыпля́|ть, ю *impf. of* ▸ **усыпи́ть**

усыха́|ть, ю *impf. of* ▸ **усо́хнуть**

ута́ива|ть, ю *impf. of* ▸ **утаи́ть**

утаи́|ть, ю́, и́шь *pf.* (*of* ▸ **ута́ивать**) **1** (*скрыть*) to conceal; (*умолчать*) to keep to oneself, keep secret **2** (*присвоить*) to appropriate

ута́птыва|ть, ю *impf. of* ▸ **утопта́ть**

утащ|и́ть, у́, ~ишь *pf.* **1** to drag away, off (*also fig.*) **2** (infml, *украсть*) to steal, pinch (BrE)

у́твар|ь, и (*no pl.*) *f.* (*collect.*) utensils, equipment

утвер|ди́ть, жу́, ди́шь *pf.* (*of* ▸ **утвержда́ть** 1) **1** (*диктатуру, правила*) to establish (*securely, firmly*) **2** (*санкционировать*)

to approve; to confirm; (*договор*) to ratify; **у. пове́стку дня** to approve an agenda; **у. в до́лжности** to confirm in a job

утвер|ди́ться, жу́сь, ди́шься *pf.* (*of* ▸ **утвержда́ться**) **1** (*укрепиться*) to gain a foothold, gain a firm hold (*also fig.*); (*порядок, режим*) to become firmly established **2** (**в** + *p.*) (*поверить*) to be confirmed in (*one's resolve, etc.*); **у. в мы́сли** to become firmly convinced **3** (**за** + *i.*) (*о репутации*): **за ним ~ди́лась репута́ция хоро́шего инжене́ра** he gained a reputation for being a good engineer

ꝏ **утвержда́|ть, ю** *impf.* **1** *impf. of* ▸ **утверди́ть** **2** (*impf. only*) to assert, maintain; (*без доказательства*) to claim, allege

утвержда́|ться, юсь *impf. of* ▸ **утверди́ться**

утвержде́ни|е, я *nt.* **1** (*высказывание*) claim, allegation **2** (*санкционирование*) approval; confirmation; (*договора*) ratification; (law, *завещания*) probate **3** (*диктатуры, порядка*) establishment

утека́|ть, ю *impf. of* ▸ **уте́чь**

ут|ёнок, ёнка, *pl.* **~я́та, ~я́т** *m.* duckling

утепли́тел|ь, я *m.* (tech.) insulating material

утепл|и́ть, ю́, и́шь *pf.* (*of* ▸ **утепля́ть**) to insulate

утепля́|ть, я́ю *impf. of* ▸ **утепли́ть**

утер|е́ть, утру́, утрёшь, *past* **~, ~ла** *pf.* (*of* ▸ **утира́ть**) to wipe (off); to wipe dry; **у. пот со лба** to wipe the sweat off one's brow

утер|е́ться, утру́сь, утрёшься, *past* **~ся, ~лась** *pf.* (*of* ▸ **утира́ться**) to wipe oneself; to dry oneself

утерп|е́ть, лю́, ~ишь *pf.* to restrain oneself

утёс, а *m.* cliff, crag

уте́чк|а, и *f.* (*жидкости, информации*) leak, leakage; (*убыль*) loss, wastage, dissipation; **у. га́за** gas escape; **«у. мозго́в»** brain drain

уте́|чь, ку́, чёшь, ку́т, *past* **~к, ~кла́** *pf.* (*of* ▸ **утека́ть**) **1** to flow away; to leak; (*о газе*) to escape **2** (*о времени*) to pass, go by

утеша́|ть, а́ю *impf. of* ▸ **уте́шить**

утеша́|ться, а́юсь *impf. of* ▸ **уте́шиться**

утеше́ни|е, я *nt.* comfort, consolation

уте́ш|ить, у, ишь *pf.* (*of* ▸ **утеша́ть**) to comfort, console

уте́ш|иться, усь, ишься *pf.* (*of* ▸ **утеша́ться**) **1** to console oneself **2** (+ *i.*) (*мыслью, событием*) to take comfort (in)

утилиза́ци|я, и *f.* recycling

утил|ь, я (*no pl.*) *m.* (*collect.*) scrap, recyclable waste

утира́|ть, ю *impf. of* ▸ **утере́ть**

утира́|ться, юсь *impf. of* ▸ **утере́ться**

утиха́|ть, а́ю *impf. of* ▸ **утихнуть**

утих|нуть, ну, нешь, *past* **~, ~ла** *pf.* (*of* ▸ **утиха́ть**) **1** (*о месте*) to become quiet, still; (*о звуках*) to cease, die away **2** (*о буре, о боли*) to abate, subside; (*о ветре*) to drop; (*о споре*) to die down **3** (*о человеке*) to become calm, calm down

утихоми́рива|ть, ю *impf. of* ▸ **утихоми́рить**

у

утихоми́рива|ться, юсь *impf. of*
▶ **утихоми́риться**

утихоми́р|ить, ю, ишь *pf.* (*of*
▶ **утихоми́ривать**) to calm down; to pacify,
placate

утихоми́р|иться, юсь, ишься *pf.* (*of*
▶ **утихоми́риваться**) to calm down; to abate,
subside

у́тк|а, и *f.* duck

уткн|у́ть, у́, ёшь *pf.* (infml) to bury; to fix; **у.
нос в кни́гу** to bury oneself in a book

уткн|у́ться, у́сь, ёшься *pf.* (infml)
1 to bury oneself (in), one's head (in); **у. в
газе́ту** to bury one's head in a newspaper
2 (*натолкну́ться*) to bump (into); **ло́дка
~у́лась в бе́рег** the boat bumped into the
bank

утол|и́ть, ю́, и́шь *pf.* (*of* ▶ **утоля́ть**)
1 (*жа́жду*) to quench, slake; (*го́лод,
любопы́тство*) to satisfy **2** (*боль*) to
relieve, alleviate

утол|я́ть, я́ю *impf. of* ▶ **утоли́ть**

утоми́тел|ьный, ~ен, ~ьна *adj.*
1 (*утомля́ющий*) wearisome, tiring
2 (*ску́чный*) tiresome; tedious

утом|и́ть, лю́, и́шь *pf.* (*of* ▶ **утомля́ть**)
to tire, weary, fatigue

утом|и́ться, лю́сь, и́шься *pf.* (*of*
▶ **утомля́ться**) to get tired

утомле́ни|е, я *nt.* tiredness, weariness,
fatigue

утомлённый *p.p.p. of* ▶ **утоми́ть** *and adj.*
tired, weary, fatigued

утомля́|ть, ю *impf. of* ▶ **утоми́ть**

утомля́|ться, юсь *impf. of* ▶ **утоми́ться**

утон|у́ть, у́, ~ешь *pf.* (*of* ▶ **тону́ть** 3,
▶ **утопа́ть** 1) **1** (*поги́бнуть*) to drown, be
drowned; (*оказа́ться под водо́й*) to sink
2 (**в** + *p.*) (fig.) to be lost (in)

утончённый *adj.* refined; exquisite, subtle

утопа́|ть, ю *impf.* **1** *impf. of* ▶ **утону́ть**
2 (*impf. only*) (**в** + *p.*) (fig., *в зе́лени*) to be
covered (in); (*в ро́скоши, бога́тстве*) to
wallow (in)

утопа́ющий *pres. part. act. of* ▶ **утопа́ть**;
(*as n.* **~ий, ~его**) drowning person

утоп|и́ть, лю́, ~ишь *pf.* (*of* ▶ **топи́ть**² 2)
1 (*челове́ка, живо́тное*) to drown **2** (fig.,
infml, *погуби́ть*) to ruin **3** (*сде́лать едва́
ви́дным*) to bury, embed

утоп|и́ться, лю́сь, ~ишься *pf.* (*of*
▶ **топи́ться**³) to drown oneself

утопи́ческий *adj.* Utopian

уто́пи|я, и *f.* Utopia

уто́пленник, а *m.* drowned man

уто́пленни|ца, цы *f. of* ▶ **уто́пленник**

утоп|та́ть, чу́, ~чешь *pf.* (*of* ▶ **ута́птывать**)
to trample down, pound

уточне́ни|е, я *nt.* clarification, elaboration;
внести́ ~е/~я во что-н. to elaborate on sth

уточн|и́ть, ю́, и́шь *pf.* (*of* ▶ **уточня́ть**) to
make more precise, clarify; to elaborate

уточн|я́ть, я́ю *impf. of* ▶ **уточни́ть**

утра́ива|ть, ю, ет *impf. of* ▶ **утро́ить**

утра́ива|ться, ется *impf. of* ▶ **утро́иться**

утрамб|ова́ть, у́ю *pf.* (*of* ▶ **утрамбо́вывать**)
to ram, tamp (*road material, etc.*)

утрамбо́выва|ть, ю *impf. of* ▶ **утрамбова́ть**

утра́|тить, чу, тишь *pf.* (*of* ▶ **утра́чивать**)
to lose

утра́чива|ть, ю *impf. of* ▶ **утра́тить**

у́тренний *adj.* morning, early

утрир|овать, ую *impf. and pf.* to exaggerate

✎ **у́тр|о, а, до ~а́, с ~а́,** *d.* **~у (к ~у́),** *pl.* **~а,
~, ~ам,** *in sense 'in the mornings': d.* **по
~а́м,** *i.* **~а́ми** *nt.* morning; **в семь часо́в ~а́**
at 7 a.m.; **на сле́дующее у.** the next morning;
с ~а́ early in the morning; **с ~а́ до ве́чера**
from morning till night; **до́брое у.!** good
morning!

утро́б|а, ы *f.* womb

утро́|ить, ю, ит *pf.* (*of* ▶ **утра́ивать**) to treble

утро́|иться, ится *pf.* (*of* ▶ **утра́иваться**) to
treble

у́тром *adv.* in the morning; **сего́дня у.** this
morning

утружда́|ть, ю *impf.* to trouble; **у. кого́-н.
про́сьбами** to trouble sb with requests

утряс|а́ть, а́ю, а́ет *impf. of* ▶ **утрясти́**

утряс|а́ться, а́ется *impf. of* ▶ **утрясти́сь**

утряс|ти́, у́, ёшь *pf.* (*of* ▶ **утряса́ть**) (infml)
to settle

утряс|ти́сь, ётся, у́тся *pf.* (*of* ▶ **утряса́ться**)
(infml, *де́ло, пробле́ма*) to sort itself out; **всё
~ётся** everything will be sorted out

уты́к|ать, аю *pf.* (*of* ▶ **утыка́ть**, ▶ **уты́кивать**)
(infml) **1** (*воткну́ть*) to stick (in) all over
2 (*заби́ть*) to stop up, caulk

утык|а́ть, а́ю *impf. of* ▶ **уты́кать**

уты́кива|ть, ю *impf.* = **уты́кать**

утю́г, а́ *m.* iron (*for ironing clothes, etc.*)

уфоло́ги|я, и *f.* ufology

ух|а́, и́ *f.* ukha (*fish soup*)

уха́б, а *m.* pothole (*in road*)

уха́жива|ть, ю *impf.* (**за** + *i.*) **1** (*за больны́м*)
to nurse, tend; (*за живо́тными, расте́ниями*)
to look after **2** (*за же́нщиной*) to court; to
pay court (to), make advances (to)

ухва|ти́ть, чу́, ~тишь *pf.* **1** (*схвати́ть*) to
lay hold (of); (*захвати́ть для себя́*) to seize,
grab **2** (fig., infml, *поня́ть*) to grasp

ухва|ти́ться, чу́сь, ~тишься *pf.* (**за** + *a.*)
1 to grasp, lay hold (of); **у. за ве́тку** to grasp
a branch **2** (fig., infml, *за возмо́жность*) to
seize; to jump (at); **у. за предложе́ние** to
jump at an offer; (*за мысль, за челове́ка*) to
latch on to

ухитр|и́ться, ю́сь, и́шься *pf.* (*of*
▶ **ухитря́ться**) (+ *inf.*) to manage (to),
contrive (to)

ухитр|я́ться, я́юсь *impf. of* ▶ **ухитри́ться**

ухло́п|ать, аю *pf.* (*of* ▶ **ухло́пывать**) (infml)
1 (*уби́ть*) to kill **2** (*истра́тить*) to
squander

ухло́пыва|ть, ю *impf. of* ▶ **ухло́пать**

у

ухмыльн|у́ться, у́сь, ёшься pf. (of ▸ухмыля́ться) (infml) to smirk, grin

ухмыл|я́ться, я́юсь impf. of ▸ухмыльну́ться

у́х|о, а, pl. **у́ши, уше́й** nt. ear; **кра́ем ~а слу́шать** to listen with half an ear; **говори́ть кому́-н. на́ у.** to have a word in sb's ear, have a private word with sb

✧ **ухо́д¹, а** m. (из комнаты; с работы) leaving; (с должности) resignation; (на пенсию) retirement; (поезда) departure; (с собрания; в монастырь) withdrawal

✧ **ухо́д², а** m. (за больным, за садом) looking after; care (of); (за машиной) maintenance; (за зданием) upkeep

✧ **ухо|ди́ть, жу́, ~дишь** impf. **1** impf. of ▸уйти́ **2** (impf. only) (простираться) to stretch, extend

ухо́жен|ный, ~, ~на adj. well looked after, well cared for

ухудш|а́ть, а́ю, а́ет impf. of ▸уху́дшить

ухудш|а́ться, а́ется impf. of ▸уху́дшиться

ухудше́ни|е, я nt. worsening, deterioration

уху́дш|ить, у, ишь pf. (of ▸ухудша́ть) to make worse, worsen

уху́дш|иться, ится pf. (of ▸ухудша́ться) to become worse, worsen, deteriorate

уцеле́|ть, ю pf. (остаться целым) to remain intact, escape destruction; (остаться живым) to remain alive, survive

уцеп|и́ться, лю́сь, ~ишься pf. (за + a.) **1** to catch hold (of), seize **2** (fig., infml, за предложение) to jump (at)

✧ **уча́ств|овать, ую** impf. (в + p.) **1** to take part (in) **2** (иметь долю) to have a share (in)

✧ **уча́сти|е, я** nt. **1** participation; **у. в при́былях** profit-sharing; **при ~и, с ~ем** (+ g.) with the participation (of), featuring; **принима́ть у.** (в + p.) to take part (in) **2** (сочувствие) sympathy, concern

участ|и́ться, и́тся pf. (of ▸учаща́ться) (удары грома) to become more frequent; (шаг, пульс) to quicken

✧ **уча́стник, а** m. (+ g.) participant (in), member (of); **~и перегово́ров** negotiating parties; **~и соглаше́ния** parties to the agreement; **у. состяза́ния** competitor

✧ **уча́ст|ок, ка** m. **1** (земли) plot; parcel **2** (площади, стены, дороги) part, section **3** (в административном делении) district, area; **избира́тельный у.** (подразделение) electoral district, ward; (здание) polling station

у́част|ь, и f. lot, fate

учаща́|ться, ется impf. of ▸участи́ться

учащённый adj. quickened; faster; **у. пульс** raised pulse/heart rate

✧ **уча́щ|ийся** pres. part. of ▸учи́ться; (as n. **у., ~егося,** f. **~аяся, ~ейся**) student; (школы) pupil

учёб|а, ы f. **1** studies; studying; learning; **за ~ой** at one's studies **2** (подготовка) training

✧ **key word**

уче́бник, а m. textbook

✧ **уче́бн|ый** adj. **1** educational; school; **у. год** academic year, school year; **~ое заведе́ние** educational institution; **у. план** curriculum **2** (mil.) training, practice; **~ая стрельба́** practice shoot

уче́ни|е, я nt. **1** (mil.) exercise; (in pl.) training **2** (система взглядов) teaching, doctrine

✧ **учени́|к, а́** m. **1** (школы) pupil **2** (в ремесле) apprentice **3** (последователь) disciple, follower

учени́ц|а, ы f. of ▸учени́к

✧ **учён|ый, ~, ~а** adj. **1** (человек) learned, erudite; (infml) educated **2** (научный) scholarly; academic; **~ая сте́пень** higher (university) degree (PhD or higher) **3** (in titles of certain academic posts and institutions): **у. сове́т** academic council **4** (as m. n. **у., ~ого**) scholar; (в университете) academic; (в области естественных наук) scientist

уч|е́сть, ту́, тёшь, past **~ёл, ~ла́** pf. (of ▸учи́тывать) **1** (обстоятельства) to take into account, consideration **2** (товары) to take stock (of), make an inventory (of)

✧ **учёт, а** m. **1** (действие) accounting; **бухга́лтерский у.** accounting, bookkeeping; (товаров) stocktaking, inventory-making; (определение) calculation **2** (обстоятельств) taking into account; **без ~а** (+ g.) disregarding **3** (регистрация) registration; **взять на у.** to register

учи́лищ|е, а nt. school, college (providing specialist instruction at secondary level); **вое́нное у.** military school

✧ **учи́тел|ь, я** m. **1** (pl. **~я́**) teacher **2** (pl. **~и**) (fig.) teacher, master (= authority)

учи́тельниц|а, ы f. of ▸учи́тель

учи́тельск|ая, ой f. staff (common) room

✧ **учи́тыва|ть, ю** impf. of ▸уче́сть

✧ **уч|и́ть, у́, ~ишь** impf. **1** (pf. **вы́~, на~** and **об~**) (+ a. and d. or + inf.) (преподавать) to teach; **у. кого́-н. неме́цкому языку́** to teach sb German; **у. игра́ть на скри́пке** to teach to play the violin **2** (no pf.) (быть учителем) to be a teacher **3**: (что) (о теории) to teach (that), say (that) **4** (pf. **вы́~**) (+ a.) (усваивать, запоминать) to learn; to memorize

✧ **уч|и́ться, у́сь, ~ишься** impf. **1** (pf. **вы́~, на~** and **об~**) (+ d. or + inf.) to learn, study **2** (быть студентом) to be a student; **у. в шко́ле** to go to, be at school **3** (pf. **вы́~**) (на кого́-н.) (infml) to study (to be, to become), learn (to be)

учреди́тел|ь, я m. founder

учре|ди́ть, жу́, ди́шь pf. (of ▸учрежда́ть) (основать) to found, establish, set up; (ввести) to introduce, institute

учрежда́|ть, ю impf. of ▸учреди́ть

✧ **учрежде́ни|е, я** nt. **1** (школы, организации) founding, establishment, setting up; (ордена) introduction **2** (заведение) establishment, institution

учти́в|ый, ~, ~а *adj.* civil, courteous

уша́нк|а, и *f.* (infml) cap with ear flaps

у́ши *see* ▸ **у́хо**

уши́б, а *m.* bruise

ушиб|и́ть, у́, ёшь, *past* ~́, ~́ла *pf.* to injure (*by knocking*); (*до синяка́*) to bruise

ушиб|и́ться, у́сь, ёшься, *past* ~́ся, ~́лась *pf.* to hurt oneself; to bruise oneself

ушива́|ть, ю *impf. of* ▸ **уши́ть**

уш|и́ть, ью́, ьёшь *pf.* (*of* ▸ **ушива́ть**) (dressmaking) to take in

ушк|о́, а́, *pl.* ~и́, ~о́в *nt.* (*у иго́лки*) eye

уще́л|ье, ья, *g. pl.* ~ий *nt.* ravine, gorge

ущем|и́ть, лю́, и́шь *pf.* (*of* ▸ **ущемля́ть**) **1** (*стесни́ть*) to limit **2** (*оскорби́ть*) to wound, hurt; **у. чьё-н. самолю́бие** to hurt sb's pride

ущемле́ни|е, я *nt.* (fig.) **1** (*прав*) limitation **2** (*самолю́бия*) wounding, hurting

ущемля́|ть, ю *impf. of* ▸ **ущеми́ть**

ущерб, а *m.* (*убы́ток*) detriment; loss; (*вред*) damage, injury; **без ~а (для** + *g.*) without prejudice (to); **в у.** (+ *d.*) to the detriment (of)

ущипну́|ть, у́, ёшь *pf. of* ▸ **щипа́ть 1**

Уэ́льс, а *m.* Wales

уэ́льс|ец, ца *m.* Welshman

уэ́льский *adj.* Welsh

ую́т, а *m.* cosiness, coziness

ую́т|ный, ~ен, ~на *adj.* cosy (BrE), cozy (AmE)

уязви́м|ый, ~, ~а *adj.* vulnerable (also fig.); ~ое ме́сто (fig.) weak spot

уязв|и́ть, лю́, и́шь *pf.* (*of* ▸ **уязвля́ть**) to wound, hurt

уязвля́|ть, ю *impf. of* ▸ **уязви́ть**

уясн|и́ть, ю́, и́шь *pf.* (*of* ▸ **уясня́ть**) (*also* **у. себе́**, *or* **у. для себя́**) to comprehend

уясн|я́ть, я́ю *impf. of* ▸ **уясни́ть**

Фф

фа *nt. indecl.* (mus.) F

фа́брик|а, и *f.* factory; (*бума́жная*) mill

фабрика́нт, а *m.* manufacturer, factory owner, mill owner

фабрик|ова́ть, у́ю *impf.* (*of* ▸ **сфабрикова́ть**) (fig.) to fabricate

фабри́чн|ый *adj.* **1** factory; manufacturing; ~ое произво́дство manufacturing **2** (*произведённый на фа́брике*) factory-made

фа́бул|а, ы *f.* (liter.) plot, story

фавори́т, а *m.* favourite (BrE), favorite (AmE) (also sport)

фавори́т|ка, ки *f. of* ▸ **фавори́т**

фаго́т, а *m.* (mus.) bassoon

фаготи́ст, а *m.* bassoon player

фаготи́ст|ка, ки *f. of* ▸ **фаготи́ст**

фа́з|а, ы *f.* phase; stage

фаза́н, а *m.* pheasant

✔ **файл, а** *m.* (comput.) file

фа́кел, а *m.* torch, flare

факи́р, а *m.* fakir

факс, а *m.* fax; **посла́ть по ~у** to fax

факси́миле *nt. indecl.* facsimile

✔ **факт, а** *m.* fact

✔ **факти́чески** *adv.* in fact, actually

факти́ческ|ий *adj.* actual; real; virtual; ~ие да́нные the facts

✔ **фа́ктор, а** *m.* factor

факту́р|а, ы *f.* **1** (*строе́ние материа́ла*) texture **2** (comm.) (*usu.* **счёт-ф.**) invoice, bill

факультати́в|ный, ~ен, ~на *adj.* optional

✔ **факульте́т, а** *m.* faculty, department

фала́нг|а, и *f.* (anat.; mil., also hist.) phalanx

фа́ллос, а *m.* phallus

фальсифика́ци|я, и *f.* **1** (*подде́лывание*) falsification **2** (*подде́льный предме́т*) forgery, fake, counterfeit

фальсифици́р|овать, ую *impf. and pf.* **1** (*исто́рию*) to falsify **2** (*вино́*) to adulterate

фальце́т, а *m.* (mus.) falsetto

фальшивомоне́тчик, а *m.* counterfeiter

фальши́в|ый, ~, ~а *adj.* **1** (*зу́бы, во́лосы*) false; (*докуме́нт*) forged, fake; (*же́мчуг*) artificial, imitation **2** (*неи́скренний*) false; insincere; **ф. комплиме́нт** insincere compliment **3** (mus.) out of tune, off-key

✔ **фами́ли|я, и** *f.* **1** surname **2** (*род*) family, kin

фами́льный *adj.* family

фамилья́р|ный, ~ен, ~на *adj.* overfamiliar; unceremonious

фана́т, а *m.* (infml) fan

фанати́зм, а *m.* fanaticism

фана́тик, а *m.* fanatic

фанати́ч|ный, ~ен, ~на *adj.* fanatical

у

ф

фана́тк|а, и *f. of* ▶ **фана́т;** (*сопровождающая популярных музыкантов*) groupie

фане́р|а, ы *f.* **1** (*для облицовки*) veneer **2** (*древесный материал*) plywood

фантазёр, а *m.* dreamer, visionary

фантази́р|овать, ую *impf.* **1** (*мечтать*) to dream, indulge in fantasies **2** (*выдумывать*) to make up, dream up

фанта́зи|я, и *f.* **1** (*воображение*) fantasy; imagination; **бога́тая ф.** fertile imagination **2** (*мечта*) fantasy, fancy; **предава́ться ~ям** to indulge in fantasies **3** (*выдумка*) fabrication

фанта́ст, а *m.* fantasy writer; science fiction writer

фанта́стик|а, и *f.* (*collect.*) (liter.) fantasy; **нау́чная ф.** science fiction; sci-fi

фантасти́ческий *adj.* **1** (*пейзаж, освещение*) fantastic, fabulous, unreal; (*новость, нахал*) fantastic, incredible **2** (*литература*) fantasy

фа́нтик, а *m.* (infml) sweet wrapper

фанто́м, а *m.* phantom

фанфа́р|а, ы *f.* (mus.) **1** (*инструмент*) bugle **2** (*торжественная фраза*) fanfare

фа́р|а, ы *f.* headlight

Фаренге́йт, а *m.* Fahrenheit; **32 гра́дуса/212 гра́дусов по ~у** 32/212 degrees Fahrenheit (= 0°C/100°C)

фаринги́т, а *m.* (med.) pharyngitis

фарисе́|й, я *m.* Pharisee (also fig.)

фармаколо́ги|я, и *f.* pharmacology

фармаце́вт, а *m.* pharmacist

фармацевти́ческий *adj.* pharmaceutical

фарс, а *m.* (theatr.) farce (also fig.)

фа́ртук, а *m.* apron

фарфо́р, а *m.* **1** (*материал*) porcelain, china **2** (*collect.*) (*посуда*) china

фарш, а *m.* (*начинка*) stuffing; (*мясо*) minced meat

фарши́р|ова́ть, у́ю *impf.* (*of* ▶ **зафарширова́ть**) (cul.) to stuff

фас, а *m.* front

фаса́д, а *m.* facade, front

фасо́л|ь, и *f.* (*растение*) bean plant; (*collect.*) (*плод*) beans

фасо́н, а *m.* cut; style

фаталисти́ческий *adj.* fatalistic

фата́л|ьный, ~ен, ~ьна *adj.* (*совпадение*) fateful; (*последствия*) fatal

фа́ун|а, ы *f.* fauna

фаши́зм, а *m.* Fascism

фаши́ст, а *m.* Fascist

фаши́ст|ка, ки *f. of* ▶ **фаши́ст**

фаши́стский *adj.* Fascist

ФБР *nt. indecl.* (*abbr. of* **Федера́льное бюро́ рассле́дований**) FBI (*Federal Bureau of Investigation*)

✔ **февра́л|ь, я́** *m.* February

февра́льский *adj. of* ▶ **февра́ль**

─────────
✔ key word

✔ **федера́льный** *adj.* federal

федерати́вный *adj.* federative, federal

✔ **федера́ци|я, и** *f.* federation

фейерве́рк, а *m.* firework(s); (*событие*) firework display

Фейсбу́к, а *m.* Facebook® (*social networking site*)

фека́л|ии, ий *m. pl.* faeces (BrE), feces (AmE)

фе́льдшер, а, *pl.* **~á** *and* **~ы** *m.* medical assistant

фельето́н, а *m.* satirical article

фемини́зм, а *m.* feminism

фемини́ст, а *m.* feminist

фемини́ст|ка, ки *f. of* ▶ **фемини́ст**

фен, а *m.* hairdryer

фено́мен, а *m.* (*явление*) phenomenon; (*событие, человек*) marvel

феномена́л|ьный, ~ен, ~ьна *adj.* phenomenal

феодали́зм, а *m.* feudalism

феода́льный *adj.* feudal

ферз|ь, я́, *pl.* **~и́, ~е́й** *m.* (chess) queen

фе́рм|а, ы *f.* farm

ферме́нт, а *m.* enzyme

фе́рмер, а *m.* farmer

✔ **фестива́л|ь, я** *m.* festival

фети́ш, а *m.* fetish

фетр, а *m.* felt

фехтова́ни|е, я *nt.* fencing

фешене́бел|ьный, ~ен, ~ьна *adj.* fashionable

фе́|я, и *f.* fairy

фиа́лк|а, и *f.* viola, violet

фиа́ско *nt. indecl.* fiasco, failure

фибро́м|а, ы *f.* (med.) fibroma

фи́г|а, и *f.* (infml) fig (*gesture of derision or contempt, consisting of thumb placed between index and middle fingers*); **показа́ть кому́-н. ~у** ≈ to cock a snook, give the V-sign; **получи́ть ~у** to get nothing

фигн|я́, и́ *f.* (sl.) rubbish

✔ **фигу́р|а, ы** *f.* **1** figure **2** (*в шахматах*) piece, chessman (*excluding pawns*)

фигура́л|ьный, ~ен, ~ьна *adj.* figurative, metaphorical

фигури́ст, а *m.* figure skater

фигури́ст|ка, ки *f. of* ▶ **фигури́ст**

фигу́рн|ый *adj.* **1** figured; ornamented **2**: **~ое ката́ние (на конька́х)** figure skating

Фи́джи *indecl.* Fiji

фи́зик, а *m.* physicist

фи́зик|а, и *f.* physics

физио́лог, а *m.* physiologist

физиологи́ческий *adj.* physiological

физиоло́ги|я, и *f.* physiology

физионо́ми|я, и *f.* (infml) face; physiognomy (also joc.)

физиотерапе́вт, а *m.* physiotherapist

физиотерапи́|я, и *f.* physiotherapy

✔ **физи́ческий** *adj.* **1** physical; **~ая культу́ра**

ф

physical training, gymnastics; **ф. труд** manual labour (BrE), labor (AmE) **2** *adj. of* ▶ **фи́зика; ф. кабине́т** physics laboratory

физкульту́р|а, ы *f.* physical training (*abbr.* PT); physical education (*abbr.* PE); **уро́к ~ы** PE lesson; **лече́бная ф.** exercise therapy

физкульту́рный *adj.* gymnastic; athletic, sports; **ф. зал** gymnasium

фикси́р|овать, ую *impf. and pf.* (*pf. also* **за~**) **1** (*регистрировать*) to record (*in writing, etc.*) **2** (*внимание, взгляд*) to fix, direct

фикти́в|ный, ~ен, ~на *adj.* fictitious; **ф. брак** marriage of convenience, sham marriage

фи́кус, а *m.* (bot.) ficus; rubber plant

филантро́п, а *m.* philanthropist

филармо́ни|я, и *f.* philharmonic society; (*зал*) concert hall

филе́ *nt. indecl.* (cul.) **1** (*мясо высшего сорта*) fillet **2** (*кусок мяса или рыбы без костей*) fillet

✓ **филиа́л, а** *m.* branch (*of an organization*)

филиппи́н|ец, ца *m.* Filipino

филиппи́н|ка, ки *f. of* ▶ **филиппи́нец**

филиппи́нский *adj.* Philippine; (*язык*) Filipino

Филиппи́н|ы, ~ (*no sg.*) the Philippines

фило́лог, а *m.* philologist

филологи́ческий *adj.* philological

филоло́ги|я, и *f.* philology

филосо́ф, а *m.* philosopher

филосо́фи|я, и *f.* philosophy

филосо́фский *adj.* philosophic(al)

филосо́фств|овать, ую *impf.* to philosophize

✓ **фильм, а** *m.* (cin.) film, movie

фильтр, а *m.* filter

фильтр|ова́ть, у́ю *impf.* (*of* ▶ **профильтрова́ть**, ▶ **отфильтрова́ть**) to filter

фина́л, а *m.* **1** (*спектакля*) finale **2** (sport) final

финали́ст, а *m.* finalist

финали́ст|ка, ки *f. of* ▶ **финали́ст**

фина́льный *adj.* final; **ф. акко́рд** (mus.) final chord; **ф. матч** (sport) final

✓ **финанси́рован|ие, я** *nt.* financing

финанси́р|овать, ую *impf. and pf.* to finance

финанси́ст, а *m.* **1** (*предприниматель*) financier **2** (*специалист по финансовым наукам*) financial expert

✓ **фина́нсовый** *adj.* financial; **ф. год** fiscal year; **ф. отде́л** finance department

фина́нс|ы, ов (*no sg.*) finance(s)

фи́ник, а *m.* date (*fruit*)

фи́ниш, а *m.* (sport) finish

фи́нк|а, и *f. of* ▶ **финн**

Финля́нди|я, и *f.* Finland

финн, а *m.* Finn

фи́нский *adj.* Finnish; **Ф. зали́в** Gulf of Finland

фиоле́товый *adj.* violet

✓ **фи́рм|а, ы** *f.* (econ.) firm

фи́рм|енный *adj. of* ▶ **фи́рма**; (*хорошего качества*) high-quality; **~енная этике́тка** proprietary label; **ф. бланк** letterhead; **~енное блю́до** speciality dish

фисгармо́ни|я, и *f.* (mus.) harmonium

фиска́льный *adj.* (fin.) fiscal

фити́л|ь, я́ *m.* (*лампы, свечи*) wick; (*для воспламенения зарядов*) fuse

фи́шинг, а *m.* (comput.) phishing (*practice of sending out emails in the name of reputable companies in order to induce people to reveal personal information*)

флаг, а *m.* flag

флагшто́к, а *m.* flagstaff

флако́н, а *m.* (scent) bottle

фламе́нко *nt. indecl.* flamenco

флами́нго *m. indecl.* flamingo

фланг, а *m.* (mil.) flank

флане́л|ь, и *f.* flannel

флегма́тик, а *m.* phlegmatic person

флегмати́ч|ный, ~ен, ~на *adj.* phlegmatic

флейт|а, ы *f.* flute

флейти́ст, а *m.* flautist

флейти́ст|ка, ки *f. of* ▶ **флейти́ст**

флеш-па́мят|ь, и *f.* (comput.) flash memory

фли́гел|ь, я, *pl.* **~я́, ~е́й** *m.* **1** (*пристройка*) wing (*of building*) **2** (*отдельное здание*) outbuilding

флирт|ова́ть, у́ю *impf.* (**с** + *i.*) to flirt (with)

флома́стер, а *m.* felt-tip pen, marker

фло́р|а, ы *f.* flora

Флори́д|а, ы *f.* Florida

флот, а *m.* **1** fleet; **вое́нно-морско́й ф.** navy **2**: **возду́шный ф.** (air) fleet

флю́гер, а, *pl.* **~á** *m.* weathervane

фля́г|а, и *f.* **1** flask; (mil.) water bottle **2** (*для молока*) churn

фо́би|я, и *f.* phobia

фойе́ *nt. indecl.* foyer

фокстерье́р, а *m.* fox terrier

фо́кус[1], а *m.* (phys.) focus (also fig.)

фо́кус[2], а *m.* (*трюк*) (conjuring) trick; **пока́зывать ~ы** to do conjuring tricks

фо́кус-гру́пп|а, ы *f.* focus group

фокуси́р|овать, ую *impf.* (*of* ▶ **сфокуси́ровать**) (phys.) to focus; (fig.) (**на** + *p.*) to focus (on)

фокуси́р|оваться, уюсь *impf.* (*of* ▶ **сфокуси́роваться**) (**на** + *p.*) to focus (on), be focussed (on)

фо́кусник, а *m.* conjuror, juggler

фольг|а́, и́ *f.* foil

фолькло́р, а *m.* folklore

✓ **фон, а** *m.* **1** background (also fig.) **2** (*помехи*) background noise

фона́рик, а *m.* small lamp; torch (BrE), flashlight (AmE)

ф

фона́рный *adj. of* ▶ **фона́рь**; **ф. столб** lamp
post

фона́р|ь, **я** *m.* (*с ручкой*) lantern; (*уличный*)
lamp; light

✍ **фонд**, **а** *m.* ❶ (fin.) fund; stock, reserves,
resources; **валю́тный ф.** currency reserves;
золото́й ф. gold reserves; **о́бщий ф.** pool
❷ (*in pl.*) (fin., *ценные бумаги*) stocks;
(fig., obs.) stock ❸ (*организация*) fund,
foundation ❹ (*архив*) archive

фо́нд|овый *adj. of* ▶ **фонд**; **~овая би́ржа**
stock exchange

фоне́тик|а, **и** *f.* phonetics

фонта́н, **а** *m.* fountain; (fig.) stream;
нефтяно́й ф. oil gusher; **бить ~ом** to gush
forth

форе́л|ь, **и** *f.* trout

✍ **фо́рм|а**, **ы** *f.* ❶ form; **по ~е, ... по
содержа́нию** in form, ... in content ❷ (*для
выпечки*) cake tin; shape ❸ (tech., *внешнее
очертание*) mould (BrE), mold (AmE), cast;
отли́ть в ~у to mould (BrE), mold (AmE),
cast ❹ (*одежда*) uniform ❺: **быть в ~е**
(infml) to be in (good) form

форма́льност|ь, **и** *f.* formality

форма́льный, **~ен**, **~ьна** *adj.* formal

✍ **форма́т**, **а** *m.* format

формати́р|овать, **ую** *impf.* (*of*
▶ **отформати́ровать**) (comput.) to format

фо́рменный *adj.* ❶ (*платье, фуражка*)
uniform ❷ (infml, *настоящий*) proper,
regular, positive

✍ **формирова́ни|е**, **я** *nt.* ❶ (*действие*)
forming; organizing ❷ (mil.) unit

формир|ова́ть, **у́ю** *impf.* (*of*
▶ **сформирова́ть**) to form; to organize;
ф. хара́ктер to form character; **ф. батальо́н**
to raise a battalion

формир|ова́ться, **у́юсь** *impf.* (*of*
▶ **сформирова́ться**) ❶ to form, develop
❷ *pass. of* ▶ **формирова́ть**

фо́рмул|а, **ы** *f.* formula; formulation

формули́р|овать, **ую** *impf. and pf.* (*pf. also*
с~) to formulate

формулиро́вк|а, **и** *f.* ❶ formulation
❷ (*сформулированная мысль*) wording

форпо́ст, **а** *m.* (mil.) advanced post; outpost
(also fig.)

форс-мажо́р, **а** *m.* (*also* **~ные
обстоя́тельства**) force majeure

форт, **а**, **о ~е**, **в ~у́**, *pl.* **~ы́** *m.* (mil.) fort

форте|пиа́но and **фортепья́но** *nt. indecl.*
piano

фо́рточк|а, **и** *f.* little window (*small hinged
pane for ventilation in windows of Russian
houses*)

✍ **фо́рум**, **а** *m.* forum

фосфа́т, **а** *m.* (chem.) phosphate

фо́сфор, **а** *m.* phosphorus

✍ **фо́то** *nt. indecl.* (infml) photo

фото... *comb. form* photo-

✍ key word

фотоальбо́м, **а** *m.* photograph album

фотоаппара́т, **а** *m.* camera

фотогени́ч|ный, **~ен**, **~на** *adj.* photogenic

фото́граф, **а** *m.* photographer

фотографи́р|овать, **ую** *impf.* (*of*
▶ **сфотографи́ровать**) to photograph

фотографи́р|оваться, **у́юсь** *impf.*
(*of* ▶ **сфотографи́роваться**) to be
photographed, have one's photo taken

фотографи́ческий *adj.* photographic

✍ **фотогра́фи|я**, **и** *f.* ❶ (*получение
изображений*) photography ❷ (*снимок*)
photograph

фотокопирова́льный *adj.*: **ф. аппара́т**
photocopier

фотоко́пи|я, **и** *f.* photocopy

фоторобо́т, **а** *m.* identikit (picture)®

фотоси́нтез, **а** *m.* (bot.) photosynthesis

фотоэлеме́нт, **а** *m.* (elec.) photoelectric cell

фрагме́нт, **а** *m.* fragment; detail (*of painting,
etc.*); **ф. фи́льма** film clip

фра́з|а, **ы** *f.* ❶ (*предложение*) sentence
❷ (*выражение*) phrase

фразеологи́ческий *adj.* phraseological;
ф. оборо́т idiom; **ф. слова́рь** dictionary of
idioms

фрак, **а** *m.* tailcoat, tails

фра́кци|я, **и** *f.* (pol.) fraction; faction, group

фраму́г|а, **и** *f.* transom

франкоязы́чный *adj.* francophone

франт, **а** *m.* dandy

Фра́нци|я, **и** *f.* France

францу́женк|а, **и** *f.* Frenchwoman

францу́з, **а** *m.* Frenchman

✍ **францу́зский** *adj.* French

фрахт, **а** *m.* freight

фрахт|ова́ть, **у́ю** *impf.* (*of* ▶ **зафрахтова́ть**)
to charter

фрега́т, **а** *m.* ❶ (naut.) frigate ❷ (zool.) frigate
bird

фре́зерный *adj.* (tech.) milling; **ф. стано́к**
milling machine

фрео́н|ы, **ов** *m. pl.* (*sg.* **~**, **~а**) CFCs (*abbr. of*
chlorofluorocarbons)

фре́ск|а, **и** *f.* fresco

фриво́льный, **~ен**, **~ьна** *adj.* frivolous

фриги́д|ный, **~ен**, **~на** *adj.* (med.) frigid

фрикаде́льк|а, **и** *f.* (*мясная*) meatball;
(*рыбная*) fishball (*in soup*)

фронт, **а**, *pl.* **~ы́** *m.* (mil., meteor., fig.) front;
на два ~а on two fronts

фрукт, **а** *m.* fruit; (*in pl.*) fruit (*collect.*)

фрукто́вый *adj.* fruit; **ф. сад** orchard

ФСБ *f. indecl.* (*abbr. of* **Федера́льная
слу́жба безопа́сности**) Federal Security
Service

фтори́д, **а** *m.* fluoride

фу́г|а, **и** *f.* (mus.) fugue

фуга́с, **а** *m.* (mil.) landmine

фуже́р, **а** *m.* tall wineglass

фунда́мент, **а** *m.* foundation, base (also fig.)

фундаментали́зм, а *m.* fundamentalism
фундаментали́ст, а *m.* fundamentalist
фундамента́л|ьный, ∼ен, ∼ьна *adj.*
  1 (*прочный*) solid, sound; (*основательный*) thorough(going) **2** (*основной, главный*) main, basic
функулёр, а *m.* funicular (railway)
функциона́льн|ый *adj.* functional; ∼ая кла́виша (comput.) function key
функциони́ровани|е, я *nt.* functioning
✐ **фу́нкци|я, и** *f.* function
фунт¹, а *m.* (*мера веса*) pound (*453.6 grams*)
фунт², а *m.* (fin.): **ф. (сте́рлингов)** pound (sterling)
функциони́р|овать, ую *impf.* to function
фу́р|а, ы *f.* (*фургон*) van; (*прицеп*) (truck) trailer
фура́жк|а, и *f.* peak cap; (mil.) service cap
фурго́н, а *m.* van

фурниту́р|а, ы *f.* accessories
фуро́р, а *m.* furore
фут, а *m.* foot (*measure of length, = 30.48 cm*)
футбо́л, а *m.* football (BrE), soccer
футболи́ст, а *m.* football player (BrE), soccer player
✐ **футбо́лк|а, и** *f.* T-shirt
футбо́л|ьный *adj. of* ▶ **футбо́л**; ∼ьные бу́тсы football boots; **ф. мяч** football
футля́р, а *m.* case; **ф. для очко́в** spectacle case; **ф. для скри́пки** violin case
футури́зм, а *m.* futurism
футури́ст, а *m.* futurist
фы́рк|ать, аю *impf.* (*of* ▶ **фы́ркнуть**) **1** (*о животном; о машине*) to snort **2** (fig., infml, *брюзжать*) to grouse
фы́рк|нуть, ну, нешь *inst. pf. of* ▶ **фы́ркать**
фэн-шу́й *m. & nt. indecl.* feng shui
фюзеля́ж, а *m.* fuselage

Xx

хаб, а *m.* (comput.) hub
ха́кер, а *m.* (comput.) hacker
ха́ки *nt. indecl. and adj. indecl.* khaki
хала́т, а *m.* **1** (*домашний*) dressing gown; (*купальный*) bathrobe **2** (*рабочий*) overall; **до́кторский х.** doctor's smock **3** (*восточный*) robe
хала́т|ный, ∼ен, ∼на *adj.* careless, negligent
халту́р|а, ы *f.* (infml) **1** (*небрежная работа*) poor-quality work **2** (*работа на стороне*) work done on the side; (*деньги*) money earned on the side
халя́в|а, ы *f.*: **на ∼у** (sl.) free of charge; for free
хам, а *m.* (infml) boor, lout
хамеле́он, а *m.* chameleon (also fig.)
хам|и́ть, лю́, и́шь *impf.* (*of* ▶ **нахами́ть**) (+ *d.*) to be rude (to)
ха́мств|о, а *nt.* (infml) boorishness, loutishness
хандр|а́, ы́ *f.* depression
ханж|а́, и́, g. pl. ∼е́й *c.g.* sanctimonious person; hypocrite
ха́нжеский *adj.* sanctimonious; hypocritical
Хано́|й, я *m.* Hanoi
ха́ос, а *m.* chaos
хаоти́ческий *adj.* chaotic
хаоти́ч|ный, ∼ен, ∼на *adj.* = **хаоти́ческий**
✐ **хара́ктер, а** *m.* **1** (*человека*) character, personality; **они́ не сошли́сь ∼ами** they could not get on (together) **2** (*твёрдый характер*) (strong) character; **челове́к с**

∼ом determined person, strong character **3** (*свойство*) character, type; **х. рабо́ты** type of work
✐ **характери́стик|а, и** *f.* **1** (*описание*) description **2** (*отзыв*) reference
характе́рно *as pred.* it is characteristic; it is typical
характе́р|ный, ∼ен, ∼на *adj.*
  1 (*свойственный*) characteristic; typical; **э́то для него́ ∼но** it is typical of him **2** (*своеобразный*) distinctive
хари́зм|а, ы *f.* charisma
харизмати́ческий *adj.* charismatic
ха́рк|ать, аю *impf.* (*of* ▶ **ха́ркнуть**) (infml) to spit, expectorate; **х. кро́вью** to spit blood
ха́рк|нуть, ну, нешь *pf. of* ▶ **ха́ркать**
ха́рти|я, и *f.* charter
харчо́ *nt. indecl.* kharcho (*Caucasian highly seasoned mutton soup*)
ха́р|я, и *f.* (sl.) mug (= *face*)
ха́т|а, ы *f.* **1** peasant house (*in Southern Russia, Ukraine, and Byelorussia*); **моя́ х. с кра́ю** it's no concern of mine; that's your, their, *etc.*, funeral **2** (sl.) home, 'pad'
хвале́б|ный, ∼ен, ∼на *adj.* laudatory, eulogistic
хвал|и́ть, ю́, ∼́ишь *impf.* (*of* ▶ **похвали́ть**) to praise
хва́ста|ть, ю *impf.* = **хва́статься**
хва́ста|ться, юсь *impf.* (*of* ▶ **похва́статься**) (+ *i.*) to boast (of)

ф

х

хвастли́в|ый, ~, ~а *adj.* boastful

хвастовств|о́, á *nt.* boasting

⚔ **хват|а́ть¹**, а́ю *impf.* (*of* ▶ схвати́ть 1) **1** to snatch, seize, catch hold (of); to grab, grasp **2** (*impf. only*) (*infml*, *вора*) to pick up

⚔ **хват|а́ть²**, а́ет *impf.* (*of* ▶ хвати́ть) (*impers.* + *g.*) (*быть доста́точным*) to suffice, be enough; to last out; **у меня́ и т. п. не ~а́ет** I am, *etc.*, short (of); **у нас не ~а́ет де́нег** we don't have enough money; **э́того ещё не ~а́ло!** that's all we need, *etc.*!

хват|а́ться, а́юсь *impf.* (*of* ▶ схвати́ться 1) (*за* + *a.*) **1** to snatch (at), catch (at); **х. за соло́минку** to clutch at straws **2** (*принима́ться за де́ло*) to start doing, take up

хват|и́ть, ~ит *pf.* (*of* ▶ хвата́ть²): ~ит! that will do!; that's enough!; **с меня́ ~ит!** I've had enough!

хва|ти́ться, чу́сь, ~тишься *pf.* (+ *g.*) (*infml*) to miss, notice the absence (of); **по́здно ~ти́лись!** you thought of it too late!

хва́тк|а, и *f.* grasp, grip

хво́йн|ый *adj.* **1** *adj. of* ▶ хвоя **2** (*де́рево*) coniferous; (*as pl. n.* ~ые, ~ых) (bot.) conifers

хвора́|ть, ю *impf.* (*infml*) to be ill (BrE), sick (AmE)

хво́рост, а *m.* (*collect.*) **1** (*ве́тки*) brushwood **2** (cul.) (pastry) straws, twiglets

хвост, á *m.* **1** tail (also fig.); **маха́ть ~о́м** to wag one's tail **2** (fig., *за́дняя часть*) tail, rear, tail end; **быть, плести́сь в ~é** to get behind, lag behind

хвоста́т|ый, ~, ~а *adj.* **1** (*име́ющий хвост*) having a tail; caudate **2** (*с больши́м хвосто́м*) having a large tail

хво́стик, а *m. dim. of* ▶ хвост; (*причёска*) ponytail

хво́|я, и *f.* **1** needle(s) (*of conifer*) **2** (*collect.*) (*ве́тви*) branches (*of conifer*)

Хе́льсинки *m. indecl.* Helsinki

хеппи-э́нд, а *m.* happy ending

хер, ~á, ~у *m.* (sl., euph. of) ▶ хуй

хе́рес, а *m.* sherry

хеште́г, а *m.* (comput.) hashtag

хижин|а, ы *f.* shack, hut

хи́л|ый, ~, ~á, ~о *adj.* weak, sickly; puny

химе́р|а, ы *f.* chimera

хи́мик, а *m.* chemist

химика́т|ы, ов *m. pl.* chemicals

химиотерапи́|я, и *f.* chemotherapy

⚔ **хими́ческ|ий** *adj.* **1** chemical; **~ие препара́ты** chemicals; **~ая чи́стка (оде́жды)** dry-cleaning; **х. элеме́нт** chemical element **2** chemistry; **х. кабине́т** chemistry laboratory

хи́ми|я, и *f.* chemistry

химчи́стк|а, и *f.* dry-cleaner's

хи́нди *m. indecl.* Hindi (*language*)

хи́ппи *c.g. indecl.* hippy

хирома́нти|я, и *f.* palmistry

хиру́рг, а *m.* surgeon

хирурги́ческий *adj.* surgical

хирурги́|я, и *f.* surgery

хит, á *m.* (*infml*, mus., etc.) hit

хит-пара́д, а *m.* (mus.) the charts

хитре́ц, á *m.* cunning person; (*infml*) slyboots

хитр|и́ть, ю́, и́шь *impf.* (*of* ▶ схитри́ть) to use cunning, guile; to dissemble

хи́трост|ь, и *f.* **1** (*сво́йство*) cunning, slyness **2** (*уло́вка*) ruse, stratagem

хитроу́м|ный, ~ен, ~на *adj.* **1** (*изобрета́тельный*) cunning; resourceful **2** (*сло́жный*) intricate, complicated

хи́т|рый, ~ёр, ~ра́, ~ро́ *adj.* **1** (*лука́вый*) cunning, sly **2** (*infml*, *изобрета́тельный*) cunning, resourceful **3** (*infml*, *замыслова́тый*) intricate

хихи́к|ать, аю *impf.* (*of* ▶ хихи́кнуть) to giggle, snigger

хихи́к|нуть, ну, нешь *inst. pf. of* ▶ хихи́кать

хище́ни|е, я *nt.* theft; embezzlement, misappropriation

хи́щник, а *m.* predator; (*живо́тное*) beast of prey; (*пти́ца*) bird of prey

хи́щ|ный, ~ен, ~на *adj.* **1** predatory; **~ные зве́ри, пти́цы** beasts of prey, birds of prey **2** (fig.) rapacious, grasping

хладнокро́ви|е, я *nt.* composure, sangfroid

хладнокро́в|ный, ~ен, ~на *adj.* **1** cool, composed; (*жесто́кий*) cold-blooded

хлам, а *m.* (*collect.*) rubbish, trash

хлеб, а, *pl.* ~ы *and* ~á *m.* **1** (*sg. only*) bread (also fig.) **2** (*pl.* ~ы) (*буха́нка*) loaf **3** (*pl.* ~á) (*семена́ зла́ков*) bread grain; (*usu. in pl.*) (*зла́ки*) corn, crops; cereals

хле́б|ец, ца *m.* rusk, dry toast

хле́бниц|а, ы *f.* bread basket

хлебн|у́ть, у́, ёшь *pf.* (*infml*) **1** (*вы́пить*) to drink down **2** (+ *g.*) (*перенести́*) to go through, endure, experience

хле́б|ный *adj.* **1** *adj. of* ▶ хлеб 1; **~ые дро́жжи** baker's yeast; **х. магази́н** baker's shop **2** *adj. of* ▶ хлеб 3; **х. амба́р** granary **3** (*урожа́йный*) rich (*in grain*); abundant; grain-producing

хлебозаво́д, а *m.* bread-baking plant, bakery

хлеборо́б, а *m.* peasant (engaged in arable farming)

хлев, а, в ~е *or* в ~ý, *pl.* ~á *m.* cowshed; (fig., *infml*) pigsty

хле|ста́ть, щу́, ~щешь *impf.* (*of* ▶ хлестну́ть) **1** (+ *a. or* по + *d.*) to lash; to whip **2** (*о дожде́*) to lash (down), beat (down), pour; to stream, gush

хлестн|у́ть, ну́, нёшь *inst. pf. of* ▶ хлеста́ть

хли́п|кий, ~ок, ~ка́, ~ко *adj.* (*infml*) **1** (*стол, мост*) rickety **2** (fig., *челове́к, здоро́вье*) weak, fragile

хло́па|ть, ю *impf.* (*of* ▶ хло́пнуть) **1** (+ *i. or* по + *d.*) to bang; to slap; **х. кали́ткой** to bang the gate; **х. кого́-н. по спине́** to slap sb on the back **2**: х. (в ладо́ши) (+ *d.*) to clap, applaud

хлопкоро́б, а *m.* cotton grower

хло́п|нуть, ну, нешь *inst. pf. of* ▶ **хло́пать**

хло́п|ок, ка *m.* cotton; **х.-сыре́ц** raw cotton

хлоп|о́к, ка́ *m.* (в ладо́ши) clap; (*выстрела*) bang

хло́пот|ы, хлопо́т, ~ам (*no sg.*) **1** (*занятия по до́му, по рабо́те*) jobs, chores; (*заботы*) trouble **2** (о + *p.*) (*старания доби́ться чего-н.*) efforts (on behalf of, for); pains

хлопу́шк|а, и *f.* (Christmas) cracker

хлопчатобума́жный *adj.* cotton

хло́пь|я, ев (*no sg.*) flakes (*of snow, etc., also of certain cereal foods*); **кукуру́зные х., пшени́чные х.** cornflakes

хлор, а *m.* (chem.) chlorine

хлы́н|уть, у, ешь *pf.* **1** (*о крови, дожде*) to gush, pour **2** (fig.) to pour, rush, surge; **толпа́ ~ула на пло́щадь** a crowd poured into the square

хлыст, а́ *m.* (*прут*) whip, switch

хлю́па|ть, ю *impf.* (infml) **1** (*грязи*) to squelch; **х. по грязи́** to squelch through the mud **2** (*плача, всхли́пывать*) to snivel; **х. но́сом** to sniff

хля́стик, а *m.* half belt (*on back of coat*)

хме́л|ь, я *m.* (bot.) (*семена*) hops; (*растение*) hop plant

хму́р|ить, ю, ишь *impf.* (*of* ▶ **нахму́рить**): **х. бро́ви** to knit one's brows

хму́р|иться, юсь, ишься *impf.* (*of* ▶ **нахму́риться**) **1** (*хму́рить бро́ви*) to frown **2** (*о пого́де, о дне*) to become gloomy; (*о не́бе*) to be overcast, cloudy

хму́р|ый, ~, ~á, ~о *adj.* **1** (*челове́к*) gloomy, sullen **2** (*небо, день*) overcast, cloudy; **х. день** dull day

хмы́ка|ть, ю *impf.* (infml) to hem (*expr. surprise, annoyance, doubt, etc.*)

хо́бби *nt. indecl.* hobby

хо́бот, а *m.* (zool.) trunk, proboscis

⚔ **ход, а (у), о ~е, в/на ~е и ~у́** *m.* **1** (в ~е, на ~у́) motion, movement, travel, going; speed, pace; **три часа́ ~у** three hours' walk; **за́дний х.** backing, reversing; **дать х.** (+ *d.*) to set in motion, set going; **пойти́ в х.** to come to be widely used; **пусти́ть в х.** to start, set in motion, set going (also fig.), put into service **2** (в ~е) (fig., *развитие*) course, progress; **х. мы́слей** train of thought; **х. собы́тий** course of events **3** (в ~е, на ~у́) (tech.) work, operation, running; **на холосто́м ~у́** idling **4** (на ~е, *pl.* ~ы́) (*в ша́хматах*) move; (*в ка́ртах*) lead; **х. бе́лых** white's move **5** (в ~е, *pl.* ~ы́) (fig.) move, gambit; **ло́вкий х.** shrewd move **6** (в, на ~е *и* ~у́, *pl.* ~ы́) (*путь*) passage(way), thoroughfare

хода́тайств|о, а *nt.* **1** (*действие*) petitioning; entreaty, pleading **2** (*про́сьба*) petition; application

⚔ **хо|ди́ть, жу́, ~дишь** *impf.* **1** (*передвига́ться, ша́гая*) to (be able to) walk **2** (indet. of ▶ **идти́**) to go (*on foot*); **х. в кино́** to go to

the cinema; **х. под па́русом** to go sailing **3** (*о поезда́х*) to run **4** (*о слу́хах, новостя́х*) to pass, go round **5** (*в ка́ртах*) to lead, play; (*в ша́хматах*) to move; **х. ферзём** to move one's queen **6** (в + *p.*) (*носи́ть*) to wear

ходу́л|и, ей и ~ь *f. pl.* (*sg.* ~я, ~и) stilts

ходьб|а́, ы́ *f.* walking; **це́рковь нахо́дится в пяти́ мину́тах ~ы́ отсю́да** the church is five minutes' walk from here

ходя́ч|ий *adj.* walking; able to walk; ~ая энциклопе́дия walking encyclopedia

⚔ **хозя́|ин, ина,** *pl.* ~ева, ~ев *m.* **1** (*владе́лец*) owner, proprietor **2** (*свое́й судьбы́; в до́ме*) master; (*предприя́тия*) boss **3** (*по отноше́нию к жильцу́*) landlord **4** (*по отноше́нию к гостя́м*) host

хозя́йк|а, и, *g. pl.* **хозя́ек** *f.* **1** (*владе́лица*) owner, proprietress **2** (*свое́й судьбы́; в до́ме*) mistress **3** (*по отноше́нию к жильцу́*) landlady **4** (*по отноше́нию к гостя́м*) hostess

хозя́йствен|ный, ~, ~на *adj.* **1** economic, of the economy; ~ная жизнь страны́ the country's economy **2** (*това́ры, инвента́рь*) household; home management **3** (*эконо́мный*) economical, thrifty

⚔ **хозя́йств|о, а** *nt.* **1** (*эконо́мика*) economy; **се́льское х.** agriculture; **дома́шнее х.** housekeeping; **вести́ х.** to manage, carry on management **2** (agric.) farm, holding **3** (*рабо́ты по хозя́йству*) housekeeping; **хлопота́ть по ~у** to be busy about the house

хоккеи́ст, а *m.* hockey player

хоккеи́ст|ка, ки *f. of* ▶ **хоккеи́ст**

хокке́|й, я *m.* hockey; **с мячо́м, ру́сский х.** bandy; **х. с ша́йбой** ice hockey; **х. на траве́** hockey (BrE), field hockey (AmE)

холе́р|а, ы *f.* (med.) cholera

холестери́н, а *m.* cholesterol

холл, а *m.* hall, vestibule, foyer

холм, а́ *m.* hill

холми́ст|ый, ~, ~а *adj.* hilly

хо́лод, а (у), *pl.* ~á, ~о́в *m.* **1** cold; coldness (also fig.); **ди́кий х.** bitter cold **2** (*in pl.*) cold (spell of) weather

холода́|ть, ет *impf.* (*of* ▶ **похолода́ть**) (*impers.*) (*станови́ться холодне́е*) to turn cold

холоде́|ть, ю *impf.* (*of* ▶ **похолоде́ть**) (*ру́ки*) to get cold

холоде́|ц, ца́ *m.* (cul.) meat in jelly

холоди́льник, а *m.* refrigerator; **ваго́н-х.** refrigerator van

хо́лодно¹ *adv.* (fig.) coldly

хо́лодно² *as pred.* it is cold; **мне,** *и т. п.* **х.** I am, etc., cold, feel cold

⚔ **холо́д|ный, хо́лоден, ~на́, хо́лодно, хо́лодны́** *adj.* **1** cold; **х. отве́т** cold reply; **х. по́яс** (geog.) frigid zone; ~ная война́ cold war; ~ное ору́жие side arms, cold steel **2** (*оде́жда*) light, thin

холост|о́й, хо́лост, ~а́, хо́лосто *adj.* **1** unmarried, single; bachelor **2** (tech.) idle,

X

free-running; **на** ~**óм ходу́** idling **3** (mil.) blank, dummy; **x. патро́н** blank cartridge

холостя́|к, á *m.* bachelor

холст, á *m.* **1** (*ткань*) coarse linen, canvas, burlap **2** (art) canvas

холу́|й, я́ *m.* (infml obs. and fig., pej.) lackey

хому́т, á *m.* **1** (*на лоша́ди*) collar **2** (tech.) clamp, ring

хомя́к, á *m.* hamster

хор, а, *pl.* ~**ы́** *m.* **1** choir **2** (mus., also fig.) chorus; ~**óм** all together

хора́л, а *m.* chorale

хорва́т, а *m.* Croat

Хорва́ти|я, и *f.* Croatia

хорва́т|ка, ки *f. of* ▶ **хорва́т**

хорва́тский *adj.* Croatian, Croat

хор|ёк, ька́ *m.* ferret

хорео́граф, а *m.* choreographer

хореогра́фи|я, и *f.* choreography

хорово́д, а *m.* round dance (*traditional Slavonic folk dance*)

хорон|и́ть, ю́, ~ишь *impf.* (*of* ▶ **похорони́ть**, ▶ **захорони́ть**) to bury (also fig.)

хоро́шенький *adj.* pretty, nice (also iron.)

хоро́шенько *adv.* (infml) properly, thoroughly, well and truly

⚔ **хоро́ш|ий, ~, ~á** *adj.* **1** good **2** (*прия́тный*) nice **3** (*only short forms*) (*краси́вый*) pretty, good-looking

⚔ **хорошо́[1] 1** *adv.* well; nicely **2** *particle* (*выража́ет согла́сие*) all right!; OK! **3** *n., nt. indecl.* (*отме́тка*) 'good' (*mark*)

⚔ **хорошо́[2]** *as pred.* it is good; it is nice; **x., что вы успе́ли прие́хать** it is good that you managed to come

хо́спис, а *m.* hospice

хот-до́г, а *m.* hot dog

⚔ **хоте́|ть, хочу́, хо́чешь, хо́чет, хоти́м, хоти́те, хотя́т** *impf.* (*of* ▶ **захоте́ть**) (+ *g.* or *inf.* or **чтобы** + *past*) to want, desire; **я** ~**л бы** I would like; **x. пить** to be thirsty; **x. сказа́ть** to mean; **е́сли хоти́те** if you like (*also = perhaps*)

⚔ **хоте́|ться, хо́чется** (*no pl.*) *impf.* (*of* ▶ **захоте́ться**) (*impers.* + *d.*) to want; **мне хо́чется** I want; **мне** ~**лось бы** I would like

⚔ **хоть** *conj.* **1** (*хотя́*) although **2** (*да́же е́сли*) even if (*esp. in set phrr.*) **3** (*as particle*) (*also* **x. бы**) (*по кра́йней ме́ре*) at least, if only **4**: **x. бы** if only

⚔ **хотя́** *conj.* **1** although, though **2**: **x. бы** even if **3** (*as particle*): **x. бы** if only; **э́то я́вно ви́дно x. бы из заключи́тельной фра́зы его́ ре́чи** this is evident if only from the final sentence of his speech

хо́хм|а, ы *f.* (infml) joke, quip, gag

хо́хот, а *m.* guffaw, loud laugh

хохо|та́ть, чу́, ~чешь *impf.* to guffaw, laugh loudly

храбре́ц, á *m.* brave person

хра́брост|ь, и *f.* bravery, courage

хра́бр|ый, ~, ~á, ~о, ~ы́ *adj.* brave, courageous

⚔ **храм, а** *m.* temple, church, place of worship

⚔ **хране́ни|е, я** *nt.* keeping, custody; storage, conservation; **ка́мера** ~**я** left luggage office (BrE), baggage room (AmE)

храни́лищ|е, а *nt.* storehouse, depository

храни́тел|ь, я *m.* **1** keeper, custodian; (fig.) repository **2** (*музе́я*) curator

хран|и́ть, ю́, и́шь *impf.* (*ста́рые пи́сьма, де́ньги в ба́нке*) to keep; (*тради́ции, до́брое и́мя*) to preserve; (*молча́ние, го́рдый вид*) to maintain; **x. в та́йне** to keep secret

хран|и́ться, ~ся *impf.* **1** (*находи́ться*) to be, be kept **2** (*быть в сохра́нности*) to be preserved

храп|е́ть, лю́, и́шь *impf.* **1** to snore **2** (*о лоша́ди*) to snort

хреб|е́т, та́ *m.* **1** (anat.) spine, spinal column; (fig., infml, *спина́*) back **2** (*го́рная цепь*) (mountain) range; ridge; (fig.) crest, peak

хрен, а (у) *m.* horseradish; **x. с** (+ *i.*) (infml) to hell (with); **ни** ~**á** (infml) nothing, bugger all

хре́новый *adj. of* ▶ **хрен**; (infml) rotten, lousy

хризанте́м|а, ы *f.* chrysanthemum

хрип, а *m.* wheeze, wheezing sound

хрип|е́ть, лю́, и́шь *impf.* to wheeze

хри́пл|ый, ~, ~á, ~о *adj.* hoarse; wheezy

хри́п|нуть, ну, нешь, *past* ~, ~**ла** *impf.* (*of* ▶ **охри́пнуть**) to become hoarse, lose one's voice

христиа|ни́н, ани́на, *pl.* ~**не,** ~**н** *m.* Christian

христиа́н|ка, ки *f. of* ▶ **христиани́н**

христиа́нский *adj.* Christian

христиа́нств|о, а *nt.* Christianity

⚔ **Христ|о́с, á** *m.* Christ

хром, а *m.* (chem.) chromium, chrome

хрома́|ть, ю *impf.* to limp; (*о живо́тном*) to limp, to be lame

хром|о́й, ~, ~á, ~о *adj.* **1** (*о челове́ке*) limping; (*о живо́тном*) limping, lame; **x. на ле́вую но́гу** lame in the left leg; (*as n.* **x.,** ~**óго,** *f.* ~**áя,** ~**óй**) man/woman with walking difficulties **2** (infml, *нога́*) gammy

хромосо́м|а, ы *f.* (biol.) chromosome

хро́ник|а, и *f.* **1** (*ле́топись*) chronicle **2** (*в газе́те*) news items **3** (cin.) newsreel

хрони́ческий *adj.* chronic

хронологи́ческий *adj.* chronological

хроноло́ги|я, и *f.* chronology

хроно́метр, а *m.* chronometer

хру́п|кий, ~ок, ~ка́, ~ко *adj.* **1** (*стекло́*) fragile, brittle **2** (fig., *здоро́вье, ребёнок*) fragile, frail; delicate

хруст, а *m.* crunch; crunching sound

хруста́л|ь, я́ *m.* cut glass, crystal; **го́рный x.** rock crystal

хруста́льный *adj.* **1** cut glass, crystal **2** (fig.) crystal clear

X

хру|сте́ть, щу́, сти́шь *impf.* (*of* ▸ хру́стнуть) to crunch

хру́ст|нуть, ну, нешь *inst. pf. of* ▸ хрусте́ть

хрустя́щий *pres. part. of* ▸ хрусте́ть *and adj.*: **х. карто́фель** potato crisps (BrE), chips (AmE)

хрю́к|ать, аю *impf.* (*of* ▸ хрю́кнуть) to grunt

хрю́к|нуть, ну, нешь *inst. pf.* (*of* ▸ хрю́кать) to give a grunt

хряк, а́ *m.* hog

хрящ, а́ *m.* (anat.) cartilage, gristle

худе́е *comp. of* ▸ худо́й¹, ▸ худо́й²

худе́|ть, ю *impf.* (*of* ▸ похуде́ть) to grow thin, lose weight

⚬ **худо́жествен|ный, ~, ~на** *adj.* **1** of art, of the arts; **~ная литерату́ра** fiction; **х. фильм** feature film; **~ная шко́ла** art school **2** (*красивый*) artistic; tasteful

⚬ **худо́жник, а** *m.* artist; **х. по костю́мам/све́ту** costume/lighting designer

худо́жни|ца, цы *f. of* ▸ худо́жник

⚬ **худ|о́й¹, ~, ~а́, ~о, ~ы** *adj.* (*не толстый*) thin, lean

⚬ **худ|о́й², ~, ~а́, ~о** *adj.* (*плохой*) bad; **на х. коне́ц** if the worst comes to the worst

худоща́в|ый, ~, ~а *adj.* thin, lean

ху́дший *superl. of* ▸ худо́й², ▸ плохо́й; (the) worst

хуёвый *adj.* (vulg.) shitty, crap(py)

ху́же *comp. of* ▸ худо́й², ▸ плохо́й, ▸ пло́хо; worse

худ, ху́я, *pl.* **ху́и, ху́ёв** *m.* (vulg.) prick, cock (= *penis*); **ни ху́я** nothing, fuck all; **пошёл/ иди́ на́ х.!** fuck off!

хуйн|я́, и́ *f.* (vulg.) (*бессмыслица*) (a load of) bollocks, crap; (*что-л. некачественное, ненужное*) crap

хулига́н, а *m.* hooligan

хулига́нств|о, а *nt.* hooliganism

ху́нт|а, ы *f.* (pol.) junta

хурм|а́, ы́ *f.* persimmon, sharon fruit (*Diospyros*)

Цц

ца́п|ать, аю *impf.* (*of* ▸ ца́пнуть) (infml) to snatch, grab

ца́п|ля, ли, *g. pl.* **~ель** *f.* heron

ца́п|нуть, ну, нешь *pf. of* ▸ ца́пать

цара́п|ать, аю *impf.* (*of* ▸ оцара́пать) to scratch

цара́па|ться, юсь *impf.* to scratch (oneself); (*друг друга*) to scratch one another

цара́пин|а, ы *f.* scratch

цар|и́ть, ю́, и́шь *impf.* **1** (*первенствовать*) to hold sway, reign supreme **2** (fig., *господствовать*) to reign, prevail; **~и́ла тишина́** silence reigned

цари́ц|а, ы *f.* **1** (*жена царя*) tsarina **2** (fig.) queen

ца́рск|ий *adj.* **1** tsar's, of the tsar; royal **2** (pol.) tsarist **3** (fig.) regal, kingly; **~ая ро́скошь** regal splendour

ца́рств|о, а *nt.* **1** (*государство*) kingdom, realm **2** (*царствование*) reign **3** (fig., *область деятельности*) realm, domain; **живо́тное ц.** animal kingdom

ца́рствовани|е, я *nt.* reign; **в ц.** (+ *g.*) during the reign (of)

ца́рств|овать, ую *impf.* to reign (also fig.)

⚬ **цар|ь, я́** *m.* **1** tsar **2** (fig.) king, ruler

цве|сти́, ту́, тёшь, *past* **~л, ~ла́** *impf.* **1** to flower, bloom, blossom (also fig.); **ц.** **здоро́вьем** to be radiant with health **2** (fig.) to prosper, flourish

⚬ **цвет¹, а,** *pl.* **~а́** *m.* (*окраска*) colour (BrE), color (AmE); **ц. лица́** complexion

⚬ **цвет², а** *m.* **1** (fig., *лучшая часть*) flower, cream, pick **2** (*расцвет*) blossoming; (fig.) prime; **в ~у́** in blossom **3** (*collect.*) (*цветы на растении*) blossom

цвете́ни|е, я *nt.* (bot.) flowering, blossoming

цветни́к, а́ *m.* flower bed

цветн|о́й *adj.* **1** (*не чёрный, не белый*) coloured (BrE), colored (AmE); colour (BrE), color (AmE); (*о людях*) (wholly or partly) of non-white descent; **~о́е стекло́** stained glass; **~ая капу́ста** cauliflower; **~о́е телеви́дение** colour (BrE), color (AmE) television; (*as m. n.* **ц., ~о́го**) (offensive) coloured (BrE), colored (AmE) person **2** (*о металлах*) non-ferrous

цветов|о́й *adj. of* ▸ цвет¹; **~а́я га́мма** colour (BrE), color (AmE) spectrum

⚬ **цвет|о́к, ка́,** *pl.* **~ы́, ~о́в** *m.* flower; (*pl. also* **~ки́, ~ко́в**) (*орган размножения*) flower

цвето́чн|ый *adj. of* ▸ цвето́к; **~ая клу́мба** flower bed; **ц. магази́н** flower shop, florist's

цвету́щий *pres. part. act. of* ▸ цвести́ *and adj.* **1** (*растение*) flowering, blossoming, blooming; (*здоровье, юноша*) blooming **2** (fig., *страна*) flourishing

х

ц

це|ди́ть, жу́, ~дишь *impf.* **1** (*через сито*) to strain, filter **2** (infml, *говорить*) to say (through clenched teeth)

целе́б|ный, ~ен, ~на *adj.* healing, medicinal

целево́й *adj.* **1** *adj. of* ▶ **цель 2** having a special purpose; **~евы́е сбо́ры** funds earmarked/ring-fenced for a special purpose **3** (*постройка*) special

целенапра́влен|ный, ~, ~на *adj.* purposeful, single-minded

целесообра́з|ный, ~ен, ~на *adj.* expedient

целеустремлён|ный, ~, ~на *adj.* purposeful

целико́м *adv.* **1** (*в це́лом ви́де*) whole; **проглоти́ть ц.** to swallow whole **2** (*полностью*) wholly, entirely; **ц. и по́лностью** utterly and completely

цели́н|а́, ы́ *f.* virgin lands

цели́тель|ь, я *m.* healer

це́л|ить, ю, ишь *impf.* (*of* ▶ **наце́лить 1**) to take aim; (**в** + *a.*) to aim (at)

це́л|иться, юсь, ишься *impf.* = **це́лить**

целлофа́н, а *m.* cellophane®

целлофа́новый *adj. of* ▶ **целлофа́н**

целлюло́з|а, ы *f.* cellulose

цел|ова́ть, у́ю *impf.* (*of* ▶ **поцелова́ть**) to kiss

цел|ова́ться, у́юсь *impf.* (*of* ▶ **поцелова́ться**) to kiss (one another)

це́л|ое, ого *nt.* **1** whole **2** (math.) integer

целому́дрен|ный, ~, ~на *adj.* chaste

целому́дри|е, я *nt.* chastity

це́лост|ный, ~ен, ~на *adj.* integrated; complete

це́л|ый *adj.* **1** (*полный*) whole, entire; **~ое число́** whole number, integer; **в ~ом** as a whole **2** (**~, ~а́, ~о**) (*неповреждённый*) safe, intact; **~ и невреди́м** safe and sound

цель|ь, и *f.* **1** (*мише́нь*) target; **бить в ц., попа́сть в ц.** to hit the target; **бить ми́мо ~и** to miss **2** (*предме́т стремле́ния*) aim, object, goal, end, purpose; **с ~ью** (+ *inf.*) with the object (of), in order (to); **пресле́довать ц.** to pursue a goal

це́ль|ный *adj.* **1** (*из одного́ куска́*) of one piece, solid **2** (**~ен, ~ьна́, ~ьно**) (*це́лостный*) entire, integral; single

Це́льси|й, я *m.* Celsius, centigrade; **10° по ~ю** 10° Celsius

цеме́нт, а *m.* cement

цен|а́, ы́, *a.* **~у,** *pl.* **~ы** *f.* **1** price, cost; **~о́й** (+ *g.*) at the price (of), at the cost (of); **любо́й ~о́й** at any cost; **э́тому ~ы́ нет** it is invaluable **2** (fig., *значе́ние*) worth, value; **знать ~у** (+ *d.*) to know the value/worth (of); **знать себе́ ~у** to be self-assured, self-possessed, to know one's own value/worth

цензу́р|а, ы *f.* censorship

цени́тель|ь, я *m.* judge, connoisseur, expert

цени́тель|ница, ницы *f. of* ▶ **цени́тель**

цен|и́ть, ю́, ~ишь *impf.* to value, appreciate; **высоко́ ц.** to rate highly

це́нник, а *m.* price tag

⚔ **це́нност|ь, и** *f.* **1** (*цена́, сто́имость*) price, value **2** (fig., *значе́ние*) value, importance **3** (*in pl.*) (*предме́ты*) valuables; (*духо́вные*) values

⚔ **це́н|ный, ~ен, ~на** *adj.* **1** (*с обозна́ченной цено́й*) containing valuables; representing a stated value; **~ные бума́ги** (fin.) securities **2** (*дорого́й*) valuable, costly; **~ная вещь** valuable object **3** (fig., *ва́жный*) valuable; precious; important

цент, а *m.* cent (*unit of currency*)

це́нтнер, а *m.* quintal (= *100 kilograms*)

⚔ **центр, а** *m.* centre (BrE), center (AmE)

централиза́ци|я, и *f.* centralization

централиз|ова́ть, у́ю *impf. and pf.* to centralize

⚔ **центра́льн|ый** *adj.* central; **~ые газе́ты** national newspapers; **~ое отопле́ние** central heating

центри́зм, а *m.* centrism

центри́ст, а *m.* centrist

центрифу́г|а, и *f.* (tech.) centrifuge

це́п|кий, ~ок, ~ка́, ~ко *adj.* **1** (*ру́ки, ко́гти*) tenacious, strong (also fig.) **2** (infml, *упо́рный*) obstinate, persistent, strong-willed

цепля́|ть, ю *impf.* **1** (**за** + *a.*) (infml) to hang on to, cling to **2** (*задева́ть чем-н. загну́тым*) to hook **3** (*прицепля́ть*) to hook on (to); to attach (to)

цепля́|ться, юсь *impf.* **1** (**за** + *a.*) (*зацепля́ться*) to hang on to, cling to **2** (**за** + *a.*) (infml, *стреми́ться удержа́ть, сохрани́ть что-н.*) to cling (to), stick (to) **3** (**к** + *d.* **or за** + *a.*) (infml, *придира́ться*) to pick (on) (*to carp at, complain of*)

цепо́чк|а, и *f.* **1** (small) chain **2** (*ряд*) file, series; **идти́ ~ой** to walk in file

цеп|ь, и, о ~и, на/в ~й, *pl.* **~и, ~е́й** *f.* **1** chain; (*in pl.*) chains (= fetters; also fig.); **посади́ть на ц.** to chain (up), shackle **2** (*гор, острово́в*) chain **3** (mil.) line, rank **4** (fig., *ряд*) series, succession; **ц. катастро́ф** succession of disasters **5** (elec.) circuit

церемо́ни|я, и *f.* ceremony

церемо́н|ный, ~ен, ~на *adj.* ceremonious

церко́вник, а *m.* churchman, clergyman

церко́вный *adj.* church; **ц. ста́роста** churchwarden; **ц. сто́рож** sexton

⚔ **це́рк|овь, ви, i. ~овью,** *pl.* **~ви, ~ве́й, ~ва́м** *and* **~вя́м** *f.* church

цех, а, в ~е *and* **в ~у́** *m.* **1** (*pl.* **~а́**) (*на заво́де*) shop, section **2** (*pl.* **~и**) (hist.) guild

цивилиза́ци|я, и *f.* civilization

цивилизо́ван|ный, ~, ~на *adj.* civilized

цика́д|а, ы *f.* cicada

⚔ **цикл, а** *m.* cycle; (*ле́кций, конце́ртов*) series

цикли́ческий *adj.* cyclic(al)

цикло́н, а *m.* (meteor.) cyclone

ц

цили́ндр, а *m.* **1** cylinder **2** (*шляпа*) top hat
цилиндри́ческий *adj.* cylindrical
цини́зм, а *m.* cynicism
ци́ник, а *m.* cynic
цини́ч|ный, ~ен, ~на *adj.* cynical
цинк, а *m.* (chem.) zinc
ци́нковый *adj.* zinc
цирк, а *m.* circus
циркáч, á *m.* (infml) circus artiste
циркáч|ка, ки *f. of* ▶ циркáч
цирково́й *adj. of* ▶ цирк
циркули́р|овать, ую *impf.* **1** (*о жидкостях*) to circulate; ~овáли слу́хи (infml) rumours (BrE), rumors (AmE) were circulating **2** (infml, *ходить*) to pass, go to and fro
ци́ркул|ь, я *m.* (pair of) compasses; dividers
циркуля́р, а *m.* circular (*official*)
циркуля́ци|я, и *f.* circulation
цирро́з, а *m.* (med.) cirrhosis
цисте́рн|а, ы *f.* (*резервуар*) cistern, tank; (*вагон*) tank car; (*автомобиль*) tanker
цитаде́л|ь, и *f.* citadel; (fig.) bulwark, stronghold
цитáт|а, ы *f.* quotation

цити́р|овать, ую *impf.* (*of* ▶ процити́ровать) to quote
ци́трус|овый *adj.* (as pl. n. ~овые, ~овых) citrus plants
циферблáт, а *m.* dial; (*часов*) face
⚬ **ци́фр|а, ы** *f.* **1** figure; digit, number, numeral **2** (*in pl.*) (*данные*) figures
⚬ **цифров|о́й** *adj.* **1** numerical **2** (electronics, comput.) digital; ~áя зáпись digital recording
цо́кол|ь, я *m.* **1** (archit.) socle, plinth, pedestal **2** (elec.) cap (*metal extremity of light bulb which is fitted into socket*)
ЦРУ *nt. indecl.* (*abbr. of* Центрáльное разве́дывательное управле́ние*) CIA (*Central Intelligence Agency*)
цунáми *nt. indecl.* tsunami
цыгáн, а, *pl.* ~е, ~ *m.* Gypsy
цыгáн|ка, ки *f. of* ▶ цыгáн
цыгáнский *adj.* Gypsy
цы́к|ать, аю *impf.* (*of* ▶ цы́кнуть) (на кого́-н.) (infml) to shout at; to silence
цы́к|нуть, ну *pf. of* ▶ цы́кать
цыпл|ёнок, ёнка, *pl.* ~я́та, ~я́т *m.* chick(en)
цы́поч|ки, ек (*no sg.*) tiptoe; на ~ках on tiptoe

Чч

ч (*abbr. of* час(ы́)) hour; o'clock
ч. (*abbr. of* часть) part
чабре́ц, á *m.* (bot., cul.) thyme
чáвк|ать, аю *impf.* to champ; to munch noisily
чаевы́|е, ых (*no sg.*) tip, gratuity
чаепи́ти|е, я *nt.* tea-drinking
⚬ **ча|й, я ю** *pl.* ~и́, ~ёв и. **1** tea **2** (*чаепитие*) tea(-drinking); за ~ем, за чáшкой ~я over (a cup of) tea **3:** дать (+ *d.*) на ч. to tip
чáйк|а, и, *g. pl.* чáек *f.* (sea)gull
чáйн|ая, ой *f.* tea room, tea shop
чáйник, а *m.* (*для заварки*) teapot; (*для кипячения воды*) kettle
чáйн|ый *adj.* tea; ч. куст tea plant; ~ая ло́жка teaspoon; ~ая чáшка teacup
чалм|á, ы́ *f.* turban
чан, а, в ~е *and* в ~у́, *pl.* ~ы́ *m.* vat, tub, tank
чароде́|й, я *m.* sorcerer, magician (also fig.)
чáртер, а *m.* charter
чáр|ы, ~ (*no sg.*) (infml) magic, charms (also fig.)
⚬ **час, а, о** ~е, в ~у́ *and* в ~е, *pl.* ~ы́ *m.*
　1 hour (also fig.); че́тверть ~á a quarter of an hour **2** (*время по часам*) (*g. sg. after*

numerals 2, 3, 4 ~á) o'clock; час one o'clock; два ~á two o'clock; во втором ~у́ between one and two (o'clock); кото́рый ч.? what is the time? **3** (*usu. in pl.*) (*время*) hours, time, period; ч. пик, ~ы́ пик rush hour
часáми *adv.* for hours
часо́в|ня, ни, *g. pl.* ~ен *f.* chapel
часов|о́й¹, о́го *m.* sentry, guard
часово́й² adj. (*of* ▶ час) **1** (*продолжающийся один час*) of one hour's duration; ч. переры́в one hour's interval **2** (*по часам*) (measured) by the hour; ч. по́яс time zone
часов|о́й³ adj. of ▶ часы́; ч. магази́н watch shop, watchmaker's, watch repair shop; ч. механи́зм clockwork; ~áя стре́лка clock hand, hour hand; по ~о́й стре́лке clockwise
часовщи́к, á *m.* watchmaker
части́ц|а, ы *f.* **1** small part, element **2** (phys.) particle **3** (gram.) particle
части́чно *adv.* partly, partially
части́ч|ный, ~ен, ~на *adj.* partial
⚬ **чáстност|ь, и** *f.* detail; в ~и in particular
⚬ **чáстн|ый** *adj.* **1** (*личный*) private, personal; ~ым о́бразом privately **2** (econ.) private, privately-owned; ~ая со́бственность private property **3** (*отдельный, особый*)

ц
ч

particular, individual; (*as nt. n.* ~ое, ~ого)
the particular

◇ ча́сто *adv.* often, frequently

◇ частот|а́, ы́, *pl.* ~ы f. frequency

◇ част|ый, ~, ~а́, о *adj.* **1** frequent; он у
нас ч. гость he is a frequent visitor at our
house **2** (*густой*) close (together); dense,
thick; ч. дождь steady rain **3** (*быстрый*)
quick, rapid; ч. ого́нь (mil.) rapid fire

◇ част|ь, и, *pl.* ~и, ~е́й f. **1** part; portion;
бо́льшей ~ью, по бо́льшей ~и for the
most part, mostly **2** (*отдел*) section,
department **3** (infml, *область*) sphere, field;
э́то не по мое́й ~и this is not my province;
по ~и (+ g.) in connection (with) **4** (mil.)
unit

ча́стью *adv.* partly, in part

час|ы́, о́в (*no sg.*) clock, watch

чат, а *m.* (comput.) IRC (abbr. of *Internet Relay
Chat*)

ча́хл|ый, ~, ~а *adj.* stunted; poor

ча́х|нуть, ну, нешь, *past* ~, ~ла *impf.* (*of*
▶ зача́хнуть) **1** (*о растительности*) to
wither away **2** (*о человеке*) to fade away

чахо́тк|а, и f. (infml) consumption

ча́ш|а, и f. cup, bowl (also fig.); (eccl.) chalice;
ч. весо́в scale pan

ча́шк|а, и f. (*для питья*) cup

ча́щ|а, и f. thicket

ча́ще *comp. of* ▶ ча́стый, ▶ ча́сто; more often;
ч. всего́ most often, mostly

чебуре́к, а *m.* cheburek (*a kind of lamb
pasty*)

чего́[1] *interrog. adv.* (infml) why? what for?

чего́[2] *g. of* ▶ что[1]

чей, чья, чьё, *pl.* чьи *interrog. pron. and rel.
pron.* whose

чей-либо *pron.* = чей-нибудь

чей-нибудь *pron.* (*в утверждениях*)
someone's, somebody's; (*в вопросах*)
anyone's, anybody's

чей-то *pron.* someone's, somebody's

чек, а *m.* **1** (*банковский*) cheque (BrE), check
(AmE); вы́писать ч. to write a cheque
2 (*с указанием суммы, которую следует
уплатить*) chit; (*удостоверяющий, что
товар оплачен*) receipt

чеки́ст, а *m.* (hist.) agent of the Cheka (*state
security organ 1918-22*)

че́к|овый *adj. of* ▶ чек; ~овая кни́жка
chequebook (BrE), checkbook (AmE)

чёлк|а, и f. fringe (BrE), bangs (AmE); (*лошади*)
forelock

челно́к, а́ *m.* **1** (*лодка*) dugout (canoe) **2** (sl.)
small trader (*travelling to buy things to resell
at home*)

◇ челове́к, а, *pl.* лю́ди, *in combination with
nums., g. pl., etc.* челове́к, ~ам, ~ами, о
~ах *m.* man, person, human being

человеконенави́стнический *adj.*
misanthropic

человекообра́з|ный, ~ен, ~на *adj.*
anthropomorphous; (zool.) anthropoid

◇ челове́ческий *adj.* **1** (*относящийся к
человеку*) human **2** (*гуманный*) humane

челове́чество, а *nt.* humanity, mankind

челове́чность, и f. humaneness, humanity

челове́ч|ный, ~ен, ~на *adj.* humane

че́люст|ь, и f. **1** jaw **2** (*зубной протез*)
dentures

◇ чем *conj.* **1** than **2** (+ *comp.*): ч. ..., тем... the
more ..., the more ...; ч. скоре́е, тем лу́чше
the sooner, the better

чемода́н, а *m.* suitcase

чемпио́н, а *m.* champion

◇ чемпиона́т, а *m.* championship

чемпио́н|ка, ки f. *of* ▶ чемпио́н

чепух|а́, и́ f. (infml) **1** (*вздор*) nonsense,
rubbish **2** (*незначительное дело*) a trifle,
trifling matter; (*пустяки*) trivialities
3 (*незначительное количество*) trifling
amount

че́рв|и[1], е́й and че́рвы, ~ f. pl. (*sg.* ~а,
~ы) (*в картах*) hearts; коро́ль ~е́й king
of hearts

че́рви[2] *pl. of* ▶ червь

черво́вый *adj. of* ▶ че́рви[1]

черв|ь, я́, *pl.* ~и, ~е́й *m.* worm; maggot

червя́к, а́ *m.* **1** = червь **2** (tech.) worm

черда́к, а́ *m.* attic, loft

чередова́ни|е, я *nt.* alternation,
interchange, rotation

черед|ова́ть, у́ю *impf.* (с + i.) to alternate
(with)

черед|ова́ться, у́юсь *impf.* to alternate; to
take turns

◇ че́рез *prep.* (+ *a.*) **1** (*улицу, забор*) across;
over; (*лес, окно*) through **2** (*о пунктах
следования*) via **3** (*посредством*) through;
ч. перево́дчика through an interpreter
4 (*по прошествии*) in; ч. полчаса́ in
half an hour's time; я верну́сь ч. год
I shall be back in a year's time **5** (*минуя
какое-н. пространство*) after; (*further*)
on; ч. три киломе́тра three kilometres
(further) on **6** (*повторяя в регулярные
промежутки*): ч. ка́ждые три страни́цы
every three pages; дежу́рить ч. день to be
on duty every other day, on alternate days

черен|о́к, ка́ *m.* **1** (*рукоятка*)
handle **2** (hort.) cutting

че́реп, а, *pl.* ~а́ *m.* skull, cranium

черепа́х|а, и f. **1** tortoise; (*морская*)
turtle; ползти́ как ч. to go at a snail's
pace **2** (*панцирь в качестве материала*)
tortoiseshell

черепи́ц|а, ы f. tile; (*collect.*) tiles

черепи́чный *adj.* tile; tiled

черепн|о́й *adj. of* ▶ че́реп; ~а́я коро́бка
cranium

череп|о́к, ка́ *m.* broken piece of pottery

чересчу́р *adv.* too; (*перед глаголом*) too much

чере́шн|я, и f. cherry (tree) (*Cerasus avium*)

ч

черкéс, а *m.* Circassian

черкéсский *adj.* Circassian

черкéшенк|а, и *f. of* ▶ черкéс

черне́|ть, ю *impf.* **1** (*pf.* **по∼**) (*становиться чёрным*) to turn black, grow black **2** (*виднеться*) to show up black

черни́к|а, и *f.* bilberry

черни́л|а, ∼ (*no sg.*) ink

черни́льниц|а, ы *f.* inkpot, inkwell

чернобу́рк|а, и *f.* (infml) silver fox (fur)

черновиќ, á *m.* rough copy, draft

чернов|óй *adj.* **1** rough, draft; preparatory **2**: ∼áя рабóта (infml) heavy, rough, dirty work

черноволóс|ый, ∼, ∼а *adj.* black-haired

черноглáз|ый, ∼, ∼а *adj.* black-eyed

черногóр|ец, ца *m.* Montenegrin

Черногóри|я, и *f.* Montenegro

черногóр|ка, ки *f. of* ▶ черногóрец

черногóрский *adj.* Montenegrin

чернокóж|ий, ∼, ∼а *adj.* black; (*as m. n.* ч., ∼его) black (man)

чернорабóч|ий, его *m.* unskilled labourer (BrE), laborer (AmE)

черносли́в, а *m.* (*collect.*) prunes

черносóтен|ец, ца *m.* (hist.) member of 'Black Hundred' (*name of armed monarchist anti-Semitic groups in Russia, active 1905-7*); (fig.) extreme reactionary, chauvinist

чернот|á, ы́ *f.* blackness (also fig.); darkness

♂ **чёр|ный, ∼ен, черна́** *adj.* **1** black; ч. ры́нок black market; (*отложи́ть на*) ч. день (to put by for) a rainy day; ∼ное де́рево ebony; Ч∼ное мóре Black Sea; ∼ная сморóдина blackcurrant; (*черножóжий*) black; (*as m. n.* ч., ∼ного) (offensive, esp. when referring to person of Caucasian or Central Asian origin) black (man) **2** (*задний*) back; ч. ход back entrance, back door **3** (fig., *мы́сли, дни*) gloomy, melancholy

черпáк, á *m.* scoop, ladle

чéрп|ать, аю *impf.* (*of* ▶ черпну́ть) **1** to draw (up); to scoop; to ladle **2** (fig., *извлекáть*) to extract, derive

черп|ну́ть, ну́, нёшь *inst. pf. of* ▶ чéрпать

чёрств|ый, ∼, черствá, ∼о *adj.* **1** stale **2** (fig., *бездýшный*) hard, callous

чёрт, а, *pl.* чéрти, чертéй *m.* devil; ч. возьми́/поберú! (infml) damn!; до ∼а (infml) hellishly; какóго ∼а? (infml) why the hell?

♂ **черт|á, ы́** *f.* **1** (*ли́ния*) line; провести́ ∼у́ to draw a line **2** (*грани́ца*) boundary **3** (*свóйство*) trait, characteristic; ∼ы́ лицá features; в óбщих ∼áх in general outline

черт|ёж, ежá *m.* draft, drawing, sketch

чертёжник, а *m.* draughtsman

чер|ти́ть, чу́, ∼тишь *impf.* (*of* ▶ начерти́ть) (*кáрту*) to draw; (*план*) to draw up

чертополóх, а *m.* thistle

черчéни|е, я *nt.* drawing; sketching

че|сáть, шу́, ∼шешь *impf.* (*of* ▶ почесáть) to scratch

че|сáться, шу́сь, ∼шешься *impf.* (*of* ▶ почесáться) **1** to scratch oneself **2** (*impf. only*) (*об ощущéнии зудá*) to itch; ру́ки у негó *и т. п.* ∼шутся (+ *inf.*) he is, *etc.*, itching to ...

чеснóк, á у́ *m.* garlic

чесóтк|а, и *f.* (med.) scabies

чéств|овать, ую *impf.* to honour (BrE), honor (AmE); to pay tribute to

чéстност|ь, и *f.* honesty, integrity

чéст|ный, ∼ен, ∼нá, ∼но, ∼ны́ *adj.* honest; (*справедли́вый*) fair; ∼ное слóво! honestly!, truly!

честолюби́в|ый, ∼, ∼а *adj.* ambitious

честолюби|е, я *nt.* ambition

♂ **чест|ь, и** *f.* honour (BrE), honor (AmE); в ч. (+ *g.*) in honour (BrE), honor (AmE) of

чет|á, ы́ *f.* pair, couple; не ч. комý-н. no match for sb

четвéрг, á *m.* Thursday

четверéньк|и (infml) на ч., на ∼ах on all fours, on one's hands and knees; стать на ч. to go down on all fours

четвёрк|а, и *f.* **1** (*ци́фра, игрáльная кáрта*) four **2** (*отмéтка*) four (*out of five*) **3** (infml, *автóбус, трамвáй*) No. 4 (*bus, tram, etc.*) **4** (*грýппа из четверы́х*) (group of) four; (*четы́ре человéка*) foursome

чéтвер|о, ы́х *num.* (*collect.*) four; нас бы́ло ч. there were four of us

четвероно́г|ий *adj.* four-legged; (*as nt. n.* ∼ое, ∼ого) quadruped

четвёртый *adj.* fourth

чéтверт|ь, и, *g. pl.* ∼éй *f.* **1** (*четвёртая часть цéлого*) quarter **2** (*чéтверть часá*) quarter (of an hour); без ∼и час a quarter to one; ч. деся́того a quarter past nine **3** (*учéбного гóда*) term **4** (mus.) crotchet (BrE), quarter note (AmE)

четвертьфинáл, а *m.* (sport) quarter-final

чёт|ки, ок (*no sg.*) (eccl.) rosary

чёт|кий, ∼ок, ∼ка *and* четкá, ∼ко *adj.* **1** (*отчётливый*) precise; clear-cut **2** (*изложéние*) clear, well defined; (*пóчерк*) legible; (*звук*) plain, distinct; (*речь*) articulate

чёткост|ь, и *f.* **1** (*движéния*) precision, preciseness **2** (*изложéния*) clarity, clearness

чётный *adj.* even (*of numbers*)

♂ **четы́р|е, ёх, ём, ьмя́, о ∼ёх** *num.* four

четы́режды *adv.* four times

четы́р|еста, ёхсóт, ёмстáм, ьмястáми, о ∼ехстáх *num.* four hundred

четырёхлéтний *adj.* **1** (*срок*) four-year **2** (*ребёнок*) four-year-old

четырёхсóтый *adj.* four-hundredth

четырёхугóльник, а *m.* quadrangle

четырёхугóльный *adj.* quadrangular

четы́рнадцатый *adj.* fourteenth

четы́рнадцат|ь, и *и num.* fourteen

чех, а *m.* Czech

чехардá, ы́ *f.* (*игрá*) leapfrog; (fig.) reshuffle

Че́хи|я, и *f.* Czech Republic

чех|о́л, ла́ *m.* (*подушки, кресла*) cover; (*контрабаса*) case

чечеви́ц|а, ы *f.* lentil; (*collect.*) lentils

чече́н|ец, ца *m.* Chechen

чече́н|ка, ки *f. of* ▶ **чече́нец**

чече́нский *adj.* Chechen

Чечн|я́, и́ *f.* Chechnya

че́шк|а, и *f. of* ▶ **чех**

че́шский *adj.* Czech

чешу|я́, и́ (*no pl.*) *f.* (zool.) scales

чизке́йк, а, *m.* cheesecake

Чи́ли *f. indecl.* Chile

чили́|ец, йца *m.* Chilean

чили́|йка, йки *f. of* ▶ **чили́ец**

чили́йский *adj.* Chilean

чин, а, *pl.* **~ы́** *m.* **1** (*разряд*) rank; **в ~е/~а́х** high-ranking **2** (*чиновник*) official

чин|и́ть, ю́, ~ишь *impf.* (*of* ▶ **починя́ть**) (*обувь, велосипед*) to repair, mend

чи́н|ный, ~ен, ~на́, ~но *adj.* decorous, proper, orderly

✍ **чино́вник, а** *m.* official, functionary

чип, а *m.* (micro)chip

чи́пс|ы, ов (*no sg.*) (potato) crisps (BrE), chips (AmE)

чири́ка|ть, ю *impf.* to chirp, twitter

чири́кн|уть, у, ешь *inst. pf.* to give a chirp

чи́рк|ать, аю *impf.* (*of* ▶ **чи́ркнуть**) (+ *i.*) (*по* + *d.*) to strike sharply (against, on); **ч. спи́чкой** to strike a match

чи́ркн|уть, ну, нешь *inst. pf. of* ▶ **чи́ркать**

чи́сленност|ь, и *f.* numbers; **ч. населе́ния** population size; (mil.) strength

чи́сленный *adj.* numerical

числи́тельн|ое, ого *nt.* (gram.) numeral

чи́сл|иться, юсь, ишься *impf.* **1** to be (*in context of calculation or official records*); **в на́шей дере́вне ~ится три́ста жи́телей** there are three hundred inhabitants in our village **2** (+ *i.*) to be officially, be on paper; **он ещё ~ился заве́дующим отде́лом, а все обя́занности исполня́ли его́ замести́тели** he was still head of the department on paper, but all the duties were being performed by his deputies **3** (*за* + *i.*) to be attributed (to), have; **за ним ~ится мно́го недоста́тков** he has many failings

✍ **чис|ло́, ла́,** *pl.* **~ла, ~ел** *nt.* **1** number; **~ло́м** in number; **без ~ла́** without number, in great numbers; **в том ~не́** including **2** (*дата*) date, day (*of month*); **како́е сего́дня ч.?** what is the date today? **3** (gram.) number; **еди́нственное, мно́жественное ч.** singular, plural

числово́й *adj.* numerical

чисти́лищ|е, а *nt.* (relig.) purgatory

чи́стильщик, а *m.* cleaner

чи́|стить, щу, стишь *impf.* **1** (*pf.* **по~, вы́~**) to clean; (*щёткой*) to brush **2** (*pf.* **по~, вы́~**) (*дорожки*) to clear; (*канал*)

---

to dredge **3** (*pf.* **о~** *and* infml **по~**) (*овощи, фрукты*) to peel; (*орехи*) to shell; (*рыбу*) to clean

чи́стк|а, и *f.* **1** cleaning; **отда́ть в ~у** to have cleaned, send to be cleaned **2** (pol.) purge; **этни́ческая ч.** ethnic cleansing

чи́сто¹ *as pred.* it is clean

чи́сто² *adv.* **1** *adv. of* ▶ **чи́стый**; **ч.-на́чисто** spotlessly clean **2** (*as conj.*) (infml) just like, just as if

чистово́й *adj.* fair, clean; **ч. экземпля́р** fair copy

чистокро́в|ный, ~ен, ~на *adj.* thoroughbred

чистописа́ни|е, я *nt.* calligraphy

чистопло́т|ный, ~ен, ~на *adj.* clean; neat, tidy

чистот|а́, ы́ *f.* **1** cleanliness; (*опрятность*) neatness, tidiness **2** (*безупречность; отсутствие примесей*) purity

✍ **чи́ст|ый, ~, ~а́, ~о, ~ы́** *adj.* **1** clean; (*опрятный*) neat, tidy; (*голос, речь*) clear; **экологи́чески ч.** eco-friendly **2** (fig., *безупречный*) pure **3** (*без примесей*) pure **4** (*открытый*) clear; open; **ч. лист** blank sheet **5** (fin., etc.) net, clear; **~ая при́быль** clear profit **6** (infml, *сущий*) pure, utter; sheer; complete; **~ая случа́йность** pure chance

чита́льный *adj.*: **ч. зал** reading room

✍ **чита́тел|ь, я** *m.* reader

✍ **чита́тель|ница, ницы** *f. of* ▶ **чита́тель**

✍ **чита́|ть, ю** *impf.* (*of* ▶ **прочита́ть**, ▶ **проче́сть**) **1** to read **2**: **ч. ле́кцию** to give a lecture; **ч. стихи́** to recite poetry

чих|а́ть, а́ю *impf.* (*of* ▶ **чихну́ть**) to sneeze

чих|ну́ть, ну́, нёшь *inst. pf. of* ▶ **чиха́ть**

чи́ще *comp. of* ▶ **чи́стый**, ▶ **чи́сто¹**, ▶ **чи́сто²**

✍ **член, а** *m.* **1** member; (*академик*) Fellow; **ч.-корреспонде́нт** corresponding member (*of an Academy*) **2** (math.) term; (gram.) part (*of sentence*) **3** (*конечность*) limb; (*половой*) penis

членоразде́л|ьный, ~ен, ~ьна *adj.* articulate

чле́нств|о, а *nt.* membership

чмо́к|ать, аю *impf.* (*of* ▶ **чмо́кнуть**) (infml) **1** to smack one's lips **2** (*целовать*) to give a smacking kiss **3** (*о грязи*) to squelch

чмо́к|нуть, ну, нешь *pf. of* ▶ **чмо́кать**

чо́к|аться, аюсь *impf.* (*of* ▶ **чо́кнуться**) to clink glasses (*when drinking toasts*)

чо́кнутый *adj.* (infml) odd, crazy

чо́к|нуться, нусь, нешься *pf. of* ▶ **чо́каться**

чо́пор|ный, ~ен, ~на *adj.* prim; stuck-up; stand-offish

ЧП *nt. indecl.* (*abbr. of* **чрезвыча́йное происше́ствие**) incident, emergency; (*катастрофа*) disaster

чрева́т|ый, ~, ~а *adj.* (+ *i.*) fraught (with)

чрезвыча́йно *adv.* extremely, extraordinarily

чрезвыча́|йный, ~ен, ~йна *adj.* **1** extraordinary **2** (*экстренный*) special, emergency; **~йные ме́ры** emergency

---

ч

✍ key word

measures; ∼йное положе́ние state of emergency

чрезме́р|ный, ∼ен, ∼на *adj.* excessive, inordinate

✓ **чте́ни|е, я** *nt.* reading

чти́в|о, а *nt.* (infml, pej.) reading matter

чтить, чту, чтишь, чтят *and* чтут *impf.* to honour (BrE), honor (AmE)

✓ **что¹**, чего́, чему́, чем, о чём *interrog. pron.* **1** what?, ∼? what's the matter (with you)?; что де́лать, что поде́лаешь? it can't be helped; для чего́? why?, what ... for?; что ты (вы)! (*выражает удивление, страх*) you don't mean to say so! **2** (*почему*) why?; что вы не еди́те? why aren't you eating?

✓ **что²**, (*sometimes printed* что) *rel. pron.* which, that; (infml, *который*) who; я зна́ю, что вы име́ете в виду́ I know what you mean; па́рень, что стоя́л ря́дом со мно́й the fellow (who was) standing next to me; он всё молча́л, что для него́ не характе́рно he said nothing the whole time, which is unlike him

что³ as far as; что до, что каса́ется (+ *g.*) as for, with regard (to), as far as ... is concerned

✓ **что⁴** *conj.* that; то, что... the fact that ...

✓ **чтоб** *conj.* = чтобы

✓ **что́бы** *conj.* **1** (*выражает цель*) in order to, in order that; ч. ... не lest **2** (that); он хо́чет, ч. она́ пришла́ в шесть часо́в he wants her to come at 6 o'clock **3** (*as particle*) (*выражает требование, пожелание*): ч. я тебя́ бо́льше не ви́дел! may I never see your face again!

что за (infml) **1** (*interrog.*) what? what sort of ... ?; что э́то за пти́ца? what sort of bird is that? **2** (*as int.*): что за день! what a (marvellous) day!

что́-либо, чего́-либо *indefinite pron.* anything

что́-нибудь, чего́-нибудь *indefinite pron.* anything

✓ **что́-то¹**, чего́-то *indefinite pron.* something

что́-то² *adv.* (infml) **1** (*несколько*) somewhat, slightly **2** (*почему-то*) somehow, for no obvious reason; что́-то мне не хо́чется идти́ I don't feel like going for some reason

чуб, а, *pl.* ∼ы́ *m.* forelock

чува́к, á *m.* (sl.) guy, fellow (both infml)

чува́ш, á, *pl.* ∼и́, ∼е́й *m.* Chuvash

чува́ш|ка, ки *f. of* ▶ чува́ш

чува́шский *adj.* Chuvash

чуви́х|а, и *f.* (sl.) chick (infml) (*girl*)

чу́вствен|ный *adj.* **1** (∼, ∼на) sensual **2** (phil.) perceptible; ∼ное восприя́тие perception

чувстви́тельност|ь, и *f.* **1** (*кожи, прибора, человека*) sensitivity, sensitiveness **2** (*сентиментальность*) sentimentality

чувстви́тел|ьный, ∼ен, ∼ьна *adj.* **1** (*прибор, человек*) sensitive **2** (*сентиментальный*) sentimental

3 (*толчок, урон*) perceptible

✓ **чу́вств|о, а** *nt.* **1** (physiol.) sense; ч. вку́са sense of taste; о́рганы ∼ senses, organs of sense **2** (*sg. or pl.*) (*сознание*) senses; лиши́ться ∼, упа́сть без ∼ to faint, lose consciousness; прийти́ в ч. to come round, regain consciousness, come to one's senses **3** (*ощущение*) feeling; sense; ч. ю́мора sense of humour (BrE), humor (AmE); пита́ть к кому́-н. не́жные ∼а to have a soft spot for sb

✓ **чу́вств|овать, ую** *impf.* (*of* ▶ почу́вствовать) **1** to feel, sense; ч. себя́ to feel; как вы себя́ ∼уете? how do you feel? **2** (*уметь воспринимать*) to appreciate, have a feeling (for) (*music, etc.*)

чу́вств|оваться, уется *impf.* **1** to be perceptible; to make itself felt **2** *pass. of* ▶ чу́вствовать

чугу́н, á *m.* cast iron

чугу́нный *adj.* cast-iron (also fig.)

чуда́к, á *m.* eccentric, crank

чуде́с|ный, ∼ен, ∼на *adj.* **1** (*сверхъесте́ственный*) miraculous; ∼ное исцеле́ние miraculous healing **2** (*чудный*) marvellous (BrE), marvelous (AmE), wonderful

чуд|но́й, ∼ён, ∼на́, ∼но́ *adj.* (*странный*) strange, odd

чу́д|ный, ∼ен, ∼на *adj.* marvellous (BrE), marvelous (AmE), wonderful, lovely

✓ **чу́д|о, а**, *pl.* ∼еса́, ∼е́с *nt.* **1** (*сверхъесте́ственное явле́ние*) miracle **2** (*нечто поразительное*) wonder, marvel

чудо́вищ|е, а *nt.* monster

чудо́вищ|ный, ∼ен, ∼на *adj.* **1** monstrous (also fig., pej.) **2** (*огромный*) enormous

чу́дом *adv.* miraculously; ч. спасти́сь to be saved by a miracle

чудотво́р|ец, ца *m.* miracle-worker

чужда́|ться, юсь *impf.* (+ *g.*) (*друзей*) to shun, avoid; (*славы*) to stand aloof (from), remain unaffected (by)

чу́жд|ый, ∼, ∼á, ∼о *adj.* **1** (+ *d.*) (*идеоло́гия, взгля́ды*) alien (to); extraneous **2** (+ *g.*) (*лишенный*) free (from), devoid (of); он ∼ зло́бы he is devoid of malice

✓ **чуж|о́й** *adj.* **1** (*не свой*) sb else's, another's, others'; на ч. счёт at sb else's expense; (*as nt. n.* ∼о́е, ∼о́го) sb else's belongings **2** (*посторонний*) strange, alien; foreign; (*as m. n.* ∼о́й, ∼о́го) stranger

чула́н, а *m.* (*для вещей*) storeroom, lumber room; (*для продуктов*) larder

чул|о́к, ка́, *g. pl.* ч. *m.* stocking

чум|á, ы́ *f.* plague

чума́з|ый, ∼, ∼а *adj.* (infml) grubby, dirty

чурба́н, а *m.* **1** block, log **2** (infml, *тупой человек*) blockhead

чу́рк|а, и *f.* block, lump

чу́т|кий, ∼ок, ∼ка́, ∼ко *adj.* **1** keen, sharp; ч. нюх keen sense of smell; ч. сон light sleep **2** (fig., *отзывчивый*) sensitive; sympathetic; tactful

ч

⚘ **чуть** **1** *adv.* (*едва*) hardly, scarcely; just; **ч. (бы́ло) не, ч. ли не** almost, nearly **2** *adv.* (*немного*) (just) a little, very slightly **3** *conj.* (*как то́лько*) as soon as; **ч. что** at the slightest provocation

чуть|ё, я́ *nt.* **1** (*у живо́тных*) scent **2** (**к** + *d.* or **на** + *a.*) (fig., *спосо́бность*) flair, feeling (for)

чуть-чу́ть *adv.* (infml) a tiny bit; **ч.-ч. не; = чуть не**

чу́чел|о, а *nt.* **1** (*живо́тное*) stuffed animal **2** (*пуга́ло*) scarecrow (also fig.)

чушь, и *f.* (infml) nonsense

чу́|ять, ю, ешь *impf.* to scent, smell; (fig.) to sense, feel

шабло́н, а *m.* **1** (tech.) template, pattern; (*фо́рма*) mould (BrE), mold (AmE) **2** (fig., pej.) cliché; routine

⚘ **шаг, а (у)**, *after numerals 2, 3, 4* ~а́, о ~е, в/на ~у́/~е, *pl.* ~и́, ~о́в *m.* step (also fig.); (*похо́дка*) pace; (*большо́й*) stride; **ш. на ме́сте** marking time; **идти́ бы́стрыми** ~а́ми make rapid strides; **заме́длить ш.** to slow down; **в двух** ~а́х, **в не́скольких** ~а́х a stone's throw away; **на ка́ждом** ~у́ everywhere, at every turn, continually

шага́|ть, а́ю *impf.* (*of* ▶ шагну́ть) **1** (*ступа́ть*) to step; (*ходи́ть*) to walk; (*больши́ми шага́ми*) to stride; (*ме́рными шага́ми*) to pace **2** (infml, *идти́*) to go, come

шаг|ну́ть, ну́, нёшь *inst. pf.* (*of* ▶ шага́ть) to take a step; (fig.) to make progress

ша́гом *adv.* at a walk, at a walking pace; slowly; **ш. марш!** (mil.) quick march!

ша́йб|а, ы *f.* **1** (tech.) washer **2** (sport) puck; **хокке́й с** ~ой ice hockey

ша́йк|а, и, *g. pl.* ша́ек *f.* gang, band

шака́л, а *m.* jackal

шала́ш, а́ *m.* (*hunter's or fisherman's*) cabin (*made of branches and straw, etc.*)

шал|и́ть, ю́, и́шь *impf.* to be naughty; to play up, play tricks (*also of inanimate objects*)

ша́лост|ь, и *f.* prank; (*in pl.*) mischief

шалу́н, а́ *m.* naughty child

шалу́н|ья, ьи *f. of* ▶ шалу́н

шалфе́|й, я *m.* (bot.) sage

шаль, и *f.* shawl

шальн|о́й *adj.* mad, crazy; wild; ~ые де́ньги easy money; ~ая пу́ля stray bullet

шама́н, а *m.* (relig.) shaman

шампа́нск|ое, ого *nt.* champagne

шампиньо́н, а *m.* field mushroom

шампу́н|ь, я *m.* shampoo

шампу́р, а *m.* skewer

⚘ **шанс, а** *m.* chance; **име́ть мно́го** ~ов, **больши́е** ~ы (**на** + *a.*) to have a good chance (of)

шансо́н, а *m.* ballad (*also as a genre*)

шансонье́ *m. indecl.* balladeer; singer-songwriter

шанта́ж, а́ *m.* blackmail

шантажи́р|овать, ую *impf.* to blackmail

шантажи́ст, а *m.* blackmailer

шантажи́ст|ка, ки *f. of* ▶ шантажи́ст

ша́пк|а, и *f.* **1** hat, cap **2** (*заголо́вок*) banner headline(s)

шар, а, *after numerals 2, 3, 4* ~а́, *pl.* ~ы́ *m.* **1** (math.) sphere; **земно́й ш.** the Earth, globe **2** (*шарови́дный предме́т*) spherical object, ball; **возду́шный ш.** balloon

шара́х|аться, аюсь *impf.* (*of* ▶ шара́хнуться) (infml) (*о ло́шади*) to shy; (*о толпе́*) to start (up); (*броса́ться*) to rush, dash

шара́х|нуться, нусь, нешься *pf. of* ▶ шара́хаться

шарж, а *m.* caricature, cartoon

шариа́т, а *m.* sharia (*Islamic canonical law*)

ша́риков|ый *adj.*: ~ая ру́чка biro®, ballpoint (pen)

ша́р|ить, ю, ишь *impf.* (**в** + *p.* or **по** + *d.*) (*иска́ть о́щупью*) to grope about, feel, fumble (in, through); (*о проже́кторе*) to sweep (*in order to locate a target*)

ша́рк|ать, аю *impf.* (+ *i.*) to shuffle

шарлата́н, а *m.* charlatan, fraud; quack

шарлата́н|ка, ки *f. of* ▶ шарлата́н

шарм, а *m.* charm

шарни́р, а *m.* (tech.) hinge, joint

шарф, а *m.* scarf

шасси́ *nt. indecl.* **1** (*автомоби́ля*) chassis **2** (aeron.) undercarriage

ша́ста|ть, ю *impf.* (infml) to roam, hang about

шата́|ть, ю *impf.* to rock, shake

шата́|ться, юсь *impf.* **1** (*о челове́ке, о ваго́не*) to rock, sway, reel **2** (*о гвозде́*) to be, come loose; (*о сту́ле, забо́ре*) to wobble, be unsteady **3** (infml, *броди́ть*) to roam; to loaf, lounge about

шатён, а *m.* man/boy with auburn/brown/chestnut hair

Ч

Ш

шате́н|ка, ки *f.* woman/girl with auburn/brown/chestnut hair

шат|ёр, ра́ *m.* tent, marquee

ша́т|кий, ~ок, ~ка́, ~ко *adj.* **1** (*стол*) unsteady; shaky; (*га́йка*) loose **2** (fig.) unstable, insecure, shaky

ша́фер, а, *pl.* ~а́ *m.* best man (*at wedding*)

шафра́н, а *m.* (bot.) saffron

шах¹, а *m.* (*мона́рх*) Shah

шах², а *m.* (chess) check; **ш. и мат** checkmate; **вам ш.** you're in check

шахмати́ст, а *m.* chess player

шахмати́ст|ка, ки *f.* of ▶ шахмати́ст

ша́хматн|ый *adj.* **1** chess; ~ая доска́ chessboard; ~ая па́ртия game of chess **2** (*с квадра́тами кле́ток*) check(ed); chequered (BrE), checkered (AmE); **в ~ом поря́дке** staggered

ша́хмат|ы, ~ (*no sg.*) **1** (*игра́*) chess **2** (*фигу́ры*) chessmen

ша́хт|а, ы *f.* **1** (*го́рная вы́работка*) mine, pit **2** (tech., *ли́фта, вентиляцио́нная*) shaft

шахтёр, а *m.* miner

ша́шк|а¹, и *f.* (*взрывча́тка*) charge (*of explosive*)

ша́шк|а², и *f.* **1** (*в игре́*) draught (BrE), checker (AmE) (*piece in game of draughts*) **2** (*in pl.*) (*игра́*) draughts (BrE), checkers (AmE)

шашлы́к, а́ *m.* (cul.) kebab, shashlik

шва *g. sg.* of ▶ шов

шва́бр|а, ы *f.* mop, swab

шварт|ова́ть, у́ю *impf.* (*of* ▶ пришвартова́ть) (naut.) to moor

шварт|ова́ться, у́юсь *impf.* (*of* ▶ пришвартова́ться) (naut.) to moor

швед, а *m.* Swede

шве́д|ка, ки *f.* of ▶ швед

шве́дский *adj.* Swedish

швейн|ый *adj.* sewing; ~ая маши́на sewing machine

швейца́р, а *m.* porter, doorman

швейца́р|ец, ца *m.* Swiss

Швейца́ри|я, и *f.* Switzerland

швейца́р|ка, ки *f.* of ▶ швейца́рец

швейца́рский *adj.* Swiss

Шве́ци|я, и *f.* Sweden

шве|я́, и́ *f.* seamstress

швыр|ну́ть, ну́, нёшь *inst. pf.* of ▶ швыря́ть

швыр|я́ть, я́ю *impf.* (*of* ▶ швырну́ть) (+ *a.* or *i.*) to throw, fling, chuck, hurl

швыря́|ться, юсь *impf.* (infml) (+ *i.*) **1** (*камня́ми*) to throw, fling, hurl (at one another) **2** (*деньга́ми, друзья́ми*) to make light (of), trifle (with)

шевел|и́ть, ю́, и́шь *impf.* (*of* ▶ шевельну́ть, ▶ пошевели́ть) **1** (*перевора́чивать*) to turn over **2** (+ *i.*) (*слегка́ сдвига́ть*) to move, stir; **ш. мозга́ми** (infml, joc.) to use one's brains

шевел|и́ться, ю́сь, и́шься *impf.* (*of* ▶ шевельну́ться, ▶ пошевели́ться) **1** (*слегка́ сдвига́ться*) to move, stir **2** (fig., *о наде́жде, сомне́ниях*) to stir

шевель|ну́ть, ну́, нёшь *inst. pf.* (*of* ▶ шевели́ть): **па́льцем не ш.** to not lift a finger

шевель|ну́ться, ну́сь, нёшься *inst. pf.* of ▶ шевели́ться

шевелю́р|а, ы *f.* (head of) hair

шеде́вр, а *m.* masterpiece

шезло́нг, а *m.* deckchair; lounger

ше́йк|а, и, *g. pl.* ше́ек *f.* **1** *dim.* of ▶ ше́я **2** (anat.): **ш. ма́тки** cervix

ше́йный *adj.* of ▶ ше́я; (anat.) cervical

шейх, а *m.* sheikh

шёл *see* ▶ идти́

ше́лест, а *m.* rustle, rustling

шелест|е́ть (*1st pers. not used*) и́шь *impf.* to rustle

шёлк, а (у), о ~е, на/в шелку́/~е, *pl.* шелка́ *m.* silk

шёлковый *adj.* silk

шелохн|у́ться, у́сь, ёшься *pf.* to stir, move

шелух|а́, и́ *f.* (*плодо́в, овоще́й*) skin; peel; (*горо́ха*) pod

шелуш|и́ться, и́тся *impf.* to peel (off)

шепеля́в|ить, лю, ишь *impf.* to lisp

шеп|ну́ть, ну́, нёшь *inst. pf.* of ▶ шепта́ть

шёпот, а *m.* whisper (also fig.)

шёпотом *adv.* in a whisper

шеп|та́ть, чу́, ~чешь *impf.* (*of* ▶ шепну́ть, ▶ прошепта́ть) to whisper

шеп|та́ться, чу́сь, ~чешься *impf.* to whisper, converse in whispers

шере́нг|а, и *f.* **1** (mil.) rank; file, column **2** (fig.) line, row

шери́ф, а *m.* sheriff

шерохова́т|ый, ~, ~а *adj.* rough (also fig.); (*неро́вный*) uneven

шерст|ь, и *f.* **1** (*на живо́тных*) hair **2** (*волокно́*) wool

шерстяно́й *adj.* wool, woollen (BrE), woolen (AmE)

шерша́в|ый, ~, ~а *adj.* rough

шест, а́ *m.* pole

ше́стви|е, я *nt.* procession

шестерёнк|а, и *f.* (tech.) gear (wheel), cogwheel, pinion

шестёрк|а, и *f.* **1** (*ци́фра, игра́льная ка́рта*) six **2** (infml, *авто́бус, трамва́й*) No. 6 (*bus, tram, etc.*) **3** (*гру́ппа из шестеры́х*) (group of) six **4** (sl., *подчинённый*) slave, dogsbody (BrE), gofer

ше́стер|о, ы́х *num.* (collect.) six

шестидеся́тый *adj.* sixtieth

шестисо́тый *adj.* six-hundredth

шестиуго́льник, а *m.* (math.) hexagon

шестна́дцат|ый *adj.* sixteenth; ~ая но́та (mus.) semiquaver (BrE), sixteenth note (AmE)

шестна́дцат|ь, и *num.* sixteen

шест|о́й *adj.* sixth; **одна́ ~а́я** one sixth

ш

шест|ь, й, *i.* **∼ью** *num.* six

шестьдеся́т, шести́десяти, *i.* **шестью́десятью, о шести́десяти** *num.* sixty

шест|ьсо́т, исо́т, иста́м, ьюста́ми, о ∼иста́х *num.* six hundred

шеф, а *m.* **1** (*infml*, *нача́льник*) boss, chief **2** (*покрови́тель*) patron, sponsor

шеф-по́вар, а, *pl.* **∼á, ∼óв** *m.* chef

ше́|я, и *f.* neck; **сиде́ть на ∼е у кого́-н.** (*infml*) to live off sb

ши́ворот, а *m.* (*infml*): **за ш.** by the collar, by the scruff of the neck

шизофре́ник, а *m.* (*med.*) schizophrenic; (*infml, offensive*) crazy person

шизофрени́|я, и *f.* (*med.*) schizophrenia

шии́т, а *m.* Shiite (Muslim)

шик, а (у) *m.* stylishness; style

шика́р|ный, ∼ен, ∼на *adj.* (*infml*) (*роско́шный*) chic, smart, stylish; (*отли́чный*) gorgeous

ши́к|ать, аю *impf.* (*of* ▶ **ши́кнуть**) (*infml*) (**на** + *a.*) to hush (*by crying 'sh'*); (*в знак неодобре́ния*) to hiss (at), boo, catcall

ши́к|нуть, ну, нешь *pf. of* ▶ **ши́кать**

шимпанзе́ *m. indecl.* chimpanzee

ши́н|а, ы *f.* **1** tyre (BrE), tire (AmE) **2** (*med.*) splint

шине́л|ь, и *f.* greatcoat

шинк|ова́ть, у́ю *impf.* (*of* ▶ **нашинкова́ть**) (*cul.*) to shred

шинши́лл|а, ы *f.* chinchilla

шип, á *m.* **1** (*bot.*) thorn **2** (*на спорти́вной обу́ви*) spike; (*на боти́нках альпини́ста*) crampon

шипе́ни|е, я *nt.* hissing; sizzling; sputtering

шип|е́ть, лю́, и́шь *impf.* **1** (*о змее́*) to hiss; (*при жа́рке*) to sizzle; (*о напи́тке*) to fizz **2** (*от зло́сти*) to hiss

шипу́чий *adj.* (*вино́*) sparkling; (*напи́ток, пи́во, вода́*) fizzy

ши́ре *comp. of* ▶ **широ́кий,** ▶ **широ́ко**

ширин|á, ы́ *f.* width, breadth; (*коле́и*) gauge (*of railway track*)

шири́нк|а, и *f.* fly (*of trousers*)

ши́рм|а, ы *f.* screen (also fig.)

широ́к|ий, ∼, ∼á, ∼ó, *pl.* **∼й** *adj.* **1** wide, broad (also fig.); **в ∼ом смы́сле** in a broad sense **2** (*fig.*) big, extensive, general; **това́ры ∼ого потребле́ния** (*econ.*) consumer goods; **ш. круг чита́телей** the average reader, the general reading public; **жить на ∼ую но́гу** to live in grand style

широко́ *adv.* **1** wide, widely, broadly (also fig.); **ш. раскры́ть глаза́** to open one's eyes wide; **ш. толкова́ть** to interpret loosely **2** (*в широ́ком масшта́бе*) extensively, on a large scale

широкопле́ч|ий, ∼, ∼a *adj.* broad-shouldered

широт|á, ы́, *pl.* **∼ы, ∼** *f.* **1** width, breadth **2** (*geog.*) latitude

широча́йший *superl. of* ▶ **широ́кий**

ширпотре́б, а *m.* (*collect.*) mass-market goods

шить, шью, шьёшь *impf.* (*of* ▶ **сшить** 1) **1** to sew **2** (*изготовля́ть*) to make (*by sewing*); **ш. себе́ что-н.** to have sth made

ши́фер, а *m.* slate

шифр, а *m.* **1** cipher; code **2** (*библиоте́чный*) shelf mark (BrE), call number (AmE)

шифр|ова́ть, у́ю *impf.* (*of* ▶ **зашифрова́ть**) to encipher

ши́шк|а, и *f.* **1** (bot.) cone **2** (*буго́рок*) bump; lump

шишкова́т|ый, ∼, ∼а *adj.* knobbly; bumpy

шкал|á, ы́, *pl.* **∼ы** *f.* (*зарпла́ты, термо́метра*) scale; (*приёмника*) dial

шкату́лк|а, и *f.* box, casket, case

шкаф, а, о ∼е, в/на ∼у́, *pl.* **∼ы́** *m.* cupboard; (*платяно́й*) wardrobe; (*ку́хонный*) dresser; **кни́жный ш.** bookcase (*with doors*); **несгора́емый ш.** safe

шквал, а *nt.* squall; (fig., *огня́, возмуще́ния*) burst

шко́л|а, ы *f.* **1** (*учрежде́ние*) school; **ходи́ть в ∼у** to go to school; **око́нчить ∼у** to leave school; **ш.-интерна́т** boarding school **2** (*вы́учка*) schooling, training

шко́льник, а *m.* schoolboy

шко́льниц|а, ы *f.* schoolgirl

шко́льный *adj.* school; **ш. во́зраст** school age

шку́р|а, ы *f.* skin (also fig.), hide, pelt; **быть в чьей-н. ∼е** to be in sb's shoes

шку́рк|а, и *f.* **1** (*шку́ра*) skin **2** (*infml, плода́*) rind **3** (*бума́га*) emery paper, sandpaper

шла *see* ▶ **идти́**

шлагба́ум, а *m.* barrier (*of swing beam type, at road or rail crossing*)

шлак, а *m.* slag; clinker

шланг, а *m.* hose

шлем, а *m.* helmet; **защи́тный ш.** hard hat (*on building site, etc.*)

шлёпан|цы, цев, *pl. m. pl.* (*sg.* **∼ец, ∼ца**) (*infml*) backless shoes/slippers; (*вьетна́мки*) flip-flops

шлёп|ать, аю *impf.* (*of* ▶ **отшлёпать,** ▶ **шлёпнуть**) to smack, slap, spank

шлёп|аться, аюсь *impf.* (*of* ▶ **шлёпнуться**) (*infml*) to fall with a plop, thud

шлёп|нуть, ну, нешь *inst. pf. of* ▶ **шлёпать**

шлёп|нуться, нусь, нешься *inst. pf. of* ▶ **шлёпаться**

шлёшь, шлёт *etc., see* ▶ **слать**

шли[1] *see* ▶ **идти́**

шли[2] *see* ▶ **слать**

шлиф|ова́ть, у́ю *impf. of* ▶ **отшлифова́ть**

шло *see* ▶ **идти́**

шлю, шлют *see* ▶ **слать**

шлюз, а *m.* lock, sluice, floodgate

шлю́пк|а, и *f.* launch, boat; **спаса́тельная ш.** lifeboat

шлю́х|а, и *f.* (*vulg.*) tart

шля́п|а, ы *f.* hat; **де́ло в ∼е** (*infml*) it's in the bag

ш

шля́пк|а, и *f.* **1** (*woman's*) hat **2** (*гвоздя́*) head (*of nail, etc.*)

шля́|ться, юсь *impf.* (infml) to loaf about

шмел|ь, я́ *m.* bumblebee

шмо́т|ки, ок (*no sg.*) (infml) clothes

шмы́г|ать, аю *impf.* (*of* ▸ шмыгну́ть 1) (infml) **1** (+ *i.*) (*нога́ми, ту́флями*) to scrape; (*щёткой*) to brush; ш. но́сом to sniff **2** (*бы́стро дви́гаться*) to rush around; to scurry

шмыг|ну́ть, ну́, нёшь *pf.* (infml) **1** *inst. pf. of* ▸ шмы́гать **2** (*бы́стро убежа́ть*) to dart, nip, sneak (*in order to escape notice*)

шни́цел|ь, я *m.* (cul.) schnitzel

шнур, а́ *m.* **1** (*верёвка*) cord; lace **2** (elec.) flex, cable

шнур|ова́ть, у́ю *impf.* (*of* ▸ зашнурова́ть) (*боти́нки*) to lace up

шнур|о́к, ка́ *m.* lace

шныр|я́ть, я́ю *impf.* (infml) to dart about

шов, шва *m.* **1** (*шве́йный*) seam; без шва seamless **2** (*в выши́вании*) stitch **3** (*хирурги́ческий*) stitch, suture; наложи́ть, снять швы to put in, remove stitches **4** (tech., *ме́сто соедине́ния*) joint, seam, junction

шовини́зм, а *m.* chauvinism

шовини́ст, а *m.* chauvinist

шовинисти́ческий *adj.* chauvinistic

шовини́ст|ка, ки *f. of* ▸ шовини́ст

шок, а *m.* (med., fig.) shock

шоки́р|овать, ую *impf.* to shock

шокола́д, а *m.* chocolate

шокола́д|ка, и *f.* (infml, *пли́тка шокола́да*) bar of chocolate

шокола́дный *adj. of* ▸ шокола́д

шо́рох, а *m.* rustle

шо́рт|ы, ~ and ~ов (*no sg.*) shorts

шоссе́ *nt. indecl.* highway; surfaced road

шотла́нд|ец, ца *m.* Scotsman, Scot

Шотла́нди|я, и *f.* Scotland; Но́вая Ш. (*прови́нция Кана́ды*) Nova Scotia

шотла́нд|ка¹, ки *f. of* ▸ шотла́ндец

шотла́нд|ка², ки *f.* (text.) tartan, plaid

шотла́ндский *adj.* Scottish, Scots

шо́у *nt. indecl.* show

шо́у-би́знес, а *m.* show business

шофёр, а *m.* driver; (*персона́льный*) chauffeur

шпа́г|а, и *f.* sword; (sport) épée; скрести́ть ~и to cross swords (also fig.)

шпага́т, а *m.* **1** string, cord; (agric.) binder twine **2** (*в гимна́стике*) the splits

шпаклёвк|а, и *f.* **1** (*де́йствие*) filling, puttying **2** (*вещество́*) putty, filler

шпа́л|а, ы *f.* (rail.) sleeper (BrE), cross tie (AmE)

шпан|а́, ы́ *f.* (infml) hooligan; (*also collect.*) rabble

шпарга́лк|а, и *f.* (infml) crib (sheet), cheat sheet (AmE) (*in school, university*)

шпа́р|ить, ю, ишь *impf.* (infml) **1** (*pf.* о~) (*облива́ть кипятко́м*) to scald, pour boiling water on **2** (*де́лать, говори́ть бы́стро, энерги́чно*) to do, say, etc., in a rush, energetically

шпа́тел|ь, я *m.* (tech., art) palette knife

шпик, а *m.* (cul.) lard

шпил|ь, я *m.* spire, steeple

шпи́льк|а, и *f.* **1** (*для воло́с*) hairpin **2** (*каблу́к*) stiletto

шпина́т, а *m.* spinach

шпио́н, а *m.* spy

шпиона́ж, а *m.* espionage

шпио́н|ить, ю, ишь *impf.* (за + *i.*) to spy (on)

шпио́н|ка, ки *f. of* ▸ шпио́н

шпио́нский *adj. of* ▸ шпио́н

шпо́р|а, ы *f.* spur

шприц, а *m.* (med.) syringe

шпро́т|ы, ~ and ~ов *f. and m. pl.* (*sg.* ~а, ~ы and ~, ~а) sprats

шрам, а *m.* scar

шрапне́л|ь, и *f.* shrapnel

Шри-Ланк|а́, и́ *f.* Sri Lanka

шрифт, а, *pl.* ~ы́ *m.* type, type face; (comput.) font

штаб, а, *pl.* ~ы́ *m.* (mil.) (*ли́ца*) staff; (*ме́сто*) headquarters

шта́бел|ь, я, *pl.* ~я́, ~е́й *m.* stack, pile

штаб-кварти́р|а, ы *f.* (mil.) headquarters

штамп, а *m.* **1** (tech., *фо́рма*) die, punch **2** (*печа́ть*) stamp **3** (fig., pej., *бана́льность*) cliché, stock phrase

штамп|ова́ть, у́ю *impf.* **1** (tech., *дета́ли*) to punch, press **2** (*докуме́нты*) to stamp **3** (fig.) (*стихи́*) to churn out; (*реше́ния*) to rubber-stamp

шта́нг|а, и *f.* **1** (sport, *сте́ржень с тя́жестями*) weight **2** (sport, *во́рот*) goalpost

штангенци́ркул|ь, я *m.* (tech.) sliding callipers, slide gauge

штанги́ст, а *m.* (sport) weightlifter

штан|ы́, о́в (*no sg.*) trousers

✍ штат¹, а *m.* state; Соединённые Ш~ы Аме́рики United States of America

✍ штат², а *m.* (*sg. or pl.*) (*сотру́дники*) staff

штати́в, а *m.* tripod, base, support, stand

шта́тск|ий *adj.* civilian; (*as m. n.* ш., ~ого) civilian

штемпел|ь, я, *pl.* ~я́ *m.* stamp; почто́вый ш. postmark

ште́псел|ь, я, *pl.* ~я́ *m.* (elec., *ви́лка*) plug

штил|ь, я *m.* (naut.) calm

што́па|ть, ю *impf.* (*of* ▸ зашто́пать) to darn

што́пор, а *m.* corkscrew

што́р|а, ы *f.* curtain; (*твёрдого материа́ла или поднима́емая вверх*) blind

шторм, а *m.* (naut.) strong gale (*wind force 9*); (infml) gale

штормо́вк|а, и *f.* (infml) anorak; parka

штраф, а *m.* fine; наложи́ть ш. to impose a fine

штраф|но́й *adj.* **1** *adj. of* ▸ штраф **2** penal, penalty; ~на́я площа́дка (sport) penalty area; ш. уда́р (sport) penalty kick

штраф|ова́ть, у́ю *impf.* (*of* ▶ **оштрафова́ть**) to fine

штрих, а́ *m.* **1** (*черта*) stroke (*in drawing*) **2** (fig., *частность*) feature, trait

штрихко́д, а *m.* bar code

шту́к|а, и *f.* **1** (*отдельный предмет*) item, one of a kind (*often not translated*); **по рублю́ ш.** one rouble each; **я возьму́ шесть ~** I'll have six (*of item in question*) **2** (infml, *вещь*) thing

штукату́р, а *m.* plasterer

штукату́р|ить, ю, ишь *impf.* (*of* ▶ **оштукату́рить**) to plaster

штукату́рк|а, и *f.* **1** (*действие*) plastering **2** (*раствор, слой раствора*) plaster

штурва́л, а *m.* steering wheel; controls; **стоя́ть за ~ом** to be at the wheel, helm, controls

штурм, а *m.* (mil.) storm, assault

шту́рман, а *m.* (naut., aeron.) navigator

штурм|ова́ть, у́ю *impf.* to storm, assault

штык, а́ *m.* bayonet; **встре́тить, приня́ть в ~й** (fig.) to give a hostile reception (to), oppose adamantly

штыр|ь, я́ *m.* (tech.) pin, dowel

шу́б|а, ы *f.* fur coat

шу́лер, а, *pl.* **~á** *m.* card sharper, cheat

шум, а (у) *m.* **1** (*звуки*) noise **2** (infml, *брань, скандал*) din, uproar, racket; **подня́ть ш.** to kick up a racket **3** (fig., *оживлённое обсуждение*) sensation, stir

шум|е́ть, лю́, и́шь *impf.* **1** (*издавать шум*) to make a noise **2** (infml, *брани́ться,* *кричать*) to row **3** (fig., *оживлённо обсуждать*) to create a stir, fuss, sensation

шу́м|ный, ~ен, ~на́, ~но, ~ны́ *adj.* **1** noisy; loud **2** (fig.) sensational

шумо́вк|а, и *f.* (cul.) perforated spoon, straining ladle

шу́рин, а *m.* brother-in-law (*wife's brother*)

шуру́п, а *m.* (tech.) screw

шурш|а́ть, у́, и́шь *impf.* to rustle (*also + i.,* *trans.*)

шу́ст|рый, ~ёр, ~ра́, ~ро, ~ры́ *adj.* (infml) smart, bright, sharp

шут, а́ *m.* **1** (hist., *при дворе*) fool, jester **2** (fig., infml, *паяц*) fool, buffoon, clown

шу|ти́ть, чу́, ~тишь *impf.* (*of* ▶ **пошути́ть**) **1** to joke, jest; **я же не ~чу́** but I'm not joking **2** (**с** + *i.*) (*несерьёзно относиться*) to play (with), trifle (with); **ш. с огнём** to play with fire **3** (**над** + *i.*) (*смеяться*) to laugh (at), make fun (of)

шу́тк|а, и *f.* joke, jest; **не ш.** it's no joke; **с ней ~и плóхи** she is not to be trifled with; **без шу́ток** joking apart; **сказа́ть в ~у** to say as a joke; **не на ~у** in earnest

шутли́в|ый, ~, ~а *adj.* **1** (*человек, характер*) jokey **2** (*тон, замечание*) joking, light-hearted; (*рассказ, песня*) humorous

шутни́к, а́ *m.* joker

шушу́ка|ться, юсь *impf.* (infml) to whisper; (fig.) to gossip

шху́н|а, ы *f.* schooner

Щщ

ща|ди́ть, жу́, ди́шь *impf.* (*of* ▶ **пощади́ть**) to spare

ще́б|ень, ня *m.* crushed stone, ballast (*as road surfacing*)

щебе|та́ть, чу́, ~чешь *impf.* to twitter, chirp

щегольну́|ть, у́, ёшь *inst. pf. of* ▶ **щеголя́ть 2**

щегол|я́ть, я́ю *impf.* (infml) **1** (**в** + *p.*) (*в новом пла́тье*) to strut around in; to sport **2** (*pf.* **~ьну́ть**) (+ *i.*) (*своими знаниями*) to show off, parade, flaunt

ще́дрост|ь, и *f.* generosity

ще́др|ый, ~, ~а́, ~о, ~ы́ *adj.* generous; (**на** + *a.*) generous/lavish with

щек|а́, и́, а. **~у/~ý, *pl.* ~и, ~, ~ám** *f.* cheek; **уда́рить кого́-н. по ~é** to slap sb's face

щеко́лд|а, ы *f.* latch; catch

щеко|та́ть, чу́, ~чешь *impf.* (*of* ▶ **пощекота́ть**) **1** to tickle (also fig.) **2** (*impers.*): **у меня́ в го́рле** *и т. п.* **~чет** I have a tickle in my throat, *etc.*

щеко́тк|а, и *f.* tickling; **боя́ться ~и** to be ticklish

щекотли́в|ый, ~, ~а *adj.* delicate, sensitive; **~ая те́ма** delicate subject

щеко́тно *as pred.* (*impers. + d.*) it tickles

щёлк|ать, аю *impf.* (*of* ▶ **щёлкнуть**) **1** (*человека, по лбу и т. п.*) to flick **2** (+ *i.*) (*производить звук*) to click, snap, crack; (comput.) to click; **два́жды щ.** to double-click **3** (*pf. only*) (*оре́хи*) to crack

щёлк|нуть, ну, нешь *inst. pf. of* ▶ **щёлкать 1,** ▶ **щёлкать 2**

щелочно́й *adj.* (chem.) alkaline

щёлоч|ь, и, *pl.* **~и, щелоче́й** *f.* (chem.) alkali

щелч|óк, ка́ *m.* flick (of the fingers); (comput., *мышью*) click; **двойнóй щ.** double click

щель, и, *pl.* **~и, ~éй** *f.* crack; chink; slit; (*в игровом, торговом автомате*) slot

щен|óк, ка́ *m.* puppy, pup (*also* fig.); whelp, cub

щепети́л|ьный, ~ен, ~ьна *adj.* **1** (*человек*) punctilious; (over)scrupulous **2** (*вопрос*) delicate

щéпк|а, и *f.* splinter, chip (*of wood*); (collect.) kindling

щепóт|ка, ки *f.* pinch (*of salt, snuff, etc.*)

щети́н|а, ы *f.* bristle; (infml, *борода*) stubble

щети́н|иться, юсь, ишься *impf. of* ▶ ощети́ниться

щётк|а, и *f.* brush; **зубна́я щ.** toothbrush; **щ. для волóс** hairbrush

щи, щей, щам, ща́ми, о щах (*no sg.*) shchi (*cabbage soup*)

щи́колотк|а, и *f.* ankle

щип|а́ть, лю́, ~лешь *impf.* **1** (*pf.* **ущипну́ть**) (*защемлять до боли*) to pinch, nip, tweak **2** (*impf. only*) (*о морозе*) to sting, bite; (*о горчице*) to burn **3** (*pf.* **о~**) (*птицу*) to pluck

щипц|ы́, óв (*no sg.*) (*каминные*) tongs; (tech.) pincers; (*плоскогубцы*) pliers; (*хирургические*) forceps

щи́пчик|и, ов (*no sg.*) tweezers

щит, а́ *m.* **1** shield; **живóй щ.** human shield **2** (*ограждение*) shield, screen **3** (*рекламный*) (display) board **4** (tech., *пульт*) panel (*see also* ▶ распредели́тельный)

щитови́дн|ый *adj.* (anat.): **~ая железа́** thyroid gland

щит|óк, ка́ *m.* **1** *dim. of* ▶ щит 2, ▶ щит 3, ▶ щит 4; (*у машины*) dashboard **2** (sport) shin pad **3** (elec.) *see* ▶ распредели́тельный

щу́к|а, и *f.* pike (*fish*)

щу́пальц|е, а, *g. pl.* **щу́палец** *nt.* (zool.) tentacle; antenna

щу́па|ть, ю *impf.* (*of* ▶ пощу́пать) to feel (for), touch; (fig., infml) to size up, suss out; **щ. пульс** (med.) to feel the pulse

щу́пл|ый, ~, ~а́, ~о *adj.* weak, puny, frail

щу́р|иться, юсь, ишься *impf.* to screw up one's eyes, squint

Ээ

эвакуа́ци|я, и *f.* evacuation

эваку́и́р|овать, ую *impf. and pf.* to evacuate (*trans.*)

эваку́и́р|оваться, уюсь *impf. and pf.* to be evacuated

Эверéст, а *m.* (Mt) Everest

эвкали́пт, а *m.* (bot.) eucalyptus

ЭВМ *f. indecl.* (*abbr. of* **электрóнно-вычисли́тельная маши́на**) computer

эволю́ци|я, и *f.* evolution

эвтана́зи|я, и *f.* euthanasia

эвфеми́зм, а *m.* euphemism

эги́д|а, ы *f.* aegis; **под ~ой** (+ *g.*) under the aegis (of)

эгои́зм, а *m.* egoism, selfishness

эгои́ст, а *m.* egoist

эгоисти́ческий *adj.* egoistic, selfish

эгоисти́ч|ный, ~ен, ~на *adj.* = эгоисти́ческий

эгои́ст|ка, ки *f. of* ▶ эгои́ст

эгоцентри́ч|ный, ~ен, ~на *adj.* egocentric

Эдинбýрг, а *m.* Edinburgh

эй *int.* hey!

эйфори́|я, и *f.* euphoria

Эквадóр, а *m.* Ecuador

эквадóр|ец, ца *m.* Ecuadorean

эквадóр|ка, ки *f. of* ▶ эквадóрец

эквадóрский *adj.* Ecuadorean

эква́тор, а *m.* equator

эквивалéнт, а *m.* equivalent

эквивалéнт|ный, ~ен, ~на *adj.* equivalent

экза́мен, а *m.* examination; **сдава́ть э.** to take, sit an examination; **сдать э.** to pass an examination; **провали́ться на ~е** to fail an examination; **э. на води́тельские права́** driving test

экзамена́тор, а *m.* examiner

экзаменацио́нн|ый *adj. of* ▶ экза́мен; **э. билéт** examination paper; **~ая сéссия** examination period, exams

экзамен|ова́ть, у́ю *impf.* (*of* ▶ проэкзаменова́ть) to examine

экзéм|а, ы *f.* (med.) eczema

экземпля́р, а *m.* **1** copy; **переписа́ть в двух ~ах** to make two copies **2** (*животного, растения*) specimen, example

экзистенциали́зм, а *m.* existentialism

экзистенциа́льный *adj.* existential

экзóтик|а, и *f.* exotica, exotic objects

экзоти́ческий *adj.* exotic

экипа́ж¹, а *m.* (*повозка*) carriage

экипа́ж², а *m.* (*команда*) crew (*of ship, aircraft, tank*)

экипиро́вк|а, и f. 1 (*де́йствие*) equipping **2** (*снаряже́ние*) equipment

эклекти́ч|ный, ~ен, ~на *adj.* eclectic

эко́лог, а *m.* ecologist

⚔ **экологи́ческий** *adj.* ecological

эколо́ги|я, и f. ecology

⚔ **эконо́мик|а, и f. 1** (*нау́ка*) economics **2** (*страны́*) economy; **ры́ночная э.** market economy

экономи́ст, а *m.* economist

эконо́м|ить, лю, ишь *impf.* (*of* ▸ **сэконо́мить**) **1** (*де́ньги, си́лы*) to use sparingly; to save **2** (**на** + *p.*) to economize (on), save (on)

⚔ **экономи́ческий** *adj.* economic

экономи́ч|ный, ~ен, ~на *adj.* economical

эконо́ми|я, и f. 1 economy, saving **2: полити́ческая э.** political economy

эконо́м|ный, ~ен, ~на *adj.* economical; careful, thrifty

экосисте́м|а, ы f. ecosystem

экотури́зм, а *m.* ecotourism

экотури́ст, а *m.* ecotourist

⚔ **экра́н, а** *m.* **1** (cin., TV, comput.) screen **2** (fig., *киноиску́сство*) screen **3** (phys., tech.) screen, shield, shade

экраниза́ци|я, и f. (cin.) filming, screening; (*рома́на*) film adaptation

экс-... *pref.* ex-

экскава́тор, а *m.* (tech.) excavator, mechanical digger

эксклюзи́в|ный, ~ен, ~на *adj.* exclusive

экскреме́нт|ы, ов (*no sg.*) excrement

экску́рси|я, и f. excursion, (conducted) tour, trip

экскурсово́д, а *m.* guide

экспанси́в|ный, ~ен, ~на *adj.* effusive

экспа́нси|я, и f. (pol.) expansion

экспатриа́нт, а *m.* expatriate

экспатриа́нт|ка, ки f. of ▸ **экспатриа́нт**

экспеди́тор, а *m.* forwarding agent, shipping clerk

экспеди́ци|я, и f. 1 (*де́йствие*) dispatch, forwarding **2** (*пое́здка; уча́стники э́той пое́здки*) expedition

экспериме́нт, а *m.* experiment

эксперимента́льный *adj.* experimental

эксперимента́тор, а *m.* experimenter

эксперименти́р|овать, ую *impf.* (**над, с** + *i.*) to experiment (on, with)

⚔ **экспе́рт, а** *m.* expert

эксперти́з|а, ы f. (law, med.) (expert) examination, expert opinion; **произвести́ ~у** to make an examination

экспе́рт|ный *adj. of* ▸ **экспе́рт**; **~ная коми́ссия** commission of experts

Э ⚔ **эксплуата́ци|я, и f. 1** (pol., pej.) exploitation **2** (*приро́дных бога́тств*) exploitation; (*средств произво́дства*) utilization; (*маши́н*) operation, running; **сдать в ~ю**
to commission, put into operation

эксплуати́р|овать, ую *impf.* **1** (pol., pej.) to exploit **2** (*приро́дные бога́тства*) to exploit; (*маши́ны*) to operate, run, work

экспози́ци|я, и f. 1 (*музе́йная*) display **2** (liter., mus.) exposition **3** (phot.) exposure

экспона́т, а *m.* exhibit

экспони́р|овать, ую *impf. and pf.* (*для обозре́ния*) to exhibit

э́кспорт, а *m.* export

экспортёр, а *m.* exporter

экспорти́р|овать, ую *impf. and pf.* to export

э́кспортный *adj. of* ▸ **э́кспорт**

экспре́сс, а *m.* express (*train, motor coach, etc.*)

экспресси́в|ный, ~ен, ~на *adj.* expressive

экспрессиони́зм, а *m.* expressionism

экспрессиони́ст, а *m.* expressionist

экспре́сси|я, и f. expression

экспро́мт, а *m.* improvisation; (mus.) impromptu

экста́з, а *m.* ecstasy

э́кстези *m. indecl.* (sl.) ecstasy (*the drug*)

экстенси́в|ный, ~ен, ~на *adj.* extensive

эксте́рн, а *m.* external student; **око́нчить университе́т ~ом** to take an external degree

экстравага́нт|ный, ~ен, ~на *adj.* eccentric, bizarre

экстраве́рт, а *m.* extrovert

экстради́ци|я, и f. (law) extradition

экстраордина́р|ный, ~ен, ~на *adj.* extraordinary

экстрасе́нс, а *m.* psychic

экстрема́л|ьный, ~ен, ~ьна *adj.* extreme

экстреми́зм, а *m.* extremism

экстреми́ст, а *m.* extremist

экстреми́стский *adj.* extremist

э́кстрен|ный, ~, ~на *adj.* **1** (*сро́чный*) urgent; emergency; **э. вы́зов** urgent summons; **в ~ном слу́чае** in case of emergency **2** (*чрезвыча́йный*) extra, special; **~ное заседа́ние** extraordinary session

эксцентри́ч|ный, ~ен, ~на *adj.* eccentric

эласти́ч|ный, ~ен, ~на *adj.* elastic (also fig.); **~ные брю́ки** stretch trousers

элева́тор, а *m.* **1** (agric.) grain store (BrE), elevator (AmE) **2** (tech.) hoist

элега́нт|ный, ~ен, ~на *adj.* elegant, smart

электора́т, а *m.* electorate

эле́ктрик, а *m.* electrician

⚔ **электри́ческий** *adj.* electric(al)

электри́честв|о, а *nt.* **1** electricity **2** (*освеще́ние*) electric light; **заже́чь э.**
to turn on the light

электри́чк|а, и f. (infml) (suburban) electric train

электрово́з, а *m.* electric locomotive

электрогита́р|а, ы f. electric guitar

электродви́гател|ь, я *m.* electric motor

электромонтёр, а *m.* electrician

электро́н, а *m.* (phys.) electron

электро́ник|а, и *f.* electronics

⚔ **электро́н|ный** *adj.* **1** *adj. of* ▶ электро́н; **э. микроско́п** electron microscope **2** electronic; **∼ная по́чта** electronic mail, email (*the system*); **∼ное письмо́** email (*letter*); **э. а́дрес** email address; **∼ная табли́ца** spreadsheet

электропо́езд, а *m.* electric train

электроприбо́р, а *m.* electrical appliance

электропрово́дк|а, и *f.* electric wiring

электроста́нци|я, и *f.* power station

электроте́хник, а *m.* electrical engineer

электроэне́рги|я, и *f.* electric power

⚔ **элеме́нт, а** *m.* **1** (*компонент, доля*) element; **э. изображе́ния** (comput.) pixel **2** (chem.) element

элемента́р|ный, ∼ен, ∼на *adj.* elementary

эли́т|а, ы *f.* elite

элита́р|ный, ∼ен, ∼на *adj.* elite; (pej.) elitist

эли́тный *adj.* best-quality

эльф, а *m.* elf

эмалиро́ванн|ый *adj.* enamelled (BrE), enameled (AmE); **∼ая посу́да** enamel ware

эма́л|ь, и *f.* enamel

эмансипа́ци|я, и *f.* (also law) emancipation

эмба́рго *nt. indecl.* (econ.) embargo

эмбле́м|а, ы *f.* emblem; (mil.) insignia

эмбрио́н, а *m.* (biol.) embryo

эмигра́нт, а *m.* émigré, emigrant

эмигра́нт|ка, ки *f. of* ▶ эмигра́нт

эмигра́ци|я, и *f.* **1** emigration **2** (*collect.*) emigration, émigrés

эмигри́р|овать, ую *impf. and pf.* to emigrate

эмо́тикон, а *m.* emoticon

эмоциона́л|ьный, ∼ен, ∼ьна *adj.* emotional

эмо́ци|я, и *f.* emotion

эмпири́ческий *adj.* empirical

эму́льси|я, и *f.* emulsion

энерге́тик, а *m.* energy specialist

энерге́тик|а, и *f.* energy sector (of the economy), power industry

энергети́ческий *adj. of* ▶ энерге́тика; **э. напи́ток** energy drink

энерги́ч|ный, ∼ен, ∼на *adj.* energetic, vigorous, forceful

⚔ **эне́рги|я, и** *f.* **1** (phys.) energy; power; **затра́та ∼и** energy consumption **2** (fig.) energy; vigour (BrE), vigor (AmE), effort

энергосисте́м|а, ы *f.* power (supply) system

энтомо́лог, а *m.* entomologist

энтомоло́ги|я, и *f.* entomology

энтузиа́зм, а *m.* enthusiasm

энтузиа́ст, а *m.* (+ *g.*) enthusiast (about, for), devotee (of)

энциклопе́ди|я, и *f.* encyclopedia

эпиде́ми|я, и *f.* epidemic

эпизо́д, а *m.* episode

эпизоди́ческий *adj.* episodic; occasional, sporadic

эпиле́пси|я, и *f.* epilepsy

эпиле́птик, а *m.* epileptic

эпилепти́ческий *adj.* epileptic

эпило́г, а *m.* epilogue (BrE), epilog (AmE)

эпита́фи|я, и *f.* epitaph

эпи́тет, а *m.* epithet

эпопе́|я, и *f.* epic

э́пос, а *m.* epic literature

⚔ **эпо́х|а, и** *f.* epoch, age, era

э́р|а, ы *f.* era; **до на́шей ∼ы** BC (*before Christ*); **на́шей ∼ы** AD (*Anno Domini*)

эргономи́ч|ный, ∼ен, ∼на *adj.* ergonomic

эре́кци|я, и *f.* (physiol.) erection

эрза́ц, а *m.* ersatz, substitute

Эритре́|я, и *f.* Eritrea

эритроци́т, а *m.* (physiol.) erythrocyte, red corpuscle

эро́зи|я, и *f.* erosion

эро́тик|а, и *f.* **1** (*чувственность*) sensuality **2** (*collect.*) (*искусство*) erotica

эроти́ческий *adj.* erotic, sensual

Эр-Рия́д, а *m.* Riyadh

эруди́рован|ный, ∼, ∼на *adj.* erudite

эруди́ци|я, и *f.* erudition

эскадри́л|ья, ьи, *g. pl.* ∼ий *f.* (aeron.) squadron

эскадро́н, а *m.* (mil.) squadron

эскала́тор, а *m.* escalator

эскало́п, а *m.* (cul.) escalope

эски́з, а *m.* (*к картине*) sketch, study; (*чертёж*) draft, outline

эскимо́с, а *m.* Eskimo, Inuit

эскимо́с|ка, ки *f. of* ▶ эскимо́с

эскимо́сский *adj.* Eskimo, Inuit

эско́рт, а *m.* (mil.) escort

эссе́ *nt. indecl.* essay

эссе́нци|я, и *f.* essence

эстака́д|а, ы *f.* **1** (*на железной дороге*) viaduct **2** (*на шоссе*) flyover (BrE), overpass

эстафе́т|а, ы *f.* **1** (sport) relay race **2** (*палочка*) baton (*in relay race*)

эсте́т, а *m.* aesthete

эсте́тик|а, и *f.* **1** aesthetics **2** (*художественность*) design

эстети́ческий *adj.* aesthetic

эстети́ч|ный, ∼ен, ∼на *adj.* aesthetic

эсто́н|ец, ца *m.* Estonian

Эсто́ни|я, и *f.* Estonia

эсто́н|ка, ки *f. of* ▶ эсто́нец

эсто́нский *adj.* Estonian

эстра́д|а, ы *f.* **1** stage, platform; **вы́йти на ∼у** to come on stage **2** (*представление*) variety; **арти́ст ∼ы** variety performer, artiste

эстра́д|ный *adj. of* ▶ эстра́да; **э. конце́рт** variety show; **∼ная му́зыка** popular music

⚔ **эта́ж, а́** *m.* storey (BrE), story (AmE), floor; **пе́рвый, второ́й** *и т. п.* **э.** ground floor, first floor, *etc.* (BrE); first floor, second floor, *etc.* (AmE)

этало́н, а *m.* standard (*of weights and measures*); (fig., *мерило*) benchmark

э

эта́п, *a m.* stage, phase

э́тик|а, и *f.* ethics

этике́т, *a m.* etiquette

этике́тк|а, и *f.* label

этимоло́ги|я, и *f.* etymology

эти́ч|ный, ~ен, ~на *adj.* ethical

этни́ческий *adj.* ethnic

этнографи́ческий *adj.* ethnographic(al)

этногра́фи|я, и *f.* ethnography, social anthropology

э́то¹ *see* ▶ э́тот

э́то² *emph. particle* (infml): куда́ э. он де́лся? wherever has he got to?; э. *вы* спра́шивали? was it *you* who was asking?

э́то³ *pron.* (*as n.*) this (is), that (is); э. наш дом this is our house; э. ве́рно that is true; не в ~м де́ло that's not the point

э́тот, э́та, э́то, *pl.* э́ти *pron.* this (these); (*as n.*) this one; (*после́днее из на́званных лиц*) the latter

этю́д, *a m.* 1 (art, liter.) study, sketch 2 (mus., *произведе́ние*) étude 3 (mus., *упражне́ние*) exercise

эфе́с, *a m.* hilt, handle (*of sword, sabre, etc.*)

эфио́п, *a m.* Ethiopian

Эфио́пи|я, и *f.* Ethiopia

эфио́п|ка, ки *f. of* ▶ эфио́п

эфио́пский *adj.* Ethiopian

эфи́р, *a m.* 1 ether; (fig.) air; прямо́й э. live broadcast 2 (chem.) ether

эффе́кт, *a m.* 1 effect, impact; произвести́ э. (на + *a.*) to have an effect (on), make an impression (on) 2 (econ.) result, consequences 3 (*in pl.*) (theatr.) effects; шумовы́е ~ы sound effects

эффекти́вност|ь, и *f.* effectiveness

эффекти́в|ный, ~ен, ~на *adj.* effective

эффе́кт|ный, ~ен, ~на *adj.* effective, striking; eye-catching

э́х|о, а *nt.* echo

эшело́н, *a m.* 1 (mil.) echelon 2 (*по́езд*) special train

эякуля́ци|я, и *f.* (physiol.) ejaculation

Юю

юа́н|ь, я *m.* yuan (*Chinese currency unit*)

ЮАР *f. indecl.* (*abbr. of* Ю́жно-Африка́нская Респу́блика) RSA (Republic of South Africa)

юбиле́|й, я *m.* 1 (*годовщина*) anniversary; jubilee 2 (*празднование*) anniversary celebrations

ю́бк|а, и *f.* skirt; шотла́ндская ю. kilt; ю.-брю́ки culottes; держа́ться за чью-н. ~y to cling to sb's apron strings

ювели́р, *a m.* jeweller (BrE), jeweler (AmE)

ювели́р|ный *adj.* 1 *adj. of* ▶ ювели́р; ~ные изде́лия jewellery (BrE), jewelry (AmE); ю. магази́н jeweller's (BrE), jeweler's (AmE) 2 (fig., *тща́тельный*) fine, intricate

юг, *a m.* south (of Russia, etc.); на ю́ге in the south; к ю́гу от to the south of

ю́го-восто́к, *a m.* south-east

ю́го-восто́чный *adj.* south-east(ern)

ю́го-за́пад, *a m.* south-west

ю́го-за́падный *adj.* south-west(ern)

Югосла́ви|я, и *f.* (hist.) Yugoslavia

югосла́вский *adj.* (hist.) Yugoslav(ian)

южа́н|ин, ина, *pl.* ~е, ~ *m.* southerner

южа́н|ка, ки *f. of* ▶ южа́нин

южне́е *comp. of* ▶ ю́жный; ю. Ло́ндона (to the) south of London

южноамерика́н|ец, ца *m.* South American

южноамерика́н|ка, ки *f. of*
▶ южноамерика́нец

южноамерика́нский *adj.* South American

южноафрика́н|ец, ца *m.* South African

южноафрика́н|ка, ки *f. of* ▶ южноафрика́нец

южноафрика́нский *adj.* South African

ю́жный *adj.* south, southern; Ю́жная Аме́рика South America; Ю́жная Африка (*государство*) South Africa; Ю. по́люс South Pole

юл|а́, ы́ top (*child's toy*)

юл|и́ть, ю́, и́шь *impf.* (infml) 1 (*суетиться*) to fuss, fidget 2 (*пе́ред* + *i.*) (*лебезить*) to play up (to)

ю́мор, *a m.* humour (BrE), humor (AmE); чу́вство ~a a sense of humour (BrE), humor (AmE)

юмори́ст, *a m.* humorist

юмористи́ческий *adj.* humorous, comic, funny

юмори́ст|ка, ки *f. of* ▶ юмори́ст

ю́нг|а, и *m.* cabin boy; sea cadet

ЮНЕ́СКО *f. indecl.* UNESCO (*abbr. of United Nations Educational, Scientific and Cultural Organization* — Организа́ция Объединённых На́ций по вопро́сам образова́ния, нау́ки и культу́ры)

юн|е́ц, ца́ *m.* (infml) youth

✧ key word

юнио́р, а *m.* (sport) junior

юнио́р|ка, ки *f. of* ▸ **юнио́р**

ю́ность|ь, и *f.* youth (*age*)

ю́нош|а, и *m.* youth (*person*)

ю́ношеский *adj.* youthful

ю́н|ый, ~, ~á, ~о *adj.* **1** young
2 (*свойственный молодости*) youthful

юпи́тер, а *m.* (*осветительный прибор*) floodlight

✔ **юриди́ческ|ий** *adj.* legal; ~ое лицо́ corporation

юрисди́кци|я, и *f.* jurisdiction

юриспруде́нци|я, и *f.* jurisprudence, law (*as academic discipline*)

юри́ст, а *m.* legal expert, lawyer

юр|кий, ~ок, ~ка́, ~ко *adj.* quick-moving, brisk

юркну́|ть, у, ешь *or* **ý, ёшь** *pf.* to scamper away, dart away, plunge

юро́див|ый *adj.* **1** crazy, simple, touched
2 (*as m. n.* **ю.**, ~ого) holy fool (*person with mental disability, etc., believed to possess divine gift of prophecy*)

ю́рт|а, ы *f.* yurt (*nomad's tent in Central Asia*)

юсти́ци|я, и *f.* justice

ю|ти́ться, чу́сь, ти́шься *impf.* to huddle (together); (*иметь пристанище*) to take shelter

Яя

✔ **я, меня́, мне, мной мно́ю, обо мне 1** *pers. pron.* I (me) **2** *n.; nt. indecl.* the self, the ego; второе я alter ego

я́бед|а, ы *f. and c.g.* **1** (*f.*) (obs., *клевета*) slander **2** (*c.g.*) (infml) informer, telltale (BrE)

я́блок|о, а, *pl.* ~и, ~ *nt.* apple; глазно́е я. eyeball

я́блон|я, и *f.* apple tree

я́блочк|о, а *nt.* **1** *dim. of* ▸ **я́блоко 2** (*на мишени*) bull's eye

я́блочный *adj. of* ▸ **я́блоко**

яв|и́ться, лю́сь, ~ишься *pf.* (*of* ▸ **явля́ться**) 1) **1** (*прийти по вызову*) to appear, present oneself; to report; я. в суд to appear before the court; я. на слу́жбу to report for duty **2** (*прибыть*) to turn up, arrive, show up

✔ **явле́ни|е, я** *nt.* **1** phenomenon; (*событие*) occurrence; приро́дное я. natural phenomenon **2** (theatr.) scene

✔ **явля́|ться, юсь** *impf.* **1** *impf. of* ▸ **яви́ться 2** (*impf. only*) (+ *i.*) (*быть*) to be; to represent

✔ **я́вно¹** *adv.* manifestly, patently; obviously

я́вно² *as pred.* it is manifest, patent; it is obvious

я́в|ный, ~ен, ~на *adj.* **1** (*открытый*) manifest, patent; overt **2** (*очевидный*) obvious

я́вор, а *m.* sycamore (*tree*)

я́вствен|ный, ~, ~на *adj.* clear, distinct

ягн|ёнок, ёнка, *pl.* ~я́та, ~я́т *m.* lamb

я́год|а, ы *f.* berry; (*collect.*) soft fruit; пойти́ по ~ы to go berry-picking

я́годиц|а, ы *f.* buttock

ягуа́р, а *m.* jaguar

яд, а (у) *m.* poison; venom (also fig.)

я́дерный *adj.* (phys.) nuclear; я. реа́ктор nuclear reactor

ядови́т|ый, ~, ~а *adj.* **1** poisonous; toxic; я. газ poison gas; ~ая змея́ poisonous snake **2** (fig., *человек, замечание*) venomous

ядр|о́, а́, *pl.* ~а, я́дер, ~ам *nt.* **1** (*ореха*) kernel; (*Земли*) core **2** (phys., biol.) nucleus **3** (*основная группа*) main body (*of a unit, group*) **4** (hist., mil.) ball, shot **5** (sport) shot; толка́ние ~á putting the shot

я́зв|а, ы *f.* **1** ulcer, sore; я. желу́дка stomach ulcer **2** (fig., *вред*) plague, curse

язви́тел|ьный, ~ен, ~ьна *adj.* caustic, biting, sarcastic

✔ **язы́к¹, á, *pl.* ~и́** *m.* **1** (anat.) tongue; держа́ть я. за зуба́ми, придержа́ть я. to hold one's tongue **2** (cul.) tongue; копчёный я. smoked tongue

✔ **язы́к², á, *pl.* ~и́,** *m.* (*речь*) language (also fig.); владе́ть мно́гими ~áми to know many languages

языкове́д, а *m.* linguist

языково́й *adj.* linguistic

языкозна́ни|е, я *nt.* linguistics

язы́ческий *adj.* heathen, pagan

язы́чник, а *m.* heathen, pagan

язы́чни|ца, цы *f. of* ▸ **язы́чник**

язы́чк|о, а, *pl.* ~и *nt.* (anat.) testicle

яи́чник, а *m.* (anat.) ovary

яи́чниц|а, ы and **яи́чница-глазу́нья** *f.* (cul.) fried eggs; я.-болту́нья scrambled eggs

яи́чный *adj. of* ▸ **яйцо́**; я. бело́к white of eggs; я. желто́к yolk of egg

яйц|о́, á, *pl.* ~а, яйц, ~ам *nt.* **1** egg; (biol.) ovum; нести́ ~а to lay eggs; я. вкруту́ю hard-boiled egg **2** (*in pl.*) (infml, *у мужчины*) balls, nuts (= *testicles*)

я́кобы **1** *conj.* (*что*) that (*expr. doubt about validity of another's statement*); **говоря́т, я. он у́мер** they say (= *they claim*) that he has died **2** *particle* (*мнимо*) supposedly, allegedly; **мы посмотре́ли э́ту я. стра́шную карти́ну** we have seen this supposedly terrifying film

я́кор|ь, я, *pl.* **~я́, ~е́й** *m.* (naut.) anchor; **стать на я.** to anchor; **бро́сить я.** to cast, drop anchor

яку́т, а *m.* Yakut

яку́т|ка, ки *f. of* ▸ **яку́т**

яку́тский *adj.* Yakut

якша́|ться, юсь *impf.* (**с** + *i.*) (infml) to consort (with), hobnob (with)

я́лик, а *m.* skiff, dinghy; yawl

я́м|а, ы *f.* **1** pit, hole; **выгребна́я я.** cesspit; **оркестро́вая я.** orchestra pit **2** (infml, *впадина*) hollow

яма́|ец, йца *m.* Jamaican

Яма́йк|а, и *f.* Jamaica; (**я.**) Jamaica woman

яма́йский *adj.* Jamaican; **я. ром** Jamaica rum

я́мк|а, и *f. dim. of* ▸ **я́ма; я. на щека́х** dimple

ямщи́к, á *m.* coachman

янва́рский *adj. of* ▸ **янва́рь**

⚹ **янва́р|ь, я́** *m.* January

я́нки *m. indecl.* Yank

янта́р|ь, я́ *m.* amber

япо́н|ец, ца *m.* Japanese

Япо́ни|я, и *f.* Japan

япо́н|ка, ки *f. of* ▸ **япо́нец**

⚹ **япо́нский** *adj.* Japanese; **я. лак** japan

ярд, а *m.* yard (*measure*, = *0.9144 metre*)

⚹ **я́р|кий, ~ок, ~ка́, ~ко** *adj.* **1** bright (*of light, colours, etc.*) **2** (fig.) (*впечатляющий*) colourful (BrE), colorful (AmE), striking; (*живой*) vivid, graphic; **я. приме́р** striking example **3** (fig., *блестящий*) brilliant, outstanding; impressive; **~кая речь** brilliant speech

я́ркост|ь, и *f.* **1** brightness **2** (fig., *живость*) vividness **3** (*блеск*) brilliance

ярлы́к, á *m.* label, tag

я́рмарк|а, и *f.* (trade) fair

ярм|о́, á, *pl.* **~а** *nt.* yoke (also fig.); **сбро́сить с себя́ я.** (fig.) to cast off the yoke

я́рост|ный, ~ен, ~на *adj.* furious, fierce, savage

я́рост|ь, и *f.* fury, rage

я́рус, а *m.* **1** (theatr.) circle **2** (*ряд*) tier

ярча́йший *superl. of* ▸ **я́ркий**

я́рче *comp. of* ▸ **я́ркий**

я́р|ый, ~, ~а *adj.* **1** furious, raging; violent **2** (*рьяный*) passionate, fervent; **я. сторо́нник/приве́рженец** strong/staunch supporter, stalwart

я́сень, я *m.* ash tree

я́сл|и, ей (*no sg.*) (*детские*) crèche (BrE), day nursery

⚹ **я́сно¹** *adv. of* ▸ **я́сный**

я́сно² *as pred.* **1** (*о погоде*) it is fine **2** (fig.) it is clear **3** (*as affirmative particle*) (*да; понял*) yes, of course

яснови́дящ|ий *adj.* (*also as n.* **я.**, *f.* **~ая**) clairvoyant

я́сност|ь, и *f.* (*ночи, неба*) clearness; (*солнца, погоды*) brightness; (*звука*) distinctness; (fig., *вопроса*) clarity; (*речи, ума*) lucidity, preciseness; **внести́ я. во что-н.** to clarify sth

я́с|ный, ~ен, ~на́, ~но, ~ны́ *adj.* **1** (*ночь, небо*) clear; (*солнце, месяц*) bright; (*погода*) fine **2** (*звук, дальний берег*) distinct **3** (*глаза, счастье*) serene **4** (fig., *вопрос, намерение*) clear, plain; **~ное де́ло** of course **5** (*ум, изложение*) lucid; precise, logical

я́стреб, а, *pl.* **~á** *and* **~ы** *m.* hawk

ятага́н, а *m.* yataghan, scimitar

я́хт|а, ы *f.* yacht

яхтсме́н, а *m.* yachtsman

яхтсме́нк|а, и *f.* yachtswoman

яче́йк|а, и, *g. pl.* **яче́ек** *f.* (biol., pol., comput.) cell

ячме́н|ь¹, я́ *m.* (*злак*) barley

ячме́н|ь², я́ *m.* (*на глазу*) sty (*in the eye*)

я́шм|а, ы *f.* (min.) jasper

я́щериц|а, ы *f.* lizard

я́щик, а *m.* **1** box; (*большой*) chest **2** (*выдвижной*) drawer

я́щур, а *m.* (*заболевание скота*) foot-and-mouth disease

⚹ key word

Contents

Russian life and culture

автоно́мная о́бласть — autonomous oblast (region) One of the six types of administrative unit into which **Росси́йская Федера́ция** is divided. Of the 83 units, only one is *автоно́мная о́бласть* (the *Jewish Autonomous Oblast*). Like **автоно́мный о́круг, го́род федера́льного значе́ния, край,** and **о́бласть**, this type of unit is not allowed to have its own constitution (Russian *конститу́ция*), unlike the 21 republics. Instead, it has its own charter (Russian *уста́в*). In common with Russia's 82 other constituent units, the single *автоно́мная о́бласть* has its own

legislature. Formerly, there were four more autonomous oblasts on the territory of the modern Russian Federation. In 1991 they all changed their status to that of republic (**респу́блика**).

автоно́мный о́круг — autonomous okrug (district) One of the six types of administrative unit into which **Росси́йская Федера́ция** is divided. Of the 83 units, four are autonomous okrugs (districts). The autonomous okrugs are all located in sparsely populated areas of Siberia and Russia's Far East, where indigenous peoples form a small part of the entire population and Russians usually make up 60–70% of the population.

For more details ► **автоно́мная о́бласть**

аттеста́т об основно́м о́бщем образова́нии — basic study course school-leaving certificate A document awarded to students who successfully finish a 9-year course of study at school (without low marks such as 2 (*дво́йка*)) and pass all their final examinations. With this, students can enter any educational institution below the level of a **вуз**.

аттеста́т о сре́днем (по́лном) о́бщем образова́нии — full study course school-leaving certificate A document awarded to students who successfully finish an 11-year course of study at school (without low marks such as 2 (*дво́йка*)) and pass all their final examinations. With this, students can enter a **вуз**.

Бе́лый дом — the White House (*in Moscow*) The generally accepted unofficial name of the seat of the Russian government. *Бе́лый дом* is situated near the centre of Moscow on the left bank of the Moskva River and together with the buildings of the US and UK embassies it forms an equilateral triangle within which the town hall is located.

ближнее зарубежье (literally 'close foreign countries') — the former Soviet republics The collective unofficial name for all the former Soviet republics, used especially by telephone operators. Outside Russia it is sometimes considered offensive, mainly because translations of the term in European languages are not quite accurate in register.

Великая Отечественная война (1941–1945) (literally 'the Great Patriotic War') The Soviet name for the Second World War in the context of the Soviet Union's involvement in it.

Восьмое марта, 8-е Марта — 8 March Women's day in Russia (men's day is **23-е Февраля** or **День защитника Отечества**). It is still sometimes referred to as *Международный женский день* (since Communist times) but this is much disputed. Men and boys give flowers (especially blossoming branches of mimosa) and other presents to their female relatives and friends of any age.

вуз — institution of higher education Any type of institution of higher education forming part of the Russian educational system, including *университет* (university), *академия* (academy), and *институт* (institute/college). The word *вуз* is an abbreviation of *высшее учебное заведение*.

Герой Российской Федерации — Hero of the Russian Federation The highest honorary title in Russia, awarded for heroic deeds. Holders of this title receive a medal *Золотая звезда Героя Российской Федерации* (Gold Star of the Hero of the Russian Federation), the highest government award of the Russian Federation.

город федерального значения — city with federal status One of the six types of administrative unit into which **Российская Федерация** is divided. Of the 83 units, two are cities with federal status, *Moscow* and *St Petersburg*.
     For more details ► **автономная область**

Государственная дума — the State Duma The lower house of **Федеральное Собрание Российской Федерации** (the bicameral parliament of the Russian Federation). *Государственная дума* has 450 members serving four-year terms.

Двадцать третье февраля, 23-е Февраля ► **День защитника Отечества**

День защитника Отечества, 23-е Февраля — Day of the Defender of the Fatherland, 23 February Men's day in Russia, similar to **Восьмое марта** for women. It is a national holiday for everyone although, nominally, it is a holiday for military men only. Women and girls give presents to their male relatives or friends of any age, whether they serve or have served in the Soviet/Russian forces or not.

День Побе́ды — Victory Day (*in the Second World War*) VE Day as celebrated in Russia and some other former Soviet republics on 9 May. It is a national holiday in Russia. The date of 9 May (one day later than in western Europe) results from difference in time zones between Russia and western Europe. *День Побе́ды* is undoubtedly the most respected date in Russian history.

дипло́м о вы́сшем образова́нии — college/university degree certificate A document verifying that a student has graduated from a university or college. In order to qualify for this, students must pass their final exams (*госуда́рственные экза́мены*) and complete and defend a dissertation (*дипло́мная рабо́та*).

край — krai (territory) One of the six types of administrative unit into which **Росси́йская Федера́ция** is divided. Of the 83 units, nine are krais (territories). They were originally (and now they are once more) border areas of Russia (Russian *окра́ины* (sg. *окра́ина*) and *край* having the same stem).

For more details ▶ **автоно́мная о́бласть**

мат — foul language This includes the words *еба́ть*, *хуй*, *пизда́*, and *блядь* (see the main Dictionary text) and all their numerous derivatives. In informal situations, these taboo words are very common among people of low social status, whereas cultured, well-educated, and well-brought-up people (almost) never use them. Traditionally, it is considered unacceptable to utter any of the four words of *мат* in front of women or children, and using *мат* in public is a violation of the law. Violators are liable to a fine or, in exceptional cases, they can even be prosecuted.

национа́льность — (ethnic) nationality In the countries of the former Soviet Union, this traditionally means a person's ethnicity rather than their legal or political status. So if a Russian native speaker refers to someone as *ру́сский по национа́льности*, they usually mean that the person is Russian by language, culture, ethnicity, and even religion (e.g. Russian Orthodox), but the person could be a citizen of any country (the US, Ukraine, Germany, etc.).

нача́льная шко́ла — elementary school The first three or, now usually, four years of schooling that Russian children undergo. Separate institutions of such a kind are now rare in Russia and children usually continue at the same school after their first four years.

Но́вый год — New Year's Day This is the favourite holiday in Russia and some other former Soviet republics, celebrated on 1 January as

elsewhere in Europe. New Year's Day and 2–4 January are national
holidays.

область — oblast (region) One of the six types of administrative unit
into which **Российская Федерация** is divided. Of the 83 units, 46 are
oblasts (regions).
   For more details ▶ **автономная область**

Парламент Российской Федерации ▶ **Федеральное Собрание
Российской Федерации**

**Председатель Правительства Российской Федерации — Prime
Minister of the Russian Federation** The official (and only correct)
title of the Prime Minister of the Russian Federation. *Председатель
Правительства Российской Федерации* is appointed by **Президент
Российской Федерации** with the consent of **Государственная дума**
(the lower house of Russia's national parliament).

**Президент Российской Федерации — President of
the Russian Federation** Under the current Russian
Constitution of 1993, *Президент Российской Федерации*
is head of the state and has very extensive powers. He or
she is directly elected by the citizens of Russia for a term
of four years and cannot serve more than two consecutive
terms. *Президент Российской Федерации* is also Supreme
Commander-in-Chief of the Armed Forces of the Russian
Federation.

республика — republic One of the six types of
administrative unit into which **Российская Федерация**
is divided. Of the 83 units, 21 are republics. Unlike
**автономная область, автономный округ, город федерального
значения, край**, and **область**, each of the 21 republics has its own
constitution (other constituent units have only charters (Russian
устав)), and is entitled to introduce its own official language(s)
(*государственный язык*) in addition to Russian.
   For more details ▶ **автономная область**

Рождество — Christmas Members of the Orthodox Church celebrate
this festival on 7 January and it is a national holiday in Russia. The
Russian Orthodox Church still uses the Julian calendar in which
7 January corresponds to 25 December in the Gregorian calendar.

**Российская Федерация, Россия — the Russian Federation,
Russia** Russia is a federal state consisting of 83 political (constituent)
units (Russian *субъекты Федерации*). They are (January 2013):
   — 21 republics (Russian **республика**) ((*the Republic of*) *Adygea, the
Republic of Altai, the Republic of Bashkortostan, the Republic of Buryatia,
the Chechen Republic, the Chuvash Republic* (also *Chuvashia*), *the
Republic of Dagestan, the Ingush Republic, the Kabarda-Balkar Republic,*

the Republic of Kalmykia, the Karachay-Cherkess Republic, the Republic of Karelia, the Republic of Khakassia, the Republic of Komi, the Republic of Mari El, the Republic of Mordovia, the Republic of North Ossetia-Alania, the Republic of Sakha (also Yakutia), the Republic of Tatarstan (also Tatarstan), the Republic of Tuva (Russian Tyva), and the Udmurt Republic;

— 9 krais (Russian **край**) (Altai Krai, Kamchatka Krai, Khabarovsk Krai, Krasnodar Krai, Krasnoyarsk Krai, Perm Krai, Primorskiy Krai, Stavropol Krai, and Zabaikal Krai);

— 46 oblasts (Russian **область**) (Amur Oblast, Arkhangelsk Oblast, Astrakhan Oblast, Belgorod Oblast, Bryansk Oblast, Chelyabinsk Oblast, Irkutsk Oblast, Ivanovo Oblast, Kaliningrad Oblast, Kaluga Oblast, Kemerovo Oblast, Kirov Oblast, Kostroma Oblast, Kurgan Oblast, Kursk Oblast, Leningrad Oblast, Lipetsk Oblast, Magadan Oblast, Moscow Oblast, Murmansk Oblast, Nizhniy Novgorod Oblast, Novgorod Oblast, Novosibirsk Oblast, Omsk Oblast, Orel Oblast, Orenburg Oblast, Penza Oblast, Pskov

Oblast, Rostov Oblast, Ryazan Oblast, Sakhalin Oblast, Samara Oblast, Saratov Oblast, Smolensk Oblast, Sverdlovsk Oblast, Tambov Oblast, Tomsk Oblast, Tver Oblast, Tula Oblast, Tyumen Oblast, Ulyanovsk Oblast, Vladimir Oblast, Volgograd Oblast, Vologda Oblast, Voronezh Oblast, and Yaroslavl Oblast);

— 2 cities with federal status (Russian **город федера́льного значе́ния**) (Moscow and St Petersburg);

— 1 autonomous oblast (Russian **автоно́мная о́бласть**) (Jewish Autonomous Oblast);

— 4 autonomous okrugs (Russian **автоно́мный о́круг**) (Chukot Autonomous Okrug, Khanty-Mansi Yugra Autonomous Okrug, Nenets Autonomous Okrug, and Yamalo-Nenets Autonomous Okrug).

Under the current Russian Constitution of 1993, both names — *Росси́я* and *Росси́йская Федера́ция* — can be used as an official name of the country.

Росси́я ▶ Росси́йская Федера́ция

СНГ ▶ Содру́жество Незави́симых Госуда́рств

Сове́т Федера́ции — the Council of the Federation The upper house of **Федера́льное Собра́ние Росси́йской Федера́ции** (the bicameral parliament of the Russian Federation). Each of the 83 constituent units of **Росси́йская Федера́ция** has two representatives in *Сове́т Федера́ции*.

Сово́к, сово́к (often written in inverted commas) The former Soviet Union in a pejorative or ironical sense. The term *сово́к* can also mean **1.** a typical Soviet citizen; **2.** the Soviet system as a whole; **3.** the Soviet ideology, lifestyle, etc.; **4.** a person of antiquated ideas living in modern Russia or any of the former Soviet republics.

► 7   Russian life and culture

Содру́жество Незави́симых Госуда́рств, СНГ — the Commonwealth of Independent States, CIS The political alliance of 11 former Soviet republics (January 2013: Armenia, Azerbaijan, Belarus, Kazakhstan, Kyrgyzstan, Moldova, Russia, Tajikistan, Turkmenistan, Ukraine, and Uzbekistan).

сре́дняя общеобразова́тельная шко́ла — secondary school Russian children go to this school until they are 15 so as to get *основно́е о́бщее образова́ние* and **аттеста́т об основно́м о́бщем образова́нии** or until they are 17 so as to get *сре́днее (по́лное) о́бщее образова́ние* and **аттеста́т о сре́днем (по́лном) о́бщем образова́нии.**

субботник — subbotnik A Soviet invention, consisting of a day of unpaid work, originally on Saturdays (its name derives from *суббо́та* 'Saturday'). The first one took place on 12 April 1919 in the locomotive depot of a Moscow railway station called Moskva-Sortirovochnaya, while the first mass *субботник* was held on 10 May 1919 on the Moscow–Kazan railway. They were a quasi-voluntary show of socially useful work. Nowadays the word is still used to denote some kinds of unpaid work such as cleaning areas of communal use, both indoors and outdoors. When performed on Sundays it is also called *воскре́сник.*

триколо́р, росси́йский триколо́р — the Russian tricolour Popular unofficial name of the national flag of the Russian Federation. It has three horizontal bands of red (lower band), blue, and white (upper band). The surest way to memorize order of colours of the Russian tricolour is to remember the name of the Soviet security police *Комите́т госуда́рственной безопа́сности*, usually abbreviated to *КГБ* (*кра́сный* (red), *голубо́й* (blue), *бе́лый* (white)).

Федера́льное Собра́ние Росси́йской Федера́ции — the Federal Assembly of the Russian Federation The official name of the bicameral national legislature of the Russian Federation. The upper house is called **Сове́т Федера́ции** (the Council of the Federation), while the lower house is called **Госуда́рственная ду́ма** (the State Duma).

Culture

Британские и американские культурные реалии

ACT — American College Test Экзамен, который сдают школьники в большинстве американских штатов после окончания средней школы. Он включает ряд предметов, в том числе английский язык и математику. Успешная сдача экзамена даёт право на поступление в университет.

African American — афроамериканец В Америке так называют американцев африканского происхождения. Данный термин является более нейтральным, чем слово «чёрный», которое подразумевает цвет кожи.

Afro-Caribbean — афрокариб В Великобритании и Америке так называют людей африканского происхождения, которые живут или ранее проживали на Карибских островах (к последним относятся Большие и Малые Антильские острова, а также Багамы).

A level — advanced level Выпускной экзамен, который сдают школьники в возрасте 18 лет в Англии и Уэльсе. Ученики, планирующие поступать в университет, должны сдать такой экзамен по трём или четырём предметам. За каждый экзамен ставится отдельная оценка. Университеты и другие вузы отбирают студентов на основе оценок, полученных ими за эти экзамены. Предпочтение отдаётся предметам, которые являются профилирующими для избранного абитуриентом факультета.

American dream — американская мечта Основополагающий принцип американской жизни. В соответствии с ним каждый может добиться успеха, особенно материального, если он будет много трудиться. Для иммигрантов американская мечта предполагает также надежду на свободу и равенство.

Asian-American В Америке так принято называть американцев, которые происходят из стран азиатского региона.

AS level — advanced subsidiary level Экзамен, занимающий промежуточное положение между **GCSE** и **A level**. Приёмные комиссии университетов приравнивают его к половине экзамена на **A level**. После окончания средней школы многие учащиеся сдают экзамены и на **AS level**, и на **A level**.

bed and breakfast Весьма распространённая в Великобритании разновидность гостиничного бизнеса. *Bed and breakfasts* функционируют на базе частных домов и маленьких гостиниц. В них можно переночевать и позавтракать за умеренную цену.

The Big Issue Журнал, освещающий серьёзные общественно-политические темы и отличающийся высоким уровнем журналистики. Его можно купить на улицах британских городов. Журнал распространяют бездомные люди, которые покупают его у издательства за установленную цену. Впоследствии они продают журнал с небольшой наценкой. Вырученные средства позволяют им жить, не прося подаяния.

Britannia Так древние римляне называли Великобританию. В наше время это обозначение стало частью национальной символики. Другим важным элементом этой символики является эмблема, на которой Великобритания изображена в виде женщины в шлеме, держащей в руках щит и трезубец. Данная эмблема воспроизводится на монетах достоинством в 50 пенсов. *Rule, Britannia!* («Правь, Британия!») — патриотическая песня, исполняемая обычно на заключительном вечере променадных концертов (**Proms**).

the British Isles — Британские острова В число этих островов входит 2 крупных острова — Великобритания (государство Великобритания) и Ирландия (Ирландская Республика и Северная Ирландия) — и более мелкие острова, располагающиеся вокруг, — Оркнейские, Гебридские, Шетлендские, Нормандские, острова Мэн и Силли.

broadsheet — широкополосная газета В Великобритании газеты, печатающиеся на широких полосах, противопоставляются таблоидам. Различие проводится не только и не столько по формату газеты, сколько по значимости освещаемого материала и по качеству журналистики. Широкополосные газеты, как правило, обсуждают серьёзные общественно-политические вопросы и демонстрируют высокий уровень журналистики.

Cabinet — Кабинет министров Данный правительственный орган Великобритании включает 20 министров, назначаемых премьер-министром. На заседаниях кабинета обсуждаются политика правительства и административные вопросы. Каждый из министров отвечает за одну определённую сферу государственной жизни. Кабинет в целом принимает решения, касающиеся общей политики правительства. Лидер главной оппозиционной партии назначает свой кабинет, называемый теневым кабинетом (**Shadow Cabinet**).

Culture

the Capitol — Капитолий Здание конгресса США. Оно находится на Капитолийском холме в Вашингтоне.

the City — Сити Финансовый и торговый центр Лондона. Он располагается в пределах исторического ядра города. В Сити сосредоточены головные офисы многих банков, страховых компаний, брокерских фирм и других финансовых организаций. В Сити работает около 500 тысяч человек.

city technology college (CTC) Школы, дающие специальное среднее образование. Они явились результатом сотрудничества между правительством и различными компаниями. Учебная программа предполагает углублённое изучение точных наук. Такого рода школы часто находятся в центре города.

cockney — кокни Диалект, на котором говорят уроженцы нескольких восточных районов Лондона. Основная черта данного диалекта — так называемый рифмованный сленг (**rhyming slang**). Кокни означает также носителей этого диалекта.

college of further education (CFE) Учебное заведение аналогичное профессионально-техническому училищу в России. В него можно поступить по достижении 16 лет. Такие училища дают как специальное, так и общее среднее образование. Учащиеся имеют возможность подготовиться к сдаче **GCSE** или **A Levels** или получить профессиональную квалификацию. Учебная программа предполагает как полные, так и сокращённые учебные дни.

colleges — колледжи В Америке слово *college* применяется как к средним специальным, так и к высшим учебным заведениям. Учебные заведения, где можно получить среднее специальное образование, проводят обучение на базе двухгодичной программы. Для получения высшего образования и степени бакалавра необходимо пройти 4-годичный курс в университете или в так называемом 4-годичном колледже. Приём в колледжи всех категорий производится на основе результатов выпускных экзаменов и текущих оценок, полученных в средней школе.

the Commonwealth — Британское Содружество Объединение в составе Великобритании и 52 стран — в основном её бывших колоний. По состоянию на январь 2013 года членами Содружества являлись: Австралия, Антигуа и Барбуда, Багамские Острова, Бангладеш, Барбадос, Белиз, Ботсвана, Бруней, Вануату, Великобритания, Гайана, Гамбия, Гана, Гренада, Доминика, Замбия, Индия, Камерун, Канада, Кения, Кипр, Кирибати, Лесото, Маврикий, Малави, Малайзия, Мальдивские Острова, Мальта, Мозамбик, Намибия, Науру, Нигерия, Новая Зеландия, Пакистан,

Папуа – Новая Гвинея, Руанда, Самоа, Свазиленд, Сейшельские Острова, Сент-Винсент и Гренадины, Сент-Китс и Невис, Сент-Люсия, Сингапур, Соломоновы Острова, Сьерра-Леоне, Танзания, Тонга, Тринидад и Тобаго, Тувалу, Уганда, Шри-Ланка, Южно-Африканская Республика, Ямайка.

Премьер-министры стран Содружества собираются каждые 2 года на конференцию для обсуждения вопросов экономического и культурного сотрудничества и взаимопомощи. Каждые 4 года проводятся спортивные Игры стран Содружества.

Термин *содружество* является также частью официального названия некоторых американских штатов, например, Кентукки, Вирджинии (Виргинии), Пенсильвании, Массачусетса.

community college Разновидность американских университетов. Учебная программа таких университетов нацелена на получение специального образования, в наибольшей степени удовлетворяющего нуждам местной экономики. Данный термин иногда используется в Англии в названиях средних школ.

comprehensive school — средняя общеобразовательная школа В Великобритании дети учатся в такой школе с 11 и до 18 лет.

Congress — конгресс Законодательный орган США. Он состоит из двух палат: палаты представителей и сената. В палату представителей входит 435 членов, избираемых на 2 года. В сенат входит 100 сенаторов (по два от каждого штата), избираемых на 6 лет. Одна треть сенаторов переизбирается или замещается каждые два года. Чтобы провести закон, иначе называемый актом, его проект (билль) должен быть рассмотрен и одобрен обеими палатами, а затем ратифицирован президентом. Конгресс заседает в Вашингтоне в Капитолии на Капитолийском холме. Слова **The Capitol** (Капитолий) и *The Hill* (холм) также относятся к конгрессу.

council tax — местный налог Налог, взимаемый районным советом с местных жителей. Размер налогового взноса зависит от стоимости дома, находящегося во владении налогоплательщика, и количества людей, проживающих в нём.

Downing Street — Даунинг-стрит Улица в центре Лондона, в районе Вестминстер. Дом номер 10 по этой улице является официальной резиденцией премьер-министра Великобритании, дом номер 11 — резиденцией канцлера казначейства (министра финансов). Выражения *Downing Street* и *Number 10* часто означают офис премьер-министра.

elementary school Начальная школа в США. Дети учатся в таких школах с 6 до 12 лет. Иногда их также называют *grade school*.

football pool — футбольный тотализатор Популярная в Великобритании азартная игра. Игроки пытаются предугадать результаты футбольных матчей, ставят определённые суммы на свои прогнозы и заносят предполагаемые результаты на специальные бланки. Выигрыши выплачиваются тем игрокам, чьи прогнозы оказались наиболее точными. Размер выигрыша прямо пропорционален ставке игрока.

further education В Великобритании данный термин применяется ко всем видам образования (кроме университетского) для учащихся от 16 лет и старше. Обязательное школьное образование ограничено возрастом 16 лет. Если учащиеся решили не поступать в университет, то они могут продолжать обучение в системе профессионально-технического и среднего специального образования. В Америке, однако, термин *further education* применяется и к университетскому образованию.

GCSE — General Certificate of Secondary Education

Школьный экзамен в Англии и Уэльсе. Все учащиеся сдают эти экзамены после 5 лет обучения в средней школе независимо от их способностей. Большинство сдают экзамены по нескольким предметам. Экзаменационная оценка ставится за каждый предмет в отдельности.

Учащиеся, намеревающиеся продолжать обучение на последней ступени средней школы и сдавать экзамены на **A Level**, должны успешно сдать определённое количество *GCSE*. Школьники могут сочетать *GCSE* с **GNVQ**.

GNVQ — General National Vocational Qualification

Школьный экзамен, альтернативный GCSE. Эти экзамены были введены в 1992 году. Предметы, по которым они сдаются, имеют профессионально-техническую направленность. Цель такого обучения — дать учащимся определённые профессиональные знания, сориентировав их таким образом на рынке труда. Многие школьники сочетают *GNVQ* с **GCSE**.

God Save the Queen/King — Боже, храни королеву/короля

Государственный гимн Великобритании. Песня, сочинённая неизвестным автором и впервые исполненная в 1745 году в Лондоне. В качестве государственного гимна принята в начале 19 века.

GP (General Practitioner) — врач общей практики/семейный врач

Эквивалент участкового врача в России. Такие врачи обслуживают жителей определённого района, зарегистрированных в местной поликлинике. Консультация для пациентов Национальной службы здравоохранения (**National Health Service**) бесплатная. В случае необходимости врач общей практики направляет их на консультацию к врачу-специалисту.

grade school = elementary school

graduate school — аспирантура Этот термин применяется в американском варианте английского языка. Студенты могут поступить в аспирантуру после 3 или 4 лет обучения в университете.

grammar school Тип средней школы в Великобритании, эквивалентный гимназиям в России. В них могут поступать одарённые дети по достижении 11—12 лет при условии успешной сдачи конкурсных экзаменов. На данный момент таких школ осталось очень мало, так как с 1965 года их стали заменять общеобразовательными школами, в которые детей принимают независимо от способностей.

green card — грин-карта, зелёная карта Документ, разрешающий жить и работать в Америке людям, не имеющим американского гражданства. Этот документ обязателен для тех, кто хочет жить и работать в Америке постоянно.

Greyhound Bus Название автобусов самой большой в Америке автобусной компании. Сеть обслуживания данной компании охватывает большинство городов Америки. Наибольшей популярностью этот вид транспорта пользуется у молодёжи и туристов.

high school Средняя школа в Америке. Такие школы имеют две ступени. Первая ступень — так называемая младшая школа (**junior high school**) для детей от 12 до 14 лет. Вторая ступень — так называемая старшая школа (**senior high school**) для детей от 15 до 18 лет. После окончания средней школы учащиеся сдают выпускные экзамены (**ACT, SAT®**), по результатам которых они могут поступить в университет.

Данный термин иногда используется и в Великобритании.

the House of Commons — палата общин Нижняя палата британского парламента. Члены парламента, заседающие в этой палате, избираются на всеобщих выборах. В палате общин обсуждают вопросы внутренней и внешней политики и принимают новые законы.

the House of Lords — палата лордов Верхняя палата британского парламента. Члены этой палаты не избираются на выборах, а назначаются от главных политических партий страны. Кроме того, часть мест в палате передаётся по наследству членам аристократических фамилий. В 1999 году количество таких мест было ограничено 92. В функции палаты входит обсуждение и ратификация законов, ранее одобренных палатой общин. Одновременно палата лордов является высшим апелляционным судом страны.

the House of Representatives — палата представителей Нижняя палата конгресса США. В неё входит 435 представителей от американских штатов, которые избираются каждые два года. Число представителей от штатов зависит от численности их населения. Палата представителей принимает новые законы. Все принимаемые законы должны быть одобрены этим органом.

the Houses of Parliament — Британский парламент Двухпалатный орган, состоящий из палаты общин и палаты лордов. Обе палаты заседают в Вестминстерском дворце. Этот дворец представляет собой комплекс зданий в центре Лондона.

independent school — независимая/частная школа В Великобритании так называют школы, которые финансируются не государством, а родителями учеников, вносящими ежегодную плату за их обучение. В эту категорию входят **public school** и **preparatory school**.

infant school Первая ступень начальной школы в Великобритании. Эти школы получили распространение главным образом в Англии. Дети учатся в них три года. Они могут быть самостоятельными или являться частью полной начальной школы, в которой дети учатся до 11 лет.

the Ivy League Это общее название применяется к восьми старейшим и самым престижным университетам США. Все они находятся на восточном побережье страны. В их число входят Гарвардский, Йельский, Колумбийский, Корнеллский, Дартмутский, Браунский, Принстонский и Пенсильванский университеты. Название, принятое для этих университетов — буквально «Лига плюща» — основано на представлении о том, что старые здания этих университетов со временем заросли плющом. Обучение в этих университетах очень дорогое, но некоторые, одарённые студенты получают стипендии.

jobcentre — биржа труда Государственная служба, содействующая людям, ищущим работу. В число услуг, предоставляемых биржами труда, входит реклама вакансий, организация собеседований с работодателями. Биржи труда есть почти во всех городах Великобритании.

junior high school Младшая средняя школа. В Америке так называют первую ступень средней школы. Дети учатся в таких школах после окончания начальной школы (**elementary school**).

Medicaid Тип медицинского страхования, предоставляемого правительством США малоимущим людям моложе 65 лет.

Medicare Тип медицинского страхования, предоставляемого правительством США людям старше 65 лет.

Middle England — средняя Англия Это выражение часто применяется к среднему классу Великобритании. Так как эта группа населения составляет самую большую часть электората, политические партии стремятся получить на выборах их голоса. Выражение *middle income Britain* имеет аналогичное употребление.

MP (Member of Parliament) — член парламента Это выражение применяется только к членам палаты общин. Они представляют 659 избирательных округов Англии, Уэльса, Шотландии и Северной Ирландии.

the National Health Service (NHS) — Национальная служба здравоохранения В Великобритании система здравоохранения финансируется государством и медицинская помощь в основном бесплатная. Однако пациенты должны платить за зубоврачебные услуги и лекарства. Исключение составляют дети до 18 лет и беременные женщины. Им эти услуги предоставляются бесплатно.

National Insurance (NI) — национальное страхование Взносы по этому страхованию обязательны для работающей части населения и для работодателей. Они отчисляются из заработной платы и идут в фонд оплаты различных социальных услуг — медицинского обслуживания, пособий по безработице, пенсий и т. д.

the National Lottery — национальная лотерея В Великобритании доходы, получаемые от розыгрышей лотереи, идут на финансирование культурных и спортивных проектов, на охрану памятников и на разного рода благотворительные цели.

the National Trust Добровольная общественная организация по охране архитектурных, исторических и природных памятников Великобритании. Она функционирует за счёт взносов членов организации и доходов, получаемых от её владений. За годы своего существования эта организация выкупила или получила в дар огромные земельные угодья, целые деревни и большое количество зданий, представляющих архитектурную или историческую ценность. Несколько месяцев в году дома-музеи и другие владения организации открыты для посещения.

Native American — коренной американец В настоящее время в Америке так принято называть коренных жителей Северной и Южной Америки, а также Карибских островов. Этому термину отдаётся предпочтение в официальных контекстах, так как он считается более точным, чем слово «индеец», которое появилось в результате ошибки, сделанной Х. Колумбом. Уверенный в том, что он достиг Индии, он

Culture

назвал местных жителей индейцами. Тем не менее, слово *индеец* имеет широкое распространение, и коренные жители обеих Америк не считают его оскорбительным.

NBC — National Broadcasting Company Национальная вещательная компания. Первая вещательная компания США. Она была основана в 1926 году. Первый телевизионный канал *NBC* начал свою работу в 1940 году.

the Open University Заочный университет в Великобритании. Обучение на всех факультетах проводится на заочной основе. В этом университете учатся студенты всех возрастов. Они работают самостоятельно и отсылают письменные работы своим преподавателям. Степень, полученная в этом университете, равноценна степени любого другого университета.

Oxbridge Сращение, образованное от названий *Oxford* и *Cambridge*. Оно относится к университетам Оксфорда и Кембриджа и подчёркивает их престиж и особое положение среди других университетов.

Parliament — парламент Британский парламент — высший законодательный орган страны. Он состоит из двух палат: палаты общин и палаты лордов. Парламент собирается в Вестминстерском дворце. Выборы в парламент проходят каждые 5 лет. Все члены палаты общин должны переизбираться. Царствующий монарх открывает новые сессии парламента и подписывает законы.

the Pledge of Allegiance — клятва верности В американских школах каждый учебный день начинается с переклички и с клятвы американскому флагу. Ученики произносят клятву верности и преданности Америке: «Я клянусь в верности флагу Соединённых Штатов Америки и республике, которую он представляет, её народу, единому перед Богом, свободе и справедливости для всех».

Иммигранты, принимающие американское гражданство приносят такую же клятву.

politically correct, PC — политически корректный, политкорректный Идея политической корректности появилась в 80-х годах двадцатого века. Суть её заключается в выработке и повсеместном закреплении языковых и поведенческих норм, лишённых любых предрассудков: будь то предрассудки расовые, половые, национальные или иные. В процессе замены старых выражений новыми — политически корректными — в языке наметилась тенденция к избавлению от многих спорных терминов. Очевидно, что слова *афроамериканец* и *коренной американец* в большей мере соответствуют исторической правде, нежели употребляемые в тех же значениях, соответственно, *чёрный* (или *негр*) и *индеец*. Однако некоторые эвфемизмы, возникшие на этой почве, грешат неопределённостью. Таким, например, является выражение *involuntarily leisured* (дословно «на вынужденном отдыхе»), используемое вместо слова *unemployed* (безработный).

Poppy Day — День маков В Великобритании так называют день, в который страна отмечает годовщину окончания Первой мировой войны. В этот день, называемый также *Remembrance Sunday* (Памятное воскресенье) или *Armistice Day* (День перемирия), поминают жертв обеих мировых войн. Многие люди вдевают в петлицы красные бумажные маки. Маки символизируют цветочные поля Франции и Бельгии, на которых похоронены солдаты, павшие в Первой и Второй мировых войнах. Бумажные маки продаются благотворительными организациями. Средства, вырученные от их продажи, идут на помощь ветеранам войны.

prep/preparatory school В Великобритании так называют частные начальные школы. Дети учатся в них с 7 и до 13 лет. Некоторые из этих школ являются интернатами. Обучение в них, как правило, раздельное для мальчиков и девочек. Ученики, окончившие такие школы, обычно поступают в частные средние школы.

В Америке данное выражение относится к очень престижным частным средним школам, которые готовят учащихся к поступлению в лучшие университеты страны.

primaries — праймериз В США так называют выборы делегатов, направляемых на партийные съезды, во время которых выдвигаются кандидаты в президенты и в вице-президенты.

prom В Америке так называют школьный бал в конце учебного года.

the Proms — promenade concerts — променадные концерты Ежегодный фестиваль классической музыки, проходящий в королевском Альберт-холле в Лондоне. Заключительный вечер променадных концертов являет собой шумное зрелище. Зрители поют под аккомпанемент оркестра традиционные песни *Land of Hope and Glory* и *Rule Britannia!* Слово *Proms* является сокращением от выражения *promenade concert* — променадные концерты, которые называются так, потому что значительная часть зрителей слушает концерты стоя.

public school — частная школа Несмотря на своё название, эти школы являются частными. Обычно в них учатся дети из привилегированных и богатых семей. Это связано с тем, что плата за обучение в таких школах чрезвычайно высокая. В особенности это относится к наиболее престижным из них: Итону (*Eton*), Хэрроу (Харроу) (*Harrow*), Винчестеру (*Winchester*), Рагби (*Rugby*). Все эти школы предоставляют стипендии одарённым детям

Culture

из малоимущих семей. Большинство этих школ является интернатами. Кроме того, обучение в них раздельно для мальчиков и девочек.

В Америке выражение *public school* относится к государственным школам.

the Queen's Speech — речь королевы Эта речь готовится для королевы британским правительством. Она произносит её в палате лордов на ежегодной церемонии официального открытия парламента. Речь королевы — важное событие в политическом календаре, так как в ней освещаются планы правительства на ближайший год.

received pronunciation (RP) — нормативное произношение Произношение английского языка, принятое за норму в Великобритании. Это произношение свободно от влияния каких-либо региональных диалектов и часто ассоциируется с речью людей из привилегированных слоёв. Произношение, принятое на радио и телевидении, часто ориентируется на эту норму, хотя в последние годы произносительный диапазон дикторов стал включать и региональные варианты.

rhyming slang — рифмованный сленг Особенность диалекта кокни, которая делает его совершенно непонятным для непосвящённых. Суть его состоит в том, что отдельные слова заменяются выражениями, которые с ними рифмуются. Например, вместо слова *believe* употребляется сочетание *Adam and Eve*, вместо слова *head* употребляется сочетание *loaf of bread*.

Трудность понимания такой речи усугубляется тем обстоятельством, что носители кокни часто сокращают эти сочетания до отдельных слов. Например, выражение *Use your loaf* означает на самом деле *Use your head*.

SAT 1. Scholastic Aptitude Test. Тест, успешная сдача которого необходима для поступления в американские университеты. Обычно его сдают при окончании средней школы. **2. Standard Assessment Test.** Экзамен, который сдают все школьники Англии и Уэльса в возрасте 7, 11 и 14 лет.

the Scottish Parliament — парламент Шотландии Он открылся в 1999 году после всеобщих шотландских выборов. Парламент уполномочен решать многие вопросы экономической, социальной и культурной политики самостоятельно, без вмешательства парламента Великобритании. Члены шотландского парламента заседают в Эдинбурге, в Холирудхаус (*Holyrood House*).

secondary schools — средние школы В Великобритании существует ряд учебных заведений, дающих среднее образование:

Culture

общеобразовательные школы (*comprehensive schools*) — бесплатные школы для мальчиков и девочек, в которых дети учатся независимо от способностей. Эти школы составляют 85% всех средних учебных заведений;

гимназии (*grammar schools*) — школы для более одарённых детей. Они могут быть как частными, так и государственными. Обучение в них обычно раздельное для мальчиков и девочек. Для поступления в такие школы необходимо сдавать вступительный экзамен;

частные школы (*public schools*) — в большинстве случаев это школы-интернаты. Обучение в таких школах очень дорогое.

the Senate — сенат Верхняя палата американского конгресса. В нём заседает 100 сенаторов — по два от каждого штата. Они избираются на 6 лет. Все новые законы должны быть утверждены как сенатом, так и палатой представителей.

Однако сенат отвечает за внешнюю политику и уполномочен «оценивать и одобрять» назначения, сделанные президентом.

senior high school В Америке так называют вторую ступень средней школы. Дети учатся в ней по завершении младшей средней школы (**junior high school**).

Shadow Cabinet ► Cabinet

Silicon Valley — Силиконовая долина Так называют долину Санта-Клара в Калифорнии, в которой располагается большое количество компьютерных компаний. Данное название связано с тем, что силикон (кремний) широко используется в электронной промышленности.

the Stars and Stripes Флаг США.

the Star-Spangled Banner **1.** Гимн США. **2.** Одно из названий американского флага.

tabloid — таблоид Малоформатная (бульварная) газета. Такие газеты противопоставляются широкоформатным (широкополосным) газетам (**broadsheet**), которые печатаются на больших листах. Таблоиды ассоциируются с жёлтой прессой, в особенности такие, как *The Sun* и *Daily Mirror*. В последнее время таблоидный формат печати, как более удобный, стал использоваться и некоторыми серьёзными газетами, например, *The Independent, The Times*.

Thanksgiving — День благодарения Зима 1620 года в Новом Свете обернулась катастрофой для английских колонистов. Половина колонии, основанной *отцами-пилигримами*, — первыми поселенцами Северной Америки — погибла в результате болезней. Однако осень 1621 года была урожайной, и это позволило оставшимся колонистам выжить. Они решили отпраздновать это событие обедом. На обед были приглашены индейцы, научившие их охотиться и выращивать кукурузу. В наши дни День благодарения отмечается ежегодно в четвёртый четверг ноября. На обед готовится индейка со сладким картофелем и клюквенным соусом. На десерт подаётся тыквенный пирог. В Канаде День благодарения отмечается во второй понедельник октября.

the three Rs Так называются главные предметы в начальной школе: чтение, письмо, арифметика. В английском произношении этих слов — *Reading, wRiting, aRithmetic* — первым звуком является *R*.

TOEFL — Test of English as a Foreign Language Экзамен по английскому языку, который должны сдавать иностранцы, поступающие в американские университеты.

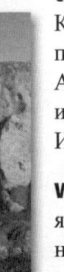

the Union Jack Так называется флаг Соединённого Королевства Великобритании и Северной Ирландии. На полотнище флага крест св. Георгия, символизирующего Англию, крест св. Андрея, символизирующего Шотландию, и крест св. Патрика, символизирующего Северную Ирландию, объединены в одном изображении.

Wall Street — Уолл-стрит Улица в Нью-Йорке, являющаяся финансовым и торговым центром США. Здесь находится фондовая биржа, головные офисы многих банков и страховых компаний и других финансовых учреждений.

Washington DC — Вашингтон Столица США, названная так в честь первого президента страны Джорджа Вашингтона. В административно-территориальном отношении этот город полностью совпадает с федеральным округом Колумбия. В Вашингтоне находятся Белый дом, конгресс, Верховный суд, национальные музеи.

welfare Система социальной защиты в США. Эта программа оказывает поддержку людям с низким доходом. Основными элементами программы являются **Medicaid** (оказание бесплатной медицинской помощи), *food stamps* (талоны на продукты питания) и *Head Start* (финансовая поддержка, оказываемая школьникам из бедных семей).

welfare state — государство всеобщего благосостояния В Великобритании данное понятие включает в себя систему социального обеспечения, нацеленную на поддержание высокого уровня жизни всех граждан. Основными элементами данной системы являются бесплатная медицинская помощь (**the National Health Service**), государственное страхование (**National Insurance**) и социальная защита безработных (*Social Security*).

the Welsh Assembly — Ассамблея Уэльса Так называется парламент Уэльса, учреждённый в 1999 году. Он заседает в столице Уэльса Кардиффе. Парламент даёт Уэльсу значительную автономию от британского правительства.

Westminster — Вестминстер Район в центре Лондона. Здесь находятся правительственные учреждения, в том числе британский парламент (**Houses of Parliament**), резиденция премьер-министра (**Downing Street**), Букингемский дворец (*Buckingham Palace*) (резиденция правящего монарха), дворец св. Джеймса (*St James's Palace*) (резиденция принца Уэльского) и др. Слово *Westminster* также означает британский парламент.

Whitehall — Уайтхолл Улица в центре Лондона, на которой расположены многие правительственные учреждения. В средствах массовой информации словом *Whitehall* часто называют британское правительство.

Correspondence

Letters/Письма

1. Запрос вакансии

Начальнику Отдела кадров
Медицинского училища № 2
г. Санкт-Петербурга
Иванову Петру Трофимовичу
от Григорьевой Ольги Николаевны,
проживающей по адресу:
Московский проспект, д. 147, кв. 3
телефон (812) 824-73-54

Уважаемый Пётр Трофимович!

Прошу Вас сообщить о наличии вакансии преподавателя биологии в Вашем училище. В настоящий момент я преподаю биологию и химию в средней школе № 396 Кировского района Санкт-Петербурга. В связи с переменой места жительства я ищу работу преподавателя в новом районе. После окончания Педагогического института им. Герцена в 1997 году я преподавала химию и биологию в средней школе. При наличии вакансии преподавателя в Вашем училище прошу Вас назначить мне собеседование в удобное для Вас время.

С уважением,   Григорьева О. Н.
14.01.2013

1. Enquiry to an employer about jobs

73 Brighton Road
Eastbourne
East Sussex
BN21 3YR

4 April 2013

Manager
Rose and Crown Hotel
Eastbourne
East Sussex
BN22 7AP

Dear Mr Davis

I am writing to enquire whether you have any vacancies for bar or restaurant staff over the summer.

I have worked at other hotels in the town in my school holidays over the past few years and have quite a lot of experience at serving behind a bar and waiting at table.

My university term ends on 19 June and I shall then be available until the middle of September when I plan to take two weeks' holiday before returning to Leeds in October.

I would prefer work in the bar or restaurant but would also consider any other jobs you can offer.

I enclose references from two previous employers and a character reference from my university tutor. I look forward to hearing from you.

Yours sincerely

Giles Goodall

2. Ответ на объявление о наличии вакансии

Директору фирмы «Заря»
Логинову Борису Аркадьевичу
от Каца Алексея Владиславовича,
проживающего по адресу:
ул. Сергея Потапова, д. 12/4, кв. 264
г. Калуга, 248921
телефон (0842) 93-14-55

Уважаемый господин директор!

В ответ на объявление в газете «Курьер» от 15 января
этого года направляю Вам свое резюме, копию
свидетельства об окончании курсов повышения
квалификации и справку с настоящего места работы.
Меня интересует должность инженера по наладке
электронной аппаратуры. В случае если моё предложение
заинтересует Вас, я бы хотел узнать подробнее об
условиях работы.

С уважением,   Кац А. В.
01.02.2012

2. Reply to a job advertisement

23 Church Road
Blundesdon
LOWESTOFT
Norfolk
NR32 3LS

19.6.12

Personnel Manager
The Norfolk Echo
5 High Street
NORWICH
Norfolk
NR3 2HF

Dear Mr Williams

I am writing in response to the advertisement that appeared last week in *The Guardian* for an Assistant Features Editor on the *Norfolk Echo*.

As you will see from my CV, I successfully completed a Media Studies degree at Lancaster University the year before last, since when I have worked in a freelance capacity for my local radio station and my local paper. I am now keen to move on to more permanent employment and believe that the experience I have gained will be relevant to the job advertised.

Apart from my CV, I enclose some examples of my work in the form of articles I have written and a CD of some interviews that I have conducted with people of local interest.

I am available for interview at any time and could take up the post immediately, should I be appointed. Thank you for considering my application.

Yours sincerely

Louise Ashby

3. Просьба о рекомендательном письме

Уважаемый Николай Константинович!

У меня к Вам большая просьба. Не могли бы Вы написать рекомендательное письмо для меня? С тех пор как меня перевели в *СУ-13, я продолжал работать в должности прораба и заочно учился в Петербургском политехническом институте. В июне я наконец получил диплом, а недавно нашёл место инженера на соседнем предприятии. Для поступления на работу в Отделе кадров у меня попросили кроме обычных документов рекомендательное письмо с предыдущего места работы. Поскольку я проработал под Вашим руководством последние шесть лет, я бы хотел попросить написать такое письмо именно Вас. Пожалуйста, направьте письмо на имя начальника Отдела кадров завода «Оптика» Малинина Георгия Сергеевича по адресу: завод «Оптика», ул. Генерала Петрова, д. 1, г. Самара, 443003.

Заранее Вам благодарен,

12.03.2013   Андреев Николай Захарович

*СУ = строительное управление 'construction company'

3. Asking for a reference

6 Highworth Cottages
Inhurst
Tadley
Hants RG26 5JP

1 February 2006

Dear Fiona

I'm sorry I haven't been in touch lately. How are you, and how's life at Basingstoke Comprehensive?

The reason I'm writing is that I was wondering if you would be willing to act as a referee with regard to several jobs I'm applying for at the moment.

After spending the past ten years in industry, I've decided to return to teaching, preferably this time in higher education. As you were my most recent Head of Department I thought that you would be the most suitable person to ask for a reference.

I'm hoping that my practical experience in the food industry will make me better qualified now than I was when I left Basingstoke. So far I have applied for posts at the Oxford & Cherwell Valley College and Kingston University, both involving teaching the catering part of the HND leisure industry course.

Please get in touch if you would like further information about what I have been doing or about the requirements for these jobs.

Best wishes

Debbie Brooks

4. Письмо в отдел кадров

Начальнику Отдела кадров

ООО «Огни»

Фокиной Марии Ивановне

Благодарю Вас за письмо от 15 марта с уведомлением о зачислении меня в фирму «Огни» на должность главного механика по наладке оборудования. К сожалению, мои попытки немедленно уволиться с настоящего места работы не привели к успеху, и я вынужден ждать положенные по закону две недели после подачи заявления об увольнении. Таким образом, я смогу приступить к исполнению своих обязанностей на Вашем предприятии не ранее 1 апреля 2012 г. Сожалею о задержке и надеюсь, что это обстоятельство не повлияет на Ваше решение о предоставлении мне рабочего места.

С уважением,

16.03.2012   Григорьев И. П.

4. Accepting a job

19 Ryden Lane
Clevelode
MALVERN
Worcestershire
WR13 8PD

22/3/12

Personnel Department
Warwickshire College
Warwick New Rd
Leamington Spa
CV32 5JE

Dear Ms Elliott

I was extremely pleased to receive your letter offering me the job of Admissions Secretary at Warwickshire College, and am glad to inform you that I accept the offer.

As discussed at my interview, I need to give a month's notice at my present job and would therefore like to start work at the beginning of May. This will give me a few days for the move and allow me to get settled into my new flat before starting.

I would be grateful if you could let me know who I should report to or where I should go when I first arrive. Please could you also send me a copy of the Terms and Conditions of Employment that you mentioned at the interview, and details of the pension scheme.

I look forward to seeing you in the near future.

Yours sincerely

Amanda Walker

РЕЗЮМЕ

Ф.И.О.	Михайлова Марина Александровна
Дата рождения, возраст	05.04.1985, 25 лет
Адрес	пр. Байрона, д. 66, кв. 6 г. Петрозаводск, 185000, Республика Карелия
Телефон	(домашний) (8242) 82-32-22, (сотовый) +79217003522
E-mail	mariners@mail.ru
Семейное положение, дети	не замужем, детей нет
Претендую на должность	переводчик (полная занятость)
Заработная плата	от 30 000 рублей

Образование

2005—2010	Петрозаводский государственный университет, филологический факультет, специальность «Английский язык и литература» (диплом с отличием)
январь-август 2008	Университет штата Канзас, практика для студентов, обучающихся по обмену, специальность «Английский язык» (почётный лист со средним баллом 3,65 из 4)
июнь-август 2007	Летняя школа Университета Осло, специальность «Норвежский язык»
1995—2005	Средняя школа №17 г. Петрозаводска с углублённым изучением английского и финского языков (серебряная медаль)

Иностранные языки	свободное владение английским языком (навыки синхронного перевода), разговорный финский, базовые знания норвежского (чтение и перевод неспециальных текстов)

Опыт работы

июль-сентябрь 2010	переводчик делегации ЮНЕСКО в Республике Карелия
июнь-август 2009	преподаватель русского языка как иностранного в Летней школе Петрозаводского государственного университета

Дополнительные навыки	компьютер на уровне уверенного пользователя, водительские права категории «В»

CURRICULUM VITAE

Name: John Phillip Hunt

Address: 24 Mulberry Rd
Brixton
LONDON SW14 5HU

Telephone: 020-592284; mobile 07905339242

Email: jp_hunt@compuserve.com

Nationality: British

Date of birth: 22/5/88

Marital Status: Single

Education/Qualifications:

2010–2011 University of Bristol: MSc in Management

2006–2010 King's College, London: BA (hons.) Russian and German, class 2:1

1999–2006 Burford Community College, Oxford Rd, Burford, Oxon.
9 GCSEs (English, Mathematics, Physics, History, Technology, German, Russian, French, Music)
4 A levels: German (A), Russian (B), History (B), English (C)

Work Experience:

September 2008– June 2009 10 months working in Personnel Department of the Max-Planck-Institut für Informatik in Saarbrücken, Germany

July–August 2007 6 weeks teaching English to foreign students at Swan School of English, Oxford

March 2005 1 week's 'shadowing' experience to Assistant Marketing Manager, EAA Technology (Environmental Energy), Didcot

June 2003 2 weeks' work experience at Marks and Spencer, Oxford

Skills: Computer literate; clean driving licence

Referees: Dr Michael Edwards (Arts Faculty)
King's College
London EC12 4HR

Dr Elaine Grigson
(Management Research Centre)
University of Bristol
Bristol BS8 1TH

SMS (electronic text messaging)

SMS is the English abbreviation for "Short Message/Messaging Service". Sending an English text message is the same procedure as sending a Russian text message, but abbreviations are used far more often. In English there are countless abbreviations which allow a lot of information to be transmitted using few letters and numbers, e.g. 2l8 = 'too late'. For many messages people type only the initial letters of each word, e.g. ttyl = 'talk to you later', or fyi = 'for your information'. Experienced senders of text messages have no problems in understanding a whole range of such abbreviations.

So-called emoticons or smileys, witty symbols created using punctuation marks, brackets, etc., are popular in text messaging. Some of the more established ones are included below.

Обмен SMS-сообщениями

Аббревиатура SMS расшифровывается как Short Message/Messaging Service, что переводится с английского как «служба обмена короткими сообщениями». Отправка текстового сообщения (SMS) на английском языке такая же тривиальная процедура, как и отправка SMS на русском языке с той лишь разницей, что англоязычные пользователи при написании SMS намного чаще прибегают к различного рода сокращениям. Их число, в силу фонетико-морфологических особенностей английского языка, не поддаётся счёту. Использование сокращений позволяет существенно упростить и ускорить набор, а заодно увеличить объём полезной информации, передаваемой в рамках одного сообщения. Нередко ту или иную мысль получается выразить при помощи всего нескольких букв или цифр. Например, 2l8 означает too late «слишком/уже поздно», где цифра 2 (two) заменяет созвучное ей слово too, буква l соответствует самой себе, а цифра 8 (eight) образует слоговой элемент слова late. Другой распространённый приём пользователей SMS — это образование сокращений из первых букв слов, входящих в состав фразы или предложения. Например, ttyl означает talk to you later «увидимся» или «до встречи» (буквально, «поговорим позже»), a fyi — for your information «к твоему/вашему сведению». Опытные отправители SMS без труда понимают всё множество подобных аббревиатур.

Т. н. эмотиконы или смайлики — остроумные обозначения, состоящие из знаков пунктуации, букв и прочих символов, — также широко применяются в языке SMS. Наиболее устоявшиеся из них приводятся ниже.

Glossary of English SMS abbreviations/Английские SMS-сокращения

(Русский перевод даётся только у выражений, значение которых нельзя получить пословным буквальным переводом. Перевод остальных выражений, а также одиночных слов следует искать в статьях к соответствующим словам в основном корпусе Словаря.)

Abbreviation	Meaning	Значение
@	at	
adn	any day now	(в самое ближайшее время)
afaik	as far as I know	(насколько я знаю, насколько мне известно)
atb	all the best	
b	be	
b4	before	
b4n	bye for now	(ну, пока!)
bbl	be back late(r)	
bcnu	be seeing you	(увидимся!, до встречи!)
bfn	bye for now	(ну, пока!)
brb	be right back	(обязательно вернусь (но не знаю когда точно))
btw	by the way	(кстати, между прочим)
bwd	backward	
c	see	
cu	see you	(увидимся!, до встречи!)
cul8r	see you later	(увидимся!, до встречи!)
f2f	face to face	(лицом к лицу)
f2t	free to talk	(есть время поболтать/поговорить)
fwd	forward	
fwiw	for what it's worth	(если это имеет (какое-то) значение)
fyi	for your information	(к твоему/вашему сведению)
gal	get a life	((1) займись (лучше) делом!; (2) займись чем-нибудь (более) интересным, ≈ живи полной жизнью!)
gr8	great	
h8	hate	
hand	have a nice day	(всего доброго/хорошего!, до свидания! (традиционная формула прощания))
hth	hope this helps	
ic	I see	((я) понял!; (я) вижу!)
iluvu, ilu	I love you	
imho	in my humble opinion	(по моему скромному мнению)
imo	in my opinion	(по-моему)
iow	in other words	(другими словами)
jic	just in case	(на всякий случай)
jk	just kidding	(шучу)
kit	keep in touch	((не пропадай! (= звони!, пиши! и т. п.))
kwim	know what I mean?	
l8	late	
l8r	later	
lol	lots of luck; laughing out loud; lots of love	(удачи!; заливаюсь смехом (громко смеюсь); много(-много) любви! (как пожелание))
mob	mobile	
msg	message	
myob	mind your own business	((а) тебе какое дело?, ≈ не будь таким любопытным (-ой -ой)!)
ne	any	
ne1	anyone	

SMS

Abbreviation	Meaning	Значение
no1	no one	
oic	oh, I see	((я) по́нял!; (я) ви́жу!)
otoh	on the other hand	(с друго́й стороны́)
pcm	please call me	
pls	please	
ppl	people	
r	are	
rofl	rolling on the floor, laughing	(ката́юсь по́ полу от сме́ха)
ru	are you	
ruok	are you OK?	(с тобо́й/ва́ми всё в поря́дке?)
sit	stay in touch	(не пропада́й! (= звони́!, пиши́! и т. п.))
som1	someone	
spk	speak	
thkq	thank you	
thx	thanks	
ttyl	talk to you later	(уви́димся!, до встре́чи!; поговори́м по́зже)
tx	thanks	
u	you	
ur	you are	
w/	with	
wan2	want to	
wan2tlk	want to talk?	
werv u bin	where have you been?	(где пропада́л(а)/был(а́)?)
wknd	weekend	
wot	what	
wu	what's up?	(как дела́?)
x	kiss	
xlnt	excellent	
xoxoxo	hugs and kisses	((кре́пко) целу́ю и обнима́ю)
yr	your; you're	
1	one	
2	to; too	
2day	today	
2moro	tomorrow	
2nite	tonight	
3sum	threesome	
4	for	

Emoticon	Meaning	Значение
:-)	smiling, happy face	улыба́ющаяся, счастли́вая ро́жица
:-|	frowning; bored	нахму́рил бро́ви; ску́чно
:-e	disappointed	разочаро́ван/огорчён
:-(	unhappy face	несча́стная ро́жица
%-)	confused	смущён, озада́чен
:~(or **:'-(**	crying	пла́чу
;-)	winking happy face	подми́гивающая дово́льная ро́жица
|-o	tired; asleep	уста́л; сплю/усну́л
:-	sceptical	с недове́рием/сомне́нием

Emoticon	Meaning	Значение
:-D	big smile, laughing face	улыбка во весь рот, смеющаяся рожица
:-<>	amazed	изумлён/поражён
X=	fingers crossed	скрестив пальцы (*наудачу*)
:-p	tongue sticking out	с высунутым языком, показывая язык
:-O	shouting; surprised	кричу; удивлён
:-Q	I don't understand	не понимаю, не понял
:-X	my lips are sealed, I won't tell anyone	держу рот на замке, никому не скажу
O:-)	angel	ангел
:-* *or* :-x	big kiss!	крепкий поцелуй
:-o	"Oooh!"; shocked face	ух ты! (*от удивления/восхищения*), ой/уй! (*от боли*); шокированная рожица
@}-,-'—	a rose	роза (*как знак любви*)

*NB: the '-' which represents the nose is often omitted or replaced by an 'o', e.g. :) or :o).

*NB Дефис «-», обозначающий нос, часто опускается или заменяется буквой «о», например, :) или :o).

Email and the Internet
Электронная почта и Интернет

to be on email	име́ть до́ступ к электро́нной по́чте (*or* к Интернéту)
an email	электро́нное письмо́, e-mail, име́йл
a mailbox	почто́вый я́щик
an 'at' sign (@)	соба́ка (знак @)
an address book	а́дресная кни́га
an email address	электро́нный а́дрес, e-mail, име́йл
a mailing list	спи́сок адреса́тов
to send (*someone*) an email	пос|ыла́ть, -ла́ть электро́нное письмо́ (*кому-н.*)
to send (*something*) by email	пос|ыла́ть, -ла́ть (*что-н.*) по электро́нной по́чте
to receive an email	получ|а́ть, -и́ть электро́нное письмо́
to forward an email	перес|ыла́ть, -ла́ть электро́нное письмо́
to copy somebody in, to cc somebody	отпр|авля́ть, -а́вить ко́пию (*письма́, сообще́ния и т. п.*) кому́-н.
cc (carbon copy)	ко́пия (*письма́*) (*отправляемая другому адресату в дополнение к основному, так что всем получателям письма становятся известными адреса друг друга*)
bcc (blind carbon copy)	скры́тая ко́пия (*письма́*) (*отправляемая другому адресату в дополнение к основному, так что другие получатели письма не знают, что этому адресату отправлена копия*)
a file	файл
a folder	па́пка
an emoticon, a smiley (:-))	эмо́тикон, сма́йл(ик)
to attach a file	вкла́дывать, вложи́ть (*or* прикреп|ля́ть, -и́ть *or* присоедин|я́ть, -и́ть) файл
to receive an attachment	получ|а́ть, -и́ть вложе́ние (*к письму́*) (*or* ат(т)а́чмент *or* присоединённый/прикреплённый (*к письму́*) файл)
to open an attachment	откр|ыва́ть, -ы́ть вложе́ние (*к письму́*) (*or* ат(т)а́чмент *or* присоединённый/прикреплённый (*к письму́*) файл)
to save a message on the desktop, on the hard disk	сохран|я́ть, -и́ть сообще́ние на рабо́чем столе́, на жёстком ди́ске
to delete a message	удал|я́ть, -и́ть сообще́ние
an inbox	входя́щие (сообще́ния)
an outbox	исходя́щие (сообще́ния)
snail mail (*infml*)	обы́чная по́чта, «ме́дленная по́чта», «черепа́шья по́чта» (*в противоположность электронной*)
to get spam	получ|а́ть, -и́ть спам
to send spam	рассыла́ть, разосла́ть спам
a modem	моде́м
an ADSL modem	ADSL-моде́м
toolbar	пане́ль инструме́нтов
to copy	копи́ровать, с-
to cut	выреза́ть, вы́резать
to paste	вст|авля́ть, -а́вить
to print	распеча́т|ывать, -ать

Toolbar menu buttons on emails	Назва́ния кно́пок меню́ в почто́вых програ́ммах
File	Файл
Edit	Пра́вка
View	Вид
Insert	Вста́вка
Format	Форма́т
Tools	Се́рвис
Actions	Де́йствия
Help	Спра́вка

Internet

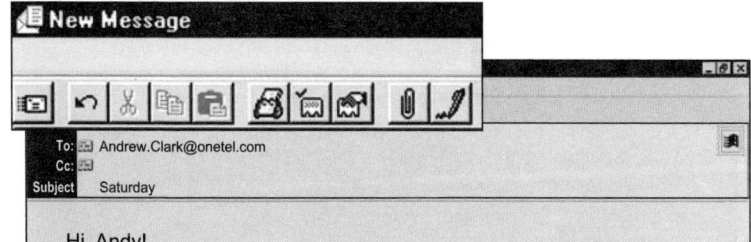

New Message

To: Andrew.Clark@onetel.com
Cc:
Subject   Saturday

Hi, Andy!

I spent the afternoon at the Internet cafe on the High Street, and I found this really interesting website: http://www.list.co.uk. You should add it to your favourites. On the home page you can select any town in the UK and it gives you all the bars/restaurants/concert venues etc. in the town you choose. When you double-click on the name of a bar, a map automatically pops up and the place you've selected is highlighted. Mail me when you've had a chance to browse! I'm sure we could find something for Saturday night.

I also attach a joke that Anna sent me this morning. She bought an ADSL modem so she's on email now. It made me laugh. (Don't worry about opening the file: I ran my antivirus over it and got the all-clear.) Speak to you soon!

Tim

PS Can you forward this to Mark? I wanted to copy him in, but I can't find his email address and I deleted his latest email from my inbox. I'm sure he'd be interested as well.

Internet

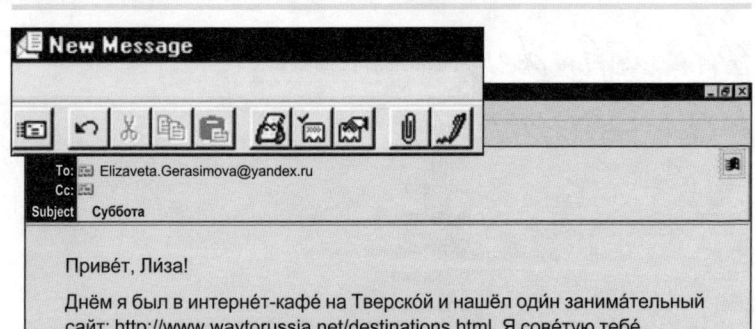

New Message

To: Elizaveta.Gerasimova@yandex.ru
Cc:
Subject: Суббота

Привет, Лиза!

Днём я был в интернет-кафе на Тверской и нашёл один занимательный сайт: http://www.waytorussia.net/destinations.html. Я советую тебе добавить его в «Избранное» твоего браузера. На главной странице ты можешь выбрать из списка российский город, и тебе будут показаны бары, рестораны, концертные площадки, расположенные в нём. Если дважды щёлкнуть на названии заведения, то автоматически во всплывающем окне откроется карта, а искомое место на ней будет выделено цветом. В общем, пиши мне, когда будет возможность. Уверен, мы найдём, где провести время в эту субботу ночью.

Я прикрепляю к письму шутку, которую мне прислал Слава сегодня утром. Он купил ADSL-модем, так что теперь он может переписываться с нами по электронной почте. (Не бойся открывать этот файл: я проверил его антивирусом — вирусов там нет.)

До скорого! Пиши!

Илья

PS Ты не могла бы переслать это письмо Юле? Я хотел отправить ей копию, но не могу найти её электронный адрес, а последнее письмо от неё я удалил из своего почтового ящика. Не сомневаюсь, ей также будет это интересно.

Phrasefinder / Разговóрник

Useful phrases / Полéзные фрáзы

yes, please	да, пожáлуйста
no, thank you	нет, спаси́бо
sorry	прости́те
excuse me	извини́те (меня́)
I'm sorry, I don't understand	прости́те, я не понимáю

Meeting people / Встрéча

hello/goodbye	здрáвствуйте/до свидáния
how are you?	как поживáете?
nice to meet you	рад/рáда с вáми познакóмиться

Asking questions / Вопрóсы

do you speak English/Russian?	вы говори́те по-англи́йски/ по-ру́сски?
what's your name?	как вас зову́т?/как вáше и́мя?
where are you from?	откýда вы?
how much is it?	скóлько э́то стóит?
where is…?	где… ?
can I have…?	мóжно мне… ?
would you like…?	не хоти́те ли… ?

Phrasefinder

Statements about yourself	**Немно́го о себе́**
my name is…	меня́ зову́т… , моё и́мя…
I'm American/Russian	я америка́нец/америка́нка/ру́сский/ру́сская
I don't speak Russian/English	я не говорю́ по-ру́сски/по-англи́йски
I live near Chester/Moscow	я живу́ недалеко́ от Че́стера/Москвы́
I'm a student	я студе́нт/студе́нтка
I work in an office	я рабо́таю на фи́рме
Emergencies	**Э́кстренные слу́чаи**
can you help me, please?	не могли́ бы вы мне помо́чь?
I'm lost	я заблуди́лся/заблуди́лась
I'm ill	я бо́лен/больна́
call an ambulance	вы́зовите ско́рую по́мощь
Reading signs	**Чита́ем на́дписи**
no entry	нет вхо́да
no smoking	не кури́ть
fire exit	запа́сный вы́ход
for sale	продаётся

Going places / Тра́нспорт, пое́здки

On the road — На шоссе́

where's the nearest service station?	где ближа́йшая бензозапра́вочная ста́нция?/где ближа́йший автосе́рвис?
what's the best way to get there?	как быстре́е туда́ добра́ться?
I've got a puncture	у меня́ проко́л ши́ны
I'd like to hire a bike/car	я хоте́л/хоте́ла бы взять напрока́т велосипе́д/автомоби́ль
there's been an accident	произошла́ ава́рия/произошло́ ДТП
my car's broken down	у меня́ слома́лась маши́на
the car won't start	мото́р не заво́дится

By rail   Пóезд

where can I buy a ticket?	где я могý купи́ть биле́т?
what time is the next train to Orel/Oxford?	когда́ сле́дующий пóезд на Орёл/Óксфорд?
do I have to change?	нýжно ли мне де́лать переса́дку?
can I take my bike on the train?	меня́ пýстят в вагóн с велосипе́дом?
which platform for the train to Kiev/London?	с какóй платфóрмы идёт пóезд на Ки́ев/Лóндон?
there's a train to London at 10 o'clock	пóезд на Лóндон отправля́ется в 10 часóв
a single/return to Leeds/Zvenigorod, please	биле́т в оди́н конéц/биле́т туда́ и обра́тно до Ли́дса/Звени́города, пожа́луйста
I'd like an all-day ticket	мне нýжен биле́т на сýтки
I'd like to reserve a seat	я хоте́л/хоте́ла бы зарезерви́ровать ме́сто

At the airport   В аэропортý

when's the next flight to Vladivostok/Manchester?	когда́ сле́дующий рейс во Владивостóк/в Ма́нчестер?
where do I check in?	где регистра́ция пассажи́ров?
I'd like to confirm my flight	я хоте́л/хоте́ла бы подтверди́ть свой рейс
I'd like a window seat/an aisle seat	мне хоте́лось бы взять ме́сто у окна́/у прохóда
I want to change/cancel my reservation	я хочý измени́ть/отмени́ть зака́з биле́та

Getting there   Как проéхать?

could you tell me the way to the castle (on foot/by transport)?	не подска́жете мне, как пройти́/проéхать к за́мку?
how long will it take to get there?	дóлго ли туда́ добира́ться?
how far is it from here?	как далекó э́то отсю́да?
which bus do I take for the cathedral?	какóй автóбус идёт до собóра?
can you tell me where to get off?	вы ска́жете мне, где вы́йти?
what time is the last bus?	до какóго ча́са хóдит автóбус?
how do I get to the airport?	как мне проéхать до аэропóрта?
where's the nearest underground station, (AmE) subway station?	где ближа́йшая ста́нция метрó?
I'll take a taxi	я возьмý такси́
can you call me a taxi?	мóжете мне вы́звать такси́?

take the first turning on the right	поверни́те на пе́рвом поворо́те напра́во
turn left at the traffic lights/just past the church	поверни́те нале́во у светофо́ра/ сра́зу за це́рковью

Keeping in touch / Сре́дства свя́зи. Отноше́ния

On the phone	Говори́м по телефо́ну
may I use your phone?	мо́жно позвони́ть по ва́шему телефо́ну?
do you have a mobile, (AmE) cell phone?	у вас есть моби́льный телефо́н?
what is the code for St Petersburg/ Edinburgh?	како́й код (телефо́на) в Санкт-Петербу́рг/Эдинбу́рг?
I want to make a phone call	мне ну́жно сде́лать звоно́к
I'd like to reverse the charges, (AmE) call collect	мне ну́жно, что́бы звоно́к оплати́ла вызыва́емая сторона́
I need to top up my mobile, (AmE) cell phone	мне ну́жно доплати́ть за моби́льный телефо́н
the line's engaged, (AmE) busy	ли́ния заня́та
there's no answer	отве́та нет
hello, this is John/Igor	алло́, э́то Джон/И́горь
is Oleg/Richard there, please?	пожа́луйста, позови́те Оле́га/Ри́чарда
who's calling?	кто говори́т?
sorry, wrong number	извини́те, не туда́ попа́ли
just a moment, please	одну́ мину́тку, пожа́луйста
please hold the line	не ве́шайте тру́бку, пожа́луйста
please tell him/her I called	пожа́луйста, переда́йте ему́/ей, что я звони́л/звони́ла
I'd like to leave a message for him/her	я хоте́л/хоте́ла бы оста́вить сообще́ние для него́/неё
…I'll try again later	…я ещё поздне́е позвоню́
please tell him/her that Elena called	пожа́луйста, переда́йте ему́/ей, что звони́ла Еле́на
can he/she ring me back?	мо́жет он/она́ мне перезвони́ть?
my home number is…	мой дома́шний телефо́н…
my business number is…	мой рабо́чий телефо́н…
my mobile, (AmE) cell phone number is…	но́мер моего́ моби́льного…
we were cut off	нас прерва́ли

Writing   Пúшем письмó

what's your address?	ваш áдрес?
where is the nearest post office?	где ближáйшая пóчта?
could I have a stamp for Russia, please?	пожáлуйста, дáйте мне мáрку для письмá в Россúю
I'd like to send a parcel/a fax	я хотéл/хотéла бы послáть посы́лку/факс

Online   Онлáйн

are you on the Internet?	вы подключены́ к Интернéту?
what's your email address?	какóй ваш электрóнный áдрес?
we could send it by email	мы моглú бы послáть э́то по электрóнной пóчте
I'll email it to you on Tuesday	я пошлю́ это вам по электрóнной пóчте во втóрник
I looked it up on the Internet	я посмотрéл/посмотрéла э́то по Интернéту
the information is on their website	информáция есть на их веб-сáйте

Meeting up   Встрéчи

what shall we do this evening?	что мы бýдем дéлать сегóдня вéчером?
where shall we meet?	где мы встрéтимся?
I'll see you outside the cafe at 6 o'clock	я вас встрéчу у кафé в 6 часóв
see you later	до встрéчи
I can't today, I'm busy	сегóдня не могý, я зáнят/занятá

Phrasefinder

Food and drink / Еда́ и напи́тки

Reservations	Зака́з в рестора́не
can you recommend a good restaurant?	мо́жете ли порекомендова́ть хоро́ший рестора́н?
I'd like to reserve a table for four	я хоте́л/хоте́ла бы заказа́ть сто́лик на четверы́х
a reservation for tomorrow evening at eight o'clock	зака́з на за́втра на во́семь часо́в ве́чера

Ordering	Зака́з блюд
could we see the menu/wine list, please?	мо́жно нам меню́/ка́рту вин?
do you have a vegetarian/children's menu?	у вас есть вегетариа́нское/де́тское меню́?
as a starter… and to follow…	на заку́ску… и зате́м…
could we have some more bread/rice?	мо́жно ещё хле́ба/ри́са?
what would you recommend?	что вы порекоменду́ете?
I'd like a	я хоте́л/хоте́ла бы заказа́ть
…white coffee, (AmE) coffee with cream	…ко́фе с молоко́м
…black coffee	…чёрный ко́фе
…decaffeinated coffee	…ко́фе без кофеи́на
…liqueur	…ликёр
could I have the bill, (AmE) check	счёт, пожа́луйста

YOU WILL HEAR	Что вы слы́шите
вы гото́вы зака́зывать?	are you ready to order?
хоти́те заказа́ть аперити́в?	would you like an aperitif?
бу́дете зака́зывать заку́ску?	would you like a starter?
како́е блю́до бу́дете зака́зывать?	what will you have for the main course?
зака́зываете десе́рт?	would you like a dessert?
ко́фе?/ликёр?	would you like coffee/liqueurs?
что ещё зака́жете?	anything else?
прия́тного аппети́та!	enjoy your meal!
обслу́живание (не) включено́	service is (not) included

The menu   Меню́

starters	заку́ски		заку́ски	starters
hors d'oeuvres	заку́ски		заку́ски	hors d'oeuvres
omelette	омле́т		омле́т	omelette
soup	суп		суп	soup

fish	ры́ба		ры́ба	fish
bass	морско́й о́кунь		кальма́р	squid
cod	треска́		карп	carp
eel	у́горь		кефа́ль	mullet
hake	хек		креве́тки	prawns, shrimps
herring	се́льдь		лосо́сь	salmon
monkfish	морско́й чёрт		ми́дии	mussels
mullet	кефа́ль		морско́й о́кунь	bass
mussels	ми́дии		морско́й язы́к	sole
oyster	у́стрица		осетри́на	sturgeon
prawns	короле́вские креве́тки		па́лтус	turbot
salmon	лосо́сь, сёмга		сарди́ны	sardines
sardines	сарди́ны		се́льдь	herring
shrimps	креве́тки		сёмга	salmon
sole	морско́й язык		треска́	cod
squid	кальма́р		туне́ц	tuna
trout	форе́ль		хек	hake
tuna	туне́ц		у́горь	eel
turbot	па́лтус		у́стрица	oyster
			форе́ль	trout

meat	мя́со		мя́со	meat
beef	говя́дина		(молода́я) бара́нина	lamb
chicken	цыплёнок		бифште́кс	steak
chop	отбивна́я		ветчина́	ham
duck	у́тка		вы́резка	steak
goose	гусь		говя́дина	beef
hare	за́яц		гусь	goose
ham	ветчина́		колба́ски	sausages
kidneys	по́чки		олени́на	venison
lamb	(молода́я) бара́нина		отбивна́я	chop
liver	печёнка		печёнка	liver
pork	свини́на		по́чки	kidneys
rabbit	крольча́тина		свини́на	pork
sirloin	филе́		теля́тина	veal
steak	бифште́кс, вы́резка		у́тка	duck
turkey	инде́йка		филе́	sirloin steak
veal	теля́тина		цыплёнок	chicken
venison	олени́на			

Phrasefinder

vegetables	о́вощи
asparagus	спа́ржа
aubergine	баклажа́н
beans	бобы́; фасо́ль
beetroot	свёкла
broccoli	бро́кколи
carrots	морко́вь
cabbage	капу́ста
celery	сельдере́й
courgettes (BrE)	цуки́ни
French beans (BrE)	стручко́вая фасо́ль
lettuce	сала́т-лату́к
mushrooms	грибы́
peas	горо́шек
(sweet) pepper	сла́дкий пе́рец
potatoes	карто́фель
runner beans	вью́щаяся фасо́ль
tomato	помидо́р
sweet potato	сла́дкий карто́фель, бата́т
zucchini (AmE)	цуки́ни

о́вощи	vegetables
баклажа́н	aubergine
бобы́	beans
горо́шек	peas
грибы́	mushrooms
зелёный лук	spring onions
капу́ста	cabbage
карто́фель	potatoes
лук	onions
морко́вь	carrots
огуре́ц	cucumber
(сла́дкий) пе́рец	(sweet) pepper
помидо́р	tomato
реди́с	radish
свёкла	beetroot
сельдере́й	celery
спа́ржа	asparagus
фасо́ль	beans
цветна́я капу́ста	cauliflower

the way it's cooked	как э́то пригото́влено
baked	запечённый
boiled	отварно́й, варёный
fried	жа́реный
griddled	пригото́вленный на пло́ской сковороде́
grilled	(жа́реный) на гри́ле
poached	припу́щенный
pureed	пюре́, пюри́рованный
rare	с кро́вью (о мясе)
roast	жа́реный
stewed	тушёный
well done	хорошо́ прожа́ренный

как э́то пригото́влено	the way it's cooked
варёный	boiled
в горшо́чке	casseroled
жа́реный	(в духовке) roast; (на сковороде) fried
жа́реный на гри́ле	grilled
запечённый	baked
отварно́й	boiled
пригото́вленный на пло́ской сковороде́	griddled
припу́щенный	poached
с кро́вью (о мясе)	rare
тушёный	stewed
хорошо́ прожа́ренный	well done

desserts	**десе́рты**
ice cream	моро́женое
fruit	фру́кты
gateau	торт
pie	пиро́г

десе́рты	**desserts**
моро́женое	ice cream
пиро́г	pie
торт	gateau
фру́кты	fruit

other	**друго́е**
bread	хлеб
butter	сли́вочное ма́сло
cheese	сыр
cheeseboard	доска́/блю́до с сы́ром
garlic	чесно́к
mayonnaise	майоне́з
mustard	горчи́ца
olive oil	оли́вковое ма́сло
pepper	пе́рец
rice	рис
salt	соль
sauce	со́ус
seasoning	припра́ва
vinegar	у́ксус

друго́е	**other**
горчи́ца	mustard
майоне́з	mayonnaise
оли́вковое ма́сло	olive oil
пе́рец	pepper
припра́ва	seasoning
сли́вочное ма́сло	butter
соль	salt
со́ус	sauce
сыр	cheese
у́ксус	vinegar
хлеб	bread
хрен	horseradish
чесно́к	garlic

drinks	**напи́тки**
beer	пи́во
bottle	буты́лка
carbonated	газиро́ванный
fizzy	шипу́чий
half-bottle	полбуты́лки
liqueur	ликёр
mineral water	минера́льная вода́
red wine	кра́сное вино́
rosé	ро́зовое вино́
soft drink	безалкого́льный напи́ток
still	негазиро́ванный
house wine	дома́шнее вино́
table wine	столо́вое вино́
tap water	водопрово́дная вода́
white wine	бе́лое вино́
wine	вино́

напи́тки	**drinks**
безалкого́льный напи́ток	soft drink
бе́лое вино́	white wine
буты́лка	bottle
вино́	wine
водопрово́дная вода́	tap water
газиро́ванный	carbonated
дома́шнее вино́	house wine
кра́сное вино́	red wine
ликёр	liqueur
минера́льная вода́	mineral water
негазиро́ванный	still
пи́во	beer
полбуты́лки	half-bottle
ро́зовое вино́	rosé
столо́вое вино́	table wine
шипу́чий	fizzy

Phrasefinder

Places to stay / Где останови́ться

Camping / Ке́мпинг

can we pitch our tent here?	мы мо́жем здесь разби́ть пала́тку?
can we park our caravan here?	мо́жем здесь припаркова́ть наш карава́н?
what are the facilities like?	каки́е здесь усло́вия?
how much is it per night?	ско́лько здесь беру́т за су́тки?
where do we park the car?	где мо́жно припаркова́ть маши́ну?
we're looking for a campsite	мы и́щем ке́мпинг
this is a list of local campsites	вот спи́сок ме́стных ке́мпингов
we go on a camping holiday every year	мы ка́ждый год отдыха́ем в ке́мпинге

At the hotel / В гости́нице

I'd like a double/single room with bath	мне ну́жен двухме́стный/одноме́стный но́мер с ва́нной
we have a reservation in the name of Morris	мы зарезерви́ровали но́мер на фами́лию Мо́ррис
we'll be staying three nights, from Friday to Sunday	мы бу́дем здесь тро́е су́ток, с пя́тницы по воскресе́нье
how much does the room cost?	ско́лько сто́ит но́мер?
I'd like to see the room	я хоте́л/хоте́ла бы посмотре́ть но́мер
what time is breakfast?	когда́ здесь за́втрак?
can I leave this in your safe?	могу́ я э́то оста́вить в ва́шем се́йфе?
bed and breakfast	ночле́г и за́втрак
we'd like to stay another night	мы хоте́ли бы оста́ться ещё на су́тки
please call me at 7.30	пожа́луйста, позвони́те мне в 7.30
are there any messages for me?	есть ли мне сообще́ние?

Hostels / Молодёжные гости́ницы

could you tell me where the youth hostel is?	скажи́те мне, пожа́луйста, где молодёжная гости́ница?
what time does the hostel close?	когда́ молодёжную гости́ницу закрыва́ют?
I'll be staying in a hostel	я остановлю́сь в молодёжной гости́нице
the hostel we're staying in is great value	молодёжная гости́ница, где мы останови́лись, недорога́я и о́чень удо́бная

I know a really good hostel in Dublin	я зна́ю в Ду́блине весьма́ прили́чную молодёжную гости́ницу
I'd like to go backpacking in Australia	я хоте́л/хоте́ла бы попутеше́ствовать с рюкзако́м по Австра́лии

Rooms to rent — Жильё внаём

I'm looking for a room with a reasonable rent	я ищу́ ко́мнату за уме́ренную це́ну
I'd like to rent an apartment for a few weeks	я хоте́л/хоте́ла бы снять кварти́ру на не́сколько неде́ль
where do I find out about rooms to rent?	где мне узна́ть о ко́мнатах, кото́рые сдаю́тся?
what's the weekly rent?	ско́лько плати́ть за жильё в неде́лю?
I'm staying with friends at the moment	я сейча́с живу́ у друзе́й
I rent an apartment on the outskirts of town	я снима́ю кварти́ру на окра́ине го́рода
the room's fine—I'll take it	ко́мната мне подхо́дит—я сниму́ её
the deposit is one month's rent in advance	зада́ток вперёд в су́мме ме́сячной опла́ты

Shopping and money / Поку́пки и де́ньги

Banking — В ба́нке

I'd like to change some money	я хоте́л/хоте́ла бы поменя́ть де́ньги
I want to change some dollars into euros	я хочу́ поменя́ть до́ллары на е́вро
do you need identification?	вам ну́жно удостовере́ние ли́чности?
what's the exchange rate today?	како́й курс обме́на на сего́дня?
do you accept traveller's cheques, (AmE) traveler's checks?	вы принима́ете доро́жные че́ки?
I'd like to transfer some money from my account	я хоте́л/хоте́ла бы перевести́ не́которую су́мму с моего́ счёта
where is there an ATM/a cash machine?	где здесь банкома́т?
I'd like high denomination notes, (AmE) bills	мне нужны́ кру́пные купю́ры
I'm with another bank	у меня́ счёт в друго́м ба́нке

Finding the right shop | Ну́жный магази́н

where's the main shopping district?	где здесь торго́вый центр?
where can I buy batteries/postcards?	где я могу́ купи́ть батаре́йки/ откры́тки?
where's the nearest pharmacy/ bookshop?	где ближа́йшая апте́ка/ближа́йший кни́жный магази́н?
is there a good food shop around here?	есть здесь побли́зости хоро́ший продово́льственный магази́н?
what time do the shops open/close?	когда́ магази́ны открыва́ются/ закрыва́ются?
where did you get those?	где вы э́то купи́ли?
I'm looking for presents for my family	я ищу́ пода́рки для мои́х родны́х
we'll do our shopping on Saturday	мы пойдём по магази́нам в суббо́ту
I love shopping	я люблю́ ходи́ть по магази́нам

Are you being served? | Вас обслу́живают?

how much does that cost?	ско́лько э́то сто́ит?
can I try it on?	могу́ я э́то приме́рить?
could you wrap it for me, please?	заверни́те, пожа́луйста
can I pay by credit card?	я могу́ плати́ть креди́тной ка́ртой?
do you have this in another colour, (AmE) color?	есть у вас э́то друго́й расцве́тки?
could I have a bag, please?	бу́дьте добры́, да́йте мне паке́т
I'm just looking	я про́сто смотрю́
I'll think about it	я до́лжен/должна́ поду́мать
I'd like a receipt, please	мне нужна́ квита́нция/мне ну́жен чек
I need a bigger/smaller size	мне ну́жен бо́льший/ме́ньший разме́р
I take a size 10/a medium	ношу́ разме́р 10/сре́дний разме́р
it doesn't suit me	мне э́то не подхо́дит
I'm sorry, I don't have any change/ anything smaller	прости́те, у меня́ нет ме́лочи/ме́лких де́нег
that's all, thank you	э́то всё, спаси́бо

Changing things | Заме́на това́ра

I'd like to change it, please	я хоте́л/хоте́ла бы э́то поменя́ть
I bought this here yesterday	я купи́л/купи́ла э́то здесь вчера́
can I have a refund?	могу́ я рассчи́тывать на возмеще́ние?/мне верну́т де́ньги?
can you mend it for me?	мо́жете э́то испра́вить/почини́ть?
it doesn't work	э́то не рабо́тает
can I speak to the manager?	могу́ я поговори́ть с ме́неджером?

Sport and leisure / Спорт и досу́г

Keeping fit	Заня́тия спо́ртом
where can we play football/squash?	где мы мо́жем поигра́ть в футбо́л/сквош?
where is the local sports centre, (AmE) center?	где здесь ме́стный спорти́вный центр?
what's the charge per day?	ско́лько сто́ит день заня́тий?
is there a reduction for children/ a student discount?	есть ли ски́дка для дете́й/студе́нтов?
I'm looking for a swimming pool/ tennis court	я ищу́ бассе́йн/те́ннисный корт
you have to be a member	вы должны́ быть чле́ном (клу́ба)
I play tennis on Mondays	я игра́ю в те́ннис по понеде́льникам
I would like to go fishing/riding	я хоте́л/хоте́ла бы заня́ться ры́бной ло́влей/верхово́й ездо́й
I want to do aerobics	я хочу́ заня́ться аэро́бикой
I love swimming/roller skating	я люблю́ пла́вание/ката́ние на ро́ликовых конька́х
we want to hire skis/snowboards	мы хоте́ли бы взять напрока́т лы́жи/сноубо́рды

Watching sport	Спорти́вные зре́лища
is there a football match on Saturday?	есть футбо́льный матч в воскресе́нье?
which teams are playing?	каки́е кома́нды игра́ют?
where can I get tickets?	где я могу́ купи́ть биле́ты?
I'd like to see a rugby/football match	я хоте́л/хоте́ла бы попа́сть на ре́гби/футбо́л
my favourite, (AmE) favorite team is…	моя́ люби́мая кома́нда…
let's watch the game on TV	дава́йте посмо́трим игру́ по телеви́зору

Going out in the evening	В теа́тре, на конце́рте
what's on?	что идёт?
when does the box office open/close?	когда́ открыва́ется/закрыва́ется биле́тная ка́сса?
what time does the concert/ performance start?	когда́ нача́ло конце́рта/спекта́кля?
when does it finish?	когда́ конча́ется (спекта́кль)?
are there any seats left for tonight?	есть ли свобо́дные места́ на сего́дня?

how much are the tickets?	ско́лько сто́ят биле́ты?
where can I get a programme, (AmE) program?	где я могу́ купи́ть програ́мму?
I want to book tickets for tonight's performance	я хочу́ заказа́ть биле́ты на сего́дняшний конце́рт/спекта́кль
I'll book seats in the circle	я закажу́ биле́ты на балко́н
I'd rather have seats in the stalls	я бы хоте́л/хоте́ла купи́ть биле́ты на места́ в парте́ре
somewhere in the middle, but not too far back	где-нибу́дь в середи́не, но не о́чень далеко́
four, please	четы́ре биле́та, пожа́луйста
for Saturday	на суббо́ту
we'd like to go to a club	мы бы хоте́ли сходи́ть в ночно́й клуб
I go clubbing every weekend	я хожу́ в ночно́й клуб ка́ждый уи́к-э́нд

Hobbies Хо́бби

what do you do at the weekend?	что вы де́лаете по суббо́там и воскресе́ньям?
I like yoga/listening to music	мне нра́вится занима́ться йо́гой/ слу́шать му́зыку
I spend a lot of time surfing the Net	я мно́го вре́мени провожу́ в Интерне́те/я мно́го брожу́ по Интерне́ту
I read a lot	я мно́го чита́ю
I collect old coins	я собира́ю стари́нные моне́ты

Time / Вре́мя

Telling the time Ско́лько вре́мени?

what time is it?	ско́лько вре́мени?
it's 2 o'clock	два часа́
at about 8 o'clock	о́коло 8 (восьми́) часо́в
from 10 o'clock onwards	по́сле 10 (десяти́) часо́в
at 5 o'clock in the morning/afternoon	в 5 (пять) (часо́в) утра́/ве́чера
it's five past/quarter past/half past one	пять мину́т/че́тверть/полови́на второ́го
it's twenty-five to/quarter to one	без двадцати́ пяти́/че́тверти час
a quarter/three quarters of an hour	че́тверть часа́/со́рок пять мину́т

Days and dates — Дни и чи́сла

Sunday, Monday, Tuesday, Wednesday, Thursday, Friday, Saturday	воскресéнье, понедéльник, вто́рник, средá, четвéрг, пя́тница, суббóта
January, February, March, April, May, June, July, August, September, October, November, December	янва́рь, февра́ль, март, апрéль, май, ию́нь, ию́ль, а́вгуст, сентя́брь, октя́брь, ноя́брь, дека́брь
what's the date?	какóе сегóдня числó?
it's the second of June	сегóдня вторóе ию́ня
we meet up every Monday	мы ви́димся ка́ждый понедéльник
we're going away in August	мы уезжа́ем в а́вгусте
on November 8th	восьмóго ноября́

Public holidays and special days — Пра́здники, нерабóчие дни

bank holiday	нерабóчий день
bank holiday Monday	нерабóчий понедéльник
New Year's Day (1 Jan.)	Нóвый год (1-е января́)
Epiphany (6 Jan.)	Крещéние Госпóдне, Богоявлéние (19-е января́)
St Valentine's Day (14 Feb.)	День святóго Валенти́на (14-е февраля́)
Day of the Defender of the Fatherland	День защи́тника Отéчества (23-е февраля́)
Shrove Tuesday/Pancake Day	вто́рник на ма́сленой недéле
Ash Wednesday	пéрвый день Вели́кого постá
International Women's Day (8 March)	Восьмóе ма́рта, Междунарóдный жéнский день (8-е ма́рта)
Maundy Thursday	Вели́кий четвéрг (на Страстнóй недéле)
Good Friday	Страстна́я пя́тница
Easter	Па́сха
May Day (1 May)	Пéрвое ма́я (1-е ма́я)
VE Day (8 May)	День Побéды (9-е ма́я)
Whit Sunday, Pentecost (7th Sunday after Easter)	Трóица, Трóицын день
Russian Defenders' Memorial Day (marking the beginning of the Great Patriotic War (1941–45))	День па́мяти защи́тников Отéчества (22-е ию́ня)
Fourth of July/Independence Day (US)	День незави́симости
Assumption/Dormition of the Virgin Mary (15 Aug.)	Успéние Пресвятóй Богорóдицы (28-е а́вгуста)

Phrasefinder

Protecting Veil/Intercession of the Virgin Mary (*people pray for protection from evil and hardships and help in view of the long winter ahead*)	Покро́в Пресвято́й Богоро́дицы (*14-е октября́*)
Halloween (*31 Oct.*)	Ка́нун Дня Всех Святы́х
All Saints' Day (*1 Nov.*)	День Всех Святы́х
Guy Fawkes Day/Bonfire Night (*5 Nov., UK*)	день Га́я Фо́кса, день годовщи́ны раскры́тия «порохово́го за́говора»
National Unity Day	День наро́дного еди́нства (*4-е ноября́*)
Remembrance Sunday (*anniversary of the armistice of 11 November 1918*)	Помина́льное воскресе́нье
Thanksgiving (*4th Thursday in November, US*)	День благодаре́ния
Christmas Eve (*24 Dec.*)	Рожде́ственский соче́льник (*6-е января́*)
Christmas Day (*25 Dec.*)	Рождество́ Христо́во (*7-е января́*)
New Year's Eve (*31 Dec.*)	Нового́дняя ночь (*31-е декабря́*)

Weights and measures / Меры длины, веса, объёма

Length/Длина́

inches/дю́ймы	0.39	3.9	7.8	11.7	15.6	19.7	39
centimetres/сантиме́тры	1	10	20	30	40	50	100

Distance/Расстоя́ние

miles/ми́ли	0.62	6.2	12.4	18.6	24.9	31	62
kilometres/киломе́тры	1	10	20	30	40	50	100

Weight/Вес

pounds/фу́нты	2.2	22	44	66	88	110	220
kilos/килогра́ммы	1	10	20	30	40	50	100

Capacity/Объём

(UK) gallons/галло́ны	0.22	2.2	4.4	6.6	8.8	11	22
(US) gallons/галло́ны	0.26	2.64	5.28	7.92	10.56	13.2	26.4
litres/ли́тры	1	10	20	30	40	50	100

Temperature/Температу́ра

°C (Celsius)/ °C (по Це́льсию)	0	5	10	15	20	25	30	37	38	40
°F (Fahrenheit)/ °F (по Фаренге́йту)	32	41	50	59	68	77	86	98.4	100	104

Clothing and shoe sizes/Разме́ры оде́жды и о́буви

Women's clothing sizes/Же́нская оде́жда

UK	8	10	12	14	16	18
US	6	8	10	12	14	16
Russia	40	42	44	46	48	50

Men's clothing sizes (chest sizes)/Мужска́я оде́жда (костю́мы, пиджаки́)

UK/US	36	38	40	42	44	46
Russia	46	48	50	52	54	56

Women's shoes/Же́нская о́бувь

UK	2.5	3	3.5	4	4.5	5	5.5	6	6.5	7	7.5	8
US	5	5.5	6	6.5	7	7.5	8	8.5	9	9.5	10	10.5
Russia	35	35.5	36	37	37.5	38	39	39.5	40	40.5	41	42

Men's shoes/Мужска́я о́бувь

UK	6	6.5	7	7.5	8	8.5	9	9.5	10	10.5	11	11.5	12
US	6.5	7	7.5	8	8.5	9	9.5	10	10.5	11	11.5	12	12.5
Russia	39.5	40	40.5	41	42	42.5	43	44	44.5	45	46	46.5	47

Aa

A¹ /eɪ/ *letter*: **from ~ to Z** от нача́ла до конца́
■ **~ road** *n.* магистра́льная доро́га, (авто)магистра́ль
A² /eɪ/ *n.* **1** (mus.) ля (*nt. indecl.*) **2** (academic mark) «отли́чно», пятёрка

✍ **a** /ə, eɪ/, **an** /æn, ən/ *indefinite article* **1** (*not usu. translated*): **it's an elephant** э́то слон **2** (~ certain): **in ~ sense** в како́м-то смы́сле; **an old friend of mine** оди́н мой ста́рый знако́мый **3** (distributive, in each) в + *a.*; **twice ~ week** два ра́за в неде́лю; **10 miles an hour** де́сять миль в час; (for each) за + *a.*; **10p ~ pound** 10 пе́нсов за фунт; (from each) с + *g.*; **they charged £1 ~ head** они́ взя́ли по фу́нту с челове́ка

A & E *n.* (*abbr. of* **Accident and Emergency**) (BrE) отделе́ние неотло́жной по́мощи (*в больни́це*)

aback /ə'bæk/ *adv.*: **we were taken ~ by the news** но́вость нас порази́ла

abacus /'æbəkəs/ *n.* (*pl.* **~es**) счёт|ы (-ов)

✍ **abandon** /ə'bænd(ə)n/ *v.t.* **1** (forsake, desert) пок|ида́ть, -и́нуть; ост|авля́ть, -а́вить; **~ ship!** поки́нуть кора́бль! **2** (renounce) отка́з|ываться, -а́ться от + *g.*; **we must ~ the idea** мы должны́ отказа́ться от э́той иде́и; **they had ~ed all hope** они́ оста́вили вся́кую наде́жду **3** (discontinue) прекра|ща́ть, -ти́ть; **the search was ~ed** по́иски бы́ли прекращены́

abandoned /ə'bænd(ə)nd/ *adj.* оста́вленный, поки́нутый

abandonment /ə'bændənmənt/ *n.* **1** (desertion) оставле́ние **2** (of a belief, lawsuit, right) отка́з (of: от + *g.*) **3** (neglect) забро́шенность **4** (of a project) прекраще́ние **5**: **~ of a ship** оставле́ние (*or* ухо́д с) корабля́

abase /ə'beɪs/ *v.t.* ун|ижа́ть, -и́зить

abashed /ə'bæʃt/ *adj.* смущённый; **she felt ~** она́ была́ смущена́

abate /ə'beɪt/ *v.i.* (of storm, feelings, pain) ут|иха́ть, -и́хнуть; (of noise) ум|енша́ться, -е́ншиться

abattoir /'æbətwɑː(r)/ *n.* скотобо́йня

abbey /'æbɪ/ *n.* (*pl.* **~s**) абба́тство

abbot /'æbət/ *n.* абба́т

abbreviate /ə'briːvɪeɪt/ *v.t.* сокра|ща́ть, -ти́ть

abbreviation /əbriːvɪ'eɪʃ(ə)n/ *n.* сокраще́ние, аббревиату́ра

abdicate /'æbdɪkeɪt/ *v.t.* отка́з|ываться, -а́ться от + *g.*

abdication /æbdɪ'keɪʃ(ə)n/ *n.* отка́з (*от чего*); отрече́ние (от престо́ла)

abdomen /'æbdəmən/ *n.* брюшна́я по́лость; живо́т

abdominal /æb'dɒmɪn(ə)l/ *adj.* брюшно́й; **~ pain** боль в животе́; **~ wound** ране́ние в живо́т

abduct /əb'dʌkt/ *v.t.* пох|ища́ть, -и́тить

abduction /əb'dʌkʃ(ə)n/ *n.* похище́ние

aberration /æbə'reɪʃ(ə)n/ *n.* **1** (error of judgement or conduct) заблужде́ние; **mental ~** помраче́ние рассу́дка, психи́ческое расстро́йство **2** (deviation) отклоне́ние от но́рмы, аберра́ция

abeyance /ə'beɪəns/ *n.*: **in ~** приостано́вленный; **the matter is in ~** де́ло вре́менно приостано́влено

abhor /əb'hɔː(r)/ *v.t.* испы́т|ывать, -а́ть, отвраще́ние к + *d.*

abhorrent /əb'hɒrənt/ *adj.* омерзи́тельный, отврати́тельный; **the very idea is ~ to me** мне проти́вно да́же ду́мать об э́том

abide /ə'baɪd/ *v.i.*: **~ by** (comply with) соблю|да́ть, -сти́; приде́рживаться (*impf.*) + *g.*

abiding /ə'baɪdɪŋ/ *adj.* постоя́нный, неизме́нный

✍ **ability** /ə'bɪlɪtɪ/ *n.* **1** (capacity in general) спосо́бность; **to the best of one's ~** по ме́ре спосо́бностей **2** (*in pl.*) (gifts) спосо́бности (*f. pl.*)

abject /'æbdʒekt/ *adj.* (humble) уни́женный; **an ~ apology** уни́женная мольба́ о проще́нии; (craven): **~ fear** малоду́шный страх; (despicable) презре́нный; (pitiful, wretched) жа́лкий; **in ~ poverty** в кра́йней нищете́

ablaze /ə'bleɪz/ *pred. adj.*: **to be ~** пыла́ть, полыха́ть (*both impf.*); **the buildings were ~** зда́ния полыха́ли *or* пыла́ли в огне́

✍ **able** /'eɪb(ə)l/ *adj.* (**abler**, **ablest**) **1**: **be ~ to** мочь, с-; быть в состоя́нии; (have the strength or power to): **he was not ~ to walk any further** он был не в си́лах (*or* не в состоя́нии) идти́ да́льше; (know how to) уме́ть (*impf.*); **he is ~ to swim** он уме́ет пла́вать **2** (skilful) уме́лый; (capable) спосо́бный
■ **~-bodied** *adj.* здоро́вый, кре́пкий

ablution /ə'bluːʃ(ə)n/ *n.* (*usu. in pl.*) (act of washing oneself) (also iron.) омове́ние; **perform one's ~s** соверш|а́ть, -и́ть омове́ние

abnormal /æb'nɔːm(ə)l/ *adj.* ненорма́льный

abnormality /æbnɔː'mælɪtɪ/ *n.* ненорма́льность

aboard /ə'bɔːd/ *adv.* **1** (on a ship or aircraft) на борту́; (on a train) в по́езде **2** (on a ship or aircraft) на́ борт; (on a train) в по́езд
● *prep.*: **~ ship** на борту́ корабля́

abode /ə'bəʊd/ *n.* жили́ще; **of no fixed ~** без постоя́нного местожи́тельства

abolish /ə'bɒlɪʃ/ *v.t.* отмен|я́ть, -и́ть

abolition /æbə'lɪʃ(ə)n/ *n.* отме́на; **the ~ of capital punishment** отме́на сме́ртной ка́зни

a

abominable /əˈbɒmɪnəb(ə)l/ *adj.*
отврати́тельный, ме́рзкий

abomination /əbɒmɪˈneɪʃ(ə)n/ *n.* (detestation)
отвраще́ние, омерзе́ние; (detestable thing)
ме́рзость; **this hotel is an ~** э́та гости́ница —
ме́рзость

aboriginal /æbəˈrɪdʒɪn(ə)l/ *n.* = aborigine
• *adj.* тузе́мный, коренно́й

aborigine /æbəˈrɪdʒɪnɪ/ *n.* тузе́м|ец (-ка);
абориге́н; коренно́й жи́тель

abort /əˈbɔːt/ *v.t.* (fig., terminate or cancel
prematurely) приостан|а́вливать, -ови́ть

abortion /əˈbɔːʃ(ə)n/ *n.* (miscarriage) або́рт;
have an ~ де́лать, с- або́рт

abortive /əˈbɔːtɪv/ *adj.* (fig.) неуда́вшийся

abound /əˈbaʊnd/ *v.i.* (exist in large numbers or
quantities) быть в изоби́лии; изоби́ловать
(*impf.*)

⚔ **about** /əˈbaʊt/ *adv.* **1** (in the vicinity; in circulation)
вокру́г, круго́м; **is he anywhere ~?** он где́-то
здесь?; **up and ~** на нога́х **2** (almost) почти́;
it's ~ time we went нам пора́ идти́; **and
~ time too!** давно́ пора́! **3** (approximately)
о́коло + *g.*; приблизи́тельно; **~ 3 o'clock**
о́коло трёх часо́в; **he is ~ your height** он
приблизи́тельно ва́шего ро́ста; **in ~ half
an hour** приме́рно че́рез полчаса́ **4** (~ to)
(ready to, just going to): **he was ~ to leave when
I arrived** он собира́лся уходи́ть, когда́ я
пришёл
• *prep.* **1** (at or to var. places in) по + *d.*; **walk ~
the room** ходи́ть (*indet.*) по ко́мнате
2 (concerning) о + *p.*; насчёт + *g.*; относи́тельно
+ *g.*; **what are you talking ~?** о чём вы
говори́те?; **how ~ a game of cards?** не
сыгра́ть ли нам в ка́рты?; **he has called ~ the
rent** он зашёл насчёт квартпла́ты; **she is mad
~ him** она́ без ума́ от него́; **there is no doubt
~ it** в э́том нет сомне́ния
■ **~-face, ~-turn** *nn.* (mil.) поворо́т круго́м;
(fig.) ре́зкий поворо́т

⚔ **above** /əˈbʌv/ *prep.* **1** (over; higher than) над + *i.*
2 (more than) свы́ше + *g.*; **~ 30 tons** свы́ше
30 тонн **3** (fig.): **he is getting ~ himself** он
начина́ет зазнава́ться; **~ all** пре́жде всего́;
са́мое гла́вное; **over and ~** вдоба́вок к + *d.*
• *adv.* **1** (overhead; upstairs) наверху́; **we live
in the flat ~** мы живём в кварти́ре этажо́м
вы́ше; (expr. motion) наве́рх; **from ~** све́рху
2 (in text, speech, etc.) вы́ше; ра́нее
• *n.*: **the ~** вышеска́занное; вышеупомя́нутое
• *adj.* (~-mentioned) вышеупомя́нутый;
(foregoing) предыду́щий
■ **~-board** *adj.* (honourable) че́стный; (open,
frank) откры́тый; **~-mentioned** *adj.*
вышеупомя́нутый

abracadabra /æbrəkəˈdæbrə/ *n.* абракада́бра

abrasion /əˈbreɪʒ(ə)n/ *n.* сса́дина

abrasive /əˈbreɪsɪv/ *adj.* абрази́вный; (fig.)
ре́зкий, колю́чий

abreast /əˈbrest/ *adv.* в ряд, на одно́й ли́нии;
three ~ по́ трое/три в ряд; (fig.): **~ of events**
в ку́рсе собы́тий

⚔ ключева́я ле́ксика

abridge /əˈbrɪdʒ/ *v.t.* сокра|ща́ть, -ти́ть

⚔ **abroad** /əˈbrɔːd/ *adv.* за грани́цей, за
рубежо́м; (motion) за грани́цу, за рубе́ж; **from
~** из-за грани́цы, из-за рубежа́

abrupt /əˈbrʌpt/ *adj.* **1** (brusque) ре́зкий
2 (sudden) внеза́пный

abscess /ˈæbsɪs/ *n.* абсце́сс

abscond /əbˈskɒnd/ *v.i.* скр|ыва́ться, -ы́ться;
he ~ed with the takings он скры́лся с
вы́ручкой

abseil /ˈæbseɪl/ (BrE) *n.* спуск на верёвке
• *v.i.* спус|ка́ться, -ти́ться на верёвке

⚔ **absence** /ˈæbs(ə)ns/ *n.* отсу́тствие; **in his ~** в
его́ отсу́тствие

absent /ˈæbs(ə)nt/ *adj.* отсу́тствующий; **he
was ~ from school** он отсу́тствовал в шко́ле
■ **~-minded** *adj.* рассе́янный

absentee /æbsənˈtiː/ *n.* отсу́тствующий

absenteeism /æbsənˈtiːɪz(ə)m/ *n.* (from work,
school) (системати́ческие) прогу́лы (*m. pl.*);
(from voting) абсентеи́зм

absolute /ˈæbsəluːt/ *adj.* соверше́нный;
абсолю́тный

⚔ **absolutely** /ˈæbsəluːtlɪ/ *adv.* (completely)
абсолю́тно; соверше́нно; (unquestionably)
безусло́вно

absolutism /ˈæbsəluːtɪz(ə)m/ *n.* абсолюти́зм

absolve /əbˈzɒlv/ *v.t.* (of blame) призн|ава́ть,
-а́ть невино́вным; **he was ~d of all blame**
он был при́знан по́лностью невино́вным;
(of sins) отпус|ка́ть, -ти́ть грехи́ + *d.*; **his sins
were ~d** он получи́л отпуще́ние грехо́в;
(of obligation) освобо|жда́ть, -ди́ть

absorb /əbˈzɔːb/ *v.t.* **1** (soak up) впи́т|ывать,
-а́ть **2** (engross) погло|ща́ть, -ти́ть

absorbent /əbˈzɔːbənt/ *adj.* вса́сывающий,
поглоща́ющий

absorption /əbˈzɔːpʃ(ə)n/ *n.* (engrossment):
his ~ in his studies его́ погружённость в
заня́тия

abstain /əbˈsteɪn/ *v.i.* возде́рж|иваться,
-а́ться; **he ~ed (from drinking) on principle** он
возде́рживался (от спиртно́го) из при́нципа;
the Opposition decided to ~ (from voting)
оппози́ция реши́ла воздержа́ться (от
голосова́ния)

abstainer /əbˈsteɪnə(r)/ *n.* (from drinking)
тре́звенник, непью́щий; (from voting)
воздержа́вшийся

abstemious /æbˈstiːmɪəs/ *adj.* возде́ржанный

abstention /əbˈstenʃ(ə)n/ *n.* воздержа́ние
(from: от + *g.*); **the resolution was passed
with three ~s** резолю́ция была́ при́нята при
трёх воздержа́вшихся

abstinence /ˈæbstɪnəns/ *n.* воздержа́ние
(from: от + *g.*); (moderation) уме́ренность

abstract /ˈæbstrækt/ *n.*: **in the ~** абстра́ктно,
отвлечённо
• *adj.* абстра́ктный, отвлечённый; **~ art**
абстра́ктное иску́сство

absurd /əbˈsɜːd/ *adj.* неле́пый, абсу́рдный

absurdity /əbˈsɜːdɪtɪ/ *n.* неле́пость, абсу́рд,
абсу́рдность; **reduce to ~** дов|оди́ть, -ести́

до абсу́рда
abundance /əˈbʌnd(ə)ns/ *n.* (plenty) изоби́лие
abundant /əˈbʌnd(ə)nt/ *adj.* (plentiful)
оби́льный; ~ **in** бога́тый, изоби́лующий (*чем*)
✧ **abuse¹** /əˈbjuːs/ *n.* **1** (misuse) злоупотребле́ние;
drug ~ злоупотребле́ние нарко́тиками;
sexual ~ сексуа́льное наси́лие; **child** ~ (sexual)
совраще́ние малоле́тних; (physical) жесто́кое
обраще́ние с детьми́; **human rights** ~
наруше́ние прав челове́ка **2** (reviling) брань;
издева́тельство; **term of** ~ оскорбле́ние
abuse² /əˈbjuːz/ *v.t.* **1** (misuse) злоупотреб|ля́ть,
-и́ть + *i.* **2** (revile) руга́ть (*impf.*); оскорб|ля́ть,
-и́ть
abusive /əˈbjuːsɪv/ *adj.* бра́нный, руга́тельный
abut /əˈbʌt/ *v.i.* (**abutted, abutting**):
~ **on** (border on) прилега́ть (*impf.*) к + *d.*;
примыка́ть (*impf.*) к + *d.*; (lean against)
уп|ира́ться, -ере́ться в + *a.*
abysmal /əˈbɪzm(ə)l/ *adj.* ужа́сный
abyss /əˈbɪs/ *n.* бе́здна, про́пасть
AC *abbr.* (*of* **alternating current**)
переме́нный ток
a/c /əˈkaʊnt/ *n.* (*abbr. of* **account**) счёт
✧ **academic** /ækəˈdemɪk/ *n.* учёный, нау́чный
рабо́тник
● *adj.* академи́ческий, нау́чный; (unpractical)
академи́чный; теорети́ческий; нереа́льный
academician /əkædəˈmɪʃ(ə)n/ *n.* акаде́мик
academy /əˈkædəmɪ/ *n.* акаде́мия; (police,
military, etc.) учи́лище
accede /ækˈsiːd/ *v.i.* **1** (agree, assent)
согла|ша́ться, -си́ться (to: с + *i.*) **2**: ~ **to**
(grant): ~ **to a request** удовлетвор|я́ть, -и́ть
про́сьбу; (take up, enter upon) вступ|а́ть, -и́ть
в + *a.*; ~ **to the throne** всходи́ть, взойти́ на
престо́л
accelerate /əkˈseləreɪt/ *v.t. & i.* уск|оря́ть(ся),
-о́рить(ся); (motoring) наб|ира́ть, -ра́ть
ско́рость
acceleration /əkseləˈreɪʃ(ə)n/ *n.* ускоре́ние
accelerator /əkˈseləreɪtə(r)/ *n.* **1** (of car) педа́ль
га́за; акселера́тор **2** (tech.) ускори́тель (*m.*)
accent /ˈæks(ə)nt/ *n.* **1** (orthographical sign;
emphasis) ударе́ние; акце́нт **2** (mode of speech)
акце́нт; **he speaks with a slight** ~ он говори́т
с лёгким акце́нтом
accentuate /əkˈsentʃʊeɪt/ *v.t.* (fig.)
акценти́ровать (*impf.*); подч|ёркивать,
-еркну́ть
✧ **accept** /əkˈsept/ *v.t.* **1** (agree to receive)
прин|има́ть, -я́ть **2** (recognize, admit)
призн|ава́ть, -а́ть; **you must** ~ **this fact** вы
должны́ смири́ться с э́тим фа́ктом
acceptable /əkˈseptəb(ə)l/ *adj.* прие́млемый
acceptance /əkˈsept(ə)ns/ *n.* (willing receipt)
приня́тие; (approval) одобре́ние
✧ **access** /ˈækses/ *n.* (to person or thing) до́ступ
(к + *d.*)
● *v.t.* (comput.): ~ **data** получа́ть, -и́ть до́ступ
к да́нным
■ ~ **road** *n.* подъездно́й путь
accessible /əkˈsesɪb(ə)l/ *adj.* досту́пный

accession /əkˈseʃ(ə)n/ *n.* вступле́ние
accessory /əkˈsesərɪ/ *n.* **1** (law) соуча́стник
2 (*in pl.*) (ancillary parts) принадле́жности
(*f. pl.*); (of clothing) аксессуа́ры (*m. pl.*)
✧ **accident** /ˈæksɪd(ə)nt/ *n.* **1** (chance) слу́чай,
случа́йность; **by** ~ случа́йно **2** (unintentional
action): **I'm sorry, it was an** ~ прости́те,
я неча́янно **3** (mishap) несча́стный
слу́чай; (rail.) круше́ние, ава́рия; **car** ~
автомоби́льная катастро́фа, автокатастро́фа,
ава́рия; **he had an** ~ он попа́л в ава́рию
accidental /æksɪˈdent(ə)l/ *adj.* **1** (chance)
случа́йный; ~ **death** смерть в результа́те
несча́стного слу́чая **2** (incidental) побо́чный
acclaim /əˈkleɪm/ *n.* (public recognition) призна́ние
acclamation /ækləˈmeɪʃ(ə)n/ *n.* (public
recognition) призна́ние; (loud approval) шу́мное
одобре́ние; (enthusiasm) энтузиа́зм; (*in pl.*)
(shouts of welcome or applause) приве́тственные
во́згласы (*m. pl.*); **his books won the** ~ **of
critics** его́ кни́ги вы́звали шу́мное одобре́ние
кри́тиков
acclimate /əˈklaɪmət/ *v.t. & i.* (AmE) = acclimatize
acclimatize /əˈklaɪmətaɪz/ *v.t. & i.*
акклиматизи́ровать(ся) (*impf., pf.*)
accolade /ˈækəleɪd/ *n.* (praise) похвала́;
(reward) награ́да
accommodat|e /əˈkɒmədeɪt/ *v.t.* **1** (house)
разме|ща́ть, -сти́ть; (single person) поме|ща́ть,
-сти́ть; предост|авля́ть, -а́вить жильё + *d.*
2 (hold, seat) вме|ща́ть, -сти́ть; **the car will** ~**e
6 persons** маши́на вмеща́ет шесть челове́к; **a
hall** ~**ing 500** зал на пятьсо́т челове́к
accommodating /əˈkɒmədeɪtɪŋ/ *adj.*
сгово́рчивый, услу́жливый
accommodation /əkɒməˈdeɪʃ(ə)n/ *n.*
жильё; **can you provide a night's** ~? мо́жно
останови́ться у вас на́ ночь?
accompaniment /əˈkʌmpənɪmənt/ *n.*
1 (accompanying) сопровожде́ние **2** (mus.)
аккомпанеме́нт
accompanist /əˈkʌmpənɪst/ *n.* (mus.)
аккомпаниа́тор
✧ **accompany** /əˈkʌmpənɪ/ *v.t.* **1** (go or
be with) сопровожда́ть (*impf.*) **2** (occur
with) сопровожда́ть (*impf.*) **3** (mus.)
аккомпани́ровать (*impf.*) + *d.*
accomplice /əˈkʌmplɪs/ *n.* соуча́стни|к (-ца);
соо́бщни|к (-ца)
accomplish /əˈkʌmplɪʃ/ *v.t.* (complete)
заверш|а́ть, -и́ть; (fulfil, perform) выполн|я́ть,
вы́полнить; сов|ерш|а́ть, -и́ть
accomplished /əˈkʌmplɪʃt/ *adj.*
соверше́нный, иску́сный
accomplishment /əˈkʌmplɪʃmənt/ *n.*
заверше́ние; выполне́ние; (achievement)
достиже́ние
accord /əˈkɔːd/ *n.* **1** (agreement) согла́сие,
соглаше́ние; **with one** ~ единоду́шно
2 (volition) of one's own ~ по со́бственному
жела́нию, по со́бственной во́ле
accordance /əˈkɔːd(ə)ns/ *n.* соотве́тствие; **in**
~ **with** в соотве́тствии с + *i.*, согла́сно + *d.*

a

according /əˈkɔːdɪŋ/ adv.: ~ **to** (in keeping or conformity with) согла́сно + d.; ~ **to the law(s)** в соотве́тствии с законода́тельством; по зако́ну; (on the authority or information of) по + d., согла́сно + d.; по мне́нию/слова́м/ сообще́нию + g.

accordingly /əˈkɔːdɪŋlɪ/ adv. **1** (appropriately) соотве́тственно **2** (therefore) поэ́тому; таки́м о́бразом

accordion /əˈkɔːdɪən/ n. аккордео́н

accost /əˈkɒst/ v.t. прист┃ава́ть, -а́ть к + d. (с разгово́рами)

✓ **account** /əˈkaʊnt/ n. **1** (comm.) счёт (-á); **current** ~ теку́щий счёт; **deposit** ~ депози́тный счёт; **joint** ~ о́бщий счёт; **do the** ~**s** пров┃оди́ть, -ести́ счета́; **balance** ~**s** св┃оди́ть, -ести́ бала́нс **2** (statement, report) отчёт; (description) описа́ние; **by all** ~**s** су́дя по всему́ **3** (estimation, consideration) расчёт; **take into** ~, **take** ~ **of** уч┃и́тывать, -е́сть; прин┃има́ть, -я́ть во внима́ние **4** (reason, cause): **on** ~ **of** (because of) из-за + g.; (in consequence of) по причи́не + g.; (as a result of) всле́дствие + g.; **on no** ~ ни в ко́ем слу́чае

● v.i.: ~ **for** (lit., fig., give a reckoning of) отчи́т┃ываться, -а́ться в + p.; да┃ва́ть, -а́ть отчёт в + p.; (fig., answer for) отв┃еча́ть, -е́тить за + a.; **is everyone** ~**ed for?** никого́ не забы́ли?; (explain) объясн┃я́ть, -и́ть; (be reason for) явля́ться (impf.) + g.

accountable /əˈkaʊntəb(ə)l/ adj. отве́тственный; **he is** ~ **to me** он отчи́тывается пе́редо мной

accountancy /əˈkaʊnt(ə)nsɪ/ n. (profession) бухга́лтерское де́ло

accountant /əˈkaʊnt(ə)nt/ n. бухга́лтер, счетово́д

accounting /əˈkaʊntɪŋ/ n. бухгалте́рия, счетово́дство

accrue /əˈkruː/ v.i. (**accrues, accrued, accruing**) **1** (accumulate) нараст┃а́ть, -и́; ~**d interest** наро́сшие проце́нты (m. pl.) **2** (come about): **certain advantages will** ~ **from this** э́то даст определённые преиму́щества **3**: ~ **to** (fall to the lot of) дост┃ава́ться, -а́ться + d.

accumulate /əˈkjuːmjʊleɪt/ v.t. нак┃а́пливать, -опи́ть; соб┃ира́ть, -ра́ть

● v.i. нак┃а́пливаться, -опи́ться; ск┃а́пливаться, -опи́ться

accumulation /əkjuːmjʊˈleɪʃ(ə)n/ n. накопле́ние

accuracy /ˈækjʊrəsɪ/ n. то́чность; (of aim or shot) ме́ткость

accurate /ˈækjʊrət/ adj. (of persons, statements, instruments, etc.) то́чный; (of aim or shot) ме́ткий

accusation /ækjuːˈzeɪʃ(ə)n/ n. обвине́ние

accusative /əˈkjuːzətɪv/ adj. & n. вини́тельный (паде́ж)

✓ **accuse** /əˈkjuːz/ v.t. обвин┃я́ть, -и́ть; **he was** ~**d of stealing** его́ обвини́ли в кра́же

accused /əˈkjuːzd/ n.: **the** ~ обвиня́емый, подсуди́мый

accuser /əˈkjuːzə(r)/ n. обвини́тель (m.)

accustom /əˈkʌstəm/ v.t. приуч┃а́ть, -и́ть (**to:** к + d.); **become** ~**ed** прив┃ыка́ть, -ы́кнуть (**to:** к + d.)

accustomed /əˈkʌstəmd/ adj. (usual) обы́чный, привы́чный

ace /eɪs/ n. туз

acerbic /əˈsɜːbɪk/ adj. (astringent) те́рпкий; (of speech, manner, etc.) язви́тельный

acetate /ˈæsɪteɪt/ n. ацета́т; уксуснокѝслая соль

ache /eɪk/ n. боль

● v.i. боле́ть (impf.); ныть (impf.); **my head** ~**s** у меня́ боли́т голова́

achievable /əˈtʃiːvəb(ə)l/ adj. достижи́мый

✓ **achieve** /əˈtʃiːv/ v.t. **1** (attain) дост┃ига́ть, -и́чь + g.; доб┃ива́ться, -и́ться + g. **2** (carry out) выполня́ть, вы́полнить

✓ **achievement** /əˈtʃiːvmənt/ n. (attainment) достиже́ние; (carrying out) выполне́ние; (success) достиже́ние, завоева́ние

acid /ˈæsɪd/ n. кислота́

● adj. ки́слый

■ ~ **rain** n. кисло́тный дождь; ~ **test** n. (fig.) про́бный ка́мень

acidic /əˈsɪdɪk/ adj. ки́слый

acidity /əˈsɪdɪtɪ/ n. кисло́тность

✓ **acknowledge** /əkˈnɒlɪdʒ/ v.t. **1** (recognize; admit) призн┃ава́ть, -а́ть **2** (confirm receipt of; reply to): ~ **a letter** подтвер┃жда́ть, -ди́ть получе́ние письма́ **3** (indicate recognition of): **he did not even** ~ **me as we passed** он прошёл ми́мо и да́же не поздоро́вался

acknowledgement, acknowledgment /əkˈnɒlɪdʒmənt/ n. **1** (recognition, admission) призна́ние **2** (confirmation) подтвержде́ние

acme /ˈækmɪ/ n. верх, верши́на

acne /ˈæknɪ/ n. угри́ (m. pl.)

acorn /ˈeɪkɔːn/ n. жёлудь (m.)

acoustic /əˈkuːstɪk/ adj. акусти́ческий; звуково́й; **an** ~ **guitar** класси́ческая гита́ра

acoustics /əˈkuːstɪks/ n. (science; acoustic properties) аку́стика

acquaint /əˈkweɪnt/ v.t. знако́мить, по-; **I** ~**ed him with the facts** я ознако́мил его́ с фа́ктами; **he soon got** ~**ed with the situation** он бы́стро ознако́мился с положе́нием дел; **be** ~**ed with sb** быть знако́мым с кем-н.

acquaintance /əˈkweɪnt(ə)ns/ n. знако́мство; **make the** ~ **of** знако́миться, по- с + i.; (person) знако́мый; **an** ~ **of mine** оди́н мой знако́мый

acquiescence /ækwɪˈes(ə)ns/ n. (agreement) согла́сие; (tractability) усту́пчивость

acquiescent /ækwɪˈes(ə)nt/ adj. усту́пчивый

✓ **acquire** /əˈkwaɪə(r)/ v.t. приобре┃та́ть, -сти́; **asparagus is an** ~**d taste** к спа́рже на́до привы́кнуть

acquisition /ækwɪˈzɪʃ(ə)n/ n. приобрете́ние; **the library's new** ~**s** но́вые библиоте́чные поступле́ния

acquisitive /əˈkwɪzɪtɪv/ adj. стяжа́тельский; жа́дный

acquisitiveness /əˈkwɪzɪtɪvnɪs/ n. стяжа́тельство; жа́дность

✓ ключева́я ле́ксика

acquit /ə'kwɪt/ *v.t.* (**acquitted, acquitting**) (declare not guilty) опра́вд|ывать, -а́ть; **he was ~ted of murder** с него́ сня́ли обвине́ние в уби́йстве

acquittal /ə'kwɪt(ə)l/ *n.* (in court of law) оправда́ние

acre /'eɪkə(r)/ *n.* акр

acreage /'eɪkərɪdʒ/ *n.* пло́щадь земли́ в а́крах

acrid /'ækrɪd/ *adj.* е́дкий

acrimonious /ækrɪ'məʊnɪəs/ *adj.* ожесточённый, го́рький

acrobat /'ækrəbæt/ *n.* акроба́т

acrobatic /ækrə'bætɪk/ *adj.* акробати́ческий

acrobatics /ækrə'bætɪks/ *n.* акроба́тика

⚡ **across** /ə'krɒs/ *adv.* **1** (crosswise) поперёк; (in crosswords) по горизонта́ли **2** (on the other side) на той стороне́ **3** (to the other side) на ту сто́рону **4** (in width): **the river here is more than six miles ~** ширина́ реки́ здесь бо́льше шести́ миль
• *prep.* **1** (from one side of to the other) че́рез + *a.* (*sometimes omitted with vv. compounded with* пере...); **he went ~ the street** он перешёл у́лицу **2** (over the surface of) по + *d.*; **he hit me ~ the face** он уда́рил меня́ по лицу́ **3** (athwart) поперёк + *g.*; **she lay ~ the bed** она́ лежа́ла поперёк крова́ти **4** (on the other side of) на той стороне́ + *g.*, по ту сто́рону + *g.*

acrylic /ə'krɪlɪk/ *n.* акри́л
• *adj.* акри́ловый

⚡ **act** /ækt/ *n.* **1** (action) посту́пок; (feat) по́двиг; **catch in the ~** пойма́ть (*pf.*) на ме́сте преступле́ния; **an ~ of kindness** до́брое де́ло **2** (law) акт, зако́н **3** (of drama) де́йствие **4** (performance) но́мер; (fig., infml): **put on an ~** притвор|я́ться, -и́ться
• *v.t.* игра́ть (*impf.*); **~ a part** (lit., fig.) игра́ть роль; **~ the fool** валя́ть (*impf.*) дурака́
• *v.i.* **1** (behave) поступ|а́ть, -и́ть; вести́ (*det.*) себя́; (take action, intervene) прин|има́ть, -я́ть ме́ры **2** (serve, function) де́йствовать (*impf.*); **~ for sb** де́йствовать от и́мени кого́-л.; **he is ~ing as interpreter** он выступа́ет в ро́ли перево́дчика **3** (have effect) де́йствовать, по- (**on:** на + *a.*) **4** (theatr.) игра́ть
□ **~ out** *v.t.* разы́гр|ывать, -а́ть
□ **~ up** *v.i.* (infml, misbehave) шали́ть (*impf.*); (give trouble): **my car has been ~ing up** моя́ маши́на барахли́т

acting /'æktɪŋ/ *n.* (theatr.) игра́; (as skill) актёрское мастерство́
• *adj.* (doing duty temporarily): **~ manager** исполня́ющий обя́занности (*or* и. о.) заве́дующего

⚡ **action** /'ækʃ(ə)n/ *n.* **1** (acting; activity; effect) де́йствие; **in ~** в де́йствии; **come into ~** вступ|а́ть, -и́ть в де́йствие; **put out of ~** выводи́ть, вы́вести из стро́я; **out of ~** него́дный к употребле́нию; **take ~** прин|има́ть, -я́ть ме́ры **2** (deed) посту́пок; **~s speak louder than words** дела́ говоря́т са́ми за себя́ **3** (physical movement) движе́ние **4** (theatr.): **the ~ takes place in London** де́йствие происхо́дит в Ло́ндоне **5** (law)

иск, суде́бное де́ло; **bring an ~ against** предъяв|ля́ть, -и́ть иск к + *d.* **6** (mil.) бой, де́йствие; **killed in ~** па́вший, поги́бший в бою́

activate /'æktɪveɪt/ *v.t.* (make operative) прив|оди́ть, -ести́ в де́йствие; активизи́ровать (*impf., pf.*)

⚡ **active** /'æktɪv/ *adj.* **1** (lively; energetic; displaying activity) акти́вный, де́ятельный; **an ~ volcano** де́йствующий вулка́н **2** (gram.) действи́тельный **3** (mil.): **on ~ service** на действи́тельной слу́жбе

activism /'æktɪvɪz(ə)m/ *n.* полити́ческая акти́вность

⚡ **activist** /'æktɪvɪst/ *n.* активи́ст (-ка)

⚡ **activity** /æk'tɪvɪtɪ/ *n.* **1** (being active; exertion of energy) акти́вность **2** (*usu. in pl.*) (pursuit, sphere of action; doings) де́ятельность

⚡ **actor** /'æktə(r)/ *n.* актёр

actress /'æktrɪs/ *n.* актри́са

⚡ **actual** /'æktʃʊəl/ *adj.* (real) действи́тельный; факти́ческий; **in ~ fact** в действи́тельности; **those were his ~ words** э́то его́ по́длинные слова́

⚡ **actually** /'æktʃʊəlɪ/ *adv.* (really; in fact) действи́тельно; на (са́мом) де́ле; (in sense 'to tell the truth') со́бственно (говоря́)

actuary /'æktʃʊərɪ/ *n.* актуа́рий (*сотру́дник компа́нии, производя́щий страховы́е расчёты на осно́ве статисти́ческого ана́лиза*)

acumen /'ækjʊmən/ *n.* (judgement) сообрази́тельность; (penetration) проница́тельность; **business ~** делова́я хва́тка

acupuncture /'ækjuː.pʌŋktʃə(r)/ *n.* акупункту́ра, иглоука́лывание

acupuncturist /'ækjuː.pʌŋktʃərɪst/ *n.* иглотерапе́вт

acute /ə'kjuːt/ *adj.* (**acuter, acutest**) (in var. senses) о́стрый; **~ shortage** о́страя нехва́тка; **~ sense of smell** то́нкое обоня́ние
■ **~ accent** *n.* (ling.) аку́т; **~ angle** *n.* о́стрый у́гол

AD *abbr.* (*of* **Anno Domini**) н. э. (на́шей э́ры)

⚡ **ad** /æd/ *n.* (infml) = **advertisement**

adage /'ædɪdʒ/ *n.* погово́рка, посло́вица; наро́дная му́дрость; **as the old ~ goes: money talks** как гласи́т дре́вняя му́дрость: де́ньги реша́ют всё

adagio /ə'dɑːdʒɪəʊ/ *n., adj. & adv.* (*pl.* **~s**) (mus.) ада́жио (*nt. indecl.*)

adamant /'ædəmənt/ *adj.* (fig.) непрекло́нный

adapt /ə'dæpt/ *v.t.* **1** приспос|а́бливать, -о́бить **2** (text, book) адапти́ровать (*impf., pf.*); **~ for the stage** инсцени́ровать (*impf., pf.*)
• *v.i.* приспос|а́бливаться, -о́биться; адапти́роваться (*impf., pf.*)

adaptable /ə'dæptəb(ə)l/ *adj.* приспособля́емый; (of person) легко́ приспособля́ющийся

adaptation /ædæp'teɪʃ(ə)n/ *n.* приспособле́ние; (of book etc.) адапта́ция; (for stage) инсцениро́вка

a

adapter, adaptor /ə'dæptə(r)/ n. (tech.)
адаптер

⚡ **add** /æd/ v.t. **1** (make an addition of) прибавля́ть,
-а́вить; **you must ~ water** на́до доба́вить
воды́; **~ed to this is the fact that …** к э́тому
ну́жно приба́вить/доба́вить тот факт, что…
2 (say in addition) добавля́ть, -а́вить; **I have
nothing to ~** мне не́чего доба́вить **3** (math.)
скла́дывать, сложи́ть; **~ two and/to three!**
сложи́те два и три!
• v.i. **1**: **~ to** (increase, enlarge) увели́чи|вать,
-ть; уси́ли|вать, -ть; (knowledge etc.) углуб|ля́ть,
-и́ть **2** (perform addition) see ▶ add up
□ **~ on** v.t. прибавля́ть, -а́вить; доб|авля́ть,
-а́вить; **the tip was ~ed on to the bill** чаевы́е
бы́ли включены́ в счёт
□ **~ together** v.t. скла́дывать, сложи́ть
□ **~ up** v.t. (find sum of) подсчи́т|ывать, -ита́ть;
подыто́жи|вать, -ть
• v.i. (perform addition): **you can't ~ up!** вы не
уме́ете счита́ть!; (total): **it ~s up to 50** э́то в
су́мме составля́ет 50
■ **~-ons** n. pl. (comput.) дополни́тельный
встро́енный/встра́иваемый мо́дуль

addend|um /ə'dendəm/ n. (pl. **~a**)
приложе́ние, дополне́ние

adder /'ædə(r)/ n. (snake) гадю́ка

addict[1] /'ædɪkt/ n. (in full **drug ~**) наркома́н
(-ка)

addict[2] /ə'dɪkt/ v.t.: **be, become ~ed to**
пристрасти́ться (pf.) к + d.

addiction /ə'dɪkʃ(ə)n/ n. пристра́стие
(**to**: к + d.); **~ to drugs** наркома́ния

addictive /ə'dɪktɪv/ adj. вызыва́ющий
привыка́ние

⚡ **addition** /ə'dɪʃ(ə)n/ n. **1** (act of adding; thing
added) прибавле́ние; добавле́ние; **in ~ to** в
дополне́ние к + d.; **in ~** (as well) вдоба́вок;
(moreover) к тому́ же **2** (math.) сложе́ние

⚡ **additional** /ə'dɪʃən(ə)l/ adj. доба́вочный,
дополни́тельный

additive /'ædɪtɪv/ n. доба́вка, добавле́ние

⚡ **address** /ə'dres/ n. а́дрес
• v.t. **1** (a letter) адресова́ть (impf., pf.) **2** (speak
to) обра|ща́ться, -ти́ться к + d.
■ **~ book** n. (also comput.) записна́я кни́жка

addressee /ædre'si:/ n. адреса́т

adenoids /'ædɪnɔɪdz/ n. pl. адено́иды (m. pl.)

adept /ə'dept/ adj. уме́лый; **he is ~ at finding
excuses** он ма́стер находи́ть оправда́ния
(or опра́вдываться)

adequate /'ædɪkwət/ adj. **1** (sufficient)
доста́точный **2** (suitable) адеква́тный

ADHD abbr. (of **attention deficit
hyperactivity disorder**) СДВГ (синдро́м
дефици́та внима́ния и гиперакти́вности)

adhere /əd'hɪə(r)/ v.i. прил|ипа́ть, -и́пнуть
(**to**: к + d.)

adherence /əd'hɪərəns/ n. (lit.) прилипа́ние;
(fig.) приве́рженность

adherent /əd'hɪərənt/ n. приве́рженец

adhesive /əd'hi:sɪv/ n. клей; кле́йкое вещество́

⚡ ключева́я ле́ксика

• adj. ли́пкий; (sticky) кле́йкий
■ **~ tape** n. кле́йкая ле́нта, скотч

ad hoc /æd 'hɒk/ adv. для да́нного слу́чая;
(attr.) специа́льный; **~ committee** вре́менный
комите́т

ad infinitum /æd ɪnfɪ'naɪtəm/ adv. до
бесконе́чности

adjacent /ə'dʒeɪs(ə)nt/ adj. (neighbouring)
сосе́дний; сме́жный; (to: примыка́ющий к
+ d.; (geom.): **~ angles** сме́жные углы́

adjectival /ædʒɪk'taɪv(ə)l/ adj. (gram.)
адъекти́вный

adjective /'ædʒɪktɪv/ n. (и́мя) прилага́тельное

adjourn /ə'dʒɜ:n/ v.t. (postpone) от|кла́дывать,
-ложи́ть; **the meeting was ~ed till Monday**
заседа́ние бы́ло отло́жено до понеде́льника

adjournment /ə'dʒɜ:nmənt/ n. (postponement)
отсро́чка; (break in proceedings) переры́в

adjudicate /ə'dʒu:dɪkeɪt/ v.t. (a claim)
рассм|а́тривать, -отре́ть

adjudication /ədʒu:dɪ'keɪʃ(ə)n/ n. (judgement)
суде́бное/арбитра́жное реше́ние

adjudicator /ə'dʒu:dɪkeɪtə(r)/ n. арби́тр; (judge)
судья́ (m.)

adjunct /'ædʒʌŋkt/ n. (appendage) приложе́ние;
(addition) дополне́ние; (gram.) обстоя́тельство

adjust /ə'dʒʌst/ v.t. **1** (arrange; put right or straight)
прив|оди́ть, -ести́ в поря́док; попр|авля́ть,
-а́вить; **he ~ed his tie** он попра́вил га́лстук;
(mechanism) регули́ровать, от-; нала́живать,
-дить **2** (fit, adapt) приг|оня́ть, -на́ть;
под|гоня́ть, -огна́ть; **well ~ed** (of person)
уравнове́шенный

adjustable /ə'dʒʌstəb(ə)l/ adj. регули́руемый;
подвижно́й

adjustment /ə'dʒʌstmənt/ n. (regulation)
регули́рование, -иро́вка; (correction)
исправле́ние, попра́вка; (fitting) подго́нка;
(adaptation) приспособле́ние

ad-lib /æd 'lɪb/ (infml) n. экспро́мт; **his speech
was full of ~s** в свое́й ре́чи он мно́го
импровизи́ровал
• v.i. (**ad-libbed, ad-libbing**) говори́ть
(impf.) экспро́мтом

administer /əd'mɪnɪstə(r)/ v.t. (manage, govern)
управля́ть (impf.) + i.; заве́довать (impf.) + i.

⚡ **administration** /ədmɪnɪ'streɪʃ(ə)n/ n.
1 (management) управле́ние **2** (of public affairs)
администра́ция; **the A~** администра́ция,
прави́тельство

administrative /əd'mɪnɪstrətɪv/ adj.
администрати́вный, организацио́нный

administrator /əd'mɪnɪstreɪtə(r)/ n.
администра́тор

admirable /'ædmərəb(ə)l/ adj. замеча́тельный,
прекра́сный

admiral /'ædmər(ə)l/ n. адмира́л

admiration /ædmɪ'reɪʃ(ə)n/ n. восхище́ние,
восто́рг

admire /əd'maɪə(r)/ v.t. (view with pleasure)
любова́ться (impf.) + i.; (respect) восхи|ща́ться,
-ти́ться + i.; восторга́ться (impf.) + i.

admirer /əd'maɪərə(r)/ *n.* покло́нни|к (-ца)

admissible /əd'mɪsɪb(ə)l/ *adj.* прие́млемый, допусти́мый

admission /əd'mɪʃ(ə)n/ *n.* **1** (permitted entry or access) вход; до́ступ **2** (acknowledgement) призна́ние

♂ **admit** /əd'mɪt/ *v.t. & i.* (**admitted, admitting**) **1** (allow, accept) допус|ка́ть, -ти́ть; призн|ава́ть, -а́ть; **you must ~ he is right** вы должны́ призна́ть, что он прав (*or* его́ правоту́) **2** (let in) впус|ка́ть, -ти́ть; (to organization) прин|има́ть, -я́ть; **the public are not ~ted to the gardens** э́тот парк закры́т для посеще́ния; **this ticket ~s one (person)** э́то биле́т на одно́ лицо́ **3** (confess) призн|ава́ть, -а́ть; **he ~s his guilt** он признаёт свою́ вину́; **~ to feeling ashamed** призн|ава́ться, -а́ться, что сты́дно

admittance /əd'mɪt(ə)ns/ *n.* (entry) вход; **no ~!** вход воспрещён!

admittedly /əd'mɪtɪdlɪ/ *adv.* пра́вда; призна́ться

admixture /əd'mɪkstʃə(r)/ *n.* (mixing) сме́шивание; (addition) при́месь

admonish /əd'mɒnɪʃ/ *v.t.* **1** (reprimand) де́лать, с- внуше́ние/замеча́ние + *d.*; **the boys were ~ed for being late** ма́льчикам сде́лали замеча́ние за опозда́ние **2** (advise, urge) насто́ятельно сове́товать, по-; убеди́тельно проси́ть, по-

ad nauseam /æd 'nɔːzɪæm/ *adv.* до тошноты́

ado /ə'duː/ *n.* (fuss) суета́; **without further ~** без дальне́йших церемо́ний

adolescence /ædə'les(ə)ns/ *n.* подростко́вый во́зраст

adolescent /ædə'les(ə)nt/ *n.* подро́сток
  • *adj.* подростко́вый

♂ **adopt** /ə'dɒpt/ *v.t.* **1** (a son) усынов|ля́ть, -и́ть; (a daughter) удочер|я́ть, -и́ть **2** (accept) прин|има́ть, -я́ть; (take over) перен|има́ть, -я́ть; **his methods should be ~ed** сле́дует воспо́льзоваться его́ мето́дикой

adoption /ə'dɒpʃ(ə)n/ *n.* **1** (of a son) усыновле́ние; (of a daughter) удочере́ние **2** (acceptance) приня́тие

adoptive /ə'dɒptɪv/ *adj.* приёмный; **~ parent** усынови́тель (-ница)

adorable /ə'dɔːrəb(ə)l/ *adj.* преле́стный, восхити́тельный

adoration /ædə'reɪʃ(ə)n/ *n.* обожа́ние

ador|e /ə'dɔː(r)/ *v.t.* (worship) обожа́ть (*impf.*); поклоня́ться (*impf.*) + *d.*; **her ~ing husband** её любя́щий муж

adorn /ə'dɔːn/ *v.t.* укр|аша́ть, -а́сить

adornment /ə'dɔːnmənt/ *n.* украше́ние

adrenalin /ə'drenəlɪn/ *n.* адренали́н

adrift /ə'drɪft/ *pred. adj. & adv.*: **be ~** дрейфова́ть (*impf.*)

adroit /ə'drɔɪt/ *adj.* ло́вкий

adulation /ædjʊ'leɪʃ(ə)n/ *n.* низкопокло́нство, лесть

♂ **adult** /'ædʌlt/ *n. & adj.* **1** взро́слый **2** (mature) зре́лый
  ■ **~ education** *n.* обуче́ние взро́слых

adulterate /ə'dʌltəreɪt/ *v.t.* (debase) по́ртить, ис-; (dilute) разб|авля́ть, -а́вить

adulterous /ə'dʌltərəs/ *adj.* неве́рный

adultery /ə'dʌltərɪ/ *n.* адюльте́р, супру́жеская изме́на

adulthood /'ædʌlthʊd/ *n.* зре́лость; (of men) возмужа́лость

♂ **advance** /əd'vɑːns/ *n.* **1** (forward move) продвиже́ние; (mil. also) наступле́ние; (*in pl.*) (overtures to a person): **make ~s to** заи́грывать (*impf.*) с + *i.* **2** (progress) прогре́сс; (in rank, social position etc.) продвиже́ние **3** (increase) повыше́ние; **an ~ on his original offer** надба́вка к первонача́льному предложе́нию **4** (loan) ссу́да; (payment beforehand) ава́нс; **an ~ on salary** ава́нс под зарпла́ту **5**: **in ~** (in front) впереди́; (beforehand) зара́нее; **in ~ of** впереди́ + *g.* **6** (*attr.*): **~ booking** предвари́тельный зака́з
  • *v.t.* **1** (move forward) продв|ига́ть, -и́нуть **2** (fig., put forward): **~ an opinion** выска́зывать, вы́сказать мне́ние **3** (fig., further): **~ sb's interests** отста́ивать (*impf.*) чьи-н. интере́сы; служи́ть, по- чьим-н. интере́сам **4** (of payment) плати́ть, за- ава́нсом; (lend) ссу|жа́ть, -ди́ть
  • *v.i.* **1** (move forward) продв|ига́ться, -и́нуться; **~ on** наступа́ть (*impf.*) на + *a.* **2** (progress) разв|ива́ться, -и́ться; де́лать, с- успе́хи

advanced /əd'vɑːnst/ *adj.* **1** (far on): **~ age, years** прекло́нный во́зраст **2** (opp. elementary): **an ~ course** курс для продви́нутого эта́па (обуче́ния) **3** (progressive) передово́й

advancement /əd'vɑːnsmənt/ *n.* (moving forward) продвиже́ние; (promotion) продвиже́ние по слу́жбе; (progress) прогре́сс

♂ **advantage** /əd'vɑːntɪdʒ/ *n.* **1** (superiority; more favourable position) преиму́щество, досто́инство **2** (profit, benefit) вы́года, по́льза; **take ~ of sth** воспо́льзоваться (*pf.*) чем-н.; (abuse) злоупотреб|ля́ть, -и́ть чем-н.; **take ~ of sb** эксплуати́ровать (*impf.*); **you may learn sth to your ~** вы мо́жете узна́ть/почерпну́ть для себя́ что́-то поле́зное **3** (tennis): **~ Henman** бо́льше у Хэ́нмена

advantageous /ædvən'teɪdʒəs/ *adj.* (favourable) благоприя́тный; (profitable) вы́годный

advent /'ædvent/ *n.* **1** (appearance; occurrence) появле́ние **2** (**A~**) (eccl.) Рожде́ственский пост

adventure /əd'ventʃə(r)/ *n.* приключе́ние
  ■ **~ story** *n.* приключе́нческий рома́н

adventurous /əd'ventʃərəs/ *adj.* **1** (of person) сме́лый; (enterprising) предприи́мчивый **2** (of actions) риско́ванный, авантю́рный

adverb /'ædvɜːb/ *n.* наре́чие

adverbial /əd'vɜːbɪəl/ *adj.* (gram.) наре́чный, адвербиа́льный

adversary /'ædvəsərɪ/ *n.* проти́вник

adverse /'ædvɜːs/ *adj.* неблагоприя́тный

adversity /əd'vɜːsɪtɪ/ *n.* беда́, несча́стье; **show courage in, under ~** прояв|ля́ть, -и́ть му́жество в беде́; **companions in ~** това́рищи по несча́стью

advert /'ædvɜːt/ *n.* (BrE, infml) = **advertisement**

a

advertise /'ædvətaɪz/ *v.t.* (publicize)
реклами́ровать (*impf., pf.*); (in newspaper)
да|ва́ть, -ть (*or* поме|ща́ть, -сти́ть)
объявле́ние о + *p.*
• *v.i.*: she ~d for a secretary она́ дала́
объявле́ние о вака́нсии секретаря́
advertisement /əd'vɜ:tɪsmənt/ *n.* рекла́ма;
(classified ~) объявле́ние
advertising /'ædvətaɪzɪŋ/ *n.*
реклами́рование; рекла́мный би́знес
■ ~ **agent** *n.* рекла́мный аге́нт
✓ **advice** /əd'vaɪs/ *n.* (*also* **piece of** ~) сове́т;
give sb a piece of ~ сове́товать, по- кому́-н.
advisable /əd'vaɪzəb(ə)l/ *adj.* целесообра́зный;
it may be ~ **to wait** сто́ит, наве́рное,
подожда́ть
✓ **advise** /əd'vaɪz/ *v.t.* **1** (counsel) сове́товать, по-
+ *d.*; рекомендова́ть (*impf., pf.*) + *d.*; **what
do you** ~ **(me to do)?** что вы посове́туете
мне предприня́ть?; **the doctor** ~**d complete
rest** врач рекомендова́л по́лный поко́й;
I ~**d him against going** я посове́товал ему́
не ходи́ть туда́; (give professional advice to)
консульти́ровать, про- **2** (comm., notify)
изве|ща́ть, -сти́ть (*кого о чём*); **please** ~ **me
of receipt** уве́домите меня́ о получе́нии
adviser, advisor /əd'vaɪzə(r)/ *nn.*
(professional) консульта́нт; (to president etc.)
сове́тник (**to:** + *g.*); **legal** ~ юрисконсу́льт;
medical ~ врач
advisory /əd'vaɪzərɪ/ *adj.* совеща́тельный,
консультати́вный
advocate¹ /'ædvəkət/ *n.* **1** (defender) защи́тник;
(supporter) сторо́нни|к (-ца) **2** (lawyer) адвока́т;
devil's ~ (fig.) «адвока́т дья́вола»
advocate² /'ædvəkeɪt/ *v.t.* (speak in favour of)
выступа́ть, вы́ступить за + *a.*; (advise,
recommend) сове́товать, по-; рекомендова́ть
(*impf., pf.*)
aegis /'i:dʒɪs/ *n.*: **under the** ~ **of** под эги́дой + *g.*
aeration /eə'reɪʃ(ə)n/ *n.* прове́тривание;
(of the soil) аэра́ция
aerial /'eərɪəl/ *n.* анте́нна
• *adj.* возду́шный
■ ~ **photography** *n.* аэрофотосъёмка
aerobatics /eərə'bætɪks/ *n.* вы́сший пилота́ж;
фигу́ры вы́сшего пилота́жа
aerobic /eə'rəʊbɪk/ *adj.* аэро́бный
aerobics /eə'rəʊbɪks/ *n.* аэро́бика
aerodrome /'eərədrəʊm/ *n.* (BrE) аэродро́м
aerodynamic /eərəʊdaɪ'næmɪk/ *adj.*
аэродинами́ческий
aerodynamics /eərəʊdaɪ'næmɪks/ *n.*
аэродина́мика
aeronautics /eərə'nɔ:tɪks/ *n.* аэрона́втика,
воздухопла́вание
aeroplane /'eərəpleɪn/ *n.* (BrE) самолёт,
аэропла́н
aerosol /'eərəsɒl/ *n.* аэрозо́ль (*m.*)
aerospace /'eərəspeɪs/ *n.* возду́шно-
косми́ческое простра́нство

✓ ключева́я ле́ксика

aesthetic /i:s'θetɪk/ (AmE *also* **esthetic**) *adj.*
эстети́ческий
aesthetics /i:s'θetɪks/ (AmE *also* **esthetics**)
n. эсте́тика
afar /ə'fɑ:(r)/ *adv.* вдалеке́; **from** ~ и́здали,
издалека́
affable /'æfəb(ə)l/ *adj.* приве́тливый;
любе́зный
✓ **affair** /ə'feə(r)/ *n.* **1** (business, matter) де́ло;
that's my ~ э́то моё де́ло; **Ministry of Foreign
A**~**s** министе́рство иностра́нных дел
2 (*also* **love** ~) любо́вная связь; рома́н;
they are having an ~ у них рома́н
■ ~**s of state** *n. pl.* госуда́рственные дела́
✓ **affect** /ə'fekt/ *v.t.* **1** (act on) де́йствовать, по-
на + *a.*; влия́ть, по- на + *a.*; **the climate** ~**ed
his health** кли́мат повлия́л на его́ здоро́вье
2 (concern) каса́ться, косну́ться + *g.*;
затр|а́гивать, -о́нуть **3** (touch emotionally)
тро́|гать, -нуть; волнова́ть, вз- **4** (of disease):
the lung is ~**ed** лёгкое поражено́
affectation /æfek'teɪʃ(ə)n/ *n.* **1** (pretence)
притво́рство **2** (unnatural behaviour) аффекта́ция
3 (of language or style) иску́сственность
affected /ə'fektɪd/ *adj.* жема́нный,
неесте́ственный
affection /ə'fekʃ(ə)n/ *n.* привя́занность
(**for:** к + *d.*); любо́вь (**for:** к + *d.*)
affectionate /ə'fekʃənət/ *adj.* не́жный
affidavit /æfɪ'deɪvɪt/ *n.* (law) пи́сьменное
показа́ние под прися́гой, аффиде́вит; **make,
swear an** ~ да|ва́ть, -ть показа́ние под
прися́гой
affiliate /ə'fɪlɪeɪt/ *v.t.* **1** (join, attach)
присоедин|я́ть, -и́ть (**to:** к + *d.*); ~**d company**
доче́рняя компа́ния **2** (adopt as member)
прин|има́ть, -я́ть в чле́ны
• *v.i.* присоедин|я́ться, -и́ться (**with:** к + *d.*)
affiliation /əfɪlɪ'eɪʃ(ə)n/ *n.* **1** присоедине́ние
2 приня́тие в чле́ны **3** (connection) связь
affinity /ə'fɪnɪtɪ/ *n.* **1** (resemblance) схо́дство;
(relationship) родство́; (connection) связь;
(closeness) бли́зость **2** (liking, attraction)
влече́ние, скло́нность
affirm /ə'fɜ:m/ *v.t.* (assert) утвер|жда́ть, -ди́ть
affirmation /æfə'meɪʃ(ə)n/ *n.* утвержде́ние
affirmative /ə'fɜ:mətɪv/ *n.*: **he answered in
the** ~ он отве́тил утверди́тельно
• *adj.* утверди́тельный
afflict /ə'flɪkt/ *v.t.* **1** (distress: of misfortune etc.)
пост|ига́ть, -и́чь (*or* -и́гнуть); **he was** ~**ed
by a great misfortune** его́ пости́гло большо́е
несча́стье **2** (*pass.*) (suffer from): **be** ~**ed
with** страда́ть (*impf.*) + *i.*; **he is** ~**ed with
rheumatism** он страда́ет ревмати́змом; **the**
~**ed** стра́ждущие (*pl.*)
affliction /ə'flɪkʃ(ə)n/ *n.* (grief) го́ре; (misfortune)
несча́стье; бе́дствие; (illness) боле́знь
affluence /'æfluəns/ *n.* (wealth) бога́тство;
(plenty) изоби́лие
affluent /'æfluənt/ *adj.* бога́тый
✓ **afford** /ə'fɔ:d/ *v.t.* (*with* **can**) (expr. possibility):
I can't ~ **all these books** все э́ти кни́ги мне
не по карма́ну; **they can** ~ **a new car** они́

мо́гут позво́лить себе́ но́вую маши́ну; **I can't ~ the time** мне не́когда

affront /əˈfrʌnt/ *v.t.* оскорбля́ть, -и́ть

Afghan /ˈæfɡæn/ *n.* афга́н|ец (-ка); (*in full ~* **hound**) афга́нская борза́я
● *adj.* афга́нский

Afghanistan /æfˈɡænɪstɑːn/ *n.* Афганиста́н

aficionado /əfɪsjəˈnɑːdəʊ/ *n.* (*pl. ~s*) покло́нни|к (-ца)

afield /əˈfiːld/ *adv.*: **far ~** вдалеке́, вдали́; (expr. motion) вдаль

afloat /əˈfləʊt/ *pred. adj. & adv.* (floating on water) на воде́

afoot /əˈfʊt/ *pred. adj. & adv.*: **there is a plan ~** гото́вится план; **there is sth ~** что́-то затева́ется

aforementioned /əˈfɔːmenʃ(ə)nd/ *adj.* вышеупомя́нутый

aforesaid /əˈfɔːsed/ *adj.* вышеска́занный

✍ **afraid** /əˈfreɪd/ *pred. adj.* испу́ганный; **be ~ of** боя́ться (*impf.*) + *g.*; **don't be ~!** не бо́йтесь!; **I'm ~ he will die** бою́сь, что он умрёт; **I'm ~ he is out** к сожале́нию, его́ нет

afresh /əˈfreʃ/ *adv.* за́ново

Africa /ˈæfrɪkə/ *n.* А́фрика

✍ **African** /ˈæfrɪkən/ *n.* африка́н|ец (-ка)
● *adj.* африка́нский
■ **~ American** *n.* афроамерика́н|ец (-ка); **~-American** *adj.* афроамерика́нский

Afrikaans /æfrɪˈkɑːns/ *n.* (язы́к) африка́анс

Afrikaner /æfrɪˈkɑːnə(r)/ *n.* африка́нер, жи́тель Ю́жно-Африка́нской Респу́блики голла́ндского происхожде́ния

Afro-Caribbean /æfrəʊkærɪˈbiːən/ *adj.* афрокари́бский
● *n.* афрокари́б (-ка); уроже́н|ец (-ка) Кари́бских острово́в африка́нского происхожде́ния

✍ **after** /ˈɑːftə(r)/ *adv.* **1** (subsequently; then) пото́м, зате́м; **soon ~** вско́ре по́сле э́того **2** (later) поздне́е, по́зже; **3 days ~** спустя́ три дня
● *prep.* **1** (in expressions of time) по́сле + *g.*; за + *i.*; че́рез + *a.*; спустя́ + *a.*; **~ dinner** по́сле обе́да; **~ you!** то́лько по́сле вас!; **~ that** пото́м, зате́м; **the day ~ tomorrow** послеза́втра; **the week ~ next** (in adv. sense) че́рез две неде́ли; **they met ~ 10 years** они́ встре́тились че́рез де́сять лет; **~ passing his exams, he …** сдав экза́мены, он…; **~ all** (in the end) в коне́чном счёте; в конце́ концо́в; (nevertheless) всё-таки **2** (in expressions of place) за + *i.*; **run ~ sb** бежа́ть за кем-н. **3** (in search of; trying to get): **the police are ~ him** его́ разы́скивает поли́ция; **what is he ~?** куда́ он ме́тит?; что он замышля́ет? **4** (in accordance with) по + *d.*, согла́сно + *d.*; **named ~** на́званный по + *d. or* в честь + *g.*; **he takes ~ his father** он похо́ж на отца́
● *conj.* по́сле того́ как; **I arrived ~ he had left** я пришёл по́сле того́, как он ушёл
■ **~-effect** *n.* после́дствие; **~math** *n.* после́дствия (*nt. pl.*); **~noon** *n.*

послеполу́денное вре́мя; **in the ~noon** днём; по́сле обе́да; во второ́й полови́не дня; **at 3 in the ~noon** в три часа́ дня; **good ~noon!** (in greeting) до́брый день!; (in leave-taking) до свида́ния!; **~shave** *n.* лосьо́н по́сле бритья́; **~shock** *n.* повто́рные толчки́; **~taste** *n.* при́вкус; **~thought** *n.* запозда́лая мысль

afterward /ˈɑːftəwəd/ *adv.* (AmE) = **afterwards**

afterwards /ˈɑːftəwədz/ *adv.* (then) пото́м; (subsequently) впосле́дствии; (later) по́зже

✍ **again** /əˈɡen/ *adv.* **1** (expr. repetition) опя́ть, сно́ва; (afresh, anew) вновь; (once more) ещё раз; (with certain vv., by use of pref.) пере…; **read ~** перечи́т|ывать, -а́ть; **say ~** повтор|я́ть, -и́ть; **start ~** нач|ина́ть, -а́ть сно́ва; **~ and ~** сно́ва и сно́ва; **now and ~** вре́мя от вре́мени; **once ~** ещё раз **2** (*with neg.*) (any more) бо́льше; **never ~** никогда́ бо́льше; **don't do it ~!** бо́льше э́того не де́лай! **3** (expr. return to original state or position): **back ~** обра́тно; **you'll soon be well ~** вы ско́ро попра́витесь

✍ **against** /əˈɡenst/ *prep.* **1** (in opposition to) про́тив + *g.*; **I have nothing ~ it** я не име́ю ничего́ про́тив; **I acted ~ my will** я де́йствовал про́тив свое́й во́ли; **~ the rules** не по пра́вилам **2** (to oppose or combat) на + *a.*; **march ~ the enemy** наступа́ть (*impf.*) на врага́ **3** (compared with): **3 deaths this year ~ 20 last year** три сме́рти в э́том году́ про́тив двадцати́ в про́шлом **4** (in contrast with): **it shows up ~ a dark background** э́то выделя́ется на тёмном фо́не **5** (in collision with) о + *a.*; **knock ~ sth** уда́ряться, уда́риться о что-н.

✍ **age** /eɪdʒ/ *n.* **1** (time of life) во́зраст; **he is 40 years of ~** ему́ со́рок лет; **when I was your ~** когда́ я был в ва́шем во́зрасте; **she doesn't look her ~** она́ вы́глядит моло́же свои́х лет; (of inanimate objects): **what is the ~ of this house?** ско́лько лет э́тому до́му? **2** (majority): **he is under ~** он несовершенноле́тний **3** (old ~) ста́рость **4** (period) пери́од; (century) век; **Ice A~** леднико́вый пери́од; **Stone A~** ка́менный век; **the Middle A~s** Сре́дние века́; (often in pl.) (infml, long time): **the bus left ~s ago** авто́бус ушёл давны́м-давно́; **we have not seen each other for ~s** мы не ви́делись сто лет (*or* це́лую ве́чность)
● *v.t.* (*pres. part.* **ageing, aging**) ста́рить, со-
● *v.i.* (*pres. part.* **ageing, aging**) (of person) старе́ть, по-; ста́риться, со-; (of thing) старе́ть, у-
■ **~ group** *n.* возрастна́я гру́ппа; **~ limit** *n.* преде́льный во́зраст; **~ of consent** *n.* бра́чный во́зраст

aged¹ /eɪdʒd/ *adj.* (of/at the age of): **~ six** шести́ лет

aged² /ˈeɪdʒɪd/ *adj.* (very old) престаре́лый
● *n.*: **the ~** пожилы́е лю́ди, престаре́лые

ageism /ˈeɪdʒɪz(ə)m/ *n.* дискримина́ция по во́зрасту

ageist /ˈeɪdʒɪst/ *adj.* дискримини́рующий по во́зрасту

✍ **agency** /ˈeɪdʒənsɪ/ *n.* аге́нтство;

a

employment ~ аге́нтство по на́йму; **news ~** информацио́нное аге́нтство; **travel ~** туристи́ческое аге́нтство, тураге́нтство

✓ **agenda** /əˈdʒendə/ *n.* пове́стка дня

✓ **agent** /ˈeɪdʒ(ə)nt/ *n.* (person acting for others) аге́нт; (representative) представи́тель (*m.*)

agent provocateur /ɑːˈʒɑ̃ prəvɒkəˈtɜː(r)/ *n.* (*pl.* **agents provocateurs** *pronunc. same*) провока́тор

aggravate /ˈæɡrəveɪt/ *v.t.* **1** (make worse) усугубл|я́ть, -и́ть **2** (infml, exasperate) раздраж|а́ть, -и́ть

aggravation /æɡrəˈveɪʃ(ə)n/ *n.* **1** (of an illness, situation) усугубле́ние **2** (exasperation) раздраже́ние

aggregate¹ /ˈæɡrɪɡət/ *n.* **1** (total, mass) совоку́пность; **in the ~** в совоку́пности **2** (phys.) скопле́ние **3** (ingredient of concrete) заполни́тель (*m.*) (бето́на)
● *adj.* (total) совоку́пный; **~ membership** о́бщее число́ чле́нов

aggregate² /ˈæɡrɪɡeɪt/ *v.t.* (collect into a mass) соб|ира́ть, -ра́ть в це́лое

aggression /əˈɡreʃ(ə)n/ *n.* агре́ссия

aggressive /əˈɡresɪv/ *adj.* агресси́вный

aggressor /əˈɡresə(r)/ *n.* агре́ссор

aggrieved /əˈɡriːvd/ *adj.* оби́женный, огорчённый

aghast /əˈɡɑːst/ *pred. adj.* (amazed) потрясённый

agile /ˈædʒaɪl/ *adj.* прово́рный; **an ~ mind** живо́й ум

agility /əˈdʒɪlɪtɪ/ *n.* прово́рство; **~ of mind** жи́вость ума́

agitate /ˈædʒɪteɪt/ *v.t.* (excite) волнова́ть, вз-; **be ~d about sth** волнова́ться (*impf.*) из-за чего́-н.

agitator /ˈædʒɪteɪtə(r)/ *n.* **1** (pol.) агита́тор **2** (apparatus) меси́тель (*m.*); меша́лка (infml)

AGM (BrE) *abbr.* (*of* **Annual General Meeting**) ежего́дное о́бщее собра́ние

agnostic /æɡˈnɒstɪk/ *n.* агно́стик
● *adj.* агности́ческий

✓ **ago** /əˈɡəʊ/ *adv.* тому́ наза́д; **long ~** давно́; **not long ~** неда́вно

agonize /ˈæɡənaɪz/ *v.i.* (fig.): **he ~d over his speech** он му́чился над свое́й ре́чью

agony /ˈæɡənɪ/ *n.* (torment) муче́ние, страда́ние; **I was in ~** я испы́тывал си́льные страда́ния; я му́чился от бо́ли

agoraphobia /æɡərəˈfəʊbɪə/ *n.* агорафо́бия, боя́знь откры́того простра́нства

agoraphobic /æɡərəˈfəʊbɪk/ *adj.* страда́ющий агорафо́бией

✓ **agree** /əˈɡriː/ *v.t.* (**agrees, agreed, agreeing**) (BrE) согласо́в|ывать, -а́ть (*что с кем*)
● *v.i.* (**agrees, agreed, agreeing**)
1 (concur; be of like opinion) согла|ша́ться, -си́ться (*с кем*) (*used mainly for past and future*); **I quite ~ with you** я соверше́нно с ва́ми согла́сен **2** (reach agreement; make common decision): **we ~d to go together** мы

договори́лись е́хать вме́сте; **~ on a price** догов|а́риваться, -ори́ться о цене́ **3** (consent) согла|ша́ться, -си́ться (*на что*) (*used mainly for past and future*) **4** (accept): **I ~ that it was wrong** согла́сен, что э́то бы́ло непра́вильно **5** **~ with** (accept as correct or right): **I don't ~ with his policy** я не согла́сен с его́ поли́тикой **6** **~ with** (suit): (usu.)|ходи́ть, -ойти́ + *d.*; годи́ться (*impf.*) + *d.*; **fish doesn't ~ with me** от ры́бы мне быва́ет пло́хо **7** **~ with** (conform; tally): **the adjective ~s with the noun** прилага́тельное согласу́ется с существи́тельным; **his story ~s with mine** его́ расска́з схо́дится с мои́м

agreeable /əˈɡriːəb(ə)l/ *adj.* прия́тный

✓ **agreement** /əˈɡriːmənt/ *n.* **1** (consent) согла́сие; **be in ~ with** согла|ша́ться, -си́ться с + *i.* **2** (treaty) соглаше́ние, догово́р; **come to an ~** при|ходи́ть, -йти́ к соглаше́нию **3** (gram.) согласова́ние

agricultural /æɡrɪˈkʌltʃər(ə)l/ *adj.* сельскохозя́йственный

agriculture /ˈæɡrɪkʌltʃə(r)/ *n.* се́льское хозя́йство

aground /əˈɡraʊnd/ *adv.*: **run ~** *v.i.* сади́ться, сесть на мель

✓ **ahead** /əˈhed/ *adv.* впереди́; (expr. motion) вперёд; **be, get ~ of** опере|жа́ть, -ди́ть; **go ~!** (ну) дава́й(те)!

ahoy /əˈhɔɪ/ *int.*: **~ there!**, **ship ~!** эй, на корабле́/су́дне!; **land ~!** земля́!

✓ **aid** /eɪd/ *n.* **1** (help, assistance) по́мощь; (support) подде́ржка; **first ~** пе́рвая по́мощь; **with the ~ of** при по́мощи + *g.*; **in ~ of** в по́мощь + *d.* **2** (appliance) посо́бие; **visual ~s** нагля́дные посо́бия
● *v.t.* (help) пом|ога́ть, -о́чь + *d.*; (promote) спосо́бствовать (*impf.*) + *d.*
■ **~ agency** *n.* организа́ция по оказа́нию по́мощи; **~ worker** *n.* рабо́тн|ик (-ица) организа́ции по оказа́нию по́мощи

aide /eɪd/ *n.* помо́щни|к (-ца)

Aids, AIDS /eɪdz/ *n.* (*abbr. of* **acquired immune deficiency syndrome**) СПИД (синдро́м приобретённого иммунодефици́та)

ailing /ˈeɪlɪŋ/ *adj.* больно́й; **an ~ economy** больна́я эконо́мика

ailment /ˈeɪlmənt/ *n.* неду́г, хворь

✓ **aim** /eɪm/ *n.* **1** (purpose) цель; **with the ~ of** с це́лью + *g.* **2** (of a gun, etc.) прице́л; **take ~ at** прице́л|иваться, -иться в + *a.*
● *v.t.* наво́|дить, -ести́; **~ a blow at** зама́х|иваться, -ну́ться на + *a.*; (fig.): **~ one's remarks at** предназн|а́чить, -а́чить свои́ замеча́ния + *d.*
● *v.i.* це́лить (*impf.*); **~ at** (with rifle) прице́л|иваться, -иться в + *a.*; (fig.): **~ at** (aspire to) це́литься, на- на + *a.*; стреми́ться (*impf.*) к + *d.*; **~ for** напр|авля́ться, -а́виться в/на + *a.*

aimless /ˈeɪmlɪs/ *adj.* бесце́льный

✓ **air** /eə(r)/ *n.* **1** во́здух; **get some fresh ~** подыша́ть (*pf.*) све́жим во́здухом; **in the open ~** на откры́том во́здухе; **travel by ~** лета́ть (*impf.*) (самолётом) **2** (in fig. phr.):

clear the ~ разря|жа́ть, -ди́ть атмосфе́ру;
he vanished into thin ~ его́ и след просты́л;
he was walking on ~ он ног под собо́й
не чу́вствовал **3** (appearance, manner) (of
person) вид; (of place) дух; ~s and graces
мане́рность; **put on** (or **give oneself**) ~s
задава́ться, ва́жничать (both impf.) **4** (radio,
TV): **go on the** ~ выходи́ть, вы́йти в эфи́р;
go off the ~ (of station) зак|а́нчивать,
-о́нчить переда́чу **5** (attr.) (pert. to aviation)
возду́шный; авиацио́нный, авиа…; (mil.)
вое́нно-возду́шный
● v.t. **1** (ventilate) прове́три|вать, -ть; (BrE,
dry) суши́ть, вы́- **2** (fig., opinions, feelings)
выска́зывать, вы́сказать
● v.i. про|су́шивать, -суши́ть
■ ~ **bag** n. авари́йная поду́шка безопа́сности;
~ **bed** n. (BrE) надувно́й матра́ц;
~-**conditioned** adj. с кондициони́рованным
во́здухом; ~ **conditioning** n.
кондициони́рование во́здуха; ~**crew** n.
экипа́ж; ~**field** n. лётное по́ле; ~ **force** n.
вое́нно-возду́шные си́лы; ~ **gun** n. духово́е
ружьё; ~ **hostess** n. (BrE) бортпроводни́ца,
стюарде́сса; ~ **letter** n. авиаписьмо́; ~**lift** n.
возду́шная перебро́ска ● v.t. перебр|а́сывать,
-о́сить (or перев|ози́ть, -езти́) по во́здуху;
~**line** n. (company) авиакомпа́ния; ~**mail**
n. авиапо́чта; ~**plane** n. (AmE) = **aeroplane**
~ **raid** n. возду́шный налёт; ~-**raid**
warning возду́шная трево́га; ~-**raid shelter**
бомбоубе́жище; ~-**raid warden** ≈ нача́льник
шта́ба гражда́нской оборо́ны; ~ **rifle**
n. пневмати́ческая винто́вка; ~**ship** n.
возду́шный кора́бль; дирижа́бль (m.);
~**sick** adj.: I was ~**sick** меня́ укача́ло в
самолёте; ~**strip** n. взлётно-поса́дочная
полоса́; ~ **terminal** n. аэровокза́л; ~**tight**
adj. гермети́ческий; ~ **traffic control**
n. авиадиспе́тчерская слу́жба; ~ **traffic**
controller n. авиадиспе́тчер; ~**waves** n.
pl. радиово́лны
aircraft /'eəkrɑːft/ n. самолёт, (collect.)
самолёты, авиа́ция
■ ~-**carrier** n. авиано́сец
airing /'eərɪŋ/ n. прове́тривание
■ ~ **cupboard** n. (BrE) суши́льный шкаф
airless /'eəlɪs/ adj. (stuffy) ду́шный; (still)
безве́тренный
airport /'eəpɔːt/ n. аэропо́рт
airy /'eərɪ/ adj. (**airier, airiest**) **1** (well ventilated)
све́жий; (spacious) просто́рный **2** (superficial;
light-hearted) ве́треный, беспе́чный
aisle /aɪl/ n. прохо́д (между ряда́ми)
ajar /ə'dʒɑː(r)/ pred. adj. приоткры́тый
aka abbr. (of **also known as**) изве́стный
та́кже под и́менем
akin /ə'kɪn/ pred. adj. & adv. (related)
ро́дственный; ~ **to** сродни́ + d.
alarm /ə'lɑːm/ n. **1** (warning; warning signal)
трево́га; **false** ~ ло́жная трево́га; **fire** ~
пожа́рная трево́га **2** (~ clock) буди́льник
3 (fright): **he ran away in** ~ он убежа́л в
испу́ге
● v.t. трево́жить; **to be** ~**ed** трево́житься, вс-

alarmist /ə'lɑːmɪst/ n. паникёр (-ша)
alas /ə'læs/ int. увы́!
Albania /æl'beɪnɪə/ n. Алба́ния
Albanian /æl'beɪnɪən/ n. **1** (person) алба́н|ец
(-ка) **2** (language) алба́нский язы́к
● adj. алба́нский
albeit /ɔːl'biːɪt/ conj. пусть (и), хотя́ и
✍ **album** /'ælbəm/ n. (book; recordings) альбо́м
alchemist /'ælkəmɪst/ n. алхи́мик
alchemy /'ælkəmɪ/ n. алхи́мия
✍ **alcohol** /'ælkəhɒl/ n. (chem.) алкого́ль (m.);
(spirit) спирт
■ ~-**free** adj. безалкого́льный
alcoholic /ælkə'hɒlɪk/ n. алкого́лик
● adj. алкого́льный; ~ **beverages** спиртно́е;
спиртны́е напи́тки (m. pl.)
alcoholism /'ælkəhɒlɪz(ə)m/ n. алкоголи́зм
alcove /'ælkəʊv/ n. алько́в, ни́ша
ale /eɪl/ n. эль (m.); (beer) пи́во
alert /ə'lɜːt/ adj. (vigilant) чу́ткий; (lively) живо́й
● v.t. прив|оди́ть, -ести́ в состоя́ние гото́вности;
~ **sb to a situation** предупре|жда́ть, -ди́ть
кого́-н. о созда́вшейся ситуа́ции
A level n. (BrE) выпускно́й экза́мен в сре́дней
шко́ле по профили́рующим предме́там
(с повы́шенным у́ровнем сло́жности)
algebra /'ældʒɪbrə/ n. а́лгебра
Algeria /æl'dʒɪərɪə/ n. Алжи́р
Algerian /æl'dʒɪərɪən/ n. алжи́р|ец (-ка)
● adj. алжи́рский
alias /'eɪlɪəs/ n. кли́чка, про́звище;
вы́мышленное и́мя
alibi /'ælɪbaɪ/ n. (pl. ~s) **1** (plea or proof of being
elsewhere) а́либи (nt. indecl.); **establish an** ~
устан|а́вливать, -ови́ть а́либи; **produce an** ~
предст|авля́ть, -а́вить а́либи **2** (infml, excuse)
отгово́рка
alien /'eɪlɪən/ n. (foreigner) иностра́н|ец
(-ка); (extraterrestrial) инопланетя́н|ин (-ка),
прише́лец (из ко́смоса)
● adj. **1** (foreign) иностра́нный; (extraterrestrial)
инопланетный **2**: ~ **to** чужды́й + d.
alienate /'eɪlɪəneɪt/ v.t. (estrange, antagonize)
отвра|ща́ть, -ти́ть; отчужда́ть (impf.)
alight¹ /ə'laɪt/ pred. adj. & adv. (on fire)
горя́щий, в огне́; **set** ~ зажига́ть, -е́чь
alight² /ə'laɪt/ v.i. (**alighted**) **1** (BrE, from
vehicle) сходи́ть, сойти́ (from: с + g.) **2** (come
to earth) сади́ться, сесть
align /ə'laɪn/ v.t. выра́внивать, вы́ровнять
alignment /ə'laɪnmənt/ n. выра́внивание;
out of ~ неро́вно, не в ряд
alike /ə'laɪk/ pred. adj. (similar) (of people)
похо́жий (на + a.); (of objects) схо́жий (с + i.)
● adv. одина́ково; **treat everyone** ~ обраща́ться
(impf.) со все́ми одина́ково; **winter and**
summer ~ как зимо́й, так и ле́том
alimony /'ælɪmənɪ/ n. (law) алиме́нт|ы (-ов)
✍ **alive** /ə'laɪv/ pred. adj. & adv. **1** (living) живо́й;
в живы́х; **buried** ~ похоро́ненный за́живо; ~
and kicking жив-здоро́в (infml) **2** (alert): **look**

a

~! живе́е! **3** (infested): **the bed was ~ with fleas** крова́ть кише́ла бло́хами

alkali /'ælkəlaɪ/ n. (pl. ~s) щёлочь; (attr.) щелочно́й

alkaline /'ælkəlaɪn/ adj. щелочно́й

✦ **all** /ɔːl/ pron. (everybody) все; (everything) всё; **~ of us** мы все; **the score is 2 ~** счёт 2:2; **~ but** (almost) почти, чуть не; **~ in ~** (in general) в о́бщем и це́лом; **above ~** пре́жде всего́; **after ~** в конце́ концо́в; в коне́чном счёте; **he came after ~** он всё же пришёл; **not at ~** совсе́м/во́все не; ниско́лько, ничу́ть; '**Thank you.' — 'Not at ~!'** «Спаси́бо.» — «Не за что!»; **he has no money at ~** у него́ совсе́м нет де́нег; **once and for ~** раз и навсегда́
● adj. весь; (every) вся́кий; **~ his life** всю свою́ жизнь; **~ day long** весь день; **~ the time** всё вре́мя; **at ~ times** в любо́е вре́мя; всегда́; **for ~ that** всё-таки
● adv. (quite) совсе́м, соверше́нно; целико́м; **~ dressed up** наряди́вшись; разряди́вшись в пух и прах; **I got ~ excited** я разволнова́лся; **I knew it ~ along** я э́то знал; **she lived ~ by herself** она́ жила́ совсе́м одна́; **she did it ~ by herself** она́ сде́лала э́то сама́; **I am ~ ears** я весь (m.) /вся (f.) внима́ние; **~ in** (exhausted) вы́бившийся из сил; (inclusive of everything) включа́я всё; **~ over again** (всё) сно́ва; **~ right!** ла́дно!, хорошо́!; '**How are you?' — 'A~ right!'** «Как дела́?» — «Норма́льно!»; **the film was ~ right** фильм был неплохо́й; **are you ~ right?** с ва́ми всё в поря́дке?; **~ the same** (however) всё-таки; **he's not ~ there** у него́ не все до́ма
■ **~-clear** n. отбо́й (трево́ги); **~-important** adj. чрезвыча́йно ва́жный; **~-night** adj.: **~-night session** заседа́ние, продолжа́ющееся всю ночь; **~-out** adj.: **an ~-out effort** максима́льное уси́лие; **~-star** adj.: **with an ~-star cast** с уча́стием звёзд; **~-time** adj.: **at an ~-time low** на небыва́ло ни́зком у́ровне; **~-time record** непревзойдённый реко́рд; **~-weather** adj. всепого́дный

Allah /'ælə/ n. Алла́х

allay /ə'leɪ/ v.t. (doubts, suspicions) рассе́|ивать, -ять; (fears) разве́|ивать, -ять; **~ thirst/hunger** утол|я́ть, -и́ть жа́жду/го́лод

allegation /ælɪ'geɪʃ(ə)n/ n. заявле́ние, утвержде́ние

✦ **allege** /ə'ledʒ/ v.t. утвержда́ть (impf.); **an ~d murderer** подозрева́емый в уби́йстве

allegedly /ə'ledʒɪdlɪ/ adv. бу́дто бы, я́кобы

allegiance /ə'liːdʒ(ə)ns/ n. (loyalty) ве́рность; (devotion) пре́данность

allegorical /ælɪ'gɒrɪk(ə)l/ adj. аллегори́ческий

allegory /'ælɪgərɪ/ n. аллего́рия

allegro /ə'legrəʊ/ n., adj., & adv. (pl. ~s) алле́гро (nt. indecl.)

alleluia /ælɪ'luːjə/ n. & int. аллилу́йя

allergic /ə'lɜːdʒɪk/ adj. аллерги́ческий; **I'm ~ to strawberries** у меня́ аллерги́я на клубни́ку

allergy /'ælədʒɪ/ n. аллерги́я

✦ ключева́я ле́ксика

alleviate /ə'liːvɪeɪt/ v.t. (relieve, lighten) облегч|а́ть, -и́ть; (mitigate, soften) смягч|а́ть, -и́ть

alley /'ælɪ/ n. (pl. ~s) переу́лок; **blind ~** тупи́к

alliance /ə'laɪəns/ n. сою́з; (pol.) алья́нс

allied /'ælaɪd/ adj. сою́зный

allocate /'æləkeɪt/ v.t. (money) ассигнова́ть (impf., pf.); (distribute) разме|ща́ть, -сти́ть; (assign) назн|ача́ть, -а́чить

allocation /ælə'keɪʃ(ə)n/ n. (allocating) выделе́ние; ассигнова́ние; размеще́ние; назначе́ние; (sum allocated) ассигнова́ние

allot /ə'lɒt/ v.t. (**allotted, allotting**) (distribute) распредел|я́ть, -и́ть; (assign) назн|ача́ть, -а́чить; **~ a task** дава́ть, -ть зада́ние

allotment /ə'lɒtmənt/ n. (BrE, plot of land) (земе́льный) уча́сток

✦ **allow** /ə'laʊ/ v.t. **1** (permit) позв|оля́ть, -о́лить; разреш|а́ть, -и́ть; **~ me!** разреши́те!; **he was ~ed to smoke** ему́ позво́лили кури́ть; **smoking is not ~ed** кури́ть воспреща́ется; **no dogs ~ed** вход с соба́ками воспрещён **2** (grant, provide) дава́ть, -ть; предост|авля́ть, -а́вить; допус|ка́ть, -ти́ть
● v.i. **~ for** (take into account) учи́тывать, -е́сть; **not ~ing for expenses** не принима́я в расчёт изде́ржек; **~ £50 for emergencies** выдел|я́ть, вы́делить 50 фу́нтов на непредви́денный слу́чай

allowance /ə'laʊəns/ n. **1** (amount provided): **monthly ~** ме́сячное посо́бие; **make sb an ~** назнача́ть, назна́чить содержа́ние кому́-н.; (mil.) дово́льствие **2** (concession): **we will make an ~ in your case** мы сде́лаем для вас исключе́ние; **make ~(s) for** учи́тывать, -е́сть; прин|има́ть, -я́ть во внима́ние

alloy /'ælɔɪ/ n. сплав

allude /ə'luːd/ v.i.: **~ to** ссыла́ться, сосла́ться на + a.; упом|ина́ть, -яну́ть; (mean) **what are you ~ing to?** на что вы намека́ете?

allure /ə'ljʊə(r)/ n. привлека́тельность, пре́лесть
● v.t. (entice, attract) зама́н|ивать, -и́ть; (charm) завл|ека́ть, -е́чь; очаро́в|ывать, -а́ть

allusion /ə'luːʒ(ə)n/ n. намёк; ссы́лка

ally¹ /'ælaɪ/ n. сою́зник

ally² /ə'laɪ/ v.t. (connect) соедин|я́ть, -и́ть; **~ oneself with** вступ|а́ть, -и́ть в сою́з с + i.

almanac /'ɔːlmənæk/ n. альмана́х

almighty /ɔːl'maɪtɪ/ n.: **the A~** Всемогу́щий
● adj. Всемогу́щий; (infml, huge) огро́мный

almond /'ɑːmənd/ n. минда́ль (m.)

✦ **almost** /'ɔːlməʊst/ adv. почти́; (with vv.) почти́, чуть не, едва́ не

✦ **alone** /ə'ləʊn/ adj. **1** (by oneself, itself) оди́н; еди́нственный **2** (… and no other(s)): **in the month of June ~** то́лько в ию́не ме́сяце; **she and I are ~** (together) мы с ней вдвоём/одни́ **3** **let, leave ~**: **his parents left him ~ all day** роди́тели оста́вили его́ на це́лый день одного́; (see also ▶ let alone ▶ let²))

✦ **along** /ə'lɒŋ/ adv. **1** (on; forward): **move ~** продв|ига́ться, -и́нуться; **come ~!** пошли́!; **a few doors ~ from the station** в не́скольких

шага́х от вокза́ла **2** (denoting accompaniment):
he brought a book ～ он принёс с собо́й
кни́гу **3** (over there; over here): **he'll be** ～ **in
10 minutes** он бу́дет че́рез де́сять мину́т
4: **all** ～ (the whole time) всё вре́мя
● *prep.* вдоль + *g.*; по + *d.*; **she was walking**
～ **the river** она́ шла вдоль реки́

alongside /əlɒŋ'saɪd/ *adv.* ря́дом, сбо́ку; **we
stopped and the police car drew up** ～ мы
останови́лись, и подъе́хавшая полице́йская
маши́на вста́ла ря́дом
● *prep.* (*also* ～ **of**) ря́дом с + *i.*; у + *g.*

aloof /ə'luːf/ *adj.* сде́ржанный, отчуждённый

aloofness /ə'luːfnɪs/ *n.* сде́ржанность,
отчуждённость

aloud /ə'laʊd/ *adv.* вслух; **read** ～ чита́ть вслух

alphabet /'ælfəbet/ *n.* алфави́т, а́збука

alphabetical /ælfə'betɪk(ə)l/ *adj.* алфави́тный;
in ～ **order** в алфави́тном поря́дке

alpine /'ælpaɪn/ *adj.* альпи́йский

Alps /ælps/ *n. pl.* (*in full* **the** ～) А́льп|ы
(*pl., g.* —)

ǰ **already** /ɔːl'redɪ/ *adv.* уже́

Alsatian /æl'seɪʃ(ə)n/ *n.* (BrE) неме́цкая овча́рка

ǰ **also** /'ɔːlsəʊ/ *adv.* то́же; та́кже; (moreover)
к тому́ же

altar /'ɔːltə(r)/ *n.* престо́л, алта́рь

alter /'ɔːltə(r)/ *v.t. & i.* меня́ть(ся) (*impf.*);
измен|я́ть(ся), -и́ть(ся); (remake) переде́л|ывать,
-ать; **the dress needs** ～**ing** э́то пла́тье на́до
переде́лать

alteration /ɔːltə'reɪʃ(ə)n/ *n.* (change)
измене́ние; (remaking, e.g. of clothes) переде́лка

altercation /ɔːltə'keɪʃ(ə)n/ *n.* ссо́ра,
перебра́нка

alternate[1] /ɔːl'tɜːnət/ *adj.* **1** (taking turns)
череду́ющийся; **on** ～ **Saturdays** ка́ждую
втору́ю суббо́ту **2** (AmE, alternative)
альтернати́вный

alternate[2] /'ɔːltəneɪt/ *v.t. & i.* чередова́ть(ся)
(*impf.*); переме́ж|а́ть(ся) (*impf.*)

ǰ **alternative** /ɔːl'tɜːnətɪv/ *n.* альтернати́ва;
there is no ～ друго́го вы́бора нет
● *adj.* альтернати́вный
■ ～ **medicine** *n.* нетрадицио́нная медици́на;
～ **technology** *n.* техноло́гия безотхо́дного
произво́дства

alternatively /ɔːl'tɜːnətɪvlɪ/ *adv.* (indicating
choice): **a £5,000 fine,** ～ **one month's
imprisonment** штраф 5000 фу́нтов и́ли оди́н
ме́сяц тюре́много заключе́ния

alternator /'ɔːltəneɪtə(r)/ *n.* (elec.) генера́тор
переме́нного то́ка

ǰ **although** /ɔːl'ðəʊ/ *conj.* хотя́; (despite the fact
that) несмотря́ на то, что

altitude /'æltɪtjuːd/ *n.* (of flight) высота́; (of a
place) высота́ над у́ровнем мо́ря

alto /'æltəʊ/ *n.* (*pl.* **altos**) альт; (*attr.*) альто́вый

altogether /ɔːltə'geðə(r)/ *adv.* **1** (entirely)
вполне́; соверше́нно; (completely) совсе́м
2 (in all, in general; as a whole) в це́лом, в о́бщем,
всего́; **how much is that** ～**?** ско́лько всего́?

altruism /'æltruːɪz(ə)m/ *n.* альтруи́зм

altruistic /æltruː'ɪstɪk/ *adj.* альтруисти́ческий

aluminium /ælju'mɪnɪəm/ (AmE **aluminum**
/ə'luːmɪnəm/) *n.* алюми́ний

ǰ **always** /'ɔːlweɪz/ *adv.* всегда́; (constantly)
постоя́нно, всё вре́мя; **he is** ～ **after money**
он всегда́/постоя́нно ду́мает о деньга́х

Alzheimer's /'æltshaɪməz/ *n.* (*in full* ～
disease) боле́знь Альцге́ймера

am /æm/ *1st pers. sing. pres. of* ▶ **be**

a.m. *abbr.* (*of* **ante meridiem**) утра́; (in the
morning) у́тром; **6** ～ шесть часо́в утра́

amalgam /ə'mælgəm/ *n.* амальга́ма; (fig.) смесь

amalgamate /ə'mælgəmeɪt/ *v.t. & i.*
(companies) слива́ть(ся), слить(ся)

amass /ə'mæs/ *v.t.* накоп|ля́ть, -и́ть

amateur /'æmətə(r)/ *n.* люби́тель (*m.*); (*attr.*)
люби́тельский

amateurish /'æmətərɪʃ/ *adj.* дилета́нтский;
непрофессиона́льный

amaz|e /ə'meɪz/ *v.t.* изум|ля́ть, -и́ть; **be
** ～**ed at** изум|ля́ться, -и́ться + *d.*; ～**ing**
изуми́тельный, удиви́тельный

amazement /ə'meɪzmənt/ *n.* изумле́ние

Amazon /'æməz(ə)n/ *n.* (myth., fig.) амазо́нка;
(river) Амазо́нка

ambassador /æm'bæsədə(r)/ *n.* посо́л;
(representative) представи́тель (*m.*)

amber /'æmbə(r)/ *n.* **1** (resin) янта́рь (*m.*)
2 (colour) янта́рный цвет, цвет янтаря́

ambidextrous /æmbɪ'dekstrəs/ *adj.*
одина́ково владе́ющий обе́ими рука́ми

ambience /'æmbɪəns/ *n.* среда́; атмосфе́ра

ambient /'æmbɪənt/ *adj.* окружа́ющий; ～
temperature температу́ра окружа́ющего
во́здуха

ambiguity /æmbɪ'gjuːɪtɪ/ *n.* двусмы́сленность;
нея́сность

ambiguous /æm'bɪgjʊəs/ *adj.* двусмы́сленный;
нея́сный

ambition /æm'bɪʃ(ə)n/ *n.* (desire for distinction)
честолю́бие, амби́ция; (aspiration) стремле́ние

ambitious /æm'bɪʃəs/ *adj.* честолюби́вый;
амбицио́зный; **an** ～ **plan** грандио́зный план

ambivalence /æm'bɪvələns/ *n.* дво́йственность

ambivalent /æm'bɪvələnt/ *adj.* дво́йственный

amble /'æmb(ə)l/ *n. v.i.* идти́ (*det.*) лёгкой
похо́дкой; прогу́ливаться (*impf.*)

ambulance /'æmbjʊləns/ *n.* маши́на ско́рой
по́мощи

ambush /'æmbʊʃ/ *n.* заса́да
● *v.t.* нап|ада́ть, -а́сть на (*кого*) из заса́ды

ameba /ə'miːbə/ *n.* (AmE) = amoeba

ameliorate /ə'miːlɪəreɪt/ *v.t. & i.* ул|учша́ть(ся),
-у́чшить(ся)

amen /ɑː'men/ *int.* ами́нь

amend /ə'mend/ *v.t.* **1** (correct) испр|авля́ть,
-а́вить **2** (make changes to) вн|оси́ть, -ести́
попра́вки/измене́ния в + *a.*

amendment /ə'mendmənt/ *n.* **1** (reform)
исправле́ние **2** (of document etc.) попра́вка

amends /ə'mendz/ *n. pl.* возмеще́ние;
исправле́ние; **make** ～ **to sb** загла́|живать,

a

-дить вину́ пе́ред (+ *i.*) (*за что*); he made ~
for his rudeness он загла́дил свою́ гру́бость

amenity /əˈmiːnɪti/ *n.* (*usu. in pl.*) удо́бства
(*nt. pl.*)

America /əˈmerɪkə/ *n.* Аме́рика

✓ **American** /əˈmerɪkən/ *n.* америка́н|ец (-ка)
● *adj.* америка́нский
■ ~ **English** *n.* америка́нский вариа́нт
англи́йского языка́; ~ **Indian** *n.*
америка́нск|ий инде́ец (-ая индиа́нка)

Americanism /əˈmerɪkənɪz(ə)m/ *n.*
американи́зм

amethyst /ˈæmɪθɪst/ *n.* амети́ст; (*attr.*)
амети́стовый

amiable /ˈeɪmɪəb(ə)l/ *adj.* приве́тливый;
добро́душный

amicable /ˈæmɪkəb(ə)l/ *adj.* дружелю́бный;
(agreement, separation) дру́жеский; (divorce)
ми́рный

amid /əˈmɪd/ *prep.* среди́ + *g.*

amidst /əˈmɪdst/ *prep.* (literary) = amid

amino acid /əˈmiːnəʊ/ *n.* аминокислота́

amiss /əˈmɪs/ *pred. adj.* непра́вильный;
something is ~ что́-то нела́дно

ammeter /ˈæmɪtə(r)/ *n.* амперме́тр

ammonia /əˈməʊnɪə/ *n.* (gas) аммиа́к; (*attr.*)
аммиа́чный

ammunition /æmjʊˈnɪʃ(ə)n/ *n.* боевы́е
припа́сы, боеприпа́сы (*m. pl.*)

amnesia /æmˈniːzɪə/ *n.* амнези́я

amnesty /ˈæmnɪsti/ *n.* амни́стия

amniocentesis /æmnɪəʊsenˈtiːsɪs/ *n.* (med.)
амниоцентёз (*пункция плодного пузыря*)

amoeba /əˈmiːbə/ (AmE also **ameba**) *n.* (*pl.*
amoebas *or* **amoebae** /-biː/) амёба

amok /əˈmɒk/ *adv.*: run ~ бу́йствовать (*impf.*);
беси́ться (*impf.*)

✓ **among** /əˈmʌŋ/ *prep.* **1** (between) ме́жду + *i.*;
conversation ~ friends разгово́р ме́жду
друзья́ми **2** (in the midst of) среди́ + *g.*; ме́жду
+ *g.*; ~ the trees среди́ дере́вьев **3** (expr. one
of a number) из + *g.*

amongst /əˈmʌŋst/ *prep.* (BrE) = among

amoral /eɪˈmɒr(ə)l/ *adj.* амора́льный

amorphous /əˈmɔːfəs/ *adj.* (shapeless)
бесфо́рменный

amortize /əˈmɔːtaɪz/ *v.t.* амортизи́ровать
(*impf., pf.*)

✓ **amount** /əˈmaʊnt/ *n.* **1** (sum) су́мма
2 (quantity) коли́чество; he spent a huge ~
of money он истра́тил ку́чу де́нег
● *v.i.*: ~ to (add up to) сост|авля́ть, -а́вить + *g.*;
дост|ига́ть, -и́чь + *g.*; the expenses ~ to £600
расхо́ды составля́ют шестьсо́т фу́нтов; (be
equivalent to) быть ра́вным/равноси́льным +
d.; it ~s to the same thing э́то сво́дится всё
к тому́ же

amp /æmp/ *n.* (*abbr. of* **ampere**) A (ампе́р)

ampere /ˈæmpeə(r)/ *n.* ампе́р

ampersand /ˈæmpəsænd/ *n.* амперса́нд (*знак*
«&»)

amphetamine /æmˈfetəmiːn/ *n.* амфетами́н

amphibian /æmˈfɪbɪən/ *n.* земново́дное;
амфи́бия

amphitheatre /ˈæmfɪθɪətə(r)/ (AmE
amphitheater) *n.* амфитеа́тр

ample /ˈæmp(ə)l/ *adj.* (**ampler**, **amplest**)
(sufficient) доста́точный; (abundant) оби́льный

amplifier /ˈæmplɪfaɪə(r)/ *n.* усили́тель (*m.*)

amplify /ˈæmplɪfaɪ/ *v.t.* уси́ли|вать, -ть

amputate /ˈæmpjʊteɪt/ *v.t.* ампути́ровать
(*impf., pf.*); отн|има́ть, -я́ть

amuse /əˈmjuːz/ *v.t.* (entertain, divert) развл|ека́ть,
-е́чь; (make laugh) смеши́ть (*impf.*); позаба́вить
(*pf.*)

amusement /əˈmjuːzmənt/ *n.* **1** (diversion)
развлече́ние, заба́ва **2** (tendency to laughter):
to everyone's ~ the clown fell over ко
всео́бщему удово́льствию кло́ун упа́л
■ ~ **park** *n.* парк с аттракцио́нами; лу́на-па́рк

amusing /əˈmjuːzɪŋ/ *adj.* заба́вный; (funny)
смешно́й

an /æn, ən/ *see* ▸ a

anachronism /əˈnækrənɪz(ə)m/ *n.* анахрони́зм

anaemia /əˈniːmɪə/ (AmE **anemia**) *n.*
малокро́вие, анеми́я

anaesthesia /ænɪsˈθiːzɪə/ (AmE **anesthesia**)
n. анестези́я, обезбо́ливание

anaesthetic /ænɪsˈθetɪk/ (AmE **anesthetic**)
n. анестези́рующее сре́дство; анесте́тик;
general/local ~ о́бщий/ме́стный нарко́з;
under ~ под нарко́зом

anaesthetist /əˈniːsθətɪst/ (AmE
anesthetist) *n.* анестезио́лог

anaesthetize /əˈniːsθətaɪz/ (AmE **anesthetize**)
v.t. анестези́ровать (*impf., pf.*); обезбо́ли|вать,
-ть

anal /ˈeɪn(ə)l/ *adj.* заднепрохо́дный, ана́льный

analgesic /ænəlˈdʒiːzɪk/ *adj.* болеутоля́ющий

analogous /əˈnæləgəs/ *adj.* аналоги́чный

analogy /əˈnælədʒi/ *n.* анало́гия; схо́дство

analyse /ˈænəlaɪz/ (AmE **analyze**) *v.t.*
анализи́ровать (*impf., pf.*) (*pf. also* про-)

✓ **analysis** /əˈnælɪsɪs/ *n.* (*pl.* **analyses** /-siːz/)
ана́лиз; (psycho~) психоана́лиз

✓ **analyst** /ˈænəlɪst/ *n.* анали́тик; (political)
коммента́тор; (psych.) психоанали́тик

analytical /ænəˈlɪtɪk(ə)l/, **analytic**
/ænəˈlɪtɪk/ *adjs.* аналити́ческий

analyze /ˈænəlaɪz/ *v.t.* (AmE) = analyse

anarchic /əˈnɑːkɪk/, **anarchical** /əˈnɑːkɪk(ə)l/
adjs. анархи́ческий

anarchist /ˈænəkɪst/ *n.* анархи́ст (-ка)

anarchy /ˈænəki/ *n.* ана́рхия

anathema /əˈnæθəmə/ *n.* (*pl.* ~**s**) (hated
thing): it's ~ to me я непримири́мый/
я́рый проти́вник э́того; я органи́чески не
прие́млю э́того

✓ ключевая лексика

anatomical /ænə'tɒmɪk(ə)l/ *adj.*
анатоми́ческий

anatomy /ə'nætəmɪ/ *n.* анато́мия

ancestor /'ænsestə(r)/ *n.* пре́док

ancestral /æn'sestr(ə)l/ *adj.* родово́й; ∼ **home**
родово́е име́ние

ancestry /'ænsestrɪ/ *n.* (lineage) родосло́вная,
происхожде́ние; **he comes of distinguished** ∼
он благоро́дного происхожде́ния

anchor /'æŋkə(r)/ *n.* я́корь (*m.*)

anchovy /'æntʃəvɪ/ *n.* анчо́ус

ⁱ **ancient** /'eɪnʃ(ə)nt/ *adj.* дре́вний; анти́чный;
(very old) стари́нный; веково́й
∎ ∼ **history** *n.* дре́вняя исто́рия; ∼
monument *n.* (BrE) па́мятник старины́

ⁱ **and** /ænd/ *conj.* **1** (connecting words or clauses) и;
(in addition) и, да; (with certain closely linked pairs,
esp. of persons) с + *i.*; **bread** ∼ **butter** хлеб с
ма́слом; **you** ∼ **I** мы с ва́ми; (with nums. denoting
addition) и, плюс; **2** ∼ **2 are 4** два и/плюс
два — четы́ре; (to form compound num., omitted):
260 две́сти шестьдеся́т; (with following fraction)
с + *i.* **2** (intensive): **he ran** ∼ **ran** он всё бежа́л
и бежа́л; **they talked for hours** ∼ **hours** они́
разгова́ривали часа́ми **3** (in order to, omitted
before inf.): **try** ∼ **find out** постара́йтесь узна́ть;
wait ∼ **see!** погоди́те — ещё уви́дите!

andante /æn'dæntɪ/ *n.*, *adj.*, *and adv.* (mus.)
анда́нте (*nt. indecl.*)

androgynous /æn'drɒdʒɪnəs/ *adj.* двупо́лый;
(bot.) обоепо́лый

anecdotal /ænɪk'dəʊt(ə)l/ *adj.* анекдоти́ческий

anecdote /'ænɪkdəʊt/ *n.* исто́рия; (joke) анекдо́т

anemia /ə'niːmɪə/ *n.* (AmE) = anaemia

anemone /ə'nemənɪ/ *n.* анемо́н; (wood ∼)
ветре́ница; **sea** ∼ морско́й анемо́н; акти́ния

anesthesia /ænɪs'θiːzɪə/ *n.* (AmE) = anaesthesia

anesthetic /ænɪs'θetɪk/ *n.* (AmE) = anaesthetic

anesthetist /ə'niːsθətɪst/ *n.* (AmE) = anaesthetist

anesthetize /ə'niːsθətaɪz/ *v.t.* (AmE)
= anaesthetize

anew /ə'njuː/ *adj.* (again) сно́ва; (in a different way)
за́ново, по-но́вому

angel /'eɪndʒ(ə)l/ *n.* (lit., fig.) а́нгел

angelic /æn'dʒelɪk/ *adj.* а́нгельский

anger /'æŋɡə(r)/ *n.* гнев
● *v.t.* серди́ть, рас-; разгне́вать (*pf.*)

angina /æn'dʒaɪnə/ *n.* (*also* ∼ **pectoris**
/'pektərɪs/) стенокарди́я, грудна́я жа́ба

angle¹ /'æŋɡ(ə)l/ *n.* у́гол; **right** ∼ прямо́й
у́гол; **at right** ∼**s** под прямы́м угло́м; (fig.,
viewpoint) то́чка зре́ния, подхо́д
● *v.t.* ста́вить, по- под угло́м; (fig.): **the news
was** ∼**d** но́вости бы́ли по́даны тенденцио́зно

angle² /'æŋɡ(ə)l/ *v.i.* (fish) уди́ть (*impf.*) ры́бу;
(fig.): ∼ **for compliments** напра́шиваться
(*impf.*) на комплиме́нты

angler /'æŋɡlə(r)/ *n.* рыболо́в

Anglican /'æŋɡlɪkən/ *n.* англика́н|ец (-ка)
● *adj.* англика́нский

Anglo-Saxon /æŋɡləʊ'sæks(ə)n/ *n.*
англосаксо́нский/древнеангли́йский язы́к
● *adj.* англосаксо́нский, древнеангли́йский

Angola /æn'ɡəʊlə/ *n.* Анго́ла

Angolan /æn'ɡəʊlən/ *n.* анго́л|ец (-ка)
● *adj.* анго́льский

angora /æn'ɡɔːrə/ *n.* (cloth) анго́рская шерсть
● *adj.* анго́рский

ⁱ **angry** /'æŋɡrɪ/ *adj.* (**angrier**, **angriest**)
серди́тый; **be** ∼ **with** серди́ться (*impf.*) на
+ *a.* (over, about sth: за + *a.*); **get** ∼ **with**
рассерди́ться (*pf.*) на + *a.*

anguish /'æŋɡwɪʃ/ *n.* муче́ние; му́ка

angular /'æŋɡjʊlə(r)/ *adj.* углова́тый

ⁱ **animal** /'ænɪm(ə)l/ *n.* живо́тное
● *adj.* живо́тный
∎ ∼ **rights** *n. pl.* права́ (*nt. pl.*) живо́тных

animate /'ænɪmeɪt/ *v.t.* ожив|ля́ть, -и́ть;
become ∼**d** ожив|ля́ться, -и́ться

animation /ænɪ'meɪʃ(ə)n/ *n.* (enthusiasm)
воодушевле́ние; (cin.) мультипликация,
анима́ция

animosity /ænɪ'mɒsɪtɪ/ *n.* (hostility)
вражде́бность; **feel** ∼ **against** пита́ть (*impf.*)
вражду́ к + *d.*

aniseed /'ænɪsiːd/ *n.* ани́с, ани́совое се́мя

ankle /'æŋk(ə)l/ *n.* лоды́жка, щи́колотка
∎ ∼ **socks** *n. pl.* носки́ (*m. pl.*)

annex¹ /'æneks/ *n.* (to a building) пристро́йка,
фли́гель (*m.*)

annex² /æ'neks/ *v.t.* присоедин|я́ть, -и́ть;
(territory etc.) аннекси́ровать (*impf., pf.*)

annexation /ænek'seɪʃ(ə)n/ *n.*
присоедине́ние; анне́ксия, аннекси́рование

annexe /'æneks/ *n.* (BrE) = annex¹

annihilate /ə'naɪəleɪt/ *v.t.* (destroy)
уничт|ожа́ть, -о́жить

anniversary /ænɪ'vɜːsərɪ/ *n.* годовщи́на

annotate /'ænəteɪt/ *v.t.* снаб|жа́ть, -ди́ть
коммента́риями *or* примеча́ниями; ∼**d text**
текст с коммента́риями *or* примеча́ниями

annotation /ænə'teɪʃ(ə)n/ *n.* (annotating)
комменти́рование; (added note) коммента́рий,
примеча́ние

ⁱ **announce** /ə'naʊns/ *v.t.* (state; declare)
объяв|ля́ть, -и́ть (*что or о чём*); заяв|ля́ть,
-и́ть (*что or о чём*); (notify, tell) сообщ|а́ть,
-и́ть (*о чём ному*); **he** ∼**d the results of his
researches** он огласи́л результа́ты свои́х
иссле́дований

announcement /ə'naʊnsmənt/ *n.*
объявле́ние, заявле́ние; **put an** ∼ **in the
newspaper** поме|ща́ть, -сти́ть объявле́ние в
газе́те; (written notification) извеще́ние; (on radio
etc.) сообще́ние

announcer /ə'naʊnsə(r)/ *n.* ди́ктор

annoy /ə'nɔɪ/ *v.t.* (vex) доса|жда́ть, -ди́ть + *d.*;
(irritate) раздража́ть (*impf.*); де́йствовать
(*impf.*) на не́рвы + *d.*; (pester) докуча́ть (*impf.*)
+ *d.*; **I was** ∼**ed with him** я был серди́т на него́

annoyance /ə'nɔɪəns/ *n.* раздраже́ние

annoying /ə'nɔɪɪŋ/ *adj.* доса́дный; **how** ∼!
кака́я доса́да!, вот доса́да!

ⁱ **annual** /'ænjʊəl/ *n.* **1** (publication) ежего́дник
2 (plant) одноле́тнее расте́ние
● *adj.* **1** (happening once a year) ежего́дный

a

2 (pert. to whole year) годово́й; ~ **income** годово́й дохо́д

annually /'ænjʊəlɪ/ *adv.* ежего́дно

annul /ə'nʌl/ *v.t.* (**annulled, annulling**) аннули́ровать (*impf., pf.*); отмен|я́ть, -и́ть; **the marriage was ~led** брак был при́знан недействи́тельным

annulment /ə'nʌlmənt/ *n.* аннули́рование, отме́на

anodyne /'ænədaɪn/ *adj.* безоби́дный

anomaly /ə'nɒməlɪ/ *n.* анома́лия

anonymous /ə'nɒnɪməs/ *adj.* анони́мный; безымя́нный

anorak /'ænəræk/ *n.* аля́ска, ку́ртка с капюшо́ном

anorexia /ænə'reksɪə/ *n.* аноре́ксия

anorexic /ænə'reksɪk/ *adj.* страда́ющий аноре́ксией

⚜ **another** /ə'nʌðə(r)/ *pron. & adj.* **1** (additional) ещё; ~ **cup of tea?** ещё ча́шку ча́я?; **have** ~ **go!** попыта́йтесь ещё раз!; **in** ~ **10 years** ещё че́рез де́сять лет; **and** ~ **thing** и вот ещё что **2** (similar): ~ **Tolstoy** второ́й Толсто́й **3** (different) друго́й; ~ **time** в друго́й раз

⚜ **answer** /'ɑːnsə(r)/ *n.* **1** (reply) отве́т; **what was his** ~? что он отве́тил?; **in** ~ **to your letter** в отве́т на Ва́ше письмо́; (retort) возраже́ние **2** (solution) отве́т; реше́ние
● *v.t.* **1** (reply to) отв|еча́ть, -е́тить (*кому, на что*); ~ **the door** откр|ыва́ть, -ы́ть дверь; ~ **the telephone** под|ходи́ть, -ойти́ к телефо́ну; отв|еча́ть, -е́тить на телефо́нные звонки́ **2** (correspond to): **he** ~**s the description exactly** он то́чно соотве́тствует описа́нию **3** (satisfy, grant): **our prayers were** ~**ed** на́ши моли́твы бы́ли услы́шаны
● *v.i.* **1** (reply) отв|еча́ть, -е́тить **2**: ~ **for** руча́ться, поручи́ться за + *a.*; **I will** ~ **for his honesty** я руча́юсь за его́ че́стность **3** (give an account): **I** ~ **to no one** я никому́ не обя́зан отчи́тываться **4**: ~ **back** дерзи́ть, на-
■ ~**phone** *n.* (BrE) автоотве́тчик

answerable /'ɑːnsərəb(ə)l/ *adj.* (responsible) отве́тственный (**to:** пе́ред + *i.*, **for:** за + *a.*)

answering /'ɑːnsərɪŋ/ *adj.*: ~ **machine** автоотве́тчик

ant /ænt/ *n.* мураве́й

antagonism /æn'tægənɪz(ə)m/ *n.* антагони́зм

antagonistic /æntægə'nɪstɪk/ *adj.* антагонисти́ческий

antagonize /æn'tægənaɪz/ *v.t.* вызыва́ть, вы́звать чьё-л. отчужде́ние; отчужда́ть (*impf.*)

Antarctic /æn'tɑːktɪk/ *n.* (*in full* **the** ~) Анта́рктика
● *adj.* антаркти́ческий

Antarctica /æn'tɑːktɪkə/ *n.* Антаркти́да

antelope /'æntɪləʊp/ *n.* (*pl.* ~ *or* ~**s**) антило́па

antenatal /æntɪ'neɪt(ə)l/ *adj.* (BrE, of care) дородово́й
■ ~ **clinic** *n.* же́нская консульта́ция

⚜ ключева́я ле́ксика

antenna /æn'tenə/ *n.* (*pl.* **antennae** /-niː/) (radio) анте́нна; (of insect) у́сик

anteroom /'æntɪruːm/ *n.* пере́дняя, прихо́жая

anthem /'ænθəm/ *n.* гимн; **national** ~ госуда́рственный гимн

anthology /æn'θɒlədʒɪ/ *n.* антоло́гия

anthrax /'ænθræks/ *n.* сиби́рская я́зва

anthropological /ænθrəpə'lɒdʒɪk(ə)l/ *adj.* антропологи́ческий

anthropologist /ænθrə'pɒlədʒɪst/ *n.* (biological) антропо́лог; **social** ~ этно́граф

anthropology /ænθrə'pɒlədʒɪ/ *n.* (biological) антрополо́гия; **social** (*or* **cultural**) ~ социа́льная антрополо́гия

anti- /'æntɪ/ *pref.* анти…, противо…

antibiotic /æntɪbaɪ'ɒtɪk/ *n.* антибио́тик

antibody /'æntɪbɒdɪ/ *n.* антите́ло

anticapitalist /æntɪ'kæpɪtəlɪst/ *n.* проти́вник капитали́зма
● *adj.* антикапиталисти́ческий

anticipate /æn'tɪsɪpeɪt/ *v.t.* (foresee) предви́деть (*impf.*); предчу́вствовать (*impf.*); (expect) ожида́ть (*impf.*); (with pleasure) предвку|ша́ть, -си́ть

anticipation /æntɪsɪ'peɪʃ(ə)n/ *n.* **1** (looking forward to) ожида́ние **2** (foreseeing) предви́дение, предвосхище́ние; **in** ~ **of a cold winter** предви́дя холо́дную зи́му **3** (foretasting) предвкуше́ние

anticlimax /æntɪ'klaɪmæks/ *n.* (ре́зкий) спад (интере́са *и т. п.*); разочарова́ние

anticlockwise /æntɪ'klɒkwaɪz/ *adj. & adv.* (BrE) про́тив часово́й стре́лки

antics /'æntɪks/ *n. pl.* проде́лки (*f. pl.*)

antidepressant /æntɪdɪ'pres(ə)nt/ *n.* антидепресса́нт

antidote /'æntɪdəʊt/ *n.* противоя́дие, антидо́т

antifreeze /'æntɪfriːz/ *n.* антифри́з

antiglobalization /æntɪɡləʊbəlaɪ'zeɪʃ(ə)n/ *n.* антиглобализа́ция

antihistamine /æntɪ'hɪstəmiːn/ *n.* антигистами́н; (*attr.*) антигистами́нный

antipathy /æn'tɪpəθɪ/ *n.* антипа́тия; **have, feel an** ~ **to, against, for** испы́тывать (*impf.*) антипа́тию к + *d.*

Antipodean /æntɪpə'diːən/ *adj.* (geog.) относя́щийся к Австра́лии и Но́вой Зела́ндии
● *n.* антипо́д, жи́тель Австра́лии и́ли Но́вой Зела́ндии

Antipodes /æn'tɪpədiːz/ *n. pl.* регио́н Австра́лии и Но́вой Зела́ндии

antiquated /'æntɪkweɪtɪd/ *adj.* (obsolete) устаре́лый; (old-fashioned) старомо́дный

antique /æn'tiːk/ *n.* антиква́рная вещь
● *adj.* (vase, table) антиква́рный
■ ~ **dealer** *n.* антиква́р; ~ **shop** *n.* антиква́рный магази́н

antiquity /æn'tɪkwɪtɪ/ *n.* (great age; olden times) дре́вность; (classical times) анти́чность; (*in pl.*) (ancient objects) антиквариа́т

anti-Semitic /æntɪsɪ'mɪtɪk/ *adj.* антисеми́тский

anti-Semitism /ˌæntɪˈsemɪtɪz(ə)m/ *n.* антисемитизм

antiseptic /ˌæntɪˈseptɪk/ *n.* антисептик
● *adj.* антисептический

antisocial /ˌæntɪˈsəʊʃ(ə)l/ *adj.* антиобщественный

antiterrorist /ˌæntɪˈterərɪst/ *adj.* антитеррористический

antithesis /ænˈtɪθəsɪs/ *n.* (*pl.* **antitheses** /-siːz/) (*contrast of opposite ideas*) антитеза; (*contrast*) контраст; (*opposite*) противоположность; **he is the ~ of his brother** он полная противоположность своему брату

anti-war /ˌæntɪˈwɔː(r)/ *adj.* антивоенный

antlers /ˈæntləz/ *n. pl.* оленьи/лосиные рога

anus /ˈeɪnəs/ *n.* задний проход, анус

anxiety /æŋˈzaɪətɪ/ *n.* **1** (*uneasiness*) беспокойство **2** (*desire; keenness*) желание/стремление (+ *inf.*) **3** (*in pl.*) (*cares, worries*) заботы (*f. pl.*)

anxious /ˈæŋkʃəs/ *adj.* **1** (*worried, uneasy*) озабоченный; беспокоиться о + р.; беспокоиться (*impf.*) за + а.; беспокоиться (*impf.*) о + р. **2** (*causing anxiety*) тревожный, беспокойный **3** (*keen, desirous*): **I am ~ to see him** мне очень хочется повидаться с ним

◆' **any** /ˈenɪ/ *pron.* **1** (*in interrog. or conditional sentences, with animates*) кто-нибудь; (*with inanimates*) что-нибудь; **if ~ of them should see him** если кто-нибудь из них увидит его **2** (*in neg. sentences*) (*with animates*) никто; (*with inanimates*) ничто; **I don't like ~ of these actors** никто/ни один из этих артистов мне не нравится; **he never spoke to ~ of our friends** ни с кем из наших друзей он (никогда) не говорил **3** (*in affirmative sentences*) любой; **take ~ of these books** возьмите любую/любые из этих книг **4**: **he has little money, if ~** денег у него мало, если (они) вообще есть
● *adj.* **1** (*in interrog. or conditional sentences*) *untranslated*: **have you ~ children?** у вас есть дети?; **have you ~ matches?** (*request*) у вас не будет спичек?; (*no matter what*) любой, какой угодно **2** (*in neg. sentences*): **we haven't ~ milk** у нас нет молока; **haven't you ~ cigarettes?** разве у вас нет сигарет?; (*not ~ at all*) никакой, ни один; **there isn't ~ man who would ... ** нет такого человека, который бы ...; (*with hardly*, vv. *of prevention etc.*): **there is hardly ~ doubt** нет почти никакого сомнения; **without ~ doubt** без/безо всякого сомнения; **they stopped us from scoring ~ goals** они не дали нам забить ни одного гола **3** (*no matter which*) любой; **at ~ time** в любое время; (*every*) любой, всякий; **in ~ case** во всяком случае
● *adv.* **1** (*in interrog. or conditional sentences*) *untranslated* or сколько-нибудь; **do you want ~ more tea?** хотите ещё чаю?; **if you stay here ~ longer** если вы ещё хоть немного задержитесь здесь **2** (*in neg. sentences*) *untranslated* or нисколько; ничуть; **I can't go ~ farther** я не могу идти дальше; **he doesn't live here ~ more** он здесь больше не живёт

◆' **anybody** /ˈenɪbɒdɪ/, **anyone** /ˈenɪwʌn/ *nn. & prons.* **1** (*in interrog. or conditional sentences*) кто-нибудь; кто-либо; **did you meet ~?** вы кого-нибудь встретили?; **if ~ rings, don't answer** если кто позвонит, не отвечайте; **is this ~'s seat?** это место занято? **2** (*in neg. sentences*) никто; **I didn't speak to ~** я ни с кем не говорил **3** (*~ at all; no matter who*) всякий, любой; **~ will tell you** любой/всякий вам скажет; **~ who says that is a liar** кто бы это ни сказал, он лжец; **~ else** кто-нибудь ещё; **there was hardly ~ there** там почти никого не было

anyhow /ˈenɪhaʊ/ *adv.* **1** (*haphazardly; carelessly*) кое-как; как-нибудь; **the work was done ~** работа была сделана кое-как **2** (*anyway, in any case*) во всяком случае; так или иначе; (*nevertheless*) всё равно, всё же; **I shall go ~** я всё равно пойду

◆' **anyone** /ˈenɪwʌn/ *n. & pron.* = **anybody**

◆' **anything** /ˈenɪθɪŋ/ *n. & pron.* **1** (*in interrog. or conditional sentences*) что-нибудь; что-либо; что; **is there ~ I can get for you?** вам что-нибудь принести?; **have you ~ to say?** у вас (*or* вам) есть, что сказать? **2** (*in neg. sentences*) ничто; **I haven't ~ to say to that** мне нечего сказать на это **3** (*everything*) всё; **I'd give ~ to see him again** я отдал бы всё, чтобы опять увидеть его; **more, better than ~** больше всего **4** (*~ at all*) что угодно **5** (*whatever*): **I will do ~ you suggest** я сделаю всё, что вы скажете

◆' **anyway** /ˈenɪweɪ/ *adv.* = **anyhow** 2

◆' **anywhere** /ˈenɪweə(r)/ *adv.* **1** (*in interrog. and conditional sentences*) где-нибудь; где-либо; (*of motion*) куда-нибудь; куда-либо; **is there a chemist's ~?** здесь есть аптека где-нибудь?; **have you ~ to stay?** у вас есть где остановиться? **2** (*in neg. sentences*) нигде; (*of motion*) никуда; **we haven't been ~ for ages** мы уже сто лет нигде не были **3** (*in any place at all; everywhere*) где угодно; везде; (по)всюду; **it is miles from ~** это чёрт-те где (*находится*)

AOB (BrE) *abbr.* (*of* **any other business**) разное

◆' **apart** /əˈpɑːt/ *adv.* **1** (*position*) в стороне; (*motion*) в сторону; **joking ~** шутки в сторону; **~ from** (*with the exception of*) за исключением + g.; кроме + g.; (*other than; besides*) кроме/помимо + g. **2** (*separate(ly); asunder*) отдельно; **they lived ~ for 2 years** два года они жили порознь; **I could not tell them ~** я не мог их различить/отличить **3** (*distant*): **the houses are a mile ~** дома находятся в миле друг от друга

apartheid /əˈpɑːteɪt/ *n.* апартеид

◆' **apartment** /əˈpɑːtmənt/ *n.* (AmE) квартира
■ **~ block, ~ house** *nn.* многоквартирный дом

apathetic /ˌæpəˈθetɪk/ *adj.* равнодушный, апатичный

apathy /ˈæpəθɪ/ *n.* апатия

ape /eɪp/ *n.* обезьяна

aperitif /əˈperɪtiːf/ *n.* аперитив

apex /ˈeɪpeks/ *n.* (*pl.* **apexes** or **apices**) (lit., fig.) вершина, верх

a

aphid /ˈeɪfɪd/ *n.* тля

aphorism /ˈæfərɪz(ə)m/ *n.* афори́зм

aphrodisiac /ˌæfrəˈdɪziæk/ *n.* сре́дство, уси́ливающее полово́е влече́ние; афродизиа́к ● *adj.* уси́ливающий полово́е влече́ние

apiary /ˈeɪpɪərɪ/ *n.* па́сека, пче́льник

apocalypse /əˈpɒkəlɪps/ *n.* апока́липсис

apocalyptic /əˌpɒkəˈlɪptɪk/ *adj.* апокалипти́ческий

apocryphal /əˈpɒkrɪf(ə)l/ *adj.* **1** (bibl.) апокрифи́ческий **2** (of doubtful authenticity) недостове́рный

apologetic /əˌpɒləˈdʒetɪk/ *adj.* извиня́ющийся; he was very ~ он о́чень извиня́лся; an ~ smile винова́тая улы́бка

apologize /əˈpɒlədʒaɪz/ *v.i.* извин|я́ться, -и́ться (to: пе́ред + *i.*, for: за + *a.*)

apolog|y /əˈpɒlədʒɪ/ *n.* извине́ние; make an ~y to sb for sth прин|оси́ть, -ести́ извине́ния кому́-н. за что-н.; please accept my ~ies прими́те мои́ извине́ния

apostle /əˈpɒs(ə)l/ *n.* апо́стол

apostrophe /əˈpɒstrəfɪ/ *n.* (gram.) апостро́ф

app /æp/ *n.* (comput.) = **application** 5

appal /əˈpɔːl/ (AmE also **appall**) *v.t.* (**appalled**, **appalling**) ужас|а́ть, -ну́ть; устраш|а́ть, -и́ть; I was ~led at the cost цена́ меня́ ужасну́ла

appall /əˈpɔːl/ *v.t.* (AmE) = **appal**

appalling /əˈpɔːlɪŋ/ *adj.* ужа́сный, жу́ткий

apparatus /ˌæpəˈreɪtəs/ *n.* **1** (instrument; appliance) прибо́р, инструме́нт **2** (in laboratory) аппарату́ра; обору́дование **3** (gymnastic) снаря́ды (*m. pl.*)

apparel /əˈpær(ə)l/ *n.* одея́ние, наря́д

✐ **apparent** /əˈpærənt/ *adj.* **1** (plain, obvious) очеви́дный; я́вный **2** (seeming) ка́жущийся, мни́мый

✐ **apparently** /əˈpærəntlɪ/ *adv.* (seemingly) по-ви́димому; вероя́тно; (как) бу́дто

apparition /ˌæpəˈrɪʃ(ə)n/ *n.* виде́ние, при́зрак

✐ **appeal** /əˈpiːl/ *n.* **1** (earnest request, plea) обраще́ние (с про́сьбой); (official) воззва́ние; an ~ on behalf of the Red Cross обраще́ние от и́мени Кра́сного Креста́; an ~ for support про́сьба о по́мощи **2** (reference to higher authority) апелля́ция, обжа́лование; Court of A~ (in England and Wales) апелляцио́нный суд; court of ~s (AmE) апелляцио́нный суд **3** (attraction) привлека́тельность; this life has little ~ for me э́та жизнь меня́ ма́ло привлека́ет
● *v.i.* **1** (make earnest request) обра|ща́ться, -ти́ться (to: к + *d.*, for: за + *i.*); he ~ed to us for help он обрати́лся к нам за по́мощью; (address oneself to) апелли́ровать (*impf., pf.*) (to: к + *d.*) **2** (law) апелли́ровать (*impf., pf.*); под|ава́ть, -а́ть апелля́цию; обжа́ловать (*pf.*) пригово́р **3**: ~ to (attract) привлека́ть (*impf.*); нра́виться (*impf.*) + *d.*

appealing /əˈpiːlɪŋ/ *adj.* (attractive) привлека́тельный; (imploring) умоля́ющий

✐ **appear** /əˈpɪə(r)/ *v.i.* **1** (become visible; arrive) появл|я́ться, -и́ться **2** (present oneself) выступ|а́ть, вы́ступить; ~ in court предст|ава́ть, -а́ть пе́ред судо́м; (of actor) игра́ть (*impf.*) на сце́не; сним|а́ться, сня́ться в кино́; (of book) выходи́ть, вы́йти (в свет); быть и́зданным **3** (seem) каза́ться, по-; he ~s to have left он, ка́жется, уе́хал **4** (turn out) ока́з|ываться, -а́ться; it ~s his wife is a Swede ока́зывается, его́ жена́ шве́дка

✐ **appearance** /əˈpɪərəns/ *n.* **1** (act of appearing) появле́ние; (in public) выступле́ние; ~ in court я́вка в суд **2** (look, aspect) (of thing) вид; (of person) нару́жность, вне́шность; judge by ~(s) (*impf.*) по вне́шнему ви́ду; to, by all ~s по всем при́знакам; су́дя по всему́

appease /əˈpiːz/ *v.t.* (one's conscience) успок|а́ивать, -о́ить; (person) умиротвор|я́ть, -и́ть; (appetites, passions) утол|я́ть, -и́ть

appeasement /əˈpiːzmənt/ *n.* **1** успокое́ние; умиротворе́ние **2** (of hunger, desire, etc.) утоле́ние

appendage /əˈpendɪdʒ/ *n.* (anat.) отро́сток, прида́ток; (fig.) прида́ток

appendectomy /ˌæpenˈdektəmɪ/ *n.* удале́ние аппе́ндикса

appendices /əˈpendɪsiːz/ *pl. of* ▶ **appendix**

appendicitis /əˌpendɪˈsaɪtɪs/ *n.* аппендици́т

appendi|x /əˈpendɪks/ *n.* (*pl.* ~**ces** *or* ~**xes**) **1** (anat.) аппе́ндикс **2** (of a book etc.) приложе́ние

appetite /ˈæpɪtaɪt/ *n.* аппети́т

appetizer /ˈæpɪtaɪzə(r)/ *n.* (hors d'oeuvre) заку́ска

appetizing /ˈæpɪtaɪzɪŋ/ *adj.* аппети́тный

applaud /əˈplɔːd/ *v.t.* (*also v.i.*) (clap) аплоди́ровать (*impf.*) + *d.*

applause /əˈplɔːz/ *n.* аплодисме́нты (*m. pl.*); рукоплеска́ния (*nt. pl.*)

apple /ˈæp(ə)l/ *n.* я́блоко
■ ~ **sauce** *n.* я́блочное пюре́ (*indecl.*); ~ **tree** *n.* я́блоня

appliance /əˈplaɪəns/ *n.* (instrument) прибо́р, приспособле́ние; domestic ~ бытово́й прибо́р

applicant /ˈæplɪk(ə)nt/ *n.* кандида́т, претенде́нт; ~ for a job кандида́т, претенде́нт на до́лжность

✐ **application** /ˌæplɪˈkeɪʃ(ə)n/ *n.* **1** (applying) прикла́дывание; наложе́ние **2** (employment; use) примене́ние; приложе́ние **3** (diligence) прилежа́ние; (concentration) сосредото́ченность **4** (request) (for work) заявле́ние; (for a grant) зая́вка; (for permission) проше́ние **5** (comput.) (*also* **application program**) приложе́ние
■ ~ **form** *n.* бланк заявле́ния

✐ **apply** /əˈplaɪ/ *v.t.* **1** (lay, put on) при|кла́дывать, -ложи́ть; (dressing, plaster) накла́дывать, наложи́ть; (paint, cream) наноси́ть, нанести́ **2** (bring into action) прил|ага́ть, -ожи́ть; ~ the brakes тормози́ть, за- **3** (make use of) примен|я́ть, -и́ть
● *v.i.*: ~ **for** (a job, grant, pass) под|ава́ть, -а́ть заявле́ние на + *a.*; ~ **to** (concern; relate to)

относи́ться (*impf.*) к + *d.*

appoint /ə'pɔɪnt/ *v.t.* (nominate) назн|ача́ть, -а́чить; **he was ~ed ambassador** он был назна́чен посло́м

appointment /ə'pɔɪntmənt/ *n.* **1** (act of appointing) назначе́ние **2** (office) до́лжность **3** (at doctor's etc.): **to make an ~ with** запи́|сываться, -са́ться на приём к + *d.*; полу|ча́ть, -чи́ть назначе́ние к + *d.*; (business) встре́ча

apportion /ə'pɔ:ʃ(ə)n/ *v.t.* распредел|я́ть, -и́ть; раздел|я́ть, -и́ть

apposite /'æpəzɪt/ *adj.* (suitable) подходя́щий; (to the point) уме́стный; уда́чный

appraisal /ə'preɪz(ə)l/ *n.* оце́нка; (of performance, of a worker) аттеста́ция

appreciable /ə'pri:ʃəb(ə)l/ *adj.* (perceptible) заме́тный; (considerable) значи́тельный

appreciate /ə'pri:ʃɪeɪt/ *v.t.* **1** (value) оц|е́нивать, -ени́ть; цени́ть (*impf.*); **we ~ your help** мы це́ним ва́шу по́мощь **2** (understand) пон|има́ть, -я́ть **3** (enjoy): **he has learnt to ~ music** он научи́лся понима́ть и цени́ть му́зыку
  ● *v.i.* (rise in value) пов|ыша́ться, -ы́ситься

appreciation /əpri:ʃɪ'eɪʃ(ə)n/ *n.* **1** (estimation, judgement) оце́нка **2** (understanding) понима́ние, призна́ние досто́инств **3** (rise in value) повыше́ние в цене́/сто́имости **4** (gratitude) призна́тельность

appreciative /ə'pri:ʃətɪv/ *adj.* **1** (perceptive of merit): **an ~ audience** понима́ющая аудито́рия **2** (grateful) благода́рный, призна́тельный (**of:** за + *a.*)

apprehend /æprɪ'hend/ *v.t.* **1** (understand) уясн|я́ть, -и́ть **2** (arrest) арестов|ывать, -а́ть; заде́рж|ивать, -а́ть

apprehension /æprɪ'henʃ(ə)n/ *n.* **1** (fear) опасе́ние **2** (arrest) аре́ст, задержа́ние **3** (understanding) уясне́ние

apprehensive /æprɪ'hensɪv/ *adj.* озабо́ченный; беспоко́йный; по́лный трево́ги

apprentice /ə'prentɪs/ *n.* подмасте́рье (*m.*)

apprenticeship /ə'prentɪsʃɪp/ *n.* уче́ние, учени́чество

approach /ə'prəʊtʃ/ *n.* **1** (drawing near; advance) приближе́ние; наступле́ние **2** (fig.) подхо́д; **his ~ to the subject** его́ подхо́д к предме́ту **3** (access) по́дступ **4** (fig., overture) предложе́ние; **they made unofficial ~es** они́ де́лали неофициа́льные предложе́ния
  ● *v.t.* **1** (come near to) прибл|ижа́ться, -и́зиться к + *d.* **2** (make overtures to) обра|ща́ться, -ти́ться к + *d.*
  ● *v.i.* прибл|ижа́ться, -и́зиться; под|ходи́ть, -ойти́; подъ|езжа́ть, -е́хать

approachable /ə'prəʊtʃəb(ə)l/ *adj.* досту́пный

approbation /æprə'beɪʃ(ə)n/ *n.* одобре́ние

appropriate[1] /ə'prəʊprɪət/ *adj.* соотве́тствующий; (suitable) подходя́щий

appropriate[2] /ə'prəʊprɪeɪt/ *v.t.* **1** (funds) ассигнова́ть (*impf., pf.*) **2** (take possession of) присв|а́ивать, -о́ить

approval /ə'pru:v(ə)l/ *n.* одобре́ние; (confirmation) утвержде́ние; (consent) согла́сие;

(sanction) апроба́ция; **on ~** на про́бу

approv|e /ə'pru:v/ *v.t.* од|обря́ть, -о́брить; (confirm) утвер|жда́ть, -ди́ть
  ● *v.i.*: **~e of** од|обря́ть, -о́брить; **an ~ing glance** одобри́тельный взгля́д

approximate[1] /ə'prɒksɪmət/ *adj.* приблизи́тельный

approximate[2] /ə'prɒksɪmeɪt/ *v.i.*: **~ to** прибл|ижа́ться, -и́зиться к + *d.*

approximation /əprɒksɪ'meɪʃ(ə)n/ *n.* приближе́ние; **this is an ~ to the truth** э́то бли́зко к и́стине

apricot /'eɪprɪkɒt/ *n.* абрико́с

April /'eɪprɪl/ *n.* апре́ль (*m.*); **~ Fool!** пе́рвое апре́ля — никому́ не ве́рю!; **~ Fool's Day** пе́рвое апре́ля

apron /'eɪprən/ *n.* (garment) пере́дник; фа́ртук

apt /æpt/ *adj.* **1** (suitable) подходя́щий **2**: **~ to** скло́нный к + *d.*

aptitude /'æptɪtju:d/ *n.* (capacity) спосо́бность
  ■ **~ test** *n.* прове́рка спосо́бностей

aquaria /ə'kweərɪə/ *pl. of* ▶ **aquarium**

aquari|um /ə'kweərɪəm/ *n.* (*pl.* **~a** *or* **~ums**) аква́риум

Aquarius /ə'kweərɪəs/ *n.* Водоле́й; **she's (an) Aquarius** она́ — Водоле́й

aquatic /ə'kwætɪk/ *adj.* водяно́й

aqueduct /'ækwɪdʌkt/ *n.* акведу́к

Arab /'ærəb/ *n.* (person) ара́б (-ка)
  ● *adj.* ара́бский
  ■ **~ Spring** *n.* (pol.) Ара́бская весна́

Arabian /ə'reɪbɪən/ *adj.* арави́йский

Arabic /'ærəbɪk/ *n.* ара́бский язы́к
  ● *adj.* ара́бский

arable /'ærəb(ə)l/ *adj.* па́хотный
  ■ **~ farming** *n.* земледе́лие

arbitrary /'ɑ:bɪtrərɪ/ *adj.* произво́льный

arbitrate /'ɑ:bɪtreɪt/ *v.i.* (act as arbiter) быть арби́тром; быть трете́йским судьёй

arbitration /ɑ:bɪ'treɪʃ(ə)n/ *n.* арбитра́ж; трете́йский суд

arbor /'ɑ:bə(r)/ *n.* (AmE) = **arbour**

arboret|um /ɑ:bə'ri:təm/ *n.* (*pl.* **~ums** *or* **~a**) дендра́рий

arbour /'ɑ:bə(r)/ (AmE **arbor**) *n.* бесе́дка

arc /ɑ:k/ *n.* дуга́

arcade /ɑ:'keɪd/ *n.* (covered passage) арка́да; (with shops) пасса́ж

arcane /ɑ:'keɪn/ *adj.* таи́нственный, та́йный

arch /ɑ:tʃ/ *n.* (curved shape) а́рка; (**~ed roof; vault**) свод
  ● *v.t.* (part of the body) выгиба́ть, вы́гнуть; **the cat ~ed its back** ко́шка вы́гнула спи́ну

arch- /ɑ:tʃ/ *comb. form* архи…; гла́вный

archaeological /ɑ:kɪə'lɒdʒɪk(ə)l/ (AmE *also* **archeological**) *adj.* археологи́ческий

archaeologist /ɑ:kɪ'ɒlədʒɪst/ (AmE *also* **archeologist**) *n.* архео́лог

archaeology /ɑ:kɪ'ɒlədʒɪ/ (AmE *also* **archeology**) *n.* археоло́гия

archaic /ɑ:'keɪɪk/ *adj.* архаи́чный; устаре́вший

archangel /'ɑ:keɪndʒ(ə)l/ *n.* арха́нгел

a

archbishop /ɑːtʃˈbɪʃəp/ *n.* архиепископ
arch-enemy /ɑːtʃˈenəmɪ/ *n.* заклятый враг
archeological /ɑːkɪəˈlɒdʒɪk(ə)l/ *adj.* (AmE)
= archaeological
archeologist /ɑːkɪˈɒlədʒɪst/ *n.* (AmE)
= archaeologist
archeology /ɑːkɪˈɒlədʒɪ/ *n.* (AmE) = archaeology
archery /ˈɑːtʃərɪ/ *n.* стрельба из лука
archetypal /ɑːkɪˈtaɪp(ə)l/ *adj.* (typical) типичный
archipelago /ɑːkɪˈpeləgəʊ/ *n.* (*pl.* ∼s or ∼es)
архипелаг
architect /ˈɑːkɪtekt/ *n.* архитектор
architectural /ɑːkɪˈtektʃər(ə)l/ *adj.*
архитектурный; строительный
architecture /ˈɑːkɪtektʃə(r)/ *n.* архитектура
architrave /ˈɑːkɪtreɪv/ *n.* (archit.) архитрав
archive /ˈɑːkaɪv/ *n.* (*also in pl.*) (also comput.)
архив
  • *v.t.* поме|щать, -стить в архив; архивировать
  (*impf., pf.*)
archivist /ˈɑːkɪvɪst/ *n.* архивариус
Arctic /ˈɑːktɪk/ *n.* (*in full* **the** ∼) Арктика
  • *adj.* Арктический; (**a**∼) (very cold) ледяной,
  студёный
  ■ ∼ **Circle** *n.* Северный полярный круг; ∼
  Ocean *n.* Северный Ледовитый океан
ardent /ˈɑːd(ə)nt/ *adj.* (fervent) горячий,
  пылкий; (passionate) страстный
ardour /ˈɑːdə(r)/ (AmE **ardor**) *n.* жар, пыл,
  рвение
arduous /ˈɑːdjʊəs/ *adj.* тяжёлый
are /ɑː(r)/ *2nd pers. sing. pres. and pl. pres. of*
  ▶ be
✓ **area** /ˈeərɪə/ *n.* **1** (measurement) площадь; **a room**
  12 square metres in ∼ комната площадью в
  12 м² (= *12 квадратных метров*) **2** (defined
  or designated space) площадь; (expanse)
  пространство; **vast** ∼**s of forest** обширные
  лесные пространства **3** (region) район, край,
  зона; **residential** ∼ жилой район; **wheat-**
  growing ∼ площадь под пшеницей **4** (sphere)
  область, сфера; **in the** ∼ **of research** в области
  исследования
arena /əˈriːnə/ *n.* (lit., fig.) арена
aren't /ɑːnt/ *neg. of* ▶ are
Argentina /ɑːdʒənˈtiːnə/ (*also* **the**
  Argentine /ˈɑːdʒəntaɪn/) *n.* Аргентина
Argentine /ˈɑːdʒəntaɪn/, **Argentinian**
  /ɑːdʒənˈtɪnɪən/ *nn.* аргентин|ец (-ка)
  • *adjs.* аргентинский
✓ **argue** /ˈɑːgjuː/ *v.t.* (**argues, argued,**
  arguing) **1** (discuss) обсу|ждать, -дить;
  (debate) дебатировать (*impf.*); спорить
  (*impf.*) о + *p.* **2** (contend) доказывать (*impf.*)
  • *v.i.* **1** (debate; disagree; quarrel) спорить (*impf.*);
  препираться (*impf.*); (object) возражать
  (*impf.*); **they** ∼**d over who should drive** они
  спорили, кому вести машину **2** (give reasons)
  прив|одить, -ести доводы, выступать,
  выступить (**against:** против + *g.*, **for, in favour**
  of: в защиту + *g.*, за + *a.*)

✓ ключевая лексика

✓ **argument** /ˈɑːgjʊmənt/ *n.* **1** (reason) аргумент;
  довод; **it's an** ∼ **for staying at home** это довод в
  пользу того, чтобы остаться дома **2** (discussion,
  debate) спор; **have an** ∼ **over, about** спорить
  (*impf.*) о + *p.*
argumentative /ɑːgjʊˈmentətɪv/ *adj.*
  сварливый
aria /ˈɑːrɪə/ *n.* ария
arid /ˈærɪd/ *adj.* (of soil etc.) сухой, пересохший;
  (of climate, also fig., dry) сухой
Aries /ˈeəriːz/ *n.* (*pl.* ∼) (astron., astrol.) Овен;
  she's (an) Aries она — Овен
✓ **arise** /əˈraɪz/ *v.i.* (*past* **arose,** *p.p.* **arisen**
  /əˈrɪz(ə)n/) (fig., come into being) возн|икать,
  -икнуть; **if the need should** ∼ если возникнет
  необходимость; **the question arose** возник
  вопрос
aristocracy /ærɪˈstɒkrəsɪ/ *n.* аристократия
aristocrat /ˈærɪstəkræt/ *n.* аристократ
aristocratic /ærɪstəˈkrætɪk/ *adj.*
  аристократический
arithmetic /əˈrɪθmətɪk/ *n.* арифметика
arithmetical /ærɪθˈmetɪk(ə)l/ *adj.*
  арифметический
✓ **arm¹** /ɑːm/ *n.* **1** (of person) рука; **he broke his**
  ∼ он сломал руку; ∼ **in** ∼ под руку **2** (of
  garment) рукав; (of chair) ручка
  ■ ∼**band** *n.* нарукавная повязка; ∼**chair** *n.*
  кресло; ∼**pit** *n.* подмышка
✓ **arm²** /ɑːm/ *n.* (*in pl.*) (weapons) оружие
  • *v.t.* вооруж|ать, -ить; (equip) снаб|жать,
  -дить; ∼**ed forces** вооружённые силы
  ■ ∼**s race** *n.* гонка вооружений
armament /ˈɑːməmənt/ *n.* (*also in pl.*)
  (weapons; military equipment) вооружение
Armenia /ɑːˈmiːnɪə/ *n.* Армения
Armenian /ɑːˈmiːnɪən/ *n.* **1** (person) арм|янин
  (-янка) **2** (language) армянский язык
  • *adj.* армянский
armistice /ˈɑːmɪstɪs/ *n.* перемирие
armor /ˈɑːmə(r)/ *n.* (AmE) = armour
armored /ˈɑːməd/ *adj.* (AmE) = armoured
armory /ˈɑːmərɪ/ *n.* (AmE) = armoury
armour /ˈɑːmə(r)/ (AmE **armor**) *n.* (for body)
  доспехи (*m. pl.*)
  ■ ∼**-plated** *adj.* бронированный
armoured /ˈɑːməd/ (AmE **armored**) *adj.*
  бронированный, бронеосный
armoury /ˈɑːmərɪ/ (AmE **armory**) *n.* арсенал
✓ **army** /ˈɑːmɪ/ *n.* армия; **join the** ∼ идти, пойти
  в армию; (*attr.*) армейский
aroma /əˈrəʊmə/ *n.* аромат
aromatherapist /ərəʊməˈθerəpɪst/ *n.*
  ароматерапевт
aromatherapy /ərəʊməˈθerəpɪ/ *n.*
  ароматерапия
aromatic /ærəˈmætɪk/ *adj.* (smell) ароматный;
  (substance) ароматический
arose /əˈrəʊz/ *past of* ▶ arise
✓ **around** /əˈraʊnd/ (*see also* ▶ round) *adv.*
  вокруг; кругом; **all** ∼ повсюду; **for miles** ∼
  на мили вокруг; **they were standing** ∼ они
  стояли поблизости; **this singer has been** ∼

a

for 30 years э́тот певе́ц уже́ 30 лет поёт
● *prep.* **1** (encircling) вокру́г + g.; круго́м
+ g.; **they stood ~ the table** они́ стоя́ли
вокру́г стола́; **the path goes ~ the garden**
доро́жка огиба́ет сад **2** (over): **he looked ~
the house** он осмотре́л дом **3** (in the vicinity
of) о́коло + g. **4** (approximately) о́коло + g.;
приблизи́тельно

arouse /əˈraʊz/ *v.t.* (awaken from sleep) буди́ть,
раз-; (fig.) пробу|жда́ть, -ди́ть; (also sexually)
возбу|жда́ть, -ди́ть

arrang|e /əˈreɪndʒ/ *v.t.* **1** (put in order)
прив|оди́ть, -ести́ в поря́док; **she was ~ing
flowers** она́ расставля́ла цветы́ **2** (put in
a certain order; group) распол|ага́ть, -ожи́ть;
расст|авля́ть, -а́вить **3** (settle) ула́|живать,
-дить **4** (organize) устра́|ивать, -о́ить;
организо́в|ывать, -а́ть; (prepare; plan in advance)
подгот|а́вливать, -о́вить; организо́в|ывать,
-а́ть; нала́|живать, -дить
● *v.i.* догова́риваться, -ори́ться; усла́вливаться,
-о́виться; **I have ~ed for somebody to meet
him at the station** я распоряди́лся, что́бы его́
встре́тили на ста́нции

 arrangement /əˈreɪndʒmənt/ *n.* **1** (setting in
order) приведе́ние в поря́док **2** (specific order)
расположе́ние **3** (*in pl.*) (planning, preparation)
ме́ры (*f. pl.*), приготовле́ния (*nt. pl.*); **make
~s for** организо́в|ывать, -а́ть; устр|а́ивать,
-о́ить **4** (agreement, understanding) соглаше́ние,
договорённость

array /əˈreɪ/ *n.* **1** (order): **in battle ~** в боево́м
поря́дке **2** (display) мно́жество **3** (dress,
apparel) облаче́ние, одея́ние
● *v.t.* **1** (place in order or line) выстра́ивать,
вы́строить; **the troops were ~ed for battle**
войска́ бы́ли вы́строены в боево́м поря́дке
2 (set out, display) выставля́ть, вы́ставить
3 (adorn) укр|аша́ть, -а́сить; **she was ~ed
in all her finery** она́ облачи́лась в са́мое
лу́чшее; (deck out, dress) над|ева́ть, -е́ть

arrears /əˈrɪəz/ *n. pl.* (of payment)
задо́лженность; просро́чка; **be in ~**
просро́чи|вать, -ть платёж

 arrest /əˈrest/ *n.* аре́ст; **be under ~** быть
(*impf.*) под аре́стом
● *v.t.* аресто́в|ывать, -а́ть

arrival /əˈraɪv(ə)l/ *n.* прибы́тие; **on his ~** по
его́ прибы́тии; (of person etc. on foot) прихо́д;
(of person by vehicle) прие́зд; (by air) прилёт

 arrive /əˈraɪv/ *v.i.* **1** (reach destination) приб|ыва́ть,
-ы́ть; (of persons on foot, also fig.) при|ходи́ть, -йти́
2: **~ at a decision/conclusion** приходи́ть,
прийти́ к реше́нию/заключе́нию

arrogance /ˈærəg(ə)ns/ *n.* высокоме́рие

arrogant /ˈærəg(ə)nt/ *adj.* высокоме́рный

arrow /ˈærəʊ/ *n.* стрела́; (as symbol or indicator)
стре́лка

arse /ɑːs/ (AmE **ass**) *n.* (vulg.) жо́па (vulg.)

arsenal /ˈɑːs(ə)n(ə)l/ *n.* (lit., fig.) арсена́л

arsenic /ˈɑːsənɪk/ *n.* мышья́к

arson /ˈɑːs(ə)n/ *n.* поджо́г

 art /ɑːt/ *n.* **1** (skill, craft) иску́сство; **a work of
~** произведе́ние иску́сства **2** (decorative)

иску́сство; **fine ~s** изя́щные/изобрази́тельные
иску́сства

■ **~ critic** *n.* искусствове́д; **~ gallery** *n.*
карти́нная галере́я; **~ school** *n.*
худо́жественное учи́лище

artefact, **artifact** /ˈɑːtɪfækt/ *n.* худо́жественное
изде́лие; (sth small or of little historical/cultural interest)
подде́лка

arterial /ɑːˈtɪərɪəl/ *adj.* **1** (anat.) артериа́льный
2: **~ road** магистра́льная доро́га; магистра́ль

artery /ˈɑːtəri/ *n.* (anat.) арте́рия

artful /ˈɑːtfʊl/ *adj.* хи́трый

arthritic /ɑːˈθrɪtɪk/ *adj.* (of pain) артри́тный; (of
person) страда́ющий (-ая) артри́том; **~ joints**
артри́т суста́вов

arthritis /ɑːˈθraɪtɪs/ *n.* артри́т

artichoke /ˈɑːtɪtʃəʊk/ *n.* артишо́к

 article /ˈɑːtɪk(ə)l/ *n.* **1** (item) предме́т;
(manufactured) изде́лие; **~ of clothing** предме́т
оде́жды **2** (piece of writing) статья́ **3** (gram.):
(in)definite ~ (не)определённый арти́кль

articulate¹ /ɑːˈtɪkjʊlət/ *adj.* (of speech)
членоразде́льный; (of thoughts) отчётливый;
(of person) чётко выража́ющий свои́ мы́сли

articulate² /ɑːˈtɪkjʊleɪt/ *v.t.* (ideas) я́сно
выража́ть, вы́разить; (words) отчётливо
произн|оси́ть, -ести́

articulated /ɑːˈtɪkjʊleɪtɪd/ *adj.*: **~ lorry** (BrE)
грузови́к с прице́пом; автопо́езд

artifact /ˈɑːtɪfækt/ *n.* = artefact

artifice /ˈɑːtɪfɪs/ *n.* хи́трость

artificial /ɑːtɪˈfɪʃ(ə)l/ *adj.* (not natural)
иску́сственный; (feigned) притво́рный
■ **~ respiration** *n.* иску́сственное дыха́ние

artillery /ɑːˈtɪləri/ *n.* артилле́рия

artisan /ˌɑːtɪˈzæn, ˈɑːtɪzæn/ *n.* реме́сленн|ик
(-ица)

 artist /ˈɑːtɪst/ *n.* худо́жн|ик (-ица)

artiste /ɑːˈtiːst/ *n.* арти́ст (-ка);
профессиона́льный музыка́нт, танцо́р
и т. п.

artistic /ɑːˈtɪstɪk/ *adj.* (person) худо́жественный;
(work) артисти́ческий, артисти́чный

artless /ˈɑːtlɪs/ *adj.* (unskilled) неиску́сный;
(ingenuous) простоду́шный; (natural)
безыску́сственный

arty /ˈɑːti/ *adj.* (**artier**, **artiest**) (infml)
вы́чурный; претенцио́зно-боге́мный
■ **~-farty** /ˈfɑːti/ *adj.* претенцио́зный

 as /æz/ *adv. & conj.* **1** (expr. comparison or
conformity) как; **~ I was saying** как я говори́л;
do ~ follows де́лайте сле́дующее; **do it ~
follows** де́лайте э́то так/вот как/сле́дующим
о́бразом; **such countries ~ Spain** таки́е
стра́ны, как Испа́ния; **the same ~ ...** то же
са́мое, что…; **~ heavy ~ lead** тяжёлый,
как свине́ц; **I am ~ tall ~** он мы с ним
одного́ ро́ста; **walk ~ fast ~ you can** иди́те
как мо́жно быстре́е; **~ quickly ~ possible**
как мо́жно скоре́е; **just ~** так же, как; **~
usual** как всегда́; **he pictured the room ~
it would be** он представля́л себе́, како́й
бу́дет ко́мната; **so ~ to** (expr. purpose) что́бы;
(expr. manner) так, что́бы **2** (expr. capacity or

a

category) как; **I regard him** ~ **a fool** я считаю его дураком; **his appointment** ~ **colonel** присвоение ему звания полковника; ~ **your guardian, I ...** как ваш опекун, я...; ~ **a rule** как правило; **I said it** ~ **a joke** я сказал это в шутку **3** (concessive): **young** ~ **I am** хоть я и молод; **much** ~ **I should like to** как бы мне ни хотелось **4** (temporal) когда; пока, в то время как; **(just)** ~ **I reached the door** когда я подошёл к двери **5** (causative) так как, поскольку; ~ **you are ready, let us begin** поскольку вы уже готовы, давайте начнём **6** (var.): ~ **far** ~ **I know** насколько мне известно; ~ **if** будто (бы); как будто (бы); **it is not** ~ **if I was poor** не то, чтобы я был беден; ~ **much** ~ ... столько, сколько...; **I thought** ~ **much!** так я и думал!; **no one so much** ~ **looked at us** на нас никто даже не посмотрел; ~ **soon** ~ как только; **I would just** ~ **soon go** я предпочёл бы пойти; ~ **though** будто (бы); как будто (бы); ~ **well** (in addition) также, тоже; **he came** ~ **well** ~ **John** и он, и Джон пришли; **you might** ~ **well help me** вы могли бы мне помочь; **it is just** ~ **well you came** хорошо, что вы пришли

a.s.a.p. *abbr.* (of **as soon as possible**) как можно скорее

asbestos /æz'bestɒs/ *n.* асбест

ascend /ə'send/ *v.t.* подн|иматься, -яться по + *d.* (*or* на + *a.*)

ascendancy /ə'send(ə)nsɪ/ *n.* власть, господство; **gain, obtain** ~ **over** доб|иваться, -иться власти/господства над + *i.*

ascent /ə'sent/ *n.* восхождение, подъём; ~ **of a mountain** восхождение на́ гору

ascertain /æsə'teɪn/ *v.t.* устан|авливать, -овить; выясн|ять, -выяснить

ascribe /ə'skraɪb/ *v.t.* припис|ывать, -ать (to: + *d.*)

asexual /eɪ'sekʃʊəl/ *adj.* бесполый

ash¹ /æʃ/ *n.* (bot.) ясень (*m.*)

ash² /æʃ/ *n.* **1** (also in pl.) зола́; пе́пел **2** (in pl.) (human remains) прах

■ ~**tray** *n.* пепельница

ashamed /ə'ʃeɪmd/ *adj.* пристыжённый; **I am, feel** ~ мне стыдно; **be** ~ **of** стыди́ться (*impf.*) + *g.*

ashen /'æʃ(ə)n/ *adj.* (pale) мёртвенно-бледный

ashore /ə'ʃɔː(r)/ *adv.* (position) на берегу́; (motion) на́ берег; **go** ~ сходи́ть, сойти́ на́ берег

Asia /'eɪʃə/ *n.* Азия

■ ~ **Minor** *n.* (peninsula) Малая Азия

Asian /'eɪʃ(ə)n/ *n.* азиа́т (-ка)
● *adj.* азиа́тский

⚐ **aside** /ə'saɪd/ *adv.* (place) в стороне́; (motion) в сто́рону; (in reserve) отде́льно, в резе́рве; **take sb** ~ отв|оди́ть, -ести́ кого́-н. в сто́рону; **set, put** ~ (reserve) от|кла́дывать, -ложи́ть

asinine /'æsɪnaɪn/ *adj.* (lit., fig.) осли́ный

⚐ **ask** /ɑːsk/ *v.t.* **1** (enquire) спр|а́шивать, -оси́ть (что у кого *or* кого о чём); **he** ~**ed me the**

time он спроси́л меня́, кото́рый час **2** (pose): ~ **a question** зад|ава́ть, -а́ть вопро́с **3** (request permission): **he** ~**ed to leave the room** он попроси́л разреше́ния вы́йти из ко́мнаты **4** (request) проси́ть, по- (что у кого *or* кого о чём); **I** ~**ed him to do it** я попроси́л его́ сде́лать это **5** (charge) проси́ть, за- **6** (invite) звать, по-; пригла|ша́ть, -си́ть; ~ **a girl out** пригла|ша́ть, -си́ть де́вушку на свида́ние
● *v.i.* **1** (make enquiries) спр|а́шивать, -оси́ть (о + *p.*); спр|авля́ться, -а́виться (о + *p.*); **she** ~**ed after your health** она́ справля́лась о ва́шем здоро́вье **2** (make a request) проси́ть, по-; **for help** проси́ть, по- о по́мощи; **he** ~**ed him for a pencil** он попроси́л у него́ каранда́ш; **he** ~**ed for advice** он попроси́л сове́та

■ ~**ing price** *n.* запра́шиваемая цена́

askance /ə'skæns/ *adv.* ко́со, и́скоса; **he looked at me** ~ он посмотре́л на меня́ и́скоса

askew /ə'skju:/ *adv.* кри́во, ко́со
● *pred. adj.* криво́й

asleep /ə'sli:p/ *pred. adj.* спя́щий; **he was sound, fast** ~ он спал кре́пким сном; **fall** ~ зас|ыпа́ть, -ну́ть

AS level *n.* (BrE) экза́мен в сре́дней шко́ле (ме́жду **GCSE** и **A level**)

asparagus /ə'spærəgəs/ *n.* спа́ржа

⚐ **aspect** /'æspekt/ *n.* **1** (look, appearance; expression) вид, выраже́ние **2** (fig., facet) аспе́кт, сторона́; (point of view) то́чка зре́ния **3** (outlook) вид

Asperger's syndrome /'æspə:dʒəz/ *n.* (med.) синдро́м Аспе́ргера (форма аутизма)

aspersion /ə'spə:ʃ(ə)n/ *n.* (slur) клевета́; **cast** ~**s on** возв|оди́ть, -ести́ клевету́ на + *a.*; клевета́ть (*impf.*) на + *a.*

asphalt /'æsfælt/ *n.* асфа́льт

asphyxiation /æsfɪksɪ'eɪʃ(ə)n/ *n.* уду́шье

aspic /'æspɪk/ *n.* заливно́е; **veal in** ~ заливна́я теля́тина

aspiration /æspɪ'reɪʃ(ə)n/ *n.* стремле́ние

aspire /ə'spaɪə(r)/ *v.i.* стреми́ться (*impf.*); **he** ~**s to be a leader** он стреми́тся стать ли́дером

aspirin /'æsprɪn/ *n.* (pl. ~ or ~**s**) аспири́н; (tablet) табле́тка аспири́на

ass¹ /æs/ осёл

ass² /æs/ *n.* (AmE, vulg.) = **arse**

assail /ə'seɪl/ *v.t.* (lit., fig.) нап|ада́ть, -а́сть на + *a.*; атак|ова́ть (*impf., pf.*); **I was** ~**ed by doubts** меня́ одолева́ли сомне́ния; ~ **with criticism** обру́ши|ваться, -ться с кри́тикой на + *a.*; ~ **with questions** зас|ыпа́ть, -ыпа́ть вопро́сами

assailant /ə'seɪlənt/ *n.* напада́ющ|ий (-ая)

assassin /ə'sæsɪn/ *n.* уби́йца (*c.g.*)

assassinate /ə'sæsɪneɪt/ *v.t.* уб|ива́ть, -и́ть (по полити́ческим моти́вам)

assassination /əsæsɪ'neɪʃ(ə)n/ *n.* полити́ческое уби́йство

assault /ə'sɒlt/ *n.* (in general) нападе́ние; (mil.) ата́ка, штурм, при́ступ; (law): **indecent** ~ оскорбле́ние де́йствием на сексуа́льной по́чве
● *v.t.* нап|ада́ть, -а́сть на + *a.*; (mil.) атак|ова́ть

(*impf., pf.*); (law) оскорб|ля́ть, -и́ть де́йствием

assemble /ə'semb(ə)l/ *v.t.* (gather together) соб|ира́ть, -ра́ть; (tech., fit together) монти́ровать, с-
● *v.i.* соб|ира́ться, -ра́ться

assembly /ə'semblɪ/ *n.* **1** (assembling) собира́ние, сбор **2** (company of persons) собра́ние **3** (of machine parts) сбо́рка
■ ~ **hall** *n.* (in school) а́ктовый зал; ~ **line** *n.* сбо́рочный конве́йер

assent /ə'sent/ *v.i.* согла|ша́ться, -си́ться (**to:** с *чем or* на *что*)

assert /ə'sə:t/ *v.t.* **1** (declare; affirm) утвер|жда́ть, -ди́ть; заяв|ля́ть, -и́ть **2** (stand up for) отст|а́ивать, -оя́ть; ~ **oneself** самоутвер|жда́ться, -ди́ться

assertion /ə'sə:ʃ(ə)n/ *n.* утвержде́ние

assertive /ə'sə:tɪv/ *adj.* (self-assured) самоуве́ренный

✍ **assess** /ə'ses/ *v.t.* **1** (estimate value of; appraise) (also fig.) оцен|ивать, -и́ть **2** (determine amount of) определ|я́ть, -и́ть су́мму/разме́р + *g.*

✍ **assessment** /ə'sesmənt/ *n.* (valuation) оце́нка; (for taxation) определе́ние

✍ **asset** /'æset/ *n.* **1** (advantage; useful quality) це́нность **2** (*in pl.*) (fin) акти́вы

assiduous /ə'sɪdjʊəs/ *adj.* приле́жный; усе́рдный

assign /ə'saɪn/ *v.t.* **1** (task) возл|ага́ть, -ожи́ть; пору|ча́ть, -чи́ть; (person) назн|ача́ть, -а́чить; (resources) предназн|ача́ть, -а́чить **2** (ascribe) припи́с|ывать, -а́ть **3** (law, transfer) перед|ава́ть, -а́ть

assignation /æsɪg'neɪʃ(ə)n/ *n.* **1** (of person) назначе́ние; (of resources) предназначе́ние; (of task) поруче́ние **2** (illicit meeting) та́йное свида́ние **3** (law, transfer) переда́ча

assignment /ə'saɪnmənt/ *n.* (task, duty) поруче́ние; зада́ние; (schoolwork) зада́ние

assimilate /ə'sɪmɪleɪt/ *v.t.* (absorb by digestion etc., also fig.) ассимили́ровать (*impf., pf.*)

✍ **assist** /ə'sɪst/ *v.t.* (help) пом|ога́ть, -о́чь + *d.*; (cooperate with) соде́йствовать (*impf., pf.*) + *d.*
● *v.i.* (help) пом|ога́ть, -о́чь; прин|има́ть, -я́ть уча́стие

✍ **assistance** /ə'sɪst(ə)ns/ *n.* по́мощь; соде́йствие

✍ **assistant** /ə'sɪst(ə)nt/ *n.* помо́щни|к (-ца); ассисте́нт (-ка); (BrE, in shop) продав|е́ц (-щи́ца)
■ ~ **manager** *n.* замести́тель (*m.*) заве́дующего

associate¹ /ə'səʊsɪət/ *n.* **1** (colleague) колле́га (*c.g.*) това́рищ; (in business) партнёр **2** (of a society) член о́бщества

✍ **associate**² /ə'səʊsɪeɪt/ *v.t.* соедин|я́ть, -и́ть; свя́з|ывать, -а́ть; (esp. psych.) ассоции́ровать (*impf., pf.*); **his name was ~d with the cause of reform** его́ и́мя ассоции́ровалось с реформа́торской де́ятельностью

✍ **association** /əsəʊsɪ'eɪʃ(ə)n/ *n.* **1** (uniting; joining) объедине́ние; соедине́ние **2** (connection) связь; ассоциа́ция **3** (group) ассоциа́ция, о́бщество

assorted /ə'sɔ:tɪd/ *adj.* (varied) разнообра́зный

assortment /ə'sɔ:tmənt/ *n.* ассортиме́нт

assuage /ə'sweɪdʒ/ *v.t.* (soothe) успок|а́ивать, -о́ить; (alleviate) смягч|а́ть, -и́ть; (appetite etc.) утол|я́ть, -и́ть

✍ **assume** /ə'sju:m/ *v.t.* **1** (take on) прин|има́ть, -я́ть; ~**e control of** брать, взять на себя́ управле́ние/руково́дство + *i.* **2** (feign) напус|ка́ть, -ти́ть на себя́; **he went under an ~ed name** он был изве́стен под вы́мышленным и́менем **3** (suppose) предпол|ага́ть, -ожи́ть; допус|ка́ть, -ти́ть; ~**ing that ...** при усло́вии, что...

assumption /ə'sʌmpʃ(ə)n/ *n.* предположе́ние; допуще́ние

assurance /ə'ʃʊərəns/ *n.* завере́ние, увере́ние

assure /ə'ʃʊə(r)/ *v.t.* **1** (ensure) обеспе́чи|вать, -ть **2** (assert confidently) ув|еря́ть, -е́рить; **I can ~ you of this** (я) могу́ вас в э́том уве́рить

asterisk /'æstərɪsk/ *n.* (typ.) звёздочка

asteroid /'æstərɔɪd/ *n.* астеро́ид

asthma /'æsmə/ *n.* а́стма

asthmatic /æs'mætɪk/ *adj.* (pertaining to asthma) астмати́ческий; (suffering from asthma) страда́ющий а́стмой

astigmatism /ə'stɪgmətɪz(ə)m/ *n.* астигмати́зм

astonish /ə'stɒnɪʃ/ *v.t.* пора|жа́ть, -зи́ть; изум|ля́ть, -и́ть; **be ~ed at** пора|жа́ться, -зи́ться + *d.*; изум|ля́ться, -и́ться + *d.*; **his success was ~ing** он име́л порази́тельный успе́х

astonishment /ə'stɒnɪʃmənt/ *n.* изумле́ние

astound /ə'staʊnd/ *v.t.* изум|ля́ть, -и́ть; пора|жа́ть, -зи́ть

astray /ə'streɪ/ *pred. adj. & adv.*: **go ~** (lit., miss one's way) заблуди́ться (*pf.*); (fig.) сб|ива́ться, -и́ться с пути́; **lead ~** (fig.) сб|ива́ть, -ить с пути́ (и́стинного)

astride /ə'straɪd/ *adv.* верхо́м
● *prep.*: ~ **a horse** верхо́м на ло́шади

astrologer /ə'strɒlədʒə(r)/ *n.* астро́лог

astrological /æstrə'lɒdʒɪk(ə)l/ *adj.* астрологи́ческий

astrology /ə'strɒlədʒɪ/ *n.* астроло́гия

astronaut /'æstrənɔ:t/ *n.* астрона́вт, космона́вт

astronomer /ə'strɒnəmə(r)/ *n.* астроно́м

astronomical /æstrə'nɒmɪk(ə)l/ *adj.* (lit., fig.) астрономи́ческий

astronomy /ə'strɒnəmɪ/ *n.* астроно́мия

astrophysicist /æstrəʊ'fɪzɪsɪst/ *n.* астрофи́зик

astrophysics /æstrəʊ'fɪzɪks/ *n.* астрофи́зика

astute /ə'stju:t/ *adj.* проница́тельный

asylum /ə'saɪləm/ *n.* прию́т; **political ~** полити́ческое убе́жище
■ ~ **seeker** *n.* претенде́нт (-ка) на получе́ние (полити́ческого) убе́жища

asymmetrical /eɪsɪ'metrɪk(ə)l/ *adj.* асимметри́чный, асимметри́ческий

✍ **at** /æt/ *prep.* **1** (denoting place) в/на + *p.*; (near, by) у + *g.*, при + *p.*; ~ **home** до́ма; ~ **school** в шко́ле; ~ **the station** на вокза́ле/ста́нции; ~ **the concert** на конце́рте; ~ **my aunt's** у мое́й тёти **2** (denoting motion or direction, lit., fig.): **he sat down ~ the table** он сел за стол; **he arrived ~ Moscow** он при́был в Москву́

3 (denoting time or order): ~ **night** но́чью; ~ **2 o'clock** в два часа́; ~ **Easter** на Па́сху; ~ **the beginning** в нача́ле; ~ **first** снача́ла **4** (of activity, state, manner, rate, etc.): ~ **work** на рабо́те; за рабо́той; **good** ~ **languages** спосо́бный к языка́м; ~ **war** в состоя́нии войны́; ~ **60 mph** со ско́ростью шестьдеся́т миль в час; ~ **best** в лу́чшем слу́чае; ~ **least** по кра́йней ме́ре; ~ **most** са́мое бо́льшее; ~ **all** вообще́; (with neg.) совсе́м

ate /et, eɪt/ *past of* ▶ **eat**

atheism /ˈeɪθɪɪz(ə)m/ *n.* атеи́зм

atheist /ˈeɪθɪɪst/ *n.* атеи́ст (-ка)

athlete /ˈæθliːt/ *n.* спортсме́н (-ка)
■ ~**'s foot** *n.* грибко́вое заболева́ние ног

athletic /æθˈletɪk/ *adj.* атлети́ческий

athletics /æθˈletɪks/ *n.* атле́тика

Atlantic /ətˈlæntɪk/ *n.* (*in full* **the** ~ **(Ocean)**) Атланти́ческий океа́н
● *adj.* атланти́ческий

atlas /ˈætləs/ *n.* а́тлас

ATM *n.* (*abbr. of* **Automated Teller Machine**) банкома́т

atmosphere /ˈætməsfɪə(r)/ *n.* атмосфе́ра

atmospheric /ætməsˈferɪk/ *adj.* атмосфе́рный

atom /ˈætəm/ *n.* а́том
■ ~ **bomb** *n.* а́томная бо́мба

atomic /əˈtɒmɪk/ *adj.* а́томный

atonal /eɪˈtəʊn(ə)l/ *adj.* (mus.) атона́льный

atone /əˈtəʊn/ *v.i.:* ~ **for** искуп|а́ть, -и́ть

atrocious /əˈtrəʊʃəs/ *adj.* ужа́сный

atrocity /əˈtrɒsɪtɪ/ *n.* зве́рство

✍ **attach** /əˈtætʃ/ *v.t.* **1** (fasten) прикреп|ля́ть, -и́ть; **the** ~**ed document** прилага́емый докуме́нт **2**: ~ **oneself to** присоедин|я́ться, -и́ться к + *d.* **3** (assign) прид|ава́ть, -а́ть **4** (of affection): **she is very** ~**ed to her brother** она́ о́чень привяза́на к своему́ бра́ту

attaché /əˈtæʃeɪ/ *n.* атташе́ (*m. indecl.*)
■ ~ **case** *n.* диплома́т

attachment /əˈtætʃmənt/ *n.* **1** (comput., file) приложе́ние, вло́женный файл **2** (affection) привя́занность

✍ **attack** /əˈtæk/ *n.* **1** нападе́ние; (mil.) ата́ка, нападе́ние; **our troops were under** ~ на́ши войска́ бы́ли атако́ваны **2** (fig., criticism) напа́д|ки (-ок) **3** (of illness) при́ступ; припа́док; **he had a heart** ~ с ним случи́лся серде́чный при́ступ
● *v.t.* **1** (lit., fig.) нап|ада́ть, -а́сть на + *a.*; атакова́ть (*impf., pf.*); обру́ши|ваться, -ться на + *a.* **2** (a task etc.) набр|а́сываться, -о́ситься на + *a.*

attacker /əˈtækə(r)/ *n.* напада́ющий

attain /əˈteɪn/ *v.t.* дост|ига́ть, -и́гнуть (*or* -и́чь) + *g.*; доб|ива́ться, -и́ться + *g.*

attainment /əˈteɪnmənt/ *n.* достиже́ние

✍ **attempt** /əˈtempt/ *n.* **1** (endeavour) попы́тка; **they made no** ~ **to escape** они́ не предприня́ли попы́тки убежа́ть **2** (product of trying to make sth): **her** ~ **at producing a meal** плод её тще́тных

кулина́рных стара́ний **3** (assault): **an** ~ **was made on his life** на его́ жизнь покуша́лись
● *v.t.* (try; try to do) пыта́ться, по-; **he was charged with** ~**ed murder** его́ обвини́ли в покуше́нии на уби́йство

✍ **attend** /əˈtend/ *v.t.* прису́тствовать (*impf.*) на + *p.*; **the concert was well** ~**ed** конце́рт собра́л большо́е коли́чество зри́телей; ~ **school** посеща́ть (*impf.*) шко́лу
● *v.i.* **1** (be present) прису́тствовать (*impf.*) **2** ~ **to** (take care of, look after) следи́ть (*impf.*) за + *i.*; забо́титься, по- о + *p.*; (deal with) зан|има́ться, -я́ться + *i.*; **are you being** ~**ed to?** (in shop) вас (уже́) обслу́живают?

attendance /əˈtend(ə)ns/ *n.* **1** (presence) прису́тствие **2**: **in** ~ (present) прису́тствующий

attendant /əˈtend(ə)nt/ *n.* (in museum, car park) служи́тель (*m.*)

✍ **attention** /əˈtenʃ(ə)n/ *n.* **1** (heed) внима́ние; **pay** ~ **to** обра|ща́ть, -ти́ть внима́ние на + *a.*; **draw** ~ **to** привл|ека́ть, -е́чь внима́ние к + *d.* **2** (mil. command) сми́рно!; (posture): **stand to** ~ стоя́ть (*impf.*) сми́рно
■ ~ **deficit disorder** *n.* синдро́м наруше́ния внима́ния

attentive /əˈtentɪv/ *adj.* **1** (heedful) внима́тельный **2** (solicitous) забо́тливый

attest /əˈtest/ *v.t.* (certify) удостов|еря́ть, -е́рить; (bear witness to) свиде́тельствовать, за-; (confirm) подтвер|жда́ть, -ди́ть
● *v.i.:* ~ **to** свиде́тельствовать (*impf.*) о + *p.*

attic /ˈætɪk/ *n.* манса́рда, чердо́к

attire /əˈtaɪə(r)/ *n.* облаче́ние, одея́ние; **in night** ~ в ночно́м облаче́нии
● *v.t.* (dress) облач|а́ть, -и́ть; над|ева́ть, -е́ть; **she was** ~**d in white** она́ была́ вся в бе́лом

✍ **attitude** /ˈætɪtjuːd/ *n.* отноше́ние

✍ **attorney** /əˈtɜːnɪ/ *n.* (*pl.* ~**s**) (AmE, lawyer) адвока́т

✍ **attract** /əˈtrækt/ *v.t.* **1** (of physical forces) притя́|гивать, -ну́ть; (fig.) привл|ека́ть, -е́чь (к себе́) **2** (captivate) привл|ека́ть (*impf.*), притя́гивать (*impf.*); **he found himself** ~**ed to her** он почу́вствовал, что увлечён е́ю

attraction /əˈtrækʃ(ə)n/ *n.* **1** (phys.) притяже́ние, тяготе́ние **2** (charm) привлека́тельность **3** (thing of interest) достопримеча́тельность; (amusement) аттракцио́н

attractive /əˈtræktɪv/ *adj.* привлека́тельный; притяга́тельный

attribute¹ /ˈætrɪbjuːt/ *n.* сво́йство

attribute² /əˈtrɪbjuːt/ *v.t.:* ~ **sth to** (work of art, quality) припи́с|ывать, -а́ть что-н. + *d.*; (event, result) отн|оси́ть, -ести́ что-н. к + *d.*

attributive /əˈtrɪbjʊtɪv/ *adj.* (gram.) определи́тельный, атрибути́вный

attrition /əˈtrɪʃ(ə)n/ *n.* тре́ние; истира́ние; (fig.) истоще́ние; измо́р; **war of** ~ война́ на истоще́ние

atypical /eɪˈtɪpɪk(ə)l/ *adj.* нетипи́чный

aubergine /ˈəʊbəʒiːn/ *n.* (BrE) баклажа́н

auburn /ˈɔːbən/ *adj.* тёмно-ры́жий

auction /ˈɔːkʃ(ə)n/ *n.* аукцио́н

● *v.t.* (*also* ~ **off**) прод|ава́ть, -а́ть с аукцио́на

■ ~ **room** *n.* аукцио́нный зал

auctioneer /ɔːkʃəˈnɪə(r)/ *n.* аукциони́ст

audacious /ɔːˈdeɪʃəs/ *adj.* (bold) сме́лый; (daring) отва́жный; (impudent) де́рзкий

audacity /ɔːˈdæsɪtɪ/ *n.* сме́лость; отва́га; де́рзость

audible /ˈɔːdɪb(ə)l/ *adj.* слы́шимый, слы́шный

✓ **audience** /ˈɔːdɪəns/ *n.* (listeners) аудито́рия; слу́шатели (*m. pl.*); (spectators) зри́тели (*m. pl.*); пу́блика

audiobook /ˈɔːdɪəʊbʊk/ *n.* аудиокни́га

audio-visual /ˌɔːdɪəʊˈvɪʒʊəl/ *adj.* аудиовизуа́льный

audit /ˈɔːdɪt/ *n.* реви́зия, ауди́т
● *v.t.* (**audited, auditing**) пров|еря́ть, -е́рить отчётность + *d.*; ревизова́ть (*impf., pf.*)

audition /ɔːˈdɪʃ(ə)n/ *n.* прослу́шивание, про́ба
● *v.t.* прослу́ш|ивать, -ать

auditor /ˈɔːdɪtə(r)/ *n.* ауди́тор

auditori|um /ˌɔːdɪˈtɔːrɪəm/ *n.* (*pl.* ~**ums** *or* ~**a**) (where audience sits) зри́тельный зал

augment /ɔːɡˈment/ *v.t.* приумн|ожа́ть, -о́жить; увели́чи|вать, -ть

augur /ˈɔːɡə(r)/ *n.* (hist.) авгу́р (*жрец, толковавший волю богов*)
● *v.t.* (portend) предвеща́ть (*impf.*)
● *v.i.* (of things) служи́ть (*impf.*)
предзнаменова́нием + *g.*; **the exam results** ~ **well for his future** результа́ты его́ экза́менов — хоро́шая зая́вка на бу́дущее

✓ **August** /ˈɔːɡəst/ *n.* а́вгуст

aunt /ɑːnt/ *n.* тётя, тётка

auntie, aunty /ˈɑːntɪ/ *n.* тётушка, тётенька

au pair /əʊ ˈpeə(r)/ *n.* ≈ ня́ня-иностра́нка

aural /ˈɔːr(ə)l/ *adj.* слухово́й

auspices /ˈɔːspɪsɪz/ *n. pl.* (patronage) покрови́тельство; эги́да; **under UN** ~ под эги́дой ООН

auspicious /ɔːˈspɪʃəs/ *adj.* благоприя́тный; **on this** ~ **day** в э́тот знамена́тельный день

austere /ɒˈstɪə(r)/ *adj.* (**austerer, austerest**) стро́гий, суро́вый

austerity /ɒˈsterɪtɪ/ *n.* стро́гость, суро́вость

Australia /ɒˈstreɪlɪə/ *n.* Австра́лия

✓ **Australian** /ɒˈstreɪlɪən/ *n.* австрали́|ец (-йка)
● *adj.* австрали́йский

Austria /ˈɒstrɪə/ *n.* А́встрия

Austrian /ˈɒstrɪən/ *n.* австри́|ец (-йка)
● *adj.* австри́йский

authentic /ɔːˈθentɪk/ *adj.* по́длинный

authenticate /ɔːˈθentɪkeɪt/ *v.t.* удостов|еря́ть, -е́рить по́длинность + *g.*

authenticity /ˌɔːθenˈtɪsɪtɪ/ *n.* по́длинность

✓ **author** /ˈɔːθə(r)/ *n.* (of specific work) а́втор; (writer in general) писа́тель (*m.*) (-ница)

authoritarian /ɔːˌθɒrɪˈteərɪən/ *adj.* авторита́рный

authoritative /ɔːˈθɒrɪtətɪv/ *adj.* авторите́тный

✓ **authority** /ɔːˈθɒrɪtɪ/ *n.* **1** (power; right) власть; (legal) полномо́чие; **who is in** ~ **here?** кто

здесь ста́рший/нача́льник?; **who gave you** ~ **over me?** кто вам дал пра́во мне прика́зывать? **2** (*usu. in pl.*) (public bodies) вла́сти (*f. pl.*); о́рганы (*m. pl.*) вла́сти

authorization /ˌɔːθəraɪˈzeɪʃ(ə)n/ *n.* (authorizing) уполномо́чивание; санкциони́рование; (sanction) разреше́ние; са́нкция

authorize /ˈɔːθəraɪz/ *v.t.* **1** (give authority to) уполномо́чи|вать, -ть **2** (sanction) разреш|а́ть, -и́ть; дозв|оля́ть, -о́лить; санкциони́ровать (*impf., pf.*)

autism /ˈɔːtɪz(ə)m/ *n.* аути́зм

autistic /ɔːˈtɪstɪk/ *adj.* аутисти́ческий; страда́ющий аути́змом

auto /ˈɔːtəʊ/ *n.* (*pl.* ~**s**) (AmE, infml) а́вто

autobiographical /ˌɔːtəbaɪəˈɡræfɪk(ə)l/ *adj.* автобиографи́ческий

autobiography /ˌɔːtəbaɪˈɒɡrəfɪ/ *n.* автобиогра́фия

autocracy /ɔːˈtɒkrəsɪ/ *n.* самодержа́вие, автокра́тия

autocrat /ˈɔːtəkræt/ *n.* самоде́ржец, автокра́т

autocratic /ˌɔːtəˈkrætɪk/ *adj.* самодержа́вный; (dictatorial) деспоти́ческий

autocue® /ˈɔːtəʊkjuː/ *n.* (BrE) автосуфлёр

autograph /ˈɔːtəɡrɑːf/ *n.* авто́граф
● *v.t.* надпи́с|ывать, -а́ть

automated /ˈɔːtəmeɪtɪd/ *adj.* автоматизи́рованный

✓ **automatic** /ˌɔːtəˈmætɪk/ *n.* (firearm) автомати́ческое ору́жие
● *adj.* автомати́ческий

automation /ˌɔːtəˈmeɪʃ(ə)n/ *n.* автоматиза́ция

automat|on /ɔːˈtɒmət(ə)n/ *n.* (*pl.* ~**a** *or* ~**ons**) автома́т (*робот; человек*)

automobile /ˈɔːtəməbiːl/ *n.* автомоби́ль (*m.*)

autonomous /ɔːˈtɒnəməs/ *adj.* автоно́мный

autonomy /ɔːˈtɒnəmɪ/ *n.* автоно́мия

autopilot /ˈɔːtəʊpaɪlət/ *n.* автопило́т

autopsy /ˈɔːtɒpsɪ/ *n.* вскры́тие тру́па, аутопси́я

✓ **autumn** /ˈɔːtəm/ *n.* о́сень; (*attr.*) осе́нний

autumnal /ɔːˈtʌmn(ə)l/ *adj.* осе́нний

auxiliary /ɔːɡˈzɪljərɪ/ *n.* (assistant) помо́щник; (*in full* ~ **verb**) (gram.) вспомога́тельный глаго́л
● *adj.* доба́вочный

avail /əˈveɪl/ *n.* (use) по́льза; **his entreaties were of no** ~ его́ мольбы́ бы́ли безуспе́шны; **his intervention was of little** ~ от его́ вмеша́тельства бы́ло ма́ло по́льзы; **to no** ~ напра́сно
● *v.t.* **1** (benefit) быть поле́зным/вы́годным + *d.*; **our efforts** ~**ed us nothing** на́ши уси́лия ни к чему́ не привели́ **2**: ~ **oneself of** воспо́льзоваться (*pf.*) + *i.*

availability /əˌveɪləˈbɪlɪtɪ/ *n.* (presence) нали́чие; (accessibility) досту́пность

✓ **available** /əˈveɪləb(ə)l/ *adj.* (product) име́ющийся в прода́же, досту́пный; **it is not** ~ **in your size** ва́шего разме́ра нет; (information): **the information was not** ~ информа́ция была́ недосту́пна; (person)

a

свобо́дный; **she's not ~** она́ занята́
avalanche /'ævəlɑːntʃ/ *n.* лави́на
avarice /'ævərɪs/ *n.* жа́дность
avaricious /ævə'rɪʃəs/ *adj.* жа́дный
avenge /ə'vendʒ/ *v.t.* мстить, ото- за + *a.*;
    she ~d her friend она́ отомсти́ла за дру́га
avenue /'ævənjuː/ *n.* (tree-lined road) алле́я;
    (wide street) проспе́кт
✔ **average** /'ævərɪdʒ/ *n.* (mean) сре́днее число́;
    (norm) сре́днее; **above/below ~** вы́ше/ни́же
    сре́днего; **on ~** в сре́днем
    ● *adj.* сре́дний
    ● *v.t. & i.:* **my expenses ~ £10 a day** мои́
    расхо́ды составля́ют в сре́днем де́сять
    фу́нтов в день; (do on **~**): **he ~s 6 hours'
    work a day** он рабо́тает в сре́днем шесть
    часо́в в день
averse /ə'vɜːs/ *pred. adj.:* **~ to** не
    располо́женный к + *d.*; **I am not ~ to a
    good dinner** я не прочь хорошо́ пообе́дать
aversion /ə'vɜːʃ(ə)n/ *n.* отвраще́ние,
    антипа́тия
avert /ə'vɜːt/ *v.t.:* **~ one's gaze, eyes** отв|оди́ть,
    -ести́ взгляд
aviary /'eɪvɪərɪ/ *n.* пти́чник; вольер(а) для птиц
aviation /eɪvɪ'eɪʃ(ə)n/ *n.* авиа́ция
avid /'ævɪd/ *adj.* жа́дный, а́лчный
avocado /ævə'kɑːdəʊ/ *n.* (*pl.* **~s**) (*in full ~
    pear*) авока́до (*nt. indecl.*)
✔ **avoid** /ə'vɔɪd/ *v.t.* (drive round) объезжа́ть,
    объе́хать; (escape, evade) избе|га́ть, -жа́ть + *g.*;
    I could not ~ meeting him я не мог избежа́ть
    встре́чи с ним
avoidable /ə'vɔɪdəb(ə)l/ *adj.:* **delays are ~**
    заде́ржек мо́жно избежа́ть; **without ~ delay**
    без нену́жных/изли́шних заде́ржек
avuncular /ə'vʌŋkjʊlə(r)/ *adj.* (manner, tone)
    оте́ческий; (person) дружелю́бный
await /ə'weɪt/ *v.t.* ожида́ть (*impf.*) + *g.*
awake /ə'weɪk/ *pred. adj.:* **are you ~ or
    asleep?** вы спи́те и́ли нет?; **is he ~ yet?** он
    просну́лся?; **the baby was wide ~** у ребёнка
    сна́ не́ было ни в одно́м глазу́
    ● *v.t.* (*past* **awoke**, *p.p.* **awoken**) буди́ть,
    раз-
    ● *v.i.* (*past* **awoke**, *p.p.* **awoken**)
    прос|ыпа́ться, -ну́ться
awaken /ə'weɪkən/ *v.t.* пробу|жда́ть, -ди́ть
✔ **award** /ə'wɔːd/ *n.* награ́да, приз
    ● *v.t.* прису|жда́ть, -ди́ть (*что кому*)
✔ **aware** /ə'weə(r)/ *pred. adj.:* **be ~ of**
    сознава́ть (*impf.*); (realize) осозн|ава́ть,
    -а́ть; **you are probably ~ that ...** вам,

вероя́тно, изве́стно, что...
awareness /ə'weənɪs/ *n.* созна́ние
✔ **away** /ə'weɪ/ *adv.* **1** (at a distance): **the shops are
    ten minutes' walk ~** магази́ны нахо́дятся в
    десяти́ мину́тах ходьбы́ отсю́да **2** (not present
    or near): **he is ~** он в отъе́зде; **our team are
    playing ~ (from home)** на́ша кома́нда игра́ет
    на вы́езде *or* на чужо́м по́ле *or* в гостя́х
    3 (of time or degree): **the wedding is three
    weeks ~** до сва́дьбы (оста́лось) три неде́ли
awe /ɔː/ *n.* благогове́ние, тре́пет
    ■ **~-inspiring** *adj.* внуша́ющий благогове́ние
awesome /'ɔːsəm/ *adj.* (impressive)
    впечатля́ющий; (AmE, infml, excellent)
    потряса́ющий
awful /'ɔːfʊl/ *adj.* ужа́сный, стра́шный
awfully /'ɔːfəlɪ/ *adv.* ужа́сно; **~ nice** (infml)
    ужа́сно ми́лый
awkward /'ɔːkwəd/ *adj.* **1** (clumsy) неуклю́жий
    2 (inconvenient, uncomfortable) неудо́бный
    3 (difficult): **an ~ problem** ка́верзная пробле́ма
    4 (embarrassing): **an ~ silence** нело́вкое
    молча́ние **5** (BrE, of person, hard to manage)
    тру́дный; **he's being ~ (about it)** он чини́т
    препя́тствия
awning /'ɔːnɪŋ/ *n.* наве́с; тент
awoke /ə'wəʊk/ *past of* ▸ **awake**
awoken /ə'wəʊk(ə)n/ *p.p. of* ▸ **awake**
AWOL /'eɪwɒl/ *pred. adj.* (*abbr. of* **absent
    without leave**) в самово́льной отлу́чке
awry /ə'raɪ/ *pred. adj.* криво́й; (distorted)
    искажённый
    ● *adv.* ко́со; (fig.): **things went ~** дела́ пошли́
    скве́рно
axe /æks/ (AmE *also* **ax**) *n.* топо́р
    ● *v.t.* (**axing**) (fig., staff, budgets) уреза́ть,
    уре́зать; (a project) заруб|а́ть, -и́ть
axes /'æksiːz/ *pl. of* ▸ **axis**
axis /'æksɪs/ *n.* (*pl.* **axes**) ось, вал
axle /'æks(ə)l/ *n.* ось
azalea /ə'zeɪlɪə/ *n.* аза́лия
Azerbaijan /æzəbaɪ'dʒɑːn/ *n.* Азербайджа́н
Azerbaijani /æzəbaɪ'dʒɑːnɪ/ *n.* (*pl.* **~s**)
    (person) азербайджа́н|ец (-ка); (language)
    азербайджа́нский язы́к
    ● *adj.* азербайджа́нский
Azov /'æzɒf/ *n.* (*in full* **Sea of ~**) Азо́вское
    мо́ре
Aztec /'æztek/ *n.* ацте́к
    ● *adj.* ацте́кский
azure /'æʒə(r)/ *n.* лазу́рь
    ● *adj.* лазу́рный, голубо́й

✔ ключева́я ле́ксика

Bb

B /biː/ *n.* **1** (mus.) си (*nt. indecl.*) **2** (academic mark) «хорошо», четвёрка

BA *abbr.* (*of* **Bachelor of Arts**) бакала́вр гуманита́рных нау́к

babble /'bæb(ə)l/ *v.t. & i.* болта́ть (*impf.*); лепета́ть (*impf.*); babbling brook журча́щий руче́й

babe /beɪb/ *n.* (sl.) де́вушка

baboon /bə'buːn/ *n.* бабуи́н, павиа́н

✤ **baby** /'beɪbɪ/ *n.* **1** младе́нец; (*of animals etc.*) детёныш **2** (*attr.*): ~ **elephant** слонёнок ■ ~**sit** *v.i.* присма́тривать (*impf.*) за детьми́ в отсу́тствие роди́телей; ~**sitter** *n.* приходя́щая ня́ня; ~**sitting** *n.* присмо́тр за детьми́

babyish /'beɪbɪʃ/ *adj.* де́тский

baccalaureate /bækə'lɔːrɪət/ *n.* сте́пень бакала́вра

bachelor /'bætʃələ(r)/ *n.* **1** холостя́к **2** (academic) бакала́вр

✤ **back** /bæk/ *n.* **1** (part of body) спина́; ~ **to** ~ спино́й к спине́; **as soon as my** ~ **was turned** не успе́л я отверну́ться **2** (fig.): behind my ~ за мое́й спино́й **3** (of chair) спи́нка **4** (other side, rear): ~ **of an envelope** обра́тная сторона́ конве́рта; **at the** ~ **of one's mind** подсозна́тельно; в глубине́ души́ **5** (sport) защи́тник **6** (*attr.*): ~ **door** чёрный ход; ~ **seat** за́днее сиде́нье; ~ **street** глуха́я у́лица
● *adv.* **1** (to or at the rear) наза́д, сза́ди **2** (returning to former position etc.) обра́тно; **he is** ~ **again** он сно́ва здесь; **we shall be** ~ **before dark** мы вернёмся за́светло; **get one's own** ~ отплати́ть (*pf.*) (*кому*)
● *v.t.* **1** (move backwards) дви́|гать, -нуть наза́д (*or* в обра́тном направле́нии); **she** ~**ed the car into the garage** она́ въе́хала за́дним хо́дом в гара́ж **2** (support) (*also* ~ **up**) подде́рж|ивать, -а́ть **3** (finance) финанси́ровать (*impf., pf.*) **4**: ~ **up** (comput.) резерви́ровать (*impf., pf.*)
● *v.i.* **1** (of motor vehicle) идти́ (*det.*) за́дним хо́дом **2**: ~ **down (from)** отступ|а́ться, -и́ться (*от чего*); ~ **out (of)** уклон|я́ться, -и́ться (*от чего*)

backache /'bækeɪk/ *n.* боль в спине́/поясни́це

backbencher /bæk'bentʃə(r)/ *n.* (BrE) рядово́й член парла́мента; заднескамее́чник

backbiting /'bækbaɪtɪŋ/ *n.* злосло́вие

backbone /'bækbəʊn/ *n.* позвоно́чник

backchat /'bæktʃæt/ *n.* (BrE) де́рзкий отве́т, де́рзость

backcloth /'bækklɒθ/ *n.* (BrE, theatr.) за́дник

backdate /bæk'deɪt/ *v.t.* (letter) пом|еча́ть, -е́тить за́дним число́м; (pay) пров|оди́ть, -ести́ за́дним число́м

backdrop /'bækdrɒp/ *n.* **1**: against the ~ of crisis на фо́не кри́зиса **2** = backcloth

backer /'bækə(r)/ *n.* ока́зывающий подде́ржку; субсиди́рующий

backfire /'bækfaɪə(r)/ *v.t.* (of a car, engine) изда|ва́ть, -ть обра́тную вспы́шку; (fig.) прив|оди́ть, -ести́ к обра́тным результа́там

✤ **background** /'bækɡraʊnd/ *n.* **1** за́дний план, фон; (*attr.*) фо́новый; **in the** ~ of the picture на за́днем пла́не карти́ны; on a dark ~ на тёмном фо́не; keep in the ~ (fig.) держа́ть(ся) (*impf.*) в тени́ **2** (of person) (parentage) происхожде́ние; (education) образова́ние; (experience) о́пыт **3** (to a situation) предысто́рия **4**: ~ music музыка́льное сопровожде́ние/оформле́ние

backhand /'bækhænd/ *n.* (sport) уда́р сле́ва

backhanded /bæk'hændɪd/ *adj.* (fig.) сомни́тельный, двусмы́сленный

backhander /'bækhændə(r)/ *n.* (BrE, bribe) взя́тка

backing /'bækɪŋ/ *n.* **1** (assistance) подде́ржка; (subsidy) субсиди́рование **2** (of cloth) подкла́дка

backlash /'bæklæʃ/ *n.* (fig.) реа́кция

backlog /'bæklɒɡ/ *n.* го́ры (*f. pl.*) накопи́вшейся рабо́ты

backpack /'bækpæk/ *n.* рюкза́к

backpacker /'bækpækə(r)/ *n.* челове́к, путеше́ствующий с рюкзако́м

back-pedal /'bækped(ə)l/ *v.i.* (fig.) идти́ (*det.*), пойти́ на попя́тную

backside /bæk'saɪd/ *n.* зад, за́дница

backslash /'bækslæʃ/ *n.* (typ.) обра́тная коса́я черта́

backslide /'bækslaɪd/ *v.t.* вновь подда́ться (*pf.*) искуше́нию; верну́ться (*pf.*) к дурны́м привы́чкам

backstage /'bæksteɪdʒ/ *adv.* за кули́сами

backstreet /'bækstriːt/ *adj.* (illicit) подпо́льный

backstroke /'bækstrəʊk/ *n.* пла́вание на спине́

backtrack /'bæktræk/ *v.i.* (fig.) идти́ (*det.*), пойти́ на попя́тную

back-up /'bækʌp/ *n.* (comput.) резе́рвная ко́пия; бэкап
● *adj.* (comput.) резе́рвный

backward /'bækwəd/ *adj.* **1** (towards the back) обра́тный; **a** ~ **glance** взгля́д наза́д **2** (lagging) отста́лый

backwardness /'bækwədnɪs/ *n.* отста́лость; (disinclination) неохо́та

b

backwards /'bækwədz/ adv. (in backward direction) наза́д; (in reverse order) в обра́тном поря́дке; **walk ~** пя́титься, по-; **~ and forwards** взад и вперёд; туда́ и обра́тно

backwater /'bækwɔː(r)/ n. боло́то, ти́хая за́водь

backyard /bæk'jɑːd/ n. **1** (BrE) за́дний двор **2** (AmE) са́д(ик) за до́мом

bacon /'beɪkən/ n. беко́н
■ **~ and eggs** n. яи́чница с беко́ном

bacteria /bæk'tɪərɪə/ pl. of ▶ **bacterium**

bacterial /bæk'tɪərɪəl/ adj. бактериа́льный

bacteriology /bæktɪərɪ'ɒlədʒɪ/ n. бактериоло́гия

bacteri|um /bæk'tɪərɪəm/ n. (pl. ~a) бакте́рия

bad /bæd/ n. (evil) дурно́е, плохо́е
● adj. (**worse, worst**) **1** плохо́й, дурно́й, скве́рный; **not ~!** непло́хо!; **too ~!** о́чень жаль! **2** (morally bad) плохо́й, дурно́й; **a ~ name** дурна́я репута́ция **3** (spoilt) испо́рченный; **go ~** по́ртиться, ис- **4** (severe) си́льный; **I caught a ~ cold** я си́льно простуди́лся **5** (harmful) вре́дный; **smoking is ~ for one** куре́ние вре́дно для здоро́вья
■ **~-mannered** adj. невоспи́танный; **~-tempered** adj. раздражи́тельный

badge /bædʒ/ n. значо́к; (fig.) си́мвол

badger /'bædʒə(r)/ n. барсу́к

badly /'bædlɪ/ adv. (**worse, worst**) **1** (not well) пло́хо **2** (very much) о́чень; си́льно **3**: **~ off** в нужде́

badminton /'bædmɪnt(ə)n/ n. бадминто́н

baffle /'bæf(ə)l/ v.t. (perplex) сби|ва́ть, -ть с то́лку; озада́чи|вать, -ть

bag /bæg/ n. **1** су́мка; (small **~**, hand**~**) су́мочка; (paper **~**, plastic **~**) паке́т **2** (large **~**, sack) мешо́к **3** (luggage) чемода́н; **pack one's ~s** собра́ть (pf.) ве́щи пе́ред отъе́здом **4** (var.): **~s under the eyes** мешки́ под глаза́ми
■ **~pipe(s)** n. (pl.) волы́нка

baggage /'bægɪdʒ/ n. бага́ж
■ **~ handler** n. опера́тор на приёме/вы́даче бага́жа; **~ reclaim** n. пункт вы́дачи бага́жа

baggy /'bægɪ/ adj. (**baggier, baggiest**) мешкова́тый

Baghdad /bæg'dæd/ n. Багда́д

Bahamas /bə'hɑːməz/ n. pl. (in full the **~**) Бага́мские острова́ (m. pl.)

bail¹ /beɪl/ n. (pledge) зало́г; поручи́тельство; **release on ~** отпус|ка́ть, -ти́ть на пору́ки
● v.t.: **~ sb out** (of detention) брать, взять кого́-н. на пору́ки

bail² /beɪl/ v.t. **1** (also **~ out**) выче́рпывать, вы́черпать (воду из лодки) **2**: **~ sb out** пом|ога́ть, -о́чь + d. (в трудном положении)
● v.i.: **~ out** (aeron.) катапульти́роваться (impf., pf.)
■ **~out** n. (econ.) фина́нсовая по́мощь

bailiff /'beɪlɪf/ n. (law) суде́бный при́став; бе́йлиф

bait /beɪt/ n. (hunting) прима́нка; (fishing) наса́дка

bake /beɪk/ v.t. печь, ис-
● v.i. пе́чься, ис-

baker /'beɪkə(r)/ n. пе́карь (m.)

bakery /'beɪkərɪ/ n. пека́рня; (shop) бу́лочная

Baku n. Баку́ (m. indecl.)

balalaika /bælə'laɪkə/ n. балала́йка

balance /'bæləns/ n. **1** (machine) весы́ (-о́в) **2** (equilibrium) равнове́сие; **lose one's ~** (fig.) теря́ть, по- душе́вное равнове́сие; **hang in the ~** висе́ть (impf.) на волоске́ **3** (bookkeeping) бала́нс; са́льдо (indecl.)
● v.t. **1** (lit.): **he ~d a pole on his chin** он баланси́ровал шест на подборо́дке **2** (make equal) уравнове́|шивать, -сить **3** (weigh one thing against another) взве́|шивать, -сить; сопост|авля́ть, -а́вить (что с чем)
● v.i. (of accounts) сходи́ться (impf.); (be in equilibrium) баланси́ровать (impf.)
■ **~ of payments** n. платёжный бала́нс; **~ of trade** n. торго́вый бала́нс

balanced /'bælənst/ adj. (of person) уравнове́шенный; **~ judgement** проду́манное сужде́ние; **~ diet** сбаланси́рованная/рациона́льная дие́та

balcony /'bælkənɪ/ n. балко́н

bald /bɔːld/ adj. лы́сый

bale¹ n. (of hay) тюк; (of cotton) ки́па

bale² /beɪl/ v.i. (BrE) = **bail²**

Balkan /'bɔːlkən/ n.: the **~s** Балка́н|ы (pl., g. —); Балка́нский полуо́стров
● adj. балка́нский

ball¹ /bɔːl/ n. (dance) бал
■ **~room** n. танцева́льный зал; **~room dancing** n. ба́льные та́нцы (m. pl.)

ball² /bɔːl/ n. **1** (sphere) шар **2** (in football, rugby, tennis) мяч; (in golf, table tennis) мя́чик **3** (of wool) клубо́к **4** (in pl.) (vulg., testicles) я́йца (nt. pl.); (BrE, nonsense) чепуха́
■ **~park** adj.: **a ~park figure** приме́рная ци́фра; **~point (pen)** n. ша́риковая ру́чка

ballad /'bæləd/ n. балла́да

ballast /'bæləst/ n. балла́ст
● v.t. грузи́ть, на- балла́стом

ballerina /bælə'riːnə/ n. балери́на

ballet /'bæleɪ/ n. бале́т
■ **~ dancer** n. арти́ст (-ка) бале́та

ballistic /bə'lɪstɪk/ adj. баллисти́ческий

ballistics /bə'lɪstɪks/ n. балли́стика

balloon /bə'luːn/ n. аэроста́т; (also child's) возду́шный шар
● v.i. (fly in **~**) лета́ть (indet.) на возду́шном ша́ре

ballot /'bælət/ n. (**~ paper**) избира́тельный бюллете́нь; (vote) голосова́ние
● v.t. (**balloted, balloting**) пров|оди́ть, -ести́ голосова́ние ме́жду + i.
■ **~ box** n. избира́тельная у́рна

Baltic /'bɔːltɪk/ n. (in full the **~ (Sea)**) Балти́йское мо́ре, Ба́лтика
● adj. балти́йский; прибалти́йский
■ **~ States** n. (при)балти́йские госуда́рства, Прибалти́ка

balustrade /ˌbælə'streɪd/ *n.* балюстра́да

bamboo /bæm'buː/ *n.* бамбу́к

bamboozle /bæm'buːz(ə)l/ *v.t.* (infml) одура́чи|вать, -ть; над|ува́ть, -у́ть

ɗ **ban** /bæn/ *n.* (prohibition) запреще́ние, запре́т
● *v.t.* (**banned**, **banning**) запре|ща́ть, -ти́ть

banal /bə'nɑːl/ *adj.* бана́льный

banana /bə'nɑːnə/ *n.* бана́н

ɗ **band¹** /bænd/ *n.* **1** (braid) тесьма́; **rubber ~** рези́нка **2** (strip) полоса́ **3** (radio): **frequency ~** диапазо́н часто́т

ɗ **band²** /bænd/ *n.* (gang) ба́нда, ша́йка; (mus.) орке́стр; **jazz ~** джаз-ба́нд, джаз-орке́стр
● *v.i.*: **~ together** объедин|я́ться, -и́ться

bandage /'bændɪdʒ/ *n.* бинт
● *v.t.* бинтова́ть, за-; перевя́з|ывать, -а́ть

bandanna, **bandana** /bæn'dænə/ *n.* цветно́й плато́к, банда́на

bandit /'bændɪt/ *n.* разбо́йник, банди́т

bane /beɪn/ *n.* прокля́тие; **it is the ~ of my life** э́то отравля́ет мне жизнь

bang /bæŋ/ *n.* **1** (blow) уда́р **2** (crash) гро́хот; стук **3** (explosion) взрыв
● *v.t.* (strike, thump) уд|аря́ть, -а́рить; **~ one's fist on the table** сту́кнуть (*pf.*) кулако́м по́ столу; **~ the door** хло́пнуть (*pf.*) две́рью
● *v.i.* (of door, window, etc.) захло́пнуться (*pf.*); **the door is ~ing** дверь хло́пает
● *adv.* (suddenly) вдруг; (BrE, just, exactly) пря́мо; как раз

banger /'bæŋə(r)/ *n.* (BrE, infml) (sausage) соси́ска; (car) драндуле́т

Bangkok /bæŋ'kɒk/ *n.* Бангко́к

Bangladesh /ˌbæŋglə'deʃ/ *n.* Бангладе́ш

Bangladeshi /ˌbæŋglə'deʃɪ/ *n.* (*pl.* **~ or ~s**) бангладе́ш|ец (-ка)
● *adj.* бангладе́шский

bangle /'bæŋg(ə)l/ *n.* брасле́т

banish /'bænɪʃ/ *v.t.* (exile) высыла́ть, вы́слать; (from one's mind) от|гоня́ть, -огна́ть

banisters /'bænɪstəz/ *n. pl.* пери́л|а (*pl., g.* —)

banjo /'bændʒəʊ/ *n.* (*pl.* **~s or ~es**) ба́нджо (*nt. indecl.*)

bank¹ /bæŋk/ *n.* (of river) бе́рег

ɗ **bank²** /bæŋk/ *n.* (fin.) банк
● *v.t.* (put money in **~**) класть, положи́ть в банк
● *v.i.* (keep money in **~**) держа́ть (*impf.*) де́ньги в ба́нке; **~ on** (fig., rely on) пол|ага́ться, -ожи́ться на + *a.*; де́лать, с- ста́вку на + *a.*
■ **~ account** *n.* ба́нковский счёт; **~ card** *n.* ба́нковская креди́тная ка́рта; **~ clerk** *n.* ба́нковский служа́щий; **~ holiday** *n.* ≈ официа́льный нерабо́чий день; **~note** *n.* банкно́та

banker /'bæŋkə(r)/ *n.* банки́р

banking /'bæŋkɪŋ/ *n.* (fin.) ба́нковское де́ло

bankroll /'bæŋkrəʊl/ *v.t.* финанси́ровать (*impf., pf.*)

bankrupt /'bæŋkrʌpt/ *adj.* (also fig.) обанкро́тившийся; несостоя́тельный; **go ~** обанкро́титься (*pf.*)

bankruptcy /'bæŋkrʌptsɪ/ *n.* банкро́тство, несостоя́тельность

banner /'bænə(r)/ *n.* (lit., fig.) зна́мя (*nt. pl.*); (with slogan) плака́т

banns /bænz/ *n. pl.* оглаше́ние (предстоя́щего бра́ка); **ask, call, read the ~** огла|ша́ть, -си́ть имена́ жениха́ и неве́сты

banquet /'bæŋkwɪt/ *n.* пир; (formal occasion) банке́т

banter /'bæntə(r)/ *n.* подшу́чивание, подтру́нивание
● *v.i.* шути́ть, по-

baptism /'bæptɪz(ə)m/ *n.* креще́ние

Baptist /'bæptɪst/ *n.* **1**: **St John the ~** Иоа́нн Крести́тель (*m.*) **2** (member of denomination) бапти́ст (-ка)

baptize /bæp'taɪz/ *v.t.* крести́ть, о-; нар|ека́ть, -е́чь

ɗ **bar¹** /bɑː(r)/ *n.* **1** (rod) прут; (of chocolate) пли́тка; (of soap) кусо́к; (strip, flat piece) полоса́ **2** (*usu. in pl.*) решётка; **behind ~s** за решёткой **3** (mus.) такт
● *v.t.* (**barred, barring**) (bolt) зап|ира́ть, -ере́ть на засо́в; (obstruct) прегра|жда́ть, -ди́ть; (exclude) исключ|а́ть, -и́ть; **soldiers ~red the way** солда́ты блоки́ровали доро́гу
■ **~ code** *n.* штрихко́д

bar² /bɑː(r)/ *n.* (legal profession) адвокату́ра

ɗ **bar³** /bɑː(r)/ *n.* (room) бар, буфе́т; (counter) прила́вок
■ **~maid** *n.* буфе́тчица, ба́рмен; **~man**, **~tender** *nn.* буфе́тчик, ба́рмен

bar⁴ /bɑː(r)/ *prep.* (BrE, infml, excluding) исключа́я, не счита́я; **~ none** без исключе́ния

barbarian /bɑː'beərɪən/ *n.* ва́рвар

barbaric /bɑː'bærɪk/ *adj.* ва́рварский

barbarism /'bɑːbərɪz(ə)m/ *n.* ва́рварство; (ling.) варвари́зм

barbarity /bɑː'bærɪtɪ/ *n.* ва́рварство

barbarous /'bɑːbərəs/ *adj.* ва́рварский; (cruel) бесчелове́чный

barbecue /'bɑːbɪkjuː/ *n.* (party) барбекю́; пикни́к, где подаю́т мя́со, зажа́ренное на ве́ртеле/жаро́вне

barbed /bɑːbd/ *adj.*: **~ wire** колю́чая про́волока

barber /'bɑːbə(r)/ *n.* парикма́хер (*мужско́й*); **~'s (shop)** парикма́херская (*мужска́я*)

barbiturate /bɑː'bɪtjʊrət/ *n.* барбитура́т

bare /beə(r)/ *adj.* **1** (naked, not covered) го́лый, наго́й; обнажённый; **with one's ~ hands** го́лыми рука́ми; **~ feet** босы́е но́ги **2** (empty) пусто́й
● *v.t.*: **~ one's teeth** ска́лить, о- зу́бы
■ **~back** *adv.* без седла́; **~foot** *adj.* босо́й
● *adv.* босико́м

barely /'beəlɪ/ *adv.* едва́

Barents Sea /'bærənts/ *n.* Ба́ренцево мо́ре

bargain /'bɑːgɪn/ *n.* **1** (deal) сде́лка, соглаше́ние; **make a ~** заключ|а́ть, -и́ть сде́лку; **it's a ~!** по рука́м! **2** (thing cheaply acquired) вы́годная поку́пка
● *v.i.* торгова́ться, с-; **~ for** (expect) ожида́ть (*impf.*); **it was more than I ~ed for** на э́то я

b

не рассчитывал

barge /bɑːdʒ/ *n.* ба́ржа
• *v.i.* (infml): ~ **in** (intrude) вва́л|иваться, -и́ться

baritone /ˈbærɪtəʊn/ *n.* (voice, singer) барито́н

barium /ˈbeərɪəm/ *n.* ба́рий

bark¹ /bɑːk/ *n.* (of tree etc.) кора́

bark² /bɑːk/ *n.* (of dog) лай
• *v.i.* (of dog etc.) ла́ять (*impf.*) (**at:** на + *a.*)

barley /ˈbɑːlɪ/ *n.* ячме́нь (*m.*) (*злак*)

bar mitzvah /bɑː ˈmɪtzvə/ *n.* (ceremony and boy undergoing this) бар-ми́цва (*m.*) (*в иудаизме*)

barmy /ˈbɑːmɪ/ *adj.* (**barmier, barmiest**) (BrE, infml) чо́кнутый, тро́нутый; **go** ~ тро́нуться (*pf.*); спя́тить (*pf.*) (both infml)

barn /bɑːn/ *n.* амба́р, сара́й

barometer /bəˈrɒmɪtə(r)/ *n.* баро́метр

baron /ˈbærən/ *n.* баро́н

baroness /ˈbærənes/ *n.* бароне́сса

baroque /bəˈrɒk/ *n.* баро́кко (*nt. indecl.*)
• *adj.* баро́чный

barrack /ˈbærək/ *n.* (*usu. in pl.*) каза́рма

barrage /ˈbærɑːʒ/ *n.* (mil.) загражде́ние; (fig.): **a** ~ **of questions** град/шквал вопро́сов

barrel /ˈbær(ə)l/ *n.* **1** бо́чка **2** (of firearm) ствол

barren /ˈbærən/ *adj.* (**barrener, barrenest**) беспло́дный

barricade /ˌbærɪˈkeɪd/ *n.* баррика́да
• *v.t.* баррикади́ровать, за-; ~ **oneself in** баррикади́роваться, за-

barrier /ˈbærɪə(r)/ *n.* барье́р; (obstacle) поме́ха, прегра́да

barring /ˈbɑːrɪŋ/ *prep.* за исключе́нием + *g.*

barrister /ˈbærɪstə(r)/ *n.* (BrE) адвока́т

barrow /ˈbærəʊ/ *n.* (BrE) (handcart) ручна́я теле́жка; (wheel~) та́чка
■ ~ **boy** *n.* у́личный торго́вец (*с тележкой*)

barter /ˈbɑːtə(r)/ *v.i.* обме́н|иваться, -я́ться + *i.*; меня́ться (*impf.*) + *i.*

base¹ /beɪs/ *n.* **1** (of structure) фунда́мент, пьедеста́л, основа́ние, ба́зис **2** (mil. etc.) ба́за
• *v.t.* осно́в|ывать, -а́ть; **the legend is** ~**d on fact** в осно́ве э́той леге́нды лежа́т действи́тельные собы́тия
■ ~**ball** *n.* бейсбо́л; ~ **camp** *n.* ба́за

base² /beɪs/ *adj.* ни́зкий

basement /ˈbeɪsmənt/ *n.* подва́л

bases /ˈbeɪsiːz/ *pl. of* ▶ basis

bash /bæʃ/ (infml) *n.* (BrE, attempt) попы́тка; **have a** ~ попыта́ться (*pf.*); (bang): **give sb a** ~ **on the head** дава́ть, дать, кому́-н. по ба́шке (infml)
• *v.t.* си́льно ударя́ть, уда́рить

bashful /ˈbæʃfʊl/ *adj.* засте́нчивый

✍ **basic** /ˈbeɪsɪk/ *adj.* основно́й

✍ **basically** /ˈbeɪsɪkəlɪ/ *adv.* в основно́м

basil /ˈbæz(ə)l/ *n.* базили́к

basin /ˈbeɪs(ə)n/ *n.* (for food) ми́ска; (washbasin) умыва́льник, ра́ковина

✍ **basis** /ˈbeɪsɪs/ *n.* (*pl.* **bases**) осно́ва, ба́зис; **lay the** ~ **for** заложи́ть (*pf.*) осно́ву + *g.*

bask /bɑːsk/ *v.i.*: ~ **in the sun** гре́ться (*impf.*) на со́лнце; (fig.): ~ **in glory** купа́ться (*impf.*) в луча́х сла́вы

basket /ˈbɑːskɪt/ *n.* корзи́на, корзи́нка
■ ~**ball** *n.* (the sport) баскетбо́л; (*attr.*) баскетбо́льный; ~ **case** *n.* (infml) (useless person) никчёмный челове́к; (useless thing) бесполе́зная вещь

Basque /bæsk/ *n.* баск (-о́нка)
• *adj.* ба́скский

bass /beɪs/ *n.* (voice, singer) бас; (~ guitar) бас-гита́ра; (double ~) контраба́с

bassoon /bəˈsuːn/ *n.* фаго́т

bassoonist /bəˈsuːnɪst/ *n.* фаготи́ст (-ка)

bastard /ˈbɑːstəd/ *n.* **1** (child) внебра́чный ребёнок **2** (as term of abuse) уро́д

bastion /ˈbæstɪən/ *n.* бастио́н

bat¹ /bæt/ *n.* (zool.) лету́чая мышь

bat² /bæt/ *n.* (sport) би́та, лапта́
• *v.t.* (**batted, batting**) бить (*impf.*) (*or* удар|я́ть, -я́ть) би́той/лапто́й

batch /bætʃ/ *n.* **1** (of bread) вы́печка **2** (consignment) па́чка; гру́ппа

bated /ˈbeɪtɪd/ *adj.*: with ~ **breath** затаи́в дыха́ние

bath /bɑːθ/ *n.* ва́нна; **take, have a** ~ прин|има́ть, -я́ть ва́нну; купа́ться, ис-
• *v.t. & i.* купа́ть(ся), ис-
■ ~**robe** *n.* купа́льный хала́т; ~**room** *n.* ва́нная (ко́мната); ~**tub** *n.* ва́нна

bathe /beɪð/ *v.t.* **1** (one's face etc.) мыть, по-; обм|ыва́ть, -ы́ть; ~ **one's eyes, a wound** пром|ыва́ть, -ы́ть глаза́/ра́ну **2**: **he was** ~**d in sweat** он облива́лся по́том
• *v.i.* купа́ться, ис-

bather /ˈbeɪðə(r)/ *n.* купа́льщи|к (-ца)

bathing /ˈbeɪðɪŋ/ *n.* купа́ние

baton /ˈbæt(ə)n/ *n.* **1** (mus.) дирижёрская па́лочка **2** (sport) эстафе́тная па́лочка **3** (BrE, policeman's) дуби́нка

batsman /ˈbætsmən/ *n.* (sport) бью́щий игро́к, бэ́тсмен

battalion /bəˈtælɪən/ *n.* баталио́н

batten /ˈbæt(ə)n/ *n.* ре́йка, пла́нка
• *v.t.*: ~ **down** (naut.) задра́и|вать, -ть

batter¹ /ˈbætə(r)/ *n.* (cul.) взби́тое те́сто

batter² /ˈbætə(r)/ *v.t. & i.* **1** (beat) колоти́ть, по-; дуба́сить, от-; громи́ть, раз- **2** (knock about): **a** ~**ed old car/hat** потрёпанная ста́рая маши́на/шля́па

battery /ˈbætərɪ/ *n.* (elec.) (in car) батаре́я; (in torch) батаре́йка

✍ **battle** /ˈbæt(ə)l/ *n.* би́тва, сраже́ние, бой; (struggle) борьба́
• *v.i.* боро́ться (*impf.*); сража́ться (*impf.*)
■ ~**field**, ~**ground** *nn.* по́ле сраже́ния/бо́я; ~**ship** *n.* лине́йный кора́бль, линко́р

batty /ˈbætɪ/ *adj.* (**battier, battiest**) (esp. BrE, infml) чо́кнутый, тро́нутый

bauble /ˈbɔːb(ə)l/ *n.* (on Christmas tree) ёлочный шар; (trinket) безделу́шка

✍ ключевая лексика

bawdy /'bɔːdɪ/ adj. (**bawdier**, **bawdiest**) непристо́йный, поха́бный

bawl /bɔːl/ v.t. & i. ора́ть (impf.); выкри́кивать, вы́крикнуть; ~ **at sb** ора́ть на кого́-н.; ~ **sb out** (infml) наора́ть (pf.) на кого́-н.

bay¹ /beɪ/ n. (bot.) лавр
■ ~ **leaf** n. лавро́вый лист

bay² /beɪ/ n. (geog.) зали́в, бу́хта

bay³ /beɪ/ n. (fig. uses): **keep sb at** ~ держа́ть (impf.) кого́-н. на расстоя́нии
● v.i. ла́ять (impf.); залива́ться (impf.) ла́ем; выть (impf.)

bayonet /'beɪənet/ n. штык

bazaar /bə'zɑː(r)/ n. база́р

BC abbr. (of **before Christ**) до н. э. (до на́шей э́ры), до рождества́ Христо́ва

be /biː/ v.i. (sg. pres. **am**, **are**, **is**, pl. pres. **are**, 1st and 3rd pers. **am**, 2nd pers. **are**, past and pl. past **were**, pres. subjunctive **be**, past subjunctive **were**, pres. part. **being**, p.p. **been**) **1** быть (impf.); (exist) существова́ть (impf.); (as copula in the pres. tense, usu. omitted or expr. by dash): **the world is round** земля́ кру́глая; **that is a dog** э́то соба́ка **2** (more emphatic uses): **an order is an order** прика́з есть прика́з; **there is a God** Бог есть **3** (expr. frequency) быва́ть (impf.); **he is in London every Tuesday** он быва́ет в Ло́ндоне по вто́рникам **4** (more formally, with complement) явля́ться (impf.) + i.; представля́ть (impf.) собо́й **5** (expr. present continuous): **she is crying** она́ пла́чет **6** (of place, time, cost, etc.): **it is a mile away** э́то в ми́ле отсю́да; **where is the office?** где нахо́дится о́фис?; **he is 21 today** ему́ сего́дня исполня́ется два́дцать оди́н год; **it is 25 pounds a yard** э́то сто́ит два́дцать пять фу́нтов за ярд; (of person or obj. in a certain position) стоя́ть, лежа́ть, сиде́ть (according to sense; all impf.); **the books are on the floor** кни́ги лежа́т на полу́; **Paris is on the Seine** Пари́ж стои́т на Се́не; **he is in hospital** он лежи́т в больни́це; **I was at home all day** я сиде́л до́ма весь день; (of continuing states): **the heat was unbearable** жара́ стоя́ла невыноси́мая **7** (expr. motion): **has the postman been?** по́чта уже́ была́? **8** (become): **what are you going to** ~ **when you grow up?** кем ты ста́нешь/бу́дешь, когда́ вы́растешь? **9** (expr. pass.): **the house is** ~**ing built** дом стро́ится; **I am told** мне сказа́ли **10** (behave, act a part): **you are** ~**ing silly** ты ведёте себя́ глу́по; **am I** ~**ing a bore?** я вам надое́л? **11** (uses of pres. part. and gerund): ~**ing a doctor**, **he knew what to do** бу́дучи врачо́м, он знал, что де́лать; **for the time** ~**ing** пока́ что, на вре́мя **12** (**be to**): **I am to inform you** я до́лжен сообщи́ть вам; **he is to** ~ **married today** он сего́дня же́нится; **his wife to** ~ его́ бу́дущая жена́ **13** (var.): **how are you?** как пожива́ете?; ~ **that as it may** как бы то ни́ было

beach /biːtʃ/ n. пляж

beacon /'biːkən/ n. (signal light, fire) сигна́льный ого́нь

bead /biːd/ n. **1** бу́син(к)а; **string of** ~**s** бу́с|ы (pl., g. —) **2** (drop) ка́пля

beady /'biːdɪ/ adj. (**beadier**, **beadiest**): ~ **eyes** глаза́-бу́синки

beak /biːk/ n. клюв

beaker /'biːkə(r)/ n. (BrE) (for drinking) пластма́ссовый стака́н (с но́сиком); (in laboratory) мензу́рка

beam¹ /biːm/ n. (of timber etc.) брус, ба́лка

beam² /biːm/ n. (ray) луч
● v.i. (shine) свети́ть (impf.), сия́ть (impf.)

bean /biːn/ n. боб; French ~**s** фасо́ль; string ~**s** зелёная фасо́ль
■ ~**bag** n. больша́я поду́шка, напо́лненная ша́риками полистиро́ла

bear¹ /beə(r)/ n. медве́дь (m.)

bear² /beə(r)/ v.t. (past **bore**, p.p. **borne**, **born**) **1** (carry) носи́ть (indet.), нести́ (det.); ~ **in mind** име́ть (impf.) в виду́ **2** (sustain, support): **the ice will** ~ **his weight** лёд вы́держит его́ **3** (endure, tolerate) терпе́ть, с-; выноси́ть, вы́нести; сн|оси́ть, -ести́; **I cannot** ~ **him** я его́ не выношу́ **4** (be capable of): ~ **comparison** выде́рживать (impf.) сравне́ние **5** (give birth to): **be born** роди́ться (impf., pf.) **6** (yield): **trees/efforts** ~ **fruit** дере́вья/уси́лия прино́сят плоды́
● v.i. (past **bore**, p.p. **borne**, **born**) **1** (of direction): **the road** ~**s to the right** доро́га идёт впра́во **2** (exert pressure, affect): **bring one's energy to** ~ **on** напра́вить (pf.) эне́ргию на + a.; ~ **with** терпе́ть (impf.), переноси́ть (impf.)
□ ~ **out** v.t. (confirm) подтвер|жда́ть, -ди́ть
□ ~ **up** v.i. (endure) держа́ться (impf.)

bearable /'beərəb(ə)l/ adj. терпи́мый, сно́сный

beard /'bɪəd/ n. борода́

bearer /'beərə(r)/ n. (one who carries) несу́щий, нося́щий; ~ **of good news** до́брый ве́стник; (of a cheque) предъяви́тель (m.)

bearing /'beərɪŋ/ n. **1** (deportment) мане́ра держа́ться **2** (relevance) отноше́ние (on: к + d.) **3** (direction): **get one's** ~**s** определя́ть, -и́ть своё местонахожде́ние; ориенти́роваться (impf., pf.)

beast /biːst/ n. **1** (animal) живо́тное; (wild animal) зверь (m.) **2** (nasty person) ското́ина (c.g.)

beastly /'biːstlɪ/ adj. (**beastlier**, **beastliest**) (unpleasant) отврати́тельный; ~ **weather** ужа́сная пого́да; **a** ~ **headache** ме́рзкая/ гну́сная головна́я боль

beat /biːt/ n. **1** (of drum) бой; (of heart) бие́ние; (rhythm) ритм; (mus.) такт **2** (policeman's) райо́н обхо́да
● v.t. (past **beat**, p.p. **beaten**) **1** (strike) бить, по-; ~ **eggs** взби|ва́ть, -ть я́йца; ~ **time** отбива́ть (impf.) такт; ~ **about the bush** (fig.) ходи́ть (indet.) вокру́г да о́коло **2** (defeat, surpass) поб|ива́ть, -и́ть; побе|жда́ть, -ди́ть; **he** ~ **me at chess** он обыгра́л меня́ в ша́хматы; **he** ~ **the record** он поби́л реко́рд
● v.i. (past **beat**, p.p. **beaten**): **his heart is** ~**ing** его́ се́рдце бьётся; **he heard drums** ~**ing** он слы́шал бараба́нный бой; **the rain** ~ **against the windows** дождь стуча́л в о́кна
□ ~ **back** v.t. отби|ва́ть, -и́ть
□ ~ **down** v.i.: **the sun** ~ **down on us** со́лнце

нещáдно пали́ло нас

□ ~ **off** *v.t.:* ~ **off an attack** отб|ивáть, -и́ть атáку

□ ~ **up** *v.t.:* ~ **sb up** изб|ивáть, -и́ть когó-н.

beating /'biːtɪŋ/ *n.* **1** (of heart) бие́ние **2** (thrashing) пóрка

beautician /bjuː'tɪʃ(ə)n/ *n.* космето́лог

✦ **beautiful** /'bjuːtɪfʊl/ *adj.* краси́вый; (excellent) прекрáсный

✦ **beauty** /'bjuːtɪ/ *n.* (quality) красотá ■ ~ **salon** *n.* космети́ческий кабине́т; ~ **spot** *n.* (BrE, place) живопи́сная ме́стность

beaver /'biːvə(r)/ *n.* (*pl.* ~ *or* ~**s**) (zool.) бобр

becalm /bɪ'kɑːm/ *v.t.:* **be** ~**ed** (naut.) штилевáть (*impf.*); заштил|евáть, -е́ть; **a** ~**ed ship** корáбль, попáвший в штиль

became /bɪ'keɪm/ *past of* ▶ become

✦ **because** /bɪ'kɒz/ *conj.* потомý что; ~ **of** из-за + *g.*, (thanks to) благодаря́ + *d.*

beckon /'bekən/ *v.t. & i.* мани́ть, по-; зазы́|вать, -вáть; **I** ~**ed (to) him to approach** я поманил его́ к себе́

✦ **become** /bɪ'kʌm/ *v.i.* (*past* **became**, *p.p.* **become**) (come to be) ста|нови́ться, -ть + *i.*; (often expr. by v. in ...еть): ~ **smaller** умéньшиться (*pf.*); **what became of him?** что с ним стáлось?; **he became a waiter** он стал официáнтом

✦ **bed** /bed/ *n.* **1** (esp. bedstead) кровáть; (esp. bedding) постéль; **go to** ~ ложи́ться, лечь спать; (in sexual sense) переспáть (*pf.*) (**with:** с + *i.*); **get into** ~ ложи́ться, лечь в постéль/кровáть; **get out of** ~ вста|вáть, -ть с постéли/кровáти; **make a** ~ уб|ирáть, -рáть, постéль **2** (of the sea) дно; (of a river) рýсло **3**: ~ **of flowers** клýмба ■ ~ **and breakfast** *n.* (guest house) мáленькая гости́ница; ~**ridden** *adj.* прикóванный к постéли; ~**room** *n.* спáльня; ~**side** *n.*: **keep books at one's** ~**side** держáть (*impf.*) кни́ги на ночнóм стóлике; ~**sit** *n.* (BrE) однокóмнатная квартира; ~**spread** *n.* покрывáло; ~**time** *n.* врéмя ложи́ться/идти́ спать

bedevil /bɪ'dev(ə)l/ *v.t.* (**bedevilled**, **bedevilling**, AmE **bedeviled**, **bedeviling**) (confuse) спýт|ывать, -ать; вн|оси́ть, -ести́ неразбери́ху в + *a.*

bedlam /'bedləm/ *n.* (fig.) бедлáм (infml)

bedraggled /bɪ'dræɡ(ə)ld/ *adj.* забры́зганный

bee /biː/ *n.* пчелá ■ ~**hive** *n.* ýлей

beech /biːtʃ/ *n.* бук

beef /biːf/ *n.* говя́дина ■ ~**burger** *n.* рýбленый бифштéкс

beefy /'biːfɪ/ *adj.* (**beefier**, **beefiest**) мускули́стый

been /biːn/ *p.p. of* ▶ be

beep /biːp/ *n.* гудóк ● *v.i.* гудéть, про-

beer /bɪə(r)/ *n.* пи́во

beet /biːt/ *n.* свёкла ■ ~**root** *n.* (BrE) свёкла

✦ ключевáя лéксика

beetle /'biːt(ə)l/ *n.* (zool.) жук

befall /bɪ'fɔːl/ *v.t. & i.* (*past* **befell** /bɪ'fel/; *p.p.* **befallen** /bɪ'fɔːlən/) (liter.) приключ|áться, -и́ться (с + *i.*); пост|игáть, -и́гнуть (*когó/ что*); **what** ~**en him?** что с ним стáло?

befit /bɪ'fɪt/ *v.t.* (**befitting**, **befitting**) под|ходи́ть, -ойти́ + *d.*

✦ **before** /bɪ'fɔː(r)/ *adv.* рáньше; **six weeks** ~ шестью́ недéлями рáньше ● *prep.* **1** (of time) пéред + *i.*; ~ **leaving** пéред отъéздом; (earlier than) до + *g.*; ~ **the war** до войны́; **the week** ~ **last** позапрóшлая недéля; **don't come** ~ **I call you** не приходи́те, покá я вас не позовý **2** (of place) пéред + *i.*; впереди́ + *g.*; ~ **my eyes** на мои́х глазáх ● *conj.* (earlier than) рáньше чем; (immediately ~) прéжде/пéред тем, как; (at a previous time) до тогó как; **do it** ~ **you forget** сдéлайте э́то, покá не забы́ли; **it will be years** ~ **we meet** пройдýт гóды, покá мы встрéтимся; **just** ~ **you arrived** пéред сáмым вáшим прихóдом ■ ~**hand** *adv.* зарáнее

befriend /bɪ'frend/ *v.t.* дрýжески отн|оси́ться, -ести́сь к + *d.*; помогáть (*impf.*) + *d.*

befuddle /bɪ'fʌd(ə)l/ *v.t.* одурмáни|вать, -ть

beg /beɡ/ *v.t.* (**begged**, **begging**) проси́ть, по-; умоля́ть (*impf.*); ~ **sb to do sth** умоля́ть (*impf.*) когó-н. сдéлать что-н. ● *v.i.* (**begged**, **begging**) **1** (ask for charity) проси́ть ми́лостыню, ни́щенствовать (*both impf.*) **2**: ~ **for** sth умоля́ть, -и́ть о + *p.*; выпрáшивать, вы́просить что-н.

began /bɪ'ɡæn/ *past of* ▶ begin

beggar /'beɡə(r)/ *n.* ни́щий

✦ **begin** /bɪ'ɡɪn/ *v.t.* (**beginning**, *past* **began**, *p.p.* **begun**) нач|инáть, -áть; **he began the meeting** он откры́л собрáние; (often translated by prefix за-): ~ **to sing** запéть (*pf.*); **he began to cry** он заплáкал ● *v.i.* нач|инáть(ся), -áть(ся); **the meeting began** собрáние началóсь; **he began as a reporter** он начинáл репортёром; **to** ~ **with** во-пéрвых

beginner /bɪ'ɡɪnə(r)/ *n.* начинáющий

✦ **beginning** /bɪ'ɡɪnɪŋ/ *n.* начáло; **at the** ~ **of April** в начáле (*or* в пéрвых чи́слах) апрéля

begonia /bɪ'ɡəʊnɪə/ *n.* бегóния

begrudge /bɪ'ɡrʌdʒ/ *v.t.* (envy sb for having sth) зави́довать, по- (*чему*); **I** ~ **him his success** я зави́дую егó успéхам; (give resentfully): **I** ~ **the time** мне жаль врéмени

beguile /bɪ'ɡaɪl/ *v.t.* (charm) очарóв|ывать, -áть

begun /bɪ'ɡʌn/ *p.p. of* ▶ begin

✦ **behalf** /bɪ'hɑːf/ *n.*: **on my** ~ (as my representative) от моегó и́мени/лицá; (for my benefit) в мои́х интерéсах, в мою́ пóльзу

behave /bɪ'heɪv/ *v.i.* вести́ (*det.*) себя́, держáться (*impf.*); ~ **well**, ~ **oneself** вести́ себя́ хорошó; ~ **badly** плóхо поступ|áть, -и́ть

behaviour /bɪ'heɪvjə(r)/ (AmE **behavior**) *n.* поведéние; отношéние (*к кому*); обращéние (*с кем*)

behead /bɪ'hed/ *v.t.* обезглáв|ливать, -ить

beheld /bɪˈheld/ *past and p.p. of* ▸ **behold**

ↄ **behind** /bɪˈhaɪnd/ *n.* (infml) зад, за́дница
● *adv.* сза́ди, позади́; **he is ~ in his studies** он отста́л в учёбе; **he is ~ with his payments** он запа́здывает с упла́той
● *prep.* (expr. place) за + *i.*; (expr. motion) за + *a.*; (more emphatic) сза́ди, позади́ + *g.*; (after) по́сле + *g.*; **he walked (just) ~ me** он шёл сле́дом за мной

behold /bɪˈhəʊld/ *v.t.* (*past and p.p.* **beheld**) (archaic) узре́ть (*pf.*); **lo and ~!** о чу́до!

beige /beɪʒ/ *adj.* бе́жевый

Beijing /beɪˈdʒɪŋ/ *n.* Пеки́н

ↄ **being** /ˈbiːɪŋ/ *n.* **1** (existence) бытие́, существова́ние; **come into ~** возн|ика́ть, -и́кнуть **2** (creature, person) существо́; **human ~** челове́к

Beirut /beɪˈruːt/ *n.* Бейру́т

Belarus /beləˈruːs/ *n.* Белару́сь, Белору́ссия

Belarusian /beləˈruːsɪən, belaˈrʌʃ(ə)n/ *n.* (person) белору́с (-ка); (language) белору́сский язы́к
● *adj.* белору́сский

belated /bɪˈleɪtɪd/ *adj.* запозда́лый

belch /beltʃ/ *n.* отры́жка
● *v.t.* (*also* ~ **forth, out**) (smoke etc.) выбра́сывать, вы́бросить
● *v.i.* рыг|а́ть, -ну́ть

beleaguered /bɪˈliːgəd/ *adj.* осаждённый

belfry /ˈbelfrɪ/ *n.* колоко́льня

Belgian /ˈbeldʒ(ə)n/ *n.* бельги́|ец (-йка)
● *adj.* бельги́йский

Belgium /ˈbeldʒəm/ *n.* Бе́льгия

Belgrade /belˈgreɪd/ *n.* Белгра́д

ↄ **belief** /bɪˈliːf/ *n.* **1** (trust) ве́ра (in: в + *a.*); дове́рие (in: к + *d.*) **2** (acceptance as true; thing believed) ве́ра, верова́ние; **the ~s of the Christian church** до́гмы (*nt. pl.*) христиа́нской це́ркви

ↄ **believe** /bɪˈliːv/ *v.t.* ве́рить, по- (*кому, чему*); ду́мать (*impf.*); **I ~ so** ду́маю, что э́то так
● *v.i.* ве́рить (*impf.*) (*во что, кого*); **~ in God** ве́рить (*impf.*) в Бо́га; (be a religious believer) ве́ровать (*impf.*); **I ~ in taking exercise** я ве́рю в по́льзу заря́дки

believer /bɪˈliːvə(r)/ *n.* **1** (relig.) ве́рующий **2** (advocate) сторо́нни|к (-ца) + *g.*

belittle /bɪˈlɪt(ə)l/ *v.t.* преум|еньша́ть, -е́ньшить; умал|я́ть, -и́ть

bell /bel/ *n.* ко́локол; (smaller) колоко́льчик; (of door, telephone, bicycle, etc.) звоно́к; **ring the ~** звони́ть (*impf.*) в звоно́к/ко́локол; **that rings a ~** (fig., infml) да, я что́-то припомина́ю

bellicose /ˈbelɪkəʊz/ *adj.* вои́нственный

belligerent /bɪˈlɪdʒərənt/ *adj.* вои́нственный

bellow /ˈbeləʊ/ *v.i.* **1** (of animal) мыча́ть, про-; реве́ть (*impf.*) **2** (shout) ора́ть (*impf.*)

bellows /ˈbeləʊz/ *n. pl.* мехи́ (*m. pl.*)

belly /ˈbelɪ/ *n.* живо́т, брю́хо (infml)
■ **~ button** *n.* (infml) пупо́к

ↄ **belong** /bɪˈlɒŋ/ *v.i.* **1**: **~ to** (be the property of) принадлежа́ть (*impf.*) + *d.*; (be a member of) состоя́ть (*impf.*) в + *p.* **2** (of place): **these**

books ~ here э́ти кни́ги стоя́т здесь; э́ти кни́ги отсю́да

belongings /bɪˈlɒŋɪŋz/ *n. pl.* ве́щи (*f. pl.*), пожи́тк|и (-ов)

Belorussia /beləʊˈrʌʃə/ *n.* = **Belarus**

Belorussian /beləʊˈrʌʃən/ *n., adj.* = **Belarusian**

beloved /bɪˈlʌvɪd/ *n.* возлю́бленн|ый (-ая)
● *adj.* возлю́бленный, люби́мый

ↄ **below** /bɪˈləʊ/ *adv.* (of place) внизу́; (of motion) вниз; (in text etc.) ни́же; **from ~** сни́зу
● *prep.* (of place) под + *i.*; (of motion) под + *a.*; (lower, downstream) ни́же + *g.*; **he is ~ average height** он ни́же сре́днего ро́ста

belt /belt/ *n.* **1** (of leather etc.) реме́нь (*m.*); (of cloth) по́яс (-á) **2** (zone) по́яс, полоса́; **green ~** зелёный по́яс, зелёная зо́на **3** (tech.) (приводно́й) реме́нь
● *v.t.* **1** (thrash) поро́ть, вы- **2**: **~ out a song** горла́нить (*impf.*) пе́сню

bemuse /bɪˈmjuːz/ *v.t.* ошелом|ля́ть, -и́ть

bench /bentʃ/ *n.* **1** (seat) скамья́, ла́вка **2** (work table) верста́к, стано́к **3** (judges) су́дьи (*m. pl.*), суде́йская колле́гия
■ **~mark** *n.* эталон, станда́рт; **~mark test** эталонный тест

bend /bend/ *n.* (curve) изги́б; (in road) поворо́т; (in river) излу́чина
● *v.t.* (*past and p.p.* **bent**) (twist, incline): **~ an iron bar** изг|иба́ть, -огну́ть желе́зный брус; **the axle is bent** ось погну́лась; **~ one's head over a book** скло|ня́ться, -и́ться над кни́гой
● *v.i.*: **the trees bent in the wind** дере́вья гну́лись на ветру́; **~ at the knees** сгиба́ться, согну́ться в коле́нях; **~ forward** накло|ня́ться, -и́ться (вперёд)
□ **~ down** *v.t.* наг|иба́ть, -ну́ть; сгиба́ть, согну́ть; прекло|ня́ть, -и́ть
● *v.i.* (*also* **~ over**) наг|иба́ться, -ну́ться; перег|иба́ться, -ну́ться

beneath /bɪˈniːθ/ *adv.* внизу́
● *prep.* (of place) под + *i.*; (of motion) под + *a.*; (lower than) ни́же + *g.*; **it is ~ you to complain** жа́ловаться — недосто́йно вас

benefactor /ˈbenɪfæktə(r)/ *n.* благотвори́тель (*m.*) (-ница)

beneficial /benɪˈfɪʃ(ə)l/ *adj.* благотво́рный, поле́зный, вы́годный

beneficiary /benɪˈfɪʃərɪ/ *n.* (law) бенефициа́р(ий) (*получа́тель де́нег/дохо́дов от чего-л./кого-л.*)

ↄ **benefit** /ˈbenɪfɪt/ *n.* **1** (advantage) по́льза, вы́года, преиму́щество; **give sb the ~ of one's advice** помо́чь (*pf.*) кому́-н. сове́том; **I gave him the ~ of the doubt** я ему́ пове́рил (на э́тот раз) **2** (grant) посо́бие; **unemployment ~** посо́бие по безрабо́тице
● *v.t.* (**benefited, benefiting,** AmE **benefitted, benefitting**) прин|оси́ть, -ести́ по́льзу + *d.*, идти́ (*det.*) на по́льзу + *d.*
● *v.i.* (**benefited, benefiting,** AmE **benefitted, benefitting**) извл|ека́ть, -е́чь по́льзу (from: из + *g.*)

benevolent /bəˈnevələnt/ *adj.* благожела́тельный

b

benign /bɪˈnaɪn/ adj. (of person) добросердечный; (med.) доброкачественный

bent /bent/ past and p.p. of ▶ **bend**

bequeath /bɪˈkwiːð/ v.t. завещать (impf., pf.)

bequest /bɪˈkwest/ n. (object) вещь, оставленная в наследство; (as part of museum collection) фонд, посмертный дар; (act) акт завещания; **make a** ~ **of** завещать (impf., pf.)

berate /bɪˈreɪt/ v.t. бранить (impf.)

bereave /bɪˈriːv/ v.t.: **a** ~**d husband** недавно овдовевший муж; **the** ~**d** (as pl.) родственники покойного

bereavement /bɪˈriːvmənt/ n. тяжёлая утрата/потеря

beret /ˈbereɪ/ n. берет

Bering Sea /ˈberɪŋ/ n. Берингово море

Berlin /bəːˈlɪn/ n. Берлин

Bermuda /bəˈmjuːdə/ n. (also (pl.) **the** ~**s**) Бермудские острова (m. pl.)
■ ~ **shorts** n. pl. шорты-бермуды

berry /ˈberɪ/ n. ягода

berserk /bəˈzəːk/ n.: **go** ~ разъяриться (pf.), обезуметь (pf.)

berth /bəːθ/ n. **1** (place at wharf) пристань, причал **2** : **give sb a wide** ~ (fig.) обходить (impf.) кого-н. стороной (or за версту) **3** (sleeping place on ship) койка; (on train) спальное место
● v.t. ставить (impf.) к причалу
● v.i. причали|вать, -ть

beseech /bɪˈsiːtʃ/ v.t. (past and p.p. **besought** /bɪˈsɔːt/ or **beseeched**) умол|ять, -ить; молить (impf.)

beset /bɪˈset/ v.t. (**besetting**, past and p.p. **beset**) окруж|ать, -ить; оса|ждать, -дить

beside /bɪˈsaɪd/ prep. **1** (alongside) рядом с + i.; (near) около + g., у + g. **2** (compared with) по сравнению с + i.; перед + i.; ~ **him all novelists are insignificant** по сравнению с ним все романисты ничего не стоят **3** : ~ **oneself** вне себя

besides /bɪˈsaɪdz/ adv. сверх того; кроме того
● prep. кроме + g.

besiege /bɪˈsiːdʒ/ v.t. оса|ждать, -дить

besotted /bɪˈsɒtɪd/ adj. одурманенный; во власти (**with**: + g.)

besought /bɪˈsɔːt/ past and p.p. of ▶ **beseech**

best /best/ adj. лучший; **we are the** ~ **of friends** мы близкие друзья; **at** ~ в лучшем случае; **do one's** ~ сделать (pf.) всё возможное; **all the** ~! всего наилучшего!; **hope for the** ~ надеяться (impf.) на лучшее
● adv. лучше всего; **I work** ~ **in the evening** мне лучше всего работается по вечерам; **you know** ~ вам лучше знать; **which town did you like** ~? какой город вам больше всего понравился?
■ ~ **man** n. (at wedding) шафер; ~**seller** n. (book) бестселлер; (BrE, author) автор бестселлера; ~**selling** adj. ходовой

bestow /bɪˈstəʊ/ v.t.: ~ **a title on sb** присв|аивать, -оить кому-н. титул

bet /bet/ n. пари (nt. indecl.), ставка
● v.t. & i. (**betting**, past and p.p. **bet** or **betted**) держать (impf.) пари; **he** ~ **£5 on a horse** он поставил 5 фунтов на лошадь; **he** ~ **me £10 I wouldn't do it** он поспорил со мной на 10 фунтов, что я не сделаю этого
■ ~**ting shop** n. (BrE) букмекерская контора

betray /bɪˈtreɪ/ v.t. измен|ять, -ить + d.; пред|авать, -ать

betrayal /bɪˈtreɪəl/ n. предательство, измена

better /ˈbetə(r)/ adj. лучший, лучше; **all the** ~ тем лучше; **get** ~ ул|учшаться, -учшиться; (in health) попр|авляться, -авиться; **things are getting** ~ дела идут лучше; **get the** ~ **of sb** взять (pf.) верх над кем-н.; превзойти (pf.) кого-н.
● adv. лучше; (more) больше; **you had** ~ **stay here** вам бы лучше остаться здесь; **I thought** ~ **of it** я раздумал/передумал; ~ **off** более состоятельный
● v.t. (improve on) превзойти (pf.)

✒ **between** /bɪˈtwiːn/ adv.: **I attended the two lectures and had lunch in** ~ я посетил две лекции и пообедал в перерыве
● prep. между + i.; ~ **you and me** между нами; ~ **two and three months** от двух до трёх месяцев; **choose** ~ **the two** выбирать, выбрать одно из двух; **we bought a car** ~ **us** мы сообща купили машину

beverage /ˈbevərɪdʒ/ n. напиток

bevy /ˈbevɪ/ n. группа

beware /bɪˈweə(r)/ v.t. & i. остер|егаться, -ечься (impf.) + g.; ~ **of the dog** осторожно, злая собака

bewilder /bɪˈwɪldə(r)/ v.t. сби|вать, -ть с толку; прив|одить, -ести в замешательство; ~**ed** смущённый, озадаченный

bewilderment /bɪˈwɪldəmənt/ n. замешательство, озадаченность

bewitch /bɪˈwɪtʃ/ v.t. околдов|ывать, -ать

✒ **beyond** /bɪˈjɒnd/ n.: **he lives at the back of** ~ он живёт на краю света
● adv. вдали; вдаль
● prep. (of place) за + i.; (of motion) за + a.; (later than) после + g.; ~ **dispute** бесспорно; ~ **belief** невероятно; **live** ~ **one's means** жить (impf.) не по средствам

biannual /baɪˈænjʊəl/ adj. выходящий дважды в год; полугодовой

bias /ˈbaɪəs/ n. предрассудок, предвзятое отношение (к чему)
● v.t. (**biased**, **biasing** or **biassed**, **biassing**) (influence) склон|ять, -ить; (prejudice) предубе|ждать, -дить; **a** ~**(s)ed opinion** предвзятое мнение

bib /bɪb/ n. (детский) нагрудник

Bible /ˈbaɪb(ə)l/ n. Библия; (fig.) библия

biblical /ˈbɪblɪk(ə)l/ adj. библейский

bibliographer /bɪblɪˈɒɡrəfə(r)/ n. библиограф

bibliographic /bɪblɪəˈɡræfɪk/, **bibliographical** /bɪblɪəˈɡræfɪk(ə)l/ adjs. библиографический

bibliography /bɪblɪˈɒɡrəfɪ/ n. библиография

bicentenary /ˌbaɪsenˈtiːnərɪ/ n. двухсотлѐтие

bicentennial /ˌbaɪsenˈtenɪəl/ n. двухсотлѐтие

biceps /ˈbaɪseps/ n. (pl. ~) бѝцепс

bicker /ˈbɪkə(r)/ v.t. (squabble) перебра́ниваться (impf.), препира́ться (impf.)

bicycle /ˈbaɪsɪk(ə)l/ n. велосипѐд

⚬ **bid** /bɪd/ n. **1** (at auction) зая́вка; предложѐние цены́ **2** (tender) зая́вка **3** (attempt) ста́вка; попы́тка; **make a ~ for power** сдѐлать (pf.) ста́вку на захва́т вла́сти
● v.t. & i. (**bidding**, past **bid**, p.p. **bid**) **1** (at auction) предл|ага́ть, -ожи́ть цѐну (за что); **~ against sb** наб|авля́ть, -а́вить цѐну про́тив кого́-н. **2** (tender): **~ for a contract** дѐлать, с- зая́вку на контра́кт

bidder /ˈbɪdə(r)/ n. (at auction) аукционѐр; **the highest ~** предложи́вший наивы́сшую цѐну

bide /baɪd/ v.t.: **~ one's time** ждать (impf.) благоприя́тного слу́чая

bidet /ˈbiːdeɪ/ n. бидѐ (nt. indecl.)

biennial /baɪˈenɪəl/ n. (bot.) двулѐтник
● adj. двухлѐтний

bifocal /baɪˈfəʊk(ə)l/ adj.: **~ spectacles** (also **~s** pl.) бифока́льные очки́

⚬ **big** /bɪɡ/ adj. (**bigger**, **biggest**) (in size) большо́й, кру́пный; (great) кру́пный; (magnanimous) великоду́шный; (important) ва́жный; **a ~ man** (in stature) кру́пный мужчи́на; (in importance) кру́пная фигу́ра; **as ~ as** величино́й в + a.; **think ~** мы́слить (impf.) смѐло/дѐрзко; **a ~ noise** (person) ши́шка (infml); **my ~ brother** мой ста́рший брат; **a ~ name** (celebrity) знамени́тость
■ **~-headed** adj. (conceited) зазна́вшийся; возомни́вший о себѐ; **~-hearted** adj. великоду́шный; **~ society** n. (pol.) концепция управления общественной жизни в стране посредством органов добровольного местного самоуправления; **~wig** n. (infml) ши́шка (важный человек)

bigamy /ˈbɪɡəmɪ/ n. бига́мия; (of man) двоежѐнство; (of woman) двоему́жие

bigoted /ˈbɪɡətɪd/ adj. фанати́ческий, фанати́чный

bike /baɪk/ n. **1** (infml) = **bicycle 2** (motorcycle) мотоци́кл
● v.i. ѐздить (indet.) на мотоци́кле

biker /ˈbaɪkə(r)/ n. мотоцикли́ст (-ка); (member of a gang) ба́йкер

bikini /bɪˈkiːnɪ/ n. (pl. ~s) бики́ни (nt. indecl.)

bilateral /baɪˈlætər(ə)l/ adj. двусторо́нний

bilberry /ˈbɪlbərɪ/ n. черни́ка (collect.); (single berry) я́года черни́ки

bilingual /baɪˈlɪŋɡw(ə)l/ adj. двуязы́чный

bill¹ /bɪl/ n. (beak) клюв

⚬ **bill²** /bɪl/ n. **1** (comm.) счёт **2** (pol.) законопроѐкт, билль (m.) **3** (advertisement): **theatre ~** театра́льная афи́ша **4** (AmE, banknote) банкно́та; **dollar ~** до́лларовая банкно́та
■ **~board** n. доска́ объявлѐний

billet /ˈbɪlɪt/ v.t. (**billeted**, **billeting**) (assign to ~) расквартиро́в|ывать, -а́ть; назн|ача́ть,

-а́чить (or ста́вить, по-) на посто́й (**on sb:** к + d.)

billiards /ˈbɪljədz/ n. билья́рд

⚬ **billion** /ˈbɪljən/ n. (pl. ~s or (with numeral or qualifying word) ~) (10^9, thousand million) миллиа́рд

billionaire /ˌbɪljəˈneə(r)/ n. миллиардѐр

billow /ˈbɪləʊ/ v.i. (of smoke) вздыма́ться (impf.); (of fabric) над|ува́ться, -у́ться

bin /bɪn/ n. (BrE) му́сорное ведро́

binary /ˈbaɪnərɪ/ adj. (math.) двои́чный

bind /baɪnd/ v.t. (past and p.p. **bound**) **1** (tie, fasten) свя́з|ывать, -а́ть; **~ together** свя́з|ывать, -а́ть **2** (books etc.) переплѐ|та́ть, -сти́ **3** (oblige, exact promise) обя́з|ывать, -а́ть; **I am bound to say** я до́лжен сказа́ть

binder /ˈbaɪndə(r)/ n. па́пка

binding /ˈbaɪndɪŋ/ n. переплёт
● adj. обя́зывающий; имѐющий обяза́тельную си́лу

binge /bɪndʒ/ n. (infml) пья́нка; **go on the ~** закути́ть, запи́ть (both pf.)
■ **~ drinking** n. попо́йка, пья́нка

bingo /ˈbɪŋɡəʊ/ n. лото́ (nt. indecl.)

binoculars /bɪˈnɒkjʊləz/ n. pl. бино́кль (m.)

biochemist /ˌbaɪəʊˈkemɪst/ n. биохи́мик

biochemistry /ˌbaɪəʊˈkemɪstrɪ/ n. биохи́мия

biodegradable /ˌbaɪəʊdɪˈɡreɪdəb(ə)l/ adj. по́ртящийся под дѐйствием микрооргани́змов

biodiversity /ˌbaɪəʊdaɪˈvɜːsɪtɪ/ n. биологи́ческое разнообра́зие

bioengineering /ˌbaɪəʊendʒɪˈnɪərɪŋ/ n. биоинженѐрия

biographer /baɪˈɒɡrəfə(r)/ n. био́граф

biographical /ˌbaɪəˈɡræfɪk(ə)l/ adj. биографи́ческий

biography /baɪˈɒɡrəfɪ/ n. биогра́фия

biological /ˌbaɪəˈlɒdʒɪk(ə)l/ adj. биологи́ческий
■ **~ clock** n. биологи́ческие часы́; **~ warfare** n. бактериологи́ческая война́

biologist /baɪˈɒlədʒɪst/ n. био́лог

biology /baɪˈɒlədʒɪ/ n. биоло́гия

biometric /ˌbaɪəʊˈmetrɪk/ adj. биометри́ческий

biopsy /ˈbaɪɒpsɪ/ n. биопси́я

biotechnology /ˌbaɪəʊtekˈnɒlədʒɪ/ n. биотехноло́гия

bipartisan /ˌbaɪpɑːtɪˈzæn/ adj. двухпарти́йный

bipartite /baɪˈpɑːtaɪt/ adj. (divided into two parts) состоя́щий из двух частѐй; (shared by two parties) двусторо́нний

bipolar /baɪˈpəʊlə(r)/ adj. (phys.) двухполя́рный, биполя́рный
■ **~ disorder** n. (med.) биполя́рное аффекти́вное расстро́йство

birch /bɜːtʃ/ n. берёза

⚬ **bird** /bɜːd/ n. пти́ца
■ **~ flu** n. пти́чий грипп; **~ of prey** n. хи́щная пти́ца; **~'s-eye view** n. вид с высоты́ пти́чьего полёта; о́бщая перспекти́ва; **~watcher** n. орнито́лог-люби́тель (m.)

biro® /ˈbaɪərəʊ/ n. (pl. ~s) (BrE) ша́риковая ру́чка

b

✐ **birth** /bɜ:θ/ n. **1** (being born) рожде́ние; (giving birth) ро́ды (pl.) **2** (descent): **an Englishman by ~** англича́нин по происхожде́нию

■ **~ certificate** n. свиде́тельство о рожде́нии; **~ control** n. регули́рование рожда́емости; (contraception) противозача́точные ме́ры (f. pl.); **~mark** n. роди́мое пятно́; **~place** n. ме́сто рожде́ния; ро́дина; **~ rate** n. рожда́емость

birthday /ˈbɜ:θdeɪ/ n. день рожде́ния

✐ **biscuit** /ˈbɪskɪt/ n. (BrE) пече́нье; (AmE) ≈ бу́лочка

bisect /baɪˈsekt/ v.t. дели́ть, раз- попола́м

bisexual /baɪˈseksjʊəl/ adj. бисексуа́льный

bishop /ˈbɪʃəp/ n. (eccl.) епи́скоп; (chess) слон

bison /ˈbaɪs(ə)n/ n. (pl. ~) бизо́н

bistro /ˈbi:strəʊ/ n. (pl. ~s) бистро́ (nt. indecl.)

✐ **bit¹** /bɪt/ n. **1** кусо́к, кусо́чек; **a ~ of paper** листо́к бума́ги **2** (abstract uses): **a ~ of news** но́вость; **a ~ of advice** сове́т; **I am a ~ late** я немно́го опозда́л; **~ by ~** ма́ло-пома́лу; **a ~ of a coward** труслова́тый

bit² /bɪt/ n. (comput.) бит

bit³ /bɪt/ n. (of bridle) удила́ (-и́л)

bit⁴ /bɪt/ past of ▸ bite

bitch /bɪtʃ/ n. **1** (female dog) су́ка **2** (infml, spiteful woman) дрянь (vulg.), сте́рва (sl.)

bitchy /ˈbɪtʃɪ/ adj. (**bitchier, bitchiest**) (infml) стервозный

bite /baɪt/ n. **1** (act of biting) куса́ние **2** (mouthful): **I haven't had a ~ to eat** у меня́ куска́ во рту не́ было **3** (wound caused by biting) уку́с

• v.t. (past **bit**, p.p. **bitten**) **1** куса́ть, укуси́ть **2** (fig.): **~ sb's head off** откуси́ть (pf.) кому́-н. го́лову

• v.i. (past **bit**, p.p. **bitten**): **does your dog ~?** ва́ша соба́ка куса́ется?; **the fish won't ~** ры́ба не клюёт

biting /ˈbaɪtɪŋ/ adj. (of wind) ре́зкий; (of satire) е́дкий, язви́тельный

bitten /ˈbɪt(ə)n/ p.p. of ▸ bite

bitter /ˈbɪtə(r)/ adj. (lit., fig.) го́рький; **a ~ wind** ре́зкий ве́тер; **~ enemy** злейший/закля́тый враг; **to the ~ end** до са́мого конца́

bivouac /ˈbɪvʊæk/ n. откры́тый ла́герь (без пала́ток и пала́ток), бива́к

• v.i. (**bivouacked, bivouacking**) распол|ага́ться, -ожи́ться откры́тым ла́герем, бива́ком

bizarre /bɪˈzɑ:(r)/ adj. чудно́й; (behaviour) чудакова́тый

✐ **black** /blæk/ n. **1** (colour) чернота́, чёрное; **be in the ~** не име́ть долго́в **2** (person) черноко́жий

• adj. **1** (colour) чёрный; **a ~ eye** подби́тый глаз **2** (person) черноко́жий **3**: **~ and white** чёрно-бе́лый; **in ~ and white** (in writing) чёрным по бе́лому

• v.i.: **~ out** (lose consciousness) теря́ть, по- созна́ние

■ **~berry** n. (plant; berries) ежеви́ка (collect.); (single berry) я́года ежеви́ки; **~bird** n. чёрный дрозд; **~board** n. кла́ссная доска́; **~currant**

n. чёрная сморо́дина; **~head** n. у́горь (m.); **~ ice** n. гололе́дица; **~mail** n. шанта́ж, вымога́тельство • v.t. шантажи́ровать (impf.); **~mailer** n. шантажи́ст, вымога́тель (m.); **~ market** n. чёрный ры́нок; **~out** n. (in wartime) затемне́ние; (electricity failure) авари́йное отключе́ние электроэне́ргии; (loss of consciousness) поте́ря созна́ния; **B~ Sea** n. Чёрное мо́ре; **~smith** n. кузне́ц; **~ tie** n. (bow tie) чёрный га́лстук-ба́бочка; (evening dress) стро́гий вече́рний костю́м

blacken /ˈblækən/ v.t. (reputation) черни́ть, о-

bladder /ˈblædə(r)/ n. пузы́рь (m.)

blade /bleɪd/ n. **1** (of knife etc.) ле́звие **2** (of oar etc.) ло́пасть, лопа́тка **3** (of grass etc.) были́нка, стебелёк

✐ **blame** /bleɪm/ n. (censure) порица́ние; осужде́ние; (fault) вина́

• v.t. порица́ть (impf.); вини́ть (impf.); осу|жда́ть, -ди́ть (кого за что); **he was ~d for the mistake** вину́ за оши́бку возложи́ли на него́; **he is entirely to ~** э́то по́лностью его́ вина́; **~ sth on sb** взва́л|ивать, -и́ть вину́ за что-н. на кого́-н.

blameless /ˈbleɪmlɪs/ adj. безупре́чный; неви́нный

bland /blænd/ adj. (mild) мя́гкий; (insipid) пре́сный

blank /blæŋk/ n. про́пуск; **my mind is a ~ on this subject** у меня́ э́то вы́летело из головы́

• adj. **1** (empty): **a ~ sheet of paper** чи́стый лист бума́ги; **a ~ cheque** незапо́лненный чек; (fig.) карт-бла́нш **2** (fig.): **look ~** (of person) вы́глядеть (impf.) озада́ченным

blanket /ˈblæŋkɪt/ n. одея́ло; (horse ~) попо́на; **the hills lay under a ~ of snow** холмы́ бы́ли покры́ты сло́ем сне́га

blankly /ˈblæŋklɪ/ adv. бессмы́сленно, ту́по

blare /bleə(r)/ v.t. (**~ out**) труби́ть, про- • v.i. труби́ть, про-; реве́ть (impf.)

blaspheme /blæsˈfi:m/ v.t. (revile) поноси́ть (impf.), хули́ть (impf.)

• v.i. богоху́льствовать (impf.), богоху́льничать (impf.)

blasphemous /ˈblæsfɪməs/ adj. богоху́льный

blasphemy /ˈblæsfəmɪ/ n. богоху́льство

blast /blɑ:st/ n. **1**: **~ of wind** поры́в ве́тра **2** (from explosion) взрыв **3**: **at full ~** (fig.) в по́лном разга́ре; по́лным хо́дом

• v.t. взр|ыва́ть, -орва́ть

• v.i.: **~ off** (rocketry) взлет|а́ть, -е́ть; стартова́ть (impf., pf.)

■ **~off** n. взлёт; моме́нт ста́рта

blatant /ˈbleɪt(ə)nt/ adj. (flagrant) я́вный, вопию́щий

blaze¹ /bleɪz/ n. **1** (of fire) пла́мя (nt.) **2** (fig.): **~e of publicity** шу́мная рекла́ма

• v.i.: **a fire was ~ing in the hearth** в ками́не пыла́л ого́нь; **the building was ~ing** зда́ние полыха́ло

□ **~e up** v.i. (lit., fig.) вспы́хивать, -ы́хнуть

blaze² /bleɪz/ v.t.: **~ a trail** про|кла́дывать, -ложи́ть путь

blazer /ˈbleɪzə(r)/ *n.* ≈ ку́ртка, (клу́бный/ шко́льный) пиджа́к, бле́йзер

bleach /bliːtʃ/ *n.* отбе́ливатель (*m.*)
- *v.t.* бели́ть (*impf.*); отбе́л|ивать, -и́ть; (hair) обесцве́|чивать, -тить
- *v.i.* беле́ть (*impf.*)

bleak /bliːk/ *adj.* уны́лый, безра́достный; (gloomy) мра́чный

bleary-eyed /blɪə(r)/ *adj.* с затума́ненными/ му́тными глаза́ми

bleat /bliːt/ *v.t. & i.* мыча́ть (*impf.*), бле́ять (*impf.*)

bleed /bliːd/ *v.t.* (*past and p.p.* **bled** /bled/): ~ sb (for money) об|ира́ть, -обра́ть кого́-н.
- *v.i.* (*past and p.p.* **bled** /bled/) (of person) ист|ека́ть, -е́чь кро́вью; (of wound) кровоточи́ть (*impf.*); **his nose is** ~**ing** у него́ но́сом идёт кровь

bleep /bliːp/ *n.* сигна́л
- *v.i.* сигна́лить, про-
- *v.t.* (summon) вызыва́ть, вы́звать сигна́лом

bleeper /ˈbliːpə(r)/ *n.* (BrE) пе́йджер

blemish /ˈblemɪʃ/ *n.* недоста́ток, изъя́н

blend /blend/ *n.* смесь
- *v.t.* сме́ш|ивать, -а́ть; (colours, ideas) сочета́ть (*impf.*)
- *v.i.* сме́ш|иваться, -а́ться; (of colours, ideas) сочета́ться (*impf.*); гармони́ровать (*impf.*)

blender /ˈblendə(r)/ *n.* (cul.) смеси́тель (*m.*), ми́ксер, бле́ндер

bless /bles/ *v.t.* (*past and p.p.* **blessed**)
1 (relig.) благослов|ля́ть, -и́ть; ~ **you!** дай вам Бог здоро́вья!; (after sneeze) бу́дьте здоро́вы! **2** (prosper, favour): **he was** ~**ed with good health** Бог награди́л его́ здоро́вьем

blessing /ˈblesɪŋ/ *n.* **1** благослове́ние **2**: **it is a** ~ **in disguise** ≈ не́ было бы сча́стья, да несча́стье помогло́!

blew /bluː/ *past of* ▶ **blow**[1]

blight /blaɪt/ *n.* головня́
- *v.t.*: ~ **sb's hopes** разр|уша́ть, -у́шить чьи-н. наде́жды

blind /blaɪnd/ *n.* што́ра, ста́вень (*m.*); **Venetian** ~ жалюзи́ (*nt. indecl.*)
- *adj.* **1** слепо́й; **the** ~ (*as n.*) слепы́е, слепцы́ (*m. pl.*); **go** ~ осле́пнуть, о-; **a** ~ **spot** слепо́е пятно́; (fig.) пробе́л; **turn a** ~ **eye to sth** закр|ыва́ть, -ы́ть глаза́ на что-н. **2** (concealed): **a** ~ **corner** непросма́триваю́щийся, закры́тый поворо́т; **a** ~ **spot** (on the road) мёртвая зо́на; **a** ~ **date** (infml) свида́ние с незнако́мым/ незнако́мой **3** (closed up): **a** ~ **alley** (lit., fig.) тупи́к
- *v.t.* ослеп|ля́ть, -и́ть; (also fig., temporarily) слепи́ть (*impf.*)
- ~**fold** *adv.* с завя́занными глаза́ми • *v.t.* завя́з|ывать, -а́ть глаза́ + *d.*

blindly /ˈblaɪndli/ *adv.* (gropingly) на о́щупь; (recklessly) слепо́

blindness /ˈblaɪndnɪs/ *n.* слепота́; (fig.) слепота́, ослепле́ние

bling /blɪŋ/ *n.* (infml) (clothing) гламу́рная оде́жда; (jewellery) ца́цки (*f. pl.*) (sl.),

побряку́шки (*f. pl.*) (infml); ((containing) diamonds) брю́лики (*m. pl.*) (infml)

blink /blɪŋk/ *n.* морга́ние, мига́ние
- *v.t. & i.* (of person) миг|а́ть, -ну́ть; морг|а́ть, -ну́ть; (of light) мерца́ть (*impf.*)

blinkers /ˈblɪŋkəz/ *n. pl.* (BrE) шо́р|ы (*pl.*, *g.* —) (also fig.)

blip /blɪp/ *n.* (on screen) отражённый и́мпульс

bliss /blɪs/ *n.* блаже́нство

blissful /ˈblɪsfʊl/ *adj.* блаже́нный

blister /ˈblɪstə(r)/ *n.* волды́рь (*m.*)
- *v.i.* покр|ыва́ться, -ы́ться волдыря́ми/ пузыря́ми

blithe /blaɪð/, **blithesome** /ˈblaɪðsəm/ *adjs.* жизнера́достный, беспе́чный

blitz /blɪts/ *n.* бомбёжка
- *v.t.* разбомби́ть (*pf.*)

blizzard /ˈblɪzəd/ *n.* бура́н, вьюга

bloated /ˈbləʊtɪd/ *adj.* разду́тый, разду́вшийся

blob /blɒb/ *n.* (small mass) ка́пля; ша́рик; (spot of colour) кля́кса

block /blɒk/ *n.* **1** (of wood) чурба́н, коло́да; (of stone, marble) глы́ба **2** (for execution) пла́ха **3** (of houses) кварта́л; ~ **of flats** (BrE) многокварти́рный дом **4** (typ.): ~ **capitals** печа́тные бу́квы
- *v.t.* (obstruct physically): **roads** ~**ed by snow** доро́ги, занесённые сне́гом; **the sink is** ~**ed** ра́ковина засори́лась
- ■ ~**buster** *n.* (infml) блокба́стер, ка́ссовый фильм

blockade /blɒˈkeɪd/ *n.* блока́да
- *v.t.* блоки́ровать (*impf., pf.*)

blog /blɒg/ *n.* (comput.) блог

blogger /ˈblɒɡə(r)/ *n.* (comput.) бло́ггер, бло́гер

blogosphere /ˈblɒɡəsfɪə(r)/ *n.* (comput.) блогосфе́ра

bloke /bləʊk/ *n.* (BrE, infml) тип; па́рень (*m.*)

blonde, **blond** /blɒnd/ *n.* блонди́нка
- *adj.* белоку́рый, све́тлый

blood /blʌd/ *n.* **1** кровь **2** (*attr.*): ~ **bank** до́норский пункт; ~ **donor** до́нор; ~ **group** гру́ппа кро́ви; ~ **test** ана́лиз кро́ви; (for paternity) иссле́дование кро́ви **3** (var. fig. uses): **in cold** ~ хладнокро́вно; **we need new** ~ нам нужны́ но́вые си́лы
- ■ ~ **pressure** *n.* кровяно́е давле́ние; ~**shed** *n.* кровопроли́тие; ~**shot** *adj.* нали́тый кро́вью; ~**stained** *adj.* запа́чканный кро́вью; ~**stream** *n.* ток кро́ви; ~**thirsty** *adj.* кровожа́дный

bloody /ˈblʌdi/ *adj.* (**bloodier**, **bloodiest**)
1 крова́вый **2** (BrE, sl.): **a** ~ **liar** отча́янный лгун
- *adv.* (sl.): ~ **awful** чертóвский; скве́рный, дрянно́й

bloom /bluːm/ *n.* (single flower) цвето́к; **in** ~ в цвету́
- *v.i.* цвести́ (*impf.*); (come into ~) расцве|та́ть, -сти́

blossom /ˈblɒsəm/ *n.* цвет, цвете́ние
- *v.i.* цвести́ (*impf.*)

b

blot /blɒt/ *n.* (on paper) кля́кса; (blemish) пятно́
• *v.t.* (**blotted, blotting**) (sully): ~ **one's copybook** (BrE, fig.) пятна́ть, за- свою́ репута́цию
□ ~ **out** *v.t.* (from one's memory) изгла́|живать, -дить (*or* ст|ира́ть, -ере́ть) из па́мяти

blouse /blaʊz/ *n.* ко́фточка, блу́зка

✎ **blow¹** /bləʊ/ *v.t.* (*past* **blew**, *p.p.* **blown**)
1 дуть, ду́нуть; ~ **a whistle** свисте́ть, за- в свисто́к; дава́ть, дать свисто́к; ~ **one's nose** сморка́ться, вы- **2** (of wind): **the wind blew the papers out of my hand** ве́тер вы́рвал бума́ги у меня́ из рук **3** (elec.): ~ **a fuse** переж|ига́ть, -е́чь про́бку
• *v.i.* (*past* **blew**, *p.p.* **blown**) **1** (of wind or person) дуть, по-, ду́нуть **2** (of thing): **the door blew open** дверь распахну́лась; **the fuse blew** про́бка перегоре́ла
□ ~ **away** *v.t. & i.* ун|оси́ть(ся), -ести́(сь)
□ ~ **down** *v.t.* вали́ть, по-
• *v.i.*: **the tree blew down** бу́ря повали́ла де́рево
□ ~ **out** *v.t.*: **he blew the candle out** он заду́л свечу́
□ ~ **over** *v.i.*: **the storm blew over** бу́ря ути́хла
□ ~ **up** *v.t.*: ~ **up a bridge** взрыва́ть, взорва́ть мост; ~ **up a tyre** нака́ч|ивать, -а́ть ши́ну/колесо́; ~ **up a photograph** увели́чи|вать, -ть фотогра́фию
• *v.i.*: **the mine blew up** ми́на взорвала́сь
■ ~**out** *n.* (of tyre) разры́в; (infml, feast) оби́льное засто́лье, кутёж; ~**torch** *n.* пая́льная ла́мпа

blow² /bləʊ/ *n.* уда́р

blown /bləʊn/ *p.p. of* ▸ **blow¹**

blub /blʌb/ *v.i.* (**blubbed, blubbing**) (infml) реве́ть (*impf.*)

blubber¹ /ˈblʌbə(r)/ *n.* (whale fat) во́рвань

blubber² /ˈblʌbə(r)/ *v.i.* = **blub**

bludgeon /ˈblʌdʒ(ə)n/ *v.t.* бить (*impf.*) дуби́нкой; (fig.) принужда́ть, -уди́ть

✎ **blue** /bluː/ *n.* **1** (colour) синева́, голубизна́ **2** (sky): **out of the** ~ (fig.) ни с того́ ни с сего́; **he arrived out of the** ~ он нагря́нул неожи́данно **3**: **the** ~**s** (infml) тоска́, уны́ние, хандра́ **4**: ~**s** (mus.) блюз
• *adj.* (**bluer, bluest**) **1** (colour) (dark) си́ний; (light) голубо́й **2** (infml, sad): **feel** ~ хандри́ть (*impf.*) **3** (infml, obscene) неприли́чный, непристо́йный
■ ~**bell** *n.* ди́кий/лесно́й гиаци́нт; ~**collar worker** *n.* произво́дственный рабо́чий; ~**print** *n.* (phot.) светоко́пия, си́нька; (fig.) план

bluff /blʌf/ *n.*: **call sb's** ~ заст|авля́ть, -а́вить кого́-н. раскры́ть ка́рты
• *v.i.* блефова́ть (*impf.*)
• *v.t.* втира́ть (*impf.*) очки́ + *d.*; ~ **one's way out of sth** вы́крутиться (*pf.*) из чего́-л.

bluish /ˈbluːɪʃ/ *adj.* (dark) синева́тый; (light) голубова́тый

blunder /ˈblʌndə(r)/ *n.* оши́бка, опло́шность
• *v.i.* блужда́ть (*impf.*); (grope) пробира́ться/

дви́гаться (*impf.*) о́щупью; ~ **into a table** нат|ыка́ться, -кну́ться на стол

blunt /blʌnt/ *adj.* (not sharp) тупо́й; (plain-spoken) прямо́й
• *v.t.* тупи́ть (*impf.*)

blur /blɜː(r)/ *n.* ды́мка
• *v.t.* (**blurred, blurring**) сма́з|ывать, -ать

blurb /blɜːb/ *n.* (infml) (изда́тельская) анно́та́ция

blurt /blɜːt/ *v.t.*: ~ **out** выпа́ливать, вы́палить

blush /blʌʃ/ *v.i.* красне́ть, по-

blusher /ˈblʌʃə(r)/ *n.* (cosmetic) румя́на

bluster /ˈblʌstə(r)/ *n.* (of storm) рёв; (of person) гро́мкие слова́ (*nt. pl.*), угро́зы (*f. pl.*)
• *v.i.* (of storm) реве́ть (*impf.*); (of person) расшуме́ться (*pf.*), разбушева́ться (*pf.*)

BO *abbr.* (of **body odour**) за́пах по́та

boar /bɔː(r)/ *n.* каба́н

✎ **board** /bɔːd/ *n.* **1** (piece of wood) доска́ (*also for chess etc.*) **2** (food) стол; ~ **and lodging, bed and** ~ пита́ние и прожива́ние; ночле́г и пита́ние **3**: **above** ~ в откры́тую, че́стно **4** (council) правле́ние; ~ **of directors** правле́ние директоро́в **5** (naut. etc.): **on** ~ на борту́
• *v.t.* **1** (cover with ~s) (*also* ~ **up**) обш|ива́ть, -и́ть (*or* покр|ыва́ть, -ы́ть) доска́ми **2**: ~ **a ship** (go on ~) сади́ться, сесть на кора́бль
■ ~ **game** *n.* насто́льная игра́; ~**room** *n.* зал заседа́ний сове́та директоро́в

boarder /ˈbɔːdə(r)/ *n.* (lodger) жиле́ц, посто́ялец; (at school) учени́|к (-ца), живу́щий (-ая) в шко́ле-интерна́те

boarding /ˈbɔːdɪŋ/ *n.* (naut.) аборда́ж; (aeron.) поса́дка
■ ~ **card**, ~ **pass** *nn.* поса́дочный биле́т/тало́н; ~ **school** *n.* шко́ла-интерна́т

boast /bəʊst/ *n.* хвастовство́
• *v.t. & i.* (~ of) хва́стать(ся), по- + *i.*; хвали́ться, по- + *i.*

boastful /ˈbəʊstfʊl/ *adj.* хвастли́вый

✎ **boat** /bəʊt/ *n.* (small, rowing ~) ло́дка, шлю́пка; (vessel) су́дно; (large) кора́бль (*m.*), парохо́д; **in the same** ~ (fig.) в одина́ковом положе́нии
• *v.i.* (go ~ing) ката́ться (*indet.*) на ло́дке
■ ~**house** *n.* сара́й для ло́док

boater /ˈbəʊtə(r)/ *n.* соло́менная шля́па

bob¹ /bɒb/ *n.* (hairstyle) коро́ткая стри́жка

bob² /bɒb/ *v.i.* (**bobbed, bobbing**) (move up and down) подпры́г|ивать, -нуть; подск|а́кивать, -очи́ть

bobsled /ˈbɒbsled/ *n.* (AmE) = **bobsleigh**

bobsleigh /ˈbɒbsleɪ/ *n.* (BrE) бобсле́й

bode /bəʊd/ *v.t. & i.*: ~ **ill/well** предвеща́ть/сули́ть (*impf.*) недо́брое/хоро́шее

bodice /ˈbɒdɪs/ *n.* корса́ж, лиф

bodily /ˈbɒdɪlɪ/ *adj.* теле́сный, физи́ческий

✎ **body** /ˈbɒdɪ/ *n.* **1** (of person or animal) те́ло **2** (dead person) мёртвое те́ло; уби́т|ый (-ая) **3** (of ship) ко́рпус; (of car) ку́зов; (of aircraft) фюзеля́ж **4** (quantity) ма́сса, гру́ппа; ~ **of**

✎ ключева́я ле́ксика

evidence совоку́пность доказа́тельств
5 (group): **public** ~ обще́ственная
организа́ция **6** (strength, consistency)
консисте́нция, вя́зкость
■ ~**builder** *n.* (person) культури́ст; (apparatus)
эспа́ндер; ~**building** *n.* культури́зм,
бодиби́лдинг; ~**guard** *n.* (group) ли́чная
охра́на; (individual) телохрани́тель (*m.*); ~
piercing *n.* пи́рсинг; ~**work** *n.* (of vehicle)
ку́зов

bog /bɒg/ *n.* боло́то, тряси́на
● *v.t.* (**bogged, bogging**): get ~ged down
(fig.) вя́знуть, за-, у-

boggle /'bɒg(ə)l/ *v.i.*: the mind ~s уму́
непостижи́мо

boggy /'bɒgɪ/ *adj.* (**boggier, boggiest**)
боло́тистый

bogus /'bəʊgəs/ *adj.* фикти́вный, притво́рный

bohemian /bəʊ'hiːmɪən/ *n.* представи́тель
(-ница) боге́мы

boil[1] /bɔɪl/ *n.* (swelling) гно́йный нары́в,
фуру́нкул

boil[2] /bɔɪl/ *n.* (state of ~ing) кипе́ние; **bring to
the** ~ довести́ (*pf.*) до кипе́ния; вскипяти́ть
(*pf.*)
● *v.t.*: ~ **water** кипяти́ть, вс- во́ду; ~ **fish/an
egg** вари́ть, с- ры́бу/яйцо́
● *v.i.*: **the water is** ~**ing** вода́ кипи́т; **the egg
has** ~**ed** яйцо́ свари́лось
□ ~ **down** *v.i.*: it ~s down to this, that … э́то
сво́дится к тому́, что…
□ ~ **over** *v.i.* (lit.) уходи́ть, уйти́ (*or* убе|га́ть,
-жа́ть) че́рез край

boiler /'bɔɪlə(r)/ *n.* отопи́тельный котёл;
бо́йлер
■ ~ **suit** *n.* (BrE) комбинезо́н

boiling /'bɔɪlɪŋ/ *adj.* кипя́щий; ~ **hot**
горя́чий, как кипято́к
■ ~ **point** *n.* то́чка кипе́ния

boisterous /'bɔɪstərəs/ *adj.* бу́йный,
шумли́вый, шу́мный

bold /bəʊld/ *n.* (typ.) жи́рный шрифт
● *adj.* **1** сме́лый, отва́жный; (impudent)
наха́льный **2**: ~ **strokes** (in painting) широ́кие
мазки́

Bolivia /bəˈlɪvɪə/ *n.* Боли́вия

Bolivian /bəˈlɪvɪən/ *n.* боливи́|ец (-йка)
● *adj.* боливи́йский

bollard /'bɒlɑːd/ *n.* (BrE) ту́мба

Bolshevik /'bɒlʃəvɪk/ *n.* большеви́|к (-чка)
● *adj.* большеви́стский

Bolshevism /'bɒlʃəvɪz(ə)m/ *n.* большеви́зм

bolster /'bəʊlstə(r)/ *n.* ва́лик
● *v.t.* подп|ира́ть, -ере́ть

bolt[1] /bəʊlt/ *n.* **1** (on door etc.) засо́в **2** (screw)
болт
● *adv.*: ~ **upright** пря́мо; вы́тянувшись
● *v.t.*: ~ **the door** зап|ира́ть, -ере́ть дверь на
засо́в

bolt[2] /bəʊlt/ *v.t.* (gulp down) глота́ть, проглоти́ть
● *v.i.* (of horse) понести́ (*pf.*); (of person)
ри́нуться (*pf.*), помча́ться (*pf.*), удра́ть (*pf.*)

✧ **bomb** /bɒm/ *n.* бо́мба
● *v.t. & i.* бомби́ть, раз-

■ ~ **disposal** *n.* обезвре́живание
неразорва́вшихся бомб; ~**shell** *n.*
артиллери́йский снаря́д; **the news came
as a** ~**shell to them** весть их как гро́мом
порази́ла; ~**site** *n.* райо́н разру́шенный
бомбардиро́вк|ой/-ами

bombard /bɒm'bɑːd/ *v.t.* **1** бомби́ть, раз-;
бомбардирова́ть (*impf.*); обстре́л|ивать, -я́ть
2 (fig.): ~ **sb with questions** бомбардирова́ть
(*impf.*) кого́-н. вопро́сами

bombardment /bɒm'bɑːdmənt/ *n.*
бомбардиро́вка, бомбёжка; (with shells)
артиллери́йский обстре́л

bombastic /bɒm'bæstɪk/ *adj.* высокопа́рный,
напы́щенный

bomber /'bɒmə(r)/ *n.* (aircraft)
бомбардиро́вщик; (person) террори́ст

bombing /'bɒmɪŋ/ *n.* бомбомета́ние,
бомбардиро́вка

bona fide /ˌbəʊnə 'faɪdɪ/ *adj.*
добросо́вестный, че́стный

bond /bɒnd/ *n.* **1** (link) связь **2** (fin.)
облига́ция; (*in pl.*) бо́ны (*f. pl.*)
● *v.t.* (form a relationship) уста́н|а́вливать, -ови́ть
кре́пкие отноше́ния (с + *i.*)

✧ **bone** /bəʊn/ *n.* **1** кость; I have a ~ **to pick with
you** у меня́ к вам прете́нзия **2** (substance) кость
● *v.t.*: ~ **fish/meat** отдел|я́ть, -и́ть ры́бу/мя́со
от косте́й
■ ~ **china** *n.* твёрдый англи́йский фарфо́р;
~ **dry** *adj.* соверше́нно сухо́й; ~ **idle** *adj.*
ужа́сно лени́вый

bonfire /'bɒnfaɪə(r)/ *n.* костёр

bonk /bɒnk/ *v.i.* (BrE, vulg.) тра́х|аться, -нуться

bonnet /'bɒnɪt/ *n.* **1** (woman's hat) ка́пор;
чепе́ц, че́пчик **2** (BrE, of car) капо́т

bonny /'bɒnɪ/ *adj.* (**bonnier, bonniest**) (Sc.,
attractive, beautiful) хоро́шенький; (healthy): **a** ~
baby кре́пкий ребёнок

bonus /'bəʊnəs/ *n.* пре́мия, премиа́льные
(*pl.*); (fig.) дополни́тельное преиму́щество,
бо́нус

bony /'bəʊnɪ/ *adj.* (**bonier, boniest**)
костяно́й, кости́стый

boo /buː/ *n.* гул/свист неодобре́ния
● *v.t.* (**boos, booed**) освист|ывать, -а́ть;
~ **an actor off the stage** гу́лом/сви́стом
неодобре́ния прогна́ть (*pf.*) актёра со сце́ны
● *v.i.* (**boos, booed**) улюлю́кать (*impf.*)
● *int.* фу!

boob[1] /buːb/ *n.* **1** (BrE, infml, mistake) прома́шка
2 (AmE, infml, simpleton) простофи́ля (*c.g.*),
дуралей
● *v.i.* (BrE, infml) оплоша́ть (*pf.*); дать (*pf.*)
прома́шку

boob[2] /buːb/ *n.* (*usu. in pl.*) (sl., breasts) буфера́
(*m. pl.*) (sl.)

booby trap /'buːbɪ/ *n.* (mil.) ми́на-лову́шка
● *v.t.* (**booby-trap**) устан|а́вливать, -ови́ть
ми́ны-лову́шки в/на + *p.*

✧ **book** /bʊk/ *n.* **1** кни́га; (small) кни́жка **2** (set):
~ **of matches/stamps** кни́жечка спи́чек/
ма́рок **3** (account): **keep the** ~**s** вести́ (*det.*)
бухга́лтерские/счётные кни́ги; **in sb's good/**

b

bad ∼s на хорошем/плохом счету у кого-н.
● *v.t.* (ticket, table, taxi) заказ|ывать, -ать; (hotel room, seat) брони́ровать, за-; ∼ **sb in at a hotel** брони́ровать, за- для кого-н. но́мер в гости́нице
■ ∼**case** *n.* кни́жный шкаф; (open-fronted) кни́жные по́лки (*f. pl.*); ∼ **club** *n.* клуб книголю́бов; ∼**keeping** *n.* бухгалте́рия, счетово́дство; ∼**maker** *n.* букме́кер; ∼**mark** *n.* (also comput.) закла́дка; ∼**seller** *n.* книготорго́вец; ∼**shelf** *n.* кни́жная по́лка; ∼**shop**, (AmE) ∼**store** *nn.* кни́жный магази́н

bookie /ˈbʊkɪ/ *n.* (infml) букме́кер

booking /ˈbʊkɪŋ/ *n.* зака́з
■ ∼ **office** *n.* (BrE) биле́тная ка́сса

booklet /ˈbʊklɪt/ *n.* брошю́ра, букле́т

boom¹ /buːm/ *n.* (of gun, thunder) гул, ро́кот; (of voice) гул
● *v.t. & i.* (of gun) бу́хать (*impf.*), грохота́ть (*impf.*); (of thunder) глу́хо грохота́ть (*impf.*)

boom² /buːm/ *n.* (comm.) бум, оживле́ние
● *v.i.*: **business is** ∼**ing** де́ло процвета́ет

boomerang /ˈbuːməræŋ/ *n.* бумера́нг

boorish /ˈbʊərɪʃ/ *adj.* ха́мский, мужи́цкий

boost /buːst/ *n.* (increase) увеличе́ние; (stimulus) толчо́к, сти́мул; **give a** ∼ **to the economy** стимули́ровать (*impf., pf.*) эконо́мику
● *v.t.* (increase) увели́чи|вать, -ть

booster /ˈbuːstə(r)/ *n.*: ∼ **injection** (med.) повто́рная приви́вка

boot /buːt/ *n.* **1** (footwear) боти́нок, башма́к; (knee-length) сапо́г; **football** ∼**s** бу́тсы (*f. pl.*) **2** (BrE, of a car) бага́жник
● *v.t.* (comput.) загру|жа́ть, -зи́ть
■ ∼**leg** *adj.* (fig.): ∼**leg whisky** контраба́ндное ви́ски; ∼**legger** *n.* самого́нщик

booth /buːð/ *n.* (for telephoning) бу́дка; (polling ∼) каби́на для голосова́ния

booty /ˈbuːtɪ/ *n.* добы́ча

booze /buːz/ *n.* вы́пивка; попо́йка
● *v.i.* пья́нствовать (*impf.*), выпива́ть (*impf.*)

bop /bɒp/ (BrE, infml) *n.* та́нец под популя́рную му́зыку; (party) та́нцы под популя́рную му́зыку (*m. pl.*)
● *v.i.* танцева́ть, с- под популя́рную му́зыку

◆ **border** /ˈbɔːdə(r)/ *n.* **1** (side, edging): ∼ **of a lake** бе́рег о́зера; **herbaceous** ∼ бордю́р из многоле́тних цвето́в **2** (frontier) грани́ца; (fig.) грань
● *v.t.*: **our garden** ∼**s his field** наш сад грани́чит с его́ по́лем
● *v.i.*: **these countries** ∼ **on one another** э́ти стра́ны грани́чат друг с дру́гом; **this** ∼**s on fanaticism** э́то грани́чит с фанати́змом
■ ∼**line** *n.* (fig.) грань; **a** ∼**line case** промежу́точный слу́чай

bore¹ /bɔː(r)/ *n.* кали́бр, кана́л ствола́
● *v.t.* сверли́ть, про-; бури́ть, про-

bore² /bɔː(r)/ *n.* (person) ску́чный челове́к; зану́да (*c.g.*); (thing): **it's such a bore cooking every day** така́я тоска́ ка́ждый день гото́вить

● *v.t.* надо|еда́ть, -е́сть + *d.*; ∼ **sb to death, tears** надо|еда́ть, -е́сть кому́-н. до́ сме́рти

bore³ /bɔː(r)/ *past of* ▶ **bear**²

bored /bɔːd/ *adj.* скуча́ющий; **I am** ∼ мне ску́чно; **in a** ∼ **voice** ску́чным/скуча́ющим го́лосом; **I am** ∼ **with him** он мне надое́л

boredom /ˈbɔːdəm/ *n.* ску́ка, тоска́

boring /ˈbɔːrɪŋ/ *adj.* ску́чный, надое́дливый

◆ **born** /bɔːn/ *adj. and p.p. of* ▶ **bear**² **1**: a ∼ **poet** прирождённый поэ́т **2**: **be** ∼ роди́ться (*pf.*)

borne /bɔːn/ *p.p. of* ▶ **bear**²

Borneo /ˈbɔːnɪəʊ/ *n.* Борне́о (*nt. indecl.*)

borough /ˈbʌrə/ *n.* райо́н

borrow /ˈbɒrəʊ/ *v.t. & i.* (take for a time) брать, взять на вре́мя; заи́мствовать, по-; зан|има́ть, -я́ть; (money) брать, взять взаймы́

borscht /bɔːʃt/, **borsch** /bɔːʃ/ *n.* борщ

Bosnia /ˈbɒznɪə/ *n.* Бо́сния

Bosnia-Herzegovina /ˈbɒznɪə hɜːtsəˈɡɒvɪnə/ *n.* (*also* **Bosnia and Herzegovina**) Бо́сния и Герцегови́на

bosom /ˈbʊz(ə)m/ *n.* **1** (breast) грудь **2** (fig.) се́рдце, душа́
■ ∼ **friend** *n.* закады́чный друг

Bosporus /ˈbɒspərəs/ *n.* Босфо́р

◆ **boss** /bɒs/ *n.* (master) босс, хозя́ин, нача́льник
● *v.t.*: ∼ **sb about** кома́ндовать (*impf.*) кем-н.

bossy /ˈbɒsɪ/ *adj.* (**bossier**, **bossiest**) (voice, tone) команди́рский; **your husband is really** ∼ твой муж привы́к и́м кома́ндовать

botanical /bəˈtænɪk(ə)l/ *adj.* ботани́ческий

botanist /ˈbɒtənɪst/ *n.* бота́ник

botany /ˈbɒtənɪ/ *n.* бота́ника

botch /bɒtʃ/ *v.t.* зава́л|ивать, -и́ть

◆ **both** /bəʊθ/ *pron. & adj.* о́ба (*m., nt.*), о́бе (*f.*); и тот и друго́й; ∼ **sledges** о́бе па́ры сане́й; ∼ **of us** мы о́ба
● *adv.*: ∼ **... and ...** и... и...; **my sister and I** ∼ **helped him** мы о́ба помогли́ ему́, и я, и сестра́

bother /ˈbɒðə(r)/ *n.* беспоко́йство; хло́п|оты (-о́т); возня́; **I had no** ∼ **finding the book** я нашёл кни́гу без труда́
● *v.t.* (disturb) беспоко́ить, по-; трево́жить, по-; (pester): **he is always** ∼**ing me to lend him money** он ве́чно пристаёт ко мне с про́сьбой одолжи́ть ему́ де́нег; ∼ **(it)!** (BrE) чёрт возьми́!; **I can't be** ∼**ed** мне лень, мне недосу́г
● *v.i.* беспоко́иться, по-; **don't** ∼ **to make tea** не вози́тесь с ча́ем

Botox® /ˈbəʊtɒks/ *n.* (med.) бо́токс (*медици́нский/космети́ческий препара́т*)

◆ **bottle** /ˈbɒt(ə)l/ *n.* буты́лка; (BrE, for infants) буты́лочка, рожо́к
● *v.t.* (preserve in ∼s) храни́ть в буты́лках; ∼ **up** (put in ∼s) разл|ива́ть, -и́ть по буты́лкам; (conceal) скрыва́ть, -ть
■ ∼**-fed** *adj.* иску́сственно вско́рмленный; ∼**neck** *n.* (fig.) зато́р; про́бка; у́зкое ме́сто; ∼**opener** *n.* открыва́лка (infml); ∼**top** *n.* колпачо́к на буты́лку

bottled /ˈbɒt(ə)ld/ *adj.*: ∼ **beer** буты́лочное пи́во

b

bottom /'bɒtəm/ n. **1** (lowest part) дно; (of mountain) подно́жие, подо́шва; (of page) низ, коне́ц; (of stairs) низ, основа́ние; ~ shelf ни́жняя по́лка; at the ~ of the class отстаю́щий в кла́ссе **2** (further end): ~ of the garden/street коне́ц са́да/у́лицы **3** (BrE, buttocks) зад; за́дняя часть **4** (fig.): get to the ~ of sth доб|ира́ться, -ра́ться до су́ти чего́-н.; he came ~ in algebra он был са́мым неуспева́ющим по а́лгебре
■ ~ line n. (crux of the matter) суть де́ла

boudoir /'bu:dwɑ:(r)/ n. будуа́р

bougainvillea, bougainvillaea /bu:gən'vɪlɪə/ n. (bot.) бугенвилле́я (*scientific name*), бугенви́ллия

bough /baʊ/ n. сук

bought /bɔːt/ past and p.p. of ▶ buy

boulder /'bəʊldə(r)/ n. валу́н

boulevard /'buːləvɑːd/ n. бульва́р

bounce /baʊns/ n. подпры́гивание, отско́к
• *v.t.*: ~ a ball бить (*impf.*) мячо́м об пол (о зе́млю, об сте́нку *u m. n.*)
• *v.i.* (of ball etc.) отск|а́кивать, -очи́ть; подпры́г|ивать, -нуть; (infml, of cheque) верну́ться (*pf.*); ~ back (fig.) бы́стро опра́виться

bouncer /'baʊnsə(r)/ n. вышиба́ла (*m.*)

bound[1] /baʊnd/ n. (*usu. in pl.*) (limit) грани́ца, преде́л; the town is out of ~s to troops вход в го́род солда́там воспрещён

bound[2] /baʊnd/ *v.i.* пры́г|ать, -нуть; скак|а́ть, -ну́ть; he ~ed off to fetch the book он подпры́гнул, чтобы доста́ть кни́гу

bound[3] /baʊnd/ *adj.* **1** (certain): he is ~ to win он непреме́нно вы́играет **2** (obliged): you are not ~ to go вам не обяза́тельно идти́ **3** (en route): the ship is ~ for New York парохо́д направля́ется в Нью-Йо́рк

bound[4] /baʊnd/ past and p.p. of ▶ bind

boundary /'baʊndrɪ/ n. (of a field etc.) грани́ца, рубе́ж; (fig.) преде́л; (*attr.*) пограни́чный

boundless /'baʊndlɪs/ *adj.* безграни́чный, беспреде́льный

bountiful /'baʊntɪfʊl/ *adj.* ще́дрый; оби́льный

bouquet /buˈkeɪ/ n. (of flowers, wine) буке́т

bourbon /'bɜːbən/ n. (whisky) бурбо́н

bourgeois /'bʊəʒwɑ/ *adj.* буржуа́зный

bourgeoisie /bʊəʒwɑ:'zi:/ n. буржуази́я

bout /baʊt/ n. **1** (at games) бой, встре́ча, схва́тка **2** (of illness) при́ступ

boutique /bu:'ti:k/ n. (небольшо́й) мо́дный магази́н; бути́к

bow[1] /bəʊ/ n. **1** (weapon) лук **2** (of violin etc.) смычо́к **3** (knot) бант
■ ~-legged *adj.* кривоно́гий; ~ tie n. (га́лстук-)ба́бочка

bow[2] /baʊ/ n. (salutation) покло́н
• *v.t.* (bend): ~ one's head склон|я́ть, -и́ть го́лову; the wind ~ed the trees ве́тер гнул/ клони́л дере́вья
• *v.i.* **1** (salute) кла́няться, поклони́ться **2** (defer) склон|я́ться, -и́ться (to, before: пе́ред + *i.*)

bow[3] /baʊ/ n. (naut.) нос

bowel /'baʊəl/ n. **1** кишка́ **2**: ~s of the earth не́др|а (*pl., g.* —) земли́

bowl[1] /bəʊl/ n. ча́ша, ва́за, ми́ска

bowl[2] /bəʊl/ n.: play ~s игра́ть (*impf.*) в бо́улинг/ке́гли/шары́
• *v.t.*: ~ over (lit.) сшиб|а́ть, -и́ть; (fig.): he was ~ed over by her она́ срази́ла его́
• *v.i.* **1** (cricket) под|ава́ть, -а́ть мяч **2** (play bowls) игра́ть (*impf.*) в бо́улинг/ке́гли/шары́
■ ~ing alley n. зал для игры́ в бо́улинг; кегельба́н; ~ing green n. лужа́йка для игры́ в бо́улинг/шары́

bowler[1] /'bəʊlə(r)/ n. (at games) подаю́щий/ броса́ющий мяч

bowler[2] /'bəʊlə(r)/ n. (*in full* ~ hat) котело́к

box[1] /bɒks/ n. **1** (receptacle) коро́бка, я́щик **2** (theatr.) ло́жа **3** (typ.) ра́мка
• *v.t.* класть, положи́ть в коро́бку/я́щик
■ ~ number n. но́мер абоне́нтского я́щика; ~ office n. (театра́льная) ка́сса

box[2] /bɒks/ *v.t.*: ~ sb's ears да|ва́ть, -ть кому́-н. оплеу́ху (*or* по́ уху)
• *v.i.* (sport) бокси́ровать (*impf.*)

boxer /'bɒksə(r)/ n. (sportsman; dog) боксёр
■ ~ shorts n. pl. боксёрские трусы́

boxing /'bɒksɪŋ/ n. (sport) бокс

Boxing Day /'bɒksɪŋ/ n. (BrE) второ́й день Рождества́

boy /bɔɪ/ n. **1** (child) ма́льчик **2** (son) сын
■ ~friend n. ≈ па́рень (*m.*), ≈ молодо́й челове́к, бойфре́нд; B~ Scout n. бойска́ут

boycott /'bɔɪkɒt/ n. бойко́т
• *v.t.* бойкоти́ровать (*impf., pf.*)

boyish /'bɔɪʃ/ *adj.* мальчи́шеский

bra /brɑ:/ n. (*pl.* bras) (infml) ли́фчик, бюстга́льтер

brace /breɪs/ n. **1** (support) подпо́рка, распо́рка **2**: ~s (BrE, for trousers) подтя́ж|ки (~ек) **3** (dentistry etc.) ши́на
• *v.t.* **1** (support) подп|ира́ть, -ере́ть; he ~d himself against the wall он опёрся о сте́ну **2** (of nerves): he ~d himself to do it он собра́лся с ду́хом чтобы сде́лать э́то

bracelet /'breɪslɪt/ n. брасле́т

bracing /'breɪsɪŋ/ *adj.* бодря́щий, укрепля́ющий

bracken /'brækən/ n. па́поротник-орля́к

bracket /'brækɪt/ n. **1** (support) кронште́йн **2** (typ.) ско́бка **3** (fig.): the higher income ~s гру́ппа населе́ния с бо́лее высо́кими дохо́дами
• *v.t.* (**bracketed, bracketing**) **1** (enclose in ~s) заключ|а́ть, -и́ть в ско́бки **2** (fig.): do not ~ me with him не равня́йте меня́ с ним

brag /bræg/ *v.i.* (**bragged, bragging**) хва́стать(ся), по- (*чем*)

braid /breɪd/ n. (of hair) коса́; (decorative) галу́н

Braille /breɪl/ n. шрифт Бра́йля; а́збука Бра́йля

brain /breɪn/ n. (anat.) мозг; (*in pl.*) (cul.) мозги́
■ ~child n. плод ра́зума/воображе́ния; ~ drain n. «уте́чка мозго́в»; ~storming session n. коллекти́вное обсужде́ние

b

проблём; **~wash** *v.t.* пром|ыва́ть, -ы́ть мозги́ (+ *d.*); **~washing** *n.* промыва́ние мозго́в; **~wave** *n.*: he had a **~wave** ему́ пришла́ счастли́вая мысль; его́ осени́ла иде́я

brainy /'breɪnɪ/ *adj.* (**brainier, brainiest**) (infml) башкови́тый, мозгови́тый

braise /breɪz/ *v.t.* туши́ть (*impf.*)

brake /breɪk/ *n.* (on vehicle) то́рмоз
● *v.t. & i.* тормози́ть, за-

bramble /'bræmb(ə)l/ *n.* ежеви́ка

bran /bræn/ *n.* о́труб|и (-ей)

✐ **branch** /brɑːntʃ/ *n.* (of tree) ветвь; ве́тка; (of family, genus) ли́ния, ветвь; (of railway line) ве́тка; (comm.) филиа́л, отделе́ние; (of knowledge, subject, industry) о́трасль
● *v.i.* (of organization): **~ out** разветв|ля́ться, -и́ться; (of road or railway) (*also* **~ off**) разветв|ля́ться, -и́ться; ответв|ля́ться, -и́ться

✐ **brand** /brænd/ *n.* сорт, ма́рка, бренд
● *v.t.* **1** (cattle etc.) клейми́ть, за- **2** (stigmatize) клейми́ть, за- **3** (comm.): **~ed goods** фи́рменные това́ры
■ **~ name** *n.* фи́рменное назва́ние; **~ new** *adj.* соверше́нно но́вый, с иго́лочки

branding /'brændɪŋ/ *n.* (comm.) бре́ндинг (*создание и продвижение на рынке торговых марок*)

brandish /'brændɪʃ/ *v.t.* разма́хивать (*impf.*) + *i.*

brandy /'brændɪ/ *n.* конья́к; бре́нди (*nt. indecl.*)

brash /bræʃ/ *adj.* наха́льный, наглова́тый, де́рзкий

brass /brɑːs/ *n.* **1** (metal) лату́нь, жёлтая медь **2** (mus.): the **~** духовы́е инструме́нты (*m. pl.*); медь
■ **~ band** *n.* духово́й орке́стр

brat /bræt/ *n.* (pej.) невоспи́танный ребёнок

bravado /brə'vɑːdəʊ/ *n.* брава́да

brave /breɪv/ *adj.* хра́брый, сме́лый
● *v.t.* бр|оса́ть, -о́сить вы́зов + *d.*; **~ publicity** не боя́ться (*impf.*) гла́сности

bravery /'breɪvərɪ/ *n.* хра́брость, сме́лость

bravo /brɑː'vəʊ/ *int.* бра́во!

brawl /brɔːl/ *n.* сканда́л
● *v.i.* сканда́лить (*impf.*)

brawny /'brɔːnɪ/ *adj.* (**brawnier, brawniest**) мускули́стый

brazen /'breɪz(ə)n/ *adj.* на́глый, бессты́дный
● *v.t.*: **~ sth out** на́гло выкру́чиваться, вы́крутиться из чего́-н.

brazier /'breɪzɪə(r)/ *n.* (portable heater) жаро́вня

Brazil /brə'zɪl/ *n.* Брази́лия

Brazilian /brə'zɪljən/ *n.* брази́л|ец (-ья́нка)
● *adj.* брази́льский

breach /briːtʃ/ *n.* **1** (violation, interruption) наруше́ние; **~ of trust** злоупотребле́ние дове́рием **2** (gap) проло́м, брешь
● *v.t.* прор|ыва́ть, -ва́ть

bread /bred/ *n.* хлеб; **~ and butter** (fig.) хлеб с ма́слом
■ **~-and-butter** *adj.* насу́щный; **~ bin** *n.* (BrE) хле́бница; **~board** *n.* хле́бная доска́;

✐ ключева́я ле́ксика

~crumb *n.* кро́шка; (*in pl.*) (cul.) толчёные сухари́ (*m. pl.*); **~line** *n.*: on the **~line** (BrE) в тяжёлом материа́льном положе́нии; **~winner** *n.* корми́лец

breadth /bredθ/ *n.* **1** (width) ширина́ **2** (fig.): **~ of mind** широта́ ума́

✐ **break** /breɪk/ *n.* **1** (broken place, gap) тре́щина, разры́в **2** (interval) переры́в, па́уза; (rest) переды́шка **3** (change) переме́на **4** (infml, opportunity) возмо́жность; **lucky ~** счастли́вый слу́чай
● *v.t.* (*past* **broke**, *p.p.* **broken**) **1** (fracture, destroy) лома́ть, с-; (glass, china) бить (*or* разбива́ть), раз-; **he broke his leg** он слома́л но́гу **2** (fig.): **~ a record** поби́ть (*pf.*) реко́рд **3** (convey): **~ the news** сообщ|а́ть, -и́ть (неприя́тные) но́вости **4** (weaken): **~ a fall** осл|абля́ть, -а́бить си́лу паде́ния **5** (violate) нар|уша́ть, -у́шить; **~ a secret** разглаша́ть, -аси́ть та́йну **6** (interrupt, put an end to): **~ one's journey** прер|ыва́ть, -ва́ть путеше́ствие
● *v.i.* (*past* **broke**, *p.p.* **broken**) **1** (fracture, disperse) лома́ться, с-; обл|а́мываться, -ома́ться; (of glass, china) би́ться (*or* разбива́ться), раз-; **~ in two** лома́ться, с-попола́м **2** (fig.): **~ing point** преде́л **3** (burst, dawn): **the storm broke** разрази́лась гроза́; **the news broke at 5 o'clock** об э́том ста́ло изве́стно в 5 часо́в **4** (change): **his voice broke** (at puberty) у него́ слома́лся го́лос; **the weather broke** пого́да испо́ртилась **5** (var.): **~ even** ост|ава́ться, -а́ться при свои́х; **we broke for lunch** мы сде́лали переры́в на обе́д
● (*with preps.*): **burglars broke into the house** граби́тели ворвали́сь в дом; **the house was broken into** в до́ме произошла́ кра́жа со взло́мом
□ **~ away** *v.i.*: **~ away from one's jailers** вырыва́ться, вы́рваться из рук тюре́мщиков; **~ away from a group** отк|а́лываться, -оло́ться от гру́ппы
□ **~ down** *v.t.*: **~ down a door** выла́мывать, вы́ломать дверь; **~ down resistance** сломи́ть (*pf.*) сопротивле́ние; **~ down expenditure** разб|ива́ть, -и́ть расхо́ды по статья́м
● *v.i.*: **the car broke down** маши́на слома́лась; **he broke down** он не вы́держал
□ **~ in** *v.t.*: **~ in a door** вл|а́мываться, -оми́ться в дверь; **~ in a horse** выезжа́ть, вы́ездить ло́шадь; **~ in a new pair of shoes** разн|а́шивать, -оси́ть но́вые ту́фли
● *v.i.*: **~ in on a conversation** вме́ш|иваться, -а́ться в разгово́р
□ **~ off** *v.t.*: **~ off a twig** отл|а́мывать, -оми́ть ве́точку; **~ off relations** пор|ыва́ть, -ва́ть отноше́ния (с + *i.*); **~ off an engagement** раст|орга́ть, -о́ргнуть помо́лвку
● *v.i.* (be severed) отл|а́мываться, -оми́ться ве́точку; **he broke off** (speaking) он замолча́л
□ **~ out** *v.i.*: **the prisoner broke out** заключённый сбежа́л; **war broke out** разрази́лась/вспы́хнула война́; **his face broke out in pimples** на его́ лице́ вы́сыпали прыщи́
□ **~ up** *v.t.*: **~ up the ground** взры́|ва́ть, -ть зе́млю; **~ up a meeting** прекра|ща́ть, -ти́ть собра́ние; **~ up a family** (separate) разб|ива́ть,

-и́ть семью́

● *v.i.*: **school ~s up tomorrow** (BrE) уча́щихся за́втра распуска́ют на кани́кулы; **she broke up with her boyfriend** она́ разошла́сь с дру́гом

■ **~away** *n.*: **a ~away faction** отколо́вшаяся фра́кция; (sport) отры́в; **~down** *n.* (mechanical) поло́мка; (of health) расстро́йство; (of negotiations) срыв; (analysis) подразделе́ние, разби́вка; **~in** *n.* взлом; **~neck** *adj.*: **~neck speed** головокружи́тельная ско́рость; **~through** *n.* (mil.) проры́в; (fig.) скачо́к, перело́м, проры́в; **~up** *n.* разва́л, распа́д; (of friendship) разры́в; **~water** *n.* волноре́з

♂ **breakfast** /'brekfəst/ *n.* за́втрак
● *v.i.* за́втракать, по-

breast /brest/ *n.* **1** грудь **2** (cul.): **~ of lamb** бара́нья груди́нка

■ **~fed** *adj.* вскóрмленный гру́дью; **~feeding** *n.* кормле́ние гру́дью; **~stroke** *n.* брасс

breath /breθ/ *n.* дыха́ние; (single ~) вздох; **out of ~** задыха́ясь; **bad ~** дурно́й за́пах изо рта; **catch, hold one's ~** затаи́вать, -и́ть дыха́ние; **take sb's ~ away** захва́т|ывать, -и́ть дух у кого́-н.

■ **~taking** *adj.* захва́тывающий

breathalyse /'breθəlaɪz/ (AmE **breathalyze**) *v.t.* пров|еря́ть, -е́рить на алкого́ль

breathalyser /'breθəlaɪzə(r)/ (AmE **Breathalyzer®**) *n.* алкóметр, алкого́льно-респира́торная тру́бка

breathe /briːð/ *v.t.* **1**: **~ fresh air** дыша́ть (*impf.*) све́жим во́здухом **2** (utter softly): **~ a sigh** изд|ава́ть, -а́ть вздох; **don't ~ a word!** ни сло́ва бо́льше!
● *v.i.* дыша́ть (*impf.*)

breather /'briːðə(r)/ *n.* переды́шка

breathing /'briːðɪŋ/ *n.* дыха́ние

■ **~ space** *n.* переды́шка

breathless /'breθlɪs/ *adj.* задыха́ющийся, запыха́вшийся

bred /bred/ *past and p.p. of* ▸ **breed**

breed /briːd/ *n.* поро́да
● *v.t.* (*past and p.p.* **bred**) **1** (cause) поро|жда́ть, -ди́ть **2** (animals) раз|води́ть, -вести́
● *v.i.* (*past and p.p.* **bred**) размн|ожа́ться, -о́житься; плоди́ться, рас-

breeder /'briːdə(r)/ *n.* животново́д, ското́вод

breeding /'briːdɪŋ/ *n.* **1** (by stockbreeders) разведе́ние **2** (manners etc.) воспи́танность

■ **~ ground** *n.* (fig.) расса́дник, оча́г

breeze /briːz/ *n.* ветеро́к; бриз
● *v.i.*: **~ in/out** (infml) влете́ть/вы́лететь (*pf.*)

breezy /'briːzɪ/ *adj.* (**breezier, breeziest**) (of weather) све́жий; (fig., of person) живо́й, беззабо́тный

brevity /'brevɪtɪ/ *n.* кра́ткость

brew /bruː/ *v.t.* (beer) вари́ть, с-; (tea) зава́р|ивать, -и́ть
● *v.i.* **1** (of tea etc.) зава́р|иваться, -и́ться **2**: **a storm is ~ing** (lit. and fig.) гроза́ надвига́ется; **there's trouble ~ing** быть беде́

brewer /'bruːə(r)/ *n.* пивова́р

brewery /'bruːərɪ/ *n.* пивова́ренный заво́д

bribe /braɪb/ *n.* взя́тка, по́дкуп
● *v.t.* да|ва́ть, -ть взя́тку + *d.*; **~ sb to do sth** по́дкупом доб|ива́ться, -и́ться чего́-н. от кого́-н.

bribery /'braɪbərɪ/ *n.* взя́точничество

brick /brɪk/ *n.* кирпи́ч; **~s** (collect.) кирпи́ч; (attr.) кирпи́чный
● *v.t.*: **~ up** за|кла́дывать, -ложи́ть кирпичо́м

■ **~layer** *n.* ка́менщик

bridal /'braɪd(ə)l/ *adj.* сва́дебный

bride /braɪd/ *n.* неве́ста

■ **~groom** *n.* жени́х; **~smaid** *n.* подру́жка неве́сты

♂ **bridge¹** /brɪdʒ/ *n.* **1** (also dentistry) мост **2** (naut.) капита́нский мо́стик **3** (of nose) перено́сица **4** (of violin) подста́вка
● *v.t.*: **~ a river** наво|ди́ть, -ести́ мост че́рез ре́ку; (join by bridging) соедин|я́ть, -и́ть мосто́м; (fig.): **~ a gap** восп|олня́ть, -о́лнить пробе́л

bridge² /brɪdʒ/ *n.* (game) бридж

bridle /'braɪd(ə)l/ *n.* узда́, узде́чка
● *v.t.* (a horse) взну́зд|ывать, -а́ть; (fig.) обу́зд|ывать, -а́ть
● *v.i.* (fig.) зад|ира́ть, -ра́ть нос

■ **~ path** *n.* (BrE) верхова́я тропа́

brief /briːf/ *n.* **1** (lawyer's) изложе́ние де́ла **2** (BrE, instructions) инстру́кция **3** (in pl.) (infml, underpants) трус|ы́ (-о́в)
● *adj.* коро́ткий, недо́лгий; **in ~** вкра́тце
● *v.t.* **1**: **~ a lawyer** (BrE) поруч|а́ть, -и́ть адвока́ту веде́ние де́ла **2** (mil. etc.) инструкти́ровать (*impf., pf.*)

■ **~case** *n.* портфе́ль (*m.*)

briefing /'briːfɪŋ/ *n.* инструкта́ж; (press) бри́финг

briefly /'briːflɪ/ *adv.* кра́тко, сжа́то

brigade /brɪ'ɡeɪd/ *n.* брига́да

brigadier /brɪɡə'dɪə(r)/ *n.* (also **~ general**) брига́дный генера́л

brigand /'brɪɡənd/ *n.* разбо́йник

♂ **bright** /braɪt/ *adj.* **1** (clear, shining) я́ркий, све́тлый; **a ~ day** я́сный день; **~ red** я́рко-кра́сный; **a ~ room** све́тлая ко́мната **2** (cheerful): **look on the ~ side** смотре́ть (*impf.*) на ве́щи оптимисти́чески **3** (clever): **a ~ girl** толко́вая де́вочка; **a ~ idea** блестя́щая мысль

brighten /'braɪt(ə)n/ *v.t.* (also **~ up**) ожив|ля́ть, -и́ть
● *v.i.* (also **~ up**): **the weather ~ed (up)** пого́да проясни́лась

brightness /'braɪtnɪs/ *n.* (lustre) я́ркость; (cleverness) блеск, смышлёность

brilliance /'brɪlɪəns/ *n.* (brightness) я́ркость; (intelligence) блеск (ума́)

brilliant /'brɪlɪənt/ *adj.* (lit., fig.) сверка́ющий, блестя́щий; (BrE, infml, excellent) замеча́тельный

brim /brɪm/ *n.* край; (of hat) поля́ (*nt. pl.*)

brine /braɪn/ *n.* рассо́л

♂ **bring** /brɪŋ/ *v.t.* (*past and p.p.* **brought**)

b

(cause to come, deliver) (a thing) прин|оси́ть,
-ести́; (a person) прив|оди́ть, -ести́; **it
brought tears to my eyes** э́то вы́звало у
меня́ слёзы

□ ~ **about** v.t. (cause) вызыва́ть, вы́звать;
произв|оди́ть, -ести́

□ ~ **back** v.t. прин|оси́ть, -ести́ (or прив|оди́ть,
-ести́) наза́д

□ ~ **down** v.t. (an aircraft) сби|ва́ть, -ть; ~ **prices
down** сн|ижа́ть, -и́зить це́ны

□ ~ **forward** v.t. (advance date of) перен|оси́ть,
-ести́ на бо́лее ра́нний срок

□ ~ **in** v.t. вн|оси́ть, -ести́; вв|оди́ть, -ести́; ~ **in
a verdict** выноси́ть, вы́нести верди́кт

□ ~ **off** v.t.: ~ **off a manoeuvre** успе́шно
заверш|а́ть, -и́ть опера́цию

□ ~ **on** v.t.: **this brought on a bad cold** э́то
вы́звало си́льный на́сморк

□ ~ **out** v.t. выноси́ть, вы́нести; выводи́ть,
вы́вести; (make evident) выявля́ть, вы́явить;
(publish) выпуска́ть, вы́пустить; **the curtains
~ out the green in the carpet** занаве́ски
оттеня́ют зе́лень ковра́

□ ~ **round** v.t. (restore to consciousness) прив|оди́ть,
-ести́ в себя́; (persuade) убе|жда́ть, -ди́ть

□ ~ **up** v.t. (educate) воспи́т|ывать, -а́ть; (vomit):
he brought up his dinner его́ вы́рвало по́сле
обе́да; ~ **up a subject** подн|има́ть, -я́ть
вопро́с; зав|оди́ть, -ести́ разгово́р о чём-н.

brink /brɪŋk/ n. край (also fig.)

brisk /brɪsk/ adj. (of movement) ско́рый; (of air,
wind) све́жий

bristle /ˈbrɪs(ə)l/ n. щети́на
● v.i. (of hair) стоя́ть (impf.); ды́бом; вста́ть
(pf.) ды́бом; (of animal, also fig., of person)
ощети́ни|ваться, -ться

Britain /ˈbrɪt(ə)n/ n. Брита́ния

✍ **British** /ˈbrɪtɪʃ/ n.: **the** ~ брита́нцы (m. pl.)
● adj. брита́нский
■ ~ **Isles** n. pl. Брита́нские острова́

Briton /ˈbrɪt(ə)n/ n. брита́н|ец (-ка)

brittle /ˈbrɪt(ə)l/ adj. ло́мкий, хру́пкий

broach /brəʊtʃ/ v.t.: ~ **a subject** подн|има́ть,
-я́ть вопро́с

✍ **broad** /brɔːd/ adj. **1** (wide) широ́кий **2**: in
~ **daylight** средь бе́ла дня **3** (decided): a ~
hint то́лстый намёк; a ~ **accent** си́льный
акце́нт **4** (approximate): in ~ **outline** в о́бщих
черта́х
■ ~ **band** n. (comput.) широкополо́сная
переда́ча да́нных; ~ **bean** n. фасо́ль;
~ **cast** n. трансля́ция ● v.t. (on radio/TV)
трансли́ровать (impf., pf.); перед|ава́ть,
-а́ть по ра́дио, телеви́дению; (spread news
etc.) распростран|я́ть, -и́ть ● v.i. (on radio/TV)
вести́ (det.) радиопереда́чу, телепереда́чу;
~ **caster** n. (radio) радиожурнали́ст;
(TV) тележурнали́ст; ~ **casting** n. (radio)
радиовеща́ние; (TV) телевеща́ние;
трансля́ция; ~ **minded** adj. широ́ких
взгля́дов; ~ **sheet** n. газе́та большо́го
форма́та

✍ ключева́я ле́ксика

broaden /ˈbrɔːd(ə)n/ v.t. & i. расш|иря́ть(ся),
-и́рить(ся)

broadly /ˈbrɔːdlɪ/ adv. (in the main) в основно́м;
~ **speaking** вообще́ говоря́

broccoli /ˈbrɒkəlɪ/ n. бро́кколи (nt. indecl.)

brochure /ˈbrəʊʃə(r)/ n. брошю́ра

broil /brɔɪl/ v.t. (AmE, cul.) жа́рить, за- на
откры́том огне́

broke /brəʊk/ adj. (infml) разори́вшийся,
безде́нежный

broken /ˈbrəʊkən/ adj. **1**: a ~ **leg** сло́манная
нога́; ~ **English** ло́маный англи́йский язы́к
2 (~-down): a ~ **marriage** расстро́енный
брак; a ~ **home** разби́тая семья́ **3** (crushed): a
~ **man** сло́мленный челове́к
■ ~ **down** adj. (of machine) сло́манный;
~ **hearted** adj. с разби́тым се́рдцем

broker /ˈbrəʊkə(r)/ n. ма́клер, бро́кер

brolly /ˈbrɒlɪ/ n. (BrE, infml) = **umbrella**

bronchitis /brɒŋˈkaɪtɪs/ n. бронхи́т

bronze /brɒnz/ n. бро́нза; (attr.) бро́нзовый

brooch /brəʊtʃ/ n. брошь

brood /bruːd/ n. пото́мство
● v.i. **1** (of bird) сиде́ть (impf.) на я́йцах **2**: ~
over an insult копи́ть (impf.) в себе́ оби́ду

broody /ˈbruːdɪ/ adj. (**broodier**, **broodiest**)
1 (thoughtful) заду́мчивый; (morose) угрю́мый
2: a ~ **hen** (хоро́шая) насе́дка **3** (of a
woman): **she's feeling** ~ в ней просну́лся
матери́нский инсти́нкт

brook /brʊk/ n. (stream) руче́й

broom /bruːm/ n. метла́
■ ~ **stick** n. (witch's) помело́

brothel /ˈbrɒθ(ə)l/ n. борде́ль (m.),
публи́чный дом

✍ **brother** /ˈbrʌðə(r)/ n. брат
■ ~ **in-law** n. (sister's husband, husband's sister's
husband) зять (m.); (wife's ~) шу́рин; (husband's
~) де́верь (m.); (wife's sister's husband) своя́к

brotherly /ˈbrʌðəlɪ/ adj. бра́тский

brought /brɔːt/ past and p.p. of ▶ **bring**

brow /braʊ/ n. (forehead) лоб, чело́; (of hill)
гре́бень (m.)

brown /braʊn/ n. кори́чневый цвет
● adj. **1** кори́чневый; (grey-~) бу́рый **2** (tanned)
загоре́лый
● v.t. поджа́ри|вать, -ть
■ ~ **bread** n. се́рый хлеб; ~ **paper** n.
обёрточная бума́га

brownish /ˈbraʊnɪʃ/ adj. коричнева́тый

browse /braʊz/ v.i. щипа́ть (impf.) траву́

browser /ˈbraʊzə(r)/ n. (comput.) бра́узер

bruise /bruːz/ n. синя́к, кровоподтёк; (on fruit)
вмя́тина
● v.t. ста́вить, по- синя́к + d.; (fruit) помя́ть,
поби́ть (both pf.); **I** ~**d my shoulder** я уши́б
плечо́

brunette /bruːˈnet/ n. брюне́тка

brunt /brʌnt/ n. гла́вный уда́р; **bear the** ~ **of
the work** выноси́ть, вы́нести всю тя́жесть
рабо́ты

brush /brʌʃ/ n. (for sweeping) щётка; (painter's)
кисть

b

● *v.t.* (clean) чи́стить, по-; (touch slightly): **the branches ~ed my cheek** ве́тви слегка́ косну́лись мое́й щеки́

● *v.i.*: **~ against sth** слегка́ каса́ться, косну́ться чего́-н.; **~ past sb** прон|оси́ться, -ести́сь ми́мо кого́-н.

□ **~ aside** *v.t.*: **~ aside difficulties** отме|та́ть, -сти́ тру́дности

□ **~ up** *v.t.*: **~ up one's French** освеж|а́ть, -и́ть в па́мяти францу́зский

● *v.i.*: **~ up on a subject** освеж|а́ть, -и́ть зна́ния по како́му-н. предме́ту

■ **~wood** *n.* хво́рост, вале́жник

brusque /bruːsk/ *adj.* ре́зкий

Brussels /'brʌs(ə)lz/ *n.* Брюссе́ль (*m.*)

■ **~ sprouts** *n. pl.* брюссе́льская капу́ста

brutal /'bruːt(ə)l/ *adj.* жесто́кий

brutality /bruːˈtælɪtɪ/ *n.* жесто́кость

brutalize /'bruːtəlaɪz/ *v.t.* ожесточ|а́ть, -и́ть; огруб|ля́ть, -и́ть

brute /bruːt/ *n.* (animal) живо́тное, зверь (*m.*); (person) скоти́на (*c.g.*)

● *adj.*: **~ force** гру́бая, физи́ческая си́ла

B.Sc. *abbr.* (*of* **Bachelor of Science**) бакала́вр (есте́ственных) нау́к

BSE *abbr.* (*of* **bovine spongiform encephalopathy**) бы́чья губкови́дная энцефалопати́я

bubble /'bʌb(ə)l/ *n.* пузы́рь (*m.*); (of air, gas) пузырёк

● *v.i.* (of water) пузыри́ться (*impf.*), кипе́ть (*impf.*)

■ **~ bath** *n.* пе́на для ва́нны

Bucharest /buːkəˈrest/ *n.* Бухаре́ст

buck¹ /bʌk/ *n.* **1** (male animal) саме́ц **2** (AmE, infml, dollar) до́ллар **3**: **pass the ~** (infml) снима́ть, снять с себя́ отве́тственность

buck² /bʌk/ *v.i.* (of horse) брыка́ться (*impf.*)

bucket /'bʌkɪt/ *n.* ведро́

● *v.i.* (**bucketed, bucketing**) (BrE, rain): **it's ~ing down** льёт как из ведра́

■ **~ list** *n.* спи́сок всех дел, кото́рые челове́к хоте́л бы сде́лать пе́ред сме́ртью

buckle /'bʌk(ə)l/ *n.* пря́жка

● *v.t.* **1** (coat, shoe) застёг|ивать, -ну́ть **2** (wheel) гнуть, по-; деформи́ровать (*impf., pf.*)

● *v.i.* **1** (of coat, shoe) застёг|иваться, -ну́ться **2** (of wheel) гну́ться, по-; деформи́роваться (*impf., pf.*) **3** (of knees) под|гиба́ться, -огну́ться

buckwheat /'bʌkwiːt/ *n.* гречи́ха; (*attr.*) гре́чневый

bud /bʌd/ *n.* по́чка; (flower not fully opened) буто́н

● *v.i.* (**budded, budding**) (of plant) покр|ыва́ться, -ы́ться по́чками; (fig.) распус|ка́ться, -ти́ться; **he's a ~ding musician** он многообеща́ющий музыка́нт

Budapest /buːdəˈpest/ *n.* Будапе́шт

Buddhism /'bʊdɪz(ə)m/ *n.* будди́зм

Buddhist /'bʊdɪst/ *n.* будди́ст

● *adj.* будди́йский, будди́стский

buddleia /'bʌdlɪə/ *n.* (bot.) буд(д)ле́я

buddy /'bʌdɪ/ *n.* (AmE, infml) дружи́ще (*m.*), прия́тель (*m.*)

budge /bʌdʒ/ *v.t.*: **I cannot ~ this rock** я не могу́ сдви́нуть э́тот ка́мень

● *v.i.*: **the bookcase won't ~ an inch** кни́жный шкаф невозмо́жно сдви́нуть с ме́ста

budgerigar /'bʌdʒərɪɡɑː(r)/ *n.* волни́стый попуга́йчик

✧ **budget** /'bʌdʒɪt/ *n.* бюдже́т

● *v.t. & i.* (**budgeted, budgeting**): **~ (funds) for a project** ассигнова́ть (*impf., pf.*) определённую су́мму на прое́кт

budgie /'bʌdʒɪ/ *n.* (infml) = **budgerigar**

Buenos Aires /bweɪnɒs 'aɪrɪz/ *n.* Буэ́нос-А́йрес

buff /bʌf/ *n.* (colour) тёмно-жёлтый цвет

buffalo /'bʌfələʊ/ *n.* (*pl.* **~** *or* **~es**) (wild ox) бу́йвол

buffer /'bʌfə(r)/ *n.* (rail., comput., also fig.) бу́фер

buffet¹ /'bʌfɪt/ *v.t.* (**buffeted, buffeting**) уд|аря́ть, -а́рить в + *a.*

buffet² /'bʊfeɪ/ *n.* (refreshment bar) буфе́т; (meal) а-ля фурше́т

bug /bʌɡ/ *n.* (small insect) бука́шка, жучо́к; (infml, germ) зара́за; (microphone) жучо́к; (comput., error) оши́бка, баг (sl.)

● *v.t.* (**bugged, bugging**): **the room was ~ged** (infml) в ко́мнате бы́ли устано́влены подслу́шивающие устро́йства; (infml, annoy) раздраж|а́ть, -и́ть

bugger /'bʌɡə(r)/ *n.* (BrE, vulg.) **1** (as term of abuse) сво́лочь; **poor ~** несча́стный

● *v.t.*: **~ (it)!** чёрт возьми́!; **~ them!** да хрен с ни́ми!; **~ all** ни хрена́

● *v.i.*: **~ off!** прова́ливай!; убира́йся!

buggy /'bʌɡɪ/ *n.* (*in full* **baby ~**) лёгкая де́тская коля́ска

bugle /'bjuːɡ(ə)l/ *n.* горн

✧ **build** /bɪld/ *n.* телосложе́ние

● *v.t.* (*past and p.p.* **built**) **1** стро́ить, по-; выстра́ивать, вы́строить; **~ a nest** вить, с- гнездо́ **2**: **a well-built man** хорошо́ сло́жённый челове́к **3** (fig.): **~ a new world** созд|ава́ть, -а́ть но́вый мир

□ **~ up** *v.t.*: **~ sb up** (in health) укреп|ля́ть, -и́ть кому́-н. здоро́вье; (in prestige) популяризи́ровать (*impf., pf.*) кого́-н.; созд|ава́ть, -а́ть и́мя кому́-н.; **~ up a business** созд|ава́ть, -а́ть де́ло

● *v.i.*: **work has built up over the past year** за после́дний год накопи́лось мно́го рабо́ты

■ **~-up** *n.* (accumulation) скопле́ние; рост, разви́тие, нара́стывание; (infml, boosting) популяриза́ция, созда́ние и́мени

builder /'bɪldə(r)/ *n.* строи́тель (*m.*)

✧ **building** /'bɪldɪŋ/ *n.* **1** (structure) зда́ние, постро́йка, строе́ние; (premises) помеще́ние **2** (activity) (по)стро́йка; (esp. large-scale) строи́тельство

■ **~ site** *n.* стро́йка; **~ society** *n.* (BrE) (жили́щно-)строи́тельное о́бщество; ≈ ипоте́чный банк

built *past and p.p. of* ▶ **build**

■ **~-in** *adj.*: **a ~ cupboard** встро́енный/стенно́й шкаф; **~-up** *adj.*: **~ area** застро́енный райо́н

bulb /bʌlb/ *n.* (bot., anat.) лу́ковица; (of lamp) ла́мпочка

b

Bulgaria /bʌlˈgeərɪə/ n. Болга́рия

Bulgarian /bʌlˈgeərɪən/ n. (person) болга́р|ин (-ка); (language) болга́рский язы́к
● adj. болга́рский

bulge /bʌldʒ/ n. вы́пуклость
● v.i. (swell) выпя́чиваться, вы́пятиться; (of bag etc.) над|ува́ться, -у́ться

bulimia /bʊˈlɪmɪə/ n. булими́я

bulimic /bʊˈlɪmɪk/ adj. страда́ющий булими́ей

bulk /bʌlk/ n. **1** (size) величина́, ма́сса, объём **2** (greater part) основна́я ма́сса/часть
■ ~ buying n. опто́вые заку́пки

bulky /ˈbʌlkɪ/ adj. (**bulkier**, **bulkiest**) громо́здкий

bull /bʊl/ n. (ox) бык; (elephant, whale, etc.) саме́ц
■ ~dog n. бульдо́г; ~dozer n. бульдо́зер; ~fight n. бой быко́в; ~fighter n. тореадо́р; ~ring n. аре́на для бо́я быко́в; ~seye n. (of target) я́блочко

bullet /ˈbʊlɪt/ n. пу́ля
■ ~proof adj. пуленепробива́емый; ~proof vest бронежиле́т

bulletin /ˈbʊlɪtɪn/ n. (official statement) бюллете́нь (m.); (news report) сво́дка (новосте́й), вы́пуск, сообще́ние

bullock /ˈbʊlək/ n. вол

bully /ˈbʊlɪ/ n. громи́ла (m.), задира (c.g.)
● v.t. запу́г|ивать, -а́ть

bum /bʌm/ n. (infml) **1** (BrE, buttocks) зад, за́дница **2** (AmE, vagrant) бродя́га (m.)

bumblebee /ˈbʌmb(ə)lbiː/ n. шмель (m.)

bump /bʌmp/ n. **1** (thump) глухо́й уда́р; (collision) толчо́к **2** (swelling, protuberance) ши́шка
● v.t. уд|аря́ть, -а́рить; ушиб|а́ть, -и́ть; I ~ed my knee as I fell я уши́б коле́но при паде́нии
● v.i.: his car ~ed into ours его́ маши́на вре́залась в на́шу; I ~ed into him in London я наткну́лся на него́ в Ло́ндоне

bumper /ˈbʌmpə(r)/ n. **1** (of car) ба́мпер **2**: ~ crop небыва́лый/неви́данный урожа́й

bumpkin /ˈbʌmpkɪn/ n. мужла́н

bumptious /ˈbʌmpʃəs/ adj. самоуве́ренный, зазна́вшийся

bumpy /ˈbʌmpɪ/ adj. (**bumpier**, **bumpiest**) (of road) уха́бистый, тря́ский; a ~ flight ≈ болта́нка

bun /bʌn/ n. **1** (cul.) бу́лочка, плю́шка **2** (of hair) пучо́к

bunch /bʌntʃ/ n. **1** (of flowers) буке́т; (of grapes) кисть, гроздь; (of bananas) гроздь; ~ of keys свя́зка ключе́й **2** (infml, group) компа́ния, гру́ппа

bundle /ˈbʌnd(ə)l/ n. **1** (of clothes etc.) у́зел; (of sticks) вяза́нка; (of hay) оха́пка **2**: she is a ~ of nerves она́ о́чень не́рвная
● v.t. **1**: ~ up свя́з|ывать, -а́ть в у́зел/вяза́нку **2** (shove) запи́х|ивать, -а́ть

bung /bʌŋ/ n. заты́чка, втулка
● v.t. **1** (cask etc.) зат|ыка́ть, -кну́ть; закупо́ри|вать, -ть; the sink is ~ed up

ра́ковина засори́лась; my nose is ~ed up у меня́ заложен нос **2** (BrE, sl., throw) швыр|я́ть, -ну́ть

bungalow /ˈbʌŋgələʊ/ n. бу́нгало (nt. indecl.)

bungle /ˈbʌŋg(ə)l/ v.t. по́ртить, на-; пу́тать, с-

bunk¹ /bʌŋk/ n. (sleeping berth) ко́йка
■ ~ bed n. двухъя́русная крова́ть

bunk² /bʌŋk/ v.i. (BrE, infml, slip away) см|ыва́ться, -ы́ться; to ~ off lessons/school прог|у́ливать, -уля́ть уро́ки, сачкова́ть (impf.)

bunker /ˈbʌŋkə(r)/ n. (underground shelter) бу́нкер, блинда́ж; (golf) я́ма

buoy /bɔɪ/ n. буй, ба́кен; (life~) спаса́тельный буй/круг
● v.t.: ~ up (fig., support) подде́рж|ивать, -а́ть; (cheer up) подб|а́дривать, -одри́ть

buoyant /ˈbɔɪənt/ adj. плаву́чий; (of person) жизнера́достный; (of hopes, market) оживлённый; (of prices) име́ющий тенде́нцию к повыше́нию

burden /ˈbəːd(ə)n/ n. (load) но́ша, груз; (fig.) бре́мя (nt.); обу́за
● v.t. (load) нагру|жа́ть, -зи́ть; (fig.) обремен|я́ть, -и́ть

bureau /ˈbjʊərəʊ/ n. (pl. ~x or ~s) (BrE, desk) бюро́ (indecl.), конто́рка; (AmE, chest) комо́д; (office) бюро́; ~ de change обме́нный пункт

bureaucracy /bjʊəˈrɒkrəsɪ/ n. бюрокра́тия

bureaucrat /ˈbjʊərəkræt/ n. бюрокра́т, чино́вник

bureaucratic /bjʊərəˈkrætɪk/ adj. бюрократи́ческий

bureaux /ˈbjʊərəʊz/ pl. of ▶ bureau

burgeon /ˈbəːdʒ(ə)n/ v.i. да|ва́ть, -ть по́чки; распус|ка́ться, -ти́ться

burger /ˈbəːgə(r)/ n. га́мбургер, котле́та
■ ~ bar n. га́мбургерная, котле́тная

burglar /ˈbəːglə(r)/ n. кварти́рный вор, взло́мщик

burglarize /ˈbəːgləraɪz/ v.t. (AmE) = burgle

burglary /ˈbəːglərɪ/ n. ограбле́ние (до́ма/ о́фиса), кра́жа с взло́мом

burgle /ˈbəːg(ə)l/ v.t. гра́бить, о-

burial /ˈberɪəl/ n. погребе́ние, захороне́ние

burly /ˈbəːlɪ/ adj. (**burlier**, **burliest**) здорове́нный, дю́жий

Burma /ˈbəːmə/ n. Би́рма

burn /bəːn/ n. ожо́г
● v.t. (past and p.p. **burnt** or **burned**) (destroy by fire) сж|ига́ть, -ечь; ~ oneself обж|ига́ться, -е́чься; the meat is ~t мя́со сгоре́ло/подгоре́ло
● v.i. (past and p.p. **burnt** or **burned**) горе́ть (impf.)
□ ~ down v.t. сж|ига́ть, -ечь
● v.i.: the house ~t down дом сгоре́л дотла́
□ ~ out v.t.: the fire ~t itself out пожа́р вы́жег всё дотла́ и стих/костёр догоре́л (до угле́й) и поту́х; ~ oneself out (fig.) сгоре́ть (pf.)

burner /ˈbəːnə(r)/ n. **1** (of stove etc.) горе́лка, конфо́рка; to put on the back burner отодвиг|а́ть, -и́нуть на за́дний план **2** (for CDs/DVDs) (CD/DVD-)реза́к (sl.) (*устро́йство для за́писи информа́ции на компа́кт-диск*)

burning /'bɜːnɪŋ/ *n.* горе́ние
● *adj.* (of fever) сжига́ющий; (of shame) жгу́чий; (of zeal) нои́стовый

burnt /bɜːnt/ *past and p.p. of* ▶ **burn**

burp /bɜːp/ (infml) *n.* отры́жка, рыга́ние
● *v.i.* рыг|а́ть, -ну́ть

burrow /'bʌrəʊ/ *n.* нора́
● *v.i.* рыть, вы́- нору; рыть, про- ходы́

bursary /'bɜːsərɪ/ *n.* (BrE, grant) стипе́ндия

burst /bɜːst/ *n.* взрыв; а ~ of energy вспы́шка/взрыв эне́ргии; ~ of applause взрыв аплодисме́нтов; ~ of machine-gun fire пулемётная о́чередь
● *v.t.* (*past and p.p.* **burst**) разрыва́ть, -орва́ть; the river ~ its banks река́ вы́шла из берего́в
● *v.i.* (*past and p.p.* **burst**): the balloon ~ возду́шный шар ло́пнул; he is ~ing with health он пы́шет здоро́вьем; he was ~ing with pride его распира́ло от го́рдости; the door ~ open дверь распахну́лась
● *with preps.*: ~ into tears разрыда́ться (*pf.*); ~ into a room врыва́ться, ворва́ться в ко́мнату; ~ into flame(s) вспы́х|ивать, -нуть
□ ~ **out** *v.i.* (exclaim) вы́палить (*pf.*); ~ out laughing расхохота́ться (*pf.*)

bury /'berɪ/ *v.t.* **1** (inter) хорони́ть, по- **2** (hide in earth) зар|ыва́ть, -ы́ть

ℐ **bus** /bʌs/ *n.* (*pl.* **buses** or AmE **busses**) авто́бус
■ ~ **conductor** *n.* конду́ктор авто́буса; ~ **driver** *n.* води́тель (*m.*) авто́буса; ~ **station** *n.* авто́бусная ста́нция; ~ **stop** *n.* авто́бусная остано́вка

bush /bʊʃ/ *n.* (shrub) куст; (wild land) некультиви́рованная земля́

bushy /'bʊʃɪ/ *adj.* (**bushier, bushiest**) (of beard etc.) густо́й; (of plant) кусти́стый; (of tail) пуши́стый

ℐ **business** /'bɪznɪs/ *n.* **1** (affair) де́ло; it is none of your ~ э́то не ва́ше де́ло; э́то вас не каса́ется; mind your own ~ не вме́шивайтесь/су́йтесь не в своё де́ло **2** (work): get down to ~ бра́ться, взя́ться за де́ло **3** (comm. etc.): ~ hours, hours of ~ (of an office) часы́ приёма/заня́тий/рабо́ты; he is in the wool ~ он занима́ется торго́влей шерстью; go into ~ заня́ться (*pf.*) комме́рцией; on ~ по де́лу **4** (establishment) фи́рма, предприя́тие
■ ~ **card** *n.* визи́тка, визи́тная ка́рточка; ~**like** *adj.* делово́й, практи́чный; ~**man** *n.* коммерса́нт, бизнесме́н, деле́ц; ~**woman** *n.* бизнес-ле́ди, бизнесву́мен (*both f. indecl.*), делова́я же́нщина

busker /'bʌskə(r)/ *n.* у́личный музыка́нт

busses /'bʌsɪz/ (AmE) *pl. of* ▶ **bus**

bust[1] /bʌst/ *n.* (sculpture; bosom) бюст

bust[2] /bʌst/ (infml) *v.t.* (*past and p.p.* **busted** *or* **bust**) (fracture, destroy) лома́ть, с-
● *v.i.* (*past and p.p.* **busted** *or* **bust**) лома́ться, с-; (*also* **go** ~) the business went

~ де́ло ло́пнуло

bustle /'bʌs(ə)l/ *n.* сумато́ха, суета́
● *v.i.* (*also* ~ **about**) суети́ться, тормоши́ться (*both impf.*)

bustling /'bʌslɪŋ/ *adj.* суетли́вый; а ~ city оживлённый го́род

ℐ **busy** /'bɪzɪ/ *adj.* (**busier, busiest**)
1 (occupied) за́нятый; I had a ~ day я весь день был за́нят упако́вкой; he was ~ packing он был за́нят упако́вкой; the line is ~ (AmE) но́мер за́нят **2**: а ~ street шу́мная/оживлённая у́лица
● *v.t.*: ~ oneself зан|има́ться, -я́ться

ℐ **but** /bʌt/ *adv.*: we can ~ try попы́тка — не пы́тка
● *prep. & conj.* (except): no one ~ me никто́, кроме меня́; she is anything ~ beautiful она́ далеко́ не краса́вица; the last ~ one предпосле́дний; next door ~ one че́рез одну́ дверь; ~ for me he would have stayed е́сли бы не я, он бы оста́лся; I cannot help ~ think … я не могу́ не ду́мать, что…
● *conj.* но

butcher /'bʊtʃə(r)/ *n.* мясни́к; ~'s (shop) мясна́я ла́вка, мясно́й павильо́н
● *v.t.* (cattle) забива́ть (*impf.*); (people) истреб|ля́ть, -и́ть

butchery /'bʊtʃərɪ/ *n.* (trade) торго́вля мя́сом; (massacre) резня́

butler /'bʌtlə(r)/ *n.* дворе́цкий

butt[1] /bʌt/ *n.* (fig., target): a ~ for ridicule мише́нь для насме́шек

butt[2] /bʌt/ *n.* (of rifle) прикла́д; (of cigarette) оку́рок; (AmE, infml, buttocks) зад, за́дница

butt[3] /bʌt/ *v.i.*: ~ in (interrupt) встр|ева́ть, -я́ть

butter /'bʌtə(r)/ *n.* ма́сло
● *v.t.* нама́з|ывать, -ать ма́слом; ~ up (fig.) льсти́ть, по- + *d.*
■ ~**cup** *n.* лю́тик; ~**fingers** *n.* растя́па (*c.g.*)

butterfly /'bʌtəflaɪ/ *n.* **1** ба́бочка; I have butterflies in my stomach у меня́ се́рдце ёкает **2** (swimming): ~ stroke баттерфля́й

buttock /'bʌtək/ *n.* я́годица

button /'bʌt(ə)n/ *n.* **1** пу́говица **2** (knob) кно́пка; press a ~ наж|има́ть, -а́ть кно́пку **3** (AmE, badge) значо́к
● *v.t.* (*also* ~ **up**) застёг|ивать, -ну́ть
■ ~**hole** *n.* петля́, петли́ца; (BrE, flower) цвето́к в петли́це ● *v.t.* (fig.) заде́рж|ивать, -а́ть разгово́ром

buttress /'bʌtrɪs/ *n.* (archit.) подпо́р(к)а; (fig.) опо́ра

ℐ **buy** /baɪ/ *n.*: a good ~ вы́годная поку́пка
● *v.t.* (**buys, buying**, *past and p.p.* **bought**) покупа́ть, купи́ть; ~ sb a drink ста́вить, по- кому́-н. вы́пивку
□ ~ **off** *v.t.* откуп|а́ться, -и́ться (*от кого́*)
□ ~ **out** *v.t.*: ~ sb out выкупа́ть, вы́купить чью-н. до́лю
□ ~ **up** *v.t.* скуп|а́ть, -и́ть
■ ~**out** *n.* (comm.) вы́куп

buyer /'baɪə(r)/ *n.* покупа́тель (*m.*)

buzz /bʌz/ *n.* жужжа́ние; (of talk) гул, жужжа́ние

● *v.t.* (summon with buzzer) звони́ть, по-; вызыва́ть, вы́звать сигна́лом

● *v.i.* (of insect, projectile) жужжа́ть (*impf.*)

buzzard /'bʌzəd/ *n.* сары́ч, каню́к; (AmE, turkey vulture) гриф-инде́йка

buzzer /'bʌzə(r)/ *n.* (elec.) зу́ммер

✔ **by** /baɪ/ *adv.* (near) побли́зости; (alongside) ря́дом; (past) ми́мо; **the days went ~** дни шли оди́н за други́м

● *prep.* **1** (near): **sit ~ the fire** сиде́ть (*impf.*) у ками́на; **I was going ~ the house** я шёл ми́мо до́ма; **~ oneself** (alone) (соверше́нно) оди́н/одна́; (unaided) сам/сама́, самостоя́тельно; **a path ~ the river** доро́жка у/вдоль реки́; **~ the way** кста́ти **2** (along, via): **~ land and sea** по су́ше и по мо́рю; **~ the nearest road** ближа́йшей доро́гой **3** (of time limit): **~ Thursday** к четвергу́; **~ now** тепе́рь; **he should know ~ now** пора́ бы уж ему́ зна́ть; **~ then** к тому́ вре́мени **4** (means) (*often expr. by i. case*) (**~ means of**) при по́мощи + *g.*; **a book ~ Tolstoy** кни́га Толсто́го; **~ my watch** по мои́м часа́м; **~ rail** по желе́зной доро́ге; **~ taxi** на/в такси́; **~ law** по зако́ну; **a letter written ~ hand** письмо́, напи́санное от руки́ **5** (of rate or measurement): **little ~ little** ма́ло-пома́лу; **bread came down in price ~**1

rouble хлеб подешеве́л на оди́н рубль; **sell sth ~ the yard** прод|ава́ть, -а́ть с я́рды; **one ~ one** оди́н за други́м; по одному́, поодино́чке; **day ~ day** день за днём; **you must divide thirty ~ five** вам на́до раздели́ть 30 на́ 5; **a room 13 feet ~ 12** ко́мната трина́дцать фу́тов на двена́дцать

bye-bye /'baɪbaɪ, bə'baɪ/ *int.* пока́!; всего́ хоро́шего!

by-election /'baɪlekʃ(ə)n/ *n.* (BrE) дополни́тельные вы́боры (*m. pl.*)

bygone /'baɪgɒn/ *n.* (*usu. in pl.*): **let ~s be ~s** что бы́ло, то прошло́

● *adj.* проше́дший, мину́вший

bypass /'baɪpaːs/ *n.* объе́зд, обхо́д; (med.) шунт; **heart ~** корона́рное шунти́рование

● *v.t.* об|ходи́ть, -ойти́ (also fig.)

by-product /'baɪprɒdʌkt/ *n.* побо́чный проду́кт

bystander /'baɪstændə(r)/ *n.* зри́тель (*m.*)

byte /baɪt/ *n.* (comput.) байт

Byzantine /baɪ'zæntaɪn/ *adj.* (lit., fig.) византи́йский

■ **~ Empire** *n.* Византи́я, Византи́йская импе́рия

Byzantium /bɪ'zæntɪəm/ *n.* (city) Виза́нтий

Cc

C¹ /siː/ *n.* **1** (mus.) до (*nt. indecl.*) **2** (academic mark) «удовлетвори́тельно», тро́йка

C² /siː/ *n.* (abbr. of **Celsius** or **centigrade**) C (= *градусов по Цельсию*)

c. *abbr. of* **1** (**century**) в. (век); столе́тие **2** (**circa**) ок. (о́коло) **3** (**cent(s)**) цент(ы)

cab /kæb/ *n.* **1** (taxi) такси́ (*nt. indecl.*); кеб **2** (of lorry etc.) каби́на води́теля

■ **~ driver** *n.* шофёр такси́

cabaret /'kæbəreɪ/ *n.* кабаре́ (*nt. indecl.*), эстра́дное представле́ние

cabbage /'kæbɪdʒ/ *n.* капу́ста

cabby /'kæbɪ/ *n.* (infml) такси́ст

cabin /'kæbɪn/ *n.* каби́на; (in ship etc.) каю́та

cabinet /'kæbɪnɪt/ *n.* **1** (piece of furniture) го́рка, (застеклённый) шкаф(чик) **2** (pol.) кабине́т (мини́стров)

cable /'keɪb(ə)l/ *n.* (elec.) ка́бель (*m.*)

■ **~ TV** *n.* ка́бельное телеви́дение

cackle /'kæk(ə)l/ *v.t. & i.* гогота́ть

cactus /'kæktəs/ *n.* (*pl.* **cacti** /-taɪ/ or **cactuses**) ка́ктус

✔ ключева́я ле́ксика

CAD *abbr.* (*of* **computer-aided design**) автоматизи́рованное проекти́рование

caddy /'kædɪ/ *n.* ча́йница

cadet /kə'det/ *n.* (mil.) каде́т, курса́нт

cadge /kædʒ/ *v.t. & i.* выкля́нчивать, вы́клянчить; (infml) стрел|я́ть, -ьну́ть (*что у кого*)

Caesarean /sɪ'zeərɪən/ (AmE *also* **Cesarean**) *adj.*: **~ birth, operation, section** ке́сарево сече́ние

✔ **cafe** /'kæfeɪ/ *n.* кафе́ (*nt. indecl.*)

cafeteria /kæfɪ'tɪərɪə/ *n.* кафете́рий

caffeine /'kæfiːn/ *n.* кофеи́н

cage /keɪdʒ/ *n.* кле́тка

Cairo /'kaɪrəʊ/ *n.* Каи́р

cajole /kə'dʒəʊl/ *v.t.* обха́живать (*impf.*)

✔ **cake** /keɪk/ *n.* **1** (sponge ~) кекс; (with cream) торт **2** (fig.): **a piece of ~** (infml) пустяко́вое де́ло

calamity /kə'læmɪtɪ/ *n.* бе́дствие

calcium /'kælsɪəm/ *n.* ка́льций

calculate /'kælkjʊleɪt/ *v.t.* **1** (compute) вычисля́ть, вы́числить **2** (estimate) рассчи́т|ывать, -а́ть **3** (plan): **a ~ed risk** обду́манный риск

calculating /'kælkjʊleɪtɪŋ/ *adj.* расчётливый, себе на уме

calculation /kælkjʊ'leɪʃ(ə)n/ *n.* вычисление

calculator /'kælkjʊleɪtə(r)/ *n.* калькулятор

Calcutta /kæl'kʌtə/ *n.* Калькутта

calendar /'kælɪndə(r)/ *n.* календарь

calf¹ /kɑːf/ *n.* (*pl.* **calves**) (of cattle) телёнок
■ ~**skin** *n.* опоек

calf² /kɑːf/ *n.* (*pl.* **calves**) (of leg) икра

calibrate /'kælɪbreɪt/ *v.t.* калибровать (*impf.*, *pf.*), градуировать (*impf.*, *pf.*)

calibre /'kælɪbə(r)/ (AmE **caliber**) *n.* калибр

California /kælɪ'fɔːnɪə/ *n.* Калифорния

⚬ **call** /kɔːl/ *n.* **1** (cry) зов, оклик **2** (of bird) крик **3** (teleph.): **telephone** ~ звонок по телефону **4** (visit): **pay a** ~ нан|осить, -ести визит **5** (summons, demand) зов, клич, призыв; **the doctor is on** ~ врач на вызове **6** (need): **there is no** ~ **for** him to worry ему нечего волноваться
● *v.t.* **1** (name) назыв|ать, -вать; **he is** ~**ed John** его зовут Джон(ом); ~ **a strike** приз|ывать, -вать к забастовке **2** (summon): ~ **a doctor/taxi!** вызовите врача/такси! **3** (announce): ~ **a meeting** соз|ывать, -вать собрание
● *v.i.* **1** (cry) звать, по-; окл|икать, -икнуть **2** (visit) за|ходить, -йти; **I** ~**ed on him** я зашёл к нему; **the train** ~**s at every station** поезд останавливается на каждой станции **3** ~ **for** (pick up): **I** ~**ed for him at 6** я зашёл за ним в 6 часов; (demand): **the situation** ~**s for courage** обстоятельства требуют мужества **4** ~ **on: the president** ~**ed on the world community for help** президент призвал на помощь мировое сообщество
□ ~ **back** *v.t. & i.* (on telephone) позвонить (*pf.*) снова + *d.*
□ ~ **in** *v.t.* (a specialist) вызывать, вызвать
□ ~ **off** *v.t.* (cancel) отмен|ять, -ить
□ ~ **out** *v.t.* (summon away) от|зывать, -озвать; (doctor) вызыв|ать, вызвать
● *v.i.* выклик|ать, выкликнуть
□ ~ **up** *v.t.* (telephone) звони́ть, по- (*кому*) по телефону; (evoke) вызыв|ать, вызвать; (for mil. service) приз|ывать, -вать
■ ~ **box** *n.* (BrE) телефонная будка; ~ **centre** *n.* колл-центр, информационно-справочная служба

caller /'kɔːlə(r)/ *n.* (visitor) посетитель (-ница); (telephone) позвонивший (по телефону)

calligraphy /kə'lɪgrəfɪ/ *n.* каллиграфия

callous /'kæləs/ *adj.* чёрствый

calm /kɑːm/ *n.* спокойствие, тишина
● *adj.* спокойный
● *v.t. & i.* (*also* ~ **down**) успок|аивать(ся), -оить(ся)

calorie /'kælərɪ/ *n.* калория

calves /kɑːvz/ *pl. of* ▸ **calf¹**, ▸ **calf²**

camaraderie /kæmə'rɑːdərɪ/ *n.* товарищеские отношения

Cambodia /kæm'bəʊdɪə/ *n.* Камбоджа

Cambodian /kæm'bəʊdɪən/ *n.* (person) камбоджи|ец (-йка)

● *adj.* камбоджийский

camcorder /'kæmkɔːdə(r)/ *n.* портативная видеокамера

came /keɪm/ *past of* ▸ **come**

camel /'kæm(ə)l/ *n.* верблюд

camellia /kə'miːlɪə/ *n.* камелия

⚬ **camera** /'kæmrə/ *n.* фотоаппарат
■ ~**man** *n.* оператор; ~ **phone** *n.* камерофон, мобильный телефон с фото-/видео|камерой

camomile /'kæməmaɪl/ *n.* ромашка

camouflage /'kæməflɑːʒ/ *n.* маскировка
● *v.t.* маскировать, за-

⚬ **camp¹** /kæmp/ *n.* лагерь
● *v.i.* (pitch camp) разб|ивать, -ить лагерь
■ ~ **bed** *n.* (BrE) раскладушка; ~**fire** *n.* походный костёр; ~**site** *n.* кемпинг, турбаза

camp² /kæmp/ *adj.* женоподобный

⚬ **campaign** /kæm'peɪn/ *n.* кампания
● *v.i.* участвовать (*impf.*) в походе; (fig.) вести (*det.*) кампанию

campaigner /kæm'peɪnə(r)/ *n.* участник кампании

camper /'kæmpə(r)/ *n.* (person) ночующий на открытом воздухе; (vehicle) (BrE *also* ~ **van**) автодом (*автомобиль, не прицеп*); (AmE) жилой/туристский автоприцеп

camping /'kæmpɪŋ/ *n.* кемпинг; **go** ~ жить (*impf.*) в палатках

campus /'kæmpəs/ *n.* (*pl.* ~**es**) университетский городок

can¹ /kæn/ *n.* **1** (for liquids) бидон **2** (for food) (консервная) банка
● *v.t.* (**canned**, **canning**) консервировать (*impf.*, *pf.*)
■ ~ **opener** *n.* консервный нож

⚬ **can²** /kæn/ *v.i.* (*3rd pers. sg. pres.* **can**, *past* **could**, *neg.* **cannot**, **can't**) (expr. ability or permission) мочь (*impf.*); (expr. capability) уметь (*impf.*); **he can't clean his teeth yet** он ещё не умеет чистить зубы; **I** ~ **see him** я вижу его; **I** ~ **understand that** я понимаю (*or* могу понять) это; **as soon as you** ~ как только сможете; как можно скорее

Canada /'kænədə/ *n.* Канада

⚬ **Canadian** /kə'neɪdɪən/ *n.* (person) канад|ец (-ка)
● *adj.* канадский

canal /kə'næl/ *n.* канал

canary /kə'neərɪ/ *n.* канарейка
■ **C**~ **Islands** *n. pl.* Канарские острова

Canberra /'kænbərə/ *n.* Канберра

cancel /'kæns(ə)l/ *v.t.* (**cancelled**, **cancelling**, AmE *also* **canceled**, **canceling**) отмен|ять, -ить. (*impf.*)

cancellation /kænsə'leɪʃ(ə)n/ *n.* отмена, аннулирование

⚬ **cancer** /'kænsə(r)/ *n.* **1** (med.) рак **2** (**C**~) (astron., astrol.) Рак

candid /'kændɪd/ *adj.* искренний

⚬ **candidate** /'kændɪdət/ *n.* кандидат

candle /'kænd(ə)l/ *n.* свеча
■ ~**light** *n.* свет свечи/свечей; ~**stick** *n.* подсвечник

candour /'kændə(r)/ (AmE **candor**)
n. открове́нность, и́скренность;
беспристра́стность

candy /'kændɪ/ *n.* (AmE) конфе́ты, сла́сти (*f. pl.*)

cane /keɪn/ *n.* **1** (bot.) камы́ш, тростни́к **2** (for punishment) ро́зга

canine /'keɪnaɪn/ *adj.* соба́чий
■ ~ **tooth** *n.* клык

cannabis /'kænəbɪs/ *n.* (resin) гаши́ш; (dried leaves) анаша́, марихуа́на

cannibal /'kænɪb(ə)l/ *n.* канниба́л

cannibalism /'kænɪbəlɪz(ə)m/ *n.*
каннибали́зм, людое́дство

cannon /'kænən/ *n.* пу́шка, ору́дие
■ ~**ball** *n.* пу́шечное ядро́

⚷ **cannot** /'kænɒt, kə'nɒt/ *neg. of* ▸ **can²**

canoe /kə'nu:/ *n.* кано́э (*nt. indecl.*)
● *v.i.* (**canoes, canoed, canoeing**) плыть (*det.*) в челноке́ (*or* на кано́э)

canopy /'kænəpɪ/ *n.* **1** (covering over bed etc.) балдахи́н, по́лог **2** (of parachute) ку́пол **3** (fig.) по́лог, покро́в

⚷ **can't** /'kɑ:nt/ *neg. of* ▸ **can²**

cantankerous /kæn'tæŋkərəs/ *adj.*
сварли́вый

canteen /kæn'ti:n/ *n.* **1** (eating place) столо́вая **2** (water container) фля́га

canter /'kæntə(r)/ *v.i.* е́хать (*impf.*) лёгким гало́пом

canvas /'kænvəs/ *n.* холст

canvass /'kænvəs/ *v.t. & i.:* ~ **a constituency**
вести́ (*det.*) предвы́борную агита́цию
в избира́тельном о́круге; ~ **opinions**
соб|ира́ть, -ра́ть мне́ния

canvasser /'kænvəsə(r)/ *n.* агита́тор

canyon /'kænjən/ *n.* каньо́н

cap /kæp/ *n.* **1** (of uniform) фура́жка; (baseball ~) ке́пка **2** (of bottle) кры́шка; (of pen) колпачо́к
● *v.t.* (**capped, capping**) (excel)
прев|осходи́ть, -зойти́; **to** ~ **it all** в
доверше́ние ко всему́

capability /keɪpə'bɪlɪtɪ/ *n.* спосо́бность

⚷ **capable** /'keɪpəb(ə)l/ *adj.* **1** (gifted) спосо́бный **2**: ~ **of** спосо́бный на + *a.*

capacious /kə'peɪʃəs/ *adj.* просто́рный

⚷ **capacity** /kə'pæsɪtɪ/ *n.* **1** (ability to hold)
вмести́мость; **the hall's seating** ~ **is 500**
вмести́мость за́ла — пятьсо́т мест; **the room was filled to** ~ ко́мната была́ запо́лнена до отка́за **2** (of engine) (наибо́льшая) мо́щность **3** (position): **in my** ~ **as critic** как кри́тик

cape¹ /keɪp/ *n.* (garment) наки́дка, плащ

cape² /keɪp/ *n.* (geog.) мыс

capers /'keɪpəz/ *n. pl.* (cul.) ка́персы (*m. pl.*)

capillary /kə'pɪlərɪ/ *adj.* капилля́рный
■ ~ **action** *n.* капилля́рное притяже́ние,
капилля́рность

⚷ **capital** /'kæpɪt(ə)l/ *n.* **1** (principal city) столи́ца **2** (upper-case letter) прописна́я/загла́вная

бу́ква **3** (wealth) капита́л
● *adj.* **1** (involving death penalty): ~ **punishment**
сме́ртная казнь **2** (econ.): ~ **expenditure**
капита́льные затра́ты **3** (upper-case)
прописно́й

capitalism /'kæpɪtəlɪz(ə)m/ *n.* капитали́зм

capitalist /'kæpɪtəlɪst/ *n.* капитали́ст
● *adj.* капиталисти́ческий

capitalize /'kæpɪtəlaɪz/ *v.t.* & *i.:* ~ **on sb's misfortune** наж|ива́ться, -и́ться на чьём-н.
несча́стье

capitulate /kə'pɪtjʊleɪt/ *v.t.* капитули́ровать
(*impf., pf.*)

cappuccino /kæpʊ'tʃi:nəʊ/ *n.* (*pl.* ~**s**)
капуч(ч)и́но (*m. & nt. indecl.*)

capricious /kə'prɪʃəs/ *adj.* прихотли́вый,
капри́зный

Capricorn /'kæprɪkɔ:n/ *n.* Козеро́г

capsize /kæp'saɪz/ *v.t. & i.* опроки́|дывать(ся),
-нуть(ся)

capsule /'kæpsju:l/ *n.* (med.) ка́псула

captain /'kæptɪn/ *n.* **1** (head of team) капита́н
кома́нды **2** (army rank) капита́н **3** (naval rank)
капита́н пе́рвого ра́нга

caption /'kæpʃ(ə)n/ *n.* (title) по́дпись к
карти́нке

captivating /'kæptɪveɪtɪŋ/ *adj.* плени́тельный

captive /'kæptɪv/ *n.* пле́нник, пле́нный

captivity /kæp'tɪvɪtɪ/ *n.* плен, пленéние

⚷ **capture** /'kæptʃə(r)/ *n.* пои́мка, захва́т
● *v.t.* брать, взять в плен; ~ **sb's attention**
прико́в|ывать, -а́ть чьё-н. внима́ние

⚷ **car** /kɑ:(r)/ *n.* (легково́й) автомоби́ль, маши́на
■ ~ **boot sale** *n.* (BrE) прода́жа (пря́мо) из
бага́жника; ~ **ferry** *n.* автопаро́м; ~ **hire** *n.*
прока́т автомоби́лей; ~ **park** *n.* (BrE) па́ркинг,
автостоя́нка; ~**sick** *adj.*: **do you get** ~**sick?**
вас ука́чивает в маши́не?

carafe /kə'ræf/ *n.* графи́н

caramel /'kærəmel/ *n.* караме́ль

carat /'kærət/ (AmE *also* **karat**) *n.* кара́т

caravan /'kærəvæn/ *n.* (horse-drawn) фурго́н,
кры́тая теле́га; (BrE, trailer) жило́й/тури́стский
автоприце́п, тре́йлер
● *v.i.* (**caravanned, caravanning**) (BrE):
go ~**ning** путеше́ствовать (*impf.*) в тре́йлере

caraway /'kærəweɪ/ *n.* тмин
■ ~ **seed** *n.* тми́нное се́мя

carbohydrate /kɑ:bə'haɪdreɪt/ *n.* углево́д

carbon /'kɑ:bən/ *n.* **1** (element) углеро́д **2**: ~
copy (fig.) (то́чная) ко́пия
■ ~ **dioxide** *n.* углеки́слый газ; ~
monoxide *n.* уга́рный газ; ~**-neutral** *adj.*
углеро́дно-нейтра́льный; ~ **offsetting**
n. компенсацио́нное сниже́ние вы́бросов
двуо́киси углеро́да

carburettor /kɑ:bə'retə(r)/ (AmE
carburetor) *n.* карбюра́тор

carcass /'kɑ:kəs/ *n.* **1** (of animal) ту́ша; ~
meat (BrE) парно́е мя́со **2** (of building, ship, etc.)
карка́с, о́стов, ко́рпус

carcinogenic /kɑ:sɪnə'dʒenɪk/ *adj.*
канцероге́нный

⚷ ключевая лексика

carcinoma /ˌkɑːsɪˈnəʊmə/ *n.* (*pl.* ~s *or* ~ta) карцинóма, рáковое новообразовáние

♂ **card** /kɑːd/ *n.* **1** (material) картóн; (piece) кáрточка; (postcard) откры́тка **2** (playing ~) игрáльная кáрта; **play** ~s игрáть, сыгрáть в кáрты

cardboard /ˈkɑːdbɔːd/ *n.* картóн

■ ~ **box** *n.* картóнная корóбка

cardiac /ˈkɑːdɪæk/ *adj.* сердéчный

■ ~ **arrest** *n.* останóвка сéрдца

cardigan /ˈkɑːdɪgən/ *n.* шерстянáя кóфта, кардигáн; (man's) вя́заная кýртка

cardinal /ˈkɑːdɪn(ə)l/ *n.* (eccl.) кардинáл

● *adj.* (principal) кардинáльный; **a matter of** ~ **importance** дéло чрезвычáйной вáжности

■ ~ **number** *n.* колúчественное числúтельное

cardiologist /ˌkɑːdɪˈɒlədʒɪst/ *n.* кардиóлог

cardiology /ˌkɑːdɪˈɒlədʒɪ/ *n.* кардиолóгия

♂ **care** /keə(r)/ *n.* **1** (serious attention) осторóжность; **handle this with** ~ обращáйтесь с э́тим осторóжно; **take** ~ **you don't fall** смотрúте, не упадúте **2** (charge) забóта, попечéние; **take a child into** ~ (BrE) взять (*pf.*) ребёнка под опéку госудáрства **3** (anxiety): **free from** ~ свобóдный от забóт

● *v.i.* **1** (feel anxiety): **I don't** ~ **what they say** мне всё равнó, что онú скáжут; **who** ~**s?** не всё ли равнó?; **I couldn't** ~ **less** (infml) мне-то что?; мне наплевáть **2** (feel inclination): **would you** ~ **for a walk?** не хотúте ли пойтú погуля́ть? **3** (look after): **he is well** ~**d for** за ним хорóший ухóд

■ ~**free** *adj.* беззабóтный; ~**taker** *n.* стóрож, смотрúтель (*m.*) здáния

♂ **career** /kəˈrɪə(r)/ *n.* карьéра, профéссия

● *v.i.* мчáться (*impf.*)

careful /ˈkeəfʊl/ *adj.* **1** (attentive) осторóжный; **be** ~ **not to fall** бýдьте осторóжны, не упадúте; **he is** ~ **with his money** он не трáтит дéнег зря **2** (of work) тщáтельный

careless /ˈkeəlɪs/ *adj.* (thoughtless) неосторóжный; **a** ~ **mistake** ошúбка по невнимáтельности; (negligent) небрéжный

carer /ˈkeərə(r)/ *n.* (BrE) человéк, ухáживающий за ребёнком, больны́м, инвалúдом *и т. д.*

caress /kəˈres/ *v.t.* ласкáть (*impf.*)

cargo /ˈkɑːgəʊ/ *n.* (*pl.* ~**es** *or* ~**s**) груз

■ ~ **ship** *n.* торгóвое сýдно

Caribbean /ˌkærɪˈbiːən, kəˈrɪbɪən/ *adj.* карúбский; (*as n.*) **the** ~ (**Sea**) Карúбское мóре

caricature /ˈkærɪkətjʊə(r)/ *n.* карикатýра

caring /ˈkeərɪŋ/ *adj.* забóтливый

carnage /ˈkɑːnɪdʒ/ *n.* бóйня

carnation /kɑːˈneɪʃ(ə)n/ *n.* гвоздúка (*декоративное растение*)

carnival /ˈkɑːnɪv(ə)l/ *n.* (annual merrymaking) ежегóдный карнавáл; (Shrovetide) Мáсленица

carnivore /ˈkɑːnɪvɔː(r)/ *n.* плотоя́дное/ хúщное живóтное

carnivorous /kɑːˈnɪvərəs/ *adj.* плотоя́дный

carol /ˈkær(ə)l/ *n.* ≈ коля́дка; рождéственская пéсня

■ ~**-singing** *n.* рождéственские песнопéния; ≈ коля́дки

carousel /ˌkærəˈsel/ *n.* карусéль

carpenter /ˈkɑːpɪntə(r)/ *n.* плóтник

carpentry /ˈkɑːpɪntrɪ/ *n.* (occupation) плóтничество, плóтницкое дéло

carpet /ˈkɑːpɪt/ *n.* ковёр

● *v.t.* (**carpeted**, **carpeting**) уст|илáть, -лáть коврáми

carriage /ˈkærɪdʒ/ *n.* **1** (road vehicle) экипáж **2** (BrE, of train) пассажúрский вагóн **3** (BrE, transport of goods) перевóзка, достáвка

■ ~**way** *n.* (BrE) проéзжая часть (дорóги)

carrier /ˈkærɪə(r)/ *n.* **1** (transport agent) транспортёр **2** (of disease) перенóсчик (болéзни)

■ ~ **bag** *n.* (BrE) сýмка для покýпок

carrot /ˈkærət/ *n.* морквь

♂ **carry** /ˈkærɪ/ *v.t.* **1** (transport) носúть (*indet.*), нестú (*det.*); (of or by vehicle) возúть (*indet.*), везтú(*det.*); **pipes** ~ **water** водá идёт по трубáм; **wires** ~ **sound** звук передаётся по проводáм; **what weight will the bridge** ~? на какóй вес рассчúтан э́тот мост? **2** (have): **I always** ~ **an umbrella** (**money**) **with me** у меня́ всегдá с собóй зóнтик (всегдá при себé есть дéньги); **this crime carries a heavy penalty** э́то преступлéние влечёт за собóй тяжёлое наказáние

● *v.i.*: **the shot carried 200 yards** снаря́д пролетéл 200 я́рдов

□ ~ **away** *v.t.* (fig.): **he was carried away by his feelings** он оказáлся во влáсти чувств; он увлёкся

□ ~ **forward, over** *vv.t.* (transfer) перен|осúть, -естú

□ ~ **off** *v.t.* (remove) ун|осúть, -естú; **he carried the situation off well** он удáчно вы́шел из положéния

□ ~ **on** *v.t.* (conduct, perform): ~ **on a conversation/ business** вестú (*det.*) разговóр/дéло

● *v.i.* (continue) прод|олжáть, -óлжить; ~ **on with your work** продолжáйте рабóту; (talk, behave excitedly) волновáться (*impf.*)

□ ~ **out** *v.t.* (execute) выполня́ть, вы́полнить

■ ~**cot** *n.* (BrE) переноснáя дéтская кровáтка

cart /kɑːt/ *n.* телéжка

■ ~**wheel** *n.* колесó телéги; **turn** ~**wheels** кувыркáться, -нýться колесóм

carte blanche /ˌkɑːt ˈblɑ̃ʃ/ *n.* карт-блáнш (*m. indecl.*)

cartel /kɑːˈtel/ *n.* (comm.) картéль (*m.*)

cartilage /ˈkɑːtɪlɪdʒ/ *n.* хрящ

cartographer /kɑːˈtɒɡrəfə(r)/ *n.* картóграф

cartography /kɑːˈtɒɡrəfɪ/ *n.* картогрáфия

carton /ˈkɑːt(ə)n/ *n.* (large box) картóнка; (for milk etc.) пакéт

cartoon /kɑːˈtuːn/ *n.* (in newspaper) карикатýра; (film) мультфúльм

cartoonist /kɑːˈtuːnɪst/ *n.* карикатурúст

cartridge /ˈkɑːtrɪdʒ/ *n.* (mil.) патрóн; (for printer) кáртридж; (for camera) кассéта

carve /kɑːv/ *v.t.* (cut) рéзать (*impf.*); (shape by cutting): ~ **a statue out of wood** вы́резать, вы́резать ста́тую из де́рева; **he** ~**d out a career for himself** он сде́лал карье́ру; ~ **meat** ре́зать, на- мя́со

□ ~ **up** *v.t.* (fig.) разде́л|ять, -и́ть

carving /ˈkɑːvɪŋ/ *n.* (object) резна́я рабо́та, резьба́

[♂] **cascade** /kæsˈkeɪd/ *n.* каска́д; водопа́д
● *v.i.* па́дать/ниспада́ть (*both impf.*) каска́дом

[♂] **case**[1] /keɪs/ *n.* **1** (instance) слу́чай, обстоя́тельство, де́ло; **in that** ~ в тако́м/ э́том слу́чае; **in any** ~ во вся́ком слу́чае; **in** ~ **of fire** в слу́чае пожа́ра **2** (med.) слу́чай, заболева́ние **3** (hypothesis): **take an umbrella in** ~ **it rains** (*or* **in** ~ **of rain**) возьми́те зо́нтик на слу́чай дождя́; **just in** ~ на вся́кий слу́чай **4** (law) суде́бное де́ло **5** (gram.) паде́ж
■ ~ **history** *n.* (med.) исто́рия боле́зни

[♂] **case**[2] /keɪs/ *n.* (container) я́щик, ларе́ц, коро́бка; (for spectacles, violin, etc.) футля́р; (BrE, suitcase) чемода́н; **glass** ~ витри́на

[♂] **cash** /kæʃ/ *n.* нали́чные (де́ньги (*pl.*, *g.* -ег)); ~ **on delivery** нало́женным платежо́м
● *v.t.*: ~ **a cheque** получ|а́ть, -и́ть де́ньги по че́ку; ~ **in** получ|а́ть, -и́ть де́ньги по + *d.*
● *v.i.*: ~ **in on** (fig.) воспо́льзоваться (*pf.*) (+ *i.*)
■ ~ **desk** *n.* (BrE) ка́сса; ~ **machine** *n.* банкома́т, де́нежный автома́т; ~ **register** *n.* ка́ссовый аппара́т, ка́сса

cashback /ˈkæʃbæk/ *n.* кешбэ́к (*получе́ние нали́чных де́нег с дебето́вой ка́рточки в предприя́тии рознично́й торго́вли при опла́те поку́пки; компенсацио́нная ски́дка с цены́ поку́пки*)

cashcard /ˈkæʃkɑːd/ *n.* (BrE) ка́рточка для банкома́та

cashew /ˈkæʃuː/ *n.* (оре́х) кешью́ (*m. indecl.*)

cashier /kæˈʃɪə(r)/ *n.* касси́р

cashmere /ˈkæʃmɪə(r)/ *n.* кашеми́р

cashpoint /ˈkæʃpɔɪnt/ *n.* (BrE) банкома́т

casino /kəˈsiːnəʊ/ *n.* (*pl.* ~**s**) казино́ (*nt. indecl.*)

casket /ˈkɑːskɪt/ *n.* шкату́лка; (AmE, coffin) гроб

Caspian /ˈkæspɪən/ *n.* (*in full* **the** ~ (**Sea**)) Каспи́йское мо́ре

casserole /ˈkæsərəʊl/ *n.* (container) кастрю́ля для туше́ния; (food) рагу́ (*nt. indecl.*)

cassette /kəˈset/ *n.* кассе́та
■ ~ **player** *n.* пле́ер; ~ **recorder** *n.* кассе́тный магнитофо́н

cassock /ˈkæsək/ *n.* ря́са

[♂] **cast** /kɑːst/ *n.* **1** (mould) фо́рма для отли́вки; (object): **plaster** ~ ги́псовый сле́пок **2** (theatr., cin.) соста́в актёров
● *v.t.* (*past and p.p.* ~) **1** (throw) бр|оса́ть, -о́сить **2** (fig.): ~ **a vote** проголосова́ть (*pf.*); отда́ть (*pf.*) го́лос; ~ **doubt on** подв|ерга́ть, -е́ргнуть сомне́нию; ~ **a spell (up)on** околд|о́вывать, -ова́ть **3** (pour) отл|ива́ть, -и́ть **4** (theatr.): ~ **a play** распредел|я́ть, -и́ть ро́ли в пье́се
■ ~**away** *n. & adj.* потерпе́вший кораблекруше́ние; ~ **iron** *n.* чугу́н; ~**iron**

[♂] ключева́я ле́ксика

adj. чугу́нный; (fig.) стально́й, желе́зный; ~-**off** *n. & adj.*: ~-**off clothing** обно́ск|и (-ов), старьё

castanets /kæstəˈnets/ *n. pl.* кастанье́ты (*f. pl.*) (*уда́рный музыка́льный инструме́нт в ви́де скреплённых пласти́н, надева́емых на па́льцы рук*)

caste /kɑːst/ *n.* ка́ста

caster /ˈkɑːstə(r)/ *n.*: ~ **sugar** (BrE) са́харный песо́к

castigate /ˈkæstɪgeɪt/ *v.t.* бичева́ть (*impf.*)

casting /ˈkɑːstɪŋ/ *n.* (theatr., cin.) распределе́ние роле́й

castle /ˈkɑːs(ə)l/ *n.* за́мок; (at chess) ладья́

castrate /kæˈstreɪt/ *v.t.* кастри́ровать (*impf., pf.*)

[♂] **casual** /ˈkæʒʊəl/ *adj.* **1** (chance) случа́йный **2** (careless) небре́жный, беспе́чный; (familiar) развя́зный; **clothes for** ~ **wear** проста́я/ повседне́вная оде́жда

casualty /ˈkæʒʊəltɪ/ *n.* (person) пострада́вший от несча́стного слу́чая; (mil.) уби́тый
■ ~ **department** *n.* (BrE) травматологи́ческое отделе́ние

[♂] **cat** /kæt/ *n.* **1** ко́шка **2** (idioms): **let the** ~ **out of the bag** проб|а́лтываться, -олта́ться; выба́лтывать, вы́болтать секре́т; **it's raining** ~**s and dogs** дождь льёт как из ведра́
■ ~**nap** *v.i.* вздремну́ть (*pf.*); ~**walk** *n.* рабо́чие мостк|и́ (-о́в); (in fashion house) по́диум

catalogue /ˈkætəlɒg/ (AmE **catalog**) *n.* катало́г
● *v.t.* (**catalogues, catalogued, cataloguing**, AmE **catalogs, cataloged, cataloging**) каталогизи́ровать (*impf., pf.*)

catalyst /ˈkætəlɪst/ *n.* катализа́тор

catalytic /kætəˈlɪtɪk/ *adj.*: ~ **converter** каталити́ческий нейтрализа́тор (выхлопны́х га́зов)

catapult /ˈkætəpʌlt/ *n.* (BrE, toy) рога́тка

cataract /ˈkætərækt/ *n.* (med.) катара́кта

catarrh /kəˈtɑː(r)/ *n.* ката́р

catastrophe /kəˈtæstrəfɪ/ *n.* катастро́фа

catastrophic /kætəˈstrɒfɪk/ *adj.* катастрофи́ческий

[♂] **catch** /kætʃ/ *n.* **1** (act of catching) пои́мка, захва́т **2** (amount caught) уло́в, добы́ча **3** (trap) уло́вка, лову́шка; **there must be a** ~ **in it** здесь есть како́й-то подво́х **4** (fastener) щеко́лда, защёлка, шпингале́т
● *v.t. & i.* (*past and p.p.* **caught**) **1** (seize) лови́ть, пойма́ть; **he caught the ball** он пойма́л мяч; ~ **a fish** пойма́ть (*pf.*) ры́бу; ~ **a fugitive** пойма́ть (*pf.*) беглеца́ **2** (of entanglement, fastening, etc.): **her dress caught on a nail** она́ зацепи́лась пла́тьем за гвоздь; **he caught his foot** у него́ застря́ла нога́ **3** (intercept, detect): **I caught him stealing** я заста́л его́, за воровство́м; **we were caught in the storm** нас засти́гла бу́ря **4** (be in time for): ~ **a train** успе́ть (*pf.*) на по́езд **5** (fig.): **I didn't** ~ **what you said** я прослу́шал, что вы сказа́ли; ~ **sb's eye** привле́чь (*pf.*) чьё-н. внима́ние; ~ **fire** загоре́ться (*pf.*); ~ **a glimpse of** уви́деть (*pf.*) ме́льком; ~ **hold of** схвати́ть, улови́ть (*both pf.*) **6** (be infected

by) схвати́ть, получи́ть (*both pf.*); ~ **cold** простуди́ться (*pf.*)

□ ~ **on** *v.i.*: **the fashion did not** ~ **on** э́та мо́да не привила́сь

□ ~ **out** *v.t.* (BrE): **he was caught out in a mistake** его́ пойма́ли/подлови́ли на оши́бке

□ ~ **up** *v.t. & i.*: **he caught the others up; he caught up with the others** он догна́л остальны́х; **I must** ~ **up on my work** я запусти́л рабо́ту — тепе́рь на́до нагоня́ть

■ ~**phrase** *n.* мо́дное выраже́ние, слове́чко; ~**-22 situation** *n.* безвы́ходное положе́ние; парадокса́льная ситуа́ция

catching /ˈkætʃɪŋ/ *adj.* зара́зный

catchy /ˈkætʃɪ/ *adj.* (**catchier, catchiest**) легко́ запомина́ющийся, прили́пчивый

categorical /ˌkætɪˈɡɒrɪk(ə)l/ *adj.* категори́ческий

categorize /ˈkætɪɡəraɪz/ *v.t.* распредел|я́ть, -и́ть по катего́риям

⚹ **category** /ˈkætɪɡərɪ/ *n.* катего́рия

cater /ˈkeɪtə(r)/ *v.i.*: ~ **for** (BrE) пост|авля́ть, -а́вить прови́зию для + *g.*; (fig.) обслу́ж|ивать, -и́ть

caterer /ˈkeɪtərə(r)/ *n.* (*often in pl.*) (company) фи́рма, обслу́живающая банке́ты, сва́дьбы *и т. п.*

caterpillar /ˈkætəpɪlə(r)/ *n.* гу́сеница

catharsis /kəˈθɑːsɪs/ *n.* (*pl.* **catharses** /-siːz/) ка́тарсис

cathartic /kəˈθɑːtɪk/ *adj.* очища́ющий

cathedral /kəˈθiːdr(ə)l/ *n.* (кафедра́льный) собо́р

⚹ **Catholic** /ˈkæθəlɪk/ *n.* като́л|ик (-и́чка)
● *adj.* (relig.) католи́ческий; **Roman** ~ ри́мско-католи́ческий

Catholicism /kəˈθɒlɪsɪz(ə)m/ *n.* католици́зм, католи́чество

cattle /ˈkæt(ə)l/ *n.* скот, скоти́на

catty /ˈkætɪ/ *adj.* (**cattier, cattiest**) ехи́дный

Caucasus /ˈkɔːkəsəs/ *n.* Кавка́з

caught /kɔːt/ *past and p.p. of* ▶ **catch**

cauldron /ˈkɔːldrən/ *n.* котёл

cauliflower /ˈkɒlɪflaʊə(r)/ *n.* цветна́я капу́ста

⚹ **cause** /kɔːz/ *n.* **1** (reason) причи́на, по́вод **2** (need) причи́на, основа́ние; **there is no** ~ **for alarm** нет основа́ний/причи́н для беспоко́йства **3** (purpose): **the** ~ **of peace** де́ло ми́ра; **a good** ~ пра́вое де́ло
● *v.t.* вызыва́ть, вы́звать; ~ **sb trouble** (*or a loss*) причин|я́ть, -и́ть кому́-н. беспоко́йство/ убы́тки; **what** ~**d the accident?** что послужи́ло причи́ной несча́стного слу́чая?

caution /ˈkɔːʃ(ə)n/ *n.* **1** (prudence) осторо́жность **2** (BrE, warning) предостереже́ние, предосторо́жность
● *v.t.* предостер|ега́ть, -е́чь

cautious /ˈkɔːʃəs/ *adj.* осторо́жный, осмотри́тельный

cavalier /ˌkævəˈlɪə(r)/ *n.* (gallant; royalist) кавале́р
● *adj.* бесцеремо́нный, надме́нный

cavalry /ˈkævəlrɪ/ *n.* кавале́рия, ко́нница

cave¹ /keɪv/ *n.* пеще́ра

■ ~**man** *n.* пеще́рный челове́к, троглоди́т

cave² /keɪv/ *v.i.*: ~ **in** (lit.) прова́л|иваться, -и́ться; (fig.) сд|ава́ться, -а́ться

cavernous /ˈkæv(ə)nəs/ *adj.* пещери́стый

caviar /ˈkævɪɑː(r)/ *n.* икра́

cavity /ˈkævɪtɪ/ *n.* по́лость; (in tooth) дупло́

cavort /kəˈvɔːt/ *v.i.* скака́ть (*impf.*)

caw /kɔː/ *v.t. & i.* ка́рк|ать, -нуть

cayenne /keɪˈen/ *n.*: ~ **pepper** кайе́нский пе́рец

CCTV *abbr.* (*of* **closed-circuit TV**) систе́ма видеонаблюде́ния, видеонаблюде́ние

CD *abbr.* (*of* **compact disc**) компа́кт-ди́ск

■ ~ **player** *n.* прои́грыватель (*m.*) компа́кт-ди́сков, CD-пле́ер

CD-ROM *abbr.* (*of* **compact disc — read-only memory**) компа́кт-ди́ск (*штампо́ванный*)

■ ~ **drive** *n.* при́вод компа́кт-ди́сков

cease /siːs/ *v.t.* прекра|ща́ть, -ти́ть
● *v.i.* прекра|ща́ться, -ти́ться

■ ~**fire** *n.* прекраще́ние огня́

ceaseless /ˈsiːslɪs/ *adj.* непреста́нный, непреры́вный

cedar /ˈsiːdə(r)/ *n.* кедр

cede /siːd/ *v.t.* сд|ава́ть, -ть

ceilidh /ˈkeɪlɪ/ *n.* вечери́нка с шотла́ндской и́ли ирла́ндской наро́дной му́зыкой и та́нцами

ceiling /ˈsiːlɪŋ/ *n.* потоло́к

⚹ **celebrate** /ˈselɪbreɪt/ *v.t. & i.* **1** (mark an occasion) пра́здновать, от- **2**: ~ **a marriage** соверш|а́ть, -и́ть обря́д бракосочета́ния

celebrated /ˈselɪbreɪtɪd/ *adj.* знамени́тый

celebration /ˌselɪˈbreɪʃ(ə)n/ *n.* пра́зднование, торжества́ (*nt. pl.*), прославле́ние; ~ **of marriage** соверше́ние обря́да бракосочета́ния

celebrity /sɪˈlebrɪtɪ/ *n.* (fame) знамени́тость; (person) знамени́тость

■ ~ **culture** *n.* культ знамени́тостей; культу́ра, сформиро́ванная ку́льтом знамени́тостей

celery /ˈselərɪ/ *n.* (листово́й) сельдере́й

celestial /sɪˈlestɪəl/ *adj.* (astron., fig.) небе́сный

■ ~ **globe** *n.* гло́бус звёздного не́ба

celibate /ˈselɪbət/ *adj.* безбра́чный, да́вший обе́т безбра́чия

⚹ **cell** /sel/ *n.* **1** (in prison) ка́мера **2** (biol.) кле́тка

■ ~**phone** *n.* со́товый телефо́н

cellar /ˈselə(r)/ *n.* по́греб, подва́л

cellist /ˈtʃelɪst/ *n.* виолончели́ст (-ка)

cello /ˈtʃeləʊ/ *n.* (*pl.* ~**s**) виолонче́ль

cellophane® /ˈseləfeɪn/ *n.* целлофа́н; (*attr.*) целлофа́новый

Celt /kelt/ *n.* кельт

Celtic /ˈkeltɪk/ *adj.* ке́льтский

cement /sɪˈment/ *n.* цеме́нт

■ ~ **mixer** *n.* бетономеша́лка

cemetery /ˈsemɪtərɪ/ *n.* кла́дбище

censor /ˈsensə(r)/ *n.* це́нзор
● *v.t.* подв|ерга́ть, -е́ргнуть цензу́ре

censorious /sen'sɔːrɪəs/ *adj.*
сверхкрити́чный, придирчивый
censorship /'sensəʃɪp/ *n.* цензу́ра
censure /'senʃə(r)/ *n.* кри́тика
• *v.t.* критикова́ть (*impf.*)
census /'sensəs/ *n.* (*pl.* ~**es**) пе́репись (населе́ния)
cent /sent/ *n.* цент
centenary /sen'tiːnərɪ/ *n.* (BrE) столе́тие
centennial /sen'tenɪəl/ *n.* (AmE) = centenary
center /'sentə(r)/ *n., v.t., & v.i.* (AmE) = centre
centigrade /'sentɪɡreɪd/ *adj.*: 20° ~ 20 гра́дусов Це́льсия (*or* по Це́льсию)
centilitre /'sentɪliːtə(r)/ (AmE **centiliter**) *n.* сантили́тр
centimetre /'sentɪmiːtə(r)/ (AmE **centimeter**) *n.* сантиме́тр
centipede /'sentɪpiːd/ *n.* многоно́жка
⚘ **central** /'sentr(ə)l/ *adj.* **1** (pert. to a centre) центра́льный; **the house is very** ~ дом нахо́дится в са́мом це́нтре го́рода **2** (principal) центра́льный, гла́вный
■ C~ **America** *n.* Центра́льная Аме́рика; **C~ Asia** *n.* Сре́дняя А́зия
centralize /'sentrəlaɪz/ *v.t.* централизова́ть (*impf., pf.*)
⚘ **centre** /'sentə(r)/ (AmE **center**) *n.* **1** (middle) центр; ~ **of gravity** центр тя́жести **2** (fig.): **shopping** ~ торго́вый центр **3** (pol.) центр
• *v.t.* помеща́ть, -сти́ть в це́нтре
• *v.i.* сосредото́чи|ваться, -ться; **the discussion** ~**d round this point** дискуссия сосредото́чилась вокру́г э́того вопро́са
■ ~ **forward** *n.* (sport) центра́льный напада́ющий; ~**piece** *n.* орнамента́льная ва́за в середи́не стола́; (fig.) гла́вное украше́ние
⚘ **century** /'sentʃərɪ/ *n.* столе́тие, век
CEO *abbr.* (*of* **chief executive officer**) гла́вный исполни́тельный дире́ктор
ceramic /sɪ'ræmɪk/ *adj.* керами́ческий
ceramics /sɪ'ræmɪks/ *n.* кера́мика
cereal /'sɪərɪəl/ *n.* хле́бный злак; (*in full* **breakfast** ~) хло́пья (к за́втраку) (*корнфлекс и т. п.*)
cerebral /'serɪbr(ə)l/ *adj.* мозгово́й, церебра́льный
■ ~ **palsy** *n.* (med.) де́тский церебра́льный парали́ч, ДЦП
ceremonial /serɪ'məʊnɪəl/ *adj.* церемониа́льный, обря́довый
ceremonious /serɪ'məʊnɪəs/ *adj.* церемо́нный
ceremony /'serɪmənɪ/ *n.* (rite) обря́д, церемо́ния; (formal behaviour) церемо́нность; **stand (up)on** ~ церемо́ниться (*impf.*)
⚘ **certain** /'sɜːt(ə)n/ *adj.* **1** (undoubted) несомне́нный; **I cannot say for** ~ я не могу́ сказа́ть наверняка́; **make** ~ **of** (ascertain) удостов|еря́ться, -е́риться в чём-н.; **he is** ~ **to succeed** наверняка́ он добьётся

успе́ха **2** (confident) уве́ренный; **I am** ~ **he will come** я уве́рен, что он придёт **3** (unspecified) изве́стный, не́который; **a** ~ **person** не́кто, не́кое лицо́; **under** ~ **conditions** при изве́стных усло́виях; **a** ~ (*sc. some*) **pleasure** не́которое удово́льствие
⚘ **certainly** /'sɜːt(ə)nlɪ/ *adv.* (without doubt) несомне́нно, наверняка́, наве́рно(е); (expr. obedience or consent) коне́чно, безусло́вно
certainty /'sɜːt(ə)ntɪ/ *n.* **1** (being certainly true) несомне́нность **2** (certain fact) несомне́нный факт
certificate /sə'tɪfɪkət/ *n.* удостовере́ние, свиде́тельство, сертифика́т
certify /'sɜːtɪfaɪ/ *v.t.* удостов|еря́ть, -ери́ть
cervical /sɜː'vaɪk(ə)l/ *adj.* ше́йный
■ ~ **smear** *n.* (BrE) мазо́к с ше́йки ма́тки
cervix /'sɜːvɪks/ *n.* (*pl.* **cervices** /-siːz/) ше́я; (of womb) ше́йка (ма́тки)
Cesarean /sɪ'zeərɪən/ *adj.* (AmE) = Caesarean
cessation /se'seɪʃ(ə)n/ *n.* прекраще́ние, остано́вка; ~ **of hostilities** прекраще́ние вое́нных де́йствий
cf. *abbr.* (*of Latin* **confer**) (= **compare with**) ср., сравни́
CFCs *abbr.* (*of* **chlorofluorocarbons**) фрео́ны (*m. pl.*)
chafe /tʃeɪf/ *v.i.* нат|ира́ться, -ере́ться
chaffinch /'tʃæfɪntʃ/ *n.* зя́блик
⚘ **chain** /tʃeɪn/ *n.* цепь; (*in pl.*) (fetters) це́пи (*f. pl.*), око́в|ы (*pl., g.* —); (fig.): ~ **of events, consequences** цепь собы́тий/после́дствий
• *v.t.* прико́в|ывать, -а́ть цепью
■ ~ **reaction** *n.* цепна́я реа́кция; ~-**smoke** *v.t.* кури́ть (*impf.*) одну́ сигаре́ту за друго́й; ~-**smoker** *n.* зая́длый кури́льщик; ~ **store** *n.* оди́н из се́ти фи́рменных магази́нов
⚘ **chair** /tʃeə(r)/ *n.* **1** стул **2** (~**man**) председа́тель (*m.*)
• *v.t.* (preside over) председа́тельствовать (*impf.*) на + *p.*
■ ~**lift** *n.* подвесно́й подъёмник; ~**man**, ~**person** *nn.* = chair *n.* 2
chaise longue /ʃeɪz 'lɒŋ(ɡ)/ *n.* (*pl.* **chaise longues** *or* **chaises longues** *pronunc. same*) шезло́нг
chalet /'ʃæleɪ/ *n.* шале́ (*nt. indecl.*)
chalk /tʃɔːk/ *n.* мел
⚘ **challenge** /'tʃælɪndʒ/ *n.* вы́зов
• *v.t.* вызыва́ть, вы́звать; (dispute) оспа́ривать (*impf.*); ~ **sb to a race** вызыва́ть, вы́звать кого́-н. на состяза́ние
challenger /'tʃælɪndʒə(r)/ *n.* претенде́нт (-ка)
challenging /'tʃælɪndʒɪŋ/ *adj.* тру́дный, но интере́сный
chamber /'tʃeɪmbə(r)/ *n.* **1** (room) ко́мната; (*in pl.*) (apartment) кварти́ра **2** (hall, e.g. of parliament) зал, за́ла **3** (official body) пала́та; C~ **of Commerce** торго́вая пала́та
■ ~**maid** *n.* го́рничная; ~ **music** *n.* ка́мерная му́зыка
chameleon /kə'miːlɪən/ *n.* хамелео́н
champagne /ʃæm'peɪn/ *n.* шампа́нское

ꟼ champion /ˈtʃæmpɪən/ *n.* **1** (defender) побо́рни|к, защи́тни|к (-ца) **2** (prizewinner) чемпио́н (-ка) (infml)

championship /ˈtʃæmpɪənʃɪp/ *n.* (advocacy) защи́та; (sport) (contest) чемпиона́т, пе́рвенство; (title) чемпио́нство

ꟼ chance /tʃɑːns/ *n.* **1** (casual occurrence) слу́чай, случа́йность; **by ~** случа́йно; **game of ~** аза́ртная игра́ **2** (possibility, opportunity) шанс, возмо́жность; **the ~s are that he will come** все ша́нсы за то, что он придёт; **I had no ~ of winning** у меня́ не́ было никаки́х ша́нсов на успе́х

chancellor /ˈtʃɑːnsələ(r)/ *n.* ка́нцлер; (BrE, of university) ре́ктор; **C~ of the Exchequer** ка́нцлер казначе́йства, мини́стр фина́нсов

chancy /ˈtʃɑːnsɪ/ *adj.* (**chancier**, **chanciest**) (infml) риско́ванный

chandelier /ˌʃændəˈlɪə(r)/ *n.* лю́стра

ꟼ change /tʃeɪndʒ/ *n.* **1** (alteration) измене́ние; (substitution) переме́на; **~ of air, scene** переме́на обстано́вки; **for a ~** для разнообра́зия **2** (spare set) сме́на; **he took a ~ of underwear with him** он взял с собо́й сме́ну белья́ **3** (money) ме́лкие де́н|ьги (-ег); (returned as balance) сда́ча; **have you ~ for a pound?** вы не разменя́ете оди́н фунт (ме́лочью)? **4** (of trains etc.) переса́дка
● *v.t.* **1** (alter, replace) меня́ть, по-; **~ (one's) clothes** переоде|ва́ться, -́ться; **~ one's mind** разду́м|ывать, -ать; переду́м|ывать, -ать; **~ the subject** смени́ть/перемени́ть (*both pf.*) те́му разгово́ра; **~ trains** переса́|живаться, -́сть на друго́й по́езд **2** (reclothe etc.): **~ a baby** перепел|ёнывать, -ена́ть; **~ a bed** меня́ть, по- посте́льное бельё **3** (money): **~ a five pound note** разменя́ть (*pf.*) пятифу́нтовую бума́жку; **~ euros into pounds** обменя́ть (*pf.*) е́вро на фу́нты (сте́рлингов) **4** (exchange): **~ places with sb** (lit.) поменя́ться (*pf.*) места́ми с кем-н.
● *v.i.* **1**: **he has ~d a lot** он си́льно измени́лся/перемени́лся; **caterpillars ~ into butterflies** гу́сеницы превраща́ются в ба́бочек **2** (rail.) переса́|живаться, -́сть
■ **~over** *n.* (of leader etc.) сме́на

changeable /ˈtʃeɪndʒəb(ə)l/ *adj.* (of person, weather) изме́нчивый

changing room /ˈtʃeɪndʒɪŋ/ *n.* (sport) раздева́лка; (BrE, in shop) приме́рочная

ꟼ channel /ˈtʃæn(ə)l/ *n.* **1** (strait) проли́в, кана́л; **the English C~** Ла-Ма́нш; **the C~ Islands** Норма́ндские острова́ **2** (fig.) **through the usual ~s** обы́чным путём **3** (television) кана́л
● *v.t.* (**channelled**, **channelling**, AmE **channeled**, **channeling**) (fig.): **his energies are ~led into sport** вся его́ эне́ргия ухо́дит на спорт
■ **C~ Tunnel** *n.* тонне́ль под Ла-Ма́ншем

channel-hop /ˈtʃæn(ə)lhɒp/ *v.i.* (infml) **1** (television) (ча́сто) переключа́ть (*impf.*) телевизио́нные кана́лы **2** (across the English Channel) (ча́сто) пересека́ть (*impf.*) Ла-Ма́нш

chant /tʃɑːnt/ *n.* песнь; (eccl.) пе́ние
● *v.t.* восп|ева́ть, -е́ть

● *v.i.* петь (*impf.*)

chaos /ˈkeɪɒs/ *n.* ха́ос

chaotic /keɪˈɒtɪk/ *adj.* хаоти́ческий, хаоти́чный

chap¹ /tʃæp/ *v.t.* (**chapped**, **chapping**): **~ped hands** потре́скавшиеся ру́ки

chap² /tʃæp/ *n.* (BrE, infml) па́рень (*m.*), ма́лый

chapel /ˈtʃæp(ə)l/ *n.* часо́вня, моле́льня

chaperone, **chaperon** /ˈʃæpərəʊn/ *n.* компаньо́нка
● *v.t.* сопрово|жда́ть, -ди́ть

chaplain /ˈtʃæplɪn/ *n.* капелла́н, свяще́нник

ꟼ chapter /ˈtʃæptə(r)/ *n.* глава́

char /tʃɑː(r)/ *v.t.* (**charred**, **charring**) обу́гли|вать, -ть

ꟼ character /ˈkærɪktə(r)/ *n.* **1** (nature) сво́йство, ка́чество **2** (personal qualities) хара́ктер **3** (distinctive person): **she is quite a ~** она́ оригина́льная ли́чность **4** (fictional) персона́ж **5** (letter, symbol) бу́ква, ли́тера, знак; **Chinese ~s** кита́йские иеро́глифы (*m. pl.*)

characteristic /ˌkærɪktəˈrɪstɪk/ *n.* характе́рная черта́
● *adj.* характе́рный, типи́чный

characterization /ˌkærɪktəraɪˈzeɪʃ(ə)n/ *n.* **1** (description) характери́стика **2** (by author or actor) созда́ние о́браза; тракто́вка

characterize /ˈkærɪktəraɪz/ *v.t.* **1** (describe) характеризова́ть (*impf., pf.*) **2** (distinguish) отлича́ть, -и́ть

characterless /ˈkærɪktəlɪs/ *adj.* (undistinguished) бесхара́ктерный, заура́дный

charade /ʃəˈrɑːd/ *n.* шара́да

charcoal /ˈtʃɑːkəʊl/ *n.* древе́сный у́голь
■ **~-grey** *n. & adj.* тёмно-се́рый, пе́пельный (цвет)

ꟼ charge /tʃɑːdʒ/ *n.* **1** (for gun) заря́д **2** (elec.) заря́д **3** (expense) цена́, расхо́ды (*m. pl.*); **what is the ~?** ско́лько э́то сто́ит?; **a ~ account** счёт в магази́не; **free of ~** беспла́тно **4** (duty, care): **she's in ~ of the hospital** она́ возглавля́ет больни́цу; **take ~ of a business** взять (*pf.*) на себя́ руково́дство де́лом **5** (person entrusted): **the nurse took her ~s for a walk** ня́ня повела́ свои́х пито́мцев на прогу́лку **6** (accusation) обвине́ние; **bring a ~ against sb** выдвига́ть, вы́двинуть обвине́ние про́тив кого́-н. **7** (attack) нападе́ние, ата́ка
● *v.t.* **1** (accuse) обвин|я́ть, -и́ть; **he is ~d with murder** его́ обвиня́ют в уби́йстве **2** (debit): **~ the amount/goods to me** запиши́те су́мму/ това́ры на мой счёт **3** (ask price): **he ~d £5 for the book** он запроси́л 5 фу́нтов за э́ту кни́гу **4** (*also v.i.*) (attack): **the troops ~d the enemy** войска́ атакова́ли неприя́теля
■ **~ card** *n.* креди́тная ка́рточка

chariot /ˈtʃærɪət/ *n.* колесни́ца

charisma /kəˈrɪzmə/ *n.* хари́зма, обая́ние

charismatic /ˌkærɪzˈmætɪk/ *adj.* харизмати́ческий

charitable /ˈtʃærɪtəb(ə)l/ *adj.* ми́лостивый, снисходи́тельный

ꟼ charity /ˈtʃærɪtɪ/ *n.* **1** (kindness) любо́вь к бли́жнему **2** (institution) благотвори́тельная организа́ция

c

■ ~ **concert** *n.* благотвори́тельный конце́рт; ~ **shop** *n.* благотвори́тельный магази́н поде́ржанных веще́й

charlatan /'ʃɑːlət(ə)n/ *n.* шарлата́н

charm /tʃɑːm/ *n.* **1** (attraction) обая́ние, очарова́ние **2** (talisman) амуле́т
• *v.t.* очаро́в|ывать, -а́ть

charming /'tʃɑːmɪŋ/ *adj.* очарова́тельный

chart /tʃɑːt/ *n.* **1** (record) табли́ца, гра́фик **2** (*in pl.*) (hit parade) хит-пара́д
• *v.t.* черти́ть, на- ка́рту + *g.*; ~ sb's progress де́лать, с- диагра́мму чьего́-н. продвиже́ния

charter /'tʃɑːtə(r)/ *n.* **1** (grant of rights) ха́ртия, гра́мота **2** (hire) фрахто́вка, наём
• *v.t.* **1** (grant diploma to): ~ed accountant (BrE) бухга́лтер-экспе́рт, ауди́тор **2** (hire) фрахтова́ть, за-
■ ~ **flight** *n.* ча́ртерный рейс

chase /tʃeɪs/ *n.* пого́ня
• *v.t.* гоня́ться (*indet.*), гна́ться (*det.*), погна́ться (*pf.*) за (+ *i.*); ~ away отгоня́ть, отогна́ть; he owes us a reply — please ~ him up! (infml) мы ждём его́ отве́та — поторопи́те-ка его́!
• *v.i.*: ~ after гна́ться, по- за (+ *i.*); охо́титься (*impf.*) за + *i.*

chasm /'kæz(ə)m/ *n.* бе́здна, про́пасть (also fig.)

chassis /'ʃæsɪ/ *n.* (*pl.* ~ /-sɪz/) шасси́ (*nt. indecl.*)

chaste /tʃeɪst/ *adj.* целому́дренный

chasten /'tʃeɪs(ə)n/ *v.t.* (punish, subdue) смир|я́ть, -и́ть; the rebuke had a ~ing effect упрёк поде́йствовал отрезвля́юще

chastise /tʃæs'taɪz/ *v.t.* наказ|ывать, -а́ть; кара́ть, по-

chastity /'tʃæstɪtɪ/ *n.* целому́дрие

chat /tʃæt/ *n.* болтовня́, бесе́да
• *v.t.* (**chatted, chatting**): ~ sb up (BrE, infml) зайгрывать (*impf.*) с кем-н.
• *v.i.* (**chatted, chatting**) болта́ть, по-
■ ~**line** *n.* кана́л многосторо́нней свя́зи (*для общения по телефону или в Интернете*); ~ **room** *n.* (comput.) разде́л ча́та; ~ **show** *n.* (BrE) бесе́да/интервью́ (*nt. indecl.*) со знамени́тостями

château /'ʃætəʊ/ *n.* (*pl.* ~x pronunc. same or /-təʊz/) за́мок

chatter /'tʃætə(r)/ *n.* болтовня́, трескотня́
• *v.i.* **1** болта́ть, тарато́рить (*both impf.*) **2**: his teeth are ~ing у него́ зу́бы стуча́т (от хо́лода/испу́га)

chatty /'tʃætɪ/ *adj.* (**chattier, chattiest**) болтли́вый, говорли́вый; (style) разгово́рный

chauffeur /'ʃəʊfə(r)/ *n.* (персона́льный) шофёр

chauvinism /'ʃəʊvɪnɪz(ə)m/ *n.* шовини́зм

chauvinist /'ʃəʊvɪnɪst/ *n.* шовини́ст (-ка); male ~ сторо́нник дискримина́ции же́нщин; мужско́й шовини́ст

chauvinistic /ʃəʊvɪ'nɪstɪk/ *adj.* шовинисти́ческий

chav /tʃæv/ *n.* (BrE, sl.) го́пни|к (-ца) (*особенно по внешним атрибутам*) (sl.), (collect.

also) гопота́ (sl.); па́рень (*m.*) /де́вушка из рабо́чего райо́на (*по интересам*)

✎ **cheap** /tʃiːp/ *adj.* дешёвый

cheapen /'tʃiːpən/ *v.t.* (degrade) ун|ижа́ть, -и́зить; ~ oneself (fig.) роня́ть (*impf.*) себя́

cheat /tʃiːt/ *n.* (person) обма́нщик, плут, жу́лик
• *v.t. & i.* обма́н|ывать, -у́ть

Chechen /'tʃetʃen/ *n.* чече́н|ец (-ка)
• *adj.* чече́нский

Chechnya /'tʃetʃnjə/ *n.* Чечня́

✎ **check¹** /tʃek/ *n.* **1** (restraint) заде́ржка **2** (verification) контро́ль (*m.*) **3** (at chess) шах (*also as int.*) **4** (AmE, used for paying) чек **5** (AmE, bill in restaurant) счёт (-а́) **6** (AmE, for hat, luggage, etc.) номеро́к; квита́нция **7** (AmE, tick) га́лочка
• *v.t.* **1** (restrain) сде́рж|ивать, -а́ть **2** (verify) контроли́ровать, про-; пров|еря́ть, -е́рить **3** (AmE, tick) отм|еча́ть, -е́тить га́лочкой
□ ~ **in** *v.i.* (at hotel) регистри́роваться, за-
• *v.t.* (baggage) сд|ава́ть, -ать
□ ~ **out** *v.i.* (from hotel) выпи́сываться, вы́писаться
□ ~ **up** *v.i.*: ~ up on sth пров|еря́ть, -е́рить что-н.
■ ~**list** *n.* контро́льный спи́сок, пе́речень (*m.*); ~**out** *n.* ка́сса; ~**point** *n.* контро́льный пункт; ~**up** *n.* прове́рка

check² /tʃek/ *n.* (pattern) кле́тка
• *attr. adj.* (*also* ~ed) кле́тчатый

checker /'tʃekə(r)/ *v.t.* (AmE) = chequer

checkers /'tʃekəz/ *n.* (AmE) ша́ш|ки (-ек)

checkmate /'tʃekmeɪt/ *n.* шах и мат

cheek /tʃiːk/ *n.* **1** (part of face) щека́ **2** (impudence) на́глость
■ ~**bone** *n.* скула́

cheeky /'tʃiːkɪ/ *adj.* (**cheekier, cheekiest**) наха́льный

cheer /'tʃɪə(r)/ *n.* **1** (shout): three ~s for our visitors! троекра́тное ура́ на́шим гостя́м!; ~s! (as toast) (за) ва́ше здоро́вье! **2** (*in pl., as int.*) (BrE, infml) спаси́бо
• *v.t.* приве́тствовать (*impf.*)
• *v.i.* (utter ~s) изд|ава́ть, -а́ть восто́рженные кри́ки
□ ~ **up** *v.t. & i.* ободр|я́ть(ся), -и́ть(ся)
• *v.i.* повеселе́ть (*pf.*); ~ up! не уныва́йте!
■ ~**leader** *n.* де́вушка из гру́ппы подде́ржки (спорти́вной кома́нды), чирли́дер

cheerful /'tʃɪəfʊl/ *adj.* весёлый, ра́достный

cheese /tʃiːz/ *n.* сыр
■ ~**burger** *n.* чи́збургер; ~**cake** *n.* чизке́йк

cheetah /'tʃiːtə/ *n.* гепа́рд

chef /ʃef/ *n.* шеф-по́вар

✎ **chemical** /'kemɪk(ə)l/ *n.* хими́ческий проду́кт; (*in pl.*) химика́ты (*m. pl.*)
• *adj.* хими́ческий

chemist /'kemɪst/ *n.* **1** (scientist) хи́мик **2** (BrE, pharmacist) апте́карь (*m.*)
■ ~'s shop *n.* (BrE) апте́ка

chemistry /'kemɪstrɪ/ *n.* хи́мия

chemo /'kiːməʊ/ *n.* (infml) химиотерапи́я

chemotherapy /kiːmə'θerəpɪ/ *n.* химиотерапи́я

✎ ключева́я ле́ксика

cheque /tʃek/ (AmE **check**) n. чек; **he made the ~ out to me** он вы́писал чек на моё и́мя
■ **~book** n. че́ковая кни́жка; **~book journalism** n. заказна́я журнали́стика

chequer /'tʃekə(r)/ (AmE **checker**) v.t. (fig.): **~ed career** бу́рная жизнь
■ **~ed flag** n. кле́тчатый, ша́хматный флажо́к

cherish /'tʃerɪʃ/ v.t. **1** (love) не́жно люби́ть (impf.) **2** (of hopes etc.) леле́ять (impf.)

cherry /'tʃerɪ/ n. **1** (sour) (fruit) ви́шня; (tree) ви́шня, вишнёвое де́рево **2** (sweet) (fruit) чере́шня; (tree) чере́шня, чере́шневое де́рево
■ **~-pick** v.t. & i. (things) от|бира́ть, -обра́ть лу́чшее; (people, animals) от|бира́ть, -обра́ть лу́чших

cherub /'tʃerəb/ n. херуви́м

chess /tʃes/ n. ша́хмат|ы (pl., g. —)
■ **~board** n. ша́хматная доска́; **~ player** n. шахмати́ст (-ка)

chest /tʃest/ n. **1** (furniture) сунду́к; **~ of drawers** шкаф с выдвижны́ми я́щиками **2** (anat.) грудна́я кле́тка; **get sth off one's ~** облегчи́ть (pf.) ду́шу

chestnut /'tʃesnʌt/ n. (tree, fruit) кашта́н

chew /tʃuː/ v.t. & i. жева́ть (impf.); **~ upon, ~ over** (fig.) пережёвывать (impf.); **~ing gum** жева́тельная рези́нка, жва́чка (infml)

chewy /'tʃuːɪ/ adj. (**chewier, chewiest**) (infml) тягу́чий

chic /ʃiːk/ adj. (**chicer, chicest**) элега́нтный, шика́рный

chick /tʃɪk/ n. птене́ц
■ **~peas** n. pl. (bot.) нут (обыкнове́нный/культу́рный), туре́цкий/бара́ний горо́х

chicken /'tʃɪkɪn/ n. цыплёнок; (as food) куря́тина, цыплёнок, ку́рица
■ **~pox** n. ветряна́я о́спа, ветря́нка (infml)

chicory /'tʃɪkərɪ/ n. (bot.) цико́рий (корнево́й)

✍ **chief** /tʃiːf/ n. **1** (leader) вождь (m.), глава́ (m.) **2** (senior official) шеф, нача́льник; **~ of staff** нача́льник шта́ба
● adj. **1** (most important) гла́вный, основно́й, важне́йший **2** (senior) гла́вный, ста́рший

chiefly /'tʃiːflɪ/ adv. гла́вным о́бразом

chiffon /'ʃɪfɒn/ n. шифо́н

chilblain /'tʃɪlbleɪn/ n. обморо́женное ме́сто

✍ **child** /tʃaɪld/ n. (pl. **children**) дитя́ (nt.), ребёнок
■ **~ benefit** n. посо́бие на ребёнка; **~birth** n. ро́д|ы (-ов); **~care** n. ухо́д за детьми́ (особенно в детских садах и яслях)

childhood /'tʃaɪldhʊd/ n. де́тство

childish /'tʃaɪldɪʃ/ adj. де́тский, ребя́ческий

childless /'tʃaɪldlɪs/ adj. безде́тный

childlike /'tʃaɪldlaɪk/ adj. де́тский

children /'tʃɪldr(ə)n/ pl. of ▶ child

Chile /'tʃɪlɪ/ n. Чи́ли (f. indecl.)

Chilean /'tʃɪlɪən/ n. чили́|ец (-йка)
● adj. чили́йский

chill /tʃɪl/ n. **1** (physical) (also fig.) хо́лод **2** (med.) просту́да; **catch a ~** просту|жа́ться, -ди́ться
● adj. холо́дный

● v.t. (lit.) охла|жда́ть, -ди́ть; (fig.) осту|жа́ть, -ди́ть
● v.i.: **~ out** (infml) рассл|абля́ться, -а́биться

chilled /tʃɪld/ adj. (of wine etc.) охлаждённый; (infml, relaxed) рассла́бленный

chilli /'tʃɪlɪ/ (AmE **chili**) n. (pl. **-es**) кра́сный стручко́вый пе́рец

chilly /'tʃɪlɪ/ adj. (**chillier, chilliest**) холо́дный

chime /tʃaɪm/ n. перезво́н
● v.t.: **the clock ~d midnight** часы́ проби́ли по́лночь

chimney /'tʃɪmnɪ/ n. труба́, дымохо́д

chimpanzee /tʃɪmpæn'ziː/ n. шимпанзе́ (m. indecl.)

chin /tʃɪn/ n. подборо́док

China /'tʃaɪnə/ n. Кита́й

china /'tʃaɪnə/ n. фарфо́р

♂ **Chinese** /tʃaɪ'niːz/ n. (pl. **~**) (person) кита́|ец (-я́нка); (language) кита́йский язы́к
● adj. кита́йский

chink¹ /tʃɪŋk/ n. (crevice) щель; **a ~ of light** у́зкая полоска све́та

chink² /tʃɪŋk/ n. (sound) звя́канье

chintz /tʃɪnts/ n. си́тец; (attr.) си́тцевый

chip /tʃɪp/ n. **1** (of wood) ще́пка; стру́жка; (of china) оско́лок **2** (fig.): **he has a ~ on his shoulder** он де́ржится вызыва́юще **3** (piece missing): **the cup has a ~** у ча́шки отко́лот кусо́к **4** (food) (BrE) карто́фель (m.) соло́мкой/фри; (AmE) чи́псы (m. pl.) **5** (at games) фи́шка, ма́рка **6** (in microelectronics) чип, микросхе́ма
● v.t. (**chipped, chipping**) струга́ть, вы́стругать; отк|а́лывать, -оло́ть; отб|ива́ть, -и́ть; обб|ива́ть, -и́ть
● v.i. (**chipped, chipping**): **~ in** (infml) вме́ш|иваться, -а́ться; влез|а́ть, -ть (в разгово́р)
■ **~board** n. фиброли́т; (attr.) фиброли́товый

chipmunk /'tʃɪpmʌŋk/ n. бурунду́к

chiropodist /kɪ'rɒpədɪst/ n. специали́ст (-ка) по лече́нию заболева́ний стопы́

chiropody /kɪ'rɒpədɪ/ n. лече́ние заболева́ний стопы́

chiropractor /'kaɪərəʊpræktə(r)/ n. хиропра́ктик

chirp /tʃə:p/ v.t. & i. чири́кать (impf.); щебета́ть (impf.)

chirpy /'tʃə:pɪ/ adj. (**chirpier, chirpiest**) (infml) бо́дрый

chisel /'tʃɪz(ə)l/ n. долото́, стаме́ска
● v.t. (**chiselled, chiselling**, AmE **chiseled, chiseling**) вая́ть, из-

chit-chat /'tʃɪttʃæt/ n. болтовня́, пересу́д|ы (-ов)

chivalrous /'ʃɪvəlrəs/ adj. ры́царский

chivalry /'ʃɪvəlrɪ/ n. ры́царство

chive /tʃaɪv/ n. лук-ре́занец

chivvy /'tʃɪvɪ/ v.t. (BrE, infml) гоня́ть (impf.)

chloride /'klɔːraɪd/ n. хлори́д

chlorine /'klɔːriːn/ n. хлор

chock /tʃɒk/ n. клин; подпо́рка
■ **~-a-block** adj. загромождённый; **~-full** adj. битко́м наби́тый

C

c

chocolate /'tʃɒkələt/ n. (also drink) шокола́д; (∼-coated sweet) шокола́дная конфе́та; ∼ **biscuit** шокола́дное пече́нье
■ ∼ **bar** n. пли́тка шокола́да

✧ **choice** /tʃɔɪs/ n. **1** (choosing) вы́бор, отбо́р **2** (thing chosen) вы́бор **3** (variety) вы́бор

choir /'kwaɪə(r)/ n. хор
■ ∼**boy** n. пе́вчий; ∼**master** n. хорме́йстер

choke /tʃəʊk/ n. (in car) возду́шная засло́нка; дро́ссель (m.)
• v.t. **1** (throttle) души́ть, за- **2** (block) заку́пор|ивать, -ить; the garden is ∼d with weeds сорняки́ заглуши́ли сад
• v.i. зад|ыха́ться, -охну́ться

choker /'tʃəʊkə(r)/ n. коро́ткое ожере́лье, колье́ (nt. indecl.)

cholera /'kɒlərə/ n. холе́ра

cholesterol /kə'lestərɒl/ n. холестери́н

✧ **choose** /tʃuːz/ v.t. (past **chose**, p.p. **chosen**) выбира́ть, вы́брать; there are five to ∼ from мо́жно выбира́ть из пяти́; I chose to remain я предпочёл оста́ться

choosy /'tʃuːzɪ/ adj. (**choosier**, **choosiest**) разбо́рчивый

chop /tʃɒp/ n. **1** (cut) ру́бящий уда́р **2** (of meat) отбивна́я котле́та
• v.t. (**chopped**, **chopping**) (also ∼ **up**) (wood) руби́ть (impf.); (food) нар|еза́ть, -е́зать; кроши́ть (impf.); ∼ a tree down руби́ть, с- де́рево

choppy /'tʃɒpɪ/ adj. (**choppier**, **choppiest**) (of sea) неспоко́йный

chopstick /'tʃɒpstɪk/ n. па́лочка для еды́

choral /'kɔːr(ə)l/ adj. хорово́й

chord /kɔːd/ n. (mus.) акко́рд

chore /tʃɔː(r)/ n. (usu. in pl.) (routine task) рути́нная рабо́та; household ∼s дома́шняя рабо́та; (tedious task) бре́мя (nt.)

choreographer /kɒrɪ'ɒɡrəfə(r)/ n. балетме́йстер, хорео́граф

choreography /kɒrɪ'ɒɡrəfɪ/ n. хореогра́фия

chorister /'kɒrɪstə(r)/ n. хори́ст (-ка)

chortle /'tʃɔːt(ə)l/ v.i. фы́ркать (impf.); дави́ться (impf.) от сме́ха

chorus /'kɔːrəs/ n. (pl. ∼es) **1** (singers) хор **2** (refrain) припе́в, рефре́н

chose /tʃəʊz/ past of ▶ choose

chosen /'tʃəʊz(ə)n/ p.p. of ▶ choose

Christ /kraɪst/ n. Христо́с

christen /'krɪs(ə)n/ v.t. крести́ть (impf., pf.); he was ∼ed John при креще́нии ему́ да́ли и́мя Джон

christening /'krɪs(ə)nɪŋ/ n. креще́ние

✧ **Christian** /'krɪstɪən/ n. христиа́н|ин (-а́нка)
• adj. христиа́нский
■ ∼ **name** n. и́мя (nt.) (в противоположность фамилии)

Christianity /krɪstɪ'ænɪtɪ/ n. христиа́нство

✧ **Christmas** /'krɪsməs/ n. (pl. ∼es) Рождество́
■ ∼ **cake** n. (BrE) рожде́ственский пиро́г; ∼ **card** n. рожде́ственская откры́тка; ∼ **Day**

n. пе́рвый день Рождества́; ∼ **Eve** n. кану́н Рождества́; ∼ **tree** n. рожде́ственская, нового́дняя ёлка

chrome /krəʊm/ n. хром

chromosome /'krəʊməsəʊm/ n. хромосо́ма

chronic /'krɒnɪk/ adj. **1** (med.) хрони́ческий **2** (fig., incessant) хрони́ческий, постоя́нный

chronicle /'krɒnɪk(ə)l/ n. хро́ника, ле́топись
• v.t. вести́ (det.) хро́нику + g.

chronological /krɒnə'lɒdʒɪk(ə)l/ adj. хронологи́ческий

chronology /krə'nɒlədʒɪ/ n. хроноло́гия

chrysanthemum /krɪ'sænθəməm/ n. хризанте́ма

chubby /'tʃʌbɪ/ adj. (**chubbier**, **chubbiest**) то́лстенький, пу́хленький

chuck /tʃʌk/ v.t. (infml, throw) швыр|я́ть, -ну́ть
□ ∼ **away** v.t. (lit.) выбра́сывать, вы́бросить
□ ∼ **out** v.t. (thing or person) вы́кинуть (pf.); вы́швырнуть (pf.)

chuckle /'tʃʌk(ə)l/ n. сда́вленный смешо́к, смех
• v.i. фы́ркать (impf.) от сме́ха, посме́иваться (impf.)

chuffed /tʃʌft/ adj. (BrE, infml) дово́льный

chum /tʃʌm/ n. прия́тель (m.), дружо́к

chunk /tʃʌŋk/ n. то́лстый кусо́к/ломо́ть (m.)

chunky /'tʃʌŋkɪ/ adj. (**chunkier**, **chunkiest**) (person) корена́стый; (jumper) то́лстый

✧ **church** /tʃɜːtʃ/ n. це́рковь; (building) це́рковь; (esp. Orthodox) храм
■ ∼**goer** n.: he is a regular ∼goer он регуля́рно хо́дит в це́рковь; ∼**yard** n. пого́ст, кла́дбище при це́ркви

churlish /'tʃɜːlɪʃ/ adj. ха́мский, гру́бый

churn /tʃɜːn/ n. (tub) маслобо́йка; (BrE, can) бидо́н
• v.t.: ∼ **butter** сби|ва́ть, -ть ма́сло; (fig.): he ∼s out novels он печёт рома́ны (как блины́); the propeller ∼ed up the waves винт взвихри́л во́лны

chute /ʃuːt/ n. (slide, slope) жёлоб, спуск; (for amusement) гора́, го́рка; (for rubbish) мусоропрово́д

chutney /'tʃʌtnɪ/ n. ча́тни (nt. indecl.) (индийская приправа из фруктов или овощей с добавлением уксуса, острых специй и сахара)

CIA abbr. (of **Central Intelligence Agency**) ЦРУ (Центра́льное разве́дывательное управле́ние)

cicada /sɪ'kɑːdə/ n. (zool.) цика́да

cider /'saɪdə(r)/ n. (BrE, alcoholic drink) сидр; (AmE, non-alcoholic drink) я́блочный напи́ток

cigar /sɪ'ɡɑː(r)/ n. сига́ра

cigarette /sɪɡə'ret/ n. сигаре́та; (of Russian type) папиро́са
■ ∼**-lighter** n. зажига́лка

cinder /'sɪndə(r)/ n. (in pl.) шлак, зола́, пе́пел

cine camera /'sɪnɪkæmrə/ n. (BrE) кинока́мера, киноаппара́т

cinema /'sɪnɪmə/ n. кино́ (nt. indecl.)

✧ ключева́я ле́ксика

cinematography /sɪnɪmə'tɒgrəfɪ/ *n.*
кинематогра́фия

cinnamon /'sɪnəmən/ *n.* кори́ца

circa /'sɜːkə/ *prep.* приблизи́тельно; о́коло + *g.*

⚔ **circle** /'sɜːk(ə)l/ *n.* **1** (math.) (*also* fig.)
круг, окру́жность; **a ~ of trees** кольцо́
дере́вьев; **go round in a ~** (fig., e.g. argument)
возвраща́ться (*impf.*) к исхо́дной то́чке
2 (theatr.): **dress ~** бельэта́ж; **upper ~** балко́н
• *v.t.:* **the earth ~s the sun** земля́ враща́ется
вокру́г со́лнца
• *v.i.:* **the hawk ~d** я́стреб кружи́л в не́бе (*or*
опи́сывал круги́)

circuit /'sɜːkɪt/ *n.* **1** (distance, journey round): **he**
made a ~ of the camp он обошёл ла́герь
2 (elec.) цепь
■ **~-breaker** *n.* автомати́ческий выключа́тель

circuitous /sɜː'kjuːɪtəs/ *adj.* кру́жный,
око́льный

circular /'sɜːkjʊlə(r)/ *n.* циркуля́р
• *adj.* кругово́й

circulate /'sɜːkjʊleɪt/ *v.i.* циркули́ровать
(*impf., pf.*); **she ~d among the guests** она́
обходи́ла госте́й

circulation /sɜːkjʊ'leɪʃ(ə)n/ *n.* (of blood)
кровообраще́ние; (of air) циркуля́ция

circumcise /'sɜːkəmsaɪz/ *v.t.* соверш|а́ть, -и́ть
обреза́ние + *d.*

circumcision /sɜːkəm'sɪʒ(ə)n/ *n.* обреза́ние

circumference /sə'kʌmfərəns/ *n.*
окру́жность

circumnavigate /sɜːkəm'nævɪgeɪt/ *v.t.*
пла́вать (*indet.*) вокру́г + *g.*; **Drake ~d**
the globe Дрейк соверши́л кругосве́тное
пла́вание

circumspect /'sɜːkəmspekt/ *adj.*
осмотри́тельный

⚔ **circumstance** /'sɜːkəmst(ə)ns/ *n.* **1** (fact,
detail) обстоя́тельство, усло́вие; **in, under the**
~s в да́нных усло́виях/обстоя́тельствах;
under no ~s ни при каки́х усло́виях/
обстоя́тельствах **2** (condition of life)
материа́льное положе́ние

circumstantial /sɜːkəm'stænʃ(ə)l/ *adj.:* **~**
evidence ко́свенные ули́ки (*f. pl.*)

circumvent /sɜːkəm'vent/ *v.t.* об|ходи́ть,
-ойти́; (outwit, cheat) перехитри́ть (*pf.*)

circus /'sɜːkəs/ *n.* (*pl.* **~es**) цирк; (fig.) балага́н

cirrhosis /sɪ'rəʊsɪs/ *n.* цирро́з

CIS *abbr.* (*of* **Commonwealth of**
Independent States) СНГ (Содру́жество
Незави́симых Госуда́рств); (*attr.*) эсэнгэ́шный
(*infml*)

cistern /'sɪst(ə)n/ *n.* цисте́рна, бак

citadel /'sɪtədel/ *n.* (lit., fig.) цитаде́ль

⚔ **cite** /saɪt/ *v.t.* (quote) цити́ровать, про-

⚔ **citizen** /'sɪtɪz(ə)n/ *n.* гражд|ани́н (-а́нка); (of
city) жи́тель (-ница)

citizenship /'sɪtɪzənʃɪp/ *n.* гражда́нство,
по́дданство

citrus /'sɪtrəs/ *n.:* **~ fruit** ци́трусовые (*nt. pl.*)

⚔ **city** /'sɪtɪ/ *n.* го́род; (of London) Си́ти (*m. indecl.*)
■ **~ centre,** (AmE) **~ center** *n.* центр го́рода

civic /'sɪvɪk/ *adj.* гражда́нский

⚔ **civil** /'sɪv(ə)l/ *adj.* **1** (relating to citizens)
гражда́нский; **~ rights** гражда́нские права́;
~ war гражда́нская война́; **~ partner**
гражда́нский супру́г/гражда́нская супру́га,
партнёр однопо́лого бра́ка; **~ partnership**
гражда́нский брак, однопо́лый брак
2 (relating to the state) госуда́рственный;
~ servant госуда́рственный слу́жащий,
чино́вник; **~ service** госуда́рственная
слу́жба **3** (polite) ве́жливый

⚔ **civilian** /sɪ'vɪlɪən/ *n. & adj.* шта́тский

⚔ **civilization** /sɪvɪlaɪ'zeɪʃ(ə)n/ *n.* цивилиза́ция

civilize /'sɪvɪlaɪz/ *v.t.* цивилизова́ть (*impf., pf.*)

⚔ **claim** /kleɪm/ *n.* **1** (assertion of right) притяза́ние
2 (assertion) утвержде́ние, заявле́ние
3 (demand) тре́бование
• *v.t.* **1** (demand) тре́бовать, по- + *g.* **2** (assert
as fact) утвер|жда́ть, -ди́ть; **he ~s to own the**
land он заявля́ет, что э́та земля́ принадлежи́т
ему́

claimant /'kleɪmənt/ *n.* претенде́нт (-ка)
(*на что*)

clairvoyant /kleə'vɔɪənt/ *n. & adj.*
яснови́дящ|ий (-ая)

clam /klæm/ *n.* двуство́рчатый морско́й
моллю́ск
• *v.i.* (**clammed, clamming**): **~ up** (infml)
уходи́ть, уйти́ в себя́

clamber /'klæmbə(r)/ *v.i.* кара́бкаться, вс- (*на*
что)

clammy /'klæmɪ/ *adj.* (**clammier,**
clammiest) холо́дный и ли́пкий

clamour /'klæmə(r)/ (AmE **clamor**) *n.* шум
(*m. pl.*)
• *v.i.* шуме́ть (*impf.*)

clamp /klæmp/ *n.* (implement) зажи́м
• *v.t.* заж|има́ть, -а́ть
• *v.i.:* **~ down on** (fig.) заж|има́ть, -а́ть
■ **~-down** *n.* стро́гий запре́т, стро́гие ме́ры
(*против чего*)

clan /klæn/ *n.* клан

clandestine /klæn'destɪn/ *adj.* та́йный

clang /'klæŋ/ *n.* лязг
• *v.t. & i.* ля́зг|ать, -нуть; звене́ть (*impf.*)

clap /klæp/ *n.* (of thunder) уда́р; (of applause)
хлопо́к, хло́панье; **let's give him a ~!**
похло́паем ему́!
• *v.t.* (**clapped, clapping**) (strike, slap): **~**
one's hands хло́п|ать, -нуть в ладо́ши
• *v.i.* (**clapped, clapping**) хло́пать (*impf.*)

clarification /klærɪfɪ'keɪʃ(ə)n/ *n.* проясне́ние

clarify /'klærɪfaɪ/ *v.t.* вн|оси́ть, -ести́ я́сность
в + *a.*

clarinet /klærɪ'net/ *n.* кларне́т

clarinettist /klærɪ'netɪst/ *n.* кларнети́ст (-ка)

clarity /'klærɪtɪ/ *n.* я́сность

clash /klæʃ/ *n.* **1** (sound) гул **2** (conflict): **~ of**
views расхожде́ние во взгля́дах
• *v.t.:* **he ~ed the cymbals** он уда́рил в
цимба́лы
• *v.i.* **1** (sound): **the cymbals ~ed** зазвене́ли
цимба́лы **2** (conflict): **the armies ~ed** а́рмии
столкну́лись; (coincide inconveniently): **the**

two concerts ~ о́ба конце́рта совпада́ют по вре́мени; **the colours** ~ э́ти цвета́ не гармони́руют друг с дру́гом

clasp /klɑːsp/ *n.* пря́жка
● *v.t.*: ~ **sb by the hand** сж|има́ть, -а́ть кому́-н. ру́ку

✓ **class** /klɑːs/ *n.* **1** (group) класс, разря́д; (railway etc.): **he went first** ~ он е́хал пе́рвым кла́ссом **2** (social) класс **3** (scholastic) класс; (period of instruction): **a maths** ~ уро́к матема́тики; **he attended** ~**es in French** он посеща́л заня́тия по францу́зскому (языку́); (AmE, graduates): **the** ~ **of 1955** вы́пуск 1955 го́да **4** (distinction) класс, шик
● *v.t.* классифици́ровать (*impf., pf.*)
■ ~**-conscious** *adj.* кла́ссово-созна́тельный; ~**mate** *n.* однокла́ссни|к (-ца); ~**room** *n.* кла́ссная ко́мната, класс

✓ **classic** /ˈklæsɪk/ *n.* **1** кла́ссик **2** (*in pl.*) (studies): **he studied** ~**s** он изуча́л класси́ческую филоло́гию
● *adj.* класси́ческий

classical /ˈklæsɪk(ə)l/ *adj.* класси́ческий

classifiable /ˈklæsɪfaɪəb(ə)l/ *adj.* поддаю́щийся классифика́ции

classification /ˌklæsɪfɪˈkeɪʃ(ə)n/ *n.* классифика́ция

classif|y /ˈklæsɪfaɪ/ *v.t.* классифици́ровать (*impf., pf.*); ~**ied** (secret) засекре́ченный
■ ~**ied ad** *n.* темати́ческое объявле́ние

classy /ˈklɑːsɪ/ *adj.* (**classier, classiest**) сти́льный (infml)

clatter /ˈklætə(r)/ *n.* (of metal) гро́хот; (of hoofs, plates, cutlery, etc.) стук, звон, звя́канье
● *v.i.* греме́ть; грохота́ть (*both impf.*)

clause /klɔːz/ *n.* **1** (gram.) предложе́ние **2** (law) статья́

claustrophobia /ˌklɔːstrəˈfəʊbɪə/ *n.* клаустрофо́бия

claustrophobic /ˌklɔːstrəˈfəʊbɪk/ *adj.*: **I'm** ~ я страда́ю клаустрофо́бией

claw /klɔː/ *n.* (of animal, bird) ко́готь (*m.*); (of crustacean) клешня́; (of machinery) кула́к, ла́па, кле́щ|и (-е́й)

clay /kleɪ/ *n.* гли́на

✓ **clean** /kliːn/ *adj.* **1** (not dirty) чи́стый; **keep a room** ~ содержа́ть (*impf.*) ко́мнату в чистоте́ **2** (fresh): **a** ~ **sheet of paper** чи́стый лист бума́ги **3** (pure, unblemished) чи́стый, незапя́тнанный **4** (neat, smooth): ~ **lines** чёткие очерта́ния; чи́стые ли́нии
● *v.t.* чи́стить (*impf.*); ~ **one's teeth** чи́стить, по- зу́бы; ~ **a car** мыть, вы́- маши́ну; ~ **a window** прот|ира́ть, -ере́ть окно́; **he had his suit** ~**ed** он о́тдал костю́м в чи́стку
□ ~ **out** *v.t.*: ~ **out a room** убра́ть (*pf.*) ко́мнату
□ ~ **up** *v.t.*: ~ **oneself up** прив|оди́ть, -ести́ себя́ в поря́док; ~ **up a city** (fig.) очи́стить (*pf.*) го́род
■ ~**-cut** *adj.* ре́зко оче́рченный; ~**-shaven** *adj.* чи́сто вы́бритый

✓ ключева́я ле́ксика

---

cleaner /ˈkliːnə(r)/ *n.* (person) убо́рщи|к (-ца); **he sent the suit to the** ~**'s** он о́тдал костю́м в чи́стку; (substance) мо́ющее сре́дство; очисти́тель (*m.*)

cleanliness /ˈklenlɪnɪs/ *n.* чистота́

cleanse /klenz/ *v.t.* оч|ища́ть, -и́стить

cleanser /ˈklenzə(r)/ *n.* сре́дство для очище́ния ко́жи

✓ **clear** /klɪə(r)/ *adj.* **1** (easy to see) я́сный, отчётливый; (evident) я́вный, очеви́дный **2** (bright) я́ркий, я́сный; **on a** ~ **day** в пого́жий день **3** (transparent) прозра́чный **4** (of sound) чи́стый **5** (intelligible, certain): **make sth** ~ **to sb** объясн|я́ть, -и́ть что-н. кому́-н.; **make oneself** ~ объясн|я́ться, -и́ться; **I am not** ~ **what he wants** мне нея́сно, чего́ он хо́чет **6** (safe, free) свобо́дный; ~ **of debt** свобо́дный от долго́в; ~ **of suspicion** вне подозре́ний; **my conscience is** ~ моя́ со́весть чиста́; **keep a** ~ **head** сохраня́ть (*impf.*) я́сный ум
● *adv.*: **stand** ~ **of the gates** стоя́ть (*impf.*) в стороне́ от воро́т; **keep** ~ **of** держа́ться (*impf.*) в стороне́ от + *g.*
● *v.t.* **1** (make ~) оч|ища́ть, -и́стить; **the streets were** ~**ed of snow** у́лицы очи́стили от сне́га; ~ **land** расч|ища́ть, -и́стить зе́млю; **she** ~**ed the table** она́ убрала́ со стола́; **he was** ~**ed for security** его́ засекре́тили; **he** ~**ed his throat** он отка́шлялся; **he** ~**ed the things out of the drawer** он освободи́л я́щик **2** (jump over; get past): **the horse** ~**ed the hedge** ло́шадь взяла́ барье́р **3** (make profit of): **we** ~**ed £50** мы получи́ли 50 фу́нтов при́были **4**: ~ **a debt** погаси́ть (*pf.*) долг
● *v.i. see* ► **clear up**
□ ~ **away** *v.t.* уб|ира́ть, -ра́ть
● *v.i.* (disperse) рассе́|иваться, -яться
□ ~ **off** *v.i.* (infml, go away) уб|ира́ться, -ра́ться
□ ~ **out** *v.t.*: **she** ~**ed out the cupboard** она́ очи́стила шкаф
● *v.i.* (infml, go away) убра́ться (*pf.*)
□ ~ **up** *v.t.* (tidy, remove) уб|ира́ть, -ра́ть; ~ **up a mystery** разгада́ть (*pf.*) та́йну
● *v.i.*: **the weather** ~**ed up** пого́да проясни́лась
■ ~**-cut** *adj.* чёткий; ~**-headed** *adj.* толко́вый

clearance /ˈklɪərəns/ *n.* **1** (removal of obstruction etc.) очи́стка, расчи́стка **2**: **security** ~ до́пуск к секре́тной рабо́те
■ ~ **sale** *n.* распрода́жа

clearing /ˈklɪərɪŋ/ *n.* про́сека, поля́на

✓ **clearly** /ˈklɪəlɪ/ *adv.* (distinctly) я́сно; (evidently) очеви́дно, коне́чно

cleavage /ˈkliːvɪdʒ/ *n.* «ручеёк», ложби́нка бю́ста

cleaver /ˈkliːvə(r)/ *n.* нож мясника́

clef /klef/ *n.* (mus.) ключ; **treble** ~ скрипи́чный ключ

cleft /kleft/ *adj.* расщеплённый
■ ~ **palate** *n.* расщеплённое нёбо

clematis /ˈklemətɪs/ *n.* клема́тис, ломоно́с

clench /klentʃ/ *v.t.*: ~ **one's teeth** сти́снуть (*pf.*) зу́бы; ~ **one's fists** сж|има́ть, -а́ть кулаки́

clergy /ˈklɜːdʒɪ/ *n.* духове́нство, клир
■ **~man** *n.* духо́вное лицо́; (Protestant) па́стор
cleric /ˈklerɪk/ *n.* церко́вник, духо́вное лицо́
clerical /ˈklerɪk(ə)l/ *adj.* **1** (of clergy) клерика́льный **2** (of clerks) канцеля́рский, конто́рский
■ **~ error** *n.* канцеля́рская оши́бка
clerk /klɑːk/ *n.* **1** (in office) секрета́рь (*m.*), делопроизводи́тель (*m.*); **bank ~** ба́нковский слу́жащий **2** (official) слу́жащий; (of court) регистра́тор **3** (AmE, shop assistant) продаве́ц; (AmE, hotel receptionist) (дежу́рный) администра́тор
clever /ˈklevə(r)/ *adj.* (**cleverer**, **cleverest**) у́мный; (skilful) ло́вкий; **he is ~ with his fingers** у него́ уме́лые ру́ки
cliché /ˈkliːʃeɪ/ *n.* клише́ (*nt. indecl.*)
ᵈ **click** /klɪk/ *n.* щёлканье, щелчо́к
  ● *v.t.* щёлк|ать, -нуть + *i.*
  ● *v.i.* щёлк|ать, -нуть; (comput.): **~ on an icon** щёлк|ать, -нуть (мы́шкой) на ико́нке
ᵈ **client** /ˈklaɪənt/ *n.* клие́нт (-ка)
clientele /kliːɒnˈtel/ *n.* клиенту́ра
cliff /klɪf/ *n.* утёс, скала́
climactic /klaɪˈmæktɪk/ *adj.* кульминацио́нный
ᵈ **climate** /ˈklaɪmət/ *n.* кли́мат; (fig.) атмосфе́ра
■ **~ change** *n.* измене́ние кли́мата
climatic /klaɪˈmætɪk/ *adj.* климати́ческий
climatologist /klaɪməˈtɒlədʒɪst/ *n.* климато́лог
climax /ˈklaɪmæks/ *n.* кульмина́ция
  ● *v.i.* (culminate) дост|ига́ть, -и́чь кульмина́ции, апоге́я
ᵈ **climb** /klaɪm/ *n.* подъём, восхожде́ние
  ● *v.t.* вл|еза́ть, -езть на + *a.*
  ● *v.i.* ла́зить (*indet.*), лезть (*det.*); **~ up a tree** влез|а́ть, -ть на де́рево; **~ over a wall** перел|еза́ть, -е́зть че́рез сте́ну; **~ down a ladder** слез|а́ть, -ть с ле́стницы; **~ on to a table** зал|еза́ть, -е́зть на стол
■ **~down** *n.* (BrE) отступле́ние, усту́пка
climber /ˈklaɪmə(r)/ *n.* альпини́ст (-ка); (plant) вью́щееся расте́ние
climbing /ˈklaɪmɪŋ/ *n.* альпини́зм
clime /klaɪm/ *n.* (poet., region) край, сторона́
clinch /klɪntʃ/ *v.t.*: **~ a bargain** заключи́ть (*pf.*) сде́лку (*окончательно согласовав все условия*)
cling /klɪŋ/ *v.i.* (past and p.p. **clung**) (adhere) цепля́ться (*impf.*) (**to**: за + *a.*); (fig.): **they clung together** они́ держа́лись вме́сте; **a ~ing dress** облега́ющее пла́тье
clinic /ˈklɪnɪk/ *n.* кли́ника
ᵈ **clinical** /ˈklɪnɪk(ə)l/ *adj.* **1** клини́ческий **2** (fig.) бесстра́стный
clink /klɪŋk/ *n.* звень/ка звене́ть (*impf.*) + *i.*
  ● *v.i.* звене́ть (*impf.*); чо́к|аться, -нуться
clip¹ /klɪp/ *n.* (for hair) зако́лка
  ● *v.t.* (**clipped**, **clipping**) (secure) заж|има́ть, -а́ть
■ **~board** *n.* доска́ с зажи́мом для бума́ги; **~-on** *adj.* пристёгивающийся

clip² /klɪp/ *n.* (cin.) отры́вок (из фи́льма)
  ● *v.t.* (**clipped**, **clipping**) (cut): **~ a hedge** подстр|ига́ть, -и́чь живу́ю и́згородь; **~ sb's wings** (fig.) подре́зать (*pf.*) кому́-н. кры́лышки
clipper /ˈklɪpə(r)/ *n.* (*in pl.*) (for nails) куса́ч|ки (-ек)
clipping /ˈklɪpɪŋ/ *n.* (from newspaper) газе́тная вы́резка
cloak /kləʊk/ *n.* плащ, ма́нтия
  ● *v.t.* (fig.) прикр|ыва́ть, -ы́ть
■ **~room** *n.* (for clothes) гардеро́б, раздева́лка; (BrE, lavatory) убо́рная
clock /klɒk/ *n.* час|ы́ (-о́в); **he works round the ~** он рабо́тает кру́глые су́тки; **put the ~ forward** ста́вить, по- часы́ вперёд; **put the ~ back** (lit.) перев|оди́ть, -ести́ часы́ наза́д; (fig.) поверну́ть (*pf.*) вре́мя вспять
  ● *v.i.*: **~ in, on** (BrE) отм|еча́ться, -е́титься по прихо́де на рабо́ту; **~ out, off** (BrE) отм|еча́ться, -е́титься при ухо́де с рабо́ты
■ **~work** *n.* часово́й механи́зм; **the ceremony went like ~work** церемо́ния прошла́ без сучка́, без задо́ринки
clockwise /ˈklɒkwaɪz/ *adj. & adv.* (дви́жущийся) по часово́й стре́лке
clog¹ /klɒg/ *n.* (shoe) башма́к на деревя́нной подо́шве; сабо́ (*nt. indecl.*)
clog² /klɒg/ *v.t.* (**clogged**, **clogging**) засор|я́ть, -и́ть; **the sink is ~ged** ра́ковина засори́лась
cloister /ˈklɔɪstə(r)/ *n.* арка́да
clone /kləʊn/ *n.* клон
  ● *v.t.* размн|ожа́ть, -о́жить вегетати́вным путём; клони́ровать (*impf.*, *pf.*)
cloning /ˈkləʊnɪŋ/ *n.* клони́рование
ᵈ **close¹** /kləʊs/ *adj.* **1** (near) бли́зкий; **he had a ~ shave, call** он был на волосо́к от ги́бели; **~ resemblance** большо́е схо́дство **2** (intimate) бли́зкий; **a ~ friend** бли́зкий друг **3** (compact): **~ texture** пло́тная ткань **4** (attentive): **keep a ~ watch on sb** тща́тельно следи́ть (*impf.*) за кем-н.; **~ examination** тща́тельное обсле́дование; **~ attention** при́стальное внима́ние **5** (of games etc.): **a ~ contest** упо́рная борьба́ **6** (stuffy) ду́шный
  ● *adv.*: **he lives ~ to, by the church** он живёт побли́зости от це́ркви; **follow ~ behind sb** сле́довать (*impf.*) непосре́дственно за кем-н.
■ **~-fitting** *adj.* облега́ющий; **~-up** *n.* (cin.) кру́пный план
ᵈ **close²** /kləʊz/ *n.* (end) коне́ц; **bring to a ~** заверш|а́ть, -и́ть, зак|а́нчивать, -о́нчить; **the meeting drew to a ~** собра́ние подошло́ к концу́
  ● *v.t.* **1** (shut) закр|ыва́ть, -ы́ть; **the museum is ~d** музе́й не рабо́тает **2** (end, complete): **~ a meeting** закр|ыва́ть, -ы́ть собра́ние; **~ a deal** заключ|а́ть, -и́ть сде́лку; **the closing scene of the play** заключи́тельная сце́на пье́сы; **the closing date is December 1** после́дний срок — пе́рвое декабря́
  ● *v.i.* **1** (shut) закр|ыва́ться, -ы́ться; **the door ~d** дверь закры́лась **2** (cease): **he**

~d with this remark он зако́нчил э́тим замеча́нием **3** (come closer) сбл|ижа́ться, -и́зиться; the soldiers ~d up солда́ты сомкну́ли ряды́
□ ~ **down** v.t. закр|ыва́ть, -ы́ть
• v.i. (e.g. of a factory) закр|ыва́ться, -ы́ться
□ ~ **off** v.t. блоки́ровать (impf., pf.)
□ ~ **up** v.t. & i. закр|ыва́ть(ся), -ы́ть(ся)

✎ **closely** /ˈkləʊslɪ/ adv.: it ~ resembles pork э́то о́чень напомина́ет свини́ну; (attentively) внима́тельно; watch ~ при́стально следи́ть (impf.) за + i.; ~ connected те́сно/про́чно свя́занный

closet /ˈklɒzɪt/ n. (AmE) (стенно́й) шкаф

closure /ˈkləʊʒə(r)/ n. закры́тие

clot /klɒt/ n. сгу́сток, комо́к; (BrE, sl., stupid person) болва́н, тупи́ца (c.g.)
• v.i. (**clotted, clotting**) свёртываться, сверну́ться

cloth /klɒθ/ n. **1** (material) ткань, мате́рия **2** (piece of ~) тря́пка

✎ **clothes** /kləʊðz/ n. pl. пла́тье, оде́жда
■ ~ **brush** n. платяна́я щётка; ~ **line** n. верёвка для белья́; ~**peg** (BrE), ~**pin** (AmE) nn. прище́пка

clothing /ˈkləʊðɪŋ/ n. оде́жда

cloud /klaʊd/ n. **1** (in the sky) о́блако; ту́ча **2** (of unhappiness etc.): this cast a ~ over our meeting э́то омрачи́ло на́шу встре́чу
• v.t. покр|ыва́ть, -ы́ть облака́ми; (fig.) омрач|а́ть, -и́ть; eyes ~ed with tears глаза́, помутне́вшие от слёз
• v.i.: the sky ~ed over, up (AmE) не́бо затяну́ло облака́ми/ту́чами

cloudy /ˈklaʊdɪ/ adj. (**cloudier, cloudiest**) о́блачный; (of liquid) му́тный

clout /klaʊt/ n. (blow) затре́щина; (influence) влия́ние
• v.t. (hit) тре́снуть (pf.)

clove /kləʊv/ n.: a ~ of garlic зу́бчик чеснока́

clover /ˈkləʊvə(r)/ n. кле́вер

cloves /kləʊvz/ n. pl. (aromatic) гвозди́ка (пря́ность)

clown /klaʊn/ n. кло́ун
• v.i. стро́ить (impf.) из себя́ шута́

club¹ /klʌb/ n. (weapon) дуби́нка; (at golf) клю́шка; (in pl.) (at cards) тре́фы (f. pl.)

✎ **club²** /klʌb/ n. (society) клуб
• v.i. (**clubbed, clubbing**): they ~bed together to pay the fine они́ сложи́лись и уплати́ли штраф; they're always going out ~bing (infml) они́ — постоя́нные посети́тели ночны́х клу́бов

cluck /klʌk/ v.i. куда́хтать, клохта́ть (both impf.)

clue /kluː/ n. ключ, нить; (for crossword) определе́ние; the police found a ~ поли́ция нашла́ ули́ку; I haven't a ~ (infml) поня́тия не име́ю

clueless /ˈkluːlɪs/ adj. (infml) бестолко́вый; не в ку́рсе

clump /klʌmp/ n. (cluster) гру́ппа
• v.t. (plant in groups) сажа́ть, посади́ть

✎ ключева́я ле́ксика

гру́ппами; (gather into a group) соб|ира́ть, -ра́ть в ку́чу

clumsy /ˈklʌmzɪ/ adj. (**clumsier, clumsiest**) неуклю́жий, нело́вкий

clung /klʌŋ/ past and p.p. of ▶ **cling**

cluster /ˈklʌstə(r)/ n. скопле́ние
• v.i. соб|ира́ться, -ра́ться гру́ппами; the children ~ed round the teacher де́ти столпи́лись вокру́г учи́теля

clutch /klʌtʃ/ n. **1** (in pl.) (grasp) ла́пы (f. pl.), ко́гти (m. pl.) **2** (of car) сцепле́ние
• v.t. & i. хвата́ться, схвати́ться (at: за + a.); he ~ed (at) the rope он ухвати́лся за верёвку
■ ~ **pedal** n. педа́ль сцепле́ния

clutter /ˈklʌtə(r)/ n. сумато́ха, суета́
• v.t. (also ~ up) загромо|жда́ть, -зди́ть

cm /ˈsentiːmiːtə(r)(z)/ n. (abbr. of **centimetre(s)**) см (сантиме́тр(ы))

Co. /kəʊ/ n. (abbr. of **company**) К° (компа́ния)

c/o abbr. (of **care of**) че́рез; John Smith c/o David Green Дэ́виду Гри́ну для переда́чи Джо́ну Сми́ту

coach¹ /kəʊtʃ/ n. **1** (horse-drawn) каре́та, экипа́ж **2** (railway) пассажи́рский ваго́н **3** (BrE, bus) (туристи́ческий, междугоро́дный) авто́бус
■ ~ **tour** n. авто́бусная экску́рсия

✎ **coach²** /kəʊtʃ/ n. (trainer) тре́нер
• v.t. репети́ровать (impf.); (train) тренирова́ть, на-

coagulate /kəʊˈægjʊleɪt/ v.t. сгу|ща́ть, -сти́ть; (phys., chem.) коагули́ровать (impf., pf.); (med., blood) свёртывать, сверну́ть
• v.i. сгу|ща́ться, -сти́ться; (phys., chem.) коагули́роваться (impf., pf.); (med., of blood) свёртываться, сверну́ться

coal /kəʊl/ n. (mineral) ка́менный у́голь; (BrE, piece of ~) у́голь (m.); (fig.): haul sb over the ~s да|ва́ть, -ть нагоня́й кому́-н.
■ ~**field** n. каменноуго́льный бассе́йн; ~ **mine** n. у́гольная ша́хта; ~ **miner** n. шахтёр

coalition /kəʊəˈlɪʃ(ə)n/ n. (pol.) коали́ция

coarse /kɔːs/ adj. (of material) гру́бый; (of sand, sugar) кру́пный; ~ **manners** гру́бые/вульга́рные мане́ры

coast /kəʊst/ n. морско́й бе́рег
• v.i. **1** (bicycle downhill) кати́ться (impf.) на велосипе́де с горы́ **2** (do sth with little effort) де́лать (impf.) что-л. без осо́бых уси́лий
■ ~**guard** n. (officer) сотру́дник (тамо́женной) берегово́й охра́ны; (collect.) берегова́я охра́на; ~**line** n. берегова́я ли́ния

coastal /ˈkəʊst(ə)l/ adj. берегово́й, прибре́жный

coaster /ˈkəʊstə(r)/ n. подно́с, подста́вка

coat /kəʊt/ n. **1** (overcoat) пальто́ (nt. indecl.); ~ **of arms** герб **2** (of animal) шерсть, мех **3** (of paint etc.) слой
• v.t. покр|ыва́ть, -ы́ть; the pill is ~ed with sugar пилю́ля в са́харной оболо́чке
■ ~ **hanger** n. ве́шалка

coating /ˈkəʊtɪŋ/ n. (layer) слой

co-author /kəʊˈɔːθə(r)/ n. соа́втор

coax /kəʊks/ v.t. угова́р|ивать, -ори́ть

cobble¹ /ˈkɒb(ə)l/ *n.* (*also* **cobblestone**) булыжник

cobble² /ˈkɒb(ə)l/ *v.t.* (*usu.* ~ **together**) делать (*impf.*) кое-как

cobbled /ˈkɒb(ə)ld/ *adj.*: ~ **street** булыжная мостовая

cobra /ˈkəʊbrə/ *n.* кобра; очковая змея

cobweb /ˈkɒbweb/ *n.* паутина

cocaine /kəˈkeɪn/ *n.* кокаин

cock¹ /kɒk/ *n.* ▮ (male domestic fowl) петух ▮ (male bird) петух, самец
■ ~ **and bull** *adj.*: ~ **and bull story** вздор, небылица; ~**pit** *n.* (aeron.) кабина; ~**roach** *n.* таракан; ~**tail** *n.* (drink) коктейль (*m.*)

cock² /kɒk/ *v.t.* ▮ (stick up etc.): **the horse** ~**ed (up) its ears** лошадь навострила уши ▮ (of gun) взводить, -ести курок + *g.*

cockerel /ˈkɒkər(ə)l/ *n.* петушок

cockle /ˈkɒk(ə)l/ *n.* сердцевидка, съедобный моллюск

cockney /ˈkɒknɪ/ *n. & adj.* (person) кокни (*c.g. indecl.*); (language) кокни (*m. indecl.*); ~ **accent** акцент кокни

cocky /ˈkɒkɪ/ *adj.* (**cockier, cockiest**) нахальный

cocoa /ˈkəʊkəʊ/ *n.* какао (*nt. indecl.*)

coconut /ˈkəʊkənʌt/ *n.* кокос, кокосовый орех

cocoon /kəˈkuːn/ *n.* кокон

COD *abbr.* (*of* **cash on delivery**) уплата при доставке

cod /kɒd/ *n.* (*pl.* ~) треска

coda /ˈkəʊdə/ *n.* (mus.) кода

⚘ **code** /kəʊd/ *n.* (of laws, conduct) кодекс; (set of symbols) код
● *v.t.* (encode) кодировать (*impf., pf.*)

codeine /ˈkəʊdiːn/ *n.* кодеин

co-educational /kəʊedjuːˈkeɪʃən(ə)l/ *adj.* совместного обучения

coerce /kəʊˈɜːs/ *v.t.* принуждать, -удить

coercion /kəʊˈɜːʃ(ə)n/ *n.* принуждение; **he paid under** ~ он заплатил под давлением; **его принудили заплатить**

coercive /kəʊˈɜːsɪv/ *adj.* принудительный

coexist /kəʊɪɡˈzɪst/ *v.i.* сосуществовать (*impf.*)

coexistence /kəʊɪɡˈzɪst(ə)ns/ *n.* сосуществование

C. of E. *abbr.* (*of* **Church of England**) Англиканская церковь

⚘ **coffee** /ˈkɒfɪ/ *n.* кофе (*m. indecl.*); **two** ~**s** два кофе; **black** ~ чёрный кофе; **white** ~ кофе с молоком
■ ~ **bar** *n.* буфет; ~ **bean** *n.* (on tree) кофейный боб; (as product) кофейное зерно; (*in pl.*) кофе в зёрнах; ~ **break** *n.* перерыв на кофе; ~ **pot** *n.* кофейник; ~ **table** *n.* кофейный/журнальный столик

coffer /ˈkɒfə(r)/ *n.* (chest) сундук; (*in pl.*) (fig., funds) казна

coffin /ˈkɒfɪn/ *n.* гроб

cog /kɒɡ/ *n.* зуб (-ья); зубец

cogent /ˈkəʊdʒ(ə)nt/ *adj.* убедительный

cogitate /ˈkɒdʒɪteɪt/ *v.i.* размышлять (*impf.*) (on/over: о чём *or* над чем)

cognac /ˈkɒnjæk/ *n.* коньяк

cognizant /ˈkɒɡnɪz(ə)nt/ *adj.* знающий, осведомлённый

cohabit /kəʊˈhæbɪt/ *v.i.* (**cohabited, cohabiting**) сожительствовать (*impf.*)

coherent /kəʊˈhɪərənt/ *adj.* связный, последовательный

cohesion /kəʊˈhiːʒ(ə)n/ *n.* сцепление; сплочённость

cohort /ˈkəʊhɔːt/ *n.* когорта

coil /kɔɪl/ *n.* виток; кольцо
● *v.t. & i.* (*also* ~ **up**) свёртывать(ся), свернуть(ся) кольцом (*or* в кольцо)

coin /kɔɪn/ *n.* монета
● *v.t.*: ~ **a phrase** создавать, -ать выражение
■ ~ **box** *n.* (BrE, telephone) телефон-автомат; ~-**operated** *adj.* монетный

coincide /kəʊɪnˈsaɪd/ *v.i.* совпадать, -асть

coincidence /kəʊˈɪnsɪd(ə)ns/ *n.* совпадение

coincidental /kəʊɪnsɪˈdent(ə)l/ *adj.* случайный

coke¹ /kəʊk/ *n.* (fuel) кокс

coke² /kəʊk/ *n.* (sl., cocaine) кокаин

colander /ˈkʌləndə(r)/ *n.* дуршлаг

⚘ **cold** /kəʊld/ *n.* ▮ холод ▮ (illness) простуда; **catch (a)** ~ просту|жаться, -диться
● *adj.* ▮ (at low temperature) холодный; **I am, feel** ~ мне холодно ▮ (fig.): **in** ~ **blood** хладнокровно; **get** ~ **feet** (infml) трусить, с- ▮ (unfeeling): **a** ~ **person** холодный человек
■ ~-**blooded** *adj.* (of reptile, fish) холоднокровный; (fig.) бесчувственный, безжалостный; ~-**shoulder** *v.t.* оказ|ывать, -ать кому-н. холодный приём

coleslaw /ˈkəʊlslɔː/ *n.* капустный салат (*свежие капуста, морковь, лук под майонезом*)

colic /ˈkɒlɪk/ *n.* колик|и (*pl., g.* —)

collaborate /kəˈlæbəreɪt/ *v.i.* сотрудничать (*impf.*)

collaboration /kəlæbəˈreɪʃ(ə)n/ *n.* сотрудничество

⚘ **collapse** /kəˈlæps/ *n.* (of a building; of prices, market, etc.) обвал; (of negotiations etc.) провал; (of hopes etc.) крушение; (of resistance etc.) развал; (med.) коллапс
● *v.i.* (of a building etc.) обвал|иваться, -иться; (of person) валиться, с-

collapsible /kəˈlæpsɪb(ə)l/ *adj.* складной

collar /ˈkɒlə(r)/ *n.* ▮ (of garment) воротник; **hot under the** ~ (fig., excited, vexed) рассерженный ▮ (of dog) ошейник
● *v.t.* (seize) схват|ывать, -ить
■ ~**bone** *n.* (anat.) ключица

collate /kəˈleɪt/ *v.t.* слич|ать, -ить

collateral /kəˈlætər(ə)l/ *adj.* побочный, дополнительный; ~ **security** (fin.) дополнительное обеспечение (*кредита*)

⚘ **colleague** /ˈkɒliːɡ/ *n.* коллега (*c.g.*)

⚘ **collect** /kəˈlekt/ *v.t.* ▮ (gather together) соб|ирать, -рать; ~**ed works** (полное) собрание

сочине́ний **2** (debts, taxes) соб|ира́ть, -ра́ть **3** (stamps etc.) коллекциони́ровать (*impf.*) **4** (fetch) заб|ира́ть, -ра́ть
• *v.i.* соб|ира́ться, -ра́ться

collected /kə'lektɪd/ *adj.* (calm) со́бранный

C

✔ **collection** /kə'lekʃ(ə)n/ *n.* (of valuables etc.) колле́кция; (accumulation) скопле́ние; (for charity) сбор; (of mail) вы́емка

collective /kə'lektɪv/ *n.* (cooperative unit) коллекти́в
• *adj.* коллекти́вный
■ ~ **farm** *n.* колхо́з

collector /kə'lektə(r)/ *n.* (of stamps etc.) коллекционе́р; **a ~'s piece** ре́дкий/уника́льный экземпля́р; (of taxes, debts) сбо́рщик

✔ **college** /'kɒlɪdʒ/ *n.* **1** (school) ко́лледж **2** (university) университе́т; институ́т **3** (within university) университе́тский ко́лледж

collide /kə'laɪd/ *v.i.* ст|а́лкиваться, -олкну́ться

colliery /'kɒlɪərɪ/ *n.* каменноу́гольная ша́хта

collision /kə'lɪʒ(ə)n/ *n.* столкнове́ние

colloquial /kə'ləʊkwɪəl/ *adj.* разгово́рный

colloquialism /kə'ləʊkwɪəlɪz(ə)m/ *n.* разгово́рное выраже́ние/сло́во

collusion /kə'lu:ʒ(ə)n/ *n.* сго́вор; **act in ~** де́йствовать (*impf.*) по сго́вору

Colombia /kə'lɒmbɪə/ *n.* Колу́мбия

Colombian /kə'lɒmbɪən/ *n.* колумби́|ец (-йка)
• *adj.* колумби́йский

colon[1] /'kəʊlɒn/ *n.* (anat.) то́лстая/ободо́чная кишка́

colon[2] /'kəʊlɒn/ *n.* (gram.) двоето́чие

colonel /'kə:n(ə)l/ *n.* полко́вник

colonial /kə'ləʊnɪəl/ *adj.* колониа́льный

colonialism /kə'ləʊnɪəlɪz(ə)m/ *n.* колониали́зм

colonist /'kɒlənɪst/ *n.* колони́ст (-ка)

colonization /kɒlənaɪ'zeɪʃ(ə)n/ *n.* колониза́ция

colonize /'kɒlənaɪz/ *v.t.* колонизова́ть, колонизи́ровать (*both impf., pf.*)

colonizer /'kɒlənaɪzə(r)/ *n.* колониза́тор

colony /'kɒlənɪ/ *n.* коло́ния

colossal /kə'lɒs(ə)l/ *adj.* колосса́льный, грома́дный

✔ **colour** /'kʌlə(r)/ (AmE **color**) *n.* **1** (lit.) цвет; **change ~** (lit.) меня́ть, по- цвет; (fig.) (go pale) бледне́ть, по-; (blush) красне́ть, по-; **the film is in ~** э́то цветно́й фильм **2** (of face) цвет лица́ **3** (*in pl.*) (paints) кра́ски **4** (of race): **a person of ~** представи́тель (-ница) небе́лой ра́сы
• *v.t.* **1** (paint) кра́сить, по- **2** (imbue): **his action was ~ed by envy** его́ посту́пок был отча́сти продикто́ван за́вистью
• *v.i.* (blush) красне́ть, по-
■ **~-blind** *adj.* страда́ющий дальтони́змом; **~ film** *n.* цветна́я плёнка; **~ scheme** *n.* цветова́я га́мма; **~ television** *n.* цветно́е телеви́дение

✔ ключевая лексика

coloured /'kʌləd/ (AmE **colored**) *adj.* (not black or white) цветно́й

colourful /'kʌləfʊl/ (AmE **colorful**) *adj.* кра́сочный, я́ркий; **a ~ personality** я́ркая/колори́тная ли́чность

colouring /'kʌlərɪŋ/ (AmE **coloring**) *n.* окра́ска; (complexion) цвет лица́

colourless /'kʌləlɪs/ (AmE **colorless**) *adj.* (lit., fig.) бесцве́тный

colt /kəʊlt/ *n.* (young horse) жеребёнок

✔ **column** /'kɒləm/ *n.* **1** (pillar) коло́нна **2** (in book etc.) столбе́ц **3** (regular feature in newspaper): **weekly ~** еженеде́льная коло́нка/ру́брика **4** (mil. etc.) коло́нна

columnist /'kɒləmnɪst/ *n.* обозрева́тель (*m.*)

coma /'kəʊmə/ *n.* (*pl.* **~s**) ко́ма

comb /kəʊm/ *n.* расчёска
• *v.t.* расчёс|ывать, -а́ть; причёс|ывать, -а́ть

combat /'kɒmbæt/ *n.* бой
• *v.t.* (**combated**, **combating**) боро́ться (*impf.*) с + *i.* (*or* про́тив + *g.*)

combatant /'kɒmbət(ə)nt/ *n.* бое́ц; вою́ющая сторона́

✔ **combination** /kɒmbɪ'neɪʃ(ə)n/ *n.* сочета́ние

combine[1] /'kɒmbaɪn/ *n.* **1** (group of people or companies) объедине́ние **2** (*in full* **~ harvester**) комба́йн

✔ **combine**[2] /kəm'baɪn/ *v.t.* сочета́ть (*impf.*); **~ forces** объедин|я́ть, -и́ть (*or* соедин|я́ть, -и́ть) си́лы

combustion /kəm'bʌstʃ(ə)n/ *n.* воспламене́ние; сгора́ние; **spontaneous ~** самовоспламене́ние; **internal ~ engine** дви́гатель (*m.*) вну́треннего сгора́ния

✔ **come** /kʌm/ *v.i.* (*past* **came**, *p.p.* **come**) **1** (move near, arrive) при|ходи́ть, -йти́; **he has ~ a hundred miles** он прие́хал за сто миль; **~ along!** пойдёмте!; **~ into the house!** заходи́те/зайди́те в дом! **2** (of inanimate things, lit., fig.): **the dress ~s to her knees** пла́тье дохо́дит ей до коле́н; **the feeling ~s and goes** э́то чу́вство то появля́ется, то исчеза́ет; **it came as a shock to me** э́то бы́ло для меня́ уда́ром **3** (fig. uses with 'into'): **he has ~ into a fortune** он получи́л большо́е насле́дство; **the party came into power** па́ртия пришла́ к вла́сти **4** (happen) случа́ться, быва́ть (*both impf.*); **Christmas ~s once a year** Рождество́ быва́ет раз в году́; **how ~ he was late?** как получи́лось, что он опозда́л?; **in years to ~** в после́дующие го́ды; в бу́дущем; **~ what may** будь, что бу́дет; **how ~?** (infml) э́то почему́ же?; как так? **5** (amount): **the bill ~s to £5** счёт равня́ется пяти́ фу́нтам; **his plans came to nothing** из его́ пла́нов ничего́ не вы́шло **6** (become, prove to be): **her dreams came true** её мечты́ осуществи́лись/сбыли́сь; **his shoelace came undone** у него́ шнуро́к развяза́лся **7** (fig., find oneself in a position): **I have ~ to see that he is right** я убеди́лся, что он прав **8** (of person, originate) прои|сходи́ть, -зойти́; **he ~s from Scotland** он уроже́нец Шотла́ндии; (of thing, originate): **wine ~s from grapes** вино́ получа́ется из виногра́да

● *with preps.*: ∼ **across** (encounter) нат|а́лкиваться, -олкну́ться на + *a.*; ∼ **into** (inherit): she came into a large estate ей доста́лось большо́е име́ние; ∼ **off** (become detached (from)): a button came off my coat от моего́ пальто́ оторвала́сь пу́говица; ∼ **over** (fig.): what came over you? что на вас нашло́?; ∼ **under** (be categorized): what heading does this ∼ under? к како́й ру́брике э́то отно́сится?

□ ∼ **across (as)** показа́ться (*pf.*) + *i.*

□ ∼ **apart** *v.i.* (become unfastened) ра|сходи́ться, -зойти́сь

□ ∼ **away** *v.i.* (become detached) отл|а́мываться, -ома́ться *or* -оми́ться (**from:** от + *g.*)

□ ∼ **back** *v.i.* (return) возвра|ща́ться, -ти́ться; верну́ться (*pf.*)

□ ∼ **down** *v.i.*: her hair ∼s down to her waist её во́лосы дохо́дят до по́яса; (of prices) па́дать, упа́сть; (fig.): he came down with influenza он слёг с гри́ппом

□ ∼ **forward** *v.i.* (offer one's services) предл|ага́ть, -ожи́ть свои́ услу́ги

□ ∼ **in** *v.i.* (lit.) входи́ть, войти́; the tide came in наступи́л прили́в; it came in handy э́то пригоди́лось

□ ∼ **off** *v.i.* (become detached) отва́л|иваться, -и́ться; (happen, succeed): the experiment came off о́пыт уда́лся; (finish work): he ∼s off at 10 он ухо́дит со слу́жбы в 10

□ ∼ **on** *v.i.* (follow) сле́довать (*impf.*); (progress) де́лать (*impf.*) успе́хи; (start, set in): I have a cold coming on у меня́ начина́ется просту́да; (*in imper.*) ∼ **on!** (expr. encouragement) ну́-ка!; (expr. impatience) ну́!; ну́ же!; (of actor; appear) появ|ля́ться, -и́ться

□ ∼ **out** *v.i.* (lit.) выходи́ть, вы́йти; the sun came out появи́лось/вы́глянуло со́лнце; (become known, appear): the book came out кни́га вы́шла; (disappear): the stains came out пятна́ сошли́; (declare oneself): he came out against the plan он вы́ступил про́тив пла́на; (publicly acknowledge one's homosexuality) откры́то признава́ть, -а́ть свою́ гомосексуа́льность; (BrE, go on strike) забастова́ть (*pf.*); she came out in a rash (BrE) она́ покры́лась сы́пью

□ ∼ **over** *v.i.*: they came over to England они́ прие́хали в А́нглию

□ ∼ **round** *v.i.* (change mind): he came round to my view он пришёл-таки к мое́й то́чке зре́ния; (yield): she'll ∼ round (BrE) она́ усту́пит/согласи́тся; (recover consciousness) при|ходи́ть, -йти́ в себя́; очну́ться (*pf.*)

□ ∼ **through** *v.i.* (survive experience) пережи́ть (*pf.*)

□ ∼ **to** *v.i.* (recover one's senses) при|ходи́ть, -йти́ в себя́

□ ∼ **up** *v.i.*: the sun came up со́лнце взошло́; the seeds came up семена́ взошли́; the water came up to my waist вода́ доходи́ла мне до по́яса; the question came up встал вопро́с; the case ∼s up tomorrow э́то де́ло разбира́ется за́втра; he came up against a difficulty он столкну́лся с тру́дностями; he came up with a suggestion он внёс предложе́ние

■ ∼**back** *n.* (return) возвраще́ние; ∼**uppance** /kʌm'ʌpəns/ *n.* (infml): he got his ∼**uppance** он

получи́л по заслу́гам

comedian /kə'miːdɪən/ *n.* ко́мик

comedy /'kɒmɪdɪ/ *n.* коме́дия

comet /'kɒmɪt/ *n.* коме́та

comfort /'kʌmfət/ *n.* **1** (physical ease) комфо́рт **2** (relief of suffering) утеше́ние, отра́да **3** (thing that brings ∼) утеше́ние, успокое́ние
● *v.t.* ут|еша́ть, -е́шить

✧ **comfortabl|e** /'kʌmftəb(ə)l/ *adj.* удо́бный, ую́тный, комфорта́бельный, комфо́ртный; the car holds six people ∼y э́та маши́на свобо́дно вмеща́ет шесть челове́к; he is ∼y off он живёт в доста́тке

comforter /'kʌmfətə(r)/ *n.* (AmE, quilt for bed) стёганое одея́ло

comforting /'kʌmfətɪŋ/ *adj.* утеши́тельный, успокои́тельный

comfy /'kʌmfɪ/ *adj.* (infml) удо́бный, ую́тный

comic /'kɒmɪk/ *n.* **1** (infml, comedian) ко́мик, юмори́ст **2** (magazine) ко́микс
● *adj.* коми́ческий, юмористи́ческий
■ ∼ **strip** *n.* ко́микс

comical /'kɒmɪk(ə)l/ *adj.* коми́чный, смешно́й

coming /'kʌmɪŋ/ *n.* прие́зд, прихо́д; ∼ **and going** движе́ние взад-вперёд
● *adj.* бу́дущий, наступа́ющий

comma /'kɒmə/ *n.* запята́я

✧ **command** /kə'mɑːnd/ *n.* **1** (order, also comput.) кома́нда **2** (authority) кома́ндование; he is in ∼ of the army он кома́ндует а́рмией **3** (control) контро́ль (*m.*) **4** (knowledge): she has a good ∼ of French она́ непло́хо владе́ет францу́зским (языко́м) **5** (mil.) кома́ндование
● *v.t.* **1** (give orders to) прика́з|ывать, -а́ть + *d.* **2** (have authority over) кома́ндовать (*impf.*) + *i.* **3** (be able to use or enjoy) располага́ть (*impf.*) + *i.*; he ∼s respect он заслу́живает уваже́ния
■ ∼ **post** *n.* кома́ндный пункт, КП

commandant /kɒmən'dant/ *n.* коменда́нт

commandeer /kɒmən'dɪə(r)/ *v.t.* реквизи́ровать (*impf., pf.*)

commander /kə'mɑːndə(r)/ *n.* команди́р, кома́ндующий

commanding /kə'mɑːndɪŋ/ *adj.*: ∼ **officer** команди́р; a ∼ **presence** внуши́тельная оса́нка

commando /kə'mɑːndəʊ/ *n.* (pl. ∼**s**) деса́нтник-диверса́нт, диверса́нт-разве́дчик; (in pl.) кома́ндос (*indecl., pl.*)

commemorate /kə'meməreɪt/ *v.t.* (celebrate memory of) отм|еча́ть, -е́тить (*годовщину, событие*)

commemorative /kə'memərətɪv/ *adj.* па́мятный, мемориа́льный

commence /kə'mens/ *v.t. & i.* нач|ина́ть(ся), -а́ть(ся)

commend /kə'mend/ *v.t.* **1** (entrust) вв|еря́ть, -е́рить; поруч|а́ть, -и́ть; he ∼ed his soul to God он посвяти́л себя́ Бо́гу **2** (praise) хвали́ть, по-

commendable /kə'mendəb(ə)l/ *adj.* похва́льный

commensurate /kə'menʃərət/ *adj.* разме́рный

✧ **comment** /'kɒment/ *n.* замеча́ние,

коммента́рий; **no ~!** без коммента́риев!
● *v.t. & i.* комменти́ровать (*impf., pf.*);
толкова́ть (*impf.*)

commentary /ˈkɒməntəri/ *n.* коммента́рий

commentator /ˈkɒmənteɪtə(r)/ *n.*
коммента́тор

commerce /ˈkɒmɜːs/ *n.* комме́рция

ꜰ **commercial** /kəˈmɜːʃ(ə)l/ *n.* рекла́ма,
рекла́мная переда́ча
● *adj.* комме́рческий, торго́вый

commercialize /kəˈmɜːʃəlaɪz/ *n.* ста́вить, по-
на комме́рческую осно́ву; вн|оси́ть, -ести́
комме́рческий дух в + *a.*

commiserate /kəˈmɪzəreɪt/ *v.i.* выража́ть,
вы́разить соболе́знование (**with:** + *d.*)

commissar /ˈkɒmɪsɑː(r)/ *n.* комисса́р

ꜰ **commission** /kəˈmɪʃ(ə)n/ *n.* **1** (authorization)
полномо́чие **2** (comm.) комиссио́нн|ые (-ых)
3 (committee) коми́ссия
● *v.t.* поруч|а́ть, -и́ть (*что кому*); **he ~ed
me to buy this** он поручи́л мне купи́ть э́то;
he ~ed a portrait from the artist он заказа́л
худо́жнику портре́т; **a ~ed officer** офице́р

commissioner /kəˈmɪʃənə(r)/ *n.* член
коми́ссии

ꜰ **commit** /kəˈmɪt/ *v.t.* (**committed,
committing**) **1** (perform) соверш|а́ть, -и́ть
2 (pledge): **he ~ted himself to helping her** он
взя́лся помо́чь ей **3**: **a ~ted writer** иде́йный
писа́тель

ꜰ **commitment** /kəˈmɪtmənt/ *n.* обяза́тельство

ꜰ **committee** /kəˈmɪti/ *n.* комите́т, коми́ссия

commodity /kəˈmɒdɪti/ *n.* това́р, предме́т
потребле́ния

commodore /ˈkɒmədɔː(r)/ *n.* (in navy or
merchant marine) коммодо́р, капита́н пе́рвого
ра́нга; (of yacht club) командо́р

ꜰ **common** /ˈkɒmən/ *n.* **1** (land) пусты́рь (*m.*),
вы́гон **2** (sth usual or shared): **you have a lot in
~ with her** у вас с ней мно́го о́бщего
● *adj.* (**commoner, commonest**)
1 (belonging to more than one, general) о́бщий;
it is ~ knowledge that … общеизве́стно,
что… **2** (belonging to the public): **~ land**
обще́ственная земля́ **3** (ordinary, usual)
обы́чный, обы́денный, обыкнове́нный;
the ~ people (просто́й) наро́д **4** (vulgar)
вульга́рный, по́шлый
■ **~-law** *adj.*: **~-law marriage**
незарегистри́рованный брак; **~-law wife**
сожи́тельница; **~place** *n.* бана́льность
● *adj.* бана́льный; **~ room** *n.* (BrE) (senior)
учи́тельская, преподава́тельская; (junior)
студе́нческая ко́мната о́тдыха; **~ sense** *n.*
здра́вый смысл

commonly /ˈkɒmənli/ *adv.* (usually) обы́чно,
обыкнове́нно

Commonwealth /ˈkɒmənwelθ/ *n.*: **the ~ (of
Nations)** Брита́нское Содру́жество (на́ций);
the ~ of Independent States Содру́жество
Незави́симых Госуда́рств

commotion /kəˈməʊʃ(ə)n/ *n.* волне́ние, возня́

ꜰ ключева́я ле́ксика

communal /ˈkɒmjʊn(ə)l/ *adj.*
обще́ственный, коммуна́льный

commune /ˈkɒmjuːn/ *n.* (administrative unit)
общи́на, комму́на; (Russian hist., peasant ~) мир

ꜰ **communicate** /kəˈmjuːnɪkeɪt/ *v.t.* сообщ|а́ть,
-и́ть
● *v.i.* свя́з|ываться, -а́ться; сообщ|а́ть, -и́ть
(*кому о чём*); **~ with sb** обща́ться (*impf.*)
с кем-н.

ꜰ **communication** /kəmjuːnɪˈkeɪʃ(ə)n/ *n.*
обще́ние; связь, сообще́ние, коммуника́ция

communicative /kəˈmjuːnɪkətɪv/ *adj.*
общи́тельный, разгово́рчивый

communion /kəˈmjuːnɪən/ *n.* прича́стие

communism /ˈkɒmjʊnɪz(ə)m/ *n.* коммуни́зм

communist /ˈkɒmjʊnɪst/ *n.* коммуни́ст (-ка)
● *adj.* коммунисти́ческий

ꜰ **community** /kəˈmjuːnɪti/ *n.* (political, social, etc.
group) общи́на, гру́ппа населе́ния; (society)
о́бщество

commute /kəˈmjuːt/ *v.i.* (to work) е́здить
(*indet.*) ка́ждый день на значи́тельное
расстоя́ние на рабо́ту
● *v.t.* замен|я́ть, -и́ть; (law) смягч|а́ть, -и́ть
(*приговор*)

commuter /kəˈmjuːtə(r)/ *n.* (traveller) жи́тель
(-ница) при́города, (регуля́рно) е́здящ|ий
(-ая) на рабо́ту в го́род (на авто́бусе, по́езде
и т. п.)

compact /kəmˈpækt/ *adj.* (concise) сжа́тый,
компа́ктный
■ **~ disc** /ˈkɒmpækt/ *n.* компа́кт-ди́ск; **~ disc
player** прои́грыватель (*m.*) компа́кт-ди́сков

companion /kəmˈpænjən/ *n.* спу́тни|к (-ца)

companionship /kəmˈpænjənʃɪp/ *n.*
дру́жеское обще́ние; дру́жеские отноше́ния

ꜰ **company** /ˈkʌmpəni/ *n.* **1** (companionship):
I was glad of his ~ я был рад его́ о́бществу;
keep sb ~ сост|авля́ть, -а́вить кому́-н.
компа́нию **2** (associates, guests): **we have ~
this evening** у нас сего́дня бу́дут го́сти
3 (commercial firm) това́рищество, компа́ния;
~ car служе́бная маши́на **4** (theatr.) тру́ппа
5 (mil.) ро́та

comparable /ˈkɒmpərəb(ə)l/ *adj.* сравни́мый

comparative /kəmˈpærətɪv/ *adj.*
1 сравни́тельный **2** (relative) относи́тельный

ꜰ **compare** /kəmˈpeə(r)/ *v.t.* сра́вн|ивать, -и́ть
● *v.i.* сра́вн|иваться, -и́ться

ꜰ **comparison** /kəmˈpærɪs(ə)n/ *n.* сравне́ние;
in, by ~ with по сравне́нию с + *i.*

compartment /kəmˈpɑːtmənt/ *n.* (section)
отделе́ние, отсе́к; (on train) купе́ (*nt. indecl.*)

compass /ˈkʌmpəs/ *n.* **1** (mariner's) ко́мпас;
points of the ~ стра́ны све́та **2** (in full **pair
of ~es**) (geom.) ци́ркуль (*m.*)

compassion /kəmˈpæʃ(ə)n/ *n.* сострада́ние

compassionate /kəmˈpæʃənət/ *adj.*
сострада́тельный

compatible /kəmˈpætɪb(ə)l/ *adj.* совмести́мый

compatriot /kəmˈpætrɪət/ *n.* сооте́чественник

compel /kəmˈpel/ *v.t.* (**compelled,
compelling**) заст|авля́ть, -а́вить

compelling /kəm'pelɪŋ/ *adj.* непреодоли́мый, неотрази́мый

compensate /'kɒmpenseɪt/ *v.t.*: ~ sb for sth компенси́ровать (*impf., pf.*) (*кому что*); **they expressed a willingness to ~ fans for their expenditure** они́ вы́разили гото́вность компенси́ровать боле́льщикам затра́ты; **he was ~d for his injuries** он получи́л компенса́цию за свои́ уве́чья

• *v.i.*: ~ **for** возме|ща́ть, -сти́ть; компенси́ровать (*impf., pf.*); **his personality ~s for his appearance** его́ ли́чные ка́чества компенси́руют его́ вне́шность

compensation /kɒmpen'seɪʃ(ə)n/ *n.* компенса́ция; **pay ~** выпла́чивать, вы́платить компенса́цию

⚬ **compete** /kəm'piːt/ *v.i.* (vie) конкури́ровать (*impf.*); ~ **with, against sb for sth** конкури́ровать (*impf.*) с кем-н. из-за чего́-н.; (in sport) состяза́ться (*impf.*)

competence /'kɒmpɪt(ə)ns/, **competency** /'kɒmpɪtənsɪ/ *nn.* уме́ние, компете́нтность

competent /'kɒmpɪt(ə)nt/ *adj.* компете́нтный

⚬ **competition** /kɒmpə'tɪʃ(ə)n/ *n.* **1** (rivalry) сопе́рничество **2** (contest) состяза́ние

competitive /kəm'petɪtɪv/ *adj.* (person) честолюби́вый; ~ **prices** конкурентоспосо́бные це́ны

competitor /kəm'petɪtə(r)/ *n.* конкуре́нт (-ка)

compilation /kɒmpɪ'leɪʃ(ə)n/ *n.* (act) собира́ние; (result) сбо́рник

compile /kəm'paɪl/ *v.t.* соб|ира́ть, -ра́ть

complacent /kəm'pleɪs(ə)nt/ *adj.* самодово́льный

⚬ **complain** /kəm'pleɪn/ *v.i.* жа́ловаться, по- (**about, of:** на + *a.*); **he ~s of frequent headaches** он жа́луется на ча́стые головны́е бо́ли

⚬ **complaint** /kəm'pleɪnt/ *n.* жа́лоба

complement /'kɒmplɪmənt/ *v.t.* доп|олня́ть, -о́лнить

complementary /kɒmplɪ'mentərɪ/ *adj.* дополни́тельный; ~ **medicine** (BrE) альтернати́вная, нетрадицио́нная медици́на

⚬ **complete** /kəm'pliːt/ *adj.* **1** (whole) по́лный **2** (finished) зако́нченный, завершённый; **when will the work be ~?** когда́ бу́дет завершён э́тот труд? **3** (thorough) соверше́нный

• *v.t.* зак|а́нчивать, -о́нчить; (fill in) зап|олня́ть, -о́лнить

⚬ **completely** /kəm'pliːtlɪ/ *adv.* соверше́нно, по́лностью

completion /kəm'pliːʃ(ə)n/ *n.* заверше́ние

⚬ **complex** /'kɒmpleks/ *n.* ко́мплекс

• *adj.* сло́жный, ко́мплексный

complexion /kəm'plekʃ(ə)n/ *n.* цвет лица́

complexity /kəm'pleksɪtɪ/ *n.* сло́жность

compliance /kəm'plaɪəns/ *n.* усту́пчивость

compliant /kəm'plaɪənt/ *adj.* усту́пчивый

complicate /'kɒmplɪkeɪt/ *v.t.* осложн|я́ть, -и́ть

complicated /'kɒmplɪkeɪtɪd/ *adj.* сло́жный

complication /kɒmplɪ'keɪʃ(ə)n/ *n.* (complicating circumstance) осложне́ние; (med.):

~s **set in** после́довали осложне́ния

complicity /kəm'plɪsɪtɪ/ *n.* соуча́стие

compliment *n.* /'kɒmplɪmənt/ комплиме́нт; похвала́

• *v.t.* /'kɒmplɪment/ говори́ть (*impf.*) комплиме́нты (+ *d.*) (*по поводу чего*)

complimentary /kɒmplɪ'mentərɪ/ *adj.* **1** (laudatory) похва́льный, ле́стный **2**: ~ **ticket** контрама́рка, пригласи́тельный биле́т

comply /kəm'plaɪ/ *v.i.*: ~ **with** уступ|а́ть, -и́ть + *d.*

⚬ **component** /kəm'pəʊnənt/ *n.* компоне́нт

• *adj.* составно́й

compose /kəm'pəʊz/ *v.t. & i.* **1** (make up) сост|авля́ть, -а́вить; **the party was ~d of teachers** гру́ппа состоя́ла из учителе́й **2** (liter., mus.) сочин|я́ть, -и́ть **3** (calm): ~ **oneself** успок|а́иваться, -о́иться; **a ~d manner** сде́ржанная мане́ра

composer /kəm'pəʊzə(r)/ *n.* (mus.) компози́тор

composite /'kɒmpəzɪt/ *adj.* составно́й

composition /kɒmpə'zɪʃ(ə)n/ *n.* **1** (act of composing) сочине́ние, составле́ние **2** (lirerary or musical work) произведе́ние, сочине́ние **3** (school exercise) сочине́ние **4** (make-up) соста́в; ~ **of the soil** соста́в по́чвы

compost /'kɒmpɒst/ *n.* компо́ст

composure /kəm'pəʊʒə(r)/ *n.* споко́йствие

compound[1] /'kɒmpaʊnd/ *n.* (enclosure) огоро́женное ме́сто

compound[2] *n.* /'kɒmpaʊnd/ (mixture) смесь; (gram.) сло́жное сло́во; (chem.) соедине́ние

• *adj.* /'kɒmpaʊnd/ составно́й, сло́жный

• *v.t.* /kəm'paʊnd/ (worsen) обостр|я́ть, -и́ть; **her interference ~ed the problem** её вмеша́тельство то́лько обостри́ло пробле́му

■ ~ **fracture** *n.* осложнённый перело́м

comprehend /kɒmprɪ'hend/ *v.t.* пон|има́ть, -я́ть

comprehensible /kɒmprɪ'hensɪb(ə)l/ *adj.* поня́тный, постижи́мый

comprehension /kɒmprɪ'henʃ(ə)n/ *n.* понима́ние, постиже́ние

comprehensive /kɒmprɪ'hensɪv/ *adj.* (of wide scope) всеобъе́млющий, исче́рпывающий

■ ~ **school** *n.* (BrE) общеобразова́тельная шко́ла со ста́ршими кла́ссами

compress[1] /'kɒmpres/ *n.* (to relieve inflammation) компре́сс

compress[2] /kəm'pres/ *v.t.* (physically) сж|има́ть, -а́ть

comprise /kəm'praɪz/ *v.t.* включ|а́ть, -и́ть в себя́

compromise /'kɒmprəmaɪz/ *n.* компроми́сс

• *v.t.* компромети́ровать, с-

• *v.i.* при|ходи́ть, -йти́ к компроми́ссу

compulsion /kəm'pʌlʃ(ə)n/ *n.* принужде́ние; **on, under ~** по принужде́нию

compulsive /kəm'pʌlsɪv/ *adj.* (irresistible) непреодоли́мый; (inveterate) зая́длый

compulsory /kəm'pʌlsərɪ/ *adj.* обяза́тельный

⚬ **computer** /kəm'pjuːtə(r)/ *n.* компью́тер

■ ~**-aided design** *n.* автоматизи́рованное

проекти́рование; ~**-aided learning** n. маши́нное обуче́ние; ~ **dating** n. подбо́р супру́гов с по́мощью компью́тера; ~ **game** n. компью́терная игра́; ~ **graphics** n. pl. компью́терная гра́фика; ~**-literate** adj. со зна́нием компью́тера; ~ **programmer** n. программи́ст (-ка); ~ **programming** n. программи́рование; ~ **science** n. вычисли́тельная те́хника

computerize /kəm'pjuːtəraɪz/ v.t. компьютеризи́ровать (impf., pf.)

comrade /'kɒmreɪd/ n. това́рищ

comradeship /'kɒmreɪdʃɪp/ n. това́рищество

con /kɒn/ (infml) v.t. (**conned**, **conning**) над|ува́ть, -у́ть
● n. жу́льничество, моше́нничество

conceal /kən'siːl/ v.t. ута́|ивать, -и́ть

concede /kən'siːd/ v.t. уступ|а́ть, -и́ть

conceit /kən'siːt/ n. самомне́ние, самонаде́янность

conceited /kən'siːtɪd/ adj. самонаде́янный

conceivabl|e /kən'siːvəb(ə)l/ adj. мы́слимый, постижи́мый; **he may** ~**y be right** не исключено́, что он прав

conceive /kən'siːv/ v.t. (imagine) заду́м|ывать, -ать
● v.i. зач|ина́ть, -а́ть, забере́менеть (pf.)

⚐ **concentrate** /'kɒnsəntreɪt/ v.t. сосредото́чи|вать, -ть
● v.i. сосредото́чи|ваться, -ться; **she** ~**d on her work** она́ сосредото́чилась на свое́й рабо́те

⚐ **concentration** /kɒnsən'treɪʃ(ə)n/ n. 1 (of attention) сосредото́ченность 2 (of people or things) сосредото́чение, концентра́ция
■ ~ **camp** n. концентрацио́нный ла́герь, концла́герь (m.)

⚐ **concept** /'kɒnsept/ n. поня́тие

conception /kən'sepʃ(ə)n/ n. 1 (notion) конце́пция 2 (physiol.) зача́тие

conceptual /kən'septʃʊəl/ adj. концептуа́льный
■ ~ **art** n. концептуа́льное иску́сство

⚐ **concern** /kən'sɜːn/ n. 1 (anxiety, worry) беспоко́йство 2 (matter) де́ло; (matter of interest) заинтересо́ванное отноше́ние 3 (business) конце́рн; **a going** ~ де́йствующее предприя́тие
● v.t. 1 (have to do with) каса́ться (impf.) + g.; ~**ed** (involved) заинтересо́ванный; **the parties** ~**ed** заинтересо́ванные сто́роны; **as far as that is** ~**ed** что каса́ется э́того 2 (cause anxiety to) беспоко́ить (impf.); ~**ed** (anxious) озабо́ченный; **I am** ~**ed about the future** меня́ беспоко́ит бу́дущее

concerning /kən'sɜːnɪŋ/ prep. относи́тельно + g.

concert /'kɒnsət/ n. конце́рт
■ ~ **hall** n. конце́ртный зал

concerted /kən'sɜːtɪd/ adj.: **a** ~ **effort to eradicate poverty** совме́стные уси́лия, напра́вленные на искорене́ние бе́дности

concertina /kɒnsə'tiːnə/ n. концерти́но (nt. indecl.), гармо́ника

concerto /kən'tʃeətəʊ/ n. (pl. ~**s**) конце́рт

concession /kən'seʃ(ə)n/ n. 1 (yielding; thing yielded) усту́пка; **as a special** ~ идя́ навстре́чу 2 (preferential rate) льго́та; (reduction) ски́дка

conciliation /kənsɪlɪ'eɪʃ(ə)n/ n. примире́ние

conciliatory /kən'sɪlɪətərɪ/ adj. примири́тельный

concise /kən'saɪs/ adj. кра́ткий, сжа́тый

conclave /'kɒŋkleɪv/ n. конкла́в; (fig.) та́йное совеща́ние

⚐ **conclud|e** /kən'kluːd/ v.t. 1 (terminate) зак|а́нчивать, -о́нчить; ~**ing** заключи́тельный, заверша́ющий; (session etc.) закр|ыва́ть, -ы́ть 2 (infer) де́лать, с- вы́вод, что…
● v.i. (end) зак|а́нчиваться, -о́нчиться

⚐ **conclusion** /kən'kluːʒ(ə)n/ n. заключе́ние; **in** ~ в заключе́ние

conclusive /kən'kluːsɪv/ adj. реша́ющий

concoct /kən'kɒkt/ v.t. (a drink etc.) стря́пать, со-; (a story etc.) стря́пать, со-

concoction /kən'kɒkʃ(ə)n/ n. (drink etc.) смесь; (story invented) вы́думка

concrete /'kɒŋkriːt/ n. бето́н
● adj. 1 (made of ~) бето́нный 2 (specific, definite) конкре́тный

concur /kən'kɜː(r)/ v.i. (**concurred**, **concurring**) 1 (of circumstance etc.) совп|ада́ть, -а́сть; сходи́ться, сойти́сь 2 (agree, consent) согла|ша́ться, -си́ться (with: с + i.)

concurrent /kən'kʌrənt/ adj. (simultaneous) одновре́менный; ~**ly** одновре́менно

concuss /kən'kʌs/ v.t. (med.) вызыва́ть, вы́звать сотрясе́ние мо́зга y + g.

concussion /kən'kʌʃ(ə)n/ n. (med.) сотрясе́ние мо́зга

condemn /kən'dem/ v.t. осу|жда́ть, -ди́ть; (blame) порица́ть (impf.); (declare unfit for use) призн|ава́ть, -а́ть непригодным
■ ~**ed cell** n. (BrE) ка́мера сме́ртника

condemnation /kɒndem'neɪʃ(ə)n/ n. осужде́ние; порица́ние; (of building) призна́ние него́дным

condensation /kɒnden'seɪʃ(ə)n/ n. (water droplets): **the inside of the tent was covered in** ~ пала́тка изнутри́ запоте́ла

condense /kən'dens/ v.t. 1 (phys.) конденси́ровать (impf., pf.) 2 (fig.): **a** ~**d account of events** сжа́тый отчёт о собы́тиях
● v.i. (phys.) конденси́роваться (impf., pf.)
■ ~**d milk** n. сгущённое молоко́

condescend /kɒndɪ'send/ v.i. сни|сходи́ть, -зойти́

condescending /kɒndɪ'sendɪŋ/ adj. снисходи́тельный

condescension /kɒndɪ'senʃ(ə)n/ n. снисхожде́ние, снисходи́тельность

⚐ **condition** /kən'dɪʃ(ə)n/ n. 1 (state) состоя́ние, положе́ние 2 (fitness): **the athlete is out of** ~ спортсме́н не в фо́рме 3 (in pl.) (circumstances) усло́вия (nt. pl.) 4 (requisite, stipulation) усло́вие; **on** ~ **that …** при усло́вии, что…

conditional /kən'dɪʃən(ə)l/ adj.: **the** ~ (**mood**) (gram.) усло́вное наклоне́ние

conditioner /kən'dɪʃənə(r)/ *n.* бальза́м для воло́с

condolence /kən'dəʊləns/ *n.* (also in pl.) соболе́знование

condom /'kɒndɒm/ *n.* презервати́в

condominium /kɒndə'mɪnɪəm/ *n.* (AmE) кондоми́ниум

condone /kən'dəʊn/ *v.t.* про|ща́ть, -сти́ть

conducive /kən'dju:sɪv/ *adj.* спосо́бствующий

conduct¹ /'kɒndʌkt/ *n.* поведе́ние

⚲ **conduct²** /kən'dʌkt/ *v.t.* **1** (lead, guide) води́ть (indet.), вести́ (det.) **2** (manage) вести́ (det.); ∼ **an experiment** ста́вить, по- о́пыт **3** (mus.) (also v.i.) дирижи́ровать (impf.) + i. **4** (phys.) проводи́ть (impf.)

conductive /kən'dʌktɪv/ *adj.* (tech.) проводя́щий

conductor /kən'dʌktə(r)/ *n.* **1** (mus.) дирижёр **2** (of bus, tram) конду́ктор; (AmE, of train) проводни́к **3** (phys.) проводни́к

cone /kəʊn/ *n.* **1** (geom.) ко́нус **2** (for ice cream) ва́фельная тру́бочка

confectioner /kən'fekʃənə(r)/ *n.* конди́тер

confectionery /kən'fekʃən(ə)rɪ/ *n.* (wares) конди́терские изде́лия

confederation /kənfedə'reɪʃ(ə)n/ *n.* сою́з; федера́ция; конфедера́ция

confer¹ /kən'fə:(r)/ *v.t.* (**conferred**, **conferring**) (grant) присв|а́ивать, -о́ить (on + d.)

confer² /kən'fə:(r)/ *v.i.* (**conferred**, **conferring**) (consult) совеща́ться (impf.) (with: c + i.)

⚲ **conference** /'kɒnfərəns/ *n.* конфере́нция, совеща́ние

▪ ∼ **call** *n.* телеконфере́нция, селе́кторное совеща́ние

confess /kən'fes/ *v.t. & i.* **1** призн|ава́ть, -а́ть; **he** ∼**ed to the crime** он созна́лся в преступле́нии **2** (relig., ∼ one's sins) испове́д|оваться, -аться

confession /kən'feʃ(ə)n/ *n.* **1** (avowal) призна́ние, созна́ние **2** (relig.) и́споведь

confetti /kən'fetɪ/ *n.* конфетти́ (nt. indecl.)

confidant, *fem.* **confidante** /'kɒndænt/ *n.* дове́ренное лицо́

confide /kən'faɪd/ *v.i.:* ∼ **in sb** (impart secrets to) дели́ться, по- (свои́ми пла́нами и т. п.) с + i.

⚲ **confidence** /'kɒnfɪd(ə)ns/ *n.* **1** (confiding of secrets) дове́рие; **I tell you this in** ∼ я говорю́ вам э́то конфиденциа́льно (or по секре́ту) **2** (secret) та́йна; конфиденциа́льное сообще́ние **3** (trust): **I have** ∼ **in him** я уве́рен в нём; я ве́рю в него́ **4** (certainty, assurance) уве́ренность **5**: ∼ **trick** моше́нничество

confident /'kɒnfɪd(ə)nt/ *adj.* уве́ренный; (self-confident) самоуве́ренный

confidential /kɒnfɪ'denʃ(ə)l/ *adj.* конфиденциа́льный

confidentiality /kɒnfɪdenʃɪ'ælɪtɪ/ *n.* конфиденциа́льность

configuration /kənfɪgə'reɪʃ(ə)n/ *n.* конфигура́ция

confine¹ /'kɒnfaɪn/ *n.* (usu. in pl.) грани́цы (f. pl.)

confine² /kən'faɪn/ *v.t.* ограни́чи|вать, -ть

confinement /kən'faɪnmənt/ *n.* (imprisonment) заключе́ние; **solitary** ∼ одино́чное заключе́ние

⚲ **confirm** /kən'fə:m/ *v.t.* **1** (establish as certain) утвер|жда́ть, -ди́ть; подтвер|жда́ть, -ди́ть; **his appointment was** ∼**ed** его́ назначе́ние бы́ло утверждено́ **2** (of person): **a** ∼**ed drunkard** го́рький пья́ница; **a** ∼**ed bachelor** убеждённый холостя́к **3** (relig.): **be** ∼**ed** про|ходи́ть, -йти́ обря́д конфирма́ции

confirmation /kɒnfə'meɪʃ(ə)n/ *n.* **1** (of report etc.) подтвержде́ние **2** (relig.) конфирма́ция

confiscate /'kɒnfɪskeɪt/ *v.t.* конфискова́ть (impf., pf.)

⚲ **conflict¹** /'kɒnflɪkt/ *n.* конфли́кт

conflict² /kən'flɪkt/ *v.i.* быть в конфли́кте (with: c + i.); ∼**ing reports** противоречи́вые сообще́ния

conform /kən'fɔ:m/ *v.i.* подчин|я́ться, -и́ться + d.

conformist /kən'fɔ:mɪst/ *n.* конформи́ст

conformity /kən'fɔ:mɪtɪ/ *n.* (correspondence, accordance) соотве́тствие; (compliance) подчине́ние; (conformism) конформи́зм

confound /kən'faʊnd/ *v.t.* **1** (amaze) пора|жа́ть, -зи́ть; потряс|а́ть, -ти́ **2** (confuse) сме́ш|ивать, -а́ть; спу́т|ывать, -ать **3** (as expletive): ∼ **it!** чёрт возьми́!; **he is a** ∼**ed nuisance** он ужа́сно доку́члив

confront /kən'frʌnt/ *v.t.* смотре́ть (impf.) в лицо́ + d.; встр|еча́ть, -е́тить

confrontation /kɒnfrʌn'teɪʃ(ə)n/ *n.* конфронта́ция

confuse /kən'fju:z/ *v.t.* **1** (throw into confusion) сму|ща́ть, -ти́ть; **his question** ∼**d me** его́ вопро́с смути́л меня́ **2** (mistake) спу́т|ывать, -ать; **he** ∼**d Austria with Australia** он спу́тал А́встрию с Австра́лией

confusion /kən'fju:ʒ(ə)n/ *n.* смуще́ние; (mix-up) пу́таница

congeal /kən'dʒi:l/ *v.i.* свёр|тываться, -ну́ться

congenial /kən'dʒi:nɪəl/ *adj.* бли́зкий по ду́ху

congenital /kən'dʒenɪt(ə)l/ *adj.:* ∼ **defect** врождённый дефе́кт

congested /kən'dʒestɪd/ *adj.* (roads) перегру́женный

congestion /kən'dʒestʃ(ə)n/ *n.* перегру́женность

▪ **congestion charge** *n.* пла́та за въезд в центр го́рода

conglomerate /kən'glɒmərət/ *n.* конгломера́т

conglomeration /kənglɒmə'reɪʃ(ə)n/ *n.* конгломера́т

Congo /'kɒngəʊ/ *n.* (country) Ко́нго (nt. indecl.); **Democratic Republic of the Congo** (formerly Zaire) Демократи́ческая Респу́блика Ко́нго

Congolese /kɒŋgə'li:z/ *n.* (native of Congo or Democratic Republic of the Congo) конголе́з|ец (-ка)

c

• *adj.* конголе́зский
congratulate /kən'grætjʊleɪt/ *v.t.*
поздр|авля́ть, -а́вить (*кого с чем*)
congratulation /kəngrætjʊ'leɪʃ(ə)n/ *n.*
поздравле́ние; ∼s! поздравля́ю!
congratulatory /kən'grætjʊlətərɪ/ *adj.*
поздрави́тельный
congregate /'kɒŋgrɪgeɪt/ *v.i.* соб|ира́ться,
-ра́ться; сходи́ться, сойти́сь
congregation /kɒŋgrɪ'geɪʃ(ə)n/ *n.*
прихожа́не (*m. pl.*)
congress /'kɒŋgres/ *n.* **1** (organized meeting)
конгре́сс, съезд **2** (pol., hist.) конгре́сс; C∼
(AmE) конгре́сс США
■ C∼man *n.* член конгре́сса, конгрессме́н;
C∼woman *n.* же́нщина-член конгре́сса
conifer /'kɒnɪfə(r)/ *n.* хво́йное де́рево
coniferous /kə'nɪfərəs/ *adj.* хво́йный
conjecture /kən'dʒektʃə(r)/ *n.*
предположе́ние, дога́дка
• *v.t. & i.* предпол|ага́ть, -ожи́ть; гада́ть (*impf.*)
conjugal /'kɒndʒʊg(ə)l/ *adj.* супру́жеский,
бра́чный
conjugate /'kɒndʒʊgeɪt/ *v.t.* (gram.) спряга́ть,
про-
conjugation /kɒndʒʊ'geɪʃ(ə)n/ *n.* (gram.)
спряже́ние
conjunction /kən'dʒʌŋkʃ(ə)n/ *n.* (gram.) сою́з
conjunctivitis /kəndʒʌŋktɪ'vaɪtɪs/ *n.* (med.)
конъюнктиви́т
conjure /'kʌndʒə(r)/ *v.t. & i.* **1** (fig.): ∼ up
вызыва́ть, вы́звать в воображе́нии **2** (perform
tricks) пока́з|ывать, -а́ть фо́кусы
conjurer, conjuror /'kʌndʒərə(r)/ *n.*
фо́кусник
connect /kə'nekt/ *v.t.* (join) соедин|я́ть, -и́ть;
the towns are ∼ed by railway э́ти города́
соединены́ желе́зной доро́гой; (associate)
свя́з|ывать, -а́ть
• *v.i.* соедин|я́ться, -и́ться; the train ∼s with
the one from London э́тот по́езд согласо́ван
по расписа́нию с ло́ндонским (по́ездом)
connection /kə'nekʃ(ə)n/ *n.* **1** (joining up)
соедине́ние, связь **2** (fig., link) связь **3** (of
transport) согласо́ванность расписа́ния; I
missed my ∼ я не успе́л сде́лать переса́дку
4 (association) связь **5** (teleph.): the ∼ was bad
телефо́н пло́хо рабо́тал
connive /kə'naɪv/ *v.i.*: ∼ at потво́рствовать
(*impf.*) + *d.*; ∼ with сгов|а́риваться, -ори́ться
с + *i.*
connoisseur /kɒnə'sə:(r)/ *n.* знато́к,
цени́тель (*m.*)
connotation /kɒnə'teɪʃ(ə)n/ *n.* побо́чное
значе́ние
conquer /'kɒŋkə(r)/ *v.t. & i.* (overcome; obtain by
conquest) завоёв|ывать, -а́ть
conqueror /'kɒŋkərə(r)/ *n.* завоева́тель (*m.*)
conquest /'kɒŋkwest/ *n.* завоева́ние
conscience /'kɒnʃ(ə)ns/ *n.* со́весть; clear ∼
чи́стая со́весть; guilty ∼ нечи́стая со́весть

conscientious /kɒnʃɪ'enʃəs/ *adj.* созна́тельный
■ ∼ objector *n.* отка́зывающийся от вое́нной
слу́жбы по убежде́нию
conscious /'kɒnʃəs/ *adj.* **1** (physically aware)
созна́ющий, ощуща́ющий **2** (mentally aware)
созна́ющий, понима́ющий; I was ∼ of having
offended him я сознава́л, что оскорби́л его́
3 (realized) созна́ющий, созна́тельный; a ∼
effort созна́тельное уси́лие
consciousness /'kɒnʃəsnɪs/ *n.* **1** (physical)
созна́ние; he lost ∼ он потеря́л созна́ние;
she regained ∼ она́ пришла́ в себя́/
созна́ние **2** (mental) созна́тельность
conscript /'kɒnskrɪpt/ *n.* новобра́нец,
призывни́к
conscription /kən'skrɪpʃ(ə)n/ *n.* во́инская
пови́нность
consecrate /'kɒnsɪkreɪt/ *v.t.* освя|ща́ть, -ти́ть
consecutive /kən'sekjʊtɪv/ *adj.*
после́довательный
consensus /kən'sensəs/ *n.* согла́сие,
единоду́шие; (pol.) консе́нсус
consent /kən'sent/ *n.* согла́сие
• *v.i.* согла|ша́ться, -си́ться
⚜ **consequence** /'kɒnsɪkwəns/ *n.* **1** (result)
сле́дствие, после́дствие **2** (importance)
ва́жность, значе́ние
consequential /kɒnsɪ'kwenʃ(ə)l/ *adj.*
1 (consequent) сле́дующий/вытека́ющий (*из
чего*) **2** (important) ва́жный, значи́тельный
consequently /'kɒnsɪkwentlɪ/ *adv.*
сле́довательно, зна́чит, (infml) ста́ло быть
conservation /kɒnsə'veɪʃ(ə)n/ *n.*
сохране́ние, охра́на
■ ∼ area *n.* запове́дник
conservationist /kɒnsə'veɪʃənɪst/ *n.* боре́ц
за охра́ну приро́ды
⚜ **conservative** /kən'sə:vətɪv/ *n.* консерва́тор
• *adj.* консервати́вный
conservatory /kən'sə:vətərɪ/ *n.* **1** (BrE,
room) застеклённая вера́нда **2** (mus.)
консервато́рия
⚜ **conserve** /kən'sə:v, *n. only also* 'kɒnsə:v/ *n.*
(preserved fruit) варе́нье
• *v.t.* (fruit) консерви́ровать, за-; (protect)
сохран|я́ть, -и́ть; ∼ one's strength бере́чь
(*impf.*) свои́ си́лы
⚜ **consider** /kən'sɪdə(r)/ *v.t. & i.* рассм|а́тривать,
-отре́ть; we are ∼ing going to Canada
мы поду́мываем о пое́здке в Кана́ду; ∼
yourself under arrest счита́йте, что вы
аресто́ваны; he is ∼ed clever его́ счита́ют
у́мным; он счита́ется у́мным; (make allowance
for) счита́ться (*impf.*) с + *i.*; we must ∼
his feelings мы должны́ счита́ться с его́
чу́вствами
⚜ **considerable** /kən'sɪdərəb(ə)l/ *adj.*
значи́тельный
considerate /kən'sɪdərət/ *adj.*
внима́тельный, забо́тливый
⚜ **consideration** /kənsɪdə'reɪʃ(ə)n/ *n.*
1 (reflection) рассмотре́ние; take into ∼
прин|има́ть, -я́ть во внима́ние **2** (making
allowance): he showed ∼ for my feelings он

─────────────

⚜ ключевая лексика

считался с мои́ми чу́вствами; он щади́л мои́ чу́вства **3** (reason, factor) соображе́ние

considering /kən'sɪdərɪŋ/ *prep. & adv.* учи́тывая, принима́я во внима́ние; **that is not so bad, ~** (infml) в о́бщем, э́то не так уж пло́хо

consign /kən'saɪn/ *v.t.* (send) пос|ыла́ть, -ла́ть; (to hand over (to), commit (to)): **~ to oblivion** преда|ва́ть, -ть забве́нию

consignment /kən'saɪnmənt/ *n.* (consigning) отпра́вка; (goods) груз, па́ртия това́ра

♂ **consist** /kən'sɪst/ *v.i.:* **~ of** состоя́ть (*impf.*) из + *g.*; **~ in** состоя́ть (*impf.*) в + *i.*; **his task ~s in defining work norms** его́ рабо́та состои́т в определе́нии норм вы́работки

consistency /kən'sɪst(ə)nsɪ/ *n.* **1** (of mixture etc.) консисте́нция **2** (adherence to logic) после́довательность

♂ **consistent** /kən'sɪst(ə)nt/ *adj.* (of argument etc.) после́довательный; (of person) после́довательный

consolation /kɒnsə'leɪʃ(ə)n/ *n.* утеше́ние, отра́да

console[1] /'kɒnsəʊl/ *n.* (panel) пульт управле́ния

console[2] /kən'səʊl/ *v.t.* ут|еша́ть, -е́шить

consolidate /kən'sɒlɪdeɪt/ *v.t.* укреп|ля́ть, -и́ть

consonant /'kɒnsənənt/ *n.* (ling.) согла́сный (звук)

consorti|um /kən'sɔ:tɪəm/ *n.* (*pl.* **~a** or **~ums**) консо́рциум

conspicuous /kən'spɪkjʊəs/ *adj.* заме́тный

conspiracy /kən'spɪrəsɪ/ *n.* за́говор; конспира́ция

conspirator /kən'spɪrətə(r)/ *n.* загово́рщик

conspiratorial /kənspɪrə'tɔ:rɪəl/ *adj.* загово́рщический, конспира́торский

conspire /kən'spaɪə(r)/ *v.t. & i.* устр|а́ивать, -о́ить за́говор

constable /'kʌnstəb(ə)l/ *n.* (BrE) полице́йский

♂ **constant** /'kɒnst(ə)nt/ *adj.* постоя́нный

constantly /'kɒnst(ə)ntlɪ/ *adj.* постоя́нно

constellation /kɒnstə'leɪʃ(ə)n/ *n.* созве́здие

consternation /kɒnstə'neɪʃ(ə)n/ *n.* смяте́ние, у́жас

constipate /'kɒnstɪpeɪt/ *v.t.:* **I am ~d** у меня́ запо́р

constipation /kɒnstɪ'peɪʃ(ə)n/ *n.* запо́р

constituency /kən'stɪtjʊənsɪ/ *n.* избира́тельный о́круг

constituent /kən'stɪtjʊənt/ *n.* (elector) избира́тель (-ница); (element) составна́я часть

constitute /'kɒnstɪtjuːt/ *v.t.* сост|авля́ть, -а́вить

constitution /kɒnstɪ'tjuːʃ(ə)n/ *n.* **1** (make-up) строе́ние, структу́ра **2** (pol.) конститу́ция

constitutional /kɒnstɪ'tjuːʃən(ə)l/ *adj.* (pol.) конституцио́нный

constrain /kən'streɪn/ *v.t.* (force) прин|ужда́ть, -у́дить; заст|авля́ть, -а́вить; вынужда́ть, вы́нудить; (restrict) ограни́чи|вать, -ть; **~ed**

(embarrassed) стеснённый

constraint /kən'streɪnt/ *n.* ограниче́ние

constrict /kən'strɪkt/ *v.t.* сж|има́ть, -а́ть

constriction /kən'strɪkʃ(ə)n/ *n.* сжа́тие, суже́ние

♂ **construct** /kən'strʌkt/ *v.t.* стро́ить, по-

♂ **construction** /kən'strʌkʃ(ə)n/ *n.* построе́ние, строи́тельство, стро́йка; (thing constructed) постро́йка, сооруже́ние; **the road is under ~** доро́га стро́ится

constructive /kən'strʌktɪv/ *adj.* (pert. to construction; helpful) конструкти́вный

construe /kən'struː/ *v.t.* (**construes, construed, construing**) (interpret) истолко́в|ывать, -а́ть

consul /'kɒns(ə)l/ *n.* ко́нсул

consulate /'kɒnsjʊlət/ *n.* ко́нсульство

consult /kən'sʌlt/ *v.t.:* **~ a book** спр|авля́ться, -а́виться в кни́ге; **~ a lawyer** сове́товаться, по- с юри́стом
  ● *v.i.* сове́товаться, по-, консульти́роваться (*impf., pf.*) (**with:** с + *i.*)
  ■ **~ing room** *n.* кабине́т (врача́)

consultancy /kən'sʌlt(ə)nsɪ/ *n.* (company) консульти́рующая фи́рма; (job) до́лжность консульта́нта

consultant /kən'sʌlt(ə)nt/ *n.* консульта́нт

consultation /kɒnsəl'teɪʃ(ə)n/ *n.* консульта́ция

consultative /kən'sʌltətɪv/ *adj.* консультати́вный, совеща́тельный

consume /kən'sjuːm/ *v.t.* **1** (eat or drink) съ|еда́ть, -есть **2** (use up) потреб|ля́ть, -и́ть **3** (destroy) истреб|ля́ть, -и́ть; **the fire ~d the huts** пожа́р уничто́жил лачу́ги **4**: **he was ~d with envy/curiosity** его́ снеда́ла за́висть; его́ снеда́ло любопы́тство

♂ **consumer** /kən'sjuːmə(r)/ *n.* потреби́тель (*m.*)
  ■ **~ goods** *n. pl.* потреби́тельские това́ры; **~ society** *n.* о́бщество потребле́ния

consummate *v.t.* /'kɒnsjʊmeɪt/ (marriage) осуществ|ля́ть, -и́ть (*бра́чные отноше́ния*)
  ● *adj.* /'kɒns(j)əmət/ зако́нченный

consumption /kən'sʌmpʃ(ə)n/ *n.* потребле́ние, поглоще́ние

♂ **contact** /'kɒntækt/ *n.* **1** (lit., fig.) конта́кт, соприкоснове́ние; **bring, come into ~ with** установи́ть (*pf.*) конта́кт с + *i.* **2** (of person): **he made useful ~s** он завяза́л поле́зные знако́мства
  ● *v.t.* связа́ться (*pf.*) с + *i.*
  ■ **~ lenses** *n. pl.* конта́ктные ли́нзы

contagion /kən'teɪdʒ(ə)n/ *n.* зара́за

contagious /kən'teɪdʒəs/ *adj.* зара́зный

♂ **contain** /kən'teɪn/ *v.t.* **1** (hold within itself) содержа́ть (*impf.*) в себе́ **2** (be capable of holding) вмеща́ть (*impf.*); **how much does this bottle ~?** ско́лько вмеща́ет э́та буты́лка? **3** (control) сде́рж|ивать, -а́ть; **he could not ~ his enthusiasm** он не мог сдержа́ть своего́ восто́рга

container /kən'teɪnə(r)/ *n.* **1** (receptacle) сосу́д **2** (for transport) конте́йнер
  ■ **~ ship, ~ truck** *nn.* контейнерово́з

contaminate /kən'tæmɪneɪt/ v.t. зара|жа́ть, -зи́ть

contamination /kəntæmɪ'neɪʃ(ə)n/ v.t. зараже́ние

contemplate /'kɒntəmpleɪt/ v.t. **1** (gaze at) созерца́ть (impf.) **2** (envisage, plan) обду́м|ывать, -ать

contemplation /kɒntəm'pleɪʃ(ə)n/ n. (gazing) созерца́ние; (thought) размышле́ние, обду́мывание

contemplative /kən'templətɪv/ adj. созерца́тельный

✧ **contemporary** /kən'tempərərɪ/ n. совреме́нни|к, све́рстни|к (-ца)
• adj. совреме́нный

contempt /kən'tempt/ n. презре́ние; ~ of court оскорбле́ние суда́, неуваже́ние к суду́

contemptible /kən'temptɪb(ə)l/ adj. презре́нный

contemptuous /kən'temptʃʊəs/ adj. презри́тельный

contend /kən'tend/ v.t. (maintain) утвержда́ть (impf.)
• v.i. (compete) состяза́ться (impf.); сопе́рничать (impf.)

✧ **content¹** /'kɒntent/ n. (lit., fig.) содержа́ние; (in pl.) содержи́мое; (in full table of ~s) оглавле́ние, содержа́ние

content² /kən'tent/ adj. дово́льный
• v.t. удовлетвор|я́ть, -и́ть; a ~ed look дово́льный вид

contention /kən'tenʃ(ə)n/ n. (strife) спор

contentious /kən'tenʃəs/ adj. вздо́рный, задири́стый

contentment /kən'tentmənt/ n. удовлетворённость

contest n. /'kɒntest/ ко́нкурс, состяза́ние
• v.t. & i. /kən'test/ **1** (dispute) осп|а́ривать, -о́рить **2** (contend for) отст|а́ивать, -оя́ть; боро́ться (impf.) за + a.

contestant /kən'test(ə)nt/ n. конкуре́нт (-ка)

✧ **context** /'kɒntekst/ n. конте́кст; in the ~ of today's America в усло́виях совреме́нной Аме́рики

continent /'kɒntɪnənt/ n. контине́нт

continental /kɒntɪ'nent(ə)l/ adj. континента́льный
■ ~ breakfast n. лёгкий у́тренний за́втрак; ~ quilt n. (BrE) стёганое одея́ло

contingency /kən'tɪndʒənsɪ/ n. возмо́жное обстоя́тельство
■ ~ plan n. вариа́нт пла́на; альтернати́вный план

contingent /kən'tɪndʒ(ə)nt/ n. (mil.) континге́нт

continual /kən'tɪnjʊəl/ adj. постоя́нный

continuation /kəntɪnjʊ'eɪʃ(ə)n/ n. продолже́ние

✧ **continue** /kən'tɪnjuː/ v.t. (continues, continued, continuing) продолжа́ть,

-о́лжить; 'to be ~d' (of story etc.) продолже́ние сле́дует
• v.i. (continues, continued, continuing) прод|олжа́ться, -о́лжиться; the wet weather ~s сыра́я пого́да де́ржится

continuity /kɒntɪ'njuːɪtɪ/ n. непреры́вность

continuous /kən'tɪnjʊəs/ adj. непреры́вный; (gram.) дли́тельный

continu|um /kən'tɪnjʊəm/ n. (pl. ~a) конти́нуум

contort /kən'tɔːt/ v.t. иска|жа́ть, -зи́ть

contortion /kən'tɔːʃ(ə)n/ n. искаже́ние; искривле́ние

contour /'kɒntʊə(r)/ n. ко́нтур
■ ~ line n. горизонта́ль

contraband /'kɒntrəbænd/ n. контраба́нда

contraception /kɒntrə'sepʃ(ə)n/ n. предупрежде́ние бере́менности

contraceptive /kɒntrə'septɪv/ n. противозача́точное сре́дство
• adj. противозача́точный

✧ **contract¹** /'kɒntrækt/ n. (agreement) контра́кт, догово́р
■ ~ killer n. ки́ллер, наёмный уби́йца; ~ killing n. заказно́е уби́йство

contract² /kən'trækt/ v.t. (an illness) подхв|а́тывать, -ати́ть
• v.i. (agree) прин|има́ть, -я́ть на себя́ обяза́тельство; he ~ed to build a bridge он подряди́лся постро́ить мост

contract³ /kən'trækt/ v.t. (shorten) сокра|ща́ть, -ти́ть; (tighten) сж|има́ть, -ать
• v.i. (shorten) сокра|ща́ться, -ти́ться; metal ~s мета́лл сжима́ется; (tighten) сж|има́ться, -а́ться

contraction /kən'trækʃ(ə)n/ n. (of metal) сжа́тие; (med.) родова́я схва́тка

contractor /kən'træktə(r)/ n. (person) подря́дчик

contradict /kɒntrə'dɪkt/ v.t. противоре́чить (impf.) + d.

contradiction /kɒntrə'dɪkʃ(ə)n/ n. противоре́чие

contradictory /kɒntrə'dɪktərɪ/ adj. противоречи́вый

contralto /kən'træltəʊ/ n. (pl. ~s) (singer) контра́льто (f. indecl.); (voice) контра́льто (nt. indecl.)

contraption /kən'træpʃ(ə)n/ n. (infml) приспособле́ние

contrary /'kɒntrərɪ/ n. противополо́жность; on the ~ (как раз) наоборо́т; there is no evidence to the ~ нет доказа́тельств проти́вного/обра́тного
• adj. **1** противополо́жный, проти́вный, обра́тный **2** /kən'treərɪ/ своево́льный, своенра́вный
• adv.: ~ to my expectations вопреки́ мои́м ожида́ниям

✧ **contrast** n. /'kɒntrɑːst/ контра́ст; in ~ to в противополо́жность + d.; by ~ with по сравне́нию с + i.
• v.t. /kən'trɑːst/ противопост|авля́ть, -а́вить
• v.i. /kən'trɑːst/ контрасти́ровать (impf., pf.)

✧ ключева́я ле́ксика

contravene /ˌkɒntrəˈviːn/ *v.t.* противоре́чить (*impf.*) + *d.*; he ~d the law он нару́шил зако́н

contravention /ˌkɒntrəˈvenʃ(ə)n/ *n.* наруше́ние; in ~ of в наруше́ние + *g.*

♂ **contribute** /kənˈtrɪbjuːt/ *v.t.* (money etc.) же́ртвовать, по-; he ~d £5 он внёс 5 фу́нтов ● *v.i.* соде́йствовать (*impf.*) (to: + *d.*); she ~s to our magazine она́ пи́шет для на́шего журна́ла

♂ **contribution** /ˌkɒntrɪˈbjuːʃ(ə)n/ *n.*: a ~ of £5 поже́ртвование/взнос в пять фу́нтов; his ~ to our success его́ вклад в наш успе́х

contributor /kənˈtrɪbjʊtə(r)/ *n.* (writer) (постоя́нный) сотру́дник; (of funds) же́ртвователь (*m.*)

contributory /kənˈtrɪbjʊtərɪ/ *adj.* соде́йствующий, спосо́бствующий; ~ factor спосо́бствующий фа́ктор; a ~ pension scheme (BrE) пенсио́нная систе́ма, осно́ванная на отчисле́ниях из за́работка рабо́тающих

■ ~ **negligence** *n.* (law) встре́чная вина́, вина́ потерпе́вшего

contrite /kənˈtraɪt/ *adj.* ка́ющийся

contrition /kənˈtrɪʃ(ə)n/ *n.* раска́яние

contrive /kənˈtraɪv/ *v.t.* (devise) заду́м|ывать, -ать; (succeed): he ~d to offend everybody он умудри́лся оби́деть всех; ~d (artificial) иску́сственный

♂ **control** /kənˈtrəʊl/ *n.* **1** (power to direct etc.) управле́ние, регули́рование; he lost ~ of the car он потеря́л управле́ние автомоби́лем; he is in ~ of the situation он хозя́ин положе́ния; the situation is under ~ ситуа́ция нормализова́лась/нахо́дится под контро́лем; the children are out of ~ де́ти не слу́шаются **2** (means of regulating) контро́ль (*m.*) **3** (*in pl.*) (of a machine etc.) рычаги́ (*m. pl.*) управле́ния **4**: ~ panel прибо́рная доска́; пульт управле́ния; ~ room пункт управле́ния; ~ tower (aeron.) контро́льно-диспе́тчерский пункт

● *v.t.* (**controlled**, **controlling**) контроли́ровать, про-; регули́ровать (*impf., pf.*); ~ one's temper владе́ть (*impf.*) собо́й; ~ prices регули́ровать це́ны

controversial /ˌkɒntrəˈvɜːʃ(ə)l/ *adj.* спо́рный

controversy /ˈkɒntrəvɜːsɪ/ *n.* поле́мика, спор

convalesce /ˌkɒnvəˈles/ *v.i.* выздора́вливать, поправля́ться (*both impf.*)

convalescence /ˌkɒnvəˈles(ə)ns/ *n.* выздоровле́ние

convalescent /ˌkɒnvəˈles(ə)nt/ *adj.* выздора́вливающий, поправля́ющийся

convene /kənˈviːn/ *v.t.* (people) соб|ира́ть, -ра́ть; (meeting) созыва́ть, -ва́ть ● *v.i.* соб|ира́ться, -ра́ться

convenience /kənˈviːnɪəns/ *n.* удо́бство; at your ~ когда́ вам бу́дет удо́бно; marriage of ~ фикти́вный брак

■ ~ **foods** *n. pl.* пищевы́е полуфабрика́ты; ~ **store** *n.* магази́н ша́говой досту́пности, (круглосу́точный) магази́н това́ров

convenient /kənˈviːnɪənt/ *adj.* удо́бный; if it is ~ for you е́сли вам удо́бно

convent /ˈkɒnv(ə)nt/ *n.* (же́нский) монасты́рь

convention /kənˈvenʃ(ə)n/ *n.* **1** (congress) съезд **2** (treaty) конве́нция **3** (custom) обы́чай

conventional /kənˈvenʃən(ə)l/ *adj.* обы́чный; a ~ person челове́к, кото́рый приде́рживается усло́вностей

converge /kənˈvɜːdʒ/ *v.i.* сходи́ться, сойти́сь

conversant /kənˈvɜːs(ə)nt/ *adj.* знако́мый (with: c + *i.*); осведомлённый (with: в + *p.*)

♂ **conversation** /ˌkɒnvəˈseɪʃ(ə)n/ *n.* разгово́р, бесе́да, речь

converse /kənˈvɜːs/ *v.i.* бесе́довать (*impf.*)

conversion /kənˈvɜːʃ(ə)n/ *n.* **1** (transformation) превраще́ние, обраще́ние **2** (relig. etc.) обраще́ние (to: в + *a.*) **3** (comm.): ~ of pounds into dollars перево́д фу́нтов в до́ллары

convert¹ /ˈkɒnvɜːt/ *n.* (ново)обращённый

convert² /kənˈvɜːt/ *v.t.* **1** (change) превра|ща́ть, -ти́ть; the house was ~ed into flats дом был разби́т на кварти́ры **2** (relig. etc.) обра|ща́ть, -ти́ть **3** (comm.): ~ pounds into euros перевести́ (*pf.*) фу́нты (сте́рлингов) в е́вро ● *v.i.*: he ~ed to Buddhism он обрати́лся в будди́зм

convertible /kənˈvɜːtɪb(ə)l/ *n.* (car) автомоби́ль (*m.*) с откидны́м/открыва́ющимся ве́рхом

convex /ˈkɒnveks/ *adj.* вы́пуклый

convey /kənˈveɪ/ *v.t.* **1** (carry, transmit) перев|ози́ть, -езти́ **2** (impart) перед|ава́ть, -а́ть

conveyancing /kənˈveɪənsɪŋ/ *n.* (law) составле́ние нотариа́льных а́ктов о переда́че иму́щества

conveyor /kənˈveɪə(r)/ *n.*: ~ belt конве́йерная ле́нта

convict¹ /ˈkɒnvɪkt/ *n.* осуждённый

convict² /kənˈvɪkt/ *v.t.* (law) осу|жда́ть, -ди́ть (of: за + *a.*)

conviction /kənˈvɪkʃ(ə)n/ *n.* **1** (law) осужде́ние **2** (settled opinion) убежде́ние, убеждённость **3** (persuasive force) убежде́ние

convince /kənˈvɪns/ *v.t.* убе|жда́ть, -ди́ть

convincing /kənˈvɪnsɪŋ/ *adj.* убеди́тельный

convivial /kənˈvɪvɪəl/ *adj.* весёлый

convoy /ˈkɒnvɔɪ/ *n.* тра́нспортная коло́нна с конво́ем

convulsion /kənˈvʌlʃ(ə)n/ *n.* (*in pl.*) (med.) конву́льсия, су́дорога

coo /kuː/ *v.t. & i.* (**coos**, **cooed**) воркова́ть (*impf.*)

cook /kʊk/ *n.* (male) по́вар; (female) куха́рка ● *v.t.* гото́вить, при- ● *v.i.* (food) гото́виться, при-; (person) гото́вить (*impf.*)

■ ~**book** *n.* (AmE) повареннáя кни́га

cooker /ˈkʊkə(r)/ *n.* (BrE, stove) плита́

cookery /ˈkʊkərɪ/ *n.* кулинари́я, стряпня́

■ ~ **book** *n.* (BrE) поваре́нная кни́га

cookie /'kʊkɪ/ *n.* (AmE, sweet biscuit) пече́нье

cooking /'kʊkɪŋ/ *n.* (cuisine) ку́хня
● *adj.*: ~ **apple** я́блоко для запека́ния

⚐ **cool** /kuːl/ *n.* **1** прохла́да **2**: lose one's ~ (infml) вы́йти (*pf.*) из себя́, потеря́ть (*pf.*) самооблада́ние
● *adj.* **1** (lit.) прохла́дный, све́жий **2** (unexcited) хладнокро́вный **3** (unenthusiastic) прохла́дный **4** (infml, splendid) клёвый, кла́ссный; ~! класс!, кру́то!
● *v.t.* охла|жда́ть, -ди́ть
● *v.i.* охла|жда́ться, -ди́ться; ~ **down, off** ост|ыва́ть, -ы́ть; ~**ing-off period** пери́од обду́мывания

coop /kuːp/ *n.* куря́тник
● *v.t.*: ~ **up** (fig.) держа́ть (*impf.*) взаперти́

cooperate /kəʊ'ɒpəreɪt/ *v.i.* сотру́дничать (*impf.*)

cooperation /kəʊɒpə'reɪʃ(ə)n/ *n.* сотру́дничество

cooperative /kəʊ'ɒpərətɪv/ *n.* кооперати́в
● *adj.* кооперати́вный

co-opt /kəʊ'ɒpt/ *v.t.* коопти́ровать (*impf., pf.*)

coordinate *n.* /kəʊ'ɔːdɪnət/ (math., geog.) координа́та; (*in pl.*) о́си (*f. pl.*) координа́т
● *v.t.* /kəʊ'ɔːdɪneɪt/ координи́ровать (*impf., pf.*)

coordination /kəʊɔː'dɪneɪʃ(ə)n/ *n.* координа́ция

cop /kɒp/ *n.* (sl., policeman) полице́йский, коп

cope /kəʊp/ *v.i.* спр|авля́ться, -а́виться (**with:** c + *i.*)

Copenhagen /kəʊpən'heɪɡən/ *n.* Копенга́ген

copious /'kəʊpɪəs/ *adj.* оби́льный

copper /'kɒpə(r)/ *n.* медь

copulate /'kɒpjʊleɪt/ *v.i.* совокуп|ля́ться, -и́ться

⚐ **copy** /'kɒpɪ/ *n.* **1** (version) ко́пия, ру́копись **2** (of book etc.) экземпля́р
● *v.t. & i.* перепи́с|ывать, -а́ть; (imitate) подража́ть (*impf.*) + *d.*; ~ **out a letter** переписа́ть (*pf.*) письмо́; **he copied in the examination** он спи́сывал на экза́мене
■ ~**right** *n.* а́вторское пра́во

cord /kɔːd/ *n.* (rope, string) верёвка; (flex) шнур

cordial /'kɔːdɪəl/ *n.* (BrE) подслащённый напи́ток
● *adj.* серде́чный, раду́шный

cordless /'kɔːdlɪs/ *adj.* беспроводно́й
■ ~ (**tele**)**phone** *n.* радиотелефо́н

cordon /'kɔːd(ə)n/ *n.* (of police etc.) оцепле́ние, кордо́н
● *v.t.* (also ~ **off**) оцеп|ля́ть, -и́ть

corduroy /'kɔːdərɔɪ/ *n.* вельве́т
● *adj.* вельве́товый

⚐ **core** /kɔː(r)/ *n.* (of fruit) сердцеви́на; (fig.) центр, ядро́, суть; ~ **of a problem** суть пробле́мы

Corfu /kɔː'fuː/ *n.* Ко́рфу (*m. indecl.*)

coriander /kɒrɪ'ændə(r)/ *n.* кориа́ндр; (of fresh leaves, usu.) кинза́

cork /kɔːk/ *n.* про́бка; (*attr.*) про́бковый

⚐ ключева́я ле́ксика

■ ~**screw** *n.* што́пор

corn¹ /kɔːn/ *n.* **1** (BrE, grain, seed) зерно́ **2** (BrE, wheat) пшени́ца **3** (AmE, maize) кукуру́за
■ ~**flakes** *n. pl.* кукуру́зные хло́пья; ~**flour** *n.* (BrE) кукуру́зная/ри́совая мука́; ~ **on the cob** *n.* кукуру́за в поча́тках

corn² /kɔːn/ *n.* (on foot) мозо́ль

cornea /'kɔːnɪə/ *n.* рогови́ца; рогова́я оболо́чка

⚐ **corner** /'kɔːnə(r)/ *n.* **1** (place where lines etc. meet) у́гол; **at, on the** ~ на углу́; **round the** ~ (lit.) за угло́м; (fig., near) ря́дом; **in a tight** ~ в затрудне́нии; **he looked out of the** ~ **of his eye** он следи́л кра́ешком гла́за **2** (football) углово́й уда́р, ко́рнер
● *v.t.* заг|оня́ть, -на́ть в у́гол; **the fugitive was** ~**ed** беглеца́ загна́ли в у́гол; **he** ~**ed the market** он завладе́л ры́нком, скупи́в весь това́р
■ ~**stone** *n.* (fig.) краеуго́льный ка́мень

cornet /'kɔːnɪt/ *n.* **1** (mus. instrument) корне́т, корне́т-а-писто́н **2** (BrE, for ice cream) ва́фельный рожо́к

cornice /'kɔːnɪs/ *n.* карни́з

corny /'kɔːnɪ/ *adj.* (**cornier, corniest**) (infml) пло́ский, изби́тый

coronary /'kɒrənərɪ/ *adj.* (med.): ~ **artery** вене́чная арте́рия
● *n.* (*in full* ~ **thrombosis**) коронаротромбо́з

coronation /kɒrə'neɪʃ(ə)n/ *n.* корона́ция

coroner /'kɒrənə(r)/ *n.* сле́дователь (*m.*) (*по делам о насильственной или скоропостижной смерти*)

corporal¹ /'kɔːpr(ə)l/ *n.* (officer) капра́л

corporal² /'kɔːpr(ə)l/ *adj.*: ~ **punishment** теле́сное наказа́ние

⚐ **corporate** /'kɔːpərət/ *adj.* **1** (collective) о́бщий **2** (of, forming a corporation) корпорати́вный

corporation /kɔːpə'reɪʃ(ə)n/ *n.* (company) акционе́рное о́бщество
■ ~ **tax** *n.* нало́г с дохо́дов компа́ний

corps /kɔː(r)/ *n.* (*pl.* ~ /kɔːz/) (mil., diplomacy) ко́рпус

corpse /kɔːps/ *n.* труп

corpuscle /'kɔːpʌs(ə)l/ *n.* корпу́скула, те́льце, части́ца

⚐ **correct** /kə'rekt/ *adj.* **1** (right, true) пра́вильный, ве́рный, то́чный **2** (of behaviour) корре́ктный
● *v.t.* испр|авля́ть, -а́вить

correction /kə'rekʃ(ə)n/ *n.* исправле́ние
■ ~ **fluid** *n.* корректи́рующая жи́дкость

correspond /kɒrɪ'spɒnd/ *v.i.* **1** (match, harmonize) соотве́тствовать (*impf.*) (**to:** + *d.*) **2** (exchange letters) перепи́сываться (*impf.*) (**with:** c + *i.*)

correspondence /kɒrɪ'spɒnd(ə)ns/ *n.* корреспонде́нция, перепи́ска
■ ~ **course** *n.* курс зао́чного обуче́ния

correspondent /kɒrɪ'spɒnd(ə)nt/ *n.* корреспонде́нт (-ка)

corresponding /kɒrɪ'spɒndɪŋ/ *adj.* соотве́тственный, соотве́тствующий

corridor /'kɒrɪdɔː(r)/ *n.* коридо́р

corroborate /kə'rɒbəreɪt/ v.t. подтвер|жда́ть, -ди́ть

corrode /kə'rəʊd/ v.t. разъ|еда́ть, -е́сть
● v.i. ржаве́ть, за-

corrosion /kə'rəʊʒ(ə)n/ n. корро́зия, ржа́вчина

corrosive /kə'rəʊsɪv/ adj. коррози́йный, разъеда́ющий, е́дкий; (fig.) разъеда́ющий

corrugate /'kɒrʊgeɪt/ v.t.: ~d iron волни́стое/ рифлёное желе́зо

corrupt /kə'rʌpt/ adj. **1** (depraved) развращённый **2** (dishonest) прода́жный **3** (comput.) повреждённый
● v.t. **1** (deprave) развра|ща́ть, -ти́ть **2** (comput.) иска|жа́ть, -зи́ть

corruption /kə'rʌpʃ(ə)n/ n. разложе́ние; развраще́ние

corset /'kɔːsɪt/ n. корсе́т

Corsica /'kɔːsɪkə/ n. Ко́рсика

cortisone /'kɔːtɪzəʊn/ n. (med.) кортизо́н

cosh /kɒʃ/ n. (BrE) дуби́нка

cosmetic /kɒz'metɪk/ n. косме́тика
● adj. космети́ческий

cosmic /'kɒzmɪk/ adj. косми́ческий

cosmology /kɒz'mɒlədʒɪ/ n. космоло́гия

cosmonaut /'kɒzmənɔːt/ n. космона́вт

cosmopolitan /kɒzmə'pɒlɪt(ə)n/ adj. космополити́ческий

cosmos /'kɒzmɒs/ n. ко́смос

Cossack /'kɒsæk/ n. каза́|к (-чка); (attr.) каза́цкий, каза́чий

cosset /'kɒsɪt/ v.t. (**cosseted, cosseting**) балова́ть (impf.); не́жить (impf.)

⚡ **cost** /kɒst/ n. **1** (monetary) цена́, сто́имость; ~ **price** себесто́имость; ~ **of living** прожи́точный ми́нимум **2** (expense, loss) цена́; **at all** ~**s** любо́й цено́й
● v.t. & i. **1** (past and p.p. ~) (involve expense) сто́ить (impf.); **this** ~ **me £5** э́то сто́ило мне 5 фу́нтов; э́то обошло́сь мне в 5 фу́нтов **2** (past and p.p. ~**ed**) (assess ~ of) оце́н|ивать, -и́ть изде́ржки (предприятия и т. п.)
■ ~-**effective** adj. рента́бельный

co-star /'kəʊstɑː(r)/ n. партнёр (-ша) (в другой гла́вной ро́ли)
● v.t.: **a picture** ~**ing X and Y** фильм с уча́стием двух звёзд — Х и У
● v.i.: **they** ~**red in that picture** они́ снима́лись в э́том фи́льме в гла́вных роля́х

costly /'kɒstlɪ/ adj. (**costlier, costliest**) дорого́й

costume /'kɒstjuːm/ n. костю́м
■ ~ **jewellery** n. бижуте́рия

cosy /'kəʊzɪ/ (AmE **cozy**) adj. (**cosier, cosiest**) ую́тный

cot /kɒt/ n. (BrE, child's bed) де́тская крова́тка; (AmE, camp bed) раскладу́шка
■ ~ **death** n. (BrE) внеза́пная сме́рть (ребёнка грудно́го во́зраста)

cottage /'kɒtɪdʒ/ n. котте́дж; да́ча; ~ **cheese** (прессо́ванный) творо́г

cotton /'kɒt(ə)n/ n. **1** (plant) хло́пок, хлопча́тник **2** (fabric) хло́пок **3** (thread) ни́тки (f. pl.) **4** (attr.) хлопчатобума́жный
■ ~ **wool** n. (BrE) ва́та

couch /kaʊtʃ/ n. (sofa) куше́тка, дива́н; (bed) крова́ть

couchette /kuː'ʃet/ n. спа́льное ме́сто

cough /kɒf/ n. ка́шель (m.)
● v.i. ка́шлять (impf.)
■ ~ **medicine, ~ mixture** (BrE) nn. миксту́ра от ка́шля

⚡ **could** /kʊd/ v. aux., see ▶ can²

couldn't /'kʊd(ə)nt/ neg. of ▶ could

⚡ **council** /'kaʊns(ə)l/ n. сове́т; **town** ~ городско́й сове́т; муниципалите́т
■ ~ **house** n. (BrE, dwelling) муниципа́льный дом; жило́й дом, принадлежа́щий муниципа́льному сове́ту

councillor /'kaʊnsələ(r)/ (AmE also **councilor**) n. член сове́та

counsel /'kaʊns(ə)l/ n. (barrister(s)) адвока́т
● v.t. (**counselled, counselling,** AmE **counseled, counseling**) сове́товать, по- + d.

counsellor /'kaʊnsələ(r)/ (AmE **counselor**) n. сове́тник

count¹ /kaʊnt/ n. (nobleman) граф (не брита́нский)

⚡ **count²** /kaʊnt/ n. **1** (reckoning) счёт, подсчёт; **keep** ~ вести́ (det.) счёт **2** (total) ито́г; **the** ~ **was 200** ито́г равня́лся 200 (двумста́м) **3** (law) пункт обвини́тельного заключе́ния
● v.t. (number, reckon) счита́ть, со-; ~ **your change!** прове́рьте сда́чу!; **50 people, not** ~**ing the children** 50 челове́к, не счита́я дете́й
● v.i. **1** (reckon, number) счита́ть (impf.); ~ **up to 10!** счита́йте до десяти́! **2** (be reckoned) счита́ться (impf.); **that doesn't** ~ э́то не в счёт (or не счита́ется) **3** (rely) рассчи́тывать (impf.) (on: на + a.); **I** ~ (**up)on you to help** я рассчи́тываю на ва́шу по́мощь
■ ~**down** n. (обра́тный) отсчёт вре́мени

countenance /'kaʊntɪnəns/ n. (face) лицо́, о́блик; выраже́ние лица́
● v.t. подде́рж|ивать, -а́ть

counter¹ /'kaʊntə(r)/ n. **1** (at games) фи́шка, ма́рка **2** (in shop) прила́вок; **under the** ~ (fig.) из-под полы́/прила́вка

counter² /'kaʊntə(r)/ v.t. & i. (oppose, parry) противоде́йствовать (impf.) + d.

counteract /kaʊntə'rækt/ v.t. противоде́йствовать (impf.) + d.

counter-attack /'kaʊntərətæk/ n. контрата́ка

counterclockwise /kaʊntə'klɒkwaɪz/ adj. & adv. (AmE) (дви́жущийся) про́тив часово́й стре́лки

counter-espionage /kaʊntər'espɪɒnɑːʒ/ n. контрразве́дка

counterfeit /'kaʊntəfɪt/ adj. подде́льный, подло́жный
● v.t. подде́л|ывать, -ать; (fig., simulate) подража́ть (impf.) + d.

counterfoil /'kaʊntəfɔɪl/ n. (BrE) корешо́к (че́ка, квита́нции и т. п.)

c

counterpart /'kaʊntəpɑːt/ *n.* па́ра (*к чему*), дополне́ние; (person) колле́га (*c.g.*)

counterproductive /kaʊntəprə'dʌktɪv/ *adj.* нецелесообра́зный

countersign /'kaʊntəsaɪn/ *v.t.* ста́вить, по-втору́ю по́дпись на + *p.*

countess /'kaʊntɪs/ *n.* графи́ня

countless /'kaʊntlɪs/ *adj.* бесчи́сленный

◇ **country** /'kʌntrɪ/ *n.* **1** (geog., pol.) страна́ **2** (opp. town) дере́вня; in the ~ за́ го́родом, на да́че; (~side) приро́да **3** (terrain) ме́стность; difficult ~ труднопроходи́мая ме́стность
■ ~ **club** *n.* за́городный клуб; ~ **house** (also ~ **seat**) *n.* поме́стье; ~**side** *n.* се́льская ме́стность; ландша́фт

◇ **county** /'kaʊntɪ/ *n.* гра́фство

coup /kuː/ *n.* (*pl.* **coups** /kuːz/) уда́чный ход
■ ~ **d'état** *n.* госуда́рственный переворо́т

coupé /'kuːpeɪ/ *n.* закры́тый двухдве́рный автомоби́ль

◇ **couple** /'kʌp(ə)l/ *n.* (objects or people) па́ра

coupon /'kuːpɒn/ *n.* купо́н, тало́н

courage /'kʌrɪdʒ/ *n.* хра́брость, сме́лость, му́жество; take, pluck up ~ мужа́ться (*impf.*); собира́ться, -ра́ться с ду́хом

courageous /kə'reɪdʒəs/ *adj.* хра́брый

courgette /kʊə'ʒet/ *n.* (BrE) кабачо́к

courier /'kʊrɪə(r)/ *n.* (messenger) курье́р; (travel guide) экскурсово́д

◇ **course** /kɔːs/ *n.* **1** (movement, process) ход, тече́ние; ~ of events ход собы́тий; in due ~ в до́лжное/своё вре́мя; of ~ коне́чно **2** (direction) курс, направле́ние; we are on ~ мы идём по ку́рсу **3** (race~) скаково́й круг **4** (series) курс; a ~ of lectures курс ле́кций; a ~ of treatment курс лече́ния **5** (cul.) блю́до; main ~ второ́е блю́до

◇ **court** /kɔːt/ *n.* **1** (yard) двор **2** (space for playing games) площа́дка для игр; (tennis) корт **3** (sovereign's etc.) двор **4** (law) суд; ~ of law, justice суд
● *v.t.* (a woman) уха́живать (*impf.*) за + *i.*
■ ~**house** *n.* зда́ние суда́; ~ **martial** *n.* вое́нный суд; ~-**martial** *v.t.* (-**martialled**, -**martialling**, AmE -**martialed**, -**martialing**) суди́ть (*impf.*) вое́нным судо́м; ~**room** *n.* зал суда́; ~**yard** *n.* двор

courteous /'kɜːtɪəs/ *adj.* ве́жливый, учти́вый

courtesan /kɔː'tɪzæn/ *n.* куртиза́нка

courtesy /'kɜːtɪsɪ/ *n.* ве́жливость, учти́вость
■ ~ **bus** *n.* беспла́тный авто́бус

courtier /'kɔːtɪə(r)/ *n.* придво́рный

courtship /'kɔːtʃɪp/ *n.* уха́живание

cousin /'kʌz(ə)n/ *n.* (male) двою́родный брат; (female) двою́родная сестра́; second ~ трою́родный брат (трою́родная сестра́)

cove /kəʊv/ *n.* бу́хточка

covenant /'kʌvənənt/ *n.* соглаше́ние, догово́р; C~ of the League of Nations уста́в Ли́ги На́ций; (relig.) заве́т
● *v.t. & i.* заключа́ть, -и́ть соглаше́ние;

договра́иваться, -ори́ться (*с кем о чём*)

◇ **cover** /'kʌvə(r)/ *n.* **1** (lid) кры́шка **2** (loose ~ing of chair etc.) чехо́л; (*in pl.*) (bedclothes) посте́ль **3** (of book etc.) переплёт, обло́жка **4** (shelter, protection) укры́тие, прикры́тие; take ~ укрыва́ться, -ы́ться **5** (at table): ~ charge пла́та за дополни́тельное обслу́живание (*музыку в ресторане и т. п.*) **6** (BrE, insurance) страхова́ние
● *v.t.* **1** (overspread etc.) (*also* ~ **up**, ~ **over**) покрыва́ть, -ы́ть; ~ a chair обива́ть, -и́ть стул; she ~ed her face in, with her hands она́ закры́ла лицо́ рука́ми; the roads are ~ed with snow доро́ги занесены́ сне́гом **2** (fig.) покрыва́ть, -ы́ть **3** (protect) закрыва́ть, -ы́ть; are you ~ed against theft? вы застрахо́ваны от кра́жи? **4** (aim weapon at) це́литься (*impf.*) в + *a.* **5** (meet, satisfy) покрыва́ть, -ы́ть **6** (deal with): the lectures ~ a wide field ле́кции охва́тывают широ́кий круг вопро́сов **7** (of correspondence): ~ing letter сопроводи́тельное письмо́
■ ~-**up** *n.* сокры́тие; ~ **version** *n.* (mus.) ка́вер-ве́рсия (*песни*)

◇ **coverage** /'kʌvərɪdʒ/ *n.* охва́т

covert /'kəʊvəːt/ *adj.* скры́тый

covet /'kʌvɪt/ *v.t.* (**coveted, coveting**) жа́ждать (*impf.*) + *g.*; (infml) за́риться (*impf.*) на + *a.*

cow /kaʊ/ *n.* коро́ва
■ ~**boy** *n.* ковбо́й

coward /'kaʊəd/ *n.* трус (-и́ха)

cowardice /'kaʊədɪs/ *n.* тру́сость

cowardly /'kaʊədlɪ/ *adj.* трусли́вый

cower /'kaʊə(r)/ *v.i.* съёжива|ться, -ться

cowslip /'kaʊslɪp/ *n.* первоцве́т

coy /kɔɪ/ *adj.* (**coyer, coyest**) стыдли́вый

cozy /'kəʊzɪ/ *adj.* (AmE) = cosy

crab /kræb/ *n.* краб; (astron., astrol.): the C~ Рак

crack /kræk/ *n.* **1** (in a cup, ice, etc.) тре́щина; (in wall, floor, etc.) щель **2** (sudden noise) треск, щёлканье **3** (infml, attempt) попы́тка; have a ~ at sth попыта́ть (*pf.*) свои́ си́лы в чём-н. **4**: at ~ of dawn с (пе́рвой) зарёй **5**: a ~ shot первокла́ссный стрело́к **6** (drug) крэк
● *v.t.* **1** (a plate, a bone) раска́лывать, -оло́ть; ~ a nut расколо́ть (*pf.*) оре́х; ~ a code разгада́ть (*pf.*) шифр **2**: ~ a whip щёлк|ать, -нуть кнуто́м; ~ a joke отпусти́ть (*pf.*) шу́тку
● *v.i.* **1** (get broken or fissured) дава́ть, -ть тре́щину; the glass ~ed стекло́ тре́снуло; (fig., give way): he did not ~ under torture пы́тки не сломи́ли его́ **2** (of sound) щёлк|ать, -нуть
□ ~ **down** *v.i.*: ~ down on прин|има́ть, -я́ть кру́тые ме́ры про́тив + *g.*
□ ~ **up** *v.i.* (of person: suffer collapse) надломи́ться (*pf.*); развал|иваться, -и́ться

cracker /'krækə(r)/ *n.* **1** (biscuit) кре́кер **2** (Christmas ~) хлопу́шка

crackle /'kræk(ə)l/ *n.* (sound) треск, потре́скивание
● *v.i.* (of sound) потре́скивать (*impf.*)

cradle /'kreɪd(ə)l/ *n.* (lit., fig.) колыбе́ль

● *v.t.:* ~ **a child in one's arms** держа́ть (*impf.*) ребёнка на рука́х

craft /krɑːft/ *n.* **1** (skill) ло́вкость, уме́ние **2** (occupation) ремесло́; **arts and** ~**s** иску́сства и ремёсла (*nt. pl.*) **3** (*pl.* ~) (boat) су́дно

■ ~**sman** *n.* реме́сленник, ма́стер

crafty /'krɑːftɪ/ *adj.* (**craftier, craftiest**) хи́трый

crag /kræg/ *n.* скала́, утёс

cram /kræm/ *v.t.* (**crammed, cramming**) **1** (insert forcefully) запи́х|ивать, -а́ть/-ну́ть; (fill): **the shelves are** ~**med with books** по́лки ло́мятся от кни́г **2** *v.t. & i.* (study intensively) уси́ленно занима́ться (пе́ред экза́меном) (*impf.*)

cramp /kræmp/ *n.* су́дорога
● *v.t.* стесн|я́ть, -и́ть

cranberry /'krænbərɪ/ *n.* клю́ква (*collect.*)

crane /kreɪn/ *n.* (bird) жура́вль (*m.*); (machine) (грузо)подъёмный кран

crank[1] /kræŋk/ *n.* (handle) кривоши́п

crank[2] /kræŋk/ *n.* (person) чуда́|к (-чка)

cranny /'krænɪ/ *n.* тре́щина

crap /kræp/ *n.* (vulg.) (sth of poor quality) говно́ (vulg.); (nonsense) вздор, чепуха́

♂ **crash** /kræʃ/ *n.* **1** (noise) гро́хот **2** (smash) ава́рия, круше́ние; **he was killed in a car/plane** ~ он поги́б в автомоби́льной/авиацио́нной катастро́фе; (comput.) фата́льный сбой **3**: **a** ~ (*sc. intensive*) **course** уско́ренный курс
● *v.t.* разб|ива́ть, -и́ть; гро́хнуть (*pf.*); **he** ~**ed the aircraft** он разби́л самолёт
● *v.i.* **1**: **the plane** ~**ed** самолёт потерпе́л ава́рию (*or* разби́лся) **2** (comput.) зав|иса́ть, -и́снуть

■ ~ **helmet** *n.* шлем автого́нщика/мотоцикли́ста; мотошле́м; ~**-land** *v.i.* соверш|а́ть, -и́ть авари́йную поса́дку; ~**-landing** *n.* авари́йная поса́дка

crass /kræs/ *adj.* глу́пый; ~ **stupidity** непроходи́мая ту́пость, полне́йшая глу́пость

crate /kreɪt/ *n.* я́щик

crater /'kreɪtə(r)/ *n.* кра́тер; (bomb ~) воро́нка

cravat /krə'væt/ *n.* широ́кий га́лстук; шёйный плато́к

crave /kreɪv/ *v.t. & i.* (desire) жа́ждать (*impf.*) + *g.*

craving /'kreɪvɪŋ/ *n.* стра́стное жела́ние

crawfish *see* ▸ **crayfish**

crawl /krɔːl/ *n.* **1** (~ing motion) по́лзание; **traffic was reduced to a** ~ тра́нспорт тащи́лся е́ле-е́ле **2** (swimming stroke) кроль (*m.*)
● *v.i.* **1** по́лзать (*indet.*), ползти́ (*det.*); **he** ~**ed on his hands and knees** он полз на четвере́ньках **2** (kowtow) пресмыка́ться (*impf.*) (**to:** пе́ред + *i.*) **3**: **the ground is** ~**ing with ants** земля́ кишмя́ киши́т муравья́ми

crayfish /'kreɪfɪʃ/, **crawfish** /'krɔːfɪʃ/ *nn.* (freshwater) речно́й рак; (marine) лангу́ст

crayon /'kreɪən/ *n.* цветно́й каранда́ш; цветно́й мело́к; пасте́ль

craze /kreɪz/ *n.* ма́ния, помеша́тельство

crazy /'kreɪzɪ/ *adj.* (**crazier, craziest**) безу́мный, сумасше́дший; ~ **about sth** поме́шанный на чём-н.; **he is** ~ **about her** он без ума́ от неё

creak /kriːk/ *v.i.* скрипе́ть (*impf.*)

cream /kriːm/ *n.* **1** (top part of milk) сли́в|ки (-ок) **2** (dish or sweet) крем (polish, cosmetic, etc.) крем, мазь; **face** ~ крем для лица́ **4** (*attr.*) (~-coloured) кре́мового цве́та
● *v.t.* (apply ~ to) на|кла́дывать, -ложи́ть крем на (+ *a*); ~ **off** от|бира́ть, -обра́ть

■ ~ **cake** *n.* торт с кре́мом; кре́мовое пиро́жное

creamy /'kriːmɪ/ *adj.* (**creamier, creamiest**) жи́рный

crease /kriːs/ *n.* скла́дка
● *v.t.* (newspaper, trousers) мять, с-/из-
● *v.i.* (form) мя́ться, с-/из-

♂ **create** /kriː'eɪt/ *v.t.* созд|ава́ть, -а́ть

♂ **creation** /kriː'eɪʃ(ə)n/ *n.* **1** (act, process) созда́ние, созида́ние **2** (product of imagination) творе́ние

♂ **creative** /kriː'eɪtɪv/ *adj.* тво́рческий

creativity /kriːeɪ'tɪvɪtɪ/ *n.* тво́рческий дар

creator /kriː'eɪtə(r)/ *n.* созда́тель (*m.*)

creature /'kriːtʃə(r)/ *n.* созда́ние, тварь, существо́

crèche /kreʃ/ *n.* (BrE) (де́тские) я́сл|и (-ей)

credential /krɪ'denʃ(ə)l/ *n.* (*usu. in pl.*) квалифика́ция

credibility /kredɪ'bɪlɪtɪ/ *n.* убеди́тельность

credible /'kredɪb(ə)l/ *adj.* (of person) заслу́живающий дове́рия

♂ **credit** /'kredɪt/ *n.* **1** (belief, trust, confidence) ве́ра, дове́рие **2** (honour): **the work does you** ~ э́та рабо́та де́лает вам честь **3** (fin.) креди́т; **buy on** ~ покупа́ть (*pf.*) в креди́т
● *v.t.* (**credited, crediting**) **1** (believe sth) ве́рить, по- + *d.* **2**: **I** ~**ed him with more sense** я счита́л его́ бо́лее благоразу́мным

■ ~ **card** *n.* креди́тная ка́рточка; ~ **crisis** *n.* (fin.) креди́тный кри́зис, фина́нсовый кри́зис; ~ **crunch** *n.* (fin.) нехва́тка ба́нковских креди́тов; ~**worthiness** *n.* кредитоспосо́бность; ~**worthy** *adj.* кредитоспосо́бный

creditable /'kredɪtəb(ə)l/ *adj.* (praiseworthy) похва́льный; (believable) правдоподо́бный, вероя́тный

creditor /'kredɪtə(r)/ *n.* кредито́р

credulous /'kredjʊləs/ *adj.* легкове́рный, дове́рчивый

creed /kriːd/ *n.* вероуче́ние; (fig.) убежде́ния (*nt. pl.*)

creek /kriːk/ *n.* (inlet) зали́в, бу́хта; (small river) ре́чка

creep /kriːp/ *n.* (infml) несно́сный/отврати́тельный тип
● *v.i.* (*past and p.p.* **crept**) по́лзать (*indet.*), ползти́ (*det.*); **old age** ~**s up on one unnoticed** ста́рость подкра́дывается незаме́тно

creeper /'kriːpə(r)/ *n.* (plant) ползу́чее/вью́щееся расте́ние

creepy /'kriːpɪ/ adj. (**creepier, creepiest**)
1 жу́ткий **2** (of flesh) в мура́шках
■ ~-**crawly** n. бука́шка

cremate /krɪ'meɪt/ v.t. кремировáть (impf., pf.)

cremation /krɪ'meɪʃ(ə)n/ n. кремáция

crematori|um /kremə'tɔːrɪəm/ n. (pl. ~a or ~ums) кремато́рий

crept /krept/ past and p.p. of ▶ creep

crescent /'krez(ə)nt/ n. **1** (moon) лу́нный серп **2** (symbol of Islam) полуме́сяц

cress /kres/ n. кресс-салáт

crest /krest/ n. **1** (tuft of feathers; top of a wave, hill) гре́бень (m.) **2** (heraldic device) герб

crevasse /krə'væs/ n. рассе́лина в леднике́

crevice /'krevɪs/ n. щель, расще́лина

✒ **crew** /kruː/ n. **1** (of vessel) кома́нда, экипа́ж; (of aircraft) экипа́ж **2** (team) брига́да, арте́ль **3**: ~ cut стри́жка ёжиком

crib /krɪb/ n. де́тская крова́тка с се́ткой

cricket¹ /'krɪkɪt/ n. (insect) сверчо́к

cricket² /'krɪkɪt/ n. (game) кри́кет

✒ **crime** /kraɪm/ n. (offence) преступле́ние; (collect.) престу́пность

Crimea /kraɪ'mɪə/ n. Крым

Crimean /kraɪ'mɪən/ adj. кры́мский

✒ **criminal** /'krɪmɪn(ə)l/ n. престу́пни|к (-ца)
● adj. **1** (guilty) престу́пный; he has a ~ history у него́ престу́пное про́шлое **2** (pert. to crime) уголо́вный, кримина́льный

criminologist /krɪmɪ'nɒlədʒɪst/ n. кримино́лог

criminology /krɪmɪ'nɒlədʒɪ/ n. криминоло́гия

crimson /'krɪmz(ə)n/ n. мали́новый цвет
● adj. мали́новый

cringe /krɪndʒ/ v.i. (**cringing**) раболе́пствовать (impf.)

crippl|e /'krɪp(ə)l/ n. (archaic or offens.) кале́ка (c.g.)
● v.t. кале́чить, ис-; (fig.): strikes are ~ing industry забасто́вки расша́тывают промы́шленность

✒ **crisis** /'kraɪsɪs/ n. (pl. **crises** /-siːz/) кри́зис

crisp /krɪsp/ n. (BrE) (in pl.) хрустя́щий карто́фель, чи́псы (-ов)
● adj. (of substance) хрустя́щий; a ~ biscuit рассы́пчатое пече́нье; a ~ lettuce све́жий салáт; (of style, orders, etc.) чека́нный
■ ~**bread** n. сухари́ (m. pl.); хрустя́щие хле́бцы (m. pl.)

criss-cross /'krɪskrɒs/ adj. перекре́щивающийся
● v.t. расче́р|чивать, -ти́ть крест-на́крест

criteri|on /kraɪ'tɪərɪən/ n. (pl. ~a) крите́рий

✒ **critic** /'krɪtɪk/ n. кри́тик

✒ **critical** /'krɪtɪk(ə)l/ adj. **1** (decisive) крити́ческий; the patient's condition is ~ больно́й в крити́ческом состоя́нии **2** (fault-finding) крити́ческий, крити́чный

✒ **criticism** /'krɪtɪsɪz(ə)m/ n. кри́тика; I have only one ~ to make у меня́ то́лько одно́

✒ ключевая лексика

✒ **criticize** /'krɪtɪsaɪz/ v.t. (adversely) критикова́ть (impf.)

critique /krɪ'tiːk/ n. кри́тика; (review) реце́нзия, крити́ческая статья́

croak /krəʊk/ v.t. & i. ква́кать (impf.)

Croat /'krəʊæt/ n. хорва́т (-ка)

Croatia /krəʊ'eɪʃə/ n. Хорва́тия

Croatian /krəʊ'eɪʃ(ə)n/ adj. хорва́тский

crochet /'krəʊʃeɪ/ n. вя́зка крючко́м
● v.t. & i. (**crocheted** /-ʃeɪd/, **crocheting** /-ʃeɪŋ/) вяза́ть (impf.) крючко́м

crockery /'krɒkərɪ/ n. гли́няная/фая́нсовая посу́да

crocodile /'krɒkədaɪl/ n. крокоди́л

crocus /'krəʊkəs/ n. (pl. **crocuses** or **croci** /-kaɪ/) кро́кус, шафра́н

croissant /'krwʌsɒ̃/ n. круасса́н, францу́зский рога́лик

crony /'krəʊnɪ/ n. дружо́к, закады́чный друг

crook /krʊk/ n. моше́нник, жу́лик

crooked /'krʊkɪd/ adj. (**crookeder, crookedest**) **1** (bent) со́гнутый, изо́гнутый **2** (infml, dishonest) бесче́стный

crop /krɒp/ n. урожа́й, жа́тва
● v.i. (**cropped, cropping**) (fig.): difficulties ~ped up появи́лись/возни́кли тру́дности

croquet /'krəʊkeɪ/ n. кроке́т

✒ **cross** /krɒs/ n. **1** крест **2** (mixing of breeds) по́месь, гибри́д
● adj. **1** (transverse) попере́чный, перекре́стный **2** (angry) серди́тый; злой (with: на + a.)
● v.t. **1** (go across, traverse) (also ~ **over**) ~ a road/bridge пере|ходи́ть, -йти́ че́рез доро́гу/мост; ~ the Channel перепл|ыва́ть, -ы́ть Ла-Ма́нш; the idea never ~ed my mind э́та мысль никогда́ не приходи́ла мне в го́лову **2** (draw lines across): ~ a cheque (BrE) перече́рк|ивать, -ну́ть чек **3** (place across) скре́|щивать, -сти́ть; ~ one's legs скрести́ть (pf.) но́ги **4**: ~ oneself крести́ться, пере-
● v.i.: he ~ed to where I was sitting он перешёл к тому́ ме́сту, где я сиде́л; he ~ed from Dover to Calais он перепра́вился из Ду́вра в Кале́
□ ~ **off, out** vv.t. вычёркивать, вы́черкнуть
■ ~-**check** n. све́рка ● v.t. све́р|ять, -ерить; ~-**country** adj.: a ~-country race бег по пересечённой ме́стности, кросс; ~-**country runner** кроссме́н; ~-**examine** v.t. подв|ерга́ть, -е́ргнуть перекрёстному допро́су; (fig.) допр|а́шивать, -оси́ть; ~-**eyed** adj. косогла́зый, косо́й; ~-**fire** n. (mil.) перекрёстный ого́нь; ~-**legged** adj. (сидя́щий) положи́в но́гу на́ ногу; ~-**purposes** n. pl. недоразуме́ние; ~-**question** v.t. допр|а́шивать, -оси́ть; ~-**reference** n. перекрёстная ссы́лка; ~-**road** n. перекрёсток; пересека́ющая доро́га; at the ~ **roads** (fig.) на распу́тье; ~ **section** n. попере́чное сече́ние; ~**word** n. кроссво́рд

crossing /'krɒsɪŋ/ n. перехо́д

crotch /krɒtʃ/ n. промежность

crotchet /'krɒtʃɪt/ n. (BrE, mus.) четвертная нота

crouch /kraʊtʃ/ v.i. сгибаться, согнуться

croupier /'kru:pɪeɪ/ n. (at gambling) крупье (m. indecl.)

crouton /'kru:tɒn/ n. (cul.) гренка

crow¹ /krəʊ/ n. ворона
■ ~'s-nest n. (naut.) наблюдательный пост на мачте, «воронье гнездо»

crow² /krəʊ/ n. (of cock) кукареканье
● v.i. кукарекать (impf.)

crowbar /'krəʊbɑ:(r)/ лом

✧ **crowd** /kraʊd/ n. толпа
● v.t. запол|нять, -нить; ~ed street многолюдная улица; the room was ~ed with furniture комната была загромождена мебелью
● v.i. (assemble in a ~) толпиться, с-; they ~ed into the room они набились в комнату
■ ~sourcing n. краудсорсинг (осуществление каких-л. работ с помощью большого числа людей, привлечённых через Интернет)

crown /kraʊn/ n. ❶ корона, венец ❷ (dental work) коронка ❸ (attr.): C~ jewels королевские/царские регалии (f. pl.)
● v.t. ❶: he was ~ed king его короновали (на царство) ❷: ~ a tooth ставить, по- коронку на зуб

✧ **crucial** /'kru:ʃ(ə)l/ adj. (decisive) решающий

crucible /'kru:sɪb(ə)l/ n. тигель (m.); (fig.) горнило (rhet.)

crucifix /'kru:sɪfɪks/ n. распятие, крест

crucifixion /kru:sɪ'fɪkʃ(ə)n/ n. распятие (на кресте)

crucify /'kru:sɪfaɪ/ v.t. расп|инать, -ять

crude /kru:d/ adj. ❶ (of materials): ~ oil сырая нефть ❷ (graceless) грубый, неотёсанный ❸ (ill-made): ~ paintings аляповатые картины

cruel /'kru:əl/ adj. (**crueller, cruellest** or **cruel, cruelest**) жестокий

cruelty /'kru:əltɪ/ n. жестокость

cruise /kru:z/ n. (pleasure voyage) морское путешествие, круиз
● v.i. (sail or drive about) курсировать (impf.); (go on cruise(s)) соверша́ть (impf.) круиз(ы)
■ ~ missile n. крылатая ракета

cruiser /'kru:zə(r)/ n. (warship) крейсер; **cabin** ~ прогулочный катер с каютой

crumb /krʌm/ n. крошка

crumble /'krʌmb(ə)l/ v.t. (bread etc.) крошить, рас-
● v.i. крошиться (impf.); (of a wall) обвал|иваться, -иться; (fig., of hopes etc.) рушиться (impf., pf.)

crumpet /'krʌmpɪt/ n. ≈ сдобная лепёшка

crumple /'krʌmp(ə)l/ v.t. мять, с-/из-; ~ up a sheet of paper скомкать (pf.) лист бумаги

crunch /krʌntʃ/ v.t. & i. грызть (impf.) с хрустом

crusade /kru:'seɪd/ n. (lit., fig.) крестовый поход

crusader /kru:'seɪdə(r)/ n. крестоносец; (fig.) борец

crush /krʌʃ/ n. ❶ (crowd) давка ❷ (infatuation): she has a ~ on him она без ума от него
● v.t. ❶ (squash) разда́в|ливать, -и́ть ❷ (crumple) мять, из-/с- ❸ (defeat) сокруш|а́ть, -и́ть; our hopes were ~ed наши надежды рухнули; a ~ing defeat полное поражение, разгром

crust /krʌst/ n. (of bread) корка; (of pastry) корочка; the earth's ~ земная кора

crustacean /krʌ'steɪʃ(ə)n/ n. ракообразное

crutch /krʌtʃ/ n. костыль (m.)

crux /krʌks/ n. (pl. ~es or **cruces** /'kru:si:z/) суть

✧ **cry** /kraɪ/ n. крик
● v.i. ❶ (weep) плакать (impf.) ❷ (shout) кричать (impf.)
□ ~ **off** v.t. & i. (an engagement) отмен|ять, -ить (свидание)
□ ~ **out** v.i. (in pain or distress) вскрик|ивать, -нуть

crypt /krɪpt/ n. склеп

cryptic /'krɪptɪk/ adj. таинственный, загадочный

crystal /'krɪst(ə)l/ n. ❶ (substance) горный хрусталь ❷ (glassware) хрусталь (m.)
■ ~ **ball** n. магический хрусталь; ~ **clear** adj. (fig.) ясный как божий день

crystallize /'krɪstəlaɪz/ v.t. ❶ (form into crystals) кристаллизовать (impf., pf.), за- (pf.) ❷ (clarify) воплощ|ать, -ти́ть в определённую форму ❸: ~d fruit засахаренные фрукты
● v.i. ❶ (form into crystals) кристаллизоваться (impf., pf.); вы́- (pf.) ❷: our plans ~d наши планы определились

CT abbr. (of **computerized tomography**) (med.) компьютерная томография; ~ **scan** исследование с помощью компьютерной томографии

cub /kʌb/ n. детёныш

Cuba /'kju:bə/ n. Куба; **in** ~ на Кубе

Cuban /'kju:bən/ n. куби́н|ец (-ка)
● adj. кубинский

cube /kju:b/ n. ❶ (math.) куб ❷ (solid) кубик
● v.t. (cut into ~s) нар|еза́ть, -е́зать кубиками

cubic /'kju:bɪk/ adj. кубический

cubicle /'kju:bɪk(ə)l/ n. (at a swimming pool; in a toilet) кабинка; (in a shop) примерочная

cubism /'kju:bɪz(ə)m/ n. кубизм

cubist /'kju:bɪst/ n. кубист (-ка)

cuckoo /'kʊku:/ n. кукушка

cucumber /'kju:kʌmbə(r)/ n. огурец

cuddle /'kʌd(ə)l/ v.t. обнимать
● v.i. обниматься

cue¹ /kju:/ n. (theatr.) реплика

cue² /kju:/ n. (sport) кий

cuff /kʌf/ n. ❶ (part of sleeve) манжета; **off the** ~ (fig.) экспромтом ❷ (AmE, trouser turn-up) отворот
■ ~links n. pl. запонки (f. pl.)

cuisine /kwɪ'zi:n/ n. (национальная) кухня

cul-de-sac /'kʌldəsæk/ n. (also fig.) тупик

culinary /'kʌlɪnərɪ/ adj. кулинарный

cull /kʌl/ n. (of wild animals) отстрел
● v.t. ❶ (slaughter) бить (impf.) ❷ (select) от|бирать, -обрать; под|бирать, -обрать

culminate /'kʌlmɪneɪt/ *v.i.:* ~ **in**
заверш|а́ться, -и́ться + *i.*

culpable /'kʌlpəb(ə)l/ *adj.* вино́вный

culprit /'kʌlprɪt/ *n.* престу́пник

cult /kʌlt/ *n.* культ

cultivate /'kʌltɪveɪt/ *v.t.* (land) возде́л|ывать,
-ать; (crops) культиви́ровать (*impf.*)

cultivator /'kʌltɪveɪtə(r)/ *n.* (person)
земледе́лец; (implement) культива́тор

cultural /'kʌltʃər(ə)l/ *adj.* культу́рный

culture /'kʌltʃə(r)/ *n.* (civilization) культу́ра,
быт

cultured /'kʌltʃəd/ *adj.* (of person)
интеллиге́нтный, культу́рный

cumbersome /'kʌmbəsəm/ *adj.* громо́здкий,
обремени́тельный

cumin /'kju:mɪn/ *n.* тмин

cumulative /'kju:mjʊlətɪv/ *adj.* кумуляти́вный

cunning /'kʌnɪŋ/ *n.* хи́трость
• *adj.* (**cunninger, cunningest**) хи́трый

cunt /kʌnt/ *n.* (vulg., genitals) пизда́ (vulg.); (as
term of abuse) су́ка

cup /kʌp/ *n.* **1** ча́шка, (liter.) ча́ша **2** (as prize)
ку́бок
• *v.t.* (**cupped, cupping**): ~ one's hand
держа́ть (*impf.*) ру́ку го́рстью

cupboard /'kʌbəd/ *n.* шкаф, буфе́т

cupola /'kju:pələ/ *n.* ку́пол

curable /'kjʊərəb(ə)l/ *adj.* излечи́мый

curate /'kjʊərət/ *n.* вика́рий

curator /kjʊə'reɪtə(r)/ *n.* (of museum etc.)
храни́тель (*m.*)

curb /kə:b/ *n.* **1** узда́ **2** = **kerb**
• *v.t.* (fig.) обу́зд|ывать, -а́ть

curd /kə:d/ *n.* творо́г
■ ~ **cheese** *n.* (BrE) творо́г

curdle /'kə:d(ə)l/ *v.i.* свёр|тываться, -ну́ться

cure /'kjʊə(r)/ *n.* (medicine, remedy) лека́рство,
сре́дство; (treatment) лече́ние
• *v.t.* **1** (a person) выле́чивать, вы́лечить; he
was ~d of asthma он вы́лечился от а́стмы
2 (a disease) выле́чивать, вы́лечить **3** (meat)
соли́ть, по-; вя́лить, про-

curfew /'kə:fju:/ *n.* коменда́нтский час

curiosity /kjʊərɪ'ɒsɪtɪ/ *n.* любопы́тство,
любозна́тельность

curious /'kjʊərɪəs/ *adj.* **1** (inquisitive)
любопы́тный, любозна́тельный **2** (odd)
стра́нный; ~ly enough как ни стра́нно

curl /kə:l/ *n.* (of hair) ло́кон, завито́к
• *v.t.*: ~ one's hair зави|ва́ть, -и́ть во́лосы
• *v.i.*: her hair ~s naturally у неё во́лосы
вью́тся от приро́ды; the dog ~ed up by the
fire соба́ка сверну́лась клубко́м у ками́на

curlers /'kə:ləz/ *n. pl.* бигуди́ (*nt. pl., indecl.*)

curly /'kə:lɪ/ *adj.* (**curlier, curliest**)
кудря́вый

currant /'kʌrənt/ *n.* изю́м, кори́нка

currency /'kʌrənsɪ/ *n.* валю́та; де́н|ьги (-ег)

ᕍ **current** /'kʌrənt/ *n.* **1** (of air, water) струя́, пото́к

2 (elec.) ток
• *adj.* теку́щий; the ~ issue of a magazine
теку́щий/очередно́й но́мер журна́ла
■ ~ **account** *n.* (BrE, comm.) теку́щий счёт;
теку́щие собы́тия; ~ **affairs** (also ~
events) *n. pl.* теку́щие собы́тия

ᕍ **currently** /'kʌrəntlɪ/ *adv.* тепе́рь, в настоя́щее
вре́мя

curricul|um /kə'rɪkjʊləm/ *n.* (*pl.* ~**a**) курс
обуче́ния
■ ~**um vitae** *n.* (кра́ткая) биогра́фия

curry[1] /'kʌrɪ/ *n.* (cul.) ка́рри (*nt. indecl.*)

curry[2] /'kʌrɪ/ *v.t.:* ~ **favour with sb**
подли́з|ываться, -а́ться к кому́-н.

curse /kə:s/ *n.* **1** (execration) прокля́тие **2** (bane)
прокля́тие, бич **3** (oath) богоху́льство
• *v.t.* **1** (pronounce ~ on) прокл|ина́ть, -я́сть
2 (abuse, scold) руга́ть (*impf.*) **3**: he is ~d
with a violent temper Госпо́дь награди́л его́
необу́зданным нра́вом
• *v.i.* (swear, utter ~s) руга́ться (*impf.*)

cursor /'kə:sə(r)/ *n.* (comput.) курсо́р

cursory /'kə:sərɪ/ *adj.* бе́глый, пове́рхностный

curt /kə:t/ *adj.* отры́вистый, ре́зкий

curtail /kə:'teɪl/ *v.t.* сокра|ща́ть, -ти́ть

curtain /'kə:t(ə)n/ *n.* занаве́ска, што́ра

curtsy, curtsey /'kə:tsɪ/ *n.* ревера́нс,
приседа́ние
• *v.i.* прис|еда́ть, -е́сть

curve /kə:v/ *n.* (line) крива́я; (bend in road) изги́б
• *v.t.* сгиба́ть, согну́ть
• *v.i.* из|гиба́ться, -огну́ться; the road ~s
доро́га извива́ется

cushion /'kʊʃ(ə)n/ *n.* (дива́нная) поду́шка
• *v.t.*: ~ a blow смягч|а́ть, -и́ть уда́р

cushy /'kʊʃɪ/ *adj.* (**cushier, cushiest**) (infml):
~ job непыльная рабо́та

cusp /kʌsp/ *n.* **1** (of moon) рог; (of leaf) о́стрый
коне́ц; (of tooth) ко́нчик **2** (beginning) поро́г

custard /'kʌstəd/ *n.* сла́дкий крем/со́ус из
яи́ц и молока́

custodian /kʌ'stəʊdɪən/ *n.* (of property etc.)
администра́тор; (of museum etc.) храни́тель
(*m.*)

custody /'kʌstədɪ/ *n.* **1** (guardianship) опе́ка,
попече́ние **2** (arrest): take, give into ~ брать,
взять под стра́жу

custom /'kʌstəm/ *n.* **1** (habit) обы́чай **2** (BrE,
clientele) клиенту́ра **3** (in pl.) (establishment)
тамо́жня; (in pl.) (duties) тамо́женные
по́шлины (*f. pl.*)
■ ~-**made** *adj.* сде́ланный/изгото́вленный на
зака́з; ~s officer *n.* тамо́женник

customary /'kʌstəmərɪ/ *adj.* обы́чный,
привы́чный

ᕍ **customer** /'kʌstəmə(r)/ *n.* (purchaser)
покупа́тель (*m.*)

customize /'kʌstəmaɪz/ *v.t.* под|гоня́ть,
-огна́ть в соотве́тствии с тре́бованиями
зака́зчика; изгот|а́вливать, -о́вить по
индивидуа́льному зака́зу

ᕍ **cut** /kʌt/ *n.* **1** (act of ~ting) ре́зка; (in finger)
поре́з; (slit) разре́з **2** (reduction) сниже́ние

3 (omission) купю́ра

• *v.t.* (**cutting**, *past and p.p.* **cut**) **1** (divide, separate, wound, extract by ∼ting) ре́зать (*impf.*); разр|еза́ть, -е́зать; отр|еза́ть, -е́зать; **he ∼ himself on the tin** он поре́зался/пора́нился о консе́рвную ба́нку; **∼ sth in two** разр|еза́ть, -е́зать что-н. попола́м **2** (make by ∼ting): **∼ me a piece of cake** отре́жьте мне кусо́к то́рта; **∼ a key** выта́чивать, вы́точить ключ; **∼ a jewel** грани́ть, о-, драгоце́нный ка́мень **3** (trim) подстр|ига́ть, -и́чь; **∼ one's nails** подстр|ига́ть, -и́чь но́гти; **have one's hair ∼** стри́чься, по- **4** (reduce) сн|ижа́ть, -и́зить **5**: **the baby ∼ a tooth** у ребёнка проре́зался зуб

• *v.i.* (**cutting**, *past and p.p.* **cut**) **1** (make incision) ре́зать (*impf.*); **this knife doesn't ∼** э́тот нож не ре́жет **2** (in pass. sense) ре́заться (*impf.*); **sandstone ∼s easily** песча́ник легко́ ре́жется **3** (run, take short ∼): **we ∼ across the fields** мы прошли́ кратча́йшим путём, напряму́ю че́рез поля́

□ **∼ back** *v.t.* (prune) подр|еза́ть, -е́зать; (fig., reduce, limit) сокра|ща́ть, -ти́ть

□ **∼ down** *v.t.* (e.g. a tree) руби́ть, с-; **∼ down expenses** сокра|ща́ть, -ти́ть расхо́ды

□ **∼ off** *v.t.*: **she ∼ the chicken's head off** она́ отруби́ла цыплёнку го́лову; **I was ∼ off while talking** меня́ разъедини́ли/прерва́ли во вре́мя разгово́ра; **they ∼ off our electricity** у нас отключи́ли/вы́ключили электри́чество; **we were ∼ off by the tide** прили́в отре́зал нас от су́ши; **he ∼ himself off from the world** он отгороди́лся от ми́ра

□ **∼ out** *v.t.*: **she ∼ out a picture from the paper** она́ вы́резала карти́нку из газе́ты; **∼ out smoking** бро́сить (*pf.*) кури́ть

□ **∼ up** *v.t.*: **he ∼ up his meat** он наре́зал мя́со

■ **∼ and paste** *v.t.* (comput.) вы́резать и вста́вить; **∼back** *n.* (reduction) сокраще́ние; **∼ glass** *n.* гранёное стекло́; хруста́ль (*m.*); **∼-price** *adj.* продава́емый по сни́женной цене́; **∼-rate** (AmE) = cut-price; **∼-throat** *n.* головоре́з; (*attr.*) **∼-throat competition** ожесточённая/беспоща́дная конкуре́нция

cute /kju:t/ *adj.* симпати́чный, ми́лый

cutlery /'kʌtləri/ *n.* столо́вые прибо́ры

cutlet /'kʌtlɪt/ *n.* отбивна́я котле́та

cutting /'kʌtɪŋ/ *n.* **1** (BrE, press ∼) вы́резка **2** (of plant) отро́сток

• *adj.*: **a ∼ retort** язви́тельный/ре́зкий отве́т; **the ∼ edge of technology** са́мая совреме́нная те́хника

C.V. *abbr.* (*of* **curriculum vitae**) (кра́ткая) автобиогра́фия

cyanide /'saɪənaɪd/ *n.* циани́д

cyberattack /'saɪbərətæk/ *n.* кибериата́ка

cyberbullying /'saɪbəbʊliŋ/ *n.* киберзапу́гивание (*использование информационных технологий, чтобы запугивать или унижать других*)

cybercafe /'saɪbəkəfeɪ/ *n.* интерне́т-кафе́

cybercrime /'saɪbəkraɪm/ *n.* **1** (offence) киберпреступле́ние **2** (*collect.*) киберпресту́пность

cybernetics /saɪbə'netɪks/ *n.* киберне́тика

cyberspace /'saɪbəspeɪs/ *n.* киберпростра́нство

cyclamen /'sɪkləmən/ *n.* (*pl.* **∼ or ∼s**) цикламе́н

✎ **cycle** /'saɪk(ə)l/ *n.* **1** (series, rotation) цикл, круг **2** (bicycle) велосипе́д

• *v.i.* е́здить (*indet.*) на велосипе́де

■ **∼ lane** *n.* (BrE) велосипе́дная доро́жка

cyclic /'sɪklɪk/, **cyclical** /'sɪklɪk(ə)l/ *adjs.* цикли́ческий

cycling /'saɪklɪŋ/ *n.* езда́ на велосипе́де

cyclist /'saɪklɪst/ *n.* велосипеди́ст

cyclone /'saɪkləʊn/ *n.* цикло́н

cygnet /'sɪgnɪt/ *n.* молодо́й ле́бедь

cylinder /'sɪlɪndə(r)/ *n.* цили́ндр

cylindrical /sɪ'lɪndrɪk(ə)l/ *adj.* цилиндри́ческий

cymbal /'sɪmb(ə)l/ *n.* таре́лка (*музыкальный инструмент*)

cynic /'sɪnɪk/ *n.* ци́ник

cynical /'sɪnɪk(ə)l/ *adj.* цини́чный

cynicism /'sɪnɪsɪz(ə)m/ *n.* цини́зм

cypress /'saɪprəs/ *n.* кипари́с

Cypriot /'sɪprɪət/ *n.* киприо́т (-ка)

• *adj.* ки́прский

Cyprus /'saɪprəs/ *n.* Кипр

Cyrillic /sɪ'rɪlɪk/ *adj.* кирилли́ческий

■ **∼ alphabet** *n.* кири́ллица

cyst /sɪst/ *n.* киста́

cystitis /sɪ'staɪtɪs/ *n.* цисти́т

cytology /saɪ'tɒlədʒɪ/ *n.* цитоло́гия

czar /zɑ:(r)/ *n.* = tsar

Czech /tʃek/ *n.* чех (че́шка); (language) че́шский язы́к

• *adj.* че́шский; **∼ Republic** Че́хия

Dd

d

D /diː/ *n.* **1** (mus.) pe (*nt. indecl.*) **2** (academic mark) «неудовлетворительно», двойка
■ **∼-Day** *n.* день (*m.*) начала военной операции, день «Д»

dab /dæb/ *n.* (small quantity) мазок
● *v.t. & i.* (**dabbed, dabbing**)
при|кладывать, -ложить; **she ∼bed (at) her eyes with a handkerchief** она прикладывала к глазам платок

dabble /'dæb(ə)l/ *v.i.*: **he ∼s in politics** он играет в политику

dacha /'dætʃə/ *n.* дача

dachshund /'dækshʊnd/ *n.* такса (*порода собак*)

dad /dæd/, **daddy** /'dædɪ/ *nn.* (infml) папа (*m.*), папочка (*m.*)

daddy /'dædɪ/ *n.* = **dad**

daffodil /'dæfədɪl/ *n.* нарцисс жёлтый

daft /dɑːft/ *adj.* (BrE, person) тронутый (infml); (action) бестолковый, глупый

Dagestan /dægɪ'stɑːn/ *n.* Дагестан

Dagestani /dægɪ'stɑːnɪ/ *n.* (*pl.* **∼s**) дагестан|ец (-ка)
● *adj.* дагестанский

dagger /'dægə(r)/ *n.* кинжал; **she looked ∼s at him** она пронзила его взглядом

dahlia /'deɪlɪə/ *n.* георгин

daily /'deɪlɪ/ *n.* (newspaper) ежедневная газета
● *adj.* ежедневный
● *adv.* ежедневно, каждый день

dainty /'deɪntɪ/ *n.* лакомство, деликатес
● *adj.* (**daintier, daintiest**) изящный, изысканный

dairy /'deərɪ/ *n.* **1** (room or building) маслодельня **2** (shop) молочный магазин; (*attr.*) молочный

daisy /'deɪzɪ/ *n.* маргаритка

dally /'dælɪ/ *v.i.* **1** (play, toy) баловаться (*impf.*) (with: + *i.*) **2** (flirt) флиртовать (*impf.*) **3** (waste time) тратить (*impf.*) время попусту

Dalmatian /dæl'meɪʃ(ə)n/ *n.* (dog) далматский дог, далматин

dam /dæm/ *n.* дамба, плотина, запруда

damage /'dæmɪdʒ/ *n.* **1** (harm, injury) вред, повреждение **2** (in pl.) (law) убытк|и (-ов)
● *v.t.* (physically) повре|ждать, -дить + *d.*; (morally) вредить, на-, причин|ять, -ить вред + *d.*

dame /deɪm/ *n.* **1** (female equivalent of knight) дейм, кавалерственная дама **2** (AmE, infml, woman) бабёнка (infml)

damn /dæm/ *n.* (negligible amount): **I don't care a ∼** мне наплевать
● *v.t.* **1** (doom to hell) прокл|инать, -ясть

2 (as expletive): **∼ (it all)!** чёрт возьми!

damned /dæmd/ *n., adj., & adv.*: **a ∼ fool** полный дурак; **it's a ∼ nuisance** (это) чертовски досадно

damp /dæmp/ *n.* влажность, сырость
● *adj.* влажный, сырой
● *v.t.* (*also* **dampen**) **1** (lit.) см|ачивать, -очить; увлажн|ять, -ить **2** (fig.): **∼ sb's ardour** осту|жать, -дить чей-н. пыл

♂ **dance** /dɑːns/ *n.* **1** танец **2** (party) танцевальный вечер; танцы (*m. pl.*)
● *v.t.* танцевать, с-
● *v.i.* танцевать, с-; плясать, с-

dancer /'dɑːnsə(r)/ *n.* (professional) танцор, танцовщи|к (-ца); (non-professional): **she's a good ∼** она хорошо танцует

dancing /'dɑːnsɪŋ/ *n.* танцы (*m. pl.*)

dandelion /'dændɪlaɪən/ *n.* одуванчик

dandruff /'dændrʌf/ *n.* перхоть

dandy /'dændɪ/ *n.* щёголь (*m.*), франт
● *adj.* (**dandier, dandiest**) (AmE, infml) превосходный; первый класс (*pred.*)

Dane /deɪn/ *n.* датчан|ин (-ка)

♂ **danger** /'deɪndʒə(r)/ *n.* опасность; **in ∼** в опасности; **he is in ∼ of falling** он рискует упасть

♂ **dangerous** /'deɪndʒərəs/ *adj.* опасный, рискованный

dangle /'dæŋg(ə)l/ *v.t.* болтать (*impf.*) + *i.*
● *v.i.* болтаться (*impf.*)

Danish /'deɪnɪʃ/ *n.* (language) датский язык
● *adj.* датский

dank /dæŋk/ *adj.* влажный, сырой

dapper /'dæpə(r)/ *adj.* щеголеватый

dare /deə(r)/ *n.* вызов
● *v.t.* бр|осать, -осить вызов + *d.*; **I ∼ you to jump over the wall!** а ну, перепрыгни через эту стену!
● *v.i.* **1** (have courage) осмели|ваться, -ться **2** (have impudence) сметь, по- **3**: **I ∼ say (that)** … надо думать (*or* полагаю), что…
■ **∼devil** *adj.* отчаянный, бесшабашный

daring /'deərɪŋ/ *adj.* отважный, дерзкий

♂ **dark** /dɑːk/ *n.* темнота, тьма; **before/after ∼** до/после наступления темноты; (ignorance): **I am in the ∼ as to his plans** я в неведении относительно его планов
● *adj.* **1** (lacking light) тёмный **2** (in colour) тёмный; тёмного цвета; (with names of colours) тёмно- **3** (of complexion) смуглый **4** (fig.) тёмный, покрытый мраком
■ **∼ blue** *n.* тёмно-синий; **∼ glasses** *n. pl.* (spectacles) тёмные/солнечные очки; **∼ green** *n.* тёмно-зелёный; **∼-haired** *adj.* темноволосый; **∼-skinned** *adj.* темнокожий

♂ ключевая лексика

darken /ˈdɑːkən/ *v.t.* затемн|я́ть, -и́ть
● *v.i.* темне́ть, по-

darkness /ˈdɑːknɪs/ *n.* темнота́

darling /ˈdɑːlɪŋ/ *n.* дорого́й, родно́й, люби́мый; **she's a ~** оно́ пре́лесть

darn /dɑːn/ *v.t. & i.* (mend) што́пать, за-

dart /dɑːt/ *n.* стрела́, дро́тик
■ **~board** *n.* мише́нь для стрел

dash /dæʃ/ *n.* **1** (sudden rush, race) рыво́к, бросо́к; **let's make a ~ for it** дава́й(те) побежи́м туда́ **2** (admixture): **a ~ of pepper** щепо́тка пе́рца **3** (written stroke) тире́ (*nt. indecl.*)
● *v.t.* **1** (hurl) швыр|я́ть, -ну́ть; **the ship was ~ed against the rocks** су́дно вы́бросило на ска́лы **2** (perform rapidly): **he ~ed off a sketch** он сде́лал набро́сок **3** (fig., disappoint) разр|уша́ть, -у́шить; **his hopes were ~ed** его́ наде́жды ру́хнули
● *v.i.* (rush) мча́ться (*impf.*); **she ~ed into the shop** она́ ворвала́сь в магази́н; **he ~ed off to town** он умча́лся в го́род

dashboard /ˈdæʃbɔːd/ *n.* прибо́рная пане́ль/доска́

dashing /ˈdæʃɪŋ/ *adj.* сти́льный

⚡ **data** /ˈdeɪtə/ *n.* (with sg. or pl. v.) да́нные (*nt. pl.*); **~ capture** сбор да́нных; **~ processing** обрабо́тка информа́ции

database /ˈdeɪtəbeɪs/ *n.* ба́за да́нных

date¹ /deɪt/ *n.* (fruit) фи́ник

⚡ **date²** /deɪt/ *n.* **1** (indication of time) да́та, число́; **what's the ~ today?** како́е сего́дня число́? **2** (period) пери́од; **at an early ~** (soon) в ближа́йшем бу́дущем; **out of ~** устаре́лый; **up to ~** нове́йший, совреме́нный **3** (appointment) свида́ние
● *v.t.* **1** (indicate ~ on) дати́ровать (*impf., pf.*) **2** (AmE, go out with) встреча́ться (*impf.*) с + *i.*; **dating agency** аге́нтство знако́мств
● *v.i.*: **this church ~s from the 14th century** э́та це́рковь отно́сится к XIV ве́ку

dated /ˈdeɪtɪd/ *adj.* (out of date) устаре́вший, устаре́лый

dative /ˈdeɪtɪv/ *adj. & n.* да́тельный (паде́ж)

⚡ **daughter** /ˈdɔːtə(r)/ *n.* дочь
■ **~-in-law** *n.* неве́стка, сноха́

daunt /dɔːnt/ *v.t.* устраш|а́ть, -и́ть; обескура́жи|вать, -ть

dawdle /ˈdɔːd(ə)l/ *v.i.* ме́шкать (*impf.*)

dawn /dɔːn/ *n.* рассве́т, заря́; **at ~** на рассве́те; на заре́
● *v.i.* **1** (of daybreak) света́ть (*impf.*) **2** (fig.): **it ~ed on me that...** меня́ осени́ло, что...

⚡ **day** /deɪ/ *n.* **1** (time of daylight) день (*m.*); (*attr.*) дневно́й; **twice a ~** два ра́за в день **2** (24 hours) день (*m.*), су́т|ки (-ок); **a ~ and a half** полтора́ дня **3** (as point of time): **what ~ (of the week) is it?** како́й сего́дня день (неде́ли)?; **one ~** (past) одна́жды; (future) когда́-нибудь; **every other ~** че́рез день; **some ~** когда́-нибудь; **~ in, ~ out** день ~ изо дня в день; **(on) the ~ I met you** в день на́шей встре́чи; **(on) the ~ before** накану́не (*чего*); **I took a ~ off** я взял выходно́й; **we**

had a ~ out (BrE) мы провели́ день вне до́ма **4** (as work period): **he works a 5-hour ~** у него́ пятичасово́й рабо́чий день **5** (period) пора́, вре́мя (*nt.*); **these ~s** (nowadays) тепе́рь, в на́ши дни; **in those ~s** в те дни; в то вре́мя **6** (denoting contest): **his arrival saved the ~** его́ прие́зд спас положе́ние
■ **~break** *n.* рассве́т; **~care** *adj.*: **~-care facilities** (for children) детса́д; (for babies, toddlers) я́сл|и (-ей); **~dream** *n.* грёза, мечта́ ● *v.i.* мечта́ть (*impf.*); **~light** *n.* (period): **in broad ~light** средь бе́ла дня; **~ nursery** *n.* (crèche) де́тские я́сл|и (-ей); **~time** *n.* день (*m.*); **in the ~time** днём; (*attr.*) дневно́й; **~-to-~** *adj.* повседне́вный

daze /deɪz/ *n.*: **he was in a ~** он был поражён/как в тума́не
● *v.t.* пора|жа́ть, -зи́ть

dazzle /ˈdæz(ə)l/ *v.t.* **1** (lit.) ослеп|ля́ть, -и́ть **2** (fig.) пора|жа́ть, -зи́ть

dB *abbr.* (*of* **decibel(s)**) дБ (дециб́ел)

DC *abbr.* (*of* **direct current**) постоя́нный ток

deacon /ˈdiːkən/ *n.* дья́кон

⚡ **dead** /ded/ *n.*: **at ~ of night** глубо́кой но́чью
● *adj.* **1** (no longer living) мёртвый, уме́рший; (in accident etc.) поги́бший, уби́тый; (of animal) до́хлый; **~ body** труп, мёртвое те́ло; **~ flowers/leaves** увя́дшие цветы́/ли́стья; **he is ~** он у́мер; (killed) он уби́т; (as n.) **the ~** уме́ршие, поко́йные **2** (inert): **~ end** (lit., fig.) тупи́к; **a ~-end job** бесперспекти́вная рабо́та **3** (spent, uncharged): **the telephone went ~** телефо́н отключи́лся **4** (abrupt, exact, complete) внеза́пный; **a ~ certainty** по́лная уве́ренность
● *adv.*: **he stopped ~** он останови́лся как вко́панный; **~ on time** мину́та в мину́ту; **~ tired** смерте́льно уста́лый; **he is ~ set on going to London** он реши́л пое́хать в Ло́ндон во что бы то ни ста́ло
■ **~line** *n.* преде́льный/кра́йний срок; **~lock** *n.* мёртвая то́чка; тупи́к; **~ loss** *n.* (fig., failure) по́лный прова́л; **he's a ~ loss** он неуда́чник, от него́ то́лку не бу́дет; **~pan** *adj.* (infml) невырази́тельный

deaden /ˈded(ə)n/ *v.t.* осл|абля́ть, -а́бить; **the drug ~s pain** лека́рство притупля́ет боль

deadly /ˈdedlɪ/ *adj.* (deadlier, deadliest) смерте́льный; **~ enemy** смерте́льный враг

deaf /def/ *adj.* **1** глухо́й; (as n.) **the ~** глухи́е **2** (fig.): **turn a ~ ear** не слу́шать (*impf.*); не обраща́ть (*impf.*) внима́ния на + *a.*
■ **~ aid** *n.* (BrE) слухово́й аппара́т; **~ mute** *n.* (often offens.) глухонемо́й

deafening /ˈdefənɪŋ/ *adj.* оглуши́тельный

⚡ **deal** /diːl/ *n.* **1** (amount) коли́чество; **a great, good ~ (of)** мно́го + *g.* **2** (business agreement) сде́лка; **it's a ~!** договори́лись!; по рука́м!
● *v.t.* (past and p.p. **dealt**) (cards) сда|ва́ть, -ть
● *v.i.* (past and p.p. **dealt**) **1** (do business) торгова́ть (*impf.*); **he ~s in** он торгу́ет меха́ми **2**: **~ with** (treat) обраща́ться (*impf.*) с + *i.*; (cope with) справля́ться, спра́виться с + *i.*; **he ~t with the problem skilfully** он

d

уме́ло подошёл к э́тому вопро́су **3**: ~ **with** (discuss a subject etc.) (of person) зан|има́ться, -я́ться (*impf.*) + i.; (of book) рассм|а́тривать, -отре́ть

dealer /'di:lə(r)/ *n.* торго́вец, ди́лер

dealing /'di:lɪŋ/ *n.* **1** (trade): ~ **in real estate** торго́вля недви́жимостью **2** (*in pl.*) (association) торго́вые дела́; сде́лки (*f. pl.*)

dealt /delt/ *past and p.p of* ▶ **deal**

dean /di:n/ *n.* (eccl.) дека́н, настоя́тель (*m.*); (academic) дека́н

dear /dɪə(r)/ *n.* ми́лый, дорого́й
• *adj.* **1** (beloved) люби́мый, дорого́й **2** (lovable) сла́вный, ми́лый **3** (in informal letters) дорого́й; (in formal letters) уважа́емый **4** (costly) дорого́й
• *int.:* **oh** ~!/~ **me!** о, Го́споди!; Бо́же ты мой!

dearly /'dɪəlɪ/ *adv.* (very much) о́чень; (at a high price) до́рого

dearth /də:θ/ *n.* нехва́тка, недоста́ток

✓ **death** /deθ/ *n.* **1** (act or fact of dying) смерть; **drink oneself to** ~ ум|ира́ть, -ере́ть от пья́нства; **work oneself to** ~ рабо́тать (*impf.*) на изно́с; **at** ~**'s door** на поро́ге сме́рти **2** (instance of dying) ги́бель **3** (utmost limit): **he was bored to** ~ ему́ бы́ло до сме́рти ску́чно; **I'm sick to** ~ **of it** мне э́то надое́ло до сме́рти ■ ~**bed** *n.* сме́ртное ло́же; ~ **penalty** *n.* сме́ртная казнь; ~ **toll** *n.* число́ поги́бших; ~ **trap** *n.:* **this theatre is a** ~ **trap in case of fire** в слу́чае пожа́ра э́тот теа́тр су́щая западня́

deathly /'deθlɪ/ *adj. & adv.* (**deathlier**, **deathliest**) смерте́льный; ~ **pale** смерте́льно бле́дный; ~ **silence** мёртвая тишина́

debar /dɪ'bɑ:(r)/ *v.t.* (**debarred**, **debarring**) препя́тствовать, вос- + d.

debarkation /di:bɑ:'keɪʃ(ə)n/ *n.* = disembarkation

debatable /dɪ'beɪtəb(ə)l/ *adj.* спо́рный

✓ **debate** /dɪ'beɪt/ *n.* диску́ссия; (in parliament) деба́т|ы (-ов)

debauched /dɪ'bɔ:tʃt/ *adj.* (dissolute) распу́тный

debauchery /dɪ'bɔ:tʃərɪ/ *n.* развра́т, распу́щенность

debit /'debɪt/ *n.* дебе́т
• *v.t.* (**debited**, **debiting**) дебетова́ть (*impf., pf.*)
■ ~ **card** *n.* дебе́товая ка́рточка

debonair /debə'neə(r)/ *adj.* обходи́тельный, учти́вый

debrief /di:'bri:f/ *v.t.* расспр|а́шивать, -оси́ть; ~ **sb** заслу́ш|ивать, -ать чей-н. отчёт

debris /'debri:/ *n.* оско́лки (*m. pl.*); обло́мки (*m. pl.*)

✓ **debt** /det/ *n.* долг; **get into** ~ входи́ть, войти́ в долги́

debtor /'detə(r)/ *n.* должни́к

debugger /di:'bʌɡə(r)/ *n.* (comput.) програ́мма отла́дки, отла́дчик

debunk /di:'bʌŋk/ *v.t.* (infml) развенч|ивать, -а́ть

<hr>

✓ ключева́я ле́ксика

debut /'debju:/ *n.* дебю́т

debutante /'debju:tɑ:nt/ *n.* (making first appearance in fashionable society) де́вушка, впервы́е выезжа́ющая в свет; (theatr., sport) дебюта́нтка

✓ **decade** /'dekeɪd/ *n.* десятиле́тие

decadence /'dekəd(ə)ns/ *n.* упа́док, декаде́нтство

decadent /'dekəd(ə)nt/ *adj.* упа́дочный, декаде́нтский

decaffeinated /di:'kæfɪneɪtɪd/ *adj.* без кофеи́на

decant /dɪ'kænt/ *v.t.* (pour wine) сце|́живать, -ди́ть; перел|ива́ть, -и́ть (*из буты́лки в графи́н*)

decanter /dɪ'kæntə(r)/ *n.* графи́н

decapitate /dɪ'kæpɪteɪt/ *v.t.* обезгла́в|ливать, -ить

decay /dɪ'keɪ/ *n.* разложе́ние; **tooth** ~ разруше́ние зубо́в
• *v.i.* разл|ага́ться, -ожи́ться

deceased /dɪ'si:st/ *adj.* поко́йный; (*as n.*) **the** ~ поко́йник

deceit /dɪ'si:t/ *n.* обма́н, ложь

deceitful /dɪ'si:tfʊl/ *adj.* обма́нчивый, лжи́вый

deceive /dɪ'si:v/ *v.t.* обма́н|ывать, -у́ть; ~ **oneself** обма́н|ываться, -у́ться

✓ **December** /dɪ'sembə(r)/ *n.* дека́брь (*m.*)

decency /'di:s(ə)nsɪ/ *n.* прили́чие

decent /'di:s(ə)nt/ *adj.* **1** (not obscene) прили́чный, присто́йный **2** (proper, adequate) прили́чный, подходя́щий **3** (honest, moral) поря́дочный **4** (good, satisfactory) хоро́ший, неплохо́й **5** (BrE, infml, kind, generous) до́брый, любе́зный

decentralize /di:'sentrəlaɪz/ *v.t.* децентрализова́ть (*impf., pf.*)

deception /dɪ'sepʃ(ə)n/ *n.* обма́н

deceptive /dɪ'septɪv/ *adj.* обма́нчивый

decibel /'desɪbel/ *n.* деци090бе́л

✓ **decide** /dɪ'saɪd/ *v.t.* реш|а́ть, -и́ть; ~ **a question** реш|а́ть, -и́ть вопро́с
• *v.i.* реш|а́ться, -и́ться; ~ **between alternatives** де́лать, с- вы́бор; ~ **on going** реши́ть (*pf.*) пое́хать; ~ **against going** реши́ть (*pf.*) не е́хать

deciduous /dɪ'sɪdjʊəs/ *adj.* ли́ственный, листопа́дный

decimal /'desɪm(ə)l/ *adj.* десяти́чный
■ ~ **point** *n.* запята́я, отделя́ющая це́лое от дро́би (*в стра́нах англи́йского языка́ в чи́слах с десяти́чными дробя́ми вме́сто запято́й испо́льзуется то́чка: 7,1 пи́шется как 7.1*)

decipher /dɪ'saɪfə(r)/ *v.t.* (fig., make out) раз|бира́ть, -обра́ть

✓ **decision** /dɪ'sɪʒ(ə)n/ *n.* реше́ние; **make, take, come to a** ~ прин|има́ть, -я́ть реше́ние

decisive /dɪ'saɪsɪv/ *adj.* реши́тельный

decisiveness /dɪ'saɪsɪvnɪs/ *n.* реши́тельность

deck /dek/ *n.* **1** (of ship) па́луба **2** (AmE, of cards) коло́да
■ ~**chair** *n.* шезло́нг

declaim /dɪˈkleɪm/ v.t. & i. декламировать (impf.)

declaration /deklaˈreɪʃ(ə)n/ n. декларация

✓ **declare** /dɪˈkleə(r)/ v.t. & i. **1** (say solemnly) заяв|лять, -и́ть; **he ~d that he was innocent** он заяви́л о свое́й невино́вности **2** (pronounce) объяв|ля́ть, -и́ть; **I ~ the meeting open** объявля́ю собра́ние откры́тым **3** (at customs) деклари́ровать (impf., pf.)

declassify /diːˈklæsɪfaɪ/ v.t. рассекре́|чивать, -тить (документы)

declension /dɪˈklenʃ(ə)n/ n. (gram.) склоне́ние

✓ **decline** /dɪˈklaɪn/ n. **1** (fall) паде́ние **2** (decay) упа́док, зака́т
● v.t. **1** отклон|я́ть, -и́ть; **he ~d the invitation** он отклони́л приглаше́ние **2** (gram.) склоня́ть, про-
● v.i. **1** (sink) па́дать, упа́сть; при|ходи́ть, -йти́ в упа́док **2** (refuse) отка́з|ываться, -а́ться

declutter /diːˈklʌtə(r)/ v.t. (tidy up) убира́ть, убра́ть, приводи́ть, привести́ в поря́док (комнату, рабочее пространство, и т. п.)

decode /diːˈkəʊd/ v.t. расшифро́в|ывать, -а́ть

decompose /diːkəmˈpəʊz/ v.i. (decay) разл|ага́ться, -ожи́ться

decontaminate /diːkənˈtæmɪneɪt/ v.t. обеззара́|живать, -зить; (remove radioactivity from) дезактиви́ровать (impf., pf.)

decor /ˈdeɪkɔː(r)/ n. (of room) убра́нство; (of stage) декора́ции (f. pl.)

decorate /ˈdekəreɪt/ v.t. **1** (adorn) укр|аша́ть, -а́сить (impf.) **2** (paint, furnish, etc.) отде́л|ывать, -ать

decoration /dekəˈreɪʃ(ə)n/ n. украше́ние, убра́нство

decorative /ˈdekərətɪv/ adj. декорати́вный

decorator /ˈdekəreɪtə(r)/ n. (painter) маля́р; (paperer) окле́йщик обо́ев

decorum /dɪˈkɔːrəm/ n. вне́шнее прили́чие; этике́т, деко́рум

decoy /ˈdiːkɔɪ/ n. прима́нка
● v.t. прима́н|ивать, -и́ть

decrease n. /ˈdiːkriːs/ уменьше́ние, убыва́ние
● v.i. /dɪˈkriːs/ ум|еньша́ться, -е́ньшиться; уб|ыва́ть, -ы́ть

decree /dɪˈkriː/ n. **1** (pol.) ука́з **2** (law) суде́бное реше́ние

decrepit /dɪˈkrepɪt/ adj. дря́хлый, ве́тхий

dedicate /ˈdedɪkeɪt/ v.t. (devote) посвя|ща́ть, -ти́ть (что-н. кому-н.); (assign) предназн|ача́ть, -а́чить (что-н. кому-н.)

dedicated /ˈdedɪkeɪtɪd/ adj. пре́данный, беззаве́тный

dedication /dedɪˈkeɪʃ(ə)n/ n. (devotion) пре́данность, самоотве́рженность; (inscription) посвяще́ние

deduce /dɪˈdjuːs/ v.t. выводи́ть, вы́вести; заключ|а́ть, -и́ть

deduct /dɪˈdʌkt/ v.t. вычита́ть, вы́честь

deduction /dɪˈdʌkʃ(ə)n/ n. (subtraction) вы́чет; (inference) вы́вод, заключе́ние

deed /diːd/ n. **1** (sth done) де́йствие, посту́пок **2** (law) акт, докуме́нт

deem /diːm/ v.t. полага́ть (impf.), счита́ть, счесть

✓ **deep** /diːp/ adj. **1** глубо́кий **2** (with measurement): **a hole 6 feet ~** я́ма глубино́й в 6 фу́тов **3** (submerged, lit., fig.): **~ in thought** заду́мавшийся; погружённый в разду́мья **4** (extreme) глубо́кий **5** (of colour) тёмный, насы́щенный **6** (low-pitched) ни́зкий
● adv. глубоко́
■ **~-freeze** n. морози́льник; **~-frozen** adj. заморо́женный; **~-fry** v.t. зажа́ри|вать, -ть; **~-rooted** adj.: **~-rooted belief** глубоко́ укорени́вшееся мне́ние; **~-sea** adj.: **~-sea fishing** глубоково́дный лов; **~-vein thrombosis** n. (med.) тромбо́з глубо́ких вен

deepen /ˈdiːpən/ v.t. & i. **1** (make, become deeper) углуб|ля́ть(ся), -и́ть(ся) **2** (intensify) уси́ли|вать(ся), -ть(ся) **3** (make, become lower in pitch) пон|ижа́ть(ся), -и́зить(ся)

✓ **deeply** /ˈdiːplɪ/ adv. глубоко́; **he is ~ in debt** он влез в долги́ по́ уши

deer /dɪə(r)/ n. (pl. **~**) оле́нь (m.)

deface /dɪˈfeɪs/ v.t. иска|жа́ть, -зи́ть

defamatory /dɪˈfæmətərɪ/ adj. клеветни́ческий

default n. /dɪˈfɔːlt, ˈdiːfɔːlt/ **1** (neglect): **he won the match by ~** он вы́играл матч из-за нея́вки проти́вника **2** (comput.) значе́ние по умолча́нию; **~ font** шрифт по умолча́нию **3** (fin.) дефо́лт
● v.i. /dɪˈfɔːlt/ не выполня́ть, вы́полнить обяза́тельства

✓ **defeat** /dɪˈfiːt/ n. пораже́ние
● v.t. нан|оси́ть, -ести́ пораже́ние + d.; **they were ~ed** они́ потерпе́ли пораже́ние

defeatism /dɪˈfiːtɪz(ə)m/ n. пораже́нчество

defeatist /dɪˈfiːtɪst/ n. пессими́ст
● adj. пораже́нческий, пессимисти́ческий

defecate /ˈdefɪkeɪt/ v.i. испражн|я́ться, -и́ться

defect¹ /ˈdiːfekt/ n. дефе́кт; поро́к

defect² /dɪˈfekt/ v.i. перебе|га́ть, -жа́ть (from: от + g.) (to: к + d., на + a.)

defection /dɪˈfekʃ(ə)n/ n. дезерти́рство; **there were several ~s from the party** не́сколько челове́к вы́шло/вы́шли из па́ртии

defective /dɪˈfektɪv/ adj. несоверше́нный

defector /dɪˈfektə(r)/ n. перебе́жчи|к (-ца)

✓ **defence** /dɪˈfens/ (AmE **defense**) n. оборо́на, защи́та; **in ~ of** в защи́ту + g.

defenceless /dɪˈfenslɪs/ (AmE **defenseless**) adj. беззащи́тный

✓ **defend** /dɪˈfend/ v.t. обороня́ть (impf.)

defendant /dɪˈfend(ə)nt/ n. отве́тчик

defender /dɪˈfendə(r)/ n. защи́тник

defense /dɪˈfens/ n. (AmE) = **defence**

defenseless /dɪˈfenslɪs/ adj. (AmE) = **defenceless**

defensive /dɪˈfensɪv/ adj. оборони́тельный; **he has a ~ manner** он как бу́дто опра́вдывается

defer¹ /dɪˈfɜː(r)/ v.t. (**deferred**, **deferring**) (postpone) отсро́чи|вать, -ть

defer² /dɪˈfɜː(r)/ v.i. (**deferred**, **deferring**): **~ to** счита́ться (impf.) с + i.

d

deference /'defərəns/ n. уваже́ние, почти́тельность

deferential /defə'renʃ(ə)l/ adj. почти́тельный

defiance /dɪ'faɪəns/ n. вы́зов; in ~ of вопреки́ + d.

defiant /dɪ'faɪənt/ adj. вызыва́ющий

deficiency /dɪ'fɪʃənsɪ/ n. **1** (lack) нехва́тка, отсу́тствие **2** (in pl.) (shortcomings) недоста́тки (m. pl.)

deficient /dɪ'fɪʃ(ə)nt/ adj. недоста́точный, непо́лный

deficit /'defɪsɪt/ n. дефици́т, недочёт

defile /dɪ'faɪl/ v.t. оскверн|я́ть, -и́ть

⚔ **define** /dɪ'faɪn/ v.t. определ|я́ть, -и́ть

definite /'defɪnɪt/ adj. **1** (specific) определённый **2** (clear, exact) то́чный, чёткий ■ ~ **article** n. (gram.) определённый арти́кль

⚔ **definitely** /'defɪnɪtlɪ/ adv. определённо, то́чно; he is ~ coming он непреме́нно/то́чно придёт

⚔ **definition** /defɪ'nɪʃ(ə)n/ n. (clearness of outline) я́сность, чёткость; (statement of meaning) определе́ние

definitive /dɪ'fɪnɪtɪv/ adj. оконча́тельный

deflect /dɪ'flekt/ v.t. & i. отклон|я́ть(ся), -и́ть(ся)

deflection /dɪ'flekʃ(ə)n/ n. отклоне́ние

deforestation /di:fɒrɪ'steɪʃ(ə)n/ n. обезле́сение

deform /dɪ'fɔ:m/ v.t. уро́довать, из-

deformity /dɪ'fɔ:mɪtɪ/ n. уро́дливость, уро́дство

defraud /dɪ'frɔ:d/ v.t. обма́н|ывать, -у́ть

defrost /di:'frɒst/ v.t. (food, refrigerator) размор|а́живать, -о́зить

deft /deft/ adj. ло́вкий, иску́сный

defunct /dɪ'fʌŋkt/ adj. несуществу́ющий, исче́знувший

defuse /di:'fju:z/ v.t. сн|има́ть, -ять взрыва́тель (m.) + g.; (fig.) разря|жа́ть, -ди́ть

defy /dɪ'faɪ/ v.t. **1** (challenge) вызыва́ть, вы́звать **2** (fig.): the problem defies solution пробле́ма неразреши́ма

degenerate adj. /dɪ'dʒenərət/ вы́родившийся, дегенерати́вный
● v.i. /dɪ'dʒenəreɪt/ вырожда́ться, вы́родиться (impf.)

degradation /degrə'deɪʃ(ə)n/ n. (moral) упа́док, деграда́ция

degrade /dɪ'greɪd/ v.t. прин|ижа́ть, -и́зить

degrading /dɪ'greɪdɪŋ/ adj. унизи́тельный

⚔ **degree** /dɪ'gri:/ n. **1** (unit of measurement) гра́дус **2** (step, stage) сте́пень; у́ровень (m.); by ~s постепе́нно; to a ~ до изве́стной сте́пени **3** (academic) (учёная) сте́пень

dehumanize /di:'hju:mənaɪz/ v.t. дегуманизи́ровать (impf., pf.)

dehydrate /di:haɪ'dreɪt/ v.t. обезво́|живать, -дить

de-icer /dɪ'aɪsə(r)/ n. антиобледени́тель (m.)

deify /'deɪfaɪ/ v.t. обожеств|ля́ть, -и́ть; боготвори́ть, о-

deign /deɪn/ v.t.: he did not ~ to answer us он не соизво́лил отве́тить нам

deity /'deɪtɪ/ n. божество́

dejected /dɪ'dʒektɪd/ adj. удручённый, пода́вленный

⚔ **delay** /dɪ'leɪ/ n. заде́ржка, отсро́чка, промедле́ние; without ~ неме́дленно
● v.t. отк|ла́дывать, -ложи́ть

delegate n. /'delɪgət/ делега́т, представи́тель (m.)
● v.t. /'delɪgeɪt/ ~ sb делеги́ровать (impf., pf.) кого́-н.; ~ a task поруч|а́ть, -и́ть рабо́ту (кому)

delegation /delɪ'geɪʃ(ə)n/ n. делега́ция

delete /dɪ'li:t/ v.t. вычёркивать, вы́черкнуть; (comput.) удал|я́ть, -и́ть

Delhi /'delɪ/ n. Де́ли (m. indecl.)

deliberate /dɪ'lɪbərət/ adj. (intentional) наме́ренный; (slow) осмотри́тельный

deliberately /dɪ'lɪbərətlɪ/ adv. наме́ренно

deliberation /dɪlɪbə'reɪʃ(ə)n/ n. (pondering) обду́мывание; (in pl.) диску́ссия; (slowness) медли́тельность, неторопли́вость

delicacy /'delɪkəsɪ/ n. (exquisiteness) утончённость, то́нкость; (proneness to injury) хру́пкость; (critical nature) щекотли́вость, делика́тность

delicate /'delɪkət/ adj. **1** (fine, exquisite) то́нкий **2** (easily injured) хру́пкий **3** (ticklish) щекотли́вый

delicatessen /delɪkə'tes(ə)n/ n. гастроно́м

delicious /dɪ'lɪʃəs/ adj. о́чень вку́сный

delight /dɪ'laɪt/ n. удово́льствие, наслажде́ние; take ~ in sth на|ходи́ть, -йти́ удово́льствие в чём-н.
● v.t. дост|авля́ть, -а́вить наслажде́ние + d.; I am ~ed to accept the invitation я с ра́достью принима́ю приглаше́ние

delightful /dɪ'laɪtfʊl/ adj. восхити́тельный, очарова́тельный

delineate /dɪ'lɪnɪeɪt/ v.t. (e.g. a frontier) оче́р|чивать, -ти́ть; (e.g. character) изобра|жа́ть, -зи́ть

delinquency /dɪ'lɪŋkwənsɪ/ n. престу́пность

delinquent /dɪ'lɪŋkwənt/ n. правонаруши́тель (-ница)

delirious /dɪ'lɪrɪəs/ adj. в бреду́ (pred.)

delirium /dɪ'lɪrɪəm/ n. бред
■ ~ **tremens** n. /'tri:menz/ бе́лая горя́чка

⚔ **deliver** /dɪ'lɪvə(r)/ v.t. **1** (of birth): she delivered a child (assisted at birth) она́ приняла́ ребёнка **2** (give, present): ~ judgement выноси́ть, вы́нести реше́ние; ~ a speech произн|оси́ть, -ести́ речь **3** (send out, convey) дост|авля́ть, -а́вить

⚔ **delivery** /dɪ'lɪvərɪ/ n. **1** (childbirth) ро́д|ы (-ов) **2** (distribution) доста́вка; charges payable on ~ опла́та при доста́вке

delphinium /del'fɪnɪəm/ n. (pl. ~s) (bot.) дельфи́ниум

delta /'deltə/ n. де́льта

delude /dɪ'lu:d/ v.t. вв|оди́ть, -ести́ в заблужде́ние; he ~d himself into believing that ... он уве́рил себя́ в то́м, что...

deluge /'delju:dʒ/ n. **1** (lit.) пото́п **2** (fig.) пото́к

delusion /dɪ'luːʒ(ə)n/ *n.* заблуждéние

de luxe /də 'lʌks/ *adj.* роскóшный; a ∼ **cabin** каюта люкс

_ℐ **demand** /dɪ'mɑːnd/ *n.* **1** (claim) трéбование; there are many ∼s on my time у меня мнóго дел **2** (desire to obtain) потрéбность, спрóс; there is no ∼ for this article на э́тот товáр нет спрóса
● *v.t.* трéбовать, по- + *g. or a.*

demanding /dɪ'mɑːndɪŋ/ *adj.* трéбовательный

demean /dɪ'miːn/ *v.t.:* ∼ oneself роня́ть, урони́ть своё достóинство

demented /dɪ'mentɪd/ *adj.* сумасшéдший

dementia /dɪ'menʃə/ *n.* слабоýмие

demilitarize /diː'mɪlɪtəraɪz/ *v.t.* демилитаризовáть (*impf., pf.*)

demise /dɪ'maɪz/ *n.* кончи́на

demo /'deməʊ/ *n. (pl.* ∼s) (infml) = demonstration

demobilize /diː'məʊbɪlaɪz/ *v.t.* демобилизовáть (*impf., pf.*)

_ℐ **democracy** /dɪ'mɒkrəsɪ/ *n.* демокрáтия

democrat /'deməkræt/ *n.* демокрáт

_ℐ **democratic** /demə'krætɪk/ *adj.* демократи́ческий

demographic /demə'græfɪk/ *adj.* демографи́ческий

demography /dɪ'mɒgrəfɪ/ *n.* демогрáфия

demolish /dɪ'mɒlɪʃ/ *v.t.* сн|осúть, -ести́

demolition /demə'lɪʃ(ə)n/ *n.* разрушéние, снос

demon /'diːmən/ *n.* дéмон

demonic /dɪ'mɒnɪk/ *adj.* дья́вольский

demonize /'diːmənaɪz/ *v.t.* демонизи́ровать (*impf., pf.*)

demonstrable /'demɒnstrəb(ə)l/ *adj.* доказýемый

_ℐ **demonstrate** /'demənstreɪt/ *v.t.* **1** (prove) докáз|ывать, -áть **2** (show in operation) демонстри́ровать, про-
● *v.i.* учáствовать (*impf.*) в демонстрáции

demonstration /demən'streɪʃ(ə)n/ *n.* (proof) доказáтельство; (public manifestation) демонстрáция

demonstrative /dɪ'mɒnstrətɪv/ *adj.* экспанси́вный

demonstrator /'demənstreɪtə(r)/ *n.* демонстрáнт

demoralize /dɪ'mɒrəlaɪz/ *v.t.* деморализовáть (*impf., pf.*)

demote /dɪ'məʊt/ *v.t.* пон|ижáть, -и́зить (в дóлжности)

demure /dɪ'mjʊə(r)/ *adj.* (**demurer**, **demurest**) скрóмный

den /den/ *n.* **1** (animal's lair) берлóга **2** (of thieves) притóн **3** (study) кабинéт

denationalization /diː'næʃənəlaɪ'zeɪʃ(ə)n/ *n.* денационализáция

denationalize /diː'næʃənəlaɪz/ *v.t.* денационализи́ровать (*impf., pf.*)

denial /dɪ'naɪəl/ *n.* отрицáние; ∼ of justice откáз в правосýдии

denim /'denɪm/ *n.* джинсóвая ткань
● *adj.* джинсóвый

Denmark /'denmɑːk/ *n.* Дáния

denomination /dɪnɒmɪ'neɪʃ(ə)n/ *n.* **1** (name, nomenclature) наименовáние **2** (relig.) вероисповéдание **3**: money of small ∼s дéнежные знáки (*m. pl.*) мáлого достóинства

denote /dɪ'nəʊt/ *v.t.* обозн|ачáть, -áчить

denounce /dɪ'naʊns/ *v.t.* **1** (speak against) осу|ждáть, -ди́ть **2** (inform against) дон|осúть, -ести́ на + *a.*

dense /dens/ *adj.* густóй

density /'densɪtɪ/ *n.* густотá

dent /dent/ *n.* (mark) вмя́тина; (hollow) вы́боина
● *v.t.* ост|авля́ть, -áвить вмя́тину в/на + *p.*

dental /'dent(ə)l/ *adj.* (of teeth) зубнóй
■ ∼ **floss** *n.* зубнáя нить; ∼ **surgeon** *n.* = dentist

dentist /'dentɪst/ *n.* зубнóй врач, данти́ст, стоматóлог

dentistry /'dentɪstrɪ/ *n.* стоматолóгия

dentures /'dentʃəz/ *n. pl.* зубнóй протéз

_ℐ **deny** /dɪ'naɪ/ *v.t.* **1** (contest truth of) отрицáть (*impf.*) **2** (repudiate) отр|екáться, -éчься от + *g.* **3** (refuse) откáз|ывать, -áть (*кому в чём*)

deodorant /diː'əʊdərənt/ *n.* дезодорáнт

depart /dɪ'pɑːt/ *v.i.* **1** (go away) отпр|авля́ться, -áвиться **2**: ∼ from (custom, plan, etc.) отступ|áть, -и́ть от + *g.*

_ℐ **department** /dɪ'pɑːtmənt/ *n.* **1** отдéл **2** (of government) департáмент, вéдомство **3** (of university) кáфедра
■ ∼ **store** *n.* универмáг

departmental /diː'pɑːtment(ə)l/ *adj.* вéдомственный

departure /dɪ'pɑːtʃə(r)/ *n.* (going away) отъéзд; (of train) отправлéние

_ℐ **depend** /dɪ'pend/ *v.i.* **1** (be conditional) зави́сеть (*impf.*) (on: от + *g.*); that ∼s; it all ∼s как сказáть **2** (rely) пол|агáться, -ожи́ться (on: на + *a.*)

dependable /dɪ'pendəb(ə)l/ *adj.* надёжный

dependant /dɪ'pend(ə)nt/ (AmE **dependent**) *n.* иждивéн|ец (-ка)

dependence /dɪ'pend(ə)ns/ *n.* зави́симость (on: от + *g.*); (reliance) довéрие (on: к + *d.*)

dependency /dɪ'pendənsɪ/ *n.* (pol.) колóния

dependent /dɪ'pend(ə)nt/ *adj.* зави́симый

depict /dɪ'pɪkt/ *v.t.* изобра|жáть, -зи́ть

depiction /dɪ'pɪkʃ(ə)n/ *n.* описáние, изображéние

deplete /dɪ'pliːt/ *v.t.* истощ|áть, -и́ть

deplorable /dɪ'plɔːrəb(ə)l/ *adj.* плачéвный

deplore /dɪ'plɔː(r)/ *v.t.* сожалéть (*impf.*) о + *p.*

deploy /dɪ'plɔɪ/ *v.t.* развёр|тывать, -нýть

deployment /dɪ'plɔɪmənt/ *n.* развёртывание; размещéние

depopulate /diː'pɒpjʊleɪt/ *v.t.* истреб|ля́ть, -и́ть/уничт|ожáть, -óжить/ум|еньшáть,

-éньшить населе́ние + g.

depopulation /diːpɒpjʊˈleɪʃ(ə)n/ *n.*
сокраще́ние населе́ния

deport /dɪˈpɔːt/ *v.t.* депорти́ровать (*impf., pf.*)

deportation /diːpɔːˈteɪʃ(ə)n/ *n.* депорта́ция,
вы́сылка

depose /dɪˈpəʊz/ *v.t.* свергáть, -éргнуть
(с престóла)

deposit /dɪˈpɒzɪt/ *n.* **1** (sum in bank) вклад
2 (advance payment) задáток **3** (layer)
отложéние; (of ore etc.) зáлежь; (of precious
metals and stones) рóссыпь
● *v.t.* (**deposited, depositing**) класть,
положи́ть; (place in bank) депони́ровать (*impf.,
pf.*)
■ ~ **account** *n.* (BrE) депози́тный счёт

depot /ˈdepəʊ/ *n.* (place of storage) склад; (AmE,
train or bus station) стáнция

deprave /dɪˈpreɪv/ *v.t.* развра|щáть, -ти́ть

depravity /dɪˈprævɪtɪ/ *n.* разврáт,
развращённость

depreciate /dɪˈpriːʃɪeɪt/ *v.i.* обесцéни|ваться,
-ться

depreciation /dɪpriːʃɪˈeɪʃ(ə)n/ *n.*
обесцéнивание, обесцéнение

depress /dɪˈpres/ *v.t.* **1** (push down) наж|имáть,
-áть на + *a.* **2** (fig.): ~**ed area** рáйон,
пострадáвший от экономи́ческой депрéссии
3 (make sad) удруч|áть, -и́ть

depressing /dɪˈpresɪŋ/ *adj.* удручáющий

depression /dɪˈpreʃ(ə)n/ *n.* депрéссия, тоскá

deprivation /deprɪˈveɪʃ(ə)n/ *n.* лишéние

deprive /dɪˈpraɪv/ *v.t.* лиш|áть, -и́ть (*кого
чего*); ~**d** (underprivileged) обездóленный

depth /depθ/ *n.* **1** (deepness) глубинá; **6 feet
in** ~ глубинóй в шесть фýтов; **be out of
one's** ~ не достáвать (*impf.*) ногáми до дна;
(fig.): **I am out of my** ~ **in this job** э́та рабóта
мне не по плечý **2** (extremity): ~ **of despair**
глубóкое отчáяние; ~ **of winter** глубóкая
зимá

deputize /ˈdepjʊtaɪz/ *v.i.:* ~ **for sb** замещáть
(*impf.*) когó-н.

deputy /ˈdepjʊtɪ/ *n.* **1** (substitute) замести́тель
(*m.*) **2** (member of parliament) депутáт
■ ~ **chairman** *n.* замести́тель (*m.*)
председáтеля

derail /diːˈreɪl/ *v.t.:* **be derailed** (of train)
сходи́ть, сойти́ с рéльсов

derailment /dɪˈreɪlmənt/ *n.* сход с рéльсов

derange /dɪˈreɪndʒ/ *v.t.* св|оди́ть, -ести́ с умá

deregulate /diːˈregjʊleɪt/ *v.t.* отмен|я́ть, -и́ть
(госудáрственное) регули́рование (*чего*)

deregulation /diːregjʊˈleɪʃ(ə)n/ *n.* отмéна
(госудáрственного) регули́рования

derelict /ˈderəlɪkt/ *adj.* забрóшенный

dereliction /derɪˈlɪkʃ(ə)n/ *n.* забрóшенность,
запýщенность; ~ **of duty** нарушéние
(служéбного) дóлга

deride /dɪˈraɪd/ *v.t.* высмéивать, вы́смеять;
осмé|ивать, -я́ть

derision /dɪˈrɪʒ(ə)n/ *n.* осмея́ние,
высмéивание

derisive /dɪˈraɪsɪv/ *adj.* (scornful) насмéшливый

derisory /dɪˈraɪsərɪ/ *adj.* (ludicrous) смешнóй,
ничтóжный

derive /dɪˈraɪv/ *v.t.* извл|екáть, -éчь; ~ **pleasure
from** получáть, -и́ть удовóльствие от + *g.*

dermatitis /dɜːməˈtaɪtɪs/ *n.* дермати́т

dermatologist /dɜːməˈtɒlədʒɪst/ *n.*
дерматóлог

derogatory /dɪˈrɒgətərɪ/ *adj.*
пренебрежи́тельный

descend /dɪˈsend/ *v.t.* сходи́ть, сойти́ с + *g.*
● *v.i.* **1** (go down) спус|кáться, -ти́ться
2 (originate) происходи́ть (*impf.*); **he is**
~**ed from a ducal family** он происхóдит из
гéрцогского рóда **3** (attack) набр|áсываться,
-óситься

descendant /dɪˈsend(ə)nt/ *n.* потóмок

descent /dɪˈsent/ *n.* **1** (act of descending) спуск
2 (ancestry) происхождéние

⚘ **describe** /dɪˈskraɪb/ *v.t.* опи́с|ывать, -áть; ~ **sb
as** наз|ывáть, -вáть когó-н. (кем-н./каки́м-н.)

⚘ **description** /dɪˈskrɪpʃ(ə)n/ *n.* описáние

descriptive /dɪˈskrɪptɪv/ *adj.* описáтельный

desecrate /ˈdesɪkreɪt/ *v.t.* оскверн|я́ть, -и́ть

desegregate /diːˈsegrɪgeɪt/ *v.t.*
десегреги́ровать (*impf., pf.*) (*отменять
сегрегацию*)

desert[1] /ˈdezət/ *n.* (waste land) пусты́ня
● *adj.* пусты́нный
■ ~ **island** *n.* необитáемый óстров

desert[2] /dɪˈzɜːt/ *v.t.* **1** (go away from)
ост|авля́ть, -áвить; **the streets were** ~**ed**
на ýлицах нé было ни души́ **2** (abandon)
пок|идáть, -и́нуть
● *v.i.* дезерти́ровать (*impf., pf.*)

deserter /dɪˈzɜːtə(r)/ *n.* дезерти́р

desertion /dɪˈzɜːʃ(ə)n/ *n.* дезерти́рство

deserts /dɪˈzɜːts/ *n. pl.:* **get one's** ~ получáть,
-и́ть по заслýгам

⚘ **deserve** /dɪˈzɜːv/ *v.t. & i.* заслýж|ивать, -и́ть

deserving /dɪˈzɜːvɪŋ/ *adj.* похвáльный

desiccate /ˈdesɪkeɪt/ *v.t.* высýшивать,
вы́сушить
■ ~**d coconut** *n.* сушёный кокóс

⚘ **design** /dɪˈzaɪn/ *n.* **1** (drawing, plan) план,
проéкт **2** (art of drawing) рисовáние **3** (tech.,
layout, system) констрýкция, проéкт; ~ **of
a car** констрýкция автомоби́ля; ~ **of a
building** проéкт здáния **4** (pattern) узóр,
рисýнок **5** (version of product) модéль
● *v.t.* сост|авля́ть, -áвить план + *g.*

designate /ˈdezɪgneɪt/ *v.t.* (specify a time)
etc.) обозн|ачáть, -áчить; (appoint to a post)
назн|ачáть, -áчить

designer /dɪˈzaɪnə(r)/ *n.* (of dresses, decorations)
модельéр; (tech.) констрýктор; (industrial)
дизáйнер
■ ~ **baby** *n.* ребёнок, рождённый из
эмбриóна, вы́бранного из нéскольких
эмбриóнов, котóрые бы́ли полýчены мéтодом
экстракорпорáльного оплодотворéния

⚘ ключевáя лéксика

desirable /dɪ'zaɪərəb(ə)l/ *adj.* жела́тельный; (attractive) привлека́тельный

✓ **desire** /dɪ'zaɪə(r)/ *n.* жела́ние, стремле́ние
• *v.t.* жела́ть, по-; **it leaves much to be ~d** э́то оставля́ет жела́ть лу́чшего *or* мно́гого

desk /desk/ *n.* пи́сьменный стол; (with sloping top) конто́рка; (information point) спра́вочный стол

desktop /'desktɒp/ *adj.* насто́льный
• *n.* (also comput.) рабо́чий стол

■ **~ publishing** *n.* насто́льная полиграфи́я; **~ publishing system** насто́льная изда́тельская систе́ма

desolate /'desələt/ *adj.* забро́шенный

despair /dɪ'speə(r)/ *n.* отча́яние
• *v.i.* отча́иваться, -яться; **I ~ of him** я утра́тил ве́ру в него́

despatch /dɪ'spætʃ/ *v.t.* (BrE) = **dispatch**

desperate /'despərət/ *adj.* **1** (wretched) отча́янный **2** (in extreme need): **he is ~ for money** он испы́тывает кра́йнюю нужду́ в деньга́х

desperation /despə'reɪʃ(ə)n/ *n.* отча́яние

despicable /dɪ'spɪkəb(ə)l/ *adj.* презре́нный

despise /dɪ'spaɪz/ *v.t.* презира́ть (*impf.*)

✓ **despite** /dɪ'spaɪt/ *prep.* несмотря́ на + *a.*

despondency /dɪ'spɒndənsɪ/ *n.* уны́ние

despondent /dɪ'spɒnd(ə)nt/ *adj.* уны́лый

despot /'despɒt/ *n.* де́спот

despotic /de'spɒtɪk/ *adj.* (system, rule) деспоти́ческий; (person, style) деспоти́чный

despotism /'despətɪz(ə)m/ *n.* деспоти́зм

dessert /dɪ'zɜːt/ *n.* десе́рт

■ **~spoon** *n.* десе́ртная ло́жка

destabilize /diː'steɪbɪlaɪz/ *v.t.* дестабилизи́ровать (*impf., pf.*)

destination /destɪ'neɪʃ(ə)n/ *n.* ме́сто назначе́ния

destine /'destɪn/ *v.t.* предназн|ача́ть, -а́чить; **the plan was ~d to fail** э́тот план был обречён на прова́л

destiny /'destɪnɪ/ *n.* судьба́

destitute /'destɪtjuːt/ *adj.* нужда́ющийся

✓ **destroy** /dɪ'strɔɪ/ *v.t.* (building) разр|уша́ть, -у́шить; (friendship, hope) разб|ива́ть, -и́ть; (kill) истреб|ля́ть, -и́ть

destroyer /dɪ'strɔɪə(r)/ *n.* **1** (one who destroys) разруши́тель (*m.*) **2** (naut.) эсми́нец; эска́дренный миноно́сец

✓ **destruction** /dɪ'strʌkʃ(ə)n/ *n.* уничтоже́ние, разруше́ние

destructive /dɪ'strʌktɪv/ *adj.* разруши́тельный

desultory /'dezəltərɪ/ *adj.* отры́вочный; **~ reading** бесси́стемное чте́ние

detach /dɪ'tætʃ/ *v.t.* отдел|я́ть, -и́ть

detachable /dɪ'tætʃəb(ə)l/ *adj.* съёмный, отделя́емый

detached /dɪ'tætʃt/ *adj.* (unemotional) равноду́шный, отчуждённый; **a ~ house** отде́льный дом

detachment /dɪ'tætʃmənt/ *n.* (indifference) отчуждённость, равноду́шие; (mil., body of troops etc.) отря́д

✓ **detail** /'diːteɪl/ *n.* дета́ль; **go into ~(s)** входи́ть, вдава́ться (*both impf.*) в подро́бности; **in ~** подро́бно, дета́льно
• *v.t.* входи́ть (*impf.*) в подро́бности + *g.*

detain /dɪ'teɪn/ *v.t.* заде́рж|ивать, -а́ть; **he was ~ed by the police** он был заде́ржан поли́цией

detainee /diːteɪ'niː/ *n.* заде́ржанный

detect /dɪ'tekt/ *v.t.* (discover) обнару́жи|вать, -ть; (discern) ул|а́вливать, -ови́ть

detection /dɪ'tekʃ(ə)n/ *n.* (of crime) рассле́дование, раскры́тие

detective /dɪ'tektɪv/ *n.* сы́щик, детекти́в

■ **~ novel** *n.* детекти́в, детекти́вный рома́н

detector /dɪ'tektə(r)/ *n.* (radio) дете́ктор

detention /dɪ'tenʃ(ə)n/ *n.* (at school) оставле́ние по́сле уро́ков; (confinement) заключе́ние (под стра́жу)

■ **~ centre** *n.* (for asylum seekers) приёмник-распредели́тель (*m.*) (*для (нелега́льных) мигра́нтов*)

deter /dɪ'tɜː(r)/ *v.t.* (**deterred, deterring**) уде́рж|ивать, -а́ть

detergent /dɪ'tɜːdʒ(ə)nt/ *n.* мо́ющее сре́дство; (washing powder) стира́льный порошо́к

deteriorate /dɪ'tɪərɪəreɪt/ *v.i.* ух|удша́ть(ся), -у́дшить(ся)

determination /dɪtɜːmɪ'neɪʃ(ə)n/ *n.* **1** (deciding upon) реше́ние **2** (resoluteness) реши́мость

✓ **determine** /dɪ'tɜːmɪn/ *v.t.* реш|а́ть, -и́ть; **he is ~d to go (or on going)** он твёрдо реши́л е́хать

determined /dɪ'tɜːmɪnd/ *adj.* реши́тельный

deterrent /dɪ'terənt/ *n.* сре́дство устраше́ния/сде́рживания

detest /dɪ'test/ *v.t.* ненави́деть (*impf.*)

detestable /dɪ'testəb(ə)l/ *adj.* отврати́тельный

detonate /'detəneɪt/ *v.t.* детони́ровать (*impf., pf.*)

detour /'diːtʊə(r)/ *n.* (on foot) обхо́д; (by transport) объе́зд

detract /dɪ'trækt/ *v.i.*: **~ from** ума́л|я́ть, -и́ть

detriment /'detrɪmənt/ *n.*: **he works long hours to the ~ of his health** он рабо́тает сверх но́рмы в уще́рб своему́ здоро́вью

detrimental /detrɪ'ment(ə)l/ *adj.* вре́дный

deuce /djuːs/ *n.* (tennis) ра́вный счёт

devaluation /diːvælju:'eɪʃ(ə)n/ *n.* обесце́нение; (fin.) девальва́ция

devalue /diː'væljuː/ *v.t.* (**devalues, devalued, devaluing**) обесце́ни|вать, -ть; (fin.) девальви́ровать (*impf., pf.*)
• *v.i.* (**devalues, devalued, devaluing**) пров|оди́ть, -ести́ девальва́цию

devastat|e /'devəsteɪt/ *v.t.* (fig.) убива́ть, уби́ть; **a ~ing remark** уничтожа́ющее/ уби́йственное замеча́ние

devastation /devə'steɪʃ(ə)n/ *n.* опустоше́ние, разоре́ние

✓ **develop** /dɪ'veləp/ *v.t.* (**developed,**

d

developing) **1** (cause to unfold) разв|ивать, -ить; (work up, polish) обраб|атывать, -отать **2** (phot.) проявля́ть, -и́ть **3** (contract): he ~ed a cough у него появи́лся ка́шель **4** (open up for residence etc.) разв|ива́ть, -и́ть
• *v.i.* (**developed, developing**) разв|ива́ться, -и́ться; ~ into превра|ща́ться, -ти́ться в + *a.*

developer /dɪ'veləpə(r)/ *n.* (builder) застро́йщик

ᵈ **development** /dɪ'veləpmənt/ *n.* **1** (unfolding) разви́тие, рост **2** (event) собы́тие, обстоя́тельство **3** (of land etc.) разви́тие (райо́на); (building) застро́йка

deviate /'diːvɪeɪt/ *v.i.* отклоня́ться, -и́ться (**from:** от + *g.*)

deviation /diːvɪ'eɪʃ(ə)n/ *n.* отклоне́ние, отхо́д

ᵈ **device** /dɪ'vaɪs/ *n.* **1** (method) приём; he was left to his own ~s он был предоста́влен самому́ себе́ **2** (instrument) приспособле́ние, прибо́р

devil /'dev(ə)l/ *n.* чёрт, дья́вол

devious /'diːvɪəs/ *adj.* (road) изви́листый, око́льный; (fig.) лука́вый, неи́скренний

devise /dɪ'vaɪz/ *v.t.* (think out) приду́м|ывать, -ать

devoid /dɪ'vɔɪd/ *adj.* лишённый; ~ **of fear** бесстра́шный

devolution /diːvə'luːʃ(ə)n/ *n.* переда́ча/ делеги́рование вла́сти

devolve /dɪ'vɒlv/ *v.t.* (delegate) перед|ава́ть, -а́ть
• *v.i.* пере|ходи́ть, -йти́; the work ~d on/ to me рабо́ту переда́ли мне; the estate ~d on/to a distant cousin име́ние перешло́ к да́льнему ро́дственнику

devote /dɪ'vəʊt/ *v.t.* посвя|ща́ть, -ти́ть; he ~s his time to study он посвяща́ет всё своё вре́мя учёбе; she is ~d to her children она́ ~ пре́дана свои́м де́тям; a ~d friend пре́данный друг

devotee /devə'tiː/ *n.* приве́рженец

devotion /dɪ'vəʊʃ(ə)n/ *n.* **1** (being devoted) пре́данность **2** (love) пре́данность

devour /dɪ'vaʊə(r)/ *v.t.* пож|ира́ть, -ра́ть

devout /dɪ'vaʊt/ *adj.* благочести́вый

dew /djuː/ *n.* роса́

dexterity /dek'sterɪtɪ/ *n.* ло́вкость, прово́рство

dexterous, dextrous /'dekstrəs/ *adj.* ло́вкий, прово́рный

diabetes /daɪə'biːtiːz/ *n.* диабе́т

diabetic /daɪə'betɪk/ *n.* диабе́тик
• *adj.* диабети́ческий

diabolical /daɪə'bɒlɪk(ə)l/, **diabolic** /daɪə'bɒlɪk/ *adjs.* дья́вольский

diagnose /'daɪəgnəʊz/ *v.t.* диагности́ровать (*impf., pf.*)

diagnosis /daɪəg'nəʊsɪs/ *n.* (*pl.* **diagnoses** /-siːz/) диа́гноз

diagnostic /daɪəg'nɒstɪk/ *adj.* диагности́ческий

diagonal /daɪ'æɡən(ə)l/ *n.* диагона́ль
• *adj.* диагона́льный; ~**ly** по диагона́ли

diagram /'daɪəɡræm/ *n.* диагра́мма

dial /'daɪ(ə)l/ *n.* **1** (of clock) цифербла́т **2** (of radio etc.) шкала́
• *v.t. & i.* (**dialled, dialling,** AmE **dialed, dialing**): ~ **a number** наб|ира́ть, -ра́ть но́мер; ~ **the police station** звони́ть, по- в поли́цию
■ ~**ling tone** *n.* дли́нный гудо́к; сигна́л «ли́ния свобо́дна»

dialect /'daɪəlekt/ *n.* диале́кт, го́вор

dialogue /'daɪəlɒg/ (AmE *also* **dialog**) *n.* диало́г

dialysis /daɪ'ælɪsɪs/ *n.* диа́лиз

diameter /daɪ'æmɪtə(r)/ *n.* диа́метр

diametric /daɪə'metrɪk/, **diametrical** /daɪə'metrɪk(ə)l/ *adjs.* диаметра́льный

diamond /'daɪəmənd/ *n.* **1** (precious stone) алма́з **2** (geom.) ромб **3** (at cards) бу́б|ны (-ен)

diaper /'daɪəpə(r)/ *n.* (AmE) подгу́зник

diaphragm /'daɪəfræm/ *n.* диафра́гма

diarrhoea /daɪə'rɪə/ (AmE **diarrhea**) *n.* поно́с

diary /'daɪərɪ/ *n.* (journal) дневни́к; (engagement book) календа́рь (*m.*)

diaspora /daɪ'æspərə/ *n.* диа́спора

dice /daɪs/ *n.* (cube) игра́льные ко́сти (*f. pl.*); (game of ~) игра́ в ко́сти
• *v.t.* нар|еза́ть, -е́зать ку́биками

dichotomy /daɪ'kɒtəmɪ/ *n.* дихотоми́я; (contrast) противопоставле́ние

Dictaphone® /'dɪktəfəʊn/ *n.* диктофо́н

dictate /dɪk'teɪt/ *v.t. & i.* (as dictation; command) диктова́ть, про-; I won't be ~d to я не позво́лю ста́вить мне усло́вия

dictation /dɪk'teɪʃ(ə)n/ *n.* (to class) дикта́нт; (to secretary) дикто́вка

dictator /dɪk'teɪtə(r)/ *n.* дикта́тор

dictatorial /dɪktə'tɔːrɪəl/ *adj.* дикта́торский

dictatorship /dɪk'teɪtəʃɪp/ *n.* диктату́ра

dictionary /'dɪkʃənrɪ/ *n.* слова́рь (*m.*)

did /dɪd/ *past of* ▶ **do**

didactic /daɪ'dæktɪk/ *adj.* поучи́тельный, дидакти́ческий

didn't /'dɪdn(ə)nt/ *neg. of* ▶ **did**

ᵈ **die** /daɪ/ *v.i.* (**dies, died, dying**) **1** (of person) ум|ира́ть, -ере́ть (*pf.*); (in accident, in war) ги́бнуть, по-; (of animals) под|ыха́ть, -о́хнуть; (of plants) ув|яда́ть, -я́нуть; поги|ба́ть, -и́бнуть **2** (fig.): I'm dying to see him я до́ сме́рти хочу́ его́ ви́деть
▫ ~ **down** *v.i.* (of fire) уг|аса́ть, -а́снуть; (of noise) ут|иха́ть, -и́хнуть; the wind ~d down ве́тер ути́х; (of feeling) ум|ира́ть, -ере́ть
▫ ~ **out** *v.i.* вымира́ть, вы́мереть

diesel /'diːz(ə)l/ *n.* (*also* ~ **engine**) ди́зель (*m.*); (*also* ~ **oil**) ди́зельное то́пливо

diet /'daɪət/ *n.* **1** (customary food) пи́ща, пита́ние **2** (medical régime) дие́та; go on a ~ сади́ться, сесть на дие́ту; he is on a ~ он (сиди́т) на дие́те

dietitian /daɪə'tɪʃ(ə)n/ *n.* (врач-)дието́лог

ᵈ **differ** /'dɪfə(r)/ *v.i.* **1** (be different) отлича́ться (*impf.*); they ~ in size они́ различа́ются разме́ром, по разме́ру **2** (disagree) ра|сходи́ться, -зойти́сь во мне́ниях; we agreed to ~ мы реши́ли прекрати́ть беспполе́зный спор

ᵠ **difference** /'dɪfrəns/ n. **1** (state of being unlike) отли́чие, разли́чие, ра́зница; it makes no ~ whether you go or not совершенно безразли́чно, идёте вы и́ли нет **2** (dispute) разногла́сие, спор

ᵠ **different** /'dɪfrənt/ adj. друго́й, ра́зный, разли́чный; they live in ~ houses они́ живу́т в ра́зных дома́х; she wears a ~ hat each day на ней ка́ждый день друга́я шля́па; of ~ kinds ра́зного ро́да; he became a ~ person он стал други́м челове́ком; ~ from непохо́жий на + a.; отли́чный от + g.

differentiate /dɪfə'renʃɪeɪt/ v.t. различа́|ть, -и́ть

differently /'dɪfrəntlɪ/ adv. по-ино́му; по-друго́му

ᵠ **difficult** /'dɪfɪkəlt/ adj. (of thing or person) тру́дный

ᵠ **difficulty** /'dɪfɪkəltɪ/ n. тру́дность, затрудне́ние; I have ~ in understanding him я с трудо́м его́ понима́ю

diffident /'dɪfɪd(ə)nt/ adj. неуве́ренный в себе́; засте́нчивый, стесни́тельный

diffuse¹ /dɪ'fju:s/ adj. (of light etc.) рассе́янный; (of style) расплы́вчатый

diffuse² /dɪ'fju:z/ v.t. (light, heat, etc.) рассе́|ивать, -ять; (learning, etc.) распростран|я́ть, -и́ть

dig /dɪg/ n. **1** (poke) толчо́к **2** (fig.) насме́шка **3** (archaeological expedition) раско́пки (f. pl.)
   ● v.t. & i. (**digging**, past and p.p. **dug**) копа́ть, вы́-; he dug a hole он вы́рыл я́му; they are ~ging for gold они́ и́щут зо́лото
   □ ~ out v.t. выка́пывать, вы́копать
   □ ~ up v.t. отка́п|ывать, -опа́ть

digest /daɪ'dʒest/ v.t. (food) перева́р|ивать, -и́ть; (information etc.) усв|а́ивать, -о́ить
   ● v.i. перева́р|иваться, -и́ться

digestion /daɪ'dʒestʃ(ə)n/ n. перева́ривание

digger /'dɪgə(r)/ n. (machine) экскава́тор

digit /'dɪdʒɪt/ n. (finger or toe) па́лец; (numeral) ци́фра

ᵠ **digital** /'dɪdʒɪt(ə)l/ adj. цифрово́й
   ■ ~ camera n. цифрова́я (фото)ка́мера; ~ clock n. цифровы́е/электро́нные час|ы́ (-о́в)

digitize /'dɪdʒɪtaɪz/ v.t. оцифро́в|ывать, -ова́ть; преобраз|о́вывать, -ова́ть в цифрову́ю фо́рму

dignified /'dɪgnɪfaɪd/ adj. по́лный досто́инства

dignitary /'dɪgnɪtərɪ/ n. сано́вник; высокопоста́вленное лицо́

dignity /'dɪgnɪtɪ/ n. досто́инство

digress /daɪ'gres/ v.i. отклон|я́ться, -и́ться (от те́мы)

digression /daɪ'greʃ(ə)n/ n. отклоне́ние

dilapidated /dɪ'læpɪdeɪtɪd/ adj. ве́тхий

dilate /daɪ'leɪt/ v.t. расш|иря́ть, -и́рить
   ● v.i. расш|иря́ться, -и́риться

dilemma /daɪ'lemə/ n. диле́мма

diligent /'dɪlɪdʒ(ə)nt/ adj. приле́жный

dill /dɪl/ n. укро́п
   ■ ~ pickle n. марино́ванный огуре́ц

dilute /daɪ'lju:t/ v.t. разв|оди́ть, -ести́

dim /dɪm/ adj. (**dimmer**, **dimmest**) (of light etc.) ту́склый; (of memory etc.) сму́тный
   ● v.t. (**dimmed**, **dimming**) затума́ни|вать, -ть; ~ one's headlights пере|ходи́ть, -йти́ на бли́жний свет

dime /daɪm/ n. десятице́нтовик

dimension /daɪ'menʃ(ə)n/ n. **1** (extent) разме́р **2** (direction of measurement) измере́ние

diminish /dɪ'mɪnɪʃ/ v.t. ум|еньша́ть, -е́ньшить

diminutive /dɪ'mɪnjʊtɪv/ n. (gram.) уменьши́тельное сло́во
   ● adj. (small) миниатю́рный

dimple /'dɪmp(ə)l/ n. я́мочка; (ripple) рябь

din /dɪn/ n. гам

dine /daɪn/ v.i. у́жинать, по-
   ■ ~ing car n. ваго́н-рестора́н; ~ing room n. столо́вая (ко́мната)

diner /'daɪnə(r)/ n. **1** (person) у́жинающий **2** (AmE, restaurant) дешёвый рестора́н (оформленный по типу вагона-ресторана)

dinghy /'dɪŋgɪ/ n. ма́ленькая шлю́пка, я́лик; (inflatable) надувна́я ло́дка

dingy /'dɪndʒɪ/ adj. (**dingier**, **dingiest**) тёмный, мра́чный

ᵠ **dinner** /'dɪnə(r)/ n. у́жин; have ~ обе́дать, по-/у́жинать, по-
   ■ ~ hour n. час обе́да/у́жина; ~ jacket n. смо́кинг; ~ party n. зва́ный обе́д; ~ time n. вре́мя у́жина

dinosaur /'daɪnəsɔ:(r)/ n. диноза́вр

dip /dɪp/ n. **1** (immersion) погруже́ние **2** (bathe) ныря́ние **3** (slope) спуск, укло́н **4** (cul.) со́ус
   ● v.t. (**dipped**, **dipping**) **1** (immerse) оку́н|а́ть, -у́ть; мак|а́ть, -ну́ть; погру|жа́ть, -зи́ть **2** (lower briefly) приспус|ка́ть, -ти́ть; ~ headlights (BrE) переключ|а́ть, -и́ть фа́ры на (or включ|а́ть, -и́ть) бли́жний свет
   ● v.i. (**dipped**, **dipping**) **1** (go below surface) окун|а́ться, -у́ться **2** (fig.): ~ into one's purse раскоше́ли|ваться, -ться **3** (slope away): the (plot of) land ~s to the south уча́сток име́ет накло́н к ю́гу **4** (fall slightly) пон|ижа́ться, -и́зиться
   ■ ~stick n. уровнеме́р, щуп

diphtheria /dɪf'θɪərɪə/ n. дифтери́я, дифтери́т

diphthong /'dɪfθɒŋ/ n. дифто́нг

diploma /dɪ'pləʊmə/ n. дипло́м

diplomacy /dɪp'ləʊməsɪ/ n. диплома́тия; (tact) дипломати́чность

diplomat /'dɪpləmæt/ n. (lit., fig.) диплома́т

diplomatic /dɪplə'mætɪk/ adj. (lit., fig.) дипломати́ческий

dire /daɪə(r)/ adj. ужа́сный; he is in ~ need of help он кра́йне нужда́ется в по́мощи

ᵠ **direct** /daɪ'rekt/ adj. (straight) прямо́й; (straightforward) прямо́й; he has a ~ way of speaking он говори́т всё пря́мо в лицо́
   ● adv. пря́мо
   ● v.t. **1** (indicate the way): can you ~ me to the station? вы не ска́жете, как пройти́ на

вокза́л? **2** (address) адресова́ть (*impf., pf.*); напр|авля́ть, -а́вить; **my remarks were ~ed to him** мои́ замеча́ния бы́ли адресо́ваны ему́ **3** (manage, control) руководи́ть (*impf.*) + *i.*; **he ~ed the play** он поста́вил пье́су
■ **~ flight** *n.* прямо́й/беспереса́дочный полёт/рейс

direction /daɪˈrekʃ(ə)n/ *n.* **1** (course) направле́ние; **they dispersed in all ~s** они́ разошли́сь в ра́зные сто́роны **2** (*in pl.*) (instructions) указа́ния (*nt. pl.*)

directive /daɪˈrektɪv/ *n.* директи́ва, указа́ние

directly /daɪˈrektlɪ/ *adv.* **1** (in var. senses of direct) пря́мо **2** (at once) неме́дленно, то́тчас

director /daɪˈrektə(r)/ *n.* **1** (of company etc.) дире́ктор **2** (theatr.) режиссёр

directory /daɪˈrektərɪ/ *n.* (reference work) спра́вочник, указа́тель (*m.*)
■ **~ assistance** (AmE), **~ enquiries** (BrE) *nn.* спра́вочная

dirge /dɜːdʒ/ *n.* погреба́льное пе́ние

dirt /dɜːt/ *n.* **1** (unclean matter) грязь **2** (earth) грунт, земля́
■ **~ track** *n.* мотоцикле́тный трек

dirty /ˈdɜːtɪ/ *adj.* (**dirtier, dirtiest**) **1** (not clean) гря́зный **2** (obscene) поха́бный **3** (nasty) гря́зный, га́дкий; **he played a ~ trick on me** он подложи́л мне свинью́; **he gave me a ~ look** (infml) он посмотре́л на меня́ серди́то
● *v.t.* грязни́ть, за-; па́чкать, за-

disability /dɪsəˈbɪlɪtɪ/ *n.* (a limiting mental or physical condition) дефе́кт; (being disabled) инвали́дность

disable /dɪsˈeɪb(ə)l/ *v.t.* (physically) кале́чить, ис-; **~d person** инвали́д

disadvantage /dɪsədˈvɑːntɪdʒ/ *n.* невы́годное положе́ние; **be at a ~** ока́з|ываться, -а́ться в невы́годном положе́нии
● *v.t.* де́йствовать (*impf.*) в уще́рб + *d.*; **~d** (underprivileged) обездо́ленный

disaffected /dɪsəˈfektɪd/ *adj.* недово́льный

disagree /dɪsəˈɡriː/ *v.i.* (**disagrees, disagreed, disagreeing**) **1** (differ) не соотве́тствовать (*impf.*) (**with:** + *d.*) **2** (in opinion) не согла|ша́ться, -си́ться; **I ~ with you** я с ва́ми не согла́сен **3** (have adverse effect): **oysters ~ with me** от у́стриц мне пло́хо

disagreeable /dɪsəˈɡriːəb(ə)/ *adj.* (unpleasant) неприя́тный; (of person) неприве́тливый

disagreement /dɪsəˈɡriːmənt/ *n.* разногла́сие

disallow /dɪsəˈlaʊ/ *v.t.* (reject) отклон|я́ть, -и́ть; (goal) не засч|и́тывать, -ита́ть

disappear /dɪsəˈpɪə(r)/ *v.i.* исч|еза́ть, -е́знуть

disappearance /dɪsəˈpɪərəns/ *n.* исчезнове́ние

disappoint /dɪsəˈpɔɪnt/ *v.t.* разочаро́в|ывать, -а́ть

disappointing /dɪsəˈpɔɪntɪŋ/ *adj.* разочаро́вывающий

disappointment /dɪsəˈpɔɪntmənt/ *n.* разочарова́ние; **to my ~** к моему́ огорче́нию

disapproval /dɪsəˈpruːv(ə)l/ *n.* неодобре́ние

disapprove /dɪsəˈpruːv/ *v.i.* (**~ of**) не одобря́ть (*impf.*)

disapproving /dɪsəˈpruːvɪŋ/ *adj.* неодобри́тельный

disarm /dɪsˈɑːm/ *v.t.* разоруж|а́ть, -и́ть

disarmament /dɪsˈɑːməmənt/ *n.* разоруже́ние

disarray /dɪsəˈreɪ/ *n.* смяте́ние, расстро́йство

disassociate /dɪsəˈsəʊsɪeɪt/ *v.t.* = dissociate

disaster /dɪˈzɑːstə(r)/ *n.* бе́дствие

disastrous /dɪˈzɑːstrəs/ *adj.* ги́бельный

disband /dɪsˈbænd/ *v.t.* распус|ка́ть, -ти́ть; расформиро́в|ывать, -а́ть
● *v.i.* расп|ада́ться, -а́сться; **the (theatre) company ~ed** тру́ппа распа́лась

disbelief /dɪsbɪˈliːf/ *n.* неве́рие

disbelieve /dɪsbɪˈliːv/ *v.t.* (person) не ве́рить (*impf.*) + *d.*; (account, evidence) не ве́рить (*impf.*) + *d.* (*or* в + *a.*)

disc /dɪsk/ *n.* **1** (AmE **disk**) диск **2** (disk) (comput.): **floppy disk** ги́бкий диск
■ **disk drive** *n.* дисково́д; **~ jockey** *n.* диск-жоке́й, дидже́й

discard /dɪˈskɑːd/ *v.t.* выбра́сывать, вы́бросить

discernible /dɪsəˈnɪb(ə)l/ *adj.* различи́мый

discerning /dɪˈsɜːnɪŋ/ *adj.* проница́тельный

discernment /dɪˈsɜːnmənt/ *n.* проница́тельность

discharge *n.* /ˈdɪstʃɑːdʒ/ **1** (of fluid) слив; (of gas) вы́брос **2** (med.) выделе́ния (*pl.*) **3** (performance, e.g. of duty) исполне́ние; (of a debt) упла́та **4** (release, dismissal) увольне́ние, освобожде́ние
● *v.t.* /dɪsˈtʃɑːdʒ/ **1** (emit liquid) слива́ть, слить **2** (med.) выделя́ть, вы́делить **3** (from hospital) выпи́сывать, вы́писать

disciple /dɪˈsaɪp(ə)l/ *n.* (relig.) апо́стол

disciplinarian /dɪsɪplɪˈneərɪən/ *n.* сторо́нник дисципли́ны; **she is a good ~** она́ уме́ет подде́рживать дисципли́ну

disciplinary /dɪsɪˈplɪnərɪ/ *adj.* дисциплина́рный; **take ~ action** прин|има́ть, -я́ть дисциплина́рные ме́ры

discipline /ˈdɪsɪplɪn/ *n.* дисципли́на

disclaim /dɪsˈkleɪm/ *v.t.* отр|ека́ться, -е́чься от + *g.*

disclose /dɪsˈkləʊz/ *v.t.* разоблач|а́ть, -и́ть

disco /ˈdɪskəʊ/ *n.* (*pl.* **~s**) (infml) = discotheque

discolor *v.i. & v.t.* (AmE) = discolour

discolour /dɪsˈkʌlə(r)/ (AmE **discolor**) *v.i.* (lose colour) обесцве́|чиваться, -титься
● *v.t.* (make change colour) меня́ть, по- цвет + *g.*; **rain ~ed the water** дождь поменя́л цвет воды́; **smoking had ~ed his teeth** его́ зу́бы пожелте́ли от куре́ния; (make lose colour) обесцве́|чивать, -тить

discomfort /dɪsˈkʌmfət/ *n.* неудо́бство

disconcert /dɪskənˈsɜːt/ *v.t.* волнова́ть, вз-

disconnect /dɪskə'nekt/ *v.t.* (gas etc.) отключ|áть, -и́ть; **we were ~ed** (telephone) нас разъедини́ли/прерва́ли

disconnection /dɪskə'nekʃ(ə)n/ *n.* разъедине́ние, отключе́ние

discontent /dɪskən'tent/ *n.* недово́льство

discontented /dɪskən'tentɪd/ *adj.* недово́льный

discontinue /dɪskən'tɪnju:/ *v.t.* (**discontinues**, **discontinued**, **discontinuing**) прекра|ща́ть, -ти́ть

discord /'dɪskɔ:d/ *n.* (disagreement) разногла́сие; (disharmony) разла́д, раздо́р; (mus.) диссона́нс

discotheque /'dɪskətek/ *n.* дискоте́ка

discount *n.* /'dɪskaʊnt/ ски́дка
• *v.t.* /dɪs'kaʊnt/ сни|жа́ть, сни́зить це́ну на + *a.*; (not consider) не прин|има́ть, -я́ть в расчёт

discourage /dɪ'skʌrɪdʒ/ *v.t.* обескура́жи|вать, -ть

discourteous /dɪs'kə:tɪəs/ *adj.* неве́жливый

ℱ **discover** /dɪ'skʌvə(r)/ *v.t.* (place, fact) откр|ыва́ть, -ы́ть; (find out) узн|ава́ть, -а́ть

discovery /dɪ'skʌvərɪ/ *n.* откры́тие; обнаруже́ние

discredit /dɪs'kredɪt/ *n.* (loss of repute) дискредита́ция; **bring sb into ~** (*or* **bring ~ upon sb**) компромети́ровать, с- кого́-н.; дискредити́ровать (*impf., pf.*) (*кого́-н.*)
• *v.t.* (**discredited**, **discrediting**) дискредити́ровать (*impf., pf.*)

discreditable /dɪs'kredɪtəb(ə)l/ *adj.* (shameful) позо́рный

discreet /dɪ'skri:t/ *adj.* (**discreeter**, **discreetest**) такти́чный

discrepancy /dɪs'krepənsɪ/ *n.* расхожде́ние

discrete /dɪ'skri:t/ *adj.* обосо́бленный

discretion /dɪ'skreʃ(ə)n/ *n.* **1** (prudence, good judgement) осмотри́тельность **2** (freedom to judge) усмотре́ние; **I leave this to your ~** я оставля́ю э́то на ва́ше усмотре́ние

discretionary /dɪ'skreʃənərɪ/ *adj.* дискрецио́нный (*позволяющий распоряжаться по своему усмотрению*)

discriminate /dɪ'skrɪmɪneɪt/ *v.i.*: **~ against** дискримини́ровать (*impf., pf.*)

discriminating /dɪ'skrɪmɪneɪtɪŋ/ *adj.* разбо́рчивый

discrimination /dɪskrɪmɪ'neɪʃ(ə)n/ *n.* дискримина́ция

discriminatory /dɪ'skrɪmɪnətərɪ/ *adj.* пристра́стный

discus /'dɪskəs/ *n.* (*pl.* **~es**) (sport) диск

ℱ **discuss** /dɪ'skʌs/ *v.t.* дискути́ровать (*impf.*)

ℱ **discussion** /dɪ'skʌʃ(ə)n/ *n.* обсужде́ние, диску́ссия

disdain /dɪs'deɪn/ *n.* презре́ние
• *v.t.* през|ира́ть, -ре́ть; пренебр|ега́ть, -е́чь + *i.*; **he ~ed to reply** он не соизво́лил отве́тить

disdainful /dɪs'deɪnfʊl/ *adj.* презри́тельный

ℱ **disease** /dɪ'zi:z/ *n.* боле́знь

diseased /dɪ'zi:zd/ *adj.* (lit., fig.) больно́й

disembark /dɪsɪm'bɑ:k/ *v.t. & i.* выса́живать(ся), вы́садить(ся)

disembarkation /dɪsɪmbɑ:'keɪʃ(ə)n/ *n.* вы́садка, вы́грузка

disembod|y /dɪsɪm'bɒdɪ/ *v.t.* (set free from the body) освобо|жда́ть, -ди́ть от теле́сной оболо́чки; **a ~ied spirit** освобождённая душа́

disenchant /dɪsɪn'tʃɑ:nt/ *v.t.* разочаро́в|ывать, -а́ть

disentangle /dɪsɪn'tæŋɡ(ə)l/ *v.t.* распу́т|ывать, -ать; вы́пут|ывать, вы́путать

disfigure /dɪs'fɪɡə(r)/ *v.t.* уро́довать, из-; обезобра́|живать, -зить

disfigurement /dɪs'fɪɡəmənt/ *n.* (act) обезобра́живание; (result) уро́дство

disgrace /dɪs'ɡreɪs/ *n.* **1** (loss of respect) бесче́стье, позо́р **2** (disfavour) неми́лость, опа́ла; **he is in ~** он в неми́лости **3** (cause of shame) позо́р
• *v.t.* позо́рить, о-; (bring shame upon): **he ~d the family name** он покры́л позо́ром свою́ семью́

disgraceful /dɪs'ɡreɪsfʊl/ *adj.* позо́рный, недосто́йный

disgruntled /dɪs'ɡrʌnt(ə)ld/ *adj.* недово́льный; раздражённый

disguise /dɪs'ɡaɪz/ *n.* маскиро́вка
• *v.t.* (weapons, objects, intentions) маскирова́ть, за-; (with clothing) переоде|ва́ть, -́ть; (emotions) скры|ва́ть, -ть

disgust /dɪs'ɡʌst/ *n.* отвраще́ние
• *v.t.* внуш|а́ть, -и́ть отвраще́ние + *d.*

disgusting /dɪs'ɡʌstɪŋ/ *adj.* отврати́тельный

dish /dɪʃ/ *n.* **1** (vessel, contents) блю́до; (wash, do the ~es) мыть, вы- посу́ду **2** (infml, TV satellite ~) таре́лка
• *v.t.*: **~ out** (food) ра|скла́дывать, -зложи́ть по таре́лкам (*еду*)
■ **~cloth** *n.* ку́хонная/посу́дная тря́пка; **~ towel** *n.* (AmE) ку́хонное/посу́дное полоте́нце; **~washer** *n.* посудомо́ечная маши́на

dishearten /dɪs'hɑ:t(ə)n/ *v.t.* прив|оди́ть, -ести́ в уны́ние; **I was ~ed** я упа́л ду́хом

dishevelled /dɪ'ʃev(ə)ld/ (AmE **disheveled**) *adj.* взъеро́шенный

dishonest /dɪs'ɒnɪst/ *adj.* нече́стный, бесче́стный

dishonesty /dɪs'ɒnɪstɪ/ *n.* нече́стность, бесче́стность

dishonour /dɪs'ɒnə(r)/ (AmE **dishonor**) *n.* бесче́стье, позо́р

dishonourable /dɪs'ɒnərəb(ə)l/ (AmE **dishonorable**) *adj.* бесче́стный

dishy /'dɪʃɪ/ *adj.* (**dishier**, **dishiest**) (BrE, infml) аппети́тный, привлека́тельный

disillusion /dɪsɪ'lu:ʒ(ə)n/ *v.t.* разочаро́в|ывать, -а́ть

disillusionment /dɪsɪ'lu:ʒənmənt/ *n.* разочарова́ние

disincentive /dɪsɪn'sentɪv/ *n.* сде́рживающее обстоя́тельство

d

d

disinfect /ˌdɪsɪnˈfekt/ v.t. дезинфицировать
(impf., pf.)
disinfectant /ˌdɪsɪnˈfekt(ə)nt/ n.
дезинфицирующее средство
disingenuous /ˌdɪsɪnˈdʒenjʊəs/ adj.
неискренний
disinherit /ˌdɪsɪnˈherɪt/ v.t. (**disinherited**,
disinheriting) лиш|ать, -ить наследства
disintegrate /dɪsˈɪntɪɡreɪt/ v.i. распад|аться,
-аться
disinterested /dɪsˈɪntrɪstɪd/ adj. (impartial)
бескорыстный
disjointed /dɪsˈdʒɔɪntɪd/ adj. бессвязный
disk /dɪsk/ n. (AmE and comput.) = **disc**
diskette /dɪˈsket/ n. (comput.) дискета
dislike /dɪsˈlaɪk/ n. (feeling) неприязнь; (often
in pl.) (disliked thing) антипатия; **I took a ~ to
him** я невзлюбил его
● v.t. не любить (impf.) + g.
dislocate /ˈdɪsləkeɪt/ v.t. вывихнуть (pf.)
dislodge /dɪsˈlɒdʒ/ v.t. сме|щать, -стить
disloyal /dɪsˈlɔɪəl/ adj. нелояльный
disloyalty /dɪsˈlɔɪəltɪ/ n. нелояльность,
неверность
dismal /ˈdɪzm(ə)l/ adj. мрачный, унылый,
гнетущий
dismantle /dɪsˈmænt(ə)l/ v.t. раз|бирать,
-обрать
dismay /dɪsˈmeɪ/ n. смятение
⚔ **dismiss** /dɪsˈmɪs/ v.t. **1** (send away)
распус|кать, -тить **2** (discharge from service)
ув|ольнять, -олить **3** (reject): **I ~ed the
idea** я оставил эту мысль **4** (law, a case)
прекра|щать, -тить
dismissal /dɪsˈmɪs(ə)l/ n. увольнение
dismissive /dɪsˈmɪsɪv/ adj. презрительный
dismount /dɪsˈmaʊnt/ v.i. (from horse)
спеши|ваться, -ться; (from bicycle) слез|ать, -ть
disobedient /ˌdɪsəˈbiːdɪənt/ adj.
непослушный
disobey /ˌdɪsəˈbeɪ/ v.t. не слушаться, по- + g.;
не повиноваться (impf., pf.) + d.
disorder /dɪsˈɔːdə(r)/ n. (untidiness)
беспорядок; (riot) беспорядки (m. pl.); (med.)
расстройство
disorderly /dɪsˈɔːdəlɪ/ adj. (untidy)
беспорядочный; (unruly) буйный
■ ~ **conduct** n. хулиганство
disorganized /dɪsˈɔːɡənaɪzd/ adj.
неорганизованный
disorient /dɪsˈɔːrɪənt/ v.t. дезориентировать
(impf., pf.)
disorientate /dɪsˈɔːrɪənteɪt/ v.t. (BrE)
= **disorient**
disown /dɪsˈəʊn/ v.t. отказ|ываться, -аться
от + g.
disparage /dɪˈspærɪdʒ/ v.t. (belittle)
преум|еньшать, -еньшить; говорить (impf.)
с пренебрежением о + p.

⚔ ключевая лексика

disparate /ˈdɪspərət/ adj. несхожий
disparity /dɪˈspærɪtɪ/ n. расхождение;
(incongruity) несоответствие
dispassionate /dɪˈspæʃənət/ adj.
бесстрастный
dispatch /dɪˈspætʃ/ n. сообщение
● v.t. **1** (send off) отпр|авлять, -авить **2** (deal
with) спр|авляться, -авиться с + i.
dispel /dɪˈspel/ v.t. (**dispelled, dispelling**)
рассе|ивать, -ять
dispensable /dɪˈspensəb(ə)l/ adj.
необязательный
dispensary /dɪˈspensərɪ/ n. аптека; (in hospital)
пункт раздачи лекарств
dispensation /ˌdɪspenˈseɪʃ(ə)n/ n. **1** (dealing
out) раздача **2** (order) закон; **under the
Mosaic ~** по Моисееву закону **3** (exemption)
освобождение, исключение; (permission)
разрешение
dispense /dɪˈspens/ v.t. **1** (deal out) разд|авать,
-ать **2** (medicines) пригот|овлять, -овить
● v.i.: **~ with** (do without) об|ходиться, -ойтись
без + g.
dispenser /dɪˈspensə(r)/ n. **1** (of medicines)
фармацевт **2** (machine) торговый автомат
disperse /dɪˈspɜːs/ v.t. рассе|ивать, -ять;
the policeman ~d the crowd полицейский
разогнал толпу
● v.i. рассе|иваться, -яться
displace /dɪsˈpleɪs/ v.t. сме|щать, -стить
■ ~**d persons** n. pl. перемещённые лица
⚔ **display** /dɪˈspleɪ/ n. **1** (manifestation) показ,
проявление **2** (of goods etc.) выставка **3** (of
computer) дисплей
● v.t. (quality, emotion) проявл|ять, -ить;
обнаруж|ивать, -ть; (on screen, in a picture)
демонстрировать, про-; (goods etc.)
выставл|ять, выставить
displeased /dɪsˈpliːzd/ adj. недовольный;
I am ~ with you я недоволен вами
displeasure /dɪsˈpleʒə(r)/ n. недовольство,
неудовольствие; **incur sb's ~** навл|екать,
-ечь на себя (or вызывать, вызвать) чьё-н.
недовольство
disposable /dɪˈspəʊzəb(ə)l/ adj. разовый,
одноразовый
disposal /dɪˈspəʊz(ə)l/ n. **1** (getting rid of)
удаление, устранение **2** (control): **the money
is at your ~** деньги в вашем распоряжении
dispose /dɪˈspəʊz/ v.t.: **he is well ~d towards
me** он хорошо ко мне относится
● v.i. (with prep. **of**) изб|авляться, -авиться
от + g.
disposition /ˌdɪspəˈzɪʃ(ə)n/ n. **1** (arrangement)
расположение **2** (character) нрав, характер;
he has a cheerful ~ у него весёлый нрав
dispossess /ˌdɪspəˈzes/ v.t. лиш|ать, -ить (кого
чего); от|бирать, -обрать (что у кого)
disproportionate /ˌdɪsprəˈpɔːʃənət/ adj.
непропорциональный
disprove /dɪsˈpruːv/ v.t. опров|ергать,
-ергнуть
disputable /dɪˈspjuːtəb(ə)l/ adj. спорный

ˣ **dispute** /dɪˈspjuːt/ n. **1** (argument) дⅰ́спут; (disagreement) спор **2** (quarrel) ссо́ра, разногла́сие
● v.t. (call in question, oppose) осп|а́ривать, -о́рить

disqualify /dɪsˈkwɒlɪfaɪ/ v.t. дисквалифицⅰ́ровать (impf., pf.)

disquiet /dɪsˈkwaɪət/ n. беспоко́йство, трево́га
● v.t. беспоко́ить, о-, трево́жить, вс-

disregard /dɪsrɪˈɡɑːd/ n. пренебреже́ние + i.; he showed ∼ for his teachers он проявля́л неуваже́ние к учителя́м
● v.t. игнорⅰ́ровать (impf., pf.)

disrepair /dɪsrɪˈpeə(r)/ n. неиспра́вность; fall into ∼ при|ходⅰ́ть, -йтⅰ́ в упа́док/ запусте́ние

disreputable /dɪsˈrepjʊtəb(ə)l/ adj. (behaviour) позо́рный; (company, person) по́льзующийся дурно́й сла́вой

disrepute /dɪsrɪˈpjuːt/ n. дурна́я сла́ва; fall into ∼ приобре|та́ть, -стⅰ́ дурну́ю сла́ву

disrespect /dɪsrɪˈspekt/ n. неуваже́ние (for, towards: к + d.)

disrespectful /dɪsrɪˈspektfʊl/ adj. непочтⅰ́тельный

disrupt /dɪsˈrʌpt/ v.t. (event) срыва́ть, сорва́ть; (process, system) прер|ыва́ть, -ва́ть

disruption /dɪsˈrʌpʃ(ə)n/ n. срыв

disruptive /dɪsˈrʌptɪv/ adj. разрушⅰ́тельный, подрывно́й

dissatisfaction /dɪsætɪsˈfækʃ(ə)n/ n. неудовлетворённость

dissatisfied /dɪˈsætɪsfaɪd/ adj. недово́льный; she is ∼ with her job она́ недово́льна свое́й рабо́той

dissect /dɪˈsekt/ v.t. вскр|ыва́ть, -ы́ть

disseminate /dɪˈsemɪneɪt/ v.t. распростран|я́ть, -ⅰ́ть

dissent /dɪˈsent/ n. несогла́сие

dissertation /dɪsəˈteɪʃ(ə)n/ n. диссерта́ция

disservice /dɪsˈsɜːvɪs/ n. плоха́я услу́га; уще́рб; he did me a ∼ он нанёс мне уще́рб; он навредⅰ́л мне; her words did great ∼ to the cause её слова́ нанеслⅰ́ большо́й уще́рб де́лу

dissident /ˈdɪsɪd(ə)nt/ n. (pol.) диссиде́нт
● adj. несогла́сный

dissimilar /dɪˈsɪmɪlə(r)/ adj. несхо́дный

dissipated /ˈdɪsɪpeɪtɪd/ adj. беспу́тный; (life style) разгу́льный

dissociate /dɪˈsəʊʃɪeɪt/ v.t.: ∼ oneself отмеж|ёвываться, -ева́ться (from: от + g.); I ∼ myself from what has been said я отмежёвываюсь от того́, что бы́ло ска́зано

dissolute /ˈdɪsəluːt/ adj. распу́щенный, беспу́тный, распу́тный

dissolve /dɪˈzɒlv/ v.t. **1** (phys.) раствор|я́ть, -ⅰ́ть **2**: the queen ∼d parliament короле́ва распустⅰ́ла парла́мент
● v.i. (phys.) раствор|я́ться, -ⅰ́ться

dissuade /dɪˈsweɪd/ v.t. отгов|а́ривать, -орⅰ́ть (кого от чего)

ˣ **distance** /ˈdɪst(ə)ns/ n. **1** (measure of space) диста́нция, расстоя́ние; she lives within walking ∼ of the office от её до́ма до рабо́ты мо́жно дойтⅰ́ пешко́м; in the ∼ вдалеке́; from a ∼ ⅰ́здали, издалека́ **2** (fig.): keep one's ∼ держа́ться (impf.) в стороне́ (from: от + g.)

distant /ˈdɪst(ə)nt/ adj. **1** (in space) далёкий, да́льний **2** (fig., remote): a ∼ cousin да́льний ро́дственник **3** (reserved) сде́ржанный, холо́дный

distaste /dɪsˈteɪst/ n. отвраще́ние (for: к + d.)

distasteful /dɪsˈteɪstfʊl/ adj. отвратⅰ́тельный, неприя́тный

distillery /dɪˈstɪləri/ n. ликёрово́дочный заво́д

distinct /dɪˈstɪŋkt/ adj. **1** (sound) вня́тный; (picture) отчётливый; (advantage, possibility) очевⅰ́дный **2** (different) отлⅰ́чный (from: от + g.)

distinction /dɪˈstɪŋkʃ(ə)n/ n. **1** (difference) отлⅰ́чие **2** (discrimination) разлⅰ́чие **3** (special quality) отличⅰ́тельная осо́бенность; a writer of ∼ выдаю́щийся писа́тель **4** (mark of honour) отлⅰ́чие

distinctive /dɪˈstɪŋktɪv/ adj. отличⅰ́тельный

distinguish /dɪˈstɪŋɡwɪʃ/ v.t. различ|а́ть, -ⅰ́ть

distinguished /dɪˈstɪŋɡwɪʃt/ adj. выдаю́щийся, вⅰ́дный

distort /dɪˈstɔːt/ v.t. искрив|ля́ть, -ⅰ́ть; ∼ facts извра|ща́ть, -тⅰ́ть фа́кты

distract /dɪˈstrækt/ v.t. отвл|ека́ть, -е́чь; it ∼s me from my work э́то отвлека́ет меня́ от рабо́ты

distraction /dɪˈstrækʃ(ə)n/ n. поме́ха

distraught /dɪˈstrɔːt/ adj. обезу́мевший

distress /dɪˈstres/ n. **1** (physical suffering) изнуре́ние, изнеможе́ние **2** (mental suffering) трево́га, депре́ссия **3** (danger) бе́дствие; a ship in ∼ су́дно, те́рпящее бе́дствие
● v.t. огорч|а́ть, -ⅰ́ть

distressing /dɪˈstresɪŋ/ adj. огорчⅰ́тельный

distribute /dɪˈstrɪbjuːt/ v.t. **1** (deal out) распредел|я́ть, -ⅰ́ть; (goods) распростран|я́ть, -ⅰ́ть **2** (spread) распредел|я́ть, -ⅰ́ть

ˣ **distribution** /dɪstrɪˈbjuːʃ(ə)n/ n. распределе́ние; (of goods) распростране́ние

distributor /dɪˈstrɪbjʊtə(r)/ n. (comm.) дистрибью́тор

ˣ **district** /ˈdɪstrɪkt/ n. райо́н, о́круг; (attr.) райо́нный, окружно́й
■ ∼ attorney n. (AmE) окружно́й прокуро́р

distrust /dɪsˈtrʌst/ v.t. не доверя́ть (impf.) + d.

distrustful /dɪsˈtrʌstfʊl/ adj. недове́рчивый

disturb /dɪsˈtɜːb/ v.t. беспоко́ить, о-; (peace) нар|уша́ть, -у́шить; he was ∼ed by the news он был обеспоко́ен но́востью

disturbance /dɪsˈtɜːb(ə)ns/ n. (act of troubling) наруше́ние; (riot) волне́ния (nt. pl.)

disturbing /dɪsˈtɜːbɪŋ/ adj. трево́жный

disuse /dɪsˈjuːs/ n.: fall into ∼ выходⅰ́ть, вы́йти из употребле́ния

disused /dɪsˈjuːzd/ adj.: a ∼ well забро́шенный коло́дец

ditch /dɪtʃ/ *n.* канáва; ров
• *v.t.* (infml): ~ one's plans забрáсывать, -óсить свои плáны; ~ sb брjosáть, -óсить когó-н.

dither /'dɪðə(r)/ *v.i.* (infml) колебáться, по-

ditto /'dɪtəʊ/ *n.* (*pl.* **~s**) то же

diva /'di:və/ *n.* (*pl.* **~s**) примадóнна, ди́ва

divan /dɪ'væn/ *n.* тахтá, дивáн
■ ~ **bed** *n.* дивáн-кровáть

dive /daɪv/ *n.* нырóк, ныря́ние; (of aircraft) пики́рование
• *v.i.* (*past and p.p.* **dived** or AmE *also* **dove**) (plunge into water) ныр|я́ть, -нýть; (in diving suit) погру|жáться, -зи́ться

diver /'daɪvə(r)/ *n.* ныря́льщик; водолáз

diverge /daɪ'vɜ:dʒ/ *v.i.* рa|сходи́ться, -зойти́сь

diverse /daɪ'vɜ:s/ *adj.* разнообрáзный

diversify /daɪ'vɜ:sɪfaɪ/ *v.t.* разнообрáзить (*impf.*); диверсифици́ровать (*impf., pf.*)

diversion /daɪ'vɜ:ʃ(ə)n/ *n.* **1** (turning aside) отклонéние; **traffic** ~ (BrE) объéзд **2** (amusement) развлечéние, забáва **3**: create a ~ отвл|екáть, -éчь внимáние

diversity /daɪ'vɜ:sɪtɪ/ *n.* разнообрáзие

divert /daɪ'vɜ:t/ *v.t.* (deflect) отклон|я́ть, -и́ть; (entertain) развл|екáть, -éчь

divest /daɪ'vest/ *v.t.*: ~ sb of sth лиш|áть, -и́ть (*когó чегó-л.*); ~ oneself of responsibilities слож|и́ть (*pf.*) с себя́ обя́занности

◈ **divide** /dɪ'vaɪd/ *n.* расхождéние
• *v.t.* **1** (share) дели́ть, по-, раз-; **they ~d the money equally** они́ раздели́ли дéньги пópовну **2** (math.) дели́ть, раз-; ~ **27 by 3** 27 дели́ть, раз- нá 3 **3** (separate) раздел|я́ть, -и́ть; **dividing line** разграничи́тельная ли́ния **4** (cause disagreement) разъедин|я́ть, -и́ть
• *v.i.* дели́ться, раз-; **the road ~s** дорóга разветвля́ется

dividend /'dɪvɪdend/ *n.* (fin.) дивидéнд

divine /dɪ'vaɪn/ *adj.* (**diviner, divinest**) божéственный

diving /'daɪvɪŋ/ *n.* ныря́ние
■ ~ **board** *n.* трампли́н, вы́шка (для прыжкóв в вóду); ~ **suit** *n.* скафáндр

divisible /dɪ'vɪzɪb(ə)l/ *adj.* (раз)дели́мый

◈ **division** /dɪ'vɪʒ(ə)n/ *n.* **1** (math.) делéние **2** (dividing) разделéние, раздéл **3** (mil.) диви́зия **4** (department) отдéл

divisive /dɪ'vaɪsɪv/ *adj.* вызывáющий разноглáсия

divorce /dɪ'vɔ:s/ *n.* (law) развóд
• *v.t.* (law) разв|оди́ть, -ести́; **he ~d his wife** он развёлся с женóй; **she is ~d** онá разведенá
• *v.i.* разв|оди́ться, -ести́сь

divorcee /dɪvɔ:'si:/ *n.* (AmE **divorcé**, *f.* **divorcée**) разведённый (муж), разведённая (женá)

divulge /daɪ'vʌldʒ/ *v.t.* разгла|шáть, -си́ть

DIY (BrE) *abbr.* (*of* **do it yourself**): ~ **store** магази́н «Умéлые ру́ки»

◈ ключевáя лéксика

dizzy /'dɪzɪ/ *adj.* (**dizzier, dizziest**) испы́тывающий головокружéние; **I feel** ~ у меня́ кру́жится головá

DJ *abbr.* (*of* **disc jockey**) ди́джéй

DNA *abbr.* (*of* **deoxyribonucleic acid**) ДНК (дезоксирибонуклеи́новая кислотá)

◈ **do** /du:/ *v.t. & aux.* (*3rd pers. sing. pres.* **does**, *past* **did**, *p.p.* **done**) **1** (as aux. or substitute for v. already used: not translated unless emph.): **I** ~ **not smoke** я не курю́; **did you not see me?** рáзве вы меня́ не ви́дели?; **I** ~ **want to go** я óчень хочу́ пойти́; ~ **tell me** пожáлуйста, расскажи́те мне; **they promised to help, and they did** они́ обещáли помóчь и помогли́; **so** ~ **I** я тóже **2** (perform, carry out): **what can I** ~ **for you?** чем могу́ служи́ть?; **what** ~**es he** ~ **(for a living)?** чем он занимáется?; **the team did well** комáнда вы́ступила успéшно; **easier said than** ~ легкó сказáть; **well** ~**ne!** молодéц! **3** (render): **it** ~**es him credit** э́то дéлает ему́ честь; **it won't** ~ **any good** э́то бесполéзно, э́то ничегó не даст **4** (solve): ~ **a sum** реш|áть, -и́ть арифмети́ческую задáчу **5** (attend to): **he** ~**es book reviews** он рецензи́рует кни́ги; **we did geography** сегóдня мы занимáлись геогрáфией **6** (arrange, clean, tidy): ~ **one's hair** прич|ёсываться, -есáться; ~ **the dishes** мыть, по- посýду **7** (cook): **well** ~**ne** хорошó прожáренный; **the potatoes are** ~**ne** картóшка свари́лась/готóва **8** (infml, swindle) над|увáть, -ýть **9**: ~**ne!** (agreed) по рукáм!
• *v.i.* (*3rd pers. sing. pres.* **does**, *past* **did**, *p.p.* **done**) **1** (act, behave): ~ **as I tell you** дéлай, что тебé говоря́т **2** (be satisfactory, fitting or advisable): **the scraps will** ~ **for the dog** объéдки пойдýт собáке; **this will never** ~ э́то никудá не годи́тся; **так не пойдёт; that will** ~! (is enough) хвáтит!; довóльно!; **tomorrow will** ~ мóжно и зáвтра **3** (fare, succeed): **how** ~ **you** ~? здрáвствуйте!; как поживáете?; **how did he** ~ **in his exams?** как он сдáл экзáмены?; **my roses are** ~**ing well** мои́ рóзы хорошó растýт; **the patient is** ~**ing well** больнóй поправля́ется
• *with preps.*: **what shall we** ~ **about lunch?** как насчёт обéда?; ~ **sb out of sth** (cheat, deprive of) вымáнивать, вы́манить что-н. у когó-н.; **what have you** ~**ne with the keys?** куда́ вы дéли ключи́?; **I could** ~ **with a drink** я охóтно (*or* с удовóльствием) вы́пил бы; **that coat could** ~ **with a clean** не помешáло бы вы́чистить э́то пальтó; **he** ~**esn't know what to** ~ **with himself** он не знáет, чем заня́ться; **it is nothing to** ~ **with you** э́то вас не касáется; **these books are** ~**ne with** э́ти кни́ги бóльше не нужны́; **we must** ~ **without luxuries** мы должны́ обойти́сь без рóскоши; **I can** ~ **without his silly jokes** мне надоéли его́ дурáцкие шу́тки

□ ~ **away** *v.i.*: ~ **away with** кончáть, кóнчить с + *i.*

□ ~ **in** *v.t.* (sl., kill) уб|ирáть, -рáть; (infml, exhaust): **I am** ~**ne in** я измóтан

□ ~ **out** *v.t.* (BrE, clean, e.g. a room) уб|ирáть, -рáть; (BrE, clear, e.g. a cupboard) вычищáть, вы́чистить

□ ~ **up** *v.t.* (repair, refurnish): ~ **up a room** отде́л|ывать, -ать ко́мнату; (fasten): ~ **up a parcel** завя́з|ывать, -а́ть паке́т; ~ **up a dress** застёг|ивать, -ну́ть пла́тье

■ ~**-it-yourself** *adj.* самоде́льный

Dobermann /ˈdəʊbəmən/, **Dobermann pinscher** /ˈdəʊbəmən ˈpɪnʃə(r)/ (AmE **Doberman**) *n.* добермáн(-пи́нчер)

docile /ˈdəʊsaɪl/ *adj.* послу́шный, поко́рный

dock[1] /dɒk/ *n.* (in court) скамья́ подсуди́мых

dock[2] /dɒk/ *n.* **1** (naut.) док **2** (*in pl.*) (port facilities) верфь **3** (wharf) при́стань
● *v.i.* (go into ~) входи́ть, войти́ в док; (of space vehicles) стыкова́ться, со-

■ ~**yard** *n.* верфь

dock[3] /dɒk/ *v.t.* (reduce) уре́з|ывать, -ать

docker /ˈdɒkə(r)/ *n.* до́кер; порто́вый рабо́чий

♂ **doctor** /ˈdɒktə(r)/ *n.* **1** (of medicine) врач, до́ктор **2** (academic) до́ктор
● *v.t.* (falsify) подде́л|ывать, -ать

doctoral /ˈdɒktər(ə)l/ *adj.* до́кторский

doctorate /ˈdɒktərət/ *n.* сте́пень до́ктора

doctrine /ˈdɒktrɪn/ *n.* доктри́на

♂ **document** /ˈdɒkjʊmənt/ документ
● *v.t.* /ˈdɒkjʊment/ документи́ровать (*impf., pf.*)

documentary /dɒkjʊˈmentərɪ/ *n.* документа́льный фильм

documentation /dɒkjʊmenˈteɪʃ(ə)n/ *n.* документа́ция

doddery /ˈdɒdərɪ/ *adj.* трясу́щийся от ста́рости; дря́хлый

dodge /dɒdʒ/ *n.* уве́ртка
● *v.t.* уви́л|ивать, -ьну́ть от + *g.*; ~ **a blow** увора́чиваться, уверну́ться от уда́ра
● *v.i.* уклон|я́ться, -и́ться (от + *g.*)

dodgy /ˈdɒdʒɪ/ *adj.* (**dodgier, dodgiest**) (BrE, infml) (suspicious) подозри́тельный; (risky) риско́ванный

does /dʌz/ *3rd pers. sing. pres. of* ▶ **do**

doesn't /ˈdʌz(ə)nt/ *neg. of* ▶ **does**

doff /dɒf/ *v.t.* сн|има́ть, -я́ть (шля́пу)

♂ **dog** /dɒg/ *n.* **1** соба́ка, пёс (also fig., pej.) **2** (male) кобе́ль (*m.*) **3** (fig.): **go to the ~s** разори́ться (*pf.*), пойти́ (*pf.*) пра́хом

■ ~ **collar** *n.* оше́йник; (infml, clergyman's) кру́глый стоя́чий воротни́к; ~**-eared** *adj.* потрёпанный; ~**house** *n.* (AmE) конура́; **in the ~house** (infml) в неми́лости; ~**paddle** *v.i.* пла́вать (*indet.*) по-соба́чьи; ~**sbody** *n.* (BrE) иша́к, рабо́тяга (*c.g.*)

dogged /ˈdɒgɪd/ *adj.* упо́рный

dogma /ˈdɒgmə/ *n.* до́гма; (specific) до́гмат

dogmatic /dɒgˈmætɪk/ *adj.* (views) догмати́ческий; (person) догмати́чный

dogmatism /ˈdɒgmətɪz(ə)m/ *n.* догмати́зм

doing /ˈduːɪŋ/ *n.*: **this was her ~** э́то её рук де́ло; **it will take some ~** придётся постара́ться; э́то не та́к про́сто

doldrums /ˈdɒldrəmz/ *n. pl.* (fig.) уны́ние, хандра́; **be in the ~** быть в уны́нии, хандри́ть (*impf.*)

dole /dəʊl/ *n.* (BrE, infml, benefit) посо́бие по безрабо́тице; **he is on the ~** он получа́ет посо́бие по безрабо́тице
● *v.t.*: ~ **out** разд|ава́ть, -а́ть

doleful /ˈdəʊlfʊl/ *adj.* ско́рбный

doll /dɒl/ *n.* ку́кла

♂ **dollar** /ˈdɒlə(r)/ *n.* до́ллар

dollop /ˈdɒləp/ *n.* (infml) соли́дная по́рция

dolphin /ˈdɒlfɪn/ *n.* дельфи́н

domain /dəˈmeɪn/ *n.* (fig.) о́бласть; (comput.) доме́н

dome /dəʊm/ *n.* ку́пол

domed /dəʊmd/ *adj.* куполообра́зный

♂ **domestic** /dəˈmestɪk/ *adj.* **1** (of the home; of animals) дома́шний **2** (not foreign) оте́чественный, вну́тренний

domesticate /dəˈmestɪkeɪt/ *v.t.* (tame) прируч|а́ть, -и́ть

domesticity /dɒməˈstɪsɪtɪ/ *n.* семе́йная/ дома́шняя жизнь

domicile /ˈdɒmɪsaɪl/ *n.* (dwelling) ме́сто жи́тельства
● *v.t.*: ~**d in England** име́ющий постоя́нное местожи́тельство в А́нглии

dominance /ˈdɒmɪnəns/ *n.* преоблада́ние, госпо́дство

dominant /ˈdɒmɪnənt/ *adj.* домини́рующий

♂ **dominate** /ˈdɒmɪneɪt/ *v.t. & i.* **1** (prevail) домини́ровать (*impf.*) (над + *i.*) **2** (influence) подавля́ть (*impf.*); **she ~s her daughter** она́ подавля́ет дочь

domination /dɒmɪˈneɪʃ(ə)n/ *n.* госпо́дство

domineering /dɒmɪˈnɪərɪŋ/ *adj.* вла́стный

Dominican /dəˈmɪnɪkən/ *adj.*: **the ~ Republic** Доминика́нская Респу́блика

domino /ˈdɒmɪnəʊ/ *n.* (*pl.* ~**es**) кость доми́но; (*in pl.*) (game) домино́ (*nt. indecl.*)

don /dɒn/ *n.* **1** (Spanish title) дон **2** (university teacher) преподава́тель (*m.*)

■ **D~ Juan** *n.* (fig.) донжуа́н

donate /dəʊˈneɪt/ *v.t.* дари́ть, по-

donation /dəʊˈneɪʃ(ə)n/ *n.* дар

done /dʌn/ *p.p. of* ▶ **do**

donkey /ˈdɒŋkɪ/ *n.* осёл (also fig.)

donor /ˈdəʊnə(r)/ *n.* дари́тель (-ница); (of blood, transplant) до́нор

♂ **don't** /dəʊnt/ *neg. of* ▶ **do**

doodle /ˈduːd(ə)l/ *v.i.* чи́ркать (*impf.*)

doom /duːm/ *n.* (ruin) ги́бель
● *v.t.* обр|ека́ть, -е́чь на + *a.*

♂ **door** /dɔː(r)/ *n.* **1** (of room etc.) дверь; (of cupboard etc.) две́рца; **behind closed ~s** (in secret) за закры́тыми дверя́ми **2** (fig.): **a ~ to success** путь к успе́ху

■ ~**bell** *n.* дверно́й звоно́к; ~ **handle** *n.* дверна́я ру́чка; ~**keeper** *n.* приврáтник; швейца́р; ~**knob** *n.* кру́глая дверна́я ру́чка; ~**man** *n.* = doorkeeper; ~**mat** *n.* полови́к; ~**step** *n.* поро́г; ~**-to-** *adj.*: ~**-to-~ salesman** коммивояжёр; ~**way** *n.* дверно́й проём

d

dope /dəʊp/ n. infml **1** (drug) дурма́н, нарко́тик **2** (fool) ду́рень (m.)
● v.t. **1** (make unconscious) дурма́нить, о- **2** (put narcotic in) нака́ч|ивать, -а́ть нарко́тиками

dopey /'dəʊpɪ/ adj. (dopier, dopiest) (bemused by drug or sleep) одурма́ненный; (infml, foolish) чо́кнутый

dormant /'dɔ:mənt/ adj. (of animals) в спя́чке; ∼ volcano спя́щий вулка́н

dormitory /'dɔ:mɪtərɪ/ n. о́бщая спа́льня

dormouse /'dɔ:maʊs/ n. (pl. **dormice**) со́ня

DOS /dɒs/ abbr. (of **disk operating system**) ДОС (ди́сковая операцио́нная систе́ма)

dose /dəʊs/ n. до́за

doss /dɒs/ v.i. (BrE, infml) **1** (also ∼ **down**) ночева́ть, пере- **2** (also ∼ **around**) безде́льничать (impf.)
■ ∼**house** n. ночле́жка

dossier /'dɒsɪə(r)/ n. досье́ (nt. indecl.), де́ло

dot /dɒt/ n. то́чка; on the ∼ то́чно
● v.t. (**dotted, dotting**) (place ∼ on): ∼ one's i's (lit., fig.) ста́вить, по- то́чки над «i»
■ ∼**ted line** n. пункти́р; пункти́рная ли́ния

dotage /'dəʊtɪdʒ/ n. ста́рческое слабоу́мие, мара́зм; he is in his ∼ он впал в де́тство/мара́зм

dot-com company /dɒt'kɒm/ n. интерне́т-компа́ния

dote /dəʊt/ v.i.: ∼ on (child, friend) обожа́ть (impf.)

double /'dʌb(ə)l/ n. **1** (two shots of spirits) двойна́я ме́ра **2** (person resembling another) двойни́к **3** (running pace): at the ∼ (BrE), on the ∼ (AmE) бе́глым ша́гом **4** (tennis) па́рная игра́; mixed ∼s сме́шанные па́ры (f. pl.)
● adj. (in two parts; twice as much) двойно́й; 'Anna' is spelt with a ∼ 'n' «А́нна» пи́шется с двумя́ «н»
● adv. вдво́е; bend ∼ сгиба́ть(ся), согну́ть(ся) вдво́е; pay ∼ плати́ть, за- вдвойне́; she sees ∼ у неё дво́ится в глаза́х
● v.t. удв|а́ивать, -о́ить
● v.i. **1** (become twice as great) удв|а́иваться, -о́иться **2** (turn sharply): he ∼d back on his tracks он пошёл обра́тно по своему́ сле́ду **3** (bend) ко́рчиться, с-; she ∼d up with the pain она́ ско́рчилась от бо́ли **4** (combine roles): I ∼d for him я дубли́ровал его́; the porter ∼s as waiter носи́льщик рабо́тает официа́нтом по совмести́тельству
■ ∼**-barrelled name** n. (BrE) двойна́я фами́лия; ∼ **bass** n. контраба́с; ∼ **bed** n. дву(х)спа́льная крова́ть; ∼**-breasted** adj. двубо́ртный; ∼**-check** v.t. перепров|еря́ть, -е́рить; ∼**-click** v.i. (comput.) два́жды щёлк|ать, -нуть; ∼**-cross** v.t. обма́н|ывать, -у́ть; ∼**-decker** n. (bus) двухэта́жный авто́бус; ∼**-dip recession** n. (econ.) двойно́е паде́ние; ∼ **Dutch** n. (BrE) тараба́рщина, кита́йская гра́мота; ∼**-park** v.t. & i. ста́вить, по- (маши́ну) во второ́й ряд; ∼ **room** n. (in hotel) двухме́стный но́мер; ∼ **take** n. (fig.) заме́дленная реа́кция

doubt /daʊt/ n. сомне́ние; there is no ∼ that … нет сомне́ния в том, что…; the question is in ∼ э́тот вопро́с ещё не я́сен; without ∼ вне сомне́ния; несомне́нно; no ∼ несомне́нно, безусло́вно
● v.t. & i. сомнева́ться (impf.) (в + p.); I ∼ that, whether she will come (я) сомнева́юсь, что она́ придёт

doubtful /'daʊtfʊl/ adj. **1** (feeling doubt) сомнева́ющийся **2** (causing doubt) сомни́тельный

dough /dəʊ/ n. те́сто
■ ∼**nut** n. по́нчик

dour /dʊə(r)/ adj. суро́вый

douse /daʊs/ v.t. (drench) зал|ива́ть, -и́ть; (extinguish) гаси́ть, по-

dove /dʌv/ n. го́лубь (m.)

dowdy /'daʊdɪ/ adj. (dowdier, dowdiest) неэлега́нтный

down[1] /daʊn/ n. (hair, fluff) пух, пушо́к

down[2] /daʊn/ n. невзго́да; ups and ∼s взлёты (m. pl.) и паде́ния (nt. pl.)
● adj. напра́вленный вниз/кни́зу
● adv. **1** (expr. motion/place) вниз/внизу́; the blinds are ∼ што́ры спу́щены; prices are ∼ це́ны упа́ли; (fig.): he is £15 ∼ он в убы́тке на 15 фу́нтов **2** (expr. movement to lower level): climb ∼ слез|а́ть, -ть; come ∼ спус|ка́ться, -ти́ться **3** (expr. change of position): sit ∼ сади́ться, сесть; lie ∼ ложи́ться, лечь; fall ∼ па́дать, упа́сть; knock sb ∼ сби|ва́ть, -ть; he bent ∼ он нагну́лся **4** (reduction): the wind died ∼ ве́тер ути́х; the house burnt ∼ дом сгоре́л дотла́ **5**: ∼ with the government! доло́й прави́тельство!
● prep. **1** (expr. downward direction): we walked ∼ the hill мы шли с горы́ (or по́д гору); tears ran ∼ her face слёзы текли́/кати́лись у неё по лицу́ **2** (at, to a lower or further part of): further ∼ the river да́льше вниз по реке́; we sailed ∼ the Volga мы плы́ли вниз по Во́лге; she lives ∼ the street она́ живёт да́льше по э́той у́лице **3** (along): he walked ∼ the street он шёл по у́лице

down-and-out /daʊnə'naʊt/ n. бродя́га (m.); бездо́мный

downcast /'daʊnkɑ:st/ adj. (dejected) удручённый; пода́вленный

downfall /'daʊnfɔ:l/ n. паде́ние

downgrade /'daʊngreɪd/ v.t. пон|ижа́ть, -и́зить в чи́не

downhearted /daʊn'hɑ:tɪd/ adj. пода́вленный

downhill /'daʊnhɪl/ adv. по́д гору; вниз; go ∼ (fig.) кати́ться (det.) по накло́нной пло́скости

download /daʊn'ləʊd/ v.t. (comput.) загру|жа́ть, -зи́ть; ска́|чивать, -ча́ть

downmarket /'daʊnmɑ:kɪt/ adj. (BrE) дешёвый

downpour /'daʊnpɔ:(r)/ n. ли́вень (m.)

downright /'daʊnraɪt/ adj. (straightforward, blunt) прямо́й; (absolute) соверше́нный; я́вный

downshift /'daʊnʃɪft/ v.i. **1** (AmE, motoring) переключ|а́ть, -и́ть на ни́жнюю ско́рость

2 (at work) пере|ходи́ть, -йти́ на ме́нее напряжённую, хотя́ и нижеопла́чиваемую рабо́ту

downsize /ˈdaʊnsaɪz/ *v.t. & i.* (comm.) ум|еньша́ть, -е́ньшить разме́ры (компа́нии) за счёт увольне́ния рабо́тников

Down's syndrome /daʊnz/ *n.* боле́знь/ синдро́м Да́уна

downstairs *adj.* /ˈdaʊnsteəz/: ~ **rooms** ко́мнаты пе́рвого этажа́
● *adv.* /daʊnˈsteəz/ (expr. place) внизу́; (expr. motion) вниз

downstream /daʊnˈstriːm/ *adv.* вниз по тече́нию

down-to-earth /ˈdaʊntəɜː/ *adj.* практи́чный

downtown /ˈdaʊntaʊn/ *adj.* (AmE) располо́женный в делово́й ча́сти го́рода

downtrodden /ˈdaʊntrɒd(ə)n/ *adj.* угнетённый

downturn /ˈdaʊntɜːn/ *n.* (fall, reduction) паде́ние, спад

downward /ˈdaʊnwəd/ *adj.* спуска́ющийся

downwards /ˈdaʊnwədz/ *adv.* вниз

doze /dəʊz/ *v.i.* дрема́ть (*impf.*); ~ **off** задрема́ть (*pf.*)

dozen /ˈdʌz(ə)n/ *n.* **1** (*pl.* ~) дю́жина **2**: ~s **of** мно́жество, ма́сса + *g.*

dozy /ˈdəʊzi/ *adj.* (**dozier, doziest**) сонли́вый; (BrE, not alert) рассе́янный

drab /dræb/ *adj.* (**drabber, drabbest**) се́рый

draft /drɑːft/ *n.* (*see also* ▸ **draught**) **1** (outline, rough copy) набро́сок, черновѝк **2** (order for payment) чек, тра́тта **3** (AmE, conscription) призы́в
● *v.t.* **1** (detach for duty) наря|жа́ть, -ди́ть **2** (conscript) приз|ыва́ть, -ва́ть **3** (prepare ~ of) набр|а́сывать, -оса́ть черновѝк + *g.*
■ ~ **dodger** *n.* лицо́, уклоня́ющееся от вое́нной слу́жбы

draftsman /ˈdrɑːftsmən/ *n.* (of contracts etc.) состави́тель (*m.*) (*законопроекта и т. п.*); (AmE, one who draws) чертёжник

drafty /ˈdrɑːfti/ *adj.* (AmE) = **draughty**

drag /dræɡ/ *n.* (infml, person) зану́да; (thing) тоска́ зелёная
● *v.t.* (**dragged, dragging**) (pull) тяну́ть, волочи́ть, тащи́ть (*all impf.*); **I had to** ~ **him to the party** мне пришло́сь тащи́ть его́ на вечери́нку; ~ **one's feet** (fig.) тяну́ть, ме́длить (*both impf.*)
● *v.i.* (**dragged, dragging**) **1** (trail) волочи́ться (*impf.*) **2** (be slow or tedious) тяну́ться (*impf.*)
□ ~ **on** *v.i.*: **the performance** ~**ged on till 11** представле́ние затяну́лось до оди́ннадцати часо́в

dragon /ˈdræɡən/ *n.* (fabulous beast) драко́н
■ ~**fly** *n.* стрекоза́

dragoon /drəˈɡuːn/ *v.t.* прин|ужда́ть, -у́дить; **she was** ~**ed into obeying** её заста́вили подчини́ться

drain /dreɪn/ *n.* (channel carrying off sewage etc.) водосто́к; (*in pl.*) (system of ~s) канализа́ция
● *v.t.* **1** (water etc.) отв|оди́ть, -ести́ **2** (land etc.) осуш|а́ть, -и́ть (*impf.*) **3** (exhaust) истощ|а́ть, -и́ть
● *v.i.* **1** (flow away) ут|ека́ть, -е́чь **2** (lose moisture) высыха́ть, вы́сохнуть
■ ~**ing board** (BrE), ~**board** (AmE) *nn.* суши́лка; ~**pipe** *n.* дрена́жная труба́

drainage /ˈdreɪnɪdʒ/ *n.* **1** (draining or being drained) дрена́ж, осуше́ние **2** (system of drains) канализа́ция

drake /dreɪk/ *n.* се́лезень (*m.*)

drama /ˈdrɑːmə/ *n.* дра́ма

dramatic /drəˈmætɪk/ *adj.* (pert. to drama) драмати́ческий; (exciting) драмати́чный

dramatics /drəˈmætɪks/ *n.* (staging of plays) драмати́ческое иску́сство; теа́тр; **amateur** ~ люби́тельский/самоде́ятельный теа́тр

dramatist /ˈdræmətɪst/ *n.* драмату́рг

dramatize /ˈdræmətaɪz/ *v.t.* (turn into a play) инсцени́ровать (*impf., pf.*); (exaggerate) драматизи́ровать (*impf., pf.*)

drank /dræŋk/ *past of* ▸ **drink**

drape /dreɪp/ *n.* (*usu. in pl.*) за́навес, портье́ра
● *v.t.* драпирова́ть, за-

drastic /ˈdræstɪk/ *adj.* реши́тельный, круто́й

draught /drɑːft/ (AmE **draft**) *n.* **1** (current of air) тя́га; **there is a** ~ **in here** здесь сквози́т **2** (of liquor): ~ **beer, beer on** ~ пи́во из бо́чки **3** (in pl., BrE, game) ша́шки (*f. pl.*)

draughtsman /ˈdrɑːftsmən/ *n.* чертёжник

draughty /ˈdrɑːfti/ (AmE **drafty**) *adj.* (**draughtier, draughtiest**): **this is a** ~ **room** в э́той ко́мнате постоя́нный сквозня́к

draw /drɔː/ *n.* (in lottery) ро́зыгрыш; (~n game) ничья́
● *v.t.* **1** (pull, move) тяну́ть (*impf.*); таска́ть (*indet.*), тащи́ть (*det.*); ~ **the curtains** (close) задв|ига́ть, -и́нуть занаве́ски; (open) разд|ви́гать, -и́нуть занаве́ски **2** (extract) выта́скивать, вы́тащить; ~ **a knife** выхва́тывать, вы́хватить нож; ~ **blood** ра́нить (*impf., pf.*) кого́-н. до кро́ви; ~ **lots** тяну́ть, вы́жребий **3** (obtain from a source): ~ **money out of the bank** снима́ть, снять де́ньги в ба́нке; ~ **on one's savings** тра́тить, по-свои́ сбереже́ния **4** (attract) привл|ека́ть, -е́чь; **I drew him into the conversation** я втяну́л/вовлёк его́ в разгово́р **5** (trace, depict) рисова́ть, на-; черти́ть, на- **6** (of mental operations): ~ **a distinction/comparison** пров|оди́ть, -ести́ разли́чие/сравне́ние; ~ **conclusions** при|ходи́ть, -йти́ к вы́водам **7** (of contest): **the match was** ~**n** матч зако́нчился вничью́
● *v.i.* (*past* **drew**, *p.p.* **drawn**) (move, come) придв|ига́ться, -и́нуться; **the day drew to a close** день бли́зился к концу́
□ ~ **in** *v.i.*: **the train drew in** по́езд подошёл к перро́ну; (shorten): **the days are** ~**ing in** дни стано́вятся коро́че
□ ~ **out** *v.t.* (extract) выта́скивать, вы́тащить;

d

вытя́гивать, вы́тянуть; (prolong) затя|гивать, -ну́ть; (encourage to speak): ~ sb out вызыва́ть, вы́звать кого́-н. на разгово́р
• *v.i.*: **the train drew out** по́езд отошёл
□ ~ **up** *v.t.* (plan, contract, etc.) сост|авля́ть, -а́вить
■ ~**back** *n.* (disadvantage) недоста́ток

drawer /drɔː(r)/ *n.* (in table etc.) (выдвижно́й) я́щик

drawing /'drɔːɪŋ/ *n.* **1** (technique) рисова́ние **2** (piece of ~) рису́нок
■ ~ **board** *n.* чертёжная доска́; ~ **pin** *n.* (BrE) кно́пка; ~ **room** *n.* гости́ная

drawl /drɔːl/ *n.* протя́жное произноше́ние

drawn /drɔːn/ *p.p. of* ▶ draw

dread /dred/ *v.t.* боя́ться (*impf.*) + *g.*; I ~ **to think what may happen** мне стра́шно поду́мать, что мо́жет случи́ться

dreadful /'dredfʊl/ *adj.* ужа́сный

✎ **dream** /driːm/ *n.* **1** (appearance in sleep) сон, сновиде́ние **2** (fantasy) мечта́, мечта́ние
• *v.t. & i.* (*past and p.p.* **dreamed** /dremt, driːmd/ *or* **dreamt** /dremt/) **1** (in sleep) ви́деть (*impf.*) сон; I ~t **of you** вы мне сни́лись; я ви́дел вас во сне **2** (imagine) пом|ышля́ть, -ы́слить о + *p.*; I **never** ~t **of doing so** у меня́ и в мы́слях не́ было де́лать э́того; **he** ~t **up a plan** (infml) он сочини́л план

dreamer /'driːmə(r)/ *n.* (dreamy person) мечта́тель (*m.*); (visionary) фантазёр

dreamt /dremt/ *past and p.p. of* ▶ dream

dreamy /'driːmɪ/ *adj.* (**dreamier, dreamiest**) мечта́тельный; (infml, lovely) восхити́тельный

dreary /'drɪərɪ/ *adj.* (**drearier, dreariest**) (gloomy) тоскли́вый; (dull) се́рый

dregs /dregz/ *n. pl.* отсто́й, оса́док

drench /drentʃ/ *v.t.* пром|а́чивать, -очи́ть

✎ **dress** /dres/ *n.* **1** (clothing, costume) оде́жда, наря́д, туале́т **2** (woman's garment) пла́тье
• *v.t.* **1** (clothe) од|ева́ть, -е́ть (*кого во что*) **2** (prepare) припр|авля́ть, -а́вить; ~ **a salad** запр|авля́ть, -а́вить сала́т **3** (a wound) перевя́з|ывать, -а́ть
• *v.i.* **1** (put on one's clothes) од|ева́ться, -е́ться; ~ **up** (~ elaborately) наря|жа́ться, -ди́ться; **they** ~ed **up as pirates** они́ наряди́лись пира́тами **2** (choose clothes) од|ева́ться, -е́ться; **he** ~es **well** он хорошо́ одева́ется
■ ~ **circle** *n.* бельэта́ж; ~ **code** *n.* дресс-ко́д (*правила-ограничения в отношении допустимой оде́жды*); ~**maker** *n.* портни́ха; ~ **rehearsal** *n.* генера́льная репети́ция

dresser[1] /'dresə(r)/ *n.*: **she is a stylish** ~ она́ шика́рно одева́ется

dresser[2] /'dresə(r)/ *n.* (sideboard) буфе́т; (AmE, chest of drawers) шкаф с выдвижны́ми я́щиками

dressing /'dresɪŋ/ *n.* **1** (med.) повя́зка **2** (AmE, stuffing) начи́нка **3** (of salad etc.) запра́вка

✎ ключева́я ле́ксика

■ ~ **gown** *n.* хала́т; ~ **room** *n.* (theatr.) артисти́ческая убо́рная; ~ **table** *n.* туале́тный сто́лик

dressy /'dresɪ/ *adj.* (**dressier, dressiest**) шика́рный, наря́дный

drew /druː/ *past of* ▶ draw

dribble /'drɪb(ə)l/ *n.* (trickle) стру́йка
• *v.t.*: ~ **a ball** вести́ (*det.*) мяч
• *v.i.* (of baby) пус|ка́ть, -ти́ть слю́ни

drier /'draɪə(r)/ *n.* = dryer

drift /drɪft/ *n.* **1** (of tide etc.) тече́ние **2** (heap of snow, leaves, etc.) нано́с, ку́ча **3** (meaning) смысл; I **get his** ~ я понима́ю, куда́ он кло́нит
• *v.i.* дрейфова́ть (*impf.*); **the boat** ~ed **out to sea** ло́дку отнесло́ в мо́ре; **they were friends but** ~ed **apart** они́ бы́ли друзья́ми, но их пути́ постепе́нно разошли́сь

drill[1] /drɪl/ *n.* (instrument) (small) дрель; (large) бур, бура́в; (dentist's) бормаши́на
• *v.t.* сверли́ть, про-; бури́ть, про-; ~ **a hole** сверли́ть, про- отве́рстие
• *v.i.* бури́ть (*impf.*); ~ **for oil** бури́ть (*impf.*) нефтяну́ю сква́жину

drill[2] /drɪl/ *n.* (mil.) строева́я подгото́вка
• *v.t.* (troops) обуч|а́ть, -и́ть строево́й подгото́вке

✎ **drink** /drɪŋk/ *n.* **1** (liquid) напи́ток, питьё **2** (quantity) глото́к **3** (alcoholic) вы́пивка, спиртно́й напи́ток
• *v.t. & i.* (*past* **drank**, *p.p.* **drunk**) пить, вы-
■ ~**-driving** *n.* (BrE) вожде́ние в нетре́звом состоя́нии; ~**ing water** *n.* питьева́я вода́

drinkable /'drɪŋkəb(ə)l/ *adj.* (safe to drink) питьево́й, го́дный для питья́; (tasty) вку́сный

drip /drɪp/ *n.* (action) ка́панье; (drop) ка́пля; (weak person) тря́пка; (med.) ка́пельница; **be on a** ~ быть под ка́пельницей
• *v.i.* (**dripped, dripping**) ка́пать (*impf.*)

dripping /'drɪpɪŋ/ *n.* **1** (in pl.) (AmE, liquid) ка́пли (*f. pl.*) **2** (BrE, cul.) топлёный жир

✎ **drive** /draɪv/ *n.* **1** (ride in vehicle) езда́; **go for a** ~ прокати́ться, поката́ться (*both pf.*) (на маши́не); **the station is an hour's** ~ **away** до ста́нции час езды́ **2** (private road) подъездна́я доро́га **3** (hit, stroke, at tennis etc.) драйв, си́льный уда́р **4** (energy) напо́ристость, напо́р **5** (organized effort) кампа́ния; **a** ~ **for new members** кампа́ния по привлече́нию но́вых чле́нов **6** (driving gear) переда́ча, при́вод **7** (comput.) при́вод; **disk** ~ дисково́д; **hard** ~ жёсткий диск
• *v.t.* (*past* **drove**, *p.p.* **driven**) **1** (force to move) гоня́ть (*indet.*), гнать (*det.*); выбива́ть, вы́бить **2** (operate) управля́ть (*impf.*) + *i.*; ~ **a car** води́ть (*indet.*) маши́ну **3** (impel, of objects): **he drove a nail into the plank** он вбил гвоздь в до́ску **4** (impel, fig.): ~ **sb mad** св|оди́ть, -ести́ кого́-н. с ума́
• *v.i.* (*past* **drove**, *p.p.* **driven**) **1** (operate vehicle) води́ть (*indet.*), вести́ (*det.*) маши́ну **2** (be impelled): **driving rain** проливно́й дождь

driven /'drɪv(ə)n/ *p.p. of* ▶ drive

⚘ **driver** /ˈdraɪvə(r)/ n. **1** (of vehicle) води́тель (*m.*), шофёр **2** (comput.) дра́йвер
■ ~'s license n. (AmE) води́тельские права́
driving /ˈdraɪvɪŋ/ n. езда́
■ ~ **instructor** n. преподава́тель (*m.*) автошко́лы; ~ **licence** n. (BrE) води́тельские права́; ~ **school** n. автошко́ла; ~ **test** n. экза́мен на вожде́ние
drizzle /ˈdrɪz(ə)l/ n. и́зморось
● *v.i.* мороси́ть (*impf.*)
dromedary /ˈdrɒmɪdəri/ n. дромаде́р, одного́рбый верблю́д
drone /drəʊn/ n. **1** (of bee) тру́тень (*m.*) **2** (of engine) гуде́ние; (of voice) жужжа́ние
● *v.i.* (hum) жужжа́ть (*impf.*); гуде́ть (*impf.*); (speak monotonously) бубни́ть (*impf.*) (infml)
drool /druːl/ *v.i.* пус|ка́ть, -ти́ть слю́ни
droop /druːp/ *v.i.* (of flowers, head) ни́кнуть, по-
⚘ **drop** /drɒp/ n. **1** (small quantity of liquid) ка́пля; (fig.): a ~ **in the bucket** (AmE), **ocean** ка́пля в мо́ре **2** (fall) паде́ние; ~ **in prices/ temperature** паде́ние цен; пониже́ние температу́ры; **there is a ~ of 30 feet behind this wall** за э́той стено́й 30-фу́товый обры́в
● *v.t.* (**dropped, dropping**) **1** (allow, cause to fall) роня́ть, урони́ть; ~ **a parcel at sb's house** оста́в|ля́ть, -а́вить паке́т у чьего́-н. до́ма **2** (bomb etc.) сбр|а́сывать, -о́сить **3** (lower): ~ **one's voice** пон|ижа́ть, -и́зить го́лос **4** (send, utter casually): ~ **sb a line** черкну́ть (*pf.*) кому́-н. па́ру строк; ~ **a hint** оброни́ть (*pf.*) намёк **5** (allow to descend, disembark) выса́живать, вы́садить; **please ~ me at the station** пожа́луйста, вы́садите меня́ у ста́нции
● *v.i.* (**dropped, dropping**) **1** (fall, descend) па́дать, упа́сть **2** (become weaker or lower) па́дать, упа́сть; **the wind ~ped** ве́тер стих/ ути́х **3** (sink, collapse) па́дать, упа́сть; **he ~ped (on) to his knees** он упа́л/опусти́лся на коле́ни
□ ~ **in** *v.i.* (infml): **he ~ped in on me** он загляну́л ко мне
□ ~ **off** *v.i.* (become fewer or less) ум|еньша́ться, -е́ньшиться; (infml, doze off) засну́ть (*pf.*)
□ ~ **out** *v.i.*: **five runners ~ped out** пять бегуно́в вы́были из соревнова́ния; **he ~ped out of school** он бро́сил шко́лу
■ ~**out** n. челове́к, поста́вивший себя́ вне о́бщества
droppings /ˈdrɒpɪŋz/ n. pl. (of animals and birds) помёт
dross /drɒs/ n. шлак, ока́лина; (fig.) отбро́сы (*m. pl.*)
drought /draʊt/ n. за́суха
drove /drəʊv/ *past of* ▸ **drive**
drown /draʊn/ *v.t.* **1** (kill by immersion) топи́ть, у- **2** (of sound) приглуш|а́ть, -и́ть
● *v.i.* тону́ть, у-
drowsy /ˈdraʊzi/ *adj.* (**drowsier, drowsiest**) (feeling sleepy) со́нный
drudgery /ˈdrʌdʒəri/ n. изнури́тельная рабо́та
⚘ **drug** /drʌg/ n. **1** (medicinal substance) медикаме́нт,

---

лека́рство **2** (narcotic or stimulant) нарко́тик
● *v.t.* (**drugged, drugging**) (food etc.) подме́ш|ивать, -а́ть нарко́тики в + *a.*; (person) да|ва́ть, -ть нарко́тики + *d.*
■ ~ **abuse** *adj.* употребле́ние нарко́тиков; ~ **addict** n. наркома́н; ~ **addiction** n. наркома́ния; ~**store** n. (AmE) ≈ апте́ка; ~ **trafficker** (also ~ **pusher**) n. наркоделе́ц
drum /drʌm/ n. **1** (instrument) бараба́н **2** (container for oil etc.) металли́ческая бо́чка
● *v.t.* (**drummed, drumming**) бараба́нить (*impf.*); ~ **up support** соз|ыва́ть, -ва́ть подмо́гу; ~ **sth into sb's head** вд|а́лбливать, -олби́ть что-н. кому́-н. в го́лову
● *v.i.* (**drummed, drumming**) бараба́нить (*impf.*)
■ ~**stick** n. бараба́нная па́лочка; (of fowl) но́жка
drummer /ˈdrʌmə(r)/ n. бараба́нщ|ик (-ица)
drunk¹ /drʌŋk/ n. пья́ный
● *adj.* пья́ный
drunk² /drʌŋk/ *p.p. of* ▸ **drink**
drunkard /ˈdrʌŋkəd/ n. пья́ница (*c.g.*), алкого́лик
drunken /ˈdrʌŋkən/ *adj.* пья́ный
⚘ **dry** /draɪ/ *adj.* (**drier** /ˈdraɪə(r)/, **driest** /ˈdraɪɪst/) **1** (free from moisture) сухо́й **2**: ~ **run** (trial) про́бный забе́г **3** (of humour) сухо́й; (of remark etc.) ирони́ческий
● *v.t.* суши́ть (*or* высу́шивать), вы́-; ~ **oneself** вытира́ться, вы́тереться; ~ **the dishes** вытира́ть, вы́тереть посу́ду; ~ **one's hands** вытира́ть, вы́тереть ру́ки; **dried fruit(s)** сушёные фру́кты
● *v.i.* со́хнуть, вы́-; суши́ться (*or* высу́шиваться), вы́-
■ ~**-clean** *v.t.* подв|ерга́ть, -е́ргнуть хими́ческой чи́стке
dryer /ˈdraɪə(r)/ n. суши́лка, суши́льный автома́т
DSL abbr. (of **digital subscriber line**) (teleph., comput.) (цифрова́я) вы́деленная ли́ния
DTD n. (abbr. of **Document Type Definition**) (comput.) описа́ние шабло́на докуме́нта
dual /ˈdjuːəl/ *adj.* двой́ственный, двойно́й
■ ~ **carriageway** n. (BrE) доро́га с двусторо́нним движе́нием и раздели́тельным барье́ром; ~ **nationality** n. двойно́е гражда́нство
dub /dʌb/ *v.t.* (**dubbed, dubbing**) (film) дубли́ровать (*impf.*)
dubious /ˈdjuːbɪəs/ *adj.* (feeling doubt) сомнева́ющийся; (inspiring mistrust) сомни́тельный
Dublin /ˈdʌblɪn/ n. Ду́блин
duchess /ˈdʌtʃɪs/ n. герцоги́ня
duchy /ˈdʌtʃi/ n. герцогство, кня́жество
duck¹ /dʌk/ n. (pl. ~ or ~s) (bird) у́тка; (as food) утиное мя́со
duck² /dʌk/ *v.t.* погру|жа́ть, -зи́ть; ~ **one's head** бы́стро наг|иба́ть, -ну́ть го́лову; (evade): ~ **a question** уклон|я́ться, -и́ться от отве́та
● *v.i.* окун|а́ться, -у́ться
duckling /ˈdʌklɪŋ/ n. утёнок

d

duct /dʌkt/ *n.* (anat.) канáл, протóк

dud /dʌd/ *adj.* (useless) непригóдный; (counterfeit) поддéльный

dude /duːd/ *n.* пижóн (infml)

⚘ **due** /djuː/ *n.* дóлжное
● *adj.* (payable) причитáющийся; **when is the rent ~?** когдá нáдо платúть за квартúру? **2** (proper) дóлжный, надлежáщий; **in ~ time** в своё врéмя; **in ~ course** в свою óчередь, свойм чередóм; **I am ~ for a haircut** мне порá постричься **3** (expected): **he is ~ to speak twice** он дóлжен выступить двáжды **4**: **~ to** (infml, owing to) благодаря + *d.*; (because of) из-за + *g.*
● *adv.* тóчно, прямо; **the village lies ~ south** дерéвня лежúт прямо на юг отсюда

duel /ˈdjuːəl/ *n.* дуэль

duet /djuːˈet/ *n.* дуэт

duffel, duffle /ˈdʌf(ə)l/ *n.* **1** (text.): **~ coat** пальтó из шерстянóй бáйки с капюшóном **2**: **~ bag** ≈ вещевóй мешóк

dug /dʌɡ/ *past and p.p. of* ▶ **dig**

duke /djuːk/ *n.* гéрцог

dull /dʌl/ *adj.* **1** (not clear or bright) тýсклый; **~ weather** пáсмурная погóда **2** (uninteresting) скýчный
● *v.t.* притуп|лять, -úть

duly /ˈdjuːlɪ/ *adv.* (in the proper manner) дóлжным óбразом; (at the right time) в дóлжное врéмя, своеврéменно

dumb /dʌm/ *adj.* **1** (unable to speak) немóй **2** (AmE, infml, stupid) глýпый
● *v.t.*: **~ down** (infml) популяризúровать (*impf.*, *pf.*)
■ **~-bell** *n.* гантéль

dumbfound, dumfound /dʌmˈfaʊnd/ *v.t.* ошарáш|ивать, -ить

dummy /ˈdʌmɪ/ *n.* кýкла; **tailor's ~** манекéн; **baby's ~** (BrE) сóска
● *adj.* (imitation) подставнóй
■ **~ run** *n.* прóбный забéг

dump /dʌmp/ *n.* **1** (rubbish tip) (мýсорная) свáлка **2** (ammunition store) врéменный полевóй склáд **3** (seedy place) дырá (infml)
● *v.t.* **1** (throw away) выбрáсывать, выбросить **2** (deposit carelessly) свáл|ивать, -úть **3** (infml, abandon) бросáть, брóсить

dumpy /ˈdʌmpɪ/ *adj.* (**dumpier, dumpiest**) призéмистый

dune /djuːn/ *n.* дюна

dung /dʌŋ/ *n.* (manure) навóз

dungarees /dʌŋɡəˈriːz/ *n. pl.* комбинезóн

dungeon /ˈdʌndʒ(ə)n/ *n.* темнúца

duo /ˈdjuːəʊ/ *n.* (*pl.* **~s**) дуэт

dupe /djuːp/ *n.* *v.t.* остав|лять, -áвить в дуракáх; над|увáть, -ýть

duplicate¹ /ˈdjuːplɪkət/ *n.* дубликáт; кóпия
● *adj.* запаснóй

duplicate² /ˈdjuːplɪkeɪt/ *v.t.* удв|áивать, -óить

duplicity /djuːˈplɪsɪtɪ/ *n.* двулúчность

durable /ˈdjʊərəb(ə)l/ *adj.* прóчный; долговéчный

duration /djʊəˈreɪʃ(ə)n/ *n.* продолжúтельность

duress /djʊəˈres/ *n.*: **under ~** под нажúмом/ давлéнием

⚘ **during** /ˈdjʊərɪŋ/ *prep.* (throughout) в течéние + *g.*; (at some point in) во врéмя + *g.*

dusk /dʌsk/ *n.* сýмер|ки (-ек)

dust /dʌst/ *n.* пыль
● *v.t.* **1** (remove ~ from) ст|ирáть, -ерéть пыль с + *g.* **2** (sprinkle) пос|ыпáть, -ыпать
■ **~bin** *n.* (BrE) мýсорный ящик; **~ cover** *n.* (for chair etc.) чехóл; (of book) суперобложка; **~cart** *n.* (BrE) мусоровóз; **~man** *n.* (BrE) мýсорщик; **~pan** *n.* совóк для мýсора

duster /ˈdʌstə(r)/ *n.* (BrE) тряпка для пыли

dusty /ˈdʌstɪ/ *adj.* (**dustier, dustiest**) пыльный

Dutch /dʌtʃ/ *n.* **1** (language) голлáндский/ нидерлáндский язык **2** (*as pl.*) (people) голлáндцы (*m. pl.*)
■ **~man** *n.* голлáндец; **~woman** *n.* голлáндка

dutiful /ˈdjuːtɪfʊl/ *adj.* прéданный; (obedient) послýшный

⚘ **duty** /ˈdjuːtɪ/ *n.* **1** (moral obligation) долг, обязанность **2** (official employment) служéбные обязанности; дежýрство; **on ~** на дежýрстве; **off ~** свобóдный; вне слýжбы; в свобóдное/неслужéбное врéмя **3** (fin.) пóшлина, сбор; **customs ~** тамóженная пóшлина
■ **~-free** *adj.* беспóшлинный

duvet /ˈduːveɪ/ *n.* (BrE) стёганое одеяло

DVD *abbr.* (*of* **digital versatile disk**) DVD, Ди-ви-дú (*m. indecl.*)
■ **~ player** *n.* DVD-плéер

dwarf /dwɔːf/ *n.* (*pl.* **dwarfs** *or* **dwarves**) (person, offens.) кáрлик; (in folklore) гном

dwell /dwel/ *v.i.* (*past and p.p.* **dwelt** *or* **dwelled**): **~ (up)on** (expatiate on) распространяться (*impf.*) о + *p.*

dwelling /ˈdwelɪŋ/ *n.* жильё, жилúще
■ **~ house** *n.* жилóй дом; **~ place** *n.* местожúтельство

dwelt /dwelt/ *past and p.p. of* ▶ **dwell**

dwindle /ˈdwɪnd(ə)l/ *v.i.* сокра|щáться, -тúться

dye /daɪ/ *n.* крáска
● *v.t.* (**dyeing**) крáсить, по-

dying /ˈdaɪɪŋ/ *adj.* умирáющий, предсмéртный

dynamic /daɪˈnæmɪk/ *n.* (force) движущая сúла; (*in pl.*) (science) динáмика
● *adj.* (pertaining to force) динамúческий; (energetic) динамúчный

dynamism /ˈdaɪnəmɪz(ə)m/ *n.* динамúзм

dynamite /ˈdaɪnəmaɪt/ *n.* динамúт (also fig.)

dynamo /ˈdaɪnəməʊ/ *n.* (*pl.* **~s**) динáмо (*nt. indecl.*); динáмо-машúна

dynasty /ˈdɪnəstɪ/ *n.* динáстия

dysentery /ˈdɪsəntrɪ/ *n.* дизентерúя

dyslexia /dɪsˈleksɪə/ *n.* (med.) дислéксия (*неспособность к чтению*)

dyslexic /dɪsˈleksɪk/ *adj.*: **he is ~** он дислéктик

Ee

E /iː/ *n.* **1** (mus.) ми (*nt. indecl.*) **2** (academic mark) «кол», единица

e|- *prefix* (comput.) электро́нный

■ **~-banking** *n.* ба́нковские услу́ги че́рез Интерне́т, Интерне́т-ба́нкинг; **~-book** *n.* электро́нная кни́га; **~-commerce** *n.* электро́нная комме́рция; **~-learning** *n.* электро́нное обуче́ние; **~-ticket** *n.* электро́нный биле́т (*на самолёт и т. п.*)

⚬ **each** /iːtʃ/ *pron. & adj.* ка́ждый; **he gave ~ (one) of us a book** он ка́ждому из нас дал по кни́ге; **he sat with a child on ~ side of him** он сиде́л ме́жду двумя́ детьми́; **the apples cost 20 pence ~** я́блоки сто́ят два́дцать пе́нсов шту́ка (*or* за шту́ку); **~ other** друг дру́га; **2 ~** по два/дво́е; **500 ~** по пятьсо́т

eager /ˈiːɡə(r)/ *adj.* стремя́щийся (**for:** к + *d.*); **he is ~ to go** он рвётся идти́

eagerness /ˈiːɡənɪs/ *n.* рве́ние, стремле́ние

eagle /ˈiːɡ(ə)l/ *n.* орёл

⚬ **ear¹** /ɪə(r)/ *n.* **1** (anat.) у́хо **2**: **~ for music** музыка́льный слух; **she plays by ~** она́ игра́ет на слух; **play it by ~** (fig.) пол|ага́ться, -ожи́ться на чутьё

■ **~ache** *n.* боль в у́хе; **~drum** *n.* бараба́нная перепо́нка; **~mark** *v.t.* (designate) предназн|ача́ть, -а́чить; ассигнова́ть (*impf., pf.*); **~phone, ~piece** *nn.* нау́шник; ра́ковина телефо́нной тру́бки; **~plug** *n.* заты́чка для уше́й; **~ring** *n.* серьга́

ear² /ɪə(r)/ *n.* (bot.) ко́лос

earl /ɜːl/ *n.* (брита́нский) граф

⚬ **earl|y** /ˈɜːlɪ/ *adj.* (**earlier, earliest**) ра́нний; **in one's ~y days, life** в ю́ности/мо́лодости; **in the ~y part of this century** в нача́ле э́того столе́тия; **we are ~y** мы пришли́ ра́но; **on Tuesday at (the) ~iest** не ра́ньше вто́рника ● *adv.* ра́но; **come as ~y as possible** приходи́те как мо́жно ра́ньше; **two hours ~ier** на два часа́ ра́ньше

⚬ **earn** /ɜːn/ *v.t. & i.* зараб|а́тывать, -о́тать; (deserve) заслу́ж|ивать, -и́ть; **~ one's living** зараба́тывать (*impf.*) на жизнь

earnest /ˈɜːnɪst/ *n.*: **in ~** серьёзно, всерьёз ● *adj.* серьёзный

earnings /ˈɜːnɪŋz/ *n. pl.* за́работок

⚬ **earth** /ɜːθ/ *n.* **1** (planet, world) земля́; **why on ~?** с како́й ста́ти?; заче́м то́лько?; **who on ~?** кто то́лько?; кто же?; **like nothing on ~** ни на что не похо́жий **2** (dry land) земля́ **3** (soil) земля́, по́чва **4** (BrE, elec.) земля́, заземле́ние

earthenware /ˈɜːθ(ə)nweə(r)/ *n.* гонча́рные изде́лия; гли́няная посу́да

earthly /ˈɜːθlɪ/ *adj.* земно́й; **there is no ~ reason to ...** нет ни мале́йшей причи́ны

(+ *inf.*); **he hasn't an ~** (BrE, infml) у него́ нет ни мале́йшего ша́нса

earthquake /ˈɜːθkweɪk/ *n.* землетрясе́ние

earthy /ˈɜːθɪ/ *adj.* (**earthier, earthiest**) (smell etc.) земляно́й; (fig.) приземлённый, грубова́тый

ease /iːz/ *n.* **1** (facility) лёгкость **2** (comfort) поко́й, о́тдых, досу́г; **be, feel at ~** чу́вствовать (*impf.*) себя́ непринуждённо; **put sb at his/her ~** приободри́ть (*pf.*) кого́-н. ● *v.t.*: **~ tension** осл|абля́ть, -а́бить напряжённость; **~ congestion** разгру|жа́ть, -зи́ть движе́ние; **~ sb's anxiety** успок|а́ивать, -о́ить кого́-н. ● *v.i.*: **~ off on drinking** (infml) пить (*impf.*) ме́ньше; **the pressure of work ~d (up)** напряжённость рабо́ты спа́ла

easel /ˈiːz(ə)l/ *n.* мольбе́рт

⚬ **easily** /ˈiːzɪlɪ/ *adv.* легко́, без труда́; **he is ~ the best** он безусло́вно са́мый лу́чший; **he may ~ be late** он вполне́ мо́жет опозда́ть

⚬ **east** /iːst/ *n.* восто́к; **to the ~ of London** к восто́ку от Ло́ндона ● *adv.* на восто́к, к восто́ку; **travel ~ of Moscow** к восто́ку от Москвы́ ● *adj.* восто́чный; **~ wind** восто́чный ве́тер

Easter /ˈiːstə(r)/ *n.* Па́сха; **at ~** на Па́сху

■ **~ Day/Sunday** *n.* Све́тлое/Христо́во воскресе́нье, Па́сха; **~ Monday** *n.* Све́тлый понеде́льник; **~ egg** *n.* пасха́льное яйцо́

easterly /ˈiːstəlɪ/ *adj.* (wind) восто́чный ве́тер ● *adj.* восто́чный

⚬ **eastern** /ˈiːst(ə)n/ *adj.* восто́чный

eastward /ˈiːstwəd/ *adj.* восто́чный ● *adv.* (*also* **~s**) на восто́к; к восто́ку, в восто́чном направле́нии

⚬ **easy** /ˈiːzɪ/ *adj.* (**easier, easiest**) **1** (not difficult) лёгкий; **the book is ~ to read** кни́га легко́ чита́ется; **he is ~ to get on with** у него́ лёгкий хара́ктер **2** (comfortable) споко́йный, лёгкий; **he leads an ~ life** у него́ лёгкая жизнь; **I am ~** (infml, have no preference) мне всё равно́ ● *adv.*: **take it ~!** (don't exert yourself) рассла́бьтесь!; (don't worry) не волну́йтесь!; (don't hurry) не спеши́те!

■ **~-going** *adj.* благоду́шный

⚬ **eat** /iːt/ *v.t. & i.* (*past* **ate**, *p.p.* **eaten**) есть, съ-; (politely, of others) ку́шать, по-/с-; **~ one's dinner** пообе́дать/поу́жинать (*pf.*)

□ **~ out** *v.i.* есть (*impf.*) вне до́ма

□ **~ up** *v.t.* до|еда́ть, -е́сть; (fig.): **he is ~en up with curiosity** его́ съеда́ет любопы́тство

eaten /ˈiːt(ə)n/ *p.p. of* ▸ **eat**

eavesdrop /ˈiːvzdrɒp/ *v.i.* подслу́ш|ивать, -ать

e

ebb /eb/ *n.* отли́в
● *v.i.* (of tide) уб|ыва́ть, -ы́ть; (fig.)
ослаб|ева́ть, -е́ть

ebony /'ebənɪ/ *n.* эбе́новое/чёрное де́рево;
(fig., black) чёрный как смоль

ebullient /ɪ'bʌlɪənt/ *adj.* кипу́чий, по́лный
энтузиа́зма

eccentric /ɪk'sentrɪk/ *n.* чуда́к; оригина́л
● *adj.* эксцентри́чный

eccentricity /eksen'trɪsɪtɪ/ *n.* (quality)
чуда́чество, эксцентри́чность; (eccentric habit)
стра́нность

ecclesiastical /ɪkli:zɪ'æstɪk(ə)l/ *adj.*
духо́вный, церко́вный

ECG *abbr.* (*of* **electrocardiogram**) ЭКГ
(электрокардиогра́мма)

echelon /'eʃəlɒn/ *n.* **1** (level, rank) чин, ранг
2 (mil. formation) эшело́н

echo /'ekəʊ/ *n.* (*pl.* **echoes**) э́хо
● *v.t.* (**echoes, echoed**) вто́рить (*impf.*) +
d.; ~ **sb's words** вто́рить чьим-н. слова́м
● *v.i.* (**echoes, echoed**) отд|ава́ться, -а́ться
э́хом

eclair /ɪ'kleə(r)/ *n.* экле́р

eclectic /ɪ'klektɪk/ *adj.* эклекти́ческий,
эклекти́чный

eclipse /ɪ'klɪps/ *n.* (astron.) затме́ние
● *v.t.* (lit., fig.) затм|ева́ть, -и́ть

eco-friendly /'i:kəʊfrendlɪ/ *adj.*
экологи́чески безвре́дный

eco-label /'i:kəʊleɪb(ə)l/ *n* экологи́ческий
я́рлык

ecological /i:kə'lɒdʒɪk(ə)l/ *adj.*
экологи́ческий

ecologist /ɪ'kɒlədʒɪst/ *n.* эко́лог

ecology /ɪ'kɒlədʒɪ/ *n.* эколо́гия

✦ **economic** /i:kə'nɒmɪk, ek-/ *adj.*
1 экономи́ческий, хозя́йственный
2 (profitable) рента́бельный
■ ~ **migrant** *n.* экономи́ческий мигра́нт

economical /i:kə'nɒmɪk(ə)l, ek-/ *adj.*
эконо́мный, бережли́вый

economics /i:kə'nɒmɪks, ek-/ *n. pl.* (*often
treated as sg.*) эконо́мика

economist /ɪ'kɒnəmɪst/ *n.* экономи́ст

economize /ɪ'kɒnəmaɪz/ *v.i.* эконо́мить, с-; ~
on fuel эконо́мить, с- то́пливо

✦ **economy** /ɪ'kɒnəmɪ/ *n.* **1** (thrift) эконо́мия,
хозя́йственность, бережли́вость **2** (economic
system) эконо́мика, хозя́йство
■ ~ **class** *n.* эконо́м-класс

ecosystem /'i:kəʊsɪstəm/ *n.* экосисте́ма

ecotourism /i:kəʊ'tʊərɪz(ə)m/ *n.* экотури́зм

ecotourist /i:kəʊ'tʊərɪst/ *n.* экотури́ст

ecstasy /'ekstəsɪ/ *n.* **1** (strong emotion) экста́з
2 (the drug) э́кстези (*m. indecl.*)

ecstatic /ɪk'stætɪk/ *adj.* экстати́ческий, в
экста́зе

Ecuador /'ekwədɔ:(r)/ *n.* Эквадо́р

Ecuadorean /ekwə'dɔ:rɪən/ *n.* эквадо́р|ец (-ка)
● *adj.* эквадо́рский

✦ ключева́я ле́ксика

eczema /'eksɪmə/ *n.* экзе́ма

✦ **edge** /edʒ/ *n.* **1** (sharpened side) остриё, ле́звие
2 (fig.): **be on** ~ быть в не́рвном состоя́нии
3 (border) грань; край
● *v.t. & i.* **1** (border) окайм|ля́ть, -и́ть; ~ **a
path with plants** обса́|живать, -ди́ть доро́жку
цвета́ми **2** (move obliquely): ~ **one's way
through a crowd** проб|ира́ться, -ра́ться че́рез
толпу́; **he** ~**d closer to me** он пододви́нулся
ко мне

edgeways /'edʒweɪz/, **edgewise** /'edʒwaɪz/
advs. бо́ком; **I could not get a word in** ~ я не
мог сло́ва вста́вить

edible /'edɪb(ə)l/ *adj.* съедо́бный

edifice /'edɪfɪs/ *n.* зда́ние; (fig.) структу́ра,
систе́ма

edifying /'edɪfaɪɪŋ/ *adj.* назида́тельный,
поучи́тельный

Edinburgh /'edɪnbərə/ *n.* Э́динбу́рг

edit /'edɪt/ *v.t.* (**edited, editing**) (a text,
newspaper) редакти́ровать, от-; (film etc.)
монти́ровать, с-

✦ **edition** /ɪ'dɪʃ(ə)n/ *n.* изда́ние; (e.g. of newspaper)
вы́пуск

✦ **editor** /'edɪtə(r)/ *n.* реда́ктор

editorial /edɪ'tɔ:rɪəl/ *n.* передови́ца,
передова́я статья́
● *adj.* редакцио́нный; реда́кторский
■ ~ **office** *n.* реда́кция

educate /'edjʊkeɪt/ *v.t.* да|ва́ть, -ть
образова́ние + *d.*; ~**d speech** культу́рная речь

✦ **education** /edjʊ'keɪʃ(ə)n/ *n.* образова́ние,
культу́ра; (upbringing) воспита́ние

educational /edjʊ'keɪʃən(ə)l/ *adj.* (pert.
to education) образова́тельный; (instructive)
воспита́тельный, уче́бный

EEC *abbr.* (*of* **European Economic
Community**) ЕЭС (Европе́йское
экономи́ческое соо́бщество)

eel /i:l/ *n.* у́горь (*m.*)

eerie /'ɪərɪ/ (AmE **eery**) *adj.* (**eerier, eeriest**)
жу́ткий

✦ **effect** /ɪ'fekt/ *n.* **1** (result) результа́т;
punishment had no ~ **on him** наказа́ние
на него́ не поде́йствовало; **to no** ~
безрезульта́тно; **take** ~ (e.g. medicine)
де́йствовать, по- **2** (validity) де́йствие; **come
into** ~ вступ|а́ть, -и́ть в си́лу **3** (sensual etc.
impression) впечатле́ние, эффе́кт
● *v.t.* осуществ|ля́ть, -и́ть; выполня́ть,
вы́полнить

✦ **effective** /ɪ'fektɪv/ *adj.* **1** (efficacious)
эффекти́вный **2** (operative) име́ющий си́лу;
де́йствующий

effeminate /ɪ'femɪnət/ *adj.* женоподо́бный

effervesce /efə'ves/ *v.i.* пузыри́ться (*impf.*);
(fig.) искри́ться (*impf.*)

effervescence /efə'ves(ə)ns/ *n.* шипе́ние;
(fig.) весёлое оживле́ние, кипе́ние

effervescent /efə'ves(ə)nt/ *adj.* пузыря́щийся,
шипу́чий; (fig.) искря́щийся, кипу́чий

effete /ɪ'fi:t/ *adj.* сла́бый, упа́дочный;
(degenerate) вы́родившийся

efficacious /efɪˈkeɪʃəs/ *adj.* эффекти́вный, де́йственный

efficacy /ˈefɪkəsɪ/ *n.* эффекти́вность, де́йственность

efficiency /ɪˈfɪʃənsɪ/ *n.* делови́тость; эффекти́вность, производи́тельность

efficient /ɪˈfɪʃ(ə)nt/ *adj.* делови́тый, исполни́тельный; эффекти́вный, производи́тельный

effigy /ˈefɪdʒɪ/ *n.* изображе́ние; **burn sb in ~** сжечь (*pf.*) чьё-н. изображе́ние/чу́чело

♂ **effort** /ˈefət/ *n.* уси́лие, попы́тка; (*in pl.*) рабо́та; **make an ~** приложи́ть (*pf.*) уси́лие

effortless /ˈefətlɪs/ *adj.* непринуждённый; не тре́бующий уси́лий; **with ~ skill** с непринуждённой ло́вкостью

effrontery /ɪˈfrʌntərɪ/ *n.* на́глость, наха́льство

effusive /ɪˈfjuːsɪv/ *adj.* экспанси́вный; **he was ~ in his gratitude** он рассы́пался в благода́рностях

e.g. *abbr.* (*of* **exempli gratia**) напр. (наприме́р)

egalitarian /ɪgælɪˈteərɪən/ *adj.* эгалита́рный

egalitarianism /ɪgælɪˈteərɪənɪz(ə)m/ *n.* эгалитари́зм

♂ **egg**¹ /eg/ *n.* яйцо́
■ **~ cup** *n.* рю́мка для яйца́; **~plant** *n.* (AmE) баклажа́н

egg² /eg/ *v.t.:* **~ on** подстрек|а́ть, -ну́ть

ego /ˈiːgəʊ/ *n.* (*pl.* **egos**) (self-esteem) самолю́бие

egocentric /iːgəʊˈsentrɪk/ *adj.* эгоцентри́ческий, эгоцентри́чный

egoism /ˈiːgəʊɪz(ə)m/ *n.* эгои́зм

egoist /ˈiːgəʊɪst/ *n.* эгои́ст (-ка)

egotist /ˈiːgətɪst/ *n.* эгоцентри́ст (-ка)

egotistic /iːgəˈtɪstɪk/, **egotistical** /iːgəˈtɪstɪk(ə)l/ *adjs.* эгоцентри́ческий

Egypt /ˈiːdʒɪpt/ *n.* Еги́пет

Egyptian /ɪˈdʒɪpʃ(ə)n/ *n.* египтя́н|ин (-ка)
● *adj.* еги́петский

eiderdown /ˈaɪdədaʊn/ *n.* (BrE, quilt) пухо́вое одея́ло

♂ **eight** /eɪt/ *n.* (число́/но́мер) во́семь; (figure; thing numbered 8; group of **~**) восьмёрка
● *adj.* во́семь + *g. pl.*

eighteen /eɪˈtiːn/ *n.* восемна́дцать
● *adj.* восемна́дцать + *g. pl.*

eighteenth /eɪˈtiːnθ/ *n.* (date) восемна́дцатое число́; (fraction) одна́ восемна́дцатая
● *adj.* восемна́дцатый

eighth /eɪtθ/ *n.* (date) восьмо́е (число́); (fraction) одна́ восьма́я
● *adj.* восьмо́й

eightieth /ˈeɪtɪθ/ *n.* одна́ восьмидеся́тая
● *adj.* восьмидеся́тый

eight|y /ˈeɪtɪ/ *n.* во́семьдесят; **he is in his ~ies** ему́ за во́семьдесят

♂ **either** /ˈaɪðə(r)/ *pron. & adj.* (one or other) любо́й, ка́ждый; тот и́ли друго́й; **do ~ of these roads lead to town?** кака́я-нибудь из э́тих доро́г ведёт к го́роду?; **~ book will do** люба́я из э́тих книг годи́тся; **I do not like ~**

(one) мне не нра́вится ни тот, ни друго́й; **on ~ side of the window** по обе́им сторона́м окна́
● *adv. & conj.:* **I do not like Smith, or Jones ~** я не люблю́ ни Сми́та, ни Джо́нса; (intensive): **it was not long ago ~** это бы́ло не так уж давно́; **~ ... or** и́ли... и́ли; ли́бо... ли́бо; то ли... то ли; не то... не то

ejaculate /ɪˈdʒækjʊleɪt/ *v.t.* (utter suddenly) воскл|ица́ть, -и́кнуть
● *v.i.* (physiol.) эякули́ровать (*impf., pf.*), изв|ерга́ть, -е́ргнуть се́мя

ejaculation /ɪdʒækjʊˈleɪʃ(ə)n/ *n.* (physiol.) эякуля́ция

eject /ɪˈdʒekt/ *v.t.* (lit., fig.) выбра́сывать, вы́бросить
● *v.i.* (aeron.): **the pilot ~ed** лётчик катапульти́ровался

eke /iːk/ *v.t.:* **~ out** (supplement) восп|олня́ть, -о́лнить; **~ out a livelihood** ко́е-как перебива́ться (*impf.*)

elaborate¹ /ɪˈlæbərət/ *adj.* иску́сно сде́ланный

elaborate² /ɪˈlæbəreɪt/ *v.t.* разраб|а́тывать, -о́тать; **~ on** (develop) разв|ива́ть, -и́ть; (make more precise) уточн|я́ть, -и́ть

elapse /ɪˈlæps/ *v.i.* про|ходи́ть, -йти́

elastic /ɪˈlæstɪk/ *n.* рези́нка
● *adj.* (lit.) эласти́чный; упру́гий; (fig.) ги́бкий
■ **~ band** *n.* (BrE) рези́нка

elate /ɪˈleɪt/ *v.t.:* **she was ~d at the news** но́вость окры́ли́ла её

elation /ɪˈleɪʃ(ə)n/ *n.* ликова́ние, восто́рг

elbow /ˈelbəʊ/ *n.* ло́коть (*m.*)
■ **~ grease** *n.* (joc.) уси́ленная полиро́вка

elder¹ /ˈeldə(r)/ *adj.* ста́рший

elder² /ˈeldə(r)/ *n.* (bot.) бузина́ (*красная, чёрное*)
■ **~berry** *n.* я́года бузины́

elderly /ˈeldəlɪ/ *adj.* пожило́й

eldest /ˈeldɪst/ *adj.* са́мый ста́рший

♂ **elect** /ɪˈlekt/ *adj.* и́збранный; **president-~** и́збранный президе́нт
● *v.t.* изб|ира́ть, -ра́ть; выбира́ть, вы́брать; **they ~ed him king** они́ избра́ли его́ королём; **he ~ed to go** он предпочёл пойти́

♂ **election** /ɪˈlekʃ(ə)n/ *n.* вы́боры (*m. pl.*)
■ **~ campaign** *n.* предвы́борная/ избира́тельная кампа́ния

electoral /ɪˈlektər(ə)l/ *adj.* избира́тельный

electorate /ɪˈlektərət/ *n.* (body of voters) избира́тели (*m. pl.*)

♂ **electric** /ɪˈlektrɪk/ *adj.* электри́ческий
■ **~ blanket** *n.* одея́ло-гре́лка; **~ shock** *n.* уда́р электри́ческим то́ком

electrical /ɪˈlektrɪk(ə)l/ *adj.* электри́ческий
■ **~ engineering** *n.* электроте́хника

electrician /ɪlekˈtrɪʃ(ə)n/ *n.* эле́ктрик (infml), (электро)монтёр

♂ **electricity** /ɪlekˈtrɪsɪtɪ/ *n.* электри́чество

electrify /ɪˈlektrɪfaɪ/ *v.t.* (also fig.) электризова́ть, на-

electrocardiogram /ɪlektrəʊˈkɑːdɪəgræm/ *n.* электрокардиогра́мма

electrocute /ɪ'lektrəkjuːt/ v.t. (execute)
казни́ть (impf., pf.) на электри́ческом сту́ле;
he was ~d (by accident) его́ уби́ло то́ком

electrode /ɪ'lektrəʊd/ n. электро́д

electromagnetic /ɪlektrəʊmæg'netɪk/ adj.
электромагни́тный

electron /ɪ'lektrɒn/ n. электро́н
■ ~ **microscope** n. электро́нный микроско́п

❧ **electronic** /ɪlek'trɒnɪk/ adj. электро́нный
■ ~ **tagging** n. электро́нная слёжка

electronics /ɪlek'trɒnɪks/ n. электро́ника

elegance /'elɪɡ(ə)ns/ n. элега́нтность,
изя́щество

elegant /'elɪɡ(ə)nt/ adj. элега́нтный, изя́щный

❧ **element** /'elɪmənt/ n. **1** (earth, air, etc.) стихи́я;
(fig.): in one's ~ в свое́й стихи́и **2** (chem.)
элеме́нт **3** (feature, constituent) элеме́нт;
составна́я часть **4** (elec.) элеме́нт

elementary /elɪ'mentərɪ/ adj. элемента́рный
■ ~ **school** n. нача́льная шко́ла

elephant /'elɪfənt/ n. (pl. ~ or ~s) слон

elevate /'elɪveɪt/ v.t. (lit.) подн|има́ть, -я́ть; ~d
railway надзе́мная желе́зная доро́га

elevated /'elɪveɪtɪd/ adj. (lofty) высо́кий,
возвы́шенный

elevator /'elɪveɪtə(r)/ n. **1** (machine)
грузоподъёмник, элева́тор **2** (AmE, lift) лифт

eleven /ɪ'lev(ə)n/ n. оди́ннадцать
● adj. оди́ннадцать + g. pl.

elevenses /ɪ'levənzɪz/ n. pl. (BrE, infml) лёгкий
за́втрак о́коло оди́ннадцати часо́в утра́

eleventh /ɪ'levənθ/ n. (date) оди́ннадцатое
(число́); (fraction) одна́ оди́ннадцатая
● adj. оди́ннадцатый

elf /elf/ n. (pl. **elves**) эльф

elicit /ɪ'lɪsɪt/ v.t. (**elicited**, **eliciting**)
извл|ека́ть, -е́чь; допы́т|ываться, -а́ться; ~
a fact выявля́ть, вы́явить факт; ~ a reply
доби́ться (pf.) отве́та

eligibility /elɪdʒɪ'bɪlɪtɪ/ n. пра́во на избра́ние

eligible /'elɪdʒɪb(ə)l/ adj. могу́щий быть
и́збранным; to be ~ for име́ть пра́во на + a.

eliminate /ɪ'lɪmɪneɪt/ v.t. **1** (rule out)
исключ|а́ть, -и́ть **2** (sport): he was ~d in the
first round он вы́был в пе́рвом ту́ре

elimination /ɪlɪmɪ'neɪʃ(ə)n/ n. устране́ние

elite /eɪ'liːt/ n. эли́та; an ~ regiment отбо́рный
полк

elitist /ɪ'liːtɪst/ adj. элита́рный

elixir /ɪ'lɪksɪə(r)/ n. эликси́р

Elizabethan /ɪlɪzə'biːθ(ə)n/ n. совреме́нник
эпо́хи (короле́вы) Елизаве́ты
● adj. елизаве́тинский, относя́щийся к эпо́хе
короле́вы Елизаве́ты

elk /elk/ n. (pl. ~ or ~s) лось (m.)

ellipse /ɪ'lɪps/ n. э́ллипс, ова́л

elliptical /ɪ'lɪptɪkəl/ adj. (math., gram.)
эллипти́ческий

elm /elm/ n. (tree; wood) вяз

elongate /'iːlɒŋɡeɪt/ v.t. удлин|я́ть, -и́ть

elongation /iːlɒŋ'ɡeɪʃ(ə)n/ n. удлине́ние

elope /ɪ'ləʊp/ v.i. (та́йно) бежа́ть (det.)
(с возлю́бленным)

eloquent /'eləkwənt/ adj. красноречи́вый

El Salvador /el 'sælvədɔː(r)/ n. Сальвадо́р

❧ **else** /els/ adj. & adv. друго́й; no one ~ никто́
друго́й; бо́льше никто́; everyone ~ все
остальны́е; nowhere ~ ни в како́м друго́м
ме́сте; everywhere ~ везде́, то́лько не
здесь/там; what ~ could I say? что ещё я
мог сказа́ть?; do you want anything ~? вы
хоти́те ещё что-нибу́дь?; or ~ и́ли же

elsewhere /els'weə(r)/ adv. (in another place)
где́-нибудь ещё, в друго́м ме́сте; (to another
place) куда́-нибудь ещё, в друго́е ме́сто

elude /ɪ'luːd/ v.t. изб|ега́ть, -ежа́ть, -е́гнуть +
g.; ускольз|а́ть, -ну́ть от + g.

elusive /ɪ'luːsɪv/ adj. неулови́мый

elves /elvz/ pl. of ▶ elf

emaciated /ɪ'meɪsɪeɪtɪd/ adj. истощённый

❧ **email**, **e-mail** /'iːmeɪl/ n. (system, letters)
электро́нная по́чта; (letter) электро́нное
письмо́
● v.t. (a person) пос|ыла́ть, -ла́ть электро́нное
письмо́ (кому́-н.); (information, a document)
пос|ыла́ть, -ла́ть электро́нной по́чтой
■ ~ **address** n. электро́нный а́дрес

emanate /'eməneɪt/ v.i. излуча́ться (impf.);
истека́ть (impf.)

emancipate /ɪ'mænsɪpeɪt/ v.t.
эмансипи́ровать (impf., pf.)

emancipation /ɪmænsɪ'peɪʃ(ə)n/ n.
эмансипа́ция

embalm /ɪm'bɑːm/ v.t. бальзами́ровать
(impf., pf.) (pf. also за-, на-)

embankment /ɪm'bæŋkmənt/ n. (wall etc.)
на́сыпь, гать; (roadway) на́бережная

embargo /em'bɑːɡəʊ/ n. (pl. ~es) эмба́рго
(nt. indecl.); lift, raise an ~ снима́ть, снять
эмба́рго (from: c + g.)

embark /ɪm'bɑːk/ v.i. (go on board) грузи́ться,
по-; сади́ться, сесть на кора́бль; (fig.)
пус|ка́ться, -ти́ться (on: в + a.); ~ on an
undertaking предприн|има́ть, -я́ть де́ло

embarkation /embɑː'keɪʃ(ə)n/ n. (of goods)
погру́зка; (of people) поса́дка

embarrass /ɪm'bærəs/ v.t. смущ|а́ть, -ти́ть

embarrassing /ɪm'bærəsɪŋ/ adj.
щекотли́вый, вызыва́ющий смуще́ние

embarrassment /ɪm'bærəsmənt/ n.
смуще́ние, замеша́тельство

embassy /'embəsɪ/ n. посо́льство

embattled /ɪm'bæt(ə)ld/ adj. (ready for war)
приведённый в боеву́ю гото́вность; (in
difficulties) в тру́дном положе́нии

embed /ɪm'bed/ v.t. (**embedded**,
embedding): stones ~ded in rock ка́мни,
вмуро́ванные в скалу́; facts ~ded in one's
memory фа́кты, вре́завшиеся в па́мять

embellish /ɪm'belɪʃ/ v.t. укр|аша́ть, -а́сить;
(a tale etc.) приукра́ш|ивать, -сить

embellishment /ɪm'belɪʃmənt/ n.
приукра́шивание

embers /'embəz/ *n. pl.* (coals etc.) тлеющие угольки (*m. pl.*)

embezzle /ɪm'bez(ə)l/ *v.t.* растрал|чивать, -тить

embezzlement /ɪm'bezəlmənt/ *n.* растрата

emblem /'embləm/ *n.* эмблема; (national) герб

embodiment /ɪm'bɒdɪmənt/ *n.* воплощение, олицетворение

embody /ɪm'bɒdɪ/ *v.t.* вопло|щать, -тить

embrace /ɪm'breɪs/ *n.* объятие
● *v.t.* **1** (clasp in one's arms) обн|имать, -ять
2 (include) включ|ать, -ить
● *v.i.* обн|иматься, -яться

embroider /ɪm'brɔɪdə(r)/ *v.t.* вышивать, вышить; (a story etc.) приукра|шивать, -сить

embroidery /ɪm'brɔɪdərɪ/ *n.* вышивание, вышивка

embroil /ɪm'brɔɪl/ *v.t.* впут|ывать, -ать; вовл|екать, -ечь

embryo /'embrɪəʊ/ *n.* (*pl.* ~**s**) эмбрион

embryology /embrɪ'ɒlədʒɪ/ *n.* эмбриология

embryonic /embrɪ'ɒnɪk/ *adj.* эмбриональный; (fig.) недоразвитый; в зародыше

emerald /'emər(ə)ld/ *n.* изумруд
■ ~ **green** *n.* изумрудно-зелёный

✓ **emerge** /ɪ'mɜːdʒ/ *v.i.* всплы|вать, -ть; появ|ляться, -иться; (fig.) возн|икать, -икнуть

emergence /ɪ'mɜːdʒ(ə)ns/ *n.* появление, возникновение

✓ **emergency** /ɪ'mɜːdʒənsɪ/ *n.* авария; крайняя необходимость; (for use in ~) запасной, запасный, временный
■ ~ **exit** *n.* запасный выход; ~ **landing** *n.* вынужденная посадка

emigrant /'emɪɡrənt/ *n.* эмигрант (-ка)

emigrate /'emɪɡreɪt/ *v.i.* эмигрировать (*impf., pf.*)

emigration /emɪ'ɡreɪʃ(ə)n/ *n.* эмиграция

émigré /'emɪɡreɪ/ *n.* эмигрант (-ка) (*особенно политический*)

eminence /'emɪnəns/ *n.* **1** (high ground) высота; возвышение **2** (celebrity) знаменитость; reach, win, attain ~ добиться (*pf.*) славы/известности **3** (title): His E~ Его Высокопреосвященство

eminent /'emɪnənt/ *adj.* (of person) выдающийся, знаменитый

emission /ɪ'mɪʃ(ə)n/ *n.* (of gas, heat) выделение; (of light) излучение; (*in pl.*) выбросы

emit /ɪ'mɪt/ *v.t.* (**emitted**, **emitting**) (smoke, smell) испус|кать, -тить; (light) излуч|ать, -ить; (gas, heat) выделять, выделить; (sound) изд|авать, -ать

emoticon /ɪ'məʊtɪkɒn/ *n.* эмотикон, смайл(ик)

✓ **emotion** /ɪ'məʊʃ(ə)n/ *n.* (feeling) эмоция; (agitation) волнение

✓ **emotional** /ɪ'məʊʃən(ə)l/ *adj.* эмоциональный

emotive /ɪ'məʊtɪv/ *adj.* эмоционально волнующий

empathy /'empəθɪ/ *n.* сопереживание

emperor /'empərə(r)/ *n.* император

emphasis /'emfəsɪs/ *n.* (*pl.* **emphases** /-siːz/) ударение, выразительность; lay ~ on подчёрк|ивать, -нуть

✓ **emphasize** /'emfəsaɪz/ *v.t.* подчёрк|ивать, -нуть

emphatic /ɪm'fætɪk/ *adj.* эмфатический, выразительный

emphysema /emfɪ'siːmə/ *n.* (med.) эмфизема

empire /'empaɪə(r)/ *n.* империя

empirical /ɪm'pɪrɪk(ə)l/ *adj.* эмпирический

empiricism /ɪm'pɪrɪsɪz(ə)m/ *n.* эмпиризм

✓ **employ** /ɪm'plɔɪ/ *v.t.* **1** (engage to work) нан|имать, -ять; дава|ть, дать работу + *d.*; be ~ed работать (*impf.*), служить (*impf.*) **2** (use) примен|ять, -ить

✓ **employee** /em'plɔɪ/ *n.* служащий

✓ **employer** /ɪm'plɔɪə(r)/ *n.* работодатель (*m.*)

✓ **employment** /ɪm'plɔɪmənt/ *n.* **1** (service for pay) работа, служба **2** (occupation) занятие **3** (use) применение, использование
■ ~ **agency** *n.* кадровое агентство; бюро по трудоустройству

empower /ɪm'paʊə(r)/ *v.t.* уполномочи|вать, -ть

empress /'emprɪs/ *n.* императрица

emptiness /'emptɪnɪs/ *n.* (lit., fig.) пустота

empt|y /'emptɪ/ *adj.* (**emptier**, **emptiest**) пустой; порожний; (fig.): ~y words пустые слова
● *v.t.* опорожн|ять, -ить; ~y water out of a jug вылить (*pf.*) воду из кувшина
● *v.i.* опорожн|яться, -иться; the streets ~ied улицы опустели
■ ~y-handed *adj.* с пустыми руками

EMS *abbr. of* **1** (**European Monetary System**) ЕВС (Европейская валютная система) **2** (**Enhanced Message/Messaging Service**): ~ message EMS-сообщение

emu /'iːmjuː/ *n.* эму (*m. indecl.*)

emulate /'emjʊleɪt/ *v.t.* подражать (*impf.*) + *d.*

emulsion /ɪ'mʌlʃ(ə)n/ *n.* эмульсия

✓ **enable** /ɪ'neɪb(ə)l/ *v.t.* (make able) да|вать, -ть возможность + *d.*; (make possible) делать, с-возможным

enact /ɪ'nækt/ *v.t.* (make law) вв|одить, -ести в действие; утвер|ждать, -дить; (act) игр|ать, сыгр|ать (*роль*); разыгр|ывать, -ать; (carry out) соверш|ать, -ить

enactment /ɪ'næktmənt/ *n.* введение закона в силу; утверждение (закона *и т. н.*); (of sb's fantasies) игра

enamel /ɪ'næm(ə)l/ *n.* эмаль

encampment /ɪn'kæmpmənt/ *n.* расположение лагерем; (camp) лагерь (*m.*)

encapsulate /ɪn'kæpsjʊleɪt/ *v.t.* (fig.) заключ|ать, -ить в себе

enchant /ɪn'tʃɑːnt/ *v.t.* обвор|аживать, -ожить; очаров|ывать, -ать

enchanting /ɪn'tʃɑːntɪŋ/ *adj.* чарующий, обворожительный

e

encircle /ɪn'sɜːk(ə)l/ v.t. окруж|а́ть, -и́ть

enclave /'enkleɪv/ n. анкла́в

enclos|e /ɪn'kləʊz/ v.t. **1** (surround, fence) окруж|а́ть, -и́ть; ~e a garden with a wall обн|оси́ть, -ести́ сад стено́й **2** (in letter etc.) при|кла́дывать, -ложи́ть; a letter ~ing an invoice письмо́ с приложе́нием счёта

enclosure /ɪn'kləʊʒə(r)/ n. (fence) огражде́ние, огра́да; (in letter) приложе́ние

encode /ɪn'kəʊd/ v.t. коди́ровать (impf., pf.) (pf. also за-); шифрова́ть, за-

encompass /ɪn'kʌmpəs/ v.t. (surround) окруж|а́ть, -и́ть; (contain, comprise) заключ|а́ть, -и́ть; (envelop) оку́т|ывать, -ать

encore /'ɒŋkɔː(r)/ n. & int. бис

encounter /ɪn'kaʊntə(r)/ n. встре́ча
 ● v.t. встр|еча́ться, -е́титься с + i.

ꝺ **encourage** /ɪn'kʌrɪdʒ/ v.t. ободр|я́ть, -и́ть; I ~d him to go я угова́ривал его́ идти́

encouragement /ɪn'kʌrɪdʒmənt/ n. ободре́ние, поощре́ние, подде́ржка

encouraging /ɪn'kʌrɪdʒɪŋ/ adj. ободря́ющий

encroach /ɪn'krəʊtʃ/ v.i. поку|ша́ться, -си́ться (on: на + a.); ~ on sb's rights посяг|а́ть, -ну́ть на чьи-н. права́

encrypt /en'krɪpt/ v.t. шифрова́ть, за-

encumber /ɪn'kʌmbə(r)/ v.t. (burden) обремен|я́ть, -и́ть; ~ oneself with luggage взва́л|ивать, -и́ть на себя́ бага́ж

encumbrance /ɪn'kʌmbrəns/ n. обу́за, препя́тствие

encyclopedia /ensaɪklə'piːdɪə, ɪn-/ n. энциклопе́дия

encyclopedic /ɪnsaɪklə'piːdɪk/ adj. энциклопеди́ческий

ꝺ **end** /end/ n. **1** (extremity, lit., fig.) коне́ц; two hours on ~ (in succession) два часа́ подря́д; third from the ~ тре́тий с кра́ю; at the ~ of August в конце́ (or в после́дних чи́слах) а́вгуста **2** (of elongated object) коне́ц, край; he stood the box on (its) ~ он поста́вил я́щик стоймя́ (infml) **3** (remnant, small part): candle ~ ога́рок; cigarette ~ оку́рок **4** (conclusion) оконча́ние; in the ~ в конце́ концо́в; в коне́чном счёте; come to an ~ ок|а́нчиваться, -о́нчиться; конча́ться, ко́нчиться; put an ~ to класть, положи́ть коне́ц + d.; he stayed till the bitter ~ он остава́лся на ме́сте до са́мого конца́ **5** (purpose) цель; to this ~ с э́той це́лью; any means to an ~ все сре́дства хороши́
 ● v.t. конча́ть, ко́нчить; ~ a quarrel прекра|ща́ть, -ти́ть ссо́ру; ~ one's days рассчита́ться с жи́знью
 ● v.i. конча́ться, ко́нчиться; the road ~s here доро́га конча́ется здесь; the story ~s happily э́то расска́з со счастли́вым концо́м
 □ ~ up v.i.: he ~ed up in jail он ко́нчил тюрьмо́й; he ~ed up at the opera в конце́ концо́в он попа́л-таки в о́перу
 ■ ~ product n. коне́чный проду́кт

endanger /ɪn'deɪndʒə(r)/ v.t. подв|ерга́ть, -е́ргнуть опа́сности; ста́вить (impf.) под угро́зу
 ■ ~ed species n. вымира́ющий вид

endear /ɪn'dɪə(r)/ v.t.: this speech ~ed her to me э́та речь расположи́ла меня́ к ней; an ~ing smile покоря́ющая/подкупа́ющая улы́бка

endearment /ɪn'dɪəmənt/ n. ла́ска; term of ~ ла́сковое обраще́ние

endeavour /ɪn'devə(r)/ (AmE **endeavor**) n. стара́ние, стремле́ние
 ● v.i. стара́ться, по-

ending /'endɪŋ/ n. (action) оконча́ние (also gram.); (of book, play) коне́ц

endive /'endaɪv/ n. сала́т энди́вий; (AmE, chicory crown) цико́рий (верхняя наземная часть)

endless /'endlɪs/ adj. бесконе́чный

endorse /ɪn'dɔːs/ v.t. **1** (sign) индосси́ровать (impf., pf.); ~ a cheque распи́с|ываться, -а́ться на че́ке **2** (support) подвер|жда́ть, -ди́ть

endorsement /ɪn'dɔːsmənt/ n. **1** переда́точная на́дпись; индоссаме́нт; резолю́ция (начальника на документе) **2** (support) подтвержде́ние

endow /ɪn'daʊ/ v.t. одар|я́ть, -и́ть

endowment /ɪn'daʊmənt/ n. **1** (act of endowing) поже́ртвование **2** (funds) вклад, поже́ртвование **3** (talent) одарённость

endurable /ɪn'djʊərəb(ə)l/ adj. прие́млемый, сно́сный

endurance /ɪn'djʊərəns/ n. (physical) про́чность; (mental) выно́сливость

endure /ɪn'djʊə(r)/ v.t. выноси́ть, вы́нести
 ● v.i. (last) прод|олжа́ться, -о́лжиться

enema /'enɪmə/ n. (med.) кли́зма

ꝺ **enemy** /'enəmɪ/ n. враг, не́друг

energetic /enə'dʒetɪk/ adj. энерги́чный

ꝺ **energy** /'enədʒɪ/ n. (physical or mental) эне́ргия
 ■ ~ drink n. энергети́ческий напи́ток, энерге́тик (infml)

enforce /ɪn'fɔːs/ v.t.: ~ a judg(e)ment (law) прив|оди́ть, -ести́ в исполне́ние суде́бное реше́ние; ~ a law следи́ть (impf.) за соблюде́нием зако́на

enforceable /ɪn'fɔːsəb(ə)l/ adj. осуществи́мый, обеспе́ченный правово́й са́нкцией

enforcement /ɪn'fɔːsmənt/ n. осуществле́ние; law ~ наблюде́ние за соблюде́нием зако́нов

ꝺ **engage** /ɪn'geɪdʒ/ v.t. **1** (occupy) зан|има́ть, -я́ть; he is ~d in reading он за́нят чте́нием; he ~d me in conversation он вовлёк меня́ в разгово́р; the line is ~d (teleph.) но́мер за́нят; ~d signal, tone (BrE) коро́ткие гудки́; сигна́л «за́нято»; the lavatory is ~d убо́рная занята́ **2** (pledge to marry): Tom and Mary are ~d Том и Мэ́ри помо́лвлены; they got ~d они́ обручи́лись **3** (tech.) зацеп|ля́ть, -и́ть; включ|а́ть, -и́ть
 ● v.i. **1** (undertake) бра́ться, взя́ться **2** (embark, busy oneself) зан|има́ться, -я́ться чем-н.; he ~d in this venture он взя́лся за э́то предприя́тие

ꝺ ключева́я ле́ксика

engagement /ɪnˈgeɪdʒmənt/ *n.* **1** (to marry) помо́лвка **2** (appointment to meet etc.) свида́ние, встре́ча
■ ~ **ring** *n.* обруча́льное кольцо́

engender /ɪnˈdʒendə(r)/ *v.t.* (fig.) поро|жда́ть, -ди́ть

engine /ˈendʒɪn/ *n.* дви́гатель (*m.*); мото́р
■ ~ **driver** *n.* (BrE) машини́ст

engineer /endʒɪˈnɪə(r)/ *n.* инжене́р, меха́ник
● *v.t.* (tech.) проекти́ровать, с-; (fig.) зат|ева́ть, -е́ять

engineering /endʒɪˈnɪərɪŋ/ *n.* инжене́рное де́ло; машиностро́ение; **civil** ~ гражда́нское строи́тельство

England /ˈɪŋglənd/ *n.* А́нглия

English /ˈɪŋglɪʃ/ *n.* **1** (language) англи́йский язы́к **2**: **the** ~ (people) англича́не
● *adj.* англи́йский
■ ~**man** *n.* англича́нин; ~**woman** *n.* англича́нка

engrave /ɪnˈgreɪv/ *v.t.* гравирова́ть, вы́-

engraving /ɪnˈgreɪvɪŋ/ *n.* гравю́ра

engross /ɪnˈgrəʊs/ *v.t.*: **he was ~ed in his work** он был поглощён рабо́той

engulf /ɪnˈgʌlf/ *v.t.* погло|ща́ть, -ти́ть

enhance /ɪnˈhɑːns/ *v.t.* уси́ли|вать, -ть

enhancement /ɪnˈhɑːnsmənt/ *n.* усиле́ние, повыше́ние

enigma /ɪˈnɪgmə/ *n.* зага́дка

enigmatic /enɪgˈmætɪk/ *adj.* зага́дочный

enjoy /ɪnˈdʒɔɪ/ *v.t.* **1** (get pleasure from) насла|жда́ться, -ди́ться + *i.*; **I ~ed talking to him** мне доста́вило удово́льствие говори́ть с ним; **we ~ed our holiday** мы хорошо́ прове́ли о́тпуск; ~ **oneself** весели́ться (*impf.*); наслажда́ться (*impf.*); хорошо́ пров|оди́ть, -ести́ вре́мя **2** (possess) располага́ть (*impf.*) + *i.*; ~ **good/bad health** облада́ть хоро́шим/плохи́м здоро́вьем

enjoyable /ɪnˈdʒɔɪəb(ə)l/ *adj.* прия́тный

enjoyment /ɪnˈdʒɔɪmənt/ *n.* наслажде́ние, удово́льствие

enlarge /ɪnˈlɑːdʒ/ *v.t.* увели́чи|вать, -ть
● *v.i.* расш|иря́ться, -и́риться; **he ~d on the point** он подро́бнее останови́лся на э́том

enlargement /ɪnˈlɑːdʒmənt/ *n.* увеличе́ние; расшире́ние

enlighten /ɪnˈlaɪt(ə)n/ *v.t.* просве|ща́ть, -ти́ть

enlightening /ɪnˈlaɪt(ə)nɪŋ/ *adj.* поучи́тельный

enlightenment /ɪnˈlaɪtənmənt/ *n.* просвеще́нность; **the E~** (hist.) Просвеще́ние

enlist /ɪnˈlɪst/ *v.t.* вербова́ть, за-; ~ **sb's support** заруч|а́ться, -и́ться чьей-н. подде́ржкой
● *v.i.* поступ|а́ть, -и́ть на вое́нную слу́жбу

enlistment /ɪnˈlɪstmənt/ *n.* **1** (of workers) вербо́вка **2** (mil.) поступле́ние на вое́нную слу́жбу

enliven /ɪnˈlaɪv(ə)n/ *v.t.* ожив|ля́ть, -и́ть

en masse /ɑ̃ ˈmæs/ *adv.* в ма́ссе

enmity /ˈenmɪtɪ/ *n.* вражда́

enormity /ɪˈnɔːmɪtɪ/ *n.* чудо́вищность

enormous /ɪˈnɔːməs/ *adj.* грома́дный, огро́мный; ~**ly** чрезвыча́йно

enough /ɪˈnʌf/ *n.* доста́точное коли́чество; дово́льно, доста́точно; **£5 is** ~ пяти́ фу́нтов доста́точно; **(that's)** ~! доста́точно!; дово́льно!; **there is** ~ **to go round** хва́тит на всех; **I have had** ~ **of your lies** надое́ла мне ва́ша ложь
● *adj.* доста́точный; **I have just** ~ **money** де́нег у меня́ в обре́з (**for:** на + *a.*)
● *adv.* доста́точно; **are you warm** ~? вы не замёрзли?; вам тепло́?; **curiously** ~ как ни стра́нно

enquire /ɪŋˈkwaɪə(r)/ *v.t.* спр|а́шивать, -оси́ть
● *v.i.* осв|едомля́ться, -е́домиться; ~ **into a matter** рассле́довать (*pf.*) де́ло; ~ **after sb** спр|а́шивать, -оси́ть о ком-н.

enquiring /ɪŋˈkwaɪərɪŋ/ *adj.*: **an** ~ **look** вопроси́тельный взгляд; **an** ~ **mind** пытли́вый ум

enquir|y /ɪŋˈkwaɪərɪ/ *n.* расспро́сы (*m. pl.*); **make** ~**ies** нав|оди́ть, -ести́ спра́вки

enrage /ɪnˈreɪdʒ/ *v.t.* беси́ть, вз-

enrich /ɪnˈrɪtʃ/ *v.t.* обога|ща́ть, -ти́ть

enrol /ɪnˈrəʊl/ *v t & i.* (**enrolled**, **enrolling**) зач|исля́ть(ся), -и́слить(ся)

enrolment /ɪnˈrəʊlmənt/ *n.* зачисле́ние, приём

ensconce /ɪnˈskɒns/ *v.t.*: ~ **oneself** устр|а́иваться, -о́иться, укр|ыва́ться, -ы́ться

ensemble /ɒnˈsɒmb(ə)l/ *n.* анса́мбль (*m.*)

enshrine /ɪnˈʃraɪn/ *v.t.* поме|ща́ть, -сти́ть в ра́ку; (fig.) храни́ть (*impf.*)

ensign /ˈensaɪn/ *n.* **1** (flag) (кормово́й) флаг **2** (hist., standard-bearer) пра́порщик **3** (AmE, naut.) мла́дший лейтена́нт

enslave /ɪnˈsleɪv/ *v.t.* порабо|ща́ть, -ти́ть

ensu|e /ɪnˈsjuː/ *v.i.* (**ensues**, **ensued**, **ensuing**) сле́довать (*impf.*) (*из чего*); **in** ~**ing years** в после́дующие го́ды

ensure /ɪnˈʃʊə(r)/ *v.t.* (make certain; secure) обеспе́чи|вать, -ть

entail /ɪnˈteɪl/ *v.t.* влечь (*impf.*) за собо́й

entangle /ɪnˈtæŋg(ə)l/ *v.t.* (lit.) запу́т|ывать, -ать; (fig.) впу́т|ывать, -ать; **he ~d himself with women** он запу́тался в отноше́ниях с же́нщинами

enter /ˈentə(r)/ *v.t. & i.* **1** (go into) входи́ть, войти́ в + *a.*; ~ **the army** вступ|а́ть, -и́ть в а́рмию; **the idea never ~ed my head** э́та мысль никогда́ не приходи́ла мне в го́лову **2** (include in record) запи́с|ывать, -а́ть; (comput.) вводи́ть, ввести́; ~ **a horse for a race** заяв|ля́ть, -и́ть ло́шадь для ска́чек; ~ **(oneself) for an examination** пода|ва́ть, -а́ть докуме́нты на уча́стие в экза́мене
● *with prep.*: ~ **into conversation** вступ|а́ть, -и́ть в разгово́р; **he ~ed into the spirit of the game** он прони́кся ду́хом игры́

enterprise /ˈentəpraɪz/ *n.* **1** (undertaking) предприя́тие **2** (initiative) предприи́мчивость **3** (econ.): **free** ~ свобо́дное предпринима́тельство

enterprising /ˈentəpraɪzɪŋ/ *adj.* предприи́мчивый

e

entertain /entə'teɪn/ v.t. развл|екáть, -éчь; прин|имáть, -я́ть; ~ **friends** угощáть, -сти́ть друзéй; (amuse) развл|екáть, -éчь

entertainer /entə'teɪnə(r)/ n. арти́ст эстрáды

entertaining /entə'teɪnɪŋ/ adj. интерéсный, занимáтельный

entertainment /entə'teɪnmənt/ n. **1** (social) приём гостéй **2** (amusement) развлечéние **3** (spectacle) представлéние

enthral /ɪn'θrɔ:l/ (AmE **enthrall**) v.t. (**enthralled, enthralling**) (fascinate) увл|екáть, -éчь; an ~**ling play** захвáтывающая пьéса

enthuse /ɪn'θju:z/ v.i. (infml) восторгáться (impf.) (чем)

enthusiasm /ɪn'θju:zɪæz(ə)m/ n. востóрг, энтузиáзм

enthusiast /ɪn'θju:zɪæst/ n. энтузиáст (-ка)

enthusiastic /ɪnθju:zɪ'æstɪk/ adj. востóрженный; пóлный энтузиáзма

entice /ɪn'taɪs/ v.t. соблазн|я́ть, -и́ть

enticement /ɪn'taɪsmənt/ n. (action) замáнивание; (lure) примáнка, соблáзн

✎ **entire** /ɪn'taɪə(r)/ adj. цéлый, пóлный, цéльный; ~**ly** целикóм, совершéнно

entirety /ɪn'taɪərəti/ n. полнотá, цéльность

✎ **entitle** /ɪn'taɪt(ə)l/ v.t. **1** (authorize) да|вáть, -ть прáво на + a.; **you are** ~**d to two books a month** вам полагáется две кни́ги в мéсяц **2**: **a book** ~**d 'Progress'** кни́га под заглáвием «Прогрéсс»

entitlement /ɪn'taɪt(ə)lmənt/ n. (right) прáво

entity /'entɪti/ n. существó

entomologist /entə'mɒlədʒɪst/ n. энтомóлог

entomology /entə'mɒlədʒɪ/ n. энтомолóгия

entourage /'ɒntʊərɑ:ʒ/ n. антурáж, окружéние

entrance¹ /'entrəns/ n. вход
■ ~ **examination** n. вступи́тельный экзáмен; ~ **fee** n. вступи́тельный взнóс; ~ **hall** n. прихóжая, вестибю́ль (m.)

entrance² /ɪn'trɑ:ns/ v.t. восторгáть (impf.)

entrant /'entrənt/ n. (person entering school, profession, etc.) поступáющий; (competitor) учáстник

entreat /ɪn'tri:t/ v.t. умол|я́ть, -и́ть

entreaty /ɪn'tri:ti/ n. мольбá

entrench /ɪn'trentʃ/ v.t. окруж|áть, -и́ть окóпами; **the enemy were** ~**ed nearby** враг окопáлся вблизи́; ~ **oneself** ок|áпываться, -опáться; (fig.): **customs** ~**ed by tradition** обы́чаи, закреплённые тради́цией

entrepreneur /ɒntrəprə'nə:(r)/ n. предпринимáтель (m.)

entrepreneurial /ɒntrəprə'nə:rɪəl/ adj. предпринимáтельский

entrust /ɪn'trʌst/ v.t. вв|еря́ть, -éрить; **I** ~**ed the task to him** (or ~**ed him with the task**) я дал емý, поручéние

✎ **entry** /'entri/ n. **1** (going in) вход **2** (access) дóступ; **he gained** ~ **to the house** он

пробрáлся в дом **3** (item) зáпись; **dictionary** ~ словáрная статья́; ~ **in a diary** зáпись в дневникé **4** (inscription; competitor): **there was a large** ~ **for the race** на скáчки записáлось мнóго учáстников
■ ~ **form** n. вступи́тельная анкéта

entryphone® /'entrɪfəʊn/ n. (BrE) домофóн

enunciate /ɪ'nʌnsɪeɪt/ v.t. (express) формули́ровать, с-; (pronounce) произн|оси́ть, -ести́

envelop /ɪn'veləp/ v.t. (**enveloped, enveloping**) оку́т|ывать, -ать; **hills** ~**ed in mist** холмы́, окýтанные тумáном; **a baby** ~**ed in a shawl** младéнец, завёрнутый в шаль; ~**ed in mystery** покры́тый тáйной

envelope /'ɒnvələʊp/ n. конвéрт

enviable /'envɪəb(ə)l/ adj. зави́дный

envious /'envɪəs/ adj. зави́стливый

✎ **environment** /ɪn'vaɪərənmənt/ n. окружéние, средá; **the** ~ окружáющая средá
■ ~**-friendly** adj. экологи́чески безврéдный

✎ **environmental** /ɪnvaɪərən'ment(ə)l/ adj. окружáющий
■ ~ **studies** n. pl. изучéние окружáющей среды́

environmentalism /ɪnvaɪərən'mentəlɪz(ə)m/ n. защи́та окружáющей среды́

environmentalist /ɪnvaɪərən'mentəlɪst/ n. стóронник защи́ты окружáющей среды́

environs /ɪn'vaɪərənz/ n. pl. окрéстности (f. pl.)

envisage /ɪn'vɪzɪdʒ/ v.t. (consider) рассм|áтривать, -отрéть; (visualize) предви́деть (impf.)

envoy /'envɔɪ/ n. дипломáт

envy /'envi/ n. зáвисть
● v.t. зави́довать, по- + d.; **I** ~ **him** я емý зави́дую; **I** ~ **his patience** я зави́дую его́ терпéнию

enzyme /'enzaɪm/ n. энзи́м

epaulette /'epəlet/ n. эполéт

ephemeral /ɪ'femər(ə)l/ adj. эфемéрный

epic /'epɪk/ n. эпи́ческая поэ́ма, эпопéя
● adj. эпи́ческий; (on a grand scale) грандиóзный

epicentre /'episentə(r)/ (AmE **epicenter**) n. эпицéнтр

epidemic /epɪ'demɪk/ n. эпидéмия

epidural /epɪ'djʊər(ə)l/ n. эпидурáльная инъéкция

epilepsy /'epɪlepsɪ/ n. эпилéпсия

epileptic /epɪ'leptɪk/ n. эпилéптик
● adj. эпилепти́ческий

✎ **episode** /'episəʊd/ n. (occurrence) эпизóд; (instalment) часть

episodic /epɪ'sɒdɪk/ adj. (composed of episodes) состоя́щий из отдéльных эпизóдов; (incidental, occasional) эпизоди́ческий

epitaph /'epɪtɑ:f/ n. эпитáфия, надгрóбная нáдпись

epitome /ɪ'pɪtəmɪ/ n. воплощéние

epitomize /ɪ'pɪtəmaɪz/ v.t. вопло|щáть, -ти́ть

✎ ключевáя лéксика

epoch /ˈiːpɒk/ n. эпо́ха

eponymous /ɪˈpɒnɪməs/ adj. и́менем кото́рого на́зван (-а, -о) (+ nom.); (hero) загла́вный (роль, герой)

⚐ **equal** /ˈiːkw(ə)l/ n. ро́вня; **our boss treats us all as** ~**s** наш нача́льник обраща́ется со все́ми на́ми на ра́вных
    ● adj. **1** (same, equivalent) ра́вный, одина́ковый **2** (adequate) спосо́бный; **she is** ~ **to the task** она́ вполне́ мо́жет спра́виться с э́той зада́чей
    ● v.t. & i. (**equalled, equalling,** AmE **equaled, equaling**) **1** (math.) равня́ться (impf.) (чему) **2:** **he** ~**s me in strength** мы с ним равны́ по си́ле

equality /ɪˈkwɒlɪtɪ/ n. ра́венство, равнопра́вие

equalize /ˈiːkwəlaɪz/ v.t. & i. ура́вн|ивать, -я́ть

equalizer /ˈiːkwəlaɪzə(r)/ n. (sport) гол, сра́внивающий счёт

⚐ **equally** /ˈiːkwəlɪ/ adv. **1** (to an equal extent) одина́ково **2** (also, likewise) ра́вным о́бразом; наравне́ **3** (evenly): **he divided the money** ~ он раздели́л де́ньги по́ровну

equanimity /ekwəˈnɪmɪtɪ/ n. душе́вное равнове́сие; споко́йствие; **with** ~ споко́йно

equate /ɪˈkweɪt/ v.t. отождествл|я́ть, -и́ть; **she** ~**s wealth with happiness** она́ отождествля́ет бога́тство со сча́стьем

equation /ɪˈkweɪʒ(ə)n/ n. уравне́ние

equator /ɪˈkweɪtə(r)/ n. эква́тор

equidistant /iːkwɪˈdɪst(ə)nt/ adj. равноотстоя́щий; **these towns are** ~ **from London** э́ти города́ располо́жены на одина́ковом расстоя́нии от Ло́ндона

equilibrium /iːkwɪˈlɪbrɪəm/ n. (lit., fig.) равнове́сие

equinox /ˈekwɪnɒks/ n. равноде́нствие

equip /ɪˈkwɪp/ v.t. (**equipped, equipping**) снаря|жа́ть, -ди́ть

⚐ **equipment** /ɪˈkwɪpmənt/ n. снаряже́ние, экипиро́вка

equitable /ˈekwɪtəb(ə)l/ adj. справедли́вый

equity /ˈekwɪtɪ/ n. **1** (fairness) справедли́вость **2** (in pl.) (fin.) обыкнове́нные а́кции (f. pl.)

equivalent /ɪˈkwɪvələnt/ n. эквивале́нт
    ● adj. эквивале́нтный

equivocal /ɪˈkwɪvək(ə)l/ adj. двусмы́сленный, сомни́тельный

⚐ **era** /ˈɪərə/ n. э́ра

eradicate /ɪˈrædɪkeɪt/ v.t. искорен|я́ть, -и́ть

erase /ɪˈreɪz/ v.t. ст|ира́ть, -ере́ть

eraser /ɪˈreɪzə(r)/ n. рези́нка

erect /ɪˈrekt/ adj. прямо́й
    ● v.t. (build, set up) воздв|ига́ть, -и́гнуть; сооруж|а́ть, -ди́ть

erection /ɪˈrekʃ(ə)n/ n. (setting up) сооруже́ние; (building) зда́ние; (physiol.) эре́кция

ergonomic /ɜːɡəˈnɒmɪk/ adj. эргономи́чный

Eritrea /erɪˈtreɪə/ n. Эритре́я

ERM abbr. (of **Exchange Rate Mechanism**) МВК (механи́зм валю́тных ку́рсов)

ermine /ˈɜːmɪn/ n. (pl. ~ or ~**s**) (animal, fur) горноста́й

erode /ɪˈrəʊd/ v.t. разъ|еда́ть, -е́сть; (fig.) подт|а́чивать, -очи́ть

erosion /ɪˈrəʊʒ(ə)n/ n. разъеда́ние, эро́зия; (fig.): **the** ~ **of his hopes** постепе́нное разруше́ние его́ наде́жд

erotic /ɪˈrɒtɪk/ adj. эроти́ческий

eroticism /ɪˈrɒtɪsɪz(ə)m/ n. эроти́зм

err /ɜː(r)/ v.i. ошиб|а́ться, -и́ться; заблужда́ться (impf.)

errand /ˈerənd/ n. поруче́ние

errant /ˈerənt/ adj. **1** (misbehaving) заблу́дший **2** (stray, wandering) стра́нствующий; **knight** ~ стра́нствующий ры́царь

erratic /ɪˈrætɪk/ adj. неусто́йчивый; (of person) беспоря́дочный; ~**ally** нерегуля́рно

erroneous /ɪˈrəʊnɪəs/ adj. оши́бочный

⚐ **error** /ˈerə(r)/ n. оши́бка, заблужде́ние; **the letter was sent in** ~ письмо́ бы́ло отпра́влено по оши́бке

erstwhile /ˈɜːstwaɪl/ adj. да́вний, давни́шний; **an** ~ **friend** да́вний/стари́нный друг

erudite /ˈeruːdaɪt/ adj. эруди́рованный, учёный

erudition /erʊˈdɪʃ(ə)n/ n. эруди́ция

erupt /ɪˈrʌpt/ v.i. (of volcano) изверга́ться (impf.)

eruption /ɪˈrʌpʃ(ə)n/ n. **1** (of volcano etc.) изверже́ние **2** (fig.) взрыв

escalate /ˈeskəleɪt/ v.i. разраста́ться (impf.)

escalation /eskəˈleɪʃ(ə)n/ n. эскала́ция

escalator /ˈeskəleɪtə(r)/ n. эскала́тор

escapade /ˈeskəpeɪd/ n. (экстравага́нтная) вы́ходка

⚐ **escape** /ɪˈskeɪp/ n. **1** (becoming free) побе́г, бе́гство **2** (avoidance) спасе́ние, избавле́ние; **he had a narrow** ~ **from shipwreck** он едва́ спа́сся при кораблекруше́нии
    ● v.t. избе|га́ть, -жа́ть + g.; **she** ~**d death** она́ оста́лась в живы́х; **nothing** ~**s you!** всё-(то) вы замеча́ете!
    ● v.i. бежа́ть (det.); уходи́ть, уйти́; соверши́ть (pf.) побе́г; **an** ~**d prisoner** бе́глый ареста́нт

escapism /ɪˈskeɪpɪz(ə)m/ n. бе́гство от действи́тельности; эскапи́зм

escort[1] /ˈeskɔːt/ n. (mil.) конво́й, эско́рт; **police** ~ (of criminal) конво́й; **her** ~ **to the ball** её кавале́р на балу́

escort[2] /ɪˈskɔːt/ v.t. сопрово|жда́ть, -ди́ть; (mil.) конвои́ровать (impf., pf.); **I** ~**ed him to his seat** я провёл его́ на ме́сто

Eskimo /ˈeskɪməʊ/ n. (pl. ~ or ~**s**) эскимо́с (-ка)
    ● adj. эскимо́сский

esophagus /iːˈsɒfəɡəs/ n. (AmE) = **oesophagus**

esoteric /iːsəʊˈterɪk/ adj. эзотери́ческий

⚐ **especially** /ɪˈspeʃ(ə)lɪ/ adj. осо́бенно

espionage /ˈespɪənɑːʒ/ n. шпиона́ж

espouse /ɪˈspaʊz/ v.t.: ~ **a cause** (целико́м) отд|ава́ться, -а́ться де́лу

espresso /eˈspresəʊ/ n. (pl. ~**s**) (coffee) ко́фе «эспре́ссо»

essay /'eseɪ/ n. (literary composition) о́черк, эссе́ (nt. indecl.); (in school) сочине́ние

essence /'es(ə)ns/ n. **1** (intrinsic nature) су́щность, существо́ **2** (extract) эссе́нция

essential /ɪ'senʃ(ə)l/ n. су́щность
● adj. **1** (necessary) необходи́мый; it is ∼ that I should know о́чень ва́жно, что́бы я знал **2** (fundamental) суще́ственный; ∼ly суще́ственно; по существу́; в су́щности **3**: ∼ oils эфи́рные масла́

establish /ɪ'stæblɪʃ/ v.t. **1** (found, set up) учре|жда́ть, -ди́ть; устан|а́вливать, -ови́ть **2** (prove, gain acceptance for) утвер|жда́ть, -ди́ть; ∼ one's reputation созд|ава́ть, -а́ть себе́ репута́цию
■ E∼ed Church n. госуда́рственная це́рковь

establishment /ɪ'stæblɪʃmənt/ n. **1** (setting up) учрежде́ние, установле́ние **2** (of a fact etc.) установле́ние **3** (institution) учрежде́ние, заведе́ние; educational ∼ уче́бное заведе́ние **4** (business concern) заведе́ние, де́ло **5** (set of institutions or key persons): the E∼ «исте́блишмент»

estate /ɪ'steɪt/ n. **1** (landed property) поме́стье, име́ние; housing ∼ (BrE) жило́й масси́в **2** (property) иму́щество; real ∼ недви́жимость
■ ∼ agent n. (BrE) аге́нт по прода́же недви́жимости; ∼ car n. (BrE) автомоби́ль (m.) с ку́зовом «универса́л»; универса́л (infml)

esteem /ɪ'stiːm/ n. уваже́ние

estimate[1] /'estɪmət/ n. **1** (assessment) оце́нка **2** (comm.) сме́та

estimate[2] /'estɪmeɪt/ v.t. оцен|ивать, -и́ть

estimation /estɪ'meɪʃ(ə)n/ n. (judgement) оце́нка, сужде́ние

Estonia /ɪ'stəʊnɪə/ n. Эсто́ния

Estonian /ɪ'stəʊnɪən/ n. эсто́н|ец (-ка)
● adj. эсто́нский

estrange /ɪ'streɪndʒ/ v.t. отдал|я́ть, -и́ть; his ∼d wife жена́, с кото́рой он живёт разде́льно

estrogen /'iːstrədʒ(ə)n/ n. (AmE) = oestrogen

estuary /'estjʊərɪ/ n. эстуа́рий, у́стье

etc. /et 'setərə/ adv. (abbr. of et cetera) и т. д., и т. п. (и так да́лее; и тому́ подо́бное)

etch /etʃ/ v.t. трави́ть, вы́-; гравирова́ть, вы́-; (fig.): it is ∼ed on my memory э́то запечатле́лось у меня́ в па́мяти

etching /'etʃɪŋ/ n. офо́рт, гравю́ра

eternal /ɪ'tɜː n(ə)l/ adj. ве́чный (also fig.)

eternity /ɪ'tɜː nɪtɪ/ n. ве́чность

ether /'iːθə(r)/ n. (phys., chem.) эфи́р

ethereal /ɪ'θɪərɪəl/ adj. эфи́рный, неземно́й; ∼ beauty неземна́я красота́

ethical /'eθɪk(ə)l/ adj. эти́чный

ethics /'eθɪks/ n. pl. э́тика; мора́ль

Ethiopia /iːθɪ'əʊpɪə/ n. Эфио́пия

Ethiopian /iːθɪ'əʊpɪən/ n. эфио́п (-ка)
● adj. эфио́пский

ethnic /'eθnɪk(ə)l/ adj. этни́ческий
■ ∼ cleansing n. этни́ческая чи́стка

ethos /'iːθɒs/ n. дух, хара́ктер

etiquette /'etɪket/ n. этике́т

etymological /etɪmə'lɒdʒɪk(ə)l/ adj. этимологи́ческий

etymology /etɪ'mɒlədʒɪ/ n. этимоло́гия

EU abbr. (of **European Union**) ЕС (Европе́йский сою́з)

eucalyp|tus /juːkə'lɪptəs/ n. (pl. ∼tuses or ∼ti /-taɪ/) эвкали́пт

Eucharist /'juːkərɪst/ n. евхари́стия, свято́е прича́стие

eulogy /'juːlədʒɪ/ n. хвале́бная речь, панеги́рик; (at funeral) надгро́бная речь

euphemism /'juːfɪmɪz(ə)m/ n. эвфеми́зм

euphemistic /juːfɪ'mɪstɪk/ adj. эвфемисти́ческий

euphoria /juː'fɔːrɪə/ adj. эйфори́я

euphoric /juː'fɒrɪk/ adj. в припо́днятом настрое́нии

eureka /jʊə'riːkə/ int. э́врика

euro /'jʊərəʊ/ n. (pl. ∼s) е́вро (m. indecl.)

Euro|- /'jʊərəʊ/ comb. form евро…
■ ∼-MP n. депута́т Европарла́мента; ∼sceptic n. евроске́птик; e∼zone n. Еврозо́на

Europe /'jʊərəp/ n. Евро́па

European /jʊərə'pɪən/ n. европе́|ец (-йка)
● adj. европе́йский

euthanasia /juːθə'neɪzɪə/ n. эвтана́зия, умерщвле́ние из милосе́рдия

evacuate /ɪ'vækjʊeɪt/ v.t. эвакуи́ровать (impf., pf.)

evacuation /ɪvækjʊ'eɪʃ(ə)n/ n. (removal) эвакуа́ция; (physiol.) очище́ние кише́чника, испражне́ние

evacuee /ɪvækjuː'iː/ n. эвакуи́рованный

evade /ɪ'veɪd/ v.t. избе|га́ть, -жа́ть + g.; ∼ a blow/question уклон|я́ться, -и́ться от уда́ра/отве́та

evaluate /ɪ'væljʊeɪt/ v.t. оцен|ивать, -и́ть

evaluation /ɪvæljʊ'eɪʃ(ə)n/ n. оце́нка

evangelical /iːvæn'dʒelɪk(ə)l/ adj. евангели́ческий

evangelism /ɪ'vændʒəlɪz(ə)m/ n. про́поведь Ева́нгелия; (fig.) пропове́дничество

evangelist /ɪ'vændʒəlɪst/ n. (author of gospel) евангели́ст; (preacher) пропове́дник Ева́нгелия

evaporate /ɪ'væpəreɪt/ v.t. & i. испар|я́ть(ся), -и́ть(ся) (also fig.)

evaporation /ɪvæpə'reɪʃ(ə)n/ n. испаре́ние

evasion /ɪ'veɪʒ(ə)n/ n. (avoidance) уклоне́ние; (prevarication) уве́ртка

evasive /ɪ'veɪsɪv/ adj. (of answer) укло́нчивый; (of person) уве́ртливый

eve /iːv/ n. (day or evening before) кану́н (also fig.); on the ∼ of накану́не + g.

even /'iːv(ə)n/ adj. (**evener**, **evenest**)
1 (level, smooth) ро́вный **2** (equal) ра́вный; the score is ∼ счёт ра́вный; get ∼ with sb расквита́ться (pf.) с кем-н. **3** (divisible by 2) чётный
● adv. да́же; и; хотя́ бы; she won't ∼ notice

она́ и не заме́тит; **not** ~ да́же не; **this applies** ~ **more to French** э́то ещё в бо́льшей сте́пени отно́сится к францу́зскому языку́ • *v.t.* (make even or equal) выра́внивать, выровня́ть

ⵊ **evening** /ˈiːvnɪŋ/ *n.* ве́чер; **in the** ~ ве́чером; **one** ~ одна́жды ве́чером; **this** ~ сего́дня ве́чером; **tomorrow** ~ за́втра ве́чером; ~ **dress, clothes** (of either sex) вече́рний туале́т; ~ **dress, gown** (woman's) вече́рнее пла́тье

evenness /ˈiːvənnɪs/ *n.* (physical smoothness) гла́дкость; (uniformity) равноме́рность; (of temper, tone, etc.) ро́вность, уравнове́шенность; (of odds, contest, etc.) ра́венство

ⵊ **event** /ɪˈvent/ *n.* **1** (occurrence) собы́тие **2** (hypothesis) слу́чай; **in the** ~ **of his coming** в слу́чае его́ прихо́да; **in any** ~ в любо́м слу́чае **3** (sports race) забе́г, зае́зд; (type of sport) вид спо́рта

eventful /ɪˈventfʊl/ *adj.* насы́щенный собы́тиями

eventual /ɪˈventʃʊəl/ *adj.* коне́чный

eventuality /ɪˌventʃʊˈælɪtɪ/ *n.* возмо́жность, слу́чай

ⵊ **eventually** /ɪˈventʃʊəlɪ/ *adv.* со вре́менем; в конце́ концо́в

ⵊ **ever** /ˈevə(r)/ *adv.* **1** (always) всегда́; **for** ~ навсегда́, наве́чно; ~ **after, since** с тех (са́мых) пор; ~ **since** (*as conj.*) с тех пор, как… **2** (at any time): **do you** ~ **see him?** вы его́ хоть иногда́ ви́дите?; **scarcely, hardly** ~ почти́ никогда́; о́чень ре́дко; **as good as** ~ не ху́же, чем ра́ньше; **better than** ~ лу́чше, чем когда́-либо **3** (intensive): **why** ~ **did you do it?** заче́м же вы э́то сде́лали?; ~ **so rich** (BrE) невероя́тно бога́тый; (infml): **thank you** ~ **so much** (BrE) я вам чрезвыча́йно благода́рен

　■ ~**green** (bot.) *n.* вечнозелёное расте́ние • *adj.* вечнозелёный; ~**lasting** *adj.* ве́чный

ⵊ **every** /ˈevrɪ/ *adj.* ка́ждый, вся́кий; **I have** ~ **confidence in him** я в нём соверше́нно уве́рен; ~ **ten minutes** ка́ждые де́сять мину́т; ~ **other car** ка́ждый второ́й автомоби́ль; ~ **other day** че́рез день; ~ **now and again; so often;** ~ **once in a while** вре́мя от вре́мени; по времена́м; иногда́

　■ ~**day** *adj.* повседне́вный; обыкнове́нный, бытово́й

everybody /ˈevrɪbɒdɪ/ *pron.* ка́ждый; вся́кий; все (*pl.*); ~**body else** все остальны́е

everyone /ˈevrɪwʌn/ *pron.* = **everybody**

everything /ˈevrɪθɪŋ/ *pron.* всё

everywhere /ˈevrɪweə(r)/ *adv.* везде́, повсю́ду

evict /ɪˈvɪkt/ *v.t.* выселя́ть, вы́селить

eviction /ɪˈvɪkʃ(ə)n/ *n.* выселе́ние

ⵊ **evidence** /ˈevɪd(ə)ns/ *n.* **1** (indication) доказа́тельство, свиде́тельство **2** (law) свиде́тельские показа́ния (*nt. pl.*); ули́ка; да́нные (*pl.*); **give** ~ да|ва́ть, -ть свиде́тельские показа́ния

• *v.t.* служи́ть, по- доказа́тельством, ули́кой (*чего*)

evident /ˈevɪd(ə)nt/ *adj.* очеви́дный, я́сный; **it was** ~ **from his behaviour that …** бы́ло ви́дно по его́ поведе́нию, что…

ⵊ **evil** /ˈiːvɪl/ *n.* зло • *adj.* злой, дурно́й

evocation /ˌevəˈkeɪʃ(ə)n/ *n.* вызыва́ние; воскреше́ние в па́мяти

evocative /ɪˈvɒkətɪv/ *adj.* навева́ющий воспомина́ния

evoke /ɪˈvəʊk/ *v.t.* вызыва́ть, вы́звать; пробу|жда́ть, -ди́ть; нап|омина́ть, -о́мнить

evolution /ˌiːvəˈluːʃ(ə)n/ *n.* эволю́ция

evolutionary /ˌiːvəˈluːʃənərɪ/ *adj.* эволюцио́нный

evolve /ɪˈvɒlv/ *v.i.* разв|ива́ться, -и́ться

ewe /juː/ *n.* овца́

ex /eks/ *n.* (infml) бы́вший муж, бы́вшая жена́

ex- /eks/ *pref.* (former) экс-…, бы́вший

exacerbate /ɪɡˈzæsəbeɪt/ *v.t.* (pain etc.) обостр|я́ть, -и́ть

exact /ɪɡˈzækt/ *adj.* то́чный

ⵊ **exactly** /ɪɡˈzæktlɪ/ *adv.* то́чно; (of numbers, quantities) ро́вно

exaggerate /ɪɡˈzædʒəreɪt/ *v.t.* преувели́чи|вать, -ть

exaggeration /ɪɡˌzædʒəˈreɪʃ(ə)n/ *n.* преувеличе́ние

exalt /ɪɡˈzɔːlt/ *v.t.* (make higher in rank etc.) пов|ыша́ть, -ы́сить; (praise) превоз|носи́ть, -ести́

exaltation /ˌeɡzɔːlˈteɪʃ(ə)n/ *n.* **1** (raising in rank etc.) повыше́ние **2** (worship) возвели́чение, возвели́чивание **3** (mental or emotional transport) экзальта́ция

exam /ɪɡˈzæm/ *n.* = **examination**

examination /ɪɡˌzæmɪˈneɪʃ(ə)n/ *n.* экза́мен; **take an** ~ сдава́ть (*impf.*) экза́мен; **pass an** ~ сдать (*pf.*) экза́мен

　■ ~ **paper** *n.* (written by examinee) экзаменацио́нная рабо́та; (questions set) вопро́сы (*m. pl.*) (для экзаменацио́нной рабо́ты)

ⵊ **examine** /ɪɡˈzæmɪn/ *v.t.* **1** (inspect) осм|а́тривать, -отре́ть; ~ **passports** пров|еря́ть, -е́рить паспорта́; ~ **a patient** осм|а́тривать, -отре́ть больно́го **2** (academic) экзаменова́ть, про-

examiner /ɪɡˈzæmɪnə(r)/ *n.* экзамена́тор

ⵊ **example** /ɪɡˈzɑːmp(ə)l/ *n.* **1** (illustration, model) приме́р; **for** ~ наприме́р **2** (warning) уро́к; **let this be an** ~ **to you** пусть э́то послу́жит вам уро́ком

exasperate /ɪɡˈzɑːspəreɪt/ *v.t.* изв|оди́ть, -ести́

exasperation /ɪɡˌzɑːspəˈreɪʃ(ə)n/ *n.* раздраже́ние

excavate /ˈekskəveɪt/ *v.t.* копа́ть (*impf.*); выка́пывать, вы́копать; раск|а́пывать, -опа́ть

excavation /ˌekskəˈveɪʃ(ə)n/ *n.* (site) раско́пки (*f. pl.*); (action) выка́пывание

excavator /ˈekskəveɪtə(r)/ *n.* (person) землеко́п; (machine) экскава́тор

exceed /ɪkˈsiːd/ *v.t.* превы|ша́ть, -́сить

e

exceedingly /ɪkˈsiːdɪŋlɪ/ *adv.* весьма́, чрезвыча́йно

excel /ɪkˈsel/ *v.i.* (**excelled, excelling**) выделя́ться (*impf.*); he ~s in sport он превосхо́дный спортсме́н

Excellency /ˈeksələnsɪ/ *n.*: His ~ его́ превосходи́тельство

⚹ **excellent** /ˈeksələnt/ *adj.* отли́чный

⚹ **except** /ɪkˈsept/ *prep.* (*also* **excepting**) исключа́я + *a.*; кро́ме + *g.*; за исключе́нием + *g.*; ра́зве лишь/то́лько; the essay is good ~ for the spelling mistakes сочине́ние хоро́шее, е́сли не счита́ть орфографи́ческих оши́бок

⚹ **exception** /ɪkˈsepʃ(ə)n/ *n.* **1** исключе́ние; with the ~ of за исключе́нием + *g.* **2**: take ~ to об|ижа́ться, -и́деться на + *a.*

exceptional /ɪkˈsepʃən(ə)l/ *adj.* исключи́тельный

excerpt /ˈeksəːpt/ *n.* вы́держка, цита́та

excess /ɪkˈses/ *n.* изли́шек, избы́ток; in ~ of £20 свы́ше двадцати́ фу́нтов
■ ~ **baggage** /ˈekses/ *n.* изли́шек багажа́

excessive /ɪkˈsesɪv/ *adj.* изли́шний; (extreme) чрезме́рный

⚹ **exchange** /ɪksˈtʃeɪndʒ/ *n.* **1** (act of exchanging) обме́н (of: + *g./i.*); in ~ for в обме́н на + *a.* **2** (fin.) разме́н, обме́н; ~ rate/control валю́тный курс/контро́ль **3** (teleph.) (центра́льная) телефо́нная ста́нция
● *v.t.* меня́ть, об-/по- (*что на что*); (reciprocally) меня́ться, об-/по- (+ *i.*); we ~d places мы поменя́лись места́ми

exchequer /ɪksˈtʃekə(r)/ *n.* казначе́йство, казна́

excise[1] /ˈeksaɪz/ *n.* акци́з
■ ~ **officer** *n.* акци́зный чино́вник

excise[2] /ɪkˈsaɪz/ *v.t.* выреза́ть, вы́резать; отр|еза́ть, -е́зать

excision /ɪkˈsɪʒ(ə)n/ *n.* вырезáние, отрезáние; (med.) иссече́ние, удале́ние

excitable /ɪkˈsaɪtəb(ə)l/ *adj.* легко́ возбуди́мый

excite /ɪkˈsaɪt/ *v.t.* волнова́ть, вз-; don't ~ yourself (*or* get ~d)! не волну́йтесь!

excitement /ɪkˈsaɪtmənt/ *n.* возбужде́ние, волне́ние

⚹ **exciting** /ɪkˈsaɪtɪŋ/ *adj.* захва́тывающий

exclaim /ɪkˈskleɪm/ *v.t. & i.* воскл|ица́ть, -и́кнуть

exclamation /ekskləˈmeɪʃ(ə)n/ *n.* восклица́ние
■ ~ **mark** *n.* восклица́тельный знак

exclude /ɪkˈskluːd/ *v.t.* исключ|а́ть, -и́ть

exclusion /ɪkˈskluːʒ(ə)n/ *n.* исключе́ние

exclusive /ɪkˈskluːsɪv/ *adj.* **1** (sole) исключи́тельный, еди́нственный **2**: ~ of (not counting) без + *g.*, не счита́я + *g.* **3** (high-class) эксклюзи́вный; an ~ club клуб для и́збранных

exclusivity /ekskluːˈsɪvɪtɪ/ *n.* эксклюзи́вность

excommunicate /ekskəˈmjuːnɪkeɪt/ *v.t.* отлуч|а́ть, -и́ть от це́ркви

⚹ ключева́я ле́ксика

excrement /ˈekskrɪmənt/ *n.* экскреме́нты (*m. pl.*)

excrete /ɪkˈskriːt/ *v.t.* выделя́ть, вы́делить

excruciating /ɪkˈskruːʃɪeɪtɪŋ/ *adj.* мучи́тельный

excursion /ɪkˈskəːʃ(ə)n/ *n.* (trip) экску́рсия

excuse[1] /ɪkˈskjuːs/ *n.* извине́ние, оправда́ние, отгово́рка; a poor ~ сла́бая отгово́рка; please make my ~s to the hostess пожа́луйста, переда́йте мои́ извине́ния хозя́йке

excuse[2] /ɪkˈskjuːz/ *v.t.* **1** (forgive) извин|я́ть, -и́ть; про|ща́ть, -сти́ть; please ~ my coming late (*or* me for coming late) извини́те, что я пришёл по́здно; ~ me, what time is it? прости́те, кото́рый час? **2** (release): I ~d him from attending я позво́лил ему́ не прису́тствовать

ex-directory /eksdaɪˈrektərɪ/ *adj.* (BrE) не внесённый в телефо́нную кни́гу; he's ~ его́ но́мера нет в телефо́нной кни́ге

execute /ˈeksɪkjuːt/ *v.t.* **1** (carry out) выполня́ть, вы́полнить; исп|олня́ть, -о́лнить **2** (put to death) казни́ть (*impf., pf.*)

execution /eksɪˈkjuːʃ(ə)n/ *n.* **1** (carrying out) исполне́ние, выполне́ние **2** (capital punishment) казнь

executioner /eksɪˈkjuːʃənə(r)/ *n.* пала́ч

⚹ **executive** /ɪgˈzekjʊtɪv/ *n.* (руково́дящий) рабо́тник
● *adj.* **1** (executing laws etc.) исполни́тельный **2** (managing) руководя́щий

executor /ɪgˈzekjʊtə(r)/ *n.* (of a will) исполни́тель (*m.*) завеща́ния, душеприка́зчик

exemplary /ɪgˈzemplərɪ/ *adj.* приме́рный, образцо́вый

exemplify /ɪgˈzemplɪfaɪ/ *v.t.* служи́ть, по- приме́ром + *g.*

exempt /ɪgˈzempt/ *adj.* освобождённый, свобо́дный (*от чего*)
● *v.t.* освобо|жда́ть, -ди́ть

exemption /ɪgˈzempʃ(ə)n/ *n.* освобожде́ние (*от чего*)

⚹ **exercise** /ˈeksəsaɪz/ *n.* **1** (physical activity) заря́дка, упражне́ние; you should take more ~ вам ну́жно бо́льше вре́мени уделя́ть физи́ческим упражне́ниям **2** (trial of skill): military ~s вое́нные уче́ния; (in lesson) упражне́ние; (fig.): the object of the ~ цель э́того предприя́тия
● *v.t.* **1** (exert, use) выка́зывать, вы́казать; проявля́ть, -и́ть; ~ authority примен|я́ть, -и́ть власть **2** (physically) упражня́ть (*impf.*)
● *v.i.* упражня́ться (*impf.*)
■ ~ **book** *n.* (BrE) (учени́ческая) тетра́дь

exert /ɪgˈzəːt/ *v.t.* осуществл|я́ть, -и́ть; ~ oneself постара́ться (*pf.*)

exertion /ɪgˈzəːʃ(ə)n/ *n.* напряже́ние, уси́лие

exhale /eksˈheɪl/ *v.i.* выдыха́ть, вы́дохнуть

exhaust /ɪgˈzɔːst/ *n.* (apparatus) вы́хлоп, вы́пуск; (expelled gas) отрабо́танный газ
● *v.t.* истощ|а́ть, -и́ть; изнур|я́ть, -и́ть; I feel ~ed я соверше́нно без сил

exhausting /ɪɡ'zɔ:stɪŋ/ *adj.* изнури́тельный, утоми́тельный

exhaustion /ɪɡ'zɔ:stʃ(ə)n/ *n.* переутомле́ние, изнеможе́ние

exhaustive /ɪɡ'zɔ:stɪv/ *adj.* исче́рпывающий, всесторо́нний

exhibit /ɪɡ'zɪbɪt/ *n.* (in museum etc.) экспона́т
● *v.t.* (**exhibited, exhibiting**) **1** (e.g. painting) экспони́ровать (*impf., pf.*) **2** (fig., display) прояв|ля́ть, -и́ть

✧ **exhibition** /eksɪ'bɪʃ(ə)n/ *n.* (public show) вы́ставка; he made an ~ of himself он сде́лал себя́ посме́шищем

exhibitionist /eksɪ'bɪʃənɪst/ *n.* хвасту́н (infml)

exhilarat|e /ɪɡ'zɪləreɪt/ *v.t.* весели́ть, раз-; ~ing news ра́достное изве́стие

exhilaration /ɪɡzɪlə'reɪʃ(ə)n/ *n.* весе́лье; прия́тное возбужде́ние

exhort /ɪɡ'zɔ:t/ *v.t.* приз|ыва́ть, -ва́ть (*кого к чему*); увещева́ть (*impf.*)

exhortation /eɡzɔ:'teɪʃ(ə)n/ *n.* призы́в, увещева́ние

exhume /eks'hju:m/ *v.t.* эксгуми́ровать (*impf., pf.*); выка́пывать, вы́копать

exile /'eksaɪl/ *n.* **1** (banishment) изгна́ние **2** (person) изгна́нник
● *v.t.* изг|оня́ть, -на́ть; ссыла́ть, сосла́ть

✧ **exist** /ɪɡ'zɪst/ *v.i.* существова́ть (*impf.*)

✧ **existence** /ɪɡ'zɪst(ə)ns/ *n.* существова́ние

existential /eɡzɪ'stenʃ(ə)l/ *adj.* экзистенциа́льный

existentialism /eɡzɪ'stenʃəlɪz(ə)m/ *n.* экзистенциали́зм

exit /'eksɪt/ *n.* (also comput.) вы́ход
● *v.i.* (**exited, exiting**) уходи́ть, уйти́; (comput.) выходи́ть, вы́йти

exonerate /ɪɡ'zɒnəreɪt/ *v.t.* опра́вд|ывать, -а́ть; сн|има́ть, -ять обвине́ние с (+ *g.*) (*в чём*)

exorbitant /ɪɡ'zɔ:bɪt(ə)nt/ *adj.* непоме́рный, чрезме́рный

exorcism /'eksɔ:sɪz(ə)m/ *n.* экзорци́зм, изгна́ние злых ду́хов

exorcize /'eksɔ:saɪz/ *v.t.* изг|оня́ть, -на́ть злых ду́хов из + *g.*

exotic /ɪɡ'zɒtɪk/ *adj.* экзоти́ческий

✧ **expand** /ɪk'spænd/ *v.t.* (lit., fig.) расш|иря́ть, -и́рить; heat ~s metals при нагрева́нии мета́ллы расширя́ются
● *v.i.* расш|иря́ться, -и́риться; увели́чи|ваться, -ться в объёме

expanse /ɪk'spæns/ *n.* протяже́ние

expansion /ɪk'spænʃ(ə)n/ *n.* расшире́ние; (pol.) экспа́нсия; (increase) подъём

expatriate /eks'pætrɪət/ *n. & adj.* экспатриа́нт ('-ка)

✧ **expect** /ɪk'spekt/ *v.t.* **1** (of future or probable event) ждать (*impf.*), ожида́ть (*impf.*) + *g.*; I ~ to see him я рассчи́тываю встре́титься с ним **2** (require) ожида́ть (*impf.*) + *g.*; I ~ you to be punctual я наде́юсь/рассчи́тываю, что

вы бу́дете пунктуа́льны **3** (suppose) полага́ть (*impf.*); I ~ you are hungry я полага́ю, вы голодны́ **4**: she is ~ing (infml, pregnant) она́ ожида́ет ребёнка

expectancy /ɪk'spekt(ə)nsɪ/ *n.* ожида́ние; предвкуше́ние

expectant /ɪk'spekt(ə)nt/ *adj.* выжида́ющий; an ~ mother бу́дущая мать

✧ **expectation** /ekspek'teɪʃ(ə)n/ *n.* ожида́ние; contrary to ~ вопреки́ ожида́ниям; come up to ~s оправда́ть (*pf.*) ожида́ния

expectorant /ek'spektərənt/ *n.* (med.) отха́ркивающее сре́дство

expediency /ɪk'spi:dɪənsɪ/ *n.* вы́года

expedient /ɪk'spi:dɪənt/ *n.* приём, спо́соб
● *adj.* целесообра́зный; (advantageous) вы́годный

expedition /ekspɪ'dɪʃ(ə)n/ *n.* экспеди́ция

expeditionary /ekspɪ'dɪʃənərɪ/ *adj.* экспедицио́нный
■ ~ force *n.* экспедицио́нные войска́

expel /ɪk'spel/ *v.t.* (**expelled, expelling**) (compel to leave) исключ|а́ть, -и́ть; выгоня́ть, вы́гнать

expend /ɪk'spend/ *v.t.* (money) расхо́довать, из-; тра́тить, ис-; (ammunition) расхо́довать, из-; (time, efforts) тра́тить, ис-/по-

expenditure /ɪk'spendɪtʃə(r)/ *n.* расхо́д, тра́та

✧ **expense** /ɪk'spens/ *n.* **1** (monetary cost) расхо́д; at my ~ (lit.) за мой счёт; go to ~ нести́ (*det.*) расхо́ды; spare no ~ не жале́ть (*impf.*) средств **2** (detriment): a joke at my ~ шу́тка на мой счёт
■ ~ account *n.* ава́нсовый отчёт

✧ **expensive** /ɪk'spensɪv/ *adj.* дорого́й, дорогосто́ящий

✧ **experience** /ɪk'spɪərɪəns/ *n.* **1** (process of gaining knowledge etc.) о́пыт **2** (event) слу́чай; an unpleasant ~ неприя́тный слу́чай
● *v.t.* испы́т|ывать, -а́ть

experienced /ɪk'spɪərɪənst/ *adj.* о́пытный

✧ **experiment** /ɪk'sperɪmənt/ *n.* экспериме́нт, о́пыт
● *v.i.* эксперименти́ровать (*impf.*)

experimental /ɪksperɪ'ment(ə)l/ *adj.* эксперимента́льный, про́бный

experimentation /ɪksperɪmen'teɪʃ(ə)n/ *n.* эксперименти́рование

✧ **expert** /'ekspɜ:t/ *n.* экспе́рт, знато́к, специали́ст (*по чему*)
● *adj.* квалифици́рованный; уме́лый; an ~ driver о́пытный шофёр; ~ advice сове́т специали́ста; she is ~ at persuading people она́ ма́стер угова́ривать

expertise /ekspɜ:'ti:z/ *n.* (skill, knowledge) компете́нтность

expire /ɪk'spaɪə(r)/ *v.i.* (of period, licence, etc.) ист|ека́ть, -е́чь

expiry /ɪk'spaɪərɪ/ *n.* истече́ние (сро́ка)

✧ **explain** /ɪk'spleɪn/ *v.t.* объясн|я́ть, -и́ть; изъясн|я́ть, -и́ть

e

✓ **explanation** /ekspləˈneɪʃ(ə)n/ *n.* объясне́ние

explanatory /ɪkˈsplænətərɪ/ *adj.* объясни́тельный

expletive /ɪkˈspliːtɪv/ *n.* (oath) бра́нное выраже́ние; (gram.) вставно́е сло́во

explicable /ɪkˈsplɪkəb(ə)l/ *adj.* объясни́мый

explicit /ɪkˈsplɪsɪt/ *adj.* я́сный, чёткий, то́чный

explode /ɪkˈspləʊd/ *v.t.* вз|рыва́ть, -орва́ть
• *v.i.* вз|рыва́ться, -орва́ться

exploit[1] /ˈeksplɔɪt/ *n.* по́двиг

exploit[2] /ɪkˈsplɔɪt/ *v.t.* **1** (use or develop economically; misuse) эксплуати́ровать (*impf.*) **2** (an advantage etc.) испо́льзовать (*impf., pf.*)

exploitation /eksplɔɪˈteɪʃ(ə)n/ *n.* (of person or resources) эксплуата́ция

exploitative /ɪkˈsplɔɪtətɪv/ *adj.* эксплуата́торский, эксплуатацио́нный

exploration /ekspləˈreɪʃ(ə)n/ *n.* (geog.) иссле́дование; (of possibilities etc.) изуче́ние

exploratory /ɪkˈsplɒrətərɪ/ *adj.* иссле́довательский; ~ **talks** предвари́тельные перегово́ры

✓ **explore** /ɪkˈsplɔː(r)/ *v.t.* **1** (geog.) иссле́довать (*impf., pf.*) **2** (possibilities etc.) изуч|а́ть, -и́ть

explorer /ɪkˈsplɔːrə(r)/ *n.* иссле́дователь (*m.*) (-ница)

explosion /ɪkˈspləʊʒ(ə)n/ *n.* (of bomb etc.) взрыв; (of rage etc.) вспы́шка; **population ~** демографи́ческий взрыв

explosive /ɪkˈspləʊsɪv/ *n.* взры́вчатое вещество́
• *adj.* взры́вчатый, взрывно́й; (situation) взрывоопа́сный

exponent /ɪkˈspəʊnənt/ *n.* (advocate) сторо́нник; представи́тель (*m.*)

exponential /ekspəˈnenʃ(ə)l/ *adj.* (math.) экспоненциа́льный, показа́тельный

export[1] /ˈekspɔːt/ *n.* э́кспорт, вы́воз

export[2] /ɪkˈspɔːt/ *v.t.* экспорти́ровать (*impf., pf.*); выв|ози́ть, -везти́

exportation /ekspɔːˈteɪʃ(ə)n/ *n.* экспорти́рование

exporter /ekˈspɔːtə(r)/ *n.* экспортёр

✓ **expose** /ɪkˈspəʊz/ *v.t.* **1** (physically) выставля́ть, вы́ставить; ~ **oneself** (indecently) обнаж|а́ться, -и́ться **2** (unmask) разоблач|а́ть, -и́ть

exposition /ekspəˈzɪʃ(ə)n/ *n.* (setting forth facts etc.) изложе́ние; (exhibition) экспози́ция, вы́ставка

exposure /ɪkˈspəʊʒə(r)/ *n.* **1** (physical): ~ **to light** выставле́ние на свет; **he died of ~** он поги́б от хо́лода **2** (unmasking) разоблаче́ние **3** (phot.) экспози́ция

expound /ɪkˈspaʊnd/ *v.t.* (a theory) изл|ага́ть, -ожи́ть; (a text) толкова́ть (*impf.*)

express[1] /ɪkˈspres/ *n.* (~ train) экспре́сс; курье́рский по́езд
• *adj.* (urgent, high-speed) сро́чный
• *adv.* сро́чно, спе́шно; **the goods were sent ~** (urgently) това́р был отпра́влен экспре́ссом

✓ ключева́я ле́ксика

■ ~ **letter** *n.* сро́чное письмо́; ~ **mail** *n.* э́кстренная по́чта

✓ **express**[2] /ɪkˈspres/ *v.t.* (show in words etc.) выража́ть, вы́разить; выска́зывать, вы́сказать; ~ **oneself** выража́ться, вы́разиться

✓ **expression** /ɪkˈspreʃ(ə)n/ *n.* **1** (act of expressing) выраже́ние **2** (word, term) выраже́ние (also math.)

expressionism /ɪkˈspreʃənɪz(ə)m/ *n.* экспрессиони́зм

expressionist /ɪkˈspreʃ(ə)nɪst/ *n.* экспрессиони́ст

expressive /ɪkˈspresɪv/ *adj.* вырази́тельный

expulsion /ɪkˈspʌlʃ(ə)n/ *n.* изгна́ние; исключе́ние

expurgate /ˈekspəɡeɪt/ *v.t.*: ~ **a book** исключ|а́ть, -и́ть (*or* изыма́ть, изъя́ть) нежела́тельные места́ из кни́ги

exquisite /ekˈskwɪzɪt/ *adj.* (perfected) утончённый

extemporize /ɪkˈstempəraɪz/ *v.t. & i.* и|мпровизи́ровать, сы-; **he ~d a speech** он произнёс импровизи́рованную речь

✓ **extend** /ɪkˈstend/ *v.t.* **1** (stretch out) протя́|гивать, -ну́ть **2** (make longer, wider or larger) удлин|я́ть, -и́ть; расш|иря́ть, -и́рить; ~ **a railway** продли́ть (*pf.*) железнодоро́жную ли́нию; ~ **one's premises** расш|иря́ть, -и́рить помеще́ние **3** (prolong) продл|ева́ть, -и́ть; ~ **one's leave/passport** продл|ева́ть, -и́ть о́тпуск/па́спорт; **an ~ed** (*sc.* lengthy) **visit** дли́тельный визи́т
• *v.i.* простира́ться (*impf.*); **the garden ~s to the river** сад простира́ется до реки́

extension /ɪkˈstenʃ(ə)n/ *n.* **1** (stretching out) вытя́гивание, удлине́ние **2** (enlarging in space or time) расшире́ние, увеличе́ние; ~ **of leave** продле́ние о́тпуска **3** (additional part of building etc.) пристро́йка (**to:** к + *d.*) **4** (teleph., telephone) паралле́льный телефо́н; (number) доба́вочный (но́мер); **my number is 5652, ~ 10** мой но́мер 5652, доба́вочный 10

■ ~ **lead** *n.* (elec.) удлини́тель (*m.*)

extensive /ɪkˈstensɪv/ *adj.* (wide, far-reaching) простра́нный

✓ **extent** /ɪkˈstent/ *n.* **1** (physical size, length, etc.) протяже́ние **2** (fig., range) разме́р; круг; диапазо́н **3** (degree) сте́пень; **to some** (*or* **a certain**) ~ до не́которой/изве́стной сте́пени

extenuat|e /ɪkˈstenjʊeɪt/ *v.t.* преум|еньша́ть, -е́ньшить; ~**ing circumstances** смягча́ющие обстоя́тельства

exterior /ɪkˈstɪərɪə(r)/ *n.* (of object) вне́шняя сторона́; (archit.) экстерье́р
• *adj.* вне́шний

exterminate /ɪkˈstɜːmɪneɪt/ *v.t.* истреб|ля́ть, -и́ть

extermination /ɪkstɜːmɪˈneɪʃ(ə)n/ *n.* истребле́ние

external /ɪkˈstɜːn(ə)l/ *n.* вне́шность
• *adj.* вне́шний; **for ~ use only** то́лько для нару́жного употребле́ния

extinct /ɪkˈstɪŋkt/ *adj.* (of volcano) поту́хший; (of species, custom) вы́мерший

extinction /ɪkˈstɪŋkʃ(ə)n/ *n.* угаса́ние; (of species etc.) вымира́ние

extinguish /ɪkˈstɪŋgwɪʃ/ *v.t.* (light, fire) гаси́ть, по-; (hopes etc.) уб|ива́ть, -и́ть

extinguisher /ɪkˈstɪŋgwɪʃə(r)/ *n.* огнетуши́тель (*m.*)

extol /ɪkˈstəʊl/ *v.t.* (**extolled, extolling**) превозн|оси́ть, -ести́

extort /ɪkˈstɔːt/ *v.t.* вымога́ть (*impf.*)

extortion /ɪkˈstɔːʃ(ə)n/ *n.* вымога́тельство

extortionate /ɪkˈstɔːʃənət/ *adj.* вымога́тельский

extortionist /ɪkˈstɔːʃənə(r)/ *n.* вымога́тель (*m.*)

⚔ **extra** /ˈekstrə/ *n.* **1** (additional item) что-н. дополни́тельное **2** (minor performer) стати́ст (-ка), актёр (актри́са) массо́вки
  ● *adj.* (additional) доба́вочный, дополни́тельный; **it costs £1, postage ~** э́то сто́ит 1 фунт без пересы́лки
  ● *adv.* сверх-, осо́бо; **~ strong** (e.g. drink) осо́бой кре́пости
  ■ **~ time** *n.* (sport) дополни́тельное вре́мя

extract[1] /ˈekstrækt/ *n.* вы́держка

extract[2] /ɪkˈstrækt/ *v.t.* (cork) выта́скивать, вы́тащить; (tooth) удал|я́ть, -и́ть

extra-curricular /ekstrəkəˈrɪkjʊlə(r)/ *adj.* проводи́мый сверх уче́бного пла́на

extradite /ˈekstrədaɪt/ *v.t.* (hand over) выдава́ть, вы́дать (*обвиняемого преступника*); экстради́ровать (*impf., pf.*)

extradition /ekstrəˈdɪʃ(ə)n/ *n.* вы́дача (престу́пника); экстради́ция

extramarital /ekstrəˈmærɪt(ə)l/ *adj.*: **~ affair** внебра́чная связь

extramural /ekstrəˈmjʊər(ə)l/ *adj.* (BrE, of education) зао́чный; **~ student** зао́чни|к (-ца)

extraneous /ɪkˈstreɪnɪəs/ *adj.* посторо́нний, чужо́й

extraordinary /ɪkˈstrɔːdɪnərɪ/ *adj.* (unusual) необы́чный; (impressive) необыча́йный; (specially convened) чрезвыча́йный

extrapolate /ɪkˈstræpəleɪt/ *v.t. & i.* (math.) (*also* fig.) экстраполи́ровать (*impf., pf.*)

extraterrestrial /ekstrətɪˈrestrɪəl/ *adj.* внеземно́й
  ● *n.* инопланетя́н|ин (-ка)

extravagance /ɪkˈstrævəg(ə)ns/ *n.* (lack of thrift) расточи́тельность; (luxury) изли́шество; (unusualness) экстравага́нтность

extravagant /ɪkˈstrævəg(ə)nt/ *adj.* расточи́тельный; **she was ~ with water** она́ расхо́довала сли́шком мно́го воды́

extravaganza /ɪkstrævəˈgænzə/ *n.* фее́рия

extreme /ɪkˈstriːm/ *n.* **1** (high degree) кра́йность **2** (of conduct etc.) кра́йность; **he**

went to ~s to satisfy them он пошёл на кра́йние ме́ры, чтобы угоди́ть им
  ● *adj.* кра́йний, преде́льный; **the ~ edge of the city** са́мая окра́ина го́рода

⚔ **extremely** /ɪkˈstriːmlɪ/ *adv.* кра́йне

extremism /ɪkˈstriːmɪz(ə)m/ *n.* экстреми́зм

extremist /ɪkˈstriːmɪst/ *n.* экстреми́ст
  ● *adj.* экстреми́стский

extremity /ɪkˈstremɪtɪ/ *n.* **1** (end, extreme point) край **2** (*in pl.*) (hands and feet) коне́чности (*f. pl.*) **3** (extreme quality) кра́йность; **the ~ of his grief** безме́рность его́ го́ря **4** (hardship) кра́йность; **reduced to ~** доведённый до кра́йности **5** (*in pl.*) (extreme measures) кра́йние ме́ры (*f. pl.*)

extricate /ˈekstrɪkeɪt/ *v.t.* высвобожда́ть, вы́свободить; **~ oneself from a difficulty** вы́путаться (*pf.*) из затрудне́ния

extrovert /ˈekstrəvɜːt/ *n.* экстраве́рт

exuberance /ɪgˈzjuːbərəns/ *n.* (profusion) изоби́лие; (of character) экспанси́вность

exuberant /ɪgˈzjuːbərənt/ *adj.* (of imagination etc.) бога́тый, бу́йный; (of spirits etc.) экспанси́вный

exude /ɪgˈzjuːd/ *v.i.* проступ|а́ть, -и́ть; выдел|я́ть, вы́делить; **she ~d cheerfulness** она́ излуча́ла весе́лье

exult /ɪgˈzʌlt/ *v.i.* торжествова́ть, ликова́ть (*both impf.*)

exultant /ɪgˈzʌlt(ə)nt/ *adj.* торжеству́ющий, лику́ющий

exultation /ɪgzʌlˈteɪʃ(ə)n/ *n.* торжество́, ликова́ние

⚔ **eye** /aɪ/ *n.* **1** (organ of vision) глаз **2** (var. idioms): **make ~s at sb** (infml) стро́ить (*impf.*) гла́зки кому́-н.; **keep an ~ on** (e.g. a saucepan, children, the time) следи́ть (*impf.*) за + *i.*; **an ~ for an ~** о́ко за о́ко; **before sb's very ~s** на глаза́х у кого́-н.; **he has an ~ for colour** он чу́вствует цвет; **I caught her ~** я пойма́л её взгляд; **see ~ to ~ with** сходи́ться (*impf.*) во взгля́дах с + *i.* **3** (special sense): **~ of a needle** иго́льное ушко́
  ● *v.t.* (**eyes, eyed, eyeing** *or* **eying**) разгля́д|ывать, -е́ть; наблюда́ть (*impf.*)
  ■ **~ball** *n.* глазно́е я́блоко; **~brow** *n.* бровь; **~brow pencil** каранда́ш для брове́й; **~-catching** *adj.* эффе́ктный; **~ drops** *n. pl.* глазны́е ка́пли; **~ hospital** *n.* глазна́я больни́ца; **~lash** *n.* ресни́ца; **~lid** *n.* ве́ко; **without batting an ~lid** (infml) гла́зом не моргну́в; **~liner** *n.* каранда́ш для подведе́ния глаз; **~shadow** *n.* те́ни (*f. pl.*) для век; **~sight** *n.* зре́ние; **she has good ~sight** у неё хоро́шее зре́ние; **~sore** *n.* уро́дство; **~witness** *n.* очеви́дец

-eyed /aɪd/ *comb. form*: **blue~** голубогла́зый

Ff

F¹ /ef/ *n.* (mus.) фа (*nt. indecl.*)

F² /ef/ *n.* (*abbr. of* **Fahrenheit**) F (= *градусов по Фаренгейту*)

fable /ˈfeɪb(ə)l/ *n.* ба́сня

fabric /ˈfæbrɪk/ *n.* (text.) ткань, мате́рия; (of a building etc., fig.) структу́ра

fabricate /ˈfæbrɪkeɪt/ *v.t.* **1** (invent) выду́мывать, вы́думать **2** (construct) стро́ить, по-

fabrication /fæbrɪˈkeɪʃ(ə)n/ *n.* **1** (invented story, lie) вы́думка; **complete ~** сплошна́я вы́думка **2** (manufacturing) изготовле́ние

fabulous /ˈfæbjʊləs/ *adj.* роско́шный, басносло́вный

facade /fəˈsɑːd/ *n.* (archit.) фаса́д

◆ **face** /feɪs/ *n.* **1** (front part of head) лицо́; **look sb in the ~** посмотре́ть (*pf.*) кому́-н. в глаза́; **I came ~ to ~ with him** я столкну́лся с ним лицо́м к лицу́; **I told him so to his ~** я сказа́л ему́ э́то в лицо́; **she laughed in my ~** она́ рассмея́лась мне в лицо́; **he shut the door in my ~** он захло́пнул дверь пе́ред мои́м но́сом; **in the ~ of danger** пе́ред лицо́м опа́сности **2** (facial expression) лицо́; выраже́ние лица́; **he made/pulled a ~** он сско́рчил/состро́ил ро́жу; **his ~ fell** он измени́лся в лице́; **у него́ вы́тянулось лицо́ 3** (respect): **he saved ~** он спас свою́ репута́цию **4** (physical surface) лицо́; (of clock) цифербла́т; **he laid the card ~ down** он положи́л ка́рту лицо́м вниз (*or* руба́шкой вверх)

● *v.t.* **1** (physically) стоя́ть (*impf.*) лицо́м к + *d.*; **the man facing us** челове́к, сидя́щий *и т. n.* про́тив нас **2** (confront) смотре́ть (*impf.*) в лицо́ *чему́*; **we must ~ facts** на́до смотре́ть фа́ктам в лицо́; **let's ~ it!** (infml) на́до гляде́ть пра́вде в глаза́!

● *v.i.*: **the house ~s south** дом обращён фаса́дом на юг; **their house ~s ours** их дом напро́тив на́шего; **he ~d up to the difficulties** он не испуга́лся тру́дностей

■ **F~book**® *n.* социа́льная сеть «Фейсбу́к»; **~lift** *n.* подтя́жка ко́жи на лице́; (fig.) вне́шнее обновле́ние, космети́ческий ремо́нт; **~ value** *n.* (of currency) номина́льная сто́имость; **I took his words at ~ value** я при́нял его́ слова́ за чи́стую моне́ту

faceless /ˈfeɪslɪs/ *adj.* (anonymous) безли́чный, безли́кий

facet /ˈfæsɪt/ *n.* грань; (fig.) аспе́кт

facetious /fəˈsiːʃəs/ *adj.* шутли́вый, шу́точный

facetiousness /fəˈsiːʃəsnɪs/ *n.* (неуме́стная) шутли́вость

◆ ключевая лексика

facial /ˈfeɪʃ(ə)l/ *n.* масса́ж лица́
● *adj.* лицево́й

facile /ˈfæsaɪl/ *adj.* (easy, fluent) лёгкий, свобо́дный; (superficial) пове́рхностный

facilitate /fəˈsɪlɪteɪt/ *v.t.* спосо́бствовать (*impf.*) + *d.*

◆ **facilit|y** /fəˈsɪlɪti/ *n.* (ease) лёгкость; (appliance, installation) сооруже́ние; **~ies for study** усло́вия (*nt. pl.*) для учёбы; **sports ~ies** спорти́вное обору́дование; помеще́ния (*nt. pl.*) для заня́тия спо́ртом

facsimile /fækˈsɪmɪli/ *n.* (exact copy) факси́миле (*nt. indecl.*); (fax) факс

◆ **fact** /fækt/ *n.* факт; **as a matter of ~** факти́чески; на са́мом де́ле; **the ~ is that ...** де́ло в том, что…; **in ~** (actually) факти́чески; в/на са́мом де́ле; (intensifying): **I think so, in ~** я тако́й ду́маю, бо́лее того́, я уве́рен в э́том

■ **~-finding** *adj.* занима́ющийся установле́нием фа́ктов, рассле́дованием обстоя́тельств

faction /ˈfækʃ(ə)n/ *n.* фра́кция, группиро́вка

factional /ˈfækʃən(ə)l/ *adj.* фракцио́нный

◆ **factor** /ˈfæktə(r)/ *n.* фа́ктор

factory /ˈfæktəri/ *n.* фа́брика, заво́д

factual /ˈfæktʃʊəl/ *adj.* факти́ческий

faculty /ˈfækəlti/ *n.* **1** (power, aptitude) спосо́бность **2** (BrE, part of university) факульте́т **3** (AmE, body of teachers) профе́ссорско-преподава́тельский соста́в

fad /fæd/ *n.* (craze) увлече́ние; (whim) при́хоть

fade /feɪd/ *v.t.* **1** (cause to lose colour) обесцве́|чивать, -тить **2** (cin., radio): **~ out** постепе́нно уме́нь|шать, -ьшить си́лу зву́ка; **~ in** постепе́нно увели́чи|вать, -ть си́лу зву́ка
● *v.i.* **1** (lose colour) обесцве́|чиваться, -титься **2** (fig.): **his hopes ~d** его́ наде́жды раста́яли

faeces /ˈfiːsiːz/ (AmE **feces**) *n. pl.* фека́лии (*f. pl.*); испражне́ния (*nt. pl.*)

fag¹ /fæɡ/ *n.* (BrE, infml, tedious task) изнури́тельная рабо́та

fag² /fæɡ/ *n.* (BrE, infml, cigarette) сигаре́та, папиро́са
■ **~ end** *n.* (butt) оку́рок; (fig.) коне́ц (*чего*); оста́ток (*чего*)

fagged /fæɡd/ *adj.* (BrE, infml) измо́танный; **I am ~ out** я вконе́ц вы́мотался

Fahrenheit /ˈfærənhaɪt/ *n.* (*abbr* **F**) Фаренге́йт

◆ **fail** /feɪl/ *n.*: **without ~** обяза́тельно, непреме́нно
● *v.t.* **1** (exam) не сда|ва́ть, -ть; (drugs test; of sportsman/addict) не про|ходи́ть, -йти́ (тест

на до́пинг/нарко́тики) **2** (disappoint, desert) подв|оди́ть, -ести́; **words** ∼ **me** я не нахожу́ слов
● *v.i.* **1** (decline) ух|удша́ться, -у́дшиться; (fall short) недоста|ва́ть (*impf.*); **the crops** ∼**ed** хлеб не уроди́лся; **his eyesight is** ∼**ing** его́ зре́ние слабе́ет; **he is in** ∼**ing health** его́ здоро́вье ухудша́ется **2** (not succeed): **he** ∼**ed in the exam** он провали́лся на экза́мене; **he** ∼**ed to convince her** ему́ не удало́сь (*or* он не суме́л) убеди́ть её **3** (omit) упус|ка́ть, -ти́ть; **he never** ∼**s to write** он никогда́ не забыва́ет писа́ть

failing /ˈfeɪlɪŋ/ *n.* (defect) недоста́ток
● *prep.* за неиме́нием + *g.*

◆ **failure** /ˈfeɪljə(r)/ *n.* **1** (unsuccess) неуда́ча, неуспе́х, прова́л **2** (person) неуда́чник **3** (non-functioning) ава́рия; **heart** ∼ остано́вка се́рдца **4** (omission): **his** ∼ **to answer is a nuisance** о́чень доса́дно, что он не отвеча́ет

faint /feɪnt/ *n.* (med.) о́бморок; **in a dead** ∼ в глубо́ком о́бмороке
● *adj.* **1** (weak, indistinct) сла́бый, неотчётливый; **I haven't the** ∼**est idea** я не име́ю ни мале́йшего поня́тия **2** (giddy): **I feel** ∼ мне ду́рно
● *v.i.* (lose consciousness) па́дать, упа́сть в о́бморок; (grow weak) слабе́ть (*impf.*)
■ ∼**-hearted** *adj.* трусли́вый, малоду́шный

fair¹ /feə(r)/ *n.* (trade fair) (вы́ставка-)я́рмарка; (fun fair) я́рмарка; аттракцио́ны *m.pl.*
■ ∼**ground** *n.* я́рмарочная площа́дь

◆ **fair²** /feə(r)/ *adj.* **1** (beautiful) прекра́сный, краси́вый; **the** ∼ **sex** прекра́сный пол **2** (of weather) я́сный **3** (abundant): **a** ∼ **amount** (a lot) значи́тельное/изря́дное коли́чество **4** (average) сно́сный; **she has a** ∼ **chance of success** у неё неплохи́е ша́нсы на успе́х; **her performance was only** ∼ её выступле́ние бы́ло та́к себе́ **5** (equitable): ∼ **share** зако́нная до́ля; **it is** ∼ **to say that …** со всей справедли́востью мо́жно сказа́ть, что… **6** (of hair) све́тлый; (blond) белоку́рый; **a** ∼ **complexion** све́тлый цвет лица́
■ ∼**-haired** *adj.* белоку́рый; ∼**-minded** *adj.* справедли́вый; ∼ **play** *n.* че́стная игра́; справедли́вость

◆ **fairly** /ˈfeəlɪ/ *adv.* **1** (moderately) дово́льно, сно́сно, терпи́мо **2** (justly) че́стно, справедли́во

fairness /ˈfeənɪs/ *n.* (equity) справедли́вость, че́стность; **in all** ∼ со всей справедли́востью

fairy /ˈfeərɪ/ *n.* фе́я
■ ∼ **story,** ∼ **tale** *nn.* ска́зка; (fig.) ска́зка, небыли́ца

fait accompli /feɪt əˈkɒmplɪ/ *n.* (*pl.* **faits accomplis** *pronunc. same*) сверши́вшийся факт

◆ **faith** /feɪθ/ *n.* **1** (trust) ве́ра, дове́рие; **I have no** ∼ **in doctors** я не ве́рю доктора́м **2** (relig.) ве́ра **3** (sincerity): **in good** ∼ че́стно, добросо́вестно

faithful /ˈfeɪθfʊl/ *adj.* то́чный, достове́рный; (*as n. pl.*) **the** ∼ (believers) правове́рные

faithfully /ˈfeɪθfʊlɪ/ *adv.* то́чно, ве́рно; **yours** ∼ (BrE, formal letter ending) с уваже́нием;

и́скренне Ваш

faithless /ˈfeɪθlɪs/ *adj.* вероло́мный

fake /feɪk/ *n.* (sham) подде́лка; (*attr.*) подде́льный
● *v.t.* подде́л|ывать, -ать

falcon /ˈfɔːlkən/ *n.* со́кол

◆ **fall** /fɔːl/ *n.* **1** (physical drop) паде́ние **2** (moral) паде́ние; ∼ **from grace** нра́вственное паде́ние **3** (diminution) пониже́ние; ∼ **in prices** паде́ние цен **4** (*in pl.*) (waterfall) водопа́д **5** (AmE, autumn) о́сень
● *v.i.* (*past* **fell**, *p.p.* **fallen**) **1** па́дать, упа́сть; **he fell over a chair** он упа́л, споткну́вшись о стул; **he fell off his horse** он упа́л с ло́шади **2** (drop, sink) па́дать, упа́сть; **prices fell** це́ны сни́зились/упа́ли; **the temperature fell** температу́ра упа́ла; **my spirits fell** я упа́л/пал ду́хом **3** (of defeat etc.) па́|дать, -сть; **the government fell** прави́тельство па́ло **4** (pass into a state): **he fell ill** он заболе́л; **he fell in love with her** он влюби́лся в неё **5** (come): **darkness fell** наступи́ла темнота́
□ ∼ **apart** расп|ада́ться, -а́сться
□ ∼ **back** (mil.) отступ|а́ть, -и́ть; ∼ **back on sth** приб|ега́ть, -е́гнуть к чему́-н.
□ ∼ **behind** (e.g. in walking) отст|ава́ть, -а́ть; (with rent) зап|а́здывать, -озда́ть с упла́той за кварти́ру
□ ∼ **down** па́дать, упа́сть
□ ∼ **for** (∼ in love with) увл|ека́ться, -е́чься + *i.*; (be taken in by): **he fell for her story** он пове́рил её расска́зу
□ ∼ **in** впасть (*во что*); **the roof fell in** кры́ша ру́хнула/обвали́лась; **the soldiers fell in** солда́ты постро́ились
□ ∼ **off** па́дать, упа́сть (*с чего*); **attendance is falling off** посеща́емость па́дает
□ ∼ **out** выпада́ть, вы́пасть; **his hair fell out** у него́ вы́пали во́лосы; (quarrel) поссо́риться (*pf.*)
□ ∼ **over** па́дать, упа́сть
□ ∼ **through** прова́л|иваться, -и́ться
■ ∼**out** *n.* (nuclear) радиоакти́вные оса́дки (*m. pl.*)

fallacious /fəˈleɪʃəs/ *adj.* оши́бочный, ло́жный

fallacy /ˈfæləsɪ/ *n.* (false belief) заблужде́ние

fallen /ˈfɔːl(ə)n/ *p.p. of* ▶ **fall**

fallible /ˈfælɪb(ə)l/ *adj.* подве́рженный оши́бкам

Fallopian tube /fəˈləʊpɪən/ *n.* фалло́пиева труба́

fallow /ˈfæləʊ/ *adj.* (agric.) вспа́ханный под пар; (земля́): **lie** ∼ ост|ава́ться, -а́ться под па́ром
■ ∼ **land** *n.* пар

◆ **false** /fɔːls/ *adj.* **1** (wrong) ло́жный, оши́бочный, фальши́вый **2** (deceitful) лжи́вый, фальши́вый **3** (sham) фальши́вый
■ ∼ **alarm** *n.* ло́жная трево́га; ∼ **bottom** *n.* двойно́е дно; ∼ **pretences** *n. pl.* обма́н, притво́рство; ∼ **start** *n.* (racing, also fig.) фальста́рт; срыв в са́мом нача́ле; ∼ **teeth** *n. pl.* иску́сственные зу́бы

falsehood /ˈfɔːlshʊd/ *n.* ложь, непра́вда; **he told a ~** он сказа́л непра́вду
falsify /ˈfɔːlsɪfaɪ/ *v.t.* подде́л|ывать, -а́ть
falsity /ˈfɔːlsɪtɪ/ *n.* (falsehood, inaccuracy) ло́жность, оши́бочность
falter /ˈfɔːltə(r)/ *v.i.* (move or act hesitatingly) спот|ыка́ться, -кну́ться; (in speaking) зап|ина́ться, -ну́ться
fame /feɪm/ *n.* сла́ва; репута́ция
✧ **familiar** /fəˈmɪlɪə(r)/ *adj.* **1** (common, usual) обы́чный, привы́чный **2** (of acquaintance) знако́мый; **I am ~ with the subject** я знако́м с э́тим предме́том
familiarity /fəmɪlɪˈærɪtɪ/ *n.* **1** (close acquaintance) бли́зкое знако́мство (with: c + *i.*) **2** (of manner) фамилья́рность
familiarize /fəˈmɪlɪəraɪz/ *v.t.* ознак|омля́ть, -о́мить (*кого с чем*); **~ oneself with sth** ознако́миться (*pf.*) с чем-н.
✧ **family** /ˈfæmɪlɪ/ *n.* **1** (parents and children) семья́ **2** (*attr.*) семе́йный
■ **~ name** *n.* (surname) фами́лия; **~ planning** *n.* контро́ль (*m.*) над рожда́емостью; **~ tree** *n.* родосло́вное де́рево
famine /ˈfæmɪn/ *n.* го́лод
famished /ˈfæmɪʃt/ *adj.* (infml): **I'm ~** я си́льно проголода́лся; я умира́ю с го́лоду
✧ **famous** /ˈfeɪməs/ *adj.* знамени́тый, просла́вленный
fan[1] /fæn/ *n.* ве́ер; (ventilator) вентиля́тор
  ● *v.t.* (**fanned, fanning**): **~ oneself** обма́хиваться (*impf.*) ве́ером
  ● *v.i.* (**fanned, fanning**): **~ out** (e.g. roads) расходи́ться (*impf.*) ве́ером; (e.g. soldiers) разв|ора́чиваться, -ерну́ться ве́ером
✧ **fan**[2] /fæn/ *n.* (infml, devotee) боле́льщи|к (-ца), фана́т (-ка), люби́тель (*m.*) (-ница)
■ **~ mail** *n.* пи́сьма (*nt. pl.*) от покло́нников
fanatic /fəˈnætɪk/ *n.* фана́тик
fanatical /fəˈnætɪk(ə)l/ *adj.* фанати́чный
fanaticism /fəˈnætɪsɪz(ə)m/ *n.* фанати́зм
fanciful /ˈfænsɪfʊl/ *adj.* капри́зный; причу́дливый
fancy /ˈfænsɪ/ *n.* **1** (imagination) фанта́зия **2** (thing imagined) фанта́зия **3** (liking) скло́нность; **he took a ~ to her** он увлёкся е́ю
  ● *adj.* (**fancier, fanciest**) (elaborate) прихотли́вый; **this dress is too ~ to wear to work** для рабо́ты ну́жно пла́тье поскро́мнее; (fashionable) мо́дный
  ● *v.t.* **1** (imagine): **~ (that)!** вообрази́(те)! **2** (BrE, like) хоте́ть (*impf.*) + *g.*; жела́ть (*impf.*); **she fancies him** (infml) он ей нра́вится; **what do you ~ for dinner?** чего́ бы вам хоте́лось на у́жин?
■ **~ dress** *n.* маскара́дный костю́м; **~-dress ball** костюми́рованный бал
fanfare /ˈfænfeə(r)/ *n.* фанфа́ра
fang /fæŋ/ *n.* (of wolf etc.) клык; (of snake) ядови́тый зуб
fantasize /ˈfæntəsaɪz/ *v.i.* фантази́ровать (*impf.*)

fantastic /fænˈtæstɪk/ *adj.* (wild, strange) фантасти́ческий, фантасти́чный; (infml, marvellous) потряса́ющий, изуми́тельный
fantasy /ˈfæntəsɪ/ *n.* фанта́зия; (genre) фанта́стика
FAQ *abbr.* (of **frequently asked questions**) (comput.) ча́сто задава́емые вопро́сы
✧ **far** /fɑː(r)/ *adj.* (**further, furthest** or **farther, farthest**) да́льний, далёкий, отдалённый; **the F~ East** Да́льний Восто́к; **at the ~ end of the street** на друго́м конце́ у́лицы
  ● *adv.* (**further, furthest** or **farther, farthest**) далеко́; **~ away, off** о́чень далеко́; **they came from ~ and wide** они́ съе́хались отовсю́ду (*or* со всех концо́в); **~ better** (на)мно́го/гора́здо лу́чше; **it is ~ from true** э́то совсе́м не так; **so ~** (until now) до сих пор; пока́ (что); **as, so ~ as** (of distance) до (*чего*); (of extent) наско́лько; поско́льку; **as ~ as I know** наско́лько мне изве́стно; **as ~ as I am concerned** что каса́ется меня́; **he went so ~ as to say …** он да́же сказа́л…; **how ~** (of distance) как далеко́; (of extent) наско́лько; **he will go ~** (succeed) он далеко́ пойдёт; **he has gone too ~ this time** на э́тот раз он зашёл сли́шком далеко́
■ **~-away** *adj.* (distant) далёкий, отдалённый; **~-fetched** *adj.* натя́жкой; притя́нутый за́ волосы/уши; **~-off** *adj.* отдалённый; **~-reaching** *adj.* далеко́ иду́щий; **~-sighted** *adj.* (prudent etc.) дальнови́дный, предусмотри́тельный; (long-sighted) дальнозо́ркий
farce /fɑːs/ *n.* (theatr., fig.) фарс
farcical /ˈfɑːsɪk(ə)l/ *adj.* смехотво́рный
fare /feə(r)/ *n.* (cost) пла́та за прое́зд
farewell /feəˈwel/ *n.* проща́ние
✧ **farm** /fɑːm/ *n.* фе́рма
  ● *v.t. & i.* **1** (agric.) занима́ться (*impf.*) се́льским хозя́йством **2**: **~ out work** отд|ава́ть, -а́ть рабо́ту
■ **~house** *n.* фе́рмерский дом; **~yard** *n.* двор фе́рмы
✧ **farmer** /ˈfɑːmə(r)/ *n.* фе́рмер
■ **~s' market** *n.* ры́нок сельскохозя́йственной проду́кции
farming /ˈfɑːmɪŋ/ *n.* се́льское хозя́йство, фе́рмерство
farther /ˈfɑːðə(r)/ (*see also* ▸ **further**) *adj.* бо́лее отдалённый; дальне́йший
  ● *adv.* да́льше, да́лее
farthest /ˈfɑːðɪst/ (*see also* ▸ **furthest**) *adj.* са́мый да́льний
  ● *adv.* да́льше всего́
fascinate /ˈfæsɪneɪt/ *v.t.* очаро́в|ывать, -а́ть
fascinating /ˈfæsɪneɪtɪŋ/ *adj.* очарова́тельный
fascination /fæsɪˈneɪʃ(ə)n/ *n.* очарова́ние, обая́ние, пре́лесть
Fascism /ˈfæʃɪz(ə)m/ *n.* фаши́зм
Fascist /ˈfæʃɪst/ *n.* фаши́ст (-ка)
  ● *adj.* фаши́стский
✧ **fashion** /ˈfæʃ(ə)n/ *n.* **1** (way) о́браз, мане́ра; **after a ~** (indifferently) до не́которой сте́пени

2 (prevailing style) мо́да; **in** ~ в мо́де; **out of** ~ вы́шедший из мо́ды
• *v.t.* (e.g. an object) прид|ава́ть, -а́ть фо́рму + *d.*
■ ~ **designer** *n.* модельёр; ~ **house** *n.* дом моде́лей; ~ **show** *n.* пока́з мод
fashionable /ˈfæʃənəb(ə)l/ *adj.* мо́дный
fast¹ /fɑːst/ *n.* (relig.) пост
• *v.i.* пости́ться (*impf.*)
fast² /fɑːst/ *adv.* (firmly) про́чно, кре́пко; **she was** ~ **asleep** она́ кре́пко спала́; **the car stuck** ~ маши́на застря́ла/завя́зла
⚲ **fast³** /fɑːst/ *adj.* (rapid) ско́рый, бы́стрый; **my watch is** ~ мои́ часы́ спеша́т
• *adv.* бы́стро
■ ~-**food restaurant** *n.* рестора́н бы́строго обслу́живания; ~ **lane** *n.* (on road) скоростно́й ряд
fasten /ˈfɑːs(ə)n/ *v.t.* (coat) застёг|ивать, -ну́ть; (laces) завя́з|ывать, -а́ть; (seat belt) пристёг|ивать, -ну́ть
• *v.i.* зап|ира́ться, -ере́ться; **the dress** ~**s down the back** пла́тье застёгивается на спине́
fastener /ˈfɑːsənə(r)/, **fastening** /ˈfɑːsnɪŋ/ *nn.* запо́р, задви́жка
fastidious /fæˈstɪdɪəs/ *adj.* привере́дливый, щепети́льный; разбо́рчивый
⚲ **fat** /fæt/ *n.* жир
• *adj.* (**fatter, fattest**) **1** (of person etc.) то́лстый, жи́рный, ту́чный; **get** ~ толсте́ть, по- **2** (rich): **a** ~ **profit** больша́я при́быль
fatal /ˈfeɪt(ə)l/ *adj.* **1** (causing death) смерте́льный; **a** ~ **accident** несча́стный слу́чай со смерте́льным исхо́дом **2** (disastrous) роково́й, фата́льный
fatalism /ˈfeɪtəlɪz(ə)m/ *n.* фатали́зм
fatalistic /feɪtəˈlɪstɪk/ *adj.* фаталисти́ческий
fatality /fəˈtælətɪ/ *n.* (death) смерть (*от несча́стного слу́чая и т. n.*); (fate) неотврати́мая судьба́
fate /feɪt/ *n.* судьба́, у́часть, уде́л, до́ля
fateful /ˈfeɪtfʊl/ *adj.* роково́й
⚲ **father** /ˈfɑːðə(r)/ *n.* **1** (male parent, also fig.) оте́ц, роди́тель (*m.*) **2** (in personifications): **F**~ **Christmas** Дед Моро́з **3** (priest) оте́ц, ба́тюшка
• *v.t.* поро|жда́ть, -ди́ть
■ ~-**in-law** *n.* (husband's ~) свёкор; (wife's ~) тесть (*m.*); ~**land** *n.* ро́дина
fatherhood /ˈfɑːðəhʊd/ *n.* отцо́вство
fatherly /ˈfɑːðəlɪ/ *adj.* оте́ческий
fathom /ˈfæð(ə)m/ *n.* морска́я саже́нь
• *v.t.* (fig.) пост|ига́ть, -и́гнуть
fatigue /fəˈtiːɡ/ *n.* (also, tech., metal ~) уста́лость; (mil.) (*in pl.*) (menial tasks) хозя́йственная рабо́та
fatten /ˈfæt(ə)n/ *v.t.* (animal) отк|а́рмливать, -орми́ть на убо́й
fattening /ˈfæt(ə)nɪŋ/ *adj.* калори́йный
fatty /ˈfætɪ/ *adj.* (**fattier, fattiest**) жи́рный, жирово́й
fatuous /ˈfætjʊəs/ *adj.* самодово́льно-глу́пый; бессмы́сленный
faucet /ˈfɔːsɪt/ *n.* (AmE, tap) кран
fault /fɔːlt/ *n.* **1** (imperfection) недоста́ток,

дефе́кт; **find** ~ **with sb** на|ходи́ть, -йти́ недоста́тки у кого́-н. **2** (in mechanism) дефе́кт **3** (error) оши́бка **4** (blame) вина́; **it's (all) your** ~ э́то ва́ша вина́; э́то всё из-за вас **5** (at tennis etc.) дво́йна́я оши́бка **6** (geol.) разло́м, сдвиг
• *v.t.* на|ходи́ть, -йти́ недоста́тки в + *p.*; **I could not** ~ **his argument** я не мог придра́ться к его́ аргумента́ции
faultless /ˈfɔːltlɪs/ *adj.*: ~ **precision** безупре́чная то́чность
faulty /ˈfɔːltɪ/ *adj.* (**faultier, faultiest**) повреждённый
fauna /ˈfɔːnə/ *n.* (*pl.* ~**s**) фа́уна
faux pas /fəʊ ˈpɑː/ *n.* (*pl.* ~) беста́ктность
⚲ **favour** /ˈfeɪvə(r)/ (AmE **favor**) *n.* **1** (goodwill) благоскло́нность; **find** ~ **in sb's eyes** сниска́ть (*pf.*) чьё-н. расположе́ние; **I am in** ~ **of the plan** я — за э́тот план **2** (kindly act) одолже́ние, любе́зность, услу́га; **he did me a** ~ он оказа́л мне любе́зность **3** (advantage) по́льза; **this is in his** ~ э́то говори́т в его́ по́льзу; **the exchange rate is in our** ~ курс обме́на валю́ты вы́годен для нас
• *v.t.* **1** (support) благоприя́тствовать (*impf.*) + *d.* **2** (treat with partiality) ока́з|ывать, -а́ть предпочте́ние + *d.*
favourable /ˈfeɪvərəb(ə)l/ (AmE **favorable**) *adj.* благоприя́тный, благоскло́нный; **a** ~ **report** положи́тельный отчёт
⚲ **favourite** /ˈfeɪvərɪt/ (AmE **favorite**) *n.* (person) люби́мец, фавори́т; (horse) фавори́т
• *adj.* люби́мый, излю́бленный
favouritism /ˈfeɪvərɪtɪz(ə)m/ (AmE **favoritism**) *n.*: **a teacher shouldn't show** ~ у учи́теля не должно́ быть люби́мчиков
fawn¹ /fɔːn/ *n.* (deer) оленёнок
fawn² /fɔːn/ *v.i.* (of person): ~ **on sb** подли́з|ываться, -а́ться к кому́-н.
fax /fæks/ *n.* факс
• *v.t.* пос|ыла́ть, -ла́ть фа́ксом
■ ~ **machine** *n.* факс, факси́мильный аппара́т
faze /feɪz/ *v.t.* сму|ща́ть, -ти́ть
FBI *abbr.* (*of* **Federal Bureau of Investigation**) ФБР (Федера́льное бюро́ рассле́дований)
FC *abbr.* (*of* **football club**) футбо́льный клуб, ФК
⚲ **fear** /fɪə(r)/ *n.* **1** (terror) страх, боя́знь, опасе́ние; **your** ~**s are groundless** ва́ши опасе́ния напра́сны **2** (likelihood): **I was silent for** ~ **of offending him** я молча́л, боя́сь оби́деть его́; **there is no** ~ **of my losing the money** мне нечего боя́ться, де́ньги я не потеря́ю
• *v.t. & i.* боя́ться (*impf.*) + *g.*; опаса́ться (*impf.*) + *g.*; **she** ~**s death** она́ бои́тся сме́рти; **I** ~ **the worst** я опаса́юсь ху́дшего; **I** ~ **for his life** я опаса́юсь за его́ жизнь
fearful /ˈfɪəfʊl/ *adj.* (terrible) ужа́сный; (timid) боязли́вый; **I was** ~ **of waking her** я боя́лся разбуди́ть её
fearless /ˈfɪəlɪs/ *adj.* бесстра́шный
fearsome /ˈfɪəsəm/ *adj.* устраша́ющий, гро́зный

f

feasible /ˈfiːzɪb(ə)l/ *adj.* осуществи́мый

feast /fiːst/ *n.* **1** (relig.) (церко́вный) пра́здник **2** (meal) пир
● *v.t. & i.* пирова́ть (*impf.*); пра́здновать (*impf.*); he ~ed his eyes on the scene он любова́лся э́тим зре́лищем

feat /fiːt/ *n.* по́двиг; ~ of engineering выдаю́щееся достиже́ние инжене́рного иску́сства

feather /ˈfeðə(r)/ *n.* перо́

feature /ˈfiːtʃə(r)/ *n.* **1** (part of face) черта́ **2** (aspect) черта́, осо́бенность **3** (main item): this journal makes a ~ of sport э́тот журна́л широко́ освеща́ет спорти́вные собы́тия; ~ (film) худо́жественный фильм
● *v.t.* (give prominence to) поме|ща́ть, -сти́ть на ви́дном ме́сте
● *v.i.* (figure prominently) быть/явля́ться (*impf.*) характе́рной черто́й

February /ˈfebruərɪ/ *n.* февра́ль (*m.*)

feckless /ˈfeklɪs/ *adj.* безала́берный

fed /fed/ *past and p.p. of ▸* feed

federal /ˈfedər(ə)l/ *adj.* федера́льный

federalism /ˈfedərəlɪz(ə)m/ *n.* федерали́зм

federation /fedəˈreɪʃ(ə)n/ *n.* федера́ция

fee /fiː/ *n.* (professional charge) гонора́р; school ~s пла́та за обуче́ние

feeble /ˈfiːb(ə)l/ *adj.* (feebler, feeblest) хи́лый, сла́бый

feed /fiːd/ *n.* (animal's) корм; (baby's) кормле́ние
● *v.t.* (*past and p.p.* fed) **1** (give food to) корми́ть, на-; (fig.): I am fed up (infml) я сыт по го́рло; мне надое́ло **2** (fig.): he fed information into the computer он ввёл да́нные в компью́тер
■ ~back *n.* (elec.) обра́тная связь; (fig.) о́тклик, о́тзыв(ы); реа́кция

feel /fiːl/ *n.* (sensation) ощуще́ние; (contact) осяза́ние; he has a ~ for language у него́ есть чу́вство языка́
● *v.t.* (*past and p.p.* felt) **1** (explore by touch) щу́пать, по-; ~ the edge of a knife тро́гать, по- ле́звие ножа́; ~ the weight of this box! чу́вствуете, ско́лько ве́сит э́тот я́щик! **2** (grope) пробира́ться (*impf.*) о́щупью; he felt his way in the dark он пробира́лся о́щупью в темноте́ **3** (be aware of) чу́вствовать, по-; did you ~ the earthquake? вы почу́вствовали землетрясе́ние? **4** (be affected by) чу́вствовать, по-; he ~s (or is ~ing) the heat жара́ пло́хо де́йствует на него́; он пло́хо перено́сит жару́ **5** (be of opinion) счита́ть (*impf.*); I ~ you should go по-мо́ему, вам сле́дует пойти́/сходи́ть
● *v.i.* (*past and p.p.* felt) **1** (experience sensation): I ~ cold мне хо́лодно; I ~ hungry я голоден; I ~ sure я уве́рен; I ~ bad about not inviting him мне со́вестно, что я не пригласи́л его́; I ~ like (going for) a walk мне хо́чется прогуля́ться; I don't ~ up to going я не в состоя́нии идти́; it ~s like rain похо́же, бу́дет дождь; I ~ for you я вам

сочу́вствую **2** (produce sensation) да|ва́ть, -ть ощуще́ние (*чего*); your hands ~ cold у вас холо́дные ру́ки; how does it ~ to be home? каково́ оказа́ться до́ма? **3** (grope): he felt in his pocket for a coin он пошári̇л в карма́не, ища́ моне́ту; he felt along the wall for the door он пыта́лся нащу́пать дверь в стене́

feeler /ˈfiːlə(r)/ *n.* (zool.) щу́пальце, у́сик; (fig.): he put out ~s он прозонди́ровал по́чву; он заки́нул у́дочку

feeling /ˈfiːlɪŋ/ *n.* **1** (power of sensation) ощуще́ние, чу́вство **2** (sense) созна́ние, чу́вство **3** (opinion): I have a ~ he won't come у меня́ предчу́вствие, что он не придёт **4** (emotion) чу́вство, страсть; he spoke with ~ он говори́л с чу́вством **5** (sensitivity) чувстви́тельность; you hurt his ~s вы его́ оби́дели

feet /fiːt/ *pl. of ▸* foot

feign /feɪn/ *v.t.* симули́ровать (*impf., pf.*); ~ madness симули́ровать безу́мие

feisty /ˈfaɪstɪ/ *adj.* (feistier, feistiest) (person) хра́брый, сме́лый; (dog) сме́лый, бесстра́шный; (action) сме́лый, реши́тельный; (spirit) реши́тельный

feline /ˈfiːlaɪn/ *n.* живо́тное из семе́йства коша́чьих
● *adj.* коша́чий

fell¹ /fel/ *v.t.* (person) сби|ва́ть, -ть с ног; (tree) руби́ть, с-; вали́ть, с-/по-

fell² /fel/ *past of ▸* fall

fellow /ˈfeləʊ/ *n.* **1** (chap) па́рень (*m.*) **2** (academic or professional) колле́га; сотру́дник; (BrE, of a college) член сове́та ко́лледжа
■ ~ countryman *n.* соотече́ственник; ~ countrywoman *n.* соотече́ственница

fellowship /ˈfeləʊʃɪp/ *n.* (companionship) това́рищество, бра́тство; (association) корпора́ция; колле́гия (*адвока́тов и т. п.*)

felony /ˈfelənɪ/ *n.* (тя́жкое) уголо́вное преступле́ние

felt¹ /felt/ *n.* (material) во́йлок, фетр; ~ hat фе́тровая шля́па
■ ~-tip pen *n.* флома́стер

felt² /felt/ *past and p.p. of ▸* feel

female /ˈfiːmeɪl/ *n.* (woman or girl) же́нщина; (animal) са́мка, ма́тка
● *adj.* же́нский

feminine /ˈfemɪnɪn/ *adj.* же́нский

femininity /femɪˈnɪnɪtɪ/ *n.* же́нственность

feminism /ˈfemɪnɪz(ə)m/ *n.* femини́зм

feminist /ˈfemɪnɪst/ *n.* femини́ст (-ка)

femme fatale /fæm fəˈtɑːl/ *n.* (*pl.* femmes fatales* pronunc. same*) рокова́я же́нщина

femur /ˈfiːmə(r)/ *n.* бедро́

fen /fen/ *n.* топь, боло́то

fence /fens/ *n.* забо́р, и́згородь, огра́да; sit on the ~ занима́ть (*impf.*) нейтра́льную/ выжида́тельную пози́цию
● *v.t.* (*also* ~ in, off, round) огор|а́живать, -оди́ть

fencer /ˈfensə(r)/ *n.* фехтова́льщик

fencing /ˈfensɪŋ/ *n.* фехтова́ние

fend /fend/ v.i.: ~ **for oneself** полага́ться (impf.) на себя́

fender /'fendə(r)/ n. **1** (in front of fire) ≈ ками́нная решётка **2** (AmE, of car) крыло́

feng shui /feŋ 'ʃuːɪ/ n. фэн-шу́й (m. & nt. indecl.)

fennel /'fen(ə)l/ n. фе́нхель (m.), сла́дкий укро́п

fern /fɜːn/ n. (pl. ~ or ~s) па́поротник

ferocious /fə'rəʊʃəs/ adj. свире́пый, лю́тый

ferocity /fə'rɒsɪtɪ/ n. свире́пость, лю́тость

ferret /'ferɪt/ n. (zool.) хорёк
● v.t. (**ferreted, ferreting**): ~ **out** (fig.) выи́скивать, вы́искать
● v.i. (**ferreted, ferreting**): ~ **about** (fig.) ры́скать (impf.)

Ferris wheel /'ferɪs/ n. чёртово колесо́; колесо́ обозре́ния

ferry /'ferɪ/ n. (boat) паро́м
● v.t. (convey to and fro) перев|ози́ть, -езти́ (or перепр|авля́ть, -а́вить) на паро́ме; отв|ози́ть, -езти́

fertile /'fɜːtaɪl/ adj. **1** (of soil) плодоро́дный; (of humans, animals) плодови́тый **2** (fig.): a ~ **imagination** бога́тое воображе́ние

fertility /fɜː'tɪlɪtɪ/ n. плодоро́дие; плодови́тость
■ ~ **drug** n. препара́т от беспло́дия

fertilize /'fɜːtɪlaɪz/ v.t. (biol.) оплодотвор|я́ть, -и́ть; (hort.) удо|бря́ть, -о́брить

fertilizer /'fɜːtɪlaɪzə(r)/ n. (hort.) удобре́ние

fervent /'fɜːv(ə)nt/ adj. (fig.) горя́чий, пы́лкий

fervid /'fɜːvɪd/ adj. пы́лкий, пла́менный

fervour /'fɜːvə(r)/ (AmE **fervor**) n. жар, пыл, страсть

fester /'festə(r)/ v.i. гно́иться, за-/на-; нагн|а́иваться, -ои́ться

festival /'festɪv(ə)l/ n. фестива́ль (m.)

festive /'festɪv/ adj. пра́здничный

festivity /fe'stɪvɪtɪ/ n. пра́зднество, торжество́

festoon /fe'stuːn/ n. гирля́нда
● v.t. укр|аша́ть, -а́сить гирля́ндами

fetal /'fiːt(ə)l/ adj. заро́дышевый, эмбриона́льный
■ ~ **position** n. положе́ние эмбрио́на (в ма́тке)

fetch /fetʃ/ v.t. **1** (go and get) прин|оси́ть, -ести́; (children from school, dry-cleaning) заб|ира́ть, -ра́ть; **they** ~ed **the doctor** они́ вы́звали врача́ **2** (of price): **his house** ~ed **£150,000** он вы́ручил 150 000 фу́нтов за свой дом

fetching /'fetʃɪŋ/ adj. привлека́тельный

fete /feɪt/ n. пра́зднество, пра́здник

fetid /'fetɪd/ adj. воню́чий, злово́нный

fetish /'fetɪʃ/ n. фети́ш

fetter /'fetə(r)/ n. (in pl.) ножны́е кандал|ы́ (-о́в); (fig.) око́в|ы (pl., g. —)
● v.t. зако́в|ывать, -а́ть в кандалы́; (fig.) ско́в|ывать, -а́ть

fettle /'fet(ə)l/ n.: **in fine** ~ (condition) в хоро́шем состоя́нии; (mood) в хоро́шем настрое́нии

fetus /'fiːtəs/ (pl. ~**es**) n. плод, заро́дыш

feud /fjuːd/ n. вражда́
● v.i. враждова́ть (с кем) (impf.)

feudal /'fjuːd(ə)l/ adj. феода́льный

fever /'fiːvə(r)/ n. жар; **he has a high** ~ у него́ жар

feverish /'fiːvərɪʃ/ adj. лихора́дочный

few /fjuː/ n. & adj. немно́гие (pl.); немно́го + g.; ма́ло + g.; ~ **(people) know the truth** немно́гие зна́ют пра́вду; a ~ **(people)** немно́гие (лю́ди); не́сколько челове́к; a **good** ~ (BrE), **quite a** ~ дово́льно мно́го (+ g.); ~ **and far between** ре́дкие; **every** ~ **minutes** ка́ждые не́сколько мину́т

fewer /'fjuːə(r)/ n. & adj. ме́нее, ме́ньше; **he wrote no** ~ **than 60 books** он написа́л ни мно́го ни ма́ло 60 книг

fiancé /fɪ'ɒnseɪ/ n. жени́х

fiancée /fɪ'ɒnseɪ/ n. неве́ста

fiasco /fɪ'æskəʊ/ n. (pl. ~**s**) фиа́ско (nt. indecl.), прова́л

fib /fɪb/ n. вы́думка, непра́вда
● v.i. (**fibbed, fibbing**) прив|ира́ть, -ра́ть (infml)

fibre /'faɪbə(r)/ (AmE **fiber**) n. **1** (filament) волокно́ **2** (in diet) клетча́тка
■ ~**glass** n. стекловолокно́; стеклопла́стик; ~**-optic** adj. воло́конно-опти́ческий

fickle /'fɪk(ə)l/ adj. переме́нчивый, непостоя́нный

fiction /'fɪkʃ(ə)n/ n. **1** (invention, pretence) вы́мысел, вы́думка, фи́кция **2** (novels etc.) беллетри́стика; **work of** ~ худо́жественное произведе́ние

fictional /'fɪkʃən(ə)l/ adj. вы́мышленный; беллетристи́ческий

fictitious /fɪk'tɪʃəs/ adj. подло́жный, фикти́вный; a ~ **name** вы́мышленное и́мя

fiddle /'fɪd(ə)l/ v.t. (BrE, falsify) подде́л|ывать, -ать
● v.i. (fidget, tamper) верте́ться (impf.); крути́ться (impf.); вози́ться (impf.); **he** ~**d with his tie** он тереби́л свой га́лстук; **don't** ~ **with my papers!** не тро́гайте мои́ бума́ги!

fidelity /fɪ'delɪtɪ/ n. (loyalty) ве́рность

fidget /'fɪdʒɪt/ v.i. (**fidgeted, fidgeting**) ёрзать (impf.)

fidgety /'fɪdʒɪtɪ/ adj. суетли́вый, непосе́дливый

field /fiːld/ n. **1** (piece of ground) по́ле **2** (physical range, area) по́ле **3** (area of activity or study) о́бласть; по́ле/сфе́ра де́ятельности
■ ~ **day** n. (fig., day of successful exploits) знамена́тельный/па́мятный день; ~ **events** n. pl. лёгкая атле́тика; ~**work** n. (research) иссле́дования (nt. pl.) в есте́ственных усло́виях

fiend /fiːnd/ n. (devil) дья́вол; (evil person) злоде́й, и́зверг; (fig.): **dope** ~ наркома́н; **fresh air** ~ (зая́длый) люби́тель све́жего во́здуха

fiendish /'fiːndɪʃ/ adj. дья́вольский, злоде́йский

fierce /fɪəs/ adj. (**fiercer, fiercest**) свире́пый, лю́тый; ~ **competition** жесто́кая конкуре́нция

f

fiery /ˈfaɪərɪ/ *adj.* (**fierier, fieriest**) огненный, пламенный; a ~ **temper** вспыльчивый/горячий характер; a ~ **horse** горячая лошадь

fifteen /fɪfˈtiːn/ *n.* пятнадцать; **she is** ~ **ей** пятнадцать лет
● *adj.* пятнадцать + *g. pl.*

fifteenth /fɪfˈtiːnθ/ *n.* (date) пятнадцатое (число); (fraction) одна пятнадцатая
● *adj.* пятнадцатый

fifth /fɪfθ/ *n.* (date) пятое (число); (fraction) одна пятая
● *adj.* пятый

fiftieth /ˈfɪftɪəθ/ *n.* (fraction) одна пятидесятая
● *adj.* пятидесятый

fifty /ˈfɪftɪ/ *n.* пятьдесят, полсотни; **the** ~**ies** (decade) пятидесятые годы; **he is in his** ~**ies** ему за пятьдесят (лет); ему пошёл шестой десяток; **we shared expenses** ~y-~y мы разделили расходы пополам
● *adj.* пятьдесят + *g. pl.*

fig /fɪɡ/ *n.* (fruit) инжир
■ ~ **leaf** *n.* фиговый листок; ~ **tree** *n.* инжир, фиговое дерево

⚹ **fight** /faɪt/ *n.* бой, схватка, драка
● *v.t. & i.* (past and p.p. **fought**) драться, по-; сражаться, -зиться; (wage war) воевать (*impf.*); **the boys/dogs are** ~**ing** мальчики/ собаки дерутся; ~ **a battle** вести (*det.*) бой; ~ **an election** вести (*det.*) предвыборную борьбу; ~ **a lawsuit** судиться (*impf.*); **he fought his way forward** он пробивался/ проталкивался вперёд; **he fought off a cold** он (быстро) справился с простудой; **they fought off the enemy** они отбили врага; ~ **back** *v.i.* отбиваться, -иться

fighter /ˈfaɪtə(r)/ *n.* (one who fights) боец; (fig.) борец ◻ (~ **aircraft**) истребитель (*m.*)

fighting /ˈfaɪtɪŋ/ *n.* бой, сражение
● *adj.* боевой; **we have a** ~ **chance** стоит попытаться

figment /ˈfɪɡmənt/ *n.* вымысел; a ~ **of the imagination** плод воображения

figurative /ˈfɪɡərətɪv/ *adj.* переносный

⚹ **figure** /ˈfɪɡə(r)/ *n.* ◻ (numerical sign) цифра; **double** ~**s** двузначные числа; a **six-**~ **number** шестизначное число ◻ (diagram, illustration) рисунок ◻ (human form) фигура; **I saw a** ~ **approaching** я увидел приближавшуюся ко мне фигуру; **she has a good** ~ у неё хорошая фигура ◻ (person of importance) фигура, выдающаяся личность
● *v.t.:* ~ **out** (calculate) вычислять, вычислить; (understand) понимать, -ять; **I can't** ~ **him out** я не могу его понять
● *v.i.* ◻ (appear) фигурировать (*impf.*); **this did not** ~ **in my plans** это не входило в мои планы ◻ (AmE, infml): **it** ~**s** (makes sense, is plausible) это похоже на правду; **I** ~ **they'll be late** я думаю, что они опоздают
■ ~**head** *n.* носовое украшение, фигура на носу корабля; (fig.) номинальный руководитель; ~ **skating** *n.* фигурное

катание

figurine /fɪɡjʊˈriːn/ *n.* фигурка, статуэтка

Fiji /ˈfiːdʒiː/ *n.* Фиджи (*indecl.*)

filament /ˈfɪləmənt/ *n.* (thread) волокно, нить; (elec.) нить накала

file¹ /faɪl/ *n.* (tool) напильник
● *v.t.* подпил|ивать, -ить; ~ **one's nails** подпил|ивать, -ить ногти

⚹ **file²** /faɪl/ *n.* ◻ (for papers) папка, скоросшиватель (*m.*) ◻ (set of papers etc.) дело, досье (*nt. indecl.*) ◻ (comput.) файл
● *v.t.* ◻ (documents) подши|вать, -ть ◻ (submit): ~ **a complaint** под|авать, -ать жалобу; ~ **suit against sb** возбу|ждать, -дить судебное дело против кого-н.
● *v.i.:* ~ **for divorce** под|авать, -ать на развод

file³ /faɪl/ *n.* (row) ряд, шеренга; колонна; **in single** ~ гуськом; по одному
● *v.i.* идти (*det.*) гуськом/колонной; **the prisoners** ~**d out** заключённые выходили гуськом друг за другом

filing /ˈfaɪlɪŋ/ *n.* (of papers) регистрация бумаг
■ ~ **cabinet** *n.* шкаф, сейф

Filipino /fɪlɪˈpiːnəʊ/ *n.* (*pl.* ~**s**) филиппин|ец (-ка)
● *adj.* филиппинский

⚹ **fill** /fɪl/ *v.t.* ◻ (make full) наполн|ять, -олнить; запол|нять, -олнить; **he** ~**ed the hole with sand** он заполнил яму песком; **I was** ~**ed with admiration** я был полон восхищения ◻: ~ **a tooth** пломбировать, за- ◻ (fig., of office etc.) зан|имать, -ять; ~ **a vacancy** запол|нять, -олнить вакантную должность ◻: ~ **a need** удовлетвор|ять, -ить потребность
● *v.i.* (become full) напол|няться, -олниться
◻ ~ **in** *v.t.* (BrE, complete) запол|нять, -олнить; **he** ~**ed in the form** (BrE) он заполнил бланк/ анкету; (infml, inform): **I** ~**ed him in** я ввёл его в курс дела
◻ ~ **out** *v.t.* (AmE, a form) запол|нять, -олнить
● *v.i.* расши|ряться, -ириться
◻ ~ **up** *v.t.* (make full) напол|нять, -олнить
● *v.i.* (become full) напол|няться, -олниться

fillet /ˈfɪlɪt/ *n.* филе (*nt. indecl.*)
● *v.t.* (**filleted, filleting**) (of fish, take off bone) отдел|ять, -ить мясо от костей

filling /ˈfɪlɪŋ/ *n.* (in tooth) пломба; (in pie) начинка
● *adj.* (of food) сытный
■ ~ **station** *n.* автозаправочная *or* бензозаправочная станция; (бензо)заправка

⚹ **film** /fɪlm/ *n.* ◻ (thin coating) плёнка ◻ (phot.) фотоплёнка; (cin.) киноплёнка ◻ (motion picture) фильм
● *v.t. & i.* сн|имать, -ять
■ ~ **crew** *n.* съёмочная группа; ~ **star** *n.* кинозвезда; ~ **studies** *n. pl.* киноведение; ~ **studio** *n.* киностудия

filter /ˈfɪltə(r)/ *n.* (for liquid) фильтр; (for light) светофильтр
● *v.t.* (purify) фильтрова́ть, от-/про-

filth /fɪlθ/ *n.* грязь

filthy /ˈfɪlθɪ/ *adj.* (**filthier, filthiest**) грязный

⚹ ключевая лексика

fin /fɪn/ *n.* плавни́к

◇ **final** /'faɪn(ə)l/ *n.* **1** (*in pl.*) (BrE, exam at end of degree course) выпускно́й экза́мен; (AmE, exam at end of term, year, class) ито́говый экза́мен **2** (match) фина́л
● *adj.* **1** (last in order) после́дний **2** (decisive) оконча́тельный, реша́ющий

finale /fɪ'nɑːlɪ/ *n.* (mus., fig.) фина́л

finalist /'faɪnəlɪst/ *n.* финали́ст (-ка)

finalize /'faɪnəlaɪz/ *v.t.* (give final form to) заверш|а́ть, -и́ть; (settle, e.g. arrangements) (оконча́тельно) ула́|живать, -дить

◇ **finally** *adv.* (after a long time) в конце́ концо́в; (once and for all) оконча́тельно; (lastly) наконе́ц

◇ **finance** /'faɪnæns/ *n.* фина́нсы (*m. pl.*); дохо́ды (*m. pl.*)
● *v.t.* финанси́ровать (*impf., pf.*)

◇ **financial** /faɪ'nænʃ(ə)l/ *adj.* фина́нсовый

financier /faɪ'nænsɪə(r)/ *n.* финанси́ст

finch /fɪntʃ/ *n.* зя́блик

◇ **find** /faɪnd/ *n.* (discovery, esp. valuable) нахо́дка
● *v.t.* (*past and p.p.* **found**) **1** (discover, encounter) на|ходи́ть, -йти́; (by search) раз|ы́скивать, от- (*both pf.*); pine trees are found in many countries сосна́ растёт/ встреча́ется во мно́гих стра́нах; I ~ it hard to understand him мне тру́дно поня́ть его́ **2** (judge): the jury found him guilty прися́жные призна́ли его́ вино́вным **3** (obtain) получ|а́ть, -и́ть; he found time to read он находи́л вре́мя для чте́ния **4**: ~ **out** (detect) узн|ава́ть, -а́ть; (ascertain) выясня́ть, вы́яснить; have you found out (about) the trains? вы узна́ли расписа́ние поездо́в?

◇ **finding** /'faɪndɪŋ/ *n.* (also in pl.) (conclusion) вы́вод(ы)

fine¹ /faɪn/ *n.* (punishment) штраф, пе́ня
● *v.t.* штрафова́ть, о-; he was ~d £5 его́ оштрафова́ли на 5 фу́нтов

◇ **fine²** /faɪn/ *adj.* **1** (of weather) я́сный, хоро́ший **2** (handsome, excellent) прекра́сный, замеча́тельный; a ~ view прекра́сный вид **3** (exquisite) то́нкий; a ~ workmanship то́нкая рабо́та **4** (of small particles) ме́лкий; ~ **dust** ме́лкая пыль **5** (thin) то́нкий, о́стрый; a pencil with a ~ point о́стро отто́ченный каранда́ш **6** (subtle) утончённый, то́нкий; a ~ distinction то́нкое разли́чие; the ~ arts изобрази́тельные/изя́щные иску́сства
● *adv.*: he cut it ~ (of time) он оста́вил себе́ вре́мени в обре́з; that suits me ~ (infml) э́то меня́ вполне́ устра́ивает

fineness /'faɪnnɪs/ *n.* (delicacy) то́нкость, утончённость, изя́щество

finery /'faɪnərɪ/ *n.* пы́шный наря́д

finesse /fɪ'nes/ *n.* (delicacy) деликáтность, то́нкость

◇ **finger** /'fɪŋgə(r)/ *n.* (of hand or glove) пáлец
● *v.t.* тро́гать, по-
■ ~**nail** *n.* нóготь (*m.*); ~**print** *n.* отпеча́ток пáльца ● *v.t.* (take sb's ~prints) сн|има́ть, -я́ть отпеча́тки пáльцев у + *g.*; ~**tip** *n.* кóнчик пáльца

finicky /'fɪnɪkɪ/ *adjs.* (чересчу́р) разбо́рчивый, приве́редливый

◇ **finish** /'fɪnɪʃ/ *n.* **1** (conclusion) оконча́ние, коне́ц **2** (polish) отде́лка
● *v.t.* **1** (end) зак|а́нчивать, -о́нчить; конча́ть, ко́нчить; I ~ed the book я (за)ко́нчил кни́гу; he ~ed (off, up) the pie он дое́л весь пиро́г; we will ~ the job мы зако́нчим рабо́ту **2** (perfect) соверше́нствовать (*impf.*) **3** (infml, exhaust, kill) изнур|я́ть, -и́ть; the fever ~ed him off лихора́дка докона́ла/прикончи́ла его́
● *v.i.* конча́ться, ко́нчиться; зак|а́нчиваться, -о́нчиться; have you ~ed with that book? вам бо́льше не нужна́ э́та кни́га?
■ ~**ing post** *n.* фи́ниш; ~**ing touch** *n.* после́дний штрих

finite /'faɪnaɪt/ *adj.* коне́чный; име́ющий преде́л

Finland /'fɪnlənd/ *n.* Финля́ндия

Finn /fɪn/ *n.* фин|н (-ка)

Finnish /'fɪnɪʃ/ *n.* (language) фи́нский язы́к
● *adj.* фи́нский

fiord /fjɔːd/ *n.* = **fjord**

fir /fɜː(r)/ *n.* (in full ~ **tree**) ель

◇ **fire** /'faɪə(r)/ *n.* **1** (phenomenon of combustion) ого́нь (*m.*); the house is on ~ дом загоре́лся/ гори́т; set ~ to подж|ига́ть, -е́чь; catch ~ загор|а́ться, -е́ться **2** (burning fuel) ого́нь (*m.*); light a ~ разж|ига́ть, -е́чь ками́н; топи́ть, за- печь **3** (conflagration) пожа́р; ~! пожа́р! **4** (of ~arms) ого́нь (*m.*), стрельба́; open ~ откр|ыва́ть, -ы́ть ого́нь
● *v.t.* **1** (set fire to) подж|ига́ть, -е́чь **2** (of ~arms) стреля́ть (*impf.*) из + *g.*; ~ a rifle стреля́ть (*impf.*) из ружья́; ~ a shot вы́стрелить (*pf.*)
● *v.i.* (of ~arms) стреля́ть (*impf.*); the troops ~d at the enemy войска́ стреля́ли по врагу́
■ ~ **alarm** *n.* (alert) пожа́рная трево́га; (device) автомати́ческий пожа́рный сигна́л; ~**arm** *n.* огнестре́льное ору́жие; ~ **bomb** *n.* зажига́тельная бо́мба; ~ **brigade** *n.* (BrE) пожа́рная кома́нда; ~ **engine** *n.* пожа́рная маши́на; ~ **escape** *n.* пожа́рная ле́стница; ~ **extinguisher** *n.* огнетуши́тель (*m.*); ~**fighter** *n.* пожа́рный; пожа́рник (infml); ~**guard** *n.* ками́нная решётка; ~**lighter** *n.* (BrE) расто́пка; ~**man** *n.* пожа́рный; пожа́рник (infml); ~**place** *n.* ками́н, оча́г; ~**proof** *adj.* огнеупо́рный ● *v.t.* прид|ава́ть, -а́ть огнесто́йкость + *d.*; ~**side** *n.* ме́сто о́коло ками́на; (fig.) дома́шний оча́г; ~ **station** *n.* пожа́рное депо́ (*nt. indecl.*); ~**wood** *n.* дров|а́ (*pl., g.* —); ~**work(s)** *n.* (*pl.*) фейерве́рк

firing /'faɪərɪŋ/ *n.* (shooting) стрельба́
■ ~ **line** *n.* ли́ния огня́

◇ **firm¹** /fɜːm/ *n.* фи́рма

◇ **firm²** /fɜːm/ *adj.* **1** (physically) кре́пкий, твёрдый **2** (fig.) усто́йчивый, сто́йкий, непоколеби́мый; you must be ~ with him вы должны́ быть с ним постро́же; a ~ offer твёрдое предложе́ние
● *adv.* твёрдо, усто́йчиво; stand ~ стоя́ть (*impf.*) твёрдо

firmament /ˈfɜːməmənt/ *n.* небе́сный свод
firmware /ˈfɜːmweə(r)/ *n.* (comput.)
микропрогра́мма, встро́енная програ́мма;
проши́вка (sl.)

✏ **first** /fɜːst/ *n.* **1** (beginning): **at ~** снача́ла,
сперва́ **2** (date) пе́рвое (число́); **on the ~ of
May** пе́рвого ма́я **3** (BrE, academic) вы́сшая
оце́нка/отме́тка
● *adj.* **1** (in time or place) пе́рвый; **on the ~
floor** (BrE) на второ́м этаже́; (AmE) на пе́рвом
этаже́; **at ~ glance** на пе́рвый взгляд; **hear
sth at ~ hand** дава́ть, -а́ть что-н. из
пе́рвых рук; **in the ~ place** во-пе́рвых, в
пе́рвую о́чередь; **I will go there ~ thing
tomorrow** за́втра я пе́рвым де́лом зайду́
туда́; **the ~ time I saw him** когда́ я в пе́рвый
раз уви́дел его́ **2** (in rank or importance) пе́рвый
● *adv.* **1** (before all) (*also* **~ and foremost**
or **~ of all**) пре́жде всего́; в пе́рвую
о́чередь **2** (initially) сперва́, снача́ла; (in the ~
place) во-пе́рвых; (for the ~ time) впервы́е; **I ~
met him last year** я познако́мился с ним в
про́шлом году́
■ **~ aid** *n.* пе́рвая по́мощь; **~-aid kit**
санита́рная су́мка; апте́чка; **~-class** *adj.*
(excellent) первокла́ссный ● *adv.* (of travel)
пе́рвым кла́ссом; **~ cousin** *n.* двою́родный
брат, двою́родная сестра́; **~ name** *n.* и́мя;
~ night *n.* (theatr.) премье́ра; **~-night nerves**
волне́ние пе́ред премье́рой; **~-rate** *adj.*
первокла́ссный

firstly /ˈfɜːstlɪ/ *adv.* во-пе́рвых

fiscal /ˈfɪsk(ə)l/ *adj.* фиска́льный, фина́нсовый

✏ **fish** /fɪʃ/ *n.* (*pl.* **~** *or* **~es**) ры́ба
● *v.i.* лови́ть/уди́ть (*impf.*) ры́бу; (fig.): **~
for compliments** напра́шиваться (*impf.*) на
комплиме́нты; **~ for information** выу́живать,
вы́удить све́дения
■ **~monger** *n.* торго́вец ры́бой; **~net** *n.*: **~net
stockings** ажу́рные чулки́

fisherman /ˈfɪʃəmən/ *n.* рыба́к; (angler for
pleasure) рыболо́в

fishery /ˈfɪʃərɪ/ *n.* (fish farm) рыбово́дческое
хозя́йство

fishing /ˈfɪʃɪŋ/ *n.* ры́бная ло́вля; **the boys have
gone ~** ма́льчики ушли́ на рыба́лку
■ **~ line** *n.* леска́; **~ net** *n.* рыболо́вная сеть;
~ rod *n.* уди́лище

fishy /ˈfɪʃɪ/ *adj.* (**fishier, fishiest**)
ры́бий, ры́бный; (infml, suspect) нечи́стый,
подозри́тельный

fissure /ˈfɪʃə(r)/ *n.* тре́щина, расще́лина
● *v.i.* тре́скаться, по-; тре́снуть (*pf.*)

fist /fɪst/ *n.* кула́к

fit¹ /fɪt/ *n.* **1** (attack of illness) при́ступ, припа́док
2 (outburst) ка́шля; **his jokes had us in ~s** от его́ шу́ток мы
пока́тывались со́ смеху **3**: **in ~s and starts**
уры́вками

✏ **fit²** /fɪt/ *n.* (of a garment etc.): **this jacket is a tight
~** э́тот пиджа́к узкова́т
● *adj.* (**fitter, fittest**) **1** (suitable) го́дный,
приго́дный, подходя́щий; **see, think ~**

✏ ключева́я ле́ксика

счита́ть, счесть ну́жным; **a meal ~ for a king**
ца́рская тра́пеза; **you are not ~ to be seen**
вам нельзя́ пока́зываться в тако́м ви́де
2 (in good health) здоро́вый; **keep (oneself)
~** подде́рживать (*impf.*) хоро́шую
(спорти́вную) фо́рму
● *v.t.* (**fitted, fitting**) **1** (equip) (*also* **~
out**, **~ up**) снаря|жа́ть, -ди́ть; снаб|жа́ть,
-ди́ть; экипирова́ть (*impf., pf.*); обору́довать
(*impf., pf.*) **2** (install): **he ~ted a new lock
on the door** он вста́вил но́вый замо́к в
дверь; (fig., accommodate): **I can ~ you in next
week** я могу́ назна́чить вам встре́чу на
сле́дующей неде́ле **3** (make suitable, adapt)
приспос|абливать, -о́бить; (correspond to in
dimensions) под|ходи́ть, -ойти́ + *d.*; **the dress
~s you** э́то пла́тье хорошо́ на вас сиди́т
4 (insert): **he ~ted the cigarette into the
holder** он вста́вил сигаре́ту в мундшту́к
● *v.i.* (**fitted, fitting**) **1** (be of the correct
dimensions) под|ходи́ть, -ойти́; **this dress ~s
well** э́то пла́тье сиди́т хорошо́; **that ~s
(in) with my plans** э́то вполне́ совпада́ет с
мои́ми пла́нами **2** (be inserted): **tubes that ~
into one another** тру́бки, вставля́ющиеся
одна́ в другу́ю
■ **~ted carpet** *n.* (BrE) ковёр во всю ко́мнату;
~ted kitchen *n.* (BrE) встро́енная ку́хня

fitful /ˈfɪtfʊl/ *adj.* нера́вный, преры́вистый

fitness /ˈfɪtnɪs/ *n.* хоро́шее здоро́вье

fitter /ˈfɪtə(r)/ *n.* (of machinery) монтёр,
сбо́рщик

fitting /ˈfɪtɪŋ/ *n.* **1** (of clothes) приме́рка
2 (fixture in building) обору́дование
● *adj.* подходя́щий, го́дный
■ **~ room** *n.* приме́рочная

✏ **five** /faɪv/ *n.* (число́/но́мер) пять; (~ people)
пя́теро; пять челове́к; **in ~s, ~ at a time** по
пяти́, пятёрками; (figure, thing numbered 5, group
of ~) пятёрка; (o'clock) пять (часо́в); **he
is ~ to 4 (o'clock)** без пяти́
четы́ре; **~ past 6** пять мину́т седьмо́го
● *adj.* пять + *g. pl.*; **~ sixes are thirty** пя́тью
шесть — три́дцать

fiver /ˈfaɪvə(r)/ *n.* (BrE, infml, five pounds, five-pound
note) пятёрка (infml)

✏ **fix** /fɪks/ *n.* (dilemma) затрудни́тельное
положе́ние; (infml, injection of drug) уко́л
● *v.t.* **1** (make firm) укреп|ля́ть, -и́ть; (fig.): **~
the blame on sb** взва́л|ивать, -и́ть вину́ на
кого́-н. **2** (direct steadily) напр|авля́ть, -а́вить;
~ed gaze при́стальный/неподви́жный
взгляд **3** (determine, settle) (*also v.i.*) **let
us ~ (on) a date** дава́йте договори́мся о
да́те **4** (provide) (*also* **~ up**) **can you ~
(up) a room for me?** (*or* **~ me up with a
room?**) мо́жете ли вы найти́/подыска́ть для
меня́ ко́мнату? **5** (infml, repair): **he ~ed the
radio in no time** он в два счёта починѝл
радиоприёмник; (AmE, prepare): **I will ~ the
drinks** я пригото́влю напи́тки

fixation /fɪkˈseɪʃ(ə)n/ *n.* (psych.) фикса́ция

fixed /fɪkst/ *adj.* неподви́жный,
закреплённый, постоя́нный; **~ idea**
навя́зчивая иде́я, иде́я фикс

■ ~ **rate** *n.* фикси́рованная ста́вка

fixer /ˈfɪksə(r)/ *n.* (phot.) фикса́ж; (sl., organizer) посре́дник

fixture /ˈfɪkstʃə(r)/ *n.* **1** (fitting in building) приспособле́ние **2** (BrE, sporting event) предстоя́щее спорти́вное состяза́ние/ мероприя́тие

fizzle /ˈfɪz(ə)l/ *v.i.* (~ **out**) око́нчиться (*pf.*) ниче́м

fizzy /ˈfɪzɪ/ *adj.* (**fizzier, fizziest**) шипу́чий

fjord, fiord /fjɔːd/ *n.* фьорд, фио́рд

flabby /ˈflæbɪ/ *adj.* (**flabbier, flabbiest**) вя́лый, дря́блый

flag¹ /flæɡ/ *n.* (emblem) флаг, зна́мя (*nt.*)
● *v.t.* (**flagged, flagging**) **1** (mark for attention) ме́тить, по- **2** (signal to stop): ~ (**down**) a passing car остан|а́вливать, -ови́ть проезжа́ющую маши́ну
■ ~**pole** *n.* флагшто́к

flag² /flæɡ/ *v.i.* (**flagged, flagging**) (grow weary) ослабе|ва́ть, -́ть; (fig.): the conversation was ~ging разгово́р не кле́ился

flagon /ˈflæɡən/ *n.* графи́н/кувши́н для вина́

flagrant /ˈfleɪɡrənt/ *adj.* вопию́щий, возмути́тельный

flail /fleɪl/ *v.i.* (fig.) маха́ть (*impf.*) + *i.*; he charged with his hands ~ing он наступа́л, разма́хивая рука́ми

flair /fleə(r)/ *n.* нюх, чутьё; a ~ for languages спосо́бности (*f. pl.*) к языка́м

flake /fleɪk/ *n.* (*in pl.*) хло́пь|я (-ев); ~s of snow снежи́нки (*f. pl.*)
● *v.i.* (peel) шелуши́ться (*impf.*); слои́ться (*impf.*); the rust ~d off ржа́вчина отслои́лась

flamboyance /flæmˈbɔɪəns/ *n.* цвети́стость; я́ркость

flamboyant /flæmˈbɔɪənt/ *adj.* (person, behaviour) колори́тный; (clothing) бро́ский, я́ркий; (style) цвети́стый

flame /fleɪm/ *n.* ого́нь (*m.*), пла́мя (*nt.*); **burst into** ~(**s**) вспы́х|ивать, -нуть; the house was in ~s дом был охва́чен пла́менем

flaming /ˈfleɪmɪŋ/ *adj.* **1** (ablaze) пыла́ющий, горя́щий **2** (fig., violent): they had a ~ **row** у них произошёл стра́шный сканда́л

flamingo /fləˈmɪŋɡəʊ/ *n.* (*pl.* ~**s** or ~**es**) флами́нго (*m. indecl.*)

flammable /ˈflæməb(ə)l/ *adj.* горю́чий; легко́ воспламеня́ющийся

flan /flæn/ *n.* откры́тый пиро́г

flank /flæŋk/ *n.* (mil.) фланг
● *v.t.*: he was ~ed by guards по обе сто́роны от него́ шла/стоя́ла стра́жа

flannel /ˈflæn(ə)l/ *n.* **1** (a kind of cloth) флане́ль **2**: face ~ (BrE) махро́вая салфе́тка для лица́

flap /flæp/ *n.* **1** (hinged piece etc.): the table has two ~s у стола́ две откидны́е до́ски; (of pocket, envelope) кла́пан **2** (waving motion) взмах
● *v.t. & i.* (**flapped, flapping**) взма́х|ивать, -ну́ть + *i.*; the bird ~ped its wings пти́ца взмахну́ла кры́льями

flare¹ /fleə(r)/ *n.* (effect of flame) сверка́ние; (illuminating device) сигна́льная раке́та;

осветительный патро́н
● *v.i.* сверк|а́ть, -ну́ть; горе́ть (*impf.*) неро́вным пла́менем; (fig.): she ~s up at the least thing она́ взрыва́ется из-за ка́ждого пустяка́

flare² /fleə(r)/ *n.*: ~**s** (trousers) брю́ки клёш
● *v.i.* расш|иря́ться, -и́риться; ~d skirt ю́бка клёш

flash /flæʃ/ *n.* **1** (burst of light) вспы́шка, про́блеск; a ~ of lightning вспы́шка мо́лнии; he had a ~ of inspiration на него́ нашло́ вдохнове́ние **2** (instant) мгнове́ние, миг; he answered in a ~ он мгнове́нно отве́тил
● *v.t.*: he ~ed the light in my face он напра́вил свет мне в лицо́; (fig.): he ~ed a glance at her он метну́л на неё взгляд
● *v.i.* сверк|а́ть, -ну́ть; вспы́х|ивать, -нуть; мельк|а́ть, -ну́ть; the light ~ed on and off свет то вспы́хивал, то гас; cars ~ed by маши́ны мча́лись ми́мо
■ ~**back** *n.* (cin. etc.) ретроспекти́ва; ~**bulb** *n.* (phot.) ла́мпа-вспы́шка; ~ **flood** *n.* ли́вневый па́водок; ~**light** *n.* (AmE) карма́нный/ электри́ческий фона́рь; ~ **memory** *n.* (comput.) флеш-па́мять

flashy /ˈflæʃɪ/ *adj.* (**flashier, flashiest**) крича́щий, показно́й, эффе́ктный

flask /flɑːsk/ *n.* фля́га, фля́жка

⚘ **flat** /flæt/ *n.* **1** (BrE, apartment) кварти́ра **2** (mus.) бемо́ль (*m.*) **3** (level object or area) пло́скость; the ~ of the hand ладо́нь
● *adj.* (**flatter, flattest**) **1** (level) пло́ский, ро́вный; ~ screen пло́ский экра́н; (no longer inflated or charged): ~ tyre (BrE), tire (AmE) спу́щенная ши́на; the battery is ~ (BrE) батаре́я се́ла **2** (uniform) однообра́зный **3** (unqualified) прямо́й, категори́ческий **4** (dull, insipid) ску́чный, вя́лый, бесцве́тный
● *adv.* (**flatter, flattest**) **1** (in or into a horizontal position): he fell ~ on his back он упа́л навзничь **2** (infml, with expressions of time): in ten seconds ~ ро́вно за де́сять секу́нд **3** (mus., below true pitch): she sings ~ on the high notes она́ фальши́вит на высо́ких но́тах
■ ~**bed** *adj.* (comput.) планше́тный; ~**bed scanner** планше́тный ска́нер; ~**mate** *n.* (BrE) сосе́д (-ка) по кварти́ре; ~ **out** *adv.*: drive ~ out (infml, at top speed) гнать (*impf.*) на по́лной ско́рости; ~ **rate** *n.* еди́ная ста́вка

flatly /ˈflætlɪ/ *adv.* (refuse) категори́чески

flatten /ˈflæt(ə)n/ *v.t.* **1** (make smooth) выра́внивать, вы́ровнять **2** (reduce thickness of) расплю́щи|вать, -ть; he ~ed himself against the wall он прижа́лся к стене́ **3** (lay low): the gale ~ed the corn бу́рей примя́ло хлеба́

flatter /ˈflætə(r)/ *v.t.* льсти́ть, по- + *d.*

flattering /ˈflætərɪŋ/ *adj.* ле́стный, льсти́вый; (of person) льсти́вый

flattery /ˈflætərɪ/ *n.* лесть

flatulence /ˈflætjʊləns/ *n.* скопле́ние га́зов; (fig.) напы́щенность, высокопа́рность

flaunt /flɔːnt/ *v.t.* афиши́ровать (*impf.*); щеголя́ть, -ьну́ть + *i.*

flautist /'flɔːtɪst/ n. флейти́ст (-ка)

flavour /'fleɪvə(r)/ (AmE **flavor**) n. арома́т, вкус
● v.t. припр|авля́ть, -а́вить

flavouring /'fleɪvərɪŋ/ (AmE **flavoring**) n. припра́ва; спе́ции (f. pl.)

flaw /flɔː/ n. (defect) изъя́н, недоста́ток

flawed /flɔːd/ adj. име́ющий недоста́тки

flawless /'flɔːlɪs/ adj. безупре́чный

flax /flæks/ n. (plant) лён; (fibre) куде́ль (волокно́ льна)

flea /fliː/ n. блоха́

fleck /flek/ n. кра́пинка, пятно́; (of dust) пыли́нка
● v.t. покр|ыва́ть, -ы́ть пя́тнами/кра́пинками

fled /fled/ past and p.p. of ▶ flee

fledgling, fledgeling /'fledʒlɪŋ/ n. то́лько что опери́вшийся птене́ц

flee /fliː/ v.t. (past and p.p. **fled**) избе|га́ть, -жа́ть
● v.i. (past and p.p. **fled**) бежа́ть, с-

fleece /fliːs/ n. руно́, ове́чья шерсть

fleecy /'fliːsɪ/ adj. (**fleecier, fleeciest**) шерсти́стый

fleet /fliːt/ n. **1** (collection of vessels) флоти́лия, флот **2** (of vehicles) парк

fleeting /'fliːtɪŋ/ adj. бе́глый, мимолётный; a ~ glimpse бе́глый взгляд

Flemish /'flemɪʃ/ n. (language) флама́ндский язы́к; the ~ (people) флама́ндцы (m. pl.)
● adj. флама́ндский

flesh /fleʃ/ n. **1** (bodily tissue) плоть, те́ло **2** (fig.): my own ~ and blood (children) моя́ плоть и кровь; (relatives) моя́ родня́ **3** (of fruit) мя́коть

fleshy /'fleʃɪ/ adj. (**fleshier, fleshiest**) (of persons) то́лстый, ту́чный

flew /fluː/ past of ▶ fly³

flex¹ /fleks/ n. (BrE) (ги́бкий) шнур

flex² /fleks/ v.t. сгиба́ть, согну́ть; ~ one's muscles напр|яга́ть, -я́чь му́скулы

flexibility /fleksɪ'bɪlɪtɪ/ n. эласти́чность; (fig.) ги́бкость

flexible /'fleksɪb(ə)l/ adj. эласти́чный, ги́бкий; (fig.) ги́бкий

flexitime /'fleksɪtaɪm/ n. ненорми́рованный рабо́чий день

flick /flɪk/ n. (jerk) толчо́к; (light touch) a ~ of the whip лёгкий уда́р хлысто́м
● v.t. (shake with a jerk) встр|я́хивать, -яхну́ть; (propel with finger end) щёлк|ать, -нуть; (touch, e.g. with whip) стегну́ть (pf.)
● v.i.: ~ through просм|а́тривать, -отре́ть

flicker /'flɪkə(r)/ n. (of light) мерца́ние; (fig.): a ~ of hope про́блеск наде́жды
● v.i. (flutter) трепета́ть (impf.); (burn or shine fitfully) мерца́ть (impf.)

flight¹ /flaɪt/ n. **1** полёт; (journey by air): a non-stop ~ беспоса́дочный полёт; (a particular ~) рейс; the next ~ from London to Paris сле́дующий рейс по маршру́ту

Ло́ндон — Пари́ж **2** (fig.): ~ of fancy полёт фанта́зии **3**: ~ of stairs ле́стничный марш ■ ~ attendant n. стю́ард (-е́сса); ~ engineer n. бортмеха́ник; ~ path n. курс полёта; ~ recorder n. бортово́й самопи́сец

flight² /flaɪt/ n. бе́гство, побе́г; take ~ обра|ща́ться, -ти́ться в бе́гство

flighty /'flaɪtɪ/ adj. (**flightier, flightiest**) ве́треный, капри́зный

flimsy /'flɪmzɪ/ adj. (**flimsier, flimsiest**) то́нкий, непро́чный; a ~ structure непро́чная постро́йка; a ~ excuse сла́бое оправда́ние

flinch /flɪntʃ/ v.i. вздр|а́гивать, -о́гнуть

fling /flɪŋ/ n. **1** (sexual) коро́ткий рома́н, интри́жка **2**: he had his ~ он повесели́лся/ нагуля́лся вво́лю
● v.t. (past and p.p. **flung**): ~ oneself into a chair бр|оса́ться, -о́ситься в кре́сло; she flung her arms around me она́ обняла́ меня́
● with adv.: ~ open the window распа́х|ивать, -ну́ть окно́

flint /flɪnt/ n. креме́нь (m.)

flip /flɪp/ n. щелчо́к
● adj. (flippant) де́рзкий
● v.t. (**flipped, flipping**) (a coin) подбр|а́сывать, -о́сить
● v.i. (infml, go crazy) сходи́ть, сойти́ с ума́

flip-flop /'flɪpflɒp/ n. (usu. in pl.) (footwear) вьетна́мка, сла́нец

flippancy /'flɪpənsɪ/ n. легкомы́слие, ве́треность

flippant /'flɪpənt/ adj. легкомы́сленный, ве́треный

flipper /'flɪpə(r)/ n. плавни́к, ласт; (diver's appendage) ласт

flirt /flɜːt/ n. коке́тка; люби́тель (m.) поуха́живать
● v.i. коке́тничать (impf.) (with: с + i.); (fig.): ~ with (an idea etc.) поду́мывать о + p.

flirtation /flɜː'teɪʃ(ə)n/ n. флирт; коке́тство; (fig.) игра́

flirtatious /flɜː'teɪʃəs/ adj. коке́тливый

flit /flɪt/ v.i. (**flitted, flitting**) порх|а́ть, -ну́ть

float /fləʊt/ n. **1** (for line or net) поплаво́к, буй; (for learning to swim) пла́вательная доска́ **2** (BrE, cart) платфо́рма на колёсах
● v.t. спус|ка́ть, -ти́ть на́ воду; (comm.): ~ a company учре|жда́ть, -ди́ть акционе́рное о́бщество
● v.i. **1** пла́вать (indet.), плыть (det.); the boat ~ed downriver ло́дку несло́ тече́нием вниз по реке́ **2** (in air) плыть (det.)

floating /'fləʊtɪŋ/ adj. пла́вающий, плаву́чий ■ ~ voter n. коле́блющийся избира́тель

flock /flɒk/ n. (of birds) ста́я; (of sheep or goats) ста́до
● v.i. стека́ться (impf.)

flog /flɒg/ v.t. (**flogged, flogging**) стега́ть, от-

flood /flʌd/ n. **1** (inundation) наводне́ние, полово́дье, разли́в **2** (fig.): she burst into ~s of tears она́ разрыда́лась

● *v.t.* затоп|ля́ть, -и́ть; the basement was ~ed подва́л затопи́ло
● *v.i.* разл|ива́ться, -и́ться
■ ~**gate** *n.* шлюз; **open the ~gates (to)** (fig.) да|ва́ть, -ть во́лю (*чему*); ~**light** *n.* прожёктор
● *v.t.* осве|ща́ть, -ти́ть прожёкторами

✧ **floor** /flɔː(r)/ *n.* **1** пол **2**: **take the ~** (in public assembly) брать, взять сло́во; (in dance hall) пойти́ (*pf.*) танцева́ть **3** (storey) эта́ж
● *v.t.* (infml, knock down) сби|ва́ть, -ть с ног; (fig., nonplus) сра|жа́ть, -зи́ть; **the question ~ed him** вопро́с срази́л его́
■ ~**board** *n.* полови́ца; ~**cloth** *n.* (BrE) полова́я тря́пка; ~ **lamp** *n.* (AmE) торшёр; ~ **show** *n.* представле́ние в кабаре́

flooring /ˈflɔːrɪŋ/ *n.* насти́л, пол

flop /flɒp/ *n.* (failure) прова́л
● *v.i.* (**flopped, flopping**) **1** (move limply): ~ **down in a chair** плю́х|аться, -нуться в кре́сло **2** (infml, fail) прова́л|иваться, -и́ться

floppy /ˈflɒpɪ/ *adj.* (**floppier, floppiest**) болта́ющийся, свиса́ющий
■ ~ **disk** *n.* (comput.) дискéта, ги́бкий диск

flora /ˈflɔːrə/ *n.* (*pl.* **floras** or **florae** /-riː/) фло́ра

floral /ˈflɔːr(ə)l/ *adj.* цвето́чный

florid /ˈflɒrɪd/ *adj.* (ornate) цвети́стый, витиева́тый; (ruddy) кра́сный, багро́вый

florist /ˈflɒrɪst/ *n.* продаве́ц цвето́в (цвето́чница)

floss /flɒs/ *n.*: dental ~ зубна́я нить

flotation /fləʊˈteɪʃ(ə)n/ *n.* распрода́жа а́кций компа́нии

flotilla /fləˈtɪlə/ *n.* флоти́лия (мéлких судо́в)

flotsam /ˈflɒtsəm/ *n.* (вы́брошенный и) пла́вающий на пове́рхности груз, му́сор

flounce[1] /flaʊns/ *v.i.* бр|оса́ться, -о́ситься; ~ **out (of a room)** вылета́ть, вы́лететь из ко́мнаты

flounce[2] /flaʊns/ *n.* (trimming) обо́рка

flounder /ˈflaʊndə(r)/ *v.i.* бара́хтаться (*impf.*); (fig.) пу́таться в слова́х

flour /ˈflaʊə(r)/ *n.* мука́

flourish /ˈflʌrɪʃ/ *n.* **1** (wave of hand etc.) широ́кий жест **2** (literary embellishment) цвети́стость
● *v.t.* разма́хивать (*impf.*) + *i.*
● *v.i.* процвета́ть (*impf.*)

flourishing /ˈflʌrɪʃɪŋ/ *adj.* процвета́ющий, преуспева́ющий

flout /flaʊt/ *v.t.* поп|ира́ть, -ра́ть

✧ **flow** /fləʊ/ *n.* тече́ние, пото́к; **in full ~** в разга́ре
● *v.i.* **1** течь, ли́ться (*both impf.*); **the Oka ~s into the Volga** Ока́ впада́ет в Во́лгу **2** (fig., move freely) ли́ться, течь (*both impf.*)
■ ~ **chart/diagram** *n.* блок-схе́ма

✧ **flower** /ˈflaʊə(r)/ *n.* цвето́к; цветко́вое расте́ние; **in ~** в цвету́
● *v.i.* (blossom; flourish) цвести́ (*impf.*)
■ ~ **arrangement** *n.* цвето́чная компози́ция; ~ **bed** *n.* клу́мба; ~**pot** *n.* цвето́чный горшо́к

flowery /ˈflaʊərɪ/ *adj.* покры́тый цвета́ми; (fig.) цвети́стый

flown /fləʊn/ *p.p. of* ▶ **fly**[3]

flu /fluː/ *n.* (infml) грипп

fluctuate /ˈflʌktʃʊeɪt/ *v.i.* колеба́ться (*impf.*)

fluctuation /ˌflʌktʃʊˈeɪʃ(ə)n/ *n.* колеба́ние

flue /fluː/ *n.* дымохо́д
■ ~ **pipe** *n.* (tech.) жарова́я труба́

fluency /ˈfluːənsɪ/ *n.* пла́вность, бéглость

fluent /ˈfluːənt/ *adj.* пла́вный, бéглый; **he speaks Russian ~ly** он свобо́дно говори́т по-ру́сски

fluff /flʌf/ *n.* пух, пушо́к
● *v.t.* **1** (make fluffy) взби|ва́ть, -ть **2** (infml, bungle) пу́тать, с-; ~ **one's lines** заб|ыва́ть, -ы́ть свои́ слова́

fluffy /ˈflʌfɪ/ *adj.* (**fluffier, fluffiest**) пуши́стый

fluid /ˈfluːɪd/ *n.* жи́дкость
● *adj.* жи́дкий, текучий; (fig.) неопределённый, перемéнчивый
■ ~ **ounce** *n.* жи́дкая у́нция

fluidity /fluːˈɪdɪtɪ/ *n.* текучесть; (fig.) перемéнчивость, неопределённость

fluke /fluːk/ *n.* (lucky stroke) (неожи́данная) уда́ча, случа́йность

flung /flʌŋ/ *past and p.p. of* ▶ **fling**

fluorescent /flʊəˈres(ə)nt/ *adj.* флюоресци́рующий

fluoride /ˈflʊəraɪd/ *n.* фтори́д

flurry /ˈflʌrɪ/ *n.* (gust) шквал; (agitation) волнéние, сумато́ха

flush /flʌʃ/ *n.* (flow of water) внеза́пный прили́в; (blush) прили́в кро́ви
● *v.t.* **1** (swill clean) пром|ыва́ть, -ы́ть; ~ **the lavatory** спус|ка́ть, -ти́ть во́ду в туалéт **2** (make red) зал|ива́ть, -и́ть кра́ской
● *v.i.* краснéть, по-

fluster /ˈflʌstə(r)/ *v.t.* волнова́ть, вз-; будора́жить, вз-

flute /fluːt/ *n.* (instrument) флéйта

flutter /ˈflʌtə(r)/ *n.* трепета́ние, дрожь
● *v.t.* мах|а́ть, -ну́ть + *i.*
● *v.i.* трепета́ть (*impf.*); (of birds) переп|а́рхивать, -орхну́ть

flux /flʌks/ *n.* постоя́нная смéна; **everything was in a state of ~** всё находи́лось в состоя́нии непреры́вного измене́ния

fly[1] /flaɪ/ *n.* му́ха
■ ~ **spray** *n.* (fluid) жи́дкость от мух; (instrument) аэрозо́ль (*m.*) от мух

fly[2] /flaɪ/ *n.* (on trousers) шири́нка

✧ **fly**[3] /flaɪ/ *v.t.* (*past* **flew**, *p.p.* **flown**): ~ **an aircraft** управля́ть (*impf.*) самолётом; ~ **home the wounded** дост|авля́ть, -а́вить ра́неных в тыл самолётом
● *v.i.* (*past* **flew**, *p.p.* **flown**) **1** (move through the air) летáть (*indet.*), летéть (*det.*), по-; **he has never flown on никогда́ не летáл **2** (move swiftly): **I must ~!** ну, я побежа́л!; **he flew downstairs** он ку́барем скати́лся с лéстницы; ~ **into a passion** со́рва́ться (*pf.*); ~ **off the handle** (infml) со́рва́ться (*pf.*); **send ~ing** швыр|я́ть, -ну́ть; (of person) сби|ва́ть, -ть с ног; **time flies** врéмя лети́т

f

• *with advs.*: leaves were ∼ing about повсю́ду кружи́лись ли́стья; ∼ **away** улет|а́ть, -е́ть; **the plane flew in to refuel and flew off again** самолёт прилете́л на запра́вку и вновь/сно́ва улете́л

■ ∼-**by-night** *n.* ненадёжный челове́к; ∼**over** *n.* (BrE, bridge, overpass) эстака́да; путепрово́д

flyer /'flaɪə(r)/ *n.* (handbill) рекла́мный листо́к

flying /'flaɪɪŋ/ *n.* полёт; **he likes** ∼ он лю́бит лета́ть

• *adj.*: **pass with** ∼ **colours** пройти́, сдать (*both pf.*) с блéском; **get off to a** ∼ **start** сра́зу пойти́ (*pf.*) хорошо́ (*or* в го́ру)

■ ∼ **saucer** *n.* лета́ющая таре́лка; ∼ **visit** *n.* блицвизи́т; кра́ткое посеще́ние

foal /fəʊl/ *n.* жеребёнок

foam /fəʊm/ *n.* пéна; ∼ **rubber** по́ристая рези́на

• *v.i.* пéниться (*impf.*); **he was** ∼**ing at the mouth** (fig., infml) он весь кипéл от зло́сти

fob /fɒb/ *v.t.* (**fobbed, fobbing**): ∼ **sb off with promises** корми́ть (*impf.*) кого́-н. обеща́ниями

focal /'fəʊk(ə)l/ *adj.*: ∼ **point** фока́льная то́чка; (fig.): **the** ∼ **point in his argument** гла́вный пункт его́ доказа́тельств

foci /'fəʊsaɪ/ *pl. of* ▶ **focus**

 focus /'fəʊkəs/ *n.* (*pl.* **focuses** *or* **foci** /-saɪ/) (math., phys., phot.) фо́кус; **out of** ∼ не в фо́кусе; (fig.) центр, средото́чие; **he became the** ∼ **of interest** он оказа́лся в це́нтре внима́ния

• *v.t.* (**focused, focusing** *or* **focussed, focussing**) (binoculars, camera) настра́ивать, -о́ить; (rays) фокуси́ровать, с-; (attention) сосредо|то́чивать, -то́чить

• *v.i.* (**focused, focusing** *or* **focussed, focussing**) (concentrate) сосредо|то́чиваться, -то́читься (**on:** на + *p.*)

■ ∼ **group** *n.* фо́кус-гру́ппа

fodder /'fɒdə(r)/ *n.* корм для скота́

foe /fəʊ/ *n.* враг, не́друг

foetal /'fiːt(ə)l/ *adj.* (BrE) = **fetal**

foetus /'fiːtəs/ *n.* (BrE) = **fetus**

fog /fɒg/ *n.* тума́н

• *v.t.* (**fogged, fogging**) (fig.): **the windows are** ∼**ged up** о́кна запоте́ли

■ ∼**horn** *n.* тума́нный горн, тума́нная сире́на; ∼ **lamp/light** *n.* противотума́нная фа́ра

fogey, fogy /'fəʊgɪ/ *n.* (*pl.* **fogeys** *or* **fogies**) старомо́дный/отста́лый челове́к

fogg|y /'fɒgɪ/ *adj.* (**foggier, foggiest**) тума́нный

foible /'fɔɪb(ə)l/ *n.* сла́бость; сла́бая стру́нка

foil¹ /fɔɪl/ *n.* (thin metal) фольга́, станио́ль (*m.*)

foil² /fɔɪl/ *v.t.* сби|ва́ть, -ть

foist /fɔɪst/ *v.t.* навя́з|ывать, -а́ть (*что кому*)

fold¹ /fəʊld/ *n.* скла́дка; **the** ∼**s of a dress** скла́дки пла́тья

• *v.t.* скла́д|ывать, сложи́ть; свёртывать (*or* -ора́чивать), -ерну́ть; ∼ **one's arms** скре́|щивать, -сти́ть ру́ки на груди́

• *v.i.* скла́д|ываться, сложи́ться; (fig.): **the play** ∼**ed after a week** пье́са сошла́ со сце́ны че́рез

неде́лю; **their business** ∼**ed** они́ сверну́ли де́ло

fold² /fəʊld/ *n.* (for sheep) заго́н; **return to the** ∼ (fig.) верну́ться (*pf.*) в ло́но (*церкви и т. п.*)

-**fold** /fəʊld/ *comb. form.* -кра́тный; **threefold** трёхкра́тный

folder /'fəʊldə(r)/ *n.* (container for papers) скоросшива́тель (*m.*); (also comput.) па́пка

folding /'fəʊldɪŋ/ *adj.* складно́й

foliage /'fəʊlɪɪdʒ/ *n.* листва́

 folk /fəʊk/ *n.* (*pl.* **folk** *or* **folks**) наро́д, лю́д|и (-éй)

folklore /'fəʊklɔː(r)/ *n.* фолькло́р

 follow /'fɒləʊ/ *v.t. & i.* **1** (proceed or happen after) сле́довать, по- за + *i.*; **he** ∼**ed (in) his father's footsteps** он пошёл по стопа́м отца́; **as** ∼**s** сле́дующим о́бразом; **как сле́дует ни́же; his plan was as** ∼**s** его́ план был тако́в **2** (as inference) сле́довать (*impf.*) из + *g.*; **it does not** ∼ **that …** э́то во́все не зна́чит, что… **3** (pursue) следи́ть (*impf.*) за + *i.*; **don't look now, we're being** ∼**ed** не огля́дывайтесь, за на́ми следя́т **4** (keep to) приде́рживаться (*impf.*) + *g.*; (fig., be guided by): ∼ **sb's advice/example** сле́довать, по-чьему́-н. сове́ту/приме́ру **5** (fig., keep track of): **I don't** ∼ **you** я вас не понима́ю; ∼ **the news in the papers** следи́ть (*impf.*) за новостя́ми в газе́тах

□ ∼ **through** *v.t. & i.* сле́довать (*impf.*) (за + *i.*) до конца́

□ ∼ **up** *v.t.* (look into) раз|бира́ть, -обра́ть; ∼ **up a suggestion** уч|и́тывать, -éсть чьё-н. предложе́ние

■ ∼-**up** *n.* продолже́ние; (med.) контро́ль (*m.*)

follower /'fɒləʊə(r)/ *n.* после́дователь (*m.*) (-ница); сторо́нни|к (-ца)

following /'fɒləʊɪŋ/ *n.* после́дователи (*m. pl.*); приве́рженцы (*m. pl.*)

• *adj.* (ensuing) сле́дующий; (**on) the** ∼ **day** на сле́дующий день; (about to be specified): **we shall need the** ∼ нам потре́буется сле́дующее

folly /'fɒlɪ/ *n.* глу́пость

foment /fə'ment/ *v.t.* (hatred etc.) подстрек|а́ть, -ну́ть

fond /fɒnd/ *adj.* **1** ∼ **of: he became** ∼ **of her** он привяза́лся к ней; **are you** ∼ **of music?** вы лю́бите му́зыку? **2** (loving) не́жный, любя́щий; ∼ **memories** прия́тные/до́брые воспомина́ния

fondle /'fɒnd(ə)l/ *v.t.* ласка́ть (*impf.*)

font /fɒnt/ *n.* (eccl.) купе́ль

 food /fuːd/ *n.* пи́ща, пита́ние; еда́; (fig.): ∼ **for thought** пи́ща для размышле́ний

■ ∼ **poisoning** *n.* пищево́е отравле́ние; ∼ **processor** *n.* ку́хонный комба́йн; ∼**stuff** *n.* пищево́й проду́кт

fool /fuːl/ *n.* (simpleton) дура́к, глупе́ц; (jester) шут; **play the** ∼ дура́читься (*impf.*); валя́ть (*impf.*) дурака́; **make a** ∼ **(out) of sb** дура́чить, о- кого́-н.

• *v.t.* (deceive) одура́чи|вать, -ть

• *v.i.* ∼ **about, around** валя́ть (*impf.*) дурака́

■ ∼**proof** *adj.* (reliable) безотка́зный, ве́рный

foolhardy /'fuːlhɑːdɪ/ *adj.* (**foolhardier, foolhardiest**) безрассу́дно хра́брый

foolish /'fu:lɪʃ/ *adj.* глу́пый; дура́цкий
foolishness /'fu:lɪʃnɪs/ *n.* глу́пость
⚡ **foot** /fʊt/ *n.* (*pl.* **feet**) **1** (extremity of leg)
ступня́, нога́; стопа́ ноги́; (lowest part, bottom):
at the ∼ of the hill у подно́жия холма́; **at the
∼ of the page** в конце́ страни́цы; **at the ∼
of the stairs** внизу́ ле́стницы; **at the ∼ of the
bed** в нога́х крова́ти **2** (unit of length) фут; **six
∼** (*or* **feet**) **tall** шести́ фу́тов ро́стом
● *phrr.*: **we came here on ∼** мы пришли́ сюда́
пешко́м; **put one's ∼ down** (fig.) зан|има́ть,
-я́ть твёрдую/реши́тельную пози́цию; **put
one's ∼ in it** (fig.) дать (*pf.*) ма́ху; **stand on
one's own (two) feet** стоя́ть (*impf.*) на нога́х;
быть самостоя́тельным
● *v.t.*: **∼ the bill** опла́|чивать, -ти́ть счёт
■ **∼-and-mouth disease** *n.* я́щур; **∼bridge**
n. пешехо́дный мо́стик; **∼hold** *n.* то́чка
опо́ры; **∼lights** *n. pl.* ра́мпа (*sg.*); **∼note** *n.*
сно́ска; **∼path** *n.* тропа́, тропи́нка; **∼print** *n.*
след ноги́; **∼step** *n.* шаг, по́ступь; **∼stool** *n.*
скаме́ечка для ног; **∼wear** *n.* о́бувь
footage /'fʊtɪdʒ/ *n.* киноматериа́л
football /'fʊtbɔ:l/ *n.* (BrE) футбо́л; (AmE)
америка́нский футбо́л; **∼ match** (BrE)
футбо́льный матч; **∼ player** футболи́ст
footballer /'fʊtbɔ:lə(r)/ *n.* (BrE) футболи́ст
footer /'fʊtə(r)/ *n.* (line of text) ни́жний
колонти́тул
footing /'fʊtɪŋ/ *n.* (foothold) опо́ра для ног(и́);
lose one's ∼ оступи́ться (*pf.*); (fig.) потеря́ть
(*pf.*) по́чву под нога́ми; **on an equal ∼** на
ра́вной ноге́
⚡ **for** /fɔ:(r)/ *prep.* **1** (with the object or purpose of)
для + *g.*; ра́ди + *g.*; **example** наприме́р;
they have gone ∼ a walk они́ пошли́
гуля́ть; (destination) на + *a.*; к + *d.*; **the train
∼ Moscow** по́езд на Москву́; (aspiration):
prospecting ∼ oil разве́дка нефтяны́х
месторожде́ний **2** (denoting reason; on account
of) ра́ди + *g.*, для + *g.*; **he is known ∼ his
generosity** он изве́стен свое́й ще́дростью;
(accorded to): **the penalty ∼ treason is death**
наказа́ние за госуда́рственную изме́ну —
сме́ртная казнь; (on the occasion of): **I gave
him a book ∼ his birthday** я подари́л ему́
кни́гу на день рожде́ния; **he went abroad
∼ his holidays** в о́тпуск он пое́хал за
грани́цу **3** (representative of): **A ∼ Anna «A»**
как в сло́ве «Анна»; (in support; in favour of): **a
vote ∼ freedom** го́лос за свобо́ду; (denoting
purpose): **they need premises ∼ a school** им
ну́жно помеще́ние под шко́лу; **ready ∼
departure** гото́в(ый) к отъе́зду; (on behalf of)
за + *a.*, от + *g.*; **speak ∼ yourself!** говори́те
за себя́! **4** (denoting intended recipient): **there is
a letter ∼ you** вам письмо́ **5** (denoting duration
or extent): **∼ a long time** на до́лгое вре́мя;
в тече́ние до́лгого вре́мени; **I haven't seen
him ∼ (some) days** я не ви́дел его́ не́сколько
дней; **there is no house ∼ miles** на мно́го
киломе́тров вокру́г нет ни еди́ного до́ма;
(intended duration): **∼ ever and ever** навсегда́,
на ве́ки ве́чные; **they are going away ∼
a few days** они́ уезжа́ют на не́сколько

дней **6** (denoting relationship; in respect of): **as
∼ me, myself** что каса́ется меня́; **luckily ∼
her** на её сча́стье, к сча́стью для неё; (in
relation to what is normal or suitable): **warm ∼ the
time of year** тепло́ для э́того вре́мени го́да;
it's cold enough ∼ snow хо́лодно — того́
и гляди́ пойдёт снег; **not bad ∼ a beginner**
непло́хо для новичка́ **7** (in return ∼, instead
of): **get something ∼ nothing** получ|а́ть,
-и́ть что-н. да́ром; **once (and) ∼ all** раз и
навсегда́ **8** (despite): **∼ all that, I still love him**
но несмотря́ на всё, я его́ люблю́ **9** (with
certain expressions of time): **∼ the first time** в
пе́рвый раз; **the wedding is arranged ∼ June
the 1st** сва́дьба назна́чена на пе́рвое ию́ня
forage /'fɒrɪdʒ/ *n.* фура́ж, корм
● *v.i.* (search) разы́скивать (*impf.*)
■ **∼ cap** *n.* фура́жка
foray /'fɒreɪ/ *n.* набе́г
forbade /fə'bæd, fə'beɪd/, **forbad** /fə'bæd/
past of ▶ forbid
forbearance /fɔ:'beərəns/ *n.*
возде́ржанность, терпели́вость, терпе́ние
forbid /fə'bɪd/ *v.t.* (**forbidding**, *past*
forbade *or* **forbad**, *p.p.* **forbidden**)
запре|ща́ть, -ти́ть (*кому что*)
forbidden /fə'bɪd(ə)n/ *adj.* запрещённый,
запре́тный
forbidding /fə'bɪdɪŋ/ *adj.* (unfriendly)
неприя́зненный; (threatening) гро́зный
⚡ **force** /fɔ:s/ *n.* **1** (strength, lit., fig.) си́ла; **use
∼** прибе́|га́ть, -е́гнуть к си́ле; **in full ∼** в
по́лном соста́ве; **by ∼** си́лой, наси́льно
2 (body of men, usu. armed) вооружённый
отря́д; (Police) **F∼** поли́ция; (*in pl.*) **the
(armed) F∼s** а́рмия, вооружённые си́лы
3 (binding power, validity) действи́тельность; **in ∼**
(of law etc.) в си́ле **4** (phys.) си́ла
● *v.t.* **1** (compel, constrain) заст|авля́ть,
-а́вить; **he was ∼d to sell the house** он был
вы́нужден прода́ть дом; **∼d** (laugh etc.)
принуждённый **2** (apply ∼ to): **∼ (open) the
door** выла́мывать, вы́ломать дверь
■ **∼-feed** *v.t.* корми́ть (*impf.*) наси́льно
forceful /'fɔ:sfʊl/ *adj.* си́льный, убеди́тельный
forceps /'fɔ:seps/ *n. pl.* хирурги́ческие
щипц|ы́ (-о́в)
forcible /'fɔ:sɪb(ə)l/ *adj.* наси́льственный;
(forceful) убеди́тельный; **∼ entry**
наси́льственное вторже́ние
ford /fɔ:d/ *n.* брод
● *v.t.* пере|ходи́ть, -йти́ вброд
fore /fɔ:(r)/ *n.*: **come to the ∼** выдвига́ться,
вы́двинуться
● *adj.* (*as pref.*) пред…
forearm /'fɔ:rɑ:m/ *n.* предпле́чье
foreboding /fɔ:'bəʊdɪŋ/ *n.* дурно́е
предчу́вствие
forecast /'fɔ:kɑ:st/ *n.* предсказа́ние; (*also*
weather ∼) прогно́з пого́ды
● *v.t.* (*past and p.p.* ∼ *or* **∼ed**) предска́з|ывать,
-а́ть
forecaster /'fɔ:kɑ:stə(r)/ *n.*: **weather ∼**
сино́птик

forecourt /'fɔːkɔːt/ n. передний двор
forefather /'fɔːfɑːðə(r)/ n. предок, праотец
forefinger /'fɔːfɪŋɡə(r)/ n. указательный палец
forefront /'fɔːfrʌnt/ n. авангард; **in the ~ of the battle** на передовой (линии)
forego /fɔːˈɡəʊ/ v.i.: **a ~ne conclusion** предрешённый исход
foreground /'fɔːɡraʊnd/ n. передний план
forehand /'fɔːhænd/ adj. (tennis): **~ stroke** удар справа
forehead /'fɒrɪd, 'fɔːhed/ n. лоб
foreign /'fɒrən/ adj. **1** (of or pertaining to another country or countries) иностранный, заграничный **2** (alien) чуждый, чуждый
■ **~ affairs** n. pl. международные отношения; **F~ Secretary** n. (BrE) министр иностранных дел; **~ trade** n. внешняя торговля
foreigner /'fɒrənə(r)/ n. иностран|ец (-ка)
foreleg /'fɔːleɡ/ n. передняя лапа/нога
foreman /'fɔːmən/ n. мастер, десятник; **~ of the jury** старшина (m.) присяжных
foremost /'fɔːməʊst/ adj. самый передний
● adv.: **first and ~** прежде всего; в первую очередь
forename /'fɔːneɪm/ n. имя (nt.) (в отличие от фамилии)
forensic /fəˈrensɪk/ adj. судебный; **~ expert, scientist** судебно-медицинский эксперт
foreplay /'fɔːpleɪ/ n. предварительные ласки, прелюдия (перед половым актом)
forerunner /'fɔːrʌnə(r)/ n. предшественни|к (-ца)
fore|see /fɔːˈsiː/ v.t. (past **~saw**, p.p. **~seen**) предвидеть (impf.)
foreseeable /fɔːˈsiːəb(ə)l/ adj.: **in the ~ future** в обозримом будущем
foreshadow /fɔːˈʃædəʊ/ v.t. предвещать (impf.)
foreshore /'fɔːʃɔː(r)/ n. береговая полоса, затопляемая приливом
foresight /'fɔːsaɪt/ n. предусмотрительность
foreskin /'fɔːskɪn/ n. крайняя плоть
forest /'fɒrɪst/ n. лес
forestall /fɔːˈstɔːl/ v.t. предвосх|ищать, -итить; опере|жать, -дить; предупре|ждать, -дить
forester /'fɒrɪstə(r)/ n. лесник
forestry /'fɒrɪstrɪ/ n. лесоводство
foretaste /'fɔːteɪst/ n. предвкушение
fore|tell /fɔːˈtel/ v.t. (past and p.p. **~told**) предсказ|ывать, -ать
forethought /'fɔːθɔːt/ n. предусмотрительность
forever /fəˈrevə(r)/ adv. навсегда, навечно; (continually) постоянно, вечно
forewarn /fɔːˈwɔːn/ v.t. предупре|ждать, -дить
foreword /'fɔːwɜːd/ n. предисловие
forfeit /'fɔːfɪt/ n. (penalty) штраф, конфискация

✎ ключевая лексика

● v.t. (**forfeited, forfeiting**) терять, по- (право на) + a.
forgave /fəˈɡeɪv/ past of ▸ **forgive**
forge /fɔːdʒ/ n. (workshop) кузница
● v.t. & i. **1** (shape metal) ковать (impf.) **2** (fabricate) изобре|тать, -сти; (counterfeit) подде́л|ывать, -ать **3**: **~ ahead** вырыва|ться, вырваться вперёд
forger /'fɔːdʒə(r)/ n. подделыватель (m.); фальсификатор; (of money) фальшивомонетчик
forgery /'fɔːdʒərɪ/ n. подделка
forget /fəˈɡet/ v.t. & i. (**forgetting**, past **forgot**, p.p. **forgotten** or esp. AmE **forgot**) заб|ывать, -ыть; **I forgot all about the lecture** я совершенно забыл о лекции
■ **~-me-not** n. (bot.) незабудка
forgetful /fəˈɡetfʊl/ adj. забывчивый
forgivable /fəˈɡɪvəb(ə)l/ adj. простительный
forgive /fəˈɡɪv/ v.t. (past **forgave**, p.p. **forgiven**) про|щать, -стить; **I ~ you (for) everything** я вам всё прощаю
forgiveness /fəˈɡɪvnɪs/ n. прощение
forgo /fɔːˈɡəʊ/ v.t. (**forgoes** /-ˈɡəʊz/; past **forwent**, p.p. **forgone** /-ˈɡɒn/) отказ|ываться, -аться от + g.
forgot /fəˈɡɒt/ past and (esp. AmE) p.p. of ▸ **forget**
forgotten /fəˈɡɒt(ə)n/ p.p. of ▸ **forget**
fork /fɔːk/ n. **1** (cul.) вилка **2** (hort.) вилы (f. pl.) **3** (bifurcation) развилка
● v.i. (bifurcate) разд|ваиваться, -воиться; **~ out** (sl., provide money) отвал|ивать, -ить; раскошéл|иваться, -ться (for: на + a.)
■ **~lift** n. (in full **~-lift truck**) автопогрузчик
forked /fɔːkt/ adj.: **~ lightning** зигзагообразная молния
forlorn /fəˈlɔːn/ adj. заброшенный
form /fɔːm/ n. **1** (shape) форма, вид; (figure) фигура **2** (kind, variant) вид, форма **3** (of health) состояние; **in good ~** в хорошей форме; (of spirits): **he appeared in great ~** он был в отличной форме **4** (document) бланк, анкета **5** (BrE, class in school) класс
● v.t. **1** (fashion) формировать, с-; **he ~ed the clay into a vase** глина под его руками превратилась в вазу; (by discipline, training, etc.): **his character was ~ed at school** его характер сформировался в школе **2** (organize, create) организ|овывать, -овать; **they ~ed an alliance** они создали/образовали союз; **he was unable to ~ a government** он не смог сформировать правительство **3** (conceive): **they ~ed a plan** они выработали план **4** (mil. etc.) стро|ить, по-; **~ a queue** (BrE), **line** (AmE) образ|овывать, -овать очередь **5** (constitute) сост|авлять, -авить; **this ~s the basis of our discussion** это составляет основу нашей дискуссии
● v.i. (take shape, appear): **ice ~ed on the window** на окне образовался/возник морозный узор; **an idea ~ed in his mind** в его мозгу возникла идея
formal /'fɔːm(ə)l/ adj. официальный

formality /fɔː'mælɪtɪ/ *n.* форма́льность

formalize /'fɔːməlaɪz/ *v.t.* оф|ормля́ть, -о́рмить

format /'fɔːmæt/ *n.* (also comput.) форма́т
● *v.t.* (comput.) формати́ровать, от-

formation /fɔː'meɪʃ(ə)n/ *n.* образова́ние, формирова́ние

formative /'fɔːmətɪv/ *adj.* формиру́ющий, образу́ющий; **he spent his ~ years in France** го́ды, когда́ скла́дывался/формирова́лся его́ хара́ктер, он провёл во Фра́нции

former /'fɔːmə(r)/ *adj.* **1** (earlier) предше́ствующий; **my ~ husband** мой бы́вший муж **2** (first mentioned of two) пе́рвый

formerly /'fɔːməlɪ/ *adv.* пре́жде, ра́ньше

formidable /'fɔːmɪdəb(ə)l/ *adj.* (frightening) устраша́ющий, гро́зный; (huge) огро́мный

formless /'fɔːmlɪs/ *adj.* бесфо́рменный

formula /'fɔːmjʊlə/ *n.* (*pl.* **formulas** or **formulae** /-liː/) (math., chem.) фо́рмула

formulate /'fɔːmjʊleɪt/ *v.t.* формули́ровать, с-

forsake /fə'seɪk/ *v.t.* (*past* **forsook** /-'sʊk/; *p.p.* **forsaken** /-'seɪk(ə)n/) пок|ида́ть, -и́нуть; ост|авля́ть, -а́вить; бр|оса́ть, -о́сить

fort /fɔːt/ *n.* форт

forte /'fɔːteɪ/ *n.* (strong point) си́льная сторона́

forth /fɔːθ/ *adv.* вперёд, да́льше; **and so ~** и так да́лее; **from this day ~** с э́того дня; впредь

forthcoming /fɔːθ'kʌmɪŋ/ *adj.* предстоя́щий; **the clerk was not very ~ with information** чино́вник не о́чень охо́тно дава́л све́дения

forthright /'fɔːθraɪt/ *adj.* прямо́й, прямолине́йный

fortieth /'fɔːtɪɪθ/ *n.* (fraction) одна́ сороковая
● *adj.* сороково́й

fortification /fɔːtɪfɪ'keɪʃ(ə)n/ *n.* укрепле́ние

fortif|y /'fɔːtɪfaɪ/ *v.t.* укреп|ля́ть, -и́ть; **~ied wines** креплёные ви́на

fortitude /'fɔːtɪtjuːd/ *n.* сто́йкость; си́ла ду́ха

fortnight /'fɔːtnaɪt/ (BrE) *n.* две неде́ли

fortnightly /'fɔːtnaɪtlɪ/ *adj.* двухнеде́льный
● *adv.* раз в две неде́ли

fortress /'fɔːtrɪs/ *n.* кре́пость

fortuitous /fɔː'tjuːɪtəs/ *adj.* случа́йный

fortunate /'fɔːtʃənət/ *adj.* счастли́вый, уда́чный; **~ly** к сча́стью

fortune /'fɔːtʃuːn/ *n.* **1** (chance) уда́ча, сча́стье, форту́на; **by good ~** по сча́стью **2** (fate) судьба́; **the Gypsy (woman) told my ~** цыга́нка (по/на)гада́ла мне **3** (large sum) состоя́ние, бога́тство; **make a ~** разбогате́ть (*pf.*)
■ **~ teller** *n.* гада́лка, ворожея́

fort|y /'fɔːtɪ/ *n.* со́рок; **~ies** (decade) сороковы́е го́ды (*m. pl.*); **they are both in their ~ies** им обо́им за со́рок
● *adj.* со́рок (+ *g. pl.*)

forward /'fɔːwəd/ *n.* (sport) напада́ющий
● *adj.* (situated to the fore) пере́дний; (progressive) прогресси́вный; (pert) наглова́тый, развя́зный
● *adv.* (onward; towards one) вперёд; **please come ~** пожа́луйста, вы́йдите вперёд; **the meeting has been brought ~ a day** собра́ние перенесли́ на́ день ра́ньше; (towards the future):

I look ~ to meeting her я с нетерпе́нием жду встре́чи с ней
● *v.t.* (send) пос|ыла́ть, -ла́ть; отпр|авля́ть, -а́вить; (send on) перес|ыла́ть, -ла́ть
■ **~ slash** *n.* коса́я черта́, слеш

forwards /'fɔːwədz/ *adv.* вперёд

forwent /fɔː'went/ *past of* ▶ **forgo**

fossil /'fɒs(ə)l/ *n.* окамене́лость

foster /'fɒstə(r)/ *v.t.* **1** (bring up) воспи́т|ывать, -а́ть (*чужого ребёнка*); (*also* **out**) (BrE, assign to someone else to bring up) отд|ава́ть, -а́ть на воспита́ние **2** (fig., hope) пита́ть (*impf.*); (hatred) се́ять, по-
■ **~-child** *n.* приёмный ребёнок, воспи́танник; **~-father** *n.* приёмный оте́ц; **~-mother** *n.* приёмная мать

fought /fɔːt/ *past and p.p. of* ▶ **fight**

foul /faʊl/ *n.* (sport) наруше́ние (пра́вил игры́)
● *adj.* гря́зный, отврати́тельный; **a ~ smell** злово́ние; **~ language** скверносло́вие, ру́гань; **~ weather** отврати́тельная пого́да, непого́да
● *v.t.* (defile) загрязн|я́ть, -и́ть; па́чкать, за-; засор|я́ть, -и́ть; (obstruct) образо́в|ывать, -а́ть затор в + *p.*
■ **~-mouthed** *adj.* скверносло́вящий; **~ play** *n.* (sport) гру́бая игра́; (violence) нечи́стое де́ло

found[1] /faʊnd/ *v.t.* осно́в|ывать, -а́ть; за|кла́дывать, -ложи́ть; (base) осно́в|ывать, -а́ть

found[2] /faʊnd/ *past and p.p. of* ▶ **find**

foundation /faʊn'deɪʃ(ə)n/ *n.* **1** (establishing) основа́ние, учрежде́ние **2** (base of building etc.) фунда́мент; (fig.) осно́ва **3**: **~ cream** крем под пу́дру

founder /'faʊndə(r)/ *n.* основа́тель (*m.*) (-ница)

foundry /'faʊndrɪ/ *n.* лите́йная

fountain /'faʊntɪn/ *n.* фонта́н
■ **~ pen** *n.* авторучка

four /fɔː(r)/ *n.* (число́/но́мер) четы́ре; (**~ people**) че́тверо; (figure; thing numbered 4; group of **~**) четвёрка; **he got down on all ~s** он опусти́лся на четвере́ньки
● *adj.* четы́ре + *g. sg.*
■ **~-letter** *adj.*: **~-letter word** (fig.) руга́тельство; непристо́йное сло́во; **~-wheel** *adj.*: **~-wheel drive** (*attr.*) с приводом на четы́ре колеса́; (*n.*) внедоро́жник, вездехо́д

fourteen /fɔː'tiːn/ *n.* четы́рнадцать
● *adj.* четы́рнадцать + *g. pl.*

fourteenth /fɔː'tiːnθ/ *n.* (date) четы́рнадцатое (число́); (fraction) одна́ четы́рнадцатая
● *adj.* четы́рнадцатый

fourth /fɔːθ/ *n.* **1** (date) четвёртое (число́) **2** (fraction) одна́ четвёртая
● *adj.* четвёртый

fowl /faʊl/ *n.* (*pl.* **~** or **~s**) (domestic) дома́шняя пти́ца

fox /fɒks/ *n.* лиса́, лиси́ца
■ **~hound** *n.* го́нчая; **~-hunting** *n.* (верхова́я) охо́та на лис

foyer /'fɔɪeɪ/ *n.* фойе́ (*nt. indecl.*)

fracking /'frækɪŋ/ *n.* (tech.) гидравли́ческий перело́м
fraction /'frækʃ(ə)n/ *n.* дробь
fractious /'frækʃəs/ *adj.* капри́зный
fracture /'fræktʃə(r)/ *n.* (of a bone) перело́м
  ● *v.t. & i.* лома́ть(ся), с-
fragile /'frædʒaɪl/ *adj.* хру́пкий
fragility /frə'dʒɪlɪtɪ/ *n.* ло́мкость, хру́пкость
fragment /'frægmənt/ *n.* обло́мок, оско́лок; (of writing) фрагме́нт
fragmentary /'frægməntərɪ/ *adj.* отры́вочный, фрагмента́рный
fragrance /'freɪgrəns/ *n.* арома́т
fragrant /'freɪgrənt/ *adj.* арома́тный
frail /freɪl/ *adj.* хру́пкий
✍ **frame** /freɪm/ *n.* **1** (structural skeleton) скеле́т, костя́к **2** (wood or metal surround) ра́ма, ра́мка **3**: ~ **of mind** настрое́ние; расположе́ние ду́ха **4** (cin.) кадр
  ● *v.t.* **1** (a picture) вст|авля́ть, -а́вить в ра́м(к)у **2** (a proposal, a reply) сост|авля́ть, -а́вить; созд|ава́ть, -а́ть **3** (an innocent person, infml) подст|авля́ть, -а́вить
  ■ ~**work** *n.* карка́с, о́стов, (fig.): **within the** ~**work of the constitution** в ра́мках конститу́ции
France /frɑːns/ *n.* Фра́нция
franchise /'fræntʃaɪz/ *n.* (right to vote) пра́во го́лоса; (comm.) привиле́гия, франши́за
frank /fræŋk/ *adj.* открове́нный, и́скренний
frankfurter /'fræŋkfɜːtə(r)/ *n.* соси́ска (копчёная)
frantic /'fræntɪk/ *adj.* нейстовый, безу́мный; **she became** ~ **with grief** она́ обезу́мела от го́ря
fraternal /frə'tɜːn(ə)l/ *adj.* бра́тский
fraternity /frə'tɜːnɪtɪ/ *n.* бра́тство
fraternize /'frætənaɪz/ *v.i.* брата́ться (*impf.*)
fraud /frɔːd/ *n.* (fraudulent act) обма́н, моше́нничество; (impostor) обма́нщик, моше́нник
fraudulent /'frɔːdjʊlənt/ *adj.* обма́нный, фальши́вый, моше́нический
fraught /frɔːt/ *adj.* по́лный; **the expedition is** ~ **with danger** экспеди́ция чрева́та опа́сностями; (tense) напряжённый
fray /freɪ/ *v.i.* прот|ира́ться, -ере́ться
frazzle /'fræz(ə)l/ *n.*: **worn to a** ~ доведённый до изнеможе́ния
freak /friːk/ *n.* (unusual occurrence): ~ **weather conditions** необы́чные пого́дные усло́вия; (abnormal person or thing) уро́д, вы́родок; ~ **of nature** оши́бка приро́ды; (enthusiast) фана́т; **health** ~ поме́шанный на здоро́вье
  ● *v.i.*: ~ **(out)** (infml) при|ходи́ть, -йти́ в возбужде́ние
freakish /'friːkɪʃ/ *adj.* причу́дливый, чудно́й
freckle /'frek(ə)l/ *n.* весну́шка
✍ **free** /friː/ *adj.* (**freer** /'friːə(r)/, **freest** /'friːɪst/) **1** свобо́дный, во́льный; **you are** ~ **to leave** вы мо́жете уйти́; **they gave us a** ~ **hand**

✍ ключева́я ле́ксика

они́ предоста́вили нам по́лную свобо́ду де́йствий; **set** ~ освобо|жда́ть, -ди́ть **2** (without constraint) непринуждённый, раско́ванный **3** (without payment) беспла́тный; ~ **of charge** беспла́тный **4** (unoccupied) свобо́дный, неза́нятый **5** (liberal) ще́дрый; ~ **with one's money** ще́дрый, расточи́тельный
  ● *v.t.* (release, e.g. a rope) высвобожда́ть; (liberate) освобо|жда́ть, -ди́ть
  ■ ~ **fall** *n.* свобо́дное паде́ние; ~-**for-all** *n.* (competition) откры́тый (для всех) ко́нкурс; ~ **gift** *n.* полу́ченное да́ром; ~**lance(r)** *n.* лицо́ свобо́дной профе́ссии; внешта́тный сотру́дник; **F**~**mason** *n.* масо́н; **F**~**masonry** *n.* масо́нство; **F**~**phone** *n.* (BrE) беспла́тный телефо́н; ~-**range** *adj.*: ~-**range eggs** я́йца от кур на свобо́дном вы́гуле; ~ **speech** *n.* свобо́да сло́ва; ~**way** *n.* (AmE) скоростна́я автостра́да; ~ **will** *n.* свобо́да во́ли; **he left of his own** ~ **will** он ушёл доброво́льно/сам (*or* по свое́й во́ле)
✍ **freedom** /'friːdəm/ *n.* свобо́да; ~ **of speech** свобо́да сло́ва
freesia /'friːʒə/ *n.* (bot.) фре́зия
freez|e /friːz/ *n.* (period of frost) замора́живание; **wage** ~**e** замора́живание за́работной пла́ты
  ● *v.t.* (*past* **froze**, *p.p.* **frozen**) замор|а́живать, -о́зить; **frozen food** моро́женые проду́кты; ~**e assets/prices** замор|а́живать, -о́зить фо́нды/це́ны
  ● *v.i.* (*past* **froze**, *p.p.* **frozen**) **1** (impers.) моро́зит (*impf.*); **it's** ~**ing outside** на дворе́ стра́шный моро́з **2** (congeal with cold): **the roads are frozen** доро́ги покры́лись льдом; **the pipes are frozen (up)** тру́бы промёрзли; ~**ing point** то́чка замерза́ния **3** (fig., become rigid) заст|ыва́ть, -ы́ть; (as command): ~**e!** стоя́ть!, ни с ме́ста! **4** (become chilled) зам|ерза́ть, -ёрзнуть; **I'm** ~**ing** я замёрз
freezer /'friːzə(r)/ *n.* (domestic appliance) морози́льник
  ■ ~ **compartment** *n.* морози́лка
freight /freɪt/ *n.* фрахт
freighter /'freɪtə(r)/ *n.* (vessel) грузово́е су́дно; (aircraft) грузово́й самолёт
✍ **French** /frentʃ/ *n.* (language) францу́зский язы́к; **the** ~ (people) францу́зы (*m. pl.*)
  ● *adj.* францу́зский
  ■ ~ **Canadian** *n.* франкоканáд|ец (-ка); ~ **fries** *n. pl.* карто́фель (*m.*) соло́мкой/фри; ~**man** *n.* францу́з; ~ **Riviera** *n.* Лазу́рный Бе́рег; ~ **window** *n.* двуство́рчатое окно́ до по́ла; (*in pl.*) две́ри в сад; ~**woman** *n.* францу́женка
frenetic /frə'netɪk/ *adj.* нейстовый
frenzied /'frenzɪd/ *adj.* нейстовый, взбешённый
frenzy /'frenzɪ/ *n.* нейстовство, бе́шенство
frequency /'friːkwənsɪ/ *n.* частота́
frequent /'friːkwənt/ *adj.* ча́стый
✍ **frequently** /'friːkwəntlɪ/ *adv.* ча́сто
fresco /'freskəʊ/ *n.* (*pl.* ~**s** *or* ~**es**) фре́ска
✍ **fresh** /freʃ/ *adj.* **1** (new) све́жий, но́вый **2** (recent in origin): ~ **bread** све́жий хлеб; **it is still** ~ **in my memory** э́то ещё све́жо в мое́й

па́мяти **3** (as opposed to salt) пре́сный **4** (cool, refreshing) све́жий, прохла́дный **5** (unspoilt, unsullied) све́жий, незапя́тнанный; ~ air све́жий во́здух **6** (lively) бо́дрый, живо́й **7** (impudent) развя́зный, де́рзкий
■ ~**water** adj. пресново́дный

freshen /ˈfreʃ(ə)n/ v.i.: she's gone to ~ up она́ пошла́ привести́ себя́ в поря́док

freshly /ˈfreʃlɪ/ adv. (recently) неда́вно; то́лько что

fret /fret/ v.i. (**fretted, fretting**) волнова́ться; му́читься (both impf.)

fretful /ˈfretfʊl/ adj. раздражи́тельный, капри́зный

Freudian /ˈfrɔɪdɪən/ adj.: ~ slip огово́рка по Фре́йду

friction /ˈfrɪkʃ(ə)n/ n. тре́ние; (fig.) тре́ния (nt. pl.)

⚜ **Friday** /ˈfraɪdeɪ/ n. пя́тница

fridge /frɪdʒ/ n. холоди́льник
■ ~**-freezer** n. (BrE) двухка́мерный холоди́льник

⚜ **friend** /frend/ n. (male) друг, прия́тель; (female) подру́га, прия́тельница; be ~s дружи́ть (impf.) (с кем); make ~s подружи́ться (pf.) (с кем)

friendly /ˈfrendlɪ/ adj. (**friendlier, friendliest**) дру́жеский, това́рищеский

friendship /ˈfrendʃɪp/ n. дру́жба

frieze /friːz/ n. (decorative band) бордю́р, фриз

frigate /ˈfrɪɡət/ n. (hist.) фрега́т; (small destroyer) эска́дренный миноно́сец; сторожево́й кора́бль

fright /fraɪt/ n. страх, испу́г; give sb a ~ испуга́ть (pf.) кого́-н.; напуга́ть (pf.) кого́-н.; I got the ~ of my life я жу́тко испуга́лся

frighten /ˈfraɪt(ə)n/ v.t. пуга́ть, на-/ис-; she is ~ed of the dark она́ бои́тся темноты́

frightening /ˈfraɪtnɪŋ/ adj. стра́шный

frightful /ˈfraɪtfʊl/ adj. (terrible) ужа́сный, стра́шный; (infml, hideous) безобра́зный

frigid /ˈfrɪdʒɪd/ adj. **1** (cold) холо́дный **2** (unfeeling) холо́дный, безразли́чный; (sexually) холо́дный, фриги́дный
■ ~ **zone** n. аркти́ческий по́яс

frill /frɪl/ n. обо́рочка

frilly /ˈfrɪlɪ/ adj. (**frillier, frilliest**) с обо́рками

fringe /frɪndʒ/ n. **1** (ornamental border) бахрома́ **2** (BrE, of hair) чёлка **3** (fig., edge, margin) край, кайма́
■ ~ **benefits** n. pl. дополни́тельные льго́ты (f. pl.)

frisk /frɪsk/ v.t. (search) обы́ск|ивать, -а́ть

frisky /ˈfrɪskɪ/ adj. (**friskier, friskiest**) ре́звый, игри́вый

frisson /ˈfriːsɔ̃/ n. дрожь (от предвкушаемого удово́льствия)

fritter /ˈfrɪtə(r)/ v.t.: ~ away транжи́рить, рас-

frivolity /frɪˈvɒlɪtɪ/ n. легкомы́слие

frivolous /ˈfrɪvələs/ adj. легкомы́сленный, пусто́й

frizzy /ˈfrɪzɪ/ adj. (**frizzier, frizziest**) вью́щийся, курча́вый

frock /frɒk/ n. пла́тье; party ~ вече́рнее пла́тье
■ ~ **coat** n. сюртук

frog /frɒɡ/ n. лягу́шка; I've got a ~ in my throat (fig.) я охри́п
■ ~**man** n. ныря́льщик с аквала́нгом

frolic /ˈfrɒlɪk/ v.i. (**frolicked, frolicking**) шали́ть (impf.); резви́ться (impf.)

⚜ **from** /frɒm/ prep. **1** (denoting origin of movement, measurement or distance): the train ~ London to Paris по́езд из Ло́ндона в Пари́ж; guests ~ Ukraine го́сти с Украи́ны; 10 miles ~ here в десяти́ ми́лях отсю́да; ~ the beginning of the book с нача́ла кни́ги; ~ end to end от одного́ конца́ до друго́го; far ~ it! отню́дь!; во́все нет! **2** (expr. separation): I took the key ~ him я взял у него́ ключ; released ~ prison вы́пущенный из тюрьмы́ **3** (denoting personal origin): a letter ~ my son письмо́ от моего́ сы́на **4** (expr. material origin): wine is made ~ grapes вино́ де́лается из виногра́да **5** (expr. origin in time): ~ the very beginning с са́мого нача́ла; ~ beginning to end с нача́ла до конца́; ~ now on с э́того моме́нта; ~ February to October с февраля́ по октя́брь; ~ time to time вре́мя от вре́мени **6** (expr. source or model): he quoted ~ memory он цити́ровал по па́мяти; he spoke ~ the heart он говори́л от души́ **7** (expr. cause) от/с + g.; suffer ~ arthritis страда́ть (impf.) артри́том **8** (expr. difference): I can't tell him ~ his brother я не могу́ отличи́ть его́ от его́ бра́та **9** (expr. change): things went ~ bad to worse дела́ шли всё ху́же и ху́же **10** (with numbers): ~ 1 to 10 от одного́ до десяти́; it will last ~ 10 to 15 days э́то продли́тся 10–15 дней; they cost ~ £5 (upwards) они́ сто́ят от 5 фу́нтов и вы́ше **11** (with advs.): ~ above све́рху; ~ below сни́зу; ~ inside изнутри́; ~ outside снару́жи; ~ afar издалека́; ~ under the table из-под стола́

frond /frɒnd/ n. ветвь с ли́стьями; лист (па́поротника)

⚜ **front** /frʌnt/ n. **1** (foremost side or part) перёд; пере́дняя сторона́; he walked in ~ of the procession он шёл впереди́ проце́ссии; in ~ of the house пе́ред до́мом; in ~ of the children при де́тях; ~ to back наперёд **2** (archit.) фаса́д **3** (fighting line) фронт; he was sent to the ~ его́ посла́ли на фронт; in the ~ line на передово́й ли́нии **4** (BrE, road bordering sea) на́бережная **5** (meteor.) фронт
■ ~ **benches** n. pl. (pol.) скамьи́ для мини́стров и ли́деров оппози́ции в парла́менте; ~ **door** n. пара́дная дверь; ~ **page** n. пе́рвая страни́ца/полоса́; ~ **page news** основны́е но́вости в газе́те

frontier /ˈfrʌntɪə(r)/ n. грани́ца

frost /frɒst/ n. моро́з
● v.t.: the windows were ~ed over о́кна замёрзли
■ ~**bite** n. обмороже́ние, отмороже́ние; ~**ed glass** n. ма́товое стекло́

frosting /ˈfrɒstɪŋ/ n. (AmE, cul.) глазу́рь

frosty /ˈfrɒstɪ/ adj. (**frostier, frostiest**) моро́зный; (fig., unfriendly) холо́дный, ледяно́й

froth /frɒθ/ n. пе́на

frothy /'frɒθɪ/ adj. (**frothier, frothiest**) пе́нистый; (fig.) пусто́й

frown /fraʊn/ v.i. хму́риться, на-; the authorities ~ on gambling вла́сти неодобри́тельно отно́сятся к аза́ртным и́грам

froze /frəʊz/ past of ▸ freeze

frozen /'frəʊz(ə)n/ adj. замёрзший, засты́вший; (ice-bound) ско́ванный льдо́м

frugal /'fru:g(ə)l/ adj. бережли́вый

✧ **fruit** /fru:t/ n. фрукт
■ ~ **cake** n. фрукто́вый кекс; ~ **juice** n. фрукто́вый сок; ~ **machine** n. (BrE) игрово́й автома́т; ~ **salad** n. фрукто́вый сала́т

fruitful /'fru:tfʊl/ adj. плодотво́рный

fruition /fru:'ɪʃ(ə)n/ n.: come to ~ осуществля́ться, -и́ться

fruitless /'fru:tlɪs/ adj. беспло́дный

fruity /'fru:tɪ/ adj. (**fruitier, fruitiest**) фрукто́вый

frustrate /frʌ'streɪt/ v.t. разочаро́в|ывать, -а́ть; I feel ~d я обескура́жен

frustration /frʌ'streɪʃ(ə)n/ n. **1** (thwarting) круше́ние (*планов/наде́жд*) **2** (disappointment) разочаро́вание

fr|y /fraɪ/ v.t. жа́рить, за-/из-/по-; ~ied egg(s) яи́чница; ~ied potato жа́реная карто́шка
● v.i. жа́риться (*impf.*)
■ ~ying pan n. сковорода́

ft abbr. (of **foot, feet**) фут(ы)

fuchsia /'fju:ʃə/ n. фу́ксия

fuck /fʌk/ (vulg.) n.: he doesn't give a ~ ему́ по́ хую (or по́ хуй); (euph.) ему́ по́ фигу (or по́ фиг)
● v.t. еба́ть, вы́-; (euph.) тра́х|ать, -нуть; ~ it! чёрт возьми́/побери́! (euph.); бля́дь!, (euph.) блин!; ~ all (BrE) ни хуя́, (euph.) ни хрена́; to do ~ all ни хуя́ не де́лать
● v.i. еба́ться, по-; (euph.) тра́х|аться, -нуться
● with advs.: ~ about/around занима́ться, страда́ть (*both impf.*) хуйнёй; (euph.) занима́ться, страда́ть (*both impf.*) хернёй; ~ off! отъеби́сь (от меня́)!; пошёл/иди́ на́ хуй!, (euph.) пошёл/иди́ на́ фиг!; ~ up v.t. (sth) запа́рывать, -оро́ть (no vulg. equivalent); (a game, contest, etc.) прос|ира́ть, -ра́ть; про|ёбывать, -еба́ть; (sb) док|а́нывать, -она́ть (no vulg. equivalent); (v.i.) лажа́ть (*impf.*), облажа́ться (*pf.*) (no vulg. equivalents); по́рта|чить, на- (no vulg. equivalent)

fucking /'fʌkɪŋ/ adj. (vulg.) ёбаный, (euph.) до́лбаный

fudge /fʌdʒ/ n. (sweetmeat) сли́вочная пома́дка
● v.t. & i. (an issue, question) уклон|я́ться, -и́ться от + g.; (facts, figures) подтасо́в|ывать, -а́ть; ~ accounts подде́л|ывать, -ать счета́

✧ **fuel** /'fju:əl/ n. то́пливо, горю́чее
● v.t. (**fuelled, fuelling**, AmE **fueled, fueling**) снаб|жа́ть, -ди́ть (or запр|авля́ть, -а́вить) то́пливом

fugitive /'fju:dʒɪtɪv/ n. бегл|е́ц (-я́нка)

fugue /fju:g/ n. (mus.) фу́га

✧ ключева́я ле́ксика

fulcr|um /'fʊlkrəm/ n. (pl. ~a or ~ums) то́чка опо́ры; то́чка приложе́ния си́лы

fulfil /fʊl'fɪl/ (AmE **fulfill**) v.t. (**fulfilled, fulfilling**) выполня́ть, вы́полнить

fulfilment /fʊl'fɪl mənt/ (AmE **fulfillment**) n. (accomplishment) выполне́ние, исполне́ние; (satisfaction) удовлетворе́ние

✧ **full** /fʊl/ adj. **1** (filled to capacity) по́лный; the hotel is ~ (up) все ко́мнаты в гости́нице за́няты; (having plenty): ~ of ideas по́лон иде́й/за́мыслов; ~ of life жизнера́достный; по́лон жи́зни **2** (complete): we waited a ~ hour мы жда́ли це́лый час
● adv. **1** (very): you know ~ well вы са́ми прекра́сно зна́ете **2** (completely): she turned the radio on ~ она́ включи́ла ра́дио на по́лную мо́щность/гро́мкость
■ ~back n. защи́тник; ~-grown adj. взро́слый; ~-length adj. во всю длину́; ~-length dress пла́тье до пят; ~ moon n. полнолу́ние; ~-scale adj. в по́лном объёме; ~ stop n. то́чка; ~-time adj. (of job) занима́ющий всё (рабо́чее) вре́мя

✧ **fully** /'fʊlɪ/ adv. вполне́, по́лностью, соверше́нно, до конца́

fulsome /'fʊlsəm/ adj. чрезме́рный, тошнотво́рный

fumble /'fʌmb(ə)l/ v.i. тереби́ть (*impf.*) в рука́х; ~ a ball упусти́ть (*pf.*) мяч
● v.i. ры́ться (*impf.*); he ~d in his pockets for a key он ры́лся в карма́нах, ища́ ключ

fume /fju:m/ n. дым, ко́поть
● v.i. (fig.): fuming with rage кипя́щий от гне́ва

fumigate /'fju:mɪgeɪt/ v.t. окур|ивать, -и́ть

✧ **fun** /fʌn/ n. весе́лье, заба́ва; make ~ of, poke ~ at насмеха́ться (*impf.*) над + i.; he is ~ to be with с ним не соску́чишься; we had ~ at the party в гостя́х бы́ло ве́село
■ ~fair n. (BrE) увесели́тельный парк

✧ **function** /'fʌŋkʃ(ə)n/ n. **1** (purpose) фу́нкция, назначе́ние **2** (social gathering) ве́чер **3**: ~ key (comput.) функциона́льная кла́виша
● v.i. функциони́ровать, де́йствовать (*both impf.*)

functional /'fʌŋkʃən(ə)l/ adj. функциона́льный

functionary /'fʌŋkʃənərɪ/ n. функционе́р, должностно́е лицо́

✧ **fund** /fʌnd/ n. фонд, запа́с, резе́рв; (in pl.) (resources) фо́нды (m. pl.); he is in ~s (BrE) он при деньга́х
● v.t. финанси́ровать (*impf., pf.*); (fin.) консолиди́ровать (*impf., pf.*)
■ ~-raising n. сбор средств; a ~-raising dinner (for charity) благотвори́тельный банке́т

fundamental /fʌndə'ment(ə)l/ adj. основно́й, суще́ственный

fundamentalism /fʌndə'mentəlɪz(ə)m/ n. фундаментали́зм

fundamentalist /fʌndə'mentəlɪst/ n. фундаментали́ст

funeral /'fju:nər(ə)l/ n. по́хор|оны (-о́н)
■ ~ parlour (BrE), ~ home (AmE) nn. похоро́нное бюро́

funereal /fju:'nɪərɪəl/ adj. мра́чный; тра́урный

fungi /'fʌŋgaɪ, 'fʌndʒaɪ/ *pl. of* ▶ fungus
fungicide /'fʌndʒɪsaɪd/ *n.* фунгици́д;
(med.) противогрибко́вое сре́дство,
противогрибко́вый препара́т
fungus /'fʌŋgəs/ *n.* (*pl.* **fungi** *or* **funguses**)
грибо́к; (ни́зший) гриб
funnel /'fʌn(ə)l/ *n.* воро́нка; (of ship) дымова́я
труба́
✧ **funny** /'fʌnɪ/ *adj.* (**funnier, funniest**)
1 (amusing) смешно́й, заба́вный **2** (strange)
стра́нный; **I have a ~ feeling you're right!** я
подозрева́ю, что вы пра́вы!
fur /fə:(r)/ *n.* **1** (animal hair) шерсть **2** (as worn)
мех
furious /'fjʊərɪəs/ *adj.* **1** (violent) бу́йный,
нейстовый **2** (enraged) взбешённый; **she was
~ with him** она́ разозли́лась на него́ не на
шу́тку
furnace /'fə:nɪs/ *n.* горн, оча́г, печь, то́пка
furnish /'fə:nɪʃ/ *v.t.* обставля́ть, -а́вить
furnishings /'fə:nɪʃɪŋz/ *n. pl.* обстано́вка
furniture /'fə:nɪtʃə(r)/ *n.* ме́бель
furore /fjʊə'rɔ:rɪ/ *n.* фуро́р
furrier /'fʌrɪə(r)/ *n.* меховщи́к, скорня́к
furrow /'fʌrəʊ/ *n.* **1** (in the earth etc.) борозда́,
жёлоб; **plough a lonely ~** (fig.) де́йствовать
(*impf.*) в одино́чку **2** (wrinkle) глубо́кая
морщи́на
  ● *v.t.* (fig.): **~ed brow** намо́рщенный лоб
furry /'fə:rɪ/ *adj.* (**furrier, furriest**)
покры́тый ме́хом; пушно́й
✧ **further** /'fə:ðə(r)/ (*see also* ▶ **farther**) *adj.*
1 дальне́йший; (additional) доба́вочный,
дополни́тельный; **until ~ notice** впредь до
дальне́йшего уведомле́ния **2** (more distant)
да́льний
  ● *adv.* да́лее, да́льше; **I can go no ~** я не могу́
да́льше идти́
  ● *v.t.* продв|ига́ть, -и́нуть; соде́йствовать
(*impf.*) + *d.*; спосо́бствовать (*impf.*) + *d.*
  ■ **~ education** *n.* (BrE) дальне́йшее
образова́ние (*после школы, не высшее*)
furtherance /'fə:ðərəns/ *n.* продвиже́ние; **in ~
of this plan** для осуществле́ния э́того пла́на

furthermore /fə:ðə'mɔ:(r)/ *adv.* к тому́ же;
кро́ме того́
furthest /'fə:ðɪst/ *adj.* са́мый да́льний
  ● *adv.* да́льше всего́
furtive /'fə:tɪv/ *adj.* скры́тный
fury /'fjʊərɪ/ *n.* я́рость
fuse¹ /fju:z/ *n.* (elec.) предохрани́тель (*m.*),
про́бка
  ● *v.t. & i.* (BrE, elec.): **he ~d the lights** он
пережёг про́бки; **the lights ~d** про́бки
перегоре́ли
  ■ **~ box** *n.* распредели́тельный щит(о́к)
(с предохрани́телями/про́бками); **~ wire** *n.*
про́волока для предохрани́теля
fuse², fuze /fju:z/ *n.* (igniting device) запа́л,
фити́ль (*m.*)
fuselage /'fju:zəlɑ:ʒ/ *n.* фюзеля́ж
fusion /'fju:ʒ(ə)n/ *n.* (blending, coalition) сплав,
слия́ние
fuss /fʌs/ *n.* суета́, шум (из-за пустяко́в);
make a ~ about, over sth суети́ться (*impf.*)
вокру́г чего́-н.; **make a ~ of sb** (BrE)
суетли́во опека́ть (*impf.*) кого́-н.
  ● *v.i.* суети́ться (*impf.*); **she ~es over her
children** она́ ве́чно во́зится со свои́ми
детьми́
fussy /'fʌsɪ/ *adj.* (**fussier, fussiest**)
разбо́рчивый; **I'm not ~ (about) what I eat** я
не привере́длив в еде́
futile /'fju:taɪl/ *adj.* напра́сный, тще́тный
futility /fju:'tɪlɪtɪ/ *n.* тще́тность,
беспло́дность
futon /'fu:tɒn/ *n.* япо́нский матра́с (*в
складно́й деревя́нной ра́ме; расстила́ется
на полу в ка́честве крова́ти и́ли кре́сла*)
✧ **future** /'fju:tʃə(r)/ *n.* **1** бу́дущее; **in (the) ~** в
бу́дущем **2** (gram.) бу́дущее вре́мя
  ● *adj.* бу́дущий; **belief in a ~ life** ве́ра в
загро́бную жизнь
futuristic /fju:tʃə'rɪstɪk/ *adj.*
футуристи́ческий
fuze /fju:z/ *n.* = **fuse²**
fuzzy /'fʌzɪ/ *adj.* (**fuzzier, fuzziest**) (fluffy)
пуши́стый; (blurred) расплы́вчатый

f

Gg

G /dʒiː/ *n.* (mus.) соль (*nt. indecl.*)

gab /gæb/ *n.* (infml): **he has the gift of the ~** у него хорошо подвешен язык

gabble /'gæb(ə)l/ *n.* бормотание; (sl.) трёп, болтовня
● *v.t. & i.* бормотать, про-

gaberdine /ɡæbə'diːn/ *n.* (material) габардин; (*attr.*) габардиновый

gadget /'gædʒɪt/ *n.* (infml) штуковина, хитроумное приспособление; (for a computer, mobile phone, etc.) гаджет

gaffe /gæf/ *n.* ложный шаг, оплошность

gag /gæg/ *n.* **1** (to prevent speech etc.) кляп **2** (joke) шутка, хохма
● *v.t.* (**gagged, gagging**) вставля́ть, -авить кляп + *d.*; (fig.) затыка́ть, -кну́ть рот + *d.*
● *v.i.* (**gagged, gagging**) (retch) дави́ться (*impf.*)

gaga /'gɑːgɑː/ *adj.* (sl.) чокнутый, слабоумный; **go ~** впада́ть, -сть в мара́зм; выжива́ть, вы́жить из ума́

gage /geɪdʒ/ *n. & v.t.* (AmE) = gauge

gaiety /'geɪətɪ/ (AmE **gayety**) *n.* весёлость, весе́лье

gain /geɪn/ *n.* **1** (profit) при́быль **2** (increase) увеличе́ние
● *v.t.* овлад|ева́ть, -е́ть; доб|ива́ться, -и́ться + *g.*; доб|ыва́ть, -ы́ть; приобре|та́ть, -сти́; **he ~ed 5 pounds in weight** он попра́вился на 5 фу́нтов; **the patient is ~ing strength** пацие́нт набира́ется сил
● *v.i.* **1** (reap profit, benefit, advantage) извл|ека́ть, -е́чь по́льзу/вы́году; **how do I stand to ~ from it?** кака́я мне от э́того по́льза/вы́года? **2** (move ahead): **my watch ~s (three minutes a day)** мои́ часы́ спеша́т (на три мину́ты в день); **he ~ed on his rival** он нагоня́л сопе́рника

gainful /'geɪnfʊl/ *adj.* при́быльный; дохо́дный; **~ employment** хорошо́ опла́чиваемая работа

galaxy /'gæləksɪ/ *n.* гала́ктика; (**the G~**) Гала́ктика

gale /geɪl/ *n.* бу́ря

gallant /'gælənt/ *adj.* **1** (attentive to ladies) гала́нтный **2** (brave) до́блестный

gallery /'gælərɪ/ *n.* **1** (walk, passage) галере́я **2** (picture **~**) карти́нная галере́я **3** (theatr.) балко́н

galley /'gælɪ/ *n.* (*pl.* **~s**) **1** (ship) гале́ра **2** (ship's kitchen) ка́мбуз; (in aircraft) ку́хня на борту́ самолёта

◆ ключевая лексика

■ **~ slave** *n.* раб на гале́рах

Gallic /'gælɪk/ *adj.* (Gaulish) га́лльский; (French) францу́зский

galling /'gɔːlɪŋ/ *adj.* (fig.) раздража́ющий

gallivant /'gælɪvænt/ *v.i.* (infml) шля́ться (*impf.*); слоня́ться (*impf.*)

gallon /'gælən/ *n.* галло́н

gallop /'gæləp/ *n.* гало́п
● *v.i.* скака́ть (*impf.*) (гало́пом); (fig.): **we ~ed through our work** мы в спе́шке зако́нчили (на́шу/свою́) рабо́ту

gallows /'gæləʊz/ *n. pl.* ви́селица; **send sb to the ~** отпра́вить (*pf.*) кого́-н. на ви́селицу
■ **~ humour,** (AmE) **humor** *n.* ю́мор ви́сельника

galore /gə'lɔː(r)/ *adv.* (infml) в изоби́лии, ско́лько уго́дно

galvanize /'gælvənaɪz/ *v.t.* оцинко́в|ывать, -а́ть; (fig.) побу|жда́ть, -ди́ть

Gambia /'gæmbɪə/ *n.* Га́мбия

gamble /'gæmb(ə)l/ *n.* аза́ртная игра́; (risky undertaking) риско́ванное предприя́тие
● *v.t. & i.* игра́ть (*impf.*) в аза́ртные и́гры; **~ away a fortune** проигра́ть (*pf.*) состоя́ние

gambler /'gæmblə(r)/ *n.* игро́к; картёжник

gambling /'gæmblɪŋ/ *n.* аза́ртные и́гры (*f. pl.*)

game /geɪm/ *n.* **1** игра́; **we had a ~ of golf** мы сыгра́ли па́ртию в гольф **2** (plan, trick) игра́; **he gave the ~ away** он раскры́л свои́ ка́рты **3** (hunted animal) дичь; зверь (*m.*)
■ **~keeper** *n.* охраня́ющий дичь е́герь; **~ plan** *n.* страте́гия; **~ reserve** *n.* охо́тничий зака́зник/запове́дник; **~s console** *n.* игрова́я консо́ль, игрова́я приста́вка; **~ show** *n.* телеигра́, игрово́е шо́у (*indecl.*)

gammon /'gæmən/ *n.* (BrE) о́корок

gamut /'gæmət/ *n.* (mus.) га́мма; (fig.) диапазо́н, га́мма; **she ran the ~ of the emotions** она́ передала́ всю га́мму чувств

gang /gæŋ/ *n.* (of workmen) брига́да; (of prisoners) па́ртия (заключённых); (of criminals) ша́йка, ба́нда
● *v.i.*: **they ~ed up on me** они́ ополчи́лись про́тив/на меня́
■ **~land** *n.* престу́пный мир; **~master** *n.* (BrE) бригади́р; **~way** *n.* (from ship to shore or aircraft to ground) трап

gangrene /'gæŋɡriːn/ *n.* гангре́на

gangster /'gæŋstə(r)/ *n.* банди́т

gannet /'gænɪt/ *n.* (bird) о́луша; (BrE fig., glutton) обжо́ра

gantry /'gæntrɪ/ *n.* помо́ст
■ **~ crane** *n.* эстака́дный кран

♂ **gap** /gæp/ *n.* (in a wall etc.) брешь, пролом; (in conversation) пауза; (of 5 years etc.) перерыв; (between rich and poor, theory and practice) разрыв; (in application form, sb's knowledge) пробел
■ ~ **year** *n.* (BrE) год перед поступлением в университет (*который выпускник школы проводит работая или путешествуя*)

gap|e /geɪp/ *v.i.* (stare) зевать (*impf.*) (по сторонам); a ~ing **wound** зияющая рана; **the chasm** ~ed **before him** перед ним зияла пропасть

garage /ˈgærɑːdʒ/ *n.* (for keeping a car) гараж; (where petrol is sold) бензозаправочная станция; (for repairing cars) автосервис

garbage /ˈgɑːbɪdʒ/ *n.* (AmE, rubbish) мусор (also fig.); (nonsense) чепуха, вздор
■ ~ **can** *n.* (AmE, outside) мусорный бак; (in kitchen) мусорное ведро; ~ **dump** *n.* свалка; ~ **truck** *n.* (AmE) мусоровоз

garble /ˈgɑːb(ə)l/ *v.t.* (distort) иска|жать, -зить

♂ **garden** /ˈgɑːd(ə)n/ *n.* **1** (plot of ground) сад; **vegetable** ~ огород **2** (*attr.*) садовый
● *v.i.* заниматься (*impf.*) садоводством
■ ~ **centre**, (AmE) **center** *n.* садовый центр; ~ **party** *n.* светский приём на открытом воздухе

gardener /ˈgɑːdnə(r)/ *n.* садовник

gargle /ˈgɑːg(ə)l/ *v.i.* полоскать, про- горло

garish /ˈgeərɪʃ/ *adj.* пёстрый

garland /ˈgɑːlənd/ *n.* гирлянда

garlic /ˈgɑːlɪk/ *n.* чеснок

garment /ˈgɑːmənt/ *n.* предмет одежды

garnish /ˈgɑːnɪʃ/ *n.* (cul.) гарнир
● *v.t.* (cul.) под|авать, -ать (*что с чем*)

garret /ˈgærɪt/ *n.* мансарда; чердак

garrison /ˈgærɪs(ə)n/ *n.* гарнизон

garter /ˈgɑːtə(r)/ *n.* подвязка
■ ~ **belt** *n.* (AmE) пояс с подвязками

♂ **gas** /gæs/ *n.* (*pl.* ~**es**) **1** газ **2** (*attr.*) газовый **3** (AmE, petrol) бензин, горючее
● *v.t.* (**gases**, **gassed**, **gassing**) умер|щвлять, -твить газом
■ ~ **cooker** *n.* (BrE) газовая плита; ~ **fire** *n.* (BrE) газовый камин; ~ **mask** *n.* противогаз; ~ **oven** *n.* (domestic) газовая духовка; ~ **station** *n.* (AmE) бензозаправочная станция

gash /gæʃ/ *n.* разрез
● *v.t.* разр|езать, -езать

gasoline, **gasolene** /ˈgæsəliːn/ *n.* газолин; (AmE, petrol) бензин

gasp /gɑːsp/ *n.* глоток воздуха; **at one's last** ~ при последнем издыхании
● *v.i.* зад|ыхаться, -охнуться; **he was** ~ing **for breath** он задыхался; **he** ~ed **with astonishment** он открыл рот от удивления

gastric /ˈgæstrɪk/ *adj.* желудочный
■ ~ **band** *n.* желудочный бандаж; ~ **juice** *n.* желудочный сок; ~ **ulcer** *n.* язва желудка

gastroenteritis /ˌgæstrəʊentəˈraɪtɪs/ *n.* гастроэнтерит

gastronomic /ˌgæstrəˈnɒmɪk/ *adj.* гастрономический

gastronomy /gæˈstrɒnəmɪ/ *n.* гастрономия

gate /geɪt/ *n.* ворота (-от); (city ~) городские ворота; (at airport) выход
■ ~**crash** *v.t. & i.* при|ходить, -йти (на вечеринку и т. п.) без приглашения; ~**crasher** *n.* незваный гость

gateau /ˈgætəʊ/ *n.* (*pl.* ~**s** or ~**x** /-əʊz/) (BrE) торт

♂ **gather** /ˈgæðə(r)/ *n.* (in cloth) сборки (*f. pl.*)
● *v.t.* **1** (pick, e.g. flowers, harvest) (*also* ~ **in**) соб|ирать, -рать **2** (collect) (*also* ~ **up**) соб|ирать, -рать **3** (understand) заключ|ать, -ить; I ~ **he's abroad** он как будто за границей **4** (pull together): ~ **one's thoughts, wits** соб|ираться, -раться с мыслями **5** (sewing) соб|ирать, -рать в складки
● *v.i.* соб|ираться, -раться; **a crowd** ~ed собралась толпа

gathering /ˈgæðərɪŋ/ *n.* собрание

gaudy /ˈgɔːdɪ/ *adj.* (**gaudier**, **gaudiest**) кричащий

gauge /geɪdʒ/ (AmE **gage**). *n.* **1** (thickness, diameter, etc.) размер; (rail.): **standard** ~ стандартная колея **2** (instrument) шаблон
● *v.t.* **1** (measure) изм|ерять, -ерить **2** (fig., estimate) оцен|ивать, -ить

gaunt /gɔːnt/ *adj.* (person) исхудалый

gauntlet /ˈgɔːntlɪt/ *n.* рукавица; (armoured glove) латная рукавица; **throw down the** ~ (fig.) бросить (*pf.*) перчатку/вызов; **pick up the** ~ принять (*pf.*) вызов

gauze /gɔːz/ *n.* марля, газ

gave /geɪv/ *past of* ▸ **give**

gawk /gɔːk/ *v.i.* = **gawp**

gawp /gɔːp/ *v.i.* (BrE) глазеть (*impf.*); пялить (*impf.*) глаза (**at:** на + *a.*)

♂ **gay** /geɪ/ *adj.* (**gayer**, **gayest**) весёлый; (infml, homosexual) гомосексуальный, голубой
● *n.* (infml, homosexual) гей, гомосексуалист
■ ~ **marriage** *n.* (infml) однополый гражданский брак

gayety /ˈgeɪətɪ/ *n.* (AmE) = **gaiety**

gaze /geɪz/ *n.* пристальный взгляд
● *v.i.* пристально глядеть

gazebo /gəˈziːbəʊ/ *n.* (*pl.* ~**s** or ~**es**) бельведер

gazelle /gəˈzel/ *n.* газель

GB *abbr.* (*of* **Great Britain**) Великобритания

GBH (BrE, law) *abbr.* (*of* **grievous bodily harm**) тяжёлые телесные повреждения

GCSE (BrE) *abbr.* (*of* **General Certificate of Secondary Education**) ≈ аттестат о неполном среднем образовании

GDP *abbr.* (*of* **gross domestic product**) ВВП (валовой внутренний продукт)

gear /gɪə(r)/ *n.* **1** (equipment, clothing) принадлежности (*f. pl.*), аксессуары (*m. pl.*); одежда; **hunting** ~ охотничье снаряжение **2** (of car etc.) зубчатая передача; **change** ~ переключ|ать, -ить передачу; **the car is in** ~ машина на передаче
● *v.t.*: ~ **up** готовить (*impf.*); пригот|авливать, -овить
■ ~**box** *n.* коробка передач; ~ **lever** *n.* (BrE)

g

рычаг переключения передач/скоростей; ~ **shift** n. (AmE) = gear lever

geek /giːk/ n. (infml) (computer etc. enthusiast) человек, увлечённый компьютерными технологиями и т. п.; (socially inept person) социально неловкий человек

geese /giːs/ pl. of ▸ **goose**

gel /dʒel/ n. гель (m.)

gelateria /dʒelæˈtɪərɪə/ n. кафе-мороженое

gelatine /ˈdʒelətiːn/ n. желатин

gem /dʒem/ n. драгоценный камень

Gemini /ˈdʒemɪnaɪ/ n. Близнецы (m. pl.)

gender /ˈdʒendə(r)/ n. (sex) пол; (gram.) род
■ ~ **reassignment** n. операция по изменению пола

g ✐ **gene** /dʒiːn/ n. ген
■ ~ **therapy** n. генная терапия

genealogical /dʒiːnɪəˈlɒdʒɪk(ə)l/ adj. родословный; генеалогический

genealogist /dʒiːnɪˈælədʒɪst/ n. специалист по генеалогии

genealogy /dʒiːnɪˈælədʒɪ/ n. генеалогия

genera /ˈdʒenərə/ pl. of ▸ **genus**

✐ **general** /ˈdʒenər(ə)l/ n. генерал
● adj. **1** (universal or nearly so) общий; генеральный **2** (usual) обычный; ~ **opinion** общее мнение; in ~ вообще
■ ~ **election** n. всеобщие выборы; ~ **knowledge** n. общие знания; ~ **practitioner** n. участковый врач; терапевт; ~ **strike** n. всеобщая забастовка

generalization /dʒenərəlaɪˈzeɪʃ(ə)n/ n. обобщение

generalize /ˈdʒenərəlaɪz/ v.i. обобщённо говорить (impf.)

✐ **generally** /ˈdʒenərəlɪ/ adv. **1** (usually) обычно **2** (widely) широко **3** (approximately) вообще; ~ **speaking** вообще говоря

✐ **generate** /ˈdʒenəreɪt/ v.t. поро|ждать, -дить; ~ **heat** выделять (impf.) тепло; ~ **hatred** вызывать (impf.) ненависть

✐ **generation** /dʒenəˈreɪʃ(ə)n/ n. **1** (of heat etc.) генерация **2** (of people) поколение; the ~ **gap** проблема отцов и детей

generator /ˈdʒenəreɪtə(r)/ n. генератор

generic /dʒɪˈnerɪk/ adj. (of a class) родовой; (general) общий; (of drug) непатентованный, общего типа

generosity /dʒenəˈrɒsɪtɪ/ n. великодушие

generous /ˈdʒenərəs/ adj. **1** (liberal) щедрый **2** (plentiful) обильный

genesis /ˈdʒenɪsɪs/ n. генезис; возникновение; (Book of) G~ книга Бытия

genetic /dʒɪˈnetɪk/ adj. генетический
■ ~**ally modified** adj. генетически модифицированный; ~ **engineering** n. генная инженерия; ~ **fingerprinting** n. генная дактилоскопия; ~ **modification** n. генетическая модификация; ~ **profiling** n. генетическое профилирование; ~ **screening** n. генетический скрининг

geneticist /dʒɪˈnetɪsɪst/ n. генетик

genetics /dʒɪˈnetɪks/ n. генетика

genial /ˈdʒiːnɪəl/ adj. сердечный

geniality /dʒiːnɪˈælɪtɪ/ n. радушие; добродушие

genie /ˈdʒiːnɪ/ n. джинн, дух

genital /ˈdʒenɪt(ə)l/ adj. половой; (in pl.) половые органы (m. pl.), гениталии (f. pl.)

genitive /ˈdʒenɪtɪv/ n. & adj. родительный (падеж)

genius /ˈdʒiːnɪəs/ n. гений

genocide /ˈdʒenəsaɪd/ n. геноцид

genome /ˈdʒiːnəʊm/ n. геном

genre /ˈʒɑːrə/ n. жанр

genteel /dʒenˈtiːl/ adj. благовоспитанный; «благородный»; с аристократическими замашками

Gentile /ˈdʒentaɪl/ n. нееврей
● adj. нееврейский

gentle /ˈdʒent(ə)l/ adj. (**gentler**, **gentlest**) мягкий, тихий, деликатный; a ~ **slope** пологий склон; a ~ **breeze** лёгкий ветерок; a ~ **hint** тонкий намёк

gentleman /ˈdʒent(ə)lmən/ n. джентльмен

gently /ˈdʒentlɪ/ adv. мягко; деликатно

gentry /ˈdʒentrɪ/ n. нетитулованное дворянство

Gents /dʒent/ n. (**the** ~) (sg.) (BrE, lavatory) мужской туалет

genuine /ˈdʒenjʊɪn/ adj. настоящий; подлинный; ~ **sorrow** искренняя печаль; a ~ **person** прямой/искренний человек

genus /ˈdʒiːnəs/ n. (pl. **genera**) род

geographer /dʒɪˈɒɡrəfə(r)/ n. географ

geographical /dʒɪːəˈɡræfɪk(ə)l/, **geographic** /dʒɪːəˈɡræfɪk/ adjs. географический

geography /dʒɪˈɒɡrəfɪ/ n. география

geological /dʒɪːəˈlɒdʒɪk(ə)l/ adj. геологический

geologist /dʒɪˈɒlədʒɪst/ n. геолог

geology /dʒɪˈɒlədʒɪ/ n. геология

geometric /dʒɪəˈmetrɪk/, **geometrical** /dʒɪəˈmetrɪkəl/ adjs. геометрический

geometry /dʒɪˈɒmɪtrɪ/ n. геометрия

geopolitical /dʒiːəʊpəˈlɪtɪk(ə)l/ adj. геополитический

Georgia /ˈdʒɔːdʒɪə/ n. (in Caucasus) Грузия

Georgian /ˈdʒɔːdʒ(ə)n/ n. грузин (-ка)
● adj. грузинский

geranium /dʒəˈreɪnɪəm/ n. герань

geriatric /dʒerɪˈætrɪk/ adj. гериатрический

geriatrics /dʒerɪˈætrɪks/ n. гериатрия

germ /dʒɜːm/ n. микроб, бактерия; (fig.) зачаток
■ ~ **warfare** n. бактериологическая война

✐ **German** /ˈdʒɜːmən/ n. **1** (person) немец (-ка) **2** (language) немецкий язык
● adj. немецкий; (esp. pol.) германский
■ ~ **measles** n. pl. краснуха; ~ **shepherd** (**dog**) n. немецкая овчарка

germane /dʒɜːˈmeɪn/ adj. уместный; подходящий

―――――――――――――――

✐ ключевая лексика

Germanic /dʒɜːˈmænɪk/ *adj.* герма́нский
Germany /ˈdʒɜːmənɪ/ *n.* Герма́ния
germinate /ˈdʒɜːmɪneɪt/ *v.i.* прораста́ть, -и́
germination /dʒɜːmɪˈneɪʃ(ə)n/ *n.*
прораста́ние; (fig.) зарожде́ние; разви́тие
gerontology /dʒerənˈtɒlədʒɪ/ *n.*
геронтоло́гия
gerund /ˈdʒerənd/ *n.* геру́ндий
gestation /dʒeˈsteɪʃ(ə)n/ *n.* бере́менность;
(fig.) созрева́ние
gesticulate /dʒeˈstɪkjʊleɪt/ *v.i.*
жестикули́ровать (*impf.*)
gesture /ˈdʒestʃə(r)/ *n.* жест
 ● *v.i.* жестикули́ровать (*impf.*)

✓ **get** /get/ *v.t.* (**getting**, *past* **got**, *p.p.* **got** *or*
AmE **gotten**) **1** (obtain, receive) получа́ть,
-и́ть; **I've got it!** (answer to problem, etc.) э́врика!;
I ~ you (infml, understand) по́нял!; **this room ~s**
a lot of sun э́та ко́мната о́чень со́лнечная;
I got (*sc. bought*) **a new suit** я приобрёл/
купи́л но́вый костю́м **2** (of suffering, etc.):
he got 2 years (sentence) он получи́л 2 го́да
(тюрьмы́); **he got the measles** он заболе́л
ко́рью; **he got a blow on the head** он
получи́л уда́р по голове́; **she got her feet**
wet она́ промочи́ла но́ги **3** (fetch, lay hands on)
доста|ва́ть, -а́ть; доб|ыва́ть, -ы́ть; **I got him a**
chair я принёс ему́ стул; **~ me the manager!**
позови́те мне заве́дующего! **4** (bring into
a position or state): **we got him home** мы
доста́вили его́ домо́й; **we got the piano**
through the door мы пронесли́ пиани́но
че́рез дверь **5** (p.p., expr. possession): **he has**
got a book у него́ есть кни́га **6** (p.p., expr.
obligation): **I have got to go** я до́лжен идти́
7 (persuade) заст|авля́ть, -а́вить; **I got him to**
tell me everything я заста́вил его́ рассказа́ть
мне всё; **I got the fire to burn** мне удало́сь
разже́чь ого́нь **8** (cause sth to be done):
I got my hair cut я постри́гся **9** (denoting
progress or achievement): **I got to know him** я
познако́мился с ним бли́же; **I got to like**
travelling я полюби́л путеше́ствия; **he got to**
be manager он стал дире́ктором
 ● *v.i.* (**getting**, *past* **got**, *p.p.* **got** *or* AmE
gotten) **1** (become, be) ста|нови́ться, -ть;
he got red in the face он покрасне́л; **he**
got angry он разозли́лся; **he got drunk** он
напи́лся; **he got married** он жени́лся; **he**
got ready он пригото́вился; **he got killed**
его́ уби́ли; он поги́б; **we got talking** мы
разговори́лись **2** (arrive) приб|ыва́ть,
-ы́ть; **when did you ~ here?** когда́ вы сюда́
при́были?; **where has my book got to?** куда́
де́лась/дева́лась моя́ кни́га?
 ● *with preps.*: **the officer got his troops across**
the river офице́р перепра́вил свои́ войска́
че́рез ре́ку; **I cannot ~ at the books** я не
могу́ добра́ться до э́тих книг; **we must**
~ at the truth мы должны́ добра́ться до
и́стины; **what is he ~ting at?** (trying to say) что
он хо́чет сказа́ть?; куда́ он кло́нит?; **she is**
always ~ting at me (BrE, criticizing) она́ всегда́
ко мне придира́ется; **he got in(to) the taxi** он
сел в такси́; **I cannot ~ into these shoes** я не

могу́ влезть в э́ти ту́фли; **he got into the club**
его́ при́няли в клуб; **he got off his horse** он
соскочи́л с коня́; **he got on his bicycle** он сел
на велосипе́д; **the lion got out of its cage** лев
вы́скочил из кле́тки; **I got out of going to the**
party я отверте́лся/уклони́лся от вечери́нки;
I got £6 out of him я вы́жал из него́ 6
фу́нтов; **we got over the wall** мы переле́зли
че́рез сте́ну; **I cannot ~ over his rudeness**
я не могу́ прийти́ в себя́ от его́ гру́бости;
we got round the difficulty мы спра́вились
с э́той пробле́мой; **she got round him** ей
удало́сь его́ уговори́ть/провести́; **I got**
through the work я проде́лал всю рабо́ту;
he got through his exam он сдал экза́мен;
we got to Paris by noon мы добрали́сь до
Пари́жа к полу́дню; **the children got up to**
mischief (BrE) де́ти расшали́лись; **we got up**
to chapter 5 мы дошли́ до 5-й (пя́той) главы́

▫ **~ about** *v.i.*: **he ~s about a great deal** он
постоя́нно в разъе́здах; **a car makes it easier to**
~ about с маши́ной ле́гче поспева́ть всю́ду
▫ **~ across** *v.t.*: **the speaker got his point across**
выступа́ющий чётко изложи́л свою́ то́чку
зре́ния
▫ **~ along** *v.i.*: **they ~ along** (*sc.* be agreeable to
each other) **very well** они́ отли́чно ла́дят
▫ **~ around** *v.i.* = get about, get round
▫ **~ away** *v.i.*: **the prisoner got away**
заключённый бежа́л; **he got away with**
cheating ему́ удало́сь сжу́льничать
▫ **~ back** *v.t.*: **he got his books back** он получи́л
обра́тно/наза́д свои́ кни́ги
 ● *v.i.*: **he got back from the country** он
верну́лся из дере́вни
▫ **~ by** *v.i.*: **please let me ~ by** (pass) разреши́те
мне пройти́, пожа́луйста
▫ **~ down** *v.t.*: **he got a book down from the**
shelf он снял кни́гу с по́лки
 ● *v.i.*: **he got down from his horse** он
соскочи́л/слез с коня́; **he got down to his**
work он засе́л за рабо́ту
▫ **~ in** *v.i.*: **the burglar got in through the**
window вор прони́к в дом че́рез окно́; **the**
train got in early по́езд пришёл ра́но; **we**
didn't ~ in to the concert мы не попа́ли на
конце́рт; **he got in** (*sc.* was elected) **for Chester**
он прошёл на вы́борах в Че́стере
▫ **~ off** *v.t.* (remove) сн|има́ть, -я́ть; **his lawyer**
got him off (acquitted) адвока́т доби́лся его́
оправда́ния
 ● *v.i.*: **he got off at the next station** он сошёл
(с по́езда) на сле́дующей ста́нции; **I got off**
(to sleep) early я ра́но засну́л; **we got off**
(*sc.* started) **at 9 a.m.** мы вы́шли/вы́ехали/
отпра́вились в 9 часо́в; **he got off with a fine**
он отде́лался штра́фом
▫ **~ on** *v.t.*: **~ your clothes on!** оде́ньтесь!
 ● *v.i.*: **how are you ~ting on?** как дела́?; **she**
is ~ting on (BrE) (making progress) она́ де́лает
успе́хи; (growing old) она́ старе́ет; **~ting on**
for (nearly) почти́; **~ on with your work!**
займи́тесь свое́й рабо́той!; **they ~ on (well)**
together они́ ла́дят ме́жду собо́й
▫ **~ out** *v.t.*: **he got out his spectacles** он вы́нул
очки́; **they got the book out** (published) они́
изда́ли/вы́пустили кни́гу

g

● *v.i.*: ~ **out!** убира́йтесь!; **the secret got out** секре́т стал изве́стен

□ ~ **round** *v.i.*: **I haven't got round to writing to him** я ника́к не соберу́сь написа́ть ему́

□ ~ **through** *v.t.* (an exam) выде́рживать, вы́держать экза́мен

□ ~ **together** *v.t.*: **he got an army together** он собра́л а́рмию

● *v.i.*: **we must** ~ **together and have a talk** мы должны́ встре́титься и поговори́ть

□ ~ **up** *v.t.*: **they got me up at 7** они́ по́дняли меня́ в 7 часо́в

● *v.i.* (from bed, chair, etc.) встаǀва́ть, -ть; **the wind/sea is** ~**ting up** поднима́ется ве́тер; мо́ре начина́ет волнова́ться

■ ~**-together** *n.* (meeting, gathering) встре́ча, сбо́рище

Ghana /'gɑːnə/ *n.* Га́на

Ghanaian /gɑ'neɪən/ *n.* га́нǀец (-ка)
● *adj.* га́нский

ghastly /'gɑːstlɪ/ *adj.* (**ghastlier**, **ghastliest**) ужа́сный

gherkin /'gɜːkɪn/ *n.* корнишо́н

ghetto /'getəʊ/ *n.* (*pl.* ~**s** *or* ~**es**) ге́тто (*nt. indecl.*)

■ ~ **blaster** *n.* (infml) переносно́й магнитофо́н, магнито́ла

ghost /gəʊst/ *n.* привиде́ние; дух

ghostly /'gəʊstlɪ/ *adj.* (**ghostlier**, **ghostliest**) похо́жий на привиде́ние

GI *abbr.* (of **government issue**) (American soldier) (америка́нский) солда́т

giant /'dʒaɪənt/ *n.* гига́нт

gibber /'dʒɪbə(r)/ *v.i.* тарато́рить (*impf.*); говори́ть (*impf.*) невня́тно; лопота́ть (*impf.*) (infml)

gibberish /'dʒɪbərɪʃ/ *n.* тараба́рщина

gibbon /'gɪbən/ *n.* гиббо́н

giblets /'dʒɪblɪts/ *n. pl.* потрохǀа́ (-о́в)

Gibraltar /dʒɪ'brɔːltə/ *n.* Гибралта́р

giddy /'gɪdɪ/ *adj.* (**giddier**, **giddiest**) головокружи́тельный; **I feel** ~ у меня́ кру́жится голова́

⚜ **gift** /gɪft/ *n.* **1** (thing given) пода́рок **2** (talent) дарова́ние; дар; **he has a** ~ **for languages** у него́ спосо́бности (*f. pl.*) /тала́нт к языка́м

■ ~ **shop** *n.* магази́н пода́рков; ~ **voucher** (BrE), ~ **token** (BrE), ~ **certificate** (AmE) *n.* пода́рочный тало́н/ купо́н

gifted /'gɪftɪd/ *adj.* одарённый

gig[1] /gɪg/ *n.* (infml, performance) выступле́ние, конце́рт

gig[2] /gɪg/ *n.* (*abbr. of* **gigabyte**) (comput., infml) гиг

giga- /'gɪgə/ *comb. form* гига...

■ ~**byte** *n.* гигаба́йт; ~**watt** *n.* гигава́тт

gigantic /dʒaɪ'gæntɪk/ *adj.* гига́нтский

giggle /'gɪg(ə)l/ *n.* хихи́канье
● *v.i.* хихи́кǀать, -нуть

gilt /gɪlt/ *n.* позоло́та

⚜ ключева́я ле́ксика

gimmick /'gɪmɪk/ *n.* трюк

gin /dʒɪn/ *n.* джин; ~ **and tonic** джин-то́ник

ginger /'dʒɪndʒə(r)/ *n.* (bot., cul.) имби́рь (*m.*); (*attr.*) имби́рный

gingerly /'dʒɪndʒəlɪ/ *adj.* (кра́йне) осторо́жный
● *adv.* осторо́жно

Gipsy, **Gypsy** /'dʒɪpsɪ/ *n.* цыга́н (-ка)
● *adj.* цыга́нский

giraffe /dʒɪ'rɑːf/ *n.* (*pl.* ~ *or* ~**s**) жира́ф

girder /'gɜːdə(r)/ *n.* (beam) ба́лка

girdle /'gɜːd(ə)l/ *n.* **1** (belt etc.) по́яс; куша́к **2** (corset) корсе́т

⚜ **girl** /gɜːl/ *n.* (child) де́вочка; (young woman) де́вушка; (pej.) девчо́нка

■ ~**friend** *n.* (female friend) подру́га; (female sexual partner) де́вушка; **G**~ **Guide** (also **G**~ **Scout**) *n.* де́вочка-ска́ут, гёрлска́ут

girlish /'gɜːlɪʃ/ *adj.* деви́ческий; (of a boy) изне́женный, (infml) как девчо́нка

girth /gɜːθ/ *n.* (of horse) подпру́га; (of tree, person, etc.) обхва́т; разме́р

gist /dʒɪst/ *n.* суть

⚜ **give** /gɪv/ *n.* **1** (elasticity) пода́тливость, эласти́чность **2**: ~ **and take** взаи́мные усту́пки (*f. pl.*)

● *v.t.* (*past* **gave**, *p.p.* **given** /'gɪv(ə)n/) **1** даǀва́ть, -ть; **I gave the porter my luggage** я о́тдал свой бага́ж носи́льщику; **two years,** ~ **or take a month or so** о́коло двух лет — ме́сяцем бо́льше и́ли ме́ньше **2** (as a present) дариǀть, по-; **he was** ~**n a book** ему́ подари́ли кни́гу **3** (~ in exchange): **I gave a good price for it** я за э́то хорошо́ заплати́л; **he gave as good as he got** он отплати́л той же моне́той **4** (provide, inflict): **he** ~**s me a lot of trouble** он доставля́ет мне мно́го хлопо́т; **he has** ~**n me his cold** я зарази́лся от него́ на́сморком; **he gave** (*sc. cited*) **an example** (cited) он привёл приме́р; ~ **him my regards** переда́йте ему́ приве́т от меня́; ~ **pleasure** доставǀля́ть, -а́вить удово́льствие **5** (devote) уделǀя́ть, -и́ть; посвяǀща́ть, -ти́ть; **he gave a lot of time to the work** он удели́л э́той рабо́те мно́го вре́мени; **he gave his life for her** он о́тдал за неё жизнь **6** (allow): **I** ~ **you an hour to get ready** я даю́ вам час на сбо́ры/ приготовле́ния **7** (organize) устрǀа́ивать, -о́ить; **they gave a dance** они́ устро́или танцева́льный ве́чер **8** (special uses of **given**): **at a** ~**n** (*sc. specified, agreed, particular*) **time** в определённое вре́мя; **he is** ~**n to boasting** он скло́нен к хвастовству́; ~**n that ...** при том, что...

● *v.i.* (*past* **gave**, *p.p.* **given** /'gɪv(ə)n/) (yield) поддаǀва́ться, -а́ться; подǀава́ться, -а́ться

□ ~ **away** *v.t.* дари́ть, по-; **he gave away the secret** он вы́дал секре́т; **he gave the game away** (revealed a secret) он проболта́лся; он вы́дал секре́т

□ ~ **back** *v.t.* (restore) возвраǀща́ть, -ти́ть

□ ~ **in** *v.t.* (submit): **he gave in his exam paper** (BrE) он сдал свою́ экзаменацио́нную рабо́ту
● *v.i.* (yield) поддаǀва́ться, -а́ться; уступǀа́ть, -и́ть; **he gave in to my persuasion** он подда́лся мои́м угово́рам

□ **∼ off** *v.t.* (emit) испус|ка́ть, -ти́ть; изд|ава́ть, -а́ть

□ **∼ out** *v.t.* (distribute) распредел|я́ть, -и́ть
   ● *v.i.* конча́ться, ко́нчиться; **his strength gave out** его́ си́лы исся́кли

□ **∼ up** *v.t.* ост|авля́ть, -а́вить; (resign, surrender) отка́з|ываться, -а́ться + *g.*; **he gave up his seat to her** он уступи́л ей ме́сто; **the murderer gave himself up** уби́йца сда́лся; (desist from) бр|оса́ть, -о́сить; **he gave up smoking** он бро́сил кури́ть; (abandon hope of): **they gave him up for lost** они́ реши́ли, что он пропа́л; **we gave it up as a bad job** мы махну́ли руко́й на э́то де́ло
   ● *v.i.*: **I ∼ up!** сдаю́сь!

■ **∼away** *n.* (infml, betrayal of secret etc.): **her tears were a ∼away** слёзы выдава́ли её; **∼n name** *n.* (forename) и́мя (*nt.*)

glacier /ˈɡlæsɪə(r)/ *n.* ледни́к

glad /ɡlæd/ *adj.* (**gladder**, **gladdest**) дово́льный; **I am ∼ to meet you** рад с ва́ми познако́миться

gladden /ˈɡlæd(ə)n/ *v.t.* ра́довать, об-; **flowers ∼ the scene** цветы́ оживля́ют вид; **wine ∼s the heart** вино́ весели́т ду́шу

gladiator /ˈɡlædɪeɪtə(r)/ *n.* гладиа́тор

gladio|lus /ɡlædɪˈəʊləs/ *n.* (*pl.* **∼li** /-laɪ/ *or* **∼luses**) гладио́лус

gladly /ˈɡlædlɪ/ *adv.* охо́тно

glamor /ˈɡlæmə(r)/ *n.* (AmE) = glamour

glamorize, **glamourize** /ˈɡlæməraɪz/ *v.t.* приукра́|шивать, -сить

glamorous /ˈɡlæmərəs/ *adj.* обольсти́тельный; (of job etc.) зама́нчивый

glamour /ˈɡlæmə(r)/ (AmE **glamor**) *n.* волшебство́

glanc|e /ɡlɑːns/ *n.* взгляд
   ● *v.t. & i.* **1** (look) взгля́н|у́ть (*pf.*); **he ∼ed at the clock** он взгляну́л на часы́; **he ∼ed round the room** он огляде́л ко́мнату **2** (bounce) отск|а́кивать, -очи́ть; **a ∼ing blow** скользя́щий уда́р

gland /ɡlænd/ *n.* железа́

glandular /ˈɡlændjʊlə(r)/ *adj.*: **∼ fever** воспале́ние гланд

glare /ɡleə(r)/ *n.* (fierce light) ослепи́тельный свет/блеск; (angry look) свире́пый взгляд
   ● *v.i.*: **∼ at sb** испепел|я́ть, -и́ть кого́-н. взгля́дом

glaring /ˈɡleərɪŋ/ *adj.* (e.g. headlights) слепя́щий; (of mistake etc.) гру́бый

✍ **glass** /ɡlɑːs/ *n.* **1** (substance) стекло́ **2** (for drinking) (tumbler) стака́н; (wine ∼) рю́мка, бока́л **3** (∼ware) стекля́нная посу́да **4** (BrE, mirror) зе́ркало **5** (*in pl.*) (spectacles) очк|и́ (-о́в)

glaucoma /ɡlɔːˈkəʊmə/ *n.* глауко́ма

glaze /ɡleɪz/ *n.* глазу́рь
   ● *v.t.* (pottery) покр|ыва́ть, -ы́ть глазу́рью

gleam /ɡliːm/ *n.* про́блеск
   ● *v.i.* поблёскивать (*impf.*)

glean /ɡliːn/ *v.t.* (information) соб|ира́ть, -ра́ть

glee /ɡliː/ *n.* (delight) весе́лье; ликова́ние

gleeful /ˈɡliːfʊl/ *adj.* лику́ющий

glen /ɡlen/ *n.* лощи́на

glib /ɡlɪb/ *adj.* (**glibber**, **glibbest**) бо́йкий на язы́к; **a ∼ excuse** благови́дный предло́г

glide /ɡlaɪd/ *v.i.* скольз|и́ть, -ну́ть; (in aircraft) плани́ровать, с-

glider /ˈɡlaɪdə(r)/ *n.* пла́нер

gliding /ˈɡlaɪdɪŋ/ *n.* (sport) планери́зм

glimmer /ˈɡlɪmə(r)/ *n.*: **a ∼ of hope** про́блеск/луч наде́жды

glimpse /ɡlɪmps/ *n.* про́блеск; **I caught a ∼ of him** он промелькну́л у меня́ пе́ред глаза́ми
   ● *v.t.* уви́деть (*pf.*) ме́льком

glint /ɡlɪnt/ *n.* блеск; (reflection) о́тблеск
   ● *v.i.* блесте́ть (*impf.*); (flash) вспы́х|ивать, -нуть

glisten /ˈɡlɪs(ə)n/ *v.i.* сверк|а́ть, -ну́ть

glitch /ɡlɪtʃ/ *n.* небольшо́е затрудне́ние

glitter /ˈɡlɪtə(r)/ *n.* блеск, сверка́ние
   ● *v.i.* блесте́ть (*impf.*); сверка́ть (*impf.*)

glitz /ɡlɪts/ *n.* (показно́й) блеск, лоск, шик

glitzy /ˈɡlɪtsɪ/ *adj.* (**glitzier**, **glitziest**) гламу́рный

gloat /ɡləʊt/ *v.i.* злора́дствовать (*impf.*)

✍ **global** /ˈɡləʊb(ə)l/ *adj.* (total) всео́бщий; (worldwide) глоба́льный

■ **∼ warming** *n.* глоба́льное потепле́ние

globalization /ɡləʊbəlaɪˈzeɪʃ(ə)n/ *n.* глобализа́ция

globe /ɡləʊb/ *n.* шар

■ **∼trotter** *n.* зая́длый тури́ст

globule /ˈɡlɒbjuːl/ *n.* ша́рик; ка́пелька

gloom /ɡluːm/ *n.* (dark) тьма; (despondency) мра́чность

gloomy /ˈɡluːmɪ/ *adj.* (**gloomier**, **gloomiest**) (dark) мра́чный; (depressing) гнету́щий; (depressed) хму́рый; уны́лый

glorify /ˈɡlɔːrɪfaɪ/ *v.t.* просл|авля́ть, -а́вить

glorious /ˈɡlɔːrɪəs/ *adj.* сла́вный, великоле́пный; **a ∼ day** (weather) изуми́тельный день

glory /ˈɡlɔːrɪ/ *n.* **1** (renown, honour) сла́ва **2** (splendour) великоле́пие
   ● *v.i.* упива́ться (*impf.*) + *i.*; **∼ in one's strength** упива́ться свое́й си́лой

gloss /ɡlɒs/ *n.* (lit., fig.) лоск
   ● *v.t.*: **∼ over faults** обойти́ (*pf.*) оши́бки молча́нием

■ **∼ paint** *n.* блестя́щий лак

glossary /ˈɡlɒsərɪ/ *n.* глосса́рий

glossy /ˈɡlɒsɪ/ *adj.* (**glossier**, **glossiest**) гля́нцевый; лощёный; **a ∼ photograph** гля́нцевая фотогра́фия; **∼ magazines** гля́нцевые журна́лы

glove /ɡlʌv/ *n.* перча́тка

■ **∼ compartment** *n.* (in car) бардачо́к (infml)

glow /ɡləʊ/ *n.* (of fire, sunset, etc.) за́рево; (of feelings) пыл
   ● *v.i.* (incandesce) накал|я́ться, -и́ться; (shine) свети́ться (*impf.*); **he ∼ed with pride** его́ распира́ла го́рдость; **he described the trip in ∼ing colours** он опи́сывал путеше́ствие в ра́дужных тона́х

g

glower /'glauə(r)/ *v.i.* серди́то смотре́ть (*impf.*) (**at:** на + *a.*)

glucose /'glu:kəus/ *n.* глюко́за

glue /glu:/ *n.* клей
• *v.t.* (**glues**, **glued**, **gluing** *or* **glueing**) прикле́и|вать, -ть
■ ~**-sniffer** *n.* токсикома́н; ~**-sniffing** *n.* токсикома́ния

glum /glʌm/ *adj.* (**glummer**, **glummest**) угрю́мый

glut /glʌt/ *n.* избы́ток

gluten /'glu:t(ə)n/ *n.* клейкови́на

glutton /'glʌt(ə)n/ *n.* обжо́ра (*c.g.*); a ~ **for work** жа́дный к рабо́те

gluttonous /'glʌtənəs/ *adj.* прожо́рливый

gluttony /'glʌtəni/ *n.* обжо́рство

glycerine /'glɪsəri:n/ (AmE **glycerin**) *n.* глицери́н

GM *abbr.* (*of* **genetically modified**): ~ **foods** генети́чески модифици́рованные проду́кты

GMT *n.* = Greenwich Mean time

gnarled /nɑ:ld/, **gnarly** /'nɑ:lɪ/ *adjs.* шишкова́тый; сучкова́тый

gnash /næʃ/ *v.t.*: ~ **one's teeth** скрежета́ть (*impf.*) зуба́ми

gnat /næt/ *n.* кома́р, мо́шка

gnaw /nɔ:/ *v.t. & i.* грызть (*impf.*)

gnome /nəum/ *n.* гном

GNP *abbr.* (*of* **gross national product**) ВНП (валово́й национа́льный проду́кт)

GNVQ *n.* (*abbr. of* **General National Vocational Qualification**) (BrE) Общенациона́льное свиде́тельство о профессиона́льной квалифика́ции

✐ **go** /gəʊ/ *n.* (*pl.* ~**es**) **1** (movement, animation): **she's on the** ~ **from morning to night** она́ с утра́ до ве́чера на нога́х **2** (turn, attempt): **now it's my** ~ тепе́рь моя́ о́чередь
• *v.i.* (*3rd pers. sing. pres.* **goes**, *past* **went**, *p.p.* **gone**) (*see also* ▶ **gone**) **1** (on foot) ходи́ть (*indet.*), идти́ (*det.*), пойти́ (*pf.*); (by transport) е́здить (*indet.*), е́хать (*det.*) пое́хать (*pf.*); (by plane) лета́ть (*indet.*), лете́ть (*det.*), полете́ть (*pf.*) (самолётом); **this train** ~**es to London** э́тот по́езд идёт в Ло́ндон **2** (fig., with general idea of motion or direction): **this road** ~**es to York** э́та доро́га ведёт в Йорк; **he** ~**es to school** (is a schoolboy) он хо́дит в шко́лу; **let me** ~! отпусти́те меня́!; **there is still an hour to** ~ ещё час в запа́се; **his plans went wrong** его́ пла́ны сорвали́сь **3** (with cognate etc. object): **he went a long way** он пошёл/ушёл далеко́; **they went halves** они́ раздели́ли всё попола́м; **the balloon went 'pop'** шар ло́пнул **4** (idea of progress or outcome): **how's it** ~**ing?** (health, affairs) как дела́?; как пожива́ете?; **everything is** ~**ing well** всё (идёт) хорошо́; **the party/play went well** вечери́нка/пье́са прошла́ хорошо́ **5** (expr. tenor or tendency): **the story** ~**es that …** расска́зывают, что… **6** (set out, depart): **the post** ~**es at 5 p.m.** по́чта ухо́дит в 5 часо́в

дня **7** (pass, disappear): **our holiday went in a flash** на́ши кани́кулы пролете́ли мгнове́нно; **it's** ~**ne 4** (o'clock) уже́ бо́льше четырёх; **пошёл пя́тый час**; **I wish this pain would** ~! хоть бы прошла́ э́та боль!; **all my money is** ~**ne** все мои́ де́ньги упльли́ **8** (become): **the milk went sour** молоко́ проки́сло; **she went red in the face** она́ покрасне́ла **9** (function): **I can't get my watch to** ~ у меня́ не заво́дятся часы́ **10** (sound): **come in when the bell** ~**es** входи́те, когда́ зазвони́т звоно́к **11** (be known, accepted, usual): **what he says** ~**es** его́ сло́во — зако́н; **anything** ~**es** всё сойдёт; **it** ~**es without saying** э́то само́ собо́й разуме́ется **12** (expr. impending or predicted action): **I'm** ~**ing to sneeze** я сейча́с чихну́; **it's** ~**ing to rain** собира́ется дождь **13** (expr. intention): **I am** ~**ing to ask him** я реши́л спроси́ть его́ **14** (be sold): **the picture went for a song** карти́ну про́дали за бесце́нок; **these cakes are** ~**ing cheap** э́ти пиро́жные сто́ят дёшево (*or* иду́т по дешёвке)
• *with preps.*: **how shall I** ~ **about this?** как мне за э́то взя́ться?; **he went about his business** он заня́лся свои́ми дела́ми; **the dog went after the hare** соба́ка погнала́сь за за́йцем; **the decision went against them** реше́ние бы́ло не в их по́льзу; **he went** (*sc. passed*) **by the window** он прошёл ми́мо окна́; **I went for a drink** я отпра́вился вы́пить; **the dog went for his legs** соба́ка хвата́ла его́ за́ ноги; **he will always** ~ **for the best** он всегда́ бу́дет стреми́ться к лу́чшему; **he went into the house** он вошёл в дом; **he had to** ~ **into hospital** ему́ пришло́сь лечь в больни́цу; **it won't** ~ **into the box** (is too big) э́то не войдёт в коро́бку; **I've** ~**ne off prawns** (BrE, infml) я разлюби́л креве́тки; **I am** ~**ing on a course** я поступа́ю на ку́рсы; **all his money went on food** все его́ де́ньги пошли́/ уходи́ли на еду́; **we have no evidence to** ~ **on** для э́того у нас нет никаки́х основа́ний; **I went over his work with him** вме́сте с ним я прошёлся по его́ рабо́те; **we have** ~**ne over** (*sc. discussed*) **that** мы э́то обсужда́ли; **we went round the gallery** мы обошли́ галере́ю; ~ **through the main gate!** проходи́те че́рез гла́вные воро́та!; **she went through his pockets** она́ обша́рила у него́ все карма́ны; **he has** ~**ne through a lot** ему́ довело́сь мно́гое испыта́ть; **I'll** ~ **through the main points again** я хочу́ повтори́ть гла́вные пу́нкты; **he went through the money in a week** он растра́тил де́ньги за неде́лю; **the estate went to her nephew** иму́щество перешло́ её племя́ннику; **the prize went to him** он вы́играл приз; **the money will** ~ **towards a new car** де́ньги пойду́т на поку́пку но́вой маши́ны; **he went up the stairs** он стал поднима́ться (*or* пошёл вверх) по ле́стнице; **this tie** ~**es with your suit** э́тот га́лстук подхо́дит к ва́шему костю́му; **he has been** ~**ing (out) with her for several months** он встреча́ется с ней уже́ не́сколько ме́сяцев; **we went without a holiday** мы обошли́сь без о́тпуска
▢ ~ **ahead!** вперёд!

□ ~ **along** *v.i.*: I cannot ~ along with that я не могу с этим согласиться

□ ~ **around** *v.i.* **1**: he is ~ing around with my sister он встречается с моей сестрой **2** (AmE) = go round *v.i.*

□ ~ **away** *v.i.* уходить, уйти; ~ away! уходите!

□ ~ **back** *v.i.* идти (*det.*) назад; возвра|щаться, -титься; he went back on his word он не сдержал своего слова; this custom ~es back to the 15th century этот обычай восходит к пятнадцатому веку

□ ~ **by** *v.i.*: as the years ~ by с годами

□ ~ **down** *v.i.* спус|каться, -титься; he went down on his knees он опустился на колени; the sun went down солнце село; she went down with flu (BrE) она слегла с гриппом; prices are ~ing down цены падают; his story went down well его рассказ был хорошо принят

□ ~ **in** *v.i.* (enter) входить, войти; the sun went in солнце зашло; he went in for the competition он принял участие в конкурсе

□ ~ **off** *v.i.*: he went off without a word он ушёл без единого слова; the alarm clock went off будильник зазвенел; the light has ~ne off свет погас; the fruit has ~ne off (BrE) фрукты погнили; his work has ~ne off lately в последнее время он стал работать хуже; the party went off well вечеринка прошла хорошо

□ ~ **on** *v.i.*: the lights went on загорелся свет; I can't ~ on any longer я так больше не могу; shall we ~ on to the next item? давайте перейдём к следующему пункту?; ~ on playing! продолжайте играть!; what is ~ing on here? что тут происходит?; ~ on at (nag) пилить (*impf.*); набрасываться (*impf.*) на + *a.*; he went on (*sc. stage*) after the interval он вышел на сцену после антракта; as time ~es on со временем

□ ~ **out** *v.i.* (exit) выходить, выйти; the light went out свет погас; the tide was ~ing out шёл отлив

□ ~ **over** *v.i.*: he went over to France он перепра́вился во Францию; the country went over to decimal coinage страна перешла на десятичную монетную систему

□ ~ **round** *v.i.* **1** (revolve) вращаться (*impf.*), кружиться, за- **2** (BrE): I went round to see him я пошёл его навестить; we had to ~ round by the park нам пришлось идти в обход через парк; he ~es round collecting money он обходит всех и собирает деньги; is there enough food to ~ round? хватит ли еды на всех?

□ ~ **through** *v.i.*: I cannot ~ through with the plan я не могу осуществить этот план; the deal went through сделка состоялась; has their divorce ~ne through? они уже развели́сь?

□ ~ **together** *v.i.*: they were ~ing (*keeping company*) together for years они встречались многие годы; these colours ~ together эти цвета гармонируют

□ ~ **under** *v.i.*: his business went under его дело лопнуло

□ ~ **up** *v.i.* подн|иматься, -яться; he went up to bed он пошёл спать; prices have ~ne up цены повысились

■ ~**-ahead** *n.* разрешение, «добро», «зелёная улица»; ~**-between** *n.* посредник; ~**-cart** (*also* ~**-kart**) *n.* карт; ~**-slow** *n.* (BrE) частичная забастовка

goad /ɡəʊd/ *n. v.t.* погонять (*impf.*); (prod) пришпори|вать, -ть; (tease, torment) раздражать (*impf.*)

✎ **goal** /ɡəʊl/ *n.* **1** (objective) цель **2** (sport) ворот|а (*pl., g. —*)

■ ~**keeper** *n.* вратарь (*m.*); ~**post** *n.* штанга

goalie /ˈɡəʊlɪ/ *n.* (infml) вратарь (*m.*)

goat /ɡəʊt/ *n.* коза; (male) козёл

gobble¹ /ˈɡɒb(ə)l/ *v.t.* жрать, по-/со-

gobble² /ˈɡɒb(ə)l/ *v.i.* (of a turkey) кулдыкать (*impf.*)

gobbledygook /ˈɡɒb(ə)ldɪɡuːk/ *n.* (sl.) болтология, (пустой) набор слов; (in speech of politicians, also) витиеватая демагогия; (in documents) бюрократический жаргон, канцелярит

goblin /ˈɡɒblɪn/ *n.* домовой, гоблин

✎ **god** /ɡɒd/ *n.* (a deity) бог; (G~: supreme being) Бог; божество; my G~! Боже мой!; Господи!

■ ~**child** *n.* крестник (*-ца*); ~**daughter** *n.* крестница; ~**father** *n.* крёстный (отец); ~**forsaken place** *n.* медвежий угол; ~**mother** *n.* крёстная (мать); ~**parent** *n.* крёстный (отец); крёстная (мать); ~**send** *n.* находка; ≈ сам Бог послал; ~**son** *n.* крестник

goddess /ˈɡɒdɪs/ *n.* богиня

goes /ɡəʊz/ *3rd pers. sing. pres. of* ▸ go

goggles /ˈɡɒɡ(ə)lz/ *n. pl.* тёмные/защитные очк|и (*-ов*)

going /ˈɡəʊɪŋ/ *n.* **1** (departure) отъезд, уход **2** (progress, speed) скорость; fifty miles an hour is good ~ 50 миль в час — хорошая скорость; this book is heavy ~ эта книга трудно читается; the conversation was heavy ~ разговор не клеился

● *adj.* **1** (working): a ~ concern действующее предприятие **2** (BrE, to be had): one of the best newspapers ~ одна из лучших нынешних газет

■ ~**-s-on** *n. pl.* (infml) поведение; поступки (*m. pl.*); дела (*nt. pl.*); «делишки» (*nt. pl.*)

✎ **gold** /ɡəʊld/ *n.* (metal) золото; he's as good as ~ (of child) он золото, а не ребёнок

● *adj.* (made of gold, gold-coloured) золотой; ~ medal золотая медаль

■ ~ **dust** *n.* золотой песок; ~**fish** *n.* золотая рыбка; ~ **mine** *n.* золотой рудник; (fig.): the shop is a ~ mine этот магазин — золотое дно; ~ **medal** *n.* золотая медаль; ~ **rush** *n.* золотая лихорадка

golden /ˈɡəʊld(ə)n/ *adj.* (lit., fig.) золотой; (of colour) золотистый; the ~ age золотой век; receive a ~ handshake on retirement получить (*pf.*) вознаграждение при уходе на пенсию; miss a ~ opportunity упустить (*pf.*) редчайшую возможность

golf /ɡɒlf/ *n.* гольф

■ ~ **club** *n.* (association) клуб любителей игры

в гольф; (implement) клю́шка; ~ **course** *n.*
площа́дка/по́ле для игры́ в гольф
golfer /'gɒlfə(r)/ *n.* игро́к в гольф
gondola /'gɒndələ/ *n.* (boat; airship car) гондо́ла
gone /gɒn/ *adj.* (*see also* ▸ **go**) **1** (departed, past) уе́хавший **2** (dead) уме́рший, усо́пший
gong /gɒŋ/ *n.* (instrument) гонг
gonorrhoea /ɡɒnəˈrɪə/ (AmE **gonorrhea**) *n.* гоноре́я

⚭ **good** /ɡʊd/ *n.* **1** (~ness, ~ action) добро́, бла́го; **he is up to no** ~ он заду́мал что́-то недо́брое **2** (benefit) по́льза; **drink it! it will do you** ~ вы́пейте э́то — вам поле́зно; **it's no** ~ **complaining** что то́лку жа́ловаться? **3**: **for** ~ (permanently) навсегда́ **4** (*in pl.*) (property) добро́ **5** (*in pl.*) (merchandise) това́р(ы)
● *adj.* (**better**, **best**) **1** (in most senses) хоро́ший; до́брый; (of food) вку́сный; ~ **idea!** прекра́сная мысль!; **a** ~ **player** си́льный игро́к; ~ **heavens!** Бо́же мой! **2** (of health, condition, etc.) хоро́ший; здоро́вый; **I don't feel so** ~ **today** (infml) я себя́ нева́жно чу́вствую сего́дня; **apples are** ~ **for you** я́блоки поле́зны для здоро́вья **3** (favourable, fortunate): ~ **luck!** жела́ю успе́ха!; **it's a** ~ **thing we stayed at home** хорошо́, что мы оста́лись до́ма **4** (kind) любе́зный, до́брый; **that's very** ~ **of you** э́то о́чень ми́ло с ва́шей стороны́ **5** (of skill): ~ **at** спосо́бный к + *d.*; си́льный в + *p.*; **she's** ~ **at maths** она́ спосо́бна к матема́тике; **he is no** ~ **at his job** он взя́лся не за своё де́ло **6** (suitable) подходя́щий **7** (well behaved) воспи́танный; послу́шный; **be** ~**!** веди́ себя́ прили́чно! **8** (var.): ~ **morning!** до́брое у́тро!; **it's** ~ **to see you** прия́тно вас ви́деть; **a** ~ **while ago** давны́м-давно́; **he was as** ~ **as his word** он сдержа́л своё сло́во; **he as** ~ **as refused to go** он факти́чески отказа́лся идти́
■ ~**-for-nothing** *n.* безде́льник, никчёмный челове́к; **G**~ **Friday** *n.* Страстна́я пя́тница; ~**-humoured**, (AmE) **-humored** *adj.* доброду́шный; ~**-looking** *adj.* краси́вый; хоро́ш/хороша́ собо́й; ~**-natured** *adj.* доброду́шный; ~**night** *int.* споко́йной но́чи!; ~**s train** *n.* това́рный по́езд; ~**will** *n.* (friendship) доброжела́тельность; (of business) репута́ция

goodbye /ɡʊdˈbaɪ/ *n.* проща́ние
● *int.* до свида́ния!; проща́йте!
goodness /'ɡʊdnɪs/ *n.* **1** (virtue) доброта́ **2** (kindness) любе́зность **3** (nourishment): **these apples are full of** ~ э́ти я́блоки о́чень поле́зны/пита́тельны **4** (euph., God): ~ **me!** вот те на́!; **thank** ~**!** сла́ва Бо́гу!
gooey /'ɡuːɪ/ *adj.* (**gooier**, **gooiest**) (infml) кле́йкий; ли́пкий
google /'ɡuːɡ(ə)l/ *v.t. & i.* иска́ть (*impf.*) в Интерне́те (*особенно в поисковой системе Google (propr.)*)
goose /ɡuːs/ *n.* (*pl.* **geese**) **1** гусь (*m.*) (*fem. also* гусы́ня) **2** (simpleton) простофи́ля (*c.g.*)
■ ~**berry** *n.* крыжо́вник (*collect.*); я́года

крыжо́вника; **play** ~**berry** (BrE, infml) ока́зываться, -а́ться тре́тьим ли́шним; ~**flesh** *n.* гуся́тина; **it gives me** ~**flesh** у меня́ от э́того мура́шки по те́лу бе́гают; ~**-step** *n.* (mil.) гуси́ный шаг
gorge /ɡɔːdʒ/ *n.* уще́лье
● *v.t. & i.* объ|еда́ться, -е́сться; **the lion** ~**d (itself) on its prey** лев жа́дно поглоща́л свою́ добы́чу
gorgeous /'ɡɔːdʒəs/ *adj.* (magnificent) великоле́пный; (richly coloured) кра́сочный
gorilla /ɡəˈrɪlə/ *n.* гори́лла
gormless /'ɡɔːmlɪs/ *adj.* (BrE, infml) безду́мный; дура́шливый
gorse /ɡɔːs/ *n.* (bot.) утёсник обыкнове́нный
gory /'ɡɔːrɪ/ *adj.* (**gorier**, **goriest**) кровопроли́тный; ~ **details** крова́вые подро́бности
gosh /ɡɒʃ/ *int.* (infml) Бо́же мой!
gosling /'ɡɒzlɪŋ/ *n.* гусёнок
gospel /'ɡɒsp(ə)l/ *n.* **1** Ева́нгелие **2** (*in full* **g. music**) го́спел
gossip /'ɡɒsɪp/ *n.* **1** (talk) спле́тня **2** (person) спле́тни|к (-ца) **3** (*attr.*): ~ **column** коло́нка све́тской хро́ники
● *v.i.* (**gossiped**, **gossiping**) спле́тничать, на-
got /ɡɒt/ *past and p.p. of* ▸ **get**
Gothic /'ɡɒθɪk/ *n.* го́тика, готи́ческий стиль
● *adj.* готи́ческий
gotten /'ɡɒt(ə)n/ (AmE) *p.p. of* ▸ **get**
gouache /ɡuˈɑːʃ/ *n.* гуа́шь
goulash /'ɡuːlæʃ/ *n.* гуля́ш
gourmet /'ɡʊəmeɪ/ *n.* гурма́н
gout /ɡaʊt/ *n.* пода́гра
govern /'ɡʌv(ə)n/ *v.t.* **1** (rule; also v.i.) пра́вить (*impf.*) + *i.*; (control, influence) руководи́ть (*impf.*) + *i.*; ~**ing body** (of hospital, school, etc.) дире́кция, правле́ние **2** (apply to): **the same principle** ~**s both cases** оди́н и тот же при́нцип примени́м в обо́их слу́чаях
governess /'ɡʌvənɪs/ *n.* гуверна́нтка
⚭ **government** /'ɡʌvənmənt/ *n.* (rule) правле́ние; (system) фо́рма правле́ния
governmental /ɡʌvənˈment(ə)l/ *adj.* прави́тельственный
⚭ **governor** /'ɡʌvənə(r)/ *n.* **1** (ruling official) губерна́тор **2** (member of governing body) член правле́ния
gown /ɡaʊn/ *n.* (woman's) пла́тье; (academic or official) ма́нтия
GP *abbr.* (*of* **general practitioner**) врач о́бщей пра́ктики; участко́вый врач
GPS *n.* (*abbr. of* **Global Positioning System**) глоба́льная спу́тниковая навигацио́нная систе́ма
⚭ **grab** /ɡræb/ *v.t. & i.* (**grabbed**, **grabbing**) схва́т|ывать, -и́ть; **he** ~**bed me by the lapels** он схвати́л меня́ за ла́цканы
⚭ **grace** /ɡreɪs/ *n.* **1** (elegance) гра́ция, изя́щество; **airs and** ~**s** (iron.) жема́нство **2** (dispensation) отсро́чка; **the law allows 3 days'** ~ по зако́ну полага́ется 3 дня

⚭ ключева́я ле́ксика

отсро́чки (*or* льго́тных дня); (prayer before meal) моли́тва; **say** ~ моли́ться (*impf.*) пе́ред едо́й

graceful /'greisful/ *adj.* грацио́зный; изя́щный

gracious /'greiʃəs/ *adj.* ми́лостивый; любе́зный; ~ **living** краси́вая жизнь
● *int.*: **good(ness)** ~ **(me)!** Бо́же мой!

grade /greid/ *n.* **1** (assessed category) сте́пень; (of quality) сорт; (of rank) сте́пень; класс; (AmE, class in school) класс **2** (school rating) отме́тка; оце́нка **3** (AmE): ~ **crossing** (железнодоро́жный) перее́зд
● *v.t.* сортирова́ть, рас-
■ ~ **school** *n.* (AmE) нача́льная шко́ла

gradient /'greidiənt/ *n.* градие́нт

gradual /'grædʒuəl/ *adj.* постепе́нный

gradually /'grædʒuəli/ *adv.* постепе́нно

⚷ **graduate¹** /'grædjuət/ *n.* (of university, school, etc.) выпускни́к (-ца)

⚷ **graduate²** /'grædjueit/ *v.i.* (from university) ок|а́нчивать, -о́нчить университе́т/вуз; (AmE, from school) шко́лу

graduation /grædju'eiʃ(ə)n/ *n.* (receiving degree) получе́ние дипло́ма/сте́пени; (AmE) оконча́ние шко́лы

graffiti /grə'fi:ti/ *n.* (*sing.* **graffito** /-təu/) граффи́ти (*indecl., pl.*), на́дписи (*f. pl.*) (на сте́нах/забо́рах)

graft /grɑ:ft/ *n.* (tissue) переса́женная ткань
● *v.t.* (med.) переса́|живать, -ди́ть; (hort., also fig.) прив|ива́ть, -и́ть

grain /grein/ *n.* **1** (collect.) (seed of cereal plants) зерно́; (single seed) зерно́ **2** (small particle) зёрнышко; ~ **of sand** песчи́нка; **there is not a** ~ **of truth in it** в э́том нет ни крупи́цы/гра́на/ка́пли пра́вды **3** (of wood) волокно́ **4**: **it goes against the** ~ **with me** (fig.) э́то мне не по душе́/нутру́

gram /græm/ *n.* грамм

grammar /'græmə(r)/ *n.* грамма́тика
■ ~ **school** *n.* (BrE) сре́дняя шко́ла с гуманита́рным укло́ном

grammatical /grə'mætik(ə)l/ *adj.* граммати́ческий

gramme /græm/ *n.* (BrE) = **gram**

gramophone /'græməfəun/ *n.* граммофо́н
■ ~ **record** *n.* грампласти́нка

gran /græn/ *n.* (BrE) = **granny**

granary /'grænəri/ *n.* амба́р

grand /grænd/ *adj.* **1** (great, important) вели́кий; грандио́зный **2** (elevated, imposing) вели́чественный **3** (all-embracing): ~ **total** о́бщая су́мма
■ ~**child** *n.* внук (вну́чка); ~**(d)ad** *n.* (infml) де́душка (*m.*); ~**daughter** *n.* вну́чка; ~**father** *n.* де́душка (*m.*); ~**father clock** высо́кие напо́льные часы́; ~**ma** *n.* (infml) ба́бушка; ~**mother** *n.* ба́бушка; ~**pa** *n.* (infml) де́душка (*m.*); ~**parent** *n.* де́душка (ба́бушка); ~ **piano** *n.* роя́ль (*m.*); ~**son** *n.* внук; ~**stand** *n.* трибу́на

grandeur /'grændʒə(r)/ *n.* вели́чие; великоле́пие

grandiose /'grændiəus/ *adj.* грандио́зный

granite /'grænit/ *n.* грани́т

granny /'græni/ *n.* (infml) ба́бушка

⚷ **grant** /grɑ:nt/ *n.* (sum etc. conferred) дота́ция; (to student) стипе́ндия
● *v.t.* **1** (bestow) дарова́ть (*impf., pf.*); жа́ловать, по- **2** (concede) призн|ава́ть, -а́ть; ~**ed, he has done all he could** согла́сен: он сде́лал всё, что мог **3**: **he takes my help for** ~**ed** он принима́ет мою́ по́мощь как до́лжное

granulate /'grænjuleit/ *v.t. & i.*: ~**d sugar** са́харный песо́к

granule /'grænju:l/ *n.* зерно́, гра́нула

grape /greip/ *n.* (a single fruit) виногра́дина; **bunch of** ~**s** гроздь виногра́да
■ ~**fruit** *n.* грейпфру́т; ~**vine** *n.* виногра́дная лоза́; (fig.): **I heard on the** ~**vine that … до меня́ дошли́ слу́хи (о том), что…

graph /grɑ:f/ *n.* гра́фик
■ ~ **paper** *n.* бума́га в кле́тку, миллиметро́вка (infml)

graphic /'græfik/ *adj.* **1** (pertaining to drawing etc.) изобрази́тельный **2** (vivid) кра́сочный

graphics /'græfiks/ *n.* гра́фика
■ ~ **card** *n.* (comput.) видеока́рта, графи́ческая пла́та

grapple /'græp(ə)l/ *v.i.*: ~ **with a problem** бра́ться, взя́ться за пробле́му

grasp /grɑ:sp/ *n.* **1** (grip) хва́тка **2** (comprehension) понима́ние
● *v.t.* **1**: (seize) схва́т|ывать, -и́ть; (comprehend) схва́т|ывать, -и́ть смысл + g.
● *v.i.*: ~ **at, for** (lit., fig.) ухвати́ться (*pf.*) за + a.

grass /grɑ:s/ *n.* **1** трава́ **2** (lawn) газо́н **3** (sl., marijuana) марихуа́на, «тра́вка»
■ ~**hopper** *n.* кузне́чик; ~**roots** *adj.* (infml) низово́й, из низо́в; ~**roots opinion is against the plan** рядовы́е гра́ждане настро́ены про́тив э́того пла́на; ~ **snake** *n.* уж

grassy /'grɑ:si/ *adj.* (**grassier, grassiest**) травяно́й; травяни́стый

grate¹ /greit/ *n.* (fireplace) ками́нная решётка; ками́н

grate² /greit/ *v.t.* тере́ть (*impf.*); ~**d cheese** тёртый сыр
● *v.i.* **1**: ~ **on** (fig.) раздража́ть (*impf.*) **2** (make harsh sound) скр|ипе́ть, -и́пнуть

grateful /'greitful/ *adj.* благода́рный; призна́тельный

grater /'greitə(r)/ *n.* тёрка

gratify /'grætifai/ *v.t.* дост|авля́ть, -а́вить удово́льствие + d.

grating /'greitiŋ/ *n.* решётка

gratis /'grɑ:tis/ *adj.* беспла́тный
● *adv.* беспла́тно

gratitude /'grætitju:d/ *n.* благода́рность

gratuitous /grə'tju:itəs/ *adj.* **1** (unwarranted) беспричи́нный; **a** ~ **insult** незаслу́женное оскорбле́ние **2** (free) дарово́й; безвозме́здный; ~ **advice** беспла́тный сове́т

gratuity /grə'tju:iti/ *n.* (tip) чаевы́|е (-х)

grave¹ /greiv/ *n.* моги́ла

g

grave | grind

■ **~stone** *n.* надгро́бная плита́; **~yard** *n.* кла́дбище

grave² /greɪv/ *adj.* серьёзный

gravel /'græv(ə)l/ *n.* гра́вий

gravitate /'grævɪteɪt/ *v.i.* (fig.) тяготе́ть (*impf.*) (**to(wards)**: к + *d.*)

gravity /'grævɪtɪ/ *n.* ■ (force) си́ла притяже́ния ■ (weight) тя́жесть; **centre of ~** центр тя́жести; **law of ~** зако́н всеми́рного тяготе́ния ■ (seriousness) серьёзность; тя́жесть

gravy /'greɪvɪ/ *n.* подли́вка

gray /greɪ/ *n. & adj.* (AmE) = grey

grayish /'greɪɪʃ/ *adj.* (AmE) = greyish

graze¹ /greɪz/ *n.* (abrasion) цара́пина; сса́дина
● *v.t.* зад|ева́ть, -е́ть; **he fell and ~d his knee** он упа́л и оцара́пал коле́но

graze² /greɪz/ *v.i.*: **he has 40 sheep out to ~** у него́ (в ста́де/ота́ре) пасётся 40 ове́ц

grease /griːs/ *n.* (fat) жир; (lubricant) сма́зка
● *v.t.* сма́з|ывать, -ать
■ **~paint** *n.* грим

greasy /'griːsɪ/ *adj.* (**greasier, greasiest**) жи́рный

⚜ **great** /greɪt/ *adj.* ■ большо́й, вели́кий; (famous) знамени́тый; **they are ~ friends** они́ больши́е друзья́; **a ~ many people** ма́сса наро́ду; **a ~ deal of courage** незауря́дный хра́брость ■ (infml, splendid) замеча́тельный; **we had a ~ time** мы замеча́тельно провели́ вре́мя ■ (eminent, distinguished) вели́кий; **a ~ occasion** торже́ственное собы́тие ■ **G~ Britain** Великобрита́ния
■ **~-aunt** *n.* двою́родная ба́бушка; **~-granddaughter** *n.* пра́внучка; **~-grandfather** *n.* пра́дед; **~-grandmother** *n.* праба́бушка; **~-grandson** *n.* пра́внук; **~-nephew** *n.* внуча́тый племя́нник; **~-niece** *n.* внуча́тая племя́нница; **~-uncle** *n.* двою́родный дед

greatly /'greɪtlɪ/ *adv.* о́чень, си́льно, значи́тельно; **I was ~ amused** э́то меня́ си́льно позаба́вило

Greece /griːs/ *n.* Гре́ция

greed /griːd/ *n.* жа́дность; (for food) прожо́рливость

greedy /'griːdɪ/ *adj.* (**greedier, greediest**) (for money etc.) жа́дный; (for food) прожо́рливый

Greek /griːk/ *n.* ■ (person) гре|к (-ча́нка) ■ (language) гре́ческий язы́к; **Ancient ~** древнегре́ческий язы́к; **it's (all) ~ to me** э́то для меня́ кита́йская гра́мота
● *adj.* гре́ческий

⚜ **green** /griːn/ *n.* ■ (colour) зелёный цвет; зелёное; **dressed in ~** оде́тый в зелёное ■ (*in pl.*) (vegetables) зе́лень ■ (grassy area) лужа́йка; (on golf course) площа́дка вокру́г лу́нки
● *adj.* зелёный; (unripe) незре́лый; (fig., inexperienced) «зелёный»
■ **~grocer** *n.* (BrE) продаве́ц (-щи́ца) зе́лени; **~house** *n.* тепли́ца; **~house effect**

парнико́вый *or* тепли́чный эффе́кт

greenery /'griːnərɪ/ *n.* зе́лень

greenish /'griːnɪʃ/ *adj.* зеленова́тый

Greenland /'griːnlənd/ *n.* Гренла́ндия
● *adj.* гренла́ндский

Greenwich Mean time, Greenwich time /'grenɪtʃ, 'grɪnɪdʒ/ *n.* вре́мя по Гри́нвичу

greet /griːt/ *v.t.* (socially) здоро́ваться, по- с + *i.*; (welcome) приве́тствовать (*impf.*)

greeting /'griːtɪŋ/ *n.* (on meeting) приве́тствие; **~s!** приве́т!; (on a special occasion): **birthday ~s** поздравле́ние с днём рожде́ния
■ **~s card** *n.* поздрави́тельная откры́тка

gregarious /grɪ'geərɪəs/ *adj.* ста́дный; (fig. also) общи́тельный

grenade /grɪ'neɪd/ *n.* грана́та

grew /gruː/ *past of* ▸ **grow**

grey /greɪ/ (AmE **gray**) *n.* се́рый цвет; се́рое
● *adj.* се́рый; **he has gone very ~** он си́льно посе́дел; **his face turned ~** он побледне́л
■ **~ area** *n.* (fig.) о́бласть неопределённости; **~-haired, ~-headed** *adjs.* седо́й, седовла́сый; **~hound** *n.* англи́йская борза́я

greyish /'greɪɪʃ/ (AmE **grayish**) *adj.* серова́тый

grid /grɪd/ *n.* ■ (grating) решётка ■ (map reference squares) координа́тная се́тка ■ (power supply system) энергосисте́ма

griddle /'grɪd(ə)l/ *n.* ≈ сковоро́дка

gridlock /'grɪdlɒk/ *n.* зато́р

grief /griːf/ *n.* (sorrow) го́ре, печа́ль; (disaster): **he will come to ~** он пло́хо ко́нчит

grievance /'griːv(ə)ns/ *n.* прете́нзия; недово́льство

grieve /griːv/ *v.t.* огорч|а́ть, -и́ть
● *v.i.* горева́ть (*impf.*); **she ~d for her husband** она́ горева́ла о му́же

grievous /'griːvəs/ *adj.* го́рестный; **~ bodily harm** (law) тяжёлые теле́сные поврежде́ния (*nt. pl.*)

grill /grɪl/ *n.* (BrE, on cooker) гриль (*m.*)
● *v.t.* (BrE, cook) жа́рить, за- на гри́ле; (infml, interrogate) учин|я́ть, -и́ть допро́с + *d.*

grille /grɪl/ *n.* решётка

grim /grɪm/ *adj.* (**grimmer, grimmest**) суро́вый, мра́чный, гро́зный

grimace /'grɪməs/ *n.* грима́са
● *v.i.* грима́сничать (*impf.*)

grime /graɪm/ *n.* са́жа; грязь

grimy /'graɪmɪ/ *adj.* (**grimier, grimiest**) чума́зый; гря́зный

grin /grɪn/ *n.* усме́шка; ухмы́лка
● *v.i.* (**grinned, grinning**) усмех|а́ться, -ну́ться; ухмыл|я́ться, -ну́ться

grind /graɪnd/ *n.* (infml) изнури́тельный труд
● *v.t.* (*past and p.p.* **ground**) ■ (crush) моло́ть, с-; **ground almonds** мо́лотый минда́ль ■ (wear down) изн|а́шивать, -оси́ть ■: **~ one's teeth** скрежета́ть/скрипе́ть (*both impf.*) зуба́ми
● *v.i.* (*past and p.p.* **ground**) ■ (rub, grate) тере́ть (*impf.*) ■: **~ to a halt** остан|а́вливаться, -ови́ться (с ля́згом)

⚜ ключева́я ле́ксика

■ ~**stone** *n.* точи́ло; **he kept his nose to the** ~**stone** он труди́лся без о́тдыха

grip /grɪp/ *n.* схва́тывание; (fig.) понима́ние; **come to** ~**s with a problem** вплотну́ю заня́ться (*pf.*) пробле́мой; **take a** ~ **of yourself!** возьми́те себя́ в ру́ки!; **he is losing his** ~ хва́тка у него́ уже́ не та
● *v.t.* (**gripped, gripping**) (hold tightly) схва́т|ывать, -и́ть; (hold the attention of) захва́т|ывать, -и́ть; **a** ~**ping story** захва́тывающий расска́з

gripe /graɪp/ *n.* **1** (*in pl.*) (colic pains) ко́лик|и (*pl., g.* —) **2** (grumble, complaint) ворча́ние
● *v.i.* (complain) ворча́ть (*impf.*)

grisly /ˈɡrɪzlɪ/ *adj.* (**grislier, grisliest**) ужаса́ющий

grist /ɡrɪst/ *n.* (fig.): **it will bring** ~ **to the mill** э́то принесёт дохо́д; **all is** ~ **to his mill** он из всего́ извлека́ет вы́году

gristle /ˈɡrɪs(ə)l/ *n.* хрящ

grit /ɡrɪt/ *n.* гра́вий
● *v.t.* (**gritted, gritting**) **1** (spread ~ on): **the streets were** ~**ted at the first sign of frost** при пе́рвых при́знаках моро́за у́лицы посы́пали песко́м **2**: ~ **one's teeth** (fig.) сти́снуть (*pf.*) зу́бы

gritty /ˈɡrɪtɪ/ *adj.* (**grittier, grittiest**) песча́ный; (fig., of style) шерохова́тый

grizzle /ˈɡrɪz(ə)l/ *v.i.* (BrE, infml, fret) капри́зничать (*impf.*); хны́кать (*impf.*)

groan /ɡrəʊn/ *n.* стон
● *v.i.* стона́ть, за-

grocer /ˈɡrəʊsə(r)/ *n.* бакале́йщик
■ ~**'s shop** *n.* бакале́я

grocery /ˈɡrəʊsərɪ/ *n.* (*in pl.*) (goods) бакале́я

groggy /ˈɡrɒɡɪ/ *adj.* (**groggier, groggiest**) нетвёрдо стоя́щий на нога́х

groin /ɡrɔɪn/ *n.* (anat.) пах

groom /ɡruːm/ *n.* (for horses) ко́нюх; (bride~) жени́х
● *v.t.* **1**: ~ **a horse** чи́стить, по- ло́шадь **2** (prepare, coach) гото́вить; **he is being** ~**ed for President** его́ про́чат в президе́нты

groove /ɡruːv/ *n.* желобо́к

grope /ɡrəʊp/ *v.t. & i.* идти́ (*det.*) о́щупью; ощу́п|ывать, -ать; **he** ~**d his way towards the door** он о́щупью добра́лся до две́ри

gross /ɡrəʊs/ *n.* (*pl.* ~) (number) гросс (*12 дюжин*)
● *adj.* **1** (coarse) гру́бый **2** (obese) ту́чный **3** (opp. net) валово́й; ~ **domestic product** валово́й вну́тренний проду́кт; ~ **national product** валово́й национа́льный проду́кт; ~ **weight** вес бру́тто
● *v.t.*: **we** ~**ed £1,000** мы получи́ли о́бщую при́быль в 1000 фу́нтов

grotesque /ɡrəʊˈtesk/ *adj.* гроте́скный

grotto /ˈɡrɒtəʊ/ *n.* (*pl.* ~**es** *or* ~**s**) грот

grouchy /ˈɡraʊtʃɪ/ *adj.* (**grouchier, grouchiest**) (infml) ворчли́вый; брюзгли́вый

✓ **ground¹** /ɡraʊnd/ *n.* **1** (surface of earth) земля́; грунт; **it suits me down to the** ~ э́то меня́ вполне́ устра́ивает **2** (soil, also fig.) по́чва **3** (position) положе́ние; **this opinion is gaining** ~ э́та то́чка зре́ния получа́ет всё бо́льшее распростране́ние; **they held their** ~ **well** они́ сто́йко держа́лись **4** (area, distance) расстоя́ние; **we covered a lot of** ~ (distance) мы покры́ли большо́е расстоя́ние; (fig., work) мы заме́тно продви́нулись вперёд **5** (defined area of activity) площа́дка; **football** ~ футбо́льная площа́дка; **sports** ~ спорти́вная площа́дка **6** (*in pl.*) (estate) сад, парк, зе́мли (*f. pl.*) **7** (*in pl.*) (dregs) гу́ща **8** (reason) основа́ние; **I have no** ~**s for complaint** у меня́ нет основа́ний жа́ловаться
● *v.t.* **1** (run aground) сажа́ть, посади́ть на мель **2** (prevent from flying) запре|ща́ть, -ти́ть полёты + *g.*
■ ~ **floor** *n.* (BrE) пе́рвый эта́ж; ~ **forces** *n. pl.* сухопу́тные войска́; ~**nut** *n.* земляно́й оре́х; ~**work** *n.* фунда́мент, осно́вы (*f. pl.*)

ground² /ɡraʊnd/ *past and p.p. of* ▶ grind

grounding /ˈɡraʊndɪŋ/ *n.* (basic instruction) подгото́вка

groundless /ˈɡraʊndlɪs/ *adj.* беспричи́нный, беспо́чвенный, необосно́ванный

✓ **group** /ɡruːp/ *n.* **1** (assemblage) гру́ппа; коллекти́в; (political etc. unit) группиро́вка; фра́кция **2** (*attr.*) группово́й
● *v.t. & i.* группирова́ть(ся), с-
■ ~ **therapy** *n.* группова́я психотерапи́я

grouse /ɡraʊs/ *n.* (*pl.* ~) (bird) шотла́ндская куропа́тка

grout /ɡraʊt/ *n.* (mortar) цеме́нтный раство́р
● *v.t.* зал|ива́ть, -и́ть цеме́нтом

grove /ɡrəʊv/ *n.* ро́ща

grovel /ˈɡrɒv(ə)l/ *v.i.* (**grovelled, grovelling**, AmE **groveled, groveling**) лежа́ть (*impf.*) ниц/распростёршись; (fig.) пресмыка́ться (*impf.*) (**to:** пе́ред + *i.*)

✓ **grow** /ɡrəʊ/ *v.t.* (*past* **grew**, *p.p.* **grown**) расти́ть, вы-; выра́щивать (*impf.*); разводи́ть (*impf.*); **he is** ~**ing a beard** он отра́щивает бо́роду
● *v.i.* (*past* **grew**, *p.p.* **grown**) **1** (of habitat) расти́, вы́расти; **ivy** ~**s on walls** плющ растёт на сте́нах **2** (of development): **he grew (by) 5 inches** он вы́рос на 5 дю́ймов; **she has** ~**n into a young lady** она́ преврати́лась в молоду́ю же́нщину; **she is letting her hair** ~ она́ отра́щивает во́лосы; **he looks quite** ~**n up** он вы́глядит совсе́м взро́слым; ~**n-ups** взро́слые (*pl.*); **I grew to like him** со вре́менем он стал мне нра́виться; **it's a habit I've never** ~**n out of** э́то привы́чка, от кото́рой я никогда́ не мог изба́виться; **he grew out of his clothes** он вы́рос из оде́жды; **the tune** ~**s on one** э́тот моти́в начина́ет нра́виться со вре́менем; (increase) увели́чи|ваться, -ться; уси́ли|ваться, -ться; **he listened with** ~**ing impatience** он слу́шал с расту́щим нетерпе́нием **3** (become) ста|нови́ться, -ть; **as he grew older, he ...** с во́зрастом он...; **she grew pale** она́ побледне́ла

grower /ˈɡrəʊə(r)/ *n.* (cultivator) садово́д

growl /graʊl/ *n.* рыча́ние
● *v.i.* рыча́ть (*impf.*)

grown /grəʊn/ *p.p. of ▶* grow

◆ **growth** /grəʊθ/ *n.* (development) рост; (increase) прирóст; (path.) нарóст

grubby /'grʌbɪ/ *adj.* (**grubbier, grubbiest**) гря́зный, запа́чканный

grudg|e /grʌdʒ/ *n.* прете́нзия, недоброжела́тельность; **I bear him no ~e** я на негó не в оби́де
● *v.t.* зави́довать, по- (*чему*); **I do not ~e him his success** я не зави́дую егó успе́ху; **I ~e paying** мне жаль стóлько плати́ть; **he obeyed ~ingly** он неохóтно вы́полнил приказа́ние

gruel /'gru:əl/ *n.* жи́дкая (овся́ная) ка́ша, каши́ца

gruelling /'gru:əlɪŋ/ (AmE **grueling**) *adj.* изма́тывающий

gruesome /'gru:səm/ *adj.* жу́ткий

gruff /grʌf/ *adj.* (of voice) хри́плый

grumble /'grʌmb(ə)l/ *v.i.* (complain) ворча́ть (*impf.*); (rumble) грохота́ть (*impf.*)

grumpy /'grʌmpɪ/ *adj.* (**grumpier, grumpiest**) сварли́вый

grunt /grʌnt/ *n.* (animal) хрю́канье; (human) ворча́ние
● *v.i.* (of animals) хрю́к|ать, -нуть; (of humans) ворча́ть, про-

guarantee /ɡærən'ti:/ *n.* гара́нтия
● *v.t.* (**guarantees, guaranteed**) страхова́ть, за-; **it is ~d to last 10 years** срок гóдности/гара́нтии — 10 лет; **~d against rust** гаранти́рованный от коррóзии

◆ **guard** /ɡɑ:d/ *n.* **1** (state of alertness) настороже́нность; **he was caught off his ~** егó заста́ли враспло́х; (mil.): **on ~ duty** на часа́х; в карау́ле **2** (man appointed to keep ~) охра́нник, карау́льный; (collect.) охра́на, стра́жа **3** (BrE, of a train) проводни́к **4** (protective device) защи́тное устрóйство
● *v.t.* охраня́ть (*impf.*); бере́чь (*impf.*)
● *v.i.* бере́чься (*impf.*), остерега́ться (*impf.*) (against: + *g.*); **everything was done to ~ against infection** бы́ли при́няты все ме́ры прóтив инфе́кции
■ **~ dog** *n.* сторожева́я соба́ка; **~sman** *n.* гварде́ец

guarded /'ɡɑ:dɪd/ *adj.* сде́ржанный; осторóжный

guardian /'ɡɑ:dɪən/ *n.* **1** (protector) опеку́н **2** (law) опеку́н
■ **~ angel** *n.* а́нгел-храни́тель (*m.*)

Guatemala /ɡwɑ:tə'mɑ:lə/ *n.* Гватема́ла

Guatemalan /ɡwɑ:tə'mɑ:lən/ *n.* гватема́л|ец (-ка)
● *adj.* гватема́льский

guerrilla /ɡə'rɪlə/ *n.* партиза́н
■ **~ warfare** *n.* партиза́нская война́

◆ **guess** /ɡes/ *n.* дога́дка; **at a rough ~** гру́бо/ориенти́ровочно
● *v.t.* **1** (estimate) прики́|дывать, -нуть;

I would ~ his age at 40 я бы дал ему́ лет 40 **2** (conjecture) дога́д|ываться, -а́ться (о *чём*) **3** (infml, expect, suppose) полага́ть (*impf.*); **I ~ you are right** вероя́тно, вы пра́вы
● *v.i.* гада́ть (*impf.*); **she likes to keep him ~ing** ей нра́вится держа́ть егó в неве́дении
■ **~work** *n.* дога́дки (*f. pl.*)

◆ **guest** /ɡest/ *n.* **1** (one privately entertained) гость (*m.*) **2** (at a hotel etc.) постоя́лец
■ **~ house** *n.* пансиóн; **~ room** *n.* кóмната для гостéй

guffaw /ɡʌ'fɔ:/ *n.* гóгот (*смех*)
● *v.i.* гогота́ть (*impf.*) (*смеяться*)

guidance /'ɡaɪd(ə)ns/ *n.* руковóдство

◆ **guide** /ɡaɪd/ *n.* **1** (leader) руковоdи́тель (*m.*); (for travellers, tourists, etc.) гид, экскурсовóд **2** (directing principle) руковóдство **3** (manual) уче́бник; **~ to fishing** руковóдство по ры́бной лóвле **4**: **(Girl) G~** дéвочка-ска́ут
● *v.t.* водить (*indet.*), вести́ (*det.*), по-; руководить (*impf.*) + *i.*; **be ~d by principles** руковóдствоваться (*impf.*) при́нципами
■ **~book** *n.* путеводи́тель (*m.*); **~ dog** *n.* соба́ка-поводы́рь; **~line** *n.* директи́ва

guild /ɡɪld/ *n.* **1** (hist.) ги́льдия **2** ассоциа́ция, сою́з

guillotine /'ɡɪləti:n/ *n.* **1** гильоти́на **2** (for paper, metal, etc.) ре́зальная маши́на

guilt /ɡɪlt/ *n.* вина́

◆ **guilty** /'ɡɪltɪ/ *adj.* (**guiltier, guiltiest**) винóвный; **he pleaded ~ to the crime** он призна́л себя́ винóвным в преступле́нии; **~ conscience** нечи́стая сóвесть; **a verdict of ~/not** обвини́тельный/оправда́тельный пригово́р

guinea pig /'ɡɪnɪ pɪɡ/ *n.* морска́я сви́нка; (fig.) «подóпытный крóлик»

guise /ɡaɪz/ *n.* (dress) наря́д; (pretence) предлóг; **under the ~ of friendship** под ви́дом дру́жбы

guitar /ɡɪ'tɑ:(r)/ *n.* гита́ра

guitarist /ɡɪ'tɑ:rɪst/ *n.* гитари́ст (-ка)

gulf /ɡʌlf/ *n.* **1** (deep bay) зали́в; бу́хта; **the G~ Stream** Гольфстри́м **2** (abyss) бе́здна **3** (fig.) прóпасть

gull /ɡʌl/ *n.* (bird) ча́йка

gullet /'ɡʌlɪt/ *n.* пищевóд; **it sticks in my ~** (fig.) э́то стои́т у меня́ поперёк гóрла

gullible /'ɡʌlɪb(ə)l/ *adj.* легкове́рный

gully /'ɡʌlɪ/ *n.* лощи́на

gulp /ɡʌlp/ *n.* большóй глотóк; **he took a ~ of tea** он глотну́л ча́ю
● *v.t.* глот|а́ть, -ну́ть

gum¹ /ɡʌm/ *n.* (anat.) десна́

gum² /ɡʌm/ *n.* (adhesive) клей; (resin) каме́дь; (chewing ~) жева́тельная рези́нка

gumption /'ɡʌmpʃ(ə)n/ *n.* (infml) смышлёность; нахóдчивость

◆ **gun** /ɡʌn/ *n.* (cannon) пу́шка, орýдие; (pistol) пистоле́т; (rifle) ружьё; **he stuck to his ~s** (fig.) он не сдал пози́ций; **jump the ~** (fig.) сова́ться, су́нуться ра́ньше вре́мени
● *v.t.* (**gunned, gunning**) стреля́ть (*impf.*); **the refugees were ~ned down** бе́женцев расстреля́ли

◆ ключева́я ле́ксика

■ ~**fire** *n.* оруди́йный ого́нь; ~**man** *n.* банди́т; террори́ст; ~**point** *n.*: at ~**point** угрожа́ть ору́жием; под ду́лом пистоле́та; ~**powder** *n.* по́рох; ~**shot** *n.* руже́йный вы́стрел

gunner /ˈɡʌnə(r)/ *n.* канони́р; артиллери́ст

gurgle /ˈɡəːɡ(ə)l/ *n.* бу́льканье
• *v.i.* бу́лькать (*impf.*)

guru /ˈɡʊruː/ *n.* гуру́ (*m. indecl.*)

gush /ɡʌʃ/ *v.i.* хлы́нуть (*pf.*)

gust /ɡʌst/ *n.* поры́в ве́тра

gusto /ˈɡʌstəʊ/ *n.* (relish) смак; (zeal) жар

gusty /ˈɡʌstɪ/ *adj.* (**gustier**, **gustiest**) бу́рный; поры́вистый; **a ~ day** ве́треный день

gut /ɡʌt/ *n.* **1** (intestine) кишка́ **2** (*in pl.*) (intestines, stomach) кишки́ (*f. pl.*); (fig., courage and determination) вы́держка; **he hadn't the ~s to tackle the burglar** у него́ не хвати́ло му́жества задержа́ть граби́теля; ~ **reaction** инсти́нктивная реа́кция
• *v.t.* (**gutted**, **gutting**) **1** (eviscerate) потроши́ть, вы- **2** (destroy contents of) опустош|а́ть, -и́ть

gutsy /ˈɡʌtsɪ/ *adj.* (**gutsier**, **gutsiest**) упо́рный, де́рзкий

gutter /ˈɡʌtə(r)/ *n.* (under eaves) водосто́чный жёлоб; (at roadside) сто́чная кана́ва

guttural /ˈɡʌtər(ə)l/ *adj.* горта́нный; горлово́й; (ling.) веля́рный, задненёбный

✓ **guy** /ɡaɪ/ *n.* ма́лый; **wise ~** у́мник

guzzle /ˈɡʌz(ə)l/ *v.t.* (eat) есть, съ- с жа́дностью; (drink) пить, вы- с жа́дностью; (fig., consume) про|еда́ть, -е́сть

gym /dʒɪm/ *n.* (gymnasium) гимнасти́ческий зал; (gymnastics) гимна́стика
■ ~ **shoe** *n.* спорти́вная та́почка

gymkhana /dʒɪmˈkɑːnə/ *n.* конноспорти́вные состяза́ния (*nt. pl.*)

gymnasi|um /dʒɪmˈneɪzɪəm/ *n.* (*pl.* ~**ums** or ~**a**) гимнасти́ческий зал

gymnast /ˈdʒɪmnæst/ *n.* гимна́ст (-ка)

gymnastic /dʒɪmˈnæstɪk/ *adj.* гимнасти́ческий

gymnastics /dʒɪmˈnæstɪks/ *n.* гимна́стика

gynaecological /ɡaɪnəkəˈlɒdʒɪk(ə)l/ (AmE **gynecological**) *adj.* гинекологи́ческий

gynaecologist /ɡaɪnəˈkɒlədʒɪst/ (AmE **gynecologist**) *n.* гинеко́лог

gynaecology /ɡaɪnəˈkɒlədʒɪ/ (AmE **gynecology**) *n.* гинеколо́гия

Gypsy /ˈdʒɪpsɪ/ *n. & adj.* = **Gipsy**

gyrate /dʒaɪəˈreɪt/ *v.i.* враща́ться (*impf.*)

g

h

Hh

haberdashery /ˈhæbədæʃərɪ/ *n.* (BrE) (shop) галантере́йный магази́н; (wares) галантере́я

habit /ˈhæbɪt/ *n.* **1** (settled practice) привы́чка; **get into the ~ of ...ing** прив|ыка́ть, -ы́кнуть + *inf.*; **get out of the ~ of ...ing** отв|ыка́ть, -ы́кнуть + *inf.* or от + *g.* **2** (nun's/monk's dress) ря́са

habitable /ˈhæbɪtəb(ə)l/ *adj.* приго́дный для жилья́

habitat /ˈhæbɪtæt/ *n.* есте́ственная среда́ (*растения, животного*)

habitual /həˈbɪtʃʊəl/ *adj.* привы́чный; обы́чный; **a ~ liar** неисправи́мый лгун

hack /hæk/ *v.t.* разруб|а́ть, -и́ть; руби́ть (*impf.*)
• *v.i.*: ~ **into** (comput.) прон|ика́ть, -и́кнуть в + *a.*; взл|а́мывать, -ома́ть

hacker /ˈhækə(r)/ *n.* (comput.) ха́кер

hackneyed /ˈhæknɪd/ *adj.* изби́тый

had /hæd/ *past and p.p. of* ▶ **have**

haddock /ˈhædək/ *n.* (*pl.* ~) пи́кша

hadn't /ˈhæd(ə)nt/ *neg. of* ▶ **had**

haematologist /hiːməˈtɒlədʒɪst/ (AmE **hematologist**) *n.* гемато́лог

haematology /hiːməˈtɒlədʒɪ/ (AmE **hematology**) *n.* гематоло́гия

haemoglobin /hiːməˈɡləʊbɪn/ (AmE **hemoglobin**) *n.* гемоглоби́н

haemophilia /hiːməˈfɪlɪə/ (AmE **hemophilia**) *n.* гемофили́я

haemophiliac /hiːməˈfɪlɪæk/ (AmE **hemophiliac**) *n.* гемофи́лик

haemorrhage /ˈhemərɪdʒ/ (AmE **hemorrhage**) *n.* кровоизлия́ние; (fig.) отто́к

haemorrhoids /ˈhemərɔɪdz/ (AmE **hemorrhoids**) *n. pl.* геморро́й

hag /hæɡ/ *n.* карга́, ве́дьма (usu. fig.)

haggard /ˈhæɡəd/ *adj.* измождённый

haggle /ˈhæɡ(ə)l/ *v.i.* торгова́ться (*impf.*)

hail[1] /heɪl/ *n.* (frozen rain) град
• *v.i.*: **it is** ~**ing** идёт град
■ ~**stone** *n.* гра́дина; ~**storm** *n.* гроза́ с гра́дом

hail[2] /heɪl/ *v.t.* **1** (acclaim) провозгла|ша́ть, -си́ть; (praise) превозноси́ть (*impf.*) **2** (summon) подз|ыва́ть, -озва́ть; **he** ~**ed a taxi** он подозва́л такси́

✓ **hair** /heə(r)/ *n.* **1** (single strand) во́лос, волосо́к **2** (head of ~) во́лосы (*m. pl.*) **3** (of animals) шерсть, щети́на
■ ~**brush** *n.* щётка для воло́с; ~**cut** *n.*

стри́жка; **have a ~cut** стри́чься, по-; **~do** *n.*
(infml) причёска; **~dresser** *n.* парикма́хер;
~dresser's *n.* (shop, salon) парикма́херская;
~dryer *n.* фен; **~grip** *n.* (BrE) зако́лка;
~pin *n.* шпи́лька; **~pin bend** (BrE), **turn** (AmE)
круто́й поворо́т; **~raising** *adj.* жу́ткий;
~spray *n.* лак для воло́с; **~style** *n.* причёска

hairy /'heəгɪ/ *adj.* (**hairier**, **hairiest**)
волоса́тый

Haiti /'heɪtɪ/ *n.* Гаи́ти (*m. indecl.*)

hake /heɪk/ *n.* хек

halcyon /'hælsɪən/ *attr. adj.* ти́хий,
безмяте́жный

hale /heɪl/ *adj.* кре́пкий; **~ and hearty**
кре́пкий и бо́дрый

✒ **half** /hɑːf/ *n.* (*pl.* **halves**) **1** (one of two equal
parts) полови́на; **one and a ~** полтора́; **he
cut the loaf in ~** он разре́зал хлеб попола́м;
~ an hour полчаса́; **~ past two** полови́на
тре́тьего; **they agreed to go halves** они́
согласи́лись подели́ть попола́м **2** (of a game)
перио́д, тайм
● *adv.*: **~ asleep** со́нный; **~ dead** полуживо́й;
~ as much вдво́е ме́ньше; **~ as much again** в
полтора́ ра́за бо́льше; **I ~ expected it** я почти́
ждал э́того
■ **~back** *n.* полузащи́тник; **~-brother**
n. (having same father) единокро́вный брат;
(having same mother) единоутро́бный брат;
~-hearted *adj.* нереши́тельный; без
энтузиа́зма; **~-hour** *n.* (*also* **an hour**)
полчаса́; **every ~-hour** ка́ждые полчаса́; **~
mast** *n.*: **at ~ mast** приспу́щенный (*флаг*);
~-moon *n.* полуме́сяц; **~-pound** *n. also* **~
a pound** полфу́нта; **~-price** *adj.* полцены́;
at ~-price за полцены́; **~-sister** *n.* (having
same father) единокро́вная сестра́; (having same
mother) единоутро́бная сестра́; **~-term** *n.*:
~-term (holiday) (BrE) кани́кулы (*pl., g.* —) в
середи́не триме́стра; **~-time** *n.* коне́ц та́йма;
the teams changed ends at ~-time кома́нды
поменя́лись места́ми по́сле пе́рвого та́йма;
~way *adj.* лежа́щий на полпути́; **~way
house** (fig.) компроми́сс; полуме́ра ● *adv.* на
полпути́; **we met ~way from the station** мы
встре́тились на полпути́ от вокза́ла

halibut /'hælɪbət/ *n.* (*pl.* **~**) па́лтус

halitosis /ˌhælɪ'təʊsɪs/ *n.* дурно́й за́пах изо рта́

✒ **hall** /hɔːl/ *n.* **1** (place of assembly) зал **2** (lobby)
(*also* **hallway**) пере́дняя, холл; **~ of
residence** (BrE) общежи́тие
■ **~mark** *n.* проби́рное клеймо́; (fig.)
отличи́тельный при́знак ● *v.t.* ста́вить, по-
про́бу на + *p.*

hallelujah /ˌhælɪ'luːjə/ *n. & int.* аллилу́йя

hallo *see* ▸ **hello**

Halloween /ˌhæləʊ'iːn/ *n.* кану́н Дня Всех
Святы́х (*31 октября́*)

hallucination /həˌluːsɪ'neɪʃ(ə)n/ *n.*
галлюцина́ция

halo /'heɪləʊ/ *n.* (*pl.* **~es** *or* **~s**) (round saint's
head) нимб; (fig.) орео́л

✒ ключева́я ле́ксика

halt /hɒlt/ *n.* остано́вка; **come to a ~**
остан|а́вливаться, -ови́ться; **call a ~** де́лать,
с- прива́л; (fig.) дава́ть, -ть отбо́й
● *v.t.* остан|а́вливать, -ови́ть
● *v.i.* (stop) остан|а́вливаться, -ови́ться; **~!
who goes there?** стой! кто идёт?

halter /'hɒltə(r)/ *n.* (for a horse) по́вод

halve /hɑːv/ *v.t.* (divide in two) дели́ть,
раз- попола́м; (reduce by half) ум|еньша́ть,
-е́ньшить (*or* сокра|ща́ть, -ти́ть) наполови́ну

halves /hɑːvz/ *pl. of* ▸ **half**

ham /hæm/ *n.* ветчина́

hamburger /'hæmbɜːgə(r)/ *n.* **1** га́мбургер
2 (AmE, minced beef) говя́жий фарш

hamlet /'hæmlɪt/ *n.* дереву́шка

hammer /'hæmə(r)/ *n.* молото́к
● *v.t.* (beat) удар|я́ть, -и́ть; (defeat) бить, по-;
~ in вби|ва́ть, -ть; **we ~ed out a plan** мы
разрабо́тали план
● *v.i.* стуча́ть (*impf.*); колоти́ть (*impf.*);
someone was ~ing on the door кто́-то
колоти́л в дверь

hammock /'hæmək/ *n.* гама́к

hamper[1] /'hæmpə(r)/ *n.* корзи́на с кры́шкой

hamper[2] /'hæmpə(r)/ *v.t.* меша́ть, по- + *d.*;
стесня́ть (*impf.*)

hamster /'hæmstə(r)/ *n.* хомя́к

✒ **hand** /hænd/ *n.* **1** (lit., fig.) рука́, кисть;
~ luggage (BrE), **baggage** (AmE) ручна́я
кладь; **I shall have my ~s full next week** на
сле́дующей неде́ле я бу́ду о́чень за́нят;
~ in ~ (lit., fig.) рука́ об ру́ку; (lit. only):
walk ~ in ~ ходи́ть (*impf.*) (держа́сь) за́
руку **2** (vbl. phrr.): **let me give, lend you a
~!** дава́йте я вам помогу́!; **she had a ~ in
his downfall** в его́ паде́нии она́ сыгра́ла не
после́днюю роль; **they were holding ~s**
они́ держа́лись за́ руки; **try one's ~ at sth**
про́бовать, по- себя́ в чём-н. **3** (prepositional
phrr.): **you should take that child in ~** вы
должны́ взять э́того ребёнка на́ руки; **on ~**
в нали́чии; в распоряже́нии; **he has a sick
father on his ~s** у него́ на рука́х больно́й
оте́ц; **things are getting out of ~** собы́тия
выхо́дят из-под контро́ля **4** (member of crew
or team): **all ~s on deck!** все наве́рх!; **farm ~**
рабо́тник на фе́рме **5** (side): **on the one ~ ...,
on the other ~** (fig.) с одно́й стороны́..., с
друго́й стороны́ **6** (of a clock) стре́лка **7** (set
of cards) ка́рты (*f. pl.*); **show one's ~** (fig.)
раскр|ыва́ть, -ы́ть ка́рты
● *v.t.* перед|ава́ть, -а́ть; **~ me the paper,
please** переда́йте мне газе́ту, пожа́луйста
● with *advs.*: **he ~ed back the money** он
верну́л де́ньги; **the custom was ~ed down**
э́тот обы́чай передава́лся из поколе́ния в
поколе́ние; **will you ~ in your resignation?**
вы подади́те заявле́ние об ухо́де?; **the
teacher ~ed out the books** учи́тель разда́л
кни́ги; **the king ~ed over his authority
to parliament** коро́ль пе́редал власть
парла́менту
■ **~bag** *n.* (BrE) су́мочка, да́мская су́мка;
~ball *n.* (game) ручно́й мяч, гандбо́л;
~book *n.* посо́бие; руково́дство; **~brake**

n. ручно́й то́рмоз; ~**cuff** *n.* нару́чник ● *v.t.*
над|ева́ть, -е́ть нару́чники + *d.* or на + *a.*;
~ **grenade** *n.* ручна́я грана́та; ~**made**
adj. сде́ланный вручну́ю; ручно́й рабо́ты;
~**out** *n.* (gift) подая́ние; ми́лостыня; (for
publicity) рекла́мный листо́к; ~**picked**
adj. тща́тельно ото́бранный; ~**set** *n.*
(telephone) тру́бка; ~**s-free** *adj.* (device etc.)
оставля́ющий ру́ки свобо́дными (*прибор и
т. п.*); ~**shake** *n.* рукопожа́тие; ~**s-on** *adj.*
практи́ческий, свя́занный с жи́знью; ~**s-on**
experience практи́ческий о́пыт; ~**stand**
n. сто́йка на рука́х; ~**writing** *n.* по́черк;
~**written** *adj.* напи́санный от руки́

handful /'hændfʊl/ *n.* го́рсть; (infml): **this**
child is a ~ с э́тим ребёнком хлопо́т не
оберёшься

handicap /'hændɪkæp/ *n.* поме́ха,
препя́тствие
　● *v.t.* (**handicapped, handicapping**)
чини́ть (*impf.*) препя́тствия (*кому*); ~**ped**
person (sometimes offens.) (physically) инвали́д;
челове́к с ограни́ченными возмо́жностями;
(mentally) у́мственно отста́лый челове́к

handicraft /'hændɪkrɑːft/ *n.* ремесло́, ручна́я
рабо́та

handiwork /'hændɪwɜːk/ *n.* ручна́я рабо́та

handkerchie|f /'hæŋkətʃiːf/ *n.* (*pl.* ~**fs** or
~**ves**) носово́й плато́к

⚔ **handle** /'hænd(ə)l/ *n.* (of door, cup) ру́чка; (of
sword, tool) рукоя́ть, рукоя́тка
　● *v.t.* **1** (take or hold in the hands) тро́гать (*impf.*)
　2 (manage, deal with, treat) обраща́ться (*impf.*)
с + *i.*; обходи́ться (*impf.*) с + *i.*; спр|авля́ться,
-а́виться с + *i.*; **he** ~**d the affair very well**
он прекра́сно спра́вился с э́тим де́лом;
the officer ~**d his men well** офице́р уме́ло
кома́ндовал свои́ми солда́тами
　■ ~**bars** *n. pl.* (of a bicycle) руль (*m.*)

handsome /'hænsəm/ *adj.* (**handsomer,**
handsomest) краси́вый

handy /'hændɪ/ *adj.* (**handier, handiest**)
　1 (to hand, available) (име́ющийся) под руко́й
　2 (convenient) удо́бный, (infml) сподру́чный;
it may come in ~ э́то мо́жет пригоди́ться
　■ ~**man** *n.* разнорабо́чий

⚔ **hang** /hæŋ/ *n.*: **I can't get the** ~ **of this**
machine (or of his argument) я не могу́
разобра́ться в э́той маши́не (or в его́
до́водах)
　● *v.t.* (*past and p.p.* **hung**, *except in sense 3:*
past and p.p. **hanged**) **1** (suspend) ве́шать,
пове́сить **2** (decorate) разве́|шивать, -сить
　3 (execute by ~ing) ве́шать, пове́сить; **Judas**
~**ed himself** Иу́да пове́сился
　● *v.i.* (*past and p.p.* **hung**, *except in*
sense 3: past and p.p. **hanged**) **1** (be
suspended) висе́ть (*impf.*); (fig.): **the threat of**
dismissal hung over him над ним нави́сла
угро́за увольне́ния **2** (lean) све́|шиваться,
-ситься; **don't** ~ **out of the window** не
высо́вывайтесь из окна́ **3** (be executed): **he**
will ~ **for it** он попадёт за э́то на ви́селицу
　4 (loiter, stay close): **he hung round the door** он
задержа́лся у две́ри

□ ~ **about** *v.i.* (BrE) = hang around

□ ~ **around** *v.i.* болта́ться (*impf.*); шата́ться
(*impf.*)

□ ~ **back** *v.i.* отст|ава́ть, -а́ть

□ ~ **on** *v.i.* (cling) держа́ться (*impf.*) (**to:** за +
a.); (persist) упо́рствовать (*impf.*); ~ **on!** (infml)
погоди́те!

□ ~ **out** *v.t.* выве́шивать, вы́весить; **she hung**
out the washing она́ вы́весила бельё
　● *v.i.* (protrude): **his shirt was** ~**ing out**
руба́шка вы́лезла у него́ из брюк; (infml,
relax) тусова́ться (*impf.*)

□ ~ **together** *v.i.* (make sense): **the story doesn't**
~ **together** ≈ концы́ с конца́ми не схо́дятся

□ ~ **up** *v.t.* (fasten on peg, nail, etc.) ве́шать,
пове́сить
　● *v.i.* (end telephone conversation) ве́шать,
пове́сить тру́бку

　■ ~**-glider** *n.* (craft) дельтапла́н; ~**-gliding**
n. дельтапланери́зм; ~**over** *n.* (from drink)
похме́лье, перепо́й; ~**-up** *n.* (infml) ко́мплекс

hangar /'hæŋə(r)/ *n.* анга́р

hanger /'hæŋə(r)/ *n.* (for clothes) ве́шалка
　■ ~**-on** *n.* приспе́шник

hanging /'hæŋɪŋ/ *n.* **1** висе́ние; (execution)
пове́шение **2** (*in pl.*) (tapestry etc.) портье́ры
(*f. pl.*)

hanker /'hæŋkə(r)/ *v.i.*: ~ **after/for** жа́ждать
+ *g.*

hanky /'hæŋkɪ/ *n.* (infml) = handkerchief

Hanoi /hæ'nɔɪ/ *n.* Хано́й

haphazard /hæp'hæzəd/ *adj.* случа́йный

hapless /'hæplɪs/ *adj.* несча́стный;
злополу́чный

⚔ **happen** /'hæp(ə)n/ *v.i.* **1** (occur) случ|а́ться,
-и́ться; прои|сходи́ть, -зойти́; получ|а́ться,
-и́ться; **I hope nothing has** ~**ed to him**
наде́юсь, с ним ничего́ не случи́лось
　2 (chance): **as it** ~**s I can help you** в да́нном
слу́чае я могу́ вам помо́чь; **we** ~**ed to meet**
мы неожи́данно/случа́йно встре́тились

happily /'hæpɪlɪ/ *adv.* **1** (contentedly) сча́стливо
　2 (fortunately) к сча́стью **3** (gladly) с
удово́льствием

happiness /'hæpɪnɪs/ *n.* сча́стье

⚔ **happy** /'hæpɪ/ *adj.* (**happier, happiest**)
　1 (contented) счастли́вый **2** (fortunate)
счастли́вый, уда́чливый; ~ **birthday!** с днём
рожде́ния!; ~ **Christmas!** с Рождество́м
(Христо́вым)! **3** (pleased) дово́льный (*чем*);
we shall be ~ **to come** мы с удово́льствием
придём
　■ ~**-go-lucky** *adj.* беззабо́тный; беспе́чный; ~
medium *n.* золота́я середи́на

harangue /hə'ræŋ/ *v.t.* увещева́ть (*impf.*)

harass /'hærəs/ *v.t.* изв|оди́ть, -ести́

harassment /'hærəsmənt/ *n.* тра́вля;
изма́тывание; **sexual** ~ сексуа́льное
домога́тельство

harbinger /'hɑːbɪndʒə(r)/ *n.* предве́стник

harbour /'hɑːbə(r)/ (AmE **harbor**) *n.* га́вань,
порт
　● *v.t.* да|ва́ть, -ть убе́жище + *d.*; ~**ing a**
criminal укрыва́тельство престу́пника; (fig.):

h

h

I ~ no grudge against him я не держу́ на
него́ зла

⚥ **hard** /hɑːd/ adj. **1** (firm, solid) твёрдый;
про́чный; ~ **core** (fig., nucleus of resistance etc.)
ядро́; ~ **and fast rules** жёсткие пра́вила
2 (difficult) тру́дный; **bargains are ~ to come
by** достава́ть ве́щи по невысо́ким це́нам
непро́сто **3** (unsentimental, relentless): **don't
be too ~ on her!** не бу́дьте к ней сли́шком
стро́ги! **4** (vigorous, harsh): ~ **times** тяжёлые
времена́; **it's a ~ life** жизнь трудна́; тру́дно
живётся; ~ **liquor** кре́пкие напи́тки; ~
drugs сильноде́йствующие нарко́тики; ~
water жёсткая вода́ **5** (intensive): ~ **work**
тяжёлая/тру́дная рабо́та **6** (infml, unfortunate):
~ **luck!** (BrE) не везёт!; **his parents are ~
up** его́ роди́тели — лю́ди небога́тые **7**: ~
of hearing глухова́тый; туго́й на́ ухо **8** (of
money): ~ **cash** нали́чность; нали́чные
(де́ньги); ~ **currency** твёрдая валю́та
● adv. **1** (solid): **the ground froze ~** земля́
промёрзла **2** (with force): **it is raining ~** идёт
си́льный дождь **3** (persistently): **work ~**
(study) усе́рдно занима́ться (impf.); **I tried
~ to make him understand** я изо всех сил
стара́лся разъясни́ть ему́ (что)
■ ~**back** n. (book) кни́га в жёстком переплёте
or в твёрдой обло́жке; ~**board** n. древе́сно-
волокни́стая плита́, ДВП; ~**-boiled**
adj.: **a ~-boiled egg** яйцо́ вкруту́ю; ~
copy n. (comput.) распеча́тка; ~**-core**
adj. (criminal) закоренéлый; (pornography)
открове́нный; жёсткий; ~ **disk** n.
(comput.) жёсткий диск; ~**-earned** adj.
зарабо́танный тяжёлым трудо́м; ~ **hat** n.
защи́тный шлем; ~**-headed** adj. тре́звый;
практи́чный; ~**-hearted** adj. бессерде́чный;
неумоли́мый; ~**-hitting** adj. (e.g. speech)
жёсткий; бескомпроми́ссный; ~ **labour**
n. исправи́тельно-трудовы́е рабо́ты; (fig.)
ка́торга; ~**liner** n. сторо́нник жёсткой ли́нии;
~**-nosed** adj. упря́мый, непримири́мый;
~**-pressed** adj. находя́щийся в тру́дном
положе́нии; ~**ware** n. скобяны́е изде́лия/
това́ры; (mil., infml) те́хника; (comput.)
аппарату́ра; ~**-wearing** adj. но́ский;
~**-working** adj. работя́щий; (at studies)
уси́дчивый

harden /ˈhɑːd(ə)n/ v.t. (make hard) де́лать,
с- твёрдым; (fig.) ожесточ|а́ть, -и́ть; **he
~ed his heart** его́ се́рдце ожесточи́лось;
a ~ed criminal закоренéлый престу́пник;
рециди́вист
● v.i. тверде́ть, за-; (fig.): **opinion ~ed** мне́ние
укрепи́лось

⚥ **hardly** /ˈhɑːdlɪ/ adv. **1** (with difficulty) с трудо́м
2 (only just) едва́; **I had ~ sat down when
the phone rang** едва́ я сел, как зазвони́л
телефо́н **3** (not reasonably) вряд ли; **you
can ~ expect her to agree** вы едва́ (or
вряд) ли мо́жете рассчи́тывать на её
согла́сие **4** (almost not): ~ **ever** почти́
никогда́; **I ~ know him** я его́ почти́ не зна́ю;
there's ~ any money left де́нег почти́ не

оста́лось

hardship /ˈhɑːdʃɪp/ n. невзго́ды (f. pl.)
hardy /ˈhɑːdɪ/ adj. (**hardier**, **hardiest**)
закалённый; (of plants) морозосто́йкий
hare /heə(r)/ n. за́яц
harem /ˈhɑːriːm/ n. гаре́м
haricot /ˈhærɪkəʊ/ n. (in full ~ **bean**) фасо́ль
(обыкнове́нная) (collect.)
harm /hɑːm/ n. вред, уще́рб; **there's no ~ (in)
trying** попы́тка не пы́тка
● v.t. вреди́ть, по- + d.; причин|я́ть, -и́ть (or
нан|оси́ть, -ести́) вред + d.
harmful /ˈhɑːmfʊl/ adj. вре́дный
harmless /ˈhɑːmlɪs/ adj. (not injurious)
безвре́дный; (innocent) безоби́дный
harmonic /hɑːˈmɒnɪk/ adj. гармони́ческий
harmonica /hɑːˈmɒnɪkə/ n. губна́я
гармо́ника
harmonious /hɑːˈməʊnɪəs/ adj. (lit., fig.)
гармони́чный
harmonize /ˈhɑːmənaɪz/ v.t. (mus.)
гармонизи́ровать (impf., pf.)
harmony /ˈhɑːmənɪ/ n. гармо́ния
harness /ˈhɑːnɪs/ n. у́пряжь
● v.t. запр|яга́ть, -я́чь; (fig., natural forces)
обу́зд|ывать, -а́ть; (energy etc.) мобилизова́ть
(impf., pf.)
harp /hɑːp/ n. а́рфа
● v.i. (fig.): ~ **on sth** тверди́ть (impf.) о чём-н.
harpist /ˈhɑːpɪst/ n. арфи́ст (-ка)
harpoon /hɑːˈpuːn/ n. гарпу́н
harpsichord /ˈhɑːpsɪkɔːd/ n. клавеси́н
harrowing /ˈhærəʊɪŋ/ adj.: **a ~ tale**
душераздира́ющая исто́рия
harsh /hɑːʃ/ adj. **1** (rough) гру́бый, ре́зкий
2 (severe) суро́вый
hart /hɑːt/ n. саме́ц оле́ня
harvest /ˈhɑːvɪst/ n. (yield) урожа́й; (process)
жа́тва, сбор урожа́я
● v.t. соб|ира́ть, -ра́ть; жать, с-
■ ~ **festival** n. пра́здник урожа́я
has /hæz/ 3rd pers. sg. pres. of ▶ **have**
hash[1] /hæʃ/ n.: (fig.): **he made a ~ of it** он
загуби́л всё де́ло
hash[2] /hæʃ/ n. (also ~ **sign**) си́мвол но́мера
(#), решётка, знак решётки
■ ~**tag** n. хеште́г
hashish /ˈhæʃiːʃ/ n. гаши́ш
hasn't /ˈhæz(ə)nt/ neg. of ▶ **has**
hassle /ˈhæs(ə)l/ n. (infml) каните́ль
hassock /ˈhæsək/ n. **1** (BrE) поду́шечка для
коленопреклоне́ния **2** (AmE) пуф
haste /heɪst/ n. спе́шка
hasten /ˈheɪs(ə)n/ v.t. (hurry) торопи́ть, по-
● v.i. торопи́ться, по-; спеши́ть (impf.); **I ~ to
add that ...** спешу́ доба́вить, что...
hasty /ˈheɪstɪ/ adj. (**hastier**, **hastiest**)
(hurried) поспе́шный; (rash, ill-considered)
поспе́шный
hat /hæt/ n. шля́па; (fur, knitted) ша́пка
■ ~**-trick** n.: **he scored a ~-trick** (fig., of footballer
etc.) он сде́лал хет-три́к

hatch¹ /hætʃ/ n. (opening) люк; (cover) крышка
■ ~**back** n. хетчбэк (*автомобиль с открывающейся вверх задней дверью*)

hatch² /hætʃ/ v.t. (egg) высиживать, высидеть; (fig., plot) вынашивать, выносить; зам|ышлять, -ыслить
● v.i. (*also* ~ **out**) (of bird) вылупляться, вылупиться

hatchet /'hætʃɪt/ n. топор, топорик

☞ **hate** /heɪt/ n. ненависть
● v.t. ненавидеть (*impf.*); (dislike strongly) ненавидеть (*impf.*); I ~ **getting up early** я ненавижу рано вставать

hateful /'heɪtfʊl/ adj. ненавистный

hatred /'heɪtrɪd/ n. ненависть (**for:** к + d.)

haughty /'hɔ:tɪ/ adj. (**haughtier, haughtiest**) высокомерный

haul /hɔ:l/ n. **1**: **a long** ~ (fig.) долгое дело **2**: **a** ~ **of fish** улов; (fig., booty) добыча, улов
● v.t. & i. тянуть (*impf.*); тащить (*impf.*)

haulage /'hɔ:lɪdʒ/ n. транспортировка

haulier /'hɔ:lɪə(r)/ n. (BrE) перевозчик

haunch /hɔ:ntʃ/ n. бедро

haunt /hɔ:nt/ n. излюбленное место
● v.t. неотступно преследовать (*impf.*); a ~**ed house** дом с привидениями; a ~**ing melody** навязчивая мелодия

☞ **have** /hæv/ n.: **the** ~**s and the** ~**-nots** имущие и неимущие
● v.t. (*3rd pers. sg. pres.* **has**, *past and p.p.* **had**) **1** иметь; (possess) обладать + i.; (often expr. by) y + g.; **she has blue eyes** y неё голубые глаза; I ~ **no doubt** y меня нет сомнений; **he had the courage to refuse** y него хватило мужества отказаться; I ~ **no idea** понятия не имею **2** (contain): **June has 30 days** в июне 30 дней **3** (experience): ~ **a good time!** желаю вам хорошо провести время!; (suffer from): **he has a cold** y него насморк **4** (bear) родить (*impf., pf.*); **she is having a baby in May** в мае y неё родится ребёнок **5** (receive, obtain): **we had news of him yesterday** вчера мы получили известие о нём; (tolerate): I **won't** ~ **it!** этого я не потерплю! **6** (show, exercise): ~ **pity on me** сжальтесь надо мной; **he had no mercy on** он был безжалостен **7** (undertake, perform): ~ **a game of tennis** сыграть (*pf.*) в теннис; ~ **a go** (infml) пытаться, по- **8** (partake of, enjoy): ~ **dinner** ужинать (*impf.*) **9** (infml, swindle): **you've been had** вас провели/надули **10** (with inf., be obliged to, need to): I ~ **to finish by tomorrow** я должен закончить к завтрашнему дню; I ~ **to sit down** мне надо сесть; (be obliged) быть обязанным; **you don't** ~ **to go** вы не обязаны идти; (having no choice) быть вынужденным; I **had to accept the invitation** я был вынужден принять приглашение **11** (phrr. with it): **let him** ~ **it!** (sl., attack him) дай ему хорошенько!; покажи ему!; **he has it in for me** (infml) y него зуб на меня; ~ **it out with sb** объясн|яться, -иться с кем-н.
● *with advs.*: **can I** ~ **my watch back?** могу я получить свои часы обратно?; **he had his**

coat off он был без пальто; **she had a red dress on** на ней было красное платье; ~ **sb on** (BrE) разыгр|ывать, -ать кого-н.; **he was had up for speeding** (BrE, infml) его задержали за превышение скорости
● *miscellaneous phrr.*: **you had better/best give the book back** вам не мешало бы вернуть книгу; **it has nothing to do with you** к вам это (никоим образом) не относится; вас это совершенно не касается; I'll ~ **nothing to do with it** я не желаю иметь никакого отношения к этому

haven /'heɪv(ə)n/ n. гавань; (fig.) приют

haven't /'hæv(ə)nt/ neg. of ▶ have

haversack /'hævəsæk/ n. рюкзак

havoc /'hævək/ n. (destruction) разгром; (fig.): **play** ~ **with** вн|осить, -ести беспорядок/хаос в + a.

Hawaii /hə'waɪɪ/ n. Гавайи (m. pl.)

hawk /hɔ:k/ n. ястреб (also fig., pol.)

hawthorn /'hɔ:θɔ:n/ n. боярышник

hay /heɪ/ n. сено
■ ~ **fever** n. поллиноз, аллергия на пыльцу растений; ~**stack** n. стог сена; ~**wire** n. (sl.): **everything went** ~**wire** всё пошло наперекосяк

hazard /'hæzəd/ n. опасность
● v.t. отваж|иваться, -иться + inf. or на + a.; **he** ~**ed a remark** он отважился высказать замечание
■ ~ **lights** n. pl. аварийные фары (*f. pl.*)

hazardous /'hæzədəs/ adj. рискованный
■ ~ **waste** n. вредные отходы m. pl.

haze /heɪz/ n. дымка

hazel /'heɪz(ə)l/ n. (tree) лесной орех; (colour) ореховый цвет; ~ **eyes** карие глаза
■ ~**nut** n. лесной орех

hazy /'heɪzɪ/ adj. (**hazier, haziest**) подёрнутый дымкой; (fig.) смутный, туманный

HDTV abbr. (*of* **high-definition television**) ТВЧ (телевидение высокой чёткости)

☞ **he** /hi:/ pers. pron. (*obj.* **him**) он; тот

☞ **head** /hed/ n. **1** голова; **from** ~ **to foot, toe** с головы до ног; I **cannot make** ~ **or tail of it** я не могу в этом разобраться; **this is all completely over my** ~ всё это выше моего понимания; **shake one's** ~ качать, по- головой; a ~ **cold** насморк **2** (mind, brain): **he has a good** ~ **for figures** он хорошо считает; **he's off his** ~ он спятил (infml); (faculties): **the wine went to his** ~ вино ударило ему в голову; **success went to his** ~ успех вскружил ему голову; (balance, composure): **he lost/kept his** ~ он потерял голову / он не терял головы **3** (on a coin): ~**s or tails?** орёл или решка? **4** (unit): **£5 a** ~ пять фунтов с каждого **5** (upper or principal end): **the** ~ **of the table** во главе стола **6** (principal member) глава (*c.g.*), старший; ~ **of state** глава государства; ~ **of the family** глава семьи; (*attr.*) главный; ~ **office** главная контора, центр **7** (culmination): **to come to a** ~ назр|евать, -еть
● v.t. **1** (direct): **he is** ~**ed for home** он

направля́ется домо́й **2** (strike with head): he ~ed the ball into the net он заби́л мяч в се́тку голово́й **3** (be in charge of) возглавля́ть, -а́вить; he ~ed the team он возглавля́л кома́нду
● *v.i.* (move, steer) направля́ться, -а́виться; (fig.): he is ~ing for disaster он пло́хо ко́нчит
■ ~ache *n.* головна́я боль; I have a ~ache у меня́ боли́т голова́; ~band *n.* головна́я повя́зка; ~dress *n.* (замыслова́тый/ экзоти́ческий) головно́й убо́р; ~ first *n. pl.* голово́й вперёд; ~hunter *n.* (fig.) челове́к, перема́нивающий специали́стов из други́х организа́ций; ~lamp, ~light *nn.* фа́ра; ~line *n.* заголо́вок; (*in pl.*) (гла́вные) но́вости дня; he hit the ~lines его́ и́мя не сходи́ло с пе́рвых поло́с газе́т; ~long *adv.* голово́й вперёд; (in a rush) стремгла́в; ~master, ~mistress *nn.* (BrE) дире́ктор шко́лы; ~-on *adj.* лобово́й, встре́чный; a ~-on collision лобово́е столкнове́ние; ~phone *n.* нау́шник; ~quarters *n.* штаб-кварти́ра; (mil.) штаб, ста́вка; ~rest *n.* подголо́вник; ~scarf *n.* косы́нка; ~set *n.* (pair of ~phones) нау́шники (*m. pl.*); ~stone *n.* (tombstone) надгро́бный ка́мень; ~strong *adj.* своево́льный, упря́мый; ~ teacher *n.* дире́ктор шко́лы; ~way *n.* продвиже́ние вперёд; (fig.): we are not making much ~way мы продвига́емся сли́шком ме́дленно

headed /ˈhedɪd/ *adj.*: ~ notepaper (of organization) ге́рбовая бума́га; (of person) именна́я бума́га

header /ˈhedə(r)/ *n.* **1** (in soccer) уда́р голово́й **2** (line of text) колонти́тул

heading /ˈhedɪŋ/ *n.* (title) заголо́вок, загла́вие; (section) ру́брика

heady /ˈhedɪ/ *adj.* (**headier, headiest**) хмельно́й; (also fig.) пьяня́щий

heal /hiːl/ *v.t.* (person) исцел|я́ть, -и́ть; (wound) зале́ч|ивать, -и́ть
● *v.i.* заж|ива́ть, -и́ть

healer /ˈhiːlə(r)/ *n.* ле́карь (*m.*)

healing /ˈhiːlɪŋ/ *n.* лече́ние

♂ **health** /helθ/ *n.* здоро́вье; in good ~ здоро́вый
■ ~ centre *n.* поликли́ника; ~ food *n.* натура́льная пи́ща; ~ insurance *n.* медици́нская страхо́вка; ~ service *n.* слу́жба здравоохране́ния, здравоохране́ние

♂ **healthy** /ˈhelθɪ/ *adj.* (**healthier, healthiest**) здоро́вый

heap /hiːp/ *n.* **1** (pile) ку́ча, гру́да **2** (*in pl.*) (infml, large quantity) ма́сса, ку́ча, у́йма; he has ~s of money у него́ у́йма/ку́ча де́нег
● *v.t.*: a ~ed (BrE), heaping (AmE) spoonful ло́жка с ве́рхом; they ~ed honours on him его́ осыпа́ли поче́стями

♂ **hear** /hɪə(r)/ *v.t. & i.* (*past and p.p.* **heard** /hɜːd/) **1** (perceive with ear) слы́шать, у-; I can't ~ a word я не слы́шу ни сло́ва; I ~d him shout я услы́шал, как он закрича́л; I ~ someone coming я слы́шу, что кто-то идёт

♂ ключева́я ле́ксика

or (чьи́-то) шаги́ **2** (listen to): ~ evidence слу́шать, за- показа́ния свиде́телей; his prayer was ~d его́ моли́твы бы́ли услы́шаны; I won't ~ of it! я и слы́шать об э́том не хочу́! **3** (learn) слы́шать, у-; have you ~d the news? вы слы́шали но́вости?; have you ~d from your brother? что слы́шно от ва́шего бра́та?; I've never ~d of him я о нём никогда́ не слы́шал **4**: ~!, ~! пра́вильно!; ве́рно ска́зано!
■ ~say *n.* слу́хи (*m. pl.*)

♂ **hearing** /ˈhɪərɪŋ/ *n.* **1** (perception) слух **2** (law) слу́шание
■ ~ aid *n.* слухово́й аппара́т

hearse /hɜːs/ *n.* катафа́лк

♂ **heart** /hɑːt/ *n.* **1** (organ) се́рдце **2** (soul; seat of emotions) се́рдце, душа́; he had set his ~ on winning он стра́стно жела́л вы́играть; don't take it to ~ не принима́йте э́то бли́зко к се́рдцу; (enthusiasm): his ~ is not in his work у него́ душа́ не лежи́т к рабо́те; (courage): he lost ~ он пал ду́хом; take ~! не па́дайте ду́хом!; (memory): I learnt it by ~ я вы́учил э́то наизу́сть **3** (centre) середи́на, сердцеви́на; this book gets to the ~ of the matter э́та кни́га затра́гивает са́мую суть де́ла **4** (*in pl.*) (cards) че́рв|и (-е́й)
■ ~ache *n.* серде́чная боль; ~ attack *n.* серде́чный при́ступ; инфа́ркт; ~beat *n.* сердцебие́ние; ~breaking *adj.* душераздира́ющий; ~broken *adj.* с разби́тым се́рдцем; ~burn *n.* изжо́га; ~ disease *n.* боле́знь се́рдца; ~ failure *n.* разры́в се́рдца; ~felt *adj.* душе́вный, глубоко́ прочу́вствованный; ~-throb *n.* (infml) люби́мец; ~-to-~ *adj.*: a ~-to-~ talk разгово́р по душа́м; ~ transplant *n.* переса́дка се́рдца

hearten /ˈhɑːt(ə)n/ *v.t.* ободр|я́ть, -и́ть

hearth /hɑːθ/ *n.* оча́г

heartless /ˈhɑːtlɪs/ *adj.* бессерде́чный

hearty /ˈhɑːtɪ/ *adj.* (**heartier, heartiest**) **1** (cordial) серде́чный **2** (healthy): a ~ appetite прекра́сный аппети́т **3** (cheerful) весёлый

♂ **heat** /hiːt/ *n.* **1** (hotness) жара́; (warmth) тепло́ **2** (warmth of feeling) теплота́; (passion) горя́чность; in the ~ of the moment сгоряча́ **3** (in running) забе́г; (in horse racing) зае́зд; (in swimming) заплы́в **4** (of animals) те́чка; our dog is on ~ у на́шей соба́ки те́чка
● *v.t.* **1** (raise temperature of) нагр|ева́ть, -е́ть; the potatoes were ~ed up карто́шку разогре́ли; ~ed swimming pool бассе́йн с подогре́вом **2**: a ~ed argument жа́ркий спор
■ ~stroke *n.* теплово́й уда́р; ~wave *n.* полоса́/пери́од си́льной жары́

heater /ˈhiːtə(r)/ *n.* обогрева́тель (*m.*)

heath /hiːθ/ *n.* **1** (BrE, waste land) пу́стошь **2** (shrub) ве́реск

heathen /ˈhiːð(ə)n/ *n.* язы́чник
● *adj.* язы́ческий

heather /ˈheðə(r)/ *n.* ве́реск

heating /ˈhiːtɪŋ/ *n.* обогрева́ние, отопле́ние

heave /hi:v/ *v.t.* (*past and p.p.* **heaved**) (lift) подн|има́ть, -я́ть; (throw) бр|оса́ть, -о́сить; ∼ a sigh (тяжело́) вздыха́ть, -охну́ть
● *v.i.* (*past and p.p.* **heaved** or esp. naut., **hove**) **1** (pull): they ∼d on the rope они́ выбрали кана́т **2** (retch) ту́житься (*impf.*) (при рво́те) **3** (rise and fall) вздыма́ться (*impf.*)

heaven /'hev(ə)n/ *n.* **1** (sky, firmament) не́бо, небе́сный свод **2** (paradise) рай, ца́рство небе́сное **3** (God): thank ∼ for that сла́ва Бо́гу; for ∼'s sake ра́ди Бо́га; (good) ∼s! Го́споди!; Бо́же мой!

heavenly /'hevənlı/ *adj.* **1** (in or of heaven) небе́сный **2** (infml, wonderful) изуми́тельный; ди́вный

heavily /'hevılı/ *adv.* значи́тельно, си́льно; he fell ∼ он тяжело́ ру́хнул; they were ∼ defeated они́ потерпе́ли тяжёлое пораже́ние

♂ **heavy** /'hevı/ *adj.* (**heavier**, **heaviest**) тяжёлый; a ∼ blow (lit., fig.) тяжёлый уда́р; a ∼ cold си́льный на́сморк; he is a ∼ drinker он си́льно пьёт; with a ∼ heart с тяжёлым се́рдцем; ∼ rain си́льный/проливно́й дождь; he is a ∼ sleeper у него́ кре́пкий сон; a ∼ sky хму́рое не́бо; ∼ traffic интенси́вное движе́ние
■ ∼-**handed** *adj.* неуклю́жий; ∼ metal *n.* (infml, mus.) хеви-мета́л; ∼**weight** *n.* (sport, fig.) тяжелове́с

Hebrew /'hi:bru:/ *n.* (language) древнееврейский язы́к; (modern) иври́т
● *adj.* древнееврейский; (modern) иври́тский

heckle /'hek(ə)l/ *v.t.* переб|ива́ть, -и́ть
● *v.i.* переб|ива́ть, -и́ть ора́тора

heckler /'heklə(r)/ *n.* челове́к, кото́рый пыта́ется переби́ть ора́тора; крику́н

hectare /'hekteə(r)/ *n.* (10,000 square metres) гекта́р

hectic /'hektık/ *adj.* (busy) лихора́дочный, бу́рный

hector /'hektə(r)/ *v.t.* запу́г|ивать, -а́ть

hedge /hedʒ/ *n.* жива́я и́згородь
● *v.t.*: ∼ one's bets (fig.) перестрах|о́вываться, -ова́ться
● *v.i.* (prevaricate) уви́л|ивать, -ьну́ть
■ ∼**hog** *n.* ёж; ∼**row** *n.* жива́я и́згородь, шпале́ра

hedonism /'he:dənız(ə)n/ *n.* гедони́зм

hedonist /'hedənıst/ *n.* гедони́ст

hedonistic /hedə'nıstık/ *adj.* гедонисти́ческий

heed /hi:d/ *n.* внима́ние
● *v.t.* уч|и́тывать, -е́сть; вн|има́ть, -ять + *d.*

heedless /'hi:dlıs/ *adj.* беззабо́тный, беспе́чный; she continued, ∼ of danger она́ продолжа́ла, невзира́я на опа́сность

heel /hi:l/ *n.* пя́тка; he fell head over ∼s он полете́л вверх торма́шками; he took to his ∼s он бро́сился наутёк

hefty /'heftı/ *adj.* (**heftier**, **heftiest**) (person) здорове́нный; (blow) здоро́вый

heifer /'hefə(r)/ *n.* тёлка, нетель

height /haıt/ *n.* **1** высота́; (of person) рост **2** (high ground) верши́на, верху́шка **3** (utmost degree) вы́сшая сте́пень; the ∼ of fashion после́дний крик мо́ды; the gale was at its ∼ шторм был в разга́ре

heighten /'haıt(ə)n/ *v.t.* (intensify) уси́ли|вать, -ть
● *v.i.* уси́ли|ваться, -ться

heinous /'heınəs/ *adj.* гну́сный, омерзи́тельный

heir /eə(r)/ *n.* насле́дник

heiress /'eərıs/ *n.* насле́дница

heirloom /'eəlu:m/ *n.* фами́льная рели́квия

held /held/ *past and p.p. of* ▶ **hold**

helicopter /'helıkɒptə(r)/ *n.* вертолёт

heliport /'helıpɔ:t/ *n.* вертолётный аэродро́м; (small, or at the top of building) вертолётная площа́дка

helium /'hi:lıəm/ *n.* ге́лий

hell /hel/ *n.* **1** (place or state) ад; he went through ∼ он перенёс му́ки а́да **2** (infml or sl., expr. vexation or emphasis): oh ∼! чёрт возьми́!; go to ∼! иди́ к чёрту; what the ∼ do you want? что вам ну́жно, чёрт возьми́/побери́?; they made the ∼ of a noise они́ ужа́сно шуме́ли; we had a ∼ of a time мы черто́вски хорошо́ повесели́лись; just for the ∼ of it за здоро́во живёшь, про́сто так

hellish /'helıʃ/ *adj.* а́дский

hello, hallo /hə'ləʊ/ *int.* (greeting) здра́вствуй(те)!; (infml) приве́т!; (on telephone) алло́!

helm /helm/ *n.* (tiller) руль, ру́мпель (*both m.*); take the ∼ (lit., fig.) вста|ва́ть, -ть у штурва́ла/руля́

helmet /'helmıt/ *n.* шлем; (modern soldier's or fireman's) ка́ска

♂ **help** /help/ *n.* по́мощь; he walks with the ∼ of a stick он хо́дит с па́лкой; your advice was a great ∼ to us ваш сове́т нам о́чень помо́г
● *v.t.* **1** (assist) пом|ога́ть, -о́чь + *d.*; please ∼ me up помоги́те мне, пожа́луйста, подня́ться **2** (serve with food etc.) уго́|щáть, -сти́ть; may I ∼ you to (some more) salad? могу́ я положи́ть вам (ещё) немно́го сала́та?; ∼ yourself! угоща́йтесь!; бери́те, пожа́луйста! **3** (prevent; also v.i.): I can't ∼ it я не могу́ ничего́ поде́лать; I can't ∼ laughing я не могу́ удержа́ться от сме́ха; я не могу́ не смея́ться; it can't be ∼ed ничего́ не поде́лаешь
● *v.i.* (avail, be of use) быть поле́зным; crying won't ∼ слеза́ми го́рю не помо́жешь
■ ∼**line** *n.* слу́жба/телефо́н дове́рия

helper /'helpə(r)/ *n.* помо́щник; (of a craftsman) подру́чный

helpful /'helpfʊl/ *adj.* поле́зный; (obliging) услу́жливый

helping /'helpıŋ/ *n.* по́рция

helpless /'helplıs/ *adj.* беспо́мощный

Helsinki /'helsıŋkı, hel'sıŋkı/ *n.* Хе́льсинки (*m. indecl.*)

hem /hem/ *n.* край, подо́л
● *v.t.* (**hemmed, hemming**) **1** (sew the edge of) подш|ива́ть, -и́ть **2**: ∼ in окруж|а́ть, -и́ть

hematologist etc. (AmE) see haematologist etc.

hemisphere /'hemɪsfɪə(r)/ n. полушарие

hemoglobin etc. (AmE) see haemoglobin etc.

hemp /hemp/ n. (plant) конопля; (fibre) пенька; **Indian ~** (plant) конопля индийская; (drug, dried leaves and flowers) марихуана, анаша; (resin) гашиш

hen /hen/ n. (domestic fowl) курица; (female of bird species) самка птицы
■ **~ party** n. (infml) девичник; **~pecked** adj.: **he is ~pecked** жена держит его под каблуком

hence /hens/ adv. (from here) отсюда; (from now): **3 years ~** через три года; (consequently) отсюда, следовательно

henchman /'hentʃmən/ n. приспешник

hepatitis /hepə'taɪtɪs/ n. гепатит

heptathlon /hep'tæθlən/ n. семиборье

her /hə:(r)/ pron. (obj. of ▶ she); **he loves ~** он любит её; **he looks at ~** он смотрит на неё
● poss. adj. её; **~ husband** её муж; (referring to subj. of sentence) свой; **she loves ~ husband** она любит своего мужа

herald /'her(ə)ld/ v.t. возве|щать, -стить

heraldic /he'rældɪk/ adj. геральдический

heraldry /'herəldrɪ/ n. геральдика

herb /hə:b/ n. трава
■ **~ tea** n. (camomile etc.) травяной чай; (blackcurrant etc.) фруктовый чай

herbaceous /hə:'beɪʃəs/ adj. травяной
■ **~ border** n. цветочный бордюр

herbal /'hə:b(ə)l/ n. травник
● adj. травяной
■ **~ medicine** n. траволечение; **~ tea** n. (camomile etc.) травяной чай; (blackcurrant etc.) фруктовый чай

herbalist /'hə:bəlɪst/ n. специалист по лекарственным растениям

herbivore /'hə:bɪvɔ:(r)/ n. травоядное животное

Herculean /hə:kju'li:ən/ adj. геркулесов; (fig.): **~ efforts** титанические усилия

herd /hə:d/ n. стадо
● v.t. сгонять, согнать (вместе)

here /hɪə(r)/ adv. **1** (in or at this place) здесь, тут; **my house is near ~** мой дом рядом; **from ~ to there** отсюда — туда **2** (to this place, in this direction) сюда; **come ~!** идите сюда! **3** (demonstrative) вот; **~ I am!** вот и я!; я тут!; **~ he comes!** вот и он!; **~ we are at last!** наконец-то (мы) пришли/приехали/прибыли!; **~'s to our victory!** за нашу победу! **4** (with offers): **~ you are!** пожалуйста! **5** (phr.): **he looked ~ and there** он поискал там и сям (infml)

hereabouts /hɪərə'baʊts/ adv. поблизости

hereafter /hɪər'ɑ:ftə(r)/ n.: **the ~** загробная жизнь

hereby /hɪə'baɪ/ adv. сим (archaic); этим; настоящим

hereditary /hɪ'redɪtərɪ/ adj. наследственный

heredity /hɪ'redɪtɪ/ n. наследственность

heresy /'herəsɪ/ n. ересь

heretic /'herətɪk/ n. ерети|к (-чка)

heretical /hɪ'retɪk(ə)l/ adj. еретический

heritage /'herɪtɪdʒ/ n. наследство; (fig.) наследие

hermaphrodite /hə:'mæfrədaɪt/ n. гермафродит

hermetic /hə:'metɪk/ adj. герметический; **~ally sealed** герметически закрытый

hermit /'hə:mɪt/ n. отшельник

hernia /'hə:nɪə/ n. грыжа

hero /'hɪərəʊ/ n. (pl. ~es) герой
■ **~ worship** n. преклонение перед героями

heroic /hɪ'rəʊɪk/ adj. (person, attempt) героический

heroin /'herəʊɪn/ n. героин

heroine /'herəʊɪn/ n. героиня

heroism /'herəʊɪz(ə)m/ n. героизм

heron /'herən/ n. цапля

herpes /'hə:pi:z/ n. лишай

herring /'herɪŋ/ n. сельдь; (as food) селёдка

hers /hə:z/ pron. её; **is this handkerchief ~?** это её платок?; **friends of ~** её друзья

herself /hə'self/ pron. **1** (refl.) себя (d., p. себе, i. собой); -сь (suff.); **she looked at ~ in the mirror** она посмотрела на себя в зеркало; **she fell down and hurt ~** она упала и ушиблась **2** (emph.) сама; **she said so ~** она сама это сказала **3** (after preps.) одна; сама; **she did it by ~** она сделала это сама; **she lives by ~** она живёт одна **4** (her normal state): **she is not ~ today** сегодня она сама не своя

hertz /hə:ts/ n. (pl. ~) герц

hesitant /'hezɪt(ə)nt/ adj. колеблющийся

hesitate /'hezɪteɪt/ v.i. колебаться (impf.); **don't ~ to ask** непременно спросите

hesitation /hezɪ'teɪʃ(ə)n/ n. колебание

hessian /'hesɪən/ n. (cloth) мешковина

heterogeneous /hetərəʊ'dʒi:nɪəs/ adj. неоднородный, разнохарактерный

heterosexual /hetərəʊ'sekʃʊəl/ n. гетеросексуал(ьный человек)
● adj. гетеросексуальный

hexagon /'heksəgən/ n. шестиугольник

hexagonal /hek'sægən(ə)l/ adj. шестиугольный

hey /heɪ/ int. (used to attract attention) эй!; (as an informal greeting) привет!

heyday /'heɪdeɪ/ n. расцвет, зенит

HGV (BrE) abbr. (of **heavy goods vehicle**) большегрузный автомобиль

hi /haɪ/ int. привет!

hiatus /haɪ'eɪtəs/ n. (pl. ~es) **1** (gap) пропуск, пробел **2** (between vowels) зияние

hibernate /'haɪbəneɪt/ v.i. впадать (impf.) в зимнюю спячку

hibiscus /hɪ'bɪskəs/ n. (pl. ~es) (bot.) гибискус

hiccup, hiccough /'hɪkʌp/ n. икота; (slight delay) заминка
● v.i. (**hiccuped**, **hiccuping**) ик|ать, -нуть

hid /hɪd/ *past of* ▶ hide²
hidden /'hɪd(ə)n/ *p.p. of* ▶ hide²
hide¹ /haɪd/ *n.* (skin) шкýра; (leather) кóжа
⚡ **hide²** /haɪd/ *v.t.* (*past* **hid**, *p.p.* **hidden**)
пря́тать, с-; скры|ва́ть, -ть
● *v.i.* (*past* **hid**, *p.p.* **hidden**) пря́таться, с-; скры|ва́ться, -́ться
■ ⁓**-and-seek** *n.* пря́т|ки (-ок); ⁓**away**, ⁓**out** *nn.* укры́тие
hideous /'hɪdɪəs/ *adj.* урóдливый, безобра́зный; (unpleasant) мéрзкий
hiding¹ /'haɪdɪŋ/ *n.* (infml, thrashing): she gave him a good ⁓ она́ его́ вы́порола как слéдует
hiding² /'haɪdɪŋ/ *n.* (concealment) укры́тие; he went into ⁓ он скры́лся
■ ⁓ **place** *n.* укры́тие
hierarchical /haɪə'rɑːkɪk(ə)l/ *adj.* иерархи́ческий
hierarchy /'haɪərɑːkɪ/ *n.* иера́рхия
hieroglyph /'haɪərəglɪf/ *n.* иерóглиф
hieroglyphic /haɪərə'glɪfɪk/ *adj.* иероглифи́ческий
hieroglyphics /haɪərə'glɪfɪks/ *n. pl.* иерóглифы, иероглифи́ческое письмо́
hi-fi /'haɪfaɪ/ *n.* (*abbr. of* **high fidelity**) (*pl.* ⁓**s**) (infml) (высокока́чественная) стереосистéма
higgledy-piggledy /hɪgəldɪ'pɪgəldɪ/ *adj.* беспоря́дочный; сумбу́рный
● *adv.* вперемéшку; беспоря́дочно
⚡ **high** /haɪ/ *n.*: prices reached a new ⁓ цéны дости́гли небыва́ло высóкого ýровня
● *adj.* **1** (tall, elevated) высóкий (also mus.); ten feet ⁓ высотóй в 10 фýтов **2** (chief, important): ⁓ command вы́сшее кома́ндование; in ⁓ places (fig.) в верха́х, в вы́сших сфéрах **3** (greater than average; extreme): ⁓ blood pressure высóкое (кровянóе) давлéние; in ⁓ spirits в отли́чном/припóднятом настроéнии **4** (at its peak): ⁓ noon пóлдень; ⁓ summer середи́на/разга́р лéта; it is ⁓ time давнó пора́; it is ⁓ time I was gone мне ужé давнó пора́ идти́ **5** (on drugs) под ка́йфом; to be ⁓ on cocaine быть под кокаи́ном
● *adv.*: ⁓ up вверх (of direction) ввысь
■ ⁓**brow** *n.* интеллектуа́л ● *adj.* интеллектуа́льный, серьёзный; ⁓**-class** *adj.* первокла́ссный, высóкого кла́сса; ⁓**-flyer** *n.* (person likely to succeed) подаю́щий больши́е надéжды (*or* многообеща́ющий) человéк; ⁓**-handed** *adj.* вла́стный, своевóльный; ⁓**-heeled** *adj.* на высóком каблукé; ⁓ **heels** *n. pl.* тýфли на высóком каблукé; ⁓ **jump** *n.* прыжóк в высотý; the H⁓lands *n. pl.* сéвер и сéверо-за́пад Шотла́ндии; ⁓**lighter** *n.* фломáстер; ⁓**-pitched** *adj.* высóкий; ⁓**-ranking** *adj.* высокопоста́вленный; ⁓**-rise** *adj.*: ⁓**-rise** apartment blocks высóтные многоквartíрные дома́; ⁓ **road** *n.* шоссé (*nt. indecl.*); ⁓**-speed** *adj.* скоростнóй; ⁓ **street** *n.* (BrE) гла́вная у́лица; ⁓**-tech** *adj.* высокотехнологи́чный; ⁓ **tide** *n.* больша́я вода́, прили́в; ⁓**way** *n.* шоссé (*nt. indecl.*); H⁓way Code пра́вила дорóжного движéния

higher /'haɪə(r)/ *adj.* (senior, advanced) вы́сший; ⁓ education вы́сшее образова́ние
● *adv.*: ⁓ up the hill вы́ше на холмé
highlight /'haɪlaɪt/ *n.* (*in pl.*) (in hair) цветны́е пря́ди (*f. pl.*); (fig.) кульминациóнный момéнт
● *v.t.* (fig., emphasize) выделя́ть, вы́делить (also comput.); заостр|я́ть, -и́ть внима́ние на + *p.*
⚡ **highly** /'haɪlɪ/ *adv.* весьма́, óчень; ⁓ paid высокоопла́чиваемый; he speaks ⁓ of you он о вас óчень хорошó отзыва́ется; she is ⁓ thought of её óчень цéнят
■ ⁓ strung *n.* (BrE) взви́нченный, нервóзный
Highness /'haɪnɪs/ *n.*: His Royal ⁓ Егó Королéвское Высóчество
hijack /'haɪdʒæk/ *v.t.* уг|оня́ть, -на́ть; пох|ища́ть, -и́тить
hijacker /'haɪdʒækə(r)/ *n.* угóнщик, похити́тель (*m.*)
hike¹ /haɪk/ *n.* (walk) турпохóд
● *v.i.* гуля́ть (*impf.*); ходи́ть (*indet.*), идти́ (*det.*) пешкóм
hike² /haɪk/ (infml) *n.* (rise) подъём
● *v.t.* (raise) подн|има́ть, -я́ть
hiker /'haɪkə(r)/ *n.* пéший тури́ст
hiking /'haɪkɪŋ/ *n.* пéший тури́зм
hilarious /hɪ'leərɪəs/ *adj.* весёлый
hilarity /hɪ'lærɪtɪ/ *n.* весéлье, потéха
hill /hɪl/ *n.* холм
■ ⁓**side** *n.* склон холма́; ⁓**top** *n.* верши́на холма́
hillock /'hɪlək/ *n.* хóлмик, бугóр
hilly /'hɪlɪ/ *adj.* (**hillier**, **hilliest**) холми́стый
⚡ **him** /hɪm/ *obj. of* ▶ he
Himalayas /hɪmə'leɪəz/ *n. pl.* Гимала́|и (-ев)
⚡ **himself** /hɪm'self/ *pron.* **1** (refl.) себя́ (*d.*, *p.* себé, *i.* собóй); -ся (*suff.*); I hope he behaves ⁓ надéюсь, что он бýдет вести́ себя́ прили́чно; he fell and hurt ⁓ он упа́л и уши́бся **2** (emph.) сам; he did the job ⁓ он сам сдéлал э́ту рабóту **3** (after preps.) оди́н; сам; he did it by ⁓ он сдéлал э́то сам; he lives by ⁓ он живёт оди́н **4** (in his normal state): he is not ⁓ today он сегóдня сам не свой
hind /haɪnd/ *adj.*: the dog stood on its ⁓ legs соба́ка вста́ла на за́дние ла́пы
■ ⁓**sight** *n.*: he spoke with ⁓sight он говори́л, зна́я, чем кóнчилось дéло
hinder /'hɪndə(r)/ *v.t.* меша́ть, по- + *d.*
Hindi /'hɪndɪ/ *n.* (language) хи́нди (*m. indecl.*)
hindrance /'hɪndrəns/ *n.* помéха, препя́тствие
Hindu /'hɪnduː/ *n.* (*pl.* ⁓**s**) индýс (-ка)
● *adj.* индýсский
Hinduism /'hɪnduːɪz(ə)m/ *n.* индуи́зм
Hindustani /hɪndʊ'stɑːnɪ/ *n.* (language) хиндуста́ни (*m. indecl.*)
hinge /hɪndʒ/ *n.* шарни́р; (on door) петля́
● *v.i.* (**hingeing** *or* **hinging**): it all ⁓d on this event всё бы́ло свя́зано с э́тим собы́тием

h

hint /hɪnt/ *n.* (suggestion) намёк; **he is always dropping ~s** он всегда говори́т намёками; **there was a ~ of frost** начина́ло подмора́живать; (written advice) сове́т
• *v.t. & i.* намек|а́ть, -ну́ть на + *a.*; **I ~ed that I needed a holiday** я намекну́л, что мне ну́жен о́тпуск; **what are you ~ing (at)?** на что вы намека́ете?

hip¹ /hɪp/ *n.* (anat.) бедро́

hip² /hɪp/ *int.*: **~, ~, hooray!** гип-гип, ура́!

hip³ /hɪp/ *adj.* (**hipper, hippest**) (infml) мо́дный, круто́й (sl.)

hippie, hippy /'hɪpɪ/ *n.* хи́ппи (*c.g., indecl.*)

hippo /'hɪpəʊ/ *n.* (*pl.* ~**s**) (infml) гиппопота́м, бегемо́т

hippopotamus /hɪpə'pɒtəməs/ *n.* бегемо́т

✎ **hire** /'haɪə(r)/ *n.* (engagement of person) наём; (of thing) наём, прока́т; **cars for ~** маши́ны напрока́т
• *v.t.* (BrE, a place) сн|има́ть, -я́ть; (BrE, equipment, a car) брать, взять напрока́т; (a worker) нан|има́ть, -я́ть
■ **~ purchase** *n.* (BrE) поку́пка в рассро́чку

✎ **his** /hɪz/ *pron.* его́; **is this book ~?** э́то его́ кни́га?; **friends of ~** его́ друзья́
• *poss. adj.* его́; **this is ~ book** э́то его́ кни́га; (referring to subj. of sentence) свой; **he loves ~ children** он лю́бит свои́х дете́й

Hispanic /hɪ'spænɪk/ *adj.* испа́нский; латиноамерика́нский
• *n.* латиноамерика́н|ец (-ка)

hiss /hɪs/ *n.* шипе́ние
• *v.i.* (of snake) шипе́ть, за-; (of audience) свисте́ть (*impf.*)

historian /hɪ'stɔːrɪən/ *n.* исто́рик

historic /hɪ'stɒrɪk/ *adj.* истори́ческий

✎ **historical** /hɪ'stɒrɪk(ə)l/ *adj.* истори́ческий

✎ **history** /'hɪstərɪ/ *n.* исто́рия

histrionic /hɪstrɪ'ɒnɪk/ *adj.* (theatrical) театра́льный, мелодрамати́ческий

✎ **hit** /hɪt/ *n.* (blow) уда́р, толчо́к; (infml, success) успе́х; (popular song) хит; шля́гер
• *v.t.* (**hitting**, *past and p.p.* **hit**) **1** (strike) уд|аря́ть, -а́рить; **he fell and ~ his head on a stone** он упа́л и уда́рился голово́й о ка́мень; **the bullet ~ him in the shoulder** пу́ля попа́ла ему́ в плечо́; **the car ~ a tree** маши́на вре́залась в де́рево; **to ~ the target/mark** поп|ада́ть, -а́сть в цель **2** (fig. uses): **the idea suddenly ~ me** меня́ вдруг осени́ло **3** (encounter): **he ~ a bad patch** (infml) у него́ начала́сь полоса́ неуда́ч
□ **~ back** *v.t.*: **if he ~s you, ~ him back** е́сли он вас уда́рит, уда́рьте его́ то́же; (fig., at critics etc.) да|ва́ть, -ть отпо́р + *d.*
□ **~ off** *v.t.*: **~ it off** ла́дить (*impf.*)
■ **~ man** *n.* наёмный/профессиона́льный уби́йца, ки́ллер

hitch /hɪtʃ/ *n.* заде́ржка
• *v.t.* **1** (fasten) привя́з|ывать, -а́ть; прицеп|ля́ть, -и́ть **2** (infml): **~ a lift** подъ|езжа́ть, -е́хать на попу́тной маши́не

• *v.i.* (infml) (*also* **~-hike**) е́здить автосто́пом
■ **~-hiker** *n.* путеше́ствующий автосто́пом; **~-hiking** *n.* «голосова́ние», езда́ автосто́пом (*or* на попу́тных маши́нах)

hither /'hɪðə(r)/ *adv.* сюда́
■ **~to** *adv.* до сих пор

HIV *abbr. of* (**human immunodeficiency virus**) (med.) ВИЧ (ви́рус иммунодефици́та челове́ка)
■ **~-positive** *adj.* ВИЧ-инфици́рованный

hive /haɪv/ *n.* у́лей; (fig.): **the office is a ~ of industry** рабо́та в о́фисе кипи́т

HND (BrE) *abbr.* (*of* **Higher National Diploma**) дипло́м о вы́сшем техни́ческом образова́нии

hoar /hɔː(r)/ *adj.* седо́й
■ **~ frost** *n.* и́ней, и́зморозь

hoard /hɔːd/ *n.* (та́йный) запа́с, склад
• *v.t.* припря́т|ывать, -ать

hoarding /'hɔːdɪŋ/ *n.* **1** (BrE, for poster display) рекла́мный щит **2** (BrE, fence round building site) забо́р/огра́да вокру́г стройплоща́дки

hoarse /hɔːs/ *adj.* хри́плый

hoax /həʊks/ *n.* надува́тельство

hob /hɒb/ *n.* (BrE) пове́рхность ку́хонной плиты́

hobble /'hɒb(ə)l/ *v.i.* ковыля́ть (*impf.*)

hobby /'hɒbɪ/ *n.* хо́бби (*nt. indecl.*)

hobnob /'hɒbnɒb/ *v.i.* (**hobnobbed, hobnobbing**) води́ться (*impf.*) (*с кем*), зна́ться (*impf.*) (*с кем*)

hockey /'hɒkɪ/ *n.* (on field) хокке́й на траве́; **ice ~** хокке́й (с ша́йбой/на льду)
■ **~ stick** *n.* клю́шка

hoe /həʊ/ *n.* моты́га, тя́пка
• *v.t. & i.* (**hoes, hoed, hoeing**) разрыхля́ть (*impf.*) моты́гой

hog /hɒg/ *n.* бо́ров; (AmE, also fig.) свинья́; **go the whole ~** дов|оди́ть, -ести́ де́ло до конца́; идти́, пойти́ на всё
• *v.t.* (**hogged, hogging**) (monopolize): **he ~ged the conversation** он не дава́л никому́ сло́ва вста́вить

Hogmanay /'hɒgməneɪ/ *n.* (Sc.) кану́н Но́вого го́да

hoist /hɔɪst/ *v.t.* подн|има́ть, -я́ть

✎ **hold** /həʊld/ *n.* **1** (grasp, grip) уде́рживание, захва́т; **he caught ~ of the rope** он ухвати́лся за кана́т; **he kept ~ of the reins** он не выпуска́л пово́дья из рук; **he seized, took ~ of my arm** он схвати́л/взял меня́ за́ руку; **I got ~ of a plumber** я нашёл/ отыска́л водопрово́дчика; **where did you get ~ of those tickets?** где вы доста́ли э́ти биле́ты?; **it's difficult to get ~ of her** её тру́дно заста́ть **2** (means of pressure): **she has a ~ on, over him** она́ име́ет над ним власть **3** (ship's) трюм
• *v.t.* (*past and p.p.* **held**) **1** (clasp, grip) держа́ть (*impf.*); **they sat ~ing hands** они́ сиде́ли держа́сь за́ руки **2** (maintain, keep in a certain position): **~ it!** (infml) (don't move) не дви́гайтесь!; не шевели́тесь!; (fig., keep): **they were held to a draw** их принуди́ли

к ничьéй; ~ **the line!** (teleph.) не клади́те
тру́бку! **3** (detain) заде́рж|ивать, -ержа́ть; **he
was held prisoner** его́ держа́ли в плену́
4 (contain) вмеща́ть, -сти́ть; **the hall ~s a
thousand** зал вмеща́ет ты́сячу челове́к
5 (consider) полага́ть (*impf.*), счита́ть (*impf.*);
the court held that … суд призна́л, что…; **he
was held responsible** ему́ пришло́сь держа́ть
отве́т; **I don't ~ it against him** я не ста́влю
ему́ э́то в вину́ **6** (restrain): **she held her breath**
она́ затаи́ла дыха́ние **7** (have, own) владе́ть
(*impf.*) + *i.*; ~ **the record** быть рекордсме́ном;
we ~ the same views мы приде́рживаемся
одина́ковых взгля́дов **8** (occupy, remain
in possession of): **he held his ground** он не
уступа́л; он не сдава́лся; **I can ~ my own
against anyone** я могу́ потяга́ться с кем
уго́дно **9** (carry on, conduct) пров|оди́ть, -ести́;
the meeting was held at noon собра́ние
состоя́лось (*or* провели́) в по́лдень

● *v.i.* (*past and p.p.* **held**) **1** (grasp): ~ **tight!**
держи́тесь кре́пче/кре́пко! **2** (remain):
~ **still!** не дви́гайтесь! **3** (remain unbroken,
unchanged, intact): **will the rope ~?** вы́держит
ли верёвка?; **how long will the weather ~?**
до́лго ли проде́ржится/простои́т така́я
пого́да?

□ ~ **back** *v.t.* (restrain) уде́рж|ивать, -а́ть; **I
couldn't ~ him back** я не мог его́ удержа́ть;
(withhold) уде́рж|ивать, -а́ть

● *v.i.* (refrain) возде́рж|иваться, -а́ться (*от
чего*)

□ ~ **down** *v.t.*: (fig.): **do you think you can ~ the
job down?** суме́ете ли вы удержа́ться на э́той
до́лжности?; **we will try to ~ prices down** мы
постара́емся сдержа́ть рост цен

□ ~ **forth** *v.i.* (infml, orate) разглаго́льствовать
(*impf.*); веща́ть (*impf.*)

□ ~ **off** *v.t.* (keep away, repel): **they held off the
attack** они́ отби́ли ата́ку; (postpone): **he held
off going to the doctor** он откла́дывал визи́т
к врачу́

● *v.i.* (stay away): **the rain held off all morning**
дождя́ так и не́ было всё у́тро

□ ~ **on** *v.t.* (keep in position) прикреп|ля́ть, -и́ть
● *v.i.* (cling) держа́ться (**to:** за + *a.*); **she held
on to the banisters** она́ держа́лась за пери́ла;
(fig.): **you should ~ on to those shares** вам
на́до держа́ться за э́ти а́кции; (infml, wait): ~
on a minute till I'm ready подожди́те: я бу́ду
гото́в че́рез мину́ту; (on the telephone): ~ **on,
please!** не ве́шайте тру́бку!

□ ~ **out** *v.t.* (extend) прот|я́гивать, -яну́ть;
he greeted me and held out his hand он
поздоро́вался и протяну́л мне ру́ку; (fig., offer):
I can't ~ out any hope я не могу́ вас ниче́м
обнаде́жить

● *v.i.* (endure, refuse to yield) держа́ться, про-; **the
men are ~ing out for more money** рабо́чие
наста́ивают на повыше́нии зарпла́ты; (last):
supplies cannot ~ out much longer запа́сов
хва́тит не надо́лго

□ ~ **over** *v.t.* (defer) от|кла́дывать, -ложи́ть

□ ~ **up** *v.t.* (lift, hold erect) подн|има́ть, -я́ть; **the
boy held up his hand** ма́льчик по́днял ру́ку;
(delay) заде́рж|ивать, -а́ть; **we were held up on
the way** по доро́ге нас задержа́ли; **traffic was**

held up by fog движе́ние останови́лось из-за
тума́на; (waylay): **the robbers held them up at
pistol point** банди́ты огра́били их, угрожа́я
пистоле́том

● *v.i.*: **do you think the table will ~ up under
the weight?** вы ду́маете, стол вы́держит
тако́й вес?

■ ~**all** *n.* (BrE) вещево́й мешо́к; ~**-up** *n.* (delay)
заде́ржка; (robbery) вооружённый грабёж

holder /ˈhəʊldə(r)/ *n.* **1** (possessor) владе́лец;
облада́тель (*m.*) **2** (container, also fin.)
держа́тель (*m.*)

✃ **hole** /həʊl/ *n.* **1** (cavity) дыра́ **2** (opening)
отве́рстие **3** (burrow) нора́ **4** (*phr.*): **the
purchase made a ~ in his savings** поку́пка
оста́вила брешь в его́ сбереже́ниях; ~ **in the
wall** (BrE, infml) банкома́т

■ ~ **punch(er)** *n.* дыроко́л

✃ **holiday** /ˈhɒlɪdeɪ/ *n.* (BrE) **1** (day off) выходно́й
(день); **bank ~** официа́льный нерабо́чий
день **2** (annual leave) о́тпуск, о́тдых; (school,
university vacation) кани́кул|ы (*pl., g.* —); (leisure
time) о́тдых; **he is on ~** он в о́тпуске/отпуску́;
у него́ кани́кулы

■ ~ **camp** *n.* (ле́тний) ла́герь; ~**maker** *n.*
отдыха́ющий; тури́ст (-ка)

holistic /hɒˈlɪstɪk/ *adj.* це́лостный

Holland /ˈhɒlənd/ *n.* (country or province)
Голла́ндия

hollow /ˈhɒləʊ/ *n.* вы́емка
● *adj.* **1** (not solid) пусто́й, по́лый **2** (of sounds)
глухо́й **3** (fig., false, insincere) фальши́вый,
лжи́вый; ~ **laughter** неесте́ственный
смех **4** (sunken) ввали́вшийся, впа́лый; ~
cheeks ввали́вшиеся щёки

holly /ˈhɒlɪ/ *n.* остроли́ст

hollyhock /ˈhɒlɪhɒk/ *n.* алте́й ро́зовый

holocaust /ˈhɒləkɔːst/ *n.* ма́ссовое
уничтоже́ние; **the H~** холоко́ст

holster /ˈhəʊlstə(r)/ *n.* кобура́

holy /ˈhəʊlɪ/ *adj.* (**holier, holiest**)
свяще́нный, свято́й; **the H~ Ghost, Spirit**
Свято́й Дух; **the H~ Land** Свята́я земля́ (*об
Израиле и Палестине*)

homage /ˈhɒmɪdʒ/ *n.* почте́ние,
преклоне́ние; **we pay ~ to his genius** мы
преклоня́емся пе́ред его́ ге́нием

✃ **home** /həʊm/ *n.* **1** (place where one resides or
belongs) дом; (*attr.*) дома́шний; **she left ~** она́
покинула (роди́тельский) дом; **at home** (in
one's house) до́ма; (on one's ~ ground) у себя́;
(e.g. football) на своём по́ле; **make yourself
at ~** бу́дьте как до́ма; **I feel at ~ here** я
чу́вствую себя́ здесь как до́ма **2** (institution):
a ~ for the disabled дом инвали́дов; **he put
his parents into a ~** он помести́л свои́х
роди́телей в дом престаре́лых **3** (*attr.*)
(opp. foreign; native, local): ~ **affairs** вну́тренние
дела́; ~ **team** кома́нда хозя́ев по́ля; ~ **town**
родно́й го́род

● *adv.* **1** (at or to one's own house): **he was on
his way ~** он шёл/е́хал домо́й; **is he ~ yet?**
он (уже́) до́ма? **2** (in or to one's own country):

he came ~ **from abroad** он верну́лся из-за грани́цы **3** (to the point aimed at): **bring sth ~ to sb** дов|оди́ть, -ести́ что-н. до чьего́-н. созна́ния; **his remarks struck ~** его́ замеча́ния попа́ли в цель

■ ~ **economics** n. pl. домово́дство; ~ **entertainment system** n. дома́шний развлека́тельный центр; ~**-grown** adj. (vegetables) дома́шний, с огоро́да; (not foreign) оте́чественный; ~ **help** n. (BrE) приходя́щая домрабо́тница; ~**land** n. ро́дина, родна́я страна́; ~**-made** adj. дома́шний; **H~ Office** n. (BrE) Министе́рство вну́тренних дел; ~ **page** n. (comput.) ста́ртовая страни́ца в Интерне́те; **H~ Secretary** n. (BrE) мини́стр вну́тренних дел; ~**sick** adj. скуча́ющий/ тоску́ющий по до́му/ро́дине; ~**work** n. дома́шнее зада́ние

homeless /ˈhəʊmlɪs/ adj. бездо́мный

homely /ˈhəʊmlɪ/ adj. (**homelier**, **homeliest**) **1** (BrE, cosy) дома́шний, ую́тный **2** (BrE, unpretentious): **a ~ meal** неприхотли́вая еда́ **3** (AmE, unattractive) некраси́вый

homeopath /ˈhəʊmɪəpæθ, ˈhɒm-/ n. гомеопа́т

homeopathic /ˌhəʊmɪəˈpæθɪk, ˌhɒm-/ adj. гомеопати́ческий

homeopathy /ˌhəʊmɪˈɒpəθɪ, ˌhɒmɪ-/ n. гомеопа́тия

homeward /ˈhəʊmwəd/ adv. (also **homewards**) домо́й

homicidal /ˌhɒmɪˈsaɪd(ə)l/ adj. замышля́ющий уби́йство

homicide /ˈhɒmɪsaɪd/ n. (crime) уби́йство

homogeneous /ˌhɒməˈdʒiːnɪəs/ adj. одноро́дный

homophobia /ˌhəʊməˈfəʊbɪə/ n. не́нависть к гомосексуали́стам, гомофо́бия

homosexual /ˌhɒməˈsekʃʊəl/ n. гомосексуали́ст
● adj. гомосексуа́льный

homosexuality /ˌhɒməsekʃʊˈælɪtɪ/ n. гомосексуали́зм

Honduran /hɒnˈdjʊərən/ n. гондура́с|ец (-ка)
● adj. гондура́сский

Honduras /hɒnˈdjʊərəs/ n. Гондура́с

hone /həʊn/ v.t. (sharpen) точи́ть, за-; (fig.) отт|а́чивать, -очи́ть

honest /ˈɒnɪst/ adj. (fair) че́стный; (candid): **to be ~ (with you)** че́стно говоря́

honestly /ˈɒnɪstlɪ/ adv. **1** (straightforwardly) че́стно **2** (candidly) пря́мо, чистосерде́чно; ~! че́стное сло́во!

honesty /ˈɒnɪstɪ/ n. **1** (integrity) че́стность **2** (candour) прямота́, и́скренность

honey /ˈhʌnɪ/ n. мёд; (AmE, infml, darling) дорого́й, ми́лый
■ ~**moon** n. медо́вый ме́сяц ● v.i. пров|оди́ть, -ести́ медо́вый ме́сяц

Hong Kong /hɒŋˈkɒŋ/ n. Гонко́нг

honk /hɒŋk/ v.i. гуде́ть (impf.)

honor /ˈɒnə(r)/ n. & v.t. (AmE) = honour

honorable /ˈɒnərəb(ə)l/ adj. (AmE) = honourable

honorari|um /ˌɒnəˈreərɪəm/ n. (pl. ~ums or ~a) гонора́р

honorary /ˈɒnərərɪ/ adj. почётный

⚜ **honour** /ˈɒnə(r)/ (AmE **honor**) n. **1** (good character, reputation) честь **2** (dignity, credit) честь; **the reception was held in his ~** приём был устро́ен в его́ честь **3** (as title): **Your H~** ва́ша честь **4** (in pl.) (academic distinction): ~**s degree** ≈ сте́пень балака́вра
● v.t. **1** (respect, do ~ to) ока́з|ывать, -а́ть честь + d. **2** (fulfil obligation) выполня́ть, вы́полнить; **he failed to ~ the agreement** он не вы́полнил соглаше́ния; **will the cheque be ~ed?** бу́дет ли упла́чено по э́тому че́ку?

honourable /ˈɒnərəb(ə)l/ (AmE **honorable**) adj. че́стный, досто́йный

hood /hʊd/ n. **1** (headgear) капюшо́н **2** (BrE, of car) складно́й верх **3** (AmE, of car engine) капо́т

hoodie /ˈhʊdɪ/ n. (infml) толсто́вка с капюшо́ном; молодо́й челове́к, нося́щий толсто́вку с капюшо́ном

hoodwink /ˈhʊdwɪŋk/ v.t. одура́чи|вать, -ть; пров|оди́ть, -ести́ (infml)

hoof /huːf/ n. (pl. **hoofs** or **hooves**) копы́то

hook /hʊk/ n. **1** (curved device, also for fishing and as fastening) крючо́к, крюк; **the receiver was off the ~** тру́бка была́ снята́; **get off the ~** (infml) вызволя́ть, вы́зволить; **let off the ~** (infml) выруча́ть, вы́ручить **2** (boxing blow) хук, боково́й уда́р
● v.t. (usu. with advs., fasten): **she ~ed up her dress** она́ застегну́ла пла́тье (на крючки́)

hooligan /ˈhuːlɪgən/ n. хулига́н

hooliganism /ˈhuːlɪgənɪz(ə)m/ n. хулига́нство

hoop /huːp/ n. **1** (plaything) о́бруч **2** (BrE, croquet) воро́т|а (pl., g. —)

hooray! /hʊˈreɪ/ int. ура́

hoot /huːt/ n. (owl's cry) у́ханье; (warning note) гудо́к, сигна́л
● v.i. (of a car etc.) гуде́ть, про-; (of an owl) у́х|ать, -нуть; (of a person): **we ~ed with laughter** мы пока́тывались со сме́ху

hooter /ˈhuːtə(r)/ n. **1** (BrE, of car, factory) гудо́к **2** (sl., nose) руби́льник (нос)

Hoover® /ˈhuːvə(r)/ (BrE) n. пылесо́с
● v.t. (**h~**) пылесо́сить, про-

hooves /huːvz/ pl. of ► hoof

hop[1] /hɒp/ n. подско́к, скачо́к (на одно́й ноге́)
● v.i. (**hopped**, **hopping**) пры́гать, скака́ть (both impf.)

hop[2] /hɒp/ n. (bot.) хмель (m.)

⚜ **hope** /həʊp/ n. наде́жда; **don't raise my ~s in vain** не обна́деживайте меня́ понапра́сну
● v.t. & i. наде́яться (impf.); **I ~ to see you soon** наде́юсь, ско́ро вас уви́деть; **let's ~ so!** бу́дем наде́яться!; **I ~ not** наде́юсь, что нет

hopeful /ˈhəʊpfʊl/ adj. **1** (having hope): **I am ~ of success** я наде́юсь/рассчи́тываю на успе́х **2** (inspiring hope) обнадёживающий; **a ~ sign** обнадёживающий знак

h

hopefully /ˈhəʊpfʊli/ adv.: ∼ he will arrive soon на́до наде́яться, он ско́ро прие́дет

hopeless /ˈhəʊplɪs/ adj. **1** (affording no hope) безнадёжный; a ∼ **situation** безнадёжное положе́ние **2** (infml, incapable): he's quite ∼ at science то́чные нау́ки ему́ соверше́нно не даю́тся

horde /hɔːd/ n. по́лчище

horizon /həˈraɪz(ə)n/ n. (lit., fig.) горизо́нт

horizontal /hɒrɪˈzɒnt(ə)l/ adj. горизонта́льный

hormonal /hɔːˈməʊn(ə)l/ adj. гормона́льный

hormone /ˈhɔːməʊn/ n. гормо́н; ∼ **replacement therapy** гормона́льная терапи́я

horn /hɔːn/ n. **1** (of cattle) рог **2** (mus., French horn) валто́рна; (hunting horn) рог **3** (of car) гудо́к

hornet /ˈhɔːnɪt/ n. ше́ршень (m.); his words stirred up a ∼'s nest (fig.) его́ слова́ потрево́жили оси́ное гнездо́

hornist /ˈhɔːnɪst/ n. валторни́ст (-ка)

horoscope /ˈhɒrəskəʊp/ n. гороско́п

horrendous /həˈrendəs/ adj. ужа́сный

horrible /ˈhɒrɪb(ə)l/, **horrid** /ˈhɒrɪd/ adjs. ужа́сный

horrific /həˈrɪfɪk/ adj. ужаса́ющий

horrify /ˈhɒrɪfaɪ/ v.t. потряса́ть, -ти́

horror /ˈhɒrə(r)/ n. у́жас; (extreme dislike): I have a ∼ of cats я терпе́ть не могу́ ко́шек ■ ∼ **film** n. фильм у́жасов

hors d'oeuvre /ɔːˈdəːv/ n. (pl. ∼ or ∼s pronunc. same or /-ˈdəːvz/) заку́ска

◆ **horse** /hɔːs/ n. ло́шадь, конь (m.); I had it straight from the ∼'s mouth я узна́л э́то из пе́рвых рук
■ ∼**back** n.: on ∼back верхо́м; ∼back riding (AmE) = horse riding; ∼ **chestnut** n. кашта́н ко́нский; ∼**power** n. лошади́ная си́ла; 20 ∼power 20 лошади́ных сил; ∼ **race**, ∼ **racing** nn. ска́чки (f. pl.), бега́ (m. pl.); ∼**radish** n. хрен; ∼ **riding** n. верхова́я езда́; ∼**shoe** n. подко́ва

horticultural /hɔːtɪˈkʌltʃər(ə)l/ adj. садово́дческий

horticulture /ˈhɔːtɪkʌltʃə(r)/ n. садово́дство

horticulturist /hɔːtɪˈkʌltʃərɪst/, **horticulturalist** /hɔːtɪˈkʌltʃərəlɪst/ nn. садово́д

hose /həʊz/ n. (also **hosepipe**) шланг

hosiery /ˈhəʊzɪəri/ n. чуло́чно-носо́чные изде́лия (nt. pl.)

hospice /ˈhɒspɪs/ n. хо́спис

hospitable /hɒˈspɪtəb(ə)l/ adj. гостеприи́мный

◆ **hospital** /ˈhɒspɪt(ə)l/ n. больни́ца; he is in ∼ он (лежи́т) в больни́це
■ ∼ **trust** n. (BrE) больни́чный трест (больница Национальной службы здравоохранения, управляемая на правах доверительной собственности)

hospitality /hɒspɪˈtælɪti/ n. гостеприи́мство

hospitalize /ˈhɒspɪtəlaɪz/ v.t. госпитализи́ровать (impf., pf.)

◆ **host¹** /həʊst/ n. хозя́ин
● v.t. организова́ть (impf., pf.)

host² /həʊst/ n. (multitude) мно́жество, ма́сса

hostage /ˈhɒstɪdʒ/ n. зало́жник

hostel /ˈhɒst(ə)l/ n. общежи́тие

hostelry /ˈhɒstəlri/ n. (archaic or joc.) постоя́лый двор

hostess /ˈhəʊstɪs/ n. хозя́йка

hostile /ˈhɒstaɪl/ adj. враждѐбный

hostility /hɒˈstɪlɪti/ n. враждѐбность

◆ **hot** /hɒt/ adj. (**hotter**, **hottest**) **1** (water, object) горя́чий; (weather) жа́ркий; I am ∼ мне жа́рко; a ∼ **flush** прили́в кро́ви; in the ∼ seat (infml) на отве́тственной до́лжности **2** (spicy) о́стрый **3**: ∼ on the scent, trail по горя́чему сле́ду
● v.i. (**hotted**, **hotting**) (BrE, infml, become livelier): the game ∼ted up игра́ оживи́лась
■ ∼**bed** n. парни́к; (fig.) расса́дник, оча́г; ∼**-blooded** adj. пы́лкий, стра́стный; ∼ **dog** n. хот-до́г; ∼**-headed** adj. вспы́льчивый, горя́чий; ∼**line** n. (for enquiries) горя́чая ли́ния; (between governments) пряма́я телефо́нная связь; ∼**plate** n. пли́тка; ∼**-tempered** adj. вспы́льчивый; ∼**-water bottle** n. гре́лка

◆ **hotel** /həʊˈtel/ n. гости́ница, отѐль (m.)

hotelier /həʊˈtelɪə(r)/ n. хозя́ин гости́ницы

hound /haʊnd/ n. охо́тничья соба́ка
● v.t. **1** (harrass) не дава́ть кому́-н. прохо́ду **2** (∼ out) (force to leave) выжива́ть, вы́жить

◆ **hour** /aʊə(r)/ n. **1** (period) час; boats for hire by the ∼ прока́т ло́док с почасово́й опла́той **2** (of clock time): every ∼ on the ∼ в нача́ле ка́ждого ча́са **3**: in office ∼s в рабо́чее вре́мя; out of ∼s в нерабо́чее вре́мя

hourly /ˈaʊəli/ adj. **1** (occurring once an hour) ежеча́сный **2**: an ∼ wage почасова́я опла́та
● adv. ежеча́сно; (at any time) с ча́су на час

◆ **house¹** /haʊs/ n. **1** (habitation) дом, зда́ние; (pol.): H∼ of Commons пала́та общин; H∼ of Lords пала́та ло́рдов; H∼ of Representatives пала́та представи́телей **2** (audience) зал, аудито́рия; they played to a full ∼ на их выступлѐнии зал был по́лон; (BrE, performance) представлѐние
■ ∼**boat** n. плаву́чий дом; ∼**bound** adj.: he is ∼bound он не выхо́дит из до́ма; ∼**holder** n. домовладѐлец; ∼ **husband** n. муж, веду́щий дома́шнее хозя́йство; ∼**keeper** n. эконо́мка; ∼**keeping** n. дома́шнее хозя́йство; ∼**-proud** adj. лю́бящий занима́ться благоустро́йством и украшѐнием до́ма; ∼**-to-**∼ adj.: a ∼-to-∼ search о́быск всех домо́в подря́д; пова́льный о́быск; ∼**-trained** adj. (BrE) приу́ченный жить (or не па́чкать) в до́ме (о собаке, кошке); ∼**-warming** n. новосѐлье; ∼**wife** n. домохозя́йка; ∼**work** n. дома́шние дела́

house² /haʊz/ v.t. **1** (provide house(s) for) сели́ть, по- **2** (accommodate) вмеща́ть, -сти́ть; this building ∼s the city council в э́том зда́нии размеща́ется муниципалите́т **3** (store) храни́ть (impf.)

household /ˈhaʊshəʊld/ n. дом; дома́шний круг; (attr.) ∼ appliances бытовы́е прибо́ры;

h

h

she is a ~ name её все зна́ют

☞ **housing** /'haʊzɪŋ/ *n.* жильё
■ ~ **association** *n.* жили́щно-строи́тельная ассоциа́ция; ~ **benefit** *n.* (BrE) посо́бие на вы́плату квартпла́ты; ~ **development,** ~ **estate** (BrE), ~ **project** (AmE) *nn.* жило́й микрорайо́н

hovel /'hɒv(ə)l/ *n.* лачу́га

hover /'hɒvə(r)/ *v.i.* пари́ть (*impf.*); (fig.): **to ~ around sb** ви́ться (*impf.*) вокру́г + *g.*
■ ~**craft** *n.* хо́веркрафт; су́дно на возду́шной поду́шке

☞ **how** /haʊ/ *adv.* **1** (in direct and indirect questions) как; каки́м о́бразом?; ~ **come?** (infml) как э́то?; ~ **come you are late?** почему́ э́то вы опа́здываете?; ~ **are you?** как пожива́ете?; ~ **do you know that?** отку́да вы э́то зна́ете?; ~ **about a drink?** не хоти́те ли вы́пить? **2** (with adjs. and advs.): ~ **far is it?** как далеко́ э́то нахо́дится?; ~ **many, much?** ско́лько?; ~ **old is she?** ско́лько ей лет? **3** (in indirect statements or questions): **I told him** ~ **I'd been abroad** я рассказа́л ему́, как я съе́здил за грани́цу **4** (in exclamations): ~ **I wish I were there!** как бы мне хоте́лось сейча́с быть там!

☞ **however** /haʊ'evə(r)/ *adv.* (with adj.) како́й бы ни; как ни; ~ **strong he is** како́й бы он ни был си́льный; (with adv.) как бы ни; ~ **hard he tried** как он ни стара́лся; (in questions) как же; ~ **did you find out that?** как же вы узна́ли э́то?; (nevertheless) одна́ко, и всё же; ~**, he forgot** одна́ко он забы́л

howl /haʊl/ *n.* вой
• *v.t. & i.* выть (*impf.*); **listen to the wolves** ~**ing!** послу́шайте, как во́ют во́лки!

howler /'haʊlə(r)/ *n.* (infml, error) грубе́йшая оши́бка, ля́псус

HQ *abbr.* (*of* **headquarters**) штаб-кварти́ра; (mil.) штаб, ста́вка

HR *abbr.* (*of* **human resources**) отде́л ка́дров

HRH (BrE) *abbr.* (*of* **Her/His Royal Highness**) Её/Его́ Короле́вское Высо́чество

HRT *abbr.* (*of* **hormone replacement therapy**) гормона́льная терапи́я

hub /hʌb/ *n.* ступи́ца; (fig.) центр; (comput.) хаб
■ ~**cap** *n.* колпа́к

hubbub /'hʌbʌb/ *n.* шум, го́вор, го́мон, гвалт

huddle /'hʌd(ə)l/ *v.i.* толпи́ться, с-; **they** ~**d together for warmth** они́ прижа́лись друг к дру́гу, что́бы согре́ться

hue[1] /hjuː/ *n.* (colour) отте́нок, тон (-а́)

hue[2] /hjuː/ *n.*: ~ **and cry** крик; (outcry) возмуще́ние

huff /hʌf/ *n.*: **he walked off in a** ~ он ушёл вконе́ц разоби́женный

hug /hʌg/ *n.* объя́тие
• *v.t. & i.* (**hugged, hugging**) обн|има́ть(ся), -я́ть(ся)

☞ **huge** /hjuːdʒ/ *adj.* огро́мный, грома́дный; (event) грандио́зный

hull /hʌl/ *n.* (of ship) ко́рпус; (of aircraft) фюзеля́ж

hum /hʌm/ *n.* (of insects) жужжа́ние; (of machines) гуде́ние, гул
• *v.t. & i.* (**hummed, humming**) **1** (make murmuring sound) (of insects) жужжа́ть (*impf.*); (of cars) гуде́ть (*impf.*) **2** (sing with closed lips) напева́ть (*impf.*)

☞ **human** /'hjuːmən/ *n.* челове́к
• *adj.* челове́ческий; ~ **being** челове́к; ~ **nature** челове́ческая приро́да; ~ **resources (department)** отде́л ка́дров; ~ **rights** права́ челове́ка; **human shield** живо́й щит

humane /hjuː'meɪn/ *adj.* гума́нный, челове́чный

humanism /'hjuːmənɪz(ə)m/ *n.* гумани́зм

humanist /'hjuːmənɪst/ *n.* гумани́ст

humanitarian /hjuːmænɪ'teərɪən/ *adj.* гуманита́рный; гума́нный

humanit|y /hjuː'mænɪti/ *n.* **1** (the human race) челове́чество **2** (humaneness) гума́нность **3**: **the** ~**ies** гуманита́рные нау́ки (*f. pl.*)

humble /'hʌmb(ə)l/ *adj.* (**humbler, humblest**) скро́мный, поко́рный, смире́нный

humbug /'hʌmbʌg/ *n.* (deceit, hypocrisy) надува́тельство; (fraud) обма́нщик; (nonsense) чушь, вздор; (BrE, sweet) ледене́ц

humdrum /'hʌmdrʌm/ *adj.* однообра́зный, ну́дный

humid /'hjuːmɪd/ *adj.* вла́жный

humidifier /hjuː'mɪdɪfaɪə(r)/ *n.* увлажни́тель (*m.*) во́здуха

humidity /hjuː'mɪdɪti/ *n.* вла́жность

humiliate /hjuː'mɪlɪeɪt/ *v.t.* ун|ижа́ть, -и́зить

humiliation /hjuːmɪlɪ'eɪʃ(ə)n/ *n.* униже́ние

humility /hjuː'mɪlɪti/ *n.* смире́ние; скро́мность

hummock /'hʌmək/ *n.* буго́р, приго́рок

humor /'hjuːmə(r)/ *n. & v.t.* (AmE) = **humour**

humorist /'hjuːmərɪst/ *n.* (facetious person) остря́к, весельча́к; (humorous writer etc.) юмори́ст

humorless /'hjuːmələs/ *adj.* (AmE) = **humourless**

humorous /'hjuːmərəs/ *adj.* юмористи́ческий

humour /'hjuːmə(r)/ (AmE **humor**) *n.* **1** (disposition) нрав, душе́вный склад **2** (amusement) ю́мор; **he has little sense of** ~ у него́ сла́бое чу́вство ю́мора
• *v.t.* потака́ть (*impf.*) + *d.*

humourless /'hjuːmələs/ (AmE **humorless**) *adj.* лишённый чу́вства ю́мора; ску́чный

hump /hʌmp/ *n.* горб

hunch /hʌntʃ/ *n.* чутьё, интуи́ция
• *v.t.*: **he** ~**ed (up) his shoulders** он ссуту́лился/сго́рбился

hundred /'hʌndrəd/ *n.* (*pl.* ~**s** or (with numeral or qualifying word) ~) (число́, но́мер) сто; (collect.) со́тня; **a** ~ **and fifty** сто пятьдеся́т; полтора́ста; ~**s of people** со́тни люде́й; **I'm one** ~ **per cent behind you** я стопроце́нтно на ва́шей стороне́; **in the nineteen** ~**s** в девятидеся́тые го́ды
• *adj.* сто + *g. pl.*; **a** ~ **miles away** (fig.) за ты́сячу вёрст

─────────────
☞ ключева́я ле́ксика

■ ~**weight** *n.* (BrE, approximately 50.8 kilograms) англи́йский це́нтнер; (AmE, approximately 45.4 kilograms) америка́нский це́нтнер

hundredth /'hʌndrədθ/ *n.* (fraction) одна́ со́тая
● *adj.* со́тый

hung /hʌŋ/ *past and p.p. of* ► **hang**

Hungarian /hʌŋ'geərɪən/ *n.* (person) венгр (венге́рка); (language) венге́рский язы́к
● *adj.* венге́рский

Hungary /'hʌŋgərɪ/ *n.* Ве́нгрия

hunger /'hʌŋgə(r)/ *n.* го́лод
■ ~ **strike** *n.* голодо́вка

hungry /'hʌŋgrɪ/ *adj.* (**hungrier**, **hungriest**) голо́дный

hunk /hʌŋk/ *n.* большо́й кусо́к; (of bread) ломо́ть (*m.*) хле́ба

hunt /hʌnt/ *n.* **1** (~ing expedition) охо́та **2** (search) охо́та (**for:** на + *a.*); по́иск|и (-ов) (**for:** + *g.*)
● *v.t. & i.* (pursue for food or sport) охо́титься (*impf.*) (на + *a.*); (search for) охо́титься (*impf.*) (за + *i.*); вести́ (*det.*) по́иски (+ *g.*), иска́ть (*impf.*)

hunter /'hʌntə(r)/ *n.* охо́тник

hunting /'hʌntɪŋ/ *n.* охо́та

hurdle /'hɜːd(ə)l/ *n.* (in athletics & fig.) барье́р, препя́тствие

hurl /hɜːl/ *v.t.* бр|оса́ть, -о́сить; **he** ~**ed abuse at me** он осы́пал меня́ оскорбле́ниями

hurrah /hʊ'rɑː/, **hurray** /hʊ'reɪ/ *int.* ура́!

hurricane /'hʌrɪkən/ *n.* урага́н

hurr|y /'hʌrɪ/ *n.* спе́шка, поспе́шность; **he was in no** ~**y to go** он не спеши́л уходи́ть; **in his** ~**y, he forgot his briefcase** в спе́шке он забы́л взять портфе́ль
● *v.t.* **1** (cause to move hastily) торопи́ть, по- **2** (perform hastily): **don't** ~**y the job** рабо́тайте не спеша́
● *v.i.* (move hastily) спеши́ть, по-; торопи́ться, по-; **he** ~**ied home** он спеши́л домо́й; **they** ~**ied to finish the work** они́ спеши́ли зако́нчить рабо́ту
● *with advs.*: ~**y along there, please!** потора́пливайтесь, пожа́луйста!; ~**y up!** потора́пливайтесь!

✍ **hurt** /hɜːt/ *n.* (offence) оби́да
● *v.t.* (*past and p.p.* ~) (inflict pain on) ушиб|а́ть, -и́ть; причин|я́ть, -и́ть боль + *d.*; **I won't** ~ **you** я не причиню́ вам бо́ли (*or* не сде́лаю вам бо́льно); **these shoes** ~ (**me**) э́ти ту́фли мне жмут; (injure) ушиб|а́ть, -и́ть; **he fell and** ~ **his back** он упа́л и уши́б спи́ну; ~ **oneself** ушиб|а́ться, -и́ться, ударя́ться, уда́риться; (damage) вреди́ть, по-; (offend, pain) об|ижа́ть, -и́деть; зад|ева́ть, -е́ть; **now you've** ~ **his feelings** ну вот, вы его́ и оби́дели
● *v.i.* (*past and p.p.* ~) (be sore) боле́ть (*impf.*); **my arm** ~**s** у меня́ боли́т/но́ет рука́; (do damage): **it won't** ~ **to wait** не меша́ло бы подожда́ть

hurtful /'hɜːtfʊl/ *adj.* оби́дный

hurtle /'hɜːt(ə)l/ *v.i.* нести́сь (*impf.*), мча́ться (*impf.*)

✍ **husband** /'hʌzbənd/ *n.* муж (-ья́)

hush /hʌʃ/ *v.t.*: **she** ~**ed the baby to sleep** она́ убаю́кала ребёнка; **the scandal was** ~**ed up**

сканда́л замя́ли
● *v.i.* (as int.) ~! ти́ше!; молчи́те!
■ ~-~ *adj.* (infml) та́йный, засекре́ченный

husk /hʌsk/ *n.* шелуха́; (of nuts) скорлупа́
● *v.t.* очища́ть, очи́стить; лущи́ть, об-

husky¹ /'hʌskɪ/ *n.* (dog) эскимо́сская ла́йка, ха́ски (*f. indecl.*)

husky² /'hʌskɪ/ *adj.* (**huskier**, **huskiest**) (hoarse) сухо́й, хри́плый

hustle /'hʌs(ə)l/ *n.* су́толока, да́вка
● *v.t.*: **the police** ~**d him away** его́ уволокли́ полице́йские

hut /hʌt/ *n.* (small building) хи́жина; (barrack) бара́к

hutch /hʌtʃ/ *n.* (for pets) кле́тка

hyacinth /'haɪəsɪnθ/ *n.* гиаци́нт

hybrid /'haɪbrɪd/ *n.* гибри́д

hybridize /'haɪbrɪdaɪz/ *v.t.* скре́|щивать, -сти́ть; гибридизи́ровать (*impf.*)

hydrangea /haɪ'dreɪndʒə/ *n.* горте́нзия

hydraulic /haɪ'drɒlɪk/ *adj.* гидравли́ческий

hydrochloric /haɪdrə'klɒrɪk/ *adj.*: ~ **acid** соля́ная кислота́

hydroelectric /haɪdrəʊɪ'lektrɪk/ *adj.* гидроэлектри́ческий

hydrofoil /'haɪdrəfɔɪl/ *n.* су́дно на подво́дных кры́льях; раке́та

hydrogen /'haɪdrədʒ(ə)n/ *n.* водоро́д

hyena /haɪ'iːnə/ *n.* гие́на

hygiene /'haɪdʒiːn/ *n.* гигие́на

hygienic /haɪ'dʒiːnɪk/ *adj.* гигиени́ческий

hygienist /'haɪdʒiːnɪst/ *n.* ассисте́нт зубно́го врача́ (*специалист по гигиене полости рта*)

hymn /hɪm/ *n.* (церко́вный) гимн

hype /haɪp/ *n.* (infml) крикли́вая рекла́ма
● *adj.*: ~**d-up** ду́тый, ли́повый

hyperactive /haɪpə'ræktɪv/ *adj.* чрезме́рно акти́вный

hyperbole /haɪ'pɜːbəlɪ/ *n.* гипе́рбола, преувеличе́ние

hyperlink /'haɪpəlɪŋk/ *n.* (comput.) гиперссы́лка, гиперте́кстовая ссы́лка

hypermarket /'haɪpəmɑːkɪt/ *n.* (BrE) гиперма́ркет

hypertension /haɪpə'tenʃ(ə)n/ *n.* (med.) высо́кое кровяно́е давле́ние

hypertext /'haɪpətekst/ *n.* (comput.) гиперте́кст

hyphen /'haɪf(ə)n/ *n.* дефи́с, чёрточка (infml)

hypnosis /hɪp'nəʊsɪs/ *n.* гипно́з

hypnotic /hɪp'nɒtɪk/ *adj.* гипноти́ческий

hypnotism /'hɪpnətɪz(ə)m/ *n.* гипноти́зм

hypnotist /'hɪpnətɪst/ *n.* гипнотизёр

hypnotize /'hɪpnətaɪz/ *v.t.* гипнотизи́ровать, за-

hypochondriac /haɪpə'kɒndrɪæk/ *n.* ипохо́ндрик

hypocrisy /hɪ'pɒkrɪsɪ/ *n.* лицеме́рие

hypocrite /'hɪpəkrɪt/ *n.* лицеме́р

hypocritical /hɪpə'krɪtɪk(ə)l/ *adj.* лицеме́рный, нейскренний

hypodermic /haɪpə'dɜːmɪk/ *adj.*: ~ **syringe/needle** шприц/игла́ для подко́жных

h

инъе́кций

hypothermia /haɪpəʊˈθɜːmɪə/ *n.* гипотерми́я

hypothesis /haɪˈpɒθɪsɪs/ *n. (pl.* **hypotheses** /-siːz/) гипо́теза

hypothetical /haɪpəˈθetɪk(ə)l/ *adj.* гипотети́ческий

hysterectomy /hɪstəˈrektəmɪ/ *n.* удале́ние ма́тки

hysteria /hɪˈstɪərɪə/ *n.* истери́я

hysterical /hɪˈsterɪk(ə)l/ *adj.* истери́чный

hysterics /hɪˈsterɪks/ *n.* исте́рика

Hz *abbr. (of* **hertz**) Гц (герц)

I i

✍ **I** /aɪ/ *pers. pron. (obj.* **me**) я; **he and** ∼ **were there** мы с ним бы́ли там; **he is older than** ∼ он ста́рше меня́

Iberian /aɪˈbɪərɪən/ *adj.* ибери́йский

✍ **ice** /aɪs/ *n.* лёд
• *v.t.* **1** (cover with ∼): **the pond was soon** ∼**d over** пруд вско́ре затяну́ло/скова́ло льдом **2** (cul.) глазирова́ть (*impf., pf.*)
■ ∼**-cold** *adj.* ледяно́й; ∼ **cream** *n.* моро́женое; ∼ **cube** *n.* ку́бик льда; ∼ **hockey** *n.* хокке́й (на льду); ∼**(d) lolly** *n.* (BrE) моро́женое на па́лочке; ∼ **rink** *n.* като́к; ∼ **skate** *n.* конёк; ∼**-skate** *v.i.* ката́ться (*impf.*) на конька́х

iceberg /ˈaɪsbɜːg/ *n.* а́йсберг

Iceland /ˈaɪslənd/ *n.* Исла́ндия

Icelandic /aɪsˈlændɪk/ *n.* исла́ндский язы́к
• *adj.* исла́ндский

icicle /ˈaɪsɪk(ə)l/ *n.* сосу́лька

icing /ˈaɪsɪŋ/ *n.* (on cake) са́харная глазу́рь

icon /ˈaɪkɒn/ *n.* ико́на; (comput.) ико́н(к)а, пиктогра́мма

iconoclastic /aɪkɒnəˈklæstɪk/ *adj.* иконобо́рческий

icy /ˈaɪsɪ/ *adj.* (**icier, iciest**) (cold, lit., fig.) ледяно́й; (covered with ice) покры́тый льдом

ID *abbr. (of* **identification**) удостовере́ние ли́чности

✍ **idea** /aɪˈdɪə/ *n.* **1** (mental concept; suggestion, plan) иде́я; **a good** ∼ хоро́шая иде́я **2** (thought) мысль; **I can't bear the** ∼ **of it** (одна́) мысль об э́том мне проти́вна **3** (notion; impression) поня́тие, представле́ние; **I've no** ∼ (я) поня́тия не име́ю **4** (aim, intention) иде́я, за́мысел, наме́рение **5** (opinion, belief) мне́ние, взгляд

✍ **ideal** /aɪˈdiːəl/ *n.* идеа́л
• *adj.* идеа́льный

idealism /aɪˈdɪəlɪz(ə)m/ *n.* идеали́зм

idealist /aɪˈdɪəlɪst/ *n.* идеали́ст

idealistic /aɪdɪəˈlɪstɪk/ *adj.* идеалисти́ческий

ideally /aɪˈdɪəlɪ/ *adv.* идеа́льно; (as sentence adverb) в идеа́ле

✍ ключева́я ле́ксика

identical /aɪˈdentɪk(ə)l/ *adj.* тожде́ственный, иденти́чный
■ ∼ **twins** *n. pl.* одноя́йцевые близнецы́

identification /aɪdentɪfɪˈkeɪʃ(ə)n/ *n.*: ∼ **of a body** опозна́ние тру́па; (*attr.*) опознава́тельный

✍ **identif|y** /aɪˈdentɪfaɪ/ *v.t.* **1** (establish identity of) опозна|ва́ть, -а́ть; идентифици́ровать (*impf., pf.*) **2** (associate) (*also v.i.*) (infml): **he** ∼**ied (himself) with the movement** он стал убеждённым сторо́нником э́того движе́ния

identikit® /aɪˈdentɪkɪt/ *n.*: **an** ∼ (**picture**) фоторо́бот

✍ **identity** /aɪˈdentɪtɪ/ *n.* ли́чность
■ ∼ **card** *n.* удостовере́ние ли́чности; ∼ **theft** *n.* кра́жа ли́чной информа́ции (*с це́лью получи́ть до́ступ к ба́нковскому счёту и т. п.*)

ideological /aɪdɪəˈlɒdʒɪk(ə)l/ *adj.* идеологи́ческий, иде́йный

ideology /aɪdɪˈɒlədʒɪ/ *n.* идеоло́гия

idiocy /ˈɪdɪəsɪ/ *n.* (stupidity; stupid behaviour) идио́тство

idiom /ˈɪdɪəm/ *n.* (expression) идио́ма; (language; way of speaking) наре́чие, го́вор, язы́к

idiomatic /ɪdɪəˈmætɪk/ *adj.* идиомати́ческий; **he speaks** ∼ **Russian** он свобо́дно владе́ет ру́сским языко́м; он говори́т по-ру́сски как ру́сский

idiosyncrasy /ɪdɪəʊˈsɪŋkrəsɪ/ *n.* своеобра́зие

idiosyncratic /ɪdɪəʊsɪŋˈkrætɪk/ *adj.* своеобра́зный

idiot /ˈɪdɪət/ *n.* идио́т (-ка)

idiotic /ɪdɪˈɒtɪk/ *adj.* идио́тский

idle /ˈaɪd(ə)l/ *adj.* (**idler, idlest**) **1** (not working) неработа́ющий; (unemployed) безрабо́тный; (of factories etc.) безде́йствующий; (of machinery) проста́ивающий **2** (lazy) пра́здный, лени́вый **3** (purposeless) пусто́й; **out of** ∼ **curiosity** из пра́здного/пусто́го любопы́тства; ∼ **talk** пуста́я болтовня́
• *v.t.*: **he** ∼**d away his life** он растра́тил свою́ жизнь впусту́ю
• *v.i.* **1** (be ∼) безде́льничать (*impf.*) **2** (of an engine): **the motor** ∼**s well** мото́р хорошо́ рабо́тает на холосто́м ходу́

idol /ˈaɪd(ə)l/ *n.* и́дол, куми́р

idolatry /aɪˈdɒlətrɪ/ *n.* идолопокло́нство; (fig.) обожа́ние

idolize /ˈaɪdəlaɪz/ *v.t.* (fig.) боготвори́ть (*impf.*)

idyll /ˈɪdɪl/ *n.* иди́ллия

idyllic /ɪˈdɪlɪk/ *adj.* идилли́ческий

i.e. *abbr.* (*of* **id est**) т. е. (то есть)

IED *n.* (*abbr. of* **improvized explosive device**) (mil.) самоде́льное взрывно́е устро́йство

☞ **if** /ɪf/ *conj.* **1** (condition or supposition) е́сли, е́сли бы; ~ **he comes** е́сли он придёт; ~ **I were you** на ва́шем ме́сте; **he talks as ~ he were the boss** он говори́т, как бу́дто он нача́льник **2** (though) хотя́, пусть; **a pleasant, ~ chilly, day** прия́тный, хотя́ и прохла́дный день **3** (whether): **do you know ~ he is at home?** вы не зна́ете, он до́ма?; **see ~ the door is locked** посмотри́те, заперта́ ли дверь

igloo /ˈɪɡluː/ *n.* и́глу (*nt. indecl.*)

ignite /ɪɡˈnaɪt/ *v.t.* заж|ига́ть, -е́чь
  ● *v.i.* заж|ига́ться, -е́чься

ignition /ɪɡˈnɪʃ(ə)n/ *n.* (~ system in engine) зажига́ние
  ■ ~ **key** *n.* ключ зажига́ния

ignoble /ɪɡˈnəʊb(ə)l/ *adj.* (**ignobler**, **ignoblest**) (base) по́длый, ни́зкий, посты́дный; (of lowly birth) ни́зкого происхожде́ния

ignominious /ɪɡnəˈmɪnɪəs/ *adj.* позо́рный, посты́дный; **an ~ death** бессла́вная смерть

ignominy /ˈɪɡnəmɪnɪ/ *n.* (dishonour) позо́р, бесче́стье

ignoramus /ɪɡnəˈreɪməs/ *n.* (*pl.* **~es**) неве́жда

ignorance /ˈɪɡnərəns/ *n.* (in general) неве́жество; (of certain facts) незна́ние, неве́дение

ignorant /ˈɪɡnərənt/ *adj.* неве́жественный; **I was ~ of his intentions** я не знал о его́ наме́рениях

☞ **ignore** /ɪɡˈnɔː(r)/ *v.t.* игнори́ровать (*impf., pf.*) (*pf. also* про-)

iguana /ɪɡˈwɑːnə/ *n.* игуа́на

ilk /ɪlk/ *n.*: **and others of his ~** (infml) и други́е того́ же ро́да; и ему́ подо́бные

ill /ɪl/ *n.* зло; **I meant him no ~** я не жела́л ему́ зла
  ● *adj.* **1** (unwell) больно́й, нездоро́вый; **he looks ~** он вы́глядит больны́м; **he was taken** (*or* **fell**) **~ with a fever** он заболе́л лихора́дкой; **I feel ~** мне нехорошо́; я пло́хо себя́ чу́вствую **2** (bad) дурно́й; ~ **effects** па́губные после́дствия; ~ **health** нездоро́вье, недомога́ние; ~ **humour** (BrE), **humor** (AmE), ~ **temper** (mood) дурно́е настрое́ние; ~ **-treatment** дурно́е обраще́ние; ~ **will** зла́я во́ля, зло́ба; **I bear you no ~ will** я не жела́ю вам зла
  ● *adv.* пло́хо, ду́рно; ~ **at ease** не по себе́; **to feel ~ at ease** чу́вствовать, по- себя́ нело́вко; **I can ~ afford it** я с трудо́м могу́ себе́ э́то позво́лить; **I have never spoken ~ of him** я никогда́ не отзыва́лся о нём пло́хо
  ■ ~ **-informed** *adj.* пло́хо осведомлённый; ~ **-mannered** *adj.* невоспи́танный, пло́хо

воспи́танный; ~ **-treat**, ~ **-use** *vv.t.* пло́хо об|ходи́ться, -ойти́сь с + *i.*

☞ **illegal** /ɪˈliːɡ(ə)l/ *adj.* незако́нный, нелега́льный

illegible /ɪˈledʒɪb(ə)l/ *adj.* неразбо́рчивый

illegitimate /ɪlɪˈdʒɪtɪmət/ *adj.* незаконнорождённый

illicit /ɪˈlɪsɪt/ *adj.* незако́нный, недозво́ленный

illiterate /ɪˈlɪtərət/ *adj.* негра́мотный

☞ **illness** /ˈɪlnɪs/ *n.* боле́знь

illogical /ɪˈlɒdʒɪk(ə)l/ *adj.* нелоги́чный

illuminate /ɪˈluːmɪneɪt/ *v.t.* осве|ща́ть, -ти́ть; **an ~d sign** светя́щаяся рекла́ма

illumination /ɪluːmɪˈneɪʃ(ə)n/ *n.* освеще́ние

illusion /ɪˈluːʒ(ə)n/ *n.* иллю́зия, обма́н; **I was under an ~** я был во вла́сти иллю́зии; **I have no ~s about him** относи́тельно него́ у меня́ нет никаки́х иллю́зий

illusionist /ɪˈluːʒənɪst/ *n.* иллюзиони́ст, фо́кусник

illusive /ɪˈluːsɪv/, **illusory** /ɪˈluːsərɪ/ *adjs.* иллюзо́рный, при́зрачный

illustrate /ˈɪləstreɪt/ *v.t.* иллюстри́ровать (*impf., pf.*)

illustration /ɪləˈstreɪʃ(ə)n/ *n.* иллюстра́ция

illustrative /ˈɪləstrətɪv/ *adj.* иллюстрати́вный, поясни́тельный; **a work of his genius** произведе́ние, пока́зывающее его́ гениа́льность/тала́нт

illustrator /ˈɪləstreɪtə(r)/ *n.* иллюстра́тор

illustrious /ɪˈlʌstrɪəs/ *adj.* просла́вленный, знамени́тый

☞ **image** /ˈɪmɪdʒ/ *n.* **1** (representation) изображе́ние **2** (likeness) ко́пия, портре́т; **he was the ~ of his father** он был то́чной ко́пией (*or* живы́м портре́том) своего́ отца́ **3** (impression made on others) и́мидж, репута́ция
  ■ ~ **consultant** *n.* консульта́нт по и́миджу

imagery /ˈɪmɪdʒərɪ/ *n.* (in writing) о́бразность

imaginable /ɪˈmædʒɪnəb(ə)l/ *adj.* вообрази́мый; **we had the greatest trouble ~** у нас бы́ли невообрази́мые хло́поты

imaginary /ɪˈmædʒɪnərɪ/ *adj.* вообража́емый

imagination /ɪmædʒɪˈneɪʃ(ə)n/ *n.* воображе́ние

imaginative /ɪˈmædʒɪnətɪv/ *adj.* (person) одарённый/облада́ющий (больши́м/ бога́тым) воображе́нием; (literature) худо́жественный

☞ **imagine** /ɪˈmædʒɪn/ *v.t.* **1** (form mental picture of) вообра|жа́ть, -зи́ть **2** (conceive) предст|авля́ть, -а́вить себе́; **I cannot ~ how it happened** я не могу́ предста́вить себе́, как э́то случи́лось **3** (suppose) предпол|ага́ть, -ожи́ть **4** (guess) дога́д|ываться, -а́ться; пон|има́ть, -я́ть

imam /ɪˈmɑːm/ *n.* има́м

imbalance /ɪmˈbæləns/ *n.* отсу́тствие равнове́сия, неусто́йчивость; несоотве́тствие

imbecile /ˈɪmbəsiːl/ *n.* глупе́ц, дура́к (ду́ра) (infml)
  ● *adj.* глу́пый

imbibe /ɪmˈbaɪb/ *v.t.* (drink) погло|ща́ть, -ти́ть; пить, вы́-; (fig., assimilate) усв|а́ивать, -о́ить;

впи́т|ывать, -а́ть; **he ~d new ideas** он впита́л но́вые иде́и

imbue /ɪm'bjuː/ *v.t.* (**imbues, imbued, imbuing**) **1** (lit., saturate) пропи́т|ывать, -а́ть; (dye) окра́|шивать, -сить **2** (fig., inspire) вселя́|ть, -и́ть (*что в кого*); (fill): **~d with hatred** прони́кнутый не́навистью

IMF *abbr.* (*of* **International Monetary Fund**) МВФ (Междунаро́дный валю́тный фонд)

imitate /'ɪmɪteɪt/ *v.t.* копи́ровать (*impf.*); и|мити́ровать, сы-

imitation /ɪmɪ'teɪʃ(ə)n/ *n.* имита́ция, подде́лка; **~ leather** иску́сственная ко́жа

immaculate /ɪ'mækjʊlət/ *adj.* безупре́чный

immaterial /ɪmə'tɪərɪəl/ *adj.* (unimportant) несуще́ственный

immature /ɪmə'tjʊə(r)/ *adj.* незре́лый

immeasurable /ɪ'meʒərəb(ə)l/ *adj.* неизмери́мый

𝄞 **immediate** /ɪ'miːdɪət/ *adj.* **1** (direct, closest possible) непосре́дственный; (next in order) очередно́й; **in the ~ neighbourhood** в непосре́дственной бли́зости; **my ~ neighbours** мои́ ближа́йшие сосе́ди; **on his ~ left** сра́зу нале́во от него́; **in the ~ future** в ближа́йшем бу́дущем **2** (without delay) неме́дленный, мгнове́нный **3** (urgent) безотлага́тельный

𝄞 **immediately** /ɪ'miːdɪətlɪ/ *adv.* неме́дленно, то́тчас (же), сра́зу, мгнове́нно

immemorial /ɪmɪ'mɔːrɪəl/ *adj.* незапа́мятный; **from time ~** с незапа́мятных времён

immense /ɪ'mens/ *adj.* огро́мный, грома́дный

immensity /ɪ'mensɪtɪ/ *n.* безме́рность, необъя́тность

immerse /ɪ'mɜːs/ *v.t.* погр|ужа́ть, -зи́ть

immersion /ɪ'mɜːʃ(ə)n/ *n.* (lit., fig.) погруже́ние ■ **~ heater** *n.* водонагрева́тель (*m.*) (погружа́емого ти́па)

immigrant /'ɪmɪɡrənt/ *n.* иммигра́нт (-ка)

immigration /ɪmɪ'ɡreɪʃ(ə)n/ *n.* иммигра́ция

imminent /'ɪmɪnənt/ *adj.* надвига́ющийся

immobile /ɪ'məʊbaɪl/ *adj.* неподви́жный

immobilize /ɪ'məʊbɪlaɪz/ *v.t.* лиш|а́ть, -и́ть подви́жности; **I was ~d by a broken leg** я не мог дви́гаться из-за сло́манной ноги́

immoderate /ɪ'mɒdərət/ *adj.* неуме́ренный

immoral /ɪ'mɒr(ə)l/ *adj.* безнра́вственный

immorality /ɪmə'rælɪtɪ/ *n.* безнра́вственность

immortal /ɪ'mɔːt(ə)l/ *n. & adj.* бессме́ртный

immortality /ɪmɔː'tælɪtɪ/ *n.* бессме́ртие

immortalize /ɪ'mɔːtəlaɪz/ *v.t.* увекове́чи|вать, -ть

immovable *adj.* недви́жимый

immune /ɪ'mjuːn/ *adj.*: **~ to disease** невосприи́мчивый к боле́зни; **~ to criticism** неподвла́стный кри́тике ■ **~ system** *n.* имму́нная систе́ма

immunity /ɪ'mjuːnɪtɪ/ *n.* (to disease etc.) иммуните́т, невосприи́мчивость (**to/**

against: к + *d.*, про́тив + *g.*); (in law) неприкоснове́нность, иммуните́т (**from:** от/ про́тив + *g.*); **diplomatic ~** дипломати́ческий иммуните́т

immunization /ɪmjuːnaɪ'zeɪʃ(ə)n/ *n.* иммуниза́ция

immunize /'ɪmjuːnaɪz/ *v.t.* вакцини́ровать (*impf., pf.*) (**against:** от + *g.*); де́лать, с- невосприи́мчивым (**against:** к + *d.*)

immutable /ɪ'mjuːtəb(ə)l/ *adj.* неизме́нный, непрело́жный

imp /ɪmp/ *n.* (also fig., mischievous child) дья́воленок, чертёнок, бесёнок; (fig. only) постре́л

𝄞 **impact** /'ɪmpækt/ *n.* (collision) столкнове́ние; (striking force) уда́р, толчо́к; (fig., effect, influence) возде́йствие, влия́ние

impair /ɪm'peə(r)/ *v.t.* (damage) повре|жда́ть, -ди́ть; (ruin; mar) по́ртить, ис-

impairment /ɪm'peəmənt/ *n.* (damage) поврежде́ние; (deterioration) ухудше́ние; (disability) дефе́кт

impale /ɪm'peɪl/ *v.t.* прок|а́лывать, -оло́ть; пронз|а́ть, -и́ть; прот|ыка́ть, -кну́ть; **he ~d himself on his sword** он пронзи́л себя́ мечо́м; **he fell and was ~d on the railings** он свали́лся на огра́ду и проткну́л себе́ живо́т

impart /ɪm'pɑːt/ *v.t.* перед|ава́ть, -а́ть

impartial /ɪm'pɑːʃ(ə)l/ *adj.* беспристра́стный

impartiality /ɪmpɑːʃɪ'ælɪtɪ/ *n.* беспристра́стность

impassable /ɪm'pɑːsəb(ə)l/ *adj.* (on foot) непроходи́мый; (for vehicles) непрое́зжий

impasse /'æmpɑːs/ *n.* тупи́к; **things reached an ~** дела́ зашли́ в тупи́к

impassioned /ɪm'pæʃ(ə)nd/ *adj.* стра́стный, пы́лкий

impassive /ɪm'pæsɪv/ *adj.* безмяте́жный

impatience /ɪm'peɪʃ(ə)ns/ *n.* нетерпе́ние; (irritation) раздраже́ние

impatient /ɪm'peɪʃ(ə)nt/ *adj.* нетерпели́вый; (irritable) раздражи́тельный, раздражённый; **he was getting ~** он теря́л терпе́ние, он раздража́лся; **he is ~ to begin** ему́ не те́рпится нача́ть

impeach /ɪm'piːtʃ/ *v.t.* (pol.) обвин|я́ть, -и́ть (*кого в чём*)

impeachment /ɪm'piːtʃmənt/ *n.* (pol.) импи́чмент

impeccable /ɪm'pekəb(ə)l/ *adj.* безупре́чный

impecunious /ɪmpɪ'kjuːnɪəs/ *adj.* безде́нежный, малообеспе́ченный

impedance /ɪm'piːd(ə)ns/ *n.* (elec.) по́лное сопротивле́ние, импеда́нс

impede /ɪm'piːd/ *v.t.* (obstruct) препя́тствовать (*impf.*) (+ *d.*); (hinder) меша́ть, по- (+ *d.*)

impediment /ɪm'pedɪmənt/ *n.* **1** (obstruction) препя́тствие; **an ~ to progress** препя́тствие на пути́ прогре́сса **2** (speech defect) дефе́кт ре́чи

impel /ɪm'pel/ *v.t.* (**impelled, impelling**) (drive; force) прин|ужда́ть, -уди́ть; заст|авля́ть, -а́вить; побу|жда́ть, -ди́ть; **conscience ~led**

𝄞 ключева́я ле́ксика

him to speak the truth со́весть принуди́ла его́ говори́ть пра́вду; **I feel ~led to say** я вы́нужден сказа́ть

impending /ɪm'pendɪŋ/ *adj.* предстоя́щий

impenetrable /ɪm'penɪtrəb(ə)l/ *adj.* непроница́емый

imperative /ɪm'perətɪv/ *n.* (gram.) повели́тельное наклоне́ние, императи́в
● *adj.* (essential): **it is ~ that you come at once** вам необходи́мо то́тчас яви́ться

imperceptible /ɪmpə'septɪb(ə)l/ *adj.* незаме́тный; незначи́тельный

imperfect /ɪm'pə:fɪkt/ *n.* (gram.) проше́дшее несоверше́нное вре́мя, имперфе́кт
● *adj.* несоверше́нный, дефе́ктный

imperfection /ɪmpə'fekʃ(ə)n/ *n.* (incompleteness, faultiness) несоверше́нство, неполнота́; (fault) дефе́кт, изъя́н; недоста́ток

imperfective /ɪmpə'fektɪv/ *n. & adj.* (gram.) несоверше́нный (вид)

imperial /ɪm'pɪərɪəl/ *adj.* импе́рский

imperialism /ɪm'pɪərɪəlɪz(ə)m/ *n.* империали́зм

imperialist /ɪm'pɪərɪəlɪst/ *n.* империали́ст
● *adj.* империалисти́ческий

impermeable /ɪm'pə:mɪəb(ə)l/ *adj.* непроница́емый

impersonal /ɪm'pə:sən(ə)l/ *adj.* безли́чный

impersonate /ɪm'pə:səneɪt/ *v.t.* (act the part of) игра́ть (*impf.*) роль + *g.*; (pretend to be) выдава́ть (*impf.*) себя́ за + *a.*

impersonator /ɪm'pə:səneɪtə(r)/ *n.* пароди́ст, имита́тор

impertinence /ɪm'pə:tɪnəns/ *n.* де́рзость, на́глость, наха́льство

impertinent /ɪm'pə:tɪnənt/ *adj.* де́рзкий, на́глый, наха́льный

imperturbable /ɪmpə'tə:bəb(ə)l/ *adj.* невозмути́мый

impervious /ɪm'pə:vɪəs/ *adj.* непроница́емый; (fig.): **~ to criticism** глухо́й к кри́тике

impetuous /ɪm'petʃʊəs/ *adj.* (impulsive) импульси́вный; (unpremeditated) необду́манный

impetus /'ɪmpɪtəs/ *n.* толчо́к; и́мпульс; (fig.) толчо́к, сти́мул

impinge /ɪm'pɪndʒ/ *v.i.* (**impinging**): **~ on** посяга́ть, -ну́ть на + *a.*

implacable /ɪm'plækəb(ə)l/ *adj.* неумоли́мый

implant *v.t.* /ɪm'plɑ:nt/ (med.) вв|оди́ть, -ести́; (fig., instil) внедр|я́ть, -и́ть
● *n.* /'ɪmplɑ:nt/ (med.) имплантáт

implausible /ɪm'plɔ:zɪb(ə)l/ *adj.* неправдоподо́бный

implement[1] /'ɪmplɪmənt/ *n.* ору́дие, инструме́нт; **farm ~s** сельскохозя́йственные ору́дия

✐ **implement**[2] /'ɪmplɪment/ *v.t.* выполня́ть, вы́полнить

implementation /ɪmplɪmen'teɪʃ(ə)n/ *n.* выполне́ние, осуществле́ние

implicate /'ɪmplɪkeɪt/ *v.t.* вовл|ека́ть, -е́чь; **the evidence ~d him** ули́ки пока́зывали на его́ прича́стность

implication /ɪmplɪ'keɪʃ(ə)n/ *n.* (thing implied) скры́тый смысл; (significance) значе́ние

implicit /ɪm'plɪsɪt/ *adj.* **1** (implied) подразумева́емый, недоска́занный
2 (unquestioning) безогово́рочный

implore /ɪm'plɔ:(r)/ *v.t.* умол|я́ть, -и́ть; **he ~d my forgiveness** он моли́л меня́ о проще́нии

impl|y /ɪm'plaɪ/ *v.t.* **1** (hint) намека́ть (*impf.*) на + *a.*; **he ~ied that I was wrong** он намека́л на то (*or* дал поня́ть), что я не прав **2** (mean) подразумева́ть (*impf.*); **what do his words ~y?** что означа́ют его́ слова́?

impolite /ɪmpə'laɪt/ *adj.* неве́жливый

imponderable /ɪm'pɒndərəb(ə)l/ *adj.* неулови́мый

import[1] /'ɪmpɔ:t/ *n.* (bringing from abroad) и́мпорт, ввоз; (*in pl.*) (goods introduced) и́мпортные/ввози́мые това́ры (*m. pl.*)

import[2] /ɪm'pɔ:t/ *v.t.* импорти́ровать (*impf., pf.*); вв|ози́ть, -езти́

✐ **importance** /ɪm'pɔ:t(ə)ns/ *n.* значе́ние, ва́жность; **it is of no ~** э́то не име́ет значе́ния

✐ **important** /ɪm'pɔ:t(ə)nt/ *adj.* ва́жный; **it is ~ for you to realize it** ва́жно, что́бы вы по́няли э́то

importer /ɪm'pɔ:tə(r)/ *n.* импортёр

✐ **impose** /ɪm'pəʊz/ *v.t.* (tax, penalty, etc.) нал|ага́ть, -ожи́ть (*что на кого*); **the government ~d a tax on wealth** госуда́рство обложи́ло бога́тых нало́гом; **he ~s his views on everyone** он всем навя́зывает свои́ взгля́ды
● *v.i.*: (**~ on**) (take advantage of): **he ~s on his friends** он испо́льзует свои́х друзе́й

imposing /ɪm'pəʊzɪŋ/ *adj.* внуши́тельный

imposition /ɪmpə'zɪʃ(ə)n/ *n.* **1** (imposing of obligation, burden, etc.) возложе́ние, наложе́ние **2** (of tax, etc.) обложе́ние **3** (unreasonable demand) чрезме́рное тре́бование

impossibility /ɪmpɒsɪ'bɪlɪtɪ/ *n.* невозмо́жность

✐ **impossible** /ɪm'pɒsɪb(ə)l/ *adj.* невозмо́жный; **don't ask me to do the ~** не тре́буйте от меня́ невозмо́жного

impostor /ɪm'pɒstə(r)/ *n.* обма́нщи|к (-ца)

impotence /'ɪmpət(ə)ns/ *n.* бесси́лие; (sexual) импоте́нция

impotent /'ɪmpət(ə)nt/ *adj.* бесси́льный

impound /ɪm'paʊnd/ *v.t.* конфискова́ть (*impf., pf.*)

impoverished /ɪm'pɒvərɪʃt/ *adj.* бе́дный, обедне́вший

impracticable /ɪm'præktɪkəb(ə)l/ *adj.* нереа́льный, неосуществи́мый

impractical /ɪm'præktɪk(ə)l/ *adj.* непракти́чный

imprecise /ɪmprɪ'saɪs/ *adj.* нето́чный

impregnable /ɪm'pregnəb(ə)l/ *adj.* непристу́пный

impregnate /'ɪmpregneɪt/ *v.t.* (fertilize) оплодотвор|я́ть, -и́ть; (saturate) проп́ит|ывать, -а́ть

impresario /ɪmprɪˈsɑːrɪəʊ/ n. (pl. ~s)
импреса́рио (m. indecl.), антрепенёр

impress /ɪmˈpres/ v.t. **1** (on the mind)
запечатл|ева́ть, -е́ть; **we ~ed on them
the need for caution** мы внуши́ли им
необходи́мость соблюда́ть осторо́жность
2 (have a strong effect on) произв|оди́ть,
-ести́ впечатле́ние на + a.; **he did not ~
me at all** он не произвёл на меня́ никако́го
впечатле́ния
● v.i. произв|оди́ть, -ести́ впечатле́ние

impression /ɪmˈpreʃ(ə)n/ n. **1** (imprint)
отпеча́ток, о́ттиск **2** (effect) эффе́кт,
результа́т; впечатле́ние; **make, create an ~**
произв|оди́ть, -ести́ впечатле́ние **3** (notion)
впечатле́ние, представле́ние; **I was under the
~ that … я полага́л, что…; I have a strong ~
that … я почти́ уве́рен, что…

impressionable /ɪmˈpreʃənəb(ə)l/ adj.
впечатли́тельный

impressionism /ɪmˈpreʃənɪz(ə)m/ n.
импрессиони́зм

impressionist /ɪmˈpreʃənɪst/ n. **1** (art)
импрессиони́ст **2** (mimic) пароди́ст,
имита́тор

✓ **impressive** /ɪmˈpresɪv/ adj. внуши́тельный,
впечатля́ющий, си́льный

imprint¹ /ˈɪmprɪnt/ n. (lit., fig.) отпеча́ток; (fig.)
печа́ть

imprint² /ɪmˈprɪnt/ v.t. отпеча́т|ывать, -ать;
(fig.) запечатл|ева́ть, -е́ть

imprison /ɪmˈprɪz(ə)n/ v.t. заключ|а́ть, -и́ть в
тюрьму́; заточа́ть, -и́ть

imprisonment /ɪmˈprɪzənmənt/ n.
тюре́мное заключе́ние

improbability /ɪmprɒbəˈbɪlɪtɪ/ n.
неправдоподо́бие, невероя́тность

improbable /ɪmˈprɒbəb(ə)l/ adj.
неправдоподо́бный, невероя́тный

impromptu /ɪmˈprɒmptjuː/ adj.
импровизи́рованный

improper /ɪmˈprɒpə(r)/ adj. **1** (unsuitable)
неподходя́щий, несоотве́тствующий;
неуме́стный **2** (incorrect) непра́вильный
3 (unseemly) неприли́чный, непристо́йный

impropriety /ɪmprəˈpraɪətɪ/ n.
(inappropriateness) неуме́стность; (indecency)
непристо́йность, неприли́чие; (irregularity)
непра́вильность

✓ **improv|e** /ɪmˈpruːv/ v.t. (make better)
ул|учша́ть, -у́чшить; **he has ~ed his French**
он де́лает успе́хи во францу́зском (языке́)
● v.i. **1** (become better) ул|учша́ться,
-у́чшиться; **wine ~es with age** с года́ми
вино́ стано́вится лу́чше; **his health is ~ing**
он улу́чшае (or его́ здоро́вье) поправля́ется **2** ~**e on**
(produce sth better than): **I can ~e on that** я могу́
предложи́ть не́что лу́чшее

✓ **improvement** /ɪmˈpruːvmənt/ n.
улучше́ние; **there has been an ~ in the
weather** пого́да улу́чшилась; (rebuilding etc.)

✓ ключевая лексика

improvidence /ɪmˈprɒvɪd(ə)ns/ n.
непредусмотри́тельность; расточи́тельность,
небережли́вость

improvident /ɪmˈprɒvɪd(ə)nt/ adj. (heedless of
the future) непредусмотри́тельный; (wasteful)
расточи́тельный, небережли́вый

improvisation /ɪmprəvaɪˈzeɪʃ(ə)n/ n.
импровиза́ция

improvise /ˈɪmprəvaɪz/ v.t. & i. (music, speech,
etc.) импровизи́ровать (impf.); (arrange
as makeshift) мастери́ть, с-; **an ~d dinner**
импровизи́рованный у́жин

imprudent /ɪmˈpruːd(ə)nt/ adj.
опроме́тчивый, неблагоразу́мный,
неосторо́жный

impudence /ˈɪmpjʊd(ə)ns/ n. де́рзость;
бессты́дство; наха́льство; на́глость

impudent /ˈɪmpjʊd(ə)nt/ adj. наха́льный,
на́глый

impulse /ˈɪmpʌls/ n. толчо́к

impulsive /ɪmˈpʌlsɪv/ adj. импульси́вный

impunity /ɪmˈpjuːnɪtɪ/ n.: **with ~**
безнака́занно

impure /ɪmˈpjʊə(r)/ adj. нечи́стый, гря́зный

impurity /ɪmˈpjʊərɪtɪ/ n. нечистота́, грязь; (in
pl.) (foreign substances) при́меси (f. pl.)

✓ **in** /ɪn/ adj. (infml, fashionable) популя́рный,
мо́дный; **he knows all the '~' people** он
зна́ет всех ну́жных люде́й
● adv. **1** (at home) до́ма; **tell them I'm not ~**
скажи́те, что меня́ нет до́ма; (~ one's office
etc.): **the boss is not ~ yet** нача́льника ещё
нет (у себя́ в кабине́те) **2** (arrived at station,
port, etc.): **the train has been ~ (for) 10 minutes**
по́езд пришёл 10 мину́т тому́ наза́д **3** (~
fashion): **short skirts are ~ again** коро́ткие
ю́бки опя́ть в мо́де **4** (~ power): **which party
was ~ then?** кака́я па́ртия была́ тогда́ у
вла́сти?
● prep. **1** (position) в/на + p.; (inhabited
places): **~ Moscow** в Москве́; (countries and
territories): **~ France** во Фра́нции; **~ the
Crimea** в Крыму́; (open spaces and flat areas):
~ the street на у́лице; **in the country(side)** в
дере́вне; **~ the garden** в саду́; (buildings): **~
the school** в шко́ле; (activities): **~ the lesson**
на уро́ке; **~ the war** на войне́; во вре́мя
войны́; (groups): **~ the crowd** в толпе́; (points
of compass): **~ the (Far) East** на (Да́льнем)
Восто́ке; (vehicles): **let's go ~ the car** пое́дем
на маши́не; (natural phenomena): **~ the fresh air**
на све́жем во́здухе; **~ darkness** в темноте́;
~ the rain под дождём; (books): **~ the Bible**
в Би́блии **2** (motion) в (rarely на) + a.; **they
arrived ~ the city** они́ при́были в го́род; **look
~ the mirror** посмотри́те в зе́ркало **3** (time,
specific centuries, years and decades): **~ the 20th
century** в двадца́том ве́ке; **~ 1975** в ты́сяча
девятьсо́т се́мьдесят пя́том году́; **~ May**
в ма́е; **~ (the) future** в бу́дущем; (ages of
history, events, periods): **~ the Middle Ages** в
Сре́дние века́; **3 times ~ one day** три ра́за
в/за оди́н день; (seasons): **~ spring** весно́й;
(times of day): **~ the morning** у́тром; **the**

mornings по утра́м; (at the end of): **I shall finish this book ~ 3 days' time** я зако́нчу/дочита́ю э́ту кни́гу че́рез три дня; (in the course of): **he completed it ~ 6 weeks** он зако́нчил э́то за шесть неде́ль **4** (condition, situation): **~ his absence** в его́ отсу́тствие; **~ these circumstances** при/в э́тих усло́виях; **~ power** у вла́сти **5** (manner): **~ a whisper** шёпотом; **~ detail** подро́бно; **~ secret** под секре́том, по секре́ту; **~ turn** по о́череди **6** (language): **~ Russian** по-ру́сски **7** (material): **a statue ~ marble** ста́туя из мра́мора **8** (ratio: out of): **only 1 ~ every 10 survived** из ка́ждых десяти́ вы́жил то́лько оди́н

inability /ɪnəˈbɪlɪtɪ/ *n.* неспосо́бность

in absentia /ɪn æbˈsentɪə/ *adv.* зао́чно

inaccessible /ɪnəkˈsesɪb(ə)l/ *adj.* недосту́пный, непристу́пный

inaccuracy /ɪnˈækjʊrəsɪ/ *n.* нето́чность

inaccurate /ɪnˈækjʊrət/ *adj.* нето́чный

inaction /ɪnˈækʃ(ə)n/ *n.* безде́йствие

inactive /ɪnˈæktɪv/ *adj.* безде́йственный, безде́йствующий

inactivity /ɪnækˈtɪvɪtɪ/ *n.* безде́йствие

inadequacy /ɪnˈædɪkwəsɪ/ *n.* недоста́точность; (personal) неспосо́бность, неполноце́нность

inadequate /ɪnˈædɪkwət/ *adj.* недоста́точный; (personally) неполноце́нный

inadvertent /ɪnədˈvɜːt(ə)nt/ *adj.* неумы́шленный, неча́янный, нево́льный

inadvisable /ɪnədˈvaɪzəb(ə)l/ *adj.* нецелесообра́зный, нежела́тельный

inane /ɪˈneɪn/ *adj.* глу́пый, пусто́й, неле́пый

inanimate /ɪnˈænɪmət/ *adj.* неодушевлённый

inanity /ɪnˈænɪtɪ/ *n.* глу́пость; неле́пость

inapplicable /ɪnˈæplɪkəb(ə)l, ɪnəˈplɪk-/ *adj.* неприменимый

inappropriate /ɪnəˈprəʊprɪət/ *adj.* неуме́стный, неподходя́щий

inarticulate /ɪnɑːˈtɪkjʊlət/ *adj.* косноязы́чный

inasmuch as /ɪnəzˈmʌtʃ/ *conj.* так как; ввиду́ того́, что

inattentive /ɪnəˈtentɪv/ *adj.* невнима́тельный

inaudible /ɪnˈɔːdɪb(ə)l/ *adj.* неслы́шный

inaugural /ɪˈnɔːgjʊr(ə)l/ *n.* торже́ственная речь при вступле́нии в до́лжность
• *adj.* вступи́тельный, инаугурацио́нный

inaugurate /ɪˈnɔːgjʊreɪt/ *v.t.* **1** (install with ceremony) (торже́ственно) вв|оди́ть, -ести́ в до́лжность; **the President was ~d** президе́нт вступи́л в до́лжность **2** (launch; officiate at opening of) откр|ыва́ть, -ы́ть; (fig.): **they ~d many reforms** они́ провели́ мно́го рефо́рм; **he ~d a new policy** он положи́л нача́ло но́вой поли́тике; **a new era was ~d** начала́сь но́вая э́ра

inauguration /ɪnɔːgjʊˈreɪʃ(ə)n/ *n.* (of official) вступле́ние в до́лжность

inauspicious /ɪnɔːˈspɪʃəs/ *adj.* злове́щий

inbox /ˈɪnbɒks/ *n.* (comput.) входя́щие (сообще́ния)

inbuilt /ɪnˈbɪlt/ *adj.* врождённый

incalculable /ɪnˈkælkjʊləb(ə)l/ *adj.* неисчисли́мый

incandescent /ɪnkænˈdes(ə)nt/ *adj.* (of electric light) накалённый, раскалённый; (emitting light) светя́щийся от нагре́ва; (furious) взбешённый; (passionate) пы́лкий

incantation /ɪnkænˈteɪʃ(ə)n/ *n.* заклина́ние, закля́тие

incapable /ɪnˈkeɪpəb(ə)l/ *adj.* неспосо́бный; **he is ~ of understanding** он неспосо́бен поня́ть (что); **~ of lying** неспосо́бный на ложь

incapacitate /ɪnkəˈpæsɪteɪt/ *v.t.*: **he was ~d for 3 weeks** он вы́был из стро́я на три неде́ли

incapacity /ɪnkəˈpæsɪtɪ/ *n.* неспосо́бность

incarcerate /ɪnˈkɑːsəreɪt/ *v.t.* заточ|а́ть, -и́ть (в тюрьму́)

incarceration /ɪnkɑːsəˈreɪʃ(ə)n/ *n.* заточе́ние (в тюрьму́)

incarnation /ɪnkɑːˈneɪʃ(ə)n/ *n.* воплоще́ние, олицетворе́ние

incendiary /ɪnˈsendɪərɪ/ *n.* (in full ~ **bomb**) зажига́тельная бо́мба

incense[1] /ˈɪnsens/ *n.* ла́дан, фимиа́м

incense[2] /ɪnˈsens/ *v.t.* разгне́вать (pf.); **she was ~d at, by his behaviour** его́ поведе́ние привело́ её в я́рость

incentive /ɪnˈsentɪv/ *n.* побужде́ние, сти́мул; **~ bonus** поощри́тельная пре́мия

inception /ɪnˈsepʃ(ə)n/ *n.* нача́ло, начина́ние

incessant /ɪnˈses(ə)nt/ *adj.* непреста́нный, непреры́вный

incest /ˈɪnsest/ *n.* кровосмеше́ние

incestuous /ɪnˈsestʃʊəs/ *adj.* кровосмеси́тельный

✍ **inch** /ɪntʃ/ *n.* дюйм

incidence /ˈɪnsɪd(ə)ns/ *n.* **1** (range or scope of effect) охва́т, сфе́ра де́йствия; **the ~ of a disease** число́ заболе́вших (or слу́чаев заболева́ния) **2** (phys., falling; contact) паде́ние, накло́н; **angle of ~** у́гол паде́ния

✍ **incident** /ˈɪnsɪd(ə)nt/ *n.* слу́чай, собы́тие; происше́ствие, инциде́нт

incidental /ɪnsɪˈdent(ə)l/ *adj.* (casual) случа́йный; (secondary) побо́чный
■ **~ music** *n.* музыка́льное сопровожде́ние

incidentally /ɪnsɪˈdentəlɪ/ *adv.* (in passing) попу́тно

incinerate /ɪnˈsɪnəreɪt/ *v.t.* испепел|я́ть, -и́ть

incinerator /ɪnˈsɪnəreɪtə(r)/ *n.* мусоросжига́тельная печь

incision /ɪnˈsɪʒ(ə)n/ *n.* надре́з

incisive /ɪnˈsaɪsɪv/ *adj.* ре́жущий; (fig.): **an ~ tone** ре́зкий тон; **an ~ mind** о́стрый/проница́тельный ум

incite /ɪnˈsaɪt/ *v.t.* (stir up) возбу|жда́ть, -ди́ть; (urge) побу|жда́ть, -ди́ть; **he ~d them to revolt** он подстрека́л их к мятежу́

incitement /ɪn'saɪtmənt/ *n.* (inciting) подстрека́тельство; (spur, stimulus) побужде́ние, сти́мул

inclination /ɪnklɪ'neɪʃ(ə)n/ *n.* **1** (tendency) накло́нность **2** (desire) охо́та, жела́ние; **he has lost all ~ to work** он потеря́л вся́кое жела́ние рабо́тать

incline /ɪn'klaɪn/ *v.t.* **1** (bend forward or down) склон|я́ть, -и́ть **2** (fig., dispose) склон|я́ть, -и́ть; **I am ~d to agree with you** я скло́нен согласи́ться с ва́ми; **if you feel ~d (to do so)** е́сли вы располо́жены э́то сде́лать
● *v.i.* **1** (lean, slope) наклон|я́ться, -и́ться **2** (tend) склон|я́ться, -и́ться; **he ~s to(wards) leniency** он скло́нен проявля́ть снисходи́тельность

✐ **includ|e** /ɪn'kluːd/ *v.t.* включ|а́ть, -и́ть; **5 members, ~ing the President** пять чле́нов, включа́я президе́нта; **service ~ed** включа́я услу́ги

inclusion /ɪn'kluːʒ(ə)n/ *n.* включе́ние

inclusive /ɪn'kluːsɪv/ *adj. & adv.* **1**: **~ of** (including) включа́я; включа́ющий в себя́; содержа́щий в себе́ **2**: **from February 2nd to 20th ~** со второ́го февраля́ по двадца́тое включи́тельно

incognito /ɪnkɒg'niːtəʊ/ *adv.* инко́гнито

incoherent /ɪnkəʊ'hɪərənt/ *adj.* бессвя́зный

✐ **income** /'ɪŋkʌm/ *n.* дохо́д
■ **~ tax** *n.* подохо́дный нало́г

incoming /'ɪnkʌmɪŋ/ *adj.* входя́щий, поступа́ющий, прибыва́ющий; **the ~ tide** прили́в; **~ calls** поступа́ющие/входя́щие звонки́; **~ mail** входя́щая по́чта

incommunicado /ɪnkəmjuːnɪ'kɑːdəʊ/ *adj. & adv.* лишённый пра́ва перепи́ски и сообще́ния; в изоля́ции

incomparable /ɪn'kɒmpərəb(ə)l/ *adj.* несравне́нный, беспод́обный

incompatible /ɪnkəm'pætɪb(ə)l/ *adj.* несовмести́мый

incompetence /ɪn'kɒmpɪt(ə)ns/ *n.* неспосо́бность, некомпете́нтность; неуме́ние

incompetent /ɪn'kɒmpɪt(ə)nt/ *adj.* (person) неспосо́бный, некомпете́нтный; (work) неуме́лый

incomplete /ɪnkəm'pliːt/ *adj.* (not full) непо́лный; (unfinished) незавершённый, незако́нченный

incomprehensible /ɪnkɒmprɪ'hensɪb(ə)l/ *adj.* непоня́тный, непостижи́мый

inconceivable /ɪnkən'siːvəb(ə)l/ *adj.* невообрази́мый

inconclusive /ɪnkən'kluːsɪv/ *adj.* (of argument etc.) неубеди́тельный; **the vote was ~** голосова́ние не́ дало определённых результа́тов

incongruity /ɪnkɒŋ'gruːɪtɪ/ *n.* несоотве́тствие; неуме́стность

incongruous /ɪn'kɒŋgrʊəs/ *adj.* (out of keeping) несоотве́тствующий, неподходя́щий; (out of

place) неуме́стный

inconsequential /ɪnkɒnsɪ'kwenʃ(ə)l/ *adj.* (insignificant) незначи́тельный; (irrelevant, immaterial) несуще́ственный

inconsiderate /ɪnkən'sɪdərət/ *adj.* невнима́тельный (к други́м), нечу́ткий

inconsistency /ɪnkən'sɪst(ə)nsɪ/ *n.* непосле́довательность; противоречи́вость

inconsistent /ɪnkən'sɪst(ə)nt/ *adj.* (of a person) непосле́довательный; (of an account) противоречи́вый

inconsolable /ɪnkən'səʊləb(ə)l/ *adj.* неуте́шный, безуте́шный

inconspicuous /ɪnkən'spɪkjʊəs/ *adj.* незаме́тный

incontestable /ɪnkən'testəb(ə)l/ *adj.* неоспори́мый

incontinent /ɪn'kɒntɪnənt/ *adj.* (unrestrained) несде́ржанный; (med.): **he was ~** он страда́л недержа́нием (мочи́/ка́ла)

incontrovertible /ɪnkɒntrə'vɜːtɪb(ə)l/ *adj.* неоспори́мый

inconvenience /ɪnkən'viːnɪəns/ *n.* неудо́бство, беспоко́йство
● *v.t.* причин|я́ть, -и́ть неудо́бство + *d.*

inconvenient /ɪnkən'viːnɪənt/ *adj.* неудо́бный

incorporate /ɪn'kɔːpəreɪt/ *v.t.* **1** (combine) объедин|я́ть, -и́ть **2** (include) включ|а́ть, -и́ть

incorrect /ɪnkə'rekt/ *adj.* (inaccurate) непра́вильный; (untrue) неве́рный

incorrigible /ɪn'kɒrɪdʒɪb(ə)l/ *adj.* неисправи́мый

✐ **increase¹** /'ɪnkriːs/ *n.* рост, возраста́ние; увеличе́ние; **unemployment is on the ~** безрабо́тица растёт/увели́чивается; (amount of ~) прирост; **my shares show an ~ of 5%** мои́ а́кции подняли́сь на пять проце́нтов

✐ **increase²** /ɪn'kriːs/ *v.t.* увели́чи|вать, -ть; (extend): **~ one's influence** расши|ря́ть, -и́рить своё влия́ние; (raise): **~ prices** пов|ыша́ть, -ы́сить це́ны; (intensify): **this merely ~d his determination** э́то то́лько укрепи́ло его́ реши́мость
● *v.i.* увели́чи|ваться, -ться; (grow) расти́ (*impf.*); (intensify) уси́ли|ваться, -ться; (expand) расш|иря́ться, -и́риться; (rise): **sugar ~d in price** са́хар повы́сился в цене́ (*or* подорожа́л)

✐ **increasingly** /ɪn'kriːsɪŋlɪ/ *adv.* всё бо́лее; **it becomes ~ difficult** стано́вится всё трудне́е

incredibl|e /ɪn'kredɪb(ə)l/ *adj.* невероя́тный; **he was ~y stupid** он был невероя́тно глуп

incredulous /ɪn'kredjʊləs/ *adj.* недове́рчивый

increment /'ɪnkrɪmənt/ *n.* (regular salary increase) приба́вка

incriminating /ɪn'krɪmɪneɪtɪŋ/ *adj.* изоблича́ющий

incubate /'ɪŋkjʊbeɪt/ *v.t.* (of a bird) сиде́ть (*impf.*) на (я́йцах); (hatch by artificial heat) инкуби́ровать (*impf., pf.*)
● *v.i.* (of a disease) находи́ться (*impf.*) в инкубацио́нном пери́оде

✐ ключева́я ле́ксика

incubator /'ɪŋkjʊbeɪtə(r)/ *n.* инкубáтор

inculcate /'ɪnkʌlkeɪt/ *v.t.* внедр|ять, -йть; внуш|áть, -йть

incumbent /ɪn'kʌmbənt/ *n.* **1** (eccl.) прихóдский свящéнник **2** (holder of a post) занимáющий (какую-н.) дóлжность
● *adj.* (holding office) занимáющий пост, дóлжность; **the ~ president** нынешний президéнт; (necessary as a duty): **~ upon** возлежáщий на + *p.*; возлóженный на + *a.*; **it is ~ upon you to warn them** вы обязаны предупредить их

incur /ɪn'kə:(r)/ *v.t.* (**incurred, incurring**) навл|екáть, -éчь на себя; **he ~red heavy expenses** он понёс большие расхóды

incurable /ɪn'kjʊərəb(ə)l/ *adj.* (of sick person) безнадёжный; (fig.): **an ~ optimist** неисправимый оптимист; (of disease) неизлечимый

incursion /ɪn'kə:ʃ(ə)n/ *n.* вторжéние, налёт, набéг

indebted /ɪn'detɪd/ *adj.* (owing money) в долгý, дóлжный; (owing gratitude) обязанный

indecency /ɪn'di:s(ə)nsɪ/ *n.* неприличие, непристóйность; **an act of gross ~** непристóйное дéйствие

indecent /ɪn'di:s(ə)nt/ *adj.* неприличный, непристóйный
■ **~ exposure** *n.* непристóйное обнажéние тéла

indecipherable /ɪndɪ'saɪfərəb(ə)l/ *adj.* не поддающийся расшифрóвке; (of handwriting etc.) неразбóрчивый

indecision /ɪndɪ'sɪʒ(ə)n/ *n.* нерешительность

indecisive /ɪndɪ'saɪsɪv/ *adj.* (irresolute) нерешительный; (not producing a result) не решáющий

indeclinable /ɪndɪ'klaɪnəb(ə)l/ *adj.* (gram.) несклоняемый

ɕ **indeed** /ɪn'di:d/ *adv.* **1** (really, actually) действительно; в сáмом дéле; вот именно **2** (expr. emphasis): **thanks very much ~** премнóго вам благодáрен; **"Will you come?" — "I will ~"** «Вы придёте?» — «Непремéнно/ обязáтельно» **3** (expr. intensification) к томý же; мáло/бóлее тогó; дáже

indefatigable /ɪndɪ'fætɪgəb(ə)l/ *adj.* неутомимый

indefensible /ɪndɪ'fensɪb(ə)l/ *adj.* (mil.) непригóдный для оборóны; (unjustified) не имéющий оправдáния, непростительный; **an ~ statement** неприéмлемое утверждéние

indefinable /ɪndɪ'faɪnəb(ə)l/ *adj.* неопределимый

indefinite /ɪn'defɪnɪt/ *adj.* **1** (not clearly defined) неопределённый **2** (unlimited) неограниченный **3** (gram.): **~ article** неопределённый артикль

indefinitely /ɪn'defɪnɪtlɪ/ *adv.* на неопределённое врéмя

indelible /ɪn'delɪb(ə)l/ *adj.* (lit., fig.) несмывáемый

indentation /ɪnden'teɪʃ(ə)n/ *n.* (notch, cut) зубéц, вырез, зазýбрина; (in coastline etc.)

извилина

independence /ɪndɪ'pend(ə)ns/ *n.* независимость (**from:** от + *g.*)

ɕ **independent** /ɪndɪ'pend(ə)nt/ *adj.* независимый, самостоятельный; не зависящий (**of:** от + *g.*); (*in adv. sense*) **~ of** независимо от + *g.*; помимо + *g.*

in-depth /ɪn'depθ/ *adj.* обстоятельный

indescribable /ɪndɪ'skraɪbəb(ə)l/ *adj.* неописуемый

indestructible /ɪndɪ'strʌktɪb(ə)l/ *adj.* неразрушимый

indeterminate /ɪndɪ'tə:mɪnət/ *adj.* (not fixed; indefinite) неопределённый; **an ~ sentence** неопределённый приговóр; (not settled; undecided) нерешённый; неокончáтельный; **an ~ result** неокончáтельный результáт; (vague; indefinable) неясный, смýтный

index /'ɪndeks/ *n.* **1** (indicative figure) индекс; **retail price ~** индекс рóзничных цен **2** (alphabetical) указáтель (*m.*); **card ~** картотéка **3**: **~ finger** указáтельный пáлец
● *v.t.* (econ.) (*also* **~-link**, BrE) индексировать (*impf., pf.*)
■ **~ card** *n.* (картотéчная) кáрточка

India /'ɪndɪə/ *n.* Индия

ɕ **Indian** /'ɪndɪən/ *n.* **1** (native of India) инди|ец (-áнка) **2** (*in full* **American ~**) инд|éец (-иáнка)
● *adj.* **1** (of India) индийский **2** (North American) индéйский
■ **~ Ocean** *n.* Индийский океáн; **~ summer** *n.* бáбье лéто

ɕ **indicate** /'ɪndɪkeɪt/ *v.t.* (point to) укáз|ывать, -áть; (be a sign of) свидéтельствовать (*impf.*) о + *p.*

indication /ɪndɪ'keɪʃ(ə)n/ *n.* (sign) знак, указáтель (*m.*); (hint) признак, намёк; **he gave no ~ of his feelings** он ничéм не выдал своих чувств

indicative /ɪn'dɪkətɪv/ *n.* (gram.) изъявительное наклонéние
● *adj.*: **~ of** (suggesting, showing) укáзывающий на (+ *a.*)

indicator /'ɪndɪkeɪtə(r)/ *n.* **1** (pointer of instrument) стрéлка; указáтель (*m.*) **2** (BrE, on vehicle) указáтель (*m.*) поворóта

indict /ɪn'daɪt/ *v.t.* предъяв|лять, -ить обвинéние + *d.*

indictment /ɪn'daɪtmənt/ *n.* (charge) обвинительный акт; (fig.): **these figures are an ~ of government policy** эти цифры служат обвинительным докумéнтом прóтив политики правительства

indifference /ɪn'dɪfrəns/ *n.* безразличие; равнодýшие

indifferent /ɪn'dɪfrənt/ *adj.* (without interest) безразличный; (mediocre) посрéдственный

indigenous /ɪn'dɪdʒɪnəs/ *adj.* тузéмный

indigestible /ɪndɪ'dʒestɪb(ə)l/ *adj.* трудноперевáриваемый

indigestion /ɪndɪ'dʒestʃ(ə)n/ *n.* несварéние желýдка

indignant /ɪn'dɪgnənt/ *adj.* возмущённый; **I was ~ at his remark** его замечáние возмути́ло меня́

indignation /ˌɪndɪɡˈneɪʃ(ə)n/ *n.* возмуще́ние

indignit|y /ɪnˈdɪɡnɪtɪ/ *n.* униже́ние, оскорбле́ние; **we were subjected to various ~ies** мы подве́рглись вся́ческим униже́ниям

indirect /ˌɪndaɪˈrekt/ *adj.* непрямо́й, ко́свенный

indiscreet /ˌɪndɪˈskriːt/ *adj.* беста́ктный

indiscretion /ˌɪndɪˈskreʃ(ə)n/ *n.* нескро́мность; (indiscreet act) неосторо́жный посту́пок

indiscriminate /ˌɪndɪˈskrɪmɪnət/ *adj.* **1** (undiscriminating) неразбо́рчивый **2** (random) де́йствующий без разбо́ра

indispensable /ˌɪndɪˈspensəb(ə)l/ *adj.* необходи́мый

indisposed /ˌɪndɪˈspəʊzd/ *adj.* (unwell) (немно́го) нездоро́вый; **the Queen is ~** короле́ве нездоро́вится

indisposition /ˌɪndɪspəˈzɪʃ(ə)n/ *n.* (feeling unwell) недомога́ние

indisputable /ˌɪndɪˈspjuːtəb(ə)l/ *adj.* неоспори́мый

indistinct /ˌɪndɪˈstɪŋkt/ *adj.* (of things seen or heard) нея́сный; невня́тный; (vague) сму́тный, расплы́вчатый

indistinguishable /ˌɪndɪˈstɪŋɡwɪʃəb(ə)l/ *adj.* (not recognizably different) неразличи́мый, неотличи́мый; **he is ~ from his brother** его́ невозмо́жно отличи́ть от бра́та; **the two are ~** э́ти дво́е неразличи́мы

✓ **individual** /ˌɪndɪˈvɪdʒʊəl/ *n.* **1** (single being) ли́чность, индиви́дуум, едини́ца, осо́бь **2** (type of person) челове́к, тип
● *adj.* **1** (single, particular) отде́льный **2** (of or for one person) ли́чный, ча́стный; **the teacher gave each pupil ~ attention** учи́тель уделя́л внима́ние ка́ждому ученику́ **3** (distinctive) характе́рный, осо́бенный

individualism /ˌɪndɪˈvɪdjʊəlɪz(ə)m/ *n.* индивидуали́зм

individuality /ˌɪndɪvɪdjʊˈælɪtɪ/ *n.* индивидуа́льность

indoctrinate /ɪnˈdɒktrɪneɪt/ *v.t.* внуш|а́ть, -и́ть при́нципы + *d.*

indolent /ˈɪndələnt/ *adj.* лени́вый, вя́лый

indomitable /ɪnˈdɒmɪtəb(ə)l/ *adj.* неукроти́мый

Indonesia /ˌɪndəˈniːzə/ *n.* Индоне́зия

Indonesian /ˌɪndəˈniːzɪən/ *n.* (person) индонези́|ец (-йка); (language) индонези́йский язы́к
● *adj.* индонези́йский

indoor /ˈɪndɔː(r)/ *adj.* ко́мнатный; **~ games** ко́мнатные и́гры; **~ swimming pool** закры́тый бассе́йн

indoors /ɪnˈdɔːz/ *adv.* (expr. position) в до́ме; взаперти́; (expr. motion) в дом, внутрь

induce /ɪnˈdjuːs/ *v.t.* **1** (persuade, prevail on) убе|жда́ть, -ди́ть; **nothing will ~ him to change his mind** ничто́ не заста́вит его́

измени́ть реше́ние **2** (bring about) вызыва́ть, вы́звать; **illness ~d by fatigue** боле́знь, вы́званная переутомле́нием

inducement /ɪnˈdjuːsmənt/ *n.* (motive, incentive) сти́мул; **there is no ~ for me to stay here** ничто́ не уде́рживает меня́ здесь; (bribe) по́дкуп

induction /ɪnˈdʌkʃ(ə)n/ *n.* введе́ние, вступле́ние

indulge /ɪnˈdʌldʒ/ *v.t.* (gratify, give way to) потво́рствовать (*impf.*) + *d.*; (spoil) по́ртить, ис-; балова́ть, из-
● *v.i.* (allow oneself pleasure) увлека́ться (*impf.*) (*чем*); **he ~s in a cigar** он позволя́ет себе́ вы́курить сига́ру

indulgence /ɪnˈdʌldʒ(ə)ns/ *n.* **1** (gratification) потво́рство **2** (pleasure indulged in) удово́льствие; **smoking is his only ~** куре́ние — его́ еди́нственная сла́бость

indulgent /ɪnˈdʌldʒ(ə)nt/ *adj.* потво́рствующий; **~ parents** не сли́шком стро́гие роди́тели

✓ **industrial** /ɪnˈdʌstrɪəl/ *adj.* промы́шленный, индустриа́льный; **~ accident** несча́стный слу́чай на произво́дстве
■ **~ action** *n.* (BrE) забасто́вочные де́йствия; **~ estate** (BrE) промы́шленная зо́на; **~ relations** *n. pl.* произво́дственные отноше́ния (ме́жду работода́телями и (их) рабо́тниками)

industrialist /ɪnˈdʌstrɪəlɪst/ *n.* промы́шленник; фабрика́нт

industrialization /ɪndʌstrɪəlaɪˈzeɪʃ(ə)n/ *n.* индустриализа́ция

industrialize /ɪnˈdʌstrɪəlaɪz/ *v.t.* индустриализи́ровать (*impf., pf.*)

industrious /ɪnˈdʌstrɪəs/ *adj.* трудолюби́вый

✓ **industry** /ˈɪndəstrɪ/ *n.* **1** (branch of manufacture) о́трасль **2** (the world of manufacture) индустри́я; промы́шленность; **he intends to go into ~** он хо́чет заня́ться произво́дством **3** (diligence) трудолю́бие

inebriated /ɪˈniːbrɪeɪtɪd/ *adj.* пья́ный

inedible /ɪnˈedɪb(ə)l/ *adj.* несъедо́бный

ineffective /ˌɪnɪˈfektɪv/ *adj.* неэффекти́вный

ineffectual /ˌɪnɪˈfektʃʊəl/ *adj.* безрезульта́тный

inefficiency /ˌɪnɪˈfɪʃ(ə)nsɪ/ *n.* (of persons) неуме́ние, неспосо́бность; (of organizations, etc.) неэффекти́вность

inefficient /ˌɪnɪˈfɪʃ(ə)nt/ *adj.* (of persons) неуме́лый, неспосо́бный; (of organizations, etc.) неэффекти́вный; (of machines) непроизводи́тельный

ineligible /ɪnˈelɪdʒɪb(ə)l/ *adj.* (for office) неподходя́щий; (for a benefit) не име́ющий пра́ва (**for**: на + *a.*)

inept /ɪˈnept/ *adj.* неуме́лый

ineptitude /ɪˈneptɪtjuːd/ *n.* неуме́ние; (act) глу́пая вы́ходка

inequality /ˌɪnɪˈkwɒlɪtɪ/ *n.* нера́венство

inequity /ɪnˈekwɪtɪ/ *n.* несправедли́вость

inert /ɪˈnɜːt/ *adj.* (fig.) вя́лый, безде́ятельный

✓ ключева́я ле́ксика

inertia /ɪ'nə:ʃə/ *n.* инéртность; (phys.) инéрция

inescapable /ɪnɪ'skeɪpəb(ə)l/ *adj.* неизбéжный

inevitability /ɪnevɪtə'bɪlɪtɪ/ *n.* неизбéжность

inevitable /ɪn'evɪtəb(ə)l/ *adj.* неизбéжный, неминýемый

inexcusable /ɪnɪk'skju:zəb(ə)l/ *adj.* непрости́тельный

inexhaustible /ɪnɪg'zɔ:stɪb(ə)l/ *adj.* (unfailing) неистощи́мый, неисчерпáемый

inexpensive /ɪnɪk'spensɪv/ *adj.* недорогóй

inexperienced /ɪnɪk'spɪərɪənst/ *adj.* неóпытный

inexplicable /ɪnɪk'splɪkəb(ə)l/ *adj.* необъясни́мый

in extremis /ɪn ek'stri:mɪs/ *adv.* в крáйнем слýчае

infallible /ɪn'fælɪb(ə)l/ *adj.* надёжный

infamous /'ɪnfəməs/ *adj.* (person) бесслáвный; (behaviour) позóрный

infancy /'ɪnf(ə)nsɪ/ *n.* младéнчество

infant /'ɪnf(ə)nt/ *n.* младéнец
■ ∼ **school** *n.* (BrE) шкóла для малышéй, млáдшие клáссы начáльной шкóлы

infantile /'ɪnfəntaɪl/ *adj.* **1** дéтский, младéнческий; ∼ **paralysis** дéтский парали́ч **2** (childish) инфанти́льный

infantry /'ɪnf(ə)ntrɪ/ *n.* пехóта
■ ∼**man** *n.* пехоти́нец

infatuate /ɪn'fætʃʊeɪt/ *v.t.*: **he is** ∼**d with her** онá покори́ла/плени́ла егó

infatuation /ɪnfætʃʊ'eɪʃ(ə)n/ *n.* влюблённость, увлечéние

infect /ɪn'fekt/ *v.t.* (lit., fig.) зарА|жáть, -зи́ть; **the wound became** ∼**ed** рáна загнои́лась

⚲ **infection** /ɪn'fekʃ(ə)n/ *n.* инфéкция; **he caught the** ∼ **from his brother** он зарази́лся от брáта

infectious /ɪn'fekʃəs/ *adj.* (disease) зарáзный, инфекциóнный; (person) зарáзный; (fig.) зарази́тельный

infer /ɪn'fə:(r)/ *v.t.* (**inferred**, **inferring**) заключ|áть, -и́ть; предпол|агáть, -ожи́ть

inferior /ɪn'fɪərɪə(r)/ *n.* подчинённый
● *adj.* **1** (lower in position, rank, etc.) ни́зший **2** (poorer in quality) хýдший **3** (of less importance) неполноцéнный; **he makes me feel** ∼ в егó прису́тствии у меня́ появля́ется кóмплекс неполноцéнности

inferiority /ɪnfɪərɪ'ɒrɪtɪ/ *n.* (of position) бóлее ни́зкое положéние; (of quality) низкосóртность
■ ∼ **complex** *n.* кóмплекс неполноцéнности

infernal /ɪn'fə:n(ə)l/ *adj.* **1** (of hell) áдский **2** (devilish, abominable) áдский, дья́вольский; **an** ∼ **machine** áдская маши́на **3** (infml, confounded) чертóвский; **an** ∼ **nuisance** прокля́тие

inferno /ɪn'fə:nəʊ/ *n.* (*pl.* ∼**s**) (lit., fig.) ад

infertile /ɪn'fə:taɪl/ *adj.* (soil) неплодорóдный; (woman, man) бесплóдный

infertility /ɪnfə'tɪlɪtɪ/ *n.* неплодорóдность; бесплóдность

infest /ɪn'fest/ *v.t.* наводн|я́ть, -и́ть; **the house is** ∼**ed with rats** дом наводнён кры́сами

infidel /'ɪnfɪd(ə)l/ *n. & adj.* (relig.) невéрный

infidelity /ɪnfɪ'delɪtɪ/ *n.* невéрность, измéна (*супружеская*)

in-fighting /'ɪnfaɪtɪŋ/ *n.* междоусóбица, внýтренняя борьбá

infiltrate /'ɪnfɪltreɪt/ *v.t.* прон|икáть, -и́кнуть

infinite /'ɪnfɪnɪt/ *adj.* бесконéчный, беспредéльный

infinitesimal /ɪnfɪnɪ'tesɪm(ə)l/ *adj.* бесконéчно мáлый

infinitive /ɪn'fɪnɪtɪv/ *n.* инфинити́в, неопределённая фóрма глагóла

infinity /ɪn'fɪnɪtɪ/ *n.* бесконéчность

infirm /ɪn'fə:m/ *adj.* (physically) нéмощный, дря́хлый

infirmary /ɪn'fə:mərɪ/ *n.* больни́ца

inflame /ɪn'fleɪm/ *v.t.*: **the wound became** ∼**d** рáна воспали́лась

inflammable /ɪn'flæməb(ə)l/ *adj.* легкó воспламеня́ющийся, горю́чий

inflammation /ɪnflə'meɪʃ(ə)n/ *n.* воспалéние

inflammatory /ɪn'flæmətərɪ/ *adj.* **1** (seditious) зажигáтельный; подстрекáтельский **2** (med.) воспали́тельный

inflatable /ɪn'fleɪtəb(ə)l/ *adj.* надувнóй

inflate /ɪn'fleɪt/ *v.t.* над|увáть, -ýть

inflation /ɪn'fleɪʃ(ə)n/ *n.* (econ.) инфля́ция

inflection /ɪn'flekʃ(ə)n/ *n.* (gram.) флéксия

inflexible /ɪn'fleksɪb(ə)l/ *adj.* неги́бкий, жёсткий; (fig.) непреклóнный, непоколеби́мый

inflict /ɪn'flɪkt/ *v.t.* (a blow) нан|оси́ть, -ести́; (pain) причин|я́ть, -и́ть

⚲ **influence** /'ɪnflʊəns/ *n.* (power to affect or change) влия́ние, воздéйствие; **she is a good** ∼ **on him** онá на негó хорошó влия́ет; **under the** ∼ (of drink) под воздéйствием (алкогóля)
● *v.t.* влия́ть, по- на *a.*; окáз|ывать, -áть влия́ние на + *a.*; **he was a** ∼**d by what he saw** уви́денное повлия́ло на негó

influential /ɪnflʊ'enʃ(ə)l/ *adj.* влия́тельный

influenza /ɪnflʊ'enzə/ *n.* грипп

influx /'ɪnflʌks/ *n.* (fig.) наплы́в

⚲ **inform** /ɪn'fɔ:m/ *v.t.* сообщ|áть, -и́ть + *d.*; информи́ровать (*impf., pf.*); осв|едомля́ть, -éдомить; стáвить, по- в извéстность; **I was not** ∼**ed of the facts** мне не сообщи́ли о фáктах; **keep me** ∼**ed** держи́те меня́ в кýрсе дел
● *v.i.* дон|оси́ть, -ести́; **he** ∼**ed against, on his comrades** он доноси́л на свои́х товáрищей

informal /ɪn'fɔ:m(ə)l/ *adj.* неофициáльный; непринуждённый; **it will be an** ∼ **party** вéчер бýдет дрýжеский; ∼ **dress** повседнéвная одéжда

⚲ **information** /ɪnfə'meɪʃ(ə)n/ *n.* информáция; свéдения (*nt. pl.*); спрáвка; дáнные (*nt. pl.*); **a useful piece of** ∼ полéзная информáция
■ ∼ **desk** *n.* спрáвочный стол; ∼ **technology** *n.* информáтика

informative /ɪnˈfɔːmətɪv/ *adj.*
информати́вный

informer /ɪnˈfɔːmə(r)/ *n.* (police ∼)
осведоми́тель (-ница); (against sb) доно́счи|к
(-ца)

infra-red /ˌɪnfrəˈred/ *adj.* инфракра́сный

infrastructure /ˈɪnfrəstrʌktʃə(r)/ *n.*
инфраструкту́ра

infrequent /ɪnˈfriːkwənt/ *adj.* ре́дкий

infringe /ɪnˈfrɪndʒ/ *v.t. & i.* нар|уша́ть,
-у́шить; this does not ∼ on your rights э́то не
ущемля́ет ва́ших прав

infringement /ɪnˈfrɪndʒmənt/ *n.* наруше́ние

infuriat|e /ɪnˈfjʊərɪeɪt/ *v.t.* прив|оди́ть, -ести́ в
я́рость/бе́шенство; разъяр|я́ть, -и́ть; an ∼ing
delay возмути́тельная заде́ржка

ingenious /ɪnˈdʒiːnɪəs/ *adj.*
изобрета́тельный; остроу́мный

ingenuity /ˌɪndʒɪˈnjuːɪti/ *n.*
изобрета́тельность; оригина́льность

ingenuous /ɪnˈdʒenjʊəs/ *adj.* простоду́шный,
наи́вный

ingot /ˈɪŋgət/ *n.* сли́ток

ingrained /ɪnˈɡreɪnd/ *adj.* **1** ∼ dirt въе́вшаяся
грязь **2** (fig.) закоренéлый, врождённый

ingratitude /ɪnˈɡrætɪtjuːd/ *n.*
неблагода́рность

ingredient /ɪnˈɡriːdɪənt/ *n.* (of mixture)
компоне́нт; (cul.) ингредие́нт; hard work is
an important ∼ of success упо́рный труд —
ва́жная составля́ющая успе́ха

inhabit /ɪnˈhæbɪt/ *v.t.* (**inhabited,
inhabiting**) жить (*impf.*) в + *p.*; обита́ть
(*impf.*) в + *p.*; is the island ∼ed? э́тот о́стров
обита́ем?

inhabitant /ɪnˈhæbɪt(ə)nt/ *n.* жи́тель
(-ница); жиле́ц

inhale /ɪnˈheɪl/ *v.t.* вд|ыха́ть, -охну́ть
● *v.i.* затя́гиваться (*сигаре́той и т. п.*)

inhaler /ɪnˈheɪlə(r)/ *n.* (device) ингаля́тор

inherent /ɪnˈherənt/ *adj.* сво́йственный,
прису́щий

inherit /ɪnˈherɪt/ *v.t.* (**inherited, inheriting**)
насле́довать (*impf., pf.*) (*pf. also* y-)
● *v.i.* (**inherited, inheriting**) получ|а́ть,
-и́ть насле́дство

inheritance /ɪnˈherɪt(ə)ns/ *n.* (inheriting)
насле́дование; (sth inherited) насле́дство

inhibit /ɪnˈhɪbɪt/ *v.t.* (**inhibited, inhibiting**)
(restrain) угнета́ть (*impf.*); ско́в|ывать, -а́ть;
an ∼ed person ско́ванный челове́к

inhibition /ˌɪnhɪˈbɪʃ(ə)n/ *n.* торможе́ние

inhospitable /ˌɪnhɒˈspɪtəb(ə)l/ *adj.*
негостеприи́мный

inhuman /ɪnˈhjuːmən/ *adj.* бесчелове́чный

inhumane /ˌɪnhjuːˈmeɪn/ *adj.* негума́нный

inhumanity /ˌɪnhjuːˈmænɪti/ *n.*
бесчелове́чность, жесто́кость

⚜ **initial** /ɪˈnɪʃ(ə)l/ *n.* нача́льная бу́ква; (in pl.)
(as signature) инициа́лы (*m. pl.*)
● *adj.* нача́льный

───────────────

⚜ ключева́я ле́ксика

● *v.t.* (**initialled, initialling**, AmE
initialed, initialing): ∼ a document
ста́вить, по- инициа́лы под докуме́нтом

⚜ **initially** /ɪˈnɪʃəli/ *adv.* внача́ле, снача́ла

initiate¹ /ɪˈnɪʃɪət/ *n.* посвящённый

initiate² /ɪˈnɪʃɪeɪt/ *v.t.* **1** (set in motion)
нач|ина́ть, -а́ть **2** (introduce) приобщ|а́ть, -и́ть
(into: к + *d.*); he was ∼d into the mysteries of
science его́ посвяти́ли в та́йны нау́ки

⚜ **initiative** /ɪˈnɪʃətɪv/ *n.* инициати́ва; he took
the ∼ он взял инициати́ву на себя́

inject /ɪnˈdʒekt/ *v.t.* вв|оди́ть, -ести́;
впры́с|кивать, -нуть; the drug was ∼ed into
the bloodstream лека́рство ввели́ в ве́ну; he
learned to ∼ himself with insulin он научи́лся
де́лать себе́ уко́лы/инъе́кции инсули́на

injection /ɪnˈdʒekʃ(ə)n/ *n.* впры́скивание;
инъе́кция

injunction /ɪnˈdʒʌŋkʃ(ə)n/ *n.* (law) суде́бный
запре́т

⚜ **injure** /ˈɪndʒə(r)/ *v.t.* (physically) ушиб|а́ть,
-и́ть; повре|жда́ть, -ди́ть; ра́нить (*impf., pf.*);
(fig.): he will ∼ his own reputation он сам
испо́ртит себе́ репута́цию

injured /ˈɪndʒəd/ *adj.* (suffering injury) ра́неный;
(as n. pl.) the dead and ∼ уби́тые и ра́неные;
(offended) оби́женный

⚜ **injury** /ˈɪndʒərɪ/ *n.* ра́на, ране́ние, уши́б, тра́вма

injustice /ɪnˈdʒʌstɪs/ *n.* несправедли́вость

ink /ɪŋk/ *n.* черни́л|а (*pl., g.* —)
■ ∼jet *adj.*: ∼jet printer (comput.) стру́йный
при́нтер

inkling /ˈɪŋklɪŋ/ *n.* (hint) намёк; (suspicion)
подозре́ние

inland /ˈɪnlənd/ *adj.* располо́женный внутри́
страны́
● *adv.* (motion) внутрь/вглубь страны́; (place)
внутри́ страны́
■ I∼ Revenue *n.* (BrE) Госуда́рственная
нало́говая слу́жба

in-law /ˈɪnlɔː/ *n.*: ∼s ро́дственники (*m. pl.*) со
стороны́ му́жа/жены́, своя́ки (infml) (*m. pl.*)

inla|y /ˈɪnleɪ/ *n.* инкруста́ция
● *v.t.* инкрусти́ровать (*impf., pf.*); an ∼id
floor парке́тный пол с инкруста́цией

in loco parentis /ɪn ˈləʊkəʊ pəˈrentɪs/ *adv.* в
ка́честве роди́телей

inmate /ˈɪnmeɪt/ *n.* (of hospital, home, etc.)
больно́й, пацие́нт; (of prison) заключённый

inn /ɪn/ *n.* тракти́р

innate /ɪˈneɪt/ *adj.* врождённый

inner /ˈɪnə(r)/ *adj.* вну́тренний

innocence /ˈɪnəs(ə)ns/ *n.* невино́вность

innocent /ˈɪnəs(ə)nt/ *adj.* **1** (law) невино́вный
2 (harmless) невинный **3** (without sin)
неви́нный, безгре́шный

innocuous /ɪˈnɒkjʊəs/ *adj.* безвре́дный,
безоби́дный

innovation /ˌɪnəˈveɪʃ(ə)n/ *n.* нововведе́ние

innovative /ˈɪnəvətɪv/ *adj.* нова́торский

innovator /ˈɪnəveɪtə(r)/ *n.* нова́тор

innuendo /ˌɪnjʊˈendəʊ/ *n.* (*pl.* ∼es or ∼s)
инсинуа́ция; (hint) намёк

inoculate /ɪ'nɒkjʊleɪt/ *v.t.* де́лать, с-приви́вку; прив|ива́ть, -и́ть; **he was ~d against smallpox** ему́ сде́лали приви́вку от о́спы/ему́ приви́ли о́спу

inoculation /ɪnɒkjʊ'leɪʃ(ə)n/ *n.* приви́вка

inoffensive /ɪnə'fensɪv/ *adj.* необи́дный

inoperable /ɪn'ɒpərəb(ə)l/ *adj.* (untreatable by surgery) неопера́бельный; (unworkable) непримени́мый; **the plan proved to be ~** план оказа́лся невыполни́мым

inordinate /ɪn'ɔ:dɪnət/ *adj.* непоме́рный, чрезме́рный, неуме́ренный

inorganic /ɪnɔ:' gænɪk/ *adj.* неоргани́ческий

inpatient /'ɪnpeɪʃ(ə)nt/ *n.* стациона́рный/ко́ечный больно́й

input /'ɪnpʊt/ *n.* (investment, resources) вложе́ние; (contribution) вклад; (comput., of data) ввод
●*v.t.* (comput.) вв|оди́ть, -ести́ (into: в + *a.*)

inquest /'ɪŋkwest/ *n.* (in criminal case) сле́дствие; (investigation) рассле́дование

inquire /ɪn'kwaɪə(r)/ (*see also* ▸ enquire) *v.i.* спр|авля́ться, -а́виться; нав|оди́ть, -ести́ спра́вки

ɟ **inquiry** /ɪn'kwaɪərɪ/ (*see also* ▸ enquiry) *n.* (investigation) рассле́дование; (in criminal case) сле́дствие; **court of ~** сле́дственная коми́ссия

inquisition /ɪnkwɪ'zɪʃ(ə)n/ *n.* (questioning) допро́с; **he was subjected to an ~** он был под сле́дствием; (hist.) инквизи́ция

inquisitive /ɪn'kwɪzɪtɪv/ *adj.* любопы́тный

inroad /'ɪnrəʊd/ *n.* (*usu. in pl.*) (encroachment) посяга́тельство; **the holiday will make large ~s into/on my savings** кани́кулы поглотя́т бо́льшую часть мои́х сбереже́ний

insane /ɪn'seɪn/ *adj.* безу́мный, сумасше́дший; (law) невменя́емый

insanitary /ɪn'sænɪtərɪ/ *adj.* антисанита́рный, негигиени́чный

insanity /ɪn'sænɪtɪ/ *n.* (madness) сумасше́ствие; безу́мие; (law) невменя́емость

insatiable /ɪn'seɪʃəb(ə)l/ *adj.* ненасы́тный

inscribe /ɪn'skraɪb/ *v.t.* **1** (engrave) высека́ть, вы́сечь; выреза́ть, вы́резать; начерта́ть (*pf.*); **the stone was~d with their names** их имена́ бы́ли вы́сечены на ка́мне; **a verse is~d on his tomb** на его́ надгро́бном ка́мне вы́сечена стихотво́рная эпита́фия **2** (autograph) надпи́с|ывать, -а́ть; **please ~ your name in the book** пожа́луйста, распиши́тесь в кни́ге

inscription /ɪn'skrɪpʃ(ə)n/ *n.* на́дпись

inscrutable /ɪn'skru:təb(ə)l/ *adj.* (smile) зага́дочный; (face) непроница́емый

insect /'ɪnsekt/ *n.* насеко́мое; **~ bite** уку́с насеко́мого

insecticide /ɪn'sektɪsaɪd/ *n.* инсектици́д

insecure /ɪnsɪ'kjʊə(r)/ *adj.* **1** (unsafe; unreliable) ненадёжный, небезопа́сный; **his position in the firm is ~** его́ положе́ние в фи́рме ша́ткое **2** (lacking confidence) неуве́ренный (в себе́)

insecurity /ɪnsɪ'kjʊrɪtɪ/ *n.* ненадёжность, небезопа́сность; неуве́ренность

insemination /ɪnsemɪ'neɪʃ(ə)n/ *n.* оплодотворе́ние; **artificial ~** иску́сственное оплодотворе́ние

insensible /ɪn'sensɪb(ə)l/ *adj.* (numb) нечувстви́тельный; **his hands were ~ with cold** от хо́лода его́ ру́ки потеря́ли чувстви́тельность; (unconscious) бесчу́вственный; (unaware) не сознаю́щий; **he was ~ of the danger** он не сознава́л опа́сности

insensitive /ɪn'sensɪtɪv/ *adj.* нечувстви́тельный; невосприи́мчивый, равноду́шный

inseparable /ɪn'sepərəb(ə)l/ *adj.* неразде́льный, неразры́вный

insert /ɪn'sɜ:t/ *v.t.* вст|авля́ть, -а́вить; поме|ща́ть, -сти́ть; **he ~ed the key in(to) the lock** он вста́вил ключ в замо́к

insertion /ɪn'sɜ:ʃ(ə)n/ *n.* (inserting) вкла́дывание, помеще́ние, введе́ние; (sth inserted) вста́вка

ɟ **inside** /ɪn'saɪd/ *n.* **1** (interior) вну́треннее простра́нство; вну́тренняя часть **2** (of road): **it is forbidden to pass on the ~** (when driving on the right/left) обго́н спра́ва/сле́ва запрещён
●*adj.* вну́тренний; **~ pocket** вну́тренний карма́н; **he received ~ information** он получи́л информа́цию из вну́тренних исто́чников
●*adv.* **1** (in the interior) внутри́; **I opened the box and there was nothing ~** я откры́л коро́бку — внутри́ бы́ло пу́сто **2** (indoors) внутри́, в помеще́нии, до́ма
●*prep.* **1** (of motion into a place) в + *a.*, внутрь + *g.*; **dogs are not allowed ~ the shop** с соба́ками вход в магази́н запрещён; (of position) в + *p.*, внутри́ + *g.*; **have you seen ~ the house?** вы ви́дели дом изнутри́? **2** (of time) в преде́лах + *g.*, в тече́ние + *g.*; **I shall be back ~ (of) a week** я верну́сь не позднее, чем че́рез неде́лю
■ **~ out** *adv.* наизна́нку; **the thieves turned everything ~ out** во́ры переверну́ли всё вверх дном; **he knows the subject ~ out** он зна́ет предме́т вдоль и поперёк

insider /ɪn'saɪdə(r)/ *n.* (comm.) свой/непосторо́нний челове́к; **~ trading** инса́йдерская торго́вля (*незаконное участие в биржевых сделках с использованием информации из внутренних источников*)

insight /'ɪnsaɪt/ *n.* проница́тельность; понима́ние; **gain an ~ into sth** пости́|гнуть, -чь (*both pf.*) что-н.

insignificant /ɪnsɪg'nɪfɪk(ə)nt/ *adj.* малова́жный, ничто́жный

insincere /ɪnsɪn'sɪə(r)/ *adj.* неи́скренний

insinuate /ɪn'sɪnjʊeɪt/ *v.t.* (hint) намек|а́ть, -ну́ть на + *a.*

insinuation /ɪnsɪnjʊ'eɪʃ(ə)n/ *n.* (hint) намёк; инсинуа́ция

insipid /ɪn'sɪpɪd/ *adj.* скуч́ный, вя́лый

ɟ **insist** /ɪn'sɪst/ *v.t. & i.* наст|а́ивать, -оя́ть на + *p.*; тре́бовать, по- + *g.*; **he ~ed on his rights** он наста́ивал на свои́х права́х; **he ~ed on my accompanying him** он наста́ивал на том, чтобы я его́ сопровожда́л

insistence /ɪn'sɪst(ə)ns/ *n.* (quality) насто́йчивость; (act) настоя́ние,

i

настойчивое требование

insistent /ɪnˈsɪst(ə)nt/ *adj.* настойчивый; **he was ~ that I should go** он настаивал на том, чтобы я пошёл

insofar as /ɪnsəʊˈfɑː(r)/ *conj.* (постольку) поскольку

insole /ˈɪnsəʊl/ *n.* стелька

insolence /ˈɪnsələns/ *n.* нахальство

insolent /ˈɪnsələnt/ *adj.* нахальный

insolvent /ɪnˈsɒlv(ə)nt/ *adj.* неплатёжеспособный; несостоятельный

insomnia /ɪnˈsɒmnɪə/ *n.* бессонница

insomniac /ɪnˈsɒmnɪæk/ *n.* страдающий бессонницей

insouciance /ɪnˈsuːsɪəns/ *n.* небрежность

insouciant /ɪnˈsuːsɪənt/ *adj.* небрежный

inspect /ɪnˈspekt/ *v.t.* осматривать, -отреть

inspection /ɪnˈspekʃ(ə)n/ *n.* осмотр, инспекция

inspector /ɪnˈspektə(r)/ *n.* (inspecting official) инспектор; (police officer) инспектор (полиции)

inspiration /ɪnspɪˈreɪʃ(ə)n/ *n.* вдохновение

ꞔ **inspire** /ɪnˈspaɪə(r)/ *v.t.* **1** (influence creatively) вдохнов|лять, -ить; **he is an ~d musician** он вдохновенный музыкант **2** (instil) всел|ять, -ить; **his work does not ~ me with confidence** его работа не вызывает у меня доверия

instability /ɪnstəˈbɪlɪtɪ/ *n.* нестабильность, неустойчивость; (of character) неуравновешенность

ꞔ **install** /ɪnˈstɔːl/ *v.t.* (**installed, installing**) **1** (a person in office) вво|дить, -ести в должность **2** (machine, also comput.) устан|авливать, -овить

installation /ɪnstəˈleɪʃ(ə)n/ *n.* (of thing) установка; (art) инсталляция; (comput.) инсталляция, установка

instalment /ɪnˈstɔːlmənt/ (AmE also **installment**) *n.* **1** (partial payment) взнос; **we are paying for our carpet in ~s** мы платим за ковёр в рассрочку **2** (of published work) отрывок, выпуск

ꞔ **instance** /ˈɪnst(ə)ns/ *n.* **1** (example) пример; **for ~** например **2** (particular case) случай; **in this ~** в этом/данном случае

instant /ˈɪnst(ə)nt/ *n.* мгновение; **come here this ~!** иди сюда сию же минуту! ● *adj.* **1** (immediate) мгновенный; немедленный **2** (cul.): **~ coffee** растворимый кофе

instantaneous /ɪnstənˈteɪnɪəs/ *adj.* мгновенный

ꞔ **instead** /ɪnˈsted/ *adv.* взамен + *g.*; **~ of** вместо + *g.*; **let me go ~ (of you)** давайте я пойду вместо вас; **if the steak is off I'll have chicken ~** если бифштексов нет, я возьму курицу

instep /ˈɪnstep/ *n.* подъём (ноги)

instigate /ˈɪnstɪɡeɪt/ *v.t.* подстрекать (*impf.*), провоцировать, с-

instil /ɪnˈstɪl/ *v.t.* (**instilled, instilling**) внуш|ать, -ить; прив|ивать, -ить

ꞔ ключевая лексика

instinct /ˈɪnstɪŋkt/ *n.* инстинкт

instinctive /ɪnˈstɪŋktɪv/ *adj.* инстинктивный, безотчётный

institute /ˈɪnstɪtjuːt/ *n.* институт ● *v.t.* устан|авливать, -овить; учре|ждать, -дить

ꞔ **institution** /ɪnstɪˈtjuːʃ(ə)n/ *n.* учреждение, организация, заведение, институт; **charitable ~** благотворительное учреждение

institutional /ɪnstɪˈtjuːʃən(ə)l/ *adj.* институциональный; **she is in need of ~ care** её следует госпитализировать; **~ reform** реформа учреждений

instruct /ɪnˈstrʌkt/ *v.t.* **1** (teach) учить, на- (*кого чему*) **2** (order) инструктировать (*impf., pf.*) (*pf. also* про-); **I was ~ed to call on you** мне было приказано зайти к вам

instruction /ɪnˈstrʌkʃ(ə)n/ *n.* (direction) указание; руководство; **follow the ~s on the packet** следуйте указаниям на пакете; (order) распоряжение, приказ ■ **~ book** *n.* руководство

instructive /ɪnˈstrʌktɪv/ *adj.* поучительный

instructor /ɪnˈstrʌktə(r)/ *n.* (sport) инструктор; (teacher) учитель (-ница)

ꞔ **instrument** /ˈɪnstrəmənt/ *n.* **1** (implement) инструмент **2** (mus.) (музыкальный) инструмент ■ **~ panel** *n.* пульт управления

instrumental /ɪnstrəˈment(ə)l/ *n.* (gram.) творительный падёж ● *adj.* **1** (serving as means): **~ to our purpose** полезный для нашей цели **2** (mus.) инструментальный **3** (gram.) творительный

instrumentalist /ɪnstrəˈmentəlɪst/ *n.* инструменталист

insubordinate /ɪnsəˈbɔːdɪnət/ *adj.* непокорный

insubordination /ɪnsəbɔːdɪˈneɪʃ(ə)n/ *n.* неподчинение; непокорность

insubstantial /ɪnsəbˈstænʃ(ə)l/ *adj.* (not real, imaginary) нереальный, иллюзорный; (building, structure) непрочный; (evidence) слабый, неубедительный; (meal) несытный

insufferable /ɪnˈsʌfərəb(ə)l/ *adj.* невыносимый

insufficient /ɪnsəˈfɪʃ(ə)nt/ *adj.* недостаточный

insular /ˈɪnsjʊlə(r)/ *adj.* островной; (fig.) ограниченный, узкий

insulate /ˈɪnsjʊleɪt/ *v.t.* (protect from escape of electricity) изолировать (*impf., pf.*); (protect from escape of heat) утепл|ять, -ить, теплоизоли|ровать (*impf., pf.*)

insulation /ɪnsjʊˈleɪʃ(ə)n/ *n.* (against escape of electricity) изоляция; (against escape of heat) теплоизоляция

insulin /ˈɪnsjʊlɪn/ *n.* инсулин

insult[1] /ˈɪnsʌlt/ *n.* оскорбление; обида

insult[2] /ɪnˈsʌlt/ *v.t.* оскорб|лять, -ить; **~ing language** оскорбительные выражения

insuperable /ɪnˈsuːpərəb(ə)l/ *adj.* непреодолимый

insupportable /ˌɪnsəˈpɔːtəb(ə)l/ *adj.*
нестерпи́мый, невыноси́мый, несно́сный

ᵒ⁺ **insurance** /ɪnˈʃʊərəns/ *n.* страхова́ние,
страхо́вка; **National I~** (BrE) госуда́рственное
страхова́ние; **take out ~** страхова́ться, за-
■ **~ company** *n.* страхова́я компа́ния; **~
policy** *n.* страхово́й по́лис

insure /ɪnˈʃʊə(r)/ *v.t.* страхова́ть, за-

insurgent /ɪnˈsɜːdʒ(ə)nt/ *n.* повста́нец

insurmountable /ˌɪnsəˈmaʊntəb(ə)l/ *adj.*
непреодоли́мый

insurrection /ˌɪnsəˈrekʃ(ə)n/ *n.* восста́ние

intact /ɪnˈtækt/ *adj.* нетро́нутый, це́лый

intake /ˈɪnteɪk/ *n.* (BrE, of recruits, students, etc.)
набо́р; (amount taken into body) потребле́ние; **~
of breath** вздох

intangible /ɪnˈtændʒɪb(ə)l/ *adj.* **1** (non-
material) неося́заемый, неулови́мый **2** (vague,
obscure): **~ ideas** сму́тные/нея́сные
представле́ния

integral /ˈɪntɪɡr(ə)l/ *adj.* неотъе́млемый,
суще́ственный

integrate /ˈɪntɪɡreɪt/ *v.t.* интегри́ровать
(*impf., pf.*)
● *v.i.* объедин|я́ться, -и́ться

integration /ˌɪntɪˈɡreɪʃ(ə)n/ *n.* интегра́ция

integrity /ɪnˈteɡrɪtɪ/ *n.* че́стность, це́льность

intellect /ˈɪntəlekt/ *n.* интелле́кт, ум, рассу́док;
the great ~s of the age вели́кие умы́ эпо́хи

intellectual /ˌɪntɪˈlektʃʊəl/ *n.* интеллиге́нт
(-ка), интеллектуа́л (-ка)
● *adj.* интеллектуа́льный, у́мственный

ᵒ⁺ **intelligence** /ɪnˈtelɪdʒ(ə)ns/ *n.* **1** (mental
power) ум, интелле́кт; **I had the ~ to refuse
his offer** у меня́ хвати́ло ума́ не приня́ть его́
предложе́ния **2** (mil.) разве́дка

intelligent /ɪnˈtelɪdʒ(ə)nt/ *adj.* у́мный,
смышлёный, сообрази́тельный

intelligentsia /ɪnˌtelɪˈdʒentsɪə/ *n.*
интеллиге́нция

intelligible /ɪnˈtelɪdʒɪb(ə)l/ *adj.* поня́тный,
вня́тный

ᵒ⁺ **intend** /ɪnˈtend/ *v.t.* **1** (have in mind)
намерева́ться, хоте́ть, собира́ться (*all impf.*)
2 (mean) предназн|ача́ть, -а́чить; **a book ~ed
for advanced students** кни́га, рассчи́танная
на продви́нутый эта́п обуче́ния

intense /ɪnˈtens/ *adj.* (**intenser, intensest**)
1 (extreme) си́льный, интенси́вный **2** (ardent)
напряжённый

intensify /ɪnˈtensɪfaɪ/ *v.t.* уси́ли|вать, -ть;
увели́чи|вать, -ть

intensity /ɪnˈtensɪtɪ/ *n.* си́ла, интенси́вность

intensive /ɪnˈtensɪv/ *adj.* интенси́вный; **~
care unit** отделе́ние реанима́ции

intent¹ /ɪnˈtent/ *n.*: **to all ~s and purposes**
факти́чески, на са́мом де́ле

intent² /ɪnˈtent/ *adj.* **1** (earnest, eager)
увлечённый, ре́вностный; (expression)
сосредото́ченный **2** (resolved): **he was ~
on getting a first** он был по́лон реши́мости
получи́ть дипло́м с отли́чием

ᵒ⁺ **intention** /ɪnˈtenʃ(ə)n/ *n.* наме́рение; у́мысел;

I have no ~ of going to the party у меня́ нет
наме́рения идти́ на вечери́нку

intentional /ɪnˈtenʃən(ə)l/ *adj.*
умы́шленный, наме́ренный; **he ignored me
~ly** он наме́ренно не заме́тил меня́

interact /ˌɪntərˈækt/ *v.i.* взаимоде́йствовать
(*impf.*)

ᵒ⁺ **interaction** /ˌɪntərˈækʃ(ə)n/ *n.* взаимоде́йствие

interactive /ˌɪntərˈæktɪv/ *adj.* (comput.)
интеракти́вный, диало́говый

intercept /ˌɪntəˈsept/ *v.t.* перехва́т|ывать, -и́ть

interchange /ˈɪntətʃeɪndʒ/ *n.* **1** обме́н; **~
of views** обме́н мне́ниями **2** (road junction)
перекрёсток с эстака́дой; **~ of views** обме́н
мне́ниями

interchangeable /ˌɪntəˈtʃeɪndʒəb(ə)l/ *adj.*
взаимозаменя́емый

intercity /ˌɪntəˈsɪtɪ/ *adj.* междугоро́дный

intercom /ˈɪntəkɒm/ *n.* (in an office, plane)
селе́ктор; (to get into a house) домофо́н

interconnect /ˌɪntəkəˈnekt/ *v.i.* соедин|я́ться,
-и́ться

intercontinental /ˌɪntəkɒntɪˈnent(ə)l/ *adj.*
межконтинента́льный; **~ ballistic missile**
межконтинента́льная баллисти́ческая
раке́та

intercourse /ˈɪntəkɔːs/ *n.* (sexual) (полово́е)
сноше́ние

interdependent /ˌɪntədɪˈpend(ə)nt/ *adj.*
взаимозави́симый

ᵒ⁺ **interest** /ˈɪntrest/ *n.* **1** (attention, curiosity)
интере́с; **show a great ~ in sth** проявля́ть,
-и́ть большо́й интере́с к чему́-н. **2** (quality
arousing ~) занима́тельность; **his books
lack ~ for me** его́ кни́ги не
занима́ют **3** (pursuit) интере́с; **a man of
wide ~s** челове́к с широ́ким кру́гом
интере́сов **4** (often in pl.) (advantage)
интере́сы (*m. pl.*), по́льза, вы́года; **it is
in your ~ to listen to his advice** в ва́ших
же интере́сах прислу́шаться к его́
сове́там **5** (charge on loan) (paid) ссу́дный
проце́нт; проце́нты (*m. pl.*); (received)
проце́нтный дохо́д; **rate of ~, ~ rate**
проце́нтная ста́вка; (fig.): **my kindness was
repaid with ~** меня́ щедро вознаградили за
мою́ доброту́
● *v.t.* интересова́ть (*impf.*); (cause a person to
take interest) заинтересова́ть (*pf.*)
■ **~-free** *adj.* беспроце́нтный

interested /ˈɪntrestɪd/ *adj.* **1** (having interest)
интересу́ющийся; **are you ~ in football?**
вы интересу́етесь футбо́лом? **2** (not
impartial) заинтересо́ванный; **an ~ party**
заинтересо́ванная сторона́

ᵒ⁺ **interesting** /ˈɪntrestɪŋ/ *adj.* интере́сный

interface /ˈɪntəfeɪs/ *n.* (comput.) интерфе́йс;
(fig.) взаимосвя́зь, взаимоде́йствие

interfer|e /ˌɪntəˈfɪə(r)/ *v.i.* вме́ш|иваться,
-а́ться; **don't ~e in my affairs** не
вме́шивайтесь в мои́ дела́; **she is an ~ing old
lady** она́ назо́йливая стару́ха

interference /ˌɪntəˈfɪərəns/ *n.* вмеша́тельство,
поме́ха; (radio, TV) поме́хи (*f. pl.*)

i

intergovernmental /ɪntəɡʌvən'ment(ə)l/ *adj.* межправи́тельственный

interim /'ɪntərɪm/ *n.* промежу́ток вре́мени; **in the ~** тем вре́менем
● *adj.* (temporary) вре́менный; (provisional) промежу́точный

interior /ɪn'tɪərɪə(r)/ *n.* **1** (inside) вну́тренняя часть, простра́нство внутри́ **2** (of building) интерье́р **3** (home affairs): **Minister of the I~** мини́стр вну́тренних дел
● *adj.* вну́тренний
■ **~ decorator** *n.* худо́жник по интерье́ру

interject /ɪntə'dʒekt/ *v.t.* вста|вля́ть, -а́вить; 'It's not true,' he **~ed** «Э́то непра́вда», — вста́вил он

interjection /ɪntə'dʒekʃ(ə)n/ *n.* восклица́ние; (gram.) междоме́тие

interlock /ɪntə'lɒk/ *v.t. & i.* соедин|я́ть(ся), -и́ть(ся), сцеп|ля́ть(ся), -и́ть(ся)

interloper /'ɪntələʊpə(r)/ *n.* незва́ный гость

interlude /'ɪntəluːd/ *n.* переры́в; (theatr.) антра́кт

intermarry /ɪntə'mærɪ/ *v.i.* сме́ш|иваться, -а́ться; родни́ться, по- путём бра́ка

intermediary /ɪntə'miːdɪərɪ/ *n.* посре́дни|к (-ца)
● *adj.* посре́днический

intermediate /ɪntə'miːdɪət/ *adj.* промежу́точный

interminable /ɪn'tɜːmɪnəb(ə)l/ *adj.* бесконе́чный, несконча́емый, ве́чный

intermission /ɪntə'mɪʃ(ə)n/ *n.* антра́кт

intermittent /ɪntə'mɪt(ə)nt/ *adj.* преры́вистый

intern[1] /'ɪntɜːn/ *n.* (trainee) стажёр, практика́нт; (AmE, medical student) молодо́й врач, интёрн

intern[2] /ɪn'tɜːn/ *v.t.* интерни́ровать (*impf., pf.*)

♂ **internal** /ɪn'tɜːn(ə)l/ *adj.* вну́тренний; **I~ Revenue Service** (AmE) *see* ▶ **IRS**

♂ **international** /ɪntə'næʃən(ə)l/ *n.* (BrE, sporting event) междунаро́дные соревнова́ния (*nt. pl.*)
● *adj.* междунаро́дный, интернациона́льный; **I~ Monetary Fund** Междунаро́дный валю́тный фонд

internee /ɪntɜː'niː/ *n.* интерни́рованный

♂ **Internet** *n.* (**the ~**) Интерне́т; **on the ~** в Интерне́те; **~ service provider** (интерне́т-)провайдер

internment /ɪn'tɜːnmənt/ *n.* интерни́рование
■ **~ camp** *n.* ла́герь (*m.*) для интерни́рованных (лиц)

interplay /'ɪntəpleɪ/ *n.* взаимоде́йствие, взаимосвя́зь

interpolate /ɪn'tɜːpəleɪt/ *v.t.* интерполи́ровать (*impf., pf.*); вст|авля́ть, -а́вить

interpret /ɪn'tɜːprɪt/ *v.t.* (**interpreted**, **interpreting**) **1** (explain) толкова́ть (*impf.*); истолк|о́вывать, -ова́ть; **how do you ~ this dream?** как вы объясня́ете э́тот сон? **2** (understand) истолко́в|ывать, -а́ть

♂ ключева́я ле́ксика

● *v.i.* перев|оди́ть, -ести́ (у́стно)

interpretation /ɪntɜːprɪ'teɪʃ(ə)n/ *n.* интерпрета́ция, толкова́ние

interpreter /ɪn'tɜːprɪtə(r)/ *n.* (у́стный) перево́дчи|к (-ца)

interracial /ɪntə'reɪʃ(ə)l/ *adj.* межра́совый

interregn|um /ɪntə'regnəm/ *n.* (*pl.* **~ums** *or* **~a**) междуца́рствие; междувла́стие

interrogate /ɪn'terəgeɪt/ *v.t.* допр|а́шивать, -оси́ть

interrogation /ɪnterə'geɪʃ(ə)n/ *n.* допро́с

interrogative /ɪntə'rɒgətɪv/ *adj.* вопроси́тельный

interrupt /ɪntə'rʌpt/ *v.t. & i.* прер|ыва́ть, -ва́ть; переб|ива́ть, -и́ть; **don't ~ when I am speaking** не перебива́йте, когда́ я говорю́; **he ~ed me as I was reading** он прерва́л моё чте́ние

interruption /ɪntə'rʌpʃ(ə)n/ *n.* поме́ха; наруше́ние; вторже́ние

intersect /ɪntə'sekt/ *v.t. & i.* перес|ека́ть(ся), -е́чь(ся)

intersection /ɪntə'sekʃ(ə)n/ *n.* (crossroads) перекрёсток; (intersecting) пересече́ние

intersperse /ɪntə'spɜːs/ *v.t.* разбр|а́сывать, -оса́ть; рас|сыпа́ть, -ы́пать; **red flowers ~d with yellow ones** кра́сные цветы́ впереме́жку с жёлтыми; **his talk was ~d with anecdotes** он пересыпа́л/разбавля́л (*infml*) своё выступле́ние анекдо́тами

interstate /'ɪntəsteɪt/ *adj.* (between regions of country) межшта́тный; (between countries) межгосуда́рственный

interval /'ɪntəv(ə)l/ *n.* **1** (of time) промежу́ток, отре́зок вре́мени; интерва́л; **we see each other at ~s** мы ви́димся вре́мя от вре́мени; **at ~s of an hour** с интерва́лами в час **2** (of place) расстоя́ние; **the posts were set at ~s of 10 feet** столбы́ бы́ли расста́влены на расстоя́нии десяти́ фу́тов (друг от дру́га) **3** (BrE, theatr.) антра́кт

intervene /ɪntə'viːn/ *v.i.* вме́ш|иваться, -а́ться; **the government ~d in the dispute** в конфли́кт вмеша́лось прави́тельство

♂ **intervention** /ɪntə'venʃ(ə)n/ *n.* вмеша́тельство

♂ **interview** /'ɪntəvjuː/ *n.* делова́я встре́ча; собесе́дование; (with the media) интервью́ (*nt. indecl.*); **an ~ for a job** собесе́дование при приёме на рабо́ту; **he gave an ~ to the press** он дал интервью́ журнали́стам
● *v.t.* (with the media) интервьюи́ровать (*impf., pf.*); **only certain candidates were ~ed** собесе́дование провели́ то́лько с не́сколькими кандида́тами

interviewee /ɪntəvjuː'iː/ *n.* интервьюи́руемый, даю́щий интервью́

interviewer /ɪntəvjuːə(r)/ *n.* (for media) интервьюе́р; (for job) проводя́щий собесе́дование

interwar /ɪntə'wɔː(r)/ *adj.*: **~ period** пери́од ме́жду двумя́ мировы́ми во́йнами

intestate /ɪn'testeɪt/ *adj.*: **to die ~** умир|а́ть, -е́ть, не оста́вив завеща́ния

intestine /ɪn'testɪn/ *n.* кише́чник

intimacy /'ɪntɪməsɪ/ *n.* инти́мность, бли́зость

intimate /'ɪntɪmət/ *adj.* **1** (close) бли́зкий **2** (private, personal) инти́мный, ли́чный; **the ～ details of his life** подро́бности его́ ли́чной жи́зни **3** (detailed) основа́тельный; **he has an ～ knowledge of the subject** он доскона́льно зна́ет предме́т

intimidate /ɪn'tɪmɪdeɪt/ *v.t.* запу́г|ивать, -а́ть; угрожа́ть (*impf.*) + *d.*

⚲ **into** /'ɪntʊ/ *prep.* **1** (expr. motion to a point within) в + *a.* **2** (expr. extent) до; **far ～ the night** до по́здней но́чи **3** (expr. change or process) в + *a. or* на + *a.*; **the rain turned ～ snow** дождь перешёл в снег; **translate ～ French** перев|оди́ть, -ести́ на францу́зский **4** (infml, of a devotee): **he's ～ jazz** он увлека́ется джа́зом

intolerable /ɪn'tɒlərəb(ə)l/ *adj.* невыноси́мый

intolerance /ɪn'tɒlərəns/ *n.* нетерпи́мость

intolerant /ɪn'tɒlərənt/ *n.* нетерпи́мый; **～ of** (unable to bear) не вынося́щий + *g.*

intone /ɪn'təʊn/ *v.t.* (utter in particular tone) интони́ровать (*impf.*); (recite with prolonged sounds) чита́ть нараспе́в (*impf.*)

intoxicate /ɪn'tɒksɪkeɪt/ *v.t.* (lit., fig.) опьян|я́ть, -и́ть

intoxication /ɪntɒksɪ'keɪʃ(ə)n/ *n.* опьяне́ние

intractable /ɪn'træktəb(ə)l/ *adj.* (of person) упря́мый, непоко́рный, несговорчивый; (of problems, metal) непода́тливый; **～ illness** труднои́злечи́мое заболева́ние; **～ pain** неустрани́мая боль

intransigent /ɪn'trænsɪdʒ(ə)nt/ *adj.* непрекло́нный

intransitive /ɪn'trænsɪtɪv/ *adj.* (gram.) непереходный

intravenous /ɪntrə'vi:nəs/ *adj.* внутриве́нный

in tray /'ɪntreɪ/ *n.* (BrE) насто́льная корзи́на для входя́щей корреспонде́нции

intrepid /ɪn'trepɪd/ *adj.* неустраши́мый, бесстра́шный

intricate /'ɪntrɪkət/ *adj.* запу́танный, сло́жный

intrigu|e *n.* /'ɪntri:g/ интри́га; про́иски (*m. pl.*) ● *v.t.* /ɪn'tri:g/ (**intrigues, intrigued, intriguing**) интригова́ть, за-; интересова́ть, за-; **I was ～ed to learn** мне бы́ло интере́сно узна́ть; **an ～ing prospect** зама́нчивая перспекти́ва

intrinsic /ɪn'trɪnzɪk/ *adj.* прису́щий, по́длинный; **～ value** по́длинная це́нность

⚲ **introduce** /ɪntrə'dju:s/ *v.t.* **1** (bring in) вв|оди́ть, -ести́; (при)вн|оси́ть, -ести́; **many improvements have been ～d** ввели́ мно́го усоверше́нствований **2** (present) предст|авля́ть, -а́вить; знако́мить, по- (*кого с кем*); **may I ～ my fiancée?** разреши́те предста́вить (вам) мою́ неве́сту

⚲ **introduction** /ɪntrə'dʌkʃ(ə)n/ *n.* **1** (bringing in) введе́ние, установле́ние **2** (sth brought in) но́вшество, нововведе́ние **3** (presentation) представле́ние; **letter of ～** рекоменда́тельное письмо́ **4** (preliminary matter in book, speech, etc.) введе́ние, вступле́ние

introductory /ɪntrə'dʌktərɪ/ *adj.* вступи́тельный, вво́дный

introspection /ɪntrə'spekʃ(ə)n/ *n.* интроспе́кция, самоана́лиз

introvert /'ɪntrəvɜ:t/ *n.* за́мкнутый челове́к, интрове́рт

intrud|e /ɪn'tru:d/ *v.t.* нав|я́зывать, -яза́ть ● *v.i.* вт|орга́ться, -о́ргнуться; **you are ～ing on my time** вы посяга́ете на моё вре́мя

intruder /ɪn'tru:də(r)/ *n.* граби́тель (*m.*)

intrusion /ɪn'tru:ʒ(ə)n/ *n.* вторже́ние

intrusive /ɪn'tru:sɪv/ *adj.* назо́йливый

intuition /ɪntju:'ɪʃ(ə)n/ *n.* интуи́ция; чутьё

intuitive /ɪn'tju:ɪtɪv/ *adj.* интуити́вный

inundate /'ɪnʌndeɪt/ *v.t.* наводн|я́ть, -и́ть; **I was ～d with letters** меня́ засы́пали пи́сьмами

invade /ɪn'veɪd/ *v.t.* вторга́ться, вто́ргнуться в + *a.*

invader /ɪn'veɪdə(r)/ *n.* захва́тчик

invalid¹ /'ɪnvəlɪd/ *n.* больно́й

invalid² /ɪn'vælɪd/ *adj.* недействи́тельный, не име́ющий (зако́нной) си́лы

invalidate /ɪn'vælɪdeɪt/ *v.t.* аннули́ровать (*impf., pf.*)

invaluable /ɪn'væljʊəb(ə)l/ *adj.* неоцени́мый, бесце́нный

invariable /ɪn'veərɪəb(ə)l/ *adj.* неизме́нный, постоя́нный

invariably /ɪn'veərɪəblɪ/ *adv.* неизме́нно

invasion /ɪn'veɪʒ(ə)n/ *n.* вторже́ние, наше́ствие; **～ of privacy** вторже́ние в ли́чную жизнь

inveigle /ɪn'veɪg(ə)l/ *v.t.* соблазн|я́ть, -и́ть; оболь|ща́ть, -сти́ть; **they ～d him into the conspiracy** они́ вовлекли́ его́ в за́говор; **he was ～d into signing a cheque** его́ обма́ном заста́вили подписа́ть чек

invent /ɪn'vent/ *v.t.* изобре|та́ть, -сти́; (think up) приду́м|ывать, -ать

invention /ɪn'venʃ(ə)n/ *n.* изобрете́ние

inventive /ɪn'ventɪv/ *adj.* изобрета́тельный, нахо́дчивый

inventor /ɪn'ventə(r)/ *n.* изобрета́тель (*m.*)

inventory /'ɪnvəntərɪ/ *n.* инвента́рь (*m.*)

invert /ɪn'vɜ:t/ *v.t.* (turn upside down) перев|ора́чивать, -ерну́ть; **～ed commas** (BrE, gram.) кавы́чки (*f. pl.*)

invertebrate /ɪn'vɜ:tɪbrət/ *n.* беспозвоно́чное (живо́тное)

⚲ **invest** /ɪn'vest/ *v.t.* вкла́дывать, вложи́ть; инвести́ровать (*impf., pf.*) ● *v.i.* вкла́дывать, вложи́ть де́ньги/капита́л; (infml, spend money usefully): **I must ～ in a new hat** мне придётся потра́титься на но́вую шля́пу

⚲ **investigate** /ɪn'vestɪgeɪt/ *v.t.* (crime, facts) рассле́довать (*impf., pf.*); (study) иссле́довать (*impf., pf.*)

⚲ **investigation** /ɪnvestɪ'geɪʃ(ə)n/ *n.* (criminal) рассле́дование, сле́дствие; (study) иссле́дование

investigative /ɪn'vestɪgətɪv/ *adj.*: **～ journalism** журнали́стика рассле́дований

investigator /ɪn'vestɪgeɪtə(r)/ *n.* (in police) сле́дователь (*m.*); (researcher) иссле́дователь (*m.*)

✓ **investment** /ɪn'vestmənt/ *n.* (investing) инвести́рование; (sum invested) инвести́ция
■ ~ **bank** *n.* инвестицио́нный банк

✓ **investor** /ɪn'vestə(r)/ *n.* вкла́дчик, инве́стор

inveterate /ɪn'vetərət/ *adj.* закорене́лый, зая́длый

invidious /ɪn'vɪdɪəs/ *adj.* оскорби́тельный; оби́дный; an ~ **comparison** оби́дное/оскорби́тельное сравне́ние

invigilate /ɪn'vɪdʒɪleɪt/ *v.i.* (*impf.*) за экзамену́ющимися наблюда́ть

invigilator /ɪn'vɪdʒɪleɪtə(r)/ *n.* официа́льный наблюда́тель (*на экзамене*)

invigorating /ɪn'vɪgəreɪtɪŋ/ *adj.* бодря́щий

invincible /ɪn'vɪnsɪb(ə)l/ *adj.* непобеди́мый

invisible /ɪn'vɪzɪb(ə)l/ *adj.* невиди́мый, незри́мый

invitation /ɪnvɪ'teɪʃ(ə)n/ *n.* приглаше́ние

✓ **invite** /ɪn'vaɪt/ *v.t.* **1** (request to come) пригла|ша́ть, -си́ть; she ~d him into her flat она́ пригласи́ла его́ к себе́ на кварти́ру; I am seldom ~d out меня́ ре́дко куда́-либо приглаша́ют **2** (request) предл|ага́ть, -ожи́ть; we were ~d to choose нам был предоста́влен вы́бор

invoice /'ɪnvɔɪs/ *n.* счёт, счёт-факту́ра
● *v.t.* выпи́сывать, вы́писать счёт кому́-н. (на това́ры)

invoke /ɪn'vəʊk/ *v.t.* взыва́ть, воззва́ть; приз|ыва́ть, -ва́ть; ~ **the law** взыва́ть, воззва́ть к зако́ну

involuntary /ɪn'vɒləntəri/ *adj.* (accidental) неча́янный; (uncontrollable) непроизво́льный

✓ **involve** /ɪn'vɒlv/ *v.t.* **1** (implicate) вовл|ека́ть, -е́чь; it will not ~ you in any expense э́то не потре́бует от вас никаки́х расхо́дов **2** (entail) влечь, по- за собо́й; вызыва́ть, вы́звать; it would ~ my living in London в тако́м слу́чае мне бы пришло́сь жить в Ло́ндоне

involved /ɪn'vɒlvd/ *adj.* сло́жный, запу́танный

involvement /ɪn'vɒlvmənt/ *n.* (participation) прича́стность; (personal) связь, вовлечённость

invulnerable /ɪn'vʌlnərəb(ə)l/ *adj.* неуязви́мый

inward /'ɪnwəd/ *adj.* (lit., fig.) вну́тренний
● *adv.* = inwards

inwards /'ɪnwədz/ *adv.* (expr. motion) внутрь

in-your-face /ɪnjɔː'feɪs/ *adj.* (infml) жёсткий, провокацио́нный

iodine /'aɪədiːn/ *n.* йод

iota /aɪ'əʊtə/ *n.* йо́та; we will not yield one ~ мы не отсту́пим ни на йо́ту; I don't care one ~ мне реши́тельно всё равно́

IOU /aɪəʊ'juː/ *n.* долгова́я распи́ска

IQ *abbr.* (*of* **intelligence quotient**) коэффицие́нт интелле́кта/у́мственного развития

IRA *abbr. of* **1** (**Irish Republican Army**) ИРА́ (Ирла́ндская республика́нская а́рмия) **2** (**individual retirement account**) (AmE) индивидуа́льные пенсио́нные вкла́ды (*m. pl.*)

Iran /ɪ'rɑːn/ *n.* Ира́н

Iranian /ɪ'reɪnɪən/ *n.* ира́н|ец (-ка)
● *adj.* ира́нский

Iraq /ɪ'rɑːk/ *n.* Ира́к

Iraqi /ɪ'rɑːki/ *n.* (*pl.* ~**s**) ира́кец, жи́тель (-ница) Ира́ка
● *adj.* ира́кский

irascible /ɪ'ræsɪb(ə)l/ *adj.* раздражи́тельный, вспы́льчивый

irate /aɪ'reɪt/ *adj.* серди́тый, гне́вный

Ireland /'aɪələnd/ *n.* Ирла́ндия

iridescent /ɪrɪ'des(ə)nt/ *adj.* ра́дужный, перели́вчатый

iris /'aɪərɪs/ *n.* **1** (plant) и́рис **2** (of eye) ра́дужная оболо́чка

✓ **Irish** /'aɪərɪʃ/ *n.* **1** (language) ирла́ндский язы́к **2**: the ~ ирла́ндцы (*m. pl.*)
● *adj.* ирла́ндский
■ ~**man** *n.* ирла́ндец; ~**woman** *n.* ирла́ндка

iron /'aɪən/ *n.* **1** (metal) желе́зо **2** (for ironing) утю́г
● *adj.* (lit., fig.) желе́зный
● *v.t.* (clothes) гла́дить, по-/вы́-; ~ **out** (fig.) сгла́|живать, -дить
● *v.i.* гла́дить (*impf.*); she spent the whole evening ~**ing** она́ гла́дила весь ве́чер
■ ~**monger** *n.* (BrE) торго́вец скобяны́ми изде́лиями; ~**monger's (shop)** *n.* (BrE) магази́н скобяны́х изде́лий/това́ров

ironic /aɪ'rɒnɪk/, **ironical** /aɪ'rɒnɪk(ə)l/ *adjs.* ирони́ческий

ironing /'aɪənɪŋ/ *n.* **1** (action) гла́женье **2** (linen) бельё для гла́женья
■ ~ **board** *n.* гла́дильная доска́

irony /'aɪərəni/ *n.* иро́ния

irrational /ɪ'ræʃən(ə)l/ *adj.* (not endowed with reason) неразу́мный; (illogical; absurd) иррациона́льный

irreconcilable /ɪ'rekənsaɪləb(ə)l/ *adj.* непримири́мый

irrefutable /ɪrɪ'fjuːtəb(ə)l/ *adj.* неопроверж́имый

irregular /ɪ'regjʊlə(r)/ *adj.* **1** (contrary to rule) непра́вильный; (contrary to custom, norm) непри́нятый **2** (variable in occurrence) нерегуля́рный; he keeps ~ hours у него́ неупоря́доченный режи́м **3** (uneven) неро́вный; ~ **teeth** неро́вные зу́бы **4** (unequal) неодина́ковый; at ~ **intervals** с неодина́ковыми интерва́лами **5** (gram.) непра́вильный

irregularity /ɪregjʊ'lærɪti/ *n.* непра́вильность, нерегуля́рность

irrelevant /ɪ'relɪv(ə)nt/ *adj.* неуме́стный, неподходя́щий

irreparable /ɪ'repərəb(ə)l/ *adj.*: an ~ **mistake** непоправи́мая оши́бка; an ~ **loss** безвозвра́тная поте́ря/утра́та; **my watch**

suffered ~ damage мои часы́ оконча́тельно
слома́лись

irreplaceable /ɪrɪ'pleɪsəb(ə)l/ *adj.*
незамени́мый

irrepressible /ɪrɪ'presɪb(ə)l/ *adj.*
неукроти́мый, неугомо́нный, неудержи́мый

irreproachable /ɪrɪ'prəʊtʃəb(ə)l/ *adj.*
безупре́чный

irresistible /ɪrɪ'zɪstɪb(ə)l/ *adj.* неотрази́мый

irresolute /ɪ'rezəluːt/ *adj.* нереши́тельный

irrespective /ɪrɪ'spektɪv/ *adj.*: ~ of невзира́я/
несмотря́ на + *a.*

irresponsible /ɪrɪ'spɒnsɪb(ə)l/ *adj.*
безотве́тственный

irreverence /ɪ'revərəns/ *n.*
непочти́тельность, неуваже́ние

irreverent /ɪ'revərənt/ *adj.* непочти́тельный

irreversible /ɪrɪ'vɜːsɪb(ə)l/ *adj.* (process)
необрати́мый; (decision) неотменя́емый

irrevocable /ɪ'revəkəb(ə)l/ *adj.*
бесповоро́тный

irrigate /'ɪrɪɡeɪt/ *v.t.* оро|ша́ть, -си́ть

irrigation /ɪrɪ'ɡeɪʃ(ə)n/ *n.* ороше́ние,
иррига́ция

irritability /ɪrɪtə'bɪlɪtɪ/ *n.* раздражи́тельность;
(of skin etc.) чувстви́тельность

irritable /'ɪrɪtəb(ə)l/ *adj.* **1** (easily
annoyed) раздражи́тельный **2** (of skin etc.)
чувстви́тельный

irritant /'ɪrɪt(ə)nt/ *n.* раздражи́тель (*m.*)

irritate /'ɪrɪteɪt/ *v.t.* раздража́ть (*impf.*)

irritation /ɪrɪ'teɪʃ(ə)n/ *n.* раздраже́ние

IRS (AmE) *abbr.* (*of* **Internal Revenue
Service**) Госуда́рственная нало́говая
слу́жба

is /ɪz/ *3rd pers. sing. pres. of* ▸ **be**

Islam /'ɪzlɑːm/ *n.* исла́м, мусульма́нство

Islamic /ɪz'læmɪk/ *adj.* мусульма́нский,
исла́мский

◆ **island** /'aɪlənd/ *n.* о́стров; **traffic** ~ острово́к
безопа́сности

islander /'aɪləndə(r)/ *n.* островитя́н|ин (-ка)

isle /aɪl/ *n.* о́стров

isn't /'ɪz(ə)nt/ *neg. of* ▸ **is**

isolate /'aɪsəleɪt/ *v.t.* изоли́ровать (*impf., pf.*)
(also med.); разобщ|а́ть, -и́ть; **an** ~**d village**
отдалённая дере́вня

isolation /aɪsə'leɪʃ(ə)n/ *n.* изоля́ция,
разобще́ние; **a case considered in** ~ отде́льно
взя́тый слу́чай

isolationism /aɪsə'leɪʃənɪz(ə)m/ *n.*
изоляциони́зм

ISP *abbr.* (*of* **Internet service provider**)
(интерне́т-)провайдер

Israel /'ɪzreɪl/ *n.* (bibl., pol.) Изра́иль (*m.*)

Israeli /ɪz'reɪlɪ/ *n.* (*pl.* ~**s**) израильтя́н|ин (-ка)
● *adj.* изра́ильский

◆ **issue** /'ɪʃuː/ *n.* **1** (publication, production) вы́пуск,

изда́ние; (sth published or produced) вы́пуск,
изда́ние; **recent** ~**s of a magazine** после́дние
номера́ журна́ла **2** (topic) вопро́с; предме́т
обсужде́ния; **I don't want to make an** ~ **of it**
я не хочу́ де́лать из э́того пробле́му
● *v.t.* (**issues, issued, issuing**) **1** (publish)
выпуска́ть, вы́пустить; изд|ава́ть, -а́ть;
a book ~**d last year** кни́га, и́зданная в
про́шлом году́ **2** (supply) выдава́ть, вы́дать;
снаб|жа́ть, -ди́ть

Istanbul /ɪstæn'bʊl/ *n.* Стамбу́л

isthmus /'ɪsθməs/ *n.* (*pl.* ~**es**) перешеек,
перемы́чка

IT *abbr.* (*of* **information technology**)
информа́тика

◆ **it** /ɪt/ *pers. pron.* **1** он (она́, оно́); (impersonal,
often untranslated) э́то; **who is** ~? кто э́то?; ~'s
the postman э́то почтальо́н; **I don't speak
Russian but I understand** ~ я не говорю́ по-
ру́сски, но понима́ю **2** (impersonal or indefinite):
~ **is cold** хо́лодно; ~ **is 6 o'clock** (сейча́с)
шесть часо́в; ~ **is raining** идёт дождь; ~
is 5 miles to Oxford до О́ксфорда пять
миль **3** (emph. another word): ~ **was John who
laughed** э́то Джон смея́лся

Italian /ɪ'tæljən/ *n.* (person) италья́н|ец (-ка);
(language) италья́нский язы́к
● *adj.* италья́нский

italics /ɪ'tælɪks/ *n.* курси́в; **in** ~ курси́вом

Italy /'ɪtəlɪ/ *n.* Ита́лия

itch /ɪtʃ/ *n.* зуд
● *v.i.* чеса́ться (*impf.*)

itchy /'ɪtʃɪ/ *adj.* (**itchier, itchiest**) (skin)
зудя́щий; (causing itchiness) вызыва́ющий зуд

◆ **item** /'aɪtəm/ *n.* пункт, но́мер; **news** ~
(коро́ткое) сообще́ние

itemize /'aɪtəmaɪz/ *v.t.* переч|исля́ть, -и́слить;
сост|авля́ть, -а́вить пе́речень + *g.*; **an** ~**d
account** подро́бный счёт

itinerary /aɪ'tɪnərərɪ/ *n.* маршру́т, план пути́
(*m.*)

◆ **its** /ɪts/ *poss. adj.* его́, её; (pert. to subject of
sentence) свой; **the horse broke** ~ **leg** ло́шадь
слома́ла но́гу

◆ **itself** /ɪt'self/ *n.* **1** (refl.) себя́ (*d., p.* себе́, *i.*
собо́й); -ся/-сь (*suff.*); **the cat was washing**
~ кот умыва́лся; **the monkey saw** ~
in the mirror обезья́на уви́дела себя́ в
зеркале **2** (emph.) сам; **she is kindness** ~ она́
сама́ доброта́; **by** ~ (alone) оди́н, одино́ко, в
отдале́нии; (automatically) самостоя́тельно

ITV (BrE) *abbr.* (*of* **Independent
Television**) Незави́симое (комме́рческое)
телеви́дение (*телеканал в Великобритании*)

IVF *n.* (*abbr. of* **in vitro fertilization**)
экстракорпора́льное оплодотворе́ние

ivory /'aɪvərɪ/ *n.* **1** (substance) слоно́вая кость;
the I~ **Coast** Кот-д'Ивуа́р **2** (colour) цвет
слоно́вой кости

ivy /'aɪvɪ/ *n.* плющ

Jj

jab /dʒæb/ *n.* **1** (sharp blow) тычо́к **2** (BrE, infml, injection) уко́л
● *v.t.* (**jabbed, jabbing**) **1** (poke) ты́кать, ткнуть **2** (thrust) втыка́ть, воткну́ть
jabber /'dʒæbə(r)/ *n.* трескотня́
● *v.t.* тарато́рить, про-
● *v.i.* треща́ть (*impf.*), тарато́рить (*impf.*)
jack /dʒæk/ *n.* **1** (name): ~ of all trades ма́стер на все ру́ки **2** (card) валёт **3** (lifting device) домкра́т
● *v.t.*: ~ in (BrE, infml, give up) бр|оса́ть, -о́сить
■ **~daw** *n.* га́лка; ~**knife** *v.i.*: **the lorry ~knifed** грузови́к занесло́; ~**pot** *n.* джекпо́т; **he hit the ~pot** (fig.) ему́ кру́пно повезло́
jackal /'dʒæk(ə)l/ *n.* шака́л
jacket /'dʒækɪt/ *n.* (informal style) ку́ртка; (part of suit) пиджа́к
jade /dʒeɪd/ *n.* (min.) нефри́т
jaded /'dʒeɪdɪd/ *adj.*: **you look ~** у вас утомлённый вид
jagged /'dʒægɪd/ *adj.* зубча́тый
jaguar /'dʒægjʊə(r)/ *n.* ягуа́р
jail /dʒeɪl/ *n.* тюрьма́
● *v.t.* заключ|а́ть, -и́ть в тюрьму́
jailer /'dʒeɪlə(r)/ *n.* тюре́мщик
jam¹ /dʒæm/ *n.* (BrE, preserve) джем
jam² /dʒæm/ *n.* (crush) да́вка; **traffic ~** про́бка
● *v.t.* (**jammed, jamming**) **1** (cram) зап|и́хивать, -ихну́ть; **she ~med everything into the cupboard** она́ всё запихну́ла в шкаф; (force): **he ~med the brakes on** он ре́зко затормози́л **2** (cause to stick or stop): **the machine got ~med** стано́к засто́порило/ закли́нило **3** (obstruct) заб|ива́ть, -и́ть; **the crowds ~med every exit** толпа́ заби́ла все вы́ходы; (radio) глуши́ть, за-
● *v.i.* (**jammed, jamming**) (get stuck) застр|ева́ть, -я́ть
■ **~-packed** *adj.* наби́тый до отка́за
Jamaica /dʒə'meɪkə/ *n.* Яма́йка
Jamaican /dʒə'meɪkən/ *n.* яма́|ец (-йка)
● *adj.* яма́йский
jangle /'dʒæŋg(ə)l/ *n.* ре́зкий звук
● *v.i.* бренча́ть (*impf.*)
● *v.t.* звя́к|ать, -нуть в + *a.*
janitor /'dʒænɪtə(r)/ *n.* вахтёр
♂ **January** /'dʒænjʊərɪ/ *n.* янва́рь (*m.*)
♂ **Japan** /dʒə'pæn/ *n.* Япо́ния
♂ **Japanese** /dʒæpə'niːz/ *n.* (*pl.* ~) (person) япо́н|ец (-ка); (language) япо́нский язы́к
● *adj.* япо́нский
japonica /dʒə'pɒnɪkə/ *n.* айва́ япо́нская

jar¹ /dʒɑː(r)/ *n.* (vessel) ба́нка
jar² /dʒɑː(r)/ *v.t.* (**jarred, jarring**) сотряс|а́ть, -ти́
● *v.i.* (**jarred, jarring**) **1** (sound discordantly) дисгармони́ровать (*impf.*) **2**: ~ **on** (irritate) раздраж|а́ть, -и́ть
jargon /'dʒɑːgən/ *n.* жарго́н
jasmine /'dʒæzmɪn/ *n.* жасми́н
jaundice /'dʒɔːndɪs/ *n.* желту́ха
● *v.t.* (*usu. p.p.*): **he took a ~d view of the affair** он мра́чно смотре́л на э́то де́ло
jaunt /dʒɔːnt/ *n.* увесели́тельная пое́здка/ прогу́лка
jaunty /'dʒɔːntɪ/ *adj.* (**jauntier, jauntiest**) бо́йкий
javelin /'dʒævəlɪn/ *n.* (мета́тельное) копьё
jaw /dʒɔː/ *n.* че́люсть
jay /dʒeɪ/ *n.* со́йка
■ **~walk** *v.i.* пере|ходи́ть, -йти́ у́лицу неосторо́жно; ~**walker** *n.* неосторо́жный пешехо́д
jazz /dʒæz/ *n.* джаз
● *v.t.*: ~ **up** (fig., enliven) оживл|я́ть, -и́ть
■ ~ **band** *n.* джаз-орке́стр, джаз-ба́нд
jazzy /'dʒæzɪ/ *adj.* (**jazzier, jazziest**) бро́ский, я́ркий
JCB® /dʒeɪsiː'biː/ *n.* (BrE) экскава́тор
JCR (BrE) *abbr.* (*of* **Junior Common Room**) студе́нческая ко́мната о́тдыха
jealous /'dʒeləs/ *adj.* **1** (of affection etc.) ревни́вый; **she was ~ of her husband's secretary** она́ ревнова́ла му́жа к секрета́рше **2** (envious) зави́стливый; **I am ~ of his success** я зави́дую его́ успе́ху
jealousy /'dʒeləsɪ/ *n.* ре́вность; (envy) за́висть
jeans /dʒiːnz/ *n. pl.* джи́нс|ы (-ов)
jeep® /dʒiːp/ *n.* джип
jeer /dʒɪə(r)/ *v.t. & i.* (taunt) глуми́ться (*impf.*) (**at**: над + *i.*); (deride) насмеха́ться (*impf.*) (**at**: над + *i.*)
jelly /'dʒelɪ/ *n.* **1** (BrE) желе́ (*nt. indecl.*) **2** (AmE, jam) джем
■ ~**fish** *n.* меду́за
jeopardize /'dʒepədaɪz/ *v.t.* (endanger) подв|ерга́ть, -е́ргнуть опа́сности; (put at risk) рискова́ть (*impf.*) + *i.*
jeopardy /'dʒepədɪ/ *n.* опа́сность; **his life was in ~** его́ жизнь была́ в опа́сности
jerk /dʒəːk/ *n.* **1** (pull) рыво́к; (jolt) уда́р **2** (twitch) су́дорожное вздра́гивание **3** (infml, idiot) ду́рень (*m.*), тупи́ца (*c.g.*)
● *v.t.* дёр|гать, -нуть
● *v.i.*: **the train ~ed to a halt** по́езд ре́зко

остановился

jerky /ˈdʒɜːkɪ/ *adj.* (**jerkier, jerkiest**)
судорожный

jersey /ˈdʒɜːzɪ/ *n.* (*pl.* ~s) свитер

jest /dʒest/ *n.* шутка; **in** ~ в шутку
● *v.i.* шутить, по-

jester /ˈdʒestə(r)/ *n.* (hist.) шут

Jesus /ˈdʒiːzəs/ *n.* Иисус; (as expletive): ~
(**Christ**)! Боже!

jet¹ /dʒet/ *n.* (min.) гагат
● *adj.* (~-black) чёрный как смоль

jet² /dʒet/ *n.* **1** (stream of water etc.) струя **2** (*in*
full ~ **engine**) реактивный двигатель; (*in*
full ~ **aircraft**) реактивный самолёт
● *v.i.* (**jetted, jetting**) летать (*indet.*) на
реактивном самолёте
■ ~ **lag** *n.* нарушение суточного ритма; ~ **set**
n. международная элита

jettison /ˈdʒetɪs(ə)n/ *v.t.* (lit., fig.)
выбрасывать, выбросить (за борт)

jetty /ˈdʒetɪ/ *n.* пристань, мол

Jew /dʒuː/ *n.* еврей (-ка)

jewel /ˈdʒuːəl/ *n.* (precious stone) драгоценный
камень; (fig.) сокровище

jeweller /ˈdʒuːələ(r)/ (AmE **jeweler**) *n.*
ювелир

jewellery /ˈdʒuːəlrɪ/ (AmE *also* **jewelry**) *n.*
ювелирные изделия; драгоценности (*f. pl.*)

ⵣ **Jewish** /ˈdʒuːɪʃ/ *adj.* еврейский

jib /dʒɪb/ *n.* **1** (naut.) кливер **2** (of crane) стрела

jibe /dʒaɪb/ *n.* (taunt) насмешка

jiffy /ˈdʒɪfɪ/ *n.* (infml) миг; **in a** ~ мигом

jig /dʒɪg/ *n.* (dance) джига

jiggle /ˈdʒɪg(ə)l/ *v.t.* покачивать (*impf.*)

jigsaw /ˈdʒɪgsɔː/ *n.* (puzzle) (составная)
картинка-загадка, пазл

jihad *n.* (relig.) джихад

jilt /dʒɪlt/ *v.t.* бросать, -осить

jingle /ˈdʒɪŋg(ə)l/ *n.* (ringing sound) звяканье;
(advertising tune) рекламная песенка
● *v.t. & i.* звякать, -нуть + *i.*

jingoistic /ˌdʒɪŋgəʊˈɪstɪk/ *adj.*
шовинистический

jinx /dʒɪŋks/ *n.* (infml) злые чары (*f. pl.*); **put a**
~ **on** сглазить (*pf.*)

jitter /ˈdʒɪtə(r)/ *n.* (infml): **have the** ~s
нервничать (*impf.*)

jittery /ˈdʒɪtərɪ/ *adj.* (infml) нервный

jive /dʒaɪv/ *n.* джайв (*танец*)
● *v.i.* исполнять, -олнить (*impf.*) джайв

ⵣ **job** /dʒɒb/ *n.* **1** (piece of work) работа;
задание; **my** ~ **is to wash the dishes** моя
обязанность — мыть посуду; (difficult task):
we had a ~ **finding them** мы с трудом
их отыскали **2** (product of work): **you've**
made a good ~ **of that** вы сделали это
хорошо **3** (employment; position) работа; место;
what is your ~? какая у вас работа?; **get**
a ~ на|ходить, -йти работу **4** (circumstance,
fact): **it's a good** ~ **you stayed at home** (BrE)
хорошо, что вы остались дома
■ ~-**seeker** *n.* лицо, ищущее работу; ~-**share**
v.i. делить (*impf.*) рабочее место и зарплату

jobcentre /ˈdʒɒbsentə(r)/ *n.* (BrE) центр по
трудоустройству, биржа труда

jobless /ˈdʒɒblɪs/ *adj.* безработный

jockey /ˈdʒɒkɪ/ *n.* (*pl.* ~s) жокей

jockstrap /ˈdʒɒkstræp/ *n.* суспензорий

jocular /ˈdʒɒkjʊlə(r)/ *adj.* весёлый

jodhpurs /ˈdʒɒdpəz/ *n. pl.* брюк|и (*pl., g.* —)
для верховой езды

jog /dʒɒg/ *n.* **1** (nudge) толчок **2** (trot) бег
трусцой
● *v.t.* (**jogged, jogging**): ~ **sb's elbow**
толк|ать, -нуть кого-н. под локоть; ~ **sb's**
memory освеж|ать, -ить чью-н. память
● *v.i.* (**jogged, jogging**) бегать (*indet.*)
трусцой

jogger /ˈdʒɒgə(r)/ *n.* любитель (*m.*)
оздоровительного бега

jogging /ˈdʒɒgɪŋ/ *n.* оздоровительный бег;
бег трусцой

ⵣ **join** /dʒɔɪn/ *n.* связь, соединение
● *v.t.* **1** (connect) соедин|ять, -ить; **the towns**
are ~**ed by a railway** эти города соединяет
железная дорога **2** (enter) вступ|ать, -ить
в + *a.*; ~ **a club** вступ|ать, -ить в клуб; ~
the army идти, пойти в армию **3** (enter sb's
company) присоедин|яться, -иться к + *d.*;
(meet) встр|ечаться, -етиться с + *i.*; **may**
I ~ **you?** разрешите присоединиться к
вам? **4** (flow or lead into) соедин|яться, -иться
с + *i.*; сли|ваться, -иться с + *i.*
● *v.i.* **1** (be connected) соедин|яться, -иться; (be
united) объедин|яться, -иться; (come together)
сходиться, сойтись; (flow together) сли|ваться,
-иться **2** (become a member) стать (*impf.*)
членом (*чего*)
◻ ~ **in** *v.i.* (take part) прин|имать, -ять участие;
(in conversation, discussion, etc.) вступ|ать, -ить в
+ *a.*
◻ ~ **up** *v.t. & i.* (unite) соедин|ять(ся), -ить(ся)
● *v.i.* (infml, enlist) идти, пойти в армию

joiner /ˈdʒɔɪnə(r)/ *n.* столяр

joinery /ˈdʒɔɪnərɪ/ *n.* столярная работа; **do,**
practise ~ столярничать (*impf.*)

ⵣ **joint** /dʒɔɪnt/ *n.* **1** (place of juncture; means of
joining) соединение; стык **2** (anat.) сустав,
сочленение **3**: **a** ~ **of meat** (BrE) кусок
мяса (*к обеду*) **4** (infml, place) притон **5** (sl.,
marijuana cigarette) косяк
● *adj.* **1** (combined; shared) совместный;
(common) общий; ~ **efforts** общие/
совместные усилия **2** (sharing): ~ **owner**
совладелец
■ ~ **account** *n.* общий/совместный счёт; ~
action *n.* совместные действия (*nt. pl.*); ~
venture *n.* совместное предприятие

joist /dʒɔɪst/ *n.* балка

jok|e /dʒəʊk/ *n.* шутка; (story) анекдот;
(witticism) острота; (laughing stock) посмешище;
it's no ~**e!** это не шутка!; **crack, make a** ~**e**
шутить, по-; **play a** ~**e on sb** сыграть (*pf.*)
шутку с кем-н.
● *v.i.* шутить, по-; **I was only** ~**ing** я всего
лишь пошутил

joker /ˈdʒəʊkə(r)/ *n.* (one who jokes) шутник;
(cards) джокер

jollity /'dʒɒlɪtɪ/ *n.* весéлье, увеселéние

jolly /'dʒɒlɪ/ *adj.* (**jollier, jolliest**) (cheerful) весёлый; (entertaining) рáдостный
● *adv.* (BrE, infml, very) óчень

jolt /dʒɒlt/ *n.* толчóк; (fig.) удáр, потрясéние
● *v.t. & i.* трясти́(сь) (*impf.*)

Jordan /'dʒɔːd(ə)n/ *n.* (country) Иордáния; (river) Иордáн

Jordanian /dʒɔː'deɪnɪən/ *n.* иордáн|ец (-ка)
● *adj.* иордáнский

jostle /'dʒɒs(ə)l/ *v.t.* толк|áть, -нýть

jot /dʒɒt/ *v.t.* (**jotted, jotting**): ~ down набр|áсывать, -осáть

journal /'dʒɜːn(ə)l/ *n.* журнáл

journalism /'dʒɜːnəlɪz(ə)m/ *n.* журнали́стика

✓ **journalist** /'dʒɜːnəlɪst/ *n.* журнали́ст (-ка)

✓ **journey** /'dʒɜːnɪ/ *n.* (*pl.* ~**s**) (expedition; trip) (long) путешéствие; (shorter) поéздка; **be, go on a** ~ путешéствовать (*impf.*); (travel; travelling time) путь
● *v.i.* (**journeys, journeyed**) путешéствовать (*impf.*)

joust /dʒaʊst/ *n.* (ры́царский) турни́р
● *v.i.* состязáться (*impf.*) на турни́ре

jovial /'dʒəʊvɪəl/ *adj.* весёлый

joy /dʒɔɪ/ *n.* (gladness) рáдость
■ ~**rider** *n.* лихáч, управля́ющий ýгнанным автомоби́лем; ~**riding** *n.* риско́ванная eздá на ýгнанном автомоби́ле

joyful /'dʒɔɪfʊl/ *adj.* рáдостный

joyless /'dʒɔɪlɪs/ *adj.* безрáдостный

joyous /'dʒɔɪəs/ *adj.* рáдостный; (happy) весёлый

jubilant /'dʒuːbɪlənt/ *adj.* лику́ющий

jubilee /'dʒuːbɪliː/ *n.* юбилéй

Judaism /'dʒuːdeɪɪz(ə)m/ *n.* иудаи́зм

✓ **judge** /dʒʌdʒ/ *n.* **1** (legal functionary) судья́ (*m.*) **2** (arbiter) арби́тр, судья́ **3** (expert) знатóк, цени́тель (*m.*)
● *v.t.* **1** (pass judgement on) суди́ть (*impf.*) о + *i.*; (assess) оцéн|ивать, -и́ть **2** (consider) считáть (*impf.*); **he was** ~**d to be innocent** его́ сочли́ невинóвным
● *v.i.* суди́ть (*impf.*); **to** ~ **from what you say** су́дя по тому́, что вы сказáли

✓ **judgement, judgment** /'dʒʌdʒmənt/ *n.* **1** (sentence) судéбное решéние, пригово́р **2** (opinion; estimation) мнéние; суждéние

judicial /dʒuː'dɪʃ(ə)l/ *adj.* судéбный

judiciary /dʒuː'dɪʃərɪ/ *n.* су́дьи (*m. pl.*); судéбная власть

judicious /dʒuː'dɪʃəs/ *adj.* рассуди́тельный

judo /'dʒuːdəʊ/ *n.* дзюдó (*nt. indecl.*)

jug /dʒʌg/ *n.* кувши́н

juggernaut /'dʒʌgənɔːt/ *n.* (BrE, lorry) многотóнный грузови́к

juggle /'dʒʌg(ə)l/ *v.i.* (lit., fig.) жонгли́ровать (*impf.*)

juggler /'dʒʌglə(r)/ *n.* жонглёр

✓ ключевáя лéксика

jugular /'dʒʌgjʊlə(r)/ *n.* (*in full* ~ **vein**) ярéмная вéна

juice /dʒuːs/ *n.* сок

juicer /'dʒuːsə(r)/ *n.* соковыжимáлка

juicy /'dʒuːsɪ/ *adj.* (**juicier, juiciest**) сóчный; (infml, scandalous) смáчный

jukebox /'dʒuːkbɒks/ *n.* музыкáльный автомáт (*для проигрывания дисков*)

✓ **July** /dʒuː'laɪ/ *n.* ию́ль (*m.*)

jumble /'dʒʌmb(ə)l/ *n.* (untidy heap) ку́ча; (muddle) беспоря́док, пу́таница; (infml, unwanted articles) хлам
● *v.t.* (*also* ~ **up**) перемéш|ивать, -áть
■ ~ **sale** *n.* (BrE) дешёвая распродáжа (*в благотворительных целях*)

jumbo /'dʒʌmbəʊ/ *n.* (*pl.* ~**s**) (*also* ~ **jet**) реакти́вный лáйнер; (*attr.*) (huge) гигáнтский

✓ **jump** /dʒʌmp/ *n.* прыжóк, скачóк; (obstacle) препя́тствие; (fig., abrupt rise) скачóк; (fig., start, shock) вздрáгивание
● *v.t.* **1** (~ over, across) перепры́г|ивать, -нуть чéрез + *a.* **2** (var. fig. uses): ~ **the queue** про|ходи́ть, -йти́ без óчереди; **you've** ~**ed a few lines** вы пропусти́ли (*or* перескочи́ли чéрез) нéсколько строк
● *v.i.* **1** пры́г|ать, -нуть; (on horseback) вск|áкивать, -очи́ть **2** (fig.) перескáкивать (*impf.*); **he** ~**ed from one topic to another** он перескáкивал с однóй тéмы на другу́ю **3** (start) подск|áкивать, -очи́ть; **the noise made me** ~ звук застáвил меня́ подскочи́ть **4** (make sudden movement) подск|áкивать, -очи́ть; **shares** ~**ed to a new level** áкции подскочи́ли в ценé **5** (fig. uses): **I would** ~ **at the chance** я бы ухвати́лся за э́ту возмóжность; ~ **on sb** (attack) набр|áсываться, -óситься на когó-н.; (rebuke) рéзко осаж|дáть, -ди́ть когó-н.
● *with advs.*: **he** ~**ed back in surprise** он отпря́нул в удивлéнии; **she** ~**ed down from the fence** онá спры́гнула с забóра; **if you want a lift,** ~ **in!** éсли хоти́те, чтóбы я вас подбрóсил, залезáйте (в маши́ну)!; ~ **up from one's chair** вск|áкивать, -очи́ть со сту́ла; ~ **up and down** пры́гать/подпры́гивать (*impf.*) вверх и вниз
■ ~ **lead** *n.* (BrE) электри́ческий кáбель (для зáпуска дви́гателя автомоби́ля от постороннего источника энéргии)

jumper /'dʒʌmpə(r)/ *n.* (BrE, sweater) джéмпер; (AmE, pinafore dress) сарафáн

jumpy /'dʒʌmpɪ/ *adj.* (**jumpier, jumpiest**) нéрвный, дёрганый

junction /'dʒʌŋkʃ(ə)n/ *n.* (meeting point: of railways) у́зел; (of roads) пересечéние (дорóг); (of rivers) слия́ние

juncture /'dʒʌŋktʃə(r)/ *n.* (joining) соединéние; **at a critical** ~ в крити́ческий момéнт; **at this** ~ в дáнный момéнт

✓ **June** /dʒuːn/ *n.* ию́нь (*m.*)

jungle /'dʒʌŋg(ə)l/ *n.* джу́нгл|и (-ей)

junior /'dʒuːnɪə(r)/ *n.*: **he is my** ~ **by 5 years** он на пять лет млáдше меня́
● *adj.* млáдший; ~ **partner** млáдший партнёр
■ ~ **high school** *n.* (AmE) непóлная срéдняя

шко́ла (*7, 8, 9 кла́ссы*); ~ **school** *n.* (BrE) нача́льная шко́ла (*для дете́й 7—11 лет*)

juniper /ˈdʒuːnɪpə(r)/ *n.* можжеве́льник; (*attr.*) можжеве́ловый

junk /dʒʌŋk/ *n.* (rubbish) хлам ■ ~ **food** *n.* неполноце́нная пи́ща; ~ **mail** *n.* рекла́мные рассы́лки; ~ **shop** *n.* ла́вка старьёвщика

junkie, junky /ˈdʒʌŋkɪ/ *n.* (sl., drug addict) наркома́н

Jupiter /ˈdʒuːpɪtə(r)/ *n.* (myth., astron.) Юпи́тер

jurisdiction /ˌdʒʊərɪsˈdɪkʃ(ə)n/ *n.* (legal authority) юрисди́кция; **have** ~ **over** име́ть (*impf.*) юрисди́кцию над + *i.*

jurisprudence /ˌdʒʊərɪsˈpruːd(ə)ns/ *n.* юриспруде́нция

juror /ˈdʒʊərə(r)/ *n.* прися́жный (заседа́тель)

jury /ˈdʒʊərɪ/ *n.* прися́жные (заседа́тели) (*m. pl.*) ■ ~ **box** *n.* скамья́ прися́жных

⚡ **just** /dʒʌst/ *adj.* (equitable) справедли́вый; (deserved) справедли́вый, заслу́женный • *adv.* **1** то́чно, как раз, и́менно; **it was** ~ **3 o'clock** бы́ло ро́вно три часа́ **2**: ~ **like, as** (expr. comparison) то́чно так же, как (и); то́чно, как; **that's** ~ **like him** (typical) э́то так похо́же на него́; **he is** ~ **as lazy as ever** он всё тако́й же лени́вый; **it's** ~ **as well I warned you** хорошо́, что я вас предупреди́л **3** ~ **about** (approximately): ~ **about right** почти́ так/пра́вильно; (almost): **I've** ~ **about finished** я почти́ (за)ко́нчил **4** (expr. time) то́лько что; (very recently): **I saw him** ~ **now** я то́лько что ви́дел его́; ~ **as** (expr. time) (как) то́лько; ~ **as he entered the room** то́лько он вошёл в ко́мнату; (at this moment): **I'm** ~ **off** я ухожу́ пря́мо сейча́с/как раз сейча́с **5** (barely) едва́; **I** ~ **caught the train** я едва́ успе́л на по́езд; **he had** ~ **come in when the phone rang** то́лько

он вошёл, как зазвони́л телефо́н; **(wait)** ~ **a minute!** (одну́) мину́т(к)у! **6** (merely) то́лько; ~ **listen to this!** вы то́лько послу́шайте!; **I went** ~ **to hear him** я пошёл то́лько, что́бы послу́шать его́; ~ **fancy!** поду́мать то́лько!; ~ **you wait!** ну, погоди́!; ~ **in case** на вся́кий слу́чай **7** (positively, absolutely) так и; про́сто(-на́просто); **it's** ~ **splendid!** э́то про́сто велико́лепно!; **not** ~ **yet** ещё не/нет

⚡ **justice** /ˈdʒʌstɪs/ *n.* **1** (fairness; equity) справедли́вость; **to do him** ~ отдава́я ему́ до́лжное **2** (system of institutions) правосу́дие, юсти́ция; **bring sb to** ~ отд|ава́ть, -а́ть кого́-н. под суд **3**: **J~ of the Peace** (BrE) мирово́й судья́

justifiable /ˈdʒʌstɪfaɪəb(ə)l/ *adj.* опра́вданный

justification /ˌdʒʌstɪfɪˈkeɪʃ(ə)n/ *n.* оправда́ние; **he objected, and with** ~ он возрази́л и не без основа́ний

⚡ **justif|y** /ˈdʒʌstɪfaɪ/ *v.t.* опра́вд|ывать, -а́ть; **I was** ~**ied in suspecting ...** я име́л все основа́ния подозрева́ть...; ~**y oneself** опра́вд|ываться, -а́ться

jut /dʒʌt/ *v.i.* (**jutted, jutting**) (*usu.* ~ **out**) выступа́ть (*impf.*); выдава́ться (*impf.*)

juvenile /ˈdʒuːvənaɪl/ *n.* подро́сток • *adj.* ю́ный, ю́ношеский ■ ~ **delinquency** *n.* престу́пность среди́ несовершенноле́тних, подростко́вая престу́пность; ~ **delinquent** *n.* несовершенноле́тний престу́пник/правонаруши́тель

juxtapose /ˌdʒʌkstəˈpəʊz/ *v.t.* поме|ща́ть, -сти́ть бок о́ бок; (for comparison) сопост|авля́ть, -а́вить (*кого с кем or что с чем*)

juxtaposition /ˌdʒʌkstəpəˈzɪʃ(ə)n/ *n.* сосе́дство, бли́зость; (for comparison) сопоставле́ние

Kk

Kabul /ˈkɑːbʊl/ *n.* Кабу́л

kale /keɪl/ *n.* листова́я капу́ста

kaleidoscope /kəˈlaɪdəskəʊp/ *n.* калейдоско́п

kangaroo /ˌkæŋɡəˈruː/ *n.* кенгуру́ (*m. indecl.*)

karaoke /ˌkærɪˈəʊkɪ/ *n.* карао́ке (*nt. indecl.*)

karate /kəˈrɑːtɪ/ *n.* карате́ (*nt. indecl.*)

Kashmir /kæʃˈmɪə(r)/ *n.* Кашми́р

kayak /ˈkaɪæk/ *n.* кая́к (*эскимо́сская ло́дка; лёгкая спорти́вная одноме́стная ло́дка*)

Kazakh /kəˈzæk/ *n.* (*pl.* ~**s**) (person) каза́|х (-шка); (language) каза́хский язы́к

Kazakhstan /ˌkæzəkˈstɑːn/ *n.* Казахста́н

kebab /kɪˈbæb/ *n.* шашлы́к

keel /kiːl/ *n.* киль (*m.*) • *v.i.*: ~ **over** опроки́|дываться, -нуться

keen /kiːn/ *adj.* (lit., fig., sharp, acute) о́стрый; ~ **eyesight** о́строе зре́ние; (piercing) пронзи́тельный; (strong, intense) си́льный; ~ **interest** живо́й интере́с; (eager; energetic) ре́вностный; **a** ~ **pupil** усе́рдный учени́к; ~ **competition** тру́дное соревнова́ние; (enthusiastic) стра́стный; **a** ~ **sportsman** стра́стный спортсме́н; **be** ~ **on** си́льно/стра́стно увл|ека́ться, -е́чься + *i.*; **I am not** ~ **on chess** я не осо́бенно увлека́юсь ша́хматами; **he is** ~ **on your coming** ему́ очень хо́чется, что́бы вы пришли́

⚔ **keep** /kiːp/ *n.* **1** (sustenance) пропита́ние; **earn one's** ~ зараба́тывать, -о́тать себе́ на пропита́ние **2**: **for** ~**s** насовсе́м (infml) • *v.t.* (*past and p.p.* **kept**) **1** (retain possession of) держа́ть (*impf.*), не отдава́ть (*impf.*); ост|авля́ть, -а́вить (себе́ *or* при себе́); (preserve) храни́ть (*impf.*); сохран|я́ть, -и́ть; (save, put by): **I shall** ~ **this paper to show my mother** я сохраню́ э́ту газе́ту, что́бы показа́ть ма́тери **2** (cause to remain): **the traffic kept me awake** у́личное движе́ние не дава́ло мне спать; **the garden** ~**s me busy** сад не даёт мне сиде́ть сложа́ ру́ки; ~ **the house clean** содержа́ть (*impf.*) дом в чистоте́/поря́дке; ~ **it to yourself** пома́лкивайте об э́том; (infml): ~ **an eye on sth** пригля́дывать (*impf.*) за чем-н.; **where do you** ~ **the salt?** где вы храни́те соль? **3** (cause to continue): **I don't like to be kept waiting** я не люблю́, когда́ меня́ заставля́ют ждать; **that will** ~ **you going till lunchtime** тепе́рь вы проде́ржитесь до обе́да **4** (remain in, on): ~ **one's seat** (remain sitting) не встава́ть (*impf.*); (retain, preserve): ~ **one's balance** сохраня́ть/уде́рживать (*both impf.*) равнове́сие **5** (have charge of; manage; maintain) име́ть, держа́ть, содержа́ть (*all impf.*); **the shop was kept by an Italian** владе́льцем ла́вки был италья́нец; **he wants to** ~ **pigs** он хо́чет держа́ть свине́й **6** (accounts, records, diary) вести́ (*det.*) **7** (detain) задерж|ивать, -а́ть; **I won't** ~ **you** я вас не задержу́ **8** (fulfil, be faithful to) сде́рж|ивать, -а́ть; соблю|да́ть, -сти́; ~ **the law** соблюда́ть зако́н; ~ **one's word** держа́ть, с- сло́во; **I can't** ~ **the appointment** я не могу́ прийти́ на встре́чу • *v.i.* (*past and p.p.* **kept**) **1** (remain) держа́ться (*impf.*); остава́ться (*impf.*); **the weather kept fine** стоя́ла хоро́шая пого́да; **I can't** ~ **warm here** я не могу́ здесь согре́ться; **how are you** ~**ing?** (BrE) как пожива́ете?; как жизнь? (infml); **I exercise to** ~ **fit** я занима́юсь гимна́стикой/спо́ртом, что́бы быть в фо́рме; **we still** ~ **in touch** мы всё ещё подде́рживаем отноше́ния/связь **2** (continue) продолжа́ть (*impf.*) (+ *inf.*); **she** ~**s giggling** она́ всё хихи́кает **3** (remain fresh): **the food will** ~ **in the refrigerator** еда́ в холоди́льнике не испо́ртится • *with preps.*: **you must** ~ **at it till it's finished** не отвлека́йтесь, пока́ не (за)ко́нчите; **what are you trying to** ~ **from me?** что вы скрыва́ете от меня́?; '~ **off the grass!'** «по газо́нам не ходи́ть»; ~ **out of sb's way** (avoid him) избега́ть (*impf.*) кого́-н.; **he cannot** ~ **out of trouble for long** он ве́чно попада́ет в исто́рии; **he** ~**s himself to himself** он замыка́ется в себе́; ~ **to the path** держа́ться (*impf.*) тропи́нки; ~ **to the point** не отклоня́ться (*impf.*) от те́мы
□ ~ **away** *v.t.*: **the rain kept people away** дождь отпугну́л наро́д; **she kept her daughter away from school** она́ не пуска́ла дочь в шко́лу

• *v.i.*: **he tried to** ~ **away from them** он стара́лся их избега́ть
□ ~ **back** *v.t.* (restrain) сде́рж|ивать, -а́ть; (retain): **they** ~ **back £100 from my wages** из мое́й зарпла́ты уде́рживают сто фу́нтов; (repress): **she could hardly** ~ **back her tears** она́ едва́ сде́рживала слёзы
□ ~ **down** *v.t.*: ~ **your voice down!** не повыша́йте го́лос!; (limit, control): **they tried to** ~ **down expenses** они́ стара́лись расхо́довать как мо́жно ме́ньше; (oppress) держа́ть (*impf.*) в подчине́нии; (digest): **he can't** ~ **anything down** его́ желу́док ничего́ не принима́ет
□ ~ **off** *v.t.* (ward off, repel): **my hat will** ~ **the rain off** моя́ шля́па защити́т меня́ от дождя́ • *v.i.* (stay at a distance): **I hope the rain** ~**s off** я наде́юсь, что дождь не начнётся
□ ~ **on** *v.t.* (continue to wear): **women** ~ **their hats on in church** в це́ркви же́нщины не снима́ют шляп; (continue to employ): **they won't** ~ **you on after 60** они́ уво́лят вас, когда́ вам испо́лнится 60 лет; (leave in place): ~ **the lid on** не снима́йте кры́шку • *v.i.* (*with pres. part.*) (continue): **he kept on reading** он продолжа́л чита́ть; **she kept on glancing out of the window** она́ то и де́ло выгля́дывала из окна́; **she kept on (working) till the job was finished** она́ рабо́тала, пока́ всё не зако́нчила
□ ~ **out** *v.t.* (exclude): **we put up a fence to** ~ **out trespassers** мы постро́или/поста́вили забо́р, что́бы посторо́нние не заходи́ли на террито́рию • *v.i.*: '**Private** — ~ **out!'** (notice) «посторо́нним вход воспрещён!»
□ ~ **up** *v.t.* (prevent from falling or sinking): **he could not** ~ **his trousers up** у него́ всё вре́мя сва́ливались брю́ки; (fig., sustain, maintain): ~ **one's strength up** подкрепля́ть (*impf*) си́лы; **the house is expensive to** ~ **up** э́тот дом до́рого содержа́ть; (continue): ~ **up the good work!** продолжа́йте в том же ду́хе!; **he could not** ~ **up the payments** он был не в состоя́нии регуля́рно плати́ть; (prevent from going to bed): **the baby kept us up half the night** ребёнок не дава́л нам спать полно́чи • *v.i.* (stay level): **we kept up with them the whole way** всю доро́гу мы не отстава́ли от них; ~ **up with the times** не отстава́ть (*impf*) от собы́тий; шага́ть (*impf*) в но́гу со вре́менем; (remain in touch): **I** ~ **up with several old friends** я подде́рживаю отноше́ния ко́е с кем из ста́рых друзе́й

keeper /ˈkiːpə(r)/ *n.* (in zoo) служи́тель (*m.*) (зоопа́рка); (BrE, museum ~) смотри́тель (*m.*)

keeping /ˈkiːpɪŋ/ *n.* **1**: **in safe** ~ в надёжных рука́х **2**: **be in** ~ **with** соотве́тствовать (*impf.*) + *d.*

keg /keg/ *n.* бочо́нок

kennel /ˈken(ə)l/ *n.* конура́

Kenya /ˈkenjə/ *n.* Ке́ния

Kenyan /ˈkenjən/ *n.* кени́|ец (-йка) • *adj.* кени́йский

kept /kept/ *past and p.p. of* ▶ **keep**

kerb /kəːb/ (AmE **curb**) *n.* обо́чина

kerfuffle /kə'fʌf(ə)l/ n. (BrE, infml) шум, завару́ха

kernel /'kɜ:n(ə)l/ n. (of nut or fruit stone) ядро́

kerosene, kerosine /'kerəsi:n/ n. кероси́н; (attr.) кероси́новый

kestrel /'kestr(ə)l/ n. (zool.) пустельга́

ketchup /'ketʃʌp/ n. ке́тчуп

kettle /'ket(ə)l/ n. ча́йник

ơ **key** /ki:/ n. (pl. **keys**) **1** ключ **2** (fig.) ключ; the ~ to understanding the political situation ключ к понима́нию полити́ческой ситуа́ции **3** (attr.) (important, essential) ключево́й, важне́йший **4** (of piano or computer) кла́виша; (in pl.) клавиату́ра **5** (mus.) тона́льность
• v.t. (**keys, keyed**) (comput.) вв|оди́ть, -ести́ (into: в + a.); ~ **up** взви́н|чивать, -ти́ть
■ ~**board** n. (mus., comput.) клавиату́ра; ~**boarder** n. опера́тор компью́тера; ~**board(s)** n. (mus. instrument) кла́вишные (pl.); ~**hole** n. замо́чная сква́жина; ~**hole surgery** n. (BrE) полостна́я опера́ция с мини́ма́льным вскры́тием; ~ **ring** n. кольцо́ для ключе́й

kg /'kɪləgræm(z)/ n. (abbr. of **kilogram(s)**) кг (килогра́мм)

KGB abbr. (hist.) КГБ (Комите́т госуда́рственной безопа́сности)

khaki /'kɑ:kɪ/ n. (pl. ~**s**) ха́ки (nt. indecl.)
• adj.: a ~ shirt руба́шка цве́та ха́ки

ơ **kick** /kɪk/ n. **1** уда́р, пино́к **2** (recoil) отда́ча **3** (infml, stimulus): **get a ~ out of sth** получ|а́ть, -и́ть удово́льствие от чего́-н.
• v.t. удар|я́ть, -а́рить ного́й; **he ~ed me on the shin** он уда́рил меня́ по го́лени; **he ~ed the ball** он уда́рил по мячу́; **I could have ~ed myself** я рвал на себе́ во́лосы; ~ **the habit** (infml, give up addiction) бро́сить (pf.) употребля́ть нарко́тики/кури́ть/пить и т. д.
• v.i. (of animals) ляга́ться (impf.); брыка́ться (impf.)
□ ~ **about, around** vv.t.: **they were** ~**ing a ball about** они́ гоня́ли мяч
□ ~ **off** v.i. (football) нач|ина́ть, -а́ть игру́; (infml, begin) нач|ина́ть, -а́ть
□ ~ **out** v.t. (infml, eject, expel) выгоня́ть, вы́гнать
□ ~ **up** v.t. (infml, create): ~ **up a row** устр|а́ивать, -о́ить сканда́л
■ ~-**boxing** n. кикбо́ксинг; ~-**off** n. нача́ло (игры́); ~-**start** v.t. (lit. and fig.): **to** ~-**start the economy** дать толчо́к эконо́мике

ơ **kid¹** /kɪd/ n. **1** (young goat) козлёнок **2** (leather) ла́йка **3** (infml, child) малы́ш; **my** ~ **brother** мой мла́дший брат
■ ~ **gloves** n. pl. ла́йковые перча́тки

kid² /kɪd/ v.t. (**kidded, kidding**) **1** (infml, deceive) над|ува́ть, -у́ть; **who are you** ~**ding?** кого́ вы хоти́те обману́ть? **2** (tease) дразни́ть (impf.)
• v.i. (**kidded, kidding**) (tease with untruths): **you're** ~**ding!** врёшь!

kidnap /'kɪdnæp/ v.t. (**kidnapped, kidnapping**, AmE **kidnaped, kidnaping**) пох|ища́ть, -и́тить

kidnapper /'kɪdnæpə(r)/ n. похити́тель (m.)

kidney /'kɪdnɪ/ n. (pl. ~**s**) по́чка
■ ~ **bean** n. фасо́ль (collect.)

Kiev /'ki:ef/ n. Ки́ев

ơ **kill** /kɪl/ v.t. **1** уб|ива́ть, -и́ть; (rats etc.) трави́ть (impf.); ~ **oneself** ко́нчить самоуби́йством; (fig., infml): **my feet are** ~**ing me** я без за́дних ног; ~ **time** уб|ива́ть, -и́ть вре́мя **2** (animals for food) ре́зать, за- **3** (destroy) уничт|ожа́ть, -о́жить; **this drug** ~**s the pain** э́то лека́рство снима́ет боль
■ ~-**joy** n. брюзга́ (c.g.)

killer /'kɪlə(r)/ n. (murderer) уби́йца (c.g.); (infml, sth hilarious) что-н. умори́тельное
■ ~ **whale** n. коса́тка

killing /'kɪlɪŋ/ n. (murder) уби́йство; (slaughter of animals) убо́й, забо́й

kiln /kɪln/ n. печь

kilo /'ki:ləʊ/ n. (pl. ~**s**) кило́ (nt. indecl.)

kilobyte /'kɪləbaɪt/ n. килоба́йт

kilogram /'kɪləgræm/ n. килогра́мм

kilohertz /'kɪləhə:ts/ n. килоге́рц

kilometre /'kɪləmi:tə(r)/ (AmE **kilometer**) n. киломе́тр

kilowatt /'kɪləwɒt/ n. килова́тт

kilt /kɪlt/ n. (шотла́ндская) ю́бка, килт

kimono /kɪ'məʊnəʊ/ n. (pl. ~**s**) кимоно́ (nt. indecl.)

kin /kɪn/ n. (family) семья́; (relations) родня́ (collect.); ро́дственники (m. pl.); **kith and** ~ родны́е и бли́зкие; **next of** ~ ближа́йш|ий ро́дственни|к (-ая -ца)

ơ **kind** /kaɪnd/ n. **1** (sort, variety) род, сорт, разнови́дность; **all** ~**s of goods** вся́кие/ра́зные това́ры; **a** ~ **of** своего́ ро́да; **what** ~ **of?** что за?; како́й?; **what** ~ **of a painter is he?** что он за худо́жник? **2** ~ **of** (infml, to some extent): **I** ~ **of expected it** я как бы ожида́л э́того **3**: **in** ~ нату́рой; **pay in** ~ плати́ть, за- нату́рой
• adj. до́брый, любе́зный
■ ~-**hearted** adj. добросерде́чный

kindergarten /'kɪndəgɑ:t(ə)n/ n. де́тский сад

kindle /'kɪnd(ə)l/ v.t. разж|ига́ть, -е́чь; (fig., arouse) возбу|жда́ть, -ди́ть

kindliness /'kaɪndlɪnɪs/ n. доброта́

kindling /'kɪndlɪŋ/ n. (firewood) раст|о́пка; ще́пки (f. pl.)

kindly /'kaɪndlɪ/ adj. (**kindlier, kindliest**) до́брый, доброду́шный
• adv. **1** (in a kind manner) любе́зно, ми́ло **2** (please): ~ **ring me tomorrow** бу́дьте добры́, позвони́те мне за́втра **3**: **he does not take** ~ **to criticism** он не лю́бит кри́тики

kindness /'kaɪndnɪs/ n. **1** (benevolence) доброта́ **2** (kind act) любе́зность

kindred /'kɪndrɪd/ adj. (lit., fig.) ро́дственный; ~ **ideas** ро́дственные иде́и; **a** ~ **spirit** родна́я душа́

kinetic /kɪ'netɪk/ adj. кинети́ческий

ơ **king** /kɪŋ/ n. **1** коро́ль (m.) **2** (chess) коро́ль (m.); (draughts, checkers) да́мка; (cards): ~ **of diamonds** бубно́вый коро́ль
■ ~**fisher** n. (голубо́й) зиморо́док

k

kingdom /'kɪŋdəm/ *n.* короле́вство; **the animal** ~ живо́тное ца́рство

kink /kɪŋk/ *n.* (in rope etc.) переги́б; (in metal) изги́б

kinky /'kɪŋkɪ/ *adj.* (**kinkier, kinkiest**) (twisted) кручёный; (infml, perverted) извращённый; со стра́нностями

kinsfolk /'kɪnzfəʊk/ *n.* родня́ (*collect.*)

kinsman /'kɪnzmən/ *n.* ро́дственник

kinswoman /'kɪnzwʊmən/ *n.* ро́дственница

kiosk /'ki:ɒsk/ *n.* кио́ск; **telephone** ~ (BrE) телефо́нная бу́дка, автома́т

kip /kɪp/ (BrE) *n.* (infml, sleep) сон
　● *v.i.* (**kipped, kipping**) **1**: ~ **down for the night** устро́иться (*pf.*) на ночь **2** (sleep) кема́рить, по- (infml)

kipper /'kɪpə(r)/ *n.* копчёная селёдка

Kirghiz /'kɜ:gɪz/ *n.* = **Kyrgyz**

Kirghizia /kɜ:'gɪzɪə/ *n.* = **Kyrgyzstan**

kiss /kɪs/ *n.* поцелу́й; **give sb a** ~ **on the cheek** поцелова́ть (*pf.*) кого́-н. в щёку; ~ **of life** иску́сственное дыха́ние
　● *v.t.* целова́ть, по-; **they** ~**ed each other goodbye** они́ поцелова́лись на проща́ние
　● *v.i.* целова́ться, по-

kit /kɪt/ *n.* (BrE, personal equipment, esp. clothing) снаряже́ние; (for particular activity) набо́р/ компле́кт (спорти́вных) принадле́жностей; (set of parts for assembly) констру́ктор
　● *v.t.* (**kitted, kitting**) (BrE) (*usu.* ~ **out**) снаряжа́ть, -ди́ть
　■ ~**bag** *n.* вещмешо́к

⚜ **kitchen** /'kɪtʃɪn/ *n.* ку́хня

kite /kaɪt/ *n.* (воздушный/бума́жный) змей; **fly a** ~ (lit.) запуска́ть, -ти́ть зме́я

kitsch /kɪtʃ/ *n.* китч

kitten /'kɪt(ə)n/ *n.* котёнок

kitty /'kɪtɪ/ *n.* (at cards etc.) банк

kiwi /'ki:wi:/ *n.* (*pl.* **kiwis**) ки́ви (*m. indecl.*)
　■ ~ **fruit** *n.* ки́ви (*m. & nt. indecl.*)

kleptomania /kleptəʊ'meɪnɪə/ *n.* клептома́ния

kleptomaniac /kleptəʊ'meɪnɪæk/ *n.* клептома́н (-ка)

km /'kɪləmi:tə(r)(z)/ *n.* (*abbr. of* **kilometre(s)**) км (киломе́тр)

knack /næk/ *n.* (skill, faculty) сноро́вка, уме́ние; **have the** ~ име́ть (*impf.*) сноро́вку (**of/for:** в + *p.*)

knacker /'nækə(r)/ *n.* (BrE) ску́пщик ста́рых живо́тных
　■ ~**'s yard** *n.* живодёрня

knackered /'nækəd/ *adj.* (BrE, infml) измо́танный

knapsack /'næpsæk/ *n.* ра́нец

knead /ni:d/ *v.t.* меси́ть, за-

knee /ni:/ *n.* коле́но (*pl.* -и); **he was on his** ~**s** он стоя́л на коле́нях
　● *v.t.* (**knees, kneed, kneeing**) ударя́ть, -а́рить коле́ном
　■ ~**cap** *n.* коле́нная ча́шечка; ~-**deep** *pred.*

⚜ ключевая лексика

adj. & adv.: **he stood** ~-**deep in water** он стоя́л по коле́но в воде́; ~-**length** *adj.* до коле́н

kneel /ni:l/ *v.i.* (*past and p.p.* **knelt** *or esp. AmE* **kneeled**) **1** (*also* ~ **down**) (go down on one's knees) станови́ться, -ть на коле́ни **2** (be in ~ing position) стоя́ть (*impf.*) на коле́нях

knelt /nelt/ *past and p.p. of* ▶ **kneel**

knew /nju:/ *past of* ▶ **know**

knickers /'nɪkəz/ *n. pl.* (BrE, undergarment) тру́сик|и (-ов)

knick-knack /'nɪknæk/ *n.* безделу́шка

knife /naɪf/ *n.* (*pl.* **knives**) нож
　● *v.t.* (kill) зак|а́лывать, -оло́ть ножо́м; (injure) ра́нить (*impf.*)
　■ ~-**edge** *n.*: **on a** ~-**edge** (fig.) вися́щий на волоске́; ~**point** *n.*: **at** ~**point** угрожа́я ножо́м

knight /naɪt/ *n.* **1** (hist.) ры́царь (*m.*) **2** (member of order) кавале́р **3** (chess) конь (*m.*)
　● *v.t.* ≈ присв|а́ивать, -о́ить (*кому*) ры́царское (ненасле́дственное дворя́нское) зва́ние

knighthood /'naɪthʊd/ *n.* ры́царство; ры́царское зва́ние

knit /nɪt/ *v.t.* (**knitting**, *past and p.p.* **knitted** *or* **knit**) вяза́ть, с-
　● *v.i.* (**knitting**, *past and p.p.* **knitted** *or* **knit**) **1** (do ~ting) вяза́ть (*impf.*) **2** (of bones) сраст|а́ться, -и́сь
　■ ~**wear** *n.* трикота́жные изде́лия

knitting /'nɪtɪŋ/ *n.* (action) вяза́ние; (thing being knitted) вяза́ние
　■ ~ **needle** *n.* вяза́льная спи́ца

knives /naɪvz/ *pl. of* ▶ **knife**

knob /nɒb/ *n.* (handle) ру́чка; (button) кно́пка

knobbly /'nɒblɪ/ *adj.* шишкова́тый, бугорча́тый

knock /nɒk/ *n.* **1** (rap) стук **2** (blow) уда́р **3** (fig.): **the pound has taken some** ~**s lately** в после́днее вре́мя положе́ние фу́нта (сте́рлингов) си́льно пошатну́лось
　● *v.t.* **1** (hit) удар|я́ть, -а́рить; **the blow** ~**ed him flat** уда́р сбил его́ с ног; **he** ~**ed the glass off the table** он смахну́л стака́н со стола́; **I** ~**ed the gun out of his hand** я вы́бил из его́ руки́ пистоле́т **2** (fig. uses): ~ **into shape** прив|оди́ть, -ести́ в поря́док; **I'll** ~ **a pound off the price** я сбро́шу/ски́ну/сба́влю фунт с цены́ **3** (criticize) ха́ять (*impf.*) (infml)
　● *v.i.* **1** (rap) стуча́ть; ~ **at the door** стуча́ть(ся), по- в дверь **2**: ~ **against** (collide with) нат|ыка́ться, -кну́ться на + *a.* **3** (of engine) стуча́ть (*impf.*)
　□ ~ **back** *v.t.* (BrE, disconcert): **the news** ~**ed me back** изве́стие привело́ меня́ в замеша́тельство; (infml, consume): **he can** ~ **back 5 pints in as many minutes** он за пять мину́т мо́жет опроки́нуть/вы́лакать пять кру́жек (пи́ва); (BrE, infml, cost): **that will** ~ **me back a bit** э́то вста́нет/вле́тит мне в копе́ечку
　□ ~ **down** *v.t.* (strike to ground) сби|ва́ть, -ть с ног; вали́ть, с-; **he was** ~**ed down by a car** его́ сби́ла маши́на; (demolish) сн|оси́ть, -ести́
　□ ~ **off** *v.t.* (lit.) сби|ва́ть, -ть; (infml uses) (deduct from price) сб|авля́ть, -а́вить; (BrE, steal)

тащи́ть, с-/у-
● *v.i.* (infml, stop work) свора́чиваться, сверну́ться (sl.)

□ **~ out** *v.t.* (make unconscious) оглуш|а́ть, -и́ть; **the blow on his head ~ed him out** он был оглушён уда́ром по голове́; (eliminate from contest): **he was ~ed out in the first round** он вы́был в пе́рвом ту́ре

□ **~ over** *v.t.* опроки́|дывать, -нуть

■ **~-down** *adj.*: **at a ~-down price** по дешёвке (infml); **~out** *n.* (boxing) нока́ут; (BrE, competition) соревнова́ния (*nt. pl.*) по олимпи́йской систе́ме; (*attr.*) **~out blow** сокруши́тельный уда́р

knocker /'nɒkə(r)/ *n.* (on door) (дверно́й) молото́к

knocking /'nɒkɪŋ/ *n.* (noise) стук

knot /nɒt/ *n.* (in rope etc.; in wood; measure of speed) у́зел; **tie a ~ in a rope** завя́з|ывать, -а́ть у́зел на верёвке; **tie sth in a ~** завя́з|ывать, -а́ть что-н. узло́м
● *v.t.* (**knotted, knotting**) завя́з|ывать, -а́ть

⚥ **know** /nəʊ/ *n.*: **be in the ~** быть в ку́рсе де́ла
● *v.t.* (*past* **knew**, *p.p.* **known**) **1** (be aware, have knowledge of) знать (*impf.*); **I ~ nothing about it** я об э́том ничего́ не зна́ю; **for all I ~** кто его́ зна́ет; **who ~s?** как знать?; **I knew it!** (я) так и знал! **2** (recognize, distinguish) знать (*impf.*); узн|ава́ть, -а́ть; отлич|а́ть, -и́ть; **I ~ him by sight** я зна́ю его́ в лицо́; **he knew her at once** он сра́зу её узна́л **3** (be acquainted, familiar with) знать (*impf.*); быть знако́мым с + *i.*; **get to ~ sb** знако́миться, по- с кем-н.; **I have ~n him since childhood** я знако́м с ним с де́тства **4** (be versed in; understand; have experience in) знать (*impf.*), понима́ть (*impf.*), разбира́ться (*impf.*) в + *p.*; **he ~s Russian** он зна́ет ру́сский язы́к; он владе́ет ру́сским языко́м; **~ how** ты уме́ть, с-
● *v.i.* (*past* **knew**, *p.p.* **known**): **let sb ~** сообщ|а́ть, -и́ть (*or* да|ва́ть, -ть знать) кому́-н.; **will you let me ~?** вы сообщи́те мне́?; **do you ~ of a good restaurant?** вы зна́ете (*or* вы мо́жете порекомендова́ть) хоро́ший рестора́н?; **I don't ~ him, but I ~ of him** ли́чно я с ним не знако́м, но наслы́шан о нём; **did you ~ about the accident?** вы зна́ли об э́том несча́стном слу́чае?

■ **~-all** (BrE), **~-it-all** (AmE) *nn.* всезна́йка (*c.g.*);

~-how *n.* уме́ние; но́у-ха́у (*nt. indecl.*); о́пыт

knowing /'nəʊɪŋ/ *adj.* (significant): **a ~ look** понима́ющий/многозначи́тельный взгляд

⚥ **knowledge** /'nɒlɪdʒ/ *n.* зна́ние; (understanding): **our ~ of the subject is as yet limited** на́ши позна́ния в э́той о́бласти пока́ ограни́чены; (range of information or experience): **to the best of my ~** наско́лько мне изве́стно

knowledgeable /'nɒlɪdʒəb(ə)l/ *adj.* хорошо́ осведомлённый

known /nəʊn/ *adj.* изве́стный; *see also* ▸ **know**

knuckle /'nʌk(ə)l/ *n.* (anat.) костя́шка (па́льца)
● *v.i.*: **~ down to one's work** прин|има́ться, -я́ться за де́ло

koala /kəʊ'ɑːlə/ *n.* (*in full* **~ bear**) коа́ла (*m.*), су́мчатый медве́дь

Kolkata /kɒl'kɑːtə/ *n.* Кальку́тта

kopek /'kəʊpek/ *n.* копе́йка

Koran /kə'rɑːn/ *n.* Кора́н

Korea /kə'riːə/ *n.* Коре́я

Korean /kə'riːən/ *n.* (person) коре́|ец (-я́нка); (language) коре́йский язы́к
● *adj.* коре́йский

kosher /'kəʊʃə(r)/ *adj.* (relig.) коше́рный

Kosovo /'kɒsəvə/ *n.* Ко́сово

kowtow, kotow /kaʊ'taʊ/ *n.* ни́зкий покло́н
● *v.i.* де́лать, с- ни́зкий покло́н; (fig.) раболе́пствовать (*impf.*), пресмыка́ться (*impf.*) (**to:** пе́ред + *i.*)

kudos /'kjuːdɒs/ *n.* сла́ва

kumquat /'kʌmkwɒt/ *n.* кумква́т (*дерево семейства цитрусовых с очень маленькими плодами оранжевого цвета; плоды этого дерева*)

kung fu /kʊŋ 'fuː/ *n.* кун-фу́ (*nt. indecl.*)

Kurd /kɜːd/ *n.* курд (-я́нка)

Kurdish /'kɜːdɪʃ/ *n.* ку́рдский язы́к
● *adj.* ку́рдский

Kurdistan /kɜːdɪ'stɑːn/ *n.* Курдиста́н

Kuwait /kʊ'weɪt/ *n.* Куве́йт

Kuwaiti /kʊ'weɪtɪ/ *n.* (*pl.* **~s**) куве́йт|ец (-ка)
● *adj.* куве́йтский

kvass /kvɑːs/ *n.* квас

Kyrgyz /'kɜːɡɪz/ *n.* (*pl.* **~**) (person) кирги́з (-ка); (language) кирги́зский язы́к
● *adj.* кирги́зский

Kyrgyzstan /kɜːɡɪ'stɑːn/ *n.* Кыргызста́н

k

L (BrE) *abbr.* (*of* **learner**): ∼-plate ≈ «У» (*на учебной машине*)

l /'li:tə(r)(z)/ *n.* (*abbr. of* **litre(s)**) л (литр)

lab /læb/ *n.* (infml) = laboratory

♂ **label** /'leɪb(ə)l/ *n.* ярлы́к, этике́тка
 • *v.t.* (**labelled, labelling**, AmE **labeled, labeling**) (stick ∼ on) накле́и|вать, -ть ярлы́к на + *a.*; (fig.): he was ∼led a fascist ему́ прикле́или ярлы́к фаши́ста

labor /'leɪbə(r)/ *etc.* see ▶ **labour** *etc.* ∼ **union** (AmE) профсою́з

laboratory /ləˈbɒrətərɪ/ *n.* лаборато́рия
 ■ ∼ **assistant** *n.* лабора́нт (-ка)

laborious /ləˈbɔːrɪəs/ *adj.* (difficult) тру́дный, тяжёлый; (toilsome) трудоёмкий

♂ **labour** /'leɪbə(r)/ (AmE **labor**) *n.* **1** (toil, work) труд, рабо́та **2** (workforce) рабо́чие (*pl.*) **3** (*in full* **L∼ Party**) лейбори́стская па́ртия, лейбори́сты (*m. pl.*); the L∼ government лейбори́стское прави́тельство **4** (childbirth) ро́д|ы (-ов); be in ∼ рожа́ть (*impf.*)
 • *v.t.*: ∼ a point вдава́ться (*impf.*) в изли́шние подро́бности
 • *v.i.* **1** (toil) труди́ться (*impf.*) **2** (strive): he is ∼ing to finish his book он прилага́ет все уси́лия, чтобы (за)ко́нчить кни́гу
 ■ ∼-**intensive** *adj.* трудоёмкий; ∼-**saving** *adj.* рационализа́торский

labourer /'leɪbərə(r)/ (AmE **laborer**) *n.* рабо́чий

Labrador /'læbrədɔ:(r)/ *n.* Лабрадо́р; (dog) лабрадо́р

laburnum /ləˈbɜːnəm/ *n.* (bot.) бобо́вник, золото́й дождь

labyrinth /'læbərɪnθ/ *n.* (lit., fig.) лабири́нт

labyrinthine /læbəˈrɪnθaɪn/ *adj.* (lit.) лабири́нтный; (fig.) запу́танный

♂ **lace** /leɪs/ *n.* **1** (openwork fabric) кру́жево, кружева́ (*nt. pl.*) **2** (of shoe etc.) шнуро́к
 • *v.t.* (fasten or tighten with ∼) шнурова́ть, за-; he ∼d up his shoes он зашнурова́л боти́нки
 ■ ∼-**ups** *n. pl.* (BrE) о́бувь на шнуро́вке/шнурка́х

lacerate /'læsəreɪt/ *v.t.* (lit., fig.) терза́ть, рас-/ис-; растерз|ывать, -а́ть; (wound) ра́нить (*impf., pf.*)

♂ **lack** /læk/ *n.* недоста́ток
 • *v.t. & i.*: he ∼s sth ему́ чего́-то недостаёт; he ∼s, is ∼ing in courage у него́ не хвата́ет хра́брости
 ■ ∼**lustre,** (AmE) ∼**luster** *adj.* ту́склый, без бле́ска

lackadaisical /lækəˈdeɪzɪk(ə)l/ *adj.* вя́лый, апати́чный

lackey /'lækɪ/ *n.* (*pl.* ∼**s**) (lit., fig.) лаке́й; (fig.) подхали́м

laconic /ləˈkɒnɪk/ *adj.* лакони́чный

lacquer /'lækə(r)/ *n.* политу́ра (*no pl.*); лак

lad /læd/ *n.* (boy) ма́льчик; (fellow, youth) па́рень (*m.*)

ladder /'lædə(r)/ *n.* **1** ле́стница **2** (BrE, in stocking) спусти́вшаяся петля́
 • *v.t. & i.* (BrE): I have ∼ed my stocking; my stocking has ∼ed у меня́ спусти́лась петля́ на чулке́

laden /'leɪd(ə)n/ *adj.*: he returned ∼ with books он верну́лся нагру́женный кни́гами; the table was ∼ with food стол ломи́лся от еды́; she was ∼ with cares она́ была́ обременена́ забо́тами

ladies /'leɪdɪz/ *n. see* ▶ **lady** 2

ladle /'leɪd(ə)l/ *n.* поло́вник

♂ **lady** /'leɪdɪ/ *n.* **1** (woman) да́ма; (as title) ле́ди (*f. indecl.*); Ladies and Gentlemen да́мы и господа́ **2**: the Ladies (*sg.*), (AmE) ladies' room (lavatory) же́нский туале́т
 ■ ∼**bird** (BrE), ∼**bug** (AmE) *nn.* бо́жья коро́вка

lag¹ /læg/ *n.* (delay) запа́здывание
 • *v.i.* (**lagged, lagging**) отст|ава́ть, -а́ть; the children are ∼ging (behind) де́ти плели́сь позади́

lag² /læg/ *v.t.* (**lagged, lagging**) (wrap in felt etc.) изоли́ровать/покрыва́ть (*impf.*) (во́йлоком)

lager /'lɑːgə(r)/ *n.* све́тлое пи́во

lagoon /ləˈguːn/ *n.* лагу́на

laid /leɪd/ *past and p.p. of* ▶ **lay²**

laid-back /leɪdˈbæk/ *adj.* непринуждённый, споко́йный

lain /leɪn/ *p.p. of* ▶ **lie²**

lair /leə(r)/ *n.* ло́гово

laissez-faire /leseɪˈfeə(r)/ *n.* невмеша́тельство (*политика невмеша́тельства прави́тельства в эконо́мику*)

lake /leɪk/ *n.* о́зеро

lama /'lɑːmə/ *n.* (relig.) ла́ма (*m.*)

lamb /læm/ *n.* ягнёнок, бара́шек; (meat) бара́шек
 ■ ∼ **chop** *n.* бара́нья котле́та

lambaste /læmˈbeɪst/ *v.t.* дуба́сить, от- (infml)

lame /leɪm/ *adj.* **1** (archaic when used of people) хромо́й **2** (fig., of excuse etc.) сла́бый

lament /ləˈment/ *n.* плач
 • *v.t.* опла́к|ивать, -ать

lamentable /ˈlæməntəb(ə)l/ *adj.* плаче́вный

lamentation /læmənˈteɪʃ(ə)n/ *n.* (lamenting) сето́вание; (lament) плач

─────────────────
♂ ключева́я ле́ксика

laminate /'læmɪneɪt/ *v.t.* (overlay with protective layer) ламини́ровать (*impf., pf.*)

lamp /læmp/ *n.* ла́мпа
■ ~ **post** *n.* фона́рный столб; ~**shade** *n.* абажу́р

lampoon /læm'puːn/ *n.* па́сквиль (*m.*)
● *v.t.* писа́ть, на- па́сквиль на + *a.*

LAN *abbr.* (*of* **local area network**) (comput.) лока́льная сеть

lance /lɑːns/ *n.* пи́ка
● *v.t.* (med.) вскры|ва́ть, -ть ланце́том

◆ **land** /lænd/ *n.* **1** земля́; (dry ~) су́ша; **travel by** ~ е́хать (*det.*) су́шей (*or* по су́ше); **reach** ~ дост|ига́ть, -и́гнуть бе́рега **2** (ground, soil) грунт, по́чва; **work the** ~ обраба́тывать (*impf.*) зе́млю; **buy a house with some** ~ дом с земе́льным уча́стком **3** (country) земля́, страна́; (state) госуда́рство **4** (property) земля́, име́ние; **his** ~**s extend for several miles** его́ владе́ния простира́ются на не́сколько миль
● *v.t.* **1** : ~ **an aircraft** сажа́ть, посади́ть (*or* приземл|я́ть, -и́ть) самолёт **2** : ~ **a fish** выта́скивать, вы́тащить ры́бу на бе́рег **3** (win) выи́грывать, вы́играть; (secure): **he** ~**ed himself a good job** он пристро́ился на хоро́шую рабо́ту **4** (get, involve): **he** ~**ed himself with a lot of work** он загрузи́л себя́ рабо́той
● *v.i.* **1** (of passengers) выса́живаться, вы́садиться **2** (of aircraft) приземл|я́ться, -и́ться; (spacecraft on moon) прилун|я́ться, -и́ться **3** (of athlete, after jump) приземл|я́ться, -и́ться **4** (fall, lit. or fig.): **she** ~**ed in trouble** она́ попа́ла в беду́; **the ball** ~**ed on his head** мяч попа́л ему́ в го́лову **5** : ~ **up** (infml, arrive) прибы́ва́ть, -ы́ть; **I** ~**ed up in the wrong street** я очути́лся не на той у́лице
■ ~**lady** *n.* (BrE, of pub) хозя́йка; (of building) домовладе́лица, хозя́йка; ~**line** *n.* назе́мная ли́ния свя́зи; ~**lord** *n.* (BrE, of pub) хозя́ин; (owner of ~) землевладе́лец; (of building) домовладе́лец, хозя́ин; ~**mark** *n.* (prominent feature) заме́тный объе́кт на ме́стности, ориенти́р; (fig.) ве́ха; ~**mine** *n.* фуга́с; ~**owner** *n.* землевладе́л|ец (-ица); ~**slide** *n.* о́ползень (*m.*); (pol.) **they won by a** ~**slide** они́ победи́ли с огро́мным переве́сом (голосо́в)

landed /'lændɪd/ *adj.* **1** (possessing land) землевладе́льческий **2** (consisting of land): ~ **property** земе́льные владе́ния
■ ~ **gentry** *n. pl.* поме́щики (*m. pl.*)

landing /'lændɪŋ/ *n.* **1** (bringing or coming to earth) поса́дка, приземле́ние; (on the moon) прилуне́ние **2** (putting ashore; depositing by air) вы́садка **3** (mil.) деса́нт **4** (on stairs) (ле́стничная) площа́дка
■ ~ **gear** *n.* шасси́ (*nt. indecl.*); ~ **strip** *n.* поса́дочная полоса́

landscape /'lændskeɪp/ *n.* (picture) пейза́ж; (scenery) ландша́фт
■ ~ **gardening** *n.* ландша́фтный диза́йн

lane /leɪn/ *n.* **1** (narrow street) переу́лок; (country road) доро́жка **2** (of traffic) ряд **3** (air route) тра́сса **4** (for shipping) морско́й путь **5** (on racetrack, swimming pool) доро́жка

◆ **language** /'læŋgwɪdʒ/ *n.* язы́к; (esp. spoken) речь; **bad** ~ скверносло́вие
■ ~ **laboratory** *n.* лингафо́нный кабине́т

languid /'læŋgwɪd/ *adj.* то́мный, вя́лый

languish /'læŋgwɪʃ/ *v.i.* томи́ться (*impf.*)

languor /'læŋgə(r)/ *n.* то́мность, вя́лость; (pleasant) исто́ма

languorous /'læŋgərəs/ *adj.* то́мный; по́лный исто́мы

lank /læŋk/ *adj.*: ~ **hair** гла́дкие/прямы́е во́лосы

lanky /'læŋkɪ/ *adj.* (**lankier**, **lankiest**) долговя́зый

lantern /'læntən/ *n.* фона́рь (*m.*)

lap¹ /læp/ *n.*: **the boy sat on his mother's** ~ ма́льчик сиде́л у ма́тери на коле́нях; **he lives in the** ~ **of luxury** ≈ он живёт в (обстано́вке) ро́скоши
■ ~ **dance** *n.* эроти́ческий та́нец, исполня́емый в непосре́дственной бли́зости к клие́нту, зака́з́вшему его́; ~**top** (**computer**) *n.* портати́вный компью́тер; лэптоп

lap² /læp/ *n.* (circuit of racetrack) круг

lap³ /læp/ *v.t.* (**lapped**, **lapping**) **1** (drink with tongue) лака́ть, вы́-; **the cat** ~**ped up the milk** ко́шка вы́лакала молоко́ **2** (fig., accept eagerly) жа́дно глота́ть (*impf.*); **he** ~**ped up their compliments** он жа́дно лови́л их комплиме́нты

lapel /lə'pel/ *n.* ла́цкан, отворо́т

Lapp /læp/ *n.* **1** (person) саа́ми (*m. & f. indecl.*); лопа́р|ь (-ка) **2** (language) (*also* ~**ish**) саа́мский/лопа́рский язы́к; язы́к саа́ми
● *adj.* **1** (*also* ~**ish**) лопа́рский, саа́мский **2** (of Lapland) лапла́ндский

lapse /læps/ *n.* **1** (slight mistake) упуще́ние; (of memory) прова́л (в) па́мяти **2** (interval) промежу́ток
● *v.i.* **1** (decline morally) пасть (*pf.*); **he** ~**d into his old ways** он принялся́ за ста́рое; ~ **into silence** зам|олка́ть, -о́лкнуть **2** (law, become void) теря́ть, по- си́лу

larch /lɑːtʃ/ *n.* (tree) ли́ственница

lard /lɑːd/ *n.* са́ло

larder /'lɑːdə(r)/ *n.* кладова́я

◆ **large** /lɑːdʒ/ *n.*: **at** ~ (free) на во́ле, на свобо́де; (in general) целико́м; во всём объёме; **the public at** ~ широ́кая пу́блика
● *adj.* большо́й, кру́пный
● *adv.*: **by and** ~ вообще́ говоря́
■ ~**scale** *adj.* крупномасшта́бный

◆ **largely** /'lɑːdʒlɪ/ *adv.* (to a great extent) по бо́льшей ча́сти; в значи́тельной сте́пени

lark¹ /lɑːk/ *n.* (bird) жа́воронок

lark² /lɑːk/ *n.* (infml, amusement) заба́ва; **for a** ~ шу́тки ра́ди

larva /'lɑːvə/ *n.* (*pl.* **larvae** /-viː/) личи́нка

laryngitis /lærɪn'dʒaɪtɪs/ *n.* ларинги́т

larynx /'lærɪŋks/ *n.* (*pl.* **larynges**) горта́нь

lascivious /lə'sɪvɪəs/ *adj.* похотли́вый

laser /'leɪzə(r)/ *n.* ла́зер; (*attr.*) ла́зерный

lash¹ /læʃ/ *n.* (*in full* **eye** ~) ресни́ца

lash² /læʃ/ n. (stroke) уда́р (пле́тью)
- v.t. (with whip, wind, rain) хлеста́ть, -ну́ть
- v.i.: the rain ~ed against the window дождь хлеста́л в окно́
□ ~ **out** v.i. (with fists) наки́|дываться, -ну́ться (на кого); (verbally) набра́|сываться, -о́ситься (с кри́тикой) (на кого)

lasso /læ'su:/ n. (pl. ~s or ~es) арка́н, лассо́ (nt. indecl.)
- v.t. (**lassoes, lassoed**) арка́нить, за-

✎ **last** /lɑːst/ n. (final or most recent person or thing): he was the ~ of his line он был после́дним в роду́; our house is the ~ in the road наш дом после́дний/кра́йний на у́лице; at ~ наконе́ц; (as excl.) наконе́ц-то!
- adj. **1** (latest; final; ~ of series) после́дний; in the ~ 7 years в после́дние 7 лет; at the very ~ moment в са́мый после́дний моме́нт; ~ but one предпосле́дний **2** (preceding, of time) про́шлый; ~ week на про́шлой неде́ле; ~ night we got home late вчера́ ве́чером мы по́здно верну́лись (домо́й) **3** (least likely or suitable): she is the ~ person to help от неё ме́ньше всего́ мо́жно ожида́ть по́мощи; that's the ~ thing I would have expected э́того я ника́к не ожида́л
- adv. **1** (in order) по́сле всех; he finished ~ он ко́нчил после́дним **2** (on the ~ occasion) в после́дний раз **3** (~ly, in the ~ place) на после́днем ме́сте
- v.i. **1** (go on, continue) дли́ться, про-; прод|олжа́ться, -о́лжиться; the rain won't ~ long дождь ско́ро пройдёт **2** (endure, be sustained) выде́рживать, вы́держать; as long as my health ~s (out) пока́ у меня́ хва́тит здоро́вья; (be preserved, survive) сохран|я́ться, -и́ться; the tradition has ~ed until today э́та тради́ция сохрани́лась до настоя́щего вре́мени **3** (remain usable): this suit has ~ed well э́тот костю́м хорошо́ но́сится; this car is built to ~ **4** (of the dying): he won't ~ long он до́лго не протя́нет (infml)
- v.i. & t. (be sufficient) хват|а́ть, -и́ть (for sb: + d.; for a certain amount of time: на + a.); £100 ~s (me) a week ста фу́нтов (мне) хвата́ет на неде́лю; the bread won't ~ us today хле́ба нам на сего́дня не хва́тит
- ■ ~-ditch adj. отча́янный; ~-minute adj. (сде́ланный) в после́днюю мину́ту; ~ name n. фами́лия; ~ rites n. pl. причаще́ние пе́ред сме́ртью

lasting /ˈlɑːstɪŋ/ adj. (enduring) про́чный, продолжи́тельный

lastly /ˈlɑːstlɪ/ adv. в заключе́ние; наконе́ц

latch /lætʃ/ n. (bar) щеко́лда; (lock) защёлка
- v.i.: ~ on to смекну́ть (pf.) (infml)

✎ **late** /leɪt/ adj. **1** (far on in time) по́здний; it is ~ по́здно; in ~ May к концу́/в конце́ ма́я; the ~ 19th century коне́ц 19 ве́ка; he is in his ~ 40s ему́ почти́/под пятьдеся́т **2** (behind time) be ~ for the train оп|а́здывать, -озда́ть на по́езд; he was an hour ~ он опозда́л на час; I was ~ in replying я опозда́л отве́тить (or с отве́том) **3** (recent) неда́вний; после́дний; his

~st book его́ после́дняя кни́га **4** (deceased) поко́йный
- adv. по́здно; stay up ~ по́здно ложи́ться (impf.); a year ~r спустя́ год

latecomer /ˈleɪtkʌmə(r)/ n. опозда́вший

lately /ˈleɪtlɪ/ adv. в после́днее вре́мя

latent /ˈleɪt(ə)nt/ adj. скры́тый

lateral /ˈlætər(ə)l/ adj. боково́й, горизонта́льный; ~ section попере́чный разре́з

latest /ˈleɪtɪst/ adj. после́дний; са́мый но́вый

lathe /leɪð/ n. тока́рный стано́к

lather /ˈlɑːðə(r)/ n. (мы́льная) пе́на

Latin /ˈlætɪn/ n. латы́нь; лати́нский язы́к
- adj. лати́нский
- ■ ~ **America** n. Лати́нская Аме́рика; ~ **American** adj. латиноамерика́нский ● n. латиноамерика́н|ец (-ка)

Latino /ləˈtiːnəʊ/ n. (pl. ~s) вы́ходец из Лати́нской Аме́рики

latitude /ˈlætɪtjuːd/ n. (geog., also fig.) широта́

✎ **latter** /ˈlætə(r)/ pron. & adj. после́дний, второ́й; of cream and yogurt, the ~ is healthier что каса́ется сли́вок и йо́гурта, то после́дний поле́знее

latterly /ˈlætəlɪ/ adv. (of late) (в/за) после́днее вре́мя; (towards the end) к концу́, под коне́ц

lattice /ˈlætɪs/ n. решётка; (attr.; also ~d) решётчатый

Latvia /ˈlætvɪə/ n. Ла́твия

Latvian /ˈlætvɪən/ n. (person) латви́|ец (-йка); латы́ш (-ка); (language) латы́шский язы́к
- adj. латви́йский; латы́шский

laudable /ˈlɔːdəb(ə)l/ adj. похва́льный

✎ **laugh** /lɑːf/ n. смех; we had a good ~ over it мы от души́ посмея́лись над э́тим
- v.t.: he was ~ing his head off он хохота́л как безу́мный
- v.i. смея́ться (impf.) (at: над + i.); burst out ~ing рассмея́ться (pf.); расхохота́ться (pf.); he ~s at my jokes он смеётся, когда́ я шучу́; it's nothing to ~ at ничего́ смешно́го; I couldn't stop ~ing я смея́лся так, что не мог останови́ться
□ ~ **off** v.t.: ~ sth off отде́л|ываться, -аться от чего́-н. шу́ткой

laughable /ˈlɑːfəb(ə)l/ adj. смешно́й, смехотво́рный

laughing /ˈlɑːfɪŋ/ n. смех
- ■ ~ **stock** n. посме́шище

laughter /ˈlɑːftə(r)/ n. смех

launch¹ /lɔːntʃ/ n. (motor boat) ка́тер

✎ **launch²** /lɔːntʃ/ n. (of ship) спуск (на́ воду); (of rocket or spacecraft) за́пуск; (of product) вы́пуск
- v.t. (set afloat): ~ a ship спус|ка́ть, -ти́ть кора́бль на́ воду; (send into air): ~ a rocket запус|ка́ть, -ти́ть раке́ту; (initiate): ~ a campaign нач|ина́ть, -а́ть (or откр|ыва́ть, -ы́ть) кампа́нию; ~ an enterprise/product пус|ка́ть, -ти́ть предприя́тие/проду́кт в прода́жу
- ■ ~(ing) pad n. ста́ртовая площа́дка

launder /ˈlɔːndə(r)/ v.t. **1** стира́ть, вы- **2** (fig.): ~ money отм|ыва́ть, -ы́ть де́ньги

launderette, laundrette /lɔːnˈdret/ *n.* (BrE) пра́чечная самообслу́живания

laundry /ˈlɔːndrɪ/ *n.* **1** (establishment) пра́чечная **2** (clothes) бельё (для сти́рки *or* из сти́рки)

laurel /ˈlɒr(ə)l/ *n.* лавр

lava /ˈlɑːvə/ *n.* ла́ва

lavatory /ˈlævətərɪ/ *n.* убо́рная, туале́т

lavender /ˈlævɪndə(r)/ *n.* лава́нда

lavish /ˈlævɪʃ/ *adj.* ще́дрый
 ● *v.t.:* ~ **money on sth** прома́тывать, -ота́ть де́ньги на что-н.; ~ **praise on sb** расточа́ть (*impf.*) похвалы́ кому́-н.

✿ **law** /lɔː/ *n.* **1** (rule or body of rules for society) зако́н; **by** ~ по зако́ну; **break the** ~ нар|уша́ть, -у́шить зако́н **2** (as subject of study, profession, system) пра́во, юсти́ция; ~ **and order** правопоря́док; **read, study** ~ изуча́ть, -и́ть пра́во **3** (phys., math.): ~ **of gravity** зако́н всеми́рного тяготе́ния; ~ **of probability** тео́рия вероя́тностей
 ■ ~**-abiding** *adj.* законопослу́шный; ~ **court** *n.* суд; ~**-enforcement** *n.* (*attr.*): ~**-enforcement agencies** правоохрани́тельные о́рганы; ~**giver**, ~**maker** *nn.* законода́тель (*m.*); ~ **school** *n.* юриди́ческий вуз; ~**suit** *n.* суде́бный проце́сс

lawful /ˈlɔːfʊl/ *adj.* зако́нный

lawless /ˈlɔːlɪs/ *adj.* (of country etc.) ди́кий; (of person) непоко́рный

lawn /lɔːn/ *n.* газо́н
 ■ ~**mower** *n.* газонокоси́лка

✿ **lawyer** /ˈlɔːjə(r)/ *n.* юри́ст; (advocate, barrister) адвока́т

lax /læks/ *adj.* нестро́гий

laxative /ˈlæksətɪv/ *n.* слаби́тельное (сре́дство)

lay¹ /leɪ/ *past of* ▶ **lie²**

✿ **lay²** /leɪ/ *v.t.* (*past and p.p.* **laid**) **1** (put down, deposit) класть, положи́ть; ~ **an egg** нести́, с- яйцо́; (set in position): ~ **bricks** класть (*impf.*) кирпичи́; ~ **a foundation** (lit., fig.) за|кла́дывать, -ложи́ть фунда́мент; ~ **a trap** ста́вить, по- лову́шку **2** (prepare): ~ **a fire** пригото́вить (*pf.*) всё, чтобы развести́ ого́нь; ~ **the table for dinner** накр|ыва́ть, -ы́ть стол к обе́ду
 ● *v.i.* (*past and p.p.* **laid**) (sc. eggs) нести́сь (*impf.*)
 □ ~ **down** *v.t.:* ~ **down one's arms** (surrender) скла́дывать, сложи́ть ору́жие; (formulate, prescribe): ~ **down conditions/rules** устана́|вливать, -ови́ть (*or* формули́ровать, с-) усло́вия/пра́вила; (sacrifice): ~ **down one's life for one's friends** же́ртвовать, по- жи́знью (*or* отда|ва́ть, -а́ть жизнь) за друзе́й
 □ ~ **off** *v.t.* (suspend from work) ув|ольня́ть, -о́лить (со слу́жбы)
 □ ~ **on** *v.t.* (BrE, provide supply of) пров|оди́ть, -ести́; (infml): **he promised to** ~ **on some drinks** он обеща́л поста́вить вы́пивку; (arrange) устра́|ивать, -о́ить
 □ ~ **out** *v.t.* (arrange for display etc.) выставля́ть, вы́ставить; (spread out) разб|ива́ть, -и́ть
 ■ ~**about** *n.* (infml) лентя́й (-ка); ~**-by** *n.* (BrE) придоро́жная площа́дка для стоя́нки автомоби́лей; ~**-off** *n.* (of workers) сокраще́ние

шта́тов; ~**out** *n.* (arrangement) расположе́ние; (of town etc.) плани́ровка; (of garden etc.) разби́вка; (plan) чертёж, план

lay³ /leɪ/ *adj.* **1** (opp. clerical) мирско́й **2** (opp. professional): ~ **opinion** непрофессиона́льное мне́ние
 ■ ~**man** *n.* (non-specialist) непрофессиона́л, неспециали́ст

✿ **layer** /ˈleɪə(r)/ *n.* слой, пласт

laze /leɪz/ *v.i.:* ~ **about** слоня́ться (*impf.*) без де́ла

laziness /ˈleɪzɪnɪs/ *n.* лень, ле́ность

lazy /ˈleɪzɪ/ *adj.* (**lazier**, **laziest**) лени́вый; **be** ~ лени́ться (*impf.*); **I was too** ~ **to write to him** мне бы́ло лень ему́ (на)писа́ть

lb /paʊnd(z)/ *n.* (*abbr. of* **libra**) фунт

LCD *abbr.* (*of* **liquid crystal display**) ЖК-дисплей (жидкокристалли́ческий дисплей)

leach /liːtʃ/ *v.t. & i.* выщела́чивать(ся), вы́щелочить(ся) (*о почве, горной породе*)

lead¹ /led/ *n.* **1** (metal) свине́ц **2** (in pencil) графи́т, гри́фель (*m.*)
 ■ ~**-free** *adj.* неэтили́рованный

✿ **lead²** /liːd/ *n.* **1** (direction, guidance; initiative) руково́дство; **take the** ~ брать, взять на (себя́) руково́дство/инициати́ву **2** (first place): **be in the** ~ стоя́ть (*impf.*) во главе́; (sport) быть впереди́; вести́ (*det.*); (fig.) стоя́ть (*impf.*) во главе́, пе́рвенствовать (*impf.*); **take the** ~ (sport) выходи́ть, вы́йти вперёд **3** (clue): **the police are looking for a** ~ поли́ция пыта́ется напа́сть на след **4** (BrE, cord, strap) поводо́к, при́вязь **5** (elec.) про́вод (-а́)
 ● *v.t.* (*past and p.p.* **led**) **1** (conduct) води́ть (*indet.*), вести́ (*det.*), повести́(*pf.*); **he led his troops into battle** он повёл солда́т в бой **2** (fig., bring, incline, induce): ~ **sb to believe** созда́ть (*pf.*) впечатле́ние у кого́-н., что... **3** (be in charge of): ~ **an expedition/ orchestra** руководи́ть (*impf.*) экспеди́цией/ орке́стром; (command) кома́ндовать (*impf.*) (+ *i.*); (act as chief or head of) возгла|вля́ть, -а́вить **4** (pass, spend): ~ **an idle life** вести́ (*det.*) пра́здную жизнь
 ● *v.i.* (*past and p.p.* **led**) **1** (of a road etc.) вести́ (*det.*) **2** (be first or ahead) быть впереди́
 □ ~ **away** *v.t.* отв|оди́ть, -ести́; ув|оди́ть, -ести́
 □ ~ **in** *v.t.* вв|оди́ть, -ести́
 □ ~ **up** *v.t.* ~ **up to** (lit.) подв|оди́ть, -ести́ к + *d.*; (precede, form preparation for) подгот|овля́ть, -о́вить; **the events that led up to the war** собы́тия, приве́дшие к войне́

leaded /ˈledɪd/ *adj.* (petrol) этили́рованный

leaden /ˈled(ə)n/ *adj.* (lit., fig.) свинцо́вый

✿ **leader** /ˈliːdə(r)/ *n.* **1** руководи́тель (*m.*), ли́дер; (comm.) ли́дер **2** (mil.) команди́р **3** (BrE, in newspaper) передова́я (статья́)

✿ **leadership** /ˈliːdəʃɪp/ *n.* (role of leader; group of leaders) руково́дство; (qualities of a leader) ли́дерство

leading /ˈliːdɪŋ/ *adj.* (foremost) веду́щий; (outstanding) выдаю́щийся; ~ **question** наводя́щий вопро́с
 ■ ~ **lady** *n.* исполни́тельница гла́вной ро́ли

leaf /liːf/ *n.* (*pl.* **leaves**) **1** (of tree or plant) лист (-ья) **2** (of book) лист (-ы́); (fig.): **turn over a new ~** начи|на́ть, -а́ть но́вую жизнь, испра́виться (*pf.*)
● *v.t.*: **~ through** перели́ст|ывать, -а́ть
leaflet /ˈliːflɪt/ *n.* листо́вка
leafy /ˈliːfɪ/ *adj.* (**leafier**, **leafiest**) густоли́ственный
⚘ **league** /liːɡ/ *n.* (alliance) ли́га; **in ~ with** в сою́зе с + *i.*; (pej.) в сго́воре с + *i.*; **be not in the same ~ as sb** быть не того́ кла́сса; **football ~** футбо́льная ли́га
■ **~ table** *n.* (BrE) (sport) табли́ца результа́тов; (fig.) сравни́тельный гра́фик
leak /liːk/ *n.* (hole) течь; (escape of fluid) уте́чка; (fig., of information) уте́чка информа́ции
● *v.t.* (fig.) выдава́ть, вы́дать
● *v.i.* (roof, boat) течь (*impf.*); **leak out** (liquid, gas) прос|а́чиваться, -очи́ться; (fig.): **the affair ~ed out** де́ло вы́плыло нару́жу
■ **~-proof** *adj.* непроница́емый
leakage /ˈliːkɪdʒ/ *n.* (lit., fig.) уте́чка
leaky /ˈliːkɪ/ *adj.* (**leakier**, **leakiest**) дыря́вый, име́ющий течь; **a ~ pipe/roof** протека́ющая труба́/кры́ша
lean[1] /liːn/ *adj.* **1** (thin) то́щий; (fig.): **~ years** ску́дные го́ды **2** (of meat) нежи́рный
lean[2] /liːn/ *v.t.* (*past and p.p.* **leaned** /liːnd, lent/ *or esp.* BrE **leant**) прислон|я́ть, -и́ть (*что к чему*); оп|ира́ть, -ере́ть (*что обо что*)
● *v.i.* (*past and p.p.* **leaned** /liːnd, lent/ *or esp.* BrE **leant**) **1** (incline from vertical) наклон|я́ться, -и́ться; **~ out of the window** высо́вываться, вы́сунуться из окна́ **2** (support oneself) прислон|я́ться, -и́ться; оп|ира́ться, -ере́ться; **he was ~ing against a tree** он стоя́л, прислони́вшись к де́реву; (fig.): **he ~s** (*sc. depends*) **on his wife for support** он опира́ется на подде́ржку жены́; (infml, put pressure): **I had to ~ on him to get results** мне пришло́сь нажа́ть на него́, чтобы доби́ться результа́тов
leaning /ˈliːnɪŋ/ *n.* (inclination) скло́нность; (tendency) пристра́стие
leant /lent/ (*esp.* BrE) *past and p.p. of* ▶ **lean**[2]
leap /liːp/ *n.* прыжо́к, скачо́к
● *v.t.* (*past and p.p.* **leaped** /liːpt, lept/ *or* **leapt** /lept/) (**~ over**) переск|а́кивать, -очи́ть (*or* перепры́г|ивать, -нуть) че́рез + *a.*
● *v.i.* (*past and p.p.* **leaped** /liːpt, lept/ *or* **leapt** /lept/) пры́г|ать, -нуть; **my heart ~t for joy** у меня́ се́рдце подскочи́ло от ра́дости; **~ to one's feet** вск|а́кивать, -очи́ть; (fig.): **he ~t at my offer** он ухвати́лся за моё предложе́ние
■ **~frog** *n.* чехарда́; **~ year** *n.* високо́сный год
⚘ **learn** /lɜːn/ *v.t.* (*past and p.p.* **learned** /lɜːnt, lɜːnd/ *or esp.* BrE **learnt** /lɜːnt/) учи́ться, на- (+ *d. or inf.*); изуч|а́ть, -и́ть; (study) занима́ться (*impf.*) (+ *i.*); **he ~ed** (how) **to ride** он научи́лся е́здить верхо́м; **he is ~ing to be an interpreter** он у́чится на

переводчика; **where did you ~ Russian?** где вы изуча́ли ру́сский язы́к?
● *v.i.* (*past and p.p.* **learned** /lɜːnt, lɜːnd/ *or esp.* BrE **learnt** /lɜːnt/) or **learnt** /lɜːnt/: **you can ~ from his mistakes** учи́тесь на его́ оши́бках
learned /ˈlɜːnɪd/ *adj.* учёный
learner /ˈlɜːnə(r)/ *n.* начина́ющий; (**~ driver**) начина́ющий води́тель(, не име́ющий води́тельских прав)
⚘ **learning** /ˈlɜːnɪŋ/ *n.* (process) уче́ние; изуче́ние; (body of knowledge) нау́ка
■ **~ curve** *n.* ско́рость приобрете́ния на́выка; **~ difficulty/disability** *n.* у́мственный недоста́ток; **person with ~ difficulties/ disabilities** у́мственно отста́лый челове́к
learnt /lɜːnt/ (*esp.* BrE) *past and p.p. of* ▶ **learn**
lease /liːs/ *n.* аре́нда
● *v.t.* (of lessee) аренд|ова́ть (*impf., pf.*); брать, взять в аре́нду/внаём; (of lessor) сд|ава́ть, -а́ть в аре́нду
■ **~hold** *n.* аре́нда; **~holder** *n.* аренда́тор
leash /liːʃ/ *n.* поводо́к
⚘ **least** /liːst/ *n.*: **to say the ~** мя́гко говоря́; **the ~ he could do is to pay for the damage** он мог бы по кра́йней ме́ре возмести́ть уще́рб; **at ~** по кра́йней ме́ре; не ме́ньше + *g.*; **at ~ once a year** не ре́же, чем раз в год; **he is ~ as tall as you** он ва́шего ро́ста, а мо́жет быть и вы́ше; **you should at ~ have warned me** вы бы хоть предупреди́ли меня́; **not in the ~** ничу́ть, ниско́лько; **he is not in the ~ interested** он совсе́м не заинтересо́ван (*pred.*)
● *adj.* (smallest) наиме́ньший; **that's the ~ of my worries** э́то меня́ ме́ньше всего́ волну́ет; (slightest) мале́йший; **he hasn't the ~ idea about it** он не име́ет ни мале́йшего поня́тия об э́том
● *adv.* ме́ньше всего́; **it is the ~ successful of his books** э́то наиме́нее уда́чная из его́ книг; **with the ~ possible trouble** с наиме́ньшими хло́потами; **с наиме́ньшей затра́той сил
leather /ˈleðə(r)/ *n.* ко́жа
● *adj.* ко́жаный
⚘ **leave** /liːv/ *n.* о́тпуск; **he is on ~** он в о́тпуске
● *v.t.* (*past and p.p.* **left**) **1** (allow or cause to remain) ост|авля́ть, -а́вить; **the wound left a scar** от ра́ны оста́лся шрам; **has anyone left a message?** никто́ ничего́ не передава́л?; (with indication of state or circumstances): **~ me alone!** оста́вьте меня́ (в поко́е)!; **~ the door open!** оста́вьте дверь откры́той!; (*p.p.*) (remaining): **I have no money left** у меня́ не оста́лось де́нег **2** (~ behind by accident) заб|ыва́ть, -ы́ть; **I left my umbrella at home** я забы́л зо́нтик до́ма **3** (bequeath) завеща́ть (*impf., pf.*); **she was left a large inheritance by her uncle** дя́дя оста́вил ей большо́е насле́дство **4** (abandon) бр|оса́ть, -о́сить; пок|ида́ть, -и́нуть; **he left his wife for another woman** он бро́сил свою́ жену́ ра́ди друго́й же́нщины **5** (entrust) предост|авля́ть, -а́вить; **~ it to him** пусть он э́то сде́лает; **~ it to me** я э́тим займу́сь **6** (go away from) выходи́ть, вы́йти из + *g.*; (by vehicle) выезжа́ть, вы́ехать из + *g.*; (by air) вылета́ть,

вы́лететь из + g.; I ~ the house at eight я
выхожу́ и́з дому в во́семь часо́в; (~ for good,
quit) бр|оса́ть, -о́сить; пок|ида́ть, -и́нуть; he
left his job он бро́сил свою́ рабо́ту; he ~s
school this year он конча́ет шко́лу в э́том
году́
• v.i. (past and p.p. left) **1** (of person on foot)
уход|и́ть, уйти́; (by transport) уезж|а́ть, уе́хать;
(by air) улет|а́ть, -е́ть; **2** (of train) от|ходи́ть,
-ойти́; (of boat) от|ходи́ть, -ойти́; отпл|ыва́ть,
-ы́ть; (of aircraft) вылета́ть, вы́лететь
▫ ~ behind v.t. оставля́ть, -а́вить по́сле себя́;
(forget to take): he left his hat behind он забы́л
свою́ шля́пу; (abandon): he was left behind
on the island он оказа́лся бро́шенным на
о́строве; (outstrip): we left him far behind мы
оста́вили его́ далеко́ позади́
▫ ~ on v.t.: I left the light on я оста́вил свет
включённым
▫ ~ out v.t.: she left the washing out in
the rain она́ оста́вила бельё под дождём;
(omit) пропус|ка́ть, -ти́ть; I felt left out я
почу́вствовал себя́ ли́шним
▫ ~ over v.t. (pass.) (remain) ост|ава́ться,
-а́ться; a lot was left over after dinner по́сле
обе́да оста́лось ещё мно́го еды́

leaves /li:vz/ pl. of ▸ leaf
Lebanese /lebə'ni:z/ n. (pl. ~) лива́н|ец (-ка)
• adj. лива́нский
Lebanon /'lebənən/ n. Лива́н
lecher /'letʃə(r)/ n. развра́тник, распу́тник
lecherous /'letʃərəs/ adj. развра́тный,
распу́тный
lechery /'letʃəri/ n. развра́т
lectern /'lektə:n/ n. анало́й (в це́ркви); (in
lecture room) пюпи́тр
lecture /'lektʃə(r)/ n. ле́кция
• v.t. чита́ть, про- ле́кцию/нота́цию + d.
• v.i.: he ~s in Russian он чита́ет ле́кции по
ру́сскому языку́
■ ~ hall, ~ room, ~ theatre nn. аудито́рия
lecturer /'lektʃərə(r)/ n. ле́ктор; (BrE, in
university) преподава́тель (m.)
led /led/ past and p.p. of ▸ lead²
ledge /ledʒ/ n. (shelf) пла́нка, по́лочка;
(projection) вы́ступ
ledger /'ledʒə(r)/ n. (book) гроссбу́х; (гла́вная)
учётная кни́га
leech /li:tʃ/ n. пия́вка
leek /li:k/ n. лук-поре́й
leer /lɪə(r)/ n. ухмы́лка
• v.i. ухмыл|я́ться, -ьну́ться; ~ at хи́тро/
зло́бно смотре́ть, по- на + a.
leeway /'li:weɪ/ n. свобо́да де́йствий
∿ **left¹** /left/ n. **1** (side, direction): from the ~
сле́ва; to the ~ нале́во; on, to my ~ нале́во
от меня́; on, from my ~ сле́ва от меня́
2 (pol.): the L~ ле́вые (pl.)
• adj. ле́вый; ~ wing (pol.) ле́вое крыло́
• adv. нале́во; turn ~ свｏора́чивать, -ерну́ть
нале́во
■ ~-hand adj. ле́вый; on the ~-hand side of
the street по ле́вой стороне́ у́лицы; car with
~-hand drive маши́на с левосторо́нним

управле́нием (or с рулём сле́ва); ~-handed
adj. де́лающий всё ле́вой руко́й, левору́кий;
~-handed person левша́ (c.g.); ~-wing adj.
ле́вый
left² /left/ past and p.p. of ▸ leave
leftovers /'leftəʊvəz/ n. pl. оста́тк|и (-ов);
(food) объе́дк|и (-ов)
∿ **leg** /leg/ n. **1** нога́; (dim.) но́жка; pull sb's
~ разы́гр|ывать, -а́ть кого́-н. **2** (meat):
~ of lamb бара́нья нога́ **3** (of furniture etc.)
но́жка **4** (of garment): trouser ~ штани́на
5 (stage of journey etc.) эта́п
legacy /'legəsɪ/ n. насле́дство, насле́дие
∿ **legal** /'li:g(ə)l/ adj. **1** (pert. to or based on law)
юриди́ческий, правово́й; take ~ advice
консульти́роваться, про- с юри́стом
2 (permitted or ordained by law) зако́нный,
лега́льный; within one's ~ rights (to)
впра́ве (по зако́ну) (+ inf.) **3** (involving court
proceedings) суде́бный
■ ~ action n. суде́бный иск; take ~ action
against возбу|жда́ть, -ди́ть де́ло про́тив
+ g.; предъяв|ля́ть, -и́ть иск (к) + d.; ~
aid n. (BrE) беспла́тная юриди́ческая
по́мощь неиму́щим; ~ holiday n. (AmE)
официа́льный нерабо́чий день; ~ tender n.
зако́нное платёжное сре́дство
legality /lɪ'gælɪtɪ/ n. зако́нность, лега́льность
legalization /li:gəlaɪ'zeɪʃ(ə)n/ n.
узако́нивание, легализа́ция
legalize /'li:gəlaɪz/ v.t. узако́ни|вать, -ть;
легализова́ть (impf., pf.)
legato /lɪ'gɑːtəʊ/ n. & adv. (pl. ~s) (mus.)
лега́то (nt. indecl.)
legend /'ledʒ(ə)nd/ n. леге́нда
legendary /'ledʒəndərɪ/ adj. легенда́рный
leggings /'legɪŋz/ n. pl. (stretch trousers)
ле́гинс|ы (-ов)
legible /'ledʒɪb(ə)l/ adj. разбо́рчивый
legislate /'ledʒɪsleɪt/ v.i. изд|ава́ть, -а́ть зако́ны
∿ **legislation** /ledʒɪs'leɪʃ(ə)n/ n. законода́тельство
legislative /'ledʒɪslətɪv/ adj. законода́тельный
legislature /'ledʒɪslətʃə(r)/ n. (assembly)
законода́тельный о́рган; (institutions)
законода́тельные учрежде́ния
legitimacy /lɪ'dʒɪtɪməsɪ/ n. зако́нность
legitimate /lɪ'dʒɪtɪmət/ adj. (lawful)
зако́нный; (justifiable): ~ demands
справедли́вые тре́бования
legitimize /lɪ'dʒɪtɪmaɪz/ v.t. узако́ни|вать, -ть
leisure /'leʒə(r)/ n. свобо́дное вре́мя; at one's
~ (in free time) в свобо́дное вре́мя; (unhurriedly)
не спеша́
■ ~ centre n. спорти́вно-развлека́тельный
ко́мплекс; ~ time n. вре́мя досу́га
leisured /'leʒəd/ adj. досу́жий, пра́здный;
the ~ classes нерабо́тающие кла́ссы/сло́и
о́бщества
leisurely /'leʒəlɪ/ adj. неспе́шный,
нетороплйвый
leitmotif, leitmotiv /'laɪtməʊtiːf/ n.
лейтмоти́в
lemon /'lemən/ n. лимо́н; (attr.) лимо́нный

lemonade /lemə'neɪd/ *n.* **1** (BrE, carbonated drink) лимона́д **2** (drink of lemon juice and water) напи́ток из со́ка лимо́на с водо́й

lemur /'li:mə(r)/ *n.* лему́р

lend /lend/ *v.t.* (*past and p.p.* **lent**) **1** да|ва́ть, -ть взаймы́; одалживать,-олжи́ть; ссу|жа́ть, -ди́ть (*кого чем or что кому*); ~ me £5 одолжи́те мне (*or* да́йте мне взаймы́) пять фу́нтов; ~ me the book for a while да́йте мне кни́гу на вре́мя **2** (impart) прид|ава́ть, -а́ть **3** (proffer): ~ a hand (help) ока́з|ывать, -а́ть по́мощь (*кому*); (help out in difficulty) выруча́ть, вы́ручить

lender /'lendə(r)/ *n.* заимода́вец, кредито́р

length /leŋkθ/ *n.* **1** (dimension, measurement) длина́; two metres in ~ два ме́тра длино́й **2** (racing etc.): the horse won by a ~ ло́шадь опереди́ла други́х на ко́рпус **3** (of time) продолжи́тельность, дли́тельность, срок; the chief fault of this film is its ~ гла́вный недоста́ток э́того фи́льма — его́ растя́нутость; at ~ (finally) наконе́ц; (in detail) во всех подро́бностях **4** (extent, degree): he went to great ~s not to offend them он сде́лал всё возмо́жное, что́бы не оби́деть их **5** (piece of material) кусо́к; отре́з

lengthen /'leŋkθ(ə)n/ *v.t. & i.* удлин|я́ть(ся), -и́ть(ся)

lengthy /'leŋkθɪ/ *adj.* (**lengthier, lengthiest**) дли́нный, затя́нутый; (in time) дли́тельный

leniency /'li:nɪənsɪ/ *n.* снисхожде́ние; мя́гкость

lenient /'li:nɪənt/ *adj.* (of person) снисходи́тельный; (of punishment etc.) мя́гкий

Leningrad /'leniŋgræd/ *n.* (hist.) Ленингра́д; (*attr.*) ленингра́дский

lens /lenz/ *n.* (anat., optics) ли́нза; (phot.) объекти́в

Lent /lent/ *n.* Вели́кий пост

lent /lent/ *past and p.p. of* ▶ **lend**

lentil /'lentɪl/ *n.* чечеви́ца

Leo /'li:əʊ/ *n.* (*pl.* ~**s**) (astron., astrol.) Лев

leopard /'lepəd/ *n.* леопа́рд

leotard /'lepɑ:d/ *n.* трико́ (*nt. indecl.*)

leper /'lepə(r)/ *n.* прокажённый

leprosy /'leprəsɪ/ *n.* прока́за

lesbian /'lezbɪən/ *n.* лесбия́нка
• *adj.* лесби́йский

lesion /'li:ʒ(ə)n/ *n.* повреде́ние, пораже́ние

✎ **less** /les/ *n.* ме́ньшее коли́чество; you should eat ~ вам сле́дует ме́ньше есть; ~ than £50 ме́нее 50 фу́нтов; in ~ than an hour ме́ньше чем за час
• *adj.* **1** (smaller) ме́ньший **2** (not so much) ме́ньше; eat ~ meat! е́шьте ме́ньше мя́са!
• *adv.* ме́ньше, ме́нее; не так, не сто́лько; he is ~ intelligent than his sister он не так умён, как его́ сестра́; the ~ you think about it the better чем ме́ньше об э́том ду́мать, тем лу́чше; ~ and ~ всё ме́ньше и ме́ньше
• *prep.* ми́нус; за вы́четом + *g.*; I paid him

his wages, ~ what he owed me за вы́дал ему́ зарпла́ту за вы́четом су́ммы, кото́рую он мне задолжа́л

lessen /'les(ə)n/ *v.t. & i.* ум|еньша́ть(ся), -е́ньшить(ся)

lesser /'lesə(r)/ *adj.* ме́ньший

✎ **lesson** /'les(ə)n/ *n.* уро́к, заня́тие; English ~s уро́ки англи́йского языка́; teach sb a ~ (rebuke, punish) дать (*pf.*) уро́к кому́-н.

let¹ /let/ *n.* (BrE, of property) аре́нда; take a house on a long ~ снять (*pf.*) дом на дли́тельный срок
• *v.t.* (**letting**, *past and p.p.* **let**) (*also* ~ **out**) сда|ва́ть, -ть внаём

✎ **let²** /let/ *v.t.* (**letting**, *past and p.p.* **let**) **1** (allow) позв|оля́ть, -о́лить + *d.*; разреш|а́ть, -и́ть + *d.*; ~ me help you позво́льте вам помо́чь; he won't ~ me work он не даёт мне рабо́тать; ~ go (relax grip on) выпуска́ть, вы́пустить из рук; отпус|ка́ть, -ти́ть; ~ oneself go увл|ека́ться, -е́чься; (set free) выпуска́ть, вы́пустить; ~ one's hair grow отпус|ка́ть, -ти́ть во́лосы **2** (cause to): ~ sb know да|ва́ть, -ть кому́-н. знать; сообщ|а́ть, -и́ть кому́-н. **3** (in imper. or hortatory sense): ~ me see (reflect) погоди́те; да́йте поду́мать; just ~ him try it! пусть то́лько попро́бует! **4** (~ come or go): shall I ~ you into a secret? хоти́те я раскро́ю вам та́йну?; he was ~ out of prison его́ вы́пустили из тюрьмы́

□ ~ **alone** *v.t.*: ~ alone (not to mention) не то́лько что, не говоря́ уже́ о + *p.*; they haven't got a radio, ~ alone television у них и ра́дио нет, не говоря́ уже́ о телеви́зоре

□ ~ **down** *v.t.* (disappoint) разочаро́в|ывать, -а́ть; (fail to support) под|води́ть, -вести́ (infml); (BrE, deflate): ~ down tyres спус|ка́ть, -ти́ть ши́ны; (lengthen): ~ down a dress отпуска́ть, отпусти́ть пла́тье

□ ~ **in** *v.t.* (admit) впус|ка́ть, -ти́ть; the window doesn't ~ in much light че́рез э́то окно́ проника́ет ма́ло све́та; my shoes ~ in water мои́ ту́фли протека́ют/промока́ют; he ~ himself in он сам откры́л дверь и вошёл; what have I ~ myself in for? во что я вяза́лся?

□ ~ **off** *v.t.* (discharge) разря|жа́ть, -ди́ть; ~ off fireworks запуска́ть (*impf.*) фейерве́рк; (not punish) не нака́зывать (*impf.*); he was ~ off lightly он легко́ отде́лался; (excuse) про|ща́ть, -сти́ть + *d.*; they ~ him off his debt ему́ прости́ли долг

□ ~ **on** *v.i.* (infml, divulge) прогов|а́риваться, -ори́ться

□ ~ **out** *v.t.*: ~ out a scream завизжа́ть (*pf.*); взви́згнуть (*pf.*); ~ out a secret прогов|а́риваться, -ори́ться; проболта́ться (*pf.*)

□ ~ **up** *v.i.* (weaken, diminish) ослаб|ева́ть, -е́ть; (stop for a while) приостан|а́вливаться, -ови́ться; (relax) перед|ыха́ть, -охну́ть

■ ~-**down** *n.* (disappointment, anticlimax) разочарова́ние

lethal /'li:θ(ə)l/ *adj.* (fatal) смерте́льный; (designed to kill) смертоно́сный

lethargic /lɪ'θɑ:dʒɪk/ *adj.* вя́лый

lethargy /'leθədʒɪ/ *n.* вя́лость

✎ ключева́я ле́ксика

⚲ **letter** /ˈletə(r)/ n. **1** (of alphabet) бу́ква **2** (written communication) письмо́

■ ~ **bomb** n. бо́мба в конве́рте; ~ **box** n. (BrE) почто́вый я́щик

lettuce /ˈletɪs/ n. сала́т (*растение*)

leukaemia /luːˈkiːmɪə/ (AmE **leukemia**) n. белокро́вие, лейкеми́я

⚲ **level** /ˈlev(ə)l/ n. у́ровень; **on a ~ with** на одно́м у́ровне с + i.; **talks at Cabinet ~** перегово́ры на прави́тельственном у́ровне
   ● adj. (even) ро́вный; (flat) пло́ский; (horizontal) горизонта́льный; **the water was ~ with the banks** вода́ была́ вро́вень с берега́ми; **draw ~ with** наг|оня́ть, -на́ть
   ● v.t. (**levelled**, **levelling**, AmE **leveled**, **leveling**) **1** (make ~) ур|а́внивать, -овня́ть; выра́внивать, вы́ровнять **2** (raze to ground) ср|а́внивать, -овня́ть с землёй **3** (aim) нав|оди́ть, -ести́; нацели|вать, -ть; **she ~led a gun at his head** она́ прице́лилась ему́ в го́лову; (criticism, accusation) напр|авля́ть, -а́вить (**at:** про́тив + g.)
   □ ~ **off**, ~ **out** vv.i. (smooth out) сгла́|живать, -дить; (make ~, even, identical) ур|а́внивать, -овня́ть

■ ~ **crossing** n. (BrE) (железнодоро́жный) перее́зд; **~-headed** adj. тре́звый, рассуди́тельный

lever /ˈliːvə(r)/ n. рыча́г

leverage /ˈliːvərɪdʒ/ n. (action) де́йствие/ уси́лие рычага́; **use ~ on sb** (fig.) повлия́ть (*pf.*) на кого́-н.

levitation /levɪˈteɪʃ(ə)n/ n. левита́ция

levity /ˈlevɪtɪ/ n. легкомы́слие

levy /ˈlevɪ/ n. обложе́ние
   ● v.t. взима́ть (*impf.*) (**on:** с + g.)

lewd /ljuːd/ adj. (of person) развра́тный; (of joke, suggestion) непристо́йный, гря́зный

lexical /ˈleksɪk(ə)l/ adj. лекси́ческий

lexicon /ˈleksɪkən/ n. (dictionary) словарь, лексико́н; (vocabulary of writer etc.) ле́ксика

liability /laɪəˈbɪlɪtɪ/ n. **1** (responsibility) отве́тственность **2** (*in pl.*) (debts) долги́ (*m. pl.*) **3** (handicap): **he's nothing but a ~** он про́сто обу́за

liable /ˈlaɪəb(ə)l/ adj. **1** (answerable) отве́тственный (**for:** за + a.) **2** (subject): **he is ~ to a heavy fine** его́ мо́гут подве́ргнуть большо́му штра́фу **3** (apt, likely): **she is ~ to forget it** она́ скло́нна забыва́ть об э́том

liaise /lɪˈeɪz/ v.i. устана́вливать/подде́рживать (*impf.*) связь (**with:** с + i.)

liaison /lɪˈeɪzɒn/ n. связь

liar /ˈlaɪə(r)/ n. лгун (-ья)

libel /ˈlaɪb(ə)l/ n. клевета́
   ● v.t. (**libelled**, **libelling**, AmE **libeled**, **libeling**) клевета́ть (*на кого*), о- (*кого*), на- (*на кого*); **they ~led me** они́ оклевета́ли меня́, они́ наклевета́ли на меня́

libellous /ˈlaɪbələs/ (AmE **libelous**) adj. клеветни́ческий

liberal /ˈlɪbər(ə)l/ n. либера́л
   ● adj. **1** (generous) ще́дрый; (abundant) оби́льный **2** (broadminded): **a man of ~**

views челове́к широ́ких взгля́дов **3** (pol.) либера́льный

■ **L~ Democrat** n. (pol.) либера́л-демокра́т

liberalization /lɪbərəlaɪˈzeɪʃ(ə)n/ n. демократиза́ция, либерализа́ция

liberalize /ˈlɪbərəlaɪz/ v.t. либерализова́ть (*impf.*, *pf.*)

liberate /ˈlɪbəreɪt/ v.t. освобо|жда́ть, -ди́ть

liberation /lɪbəˈreɪʃ(ə)n/ n. освобожде́ние

liberator /ˈlɪbəreɪtə(r)/ n. освободи́тель (-ница)

Liberia /laɪˈbɪərɪə/ n. Либе́рия

Liberian /laɪˈbɪərɪən/ n. либери́|ец (-йка)
   ● adj. либери́йский

libertarian /lɪbəˈteərɪən/ n. (advocate of freedom) боре́ц за демократи́ческие свобо́ды

liberty /ˈlɪbətɪ/ n. свобо́да; **at ~** находя́щийся на свобо́де; **you are at ~ to go** вы вольны́ уйти́

libido /lɪˈbiːdəʊ/ n. (*pl.* **~s**) либи́до (*nt. indecl.*)

Libra /ˈliːbrə/ n. (astron., astrol.) Весы́ (-о́в)

librarian /laɪˈbreərɪən/ n. библиоте́карь (*m.*)

⚲ **library** /ˈlaɪbrərɪ/ n. библиоте́ка

Libya /ˈlɪbɪə/ n. Ли́вия

Libyan /ˈlɪbɪən/ n. ливи́|ец (-йка)
   ● adj. ливи́йский

licence /ˈlaɪs(ə)ns/ (AmE also **license**) n. **1** (permission) разреше́ние; (for trade) лице́нзия **2** (permit) свиде́тельство; **driving ~** води́тельские права́ **3** (freedom) во́льность

■ ~ **plate** n. (AmE) номерно́й знак

⚲ **license** /ˈlaɪs(ə)ns/ (AmE also **licence**) v.t. **1** (authorize) разреша́ть, -и́ть *что*; да|ва́ть, -ть разреше́ние на *что* **2** (grant permit, permission to) разреш|а́ть, -и́ть + d.; **~d premises** заведе́ние, облада́ющее лице́нзией на прода́жу спиртны́х напи́тков

licensee /laɪsənˈsiː/ n. облада́тель (-ница) разреше́ния/лице́нзии; (of public house) хозя́|ин (-йка) ба́ра

licensing /ˈlaɪsənsɪŋ/ n. лицензи́рование

licentious /laɪˈsenʃəs/ adj. распу́щенный

lichen /ˈlaɪkən/ n. лиша́йник

lick /lɪk/ v.t. **1** лиз|а́ть, -ну́ть; ~ **one's lips/** (infml) **chops** обли́з|ывать, -а́ть гу́бы; обли́з|ываться, -а́ться; (fig.): ~ **one's wounds** зали́з|ывать, -а́ть ра́ны **2** (infml, defeat) поб|ива́ть, -и́ть

licorice /ˈlɪkərɪs, -rɪʃ/ n. (AmE) = **liquorice**

lid /lɪd/ n. кры́шка

lido /ˈliːdəʊ, ˈlaɪ-/ n. (*pl.* **~s**) (обще́ственный) пляж

lie¹ /laɪ/ n. (falsehood) ложь; **tell a ~** лгать, со-
   ● v.i. (**lies**, **lied**, **lying**) лгать, со-; врать, со-/на-; **he ~d to me** он мне солга́л

⚲ **lie²** /laɪ/ v.i. (**lying**, *past* **lay**, *p.p.* **lain**) **1** (repose) лежа́ть, по-; ~ **low** притаи́ться (*pf.*) **2** (be; be situated) находи́ться (*impf.*); быть располо́женным **3** (fig., reside, rest): **the choice ~s with you** вы́бор зави́сит от вас; вам выбира́ть; **she knows where her interests ~** она́ своего́ не упу́стит **4** (~ **down**) ложи́ться,

лечь; приле́чь (*pf.*); **he went and lay on the bed** он лёг на крова́ть
□ **~ about, ~ around** *vv.i.* валя́ться (*impf.*)
□ **~ ahead** *v.i.* предстоя́ть (*impf.*)
□ **~ down** *v.i.* ложи́ться, лечь; **I shall ~ down for an hour** я приля́гу на час/часо́к
■ **~-down** *n.* (BrE): **she had a ~-down** она́ полежа́ла; **~-in** *n.* (BrE): **we had a ~-in** мы вста́ли по́здно

lieu /luː/ *n.*: **in ~ of** вме́сто + *g.*

lieutenant /lefˈtenənt/ *n.* лейтена́нт

✍ **life** /laɪf/ *n.* (*pl.* **lives**) **1** (being alive) жизнь; **save sb's ~** спасти́ (*pf.*) жизнь кому́-н.; (existence): **that's ~!** такова́ жизнь!; (way or style of ~) быт; **family ~** дома́шний быт; **country, village ~** дереве́нская жизнь **2** (period, span of ~): **have the time of one's ~** прекра́сно проводи́ть (*impf.*) вре́мя; **he has had a good/ quiet ~** он прожи́л хоро́шую/споко́йную жизнь **3** (animation) жи́вость; **the ~ and soul of the party** душа́ о́бщества; **the child is full of ~** ребёнок о́чень живо́й; **the play came to ~ in the third act** к тре́тьему де́йствию пье́са оживи́лась **4** (living things) жизнь; **is there ~ on Mars?** есть ли жизнь на Ма́рсе?; **animal ~** живо́тный мир
■ **~belt** *n.* (BrE) спаса́тельный круг; **~boat** *n.* спаса́тельная ло́дка; **~ coach** *n.* персона́льный наста́вник; **~ expectancy** *n.* вероя́тная продолжи́тельность жи́зни; **~guard, ~saver** *nn.* спаса́тель (-ница) (на пля́же); **~ insurance** *n.* страхова́ние жи́зни; **~ jacket** *n.* спаса́тельный жиле́т; **~like** *adj.* реалисти́чный; **~line** *n.* (fig.) еди́нственная наде́жда; спаси́тельное сре́дство; (of communication line) связу́ющий мост (**to:** с + *i.*); **~long** *adj.* пожи́зненный; **they were ~long friends** они́ бы́ли друзья́ми всю жизнь; **~saving** *n.* спасе́ние; **~ sentence** *n.* пожи́зненное заключе́ние (*как приговор*); (of inanimate things, durability) долгове́чность; срок слу́жбы; **~-size(d)** *adjs.* в натура́льную величину́; **~span** *n.* (of person, animal) продолжи́тельность жи́зни; (of machine, tool) срок эксплуата́ции; **~style** *n.* о́браз жи́зни; **~support** *adj.*: **~-support system** систе́ма жизнеобеспе́чения; **~time** *n.* жизнь; **in sb's ~time** при жи́зни кого́-н.; **the chance of a ~time** ре́дкий/исключи́тельный слу́чай; **it's a ~time since I saw her** я не ви́дел её це́лую ве́чность

lifeless /ˈlaɪflɪs/ *adj.* (dead) мёртвый; (inanimate) неживо́й; (inert) безжи́зненный

✍ **lift** /lɪft/ *n.* **1** (in car etc.): **give sb a ~** подв|ози́ть, -езти́ кого́-н. **2** (fig., of spirits): **the news gave her a ~** от э́той но́вости она́ воспря́нула ду́хом **3** (BrE, apparatus) лифт
● *v.t.* **1** (raise) подн|има́ть, -я́ть **2** (remove): **~ a ban** сн|има́ть, -ять запре́т
● *v.i.* (disperse) рассе́|иваться, -яться; (cease) прекра|ща́ться, -ти́ться
□ **~ off** *v.t.* сн|има́ть, -ять
● *v.i.* (of rocket) от|рыва́ться, -орва́ться от земли́
□ **~ up** *v.t.* подн|има́ть, -я́ть

✍ ключева́я ле́ксика

■ **~-off** *n.* отры́в от земли́

ligament /ˈlɪɡəmənt/ *n.* свя́зка

✍ **light¹** /laɪt/ *n.* **1** свет; **stand against the ~** стоя́ть (*impf.*) про́тив све́та; **bring to ~** выводи́ть, вы́вести на чи́стую во́ду; **come to ~** обнару́жи|ваться, -ться; вы́плыть, выплыва́ть; **shed, throw ~ on sth** прол|ива́ть, -и́ть свет на что-н.; (in a picture): **effects of ~ and shade** эффе́кты све́та и те́ни; (lighting) освеще́ние; (fig.): **this book shows him in a bad ~** э́та кни́га пока́зывает его́ в невы́годном све́те; (point of ~): **the ~s of the town** огни́ го́рода **2** (lamp) ла́мпа; (of car) фа́ра; **traffic ~s** светофо́р **3** (flame) ого́нь (*m.*); **have you a ~?** у вас огонька́ не бу́дет?
● *adj.* **1** (opp. dark) све́тлый; **get ~** рассве|та́ть, -сти́ **2** (in colour) све́тлый; све́тлого цве́та; **~-haired** светловоло́сый; **~-skinned** светлоко́жий; (with names of colours) све́тло-; **~ green** све́тло-зелёный; **~ blue** све́тло-голубо́й
● *v.t.* (*past* **lit**, *p.p.* **lit** or (*attr.*) **lighted**) (*also* **~ up**) **1** (kindle) заж|ига́ть, -е́чь; **~ a fire** разв|оди́ть, -ести́ ого́нь; **~ (up) a cigarette** заку́р|ивать, -и́ть папиро́су **2** (illuminate) осве|ща́ть, -ти́ть; **~ the way for sb** свети́ть, по- кому́-н.; (fig.): **a smile lit up his face** улы́бка озари́ла его́ лицо́
■ **~ bulb** *n.* ла́мпочка; **~house** *n.* мая́к; **~weight** *n.* (sport, also fig.) легкове́с; **~ year** *n.* светово́й год

✍ **light²** /laɪt/ *adj.* (opp. heavy) лёгкий; **our casualties were ~** на́ши поте́ри бы́ли незначи́тельны; **a ~ sentence** мя́гкий пригово́р; **I am a ~ sleeper** я чу́тко сплю
■ **~-headed** *adj.*: **she felt ~-headed** у неё закружи́лась голова́; **~-hearted** *adj.* (carefree) беспе́чный; (of action) необду́манный; **~ music** *n.* лёгкая му́зыка; **~ reading** *n.* лёгкое чте́ние; **~weight** *adj.* (suit) лёгкий; (fig.) несерьёзный, легкове́сный

lighten¹ /ˈlaɪt(ə)n/ *v.t.* (make less heavy or easier) облегч|а́ть, -и́ть

lighten² /ˈlaɪt(ə)n/ *v.i.* (grow brighter) светле́ть, по-

lighter /ˈlaɪtə(r)/ *n.* (for cigarettes etc.) зажига́лка

lighting /ˈlaɪtɪŋ/ *n.* освеще́ние

lightly /ˈlaɪtlɪ/ *adv.* легко́; **you have got off ~** вы легко́ отде́лались

lightning /ˈlaɪtnɪŋ/ *n.* мо́лния; **he was struck by ~** в него́ уда́рила мо́лния
● *attr. adj.*: **with ~ speed** молниено́сно

✍ **like¹** /laɪk/ *n.* (sth equal or similar) подо́бное; **music, dancing and the ~** му́зыка, та́нцы и тому́ подо́бное; (person) подо́бный; **the ~s of me, us** наш брат
● *adj.* (**more like, most like**) подо́бный, похо́жий
● *prep.* **1** (similar to, characteristic of) похо́жий на + *a.*; **she is ~ her mother** она́ похо́жа на мать; **what's she ~?** что она́ за челове́к?; **a house ~ yours** дом вро́де ва́шего; **it sounds ~ thunder** как бу́дто гром греми́т; **it sounds ~ a good idea** э́то, пожа́луй, хоро́шая иде́я; **a person ~ that** тако́й челове́к **2** (inclined towards): **I don't feel ~ it** мне (что́-то) не

хо́чется; **I felt ~ crying** мне хоте́лось
пла́кать; **I feel ~ an ice cream** я бы не прочь
съесть моро́женое

■ **~-minded** *adj.* приде́рживающийся тех же
взгля́дов

♂ **like²** /laɪk/ *v.t.* (take pleasure in) люби́ть (*impf.*),
цени́ть (*impf.*); **he ~s living in Paris** ему́
нра́вится жить в Пари́же; **she ~d dancing**
она́ люби́ла танцева́ть; **I ~ him** он мне
нра́вится; **we ~d the play** пье́са нам
понра́вилась; **would you ~ a drink?** хоти́те
вы́пить (чего́-нибудь)?; **if you ~** е́сли
хоти́те; **I should ~ to meet him** мне хоте́лось
бы познако́миться с ним; **he would ~ to
come** он хоте́л бы прийти́; **as you ~** как
уго́дно

likeable /ˈlaɪkəb(ə)l/ *adj.* симпати́чный

likelihood /ˈlaɪklɪhʊd/ *n.* вероя́тность; **in all
~** по всей вероя́тности

♂ **likely** /ˈlaɪklɪ/ *adj.* (**likelier, likeliest**)
1 (probable) вероя́тный; (plausible)
правдоподо́бный **2** (to be expected): **he is ~ to
come** он, вероя́тно, придёт

liken /ˈlaɪkən/ *v.t.* упод|обля́ть, -о́бить (*кого/
что кому/чему*)

likeness /ˈlaɪknɪs/ *n.* схо́дство, подо́бие; **a
family ~** фами́льное схо́дство

likewise /ˈlaɪkwaɪz/ *adv.* подо́бно

liking /ˈlaɪkɪŋ/ *n.* симпа́тия (*к кому*); **I took a
~ to him** я почу́вствовал к нему́ симпа́тию;
is the meat done to your ~? э́то мя́со
пригото́влено, как вы лю́бите?

lilac /ˈlaɪlək/ *n.* сире́нь

lilt /lɪlt/ *n.* (tune) напе́в; (rhythm) ритм
● *v.i.* **a ~ing melody** мелоди́чный напе́в

lily /ˈlɪlɪ/ *n.* ли́лия
■ **~ of the valley** *n.* ла́ндыш

limb /lɪm/ *n.* **1** (of body, also fig.) член;
коне́чность **2** (branch of tree) сук, ветвь

limber /ˈlɪmbə(r)/ *v.i.:* **~ up** разм|ина́ться,
-я́ться

limbo /ˈlɪmbəʊ/ *n.* (*pl.* **~s**) **1** (relig.) лимб
2 (fig.): **our plans are in ~** на́ши пла́ны вися́т
в во́здухе

lime¹ /laɪm/ *n.* (fruit) лайм
■ **~ juice** *n.* сок ла́йма

lime² /laɪm/ *n.* (tree) ли́па

lime³ /laɪm/ *n.* (calcium oxide) и́звесть
■ **~light** *n.* (lit.) свет ра́мпы; (fig.): **be in the
~light** быть знамени́тостью; **~stone** *n.*
известня́к

♂ **limit** /ˈlɪmɪt/ *n.* **1** (terminal point) преде́л;
set, fix a ~ to sth устан|а́вливать, -ови́ть
преде́л чему́-н.; **I am willing to help you,
within ~s** я гото́в помо́чь вам в преде́лах
возмо́жного **2** (boundary) грани́ца **3** (time
~) (преде́льный) срок; **age ~** преде́льный
во́зраст
● *v.t.* (**limited, limiting**) ограни́чи|вать,
-ть (*кого/чего чем*)

■ **~ed (liability) company** *n.* (BrE) компа́ния
с ограни́ченной отве́тственностью

limitation /lɪmɪˈteɪʃ(ə)n/ *n.* (condition)
огово́рка; (drawback) недоста́ток; **he has his**

~s он не лишён недоста́тков; (limiting, being
limited) ограниче́ние

limitless /ˈlɪmɪtlɪs/ *adj.* безграни́чный,
беспреде́льный; (of time) бесконе́чный

limousine /ˈlɪmʊˈziːn/ *n.* лимузи́н

limp¹ /lɪmp/ *n.* хромота́; **he has a ~** он
хрома́ет/прихра́мывает
● *v.i.* хрома́ть (*impf.*)

limp² /lɪmp/ *adj.* **1** (flexible) мя́гкий **2** (flabby)
вя́лый

linchpin, lynchpin /ˈlɪntʃpɪn/ *n.* чека́;
(fig., of person or thing) тот/то, на ком/чём всё
де́ржится

♂ **line¹** /laɪn/ *n.* **1** (cord) верёвка; **hang washing
on the ~** разве́сить (*pf.*) бельё на верёвке;
(fishing ~) ле́ска **2** (wire, cable for communication)
ли́ния (свя́зи); ка́бель (*m.*); про́вод; **he is
on the ~** он говори́т по телефо́ну; он у
телефо́на **3** (rail.) ли́ния; (track) полотно́;
ре́льсы (*m. pl.*) **4** (transport system) ли́ния;
air ~s возду́шные ли́нии **5** (long narrow
mark) ли́ния, черта́; (imagined straight **~**):
~ of fire направле́ние стрельбы́ **6** (on
face, etc.) скла́дка **7** (drawn, painted, etc.)
штрих **8** (boundary) грани́ца, преде́л,
черта́ **9** (row) ряд, ли́ния; **stand in a ~**
стоя́ть (*impf.*) в ряд; **stand in ~** (AmE, queue)
стоя́ть (*impf.*) в о́череди; **in ~ with** в одну́
ли́нию (*or* в ряд) с + *i.*; (fig.) в согла́сии/
соотве́тствии с + *i.*; **bring into ~** (fig.)
привле́чь (*pf.*) (*кого*) на свою́ сто́рону;
come, fall into ~ (fig.) согласова́ться (*impf.,
pf.*) **10** (mil., entrenched position): **front ~**
ли́ния фро́нта **11** (of print or writing) строка́;
on ~ 10 there's a mistake в деся́той строке́
оши́бка; (*in pl.*) (actor's part) роль **12** (lineage)
ли́ния **13** (course, direction, track) направле́ние,
ли́ния; **take a firm, hard, strong ~** зан|има́ть,
-я́ть твёрдую пози́цию; стро́го об|ходи́ться,
-ойти́сь (*с кем*) **14** (province) **his ~ of
business** род его́ заня́тий **15** (class of goods)
сорт, род, моде́ль (това́ра)
● *v.t.* **1** (mark with **~s**): **~d paper** лино́ванная
бума́га; **his face was deeply ~d** его́ лицо́
бы́ло изборождено́ морщи́нами **2** (form a
~ along) стоя́ть (*impf.*) вдоль + *g*; **police ~d
the street** полице́йские стоя́ли по обе́им
сторона́м у́лицы
□ **~ up** *v.t.* (align) выстра́ивать, вы́строить в
ряд/ли́нию
● *v.i.* (queue up) ста|нови́ться, -ть в о́чередь

■ **~sman** *n.* (sport) боково́й судья́; **~-up**
n. (sport) соста́в кома́нды; (mus.) соста́в
анса́мбля/(поп-)гру́ппы; (TV) расписа́ние
переда́ч

line² /laɪn/ *v.t.* **1** (put lining into) ста́вить, по- на
подкла́дку; **her coat is ~d with silk** у неё
пальто́ на шёлковой подкла́дке **2** (fig.)
заст|авля́ть, -а́вить; **the wall was ~d with
books** стена́ была́ заста́влена кни́гами

lineage /ˈlɪnɪɪdʒ/ *n.* (ancestry) происхожде́ние;
(genealogy) родосло́вная

linear /ˈlɪnɪə(r)/ *adj.* лине́йный

linen /ˈlɪnɪn/ *n.* **1** (smooth) лён; (coarse) холст
2 (~ articles) бельё; (bed ~) посте́льное бельё

• *adj.* полотня́ный

liner /'laɪnə(r)/ *n.* ла́йнер

linger /'lɪŋɡə(r)/ *v.i.* (take one's time) ме́длить (*impf.*); (stay on) заде́рж|иваться, -а́ться; **I have ~ing** doubts мои́ сомне́ния не рассе́ялись

□ **~ on** *v.i.* (remain) оста|ва́ться, -а́ться

lingerie /'læʒəri/ *n.* да́мское бельё

linguist /'lɪŋɡwɪst/ *n.* лингви́ст, языкове́д

linguistic /lɪŋ'ɡwɪstɪk/ *adj.* лингвисти́ческий

linguistics /lɪŋ'ɡwɪstɪks/ *n.* лингви́стика

lining /'laɪnɪŋ/ *n.* подкла́дка

✧ **link** /lɪŋk/ *n.* **1** (of chain, also fig.) звено́ **2** (connection) связь; (comput.) ссы́лка
• *v.t.* (unite) соедин|я́ть, -и́ть; (join) свя́з|ывать, -а́ть; **~ arms with sb** идти́ (*det.*) по́д руку с кем-н.

□ **~ up** *v.t. & i.* соедин|я́ть(ся), -и́ть(ся)

■ **~-up** *n.* связь, соедине́ние

lino /'laɪnəʊ/ *n.* (*pl.* **~s**) (BrE) = **linoleum**

linoleum /lɪ'nəʊliəm/ *n.* лино́леум

linseed /'lɪnsiːd/ *n.* льняно́е се́мя

■ **~ oil** *n.* льняно́е ма́сло

lintel /'lɪnt(ə)l/ *n.* при́толока (*верхний брус дверно́й/око́нной рамы*)

lion /'laɪən/ *n.* лев

■ **~ cub** *n.* львёнок

lioness /'laɪənes/ *n.* льви́ца

lip /lɪp/ *n.* **1** губа́; (dim.) гу́бка **2** (edge of cup, wound, etc.) край

■ **~-read** *v.t. & i.* чита́ть (*impf.*) с губ; **~salve** *n.* (BrE) гигиени́ческая губна́я пома́да; **~ service** *n.*: **pay ~ service to sth** призн|ава́ть, -а́ть что-н. то́лько на слова́х; **~stick** *n.* (substance) губна́я пома́да; (applicator) тю́бик губно́й пома́ды

liqueur /lɪ'kjʊə(r)/ *n.* ликёр

liquid /'lɪkwɪd/ *n.* жи́дкость
• *adj.* жи́дкий

■ **~ assets** *n. pl.* (fin.) ликви́дные акти́вы

liquidate /'lɪkwɪdeɪt/ *v.t.* ликвиди́ровать (*impf., pf.*)

liquidation /lɪkwɪ'deɪʃ(ə)n/ *n.* ликвида́ция

liquidize /'lɪkwɪdaɪz/ *v.t.* (BrE, cul.) превра|ща́ть, -ти́ть в жи́дкость; пропус|ка́ть, -ти́ть че́рез сме́ситель/ми́ксер

liquidizer /'lɪkwɪdaɪzə(r)/ *n.* (BrE, cul.) сме́ситель (*m.*), ми́ксер

liquor /'lɪkə(r)/ *n.* (спиртно́й) напи́ток

■ **~ store** *n.* (AmE) ви́нный магази́н

liquorice /'lɪkərɪs, -rɪʃ/ (AmE **licorice**) *n.* (plant) соло́дка, лакри́чник; (substance) лакри́ца

lisp /lɪsp/ *n.* шепеля́вость; **he has a ~** он шепеля́вит

✧ **list¹** /lɪst/ *n.* (inventory, enumeration) спи́сок, пе́речень (*m.*); **~ price** цена́ по прейскура́нту
• *v.t.* (make a ~ of) сост|авля́ть, -а́вить спи́сок + *g.*; (enter on a ~) вн|оси́ть, -ести́ в спи́сок

■ **~ed building** *n.* зда́ние, находя́щееся под охра́ной госуда́рства

list² /lɪst/ *v.i.* (of ship) накреня́ться (*impf.*)

✧ **listen** /'lɪs(ə)n/ *v.i.* слу́шать, по-; **~ to** слу́шать, по- + *a.*; **do you ~ to the radio?** вы слу́шаете ра́дио?; (pay attention) прислу́ш|иваться, -аться к + *d.*; **don't ~ to him!** не обраща́йте на него́ внима́ния!; **I was ~ing for the bell** я (напряжённо) ждал звонка́; **he ~ed in on their conversation** он подслу́шал их разгово́р

listener /'lɪsənə(r)/ *n.* слу́шатель (*m.*)

listing /'lɪstɪŋ/ *n.* (list) спи́сок; (mentioning) упомина́ние

listless /'lɪstlɪs/ *adj.* вя́лый

lit /lɪt/ *past and p.p. of* ▶ **light¹**

litany /'lɪtəni/ *n.* (Orthodox) ектенья́; (Catholic) лита́ния; (fig., tedious enumeration) ску́чное перечисле́ние

literacy /'lɪtərəsi/ *n.* гра́мотность

literal /'lɪtər(ə)l/ *adj.* буква́льный

literary /'lɪtərəri/ *adj.* литерату́рный

literate /'lɪtərət/ *adj.* гра́мотный

✧ **literature** /'lɪtərətʃə(r)/ *n.* литерату́ра

lithe /laɪð/ *adj.* ги́бкий

lithograph /'lɪθəɡrɑːf/ *n.* литогра́фия

lithography /lɪ'θɒɡrəfɪ/ *n.* литогра́фия

Lithuania /lɪθjʊ'eɪniə/ *n.* Литва́

Lithuanian /lɪθjʊ'eɪniən/ *n.* (person) лито́в|ец (-ка); (language) лито́вский язы́к
• *adj.* лито́вский

litigate /'lɪtɪɡeɪt/ *v.i.* суди́ться (*impf.*)

litigation /lɪtɪ'ɡeɪʃ(ə)n/ *n.* тя́жба; суде́бный проце́сс

litigious /lɪ'tɪdʒəs/ *adj.* **1** (fond of going to law) сутя́жнический; **a ~ person** сутя́жни|к (-ца) **2** (pert. to litigation): **~ procedure** процеду́ра суде́бного разбира́тельства

litmus /'lɪtməs/ *n.* ла́кмус

■ **~ paper** *n.* ла́кмусовая бума́га

litre /'liːtə(r)/ (AmE **liter**) *n.* литр

litter /'lɪtə(r)/ *n.* **1** (refuse) сор, отбро́с|ы (-ов) **2**: **cat ~** коша́чья подсти́лка **3** (newly-born animals) помёт
• *v.t.* сори́ть, на-; **the table is ~ed with books** стол зава́лен кни́гами

■ **~ bin** *n.* (BrE) му́сорный я́щик

✧ **little** /'lɪt(ə)l/ *n.* (not much) ма́ло, немно́го, немно́жко + *g.*; **I see ~ of him now** я тепе́рь ре́дко ви́жу его́; **~ or nothing** почти́ ничего́; **~ by ~** ма́ло-пома́лу; постепе́нно
• *adj.* (**littler**, **littlest**) **1** (small) ма́ленький, небольшо́й **2** (young): **~ boy** (ма́ленький) ма́льчик; **~ girl** (ма́ленькая) де́вочка **3** (trivial) ме́лкий; незначи́тельный **4** (not tall or long) невысо́кий; недли́нный; **wait here for a ~ while** подожди́те здесь немно́жко **5** (**less**, **least**) (small, of quantity) ма́ло, немно́го, немно́жко + *g.*; **there is ~ butter left** ма́сла оста́лось ма́ло
• *adv.* (**less**, **least**) **1** (not much) ма́ло; **I see him very ~** я ма́ло/ре́дко с ним ви́жусь; **~ more** ненамно́го/немно́гим бо́льше; **he is ~ better than a thief** он про́сто-на́просто вор; (not at all): **~ did he know I was following him**

он и не подозревáл, что я идý за ним **2** (**a ∼**) (slightly, somewhat) немнóго, немнóжко; **I am a ∼ happier now** тепéрь я нéсколько успокóился; **she is a ∼ over 40** ей немнóгим бóльше сорокá

■ **∼ finger** *n.* мизи́нец

liturgy /ˈlɪtədʒɪ/ *n.* (eccl.) литурги́я

✓ **live¹** /laɪv/ *adj.* **1** (living) живóй **2** (not spent or exploded): **∼ ammunition** боевы́е патрóны; **a ∼ wire** (lit.) прóвод под тóком/напряжéнием; (fig.) человéк с изю́минкой **3** (not recorded): **∼ broadcast** прямáя передáча; прямóй эфи́р; **∼ music** живáя мýзыка; **the game was broadcast ∼** матч трансли́ровался непосрéдственно со стадиóна (*or* шёл в прямóй трансля́ции)
● *adv.* (as or at an actual event) живьём (infml); **he sang ∼** он пел живьём

■ **∼stock** *n.* домáшний скот

✓ **live²** /lɪv/ *v.i.* **1** (be alive) жить (*impf.*) **2** (subsist): **they ∼ on vegetables** они́ питáются овощáми **3** (depend on one's living) жить (*impf.*); **he ∼s off his friends** он живёт за счёт друзéй; **he ∼s on his reputation** он живёт за счёт бы́лых заслýг **4** (conduct oneself) жить (*impf.*); **he ∼d up to my expectations** он не обманýл мои́х ожидáний; (arrange one's diet, habits, etc.): **he ∼s well** он живёт хорошó (*or* на широ́кую нóгу) **5** (continue alive): **the doctors think he won't ∼** врачи́ дýмают, что он не вы́живет; **he ∼d to regret it** впослéдствии он об э́том жалéл; (fig., survive): **his fame will ∼ for ever** слáва его́ не умрёт **6** (reside) жить, проживáть (*both impf.*); обитáть (*impf.*); **where do you ∼?** где вы живёте; **∼ with** (fig., tolerate) мири́ться, при– с + *i.*

□ **∼ in** *v.i.* (of student) жить (*impf.*) в общежи́тии

□ **∼ on** *v.i.*: **his memory ∼s on** пáмять о нём живá

□ **∼ up** *v.t.*: **∼ it up** (infml) жить (*impf.*) широкó, вести́ (*impf.*) бýрную жизнь

■ **∼-in** *adj.*: **∼-in nanny** ня́ня, живýщая в семьé; **∼-in lover** сожи́тель (-ница)

livelihood /ˈlaɪvlɪhʊd/ *n.* срéдства (*nt. pl.*) к существовáнию

lively /ˈlaɪvlɪ/ *adj.* (**livelier**, **liveliest**) живóй

liven /ˈlaɪv(ə)n/ *v.t. & i.* (*also* **∼ up**) оживля́ть(ся), –и́ть(ся)

liver /ˈlɪvə(r)/ *n.* (anat.) пéчень; (food) печёнка

livery /ˈlɪvərɪ/ *n.* (of servants) ливрéя; (of a guild etc.) фóрма; (for horses) прокóрм

■ **∼ stable** *n.* плáтная коню́шня

lives¹ /laɪvz/ *pl. of* ▶ **life**

lives² /lɪvz/ *2nd pers. sg. pres. of* ▶ **live²**

livid /ˈlɪvɪd/ *adj.* (furious) в я́рости; (crimson) багрóвый

✓ **living** /ˈlɪvɪŋ/ *n.* **1** (process, manner of ∼): **∼ conditions** услóвия жи́зни; **cost of ∼** стóимость жи́зни; **standard of ∼** жи́зненный ýровень **2** (livelihood) срéдства (*nt. pl.*) к жи́зни; **earn one's ∼** зарабá|тывать, –óтать себé на жизнь
● *adj.* живóй; **within ∼ memory** на пáмяти живýщих

■ **∼ room** *n.* гости́ная

lizard /ˈlɪzəd/ *n.* я́щерица

llama /ˈlɑːmə/ *n.* лáма (*живóтное*)

✓ **load** /ləʊd/ *n.* **1** (burden) нóша; груз, нагрýзка; тя́жесть; (fig.) брéмя **2** (amount carried) груз; **a ∼ of bricks** груз кирпичéй **3** (*in pl.*) (infml, large amount) ýйма, мáсса
● *v.t.* **1** (cargo, etc.) грузи́ть, по– **2** (ship, vehicle, etc.) грузи́ть, на– **3** (fig., with cares, etc.) обременя́ть, –и́ть (*когó чем*) **4** (with gifts, praises, etc.) ос|ыпáть, –ы́пать (*когó чем*) **5** (firearm, camera, etc.) заряжá|ть, –ди́ть **6** (fig.): **a ∼ed question** провокациóнный вопрóс **7** (sl.): **he's ∼ed** (rich) он (пóлностью/хорошó) упакóван **8** (comput.) загружá|ть, –зи́ть

□ **∼ down** *v.t.* обремен|я́ть, –и́ть

□ **∼ up** *v.t.* нагружá|ть, –зи́ть
● *v.i.* грузи́ться, на-

loaf¹ /ləʊf/ *n.* (*pl.* **loaves**) бухáнка

loaf² /ləʊf/ *v.i.* (infml) (*also* **∼ about**) лóдырничать (*impf.*)

loafer /ˈləʊfə(r)/ *n.* (person) лóдырь (*m.*); (shoe) кóжаная тýфля ти́па мокаси́н

loam /ləʊm/ *n.* сугли́нок

✓ **loan** /ləʊn/ *n.* **1** (sum lent) заём, ссýда **2** (lending or being lent): **take on ∼**; **have the ∼ of** (of money) брать, взять взаймы́; (of objects) брать, взять на врéмя
● *v.t.* (lend, borrow) од|áлживать, –олжи́ть (*что-н. комý-н, что-н. у когó-н.*)

■ **∼ shark** *n.* (infml) ростовщи́к

loath /ləʊθ/ *pred. adj.*: **he was ∼ to do anything** он ничегó не хотéл дéлать

loathe /ləʊð/ *v.t.* ненави́деть (*impf.*)

loathing /ˈləʊðɪŋ/ *n.* отвращéние; **feel ∼ for** испы́тывать (*impf.*) отвращéние к + *d.*

loathsome /ˈləʊðsəm/ *adj.* отврати́тельный, омерзи́тельный

loaves /ləʊvz/ *pl. of* ▶ **loaf¹**

lob /lɒb/ *n.* (high-pitched ball) свечá
● *v.t.* (**lobbed**, **lobbing**): **∼ a ball** под|авáть, –áть свечý

lobby /ˈlɒbɪ/ *n.* вестибю́ль (*m.*); (theatr.) фойé (*nt. indecl.*); (group) лóбби (*nt. indecl.*)
● *v.i.* агити́ровать (*impf.*)
● *v.t.* агити́ровать, с- (infml)

lobbying /ˈlɒbɪɪŋ/ *n.* агитáция

lobe /ləʊb/ *n.* (of ear) мóчка

lobelia /ləˈbiːlɪə/ *n.* (bot.) лобéлия

lobster /ˈlɒbstə(r)/ *n.* омáр

✓ **local** /ˈləʊk(ə)l/ *n.* (inhabitant) мéстный жи́тель; (BrE, public house) мéстный паб, мéстная пивнáя
● *adj.* мéстный; (of this place) здéшний; **2 o'clock ∼ time** два часá по мéстному врéмени

■ **∼ anaesthetic** *n.* мéстный наркóз; **∼ authority** *n.* (BrE) мéстные влáсти; **∼ call** *n.* мéстный телефóнный разговóр; **∼ government** *n.* мéстное самоуправлéние

locale /ləʊˈkɑːl/ *n.* мéсто (дéйствия); мéстность

locality /ləʊˈkælɪtɪ/ *n.* мéстность; (neighbourhood): **there is no cinema in the ∼** нигдé побли́зости нет кинó

localize /ˈləʊkəlaɪz/ *v.t.* локализовáть (*impf., pf.*)

locally /ˈləʊkəlɪ/ *adv.*: **he is well known ∼** он извéстен в э́тих края́х; **he works ∼** он работает поблизости

✍ **locate** /ləʊˈkeɪt/ v.t. **1** be ~d (situated) находиться (impf.) **2** (determine position of) определ|ять, -и́ть ме́сто/местоположе́ние + g.; **has the fault been ~d?** нашли́ повреждение?; определи́ли ли ме́сто повреждения?

✍ **location** /ləʊˈkeɪʃ(ə)n/ n. **1** (determining of place) определе́ние (ме́ста) **2** (position) местонахожде́ние **3**: **on ~** (cin.) на нату́ре; **shooting on ~** нату́рная съёмка

locative /ˈlɒkətɪv/ n. & adj. (gram.) ме́стный (паде́ж)

loch /lɒk/ n. о́зеро (в Шотла́ндии); **L~ Ness** о́зеро Лох-Не́сс

lock¹ /lɒk/ n. (of hair) ло́кон

lock² /lɒk/ n. **1** (on door or firearm) замо́к; **under ~ and key** под замко́м; (on door or gate) запо́р **2** (on canal) шлюз
● v.t. **1** (secure; restrict movement of) зап|ира́ть, -ере́ть (на замо́к); **I was ~ed out** дверь была́ за́перта, и я не мог войти́ **2** (cause to stop moving or revolving) тормози́ть, за-; **he ~ed the steering** он заблоки́ровал руль **3** (interlace) спле|та́ть, -сти́; **his fingers were ~ed together** он сцепи́л ру́ки
● v.i.: **does this chest ~?** э́тот сунду́к запира́ется?
□ **~ in** v.t. зап|ира́ть, -ере́ть (кого) в ко́мнате/ до́ме и т.п.; **he ~ed himself in** он за́перся на ключ
□ **~ out** v.t. зап|ира́ть, -ере́ть дверь и не впуска́ть
□ **~ up** v.t. зап|ира́ть, -ере́ть на замо́к; (imprison) сажа́ть, посади́ть (в тюрьму)
■ **~smith** n. сле́сарь (m.)

locker /ˈlɒkə(r)/ n. (cupboard) шка́фчик
■ **~ room** n. раздева́лка

locket /ˈlɒkɪt/ n. медальо́н

locomotion /ləʊkəˈməʊʃ(ə)n/ n. передвиже́ние

locomotive /ləʊkəˈməʊtɪv/ n. локомоти́в

locum /ˈləʊkəm/ n. (pl. ~s) (infml) = **locum tenens**

locum tenens /ˈləʊkəm ˈtiːnenz/ n. (pl. **locum tenentes** /ˈləʊkəm trˈnentiːz/) (doctor or clergyman) вре́менный замести́тель (m.)

locust /ˈləʊkəst/ n. саранча́ (also collect.)

lodge /lɒdʒ/ n. **1** (cottage) дом привра́тника **2** (porter's apartment) сторо́жка
● v.t.: **~ a complaint/appeal** обра|ща́ться, -ти́ться с жа́лобой/апелля́цией
● v.i. **1** (live) жить (impf.); прожива́ть (impf.); **he ~s with us** он наш жиле́ц **2** (become stuck) застр|ева́ть, -я́ть; **a bone ~d in his throat** кость застря́ла у него́ в го́рле

lodger /ˈlɒdʒə(r)/ n. жиле́ц

lodging /ˈlɒdʒɪŋ/ n. прожива́ние (see ▸ **board** n. 2); (in pl.) меблиро́ванные ко́мнаты (f. pl.)

loft /lɒft/ n. черда́к

lofty /ˈlɒftɪ/ adj. (**loftier**, **loftiest**) (high) высо́кий; (exalted) возвы́шенный; (haughty)

высокоме́рный

log¹ /lɒg/ n. **1** (of wood) бревно́, чурба́н **2** (for fire) поле́но; **he slept like a ~** он спал как уби́тый
■ **~ cabin** n. (бреве́нчатая) хи́жина

log² /lɒg/ n. (in full **~book**) ва́хтенный журна́л; (of aircraft) бортово́й журна́л; (of car) формуля́р
● v.t. (**logged**, **logging**) (record) занос|и́ть, -ести́ в ва́хтенный журна́л; **~ in/on** (comput.) входи́ть, войти́ в систе́му; **~ out/off** (comput.) выходи́ть, вы́йти из систе́мы
■ **~book** n. = log² n.

loganberry /ˈləʊgənbərɪ/ n. лога́нова я́года (гибрид малины с ежевикой)

logarithm /ˈlɒgərɪð(ə)m/ n. логари́фм

loggerheads /ˈlɒgəhedz/ n. pl.: **they are at ~** они́ в ссо́ре (or не в лада́х) друг с дру́гом

logic /ˈlɒdʒɪk/ n. ло́гика

logical /ˈlɒdʒɪk(ə)l/ adj. (based on logic, e.g. conclusion, explanation) логи́ческий; (reasonable, e.g. action) логи́чный

logistic /ləˈdʒɪstɪk/ adj. организацио́нный

logistical /ləˈdʒɪstɪk(ə)l/ adj. = **logistic**

logistics /ləˈdʒɪstɪks/ n. pl. организа́ция; (mil.) материа́льно-техни́ческое обеспе́чение

logo /ˈləʊgəʊ/ n. (pl. ~s) эмбле́ма

loin /lɔɪn/ n. (meat) филе́ (nt. indecl.) (мясное)

loiter /ˈlɔɪtə(r)/ v.i. ме́шкать (impf.)

loll /lɒl/ v.i. **1** (sit or stand in lazy attitude) сиде́ть/ стоя́ть (impf.) развали́сь **2** (of tongue etc.: hang loose) выва́ливаться (impf.)

lollipop /ˈlɒlɪpɒp/ n. леденец на па́лочке

London /ˈlʌnd(ə)n/ n. Ло́ндон

lone /ləʊn/ adj. одино́кий, уединённый

lonely /ˈləʊnlɪ/ adj. (**lonelier**, **loneliest**) **1** (solitary, alone) одино́кий; **lead a ~ existence** вести́ (det.) одино́кий о́браз жи́зни **2** (isolated) уединённый

loner /ˈləʊnə(r)/ n. (infml) одино́чка (c.g.)

lonesome /ˈləʊnsəm/ adj. одино́кий

✍ **long¹** /lɒŋ/ n.: **I shan't be away for ~** я уезжа́ю ненадо́лго; я ско́ро верну́сь; **it won't take ~** э́то не займёт мно́го вре́мени
● adj. **1** (of space, measurement) дли́нный; **the table is 2 metres ~** длина́ э́того стола́ — два ме́тра; **how ~ is this river?** какова́ длина́ э́той реки́? **2** (of distance) да́льний; **a ~ journey** да́льний/до́лгий путь **3** (of time) до́лгий; **my holiday is 2 weeks ~** мой о́тпуск дли́тся две неде́ли; **for a ~ time** до́лго, давно́; надо́лго; **a ~ time ago** мно́го вре́мени тому́ наза́д; давны́м-давно́ **4** (prolonged) дли́тельный; **a ~ illness** затяжна́я боле́знь
● adv. **1** (a ~ time): **I shan't be ~** я ско́ро верну́сь; я не задержу́сь; **~ after** prep. до́лгое вре́мя по́сле + g.; **~ before** prep. задо́лго до + g.; **~ ago** (давны́м-)давно́; **before ~** вско́ре, ско́ро **2** (for a ~ time): **have you been here ~?** вы здесь давно́?; **~ live the Queen!** да здра́вствует короле́ва! **3** (throughout): **all day ~** це́лый день; **all night ~** всю ночь напролёт **4**: **as ~ as** **I live** пока́ я жив; **stay as ~ as you like**

оставáйтесь, скóлько хотúте; **as ~ as you don't mind** éсли вам всё равнó; éсли вы не возражáете **5**: **so ~!** (infml) покá! **6**: **no ~er** бóльше не; **she no ~er lives here** онá бóльше здесь не живёт; **I can't wait much ~er** намнóго дóльше ждать я не могý

■ **~-awaited** adj. долгождáнный; **~-distance** adj.: **~-distance call** междугорóдный/ междунарóдный вы́зов; **~-distance runner** бегýн на длúнные дистáнции; **~-haired** adj. длинноволóсый; **~ johns** n. pl. кальсóн|ы (pl., g. —); **~ jump** n. прыжóк в длинý; **~-range** adj. (of gun) дальнобóйный; (of forecast, policy, etc.) долгосрóчный; **~-sighted** adj. дальнозóркий; **~-standing** adj. старúнный, долголéтний; **~-term** adj. долгосрóчный; (of plans, etc.) перспектúвный; **~-winded** adj. многослóвный

long² /lɒŋ/ v.i.: **~ for sth** жáждать (impf.) чегó-н.; **~ to do sth** мечтáть (impf.) дéлать чтó-то

longevity /lɒnˈdʒɛvɪtɪ/ n. (of person) долголéтие; (of thing) долговéчность

longing /ˈlɒŋɪŋ/ n. (eager desire) жáжда (**for:** + g.); (melancholy desire) тоскá (**for:** по + d.)

longitude /ˈlɒŋɡɪtjuːd/ n. долготá

loo /luː/ n. (BrE, infml, lavatory) сортúр (infml)

✎ **look** /lʊk/ n. **1** (glance) взгляд **2**: **have, take a ~ at** (examine) осм|áтривать, -отрéть; рассм|áтривать, -отрéть **3**: **have a ~ for** (search for) искáть, по- **4** (expression) выражéние; **there was a ~ of horror on his face** егó лицó выражáло ýжас **5** (appearance) вид; **he has given the shop a new ~** он (пóлностью) преобразúл магазúн; (in pl.) (personal appearance) нарýжность, внéшность

● v.t. **1** (inspect, scrutinize): **~ sb in the face, eye** смотрéть, по- в глазá комý-н. **2** (have the appearance of) вы́глядеть (impf.) + i.; **he made me ~ a fool** он постáвил меня в дурáцкое положéние; **he ~s his age** емý вполнé дашь егó гóды; **she is thirty, but she does not ~ it** ей трúдцать, но éй стóлько не дашь

● v.i. **1** (use one's eyes; pay attention) смотрéть, по-; **he ~ed out of the window to see if she was coming** он посмотрéл в окнó, не идёт ли онá; (search) искáть, по- **2** (face) выходúть (impf.); **the windows ~ on to the garden/street** óкна выхóдят в сад/на ýлицу **3** (appear) вы́глядеть (impf.) + i.; **she is ~ing well** онá хорошó вы́глядит; **everybody ~ed tired** у всех был устáлый вид; **that ~s tasty** у э́того блю́да аппетúтный вид; **things ~ black** плóхо дéло; **that ~s suspicious** э́то подозрúтельно; **~ like** (resemble) вы́глядеть (impf.) + i.; похóдить (impf.) на + a.; **he ~s like his father** он похóж на отцá; (give expectation of): **it ~s like rain** собирáется (or похóже, (что) бýдет) дождь

□ **~ after** v.t. (care for, tend to) ухáживать (impf.) за + i.; (keep safe) хранúть (impf.); (be responsible for) занимáться (impf.) + i.

□ **~ at** v.i. (direct gaze on) смотрéть, по- на + a; **he was ~ing at a book** он смотрéл на кнúгу; (inspect, examine) смотрéть, по- на + a.; осм|áтривать, -отрéть; **the customs men ~ed**

at our luggage тамóженники осмотрéли наш багáж

□ **~ back** v.i.: **once started, there was no ~ing back** раз уж мы нáчали, отступáть бы́ло пóздно; **~ back on** вспоминáть (impf.)

□ **~ down** v.i. (lower one's gaze) опус|кáть, -тúть глазá; **~ down on** смотрéть (impf.) свысокá на + a.; презирáть (impf.)

□ **~ for** v.i. (seek) искáть, по-; **he is ~ing for a job** он úщет мéсто/рабóту

□ **~ forward** v.i.: **~ forward to** предвкушáть (impf.); ждать (impf.) + g. с нетерпéнием; **I ~ forward to meeting you** жду с нетерпéнием, когдá увúжусь с вáми

□ **~ in** v.i. (visit) загля|дывать, -нýть к комý-н., забе|гáть, -жáть к комý-н.

□ **~ into** v.i. (investigate, examine) исслéдовать (impf.); рассм|áтривать, -отрéть

□ **~ on** v.i. (watch without getting involved) наблюдáть, смотрéть (both impf.); (regard) считáть (impf.); **I ~ on him as my son** я считáю егó своúм сы́ном; **~ on to** (face) see ▶ **look** v.i. **2**

□ **~ out** v.i. (be careful) быть начекý/насторожé; **~ out!** осторóжно!; (keep one's eyes open): **she stood at the door ~ing out for the postman** онá стоя́ла в дверя́х, высмáтривая почтальóна; **we are ~ing out for a house** мы присмáтриваем себé

□ **~ round** v.i. (turn one's head) огля|дываться, -нýться; (make an inspection) осм|áтриваться, -отрéться; озирáться (impf.); (inspect) осм|áтривать, -отрéть

□ **~ through** v.i.: **they ~ed through** (sc. examined) **our papers** онú просмотрéли нáши бумáги; **he quickly ~ed through the newspaper** он бы́стро пробежáл глазáми газéту

□ **~ to** v.i. (turn to) обра|щáться, -тúться к + d.; **we ~ed to him for help** мы рассчúтывали на егó пóмощь

□ **~ up** v.t. (visit) навe|щáть, -стúть; (seek information on) оты́ск|ивать, -áть

● v.i. (raise one's eyes) подн|имáть, -я́ть глазá (**at sb:** на когó-н.); (improve) ул|учшáться, -ýчшиться; **things are ~ing up** делá идýт на попрáвку; **~ up to** (respect) уважáть (impf.)

■ **~alike** n. двойнúк; **~-in** n. (BrE, infml) шанс, возмóжность; **~out** n. (post) наблюдáтельный пункт; (watch): **be on the ~out for** (e.g. a house) присмáтривать (impf.) себé

loom¹ /luːm/ n. ткáцкий станóк

loom² /luːm/ v.i. **1** (appear indistinctly) (also **~ up**) нея́сно вырисóвываться (impf.) **2** (impend) нав|исáть, -úснуть

loop /luːp/ n. (also comput.) петля́

loophole /ˈluːphəʊl/ n. (fig.) лазéйка

loose /luːs/ n.: **on the ~** в загýле; на свобóде; на вóле

● adj. **1** (free, unconfined) свобóдный; **break ~** вырвать|ся (pf.) на свобóду; **let ~** (e.g. a dog) спус|кáть, -тúть с цепú **2** (not fastened or held together): **~ papers** отдéльные листы́ **3** (not secure or firm): **at a ~ end** (fig.) без дéла; **I have a ~ tooth** у меня зуб шатáется; **the nut is ~** гáйка разболтáлась; **the button is ~** пýговица болтáется **4** (slack) слáбо натя́нутый; **~ clothes** широ́кая/просто́рная оде́жда **5** (not compact or dense): ~ **weave** непло́тная ткань **6** (imprecise): a ~ **translation** приблизи́тельный/во́льный перево́д **7** (morally lax) распу́щенный

loosen /'luːs(ə)n/ v.t. (tongue) развя́з|ывать, -а́ть; (screw) отви́н|чивать, -ти́ть; (by shaking or pulling) расша́т|ывать, -а́ть; (tie, rope, belt, etc.) осл|абля́ть, -а́бить

loot /luːt/ n. добы́ча
• v.t. гра́бить, раз-

looter /'luːtə(r)/ n. мародёр, граби́тель (m.)

lopsided /lɒp'saɪdɪd/ adj. (grin) криво́й; (fig.) неравноме́рный, односторо́нний

loquacious /lə'kweɪʃəs/ adj. словоохо́тливый, болтли́вый

lord /lɔːd/ n. **1** (BrE, nobleman) лорд **2** (ruler, also fig.) власти́тель (m.); ~ **of the manor** владе́лец поме́стья **3** (God) Госпо́дь; Our L~ (Christ) Госпо́дь
• v.t.: ~ **it over sb** кома́ндовать (impf.) кем-н.

Lordship /'lɔːdʃɪp/ n.: Your ~ ва́ша све́тлость/ ми́лость

lorry /'lɒrɪ/ n. (BrE) грузови́к

✎ **los|e** /luːz/ v.t. (past and p.p. **lost**) **1** теря́ть, по-; ~e **patience** выходи́ть, вы́йти из терпе́ния; ~e **one's temper** серди́ться, рас- **2**: **be, get** ~t (~e one's way) заблуди́ться (pf.); **get** ~t! исче́зни!, кати́сь! (infml); (fig.): ~t **in thought** заду́мавшись **3** (in contest, sport, gambling) прои́гр|ывать, -а́ть; **he** ~t **the argument** его́ победи́ли в спо́ре; **they** ~t **the match** они́ проигра́ли **4** (of a clock) отст|ава́ть, -а́ть на + a.
• v.i. **1** прои́гр|ывать, -а́ть; теря́ть, по-; ~e **out** (infml) потерпе́ть (pf.) неуда́чу **2** (of a clock): **my watch is** ~ing мои́ часы́ отстаю́т
■ ~t **property office** (BrE), ~t **and found department** (AmE) nn. бюро́ нахо́док

loser /'luːzə(r)/ n. (at a game) проигра́вший; (person who habitually fails) неуда́чник; **he is a good (bad)** ~ он (не) уме́ет досто́йно прои́грывать

✎ **loss** /lɒs/ n. **1** поте́ря **2** (monetary) убы́ток **3**: **I am at a** ~ **to answer** я затрудня́юсь отве́тить

lost /lɒst/ past and p.p. of ▶ **lose**

✎ **lot** /lɒt/ n. **1**: **draw** ~s тяну́ть (impf.) жре́бий; (fig., destiny) судьба́, у́часть, до́ля **2** (plot of land) уча́сток **3** (in auction) лот **4**: **the** ~ (BrE, infml, everything) всё; **that's the** ~! вот и всё! **5** (**a** ~, ~s) (a large number, amount) мно́го; a ~ **of people** мно́го наро́ду; мно́гие; **I don't see a** ~ **of him nowadays** тепе́рь мы с ним ма́ло/ре́дко ви́димся; **there were** ~s **of apples left** оста́лась у́йма/ку́ча я́блок; **he plays a** ~ **of football** он мно́го игра́ет в футбо́л
• adv. (**a** ~) **1** (often) ча́сто; **we went to the theatre a** ~ мы ча́сто ходи́ли в теа́тр **2** (with comps.) (much) гора́здо, намно́го; a ~ **worse** гора́здо ху́же

lotion /'ləʊʃ(ə)n/ n. лосьо́н

lottery /'lɒtərɪ/ n. лотере́я

✎ ключева́я ле́ксика

loud /laʊd/ adj. шу́мный; (fig.): ~ **colours** крича́щие кра́ски
• adv. гро́мко; **out** ~ вслух
■ ~**speaker** n. громкоговори́тель (m.), дина́мик

lounge /laʊndʒ/ n. (BrE, sitting room) гости́ная; (at airport) зал ожида́ния; (bar) бар пе́рвого кла́сса
• v.i.: ~ **about** (idly) безде́льничать (impf.)

lousy /'laʊzɪ/ adj. (**lousier, lousiest**) (infml) парши́вый, отврати́тельный

lout /laʊt/ n. хам

loutish /'laʊtɪʃ/ adj. ха́мский; неотёсанный

lovable /'lʌvəb(ə)l/ adj. ми́лый

✎ **love** /lʌv/ n. **1** любо́вь; **he sent you his** ~ он проси́л переда́ть вам серде́чный приве́т; **be in** ~ (**with sb**) быть влюблённым в кого́-н.; **fall in** ~ **with sb** влюб|ля́ться, -и́ться в кого́-н.; **make** ~ (have sexual intercourse) зан|има́ться, -я́ться любо́вью; (BrE, in address): (**my**) ~! (мой) ми́лый!; (моя́) ми́лая! **2** (zero score) ноль (m.)
• v.t. люби́ть (impf.); **I** ~ **the way he smiles** мне ужа́сно нра́вится, как он улыба́ется; **I** ~ **walking in the rain** я обожа́ю гуля́ть под дождём
■ ~ **affair** n. рома́н; (pej.) любо́вная связь

loveless /'lʌvlɪs/ adj. нелюбя́щий, без любви́; ~ **marriage** брак без любви́

lovely /'lʌvlɪ/ adj. (**lovelier, loveliest**) (beautiful) краси́вый; (charming) преле́стный

lover /'lʌvə(r)/ n. **1** любо́вни|к (-ца); (in pl.) влюблённые **2** (devotee) люби́тель m. (-ница)

loving /'lʌvɪŋ/ adj. лю́бящий; (tender) не́жный

✎ **low** /ləʊ/ n. **1** (meteor.) цикло́н **2** (~ point or level): **the pound fell to an all-time** ~ фунт дости́г небыва́ло ни́зкого у́ровня
• adj. **1** ни́зкий, невысо́кий; (of pitch of sound) ни́зкий; (of volume of sound) негро́мкий, ти́хий; **he spoke in a** ~ **voice** он говори́л, пони́зив го́лос (or ти́хим го́лосом); **keep a** ~ **profile** вести́ себя́ сде́ржанно **2** (base) ни́зкий, по́длый; a ~ **trick** по́длая уло́вка **3** (nearly empty; scanty) ни́зкая/плоха́я посеща́емость; **we are getting** ~ **on sugar** у нас остаётся малова́то са́хара **4** (depressed): **I was feeling** ~ мне бы́ло невесе́ло
• adv. ни́зко
■ ~-**alcohol** adj. слабоалкого́льный; ~-**brow** adj. нера́звитый; ~-**calorie** adj. малокалори́йный; ~-**carb** adj. низкоуглево́дный; ~-**carbon** adj. низкоуглеро́дистый; ~-**cut** adj. с ни́зким/ глубо́ким вы́резом; ~-**down** n. (information) подного́тная (infml) • adj. по́длый, скве́рный; ~-**fat** adj. маложи́рный; ~-**key** adj. (fig.) сде́ржанный; ~-**land** n. (usu. in pl.) ни́зменность; ~-**lying** adj. ни́зменный; ~-**paid** adj. малоопла́чиваемый; ~ **tide** (also ~ **water**) n. ма́лая вода́, отли́в

lower /'ləʊə(r)/ adj. ни́жний
• v.t. **1** (e.g. boat, flag) спус|ка́ть, -ти́ть; (eyes) опус|ка́ть, -ти́ть; (price) сни|жа́ть, -и́зить; (voice) пон|ижа́ть, -и́зить **2** (decrease) ум|еньша́ть,

-е́ньшить **3** (debase) ун|ижа́ть, -и́зить

lowly /ˈləʊlɪ/ *adj.* (**lowlier, lowliest**) (humble) скро́мный; (primitive) ни́зший

loyal /ˈlɔɪəl/ *adj.* (faithful) ве́рный; (devoted) пре́данный; (pol.) лоя́льный

loyalist /ˈlɔɪəlɪst/ *n.* лоялӣст (-ка)

loyalty /ˈlɔɪəltɪ/ *n.* ве́рность, пре́данность, лоя́льность

lozenge /ˈlɒzɪndʒ/ *n.* табле́тка(-ледене́ц)

LP *abbr.* (*of* **long-playing record**) долгоигра́ющая пласти́нка

LSD *abbr. of* (chem.) (**lysergic acid diethylamide**) ЛСД (диэтиламӣд лизерги́новой кислоты́)

Ltd /ˈlɪmɪtɪd/ *abbr.* (*of* **limited liability company**) (BrE, comm.) ООО (о́бщество с ограни́ченной отве́тственностью)

lubricate /ˈluːbrɪkeɪt/ *v.t.* сма́з|ывать, -ать

lubrication /luːbrɪˈkeɪʃ(ə)n/ *n.* сма́зывание

lucid /ˈluːsɪd/ *adj.* я́сный

lucidity /luːˈsɪdɪtɪ/ *n.* я́сность

luck /lʌk/ *n.*: **good/bad** ~ сча́стье/несча́стье; **good** ~!; **the best of** ~! жела́ю сча́стья/ уда́чи/успе́ха!; **bad, hard** ~! не повезло́!

luckily /ˈlʌkɪlɪ/ *adv.* к сча́стью

✍ **lucky** /ˈlʌkɪ/ *adj.* (**luckier, luckiest**) **1** (of person) счастли́вый, уда́чливый; (of things, actions, events) уда́чный; **you're** ~ **to be alive** скажи́ спаси́бо, что оста́лся в живы́х **2** (bringing luck): **a** ~ **charm** счастли́вый талисма́н

lucrative /ˈluːkrətɪv/ *adj.* при́быльный

lucre /ˈluːkə(r)/ *n.* при́быль, нажи́ва; **filthy** ~ презре́нный мета́лл

ludicrous /ˈluːdɪkrəs/ *adj.* смехотво́рный

lug /lʌg/ *v.t.* (**lugged, lugging**) (infml) тащи́ть (*impf.*)

luggage /ˈlʌgɪdʒ/ *n.* бага́ж

■ ~ **rack** *n.* (on train, bus) се́тка/по́лка для багажа́

lugubrious /luˈguːbrɪəs/ *adj.* (mournful) скро́бный; (dismal) мрáчный

lukewarm /luːkˈwɔːm/ *adj.* теплова́тый

lull /lʌl/ *n.* (in storm, fighting, etc.) зати́шье; (in conversation) па́уза, переры́в
● *v.t.* (~ **to sleep**) убаю́к|ивать, -ать; ~ **sb into a false sense of security** усып|ля́ть, -и́ть чью-н. бди́тельность

lullaby /ˈlʌləbaɪ/ *n.* колыбе́льная (пе́сня)

lumbar /ˈlʌmbə(r)/ *adj.* поясни́чный

lumber¹ /ˈlʌmbə(r)/ *n.* (AmE, timber) пиломатериа́лы (*m. pl.*)
● *v.t.* (BrE, encumber) обремен|я́ть (*impf.*); **I'm** ~**ed with my mother-in-law** тёща сиди́т у меня́ на ше́е
■ ~**jack** *n.* лесору́б

lumber² /ˈlʌmbə(r)/ *v.i.* (*also* ~ **along**) дви́гаться (*impf.*) тяжело́

luminary /ˈluːmɪnərɪ/ *n.* свети́ло

luminous /ˈluːmɪnəs/ *adj.* светя́щийся

lump /lʌmp/ *n.* **1** (of earth, dough, etc.) ком; ~ **of sugar** кусо́к са́хара; ~ **in the throat** комо́к в го́рле **2** (swelling) ши́шка, о́пухоль
● *v.t.*: ~ **together** (treat alike) ста́вить (*impf.*)

на одну́ до́ску

■ ~ **sum** *n.* единовре́менно выпла́чиваемая су́мма

lumpectomy /lʌmˈpektəmɪ/ *n.* (med.) удале́ние о́пухоли моло́чной железы́

lumpy /ˈlʌmpɪ/ *adj.* (**lumpier, lumpiest**) комкова́тый

lunacy /ˈluːnəsɪ/ *n.* безу́мие

lunar /ˈluːnə(r)/ *adj.* лу́нный

lunatic /ˈluːnətɪk/ *n.* сумасше́дший

✍ **lunch** /lʌntʃ/ *n.* обе́д
● *v.i.* обе́дать, по-
■ ~ **break**, ~ **hour**, ~**time** *nn.* обе́денный переры́в

lung /lʌŋ/ *n.* лёгкое

lunge /lʌndʒ/ *v.i.* (**lungeing** *or* **lunging**) бро́ситься (*pf.*) (forward: вперёд; at: на + *a.*)

lupin /ˈluːpɪn/ *n.* люпи́н

lurch¹ /lɜːtʃ/ *n.*: **leave sb in the** ~ пок|ида́ть, -и́нуть кого́-н. в беде́

lurch² /lɜːtʃ/ *v.i.* шата́ться (*impf.*); **the drunken man** ~**ed across the street** пья́ный, пошатываясь, перешёл у́лицу

lure /ljʊə(r)/ *n.* (decoy) прима́нка; (fig., enticement) соблазн; **the** ~ **of foreign travel** зама́нчивость заграни́чных путеше́ствий
● *v.t.* (persons) зама́н|ивать, -и́ть; **a rival firm** ~**d him away** конкури́рующая фи́рма перемани́ла его́ (к себе́)

lurid /ˈljʊərɪd/ *adj.* (gaudy) крича́щий; (sensational) сенсацио́нный; ~ **details** жу́ткие подро́бности

lurk /lɜːk/ *v.i.* прита́|иваться, -и́ться

luscious /ˈlʌʃəs/ *adj.* (succulent) со́чный

lush /lʌʃ/ *adj.* пы́шный, роско́шный

lust /lʌst/ *n.* **1** (sexual passion) по́хоть **2** (craving): ~ **for power** жа́жда вла́сти
● *v.i.*: ~ **for, after sb** испы́т|ывать, -а́ть вожделе́ние к кому́-н.

luster /ˈlʌstə(r)/ *n.* (AmE) = lustre

lustful /ˈlʌstfʊl/ *adj.* похотли́вый

lustre /ˈlʌstə(r)/ (AmE **luster**) *n.* блеск

lustrous /ˈlʌstrəs/ *adj.* (brilliant) блестя́щий; (glossy) гля́нцевитый

lusty /ˈlʌstɪ/ *adj.* (**lustier, lustiest**) (healthy) здоро́вый; (vigorous) бо́дрый

lute /luːt/ *n.* (mus.) лю́тня

Luxembourg /ˈlʌksəmbɜːg/ *n.* Люксембу́рг
● *adj.* люксембу́ргский

Luxembourger /ˈlʌksəmbɜːgə(r)/ *n.* люксембу́рж|ец (-енка)

luxuriance /lʌgˈzjʊərɪəns/ *n.* изоби́лие; пы́шность

luxuriant /lʌgˈzjʊərɪənt/ *adj.* (of growth) бу́йный

luxuriate /lʌgˈzjʊərɪeɪt/ *v.i.* (enjoy oneself): ~ **in sth** наслажда́ться (*impf.*) чем-н.

luxurious /lʌgˈzjʊərɪəs/ *adj.* роско́шный

luxury /ˈlʌkʃərɪ/ *n.* **1** (luxuriousness) ро́скошь **2** (object of) ~ предме́т ро́скоши; ~ **apartment** роско́шная кварти́ра

lying /ˈlaɪɪŋ/ *n.* (telling lies) ложь
● *adj.* лжи́вый

lymph /lɪmf/ *n.* (physiol.) ли́мфа
■ ~ **gland/node** *nn.* лимфати́ческий у́зел
lynch /lɪntʃ/ *v.t.* линчева́ть (*impf., pf.*)
lynchpin /lɪntʃpɪn/ *n.* = linchpin
lyre /ˈlaɪə(r)/ *n.* ли́ра
■ ~**bird** *n.* пти́ца-ли́ра, лирохво́ст

lyric /ˈlɪrɪk/ *n.* (*usu. in pl.*) (words of song) слова́ (*nt. pl.*), текст
lyrical /ˈlɪrɪk(ə)l/ *adj.* лири́ческий; **he waxed ~ about, over** ... он расчу́вствовался, говоря́ о...
lyricist /ˈlɪrɪsɪst/ *n.* а́втор слов/те́кста (*песни/ мюзикла*)

Mm

m /ˈmiːtə(r)(z)/ *n.* (*abbr. of* **metre(s)**) м (метр)
m|- *pref.* моби́льный; ~-**commerce** моби́льная комме́рция
MA *abbr.* (*of Master of Arts*) маги́стр гуманита́рных нау́к
mac /mæk/ *n.* (BrE, infml) = mackintosh
macabre /məˈkɑːbr(ə)/ *adj.* мра́чный
macaroni /mækəˈrəʊnɪ/ *n.* макаро́н|ы (*pl., g.* —)
Macedonia /mæsəˈdəʊnɪə/ *n.* Македо́ния
Macedonian /mæsɪˈdəʊnɪən/ *n.* македо́н|ец (-ка)
  ● *adj.* македо́нский
machination /mækɪˈneɪʃ(ə)n/ *n.* (*usu. in pl.*) махина́ция; ко́зни (*f. pl.*); интри́га
⚹ **machine** /məˈʃiːn/ *n.* маши́на, механи́зм
■ ~ **gun** *n.* пулемёт; ~-**readable** *adj.* (comput.) машиночита́емый
machinery /məˈʃiːnərɪ/ *n.* (collect.) (machines) маши́ны (*f. pl.*); (fig.): **the ~ of government** прави́тельственные структу́ры (*f. pl.*)
machinist /məˈʃiːnɪst/ *n.* машини́ст; (BrE, sewing machine operator) шве́йник (швея́)
macho /ˈmætʃəʊ/ *adj.* мужско́й, мужи́цкий; му́жественный
macintosh *see* ▸ mackintosh
mackerel /ˈmækr(ə)l/ *n.* (*pl.* ~ *or* ~**s**) ску́мбрия
mackintosh, macintosh /ˈmækɪntɒʃ/ *n.* (BrE) дождеви́к (*плащ*)
macro /ˈmækrəʊ/ *n.* (*pl.* ~**s**) (comput.) макрокома́нда
macrocosm /ˈmækrəʊkɒz(ə)m/ *n.* макроко́см(ос)
mad /mæd/ *adj.* (**madder, maddest**)
1 (insane) сумасше́дший; **go ~** сходи́ть, сойти́ с ума́; **drive sb ~** св|оди́ть, -ести́ кого́-н. с ума́ **2** (of animals) бе́шеный **3** (wildly foolish) шально́й; ~**ly in love** безу́мно влюблённый **4** (infml, angry) серди́тый; **be, get ~** вы́йти (*pf.*) из себя́; **she was ~ with me for breaking the vase** она́ разозли́лась на меня́ за то, что я разби́л ва́зу **5**: **~ about** (infatuated with, enthusiastic for) в восто́рге (*or* без па́мяти) от + *g.*
■ ~ **cow disease** *n.* коро́вье бе́шенство; ~**man** *n.* сумасше́дший
Madagascar /mædəˈɡæskə(r)/ *n.* Мадагаска́р
madam /ˈmædəm/ *n.* (form of address) мада́м, госпожа́
maddening /ˈmædənɪŋ/ *adj.* несно́сный
made /meɪd/ *past and p.p. of* ▸ make
■ ~**-to-measure** *adj.* сде́ланный (как) на зака́з
Madeira /məˈdɪərə/ *n.* Маде́йра; (wine) маде́ра
madness /ˈmædnɪs/ *n.* (insanity) сумасше́ствие; (folly) безу́мие
Madrid /məˈdrɪd/ *n.* Мадри́д
madrigal /ˈmædrɪɡ(ə)l/ *n.* мадрига́л
maestr|o /ˈmaɪstrəʊ/ *n.* ~**i** *or* ~**os** маэ́стро (*m. indecl.*)
Mafia /ˈmæfɪə/ *n.* ма́фия
magazine¹ /mæɡəˈziːn/ *n.* (cartridge chamber) магази́н (*автома́та*)
⚹ **magazine²** /mæɡəˈziːn/ *n.* (periodical) журна́л
magenta /məˈdʒentə/ *n. & adj.* краснова́то-лило́вый/пурпу́рный цвет
maggot /ˈmæɡət/ *n.* личи́нка
magic /ˈmædʒɪk/ *n.* (lit., fig.) ма́гия, волшебство́
  ● *adj.* волше́бный, маги́ческий
magical /ˈmædʒɪk(ə)l/ *adj.* волше́бный
magician /məˈdʒɪʃ(ə)n/ *n.* (sorcerer) волше́бник; (conjurer) фо́кусник
magisterial /mædʒɪˈstɪərɪəl/ *adj.* (of a magistrate) суде́йский; (authoritative) авторите́тный
magistrate /ˈmædʒɪstreɪt/ *n.* мирово́й судья́ (*m.*)
magnanimous /mæɡˈnænɪməs/ *adj.* великоду́шный
magnate /ˈmæɡneɪt/ *n.* магна́т
magnesium /mæɡˈniːzɪəm/ *n.* ма́гний
magnet /ˈmæɡnɪt/ *n.* (lit., fig.) магни́т
magnetic /mæɡˈnetɪk/ *adj.* магни́тный
magnetism /ˈmæɡnɪtɪz(ə)m/ *n.* магнети́зм
magnetize /ˈmæɡnɪtaɪz/ *v.t.* намагни́|чивать, -тить; (fig.) гипнотизи́ровать, за-

⚹ ключева́я ле́ксика

magnification /ˌmæɡnɪfɪˈkeɪʃ(ə)n/ *n.* увеличе́ние; (of a radio signal) усиле́ние; (exaggeration) преувеличе́ние

magnificence /mæɡˈnɪfɪs(ə)ns/ *n.* великоле́пие

magnificent /mæɡˈnɪfɪs(ə)nt/ *adj.* великоле́пный

magnify /ˈmæɡnɪfaɪ/ *v.t.* увели́чи|вать, -ть
■ ~**ing glass** *n.* увеличи́тельное стекло́, лу́па

magnitude /ˈmæɡnɪtjuːd/ *n.* (size) величина́; (importance) ва́жность

magnolia /mæɡˈnəʊlɪə/ *n.* **1** (tree) магно́лия **2** (colour) кре́мовый цвет

magpie /ˈmæɡpaɪ/ *n.* соро́ка

mahogany /məˈhɒɡənɪ/ *n.* (wood, tree) кра́сное де́рево

maid /meɪd/ *n.* (domestic servant) прислу́га; (in hotel) го́рничная
■ ~**servant** *n.* прислу́га, служа́нка

maiden /ˈmeɪd(ə)n/ *n.* де́ва
● *adj.* **1** (of a girl) де́вичий **2** (first): ~ **speech** пе́рвая речь (новоизбранного чле́на парла́мента); ~ **voyage** пе́рвый рейс
■ ~ **name** *n.* де́вичья фами́лия

mail /meɪl/ *n.* **1** (postal system) по́чта **2** (letters) по́чта, пи́сьма (*nt. pl.*)
● *v.t.* отправ|ля́ть, -а́вить (по по́чте); **the firm has me on its** ~**ing list** я состою́ в спи́ске подпи́счиков фи́рмы
■ ~**box** *n.* (AmE, also comput.) почто́вый я́щик; ~**man** *n.* (AmE) почтальо́н; ~ **order** *n.* почто́вый зака́з; ~**order** *adj.* торгу́ющий по почто́вым зака́зам; ~**shot** *n.* (BrE) рекла́мная рассы́лка

maim /meɪm/ *v.t.* кале́чить, ис-

main /meɪn/ *n.* (*in sg. and* (BrE) *in pl.*) (principal supply line) магистра́ль; (sewerage) канализа́ция; (water) водопрово́д; водопрово́дная магистра́ль; (gas) газопрово́д; (electricity) ка́бель (*m.*)
● *adj.* гла́вный, основно́й; ~ **street** гла́вная у́лица
■ ~ **course** *n.* (of meal) основно́е блю́до; ~**land** *n.* (continent) матери́к; (opp. island): **they live on the** ~**land** они́ живу́т на большо́й земле́; ~ **line** *n.* (rail.) железнодоро́жная магистра́ль; ~ **road** *n.* магистра́ль, гла́вная доро́га; ~**stream** *n.* (fig.) госпо́дствующая тенде́нция

mainframe /ˈmeɪnfreɪm/ *adj.*: ~ **computer** больша́я ЭВМ

mainly /ˈmeɪnlɪ/ *adv.* гла́вным о́бразом

maintain /meɪnˈteɪn/ *v.t.* **1** (keep up) подде́рживать (*impf.*); (preserve) сохран|я́ть, -и́ть **2** (support) содержа́ть (*impf.*); **he has a wife and child to** ~ ему́ прихо́дится содержа́ть жену́ и ребёнка **3** (keep in repair) обслу́живать (*impf.*) **4** (assert as true) утвержда́ть (*impf.*); **he** ~**ed his innocence** он наста́ивал на свое́й невино́вности

maintenance /ˈmeɪntənəns/ *n.* **1** (maintaining) подде́ржание **2** (of dependants) содержа́ние **3** (of machinery etc.) (техни́ческое) обслу́живание

maisonette /ˌmeɪzəˈnet/ *n.* двухэта́жная кварти́ра

maize /meɪz/ *n.* кукуру́за, маи́с

majestic /məˈdʒestɪk/ *adj.* вели́чественный

majesty /ˈmædʒɪstɪ/ *n.* (stateliness) вели́чественность; (title): **His/Her M**~ Его́/Её Вели́чество

⚔ **major** /ˈmeɪdʒə(r)/ *n.* **1** (rank) майо́р **2** (mus.) мажо́р; **C** ~ до мажо́р **3** (AmE, main subject of study) основно́й предме́т (*в колле́дже*)
● *adj.* **1** (greater) бо́льший; (principal, more important) гла́вный; ~ **road** гла́вная доро́га **2** (significant) кру́пный; **a** ~ **operation** кру́пная опера́ция **3** (mus.) мажо́рный; ~ **key** мажо́рная тона́льность
● *v.i.*: **he** ~**ed in physics** (AmE) он специализи́ровался по фи́зике

Majorca /məˈjɔːkə/ *n.* Мальо́рка

⚔ **majority** /məˈdʒɒrɪtɪ/ *n.* **1** большинство́; бо́льшая часть; (in elections etc.): **the government has a** ~ **of 60** у прави́тельства — большинство́ в 60 голосо́в

⚔ **make** /meɪk/ *n.* (brand): **a good** ~ **of car** автомоби́ль хоро́шей ма́рки
● *v.t.* (*past and p.p.* **made**) **1** (create, construct) де́лать, с-; (build) стро́ить, по-; **what is this made of?** из чего́ э́то сде́лано? **2** (sew) шить, с-; **a suit made to order** костю́м, сши́тый на зака́з **3** (manufacture) изгот|а́вливать, -о́вить; произво|ди́ть, -ести́; **the factory** ~**s shoes** фа́брика произво́дит о́бувь **4** (prepare) гото́вить, при-; ва́рить, с-; **she made breakfast** она́ приго́товила за́втрак; ~ **a bed** (prepare it for sleeping) стели́ть, по- посте́ль; (tidy it after use) уб|ира́ть, -ра́ть посте́ль **5** (equal) равня́ться (*impf.*) + *d.*; **four plus two** ~**s six** четы́ре плюс два равня́ется шести́; (constitute): **it** ~**s sense** э́то разу́мно **6** (understand) пон|има́ть, -я́ть; **what do you** ~ **of this sentence?** как вы понима́ете э́то предложе́ние? (estimate): **what do you** ~ **the time?** кото́рый час на ва́ших часа́х? **7** (reach) дост|ига́ть, -и́чь + *g.*; **he made it** (*sc. succeeded*) **after three years** он дости́г успе́ха че́рез три го́да; (earn) зараб|а́тывать, -о́тать; **he** ~**s a good living** он хорошо́ зараба́тывает **8** (cause to be) де́лать, с- + *a. and i.*; **the rain** ~**s the road slippery** от дождя́ доро́га стано́вится ско́льзкой; ~ **sb angry** серди́ть, рас- кого́-н.; (appoint, elect): **they made him chairman** его́ вы́брали председа́телем **9** (compel, cause to) заст|авля́ть, -а́вить; **I'll** ~ **you pay for this!** вы у меня́ за э́то запла́тите!; **don't** ~ **me laugh!** не смеши́те меня́!; ~ **do with/without both** об|ходи́ться, -ойти́сь чем-н./без чего́-н.
● *v.i.* (*past and p.p.* **made**) (with ceratin preps.: move, proceed): ~ **after** пус|ка́ться, -ти́ться вслед за + *i.*; ~ **for** (head towards) напр|авля́ться, -а́виться на + *a.* or к + *d.*
□ ~ **off** *v.i.* (hurry away) сбе|га́ть, -жа́ть
□ ~ **out** *v.t.* (write out): ~ **out a bill/cheque** выпи́сывать, вы́писать счёт/чек; (assert) утвержда́ть (*impf.*); **they** ~ **out he was drunk** они́ утвержда́ют, что он был пьян; (understand) раз|бира́ться, -обра́ться в + *p.*; **I can't** ~ **him out** я не могу́ его́ поня́ть; (discern, distinguish)

m

различ|а́ть, -и́ть

□ ~ **up** *v.t.* (pay; pay the residue of) допла́|чивать, -ти́ть; **I shall ~ up the difference out of my own pocket** я доплачу́ ра́зницу из своего́ карма́на; (repay) возме|ща́ть, -сти́ть; **we must ~ it up to him somehow** мы должны́ ка́к-то возмести́ть ему́ э́то; (prepare) гото́вить, при-/ из-; ~ **up a bed** заст|ила́ть, -ели́ть посте́ль; (fig.): ~ **up one's mind** реш|а́ть, -и́ть; (form, compose) сост|авля́ть, -а́вить; **life is made up of disappointments** жизнь полна́ разочарова́ний; (invent) выду́мывать, вы́думать; сочин|я́ть, -и́ть; **the whole story was made up** вся э́та исто́рия была́ вы́думана; (assemble) соб|ира́ть, -ра́ть; ~ **(it) up** (be reconciled) мири́ться, по-; (with cosmetics) кра́сить, по-; **she was heavily made up** она́ была́ си́льно накра́шена

□ ~ **up for** (compensate for) возме|ща́ть, -сти́ть; **this will ~ up for everything** э́тим всё бу́дет компенси́ровано

■ ~**-believe** *n.*: **he lives in a world of ~-believe** он живёт в ми́ре грёз; ~**shift** *adj.*: **a ~shift shelter** на́скоро ско́лоченное укры́тие; ~**-up** *n.* (composition): **there is some cowardice in his ~-up** в нём не́сколько трусова́т; (cosmetics) макия́ж, косме́тика; (theatr., etc.) грим; ~**-up artist** *n.* визажи́ст; ~**-up room** *n.* гримёрная

maker /'meɪkə(r)/ *n.* производи́тель (*m.*)

making /'meɪkɪŋ/ *n.* **1** (potential qualities): **he has all the ~s of a general** у него́ есть все зада́тки, чтобы стать генера́лом **2** (creation) созда́ние; **the difficulties were not of my ~** э́ти тру́дности возни́кли не из-за меня́; (manufacture, production) изготовле́ние, произво́дство; (preparation) приготовле́ние

malachite /'mæləkaɪt/ *n.* малахи́т; (*attr.*) малахи́товый

maladjusted /ˌmælə'dʒʌstɪd/ *adj.* (fig., of person) пло́хо приспосо́бленный

malady /'mælədɪ/ *n.* (lit., fig.) неду́г, боле́знь

malaise /mə'leɪz/ *n.* (bodily discomfort) недомога́ние; (disquiet) беспоко́йство

malaria /mə'leərɪə/ *n.* маляри́я

Malay /mə'leɪ/ *n.* & *adj.* = Malayan

Malaya /mə'leɪə/ *n.* Мала́йя

Malayan /mə'leɪən/ *n.* (person) мала́|ец (-йка); (language) мала́йский язы́к
● *adj.* мала́йский

Malaysia /mə'leɪʒə/ *n.* Мала́йзия

Malaysian /mə'leɪʒ(ə)n/ *adj.* малайзи́йский
● *n.* малайзи́|ец (-йка)

malcontent /'mælkəntent/ *n.* & *adj.* недово́льный

♂ **male** /meɪl/ *n.* (person) мужчи́на (*m.*); (animal etc.) саме́ц
● *adj.* мужско́й; ~ **pigeon** го́лубь-саме́ц

malevolence /mə'levələns/ *n.* недоброжела́тельность, злора́дство

malevolent /mə'levələnt/ *adj.* недоброжела́тельный, злора́дный

malformation /ˌmælfɔː'meɪʃ(ə)n/ *n.* непра́вильное образова́ние, поро́к разви́тия;

уро́дство

malformed /mæl'fɔːmd/ *adj.* непра́вильно/ пло́хо сформиро́ванный

malfunction /mæl'fʌŋkʃ(ə)n/ *n.* неиспра́вная рабо́та, отка́з
● *v.i.* неиспра́вно де́йствовать (*impf.*)

malice /'mælɪs/ *n.* зло́ба; **I bear you no ~** я не пита́ю к вам зло́бы

malicious /mə'lɪʃəs/ *adj.* (of person) злой; (of thought, act, etc.) зло́бный

malign /mə'laɪn/ *v.t.* клевета́ть, о- (*кого*), на- (*на кого*); **he ~ed me** он оклевета́л меня́, он наклевета́л на меня́

malignant /mə'lɪɡnənt/ *adj.* злой, зло́бный; (med.) злока́чественный

malinger /mə'lɪŋɡə(r)/ *v.i.* симули́ровать (*impf., pf.*) боле́знь

malingerer /mə'lɪŋɡərə(r)/ *n.* симуля́нт (-ка)

mall /mæl/ *n.* торго́вый центр

mallard /'mælɑːd/ *n.* (*pl.* ~ *or* ~**s**) кря́ква

malleable /'mælɪəb(ə)l/ *adj.* пода́тливый

mallet /'mælɪt/ *n.* деревя́нный молото́к

malnutrition /ˌmælnjuː'trɪʃ(ə)n/ *n.* недоеда́ние

malpractice /mæl'præktɪs/ *n.* (of doctor) престу́пная небре́жность (врача́); (law, abuse of trust) злоупотребле́ние дове́рием

Malta /'mɔːltə/ *n.* Ма́льта

Maltese /mɔːl'tiːz/ *n.* (*pl.* ~) (person) мальти́|ец (-йка); (language) мальти́йский язы́к
● *adj.* мальти́йский

maltreat /mæl'triːt/ *v.t.* ду́рно обраща́ться (*impf.*) с + *i.*

maltreatment /mæl'triːtmənt/ *n.* дурно́е обраще́ние (*с кем*)

mammal /'mæm(ə)l/ *n.* млекопита́ющее (живо́тное)

mammogram /'mæməɡræm/ *n.* маммогра́мма

mammoth /'mæməθ/ *n.* ма́монт
● *adj.* (huge) гига́нтский, грома́дный

♂ **man** /mæn/ *n.* (*pl.* **men**) **1** (adult male) мужчи́на (*m.*); **they talked ~ to ~** они́ говори́ли как мужчи́на с мужчи́ной; **old ~** стари́к **2** (mankind) челове́к, челове́чество **3** (person) челове́к (лю́ди) **4** (husband) муж **5** (piece in chess) ша́хматная фигу́ра; (in draughts) ша́шка
● *v.t.* (**manned, manning**) **1** (a post) зан|има́ть, -я́ть **2** (guns, machines) обслу́живать (*impf.*)

■ ~**hole** *n.* люк; ~**-made** *adj.* иску́сственный; (text.) синтети́ческий; ~**power** *n.* рабо́чая си́ла

♂ **manag|e** /'mænɪdʒ/ *v.t.* **1** (control, conduct) управля́ть, руководи́ть, заве́довать (*all impf.* + *i.*); **they ~ed the business between them** они́ вдвоём управля́ли предприя́тием **2** (handle) владе́ть (*impf.*) + *i.*; **I can't ~e it** это мне не по си́лам **3** (be ~er of): **he has ~ed the team for 10 years** он руководи́л кома́ндой в тече́ние десяти́

лет; the singer was looking for someone
to ∼e him певе́ц поды́скивал себе́
импресса́рио **4** (cope with) справля́ться,
-а́виться с + *i.*; I can't ∼e this work я не
спра́влюсь с э́той рабо́той **5** (contrive)
суме́ть (*pf.*); I ∼ed to convince him мне
удало́сь убеди́ть его́
 • *v.i.* (cope) справля́ться, -а́виться; (get by,
make do) об|ходи́ться, -ойти́сь
 ■ ∼ing director *n.* дире́ктор-распоряди́тель
(*m.*)
manageable /ˈmænɪdʒəb(ə)l/ *adj.*
выполни́мый
⚹ **management** /ˈmænɪdʒmənt/ *n.* **1** (control,
controlling) управле́ние (*чем*), ме́неджмент
2 (handling person or thing) обраще́ние; staff ∼
обраще́ние с ли́чным соста́вом **3** (managers)
администра́ция, дире́кция
⚹ **manager** /ˈmænɪdʒə(r)/ *n.* (controller of business
etc.) заве́дующий (*чем*); (sport) ста́рший
тре́нер; (of sb's career) ме́неджер
manageress /mænɪdʒəˈres/ *n.* заве́дующая
(*чем*)
managerial /mænɪˈdʒɪərɪəl/ *adj.*
администрати́вный; управле́нческий
mandarin /ˈmændərɪn/ *n.* (orange) мандари́н
mandate /ˈmændeɪt/ *n.* (official order) манда́т;
(given by voters) нака́з
mandatory /ˈmændətərɪ/ *adj.* обяза́тельный
mandolin /ˈmændəlɪn/ *n.* мандоли́на
mane /meɪn/ *n.* гри́ва
maneuver /məˈnuːvə(r)/ *n.*, *v.t.*, & *v.i.* (AmE)
= manoeuvre
manful /ˈmænfʊl/ *adj.* му́жественный
manger /ˈmeɪndʒə(r)/ *n.* я́сл|и (-ей)
mangle /ˈmæŋg(ə)l/ *v.t.* (mutilate) уро́довать, из-
mango /ˈmæŋgəʊ/ *n.* (*pl.* ∼es *or* ∼s) ма́нго
(*nt. indecl.*)
mangy /ˈmeɪndʒɪ/ *adj.* (**mangier**,
mangiest) парши́вый, шелуди́вый (infml)
manhandle /ˈmænhænd(ə)l/ *v.t.* (move by
manual effort) та|ска́ть (*indet.*), -щи́ть (*det.*)
(вручну́ю); (treat roughly) изб|ива́ть, -и́ть
mania /ˈmeɪnɪə/ *n.* ма́ния
maniac /ˈmeɪnɪæk/ *n.* манья́к
manic /ˈmænɪk/ *n.* безу́мный
manicure /ˈmænɪkjʊə(r)/ *n.* маникю́р
 • *v.t.* де́лать, с- маникю́р + *d.*
manicurist /ˈmænɪkjʊərɪst/ *n.* (female)
маникю́рша
manifest /ˈmænɪfest/ *adj.* я́вный, очеви́дный
 • *v.t.* (show clearly) я́сно пока́з|ывать, -а́ть;
(exhibit) прояв|ля́ть, -и́ть
manifestation /mænɪfeˈsteɪʃ(ə)n/ *n.*
проявле́ние
manifesto /mænɪˈfestəʊ/ *n.* (*pl.* ∼s) манифе́ст
manifold /ˈmænɪfəʊld/ *adj.* (numerous)
многочи́сленный; (various) разнообра́зный
manikin /ˈmænɪkɪn/ *n.* (very small person)
челове́чек; (artist's dummy) манеке́н
Manila /məˈnɪlə/ *n.* Мани́ла
 • *adj.* мани́льский
 ■ ∼ **paper** *n.* мани́льская бума́га

⚹ **manipulate** /məˈnɪpjʊleɪt/ *v.t.* (lit., fig., also
pej.) манипули́ровать (*impf.*) (+ *i.*)
manipulation /mənɪpjʊˈleɪʃ(ə)n/ *n.*
манипуля́ция
manipulative /məˈnɪpjʊlətɪv/ *adj.* (person)
жуликова́тый (infml); (behaviour, practice)
жу́льнический (infml)
mankind /mænˈkaɪnd/ *n.* челове́чество
manliness /ˈmænlɪnɪs/ *n.* му́жественность
manly /ˈmænlɪ/ *adj.* (**manlier**, **manliest**)
подоба́ющий мужчи́не
mannequin /ˈmænɪkɪn/ *n.* (person)
манеке́нщица; (dummy) манеке́н
⚹ **manner** /ˈmænə(r)/ *n.* **1** (way, fashion, mode)
о́браз; in a ∼ of speaking в не́котором
смы́сле **2** (in pl.) (ways of life; customs) обы́чаи
(*m. pl.*) **3** (style of behaviour) мане́ра; he has
an awkward ∼ он де́ржится нело́вко **4** (in
pl.) (behaviour) мане́ры (*f. pl.*); good, bad ∼s
хоро́шие/плохи́е мане́ры; (polite behaviour):
have you no ∼s? как ты себя́ веде́шь?
mannered /ˈmænəd/ *adj.* (affected) мане́рный
mannerism /ˈmænərɪz(ə)m/ *n.* (affected
habitual gesture etc.) мане́ра; (excessive use of these)
мане́рность
manoeuvrable /məˈnuːvrəb(ə)l/ (AmE
maneuverable) *adj.* мане́вренный,
подвижно́й
manoeuvre /məˈnuːvə(r)/ (AmE **maneuver**)
n. манёвр
 • *v.t.* маневри́ровать (*impf.*) + *i.*; I ∼d him to
his chair мне удало́сь довести́ его́ к сту́лу
 • *v.i.* (lit., fig.) маневри́ровать (*impf.*)
manor /ˈmænə(r)/ *n.* (estate) поме́стье; (∼
house) особня́к
mansion /ˈmænʃ(ə)n/ *n.* особня́к
manslaughter /ˈmænslɔːtə(r)/ *n.*
непредумы́шленное уби́йство
mantel /ˈmænt(ə)l/, **mantelpiece**
/ˈmænt(ə)lpiːs/ *nn.* ками́нная по́лка
mantra /ˈmæntrə/ *n.* ма́нтра
manual /ˈmænjʊəl/ *n.* (handbook) посо́бие
 • *adj.* (operated by hand) ручно́й
 ■ ∼ **labour** *n.* физи́ческий труд
manufacture /mænjʊˈfæktʃə(r)/ *n.*
изготовле́ние; (on large scale) произво́дство
 • *v.t.* изгот|а́вливать, -о́вить; произв|оди́ть,
-ести́; ∼ed goods промтова́ры (*m. pl.*)
⚹ **manufacturer** /mænjʊˈfæktʃərə(r)/ *n.*
изготови́тель (*m.*), производи́тель (*m.*)
manure /məˈnjʊə(r)/ *n.* наво́з
manuscript /ˈmænjʊskrɪpt/ *n.* ру́копись
⚹ **many** /ˈmenɪ/ *adj.* (**more**, **most**) мно́гие; ∼
times мно́го раз; half as ∼ вдво́е ме́ньше;
twice as ∼ вдво́е бо́льше; as, so ∼ (as)
сто́лько(, ско́лько); not as ∼ не так мно́го,
как; not ∼ немно́го, не так уж мно́го
⚹ **map** /mæp/ *n.* ка́рта; (e.g. of railway system)
схе́ма; town ∼ план го́рода
 • *v.t.* (**mapped**, **mapping**): ∼ out (make
∼ of): he ∼ped out his route before leaving
он соста́вил маршру́т пе́ред отъе́здом; (fig.,
plan) плани́ровать, рас-; he ∼ped out his

m

plans он прики́нул, что ему́ ну́жно де́лать

maple /'meɪp(ə)l/ *n.* клён; (*attr.*) кле́новый

marathon /'mærəθ(ə)n/ *n.* марафо́н
■ ~ **runner** *n.* марафо́нец

maraud /mə'rɔːd/ *v.i.* мародёрствовать (*impf., pf.*)

marble /'mɑːb(ə)l/ *n.* **1** (substance) мра́мор **2** (in child's game) стекля́нный ша́рик; **play** ~s игра́ть (*impf.*) в ша́рики
● *adj.* мра́морный

✍ **March** /mɑːtʃ/ *n.* март

march /mɑːtʃ/ *n.* (mil.) марш; (pol.) марш, демонстра́ция
● *v.i.* **1** (mil.) маршировать, про-; **we watched them** ~ **past** мы смотре́ли, как они́ прошли́ стро́ем; **quick** ~**!** ша́гом марш! **2** (walk determinedly): **he** ~**ed into the room** он сме́ло вошёл в ко́мнату
□ ~ **along** *v.i.*: **they were** ~**ing along singing** они́ маршировали с пе́снями

mare /meə(r)/ *n.* кобы́ла

margarine /mɑːdʒə'riːn/ *n.* маргари́н

margin /'mɑːdʒɪn/ *n.* **1** (edge) край; (of page) по́ле (*usu. in pl.*); **in the** ~ на поля́х **2** (extra amount) запа́с; **he won by a narrow** ~ он победи́л с небольши́м преиму́ществом

marginal /'mɑːdʒɪn(ə)l/ *adj.* (insignificant) незначи́тельный; минима́льный

marguerite /mɑːgə'riːt/ *n.* нивя́ник (*крупная полевая ромашка*)

marigold /'mærɪgəʊld/ *n.* (*also called* **common/pot** ~) (genus Calendula) ноготки́ (*m. pl.*); (*also called* **French/African** ~) (genus Tagetes) ба́рхатцы (*m. pl.*)

marijuana /mærɪ'(h)wɑːnə/ *n.* марихуа́на

marina /mə'riːnə/ *n.* мари́на, при́стань для яхт

marinade /'mærɪneɪd/ *n.* марина́д
● *v.t.* (*also* **marinate**) маринова́ть, за-

marine /mə'riːn/ *n.* **1** (fleet): **mercantile, merchant** ~ торго́вый флот **2** (naval infantryman) солда́т морско́й пехо́ты, морско́й пехоти́нец
● *adj.* морско́й

marital /'mærɪt(ə)l/ *adj.*: ~ **relations** супру́жеские отноше́ния; ~ **status** семе́йное положе́ние

maritime /'mærɪtaɪm/ *adj.* (of the sea): ~ **law** морско́е пра́во; (situated by the sea) примо́рский

marjoram /'mɑːdʒərəm/ *n.* майора́н садо́вый

✍ **mark** /mɑːk/ *n.* **1** (imperfection; stain, spot, etc.) пятно́ **2** (trace) след; **you have left dirty** ~s **on the floor** вы наследи́ли на полу́ **3** (sign, symbol) знак; **as a** ~ **of goodwill** в знак расположе́ния **4** (reference point) ме́тка; (fig., standard): **his work was not up to the** ~ его́ рабо́та была́ не на высоте́ **5** (starting line) старт; **on your** ~s, **get set, go!** на старт, внима́ние, марш! **6** (assessment of performance) отме́тка; **he always gets good** ~s он всегда́ получа́ет хоро́шие отме́тки; (preceded by

number) балл
● *v.t.* **1** (stain, scar, scratch, etc.): **a tablecloth** ~**ed with coffee stains** ска́терть, забры́зганная ко́фе; **the table was badly** ~**ed** стол был си́льно запа́чкан **2** (indicate) отм|еча́ть, -е́тить; **is our village** ~**ed on this map?** на́ша дере́вня нанесена́ на э́ту ка́рту?; **the prices are clearly** ~**ed** це́ны чётко проста́влены **3** (observe and remember): **a** ~**ed man** челове́к, взя́тый на заме́тку; (BrE, football, etc.: follow closely) закр|ыва́ть, -ы́ть; (notice) зам|еча́ть, -е́тить; ~ **my words!** помяни́те моё сло́во! **4** (assign ~s to): ~ **an exercise** пров|еря́ть, -е́рить упражне́ние
□ ~ **down** *v.t.* (reduce price of): **all the goods were** ~**ed down for the sale** для распрода́жи це́ны на все това́ры бы́ли сни́жены
□ ~ **off** *v.t.* отм|еча́ть, -е́тить
□ ~ **out** *v.t.*: **a tennis court had been** ~**ed out** те́ннисный корт был расче́рчен/разме́чен; (preselect, destine): **he was** ~**ed out for promotion** его́ реши́ли повы́сить в до́лжности
□ ~ **up** *v.t.* (raise price of): **goods were** ~**ed up after the budget** це́ны бы́ли повы́шены по́сле объявле́ния фина́нсовой сме́ты

marked /mɑːkt/ *adj.* (noticeable) заме́тный

markedly /'mɑːkɪdlɪ/ *adv.*: **they were** ~ **different** они́ заме́тно отлича́лись друг от дру́га

marker /'mɑːkə(r)/ *n.* (indicator) индика́тор; (flag) сигна́льный флажо́к; (pen) флома́стер

✍ **market** /'mɑːkɪt/ *n.* **1** (gathering; event; place of business) ры́нок, база́р; (*attr.*) ры́ночный, база́рный **2** (trade) торго́вля; **there is no** ~ **for these goods** на э́ти това́ры нет спро́са. **3** (share prices) це́ны (*f. pl.*); **the** ~ **is falling** це́ны па́дают **4 on the** ~ (available for purchase): **he put his house on the** ~ он вы́ставил свой дом на прода́жу
● *v.t.* (**marketed, marketing**) (advertise) реклами́ровать (*impf.*); (sell) прода|ва́ть (*impf.*)
■ ~ **day** *n.* (BrE) база́рный день; ~ **economy** *n.* ры́ночная эконо́мика; ~ **forces** *n. pl.* ры́ночные си́лы (*f. pl.*); ~ **gardener** *n.* (BrE) владе́лец огоро́дного хозя́йства; ~ **leader** *n.* ли́дер ры́нка; ~**place** *n.* база́рная пло́щадь; (fig.) ры́нок; ~ **research** *n.* иссле́дование ры́нка; ~ **share** *n.* до́ля ры́нка; ~ **town** *n.* (небольшо́й) го́род с ры́нком; ~ **value** *n.* ры́ночная сто́имость

marketable /'mɑːkɪtəb(ə)l/ *adj.* (produced for sale) това́рный; (selling quickly) хо́дкий

✍ **marketing** /'mɑːkɪtɪŋ/ *n.* ма́ркетинг
■ ~ **manager** *n.* ме́неджер по ма́ркетингу

marking /'mɑːkɪŋ/ *n.* **1** (on animals etc.) окра́ска **2** (for identification) знак

marksman /'mɑːksmən/ *n.* стрело́к

marmalade /'mɑːməleɪd/ *n.*: **orange** ~ апельси́новый джем

maroon[1] /mə'ruːn/ *n. & adj.* (colour) тёмно-бордо́вый (цвет)

maroon[2] /mə'ruːn/ *v.t.* выса́живать, вы́садить на необита́емый о́стров *и т. п.*; (fig.) (*in pass.*) застр|ева́ть, -я́ть; **we were** ~**ed in Paris**

m

мы застря́ли в Пари́же

marquee /mɑːˈkiː/ *n.* (BrE) (больша́я) пала́тка

⚬ **marriage** /ˈmærɪdʒ/ *n.* **1** (married state) брак; ~ **of convenience** фикти́вный брак **2** (ceremony) сва́дьба; бракосочета́ние **3** (*attr.*) бра́чный; ~ **certificate** свиде́тельство о бра́ке; ~ **guidance** (BrE) семе́йная консульта́ция

married /ˈmærɪd/ *adj.* **1** (of man) жена́тый (**to:** на + *p.*); (of woman) замужняя, (*pred.*) за́мужем (**to:** за + *i.*); **they are** ~ (to each other) они́ жена́ты **2** (pert. to marriage) супру́жеский; **a** ~ **couple** супру́жеская па́ра

marrow /ˈmærəʊ/ *n.* **1** (anat.) (ко́стный) мозг **2** (*in full* **vegetable** ~) (BrE) кабачо́к

⚬ **marry** /ˈmæri/ *v.t.* **1** (of man) жени́ться (*impf.*, *pf.*) на + *p.* **2** (of woman) выходи́ть, вы́йти за́муж за + *a.* **3** (of priest) венча́ть, об-
● *v.i.* (of man) жени́ться (*impf., pf.*); (of woman) выходи́ть, вы́йти за́муж; (of couple) пожени́ться (*pf.*); (relig.) венча́ться, об-

Mars /mɑːz/ *n.* (myth., astron.) Марс

marsh /mɑːʃ/ *n.* боло́то
■ ~**land** *n.* боло́тистая ме́стность

marshal /ˈmɑːʃ(ə)l/ *n.* **1** (mil.) ма́ршал **2** (organizer) распоряди́тель (*m.*) **3** (AmE, head of police) нача́льник полице́йского уча́стка
● *v.t.* (**marshalled, marshalling**, AmE **marshaled, marshaling**) **1** (draw up in order): ~ **troops** выстра́ивать, вы́строить войска́; (fig.): ~ **one's forces** соб|ира́ть, -ра́ть си́лы **2** (direct): ~ **a crowd** напр|авля́ть, -а́вить толпу́

marshy /ˈmɑːʃi/ *adj.* (**marshier, marshiest**) боло́тистый

marsupial /mɑːˈsuːpɪəl/ *n.* су́мчатое живо́тное
● *adj.* су́мчатый

martial /ˈmɑːʃ(ə)l/ *adj.* (military) вое́нный
■ ~ **arts** *n. pl.* спорти́вная борьба́; ~ **law** *n.* вое́нное положе́ние

martyr /ˈmɑːtə(r)/ *n.* му́чени|к (-ца)
● *v.t.* му́чить, за-

martyrdom /ˈmɑːtədəm/ *n.* му́ченичество

marvel /ˈmɑːv(ə)l/ *n.* чу́до
● *v.i.* (**marvelled, marvelling**, AmE **marveled, marveling**) (wonder) диви́ться (*impf.*) + *d.*; удив|ля́ться, -и́ться + *i.*

marvellous /ˈmɑːvələs/ (AmE **marvelous**) *adj.* (astonishing) изуми́тельный; (splendid) чуде́сный

Marxism /ˈmɑːksɪz(ə)m/ *n.* маркси́зм

Marxist /ˈmɑːksɪst/ *n.* маркси́ст (-ка)
● *adj.* маркси́стский

marzipan /ˈmɑːzɪpæn/ *n.* марципа́н (*кондитерское изделие; начинка, глазурь*)

mascara /mæˈskɑːrə/ *n.* тушь для ресни́ц

mascot /ˈmæskɒt/ *n.* талисма́н

masculine /ˈmæskjʊlɪn/ *adj.* мужско́й

masculinity /mæskjʊˈlɪnɪti/ *n.* му́жественность

mash /mæʃ/ *n.* (BrE, potato) пюре́ (*nt. indecl.*)
● *v.t.* (cul.): ~**ed potatoes** карто́фельное пюре́
■ ~**-up** *n.* (mixture, fusion) (infml) смесь

несхо́дных элеме́нтов

mask /mɑːsk/ *n.* ма́ска
● *v.t.* над|ева́ть, -е́ть ма́ску на + *a.*; (fig.): **she** ~**ed her feelings** она́ скрыва́ла свои́ чу́вства

masochism /ˈmæsəkɪz(ə)m/ *n.* мазохи́зм

masochist /ˈmæsəkɪst/ *n.* мазохи́ст (-ка)

masochistic /mæsəˈkɪstɪk/ *adj.* мазохи́стский

mason /ˈmeɪs(ə)n/ *n.* ка́менщик; (M~, Free~) масо́н

masonry /ˈmeɪsənri/ *n.* ка́менная кла́дка

masquerade /mæskəˈreɪd/ *n.* (lit., fig.) маскара́д
● *v.i.*: **he** ~**d as a general** он выдава́л себя́ за генера́ла

Mass /mæs/ *n.* (relig.) ме́сса, литурги́я; (in Orthodox church) обе́дня

⚬ **mass** /mæs/ *n.* **1** (phys. etc.) ма́сса **2** (large number) мно́жество; ~**es of people** ма́сса наро́ду; **the** ~**es** (наро́дные/широ́кие) ма́ссы; (*in pl.*) (infml, a large amount): **there's** ~**es of food** полно́ еды́ **3** (*attr.*) ма́ссовый; **the** ~ **media** сре́дства ма́ссовой информа́ции (*abbr.* СМИ); масс-ме́диа (*pl. indecl.*)
● *v.t.* соб|ира́ть, -ра́ть; ~ **troops** сосредото́ч|ивать, -ть, войска́
● *v.i.* соб|ира́ться, -ра́ться; **the clouds are** ~**ing** собира́ются облака́
■ ~ **destruction** *n.* ма́ссовое уничтоже́ние; ~**-produce** *v.t.*: **these toys are** ~**-produced** э́ти игру́шки ма́ссового произво́дства; ~ **production** *n.* ма́ссовое произво́дство

massacre /ˈmæsəkə(r)/ *n.* бо́йня
● *v.t.* переб|ива́ть, -и́ть

massage /ˈmæsɑːʒ/ *n.* масса́ж
● *v.t.* масси́ровать (*impf., pf.*)

masseur /mæˈsɜː(r)/ *n.* массажи́ст

masseuse /mæˈsɜːz/ *n.* массажи́стка

⚬ **massive** /ˈmæsɪv/ *adj.* (large and heavy) масси́вный; (substantial) огро́мный

mast /mɑːst/ *n.* ма́чта

mastectomy /mæsˈtektəmi/ *n.* мастэктоми́я (*ампутация молочной железы*)

⚬ **master** /ˈmɑːstə(r)/ *n.* **1** (one in control, boss) хозя́ин; (owner) владе́лец **2** (BrE, teacher) учи́тель (*m.*); (in university): **M**~ **of Arts** маги́стр гуманита́рных нау́к **3** (skilled craftsman, expert) ма́стер **4** (original) по́длинник
● *v.t.* **1** (gain control of) спр|авля́ться, -а́виться с + *i.* **2** (acquire knowledge of, skill in) овлад|ева́ть, -е́ть + *i.*; **it is a language which can be** ~**ed in 6 months** э́тим языко́м мо́жно овладе́ть за шесть ме́сяцев **3** (overcome) овлад|ева́ть, -е́ть + *i.*; ~ **one's feelings** владе́ть, о- свои́ми чу́вствами
■ ~ **bedroom** *n.* гла́вная спа́льня; ~ **builder** *n.* строи́тель-подря́дчик; ~ **key** *n.* отмы́чка; ~**mind** *n.* руководи́тель (*m*) ● *v.t.*: **he** ~**minded the plan** он разрабо́тал весь план; ~ **of ceremonies** *n.* распоряди́тель (*m.*), конферансье́ (*nt. indecl.*); ~**piece** *n.* шеде́вр; ~ **plan** *n.* генера́льный план

masterful /ˈmɑːstəfʊl/ *adj.* вла́стный

masterly /'mɑːstəlɪ/ *adj.* ма́стерский

mastery /'mɑːstərɪ/ *n.* **1** (authority) власть **2** (skill) мастерство́ **3** (knowledge) владе́ние

masturbate /'mæstəbeɪt/ *v.i.* мастурби́ровать (*impf.*)

masturbation /mæstə'beɪʃ(ə)n/ *n.* мастурба́ция

mat¹ /mæt/ *n.* **1** (floor covering) ко́врик **2** (to protect table) подста́вка

mat² /mæt/ *v.t.* (**matted, matting**): his hair was ~ted with blood его́ во́лосы сли́плись от кро́ви

matador /'mætədɔː(r)/ *n.* матадо́р

match¹ /mætʃ/ *n.* (for producing flame) спи́чка ■ ~box *n.* спи́чечная коро́бка

✎ **match²** /mætʃ/ *n.* **1** (equal) па́ра, ро́вня; he's no ~ for her он ей не па́ра **2** (thing resembling or suiting another): these curtains are a good ~ for the carpet э́ти занаве́ски подхо́дят к ковру́ **3** (game) соревнова́ние, состяза́ние; матч, игра́; football ~ футбо́льный матч ● *v.t.* (suit; correspond to) под|ходи́ть, -ойти́ к + *d.*; гармони́ровать (*impf.*) c + *i.*; her hat doesn't ~ her dress её шля́па не подхо́дит к пла́тью; (find a ~ for): we try to ~ the jobs to the applicants мы стара́емся подбира́ть подходя́щую рабо́ту для кандида́тов ● *v.i.* (correspond: be identical): the handbag and gloves don't ~ су́мочка и перча́тки не гармони́руют друг с дру́гом ■ ~ point *n.* очко́, реша́ющее исхо́д ма́тча; матч-по́йнт

mate /meɪt/ *n.* **1** (BrE, infml, companion, also as form of address) брат, друг **2** (one of a pair of animals or birds) саме́ц (са́мка) **3** (assistant) помо́щник **4** (ship's ~) помо́щник капита́на ● *v.t. & i.* спа́ри|вать(ся), -ть(ся)

✎ **material** /mə'tɪərɪəl/ *n.* **1** (substance) материа́л; raw ~(s) сырьё; (fig., of person): he is good officer ~ из него́ вы́йдет хоро́ший офице́р; (subject matter): there is good ~ there for a novel там есть хоро́ший материа́л для рома́на **2** (fabric) мате́рия **3** (*in pl.*): writing ~s пи́сьменные принадле́жности ● *adj.* материа́льный

materialism /mə'tɪərɪəlɪz(ə)m/ *n.* материали́зм

materialist /mə'tɪərɪəlɪst/ *n.* материали́ст

materialistic /mətɪərɪə'lɪstɪk/ *adj.* материалисти́ческий

materialize /mə'tɪərɪəlaɪz/ *v.i.* материализова́ться (*impf., pf.*)

maternal /mə'tɜːn(ə)l/ *adj.* (motherly) матери́нский

maternity /mə'tɜːnɪtɪ/ *n.* матери́нство ■ ~ leave *n.* декре́тный о́тпуск

math /mæθ/ *n.* (AmE, infml) (*abbr.*) = mathematics

mathematical /mæθə'mætɪk(ə)l/ *adj.* математи́ческий

mathematician /mæθəmə'tɪʃ(ə)n/ *n.* матема́тик

mathematics /mæθə'mætɪks/ *n.* матема́тика

maths /mæθs/ *n.* (BrE, infml) (*abbr.*) = mathematics

matinee /'mætɪneɪ/ *n.* дневно́е представле́ние

mating /'meɪtɪŋ/ *n.* спа́ривание ■ ~ season *n.* сезо́н спа́ривания

matriarchal /meɪtrɪ'ɑːk(ə)l/ матриарха́льный

matriculate /mə'trɪkjʊleɪt/ *v.i.* быть при́нятым в вы́сшее уче́бное заведе́ние

matriculation /mətrɪkjʊ'leɪʃ(ə)n/ *n.* зачисле́ние в вы́сшее уче́бное заведе́ние

matrimonial /mætrɪ'məʊnɪəl/ *adj.* супру́жеский; бра́чный

matrimony /'mætrɪmənɪ/ *n.* брак

matri|x /'meɪtrɪks/ *n.* (*pl.* ~ces /-siːz/ or ~xes) ма́трица

matron /'meɪtrən/ *n.* **1** (BrE, in hospital) ста́ршая сестра́ **2** (in school) эконо́мка

matt /mæt/ *adj.* ма́товый; ~ paint ма́товая кра́ска

✎ **matter** /'mætə(r)/ *n.* **1** (phys., phil.) мате́рия; (substance) вещество́ **2** (physiol.): grey ~ се́рое вещество́; (pus) гной **3** (material for reading) материа́лы (*m. pl.*); printed ~ печа́тный материа́л **4** (question; issue) вопро́с; де́ло; that's quite another ~ э́то совсе́м друго́е де́ло; it is a ~ of course само́ собо́й разуме́ется; as a ~ of fact (to tell the truth) по пра́вде сказа́ть; (in reality) на са́мом де́ле; (incidentally) со́бственно (говоря́); it is a ~ for the police э́то де́ло поли́ции; a ~ of life and death вопро́с жи́зни и сме́рти; that's a ~ of opinion э́то спо́рный вопро́с; (*in pl.*) (affairs) дела́; to make ~s worse в доверше́ние ко всем бе́дам **5** (the ~) (sth wrong, amiss): what's the ~? в чём де́ло?; is (there) anything the ~? что́-нибудь не ла́дно?; what's the ~ with him? что с ним?; there's nothing the ~ (with me) (у меня́) всё в поря́дке **6** (importance): no ~ what I do, the result will be the same что бы я ни сде́лал, результа́т бу́дет тот же ● *v.i.* име́ть (*impf.*) значе́ние; it doesn't ~ to me э́то не име́ет для меня́ значе́ния ■ ~-of-fact *adj.* приземлённый, лишённый фанта́зии; сухо́й, делово́й

mattress /'mætrɪs/ *n.* матра́с, матра́ц

mature /mə'tjʊə(r)/ *adj.* (**maturer, maturest**) зре́лый ● *v.i.* **1** (lit., fig., ripen, develop) созр|ева́ть, -е́ть; children ~ earlier nowadays в на́ши дни де́ти развива́ются быстре́е **2** (become due for payment): the policy ~s next year в бу́дущем году́ наступа́ет срок вы́платы по страхово́му по́лису ■ ~ student *n.* (BrE) студе́нт (-ка) зре́лого во́зраста

maturity /mə'tjʊərɪtɪ/ *n.* зре́лость

maudlin /'mɔːdlɪn/ *adj.* слюня́во сентимента́льный; плакси́вый во хмелю́

maul /mɔːl/ *v.t.* терза́ть, рас-; he was ~ed to death by a tiger его́ растерза́л тигр

Mauritania /mɒrɪ'teɪnɪə/ *n.* Маврита́ния

mausoleum /mɔːsə'liːəm/ *n.* мавзоле́й

m

mauve /məʊv/ *n. & adj.* розова́то-лило́вый (цвет)

maverick /ˈmævərɪk/ *n.* (fig., dissenter) диссиде́нт; (*attr.*) неприка́янный

mawkish /ˈmɔːkɪʃ/ *adj.* при́торный

maxim /ˈmæksɪm/ *n.* (aphorism) афори́зм

maximize /ˈmæksɪmaɪz/ *v.t.* максима́льно увели́чи|вать, -ть

maximum /ˈmæksɪməm/ *n.* ма́ксимум ● *adj.* максима́льный

♂ **May** /meɪ/ *n.* май; ~ Day Пе́рвое мая; пра́здник Пе́рвого ма́я
■ ~**day** *n.* (distress signal) сигна́л бе́дствия

♂ **may** /meɪ/ *v. aux.* (3rd pers. sing. pres. **may**, *past* **might**) **1** (expr. possibility) мо́жет быть; пожа́луй; it ~ be true возмо́жно, э́то пра́вда; it ~ not be true возмо́жно, э́то не так; he might have lost his way without my help без мое́й по́мощи он мог бы заблуди́ться; you ~ well be right вполне́ возмо́жно, вы и пра́вы **2** (expr. permission): ~ **I come and see you?** мо́жно мне (*or* могу́ я) к вам зайти́?; you ~ **go if you wish** е́сли хоти́те, мо́жете идти́ **3** (expr. reproach): **you might have asked my permission** мо́жно бы́ло бы спроси́ть моего́ согла́сия **4** (in main clause, expr. wish or hope): ~ **the best man win!** да победи́т сильне́йший!
■ ~**be** *adv.* мо́жет быть

maybe /ˈmeɪbi/ *adv.* мо́жет быть

mayhem /ˈmeɪhem/ *n.* разгро́м

mayonnaise /meɪəˈneɪz/ *n.* майоне́з

mayor /meə(r)/ *n.* мэр

mayoress /ˈmeərɪs/ *n.* (mayor's wife) жена́ мэ́ра; (female mayor) же́нщина-мэр

maze /meɪz/ *n.* лабири́нт; (fig.) пу́таница

MBA *abbr.* (*of* **Master of Business Administration**) маги́стр ме́неджмента

MBE *n.* (abbr. *of* **Member of the Order of the British Empire**) кавале́р о́рдена Брита́нской импе́рии 5-й (*низшей*) сте́пени

MC *abbr.* (*of* **Master of Ceremonies**) конферансье́ (*nt. indecl.*), распоряди́тель (*m.*)

MD (BrE) *abbr.* (*of* **Managing Director**) дире́ктор-распоряди́тель (*m.*)

ME *abbr.* (*of* **myalgic encephalitis**) миалги́ческий энцефали́т, синдро́м хрони́ческой уста́лости

♂ **me** /miː/ *obj. of* ▸ **I**

meadow /ˈmedəʊ/ *n.* луг

meagre /ˈmiːgə(r)/ (AmE **meager**) *adj.* ску́дный

♂ **meal** /miːl/ *n.* еда́, тра́пеза; **we have 3** ~**s a day** мы еди́м три ра́за в день

♂ **mean**[1] /miːn/ *n.* (average) середи́на
■ ~**time** *n.*: in the ~**time** ме́жду тем

mean[2] /miːn/ *adj.* **1** (niggardly) скупо́й **2** (spiteful) злобный; **don't be** ~ **to him** не обижа́йте его́ **3** (inferior): **he is a man of no** ~ **abilities** он челове́к незауря́дных спосо́бностей

♂ **mean**[3] /miːn/ *v.t.* (*past and p.p.* **meant**) **1** (intend) име́ть (*impf.*) в виду́; намерева́ться (*impf.*); **I** ~ **to solve this problem** я наме́рен реши́ть э́тот вопро́с; **I** ~**t no harm** я не жела́л зла; **I** ~**t it as a joke** я хоте́л пошути́ть; **I didn't** ~ **to hurt you** я не хоте́л вас оби́деть **2** (design, destine) предназн|ача́ть, -а́чить; **they were** ~**t for each other** друг для дру́га **3** (of person, intend to convey) хоте́ть (*impf.*) сказа́ть; **what do you** ~? что вы э́тим хоти́те сказа́ть? **4** (of words etc., signify) зна́чить (*impf.*), означа́ть (*impf.*); **this sentence** ~**s nothing to me** э́то предложе́ние ничего́ мне не говори́т; **does my friendship** ~ **nothing to you?** неуже́ли моя́ дру́жба ничего́ для вас не зна́чит?; (entail, involve): **organizing a fete** ~**s a lot of hard work** подгото́вка к пра́зднику тре́бует мно́го уси́лий

meander /mɪˈændə(r)/ *v.i.* (of streams, roads, etc.) извива́ться, ви́ться (*both impf.*)

♂ **meaning** /ˈmiːnɪŋ/ *n.* значе́ние

meaningful /ˈmiːnɪŋfʊl/ *adj.* значи́тельный

meaningless /ˈmiːnɪŋlɪs/ *adj.* бессмы́сленный

meanness /ˈmiːnnɪs/ *n.* по́длость, ни́зость; ску́пость

means /miːnz/ *n.* **1** (instrument, method) спо́соб; **a** ~ **to an end** сре́дство для достиже́ния це́ли; **by** ~ **of** посре́дством + *g.*; с по́мощью + *g.*; **by all** ~ (AmE, without fail) непреме́нно; (expr. permission) коне́чно; пожа́луйста; **it was by no** ~ **easy** э́то бы́ло отню́дь не про́сто **2** (facilities): ~ **of communication** (transport) сре́дства сообще́ния; (telecommunication) сре́дства свя́зи **3** (resources) сре́дства; **a man of** ~ челове́к со сре́дствами; **live beyond one's** ~ жить (*impf.*) не по сре́дствам
■ ~ **test** *n.* прове́рка нужда́емости

meant /ment/ *past and p.p. of* ▸ **mean**[3]

meanwhile /ˈmiːnwaɪl/ *adv.* ме́жду тем, тем вре́менем

measles /ˈmiːz(ə)lz/ *n.* корь

measly /ˈmiːzlɪ/ *adj.* (**measlier**, **measliest**) жа́лкий

measurable /ˈmeʒərəb(ə)l/ *adj.* измери́мый

♂ **measure** /ˈmeʒə(r)/ *n.* **1** (standard unit for expressing size, quantity, degree) ме́ра; (portion, of whisky etc.) по́рция **2** (graduated rod or tape for measuring) измери́тельная лине́йка; руле́тка **3** (step) ме́ра, мероприя́тие **4** (degree, extent) сте́пень; **in some** ~ до не́которой сте́пени; **she was irritated beyond** ~ она́ пришла́ в невероя́тное раздраже́ние ● *v.t.* **1** (find size etc. of) ме́рить, с-; изм|еря́ть, -е́рить; **he was** ~**d for a suit** с него́ сня́ли ме́рку для костю́ма **2** (amount to when measured): **the room** ~**s 12 ft across** ко́мната ширино́й в двена́дцать фу́тов
□ ~ **off**, ~ **out** *vv.t.* отм|еря́ть, -е́рить
□ ~ **up** *v.i.*: **the team has not** ~**d up to our expectations** кома́нда не оправда́ла на́ших ожида́ний

measured /ˈmeʒəd/ *adj.* **1** (steps) разме́ренный; ~ **tread** ме́рная по́ступь **2** (tone) уме́ренный; (considered; careful) обду́манный, осторо́жный

m

measurement /'meʒəmənt/ *n.* (measuring) измере́ние; (dimension) разме́р; **take sb's ~s** снять (*pf.*) ме́рку с кого́-н.; **waist ~** объём та́лии

meat /miːt/ *n.* мя́со

meaty /'miːtɪ/ *adj.* (**meatier**, **meatiest**) мяси́стый

Mecca /'mekə/ *n.* Ме́кка

mechanic /mɪ'kænɪk/ *n.* меха́ник

mechanical /mɪ'kænɪk(ə)l/ *adj.* механи́ческий
■ **~ engineering** *n.* машинострое́ние

mechanics /mɪ'kænɪks/ *n.* меха́ника

✎ **mechanism** /'mekənɪz(ə)m/ *n.* механи́зм

mechanization /mekənaɪ'zeɪʃ(ə)n/ *n.* механиза́ция

mechanize /'mekənaɪz/ *v.t. & i.* механизи́ровать(ся) (*impf., pf.*)

Med /med/ *n.* (BrE, infml) (*abbr.*): **the ~** Средизе́мное мо́ре

medal /'med(ə)l/ *n.* меда́ль; (mil. award) о́рден (-á)

medallion /mə'dæljən/ *n.* медальо́н

medallist /'medəlɪst/ (AmE **medalist**) *n.* (recipient) медали́ст (-ка)

meddle /'med(ə)l/ *v.i.*: **~ in** (interfere in) вме́ш|иваться, -áться в + *a.*; **~ with** (touch, tamper with) тро́|гать, -нуть

meddlesome /'medəlsəm/ *adj.* назо́йливый; **he is a ~ person** он всё вре́мя вме́шивается не в свои́ дела́

✎ **media** /'miːdɪə/ *see* ▶ **medium** *n.* 4

mediate /'miːdɪeɪt/ *v.i.* выступа́ть, вы́ступить посре́дником

mediation /miːdɪ'eɪʃ(ə)n/ *n.* посре́дничество

mediator /'miːdɪeɪtə(r)/ *n.* посре́дник

medic /'medɪk/ *n.* (infml) (студе́нт-)ме́дик

✎ **medical** /'medɪk(ə)l/ *n.* (infml, **~ examination**): **have a ~** про|ходи́ть, -йти́ медици́нский осмо́тр (*abbr.* медосмо́тр)
● *adj.* медици́нский; враче́бный
■ **~ certificate** *n.* спра́вка от врача́

medicament /mɪ'dɪkəmənt/ *n.* лека́рство, медикаме́нт

medication /medɪ'keɪʃ(ə)n/ *n.* (medicine) лека́рство; (treatment) лече́ние

medicinal /mə'dɪsɪn(ə)l/ *adj.* (of medicine) лека́рственный; (curative) целе́бный

✎ **medicine** /'medsɪn/ *n.* 1 (science, practice) медици́на 2 (substance) лека́рство; медикаме́нт, миксту́ра
■ **~ cabinet** *n.* апте́чка; **~ man** *n.* зна́харь (*m.*)

medieval /medɪ'iːv(ə)l/ *adj.* средневеко́вый

mediocre /miːdɪ'əʊkə(r)/ *adj.* посре́дственный

mediocrity /miːdɪ'ɒkrɪtɪ/ *n.* посре́дственность

meditate /'medɪteɪt/ *v.i.* размышля́ть (*impf*) (**on**: о + *p.*); (relig.) медити́ровать (*impf.*)

meditation /medɪ'teɪʃ(ə)n/ *n.* размышле́ние; (relig.) медита́ция

meditative /'medɪtətɪv/ *adj.* заду́мчивый

Mediterranean /medɪtə'reɪnɪən/ *n.* (*in full* **~ Sea**) Средизе́мное мо́ре
● *adj.* средиземномо́рский

medium /'miːdɪəm/ *n.* (*pl.* **media** *or* **mediums**) 1 (middle quality) середи́на; **he strikes a happy ~** он приде́рживается золото́й середи́ны 2 (means, agency) сре́дство 3 (spiritualist) ме́диум 4: **the media** (mass media) сре́дства ма́ссовой информа́ции
● *adj.* (intermediate) промежу́точный; (average) сре́дний
■ **~ dry** *adj.* полусухо́й; **~-sized** *adj.* сре́днего разме́ра

medley /'medlɪ/ *n.* (*pl.* **medleys**) смесь; (mus.) попурри́ (*nt. indecl.*)

meek /miːk/ *adj.* кро́ткий

✎ **meet** /miːt/ *n.* (of sportsmen, etc.) сбор
● *v.t.* (*past and p.p.* **met**) 1 (encounter) встре|ча́ть, -éтить; (make acquaintance of) знако́миться, по- с + *i.*; **I met your sister in Moscow** я познако́мился с ва́шей сестро́й в Москве́ 2 (face): **I am ready to ~ your challenge** я гото́в приня́ть ваш вы́зов 3 (experience, suffer): **~ one's death** поги́бнуть (*pf.*) 4 (pay, settle): **this will barely ~ my expenses** э́то с трудо́м покро́ет мои́ расхо́ды
● *v.i.* (*past and p.p.* **met**) 1 (of persons, come together) встре|ча́ться, -éтиться; **our eyes met** на́ши глаза́ встре́тились; (become acquainted) знако́миться, по-; **we met at a dance** мы познако́мились на та́нцах 2 (assemble) соб|ира́ться, -ра́ться; **the council met to discuss the situation** сове́т собра́лся, что́бы обсуди́ть положе́ние 3 (of things, qualities, etc.: come into contact) сходи́ться (*impf.*); **the rivers Oka and Volga ~ at Nizhniy Novgorod** Ни́жний Но́вгород — ме́сто слия́ния рек Оки́ и Во́лги; **make (both) ends ~** (fig.) сво́|дить, -ести́ концы́ с конца́ми 4 **~ with**: **~ with difficulties** испы́т|ывать, -áть затрудне́ния; **he met with an accident** с ним произошёл несча́стный слу́чай
□ **~ up** *v.i.* (infml): **we met up** (*or* **I met up with him/her/them**) **in London** мы встре́тились в Ло́ндоне

✎ **meeting** /'miːtɪŋ/ *n.* 1 (encounter) встре́ча; (by arrangement) свида́ние 2 (gathering) собра́ние 3 (sports **~**) (спорти́вное) состяза́ние; (race **~**) ска́чки (*f. pl.*)
■ **~ place**, **~ point** *nn.* ме́сто встре́чи

meg /meg/ *n.* (comput., infml) (*abbr.*) мег (infml)

megabyte /'megəbaɪt/ *n.* (comput.) мегаба́йт

megalomania /megələ'meɪnɪə/ *n.* ма́ния вели́чия, мегалома́ния

megalomaniac /megələ'meɪnɪæk/ *n.* страда́ющий ма́нией вели́чия

megaphone /'megəfəʊn/ *n.* мегафо́н

megapixel /'megəpɪks(ə)l/ *n.* (comput.) мегапи́ксель (*m.*)

melancholy /'melənkəlɪ/ *n.* уны́ние
● *adj.* (of person) уны́лый; (of things) гру́стный

mellow /'meləʊ/ *adj.* 1 (of voice, sound, colour, light) со́чный 2 (of wine) вы́держанный 3 (of character) подобре́вший

● *v.t.*: age has ~ed him го́ды смягчи́ли его́ хара́ктер
● *v.i.* (of person) смягч|а́ться, -и́ться

melodic /mɪˈlɒdɪk/ *adj.* мелоди́чный

melodious /mɪˈləʊdɪəs/ *adj.* мелоди́чный; ~ voice певу́чий го́лос

melodrama /ˈmelədrɑːmə/ *n.* мелодра́ма

melodramatic /melədrəˈmætɪk/ *adj.* мелодрамати́ческий

melody /ˈmelədɪ/ *n.* мело́дия

melon /ˈmelən/ *n.* ды́ня

melt /melt/ *v.t.* **1** (reduce to liquid) раст|а́пливать, -опи́ть **2** (fig., soften) размягч|а́ть, -и́ть
● *v.i.* **1** (become liquid) та́ять, рас- **2** (fig., soften) смягч|а́ться, -и́ться; her heart ~ed at the sight её се́рдце смягчи́лось при ви́де э́того
□ ~ **down** *v.t.* распл|авля́ть, -а́вить

melting point /ˈmeltɪŋ pɔɪnt/ *n.* температу́ра плавле́ния

⚥ **member** /ˈmembə(r)/ *n.* член, уча́стни|к (-ца) (*о́бщества и т. п.*)

membership /ˈmembəʃɪp/ *n.* (being a member) чле́нство; (collect.) (members) чле́ны (*m. pl.*)

membrane /ˈmembreɪn/ *n.* перепо́нка, мембра́на

memento /məˈmentəʊ/ *n.* (*pl.* ~es *or* ~s) сувени́р

memo /ˈmeməʊ/ *n.* (*pl.* ~s) = memorandum

memoir /ˈmemwɑː(r)/ *n.* (in pl.) (autobiography) воспомина́ния (*nt. pl.*), мемуа́р|ы (-ов)

memorable /ˈmemərəb(ə)l/ *adj.* па́мятный; незабыва́емый

memorandum /meməˈrændəm/ *n.* запи́ска

memorial /məˈmɔːrɪəl/ *n.* па́мятник

memorize /ˈmeməraɪz/ *v.t.* зау́ч|ивать, -и́ть (наизу́сть)

⚥ **memory** /ˈmemərɪ/ *n.* **1** (faculty; its use) па́мять; I have a bad ~ for faces у меня́ плоха́я па́мять на ли́ца; in ~ of в па́мять + g. **2** (recollection) воспомина́ние **3** (comput.) па́мять
■ **Memory Stick**® *n.* (comput.) флеш-па́мять; флёшка (infml)

men /men/ *pl. of* ▶ **man**
■ ~'s **room** *n.* (AmE) мужско́й туале́т

menace /ˈmenɪs/ *n.* угро́за
● *v.t.* угрожа́ть (impf.) + d.

ménage /meɪˈnɑːʒ/ *n.* хозя́йство
■ ~ à **trois** *n.* брак втроём

menagerie /mɪˈnædʒərɪ/ *n.* звери́нец

mend /mend/ *n.*: be on the ~ идти́ (det.) на попра́вку
● *v.t.* **1** (repair) чини́ть, по-; заш|ива́ть, -и́ть **2** (improve, reform) испр|авля́ть, -а́вить; ~ one's **ways** испр|авля́ться, -а́виться
● *v.i.* (regain health) выздора́вливать, вы́здороветь; his leg is ~ing nicely его́ нога́ зажива́ет хорошо́

mendacious /menˈdeɪʃəs/ *adj.* лжи́вый

menial /ˈmiːnɪəl/ *adj.* лаке́йский
■ ~ **work** *n.* чёрная рабо́та

meningitis /menɪnˈdʒaɪtɪs/ *n.* менинги́т

menopause /ˈmenəpɔːz/ *n.* кли́макс

menstrual /ˈmenstrʊəl/ *adj.* менструа́льный

menstruate /ˈmenstrʊeɪt/ *v.i.* менструи́ровать (impf.)

menstruation /menstrʊˈeɪʃ(ə)n/ *n.* менструа́ция

menswear /ˈmenzweə(r)/ *n.* мужска́я оде́жда

⚥ **mental** /ˈment(ə)l/ *adj.* **1** (of the mind) у́мственный; ~ly handicapped (sometimes offens.) у́мственно отста́лый **2** (pert. to ~ health) психи́ческий; ~ **illness** психи́ческая боле́знь **3** (carried out in the mind) мы́сленный
■ ~ **hospital** *n.* (often offens.) психиатри́ческая больни́ца

mentality /menˈtælɪtɪ/ *n.* менталите́т

⚥ **mention** /ˈmenʃ(ə)n/ *n.* упомина́ние; there was a ~ of him in the paper в газе́те упомина́лось его́ и́мя
● *v.t.* упом|ина́ть, -яну́ть (кого/что *or* о ком/чём); I shall ~ it to him я скажу́ ему́ об э́том; ~ sb's name наз|ыва́ть, -ва́ть чьё-н. и́мя; don't ~ it! не́ за что!; ничего́; не сто́ит!; not to ~ (*or* without ~ing) не говоря́ уже́ о + p.

mentor /ˈmentɔː(r)/ *n.* наста́вник, ме́нтор

menu /ˈmenjuː/ *n.* (also comput.) меню́ (*nt. indecl.*)

MEP *abbr.* (*of* **Member of the European Parliament**) депута́т Европарла́мента

mercantile /ˈmɜːkəntaɪl/ *adj.* торго́вый
■ ~ **marine** *n.* торго́вый флот

mercenary /ˈmɜːsɪnərɪ/ *n.* наёмник
● *adj.* коры́стный

merchandise /ˈmɜːtʃəndaɪz/ *n.* **1** това́ры (*m. pl.*) **2** (of a football club etc.) атрибу́тика

merchant /ˈmɜːtʃ(ə)nt/ *n.* (hist.) купе́ц; (with qualifying word: dealer) торго́вец; wine ~ торго́вец ви́нами
■ ~ **bank** *n.* (BrE) комме́рческий банк; ~ **marine** (AmE), ~ **navy** (BrE) *nn.* торго́вый флот

merciful /ˈmɜːsɪfʊl/ *adj.* милосе́рдный, сострада́тельный; his death was a ~ release смерть была́ для него́ благо́м

merciless /ˈmɜːsɪlɪs/ *adj.* беспоща́дный, безжа́лостный

mercurial /mɜːˈkjʊərɪəl/ *adj.* **1** (of mercury) рту́тный; ~ **poisoning** отравле́ние рту́тью **2** (of person, lively) живо́й; (volatile) непостоя́нный, изме́нчивый

mercury /ˈmɜːkjʊrɪ/ *n.* ртуть

mercy /ˈmɜːsɪ/ *n.* **1** (compassion, clemency) милосе́рдие; поща́да; beg for ~ проси́ть (impf.) поща́ды; show ~ to (*or* have ~ on) щади́ть, по- **2** (power): at the ~ of во вла́сти + g.

mere /mɪə(r)/ *adj.* (**merest**) **1** (simple; pure) просто́й; чи́стый; (nothing but) не бо́лее чем; всего́ лишь; то́лько; he is a ~ **child** он всего́ лишь ребёнок **2** (alone) оди́н (то́лько); the ~ **sight** of him disgusts me оди́н его́ вид вызыва́ет у меня́ отвраще́ние

⚥ **merely** /ˈmɪəlɪ/ *adv.* (simply) про́сто; (only) то́лько

merge /mɜːdʒ/ *v.t. & i.* сл|ива́ть(ся), -и́ть(ся)

merger /'mɜ:dʒə(r)/ *n.* объединéние
meringue /mə'ræŋ/ *n.* безé (*nt. indecl.*)
merit /'merɪt/ *n.* (deserving quality, worth)
достóинство
　● *v.t.* (**merited, meriting**) заслýж|ивать,
-и́ть
meritocracy /merɪ'tɒkrəsɪ/ *n.* óбщество,
управля́емое людьми́ с наибóльшими
спосóбностями
mermaid /'mɜ:meɪd/ *n.* русáлка
merriment /'merɪmənt/ *n.* весéлье
merry /'merɪ/ *adj.* (**merrier, merriest**)
(happy, full of gaiety) весёлый; **M~ Christmas!** с
Рождествóм (Христóвым)!
■ **~-go-round** *n.* карусéль
mesh /meʃ/ *n.* **1** (space in net etc.) ячéйка **2** (*in
pl.*) (network) сеть
　● *v.i.* (interlock) зацеп|ля́ться, -и́ться
mesmerize /'mezməraɪz/ *v.t.* (lit., fig.)
гипнотизи́ровать, за-
mess¹ /mes/ *n.* **1** (disorder) беспоря́док; **the
room was in a complete ~** кóмната былá
в совершéнном беспоря́дке; **make a ~ of**
(spoil; bungle) прова́л|ивать, -и́ть **2** (confusion)
пýтаница **3** (trouble) неприя́тность, бедá,
гóре; **get oneself into a ~** вли́пнуть (*pf.*)
(infml)
　● *v.i.:* **~ with** (interfere with) вмéшиваться
(*impf.*) в + *a.*
　□ **~ about** *v.t.* (BrE, inconvenience) причиня́ть
(*impf.*) неудóбство + *d.*
　● *v.i.* (work half-heartedly or without plan)
ковыря́ться (*impf.*); (potter, idle about)
кани́телиться (*impf.*)
　□ **~ about with** (fiddle with) вози́ться (*impf.*)
с + *i.*
　□ **~ around** *v.t. & i.* = **mess about**
　□ **~ up** *v.t.* (make dirty) пáчкать, пере-; (bungle)
прова́л|ивать, -и́ть; (put into confusion)
перепýт|ывать, -ать
mess² /mes/ *n.* (eating place) столóвая
ℐ **message** /'mesɪdʒ/ *n.* (formal) сообщéние;
(informal) запи́ска, зáпись
messenger /'mesɪndʒə(r)/ *n.* курьéр,
посы́льный
Messiah /mɪ'saɪə/ *n.* Мессия (*m.*)
Messrs /'mesəz/ *pl. of* ▶ **Mr**
messy /'mesɪ/ *adj.* (**messier, messiest**)
(untidy) неубрáнный; (slovenly) неря́шливый;
(unpleasant) неприя́тный
Met /met/ *abbr. of* **1** (**the Met (Office)**)
Метеорологи́ческое бюрó (*во
Великобритании*) **2** (**the Met**) поли́ция
Лондóна **3** (**the Met**) Метрополи́тен-
óпера (*в Нью-Йóрке*)
met /met/ *past and p.p. of* ▶ **meet**
metabolic /metə'bɒlɪk/ *adj.:* **~ rate** скóрость
обмéна вещéств
metabolism /mɪ'tæbəlɪz(ə)m/ *n.* обмéн
вещéств
ℐ **metal** /'met(ə)l/ *n.* метáлл
　● *adj.* металли́ческий

────────────
ℐ ключевáя лéксика

metallic /mə'tælɪk/ *adj.* металли́ческий
metallurgist /me'tælədʒɪst/ *n.* металлýрг
metallurgy /mɪ'tælədʒɪ/ *n.* металлурги́я
metamorphosis /metə'mɔ:fəsɪs/ *n.* (*pl.*
metamorphoses /-si:z/) метаморфóза
metaphor /'metəfɔ:(r)/ *n.* метáфора
metaphorical /metə'fɒrɪk(ə)l/ *adj.*
метафори́ческий; **~ly speaking** óбразно
говоря́
metaphysical /metə'fɪzɪk(ə)l/ *adj.*
метафизи́ческий
metaphysics /metə'fɪzɪks/ *n.* метафи́зика
mete /mi:t/ *v.t.* (**~ out**) распредел|я́ть, -и́ть
meteor /'mi:tɪə(r)/ *n.* метеóр
meteoric /mi:tɪ'ɒrɪk/ *adj.* (fig.)
головокружи́тельный
meteorite /'mi:tɪəraɪt/ *n.* метеори́т
meteorological /mi:tɪərə'lɒdʒɪk(ə)l/ *adj.*
метеорологи́ческий
■ **~ office** (BrE), **~ center** (AmE) *nn.* слýжба
погóды
meteorologist /mi:tɪə'rɒlədʒɪst/ *n.*
метеорóлог
meteorology /mi:tɪə'rɒlədʒɪ/ *n.* метеороло́гия
meter¹ /'mi:tə(r)/ *n.* (apparatus) счётчик; **gas ~**
гáзовый счётчик
　● *v.t.* изм|еря́ть, -éрить; зам|еря́ть, -éрить
meter² /'mi:tə(r)/ *n.* (AmE) = **metre**
methane /'mi:θeɪn/ *n.* метáн
ℐ **method** /'meθəd/ *n.* (way) мéтод, спóсоб;
(system) систéма, метóдика
methodical /mɪ'θɒdɪk(ə)l/ *adj.*
системати́ческий
Methodist /'meθədɪst/ *n.* (relig.) методи́ст
(-ка); (*attr.*) методи́стский
methodology /meθə'dɒlədʒɪ/ *n.* методоло́гия
meths /meθs/ *n.* (BrE, infml) денатурáт
methylated /'meθɪleɪtɪd/ *adj.:* **~ spirit**
денатурáт
meticulous /mə'tɪkjʊləs/ *adj.* тщáтельный
meticulousness /mə'tɪkjʊləsnɪs/ *n.*
тщáтельность, аккурáтность
ℐ **metre** /'mi:tə(r)/ (AmE **meter**) *n.* метр
metric /'metrɪk/ *adj.* метри́ческий
metronome /'metrənəʊm/ *n.* метронóм
metropolis /mɪ'trɒpəlɪs/ *n.* столи́ца
metropolitan /metrə'pɒlɪt(ə)n/ *adj.*
столи́чный
mettle /'met(ə)l/ *n.* си́ла харáктера
mews /mju:z/ *n. pl.* (BrE) конюшни (*f. pl.*)
(передéланные в жилóе помещéние)
Mexican /'meksɪkən/ *n.* мексикáн|ец (-ка)
　● *adj.* мексикáнский
Mexico /'meksɪkəʊ/ *n.* Мéксика; **~ City**
Мéхико (*m. indecl.*)
mezzanine /'metsəni:n/ *n.* мезони́н, полуэтáж
mezzo /'metsəʊ/ *adv.* пóлу-
■ **~ forte** *adv.* довóльно грóмко; **~-soprano**
n. (*pl.* **~s**) (singer) мéццо-сопрáно (*f. indecl.*);
(voice) мéццо-сопрáно (*nt. indecl.*)
miaow /mɪ'aʊ/ *v.i.* мяýкать (*impf.*)

mice /mais/ *pl. of* ▶ mouse

microbe /'maɪkrəʊb/ *n.* микро́б

microbiologist /maɪkrəʊbaɪˈɒlədʒɪst/ *n.* микробио́лог

microbiology /maɪkrəʊbaɪˈɒlədʒɪ/ *n.* микробиоло́гия

microblog /'maɪkrəʊblɒg/ *n.* (comput.) микробло́г

microchip /'maɪkrəʊtʃɪp/ *n.* микросхе́ма, чип

microclimate /'maɪkrəʊklaɪmət/ *n.* микрокли́мат

microcosm /'maɪkrəkɒz(ə)m/ *n.* микроко́см

microfiche /'maɪkrəʊfiːʃ/ *n.* микрофи́ша (*несколько фотографий на микроплёнке*)

microfilm /'maɪkrəʊfɪlm/ *n.* микрофи́льм, микроплёнка

microlight /'maɪkrəʊlaɪt/ *n.* (BrE) сверхлёгкий персона́льный самолёт

microorganism /maɪkrəʊˈɔːgənɪz(ə)m/ *n.* микроорганизм

microphone /'maɪkrəfəʊn/ *n.* микрофо́н

microprocessor /maɪkrəʊˈprəʊsesə(r)/ *n.* микропроце́ссор

microscope /'maɪkrəskəʊp/ *n.* микроско́п

microscopic /maɪkrəˈskɒpɪk/ *adj.* микроскопи́ческий

microwave /'maɪkrəʊweɪv/ *n.*: ~ oven микроволно́вая печь

mid /mɪd/ *adj. & pref.*: in ~ air (высоко́) в во́здухе; from ~ June to ~ July с середи́ны ию́ня до середи́ны ию́ля
■ ~**day** *n.* по́лдень (*m.*); ~**night** *n.* по́лночь; ~**summer** *n.* середи́на ле́та; (*attr.*) M~summer Day Ива́нов день (*24 ию́ня*); ~**way** *adv.* на полпути́; the M~**west** *n.* Сре́дний За́пад США; ~**winter** *n.* середи́на зимы́

ℱ **middle** /'mɪd(ə)l/ *n.* **1** середи́на; in the ~ of среди́ + *g.*; (of time): in the ~ of the night посреди́ но́чи; I was in the ~ of getting ready в тот моме́нт я как раз собира́лся **2** (waist) та́лия
● *adj.* сре́дний; the M~ Ages Сре́дние века́; the ~ classes сре́дние слои́ о́бщества; сре́дний класс
■ ~-**aged** *adj.* сре́дних лет; ~-**class** *adj.* относя́щийся к сре́днему кла́ссу; M~ East *n.* Бли́жний Восто́к; ~**man** *n.* посре́дник; ~ school *n.* (BrE) сре́дняя шко́ла; ~**weight** *n. & adj.* (боксёр) сре́днего ве́са

middling /'mɪdlɪŋ/ *adj.* сре́дний, второсо́ртный; fair to ~ так себе́

midge /mɪdʒ/ *n.* кома́р, мо́шка

midget /'mɪdʒɪt/ *n.* (offens.) ка́рлик

midriff /'mɪdrɪf/ *n.* ве́рхняя часть живота́

midst /mɪdst/ *n.* середи́на; in the ~ of среди́, в разга́р + *g.*, ме́жду + *i.*; a stranger in our ~ чужо́й среди́ нас

midwife /'mɪdwaɪf/ *n.* акуше́рка

miff /mɪf/ *v.t.* (infml): he was ~ed by my remark моё замеча́ние оби́дело его́

might[1] /maɪt/ *n.* **1** (power) мощь **2** (strength) си́ла; with (all his) ~ and main изо всех сил,

что бы́ло мо́чи

ℱ **might**[2] /maɪt/ *v. aux. see* ▶ may

mighty /'maɪtɪ/ *adj.* (**mightier**, **mightiest**) мо́щный

migraine /'miːgreɪn/ *n.* мигре́нь

migrant /'maɪgrənt/ *n.* пересе́ленец
● *adj.* кочу́ющий

migrate /maɪˈgreɪt/ *v.i.* пересел|я́ться, -и́ться; (of birds) соверш|а́ть, -и́ть перелёт

migration /maɪˈgreɪʃ(ə)n/ *n.* мигра́ция; перелёт

migratory /maɪˈgreɪtərɪ/ *adj.* перелётный

mike /maɪk/ *n.* (infml) = microphone

mild /maɪld/ *adj.* мя́гкий; a ~ day тёплый день

mildew /'mɪldjuː/ *n.* пле́сень

ℱ **mile** /maɪl/ *n.* ми́ля; (fig.): I was ~s away я замеча́лся; it sticks out a ~ э́то броса́ется в глаза́
■ ~**stone** *n.* ка́мень с указа́нием расстоя́ния; (fig.) ве́ха

mileage /'maɪlɪdʒ/ *n.* **1** (distance in miles) расстоя́ние в ми́лях; (of car) пробе́г автомоби́ля в ми́лях **2** (travel expenses) проездны́е (*pl.*)

milieu /miːˈljɜː/ *n.* (*pl.* ~x *or* ~s) окруже́ние, среда́

militancy /'mɪlɪt(ə)nsɪ/ *n.* вои́нственность

militant /'mɪlɪt(ə)nt/ *n.* бое́ц, боре́ц
● *adj.* вои́нствующий

militarism /'mɪlɪtərɪz(ə)m/ *n.* милитари́зм

militaristic /mɪlɪtəˈrɪstɪk/ *adj.* милитари́стский, милитаристи́ческий

ℱ **military** /'mɪlɪtərɪ/ *n.*: the ~ военнослу́жащие (*m. pl.*), войска́ (*nt. pl.*)
● *adj.* вое́нный
■ ~ **service** *n.* вое́нная слу́жба; (as liability) во́инская пови́нность

militate /'mɪlɪteɪt/ *v.i.*: ~ against препя́тствовать (*impf.*) + *d.*; говори́ть (*impf.*) про́тив + *g.*; his age ~s against him ему́ меша́ет во́зраст

militia /mɪˈlɪʃə/ *n.* мили́ция

milk /mɪlk/ *n.* молоко́
● *v.t.* дои́ть, по-; (fig.): they ~ed him of all his cash они́ вы́качали из него́ все де́ньги
■ ~**man** *n.* продаве́ц молока́, моло́чник; ~**shake** *n.* моло́чный кокте́йль

milky /'mɪlkɪ/ *adj.* (**milkier**, **milkiest**) моло́чный; the M~ Way Мле́чный Путь

mill /mɪl/ *n.* (for grinding corn) ме́льница; (factory) фа́брика
● *v.t.* моло́ть, пере-
● *v.i.* (infml): a crowd was ~ing around the entrance лю́ди толпи́лись у вхо́да

millenni|um /mɪˈlenɪəm/ *n.* (*pl.* ~ums *or* ~a) тысячеле́тие

miller /'mɪlə(r)/ *n.* ме́льник

milligram, milligramme /'mɪlɪgræm/ *n.* миллигра́м

millimetre /'mɪlɪmiːtə(r)/ (AmE -**meter**) *n.* миллиме́тр

milliner /'mɪlɪnə(r)/ *n.* ма́стер/мастери́ца по изготовле́нию же́нских шляп

m

million /'mɪljən/ *n. & adj. (pl.* ~s *or* (*with numeral or qualifying word*) ~) миллио́н + g.

millionaire /mɪljə'neə(r)/ *n.* миллионе́р

millionth /'mɪljənθ/ *n.* миллио́нная часть
● *adj.* миллио́нный

milometer /maɪ'lɒmɪtə(r)/ *n.* (BrE) счётчик пробе́га

mime /maɪm/ *n.* (performance; technique) пантоми́ма; (artist) арти́ст пантоми́мы
● *v.t.* (act by miming) изобра|жа́ть, -зи́ть пантоми́мой
● *v.i.* (pretend to sing) петь, с-/про- под фоногра́мму

mimic /'mɪmɪk/ *n.* имита́тор
● *v.t.* (**mimicked, mimicking**) передра́зн|ивать, -и́ть

mimicry /'mɪmɪkrɪ/ *n.* (imitation) имити́рование; подража́ние + d.

minaret /mɪnə'ret/ *n.* минаре́т

minc|e /mɪns/ *n.* (BrE) фарш
● *v.t.* руби́ть (*impf.*)
■ ~**ed beef** *n.* говя́жий фарш; ~**ing machine** *n.* мясору́бка

mind /maɪnd/ *n.* **1** (intellect) ум; **you must be out of your** ~ вы с ума́ сошли́ **2** (remembrance): **bear in** ~ по́мнить (*impf.*); **the tune went clean out of my** ~ я на́чисто забы́л э́ту мело́дию **3** (opinion) мне́ние; **he spoke his** ~ **on the subject** он открове́нно вы́сказался на э́ту те́му; **he doesn't know his own** ~ он сам не зна́ет, чего́ он хо́чет; **try to keep an open** ~! постара́йтесь быть объекти́вн|ым (-ой)! **4** (intention) наме́рение; **he changed his** ~ он переду́мал; **I have made up my** ~ **to stay** я реши́л оста́ться **5** (thought) мы́сли (*f. pl.*); **I had something on my** ~ меня́ что́-то трево́жило; **I set his** ~ **at rest** я его́ успоко́ил; **it took her** ~ **off her troubles** э́то отвлекло́ её от (её) забо́т/невзго́д; **I cannot read his** ~ я не могу́ угада́ть/проче́сть его́ мы́сли; **I can see him in my** ~'**s eye** он стои́т у меня́ пе́ред глаза́ми **6** (way of thinking) настрое́ние; **to my** ~ на мой взгляд; мне ка́жется (*or* я счита́ю), что **7** (attention): **keep your** ~ **on what you are doing** не отвлека́йтесь
● *v.t.* **1** (take care, charge of) присм|а́тривать, -отре́ть за + *i.*; ~ **your own business!** не вме́шивайтесь не в своё де́ло! **2** (worry about) забо́титься (*impf.*) o + *p.*; беспоко́иться o + *p.*; **never** ~ **the expense** не ду́майте о расхо́дах; ~ **your head!** осторо́жнее, не ушиби́те го́лову! **3** (object to) возра|жа́ть, -зи́ть на + *a.*; име́ть (*impf.*) что-н. про́тив + *g.*; **I don't** ~ **the cold** я не бою́сь хо́лода; **would you** ~ **opening the door?** откро́йте, пожа́луйста, дверь; **I wouldn't** ~ **going for a walk** я не прочь прогуля́ться
● *v.i.* **1** (worry) беспоко́иться (*impf.*); трево́житься (*impf.*); **we're rather late, but never** ~! мы немно́го опа́здываем, ну, ничего́! **2** (object) возра|жа́ть, -зи́ть; **do you** ~ **if I smoke?** вы не про́тив, е́сли я закурю́?

● ключева́я ле́ксика

■ ~-**boggling** *adj.* порази́тельный

minder /'maɪndə(r)/ *n.* (BrE) (child minder) ня́ня; (infml, bodyguard) телохрани́тель (*m.*)

mindful /'maɪndfʊl/ *adj.* забо́тливый; **we must be** ~ **of the children** мы должны́ ду́мать о де́тях; **I was** ~ **of his advice** я по́мнил его́ сове́т; **he was** ~ **of his duty** он сознава́л свой долг

mindless /'maɪndlɪs/ *adj.* **1** (thoughtless) безду́мный; (stupid) глу́пый **2** (not requiring intelligence): ~ **drudgery** механи́ческий труд

mine¹ /maɪn/ *n.* **1** (excavation) ша́хта; рудни́к **2** (explosive device) ми́на
● *v.t.* **1** (excavate): ~ **coal/ore** добыва́ть (*impf.*) у́голь/руду́ **2** (mil.) мини́ровать, за-
● *v.i.* разраб|а́тывать, -о́тать рудни́к
■ ~**field** *n.* ми́нное по́ле

mine² /maɪn/ *pron.*: **that book is** ~ э́то моя́ кни́га; **a friend of** ~ (оди́н) мой друг/ знако́мый

miner /'maɪnə(r)/ *n.* (coal ~) шахтёр

mineral /'mɪnər(ə)l/ *n.* минера́л, руда́
● *adj.* минера́льный
■ ~ **water** *n.* минера́льная вода́

mineralogical /mɪnərə'lɒdʒɪk(ə)l/ *adj.* минералоги́ческий

mineralogist /mɪnə'rælədʒɪst/ *n.* минерало́г

mineralogy /mɪnə'rælədʒɪ/ *n.* минерало́гия

minestrone /mɪnɪ'strəʊnɪ/ *n.* италья́нский овощно́й суп с ме́лкими макаро́нными изде́лиями

mingle /'mɪŋɡ(ə)l/ *v.i.* сме́шиваться (*impf.*); ~ **with** (frequent) обща́ться (*impf.*) c + *i.*

mini /'mɪnɪ/ *n.* (pl. ~s) (garment) ми́ни (*юбка и т. д.*)

miniature /'mɪnɪtʃə(r)/ *n.* миниатю́ра
● *adj.* миниатю́рный

minibus /'mɪnɪbʌs/ *n.* микроавто́бус

minicab /'mɪnɪkæb/ *n.* (BrE) такси́ (*nt. indecl.*)

minidisc /'mɪnɪdɪsk/ *n.* ми́ни-ди́ск

minim /'mɪnɪm/ *n.* (BrE, mus.) полови́нная но́та

minimal /'mɪnɪm(ə)l/ *adj.* минима́льный

minimalism /'mɪnɪməlɪz(ə)m/ *n.* минимали́зм

minimalist /'mɪnɪməlɪst/ *n.* минимали́ст
● *adj.* минимали́стский

minimize /'mɪnɪmaɪz/ *v.t.* (reduce to minimum) дов|оди́ть, -ести́ до ми́нимума; (make light of) преум|еньша́ть, -е́ньшить

minimum /'mɪnɪməm/ *n.* ми́нимум; (*attr.*) минима́льный

mining /'maɪnɪŋ/ *n.* го́рное де́ло, го́рная промы́шленность

minion /'mɪnjən/ *n.* приспе́шник

miniskirt /'mɪnɪskə:t/ *n.* ми́ни-ю́бка

minister /'mɪnɪstə(r)/ *n.* **1** (head of government dept.) мини́стр **2** (clergyman) свяще́нник, па́стор
● *v.i.*: ~ **to** служи́ть (*impf.*) + *d.*; прислу́живать (*impf.*) + *d.*

ministerial /mɪnɪ'stɪərɪəl/ *adj.* министе́рский

ministry /'mɪnɪstrɪ/ *n.* министе́рство

mink /mɪŋk/ *n.* но́рка

minnow /'mɪnəʊ/ *n.* пескáрь (*m.*)

⚡ **minor** /'maɪnə(r)/ *n.* **1** (person under age) несовершеннолéтний **2** (mus.) минóр; A ∼ ля минóр
● *adj.* **1** (of lesser importance) второстепéнный; малозначи́тельный, мéлкий, небольшóй **2** (mus.) минóрный; ∼ **key** минóрная тонáльность

⚡ **minority** /maɪ'nɒrɪtɪ/ *n.* меньшинствó, мéньшая часть; (*attr.*) ∼ **group** меньшинствó

Minsk *n.* Минск

minstrel /'mɪnstr(ə)l/ *n.* менестрéль (*m.*)

mint[1] /mɪnt/ *n.* (bot.) мя́та; (a sweet) мя́тная конфéта

mint[2] /mɪnt/ *n.* (fin.) монéтный двор
● *v.t.* чекáнить (*impf.*)

minuet /mɪnjʊ'et/ *n.* менуэ́т

minus /'maɪnəs/ *n.* ми́нус
● *adj.* отрицáтельный
● *prep.* ми́нус; без + *g.*; ∼ **1** ми́нус оди́н; **he came back** ∼ **an arm** он верну́лся без руки́
■ ∼ **sign** *n.* (знак) ми́нус

minuscule /'mɪnəskjuːl/ *adj.* крóхотный, óчень мáленький

⚡ **minute**[1] /'mɪnɪt/ *n.* **1** (fraction of hour or degree) мину́та; **he left everything till the last** ∼ он отложи́л всё до послéдней мину́ты **2** (moment) мгновéние, момéнт, миг; **just a** ∼**!** (одну́) мину́тку!; **I'll tell him the** ∼ **he arrives** как тóлько он придёт, я ему́ скажу́ **3** (*usu. in pl.*) (record) протокóл

minute[2] /maɪ'njuːt/ *adj.* (**minutest**, *no comp.*) (tiny) мéлкий, крóхотный

minutiae /maɪ'njuːʃɪaɪ/ *n.* мéлочи (*f. pl.*); детáли (*f. pl.*)

minx /mɪŋks/ *n.* (joc.) озорни́ца; (coquette) кокéтка

miracle /'mɪrək(ə)l/ *n.* чу́до

miraculous /mɪ'rækjʊləs/ *adj.* чудéсный

mirage /'mɪrɑːʒ/ *n.* мирáж

mire /'maɪə(r)/ *n.* тряси́на; болóто; **his name was dragged through the** ∼ егó смешáли с гря́зью

mirror /'mɪrə(r)/ *n.* зéркало
● *v.t.* отражáть, -зи́ть

mirth /mɜːθ/ *n.* (gladness) весéлье; (laughter) смех

misadventure /mɪsəd'ventʃə(r)/ *n.* несчáстье, несчáстный слу́чай; **death by** ∼ смерть от несчáстного слу́чая

misapprehension /mɪsæprɪ'henʃ(ə)n/ *n.* преврáтное понимáние; **I was under a** ∼ я заблуждáлся

misappropriate /mɪsə'prəʊprɪeɪt/ *v.t.* (незакóнно) присвáивать, -óить

misappropriation /mɪsəprəʊprɪ'eɪʃ(ə)n/ *n.* незакóнное присвоéние

misbehave /mɪsbɪ'heɪv/ *v.i.* ду́рно себя́ вести́ (*det.*)

miscalculate /mɪs'kælkjʊleɪt/ *v.t.* плóхо рассчи́т|ывать, -áть
● *v.i.* просчи́т|ываться, -áться

miscalculation /mɪskælkjʊ'leɪʃ(ə)n/ *n.* просчёт

miscarriage /'mɪskærɪdʒ/ *n.* **1** (biol.) вы́кидыш; **she had a** ∼ у неё произошёл вы́кидыш **2**: ∼ **of justice** оши́бка правосу́дия

miscarry /mɪs'kærɪ/ *v.i.* **1** (of a woman) имéть (*impf.*) вы́кидыш **2** (fail) терпéть (*impf.*) неудáчу; **his plans** ∼**ied** егó плáны провали́лись

miscellaneous /mɪsə'leɪnɪəs/ *adj.* смéшанный; разнообрáзный

mischief /'mɪstʃɪf/ *n.* озорствó; прокáзы (*f. pl.*); **he is always getting into** ∼ он всегдá прокáзничает/шали́т

mischievous /'mɪstʃɪvəs/ *adj.* озорнóй, шаловли́вый

misconception /mɪskən'sepʃ(ə)n/ *n.* непрáвильное представлéние/понимáние

misconduct /mɪs'kɒndʌkt/ *n.* дурнóе поведéние; **professional** ∼ нарушéние профессионáльной э́тики; должностнóе преступлéние

misconstrue /mɪskən'struː/ *v.t.* непрáвильно истолкóв|ывать, -áть

misdeed /mɪs'diːd/ *n.* преступлéние

misdemeanour /mɪsdɪ'miːnə(r)/ (AmE **misdemeanor**) *n.* просту́пок

misdiagnose /mɪsdaɪəg'nəʊz/ *v.t.* (med.) стáвить, по- невéрный диáгноз; **her depression was** ∼**d as stress** у неё былá депрéссия, а ей оши́бочно постáвили диáгноз «стрéсс»

miser /'maɪzə(r)/ *n.* скря́га (*c.g.*), скуп|óй (-áя)

miserable /'mɪzərəb(ə)l/ *adj.* **1** (unhappy) жáлкий, несчáстный **2** (causing wretchedness) плохóй, сквéрный; **what** ∼ **weather!** какáя сквéрная погóда! **3** (mean): **a** ∼ **sum (of money)** ничтóжная/ми́зерная су́мма

miserly /'maɪzəlɪ/ *adj.* скупóй

misery /'mɪzərɪ/ *n.* **1** (suffering) страдáние; мучéние **2** (extreme poverty) нищетá, бéдность **3** (BrE, infml, person who complains) зану́да (*c.g.*), ны́тик

misfire /mɪs'faɪə(r)/ *v.i.* да|вáть, -ть осéчку; (tech., of ignition) выпадáть, вы́пасть; (fig.) не состоя́ться (*impf.*); **his plans** ∼**d** егó план сорвáлся

misfit /'mɪsfɪt/ *n.* неприспосóбленный человéк

misfortune /mɪs'fɔːtʃuːn/ *n.* (bad luck) бедá, несчáстье; **I had the** ∼ **to lose my purse** я имéл несчáстье потеря́ть кошелёк; (stroke of bad luck) несчáстье, неудáча

misgiving /mɪs'gɪvɪŋ/ *n.* опасéние; дурнóе предчу́вствие

misguided /mɪs'gaɪdɪd/ *adj.*: **I was** ∼ **enough to trust him** я имéл неосторóжность довéриться ему́; ∼ **enthusiasm** энтузиáзм, достóйный лу́чшего применéния

mishandle /mɪs'hænd(ə)l/ *v.t.* (ill-treat) плóхо/ ду́рно обращáться (*impf.*) с + *i.*; (manage inefficiently) плóхо вести́ (*det.*) (дéло)

mishap /'mɪshæp/ *n.* неудáча

mishear /mɪs'hɪə(r)/ *v.t.* нетóчно расслы́шать (*pf.*)

misinform /ˌmɪsɪnˈfɔːm/ v.t. непра́вильно информи́ровать (impf., pf.)

misinformation /ˌmɪsɪnfəˈmeɪʃ(ə)n/ n. неве́рная информа́ция; дезинформа́ция

misinterpret /ˌmɪsɪnˈtɜːprɪt/ v.t. непра́вильно пон|има́ть, -я́ть

misinterpretation /ˌmɪsɪntɜːprɪˈteɪʃ(ə)n/ n. непра́вильное понима́ние/толкова́ние

misjudge /mɪsˈdʒʌdʒ/ v.t. неве́рно оце́н|ивать, -и́ть

mislay /mɪsˈleɪ/ v.t. затеря́ть (pf.)

mislead /mɪsˈliːd/ v.t. вв|оди́ть, -ести́ в заблужде́ние

mismanage /mɪsˈmænɪdʒ/ v.t. пло́хо управля́ть (impf.) + i.

mismanagement /mɪsˈmænɪdʒmənt/ n. плохо́е управле́ние/руково́дство; (inefficiency) нераспоряди́тельность

misnomer /mɪsˈnəʊmə(r)/ n. непра́вильное назва́ние/и́мя

misogynist /mɪˈsɒdʒɪnɪst/ n. женоненави́стник

misogyny /mɪˈsɒdʒɪnɪ/ n. женоненави́стничество

misplaced /mɪsˈpleɪst/ adj. (inappropriate) неуме́стный; (unfounded) безоснова́тельный

misprint /ˈmɪsprɪnt/ n. опеча́тка

mispronounce /ˌmɪsprəˈnaʊns/ v.t. непра́вильно произн|оси́ть, -ести́

misquote /mɪsˈkwəʊt/ v.t. нето́чно цити́ровать, про-; **I have been ~d** мои́ слова́ исказили

misread /mɪsˈriːd/ v.t. (read incorrectly) чита́ть, про- непра́вильно; (misinterpret) непра́вильно истолко́в|ывать, -а́ть

misrepresent /ˌmɪsreprɪˈzent/ v.t. иска|жа́ть, -зи́ть

misrepresentation /ˌmɪsreprɪzenˈteɪʃ(ə)n/ n. искаже́ние (фа́ктов)

misrule /mɪsˈruːl/ n. (bad government) плохо́е правле́ние; (lawlessness) беспоря́док, ана́рхия

✍ **miss¹** /mɪs/ n. (failure to hit etc.) про́мах; **I gave the meeting a ~** (BrE) я не пошёл на собра́ние
● v.t. **1** (fail to hit or catch): **he ~ed the ball** он пропусти́л мяч; **he ~ed the bus** он опозда́л на авто́бус **2** (fig., fail to grasp) не пон|има́ть, -я́ть; не улови́ть (pf.); **you have ~ed the point** вы не по́няли су́ти **3** (fail to hear or see) не услы́шать (pf.); пропус|ка́ть, -ти́ть; **you must not ~ this film** не пропусти́те э́тот фильм **4** (fail to meet): **you've just ~ed him!** вы с ним чуть-чу́ть размину́лись! **5** (escape by chance) избе|га́ть, -жа́ть; **we just ~ed having an accident** мы чуть не попа́ли в катастро́фу **6** (regret absence of) скуча́ть (impf.), соскучи́ться (pf.) по (+ d.); **she ~es her husband** она́ скуча́ет по му́жу; **he ~ed Moscow** он соскучи́лся по Москве́
● v.i. (fail to hit target) прома́х|иваться, -ну́ться; не поп|ада́ть, -а́сть в цель
□ **~ out** v.t. упус|ка́ть, -ти́ть; пропус|ка́ть,

-ти́ть; **you have ~ed out the most important thing** вы пропусти́ли/упусти́ли са́мое ва́жное
● v.i. (infml): **he ~ed out on all the fun** он пропусти́л са́мое весе́лье; **I felt I was ~ing out** я чу́вствовал, что мно́гое упуска́ю

miss² /mɪs/ n. мисс

mis-sell /mɪsˈsel/ v.t. прод|ава́ть, -а́ть обма́нным/нече́стным путём

misshapen /mɪsˈʃeɪpən/ adj. уро́дливый

missile /ˈmɪsaɪl/ n. **1** (object thrown) мета́тельный предме́т **2** (weapon thrown or fired) снаря́д **3** (rocket weapon) раке́та

missing /ˈmɪsɪŋ/ adj. недостаю́щий; потеря́вшийся; **there is a page ~** не хвата́ет страни́цы; **he went ~** он пропа́л (бе́з вести)

✍ **mission** /ˈmɪʃ(ə)n/ n. **1** (mil.) зада́ние **2** (pol., relig.) ми́ссия

missionary /ˈmɪʃənərɪ/ n. миссионе́р (-ка)

missive /ˈmɪsɪv/ n. посла́ние

misspell /mɪsˈspel/ v.t. & i. непра́вильно написа́ть (pf.); сде́лать (pf.) орфографи́ческую оши́бку

mist /mɪst/ n. (lit., fig.) тума́н, ды́мка, мгла
● v.t. & i. затума́ни|вать(ся), -ть(ся); **my glasses have ~ed over** у меня́ запоте́ли очки́

✍ **mistake** /mɪˈsteɪk/ n. оши́бка; заблужде́ние; **by ~** по оши́бке; **make no ~ (about it)** бу́дьте уве́рены
● v.t. (misunderstand) ошиб|а́ться, -и́ться в + p.; (misrecognize): **he mistook me for my brother** он при́нял меня́ за моего́ бра́та

mistaken /mɪˈsteɪkən/ adj. **1** (in error): **if I am not ~** е́сли я не ошиба́юсь **2** (ill-judged; erroneous) неосмотри́тельный

mistletoe /ˈmɪs(ə)ltəʊ/ n. оме́ла

mistress /ˈmɪstrɪs/ n. **1** (woman in charge) хозя́йка **2** (lover) любо́вница

mistrial /mɪsˈtraɪəl/ n. непра́вильное суде́бное разбира́тельство

mistrust /mɪsˈtrʌst/ n. недове́рие
● v.t. не доверя́ть (impf.) + d.

misty /ˈmɪstɪ/ adj. (**mistier, mistiest**) тума́нный

misunderstand /ˌmɪsʌndəˈstænd/ v.t. непра́вильно пон|има́ть, -я́ть; **she felt ~stood** она́ чу́вствовала, что её не понима́ют

misunderstanding /ˌmɪsʌndəˈstændɪŋ/ n. недоразуме́ние

misuse¹ /mɪsˈjuːs/ n. непра́вильное употребле́ние; злоупотребле́ние (чем)

misuse² /mɪsˈjuːz/ v.t. (use improperly) непра́вильно употреб|ля́ть, -и́ть; (treat badly) ду́рно обраща́ться (impf.) с + i.

miter /ˈmaɪtə(r)/ n. (AmE) = mitre

mitigat|e /ˈmɪtɪgeɪt/ v.t. смягч|а́ть, -и́ть; **~ing circumstances** смягча́ющие обстоя́тельства

mitigation /mɪtɪˈgeɪʃ(ə)n/ n. смягче́ние, ослабле́ние; **a plea in ~** хода́тайство о смягче́нии пригово́ра

mitre /ˈmaɪtə(r)/ (AmE **miter**) n. (bishop's headgear) ми́тра

mitten /ˈmɪt(ə)n/ n. рукави́ца

ꝏ **mix** /mɪks/ *n.* смесь
• *v.t.* **1** (mingle) смеш|ивать, -а́ть; (combine) сочета́ть (*impf.*); I like to ~ business with pleasure я люблю́ сочета́ть прия́тное с поле́зным **2** (prepare by ~ing) смеш|ивать, -а́ть; переме́ш|ивать, -а́ть
• *v.i.* (of persons) обща́ться (*impf., pf.*); she won't ~ with her neighbours она́ не хо́чет обща́ться с сосе́дями
□ ~ **up** *v.t.* (~ thoroughly) (хорошо́) переме́ш|ивать, -а́ть; (confuse) перепу́т|ывать, -ать; I ~ed him up with his father я перепу́тал его́ с его́ отцо́м; a ~ed-up child (infml) тру́дный ребёнок; (involve) впу́т|ывать, -ать
■ ~-**up** *n.* недоразуме́ние

mixed /mɪkst/ *adj.* сме́шанный, переме́шанный; (place for) ~ bathing о́бщий пляж; I have ~ feelings about it у меня́ на э́тот счёт противоречи́вые чу́вства
■ ~-**race** *adj.* име́ющий роди́телей ра́зных рас, состоя́щий из люде́й ра́зных рас

mixer /'mɪksə(r)/ *n.* (for cement) меша́лка; (for food) ми́ксер

mixture /'mɪkstʃə(r)/ *n.* смесь

ml *abbr. of* **1** (**millilitre(s)**) /'mɪlɪlɪːtə(r)(z)/ мл (миллили́тр) **2** (**mile(s)**) /maɪl(z)/ ми́ля

mm /'mɪlɪmiːtə(r)(z)/ *n.* (*abbr. of* **millimetre(s)**)) мм (миллиме́тр)

MMR (med.) (*of* **measles, mumps, and rubella**) *abbr.*, MMR, приви́вка «корь-свинка-красну́ха»

MMS *abbr.* (*of* **Multimedia Message/ Messaging Service**): ~ message MMS-сообще́ние

moan /məʊn/ *n.* стон; (infml, complaint) стон, нытьё
• *v.i.* стона́ть (*impf.*); (infml, complain) ныть (*impf.*)

moat /məʊt/ *n.* ров с водо́й

mob /mɒb/ *n.* толпа́
• *v.t.* (**mobbed, mobbing**) нап|ада́ть, -а́сть на + *a.*

ꝏ **mobile** /'məʊbaɪl/ *n.* (BrE) моби́льный/со́товый телефо́н
• *adj.* **1** (easily moved) передвижно́й, переносно́й; (troops) подви́жный **2** (person) моби́льный
■ ~ **phone** *n.* (BrE) моби́льный/со́товый телефо́н

mobility /məˈbɪlɪtɪ/ *n.* подви́жность, моби́льность

mobilization /məʊbɪlaɪˈzeɪʃ(ə)n/ *n.* мобилиза́ция

mobilize /'məʊbɪlaɪz/ *v.t.* мобилизова́ть (*impf., pf.*)
• *v.i.* мобилизова́ться (*impf., pf.*)

moccasin /'mɒkəsɪn/ *n.* мокаси́н

mock /mɒk/ *adj.* подде́льный, фальши́вый
• *v.t.* насмеха́ться (*impf.*) над + *i.*
■ ~ **examination** *n.* (BrE) предэкзаменацио́нная прове́рка

mockery /'mɒkərɪ/ *n.* (ridicule) издева́тельство; (parody) паро́дия

MOD *abbr.* (*of* **Ministry of Defence**) Министе́рство оборо́ны

mod /mɒd/ *adj.* (*attr.*): ~ cons (BrE) совреме́нные удо́бства; with all ~ cons (BrE, in advertisement) со всеми удо́бствами

mode /məʊd/ *n.* ме́тод

ꝏ **model** /'mɒd(ə)l/ *n.* **1** (representation) моде́ль, схе́ма **2** (pattern) образе́ц, станда́рт; he is a ~ of gallantry он образе́ц гала́нтности; a ~ husband идеа́льный муж **3** (person posing for artist) нату́рщи|к (-ца) **4** (woman displaying clothes etc.) манеке́нщица, моде́ль **5** (design) моде́ль, тип
• *v.t.* (**modelled, modelling**, AmE **modeled, modeling**) де́лать, с- моде́ль + *g.*; she ~led the dress (wore it as a ~) она́ демонстри́ровала пла́тье; (fig.): he ~s himself upon his father он сле́дует приме́ру своего́ отца́

modem /'məʊdem/ *n.* моде́м

moderate[1] /'mɒdərət/ *adj.* уме́ренный; сре́дний; ~ drinker уме́ренно пью́щий челове́к

moderate[2] /'mɒdəreɪt/ *v.t.* ум|еря́ть, -е́рить; смягча́ть, -и́ть
• *v.i.* смягча́ться, -и́ться

moderation /mɒdəˈreɪʃ(ə)n/ *n.* уме́ренность; in ~ уме́ренно

ꝏ **modern** /'mɒd(ə)n/ *adj.* совреме́нный
■ ~ **languages** *n. pl.* но́вые языки́

modernism /'mɒdənɪz(ə)m/ *n.* модерни́зм

modernization /mɒdənaɪˈzeɪʃ(ə)n/ *n.* модерниза́ция

modernize /'mɒdənaɪz/ *v.t.* модернизи́ровать (*impf., pf.*)

modest /'mɒdɪst/ *adj.* скро́мный

modesty /'mɒdɪstɪ/ *n.* скро́мность

modicum /'mɒdɪkəm/ *n.* чу́точка, толи́ка

modification /mɒdɪfɪˈkeɪʃ(ə)n/ *n.* модифика́ция

modify /'mɒdɪfaɪ/ *v.t.* модифици́ровать (*impf.*)

modish /'məʊdɪʃ/ *adj.* мо́дный

modulate /'mɒdjʊleɪt/ *v.t.* (vary pitch of, also radio) модули́ровать (*impf.*)

module /'mɒdjuːl/ *n.* (independent unit) блок, се́кция; (unit of study) курс

mogul /'məʊɡ(ə)l/ *n.* (fig., tycoon) магна́т

mohair /'məʊheə(r)/ *n.* мохе́р; (*attr.*) мохе́ровый

moist /mɔɪst/ *adj.* вла́жный, сыро́й

moisten /'mɔɪs(ə)n/ *v.t.* увлажн|я́ть, -и́ть; см|а́чивать, -очи́ть

moisture /'mɔɪstʃə(r)/ *n.* вла́жность, вла́га

moisturize /'mɔɪstʃəraɪz/ *v.t.* увлажн|я́ть, -и́ть

moisturizer /'mɔɪstʃəraɪzə(r)/ *n.* увлажня́ющий крем

mold /məʊld/ (AmE) = **mould**[1], **mould**[2]

Moldova /mɒlˈdəʊvə/ *n.* Молдо́ва

Moldovan /mɒlˈdəʊv(ə)n/ *n.* молдава́н|ин (-ка)
• *adj.* молда́вский

m

moldy /ˈməʊldɪ/ *adj.* (AmE) = **mouldy**

mole¹ /məʊl/ *n.* (on skin) ро́динка

mole² /məʊl/ *n.* (zool.) крот; (secret agent) аге́нт, внедри́вшийся в иностра́нную разве́дку

molecular /məˈlekjʊlə(r)/ *adj.* молекуля́рный

molecule /ˈmɒlɪkjuːl/ *n.* моле́кула

molest /məˈlest/ *v.t.* пристǀава́ть, -а́ть к + *d.*

mollify /ˈmɒlɪfaɪ/ *v.t.* смягч|а́ть, -и́ть; успок|а́ивать, -о́ить

mollusc /ˈmɒləsk/ *n.* моллю́ск

mollycoddle /ˈmɒlɪkɒd(ə)l/ *v.t.* не́жить (*impf.*)

Molotov cocktail /ˈmɒlətɒf ˈkɒkteɪl/ *n.* буты́лка с зажига́тельной сме́сью

molt /məʊlt/ *v.i.* (AmE) = **moult**

molten /ˈməʊlt(ə)n/ *adj.* распла́вленный

⚹ **moment** /ˈməʊmənt/ *n.* моме́нт, миг; **he will be here (at) any ~ now** он здесь бу́дет с мину́ты на мину́ту; **I am busy at the ~** я сейча́с за́нят

momentarily /ˈməʊməntərɪlɪ/ *adv.* на мгнове́ние; (AmE, very soon) че́рез не́сколько мину́т

momentary /ˈməʊməntərɪ/ *adj.* мгнове́нный

momentous /məˈmentəs/ *adj.* ва́жный

momentum /məˈmentəm/ *n.* (*pl.* **momenta**) (phys.) ине́рция; (fig., impetus) дви́жущая си́ла; и́мпульс

monarch /ˈmɒnək/ *n.* мона́рх

monarchist /ˈmɒnəkɪst/ *n.* монархи́ст (-ка)
● *adj.* монархи́стский

monarchy /ˈmɒnəkɪ/ *n.* мона́рхия

monastery /ˈmɒnəstrɪ/ *n.* монасты́рь (*m.*)

monastic /məˈnæstɪk/ *adj.* (of monasteries) монасты́рский; ~ **life** мона́шеская жизнь; ~ **order** мона́шеский о́рден

⚹ **Monday** /ˈmʌndeɪ/ *n.* понеде́льник

monetarism /ˈmʌnɪtərɪz(ə)m/ *n.* монетари́зм

monetarist /ˈmʌnɪtərɪst/ *n.* монетари́ст
● *adj.* монетари́стский

monetary /ˈmʌnɪtərɪ/ *adj.* де́нежный

⚹ **money** /ˈmʌnɪ/ *n.* (*pl.* **moneys** *or* **monies**) де́ньги (-ег); **I got my ~'s worth** я получи́л сполна́ за свои́ де́ньги; **make** ~ (earn money) зараб|а́тывать, -о́тать; (become rich) разбогате́ть (*pf.*)
■ ~ **box** *n.* (BrE) копи́лка; ~ **laundering** *n.* отмыва́ние де́нег; ~**lender** *n.* ростовщи́к; ~ **order** *n.* почто́вый перево́д

Mongolia /mɒnˈɡəʊlɪə/ *n.* Монго́лия

Mongolian /mɒnˈɡəʊlɪən/ *n.* (person) монго́л (-ка); (language) монго́льский язы́к
● *adj.* монго́льский

mongrel /ˈmʌŋɡr(ə)l/ *n.* дворня́га

monitor /ˈmɒnɪt(ə)r/ *n.* (TV, comput.) монито́р
● *v.t.* следи́ть (*impf.*) за + *i.*

monk /mʌŋk/ *n.* мона́х

monkey /ˈmʌŋkɪ/ *n.* (*pl.* ~**s**) обезья́на

mono /ˈmɒnəʊ/ *n.* мо́но; **recorded in** ~ запи́санный монофони́чески

monochrome /ˈmɒnəkrəʊm/ *n.* однокра́сочное изображе́ние
● *adj.* одноцве́тный, монохро́мный

monogamous /məˈnɒɡəməs/ *adj.* монога́мный, единобра́чный

monogamy /məˈnɒɡəmɪ/ *n.* монога́мия, единобра́чие

monogram /ˈmɒnəɡræm/ *n.* моногра́мма

monograph /ˈmɒnəɡrɑːf/ *n.* моногра́фия

monolith /ˈmɒnəlɪθ/ *n.* моноли́т

monolithic /mɒnəˈlɪθɪk/ *adj.* (lit., fig.) моноли́тный

monologue /ˈmɒnəlɒɡ/ *n.* моноло́г

monopolize /məˈnɒpəlaɪz/ *v.t.*: **he ~s the conversation** он не даёт нико́му вста́вить сло́ва

monopoly /məˈnɒpəlɪ/ *n.* монопо́лия

monosodium glutamate /mɒnəˈsəʊdɪəm ˈɡluːtəmeɪt/ *n.* глутама́т на́трия (*пищева́я доба́вка*)

monosyllabic /mɒnəsɪˈlæbɪk/ *adj.* односло́жный

monotone /ˈmɒnətəʊn/ *n.*: **in a** ~ без вся́кого выраже́ния, моното́нно

monotonous /məˈnɒtənəs/ *adj.* моното́нный

monotony /məˈnɒtənɪ/ *n.* моното́нность, однообра́зие

monsoon /mɒnˈsuːn/ *n.* сезо́н дожде́й

monster /ˈmɒnstə(r)/ *n.* (misshapen creature) уро́д; (imaginary animal) чудо́вище; (person of exceptional cruelty etc.) чудо́вище, и́зверг

monstrosity /mɒnˈstrɒsɪtɪ/ *n.* (unsightly thing) чудо́вище

monstrous /ˈmɒnstrəs/ *adj.* (monsterlike) ужа́сный; (huge) грома́дный, исполи́нский

Montenegro /mɒntɪˈniːɡrəʊ/ *n.* Черного́рия

⚹ **month** /mʌnθ/ *n.* ме́сяц

monthly /ˈmʌnθlɪ/ *n.* (periodical) ежеме́сячник
● *adj.* ме́сячный
● *adv.* ежеме́сячно

monument /ˈmɒnjʊmənt/ *n.* па́мятник, монуме́нт

monumental /mɒnjʊˈment(ə)l/ *adj.* монумента́льный; (fig.) колосса́льный

moo /muː/ *v.i.* (**moos**, **mooed**) мыча́ть, про-

mooch /muːtʃ/ *v.i.* **1** (*usu.* ~ **about/ around**) (BrE, infml, loiter) слоня́ться (*impf.*) (без де́ла) **2** (AmE, infml, cadge) попроша́йничать (*impf.*)

mood /muːd/ *n.* (state of mind) настрое́ние; **I am not in the** ~ **for conversation** я не располо́жен к разгово́ру

moody /ˈmuːdɪ/ *adj.* (**moodier**, **moodiest**) (gloomy) угрю́мый; (subject to changes of mood) капри́зный; переме́нчивого настрое́ния

moon /muːn/ *n.* луна́; (astron.) Луна́; **new** ~ молодо́й ме́сяц, новолу́ние
■ ~**light** *n.* лу́нный свет; **by** ~**light** при луне́
● *v.i.* (infml) подхалту́ри|вать, -ть; ~**lighting** *n.* (infml) халту́ра; ~**lit** *adj.* за́литый лу́нным све́том

moor¹ /mʊə(r)/ *n.* ме́стность, поро́сшая ве́реском

⚹ ключева́я ле́ксика

■ ∼**land** n. вѐресковая пу́стошь

moor² /mʊə(r)/ v.t. ста́вить, по- на прича́л; швартова́ть, при-
● v.i.: they ∼ed in the harbour они́ пришвартова́лись в га́вани

mooring /'mʊərɪŋ/ n. прича́л

Moorish /'mʊərɪʃ/ adj. маврита́нский

moose /muːs/ n. (pl. ∼) америка́нский лось

moot /muːt/ adj.: a ∼ point спо́рный пункт
● v.t.: the question was ∼ed вопро́с поста́вили на обсужде́ние

mop /mɒp/ n. шва́бра; ∼ of hair копна́ воло́с
● v.t. (**mopped, mopping**) прот|ира́ть, -ере́ть; вытира́ть, вы́тереть; she ∼ped the floor она́ протёрла пол; he ∼ped his brow он вы́тер лоб
□ ∼ **up** v.t. (spilt liquid) вытира́ть, вы́тереть

mope /məʊp/ v.i. хандри́ть (impf.)

moped /'məʊped/ n. мопѐд

☞ **moral** /'mɒr(ə)l/ n. **1** мора́ль **2** (in pl.) нра́в|ы (-ов)
● adj. **1** (ethical) мора́льный; нра́вственный **2** (virtuous) нра́вственный

morale /mə'rɑːl/ n. мора́льное состоя́ние

moralist /'mɒrəlɪst/ n. морали́ст (-ка)

morality /mə'rælɪtɪ/ n. нра́вственность, э́тика

moralize /'mɒrəlaɪz/ v.i. морализи́ровать (impf.)

morass /mə'ræs/ n. боло́то; тряси́на

moratorium /mɒrə'tɔːrɪəm/ n. (pl. **moratoriums** or **moratoria**) морато́рий; impose a ∼ объяв|ля́ть, -и́ть морато́рий

morbid /'mɔːbɪd/ adj. боле́зненный, нездоро́вый

☞ **more** /mɔː(r)/ n. & adj. (greater amount or number) бо́льше, бо́лее; a little ∼ побо́льше; he received ∼ than I did он получи́л бо́льше меня́; (additional amount or number) ещё; бо́льше; ∼ tea ещё ча́ю; have you any ∼ matches? у вас ещё оста́лись спи́чки?; there is no ∼ soup су́па бо́льше нет
● adv. бо́льше, бо́лее; (rather) скоре́е; ∼ or less бо́лее и́ли ме́нее; I like beef ∼ than lamb я предпочита́ю говя́дину бара́нине; she is ∼ beautiful than her sister она́ краси́вее свое́й сестры́; ∼ and ∼ всё бо́лее и бо́лее; the ∼ the better чем бо́льше, тем лу́чше; ∼ than once не раз; once ∼ сно́ва, опя́ть, ещё раз

moreover /mɔː'rəʊvə(r)/ adv. кро́ме того́; сверх того́

morgue /mɔːg/ n. морг

moribund /'mɒrɪbʌnd/ adj. умира́ющий, отмира́ющий

☞ **morning** /'mɔːnɪŋ/ n. **1** у́тро; in the ∼ у́тром; it began to rain in the ∼ дождь пошёл с утра́; on Monday ∼ в понеде́льник у́тром; this ∼ сего́дня у́тром; good ∼! до́брое у́тро! **2** (attr.) у́тренний

Moroccan /mə'rɒkən/ n. марокка́н|ец (-ка)
● adj. марокка́нский

Morocco /mə'rɒkəʊ/ n. Маро́кко (nt. indecl.)

moron /'mɔːrɒn/ n. (infml) идио́т (-ка)

morose /mə'rəʊs/ adj. (gloomy) мра́чный; (unsociable) необщи́тельный

morphine /'mɔːfiːn/ n. мо́рфий

morris dance /'mɒrɪs/ n. мо́ррис (народный английский танец)

Morse /mɔːs/ n. (in full ∼ **code**) а́збука Мо́рзе

morsel /'mɔːs(ə)l/ n. кусо́чек

mortal /'mɔːt(ə)l/ n. сме́ртный
● adj. сме́ртельный, смертоно́сный; a ∼ wound смерте́льная ра́на

mortality /mɔː'tælɪtɪ/ n. сме́ртность

mortar /'mɔːtə(r)/ n. (building material) известко́вый раство́р

mortgage /'mɔːgɪdʒ/ n. ссу́да на поку́пку до́ма
● v.t. за|кла́дывать, -ложи́ть

mortician /mɔː'tɪʃ(ə)n/ n. (AmE) похоро́нных дел ма́стер

mortify /'mɔːtɪfaɪ/ v.t. (shame, humiliate) об|ижа́ть, -и́деть; ун|ижа́ть, -и́зить; a ∼ing defeat унизи́тельное пораже́ние

mortuary /'mɔːtjʊərɪ/ n. морг, поко́йницкая

mosaic /məʊ'zeɪk/ n. моза́ика
● adj. мозаи́чный

Moscow /'mɒskəʊ/ n. Москва́; (attr.) моско́вский

mosque /mɒsk/ n. мече́ть

mosquito /mɒ'skiːtəʊ/ n. (pl. ∼es) кома́р

moss /mɒs/ n. мох

☞ **most** /məʊst/ n. (greatest part) бо́льшая часть; I was in bed ∼ of the time бо́льшую часть вре́мени я провёл в посте́ли; (greatest amount) наибо́льшее коли́чество; £5 at the ∼ ма́ксимум 5 фу́нтов; you must make the ∼ of your chances вам ну́жно наилу́чшим о́бразом испо́льзовать свои́ возмо́жности
● adj.: ∼ people большинство́ люде́й; ∼ of us большинство́ из нас; who has the ∼ money? у кого́ бо́льше всех де́нег?
● adv. **1** (expr. comparison): what I ∼ desire чего́ я бо́льше всего́ хочу́; the ∼ beautiful са́мый краси́вый **2** (very) о́чень, весьма́

☞ **mostly** /'məʊstlɪ/ adv. гла́вным о́бразом

MOT (BrE) abbr. (of **Ministry of Transport**) Министе́рство тра́нспорта; ∼ (**test**) ≈ техосмо́тр

motel /məʊ'tel/ n. моте́ль (m.)

moth /mɒθ/ n. мотылёк, ночна́я ба́бочка

☞ **mother** /'mʌðə(r)/ n. **1** мать **2** (attr.) матери́нский
● v.t. относи́ться (impf.) по-матери́нски к + d.
■ ∼**board** n. (comput.) матери́нская пла́та; ∼ **country** n. ро́дина; ∼**-in-law** n. (wife's mother) тёща; (husband's mother) свекро́вь; ∼**-of-pearl** n. перламу́тр ● adj. перламу́тровый; ∼ **tongue** n. родно́й язы́к

motherhood /'mʌðəhʊd/ n. матери́нство

motherly /'mʌðəlɪ/ adj. нѐжный, забо́тливый

motif /məʊ'tiːf/ n. моти́в

☞ **motion** /'məʊʃ(ə)n/ n. **1** (movement) движе́ние; the car was in ∼ маши́на дви́галась; he set the plan in ∼ он приступи́л

m

к осуществле́нию пла́на **2** (proposal)
предложе́ние
● *v.t. & i.*: he ～ed to them to leave он показа́л
же́стом, что́бы они́ ушли́

motionless /'məʊʃənlɪs/ *adj.* неподви́жный

motivate /'məʊtɪveɪt/ *v.t.* (induce) побу|жда́ть,
-ди́ть; he is highly ～d у него́ есть мо́щный
сти́мул

motivation /məʊtɪ'veɪʃ(ə)n/ *n.* побужде́ние,
сти́мул

motive /'məʊtɪv/ *n.* по́вод, моти́в,
побужде́ние

motley /'mɒtlɪ/ *adj.*: a ～ crew пёстрая толпа́

motor /'məʊtə(r)/ *n.* **1** (engine) дви́гатель
(*m.*), мото́р **2** (*in full* BrE ～ **car**) (легково́й)
автомоби́ль (*m.*); the ～ trade торго́вля
автомоби́лями
■ ～**bike** *n.* мотоци́кл; ～ **boat** *n.* мото́рная
ло́дка; ～**cycle** *n.* мотоци́кл; ～**cyclist**
n. мотоцикли́ст; ～ **racing** *n.* (BrE)
автомоби́льные го́нки (*abbr.* автого́нки) (*f.
pl.*); ～ **scooter** *n.* моторо́ллер; ～ **show**
n. автосало́н; ～**way** *n.* (BrE) автостра́да,
автомагистра́ль

motorcade /'məʊtəkeɪd/ *n.* автоколо́нна

motorist /'məʊtərɪst/ *n.* автомобили́ст (-ка)

motorize /'məʊtəraɪz/ *v.t.* моторизова́ть
(*impf., pf.*)

mottled /'mɒt(ə)ld/ *adj.* пятни́стый,
кра́пчатый

motto /'mɒtəʊ/ *n.* (*pl.* ～**es** *or* ～**s**) деви́з;
ло́зунг

mould¹ /məʊld/ (AmE **mold**) *n.* (container)
фо́рма
● *v.t.* лепи́ть, с-; (fig.) формирова́ть, с-

mould² /məʊld/ (AmE **mold**) *n.* (fungus)
пле́сень

mouldy /'məʊldɪ/ (AmE **moldy**)
adj. (**mo(u)ldier, mo(u)ldiest**)
заплесневелый

moult /məʊlt/ (AmE **molt**) *v.i.* линя́ть (*impf.*)

mound /maʊnd/ *n.* (for burial or fortification)
на́сыпь; (heap) ку́ча

mount /maʊnt/ *n.*: M～ Everest гора́ Эвере́ст
● *v.t.* **1** (ascend, get on to) вз|бира́ться,
-обра́ться на + *a.*; подн|има́ться, -я́ться на +
a.; he ～ed his horse он сел на ло́шадь **2** (put,
fix on a ～) вст|авля́ть, -а́вить в опра́ву;
опр|авля́ть, -а́вить **3** (set up): the enemy ～ed
an offensive враг предприня́л наступле́ние
● *v.i.* (increase) расти́ (*impf.*); (*also* ～ **up**)
нак|а́пливаться, -опи́ться

✔ **mountain** /'maʊntɪn/ *n.* **1** гора́ **2** (*attr.*)
го́рный

mountaineer /maʊntɪ'nɪə(r)/ *n.* альпини́ст
(-ка)

mountaineering /maʊntɪ'nɪərɪŋ/ *n.*
альпини́зм

mountainous /'maʊntɪnəs/ *adj.* гори́стый

mourn /mɔːn/ *v.t.* опла́кивать (*impf.*)
● *v.i.* скорбе́ть (*impf.*); печа́литься (*impf.*);
she ～ed for her child она́ опла́кивала смерть

своего́ ребёнка

mourner /'mɔːnə(r)/ *n.* прису́тствующий на
похорона́х

mournful /'mɔːnfʊl/ *adj.* ско́рбный,
тра́урный

mourning /'mɔːnɪŋ/ *n.* скорбь; тра́ур

mouse /maʊs/ *n.* (*pl.* **mice**) мышь; (comput.
pl. also ～**s**) мышь, мы́шка
■ ～ (BrE), ～ **pad** (AmE) *nn.* (comput.)
ко́врик для мы́ши; ～**over** *n.* (comput.)
маусо́вер (sl.)

mousse /muːs/ *n.* мусс

moustache /mə'stɑːʃ/ (AmE **mustache**) *n.*
ус|ы́ (-о́в)

✔ **mouth¹** /maʊθ/ *n.* рот; (fig.): ～ of a cave вход
в пеще́ру; ～ of a river у́стье реки́
■ ～ **organ** *n.* губна́я гармо́ника; ～**wash**
n. полоска́ние для рта; ～**-watering** *adj.*
вку́сный, аппети́тный

mouth² /maʊð/ *v.t.*: the actor ～ed his words
актёр напы́щенно деклами́ровал

mouthful /'maʊθfʊl/ *n.* кусо́к, глото́к

✔ **move** /muːv/ *n.* **1** (in games) ход; it's
your ～! ваш ход!; (fig., action) посту́пок;
ход, шаг **2** (initiation of action) движе́ние;
it's time we made a ～ (BrE) нам пора́
дви́гаться; get a ～ on! дви́гайтесь!,
потора́пливайтесь! **3** (change of residence)
перее́зд
● *v.t.* **1** (change position of; put in motion) дви́гать
(*impf.*); передв|ига́ть, -и́нуть; he ～d his
chair nearer the fire он пододви́нул стул к
ками́ну **2** (affect, provoke) тро́гать, тро́нуть;
волнова́ть, вз-; the sight ～d him to tears
зре́лище тро́нуло его́ до слёз
● *v.i.* **1** (change position; be in motion) дви́|гаться,
-нуться; the lever won't ～ рыча́г не
сдвига́ется; don't ～! не дви́гайтесь!; a
moving staircase эскала́тор **2** (change one's
residence) пере|езжа́ть, -е́хать **3** (make progress)
развива́ться (*impf.*) **4** (stir) шевели́ться
(*impf.*); nobody ～d to help him никто́ не
пошевели́лся, что́бы ему́ помо́чь
□ ～ **about, ～ around** *v.i.* пере|езжа́ть, -е́хать;
разъезжа́ть (*impf.*); he ～s about a lot он
мно́го разъезжа́ет
□ ～ **along** *v.i.*: ～ along there, please!
проходи́те, пожа́луйста!
□ ～ **away** *v.t. & i.* удал|я́ть(ся), -и́ть(ся); they
～d away from here они́ перее́хали отсю́да
□ ～ **in** *v.i.* (take up abode): they ～d in next door
они́ посели́лись в сосе́днем до́ме
□ ～ **on** *v.i.* продв|ига́ться, -и́нуться; идти́ (*det.*)
да́льше; she stopped and then ～d on она́
останови́лась, а зате́м опя́ть продо́лжила
путь; he ～d on to a better job он перешёл на
бо́лее подходя́щую рабо́ту
□ ～ **out** *v.i.*: we have to ～ out tomorrow мы
должны́ съе́хать за́втра
□ ～ **over** *v.i.* (to make room) подв|ига́ться,
-и́нуться
□ ～ **up** *v.i.* подв|ига́ться, -и́нуться; ～ up and let
me sit down! подви́ньтесь и да́йте мне сесть!

✔ **movement** /'muːvmənt/ *n.* **1** (state of moving,
motion) движе́ние, перемеще́ние **2** (of the body

or part of it) жест, телодвиже́ние **3** (group united by common purpose) движе́ние

🞨 **movie** /'mu:vɪ/ *n.* (infml) фильм, кинокарти́на; **he's gone to the ~s** он пошёл в кино́

moving /'mu:vɪŋ/ *adj.* волну́ющий, тро́гательный

mow /məʊ/ *v.t. & i.* (*p.p.* **mowed** *or* **mown**) коси́ть, с-; **he ~ed the lawn** он подстри́г траву́/газо́н

mower /'məʊə(r)/ *n.* коси́лка

Mozambican /məʊzæm'bi:kən/ *n.* мозамби́кец; жи́тель (-ница) Мозамби́ка
● *adj.* мозамби́кский

Mozambique /məʊzæm'bi:k/ *n.* Мозамби́к

MP *abbr.* (*of* **Member of Parliament**) член парла́мента

MP3 *n.* (comput.) МР3, МП3 (*формат сжатия аудиоданных*); **MP3 player** МР3-пле́ер

mpg *abbr.* (*of* **miles per gallon**) миль на галло́н (бензи́на)

mph *abbr.* (*of* **miles per hour**) миль в час

🞨 **Mr** /'mɪstə(r)/ *n.* (*abbr. of* **mister**) (*pl.* **Messrs**) г-н (господи́н (*pl.* -á))

MRI *abbr.* (*of* **magnetic resonance imaging**) МРТ (магни́тно-резона́нсная томогра́фия)(); **~ scan** иссле́дование с по́мощью МРТ

🞨 **Mrs** /'mɪsɪz/ *n.* (*abbr. of* **mistress**) (*pl.* **~**) г-жа (госпожа́)

MS *abbr.* (*of* **multiple sclerosis**) рассе́янный склеро́з

🞨 **Ms** /mɪz, məz/ *n.* г-жа (госпожа́)

M.Sc. *abbr.* (*of* **Master of Science**) маги́стр (есте́ственных) нау́к

Mt /maʊnt/ *n.* (*abbr. of* **Mount**) г. (гора́)

🞨 **much** /mʌtʃ/ *n. & adj.* (**more, most**) мно́гое; мно́го + *g.*; **his work is not up to ~** его́ рабо́та не отлича́ется высо́ким ка́чеством; **too ~** сли́шком (мно́го); мно́го; **I don't see ~ of him** я его́ ре́дко ви́жу; **he doesn't read ~ of an actor** он актёр нева́жный; **how ~** ско́лько + *g.*; **very ~** о́чень (мно́го); о́чень си́льно; **as ~ again** ещё сто́лько же; **I thought as ~** я так и ду́мал; **so ~** сто́лько + *g.*
● *adv.* (**more, most**) **1** (by far) гора́здо; **~ better** гора́здо лу́чше; **~ the best** гора́здо лу́чше други́х/остальны́х **2** (greatly) о́чень; нема́ло; **I am ~ obliged to you** премно́го вам обя́зан; **it doesn't ~ matter** э́то не име́ет большо́го значе́ния; **so ~ the better** тем лу́чше; **how ~ do you love me?** как си́льно ты меня́ лю́бишь?; **~ to my surprise** к моему́ вели́кому удивле́нию; **~ as I should like to go** как бы я ни хоте́л пойти́; **not ~!** (infml, very ~) о́чень да́же!; а как же! **3** (about) приме́рно, почти́; **his condition is ~ the same** его́ состоя́ние приме́рно тако́е же

muck /mʌk/ (infml) *n.* (dirt) грязь; (anything disgusting) дрянь
□ **~ about** (BrE) *v.t.* (inconvenience) причин|я́ть, -и́ть неудо́бство + *d.*
● *v.i.*: **he was ~ing about with the radio** он вози́лся с ра́дио

mud /mʌd/ *n.* грязь; сля́коть

muddle /'mʌd(ə)l/ *n.* **1** (mess; disorder) беспоря́док; неразбери́ха; **things have got into a ~** всё перепу́талось/смеша́лось **2** (confusion of mind) пу́таница
● *v.t.* **1** (bring into disorder) перепу́т|ывать, -ать; вн|оси́ть, -ести́ беспоря́док в + *a.*; **you have ~d (up) my papers** вы смеша́ли мои́ бума́ги **2** (confuse) пу́тать, на-; сби|ва́ть, -ть с то́лку; **don't ~ me (up)** не сбива́йте меня́ с то́лку

muddy /'mʌdɪ/ *adj.* (**muddier, muddiest**) гря́зный

muesli /'m(j)u:zlɪ/ *n.* мю́сли (*смесь злаков, орехов и сухих фруктов*) (nt. indecl.)

muffin /'mʌfɪn/ *n.* ма́ффин, ма́ленький куполови́дный кекс; (AmE **English ~**) ≈ горя́чая бу́лочка, ≈ ола́дья

muffle /'mʌf(ə)l/ *v.t.* **1** (wrap up) ку́тать, за-; **he was ~d up in an overcoat** он был заку́тан в пальто́ **2** (of sound) глуши́ть, за-

mug[1] /mʌg/ *n.* (vessel) кру́жка

mug[2] /mʌg/ *n.* (BrE, infml, simpleton) балбе́с

mug[3] /mʌg/ *v.t.* (**mugged, mugging**) (BrE, infml) (attack) нап|ада́ть, -а́сть на (+ *a.*); (rob) гра́бить, о-

mugger /'mʌgə(r)/ *n.* у́личный граби́тель

mugging /'mʌgɪŋ/ *n.* у́личный грабёж

muggy /'mʌgɪ/ *adj.* (**muggier, muggiest**) (damp and warm) вла́жный и тёплый; (close) ду́шный

mulberry /'mʌlbərɪ/ *n.* (tree) ту́товое де́рево, шелкови́ца; (fruit) ту́товая я́года; (attr.) (colour) багро́вый

mulch /mʌltʃ/ *n.* му́льча (*защитная подстилка из сухой травы, листьев, навоза и т. п.*)
● *v.t.* мульчи́ровать (impf., pf.)

mule[1] /mju:l/ *n.* мул; (fig., of person) упря́мый осёл

mule[2] /mju:l/ *n.* (slipper) шлёпанец

mull[1] /mʌl/ *v.t.*: **~ wine** вари́ть, с- глинтве́йн

mull[2] /mʌl/ *v.t.*: **~ over** (ponder) размышля́ть (impf.) над + *i.*

mullah /'mʊlə/ *n.* мулла́ (*m.*)

mullet /'mʌlɪt/ *n.* кефа́ль

multicoloured /'mʌltɪkʌləd/ (AmE **multicolored**) *adj.* многоцве́тный, кра́сочный

multicultural /mʌltɪ'kʌltʃər(ə)l/ *adj.* многокульту́рный, многонациона́льный

multiculturalism /mʌltɪ'kʌltʃərəlɪz(ə)m/ *n.* мультикультурали́зм

multifarious /mʌltɪ'feərɪəs/ *adj.* разнообра́зный

multilateral /mʌltɪ'lætər(ə)l/ *adj.* многосторо́нний

multimedia /mʌltɪ'mi:dɪə/ *n.* мультиме́диа (*pl. indecl.*); (attr.) мультимеди́йный

multinational /mʌltɪ'næʃən(ə)l/ *adj.* многонациона́льный

🞨 **multiple** /'mʌltɪp(ə)l/ *n.* кра́тное число́
● *adj.* многочи́сленный

m

■ ~ **sclerosis** *n.* рассе́янный склеро́з

multiplication /ˌmʌltɪplɪˈkeɪʃ(ə)n/ *n.* умноже́ние

multiplicity /ˌmʌltɪˈplɪsɪtɪ/ *n.* многочи́сленность, разнообра́зие

multiply /ˈmʌltɪplaɪ/ *v.t.* умн|ожа́ть, -о́жить
• *v.i.* разм|ожа́ться, -о́житься

multipurpose /ˌmʌltɪˈpəːpəs/ *adj.* многоцелево́й

multiracial /ˌmʌltɪˈreɪʃ(ə)l/ *adj.* многонациона́льный, многора́совый

multistorey /ˌmʌltɪˈstɔːrɪ/ *adj.* многоэта́жный

multitask /ˈmʌltɪtɑːsk/ *v.i.* **1** (comput.) рабо́тать (*impf.*) в многозада́чном режи́ме **2** (fig.) де́лать, с- мно́го дел одновреме́нно

multitude /ˈmʌltɪtjuːd/ *n.* мно́жество, ма́сса

mum /mʌm/ *n.* (BrE, infml, mother) ма́ма

mumble /ˈmʌmb(ə)l/ *v.t. & i.* (mutter) бормота́ть, про-

mumbo-jumbo /ˌmʌmbəʊˈdʒʌmbəʊ/ *n.* тараба́рщина

mummy¹ /ˈmʌmɪ/ *n.* (embalmed corpse) му́мия

mummy² /ˈmʌmɪ/ *n.* (BrE, infml, mother) ма́ма, ма́мочка

mumps /mʌmps/ *n.* сви́нка (*заболевание*)

munch /mʌntʃ/ *v.t. & i.* жева́ть (*impf.*)

mundane /mʌnˈdeɪn/ *adj.* земно́й, мирско́й

municipal /mjuːˈnɪsɪp(ə)l/ *adj.* муниципа́льный, городско́й

municipality /mjuːnɪsɪˈpælɪtɪ/ *n.* муниципалите́т

munitions /mjuːˈnɪʃ(ə)ns/ *n. pl.* снаряже́ние, вооруже́ние
■ ~ **factory** *n.* вое́нный заво́д

♂ **murder** /ˈməːdə(r)/ *n.* уби́йство
• *v.t.* уб|ива́ть, -и́ть

murderer /ˈməːdərə(r)/ *n.* уби́йца (*c.g.*)

murderous /ˈməːdərəs/ *adj.* смертоно́сный

murky /ˈməːkɪ/ *adj.* (**murkier, murkiest**) мра́чный, тёмный

murmur /ˈməːmə(r)/ *n.* ро́пот
• *v.t. & i.* говори́ть (*impf.*) ти́хо; бормота́ть, про-; шепта́ть, про-

♂ **muscle** /ˈmʌs(ə)l/ *n.* мы́шца, му́скул
• *v.i.* (infml): **he ~d in on the conversation** он ввяза́лся в разгово́р

Muscovite /ˈmʌskəvaɪt/ *n.* москви́ч (-ка)
• *adj.* моско́вский

muscular /ˈmʌskjʊlə(r)/ *adj.* (pert. to muscle) мы́шечный; (with strong muscles) мускули́стый; си́льный

muse¹ /mjuːz/ *n.* (myth.) му́за

muse² /mjuːz/ *v.i.* размышля́ть (*impf.*); заду́мываться (*impf.*)

♂ **museum** /mjuːˈzɪəm/ *n.* музе́й

mushroom /ˈmʌʃruːm/ *n.* гриб

mushy /ˈmʌʃɪ/ *adj.* (**mushier, mushiest**) мя́гкий; (fig.) слаща́вый

♂ **music** /ˈmjuːzɪk/ *n.* му́зыка

♂ **musical** /ˈmjuːzɪk(ə)l/ *n.* мю́зикл
• *adj.* музыка́льный

musician /mjuːˈzɪʃ(ə)n/ *n.* музыка́нт

musicologist /mjuːzɪˈkɒlədʒɪst/ *n.* музыкове́д

musicology /mjuːzɪˈkɒlədʒɪ/ *n.* музыкове́дение

musket /ˈmʌskɪt/ *n.* мушке́т

♂ **Muslim** /ˈmʊzlɪm, ˈmʌ-/ *n.* мусульма́н|ин (-ка)
• *adj.* мусульма́нский

mussel /ˈmʌs(ə)l/ *n.* ми́дия

♂ **must** /mʌst/ *n.* (infml, necessary item): **the Tower of London is a ~ for visitors** тури́сты должны́ непреме́нно посмотре́ть Ло́ндонский Та́уэр
• *v. aux.* (3rd pers. sing. pres. **must**, had to *or* in indirect speech **must**) **1** (expr. necessity): **one ~ eat to live** чтобы жить, ну́жно есть; **~ you go so soon?** неуже́ли вам уже́ на́до уходи́ть?; **~ you behave like that?** неуже́ли вы ина́че не мо́жете?; (expr. obligation): **we ~ not be late** нам нельзя́ опа́здывать; **I ~ admit** я до́лжен призна́ть **2** (with neg., expr. prohibition): **cars ~ not be parked here** стоя́нка маши́н запрещена́ **3** (expr. certainty or strong probability): **you ~ be tired** вы, наве́рно, уста́ли; **you ~ have known that** не мо́жет быть, чтобы вы э́того не зна́ли

mustache /məˈstɑːʃ/ *n.* (AmE) = moustache

mustard /ˈmʌstəd/ *n.* (plant; relish) горчи́ца

muster /ˈmʌstə(r)/ *n.*: **will his work pass ~?** (fig.) его́ рабо́та годи́тся?
• *v.t.* (summon together) соб|ира́ть, -ра́ть; (fig.): **he ~ed (up) all his courage** он собра́лся с ду́хом
• *v.i.* (assemble) соб|ира́ться, -ра́ться

mustn't /ˈmʌs(ə)nt/ *neg. of* ▶ must

musty /ˈmʌstɪ/ *adj.* (**mustier, mustiest**) за́тхлый

mutant /ˈmjuːt(ə)nt/ *n.* (biol.) мута́нт

mutate /mjuːˈteɪt/ *v.i.* (biol.) мути́ровать (*impf., pf.*); (change) видоизмен|я́ться, -и́ться

mutation /mjuːˈteɪʃ(ə)n/ *n.* (biol.) мута́ция; (change) измене́ние

mute /mjuːt/ *adj.* **1** (silent) безмо́лвный **2** (unable to speak) (often offens.) немо́й
• *v.t.* приглуш|а́ть, -и́ть

mutilate /ˈmjuːtɪleɪt/ *v.t.* уве́чить, из-

mutilation /mjuːtɪˈleɪʃ(ə)n/ *n.* уве́чье

mutineer /mjuːtɪˈnɪə(r)/ *n.* мяте́жник

mutinous /ˈmjuːtɪnəs/ *adj.* мяте́жный

mutiny /ˈmjuːtɪnɪ/ *n.* мяте́ж
• *v.i.* бунтова́ть, взбунтова́ться

mutter /ˈmʌtə(r)/ *v.t. & i.* бормота́ть (*impf.*); говори́ть (*impf.*) невня́тно

mutton /ˈmʌt(ə)n/ *n.* бара́нина

mutual /ˈmjuːtʃʊəl/ *adj.* взаи́мный
■ ~ **aid** *n.* взаимопо́мощь

muzzle /ˈmʌz(ə)l/ *n.* **1** (animal's) мо́рда **2** (guard for this) намо́рдник **3** (of firearm) ду́ло
• *v.t.* надева́ть, -е́ть намо́рдник на + *a.*; (fig.) заст|авля́ть, -а́вить молча́ть

♂ **my** /maɪ/ *poss. adj.* мой; (belonging to speaker) свой; **I lost ~ pen** я потеря́л свою́ ру́чку

Myanmar /maɪənˈmɑː(r)/ *n.* Мья́нма

myopia /maɪˈəʊpɪə/ *n.* миопи́я, близору́кость

myopic /maɪˈɒpɪk/ *adj.* близору́кий

myriad /'mɪrɪəd/ *n.* несметное число; мириад|ы (*pl., g.* —)
● *adj.* несчётный
myrrh /mɜː(r)/ *n.* (fragrant resin) мирра
♂ **myself** /maɪ'self/ *pron.* **1** (refl.) себя (*d., p.* себе, *i.* собой); -ся/-сь (*suff.*); I said to ～ я сказал себе; I felt pleased with ～ я был доволен собой; I hurt ～ я ушибся/ушиблась **2** (emph.) сам; I did it ～ я сам это сделал; I did it by ～ (without help) я это сделал сам; I am not ～ today я сегодня немного не в форме (*or* сам не свой) **3** (after preps.): dancing takes me out of ～ танцы развлекают меня
mysterious /mɪ'stɪərɪəs/ *adj.* таинственный, загадочный

mystery /'mɪstərɪ/ *n.* тайна, секрет, загадка
mystic /'mɪstɪk/ *n.* мистик
● *adj.* (*also* ～al /'mɪstɪk(ə)l/) мистический
mysticism /'mɪstɪsɪz(ə)m/ *n.* мистика
mystify /'mɪstɪfaɪ/ *v.t.* озадачи|вать, -ть
mystique /mɪ'stiːk/ *n.* таинственность, загадочность
myth /mɪθ/ *n.* (lit., fig.) миф
mythical /'mɪθɪk(ə)l/ *adj.* мифический
mythological /mɪθə'lɒdʒɪk(ə)l/ *adj.* мифологический
mythology /mɪ'θɒlədʒɪ/ *n.* мифология
myxomatosis /mɪksəmə'təʊsɪs/ *n.* миксоматоз (*заболевание кроликов*)

Nn

nab /næb/ *v.t.* (**nabbed, nabbing**) захват|ывать, -ить; заст|авать, -ать
naff /næf/ *adj.* (BrE) безвкусный
nag /næg/ *v.t.* (**nagged, nagging**) пилить (*impf.*)
nagging /'nægɪŋ/ *adj.* придирчивый; a ～ pain ноющая боль
nail /neɪl/ *n.* **1** (on finger or toe) ноготь (*m.*) **2** (metal spike) гвоздь (*m.*)
● *v.t.* **1** приб|ивать, -ить (*что к чему*); пригво|ждать, -здить **2** (pin down): he tried to evade the issue but I ～ed him down он пытался уйти от проблемы, но я прижал его к стенке
■ ～ brush *n.* щёт(оч)ка для ногтей; ～ file *n.* пил(оч)ка (для ногтей); ～ polish *n.* лак для ногтей; ～ varnish *n.* (BrE) лак для ногтей
naive /naɪ'iːv/ *adj.* наивный, простодушный
naivety, naïvety /naɪ'iːvɪtɪ/ *n.* наивность, простодушие
naked /'neɪkɪd/ *adj.* голый
nakedness /'neɪkɪdnɪs/ *n.* нагота, обнажённость
♂ **name** /neɪm/ *n.* **1** (*esp.* fore～) имя (*nt.*); (surname) имя, фамилия; (of pet) кличка; what is his ～? как его зовут/фамилия? **2** (of a thing) название **3** (reputation) имя, репутация; he made a ～ for himself он создал/сделал себе имя **4**: call sb ～s ругать (*impf.*) кого-н. (нехорошими словами)
● *v.t.* **1** (give ～ to) наз|ывать, -вать, да|вать, -ть имя + *d.*; they haven't yet ～d the baby они ещё не дали ребёнку имя; he was ～d Andrew after his grandfather его назвали Андреем в честь деда **2** (recite) наз|ывать, -вать; the pupil ～d the chief cities of Europe ученик назвал/перечислил главные города

Европы; (state) наз|ывать, -вать; ～ your price! назначьте цену!; (identify): how many stars can you ～? сколько звёзд вы можете определить?
■ ～-dropping *n.* (infml) ≈ хвастовство своими знакомствами/связями; ～sake *n.* (with same first ～) тёзка (*c.g.*)
namely /'neɪmlɪ/ *adv.* (a) именно; то есть
Namibia /nə'mɪbɪə/ *n.* Намибия
Namibian /nə'mɪbɪən/ *n.* намиби|ец (-йка)
● *adj.* намибийский
nanny /'nænɪ/ *n.* (for child) няня, нянечка
■ ～ goat *n.* коза
nanotechnology /nænəʊtek'nɒlədʒɪ/ *n.* нанотехнология
nap /næp/ *n.* (short sleep) короткий сон; have, take a ～ вздремнуть (*pf.*)
napalm /'neɪpɑːm/ *n.* напалм; (*attr.*) напалмовый
nape /neɪp/ *n.* загривок
napkin /'næpkɪn/ *n.* (in full **table** ～) салфетка
nappy /'næpɪ/ *n.* (BrE, infml) подгузник
narcissistic /nɑːsɪ'sɪstɪk/ *adj.* самовлюблённый
narcis|sus /nɑː'sɪsəs/ *n.* (*pl.* ～si /-saɪ/) нарцисс
narcotic /nɑː'kɒtɪk/ *n.* наркотик
● *adj.* наркотический
narrate /nə'reɪt/ *v.t.* **1** (story) расск|азывать, -ать **2**: ～ a film/broadcast читать (*impf.*) текст от автора
narrative /'nærətɪv/ *n.* (story) рассказ
● *adj.* повествовательный
narrator /nə'reɪtə(r)/ *n.* рассказч|ик (-ица); (theatr., cin.) авторский голос, диктор
narrow /'nærəʊ/ *adj.* (**narrower, narrowest**) (lit., fig.) **1** узкий **2** (with little margin): a ～

majority незначи́тельное большинство́; he
had a ~ escape from death он чу́дом избежа́л
сме́рти
● *v.t.*: the choice was ~ed down to
two candidates вы́бор свёлся к двум
кандидату́рам
● *v.i.* (of river, road) су́живаться, -зиться
■ ~-gauge *adj.* узкоколе́йный; ~-minded *adj.*
узколо́бый, ограни́ченный

nasal /ˈneɪz(ə)l/ *adj.* (of, for the nose) носово́й;
(of the voice) гнуса́вый

nasturtium /nəˈstɜːʃəm/ *n.* насту́рция

nasty /ˈnɑːstɪ/ *adj.* (**nastier, nastiest**)
1 (offensive, e.g. smell or taste) неприя́тный,
проти́вный **2** (morally offensive) ме́рзкий,
га́дкий, гну́сный **3** (unkind, unpleasant)
злой; a ~ **remark** злое замеча́ние; a ~
temper тяжёлый хара́ктер; he played a
~ **trick on me** он сыгра́л со мной злу́ю
шу́тку; (of the elements): ~ **weather** скве́рная
пого́да **4** (threatening) опа́сный; there was
a ~ **look in his eye** его́ вид не предвеща́л
ничего́ до́брого **5** (difficult): that's a ~ **rock to
climb** на э́ту скалу́ нелегко́ взобра́ться

⚜ **nation** /ˈneɪʃ(ə)n/ *n.* (population) на́ция; (people)
наро́д; (country) страна́
■ ~wide *adj.* общенациона́льный,
всенаро́дный; a ~wide search ро́зыск/по́иски
(*m. pl.*) по всей стране́

⚜ **national** /ˈnæʃən(ə)l/ *n.* гражд|ани́н (-а́нка)
● *adj.* (of the state) госуда́рственный; (of
the country or population as a whole) наро́дный,
всенаро́дный; (central; opp. provincial)
центра́льный; (pert. to a particular nation or
ethnic group) национа́льный; ~ newspapers
центра́льные газе́ты
■ ~ **anthem** *n.* госуда́рственный гимн;
N~ **Health Service** *n.* Национа́льная
слу́жба здравоохране́ния; N~ **Insurance** *n.*
Госуда́рственное страхова́ние; ~ **service** *n.*
во́инская пови́нность

nationalism /ˈnæʃənəlɪz(ə)m/ *n.* национали́зм

nationalist /ˈnæʃənəlɪst/ *n.* национали́ст (-ка)

nationalistic /ˌnæʃənəˈlɪstɪk/ *adj.*
националисти́ческий

nationality /ˌnæʃəˈnælɪtɪ/ *n.* по́дданство;
гражда́нство; (ethnic group, e.g. within Russia)
национа́льность

nationalization /ˌnæʃənəlaɪˈzeɪʃ(ə)n/ *n.*
национализа́ция

nationalize /ˈnæʃənəlaɪz/ *v.t.*
национализи́ровать (*impf., pf.*)

native /ˈneɪtɪv/ *n.* **1** (indigenous inhabitant)
тузе́м|ец (-ка) **2**: a ~ **of** уроже́н|ец (-ка) + *g.*
3 (of animal, plant): the kangaroo/eucalyptus
is a ~ **of Australia** ро́дина кенгуру́/
эвкали́пта — Австра́лия
● *adj.* **1** (of one's birth) родно́й; ~ **language**
родно́й язы́к **2** (indigenous) тузе́мный; ~
population тузе́мное/коренно́е/ме́стное
населе́ние
■ N~ **American** *n.* америка́нск|ий инде́ец
(-ая индиа́нка)

nativity /nəˈtɪvɪtɪ/ *n.* Рождество́ Христо́во

NATO /ˈneɪtəʊ/ *n.* (*abbr. of* **North
Atlantic Treaty Organization**) НА́ТО
(Организа́ция Североатланти́ческого
догово́ра)

natter /ˈnætə(r)/ (BrE, infml) *n.*: I came in for a
~ я зашёл поболта́ть
● *v.i.* болта́ть (*impf.*)

⚜ **natural** /ˈnætʃər(ə)l/ *adj.* **1** (found in, pertaining to
nature) есте́ственный, приро́дный; стихи́йный;
~ **phenomena** явле́ния приро́ды **2** (normal, not
surprising) есте́ственный, норма́льный; it is ~
for parents to love their children для роди́телей
есте́ственно люби́ть свои́х дете́й **3** (simple,
unaffected) просто́й; простоду́шный
■ ~-born *adj.* прирождённый; ~ resources *n.
pl.* приро́дные ресу́рсы/бога́тства

naturalism /ˈnætʃərəlɪz(ə)m/ *n.* натурали́зм

naturalist /ˈnætʃərəlɪst/ *n.* натурали́ст

naturalistic /ˌnætʃərəˈlɪstɪk/ *adj.*
натуралисти́ческий

naturalization /ˌnætʃərəlaɪˈzeɪʃ(ə)n/ *n.*
натурализа́ция; акклиматиза́ция

naturalize /ˈnætʃərəlaɪz/ *v.t.* (admit to citizenship)
натурализова́ть (*impf., pf.*); (of animals, plants:
introduce to another country) акклиматизи́ровать
(*impf., pf.*)

naturally /ˈnætʃərəlɪ/ *adv.* есте́ственно

⚜ **nature** /ˈneɪtʃə(r)/ *n.* **1** (force, natural phenomena)
приро́да **2** (temperament) нату́ра, хара́ктер;
human ~ челове́ческая приро́да; it was his
~ to be proud он был го́рдым по нату́ре
3 (essential quality) приро́да, хара́ктер; by, in
the (very) ~ of things по приро́де веще́й
■ ~ reserve *n.* запове́дник

naturism /ˈneɪtʃərɪz(ə)m/ *n.* (nudism) нуди́зм

naturist /ˈneɪtʃərɪst/ *n.* (nudist) нуди́ст (-ка)

naughtiness /ˈnɔːtɪnɪs/ *n.* озорство́

naughty /ˈnɔːtɪ/ *adj.* (**naughtier,
naughtiest**) **1** (e.g. child's behaviour)
непослу́шный, шаловли́вый, озорно́й; be
~ озорнича́ть (*impf.*); you were ~ today
ты сего́дня пло́хо себя́ вёл **2** (risqué)
риско́ванный

nausea /ˈnɔːzɪə/ *n.* тошнота́

nauseat|e /ˈnɔːzɪeɪt/ *v.t.* вызыва́ть, вы́звать
тошноту́ у + *g.*; ~ing тошнотво́рный

nauseous /ˈnɔːzɪəs/ *adj.* тошнотво́рный; I feel
~ меня́ тошни́т

nautical /ˈnɔːtɪk(ə)l/ *adj.* морско́й

naval /ˈneɪv(ə)l/ *adj.* морско́й; (of the navy)
вое́нно-морско́й
■ ~ **base** *n.* вое́нно-морска́я ба́за; ~ **officer** *n.*
морско́й офице́р

nave /neɪv/ *n.* (of church) неф

navel /ˈneɪv(ə)l/ *n.* пупо́к (infml)

navigable /ˈnævɪɡəb(ə)l/ *adj.* (of river, sea)
судохо́дный

navigate /ˈnævɪɡeɪt/ *v.t.* (of person): ~ a
ship/aircraft управля́ть (*impf.*) корабля́м/
самолётом; ~ a river/sea пла́вать (*indet.*),
плыть (*det.*) по реке́/мо́рю
● *v.i.* (in ship) пла́вать (*indet.*), плыть (*det.*);

⚜ ключева́я ле́ксика

(in aircraft) лет|а́ть (*indet.*), -ёть (*det.*)

navigation /nævɪ'geɪʃ(ə)n/ *n.* навига́ция

navigator /'nævɪgeɪtə(r)/ *n.* (naut., aeron.) шту́рман, навига́тор

navy /'neɪvɪ/ *n.* **1** (naval forces) вое́нно-морски́е си́лы (*f. pl.*); (ships of war) вое́нно-морско́й флот **2** (*in full* ~ **blue**) тёмно-си́ний цвет
● *adj.* = navy-blue
■ ~-**blue** *adj.* тёмно-си́ний

Nazi /'nɑːtsɪ/ *n.* (*pl.* ~**s**) наци́ст (-ка)
● *adj.* наци́стский

Nazism /'nɑːtsɪz(ə)m/ *n.* наци́зм

⚡ **near** /nɪə(r)/ *adj.* **1** (close at hand, in space or time) бли́зкий; **the station is quite ~ (to) our house** ста́нция (нахо́дится) совсе́м бли́зко от на́шего до́ма; **in the ~ future** в ближа́йшем бу́дущем **2**: **the ~ side** (of road or vehicle in Britain) ле́вая сторона́ **3** (narrowly achieved): **a ~ miss** непрямо́е попада́ние; **we won, but it was a ~ thing** мы победи́ли, но с трудо́м
● *adv.* **1** (of place or time) бли́зко; **come a little ~er** подойди́те побли́же **2** (fig.): **the bus was nowhere ~ full** авто́бус был далеко́ не по́лный; **she is nowhere ~ as old as her husband** она́ далеко́ не так стара́, как её муж
● *v.t.* прибл|ижа́ться, -и́зиться к + *d.*; **he is ~ing his end** он при сме́рти
● *prep.* о́коло, во́зле, близ, бли́зко от, у (*all + g.*); ~ **here** недалеко́ отсю́да; **come ~er the fire!** подвига́йтесь к ками́ну!; **we are no ~er a solution** мы ничу́ть не приблизи́лись/бли́же к реше́нию
■ ~**by** *adj., adv.* располо́женный побли́зости; близлежа́щий, сосе́дний; **he was standing ~by** он стоя́л бли́зко/ря́дом; ~**sighted** *adj.* близору́кий

⚡ **nearly** /'nɪəlɪ/ *adv.* (almost) почти́; **he ~ fell** он чуть не упа́л; **we are ~ there** мы почти́ прие́хали/пришли́; **there is not ~ enough to eat** еды́ далеко́ не доста́точно

nearness /'nɪənɪs/ *n.* бли́зость

neat /niːt/ *adj.* **1** (of appearance) опря́тный, аккура́тный **2** (clear, precise) чёткий, изя́щный **3** (of liquor etc., undiluted) неразба́вленный **4** (AmE, infml, excellent) отли́чный, кла́ссный

nebulous /'nebjʊləs/ *adj.* (fig.) тума́нный

⚡ **necessarily** /nesə'serɪlɪ/ *adv.* обяза́тельно; **it is not ~ true** э́то не обяза́тельно так

⚡ **necessary** /'nesəsərɪ/ *adj.* (indispensable) необходи́мый; (compulsory) необходи́мый, обяза́тельный; (inevitable) неизбе́жный; **it is ~ to eat in order to live** чтобы жить, необходи́мо пита́ться; **it is not ~ to dress for dinner** переодева́ться к обе́ду необяза́тельно; мо́жно и не одева́ться к обе́ду

necessitate /nɪ'sesɪteɪt/ *v.t.* вызыва́ть, вы́звать; обусло́в|ливать, -ить

necessity /nɪ'sesɪtɪ/ *n.* **1** (inevitability) неизбе́жность **2** (need) нужда́, необходи́мость; **of ~** по необходи́мости **3** (necessary thing): **the telephone is a ~** телефо́н не ро́скошь, а предме́т пе́рвой необходи́мости

neck /nek/ *n.* **1** ше́я; **stick one's ~ out** (infml) ста́вить, по- себя́ под уда́р; ~ **and ~** ноздря́ в ноздрю́; голова́ в го́лову **2** (of var. objects): ~ **of a bottle** го́рлышко буты́лки; ~ **of a shirt** во́рот руба́шки
■ ~**lace** *n.* ожере́лье; ~**line** *n.* вы́рез (пла́тья); ~**tie** *n.* га́лстук

nectar /'nektə(r)/ *n.* некта́р

nectarine /'nektərɪn/ *n.* нектари́н, гла́дкий пе́рсик

née /neɪ/ *adj.* урождённая

⚡ **need** /niːd/ *n.* (want, requirement) нужда́; **the house is in ~** of repair дом нужда́ется в ремо́нте; **my ~s are few** у меня́ скро́мные потре́бности; (necessity) необходи́мость; **if ~ be** в слу́чае необходи́мости; **there's no ~ to get upset** не́зачем расстра́иваться; **there is no ~ for him to read the whole book** ему́ необяза́тельно/не́зачем чита́ть всю кни́гу
● *v.t.* **1** (require) нужда́ться (*impf.*) в + *p.*; **the grass ~s cutting** газо́н сле́дует подстри́чь; **he ~s a haircut** ему́ пора́ (по)стри́чься **2** (*with inf.*) (be obliged, under necessity): ~ **I come today?** мне ну́жно приходи́ть сего́дня?; **you ~n't do it all tomorrow** вам не обяза́тельно ко́нчить всю рабо́ту за́втра; **you ~ not have bothered** напра́сно вы беспоко́ились; **I ~ not** (have no reason to) мне не́зачем; **he ~ not come** он мо́жет не приходи́ть

needle /'niːd(ə)l/ *n.* игла́, иго́лка
● *v.t.* (irritate, tease) подд|ева́ть, -е́ть
■ ~**work** *n.* рукоде́лие

needless /'niːdlɪs/ *adj.* (unnecessary) нену́жный; (inappropriate) неуме́стный; ~ **to say** (само́ собо́й) разуме́ется

needy /'niːdɪ/ *adj.* (**needier, neediest**) нужда́ющийся

nefarious /nɪ'feərɪəs/ *adj.* злоде́йский

negate /nɪ'geɪt/ *v.t.* св|оди́ть, -ести́ на нет

negation /nɪ'geɪʃ(ə)n/ *n.* опроверже́ние

⚡ **negative** /'negətɪv/ *n.* **1** (statement, reply, word) отрица́ние **2** (phot.) негати́в
● *adj.* отрица́тельный

neglect /nɪ'glekt/ *n.* **1** (failure to attend to) пренебреже́ние + *i.*; ~ **of one's duties** пренебреже́ние свои́ми обя́занностями **2** (lack of care) запу́щенность; ~ **of one's children** отсу́тствие забо́ты о свои́х де́тях **3** (failure to notice) невнима́ние (**of:** к + *d.*) **4** (uncared-for state) запу́щенность, забро́шенность; **the house was in a state of ~** дом был запу́щен/забро́шен
● *v.t.* **1** (work) запус|ка́ть, -ти́ть; забр|а́сывать, -о́сить; (duty) пренебр|ега́ть, -е́чь + *i.* **2** (leave uncared for) забр|а́сывать, -о́сить, ост|авля́ть, -а́вить без внима́ния; **he ~ed his family** он забро́сил свою́ семью́; ~**ed children** безнадзо́рные/забро́шенные де́ти; **a ~ed garden** запу́щенный/забро́шенный сад **3** (*with inf.*) (fail) заб|ыва́ть, -ы́ть; **he ~ed to wind up the clock** он забы́л завести́ часы́

neglectful /nɪ'glektfʊl/ *adj.* небре́жный, невнима́тельный; **he is ~ of his interests** он не забо́тится о со́бственных интере́сах

n

negligence /'neglɪdʒ(ə)ns/ *n.* небре́жность
negligent /'neglɪdʒ(ə)nt/ *adj.* (careless)
небре́жный; (inattentive) невнима́тельный
negligible /'neglɪdʒɪb(ə)l/ *adj.*
незначи́тельный
negotiable /nɪ'gəʊʃəb(ə)l/ *adj.*
1: ~ **conditions, terms** усло́вия, кото́рые
мо́гут служи́ть предме́том перегово́ров
2 (navigable) проходи́мый; (of roads) прое́зжий
negotiate /nɪ'gəʊʃɪeɪt/ *v.t.* **1** (conduct
negotiations over) вести́ (*impf.*) перегово́ры о
+ *p.*; (conclude agreement on) при|ходи́ть, -йти́
к соглаше́нию о + *p.* **2** (get over or through)
проб|ира́ться, -ра́ться че́рез + *a.*; ~ **a corner**
брать, взять поворо́т
• *v.i.* догов|а́риваться, -ори́ться
negotiation /nɪgəʊʃɪ'eɪʃ(ə)n/ *n.* (process)
обсужде́ние; (in pl.) (talks) перегово́ры (*m. pl.*)
negotiator /nɪ'gəʊʃɪeɪtə(r)/ *n.* уча́стник
перегово́ров
Negro /'niːgrəʊ/ *n.* (*pl.* ~**es**) (often offens.) негр
• *adj.* негритя́нский
neigh /neɪ/ *v.i.* ржа́ть (*impf.*)
⚘ **neighbour** /'neɪbə(r)/ (AmE **neighbor**) *n.*
сосе́д (-ка)
⚘ **neighbourhood** /'neɪbəhʊd/ (AmE
neighborhood) *n.* **1** (locality) ме́стность,
окре́стность; (district) райо́н **2** (neighbours)
сосе́ди (*m. pl.*)
neighbouring /'neɪbərɪŋ/ (AmE
neighboring) *adj.* сосе́дний
neighbourly /'neɪbəlɪ/ (AmE **neighborly**)
adj. добрососе́дский; **in a** ~ **fashion** по-
сосе́дски; **that's not a** ~ **thing to do** э́то не
по-сосе́дски
⚘ **neither** /'naɪðə(r)/ *pron. & adj.* ни тот, ни
друго́й; ~ **of them knows** ни оди́н (*or* никто́)
из них не зна́ет
• *adv.* **1**: ~ ... **nor** ни... ни; ~ **he nor I went**
ни он, ни я не пошёл **2** (after neg. clause):
he didn't go and ~ **did I** он не пошёл, и я
то́же
neoclassical /niːəʊ'klæsɪk(ə)l/ *adj.*
неокласси́ческий
neon /'niːɒn/ *adj.* нео́новый
■ ~ **light** *n.* нео́новый свет; ~ **sign** *n.*
нео́новая рекла́ма
neo-Nazi /niːəʊ'nɑːtsɪ/ *n.* (*pl.* ~**s**) неонаци́ст
(-ка)
Nepal /nɪ'pɔːl/ *n.* Непа́л
Nepal|ese /nepə'liːz/, **Nepali** /nɪ'pɔːlɪ/ *nn.*
(*pl.* ~**ese**, ~**i**, ~**is**) непа́л|ец (-ка)
• *adjs.* непа́льский
nephew /'nefjuː/ *n.* племя́нник
nepotism /'nepətɪz(ə)m/ *n.*
семе́йственность, кумовство́
Neptune /'neptjuːn/ *n.* Непту́н
nerd /nɜːd/ *n.* зану́да (*c.g.*)
nerve /nɜːv/ *n.* **1** нерв; **he doesn't know what**
~**s are** он не зна́ет, что тако́е не́рвы; **he gets
on my** ~**s** он де́йствует мне на не́рвы

2 (courage, assurance) сме́лость; **lose one's** ~
робе́ть, о-; (infml, impudence) на́глость; **he's got
a** ~ **I** ну и нагле́ц!
■ ~**-racking** *adj.* (situation) нерво́зный; (time)
напряжённый
nervous /'nɜːvəs/ *adj.* **1** (pert. to nerves)
не́рвный; **he had a** ~ **breakdown** у него́
бы́ло не́рвное расстро́йство; **he's a** ~
wreck э́то челове́к с подо́рванной не́рвной
систе́мой **2** (highly strung) не́рвный
3 (agitated) не́рвный, взволно́ванный; **I'm**
~ я не́рвничаю **4** (apprehensive) не́рвный,
не́рвничающий
nervousness /'nɜːvəsnɪs/ *n.* не́рвность,
нерво́зность
nest /nest/ *n.* гнездо́; ~ **of tables** компле́кт
сто́ликов (*вставляющихся один в другой*)
• *v.i.* (of birds) гнезди́ться (*impf.*)
■ ~ **egg** *n.* (fig., savings) сбереже́ния (*nt. pl.*)
nestle /'nes(ə)l/ *v.t. & i.*: ~ (**one's head/
face**) **against sb/sth** приж|има́ться, -а́ться
(голово́й/лицо́м) к кому́/чему́-н.; **a village
(lay)** ~**d at the foot of the hill** у подно́жия
горы́ приюти́лась дере́вня
⚘ **net¹** /net/ *n.* **1** (for protecting fruit, against
mosquitoes etc.) се́тка; (snare for birds, fishing ~, also
fig.) сеть (*f. pl.*) **2** (fabric) тюль (*m.*)
3: **the Net** (comput.) Сеть, Интерне́т
• *v.t.* (**netted, netting**) (fish etc.) лови́ть,
пойма́ть в сеть/се́ти; **he netted the ball** он
закинул мяч в се́тку; (at football) он заби́л гол
■ ~**ball** *n.* нетбо́л (*род баскетбола*); ~
curtains *n. pl.* тю́левые занаве́ски; ~**work**
n. сеть • *v.t.* (BrE, TV, radio) перед|ава́ть, -а́ть
по (телевизио́нной/радиотрансляцио́нной)
се́ти; (comput.) свя́з|ывать, -а́ть в о́бщую
сеть • *v.i.* (fig.) нала́|живать, -дить конта́кты/
свя́зи
net², **nett** /net/ *adj.* чи́стый
• *v.t.* (**netted, netting**) (obtain as profit)
получ|а́ть, -и́ть чи́стыми; де́лать, с-
■ ~ **income** *n.* чи́стый дохо́д
nether /'neðə(r)/ *adj.* ни́жний
■ ~**most** *adj.* са́мый ни́жний; ~ **regions** *n. pl.*
преиспо́дняя
Netherlands /'neðələndz/ *n. pl.* Нидерла́нд|ы
(-ов)
nett /net/ *adj. & v.t.* (BrE) = **net²**
netting /'netɪŋ/ *n.* се́тка
nettle /'net(ə)l/ *n.* крапи́ва
neuralgia /njʊə'rældʒə/ *n.* невралги́я
neurological /njʊərə'lɒdʒɪk(ə)l/ *adj.*
невроло́гический
neurologist /njʊə'rɒlədʒɪst/ *n.* невропато́лог,
невро́лог
neurology /njʊə'rɒlədʒɪ/ *n.* невроло́гия
neurosis /njʊə'rəʊsɪs/ *n.* (*pl.* **neuroses**
/-siːz/) невро́з
neurotic /njʊə'rɒtɪk/ *adj.* невроти́ческий
neuter /'njuːtə(r)/ *n.* сре́дний род
• *adj.* (gram.) сре́дний; сре́днего ро́да
• *v.t.* кастри́ровать (*impf., pf.*)
neutral /'njuːtr(ə)l/ *n.* (of gears): **in** ~ в
нейтра́льном положе́нии; на нейтра́льной

⚘ ключева́я ле́ксика

переда́че; **put the car in(to)** ~ поста́вить (*pf.*) маши́ну на нейтра́льную переда́чу

● *adj.* нейтра́льный

neutrality /nju:'trælɪtɪ/ *n.* нейтралите́т

neutralize /'nju:trəlaɪz/ *v.t.* нейтрализова́ть (*impf., pf.*)

neutron /'nju:trɒn/ *n.* нейтро́н

Neva /'ni:və/ *n.* Нева́

♂ **never** /'nevə(r)/ *adv.* никогда́ (… не); (not once) ни ра́зу (… не); **you** ~ **know** как знать?; ~ **before** никогда́ ра́ньше; **I believed him once, but** ~ **again** одна́жды я ему́ пове́рил, но бо́льше никогда́ не пове́рю; (emphatic for not) так и не; **he** ~ **even tried** он да́же не попро́бовал; (BrE, expr. incredulity): ~! не мо́жет быть!

■ ~**-ending** *adj.* бесконе́чный; **it's a** ~**-ending job** э́той рабо́те конца́ нет; ~**theless** *adv.* одна́ко; (*conj.*) тем не ме́нее

♂ **new** /nju:/ *adj.* **1** но́вый; **as good as** ~ совсе́м как но́вый **2** (modern, advanced) нове́йший, после́дний; **the** ~**est fashions** нове́йшие/после́дние мо́ды **3** (fresh) молодо́й **4** (unaccustomed): **I am** ~ **to this work** я в э́том де́ле новичо́к; (unfamiliar): **this work is** ~ **to me** э́та рабо́та для меня́ непривы́чна

■ N~ **Age** *n.* филосо́фская систе́ма, бази́рующаяся на ве́ре в альтернати́вный о́браз жи́зни; ~**born** *adj.* новорождённый; ~**comer** *n.* новичо́к; ~**found** *adj.*: **a** ~**-found interest** но́вое увлече́ние + *i.*; ~ **moon** *n.* молодо́й ме́сяц, новолу́ние; ~ **potatoes** *n. pl.*: молодо́й карто́фель; **N**~ **Year** *n.* Но́вый год; **Happy N**~ **Year!** с Но́вым го́дом!; **N**~ **Year's Day** день Но́вого го́да; **N**~ **Year's Eve** кану́н Но́вого го́да

newel /'nju:əl/ *n.* **1** коло́нна винтово́й ле́стницы **2** (*also* ~ **post**) баля́сина пери́л

newly /'nju:lɪ/ *adv.* **1** (recently) неда́вно, но́во-; ~ **arrived** неда́вно прибы́вший, новоприбы́вший **2** (anew) вновь; **a** ~ **painted gate** свежевы́крашенная кали́тка

■ ~**-wed** *n.*: **the** ~**-weds** молодожён|ы (-ов)

newness /'nju:nɪs/ *n.* новизна́

♂ **news** /nju:z/ *n.* **1** но́вости (*f. pl.*); (piece of ~) но́вость, весть; **have you heard the** ~? вы слы́шали но́вость? **2** (in press or radio) но́вости (*f. pl.*), после́дние изве́стия

■ ~ **agency** *n.* информацио́нное аге́нтство; ~**agent** *n.* (shop) газе́тный кио́ск; (person) = newsvendor; ~ **bulletin** *n.* (BrE) вы́пуск новосте́й; ~**caster** *n.* ди́ктор; ~ **conference** *n.* пресс-конфере́нция; ~ **flash** *n.* экстренное сообще́ние; ~**letter** *n.* информацио́нный бюллете́нь; ~**reader** *n.* (BrE) ди́ктор (*последних известий*); ~**vendor** *n.* (BrE) продаве́ц (-щи́ца) газе́т

newspaper /'nju:speɪpə(r)/ *n.* газе́та; (*attr.*) газе́тный

newt /nju:t/ *n.* трито́н

New York /nju: 'jɔ:k/ *n.* Нью-Йо́рк

New Zealand /nju: 'zi:lənd/ *n.* Но́вая Зела́ндия

New Zealander /nju: 'zi:ləndə(r)/ *n.* новозела́нд|ец (-ка)

♂ **next** /nekst/ *n.* (in order): **the week after** ~ че́рез неде́лю; ~**, please!** сле́дующий!; ~ **of kin** ближа́йший ро́дственник

● *adj.* **1** (of place: nearest) ближа́йший; (adjacent) сосе́дний, сме́жный; **he lives** ~ **door** он живёт ря́дом **2** ~ **to** (fig., almost) почти́; **I got it for** ~ **to nothing** я купи́л э́то за бесце́нок **3** (in a series) очередно́й; (future) бу́дущий, сле́дующий; ~ **day** на друго́й/сле́дующий день; ~ **Friday** в сле́дующую пя́тницу; ~ **October** в сле́дующем октябре́; ~ **week** на бу́дущей/сле́дующей неде́ле; ~ **year** в бу́дущем году́; ~ **time we'll go to London** в сле́дующий раз мы пое́дем в Ло́ндон

● *adv.*: **what** ~? э́того ещё не хвата́ло!; **what will he do** ~? а тепе́рь что он наду́мает?; ~ **to** ря́дом с (+ *i.*); **he stood** ~ **to the fire** он стоя́л во́зле ками́на

■ ~**-door** *adj.* сосе́дний; ~**-door neighbour** ближа́йший сосе́д

NHS *abbr.* (*of* **National Health Service**) Национа́льная слу́жба здравоохране́ния

nib /nɪb/ *n.* перо́

nibble /'nɪb(ə)l/ *v.t.* поку́сывать (*impf.*)

● *v.i.*: ~ **at sth** грызть (*impf.*) что-н.

Nicaragua /nɪkə'rægjʊə/ *n.* Никара́гуа (*nt. & f. indecl.*)

Nicaraguan /nɪkə'rægjʊən/ *n.* никарагуа́н|ец (-ка)

● *adj.* никарагуа́нский

♂ **nice** /naɪs/ *adj.* (agreeable) прия́тный, ми́лый; (good) хоро́ший; (of person) прия́тный, ми́лый, симпати́чный, любе́зный; **that's very** ~ **of you** э́то о́чень ми́ло с ва́шей стороны́; **this soup tastes** ~ э́тот суп вку́сный; **the children were** ~ **and clean** де́ти бы́ли чи́стенькие

■ ~**-looking** *adj.* ми́лый, симпати́чный

nicely /'naɪslɪ/ *adv.* (well, satisfactorily) хорошо́; (agreeably) прия́тно; (kindly) ми́ло

nicety /'naɪsɪtɪ/ *n.* **1** (*usu. in pl.*) (subtle detail or distinction) то́нкость, ме́лкая подро́бность **2** (exactness) то́чность; (accuracy) аккура́тность; **to a** ~ то́чно

niche /ni:ʃ/ *n.* ни́ша

nick /nɪk/ *n.* **1** (notch) зару́бка **2**: **in the** ~ **of time** в (са́мый) после́дний моме́нт; как раз во́время

● *v.t.* **1** (cut) де́лать, с- зару́бку на + *p.*; **he** ~**ed his chin shaving** он поре́зал себе́ подборо́док во вре́мя бритья́ **2** (BrE, sl., arrest) брать, взять **3** (BrE, sl., steal) спере́ть (*pf.*) (sl.)

nickel /'nɪk(ə)l/ *n.* (metal) ни́кель (*m.*); (AmE coin) пятице́нтовик

nickname /'nɪkneɪm/ *n.* про́звище, кли́чка

● *v.t.* прозва́ть (*pf.*) (*sb sth* + *a. and i.*)

nicotine /'nɪkəti:n/ *n.* никоти́н

niece /ni:s/ *n.* племя́нница

Nigeria /naɪ'dʒɪərɪə/ *n.* Ниге́рия

Nigerian /naɪ'dʒɪərɪən/ *n.* нигери́|ец (-йка)

● *adj.* нигери́йский

niggardly /'nɪgədlɪ/ *adj.* скупо́й

niggle /'nɪg(ə)l/ *v.t.* дёргать, придира́ться (*both impf.*) к + *d.*

niggling /'nɪglɪŋ/ *adj.* придирчивый

nigh /naɪ/ *adj., adv., & prep.* (archaic) = **near**

 night /naɪt/ *n.* ночь; (waking hours of darkness) вечер; **all ~ (long)** всю ночь (напролёт); **last ~** вчера вечером/ночью; **at, by ~** ночью; **on Saturday ~** в субботу вечером; **good ~!** (infml): **~-~!** спокойной ночи!
■ **~club** *n.* ночной клуб; **~dress** *n.* ночная рубашка; **~ life** *n.* ночная жизнь (города); **~mare** *n.* (also fig.) кошмар; **have a ~mare** видеть (*impf.*) кошмарный сон; **~marish** *adj.* кошмарный; **~ school** *n.* вечерняя школа; **~ shift** *n.* ночная смена; **~-time** *n.* ночное время; **in the ~-time** ночью; **~watchman** *n.* ночной сторож

nightie /'naɪtɪ/ *n.* ночная рубашка/сорочка

nightingale /'naɪtɪŋgeɪl/ *n.* соловей

nightly /'naɪtlɪ/ *adj.* (happening every night) еженощный; ежевечерний; **~ performances** ежедневные вечерние представления
● *adv.* еженощно; каждую ночь; каждый вечер

nil /nɪl/ *n.* нуль (*m.*)

Nile /naɪl/ *n.* Нил

nimble /'nɪmb(ə)l/ *adj.* (**nimbler, nimblest**) (agile) проворный, шустрый (infml); (dextrous) ловкий

 nine /naɪn/ *n.* (число/номер) девять; (figure; thing numbered 9; group of ~) девятка; **~ (o'clock)** пять (часов); **he is ~** ему девять лет
● *adj.* девять + *g. pl.*

nineteen /naɪn'tiːn/ *n.* девятнадцать; **talk ~ to the dozen** тараторить (*impf.*)
● *adj.* девятнадцать + *g. pl.*

nineteenth /naɪn'tiːnθ/ *n.* (date) девятнадцатое число; (fraction) одна девятнадцатая
● *adj.* девятнадцатый

ninetieth /'naɪntɪθ/ *n.* одна девяностая
● *adj.* девяностый

ninety /'naɪntɪ/ *n.* девяносто; **he is in his ~ies** ему за девяносто; **in the ~ies** (decade) в девяностых годах
● *adj.* девяносто + *g. pl.*

ninth /naɪnθ/ *n.* (date) девятое число; (fraction) одна девятая
● *adj.* девятый

nip /nɪp/ *n.* **1** (pinch) щипок **2** (small bite) укус **3** (of frost): **there's a ~ in the air today** сегодня мороз пощипывает
● *v.t.* (**nipped, nipping**) **1** (pinch) щип|ать, -нуть **2** (bite) укусить, куснуть (*both pf.*)
● *v.i.* (**nipped, nipping**) **1** (pinch) щипаться (*impf.*) **2** (BrE, usu. with advs., move smartly): **I must ~ along to the shop** мне нужно сбегать в магазин; **he ~ped out to have a smoke** он выскочил покурить

nipple /'nɪp(ə)l/ *n.* сосок

nippy /'nɪpɪ/ *adj.* (**nippier, nippiest**) **1** (nimble) проворный **2** (chilly): **the weather is ~** морозит

nirvana /nə'vɑːnə/ *n.* нирвана

nit /nɪt/ *n.* гнида
■ **~pick** *v.i.* (sl.) придираться (*impf.*) к мелочам

nitrate /'naɪtreɪt/ *n.* нитрат

nitrogen /'naɪtrədʒ(ə)n/ *n.* азот

nitty-gritty /nɪtɪ'grɪtɪ/ *n.* (sl.) суть дела; **the ~ of politics** политическая кухня

nitwit /'nɪtwɪt/ *n.* олух (infml)

 no /nəʊ/ *adj.* **1** (not any) никакой; **there's ~ food in the house** в доме нет (никакой) еды; **it's ~ use complaining** нет (никакого) смысла жаловаться; **~ doubt** несомненно; **~ one** никто; **I spoke to ~ one** я ни с кем не говорил; *see also* ▶ **nobody 2** (not a; quite other than) не; **he's ~ fool** он (вовсе) не дурак; **in ~ time** (very quickly) в короткий срок, в два счёта (infml) **3** (expr. refusal or prohibition): **~ smoking** курить воспрещается; **~ entry** вход воспрещён; нет входа
● *adv.* (with comps., not at all, in no way) не; **~ better than before** ничуть не лучше, чем раньше; **he ~ longer lives there** он там больше не живёт; **there is ~ more bread** хлеба больше нет; **~ sooner said than done!** сказано — сделано!; **~ sooner had he said it than …** не успел он сказать, как…
● *particle* нет; **~ thank you** нет, спасибо; (after negative statement or question, sometimes) да; **"You don't like him, do you?" — "No, I don't"** «Ведь он вам не нравится?» — «Да, не нравится»
■ **~-fly** *adj.*: **~-fly zone** запретная воздушная зона; **~-go** *adj.*: **~-go area** (BrE) запретная область

nobble /'nɒb(ə)l/ *v.t.* (BrE, infml) **1** (horse) портить, ис- **2** (bribe) подмаз|ывать, -ать; подкуп|ать, -ить

nobility /nəʊ'bɪlɪtɪ/ *n.* (quality) благородство; (titled class) дворянство

noble /'nəʊb(ə)l/ *n.* (*in full* **~man, ~woman**) дворян|ин (-янка)
● *adj.* (**nobler, noblest**) **1** (of character) благородный **2** (belonging to the nobility) дворянский

 nobody /'nəʊbədɪ/ *n.* ничтожный человек, ничтожество
● *pron.* (*also* **no one**) никто (… не); **~ knows** никто не знает; **there was ~ present** никого не было; **I spoke to ~** я ни с кем не говорил

nocturnal /nɒk'tɜːn(ə)l/ *adj.* ночной

nod /nɒd/ *n.* кивок; **give sb a ~ of the head** кивать, -нуть головой кому-н.
● *v.t.* (**nodded, nodding**): **~ one's head** кив|ать, -нуть
● *v.i.* (**nodded, nodding**) кив|ать, -нуть

node /nəʊd/ *n.* (bot., phys.) узел; (astron., math.) точка пересечения

nodule /'nɒdjuːl/ *n.* (bot., med.) узелок

 noise /nɔɪz/ *n.* **1** (din) шум; **make a ~** шуметь, за- **2** (sound) звук

noisy /'nɔɪzɪ/ *adj.* (**noisier, noisiest**) (of thing) шумный; (of person) шумливый

nomad /'nəʊmæd/ *n.* кочевник

nomenclature /nəʊ'menklətʃə(r)/ *n.* номенклатура

nominal /'nɒmɪn(ə)l/ *adj.* номина́льный

nominate /'nɒmɪneɪt/ *v.t.* (appoint, e.g. person) назн|ача́ть, -а́чить; (propose, e.g. candidate) выставля́ть, вы́ставить кандидату́ру + *g.*; (for a prize) номини́ровать (*impf.*, *pf.*)

nomination /nɒmɪ'neɪʃ(ə)n/ *n.* назначе́ние; (for a prize) номина́ция

nominative /'nɒmɪnətɪv/ *adj. & n.* имени́тельный (паде́ж)

nominee /nɒmɪ'niː/ *n.* кандида́т; (for a prize) номина́нт

non- /nɒn/ *pref.* не…

non-alcoholic /nɒnælkə'hɒlɪk/ *adj.* безалкого́льный

non-aligned /nɒnə'laɪnd/ *adj.* (pol.) неприсоедини́вшийся (к полити́ческим бло́кам)

non-believer /nɒnbɪ'liːvə(r)/ *n.* неве́рующий

nonchalance /'nɒnʃələns/ *n.* беззабо́тность; безразли́чие

nonchalant /'nɒnʃələnt/ *adj.* беззабо́тный

non-committal /nɒnkə'mɪt(ə)l/ *adj.* (evasive) укло́нчивый

non-compliance /nɒnkəm'plaɪəns/ *n.:* ~ **with regulations** несоблюде́ние пра́вил

nonconformist /nɒnkən'fɔːmɪst/ *adj.* нонконформи́стский

non-cooperation /nɒnkəʊɒpə'reɪʃ(ə)n/ *n.* отка́з от сотру́дничества

nondescript /'nɒndɪskrɪpt/ *adj.* невзра́чный, безли́чный

♂ **none** /nʌn/ *pron.* (person) никто́; ~ **of us is perfect** никто́ из нас не явля́ется соверше́нством; ~ **of the people died** ни оди́н челове́к не у́мер; (thing) ничто́; **there is** ~ **of it left** из э́того ничего́ не оста́лось; **it's** ~ **of your business** э́то не ва́ше де́ло
● *adv.*: **he is** ~ **the worse for his accident** он ничу́ть не пострада́л по́сле ава́рии

nonentity /nɒ'nentɪtɪ/ *n.* (person) ничто́жество

non-essential /nɒnɪ'senʃ(ə)l/ *adj.* несуще́ственный

non-event /nɒnɪ'vent/ *n.* собы́тие сомни́тельной ва́жности

non-existence /nɒnɪg'zɪst(ə)ns/ *n.* небытие́

non-existent /nɒnɪg'zɪst(ə)nt/ *adj.* несуществу́ющий

non-fiction /nɒn'fɪkʃ(ə)n/ *n.* докумета́льная про́за/литерату́ра

non-interference /nɒnɪntə'fɪərəns/ *n.* невмеша́тельство

non-intervention /nɒnɪntə'venʃ(ə)n/ *n.* невмеша́тельство

non-member /nɒn'membə(r)/ *n.* не член

no-nonsense /nəʊ'nɒns(ə)ns/ *adj.* (businesslike) делово́й; (strict) стро́гий

nonplus /nɒn'plʌs/ *v.t.* (**nonplussed**, **nonplussing**) прив|оди́ть, -ести́ в замеша́тельство

non-profit /nɒn'prɒfɪt/ *adj.* некомме́рческий

non-profit-making /nɒn'prɒfɪt,meɪkɪŋ/ *adj.* (BrE) = **non-profit**

nonsense /'nɒns(ə)ns/ *n.* **1** (sth without meaning) бессмы́слица; (rubbish) вздор; ерунда́ (infml); **talk** ~ говори́ть (*impf.*) вздор/ерунду́ **2** (foolish conduct) глу́пость; **let's have no more** ~! хва́тит валя́ть дурака́!

nonsensical /nɒn'sensɪk(ə)l/ *adj.* бессмы́сленный

non-smoker /nɒn'sməʊkə(r)/ *n.* некуря́щий

non-smoking /nɒn'sməʊkɪŋ/ *adj.*: ~ **compartment** купе́ (*nt. indecl.*) для некуря́щих

non-starter /nɒn'stɑːtə(r)/ *n.* (infml, of plan, idea) до́хлый но́мер, до́хлое де́ло

non-stick /nɒn'stɪk/ *adj.*: **a** ~ **saucepan** кастрю́ля с непригора́ющим покры́тием

non-stop /nɒn'stɒp/ *adj.* **1** (of train or coach) иду́щий/е́дущий без остано́вок; (of aircraft or flight) беспоса́дочный **2** (continuous) непреры́вный
● *adv.* **1** беспоса́дочно **2**: **he talks** ~ он говори́т без у́молку

noodles /'nuːd(ə)lz/ *n. pl.* (cul.) лапша́

nook /nʊk/ *n.* уголо́к; **I searched every** ~ **and cranny** я обша́рил ка́ждый уголо́к

noon /nuːn/ *n.* по́лдень (*m.*); **12** ~ двена́дцать часо́в дня

no one /'nəʊwʌn/ *pron. see* ▶ **nobody**

noose /nuːs/ *n.* (loop) петля́; (lasso) арка́н

♂ **nor** /nɔː(r)/ *conj.*: **they had neither arms** ~ **provisions** у них не́ было ни ору́жия, ни провиа́нта; **you are not well,** ~ **am I** вам нездоро́вится, и мне то́же

norm /nɔːm/ *n.* но́рма, пра́вило

♂ **normal** /'nɔːm(ə)l/ *adj.* (regular, standard) норма́льный; (usual) обы́чный; **I** ~**ly use the bus** обы́чно я е́ду авто́бусом; (sane, well balanced) норма́льный

normality /nɔː'mælɪtɪ/ *n.* норма́льность

♂ **north** /nɔːθ/ *n.* се́вер; (naut.) норд; **the** ~ **of England** се́вер А́нглии/се́верная часть А́нглии; **in the** ~ на се́вере; **from the** ~ с се́вера; **to the** ~ на се́вер
● *adj.* се́верный
● *adv.*: **we went** ~ мы пое́хали на се́вер
■ **N**~ **America** *n.* Се́верная Аме́рика; **N**~ **American** *n.* североамерика́н|ец (-ка) ● *adj.* североамерика́нский; ~**bound** *adj.* направля́ющийся на се́вер; ~**-east** *n.* се́веро-восто́к ● *adj.* се́веро-восто́чный; ~**-east wind** норд-о́ст ● *adv.* к се́веро-восто́ку; на се́веро-восто́к; ~**-easterly** *adj.* се́веро-восто́чный; ~**-eastern** *adj.* се́веро-восто́чный; **N**~ **Pole** *n.* Се́верный по́люс; **N**~ **Sea** *n.* Се́верное мо́ре; ~**-west** *n.* се́веро-за́пад ● *adj.* се́веро-за́падный; ~**-west wind** норд-ве́ст ● *adv.* к се́веро-за́паду; на се́веро-за́пад; ~**-westerly** *adj.* се́веро-за́падный; ~**-western** *adj.* се́веро-за́падный

northerly /'nɔːðəlɪ/ *n.* (wind) се́верный ве́тер
● *adj.* се́верный

northern /'nɔ:ð(ə)n/ *adj.* се́верный
■ **N~ Ireland** *n.* Се́верная Ирла́ндия; **N~ Irish** *adj.* североирла́ндский

northerner /'nɔ:ðənə(r)/ *n.* северя́н|ин (-ка)

northward /'nɔ:θwəd/ *adj.* се́верный
● *adv.* (*also* **~s**) на се́вер; к се́веру, в се́верном направле́нии

Norway /'nɔ:weɪ/ *n.* Норве́гия

Norwegian /nɔ:'wi:dʒ(ə)n/ *n.* (person) норве́ж|ец (-ка); (language) норве́жский язы́к
● *adj.* норве́жский

nose /nəʊz/ *n.* **1** нос; (dim.) но́сик; **blow one's ~** сморка́ться, вы-; **look down one's ~ at sb** смотре́ть, по- свысока́ на кого́-н.; **rub sb's ~ in sth** ты́кать, ткнуть кого́-н. но́сом во что-н.; **turn up one's ~ at sth** вороти́ть (*impf.*) нос от чего́-н. **2** (sense of smell) нюх, чутьё
● *v.t.*: **~ into** (pry, meddle) сова́ться, су́нуться (*or* сова́ть, су́нуть нос) в + *a.*
■ **~bleed** *n.*: **he has frequent ~bleeds** у него́ ча́сто идёт но́сом (*or* из но́са) кровь; **~dive** *n.* пики́рование; **prices took a ~dive** це́ны ре́зко упа́ли ● *v.i.* пики́ровать (*impf., pf.*)

nosey /'nəʊzɪ/ *adj.* = **nosy**

nostalgia /nɒ'stældʒə/ *n.* ностальги́я

nostalgic /nɒ'stældʒɪk/ *adj.* (person): **be ~ for** тоскова́ть по + *d.*; (thing) ностальги́ческий

nostril /'nɒstrɪl/ *n.* ноздря́

nosy, nosey /'nəʊzɪ/ *adj.* (**nosier, nosiest**) (infml) любопы́тный

not /nɒt/ *adv.* **1** не; (*as pred.*) нет; **she is ~ here** её здесь нет **2** (elliptical phrr.): **guilty or ~, he is my son** вино́вен он и́ли нет, а он мой сын; **whether or ~** так и́ли ина́че; **I hope ~** наде́юсь, что нет **3** (**~ even**): **~ one of them moved** ни оди́н из них не подви́нулся **4** (**~ at all**): **'Do you mind if I smoke?' — 'N~ at all!'** «Вы не возража́ете, е́сли я закурю́?» — «Ниско́лько/ничу́ть»; **'Many thanks!' — 'N~ at all!'** «Большо́е спаси́бо!» — «Не сто́ит! (*or* Пожа́луйста!)» **5** (var. phrr.): **~ on your life** ни в ко́ем слу́чае; **~ in the least** ничу́ть; ниско́лько

notable /'nəʊtəb(ə)l/ *n.* знамени́тость
● *adj.* (perceptible) заме́тный; (remarkable) замеча́тельный; (well known) изве́стный

notably /'nəʊtəblɪ/ *adv.* заме́тно

notary /'nəʊtərɪ/ *n.* (*also* **~ public**) нота́риус

notch /nɒtʃ/ *n.* зару́бка
● *v.t.* **1** (mark with **~**) де́лать, с- зару́бку на + *p.* **2**: **~ up a point** (in game) выи́грывать, выи́грать очко́

note /nəʊt/ *n.* **1** (communication) запи́ска; **he left a ~ for you** он оста́вил вам запи́ску **2** (written record) за́пись; **make a ~ of sth** запи́с|ывать, -а́ть что-н. **3** (attention, notice) внима́ние; **take ~ of** (observe) прин|има́ть, -я́ть во внима́ние; (heed) прин|има́ть, -я́ть к све́дению **4** (mus.) но́та; (key of instrument) кла́виша **5** (BrE, currency) банкно́та
● *v.t.* **1** (observe, notice) зам|еча́ть, -е́тить;

(heed) обра|ща́ть, -ти́ть внима́ние на + *a.*
2: **~ down** (in writing) запи́с|ывать, -а́ть
■ **~book** *n.* записна́я кни́жка; **~book computer** *n.* ноутбу́к; **~pad** *n.* блокно́т; **~paper** *n.* пи́счая бума́га; **~worthy** *adj.* досто́йный внима́ния

noted /'nəʊtɪd/ *adj.* изве́стный, знамени́тый; **~ for his courage** изве́стный свои́м му́жеством

nothing /'nʌθɪŋ/ *pron.* ничто́, ничего́ (infml); **she is ~ to me** она́ для меня́ ничто́; **there's ~ to be ashamed of** в э́том нет ничего́ посты́дного; **there's ~ worse than getting wet through** нет ничего́ ху́же, чем промо́кнуть наскво́зь; **there's ~ like a hot bath** нет ничего́ лу́чше горя́чей ва́нны; **~ much** ма́ло; **there's ~ wrong with that** ничего́ в э́том плохо́го нет; **he did ~ to help** он ниче́м не помо́г; **I have ~ to do** мне не́чего де́лать; **it has ~ to do with me** э́то меня́ не каса́ется; **they had ~ to eat** им не́чего бы́ло есть, у них не́ было никако́й еды́; **I have ~ but praise for him** я не могу́ им нахвали́ться; **he had ~ on** (was naked) он был соверше́нно го́лый; **~ of the kind** ничего́ подо́бного; **he will stop at ~** он ни пе́ред чем не остано́вится; **for ~** (without cause) ни за что́, ни про что́; (to no purpose) зря, напра́сно, да́ром; (free of charge) беспла́тно
● *adv.*: **she is ~ like her sister** она́ совсе́м не похо́жа на сестру́; **this exam is ~ like as hard as the last** э́тот экза́мен гора́здо/куда́ ле́гче предыду́щего

notice /'nəʊtɪs/ *n.* **1** (intimation) предупрежде́ние **2** (time limit): **I have to give my employer a month's ~** (of resignation) я до́лжен предупреди́ть хозя́ина за ме́сяц (об ухо́де с рабо́ты); **at short ~** в после́днюю мину́ту; в сро́чном поря́дке; **till further ~** впредь до дальне́йшего уведомле́ния **3** (written announcement) объявле́ние **4** (attention) внима́ние; **he took no ~ of me** он не обраща́л на меня́ внима́ния
● *v.t.* (observe) зам|еча́ть, -е́тить
■ **~ board** *n.* (BrE) доска́ объявле́ний

noticeable /'nəʊtɪsəb(ə)l/ *adj.* заме́тный

notifiable /'nəʊtɪfaɪəb(ə)l/ *adj.* (of disease etc.) подлежа́щий регистра́ции

notification /ˌnəʊtɪfɪ'keɪʃ(ə)n/ *n.* извеще́ние

notif|y /'nəʊtɪfaɪ/ *v.t.* **1** (inform) изве|ща́ть, -сти́ть; сообщ|а́ть, -и́ть + *d.*; **I was ~ied of your arrival** мне сообщи́ли/мне сообщи́ли о ва́шем (предстоя́щем) прие́зде; **he ~ied me of his address** он сообщи́л мне свой а́дрес **2** (register) регистри́ровать (*impf., pf.*); **all births must be ~ied** все рожде́ния подлежа́т регистра́ции

notion /'nəʊʃ(ə)n/ *n.* поня́тие, представле́ние

notional /'nəʊʃən(ə)l/ *adj.* (ostensible, imaginary) вообража́емый, мни́мый

notoriety /ˌnəʊtə'raɪətɪ/ *n.* дурна́я сла́ва, печа́льная изве́стность; **his arrest won him a brief ~** его́ аре́ст созда́л/принёс ему́ на вре́мя печа́льную изве́стность

◦ ключева́я ле́ксика

notorious /nəʊˈtɔːrɪəs/ adj. (well known) (обще)изве́стный; (pej.) преслову́тый; печа́льно изве́стный

notwithstanding /nɒtwɪðˈstændɪŋ/ adv. всё-таки
● *prep.* несмотря́ на + a.

nought /nɔːt/ n. **1** (zero) нуль (m.) **2** (figure 0) ноль (m.)

noun /naʊn/ n. (и́мя) существи́тельное

nourish /ˈnʌrɪʃ/ v.t. пита́ть (impf.)

nourishment /ˈnʌrɪʃmənt/ n. пита́ние

nouveau riche /nuːˌvəʊ ˈriːʃ/ n. (pl. **nouveaux riches** pronunc. same) нувори́ш

⚘ **novel** /ˈnɒv(ə)l/ n. рома́н
● *adj.* необы́чный

novelist /ˈnɒvəlɪst/ n. писа́тель (-ница); романи́ст (-ка)

novelty /ˈnɒvəltɪ/ n. (newness) новизна́; (new thing) нови́нка; но́вшество

⚘ **November** /nəʊˈvembə(r)/ n. ноя́брь (m.)

novice /ˈnɒvɪs/ n. **1** (relig.) послу́шни|к (-ца) **2** (beginner) новичо́к

⚘ **now** /naʊ/ adv. **1** (at the present time) тепе́рь, сейча́с, ны́не; в настоя́щее вре́мя; (opp. previously): **I'm married** ~ я тепе́рь жена́т; **(every)** ~ **and then** вре́мя от вре́мени; порóй; (with preps.): **before** ~ (hitherto) до сих пор; (in the past) в про́шлом; **by** ~ к э́тому вре́мени; **he should be here by** ~ он до́лжен уже́ быть здесь; **from** ~ **on** впредь; отны́не **2** (this time): ~ **you've broken the glass** ну, вот вы и разби́ли стака́н **3** (at once; at this moment) сейча́с; **I must go** ~ мне пора́ (уходи́ть); **he was here just** ~ он то́лько что был здесь; **only** ~ то́лько тепе́рь **4** (emphatic) ну, так, ита́к; ~ **you just listen to me** нет, вы послу́шайте, что я вам скажу́; ~ **why didn't I think of that?** как же я об э́том не поду́мал?
● *conj.* (*also* ~ **that**) по́сле того́ как

nowadays /ˈnaʊədeɪz/ adv. в на́ши дни; в на́ше вре́мя; ны́не

nowhere /ˈnəʊweə(r)/ adv. нигде́; (motion) никуда́; **the house was** ~ **near the park** дом стоя́л о́чень далеко́ от па́рка; **he was** ~ **near 60** ему́ ещё бы́ло далеко́ до шести́десяти (лет); **this conversation is getting us** ~ э́тот разгово́р нас ни к чему́ не приведёт; **there's** ~ **to sit** не́где сесть

noxious /ˈnɒkʃəs/ adj. вре́дный, па́губный

nozzle /ˈnɒz(ə)l/ n. сопло́

nuance /ˈnjuːɑːs/ n. отте́нок, нюа́нс

nub /nʌb/ n. (fig., point, gist) суть

nubile /ˈnjuːbaɪl/ adj. (mature) зре́лый, созре́вший; (alluring) прельсти́тельный

⚘ **nuclear** /ˈnjuːklɪə(r)/ adj. **1** (phys.) я́дерный **2**: ~ **family** ма́лая/нуклеа́рная семья́
■ ~ **bomb** n. я́дерная бо́мба; ~ **energy** n. я́дерная эне́ргия; ~ **power station** n. а́томная электроста́нция; ~ **reactor** n. а́томный/я́дерный реа́ктор

nucleus /ˈnjuːklɪəs/ n. (pl. **nuclei**) (phys., fig.) ядро́; (biol.) заро́дыш

nude /njuːd/ n. **1** (art) обнажённая (фигу́ра) **2**: **in the** ~ в го́лом ви́де, нагишо́м (infml)

● *adj.* го́лый, обнажённый, наго́й

nudge /nʌdʒ/ v.t. подт|а́лкивать, -олкну́ть

nudist /ˈnjuːdɪst/ n. нуди́ст (-ка)

nudity /ˈnjuːdɪtɪ/ n. нагота́

nugget /ˈnʌgɪt/ n. саморо́док (зо́лота)

nuisance /ˈnjuːs(ə)ns/ n. (annoyance) доса́да; (inconvenience) неудо́бство; **what a** ~! кака́я доса́да!

null /nʌl/ adj.: **become** ~ **and void** утра́|чивать, -тить (зако́нную) си́лу

nullify /ˈnʌlɪfaɪ/ v.t. аннули́ровать (impf., pf.)

numb /nʌm/ adj. **1** (of body) онеме́лый, онеме́вший; (of extremities, ~ **with cold**) окочене́лый **2** (of mind, senses) онеме́вший, оцепене́вший; **go** ~ неме́ть, о-, цепене́ть, о-
● *v.t.*: **the cold had** ~**ed my hands** мои́ ру́ки окочене́ли от хо́лода; **morphine** ~**ed the pain** мо́рфий притупи́л боль

⚘ **number** /ˈnʌmbə(r)/ n. **1** (numeral) число́, ци́фра **2** (quantity, amount) число́, коли́чество; **the average** ~ **in a class is 30** сре́дняя чи́сленность кла́сса — три́дцать челове́к/ учени́ков; **there were a large** ~ **of people there** там бы́ло мно́го наро́ду/большо́е коли́чество люде́й; **a** ~ **of professors attended the lecture** ле́кцию слу́шали не́сколько профессоро́в **3** (identifying) но́мер; **he was** ~ **3 on the list** он шёл тре́тьим но́мером в спи́ске; **look after** ~ **one** (fig.) забо́титься (impf.) о со́бственной персо́не; **telephone** ~ но́мер телефо́на; **you have the wrong** ~ вы не туда́ звони́те/попа́ли; (song or item in stage performance) но́мер
● *v.t.* **1** (count) перечисля́ть, -и́слить; **his days are** ~**ed** его́ дни сочтены́ **2** (give ~ to) нумерова́ть, про- **3** (amount to) насчи́тываться (impf.)

■ ~ **plate** n. (BrE) номерно́й знак

numeracy /ˈnjuːmərəsɪ/ n. зна́ние арифме́тики

numeral /ˈnjuːmər(ə)l/ n. ци́фра

numerical /njuːˈmerɪk(ə)l/ adj. чи́сленный, числово́й

⚘ **numerous** /ˈnjuːmərəs/ adj. многочи́сленный

nun /nʌn/ n. мона́хиня, мона́шенка

nunnery /ˈnʌnərɪ/ n. же́нский монасты́рь

nuptial /ˈnʌpʃ(ə)l/ adj. сва́дебный

nuptials /ˈnʌpʃ(ə)lz/ n. pl. сва́дьба

⚘ **nurse** /nɜːs/ n. **1** (~ **maid**) ня́ня, ня́нька (infml) **2** (of the sick) сиде́лка; (orderly) санита́рка; (senior ~) медсестра́; **male** ~ (orderly) санита́р; (senior) медбра́т
● *v.t.* **1** (suckle) корми́ть (impf.) (гру́дью) **2** (attend to) уха́живать (impf.) за + i. **3** (fig.): ~ **hopes** леле́ять (impf.) наде́жду

nursery /ˈnɜːsərɪ/ n. **1** (room) де́тская **2** (institution etc. for care of young): **day** ~ (дневны́е) я́сл|и (-ей) **3**: ~ **nurse** (BrE) воспита́тельница я́слей/де́тского са́да; ~ **school** де́тский сад, детса́д; ~ **rhyme** де́тские сти́шки (m. pl.); де́тская пе́сенка **4** (hort.) пито́мник

nursing /ˈnɜːsɪŋ/ n. (career) профе́ссия медсестры́

■ ~ **home** *n.* (частная) лечебница, (частный) санаторий; (old people's home) дом (для) престарелых

nurture /'nɜ:tʃə(r)/ *v.t.* (nourish) питать (*impf.*); (rear) воспитывать, -ать

nut /nʌt/ *n.* **1** орех **2** (for securing bolt) гайка

■ ~**crackers** *n. pl.* щипцы (-ов) для орехов; ~**shell** *n.* ореховая скорлупа; **in a** ~**shell** (fig.) кратко; в двух словах

nutmeg /'nʌtmeg/ *n.* мускатный орех

nutrient /'nju:trɪənt/ *n.* питательное вещество

nutrition /nju:'trɪʃ(ə)n/ *n.* питание

nutritional /nju:'trɪʃən(ə)l/ *adj.* (deficiency, value) питательный; (advice) диетический

nutritious /nju:'trɪʃəs/ *adj.* питательный

nutty /'nʌtɪ/ *adj.* (**nuttier, nuttiest**) **1** (of taste) с привкусом ореха **2** (crazy) чокнутый (infml)

nuzzle /'nʌz(ə)l/ *v.t. & i.:* ~ (**against, up to**) sb/ sth тыкаться (*impf.*) носом в кого-н./что-н.

nylon /'naɪlɒn/ *n.* нейлон
• *adj.* нейлоновый

nymph /nɪmf/ *n.* нимфа

nymphomaniac /nɪmfə'meɪnɪæk/ *n.* нимфоманка

Oo

O /əʊ/ *n.* (nought) нуль (*m.*), ноль (*m.*)

oak /əʊk/ *n.* (tree; wood) дуб; (*attr.*) дубовый

OAP (BrE) *abbr.* (*of* **old-age pensioner**) пенсионер (-ка) (по старости)

oar /ɔ:(r)/ *n.* весло

oasis /əʊ'eɪsɪs/ *n.* (*pl.* **oases** /-si:z/) оазис

oast house /'əʊsthaʊs/ *n.* хмелесушильня

oat /əʊt/ *n.* (in *pl.*) овёс; **sow one's wild** ~**s** (fig.) прожигать, -ечь молодость; перебеситься (*pf.*)

■ ~**meal** *n.* толокно; овсяная крупа

oath /əʊθ/ *n.* **1** присяга; **on** (BrE), **under** ~ под присягой **2** (profanity) проклятие

obdurate /'ɒbdjʊrət/ *adj.* (stubborn) упрямый; (hard-headed) ожесточённый

OBE *abbr.* (*of* **Officer of the Order of the British Empire**) кавалер ордена Британской империи 4-й степени

obedience /ə'bi:dɪəns/ *n.* повиновение

obedient /ə'bi:dɪənt/ *adj.* послушный, покорный

obelisk /'ɒbəlɪsk/ *n.* обелиск

obese /əʊ'bi:s/ *adj.* тучный

obesity /əʊ'bi:sɪtɪ/ *n.* тучность

obey /ə'beɪ/ *v.t.* (comply with): ~ **the laws** подчиняться, -иться законам; (be obedient to): ~ **one's parents** слушаться, по- родителей
• *v.i.* повиноваться (*impf., pf.*)

obfuscate /'ɒbfʌskeɪt/ *v.t.* (darken, obscure) затемнять, -ить; (confuse) смущать, -тить

obfuscation /ɒbfʌs'keɪʃ(ə)n/ *n.* затемнение; смущение

obituary /ə'bɪtjʊərɪ/ *n.* некролог

⚔ **object¹** /'ɒbdʒɪkt/ *n.* **1** (material thing) предмет, вещь **2** (focus) предмет, объект **3** (purpose, aim) цель; **I had no particular** ~ **in view** никакой определённой цели я не преследовал **4** (gram.) дополнение

object² /əb'dʒekt/ *v.t.* возра|жать, -зить (**to**: против + *g.*); протестовать (*impf.*) (**to**: против + *g.*); выдвигать, выдвинуть возражения (**to**: против + *g.*); **I** ~ **to being treated like this** я протестую против такого обращения; **do you** ~ **to my smoking?** вам не мешает, что я курю?; **I'll open a window if you don't** ~ я открою окно, если вы не возражаете

objection /əb'dʒekʃ(ə)n/ *n.* возражение, протест; **I have no** ~ **to your going abroad** я не возражаю (*or* я ничего не имею) против вашей поездки за границу

objectionable /əb'dʒekʃənəb(ə)l/ *adj.* нежелательный; неприемлемый

objective /əb'dʒektɪv/ *n.* цель
• *adj.* объективный

objectivity /ɒbdʒek'tɪvɪtɪ/ *n.* объективность

objector /əb'dʒektə(r)/ *n.* возражающий; **conscientious** ~ человек, отказывающийся от военной службы из принципиальных соображений

obligate /'ɒblɪgeɪt/ *v.t.* обяз|ывать, -ать

obligation /ɒblɪ'geɪʃ(ə)n/ *n.* (promise, commitment) обязательство; (duty, responsibility) обязанность; **be under an** ~ **to sb** быть обязанным кому-н.

obligatory /ə'blɪgətərɪ/ *adj.* обязательный

oblige /ə'blaɪdʒ/ *v.t.* **1** (compel) вынуждать, вынудить; **we are** ~**d to remind you** мы вынуждены напомнить вам **2** (do favour to) обяз|ывать, -ать; **I am much** ~**d to you** я вам очень обязан/благодарен

obliging /ə'blaɪdʒɪŋ/ *adj.* услужливый

oblique /ə'bli:k/ *adj.* **1** (slanting) косой **2** (gram. and fig.) косвенный

⚔ ключевая лексика

obliterate /ə'blɪtəreɪt/ v.t. (lit., fig.) ст|ира́ть, -ере́ть (с лица́ земли́)

obliteration /əblɪtə'reɪʃ(ə)n/ n. стира́ние

oblivion /ə'blɪvɪən/ n. забве́ние

oblivious /ə'blɪvɪəs/ adj.: to be ~ of не име́ть никако́го поня́тия о + p.; he was ~ to her objections он был глух к её возраже́ниям

oblong /'ɒblɒŋ/ n. продолгова́тая фигу́ра
● adj. продолгова́тый

obnoxious /əb'nɒkʃəs/ adj. проти́вный

oboe /'əʊbəʊ/ n. гобо́й

oboist /'əʊbəʊɪst/ n. гобои́ст (-ка)

obscene /əb'siːn/ adj. непристо́йный

obscenity /əb'senɪtɪ/ n. непристо́йность

obscure /əb'skjʊə(r)/ adj. **1** (not easily understood) нея́сный **2** (little known) малоизве́стный
● v.t. (darken, also fig.) затемн|я́ть, -и́ть; (conceal from sight) заслон|я́ть, -и́ть

obscurity /əb'skjʊərɪtɪ/ n. (lack of clarity) нея́сность; (being unknown) безве́стность

obsequious /əb'siːkwɪəs/ adj. подобостра́стный, раболе́пный

observable /əb'zɜːvəb(ə)l/ adj. заме́тный, различи́мый

observance /əb'zɜːv(ə)ns/ n. **1** (of rule, law, custom, etc.) соблюде́ние **2** (rite, ceremony) обря́д; (ritual) ритуа́л

observant /əb'zɜːv(ə)nt/ adj. наблюда́тельный; внима́тельный

◆ **observation** /ɒbzə'veɪʃ(ə)n/ n. наблюде́ние; keep sb under ~ держа́ть (impf.) кого́-н. под наблюде́нием

observatory /əb'zɜːvətərɪ/ n. обсервато́рия

◆ **observe** /əb'zɜːv/ v.t. **1** (notice) зам|еча́ть, -е́тить; (see) ви́деть, у- **2** (watch) наблюда́ть (impf.) за + i. **3** (remark) зам|еча́ть, -е́тить

observer /əb'zɜːvə(r)/ n. наблюда́тель (m.)

obsess /əb'ses/ v.t. завлад|ева́ть, -е́ть (чьим-н.) умо́м

obsession /əb'seʃ(ə)n/ n. (being obsessed) одержи́мость; (fixed idea) навя́зчивая иде́я

obsessive /əb'sesɪv/ adj. навя́зчивый

obsolescence /ɒbsə'les(ə)ns/ n. устарева́ние; planned, built-in ~ заплани́рованная устаре́лость (товара)

obsolescent /ɒbsə'les(ə)nt/ adj. устарева́ющий

obsolete /'ɒbsəliːt/ adj. устаре́лый; become ~ выходи́ть, вы́йти из употребле́ния; отж|ива́ть, -и́ть

obstacle /'ɒbstək(ə)l/ n. препя́тствие
■ ~ course n. (sport) полоса́ препя́тствий; ~ race n. бег/ска́чки с препя́тствиями

obstetric /əb'stetrɪk/, **obstetrical** /əb'stetrɪk(ə)l/ adjs. акуше́рский, родовспомога́тельный

obstetrician /ɒbstə'trɪʃ(ə)n/ n. акуше́р (-ка)

obstetrics /əb'stetrɪks/ n. акуше́рство

obstinate /'ɒbstɪnət/ adj. (stubborn) упря́мый; (persistent) насто́йчивый

obstruct /əb'strʌkt/ v.t. меша́ть (impf.) + d., препя́тствовать (impf.) + d.; ~ the road

загра|жда́ть, -ди́ть доро́гу; ~ the view заслон|я́ть, -и́ть вид

obstruction /əb'strʌkʃ(ə)n/ n. загражде́ние; (hindrance) препя́тствие

obstructive /əb'strʌktɪv/ adj. (policy) препя́тствующий; (object) загора́живающий; (pol.) обстру́кцио́нный

◆ **obtain** /əb'teɪn/ v.t. (procure) доб|ыва́ть, -ы́ть; (acquire) приобре|та́ть, -сти́
● v.i. (formal, be current, prevalent) существова́ть (impf.)

obtainable /əb'teɪnəb(ə)l/ adj. достижи́мый, досту́пный; is this model still ~? э́ту моде́ль мо́жно ещё приобрести́?

obtrusive /əb'truːsɪv/ adj. навя́зчивый, назо́йливый

obtuse /əb'tjuːs/ adj. (lit., fig.) тупо́й

obviate /'ɒbvɪeɪt/ v.t. (evade, circumvent) избе|га́ть, -жа́ть + g.; (remove) устран|я́ть, -и́ть

◆ **obvious** /'ɒbvɪəs/ adj. очеви́дный, я́сный; ~ly очеви́дно

◆ **occasion** /ə'keɪʒ(ə)n/ n. слу́чай; on many ~s во мно́гих слу́чаях; ча́сто; on the ~ of his marriage по слу́чаю его́ бра́ка; today is a special ~ сего́дня осо́бый день; rise to the ~ ока́з|ываться, -а́ться на высоте́ положе́ния

occasional /ə'keɪʒən(ə)l/ adj. случа́йный; (infrequent) ре́дкий

occasionally /ə'keɪʒən(ə)lɪ/ adv. вре́мя от вре́мени, поро́й, иногда́, и́зредка

occult /ɒ'kʌlt/ n.: the ~ оккульти́зм

occupancy /'ɒkjʊpənsɪ/ n. заня́тие; (taking, holding possession) завладе́ние; (holding on lease) аре́нда, владе́ние

occupant /'ɒkjʊpənt/ n. **1** (tenant) жиле́ц, аренда́тор, нанима́тель (m.) **2**: the ~s of the car е́хавшие в маши́не

occupation /ɒkjʊ'peɪʃ(ə)n/ n. **1** (taking possession) завладе́ние **2** (mil.) оккупа́ция; army of ~ оккупацио́нная а́рмия **3** (pastime) заня́тие, время(пре)провожде́ние **4** (employment) заня́тие; профе́ссия

occupational /ɒkjʊ'peɪʃən(ə)l/ adj. профессиона́льный
■ ~ hazard n. риск, свя́занный с хара́ктером рабо́ты; профессиона́льный/ произво́дственный риск

occupier /'ɒkjʊpaɪə(r)/ n. (BrE) прожива́ющий

◆ **occup|y** /'ɒkjʊpaɪ/ v.t. **1** (take over; take possession of) зан|има́ть, -я́ть; завлад|ева́ть, -е́ть + i. **2** (employ): he ~ies his time with crossword puzzles он посвяща́ет всё своё вре́мя разга́дыванию/реше́нию кроссво́рдов

◆ **occur** /ə'kɜː(r)/ v.i. (**occurred**, **occurring**) **1** (take place) случ|а́ться, -и́ться **2** (of thought) при|ходи́ть, -йти́ в го́лову, на ум; it ~red to me that ... мне пришло́ в го́лову, что...

occurrence /ə'kʌrəns/ n. происше́ствие, слу́чай

OCD abbr. (of **obsessive-compulsive disorder**) (med.) ОКР (обсесси́вно-компульси́вное расстро́йство)

ocean /'əʊʃ(ə)n/ n. океа́н

o

oceanic /ˌəʊʃɪˈænɪk/ *adj.* океани́ческий, океа́нский

oceanographer /ˌəʊʃəˈnɒɡrəfə(r)/ *n.* океано́граф

oceanography /ˌəʊʃəˈnɒɡrəfɪ/ *n.* океаногра́фия

ochre /ˈəʊkə(r)/ (AmE **ocher**) *n.* о́хра

o'clock /əˈklɒk/ *adv.*: **two** ~ два часа́; **at 10** ~ **at night** в де́сять часо́в ве́чера

octagon /ˈɒktəɡən/ *n.* восьмиуго́льник

octagonal /ɒkˈtæɡən(ə)l/ *adj.* восьмиуго́льный

octave /ˈɒktɪv/ *n.* (mus.) окта́ва

☞ **October** /ɒkˈtəʊbə(r)/ *n.* октя́брь (*m.*)

☞ **octopus** /ˈɒktəpəs/ *n.* (*pl.* **octopuses**) осьмино́г; спрут

☞ **odd** /ɒd/ *adj.* **1** (not even): ~ **numbers** нечётные чи́сла **2** (not matching) непа́рный; **I was wearing** ~ **socks** я был в ра́зных носка́х **3** (not in a set) разро́зненный **4** (with some remainder) с ли́шним; **40** ~ со́рок с ли́шним (*or* с чем-то) **5** (occasional) случа́йный; ~ **jobs** случа́йная рабо́та; **he made the** ~ **mistake** (infml) ему́ случа́лось ошиба́ться **6** (strange) стра́нный, эксцентри́чный, чудно́й

oddity /ˈɒdɪtɪ/ *n.* (person) чуда́|к (-чка); (thing) причу́дливая вещь

oddly /ˈɒdlɪ/ *adv.*: ~ **enough** как (э́то) ни стра́нно; предста́вьте себе́

odds /ɒdz/ *n. pl.* **1** (balance of advantage): **the** ~ **are in our favour** переве́с на на́шей стороне́; **the** ~ **were against his winning** у него́ бы́ло ма́ло ша́нсов на вы́игрыш **2** (betting): **long** ~ нера́вные ша́нсы (*m. pl.*); **short** ~ почти́ ра́вные ша́нсы **3** (variance): **be at** ~ **with sb** не ла́дить (*impf.*) с кем-н. **4**: ~ **and ends** (leftovers) оста́тки (*m. pl.*); (sundries) вся́кая вся́чина

ode /əʊd/ *n.* о́да

odious /ˈəʊdɪəs/ *adj.* (hateful) ненави́стный, одио́зный; (foul, vile) гну́сный; (repulsive) отврати́тельный

odour /ˈəʊdə(r)/ (AmE **odor**) *n.* (smell) за́пах

odyssey /ˈɒdɪsɪ/ *n.* (*pl.* ~**s**) одиссе́я, приключе́ния (*nt. pl.*)

oedema /ɪˈdiːmə/ (AmE **edema**) *n.* отёк

oesopha|gus /iːˈsɒfəgəs/ (AmE **esophagus**) *n.* (*pl.* ~**gi** /-dʒaɪ/ *or* ~**guses**) пищево́д

oestrogen /ˈiːstrədʒ(ə)n/ (AmE **estrogen**) *n.* эстроге́н

☞ **of** /ɒv/ *prep.* (expr. by g. and/or var. preps.) **1** (origin): **Lawrence** ~ **Arabia** Ло́уренс Арави́йский **2** (cause): **he died** ~ **fright** он у́мер от испу́га **3** (material) из + g.; **what is it made** ~? из чего́ э́то сде́лано? **4** (composition): **a bunch** ~ **keys** свя́зка ключе́й; **a family** ~ **8** семья́ из восьми́ челове́к **5** (contents): **a bottle** ~ **milk** (full) буты́лка молока́ **6** (qualities): **a man** ~ **ability** спосо́бный челове́к **7** (possession): **the property** ~ **the state** госуда́рственная

со́бственность **8** (partitive): **some** ~ **us** не́которые/ко́е-кто из нас; **a quarter** ~ **an hour** че́тверть часа́; **most** ~ **all** осо́бенно; бо́льше всего́/всех; **a friend** ~ **ours** оди́н из на́ших знако́мых **9** (separation, distance): **within 10 miles** ~ **London** в десяти́ ми́лях от Ло́ндона

☞ **off** /ɒf/ *adj.* **1** (nearer to centre of road): **on the** ~ **side** (in Britain) на пра́вой стороне́ **2** (improbable): **I went on the** ~ **chance of finding him in** я пошёл туда́ науда́чу — вдруг заста́ну (его́) **3** (substandard): **it was one of my** ~ **days** в тот день я был не в са́мой лу́чшей фо́рме **4** (inactive): **the** ~ **season** мёртвый сезо́н, межсезо́нье

• *adv.* **1** (away): **two miles** ~ в двух ми́лях отту́да/отсю́да; **the elections are still two years** ~ до вы́боров ещё два го́да; **it's time I was** ~; **I must be** ~ мне пора́ (уходи́ть) **2** (disconnected): **the electricity was** ~ электри́чество бы́ло отключено́ **3** (ended, cancelled): **their engagement is** ~ их помо́лвка расто́ргнута; **the match is** ~ матч отменён **4** (not working): **day** ~ выходно́й (день); **he was** ~ **sick** он отсу́тствовал/не́ был на рабо́те по боле́зни **5** (not fresh): **the fish is** ~ ры́ба испо́ртилась (*or* с душко́м (infml))

• *prep.* (from; away from; up or down from): **the car went** ~ **the road** маши́на съе́хала с доро́ги; ~ **work** не на рабо́те; **he fell** ~ **the ladder** он упа́л с ле́стницы; **he took 50p** ~ **the price** он сни́зил це́ну на пятьдеся́т пе́нсов; он сба́вил с цены́ пятьдеся́т пе́нсов; (disinclined for): **he is** ~ **his food** он потеря́л аппети́т

offal /ˈɒf(ə)l/ *n.* (of meat) потроха́ (*m. pl.*); (entrails) требуха́

☞ **offence** /əˈfens/ (AmE **offense**) *n.* **1** (crime) правонаруше́ние, преступле́ние **2** (affront) оби́да; **cause, give** ~ **to** оскорб|ля́ть, -и́ть **3** (mil.) наступле́ние

offend /əˈfend/ *v.t.* об|ижа́ть, -и́деть • *v.i.* греши́ть (*impf.*)

offender /əˈfendə(r)/ *n.* (against law) правонаруши́тель (*m.*) (-ница)

offense /əˈfens/ *n.* (AmE) = **offence**

offensive /əˈfensɪv/ *n.* нападе́ние; (mil.) наступле́ние; **go on the** ~ пере|ходи́ть, -йти́ в наступле́ние; (fig.) зан|има́ть, -я́ть наступа́тельную пози́цию • *adj.* (causing offence) оскорби́тельный; (of person) отврати́тельный, проти́вный

☞ **offer** /ˈɒfə(r)/ *n.* **1** предложе́ние **2**: **be on** ~ (BrE, for sale at reduced price) прод|ава́ться, -а́ться со ски́дкой • *v.t.* предл|ага́ть, -ожи́ть; **he** ~**ed me a drink** он предложи́л мне вы́пить; ~ **an opinion** выража́ть, вы́разить своё мне́ние; **he did not** ~ **to help** он не предложи́л помо́чь

offering /ˈɒfərɪŋ/ *n.* **1** (sacrifice) подноше́ние, же́ртва **2** (contribution) поже́ртвование

offhand /ɒfˈhænd, ˈɒfhænd/ *adj.* развя́зный, бесцеремо́нный • *adv.* (right now, without thought) сра́зу

☞ **office** /ˈɒfɪs/ *n.* **1** (position of responsibility) до́лжность, слу́жба; **the party in** ~ па́ртия,

находя́щаяся у вла́сти; **he held ~ for
10 years** он занима́л до́лжность/пост
де́сять лет **2** (premises) о́фис, конто́ра,
канцеля́рия **3** (for services) бюро́ (*nt. indecl.*);
booking ~ биле́тная ка́сса
■ **~ block** *n.* администрати́вное зда́ние; **~
hours** *n. pl.* часы́ рабо́ты; рабо́чее/служе́бное
вре́мя

⚬ **officer** /ˈɒfɪsə(r)/ *n.* **1** (in armed forces)
офице́р **2** (official) должностно́е лицо́,
чино́вник; **customs ~** тамо́женник

⚬ **official** /əˈfɪʃ(ə)l/ *n.* должностно́е лицо́,
чино́вник
● *adj.* (authoritative) официа́льный; (relating to
office) служе́бный, должностно́й

officiate /əˈfɪʃɪeɪt/ *v.i.* (be in charge)
распоряжа́ться (*impf.*); (at church service)
соверш|а́ть, -и́ть богослуже́ние; **~
at a wedding** соверш|а́ть, -и́ть обря́д
бракосочета́ния; **~ as chairman**
председа́тельствовать (*impf.*)

officious /əˈfɪʃəs/ *adj.* навя́зчивый,
назо́йливый

offing /ˈɒfɪŋ/ *n.*: **in the ~** (fig.) в перспекти́ве

off-key /ɒfˈkiː/ *adj.* (mus., also fig.) фальши́вый

off-licence /ˈɒflaɪs(ə)ns/ *n.* (BrE) ви́нный
магази́н

offline /ɒfˈlaɪn/ *adj.* (comput.) автоно́мный,
офла́йновый; (disconnected) отключённый

offload /ɒfˈləʊd/ *v.t.* разгру|жа́ть, -зи́ть

off-peak /ˈɒfpiːk/ *adj.* непи́ковый

off-piste /ɒfˈpiːst/ *adj., adv.* вне
горнолы́жной тра́ссы; (fig.) вдали́ от
проторённых маршру́тов

off-putting /ˈɒfpʊtɪŋ/ *adj.* (infml)
отта́лкивающий

offset /ˈɒfset/ *v.t.* **1** (take into consideration)
засчи́т|ывать, -а́ть; **donations to charity
can be ~ against tax** поже́ртвования
на благотвори́тельные це́ли мо́гут
засчи́тываться при упла́те нало́гов
2 (compensate for) возме|ща́ть, -сти́ть

offshoot /ˈɒfʃuːt/ *n.* побе́г; (fig.) о́трасль

offshore /ˈɒfʃɔː(r)/ *adj.* (close to the shore)
прибре́жный; (at a distance from the shore)
морско́й; (foreign) заграни́чный; (fin.)
офшо́рный
● *adv.* (in the open sea) в откры́том мо́ре;
(abroad) за грани́цей
■ **~ wind** *n.* берегово́й ве́тер

offside /ɒfˈsaɪd/ (football) *n.* положе́ние вне
игры́, офса́йд
● *adv.* вне игры́, офса́йд

offspring /ˈɒfsprɪŋ/ *n.* (*pl.* **~**) пото́мок,
о́тпрыск; (*in pl.*) пото́мство

offstage /ɒfˈsteɪdʒ/ *adj.* закули́сный
● *adv.* за кули́сами

off-the-cuff /ɒfðəˈkʌf/ *adj.*
импровизи́рованный

off-the-record /ɒfðəˈrekɔːd/ *adj.*
неофициа́льный

off-white /ˈɒfwaɪt/ *adj. & n.* гря́зно-бе́лый
(цвет)

⚬ **often** /ˈɒf(ə)n/ *adv.* (**oftener, oftenest**)

ча́сто; **every so ~** вре́мя от вре́мени

ogle /ˈəʊɡ(ə)l/ *v.t.* пожира́ть (*impf.*) глаза́ми

ogre /ˈəʊɡə(r)/ *n.* велика́н-людое́д; (fig.)
стра́шный челове́к

⚬ **oh** /əʊ/ *int.* о!, ах!; (expr. surprise, fright, pain) ой!

ohm /əʊm/ *n.* ом

⚬ **oil** /ɔɪl/ *n.* **1** ма́сло; **engine ~** маши́нное
ма́сло **2** (petroleum) нефть
● *v.t.* (lubricate) сма́з|ывать, -ать
■ **~field** *n.* месторожде́ние не́фти; **~
painting** *n.* ма́сло, холст, карти́на; **~ rig** *n.*
нефтяна́я вы́шка; **~skin** *n.* непромока́емый
костю́м; **~ slick** *n.* плёнка не́фти на воде́; **~
tanker** *n.* (ship) та́нкер; (vehicle) нефтево́з; **~
well** *n.* нефтяна́я сква́жина

oily /ˈɔɪlɪ/ *adj.* (**oilier, oiliest**) масляны́й

ointment /ˈɔɪntmənt/ *n.* мазь

OK, okay /əʊˈkeɪ/ *n.* (*pl.* **~s**) (infml)
одобре́ние, «добро́»
● *adj.* (safe, well): **she is ~** она́ в поря́дке;
(acceptable): **are you sure it's ~?** э́то ничего́?;
I'll be back soon, ~? я ско́ро верну́сь, ла́дно?
● *adv.*: **the meeting went off ~** собра́ние
прошло́ норма́льно; **he is doing ~** у него́ всё
хорошо́/норма́льно
● *v.t.* (**OK's, OK'd, OK'ing**) од|обря́ть,
-о́брить
● *int.* ла́дно!, хорошо́!

⚬ **old** /əʊld/ *n.*: **the ~** (people) старики́ (*m. pl.*),
пожилы́е/престаре́лые (лю́ди)
● *adj.* (**older, oldest**) **1** ста́рый; (object,
house) стари́нный; **grow ~** ста́риться, со-
2 (expr. age): **how ~ is he?** ско́лько ему́ лет?;
my son is 4 years ~ моему́ сы́ну четы́ре го́да
3 (longstanding) стари́нный, да́вний(ший);
they are ~ friends они́ стари́нные/да́вние
друзья́ **4** (former) бы́вший, пре́жний
■ **~ age** *n.* ста́рость; **~-age pension** (BrE)
пе́нсия по ста́рости; **~-fashioned** *adj.*
старомо́дный; **~ man** *n.* (also infml, husband or
father) стари́к; **~ people's/folk's home** *n.*
дом престаре́лых; **~ woman** *n.* (also infml,
wife) стару́ха

oligarch /ˈɒlɪɡɑːk/ *n.* олига́рх

oligarchy /ˈɒlɪɡɑːkɪ/ *n.* олига́рхия

olive /ˈɒlɪv/ *n.* масли́на
● *adj.* оли́вковый
■ **~ oil** *n.* оли́вковое ма́сло

Olympic /əˈlɪmpɪk/ *adj.*: **~ Games, ~s**
Олимпи́йские и́гры

ombudsman /ˈɒmbʊdzmən/ *n.* о́мбудсмен;
уполномо́ченный по права́м челове́ка

omelette /ˈɒmlɪt/ (AmE *also* **omelet**) *n.*
омле́т

omen /ˈəʊmən/ *n.* знак

ominous /ˈɒmɪnəs/ *adj.* злове́щий

omission /əˈmɪʃ(ə)n/ *n.* про́пуск

omit /əˈmɪt/ *v.t.* (**omitted, omitting**)
пропус|ка́ть, -ти́ть

omnibus /ˈɒmnɪbəs/ *n.* **1** (obs.) о́мнибус,
авто́бус **2** (~ volume) сбо́рник, антоло́гия

omnipotence /ɒmˈnɪpət(ə)ns/ *n.*
всемогу́щество

omnipotent /ɒmˈnɪpət(ə)nt/ *adj.* всемогу́щий

omnipresent /ɒmnɪˈprez(ə)nt/ *adj.*
вездесу́щий

omniscience /ɒmˈnɪsɪəns/ *n.* всеве́дение

omniscient /ɒmˈnɪsɪənt/ *adj.* всеве́дущий

omnivorous /ɒmˈnɪvərəs/ *adj.* всея́дный

✧ **on** /ɒn/ *adv.* **1** (expr. continuation): straight ~
пря́мо; **and so** ~ и так да́лее; **from now** ~
(начина́я) с э́того дня; **he went** ~ **(and** ~**)**
about his dog он без конца́ говори́л о свое́й
соба́ке; (expr. extension): **further** ~ да́льше;
later ~ по́зже **2** (placed, spread, etc. ~ sth):
he had his glasses ~ он был в очка́х; он
наде́л очки́ **3** (arranged, available): **what's** ~
tonight? (TV) что сего́дня по програ́мме?;
что сего́дня пока́зывают?; **is the match still**
~**?** матч не отмени́ли/отменён? **4** (turned,
switched ~): **the kettle is** ~ ча́йник поста́влен/
включён; **the light is** ~ свет включён; **the
radio was** ~ **full blast** ра́дио бы́ло включено́
на всю мощь **5**: **it's not** ~ (infml) (not feasible)
так не пойдёт; (not acceptable) недопусти́мо
● *prep.* **1** (expr. position) на + *p.*; ~ **the table** на
столе́; (supported by): **stand** ~ **one leg** стоя́ть
(*impf.*) на одно́й ноге́; **the look** ~ **his face**
выраже́ние его́ лица́; (as means of transport) на
+ *p.*; ~ **horseback** верхо́м; ~ **foot** пешко́м;
I came ~ **the bus** я прие́хал на авто́бусе; (~
one's person): **I have no money** ~ **me** у меня́
нет при себе́ де́нег; (expr. relative position): ~
my left сле́ва от меня́ **2** (expr. final position)
на + *a.*; **he sat down** ~ **the sofa** он сел на
дива́н **3** (expr. point of contact): **he hit me** ~ **the
head** он уда́рил меня́ по голове́; **he knocked**
~ **the door** он постуча́л в дверь; **she dried
her hands** ~ **a towel** она́ вы́терла ру́ки
полоте́нцем **4** (of a medium of communication)
по + *d.*; ~ **the radio/telephone/television** по
ра́дио/телефо́ну/телеви́зору **5** (expr. time):
~ **Tuesday** во вто́рник; ~ **time** во́время;
своевре́менно; ~ **the 8th of May** восьмо́го
ма́я; ~ **Tuesdays** по вто́рникам **6** (immediately
after): ~ **his arrival** по его́ прие́зде; ~
seeing him she ran off уви́дев его́, она́
убежа́ла; (during): ~ **my way home** по доро́ге
домо́й **7** (concerning): **an article** ~ **Pushkin**
статья́ о Пу́шкине **8** (at the expense of): **drinks
are** ~ **me** я угоща́ю; **the joke was** ~ **me**
шу́тка оберну́лась про́тив меня́ **9** (taking
drugs etc.): **he's** ~ **drugs** он (регуля́рно)
принима́ет нарко́тики
■ ~**-over** *n.* (infml) **give sb/sth the** ~**-over** бе́гло
осма́тривать, -отре́ть кого́/что-н.

on-board /ˈɒnbɔːd/ *adj.* бортово́й

✧ **once** /wʌns/ *adv.* **1** (оди́н) раз; ~ **again, more**
ещё раз **2** (as soon as): ~ **you hesitate you
are lost** сто́ит (то́лько) заколеба́ться, и ты
пропа́л **3** (at one time, formerly) не́когда; одно́
вре́мя; одна́жды; когда́-то; ~ **upon a time
there was** (давны́м-давно́) жил-был **4**: **at**
~ (immediately) сейча́с же; (simultaneously) в то
же вре́мя
■ ~**-over** *n.* (infml) **give sb/sth the** ~**-over** бе́гло
осма́тривать, -отре́ть кого́/что-н.

oncologist /ɒŋˈkɒlədʒɪst/ *n.* онко́лог

oncology /ɒŋˈkɒlədʒɪ/ *n.* онколо́гия

✧ ключева́я ле́ксика

oncoming /ˈɒnkʌmɪŋ/ *adj.*
приближа́ющийся, наступа́ющий

✧ **one** /wʌn/ *n.* **1** (number) оди́н; (in counting): ~,
two, three раз/оди́н, два, три **2** (hour) час; ~
o'clock (a.m.) час но́чи; (p.m.) час дня **3** (age):
he's only ~ ему́ всего́/то́лько год(ик)
4 (person): **little** ~**s** де́ти; **our loved** ~**s** на́ши
бли́зкие; **he is not** ~ **to refuse** он не из тех,
кто отка́зывается **5** (member of a group) оди́н;
~ **of my friends** оди́н из мои́х друзе́й; **the** ~
with the beard тот(, кото́рый) с бородо́й; **I for**
~ **don't believe him** что каса́ется меня́, то
я не ве́рю ему́; ~ **of these days** ка́к-нибудь
на днях; ~ **another** друг дру́га; ~ **after the
other**; ~ **by** ~ оди́н за други́м; ~ **at a time**
по одному́; по о́череди **6** (referring to category
understood): **which book do you want, the red
or the green** ~**?** каку́ю кни́гу вы хоти́те,
кра́сную и́ли зелёную?
● *pron.*: ~ **never knows** никогда́ не зна́ешь;
~ **gets used to anything** челове́к ко всему́
привыка́ет
● *adj.* **1** оди́н; **price** ~ **rouble** цена́ (оди́н)
рубль; (with pluralia tantum) одни́; ~ **watch**
одни́ часы́ **2** (only) еди́нственный; **the** ~
way to do it еди́нственный спо́соб сде́лать
э́то **3** (the same) тот же са́мый **4** (particular
but unspecified): ~ **evening** ка́к-то/одна́жды
ве́чером; ~ **day** (in past) одна́жды; (in future)
когда́-нибудь
■ ~**-off** *adj.* (BrE, infml) уника́льный,
еди́нственный; ~**-parent family** *n.*
семья́ с одни́м роди́телем; ~**-sided** *adj.*
(prejudiced) односторо́нний, односторо́нний;
~**-time** *adj.* бы́вший; былóй; ~**-to-one** *adj.*
непосре́дственный; ~**-way** *adj.*: ~**-way traffic**
односторо́ннее движе́ние; ~**-way street** у́лица с
односторо́нним движе́нием; ~**-way ticket** биле́т
в одну́ сто́рону (*or* в одно́м направле́нии)

onerous /ˈəʊnərəs/ *adj.* обремени́тельный,
тя́гостный

oneself /wʌnˈself/ *pron.* **1** (refl.) себя́, -ся
suff.; **talk to** ~ говори́ть (*impf.*) с сами́м
собо́й **2** (emph.) сам; **it's best to do it** ~
лу́чше сде́лать э́то самому́

ongoing /ˈɒnɡəʊɪŋ/ *adj.* (continuing): ~ **process**
поступа́тельный проце́сс; (in progress) теку́щий

onion /ˈʌnjən/ *n.* лу́ковица (*pl., collect.*)
(ре́пчатый) лук

✧ **online** /ɒnˈlaɪn/ (comput.) *adj.* (information,
program) онла́йновый, диало́говый,
интеракти́вный; (connected) подключённый;
~ **dating** знако́мство в Интерне́те; ~ **dating
site** сайт знако́мств
● *adv.* (в режи́ме) онла́йн, в Интерне́те; **we
watched the film** ~ мы смотре́ли фильм в
Интерне́те

onlooker /ˈɒnlʊkə(r)/ *n.* зри́тель (*m.*)

✧ **only** /ˈəʊnlɪ/ *adj.* еди́нственный; **she was an**
~ **child** она́ была́ еди́нственным ребёнком; **I
was the** ~ **one there** кро́ме меня́ там никого́
не́ бы́ло
● *adv.* то́лько; всего́; ~ **just** (recently) то́лько
что; (barely) едва́; **I have** ~ **just arrived** я
то́лько что при́был; **he was** ~ **just in time**

он едва успе́л; if ~ you knew е́сли бы вы то́лько зна́ли; the soup was ~ warm суп был е́ле тёплый
● *conj.* но; I would go myself, ~ I'm tired я пошёл бы сам, но я уста́л

onomatopoeia /ɒnəmætə'pi:ə/ *n.* звукоподража́ние

on-screen /ɒn'skri:n/ *adj.* (comput.) экра́нный; follow the ~ instructions сле́дуйте инстру́кциям на экра́не

onset /'ɒnset/ *n.* нача́ло, наступле́ние

on-site /'ɒnsaɪt/ *adj.* на места́х/ме́сте

onslaught /'ɒnslɔ:t/ *n.* ата́ка, нападе́ние

♂ **onto** /'ɒntu:/ *prep.* (= on *prep.* 2) на + *a.*; she climbed ~ the roof она́ вле́зла на кры́шу

onus /'əʊnəs/ *n.* бре́мя, отве́тственность

onward /'ɒnwəd/ *adj.* продвига́ющийся
● *adv.* (*also* **onwards**) вперёд, да́лее; from now ~ впредь, отны́не; from then ~ с тех пор; (in future) с того́ вре́мени

oops! /ʊps/ *int.* (infml) ой!

ooze /u:z/ *v.t.* (emit): the wound ~d blood из ра́ны сочи́лась кровь; (fig.): he ~d self-confidence он источа́л самоуве́ренность
● *v.i.* ме́дленно течь (*impf.*)

opal /'əʊp(ə)l/ *n.* опа́л

opaque /əʊ'peɪk/ *adj.* (**opaquer, opaquest**) непрозра́чный

♂ **open** /'əʊpən/ *n.* ◼ (~ space; ~ air) откры́тое простра́нство; in the ~ под откры́тым не́бом ◼ (fig.): bring sth into the ~ выявля́ть, вы́явить
● *adj.* ◼ откры́тый; in the ~ air на откры́том во́здухе; ~ contempt я́вное/нескрыва́емое презре́ние; in ~ country на откры́той ме́стности; have an ~ mind on sth не име́ть предвзя́того мне́ния о + *p.*; on the ~ road на пусто́й/свобо́дной доро́ге; the door flew ~ дверь распахну́лась ◼ (accessible, available) досту́пный; the road is ~ to traffic доро́га откры́та для движе́ния ◼ (frank) откры́тый, открове́нный
● *v.t.* ◼ откр|ыва́ть, -ы́ть; (book, newspaper) откр|ыва́ть, -ы́ть; раскр|ыва́ть, -ы́ть ◼ (fig.): he ~ed an account он откры́л счёт; a new business has been ~ed откры́ли но́вый би́знес
● *v.i.* ◼ откр|ыва́ться, -ы́ться ◼ (fig., begin) нач|ина́ться, -а́ться; the play ~s with a long speech пье́са начина́ется дли́нным моноло́гом; the new play ~s on Saturday но́вая пье́са идёт с суббо́ты ◼ (of door etc.): the windows ~ on to a courtyard о́кна выхо́дят во двор
□ ~ up *v.t.*: ~ up! (command to open) откро́йте дверь!; he ~ed up the boot (of the car) он откры́л бага́жник
● *v.i.*: he ~ed up about his visit он открове́нно рассказа́л о свое́й пое́здка
◼ ~-air *adj.*: ~ air life жизнь на откры́том во́здухе; ~ competition *n.* откры́тое соревнова́ние; ~ day *n.* (BrE, at school) день откры́тых двере́й; ~-heart *adj.*: ~-heart surgery опера́ция, проводи́мая на отключённом се́рдце; ~ market *n.* откры́тый ры́нок; ~-minded *adj.*

непредвзя́тый, непредубеждённый; ~-plan *adj.* с откры́той планиро́вкой; ~ ticket *n.* биле́т с откры́той да́той

opener /'əʊpənə(r)/ *n.* (in full can ~) консе́рвный нож

opening /'əʊpənɪŋ/ *n.* ◼ (aperture) отве́рстие ◼ (beginning) нача́ло; (of play, speech) вступле́ние ◼ (job) ме́сто, вака́нсия
● *adj.* (initial) нача́льный, пе́рвый; ~ remarks вступи́тельные замеча́ния; (working): ~ hours рабо́чие часы́; часы́ рабо́ты

openly /'əʊpənli/ *adv.* откры́то; (frankly) открове́нно; (publicly) публи́чно, откры́то

openness /'əʊpənnɪs/ *n.* (frankness) откры́тость, открове́нность; (pol.) гла́сность

opera /'ɒpərə/ *n.* о́пера
◼ ~ glass *n.* театра́льный бино́кль; ~ house *n.* о́перный теа́тр

operable /'ɒpərəb(ə)l/ *adj.* ◼ (med.) опера́бельный ◼ (workable) де́йствующий, функциони́рующий

♂ **operate** /'ɒpəreɪt/ *v.t.* ◼ (control work of) управля́ть (*impf.*) + *i.*; the machine is ~d by electricity э́та маши́на рабо́тает на электри́честве ◼ (put into effect): we ~ a simple system мы применя́ем просту́ю систе́му
● *v.i.* ◼ (work, act) рабо́тать (*impf.*); the brakes failed to ~ тормоза́ отказа́ли ◼: ~ on (med.) опери́ровать (*impf., pf.*) (for: по по́воду + *g.*)

operatic /ɒpə'rætɪk/ *adj.* о́перный

operating /'ɒpəreɪtɪŋ/ *adj.* ◼ (med.): ~ room (AmE), theatre (BrE) операцио́нная ◼ (comput.): ~ system операцио́нная систе́ма

♂ **operation** /ɒpə'reɪʃ(ə)n/ *n.* ◼ (action, effect) де́йствие; рабо́та; bring into ~ прив|оди́ть, -ести́ в де́йствие ◼ (process) проце́сс, опера́ция ◼ (control) эксплуата́ция, управле́ние ◼ (med.) опера́ция ◼ (mil.) опера́ция, де́йствия (*nt. pl.*)

operational /ɒpə'reɪʃən(ə)l/ *adj.* де́йствующий; the factory is fully ~ заво́д по́лностью гото́в к эксплуата́ции

operative /'ɒpərətɪv/ *n.* (machine operator) стано́чник; квалифици́рованный рабо́чий; опера́тор (*какого-н. устро́йства*)
● *adj.* де́йственный

operator /'ɒpəreɪtə(r)/ *n.* ◼ (one who works a machine) опера́тор ◼ (telephonist) телефони́ст (-ка)

operetta /ɒpə'retə/ *n.* опере́тта

ophthalmic /ɒf'θælmɪk/ *adj.* глазно́й
◼ ~ optician *n.* (BrE) окули́ст

ophthalmologist /ɒfθæl'mɒlədʒɪst/ *n.* офтальмо́лог

ophthalmology /ɒfθæl'mɒlədʒɪ/ *n.* офтальмоло́гия

opiate /'əʊpɪət/ *n.* опиа́т; (fig.) о́пиум

♂ **opinion** /ə'pɪnjən/ *n.* (judgement) мне́ние; (view) взгляд; in my ~ по моему́ мне́нию, по-мо́ему, на мой взгляд; (estimate): have a high/low ~ of быть высо́кого/невысо́кого мне́ния о + *p.*
◼ ~ poll *n.* опро́с обще́ственного мне́ния

opinionated /ə'pɪnjəneɪtɪd/ *adj.* догмати́чный

opium /'əʊpɪəm/ *n.* о́пиум

° **opponent** /ə'pəʊnənt/ *n.* оппоне́нт,
проти́вник; (sport) проти́вник, сопе́рник

opportune /'ɒpətjuːn/ *adj.* своевре́менный,
уме́стный

opportunism /ɒpə'tjuːnɪz(ə)m/ *n.*
оппортуни́зм

opportunist /ɒpə'tjuːnɪst/ *n.* оппортуни́ст
● *adj.* оппортунисти́ческий

opportunistic /ɒpətjuː'nɪstɪk/ *adj.*
оппортунисти́ческий

° **opportunity** /ɒpə'tjuːnɪtɪ/ *n.* (favourable
circumstance) удо́бный слу́чай; (good chance)
возмо́жность; **he took the ~ to ...** он
воспо́льзовался слу́чаем, что́бы...

° **oppos|e** /ə'pəʊz/ *v.t.* ▮ (set against): **as ~ed to**
в отли́чие от + *g.*; **I am firmly ~ed to the idea**
я реши́тельно про́тив э́той иде́и ▮ (set oneself
against): **the ~ing side** проти́вная сторона́;
(sport) кома́нда проти́вника; (show opposition
to) проти́виться (*impf.*) + *d.*

opposite /'ɒpəzɪt/ *n.* противополо́жность;
just the ~ как раз наоборо́т
● *adj.* противополо́жный; **his house is ~
ours** его́ дом (стои́т) напро́тив на́шего; **in
the ~ direction** в обра́тном направле́нии;
~ number лицо́, занима́ющее таку́ю же
до́лжность в друго́й организа́ции
● *adv.* напро́тив
● *prep.* (на)про́тив (+ *g.*)

° **opposition** /ɒpə'zɪʃ(ə)n/ *n.* ▮ (resistance)
сопротивле́ние, противоде́йствие; **he
offered no ~** он не оказа́л никако́го
сопротивле́ния ▮ (BrE, pol.) оппози́ция

oppress /ə'pres/ *v.t.* угнета́ть (*impf.*)

oppression /ə'preʃ(ə)n/ *n.* (oppressing)
угнете́ние, гнёт, притесне́ние, тирани́я;
(being oppressed) угнетённость

oppressive /ə'presɪv/ *adj.* угнета́ющий,
давя́щий; **~ weather** угнета́ющая/ду́шная
пого́да

oppressor /ə'presə(r)/ *n.* угнета́тель (*m.*)

opt /ɒpt/ *v.i.* **~ for** выбира́ть, вы́брать; **~ out
of** отка́з|ываться, -а́ться от уча́стия в + *p.*
■ **~-out** *n.* отка́з от уча́стия в чём-н.

optic /'ɒptɪk/ *adj.*: **~ nerve** зри́тельный нерв

optical /'ɒptɪk(ə)l/ *adj.* опти́ческий
■ **~ illusion** *n.* опти́ческий обма́н

optician /ɒp'tɪʃ(ə)n/ *n.* окули́ст

optics /'ɒptɪks/ *n.* о́птика

optimism /'ɒptɪmɪz(ə)m/ *n.* оптими́зм

optimist /'ɒptɪmɪst/ *n.* оптими́ст (-ка)

optimistic /ɒptɪ'mɪstɪk/ *adj.*
оптимисти́ческий, оптимисти́чный

optimize /'ɒptɪmaɪz/ *v.t.* оптимизи́ровать
(*impf., pf.*)

optimum /'ɒptɪməm/ *adj.* оптима́льный

° **option** /'ɒpʃ(ə)n/ *n.* вы́бор; **I have no ~ but
to ...** у меня́ нет друго́го вы́бора, (кро́ме)
как...

optional /'ɒpʃən(ə)l/ *adj.* необяза́тельный

° ключева́я ле́ксика

optometrist /ɒp'tɒmɪtrɪst/ *n.* (AmE) окули́ст

opulence /'ɒpjʊləns/ *n.* бога́тство, оби́лие,
изоби́лие

opulent /'ɒpjʊlənt/ *adj.* (wealthy) бога́тый;
(abundant) оби́льный

° **or** /ɔː(r)/ *conj.* ▮ и́ли; **two ~ three** два-три
▮ (**~ else**) и́ли, ина́че; и́ли же; а (не) то;
we must hurry ~ we'll be late ну́жно
потора́пливаться, а то опозда́ем ▮: **there
were 20 ~ so people present** там бы́ло
челове́к 20 (*or* о́коло двадцати́ челове́к)

oral /'ɔːr(ə)l/ *n.* у́стный экза́мен
● *adj.* (by word of mouth) у́стный; (pert. to mouth)
стоматологи́ческий; (pert. to contraceptive, sex)
ора́льный
■ **~ hygiene** *n.* гигие́на по́лости рта

orange /'ɒrɪndʒ/ *n.* ▮ (fruit) апельси́н ▮ (tree)
апельси́новое де́рево ▮ (colour) ора́нжевый
цвет
● *adj.* (colour) ора́нжевый
■ **~ juice** *n.* апельси́новый сок

orang-utan /əˌræŋə'tæn/ *n.* орангута́н(г)

oration /ɔː'reɪʃ(ə)n/ *n.* речь

orator /'ɒrətə(r)/ *n.* ора́тор

orbit /'ɔːbɪt/ *n.* орби́та
● *v.t.* (**orbited**, **orbiting**) (move in ~ round)
враща́ться (*impf.*) вокру́г (+ *g.*)
● *v.i.* (**orbited**, **orbiting**) (move in ~)
враща́ться (*impf.*) по орби́те

orchard /'ɔːtʃəd/ *n.* (фрукто́вый) сад

orchestra /'ɔːkɪstrə/ *n.* орке́стр

orchestral /ɔː'kestr(ə)l/ *adj.* оркестро́вый

orchestrate /'ɔːkɪstreɪt/ *v.t.* оркестрова́ть
(*impf., pf.*); (fig.) организо́в|ывать, -а́ть

orchestration /ɔːkɪ'streɪʃ(ə)n/ *n.*
оркестро́вка

orchid /'ɔːkɪd/ *n.* орхиде́я

ordain /ɔː'deɪn/ *v.t.* ▮ (eccl.) посвя|ща́ть, -ти́ть
в духо́вный сан ▮ (destine) предпи́с|ывать,
-а́ть

ordeal /ɔː'diːl/ *n.* му́ка

° **order** /'ɔːdə(r)/ *n.* ▮ (arrangement) поря́док;
(sequence, succession) после́довательность;
in alphabetical ~ в алфави́тном
поря́дке; **in ~ of importance** по сте́пени
ва́жности ▮ (result of arrangement or control)
поря́док; **everything is in ~** всё в поря́дке;
(settled state): **restore ~** восстан|а́вливать,
-ови́ть поря́док; **out of ~** неиспра́вный, в
плохо́м состоя́нии ▮ (instruction) прика́з,
распоряже́ние, поруче́ние; **give an, the
~** отд|ава́ть, -а́ть прика́з; **under sb's ~s**
под кома́ндой кого́-н. ▮ (direction to supply)
зака́з (**for**: на + *a.*); **on ~** по зака́зу ▮ (*in
pl.*) (eccl.): **holy ~s** духо́вный сан; **take ~s**
прин|има́ть, -я́ть духо́вный сан ▮: **in ~ to**
(для того́), что́бы (+ *inf.*); **in ~ that** (для
того́), что́бы (+ *past tense*)
● *v.t.* ▮ (arrange) прив|оди́ть, -ести́ в
поря́док ▮ (command) прика́з|ывать, -а́ть;
распоря|жа́ться, -ди́ться; **he ~ed the
soldiers to leave** он приказа́л солда́там
разойти́сь ▮ (reserve; request) зака́з|ывать,
-а́ть ▮: **~ sb about** кома́ндовать (*impf.*) + *i.*

■ ～ **form** *n.* бланк зака́за

orderliness /ˈɔːdəlɪnɪs/ *n.* (order) поря́док; (methodical nature) аккура́тность

orderly /ˈɔːdəlɪ/ *n.* санита́р
  ● *adj.* **1** (organized) организо́ванный **2** (quiet, well behaved) ти́хий, послу́шный

ordinal /ˈɔːdɪn(ə)l/ *n.* (*in full* ～ **number**) поря́дковое числи́тельное

ɤ **ordinary** /ˈɔːdɪnərɪ/ *n.*: **out of the** ～ необы́чный, незауря́дный
  ● *adj.* (usual) обы́чный; (average) обыкнове́нный; (normal) норма́льный

ordination /ɔːdɪˈneɪʃ(ə)n/ *n.* (eccl.) рукоположе́ние

ore /ɔː(r)/ *n.* руда́

oregano /ɒrɪˈɡɑːnəʊ/ *n.* души́ца обыкнове́нная, ди́кий майора́н

organ /ˈɔːɡən/ *n.* **1** (mus.) орга́н **2** (biol., pol., etc.) о́рган
  ■ ～ **donor** *n.* до́нор; ～ **transplant** *n.* переса́дка о́ргана

organic /ɔːˈɡænɪk/ *adj.* органи́ческий; ～ **food** натура́льные пищевы́е проду́кты

organism /ˈɔːɡənɪz(ə)m/ *n.* органи́зм

organist /ˈɔːɡənɪst/ *n.* органи́ст (-ка)

ɤ **organization** /ɔːɡənaɪˈzeɪʃ(ə)n/ *n.* организа́ция

organizational /ɔːɡənaɪˈzeɪʃən(ə)l/ *adj.* организацио́нный

ɤ **organize** /ˈɔːɡənaɪz/ *v.t.* организо́в|ывать, -а́ть; устр|а́ивать, -о́ить; ～**d crime** организо́ванная престу́пность

organizer /ˈɔːɡənaɪzə(r)/ *n.* организа́тор

orgasm /ˈɔːɡæz(ə)m/ *n.* орга́зм

orgy /ˈɔːdʒɪ/ *n.* о́ргия; (fig.) разгу́л

Orient /ˈɔːrɪənt/ *n.* Восто́к

orient /ˈɔːrɪənt, ˈɒːr-/, **orientate** /ˈɒrɪənteɪt, ˈɔːr-/ *v.t.* (determine position of) ориенти́ровать (*impf., pf.*) (*pf. also* c-); ～ **oneself** ориенти́роваться (*impf., pf.*) (*pf. also* c-)

oriental /ɔːrɪˈent(ə)l/ *adj.* восто́чный

orientation /ɔːrɪenˈteɪʃ(ə)n/ *n.* (lit., fig.) ориенти́ровка, ориента́ция

orienteering /ɔːrɪenˈtɪərɪŋ/ *n.* спорти́вное ориенти́рование, ориенти́рование на ме́стности

orifice /ˈɒrɪfɪs/ *n.* (aperture) отве́рстие; (mouth) у́стье

ɤ **origin** /ˈɒrɪdʒɪn/ *n.* нача́ло, исто́чник

ɤ **original** /əˈrɪdʒɪn(ə)l/ *n.* по́длинник, оригина́л
  ● *adj.* **1** (first, earliest) первонача́льный; **the** ～ **inhabitants** иско́нные жи́тели **2** (inventive) оригина́льный, самобы́тный

originality /ərɪdʒɪˈnælɪtɪ/ *n.* оригина́льность, самобы́тность

ɤ **originally** /əˈrɪdʒɪnəlɪ/ *adv.* (in the first place) первонача́льно, исхо́дно; (in origin) по происхожде́нию

originate /əˈrɪdʒɪneɪt/ *v.i.* брать, взять нача́ло; (arise) возн|ика́ть, -и́кнуть

ornament /ˈɔːnəmənt/ *n.* **1** (adornment) украше́ние **2** (decorative article) орна́мент

ornamental /ɔːnəˈment(ə)l/ *adj.* декорати́вный

ornamentation /ɔːnəmenˈteɪʃ(ə)n/ *n.* украше́ние

ornate /ɔːˈneɪt/ *adj.* бога́то укра́шенный

ornithological /ɔːnɪθəˈlɒdʒɪk(ə)l/ *adj.* орнитологи́ческий

ornithologist /ɔːnɪˈθɒlədʒɪst/ *n.* орнито́лог

ornithology /ɔːnɪˈθɒlədʒɪ/ *n.* орнитоло́гия

orphan /ˈɔːf(ə)n/ *n.* сирота́ (*c.g.*)

orphanage /ˈɔːfənɪdʒ/ *n.* прию́т для сиро́т

orthodox /ˈɔːθədɒks/ *adj.* ортодокса́льный, правове́рный; **the O**～ **Church** правосла́вная це́рковь

orthodoxy /ˈɔːθədɒksɪ/ *n.* (relig.) ортодокса́льность, правове́рность; (fig.) ортодокса́льность

orthographic /ɔːθəˈɡræfɪk/, **orthographical** /ɔːθəˈɡræfɪk(ə)l/ *adjs.* орфографи́ческий

orthography /ɔːˈθɒɡrəfɪ/ *n.* правописа́ние, орфогра́фия

orthopaedic /ɔːθəˈpiːdɪk/ (AmE **orthopedic**) *adj.* ортопеди́ческий

orthopaedics /ɔːθəˈpiːdɪks/ (AmE **orthopedics**) *n.* ортопе́дия

orthopaedist /ɔːθəˈpiːdɪst/ (AmE **orthopedist**) *n.* ортопе́д

oscillate /ˈɒsɪleɪt/ *v.t.* кача́ть (*impf.*)
  ● *v.i.* (swing) кача́ться (*impf.*) (elec., radio, also fig.), колеба́ться (*impf.*); (elec., radio, also fig.) колеба́ться (*impf.*)

oscillation /ɒsɪˈleɪʃ(ə)n/ *n.* колеба́ние; (elec.) осцилля́ция

Oslo /ˈɒzləʊ/ *n.* О́сло (*m. indecl.*)

osmosis /ɒzˈməʊsɪs/ *n.* (biol., chem.) о́смос

ostensible /ɒˈstensɪb(ə)l/ *adj.* (for show) показно́й; (professed) мни́мый; **he called** ～**y to thank me** он пришёл я́кобы для того́, что́бы поблагодари́ть меня́

ostentation /ɒstenˈteɪʃ(ə)n/ *n.* (display) показна́я ро́скошь

ostentatious /ɒstenˈteɪʃəs/ *adj.* показно́й, хвастли́вый

osteopath /ˈɒstɪəpæθ/ *n.* остеопа́т

osteopathy /ɒstɪˈɒpəθɪ/ *n.* остеопа́тия

ostracize /ˈɒstrəsaɪz/ *v.t.* подв|ерга́ть, -е́ргнуть остраки́зму

ostrich /ˈɒstrɪtʃ/ *n.* стра́ус (*африка́нский*); (*attr.*) страуси́ный

ɤ **other** /ˈʌðə(r)/ *pron.* друго́й, ино́й; ～**s may disagree with you** други́е/ины́е мо́гут с ва́ми не согласи́ться; **one after the** ～ оди́н за други́м; **someone or** ～ кто́-нибудь; (expr. reciprocity): **they were in love with each** ～ они́ бы́ли влюблены́ друг в дру́га; (*in pl.*) (additional ones; more) ещё + *g.*; (remaining ones) остальны́е
  ● *adj.* **1** друго́й; **on the** ～ **side of the road** на друго́й/той стороне́ доро́ги; **some** ～ **time** в друго́й раз **2** (additional) ещё + *g.* **3** (remaining) остально́й; **we shall visit the** ～ **museums tomorrow** мы посети́м

o

остальны́е музе́и за́втра **4**: the ~ day на
днях; every ~ day че́рез день

✛ **otherwise** /'ʌðəwaɪz/ *adv.* **1** (in a different way)
ина́че, по-друго́му, други́м спо́собом **2** (in
other respects) в други́х отноше́ниях; **the house
is cold but ~ comfortable** дом холо́дный, но
в остально́м удо́бный **3** (if not; or else) ина́че,
а то; **I went, ~ I would have missed them** я
пошёл, ина́че я бы их не заста́л

Ottawa /'ɒtəwə/ *n.* Отта́ва

otter /'ɒtə(r)/ *n.* вы́дра

Ottoman /'ɒtəmən/ *n.* (*pl.* ~**s**) **1** (hist.)
оттома́н **2** (**o**~) (sofa) оттома́нка, тахта́
● *adj.* оттома́нский

ouch /aʊtʃ/ *int.* ой!, ай!

ought /ɔːt/ *v. aux.* **1** (expr. duty) до́лжен; **you
~ to go there** вы должны́ (*or* вам сле́дует)
туда́ пойти́; **you ~ to have gone yesterday**
вам сле́довало пойти́ туда́ вчера́ **2** (expr.
desirability) до́лжен; на́до + *d.*; **you ~ to
have seen his face** на́до бы́ло ви́деть его́
лицо́ **3** (expr. probability) должно́ быть,
вероя́тно; **he ~ to be there by now** сейча́с
он, вероя́тно (*or* должно́ быть), уже́ там

ounce /aʊns/ *n.* (weight) у́нция (= *28,35 г*)

✛ **our** /'aʊə(r)/ *poss. adj.* наш

ours /'aʊəz/ *pron. & pred. adj.* наш; ~ **is a blue
car** на́ша маши́на си́няя; **this tree is** ~ э́то
де́рево на́ше

✛ **ourselves** /aʊə'selvz/ *pron.* **1** (refl.) себя́ (*d.,
p.* себе́, *i.* собо́й); (*suff.*) -сь; **we washed
~** мы умы́лись; (after preps): **we can only
depend on ~** мы мо́жем полага́ться то́лько
на себя́ (сами́х); **we were not satisfied with
~** мы бы́ли недово́льны собо́й **2** (emph.)
са́ми; **we ~ were not present** са́ми мы не
прису́тствовали **3**: **by ~** (alone) са́ми (по
себе́); (without aid) са́ми, одни́

oust /aʊst/ *v.t.* (force out, also fig.) вытесня́ть,
вы́теснить; (expel) выгоня́ть, вы́гнать

✛ **out** /aʊt/ *pred. adj. & adv.* **1** (away from home,
room, usual place, etc.): **he is ~** его́ нет до́ма;
(sport) вне игры́ **2** (~ of doors) на дворе́; на
у́лице; **it is quite warm ~ today** сего́дня на
дворе́ тепло́; **he was ~ and about all day** он
был на нога́х весь день; **we were ~ in the
garden** мы бы́ли в саду́; (fig., intent): **they are
~ to get him** они́ (во что бы то ни ста́ло)
наме́рены его́ пойма́ть **3** (visible): **the stars
are ~** вы́сыпали звёзды; **the sun will be ~
this afternoon** по́сле полу́дня пока́жется/
поя́вится со́лнце; (revealed): **the secret is,
was ~** секре́т раскры́лся (*or* стал всем
изве́стен); (published): **my book is ~ at last**
моя́ кни́га наконе́ц вы́шла (из печа́ти) **4** (at
departure): **he stumbled on the way ~** вы́ходя́,
он споткну́лся; (at a distance): **the tide is ~**
сейча́с отли́в **5** (astray, wrong): **I wasn't far
~** я не намно́го оши́бся **6** (infml, of favour,
fashion): **short hair is ~** коро́ткая стри́жка
сейча́с не в мо́де **7** (over): **before the week
is ~** до оконча́ния неде́ли; (extinguished): **the
fire is ~** ого́нь поту́х **8**: ~ **of** (movement) из

+ *g.*; **he fell ~ of the window** он вы́пал из
окна́; (material): **made ~ of silk** (сши́тый) из
шёлка, шёлковый; (from among): **two students
~ of forty** два студе́нта из сорока́; (motive):
~ **of pity/love/respect** из жа́лости/любви́/
уваже́ния (**for:** к + *d.*); ~ **of grief/joy** с
го́ря/ра́дости; ~ **of boredom** от/со ску́ки;
(outside): ~ **of danger** вне опа́сности; ~ **of
doors** на у́лице, на дворе́, на во́здухе; **feel
~ of it** чу́вствовать (*impf.*) себя́ чужи́м (*or*
ни при чём); ~ **of control** вне контро́ля; ~ **of
fashion** не в мо́де; (without): ~ **of breath**
запыха́вшийся; ~ **of work** безрабо́тный
● *v.t.* (infml, expose as being homosexual)
изоблича́ть, -и́ть в гомосексуали́зме

out-and-out /aʊtənd'aʊt/ *adj.* соверше́нный,
по́лный, отъя́вленный

outback /'aʊtbæk/ *n.* глушь

outboard /'aʊtbɔːd/ *adj.*: ~ **motor** подвесно́й
мото́р

outbox /'aʊtbɒks/ *n.* (comput.) исходя́щие
(сообще́ния)

outbreak /'aʊtbreɪk/ *n.* вспы́шка

outbuilding /'aʊtbɪldɪŋ/ *n.* надво́рное
строе́ние, надво́рная постро́йка

outburst /'aʊtbɜːst/ *n.* вспы́шка, взрыв

outcast /'aʊtkɑːst/ *n.* изгна́нник,
отве́рженный

✛ **outcome** /'aʊtkʌm/ *n.* исхо́д, результа́т

outcry /'aʊtkraɪ/ *n.* проте́ст, (обще́ственное)
негодова́ние

outdo /aʊt'duː/ *v.t.* превосходи́ть, -зойти́

outdoor /'aʊtdɔː(r)/ *adj.*: ~ **games** и́гры на
откры́том во́здухе, подви́жные и́гры; ~
clothes ве́рхнее пла́тье

outdoors /aʊt'dɔːz/ *adv.* на откры́том
во́здухе, на дворе́; (expr. motion) на во́здух

outer /'aʊtə(r)/ *adj.* (external) вне́шний
■ ~ **space** *n.* ко́смос

outfit /'aʊtfɪt/ *n.* компле́кт (оде́жды)

outgoing /'aʊtɡəʊɪŋ/ *adj.* **1** (departing): **the
~ president** президе́нт, уходя́щий с поста́; ~
mail исходя́щая по́чта **2** (sociable): **an ~
person** общи́тельный/уживчивый челове́к

outgoings /'aʊtɡəʊɪŋz/ *n. pl.* (BrE) расхо́ды
(*m. pl.*)

outgrow /aʊt'ɡrəʊ/ *v.t.* **1** (grow too large for)
выраста́ть, вы́расти из + *g.* **2** (discard with
time) выраста́ть, вы́расти из + *g.*

outhouse /'aʊthaʊs/ *n.* надво́рное строе́ние;
(AmE, lavatory) убо́рная во дворе́, отхо́жее
ме́сто

outing /'aʊtɪŋ/ *n.* прогу́лка, экску́рсия

outlandish /aʊt'lændɪʃ/ *adj.* дико́винный,
чудно́й

outlast /aʊt'lɑːst/ *v.t.* (outlive) пережи|ва́ть, -и́ть

outlaw /'aʊtlɔː/ *n.* лицо́, объя́вленное вне
зако́на
● *v.t.* объявл|я́ть, -и́ть вне зако́на

outlay /'aʊtleɪ/ *n.* изде́ржки (*f. pl.*)

outlet /'aʊtlet/ *n.* **1** (lit.) выходно́е/выпускно́е
отве́рстие **2** (shop) фи́рменный магази́н
3 (for energies etc.) отду́шина, вы́ход

o

outline /'aʊtlaɪn/ n. **1** (contour) кóнтур, очертáние (*often in pl.*) **2** (of speech, article) конспéкт
• *v.t.* нам|ечáть, -éтить в óбщих чертáх

outlive /aʊt'lɪv/ *v.t.* переж|ивáть, -и́ть

outlook /'aʊtlʊk/ n. **1** (lit., fig., prospect) вид, перспекти́ва; (weather etc.) прогнóз **2** (point of view) тóчка зрéния

outlying /'aʊtlaɪɪŋ/ *adj.* отдалённый, удалённый

outmoded /aʊt'məʊdɪd/ *adj.* старомóдный, немóдный, устарéлый

outnumber /aʊt'nʌmbə(r)/ *v.t.* прев|осходи́ть, -зойти́ *кого/что* чи́сленно

out-of-court settlement /aʊtəv'kɔːt/ n. (law) мировáя сдéлка, урегули́рованная вне судá

out-of-date /aʊtəv'deɪt/ *adj.* устарéлый, старомóдный

outpatient /'aʊtpeɪʃ(ə)nt/ n. амбулатóрный больнóй
■ ~ **department** n. поликли́ника, амбулатóрная отделéние

outpost /'aʊtpəʊst/ n. отдалённое поселéние

output /'aʊtpʊt/ n. **1** (production) вы́пуск, продýкция, произвóдство **2** (productivity) производи́тельность
• *v.t.* (comput.) выводи́ть, вы́вести

outrage /'aʊtreɪdʒ/ n. (outrageous situation) безобрáзие; (outrageous act) безобрáзный постýпок; (anger) негодовáние

outrageous /aʊt'reɪdʒəs/ *adj.* безобрáзный, возмути́тельный

outrider /'aʊtraɪdə(r)/ n. (*usu. in pl.*) эскóрт

outright *adj.* /'aʊtraɪt/ (direct) прямóй, открытый; (total) совершéнный
• *adv.* /aʊt'raɪt/ (directly, openly) прямо, открыто; (totally) совершéнно; (fully) пóлностью; (instantly) срáзу

outset /'aʊtset/ n. начáло; **at the** ~ вначáле; **from the** ~ с сáмого начáла

⚹ **outside** n. /aʊt'saɪd/ нарýжная сторонá; **from, on the** ~ снарýжи; **at the (very)** ~ сáмое бóльшее
• *adj.* /'aʊtsaɪd/ **1** (external, exterior) нарýжный, внéшний **2** (extreme) крáйний; **he has an** ~ **chance of winning** у негó есть при́зрачные шáнсы на вы́игрыш
• *adv.* /aʊt'saɪd/ снарýжи; извнé; (to the ~) нарýжу
• *prep.* /aʊt'saɪd/ вне + *g.*, из + *g.*; (beyond bounds of) за предéлами + *g.*; ~ **the door/window** за двéрью/окнóм

outsider /aʊt'saɪdə(r)/ n. посторóнний; (in contest, lit., fig.) аутсáйдер

outsize /'aʊtsaɪz/ *adj.* нестандáртный

outskirts /'aʊtskɜːts/ n. pl. (of town) окрáина

outsource /aʊt'sɔːs/ *v.t.* (econ.) отд|авáть, -áть нá сторону/на субподрáд

outspoken /aʊt'spəʊkən/ *adj.* прямóй, откровéнный

outstanding /aʊt'stændɪŋ/ *adj.* (prominent, eminent) выдаю́щийся; (still to be done) невы́полненный; (unpaid) неоплáченный

outstay /aʊt'steɪ/ *v.t.:* ~ **one's welcome** загости́ться (*pf.*)

outstretched /'aʊtstretʃt, aʊt'stretʃt/ *adj.* (hand) протя́нутый

outstrip /aʊt'strɪp/ *v.t.* (lit., fig.) опере|жáть, -ди́ть

outward /'aʊtwəd/ *adj.* (external) нарýжный, внéшний

outwardly /'aʊtwədlɪ/ *adv.* внéшне, на вид

outwards /'aʊtwədz/ *adv.* нарýжу

outweigh /aʊt'weɪ/ *v.t.* перевé|шивать, -сить

outwit /aʊt'wɪt/ *v.t.* (**outwitted, outwitting**) перехитри́ть (*pf.*)

oval /'əʊv(ə)l/ n. овáл
• *adj.* овáльный

ovarian /ə'veərɪən/ *adj.* яи́чниковый
■ ~ **cancer** n. рак яи́чников

ovary /'əʊvərɪ/ n. яи́чник

ovation /əʊ'veɪʃ(ə)n/ n. овáция

oven /'ʌv(ə)n/ n. духóвка

⚹ **over** /'əʊvə(r)/ *adv.* **1** (across; to, on the other side): ~ **there** (вон) там; **I asked him** ~ я пригласи́л егó к себé **2** (covering surface): all ~ повсю́ду; **I felt hot and cold all** ~ меня́ (всегó) бросáло то в жар, то в хóлод **3** (at an end): **the meeting is** ~ собрáние кóнчилось **4** (*also* ~ **again**) (once more) опя́ть, снóва, ещё раз; ~ **and** ~ **again** ты́сячу раз, снóва и снóва **5** (in excess): **sums of £5 and** ~ сýммы в/от 5 фýнтов и вы́ше; **I had £3 (left)** ~ у меня́ ещё оставáлось три фýнта
• *prep.* **1** (above) над + *i.*; **a roof** ~ **one's head** крыша над головóй; (expr. division): **five** ~ **two** (math.) пять дробь два **2** (to the far side of) чéрез + *a.*; **a bridge** ~ **the river** мост чéрез рéку; **I threw the ball** ~ **the wall** я переки́нул мяч чéрез стéну; **he jumped** ~ **the puddles** он перепры́гнул (чéрез) лýжи; (down from): **he fell** ~ **the cliff** он упáл со скалы́; (against): **he tripped** ~ **a stone** он споткнýлся о кáмень **3** (on the far side of): **he lives** ~ **the way** он живёт чéрез ýлицу **4** (resting on): **he pulled his cap** ~ **his eyes** он надви́нул шáпку на глазá; (crossing one leg ~ the other) закинув нóгу нá ногу; (across, ~ the surface of) по + *d.*; **all** ~ **the world** по всемý свéту **5** (more than) бóльше/свы́ше + *g.*; ~ **a year ago** бóльше/свы́ше гóда (тому́) назáд; **children** ~ **5** дéти стáрше пяти́ лет; ~ **600** свы́ше шестисóт **6** (during): **much has happened** ~ **the past two years** за послéдние два гóда мнóгое случи́лось/произошлó **7** (on the subject of): **he gets angry** ~ **nothing** он зли́тся из-за пустяков; **a quarrel** ~ **money** ссóра из-за дéнег

⚹ **overall** n. /'əʊvərɔːl/ (BrE) рабóчий халáт; (*in pl.*) комбинезóн
• *adj.* /'əʊvərɔːl/ (total) пóлный; (general) (все)óбщий
• *adv.* /əʊvər'ɔːl/ (taken as a whole) в цéлом

overawe /əʊvər'ɔː/ *v.t.* внуш|áть, -и́ть благоговéйный страх + *d.*

overbalance /əʊvə'bæləns/ (BrE) *v.i.* теря́ть, по- равновéсие

overbearing /ˌəʊvəˈbeərɪŋ/ *adj.* вла́стный

overboard /ˈəʊvəbɔːd/ *adv.*: **man ~!** челове́к за бо́ртом!

overbook /ˌəʊvəˈbʊk/ *v.t.*: **the plane was ~ed** биле́тов на самолёт бы́ло про́дано бо́льше, чем име́лось мест

overcast /ˈəʊvəkɑːst/ *adj.* покры́тый облака́ми

overcharge /ˌəʊvəˈtʃɑːdʒ/ *v.t.* назн|ача́ть, -а́чить завы́шенную це́ну (*кому*) (**for:** за + *a.*)

overcoat /ˈəʊvəkəʊt/ *n.* пальто́ (*nt. indecl.*)

overcome /ˌəʊvəˈkʌm/ *v.t.* (prevail over) преодол|ева́ть, -е́ть; (of emotion) охва́т|ывать, -и́ть

overconfident /ˌəʊvəˈkɒnfɪd(ə)nt/ *adj.* самонаде́янный

overcook /ˌəʊvəˈkʊk/ *v.t.* (by roasting, frying) пережа́р|ивать, -ить; (by boiling) перева́р|ивать, -и́ть

overcrowd /ˌəʊvəˈkraʊd/ *v.t.* перепо́лн|я́ть, -о́лнить

overdo /ˌəʊvəˈduː/ *v.t.* (by roasting, frying) пережа́ри|вать, -ть; (by boiling) перева́р|ивать, -и́ть; **~ it** перестара́ться (*pf.*); переб|а́рщивать, -орщи́ть (infml); переусе́рдствовать (*pf.*) (*в чём*)

overdose /ˈəʊvədəʊs/ *n.* передозиро́вка, чрезме́рная до́за

overdraft /ˈəʊvədrɑːft/ *n.* (deficit in bank account) овердра́фт, перерасхо́д; (agreement) разреше́ние на превыше́ние креди́та

overdraw /ˌəʊvəˈdrɔː/ *v.t.*: **I am £100 ~n** я превы́сил креди́т в ба́нке на 100 фу́нтов

overdue /ˌəʊvəˈdjuː/ *adj.* запозда́лый; **the baby is 2 weeks ~** ребёнок до́лжен был роди́ться две неде́ли тому́ наза́д; (of payment) просро́ченный

overeat /ˌəʊvərˈiːt/ *v.i.* пере|еда́ть, -е́сть; объ|еда́ться, -е́сться

overestimate /ˌəʊvərˈestɪmeɪt/ *v.t.* переоце́н|ивать, -и́ть

overexcited /ˌəʊvərɪkˈsaɪtɪd/ *adj.* кра́йне возбуждённый

overflow /ˌəʊvəˈfləʊ/ *v.t. & i.* перел|ива́ться, -и́ться (*через что*); **the river ~s its banks** река́ залива́ет берега́ (*or* выхо́дит из берего́в); **~ing with** (fig.) преиспо́лненный + *g.*

overground /ˈəʊvəɡraʊnd/ *adj.* надзе́мный

overgrow /ˌəʊvəˈɡrəʊ/ *v.t.*: **be ~n (with)** зараст|а́ть, -и́ + *i.*

overhaul /ˈəʊvəhɔːl/ *n.* (of machine) осмо́тр; (of system) пересмо́тр
● *v.t.* осм|а́тривать, -отре́ть; ремонти́ровать, от-; пересм|а́тривать, -отре́ть

overhead *n.* /ˈəʊvəhed/ (*usu. in pl.*) накладны́е расхо́ды (*m. pl.*)
● *adj.*: /ˈəʊvəhed/ **~ projector** диапрое́ктор; **~ railway** надзе́мная желе́зная доро́га
● *adv.* /ˌəʊvəˈhed/ наверху́, вверху́; (in the sky) на не́бе

overhear /ˌəʊvəˈhɪə(r)/ *v.t.* неча́янно услы́шать (*pf.*)

overheat /ˌəʊvəˈhiːt/ *v.t. & i.* перегр|ева́ть(ся), -е́ть(ся)

overindulge /ˌəʊvərɪnˈdʌldʒ/ *v.i.*: **~ in sth** злоупотреб|ля́ть, -и́ть чем-н.

overjoyed /ˌəʊvəˈdʒɔɪd/ *adj.* вне себя́ от ра́дости

overkill /ˈəʊvəkɪl/ *n.* (fig.) вы́ход за преде́лы необходи́мости

overland /ˈəʊvəlænd/ *adj.* сухопу́тный
● *adv.* по су́ше

overlap /ˈəʊvəlæp/ *v.i.* за|ходи́ть, -йти́ оди́н на друго́й; (coincide) (части́чно) совп|ада́ть, -а́сть

overleaf /ˌəʊvəˈliːf/ *adv.* на оборо́те (страни́цы)

overload /ˈəʊvələʊd/ *v.t.* перегру|жа́ть, -зи́ть

overlook /ˌəʊvəˈlʊk/ *v.t.* **1** (open on to) выходи́ть (*impf.*) на + *a.*; **our house is not ~ed** наш дом защищён от посторо́нних взгля́дов; **a view ~ing the lake** вид на о́зеро **2** (fail to notice) просмотре́ть (*pf.*), прогля́деть (*pf.*), пропус|ка́ть, -ти́ть; (disregard) упус|ка́ть, -ти́ть

overly /ˈəʊvəli/ *adv.* сли́шком, чересчу́р

overnight /ˌəʊvəˈnaɪt/ *adj.*: **an ~ stay** ночёвка, ночле́г
● *adv.* (through the night) всю ночь; (during the night) за́ ночь; **stay ~** ночева́ть, за-
■ **~ bag** *n.* доро́жная су́мка, небольшо́й чемода́н

overpass /ˈəʊvəpɑːs/ *n.* эстака́да

overpayment /ˌəʊvəˈpeɪmənt/ *n.* перепла́та

overpopulated /ˌəʊvəˈpɒpjʊleɪtɪd/ *adj.* перенаселённый

overpower /ˌəʊvəˈpaʊə(r)/ *v.t.* одол|ева́ть, -е́ть; (overwhelm) сокруш|а́ть, -и́ть; **~ing smell** о́чень си́льный за́пах

overrate /ˌəʊvəˈreɪt/ *v.t.* переоце́н|ивать, -и́ть

overreach /ˌəʊvəˈriːtʃ/ *v.t.* (outwit) перехитри́ть (*pf.*); **~ oneself** (defeat one's object) перестара́ться (*pf.*)

overreact /ˌəʊvərɪˈækt/ *v.i.* реаги́ровать, от-/про- чрезме́рно ре́зко

overrid|e /ˌəʊvəˈraɪd/ *v.t.* (reject) отв|ерга́ть, -е́ргнуть; **~ing** (aim) основно́й, первостепе́нный; (consideration) гла́вный, реша́ющий

overrule /ˌəʊvəˈruːl/ *v.t.* (annul) аннули́ровать (*impf., pf.*); **I was ~d** моё возраже́ние отве́ргли

overrun /ˌəʊvəˈrʌn/ *v.t.* **1** (of enemy) соверш|а́ть, -и́ть набе́г на + *a.* **2** (infest): **the garden is ~ with weeds** сад заро́с сорняка́ми; **the house is ~ with rats** дом киши́т кры́сами
● *v.i.*: **the broadcast is ~ning by 20 minutes** переда́ча идёт на 20 мину́т до́льше поло́женного вре́мени

overseas *adj.* /ˈəʊvəsiːz/ (trip) заграни́чный; (visitor) иностра́нный
● *adv.* /ˌəʊvəˈsiːz/ за грани́цей

oversee /ˌəʊvəˈsiː/ *v.t.* надзира́ть (*impf.*) за + *i.*

overseer /ˈəʊvəsiːə(r)/ *n.* надсмо́трщик, надзира́тель (*m.*)

overshadow /ˌəʊvəˈʃædəʊ/ v.t. (lit., fig.) заслон|я́ть, -и́ть

overshoot /ˌəʊvəˈʃuːt/ v.t. (junction, traffic lights) про|езжа́ть, -е́хать; проск|а́кивать, -очи́ть; ~ the mark (lit.) брать, взять вы́ше це́ли; (fig.) за|ходи́ть, -йти́ сли́шком далеко́
● v.i.: the plane overshot on landing (при поса́дке) самолёт перелете́л то́чку приземле́ния

oversight /ˈəʊvəsaɪt/ n. недосмо́тр, упуще́ние

oversimplify /ˌəʊvəˈsɪmplɪfaɪ/ v.t. сли́шком упро|ща́ть, -сти́ть

oversleep /ˌəʊvəˈsliːp/ v.i. прос|ыпа́ть, -па́ть

overspend /ˌəʊvəˈspend/ v.i. тра́тить, по-сли́шком мно́го

overstep /ˌəʊvəˈstep/ v.t. переступ|а́ть, -и́ть

oversubscribed /ˌəʊvəsəbˈskraɪbd/ adj.: the course is ~ курс перепо́лнен

overt /ˈəʊvɜːt/ adj. я́вный, очеви́дный

overtake /ˌəʊvəˈteɪk/ v.t. об|гоня́ть, -огна́ть

over the top /ˌəʊvə ðə ˈtɒp/ adj. чрезме́рный

overthrow /ˌəʊvəˈθrəʊ/ v.t. ниспров|ерга́ть, -е́ргнуть

overtime /ˈəʊvətaɪm/ n. сверхуро́чная рабо́та
● adv. сверхуро́чно

overtone /ˈəʊvətəʊn/ n. отте́нок

overture /ˈəʊvətjʊə(r)/ n. увертю́ра

overturn /ˌəʊvəˈtɜːn/ v.t. & i. опроки́|дывать(ся), -нуть(ся)

overview /ˈəʊvəvjuː/ n. обзо́р

overweight /ˌəʊvəˈweɪt/ adj. ве́сящий бо́льше но́рмы

overwhelm /ˌəʊvəˈwelm/ v.t. (in battle) сокруш|а́ть, -и́ть; (fig.): his kindness ~ed me я был ошеломлён/потрясён его́ добро́той; ~ing majority подавля́ющее большинство́

overwork /ˌəʊvəˈwɜːk/ v.t. & i. переутом|ля́ть(ся), -и́ть(ся)

overwrought /ˌəʊvəˈrɔːt/ adj. сли́шком возбуждённый, не́рвный; she is ~ у неё

не́рвное истоще́ние

ovulate /ˈɒvjʊleɪt/ v.i. овули́ровать (impf., pf.)

ovulation /ˌɒvjʊˈleɪʃ(ə)n/ n. овуля́ция

owe /əʊ/ v.t. & i. быть до́лжным + d.; you ~ us £50 вы должны́ нам 50 фу́нтов; I ~ you for the ticket я до́лжен вам за биле́т

owing /ˈəʊɪŋ/ adj. **1** (yet to be paid) причита́ющийся **2**: ~ to (attributable to) по причи́не + g.; (on account of, because of) из-за + g.

owl /aʊl/ n. сова́

◆ **own** /əʊn/ pron.: get one's ~ back on sb поквита́ться (pf.) с кем-н.; on one's ~ (alone) в одино́честве; (independently) самостоя́тельно, сам (по себе́)
● adj. со́бственный, свой; my ~ house мой со́бственный дом; this house is not my ~ э́тот дом мне не принадлежи́т; can I have a room of my ~? мо́жно получи́ть отде́льную ко́мнату?; of one's ~ accord по со́бственному побужде́нию; по со́бственной во́ле; my ~ father мой родно́й оте́ц
● v.t. владе́ть (impf.) + i.; who ~s this bag? чья э́то су́мка?; the land was ~ed by my father (э́та) земля́ принадлежа́ла моему́ отцу́ (or э́той землёй владе́л мой оте́ц)
● v.i. **1**: ~ to (liter., acknowledge, admit) призн|ава́ть, -а́ть (что); she ~ed to feelings of jealousy она́ призна́лась в том, что ревнова́ла **2**: ~ up (to sth) призн|ава́ться, -а́ться (в чём-н.); I ~ed up to having told a lie я призна́лся, что солга́л

◆ **owner** /ˈəʊnə(r)/ n. владе́л|ец (-ица)

ownership /ˈəʊnəʃɪp/ n. владе́ние (of: + i.); со́бственность (of: на + a.)

ox /ɒks/ n. (pl. **oxen**) бык

oxide /ˈɒksaɪd/ n. о́кись, окси́д

oxidize /ˈɒksɪdaɪz/ v.t. окисл|я́ть, -и́ть

oxygen /ˈɒksɪdʒ(ə)n/ n. кислоро́д

oyster /ˈɔɪstə(r)/ n. у́стрица

ozone /ˈəʊzəʊn/ n. озо́н
■ ~ layer n. озо́нный/озо́новый слой

o

p

Pp

p abbr. **1** (of **penny, pence**) (BrE) пе́нни (nt. indecl.), пенс **2** (of **page**) с(тр). (страни́ца)

PA abbr. of **1** (BrE) (**personal assistant**) ли́чный секрета́рь **2** (**public address (system)**) звукоусили́тельная аппарату́ра

◆ **pace** /peɪs/ n. **1** (step) шаг **2** (speed): keep ~ with посп|ева́ть, -е́ть за + i.
● v.i.: he ~d up and down он ходи́л взад и вперёд
■ ~maker n. (leader) ли́дер, задаю́щий

темп; (med.) (электро)кардиостимуля́тор, электри́ческий стимуля́тор се́рдца

Pacific /pəˈsɪfɪk/ n. (in full the ~ (Ocean)) Ти́хий океа́н

pacifier /ˈpæsɪfaɪə(r)/ n. (AmE, child's dummy) со́ска

pacifism /ˈpæsɪfɪz(ə)m/ n. пацифи́зм

pacifist /ˈpæsɪfɪst/ n. пацифи́ст (-ка)

pacify /ˈpæsɪfaɪ/ v.t. успок|а́ивать, -о́ить

⚲ **pack** /pæk/ n. **1** (rucksack) рюкза́к **2** (packet) па́чка, паке́т **3** (collection) набо́р; **it's all a ~ of lies** э́то сплошна́я ложь **4** (animals): **~ of wolves** ста́я волко́в **5** (BrE, cards) коло́да
● v.t. **1** (put into container) упако́в|ывать, -а́ть; укла́дывать, уложи́ть **2** (put into small space): **they were ~ed in there like sardines** они́ наби́лись туда́ как се́льди в бо́чке **3** (cover for protection) упако́в|ывать, -а́ть; **the glass is ~ed in cotton wool** стекло́ упако́вано в ва́ту **4** (fill) зап|олня́ть, -о́лнить; **he ~ed his bags and left** он уложи́л чемода́ны и уе́хал; **the hall was ~ed** зал был битко́м наби́т
● v.i. **1** (for travelling) укла́дываться, уложи́ться **2** (crowd together): **they ~ed into the car** они́ вти́снулись в автомоби́ль
□ **~ in** v.t. (infml, stop, give up) прекра|ща́ть, -ти́ть
□ **~ up** v.t.: **have the presents been ~ed up yet?** пода́рки уже́ упако́ваны?; (infml, stop): **I ~ed up smoking last year** я бро́сил кури́ть в про́шлом году́
● v.i.: **we spent the day ~ing up** мы це́лый день укла́дывались; (infml, stop working): **the workmen ~ed up at 5** рабо́чие зако́нчили в 5 часо́в; **the engine ~ed up** (BrE) мото́р отказа́л
■ **~ed lunch** n. бутербро́ды с собо́й

⚲ **package** /'pækɪdʒ/ n. **1** (parcel) посы́лка; (comput.) паке́т; (in full ~ **deal**) ко́мплексная сде́лка
● v.t. упако́в|ывать, -а́ть
■ **~ holiday, ~ tour** nn. (BrE) организо́ванная тури́стическая пое́здка

packet /'pækɪt/ n. (of cigarettes, biscuits) па́чка; (of crisps) паке́т

packing /'pækɪŋ/ n. упако́вка

pact /pækt/ n. соглаше́ние, догово́р

pad /pæd/ n. **1** (small cushion) поду́шечка; (for protection) прокла́дка **2** (block of paper) блокно́т **3** (launching platform) ста́ртовая площа́дка
● v.t. (**padded, padding**) **1** (cushion) наб|ива́ть, -и́ть; (coat) подб|ива́ть, -и́ть **2** (also ~ **out**) (fig.) (lengthen unnecessarily) разб|авля́ть, -а́вить
● v.i. (**padded, padding**) (infml, move softly) бесшу́мно дви́гаться (impf.)

padding /'pædɪŋ/ n. наби́вка

paddle[1] /'pæd(ə)l/ n. гребо́к (весло)
● v.t. & i. грести́ (impf.)

paddle[2] /'pæd(ə)l/ n.: **the children have gone for a ~e** де́ти пошли́ поплеска́ться в воде́
● v.i. (walk in shallow water) шлёпать (impf.) по воде́
■ **~ing pool** n. (BrE) де́тский бассе́йн, лягуша́тник (infml)

paddock /'pædək/ n. (small field, esp. for horses) вы́гул; (at racecourse, track) па́ддок (техническая зона на ипподроме между конюшнями и беговой дорожкой, где лошадей готовят к забегу; аналогичное место для гоночных машин непосредственно возле трассы)

padlock /'pædlɒk/ n. вися́чий замо́к
● v.t. ве́шать, пове́сить замо́к на + a.

⚲ ключевая лексика

paediatric /pi:dɪ'ætrɪk/ (AmE **pediatric**) adj. педиатри́ческий

paediatrician /pi:dɪə'trɪʃ(ə)n/ (AmE **pediatrician**) n. педиа́тр

paediatrics /pi:dɪ'ætrɪks/ (AmE **pediatrics**) n. педиатри́я

paedophile /'pi:dəfaɪl/ (AmE **pedophile**) n. педофи́л

paedophilia /pi:də'fɪlɪə/ (AmE **pedophilia**) n. педофили́я

pagan /'peɪɡən/ n. язы́чни|к (-ца)
● adj. язы́ческий

paganism /'peɪɡənɪz(ə)m/ n. язы́чество

⚲ **page**[1] /peɪdʒ/ n. (of a book etc.) страни́ца

page[2] /peɪdʒ/ n. ма́льчик-слуга́
● v.t.: **please ~ Mr Smith!** пожа́луйста, вы́зовите господи́на Сми́та по пе́йджеру!

pageant /'pædʒ(ə)nt/ n. представле́ние, де́йство

pageantry /'pædʒəntrɪ/ n. пы́шность, пара́дность

pager /'peɪdʒə(r)/ n. пе́йджер

paid /peɪd/ past and p.p. of ▸ **pay**; **put ~ to** (infml) класть, положи́ть коне́ц + d.

pail /peɪl/ n. ведро́

⚲ **pain** /peɪn/ n. **1** (suffering) боль; **he is in great ~** его́ му́чают бо́ли; (localized): **he had severe stomach ~s** у него́ бы́ли о́стрые бо́ли в желу́дке; **he is a ~ in the neck** (infml) он стои́т всем поперёк го́рла **2** (in pl.) (trouble, effort) стара́ния (nt. pl.), хло́п|оты (-о́т); **he takes great ~s over every picture** он подо́лгу рабо́тает над ка́ждой карти́ной
■ **~killer** n. болеутоля́ющее (сре́дство)

painful /'peɪnfʊl/ adj. (of part of body) больно́й; (causing pain) боле́зненный, мучи́тельный

painless /'peɪnlɪs/ adj. безболе́зненный

painstaking /'peɪnzteɪkɪŋ/ adj. стара́тельный, усе́рдный

⚲ **paint** /peɪnt/ n. кра́ска
● v.t. **1** (portray in colours) рисова́ть, на- **2** (cover with ~) кра́сить, по-/вы́-
● v.i. рисова́ть (impf.); писа́ть (impf.) кра́сками
■ **~box** n. набо́р кра́сок; **~brush** n. кисть

painter /'peɪntə(r)/ n. (artist) худо́жник; (decorator) маля́р

⚲ **painting** /'peɪntɪŋ/ n. **1** (profession) жи́вопись **2** (work of art) карти́на

⚲ **pair** /peə(r)/ n. па́ра; **they walked along in ~s** они́ шли па́рами; **~ of scissors** но́жниц|ы (pl., g. —); **two ~s of trousers** дво́е (or две па́ры) брюк
□ **~ off** v.t. & i. разб|ива́ть(ся), -и́ть(ся) на па́ры; (infml, marry) жени́ться (impf., pf.), пожени́ться (pf.)

pajamas /pɪ'dʒɑ:məz/ n. pl. (AmE) = pyjamas

Pakistan /pɑ:kɪ'stɑ:n/ n. Пакиста́н

Pakistani /pɑ:kɪ'stɑ:nɪ/ n. (pl. ~s) пакиста́н|ец (-ка)
● adj. пакиста́нский

pal /pæl/ n. (infml) дружо́к

palace /'pælɪs/ n. дворе́ц

palaeography /ˌpælɪˈɒgrəfɪ/ (AmE **paleography**) *n.* палеогра́фия
palatable /ˈpælətəb(ə)l/ *adj.* вку́сный
palate /ˈpælət/ *n.* нёбо
palatial /pəˈleɪʃ(ə)l/ *adj.* роско́шный, великоле́пный
palaver /pəˈlɑːvə(r)/ *n.* (infml) суета́
pale /peɪl/ *adj.* (of complexion) бле́дный; she turned ∼ она́ побледне́ла; (of colours) све́тлый; ∼ **blue** све́тло-голубо́й
● *v.i.* бледне́ть, по-; (fig.): **the event** ∼**d into insignificance** э́то собы́тие отошло́ на за́дний план
Palestine /ˈpælɪstaɪn/ *n.* Палести́на
Palestinian /ˌpælɪˈstɪnɪən/ *n.* палести́н|ец (-ка)
● *adj.* палести́нский
palette /ˈpælɪt/ *n.* (lit., fig.) пали́тра
pall[1] /pɔːl/ *n.* покро́в; **a** ∼ **of smoke hung over the city** пелена́ ды́ма висе́ла над го́родом
■ ∼**-bearer** *n.* несу́щий гроб
pall[2] /pɔːl/ *v.i.* при|еда́ться, -е́сться, надо|еда́ть, -е́сть (**on:** + *d.*)
pallet /ˈpælɪt/ *n.* (for loads) поддо́н
palliative /ˈpælɪətɪv/ *n.* паллиати́в, полуме́ра
● *adj.* паллиати́вный; смягча́ющий
pallid /ˈpælɪd/ *adj.* бле́дный
pallor /ˈpælə(r)/ *n.* бле́дность
pally /ˈpælɪ/ *adj.* (**pallier, palliest**) (infml, friendly) дружелю́бный; **be** ∼ **with sb** быть с кем-н. на коро́ткой ноге́
palm[1] /pɑːm/ *n.* (tree) па́льма
■ **P**∼ **Sunday** *n.* Ве́рбное воскресе́нье
palm[2] /pɑːm/ *n.* (of hand) ладо́нь
● *v.t.*: ∼ **sth off on sb** (*or* **sb off with sth**) подс|о́вывать, -у́нуть что-н. кому́-н.
palmistry /ˈpɑːmɪstrɪ/ *n.* хирома́нтия
palpable /ˈpælpəb(ə)l/ *adj.* ощути́мый
palpitate /ˈpælpɪteɪt/ *v.i.* пульси́ровать (*impf.*)
palpitation /ˌpælpɪˈteɪʃ(ə)n/ *n.* сердцебие́ние; **just to watch him gave me** ∼**s** оди́н его́ вид приводи́л меня́ в тре́пет
paltry /ˈpɔːltrɪ/ *adj.* (**paltrier, paltriest**) (worthless) ничто́жный; (petty, mean) ме́лкий
pamper /ˈpæmpə(r)/ *v.t.* балова́ть, из-
pamphlet /ˈpæmflɪt/ *n.* (printed leaflet) брошю́ра
pan[1] /pæn/ *n.* кастрю́ля; (*in full* **frying** ∼) сковорода́
● *v.t.* (**panned, panning**) (infml, criticize severely) разн|оси́ть, -ести́
● *v.i.* (**panned, panning**) (fig.): **everything** ∼**ned out well** (всё) вы́шло как нельзя́ лу́чше
pan[2] /pæn/ *v.i.* (**panned, panning**) (of camera) повора́чиваться (*impf.*)
panacea /ˌpænəˈsiːə/ *n.* панаце́я
panache /pəˈnæʃ/ *n.* (flamboyance) рисо́вка, щегольство́
Panama /ˈpænəmɑː/ *n.* Пана́ма
■ ∼ **Canal** *n.* Пана́мский кана́л
pancake /ˈpænkeɪk/ *n.* блин; ола́дья
■ **P**∼ **Day** *n.* вто́рник на Ма́сленой неде́ле, в кото́рый пеку́т блины́
pancreas /ˈpæŋkrɪəs/ *n.* поджелу́дочная железа́
pancreatic /ˌpæŋkrɪˈætɪk/ *adj.* панкреати́ческий

panda /ˈpændə/ *n.* па́нда
pandemonium /ˌpændɪˈməʊnɪəm/ *n.* стра́шный шум; (скандал) смяте́ние, столпотворе́ние
pander /ˈpændə(r)/ *v.i.* (minister) потво́рствовать (*impf.*) (**to:** + *d.*)
pane /peɪn/ *n.* око́нное стекло́
⚘ **panel** /ˈpæn(ə)l/ *n.* **1** (of door etc.) пане́ль **2**: ∼ **of judges** жюри́ (*nt. indecl.*), суде́йская гру́ппа **3** (for instruments) пульт; **control** ∼ пульт управле́ния
■ ∼ **game** *n.* (BrE) викторина
panellist /ˈpænəlɪst/ (AmE **panelist**) *n.* (in discussion) уча́стник диску́ссии/кру́глого стола́; (judge) член жюри́
pang /pæŋ/ *n.* **1** (sharp pain) ко́лики (*f. pl.*); ∼**s of hunger** голо́дные бо́ли **2** (mental) му́ки (*f. pl.*); **a** ∼ **of conscience** угрызе́ния (*nt. pl.*) со́вести
panic /ˈpænɪk/ *n.* па́ника
● *v.t.* (**panicked, panicking**) (infml): **they were** ∼**ked into surrender** они́ впа́ли в па́нику и сдали́сь
● *v.i.* (**panicked, panicking**) паникова́ть (*impf.*)
■ ∼**-stricken** *adj.* охва́ченный па́никой
panicky /ˈpænɪkɪ/ *adj.* (infml, action) пани́ческий; (person): **he was** ∼ он паникова́л
pannier /ˈpænɪə(r)/ *n.* корзи́на
panorama /ˌpænəˈrɑːmə/ *n.* панора́ма
panoramic /ˌpænəˈræmɪk/ *adj.* панора́мный
pansy /ˈpænzɪ/ *n.* аню́тин|ы гла́з|ки (-ых -ок)
pant /pænt/ *v.i.* тяжело́ дыша́ть (*impf.*)
panther /ˈpænθə(r)/ *n.* панте́ра; (AmE) пу́ма
panties /ˈpæntɪz/ *n. pl.* (infml) тру́сик|и (-ов)
pantomime /ˈpæntəmaɪm/ *n.* (BrE, entertainment) рожде́ственское представле́ние
pantry /ˈpæntrɪ/ *n.* кладова́я
pants /pænts/ *n. pl.* (BrE, underwear) трус|ы́ (*pl., g.* -о́в); (AmE, trousers) брю́к|и (*pl., g.* —)
pantyhose /ˈpæntɪhəʊz/ *n.* (AmE) колго́т|ки *pl. g.* -ок
papacy /ˈpeɪpəsɪ/ *n.* па́пство
papara|zzo /ˌpæpəˈrætsəʊ/ *n.* (*pl.* ∼**zzi** /-tsɪ/) папара́цци (*c.g. indecl.*); фотокорреспонде́нт, рабо́тающий на бульва́рную пре́ссу
⚘ **paper** /ˈpeɪpə(r)/ *n.* **1** бума́га **2** (newspaper) газе́та **3** (*in pl.*) (documents) докуме́нты (*m. pl.*), бума́ги (*f. pl.*) **4** (*in full* **examination** ∼) (BrE) экзаменацио́нная рабо́та **5** (essay, lecture) докла́д **6** (wallpaper) обо́|и (-ев)
● *v.t.* (apply wallpaper to) окле́и|вать, -ть обо́ями
■ ∼**back** *n.* кни́га в бума́жном/мя́гком переплёте; ∼ **bag** *n.* бума́жный паке́т; ∼ **clip** *n.* канцеля́рская скре́пка; ∼ **handkerchief** *n.* бума́жная салфе́тка; ∼ **round** *n.* доста́вка газе́т (на́ дом); ∼ **shop** *n.* газе́тный кио́ск; ∼**work** *n.* канцеля́рская рабо́та
paprika /ˈpæprɪkə/ *n.* (spice) па́прика
Papua New Guinea /ˈpæpjʊə njuː ˈgɪnɪ/ *n.* Па́пуа — Но́вая Гвине́я
par /pɑː(r)/ *n.* **1** (equality) ра́венство; **this is on a** ∼ **with his other work** (э́та) рабо́та на

p

у́ровне его други́х **2** (face value) цена́; above ~ вы́ше номина́льной цены́; below ~ ни́же номина́льной цены́ **3** (standard): I feel below ~ today я сего́дня нева́жно себя́ чу́вствую

parable /'pærəb(ə)l/ n. при́тча

parabola /pə'ræbələ/ n. (pl. **parabolas** or **parabolae** /-li:/) пара́бола

parabolic /pærə'bɒlɪk/ adj. (geom.) параболи́ческий

paracetamol /pærə'si:təmɒl/ n. (BrE) парацетамо́л

parachute /'pærəʃu:t/ n. парашю́т
• v.t. сбра́сывать, сбро́сить с парашю́том
• v.i.: the pilot ~d out of the aircraft пило́т вы́бросился из самолёта с парашю́том
■ ~ **jump** n. прыжо́к с парашю́том

parachutist /'pærəʃu:tɪst/ n. парашюти́ст (-ка)

parade /pə'reɪd/ n. **1** (public procession) ше́ствие, пара́д **2** (of troops) пара́д
• v.t. выставля́ть, вы́ставить напока́з
• v.i. ше́ствовать (impf.)
■ ~ **ground** n. плац

paradise /'pærədaɪs/ n. рай

paradox /'pærədɒks/ n. парадо́кс

paradoxical /pærə'dɒksɪk(ə)l/ adj. парадокса́льный

paraffin /'pærəfɪn/ n. **1** (BrE, ~ oil) кероси́н **2** (~ wax) парафи́н

paragon /'pærəgən/ n. образе́ц

paragraph /'pærəgrɑ:f/ n. абза́ц, пара́граф

Paraguay /'pærəgwaɪ/ n. Парагва́й

parallel /'pærəlel/ n. **1** (line) паралле́льная ли́ния; (of latitude) паралле́ль **2** (fig.) паралле́ль
• adj. паралле́льный; (similar) аналоги́чный

parallelogram /pærə'leləgræm/ n. параллелогра́мм

Paralympics /pærə'lɪmpɪks/ n. pl. Параолимпи́йские и́гры f. pl.

paralyse /'pærəlaɪz/ (AmE **paralyze**) v.t. парализова́ть (impf., pf.)

paralysis /pə'rælɪsɪs/ n. (pl. **paralyses** /-si:z/) парали́ч

paralytic /pærə'lɪtɪk/ adj. (med.) паралити́ческий, парализо́ванный; (BrE, incapably drunk) мертве́цки пья́ный

paramedic /pærə'medɪk/ n. медрабо́тник (без высшего образования)

parameter /pə'ræmɪtə(r)/ n. (math., comput., also fig.) пара́метр

paramilitary /pærə'mɪlɪtəri/ adj. военизи́рованный

paramount /'pærəmaʊnt/ adj. первостепе́нный

paranoia /pærə'nɔɪə/ n. парано́йя

paranoid /'pærənɔɪd/ n. парано́ик
• adj. парано́идный

paranormal /pærə'nɔ:m(ə)l/ adj. паранорма́льный

parapet /'pærəpɪt/ n. (low wall) парапе́т; (trench defence) бру́ствер

paraphernalia /pærəfə'neɪlɪə/ n. причинда́л|ы (-ов) (infml, joc.)

paraphrase /'pærəfreɪz/ v.t. переска́з|ывать, -а́ть

paraplegic /pærə'pli:dʒɪk/ adj. парализо́ванный

parasailing n. (sport) парасе́йлинг (полёты на парашюте за катером)

parasite /'pærəsaɪt/ n. парази́т

parasitic /pærə'sɪtɪk/ adj. (lit., fig.) паразити́ческий

parasol /'pærəsɒl/ n. зо́нтик (от со́лнца)

paratrooper /'pærətru:pə(r)/ n. (авиа)деса́нтник

parcel /'pɑ:s(ə)l/ n. паке́т, бандеро́ль, посы́лка
• v.t. (parcelled, parcelling, AmE parceled, parceling) **1** (also ~ up) (pack up) пакова́ть, у- **2** (also ~ out) (divide) дроби́ть, раз-

parch /pɑ:tʃ/ v.t. иссуш|а́ть, -и́ть; the ground was ~ed земля́ вы́сохла; my lips are ~ed у меня́ запекли́сь гу́бы

parchment /'pɑ:tʃmənt/ n. перга́мент

pardon /'pɑ:d(ə)n/ n. **1** извине́ние, проще́ние **2** (law) поми́лование; they were granted a free ~ их поми́ловали
• v.t. (forgive) про|ща́ть, -сти́ть; (excuse) извин|я́ть, -и́ть; (law) ми́ловать, по-

✐ **parent** /'peərənt/ n. (father or mother) роди́тель (-ница)
■ ~ **company** n. компа́ния-учреди́тель

parentage /'peərəntɪdʒ/ n. происхожде́ние; he is of mixed ~ он происхо́дит от сме́шанного бра́ка

parental /pə'rent(ə)l/ adj. роди́тельский

parenthes|is /pə'renθəsɪs/ n. (pl. **parentheses** /-si:z/) (word) вво́дное сло́во; (sentence) вво́дное предложе́ние; (in pl.) (text mark) кру́глые ско́бки (f. pl.); in ~es в ско́бках

parenthood /'peərənthʊd/ n. (fatherhood) отцо́вство; (motherhood) матери́нство

parenting /'peərəntɪŋ/ n. воспита́ние

Paris /'pærɪs/ n. Пари́ж

parish /'pærɪʃ/ n. (eccl.) прихо́д; (BrE, civil) о́круг

parishioner /pə'rɪʃənə(r)/ n. прихожа́н|ин (-ка)

parity /'pærɪti/ n. (equality) ра́венство, парите́т

✐ **park** /pɑ:k/ n. **1** (public garden) парк **2** (protected area of countryside) парк **3** (grounds of country mansion) уго́дь|я (-ий)
• v.t. паркова́ть, при-
• v.i. паркова́ться, при-
■ **park-and-ride** n. «парку́йся и поезжа́й (да́льше)» (система периферийных автостоянок, где автовладельцы оставляют свои автомобили и пересаживаются на общественный транспорт)

parking /'pɑ:kɪŋ/ n. (авто)стоя́нка; 'no ~!' «стоя́нка запрещена́!»
■ ~ **lot** n. (AmE) стоя́нка; ме́сто стоя́нки; ~ **meter** n. счётчик на стоя́нке; ~ **place** n.

ме́сто для парко́вки; ~ **ticket** *n.* штраф за
наруше́ние пра́вил стоя́нки/парко́вки

Parkinson's disease /ˈpɑːkɪns(ə)nz/ *n.*
боле́знь Паркинсо́на

parlance /ˈpɑːləns/ *n.* язы́к; мане́ра
выраже́ния; **in common** ~ в просторе́чии

parliament /ˈpɑːləmənt/ *n.* парла́мент

parliamentarian /ˌpɑːləmenˈteərɪən/ *n.*
(member of parliament) парламента́рий

parliamentary /ˌpɑːləˈmentərɪ/ *adj.*
парла́ментский, парламента́рный

parlour /ˈpɑːlə(r)/ (AmE **parlor**) *n.* (in house)
гости́ная; **beauty** ~ космети́ческий кабине́т/
сало́н; **funeral** ~ похоро́нное бюро́ (*nt.
indecl.*); **ice cream** ~ кафе́-моро́женое

parochial /pəˈrəʊkɪəl/ *adj.* прихо́дский; (fig.)
ограни́ченный, у́зкий

parochialism /pəˈrəʊkɪəlɪz(ə)m/ *n.*
ограни́ченность, у́зость

parody /ˈpærədɪ/ *n.* паро́дия
● *v.t.* паро́дировать (*impf., pf.*)

parole /pəˈrəʊl/ *n.* че́стное сло́во; **he was
released on** ~ его́ освободи́ли под че́стное
сло́во

paroxysm /ˈpærəksɪz(ə)m/ *n.* (med., also fig.)
при́ступ

parquet /ˈpɑːkɪ, -keɪ/ *n.* парке́т
■ ~ **floor** *n.* парке́тный пол

parrot /ˈpærət/ *n.* попуга́й

parry /ˈpærɪ/ *v.t.* (blow) отра|жа́ть, -зи́ть;
(question) пари́ровать (*impf., pf.*)

parsimonious /ˌpɑːsɪˈməʊnɪəs/ *adj.* скупо́й

parsley /ˈpɑːslɪ/ *n.* петру́шка

parsnip /ˈpɑːsnɪp/ *n.* пастерна́к

parson /ˈpɑːs(ə)n/ *n.* па́стор
■ ~'s **nose** *n.* (of fowl) «архиере́йский нос»,
кури́ная гу́зка

✐ **part** /pɑːt/ *n.* **1** часть; (portion) до́ля; **for the
most** ~ бо́льшей ча́стью; **in** ~ части́чно,
отча́сти; (component): **spare** ~**s** запасны́е
ча́сти; (gram.): ~**s of speech** ча́сти ре́чи
2 (share) уча́стие; **take** ~ **in** прин|има́ть, -я́ть
уча́стие в + *p.* **3** (actor's role or lines) роль
4 (side in dispute etc.) сторона́; **for my** ~ с мое́й
стороны́, что каса́ется меня́ **5** (AmE, in one's
hair) пробо́р
● *adv.* части́чно, ча́стью, отча́сти; **the wall is**
~ **brick and** ~ **stone** стена́ сло́жена части́чно
из кирпича́, части́чно из ка́мня
● *v.t.* разде|ля́ть, -и́ть; **the policeman** ~**ed the
crowd** полице́йский раздви́нул толпу́; **his
hair was** ~**ed in the middle** его́ во́лосы бы́ли
расчёсаны на прямо́й пробо́р
● *v.i.* (of people) расст|ава́ться, -а́ться; **the
crowd** ~**ed** толпа́ расступи́лась; **she has** ~**ed
from her husband** она́ разошла́сь с му́жем;
he hates to ~ **with his money** он о́чень не
лю́бит расстава́ться с деньга́ми
■ ~ **exchange** *n.* (BrE) сде́лка, при кото́рой
ста́рая вещь обме́нивается на но́вую с
допла́той; ~**-time** *adj., adv.* на полста́вки;
I want a ~**-time job** я хочу́ рабо́тать на
полста́вки; **he works** ~**-time** он рабо́тает на
полста́вки

partial /ˈpɑːʃ(ə)l/ *adj.* **1** (opp. total) части́чный
2 (biased) пристра́стный **3**: ~ **to** (fond of)
неравноду́шный к + *d.*

✐ **participant** /pɑːˈtɪsɪpənt/ *n.* уча́стник

✐ **participate** /pɑːˈtɪsɪpeɪt/ *v.i.* уча́ствовать
(*impf.*)

participation /pɑːˌtɪsɪˈpeɪʃ(ə)n/ *n.* уча́стие

participle /ˈpɑːtɪsɪp(ə)l/ *n.* прича́стие

particle /ˈpɑːtɪk(ə)l/ *n.* (also gram.) части́ца
■ ~ **accelerator** *n.* ускори́тель части́ц

✐ **particular** /pəˈtɪkjʊlə(r)/ *n.* ча́стность; **in** ~
(specifically) в ча́стности; (especially) осо́бенно;
(*in pl.*) да́нные (*pl.*); **let me take down your**
~**s** разреши́те мне записа́ть ва́ши да́нные
● *adj.* **1** (specific) осо́бенный, осо́бый; **for no**
~ **reason** без осо́бой причи́ны **2** (fastidious)
привере́дливый; **she is not** ~ **about what she
wears** ей всё равно́, что наде́ть

✐ **particularly** /pəˈtɪkjʊləlɪ/ *adv.* осо́бенно

parting /ˈpɑːtɪŋ/ *n.* **1** (leave-taking) проща́ние
2 (BrE, of the hair) пробо́р

partisan /ˌpɑːtɪˈzæn/ *n.* партиза́н (-ка)
● *adj.* пристра́стный

partition /pɑːˈtɪʃ(ə)n/ *n.* (division) разде́л;
(dividing structure) перегоро́дка
● *v.t.* дели́ть, раз-/по-; ~ **off** отгор|а́живать,
-оди́ть

partly /ˈpɑːtlɪ/ *adv.* части́чно, отча́сти

✐ **partner** /ˈpɑːtnə(r)/ *n.* (business, sexual, cards,
dancing, etc.) партнёр (-ша (infml)); (in marriage)
супру́г (-а)

partnership /ˈpɑːtnəʃɪp/ *n.* това́рищество;
партнёрство; **to go into** ~ входи́ть, войти́ в
партнёрство (**with:** с + *i.*)

partridge /ˈpɑːtrɪdʒ/ *n.* (*pl.* ~ *or* ~**s**)
куропа́тка

✐ **party** /ˈpɑːtɪ/ *n.* **1** (political group) па́ртия
2 (group) компа́ния, гру́ппа **3** (social gathering)
вечери́нка **4** (participant in contract etc.) сторона́
■ ~ **line** *n.* (pol.) поли́тика (*or* полити́ческий
курс) па́ртии; (teleph.) о́бщая телефо́нная
ли́ния; ~ **political** *adj.* парти́йный; ~ **political
broadcast** (BrE) пропаганди́стское выступле́ние
па́ртии по ра́дио и/или телеви́дению

✐ **pass** /pɑːs/ *n.* **1** (qualifying standard in exam) сда́ча
экза́мена **2** (document) про́пуск **3** (transfer of
ball in game) пас, переда́ча **4** (lunge) вы́пад;
(infml, amorous approach): **he made a** ~ **at her**
он к ней пристава́л (infml) **5** (mountain defile)
уще́лье, перева́л
● *v.t.* **1** (go by) про|ходи́ть, -йти́ (ми́мо + *g.*);
I ~**ed him in the street** я прошёл ми́мо него́
на у́лице **2** (go, get through) про|ходи́ть, -йти́;
will your car ~ **the test** пройдёт ли ва́ша
маши́на прове́рку?; ~ **an exam** сдать (*pf.*)
экза́мен **3** (spend) пров|оди́ть, -ести́ **4** (accept)
пропус|ка́ть, -ти́ть; (approve) од|обря́ть,
-о́брить **5** (hand over) перед|ава́ть, -а́ть; ~
(me) **the salt, please!** переда́йте мне соль,
пожа́луйста! **6** (utter) произн|оси́ть, -ести́; **the
judge** ~**ed sentence** судья́ вы́нес пригово́р
● *v.i.* **1** (proceed, move) про|ходи́ть, -йти́;
перепр|авля́ться, -а́виться; (get through):
let me ~! да́йте мне пройти́!, разреши́те

пройти́! **2** (go by, elapse) про|ходи́ть, -йти́; time ~es slowly вре́мя прохо́дит ме́дленно **3** (qualify in exam etc.) про|ходи́ть, -йти́

□ ~ **away** v.i. (die) сконча́ться (pf.)

□ ~ **by** v.t. & i. про|ходи́ть, -йти́ (ми́мо + g.)

□ ~ **down** v.t. перед|ава́ть, -а́ть

□ ~ **off** v.t. (dismiss): he ~ed off the whole affair as a joke он обрати́л всё де́ло в шу́тку; (falsely represent): he tried to ~ off the picture as genuine он выдава́л карти́ну за по́длинник • v.i. (go away) прекра́|ща́ться, -ти́ться; the pain was slow to ~ off боль проходи́ла ме́дленно; (be carried through) про|ходи́ть, -йти́; the wedding ~ed off without a hitch сва́дьба прошла́ без пробле́м

□ ~ **on** v.t. перед|ава́ть, -а́ть • v.i. про|ходи́ть, -йти́; (euph., die) сконча́ться (pf.)

□ ~ **out** v.i. (infml, lose consciousness) отключ|а́ться, -и́ться

■ ~ **key** n. отмы́чка; P~**over** n. евре́йская Па́сха; ~**word** n. (also comput.) паро́ль (m.)

passable /ˈpɑːsəb(ə)l/ adj. (affording passage) проходи́мый; (tolerable) сно́сный

passage /ˈpæsɪdʒ/ n. **1** (going by) прохо́д; (going across, over) перее́зд; перелёт; a bird of ~ перелётная пти́ца; (transition, change) перехо́д; (going through, way through) прохо́д **2** (crossing by ship etc.) рейс **3** (corridor) коридо́р **4** (literary excerpt) отры́вок, текст

■ ~**way** n. коридо́р

passé /ˈpæseɪ/ adj. устаре́лый, немо́дный

ꝰ **passenger** /ˈpæsɪndʒə(r)/ n. пассажи́р

■ ~ **train** n. пассажи́рский по́езд

passer-by /pɑːsəˈbaɪ/ n. прохо́жий

passing /ˈpɑːsɪŋ/ n.: I will mention in ~ я заме́чу ме́жду про́чим • adj. (transient): a ~ fancy мимолётное увлече́ние

passion /ˈpæʃ(ə)n/ n. страсть

passionate /ˈpæʃənət/ adj. стра́стный, пы́лкий

passive /ˈpæsɪv/ n. (gram.) страда́тельный зало́г • adj. пасси́вный

■ ~ **smoking** n. пасси́вное куре́ние; (gram.) пасси́вный, страда́тельный

passivity /pæˈsɪvɪtɪ/ n. пасси́вность

passport /ˈpɑːspɔːt/ n. па́спорт

ꝰ **past** /pɑːst/ **1** про́шлое **2** (gram.) проше́дшее вре́мя • adj. **1** (bygone) мину́вший, про́шлый; (pred.) (gone by) ми́мо; the time for that is ~ вре́мя (для) э́того давно́ минова́ло **2** (preceding) про́шлый, после́дний; for the ~ few days за после́дние не́сколько дней; during the ~ week за после́днюю/э́ту неде́лю **3** (gram.) проше́дший • adv. ми́мо; the soldiers marched ~ солда́ты прошли́ ми́мо • prep. **1** (after) по́сле + g.; it is ~ eight (o'clock) сейча́с девя́тый час; ten ~ one де́сять мину́т второ́го **2** (by) ми́мо + g.; he drove ~ the house он прое́хал ми́мо

до́ма **3** (to the far side of) за + a.; (on the far side of) за + i.; you've gone ~ the turning вы прое́хали поворо́т **4** (beyond) свы́ше + g., сверх + g.; he was a fine actor, but he's ~ it now (infml) когда́-то он был хоро́шим актёром, но э́то в про́шлом; I wouldn't put it ~ him to steal the money я ду́маю, что он спосо́бен укра́сть де́ньги

■ ~ **participle** n. прича́стие проше́дшего вре́мени; ~ **tense** n. проше́дшее вре́мя

pasta /ˈpæstə/ n. макаро́н|ы (pl., g. —)

paste /peɪst/ n. (adhesive) клей • v.t. **1** (stick) накле́|ивать, -ить; прикле́|ивать, -ить **2** (comput.) вст|авля́ть, -а́вить

pastel /ˈpæst(ə)l/ n. (crayon) пасте́ль; ~ **shades** пасте́льные кра́ски

pasteurize /ˈpɑːstʃəraɪz/ v.t. пастеризова́ть (impf., pf.)

pastiche /pæˈstiːʃ/ n. (literary imitation) стилиза́ция (of: под + a.); подде́лка

pastime /ˈpɑːstaɪm/ n. время(пре)провожде́ние

pastor /ˈpɑːstə(r)/ n. па́стор

pastoral /ˈpɑːstər(ə)l/ adj. пастора́льный

pastry /ˈpeɪstrɪ/ n. (dough) те́сто; (tart) пиро́жное

pasturage /ˈpɑːstʃərɪdʒ/ n. (grazing land) па́стбище; (grazing) вы́пас

pasture /ˈpɑːstʃə(r)/ n. па́стбище

pat¹ /pæt/ n. **1** (light touch) хлопо́к; шлепо́к **2** (of butter) кусо́чек • v.t. (patted, patting) похло́п|ывать, -ать; (a dog) гла́дить, по-

pat² /pæt/ adj. гото́вый; he had his lesson off ((AmE) down) ~ он вы́учил уро́к назубо́к

patch /pætʃ/ n. **1** (covering over hole) запла́та; (over eye) повя́зка; (comput.) патч, «запла́т(к)а» **2** (distinctive area) клочо́к; ~es of blue sky клочки́ голубо́го не́ба; there were ~es of ice on the road на доро́ге места́ми была́ гололе́дица **3** (piece of ground) уча́сток **4** (scrap) лоску́т • v.t. (mend) лата́ть, за-

□ ~ **up** v.t. (repair) чини́ть, по-; (fig.) ула́|живать, -дить

patchy /ˈpætʃɪ/ adj. (fig., of knowledge) отры́вочный; (fig., of uneven quality) неро́вный

patent /ˈpeɪt(ə)nt/ n. пате́нт • adj. **1**: ~ **leather** лакиро́ванная ко́жа **2** (obvious) очеви́дный • v.t. патентова́ть, за-

paternal /pəˈtɜːn(ə)l/ adj. отцо́вский

paternalistic /pətɜːnəˈlɪstɪk/ adj. (pol.) патернали́стский; (manner, tone) покрови́тельственный

paternity /pəˈtɜːnɪtɪ/ n. отцо́вство

■ ~ **leave** n. о́тпуск по ухо́ду за ребёнком (для отца́)

ꝰ **path** /pɑːθ/ n. (track for walking) тропа́, тропи́нка; доро́жка; (fig.) путь (m.); (course, trajectory) траекто́рия; the ~ of a bullet траекто́рия полёта пу́ли

pathetic /pəˈθetɪk/ adj. жа́лкий

pathological /pæθəˈlɒdʒɪk(ə)l/ adj. патологи́ческий

p

pathologist /pə'θɒlədʒɪst/ n. пато́лог

pathology /pə'θɒlədʒɪ/ n. патоло́гия

pathos /'peɪθɒs/ n. го́речь, печа́ль

patience /'peɪʃ(ə)ns/ n. **1** терпе́ние; she lost ～ with him она́ потеря́ла с ним вся́кое терпе́ние **2** (BrE, card game) пасья́нс

patient /'peɪʃ(ə)nt/ n. пацие́нт, больно́й
● adj. терпели́вый

patio /'pætɪəʊ/ n. (pl. ～s) дво́рик

patriarchal /peɪtrɪ'ɑːk(ə)l/ adj. патриарха́льный

patriot /'peɪtrɪət/ n. патрио́т (-ка)

patriotic /pætrɪ'ɒtɪk/ adj. патриоти́ческий

patriotism /'pætrɪətɪz(ə)m/ n. патриоти́зм

patrol /pə'trəʊl/ n. **1** (action) патрули́рование, дозо́р **2** (～ling body) патру́ль (m.)
● v.t. & i. (**patrolled, patrolling**) патрули́ровать (impf.)
■ ～ **car** n. (полице́йская) патру́льная маши́на; ～ **vessel** n. сторожево́й кора́бль

patron /'peɪtrən/ n. **1** (supporter) покрови́тель (m.), патро́н; a ～ **of the arts** покрови́тель иску́сств, мецена́т **2** (customer) (постоя́нный) клие́нт
■ ～ **saint** n. свят|о́й засту́пни|к (-а́я -ца)

patronage /'pætrənɪdʒ/ n. покрови́тельство, ше́фство

patroniz|e /'pætrənaɪz/ v.t. (visit as customer) постоя́нно посеща́|ть (impf.); (treat condescendingly) отн|оси́ться, -ести́сь свысока́ к + d.; ～ing **manner** снисходи́тельная мане́ра

patronymic /pætrə'nɪmɪk/ n. о́тчество

patter[1] /'pætə(r)/ n. (of salesman) скорогово́рка

patter[2] /'pætə(r)/ n. (tapping sound) стук, посту́кивание
● v.i. (of rain) бараба́нить (impf.); (of feet) топота́ть (impf.)

pattern /'pæt(ə)n/ n. **1** (decorative design) узо́р **2** (example) образе́ц **3** (model for production) вы́кройка; dress ～ вы́кройка пла́тья **4** (system) о́браз, мане́ра; new ～s of behaviour но́вые но́рмы (f. pl.) поведе́ния
● v.t.: a ～ed dress пла́тье с узо́рами

paucity /'pɔːsɪtɪ/ n. нехва́тка, ску́дость

paunch /pɔːntʃ/ n. брюшко́, живо́т

pauper /'pɔːpə(r)/ n. бедня́к

pause /pɔːz/ n. (intermission) переры́в; (in speaking) па́уза
● v.i. остан|а́вливаться, -ови́ться

pave /peɪv/ v.t. мости́ть, вы́-; (fig.): his proposal ～d the way to a lasting peace его́ предложе́ние проложи́ло путь к про́чному ми́ру

pavement /'peɪvmənt/ n. **1** (BrE, footway) тротуа́р **2** (AmE, paved surface) мостова́я

pavilion /pə'vɪljən/ n. (BrE, sport) павильо́н

paving stone /'peɪvɪŋ stəʊn/ n. брусча́тка

paw /pɔː/ n. ла́па

pawn[1] /pɔːn/ n. (chessman, also fig.) пе́шка

pawn[2] /pɔːn/ v.t. за|кла́дывать, -ложи́ть
■ ～**broker** n. челове́к, даю́щий де́ньги под зало́г (веще́й); ～**shop** n. ломба́рд

pay /peɪ/ n. (wages) зарпла́та; жа́лованье
● v.t. (past and p.p. **paid**) **1** (give in return for sth) плати́ть, за-, у-; she always ～s cash она́ всегда́ пла́тит нали́чными; (contribute): everyone must ～ their share ка́ждый до́лжен внести́ свою́ до́лю **2** (remunerate) плати́ть, за-, опла́|чивать, -ти́ть (sb: + d.); we are paid on Fridays нам пла́тят по пя́тницам; мы получа́ем зарпла́ту по пя́тницам **3** (bestow): ～ attention to me! послу́шайте меня́!; ～ sb a compliment де́ла|ть, с- кому́-н. комплиме́нт; ～ sb a visit наве|ща́ть, -сти́ть кого́-н. **4** (benefit, profit): it will ～ you to wait вам сто́ит подожда́ть
● v.i. (past and p.p. **paid**) **1** (give money) распла́|чиваться, -ти́ться (for: за + a.) **2** (suffer) плати́ть, за-; плати́ться, по- (for: за + a.); he paid for his carelessness он поплати́лся за своё легкомы́слие **3** (yield a return) окуп|а́ться, -и́ться; дава́ть, дать при́быль
□ ～ **back** v.t. (reimburse): he paid me back in person он ли́чно верну́л мне де́ньги; (have revenge on) отплати́ть (pf.) + d.
□ ～ **in** v.t. вн|оси́ть, -ести́
□ ～ **off** v.t. рассчи́т|ывать, -а́ться с + i.; (～ wages and discharge) рассчи́т|ывать, -а́ть
   ● v.i. (bring profit) окуп|а́ться, -и́ться
□ ～ **out** v.t. (expend) выпла́|чивать, вы́платить
□ ～ **up** v.i. (～ amount due) рассчи́т|ываться, -а́ться сполна́
■ ～ **day** n. платёжный день; ～ **packet** n. (BrE) n. за́работок, (infml) полу́чка; ～**phone** n. телефо́н-автома́т; ～**slip** n. (BrE) квита́нция о вы́даче зарпла́ты; ～ **TV** n. пла́тное телеви́дение; ～**wall** n. (comput.) систе́ма пла́тного до́ступа, пла́тная подпи́ска

payable /'peɪəb(ə)l/ adj. опла́чиваемый; подлежа́щий упла́те

PAYE (BrE) abbr. (of **pay-as-you-earn**) автомати́ческое отчисле́ние подохо́дного нало́га из зарпла́ты

payment /'peɪmənt/ n. (paying) опла́та, платёж; (sum paid) пла́та; (of debt etc.) упла́та

PC abbr. of **1** (**personal computer**) ПК (персона́льный компью́тер) **2** (**politically correct**) полити́чески корре́ктный, политкорре́ктный

PDA n. (abbr. of **Personal Digital Assistant**) «электро́нный помо́щник»

PE abbr. (of **physical education**) физкульту́ра

pea /piː/ n. горо́шина
■ ～**nut** n. ара́хис, земляно́й оре́х; ～**nut butter** па́ста из тёртого ара́хиса

peace /piːs/ n. **1** (freedom from war) мир **2** (freedom from civil disorder) споко́йствие, поря́док **3** (quiet) споко́йствие, поко́й; can we have some ～ and quiet? нельзя́ ли поти́ше?; ～ **of mind** споко́йствие ду́ха
■ ～**keeping** adj.: ～keeping force миротво́рческие войска́ (nt. pl.) /си́лы (f. pl.); ～**maker** n. миротво́рец; ～ **talks** n. pl. ми́рные перегово́ры; ～**time** n. ми́рное вре́мя

peaceful /'piːsfʊl/ adj. ми́рный

p

peach /piːtʃ/ *n.* **1** (fruit) пе́рсик **2** (tree) пе́рсиковое де́рево

peacock /'piːkɒk/ *n.* павли́н

peak /piːk/ *n.* **1** (mountain top) пик, верши́на **2** (of cap) козырёк **3** (fig., highest point) пик, верши́на; ~ **viewing hours** прайм-та́йм
● *v.i.*: **demand** ~**ed** спрос дости́г вы́сшей то́чки

peaked /piːkt/ *adj.* **1** остроконе́чный; ~ **cap** (фо́рменная) фура́жка **2** (haggard) (*also* **peaky**) осу́нувшийся

peaky /'piːkɪ/ *adj.* (**peakier, peakiest**) = **peaked** 2

peal /piːl/ *n.* (of bells) трезво́н; (of laughter) взрыв

pear /peə(r)/ *n.* **1** (fruit) гру́ша **2** (tree) гру́шевое де́рево, гру́ша

pearl /pɜːl/ *n.* жемчу́жина

peasant /'pez(ə)nt/ *n.* крестья́н|ин (-ка)

peat /piːt/ *n.* торф

pebble /'peb(ə)l/ *n.* га́лька

pebbly /'peblɪ/ *adj.* покры́тый га́лькой

pecan /'piːkən/ *n.* оре́х пека́н

peck /pek/ *n.* (made by beak) клево́к; (fig., hasty kiss): **he gave her a** ~ **on the cheek** он чмо́кнул её в щё(ч)ку
● *v.t.* клева́ть, клю́нуть; поклева́ть (*pf.*)
● *v.i.* (fig.): **she** ~**ed at her food** она́ едва́ дотро́нулась до еды́
■ ~**ing order** *n.* ≈ неофициа́льная иера́рхия

peckish /'pekɪʃ/ *adj.* (BrE, infml) голо́дный

pectoral /'pektər(ə)l/ *adj.* (anat.) грудно́й

peculiar /pɪ'kjuːlɪə(r)/ *adj.* **1** (exclusive) осо́бенный, своеобра́зный **2** (strange) стра́нный

peculiarity /pɪkjuːlɪ'ærɪtɪ/ *n.* (characteristic) сво́йство; (oddity) стра́нность

pecuniary /pɪ'kjuːnɪərɪ/ *adj.* де́нежный

pedagogical /pedə'ɡɒɡɪk(ə)l/, **pedagogic** /pedə'ɡɒɡɪk/ *adjs.* педагоги́ческий

pedal /'ped(ə)l/ *n.* педа́ль
● *v.i.* (**pedalled, pedalling,** AmE **pedaled, pedaling**) е́хать (*det.*) на велосипе́де

pedant /'ped(ə)nt/ *n.* педа́нт (*fem. also* -ка)

pedantic /pɪ'dæntɪk/ *adj.* педанти́чный

pedantry /'ped(ə)ntrɪ/ *n.* педанти́чность

peddle /'ped(ə)l/ *v.t.* торгова́ть (*impf.*) вразно́с

peddler /'pedlə(r)/ *n.* (of drugs) торго́вец нарко́тиками

pedestal /'pedɪst(ə)l/ *n.* пьедеста́л

pedestrian /pɪ'destrɪən/ *n.* пешехо́д
● *adj.* пешехо́дный
■ ~ **crossing** *n.* (BrE) перехо́д; ~ **precinct** *n.* пешехо́дная зо́на

pediatric /piːdɪ'ætrɪk/ *adj.* (AmE) = **paediatric**

pediatrician /piːdɪə'trɪʃ(ə)n/ *n.* (AmE) = **paediatrician**

pediatrics /piːdɪ'ætrɪks/ *n.* (AmE) = **paediatrics**

pedicure /'pedɪkjʊə(r)/ *n.* (treatment) педикю́р; (person) педикю́рша

pedigree /'pedɪɡriː/ *n.* происхожде́ние; (*attr.*) ~ **cattle** племенно́й скот

pedophile /'piːdəfaɪl/ *n.* (AmE) = **paedophile**

pedophilia /piːdə'fɪlɪə/ *n.* (AmE) = **paedophilia**

pee /piː/ (infml) *n.* (urination) пи-пи́ (*nt. indecl.*); (urine) моча́
● *v.i.* (**pees, peed**) мочи́ться, по-

peek /piːk/ *n.* (infml) взгляд укра́дкой

peel /piːl/ *n.* (thin skin of fruit) кожура́; (of vegetables) шелуха́; (rind of orange etc.) ко́рка
● *v.t.* **1** (remove skin from) оч|ища́ть, -и́стить **2** (remove from surface) сн|има́ть, -ять
● *v.i.* **1** (lose skin) шелуши́ться (*impf.*) **2** (come away from surface) (*also* ~ **away,** ~ **off**) слез|а́ть, -ть; обл|еза́ть, -е́зть; **the paint has begun to** ~ **(off)** кра́ска начала́ облеза́ть

peeling /'piːlɪŋ/ *n.* (of fruit) кожура́; (of vegetables) шелуха́

peep[1] /piːp/ *n.* (furtive or hasty look) взгляд укра́дкой; **take, have a** ~ **at** взгляну́ть (*pf.*) на + *a.*
● *v.i.* погля́д|ывать, -е́ть; **he** ~**ed in at the window** он загляну́л в окно́
■ ~**hole** *n.* глазо́к

peep[2] /piːp/ *n.* (chirp) писк; (fig.): **not a** ~**!** ни сло́ва!
● *v.i.* (chirp) пища́ть, пи́скнуть

peer[1] /pɪə(r)/ *n.* **1** (equal) ра́вн|ый (-ая); (person of the same age) рове́сни|к (-ца), све́рстни|к (-ца) **2** (noble) пэр
■ ~ **group** *n.* рове́сники, све́рстники (*m. pl.*); ~ **(group) pressure** давле́ние гру́ппы (све́рстников)

peer[2] /pɪə(r)/ *v.i.* (look closely) всм|а́триваться, -отре́ться (**at/into:** в + *a.*)

peerage /'pɪərɪdʒ/ *n.* пэ́рство, ти́тул пэ́ра

peeved /piːvd/ *adj.* (infml): **he looks** ~ у него́ недово́льный вид

peg /peɡ/ *n.* (for holding sth down) ко́лышек; (*in full* **clothes** ~) (BrE) прище́пка; (for hat, coat) ве́шалка, крючо́к

pejorative /pɪ'dʒɒrətɪv/ *adj.* уничижи́тельный

pelican /'pelɪkən/ *n.* пелика́н

pellet /'pelɪt/ *n.* ша́рик

pelt /pelt/ *v.t.* (assail) забр|а́сывать, -оса́ть; **they** ~**ed him with stones/insults** они́ заброса́ли его́ камня́ми/оскорбле́ниями
● *v.i.* стуча́ть, бараба́нить (*both impf.*); **the rain was** ~**ing down** дождь бараба́нил вовсю́

pelvic /'pelvɪk/ *adj.* та́зовый
■ ~ **girdle** *n.* та́зовый по́яс

pelvis /'pelvɪs/ *n.* (*pl.* **pelvises**) (anat.) таз

pen[1] /pen/ *n.* (writing instrument) ру́чка
■ ~**friend** *n.* (BrE) друг (подру́га по перепи́ске); ~**knife** *n.* перочи́нный нож(ик); ~ **pal** *n.* (AmE) = **penfriend**

pen[2] /pen/ *n.* (enclosure) заго́н

penal /'piːn(ə)l/ *adj.*: ~ **code** уголо́вный ко́декс; ~ **colony** исправи́тельная коло́ния

penalize /'piːnəlaɪz/ *v.t.* нака́з|ывать, -а́ть

⚹ **penalty** /'pen(ə)ltɪ/ *n.* (punishment) наказа́ние; (fine) штраф; (football) (*in full* ~ **kick**) пена́льти (*m. indecl.*)

penance /'penəns/ *n.* епитимья́; покая́ние; he must do ~ for his sins он до́лжен замоли́ть/искупи́ть свои́ грехи́

pence /pens/ *n. see* ▶ penny

penchant /'pɑ̃ʃɑ̃/ *n.* скло́нность (for: к + *d.*)

pencil /'pensıl/ *n.* каранда́ш
• *v.t.* (**pencilled, pencilling**, AmE **penciled, penciling**): ~ **in** (arrange provisionally) де́лать, с- предвари́тельную заме́тку насчёт + *g.*
■ ~ **case** *n.* пена́л; ~ **sharpener** *n.* точи́лка

pendant /'pend(ə)nt/ *n.* куло́н

pending /'pendıŋ/ *adj.* рассма́триваемый
• *prep.* до + *g.*; в ожида́нии + *g.*

pendulous /'pendjʊləs/ *adj.* подвесно́й

pendulum /'pendjʊləm/ *n.* ма́ятник

penetrate /'penɪtreɪt/ *v.t.* прон|ика́ть, -и́кнуть в + *a.*

penetrating /'penɪtreɪtɪŋ/ *adj.* си́льный; о́стрый; a ~ **voice** пронзи́тельный го́лос

penguin /'peŋgwın/ *n.* пингви́н

penicillin /penɪ'sılın/ *n.* пеницилли́н

peninsula /pə'nınsjʊlə/ *n.* полуо́стров

penis /'pi:nıs/ *n.* (*pl.* **penises**) пе́нис, половой член

penitence /'penɪt(ə)ns/ *n.* раска́яние

penitent /'penɪt(ə)nt/ *adj.* раска́ивающийся

penitentiary /penɪ'tenʃərɪ/ *n.* тюрьма́

pennant /'penənt/ *n.* флажо́к, вы́мпел

penniless /'penılıs/ *adj.* безде́нежный, без гроша́ (*pred.*)

penny /'penı/ *n.* (*pl. for separate coins* **pennies**, *for a sum of money* **pence**) пе́нни (*nt. indecl.*), пенс; (AmE cent) цент; at last the ~ has dropped! (BrE, infml) наконе́ц-то дошло́!

pension /'penʃ(ə)n/ *n.* пе́нсия; old-age ~ пе́нсия по ста́рости

pensionable /'penʃənəb(ə)l/ *adj.*: ~ age пенсио́нный во́зраст; his job is ~ его́ рабо́та даёт ему́ пра́во на пе́нсию

pensioner /'penʃənə(r)/ *n.* пенсионе́р (-ка)

pensive /'pensıv/ *adj.* заду́мчивый

pent /pent/ *adj.*: ~-up feelings сде́рживаемые чу́вства

pentagon /'pentəgən/ *n.* пятиуго́льник; the P~ (AmE War Department) Пентаго́н

pentathlon /pen'tæθlən/ *n.* пятибо́рье

Pentecost /'pentɪkɒst/ *n.* Пятидеся́тница (*христиа́нский пра́здник*)

penthouse /'penthaʊs/ *n.* (apartment) роско́шная кварти́ра на после́днем этаже́; пентха́ус

penultimate /pɪ'nʌltımət/ *adj.* предпосле́дний

penury /'penjʊrɪ/ *n.* бе́дность, нужда́

peony /'pi:ənɪ/ *n.* пио́н

✍ **people** /'pi:p(ə)l/ *n.* ◗ (persons) лю́д|и (-е́й); few ~ ма́ло люде́й; most ~ will object большинство́ (люде́й) бу́дет про́тив ◙ (nation; proletariat) наро́д ◖ (inhabitants) жи́тели (*m. pl.*); (citizens) гра́ждане (*m. pl.*) ◗ (persons grouped by type): young ~ молодёжь,

молоды́е лю́ди; old ~ старики́ (*m. pl.*)

pep /pep/ *n.*: ~ talk нака́чка
• *v.t.* (**pepped, pepping**) (*usu.* ~ **up**) оживл|я́ть, -и́ть

pepper /'pepə(r)/ *n.* (condiment) пе́рец; (vegetable, sweet ~) (сла́дкий) пе́рец
■ ~**corn** *n.* перчи́нка; ~ **mill** *n.* ме́льница для пе́рца; ~**mint** *n.* (sweet) мя́тный ледене́ц

peptic /'peptık/ *adj.* пепти́ческий, пищевари́тельный
■ ~ **ulcer** *n.* я́зва желу́дка

✍ **per** /pə:(r)/ *prep.* в + *a.*; на + *a.*; с + *g.*; 60 miles ~ hour 60 миль в час; they collected 20 pence ~ man они́ собра́ли по 20 пе́нсов с челове́ка

per capita /pə 'kæpıtə/ *adv.* на ду́шу (населе́ния)

perceive /pə'si:v/ *v.t.* (with mind) пост|ига́ть, -и́гнуть, -и́чь; (through senses) восприн|има́ть, -я́ть

✍ **per cent** /pə 'sent/ (AmE **percent**) *n., adv.* проце́нт

percentage /pə'sentıdʒ/ *n.* (of people/things) проце́нт; (of substance) проце́нтное содержа́ние
■ ~ **point** *n.* проце́нтный пункт

perceptible /pə'septıb(ə)l/ *adj.* ощути́мый

perception /pə'sepʃ(ə)n/ *n.* (process) восприя́тие, ощуще́ние; (discernment) осозна́ние, понима́ние

perceptive /pə'septıv/ *adj.* восприи́мчивый; (observant) проница́тельный

perch /pə:tʃ/ *n.* (of bird) насе́ст
• *v.t. & i.* сади́ться, сесть; he ~ed on a stool он присе́л на табуре́т

percipient /pə'sıpıənt/ *adj.* воспринима́ющий

percolate /'pə:kəleıt/ *v.t.* про|ходи́ть, -йти́ че́рез + *a.*
• *v.i.* прос|а́чиваться, -очи́ться; water ~s through sand вода́ проса́чивается/прохо́дит сквозь песо́к; I'm waiting for the coffee to ~ я жду, пока́ ко́фе профильтру́ется; ~ through (fig., news, idea, fashion) (постепе́нно) распростран|я́ться, -и́ться, получ|а́ть, -и́ть распростране́ние (*среди люде́й, в обществе*); (of news, also) (постепе́нно) ста|нови́ться, -ть изве́стным (to: + *d.*)

percolator /'pə:kəleıtə(r)/ *n.* (cul.) перкуля́тор, кофева́рка

percussion /pə'kʌʃ(ə)n/ *n.* (in full ~ instruments) уда́рные инструме́нты (*m. pl.*)

peremptory /pə'remptərı/ *adj.* (imperious) повели́тельный; непререка́емый

perennial /pə'renıəl/ *adj.* (plant) многоле́тний; (enduring) ве́чный

perestroika /perɪ'strɔɪkə/ *n.* перестро́йка

✍ **perfect**[1] /'pə:fıkt/ *adj.* ◗ (complete; absolute) соверше́нный; по́лный; I am ~ly sure of it я соверше́нно/по́лностью уве́рен в э́том ◙ (faultless) соверше́нный, безупре́чный; he speaks ~ English он в соверше́нстве владе́ет англи́йским (языко́м) ◖ (exact, precise) абсолю́тный; ~ pitch (mus.) абсолю́тный

p

слух; (corresponding to requirements): **the dress is a ~ fit** пла́тье сиди́т безупре́чно **4** (gram.) перфе́ктный, соверше́нный
■ **~ tense** *n.* перфе́кт

perfect² /pə'fekt/ *v.t.* соверше́нствовать, у-

perfection /pə'fekʃ(ə)n/ *n.* соверше́нство; **she dances to ~** она́ безупре́чно танцу́ет

perfectionist /pə'fekʃənɪst/ *n.* взыска́тельный челове́к

perfidious /pə'fɪdɪəs/ *adj.* вероло́мный, кова́рный

perforate /'pə:fəreɪt/ *v.t.* перфори́ровать (*impf.*); **a ~d appendix** прободно́й/перфорати́вный аппендици́т

⚜ **perform** /pə'fɔːm/ *v.t.* **1** (task) выполня́ть, вы́полнить **2** (piece of music) исп|олня́ть, -о́лнить; (play) игра́ть, сыгра́ть
● *v.i.* **1** (in public) игра́ть, сыгра́ть; выступа́ть, вы́ступить **2** (function) рабо́тать (*impf.*); **my car ~s well on hills** моя́ маши́на хорошо́ идёт в го́ру

⚜ **performance** /pə'fɔːməns/ *n.* **1** (of task) выполне́ние **2** (of a machine, vehicle, etc.) ход, характери́стика **3** (public appearance) выступле́ние **4** (of play, etc.) представле́ние

performer /pə'fɔːmə(r)/ *n.* исполни́тель (*m.*) (-ница)

perfume /'pə:fjuːm/ *n.* дух|и́ (-о́в), парфю́м
● *v.t.* (impart odour to) де́лать, с- благоуха́нным

perfumery /pə'fjuːmərɪ/ *n.* (business) парфюме́рия; (shop) парфюме́рный магази́н
■ **~ department** *n.* парфюме́рия

perfunctory /pə'fʌŋktərɪ/ *adj.* (glance, inspection) пове́рхностный; (kiss, smile) небре́жный

pergola /'pə:gələ/ *n.* садо́вая а́рка, а́рка из вью́щихся расте́ний

⚜ **perhaps** /pə'hæps/ *adv.* мо́жет быть; возмо́жно; пожа́луй

peril /'perɪl/ *n.* опа́сность; риск

perilous /'perɪləs/ *adj.* опа́сный; риско́ванный

perimeter /pə'rɪmɪtə(r)/ *n.* периме́тр

⚜ **period** /'pɪərɪəd/ *n.* **1** пери́од; **she has ~s of depression** у неё быва́ют пери́оды депре́ссии; **for a long ~** до́лгое вре́мя **2** (previous age) эпо́ха; **~ furniture** стари́нная ме́бель **3** (lesson) уро́к **4** (menstruation) ме́сячные (*pl.*) **5** (AmE, full stop) то́чка
■ **~ pains** *n. pl.* (BrE) ме́сячные бо́ли (*f. pl.*)

periodic /pɪərɪ'ɒdɪk/ *adj.* периоди́ческий

periodical /pɪərɪ'ɒdɪk(ə)l/ *n.* периоди́ческое изда́ние

peripatetic /perɪpə'tetɪk/ *adj.* (teacher) приходя́щий; (itinerant) бродя́чий

peripheral /pə'rɪfər(ə)l/ *n.* (comput.) перифери́йное устро́йство
● *adj.* (lit.) перифери́йный; (fig.) несуще́ственный; побо́чный

periphery /pə'rɪfərɪ/ *n.* (boundary) грани́ца, черта́; (also fig.) перифери́я

periscope /'perɪskəʊp/ *n.* периско́п

⚜ ключева́я ле́ксика

perish /'perɪʃ/ *v.i.* **1** поги|ба́ть, -́бнуть **2**: **the rubber has ~ed** рези́на пришла́ в него́дность

perishable /'perɪʃəb(ə)l/ *adj.* скоропо́ртящийся; (*in pl., as n.*) скоропо́ртящийся това́р

perjure /'pə:dʒə(r)/ *v.t.*: **~ oneself** да|ва́ть, -ть ло́жное показа́ние под прися́гой, лжесвиде́тельствовать (*impf.*)

perjury /'pə:dʒərɪ/ *n.* лжесвиде́тельство

perk /pə:k/ *v.i. & t.*: **~ up** (liven up) ожив|ля́ть(ся), -и́ть(ся)

perky /'pə:kɪ/ *adj.* (**perkier, perkiest**) (infml) весёлый, оживлённый

perm /pə:m/ *n.* перманéнтная зави́вка, перманéнт
● *v.t.*: **she had her hair ~ed** она́ сде́лала себе́ перманéнтную зави́вку/перманéнт

permafrost /'pə:məfrɒst/ *n.* ве́чная мерзлота́

permanence /'pə:mənəns/ *n.* неизме́нность

permanent /'pə:mənənt/ *adj.* постоя́нный

permeable /'pə:mɪəb(ə)l/ *adj.* проница́емый

permeate /'pə:mɪeɪt/ *v.t.* пропи́т|ывать, -а́ть; прон|ика́ть, -и́кнуть в + *a.*

permissible /pə'mɪsɪb(ə)l/ *adj.* допусти́мый, позволи́тельный

permission /pə'mɪʃ(ə)n/ *n.* позволе́ние, разреше́ние

permissive /pə'mɪsɪv/ *adj.*: **~ society** о́бщество вседозво́ленности

permit¹ /'pə:mɪt/ *n.* разреше́ние, про́пуск (-á); **work ~** разреше́ние на рабо́ту

permit² /pə'mɪt/ *v.t.* (**permitted, permitting**) разреш|а́ть, -и́ть, позв|оля́ть, -о́лить; **smoking ~ted** кури́ть разреша́ется
● *v.i.* (**permitted, permitting**): **if circumstances ~** е́сли обстоя́тельства позво́лят

permutation /pə:mjʊ'teɪʃ(ə)n/ *n.* (math.) перестано́вка; (fig.) вариа́нт, модифика́ция

pernicious /pə'nɪʃəs/ *adj.* па́губный, вре́дный; **~ anaemia** злока́чественное малокро́вие

pernickety /pə'nɪkɪtɪ/ *adj.* (infml) приверéдливый

peroxide /pə'rɒksaɪd/ *n.* пе́рекись; **a ~ blonde** кра́шеная блонди́нка

perpendicular /pə:pən'dɪkjʊlə(r)/ *adj.* перпендикуля́рный

perpetrate /'pə:pɪtreɪt/ *v.t.* соверш|а́ть, -и́ть

perpetrator /'pə:pɪtreɪtə(r)/ *n.* вино́вник (+ *g.*), вино́вный (в + *p.*)

perpetual /pə'petʃʊəl/ *adj.* ве́чный

perpetuate /pə'petʃʊeɪt/ *v.t.* увекове́чи|вать, -ть

perpetuity /pə:pɪ'tjuːɪtɪ/ *n.* ве́чность; **in ~** навсегда́, (на)ве́чно

perplex /pə'pleks/ *v.t.* озада́чи|вать, -ть

persecute /'pə:sɪkjuːt/ *v.t.* пресле́довать (*impf.*)

persecution /pə:sɪ'kjuːʃ(ə)n/ *n.* пресле́дование

persecutor /'pə:sɪkjuːtə(r)/ *n.* пресле́дователь (*m.*) (-ница)

perseverance /pə:sɪ'vɪərəns/ *n.* упо́рство, насто́йчивость

persevere /pɜːsɪ'vɪə(r)/ *v.i.* проявля́ть, -и́ть упо́рство/насто́йчивость (в + *p.*); **you must ~ in (at, with) your work** вы должны́ прояви́ть упо́рство/насто́йчивость в свое́й рабо́те

Persian /'pɜːʃ(ə)n/ *adj.*: ~ **Gulf** Перси́дский зали́в

persist /pə'sɪst/ *v.i.* (continue stubbornly) упо́рно/ насто́йчиво продолжа́ть (*impf.*); (continue) сохран|я́ться, -и́ться; **fog will ~ all day** тума́н проде́ржится весь день

persistence /pə'sɪst(ə)ns/ *n.* упо́рство, насто́йчивость

persistent /pə'sɪst(ə)nt/ *adj.* (stubborn) упо́рный, насто́йчивый; (continuous) постоя́нный

⚭ **person** /'pɜːs(ə)n/ *n.* **1** (individual) челове́к **2** (of particular category, also gram.) лицо́; **first ~ singular** пе́рвое лицо́ еди́нственного числа́

personable /'pɜːsənəb(ə)l/ *adj.* привлека́тельный

⚭ **personal** /'pɜːsən(ə)l/ *adj.* ли́чный; **don't make ~ remarks!** не переходи́те на ли́чности!
  ■ ~ **column** *n.* (of newspaper) коло́нка ча́стных объявле́ний; ~ **computer** *n.* персона́льный компью́тер; ~ **organizer** *n.* органа́йзер; ~ **stereo** *n.* пле́ер

personality /pɜːsə'nælɪtɪ/ *n.* **1** (character) ли́чность **2** (famous person) знамени́тость

personally /'pɜːsənəlɪ/ *adv.* ли́чно

personification /pəsɒnɪfɪ'keɪʃ(ə)n/ *n.* олицетворе́ние, воплоще́ние; **he is the ~ of selfishness** он явля́ется воплоще́нием эгои́зма

personif|y /pə'sɒnɪfaɪ/ *v.t.* вопло|ща́ть, -ти́ть; **she was kindness ~ied** она́ была́ воплоще́нием доброты́

personnel /pɜːsə'nel/ *n.* персона́л; штат; ка́дры (*m. pl.*)
  ■ ~ **department** *n.* = HR

⚭ **perspective** /pə'spektɪv/ *n.* **1** перспекти́ва **2** (fig.): **you must see, get things in ~** на́до ви́деть ве́щи в их и́стинном све́те

perspex® /'pɜːspeks/ *n.* (BrE) плексигла́с, органи́ческое стекло́, оргстекло́

perspicacious /pɜːspɪ'keɪʃəs/ *adj.* проница́тельный

perspicacity /pɜːspɪ'kæsɪtɪ/ *n.* проница́тельность

perspicuous /pə'spɪkjʊəs/ *adj.* я́сный, поня́тный

perspiration /pɜːspɪ'reɪʃ(ə)n/ *n.* пот

perspire /pə'spaɪə(r)/ *v.i.* поте́ть, вс-

persuade /pə'sweɪd/ *v.t.* **1** (convince) убе|жда́ть, -ди́ть; **I ~d him of my innocence** я убеди́л его́ в мое́й неви́нновности **2** (induce) угов|а́ривать, -ори́ть; **he was ~d to sing** его́ уговори́ли спеть

persuasion /pə'sweɪʒ(ə)n/ *n.* (persuading) убежде́ние; (conviction) убежде́ние; (denomination) вероиспове́дание

persuasive /pə'sweɪsɪv/ *adj.* убеди́тельный; (of person) облада́ющий да́ром убежде́ния

pert /pɜːt/ *adj.* де́рзкий, наха́льный

pertain /pə'teɪn/ *v.i.* (relate) относи́ться (*impf.*) (**to:** к + *d.*)

pertinent /'pɜːtɪnənt/ *adj.* уме́стный

perturb /pə'tɜːb/ *v.t.* трево́жить, вс-

Peru /pə'ruː/ *n.* Перу́ (*nt. & f. indecl.*)

peruse /pə'ruːz/ *v.t.* рассм|а́тривать, -отре́ть

Peruvian /pə'ruːvɪən/ *n.* перуа́н|ец (-ка)
  ● *adj.* перуа́нский

pervade /pə'veɪd/ *v.t.* прони́з|ывать, -а́ть

pervasive /pə'veɪsɪv/ *adj.* прони́зывающий

perverse /pə'vɜːs/ *adj.* превра́тный

perversion /pə'vɜːʃ(ə)n/ *n.* (distortion; sexual deviation) извраще́ние

perversity /pə'vɜːsɪtɪ/ *n.* превра́тность

pervert[1] /'pɜːvɜːt/ *n.* (sexual deviant) извраще́нец

pervert[2] /pə'vɜːt/ *v.t.* извра|ща́ть, -ти́ть; ~ **the course of justice** иска|жа́ть, -зи́ть ход правосу́дия

pessimism /'pesɪmɪz(ə)m/ *n.* пессими́зм

pessimist /'pesɪmɪst/ *n.* пессими́ст (-ка)

pessimistic /pesɪ'mɪstɪk/ *adj.* пессимисти́ческий; (person) пессимисти́чный

pest /pest/ *n.* (harmful creature) вреди́тель (*m.*); (of person) зану́да (*c.g.*)

pester /'pestə(r)/ *v.t.* докуча́ть (*impf.*); **he keeps ~ing me for money** он всё вре́мя пристаёт ко мне насчёт де́нег

pesticide /'pestɪsaɪd/ *n.* пестици́д

pestilence /'pestɪləns/ *n.* чума́

pet /pet/ *n.* **1** (animal, bird, etc.) пито́мец, дома́шнее живо́тное **2** (favourite) люби́м|ец (-ица), ба́ловень (*m.*); **his ~ subject** его́ излю́бленная те́ма
  ● *v.t.* (**petted, petting**) (fondle) ласка́ть, при-
  ● *v.i.* (**petted, petting**) (infml, fondle each other) обнима́ться (*impf.*)
  ■ ~ **food** *n.* корм для дома́шних живо́тных; ~ **name** *n.* ласка́тельное/уменьши́тельное и́мя

petal /'pet(ə)l/ *n.* лепесто́к

peter /'piːtə(r)/ *v.i.* (*usu.* ~ **out**) (run dry, low) исс|яка́ть, -я́кнуть; (of a path) постепе́нно исч|еза́ть, -е́знуть

petite /pə'tiːt/ *adj.* миниатю́рный

petition /pɪ'tɪʃ(ə)n/ *n.* (signed by many people) пети́ция; (application to court) исково́е заявле́ние
  ● *v.t.* (a person/an organization) под|ава́ть, -а́ть проше́ние *кому or во что*
  ● *v.i.*: ~ **for divorce** под|ава́ть, -а́ть заявле́ние о разво́де

petrif|y /'petrɪfaɪ/ *v.t.* (fig.) прив|оди́ть, -ести́ в оцепене́ние; **I was ~ied** я оцепене́л

petrochemicals /petrəʊ'kemɪk(ə)ls/ *n. pl.* нефтепроду́кты (*m. pl.*), нефтехими́ческие проду́кты (*m. pl.*)

petrol /'petr(ə)l/ *n.* (BrE) бензи́н; **fill up with ~** запр|авля́ться, -а́виться бензи́ном
  ■ ~ **pump** *n.* (at garage) бензоколо́нка; ~ **station** *n.* бензозапра́вочная ста́нция, бензоколо́нка; ~ **tank** *n.* бензоба́к

petroleum /pə'trəʊlɪəm/ *n.* нефть

petticoat /'petɪkəʊt/ *n.* ни́жняя ю́бка

p

petty /ˈpetɪ/ *adj.* (**pettier, pettiest**) **1** (trivial) ме́лкий, малова́жный **2** (small-minded) ме́лочный **3** (of small amounts): ~ **cash** де́ньги на ме́лкие расхо́ды; ~ **theft** ме́лкая кра́жа

petulance /ˈpetjʊləns/ *n.* раздражи́тельность

petulant /ˈpetjʊlənt/ *adj.* раздражи́тельный

petunia /pɪˈtjuːnɪə/ *n.* пету́ния

pew /pjuː/ *n.* (церко́вная) скамья́

pewter /ˈpjuːtə(r)/ *n.* (alloy) сплав о́лова с ме́дью/со свинцо́м; (vessels made of ~) оловя́нная посу́да
● *adj.* оловя́нный

phallic /ˈfælɪk/ *adj.* фалли́ческий
■ ~ **symbol** *n.* фалли́ческий си́мвол

phallus /ˈfæləs/ *n.* (*pl.* **phalli** /-laɪ, -lɪ/ *or* **phalluses**) фа́ллос

phantom /ˈfæntəm/ *n.* фанто́м

Pharaoh /ˈfeərəʊ/ *n.* фарао́н

pharmaceutical /faːməˈsjuːtɪk(ə)l/ *adj.* фармацевти́ческий

pharmacist /ˈfaːməsɪst/ *n.* фармаце́вт

pharmacology /faːməˈkɒlədʒɪ/ *n.* фармаколо́гия

pharmacy /ˈfaːməsɪ/ *n.* (dispensary) апте́ка; (science, practice) апте́чное де́ло

pharynx /ˈfærɪŋks/ *n.* (*pl.* **pharynges** /fəˈrɪndʒiːz/) зев; гло́тка

✐ **phase** /feɪz/ *n.* фа́за; (stage) ста́дия
● *v.t.*: a ~**d withdrawal** поэта́пный вы́вод; ~ **out** (weapons) поэта́пно сн|има́ть, -я́ть с вооруже́ния

Ph.D. *abbr.* (*of Doctor of Philosophy*) ≈ сте́пень кандида́та нау́к

pheasant /ˈfez(ə)nt/ *n.* фаза́н

phenomena /fɪˈnɒmɪnə/ *pl. of* ▶ **phenomenon**

phenomenal /fɪˈnɒmɪn(ə)l/ *adj.* феномена́льный

phenomenon /fɪˈnɒmɪnən/ *n.* (*pl.* **phenomena**) фено́мен

philanderer /fɪˈlændərə(r)/ *n.* волоки́та (*m.*)

philanthropic /filənˈθrɒpɪk/ *adj.* филантропи́ческий

philanthropist /fɪˈlænθrəpɪst/ *n.* филантро́п (-ка)

philanthropy /fɪˈlænθrəpɪ/ *n.* филантро́пия

philatelist /fɪˈlætəlɪst/ *n.* филатели́ст (-ка)

philately /fɪˈlætəlɪ/ *n.* филателия

Philippines /ˈfilɪpiːnz/ *n. pl.* (*in full* **the** ~) Филиппи́н|ы (*pl., g.* —)

philistine /ˈfilɪstaɪn/ *n.* (fig.) обыва́тель (*m.*)

philological /filəˈlɒdʒɪk(ə)l/ *adj.* языкове́дческий; филологи́ческий

philologist /fɪˈlɒlədʒɪst/ *n.* языкове́д; фило́лог

philology /fɪˈlɒlədʒɪ/ *n.* (language) языкове́дение; (language and literature) филоло́гия

philosopher /fɪˈlɒsəfə(r)/ *n.* фило́соф

philosophical /filəˈsɒfɪk(ə)l/, **philosophic** /filəˈsɒfɪk/ *adjs.* филосо́фский

philosophize /fɪˈlɒsəfaɪz/ *v.i.* филосо́фствовать (*impf.*)

philosophy /fɪˈlɒsəfɪ/ *n.* филосо́фия

phishing /ˈfɪʃɪŋ/ *n.* (comput.) фи́шинг (*рассылка электронных сообщений пользователям сети Интернет от имени солидных компаний с целью получения их личных данных*)

phlegm /flem/ *n.* (secretion) мокро́та; (fig.) флегмати́чность

phlegmatic /flegˈmætɪk/ *adj.* флегмати́чный

phobia /ˈfəʊbɪə/ *n.* фо́бия, страх

phoenix /ˈfiːnɪks/ *n.* (myth.) фе́никс

✐ **phone** /fəʊn/ *n.* (*see also* ▶ **telephone**) *n.* телефо́н
● *v.t. & i.* звони́ть, по- (*кому*)
□ ~ **back** *v.t. & i.* перезвони́ть (*pf.*)
□ ~ **up** *v.t. & i.* звони́ть, по- (*кому*)
■ ~**card** *n.* телефо́нная ка́рточка; ~ **hacker** *n.* взло́мщик мобильных телефо́нов; ~ **hacking** *n.* взлом мобильных телефо́нов; ~**in** *n.* горя́чая ли́ния в прямом эфи́ре

phonetic /fəˈnetɪk/ *adj.* фонети́ческий

phoney, phony /ˈfəʊnɪ/ (sl.) *n.* (*pl.* **phoneys** *or* **phonies**) (person) шарлата́н; (thing) подде́лка
● *adj.* (**phonier, phoniest**) подде́льный

phony /ˈfəʊnɪ/ *n. & adj.* = **phoney**

phosphate /ˈfɒsfeɪt/ *n.* фосфа́т

phosphorus /ˈfɒsfərəs/ *n.* фо́сфор

✐ **photo** /ˈfəʊtəʊ/ *n.* (*pl.* **photos**) фо́то (*nt. indecl.*), сни́мок
■ ~**call** *n.* (BrE) = photo opportunity; ~**copier** *n.* фотокопирова́льный аппара́т; ~**copy** *n.* фотоко́пия, ксероко́пия ● *v.t.* сн|има́ть, -я́ть фотоко́пию (с) + *g.*; ~ **opportunity** *n.* сеа́нс фотосъёмки, фотосе́ссия (*для прессы*)

photogenic /fəʊtəʊˈdʒenɪk/ *adj.* фотогени́чный

✐ **photograph** /ˈfəʊtəɡraːf/ *n.* фотогра́фия
● *v.t.* фотографи́ровать, с-

photographer /fəˈtɒɡrəfə(r)/ *n.* фото́граф

photographic /fəʊtəˈɡræfɪk/ *adj.* фотографи́ческий

photography /fəˈtɒɡrəfɪ/ *n.* фотогра́фия, фотосъёмка

photosynthesis /fəʊtəʊˈsɪnθɪsɪs/ *n.* фотоси́нтез

phrase /freɪz/ *n.* фра́за
● *v.t.* формули́ровать, с-
■ ~ **book** *n.* разгово́рник

phraseology /freɪzɪˈɒlədʒɪ/ *n.* фразеоло́гия

✐ **physical** /ˈfɪzɪk(ə)l/ *adj.* физи́ческий; (relating to the body): ~ **education/training** физи́ческое воспита́ние/трениро́вка; физкульту́ра; ~**ly handicapped** (sometimes offens.) физи́чески неполноце́нный; **have you had your ~ (examination)?** вы прошли́ медици́нский осмо́тр?

physician /fɪˈzɪʃ(ə)n/ *n.* врач

physicist /ˈfɪzɪsɪst/ *n.* фи́зик

physics /ˈfɪzɪks/ *n.* фи́зика

physiognomy /fɪzɪˈɒnəmɪ/ *n.* (facial features) физионо́мия

✐ ключевая лексика

physiological /ˌfɪzɪəˈlɒdʒɪk(ə)l/ *adj.*
физиологи́ческий

physiology /fɪzɪˈblədʒɪ/ *n.* физиоло́гия

physiotherapist /ˌfɪzɪəʊˈθerəpɪst/ *n.*
физиотерапе́вт

physiotherapy /ˌfɪzɪəʊˈθerəpɪ/ *n.*
физиотерапи́я

physique /fɪˈziːk/ *n.* телосложе́ние

pianist /ˈpɪənɪst/ *n.* пиани́ст (-ка)

piano /pɪˈænəʊ/ *n.* (*pl.* ∼**s**) фортепиа́но,
фортепья́но (*nt. indecl.*); (upright) пиани́но
(*nt. indecl.*)

piccolo /ˈpɪkələʊ/ *n.* (*pl.* ∼**s**) пи́кколо (*nt.
indecl.*)

⚡ **pick** /pɪk/ *n.* **1** (∼axe) кирка́ **2** (selection): take
your ∼! выбира́йте!; the ∼ of the bunch
са́мый лу́чший
● *v.t.* **1** (pluck) рвать, со-; (gather) соб|ира́ть,
-ра́ть **2** (probe) ковыря́ть (*impf.*); stop ∼ing
your nose! не ковыря́й в носу́! **3** (make
by ∼ing): he ∼ed a hole in the cloth он
продыря́вил ткань **4** (select) выбира́ть,
вы́брать; she ∼ed her way through the
mud она́ осторо́жно ступа́ла по гря́зи; the
captains ∼ed sides капита́ны определи́ли
соста́в(ы) кома́нд; he's trying to ∼ a quarrel
он и́щет по́вод(а) для ссо́ры
● *v.i.* (select) выбира́ть, вы́брать; ∼ and
choose быть разбо́рчивым
● *with preps.*: ∼ at ковыря́ть, по-; the child
∼ed at (*sc. trifled with*) his food ребёнок
поковыря́л еду́ ви́лкой; ∼ on (find fault with)
прид|ира́ться, -ра́ться к + *d.*
□ ∼ **out** *v.t.* (select): he ∼ed out the best for
himself са́мое лу́чшее он отобра́л для себя́;
(distinguish): I ∼ed him out in the crowd я узна́л
его́ в толпе́
□ ∼ **up** *v.t.* (lift) подн|има́ть, -я́ть; (acquire,
gain) приобре|та́ть, -сти́; he has ∼ed up an
American accent он приобрёл америка́нский
акце́нт; the car began to ∼ up speed маши́на
начала́ набира́ть ско́рость; (provide transport
for) заб|ира́ть, -ра́ть, под|бира́ть, -обра́ть;
I never ∼ up hitch-hikers я никогда́ не
беру́ «голосу́ющих» на доро́ге; (apprehend)
заде́рж|ивать, -а́ть; the culprit was ∼ed up
by the police престу́пник был заде́ржан
поли́цией; (resume) возобнов|ля́ть, -и́ть;
he ∼ed up the thread where he had left off
он возобнови́л бесе́ду с того́ ме́ста, где
останови́лся
● *v.i.* (recover health) опр|авля́ться, -а́виться;
поп|равля́ться, -а́виться; (improve)
ул|учша́ться, -у́чшиться; trade is ∼ing up
торго́вля оживля́ется
■ ∼**axe,** (AmE) *also* ∼**ax** *n.* кирка́; ∼**-me-up**
n. тонизи́рующее сре́дство; ∼**pocket** *n.*
карма́нник, карма́нный вор; ∼**up** *n.* (van)
пика́п

picket /ˈpɪkɪt/ *n.* (of strikers) пике́т
● *v.t.* (**picketed, picketing**) пикети́ровать
(*impf.*); the workers are ∼ing the factory
рабо́чие пикети́руют фа́брику

picking /ˈpɪkɪŋ/ *n.* **1** (gathering) сбор **2** (*in pl.*)
(remains) оста́тки (*m. pl.*); объе́дки (*m. pl.*)

pickle /ˈpɪk(ə)l/ *n.* (*usu. in pl.*) (preserved
vegetables) соле́нья (*pl.*) **2** (infml, predicament)
напа́сть
● *v.t.* маринова́ть, за-

picky /ˈpɪkɪ/ *adj.* (**pickier, pickiest**) (infml)
разбо́рчивый

picnic /ˈpɪknɪk/ *n.* пикни́к

pictorial /pɪkˈtɔːrɪəl/ *n.* иллюстри́рованное
изда́ние
● *adj.* изобрази́тельный; (illustrated)
иллюстри́рованный

⚡ **picture** /ˈpɪktʃə(r)/ *n.* **1** (depiction) карти́на;
(drawing) рису́нок; (image on TV screen) карти́нка,
изображе́ние **2** (embodiment) олицетворе́ние;
he looks the ∼ of health он пы́шет здоро́вьем
3 (infml, of information): he will soon put you in
the ∼ он вско́ре введёт вас в курс (де́ла)
4 (film) (кино)фи́льм, (кино)карти́на; (*in pl.*)
(cinema show, cinema) кино́ (*nt. indecl.*)
● *v.t.*: ∼ to yourself вообрази́те/предста́вьте
себе́
■ ∼ **book** *n.* кни́жка с карти́нками

picturesque /ˌpɪktʃəˈresk/ *adj.* живопи́сный

pie /paɪ/ *n.* пиро́г; (small one) пирожо́к

⚡ **piece** /piːs/ *n.* **1** (portion, bit) кусо́к; a ∼ of
bread кусо́к хле́ба; a ∼ of paper листо́к
бума́ги, бума́жка; to pull, tear to ∼s
раз|рыва́ть, -орва́ть на ча́сти/куски́; to go
to ∼s (of person) поддава́ться, подда́ться
эмо́циям **2** (example): a ∼ of news но́вость;
a ∼ of advice сове́т; I gave him a ∼ of
my mind я его́ отчита́л **3** (object of art etc.)
произведе́ние (иску́сства); ∼ of furniture
предме́т ме́бели **4** (chess) фигу́ра **5** (coin)
моне́та
□ ∼ **together** *v.t.* соедин|я́ть, -и́ть; (fig.)
свя́з|ывать, -а́ть
■ ∼**meal** *adj.* части́чный ● *adv.* по частя́м

pier /pɪə(r)/ *n.* (structure projecting into sea) пирс;
(landing stage) прича́л; (breakwater) мол

pierc|e /pɪəs/ *v.t.* прок|а́лывать, -оло́ть; she
had her ears ∼ed она́ проколо́ла у́ши; a ∼ing
cry пронзи́тельный крик

piercing /ˈpɪəsɪŋ/ *n.* (of body) пи́рсинг

piety /ˈpaɪtɪ/ *n.* на́божность

pig /pɪg/ *n.* (animal) свинья́; (greedy person): he
made a ∼ of himself он нае́лся, как свинья́
■ ∼**-headed** *adj.* упря́мый (как осёл); ∼**sty** *n.*
(lit., fig.) свина́рник

pigeon /ˈpɪdʒɪn/ *n.* го́лубь (*m.*)
■ ∼**hole** *n.* (compartment) отделе́ние для бума́г
● *v.t.* (categorize) классифици́ровать (*impf., pf.*)

piggy /ˈpɪgɪ/ *n.* (piglet) поросёнок
■ ∼**back** *n.*: give sb a ∼**back** носи́ть (*indet.*),
нести́ (*det.*) кого́-н на спине́; ∼ **bank** *n.*
копи́лка

piglet /ˈpɪglɪt/ *n.* поросёнок

pigment /ˈpɪgmənt/ *n.* пигме́нт

pigmentation /ˌpɪgmənˈteɪʃ(ə)n/ *n.*
пигмента́ция

pike /paɪk/ *n.* (*pl.* ∼) (fish) щу́ка

pile /paɪl/ *n.* (heap) ку́ча, гру́да; (infml, large
quantity) (*often in pl.*) ку́ча, ма́сса

p

• *v.t.* **1** (heap up) свáл|ивать, -и́ть в кýчу **2** (load) навáл|ивать, -али́ть; заставл|я́ть, -áвить

□ ~ **in** *v.i.* (infml, crowd into) наб|ивáться, -и́ться

□ ~ **up** *v.i.* (accumulate) (of objects) нагромо|ждáться, -зди́ться; (of work, debts) нак|áпливаться, -опи́ться

■ ~**up** *n.* (crash) столкновéние нéскольких маши́н

piles /paɪlz/ *n. pl.* (med.) геморрóй (*see also* ▶ pile *n.*)

pilfer /'pɪlfə(r)/ *v.t. & i.* воровáть (*impf.*)

pilgrim /'pɪlgrɪm/ *n.* палóмник

pilgrimage /'pɪlgrɪmɪdʒ/ *n.* палóмничество

pill /pɪl/ *n.* пилю́ля, таблéтка; **she is on the** ~ онá принимáет противозачáточные таблéтки

pillage /'pɪlɪdʒ/ *n.* мародёрство, грабёж
• *v.t.* грáбить, раз-
• *v.i.* мародёрствовать (*impf.*); грáбить (*impf.*)

pillar /'pɪlə(r)/ *n.* столб, колóнна

pillion /'pɪljən/ *n.*: **she rode** ~ онá éхала на зáднем сидéнье мотоци́кла

pillow /'pɪləʊ/ *n.* подýшка

■ ~**case**, ~**slip** *nn.* нáволочка

⚡ **pilot** /'paɪlət/ *n.* **1** (of aircraft) лётчи|к (-ца), пилóт **2** (*attr.*) (fig.) прóбный, óпытный
• *v.t.* (**piloted, piloting**) (lit.) пилоти́ровать (*impf.*)

■ ~ **scheme** *n.* эксперимéнт

pimp /pɪmp/ *n.* сутенёр

pimple /'pɪmp(ə)l/ *n.* прыщ, пры́щик

pimply /'pɪmplɪ/ *adj.* прыщáвый

PIN /pɪn/ *n.* (*abbr. of* **personal identification number**) персонáльный код

pin /pɪn/ *n.* **1** булáвка **2** (securing peg) прищéпка
• *v.t.* (**pinned, pinning**) **1** (fasten) прик|áлывать, -олóть; (fig.): ~ **blame on sb** свáл|ивать, -и́ть винý на когó-н. **2** (immobilize) приж|имáть, -áть; **the bandits** ~**ned him against the wall** банди́ты прижáли егó к стенé

□ ~ **down** *v.t.* (lit.) прик|áлывать, -олóть; (fig., commit to an action or opinion) прип|ирáть, -ерéть к стéнке

□ ~ **up** *v.t.* прик|áлывать, -олóть; вéшать, повéсить

■ ~**ball** *n.* (game, machine) пинбóл; ~**point** *n.* (lit.) острие булáвки • *v.t.* (fig.) тóчно определ|я́ть, -и́ть; ~**stripe (suit)** *n.* костю́м в тóнкую свéтлую полóску; ~**up** *n.* фотогрáфия красóтки (в журнáле)

pinafore /'pɪnəfɔ:(r)/ *n.* (BrE, apron) фáртук

■ ~ **dress** *n.* плáтье-сарафáн

pincers /'pɪnsəz/ *n. pl.* **1** (of crab) клешн|и́ (-éй) **2** (tech.) клéщ|и (-éй)

pinch /pɪntʃ/ *n.* **1** (nip) щипóк **2** (small amount) щепóтка
• *v.t.* **1** (squeeze) (objects) прищем|ля́ть, -и́ть; (person) щипáть, ущипнýть **2** (BrE, infml, steal) стащи́ть (*pf.*)

pine¹ /paɪn/ *n.* соснá

■ ~**apple** *n.* ананáс; ~ **cone** *n.* соснóвая ши́шка

pin|e² /paɪn/ *v.i.* **1** (languish) чáхнуть, за-; томи́ться (*impf.*); **she is** ~**ing away** онá чáхнет **2** (long): ~**e for** жáждать (*impf.*) + *g.*

ping-pong /'pɪŋpɒŋ/ *n.* пинг-пóнг

pink /pɪŋk/ *n.* (flower) гвозди́ка; (colour) рóзовый цвет
• *adj.* (of colour) рóзовый

pinnacle /'pɪnək(ə)l/ *n.* (fig.) верши́на

pint /paɪnt/ *n.* пи́нта

pioneer /paɪə'nɪə(r)/ *n.* пионéр, новáтор
• *v.t. & i.* быть пионéром (*в чём*)

pious /'paɪəs/ *adj.* нáбожный

pip /pɪp/ *n.* (BrE) сéмечко; зёрнышко

pipe /paɪp/ *n.* **1** (conduit) трубá **2** (mus. instrument) дýдка; (*in pl.*) (bagpipes) волы́нка **3** (for smoking) трýбка
• *v.t.* **1** (convey by ~s) пус|кáть, -ти́ть по трубáм **2**: ~**d music** музыкáльная трансля́ция (в обществéнном мéсте)

■ ~ **dream** *n.* несбы́точная мечтá; ~**line** *n.* (for oil) нефтепровóд; (fig.): **in the** ~**line** на подхóде (infml)

piper /'paɪpə(r)/ *n.* (bagpipe player) волы́нщи|к (-ца); **he who pays the** ~ **calls the tune** кто плáтит, тот и распоряжáется

piping /'paɪpɪŋ/ *adv.*: ~ **hot** с пы́лу, с жáру

piquancy /'pi:kənsɪ/ *n.* пикáнтность

piquant /'pi:kɑ:nt/ *adj.* пикáнтный

pique /pi:k/ *n.* досáда; **in a fit of** ~ в поры́ве раздражéния

piracy /'paɪərəsɪ/ *n.* пирáтство

pirate /'paɪərət/ *n.* пирáт; (infringer of copyright) наруши́тель (*m.*) áвторского прáва, пирáт
• *v.t.* (video, software) выпус|кáть, вы́пустить пирáтскую кóпию + *g.*

pirouette /pɪru'et/ *n.* пируэ́т

Pisces /'paɪsi:z/ *n.* (*pl.* ~) (astron., astrol.) Ры́бы (*f. pl.*)

piss /pɪs/ *v.i.* (vulg.) ссать, по- (vulg.); ~ **off!** (BrE) отвали́!; провáливай!

pissed /pɪst/ *adj.* (BrE, vulg., drunk) в жóпу пья́ный (vulg.); ~ **off** (AmE *also* ~) обозлённый

pistachio /pɪ'stɑ:ʃɪəʊ/ *n.* (*pl.* ~**s**) фистáшка

piste /pi:st/ *n.* (skiing) горнолы́жная трáсса

pistol /'pɪst(ə)l/ *n.* пистолéт

piston /'pɪst(ə)n/ *n.* пóршень (*m.*)

pit¹ /pɪt/ *n.* **1** (a large hole) котловáн; (for gravel) карьéр **2**: **the** ~**s** (sl.) хýже нéкуда
• *v.t.* (**pitted, pitting**): **he** ~**ted his wits against the law** он пытáлся обойти́ закóн

■ ~**fall** *n.* западня́, капкáн

pit² /pɪt/ *n.* (AmE, fruit stone) кóсточка

pitch¹ /pɪtʃ/ *n.* **1** (of voice or instrument) высотá **2** (BrE, area for games) пóле, площáдка
• *v.t.* **1** (set up, erect): **they** ~**ed camp for the night** они́ разби́ли нá ночь лáгерь **2** (throw) бр|осáть, -óсить **3** (mus.): **the song is** ~**ed too high for me** э́та пéсня сли́шком высокá для моегó гóлоса
• *v.i.* (of ship): **the ship was** ~**ing** корáбль испы́тывал килевýю кáчку; (of person, fall

forwards) па́дать, упа́сть на́взничь
□ ~ **in** *v.i.* (join in with vigour) горячо́/энерги́чно
бра́ться, взя́ться (*за что*)
■ ~**fork** *n.* (сенны́е) ви́л|ы (*pl., g. —*)
pitch² /pɪtʃ/ *n.* (substance) смола́
■ ~**-black** *adj.* чёрный как смоль; ~**-dark** *adj.*:
it is ~**-dark here** здесь тьма кроме́шная; здесь
темны́м-темно́ (infml)
pitcher /ˈpɪtʃə(r)/ *n.* (jug) кувши́н; (at baseball)
подаю́щий
piteous /ˈpɪtɪəs/ *adj.* жа́лкий; (voice, song, words)
жа́лобный
pith /pɪθ/ *n.* (plant tissue) сердцеви́на, мя́коть;
(essential part) суть; (vigour, force) эне́ргия, си́ла
pithy /ˈpɪθɪ/ *adj.* (**pithier, pithiest**) (fig.)
сжа́тый; содержа́тельный
pitiful /ˈpɪtɪfʊl/ *adj.* жа́лкий
pitiless /ˈpɪtɪlɪs/ *adj.* безжа́лостный
pittance /ˈpɪt(ə)ns/ *n.* жа́лкие гроши́ (*m. pl.*)
pitted /ˈpɪtɪd/ *adj.* (with its stone removed) без
ко́сточки
pituitary /pɪˈtjuːɪtərɪ/ *n.* (*in full* ~ **gland**)
гипо́физ
pity /ˈpɪtɪ/ *n.* **1** (compassion) жа́лость; **have,
take** ~ **on** сжа́литься (*pf.*) над + *i.* **2** (cause
for regret) жаль; **what a** ~! как жаль/жа́лко!
● *v.t.* жале́ть, по-
pivot /ˈpɪvət/ *v.i.* (**pivoted, pivoting**)
враща́ться (*impf.*)
pixel /ˈpɪks(ə)l/ *n.* (comput.) пи́ксель (*m.*),
элеме́нт изображе́ния
pixy, pixie /ˈpɪksɪ/ *n.* эльф
pizza /ˈpiːtsə/ *n.* пи́цца
placard /ˈplækɑːd/ *n.* плака́т
placate /pləˈkeɪt/ *v.t.* умиротвор|я́ть, -и́ть
⚔ **place** /pleɪs/ *n.* **1** ме́сто; **all over the** ~
(everywhere) повсю́ду; (in confusion) повсю́ду,
в беспоря́дке; **everything is in** ~ всё на
ме́сте; **your laughter is out of** ~ ваш
смех неуме́стен; **that put him in his** ~ э́то
поста́вило его́ на ме́сто; **he took his** ~ **in
the queue** (BrE), **in (the) line** (AmE) он за́нял
ме́сто в о́череди; (seat): **he gave up his** ~
to a lady он уступи́л своё ме́сто да́ме; (fig.,
position): **put yourself in my** ~ поста́вьте
себя́ на моё ме́сто; (fig.): **take** ~ состоя́ться
(*pf.*); име́ть (*impf.*) ме́сто; **in** ~ **of** вме́сто
+ *g.* **2** (locality) ме́сто; **in** ~**s** (here and there)
места́ми **3** (building) дом; жили́ще; ~ **of
work** ме́сто рабо́ты; **come round to my** ~!
заходи́те ко мне! **4** (position) ме́сто; **our team
took first** ~ на́ша кома́нда заняла́ пе́рвое
ме́сто; **in the first** ~ во-пе́рвых
● *v.t.* **1** (stand) ста́вить, по-; (lay) класть,
положи́ть **2** (comm.): **I** ~**d an order with them**
я сде́лал у них зака́з **3** (identify) определ|я́ть,
-и́ть; **I know those lines, but I cannot** ~ **them**
мне знако́мы э́ти стро́чки, но я не могу́
вспо́мнить, отку́да они́
■ ~ **mat** *n.* подста́вка/салфе́тка под столо́вый
прибо́р; ~ **name** *n.* географи́ческое назва́ние
placebo /pləˈsiːbəʊ/ *n.* (*pl.* ~**s**) (med.) плаце́бо
(*nt. indecl.*); имита́ция лека́рственного
сре́дства

placen|ta /pləˈsentə/ *n.* (*pl.* ~**tae** /-tiː/ *or*
~**tas**) плаце́нта
placid /ˈplæsɪd/ *adj.* споко́йный
plagiarism /ˈpleɪdʒərɪz(ə)m/ *n.* плагиа́т
plagiarize /ˈpleɪdʒəraɪz/ *v.i.* занима́ться
(*impf.*) плагиа́том
● *v.t.*: **he** ~**d my book** его́ рабо́та цели́ком
спи́сана с мое́й кни́ги
plague /pleɪɡ/ *n.* **1** (pestilence) чума́
2 (infestation): **a** ~ **of rats** наше́ствие крыс
● *v.t.* (**plagues, plagued, plaguing**)
(pester) докуча́ть (*impf.*) + *d.*
plaice /pleɪs/ *n.* (*pl.* ~) ка́мбала
plaid /plæd/ *n.* (fabric) шотла́ндка (*ткань*)
plain /pleɪn/ *n.* равни́на
● *adj.* **1** (clear) я́сный, я́вный; **her distress
was** ~ **to see** она́ я́вно страда́ла **2** (easy to
understand) я́сный, поня́тный **3** (not patterned):
~ **blue shirt** одното́нная (*or* гла́дкая) голуба́я
руба́шка; ~ **paper** нелино́ванная бума́га;
(simple, ordinary) просто́й; ~ **food** проста́я
пи́ща **4** (unattractive) некраси́вый
■ ~ **chocolate** *n.* чёрный шокола́д;
~**-clothes** *adj.* оде́тый в шта́тское; ~ **flour**
n. (BrE) мука́ без доба́вок
plaintiff /ˈpleɪntɪf/ *n.* исте́ц (-и́ца)
plaintive /ˈpleɪntɪv/ *adj.* печа́льный
plait /plæt/ *n.* (BrE) коса́
● *v.t.* запле|та́ть, -сти́
⚔ **plan** /plæn/ *n.* план; (drawing) чертёж;
(schedule): **all went according to** ~ всё прошло́
по пла́ну; (project) план, прое́кт
● *v.t.* (**planned, planning**) плани́ровать,
за-; (design) проекти́ровать, с-
● *v.i.* (**planned, planning**) намерева́ться,
плани́ровать (*both impf.*); **we must** ~ **ahead**
на́до ду́мать о бу́дущем
plane¹ /pleɪn/ *n.* (tool) руба́нок, струг
● *v.t.* строга́ть, вы́-
⚔ **plane²** /pleɪn/ *n.* **1** (flat surface) пло́скость
2 (aeroplane) самолёт **3** (fig., level of existence,
thought) у́ровень (*m.*)
⚔ **planet** /ˈplænɪt/ *n.* плане́та
plank /plæŋk/ *n.* доска́
plankton /ˈplæŋkt(ə)n/ *n.* планкто́н
⚔ **planning** /ˈplænɪŋ/ *n.* плани́рование
■ ~ **permission** *n.* (BrE) разреше́ние на
строи́тельство
⚔ **plant** /plɑːnt/ *n.* **1** (vegetable organism) расте́ние
2 (industrial machinery) обору́дование
3 (factory) заво́д
● *v.t.* **1** (put in ground) сажа́ть, посади́ть;
(seeds) се́ять, по- **2** (fig.): ~ **evidence**
подбр|а́сывать, -о́сить ули́ки; подде́л|ывать,
-ать доказа́тельства
plantation /plɑːnˈteɪʃ(ə)n/ *n.* планта́ция
planter /ˈplɑːntə(r)/ *n.* (person who plants
seeds, bulbs, trees) сажа́льщик, се́ятель (*m.*);
(of seeds only, plantation owner) планта́тор;
(agricultural machine) се́ялка; (container for plants)
декорати́вный горшо́к (для расте́ний)
plaque /plæk/ *n.* (tablet) доще́чка; (on teeth)
зубно́й ка́мень
plasma /ˈplæzmə/ *n.* пла́зма

p

■ ~ **screen** n. (TV, comput.) пла́зменный экра́н

plaster /ˈplɑːstə(r)/ n. **1** (for coating walls etc.) штукату́рка **2** (BrE, med.) пла́стырь (m.)
• v.t. **1** (wall) штукату́рить, о- **2** (cover) облеп|ля́ть, -и́ть; **his boots were ~ed with mud** его́ боти́нки бы́ли обле́плены гря́зью
■ ~ **cast** n. ги́псовый слепо́к

plasterer /ˈplɑːstərə(r)/ n. штукату́р

✍ **plastic** /ˈplæstɪk/ n. пла́стик, пластма́сса; (infml, credit card) креди́тная ка́рточка
• adj. **1** (made of ~) пластма́ссовый; пла́стиковый **2** (art) пласти́ческий
■ ~ **bag** n. полиэтиле́новый мешо́к/паке́т; ~ **surgery** n. (practice) пласти́ческая хирурги́я; (operation) пласти́ческая опера́ция

plasticine® /ˈplæstɪsiːn/ n. пластили́н

✍ **plate** /pleɪt/ n. **1** (shallow dish) (ме́лкая) таре́лка **2** (sheet of metal, glass, etc.) лист, пласти́н(к)а **3** (illustration) вкладна́я иллюстра́ция, вкле́йка **4** (in full dental ~) вставна́я че́люсть
• v.t.: **silver-~d spoons** посере́брённые ло́жки
■ ~-**glass** adj. из зерка́льного стекла́

plateau /ˈplætəʊ/ n. (pl. ~**x** /-z/ or ~**s**) плато́ (nt. indecl.)

✍ **platform** /ˈplætfɔːm/ n. **1** (at station) платфо́рма, перро́н **2** (for speakers) трибу́на; (fig., pol.) (полити́ческая) платфо́рма **3** (comput.) платфо́рма

platinum /ˈplætɪnəm/ n. пла́тина

platitude /ˈplætɪtjuːd/ n. изби́тая фра́за, бана́льность

platonic /pləˈtɒnɪk/ adj. платони́ческий

platoon /pləˈtuːn/ n. взвод

platter /ˈplætə(r)/ n. блю́до

plaudit /ˈplɔːdɪt/ n. (usu. in pl.) (applause) аплодисме́нт|ы (-ов); (praise) похвала́ (sg.)

plausibility /ˌplɔːzɪˈbɪlɪti/ n. вероя́тность, правдоподо́бие

plausible /ˈplɔːzɪb(ə)l/ adj. (statement) правдоподо́бный, вероя́тный; (person) убеди́тельный

✍ **play** /pleɪ/ n. **1** (dramatic work) пье́са; (in theatre) спекта́кль (m.) **2** (recreation) игра́; ~ **on words** игра́ слов **3** (sport): **the ball was out of** ~ мяч был вне игры́ **4** (fig., action) де́йствие, де́ятельность; **all his strength was brought into** ~ он мобилизова́л все свои́ си́лы
• v.t. **1** (perform, take part in) игра́ть, сыгра́ть в + a.; ~ **football** игра́ть (impf.) в футбо́л **2** (perform on) игра́ть, сыгра́ть на + p.; **can you ~ the piano?** вы игра́ете на роя́ле? **3** (perform piece of music) исп|олня́ть, -о́лнить; (CD) про|и́грывать, -игра́ть **4** (perpetrate): **he is always ~ing tricks on me** он всегда́ надо мно́й подшу́чивает **5** (enact role of) игра́ть, сыгра́ть **6** (cards): **he ~ed the ace** он пошёл с туза́
• v.i. игра́ть, сыгра́ть; (have fun) игра́ть, забавля́ться (both impf.); (take part in game) игра́ть (impf.); **they ~ed to win** они́ игра́ли с аза́ртом

✍ ключева́я ле́ксика

□ ~ **down** v.t. (represent as not important) преум|еньша́ть, -е́ньшить

□ ~ **up** v.i. (BrE, misbehave) распус|ка́ться, -ти́ться

■ ~**boy** n. плейбо́й; ~**ground** n. площа́дка для игр; ~**group** n. (BrE) дошко́льная гру́ппа; ~**house** n. теа́тр; ~**mate** n. прия́тель (-ница); ~-**off** n. реша́ющая встре́ча; повто́рная встре́ча по́сле ниче́йей; ~**school** n. ≈ де́тский сад; ~**thing** n. игру́шка; ~**time** n. (школьная) переме́на; ~**wright** n. драмату́рг

✍ **player** /ˈpleɪə(r)/ n. **1** (of game) игро́к; спортсме́н **2** (actor) актёр **3** (musician) исполни́тель (-ница)

playful /ˈpleɪfʊl/ adj. игри́вый, шаловли́вый

playfulness /ˈpleɪfʊlnɪs/ n. игри́вость

playing /ˈpleɪŋ/ n. игра́
■ ~ **card** n. игра́льная ка́рта; ~ **field** n. спорти́вное по́ле

plaza /ˈplɑːzə/ n. пло́щадь

PLC, plc (BrE) abbr. (of **public limited company**) откры́тая/публи́чная компа́ния с ограни́ченной отве́тственностью

plea /pliː/ n. **1** (law) заявле́ние (ответчика); **he entered a ~ of guilty** он призна́л себя́ вино́вным **2** (appeal) про́сьба

plead /pliːd/ v.t. **1** (case) вести́ (impf.) **2** (offer as excuse) ссыла́ться, сосла́ться на + a.; **the defendant ~ed insanity** подсуди́мый сосла́лся на невменя́емость **3** (declare oneself): **my client ~s (not) guilty** мой клие́нт (не) признаёт себя́ вино́вным
• v.i. приз|ыва́ть, -ва́ть; умоля́ть (impf.); **he ~ed with me to stay** он умоля́л меня́ оста́ться

pleasant /ˈplez(ə)nt/ adj. (**pleasanter, pleasantest**) прия́тный

pleasantry /ˈplezəntri/ n. (amiable remark) любе́зность

✍ **please** /pliːz/ v.t. нра́виться, по- + d.; ра́довать, по-; дост|авля́ть, -а́вить удово́льствие + d.; **I was not very ~d at, by, with the results** я был не о́чень дово́лен результа́тами; **I shall be ~d to attend** я бу́ду рад приня́ть уча́стие
• v.i. **1** (give pleasure) угожда́ть, -ди́ть **2** (think fit) изво́лить (impf.); **do as you ~** де́лайте, как хоти́те **3** (polite request): ~ **shut the door** пожа́луйста, закро́йте дверь

pleasing /ˈpliːzɪŋ/ adj. прия́тный

pleasurable /ˈpleʒərəb(ə)l/ adj. прия́тный

pleasure /ˈpleʒə(r)/ n. удово́льствие; **it's a ~!** (I'm delighted to oblige) не сто́ит!

pleat /pliːt/ n. скла́дка
• v.t.: ~**ed skirt** плиссиро́ванная ю́бка

plectr|um /ˈplektrəm/ n. (pl. ~**ums** or ~**a**) (mus., for guitar etc.) медиа́тор, плектр

pledge /pledʒ/ n. обе́т, обеща́ние
• v.t. отд|ава́ть, -а́ть в зало́г

plenteous /ˈplentiəs/ adj. оби́льный

plentiful /ˈplentifʊl/ adj. оби́льный

✍ **plenty** /ˈplenti/ n. (a lot) мно́жество; **we have ~ у** нас мно́го; **we have ~ of time to spare** у нас мно́го вре́мени в запа́се; **he has ~ of money** у него́ мно́го, де́нег;

(sufficient): that will be ∼ э́того бу́дет
доста́точно

plethora /'pleθərə/ *n.* (med.) полнокро́вие;
(fig., overabundance) избы́ток

pleurisy /'plʊərɪsɪ/ *n.* (med.) плеври́т

pliable /'plaɪəb(ə)l/ *adj.* ги́бкий

pliers /'plaɪəz/ *n. pl.* кле́щ|и (-е́й)

plight /plaɪt/ *n.* (незави́дная) у́часть

plimsoll /'plɪms(ə)l/ *n.* (BrE, light shoe): ∼s
паруси́новые ту́фли *f. pl.*

plinth /plɪnθ/ *n.* цо́коль; постаме́нт

plod /plɒd/ *v.t. & i.* (**plodded, plodding**)
тащи́ться (*impf.*)

plonk /plɒŋk/ *n.* (BrE, sl., cheap wine) дешёвое
вино́, бормоту́ха (infml)
 ● *v.t.* (infml, put down heavily) гро́х|ать, -нуть;
ба́х|ать, -нуть

✎ **plot** /plɒt/ *n.* **1** (piece of ground) уча́сток
(земли́) **2** (outline of play etc.) фа́була, сюже́т
3 (conspiracy) за́говор
 ● *v.t.* (**plotted, plotting**) **1** (conspire to
achieve): they ∼ted his ruin они́ гото́вили ему́
ги́бель **2** (mark on a graph) нан|оси́ть, -ести́
(*да́нные*) на ка́рту/гра́фик
 ● *v.i.* (**plotted, plotting**) (conspire)
организо́вывать, организова́ть (*both impf.*)
за́говор

plough /plaʊ/ (AmE **plow**) *n.* плуг
 ● *v.t.* паха́ть, вс-
 ● *v.i.* (fig.) продв|ига́ться, -и́нуться; I ∼ed
through the book я с трудо́м оси́лил кни́гу
 □ ∼ **back** *v.t.*: profits are ∼ed back прибыль
вкла́дывается в де́ло/реинвести́руется
 □ ∼ **up** *v.t.* распа́х|ивать, -а́ть

ploy /plɔɪ/ *n.* уло́вка

pluck /plʌk/ *v.t.* **1** (flowers) срыва́ть, сорва́ть
2 (bird) ощи́п|ывать, -а́ть **3** (eyebrows)
выщи́пывать, вы́щипать **4** (mus.) перебира́ть
(*impf.*) стру́ны + *g.* **5** (twitch, pull at; also v.i.)
дёр|гать, -нуть
 □ ∼ **up** *v.t.*: ∼ up courage соб|ира́ться, -ра́ться
с ду́хом

plucky /'plʌkɪ/ *adj.* (**pluckier, pluckiest**)
(infml) сме́лый, отва́жный

plug /plʌg/ *n.* **1** (stopper, e.g. of bath) про́бка,
заты́чка **2** (elec.) (connector with pins) ви́лка;
(socket) розе́тка **3** (spark ∼) свеча́ зажига́ния
4 (infml, advertisement) рекла́ма
 ● *v.t.* (**plugged, plugging**) (stop
up) зат|ыка́ть, -кну́ть; (infml, advertise)
реклами́ровать (*impf., pf.*)
 □ ∼ **in** *v.t.* включ|а́ть, -и́ть

 ■ ∼**hole** *n.* (BrE) сто́чное отве́рстие; ∼**-in** *adj.*
вставно́й

plum /plʌm/ *n.* **1** (fruit, tree) сли́ва **2** (fig.): a ∼
job тёплое месте́чко

plumage /'pluːmɪdʒ/ *n.* опере́ние

plumb /plʌm/ *adj.* (vertical) вертика́льный
 ● *adv.* (infml, exactly) то́чно; (AmE, utterly)
соверше́нно, совсе́м
 ● *v.t.* (sound) изм|еря́ть, -е́рить ло́том; (fig.):
he ∼ed the depths of absurdity он дошёл до
по́лного абсу́рда

plumber /'plʌmə(r)/ *n.* водопрово́дчик

plumbing /'plʌmɪŋ/ *n.* канализа́ция,
водопрово́дно-канализацио́нная сеть

plume /pluːm/ *n.* **1** (feather) перо́; a ∼ of
smoke шлейф ды́ма **2** (in headdress) султа́н,
плюма́ж

plummet /'plʌmɪt/ *v.i.* (**plummeted,
plummeting**) об|рыва́ться, -орва́ться

plump /plʌmp/ *adj.* пу́хлый

plunder /'plʌndə(r)/ *n.* (looting) грабёж; (loot)
добы́ча
 ● *v.t.* гра́бить, раз-

plunge /plʌndʒ/ *n.* (fig.): he took the ∼ он
реши́л: была́ не была́
 ● *v.t.* погру|жа́ть, -зи́ть; the room was ∼d
into darkness ко́мната погрузи́лась во мрак
 ● *v.i.* окун|а́ться, -у́ться

pluperfect /pluː'pɜːfɪkt/ *n.* (gram.)
плюсквамперфе́кт, давнопроше́дшее вре́мя
 ● *adj.* плюсквамперфе́ктный,
давнопроше́дший

plural /'plʊər(ə)l/ *n.* мно́жественное число́
 ● *adj.*: ∼ noun существи́тельное во
мно́жественном числе́

pluralism /'plʊərəlɪz(ə)m/ *n.* плюрали́зм

✎ **plus** /plʌs/ *n.* плюс
 ● *adj.* доба́вочный
 ● *prep.* плюс; 3 ∼ 4 is 7 три плюс четы́ре —
семь
 ■ ∼ **sign** *n.* (знак) плюс

plush /plʌʃ/ *n.* плюш
 ● *adj.* **1** (made of ∼) плю́шевый **2** (sl.,
sumptuous) (*also* **plushy**) шика́рный

plutonium /pluː'təʊnɪəm/ *n.* плуто́ний

ply¹ /plaɪ/ *n.* **1** (layer) слой; (strand) нить; three-∼
(plywood) трёхсло́йная фане́ра; three-∼ yarn
трёхни́точная пря́жа
 ■ ∼**wood** *n.* фане́ра ● *adj.* фане́рный

ply² /plaɪ/ *v.t.* **1** (work at): he plies an honest
trade он зараба́тывает на хлеб че́стным
трудо́м **2** (keep supplied) корми́ть, на-; I was
plied with food меня́ хорошо́ накорми́ли
 ● *v.i.* (travel regularly) курси́ровать (*impf.*)

PM *abbr.* (*of* **Prime Minister**) премье́р-
мини́стр

p.m. *abbr.* (*of* **post meridiem**) по́сле
полу́дня; at 3 p.m. в три часа́ дня

PMT (BrE) *abbr.* (*of* **premenstrual tension**)
предменструа́льное напряже́ние

pneumatic /njuː'mætɪk/ *adj.* пневмати́ческий
 ■ ∼ **drill** *n.* пневмати́ческий отбо́йный молото́к

pneumonia /njuː'məʊnɪə/ *n.* воспале́ние
лёгких, пневмони́я

PO *abbr.* (*of* **Post Office**) по́чта
 ■ ∼ **box** *n.* абоне́нтский я́щик

poach¹ /pəʊtʃ/ *v.t.* (cul.) _вари́ть, с- на
ме́дленном огне́; ∼ed egg яйцо́-пашо́т

poach² /pəʊtʃ/ *v.t. & i.*: ∼ game занима́ться
(*impf.*) браконье́рством; браконье́рствовать
(*impf.*)

poacher /'pəʊtʃə(r)/ *n.* браконье́р

pocket /'pɒkɪt/ *n.* **1** (in clothing) карма́н **2** (at
billiards) лу́за **3** (*attr.*) (miniature) карма́нный

● *v.t.* (**pocketed, pocketing**) класть, положи́ть в карма́н
■ ~**book** *n.* (AmE, handbag) су́мочка; (AmE, wallet) бума́жник; ~**knife** *n.* карма́нный но́ж(ик); ~ **money** *n.* (BrE) карма́нные де́н｜ьги (-ег)
pod /pɒd/ *n.* стручо́к
podgy /ˈpɒdʒɪ/ *adj.* (**podgier, podgiest**) (BrE) то́лстенький, призе́мистый
podium /ˈpəʊdɪəm/ *n.* возвыше́ние/по́диум
♂ **poem** /ˈpəʊɪm/ *n.* стихотворе́ние; (long narrative) поэ́ма
poet /ˈpəʊɪt/ *n.* поэ́т
poetic /pəʊˈetɪk/ *adj.* поэти́ческий
poetry /ˈpəʊɪtrɪ/ *n.* (also fig.) поэ́зия
pogrom /ˈpɒɡrəm/ *n.* погро́м
poignant /ˈpɔɪnjənt/ *adj.* о́стрый, го́рький
♂ **point** /pɔɪnt/ *n.* **1** (sharp end) остриё **2** (tip) ко́нчик **3** (promontory) мыс **4** (dot) то́чка; **decimal** ~ (in Russian usage) запята́я (*отделяющая десятичную дробь от целого числа*); **two** ~ **five (2.5)** две це́лых (и) пять деся́тых **5** (mark, position) ме́сто, пункт; ~ **of view** то́чка зре́ния **6** (moment) моме́нт; **at this** ~ **he turned round** в э́тот моме́нт/тут он поверну́лся; **I was on the** ~ **of leaving** я уже́ собра́лся уходи́ть **7** (unit, e.g. on shares index) едини́ца; **up to a** ~ до изве́стной сте́пени **8** (unit of evaluation) пункт, очко́; **they won on** ~s они́ вы́играли по очка́м **9** (chief idea, meaning, purpose) суть, вопро́с, смысл; **that is beside the** ~ не в э́том суть/де́ло; **come to the** ~ до|ходи́ть, -йти́ до гла́вного/су́ти (де́ла); **I don't see the** ~ **of the joke** э́та шу́тка мне непоня́тна; **I made a** ~ **of seeing him** я счёл необходи́мым повида́ться с ним; **you missed the** ~ вы не по́няли су́ти (де́ла); **there was no** ~ **in staying** не име́ло смы́сла остава́ться; **what's the** ~ **of it?** како́й в э́том смысл? **10** (item) пункт; **we agree on certain** ~s по не́которым пу́нктам мы схо́димся **11** (quality) черта́; **singing is not my strong** ~ я не силён в пе́нии
● *v.t.* ука́з|ывать, -а́ть; пока́з|ывать, -а́ть; **he** ~**ed a gun at her** он навёл на неё пистоле́т
● *v.i.* ука́з|ывать, -а́ть (**at, to:** на + *a.*); **everything** ~**s to his guilt** всё ука́зывает на его́ вину́
□ ~ **out** *v.t.* ука́з|ывать, -а́ть на + *a.*
■ ~-**blank** *adj.* (lit.) прямо́й; (fig.) категори́ческий
● *adv.* пря́мо, в упо́р
pointed /ˈpɔɪntɪd/ *adj.* **1** (e.g. a stick) остроко́нечный **2** (significant) о́стрый, ко́лкий; подчёркнутый
pointer /ˈpɔɪntə(r)/ *n.* **1** (of balance etc.) стре́лка, указа́тель (*m.*) **2** (indication) намёк
pointing /ˈpɔɪntɪŋ/ *n.* (of wall etc.) расши́вка швов
pointless /ˈpɔɪntlɪs/ *adj.* бессмы́сленный
poise /pɔɪz/ *n.* уравнове́шенность, самооблада́ние
● *v.t.*: **he is** ~**d to attack** он гото́в к нападе́нию
poison /ˈpɔɪz(ə)n/ *n.* яд, отра́ва
● *v.t.* (lit., fig.) отравля́ть, -и́ть; **food** ~**ing** пищево́е отравле́ние; **he has food** ~**ing** он отрави́лся
poisonous /ˈpɔɪz(ə)nəs/ *adj.* ядови́тый; (fig.) вре́дный
poke /pəʊk/ *n.* толчо́к
● *v.t.* **1** (prod) ты́кать, ткнуть; **to** ~ **the fire** меша́ть, по- у́гли в ками́не **2** (thrust) пиха́ть, пихну́ть/сова́ть, су́нуть; **he** ~**d his tongue out** он вы́сунул язы́к; **he** ~**s his nose into other people's business** он суёт нос не в своё де́ло
● *v.i.*: **he** ~**d about among the rubbish** он ры́лся в му́соре
poker /ˈpəʊkə(r)/ *n.* **1** (for a fire) кочерга́ **2** (game) по́кер
■ ~-**faced** *adj.* с ка́менным лицо́м
poky /ˈpəʊkɪ/ *adj.* (**pokier, pokiest**) (infml) те́сный
Poland /ˈpəʊlənd/ *n.* По́льша
polar /ˈpəʊlə(r)/ *adj.* поля́рный
■ ~ **bear** *n.* бе́лый медве́дь
Pole /pəʊl/ *n.* (person) поля́к (по́лька)
pole[1] /pəʊl/ *n.* (of earth, elec., and fig.) по́люс
■ **P**~ **Star** *n.* Поля́рная звезда́
pole[2] /pəʊl/ *n.* (post) столб, шест
■ ~ **vault** *n.* прыжо́к с шесто́м; ~-**vaulter** *n.* прыгу́н (-нья) с шесто́м, шестови́к
polemic /pəˈlemɪk/ *n.* поле́мика, спор
● *adj.* (*also* **polemical**) полеми́ческий, спо́рный
♂ **police** /pəˈliːs/ *n.* поли́ция; (in Russia) мили́ция
● *v.t.* охраня́ть, подде́рживать (*both impf.*) поря́док в (+ *p.*)
■ ~ **constable** *n.* (BrE) полице́йский; ~ **force** *n.* поли́ция; ~ **man** *n.* полице́йский; (in Russia) милиционе́р; ~ **officer** *n.* полице́йский; ~ **station** *n.* (полице́йский) уча́сток; (in Russia) отделе́ние мили́ции; ~-**woman** *n.* же́нщина-полице́йский/милиционе́р
♂ **policy** /ˈpɒlɪsɪ/ *n.* (planned action) поли́тика; (insurance) (страхово́й) по́лис
■ ~-**holder** *n.* держа́тель (*m.*) страхово́го по́лиса
polio /ˈpəʊlɪəʊ/ *n.* полиомиели́т
Polish /ˈpəʊlɪʃ/ *n.* (language) по́льский язы́к
● *adj.* по́льский
polish /ˈpɒlɪʃ/ *n.* **1** (brightness) полиро́вка **2** (substance used for ~ing) полирова́льная па́ста **3** (fig., refinement) лоск, блеск
● *v.t.* полирова́ть, от-; (metal, also fig.) шлифова́ть, от-
□ ~ **off** *v.t.* (infml, finish) разде́л|ываться, -аться с + *i.*; поко́нчить (*pf.*) с + *i.*
polite /pəˈlaɪt/ *adj.* (**politer, politest**) ве́жливый
politic /ˈpɒlɪtɪk/ *adj.* **1** (prudent) благоразу́мный **2**: **the body** ~ госуда́рство
♂ **political** /pəˈlɪtɪk(ə)l/ *adj.* полити́ческий; ~**ly correct** полит(и́чески)корре́ктный
■ ~ **correctness** *n.* полит(и́ческая) корре́ктность; ~ **prisoner** *n.* полит(и́ческий) заключённый
♂ **politician** /ˌpɒlɪˈtɪʃ(ə)n/ *n.* поли́тик
politicize /pəˈlɪtɪsaɪz/ *v.t.* политизи́ровать (*impf., pf.*)

♂ ключева́я ле́ксика

✍ **politics** /'pɒlɪtɪks/ *n.* поли́тика; (political views) полити́ческие взгля́ды (*m. pl.*) /убежде́ния (*nt. pl.*)

✍ **poll** /pəʊl/ *n.* (voting process) голосова́ние; (opinion canvass) опро́с
● *v.t.* **1** (receive) получ|а́ть, -и́ть/наб|ира́ть, -ра́ть **2** (take votes of): **they ~ed the meeting** они́ поста́вили вопро́с на голосова́ние

pollen /'pɒlən/ *n.* цвето́чная пыльца́

pollinate /'pɒlɪneɪt/ *v.t.* опыл|я́ть, -и́ть

polling /'pəʊlɪŋ/ *n.* голосова́ние
■ **~ booth** *n.* (BrE) каби́на для голосова́ния; **~ day** *n.* день вы́боров; **~ station** *n.* избира́тельный уча́сток

pollutant /pə'lu:tənt/ *n.* загрязни́тель (*m.*)

pollute /pə'lu:t/ *v.t.* загрязн|я́ть, -и́ть

pollution /pə'lu:ʃ(ə)n/ *n.* загрязне́ние

polo /'pəʊləʊ/ *n.* по́ло (*nt. indecl.*)
■ **~ neck** *n.* (BrE) сви́тер с кру́глым высо́ким воротнико́м

polyester /pɒlɪ'estə(r)/ *n.* (fabric) полиэ́стер

polygamy /pə'lɪɡəmɪ/ *n.* полига́мия

polygon /'pɒlɪɡɒn/ *n.* многоуго́льник

Polynesia /pɒlɪ'ni:ʒə/ *n.* Полине́зия

Polynesian /pɒlɪ'ni:ʒ(ə)n/ *n.* полинези́|ец (~йка)
● *adj.* полинези́йский

polyp /'pɒlɪp/ *n.* (zool., med.) поли́п

polystyrene /pɒlɪ'staɪri:n/ *n.* полистиро́л

polytechnic /pɒlɪ'teknɪk/ *n.* политехни́ческий институ́т

polythene /'pɒlɪθi:n/ *n.* (BrE) полиэтиле́н; (*attr.*) полиэтиле́новый

polyurethane /pɒlɪ'jʊərəθeɪn/ *n.* полиурета́н

pomegranate /'pɒmɪɡrænɪt/ *n.* (tree, fruit) грана́т

pomp /pɒmp/ *n.* пы́шность, по́мпа

pompom /'pɒmpɒm/, **pompon** /'pɒmpɒn/ *nn.* (tuft) помпо́н

pomposity /pɒm'pɒsɪtɪ/ *n.* помпе́зность; (of person) напы́щенность

pompous /'pɒmpəs/ *adj.* помпе́зный; (of person) напы́щенный

poncho /'pɒntʃəʊ/ *n.* (*pl.* **~s**) по́нчо (*nt. indecl.*)

pond /pɒnd/ *n.* пруд

ponder /'pɒndə(r)/ *v.t.* обду́м|ывать, -ать
● *v.i.* размышля́ть (*impf.*)

pong /pɒŋ/ *n.* (BrE, infml) вонь, злово́ние

pontiff /'pɒntɪf/ *n.*: **supreme ~** (the Pope) Па́па Ри́мский

pontificate /pɒn'tɪfɪkeɪt/ *v.i.* (fig., speak pompously) веща́ть (*impf.*) (*говори́ть ва́жно, напы́щенно*)

pony /'pəʊnɪ/ *n.* (horse) по́ни (*m. indecl.*)
■ **~tail** *n.* хво́стик (*причёска*)

poodle /'pu:d(ə)l/ *n.* пу́дель (*m.*)

✍ **pool¹** /pu:l/ *n.* (small body of water) пруд; (puddle) лу́жа; (*in full* **swimming ~**) (пла́вательный) бассе́йн

pool² /pu:l/ *n.* **1** (total of staked money) совоку́пность ста́вок; (in cards) банк; **football ~s** футбо́льный тотализа́тор **2** (common reserve) о́бщий фонд **3** (billiards game) пул
● *v.t.* объедин|я́ть, -и́ть (в о́бщий фонд)

✍ **poor** /pɔ:ə(r)/ *n.* (*collect.*): **the ~** беднота́, бедняки́ (*m. pl.*), бе́дные (*pl.*)
● *adj.* **1** (indigent) бе́дный **2** (unfortunate) бе́дный, несча́стный **3** (small) ску́дный; плохо́й; **a ~ harvest** ни́зкий урожа́й **4** (of low quality) плохо́й; **~ health** плохо́е здоро́вье

poorly /'pɔ:əlɪ/ *adj.* (BrE) нездоро́вый
● *adv.* пло́хо; **this book is ~ written** э́та кни́га пло́хо напи́сана

pop¹ /pɒp/ *n.* (explosive sound) щелчо́к, хлопо́к; (infml, gaseous drink) газиро́вка
● *adv.*: **the balloon went ~** ша́рик ло́пнул
● *v.t.* (**popped**, **popping**) **1** (cause to explode): **~ a balloon** прок|а́лывать, -оло́ть ша́рик **2** (put suddenly) сова́ть, су́нуть
● *v.i.* (**popped**, **popping**) (make explosive sound) хло́п|ать, -нуть, щёлк|ать, -нуть
● *with advs.* (infml): **they ~ped in for a drink** они́ заскочи́ли/забежа́ли вы́пить; **she kept ~ping out all day** она́ весь день куда́-то выска́кивала; **he ~ped up unexpectedly** он появи́лся неожи́данно
■ **~corn** *n.* попко́рн, возду́шная кукуру́за; **~-up** *n.* (comput.) всплыва́ющее окно́

✍ **pop²** /pɒp/ *n.* (infml, music) поп-му́зыка
● *adj.*: **~ group** поп-гру́ппа; **~ star** поп-звезда́

pope /pəʊp/ *n.* (*also* **the Pope**) Па́па Ри́мский (*m.*)

poplar /'pɒplə(r)/ *n.* то́поль (*m.*)

poppy /'pɒpɪ/ *n.* мак
■ **~ seed** *n.* мак

populace /'pɒpjʊləs/ *n.* (the masses) ма́ссы (*f. pl.*)

✍ **popular** /'pɒpjʊlə(r)/ *adj.* **1** (of the people) наро́дный **2** (of or for the masses): **the ~ press** ма́ссовая пре́сса/печа́ть **3** (generally liked) по́льзующийся о́бщей симпа́тией; **he is ~ with the ladies** он име́ет успе́х у же́нщин

popularity /pɒpjʊ'lærɪtɪ/ *n.* популя́рность; успе́х

popularize /'pɒpjʊləraɪz/ *v.t.* популяризи́ровать (*impf., pf.*)

populate /'pɒpjʊleɪt/ *v.t.* насел|я́ть, -и́ть

✍ **population** /pɒpjʊ'leɪʃ(ə)n/ *n.* населе́ние; жи́тели (*m. pl.*)

populous /'pɒpjʊləs/ *adj.* многолю́дный, густонаселённый

porcelain /'pɔ:səlɪn/ *n.* фарфо́р; (*attr.*) фарфо́ровый

porch /pɔ:tʃ/ *n.* (covered entrance) крыльцо́; (AmE, veranda) вера́нда

porcupine /'pɔ:kjʊpaɪn/ *n.* дикобра́з

pore¹ /pɔ:(r)/ *n.* по́ра

pore² /pɔ:(r)/ *v.i.*: **he likes to ~ over old books** он лю́бит сиде́ть над ста́рыми кни́гами

pork /pɔ:k/ *n.* свини́на

porn /pɔ:n/, **porno** /'pɔ:nəʊ/ *nn.* (infml) порногра́фия, по́рно (*nt. indecl.*) (infml), порну́ха (infml)

pornographic /pɔ:nə'ɡræfɪk/ *adj.* порнографи́ческий

p

pornography /pɔːˈnɒgrəfɪ/ n. порногра́фия

porridge /ˈpɒrɪdʒ/ n. овся́ная ка́ша

port[1] /pɔːt/ n. (harbour) порт, га́вань; ~ of call порт захо́да

port[2] /pɔːt/ n. (wine) портве́йн

port[3] /pɔːt/ n. (comput.) порт

port[4] /pɔːt/ n. (left side) ле́вый борт
● adj. ле́вый; ~ side ле́вый борт; ~ wind ве́тер с ле́вого бо́рта

portable /ˈpɔːtəb(ə)l/ adj. портати́вный

portal /ˈpɔːt(ə)l/ n. (comput.) порта́л

portcullis /pɔːtˈkʌlɪs/ n. опускна́я решётка

portend /pɔːˈtend/ v.t. предвеща́ть (impf.)

portent /ˈpɔːt(ə)nt/ n. (omen) предзнаменова́ние; (marvel) чу́до

porter /ˈpɔːtə(r)/ n. **1** (carrier of luggage) носи́льщик **2** (AmE, sleeping car attendant) проводни́к **3** (BrE, doorkeeper) швейца́р

portfolio /pɔːtˈfəʊlɪəʊ/ n. (pl. ~s) **1** (case) портфе́ль (m.); (artist's) па́пка (с образца́ми рабо́т); (fashion model's) портфо́лио (nt. indecl.) **2** (pol., fin.) портфе́ль (m.)

porthole /ˈpɔːthəʊl/ n. иллюмина́тор

portion /ˈpɔːʃ(ə)n/ n. (part, share) часть; до́ля; (of food) по́рция

portly /ˈpɔːtlɪ/ adj. (**portlier**, **portliest**) доро́дный, по́лный, ту́чный

portrait /ˈpɔːtrɪt/ n. портре́т

portray /pɔːˈtreɪ/ v.t. (depict, describe) рисова́ть, на- портре́т + g.; (act part of) игра́ть, сыгра́ть

portrayal /pɔːˈtreɪəl/ n. изображе́ние

Portugal /ˈpɔːtjʊg(ə)l/ n. Португа́лия

Portuguese /pɔːtjʊˈgiːz/ n. (pl. ~) **1** (person) португа́л|ец (-ка) **2** (language) португа́льский язы́к
● adj. португа́льский

pose /pəʊz/ n. по́за
● v.t. (put forward) предл|ага́ть, -ожи́ть; изл|ага́ть, -ожи́ть
● v.i. **1** (take up a position) пози́ровать (impf.); he ~s as an expert он выдаёт себя́ за знатока́/специали́ста **2** (behave in an affected way) рисова́ться (impf.)

poser /ˈpəʊzə(r)/ n. (problem) головоло́мка; (person) позёр

posh /pɒʃ/ adj. (infml) шика́рный; (people) све́тский

position /pəˈzɪʃ(ə)n/ n. **1** (place occupied by sb or sth) ме́сто, положе́ние **2** (situation) положе́ние; that puts me in an awkward ~ э́то ста́вит меня́ в неудо́бное/нело́вкое положе́ние; I am not in a ~ to say я не в состоя́нии сказа́ть **3** (attitude, opinion) пози́ция **4** (post) до́лжность, ме́сто
● v.t. поме|ща́ть, -сти́ть

positive /ˈpɒzɪtɪv/ adj. **1** (definite) несомне́нный, определённый **2** (certain) уве́ренный, убеждённый; are you ~ you saw him? вы уве́рены, что ви́дели его́? **3** (assertive) самоуве́ренный **4** (practical, helpful) позити́вный, констукти́вный

5 (gram., math., elec., med.) положи́тельный
■ ~ **discrimination** n. дискримина́ция в по́льзу определённой гру́ппы

positively /ˈpɒzɪtɪvlɪ/ adv. (with conviction) с уве́ренностью; (definitely) несомне́нно; (for emphasis): she was ~ rude to me она́ была́ со мной про́сто груба́

possess /pəˈzes/ v.t. **1** (own, have) владе́ть (impf.) + i.; (good qualities) облада́ть (impf.) + i. **2** (influence) овлад|ева́ть, -е́ть; whatever ~ed him to do that? что его́ заста́вило поступи́ть таки́м о́бразом?

possession /pəˈzeʃ(ə)n/ n. **1** (ownership, occupation) владе́ние; they took ~ of the house они́ ста́ли владе́льцами до́ма **2** (property) иму́щество, со́бственность

possessive /pəˈzesɪv/ n. (gram.) притяжа́тельный паде́ж
● adj. **1** (gram.) притяжа́тельный **2** (of person) со́бственнический; (jealous) ревни́вый

⚜ **possibility** /pɒsɪˈbɪlɪtɪ/ n. возмо́жность; вероя́тность

⚜ **possible** /ˈpɒsɪb(ə)l/ adj. возмо́жный; as soon as ~ как мо́жно скоре́е; I have done everything ~ to help я сде́лал всё возмо́жное, что́бы помо́чь

⚜ **possibly** /ˈpɒsɪblɪ/ adv. возмо́жно; how can I ~ do that? как же я могу́ э́то сде́лать?; I can't ~ я ника́к не смогу́

⚜ **post**[1] /pəʊst/ n. (of wood, metal, etc.) столб
● v.t. (display publicly) выве́шивать, вы́весить; the results will be ~ed (up) on the board результа́ты бу́дут вы́вешены на доске́

⚜ **post**[2] /pəʊst/ n. (BrE, mail) по́чта; by return of ~ с обра́тной по́чтой; I must take these letters to the ~ я до́лжен отнести́ э́ти пи́сьма на по́чту; if you hurry you will catch the ~ е́сли вы поспеши́те, то успе́ете до отпра́вки по́чты; has the ~ come yet? по́чта уже́ была́/пришла́?
● v.t. **1** (BrE, dispatch by mail) отпр|авля́ть, -а́вить по по́чте **2** (fig.) изве|ща́ть, -сти́ть; keep me ~ed (of events) держи́те меня́ в ку́рсе (дел)
■ ~**box** n. почто́вый я́щик; ~**card** n. откры́тка; ~**code** n. (BrE) почто́вый и́ндекс; ~**man** n. (BrE) почтальо́н; ~**mark** n. почто́вый штемпель; ~ **office** n. по́чта; ~**woman** n. (BrE) почтальо́н, почтальо́нка (infml)

⚜ **post**[3] /pəʊst/ n. **1** (place of duty) пост; at one's ~ на посту́ **2** (job) до́лжность, пост
● v.t. **1** (assign to place of duty) назн|ача́ть, -а́чить на до́лжность **2** (mil., guard, sentry) выставля́ть, вы́ставить

postage /ˈpəʊstɪdʒ/ n. почто́вые расхо́ды (m. pl.); почто́вый сбор

postal /ˈpəʊst(ə)l/ adj. почто́вый
■ ~ **order** n. (BrE) (де́нежный) почто́вый перево́д

post-date /pəʊstˈdeɪt/ v.t. **1** (give a date later than the actual one) дати́ровать (impf.) бо́лее по́здним число́м **2** (occur later than) сле́довать, по- за + i.

poste-haste /pəʊstˈheɪst/ adv. о́чень бы́стро, неме́дленно

poster /'pəʊstə(r)/ n. (placard) афи́ша, плака́т; (advertising) по́стер

posterior /pɒ'stɪərɪə(r)/ n. зад
● adj. (subsequent) после́дующий; (behind) за́дний

posterity /pɒ'sterɪtɪ/ n. пото́мк|и (-ов)

postgraduate /pəʊst'grædjʊət/ n.: ~ student аспира́нт (-ка)
● adj. аспира́нтский

posthumous /'pɒstjʊməs/ adj. посме́ртный

post-impressionism /pəʊstɪm'preʃənɪz(ə)m/ n. постимпрессиони́зм

postmodern /pəʊst'mɒd(ə)n/ adj. постмодерни́стский

postmodernism /pəʊst'mɒdənɪz(ə)m/ n. постмодерни́зм

post-mortem /pəʊst'mɔːtəm/ n. вскры́тие (тру́па), аутопси́я

postnatal /pəʊst'neɪt(ə)l/ adj. послеродово́й

post-operative /pəʊst'ɒpərətɪv/ adj. послеоперацио́нный

postpone /pəʊs'pəʊn/ v.t. отсро́чи|вать, -ть; от|кла́дывать, -ложи́ть

postscript /'pəʊskrɪpt/ n. постскри́птум

postulate /'pɒstjʊleɪt/ v.t. постули́ровать (impf., pf.)

posture /'pɒstʃə(r)/ n. оса́нка
● v.i. пози́ровать (impf.)

post-war /pəʊst'wɔː(r)/ adj. послевое́нный

posy /'pəʊzɪ/ n. буке́т цвето́в

pot¹ /pɒt/ n. горшо́к; ~s and pans ку́хонная посу́да/у́тварь; a ~ of tea ча́йник с зава́ренным ча́ем; his work is going to ~ (infml) его́ рабо́та идёт наскма́рку
● v.t. (**potted**, **potting**) **1** (preserves) консерви́ровать, за- **2** (plants) сажа́ть, посади́ть в горшо́к **3** (fig., abridge): ~ted history кра́ткая исто́рия **4** (billiards) заг|оня́ть, -на́ть в лу́зу
■ ~ belly n. (большо́й) живо́т, пу́зо; ~hole n. (in road) вы́боина; ~holing n. (BrE) спелеоло́гия; ~ plant n. (BrE) горше́чное расте́ние

pot² /pɒt/ n. (infml, marijuana) анаша́

potash /'pɒtæʃ/ n. пота́ш, углеки́слый ка́лий

potassium /pə'tæsɪəm/ n. ка́лий; (attr.) ка́лиевый, кали́йный

potato /pə'teɪtəʊ/ n. (pl. ~es) (collect., and in pl.) карто́фель (m.); (single ~) карто́фелина
■ ~ chips (AmE), ~ crisps (BrE) nn. pl. хрустя́щий карто́фель, чи́пс|ы (pl., g. -ов)

potent /'pəʊt(ə)nt/ adj. (powerful) си́льный, могу́щественный; (of alcoholic drink) кре́пкий

potential /pə'tenʃ(ə)l/ n. потенциа́л
● adj. потенциа́льный

potion /'pəʊʃ(ə)n/ n. насто́йка, сна́добье; love ~ любо́вный напи́ток

potter¹ /'pɒtə(r)/ n. гонча́р

potter² /'pɒtə(r)/ v.i. (e.g. in garden) копа́ться, ковыря́ться (both impf.)

pottery /'pɒtərɪ/ n. кера́мика

potty¹ /'pɒtɪ/ n. (infml, chamber pot) горшо́к

potty² /'pɒtɪ/ adj. (**pottier**, **pottiest**) (BrE, crazy) чо́кнутый (infml)

pouch /paʊtʃ/ n. су́мочка, мешо́чек; (kangaroo's) су́мка

pouffe, **pouf** /puːf/ n. (seat) пуф

poultry /'pəʊltrɪ/ n. дома́шняя пти́ца (collect.)

pounce /paʊns/ v.i. набр|а́сываться, -о́ситься; the cat ~d on the mouse ко́шка бро́силась на мышь

pound¹ /paʊnd/ n. **1** (weight) фунт **2** (money) фунт (сте́рлингов)

pound² /paʊnd/ n. (enclosure) заго́н

pound³ /paʊnd/ v.t. **1** (crush) разб|ива́ть, -и́ть **2** (thump) колоти́ть (impf.)
● v.i. **1** (thump): he ~ed at the door он колоти́л в дверь; her heart was ~ing with excitement её се́рдце колоти́лось от волне́ния **2** (run heavily) мча́ться/нести́сь (both impf.) с гро́хотом

pour /pɔː(r)/ v.t. лить (impf.); нал|ива́ть, -и́ть; will you ~ me (out) a cup of tea? нале́йте мне, пожа́луйста, ча́шку ча́я; (fig.): he ~ed scorn on the idea он вы́смеял э́ту иде́ю
● v.i. ли́ться (impf.); (fig.): the crowd ~ed out of the theatre толпа́ повали́ла из теа́тра (infml); (of rain) лить (impf.); it was ~ing with rain шёл проливно́й дождь, дождь лил как из ведра́
■ with advs. (fig.): letters ~ed in посы́пались пи́сьма; she ~ed out a tale of woe она́ излила́ своё го́ре

pout /paʊt/ v.i. над|ува́ть, -у́ть гу́бы; ду́ться, на-

poverty /'pɒvətɪ/ n. бе́дность, нищета́; on the ~ line на гра́ни нищеты́
■ ~-stricken adj. ни́щий

POW abbr. (of **prisoner of war**) военнопле́нный

powder /'paʊdə(r)/ n. (chem., med., etc.) порошо́к; (cosmetic) пу́дра
● v.t. **1** (reduce to ~) превра|ща́ть, -ти́ть в порошо́к **2** (apply ~ to) пу́дрить, на-
■ ~ed milk n. порошко́вое/сухо́е молоко́

powdery /'paʊdərɪ/ adj. порошкообра́зный; рассы́пчатый

power /'paʊə(r)/ n. **1** (ability, capacity) си́ла, мощь; purchasing ~ покупа́тельная спосо́бность **2** (in pl.) (faculties): he was at the height of his ~s он был в расцве́те сил **3** (vigour) эне́ргия **4** (electrical energy) эне́ргия; there was a ~ cut электроэне́ргию вре́менно отключи́ли; (mechanical energy) мо́щность **5** (control) власть; I have him in my ~ он в мое́й вла́сти; in ~ у вла́сти **6** (right) полномо́чия (nt. pl.), пра́во **7** (influential person or organization) си́ла **8** (state) держа́ва **9** (supernatural force) си́ла **10** (infml, large amount) ма́сса, мно́жество; this medicine has done me a ~ of good э́то лека́рство принесло́ мне огро́мную по́льзу **11** (math.): two to the ~ of ten два в деся́той сте́пени
● v.t. (supply with electrical energy) снаб|жа́ть, -ди́ть эне́ргией; (supply with mechanical energy) прив|оди́ть, -ести́ в де́йствие

p

■ **~boat** *n.* мото́рный ка́тер; **~ drill** *n.* электри́ческая дрель; **~ line** *n.* ли́ния электропереда́чи; **~point** *n.* (BrE) штепсельная розе́тка; **~ plant, ~ station** *nn.* электроста́нция

✓ **powerful** /'pauəful/ *adj.* си́льный, мо́щный; **a ~ speech** я́ркая речь

powerless /'pauəlıs/ *adj.* бесси́льный

pp *abbr.* (*of* **per procurationem**): **John Brown pp A. Smith** по дове́ренности Джо́на Бра́уна подписа́л А. Смит

pp. *abbr.* (*of* **pages**) стр./сс. (страни́цы)

PR *abbr. of* **1** (**public relations**) пиа́р **2** (**proportional representation**) пропорциона́льное представи́тельство

practicable /'præktıkəb(ə)l/ *adj.* (feasible) осуществи́мый, реа́льный

✓ **practical** /'præktık(ə)l/ *adj.* **1** (concerned with practice) практи́ческий; **a ~ joke** ро́зыгрыш, шу́тка; **he is a ~ man** он практи́чный челове́к **2** (workable, feasible) осуществи́мый, реа́льный

practicality /præktı'kælıtı/ *n.* практи́чность

practically /'præktıkəlı/ *adv.* **1** (in a practical manner) практи́чески; на де́ле **2** (almost) практи́чески, факти́чески

✓ **practice** /'præktıs/ *n.* **1** (performance) пра́ктика; **the idea will not work in ~** э́та иде́я на пра́ктике неосуществи́ма **2** (habitual performance) обы́чай, обыкнове́ние **3** (repeated exercise) упражне́ние, трениро́вка, пра́ктика; **I am badly out of ~** я давно́ не упражня́лся/ практикова́лся **4** (work of doctor, lawyer, etc.) пра́ктика
● *v.t. & i.* (AmE) = **practise**

✓ **practis|e** /'præktıs/ (AmE **practice**) *v.t.* **1** (perform habitually) де́лать, с- по привы́чке; (for exercise) упражня́ть (*impf.*) отраба́|тывать, -о́тать; (sport, game, etc.) упражня́ться (*impf.*) в + *p.*; (instrument): **she was ~ing the piano** она́ упражня́лась на роя́ле/фортепиа́но **2** (a profession etc.) практикова́ть (*impf.*); **a ~ing physician** практику́ющий врач
● *v.i.* упражня́ться (*impf.*); тренирова́ться (*impf.*)

practitioner /præk'tıʃənə(r)/ *n.* практику́ющий специали́ст

pragmatic /præg'mætık/ *adj.* прагмати́ческий

pragmatism /'prægmətız(ə)m/ *n.* прагмати́зм

pragmatist /'prægmətıst/ *n.* прагма́тик

Prague /prɑːɡ/ *n.* Пра́га

prairie /'preərı/ *n.* пре́рия

✓ **praise** /preız/ *n.* похвала́
● *v.t.* (voice admiration of) хвали́ть, по-; (give glory to) восхвал|я́ть, -и́ть
■ **~worthy** *adj.* досто́йный похвалы́, похва́льный

pram /præm/ *n.* (BrE) (де́тская) коля́ска

prance /prɑːns/ *v.i.* (of horse) гарцева́ть (*impf.*); (of person) ва́жничать (*impf.*)

prank /præŋk/ *n.* вы́ходка, проде́лка

prankster /'præŋkstə(r)/ *n.* шутни́к, прока́зник

prat /præt/ *n.* (BrE, infml, idiot) идио́т (-ка)

prattle /'præt(ə)l/ *n.* болтовня́; (childish) ле́пет
● *v.i.* болта́ть (*impf.*); (of child) лепета́ть, про-

prawn /prɔːn/ *n.* креве́тка

pray /preı/ *v.i.* моли́ться, по-; **the farmers ~ed for rain** фе́рмеры моли́ли Бо́га, что́бы пошёл дождь; **we will ~ for the Queen** мы бу́дем моли́ться за короле́ву

prayer /'preə(r)/ *n.* моли́тва; **say one's ~s** моли́ться, по-

preach /priːtʃ/ *v.t.* пропове́довать (*impf.*)
● *v.i.* чита́ть про́поведь

preacher /'priːtʃə(r)/ *n.* пропове́дник

preamble /priː'æmb(ə)l/ *n.* преа́мбула

prearrange /priːə'reındʒ/ *v.t.* организо́в|ывать, -а́ть зара́нее

precarious /prı'keərıəs/ *adj.* **1** (uncertain) ненадёжный; **a ~ foothold** ненадёжная опо́ра **2** (dangerous, risky) опа́сный, риско́ванный

precaution /prı'kɔːʃ(ə)n/ *n.* предосторо́жность

precautionary /prı'kɔːʃənərı/ *adj.* предупреди́тельный

precede /prı'siːd/ *v.t.* предше́ствовать (*impf.*) + *d.*

precedence /'presıd(ə)ns/ *n.* первоочерёдность; **this question takes ~** э́тот вопро́с до́лжен рассма́триваться в пе́рвую о́чередь

precedent /'presıd(ə)nt/ *n.* прецеде́нт; **set a ~** созд|ава́ть, -а́ть прецеде́нт

precept /'priːsept/ *n.* (moral instruction) наставле́ние; (rule) пра́вило

precinct /'priːsıŋkt/ *n.* **1** (BrE, area of restricted access): **pedestrian ~** пешехо́дная зо́на; **shopping ~** торго́вый центр **2** (AmE, police or electoral district) уча́сток

precious /'preʃəs/ *adj.* (valued) це́нный; (stone) драгоце́нный

precipice /'presıpıs/ *n.* про́пасть, обры́в

precipitate¹ /prı'sıpıtət/ *adj.* (rash) опроме́тчивый

precipitate² /prı'sıpıteıt/ *v.t.* **1** вв|ерга́ть, -е́ргнуть; **the country was ~d into war** страну́ вве́ргли в войну́ **2** (bring on rapidly) уск|оря́ть, -о́рить

precipitation /prısıpı'teıʃ(ə)n/ *n.* (rain etc.) оса́д|ки (-ов)

precipitous /prı'sıpıtəs/ *adj.* (steep) обры́вистый, круто́й; (hasty) поспе́шный

precise /prı'saıs/ *adj.* то́чный, аккура́тный

precisely /prı'saıslı/ *adv.* то́чно; (with numbers or quantities) ро́вно; (as reply: 'quite so') соверше́нно ве́рно; вот и́менно

precision /prı'sıʒ(ə)n/ *n.* то́чность; аккура́тность

preclude /prı'kluːd/ *v.t.* (prevent) предотвра|ща́ть, -ти́ть; (make impossible) исключ|а́ть, -и́ть

✓ ключева́я ле́ксика

precocious /prɪˈkəʊʃəs/ *adj.* ра́но
развива́вшийся, ра́нний

preconceived /priːkənˈsiːvd/ *adj.* предвзя́тый

preconception /priːkənˈsepʃ(ə)n/ *n.*
предвзя́тое мне́ние

precondition /priːkənˈdɪʃ(ə)n/ *n.*
предвари́тельное усло́вие

precursor /priːˈkɜːsə(r)/ *n.* предше́ственни|к
(-ца); (of event) предве́стник

pre-date /priːˈdeɪt/ *v.t.* предше́ствовать
(*impf.*) + *d.*

predator /ˈpredətə(r)/ *n.* хи́щник

predatory /ˈpredətərɪ/ *adj.* хи́щный

predecease /priːdɪˈsiːs/ *v.t.:* he ~d her он
у́мер ра́ньше её

predecessor /ˈpriːdɪsesə(r)/ *n.*
предше́ственни|к (-ца)

predetermine /priːdɪˈtɜːmɪn/ *v.t.*
предреш|а́ть, -и́ть

predicament /prɪˈdɪkəmənt/ *n.* тру́дное
положе́ние

predicate /ˈpredɪkət/ *n.* (gram.) сказу́емое

predicative /prɪˈdɪkətɪv/ *adj.* (gram.)
предикати́вный

ℰ **predict** /prɪˈdɪkt/ *v.t.* предска́з|ывать, -а́ть

predictable /prɪˈdɪktəb(ə)l/ *adj.*
предсказу́емый

prediction /prɪˈdɪkʃ(ə)n/ *n.* предсказа́ние

predilection /priːdɪˈlekʃ(ə)n/ *n.* пристра́стие,
скло́нность (**for:** к + *d.*)

predispose /priːdɪˈspəʊz/ *v.t.*
предраспол|ага́ть, -ожи́ть

predominance /prɪˈdɒmɪnəns/ *n.* (control;
superiority) госпо́дство; (preponderance)
преоблада́ние

predominant /prɪˈdɒmɪnənt/ *adj.*
преоблада́ющий

predominantly /prɪˈdɒmɪnəntlɪ/ *adv.*
преиму́щественно

predominate /prɪˈdɒmɪneɪt/ *v.i.* преоблада́ть
(*impf.*)

pre-eminence /priːˈemɪnəns/ *n.*
превосхо́дство, преиму́щество

pre-eminent /priːˈemɪnənt/ *adj.* выдаю́щийся

pre-empt /priːˈempt/ *v.t.* предупре|жда́ть, -ди́ть

pre-emptive /priːˈemptɪv/ *adj.:* ~ strike
упрежда́ющий уда́р

preen /priːn/ *v.t.* (of bird): ~ one's feathers
чи́стить, по- пе́рья; (of person): ~ oneself
прихор|а́шиваться, -оши́ться (infml)

prefabricate /priːˈfæbrɪkeɪt/ *v.t.:* ~d house
(*or* (infml) **prefab**) сбо́рный дом

preface /ˈprefəs/ *n.* предисло́вие

prefect /ˈpriːfekt/ *n.* (BrE, at school) ста́роста (*c.g.*)

ℰ **prefer** /prɪˈfɜː(r)/ *v.t.* (**preferred, preferring**)
1 (like better) предпоч|ита́ть, -е́сть; I ~ juice
to water я предпочита́ю сок воде́ **2** (submit):
~ charges предъяв|ля́ть, -и́ть обвине́ния

preferable /ˈprefərəb(ə)l/ *adj.*
предпочти́тельный

preference /ˈprefərəns/ *n.* предпочте́ние

preferential /prefəˈrenʃ(ə)l/ *adj.*
предпочти́тельный; льго́тный

prefix /ˈpriːfɪks/ *n.* приста́вка, пре́фикс

pregnancy /ˈpreɡnənsɪ/ *n.* бере́менность

pregnant /ˈpreɡnənt/ *adj.* бере́менная;
become ~ забере́менеть (*pf.*)

preheat /priːˈhiːt/ *v.t.* предвари́тельно
подогр|ева́ть, -е́ть

prehistoric /priːhɪˈstɒrɪk/ *adj.*
доистори́ческий

prejudge /priːˈdʒʌdʒ/ *v.t.* предреш|а́ть, -и́ть

prejudice /ˈpredʒʊdɪs/ *n.* предрассу́док,
предубежде́ние
● *v.t.* **1** (cause to have a ~): you are ~d
against him вы отно́ситесь к нему́ с
предубежде́нием **2** (harm) нан|оси́ть, -ести́
уще́рб + *d.*

prejudiced /ˈpredʒʊdɪst/ *adj.* предубеждённый

preliminary /prɪˈlɪmɪnərɪ/ *adj.*
предвари́тельный

prelude /ˈpreljuːd/ *n.* (mus., fig.) прелю́дия

premarital /priːˈmærɪt(ə)l/ *adj.* добра́чный

premature /preməˈtjʊə(r)/ *adj.*
преждевре́менный
■ ~ **baby** *n.* недоно́шенный ребёнок

premeditate /priːˈmedɪteɪt/ *v.t.:* ~d murder
преднаме́ренное уби́йство

premenstrual /priːˈmenstrʊəl/ *adj.*
предменструа́льный

premier /ˈpremɪə(r)/ *n.* премье́р(-мини́стр)
● *adj.* пе́рвый; гла́вный

premiere /ˈpremɪeə(r)/ *n.* премье́ра

premiership /ˈpremɪəʃɪp/ *n.* премье́рство

premise /ˈpremɪs/ *n.* (phil.) посы́лка;
предположе́ние

premises /ˈpremɪsɪz/ *n. pl.* помеще́ние

premium /ˈpriːmɪəm/ *n.* (*pl.* ~**s**) **1** (payment
for insurance) (страхова́я) пре́мия **2** (additional
payment) припла́та **3**: **at a** ~ вы́ше номина́ла

premonition /preməˈnɪʃ(ə)n/ *n.* предчу́вствие

prenatal /priːˈneɪt(ə)l/ *adj.* предродово́й

preoccupation /priːɒkjʊˈpeɪʃ(ə)n/ *n.*
озабо́ченность

preoccupy /priːˈɒkjʊpaɪ/ *v.t.* забо́тить, о-

preparation /prepəˈreɪʃ(ə)n/ *n.* подгото́вка,
приготовле́ние; **she was packing in** ~ **for
the journey** она́ укла́дывала ве́щи, готовя́сь
к пое́здке; (*in pl.*) (preparatory measures)
приготовле́ния (*nt. pl.*)

preparatory /prɪˈpærətərɪ/ *adj.*
подготови́тельный

ℰ **prepare** /prɪˈpeə(r)/ *v.t.* гото́вить (*impf.*);
пригот|а́вливать, -о́вить; подгот|а́вливать,
-о́вить; **the tutor** ~d **him for his exams**
учи́тель подгото́вил его́ к экза́менам
● *v.i.* подгот|а́вливаться, -о́виться;
пригот|а́вливаться, -о́виться

preponderance /prɪˈpɒndərəns/ *n.* переве́с;
преиму́щество

preposition /prepəˈzɪʃ(ə)n/ *n.* (gram.) предло́г

prepositional /prepəˈzɪʃənəl/ *n. & adj.* (gram.)
предло́жный (паде́ж)

prepossessing /priːpəˈzesɪŋ/ *adj.*
располага́ющий, привлека́тельный

p

preposterous /prɪˈpɒstərəs/ *adj.*
возмути́тельный

prerequisite /priːˈrekwɪzɪt/ *n.* предпосы́лка

prerogative /prɪˈrɒɡətɪv/ *n.* (of ruler, etc.)
прерогати́ва; (privilege) привиле́гия

Presbyterian /prezbɪˈtɪərɪən/ *n.*
пресвитериа́н|ин (-ка)
• *adj.* пресвитериа́нский

preschool /ˈpriːskuːl/ *adj.* дошко́льный

prescribe /prɪˈskraɪb/ *v.t.* **1** (impose)
предпи́с|ывать, -а́ть **2** (med.) пропи́с|ывать,
-а́ть

prescription /prɪˈskrɪpʃ(ə)n/ *n.* (from doctor)
реце́пт; (medicine) лека́рство

prescriptive /prɪˈskrɪptɪv/ *adj.* (imposing a rule
or method) предпи́сывающий

◦ **presence** /ˈprez(ə)ns/ *n.* прису́тствие; ~ of
mind прису́тствие ду́ха

◦ **present¹** /ˈprez(ə)nt/ *n.* **1** (time now at hand)
настоя́щее (вре́мя); at ~ в настоя́щее вре́мя;
сейча́с (gram., ~ tense) настоя́щее вре́мя
• *adj.* **1** (at hand) прису́тствующий; no one
else was ~ никого́ бо́льше не́ было
2 (in question) да́нный; in the ~ case в
да́нном слу́чае **3** (existent) настоя́щий;
at the ~ time в настоя́щее вре́мя;
сейча́с; under ~ circumstances в да́нных
обстоя́тельствах **4** (gram.) настоя́щего
вре́мени
■ ~-day *adj.* совреме́нный, ны́нешний; ~
participle *n.* прича́стие настоя́щего вре́мени

present² /ˈprez(ə)nt/ *n.* (gift) пода́рок

◦ **present³** /prɪˈzent/ *v.t.* **1** (offer, put forward)
дари́ть, по-; вруч|а́ть, -и́ть; преподн|оси́ть,
-ести́; as soon as an opportunity ~s itself как
то́лько предста́вится слу́чай; he ~ed his case
well он хорошо́ изложи́л свои́ до́воды; (give)
предост|авля́ть, -а́вить; I was ~ed with a
choice мне предоста́вили вы́бор **2** (introduce)
предст|авля́ть, -а́вить

presentable /prɪˈzentəb(ə)l/ *adj.* прили́чный

◦ **presentation** /prezənˈteɪʃ(ə)n/ *n.* **1** (making a
present) подноше́ние, вруче́ние **2** (production)
предъявле́ние **3** (exposition) изложе́ние,
пода́ча

presenter /prɪˈzentə(r)/ *n.* (TV, radio) веду́щ|ий
(-ая)

presentiment /prɪˈzentɪmənt/ *n.*
предчу́вствие; he had a ~ of danger он
предчу́вствовал опа́сность

presently /ˈprezntlɪ/ *adv.* (soon) вско́ре;
(AmE, at present) сейча́с, в настоя́щее вре́мя, в
да́нный моме́нт

preservation /prezəˈveɪʃ(ə)n/ *n.* (act of
preserving) сохране́ние; консерви́рование;
(of materials) консерва́ция; (of monuments, etc.)
охра́на

preservative /prɪˈzɜːvətɪv/ *n.* (in food)
консерва́нт

preserve /prɪˈzɜːv/ **1** (jam) варе́нье **2** (area for
protection of game, etc.) запове́дник
• *v.t.* **1** (save; protect) сохран|я́ть, -и́ть **2** (keep
from decomposition, etc.) консерви́ровать, за-
3 (maintain) подде́рж|ивать, -а́ть; храни́ть, со-

preside /prɪˈzaɪd/ *v.i.* председа́тельствовать
(*impf.*)

presidency /ˈprezɪdənsɪ/ *n.* президе́нтство

◦ **president** /ˈprezɪd(ə)nt/ *n.* (of state, bank, etc.)
президе́нт

presidential /prezɪˈdenʃ(ə)l/ *adj.*
президе́нтский

◦ **press** /pres/ *n.* **1** (act of ~ing): she gave his
trousers a ~ она́ погла́дила ему́ брю́ки
2 (machine for ~ing or printing) пресс
3 (newspaper world) печа́ть, пре́сса; (newspaper
reaction) о́тклик, реце́нзия; a good ~ helps
to sell a book хоро́шие о́тклики в печа́ти
спосо́бствуют сбы́ту кни́ги
• *v.t.* **1** (exert physical pressure on) наж|има́ть,
-а́ть; ~ the button наж|има́ть, -а́ть (на)
кно́пку **2** (push) приж|има́ть, -а́ть; he ~ed
his nose against the window он прижа́л
нос к окну́ **3** (iron) гла́дить, по- **4** (clasp)
сжима́ть, сжать; he ~ed her hand он сжал
ей ру́ку **5** (fig., sustain vigorously): ~ charges
выдвига́ть, вы́двинуть обвине́ние **6** (urge):
they ~ed me to stay они́ угова́ривали меня́
оста́ться
• *v.i.*: if you ~ too hard, the pencil will
break е́сли сли́шком нажима́ть, каранда́ш
слома́ется; ~ for (reform, enqiury, etc.)
добива́ться (*impf.*) + g.
□ ~ **forward** *v.i.* прот|а́лкиваться, -олкну́ться
(вперёд)
□ ~ **on** *v.i.* продолжа́ть (*impf.*)
■ ~ **agency** *n.* аге́нтство печа́ти; ~
conference *n.* пресс-конфере́нция; ~ **stud**
n. (BrE) кно́пка (на оде́жде); ~-up *n.* (BrE)
отжима́ние; do ~-ups отж|има́ться, -а́ться
(от по́ла)

pressing /ˈpresɪŋ/ *adj.* настоя́тельный,
неотло́жный

◦ **pressure** /ˈpreʃə(r)/ *n.* **1** давле́ние
2 (compulsive influence) давле́ние, возде́йствие;
put ~ on ока́з|ывать, -а́ть давле́ние/нажи́м
на + *a.*; наж|има́ть, -а́ть на + *a.* (infml)
■ ~ **cooker** *n.* скорова́рка; ~ **group** *n.* ≈
инициати́вная гру́ппа; движе́ние

pressurize /ˈpreʃəraɪz/ *v.t.* **1** герметизи́ровать
(*impf.*) **2** (fig.) ока́з|ывать, -а́ть давле́ние на
+ *a.*; he was ~d into writing a confession его́
заста́вили написа́ть призна́ние

prestige /preˈstiːʒ/ *n.* прести́ж

prestigious /preˈstɪdʒəs/ *adj.* прести́жный

presumably /prɪˈzjuːməblɪ/ *adv.* вероя́тно

presume /prɪˈzjuːm/ *v.t.* **1** (assume) полага́ть
(*impf.*) **2** (with inf.: venture) брать, взять на
себя́ сме́лость; I would not ~ to argue with
you я не возьму́ на себя́ сме́лость с ва́ми
спо́рить

presumptuous /prɪˈzʌmptʃʊəs/ *adj.*
самонаде́янный

presuppose /priːsəˈpəʊz/ *v.t.* (зара́нее)
предпол|ага́ть, -ожи́ть; допус|ка́ть, -ти́ть

pre-tax /ˈpriːtæks/ *adj.* до вы́чета нало́гов

◦ ключева́я ле́ксика

p

pretence /prɪ'tens/ (AmE **pretense**) *n.*
  1 (pretending) притво́рство; **he made a ~
  of reading the newspaper** он притвори́лся,
  что чита́ет газе́ту; **by/under/on false ~s**
  обма́нным путём **2** (pretext, excuse) предло́г;
  he called under the ~ of asking advice он
  зашёл под предло́гом спроси́ть сове́та
pretend /prɪ'tend/ *v.t. & i.* притворя́ться
  (*impf.*); де́лать (*impf.*) вид; **she is ~ing to be
  asleep** она́ притворя́ется, что спит; **~ to be
  pirates** игра́ть в пира́тов (*о детях*)
pretense /prɪ'tens/ *n.* (AmE) = **pretence**
pretension /prɪ'tenʃ(ə)n/ *n.* претенцио́зность
pretentious /prɪ'tenʃəs/ *adj.* претенцио́зный;
  показно́й
pretext /'pri:tekst/ *n.* предло́г; **on/under the
  ~ of** под предло́гом + *g.*
✎ **pretty** /'prɪtɪ/ *adj.* (**prettier, prettiest**)
  краси́вый, хоро́шенький
  ● *adv.* доста́точно, дово́льно; **~ much** (nearly)
  почти́
prevail /prɪ'veɪl/ *v.i.* **1** (win) торжествова́ть,
  вос-; (of idea) возоблада́ть (*impf.*) **2** (be
  widespread) преоблада́ть (*impf.*); **~ing
  winds** преоблада́ющие ве́тры **3**: **~ (up)on**
  (persuade) убе|жда́ть, -ди́ть
prevalence /'prevələns/ *n.* распростране́ние
prevalent /'prevələnt/ *adj.*
  распространённый
prevaricate /prɪ'værɪkeɪt/ *v.i.* виля́ть (*impf.*)
prevarication /prɪværɪ'keɪʃ(ə)n/ *n.* уви́ливание
✎ **prevent** /prɪ'vent/ *v.t.* (stop happening)
  предотвра|ща́ть, -ти́ть; (make unable to do)
  меша́ть, по- + *d.*; **illness ~ed him from
  coming** боле́знь помеша́ла ему́ прийти́
preventable /prɪ'ventəb(ə)l/ *adj.*
  предотврати́мый
preventative /prɪ'ventətɪv/ *adj.* = **preventive**
prevention /prɪ'venʃ(ə)n/ *n.*
  предотвраще́ние, предупрежде́ние
preventive /prɪ'ventɪv/ *adj.*
  предупреди́тельный
  ■ **~ medicine** *n.* профила́ктика
preview /'pri:vju:/ *n.* (of film)
  (предвари́тельный) просмо́тр; (of exhibition)
  верниса́ж
✎ **previous** /'pri:vɪəs/ *adj.* (earlier, former)
  предыду́щий
✎ **previously** /'pri:vɪəslɪ/ *adv.* ра́ньше
pre-war /pri:'wɔ:(r)/ *adj.* довое́нный,
  предвое́нный
prey /preɪ/ *n.* добы́ча
  ● *v.i.* охо́титься (*impf.*); **owls ~ on mice** со́вы
  охо́тятся на мыше́й; (fig.): **the crime ~ed
  upon his mind** (соверше́нное) преступле́ние
  мучи́ло его́, не дава́ло ему́ поко́я
✎ **price** /praɪs/ *n.* **1** цена́; **they wanted peace
  at any ~** им ну́жен был мир любо́й цено́й
  2 (value) це́нность
  ● *v.t.* (fix ~ of) оце́н|ивать, -и́ть
  ■ **~ list** *n.* прейскура́нт; **~ tag** *n.* це́нник,
  ярлы́к (*с указа́нием цены́*)

priceless /'praɪslɪs/ *adj.* (invaluable) бесце́нный;
  (infml, amusing) бесподо́бный
pricey /'praɪsɪ/ *adj.* (**pricier, priciest**) (infml)
  дорого́й
prick /prɪk/ *n.* шип; колю́чка
  ● *v.t.* прок|а́лывать, -оло́ть
  □ **~ up** *v.t.*: **~ up one's ears** навостри́ть (*pf.*) у́ши
prickle /'prɪk(ə)l/ *n.* (thorn) колю́чка, шип; (of
  hedgehog etc.) игла́
  ● *v.t. & i.* коло́ть(ся), у-
prickly /'prɪklɪ/ *adj.* (**pricklier, prickliest**)
  (having spines or thorns) колю́чий; (causing a
  prickling sensation) ко́лкий, колю́щий(ся); (fig.,
  easily offended) оби́дчивый
pride /praɪd/ *n.* го́рдость; **he takes ~ in his
  work** он горди́тся свое́й рабо́той
  ● *v.t.*: **~ oneself on** горди́ться (*impf.*) + *i.*
priest /pri:st/ *n.* свяще́нник
priesthood /'pri:sthʊd/ *n.* свяще́нство
prig /prɪg/ *n.* педа́нт; (hypocrite) ханжа́ (*c.g.*)
priggish /'prɪgɪʃ/ *adj.* педанти́чный;
  (hypocritical) ха́нжеский
prim /prɪm/ *adj.* (**primmer, primmest**)
  (*also* **~ and proper**) чо́порный
prima /'pri:mə/ *adj.*: **~ ballerina** при́ма-
  балери́на; **~ donna** (lit.) примадо́нна, ди́ва;
  (fig.) примадо́нна
primarily /'praɪmərɪlɪ/ *adv.* (principally) в
  основно́м
✎ **primary** /'praɪmərɪ/ *n.* (AmE, election)
  предвари́тельные вы́бор|ы (-ов)
  ● *adj.* **1** (original) первонача́льный **2** (basic,
  principal) основно́й; **of ~ importance**
  первостепе́нной ва́жности
  ■ **~ colours**, (AmE) **~ colors** *n. pl.* основны́е
  цвета́; **~ school** *n.* (BrE) нача́льная шко́ла
primate /'praɪmeɪt/ *n.* (archbishop) прима́с;
  (mammal) прима́т
prime /praɪm/ *n.*: **in the ~ of life** в расцве́те
  сил; **he is past his ~** его́ лу́чшие дни/го́ды
  (оста́лись) позади́
  ● *adj.* **1** (principal) гла́вный **2** (best) лу́чший;
  ~ beef говя́дина вы́сшего со́рта
  ● *v.t.* **1** (firearm) заря|жа́ть, -ди́ть; (engine,
  pump) запр|авля́ть, -а́вить **2** (supply with facts
  etc.) инструкти́ровать (*impf., pf.*)
  ■ **~ minister** *n.* премье́р-мини́стр; **~
  number** *n.* (math.) просто́е число́; **~ time** *n.*
  (TV, radio) прайм-та́йм
primeval /praɪ'mi:v(ə)l/ *adj.* первобы́тный
primitive /'prɪmɪtɪv/ *adj.* примити́вный; (of
  earliest man, tribes) первобы́тный
primordial /praɪ'mɔ:dɪəl/ *adj.* перви́чный,
  первобы́тный; (fundamental) основно́й
primrose /'prɪmrəʊz/ *n.* первоцве́т (*лесно́е
  расте́ние*)
primula /'prɪmjʊlə/ *n.* при́мула
prince /prɪns/ *n.* князь (*m.*); (son of royalty) принц
princely /'prɪnslɪ/ *adj.* (**princelier,
  princeliest**) кня́жеский; (splendid)
  великоле́пный; (generous): **~ sum** ца́рская
  су́мма
princess /prɪn'ses/ *n.* принце́сса

p

principal /ˈprɪnsɪp(ə)l/ n. дире́ктор, ре́ктор
● adj. гла́вный, основно́й

principality /prɪnsɪˈpælɪtɪ/ n. кня́жество

principally /ˈprɪnsɪpəlɪ/ adv. гла́вным о́бразом, преиму́щественно

✓ **principle** /ˈprɪnsɪp(ə)l/ n. при́нцип, нача́ло; in ∼ в при́нципе; on ∼ из при́нципа

✓ **print** /prɪnt/ n. **1** (mark made on surface by pressure) след; отпеча́ток **2** (letters, etc.) шрифт; печа́ть; the book is in ∼ кни́га ещё продаётся; the book is out of ∼ кни́га бо́льше не продаётся **3** (picture) гравю́ра, эста́мп; (by photography) репроду́кция ● v.t. **1** (impress) печа́тать, на-/от-; (fig.) запечатл|ева́ть, -е́ть **2** (produce by ∼ing process) печа́тать, на-/от- **3** (write in imitation of ∼) писа́ть, на- печа́тными бу́квами ▢ ∼ **out** v.t. (comput.) распеча́т|ывать, -ать ■ ∼**out** n. (comput.) распеча́тка

printer /ˈprɪntə(r)/ n. (person) печа́тник, типо́граф; (printing house) типогра́фия; (comput.) при́нтер

✓ **prior** /ˈpraɪə(r)/ adj. (earlier) пре́жний; (more important) первоочередно́й ● adv.: ∼ **to** до + g.

prioritize /praɪˈɒrɪtaɪz/ v.t. (determine the order for dealing with) определ|я́ть, -и́ть свои́ приорите́ты в + p.; (designate or treat as most important) удел|я́ть, -и́ть первостепе́нное внима́ние + d.

✓ **priority** /praɪˈɒrɪtɪ/ n. приорите́т

priory /ˈpraɪərɪ/ n. монасты́рь (m.)

prise /praɪz/ (AmE **prize**) v.t. взл|а́мывать, -ома́ть; the box was ∼d open я́щик взлома́ли; (fig.) разн|има́ть, -я́ть; they ∼d the combatants apart они́ разня́ли деру́щихся

prism /ˈprɪz(ə)m/ n. при́зма

✓ **prison** /ˈprɪz(ə)n/ n. **1** тюрьма́ **2** (attr.) тюре́мный ■ ∼ **camp** n. исправи́тельно-трудово́й ла́герь; ∼ **sentence** n. тюре́мный срок

✓ **prisoner** /ˈprɪznə(r)/ n. **1** (detained by civil authorities) заключённый **2** (∼ of war) пле́нный, военнопле́нный

prissy /ˈprɪsɪ/ adj. (**prissier, prissiest**) чо́порный, жема́нный; (of style) вы́чурный

pristine /ˈprɪstiːn/ adj. чи́стый; нетро́нутый

privacy /ˈprɪvəsɪ/ n. уедине́ние

✓ **private** /ˈpraɪvət/ n. **1** (soldier) рядово́й **2**: in ∼ (meet, talk) с гла́зу на глаз ● adj. **1** (personal) ча́стный, ли́чный; in ∼ life в ли́чной жи́зни; for ∼ reasons по ли́чным причи́нам **2** (not open to the general public) закры́тый **3** (secret) та́йный, секре́тный **4** (without official status) ча́стный; неофициа́льный ■ ∼ **eye** n. (infml) ча́стный сы́щик, детекти́в; ∼ **property** n. ча́стная со́бственность

privation /praɪˈveɪʃ(ə)n/ n. (hardship) лише́ния (nt. pl.); нужда́; (loss) утра́та; лише́ние

privatization /praɪvətaɪˈzeɪʃ(ə)n/ n. приватиза́ция

privatize /ˈpraɪvətaɪz/ v.t. приватизи́ровать (impf., pf.)

privet /ˈprɪvɪt/ n. (bot.) бирючи́на

privilege /ˈprɪvɪlɪdʒ/ n. привиле́гия

privileged /ˈprɪvɪlɪdʒd/ adj. привилегиро́ванный

✓ **prize¹** /praɪz/ n. **1** (reward for merit in sport etc.) приз; (esp. monetary) пре́мия **2** (attr.) (awarded as prize) призово́й; (∼-winning) премиро́ванный; (possession) бесце́нный ■ ∼-**giving** n. (BrE) церемо́ния вруче́ния награ́д; ∼ **money** n. призовы́е де́н|ьги (-ег); ∼**winner** n. призёр

prize² /praɪz/ v.t. (AmE) = **prise**

pro¹ /prəʊ/ n. (pl. ∼s) (point in favour): ∼s and **cons** за и про́тив ● prep. (infml, in favour of) за + a.

pro² /prəʊ/ n. (pl. ∼s) (infml, professional) профессиона́л (-ка); про́фи (c.g. indecl.) (infml)

proactive /prəʊˈæktɪv/ adj. де́йственный

probability /prɒbəˈbɪlɪtɪ/ n. вероя́тность; in **all** ∼ по всей вероя́тности

probable /ˈprɒbəb(ə)l/ adj. вероя́тный

✓ **probably** /ˈprɒbəblɪ/ adv. вероя́тно

probate /ˈprəʊbeɪt/ n. утвержде́ние завеща́ния

probation /prəˈbeɪʃ(ə)n/ n.: be on ∼ (at work) про|ходи́ть, -йти́ испыта́тельный срок; (law) быть усло́вно осуждённым ■ ∼ **officer** n. должностно́е лицо́, осуществля́ющее надзо́р за усло́вно осуждёнными

probationary /prəˈbeɪʃənərɪ/ adj. испыта́тельный

probationer /prəˈbeɪʃənə(r)/ n. (trainee) стажёр; практика́нт; (offender on probation) усло́вно осуждённый

probe /prəʊb/ n. (instrument) зонд; (fig., investigation) рассле́дование ● v.t. & i. иссле́довать (impf., pf.)

✓ **problem** /ˈprɒbləm/ n. пробле́ма, вопро́с; (math. etc.) зада́ча ■ ∼ **child** n. тру́дный ребёнок

problematic /prɒbləˈmætɪk/, **problematical** /prɒbləˈmætɪkəl/ adjs. проблемати́чный

✓ **procedure** /prəˈsiːdʒə(r)/ n. процеду́ра

✓ **proceed** /prəˈsiːd/ v.i. **1** (go on) продолжа́ть, -о́лжить **2** (start) прин|има́ться, -я́ться (with: за + a.); she ∼ed to lay the table она́ приняла́сь накрыва́ть на стол

proceedings /prəˈsiːdɪŋz/ n. pl. **1** (activity) де́ятельность **2** (legal action) суде́бное де́ло, иск

proceeds /ˈprəʊsiːdz/ n. pl. вы́ручка, дохо́д

✓ **process** /ˈprəʊses/ n. **1** проце́сс **2** (course) тече́ние, ход; we're in the ∼ of buying a **house** сейча́с мы покупа́ем дом ● v.t. **1** (treat in special way, also comput.) обраб|а́тывать, -о́тать **2** (subject to routine handling) оф|ормля́ть, -о́рмить

procession /prəˈseʃ(ə)n/ n. проце́ссия, ше́ствие

processor /'prəʊsesə(r)/ *n.* (comput.) процéссор

proclaim /prə'kleɪm/ *v.t.* провозгла|шáть, -сúть

proclamation /prɒklə'meɪʃ(ə)n/ *n.*
провозглашéние

proclivity /prə'klɪvɪtɪ/ *n.* склóнность,
наклóнность

procrastinate /prəʊ'kræstɪneɪt/ *v.i.* мéдлить
(*impf.*)

procreate /'prəʊkrɪeɪt/ *v.t. & i.* произв|одúть,
-естú (потóмство)

procreation /prəʊkrɪ'eɪʃ(ə)n/ *n.*
воспроизведéние

procure /prə'kjʊə(r)/ *v.t.* дост|авáть, -áть

procurement /prə'kjʊəmənt/ *n.*
приобретéние, получéние; (of equipment etc.)
постáвка

prod /prɒd/ *n.* тычóк
  ● *v.t.* (**prodded**, **prodding**) ты́кать, ткнуть

pro-democracy /prəʊdɪ'mɒkrəsɪ/ *adj.*
продемократúческий, защищáющий
демокрáтию

prodigal /'prɒdɪg(ə)l/ *adj.* (wasteful)
расточúтельный; **the P~ Son** (bibl.) блýдный
сын; (lavish) щéдрый

prodigious /prə'dɪdʒəs/ *adj.* (amazing)
потрясáющий; (enormous) огрóмный

prodigy /'prɒdɪdʒɪ/ *n.* вундеркúнд

produce¹ /'prɒdjuːs/ *n.* продýкты (*m. pl.*)
(*пищевые*)

produce² /prə'djuːs/ *v.t.* **1** (make, manufacture)
произв|одúть, -естú; выпускáть, вы́пустить
2 (bring about) вызывáть, вы́звать; прин|осúть,
-естú **3** (present) предст|авля́ть, -áвить; **can
you ~ proof of your words?** мóжете ли вы
предстáвить чтó-либо в доказáтельство/
подтверждéние вáших слов? **4** (show)
предъяв|ля́ть, -úть; **you must ~ a ticket**
вы должны́ предъявúть билéт **5** (yield)
произв|одúть, -естú; **this soil ~s good crops**
э́та пóчва даёт хорóший урожáй **6** (theatr.)
стáвить, по-; (cin.) выпускáть, вы́пустить

producer /prə'djuːsə(r)/ *n.* **1** (of goods)
производúтель (*m.*) **2** (stage, TV) режиссёр-
постанóвщик **3** (film) продю́сер

product /'prɒdʌkt/ *n.* продýкт, издéлие; (*in
pl.*) продýкция; (*collect.*) товáры (*m. pl.*)

production /prə'dʌkʃ(ə)n/ *n.* **1** (manufacture)
произвóдство **2** (yield) производúтельность
3 (stage, film) постанóвка, режиссýра
  ■ **~ line** *n.* произвóдственная лúния

productive /prə'dʌktɪv/ *adj.* (tending to produce)
производúтельный; (yielding well) плодорóдный

productivity /prɒdʌk'tɪvɪtɪ/ *n.*
производúтельность, продуктúвность

profane /prə'feɪn/ *adj.* (secular) мирскóй;
(heathen) язы́ческий; (irreverent) богохýльный
  ● *v.t.* профанúровать (*impf., pf.*);
оскверн|я́ть, -úть

profanit|y /prə'fænɪtɪ/ *n.* (irreverence)
богохýльство; (swearing) сквернослóвие; **to
utter ~ies** сквернослóвить (*impf.*)

profess /prə'fes/ *v.t.* **1** (claim to have or feel)
заяв|ля́ть, -úть; **he ~es an interest in**

architecture он заявля́ет, что интересýется
архитектýрой **2** (claim, pretend) претендовáть
(*impf.*); **I don't ~ to know much about music**
я не претендýю на бóльшие познáния в
мýзыке; **he ~es to be an expert at chess** он
выдаёт себя́ за первоклáссного шахматúста

profession /prə'feʃ(ə)n/ *n.* профéссия

ơ **professional** /prə'feʃən(ə)l/ *n.* профессионáл
  ● *adj.* профессионáльный

professionalism /prə'feʃənəlɪz(ə)m/ *n.*
профессионалúзм

ơ **professor** /prə'fesə(r)/ *n.* (holder of university
chair) профéссор; (AmE, university teacher)
преподавáтель (-ница)

proffer /'prɒfə(r)/ *n.* предложéние
  ● *v.t.* предл|агáть, -ожúть; **he ~ed his hand**
он протянýл рýку

proficiency /prə'fɪʃ(ə)nsɪ/ *n.* мастерствó,
умéние

proficient /prə'fɪʃ(ə)nt/ *adj.* умéлый

profile /'prəʊfaɪl/ *n.* прóфиль (*m.*); **he kept a
low ~** он старáлся не выделя́ться

ơ **profit** /'prɒfɪt/ *n.* прúбыль
  ● *v.t.* (**profited**, **profiting**) прин|осúть,
-естú пóльзу + *d.*
  ● *v.i.* (**profited**, **profiting**) пóльзоваться,
вос- (from: + *g.*); извл|екáть, -éчь пóльзу
(from: из + *g.*); **he has not ~ed from his
experience** он не воспóльзовался своúм
óпытом

profitability /prɒfɪtə'bɪlɪtɪ/ *n.* дохóдность,
прúбыльность, рентáбельность

profitable /'prɒfɪtəb(ə)l/ *adj.* (advantageous)
полéзный, вы́годный; (lucrative) дохóдный

profiteer /prɒfɪ'tɪə(r)/ *n.* спекуля́нт (-ка)
  ● *v.i.* спекулúровать (*impf.*)

profligate /'prɒflɪgət/ *adj.* (extravagant)
расточúтельный; (dissolute) распýтный
  ● *n.* (dissolute person) разврáтник

profound /prə'faʊnd/ *adj.* (**profounder**,
profoundest) глубóкий

profundity /prə'fʌndɪtɪ/ *n.* глубинá

profuse /prə'fjuːs/ *adj.* (plentiful) обúльный;
(lavish) щéдрый; **he apologized ~ly** он
рассы́пался в извинéниях

profusion /prə'fjuːʒ(ə)n/ *n.* изобúлие

progesterone /prəʊ'dʒestərəʊn/ *n.*
прогестерóн

prognosis /prɒg'nəʊsɪs/ *n.* (*pl.* **prognoses**
/-siːz/) прогнóз

ơ **program** /'prəʊgræm/ *n.* (comput.) прогрáмма;
(AmE) = programme
  ● *v.t.* (**programmed**, **programming**)
(comput., also fig.) программúровать, за-; (AmE)
= programme

ơ **programme** /'prəʊgræm/ *n.* прогрáмма;
(radio, TV) передáча; (plan) прогрáмма, план
  ● *v.t.* (**programmed**, **programming**)
(schedule): **the meeting is ~d for today**
собрáние назнáчено на сегóдня

programmer /'prəʊgræmə(r)/ *n.* (comput.)
программúст (-ка)

ơ **progress¹** /'prəʊgres/ *n.* **1** (forward movement)

движе́ние вперёд **2** (advance, development)
прогре́сс; **a meeting is in ~** идёт заседа́ние
■ **~ report** *n.* докла́д о хо́де рабо́ты
progress² /prəˈgres/ *v.i.* прогресси́ровать
(*impf.*); продв|ига́ться, -и́нуться (вперёд)
progression /prəˈgreʃ(ə)n/ *n.* продвиже́ние
progressive /prəˈgresɪv/ *adj.* **1** (favouring
progress) прогресси́вный, передово́й
2 (gradual) постепе́нный, постепе́нный
prohibit /prəˈhɪbɪt/ *v.t.* (**prohibited**,
prohibiting) запре|ща́ть, -ти́ть
prohibition /prəʊhɪˈbɪʃ(ə)n, prəʊɪˈb-/ *n.*
запреще́ние
prohibitive /prəˈhɪbɪtɪv/ *adj.*
запрети́тельный, запреща́ющий
ᴥ **project¹** /ˈprɒdʒekt/ *n.* (scheme) прое́кт, план;
(at school) рабо́та
project² /prəˈdʒekt/ *v.t.* (throw) выбра́сывать,
вы́бросить; (fig.): **she ~ed a positive image**
она́ производи́ла позити́вное впечатле́ние
● *v.i.* (protrude) выдава́ться (*impf.*); выступа́ть
(*impf.*)
projectile /prəˈdʒektaɪl/ *n.* снаря́д
projection /prəˈdʒekʃ(ə)n/ *n.* **1** (planning)
проекти́рование **2** (throwing, propulsion)
отбра́сывание **3** (cin.) прое́кция
(изображе́ния) **4** (psych., geom.) прое́кция
5 (protrusion) вы́ступ
■ **~ room** *n.* (кино)проекцио́нная каби́на
projector /prəˈdʒektə(r)/ *n.* (apparatus)
прое́ктор
proletarian /prəʊlɪˈteərɪən/ *n.* пролета́рий
● *adj.* пролета́рский
proletariat /prəʊlɪˈteərɪət/ *n.* пролетариа́т
pro-life /prəʊˈlaɪf/ *adj.* возража́ющий про́тив
або́ртов
proliferate /prəˈlɪfəreɪt/ *v.i.* (бы́стро)
распростран|я́ться, -и́ться
proliferation /prəlɪfəˈreɪʃ(ə)n/ *n.* (бы́строе)
размноже́ние, пролифера́ция; (fig.)
распростране́ние
prolific /prəˈlɪfɪk/ *adj.* (lit.) плодоро́дный; (fig.)
плодови́тый
prologue /ˈprəʊlɒg/ (AmE **prolog**) *n.* проло́г
prolong /prəˈlɒŋ/ *v.t.* продл|ева́ть, -и́ть
prom /prɒm/ *n.* (infml) **1** = promenade **2** (AmE,
students' ball) бал, вы́пускно́й
promenade /prɒməˈnɑːd/ *n.* (BrE, esp. at
seaside) ме́сто для гуля́ния
prominence /ˈprɒmɪnəns/ *n.* (importance)
ви́дное положе́ние
prominent /ˈprɒmɪnənt/ *adj.* **1** (projecting)
выступа́ющий **2** (important) выдаю́щийся
promiscuity /prɒmɪˈskjuːɪtɪ/ *n.*
распу́щенность
promiscuous /prəˈmɪskjʊəs/ *adj.*
распу́щенный
ᴥ **promise** /ˈprɒmɪs/ *n.* **1** (assurance) обеща́ние;
he kept his ~ он сдержа́л своё обеща́ние
2 (ground for expectation) наде́жда; **he shows ~**

он подаёт наде́жды
● *v.t. & i.* обеща́ть, по-; **he ~d to be here by 7**
он обеща́л быть здесь к 7 часа́м; **I ~d myself
a quiet evening** я реши́л споко́йно провести́
ве́чер
promising /ˈprɒmɪsɪŋ/ *adj.* перспекти́вный;
многообеща́ющий, подаю́щий наде́жды
promontory /ˈprɒməntərɪ/ *n.* мыс
ᴥ **promote** /prəˈməʊt/ *v.t.* **1** (raise to higher rank)
продв|ига́ть, -и́нуть; повы́|ша́ть, -ы́сить (в
чи́не/зва́нии) **2** (encourage, support) поощр|я́ть,
-и́ть; подде́рж|ивать, -а́ть **3** (publicize)
реклами́ровать (*impf.*)
promoter /prəˈməʊtə(r)/ *n.* (of event) аге́нт,
промо́утер; (of cause) пропаганди́ст (-ка)
promotion /prəˈməʊʃ(ə)n/ *n.* **1** продвиже́ние,
повыше́ние; (encouragement, support) поощре́ние,
подде́ржка; (publicizing) рекла́ма, промо́ушен
prompt¹ /prɒmpt/ *v.t.* **1** (assist memory
of) подска́з|ывать, -а́ть + *d.*; (theatr.)
суфли́ровать (*impf.*) + *d.* **2** (impel)
побу|жда́ть, -ди́ть
prompt² /prɒmpt/ *adj.* бы́стрый,
неме́дленный; **he arrived ~ly at 9** он
прие́хал то́чно в де́вять
prompter /ˈprɒmptə(r)/ *n.* (theatr.) суфлёр
prone /prəʊn/ *adj.* **1** (face downwards)
лежа́щий ничко́м, лежа́щий вниз лицо́м
2: **~ to** (liable to) скло́нный к + *d.*
prong /prɒŋ/ *n.* зубе́ц
pronoun /ˈprəʊnaʊn/ *n.* местоиме́ние
pronounce /prəˈnaʊns/ *v.t.* произн|оси́ть, -ести́
pronounced /prəˈnaʊnst/ *adj.* (decided)
я́вный; **he walks with a ~ limp** он си́льно/
заме́тно хрома́ет
pronouncement /prəˈnaʊnsmənt/ *n.*
заявле́ние; выска́зывание
pronunciation /prənʌnsɪˈeɪʃ(ə)n/ *n.*
произноше́ние
proof /pruːf/ *n.* доказа́тельство; (typ.)
корректу́ра
■ **~reader** *n.* корре́ктор
prop¹ /prɒp/ *n.* (support) сто́йка; подпо́рка;
(fig.) опо́ра, подде́ржка
● *v.t.* (**propped**, **propping**) (*also* **prop
up**) **1** подп|ира́ть, -ере́ть; **~ the ladder
against the wall!** приста́вьте ле́стницу к
стене́! **2** (fig.) подде́рж|ивать, -а́ть
prop² /prɒp/ *n.* (usu. in pl.) (theatr.) бутафо́рия,
реквизи́т
propaganda /prɒpəˈgændə/ *n.* пропага́нда
propagate /ˈprɒpəgeɪt/ *v.t.* (plants) разв|оди́ть,
-ести́; (ideas) распростран|я́ть, -и́ть
propagation /prɒpəˈgeɪʃ(ə)n/ *n.*
размноже́ние; (fig.) распростране́ние
propagator /ˈprɒpəgeɪtə(r)/ *n.* (person)
распространи́тель (-ница); (for plants)
микропарни́к
propel /prəˈpel/ *v.t.* (**propelled**,
propelling) прив|оди́ть, -ести́ в движе́ние
propeller /prəˈpelə(r)/ *n.* пропе́ллер
propensity /prəˈpensɪtɪ/ *n.*
предрасполо́женность, скло́нность

p

proper /'prɒpə(r)/ *adj.* **1** (suitable) подходя́щий, ну́жный **2** (decent) (благо)присто́йный, прили́чный **3** (correct) пра́вильный; **in the ~ sense of the word** в прямо́м смы́сле сло́ва

properly /'prɒpəlɪ/ *adv.* (correctly) подоба́юще, как сле́дует; **you must be ~ dressed** вы должны́ оде́ться подоба́юще

property /'prɒpətɪ/ *n.* **1** (possession(s)) со́бственность; иму́щество **2** (house) дом; (estate) име́ние; (real estate) недви́жимость **3** (attribute) сво́йство

prophecy /'prɒfɪsɪ/ *n.* проро́чество

prophesy /'prɒfɪsaɪ/ *v.t.* проро́чить, на-

prophet /'prɒfɪt/ *n.* проро́к

prophetic /prə'fetɪk/ *adj.* проро́ческий

prophylactic /ˌprɒfɪ'læktɪk/ *n.* профилакти́ческое сре́дство
● *adj.* профилакти́ческий

proponent /prə'pəʊnənt/ *n.* пропаганди́ст, побо́рник (*чего*)

proportion /prə'pɔːʃ(ə)n/ *n.* **1** (part) часть, до́ля **2** (ratio) пропо́рция, соотноше́ние; **in ~** пропорциона́льно, соразме́рно **3** (due relation) соразме́рность; **his ambitions are out of all ~** его́ честолю́бие выхо́дит за вся́кие ра́мки **4** (*in pl.*) (dimensions) разме́р, разме́ры (*m. pl.*)

proportional /prə'pɔːʃən(ə)l/ *adj.* пропорциона́льный
■ **~ representation** *n.* (pol.) пропорциона́льное представи́тельство

proportionate /prə'pɔːʃənət/ *adj.* соразме́рный; **payment will be ~ to effort** опла́та бу́дет соотве́тствовать затра́ченным уси́лиям

proposal /prə'pəʊz(ə)l/ *n.* предложе́ние

propose /prə'pəʊz/ *v.t.* **1** (suggest) предл|ага́ть, -ожи́ть; **he ~d (marriage) to her** он сде́лал ей предложе́ние (*стать же́ной*) **2** (put forward) выдвига́ть, вы́двинуть **3** (intend) предпол|ага́ть, -ожи́ть; намерева́ться (*impf.*); **I ~ to leave tomorrow** я намерева́юсь е́хать за́втра

proposition /ˌprɒpə'zɪʃ(ə)n/ *n.* **1** (statement) заявле́ние **2** (proposed scheme) предложе́ние

propound /prə'paʊnd/ *v.t.* предл|ага́ть, -ожи́ть на обсужде́ние; изл|ага́ть, -ожи́ть

proprietor /prə'praɪətə(r)/ *n.* владе́лец, хозя́ин

proprietorial /prəˌpraɪə'tɔːrɪəl/ *adj.* со́бственнический

propriety /prə'praɪətɪ/ *n.* (fitness) уме́стность; (correctness of behaviour) пра́вила поведе́ния; пра́вила прили́чия, (благо)присто́йность

pro rata /prəʊ 'rɑːtə/ *adv.* пропорциона́льно; соотве́тственно

prosaic /prə'zeɪɪk/ *adj.* прозаи́ческий

proscribe /prə'skraɪb/ *v.t.* запре|ща́ть, -ти́ть

prose /prəʊz/ *n.* про́за

prosecute /'prɒsɪkjuːt/ *v.t.* (law) возбу|жда́ть, -ди́ть де́ло про́тив + g.

prosecution /ˌprɒsɪ'kjuːʃ(ə)n/ *n.* **1** (carrying on legal proceedings) обвине́ние; предъявле́ние и́ска **2** (prosecuting party) обвине́ние; **counsel for the ~** обвини́тель (*m.*) (в уголо́вном проце́ссе)

prosecutor /'prɒsɪkjuːtə(r)/ *n.* обвини́тель (*m.*)

prospect /'prɒspekt/ *n.* перспекти́ва; **there is no ~ of success** нет наде́жды на успе́х; **a job without ~s** рабо́та без перспекти́в

prospective /prə'spektɪv/ *adj.* бу́дущий

prospector /prə'spektə(r)/ *n.* разве́дчик, стара́тель (*m.*)

prospectus /prə'spektəs/ *n.* (*pl.* **~es**) проспе́кт (*рекла́мное изда́ние*)

prosper /'prɒspə(r)/ *v.i.* преуспе|ва́ть, -е́ть

prosperity /prɒ'sperɪtɪ/ *n.* процвета́ние

prosperous /'prɒspərəs/ *adj.* процвета́ющий

prostate /'prɒsteɪt/ *n.* (*in full* **~ gland**) проста́та, предста́тельная железа́

prosthe|sis /'prɒsθiːsɪs/ *n.* (*pl.* **~ses** /-siːz/) проте́з

prosthetic /prɒs'θetɪk/ *adj.* протéзный

prostitute /'prɒstɪtjuːt/ *n.* проститу́тка; **male ~** мужчи́на-проститу́тка
● *v.t.*: **~ oneself** зан|има́ться, -я́ться проститу́цией; (fig.) торгова́ть (*impf.*) собо́й

prostitution /ˌprɒstɪ'tjuːʃ(ə)n/ *n.* (lit., fig.) проститу́ция

prostrate /'prɒstreɪt/ *adj.* **1** (lying face down) распросте́ртый **2** (overcome): **she was ~ with grief** она́ была́ сло́млена го́рем

protagonist /prə'tægənɪst/ *n.* гла́вный геро́й

protect /prə'tekt/ *v.t.* защи|ща́ть, -ти́ть

protection /prə'tekʃ(ə)n/ *n.* **1** (defence) защи́та **2** (care) попече́ние
■ **~ racket** *n.* рэ́кет

protectionism /prə'tekʃ(ə)nɪz(ə)m/ *n.* протекциони́зм

protectionist /prə'tekʃ(ə)nɪst/ *n.* протекциони́ст
● *adj.* протекциони́стский

protective /prə'tektɪv/ *adj.* защи́тный

protégé /'prɒtɪʒeɪ/ *n.* (*f.* **protégée**) протеже́ (*c.g., indecl.*)

protein /'prəʊtiːn/ *n.* протеи́н, бело́к

pro tem /prəʊ 'tem/ *adv.* на вре́мя, вре́менно

protest¹ /'prəʊtest/ *n.* проте́ст; возраже́ние
■ **~ march** *n.* марш проте́ста

protest² /prə'test/ *v.t.* **1** (affirm) утвержда́ть (*impf.*); **he continued to ~ his innocence** он продолжа́л наста́ивать на свое́й невино́вности **2** (AmE, object to) возража́ть/протестова́ть (*impf.*) про́тив + g.
● *v.i.*: **~ against** протестова́ть (*impf.*) про́тив + g.; **~ about** выража́ть, вы́разить недово́льство + i.

Protestant /'prɒtɪst(ə)nt/ *n.* протеста́нт (-ка)
● *adj.* протеста́нтский

protestation /ˌprɒtɪ'steɪʃ(ə)n/ *n.* (affirmation) (торже́ственное) заявле́ние; **~s of innocence** торже́ственные заявле́ния о невино́вности

protester /prə'testə(r)/ *n.* протесту́ющ|ий (-ая)

protocol /'prəʊtəkɒl/ *n.* протоко́л

proton /'prəʊtɒn/ *n.* прото́н

p

prototype /'prəʊtətaɪp/ *n.* прототи́п

protract /prə'trækt/ *v.t.* затя́|гивать, -ну́ть; a ∼ed visit затяну́вшийся визи́т; a ∼ed war затяжна́я война́

protractor /prə'træktə(r)/ *n.* (geom.) транспорти́р

protrud|e /prə'tru:d/ *v.i.* выдава́ться (*impf.*); ∼ing teeth выпира́ющие зу́бы

♂ **proud** /praʊd/ *adj.* го́рдый; to be ∼ (of) горди́ться + *i.*; this is a ∼ day for the school э́то торже́ственный/ра́достный день для шко́лы; (arrogant) надме́нный

♂ **prove** /pru:v/ *v.t.* (*p.p.* **proved** or **proven** /'pru:v(ə)n, 'prəʊ-/) дока́з|ывать, -а́ть; he ∼d his worth он показа́л себя́ досто́йным челове́ком; he needs to ∼ himself to others ему́ на́до утверди́ть себя́ в глаза́х други́х
• *v.i.* (*p.p.* **proved** or **proven** /'pru:v(ə)n, 'prəʊ-/) (turn out) ока́з|ываться, -а́ться; the alarm ∼d (to be) a hoax трево́га оказа́лась ло́жной

provenance /'prɒvɪnəns/ *n.* происхожде́ние

proverb /'prɒvɜ:b/ *n.* посло́вица

proverbial /prə'vɜ:bɪəl/ *adj.* **1** (pert. to provs.) воше́дший в погово́рку/посло́вицу, как; как *кто-н./что-н.* из той погово́рки/посло́вицы; ∼ **wisdom** наро́дная му́дрость **2** (notorious) общеизве́стный

♂ **provide** /prə'vaɪd/ *v.t.* **1**: ∼ **sb with sth** обеспе́чи|вать, -ть кого́-н. чем-н.; снаб|жа́ть, -ди́ть кого́-н. чем-н. **2** (prescribe) предусм|а́тривать, -отре́ть
• *v.i.* (prepare oneself) пригот|а́вливаться, -о́виться; she had three children to ∼ for у неё на содержа́нии бы́ло тро́е дете́й

provided /prə'vaɪdɪd/, **providing** /prə'vaɪdɪŋ/ *conjs.* при усло́вии, что; е́сли

providence /'prɒvɪd(ə)ns/ *n.* **1** (foresight) предусмотри́тельность; (thrift) расчётливость **2** (divine care): he escaped by a special ∼ его́ спасло́ (то́лько) провиде́ние; (P∼: God or nature) Провиде́ние, про́мысл Бо́жий

provider /prə'vaɪdə(r)/ *n.* снабже́нец; поставщи́|к (-ца); (breadwinner): her husband is a good ∼ её муж хорошо́ обеспе́чивает семью́; (comput., Internet service ∼) прова́йдер

province /'prɒvɪns/ *n.* о́бласть; in the ∼s в прови́нции, на перифери́и

provincial /prə'vɪnʃ(ə)l/ *adj.* провинциа́льный

♂ **provision** /prə'vɪʒ(ə)n/ *n.* **1** (supplying) снабже́ние **2** (*in pl.*) (supplies, esp. food) прови́зия **3** (preparation) обеспе́чение; their father had made ∼ for them оте́ц обеспе́чил их на бу́дущее

provisional /prə'vɪʒən(ə)l/ *adj.* вре́менный

proviso /prə'vaɪzəʊ/ *n.* (*pl.* ∼s) усло́вие, огово́рка; with the ∼ that ... с усло́вием (*or* с огово́ркой), что...

provocation /prɒvə'keɪʃ(ə)n/ *n.* провока́ция; I did it under ∼ меня́ спровоци́ровали на э́то

provocative /prə'vɒkətɪv/ *adj.* (challenging) вызыва́ющий; (alluring) соблазни́тельный

provoke /prə'vəʊk/ *v.t.* **1** (cause) вызыва́ть, вы́звать; провоци́ровать, с- **2** (anger) серди́ть, рас-

prow /praʊ/ *n.* нос (*судна*)

prowess /'praʊɪs/ *n.* (skill) мастерство́; (valour) до́блесть

prowl /praʊl/ *v.t.* (a place) ры́скать (*impf.*) по + *d.*
• *v.i.* ры́скать (*impf.*)

proximity /prɒk'sɪmɪti/ *n.* бли́зость; сосе́дство

proxy /'prɒksɪ/ *n.* (authorization) полномо́чие, дове́ренность; they voted by ∼ они́ голосова́ли по дове́ренности

prude /pru:d/ *n.* ханжа́ (*c.g.*)

prudence /'pru:d(ə)ns/ *n.* благоразу́мие

prudent /'pru:d(ə)nt/ *adj.* благоразу́мный

prudish /'pru:dɪʃ/ *adj.* стыдли́вый; (pej.) ха́нжеский

prune[1] /pru:n/ *n.* черносли́в

prune[2] /pru:n/ *v.t.* (trim) обр|еза́ть, -е́зать; подр|еза́ть, -е́зать

prurient /'prʊərɪənt/ *adj.* похотли́вый

pry /praɪ/ *v.i.* вме́ш|иваться, -а́ться (в чужи́е дела́)

PS *abbr.* (*of* **postscript**) постскри́птум, припи́ска

psalm /sɑ:m/ *n.* псало́м

pseudonym /'sju:dənɪm/ *n.* псевдони́м

psych /saɪk/ *v.t.*: ∼ **oneself up** настр|а́ивать, -о́ить себя́

psyche /'saɪkɪ/ *n.* душа́; дух

psychedelic /saɪkə'delɪk/ *adj.* (experience) психодели́ческий; (clothes, colours) чудно́й; (drug) галлюциноге́нный

psychiatric /saɪkɪ'ætrɪk/ *adj.* психиатри́ческий

psychiatrist /saɪ'kaɪətrɪst/ *n.* психиа́тр

psychiatry /saɪ'kaɪətrɪ/ *n.* психиатри́я

psychic /'saɪkɪk/ *n.* экстрасе́нс
• *adj.* ≈ яснови́дящ|ий (-ая)

psychoanalyse /saɪkəʊ'ænəlaɪz/ (AmE **-analyze**) *v.t.* подв|ерга́ть, -е́ргнуть психоана́лизу

psychoanalysis /saɪkəʊə'nælɪsɪs/ *n.* психоана́лиз

psychoanalyst /saɪkəʊ'ænəlɪst/ *n.* психоанали́тик

psychological /saɪkə'lɒdʒɪk(ə)l/ *adj.* психологи́ческий

psychologist /saɪ'kɒlədʒɪst/ *n.* психо́лог

psychology /saɪ'kɒlədʒɪ/ *n.* психоло́гия

psychopath /'saɪkəpæθ/ *n.* психопа́т (-ка)

psychopathic /saɪkə'pæθɪk/ *adj.* психопати́ческий; he is ∼ он психопа́т

psychosis /saɪ'kəʊsɪs/ *n.* (*pl.* **psychoses** /-si:z/) психо́з

psychosomatic /saɪkəʊsə'mætɪk/ *adj.* психосомати́ческий

psychotherapist /saɪkəʊ'θerəpɪst/ *n.* психотерапе́вт

psychotherapy /saɪkəʊ'θerəpɪ/ *n.* психотерапи́я

---

p

psychotic /saɪˈkɒtɪk/ adj. психоти́ческий, душевнобольно́й

PTA abbr. (of **parent-teacher association**) ассоциа́ция учителе́й и роди́телей, учи́тельско-роди́тельский комите́т

PTO abbr. (of **please turn over**) см. на об. (смотри́ на оборо́те)

pub /pʌb/ n. (BrE, infml) пивна́я; паб; каба́к

puberty /ˈpjuːbəti/ n. полово́е созрева́ние

pubescent /pjuːˈbes(ə)nt/ adj. дости́гший полово́й зре́лости, половозре́лый

pubic /ˈpjuːbɪk/ adj. лобко́вый, ло́нный
■ ~ **hair** n. лобко́вые во́лосы

ᓍ **public** /ˈpʌblɪk/ n. **1** (community) обще́ственность; наро́д; **the library is open to the** ~ вход в библиоте́ку свобо́дный **2** (audience) пу́блика; **I have never spoken in** ~ я никогда́ не выступа́л пе́ред пу́бликой
● adj. **1** (pert. to people in general) обще́ственный; **in the** ~ **interest** в интере́сах о́бщества/ госуда́рства **2** (pert. to politics or the state) обще́ственный, госуда́рственный; **a** ~ **figure** обще́ственный де́ятель **3** (shared by the community) публи́чный, обще́ственный **4** (done openly, in view of others) публи́чный, гла́сный, откры́тый
■ ~ **address system** n. набо́р звукоусили́тельной аппарату́ры для выступле́ний; ~ **convenience** n. (BrE) обще́ственный туале́т; ~ **holiday** n. устано́вленный зако́ном пра́здник; ~ **house** n. (BrE) пивна́я, паб; ~ **inquiry** n. публи́чное/откры́тое рассле́дование; ~ **opinion** n. обще́ственное мне́ние; ~ **prosecutor** n. прокуро́р; ~ **relations** n. pl. свя́зи с обще́ственностью; ~ **sector** n. госуда́рственный се́ктор; ~ **school** n. (BrE) ча́стная шко́ла; (AmE) госуда́рственная шко́ла; ~ **transport** n. обще́ственный тра́нспорт

publican /ˈpʌblɪkən/ n. (BrE) содержа́тель (m.) ба́ра/па́ба

ᓍ **publication** /ˌpʌblɪˈkeɪʃ(ə)n/ n. публика́ция, опубликова́ние, изда́ние

publicity /pʌbˈlɪsɪti/ n. **1** (public notice, dissemination) гла́сность, огла́ска **2** (advertisement) реклами́рование, рекла́ма, па́блисити (nt. indecl.)
■ ~ **campaign** n. рекла́мная кампа́ния

publicize /ˈpʌblɪsaɪz/ v.t. реклами́ровать (impf.); огла|ша́ть, -си́ть

ᓍ **publish** /ˈpʌblɪʃ/ v.t. **1** (books, newspapers) изд|ава́ть, -а́ть; выпуска́ть, вы́пустить **2** (letter, article, information, author) публикова́ть, о-

publisher /ˈpʌblɪʃə(r)/ n. изда́тель (m.)

publishing /ˈpʌblɪʃɪŋ/ n. изда́тельское де́ло; ~ **house** изда́тельство

pudding /ˈpʊdɪŋ/ n. пу́динг, запека́нка; (BrE, sweet course) сла́дкое; **black** ~ кровяна́я колбаса́

puddle /ˈpʌd(ə)l/ n. (pool) лу́жа

puerile /ˈpjʊəraɪl/ adj. де́тский, инфанти́льный

Puerto Rican /pwɜːˈtəʊ ˈriːkən/ n. пуэрторика́н|ец (-ка)
● adj. пуэрторика́нский

Puerto Rico /pwɜːˈtəʊ ˈriːkəʊ/ n. Пуэ́рто-Ри́ко (nt. indecl.)

puff /pʌf/ n. **1** (of breath) вы́дох **2** (of smoke) дымо́к, клуб **3** (of air or wind) дунове́ние
● v.t. **1** (breathe out) выдыха́ть, вы́дохнуть; **he** ~**ed smoke in my face** он вы́дохнул дым мне в лицо́ **2** (make out of breath): **I was** ~**ed after the climb** по́сле подъёма у меня́ появи́лась одышка **3** ~ **out** (smoke) выпуска́ть, вы́пустить; (chest): **he** ~**ed out his chest with pride** он го́рдо вы́пятил грудь **4**: ~**ed-up** (haughty) наду́тый
● v.i. **1** (breathe quickly): **he was** ~**ing and panting** он пыхте́л **2** (emit smoke) дыми́ться (impf.) **3** ~ **up** (swell) расп|уха́ть, -у́хнуть
■ ~ **pastry** n. сло́ёное те́сто

puffin /ˈpʌfɪn/ n. ту́пик, топо́рик (птица)

puffy /ˈpʌfi/ adj. (**puffier**, **puffiest**) (eyes) опу́хший; (face) отёчный

pugnacious /pʌgˈneɪʃəs/ adj. драчли́вый, вои́нственный

puke /pjuːk/ n. (infml) рво́та, блевоти́на
● v.i. блева́ть (impf.) (infml); **he** ~**d** его́ вы́рвало

ᓍ **pull** /pʊl/ n. (traction) тя́га; (act) дёрганье; **he gave a** ~ **on the rope** он дёрнул (за) верёвку
● v.t. **1** (draw towards one, tug, jerk) тяну́ть, по-; тащи́ть, по-; **he** ~**ed me by the sleeve** он потяну́л меня́ за рука́в **2** (fig.): **she** ~**ed a face at him** она́ ско́рчила ему́ грима́су **3** (extract): **he** ~**ed a gun on me** он вы́хватил пистоле́т и навёл его́ на меня́ **4** (strain) растя́|гивать, -ну́ть
● v.i. тяну́ть, по-; **they** ~**ed on the rope** они́ потяну́ли за верёвку

□ ~ **apart** v.t. (also ~ **to pieces**) раз|рыва́ть, -орва́ть (на куски́); (fig., criticize severely) разн|оси́ть, -ести́ в пух и прах

□ ~ **away** v.i. (move off) от|ходи́ть, -ойти́

□ ~ **back** v.t. отта́|скивать, -щи́ть; оття́|гивать, -ну́ть; **he** ~**ed her back from the window** он отташи́л её от окна́
● v.i. отступ|а́ть, -и́ть

□ ~ **down** v.t. (lower by) спус|ка́ть, -ти́ть; (demolish) сн|оси́ть, -ести́

□ ~ **in** v.i. (drive or move to a standstill) остан|а́вливаться, -ови́ться; **the train** ~**ed in** по́езд подошёл к перро́ну; **he** ~**ed in to the kerb** (BrE), **up to the curb** (AmE) он подъе́хал к тротуа́ру; (drive or move towards near side of road): **he** ~**ed in to avoid a collision** он прижа́лся к обо́чине, что́бы избежа́ть столкнове́ния

□ ~ **off** v.t. (remove, detach) стя́|гивать, -ну́ть; сн|има́ть, -ять; (infml, achieve) успе́шно заверш|а́ть, -и́ть

□ ~ **on** v.t. натя́|гивать, -ну́ть

□ ~ **out** v.t. (extract) выта́скивать, вы́тащить; (withdraw) выводи́ть, вы́вести; **the troops should be** ~**ed out** войска́ сле́дует вы́вести
● v.i. (drive or move away) от|ходи́ть, -ойти́; (of driving manoeuvres) отъ|езжа́ть, -е́хать; **he** ~**ed out to overtake** он пошёл на обго́н; (withdraw, of troops) от|ходи́ть, -ойти́; (from an enterprise): **he** ~**ed out** он отказа́лся от

p

уча́стия в э́том де́ле
□ ~ **through** *v.i.* (recover from illness) поправ|ля́ться, -а́виться
□ ~ **together** *v.t.*: ~ **yourself together!** возьми́те себя́ в ру́ки!
● *v.i.* (fig.) сраба́тываться, -о́таться; **if we all ~ together, we shall win** объедини́вшись, мы победи́м
□ ~ **up** *v.t.* (uproot) вырыва́ть, вы́рвать; (raise) выта́гивать, вы́тянуть; (draw nearer) придв|ига́ть, -и́нуть; ~ **up a chair!** придви́ньте стул!; (bring to a halt) остан|а́вливать, -ови́ть; (reprimand) отчи́т|ывать, -а́ть
● *v.i.* (come to a halt) остан|а́вливаться, -ови́ться
■ ~**-up** *n.* (gymnastic exercise) подтя́гивание

pulley /ˈpʊlɪ/ *n.* (*pl.* **pulleys**) шкив
pullover /ˈpʊləʊvə(r)/ *n.* пуло́вер, сви́тер
pulp /pʌlp/ *n.* **1** (of fruit) мя́коть **2** (fig.) ме́сиво; бесфо́рменная ма́сса
pulpit /ˈpʊlpɪt/ *n.* ка́федра (*в церкви*)
pulsate /pʌlˈseɪt/ *v.i.* пульси́ровать (*impf.*)
pulse /pʌls/ *n.* пульс
pulverize /ˈpʌlvəraɪz/ *v.t.* (reduce to powder) размельч|а́ть, -и́ть; (fig., smash, demolish) уничт|ожа́ть, -о́жить
puma /ˈpjuːmə/ *n.* пу́ма
pummel /ˈpʌm(ə)l/ *v.t.* (**pummelled**, **pummelling**, AmE **pummeled**, **pummeling**) колоти́ть, по-, бить, из- (*кулака́ми*)
pump /pʌmp/ *n.* насо́с, по́мпа
● *v.t.* **1** (transfer by ~ing) кача́ть, на- **2** (fig.): **I ~ed him for information** я выспра́шивал его́; я выве́дывал у него́ све́дения **3** (*also* ~ **up**) (inflate) нака́ч|ивать, -а́ть
pumpkin /ˈpʌmpkɪn/ *n.* ты́ква
pun /pʌn/ *n.* игра́ слов, каламбу́р
punch /pʌntʃ/ *n.* **1** (blow with fist) уда́р кулако́м **2** (fig., energy) эне́ргия, ого́нь (*m.*) **3** (tool for perforating, e.g. paper) дыроко́л
● *v.t.* **1** (hit with fist) уд|аря́ть, -а́рить кулако́м **2** (perforate) компости́ровать (*impf.*)
■ ~**line** *n.* концо́вка, развя́зка (*анекдо́та и т. n.*); ~**-up** *n.* (BrE, infml) дра́ка
punctilious /pʌŋkˈtɪlɪəs/ *adj.* скрупулёзный
punctual /ˈpʌŋktʃʊəl/ *adj.* пунктуа́льный, то́чный
punctuate /ˈpʌŋktʃʊeɪt/ *v.t.* (insert punctuation marks in) ста́вить, по- зна́ки препина́ния в + *a.*; (fig., interrupt, intersperse) прер|ыва́ть, -ва́ть
punctuation /pʌŋktʃʊˈeɪʃ(ə)n/ *n.* пунктуа́ция
■ ~ **mark** *n.* знак препина́ния
puncture /ˈpʌŋktʃə(r)/ *n.* проко́л
● *v.t.* прок|а́лывать, -оло́ть
pundit /ˈpʌndɪt/ *n.* знато́к, специали́ст
pungent /ˈpʌndʒ(ə)nt/ *adj.* о́стрый
punish /ˈpʌnɪʃ/ *v.t.* нака́з|ывать, -а́ть; кара́ть, по-
punishment /ˈpʌnɪʃmənt/ *n.* наказа́ние
punitive /ˈpjuːnɪtɪv/ *adj.* кара́тельный; ~ **taxation** высо́кое налогообложе́ние

p

punk /pʌŋk/ *n.* **1** (admirer of ~ rock) панк; (~ rock) панк-ро́к **2** (AmE, infml, worthless person) дрянь
● *adj.* па́нковский
punnet /ˈpʌnɪt/ *n.* (BrE) корзи́н(оч)ка
punt /pʌnt/ *n.* (boat) плоскодо́нка
punter /ˈpʌntə(r)/ *n.* **1** (BrE) (at cards) понтёр; (at races) игро́к; (client) клие́нт (-ка) **2** (in American football and rugby) игро́к, бью́щий по подбро́шенному мячу́
puny /ˈpjuːnɪ/ *adj.* (**punier**, **puniest**) (undersized, feeble) тщеду́шный, хи́лый
pup /pʌp/ *n.* (young dog) щено́к
◌⃠ **pupil** /ˈpjuːp(ə)l/ *n.* **1** (one being taught) учени́|к (-ца) **2** (of eye) зрачо́к
puppet /ˈpʌpɪt/ *n.*: glove ~ ку́кла; string ~ марионе́тка; (fig.) марионе́тка
puppy /ˈpʌpɪ/ *n.* щено́к
■ ~ **fat** *n.* де́тская пу́хлость; ~ **love** *n.* де́тская любо́вь
◌⃠ **purchase** /ˈpəːtʃɪs/ *n.* (buying; thing bought) поку́пка, приобрете́ние
● *v.t.* (buy) покупа́ть, купи́ть
purchaser /ˈpəːtʃɪsə(r)/ *n.* покупа́тель (-ница)
pure /pjʊə(r)/ *adj.* чи́стый
purée /ˈpjʊəreɪ/ *n.* пюре́ (*nt. indecl.*)
purely /ˈpjʊəlɪ/ *adv.* исключи́тельно, соверше́нно, чи́сто
purgatory /ˈpəːgətərɪ/ *n.* чисти́лище; (fig.) ад
purge /pəːdʒ/ *n.* очище́ние
● *v.t.* (lit., fig.) оч|ища́ть, -и́стить
purify /ˈpjʊərɪfaɪ/ *v.t.* оч|ища́ть, -и́стить
purist /ˈpjʊərɪst/ *n.* пури́ст
puritan /ˈpjʊərɪt(ə)n/ *n.* (**P~**) (hist.) пурита́н|ин (-ка); (fig.) пурита́н|ин (-ка)
● *adj.* пурита́нский
puritanical /pjʊərɪˈtænɪk(ə)l/ *adj.* пурита́нский
purity /ˈpjʊərɪtɪ/ *n.* чистота́
purple /ˈpəːp(ə)l/ *n.* лило́вый/фиоле́товый цвет
● *adj.* лило́вый, фиоле́товый
purport¹ /ˈpəːpɔːt/ *n.* смысл, суть
purport² /pəˈpɔːt/ *v.t.* (state) подразумева́ть (*impf.*); (claim): **this book is not all it ~s to be** э́та кни́га не совсе́м така́я, како́й она́ претенду́ет быть
◌⃠ **purpose** /ˈpəːpəs/ *n.* (aim) цель; (intention) наме́рение; **on ~** наро́чно, специа́льно; **she went out with the ~ of buying clothes** она́ вы́шла с це́лью купи́ть оде́жду
■ ~**-built** *adj.* (BrE) вы́строенный специа́льно
purposeful /ˈpəːpəsfʊl/ *adj.* целеустремлённый
purposely /ˈpəːpəslɪ/ *adv.* наро́чно, (пред)наме́ренно, специа́льно
purr /pəː(r)/ *v.i.* мурлы́кать (*impf.*)
purse /pəːs/ *n.* (for money) кошелёк; (AmE, handbag) су́мочка
● *v.t.* мо́рщить, с-; **he ~d (up) his lips** он поджа́л гу́бы
■ ~ **strings** *n. pl.*: **her husband holds the ~ strings** (fig.) её муж распоряжа́ется деньга́ми
◌⃠ **pursue** /pəˈsjuː/ *v.t.* (**pursues**, **pursued**, **pursuing**) **1** (chase) пресле́довать (*impf.*)

2 (strive after) добива́ться (*impf.*) + g. **3** (course) сле́довать (*impf.*) + d.; (interest) занима́ться (*impf.*) + i.; (activity) предприн|има́ть, -я́ть; (policy) проводи́ть (*impf.*)

pursuer /pəˈsjuːə(r)/ n. пресле́дователь (*m.*)

pursuit /pəˈsjuːt/ n. **1** (chase) пресле́дование; пого́ня; **he escaped, with the police in hot ∼** он бежа́л, пресле́дуемый поли́цией по пята́м **2** (seeking) по́иск|и (-ов); **he will stop at nothing in ∼ of his ends** он не остано́вится ни пе́ред чем для достиже́ния свои́х це́лей **3** (recreation) заня́тие

pus /pʌs/ n. гной

♂ **push** /pʊʃ/ n. толчо́к
● v.t. **1** (exert pressure to move) толк|а́ть, -ну́ть; пих|а́ть, -ну́ть **2** (fig., urge) подт|а́лкивать, -олкну́ть; вынужда́ть, вы́нудить **3** (press) наж|има́ть, -а́ть **4** (promote) реклами́ровать (*impf.*); прот|а́лкивать, -олкну́ть
● v.i. **1** (exert force) толка́ться (*impf.*); **don't ∼!** не толка́йтесь! **2** (force one's way) прот|а́лкиваться, -олкну́ться; **he ∼ed past me** он проле́з вперёд, оттолкну́в меня́
□ **∼ around** v.t. (fig.): **I won't be ∼ed around** я не позво́лю кома́ндовать над(о) мной
□ **∼ aside/away** v.t. отт|а́лкивать, -олкну́ть
□ **∼ in** v.t. вт|а́лкивать, -олкну́ть
● v.i. втира́ться, втере́ться; **don't ∼ in!** (intrude) не ле́зьте!
□ **∼ on** v.i. продв|ига́ться, -и́нуться (вперёд)
□ **∼ over** v.t. опроки́|дывать, -нуть
□ **∼ past** v.i. прот|а́лкиваться, -олкну́ться
□ **∼ through** v.t. (lit., fig.) прот|а́лкивать, -олкну́ть
■ **∼chair** n. (BrE) (де́тская) прогу́лочная коля́ска; **∼-up** n. (AmE) отжима́ние; **do ∼-ups** отж|има́ться, -а́ться (от по́ла)

pusher /ˈpʊʃə(r)/ n. (infml, drug ∼) наркоторго́вец

pushy /ˈpʊʃɪ/ adj. (**pushier**, **pushiest**) напо́ристый

puss /pʊs/ n. (cat) ко́шечка, ки́ска

♂ **put** /pʊt/ v.t. (**putting**, past and p.p. **put**)
1 (move into a certain position) класть, положи́ть; (stand) ста́вить, по-; (set) сажа́ть, посади́ть; **∼ the money in your pocket!** положи́те де́ньги в карма́н!; **∼ yourself in my place!** поста́вьте себя́ на моё ме́сто!; **I ∼ the matter into the hands of my lawyer** я поручи́л э́то де́ло своему́ адвока́ту; **she ∼ a cloth on the table** она́ накры́ла стол ска́тертью; **she ∼ the children to bed** она́ уложи́ла дете́й; **where did I ∼ that book?** куда́ я дел э́ту кни́гу? **2** (thrust) вонз|а́ть, -и́ть; **he ∼ his fist through the window** он проби́л окно́ кулако́м **3** (bring into a certain state or relationship): **that ∼s me at a disadvantage** э́то ста́вит меня́ в невы́годное положе́ние; **he ∼ his cold ∼ him off his food** из-за просту́ды он потеря́л аппети́т; (impose, bring in): **the tax ∼s a heavy burden on the rich** нало́г ложи́тся тяжёлым бре́менем на бога́тых; (set, arrange): **∼ in order** прив|оди́ть, -ести́ в поря́док; (appoint to a job) ста́вить, по-; **∼ sb in charge of** ста́вить, по- кого́-н. во главе́ + g.; (offer): **they ∼ their house**

on the market они́ объяви́ли о прода́же до́ма; (invest) вкла́дывать, вложи́ть; поме|ща́ть, -сти́ть **4** (estimate, consider): **I would ∼ her (age) at about 65** я дал бы ей лет 65; **I wouldn't ∼ it past him to be lying** с него́ ста́нется: соврёт и де́нег не возьмёт; **he ∼s a high value on courtesy** он высоко́ це́нит ве́жливость **5** (submit) выдвига́ть, вы́двинуть; задава́ть, -а́ть; **may I ∼ a suggestion?** мо́жно мне внести́ предложе́ние? **6** (express) изл|ага́ть, -ожи́ть; **how can I ∼ it?** как бы э́то сказа́ть?; **will you ∼ that in writing?** вы мо́жете изложи́ть э́то на бума́ге?
□ **∼ across** v.t. (make clear, communicate) объясн|я́ть, -и́ть
□ **∼ away** v.t. (tidy) уб|ира́ть, -ра́ть; (save) от|кла́дывать, -ложи́ть
□ **∼ back** v.t. (replace, restore) класть, положи́ть на ме́сто; (of clock) перев|оди́ть, -ести́ наза́д; (postpone) от|кла́дывать, -ложи́ть
□ **∼ by** v.t. (save) от|кла́дывать, -ложи́ть
□ **∼ down** v.t. (place on ground, etc.) класть, положи́ть на зе́млю; **∼ your gun down** бро́сьте ору́жие!; опусти́те ружьё!; (allow to alight): **the bus stopped to ∼ down passengers** авто́бус останови́лся, что́бы вы́садить пассажи́ров; (make deposit of) вн|оси́ть, -ести́ (зада́ток); (lower) сн|ижа́ть, -и́зить; (repress) подав|ля́ть, -и́ть; **the rebellion was quickly ∼ down** восста́ние бы́ло бы́стро пода́влено; (write down) запи́с|ывать, -а́ть; (kill sick animal) усып|ля́ть, -и́ть; умерщв|ля́ть, -и́ть
□ **∼ forward** v.t. (advance) **the clocks are ∼ forward in spring** весно́й часы́ перево́дят вперёд; (propose) выдвига́ть, вы́двинуть; **his name was ∼ forward** была́ вы́двинута его́ кандидату́ра; (bring nearer) передв|ига́ть, -и́нуть вперёд
□ **∼ in** v.t. (cause to enter; insert) вст|авля́ть, -а́вить; (install) вст|авля́ть, -а́вить; (contribute): **I ∼ in a word for him** я вста́вил за него́ слове́чко; (submit, present) под|ава́ть, -а́ть; **I ∼ in an application** я по́дал заявле́ние; **in an appearance** появ|ля́ться, -и́ться; (work): **I ∼ in 6 hours today** я сего́дня отрабо́тал 6 часо́в
● v.i. (of boat or crew) за|ходи́ть, -йти́ в порт; **the ship ∼ in at Gibraltar** кора́бль зашёл в Гибралта́р; (apply): **she ∼ in for a job as secretary** она́ подала́ заявле́ние на до́лжность/ме́сто секретаря́
□ **∼ off** v.t. (postpone) от|кла́дывать, -ложи́ть; отсро́чи|вать, -ть; (fob off): **he ∼ me off with promises** он отде́лался от меня́ обеща́ниями; (deter) отпу́г|ивать, -ну́ть; **we were ∼ off by the weather** мы переду́мали из-за пого́ды; (repel) отт|а́лкивать, -олкну́ть; **me off by his tactlessness** меня́ оттолкну́ла его́ беста́ктность; (distract): **I can't recite if you keep ∼ting me off** я не могу́ деклами́ровать, когда́ вы меня́ отвлека́ете
□ **∼ on** v.t. (clothes, etc.) над|ева́ть, -е́ть; (place in position): **when the pot is full, ∼ the lid on** когда́ кастрю́ля напо́лнится, накро́йте её кры́шкой; (assume): **he ∼ on an air of innocence** он напусти́л на себя́ неви́нный вид; (increase) увели́чи|вать, -ть; **you're ∼ting on weight**

вы полне́ете/поправля́етесь; (light, radio, etc.)
включа́|ть, -и́ть; (play, concert, etc.) ста́вить, по-
□ ~ **out** *v.t.* (place outside door) выставля́ть,
вы́ставить за дверь; (extend, protrude): ~
your tongue out! покажи́те язы́к!; **he ~
out his hand in welcome** он протяну́л ру́ку
для приве́тствия; (arrange so as to be seen)
выставля́ть, вы́ставить; выкла́дывать,
вы́ложить; (hang up outside) выве́шивать,
вы́весить; **she ~ the washing out to dry**
она́ вы́весила бельё суши́ться; (extinguish)
туши́ть, по-; гаси́ть, по-; ~ **the lights out!**
потуши́те свет!; ~ **your cigarette out!**
погаси́те сигаре́ту!; (dislocate) выви́хивать,
вы́вихнуть; (inconvenience) нар|уша́ть, -у́шить
пла́ны + *g.*; **would it ~ you out to come at
3?** вас не затрудни́т прийти́ в 3 часа́?; (vex)
раздраж|а́ть, -и́ть
□ ~ **through** *v.t.* (accomplish) осуществ|ля́ть,
-и́ть; (connect by telephone) соедин|я́ть, -и́ть
□ ~ **together** *v.t.* (bring close or into contact)
соедин|я́ть, -и́ть; (assemble) сост|авля́ть,
-а́вить; (construct from components) соб|ира́ть,
-ра́ть
□ ~ **up** *v.t.* (raise, hold up) подн|има́ть, -я́ть;
~ **up your hand if you know the answer!**
кто зна́ет отве́т, подними́те ру́ку!; (display)
выставля́ть, вы́ставить; (erect) воздв|ига́ть,
-и́гнуть; стро́ить, по-; **shall we ~ the
curtains up?** бу́дем ве́шать занаве́ски?;
(increase) повы́ша́ть, -ы́сить; ~ **up prices** (BrE)
подн|има́ть, -я́ть це́ны; (offer) выдвига́ть,
вы́двинуть; **he ~ up no resistance** он не
оказа́л никако́го сопротивле́ния; **they ~
up three candidates** они́ вы́двинули трёх
кандида́тов; (supply) вн|оси́ть, -ести́; **I will
~ up £1,000 to support him** я внесу́ ты́сячу
фу́нтов в его́ по́льзу; (accommodate): **he ~ me**

up for the night я переночева́л у него́; (infml,
introduce): **I ~ him up to that trick** я его́ научи́л
э́тому приёму/трю́ку
● *v.i.* (tolerate) мири́ться, при- (*с кем/чем*); **I
won't ~ up with any nonsense** я не потерплю́
никаки́х глу́постей
■ **~-down** *n.* (snub) ре́зкость

putrefy /'pju:trɪfaɪ/ *v.i.* (go bad) гнить, с-;
(fester) разл|ага́ться, -ожи́ться

putrid /'pju:trɪd/ *adj.* (decomposed) гнило́й;
(infml, unpleasant) отврати́тельный

putt /pʌt/ *n.* уда́р, загоня́ющий мяч в лу́нку
(*в гольфе*)
● *v.i.* (**putted, putting**) заг|оня́ть, -на́ть
мяч в лу́нку
■ **~ing green** *n.* лужа́йка с лу́нками
(*в гольфе*)

putty /'pʌtɪ/ *n.* зама́зка, шпаклёвка

puzzle /'pʌz(ə)l/ *n.* зага́дка; (for entertainment)
головоло́мка, пазл
● *v.t.* озада́чи|вать, -ть; прив|оди́ть, -ести́ в
недоуме́ние

PVC *abbr.* (*of* **polyvinyl chloride**) ПВХ
(поливинилхлори́д)

pygmy /'pɪgmɪ/ *n.* пигме́й

pyjamas /pəˈdʒɑ:məz/ (AmE **pajamas**) *n. pl.*
пижа́ма; **pyjama trousers** пижа́мные штаны́

pylon /'paɪlən/ *n.* (for electricity) опо́ра (*ли́нии
электропереда́ч*)

pyramid /'pɪrəmɪd/ *n.* пирами́да

pyre /'paɪə(r)/ *n.* погреба́льный костёр

Pyrenees /pɪrəˈni:z/ *n. pl.* Пирене́|и (-ев)

pyrotechnics /paɪərəʊˈtekrɪks/ *n. pl.*
(*treated as sg. or pl.*) (art of making fireworks)
пироте́хника; (firework display, also fig.)
фейерве́рк

python /'paɪθ(ə)n/ *n.* пито́н

p

q

Qq

Qatar /ˈkæˈtɑ:(r)/ *n.* Ка́тар

QE *abbr.* (*of* **quantitative easing**) (econ.)
коли́чественное смягче́ние

quack /kwæk/ *n.* (sound) кря́канье
● *v.i.* кря́кать (*impf.*)

quadruple /ˈkwɒdrʊp(ə)l/ *adj.* учетверённый
● *v.t. & i.* увели́чи|вать(ся), -ть(ся) в четы́ре
ра́за

quagmire /ˈkwɒgmaɪə(r)/ *n.* (also fig.) боло́то

quail /kweɪl/ *v.i.* тру́сить, с-

quaint /kweɪnt/ *adj.* причу́дливый, чудно́й

quake /kweɪk/ *v.i.* дрожа́ть (*impf.*);
содрог|а́ться, -ну́ться

qualification /ˌkwɒlɪfɪˈkeɪʃ(ə)n/ *n.* **1** (skill)
квалифика́ция **2** (modification) ограниче́ние

qualifier /ˈkwɒlɪfaɪə(r)/ *n.* (match) отбо́рочное
соревнова́ние, отбо́рочный матч; (person,
team) челове́к, проше́дший (*or* кома́нда,
проше́дшая) отбо́рочные соревнова́ния

✔ **qualif|y** /ˈkwɒlɪfaɪ/ *v.t.* **1** (for job) гото́вить
(*impf.*); **I am not ~ied to advise you** я
недоста́точно компете́нтен, что́бы дава́ть
вам сове́ты; (make entitled) дава́ть, дать пра́во
(+ *d.*) (**to** + *inf.*; **for:** на + *a.*); **he is a ~ied**

doctor он дипломи́рованный врач **2** (modify)
огово|а́ривать, -ори́ть; уточни|я́ть, -и́ть; **I must
∼y my statement** я до́лжен сде́лать огово́рку
● *v.i.* (be eligible) име́ть (*impf.*) пра́во (**for:**
на + *a.*); **will you ∼y for a pension?** бу́дете
ли вы име́ть пра́во на пе́нсию?; (sport): **our
team failed to ∼y** на́ша кома́нда не прошла́
отбо́рочные соревнова́ния

qualitative /ˈkwɒlɪtətɪv/ *adj.* ка́чественный

⚘ **quality** /ˈkwɒlɪtɪ/ *n.* **1** (degree of merit)
ка́чество; (excellence) высо́кое ка́чество,
доброка́чественность **2** (characteristic)
ка́чество, сво́йство
● *adj.* (высоко)ка́чественный

qualm /kwɑːm/ *n.* сомне́ние, колеба́ние

quandary /ˈkwɒndərɪ/ *n.* затрудни́тельное
положе́ние

quango /ˈkwæŋɡəʊ/ *n.* (*pl.* **∼s**) (BrE, infml)
полуавтоно́мная организа́ция

quantifiable /ˈkwɒntɪfaɪəb(ə)l/ *adj.*
измери́мый

quantitative /ˈkwɒntɪtətɪv/ *adj.*
коли́чественный
■ **∼ easing** *n.* (econ.) коли́чественная
смягче́ние

quantity /ˈkwɒntɪtɪ/ *n.* коли́чество
■ **∼ surveyor** *n.* (BrE) инжене́р-планови́к

quantum /ˈkwɒntəm/ *n.* (*pl.* **quanta**) (phys.)
квант; **∼ leap** скачо́к; **∼ mechanics** ква́нтовая
меха́ника; **∼ theory** ква́нтовая тео́рия

quarantine /ˈkwɒrəntiːn/ *n.* каранти́н
● *v.t.* содержа́ть (*impf.*) в каранти́не

quarrel /ˈkwɒr(ə)l/ *n.* **1** (altercation) ссо́ра
2 (cause for complaint) по́вод для ссо́ры,
прете́нзия; **I have no ∼ with him on that
score** у меня́ нет к нему́ прете́нзий по э́тому
по́воду
● *v.i.* (**quarrelled, quarrelling**, AmE
quarreled, quarreling) (have an argument)
ссо́риться, по-; (take issue): **I cannot ∼ with his
logic** я не могу́ не согласи́ться с его́ ло́гикой

quarrelsome /ˈkwɒrəlsəm/ *adj.* сварли́вый

quarry[1] /ˈkwɒrɪ/ *n.* (prey) добы́ча

quarry[2] /ˈkwɒrɪ/ *n.* (for stone etc.) карье́р
● *v.t.* (extract) доб|ыва́ть, -ы́ть

⚘ **quarter** /ˈkwɔːtə(r)/ *n.* **1** (fourth part) че́тверть;
(of hour): **a ∼ to six** без че́тверти шесть;
a ∼ past six че́тверть седьмо́го; (of year)
кварта́л **2** (AmE coin) два́дцать пять це́нтов
3 (district) кварта́л **4** (*in pl.*) (lodgings) каза́рмы
(*f. pl.*); кварти́ры (*f. pl.*) **5**: **at close ∼s** в
те́сном сосе́дстве, вблизи́
● *v.t.* (divide into four) дели́ть, раз- на четы́ре
ча́сти
■ **∼-final** *n.* четвертьфина́л

quarterly /ˈkwɔːtəlɪ/ *adj.* кварта́льный
● *adv.* ежекварта́льно; раз в три ме́сяца

quartet /kwɔːˈtet/ *n.* (mus.) кварте́т

quartz /kwɔːts/ *n.* кварц

quash /kwɒʃ/ *v.t.* подав|ля́ть, -и́ть

quaver /ˈkweɪvə(r)/ *n.* **1** (trembling tone)
дрожа́ние **2** (BrE, mus.) восьма́я но́та
● *v.i.* дрожа́ть (*impf.*)

quay /kiː/ *n.* прича́л

■ **∼side** *n.* при́стань

queasy /ˈkwiːzɪ/ *adj.* (**queasier, queasiest**):
I feel a little ∼ меня́ немно́го тошни́т

queen /kwiːn/ *n.* **1** короле́ва **2** (fig.)
короле́ва, цари́ца **3** (*also* **∼ bee**) ма́тка
4 (at chess) ферзь (*m.*) **5** (at cards) да́ма
■ **Q∼'s Counsel** *n.* адвока́т вы́сшего ра́нга

queer /kwɪə(r)/ *adj.* стра́нный

quell /kwel/ *v.t.* подав|ля́ть, -и́ть

quench /kwentʃ/ *v.t.*: **∼ one's thirst** утол|я́ть,
-и́ть жа́жду

querulous /ˈkwerʊləs/ *adj.* ворчли́вый

query /ˈkwɪərɪ/ *n.* вопро́с
● *v.t.* выража́ть, вы́разить сомне́ние в + *p.*;
усомни́ться (*pf.*) в + *p.*

quest /kwest/ *n.* по́иски (*m. pl.*); **the ∼ for
happiness** по́иски сча́стья

⚘ **question** /ˈkwestʃ(ə)n/ *n.* **1** (interrogation;
problem) вопро́с; **it is only a ∼ of finding
the money** де́ло то́лько за тем, что́бы
найти́ де́ньги; **a holiday is out of the ∼** об
о́тпуске не мо́жет быть и ре́чи; **the man in
∼** челове́к, о кото́ром идёт речь **2** (doubt,
objection) сомне́ние; **his statements were called
into ∼** его́ заявле́ния бы́ли поста́влены под
сомне́ние
● *v.t.* **1** (interrogate) допр|а́шивать, -оси́ть
2 (cast doubt on) ста́вить, по- под сомне́ние
■ **∼ mark** *n.* вопроси́тельный знак

questionable /ˈkwestʃənəb(ə)l/ *adj.*
сомни́тельный

questioner /ˈkwestʃənə(r)/ *n.* задаю́щий/
задава́вший вопро́с(ы)

questionnaire /kwestʃəˈneə(r)/ *n.* анке́та

queue /kjuː/ (BrE) *n.* о́чередь; **he was trying to
jump the ∼** он пыта́лся пройти́ без о́череди
● *v.i.* (**queues, queued, queuing** or
queueing) (*also* **∼ up**) станови́ться, стать
в о́чередь

quibble /ˈkwɪb(ə)l/ *v.i.* (argue) пререка́ться
(*impf.*)

quiche /kiːʃ/ *n.* откры́тый пиро́г с сы́ром,
беко́ном, овоща́ми *и т. п.*

⚘ **quick** /kwɪk/ *n.*: **he bit his nails to the ∼** он
искуса́л все но́гти; **his words cut me to the ∼**
его́ слова́ заде́ли меня́ за живо́е
● *adj.* **1** (rapid) бы́стрый, ско́рый; **he is a ∼
worker** он бы́стро рабо́тает **2** (lively) живо́й;
(quick-minded) сообрази́тельный; **he has a ∼
temper** он о́чень вспы́льчив
● *adv.* бы́стро; **∼, get a doctor!** скоре́е
позови́те врача́!
■ **∼sand(s)** *n.* зыбу́чий песо́к; зыбу́чие пески́;
∼-tempered *adj.* вспы́льчивый; **∼-witted**
adj. смышлёный, нахо́дчивый

quicken /ˈkwɪkən/ *v.t.* (make quicker) уск|оря́ть,
-о́рить; (stimulate) возбу|жда́ть, -ди́ть
● *v.i.* (become quicker) уск|оря́ться, -о́риться

quid /kwɪd/ *n.* (*pl.* **∼**) (BrE, infml, £1) фунт
(сте́рлингов)

⚘ **quiet** /ˈkwaɪət/ *n.* (silence) тишина́; (repose)
поко́й
● *adj.* (**quieter, quietest**) **1** (making little or
no sound) ти́хий; бесшу́мный; **can't you keep**

q

~? ты не мо́жешь помолча́ть? **2** (undisturbed) споко́йный, ми́рный; **we had a ~ night** ночь прошла́ споко́йно **3** (of gentle disposition) споко́йный, ти́хий **4** (private; concealed) та́йный; скры́тый; **on the ~** (infml, secretly) тайко́м; втихомо́лку; (in confidence) под (больши́м) секре́том
● *int.* ти́ше!

quieten /'kwaɪət(ə)n/ *v.t. & i.* (BrE also ~ **down**) успок|а́ивать(ся), -о́ить(ся)

quietness /'kwaɪətnɪs/ *n.* (stillness) тишина́; (repose) поко́й; (of manner) невозмути́мость, споко́йствие

quiff /kwɪf/ *n.* (BrE) чёлка; (tuft) зачёс

quill /kwɪl/ *n.* перо́; (of porcupine) игла́ (*дикобраза*)

quilt /kwɪlt/ *n.* стёганое одея́ло
● *v.t.:* ~ed bathrobe, bedcover стёганый хала́т, стёганое покрыва́ло

quip /kwɪp/ *n.* остро́та
● *v.i.* (quipped, quipping) остри́ть, с-

quirk /kwɜːk/ *n.* причу́да

quirky /'kwɜːkɪ/ *adj.* (quirkier, quirkiest) причу́дливый

quit /kwɪt/ *v.t.* (quitting, *past and p.p.* quitted or quit) **1** (leave) ост|авля́ть, -а́вить **2** (infml, stop) прекра|ща́ть, -ти́ть
● *v.i.* (quitting, *past and p.p.* quitted or quit) **1** (leave job etc.): the maid was given notice to ~ го́рничной предупреди́ли об увольне́нии **2** (leave off) перест|ава́ть, -а́ть

♂ **quite** /kwaɪt/ *adv.* **1** (entirely) совсе́м,

соверше́нно, вполне́; **I ~ agree** я вполне́/ соверше́нно согла́сен; **~ right!** соверше́нно ве́рно!; **have you ~ finished?** ну, вы ко́нчили?; **that is ~ another matter** э́то совсе́м друго́е де́ло **2** (to a certain extent) дово́льно; **it is ~ cold here** здесь дово́льно хо́лодно; **I ~ like cycling** я не прочь поката́ться на велосипе́де; **~ a long time** дово́льно мно́го вре́мени; **~ a few** дово́льно мно́го; нема́ло

quits /kwɪts/ *pred. adj.*: **now we are ~** тепе́рь мы кви́ты

quiver /'kwɪvə(r)/ *v.i.* дрожа́ть, за-

quiz /kwɪz/ *n.* (*pl.* quizzes) (test of knowledge) викторина; (AmE, school test) контро́льная (рабо́та)
● *v.t.* (quizzed, quizzing) выспра́шивать, вы́спросить

quizzical /'kwɪzɪk(ə)l/ *adj.* насме́шливый, ирони́ческий

quorum /'kwɔːrəm/ *n.* кво́рум

quota /'kwəʊtə/ *n.* (*pl.* ~s) кво́та, но́рма

quotation /kwəʊ'teɪʃ(ə)n/ *n.* **1** (passage quoted) цита́та **2** (estimate of cost) цена́, сто́имость
■ **~ marks** *n. pl.* кавы́ч|ки (-ек)

♂ **quote** /kwəʊt/ *n.* **1** (infml, quotation) цита́та **2** (*in pl.*) (infml, quotation marks) кавы́ч|ки (-ек)
● *v.t.* **1** (repeat words of) цити́ровать, про- **2** (refer to) ссыла́ться, сосла́ться на + *a.* **3**: **~ a price** назн|ача́ть, -а́чить це́ну

Rr

rabbi /'ræbaɪ/ *n.* (*pl.* ~s) равви́н

rabbit /'ræbɪt/ *n.* кро́лик

rabble /'ræb(ə)l/ *n.* сброд, чернь
■ **~-rouser** *n.* демаго́г; **~-rousing** *adj.* демагоги́ческий

rabid /'ræbɪd/ *adj.* (with rabies, also fig.) бе́шеный

rabies /'reɪbiːz/ *n.* бе́шенство

raccoon, racoon /rə'kuːn/ *n.* ено́т

♂ **race¹** /reɪs/ *n.* бег на ско́рость, го́нка; забе́г; (horse) ~s ска́чки (*f. pl.*)
● *v.t.:* **I'll ~ you to the corner** посмо́трим, кто быстре́е добежи́т до угла́
● *v.i.* **1** (compete in speed) состяза́ться (*impf.*) в ско́рости **2** (move at speed) нести́сь (*impf.*); мча́ться
■ **~horse** *n.* скакова́я ло́шадь; **~track** *n.* трек

race² /reɪs/ *n.* (ethnic) ра́са

racer /'reɪsə(r)/ *n.* (person) го́нщик; (car, yacht, etc.) го́ночная маши́на/я́хта *и т. п.*

racial /'reɪʃ(ə)l/ *adj.* ра́совый

racing /'reɪsɪŋ/ *n.* (*in full* horse ~) ска́чки (*f. pl.*); (*in full* motor ~) автого́нки (*f. pl.*)
■ **~ car** *n.* го́ночный автомоби́ль; **~ driver** *n.* го́нщик

racism /'reɪsɪz(ə)m/ *n.* раси́зм

racist /'reɪsɪst/ *n.* раси́ст (-ка)
● *adj.* раси́стский

rack¹ /ræk/ *n.* сто́йка с по́лками; стелла́ж; (plate ~) подста́вка для посу́ды; (luggage ~) бага́жная по́лка/се́тка

rack² /ræk/ *v.t.* му́чить, из-; **he was ~ed with pain** он ко́рчился от бо́ли; (fig.): **I ~ed my brains for an answer** я лома́л го́лову над отве́том

racket¹, racquet /'rækɪt/ *n.* раке́тка

racket² /'rækɪt/ *n.* **1** (din) шум, гам **2** (infml, dishonest scheme) жу́льническое предприя́тие

♂ ключева́я ле́ксика

racketeer /ræki'tiə(r)/ *n.* рэкети́р

raconteur /rækɒn'tə:(r)/ *n.* хоро́ший
расска́зчик

racoon /rə'ku:n/ *n.* = raccoon

racy /'reisi/ *adj.* (**racier, raciest**) (piquant,
lively) о́стрый, пря́ный; a ~ style бо́йкий/
я́ркий стиль

radar /'reidɑ:(r)/ *n.* радиолока́ция; (apparatus)
рада́р; ~ screen экра́н рада́ра

radiance /'reidiəns/ *n.* сия́ние, блеск; **the
sun's** ~ со́лнечное сия́ние

radiant /'reidiənt/ *adj.* сия́ющий; **she was** ~
with happiness она́ сия́ла от сча́стья

radiate /'reidieit/ *v.t. & i.* излуч|а́ть(ся),
-и́ть(ся); (fig.): **his face** ~**d happiness** его́
лицо́ свети́лось ра́достью

radiation /reidi'eiʃ(ə)n/ *n.* радиа́ция,
излуче́ние

radiator /'reidieitə(r)/ *n.* (heating device)
батаре́я, радиа́тор; (of car) радиа́тор

radical /'rædik(ə)l/ *n.* (pol., chem., math.)
радика́л
● *adj.* (fundamental) коренно́й; (pol.)
радика́льный

radicalization /rædikəlai'zeiʃ(ə)n/ *n.*
радикализа́ция

radicalize /'rædikəlaiz/ *v.t.* радикализи́ровать
(*impf., pf.*)

◊ **radio** /'reidiəʊ/ *n.* (*pl.* ~**s**) (means of
communication) ра́дио (*nt. indecl.*); (receiving
apparatus) радиоприёмник
● *v.t.* (**radioes, radioed**) 1 (send by ~)
перед|ава́ть, -а́ть (по ра́дио) 2 (contact by ~)
ради́ровать (*pf.*) + d.
■ ~**-controlled** *adj.* радиоуправля́емый; ~
station *n.* радиоста́нция

radioactive /reidiəʊ'æktiv/ *adj.*
радиоакти́вный

radioactivity /reidiəʊæk'tiviti/ *n.*
радиоакти́вность

radiographer /reidi'ɒgrəfə(r)/ *n.*
рентгено́лог, радиографи́ст

radiography /reidi'ɒgrəfi/ *n.*
рентгеногра́фия, радиогра́фия

radiologist /reidi'ɒlədʒist/ *n.* радио́лог,
рентгено́лог

radiology /reidi'ɒlədʒi/ *n.* рентгеноло́гия,
радиоло́гия

radiotherapy /reidiəʊ'θerəpi/ *n.*
радиотерапи́я

radish /'rædiʃ/ *n.* реди́ска; (*in pl., collect.*)
реди́с

radius /'reidiəs/ *n.* ра́диус

raffle /'ræf(ə)l/ *n.* лотере́я

raft /rɑ:ft/ *n.* (сплавно́й) плот

rafter /'rɑ:ftə(r)/ *n.* стропи́ло

rag /ræg/ *n.* (cloth) тря́пка, лоску́т; (*in pl.*) (torn
or tattered clothing) лохмо́ть|я (-ев)

rag|e /reidʒ/ *n.* 1 (violent anger) я́рость, гнев
2 (dominant fashion) после́дний крик мо́ды
● *v.i.*: **he** ~**ed at his wife** он наки́нулся
на свою́ жену́; **the wind** ~**ed all day**
ве́тер бушева́л весь день; **a** ~**ing thirst**
мучи́тельная жа́жда

ragged /'rægid/ *adj.* 1 (torn) рва́ный,
потрёпанный; (wearing torn clothes) обо́рванный
2 (rough): **a** ~ **beard** косма́тая борода́; ~
clouds рва́ные облака́

raid /reid/ *n.* (by police) обла́ва, рейд; (by
criminals) налёт; (mil.) рейд, налёт
● *v.t.*: **our bombers** ~**ed Hamburg** на́ши
бомбардиро́вщики соверши́ли налёт на
Га́мбург; **the flat was** ~**ed in his absence** в
его́ отсу́тствие кварти́ру огра́били

rail /reil/ *n.* 1 (bar for support etc.) перекла́дина,
ре́йка; (of staircase) пери́л|а (*pl., g.* —); (for
hanging things on) ве́шалка 2 (of railway track)
рельс; (railway transport): **by** ~ по́ездом
■ ~**road** *n.* (AmE) желе́зная доро́га ● *v.t.* (infml):
they were ~**roaded into agreement** их с хо́ду
втяну́ли в соглаше́ние; ~**way** *n.* желе́зная
доро́га; (*attr.*) железнодоро́жный

railing /'reiliŋ/, **railings** /'reiliŋz/ *nn.* огра́да,
решётка

◊ **rain** /rein/ *n.* дождь (*m.*)
● *v.i.*: **it is** ~**ing** идёт дождь; **it was** ~**ing hard**
шёл си́льный дождь
■ ~**bow** *n.* ра́дуга; ~ **check** *n.* (AmE) обеща́ние
приня́ть приглаше́ние в друго́й раз; ~**coat**
n. плащ; ~**drop** *n.* ка́пля дождя́; ~**fall** *n.*
оса́дк|и (-ов); ~**forest** *n.* тропи́ческий лес

rainy /'reini/ *adj.* (**rainier, rainiest**)
дождли́вый; **save, keep for a** ~ **day**
откла́дывать, отложи́ть на чёрный день

◊ **raise** /reiz/ *n.* (AmE, rise in salary) приба́вка
● *v.t.* 1 (lift) подн|има́ть, -я́ть; (make higher)
повы́ша́ть, -ы́сить; **the government** ~**d the
duty on tobacco** прави́тельство повы́сило
по́шлину на таба́к; **the news** ~**d my hopes**
изве́стие укрепи́ло мои́ наде́жды; (make
louder): **don't** ~ **your voice!** не повыша́йте
го́лоса! 2 (bring up): **may I** ~ **one question?**
мо́жно мне зада́ть вопро́с?; (evoke): **you**
~**d a doubt in my mind** вы зарони́ли мне в
ду́шу сомне́ние 3 (give voice to): **she** ~**d the
alarm** она́ подняла́ трево́гу 4 (collect): **she**
~**d money for charity** она́ собрала́ де́ньги на
благотвори́тельные це́ли 5 (rear): **they** ~**d a
family** они́ вы́растили дете́й

raisin /'reiz(ə)n/ *n.* изю́минка

rake /reik/ *n.* (tool) гра́б|ли (*pl., g.* -лей/-ель)
● *v.t.*: **he** ~**d the soil level** он разрыхли́л грунт
□ ~ **in** *v.t.*: **he** ~**d in the money** (fig., infml) он
загреба́л де́ньги лопа́той
□ ~ **up** *v.t.* сгре|ба́ть, -сти́; (fig.): **why** ~ **up an
old quarrel?** зачём вороши́ть ста́рую ссо́ру?

rakish /'reikiʃ/ *adj.* (of man) распу́тный,
бесшаба́шный; (of hat) залихва́тски/ли́хо/
небре́жно наде́тый

rall|y /'ræli/ *n.* 1 (mass gathering) ми́тинг 2 (at
tennis etc.) (затяжно́й) обме́н уда́рами, се́рия
3 (motor race) автора́лли (*nt. indecl.*)
● *v.t.* (reassemble) соб|ира́ть, -ра́ть (в строй)
● *v.i.* 1 (reassemble) соб|ира́ться, -ра́ться
2 (revive): **he** ~**ied from his illness** он
опра́вился от боле́зни; **the market** ~**ied**
ры́нок о́жил/ожжи́лся

r

RAM /ræm/ *n. (abbr. of* **random-access memory**) (comput.) операти́вная па́мять, ОЗУ (операти́вное запомина́ющее устро́йство)

ram /ræm/ *n.* бара́н
  ● *v.t.* (**rammed, ramming**) **1** (drive by force): stakes were ~med into the ground ко́лья бы́ли вби́ты в зе́млю **2** (strike with force): the ship ~med the bridge кора́бль наскочи́л на мост
■ ~ **raid** *n.* ограбле́ние с испо́льзованием тяжёлой (строи́тельной) те́хники

Ramadan /ˈræmədæn/ *n.* (relig.) Рамаза́н, Рамада́н

rambl|e /ˈræmb(ə)l/ *n.* прогу́лка
  ● *v.i.* **1** (walk) прогу́л|иваться, -я́ться **2** (fig., of speech) болта́ть (*impf.*) языко́м; a ~ing speaker многосло́вный ора́тор; a ~ing speech бессвя́зная речь

rambler /ˈræmblə(r)/ *n.* (hiker) люби́тель (-ница) пешехо́дного тури́зма

ramification /ˌræmɪfɪˈkeɪʃ(ə)n/ *n.* разветвле́ние; (consequence) после́дствие

ramp /ræmp/ *n.* (slope) скат, укло́н

rampage *n.*: /ˈræmpeɪdʒ/: **go on the** ~ неи́стовствовать (*impf.*)
  ● *v.i.* /ræmˈpeɪdʒ/ бу́йствовать, буя́нить (*both impf.*)

rampant /ˈræmpənt/ *adj.* свире́пствующий, безу́держный

rampart /ˈræmpɑːt/ *n.* крепостно́й вал

ramshackle /ˈræmʃæk(ə)l/ *adj.* обветша́лый

ran /ræn/ *past of* ▶ run

ranch /rɑːntʃ/ *n.* ра́нчо (*nt. indecl.*), фе́рма

rancher /ˈrɑːntʃə(r)/ *n.* владе́лец ра́нчо; скотово́д

rancid /ˈrænsɪd/ *adj.* прого́рклый, ту́хлый

rancour /ˈræŋkə(r)/ (AmE **rancor**) *n.* зло́ба

R & B *abbr.* (*of* **rhythm and blues**) ритм-энд-блюз; (modern style) ар-эн-би́ (*m. indecl.*) (*usu. written in Roman*)

R & D *abbr.* (*of* **research and development**) нау́чно-иссле́довательская рабо́та

random /ˈrændəm/ *n.*: at ~ наобу́м, науга́д, науда́чу
  ● *adj.* случа́йный

randy /ˈrændɪ/ *adj.* (**randier, randiest**) (BrE, infml) сексуа́льно возбуждённый, похотли́вый

rang /ræŋ/ *past of* ▶ ring²

⚹ **range** /reɪndʒ/ *n.* **1** (row, series) цепь, ряд **2** (grazing area) неогоро́женное па́стбище; (hunting ground) охо́тничье уго́дье **3** (area for firing, bombing, etc.) полиго́н; **rifle** ~ стре́льбище **4** (operating distance) да́льность, ра́диус; **they fired at close** ~ они́ стреля́ли с бли́зкого расстоя́ния **5** (extent) диапазо́н **6** (selection) набо́р; (assortment) ассортиме́нт **7** (stove) ку́хонная плита́
  ● *v.i.* **1** (wander): tigers ~d through the jungle ти́гры броди́ли по джу́нглям **2** (extend)

⚹ ключева́я ле́ксика

простира́ться (*impf.*); **my research** ~s over **a wide field** мои́ иссле́дования охва́тывают широ́кую о́бласть **3** (vary between limits) колеба́ться (*impf.*)

ranger /ˈreɪndʒə(r)/ *n.* лесни́к, объе́здчик

⚹ **rank¹** /ræŋk/ *n.* **1** (row) ряд; (*in full* **taxi** ~) (BrE) стоя́нка такси́ **2** (line of soldiers) шере́нга; **the men broke** ~(s) солда́ты нару́шили строй; **among the** ~s of the unemployed в ряда́х безрабо́тных **3** (**the** ~s) (common soldiers) рядовы́е **4** (position in armed forces etc.) зва́ние, чин **5** (social position): **people of all** ~s of society представи́тели всех слоёв о́бщества
  ● *v.t.* (class) классифици́ровать (*impf., pf.*); **he was** ~ed among the great poets его́ причисля́ли к вели́ким поэ́там
  ● *v.i.* (have a place): a high-~ing officer ста́рший офице́р
■ ~ **and file** *n. pl.* (ordinary members of organization) рядовы́е

rank² /ræŋk/ *adj.* **1** (foul; offensive): the skunk gives off a ~ odour от ску́нса исхо́дит злово́ние **2** (gross) чрезме́рный; ~ outsider соверше́нно посторо́нний челове́к

rankle /ˈræŋk(ə)l/ *v.i.* терза́ть, му́чить (*both impf.*)

ransack /ˈrænsæk/ *v.t.* **1** (search) обша́ри|вать, -ть **2** (plunder) гра́бить, раз-

ransom /ˈrænsəm/ *n.* вы́куп; **he was held to** ~ (lit.) за него́ тре́бовали вы́куп; (fig.) его́ шантажи́ровали

rant /rænt/ *v.i.* разглаго́льствовать (*impf.*)

rap /ræp/ *n.* **1** (light blow) лёгкий уда́р, стук **2** (*also* ~ **music**) рэп
  ● *v.t.* (**rapped, rapping**) слегка́ уд|аря́ть, -а́рить по + *d.*
  ● *v.i.* (**rapped, rapping**) сту́ча|ть, -у́кнуть; **he** ~ped on the door он постуча́л в дверь

rapacious /rəˈpeɪʃəs/ *adj.* жа́дный, ненасы́тный

rape¹ /reɪp/ *n.* изнаси́лование
  ● *v.t.* наси́ловать, из-

rape² /reɪp/ *n.* (bot.) рапс

rapid /ˈræpɪd/ *adj.* (**rapider, rapidest**) бы́стрый, ско́рый

rapidity /rəˈpɪdɪtɪ/ *n.* быстрота́, ско́рость

rapist /ˈreɪpɪst/ *n.* наси́льник

rapper /ˈræpə(r)/ *n.* исполни́тель (*m.*) рэ́па, рэ́ппер

rapport /ræˈpɔː(r)/ *n.* взаимопонима́ние, конта́кт

rapture /ˈræptʃə(r)/ *n.* восто́рг

rapturous /ˈræptʃərəs/ *adj.* восто́рженный

⚹ **rare¹** /reə(r)/ *adj.* (**rarer, rarest**) (uncommon) ре́дкий

rare² /reə(r)/ *adj.* (**rarer, rarest**) (bloody): a ~ steak бифште́кс с кро́вью

rarefied /ˈreərɪfaɪd/ *adj.* (phys.) разрежённый; (fig.) утончённый, изы́сканный

rarely /ˈreəlɪ/ *adv.* ре́дко, неча́сто, и́зредка

raring /ˈreərɪŋ/ *adj.* (infml): he was ~ to go ему́ не терпе́лось приступи́ть к де́лу

rarity /ˈreərɪtɪ/ n. (uncommonness) редкость; (thing valued for this) (большая) редкость

rascal /ˈrɑːsk(ə)l/ n. мошенник, плут

rash[1] /ræʃ/ n. сыпь

rash[2] /ræʃ/ adj. опрометчивый

rasher /ˈræʃə(r)/ n. ломтик (бекона)

rasp /rɑːsp/ n. (file) рашпиль (m.), напильник; (grating sound) скрежет
● v.t. (scrape) скрести, скоблить, тереть (all impf.)
● v.i. скрежетать (impf.); a ~ing voice скрипучий голос
□ ~ **away**, ~ **off** vv.t. соск|абливать, -облить
□ ~ **out** v.t. (e.g. an order) гаркнуть (pf.)

raspberry /ˈrɑːzbərɪ/ n. малина (collect.)

Rastafarian /ˌræstəˈfeərɪən/ n. (relig.) растафари (c.g. indecl.)
● adj. растафарианский

rat /ræt/ n. крыса
■ ~ **race** n. бешеная погоня за успехом/ богатством

✐ **rate** /reɪt/ n. **1** (proportion) норма, размер; ~ **of exchange** курс обмена; **birth** ~ рождаемость **2** (speed) скорость; **we shall never get there at this** ~ при таких темпах мы туда никогда не доберёмся **3** (price) расценка, тариф **4** (BrE, tax on property etc.) местный налог **5**: **at any** ~ (in any case) во всяком случае
● v.t. оцен|ивать, -ить
■ ~**payer** n. (BrE) плательщик местных налогов

✐ **rather** /ˈrɑːðə(r)/ adv. **1** (by preference): **I would** ~ **die than consent** я скорее умру, чем соглашусь; **I'd** ~ **have coffee** я предпочёл бы кофе; **I'd** ~ **not say** я лучше промолчу **2** (somewhat) довольно, несколько; **the result was** ~ **surprising** результат был довольно неожиданным; **it is** ~ **a pity** а жаль всё же; **the effect was** ~ **spoiled** эффект был смазан/подпорчен

ratification /ˌrætɪfɪˈkeɪʃ(ə)n/ n. ратификация

ratify /ˈrætɪfaɪ/ v.t. ратифици|ровать (impf., pf.)

rating /ˈreɪtɪŋ/ n. рейтинг

ratio /ˈreɪʃɪəʊ/ n. (pl. ~s) отношение, соотношение

ration /ˈræʃ(ə)n/ n. рацион, паёк
● v.t.: **they were** ~**ed to one loaf a week** их паёк сводился к одной буханке в неделю; **meat was severely** ~**ed** мясо было строго нормировано

rational /ˈræʃən(ə)l/ adj. разумный, рациональный

rationale /ˌræʃəˈnɑːl/ n. основная причина

rationalism /ˈræʃənəlɪz(ə)m/ n. рационализм

rationality /ˌræʃəˈnælɪtɪ/ n. разумность, рациональность

rationalize /ˈræʃənəlaɪz/ v.t. (give reasons for) разумно объясн|ять, -ить; (make more efficient) рационализи́ровать (impf., pf.)

rattle /ˈræt(ə)l/ n. **1** (sound) треск, грохот **2** (child's toy) погремушка
● v.t.: **he** ~**d the money box** он встряхнул копилку
● v.i.: **the hail** ~**d on the roof** град барабанил по крыше
■ ~**snake** n. гремучая змея

ratty /ˈrætɪ/ adj. (**rattier, rattiest**) (BrE, infml, irritable) злой, раздражительный

raucous /ˈrɔːkəs/ adj. резкий, хриплый

raunchy /ˈrɔːntʃɪ/ adj. (**raunchier, raunchiest**) распутный

ravage /ˈrævɪdʒ/ v.t. опустош|ать, -ить

rave /reɪv/ n. (party) весёлая вечеринка
● adj.: ~ **review** восторженный отзыв
● v.i. (in delirium) бредить (impf.); (in delight): **they** ~**d about the play** они были в восторге от пьесы

raven /ˈreɪv(ə)n/ n. ворон
■ ~-**haired** adj. с волосами цвета воронова крыла (or чёрными как смоль)

ravenous /ˈrævənəs/ adj.: **I am** ~ я голоден как волк

ravine /rəˈviːn/ n. овраг, лощина

raving /ˈreɪvɪŋ/ adj. & adv. (insane): **a** ~ **lunatic** буйно помешанный; **you must be** ~ **mad** ты совсем спятил

ravioli /ˌrævɪˈəʊlɪ/ n. равиол|и (-ей)

ravishing /ˈrævɪʃɪŋ/ adj. восхитительный

raw /rɔː/ adj. **1** (uncooked) сырой **2** (unprocessed) необработанный; ~ **data** необработанные данные; ~ **materials** сырьё **3** (inexperienced) неопытный, зелёный **4** (of weather) сырой **5** (harsh): **he got a** ~ **deal** (infml) с ним сурово обошлись

Rawlplug® /ˈrɔːlplʌg/ n. (BrE) пластиковый дюбель (для вкручивания шурупов в стену и т. п.)

ray /reɪ/ n. луч

raze /reɪz/ v.t. разр|ушать, -ушить до основания

razor /ˈreɪzə(r)/ n. бритва; **electric** ~ электробритва
■ ~ **blade** n. лезвие

re /riː/ prep. касательно + g.

✐ **reach** /riːtʃ/ n. **1** (extent of stretch) размах рук, длина руки; (fig.): **we are within easy** ~ **of London** от нас легко добраться до Лондона; от нас до Лондона рукой подать **2** (usu. in pl.) (stretch of river): **the upper** ~**es of the Thames** верховья (nt. pl.) Темзы
● v.t. **1** (fetch) дотя́|гиваться, -нуться до + g.; **I can just** ~ **the shelf** я еле-еле достаю (or могу дотянуться) до полки **2** (arrive at) дост|игать, -игнуть + g.; **your letter** ~**ed me only yesterday** ваше письмо дошло до меня только вчера; ~ **agreement** прийти (pf.) к соглашению
● v.i. **1** (stretch out hand) тянуться, по- рукой; **he** ~**ed for his rifle** он потянулся к винтовке **2** (extend) простираться, тянуться (both impf.)
□ ~ **down** v.i.: **he** ~**ed down and picked up the coin** он нагнулся и поднял монету
□ ~ **up** v.i. протянуть (pf.) руку вверх

react /rɪˈækt/ v.i. реаги́ровать, от-/про-/с-

✐ **reaction** /rɪˈækʃ(ə)n/ n. реакция

reactionary /rɪˈækʃənərɪ/ n. реакционер

r

• *adj.* реакцио́нный

reactor /rɪˈæktə(r)/ *n.* (tech.) реа́ктор

✓ **read** /riːd/ *v.t.* (*past and p.p.* **read** /red/)
1 (peruse) чита́ть, про- *or* проче́сть; **have you read this book?** вы чита́ли э́ту кни́гу?; **can you ~ music?** вы уме́ете игра́ть по но́там?
2 (discern): **he read my thoughts** он (про)чита́л мои́ мы́сли **3** (BrE, study) изуча́ть (*impf.*); **he is ~ing law** он у́чится на юриди́ческом факульте́те **4** (examine): **~ a meter** сн|има́ть, -я́ть показа́ния счётчика
• *v.i.* (*past and p.p.* **read** /red/): **he can neither ~ nor write** он не уме́ет ни чита́ть, ни писа́ть
□ **~ out** *v.t.* прочи́т|ывать, -а́ть; огла|ша́ть, -си́ть
□ **~ through** *v.t.* прочи́т|ывать, -а́ть
□ **~ up on** *v.i.* мно́го чита́ть (*impf.*); **he read up on the subject** он подчита́л ко́е-что по э́тому предме́ту

readable /ˈriːdəb(ə)l/ *adj.* **1** (legible) разбо́рчивый **2** (enjoyable, infml) интере́сный

✓ **reader** /ˈriːdə(r)/ *n.* чита́тель (-ница)

readily /ˈredɪlɪ/ *adv.* (willingly) охо́тно; (without difficulty) легко́, без труда́

✓ **reading** /ˈriːdɪŋ/ *n.* **1** (pursuit) чте́ние **2** (interpretation) толкова́ние **3** (of instrument) показа́ние
■ **~ room** *n.* чита́льный зал

readjust /riːəˈdʒʌst/ *v.t.* попр|авля́ть, -а́вить
• *v.i.*: **after the war he found it hard to ~** по́сле войны́ ему́ бы́ло тру́дно приспосо́биться к ми́рной жи́зни

✓ **ready** /ˈredɪ/ *adj.* (**readier, readiest**) (prepared) гото́вый (*к чему*); пригото́вленный, подгото́вленный; **I'm just getting ~** я почти́ гото́в; **she got the children ~ for school** она́ собрала́ дете́й в шко́лу; (willing) гото́вый; **I am ~ to admit I was wrong** гото́в призна́ть, что я был непра́в
• *adv.*: **they sell meat ~ cooked** там продаётся мясна́я кулинари́я
■ **~-made** *adj.* гото́вый

✓ **real** /riːl/ *adj.* (actual) настоя́щий; реа́льный; **in ~ life** в жи́зни; **~ silver** настоя́щее серебро́
■ **~ estate** *n.* недви́жимость; **~ time** *adj.* (comput.) (рабо́тающий/происходя́щий) в режи́ме реа́льного вре́мени

realign /riːəˈlaɪn/ *v.t.* перестр|а́ивать, -о́ить

realism /ˈriːəlɪz(ə)m/ *n.* реали́зм

realist /ˈrɪəlɪst/ *n.* реали́ст (-ка)

realistic /rɪəˈlɪstɪk/ *adj.* реалисти́чный, практи́чный

✓ **reality** /rɪˈælɪtɪ/ *n.* реа́льность, действи́тельность
■ **~ TV** *n.* реа́лити-ТВ (*nt. indecl.*)

realization /rɪəlaɪˈzeɪʃ(ə)n/ *n.* осозна́ние

✓ **realize** /ˈrɪəlaɪz/ *v.t.* **1** (be aware of) осозн|ава́ть, -а́ть; (grasp mentally) сообра|жа́ть, -зи́ть; **he ~d his mistake at once** он сра́зу же осозна́л свою́ оши́бку; **do you ~ what you have done?** вы понима́ете, что вы сде́лали?; **I didn't ~ you wanted me** до меня́ не дошло́, что э́то вам

ну́жно **2** (convert into fact) осуществ|ля́ть, -и́ть; **I will help you to ~ your ambition** я помогу́ вам осуществи́ть ва́ши стремле́ния

✓ **really** /ˈrɪəlɪ/ *adv.* действи́тельно; в/на са́мом де́ле; **do you ~ mean it?** вы серьёзно?; **I am ~ sorry for you** мне вас и́скренне жаль; **~?** (expr. surprise) серьёзно?; (acknowledging information) да?, пра́вда?; **~!** (expr. indignation) ну, зна́ете!; **not ~** не о́чень, не осо́бенно

realm /relm/ *n.* короле́вство; (fig.) сфе́ра, о́бласть, мир

reap /riːp/ *v.t. & i.* жать, с-

reappear /riːəˈpɪə(r)/ *v.i.* сно́ва появ|ля́ться, -и́ться

reappraise /riːəˈpreɪz/ *v.t.* пересм|а́тривать, -отре́ть

rear[1] /rɪə(r)/ *n.* за́дняя часть, сторона́
• *adj.*: **~ entrance** чёрный ход; **~ wheel** за́днее колесо́
■ **~-view mirror** *n.* зе́ркало за́днего ви́да

rear[2] /rɪə(r)/ *v.t.* (bring up) расти́ть, вы-; (breed) разв|оди́ть, -ести́
• *v.i.* (*also* **~ up**) ста|нови́ться, -ть на дыбы́; **the horse ~ed in terror** ло́шадь (в)ста́ла на дыбы́ от испу́га

rearm /riːˈɑːm/ *v.t. & i.* перевооруж|а́ть(ся), -и́ть(ся)

rearmament /riːˈɑːməmənt/ *n.* перевооруже́ние

rearrange /riːəˈreɪndʒ/ *v.t.* (objects) перест|авля́ть, -а́вить; (a meeting) передв|ига́ть, -и́нуть вре́мя + *g.*

rearrangement /riːəˈreɪndʒmənt/ *n.* перестано́вка

✓ **reason** /ˈriːz(ə)n/ *n.* **1** (cause, ground) причи́на; **with ~** обосно́ванно **2** (good sense) благоразу́мие; **he will not listen to ~** он не прислу́шивается к го́лосу ра́зума
• *v.i.*: **it is useless to ~ with him** его́ беспле́зно убежда́ть; ло́гика на него́ не де́йствует

✓ **reasonable** /ˈriːzənəb(ə)l/ *adj.* **1** (sensible) (благо)разу́мный **2** (fairly good) дово́льно хоро́ший, неплохо́й

reasoning /ˈriːzənɪŋ/ *n.* рассужде́ние

reassert /riːəˈsɜːt/ *v.t.* сно́ва подтвер|жда́ть, -ди́ть

reassess /riːəˈses/ *v.t.* переоце́н|ивать, -и́ть

reassessment /riːəˈsesmənt/ *n.* переоце́нка

reassurance /riːəˈʃʊərəns/ *n.* (повто́рное) завере́ние, подтвержде́ние

reassure /riːəˈʃɔː(r)/ *v.t.* успок|а́ивать, -о́ить; подбодр|я́ть, -и́ть; **his words were most ~ing** его́ слова́ звуча́ли са́мым ободря́ющим о́бразом

rebate /ˈriːbeɪt/ *n.* возвра́т переплаче́нной су́ммы

rebel[1] /ˈreb(ə)l/ *n.* повста́нец

rebel[2] /rɪˈbel/ *v.i.* (**rebelled, rebelling**) восст|ава́ть, -а́ть

rebellion /rɪˈbeljən/ *n.* восста́ние, мяте́ж, бунт

rebellious /rɪˈbeljəs/ *adj.* (in revolt) восста́вший, мяте́жный; (disobedient) непоко́рный

reboot /riːˈbuːt/ v.t. (comput.) перезагру|жа́ть, -зи́ть

rebound[1] /rɪˈbaʊnd/ n. отско́к; **on the ~** на отско́ке; (fig.): **he married her on the ~** он жени́лся на ней по́сле разочарова́ния в любви́ к друго́й

rebound[2] /rɪˈbaʊnd/ v.i. отск|а́кивать, -очи́ть

rebranding /riːˈbrændɪŋ/ n. (comm.) ребре́ндинг (*пересоздание и продвижение на рынке торговых марок*)

rebuff /rɪˈbʌf/ n. отпо́р, ре́зкий отка́з
• v.t. дава́ть, дать отпо́р + d.; ре́зко отклон|я́ть, -и́ть; (mil.): **the enemy's attack was ~ed** ата́ка неприя́теля была́ отражена́

rebuild /riːˈbɪld/ v.t. сно́ва стро́ить, по-

rebuke /rɪˈbjuːk/ n. упрёк, уко́р
• v.t. упрек|а́ть, -ну́ть; укоря́ть (*impf.*)

rebut /rɪˈbʌt/ v.t. (**rebutted, rebutting**) опров|ерга́ть, -е́ргнуть

rebuttal /rɪˈbʌt(ə)l/ n. опроверже́ние

recalcitrant /rɪˈkælsɪtrənt/ adj. непоко́рный

recall[1] /ˈriːkɔːl/ n. воспомина́ние

♂ **recall**[2] /rɪˈkɔːl/ v.t. **1** (summon back) от|зыва́ть, -озва́ть **2** (to mind) нап|омина́ть, -о́мнить

recant /rɪˈkænt/ v.t. & i. публи́чно ка́яться, по- (*в чём*); отр|ека́ться, -е́чься (*от чего*)

recap /ˈriːkæp/ n. повторе́ние
• v.t. & i. (**recapped, recapping**) повтор|я́ть, -и́ть; резюми́ровать (*impf., pf.*)

recapture /riːˈkæptʃə(r)/ v.t. взять (*pf.*) обра́тно; (fig.) восстан|а́вливать, -ови́ть в па́мяти

recce /ˈrekɪ/ n. (BrE, infml) = **reconnaissance**

reced|e /rɪˈsiːd/ v.i. **1** (move back) отступ|а́ть, -и́ть; (move away) удал|я́ться, -и́ться; **the tide was ~ing** вода́ спада́ла; **~ing hair** реде́ющие во́лосы **2** (diminish) ум|еньша́ться, -е́ньшиться

receipt /rɪˈsiːt/ n. **1** (receiving) получе́ние **2** (in pl.) (money received) де́нежные поступле́ния, прихо́д **3** (written acknowledgement) распи́ска, квита́нция

♂ **receive** /rɪˈsiːv/ v.t. **1** (get, be given) получ|а́ть, -и́ть; **he ~s stolen goods** (BrE) он укрыва́ет кра́деное **2** (admit) прин|има́ть, -я́ть; (greet) прин|има́ть, -я́ть; **how was your speech ~d?** как бы́ло встре́чено ва́ше выступле́ние?

receiver /rɪˈsiːvə(r)/ n. **1** (*also* **telephone ~**) (телефо́нная) тру́бка **2** (*also* **radio ~**) (ра́дио)приёмник

♂ **recent** /ˈriːs(ə)nt/ adj. **1** (occurring lately) неда́вний **2** (modern) совреме́нный

♂ **recently** /ˈriːsəntlɪ/ adv. неда́вно, на днях, за после́днее вре́мя; **until quite ~** ещё совсе́м неда́вно

receptacle /rɪˈseptək(ə)l/ n. вмести́лище

reception /rɪˈsepʃ(ə)n/ n. **1** (of guests etc.) приём **2** (greeting) встре́ча, приём; **he was given a great ~** ему́ устро́или великоле́пный приём **3** (of radio signals) приём
■ **~ desk** n. (in hotel) регистра́ция; (in hospital) регистрату́ра

receptionist /rɪˈsepʃənɪst/ n. (in hotel, hospital) регистра́тор, дежу́рный; (in a business firm) секрета́рь (*m.*) по приёму посети́телей

receptive /rɪˈseptɪv/ adj. восприи́мчивый

recess /rɪˈses, ˈriːses/ n. **1** (vacation) переры́в; (AmE, between classes) переме́на **2** (niche) ни́ша, алько́в

recession /rɪˈseʃ(ə)n/ n. спад

recharge /riːˈtʃɑːdʒ/ v.t. перезаря|жа́ть, -ди́ть

recipe /ˈresɪpɪ/ n. реце́пт

recipient /rɪˈsɪpɪənt/ n. получа́тель (-ница)

reciprocal /rɪˈsɪprək(ə)l/ adj. взаи́мный

reciprocate /rɪˈsɪprəkeɪt/ v.t. отв|еча́ть, -е́тить взаи́мностью
• v.i. отпла́|чивать, -ти́ть

reciprocity /resɪˈprɒsɪtɪ/ n. взаи́мность; взаимоде́йствие; обме́н

recital /rɪˈsaɪt(ə)l/ n. изложе́ние

recite /rɪˈsaɪt/ v.t. деклами́ровать, про-

reckless /ˈreklɪs/ adj. безрассу́дный; **he drove ~ly** он неосторо́жно вёл маши́ну

reckon /ˈrekən/ v.t. **1** (calculate) счита́ть, по- **2** (think, consider) счита́ть (*impf.*)
• v.i. **1** (count) счита́ть (*impf.*); **he is a man to be ~ed with** с таки́м челове́ком, как он, ну́жно счита́ться **2** (rely) рассчи́тывать (*impf.*) (*на кого/что*); **he ~ed on making a clear profit** он рассчи́тывал на чи́стую при́быль

reckoning /ˈrekənɪŋ/ n. счёт, вычисле́ние

reclaim /rɪˈkleɪm/ v.t. **1** (bring under cultivation) осв|а́ивать, -о́ить **2** (demand return of) тре́бовать, по- обра́тно **3** (recycle) утилизи́ровать (*impf., pf.*)

reclamation /rekləˈmeɪʃ(ə)n/ n. (of land) освое́ние; (of waste) утилиза́ция

reclin|e /rɪˈklaɪn/ v.i. (полу)лежа́ть (*impf.*); **~ing nude** лежа́щая обнажённая

recluse /rɪˈkluːs/ n. затво́рни|к (-ца), отше́льни|к (-ца)

recognition /rekəgˈnɪʃ(ə)n/ n. **1** (knowing again) опознава́ние, узнава́ние; (comput.) распознава́ние **2** (acknowledgement) призна́ние

recognizable /ˈrekəgnaɪzəb(ə)l/ adj. опознава́емый

♂ **recognize** /ˈrekəgnaɪz/ v.t. **1** (know again) узн|ава́ть, -а́ть **2** (acknowledge) призн|ава́ть, -а́ть; **he was ~d as the lawful heir** он был при́знан зако́нным насле́дником

recoil /ˈriːkɔɪl/ v.i. отпря́нуть (*pf.*)

recollect /rekəˈlekt/ v.t. всп|омина́ть, -о́мнить

recollection /rekəˈlekʃ(ə)n/ n. па́мять

♂ **recommend** /rekəˈmend/ v.t. **1** (suggest as suitable) рекомендова́ть (*impf., pf.*), от-/по- (*pf.*) **2** (advise sb) рекомендова́ть, по- + d.

recommendation /rekəmenˈdeɪʃ(ə)n/ n. рекоменда́ция

recompense /ˈrekəmpens/ n. компенса́ция

reconcile /ˈrekənsaɪl/ v.t. **1** (make friendly) мири́ть, по- **2** (make compatible) совме|ща́ть, -сти́ть **3** (resign): **~ oneself** смир|я́ться,

r

-и́ться (**to:** с + *i.*)

reconciliation /rekənsılı'eıʃ(ə)n/ *n.*
примире́ние

reconnaissance /rı'kɒnıs(ə)ns/ *n.* разве́дка,
рекогносциро́вка

reconnoitre /rekə'nɔıtə(r)/ (AmE
reconnoiter) *v.t. & i.* разве́дывать (*impf.*);
производи́ть (*impf*) разве́дку

reconsider /ri:kən'sıdə(r)/ *v.t.*
пересм|а́тривать, -отре́ть
• *v.i.* переду́мать (*pf.*)

reconstitute /ri:'kɒnstıtju:t/ *v.t.*
воспроизв|оди́ть, -ести́

reconstruct /ri:kən'strʌkt/ *v.t.*
восстан|а́вливать, -ови́ть; воссозд|ава́ть,
-а́ть; (fig.): **the police ~ed the crime** поли́ция
воспроизвела́ карти́ну преступле́ния

reconstruction /ri:kən'strʌkʃ(ə)n/ *n.*
восстановле́ние, воссозда́ние; (of acts etc.)
воспроизведе́ние, воссозда́ние

⚐ **record¹** /'rekɔ:d/ *n.* **1** (written note, document)
за́пись, учёт; **the teacher keeps a ~
of attendance** учи́тель ведёт учёт
посеща́емости; **weather ~s** да́нные
наблюде́ний за пого́дными явле́ниями
2 (state of being recorded, esp. as evidence)
за́пись; **this is off the ~** э́то не должно́
быть пре́дано огла́ске **3** (past conduct,
achievement) про́шлое; **this firm has a
bad ~ for strikes** э́та фи́рма изве́стна
многочи́сленными забасто́вками; **the
defendant had a (criminal) ~** у обвиня́емого
ра́нее име́лись суди́мости **4** (sound recording)
(грам)пласти́нка **5** (best performance) реко́рд;
world ~ мирово́й реко́рд; (*attr.*) реко́рдный,
небыва́лый; **cars have had ~ sales** про́дано
реко́рдное коли́чество маши́н
■ **~-breaking** *adj.* реко́рдный; **~ holder**
n. рекордсме́н (-ка); **~ player** *n.*
прои́грыватель (*m.*)

⚐ **record²** /rı'kɔ:d/ *v.t.* **1** (set down in writing, also
fig.) запи́с|ывать, -а́ть **2** (on tape, film, etc.)
запи́с|ывать, -а́ть (на плёнку) **3** (of instrument:
register) регистри́ровать, за-

recorder /rı'kɔ:də(r)/ *n.* (mus.) (англи́йская)
фле́йта

recording /rı'kɔ:dıŋ/ *n.* за́пись

recount¹ /ri:'kaʊnt/ *n.* (second count) пересчёт
• *v.t.* пересчи́т|ывать, -а́ть

recount² /rı'kaʊnt/ *v.t.* (narrate) расска́з|ывать,
-а́ть

recoup /rı'ku:p/ *v.t.*: **~ one's losses** возвраща́ть,
верну́ть потеря́нное

recourse /rı'kɔ:s/ *n.*: **have ~ to** приб|ега́ть,
-е́гнуть к + *d.*

⚐ **recover** /rı'kʌvə(r)/ *v.t.* (regain) получ|а́ть,
-и́ть обра́тно; верну́ть (*pf.*); **he tried to ~
his losses** он пыта́лся верну́ть потеря́нное;
(win back) отвоёв|ывать, -а́ть
• *v.i.* попр|авля́ться, -а́виться; **we must help
the country to ~** мы должны́ помо́чь стране́
сно́ва встать на́ ноги

recovery /rı'kʌvərı/ *n.* **1** (regaining possession)
возвра́т; возмеще́ние; **the ~ of your money
will take time** пройдёт вре́мя, пре́жде чем
вы полу́чите свои́ де́ньги обра́тно **2** (revival)
выздоровле́ние; **he made a rapid ~** он
бы́стро попра́вился **3** (rehabilitation)
восстановле́ние
■ **~ vehicle** *n.* авари́йный автомоби́ль

recreate /ri:krı'eıt/ *v.t.* вновь созд|ава́ть, -а́ть

recreation /rekrı'eıʃ(ə)n/ *n.* о́тдых;
развлече́ние

recrimination /rıkrımı'neıʃ(ə)n/ *n.*
встре́чное обвине́ние

recruit /rı'kru:t/ *n.* (mil.) новобра́нец
• *v.t.* (enlist) вербова́ть, за-; наб|ира́ть, -ра́ть

recruitment /rı'kru:tmənt/ *n.* вербо́вка

rectangle /'rektæŋg(ə)l/ *n.* прямоуго́льник

rectangular /rek'tæŋɡʊlə(r)/ *adj.*
прямоуго́льный

rectify /'rektıfaı/ *v.t.* испр|авля́ть, -а́вить

rector /'rektə(r)/ *n.* (BrE, clergyman) ≈
прихо́дский свяще́нник

rectory /'rektərı/ *n.* (BrE) дом прихо́дского
свяще́нника

rectum /'rektəm/ *n.* (*pl.* **rectums** or **recta**)
пряма́я кишка́

recuperate /rı'ku:pəreıt/ *v.i.* попр|авля́ться,
-а́виться

recuperation /rıku:pə'reıʃ(ə)n/ *n.*
выздоровле́ние

recur /rı'kɜ:(r)/ *v.i.* (**recurred**, **recurring**)
повтор|я́ться, -и́ться; **a ~ring headache**
хрони́ческие головны́е бо́ли (*f. pl.*)

recurrence /rı'kʌrəns/ *n.* повторе́ние

recurrent /rı'kʌrənt/ *adj.* повторя́ющийся

recycle /ri:'saık(ə)l/ *v.t.* перераб|а́тывать, -о́тать

recycling /ri:'saıklıŋ/ *n.* повто́рное
испо́льзование, перерабо́тка

⚐ **red** /red/ *n.* **1** кра́сный цвет; **~ doesn't suit
her** кра́сное ей не идёт; **she was dressed in
~** она́ была́ оде́та в кра́сное **2** (debit side
of account) долг, задо́лженность; **in the ~** в
долга́х
• *adj.* (**redder, reddest**) кра́сный; а́лый;
she went ~ in the face она́ покрасне́ла
■ **R~ Crescent** *n.* Кра́сный Полуме́сяц;
R~ Cross *n.* Кра́сный Крест; **~currant**
n. кра́сная сморо́дина; **~-handed** *adj.*: **he
was caught ~-handed** его́ пойма́ли на ме́сте
преступле́ния (*or* с поли́чным); **~head** *n.*
ры́жий (*челове́к*); **~-headed** *adj.* ры́жий;
~-hot *adj.* раскалённый докрасна́; **~-light
district** *n.* кварта́л публи́чных домо́в; **~
tape** *n.* (fig.) (канцеля́рская) волоки́та

redden /'red(ə)n/ *v.t.* окра́|шивать, -сить в
кра́сный цвет
• *v.i.* красне́ть, по-

reddish /'redıʃ/ *adj.* краснова́тый

redecorate /ri:'dekəreıt/ *v.t.* отде́л|ывать,
-ать; ремонти́ровать, от-

redeem /rı'di:m/ *v.t.* **1** (get back, recover)
выкупа́ть, вы́купить **2** (relig.): **Christ came
to ~ sinners** Христо́с пришёл искупи́ть

грехи́ люде́й **3** (compensate): he has one ~ing feature у него́ есть одно́ положи́тельное ка́чество

redemption /rɪ'dempʃ(ə)n/ *n.* (relig.) искупле́ние; past ~ без наде́жды на спасе́ние

redeploy /ri:dɪ'plɔɪ/ *v.t. & i.* (mil.) передислоци́ровать(ся) (*impf., pf.*)

redeployment /ri:dɪ'plɔɪmənt/ *n.* передислока́ция; перераспределе́ние

redevelop /ri:dɪ'veləp/ *v.t.* перестр|а́ивать, -о́ить

redial /ri:'daɪ(ə)l/ *v.t. & i.* повто́рно наб|ира́ть, -ра́ть (но́мер)

rediscover /ri:dɪs'kʌvə(r)/ *v.t.* откр|ыва́ть, -ы́ть за́ново

redo /ri:'du:/ *v.t.* переде́л|ывать, -ать

redouble /rɪ'dʌb(ə)l/ *v.t. & i.* удв|а́ивать(ся), -о́ить(ся); he ~d his efforts он удво́ил свои́ уси́лия

redoubtable /rɪ'daʊtəb(ə)l/ *adj.* гро́зный; устраша́ющий

redress /rɪ'dres/ *n.* возмеще́ние; I shall seek ~ я бу́ду добива́ться компенса́ции
● *v.t.* возме|ща́ть, -сти́ть; their victory ~ed the balance of forces их побе́да восстанови́ла равнове́сие сил

⚡ **reduce** /rɪ'dju:s/ *v.t.* **1** (make less or smaller) ум|еньша́ть, -е́ньшить; сокра|ща́ть, -ти́ть; (lower) сн|ижа́ть, -и́зить; сб|авля́ть, -а́вить; all prices are ~d все це́ны сни́жены **2** (bring, compel) дов|оди́ть, -ести́ (*до чего́*); вы́нудить; the film ~d her to tears фильм растро́гал её до слёз; the family was ~d to begging семья́ была́ обречена́ на нищету́

⚡ **reduction** /rɪ'dʌkʃ(ə)n/ *n.* сокраще́ние; сниже́ние; a ~ in numbers коли́чественное сокраще́ние; price ~s сниже́ние цен

redundancy /rɪ'dʌnd(ə)nsɪ/ *n.* (BrE, dismissal) увольне́ние

redundant /rɪ'dʌnd(ə)nt/ *adj.* (superfluous) изли́шний; (BrE, at work): many workers were made ~ мно́гих рабо́чих уво́лили

reed /ri:d/ *n.* **1** (bot.) тростни́к, камы́ш **2** (mus.) язычо́к

reef /ri:f/ *n.* риф

reek /ri:k/ *v.i.* воня́ть, про-; his clothes ~ed of tobacco от его́ оде́жды несло́ табако́м

reel[1] /ri:l/ *n.* (winding device) кату́шка; руло́н
● *with advs.*: the fisherman ~ed in the line рыба́к смота́л у́дочку; the guide ~ed off a lot of dates гид вы́палил це́лый ряд истори́ческих дат

reel[2] /ri:l/ *v.i.* кружи́ться (*impf.*); he ~ed under the blow он зашата́лся от уда́ра

re-elect /ri:ɪ'lekt/ *v.t.* переизб|ира́ть, -ра́ть

re-emerge /ri:ɪ'mɜ:dʒ/ *v.i.* вновь появ|ля́ться, -и́ться

re-examine /ri:ɪg'zæmɪn/ *v.t.* вновь рассм|а́тривать, -отре́ть

ref /ref/ *n.* (infml) = referee *n.* 2

refectory /rɪ'fektərɪ/ *n.* (in monastery) тра́пезная; (in school, college) столо́вая

⚡ **refer** /rɪ'fɜ:(r)/ *v.t.* (**referred, referring**) (pass on, direct) от|сыла́ть, -осла́ть; the clerk ~red me to the manager слу́жащий отосла́л меня́ к нача́льнику
● *v.i.* (**referred, referring**) **1** (have recourse) спр|авля́ться, -а́виться; he ~red to the dictionary он спра́вился в словаре́; the speaker ~red to his notes ора́тор загляну́л в конспе́кт **2** (allude): ~ to (mention) упом|ина́ть, -яну́ть; (cite) ссыла́ться, сосла́ться на + *a.*

referee /refə'ri:/ *n.* **1** (arbitrator) арби́тр **2** (at games) судья́ (*m.*); ре́фери (*m. indecl.*) **3** (person supplying testimonial) поручи́тель (*m.*)
● *v.t. & i.* (**referees, refereed**): he agreed to ~ the match он согласи́лся суди́ть матч

⚡ **reference** /'refərəns/ *n.* **1** (referring for decision etc.) отсы́лка; he acted without ~ to his superiors он де́йствовал без согласова́ния с нача́льством **2** (relation) отноше́ние; with ~ to your letter в связи́ с ва́шим письмо́м **3** (allusion) упомина́ние, ссы́лка; the book contains many ~s to the Queen в кни́ге ча́сто упомина́ется короле́ва **4** (in text) ссы́лка, сно́ска **5** (referring for information) спра́вка **6** (testimonial) о́тзыв, рекоменда́ция, характери́стика; (person supplying ~) поручи́тель (*m.*)
■ ~ book *n.* спра́вочник

referend|um /refə'rendəm/ *n.* (*pl.* ~ums *or* ~a) рефере́ндум

referral /rɪ'fɜ:r(ə)l/ *n.* направле́ние

refill[1] /'ri:fɪl/ *n.* (for pen etc.) запасно́й сте́ржень

refill[2] /ri:'fɪl/ *v.t.* нап|олня́ть, -о́лнить вновь

refine /rɪ'faɪn/ *v.t.* **1** (purify) оч|ища́ть, -и́стить **2** (make more cultured) соверше́нствовать, у-; ~d manners утончённые/изы́сканные мане́ры

refinement /rɪ'faɪnmənt/ *n.* **1** (good manners) благовоспи́танность **2** (improving change, addition) улучше́ние, усоверше́нствование

refinery /rɪ'faɪnərɪ/ *n.* (oil) нефтеочисти́тельный заво́д

refit[1] /'ri:fɪt/ *n.* ремо́нт, переоборудова́ние

refit[2] /ri:'fɪt/ *v.t.* чини́ть, по-; переоборудовать (*impf., pf.*); ремонти́ровать, от-

⚡ **reflect** /rɪ'flekt/ *v.t.* отра|жа́ть, -зи́ть
● *v.i.* **1** (produce a reflection) отра|жа́ться, -зи́ться; (fig., bring discredit): your behaviour ~s on us all ва́ше поведе́ние ложи́тся пятно́м на нас всех **2** (consider) заду́маться (*pf.*) (on: над + *i.*); I ~ed (on/upon) how fortunate I had been я поду́мал о том, как мне повезло́

reflection /rɪ'flekʃ(ə)n/ *n.* **1** (of light, heat, etc.) отраже́ние **2** (consideration) on ~, I may have been wrong поразмы́слив, я реши́л, что, возмо́жно, (я) был непра́в

reflex /'ri:fleks/ *n.* (*also* ~ action) рефле́кс

reflexive /rɪ'fleksɪv/ *adj.* возвра́тный

reflexologist /ri:flek'sɒlədʒɪst/ *n.* рефлексотерапе́вт

reflexology /ri:flek'sɒlədʒɪ/ *n.* (med.) рефлексоло́гия

r

reform /rɪˈfɔːm/ *n.* рефо́рма
● *v.t.* (a system) ул|учша́ть, -у́чшить; реформи́ровать (*impf., pf.*); (a person) перевоспи́т|ывать, -а́ть; испр|авля́ть, -а́вить
● *v.i.* испр|авля́ться, -а́виться

reformat /riːˈfɔːmæt/ *v.t.* (comput.) формати́ровать, от- за́ново

Reformation /refəˈmeɪʃ(ə)n/ *n.* Реформа́ция

reformer /rɪˈfɔːmə(r)/ *n.* реформа́тор

reformist /rɪˈfɔːmɪst/ *n.* реформи́ст

refraction /rɪˈfrækʃ(ə)n/ *n.* преломле́ние; рефра́кция

refrain[1] /rɪˈfreɪn/ *n.* припе́в

refrain[2] /rɪˈfreɪn/ *v.i.* сдерж|иваться, -а́ться; **I could hardly ~ from laughing** я е́ле сде́рживался от сме́ха

refresh /rɪˈfreʃ/ *v.t.* освеж|а́ть, -и́ть; **let me ~ your memory** позво́льте напо́мнить вам

refresher /rɪˈfreʃə(r)/ *n.* (*also* **~ course**) курс переподгото́вки

refreshing /rɪˈfreʃɪŋ/ *adj.* освежа́ющий

refreshment /rɪˈfreʃmənt/ *n.* еда́; питьё; **~s are served on the train** в по́езде мо́жно перекуси́ть

refrigerate /rɪˈfrɪdʒəreɪt/ *v.t.* замор|а́живать, -о́зить

refrigeration /rɪfrɪdʒəˈreɪʃ(ə)n/ *n.* замора́живание

refrigerator /rɪˈfrɪdʒəreɪtə(r)/ *n.* холоди́льник

refuel /riːˈfjuːəl/ *v.i.* запр|авля́ться, -а́виться

refuge /ˈrefjuːdʒ/ *n.* убе́жище; приста́нище; **the cat took ~ beneath the table** кот спря́тался под столо́м

refugee /refjʊˈdʒiː/ *n.* бе́жен|ец (-ка)
■ **~ camp** *n.* ла́герь (*m.*) бе́женцев

refund[1] /ˈriːfʌnd/ *n.* возмеще́ние убы́тков

refund[2] /rɪˈfʌnd/ *v.t.* возме|ща́ть, -сти́ть (*что кому*)

refurbish /riːˈfɜːbɪʃ/ *v.t.* отде́л|ывать, -ать

refurbishment /riːˈfɜːbɪʃmənt/ *n.* (капита́льный) ремо́нт

refusal /rɪˈfjuːz(ə)l/ *n.* отка́з

refuse[1] /ˈrefjuːs/ *n.* му́сор
■ **~ collection** *n.* убо́рка му́сора

refuse[2] /rɪˈfjuːz/ *v.t. & i.* (decline to give) отка́з|ывать, -а́ть (*кому в чём*); (reject) отв|ерга́ть, -е́ргнуть; (decline sth offered) отка́з|ываться, -а́ться от + *g.*

refute /rɪˈfjuːt/ *v.t.* опров|ерга́ть, -е́ргнуть

regain /rɪˈɡeɪn/ *v.t.* получ|а́ть, -и́ть обра́тно; **he never ~ed consciousness** он так и не пришёл в созна́ние

regal /ˈriːɡ(ə)l/ *adj.* короле́вский

regale /rɪˈɡeɪl/ *v.t.* уго|ща́ть, -сти́ть; по́тчевать (*impf.*)

regard /rɪˈɡɑːd/ *n.* **1** (respect) отноше́ние; **in this ~** в э́том отноше́нии; **in, with ~ to your request** что каса́ется ва́шей про́сьбы; **2** (consideration) внима́ние, забо́та; **he paid**

no ~ to her feelings он не счита́лся с её чу́вствами; **3** (esteem) уваже́ние (**for:** к + *d.*); **he holds your opinion in high ~** он о́чень высоко́ це́нит ва́ше мне́ние; **4** (*in pl.*) (greetings) приве́т; **give him my warmest ~s** переда́йте ему́ от меня́ серде́чный приве́т
● *v.t.* **1** (consider) расце́н|ивать, -и́ть; сч|ита́ть, -есть; **he was ~ed as a hero** счита́ли геро́ем **2** (concern): **as ~s, ~ing** относи́тельно + *g.*; что каса́ется + *g.*; насчёт + *g.* **3** (look at) разгля́д|ывать, -е́ть

regardless /rɪˈɡɑːdlɪs/ *adj.* невнима́тельный (**of:** к + *d.*); **~ of expense** не счита́ясь с расхо́дами

regatta /rɪˈɡætə/ *n.* рега́та

regenerate /rɪˈdʒenəreɪt/ *v.t. & i.* возро|жда́ть(ся), -ди́ть(ся)

regent /ˈriːdʒ(ə)nt/ *n.* ре́гент

reggae /ˈreɡeɪ/ *n.* ре́гги (*m. indecl.*)

regime /reɪˈʒiːm/ *n.* режи́м, строй; **under the old ~** при ста́ром режи́ме

regiment /ˈredʒɪmənt/ *n.* полк

regimental /redʒɪˈment(ə)l/ *adj.* полково́й

region /ˈriːdʒ(ə)n/ *n.* райо́н, о́бласть; регио́н; **in the ~ of £5,000** приблизи́тельно 5000 фу́нтов

regional /ˈriːdʒən(ə)l/ *adj.* райо́нный; областно́й; региона́льный

register /ˈredʒɪstə(r)/ *n.* (record, list) рее́стр; за́пись; (in school) журна́л
● *v.t.* **1** (enter on official record) регистри́ровать, за-; оф|ормля́ть, -о́рмить; **~ed letter** заказно́е письмо́ **2** (of an instrument: record) пока́з|ывать, -а́ть; отм|еча́ть, -е́тить **3** (express) выража́ть, вы́разить
● *v.i.* (record one's name) регистри́роваться, за-

registrar /redʒɪsˈtrɑː(r)/ *n.* (keeper of records) регистра́тор; (BrE, in hospital) врач, проходя́щий пра́ктику по специа́льности

registration /redʒɪˈstreɪʃ(ə)n/ *n.* регистра́ция; **~ number of a car** (BrE) (регистрацио́нный) но́мер маши́ны

registry /ˈredʒɪstrɪ/ *n.* регистрату́ра; **~ office** (BrE): **they were married at a ~ office** они́ расписа́лись в за́гсе; они́ зарегистри́ровались

regress /rɪˈɡres/ *v.i.* дви́гаться (*impf.*) в обра́тном направле́нии, регресси́ровать (*impf.*)

regret /rɪˈɡret/ *n.* сожале́ние; **I found to my ~ that I was late** я обнаружи́л, к своему́ сожале́нию, что опозда́л; **I have no ~s** я ни о чём не жале́ю
● *v.t.* (**regretted, regretting**) сожале́ть (*impf.*); **I ~ losing my temper** я сожале́ю, что вы́шел из себя́; **I ~ to say ...** к сожале́нию, я до́лжен сказа́ть...; **you will live to ~ this** вы ещё пожале́ете об э́том

regretful /rɪˈɡretfʊl/ *adj.* опеча́ленный; по́лный сожале́ния

regrettable /rɪˈɡretəb(ə)l/ *adj.* приско́рбный

regular /ˈreɡjʊlə(r)/ *n.* **1** (in full **~ soldier**) солда́т регуля́рной а́рмии **2** (in full **~ customer**) завсегда́тай; постоя́нный

посети́тель
● *adj.* **1** (orderly in appearance, symmetrical) пра́вильный, регуля́рный **2** (steady, unvarying) регуля́рный, норма́льный; a ~ pulse ритми́чный пульс; he keeps ~ hours y него́ стро́гий/чёткий режи́м (дня) **3** (AmE, ordinary) регуля́рный, обы́чный

regularity /reɡjʊˈlærɪtɪ/ *n.* регуля́рность

regularly /ˈreɡjʊlə̆lɪ/ *adv.* регуля́рно

regulate /ˈreɡjʊleɪt/ *v.t.* регули́ровать (*impf.*)

✍ **regulation** /reɡjʊˈleɪʃ(ə)n/ *n.* **1** (control) регули́рование **2** (rule) пра́вило

regulator /ˈreɡjʊleɪtə(r)/ *n.* (person) отве́тственное лицо́; (body) отве́тственная организа́ция; (device) регуля́тор, стабилиза́тор

regulatory /reɡjʊˈleɪtərɪ/ *adj.* регули́рующий
■ ~ **body** *n.* о́рган управле́ния

regurgitate /rɪˈɡɜːdʒɪteɪt/ *v.t.* отры́г|ивать, -ну́ть

rehabilitate /riːhəˈbɪlɪteɪt/ *v.t.* перевоспи́т|ывать, -а́ть

rehabilitation /riːhəbɪlɪˈteɪʃ(ə)n/ *n.* перевоспита́ние; реабилита́ция

rehearsal /rɪˈhɜːs(ə)l/ *n.* репети́ция

rehearse /rɪˈhɜːs/ *v.t.* репети́ровать, от-

rehouse /riːˈhaʊz/ *v.t.* пересел|я́ть, -и́ть

reign /reɪn/ *n.* ца́рствование, власть
● *v.i.* ца́рствовать (*impf.*); (fig.) цари́ть (*impf.*)

reimburse /riːɪmˈbɜːs/ *v.t.* возме|ща́ть, -сти́ть (*что кому*)

reimbursement /riːɪmˈbɜːsmənt/ *n.* возмеще́ние, возвраще́ние

reincarnation /riːɪnkɑːˈneɪʃ(ə)n/ *n.* перевоплоще́ние

reindeer /ˈreɪndɪə(r)/ *n.* (*pl.* ~ *or* ~s) се́верный оле́нь

reinforce /riːɪnˈfɔːs/ *v.t.* уси́ли|вать, -ть

reinforcement /riːɪnˈfɔːsmənt/ *n.* усиле́ние; (*in pl.*) (troops) подкрепле́ние

reins /reɪnz/ *n. pl.* во́ж|жи (-же́й)

reinstate /riːɪnˈsteɪt/ *v.t.* восстан|а́вливать, -ови́ть в права́х/до́лжности/положе́нии

reinstatement /riːɪnˈsteɪtmənt/ *n.* восстановле́ние в права́х/до́лжности/ положе́нии

reissue /riːˈɪʃuː/ *v.t.* переизд|ава́ть, -а́ть

reiterate /riːˈɪtəreɪt/ *v.t.* повтор|я́ть, -и́ть

reject¹ /ˈriːdʒekt/ *n.* (discarded article) неподходя́щая вещь; (comm.) брако́ванное изде́лие; (*pl., collect.*) брак

✍ **reject²** /rɪˈdʒekt/ *v.t.* отклон|я́ть, -и́ть; отв|ерга́ть, -е́ргнуть; my offer was ~ed out of hand моё предложе́ние сра́зу же отклони́ли

rejection /rɪˈdʒekʃ(ə)n/ *n.* отка́з, отклоне́ние

rejoice /rɪˈdʒɔɪs/ *v.i.* ра́доваться, об- (*чему*)

rejuvenate /rɪˈdʒuːvəneɪt/ *v.t.* омол|а́живать, -оди́ть

rekindle /riːˈkɪnd(ə)l/ *v.t.* разж|ига́ть, -е́чь вновь

relapse *n.* /ˈriːlæps/ рециди́в
● *v.i.* /rɪˈlæps/ сно́ва преда́ться (*pf.*) (*чему*); he

~d into bad ways он сно́ва сби́лся с пути́; she ~d into silence она́ (сно́ва) замолча́ла

✍ **relate** /rɪˈleɪt/ *v.t.* **1** (narrate) расска́з|ывать, -а́ть o + *p.* **2** (establish relation between) свя́з|ывать, -а́ть (*что c чем*)
● *v.i.* относи́ться (*impf.*) (to: к + *d.*)

✍ **related** /rɪˈleɪtɪd/ *adj.* **1** (logically connected) свя́занный (c + *i.*); взаимосвя́занный (друг с дру́гом) **2** (by blood or marriage): he and I are ~ мы с ним ро́дственники

✍ **relation** /rɪˈleɪʃ(ə)n/ *n.* **1** (connection) отноше́ние; in, with ~ to относи́тельно + *g.* **2** (*in pl.*) (dealings) отноше́ния (*nt. pl.*); international ~s междунаро́дные отноше́ния **3** (family member) ро́дственни|к (-ца)

✍ **relationship** /rɪˈleɪʃənʃɪp/ *n.* (relevance) связь, отноше́ние; (between people or groups) взаимоотноше́ния (*nt. pl.*), связь; (kinship) родство́

✍ **relative** /ˈrelətɪv/ *n.* (family member) ро́дственни|к (-ца)
● *adj.* **1** (comparative) относи́тельный, сравни́тельный; he is a ~ newcomer он здесь относи́тельно неда́вно **2** (gram.): ~ pronoun относи́тельное местоиме́ние

✍ **relatively** /ˈrelətɪvlɪ/ *adv.* относи́тельно; ~ speaking вообще́ говоря́

relativity /reləˈtɪvɪtɪ/ *n.* относи́тельность; theory of ~ тео́рия относи́тельности

relax /rɪˈlæks/ *v.i.* (rest) рассл|абля́ться, -а́биться; отдыха́ть (*impf.*); I like to ~ in the sun я люблю́ посиде́ть на со́лнце; a ~ed atmosphere споко́йная атмосфе́ра; (slacken) осл|абева́ть, -абе́ть
● *v.t.* (control, attention) осл|абля́ть, -а́бить; he ~ed his grip он разжа́л ру́ку; (person) рассл|абля́ть, -а́бить

relaxation /riːlækˈseɪʃ(ə)n/ *n.* **1** (rest, recreation) о́тдых, развлече́ние **2** (of control) ослабле́ние **3** (of tension) разря́дка

relay /ˈriːleɪ/ *n.* **1** (fresh team) сме́на **2** (*in full* ~ race) эстафе́тный бег
● *v.t.* (transmit) трансли́ровать (*impf., pf.*)

✍ **release** /rɪˈliːs/ *n.* **1** (liberation) освобожде́ние **2** (unfastening) освобожде́ние **3** (device for doing this) спуск **4** (of book, recording, film) вы́пуск
● *v.t.* **1** (liberate) освобо|жда́ть, -ди́ть **2** (unfasten) отпус|ка́ть, -ти́ть; выпуска́ть, вы́пустить; do not ~ the brake не отпуска́йте то́рмоз **3** (book, CD, film) выпуска́ть, вы́пустить

relegate /ˈrelɪɡeɪt/ *v.t.* от|сыла́ть, -осла́ть; the team was ~d to the second division (BrE) кома́нду перевели́ во второ́й дивизио́н

relegation /relɪˈɡeɪʃ(ə)n/ *n.* пониже́ние, перево́д (в бо́лее ни́зкий класс *и т. п.*)

relent /rɪˈlent/ *v.i.* смягч|а́ться, -и́ться; подобре́ть (*pf.*)

relentless /rɪˈlentlɪs/ *adj.* безжа́лостный

relevance /ˈrelɪv(ə)ns/ *n.* отноше́ние к де́лу; уме́стность

✍ **relevant** /ˈrelɪv(ə)nt/ *adj.* относя́щийся к

r

де́лу; уме́стный; ~ **to** относя́щийся к + *d.*

reliability /rɪlaɪə'bɪlɪtɪ/ *n.* надёжность; достове́рность

reliable /rɪ'laɪəb(ə)l/ *adj.* надёжный; (of a statement) достове́рный

reliance /rɪ'laɪəns/ *n.* (trust) дове́рие; **I place great ~ upon him** я ему́ о́чень доверя́ю; (dependence) зави́симость; ~ **on drugs** зави́симость от нарко́тиков

reliant /rɪ'laɪənt/ *adj.* (dependent) зави́симый, зави́сящий; **they are completely ~ on their pension** они́ по́лностью зави́сят от свое́й пе́нсии

relic /'relɪk/ *n.* реликвия

✓ **relief** /rɪ'li:f/ *n.* **1** (alleviation) облегче́ние **2** (assistance) посо́бие; **a ~ fund for flood victims** фонд по́мощи же́ртвам наводне́ния **3** (sculpture etc.) рельеф
 ■ ~ **agency** *n.* организа́ция по оказа́нию по́мощи; ~ **map** *n.* рельефная ка́рта

relieve /rɪ'li:v/ *v.t.* **1** (alleviate) облегч|а́ть, -и́ть; **I was ~d to get your letter** я был рад получи́ть ва́ше письмо́ **2** (bring assistance to) при|ходи́ть, -йти́ на по́мощь + *d.* **3** (unburden) освобо|жда́ть, -ди́ть (*кого от чего*); **this ~s me of the necessity to speak** э́то освобожда́ет меня́ от необходи́мости говори́ть **4** (replace on duty) смен|я́ть, -и́ть

✓ **religion** /rɪ'lɪdʒ(ə)n/ *n.* рели́гия, ве́ра; вероисповеда́ние

✓ **religious** /rɪ'lɪdʒəs/ *adj.* религио́зный

relinquish /rɪ'lɪŋkwɪʃ/ *v.t.* (abandon) ост|авля́ть, -а́вить; (surrender) сд|ава́ть, -ать; **he ~ed his claims** он отказа́лся от свои́х тре́бований

relish /'relɪʃ/ *n.* **1** (zest) (большо́е/ нескрыва́емое) удово́льствие; **he ate with ~** он ел с аппети́том **2** (sauce) припра́ва
 ● *v.t.* получ|а́ть, -и́ть удово́льствие от + *g.*; (infml): **I don't ~ the prospect** меня́ не прельща́ет перспекти́ва

relocate /ri:ləʊ'keɪt/ *v.t. & i.* переме|ща́ть(ся), -сти́ть(ся)

relocation /ri:ləʊ'keɪʃən/ *n.* перемеще́ние

reluctance /rɪ'lʌkt(ə)ns/ *n.* нежела́ние; неохо́та

reluctant /rɪ'lʌkt(ə)nt/ *adj.* неохо́тный; **she was ~ to leave home** ей не хоте́лось покида́ть дом

✓ **rely** /rɪ'laɪ/ *v.i.* полага́ться (*impf.*); наде́яться (*impf.*) (*both* на + *a.*); **you can ~ on me** вы мо́жете на меня́ положи́ться

✓ **remain** /rɪ'meɪn/ *v.i.* ост|ава́ться, -а́ться; (stay) пребыва́ть (*impf.*); **he ~ed silent** он храни́л молча́ние

remainder /rɪ'meɪndə(r)/ *n.* (rest) оста́т|ок, -ки (*m. pl.*); (of people) остальны́е (*pl.*)

remains /rɪ'meɪnz/ *n.* оста́тки (*m. pl.*), оста́нк|и (-ов)

remand /rɪ'mɑ:nd/ *n.*: **on ~** под стра́жей
 ● *v.t.*: **he was ~ed in custody** он содержа́лся под стра́жей

✓ ключевая лексика

 ■ ~ **home** *n.* (BrE) исправи́тельный дом для несовершенноле́тних

remark /rɪ'mɑ:k/ *n.* замеча́ние
 ● *v.t.* зам|еча́ть, -е́тить

remarkable /rɪ'mɑ:kəb(ə)l/ *adj.* удиви́тельный; замеча́тельный

remarry /ri:'mærɪ/ *v.i.* вступ|а́ть, -и́ть в но́вый брак

remedial /rɪ'mi:dɪəl/ *adj.* (of education) корректи́вный

remedy /'remɪdɪ/ *n.* (cure) сре́дство, лека́рство (**for:** от + *g.*)
 ● *v.t.* испр|авля́ть, -а́вить

✓ **remember** /rɪ'membə(r)/ *v.t.* **1** (have in one's memory) по́мнить (*impf.*); **I ~ you saying it** я по́мню, что вы э́то сказа́ли; **I ~ her as a girl** я по́мню её де́вочкой **2** (recall) всп|омина́ть, -о́мнить; **he couldn't ~ how many meetings he had had in the past days** он не смог вспо́мнить число́ встреч, на кото́рых он побыва́л за после́дние дни **3** (not forget) не заб|ыва́ть, -ы́ть, име́ть (*impf.*) в виду́; ~ **to turn out the light** не забу́дьте погаси́ть свет

remembrance /rɪ'membrəns/ *n.* па́мять; **in ~ of** в па́мять о + *p.*

✓ **remind** /rɪ'maɪnd/ *v.t.* нап|омина́ть, -о́мнить (*кому что, or о чём, or + inf.*); **he ~s me of my father** он напомина́ет мне отца́; **he ~ed me to buy bread** он напо́мнил мне купи́ть хле́ба

reminder /rɪ'maɪndə(r)/ *n.* напомина́ние

reminisce /remɪ'nɪs/ *v.i.* пред|ава́ться, -а́ться воспомина́ниям

reminiscence /remɪ'nɪs(ə)ns/ *n.* воспомина́ние

reminiscent /remɪ'nɪs(ə)nt/ *adj.* **1** (of person, recalling the past): **he became ~ of** он преда́лся воспомина́ниям **2**: ~ **of** (tending to remind one of sth or suggest sth) напомина́ющий; вызыва́ющий воспомина́ния о + *p.*; **his music is ~ of Brahms** его́ му́зыка напомина́ет Бра́мса

remiss /rɪ'mɪs/ *adj.* хала́тный; неради́вый; **that was very ~ of me** с мое́й стороны́ э́то бы́ло недобросо́вестно

remission /rɪ'mɪʃ(ə)n/ *n.* (med.) реми́ссия

remit /'ri:mɪt/ *n.* зада́чи (*f. pl.*), компете́нция

remnant /'remnənt/ *n.* (remains) оста́ток; (of cloth) оста́тки

remodel /ri:'mɒd(ə)l/ *v.t.* переде́л|ывать, -ать

remonstrate /'remənstreɪt/ *v.i.* протестова́ть (*impf.*); возра|жа́ть, -зи́ть; (exhort): **he ~d with me** он увещева́л меня́

remorse /rɪ'mɔ:s/ *n.* угрызе́ния (*nt. pl.*) со́вести

remorseful /rɪ'mɔ:sfʊl/ *adj.* по́лный раска́яния

remorseless /rɪ'mɔ:slɪs/ *adj.* безжа́лостный

remortgage /ri:'mɔ:gɪdʒ/ *v.t.* (fin.) переза|кла́дывать, -ложи́ть

remote /rɪ'məʊt/ *adj.* (**remoter, remotest**) отдалённый, глухо́й; **a ~ ancestor** далёкий прéдок; **there is a ~ possibility of its happening** не исключенó, что э́то случи́тся; **I haven't the ~st idea** не име́ю ни мале́йшего поня́тия; **he was not even ~ly interested** он не прояви́л ни мале́йшего интере́са (к + *d.*)

■ **~ control** *n.* (control) дистанцио́нное управле́ние; (device) пульт ДУ, пульт дистанцио́нного управле́ния; **~-controlled** *adj.* с дистанцио́нным управле́нием

remoteness /rɪˈməʊtnɪs/ *n.* отдалённость

removal /rɪˈmuːv(ə)l/ *n.* (taking away) удале́ние; (BrE, of furniture) перево́зка

♂ **remove** /rɪˈmuːv/ *v.t.* **1** (take away, off) уб|ира́ть, -ра́ть; ун|оси́ть, -ести́; **how can I ~ these stains?** как мо́жно вы́вести э́ти пя́тна? **2** (dismiss): **he was ~d from office** его́ сня́ли с рабо́ты

remover /rɪˈmuːvə(r)/ *n.*: **furniture ~** (BrE) перево́зчик ме́бели; **stain ~** пятновыводи́тель (*m.*)

remunerate /rɪˈmjuːnəreɪt/ *v.t.* (person) вознагра|жда́ть, -ди́ть; (work) опла́|чивать, -ти́ть

remuneration /rɪmjuːnəˈreɪʃ(ə)n/ *n.* вознагражде́ние

Renaissance /rɪˈneɪs(ə)ns/ *n.* (hist.) Ренесса́нс, Возрожде́ние; (**r~**) (revival) возрожде́ние

rename /riːˈneɪm/ *v.t.* переимено́в|ывать, -а́ть

render /ˈrendə(r)/ *v.t.* (cause to be): **he was ~ed speechless** он онеме́л

rendezvous /ˈrɒndɪvuː/ *n.* (*pl.* **~** /-vuːz/) рандеву́ (*nt. indecl.*), свида́ние
● *v.i.* (**rendezvouses** /-vuːz/, **rendezvoused** /-vuːd/, **rendezvousing** /-vuːɪŋ/) встр|еча́ться, -е́титься

rendition /renˈdɪʃ(ə)n/ *n.* (performance) исполне́ние; (translation) перево́д

renegade /ˈrenɪɡeɪd/ *n.* pereга́т, отсту́пник
● *adj.* pereга́тский, отсту́пнический

renege, renegue /rɪˈneɪɡ/ *v.i.*: **he ~d on his promise** он нару́шил своё обеща́ние

renew /rɪˈnjuː/ *v.t.* возобнов|ля́ть, -и́ть

renewable /rɪˈnjuːəb(ə)l/ *adj.*: **~ resources** возобновля́емые ресу́рсы

renewal /rɪˈnjuːəl/ *n.* возобновле́ние

renounce /rɪˈnaʊns/ *v.t.* отка́з|ываться, -а́ться от + *g.*

renouncement /rɪˈnaʊnsmənt/ *n.* отрече́ние, отка́з

renovate /ˈrenəveɪt/ *v.t.* ремонти́ровать, от-; реставри́ровать (*impf., pf.*) (*pf. also* от-)

renovation /renəˈveɪʃ(ə)n/ *n.* реставра́ция; ремо́нт

renown /rɪˈnaʊn/ *n.* сла́ва; изве́стность; **a preacher of ~** пропове́дник, по́льзующийся большо́й изве́стностью; **he won ~ on the battlefield** он завоева́л сла́ву на по́ле бо́я

renowned /rɪˈnaʊnd/ *adj.* изве́стный

rent¹ /rent/ *n.* (tear, split) дыра́

♂ **rent²** /rent/ *n.* (for premises) аре́ндная пла́та; (for a flat) квартпла́та
● *v.t.* **1** (car, equipment) брать, взять напрока́т;

(a place) сн|има́ть, -ять **2**: **~ (out)** (car) дава́ть, дать напрока́т; (building) сд|ава́ть, -а́ть

■ **~ boy** *n.* (BrE, infml) мужчи́на-проститу́тка

rental /ˈrent(ə)l/ *n.* разме́р аре́ндной пла́ты

renunciation /rɪnʌnsɪˈeɪʃ(ə)n/ *n.* отрече́ние, отка́з

reorganization /riːɔːɡənaɪˈzeɪʃ(ə)n/ *n.* реорганиза́ция

reorganize /riːˈɔːɡənaɪz/ *v.t.* реорганизо́в|ывать, -а́ть

rep¹ /rep/ *n.* (infml) = **representative 1**

rep² /rep/ *n.* (infml) = **repertory 2**

repair /rɪˈpeə(r)/ *n.* **1** (restoring) ремо́нт **2** (condition): **the house is in good ~** дом в хоро́шем состоя́нии
● *v.t.* (mend) ремонти́ровать, от-; чини́ть, по-; (restore) восстан|а́вливать, -ови́ть

■ **~man** *n.* ма́стер

reparation /repəˈreɪʃ(ə)n/ *n.* компенса́ция; возмеще́ние уще́рба; (*in pl.*) (compensation for war damage) (вое́нные) репара́ции (*f. pl.*)

repartee /repɑːˈtiː/ *n.* остроу́мный разгово́р

repatriate /riːˈpætrɪeɪt/ *v.t.* репатрии́ровать (*impf., pf.*)

repatriation /riːpætrɪˈeɪʃ(ə)n/ *n.* репатриа́ция

repay /riːˈpeɪ/ *v.t.* (debt) выпла́чивать, вы́платить (*кому*)

repayable /riːˈpeɪəb(ə)l/ *adj.* подлежа́щий упла́те

repayment /riːˈpeɪmənt/ *n.* вы́плата, возмеще́ние

repeal /rɪˈpiːl/ *n.* отме́на, аннули́рование
● *v.t.* аннули́ровать (*impf., pf.*)

♂ **repeat** /rɪˈpiːt/ *n.* повторе́ние
● *v.t.* повтор|я́ть, -и́ть; **after ~ed attempts** по́сле неоднокра́тных попы́ток

repeatedly /rɪˈpiːtɪdlɪ/ *adv.* неоднокра́тно

repel /rɪˈpel/ *v.t.* (**repelled, repelling**) **1** (enemy, attack) отб|ива́ть, -и́ть **2** (be repulsive to) отта́лкивать (*impf.*)

repellent /rɪˈpelənt/ *n.*: **insect ~** сре́дство от насеко́мых
● *adj.* (repulsive) отта́лкивающий

repent /rɪˈpent/ *v.t. & i.* ка́яться (*impf.*); раска́|иваться, -яться (*в чём*)

repentance /riːˈpentəns/ *n.* раска́яние

repentant /riːˈpentənt/ *adj.* раска́ивающийся

repercussion /riːpəˈkʌʃ(ə)n/ *n.* (*usu. in pl.*) после́дствия (*nt. pl.*)

repertoire /ˈrepətwɑː(r)/ *n.* репертуа́р

repertory /ˈrepətərɪ/ *n.* **1** (repertoire) репертуа́р **2** (*also* **rep**: infml): **~ company** постоя́нная тру́ппа с определённым репертуа́ром; **~ theatre** (BrE), **theater** (AmE) репертуа́рный теа́тр **3** (fig., store) запа́с

repetition /repɪˈtɪʃ(ə)n/ *n.* повторе́ние

repetitious /repɪˈtɪʃəs/ *adj.* = **repetitive**

repetitive /rɪˈpetɪtɪv/ *adj.* повторя́ющийся; ску́чный

■ **~ strain injury** *n.* тра́вма, вы́званная повторя́ющимся движе́нием

r

⚡ **replace** /rɪ'pleɪs/ *v.t.* **1** (put back) класть, положи́ть (*or* ста́вить, по-) на ме́сто; возвра|ща́ть, -ти́ть **2** (provide substitute for) заменя́ть, -и́ть; **the vase cannot be** ~**d** э́то уника́льная ва́за **3** (take the place of) заме|ща́ть, -сти́ть; **he** ~**d me as secretary** он замеща́л/смени́л меня́ в до́лжности секретаря́

replacement /rɪ'pleɪsmənt/ *n.* (provision of substitute) замеще́ние, заме́на; (substitute) заме́на

replay[1] /'riːpleɪ/ *n.* (of a game) переигро́вка

replay[2] /riː'pleɪ/ *v.t.* (sport) переигр|ывать, -а́ть

replenish /rɪ'plenɪʃ/ *v.t.* (one's wardrobe) поп|олня́ть, -о́лнить; **he** ~**ed his glass** он сно́ва напо́лнил стака́н

replete /rɪ'pliːt/ *adj.* напо́лненный; сы́тый, бога́тый (*чем*); ~ **with food** нае́вшийся вдо́воль

replica /'replɪkə/ *n.* ко́пия

replicate /'replɪkeɪt/ *v.t.* копи́ровать, с-

⚡ **reply** /rɪ'plaɪ/ *n.* отве́т
● *v.i.* отве|ча́ть, -́тить

⚡ **report** /rɪ'pɔːt/ *n.* докла́д, отчёт; **newspaper** ~ сообще́ние, изве́стие, репорта́ж; **school** ~ (BrE), ~ **card** (AmE) отчёт об успева́емости
● *v.t.* **1** (give news or account of) сообщ|а́ть, -и́ть; сост|авля́ть, -а́вить отчёт о + *p.*; **it has been** ~**ed that ...** сообща́лось, что... **2** (inform against) жа́ловаться, по- на + *a.*; **I shall** ~ **you for insolence** я пожа́луюсь на вас за ва́шу де́рзость
● *v.i.* **1** (give information) до|кла́дывать, -ложи́ть; де́лать, с- докла́д; предст|авля́ть, -а́вить отчёт **2** (present oneself) яв|ля́ться, -и́ться (*куда-н.*)

⚡ **reporter** /rɪ'pɔːtə(r)/ *n.* репортёр

repository /rɪ'pɒzɪtərɪ/ *n.* (receptacle) храни́лище, вмести́лище; (store) склад; (fig.): **he is a** ~ **of information** он неиссяка́емый исто́чник информа́ции

repossess /riːpə'zes/ *v.t.* изыма́ть, -ъя́ть за непла́тёж

reprehensible /reprɪ'hensɪb(ə)l/ *adj.* предосуди́тельный

⚡ **represent** /reprɪ'zent/ *v.t.* **1** (speak or act for) представля́ть (*impf.*) **2** (constitute, amount to) представля́ть (*impf.*) собо́й **3** (portray) изобра|жа́ть, -зи́ть; **what does this picture** ~? что изображено́ на э́той карти́не?; (make out): **he** ~**ed himself as an expert** он выдава́л себя́ за знатока́ **4** (symbolize, correspond to) символизи́ровать (*impf., pf.*), изобража́ть (*impf.*), обознача́ть (*impf.*)

representation /reprɪzen'teɪʃ(ə)n/ *n.* **1** (portrayal) изображе́ние **2** (*in pl.*) (statements): **diplomatic** ~**s** дипломати́ческие представле́ния (*заявле́ния*) **3** (being represented) представи́тельство

⚡ **representative** /reprɪ'zentətɪv/ *n.* представи́тель (*m.*) (-ница)
● *adj.* показа́тельный, типи́чный

⚡ ключева́я ле́ксика

repress /rɪ'pres/ *v.t.* **1** (put down) подав|ля́ть, -и́ть **2** (restrain) сде́рж|ивать, -а́ть

repression /rɪ'preʃ(ə)n/ *n.* (of feelings) подавле́ние; (of people) репре́ссия

repressive /rɪ'presɪv/ *adj.* репресси́вный

reprieve /rɪ'priːv/ *n.* (law) отсро́чка исполне́ния (сме́ртного) пригово́ра

reprimand /'reprɪmɑːnd/ *n.* вы́говор, замеча́ние
● *v.t.* де́лать, с- вы́говор/замеча́ние + *d.*

reprint[1] /'riːprɪnt/ *n.* перепеча́тка

reprint[2] /riː'prɪnt/ *v.t.* перепеча́т|ывать, -ать

reprisal /rɪ'praɪz(ə)l/ *n.* отве́тное де́йствие

reproach /rɪ'prəʊtʃ/ *n.* упрёк, уко́р
● *v.t.* упрек|а́ть, -ну́ть; укоря́ть (*impf.*)

reproachful /rɪ'prəʊtʃfʊl/ *adj.* укори́зненный

reprobate /'reprəbeɪt/ *n.* негодя́й, нечести́вец
● *adj.* нечести́вый; безнра́вственный

reproduce /riːprə'djuːs/ *v.t.* (copy) воспроизв|оди́ть, -ести́
● *v.i.* (biol.) разм|ножа́ться, -о́житься

reproduction /riːprə'dʌkʃ(ə)n/ *n.* (biol.) размноже́ние; (art) репроду́кция

reproductive /riːprə'dʌktɪv/ *adj.* (biol.) полово́й

reproof /rɪ'pruːf/ *n.* порица́ние

reprove /rɪ'pruːv/ *v.t.* де́лать, с- вы́говор + *d.*

reptile /'reptaɪl/ *n.* пресмыка́ющееся, репти́лия

republic /rɪ'pʌblɪk/ *n.* респу́блика

republican /rɪ'pʌblɪkən/ *n.* республика́н|ец (-ка)
● *adj.* республика́нский

repudiate /rɪ'pjuːdɪeɪt/ *v.t.* отв|ерга́ть, -е́ргнуть

repugnance /rɪ'pʌɡnəns/ *n.* отвраще́ние

repugnant /rɪ'pʌɡnənt/ *adj.* отврати́тельный

repulse /rɪ'pʌls/ *v.t.* (drive back) отб|ива́ть, -и́ть; (refuse) отт|а́лкивать, -олкну́ть

repulsion /rɪ'pʌlʃ(ə)n/ *n.* отвраще́ние

repulsive /rɪ'pʌlsɪv/ *adj.* отврати́тельный

reputable /'repjʊtəb(ə)l/ *adj.* почте́нный

⚡ **reputation** /repjʊ'teɪʃ(ə)n/ *n.* репута́ция

repute /rɪ'pjuːt/ *n.*: **an artist of** ~ худо́жник с и́менем
● *v.t.*: **he is** ~**d to be rich** он счита́ется бога́тым; говоря́т, что он бога́т; **the** ~**d father** предполага́емый оте́ц

reputedly /rɪ'pjuːtɪdlɪ/ *adv.* по о́бщему мне́нию

⚡ **request** /rɪ'kwest/ *n.* про́сьба; **a programme of** ~**s** конце́рт по зая́вкам
● *v.t.* проси́ть, по-

requiem /'rekwɪəm/ *n.* (mus.) ре́квием; (relig.) панихи́да

⚡ **require** /rɪ'kwaɪə(r)/ *v.t.* **1** (need) нужда́ться (*impf.*) в + *p.*; **the matter** ~**s some thought** над э́тим на́до поду́мать **2** (demand) тре́бовать, по- + *g.*; **my attendance is** ~**d by law** по зако́ну я обя́зан прису́тствовать; **I have done all that is** ~**d** я сде́лал всё, что тре́буется

⚡ **requirement** /rɪ'kwaɪəmənt/ *n.* **1** (need)

потре́бность **2** (demand) тре́бование

requisite /'rekwɪzɪt/ *adj.* необходи́мый

requisition /rekwɪ'zɪʃ(ə)n/ *v.t.* реквизи́ровать (*impf., pf.*)

reschedule /ri:'ʃedju:l/ *v.t.* переноси́ть, -ести́

◇' **rescue** /'reskju/ *n.* спасе́ние, вы́ручка; **he came to my ~** он пришёл мне на по́мощь/ вы́ручку
● *v.t.* (**rescues, rescued, rescuing**) спас|а́ть, -ти́

rescuer /'reskju:ə(r)/ *n.* спаси́тель (-ница)

◇' **research** /rɪ'sɜ:tʃ/ *n.* изуче́ние, иссле́дование, изыска́ние; **~ and development** нау́чно-иссле́довательская рабо́та
● *v.t. & i.* иссле́довать (*impf., pf.*)

◇' **researcher** /rɪ'sɜ:tʃə(r)/ *n.* иссле́дователь (-ница)

resemblance /rɪ'zembləns/ *n.* схо́дство

resemble /rɪ'zemb(ə)l/ *v.t.* походи́ть (*impf.*) на + *a.*

resend /ri:'send/ *v.t.* отпр|авля́ть, -а́вить повто́рно; пос|ыла́ть, -ла́ть повто́рно

resent /rɪ'zent/ *v.t.* возму|ща́ться, -ти́ться + *i.*; **I ~ your interfering in my affairs** мне о́чень не нра́вится, что вы вме́шиваетесь в мои́ дела́

resentful /rɪ'zentfʊl/ *adj.* возмущённый

resentment /rɪ'zentmənt/ *n.* возмуще́ние

reservation /reza'veɪʃ(ə)n/ *n.* **1** (booking) (предвари́тельный) зака́з **2** (limitation) огово́рка **3** (for indigenous people) резерва́ция

◇' **reserve** /rɪ'zɜ:v/ *n.* **1** (store) запа́с, резе́рв **2** (mil.) резе́рв **3** (~ player) запасно́й (игро́к) **4** (area) запове́дник; **game ~** охо́тничий запове́дник **5** (reticence) сде́ржанность
● *v.t.* **1** (save) бере́чь, с-; прибер|ега́ть, -е́чь **2** (set aside) резерви́ровать, за-; (ticket, table) зака́з|ывать, -а́ть; (hotel room) брони́ровать, за-

reserved /rɪ'zɜ:vd/ *adj.* **1** (booked) зака́занный (зара́нее) **2** (reticent) сде́ржанный

reservist /rɪ'zɜ:vɪst/ *n.* резерви́ст

reservoir /'rezəvwɑ:(r)/ *n.* водохрани́лище, водоём

reset /ri:'set/ *v.t.* (clock) перест|авля́ть, -а́вить; (trap) сно́ва ста́вить, по-

resettle /ri:'set(ə)l/ *v.t.* пересел|я́ть, -и́ть
● *v.i.* пересел|я́ться, -и́ться

resettlement /ri:'setəlmənt/ *n.* переселе́ние

reshuffle /ri:'ʃʌf(ə)l/ *n.*: **Cabinet ~** перестано́вки в Кабине́те мини́стров

reside /rɪ'zaɪd/ *v.i.* прожива́ть (*impf.*); жить (*impf.*)

residence /'rezɪd(ə)ns/ *n.* **1** (residing) прожива́ние **2** (home, mansion) дом, резиде́нция

◇' **resident** /'rezɪd(ə)nt/ *n.* (inhabitant) (постоя́нный) жи́тель; (BrE, in hotel) постоя́лец
● *adj.* постоя́нно прожива́ющий

residential /rezɪ'denʃ(ə)l/ *adj.*: **a ~ area** жило́й райо́н

residual /rɪ'zɪdʒʊəl/ *adj.* оста́точный, оста́вшийся

residue /'rezɪdju:/ *n.* оста́ток

resign /rɪ'zaɪn/ *v.t.* **1** (give up) отка́з|ываться, -а́ться от + *g.*; **he ~ed his post as Chancellor** он по́дал в отста́вку с поста́ ка́нцлера **2** (reconcile): **he ~ed himself to defeat** он смири́лся с пораже́нием
● *v.i.* под|ава́ть, -а́ть (*or* уходи́ть, уйти́) в отста́вку; уход|и́ть, уйти́ с рабо́ты

resignation /rezɪg'neɪʃ(ə)n/ *n.* **1** (resigning of office) отста́вка; **he handed in his ~** он по́дал заявле́ние об отста́вке/ухо́де **2** (acceptance of fate) поко́рность

resigned /rɪ'zaɪnd/ *adj.* поко́рный, смири́вшийся (**to:** с + *i.*)

resilience /rɪ'zɪlɪəns/ *n.* эласти́чность, (fig.) выно́сливость

resilient /rɪ'zɪlɪənt/ *adj.* эласти́чный; (fig.) выно́сливый

resin /'rezɪn/ *n.* смола́

resist /rɪ'zɪst/ *v.t.* **1** (oppose) сопротивля́ться (*impf.*) + *d.* **2** (refrain from) возде́рж|иваться, -а́ться от + *g.*; **I could not ~ the temptation to smile** я не мог удержа́ться от улы́бки; **she cannot ~ chocolates** она́ не мо́жет устоя́ть пе́ред шокола́дом

◇' **resistance** /rɪ'zɪst(ə)ns/ *n.* сопротивле́ние; (political movement) движе́ние сопротивле́ния

resistant /rɪ'zɪst(ə)nt/ *adj.* сопротивля́ющийся

resit /ri:'sɪt/ *v.t.* (BrE): **~ an examination** пересдава́ть (*impf.*) экза́мен

resolute /'rezəlu:t/ *adj.* реши́тельный

◇' **resolution** /reza'lu:ʃ(ə)n/ *n.* **1** (firmness of purpose) реши́мость **2** (vow): **New Year ~** нового́дний заро́к **3** (expression of intent) резолю́ция **4** (comput., TV, phot., etc., of screen, camera, etc.) разреше́ние

◇' **resolve** /rɪ'zɒlv/ *n.* (determination) реши́тельность, реши́мость
● *v.t. & i.* **1** (decide) реш|а́ть, -и́ть; прин|има́ть, -я́ть реше́ние **2** (settle) (раз)реш|а́ть, -и́ть; **their quarrel was ~d** их спор разреши́лся

resonance /'rezənəns/ *n.* резона́нс, гул

resonant /'rezənənt/ *adj.* звуча́щий

resonate /'rezəneɪt/ *v.i.* резони́ровать, звуча́ть (*both impf.*)

resort /rɪ'zɔ:t/ *n.* **1** (recourse): **in the last ~** в кра́йнем слу́чае **2** (place): **holiday ~** куро́рт; **seaside ~** морско́й куро́рт
● *v.i.* (have recourse) приб|eráть, -е́гнуть (**to:** к + *d.*)

resound /rɪ'zaʊnd/ *v.i.* звуча́ть (*impf.*); **the hall ~ed with voices** в за́ле раздава́лись голоса́; (fig.): **a ~ing success** оглуши́тельный успе́х

◇' **resource** /rɪ'zɔ:s/ *n.* (source) исто́чник; (*in pl.*) запа́сы (*m. pl.*); ресу́рсы (*m. pl.*)
● *v.t.* снаб|жа́ть, -ди́ть кого́-н. (*деньга́ми, обору́дованием и т. п.*)

resourceful /rɪ'zɔ:sfʊl/ *adj.* изобрета́тельный

resourcefulness /rɪ'zɔ:sfʊlnɪs/ *n.* изобрета́тельность, нахо́дчивость

◇' **respect** /rɪ'spekt/ *n.* **1** (esteem) уваже́ние

r

2 (reference): with ~ to что касáется + g.
3 (in pl.) (polite greetings) почтéние;
he came to pay his ~s он пришёл засвидéтельствовать своё почтéние
● v.t. уважáть (impf.); почитáть (impf.)

respectability /rɪspektə'bɪlɪtɪ/ n. респектáбельность

respectable /rɪ'spektəb(ə)l/ adj. приличный

respectful /rɪ'spektfʊl/ adj. почтительный

respective /rɪ'spektɪv/ adj. соотвéтственный;
we went off to our ~ rooms мы разошлись по своим кóмнатам; the boys and girls were taught woodwork and sewing ~ly мáльчиков и дéвочек учи́ли соотвéтственно столя́рному дéлу и шитью́

respiration /respɪ'reɪʃ(ə)n/ n. дыхáние

respirator /'respɪreɪtə(r)/ n. респирáтор

respiratory /rɪ'spɪrətərɪ/ adj. дыхáтельный

respite /'respaɪt/ n. (rest) передышка

resplendent /rɪ'splend(ə)nt/ adj. блистáтельный

♂ **respond** /rɪ'spɒnd/ v.i. **1** (reply) отв|ечáть, -éтить (to: на + a.) **2** (react) реагировать, от- (to: на + a.); his illness is ~ing to treatment его болéзнь поддаётся лечéнию

♂ **response** /rɪ'spɒns/ n. **1** (reply) отвéт; in ~ to your enquiry в отвéт на ваш запрóс **2** (reaction) реáкция, óтклик

♂ **responsibility** /rɪspɒnsɪ'bɪlɪtɪ/ n. отвéтственность; I take full ~ for my actions я беру́ на себя́ пóлную отвéтственность за свои́ дéйствия

♂ **responsible** /rɪ'spɒnsɪb(ə)l/ adj. **1** (accountable) отвéтственный; she is ~ for cleaning my room убóрка моéй кóмнаты вхóдит в её обя́занности **2** (to blame): who's ~? кто винóват?; who was ~ for breaking the window? кто разбил окнó? **3** (trustworthy) надёжный **4** (involving responsibility) вáжный

responsive /rɪ'spɒnsɪv/ adj. отзывчивый

♂ **rest¹** /rest/ n. **1** (relaxation) óтдых; I'm going (up) to have a ~ (я) пойду́ приля́гу **2** (undisturbed state) покóй; I set his mind at ~ я его́ успокóил **3** (intermission) передышка; they took a short ~ они сдéлали небольшу́ю передышку **4** (prop) опóра
● v.t. **1** (give ~ to) да|вáть, -ть óтдых + d. **2** (place for support) класть, положить (on: на + a.); прислон|я́ть, -ить (что к чему)
● v.i. **1** (relax) лежáть (impf.); отд|ыхáть, -охну́ть **2** (fig., remain) ост|авáться, -áться; the decision ~s with you решéние зависит от вас **3** (be supported) опирáться (impf.) (на что)
■ ~room n. (AmE, toilet) туалéт

♂ **rest²** /rest/ n. (remainder) остáток; (remaining things, people) остальны́е (pl.)

restart /riː'stɑːt/ v.t. (begin again) вновь нач|инáть, -áть; (car) снóва зав|одить, -ести

♂ **restaurant** /'restərɒnt/ n. ресторáн
■ ~ car n. вагóн-ресторáн

restful /'restfʊl/ adj. успокáивающий

restive /'restɪv/ adj. (of horse) норовистый; (of person) стропти́вый; (restless) беспокóйный

restless /'restlɪs/ adj. беспокóйный

restock /riː'stɒk/ v.i. поп|олня́ть, -óлнить запáсы

restoration /restə'reɪʃ(ə)n/ n. реставрáция

♂ **restore** /rɪ'stɔː(r)/ v.t. **1** (goods to owner) возвра|щáть, -тить (or верну́ть); (former state or situation) восстан|áвливать, -овить; order was ~d поря́док был восстанóвлен **2** (monument, work of art) реставрировать (impf., pf.) (pf. also от-)

restorer /rɪ'stɔːrə(r)/ n. реставрáтор

restrain /rɪ'streɪn/ v.t. сдéрж|ивать, -áть; his manner was ~ed он был сдéржан

restraint /rɪ'streɪnt/ n. **1** (self-control) сдéржанность **2** (constraint) ограничéние

restrict /rɪ'strɪkt/ v.t. ограни́чи|вать, -ть

restriction /rɪ'strɪkʃ(ə)n/ n. ограничéние

restrictive /rɪ'strɪktɪv/ adj. ограничи́тельный

♂ **result** /rɪ'zʌlt/ n. результáт, слéдствие; he died as a ~ of his injuries он у́мер от ран
● v.i. **1** (arise) слéдовать (impf.) (из чего) **2** (end) конч|áться, -иться (in: + i.); the quarrel ~ed in bloodshed ссóра кончилась кровопроли́тием

resume /rɪ'zjuːm/ v.t. (continue) прод|олжáть, -óлжить; (take again): he ~d command он снóва при́нял командовáние (чем)
● v.i.: let us ~ after lunch продóлжим пóсле обéда

résumé /'rezjʊmeɪ/ n. (summary; CV) резюмé (nt. indecl.)

resumption /rɪ'zʌmpʃ(ə)n/ n. продолжéние

resurface /riː'sɜːfɪs/ v.t. меня́ть, смени́ть покры́тие + g.
● v.i. всплы|вáть, -ть

resurgence /rɪ'sɜːdʒ(ə)ns/ n. возрождéние

resurrect /rezə'rekt/ v.t. воскре|шáть, -сить

resurrection /rezə'rekʃ(ə)n/ n. (of Christ) воскресéние; (fig.) воскрешéние

resuscitate /rɪ'sʌsɪteɪt/ v.t. прив|одить, -ести в сознáние; реанимировать (impf., pf.)

resuscitation /rɪsʌsɪ'teɪʃ(ə)n/ n. реанимáция (искусственное дыхание)

retail /'riːteɪl/ n. рóзничная продáжа
● v.i. продавáться (impf.) в рóзницу

retailer /'riːteɪlə(r)/ n. рóзничный торгóвец

♂ **retain** /rɪ'teɪn/ v.t. удéрживать (impf.); сохран|я́ть, -ить

retainer /rɪ'teɪnə(r)/ n. **1** (hist.) вассáл; (servant) слугá (m.) **2** (fee) предвари́тельный гонорáр

retaliate /rɪ'tælɪeɪt/ v.i. отпла́|чивать, -тить той же монéтой

retaliation /rɪtælɪ'eɪʃ(ə)n/ n. отпла́та, возмéздие

retarded /rɪ'tɑːdɪd/ adj.: (offens.) a ~ child у́мственно отстáлый ребёнок

retentive /rɪ'tentɪv/ adj.: a ~ memory цéпкая пáмять; a soil ~ of moisture пóчва, сохраня́ющая влáгу

rethink /riː'θɪŋk/ v.t. пересм|áтривать, -отрéть

♂ ключевáя лéксика

reticent /'retɪs(ə)nt/ *adj.* молчали́вый

retina /'retɪnə/ *n.* (*pl.* **retinas** *or* **retinae** /-niː/) сетча́тка

retinue /'retɪnjuː/ *n.* сви́та

retir|e /rɪ'taɪə(r)/ *v.i.* **1** (from employment) уходи́ть, уйти́ в отста́вку **2** (withdraw) удал|я́ться, -и́ться; **he has a ~ing disposition** он засте́нчивый челове́к

retired /rɪ'taɪəd/ *adj.* (находя́щийся) на пе́нсии

retirement /rɪ'taɪəmənt/ *n.* отста́вка, вы́ход на пе́нсию (*or* в отста́вку)
■ **~ age** *n.* пенсио́нный во́зраст

retort /rɪ'tɔːt/ *n.* возраже́ние
● *v.i.* отв|еча́ть, -е́тить ре́зко (*or* тем же)

retrace /riː'treɪs/ *v.t.*: **~ one's steps** возвраща́ться, верну́ться тем же путём

retract /rɪ'trækt/ *v.t.* отка́з|ываться, -а́ться от + *g.*
● *v.i.* втя́|гиваться, -ну́ться

retrain /riː'treɪn/ *v.t. & i.* переквалифици́ровать(ся) (*impf., pf.*)

retreat /rɪ'triːt/ *n.* отступле́ние, отхо́д
● *v.i.* (withdraw) удал|я́ться, -и́ться

retrench /rɪ'trentʃ/ *v.i.* (economize) эконо́мить, с-

retrial /'riːtraɪəl/ *n.* повто́рное слу́шание де́ла

retribution /retrɪ'bjuːʃ(ə)n/ *n.* возме́здие, ка́ра

retrieval /rɪ'triːv(ə)l/ *n.* (recovery, getting back) возвраще́ние

retrieve /rɪ'triːv/ *v.t.* брать, взять обра́тно

retriever /rɪ'triːvə(r)/ *n.* охо́тничья поиско́вая соба́ка; ретри́вер

retrograde /'retrəgreɪd/ *adj.* реакцио́нный

retrogressive /retrə'gresɪv/ *adj.* регресси́рующий

retrospect /'retrəspekt/ *n.*: **in ~** ретроспекти́вно

retrospective /retrə'spektɪv/ *adj.* ретроспекти́вный; **a ~ law** зако́н, име́ющий обра́тную си́лу
● *n.* (exhibition) ито́говая вы́ставка рабо́т худо́жника

⚘ **return** /rɪ'tɜːn/ *n.* **1** (coming or going back) возвраще́ние; **many happy ~s (of the day)!** с днём рожде́ния!; **~ fare** сто́имость обра́тного прое́зда **2** (*in full* **~ ticket**) (BrE) обра́тный биле́т, биле́т в о́ба конца́ **3** (profit) дохо́д **4** (giving, sending, putting) отда́ча, возвра́т **5** (reciprocation): **in ~ (for)** взаме́н (+ *g.*); (in response to) в отве́т (на + *a.*) **6** (report) отчёт, ра́порт; **income tax ~** нало́говая деклара́ция **7** (comput.) возвра́т
● *v.t.* **1** (give, send, put, back) возвра|ща́ть, -ти́ть (*or* верну́ть); **he ~ed the ball accurately** он хорошо́ отби́л мяч **2** (declare) до|кла́дывать, -ложи́ть; **the jury ~ed a verdict of guilty** прися́жные призна́ли обвиня́емого вино́вным
● *v.i.* возвра|ща́ться, -ти́ться (*or* верну́ться)

reunion /riː'juːnjən/ *n.* (reuniting) воссоедине́ние; (meeting of old friends etc.) встре́ча (ста́рых друзе́й)

reunite /riːjuː'naɪt/ *v.t. & i.* воссоедин|я́ть(ся), -и́ть(ся)

reusable /riː'juːzəb(ə)l/ *adj.* многокра́тного по́льзования

reuse /riː'juːz/ *v.t.* сно́ва испо́льзовать (*impf., pf.*)

rev /rev/ *v.t. & i.* (**revved, revving**) (*also* **~ up**) увели́чи|вать, -ть оборо́ты (мото́ра)

revamp /riː'væmp/ *v.t.* обновля́ть, -и́ть

⚘ **reveal** /rɪ'viːl/ *v.t.* обнару́жи|вать, -ть; **this account is very ~ing** э́тот отчёт о́чень показа́телен; **she wore a ~ing dress** она́ была́ в откры́том пла́тье

revel /'rev(ə)l/ *v.i.* (**revelled, revelling**, AmE **reveled, reveling**) наслажда́ться (*impf.*) + *i.*; **she ~s in gossip** она́ обожа́ет спле́тни

revelation /revə'leɪʃ(ə)n/ *n.* откры́тие, открове́ние

reveller /'revələ(r)/ (AmE **reveler**) *n.* кути́ла (*m.*), гуля́ка (*c.g.*)

revelry /'revəlrɪ/ *n.* попо́йка, разгу́л

revenge /rɪ'vendʒ/ *n.* месть; **he took his ~ on me** он мне отомсти́л
● *v.t.*: **he ~d himself on his enemies** он отомсти́л свои́м врага́м

⚘ **revenue** /'revənjuː/ *n.* дохо́д

reverberate /rɪ'vɜːbəreɪt/ *v.i.* отра|жа́ться, -зи́ться

revere /rɪ'vɪə(r)/ *v.t.* почита́ть (*impf.*)

reverence /'revərəns/ *n.* почита́ние, почте́ние

Reverend /'revərənd/ *adj.*: **the ~ John Smith** его́ преподо́бие Джон Смит

reverent /'revərənt/, **reverential** /revə'renʃ(ə)l/ *adjs.* почти́тельный

reverie /'revərɪ/ *n.* мечта́ние

reversal /rɪ'vɜːs(ə)l/ *n.* по́лная переме́на

reverse /rɪ'vɜːs/ *n.* **1** (opposite) противополо́жность; **the ~ is true** де́ло обстои́т как раз наоборо́т **2** (~ gear): **he put the car into ~** он включи́л за́дний ход
● *adj.* обра́тный, противополо́жный; **in ~ order** в обра́тном поря́дке; **in ~ gear** за́дним хо́дом
● *v.t.* **1** (turn round, invert) пов|ора́чивать, -ерну́ть обра́тно **2** (drive backwards): **he ~d (the car) into a wall** он дал за́дний ход и вре́зался в сте́ну
● *v.i.* (of driver) да|ва́ть, -ть за́дний ход

reversible /rɪ'vɜːsɪb(ə)l/ *adj.* (process etc.) обрати́мый; (garment) двусторо́нний

revert /rɪ'vɜːt/ *v.i.* возвра|ща́ть́ся, -ти́ться; **the fields have ~ed to scrub** поля́ вновь поросли́ куста́рником; **he ~ed to his old ways** он взя́лся за ста́рое; (of property, rights, etc.) пере|ходи́ть, -йти́ (*к пре́жнему владе́льцу*)

⚘ **review** /rɪ'vjuː/ *n.* **1** (re-examination, retrospect) пересмо́тр **2** (of mil. forces etc.) пара́д **3** (of book etc.) реце́нзия **4** (periodical) обозре́ние
● *v.t.* **1** (re-examine) пересм|а́тривать, -отре́ть **2** (inspect) просм|а́тривать, -отре́ть **3** (write critical account of) рецензи́ровать, от-

reviewer /rɪ'vjuːə(r)/ *n.* реце́нзе́нт

revise /rɪ'vaɪz/ v.t. (one's views) пересм|а́тривать, -отре́ть; (correct a text, an opinion) испр|авля́ть, -а́вить
● v.i. (BrE): **I must ~ for the exams** я до́лжен повтори́ть материа́л к экза́менам

revision /rɪ'vɪʒ(ə)n/ n. (of text) прове́рка, перерабо́тка; (for exams) повторе́ние

revitalize /ri:'vaɪtəlaɪz/ v.t. вновь оживля́ть, -и́ть

revival /rɪ'vaɪv(ə)l/ n. (return to consciousness, health, etc.) возвраще́ние созна́ния; **a ~ of interest** оживле́ние интере́са; (return to use, popularity) возрожде́ние

revive /rɪ'vaɪv/ v.t. (bring back to life, enliven) оживля́ть, -и́ть; (custom, hope) возро|жда́ть, -ди́ть
● v.i. (of flowers, person) ож|ива́ть, -и́ть; (regain consciousness) при|ходи́ть, -йти́ в себя́

revoke /rɪ'vəʊk/ v.t. отменя́ть, -и́ть

revolt /rɪ'vəʊlt/ n. восста́ние
● v.t. вызыва́ть, вы́звать отвраще́ние у + g.; **a ~ing sight** отврати́тельное зре́лище
● v.i. восст|ава́ть, -а́ть; бунтова́ть (impf.); взбунтова́ться (pf.)

revolution /revə'lu:ʃ(ə)n/ n. **1** (one complete rotation) оборо́т **2** (pol., also fig.) револю́ция

revolutionary /revə'lu:ʃənərɪ/ n. революционе́р (-ка)
● adj. революцио́нный

revolutionize /revə'lu:ʃənaɪz/ v.t. революционизи́ровать (impf., pf.)

revolv|e /rɪ'vɒlv/ v.i. враща́ться (impf.); (fig.): **he thinks everything ~es around him** он мнит себя́ це́нтром вселе́нной
■ **~ing doors** n. pl. враща́ющиеся две́ри

revolver /rɪ'vɒlvə(r)/ n. револьве́р

revue /rɪ'vju:/ n. (theatr.) обозре́ние, ревю́ (nt. indecl.)

revulsion /rɪ'vʌlʃ(ə)n/ n. отвраще́ние

reward /rɪ'wɔ:d/ n. **1** (for achievement) награ́да (for: за + a.) **2** (sum offered) пре́мия
● v.t. (воз)награ|жда́ть, -ди́ть; **it was a ~ing task** де́ло сто́ило того́

rewind /ri:'waɪnd/ v.t. перем|а́тывать, -ота́ть

rewire /ri:'waɪə(r)/ v.t.: **~ a house** заменя́ть, -и́ть прово́дку в до́ме

reword /ri:'wɜ:d/ v.t. переформули́ровать (impf., pf.)

rework /ri:'wɜ:k/ v.t. перераб|а́тывать, -о́тать

rewrite /ri:'raɪt/ v.t. (copy out) перепи́с|ывать, -а́ть; (rework) перераб|а́тывать, -о́тать

rhapsod|y /'ræpsədɪ/ n. (mus.) рапсо́дия; (fig.): **he went into ~ies over her dress** он пел дифира́мбы её туале́ту/наря́ду

rhetoric /'retərɪk/ n. рито́рика

rhetorical /rɪ'tɒrɪk(ə)l/ adj. ритори́ческий

rheumatic /ru:'mætɪk/ n. (sufferer from rheumatism) ревма́тик; (in pl.) (infml, rheumatism) ревмати́зм
● adj. ревмати́ческий
■ **~ fever** n. ревмати́зм

rheumatism /'ru:mətɪz(ə)m/ n. ревмати́зм

rheumatoid /'ru:mətɔɪd/ adj. ревмато́идный, ревмати́ческий
■ **~ arthritis** n. ревмато́идный артри́т

rhino /'raɪnəʊ/ n. (pl. ~s or ~) = rhinoceros

rhinoceros /raɪ'nɒsərəs/ n. (pl. ~ or ~es) носоро́г

Rhodes /rəʊdz/ n. Ро́дос

rhododendron /rəʊdə'dendrən/ n. рододе́ндрон

rhubarb /'ru:bɑ:b/ n. реве́нь (m.)

rhyme /raɪm/ n. ри́фма; (poem) стих
● v.t. & i. рифмова́ть(ся) (impf.)

rhythm /'rɪð(ə)m/ n. ритм

rhythmic /'rɪðmɪk/ adj. ритми́чный, ритми́ческий

rib /rɪb/ n. (anat.) ребро́; **spare ~s** (of meat) рёбрышки (nt. pl.)

ribald /'rɪb(ə)ld/ adj. непристо́йный, скабрёзный

ribbon /'rɪbən/ n. ле́нта, тесьма́

rice /raɪs/ n. рис

♂ **rich** /rɪtʃ/ n. (collect.): **the ~** бога́тые (pl.)
● adj. **1** (wealthy) бога́тый **2** (fertile) плодоро́дный **3** (of food) жи́рный

riches /'rɪtʃɪz/ n. pl. бога́тство

richness /'rɪtʃnɪs/ n. бога́тство; (of food) жи́рность

Richter scale /'rɪktə/ n. шкала́ Ри́хтера

rickety /'rɪkɪtɪ/ adj. ша́ткий, неусто́йчивый

ricochet /'rɪkəʃeɪ/ n. рикоше́т; **~ fire** стрельба́ на рикоше́тах
● v.i. (**ricocheted** /-ʃeɪd/, **ricocheting** /-ʃeɪŋ/ or **ricochetted** /-ʃetɪd/, **ricochetting** /-ʃetɪŋ/) рикошети́ровать (impf., pf.); бить (impf.) рикоше́том

rid /rɪd/ v.t. (**ridding**, past and p.p. **rid**) освобо|жда́ть, -ди́ть; избавля́ть, -а́вить; **get ~ of** изб|авля́ться, -а́виться от + g.; **we were glad to be, get ~ of him** мы бы́ли ра́ды от него́ изба́виться

riddance /'rɪd(ə)ns/ n.: **good ~ to him!** ≈ ска́тертью доро́га!

ridden /'rɪd(ə)n/ p.p. of ► ride

riddle¹ /'rɪd(ə)l/ n. зага́дка

riddle² /'rɪd(ə)l/ v.t. (pierce all over) решети́ть, из-; **he was ~d with bullets** пу́ли изрешети́ли его́ те́ло

♂ **ride** /raɪd/ n. **1** (on horseback) прогу́лка верхо́м; (by vehicle) пое́здка, езда́ **2** (excursion) прогу́лка **3** (fairground attraction) аттракцио́н
● v.t. & i. (past **rode**, p.p. **ridden**) **1** (on horseback) е́здить (indet.), е́хать (det.), по-(верхо́м) (на + p.); ката́ться (impf.) (верхо́м) (на + p.) **2** (on a vehicle) е́здить (indet.), е́хать (det.), по- (на + p.); **I ~ a bicycle to work** я е́зжу на рабо́ту на велосипе́де
□ **~ out** v.t.: **we shall ~ out our present troubles** мы переживём ны́нешние тру́дности
□ **~ up** v.i. (approach on horseback) подъ|езжа́ть, -е́хать верхо́м; (of clothing) заде́ра́ться, -ра́ться

rider /'raɪdə(r)/ n. (horseman) вса́дни|к (-ца); (cyclist) велосипеди́ст (-ка)

ridge /rɪdʒ/ *n.* **1** край; спинка **2** (of high land) горный хребет

ridicule /'rɪdɪkjuːl/ *n.* насмешка
● *v.t.* подн|имать, -ять на смех

ridiculous /rɪ'dɪkjʊləs/ *adj.* (funny) смехотворный; (stupid) (*attr.*) смешной; (stupid) (*pred.*) глупый; **don't be ~!** не будь(те) посмешищем!; **~ly low prices** до смешного низкие цены

riding /'raɪdɪŋ/ *n.* верховая езда
■ **~ school** *n.* школа верховой езды

rife /raɪf/ *adj.* распространённый

riff /rɪf/ *n.* (mus.) рифф

riff-raff /'rɪfræf/ *n.* подонки (*m. pl.*) общества; сброд

rifle /'raɪf(ə)l/ *n.* винтовка

rift /rɪft/ *n.* **1** трещина, щель **2** (fig.) разлад

rig /rɪɡ/ *n.* буровая вышка
● *v.t.* (**rigged**, **rigging**) (conduct fraudulently): **the elections were ~ged** результаты выборов были подтасованы
□ **~ up** *v.t.* (наскоро) сооруж|ать, -дить

Riga /'riːɡə/ *n.* Рига

rigging /'rɪɡɪŋ/ *n.* такелаж

⚹ **right** /raɪt/ *n.* **1** (what is morally good) правота; справедливость; **the child must learn the difference between ~ and wrong** ребёнка следует научить отличать добро от зла **2** (entitlement) право; **by ~s** по справедливости; честно говоря; **~ of way** право прохода/проезда **3** (~-hand side etc.) правая сторона; **on, to the ~** направо; **on, from the ~** справа **4** (pol.): **the R~** правые (*pl.*)
● *adj.* **1** (just, morally good) правый, справедливый; **I try to do what is ~** я стараюсь поступать честно; **you were ~ to refuse** вы правильно сделали, что отказались **2** (correct, true) правильный, верный; **what is the ~ time?** вы можете сказать точное время?; **~ side up** в правильном положении; **that's ~!** правильно!; верно!; **I set him ~ on a few points** я ему кое-что разъяснил **3** (in order, good health): **I don't feel ~** я плохо себя чувствую; **this medicine will soon put you ~** от этого лекарства вы скоро поправитесь; **are you all ~?** с вами всё в порядке?; (expr. doubt) вам нехорошо?; вам плохо?; **all ~, I'll come with you!** ладно, я пойду с вами!; **~!** (expr. agreement or consent) верно!; хорошо! **4** (opp. left) правый
● *adv.* **1** (straight) прямо; **carry ~ on!** всё время прямо! **2** (exactly) точно; **~ here/there** прямо здесь/там; **~ now** сейчас; в данный момент **3** (immediately) сразу (же); **~ away** сразу (же), прямо сейчас, немедленно, сию минуту **4** (all the way) полностью; **he turned ~ round** он повернулся кругом; **I went ~ back to the beginning** я вернулся к самому началу; **he came ~ up to me** он подошёл ко мне вплотную **5** (correctly, properly) справедливо; правильно; **he can do nothing ~** у него ничего не ладится; **have I guessed ~?** я угадал? **6** (of direction) направо

● *v.t.* (correct) исправлять, -авить
■ **~ angle** *n.* прямой угол; **~-hand** *adj.* правый; **~-hand drive** правостороннее управление; **~-hand man** (fig.) верный помощник, правая рука; **~-handed** *adj.* делающий всё правой рукой, праворукий; **~-wing** *adj.* (pol.) правых взглядов; правый

righteous /'raɪtʃəs/ *adj.* праведный

rightful /'raɪtfʊl/ *adj.* законный

rightly /'raɪtlɪ/ *adv.* **1** (correctly) правильно; **~ or wrongly, I believe he is lying** так это или нет, но я думаю, он лжёт **2** (justly) справедливо

rigid /'rɪdʒɪd/ *adj.* жёсткий; (fig.) негибкий; **~ discipline** строгая дисциплина

rigidity /rɪ'dʒɪdɪtɪ/ *n.* жёсткость; (fig.) негибкость

rigmarole /'rɪɡmərəʊl/ *n.* канитель

rigorous /'rɪɡərəs/ *adj.* строгий

rigour /'rɪɡə(r)/ (AmE **rigor**) *n.* строгость

rile /raɪl/ *v.t.* (infml) сердить, рас-; раздраж|ать, -ить; **it ~d him to lose the game** его злило, что он проиграл

rim /rɪm/ *n.* обод; край

rind /raɪnd/ *n.* (of orange, cheese) корка; (of bacon) кожура, шкурка

⚹ **ring**¹ /rɪŋ/ *n.* **1** (ornament) кольцо; (with stone; signet ~) перстень (*m.*); **engagement ~** кольцо, подаренное при помолвке; **wedding ~** обручальное кольцо **2** (circle) кольцо, круг; **he had ~s under his eyes** у него были тёмные круги под глазами **3** (conspiracy) шайка, банда; **spy ~** шпионская организация **4** (of circus, boxing, etc.) арена, ринг **5** (of cooker) конфорка
■ **~ binder** *n.* скоросшиватель (*m.*); **~ leader** *n.* главарь (*m.*); **~ road** *n.* (BrE) кольцевая дорога

⚹ **ring**² /rɪŋ/ *n.* **1** (sound of bell) звонок; **there was a ~ at the door** в дверь позвонили **2** (BrE, telephone call) звонок; **give me a ~ tomorrow** позвоните мне завтра
● *v.t.* (*past* **rang**, *p.p.* **rung**) **1** звонить, по- в + *a.* **2** (BrE, telephone) (*also* **~ up**) звонить, по- + *d.*
● *v.i.* (*past* **rang**, *p.p.* **rung**) **1** звонить, по-; **the bells are ~ing** звонят колокола; **the telephone rang** зазвонил телефон; (fig.): **his words ~ true** его слова звучат правдоподобно **2** (BrE, telephone) звонить, по-; **we must ~ for the doctor** мы должны вызвать врача (по телефону) **3** (resound) оглаш|аться, -иться (*чем*)
● *with advs.*: **~ off** (BrE) повесить (*pf.*) трубку; **a shot rang out** раздался выстрел
■ **~tone** *n.* мелодия звонка, рингтон (*в мобильном телефоне*)

ringing /'rɪŋɪŋ/ *adj.* звонкий

ringlet /'rɪŋlɪt/ *n.* (curl) локон

rink /rɪŋk/ *n.* каток

rinse /rɪns/ *n.* полоскание
● *v.t.* полоскать, про-

Rio /'riːəʊ/, **Rio de Janeiro** /'riːəʊ də dʒə'nɪərəʊ/ *n.* Рио-де-Жанейро (*m. indecl.*)

riot /'raɪət/ n. **1** (revolt) мятёж, бунт **2** (fig.): she allowed her imagination to run ~ она дала́ по́лную во́лю воображе́нию; the weeds are running ~ сорняки́ бу́йно разраста́ются; the garden was a ~ of colour сад пестре́л все́ми кра́сками
• v.i. (rebel) бесчи́нствовать (impf.)

rioter /'raɪətə(r)/ n. бунта́рь (m.), мяте́жник

riotous /'raɪətəs/ adj. (rebellious) мяте́жный; (wildly enthusiastic) безуде́ржный, шу́мный

rip /rɪp/ v.t. (**ripped, ripping**) рвать, разо-; he ~ped his trousers on a nail он порва́л брю́ки о гвоздь; he ~ped open the envelope он разорва́л конве́рт; ~ off (infml, steal) об|дира́ть, -одра́ть; she ~ped up the letter она́ разорвала́ письмо́
• v.i. (**ripped, ripping**) рва́ться, разо-
■ ~-off n. (infml): it's a ~-off э́то обдира́ловка

ripe /raɪp/ adj. спе́лый, зре́лый; the corn is ~ хлеба́ поспе́ли/созре́ли; ~ cheese вы́держанный сыр

ripen /'raɪpən/ v.i. зреть (or созрева́ть), со-
• v.t.: the sun ~ed the tomatoes помидо́ры созре́ли на со́лнце

ripple /'rɪp(ə)l/ n. рябь
• v.t. & i. покр|ыва́ть(ся), -ы́ть(ся) ря́бью

⚘ **rise** /raɪz/ n. **1** (slope, also fig., ascent) подъём **2** (increase) повыше́ние, увеличе́ние; a ~ in temperature повыше́ние температу́ры; they asked for a ~ (BrE) они́ попроси́ли об увеличе́нии зарпла́ты **3** (origin): give ~ to вызыва́ть, вы́звать
• v.i. (past **rose**, p.p. **risen** /'rɪz(ə)n/) **1** (get up from bed) вста|ва́ть, -ть (на́ ноги); (from seated or kneeling position) вста|ва́ть, -ть; подн|има́ться, -я́ться; (into the air) подн|има́ться, -я́ться; (from the dead) воскре|са́ть, -е́снуть; (above the horizon) восходи́ть, взойти́; when the sun ~s когда́ восхо́дит со́лнце; he will always ~ to the occasion он не растеря́ется в любо́й ситуа́ции **2** (slope upwards) подн|има́ться, -я́ться; (tower): the cliffs rose sheer above them над ни́ми кру́то возвыша́лись ска́лы **3** (increase in amount) возраста́ть (impf.); увели́чи|ваться, -ться; rising costs увели́чивающиеся расхо́ды; (in level): the waters are rising вода́ поднима́ется/ прибыва́ет; the bread has ~n хлеб подня́лся (на дрожжа́х); the temperature is rising температу́ра повыша́ется; (in price) пов|ыша́ться, -ы́ситься в цене́; дорожа́ть, по-; (in pitch): his voice rose in anger в гне́ве он повы́сил го́лос

risible /'rɪzɪb(ə)l/ adj. смешно́й, смехотво́рный

⚘ **risk** /rɪsk/ n. риск; he takes many ~s он лю́бит рискова́ть; he ran the ~ of defeat он рискова́л потерпе́ть пораже́ние
• v.t. рискова́ть (impf.) + i.

risky /'rɪski/ adj. (**riskier, riskiest**) риско́ванный, опа́сный

risotto /rɪ'zɒtəʊ/ n. (pl. ~s) ризо́тто (nt. indecl.)

risqué /'rɪskeɪ/ adj. риско́ванный

rite /raɪt/ n. обря́д

ritual /'rɪtʃʊəl/ n. ритуа́л; (collect.) обря́дность
• adj. ритуа́льный

rival /'raɪv(ə)l/ n. сопе́рник; (in business) конкуре́нт
• adj. сопе́рничающий; the ~ team кома́нда проти́вника
• v.t. (**rivalled, rivalling**, AmE **rivaled, rivaling**) сопе́рничать (impf.) с + i.

rivalry /'raɪvəlrɪ/ n. сопе́рничество; (in business) конкуре́нция

⚘ **river** /'rɪvə(r)/ n. река́; (attr.) речно́й; up/down ~ вверх/вниз по реке́
■ ~side n. прибре́жная полоса́ • adj. прибре́жный, стоя́щий на берегу́ реки́

rivet /'rɪvɪt/ n. заклёпка
• v.t. (**riveted, riveting**) клепа́ть (impf.); склёпывать, -а́ть

riveting /'rɪvɪtɪŋ/ adj. (infml) захва́тывающий

Riyadh /'rɪːæd/ n. Эр-Рия́д

⚘ **road** /rəʊd/ n. **1** (thoroughfare) доро́га; (attr.) доро́жный **2** (fig.) путь (m.), доро́га; he is on the ~ to recovery он на пути́ к выздоровле́нию
■ ~block n. блокпо́ст; ~ map n. ка́рта (автомоби́льных) доро́г; (fig.) путеводная нить; ~ rage n. (BrE) при́ступ гне́ва/я́рости води́теля автомоби́ля; ~show n. (radio, TV) репорта́ж с ме́ста собы́тий; (pol.) вы́ездное заседа́ние, встре́ча с избира́телями; ~side n. обо́чина доро́ги; ~works n. pl. (BrE) доро́жно-ремо́нтные рабо́ты; ~worthy adj. приго́дный для езды́ по доро́гам

roam /rəʊm/ v.t. & i. броди́ть, стра́нствовать, скита́ться (all impf.); he ~ed the streets он броди́л по у́лицам

roar /rɔː(r)/ n. (of animal, people) рёв; ~s of laughter взры́вы хо́хота
• v.t. & i. реве́ть (impf.); he ~ed with laughter он хохота́л во всё го́рло

roast /rəʊst/ n. жарко́е
• v.t. жа́рить, за-, из-; ~ beef жа́реная/ запечённая говя́дина
• v.i. гре́ться (impf.)

rob /rɒb/ v.t. (**robbed, robbing**) (person) обкра́дывать, обокра́сть; гра́бить, о-; (building) гра́бить, о-; I have been ~bed меня́ обокра́ли/огра́били; the bank was ~bed банк огра́били; they ~bed him of his watch они́ укра́ли у него́ часы́; (fig., deprive) лиш|а́ть, -и́ть (кого-н. чего-н.)

robber /'rɒbə(r)/ n. граби́тель (m.), вор

robbery /'rɒbərɪ/ n. (of person, building) ограбле́ние, грабёж; (when life-threatening) разбо́й

robe /rəʊb/ n. **1** ма́нтия **2** (AmE, dressing gown) (also **bath~**) (купа́льный) хала́т

robin /'rɒbɪn/ n. мали́новка

robot /'rəʊbɒt/ n. ро́бот

robust /rəʊ'bʌst/ adj. (**robuster, robustest**) кре́пкий, си́льный

⚘ **rock**[1] /rɒk/ n. (solid part of earth's crust) го́рная

r

поро́да; (boulder) валу́н; **the firm is on the ~s** (infml) фи́рма прогоре́ла; (AmE, stone, pebble) ка́мень (*m.*); **whisky on the ~s** (infml) ви́ски со льдо́м

■ ~ **bottom** *n.* (fig.): **at ~-bottom prices** по са́мым ни́зким це́нам; ~ **climber** *n.* скалола́з; ~ **climbing** *n.* скалола́зание; ~ **face** *n.* скала́; ~**fall** *n.* камнепа́д; ~ **garden** *n.* = rockery

✧ **rock²** /rɒk/ *n.* (music) рок
• *v.t.* (sway gently) кач|а́ть, -ну́ть; ука́ч|ивать, -а́ть; **she ~ed the baby to sleep** она́ укача́ла/ убаю́кала ребёнка; (shake) трясти́, по-; **the earthquake ~ed the house** дом шата́лся от землетрясе́ния
• *v.i.* (sway gently) кача́ться (*impf.*)

■ ~**ing chair** *n.* кача́лка; ~ **'n' roll** *n.* рок-н-ро́лл; ~ **star** *n.* рок-звезда́

rockery /'rɒkərɪ/ *n.* альпина́рий, альпи́йская го́рка

rocket /'rɒkɪt/ *n.* раке́та
• *v.i.* (**rocketed, rocketing**) (fig.): **prices ~ed** це́ны ре́зко подскочи́ли

rocky /'rɒkɪ/ *adj.* (**rockier, rockiest**) **1** (of rock; full of rocks) скали́стый, камени́стый; **the R~ Mountains, the Rockies** (infml) Скали́стые го́ры (*f. pl.*); **2** (unsteady) неусто́йчивый, ша́ткий

rococo /rə'kəʊkəʊ/ *n.* рококо́ (*nt. indecl.*)
• *adj.* в сти́ле рококо́

rod /rɒd/ *n.* **1** (slender stick) прут; (fishing ~) у́дочка; (instrument of chastisement) ро́зга **2** (metal bar) сте́ржень (*m.*)

rode /rəʊd/ *past of* ▶ ride

rodent /'rəʊd(ə)nt/ *n.* грызу́н

rogue /rəʊg/ *n.* жу́лик, моше́нник
■ ~ **state** *n.* (pol.) госуда́рство-изго́й; ~ **trader** *n.* (fin.) афери́ст

roguish /'rəʊgɪʃ/ *adj.* (villainous) жуликова́тый; (playful) прока́зливый, озорно́й

✧ **role** /rəʊl/ *n.* роль; **title ~** загла́вная роль
■ ~ **model** *n.* образе́ц для подража́ния; ~**-play** *v.i.* разы́гр|ывать, -а́ть ро́ли

✧ **roll** /rəʊl/ *n.* **1** (of cloth, paper, film, etc.) руло́н **2** (list) рее́стр, спи́сок **3** (of bread) бу́лочка **4** (rumbling sound) раска́т; **bois** of drum **bar**ab́ана
• *v.t.* **1** (move by revolving) ката́ть (*indet.*), кати́ть (*det.*), по- **2** (flatten by use of cylinder) ката́ть, рас-; раска́тывать (*impf.*); **she was ~ing pastry** она́ раска́тывала те́сто **3** (shape into cylinder or sphere) свёр|тывать, -ну́ть; свора́чивать (*impf.*)
• *v.i.* **1** (move by revolving) кати́ться (*impf.*); ска́тываться (*impf.*); **the car began to ~ downhill** маши́на покати́лась вниз **2** (sway) кача́ться (*impf.*); колыха́ться (*impf.*) **3** (make deep sound) греме́ть (*impf.*); грохота́ть (*impf.*)

□ ~ **along** *v.i.*: **we were ~ing along at 30 mph** маши́на кати́лась со ско́ростью 30 миль в час
□ ~ **over** *v.i.*: **he ~ed over and went to sleep again** он переверну́лся на друго́й бок и сно́ва засну́л
□ ~ **up** *v.t.* свёр|тывать, -ну́ть; (sleeves) засу́ч|ивать, -и́ть

■ ~**ing pin** *n.* ска́лка; ~**-up** *n.* (BrE, cigarette) самокру́тка

roller /'rəʊlə(r)/ *n.* ро́лик; като́к; (for paint) ва́лик; (*in pl.*) (for hair) бигуди́ (*nt. pl., indecl.*)
■ ~ **blades®** *n. pl.* одноря́дные ро́ликовые коньки́ (*m. pl.*); ~ **coaster** *n.* америка́нские го́рки (*f. pl.*); ~ **skate** *v.i.* ката́ться (*indet.*) на ро́ликах; ~ **skates** *n. pl.* ро́ликовые коньки́ (*m. pl.*)

ROM /rɒm/ *n.* (*abbr. of* **read-only memory**) (comput.) ПЗУ (постоя́нное запомина́ющее устро́йство)

Roman /'rəʊmən/ *n.* (also hist.) ри́млян|ин (-ка)
• *adj.* (of Rome) ри́мский; **the ~ alphabet** лати́нский алфави́т
■ ~ **Catholic** *n.* като́л|ик (-и́чка) • *adj.* католи́ческий

romance /rəʊ'mæns/ *n.* **1** (novel, love affair) рома́н **2** (romantic atmosphere) рома́нтика **3** R~ **languages** рома́нские языки́

Romanesque /rəʊmə'nesk/ *n. & adj.* рома́нский (стиль)

Romania /rəʊ'meɪnɪə/ *n.* Румы́ния

Romanian /rəʊ'meɪnɪən/ *n.* (person) румы́н (-ка); (language) румы́нский язы́к
• *adj.* румы́нский

romantic /rəʊ'mæntɪk/ *n.* рома́нтик
• *adj.* романти́ческий, романти́чный

romanticism /rəʊ'mæntɪsɪz(ə)m/ *n.* романти́зм

romanticize /rəʊ'mæntɪsaɪz/ *v.t.* романтизи́ровать (*impf., pf.*)

Romany /'rɒmənɪ/ *n.* (Gypsy) цыга́н (-ка); (language) цыга́нский язы́к
• *adj.* цыга́нский

Rome /rəʊm/ *n.* Рим

romp /rɒmp/ *n.* возня́
• *v.i.* резви́ться (*impf.*)

roof /ruːf/ *n.* кры́ша; ~ **of the mouth** нёбо
■ ~ **rack** *n.* бага́жник (на кры́ше автомоби́ля)

rook /rʊk/ *n.* (bird) грач; (chess) ладья́

✧ **room** /ruːm/ *n.* **1** ко́мната **2** (space) ме́сто, простра́нство; **there's plenty of ~** полно́ ме́ста **3** (scope) возмо́жность
■ ~**-mate** *n.* сосе́д (-ка) по ко́мнате; ~ **service** *n.* обслу́живание в но́мере

roomy /'ruːmɪ/ *adj.* (**roomier, roomiest**) просто́рный, вмести́тельный

rooster /'ruːstə(r)/ *n.* (AmE) пету́х

✧ **root** /ruːt/ *n.* **1** (of plant) ко́рень (*m.*); **take ~** пус|ка́ть, -ти́ть ко́рни; **the idea took ~ in his mind** э́та мысль засе́ла у него́ в голове́ **2** (fig., source) причи́на; ~ **cause** основна́я причи́на; **money is the ~ of all evil** де́ньги — ко́рень зла
• *v.t.* **1** (fig.): **he is a man of deeply ~ed prejudices** он челове́к с укорени́вшимися предрассу́дками **2** (transfix): **he stood ~ed to the ground** он стоя́л как вко́панный
□ ~ **about** *v.i.* ры́ться (*impf.*)
□ ~ **out** *v.t.* вырыва́ть, вы́рвать с ко́рнем

rope /rəʊp/ *n.* (cord) верёвка, кана́т; (fig.): **he knows the ~s** он зна́ет все ходы́ и вы́ходы; он зна́ет, что к чему́

r

● *v.t.* привя́з|ывать, -а́ть (*что к чему*)

□ ~ **in** *v.t.* (infml, enlist) втя́г|ивать, -ну́ть; I was ~d in to help меня́ запрягли́ в э́то де́ло

rosary /'rəʊzərı/ *n.* чёт|ки (-ок)

rose¹ /'rəʊz/ *n.* ро́за

■ ~**bud** *n.* буто́н ро́зы; ~ **bush** *n.* ро́зовый куст; ~**-coloured,** (AmE) **-colored** *adj.* ро́зовый; he sees the world through ~**-coloured spectacles** (BrE), **glasses** (AmE) он смо́трит на мир че́рез ро́зовые очки́

rose² /'rəʊz/ *past of* ▶ **rise**

rosemary /'rəʊzmərı/ *n.* розмари́н

rosette /rəʊ'zet/ *n.* розе́тка (*украшение*)

roster /'rɒstə(r)/ *n.* гра́фик дежу́рств

rostrum /'rɒstrəm/ *n.* трибу́на

rosy /'rəʊzı/ *adj.* (**rosier, rosiest**) ро́зовый; ~ **cheeks** румя́ные щёки

rot /rɒt/ *n.* гние́ние; гниль
   ● *v.t.* (**rotted, rotting**) по́ртить, ис-
   ● *v.i.* (**rotted, rotting**) гнить, с-; по́ртиться, ис-

rota /'rəʊtə/ *n.* (BrE) гра́фик дежу́рств

rotary /'rəʊtərı/ *adj.* враща́ющийся

rotate /rəʊ'teıt/ *v.t. & i.* враща́ть(ся) (*impf.*)

rotation /rəʊ'teıʃ(ə)n/ *n.* враще́ние; оборо́т

rote /rəʊt/ *n.*: he learnt the poem by ~ он вы́учил стихотворе́ние наизу́сть

■ ~ **learning** *n.* механи́ческое запомина́ние

rotten /'rɒt(ə)n/ *adj.* (**rottener, rottenest**) (decayed) гнило́й; (corrupt) разложи́вшийся; испо́рченный; (very unfortunate) отврати́тельный; I'm feeling ~ я себя́ пога́но чу́вствую

Rottweiler /'rɒtvaılə(r)/ *n.* ротве́йлер

rotund /rəʊ'tʌnd/ *adj.* (spherical) округлённый; (corpulent, plump) по́лный

rouble /'ru:b(ə)l/ *n.* рубль (*m.*)

rouge /ru:ʒ/ *n.* (cosmetic) румя́н|а (*pl., g.* —)
   ● *v.t. & i.* румя́нить(ся), на-

rough /rʌf/ *adj.* **1** (opp. smooth, even, level) шерохова́тый, неро́вный **2** (opp. calm, gentle) бу́рный; a ~ **crowd** хамова́тая пу́блика; the students were ~**ly** handled by the police поли́ция гру́бо обраща́лась со студе́нтами **3** (arduous) тру́дный; he had a ~ **time** ему́ пришло́сь ту́го **4** (crude) гру́бый; a ~**-and-ready meal** еда́, пригото́вленная на ско́рую ру́ку **5** (rudimentary) черново́й; a ~ **sketch** черново́й набро́сок **6** (approximate) приблизи́тельный; at a ~ **guess** по приблизи́тельной оце́нке; ~**ly speaking** гру́бо говоря́
   ● *v.t.*: ~ **it** (infml) жить (*impf.*) без удо́бств

■ ~**shod** *adv.* (fig.): he rode ~**shod** over their feelings он соверше́нно не щади́л их чувств

roughage /'rʌfıdʒ/ *n.* гру́бая пи́ща

roughen /'rʌf(ə)n/ *v.t. & i.* де́лать(ся), с- гру́бым/шерохова́тым

roulette /ru:'let/ *n.* руле́тка

⚐ **round** /raʊnd/ *n.* **1** (circular or ~ed object) круг, окру́жность; (BrE, slice) ло́мтик **2** (regular cycle)

⚐ ключева́я ле́ксика

цикл; обхо́д; круговоро́т; the doctor is on his ~s до́ктор де́лает обхо́д **3** (stage in contest) тур, эта́п, ра́унд **4** (set, series): he bought a ~ **of drinks** он поста́вил по стака́нчику всем прису́тствующим; a ~ **of applause** аплодисме́нты (*m. pl.*) **5** (of ammunition) патро́н

● *adj.* **1** (circular, spherical) кру́глый; ~ **shoulders** суту́лые пле́чи **2** (involving circular motion) кругово́й **3** (of numbers) кру́глый; a ~ **dozen** це́лая дю́жина

● *adv.* (BrE): all the year ~ кру́глый год; the tree is six feet ~ э́то де́рево шесть фу́тов в окру́жности; he went a long way ~ он сде́лал изря́дный крюк; he was ~ **at our house** он зашёл к нам

● *prep.* (BrE) **1** (encircling) вокру́г, круго́м, о́коло (*all + g.*); they sat ~ **the table** они́ сиде́ли вокру́г стола́ **2** (to or at all points of): he looked ~ **the room** он осмотре́л (всю) ко́мнату; they went ~ **the galleries** они́ обошли́ карти́нные галере́и **3**: ~ **the corner** (of position) за угло́м; (of motion) за́ угол

● *v.t.* **1** (go ~) огиба́ть, обогну́ть; об|ходи́ть, -ойти́ круго́м; we ~**ed the corner** мы заверну́ли/сверну́ли за́ угол **2** (~ a number up or down) округл|я́ть, -и́ть

● *v.i.* (turn aggressively): he ~**ed on me with abuse** он обру́шился на меня́ с бра́нью; he ~**ed on his pursuers** он набро́сился на свои́х пресле́дователей

□ ~ **off** *v.t.* (smooth) выра́внивать, вы́ровнять; (bring to a conclusion) заверш|а́ть, -и́ть

□ ~ **up** *v.t.* сгоня́ть, согна́ть; the courier ~**ed up the party** гид собра́л свою́ гру́ппу

■ ~**about** *n.* (merry-go-round) карусе́ль; (BrE, traffic island) кольцева́я тра́нспортная развя́зка ● *adj.* око́льный; ~ **about** *adv.* приблизи́тельно; ~**-the-clock** *adj.* круглосу́точный; ~**-the-world** *adj.* кругосве́тный; ~ **trip** *n.* пое́здка в о́ба конца́; ~**-up** *n.* (of news) сво́дка новосте́й; (of cattle) заго́н скота́; (raid) обла́ва

rounders /'raʊndəz/ *n.* англи́йская лапта́ (*кома́ндная игра́, напомина́ющая бейсбо́л*)

rouse /raʊz/ *v.t.* **1** (wake) буди́ть, раз- **2** (stimulate to action, interest, etc.) подстрека́ть (*impf.*); побу|жда́ть, -ди́ть

rout /raʊt/ *n.* разгро́м
   ● *v.t.* разб|ива́ть, -и́ть на́голову

⚐ **route** /ru:t/ *n.* (of bus etc.) маршру́т; (way) путь, доро́га

routine /ru:'ti:n/ *n.* **1** (regular course of action) заведённый поря́док; (*attr.*) регуля́рный; повседне́вный **2** (theatr.) но́мер, выступле́ние

rov|e /rəʊv/ *v.i.* скита́ться (*impf.*); he has a ~**ing disposition** он лю́бит стра́нствовать; a ~**ing correspondent** разъездно́й корреспонде́нт

⚐ **row¹** /rəʊ/ *n.* (line) ряд

row² /rəʊ/ *v.t.*: he ~**ed the boat in to shore** он привёл ло́дку к бе́регу
   ● *v.i.* грести́ (*impf.*)

■ ~**boat** (AmE), ~**ing boat** (BrE) *nn.* гребна́я шлю́пка

row³ /raʊ/ *n.* (BrE) **1** (noise) шум **2** (argument)
ссо́ра; спор; (dispute) дисп́ут, дисќуссия;
I had a ~ with the neighbours я поруга́лся с
сосе́дями
● *v.i.* (quarrel) ссо́риться, по-
rowan /'rəʊən/ *n.* ряби́на
rowdy /'raʊdɪ/ *adj.* (**rowdier, rowdiest**)
гру́бый, шу́мный
rowing /'rəʊɪŋ/ *n.* (sport) гре́бля
rowlock /'rɒlək/ *n.* уклю́чина
royal /'rɔɪəl/ *adj.* короле́вский, ца́рский; **His
R~ Highness** Его́ Короле́вское Высо́чество
■ ~ **blue** *n.* я́рко-си́ний цвет
royalist /'rɔɪəlɪst/ *n.* рояли́ст (-ка)
● *adj.* роялисти́ческий
royalty /'rɔɪəltɪ/ *n.* **1** (royal person(s)) члéн(ы)
короле́вской семьи́ **2** (payment) а́вторский
гонора́р
RSI *abbr.* (*of* **repetitive strain injury**)
тра́вма, вы́званная повторя́ющимся
движе́нием
RSVP *abbr.* (*of* **répondez, s'il vous plaît**)
бу́дьте любе́зны отве́тить
rub /rʌb/ *v.t.* (**rubbed, rubbing**) (part of
the body) тере́ть (*impf.*); пот|ира́ть, -ере́ть;
(chafe) нат|ира́ть, -ере́ть; (sth with a substance)
нат|ира́ть, -ере́ть + *i.*
● *v.i.* (**rubbed, rubbing**) тере́ться (*impf.*)
□ ~ **in** *v.t.* вт|ира́ть, -ере́ть; **it was my fault;
don't ~ it in!** я винова́т, но ско́лько мо́жно
упрека́ть?!
□ ~ **off** *v.t.* ст|ира́ть, -ере́ть
□ ~ **out** *v.t.* отт|ира́ть, -ере́ть; ст|ира́ть, -ере́ть
□ ~ **up** *v.t.* нач|ища́ть, -и́стить; полирова́ть, от-;
you ~bed him (up) the wrong way вы к нему́
не так подошли́
rubber /'rʌbə(r)/ *n.* **1** (substance) рези́на;
(*attr.*) рези́новый **2** (BrE, eraser) ла́стик,
рези́нка
■ ~ **band** *n.* рези́нка; ~ **gloves** *n. pl.*
рези́новые перча́тки; **~-stamp** *v.t.* (infml)
подпи́с|ывать, -а́ть не гля́дя
rubbish /'rʌbɪʃ/ *n.* **1** (BrE) (refuse) му́сор; хлам
(also fig.); (nonsense) чепуха́, вздор
■ ~ **bin** *n.* му́сорное ведро́; ~ **dump, ~ tip**
nn. сва́лка
rubble /'rʌb(ə)l/ *n.* булы́жник, ще́бень (*m.*)
rubella /ru:'belə/ *n.* (med.) красну́ха
ruble /'ru:b(ə)l/ *n.* = **rouble**
ruby /'ru:bɪ/ *n.* руби́н
rucksack /'rʌksæk/ *n.* рюкза́к
rudder /'rʌdə(r)/ *n.* руль (*m.*)
ruddy /'rʌdɪ/ *adj.* (**ruddier, ruddiest**)
румя́ный
rude /ru:d/ *adj.* **1** (impolite) гру́бый;
невоспи́танный; **don't be ~!** не груби́те!;
he was ~ to the teacher он нагруби́л
учи́телю **2** (indecent) гру́бый, непристо́йный
rudiment /'ru:dɪmənt/ *n.* (*in pl.*)
элемента́рные зна́ния
rudimentary /ru:dɪ'mentərɪ/ *adj.*
элемента́рный
rueful /'ru:fʊl/ *adj.* печа́льный, удручённый

ruffian /'rʌfɪən/ *n.* головоре́з, банди́т
ruffle /'rʌf(ə)l/ *n.* (frill) обо́рка
● *v.t.*: **a breeze ~d the surface of the lake** от
ве́тра о́зеро покры́лось ря́бью; **she ~d his
hair** она́ взъеро́шила ему́ во́лосы; **the bird
~d up its feathers** пти́ца взъеро́шила пе́рья;
he never gets ~d он всегда́ невозмути́м
rug /rʌg/ *n.* ковёр
rugby /'rʌgbɪ/ *n.* (*also* **rugby football**)
ре́гби (*nt. indecl.*)
■ ~ **player** *n.* регби́ст; ~ **shirt** *n.* руба́шка-
ре́гби
rugged /'rʌgɪd/ *adj.* **1** (rough, uneven)
неро́вный; **a ~ coast** скали́стый бе́рег
2 (irregular) гру́бый; ~ **features** ре́зкие черты́
rugger /'rʌgə(r)/ *n.* (BrE, infml) = **rugby**
ruin /'ru:ɪn/ *n.* **1** (downfall) ги́бель, круше́ние
2 (collapsed or destroyed state; building in this state)
разва́лины, руи́ны (*both f. pl.*); **the town lay
in ~s** го́род лежа́л в руи́нах; **the house fell
into ~** дом соверше́нно развали́лся; (fig.):
their plans lay in ~s их пла́ны ру́хнули
● *v.t.* разр|уша́ть, -у́шить; уничт|ожа́ть,
-о́жить; губи́ть, по-; **he was ~ed** (in business)
он разори́лся; **the rain ~ed my suit** дождь
испо́ртил мой костю́м; **a ~ed building**
разру́шенное зда́ние
꙳ **rule** /ru:l/ *n.* **1** (regulation; principle) пра́вило;
smoking is against the ~s кури́ть не
разреша́ется **2** (normal practice) привы́чка,
обы́чай; **as a ~** как пра́вило **3** (government)
правле́ние, госпо́дство **4** (measuring stick)
лине́йка
● *v.t.* **1** (govern) управля́ть (*impf.*) + *i.*;
руководи́ть (*impf.*) + *i.* **2** (decree)
постан|а́вливать, -ови́ть; **the umpire ~d
that the ball was not out** судья́ объяви́л, что
мяч не́ был в а́уте **3**: ~**d paper** лино́ванная
бума́га
● *v.i.* (hold sway) пра́вить (*impf.*); управля́ть
(*impf.*); **ruling classes** пра́вящие кла́ссы
□ ~ **out** *v.t.* (exclude) исключ|а́ть, -и́ть
ruler /'ru:lə(r)/ *n.* (reigning person) прави́тель
(*m.*); (measuring stick) лине́йка
ruling /'ru:lɪŋ/ *n.* (decree) постановле́ние;
реше́ние
rum /rʌm/ *n.* ром
rumba /'rʌmbə/ *n.* ру́мба
● *v.i.* (**rumbas, rumbaed** /-bəd/ *or*
rumba'd, rumbaing /-bə(r)ɪŋ/) танцева́ть,
с- ру́мбу
rumbl|e /'rʌmb(ə)l/ *n.* громыха́ние, гул
● *v.i.* громыха́ть (*impf.*); греме́ть, за-/про-;
thunder was ~ing in the distance вдалеке́
греме́л гром
ruminant /'ru:mɪnənt/ *n.* жва́чное живо́тное
● *adj.* жва́чный
ruminate /'ru:mɪneɪt/ *v.i.* (ponder)
разду́мывать (*impf.*)
rumination /ru:mɪ'neɪʃ(ə)n/ *n.* (fig.)
размышле́ние
rummage /'rʌmɪdʒ/ *v.i.* ры́ться (*impf.*)
rumour /'ru:mə(r)/ (AmE **rumor**) *n.* слух;
то́лк|и (-ов)

r

● *v.t.*: the ~ed visit визи́т, о кото́ром прошёл слух

rumple /'rʌmp(ə)l/ *v.t.* (clothes) мять, по-; (hair) еро́шить, взъ-

rumpus /'rʌmpəs/ *n.* (*pl.* **rumpuses**) шум; сканда́л; **kick up a ~** подн|има́ть, -я́ть шум

■ **~ room** *n.* (AmE) ко́мната для игр и развлече́ний

⚹ **run** /rʌn/ *n.* **1** (action of ~ning) бег; пробе́г; **he went for a ~ before breakfast** он сде́лал пробе́жку пе́ред за́втраком; **the prisoner made a ~ for it** заключённый бежа́л/удра́л; **the prisoner is on the ~** заключённый нахо́дится в бега́х **2** (trip, journey, route) пое́здка, рейс, маршру́т **3** (continuous stretch) отре́зок вре́мени; **he had a ~ of good luck** у него́ была́ полоса́ везе́ния; **the play had a long ~** пье́са шла до́лго; **in the long ~** в коне́чном счёте **4** (score at cricket etc.) очко́ **5** (for fowls etc.) заго́н **6** (AmE, ladder in stocking) спусти́вшаяся петля́

● *v.t.* (**running**, *past* **ran**, *p.p.* **run**) **1** (execute): **he ran a good race** он хорошо́ пробежа́л (диста́нцию) **2** (cover) бежа́ть (*det.*), про-; **he can ~ the mile in under a minute** он мо́жет пробежа́ть ми́лю ме́ньше чем за мину́ту **3** (convey in car) подв|ози́ть, -езти́ (на маши́не); **shall I ~ you home?** хоти́те, я подвезу́ вас домо́й? **4** (cause to go): **he ran his fingers over the keys** он пробежа́л па́льцами по кла́вишам; **he ran his eye over the page** он пробежа́л глаза́ми страни́цу; **I shall ~ (water into) the bath** я напущу́ воды́ в ва́нну **5** (operate) управля́ть (*impf.*) (+ *i.*); **who is ~ning the shop?** кто ве́дает ла́вкой?; **he ~s a small business** у него́ своё небольшо́е де́ло; **she ~s the house single-handed** она́ сама́ ведёт хозя́йство; **he ran the engine for a few minutes** он завёл мото́р на не́сколько мину́т

● *v.i.* (**running**, *past* **ran**, *p.p.* **run**) **1** (move quickly) бе́гать (*indet.*), бежа́ть (*det.*), побежа́ть (*pf.*); **I had to ~ for the train** мне пришло́сь бежа́ть, что́бы поспе́ть на по́езд; **he ran for his life** он удира́л изо всех сил; **~ for it!** беги́! **2** (come by chance) столкну́ться (*pf.*) (с + *i.*); натолкну́ться (*pf.*) (на + *a.*); **I ran into, across an old friend** я случа́йно встре́тил ста́рого това́рища **3** (compete) соревнова́ться (*impf.*); (fig.): **he ran for president** он баллоти́ровался в президе́нты **4** (of public transport) ходи́ть (*indet.*); **there are no trains ~ning** поезда́ не хо́дят **5** (of machines etc.) function) де́йствовать (*impf.*); **most cars ~ on petrol** (BrE), **gasoline** (AmE) большинство́ маши́н рабо́тает на бензи́не; **leave the engine ~ning!** не выключа́йте мото́р! **6** (flow) течь, протека́ть, струи́ться (*all impf.*); **tears/sweat ran down his face** слёзы кати́лись (*or* пот струи́лся) по его́ щека́м; **his nose was ~ning** у него́ текло́ из но́су **7** (of colour, ink) линя́ть, по- **8** (extend) тяну́ться (*impf.*); **the gardens ~ down**

to the river сады́ тя́нутся до реки́; **his income ~s into five figures** его́ дохо́д измеря́ется пятизна́чной ци́фрой **9** (continue) быть действи́тельным; **the lease has seven years to ~** догово́р о на́йме действи́телен ещё семь лет; **the play has been ~ning for five years** пье́са идёт пять лет; **it ~s in their family** э́то у них насле́дственное

● *further phr. with preps.*: **~ into** (collide with) налете́ть (*impf.*) на + *a.*; (encounter): **he ran into debt** он залёз/влез в долги́; **~ over, through** (review) повтор|я́ть, -и́ть

☐ **~ about** *v.i.* бе́гать (*indet.*)

☐ **~ away** *v.i.* убе|га́ть, -жа́ть; уд|ира́ть, -ра́ть

☐ **~ back** *v.i.*: **he ran back to apologize** он прибежа́л наза́д, что́бы извини́ться

☐ **~ down** *v.t.*: **don't ~ your battery down** не тра́тьте батаре́ю; **she is always ~ning down her neighbours** она́ ве́чно поно́сит сосе́дей; **you look very ~ down** у вас о́чень утомлённый вид

☐ **~ off** *v.i.* убе|га́ть, -жа́ть; уд|ира́ть, -ра́ть; **he ran off with the jewels** он сбежа́л с драгоце́нностями

☐ **~ out** *v.i.* (come to an end) конча́ться, ко́нчиться; **he will soon ~ out of money** у него́ ско́ро ко́нчатся де́ньги

☐ **~ over** *v.t.* задави́ть (*pf.*); **he was ~ over by a car** его́ задави́ла маши́на

☐ **~ up** *v.t.*: **he ran up a bill at the tailor's** он задолжа́л портно́му

● *v.i.*: **she ran up to tell me the news** она́ прибежа́ла, что́бы сообщи́ть мне но́вость

■ **~away** *n.* (fugitive) бегле́ц (-я́нка); (*attr.*) **a ~away horse** ло́шадь, кото́рая понесла́; **~in** *n.* (fight, squabble) схва́тка; **~-of-the-mill** *adj.* обы́чный, сре́дний; **~-up** *n.* (run preparatory to action) разбе́г; (fig.): **the ~-up to the election** (BrE) предвы́борная пора́/кампа́ния; **~way** *n.* (aeron.) взлётно-поса́дочная полоса́

rung[1] /rʌŋ/ *n.* (of ladder) ступе́нька

rung[2] /rʌŋ/ *p.p. of* ▶ **ring**[2]

runner /'rʌnə(r)/ *n.* **1** (athlete) бегу́н **2** (horse in race) рыса́к, (бегова́я) ло́шадь **3** (narrow cloth, rug) доро́жка **4** (bot., shoot) побе́г

■ **~ bean** *n.* (BrE) зелёная (стручко́вая) фасо́ль; **~-up** *n.* уча́стник/кандида́т, заня́вший второ́е ме́сто

running /'rʌnɪŋ/ *n.* **1** (sport) бег; **I shall take up ~** я займу́сь бе́гом **2** (contest) состяза́ние; **they are out of the ~ for the Cup** они́ вы́были из соревнова́ний на ку́бок **3** (operation) управле́ние (*чем*)

● *adj.* **1** (performed while events proceed) теку́щий **2** (continuous) непреры́вный **3** (in succession) подря́д, кря́ду; **he won three times ~** он вы́играл три ра́за подря́д

■ **~ commentary** *n.* репорта́ж (с ме́ста собы́тия); **~ costs** *n. pl.* (of business) теку́щие расхо́ды (*m. pl.*); (of car) расхо́ды (*m. pl.*) на содержа́ние маши́ны; **~ shoes** *n. pl.* кроссо́в|ки (-ок); **~ water** *n.* водопрово́д

runny /'rʌnɪ/ *adj.* (**runnier**, **runniest**) теку́чий, жи́дкий; **a ~ nose** на́сморк

⚹ ключева́я ле́ксика

rupture /'rʌptʃə(r)/ n. проры́в; перело́м
  ● v.t. (burst, break) прор|ыва́ть, -ва́ть
  ● v.i. раз|рыва́ться, -орва́ться
ᵟ **rural** /'rʊər(ə)l/ adj. се́льский
ruse /ru:z/ n. уло́вка, ухищре́ние
rush¹ /rʌʃ/ n. (bot.) тростни́к
rush² /rʌʃ/ n. стреми́тельное движе́ние;
  he made a ~ for the goal он бро́сился к
  воро́там; (bustle) спе́шка; (increase in activity):
  the Christmas ~ предрожде́ственская суета́;
  in the ~ hour в часы́ пик
  ● v.t. **1** (speed) торопи́ть, по-; **troops were
  ~ed to the front** войска́ бы́ли сро́чно
  перебро́шены на фронт; **the order was ~ed
  through** зака́з бы́стро проверну́ли; **I refuse
  to be ~ed into a decision** я отка́зываюсь
  принима́ть реше́ние в спе́шке **2** (charge)
  брать, взять шту́рмом
  ● v.i. мча́ться, по-; бр|оса́ться, -о́ситься;
  кида́ться, ки́нуться; **she ~ed off
  without saying goodbye** она́ убежа́ла, не
  попроща́вшись; **they ~ed to congratulate
  her** они́ бро́сились её поздравля́ть
rusk /rʌsk/ n. суха́рь (m.)
Russia /'rʌʃə/ n. Росси́я
ᵟ **Russian** /'rʌʃ(ə)n/ n. **1** (person of Russian
nationality) ру́сск|ий (-ая); (person of Russian
citizenship) россия́н|ин (-ка) **2** (language)
ру́сский язы́к; **do you speak ~?** вы говори́те
по-ру́сски?
  ● adj. ру́сский
  ■ **~ doll** n. матрёшка; **~-speaking** adj.
  русскоязы́чный
rust /rʌst/ n. ржа́вчина
  ● v.i. ржаве́ть, за-
rustic /'rʌstɪk/ adj. дереве́нский, се́льский
rustle /'rʌs(ə)l/ n. ше́лест, шо́рох
  ● v.t. шелесте́ть (impf.) + i.; шурша́ть (impf.)
  + i.
  ● v.i. шелесте́ть (impf.); шурша́ть (impf.)
rusty /'rʌstɪ/ adj. (**rustier, rustiest**) ржа́вый;
  (fig., out of practice): **his Russian is ~** он
  подзабы́л ру́сский
rut /rʌt/ n. (wheel track) колея́, вы́боина; (fig.)
  рути́на; **it is easy to get into a ~** легко́
  погря́знуть в рути́не
ruthless /'ru:θlɪs/ adj. безжа́лостный,
  жесто́кий
Rwanda /rʊ'ændə/ n. Руа́нда
rye /raɪ/ n. рожь; **~ bread** ржано́й хлеб; (**~
  whisky**) ржано́е ви́ски (nt. indecl.)

Ss

sabbath /'sæbəθ/ n. (Jewish) суббо́та; (Christian)
воскресе́нье
sabbatical /sə'bætɪk(ə)l/ n. (also **~ leave**)
тво́рческий о́тпуск
sabotage /'sæbətɑ:ʒ/ n. диве́рсия, сабота́ж
  ● v.t. саботи́ровать (impf., pf.)
saboteur /sæbə'tɜ:(r)/ n. сабота́жни|к (-ца),
диверса́нт
sabre /'seɪbə(r)/ n. са́бля
saccharine /'sækəri:n/ adj. са́харный,
сахари́стый; (fig.) слаща́вый, прито́рный
sachet /'sæʃeɪ/ n. (BrE) паке́тик (шампуня и
m. n.)
sack¹ /sæk/ n. **1** (bag) мешо́к **2** (infml, dismissal)
увольне́ние; **I got the ~** меня́ вы́гнали/
уво́лили
  ● v.t. (infml, dismiss) выгоня́ть, вы́гнать;
ув|ольня́ть, -о́лить
sack² /sæk/ v.t. (plunder) гра́бить, раз-
sacrament /'sækrəmənt/ n. та́инство
sacred /'seɪkrɪd/ adj. свяще́нный, свято́й
sacrifice /'sækrɪfaɪs/ n. же́ртва
  ● v.t. (lit., at altar) прин|оси́ть, -ести́ (кого/
что) в же́ртву; (give up) же́ртвовать, по- + i.
sacrificial /sækrɪ'fɪʃ(ə)l/ adj. же́ртвенный
sacrilege /'sækrɪlɪdʒ/ n. святота́тство
sacrilegious /sækrɪ'lɪdʒəs/ adj.
святота́тственный, кощу́нственный
sacrosanct /'sækrəʊsæŋkt/ adj. свяще́нный
ᵟ **sad** /sæd/ adj. (**sadder, saddest**) гру́стный,
печа́льный; **I feel ~** мне гру́стно; **a ~
event** печа́льное собы́тие; (regrettable)
приско́рбный; **it is ~ that you failed the
exams** о́чень жаль, что вы провали́лись на
экза́менах
sadden /'sæd(ə)n/ v.t. печа́лить, о-
saddle /'sæd(ə)l/ n. седло́
  ● v.t. **1** седла́ть, о- **2** (fig.) (burden): **~ sb with
sth** взва́л|ивать, -и́ть что-н. на кого́-н.
sadism /'seɪdɪz(ə)m/ n. сади́зм
sadist /'seɪdɪst/ n. сади́ст (-ка)
sadistic /sə'dɪstɪk/ adj. сади́стский
sadness /'sædnɪs/ n. грусть, печа́ль, тоска́
sae (BrE) abbr. (of **stamped addressed
envelope**) конве́рт с ма́ркой и обра́тным
а́дресом
safari /sə'fɑ:rɪ/ n. (pl. **~s**) сафа́ри (nt. indecl.)
  ■ **~ park** n. сафа́ри-парк
safe¹ /seɪf/ n. сейф
ᵟ **safe²** /seɪf/ adj. **1** (affording security, not dangerous)

r

s

безопа́сный; (reliable) надёжный; **in sb's ~ keeping** у кого́-н. на сохране́нии; **to be on the ~ side** на вся́кий слу́чай, для (бо́льшей) ве́рности **2** (free from danger): **we are ~ from attack** мы мо́жем не опаса́ться нападе́ния; (unhurt, undamaged): **we saw them home ~ and sound** мы доста́вили их домо́й це́лыми и невреди́мыми (or в це́лости и сохра́нности) **3** (cautious, moderate) осторо́жный; **better ~ than sorry** бережёного Бог бережёт; **I decided to play ~** я реши́л не рискова́ть **4** (certain): **it's a ~ bet** мо́жно быть уве́ренным

■ ~ **conduct** n. (document) охра́нная гра́мота; ~ **deposit** n. храни́лище с се́йфами; ~**guard** n. охра́на, страхо́вка, гара́нтия (**against:** от + g.); защи́тная ме́ра, ме́ры безопа́сности ● v.t. гаранти́ровать (impf., pf.); охран|я́ть, -и́ть; ~ **house** n. конспирати́вная кварти́ра; укры́тие; ~ **sex** n. безопа́сный секс

safely /ˈseɪflɪ/ adv. **1** (unharmed) благополу́чно, в сохра́нности; **we returned ~** мы благополу́чно верну́лись; **the parcel arrived ~** посы́лка пришла́ в це́лости и сохра́нности **2** (with confidence) уве́ренно, с уве́ренностью; **I can ~ say that …** я могу́ с уве́ренностью сказа́ть, что… **3** (securely) надёжно

⚲ **safety** /ˈseɪftɪ/ n. безопа́сность; **road ~** безопа́сность на доро́гах

■ ~ **belt** n. реме́нь (m.) безопа́сности; ~ **net** n. (fig.) страхо́вка; ~ **pin** n. англи́йская була́вка

saffron /ˈsæfrən/ n. (substance) шафра́н; (colour) шафра́нный/шафра́новый цвет (*оранжево-жёлтый*)
● adj. шафра́нный

sag /sæg/ v.i. (**sagged, sagging**) (of rope, curtain) пров|иса́ть, -и́снуть; (of ceiling) прог|иба́ться, -ну́ться; (of cheeks, breasts) обв|иса́ть, -и́снуть

saga /ˈsɑːgə/ n. са́га; (fig.): **he told me the ~ of his escape** он пове́дал мне (фантасти́ческую) исто́рию своего́ побе́га

sagacious /səˈgeɪʃ(ə)s/ adj. **1** (of person) му́дрый; (of animal) у́мный **2** (perspicacious) проница́тельный, му́дрый **3** (of action: far-sighted) дальнови́дный, прозорли́вый

sage[1] /seɪdʒ/ n. (bot.) шалфе́й

sage[2] /seɪdʒ/ n. (wise man) мудре́ц

Sagittarius /sædʒɪˈteərɪəs/ n. Стреле́ц

Sahara /səˈhɑːrə/ n. Caха́ра

said /sed/ past and p.p. of ▶ **say**

sail /seɪl/ n. **1** па́рус; **in full ~** на всех паруса́х; **make, set ~ for** отпл|ыва́ть, -ы́ть в/ на + a.; отпр|авля́ться, -а́виться в/на + a. **2** (voyage on water) пла́вание
● v.t. **1** (of person or ship) пла́вать (indet.), плыть в (+ p.); (cover a distance) проплы́|ва́ть, -ы́ть; **we ~ed 150 miles** мы проплы́ли/прошли́ 150 миль **2** (control navigation of) управля́ть (impf.) (+ i.)
● v.i. **1** пл|а́вать (indet.), -ыть (det.),

попл|ы́ть (pf.); **the ship ~ed into harbour** кора́бль вошёл в га́вань; **we ~ed out to sea** мы вы́шли в мо́ре; **they ~ed up the coast** они́ плы́ли вдоль бе́рега **2** (fig., move gracefully) плыть (det.); пла́вно дви́гаться (impf.); пропл|ыва́ть, -ы́ть; **he ~ed through (sc. made light work of) the exams** он с лёгкостью (or без труда́) сдал экза́мены

■ ~**boat** n. (AmE) па́русная ло́дка

sailboard /ˈseɪlbɔːd/ n. виндсёрф(ер)

sailboarder /ˈseɪlbɔːdə(r)/ n. виндсёрфинги́ст (-ка)

sailboarding /ˈseɪlbɔːdɪŋ/ n. виндсёрфинг

sailing /ˈseɪlɪŋ/ n. (as sport) па́русный спорт

■ ~ **boat** n. (BrE) па́русная ло́дка; ~ **ship** n. па́русное су́дно, па́русник

sailor /ˈseɪlə(r)/ n. моря́к, матро́с

saint /seɪnt/ n. свято́й; **S~ Valentine's Day** день свято́го Валенти́на

sainthood /ˈseɪnthʊd/ n. свя́тость

saintly /ˈseɪntlɪ/ adj. (**saintlier, saintliest**) свято́й

sake /seɪk/ n.: **for the ~ of** ра́ди + g.; **for God's, heaven's, goodness ~** ра́ди Бо́га (or всего́ свято́го); **for old times' ~** по ста́рой па́мяти

salable /ˈseɪləb(ə)l/ adj. (AmE) = saleable

salacious /səˈleɪʃəs/ adj. (indecent) непристо́йный, скабрёзный

salad /ˈsæləd/ n. сала́т

■ ~ **dressing** n. запра́вка для сала́та

salami /səˈlɑːmɪ/ n. (pl. ~**s**) копчёная колбаса́, саля́ми (f. indecl.)

salary /ˈsælərɪ/ n. зарпла́та

⚲ **sale** /seɪl/ n. **1** прода́жа, сбыт; **be on, for ~** име́ться (impf.) в прода́же; ~ (sc. selling) **price** прода́жная цена́ **2** (event, clearance ~) распрода́жа; ~ (sc. reduced) **price** сни́женная цена́, цена́ со ски́дкой

■ ~**s assistant, ~s clerk** (AmE) nn. продав|е́ц (-щи́ца); ~**sman** n. (in shop) продаве́ц; (travelling door-to-door) коммивояжёр; ~**swoman** n. (in shop) продавщи́ца

saleable /ˈseɪləb(ə)l/ (AmE also **salable**) adj. ходово́й, хо́дкий (both infml)

salient /ˈseɪlɪənt/ adj. (noticeable, important) выдаю́щийся, я́ркий

saline /ˈseɪlaɪn/ n. (salt in water) соляно́й раство́р; (med.) физиологи́ческий раство́р
● adj. солёный, соляно́й

■ ~ **solution** n. соляно́й раство́р

saliva /səˈlaɪvə/ n. слюна́

salivate /ˈsælɪveɪt/ v.i. выделя́ть, вы́делить слюну́

salmon /ˈsæmən/ n. лосо́сь (m.); сёмга

salmonella /sælməˈnelə/ n. сальмоне́лла

salon /ˈsælɒn/ n. сало́н

saloon /səˈluːn/ n. (on ship) сало́н; (in full ~ **bar**) (BrE) бар; (in full ~ **car**) (BrE) седа́н

salt /sɔːlt/ n. соль
● adj.: ~ **water** морска́я вода́
● v.t. **1** (cure in brine) соли́ть, за- **2** (sprinkle with ~) соли́ть, по-

⚲ ключевая лексика

■ ~ **cellar** *n.* солóнка

salty /'sɔ:ltɪ/ *adj.* (**saltier, saltiest**) солёный

salubrious /sə'lu:brɪəs/ *adj.* (healthy) здорóвый; (curative) целéбный, целúтельный

salutary /'sæljʊtərɪ/ *adj.* благотвóрный

salute /sə'lu:t/ *n.* отдáние чéсти; вóинское привéтствие
 ● *v.t. & i.* отд|авáть, -áть честь (*кому*)

Salvadorean /sælvə'dɔ:rɪən/ *n.* сальвадóр|ец (-ка)
 ● *adj.* сальвадóрский

salvage /'sælvɪdʒ/ *n.* (action of saving) спасéние (имýщества); (what is saved) спасённое имýщество; спасённый груз *и т. п.*
 ● *v.t.* (save) спас|áть, -тú; (preserve) сохран|я́ть, -úть

salvation /sæl'veɪʃ(ə)n/ *n.* спасéние (душú), избавлéние

■ **S~ Army** *n.* А́рмия спасéния

salve /sælv/ *n.* (lit., fig.) бальзáм
 ● *v.t.* (fig., soothe) успок|áивать, -óить

Samaritan /sə'mærɪt(ə)n/ *n.*: **good ~** (bibl.) дóбрый самаритя́нин

samba /'sæmbə/ *n.* сáмба

✓ **same** /seɪm/ *adj.* тот же (сáмый); такóй же; одúн (и тот же); (unvarying) одинáковый, неизмéнный, рóвный; **is that the ~ man we saw yesterday?** э́то тот же человéк, котóрого мы вúдели вчерá?; **we are the ~ age** мы однúх лет (*or* однóго вóзраста); **in the ~ way** такúм же óбразом; **at the ~ time** в то же врéмя, одновремéнно; (however) в то же врéмя, мéжду тем; **the village looks just the ~ as ever** дерéвня вы́глядит такóй же, как всегдá; **it's the ~ everywhere** вездé одинáково
 ● *pron.* тот же (сáмый); **it's all the ~ to me** мне всё равнó; **~ again, please!** то же сáмое, пожáлуйста!; **... and the ~ to you!** ... и вам тáкже (*or* тогó же)!
 ● *adv.*: **I don't feel the ~ towards him** я измени́л своё отношéние к немý; **all the ~** (nevertheless) всё-таки, всё равнó; всё же; **just the ~** (despite that) тем не мéнее; **~ here!** я тóже!

samovar /'sæməvɑ:(r)/ *n.* самовáр

✓ **sample** /'sɑ:mp(ə)l/ *n.* (comm., fig.) образéц, обрáзчик, примéр; (med.) прóба
 ● *v.t.* прóбовать, по-

sanatorium /sænə'tɔ:rɪəm/ (AmE **sanitarium**) *n.* санатóрий

sanctify /'sæŋktɪfaɪ/ *v.t.* освя|щáть (*or* святи́ть) -ти́ть; (justify) опрáвд|ывать, -áть

sanctimonious /sæŋktɪ'məʊnɪəs/ *adj.* хáнжеский

sanction /'sæŋkʃ(ə)n/ *n.* сáнкция
 ● *v.t.* (authorize) санкциони́ровать (*impf., pf.*); (approve) од|обря́ть, -óбрить

sanctity /'sæŋktɪtɪ/ *n.* свя́тость

sanctuary /'sæŋktjʊərɪ/ *n.* **1** (holy place) святи́лище **2** (asylum) убéжище **3** (for wild life) заповéдник

sanctum /'sæŋktəm/ *n.* (*pl.* **~s**) святи́лище; (fig., 'den') прибéжище

sand /sænd/ *n.* песóк
 ● *v.t.* (polish) (*also* ~ **down**) шлифовáть, от-

■ ~ **dune** *n.* дю́на; **~paper** *n.* (шлифовáльная) шкýрка ● *v.t.* чи́стить, за- (*or* шлифовáть, от-) шкýркой; **~stone** *n.* песчáник

sandal /'sænd(ə)l/ *n.* сандáлия

sandwich /'sænwɪdʒ/ *n.* бутербрóд; **ham ~** бутербрóд с ветчинóй
 ● *v.t.*: **his car was ~ed between two lorries** егó маши́на былá зажáта мéжду двумя́ грузовикáми

■ ~ **bar** *n.* бутербрóдная; **~ course** *n.* (BrE) курс обучéния, чередýющий теóрию с прáктикой

sandy /'sændɪ/ *adj.* (**sandier, sandiest**) **1** (consisting of sand) песчáный; (resembling sand) песóчный **2** (hair) рыжевáтый

sane /seɪn/ *adj.* (opp. mad) нормáльный, психи́чески здорóвый; (idea, plan) здрáвый

San Francisco /sæn fræn'sɪskəʊ/ *n.* Сан-Франци́ско (*m. indecl.*)

sang /sæŋ/ *past of* ► **sing**

sanguine /'sæŋgwɪn/ *adj.* (optimistic) оптимисти́чный

sanitarium /sænɪ'teərɪəm/ *n.* (AmE) = **sanatorium**

sanitary /'sænɪtərɪ/ *adj.* санитáрный, гигиени́ческий

■ ~ **towel** (BrE), **~ napkin** (AmE) *nn.* гигиени́ческая проклáдка

sanitation /sænɪ'teɪʃ(ə)n/ *n.* санитáрия; канализациóнная систéма

sanitize /'sænɪtaɪz/ *v.t.* дéлать, с- бóлее приéмлемым

sanity /'sænɪtɪ/ *n.* (state of being sane) здрáвый ум

sank /sæŋk/ *past of* ► **sink**

Santa Claus /'sæntə klɔ:z/ *n.* (in Russia) ≈ Дед Морóз; (in Britain, US, etc.) Сáнта-Клáус

sap /sæp/ *n.* (of plants) сок
 ● *v.t.* (**sapped, sapping**) (fig.): **~ sb's strength** истощ|áть, -и́ть чьи-н. си́лы

sapling /'sæplɪŋ/ *n.* (tree) молодóе дéревце

sapphire /'sæfaɪə(r)/ *n.* (stone) сапфи́р; (colour) лазýрь

sarcasm /'sɑ:kæz(ə)m/ *n.* саркáзм

sarcastic /sɑ:'kæstɪk/ *adj.* саркасти́ческий

sarcopha|gus /sɑ:'kɒfəgəs/ *n.* (*pl.* **~gi** /-gaɪ/) саркофáг

sardine /sɑ:'di:n/ *n.* сарди́н(к)а

sardonic /sɑ:'dɒnɪk/ *adj.* злóбно-насмéшливый, язви́тельный

sari /'sɑ:rɪ/ *n.* (*pl.* **~s**) сáри (*nt. indecl.*) (*индийская национальная женская одежда*)

sarong /sə'rɒŋ/ *n.* сарóнг (*малай(зий)ская/ индонезийская национальная одежда*)

SARS /sɑ:z/ *n.* (*abbr. of* **severe acute respiratory syndrome**) атипи́чная пневмони́я, САРС (*тяжёлый óстрый респирáторный синдрóм*)

S

sash /sæʃ/ *n.* (round waist) по́яс; (over shoulder) (о́рденская) ле́нта

sat /sæt/ *past and p.p. of* ▶ **sit**

Satan /'seɪt(ə)n/ *n.* сатана́ (*m.*)

satanic /sə'tænɪk/ *adj.* сатани́нский, а́дский

satanism /'seɪtənɪz(ə)m/ *n.* сатани́зм

satchel /'sætʃ(ə)l/ *n.* ра́нец

satellite /'sætəlaɪt/ *n.* (иску́сственный) спу́тник; ~ **television broadcasting** спу́тниковое телеви́дение
■ ~ **dish** *n.* спу́тниковая анте́нна

satiate /'seɪʃɪeɪt/ *v.t.* нас|ыща́ть, -ы́тить

satin /'sætɪn/ *n.* атла́с
● *adj.* атла́сный

satire /'sætaɪə(r)/ *n.* сати́ра

satirical /sə'tɪrɪk(ə)l/ *adj.* сатири́ческий

satirist /'sætɪrɪst/ *n.* сати́рик

satirize /'sætɪraɪz/ *v.t.* высме́ивать, вы́смеять

satisfaction /sætɪs'fækʃ(ə)n/ *n.* удовлетворе́ние, удовлетворённость

satisfactory /sætɪs'fæktərɪ/ *adj.* удовлетвори́тельный, хоро́ший

↙ **satisfy** /'sætɪsfaɪ/ *v.t.* **1** удовлетвор|я́ть, -и́ть; ~**y one's hunger** утол|я́ть, -и́ть го́лод; a ~**ied customer** дово́льный клие́нт **2** (convince) убе|жда́ть, -ди́ть; I ~**ied him of my innocence** я убеди́л его в мое́й невино́вности **3** (fulfil): ~**y an obligation** выполн|я́ть, вы́полнить обяза́тельство **4** (of food): a ~**ying lunch** сы́тный обе́д

satphone /'sætfəʊn/ *n.* спу́тниковый телефо́н

satsuma /sæt'suːmə/ *n.* мандари́н

saturate /'sætʃəreɪt/ *v.t.* нас|ыща́ть, -ы́тить; **the carpet became** ~**d with water** ковёр пропита́лся водо́й; I **was** ~**d** я весь промо́к

saturation /sætʃə'reɪʃ(ə)n/ *n.* насыще́ние, насы́щенность

↙ **Saturday** /'sætədeɪ/ *n.* суббо́та

Saturn /'sæt(ə)n/ *n.* (astron., myth.) Сату́рн

sauce /sɔːs/ *n.* (cul.) со́ус, подли́вка
■ ~**pan** *n.* кастрю́ля

saucer /'sɔːsə(r)/ *n.* блю́дце

saucy /'sɔːsɪ/ *adj.* (**saucier, sauciest**) (cheeky) де́рзкий; (BrE, coquettish) коке́тливый

Saudi /'saʊdɪ/ *n.* (*pl.* ~**s**) сауд́ов|ец (-ка)
● *adj.* сау́довский
■ ~ **Arabia** *n.* Сау́довская Ара́вия

sauerkraut /'saʊəkraʊt/ *n.* ки́слая/ква́шеная капу́ста

sauna /'sɔːnə/ *n.* са́уна, фи́нская (парна́я) ба́ня

saunter /'sɔːntə(r)/ *v.i.* идти́ (*det.*) не торопя́сь

sausage /'sɒsɪdʒ/ *n.* соси́ска
■ ~ **roll** *n.* (BrE) соси́ска в те́сте

savage /'sævɪdʒ/ *n.* дика́р|ь (-ка)
● *adj.* **1** (of animals: fierce) свире́пый **2** (of attack, blow, etc.) жесто́кий, я́ростный
● *v.t.* (жесто́ко) иск|уса́ть, -уса́ть; (fig.)

раст|ерза́ть, -ерза́ть

↙ **sav|e** /seɪv/ *n.* (football etc.): **the goalkeeper made a brilliant** ~**e** врата́рь блестя́ще отби́л уда́р
● *v.t.* **1** (rescue) спас|а́ть, -ти́; изб|авля́ть, -а́вить; **he** ~**ed my life** он спас мне жизнь; **she was** ~**ed from drowning** ей не да́ли утону́ть; (protect) храни́ть (*impf.*) **2** (put by) бере́чь, с-; от|кла́дывать, -ложи́ть; копи́ть, на-; I ~**ed (up) £100 towards a holiday** я скопи́л 100 фу́нтов на о́тпуск; ~**e me something to eat!** оста́вьте мне что́-нибудь пое́сть!; (collect) соб|ира́ть, -ра́ть; (avoid using or spending) эконо́мить, с-; **he took the bus to** ~**e time** он взял авто́бус, что́бы сэконо́мить вре́мя; (obviate need for, expense of, etc.) эконо́мить, с-; **that will** ~**e me £100** я сэконо́млю на э́том сто фу́нтов; I ~**ed him the trouble of replying** я изба́вил его́ от необходи́мости отвеча́ть; (comput.) сохран|я́ть, -и́ть
● *v.i.* эконо́мить, с-; копи́ть (*impf.*); **he is** ~**ing up for a bicycle** он откла́дывает/ко́пит де́ньги (*or* он ко́пит) на велосипе́д

saver /'seɪvə(r)/ *n.* (investor) вкла́дчик

saving /'seɪvɪŋ/ *n.* **1** (salvation) спасе́ние **2** (economy) эконо́мия **3** (*in pl.*) (money laid by) сбереже́ния (*nt. pl.*)
● *adj.*: ~ **grace** поло́жи́тельное/спаси́тельное сво́йство/ка́чество
■ ~**s account** *n.* сберега́тельный счёт; ~**s bank** *n.* сберега́тельная ка́сса, сберега́тельный банк

saviour /'seɪvjə(r)/ (AmE **savior**) *n.* спаси́тель (*m.*)

savour /'seɪvə(r)/ (AmE **savor**) *n.* вкус
● *v.t.* смакова́ть (*impf.*)

savoury /'seɪvərɪ/ (AmE **savory**) *adj.* несла́дкий

saw¹ /sɔː/ *n.* (tool) пила́
● *v.t.* (*p.p.* **sawn** /sɔːn/ *or* **sawed**) пили́ть (*impf.*); распил|ивать, -и́ть
● *v.i.* (*p.p.* **sawn** /sɔːn/ *or* **sawed**) пили́ть (*impf.*)
□ ~ **off** *v.t.* отпил|ивать, -и́ть; ~**n-off** (*or* AmE ~**ed-off**) **shotgun** обре́з
■ ~**dust** *n.* опи́л|ки (-ок)

saw² /sɔː/ *past of* ▶ **see**

sax /sæks/ *n.* (infml) = **saxophone**

saxophone /'sæksəfəʊn/ *n.* саксофо́н

saxophonist /sæk'sɒfənɪst/ *n.* саксофони́ст (-ка)

↙ **say** /seɪ/ *n.* (expression of opinion): **let sb have his** ~ да|ва́ть, -ть кому́-н. вы́сказаться; **we had no** ~ **in the matter** с на́шим мне́нием в э́том де́ле не счита́лись
● *v.t. & i.* (*3rd pers. sing. pres.* **says** /sez/; *past and p.p.* **said**) **1** говори́ть, сказа́ть; **he** ~**s I am lazy** он говори́т, что я лени́в; I **must** ~ призна́ться; **she is said to be rich** говоря́т, она́ бога́та; **when all is said and done** в конце́ концо́в, в коне́чном счёте; ~ **good morning to sb** здоро́ваться, по- с кем-н.; **that is to** ~ (in other words; viz.) то есть; други́ми слова́ми; **it goes without** ~**ing** (само́ собо́й)

разуме́ется; слов нет **2** (of inanimate objects: indicate): **the signpost** ∼**s London** на указа́теле напи́сано «Ло́ндон»; **the clock** ∼**s 5 o'clock** часы́ пока́зывают пять **3** (formulate, express): ∼ **a prayer** произн|оси́ть, -ести́ моли́тву

saying /'seɪɪŋ/ n. погово́рка

scab /skæb/ n. струп, ко́рка

scaffold /'skæfəʊld/ n. **1** эшафо́т, пла́ха; **die on the** ∼ умира́ть, умере́ть на эшафо́те **2** = **scaffolding**

scaffolding /'skæfəʊldɪŋ/ n. лес|á (-о́в) (*строи́тельные*)

scald /skɔːld/ v.t. ошпа́ри|вать, -ть; ∼**ing water** круто́й кипято́к

scale[1] /skeɪl/ n. **1** (of fish, reptile, etc.) чешу́йка; (*pl., collect.*) чешуя́ **2** (on teeth) (зубно́й) ка́мень (*m.*)

scale[2] /skeɪl/ n. (*usu.* ∼ **pan**) ча́ш(к)а (весо́в)

♂ **scale**[3] /skeɪl/ n. **1** (grading) шкала́; ∼ **of charges** шкала́ расце́нок **2** (of map, also fig.) масшта́б **3** (size) разме́р **4** (mus.) га́мма ● v.t. (climb): ∼ **a wall** влез|а́ть, -ть (*or* зал|еза́ть, -е́зть) на сте́ну; ∼ **a mountain** вз|бира́ться, -обра́ться на́ гору □ ∼ **down** v.t. ум|еньша́ть, -е́ньшить; сокра|ща́ть, -ти́ть ■ ∼ **drawing** n. масшта́бный чертёж

scales /skeɪlz/ n. pl. (weighing machine) вес|ы́ (-о́в)

scalp /skælp/ n. скальп

scalpel /'skælp(ə)l/ n. ска́льпель (*m.*)

scam /skæm/ n. (sl.) обма́н, надува́тельство

scamper /'skæmpə(r)/ v.i. мча́ться (*impf.*), бе́гать (*indet.*); **the dog** ∼**ed off** соба́ка умча́лась

scampi /'skæmpɪ/ n. креве́тки (*f. pl.*) (*кру́пные, пригото́вленные*)

scan /skæn/ v.t. (**scanned**, **scanning**) **1** (survey) обв|оди́ть, -ести́ взгля́дом; (glance through) пробе|га́ть, -жа́ть (глаза́ми) **2** (comput., med.) скани́ровать (*impf.*) ● n. **1** (act of surveying or looking) внима́тельное просма́тривание **2** (med.) *see* ▸ **CT**, ▸ **MRI**, ▸ **ultrasound 3** (image obtained by scanning) изображе́ние, фотогра́фия

scandal /'skænd(ə)l/ n. сканда́л; **it is a** ∼ э́то безобра́зие

scandalize /'skændəlaɪz/ v.t. шоки́ровать (*impf., pf.*)

scandalous /'skændələs/ adj. (shocking) сканда́льный; (disgraceful) позо́рный, безобра́зный, возмути́тельный

Scandinavia /skændɪ'neɪvɪə/ n. Скандина́вия

Scandinavian /skændɪ'neɪvɪən/ n. скандина́в (-ка) ● adj. скандина́вский

scanner /'skænə(r)/ n. (comput., med.) ска́нер

scant /skænt/ adj. (inadequate) недоста́точный

scanty /'skæntɪ/ adj. (**scantier**, **scantiest**) ску́дный

scapegoat /'skeɪpɡəʊt/ n. козёл отпуще́ния

scar /skɑː(r)/ n. шрам, рубе́ц; (fig.) след, ра́на ● v.t. (**scarred**, **scarring**) (mark with ∼)

ост|авля́ть, -а́вить шра́мы на + *p.*; (fig.) ра́нить (*impf., pf.*)

scarce /skeəs/ adj. ре́дкий

scarcely /'skeəslɪ/ adv. едва́; почти́ не

scarcity /'skeəsɪtɪ/ n. **1** (insufficiency) недоста́ток, нехва́тка, дефици́т; **it was a time of great** ∼ э́то бы́ло вре́мя больши́х лише́ний **2** (rarity) ре́дкость ■ ∼ **value** n. сто́имость, определя́емая дефици́том

scare /skeə(r)/ n. (fright) испу́г; **give sb a** ∼ пуга́ть, ис- кого́-н.; (alarm, panic) па́ника ● v.t. пуга́ть, ис-; **I felt** ∼**d** я боя́лся; **they were** ∼**d stiff** они́ до́ смерти перепуга́лись □ ∼ **away**, ∼ **off** vv.t. отпу́г|ивать, -ну́ть; спу́г|ивать, -ну́ть ■ ∼**crow** n. пу́гало, (огоро́дное) чу́чело; ∼**monger** n. паникёр (-ша)

scarf /skɑːf/ n. (pl. **scarves** or ∼**s**) шарф

scarlet /'skɑːlɪt/ n. а́лый цвет ● adj. а́лый ■ ∼ **fever** n. скарлати́на

scarves /skɑːvz/ pl. of ▸ **scarf**

scary /'skeərɪ/ adj. (**scarier**, **scariest**) (infml) стра́шный, жу́ткий

scathing /'skeɪðɪŋ/ adj. е́дкий

scatter /'skætə(r)/ v.t. **1** (throw here and there) разбр|а́сывать, -оса́ть; (sprinkle) расс|ыпа́ть, -ыпа́ть; пос|ыпа́ть, -ыпа́ть **2** (*pass.*): ∼**ed villages** разбро́санные (там и тут) сёла **3** (disperse) раз|гоня́ть, -огна́ть ● v.i. (disperse) рассе́|иваться, -яться

scavenge /'skævɪndʒ/ v.i. ры́ться/копа́ться (*impf.*) в отбро́сах

scavenger /'skævɪndʒə(r)/ n. (animal) живо́тное, пита́ющееся па́далью; (person) помо́йник; челове́к, собира́ющий ве́щи и/ и́ли еду́ на помо́йках

scenario /sɪ'nɑːrɪəʊ/ n. (pl. ∼**s**) сцена́рий

♂ **scene** /siːn/ n. **1** (stage, of play) сце́на **2** (place) ме́сто; **change of** ∼ переме́на обстано́вки **3** (set, decor) декора́ция; (fig.): **behind the** ∼**s** за кули́сами **4** (view) карти́на

scenery /'siːnərɪ/ n. (theatr.) декора́ции (*f. pl.*); (landscape) пейза́ж, вид

scenic /'siːnɪk/ adj. **1** (picturesque) живопи́сный; ∼ **beauty** живопи́сность (ландша́фта) **2** (theatr.) сцени́ческий; ∼ **effects** сцени́ческие эффе́кты (*m. pl.*)

scent /sent/ n. **1** (odour) за́пах, арома́т, благоуха́ние **2** (perfume) дух|и́ (-о́в) **3** (trail, also fig.) след ● v.t.: ∼**ed candle** аромати́ческая свеча́

sceptic /'skeptɪk/ (AmE **skeptic**) n. ске́птик

sceptical /'skeptɪk(ə)l/ (AmE **skeptical**) adj. скепти́ческий

scepticism /'skeptɪsɪz(ə)m/ (AmE **skepticism**) n. скептици́зм

sceptre /'septə(r)/ (AmE **scepter**) n. ски́петр

♂ **schedule** /'ʃedjuːl/ n. **1** (list) спи́сок, пе́речень (*m.*) **2** (timetable) план, расписа́ние; **a full** ∼ больша́я програ́мма; **be behind** ∼ опа́здывать, -озда́ть; **be ahead of** ∼ опере|жа́ть, -ди́ть

s

гра́фик; **on ~** во́время/то́чно
● *v.t.* **1** (tabulate) сост|авля́ть, -а́вить спи́сок + *g.*; **a ~d flight** регуля́рный рейс **2** (time; plan) рассчи́т|ывать, -а́ть; нам|еча́ть, -е́тить; **we are ~d to finish by May** по пла́ну мы должны́ ко́нчить к ма́ю

schematic /ski:ˈmætɪk/ *adj.* схемати́ческий; (simplistic, formulaic) схемати́чный

✇ **scheme** /ski:m/ *n.* **1** (plan) прое́кт, план **2** (plot) про́иск|и (-ов)
● *v.i.* интригова́ть (*impf.*)

schism /ˈskɪz(ə)m/ *n.* раско́л; (relig. also) схи́зма

schizophrenia /ˌskɪtsəˈfriːnɪə/ *n.* шизофрени́я

schizophrenic /ˌskɪtsəˈfrenɪk/ *n.* шизофре́н|ик (-и́чка)
● *adj.* шизофрени́ческий

scholar /ˈskɒlə(r)/ *n.* учёный

scholarly /ˈskɒləlɪ/ *adj.* учёный, академи́ческий

scholarship /ˈskɒləʃɪp/ *n.* (erudition) учёность; (grant) стипе́ндия

✇ **school** /sku:l/ *n.* **1** (for educating children) шко́ла; **at ~** в шко́ле; **go to ~** ходи́ть (*indet.*) в шко́лу; учи́ться (*impf.*) в шко́ле; **we were at ~ together** мы учи́лись в одно́й шко́ле; **boys'/girls' ~** мужска́я/же́нская шко́ла **2** (AmE, university) университе́т; (department of university): **~ of law** юриди́ческий факульте́т **3** (for specialist education) учи́лище; **military ~** вое́нное учи́лище; **~ of art** худо́жественное учи́лище
■ **~bag** *n.* шко́льная су́мка; **~ book** *n.* уче́бник; **~boy** *n.* шко́льник; **~children** *n. pl.* шко́льники (*m. pl.*); **~ fees** *n. pl.* пла́та за обуче́ние; **~girl** *n.* шко́льница; **~leaver** *n.* (BrE) выпускни́|к (-ца); **~-leaving** *adj.*: **~-leaving age** (BrE) во́зраст, до кото́рого обуче́ние в шко́ле обяза́тельно; **~ report** *n.* шко́льный та́бель; **~ run** *n.* путь, кото́рый ежедне́вно проде́лывают роди́тели, отвозя́щие дете́й в шко́лу на автомоби́ле; **~ teacher** *n.* учи́тель (-ница)

schooling /ˈsku:lɪŋ/ *n.* (об)уче́ние

schooner /ˈsku:nə(r)/ *n.* (naut.) шху́на; (BrE, for sherry) фуже́р; (AmE, for beer) большо́й пивно́й бока́л

✇ **science** /ˈsaɪəns/ *n.* **1** (systematic knowledge) нау́ка **2** (natural ~s) есте́ственные нау́ки
■ **~ fiction** *n.* нау́чная фанта́стика

✇ **scientific** /ˌsaɪənˈtɪfɪk/ *adj.* нау́чный

✇ **scientist** /ˈsaɪəntɪst/ *n.* учёный (*в о́бласти есте́ственных нау́к*)

sci-fi /ˈsaɪfaɪ/ *n.* (infml) нау́чная фанта́стика

scintillating /ˈsɪntɪleɪtɪŋ/ *adj.* блестя́щий

scissors /ˈsɪzəz/ *n. pl.* но́жниц|ы (*pl., g. —*)

scoff[1] /skɒf/ *v.i.* (mock) смея́ться (*impf.*); **~ at** издева́ться/глуми́ться/насмеха́ться (*all impf.*) над + *i.*

scoff[2] /skɒf/ (BrE, infml) *v.t. & i.* жрать, со-

scold /skəʊld/ *v.t.* руга́ть, об-

✇ ключева́я ле́ксика

scone /skɒn/ *n.* ≈ небольшо́й кекс

scoop /sku:p/ *n.* **1** (for food) ло́жка **2** (journalism) ≈ сенса́ция
● *v.t.* **1** (lift with ~) зачёрп|ывать, -ну́ть; (*also* **~ out**) выче́рп|ывать, вы́черпать **2** (win) вы́игрывать, вы́играть

scooter /ˈsku:tə(r)/ *n.* (child's) самока́т; (motor **~**) мотороллер

scope /skəʊp/ *n.* **1** (range) разма́х, охва́т; **this is beyond the ~ of our enquiry** э́то выхо́дит за преде́лы/ра́мки на́шего рассле́дования **2** (outlet): **the game offers ~ for the children's imagination** э́та игра́ даёт просто́р де́тскому воображе́нию

scorch /skɔ:tʃ/ *v.t.* (burn, dry up) жечь, с-; выжига́ть, вы́жечь; (clothes etc.) подпа́л|ивать, -и́ть

✇ **score** /skɔ:(r)/ *n.* **1** (in games) счёт; **what's the ~?** како́й счёт?; **keep the ~** вести́ (*det.*) счёт **2** (mus.) партиту́ра **3** (twenty) два́дцать; (about twenty) о́коло двадцати́ **4**: **on that/this ~** на э́тот счёт
● *v.t.* **1** (scratch) цара́пать, ис-; **~ out, through** вычёрк|ивать, вы́черкнуть **2** (win) выи́грывать, вы́играть; **~ a goal** (football) заб|ива́ть, -и́ть гол
● *v.i.* вы́игрывать, вы́играть очко́; (football) заб|ива́ть, -и́ть гол

scorn /skɔ:n/ *n.* презре́ние
● *v.t.* презира́ть (*impf.*); пренебр|ега́ть, -е́чь + *i.*

scornful /ˈskɔ:nfʊl/ *adj.* (person): **he was ~ of the idea** он отнёсся к э́той иде́е с презре́нием; (glance etc.) презри́тельный

Scorpio /ˈskɔ:pɪəʊ/ *n.* (*pl.* **~s**) Скорпио́н

Scot /skɒt/ *n.* шотла́нд|ец (-ка)

Scotch /skɒtʃ/ *n.* (whisky) шотла́ндское ви́ски (*nt. indecl.*), скотч
● *adj.* шотла́ндский
■ **~ tape**® *n.* кле́йкая ле́нта, скотч

scot-free /skɒtˈfri:/ *adv.*: **go/get off ~** (unpunished) ост|ава́ться, -а́ться безнака́занным

Scotland /ˈskɒtlənd/ *n.* Шотла́ндия

Scots /skɒts/ *n.* (ling.) шотла́ндский го́вор
● *adj.* шотла́ндский
■ **~man** *n.* шотла́ндец; **~woman** *n.* шотла́ндка

✇ **Scottish** /ˈskɒtɪʃ/ *adj.* шотла́ндский

scoundrel /ˈskaʊndr(ə)l/ *n.* подле́ц

scour[1] /ˈskaʊə(r)/ *v.t.* (cleanse) чи́стить, вы-

scour[2] /ˈskaʊə(r)/ *v.t.* (range or pursuit) обры́скать (*pf.*); **he ~ed the town for his daughter** он обе́гал весь го́род в по́исках до́чери

scourer /ˈskaʊərə(r)/ *n.* (for saucepans etc.) металли́ческая моча́лка; ёж

scourge /skɜ:dʒ/ *n.* бич

scout /skaʊt/ *n.* **1** (mil.) разве́дчик **2** (Boy S~) скаут, бойска́ут; (Girl S~) де́вочка-ска́ут
● *v.i.*: **I have been ~ing about for a present** я обходи́л все магази́ны в по́исках пода́рка

scowl /skaʊl/ *n.* серди́тый/хму́рый взгляд

● *v.i.*: **he ~ed at me** он хму́ро/серди́то посмотре́л на меня́

Scrabble® /'skræb(ə)l/ *n.* скрэбл, ≈ игра «Эруди́т»

scrabble /'skræb(ə)l/ *v.i.*: **~ about** ша́рить (*impf.*); **~ about for sth** разы́скивать (*impf.*) что-н.

scramble /'skræmb(ə)l/ *n.* **1** (climb with hands and feet) кара́бканье **2** (struggle to get sth) сва́лка; (fig.) борьба́, схва́тка
● *v.t.*: **~d eggs** яи́чница-болту́нья
● *v.i.* кара́бкаться, вс-; вз|бира́ться, -обра́ться; **the boys ~d over the wall** ма́льчики переле́зли че́рез забо́р

scrap /skræp/ *n.* **1** (small piece) кусо́чек; (of metal) обло́мок; (of cloth) обре́зок; лоску́т; (fragment) обры́вок; **~s of paper** клочки́ (*m. pl.*) бума́ги **2** (*in pl.*) (waste food) объе́дк|и (-ов) **3** (waste material) ути́ль (*m.*); (~ metal) металлоло́м; (~ paper) макулату́ра
● *v.t.* (**scrapped**, **scrapping**) **1** (make into ~) перевра|ща́ть, -ти́ть в лом **2** (infml, discard, plan) отмен|я́ть, -и́ть
■ **~book** *n.* альбо́м для накле́ивания вы́резок; **~ heap** *n.* сва́лка; **~ iron** *n.* металли́ческий лом; **~yard** *n.* (BrE) сва́лка

scrape /skreɪp/ *n.*: **get into a ~** вли́пнуть (*pf.*) в исто́рию (infml)
● *v.t.* **1** (abrade) скобли́ть, вы́-; (graze) сса́|живать, -ди́ть; (scratch) **he ~d his car against a tree** он поцара́пал маши́ну о де́рево **2** (clean) выска́бливать (*or* скобли́ть) вы́скоблить
● *v.i.* **1** (rub): **my hand ~d against the wall** я ссади́л себе́ ру́ку о сте́ну **2** (get through): **she just ~d into the final** она́ с трудо́м вы́шла в фина́л
□ **~ along, ~ by** *vv.i.* (get by) переб|ива́ться, -и́ться; **we can just ~ by** мы ко́е-как перебива́емся
□ **~ through** *v.i.* проти́с|киваться, -нуться; **she ~d through (her exam)** она́ с трудо́м сдала́ экза́мен
□ **~ together** *v.t.* (money etc.) наскре|ба́ть, -сти́

scratch /skrætʃ/ *n.* **1** (mark) цара́пина **2** (noise) цара́панье **3** (wound) цара́пина, сса́дина **4** (fig.): **come up to ~** де́лать (*impf.*) то, что поло́жено; **start from ~** нач|ина́ть, -а́ть с нача́ла/нуля́
● *v.t.* **1** цара́пать, о-; **he ~ed letters on the wall** он нацара́пал бу́квы на стене́ **2** (to relieve itching) чеса́ть, по-; **~ one's head** чеса́ть (*impf.*) го́лову
● *v.i.* **1** (of person, **~ oneself**) чеса́ться, по- **2** (of animal): **does your cat ~?** ва́ша ко́шка цара́пается?
□ **~ about, ~ around** *vv.i.*: **the chickens ~ed around for food** ку́ры клева́ли зе́млю в по́исках пи́щи
□ **~ out** *v.t.*: **~ sb's eyes out** выцара́пывать, вы́цара́пать глаза́ кому́-н.

scrawl /skrɔːl/ *n.* кара́кули (*f. pl.*)
● *v.t.* черк|а́ть, -ну́ть; цара́пать, на-
● *v.i.* писа́ть (*impf.*) кара́кулями

scrawny /'skrɔːnɪ/ *adj.* (**scrawnier**, **scrawniest**) костля́вый, то́щий

scream /skriːm/ *n.* **1** пронзи́тельный крик; (shriek) вопль (*m.*); (high-pitched ~) визг **2** (infml, funny affair): **it was a ~!** (э́то была́) умо́ра!
● *v.t.* выкри́кивать, вы́крикнуть
● *v.i.* вопи́ть (*impf.*); (high-pitched) визжа́ть (*impf.*); **he was ~ing for help** он взыва́л о по́мощи

screech /skriːtʃ/ *n.* пронзи́тельный крик, визг; (of object) скрип, скре́жет
● *v.i.* пронзи́тельно крича́ть, за-; (of gears, tyres, etc.) скрежета́ть (*impf.*)

screen /skriːn/ *n.* **1** (partition) перегоро́дка **2** (furniture) ши́рма **3** (shelter) прикры́тие; **behind a ~ of trees** под прикры́тием дере́вьев **4** (cin., TV, comput.) экра́н
● *v.t.* **1** (protect) защи|ща́ть, -ти́ть **2** (hide) укр|ыва́ть, -ы́ть **3** (separate) отгор|а́живать, -оди́ть; **we ~ed off the kitchen from the dining room** мы отгороди́ли ку́хню от столо́вой **4** (fig., also med.) investigate: **be ~ed (for)** про|ходи́ть, -йти́ прове́рку на + *a.* **5** (show on ~) пока́з|ывать, -а́ть
■ **~ grab** *n.* (comput.) скриншо́т; **~play** *n.* сцена́рий; **~saver** *n.* (comput.) скринсе́йвер; **~shot** *n.* (comput.) скриншо́т; **~writer** *n.* сцена́рист

screw /skruː/ *n.* винт, шуру́п
● *v.t.* зави́н|чивать, -ти́ть; **the cupboard was ~ed to the wall** шкаф был приви́нчен к стене́
□ **~ up** *v.t.* зави́н|чивать, -ти́ть; (crumple) ко́мкать, с-; **~ up one's eyes** щу́рить, со- глаза́; **a face ~ed up with pain** лицо́, искажённое от бо́ли; **~ up one's courage** соб|ира́ться, -ра́ться с ду́хом; (sl., spoil) напорта́чить (*pf.*); зава́л|ивать, -и́ть
■ **~ cap, ~ top** *nn.* нави́нчивающаяся кры́шка; **~driver** *n.* отвёртка

scribble /'skrɪb(ə)l/ *v.i.* (make marks) исчёркивать, исчерка́ть; **the children ~d all over the wall** де́ти исчерка́ли всю сте́ну
● *v.t.* (write hastily) начерка́ть (*pf.*); **~ sth down** бы́стро написа́ть (*pf.*); (write untidily) цара́пать, на-

scribe /skraɪb/ *n.* (hist.) писе́ц

scrimp /skrɪmp/ *v.i.* = **skimp**

script /skrɪpt/ *n.* (writing system) письмо́; (text) текст; (theatr. etc.) сцена́рий; (comput.) скрипт, сцена́рий
■ **~writer** *n.* сцена́рист

scripture /'skrɪptʃə(r)/ *n.* Писа́ние

scroll /skrəʊl/ *n.* (of parchment) сви́ток; (archit.) завито́к
● *v.i.* (comput.) (**~ down/up**) прокр|у́чивать, -ути́ть (вниз/вверх)
■ **~ bar** *n.* (comput.) полоса́ прокру́тки

scrot|um /'skrəʊtəm/ *n.* (*pl.* **~a** *or* **~ums**) мошо́нка

scrounge /skraʊndʒ/ *v.t.* (infml, cadge) стрел|я́ть, -ну́ть; (*impf.*)
● *v.i.* (cadge) попроша́йничать (*impf.*)

scrounger /'skraʊndʒə(r)/ *n.* (infml) попроша́йка (*c.g.*)

scrub¹ /skrʌb/ *n.* (brushwood) куста́рник; (area) за́росли (*f. pl.*)

scrub² /skrʌb/ *n.*: give sth a ~ вычища́ть, вы́чистить что-н.
- *v.t.* (**scrubbed, scrubbing**) (scour) скрести́ (*impf.*); (wipe) тере́ть (*impf.*); (clean) чи́стить, по-; дра́ить, на-; ~ the floor мыть, вы́- пол
- ~**bing brush** *n.* жёсткая щётка

scruff /skrʌf/ *n.*: take sb by the ~ of the neck хвата́ть, схвати́ть кого́-н. за ши́ворот/ загри́вок

scruffy /ˈskrʌfɪ/ *adj.* (**scruffier, scruffiest**) (infml) неопря́тный

scrumptious /ˈskrʌmpʃəs/ *adj.* (infml) о́чень вку́сный, сма́чный

scruple /ˈskruːp(ə)l/ *n.* сомне́ния (*nt. pl.*); have ~s about doing sth со́веститься, по- сде́лать что-н.; have no ~s about doing sth не стесня́ться, по- сде́лать что-н.

scrupulous /ˈskruːpjʊləs/ *adj.* тща́тельный, скрупулёзный, педанти́чный

scrutinize /ˈskruːtɪnaɪz/ *v.t.* (examine) рассм|а́тривать, -отре́ть; (stare at) при́стально смотре́ть (*impf.*) на + *a.*

scrutiny /ˈskruːtɪnɪ/ *n.* ❶ (searching gaze) внима́тельный/испыту́ющий взгляд ❷ (close investigation) тща́тельное рассле́дование/ рассмотре́ние/иссле́дование

scuba /ˈskuːbə/ *n.* скуба, акваланг
- ~-**diver** *n.* аквалангӣ́ст; ~-**diving** *n.* подво́дное пла́вание со скубой

scud /skʌd/ *v.i.* (**scudded, scudding**) нести́сь, про-; (naut.) идти́ (*det.*) под ве́тром

scuff /skʌf/ *v.t.*: ~ (*sc. wear away*) one's shoes сн|а́шивать, -оси́ть обувь

scuffle /ˈskʌf(ə)l/ *n.* потасо́вка, схва́тка

scullery /ˈskʌlərɪ/ *n.* судомо́йня

sculpt /skʌlpt/ *v.t.* вая́ть, из-; (model in clay etc.) лепи́ть, вы́-; (in stone) высека́ть, вы́сечь; (in wood) ре́зать, вы́-
- *v.i.* быть/рабо́тать (*impf.*) ску́льптором

sculptor /ˈskʌlptə(r)/ *n.* ску́льптор

sculpture /ˈskʌlptʃə(r)/ *n.* скульпту́ра

scum /skʌm/ *n.* пе́на; (fig.) подо́нки (*m. pl.*)

scurry /ˈskʌrɪ/ *n.* суета́, спе́шка; there was a ~ towards the exit все бро́сились к вы́ходу; the ~ of mice under the floor возня́ мыше́й под по́лом
- *v.i.* (also ~ **about**) суетли́во бе́гать (*impf.*); снова́ть (*impf.*); ~ through one's work на́спех проде́л|ывать, -ать рабо́ту
- □ ~ **away**, ~ **off** *vv.i.* убе|га́ть, -жа́ть; (disperse) разбе|га́ться, -жа́ться

scuttle /ˈskʌt(ə)l/ *v.i.* юркнуть (*pf.*); снова́ть (*impf.*)

scythe /saɪð/ *n.* коса́

ᵈ **sea** /siː/ *n.* мо́ре; at ~ в мо́ре; be all at ~ не знать что де́лать; by ~ мо́рем; by the ~ у мо́ря, на мо́ре; (*attr.*) ~ air морско́й во́здух; ~ voyage морско́е путеше́ствие
- ~**food** *n.* морепроду́кты (*m. pl.*); ~**front** *n.*

примо́рский бульва́р, на́бережная; ~**gull** *n.* ча́йка; ~ **horse** *n.* морско́й конёк; ~ **level** *n.* у́ровень (*m.*) мо́ря; ~ **lion** *n.* морско́й лев; ~**man** *n.* моря́к, матро́с; ~**plane** *n.* гидросамолёт; ~**shell** *n.* морска́я ра́ковина; ~**shore** *n.* морско́й бе́рег, взмо́рье; ~**sick** *adj.*: I was ~sick меня́ укача́ло (на корабле́); ~**side** *n.* морско́е побере́жье ● *adj.* примо́рский; a ~side resort морско́й куро́рт; ~ **urchin** *n.* морско́й ёж; ~**water** *n.* морска́я вода́; ~**weed** *n.* морска́я во́доросль; ~**worthy** *adj.* морехо́дный, го́дный к пла́ванию

seal¹ /siːl/ *n.* (zool.) тюле́нь (*m.*); (*in full fur* ~) ко́тик

seal² /siːl/ *n.* (on document etc.) печа́ть
- *v.t.* ❶ (affix ~ to) при|кла́дывать, -ложи́ть печа́ть к + *d.* ❷ (confirm): ~ a bargain скреп|ля́ть, -и́ть сде́лку ❸ (close securely) запеча́т|ывать, -ать; пло́тно/ на́глухо закр|ыва́ть, -ы́ть; a ~ed envelope запеча́танный конве́рт; the police ~ed off all exits from the square поли́ция перекры́ла все вы́ходы с пло́щади ❹ (decide): his fate is ~ed его́ у́часть решена́

seam /siːm/ *n.* шов, рубе́ц

seamless /ˈsiːmlɪs/ *adj.* без шва; из одного́ куска́

seamstress /ˈsemstrɪs/ *n.* швея́

seance /ˈseɪɒns/ *n.* спирити́ческий сеа́нс

ᵈ **search** /sɜːtʃ/ *n.* ❶ (quest, also comput.) по́иск (*usu. in pl.*); make a ~ for sb/sth иска́ть (*impf.*) кого́-н./что-н.; a man in ~ of a wife мужчи́на, и́щущий себе́ жену́ ❷ (examination) о́быск
- *v.t.* ❶ (examine) обы́ск|ивать, -а́ть; пров|оди́ть, -ести́ о́быск + *g.*; (rummage through) обша́ри|вать, -ть ❷ (peer at) обв|оди́ть, -ести́ взгля́дом ❸ (penetrate): ~ing questions подро́бные вопро́сы
- *v.i.* иска́ть (*impf.*); (of police, customs) пров|оди́ть, -ести́ о́быск; ~ for иска́ть (*impf.*), разы́скивать (*impf.*); ~ through просм|а́тривать, -отре́ть; he ~ed through all his papers for the contract он перерь́л/ перебра́л все свои́ бума́ги в по́исках догово́ра
- ~ **engine** *n.* (comput.) поиско́вая систе́ма/ маши́на; ~**light** *n.* проже́ктор; ~ **party** *n.* поиско́вая гру́ппа; ~ **warrant** *n.* о́рдер на о́быск

ᵈ **season** /ˈsiːz(ə)n/ *n.* ❶ сезо́н; (of year) вре́мя го́да; strawberries are in ~ сейча́с сезо́н клубни́ки; holiday ~ сезо́н о́тпусков ❷ (BrE) (*in full* ~ **ticket**) сезо́нный/проездно́й биле́т; (for concerts, etc.) абонеме́нт
- *v.t.* ❶ (mature: of timber, wine, etc.) выде́рж|ивать, -ать ❷ (acclimatize): a ~ed traveller о́пытный путеше́ственник ❸ (spice) припр|авля́ть, -а́вить; a highly ~ed dish о́строе блю́до

seasonable /ˈsiːzənəb(ə)l/ *adj.* (suited to the season) соотве́тствующий сезо́ну; (opportune) своевре́менный

seasonal /ˈsiːzən(ə)l/ *adj.* сезо́нный

S

seasoning /'si:zənɪŋ/ n. (cul.) приправа

✓ **seat** /si:t/ n. **1** (place to sit) сиде́нье; (chair) стул; (bench) скамья́, скаме́йка **2** (place in vehicle, theatre, etc.) ме́сто; take one's ~ зан|има́ть, -я́ть ме́сто; he booked a ~ он заказа́л биле́т **3** (of chair) сиде́нье **4** (of trousers) зад (у) брюк
• v.t. **1** (make sit) сажа́ть, посади́ть **2** (provide with ~s) вме|ща́ть, -сти́ть; this table ~s twelve за э́тот стол мо́жно посади́ть двена́дцать челове́к
■ ~ **belt** n. реме́нь (m.) безопа́сности

seating /'si:tɪŋ/ n. (allocation of places) расса́живание; (placing at table) размеще́ние госте́й за столо́м

secateurs /sekə'tə:z/ n. pl. (BrE) садо́вые но́жниц|ы (pl., g. —)

secede /sɪ'si:d/ v.i. отдел|я́ться, -и́ться (from: от + g.); выходи́ть, вы́йти (from: из + g.)

secession /sɪ'seʃ(ə)n/ n. отделе́ние (from: от + g.); вы́ход (from: из + g.)

secluded /sɪ'klu:dɪd/ adj.: a ~d spot уедине́нный/укро́мный уголо́к

seclusion /sɪ'klu:ʒ(ə)n/ n. уедине́ние, изоля́ция

✓ **second** /'sekənd/ n. **1** второ́й; on the ~ of May второ́го ма́я **2** (in pl.) (imperfect goods) второсо́ртный/брако́ванный това́р **3** (measure of time) секу́нда; wait a ~! одну́ секу́нду!; ~(s) hand (of clock) секу́ндная стре́лка
• adj. второ́й; (other) друго́й; Charles the S~ Карл Второ́й; on the ~ floor, (AmE) third floor на тре́тьем этаже́; the ~ largest city второ́й по величине́ го́род; (additional) доба́вочный; ~ helping доба́вка; have ~ thoughts передумать, раздумать (both pf.)
• v.t. (support) подде́рж|ивать, -а́ть
■ ~ **best** adj. не са́мый лу́чший; (inferior) второсо́ртный; ~-class adj.: ~-class cabin каю́та второ́го кла́сса; ~-class citizens гра́ждане второ́го со́рта • adv.: we travel ~-class мы е́здим вторы́м кла́ссом; ~ cousin n. трою́родный брат (трою́родная сестра́); ~ hand n. see ▸ second n. 3; ~-hand adj. (previously used) поде́ржанный; ~-hand bookshop букинисти́ческий магази́н; (indirect): ~-hand information информа́ция из вторы́х рук • adv.: I bought the car ~-hand я купи́л поде́ржанную маши́ну; ~ name n. (BrE) фами́лия; ~-rate adj. (of goods) второсо́ртный; (mediocre) посре́дственный

secondary /'sekəndərɪ/ adj. (less important) втори́чный; (school) сре́дний

secondly /'sekəndlɪ/ adv. во-вторы́х

secondment /sɪ'kɒndmənt/ n. (BrE) командиро́вка

secrecy /'si:krɪsɪ/ n. секре́тность

✓ **secret** /'si:krɪt/ n. секре́т, та́йна; keep a ~ храни́ть, со- секре́т; in ~ секре́тно, та́йно
• adj. секре́тный, та́йный; (hidden) потайно́й, секре́тный; (undisclosed): I was ~ly glad to see him в глубине́ души́ я был рад его́ ви́деть

secretarial /sekrɪ'teərɪəl/ adj. секрета́рский

✓ **secretary** /'sekrɪtərɪ/ n. секрета́р|ь; (female typist, receptionist, etc.) секрета́рша (infml)
■ **S~ of State** n. (in UK) мини́стр; (in US) госуда́рственный секрета́рь, мини́стр иностра́нных дел

secrete /sɪ'kri:t/ v.t. **1** (physiol. etc.) выделя́ть, вы́делить **2** (conceal) укр|ыва́ть, -ы́ть; пря́тать, с-; ~ oneself укр|ыва́ться, -ы́ться; пря́таться, с-

secretive /'si:krɪtɪv/ adj. скры́тный, за́мкнутый

sect /sekt/ n. се́кта

sectarian /sek'teərɪən/ adj. секта́нтский

✓ **section** /'sekʃ(ə)n/ n. **1** (separate or distinct part) се́кция; (severed portion) кусо́к; ~ of the population часть населе́ния; ~ of a book разде́л кни́ги; (department) отде́л, отделе́ние **2** (geom. etc.) разре́з; ~ drawing чертёж в разре́зе; сече́ние

✓ **sector** /'sektə(r)/ n. се́ктор

secular /'sekjʊlə(r)/ adj. (worldly) мирско́й; (lay, non-religious) све́тский

✓ **secure** /sɪ'kjʊə(r)/ adj. **1** (free from care) споко́йный; feel ~ about sth не беспоко́иться (impf.) о чём-н. **2** (safe) про́чный, надёжный; (reliable) надёжный; (assured): a ~ income гаранти́рованный/ве́рный дохо́д
• v.t. **1** (make safe) закреп|ля́ть, -и́ть; застрахо́в|ывать, -а́ть **2** (insure) страхова́ть, за- **3** (obtain) дост|ава́ть, -а́ть

✓ **security** /sɪ'kjʊərɪtɪ/ n. **1** (safety) безопа́сность; he is a ~ risk он неблагонадёжен **2** (guarantee) гара́нтия **3** (pledge) зало́г, гара́нтия; ~ for a loan гара́нтия за́йма; закла́д **4** (in pl.) (bonds) це́нные бума́ги (f. pl.)
■ ~ **guard** n. охра́нник, секью́рити (m. indecl.)

sedate¹ /sɪ'deɪt/ adj. степе́нный, уравнове́шенный

sedate² /sɪ'deɪt/ v.t. да|ва́ть, -ть успокои́тельное + d.

sedation /sɪ'deɪʃ(ə)n/ n. успокое́ние; under ~ под де́йствием успокои́тельного

sedative /'sedətɪv/ n. успокои́тельное (сре́дство)

sedentary /'sedəntərɪ/ adj. (of posture etc.) сидя́чий; a ~ way of life сидя́чий/малоподви́жный о́браз жи́зни; (of person) неподви́жный, малоподви́жный

sediment /'sedɪmənt/ n. оса́док, отсто́й

sedimentary /sedɪ'mentərɪ/ adj. оса́дочный

sedition /sɪ'dɪʃ(ə)n/ n. подстрека́тельство к мятежу́

seduce /sɪ'dju:s/ v.t. соблазн|я́ть, -и́ть

seducer /sɪ'dju:sə(r)/ n. соблазни́тель (m.); обольсти́тель (m.)

seduction /sɪ'dʌkʃ(ə)n/ n. (act of seducing sb) обольще́ние; (temptation) собла́зн

seductive /sɪ'dʌktɪv/ adj. соблазни́тельный

✓ **see** /si:/ v.t. (past saw, p.p. seen) **1** ви́деть; I saw her arrive я ви́дел, как она́ прие́хала;

S

did you ~ anyone leaving? вы ви́дели, чтобы кто́-нибудь выходи́л? **2** (look at, watch) смотре́ть, по- на + a.; ~ **p 4** см. стр./с. 4; let me ~ that да́йте мне на э́то посмотре́ть; the film is worth ~ing э́тот фильм сто́ит посмотре́ть; ~ the sights осм|а́тривать, -отре́ть достопримеча́тельности **3** (imagine) предст|авля́ть, -а́вить себе́ (что) **4** (find out) посмотре́ть (pf.) узн|ава́ть, -а́ть; I'll ~ if I can get tickets я посмотрю́, смогу́ ли я доста́ть биле́ты **5** (comprehend) ви́деть, у-; пон|има́ть, -я́ть; I don't ~ what good that is я не ви́жу, кака́я от э́того по́льза; as far as I can ~ наско́лько я понима́ю **6** (consider) ду́мать, по-; I'll ~ я я поду́маю; посмо́трим **7** (meet) ви́деть, у-; встр|еча́ть, -е́тить; (associate) ви́деться (impf.), встреча́ться (impf.) (с кем); they stopped ~ing each other они́ разошли́сь (or переста́ли встреча́ться); (visit) посе|ща́ть, -ти́ть; наве|ща́ть, -сти́ть; we went to ~ our friends мы навести́ли на́ших друзе́й; come and ~ me, us sometime заходи́те как-нибудь; ~ you on Tuesday! до вто́рника! **8** (consult): I went to ~ him about a job я пошёл к нему́ поговори́ть о рабо́те; can I ~ you for a moment? мо́жно вас на мину́тку? **9** (escort) прово|жа́ть, -ди́ть; he saw her to the door он проводи́л её до две́ри **10** (ensure) следи́ть, про-; ~ (to it) that the door is locked проследи́те, чтобы за́перли дверь
  ● v.i. (past saw, p.p. seen) **1** ви́деть (impf.); can you ~ from where you are? вам отту́да ви́дно?; he cannot ~ (is blind) он не ви́дит; он слеп; we saw through him мы раскуси́ли его́ **2** (make provision; take care; give attention; organize) забо́титься, по- (о чём); (arrange, organize) забо́титься, по-; she ~s to the laundry она́ ве́дает сти́ркой; I have to ~ to the children мне прихо́дится забо́титься о де́тях; he saw to it that I got the money он позабо́тился о том, чтобы я получи́л де́ньги
  □ ~ off v.t. (accompany) прово|жа́ть, -ди́ть; we saw them off at the station мы проводи́ли их на по́езд
  □ ~ out v.t. прово|жа́ть, -ди́ть до вы́хода; I can ~ myself out ≈ я сам найду́ доро́гу
  □ ~ through v.t.: who will ~ the job through? кто доведёт де́ло до конца́?
  ■ ~-through adj. прозра́чный

🔹 **seed** /siːd/ n. **1** (lit., fig.) се́мя (nt.); (of apple, melon, sunflower) се́мечко; go, run to ~ (lit.) идти́, пойти́ на семена́; (fig., of person) сд|ава́ть, -а́ть **2** (sport: ~ed player) посе́янный игро́к

seedling /ˈsiːdlɪŋ/ n. се́янец

seedy /ˈsiːdɪ/ adj. (seedier, seediest) (shabby) потрёпанный; (sleazy) захуда́лый

🔹 **seek** /siːk/ v.t. (past and p.p. sought) (look for) иска́ть (impf.) (+ a./g. of concrete/abstract object); (try to get) иска́ть (impf.) (+ g.); (ask for): ~ advice проси́ть, по- сове́та; ~ out разы́скивать (pf.); отыска́ть (pf.)

🔹 **seem** /siːm/ v.i. каза́ться, по-; предст|авля́ться,

-а́виться; it ~s to me мне ка́жется; по-мо́ему; it ~s like only yesterday как бу́дто э́то бы́ло вчера́; she ~s young она́ мо́лодо вы́глядит; I ~ed to hear a voice мне показа́лось, что я слы́шал чей-то го́лос

seen /siːn/ p.p. of ▶ see

seep /siːp/ v.i. (usu. ~ out, through) прос|а́чиваться, -очи́ться

see-saw /ˈsiːsɔː/ n. (доска́-)каче́л|и (-ей)
  ● v.i. (fig.) колеба́ться (impf.)

seethe /siːð/ v.i. (of liquids, also fig.) бурли́ть (impf.); the streets were ~ing with people у́лицы кише́ли наро́дом/людьми́

segment /ˈsegmənt/ n. сегме́нт; (of fruit) до́лька

segregate /ˈsegrɪɡeɪt/ v.t. отдел|я́ть, -и́ть; раздел|я́ть, -и́ть

segregation /ˌsegrɪˈɡeɪʃ(ə)n/ n. (separation) отделе́ние, изоля́ция; (racial) (ра́совая) сегрега́ция

seismologist /saɪzˈmɒlədʒɪst/ n. сейсмологи́ческий

seismology /saɪzˈmɒlədʒɪ/ n. сейсмоло́гия

seize /siːz/ v.t. **1** (grasp; lay hold of) хвата́ть, схвати́ть; he ~d (hold of) the rope он схвати́л (or ухвати́лся за) верёвку; ~ an opportunity ухв|а́тываться, -ати́ться за возмо́жность; по́льзоваться, вос- слу́чаем **2** (power, land) захва́т|ывать, -и́ть; брать, взять
  ● v.i. (jam) (also ~ up) за|еда́ть, -е́сть; застр|ева́ть, -я́ть

seizure /ˈsiːʒə(r)/ n. (capture) захва́т; (confiscation) конфиска́ция; (attack of illness) при́ступ, припа́док; (stroke) уда́р

seldom /ˈseldəm/ adv. ре́дко

🔹 **select** /sɪˈlekt/ adj. и́збранный, элита́рный
  ● v.t. выбира́ть, вы́брать; от|бира́ть, -обра́ть; под|бира́ть, -обра́ть

🔹 **selection** /sɪˈlekʃ(ə)n/ n. **1** (choice) вы́бор **2** (assortment) подбо́р, ассортиме́нт

selective /sɪˈlektɪv/ adj. (choosing carefully) разбо́рчивый; (partial) вы́борочный

🔹 **self** /self/ n. (pl. selves) (individuality) су́щность; (personality) ли́чность; I am not my former ~ я уже́ не тот, что пре́жде

self-absorbed /ˌselfəbˈzɔːbd/ adj. поглощённый собо́й

self-addressed /ˌselfəˈdrest/ adj.: ~ envelope конве́рт с обра́тным а́дресом отправи́теля

self-adhesive /ˌselfədˈhiːsɪv/ adj. самоклея́щийся

self-assurance /ˌselfəˈʃʊərəns/ n. уве́ренность (в себе́)

self-assured /ˌselfəˈʃʊəd/ adj. (само)уве́ренный

self-awareness /ˌselfəˈweənɪs/ n. самосозна́ние

self-catering /selfˈkeɪtərɪŋ/ n. (BrE): ~ apartment жильё с самообслу́живанием; ~ holiday путёвка, включа́ющая жильё с самообслу́живанием

self-centred /self'sentəd/ (AmE **-centered**)
adj. эгоцентри́чный
self-confessed /selfkən'fest/ *adj.* открове́нный
self-confidence /self'kɒnfɪd(ə)ns/ *n.*
уве́ренность (в себе́)
self-confident /self'kɒnfɪd(ə)nt/ *adj.*
уве́ренный (в себе́)
self-conscious /self'kɒnʃəs/ *adj.* (awkward)
нело́вкий; (shy) засте́нчивый; (embarrassed)
смущённый
self-contained /selfkən'teɪnd/ *adj.* (person)
самостоя́тельный, незави́симый; (BrE, of
accommodation) отде́льный
self-control /selfkən'trəʊl/ *n.* самооблада́ние
self-controlled /selfkən'trəʊld/ *adj.*
вы́держанный
self-criticism /self'krɪtɪsɪz(ə)m/ *n.*
самокри́тика
self-defence /selfdɪ'fens/ (AmE **-defense**) *n.*
самооборо́на, самозащи́та
self-denial /selfdɪ'naɪəl/ *n.* самоотрече́ние;
practise ~ отка́зывать (*impf.*) себе́ во всём;
ограни́чивать (*impf.*) себя́
self-destruct /selfdɪ'strʌkt/ *v.i.* (tech.)
самоликвиди́роваться (*impf., pf.*)
self-destructive /selfdɪ'strʌktɪv/ *adj.*
самоуби́йственный
self-determination /selfdɪtə:mɪ'neɪʃ(ə)n/ *n.*
самоопределе́ние
self-discipline /self'dɪsɪplɪn/ *n.* вну́тренняя
дисципли́на
self-effacing /selfɪ'feɪsɪŋ/ *adj.* скро́мный
self-employed /selfɪm'plɔɪd/ *adj.*
рабо́тающий не по на́йму
self-esteem /selfɪ'sti:m/ *n.* самоуваже́ние,
самолю́бие
self-evident /self'evɪd(ə)nt/ *adj.* очеви́дный
self-explanatory /selfɪk'splænətərɪ/ *adj.* не
тре́бующий разъясне́ний
self-expression /selfɪk'spreʃ(ə)n/ *n.*
самовыраже́ние
self-fulfilling /selffʊl'fɪlɪŋ/ *adj.*: **~ prophecy**
предсказа́ние, влия́ющее на результа́т
self-governing /self'gʌvənɪŋ/ *adj.*
самоуправля́ющийся, автоно́мный
self-government /self'gʌvənmənt/ *n.*
самоуправле́ние
self-help /self'help/ *n.* самопо́мощь
self-image /self'ɪmɪdʒ/ *n.* самооце́нка,
со́бственное представле́ние о себе́
self-important /selfɪm'pɔ:t(ə)nt/ *adj.*
ва́жный, самонаде́янный
self-indulgent /selfɪn'dʌldʒ(ə)nt/ *adj.*
избало́ванный
self-inflicted /selfɪn'flɪktɪd/ *adj.* нанесённый
самому́ себе́
self-interest /self'ɪntrest/ *n.* со́бственный
интере́с; коры́сть
selfish /'selfɪʃ/ *adj.* эгоисти́чный,
эгоисти́ческий, коры́стный
selfishness /'selfɪʃnɪs/ *n.* эгоисти́чность,
эгои́зм

selfless /'selflɪs/ *adj.* самоотве́рженный,
беззаве́тный
self-made /'selfmeɪd/ *adj.*: **he is a ~ man** он
сам себя́ сде́лал; он челове́к, вы́бившийся
из низо́в
self-pity /self'pɪtɪ/ *n.* жа́лость к себе́
self-portrait /self'pɔ:trɪt/ *n.* автопортре́т
self-possessed /selfpə'zest/ *adj.*
хладнокро́вный, невозмути́мый
self-possession /selfpə'zeʃ(ə)n/ *n.*
хладнокро́вие, невозмути́мость
self-preservation /selfprezə'veɪʃ(ə)n/ *n.*
самосохране́ние
self-proclaimed /selfprə'kleɪmd/ *adj.*
самозва́ный
self-raising /self'reɪzɪŋ/ (AmE **self-rising**)
adj.: **~ flour** мука́ с разрыхли́телем
self-reliant /selfrɪ'laɪənt/ *adj.*
самостоя́тельный
self-respect /selfrɪ'spekt/ *n.* самоуваже́ние
self-righteous /selfraɪtʃəs/ *adj.* ха́нжеский
self-rule /self'ru:l/ *n.* самоуправле́ние
self-sacrifice /self'sækrɪfaɪs/ *n.*
самопоже́ртвование
self-satisfied /self'sætɪsfaɪd/ *adj.*
самодово́льный
self-sealing /self'si:lɪŋ/ *adj.*
самозакле́ивающийся
self-service /self'sə:vɪs/ *n.*
самообслу́живание
self-sufficient /selfsə'fɪʃ(ə)nt/ *adj.*
самостоя́тельный; (econ.): **Russia is 70% ~**
in oil/food production Росси́я обеспе́чивает
свои́ потре́бности в не́фти/продово́льствии
на 70% за счёт вну́тренних ресу́рсов
self-taught /self'tɔ:t/ *adj.*: **a ~ man, woman**
самоу́чка (*c.g.*)
self-willed /self'wɪld/ *adj.* своево́льный
ⅾ **sell** /sel/ *v.t.* (*past and p.p.* **sold**) **1** прод|ава́ть,
-а́ть; торгова́ть (*impf.*) + *i.*; **I'll ~ you this**
carpet for £20 я прода́м вам э́тот ковёр за
20 фу́нтов; **~ing price** прода́жная цена́; **this**
shop ~s stamps в э́том магази́не продаю́тся
почто́вые ма́рки **2** (infml, put across): **he was**
unable to ~ his idea to the management ему́
не удало́сь убеди́ть правле́ние приня́ть его́
предложе́ние
● *v.i.* (*past and p.p.* **sold**) **1** (of person): **you**
were wise to ~ when you did вы во́время
про́дали свой това́р **2** (of goods): **the house**
sold for £90,000 за дом вы́ручили 90 000
фу́нтов
□ **~ off** *v.t.* распрод|ава́ть, -а́ть; **they sold off**
the goods at a reduced price они́ распро́дали
това́р по сни́женной цене́
□ **~ out** *v.i.*: **the book sold out** э́та кни́га
разошла́сь; **the shop sold out of cigarettes**
магази́н распро́дал все сигаре́ты; **they**
have sold out of tickets все биле́ты про́даны;
they were accused of ~ing out to the enemy
их обвини́ли в том, что они́ продали́сь
врагу́
■ **~-by date** *n.* (BrE) срок го́дности; **~-out**
n. спекта́кль/конце́рт/спорти́вный матч с

пóлным зáлом/стадиóном *и т. n.*; аншлáг

seller /'selə(r)/ *n.* продав|éц (-щи́|ца); торгóв|ец (-ка)

Sellotape® /'seləteɪp/ *n.* (BrE) скотч, клéйкая лéнта

selves /selvz/ *pl. of* ▸ **self**

semantic /sɪ'mæntɪk/ *adj.* семанти́ческий, смыслово́й

semaphore /'seməfɔ:(r)/ *n.* семафóр
● *v.t. & i.* сигнализи́ровать (*impf., pf.*) флажкáми

semen /'si:mən/ *n.* сéмя (*nt.*), спéрма

semester /sɪ'mestə(r)/ *n.* семéстр

semi /'semɪ/ *n.* (*pl.* ∼**s**) (BrE, infml, house) оди́н из двух особнякóв, имéющих óбщую стéну
● *pref.* полу…
■ ∼**-automatic** *adj.* полуавтомати́ческий; ∼**breve** *n.* (BrE, mus.) цéлая нóта; ∼**circle** *n.* полукрýг; ∼**circular** *adj.* полукрýглый; ∼**colon** *n.* тóчка с запятóй; ∼**conductor** *n.* полупроводни́к; ∼**-conscious** *adj.* в полубессознáтельном состоя́нии; ∼**-detached** *adj.*: ∼**-detached house** оди́н из двух особнякóв, имéющих óбщую стéну; ∼**-final** *n.* полуфинáл; ∼**-finalist** *n.* полуфинали́ст (-ка); ∼**-skimmed** *adj.* (BrE) обезжи́ренный; ∼**tone** *n.* (mus.) полутóн

seminal /'semɪn(ə)l/ *adj.* **1** семеннóй **2** (fig., work) эпохáльный; (idea) плодотвóрный
■ ∼ **fluid** *n.* семеннáя жи́дкость

seminar /'semɪnɑ:(r)/ *n.* семинáр

seminary /'semɪnərɪ/ *n.* семинáрия

Semitic /sɪ'mɪtɪk/ *adj.* семити́ческий, семи́тский; (language) семи́тский

semolina /semə'li:nə/ *n.* мáнная крупá, мáнка (infml)

senate /'senɪt/ *n.* сенáт; (of university) совéт

senator /'senətə(r)/ *n.* сенáтор

⚔ **send** /send/ *v.t.* (*past and p.p.* **sent**) (dispatch) пос|ылáть, -лáть; отправ|ля́ть, -áвить; **he sent me a book** он присла́л мне кни́гу; **I shall** ∼ **you to bed** я отпра́влю тебя́ спать; **the teacher sent him out of the room** учи́тель вы́ставил его́ из кла́сса
● *v.i.* (*past and p.p.* **sent**): **he sent for a doctor** он вы́звал врача́; он посла́л за врачо́м
□ ∼ **away** *v.i.*: ∼ **away for sth** выпи́сывать, вы́писать что-н., зак|áзывать, -азáть что-н.
□ ∼ **back** *v.t.* (person) пос|ылáть, -лáть назáд; (thing) от|сылáть, -ослáть
□ ∼ **in** *v.t.*: **he sent in his bill** он послáл счёт; ∼ **in a report** предст|авля́ть, -áвить отчёт
□ ∼ **off** *v.t.* (dispatch) отпр|авля́ть, -áвить; **he was sent off by the referee** судья́ удали́л его́ с пóля
□ ∼ **on** *v.t.* (forward) перес|ылáть, -лáть
□ ∼ **out** *v.t.* высылáть, вы́слать; (distribute) ра|ссылáть, -зослáть; (emit): ∼ **out heat** выделя́ть, вы́делить теплó
□ ∼ **up** *v.t.* (infml, ridicule) высмéивать, вы́смеять
■ ∼**-off** *n.* прово́д|ы (-ов); **he got a marvellous** ∼**-off from his friends** друзья́ устрóили емý замечáтельные прово́ды; ∼**-up** *n.* (infml, parody,

satire) парóдия, сати́ра

sender /'sendə(r)/ *n.* отправи́тель (*m.*)

Senegal /senɪ'gɔ:l/ *n.* Сенегáл

senile /'si:naɪl/ *adj.* стáрческий
■ ∼ **dementia** *n.* стáрческое слабоýмие; (of person) дря́хлый

senility /sɪ'nɪlɪtɪ/ *n.* (physical) дря́хлость; (mental) стáрческое слабоýмие

⚔ **senior** /'si:nɪə(r)/ *n.*: **he is my** ∼ **by 5 years** он на пять лет стáрше меня́
● *adj.* (in age) стáрший (вóзрастом, годáми); (in position) стáрший (по чи́ну/звáнию)
■ ∼ **citizen** *n.* пожилóй человéк, человéк пенсиóнного вóзраста

seniority /si:nɪ'ɒrɪtɪ/ *n.* старшинствó

sensation /sen'seɪʃ(ə)n/ *n.* **1** (feeling) ощущéние **2** (exciting event) сенсáция

sensational /sen'seɪʃən(ə)l/ *adj.* сенсациóнный

sensationalism /sen'seɪʃənəlɪz(ə)m/ *n.* сенсациóнность

⚔ **sense** /sens/ *n.* **1** (faculty) чýвство; **the five** ∼**s** пять чувств; **a keen** ∼ **of hearing** óстрый слух **2** (feeling; perception; appreciation) чýвство, ощущéние; **have you no** ∼ **of shame?** у вас стыдá нет!; ∼ **of humour** чýвство ю́мора **3** (*in pl.*) (sanity) ум; **take leave of one's** ∼**s** сходи́ть, сойти́ с умá; **come to one's** ∼**s** брáться, взя́ться за ум **4** (common ∼) здрáвый смысл; **he had the** ∼ **to call the police** у негó хвати́ло умá вы́звать поли́цию **5** (meaning) смысл, значéние; **in a** ∼ в извéстном/нéкотором смы́сле; **make** ∼ **of** пон|имáть, -я́ть; разб|ирáться, -обрáться в + *p.*; **it makes** ∼ э́то разýмно
● *v.t.* чýвствовать, по-; ощущáть, -ти́ть

senseless /'senslɪs/ *adj.* **1** (foolish) бессмы́сленный **2** (unconscious) бесчýвственный; **knock sb** ∼ оглуш|áть, -и́ть когó-н.

sensible /'sensɪb(ə)l/ *adj.* (благо)разýмный; ∼ **shoes** практи́чная óбувь

sensitive /'sensɪtɪv/ *adj.* чувстви́тельный, восприи́мчивый; (tender): ∼ **skin** нéжная кóжа; (painful): ∼ **tooth** больнóй зуб; (potentially embarrassing): **a** ∼ **topic** щекотли́вая/ делика́тная тéма

sensitivity /sensɪ'tɪvɪtɪ/ *n.* чувстви́тельность

sensor /'sensə(r)/ *n.* (tech.) дáтчик

sensual /'sensjʊəl/ *adj.* чýвственный

sensuous /'sensjʊəs/ *adj.* чýвственный

sent /sent/ *past and p.p. of* ▸ **send**

⚔ **sentence** /'sent(ə)ns/ *n.* **1** (gram.) предложéние **2** (law) пригово́р
● *v.t.* пригов|áривать, -ори́ть

sentiment /'sentɪmənt/ *n.* **1** (feeling) чýвство **2** (opinion) мнéние, тóчка зрéния; **those are my** ∼**s** таковó моё мнéние

sentimental /sentɪ'ment(ə)l/ *adj.* сентиментáльный

sentimentality /sentɪmen'tælɪtɪ/ *n.* сентиментáльность

sentry /'sentrɪ/ *n.* часовóй

Seoul /səʊl/ *n.* Сеу́л

⚡ **separate¹** /'sepərət/ *adj.* отде́льный; (distinct) осо́бый; (not together) разде́льный; **two ~ questions** два самостоя́тельных/ра́зных вопро́са; **they are living ~ly** они́ живу́т/ прожива́ют отде́льно/разде́льно

separate² /'sepəreɪt/ *v.t.* (set apart) отдел|я́ть, -и́ть; (part) разлуч|а́ть, -и́ть; **he is ~d from his family** он не живёт с семьёй
● *v.i.* **1** (become detached) отдел|я́ться, -и́ться
2 (of man and wife) ра|сходи́ться, -зойти́сь

separation /sepə'reɪʃ(ə)n/ *n.* отделе́ние, разделе́ние; (of spouses) разде́льное прожива́ние

separatism /'sepərətɪz(ə)m/ *n.* сепарати́зм

separatist /'sepərətɪst/ *n.* сепарати́ст (-ка)

⚡ **September** /sep'tembə(r)/ *n.* сентя́брь (*m.*)

septic /'septɪk/ *adj.* септи́ческий; **the wound has gone ~** ра́на загнои́лась

sepulchral /sɪ'pʌlkr(ə)l/ *adj.* (of a tomb): ~ **stone** надгро́бный/моги́льный ка́мень; (gloomy): ~ **voice** замоги́льный го́лос

sepulchre /'sepəlkə(r)/ (AmE **sepulcher**) *n.* гробни́ца; (in cave) склеп

sequel /'si:kw(ə)l/ *n.* продолже́ние (**to:** + *g.*); си́квел (**to:** + *g. or* к + *d.*)

sequence /'si:kwəns/ *n.* **1** (succession) после́довательность; поря́док; ~ **of events** ход/после́довательность собы́тий **2** (part of film) эпизо́д

sequential /sɪ'kwenʃ(ə)l/ *adj.* после́довательный

sequester /sɪ'kwestə(r)/ *v.t.* **1** (isolate, detach) изоли́ровать (*impf., pf.*); ~ **oneself from the world** удал|я́ться, -и́ться от ми́ра; a ~ed **village** уединённая дере́вня **2** (law etc., confiscate) (*also* **sequestrate**) (take temporary possession) секвестрова́ть (*impf., pf.*); (confiscate) конфискова́ть (*impf., pf.*)

sequestrate /'si:kwɪstreɪt/ *v.t.* = **sequester 2**

sequestration /si:kwɪ'streɪʃ(ə)n/ *n.* секве́стр, аре́ст иму́щества

sequin /'si:kwɪn/ *n.* (spangle) блёстка

Serb /sɜːb/ *n.* серб (-ка)

Serbia /'sɜːbɪə/ *n.* Се́рбия

Serbian /'sɜːbɪən/ *n.* (person) серб (-ка); (language) се́рбский язы́к
● *adj.* се́рбский

Serbo-Croat /sɜːbəʊ'krəʊæt/, **Serbo-Croatian** /sɜːbəʊkrəʊ'eɪʃ(ə)n/ *nn.* серб(ск)охорва́тский язы́к
● *adjs.* серб(ск)охорва́тский

serenade /serə'neɪd/ *n.* серена́да
● *v.t. & i.* петь, с- серена́ду (*кому*)

serene /sɪ'riːn/ *adj.* (**serener, serenest**) безмяте́жный, споко́йный

serf /sɜːf/ *n.* крепостно́й; **emancipation of the ~s** раскрепоще́ние крестья́н

sergeant /'sɑːdʒ(ə)nt/ *n.* сержа́нт

serial /'sɪərɪəl/ *n.* (story etc.) рома́н, выходя́щий отде́льными вы́пусками; (TV) многосери́йный телефи́льм; сериа́л
● *adj.*: ~ **killer** сери́йный уби́йца; ~ **number**

сери́йный но́мер

serialize /'sɪərɪəlaɪz/ *v.t.* (publish in successive parts) изд|ава́ть, -а́ть вы́пусками; (screen in successive parts) выпуска́ть, вы́пустить се́риями

⚡ **series** /'sɪəriːz/ *n.* (*pl.* ~) **1** (succession) се́рия **2** (TV) цикл програ́мм

⚡ **serious** /'sɪərɪəs/ *adj.* **1** (thoughtful) серьёзный; **I am ~ about this** я говорю́ э́то всерьёз; **you can't be ~** вы шу́тите; **take sth ~ly** отн|оси́ться, -ести́сь серьёзно к + *d.*; (words) (вос)прин|има́ть, -я́ть что-н. всерьёз **2** (important; not slight) серьёзный, суще́ственный, ва́жный; ~ **crime** тя́жкое/ серьёзное преступле́ние; **he is ~ly ill** он серьёзно/тяжело́ бо́лен

seriousness /'sɪərɪəsnɪs/ *n.* серьёзность; ва́жность; **in all ~** без шу́ток; со всей серьёзностью

sermon /'sɜːmən/ *n.* про́поведь

serpent /'sɜːpənt/ *n.* змея́; (bibl.) змий

serrated /sə'reɪtɪd/ *adj.* зубча́тый, зазу́бренный

serum /'sɪərəm/ *n.* сы́воротка

servant /'sɜːv(ə)nt/ *n.* (male, also fig.) слуга́ (*m.*); (female) служа́нка, прислу́га

⚡ **serve** /sɜːv/ *n.* (at tennis) пода́ча
● *v.t.* **1** (be servant to; give service to) служи́ть (*impf.*) + *d.*; **if my memory ~s me correctly** е́сли па́мять мне не изменя́ет **2** (meet needs of, satisfy): ~ **a purpose** служи́ть (*impf.*) це́ли; **this box has ~d its purpose** э́та коро́бка сослужи́ла свою́ слу́жбу; (provide service to) обслу́ж|ивать, -и́ть; **the railway ~s all these villages** желе́зная доро́га обслу́живает все э́ти сёла **3** (supply with food, goods, etc.) под|ава́ть, -а́ть + *d.*; **the waiter ~d us with vegetables** официа́нт по́дал (нам) о́вощи; **are you being ~d?** вас кто́-нибудь обслу́живает? **4** (proffer) под|ава́ть, -а́ть; **dinner is ~d** обе́д по́дан; ~ **a ball** под|ава́ть, -а́ть мяч **5** (fulfil, go through): ~ **one's sentence** отб|ыва́ть, -ы́ть срок **6** (treat): **it ~s him right** так ему́ и на́до; поде́лом ему́
● *v.i.* служи́ть (*impf.*); **he ~d in the army** он служи́л в а́рмии; ~ **on a jury** быть прися́жным; **the plank ~d as a bench** доска́ служи́ла ла́вкой/скамьёй

server /'sɜːvə(r)/ *n.* (at tennis) подаю́щий; (comput.) се́рвер

⚡ **service** /'sɜːvɪs/ *n.* **1** (employment) слу́жба; **length of ~** стаж **2** (branch of public work) слу́жба; **public, civil ~** госуда́рственная слу́жба; **do one's military ~** отб|ыва́ть, -ы́ть во́инскую пови́нность; **the ~s** вооружённые си́лы (*f. pl.*) **3** (work done for sb or sth) услу́га; (by hotel staff etc.) обслу́живание, се́рвис **4** (system to meet public need): **postal ~** почто́вая слу́жба; **a frequent train ~ to London** регуля́рное железнодоро́жное сообще́ние с Ло́ндоном **5** (technical maintenance) техобслу́живание **6** (eccl.) слу́жба; обря́д; **marriage/burial ~** венча́ние/ отпева́ние **7** (in tennis) пода́ча
● *v.t.*: ~ **a vehicle** пров|оди́ть, -ести́ осмо́тр и теку́щий ремо́нт маши́ны

S

■ ~ **charge** n. пла́та за обслу́живание; ~**man** n. военнослу́жащий; ~ **station** n. (for petrol) бензозапра́вочная ста́нция, бензоколо́нка; (for repairs) ста́нция техни́ческого обслу́живания; ~**woman** n. военнослу́жащая

serviceable /ˈsəːvɪsəb(ə)l/ adj. поле́зный, го́дный

serviette /səːviˈet/ n. (BrE) салфе́тка

servile /ˈsəːvaɪl/ adj. раболе́пный, подобостра́стный

servility /səːˈvɪlɪtɪ/ n. подобостра́стие

serving /ˈsəːvɪŋ/ n. (of food) по́рция

servitude /ˈsəːvɪtjuːd/ n. ра́бство; **penal** ~ ка́торжные рабо́ты (f. pl.)

✧ **session** /ˈseʃ(ə)n/ n. (meeting) заседа́ние; (period) се́ссия

✧ **set** /set/ n. **1** (collection) набо́р; (complete set) компле́кт; (pictures, coins, etc. collected) колле́кция; **chess** ~ ша́хматы (pl., g. —); **dinner** ~ столо́вый серви́з; ~ **of teeth** (dentures) зубно́й проте́з **2** (receiving apparatus): **television** ~ телеви́зор **3** (tennis) сет, па́ртия **4** (theatr.) декора́ция **5** (cin.): **on** ~ на съёмочной площа́дке
• adj. **1** (fixed): **a** ~ **smile** засты́вшая улы́бка; **he has** ~ **opinions** у него́ установи́вшиеся взгля́ды; **he is** ~ **in his ways** он не изменя́ет свои́м привы́чкам; ~ **phrase** клише́ (indecl.); шабло́нное выраже́ние; (prearranged): **at the** ~ **time** в устано́вленное вре́мя; ~ **menu** ко́мплексное меню́; (prescribed): ~ **books** обяза́тельная литерату́ра **2** (infml, ready): **all** ~? гото́вы?; **we were all** ~ **to go** мы совсе́м уже́ собрали́сь идти́ **3** (resolved): **he is** ~ **on going to the cinema** он настро́ился идти́ в кино́; **he was dead** ~ **against the idea** он был реши́тельно/категори́чески про́тив э́того предложе́ния
• v.t. (**setting**, past and p.p. ~) **1** (lay) класть, положи́ть; (place) разме|ща́ть, -сти́ть; распол|ага́ть, -ожи́ть; (arrange; ~ **out**) расст|авля́ть, -а́вить **2** (adjust, prepare) ста́вить, по-; **I always** ~ **my watch by the station clock** я всегда́ ста́влю часы́ по станцио́нным часа́м; **they** ~ **a trap for him** они́ устро́или ему́ лову́шку; ~ **the table** накр|ыва́ть, -ы́ть (на) стол **3** (make straight or firm): ~ **a bone** впр|авля́ть, -а́вить кость; ~ **sb's hair** укла́дывать, уложи́ть кому́-н. во́лосы **4** (fig., apply): ~ **one's heart on** стра́стно жела́ть (impf.) + g. **5** (make or put into specified state) прив|оди́ть, -ести́; **he** ~ **the boat in motion** он привёл ло́дку в движе́ние; ~ **sb's mind at ease, rest** успок|а́ивать, -о́ить кого́-н.; ~ **on fire** подж|ига́ть, -е́чь; (incite): **he** ~ **his dog on me** он натрави́л на меня́ свою́ соба́ку **6** (start) заст|авля́ть, -а́вить (+ inf.); **the smoke** ~ **her coughing** она́ зака́шлялась от ды́ма **7** (present) зад|ава́ть, -а́ть **8** (establish): **he is** ~ting **his children a bad example** он подаёт свои́м де́тям дурно́й приме́р **9** (an exam) сост|авля́ть, -а́вить **10** ~ **sth to music** класть, положи́ть что-н. на му́зыку

✧ **ключевая лексика**

11 (situate): **he** ~ **the scene in Paris** ме́стом де́йствия он избра́л Пари́ж
• v.i. (**setting**, past and p.p. ~) **1** (of sun) сади́ться, сесть **2** (become firm or solid) затверд|ева́ть, -е́ть; твердёть (impf.); (of jelly) заст|ыва́ть, -ы́ть; (of cement) схва́т|ываться, -и́ться
• with preps.: ~ **about (doing)** sth прин|има́ться, -я́ться за что-н.; ~ **(up)on** sb нап|ада́ть, -а́сть на кого́-н.
□ ~ **aside** v.t. (allocate) выдел|я́ть, вы́делить; (reserve) от|кла́дывать, -ложи́ть
□ ~ **back** v.t. (delay, damage) зам|едля́ть, -е́длить; отбр|а́сывать, -о́сить наза́д; нан|оси́ть, -ести́ уро́н + d.; (infml, cost): **the trip** ~ **him back a few pounds** пое́здка влете́ла ему́ в копе́ечку
□ ~ **down** v.t. (make statement or record): **he** ~ **down his complaint in writing** он изложи́л свою́ жа́лобу в пи́сьменном ви́де; **she** ~ **down her impressions in a diary** она́ заноси́ла/запи́сывала свои́ впечатле́ния в дневни́к
□ ~ **forth** v.t. (declare) изл|ага́ть, -ожи́ть
• v.i. (leave) отпр|авля́ться, -а́виться
□ ~ **in** v.i. (take hold): **winter is** ~ting **in** наступа́ет зима́; **the rain** ~ **in early** дождь начался́ ра́но
□ ~ **off** v.t. (cause to explode): **they were** ~ting **off fireworks** они́ устро́или фейерве́рк; (cause): **his arrest** ~ **off a wave of protest** его́ аре́ст вы́звал волну́ проте́стов; (enhance): **the ribbon will** ~ **off your complexion** ле́нта оттени́т/подчеркнёт цвет ва́шего лица́; (compensate) возме|ща́ть, -сти́ть; ~ **off gains against losses** баланси́ровать, с- при́быль и убытки́; (cause to start): **the story** ~ **them off laughing** э́тот расска́з рассмеши́л их
• v.i. (leave, on foot) пойти́ (pf.); (by transport) пое́хать (pf.); отпр|авля́ться, -а́виться
□ ~ **out** v.t. (arrange, display) распол|ага́ть, -ожи́ть; (expound) изл|ага́ть, -ожи́ть
• v.i. (leave) пойти́, пое́хать (both pf.); отпр|авля́ться, -а́виться; (attempt): **he** ~ **out to conquer Europe** он заду́мал покори́ть Евро́пу
□ ~ **to** v.i. (make a start) прин|има́ться, -я́ться; (begin to fight or argue) сцеп|ля́ться, -и́ться (infml); схв|а́тываться, -ати́ться
□ ~ **up** v.t. (erect) устан|а́вливать, -ови́ть; (form) образ|о́вывать, -ова́ть; **we** ~ **up a committee** мы организова́ли комите́т; (establish): ~ **up a school** осно́в|ывать, -а́ть шко́лу; (claim, put forward): **he** ~s **himself up to be a scholar** он изобража́ет из себя́ учёного; (restore to health): **a holiday will** ~ **you up** о́тдых вас поста́вит на́ ноги
• v.i.: **she** ~ **up in business** она́ организова́ла своё де́ло
■ ~**back** n. (delay) заде́ржка; (failure) неуда́ча; (difficulty) затрудне́ние; ~**-to** n. (infml, fight) схва́тка; ~**-up** n. (infml, arrangement) поря́дки (m. pl.); обстано́вка; (comput.) устано́вка

settee /seˈtiː/ n. (небольшо́й) дива́н

✧ **setting** /ˈsetɪŋ/ n. **1** (of sun etc.) захо́д, зака́т **2** (of gems) опра́ва **3** (background) обстано́вка, окруже́ние

✧ **settle** /ˈset(ə)l/ v.t. **1** (place securely): ~ **oneself in an armchair** ус|а́живаться, -е́сться

S

в кре́сло **2** (install) поме|ща́ть, -сти́ть;
устр|а́ивать, -о́ить **3** (calm) успок|а́ивать,
-о́ить **4** (reconcile) ула́|живать, -дить; **their
differences were soon ~d** их разногла́сия
бы́ли ско́ро ула́жены **5** (decide) реш|а́ть,
-и́ть; **that ~s it** тогда́ всё (я́сно) **6** (pay): **~
a bill** плати́ть, за- по счёту; **~ a debt** гаси́ть,
по-/упл|а́чивать, -ати́ть долг
● *v.i.* **1** (sink down; come to rest) ос|еда́ть,
-е́сть; **the dust will soon ~** (fig.) шуми́ха
ско́ро уля́жется; (alight) ус|а́живаться,
-е́сться **2** (become fixed) устан|а́вливаться,
-ови́ться **3** (become comfortable, accustomed)
(*also* ~ **down**) **the dog ~d in its basket**
соба́ка улегла́сь в свое́й корзи́не **4** (make
one's home) посел|я́ться, -и́ться
□ **~ down** *v.i.* (in home) устр|а́иваться, -о́иться;
(in job) осв|а́иваться, -о́иться; (adopt sober
ways) остепен|я́ться, -и́ться; (become quiet)
успок|а́иваться, -о́иться; **he ~d down to write
letters** он принялся́/усе́лся писа́ть пи́сьма
□ **~ in** *v.i.* осв|а́иваться, -о́иться
□ **~ up** *v.i.* распла́|чиваться, -ти́ться (*с кем*)

⚥ **settlement** /ˈsetəlmənt/ *n.* **1** (colony)
поселе́ние; (settled place) посёлок **2** (agreement)
соглаше́ние; **reach a ~** дост|ига́ть, -и́чь
соглаше́ния **3** (payment) упла́та, расчёт;
~ of an account упла́та по счёту

settler /ˈsetlə(r)/ *n.* поселе́н|ец (-ка)

⚥ **seven** /ˈsev(ə)n/ *n.* (число́/но́мер) семь;
(~ people) се́меро, семь челове́к; (figure; thing
numbered 7; group of ~) семёрка
● *adj.* семь + *g. pl.*

seventeen /sevənˈtiːn/ *n.* семна́дцать
● *adj.* семна́дцать + *g. pl.*

seventeenth /sevənˈtiːnθ/ *n.* (date)
семна́дцатое (число́); (fraction) одна́
семна́дцатая
● *adj.* семна́дцатый

seventh /ˈsev(ə)nθ/ *n.* (date) седьмо́е (число́);
(fraction) одна́ седьма́я
● *adj.* седьмо́й

seventieth /ˈsevəntiəθ/ *n.* одна́ семидеся́тая
● *adj.* семидеся́тый

seventy /ˈsevəntɪ/ *n.* се́мьдесят; **he is in
his ~ies** ему́ за се́мьдесят; ему́ (пошёл)
восьмо́й деся́ток; **in the ~ies** (decade) в
семидеся́тых года́х; в семидеся́тые го́ды
● *adj.* се́мьдесят + *g. pl.*

sever /ˈsevə(r)/ *v.t.* отдел|я́ть, -и́ть; **~ a
rope** перер|еза́ть, -е́зать верёвку; **~ one's
connection with** пор|ыва́ть, -ва́ть связь с + *i.*

⚥ **several** /ˈsevr(ə)l/ *pron.*: **~ of my friends**
не́которые из мои́х друзе́й
● *adj.* не́сколько + *g. pl.*; **myself and ~ others**
я и не́сколько други́х люде́й

severance /ˈsevərəns/ *n.* отделе́ние, разры́в
■ **~ pay** *n.* выходно́е посо́бие; компенса́ция
при увольне́нии

⚥ **severe** /sɪˈvɪə(r)/ *adj.* **1** (stern, strict) стро́гий,
суро́вый **2** (violent) жесто́кий, си́льный; **~
pain** си́льная/стра́шная боль

severity /sɪˈverɪtɪ/ *n.* (strictness) стро́гость,
суро́вость; (seriousness) серьёзность

sew /səʊ/ *v.t.* & *i.* (*p.p.* **sewn** *or* **sewed**)
шить, с-; **~ a button on to a dress**
приш|ива́ть, -и́ть пу́говицу к пла́тью

sewage /ˈsuːɪdʒ/ *n.* сто́чные во́ды (*f. pl.*)

sewer /ˈsuːə(r)/ *n.* (conduit) сто́чная труба́,
канализацио́нная труба́

sewing /ˈsəʊɪŋ/ *n.* шитьё; (*attr.*) шве́йный
■ **~ machine** *n.* шве́йная маши́н(к)а

sewn /səʊn/ *p.p. of* ▶ **sew**

⚥ **sex** /seks/ *n.* **1** пол; (*attr.*) половой **2** (sexual
activity) секс; (sexual intercourse) полово́е
сноше́ние; **have ~ with sb** (infml) спать,
пере- с кем-н.
□ **~ up** *v.t.* (infml) ожив|ля́ть, -и́ть (*де́лать
бо́лее я́рким, вырази́тельным*)
■ **~ change** *n.* опера́ция по измене́нию по́ла; **~
education** *n.* полово́е воспита́ние

sexiness /ˈseksɪnɪs/ *n.* сексуа́льность

sexism /ˈseksɪz(ə)m/ *n.* сексизм

sexist /ˈseksɪst/ *adj.* секси́стский

⚥ **sexual** /ˈsekʃʊəl/ *adj.* (organ, disease, reproduction)
полово́й; (relations) сексуа́льный; **~
harassment** сексуа́льное домога́тельство; **~
relations** сексуа́льные отноше́ния (*nt. pl.*)

sexuality /seksjʊˈælɪtɪ/ *n.* сексуа́льность

sexy /ˈseksɪ/ *adj.* (**sexier**, **sexiest**) (infml)
сексуа́льный; (film, novel) эроти́ческий

shabbiness /ˈʃæbɪnɪs/ *n.* (of clothes)
изно́шенность; (of building, room, area)
убо́гость; (of behaviour) по́длость

shabby /ˈʃæbɪ/ *adj.* (**shabbier**, **shabbiest**)
(clothes, personal appearance) потрёпанный;
(building, room, area) убо́гий; (behaviour) по́длый

shack /ʃæk/ *n.* лачу́га

shackle /ˈʃæk(ə)l/ *n.* (*in pl.*) (fetters) (also fig.)
око́в|ы (*pl., g.* —)
● *v.t.* (lit., fetter) зако́в|ывать, -а́ть в око́вы;
(impede) ско́в|ывать, -а́ть; стесня́ть (*impf.*)

shade /ʃeɪd/ *n.* **1** (unilluminated area) тень; **put
in(to) the ~** (fig.) затм|ева́ть, -и́ть **2** (tint,
nuance) отте́нок, тон **3** (of lamp) абажу́р
4 (AmE, blind) што́ра
● *v.t.* **1** (screen from light) затен|я́ть, -и́ть; (shield
from light etc.) заслон|я́ть, -и́ть **2** (restrict light of)
приглуш|а́ть, -и́ть

shadow /ˈʃædəʊ/ *n.* тень; **he has ~s under
his eyes** у него́ (чёрные/тёмные) круги́ под
глаза́ми
● *v.t.* (follow secretly) (та́йно) следи́ть/
сле́довать (*impf.*) за (+ *i.*)
■ **~ cabinet** *n.* (BrE) теневой кабине́т

shadowy /ˈʃædəʊɪ/ *adj.* (shady) тени́стый;
(dim) нея́сный; (vague) сму́тный

shady /ˈʃeɪdɪ/ *adj.* (**shadier**, **shadiest**)
1 (in shadow) теневой **2** (infml, suspect)
сомни́тельный, тёмный

shaft /ʃɑːft/ *n.* **1** (of spear) дре́вко; (handle)
ру́чко, рукоя́тка **2** (of light) луч **3** (tech., rod)
вал **4** (of mine) ша́хта, ствол ша́хты

shag /ʃæg/ (BrE, vulg.) *v.t.* тра́х|ать, -нуть
● *v.i.* тра́х|аться, -нуться

shaggy /ˈʃægɪ/ *adj.* (**shaggier**, **shaggiest**)
лохма́тый

S

♂ **shake** /ʃeɪk/ n. встря́ска; give sb/sth a ~ встря́х|ивать, -ну́ть кого́-н./что-н.
● v.t. (past **shook**, p.p. **shaken** /ʃeɪk(ə)n/)
1 тряс|ти́, -хну́ть; сотряс|а́ть, -ти́ (что, чем); they shook hands они́ пожа́ли друг дру́гу ру́ки; he shook his head он покача́л голово́й **2** (shock) потряс|а́ть, -ти́; (morally) колеба́ть, по-
● v.i. (past **shook**, p.p. **shaken** /ʃeɪk(ə)n/)
1 (vibrate) трясти́сь (impf.); сотряса́ться (impf.) **2** (tremble) дрожа́ть, за-; his hands shook у него́ дрожа́ли ру́ки; he was shaking with fever его́ трясла́ лихора́дка
□ ~ **off** v.t. (fig., of pursuers, illness, habit, etc.) отде́л|ывать, -а́ться от + g.; изб|авля́ться, -а́виться от + g.
□ ~ **up** v.t. встря́х|ивать, -ну́ть; (mix by shaking): ~ **up a medicine** взб|а́лтывать, -олта́ть лека́рство
■ **~-up** n. (in cabinet, etc.) ка́дровая перестано́вка; (in a system, in a service) коренны́е переме́ны (f. pl.)

shaky /ʃeɪkɪ/ adj. (**shakier, shakiest**) ша́ткий, нетвёрдый; his position in the party is ~ его́ положе́ние в па́ртии ша́ткое/непро́чное; a ~ **voice** дрожа́щий го́лос

♂ **shall** /ʃæl/ v. aux. **1** (in 1st person, usu. translated by future tense): I ~ **go** я пойду́ **2** (interrog.): ~ **I wait?** мне подожда́ть?; ~ **we have dinner now?** не пообе́дать ли нам сейча́с?; дава́йте пообе́даем

shallot /ʃə'lɒt/ n. (лук-)шало́т

shallow /ʃæləʊ/ adj. ме́лкий; (fig.): ~ **mind** пове́рхностный/неглубо́кий ум

sham /ʃæm/ n. **1** (pretence) притво́рство; his illness is only a ~ его́ боле́знь то́лько/одно́ притво́рство; (hypocrisy) лицеме́рие **2** (counterfeit) подде́лка
● adj. **1** (feigned) притво́рный **2** (counterfeit) подде́льный; ~ **marriage** фикти́вный брак
● v.i. (**shammed, shamming**): he is ~ming он притворя́ется

shaman /ʃeɪmən/ n. шама́н

shambles /ʃæmb(ə)lz/ n. (infml, mess) беспоря́док, ха́ос, барда́к

shame /ʃeɪm/ n. **1** (sense of guilt) стыд; ~ **on you!** как тебе́ (or вам) не сты́дно! **2** (disgrace) позо́р, срам; bring ~ **on** позо́рить, о- **3** (sth regrettable) жа́лость, доса́да; what a ~! как жаль!
● v.t. **1** (cause to feel ashamed) сму|ща́ть, -ти́ть; стыди́ть, при- **2** (disgrace) позо́рить, о-

shameful /ʃeɪmfʊl/ adj. позо́рный, посты́дный

shameless /ʃeɪmlɪs/ adj. бессты́дный; (unscrupulous) бессо́вестный

shampoo /ʃæm'puː/ n. шампу́нь (m.)
● v.t. (**shampoos, shampooed**) мыть, вы- шампу́нем

shandy /ʃændɪ/ n. смесь пи́ва с лимона́дом

shan't /ʃaːnt/ neg. of ▶ shall

shanty /ʃæntɪ/ n.: ~ **town** трущо́бный посёлок

♂ **shape** /ʃeɪp/ n. **1** (outward form) фо́рма; (outline) очерта́ние; take ~ (become clear) проясн|я́ться, -и́ться **2** (vague figure) о́браз **3** (order) поря́док; put or (infml) knock sth into ~ прив|оди́ть, -ести́ что-н. в поря́док; (condition) фо́рма, состоя́ние; he is exercising to get into ~ он трениру́ется, чтобы обрести́ (спорти́вную) фо́рму
● v.t. прид|ава́ть, -а́ть фо́рму + d.; (from wood) выреза́ть, вы́резать; (from clay) лепи́ть, вы́-/с-; (fig.): ~ **sb's character** формирова́ть, с- чей-н. хара́ктер
□ ~ **up** v.i. (take ~) скла́дываться, сложи́ться

shapeless /ʃeɪplɪs/ adj. бесфо́рменный

shapely /ʃeɪplɪ/ adj. (**shapelier, shapeliest**) хорошо́ сложённый; стро́йный; ~ **legs** стро́йные но́ги

shard /ʃaːd/ n. (broken piece) черепо́к

♂ **share** /ʃeə(r)/ n. **1** (part) часть; (portion) до́ля; fair ~ справедли́вая часть **2** (of capital) а́кция
● v.t. дели́ть, раз- (что с кем); he ~s all his secrets with me (or I ~ all his secrets) он де́лится со мной все́ми свои́ми секре́тами; ~ **an office with sb** рабо́тать (impf.) с кем-н. в одно́й ко́мнате; we must all ~ the blame мы все несём отве́тственность за э́то; I ~ **your views** я разделя́ю ва́ши взгля́ды; I ~ **your grief** я разделя́ю ва́ше го́ре
● v.i.: I ~ **in your grief** я разделя́ю ва́ше го́ре
□ ~ **out** v.t. (divide) дели́ть, раз-; (allocate) распредел|я́ть, -и́ть
■ **~holder** n. акционе́р

shark /ʃaːk/ n. аку́ла

♂ **sharp** /ʃaːp/ n. (mus.) дие́з
● adj. **1** (edged, pointed) (also fig., of senses etc.) о́стрый; ре́зкий; ~ **knife** о́стрый нож; ~ **pencil** о́стрый каранда́ш; ~ **features** ре́зкие черты́ лица́; (keen): ~ **eyes** о́строе зре́ние; ~ **ears** то́нкий слух; ~ **wits** о́стрый ум; (of sounds): ~ **voice** ре́зкий го́лос; (severe): a ~ **remark** ко́лкое замеча́ние; ~ **tongue** злой/о́стрый язы́к; ~ **frost** си́льный моро́з; ~ **wind** ре́зкий ве́тер; ~ **pain** о́страя/ре́зкая боль; (sour) ки́слый **2** (abrupt) круто́й, ре́зкий; ~ **turn** круто́й поворо́т; a ~ **drop in the temperature** ре́зкое паде́ние температу́ры; a ~ **rise in prices** ре́зкое повыше́ние цен **3** (artful) хи́трый
● adv. **1** (at a ~ angle): turn ~ **right** кру́то пов|ора́чивать, -ерну́ть напра́во **2** (punctually): at four o'clock ~ то́чно/ро́вно в четы́ре (часа́) **3** (mus.): he sings ~ он поёт сли́шком высоко́

sharpen /ʃaːpən/ v.t. (knife etc.) точи́ть, на-; зат|а́чивать, -очи́ть; (pencil) заостр|я́ть, -и́ть; точи́ть, под-

sharpener /ʃaːpənə(r)/ n. (pencil ~) точи́лка

sharpness /ʃaːpnɪs/ n. (of knife, etc.) острота́; (of voice, etc.) ре́зкость; (of outline, photograph, etc.) чёткость; (astringency) те́рпкость, е́дкость

shatter /ʃætə(r)/ v.t. (breakables, hopes) разб|ива́ть, -и́ть; (of health or nerves) расстр|а́ивать, -о́ить; I was ~ed (BrE, infml, exhausted) я вы́мотался до преде́ла; I was ~ed by the news я был потрясён/уби́т э́той

S

но́востью
● *v.i.* разб|ива́ться, -и́ться

shave /ʃeɪv/ *n.* **1** бритьё; have a ~ побри́ться (*pf.*) **2** (infml, escape): we had a close ~ мы бы́ли на волосо́к от ги́бели
● *v.t.* (*p.p.* **shaved** *or* (*as adj.*) **shaven**): ~ one's chin/beard выбрива́ть, вы́брить подборо́док; брить, по- бо́роду
● *v.i.* (*p.p.* **shaved**) бри́ться, по-; he does not ~ every day он бре́ется не ка́ждый день
▫ ~ **off** *v.t.* сбри|ва́ть, -ть

shaver /ˈʃeɪvə(r)/ *n.* (razor) бри́тва; electric ~ электробри́тва

shaving /ˈʃeɪvɪŋ/ *n.* **1** (action) бритьё **2** (~s) (of wood or metal) стру́жка
■ ~ **brush** *n.* помазо́к; ~ **cream**, ~ **foam** *nn.* крем, пе́на для бритья́

shawl /ʃɔːl/ *n.* шаль

♂ **she** /ʃiː/ *pers. pron.* (*obj.* **her**) она́; ~ **and I** я и она́; мы с ней

sheaf /ʃiːf/ *n.* (*pl.* **sheaves**) (of corn) сноп; ~ **of papers** па́чка/свя́зка бума́г

shear /ʃɪə(r)/ *n.* (*in pl.*) (pair of ~s) (садо́вые) но́жниц|ы (*pl., g.* —)
● *v.t.* (*past* **sheared**) *p.p.* **shorn** *or* **sheared**) (sheep) стри́чь, о-

sheath /ʃiːθ/ *n.* (of weapon) нож|ны́ (-ен); (BrE, condom) презервати́в

sheaves /ʃiːvz/ *pl. of* ▶ **sheaf**

shed[1] /ʃed/ *n.* сара́й; (for aircraft) анга́р

shed[2] /ʃed/ *v.t.* (**shedding**, *past and p.p.* ~) **1** (load, skin) сбр|а́сывать, -о́сить; trees ~ their leaves дере́вья роня́ют ли́стья/ листву́ **2** (blood, tears) прол|ива́ть, -и́ть **3** (diffuse): ~ **light on** (lit., fig.) пролива́ть, проли́ть (*or* бр|оса́ть, -о́сить) свет на + *a.* **4**: ~ **jobs** сокра|ща́ть, -ти́ть рабо́чие места́

sheen /ʃiːn/ *n.* (gloss) лоск; (brightness) блеск, сия́ние

sheep /ʃiːp/ *n.* (*pl.* ~) овца́; (male) бара́н
■ ~**skin** *n.* овчи́на; ове́чья шку́ра; бара́нья ко́жа

sheepish /ˈʃiːpɪʃ/ *adj.* сконфу́женный

sheer /ʃɪə(r)/ *adj.* **1** (absolute) соверше́нный, су́щий, я́вный **2** (precipitous) отве́сный; перпендикуля́рный; a ~ **drop** круто́й обры́в **3** (text., diaphanous) прозра́чный

sheet /ʃiːt/ *n.* **1** (bed linen) простыня́ **2** (flat piece) лист (-ы́); ~ **of water/ice** слой воды́/льда
■ ~ **music** *n.* но́ты (*f. pl.*)

sheikh, **sheik** /ʃeɪk/ *n.* шейх

shelf /ʃelf/ *n.* (*pl.* **shelves**) **1** по́лка; set of shelves стелла́ж **2** (ledge of rock etc.) вы́ступ
■ ~ **life** *n.* срок хране́ния

shell /ʃel/ *n.* **1** (of mollusc etc.) ра́ковина, раку́шка; (of tortoise) па́нцирь (*m.*); (of egg, nut) скорлупа́ **2** (of building) нару́жные сте́ны **3** (of bomb) оболо́чка; (missile) снаря́д
● *v.t.* **1**: ~ **peas** лущи́ть, об- горо́х; ~ **eggs** чи́стить, о- я́йца **2** (bombard) обстре́л|ивать, -я́ть (артиллери́йскими снаря́дами)
▫ ~ **out** (infml) *v.i.* раскоше́ли|ваться, -ться (infml)
● *v.t.* отва́л|ивать, -и́ть (infml)

■ ~**fish** *n.* (mollusc) моллю́ск; (crustacean) ракообра́зное

shelter /ˈʃeltə(r)/ *n.* **1** (protection) укры́тие, защи́та; take ~ **from** укр|ыва́ться, -ы́ться от + *g.* **2** (building etc. providing ~) прию́т, убе́жище; (for homeless people) ночле́жка
● *v.t.* **1** (provide refuge for) приюти́ть (*pf.*) **2** (protect) оберега́ть (*impf.*); защи|ща́ть, -ти́ть
● *v.i.* укр|ыва́ться, -ы́ться; пря́таться, с- (**from**: от + *g.*)

■ ~**ed housing** *n.* (BrE) дома́, обору́дованные необходи́мыми удо́бствами для престаре́лых/ инвали́дов

shelves /ʃelvz/ *pl. of* ▶ **shelf**

shelving /ˈʃelvɪŋ/ *n.* стелла́ж

shepherd /ˈʃepəd/ *n.* пасту́х

sheriff /ˈʃerɪf/ *n.* шери́ф

sherry /ˈʃerɪ/ *n.* хе́рес

Shetland /ˈʃetlənd/ *n.* (in full **the** ~**s** *or* **the** ~ **Islands**) Шетле́ндские острова́ (*m. pl.*)

shield /ʃiːld/ *n.* щит
● *v.t.* заслон|я́ть, -и́ть; защи|ща́ть, -ти́ть; (fig.) огра|жда́ть, -ди́ть

♂ **shift** /ʃɪft/ *n.* **1** (change of position etc.) сдвиг, измене́ние, перемеще́ние **2** (of workers) сме́на; work (in) ~s рабо́тать (*impf.*) посме́нно; he is on the night ~ он рабо́тает в ночну́ю сме́ну
● *v.t.* (move) сме|ща́ть, -сти́ть; дви́|гать, -нуть; (transfer) переме|ща́ть, -сти́ть; (remove) уб|ира́ть, -ра́ть
● *v.i.* переме|ща́ться, -сти́ться
■ ~ **work** *n.* (по)сме́нная рабо́та

shifty /ˈʃɪftɪ/ *adj.* (**shiftier**, **shiftiest**): a ~ fellow ско́льзкий тип; ~ **eyes** бе́гающие гла́зки (*m. pl.*)

Shiite /ˈʃiːaɪt/ *n.* шии́т

shilly-shally /ˈʃɪlɪʃælɪ/ *v.i.* колеба́ться (*impf.*)

shimmer /ˈʃɪmə(r)/ *v.i.* мерца́ть (*impf.*)

shin /ʃɪn/ *n.* го́лень

shin|e /ʃaɪn/ *n.* **1** (brightness) блеск; (gloss) гля́нец, лоск **2** (infml): take a ~e to sb увл|ека́ться, -е́чься кем-н.
● *v.t.* (*past and p.p.* **shined**) **1** (polish) чи́стить, вы́-по-; ~e shoes чи́стить, вы́-по- ту́фли **2**: ~e a light in sb's face осве|ща́ть, -ти́ть фонарём чьё-н. лицо́
● *v.i.* (*past and p.p.* **shone** *or* **shined**) **1** (emit light) свети́ть(ся) (*impf.*); (brightly) сия́ть (*impf.*); the sun ~es со́лнце сия́ет; (fig.): his face shone with happiness его́ лицо́ сия́ло от сча́стья; ~ing eyes сия́ющие глаза́ **2** (glitter) блиста́ть (*impf.*); блес|те́ть, -ну́ть **3** (fig., excel) блиста́ть (*impf.*); блесте́ть (*impf.*); he is a ~ing example of industry он явля́ется собо́й замеча́тельный приме́р трудолю́бия

shingle /ˈʃɪŋ(ə)l/ *n.* (pebbles) га́лька

shingles /ˈʃɪŋ(ə)lz/ *n.* (med.) опоя́сывающий лиша́й

shiny /ˈʃaɪnɪ/ *adj.* (**shinier**, **shiniest**) блестя́щий

S

♂ **ship** /ʃɪp/ *n.* кора́бль (*m.*); су́дно
● *v.t.* (**shipped, shipping**) отпр|авля́ть,
-а́вить
■ ~**building** *n.* судостроéние,
кораблестроéние; ~**owner** *n.* судовладéлец;
~**wreck** *n.* кораблекрушéние ● *v.t.* (*in
pass.*) **be** ~**wrecked** терпéть, по-
кораблекрушéние; ~**yard** *n.* верфь;
судострои́тельный заво́д
shipment /ʃɪpmənt/ *n.* **1** (dispatch) отпра́вка,
отгру́зка **2** (goods shipped) па́ртия това́ра
shipping /ʃɪpɪŋ/ *n.* **1** (transport) перево́зка,
транспортиро́вка **2** (ships) флот
shirk /ʃɜːk/ *v.t.* уклон|я́ться, -и́ться от + *g.*
● *v.i.* лóдырничать (*impf.*)
shirt /ʃɜːt/ *n.* руба́шка; соро́чка
■ ~**sleeve** *n.*: in ~**sleeves** без пиджака́
shirty /ʃɜːtɪ/ *adj.* (**shirtier, shirtiest**) (BrE,
infml): **get** ~ раздраж|а́ться, -и́ться
shit /ʃɪt/ *n.* (vulg.) говно́; (as expletive) чёрт!
shitty /ʃɪtɪ/ *adj.* (**shittier, shittiest**) (vulg.)
говённый, говня́ный; (euph.) дерьмо́вый
shiver /ʃɪvə(r)/ *n.* дрожь; **it gives me the** ~**s
to think of it** от одно́й мы́сли об э́том меня́
броса́ет в дрожь
● *v.i.* дрожа́ть (*impf.*)
shoal /ʃəʊl/ *n.* (of fish) кося́к (*рыб*)
♂ **shock¹** /ʃɒk/ *n.* **1** (violent jar or blow) толчо́к,
уда́р; **I got an electric** ~ меня́ уда́рило тóком
2 (disturbing impression) потрясéние, шок; **the
news gave him a** ~ нóвость потрясла́ его́;
(distressing surprise) уда́р **3** (med.) шок
● *v.t.* **1** (distress): **I was** ~**ed to hear of the
disaster** я был потрясён сообщéнием
о катастро́фе **2** (offend sense of decency)
шоки́ровать (*impf., pf.*)
■ ~ **absorber** *n.* амортиза́тор; ~ **wave** *n.*
взрывна́я волна́
shock² /ʃɒk/ *n.* (of hair) копна́ волóс
shocking /ʃɒkɪŋ/ *adj.* (disturbing) ужаса́ющий;
(scandalous) шоки́рующий, сканда́льный
shod /ʃɒd/ *past and p.p. of* ▶ **shoe**
shoddy /ʃɒdɪ/ *adj.* (**shoddier, shoddiest**)
дрянно́й, некáчественный
shoe /ʃuː/ *n.* **1** ту́фля **2** (*in full* **horse**~)
подкóва
● *v.t.* (**shoes, shoeing,** *past and p.p.* **shod**)
(horse) подкóв|ывать, -а́ть
■ ~**lace** *n.* шнуро́к; ~ **shop** *n.* обувно́й
магази́н
shone /ʃɒn/ *past and p.p. of* ▶ **shine**
shoo /ʃuː/ *v.t.* (**shoos, shooed**) (*often* ~
away, ~ **off**) отпу́г|ивать, -ну́ть
shook /ʃʊk/ *past of* ▶ **shake**
♂ **shoot** /ʃuːt/ *n.* **1** (bot.) росто́к, побéг **2** (~**ing**
expedition) охóта
● *v.t.* (*past and p.p.* **shot**) **1** (discharge, fire):
to ~ **an arrow** пус|ка́ть, -ти́ть стрелу́;
these guns ~ **rubber bullets** э́ти ру́жья
стреля́ют рези́новыми пу́лями **2** (kill)
застрели́ть (*pf.*); (wound) ра́нить (*impf.,
pf.*); **he was shot in the head** пу́ля попáла

ему́ в гóлову **3** (propel): ~ **a bolt** (on door)
задв|ига́ть, -и́нуть засо́в **4** (cin., film, scene)
сн|има́ть, -я́ть, засня́ть (*pf.*) (*фильм, эпизод*)
● *v.i.* (*past and p.p.* **shot**) **1** (fire, of person
or weapon) стреля́ть (*impf.*) (**at:** в + *a.*);
he was shot at twice в негó два́жды
стреля́ли **2** (dart) прон|оси́ться, -ести́сь;
he shot out of the doorway он вы́скочил из
подъéзда; **a** ~**ing pain** стреля́ющая боль; **a**
~**ing star** пáдающая звездá **3** (football etc.)
бить (*impf.*) по мячу́
□ ~ **down** *v.t.*: **we shot down five enemy
aircraft** мы сби́ли пять самолётов проти́вника
□ ~ **up** *v.i.* (of prices etc.) подск|áкивать, -очи́ть;
(sl., inject drugs) ширя́ться, на-
■ ~**-out** *n.* (infml) перестрéлка
shooting /ʃuːtɪŋ/ *n.* (marksmanship; attack)
стрельбá; (hunting) охóта
■ ~ **range** *n.* тир; (outdoor) стрéльбище,
полигóн
♂ **shop** /ʃɒp/ *n.* **1** магази́н; (small ~) лáвка;
talk ~ разговáривать/говори́ть (*both impf.*)
о (свои́х профессионáльных) делáх
2 (work~) мастерскáя, цех; **on the** ~ **floor**
(BrE) в цéху/цéхе
● *v.i.* (**shopped, shopping**) дéлать, с-
покýпки; **she** ~**ped around** онá ходи́ла по
магази́нам и прицéнивалась
■ ~ **assistant** *n.* (BrE) продав|éц (-щи́ца);
~**keeper** *n.* владé|лец (-ица) магази́на;
~**lifter** *n.* магази́нный вор; ~**lifting**
n. воровствó в магази́нах; магази́нная
крáжа; ~**soiled** (BrE), ~**worn** (AmE) *adjs.*
залежáвшийся; ~ **window** *n.* витри́на
shopper /ʃɒpə(r)/ *n.* покупáтель (-ница)
shopping /ʃɒpɪŋ/ *n.* покýпки (*f. pl.*); **do
one's** ~ дéлать, с- покýпки
■ ~ **bag** *n.* хозя́йственная сýмка; ~ **centre** *n.*
торгóвый центр
shore¹ /ʃɔː(r)/ *n.* бéрег; **on the** ~ на берегý
shore² /ʃɔː(r)/ *v.t.*: ~ **up** подп|ирáть, -ерéть;
крепи́ть (*impf.*)
shorn /ʃɔːn/ *p.p. of* ▶ **shear**
♂ **short** /ʃɔːt/ *n.* **1** (~ film) короткометрáжный
фильм **2** (BrE, ~ drink) крéпкий напи́ток
● *adj.* **1** корóткий; (of duration) крáткий,
недóлгий; (of stature) невысóкого рóста;
(small) небольшóй; **this dress is too** ~ э́то
плáтье сли́шком корóтко; **the days are
getting** ~**er** дни станóвятся корóче; **a** ~
time ago недáвно; **at** ~ **range** с бли́зкого
расстоя́ния; **make** ~ **work of sth** бы́стро
расправ|ля́ться, -áвиться с чем-н.;
I want my hair cut ~ я хочý корóтко
постри́чься **2** (brief): **in** ~ корóче говоря́;
(одни́м) слóвом; **for** ~ сокращённо; **for**
крáткости **3** (curt, sharp) рéзкий **4** (insufficient):
in ~ **supply** дефици́тный; **I am 2 pounds** ~
мне не хватáет двух фýнтов **5**: **be** ~ **of sth**
(lacking) испы́тывать (*impf.*) недостáток в
чём-н.; **be** ~ **of breath** запыхáться (*impf.*)
6: ~ **of** (except) крóме + *g.* **7** (of pastry)
рассы́пчатый, песóчный
● *adv.* **1** (abruptly): **he stopped** ~ он вдруг
останови́лся; (while speaking) он вдруг
замолчáл **2** ~ **of** (without reaching): **fall** ~ **of a**

target не дост|игать, -и́чь це́ли; **we ran ~ of potatoes** у нас ко́нчилась карто́шка

■ **~bread, ~cake** nn. песо́чное пече́нье; **~-change** v.t. (infml) обсчи́т|ывать, -а́ть; **~ circuit** n. коро́ткое замыка́ние; **~-circuit** v.t. зам|ыка́ть, -кну́ть на́коротко; **~coming** n. недоста́ток; ■ **~ cut** n. (route) кратча́йший путь; **~fall** n. недоста́ток, дефици́т; **~hand** n. стеногра́фия; **~hand typist** (BrE) стенографи́стка; **~list** n. шорт-ли́ст, коро́ткий спи́сок кандида́тов, соиска́телей u m. n. ● v.t. зан|оси́ть, -ести́ в шорт-ли́ст (or коро́ткий спи́сок); **~-lived** adj. недолгове́чный, мимолётный; **~-range** adj. (of gun) с небольшо́й да́льностью стрельбы́; (of missile) бли́жнего де́йствия; (of forecast) краткосро́чный; **~-sighted** adj. (lit., fig.) близору́кий; **~-sleeved** adj. (shirt) с коро́ткими рукава́ми; **~-staffed** adj. страда́ющий недоста́тком рабо́тников; **~ story** n. расска́з; **~-term** adj. краткосро́чный; **~-wave** adj. коротковолно́вый

shortage /ˈʃɔːtɪdʒ/ n. недоста́ток, нехва́тка, дефици́т

shorten /ˈʃɔːt(ə)n/ v.t. & i. укор|а́чивать(ся), -оти́ть(ся)

shortly /ˈʃɔːtlɪ/ adv. **1** (soon) ско́ро; **~ before** незадо́лго + g.; **~ after** вско́ре по́сле + g. **2** (sharply) ре́зко

shorts /ʃɔːts/ n. pl. (short trousers) шо́рты (pl., g. —/ -о́в); (AmE, underpants) трус|ы́ (pl., g. -о́в)

♂ **shot**[1] /ʃɒt/ n. **1** (discharge of firearm) вы́стрел; **take a ~ at** вы́стрелить (pf.) в + a. or по + d. **2** (stroke, at games etc.) уда́р **3** (of person) стрело́к; **he's a good ~** он хоро́ший стрело́к **4** (phot.) сни́мок; (cin.) кадр **5** (small dose): **~ of liquor** глото́к спиртно́го; (injection) уко́л

■ **~gun** n. дробови́к; **~-put(ting)** n. (sport) толка́ние ядра́

shot[2] /ʃɒt/ past and p.p. of ▶ shoot

♂ **should** /ʃʊd/ v. aux. **1** (conditional): **I ~ say** я бы сказа́л; **I ~ have thought so** на́до полага́ть; каза́лось бы; **~ he die** (в слу́чае) е́сли он умрёт; **I ~n't think so** не ду́маю **2** (expr. duty): **you ~ tell him** вы должны́ ему́ сказа́ть **3** (expr. probability or expectation): **we ~ be there by noon** мы должны́ поспе́ть туда́ к полу́дню; **how ~ I know?** отку́да мне знать? **4** (expr. purpose): **he suggested that I ~ go** он предложи́л мне уйти́

♂ **shoulder** /ˈʃəʊldə(r)/ n. плечо́
● v.t.: (lit.): **~ a heavy load** взва́л|ивать, -и́ть на себя́ тяжёлый груз; (fig.): **~ responsibility** брать, взять на себя́ отве́тственность

■ **~ blade** n. лопа́тка

shouldn't /ˈʃʊd(ə)nt/ neg. of ▶ should

shout /ʃaʊt/ n. крик
● v.t. выкри́к|ивать, вы́крикнуть
● v.i. кр|ича́ть, -и́кнуть; **don't ~ at me** не кричи́те на меня́; **~ for help** звать, по- на по́мощь

□ **~ down** v.t.: **he was ~ed down** его́ слова́

бы́ли заглушены́ кри́ком/кри́ками

□ **~ out** v.t. выкри́кивать, вы́крикнуть
● v.i. закрича́ть (pf.)

shove /ʃʌv/ n. толчо́к; **give sb a ~** пихну́ть/толкну́ть (pf.) кого́-н.
● v.t. толк|а́ть, -ну́ть; **~ sth into one's pocket** сова́ть, су́нуть что-н. себе́ в карма́н; **he ~d his way forward** он проти́снулся вперёд

□ **~ aside, ~ away** vv.t. отт|а́лкивать, -олкну́ть

shovel /ˈʃʌv(ə)l/ n. лопа́та; (mechanical) экскава́тор
● v.t. (**shovelled, shovelling**, AmE **shoveled, shoveling**): **~ snow off a path** сгре|ба́ть, -сти́ снег с доро́жки; расч|ища́ть, -и́стить доро́жку от сне́га

♂ **show** /ʃəʊ/ n. **1** (manifestation): **make a ~ of force** демонстри́ровать, про- си́лу; (semblance) ви́димость **2** (exhibition) пока́з, вы́ставка; шо́у; **for ~** для ви́ду; напока́з; (ostentation) пы́шность, пара́дность **3** (entertainment) представле́ние; шо́у
● v.t. (p.p. **shown** or **showed**) **1** (disclose, reveal, offer for inspection) пока́з|ывать, -а́ть; **this dress will not ~ the dirt** на э́том пла́тье грязь не бу́дет заме́тна; **he has nothing to ~ for his efforts** он зря стара́лся; **~ oneself** (appear) появ|ля́ться, -и́ться; пока́з|ываться, -а́ться **2** (exhibit publicly) выставля́ть, вы́ставить; (a film) пок|а́зывать, -аза́ть **3** (display) проявля́ть, -и́ть; демонстри́ровать, про- **4** (point out) ука́з|ывать, -а́ть на + a.; (demonstrate) пок|а́зывать, -аза́ть; **he ~ed me how to play** он показа́л мне, как игра́ть; (explain) объясн|я́ть, -и́ть **5** (conduct) прово|жа́ть, -ди́ть; **he ~ed me to the door** он проводи́л меня́ до две́ри
● v.i. (p.p. **shown** or **showed**) **1** (be visible) видне́ться (impf.); **the stain will not ~** пятно́ не бу́дет заме́тно **2** (be exhibited): **what films are ~ing?** каки́е фи́льмы пока́зывают/иду́т?

□ **~ in** v.t. вв|оди́ть, -ести́/пров|оди́ть, -ести́ в ко́мнату/дом

□ **~ off** v.t. (display to advantage) вы́годно подчёркивать (impf.); **the frame ~s off the picture** в э́той ра́мке карти́на подчёркнута хорошо́ (impf.) напока́з, щеголя́ть (impf.) + i.
● v.i. рисова́ться (impf.)

□ **~ out** v.t. пров|оди́ть, -ести́ к вы́ходу

□ **~ up** v.t. (make conspicuous) выделя́ть, вы́делить
● v.i. (infml, appear) появ|ля́ться, -и́ться; (be conspicuous): **the flowers ~ed up against the white background** цветы́ выделя́лись на бе́лом фо́не

■ **~ business** n. шо́у-би́знес; **~case** n. витри́на; **~down** n. про́ба сил; оконча́тельная прове́рка; **~jumping** n. конку́р; **~-off** n. позёр (-ка); хвасту́н (-ья) (infml); **~room** n. демонстрацио́нный зал

shower /ˈʃaʊə(r)/ n. **1** (of rain/snow) кратковре́менный дождь/снег **2** (for washing oneself) душ; **take a ~** прин|има́ть, -я́ть душ

● *v.t.* **1** (with water etc.) зал|ива́ть, -и́ть **2** (with bullets etc.) ос|ыпа́ть, -ы́пать гра́дом (*пуль и m. n.*)

● *v.i.* прин|има́ть, -я́ть душ

showery /ˈʃaʊərɪ/ *adj.* дождли́вый

shown /ʃəʊn/ *p.p. of* ▶ show

showy /ˈʃəʊɪ/ *adj.* (**showier, showiest**) я́ркий, бро́ский

shrank /ʃræŋk/ *past of* ▶ shrink

shrapnel /ˈʃræpn(ə)l/ *n.* шрапне́ль

shred /ʃred/ *n.* **1** (of cloth) клочо́к; tear to ~s раз|рыва́ть, -орва́ть в кло́чья **2** (fig., bit): not a ~ of evidence ни мале́йших доказа́тельств; not a ~ of truth ни ка́пли пра́вды

● *v.t.* (**shredded, shredding**) (tear) раз|рыва́ть, -орва́ть; (cut) разр|еза́ть, -е́зать

shredder /ˈʃredə(r)/ *n.* (for documents) маши́на для уничтоже́ния бума́ги

shrew /ʃruː/ *n.* (zool.) землеро́йка; (woman) сварли́вая же́нщина

shrewd /ʃruːd/ *adj.* проница́тельный

shriek /ʃriːk/ *n.* визг; ~s of laughter визгли́вый смех

● *v.i.* визжа́ть (*impf.*); взви́зг|ивать, -нуть

shrill /ʃrɪl/ *adj.* пронзи́тельный

shrimp /ʃrɪmp/ *n.* креве́тка

shrine /ʃraɪn/ *n.* (tomb) гробни́ца; (chapel) часо́вня; (lit., fig., hallowed place) святы́ня, храм

shrink /ʃrɪŋk/ *v.t.* (*past* **shrank**, *p.p.* **shrunk** *or esp. as adj.* **shrunken**): hot water will ~ this fabric от горя́чей воды́ э́тот материа́л ся́дет

● *v.i.* (*past* **shrank**, *p.p.* **shrunk**) **1** (of clothes) сади́ться, сесть; (of wood) сс|ыха́ться, -о́хнуться **2** (grow smaller) сокра|ща́ться, -ти́ться **3** (recoil) отпря́нуть (*pf.*); he shrank (back) from the fire он отпря́нул от огня́

shrivel /ˈʃrɪv(ə)l/ *v.t.* (**shrivelled, shrivelling**, AmE **shriveled, shriveling**) (dry up) высу́шивать, вы́сушить; (wrinkle) мо́рщить, с-

● *v.i.* (**shrivelled, shrivelling**, AmE **shriveled, shriveling**) (dry up) высыха́ть, вы́сохнуть; (wrinkle up) смо́рщи|ваться, -ться

shroud /ʃraʊd/ *n.* са́ван

● *v.t.* оку́т|ывать, -ать

Shrove Tuesday /ʃrəʊv/ *n.* вто́рник на Ма́сленой неде́ле

shrub /ʃrʌb/ *n.* (bot.) куст

shrubbery /ˈʃrʌbərɪ/ *n.* куста́рник; уча́сток са́да, заса́женный куста́рником

shrug /ʃrʌɡ/ *n.*: with a ~ (of the shoulders) пожа́в плеча́ми

● *v.t. & i.* (**shrugged, shrugging**): ~ (one's shoulders) пож|има́ть, -а́ть плеча́ми; ~ sth off отм|а́хиваться, -ахну́ться от чего́-н.

shrunk /ʃrʌŋk/ *p.p. of* ▶ shrink

shrunken /ˈʃrʌŋk(ə)n/ *adj.* (*p.p. of* ▶ shrink) (old person; body, face) иссо́хший, высо́хший (infml)

shudder /ˈʃʌdə(r)/ *n.* дрожь

● *v.i.* дрожа́ть, за-; содрог|а́ться, -ну́ться

---

shuffle /ˈʃʌf(ə)l/ *v.t.* **1**: ~ one's feet ша́ркать (*impf.*) нога́ми **2**: ~ cards тасова́ть, пере-; ка́рты

● *v.i.*: ~ along, about волочи́ть (*impf.*) но́ги

shun /ʃʌn/ *v.t.* (**shunned, shunning**) избега́ть (*impf.*) + g.

shunt /ʃʌnt/ *v.t.* (rail.) перев|оди́ть, -ести́ (*поезд, вагон*)

● *v.i.* маневри́ровать (*impf.*)

✧ **shut** /ʃʌt/ *v.t.* (**shutting**, *past and p.p.* ~) закр|ыва́ть, -ы́ть

● *v.i.* (**shutting**, *past and p.p.* ~) закр|ыва́ться, -ы́ться

□ ~ **down** *v.t.* закр|ыва́ть, -ы́ть; (comput.) выключа́ть, вы́ключить; заверш|а́ть, -и́ть рабо́ту

● *v.i.* закр|ыва́ться, -ы́ться

□ ~ **off** *v.t.* (stop supply of) отключ|а́ть, -и́ть

□ ~ **out** *v.t.* (exclude) исключ|а́ть, -и́ть; ~ out light/noise не пропус|ка́ть, -ти́ть све́та/шу́ма

□ ~ **up** *v.t.* (close) зап|ира́ть, -ере́ть; their house is ~ up for the winter дом у них заколо́чен на́ зиму; (confine): the boy was ~ up in his room ма́льчик был за́перт в ко́мнате; (silence): they soon ~ him up они́ ско́ро заста́вили его́ замолча́ть

● *v.i.* (be, become silent): ~ up! замолчи́!, закни́сь! (infml)

■ ~**down** *n.* закры́тие; (comput.) выключе́ние, заверше́ние рабо́ты

shutter /ˈʃʌtə(r)/ *n.* **1** (on window) ста́вень (*m.*) **2** (phot.) затво́р

shuttle /ˈʃʌt(ə)l/ *n.*: ~ service регуля́рное движе́ние/сообще́ние

● *v.i.* снова́ть (*impf.*)

■ ~**cock** *n.* вола́н

shy /ʃaɪ/ *adj.* (**shyer, shyest**) (bashful) засте́нчивый; (timid) ро́бкий

● *v.i.* (of person): ~ away from sth шара́х|аться, -нуться от чего́-н.

Siamese /saɪəˈmiːz/ *n.* (*pl.* ~) (*also* ~ **cat**) сиа́мская ко́шка

● *adj.* сиа́мский

■ ~ **twins** *n. pl.* сиа́мские близнецы́ (*m. pl.*)

Siberia /saɪˈbɪərɪə/ *n.* Сиби́рь

Siberian /saɪˈbɪərɪən/ *n.* сибиря́|к (-чка)

● *adj.* сиби́рский

sibling /ˈsɪblɪŋ/ *n.* (brother) родно́й брат; (sister) родна́я сестра́

✧ **sick** /sɪk/ *adj.* **1** (unwell) больно́й **2** (nauseated): I feel ~ меня́ тошни́т/мути́т; he was ~ его́ вы́рвало **3** ~ of: I am ~ to death of her она́ мне надое́ла до́ смерти **4** (morbid) ме́рзкий, жу́ткий; ~ joke ме́рзкий анекдо́т

■ ~**bay** *n.* лазаре́т; ~ **leave** *n.* о́тпуск по боле́зни; he is on ~ leave он на больни́чном (infml); ~ **pay** *n.* опла́та по больни́чному листу́

sicken /ˈsɪkən/ *v.t.* (fig., disgust) вызыва́ть, вы́звать отвраще́ние у (*кого*); ~**ing** отврати́тельный, проти́вный

● *v.i.* (become ill) забол|ева́ть, -е́ть; he is ~**ing** for influenza (BrE) он заболева́ет гри́ппом

sickle /ˈsɪk(ə)l/ *n.* серп

sickly /ˈsɪklɪ/ *adj.* (**sicklier, sickliest**)
(unhealthy) боле́зненный; (inducing nausea)
тошнотво́рный

sickness /ˈsɪknɪs/ *n.* (ill health) нездоро́вье;
(nausea) тошнота́

⚲ **side** /saɪd/ *n.* **1** сторона́; **on the right/left**
~ с пра́вой/с ле́вой стороны́; спра́ва/
сле́ва; **on the** ~ (infml, additionally, illicitly) на
стороне́ **2** (edge) край; **by the** ~ **of the lake**
на берегу́ о́зера; **on the** ~ **of the mountain**
на скло́не горы́ **3** (of room, table) коне́ц **4** (of
the body) бок; **at my** ~ ря́дом со мной; **they
were standing** ~ **by** ~ они́ стоя́ли бок о́
бок/ря́дом **5** (of a building) бокова́я стена́; ~
entrance боково́й вход **6** (aspect) сторона́;
I can see the funny ~ **of the affair** мне
очеви́дна смешна́я сторона́ (де́ла) **7** (party)
сторона́; **take** ~s **with sb** прин|има́ть,
-я́ть (*or* ста|нови́ться, -ть на) чью-н.
сто́рону **8** (BrE, team) кома́нда **9** (*attr.*)
боково́й
● *v.i.:* ~ **with sb** ста|нови́ться, -ть на чью-н.
сто́рону
■ ~**board** *n.* буфе́т, серва́нт; ~**boards** (Br)
(*also* ~**burns**) *n. pl.* (infml) бакенба́рды
(*pl., g.* —); ~ **effect** *n.* побо́чное де́йствие;
~**line** *n.* (work) побо́чная рабо́та; (goods)
неходово́й това́р ● *v.t.* оттесн|я́ть -и́ть на
за́дний план; ~**long** *adj.* косо́й; ~ **plate**
n. ма́ленькая таре́лка; ~**show** *n.* (at fair)
аттракцио́н; ~**step** *v.t.* (fig.) уклон|я́ться,
-и́ться от + *g.*; ~ **street** *n.* переу́лок;
~**track** *v.t.* (distract): **I meant to finish the job,
but I was** ~**tracked** я собира́лся зако́нчить
(э́ту) рабо́ту, но меня́ отвлекли́; ~**walk** *n.*
(AmE) тротуа́р; ~**ways** *adj.* боково́й ● *adv.*
(to one ~) вбок; (of motion) бо́ком

siding /ˈsaɪdɪŋ/ *n.* (rail.) запа́сный путь

sidle /ˈsaɪd(ə)l/ *v.i.:* ~ **up to sb** под|ходи́ть,
-ойти́ к кому́-н. бочко́м

siege /siːdʒ/ *n.* оса́да, блока́да; **lay** ~ **to**
оса|жда́ть, -ди́ть

siesta /sɪˈestə/ *n.* сие́ста

sieve /sɪv/ *n.* си́то
● *v.t.* просе́|ивать, -ять

sift /sɪft/ *v.t.* просе́|ивать, -ять; (fig.): ~ **the facts**
тща́тельно рассм|а́тривать, -отре́ть фа́кты

sigh /saɪ/ *n.* вздох
● *v.i.* взд|ыха́ть, -охну́ть

⚲ **sight** /saɪt/ *n.* **1** (faculty) зре́ние **2** (seeing,
being seen) вид; **I can't bear the** ~ **of him** я
его́ ви́деть не могу́; **catch** ~ **of** зам|еча́ть,
-е́тить; **lose** ~ **of** теря́ть, по- из ви́ду; **at first**
~ с пе́рвого взгля́да; на пе́рвый взгляд;
(range of vision): **come into** ~ пока́з|ываться,
-а́ться; появ|ля́ться, -и́ться; **in** ~ на виду́;
keep out of ~ не пока́з|ываться, -а́ть(ся)
(на глаза́); **he would not let her out of his**
~ он с неё глаз не спуска́л **3** (spectacle)
вид, зре́лище; **a** ~ **for sore eyes** (infml)
прия́тное зре́лище; **see the** ~s осм|а́тривать,
-отре́ть достопримеча́тельности **4** (aiming
device) прице́л; **he set his** ~s **on becoming a
professor** он ме́тил в профессора́ (infml)
● *v.t.* (spot) зам|еча́ть, -е́тить; ви́деть, у-

■ ~**seeing** *n.* осмо́тр
достопримеча́тельностей; ~**seer** *n.* тури́ст
(-ка); экскурса́нт (-ка)

⚲ **sign** /saɪn/ *n.* **1** (mark; gesture) знак; (symbol)
си́мвол; **plus/minus/equals** ~ знак плюс/
ми́нус/ра́венства **2** (indication) при́знак;
there's still no ~ **of him** его́ всё нет и нет
3 (board with information) вы́веска; **road/traffic**
~ доро́жный знак
● *v.t. & i.* подпи́с|ывать(ся), -а́ть(ся);
распи́с|ываться, -а́ться
□ ~ **on** *v.i.* (BrE, as unemployed) регистри́роваться,
за- в спи́сках безрабо́тных; (*also* ~ **up**)
(register) регистри́роваться, за-
● *v.t. & i.* (for job) нан|има́ться, -я́ть(ся)
■ ~ **language** *n.* язы́к же́стов; ~**post** *n.*
указа́тель (*m.*)

⚲ **signal** /ˈsɪɡn(ə)l/ *n.* (also as needed for mobile phone
to work) сигна́л
● *v.i.* (**signalled, signalling**, AmE
signaled, signaling) сигнализи́ровать
(*impf., pf.*)

signatory /ˈsɪɡnətərɪ/ *n.* подписа́вшийся
● *adj.:* ~ **powers** держа́вы, подписа́вшие
догово́р

signature /ˈsɪɡnətʃə(r)/ *n.* **1** по́дпись
2 (mus.): ~ **tune** (BrE) (музыка́льная)
заста́вка

signet /ˈsɪɡnɪt/ *n.* печа́тка
■ ~ **ring** *n.* кольцо́ с печа́ткой

significance /sɪɡˈnɪfɪkəns/ *n.* значе́ние

⚲ **significant** /sɪɡˈnɪfɪk(ə)nt/ *adj.* значи́тельный;
(important) ва́жный

signify /ˈsɪɡnɪfaɪ/ *v.t.* означа́ть (*impf.*)

Sikh /siːk/ *n.* сикх
● *adj.* си́кхский

Sikhism /ˈsiːkɪz(ə)m/ *n.* сикхи́зм

silage /ˈsaɪlɪdʒ/ *n.* си́лос

silence /ˈsaɪləns/ *n.* молча́ние; тишина́; **in** ~ в
молча́нии/тишине́; мо́лча
● *v.t.* заст|авля́ть, -а́вить замолча́ть

silencer /ˈsaɪlənsə(r)/ *n.* глуши́тель (*m.*)

silent /ˈsaɪlənt/ *adj.* (saying nothing)
безмо́лвный; **keep** ~ молча́ть (*impf.*);
(taciturn) молчали́вый; **fall, become** ~
замолча́ть (*pf.*); умолка́ть, умо́лкнуть;
(mute): ~ **film** немо́й фильм

silhouette /sɪluːˈet/ *n.* силуэ́т

silicon /ˈsɪlɪkən/ *n.:* ~ **chip** кре́мниевый чип

silicone /ˈsɪlɪkəʊn/ *n.* силико́н; (*attr.*)
силико́новый

silk /sɪlk/ *n.* шёлк; (*attr.*) шёлковый

silky /ˈsɪlkɪ/ *adj.* (**silkier, silkiest**)
шелкови́стый

sill /sɪl/ *n.* подоко́нник

silly /ˈsɪlɪ/ *adj.* (**sillier, silliest**) глу́пый

silo /ˈsaɪləʊ/ *n.* (*pl.* ~**s**) (tower; pit on farm)
си́лосная ба́шня/я́ма; (for missile) ста́ртовая
ша́хта (*ракеты*)

silt /sɪlt/ *n.* ил
● *v.t. & i.* (*usu.* ~ **up**) зай|ли́|вать(ся), -ть(ся)

S

silver /'sɪlvə(r)/ *n.* **1** (metal; silverware) серебро́ **2** (colour) сере́бряный цвет
• *adj.* (made of ~) сере́бряный; (resembling ~) серебри́стый
■ ~ **birch** *n.* бе́лая берёза; ~ **paper** *n.* (BrE) фольга́

silvery /'sɪlvərɪ/ *adj.* серебри́стый

SIM /sɪm/ (*in full* **SIM card**) *n.* сим-ка́рта, SIM-ка́рта

⚷ **similar** /'sɪmɪlə(r)/ *adj.* **1** (alike) схо́дный, похо́жий **2**: ~ **to** похо́жий на + *a.*; подо́бный + *d.*

similarity /sɪmɪ'lærɪtɪ/ *n.* схо́дство

similarly /'sɪmɪləlɪ/ *adv.* так же

simile /'sɪmɪlɪ/ *n.* сравне́ние

simmer /'sɪmə(r)/ *v.i.* кипе́ть (*impf.*) на ме́дленном огне́; (fig.): ~ **with indignation** кипе́ть (*impf.*) негодова́нием; ~ **down** (fig.) успок|а́иваться, -о́иться

simper /'sɪmpə(r)/ *n.* жема́нная улы́бка
• *v.i.* жема́нно улыб|а́ться, -ну́ться

⚷ **simple** /'sɪmp(ə)l/ *adj.* (**simpler**, **simplest**) **1** просто́й **2** (easy) лёгкий

simpleton /'sɪmp(ə)lt(ə)n/ *n.* проста́к

simplicity /sɪm'plɪsɪtɪ/ *n.* простота́

simplification /sɪmplɪfɪ'keɪʃ(ə)n/ *n.* упроще́ние

simplify /'sɪmplɪfaɪ/ *v.t.* упро|ща́ть, -сти́ть

simplistic /sɪm'plɪstɪk/ *adj.* (чрезме́рно) упрощённый

⚷ **simply** /'sɪmplɪ/ *adv.* про́сто; **the weather was ~ dreadful** пого́да была́ про́сто ужа́сная

simulate /'sɪmjʊleɪt/ *v.t.* (feeling etc.) изобра|жа́ть, -зи́ть, симули́ровать (*impf., pf.*); (leather, stone) и|мити́ровать, сы-; (conditions) модели́ровать, с-

simulation /sɪmjʊ'leɪʃ(ə)n/ *n.* симуля́ция; (of conditions) модели́рование

simulator /'sɪmjʊleɪtə(r)/ *n.* (person) симуля́нт, притво́рщик; (device) модели́рующее/имити́рующее устро́йство; **flight** ~ пилота́жный тренажёр

simultaneous /sɪməl'teɪnɪəs/ *adj.* одновре́ме́нный

S

sin /sɪn/ *n.* грех
• *v.i.* (**sinned**, **sinning**) греши́ть, со-

⚷ **since** /sɪns/ *adv.* с тех пор; **the house has ~ been rebuilt** с тех пор (*or* поздне́е) дом перестро́или
• *prep.* с + *g.*; **nothing has happened ~ Christmas** с Рождества́ ничего́ не произошло́; ~ **yesterday** со вчера́шнего дня
• *conj.* **1** (from, during the time when): **how long is it ~ we last met?** ско́лько вре́мени прошло́ с на́шей после́дней встре́чи?; **I have moved house ~ I saw you** с тех пор как мы с ва́ми (после́дний раз) ви́делись, я перее́хал **2** (seeing that) так как, поско́льку; ~ **you ask** е́сли хоти́те знать

sincere /sɪn'sɪə(r)/ *adj.* (**sincerer**, **sincerest**) и́скренний; **yours ~ly** и́скренне Ваш

sincerity /sɪn'serɪtɪ/ *n.* и́скренность

sinew /'sɪnjuː/ *n.* сухожи́лие

sinful /'sɪnfʊl/ *adj.* гре́шный

⚷ **sing** /sɪŋ/ *v.t.* (*past* **sang**, *p.p.* **sung**) петь, с-; (fig.): ~ **sb's praises** восхваля́ть (*impf.*) кого́-н.
• *v.i.* (*past* **sang**, *p.p.* **sung**) петь, с-

Singapore /sɪŋə'pɔː(r)/ *n.* Сингапу́р

Singaporean /sɪŋə'pɔːrɪən/ *n.* сингапу́р|ец (-ка)
• *adj.* сингапу́рский

singe /sɪndʒ/ *v.t.* (**singeing**) пали́ть, о-; (slightly) подпа́л|ивать, -и́ть

singer /'sɪŋə(r)/ *n.* пев|е́ц (-и́ца)

singing /'sɪŋɪŋ/ *n.* пе́ние

⚷ **single** /'sɪŋg(ə)l/ *n.* (BrE, ticket) биле́т в оди́н коне́ц; (CD, vinyl) сингл; (*in pl.*) (of tennis etc.) одино́чная игра́; одино́чный разря́д
• *adj.* **1** (one) оди́н; (only one) еди́нственный, еди́ный; **in ~ file** гусько́м **2** (unmarried) одино́кий; (man) холосто́й; (woman) незаму́жняя
• *v.t.* ~ **out**: **he was ~d out** его́ вы́делили
■ ~ **bed** *n.* односпа́льная крова́ть; **~-handed** *adj. & adv.* без посторо́нней по́мощи; **~-minded** *adj.* целеустремлённый; ~ **mother** *n.* мать-одино́чка; ~ **parent** *n.* роди́тель-одино́чка; ~ **room** *n.* (in hotel) одноме́стный но́мер; **~-sex** *adj.*: **~-sex school** шко́ла разде́льного обуче́ния

singlet /'sɪŋglɪt/ *n.* (BrE) ма́йка

singular /'sɪŋgjʊlə(r)/ *n.* (gram.) еди́нственное число́
• *adj.*: ~ **noun** существи́тельное в еди́нственном числе́

sinister /'sɪnɪstə(r)/ *adj.* злове́щий

sink /sɪŋk/ *n.* (in kitchen etc.) ра́ковина
• *v.t.* (*past* **sank** *or* **sunk**, *p.p.* **sunk**) **1**: ~ **a ship** топи́ть, по-/за- су́дно **2** (plunge) вби|ва́ть, -ть; (fig.): **the dog sank its teeth into his leg** соба́ка вонзи́ла зу́бы ему́ в но́гу **3** (excavate): ~ **a well** рыть, вы- коло́дец
• *v.i.* (*past* **sank** *or* **sunk**, *p.p.* **sunk** *or as adj.* **sunken**) **1** (in water etc.) тону́ть, у-; (of objects) тону́ть, за-; **the ship sank** су́дно затону́ло **2** (below the horizon) за|ходи́ть, -йти́; **the sun ~s in the west** со́лнце захо́дит на за́паде **3** (subside, of water) спа|да́ть, -сть; (of building or soil) ос|еда́ть, -е́сть **4** (get lower) па́дать, упа́сть; **his voice sank** он пони́зил го́лос **5** (fall): **I sank into a deep sleep** я погрузи́лся в глубо́кий сон; (fig.): **my heart sank** (with a sudden shock) у меня́ се́рдце оборва́ло́сь; **his heart sank when he saw how much he had to do** ему́ ста́ло ду́рно, когда́ он уви́дел, ско́лько ему́ предстоя́ло сде́лать **6** (penetrate) впи́т|ываться, -а́ться; (fig.): **his words sank in** его́ слова́ дошли́ до меня́ *и т. п.*

sinner /'sɪnə(r)/ *n.* гре́шни|к (-ца)

sinus /'saɪnəs/ *n.* па́зуха

sinusitis /saɪnə'saɪtɪs/ *n.* (med.) синуси́т

sip /sɪp/ *n.* глото́к
• *v.t.* (**sipped**, **sipping**) потя́гивать (*impf.*)

⚷ ключевая лексика

siphon, syphon /'saɪf(ə)n/ *n.* сифо́н (*трубка для переливания жидкостей*)
● *v.t.*: ~ **off, out** выка́чивать, вы́качать сифо́ном

sir /sɜː(r)/ *n.* (form of address; title) сэр, господи́н; **Dear S~** (in letters) Уважа́емый господи́н

siren /'saɪərən/ *n.* сире́на

sirloin /'sɜːlɔɪn/ *n.* филе́ (*nt. indecl.*) (*говядины*)

♂ **sister** /'sɪstə(r)/ *n.* сестра́; (BrE, nursing ~) ста́ршая медици́нская сестра́
■ ~**-in-law** *n.* (brother's wife) неве́стка; (husband's sister) золо́вка; (wife's sister) своя́ченица

sisterly /'sɪstəlɪ/ *adj.* сё́стринский

♂ **sit** /sɪt/ *v.t.* (**sitting**, *past and p.p.* **sat**) (BrE): ~ **an examination** сдава́ть (*impf.*) экза́мен
● *v.i.* (**sitting**, *past and p.p.* **sat**) **1** (take a seat) сади́ться, сесть **2** (be seated) сиде́ть (*impf.*); **he can't ~ still** ему́ не сиди́тся (на ме́сте); ~ **on a committee** бы́ть чле́ном комите́та **3** (pose): ~ **for an artist** пози́ровать (*impf.*) худо́жнику; ~ **for one's photograph** фотографи́роваться, с- **4** (be in session) заседа́ть (*impf.*); **the committee ~s at 10** заседа́ние комите́та начина́ется в 10 (часо́в)
□ ~ **down** *v.i.* сади́ться, сесть
□ ~ **in** *v.i.*: ~ **in on a meeting** прису́тствовать (*impf.*) на собра́нии
□ ~ **up** *v.i.* (from lying position): **he sat up in bed** он приподня́лся и сел в посте́ли/крова́ти; (straighten one's back) сиде́ть (*impf.*) пря́мо
■ ~**ting duck** (also ~**ting target**) *n.* (fig.) лё́гкая добы́ча/мише́нь

sitcom /'sɪtkɒm/ *n.* (infml) коме́дия положе́ний (*комедийный сериал с участием одних и тех же героев в разных ситуациях*)

♂ **site** /saɪt/ *n.* (place) ме́сто; (position) положе́ние; (location) местоположе́ние

sitter /'sɪtə(r)/ *n.* **1** (person sitting for portrait) моде́ль; **she was his ~ many times** она́ мно́го раз ему́ пози́ровала; (paid one) нату́рщи|к (-ца) **2** (baby~) ≈ приходя́щая ня́ня

sitting /'sɪtɪŋ/ *n.* (of assembly) заседа́ние; (for serving meals) сме́на
■ ~ **room** *n.* (BrE) гости́ная

situate /'sɪtjʊeɪt/ *v.t.* распол|ага́ть, -ожи́ть

♂ **situation** /sɪtʃʊ'eɪʃ(ə)n/ *n.* **1** (place) ме́сто; (position) местоположе́ние **2** (circumstances) положе́ние, ситуа́ция; **what is the ~?** каково́ положе́ние дел? **3** (job): ~**s vacant** (BrE, as column heading) вака́нтные до́лжности

♂ **six** /sɪks/ *n.* (число́/но́мер) шесть; (~ people) ше́стеро, шесть челове́к; (figure; thing numbered 6; group of ~) шестё́рка
● *adj.* шесть + *g. pl.*

sixteen /sɪks'tiːn/ *n.* шестна́дцать
● *adj.* шестна́дцать + *g. pl.*

sixteenth /sɪks'tiːnθ/ *n.* (date) шестна́дцатое (число́); (fraction) одна́ шестна́дцатая
● *adj.* шестна́дцатый

sixth /sɪksθ/ *n.* (date) шесто́е (число́); (fraction) одна́ шеста́я
● *adj.* шесто́й; **in the ~ form** (BrE) в ста́ршем кла́ссе

■ ~**-form college** *n.* (BrE) шко́ла со ста́ршими кла́ссами; ~ **sense** *n.* шесто́е чу́вство

sixtieth /'sɪkstɪɪθ/ *n.* одна́ шестидеся́тая
● *adj.* шестидеся́тый

sixt|y /'sɪkstɪ/ *n.* шестьдеся́т; **he is in his ~ies** ему́ за шестьдеся́т(лет); **in the ~ies** (decade) в шестидеся́тых года́х; в шестидеся́тые го́ды
● *adj.* шестьдеся́т + *g. pl.*

sizable /'saɪzəb(ə)l/ *adj.* = sizeable

♂ **size** /saɪz/ *n.* **1** (dimension) разме́р; величина́; **these books are all the same ~** все э́ти кни́ги одного́ форма́та; **cut sb down to ~** (infml) ста́вить, по- кого́-н. на ме́сто **2** (of clothes etc.): **I take ~ 12** я ношу́/у меня́ двена́дцатый разме́р; **I take ~ 10 in shoes** я ношу́ о́бувь деся́того разме́ра
● *v.t.*: ~ **sb up** сост|авля́ть, -а́вить о ком-н. мне́ние; ~ **up the situation** оце́нивать, -ени́ть обстано́вку

sizeable, sizable /'saɪzəb(ə)l/ *adj.* значи́тельного разме́ра

sizzle /'sɪz(ə)l/ *v.i.* шипе́ть (*impf.*)

skate¹ /skeɪt/ *n.* (ice ~) конё́к; (*in full roller* ~) ро́лик; (*in sg. usu.*) боти́нок
● *v.i.* (on ice) ката́ться/бе́гать (*both indet.*) на конька́х; (on roller-~s) ката́ться (*indet.*) на ро́ликах
■ ~**board** *n.* скейтбо́рд; ~**boarder** *n.* скейтборди́ст (-ка); ~**boarding** *n.* скейтбо́рдинг

skate² /skeɪt/ *n.* (fish) скат

skater /'skeɪtə(r)/ *n.* (figure ~) фигури́ст (-ка)

skating /'skeɪtɪŋ/ *n.* (figure ~) ката́ние на конька́х
■ ~ **rink** *n.* като́к

skeleton /'skelɪt(ə)n/ *n.* **1** скеле́т **2** (*attr.*): ~ **key** отмы́чка

skeptic /'skeptɪk/ *n.* (AmE) = sceptic

skeptical /'skeptɪk(ə)l/ *n.* (AmE) = sceptical

skepticism /'skeptɪsɪz(ə)m/ *n.* (AmE) = scepticism

sketch /sketʃ/ *n.* **1** (artistic) эски́з, набро́сок, зарисо́вка **2** (brief outline) кра́ткое описа́ние; (of plan) о́бщее представле́ние **3** (play) скетч
● *v.t.* (draw) набр|а́сывать, -оса́ть; (fig. also) опи́с|ывать, -а́ть в о́бщих черта́х
● *v.i.* де́лать, с- эски́з/зарисо́вку
■ ~**book** *n.* альбо́м для эски́зов/рисова́ния

sketchy /'sketʃɪ/ *adj.* (**sketchier**, **sketchiest**) пове́рхностный

skewer /'skjuːə(r)/ *n.* ве́ртел
● *v.t.* наса́|живать, -ди́ть на ве́ртел

ski /skiː/ *n.* (*pl.* ~**s**) лы́жа
● *v.i.* (**skis**, **skied** /skiːd/, **skiing**) (cross-country) ходи́ть (*indet.*) на лы́жах; (downhill) ката́ться (*impf.*) на лы́жах
■ ~ **boots** *n. pl.* лы́жные боти́нки (*m. pl.*); ~ **jumping** *n.* прыжки́ (*m. pl.*) на лы́жах с трампли́на; ~ **lift** *n.* (горнолы́жный) подъё́мник

skid /skɪd/ *n.* (of car) скольже́ние; юз, зано́с; **the car went into a ~** маши́ну занесло́

S

• *v.i.* (**skidded, skidding**) (of car, wheels) пойти (*pf.*) юзом

skier /'ski:ə(r)/ *n.* лы́жник

skiing /'ski:ɪŋ/ *n.* ката́ние на лы́жах

skilful /'skɪlfʊl/ (AmE **skillful**) *adj.* иску́сный, уме́лый

ďſ **skill** /skɪl/ *n.* мастерство́, иску́сство; (specific ability) на́вык

skilled /skɪld/ *adj.* (skilful) иску́сный; (trained) квалифици́рованный

skillet /'skɪlɪt/ *n.* (AmE) сковорода́

skillful /'skɪlfʊl/ *adj.* (AmE) = skilful

skim /skɪm/ *v.t.* (**skimmed, skimming**)
1 : ~ a liquid сн|има́ть, -ять на́кипь/пе́нку с жи́дкости **2** (move lightly over) лете́ть (*det.*) над са́мой пове́рхностью + *g.* **3** (scan through) бегло́ просм|а́тривать, -отре́ть
■ ~med milk *n.* обезжи́ренное молоко́

skimp /skɪmp/ *v.i.* скупи́ться, эконо́мить (*both impf.*)

skimpy /'skɪmpɪ/ *adj.* (**skimpier, skimpiest**) (meagre, of knowledge) ску́дный; (of clothes) те́сный, у́зкий

ďſ **skin** /skɪn/ *n.* **1** ко́жа; I got soaked to the ~ я промо́к до ни́тки; escape by the ~ of one's teeth чу́дом спаса́ться, -ти́сь **2** (of animal) шку́ра **3** (of fruit) кожура́
• *v.t.* (**skinned, skinning**) (remove ~ from) сн|има́ть, -ять шку́ру с + *g.*; свежева́ть, о-
■ ~-deep *adj.* пове́рхностный; ~ diving *n.* подво́дное пла́вание (с аквала́нгом); ~flint *n.* скря́га (*c.g.*); ~head *n.* (BrE) «бритоголо́вый», скинхе́д; ~tight *adj.*: ~tight trousers брю́ки в обтя́жку

skinny /'skɪnɪ/ *adj.* (**skinnier, skinniest**) то́щий

skint /skɪnt/ *adj.* (BrE, infml): I'm ~ я без копе́йки, я на мели́

skip[1] /skɪp/ *n.* скачо́к, прыжо́к
• *v.t.* (**skipped, skipping**) (lesson etc.) пропуск|а́ть, -ти́ть
• *v.i.* (**skipped, skipping**) (use ~ping rope) скака́ть/пры́гать (*impf.*) (че́рез скака́лку); (jump): she ~ped for joy она́ подпры́гнула от ра́дости
■ ~ping rope *n.* (BrE) скака́лка

skip[2] /skɪp/ *n.* (BrE, for rubbish) конте́йнер для (перево́зки) му́сора

skipper /'skɪpə(r)/ *n.* (captain) шки́пер, капита́н

skirmish /'skɜ:mɪʃ/ *n.* схва́тка

skirt /skɜ:t/ *n.* ю́бка
• *v.t.* (go round) об|ходи́ть, -ойти́; we ~ed the town мы обошли́ го́род; (form border of): the road ~s the forest доро́га обрамля́ет лес
■ ~ing board *n.* (BrE) пли́нтус

skittish /'skɪtɪʃ/ *adj.* (of horse etc.) нарови́стый; (of person) капри́зный

skittle /'skɪt(ə)l/ *n.* ке́гля; (in pl.) (game) ке́гли (*f. pl.*)

skive /skaɪv/ *v.i.* (BrE, infml) сачкова́ть (*impf.*) (sl.)

skiver /'skaɪvə(r)/ *n.* (BrE, infml) сачо́к (sl.)

skulduggery /skʌl'dʌgərɪ/ *n.* надува́тельство

skulk /skʌlk/ *v.i.* зата́иваться (*impf.*)

skull /skʌl/ *n.* че́реп

skunk /skʌŋk/ *n.* скунс

ďſ **sky** /skaɪ/ *n.* не́бо
■ ~diving *n.* затяжны́е прыжки́ с парашю́том; ~-high *adv.* (fig.) до небе́с; ~light *n.* фона́рь (*m.*); ~line *n.* (horizon) горизо́нт; (silhouette against the sky) силуэ́т (на фо́не не́ба); ~ marshal *n.* сотру́дник слу́жбы безопа́сности, сопровожда́ющий возду́шные ре́йсы; ~scraper *n.* небоскрёб

slab /slæb/ *n.* (of stone etc.) плита́; (of cake etc.) кусо́к

slack /slæk/ *adj.* **1** (slow) ме́дленный
2 (negligent) небре́жный **3** (loose): ~ rope прови́сшая верёвка **4** (quiet): ~ season, period мёртвый сезо́н
• *v.i.* (BrE) ло́дырничать (*impf.*); we ~ed off towards five к пяти́ часа́м мы сба́вили темп (рабо́ты)

slacken /'slækən/ *v.t.* **1** (rope, rein) отпус|ка́ть, -ти́ть; (screw, nut) ослабля́ть, осла́бить
2 (diminish): ~ speed сб|авля́ть, -а́вить ско́рость
• *v.i.* **1** (of rope) пров|иса́ть, -и́снуть; (of screw, nut) слабе́ть, о- **2** (die down): demand is ~ing спрос уменьша́ется

slag /slæg/ *v.i.* (**slagged, slagging**): ~ off (BrE, infml, criticize) разн|оси́ть, -ести́
■ ~ heap *n.* гру́да шла́ка

slain /sleɪn/ *p.p. of* ▶ slay

slalom /'slɑ:ləm/ *n.* сла́лом

slam /slæm/ *v.t.* (**slammed, slamming**)
1 (shut with a bang): ~ a door хло́п|ать, -нуть две́рью **2** (other violent action): he ~med the brakes on он ре́зко нажа́л на тормоза́
• *v.i.* (**slammed, slamming**) (of door etc.) захло́п|ываться, -нуться

slander /'slɑːndə(r)/ *n.* клевета́
• *v.t.* клевета́ть (*на кого*), о- (*кого*), на- (*на кого*); he ~ed me он оклевета́л меня́, он наклевета́л на меня́

slanderous /'slɑːndərəs/ *adj.* клеветни́ческий

slang /slæŋ/ *n.* жарго́н; сленг

slant /slɑ:nt/ *n.* (oblique position) накло́н; укло́н
• *v.t.* (incline) накло́н|я́ть, -и́ть
• *v.i.*: his handwriting ~s to the right он пи́шет с накло́ном впра́во

slap /slæp/ *n.* шлепо́к; ~ in the face (lit., fig.) пощёчина
• *adv.* (exactly) пря́мо
• *v.t.* (**slapped, slapping**) шлёпать, от-; ~ sb's face да|ва́ть, -ть кому́-н. пощёчину
■ ~dash *adj.* небре́жный

slash /slæʃ/ *n.* (slit) разре́з; (oblique mark; also, forward ~) коса́я черта́
• *v.t.* **1** (wound with knife etc.) ра́нить, по- **2** (cut slits in) разреза́ть, -е́зать **3** (reduce): ~ prices ре́зко сн|ижа́ть, -и́зить це́ны

slat /slæt/ *n.* пла́нка; (of blind) пласти́нка (жалюзи́)

S

slate /sleɪt/ n. **1** (material) сла́нец **2** (piece of ~ for roofing) ши́ферная пли́тка **3** (fig.): **wipe the ~ clean** поко́нчить (pf.) с про́шлым
• v.t. **1** (cover with ~s) крыть, по- ши́фером **2** (BrE, criticize) разно́сить, -ести́
slaughter /'slɔ:tə(r)/ n. избие́ние, резня́; (of animals) убо́й
• v.t. **1** (kill animals, people) ре́зать, за- **2** (infml, defeat heavily) разби́ва́ть, -и́ть в пух и прах
■ ~**house** n. (ското)бо́йня
Slav /slɑ:v/ n. славя́ни́н (-я́нка)
• adj. славя́нский
slave /sleɪv/ n. раб (-ы́ня)
• v.i. (also ~ **away**) рабо́тать (impf.) как раб
slavery /'sleɪvərɪ/ n. ра́бство
Slavic /'slɑ:vɪk/ adj. славя́нский
slavish /'sleɪvɪʃ/ adj. ра́бский
Slavonic /slə'vɒnɪk/ adj. славя́нский
slay /sleɪ/ v.t. (past **slew**, p.p. **slain**) (liter.) умер|щвля́ть, -тви́ть
sleazy /'sli:zɪ/ adj. (**sleazier**, **sleaziest**) (infml, squalid) захуда́лый, убо́гий
sled /sled/ (AmE) n. = sledge n.
• v.i. (**sledded**, **sledding**) = sledge v.i.
sledge /sledʒ/ n. са́н|и (-е́й)
• v.i. ката́ться (indet.) на саня́х
sledgehammer /'sledʒhæmə(r)/ n. кува́лда
sleek /sli:k/ adj. (of animal) гла́дкий, лосня́щийся; (of person's hair) прили́занный
ᕼ **sleep** /sli:p/ n. сон; **have a ~** поспа́ть (pf.); **go to ~** зас|ыпа́ть, -ну́ть, усну́ть (pf.); **send to ~** усып|ля́ть, -и́ть; **we had our dog put to ~** нам пришло́сь усыпи́ть соба́ку
• v.i. **1** (past and p.p. **slept**) спать (impf.); ~ **like a log** спать (impf.) как уби́тый; **I can't ~** я не могу́ засну́ть; ~ **on a decision** откла́дывать, отложи́ть реше́ние до утра́ **2** (have sex) спать, пере- (with: c + i.)
□ ~ **around** v.i. спать (impf.) с кем попа́ло
□ ~ **in** v.i. (intentionally) поспа́ть (pf.) вдо́сталь; (oversleep) прос|ыпа́ть, -па́ть
■ ~**walk** v.i. ходи́ть (impf.) во сне; ~**walker** n. луна́тик
sleeper /'sli:pə(r)/ n. (person): **he is a light/ heavy ~** он чу́тко/кре́пко спит; (BrE, rail support) шпа́ла; (sleeping car) спа́льный ваго́н
sleeping /'sli:pɪŋ/**:**
■ ~ **bag** n. спа́льный мешо́к; ~ **pill** n. снотво́рная табле́тка, снотво́рное
sleepless /'sli:plɪs/ adj. бессо́нный
sleepy /'sli:pɪ/ adj. (**sleepier**, **sleepiest**) (lit., fig.) со́нный; сонли́вый; **I feel ~** мне хо́чется (or я хочу́) спать
sleet /sli:t/ n. мо́крый снег
• v.i.: **it is ~ing** идёт мо́крый снег
sleeve /sli:v/ n. **1** рука́в; **have sth up one's ~** (fig.) име́ть (impf.) что-н. про запа́с **2** (record cover) конве́рт (пластинки)
sleeveless /'sli:vlɪs/ adj. без рукаво́в
sleigh /sleɪ/ n. са́н|и (-е́й)
sleight of hand /slaɪt/ n. ло́вкость рук
slender /'slendə(r)/ adj. (**slenderer**, **slenderest**) **1** (thin) то́нкий; (of person, slim)

стро́йный **2** (scanty) ску́дный; ~ **means** ску́дные сре́дства
slept /slept/ past and p.p. of ▸ sleep
sleuth /slu:θ/ n. сы́щик
slew /slu:/ past of ▸ slay
slice /slaɪs/ n. **1** (of bread, meat) ломо́ть (m.); (of cake, apple) кусо́к **2** (share) часть, до́ля
• v.t. нар|еза́ть, -е́зать ломтя́ми/ло́мтиками
■ ~**d bread** n. (предвари́тельно) наре́занный хлеб
slick /slɪk/ adj. (skilful) ло́вкий, бо́йкий; (smooth, also fig.) гла́дкий; (slippery) ско́льзкий
slid|e /slaɪd/ n. **1** (chute) спуск, жёлоб **2** (of microscope) предме́тное стекло́ **3** (for projection on screen) слайд, диапозити́в **4** (BrE, hair~e) зако́лка
• v.t. (past and p.p. **slid** /slɪd/): ~**e a drawer into place** задв|ига́ть, -и́нуть я́щик на ме́сто
• v.i. (past and p.p. **slid** /slɪd/) **1** скользи́ть (impf.); ~**ing door** раздвижна́я дверь; **the papers ~ off my lap** бума́ги соскользну́ли у меня́ с коле́н **2**: ~**ing scale** (econ.) скользя́щая шкала́
■ ~**e projector** n. прое́ктор; ~**e rule** n. логарифми́ческая лине́йка
slight¹ /slaɪt/ n. (offence) оби́да
• v.t. об|ижа́ть, -и́деть
slight² /slaɪt/ adj. **1** (slender) то́нкий **2** (not serious) лёгкий; **she has a ~ cold** у неё лёгкая просту́да **3** (small): **there is a ~ risk of infection** есть не́которая опа́сность зараже́ния **4**: ~**est** мале́йший; **this is not the ~est use** от э́того ни мале́йшей по́льзы
ᕼ **slightly** /'slaɪtlɪ/ adv. слегка́; **I know them ~** я с ни́ми немно́го знако́м; ~ **younger** немно́го/чуть моло́же
slim /slɪm/ adj. (**slimmer**, **slimmest**) то́нкий, худо́й
• v.i. (**slimmed**, **slimming**) худе́ть, по-
slime /slaɪm/ n. (mud) ил; (viscous substance) слизь
slimy /'slaɪmɪ/ adj. (**slimier**, **slimiest**) **1** сли́зистый, ско́льзкий **2** (fig., infml, of person) нейскренний
sling /slɪŋ/ n. пере́вязь
• v.t. (past and p.p. **slung**) швыр|я́ть, -ну́ть
slink /slɪŋk/ v.i. (past and p.p. **slunk**): ~ **off, away** (stealthily) выска́льзывать, вы́скользнуть; (in a guilty way) уходи́ть, уйти́ поджа́в хвост
slinky /'slɪŋkɪ/ adj. (**slinkier**, **slinkiest**): a ~ **dress** облега́ющее пла́тье
slip /slɪp/ n. **1** (error) оши́бка (по небре́жности); ~ **of the tongue/pen** огово́рка/опи́ска **2** (petticoat) комбина́ция (же́нское бельё) **3** (of paper) поло́ска
• v.t. (**slipped**, **slipping**) **1** (slide; pass covertly): **he ~ped the ring on to her finger** он наде́л ей на па́лец кольцо́; **I ~ped the waiter a coin** я су́нул официа́нту моне́ту **2** (escape from): выска́льзывать, вы́скользнуть из + g.; **his name ~ped my memory/mind** его́ и́мя вы́скочило у меня́ из па́мяти/головы́
• v.i. (**slipped**, **slipping**) **1** (slide) скользи́ть

(*impf.*); (fall over) поскользну́ться (*pf.*); she ~ped on the ice она́ поскользну́лась на льду **2** (move quickly) выска́льзывать, вы́скользнуть; she ~ped out of the room она́ вы́скользнула из ко́мнаты; I'll ~ into another dress я (бы́стренько) переоде́нусь; ~ through проск|а́льзывать, -ользну́ть (че́рез *a.*)
□ ~ up *v.i.*: he ~ped up and hurt his back он поскользну́лся и повреди́л себе́ спи́ну; I ~ped up in my calculations я оши́бся в подсчётах; (fig.) я просчита́лся
■ ~ped disc *n.* сме́щенный межпозвоно́чный диск; ~ road *n.* (BrE) подъездна́я доро́га; ~shod *adj.* небре́жный; ~-up *n.* (infml) оши́бка

slipper /'slɪpə(r)/ *n.* та́почка

slippery /'slɪpərɪ/ *adj.* (also fig.) ско́льзкий

slit /slɪt/ *n.* (cut) разре́з; (slot) щель, щёлка
● *v.t.* (**slitting**, *past and p.p.* ~): ~ open an envelope вскр|ыва́ть, -ы́ть/раз|рыва́ть, -орва́ть конве́рт; ~ sb's throat пере|реза́ть, -е́зать кому́-н. го́рло

slither /'slɪðə(r)/ *v.i.*: ~ about in the mud скользи́ть (*impf.*) по грязи

sliver /'slɪvə(r)/ *n.* (of glass) оско́лок; (of cake, cheese) кусо́чек

slob /slɒb/ *n.* (sl.) недотёпа (*c.g.*)

slobber /'slɒbə(r)/ *v.i.* (lit., fig.) распус|ка́ть, -ти́ть слю́ни

slog /slɒg/ *n.* (infml, arduous work) тяжёлая работа
● *v.i.* (**slogged, slogging**) (work hard) вка́лывать (*impf.*) (infml); he was ~ging along the road он упо́рно шага́л по доро́ге; he is ~ging away at Latin он корпи́т над латы́нью (infml)

slogan /'sləʊgən/ *n.* (advertising) сло́ган; (political) ло́зунг

slop /slɒp/ *n.* (in pl.) помо́|и (-ев)
● *v.t.* (**slopped, slopping**): ~ beer over the table расплёск|ивать, -а́ть пи́во по столу́

slope /sləʊp/ *n.* (area of land) склон; (of 90 degrees etc.) укло́н, накло́н
● *v.i.*: ~ back(wards)/forwards коси́ться, поназа́д/вперёд; ~ down спуска́ться (*impf.*); ~ up(wards) поднима́ться (*impf.*)

sloping /'sləʊpɪŋ/ *adj.* (roof, shoulders) пока́тый; (surface, handwriting) накло́нный; (ground) понижа́ющийся

sloppy /'slɒpɪ/ *adj.* (**sloppier, sloppiest**) **1** (careless) неря́шливый **2** (sentimental) сентимента́льный

slot /slɒt/ *n.* **1** (slit) паз; (aperture) отве́рстие **2** (in timetable) специа́льно отведённое вре́мя; временно́й интерва́л
● *v.t.* (**slotted, slotting**) **1**: ~ together соедин|я́ть, -и́ть на шипа́х **2**: ~ in вст|авля́ть, -а́вить
■ ~ machine *n.* (BrE, vending machine) торго́вый автома́т; (fruit machine) игрово́й автома́т

sloth /sləʊθ/ *n.* **1** (zool.) лени́вец **2** (idleness) ле́ность

slothful /'sləʊθfʊl/ *adj.* лени́вый

slouch /slaʊtʃ/ *v.i.* суту́литься (*impf.*); he sat ~ed in a chair он сиде́л развали́вшись в кре́сле

Slovak /'sləʊvæk/ *n.* (person) слова́|к (-чка); (language) слова́цкий язы́к
● *adj.* слова́цкий

Slovakia /slə'vækɪə/ *n.* Слова́кия

Slovene /'sləʊviːn/, **Slovenian** /slə'viːnɪən/ *nn.* (person) слове́н|ец (-ка); (language) слове́нский язы́к
● *adjs.* слове́нский

Slovenia /slə'viːnɪə/ *n.* Слове́ния

slovenly /'slʌvənlɪ/ *adj.* неря́шливый

✧ **slow** /sləʊ/ *adj.* **1** ме́дленный; in ~ motion в заме́дленном де́йствии **2** (of clock): my watch is 10 minutes ~ мои́ часы́ отстаю́т на де́сять мину́т **3** (dull-witted) тупо́й **4** (not lively): business is ~ дела́ иду́т вя́ло
● *adv.* ме́дленно
● *v.t.* (also ~ **down**, ~ **up**) зам|едля́ть, -е́длить
● *v.i.* (also ~ **down**, ~ **up**) зам|едля́ться, -е́дляться
■ ~-**moving** *adj.* ме́дленный

sludge /slʌdʒ/ *n.* грязь

slug /slʌg/ *n.* (zool.) слизня́к

sluggish /'slʌgɪʃ/ *adj.* **1**: ~ market вя́лый ры́нок; (slow-moving) ме́дленный **2** (lazy) лени́вый

sluice /sluːs/ *n.* (in full ~ gate) шлюз

slum /slʌm/ *n.* трущо́ба

slumber /'slʌmbə(r)/ *n.* дремо́та; disturb sb's ~s нар|уша́ть, -у́шить чей-н. сон
● *v.i.* дрема́ть, за-

slump /slʌmp/ *n.* (fall in prices etc.) паде́ние; (trade recession) упа́док
● *v.i.* **1** (of person) сва́л|иваться, -и́ться **2** (of price, trade) ре́зко па́дать, упа́сть

slung /slʌŋ/ *past and p.p. of* ▶ sling

slunk /slʌŋk/ *past and p.p. of* ▶ slink

slur /slɜː(r)/ *n.* пятно́
● *v.t.* (**slurred, slurring**) (pronounce indistinctly) говори́ть, сказа́ть невня́тно

slush /slʌʃ/ *n.* **1** сля́коть **2**: ~ fund де́ньги для по́дкупа госуда́рственных чино́вников

slushy /'slʌʃɪ/ *adj.* (**slushier, slushiest**) сля́котный, мо́крый; (sentimental) сентимента́льный

slut /slʌt/ *n.* (pej.) (loose woman) шлю́ха, потаску́ха (both vulg.); (sloven) неря́ха (infml)

sly /slaɪ/ *adj.* (**slyer, slyest**) хи́трый; on the ~ укра́дкой, исподтишка́

smack[1] /smæk/ *n.* **1** (sound) хлопо́к **2** (slap) шлепо́к; ~ in the face пощёчина
● *v.t.* шлёп|ать, -нуть; шлёпать, от-

smack[2] /smæk/ *v.i.*: ~ of (lit., fig.) отдава́ть (*impf.*) + i.

✧ **small** /smɔːl/ *n.*: ~ of the back поясни́ца
● *adj.* **1** ма́ленький, небольшо́й, ма́лый; (of eggs, berries, stones, etc.) ме́лкий; (not big enough): this coat is too ~ for me э́то пальто́ мне мало́; make sb look ~ (fig.) ун|ижа́ть, -и́зить

s

кого́-н.; **I felt very** ~ я (по)чу́вствовал себя́ соверше́нно уничто́женным **2** (unimportant, of ~ value) ме́лкий, незначи́тельный
● *adv.*: **chop sth up** ~ ме́лко наруб|а́ть, -и́ть что-н.
■ ~ **ad** *n.* коро́ткое объявле́ние; ~ **change** *n.* ме́лкие де́ньги, ме́лочь; ~ **print** *n.* ме́лкий шрифт; ~**-scale** *adj.* (map, drawing) маломасшта́бный; ~ **talk** *n.* све́тский разгово́р

smarmy /'smɑːmɪ/ *adj.* (**smarmier**, **smarmiest**) (infml) льсти́вый

smart¹ /smɑːt/ *v.i.* **1** (of wound) жечь (*impf.*); **my eyes are** ~**ing** у меня́ глаза́ щи́плет **2** (of person) страда́ть (*impf.*)

◆ **smart²** /smɑːt/ *adj.* **1** (sharp) ре́зкий, суро́вый, о́стрый **2** (brisk): **he walked off at a** ~ **pace** он удали́лся бы́стрым ша́гом **3** (clever) сообрази́тельный **4** (elegant): **a** ~ **hat** элега́нтная шля́па; **you look** ~ вы вы́глядите про́сто превосхо́дно
■ ~ **card** *n.* пла́стиковая ка́рточка со встро́енным микропроце́ссором; смарт-ка́рта

smarten /'smɑːt(ə)n/ *v.t.* (*also* ~ **up**): ~ **oneself up** прихора́шиваться (*impf.*) (infml); (a room, house, ship, etc.) прив|оди́ть, -ести́ в поря́док
● *v.i.* (~ **up**) (in appearance): **he has** ~**ed up** он привёл себя́ в поря́док

smartphone /'smɑːtfəʊn/ *n.* (comput.) смартфо́н

smash /smæʃ/ *n.* **1** (sound) гро́хот; (collision) столкнове́ние **2** (at tennis etc.) смэш **3**: ~ **hit** (infml) суперхи́т; **be a** ~ **hit** име́ть (*impf.*) оглуши́тельный успе́х
● *v.t.* **1** (shatter) разб|ива́ть, -и́ть **2** (drive with force): **he** ~**ed the ball over the net** си́льным уда́ром он посла́л мяч че́рез се́тку
● *v.i.* **1** (be broken) разб|ива́ться, -и́ться **2** (crash) вр|еза́ться, -е́заться; **the car** ~**ed into a wall** маши́на вре́залась в сте́ну

smashing /'smæʃɪŋ/ *adj.* (BrE, infml): **a** ~ **film** замеча́тельный/потряса́ющий фильм

smattering /'smætərɪŋ/ *n.*: **he has a** ~ **of German** он чуть-чу́ть зна́ет неме́цкий

smear /smɪə(r)/ *n.* **1** (blotch) пятно́ **2** (infml, slander) клевета́
● *v.t.* ма́зать, на-; разма́з|ывать, -ать; **he** ~**ed grease paint on his face** он наложи́л грим (себе́) на лицо́
■ ~ **campaign** *n.* клеветни́ческая кампа́ния; ~ **test** *n.* мазо́к с ше́йки ма́тки

smell /smel/ *n.* **1** (faculty) обоня́ние **2** (odour) за́пах
● *v.t.* (*past and p.p.* **smelt** *or* **smelled**) **1** (perceive ~ of) чу́вствовать, по- за́пах + *g.*; **I** ~ **something burning** я чу́вствую за́пах га́ри; (of animals, also fig.) чу́ять (*impf.*) **2** (sniff) ню́хать, по-
● *v.i.* (*past and p.p.* **smelt** *or* **smelled**) (emit ~) па́хнуть (*impf.*); (pleasantly) издава́ть (*impf.*) арома́т; **the soup** ~**s good** суп хорошо́/вку́сно па́хнет; **the room smelt of cigarettes** в ко́мнате па́хло табако́м; (unpleasantly) ду́рно/пло́хо па́хнуть (*impf.*)

■ ~**ing salts** *n. pl.* ню́хательная соль

smelly /'smelɪ/ *adj.* (**smellier**, **smelliest**) ду́рно па́хнущий, воню́чий

smelt /smelt/ *past and p.p. of* ▶ **smell**

smidgen /'smɪdʒ(ə)n/ *n.* (infml) чуто́к, немно́го

◆ **smile** /smaɪl/ *n.* улы́бка
● *v.i.* улыб|а́ться, -ну́ться; ~ **on** (fig.): **fortune** ~**d on him** сча́стье ему́ улыба́лось

◆ **smil|ey** /'smaɪlɪ/ *n.* (*pl.* ~**eys**, ~**ies**) (symbol) сма́йл(ик)

smirk /smɜːk/ *n.* самодово́льная улы́бка, ухмы́лка
● *v.i.* ухмыл|я́ться, -ьну́ться

smith /smɪθ/ *n.* (*in full* **black**~) кузне́ц

smithereens /smɪðə'riːnz/ *n. pl.*: **to** ~ вдре́безги

smithy /'smɪðɪ/ *n.* ку́зница

smock /smɒk/ *n.* пла́тье/блу́зка со сбо́рками

smog /smɒg/ *n.* смог

◆ **smoke** /sməʊk/ *n.* дым
● *v.t.* **1** (preserve with ~) копти́ть, за-; ~**d fish** копчёная ры́ба **2** (tobacco etc.) кури́ть, вы́-
● *v.i.* **1** (of person) кури́ть (*impf.*) **2** (of chimney etc.) дыми́ться (*impf.*)
■ ~**screen** *n.* (lit., fig.) дымова́я заве́са

smokeless /'sməʊklɪs/ *adj.* безды́мный; ~ **zone** (BrE) безды́мная городска́я зо́на

smoker /'sməʊkə(r)/ *n.* куря́щий; кури́льщи|к (-ца)

smoking /'sməʊkɪŋ/ *n.* куре́ние; '**No S**~**!**' «кури́ть воспреща́ется!»; «не кури́ть!»

smoky /'sməʊkɪ/ *adj.* (**smokier**, **smokiest**) ды́мный

smolder /'sməʊldə(r)/ *v.i.* (AmE) = smoulder

smooch /smuːtʃ/ *v.i.* (infml) **1** (kiss and cuddle) обнима́ться, целова́ться, прижима́ться (infml), ти́скаться (infml) (*all impf.*) **2** (BrE, dance in close embrace) обнима́ться, прижима́ться (infml) (*both impf.*) в та́нце (*or* танцу́я)

smooth /smuːð/ *adj.* **1** (even, level) гла́дкий, ро́вный; **a** ~ **paste** те́сто без комко́в **2** (not harsh): ~ **wine** нете́рпкое вино́ **3** (suave) гала́нтный
● *v.t.* **1** (make level) выра́внивать, вы́ровнять **2** (flatten) пригла́ж|ивать, -дить **3** (make easy) смягч|а́ть, -и́ть
□ ~ **away** *v.t.*: **he** ~**ed away our difficulties** он устрани́л на́ши тру́дности
□ ~ **over** *v.t.* смягч|а́ть, -и́ть; ~ **things over** ула́ж|ивать, -дить де́ло

smother /'smʌðə(r)/ *v.t.* **1** (suffocate) души́ть, за-; ~ **a fire** туши́ть, по- ого́нь **2** (cover) покр|ыва́ть, -ы́ть **3** (suppress, conceal) подав|ля́ть, -и́ть

smoulder /'sməʊldə(r)/ (AmE *also* **smolder**) *v.i.* (lit., fig.) тлеть (*impf.*); ~**ing hatred** затаённая не́нависть

SMS *n.* (*abbr. of* **Short Message/ Messaging Service**): ~ **message** SMS/ СМС-сообще́ние, (infml) SMS (*pronounced* эс-эм-э́с)

smudge /smʌdʒ/ *n.* пятно́
● *v.t.* сма́з|ывать, -ать

smug /smʌg/ adj. (**smugger, smuggest**) самодово́льный

smuggle /'smʌg(ə)l/ v.t. пров|ози́ть, -езти́ контраба́ндой; (fig.): he was ~d into the house его́ та́йком провели́ в дом

smuggler /'smʌglə(r)/ n. контрабанди́ст (-ка)

smuggling /'smʌglɪŋ/ n. контраба́нда

smutty /'smʌtɪ/ adj. (**smuttier, smuttiest**): ~ face гря́зное/запа́чканное лицо́; ~ joke гря́зный/поха́бный (infml) анекдо́т

snack /snæk/ n. заку́ска; have a ~ перекус|ывать, -и́ть
■ ~ **bar** n. заку́сочная, буфе́т

snag /snæg/ **1** (obstacle) препя́тствие; (difficulty) затрудне́ние **2** (tear) разры́в

snail /sneɪl/ n. ули́тка

snake /sneɪk/ n. змея́

snap /snæp/ n. **1** (noise) щелчо́к, щёлканье; (of sth breaking) треск **2** (infml, photograph) сни́мок
● adj.: ~ **decision** внеза́пное реше́ние
● v.t. (**snapped, snapping**) **1** (make ~ping noise with) щёлк|ать, -нуть (+ i.) **2** (break) разл|а́мывать, -ома́ть; he ~ped the stick in two он разлома́л па́лку на́двое **3** (infml, photograph) сн|има́ть, -ять
● v.i. (**snapped, snapping**) **1** (make biting motion): ~ at огрыз|а́ться, -ну́ться на (+ a.); (speak sharply) груби́ть, на- (at: + d.); don't ~ at me! не груби́те (мне)! **2** (break) тре́снуть, слома́ться (both pf.)
□ ~ **off** v.t.: ~ sb's head off (infml) набр|а́сываться, -о́ситься на кого́-н.
□ ~ **up** v.t. (buy eagerly) расхва́т|ывать, -а́ть
■ ~**shot** n. (люби́тельский) сни́мок

snappy /'snæpɪ/ adj. (**snappier, snappiest**): make it ~! жи́во!

snare /sneə(r)/ n. западня́, лову́шка

snarl /snɑːl/ v.i. рыча́ть, за-

snatch /snætʃ/ n. обры́вок, отры́вок
● v.t. хвата́ть, схвати́ть; ~ sth from sb вырыва́ть, вы́рвать что-н. у кого́-н.
● v.i. хвата́ть (impf.); ~ at sth хвата́ться, схвати́ться за что-н.

sneak /sniːk/ v.i. (past and p.p. **sneaked** or AmE, infml **snuck**) кра́сться (impf.); ~ into a room прокра́д|ываться, -сться в ко́мнату; ~ out of a room выска́льзывать, вы́скользнуть из ко́мнаты

sneakers /'sniːkəz/ n. pl. (AmE) кроссо́вки (f. pl.)

sneaking /'sniːkɪŋ/ adj.: ~ **feeling** сму́тное подозре́ние

sneaky /'sniːkɪ/ adj. (**sneakier, sneakiest**) **1** (person) хи́трый **2** = sneaking

sneer /snɪə(r)/ n. презри́тельная усме́шка
● v.i. усмех|а́ться, -ну́ться; ~ at глуми́ться/ насмеха́ться (both impf.) над + i.

sneeze /sniːz/ n. чиха́нье
● v.i. чих|а́ть, -ну́ть

snide /snaɪd/ adj. (infml) еха́дный

---

sniff /snɪf/ n. вдох
● v.t. (inhale) вд|ыха́ть, -охну́ть; (smell at) ню́хать, по-
● v.i. шмы́г|ать, -ну́ть (но́сом) (infml)

sniffle /'snɪf(ə)l/ n. сопе́ние; (in pl.) на́сморк
● v.i. шмы́г|ать, -ну́ть (но́сом)

snigger /'snɪgə(r)/ v.i. хихи́к|ать, -нуть

snip /snɪp/ v.t. (**snipped, snipping**) подр|еза́ть, -е́зать

sniper /'snaɪpə(r)/ n. сна́йпер

snippet /'snɪpɪt/ n. (in pl.) (of news etc.) обры́вки (m. pl.)

snivel /'snɪv(ə)l/ v.i. (**snivelled, snivelling**, AmE **sniveled, sniveling**) хны́кать (impf.)

snob /snɒb/ n. сноб

snobbery /'snɒbərɪ/ n. сноби́зм

snobbish /'snɒbɪʃ/ adj. сноби́стский

snog /snɒg/ v.i. (**snogged, snogging**) (BrE, infml) лиза́ться (impf.) (infml)

snooker /'snuːkə(r)/ n. сну́кер (игра́ на билья́рде)

snoop /snuːp/ v.i. (infml) подгл|я́дывать, -яде́ть чужи́е та́йны

snooty /'snuːtɪ/ adj. (**snootier, snootiest**) (infml) наду́тый, зазна́вшийся

snooze /snuːz/ (infml) n.: have, take a ~ вздремну́ть (pf.)
● v.i. дрема́ть (impf.)

snore /snɔː(r)/ n. храп
● v.i. храпе́ть, за-

snorkel /'snɔːk(ə)l/ n. (дыха́тельная) тру́бка (для подво́дного пла́вания)

snort /snɔːt/ v.i. фы́рк|ать, -нуть

snout /snaʊt/ n. (of animal) мо́рда; (of pig) ры́ло

snow /snəʊ/ n. снег
● v.i.: it is ~ing идёт снег
□ ~ **in** v.t.: we were ~ed in наш дом занесло́ сне́гом
□ ~ **under** v.t. (fig.): we are ~ed under with work мы зава́лены рабо́той
■ ~**ball** n. снежо́к ● v.i. (fig., increase) расти́ (impf.) как сне́жный ком; ~**board** n. сноубо́рд; ~**boarding** n. сноубо́рдинг; ~**drift** n. сугро́б; ~**drop** n. подсне́жник; ~**fall** n. снегопа́д; ~**flake** n. снежи́нка; (in pl.) (large) (сне́жные) хло́пья; ~**man** n. сне́жная ба́ба; ~**plough** n. снегоубо́рочная маши́на

snowy /'snəʊɪ/ adj. (**snowier, snowiest**): ~ **weather** сне́жная пого́да; ~ **roofs** засне́женные кры́ши

snub /snʌb/ n. (rebuff) оби́да
● v.t. (**snubbed, snubbing**) ун|ижа́ть, -и́зить

snuck /snʌk/ (AmE, infml) past and p.p. of ▶ sneak

snuff /snʌf/ n. ню́хательный таба́к; pinch of ~ поню́шка; take ~ ню́хать, по- таба́к
■ ~**box** n. табаке́рка

snug /snʌg/ adj. (**snugger, snuggest**) ую́тный

snuggle /'snʌg(ə)l/ v.i.: ~ down in bed свёр|тываться, -ну́ться в посте́ли; ~ up to sb приж|има́ться, -а́ться к кому́-н.

ⳕ **so** /səʊ/ *adv.* **1** так; **is that ~?** э́то так?; (э́то) пра́вда?; **that being ~** раз так; **I'm ~ glad to see you** я так рад вас ви́деть; **would you be ~ kind as to visit her?** бу́дьте так добры́, навести́те её; **he is not ~ silly as to ask her** он не насто́лько глуп, что́бы проси́ть её; **he was ~ overworked that …** он был так/ до тако́й сте́пени загру́жен рабо́той, что…; **~ far** (up to now) до сих пор, пока́; **~ far as I know** насколько я зна́ю; **and ~ forth, on** и так да́лее; **~ long as** (provided that) е́сли то́лько; **~ many** сто́лько + *g.*, так мно́го + *g.*; **thank you ~ much!** большо́е (вам) спаси́бо!; **~ much the worse/better** тем ху́же/лу́чше; **~ to say, speak** так сказа́ть; **~ what** ну и что? **2** (also) то́же; **(and) ~ do I** и я то́же **3** (consequently, accordingly) поэ́тому, так что; ита́к, зна́чит; **he is ill, (and) ~ he can't come** он нездоро́в, поэ́тому не мо́жет прийти́; **~ you did see him after all** зна́чит/ ита́к, вы всё-таки его́ ви́дели **4** (that the foregoing is true or will happen): **I suppose/hope ~** я ду́маю/наде́юсь, что да; **do you think ~?** вы так ду́маете? **5**: **~ as to** (in order to) для того́, что́бы; (in such a way as to) так, что́бы **6** (thereabouts): **there were 100 or ~ people there** там бы́ло приме́рно сто челове́к (*or* о́коло ста челове́к)
■ **~-called** *adj.* так называ́емый; **~-so** *adj.* & *adv.* ничего́; так себе́

soak /səʊk/ *v.t.* **1** (wet) зама́чивать, -очи́ть; выма́чивать, вы́мочить; **she ~s the laundry overnight** она́ зама́чивает бельё на́ ночь **2** (wet through): **the shower ~ed me to the skin** дождь промочи́л меня́ до ни́тки/наскво́зь
• *v.i.* **1** (remain immersed) мо́кнуть (*impf.*) **2** (drain) впи́т|ываться, -а́ться; **the rain ~ed into the ground** дождь пропита́л по́чву; **the water ~ed through my shoes** вода́ просочи́лась мне в ту́фли
□ **~ up** *v.t.* (lit., fig.) впи́т|ывать, -а́ть

soaking /ˈsəʊkɪŋ/ *adj.* & *adv.*: **you are ~ (wet)** вы промо́кли наскво́зь

soap /səʊp/ *n.* мы́ло
■ **~ opera** *n.* мы́льная о́пера, телесериа́л; **~ powder** *n.* стира́льный порошо́к

soapy /ˈsəʊpɪ/ *adj.* (**soapier, soapiest**) **1** (covered with soap) мы́льный, намы́ленный **2** (resembling, containing, consisting of soap) мы́льный

soar /sɔː(r)/ *v.i.* **1** (of birds) высоко́ взлет|а́ть, -е́ть **2** (fig.): **her spirits ~ed** она́ испыта́ла душе́вный подъём **3** (of prices) (ре́зко) пов|ыша́ться, -ы́ситься **4** (of mountains, buildings) возвыша́ться (*impf.*)

sob /sɒb/ *n.* всхлип, всхли́пывание
• *v.i.* (**sobbed, sobbing**) всхли́п|ывать, -нуть

sober /ˈsəʊbə(r)/ *adj.* (**soberer, soberest**) **1** (not drunk, not fanciful) тре́звый **2** (of colour) споко́йный
• *v.t.* (*usu.* **~ up**) отрезв|ля́ть, -и́ть
• *v.i.*: **~ up** протрезв|ля́ться, -и́ться

sobriety /səˈbraɪɪtɪ/ *n.* тре́звость

soccer /ˈsɒkə(r)/ *n.* футбо́л
■ **~ match** *n.* футбо́льный матч; **~ player** *n.* футболи́ст

sociable /ˈsəʊʃəb(ə)l/ *adj.* общи́тельный

ⳕ **social** /ˈsəʊʃ(ə)l/ *adj.* **1** (pert. to the community) обще́ственный, социа́льный **2** (convivial): **~ gathering** дру́жеская встре́ча
■ **S~ Democrat** *n.* социа́л-демокра́т; **~ media** *n. pl.* социа́льные се́ти; **~ network** *n.* социа́льная сеть; **~ networking** *n.* по́льзование социа́льной се́тью; **~ sciences** *n. pl.* обще́ственные нау́ки; **~ security** *n.* (system) социа́льное обеспе́чение; (money received) посо́бие; **~ services** *n. pl.* систе́ма социа́льного обеспе́чения; **~ worker** *n.* социа́льный рабо́тник

socialism /ˈsəʊʃəlɪz(ə)m/ *n.* социали́зм

socialist /ˈsəʊʃəlɪst/ *n.* социали́ст (-ка)
• *adj.* социалисти́ческий

socialite /ˈsəʊʃəlaɪt/ *n.* све́тская знамени́тость

socialize /ˈsəʊʃəlaɪz/ *v.i.* обща́ться (*impf.*)

ⳕ **society** /səˈsaɪətɪ/ *n.* о́бщество; (association) о́бщество, объедине́ние, организа́ция

sociological /ˌsəʊsɪəˈlɒdʒɪk(ə)l/ *adj.* социологи́ческий

sociologist /ˌsəʊsɪˈɒlədʒɪst/ *n.* социо́лог

sociology /ˌsəʊsɪˈɒlədʒɪ/ *n.* социоло́гия

sock /sɒk/ *n.* носо́к

socket /ˈsɒkɪt/ *n.* **1** (anat.) впа́дина; **eye ~** глазна́я впа́дина, глазни́ца **2** (for plug) розе́тка; (slot for connecting electrical device) разъём; (for bulb) патро́н

sod /sɒd/ *n.* (BrE, sl.) *n.* сво́лочь (*f.*)
• *v.i.* (**sodded, sodding**) ~ **off: I told him to ~ off** я его́ посла́л; **~ off!** иди́ на́ фиг!
• *v.t.* (**sodded, sodding**): ~ **it!** чёрт возьми́!

soda /ˈsəʊdə/ *n.* **1** со́да; **washing ~** стира́льная/криста́ллическая со́да **2** (also ~ **water**) со́довая (вода́)

sodden /ˈsɒd(ə)n/ *adj.* промо́кший

sodium /ˈsəʊdɪəm/ *n.* на́трий

sofa /ˈsəʊfə/ *n.* дива́н
■ **~ bed** *n.* дива́н-крова́ть

Sofia /ˈsəʊfɪə/ *n.* Со́фия

ⳕ **soft** /sɒft/ *adj.* **1** мя́гкий **2** (compassionate) мя́гкий; отзы́вчивый; **have a ~ spot for sb** пита́ть (*impf.*) сла́бость к кому́-н.; (indulgent) мя́гкий, нестро́гий; **she is too ~ with her children** она́ недоста́точно строга́ с детьми́
■ **~ drink** *n.* безалкого́льный напи́ток; **~ drugs** *n. pl.* лёгкие нарко́тики; **~ sign** *n.* (gram.) мя́гкий знак; **~ toy** *n.* мя́гкая игру́шка

soften /ˈsɒf(ə)n/ *v.t.* смягч|а́ть, -и́ть
• *v.i.* смягч|а́ться, -и́ться
□ **~ up** *v.t.*: **~ sb up** (fig.) осл|абля́ть, -а́бить чьё-н. сопротивле́ние

software /ˈsɒftweə(r)/ *n.* (comput.) програ́ммное обеспе́чение

soggy /ˈsɒgɪ/ *adj.* (**soggier, soggiest**) сыро́й, вла́жный

S

soil¹ /sɔɪl/ *n.* по́чва

soil² /sɔɪl/ *v.t.* па́чкать, за-/ис-/вы́-; **~ed linen** гря́зное бельё

soirée /ˈswɑːreɪ/ *n.* зва́ный ве́чер

sojourn /ˈsɒdʒ(ə)n/ (liter.) *n.* (вре́менное) пребыва́ние
● *v.i.* пребыва́ть, (вре́менно) жить, прожива́ть (*all impf.*)

solace /ˈsɒləs/ *n.* утеше́ние, отра́да

solar /ˈsəʊlə(r)/ *adj.* со́лнечный
■ **~ system** *n.* Со́лнечная систе́ма

sold /səʊld/ *past and p.p. of* ▶ **sell**

solder /ˈsəʊldə(r)/ *v.t.* пая́ть (*impf.*); **~ sth to sth** припа́ивать, -я́ть что-н. к чему́-н.; **~ together** спая́ть (*pf.*)

soldier /ˈsəʊldʒə(r)/ *n.* солда́т
● *v.i.*: **~ on** (fig., persevere doggedly) не сдава́ться (*impf.*)

sole¹ /səʊl/ *n.* (*pl.* **~**) (fish) морско́й язы́к (*род камбалы*)

sole² /səʊl/ *n.* (of foot) ступня́, подо́шва (infml); (of shoe) подо́шва, подмётка

sole³ /səʊl/ *adj.* (only) еди́нственный; (exclusive) исключи́тельный

solecism /ˈsɒlɪsɪz(ə)m/ *n.* (of language) солеци́зм; гру́бая (языкова́я) оши́бка; (of behaviour) гру́бая вы́ходка, гру́бость

solely /ˈsəʊllɪ/ *adv.* то́лько, еди́нственно, исключи́тельно

solemn /ˈsɒləm/ *adj.* торже́ственный; (serious) серьёзный, ва́жный

solemnity /səˈlemnɪtɪ/ *n.* торже́ственность; (gravity) ва́жность; (of appearance) серьёзность

solicit /səˈlɪsɪt/ *v.t.* (soliciting) (petition): **~ sb's help** проси́ть, по- кого́-н. о по́мощи
● *v.i.* (solicited, soliciting) (of prostitute) пристава́ть (*impf.*) к мужчи́нам

solicitor /səˈlɪsɪtə(r)/ *n.* (BrE) адвока́т

solicitous /səˈlɪsɪtəs/ *adj.* забо́тливый, внима́тельный; **she is ~ for, about your safety** она́ забо́тится о ва́шей безопа́сности

solicitude /səˈlɪsɪtjuːd/ *n.* забо́тливость

solid /ˈsɒlɪd/ *n.* (phys.) твёрдое те́ло
● *adj.* (**solider, solidest**) **1** (not liquid) твёрдый; **become ~** тверде́ть, за- **2** (not hollow) це́льный **3** (homogeneous): **~ silver** чи́стое серебро́ **4** (unbroken): **a ~ line** сплошна́я черта́; **it rained for 3 ~ days** дождь лил три дня подря́д **5** (firmly built) про́чный **6** (sound, reliable) соли́дный; надёжный

solidarity /sɒlɪˈdærɪtɪ/ *n.* солида́рность

solidify /səˈlɪdɪfaɪ/ *v.i.* тверде́ть, за-

solidity /səˈlɪdɪtɪ/ *n.* твёрдость; (sturdiness) про́чность; (reliability) надёжность; (soundness) основа́тельность

soliloquy /səˈlɪləkwɪ/ *n.* моноло́г

solitary /ˈsɒlɪtərɪ/ *adj.* (secluded) уединённый; (lonely) одино́кий; (single) едини́чный, еди́нственный

■ **~ confinement** *n.* одино́чное заключе́ние

solitude /ˈsɒlɪtjuːd/ *n.* уедине́ние, одино́чество

solo /ˈsəʊləʊ/ *n.* (mus.) со́ло (*nt. indecl.*)
● *adj.* со́льный; (aeron.) самостоя́тельный

soloist /ˈsəʊləʊɪst/ *n.* соли́ст (-ка)

solstice /ˈsɒlstɪs/ *n.* солнцестоя́ние

soluble /ˈsɒljʊb(ə)l/ *adj.* раствори́мый

solution /səˈluːʃ(ə)n/ *n.* **1** (result of dissolving) раство́р **2** (solving, answer) реше́ние

solve /sɒlv/ *v.t.*: **~ an equation/problem** реша́ть, -и́ть уравне́ние/зада́чу; **~ a mystery** раскры́|вать, -ы́ть та́йну

solvent /ˈsɒlv(ə)nt/ *n.* раствори́тель (*m.*)
● *adj.* (fin.) платёжеспосо́бный
■ **~ abuse** *n.* токсикома́ния

Somali /səˈmɑːlɪ/ *n.* (*pl.* **~** *or* **~s**) (person) сомали́|ец (-йка); (language) сомали́ (*m. indecl.*)
● *adj.* сомали́йский

Somalia /səˈmɑːlɪə/ *n.* Сомали́ (*nt. indecl.*)

sombre /ˈsɒmbə(r)/ (AmE *also* **somber**) *adj.* угрю́мый

some /sʌm/ *pron.* **1** (of persons) не́которые, одни́; **~ left and others stayed** одни́ ушли́, други́е оста́лись; **~ of these girls** не́которые/ кое-кто из э́тих де́вушек **2** (of things, an indefinite number) не́сколько; **can I have ~?** мо́жно (мне) взять не́сколько?; (an indefinite amount): **have ~ more!** возьми́те ещё! **3** (a part) часть; **I agree with ~ of what you said** части́чно я согла́сен с ва́шими слова́ми
● *adj.* **1** (definite though unspecified) како́й-то; **~ fool has locked the door** како́й-то дура́к за́пер дверь; **~ day/time** когда́-нибудь **2** (no matter what) како́й-нибудь, како́й-либо **3** (one or two) кое-каки́е (*pl.*); (a certain amount, may be expr. by g.): **I bought ~ milk** я купи́л молока́; (a certain number) не́сколько; (or untranslated) **I bought ~ envelopes** я купи́л конве́рты; **for ~ time now** с не́которого вре́мени **4** (approximately) приме́рно, о́коло

somebody /ˈsʌmbədɪ/ *pron.* (*also* **someone**) (in particular) кто́-то; **there is ~ in the cellar** в по́гребе кто́-то есть; (only in nom.) не́кто; (no matter who) кто́-нибудь, кто́-либо; **~ else can do it** кто́-нибудь друго́й мо́жет э́то сде́лать

somehow /ˈsʌmhaʊ/ *adv.* (no matter how) ка́к-нибудь; так и́ли ина́че; **we shall manage ~** мы ка́к-нибудь спра́вимся; (in some unspecified way) ка́к-то, каки́м-то о́бразом; **he found out my name ~** он каки́м-то о́бразом узна́л, как меня́ зову́т; (for some reason) **~ I never liked him** он мне почему́-то никогда́ не нра́вился

someone /ˈsʌmwʌn/ *pron.* = **somebody**

someplace /ˈsʌmpleɪs/ *adv.* (AmE) = **somewhere 1**

somersault /ˈsʌməsɔlt/ *n.* (in the air) са́льто (*nt. indecl.*); (on the ground) кувыро́к
● *v.i.* кувырк|а́ться, -ну́ться; де́лать, с- са́льто

something /ˈsʌmθɪŋ/ *pron.* (definite) что́-то; (only in nom.) не́что; (indefinite) что́-нибудь, что́-либо; **I must get ~ to eat** я до́лжен что-нибудь поесть; **she lectures in** ~ **or other** она читает лекции по какому-то (там) предмету; **there is** ~ **about him** в нём что-то такое есть; **she has a cold or** ~ у неё простуда или что-то в этом роде; (expr. approximation): **he left** ~ **like a million** он оставил что-то порядка миллиона

sometime /'sʌmtaɪm/ *adv.* когда-нибудь, когда-либо; ~ **soon** как-нибудь, скоро

⟋ **sometimes** /'sʌmtaɪmz/ *adv.* иногда

⟋ **somewhat** /'sʌmwɒt/ *adv.* как-то, несколько, довольно

⟋ **somewhere** /'sʌmweə(r)/ *adv.* **1** (AmE *also* **someplace**) (place, specific) где-то; (place, anywhere) где-нибудь, где-либо; (motion, specific) куда-то; (motion, anywhere) куда-нибудь, куда-либо **2** (approximately) около + *g.*

⟋ **son** /sʌn/ *n.* сын

■ ~-**in-law** *n.* зять (*m.*) (*муж дочери*)

sonata /sə'nɑːtə/ *n.* соната

⟋ **song** /sɒŋ/ *n.* песня

sonic /'sɒnɪk/ *adj.* звуковой

sonnet /'sɒnɪt/ *n.* сонет

sonorous /'sɒnərəs/ *adj.* звучный

⟋ **soon** /suːn/ *adv.* **1** (in a short while) скоро, вскоре; **write** ~! напишите (по)скорее!; **as** ~ **as possible** как можно скорее **2** (early) рано; ~**er or later** рано или поздно **3**: **as** ~ **as** как только; **as** ~ **as I saw him, I recognized him** я узнал его, как только увидел **4** (willingly): **I would** ~**er die than permit it** я скорее умру, чем допущу это; **what would you** ~**er do: go now or wait?** что вы предпочитаете: уйти или подождать?

soot /sʊt/ *n.* сажа, копоть

soothe /suːð/ *v.t.* (calm) успок|аивать, -оить; (relieve) облегч|ать, -ить

soothing /'suːðɪŋ/ *adj.* (tone) утешительный; (cream) успокоительный

sooty /'sʊti/ *adj.* (**sootier**, **sootiest**) (blackened with soot) закопчённый, закоптелый; (black as soot) чёрный как сажа; (containing soot): ~ **deposit** слой сажи

sophisticated /sə'fɪstɪkeɪtɪd/ *adj.* **1** (complicated): ~ **techniques** сложная техника **2** (refined): ~ **taste** утончённый вкус

sophistication /səfɪstɪ'keɪʃ(ə)n/ *n.* (refinement) утончённость, искушённость

soporific /sɒpə'rɪfɪk/ *adj.* снотворный, усыпляющий

soppy /'sɒpi/ *adj.* (**soppier**, **soppiest**) (BrE, infml, sentimental) сентиментальный

soprano /sə'prɑːnəʊ/ *n.* (*pl.* ~s) (singer) сопрано (*f. indecl.*); (voice) сопрано (*nt. indecl.*)

sorbet /'sɔːbeɪ/ *n.* шербет

sorcerer /'sɔːsərə(r)/ *n.* колдун, волшебник

sorceress /'sɔːsərɪs/ *n.* колдунья, волшебница

sorcery /'sɔːsəri/ *n.* колдовство, волшебство

sordid /'sɔːdɪd/ *adj.* (squalid) убогий; (morally bad) гнусный

sore /sɔː(r)/ *n.* болячка, язва

● *adj.*: **a** ~ **tooth** больной зуб; **I have a** ~ (*sc.* grazed) **knee** я ссадил себе колено; **he has a** ~ **throat** у него болит горло; **it is a** ~ **point with him** это у него больное место

sorrow /'sɒrəʊ/ *n.* (sadness) печаль, горе; (*in pl.*) горести (*pl., f.*)

sorrowful /'sɒrəʊfʊl/ *adj.* печальный, горестный

⟋ **sorry** /'sɒri/ *adj.* (**sorrier**, **sorriest**) **1** (regretful): **be** ~ **for sth** сожалеть (*impf.*) о чём-н., жалеть, по- о чём-н.; **we were** ~ **to hear of your father's death** мы с грустью узнали о смерти вашего отца; ~! виноват!; простите!; извините!; **say you're** ~! (по)проси прощения!; ~, **I'm busy** извините, но я занят; **I'm** ~ **I came** я жалею, что пришёл **2** (expr. pity, sympathy): **I feel** ~ **for you** мне жалко/жаль тебя; **it's the children I feel** ~ **for** кого мне жалко/жаль — так это детей; **feel** ~ **for oneself** жалеть (*impf.*) себя **3** (wretched) жалкий; **in a** ~ **state** в жалком состоянии

⟋ **sort** /sɔːt/ *n.* **1** (kind, species) род, сорт, разряд, вид; **he is not the** ~ (of person) **to complain** он не из тех, кто жалуется; **what** ~ **of man is he?** что он за человек?; **what** ~ **of music do you like?** какую музыку вы любите?; **people of all** ~**s** самые разные люди **2**: ~ **of** (infml) вроде, как бы; в общем-то; **he** ~ **of suggested I took him with me** он как бы дал мне понять, что хочет пойти со мной **3**: **out of** ~**s** (BrE) не в духе

● *v.t.* раз|бирать, -обрать; **they** ~**ed themselves into groups of six** они разбились на группы по шесть человек; (letters etc., also comput.) сортиров|ать, рас-

□ ~ **out** *v.t.* (select) от|бирать, -обрать; (separate) отдел|ять, -ить; (arrange) раз|бирать, -обрать; (fig., put in order): **I have to go home to** ~ **things out** мне нужно пойти домой и во всём разобраться

sortie /'sɔːtiː/ *n.* (sally) вылазка (also fig.); (flight) вылет

SOS *n.* (*pl.* ~**s**) (радио)сигнал бедствия

sought /sɔːt/ *past and p.p. of* ▶ **seek**

⟋ **soul** /səʊl/ *n.* **1** душа **2** (music) соул

soulful /'səʊlfʊl/ *adj.* проникновенный, задушевный

soulless /'səʊlls/ *adj.* бездушный

⟋ **sound**[1] /saʊnd/ *n.* **1** звук; (of rain, sea, wind, etc.) шум **2**: **I don't like the** ~ **of it** мне это (что-то) не нравится

● *v.t.*: **they** ~**ed the bell** они позвонили в колокол; ~ **the alarm** бить, за- тревогу

● *v.i.* **1** (emit sound) звучать, про- **2** (give impression) каз|аться, по-; **it** ~**s like thunder** похоже на гром; **the statement** ~**s improbable** это заявление кажется маловероятным

■ ~ **barrier** *n.* звуковой барьер; ~ **card** *n.* (comput.) звуковая карта; ~ **effects** *n. pl.* звуковое сопровождение, шумовые эффекты; ~**proof** *adj.* звуконепроницаемый; ~**track** *n.* саундтрек

sound[2] /saʊnd/ *n.* (strait) пролив

S

$\mathscr{O}$ **sound³** /saʊnd/ v.t. (fig.): ~ (out) sb (or sb's intentions, opinions) зонди́ровать, про- кого́-н.

sound⁴ /saʊnd/ adj. **1** (healthy) здоро́вый; of ~ mind в здра́вом уме́; (in good condition) испра́вный **2** (thorough) хоро́ший; he slept ~ly он кре́пко спал; he was ~ly thrashed его́ си́льно изби́ли

soup /suːp/ n. суп
■ ~ kitchen n. беспла́тная столо́вая для нужда́ющихся

sour /'saʊə(r)/ adj. **1** (of fruit etc.) ки́слый **2** (of milk) проки́сший, ски́сший; go, turn ~ ск|иса́ть, -и́снуть **3** (of person) мра́чный, озло́бленный

$\mathscr{O}$ **source** /sɔːs/ n. **1** (of stream etc.) исто́к **2** (fig.) исто́чник

$\mathscr{O}$ **south** /saʊθ/ n. юг; (naut.) зюйд; in the ~ на ю́ге; from the ~ с ю́га; to the ~ of к ю́гу от + g.
● adj. ю́жный
● adv.: the ship sailed due ~ су́дно шло пря́мо на юг; our village is ~ of London на́ша дере́вня нахо́дится к ю́гу от Ло́ндона
■ ~-east n. юго-восто́к ● adj. юго-восто́чный; ~-east wind зюйд-о́ст ● adv. к юго-восто́ку; на юго-восто́к; ~-easterly adj. юго- восто́чный; ~-eastern adj. юго-восто́чный; S~ Pole n. Ю́жный по́люс; ~-west n. юго-за́пад ● adj. юго-за́падный; ~-west wind зюйд-ве́ст ● adv. к юго-за́паду; на юго-за́пад; ~-westerly adj. юго-за́падный; ~-western adj. юго-за́падный; ~ wind n. ю́жный ве́тер

South Africa /saʊθ 'æfrɪkə/ n. Ю́жная А́фрика
South African /saʊθ 'æfrɪkən/ n. южноафрика́н|ец (-ка)
● adj. южноафрика́нский
South America /saʊθ ə'merɪkə/ n. Ю́жная Аме́рика
South American /saʊθ ə'merɪkən/ n. южноамерика́н|ец (-ка)
● adj. южноамерика́нский
southerly /'sʌðəlɪ/ n. (wind) ю́жный ве́тер
● adj. ю́жный

$\mathscr{O}$ **southern** /'sʌð(ə)n/ adj. ю́жный
southerner /'sʌðənə(r)/ n. южан|ин (-ка)
southward /'saʊθwəd/ adj. ю́жный
● adv. (also ~s) /-wədz/ на юг; к ю́гу, в ю́жном направле́нии
souvenir /suːvə'nɪə(r)/ n. сувени́р
sovereign /'sɒvrɪn/ n. (monarch) госуда́р|ь (-ыня); (coin) совере́н
● adj. сувере́нный
sovereignty /'sɒvrɪntɪ/ n. суверените́т
$\mathscr{O}$ **Soviet** /'səʊvɪət/ (hist.) n. сове́т
● adj. сове́тский; the ~ Union Сове́тский Сою́з
sow¹ /saʊ/ n. (pig) свинья́ (самка)
sow² /səʊ/ v.t. (past sowed /səʊd/; p.p. sown or sowed) **1** (seed) се́ять, по- **2** (ground) зас|е́ивать, -е́ять

$\mathscr{O}$ ключева́я ле́ксика

soy /'sɔɪ/, **soya** /'sɔɪə/ nn. со́я
● adj. со́евый; ~ sauce со́евый со́ус
sozzled /'sɒz(ə)ld/ adj. (sl.) пья́ный вдребёзги
spa /spɑː/ n. во́ды (f. pl.); куро́рт с минера́льными исто́чниками

$\mathscr{O}$ **space** /speɪs/ n. **1** (expanse) простра́нство, просто́р **2** (outer ~) ко́смос; (attr.) косми́ческий **3** (distance, interval) расстоя́ние **4** (of time, distance) промежу́ток/пери́од вре́мени; in the ~ of an hour за час; в тече́ние ча́са **5** (area) ме́сто; blank ~ пусто́е ме́сто
● v.t. (also ~ out): the posts were ~d six feet apart столбы́ бы́ли расположёны на расстоя́нии шести́ фу́тов друг от дру́га
■ ~craft (also ~ship) n. косми́ческий кора́бль; ~suit n. скафа́ндр (космона́вта)
spacious /'speɪʃəs/ adj. просто́рный
spade /speɪd/ n. **1** (tool) лопа́та **2** (cards) пи́ка; queen of ~s пи́ковая да́ма, да́ма пик
spaghetti /spə'getɪ/ n. спаге́тти (nt. and pl. indecl.)
Spain /speɪn/ n. Испа́ния
span¹ /spæn/ n. **1** (distance between supports) пролёт **2** (of time) промежу́ток/пери́од вре́мени **3**: wing ~ разма́х кры́льев
● v.t. (spanned, spanning) перекр|ыва́ть, -ы́ть; (fig.): the movement ~s almost two centuries э́то движе́ние охва́тывает почти́ два столе́тия
span² /spæn/ past of ▶ spin
span³ /spæn/ see ▶ spick
Spaniard /'spænjəd/ n. испа́н|ец (-ка)
spaniel /'spænj(ə)l/ n. спание́ль (m.)
Spanish /'spænɪʃ/ n. **1** (language) испа́нский (язы́к) **2**: the ~ (collect.) испа́нцы (m. pl.)
● adj. испа́нский
spank /spæŋk/ v.t. шлёпать, от-
spanner /'spænə(r)/ n. (BrE) га́ечный ключ
spar /spɑː(r)/ v.i. (sparred, sparring) бокси́ровать (impf.)
spare /speə(r)/ n. **1** (in full ~ part) запасна́я часть, запча́сть **2** (in full ~ wheel) запасно́е колесо́
● adj. (extra) ли́шний; (additional, reserve) запасно́й, резе́рвный
● v.t. **1** (withhold use of) жале́ть, по- **2** (dispense with, do without) об|ходи́ться, -ойти́сь без + g.; we cannot ~ him мы не мо́жем обойти́сь без него́ **3** (afford): can you ~ a cigarette? у вас не найдётся сигаре́ты?; I can ~ you only a few minutes я могу́ удели́ть вам то́лько не́сколько мину́т **4** to ~ (available, left over): I have no time to ~ у меня́ нет ли́шнего вре́мени; we got there with an hour to ~ когда́ мы прие́хали туда́, у нас остава́лся це́лый час в запа́се **5** (show leniency to) щади́ть, по-; I tried to ~ his feelings я стара́лся щади́ть его́ чу́вства **6** (save from) изб|авля́ть, -а́вить (кого от чего); I will ~ you the trouble of replying я изба́влю вас от необходи́мости отвеча́ть
■ ~ room n. ко́мната для госте́й; ~ time n. свобо́дное вре́мя

spark /spɑːk/ *n.* и́скра
● *v.t.* (*also* ~ **off**) (cause) вызыва́ть, вы́звать; (friendship) дава́ть, -ть нача́ло + *d.*
■ ~ **plug** *n.* свеча́ зажига́ния, запа́льная свеча́

sparkl|e /'spɑːk(ə)l/ *n.* сверка́ние, блеск, блиста́ние; блёстка, и́скорка
● *v.i.* сверка́ть, за-; (flash) блесте́ть, за-; ~ing **wine** шипу́чее/игри́стое вино́

sparkler /'spɑːklə(r)/ *n.* (firework) бенга́льский ого́нь

sparrow /'spærəʊ/ *n.* воробе́й

sparse /spɑːs/ *adj.* ре́дкий; (scattered) разбро́санный; ~ly **populated** малонаселённый

Spartan /'spɑːt(ə)n/ *n.* спарта́н|ец (-ка)
● *adj.* спарта́нский

spasm /'spæz(ə)m/ *n.* (of muscles) спа́зм; (mental or physical reaction) при́ступ, припа́док

spasmodic /spæz'mɒdɪk/ *adj.* спазмати́ческий

spastic /'spæstɪk/ *n.* (often offens.) (спасти́ческий) парали́тик

spat /spæt/ *past and p.p. of* ▶ **spit**²

spate /speɪt/ *n.* (BrE, sudden flood) разли́в; (fig.) пото́к

spatial /'speɪʃ(ə)l/ *adj.* простра́нственный

spatter /'spætə(r)/, **splatter** /'splætə(r)/ *vv.t. & i.* бры́з|гать, -нуть; забры́згать (*pf.*); ~ed **with mud** забры́зганный гря́зью

spatula /'spætjʊlə/ *n.* (med.) шпа́тель (*m.*); (cul.) лопа́точка

◌⁵ **speak** /spiːk/ *v.t.* (*past* **spoke**, *p.p.* **spoken**)
1 (say) говори́ть, сказа́ть; произн|оси́ть, -ести́; (express): ~ **one's mind** выска́зывать, вы́сказать своё мне́ние **2** (converse in) говори́ть (*impf.*); **he** ~s **Russian well** он хорошо́ говори́т по-ру́сски
● *v.i.* (*past* **spoke**, *p.p.* **spoken**) говори́ть (*impf.*); (converse) говори́ть, по-; разгова́ривать (*impf.*); вести́ (*indet.*) разгово́р; (make a speech) выступа́ть, вы́ступить; произн|оси́ть, -ести́ речь; '**Smith** ~**ing**' (on telephone) «(с ва́ми) говори́т Смит»; **roughly, broadly** ~**ing** гру́бо говоря́; в о́бщих черта́х; **strictly** ~**ing** стро́го говоря́; ~ **of** (mention, refer to) упом|ина́ть, -яну́ть о + *d.*
□ ~ **out** *v.i.* (express oneself plainly) выска́зываться, вы́сказаться (открове́нно)
□ ~ **up** *v.i.* (~ louder) говори́ть (*impf.*) гро́мче; (express support): ~ **up for sb** подде́рж|ивать, -а́ть кого́-н.

◌⁵ **speaker** /'spiːkə(r)/ *n.* **1**: **the** ~ **was a man of about 40** говоря́щему бы́ло лет со́рок **2**: **a Russian** ~ челове́к, владе́ющий ру́сским языко́м **3** (public ~) ора́тор, докла́дчик, выступа́ющий **4** (*in full* **loud** ~) громкоговори́тель (*m.*) **5** (pol.) спи́кер

spear /spɪə(r)/ *n.* копьё, дро́тик
■ ~**head** *v.t.*: ~**head a movement** возгл|авля́ть, -а́вить движе́ние

spec¹ /spek/ *n.* (infml): **he went there on** ~ он пошёл туда́ науда́чу

spec² /spek/ *n.* (infml, specification) специфика́ция

◌⁵ **special** /'speʃ(ə)l/ *adj.* **1** (exceptional)

осо́бый, осо́бенный; (for a particular purpose) специа́льный **2** (extraordinary) специа́льный, э́кстренный
■ ~ **delivery** *n.* сро́чная доста́вка; ~ **effect** *n.* спецэффе́кт

specialist /'speʃəlɪst/ *n.* специали́ст (-ка) (**in:** по + *d.*)

speciality /speʃɪ'ælɪtɪ/ (AmE **specialty**) *n.* **1** (pursuit) специа́льность, специализа́ция **2** (product, recipe, etc.): ~ **of the house** фи́рменное блю́до

specialize /'speʃəlaɪz/ *v.i.* специализи́роваться (*impf., pf.*) (**in:** по + *d.*; в/на + *p.*)

specially /'speʃəlɪ/ *adv.* **1** (for specific purpose) специа́льно **2** (exceptionally) осо́бенно, исключи́тельно; **be** ~ **careful** быть осо́бенно осторо́жным

specialty /'speʃəltɪ/ *n.* (AmE) = **speciality**

◌⁵ **species** /'spiːʃiːz/ *n.* (*pl.* ~) (биологи́ческий) вид

◌⁵ **specific** /spə'sɪfɪk/ *adj.* определённый

◌⁵ **specifically** /spə'sɪfɪkəlɪ/ *adv.* (exactly) определённо; (specially) специа́льно

specification /spesɪfɪ'keɪʃ(ə)n/ *n.* (tech.) специфика́ция; (*in pl.*) техни́ческие характери́стики (*f. pl.*)

specify /'spesɪfaɪ/ *v.t.* определ|я́ть, -и́ть

specimen /'spesɪmən/ *n.* (of rock, handwriting) образе́ц; (of plant, animal) экземпля́р; (of urine) моча́ для ана́лиза

speck /spek/ *n.* (of dirt) пя́тнышко; ~ **of dust** пыли́нка

specs /speks/ *n. pl.* (infml) = **spectacle 2**

spectacle /'spektək(ə)l/ *n.* **1** (public show; sight) зре́лище **2** (BrE) (*in pl.*) (glasses) очк|и́ (-о́в)

spectacular /spek'tækjʊlə(r)/ *adj.* эффе́ктный, впечатля́ющий

spectator /spek'teɪtə(r)/ *n.* зри́тель (-ница)

spectre /'spektə(r)/ (AmE **specter**) *n.* привиде́ние, при́зрак

spectrum /'spektrəm/ *n.* спектр

speculate /'spekjʊleɪt/ *v.i.* **1** (meditate) размышля́ть (*impf.*) (*о чём*); (conjecture) гада́ть (*impf.*) **2** (risk, invest money) спекули́ровать (*impf.*), игра́ть (*impf.*) на би́рже; **he** ~s **in oil shares** он спекули́рует а́кциями нефтяны́х компа́ний

speculation /spekjʊ'leɪʃ(ə)n/ *n.* (meditation) размышле́ние; (conjecture) дога́дка; (investment) спекуля́ция

speculative /'spekjʊlətɪv/ *adj.* (investment) спекуляти́вный

speculator /'spekjʊleɪtə(r)/ *n.* спекуля́нт (-ка)

sped /sped/ *past and p.p. of* ▶ **speed** *v.i.* 1

◌⁵ **speech** /spiːtʃ/ *n.* речь; **make a** ~ произн|оси́ть, -ести́ речь
■ ~ **therapist** *n.* логопе́д

speechless /'spiːtʃlɪs/ *adj.*: **I was** ~ **with surprise** я онеме́л от удивле́ния

◌⁵ **speed** /spiːd/ *n.* (rapidity) быстрота́, ско́рость; (rate) ско́рость; **at full, top** ~ на по́лной

S

скорости
- *v.t.* (*past and p.p.* **speeded**) (*also* ~ **up**) уск|оря́ть, -о́рить
- *v.i.* **1** (*past and p.p.* **sped**) (move quickly) мча́ться, нести́сь (*impf.*); **2** (*past and p.p.* **speeded**) (go too fast): he was fined for ~ing его́ оштрафова́ли за превыше́ние ско́рости **3** ~ **up** (*past and p.p.* **speeded**) уск|оря́ться, -о́риться
- ■ ~**boat** *n.* быстрохо́дный ка́тер; ~ **camera** *n.* ка́мера-рада́р, спид-ка́мера (*фиксирует скорость автомобиля для последующего доказательства превышения скорости*); ~ **dating** *n.* экспре́сс-знако́мства (*nt. pl.*)

speedometer /spiːˈdɒmɪtə(r)/ *n.* спидо́метр

speedy /ˈspiːdɪ/ *adj.* (**speedier, speediest**) (rapid) ско́рый, бы́стрый; (hasty) поспе́шный; (prompt, undelayed) ско́рый, неме́дленный

spell[1] /spel/ *n.* (magical formula) ча́р|ы (*pl., g.* —); колдовство́; cast a ~ over заколдо́в|ывать, -а́ть
- ■ ~**bound** *adj.* очаро́ванный, зачаро́ванный

spell[2] /spel/ *n.* (interval) пери́од; промежу́ток вре́мени; we're in for a ~ of fine weather ожида́ется полоса́ хоро́шей пого́ды

spell[3] /spel/ *v.t.* (*past and p.p.* **spelled** *or esp.* BrE **spelt**) **1** (write or name letters in sequence) произн|оси́ть, -ести́ (*or* писа́ть, на-) по бу́квам; how do you ~ your name? как пи́шется ва́ша фами́лия?; he cannot ~ his own name он не мо́жет пра́вильно написа́ть свою́ фами́лию **2** (fig., signify) означа́ть (*impf.*); these changes ~ disaster э́ти переме́ны сули́т несча́стье
- *v.i.* (*past and p.p.* **spelled** *or esp.* BrE **spelt**) писа́ть (*impf.*) пра́вильно/гра́мотно
- ■ ~**checker** *n.* (comput.) програ́мма прове́рки орфогра́фии

spelling /ˈspelɪŋ/ *n.* правописа́ние, орфогра́фия

spelt /spelt/ *past and p.p. of* ▶ **spell**[3]

✍ **spend** /spend/ *v.t.* (*past and p.p.* **spent**) **1** (pay out) тра́тить, ис-; расхо́довать, из- **2** (pass) пров|оди́ть, -ести́; how do you ~ your leisure time? как вы прово́дите свой досу́г?
- *v.i.* (*past and p.p.* **spent**) (~ money) тра́титься, по-; they went on a ~ing spree они́ пошли́ транжи́рить де́ньги

spent /spent/ *past and p.p. of* ▶ **spend**

sperm /spɜːm/ *n.* (*pl.* ~ *or* ~**s**) спе́рма; (*in full* ~ **whale**) кашало́т

spew /spjuː/ (infml) *v.t.* (vomit) выблёвывать, вы́блевать (sl.); (lit., fig.) изрыга́ть (*impf.*); a machine gun ~ing out bullets пулемёт, полива́ющий (неприя́теля) огнём
- *v.i.* (vomit) блева́ть (*impf.*) (sl.)

sphere /sfɪə(r)/ *n.* сфе́ра; ~ of influence сфе́ра влия́ния

spherical /ˈsferɪk(ə)l/ *adj.* сфери́ческий

sphinx /sfɪŋks/ *n.* сфинкс

spice /spaɪs/ *n.* **1** спе́ция, пря́ность, припра́ва **2** (fig., piquancy) острота́

✍ ключева́я ле́ксика

spick /spɪk/ *adj.:* ~ **and span** (clean, tidy) сверка́ющий чистото́й

spicy /ˈspaɪsɪ/ *adj.* (**spicier, spiciest**) пря́ный; (fig.) пика́нтный

spider /ˈspaɪdə(r)/ *n.* пау́к; ~'s **web** паути́на

spike /spaɪk/ *n.* остриё

spiky /ˈspaɪkɪ/ *adj.* (**spikier, spikiest**) остроконе́чный; ~ **hairstyle** ёжик

spill /spɪl/ *v.t.* (*past and p.p.* **spilt** *or* **spilled**) (liquid) прол|ива́ть, -и́ть; (powder etc.) расс|ыпа́ть, -ы́пать
- *v.i.* (*past and p.p.* **spilt** *or* **spilled**) (of liquids) разл|ива́ться, -и́ться; (of salt etc.) расс|ыпа́ться, -ы́паться
- □ ~ **over** *v.i.* перел|ива́ться, -и́ться (че́рез край)

spin /spɪn/ *n.* **1** (whirl) круже́ние, враще́ние **2** (of ball) враще́ние; put ~ **on a ball** закру́|чивать, -ти́ть мяч **3** (outing): go for a ~ **in the car** прокати́ться/поката́ться (*both pf.*) на маши́не **4** (bias) пристра́стие
- *v.t.* (**spinning**, *past* **spun** *or* **span**, *p.p.* **spun**) **1** (yarn, wool, etc.) прясть, с-; ~**ning wheel** пря́лка; the spider ~s its **web** пау́к плетёт паути́ну **2** (cause to revolve) верте́ть, за-; крути́ть, за-; кружи́ть, за-; ~ **a coin** подбр|а́сывать, -о́сить моне́ту
- *v.i.* (**spinning**, *past* **spun** *or* **span**, *p.p.* **spun**) верте́ться, за-; крути́ться, за-; кружи́ться, за-; (of wheel) бы́стро враща́ться/крути́ться (*impf.*); (of one's head): my head is ~**ning** у меня́ голова́ идёт кру́гом
- □ ~ **out** *v.t.:* ~ **out a story** растя́|гивать, -ну́ть расска́з
- □ ~ **round** *v.t. & i.* бы́стро пов|ора́чивать(ся), -ерну́ть(ся) (круго́м)
- ■ ~ **doctor** *n.* (pol.) политтехно́лог; ~ **dryer** *n.* (BrE) суши́лка, суши́льный автома́т; ~**-off** *n.* (infml) побо́чный результа́т

spina bifida /ˌspaɪnə ˈbɪfɪdə/ *n.* расщепле́ние позвоно́чника

spinach /ˈspɪnɪdʒ/ *n.* шпина́т

spinal /ˈspaɪn(ə)l/ *adj.* спинно́й, позвоно́чный
- ■ ~ **column** *n.* позвоно́чный столб; ~ **cord** *n.* спинно́й мозг

spindle /ˈspɪnd(ə)l/ *n.* (axis, rod) ось, шпи́ндель (*m.*)

spine /spaɪn/ *n.* **1** (backbone) позвоно́чник, спинно́й хребе́т **2** (of hedgehog, plant) игла́ **3** (of book) корешо́к

spineless /ˈspaɪnlɪs/ *adj.* (fig.) бесхребе́тный, бесхара́ктерный

spinster /ˈspɪnstə(r)/ *n.* (old maid) ста́рая де́ва; (law, unmarried woman) незаму́жняя же́нщина

spiral /ˈspaɪər(ə)l/ *n.* спира́ль
- *adj.* спира́льный
- *v.i.* (**spiralled, spiralling**, AmE **spiraled, spiraling**): the crime rate is ~**ling (upwards)** престу́пность (*or* у́ровень престу́пности) растёт бы́стрыми те́мпами
- ■ ~ **staircase** *n.* винтова́я ле́стница

spire /ˈspaɪə(r)/ *n.* (of church etc.) шпиль (*m.*)

✍ **spirit** /ˈspɪrɪt/ *n.* **1** (soul) душа́; духо́вное нача́ло **2** (courage) хра́брость; show some ~

проявля́ть, -и́ть му́жество/хара́ктер **3** (*in
pl.*) (humour) настрое́ние; **he was in high ~s**
он был в припо́днятом настрое́нии; **keep
one's ~s up** мужа́ться (*impf.*); не па́дать
(*impf.*) ду́хом **4** (*in pl.*) (BrE, alcoholic drink)
спиртно́й напи́ток
■ **~ level** *n.* ватерпа́с

spirited /ˈspɪrɪtɪd/ *adj.* живо́й; **a ~ reply**
бо́йкий отве́т; **a ~ horse** горя́чий конь

spiritual /ˈspɪrɪtʃʊəl/ *adj.* духо́вный

spiritualism /ˈspɪrɪtʃʊəlɪz(ə)m/ *n.* спирити́зм

spiritualist /ˈspɪrɪtʃʊəlɪst/ *n.* спири́т (-ка)

spirituality /ˌspɪrɪtʃʊˈælɪtɪ/ *n.*
одухотворённость

spit¹ /spɪt/ *n.* (for roasting) ве́ртел

spit² /spɪt/ *n.* (spittle) слюна́
● *v.t.* (**spitting**, *past and p.p.* **spat** *or* **~**)
(*also* **~ out**) выплёвывать, вы́плюнуть
● *v.i.* (**spitting**, *past and p.p.* **spat** *or* **~**)
1 плева́ть, -ю́нуть; (of cat etc.) фы́рк|ать,
-нуть **2** (of fire) сы́пать (*impf.*) и́скрами
3 (BrE, infml, rain) накра́пывать (*impf.*)
■ **~ting image** *n.*: **the ~ting image of his
father** то́чная ко́пия своего́ отца́

spite /spaɪt/ *n.* **1** (ill will) зло́ба, злость
2: **in ~ of** несмотря́ на + *a.*
● *v.t.*: **he does it to ~ me** он де́лает э́то мне
назло́

spiteful /ˈspaɪtfʊl/ *adj.* зло́бный, злора́дный

spitefulness /ˈspaɪtfʊlnɪs/ *n.* зло́бность,
злора́дство

spittle /ˈspɪt(ə)l/ *n.* плево́к; слюна́

splash /splæʃ/ *n.* **1** (sound) всплеск, плеск
2 (liquid) бры́зги (*m. pl.*); **I felt a ~ of rain** на
меня́ упа́ли ка́пли дождя́ **3** (of blood, mud, etc.)
пятно́; **a ~ of colour** кра́сочное пятно́
● *v.t.* бры́з|гать, -нуть (*чем на что*);
забры́згать (*pf.*) (*что чем*); **he ~ed paint on
her dress** он забры́згал ей пла́тье кра́ской
● *v.i.* **1** (of liquid etc.) разбры́зг|иваться, -аться;
(of waves) плеска́ться (*impf.*) **2** (move or fall
with ~): **the ducks ~ed about in the pond**
у́тки плеска́лись в пруду́; (BrE, infml, fig.): **they
~ed out on a new carpet** они́ разори́лись на
но́вый ковёр

splatter /ˈsplætə(r)/ *v.t. & i.* = spatter

splay /spleɪ/ *v.t.*: **~ one's legs** раски́|дывать,
-нуть но́ги

spleen /spliːn/ *n.* (anat.) селезёнка

splendid /ˈsplendɪd/ *adj.* (excellent)
прекра́сный, отли́чный; **what a ~ idea!**
замеча́тельная/прекра́сная мысль!

splendour /ˈsplendə(r)/ (AmE **splendor**) *n.*
великоле́пие, пы́шность

splice /splaɪs/ *v.t.* **1** (rope) ср|а́щивать, -асти́ть
2 (tape) скле́и|вать, -ть

splint /splɪnt/ *n.* (for broken bone) ши́на, лубо́к

splinter /ˈsplɪntə(r)/ *n.* **1** (of wood) лучи́на,
ще́пка; (in finger) зано́за **2** (fig.): **~ group**
отколо́вшаяся фра́кция
● *v.t. & i.* расщеп|ля́ть(ся), -и́ть(ся)

split /splɪt/ *n.* **1** (crack, fissure) тре́щина, щель,
расще́лина **2** (fig., schism) раско́л **3**: **do the
~s** (BrE) де́лать, с- шпага́т

● *v.t.* (**splitting**, *past and p.p.* **~**) **1** коло́ть,
рас-; расщеп|ля́ть, -и́ть; (crack open)
раск|а́лывать, -оло́ть **2** (divide) раздел|я́ть,
-и́ть; (share) дели́ть, по- **3** (cause dissension in)
раск|а́лывать, -оло́ть
● *v.i.* (**splitting**, *past and p.p.* **~**) **1** (of
hard substance) раск|а́лываться, -оло́ться;
тре́снуть (*pf.*); (divide) разделя́ться, -и́ться
2 (become disunited) разъедин|я́ться, -и́ться;
раск|а́лываться, -оло́ться
□ **~ up** *v.t. & i.* (separate) ра|схо́диться, -зойти́сь;
раз|бива́ть(ся), -би́ть(ся); **we ~ up into two
groups** мы разби́лись на две гру́ппы; **he and
his wife ~ up** они́ с жено́й разошли́сь
■ **~ second** *n.* до́ля секу́нды

splutter /ˈsplʌtə(r)/ *v.t. & i.* (of person)
говори́ть (*impf.*) захлёбываясь; (of fire)
шипе́ть (*impf.*)

spoil /spɔɪl/ *v.t.* (*past and p.p.* **spoiled** *or* esp.
BrE **spoilt**) **1** (impair, ruin) по́ртить, ис-; **the
rain ~t our holiday** дождь испо́ртил нам
о́тпуск **2** (overindulge) балова́ть, из-; **a ~t
child** избало́ванный ребёнок
● *v.i.* (*past and p.p.* **spoilt**, esp. BrE or
spoiled) (go bad etc.) по́ртиться, ис-
■ **~sport** *n.* тот, кто по́ртит удово́льствие
други́м

spoilt /spɔɪlt/ *past and p.p. of* ▶ spoil

spoke¹ /spəʊk/ *n.* (of wheel) спи́ца

spoke² /spəʊk/ *past of* ▶ speak

spoken /ˈspəʊkən/ *p.p. of* ▶ speak

✍ **spokesman** /ˈspəʊksmən/ *n.* представи́тель
(*m.*)

spokesperson /ˈspəʊkspɜːs(ə)n/ *n.*
представи́тель (*m.*) (-ница)

spokeswoman /ˈspəʊkswʊmən/ *n.*
представи́тельница

sponge /spʌndʒ/ *n.* **1** (zool, toilet article) гу́бка
2 (cake) бискви́т
● *v.t.* (**sponging** *or* **spongeing**) обт|ира́ть,
-ере́ть гу́бкой
● *v.i.* (**sponging** *or* **spongeing**) (fig.): **he
~s off his brother** он сиди́т на ше́е у бра́та
■ **~ bag** *n.* (BrE) су́мка для туале́тных
принадле́жностей; **~ cake** *n.* бискви́т

✍ **sponsor** /ˈspɒnsə(r)/ *n.* **1** (guarantor)
поручи́тель (-ница); (of new member etc.)
рекоменда́тель (-ница) **2** (providing finance)
спо́нсор
● *v.t.* руча́ться, поручи́ться за + *a.*;
рекомендова́ть (*impf., pf.*); (on TV etc.)
финанси́ровать (*impf., pf.*)

sponsorship /ˈspɒnsəʃɪp/ *n.* поручи́тельство,
пору́ка; спо́нсорство

spontaneity /ˌspɒntəˈneɪɪtɪ/ *n.* спонта́нность,
стихи́йность, непосре́дственность

spontaneous /spɒnˈteɪnɪəs/
adj. спонта́нный, стихи́йный,
непосре́дственный

spoof /spuːf/ *n.* (infml) паро́дия

spook /spuːk/ *n.* (joc.) привиде́ние, при́зрак

spooky /ˈspuːkɪ/ *adj.* (**spookier**, **spookiest**)
(infml) злове́щий; **~ house** дом с
привиде́ниями

spool /spuːl/ *n.* шпу́лька, кату́шка

spoon /spuːn/ *n.* ло́жка

spoonful /'spuːnfʊl/ *n.* (по́лная) ло́жка (чего́)

sporadic /spə'rædɪk/ *adj.* споради́ческий, едини́чный, отде́льный

⚔ **sport** /spɔːt/ *n.* **1** (outdoor pastime(s)) спорт; (*in pl.*) спорт, ви́ды (*m. pl.*) спо́рта **2** (*in pl.*) (BrE, athletic events) спорти́вные и́гры (*f. pl.*) **3** (infml, person) молодчи́на (*m.*)
  ■ ~**s car** *n.* спорти́вный автомоби́ль

sporting /'spɔːtɪŋ/ *adj.* **1** (connected with, fond of sport) спорти́вный **2** (sportsmanlike) че́стный, поря́дочный

sportsman /'spɔːtsmən/ *n.* спортсме́н

sportswoman /'spɔːtswʊmən/ *n.* спортсме́нка

sporty /'spɔːtɪ/ *adj.* (**sportier, sportiest**) (person, clothing) спорти́вный

⚔ **spot** /spɒt/ *n.* **1** (patch) пятно́; (speck) пя́тнышко, кра́пинка; **come out in ~s** (rash) покрыва́ться, -ы́ться сы́пью **2** (stain) пятно́ **3** (pimple) прыщ(ик) **4** (place) ме́сто; **the police were on the ~ within minutes** поли́ция прибыла́ на ме́сто (уже́) че́рез не́сколько мину́т; **we were in a (tight) ~** нам пришло́сь ту́го **5** (BrE, infml, small amount): **I have a ~ of work to do** мне ну́жно немно́го порабо́тать; **~ of bother** небольша́я неприя́тность **6**: **~ on** (BrE, infml, exactly right) в са́мую то́чку
  • *v.t.* (**spotted, spotting**) **1** (stain) па́чкать, за-; (with liquid) зака́пать (*pf.*) **2** (*p.p.*) (covered, decorated with ~s): **a ~ted tie** га́лстук в кра́пинку **3** (infml, notice) замеча́ть, -е́тить; (catch sight of) уви́деть (*pf.*)
  ■ ~ **check** *n.* вы́борочная прове́рка; ~**light** *n.* освети́тельный проже́ктор; (fig.): **turn the ~light on sth** привлека́ть, -е́чь внима́ние к чему́-н.; **be in the ~light** быть в це́нтре внима́ния

spotless /'spɒtlɪs/ *adj.* сверка́ющий чистото́й; без еди́ного пя́тнышка

spotty /'spɒtɪ/ *adj.* (**spottier, spottiest**) (of colour) пятни́стый; (BrE, pimply) прыщева́тый

spouse /spaʊs/ *n.* супру́г (-а)

spout /spaʊt/ *n.* но́сик
  • *v.t.* **1**: **a whale ~s water** кит выбра́сывает струю́ воды́ **2** (infml, declaim) говори́ть (*impf.*) о + *p.*; ~ **poetry** деклами́ровать, про- стихи́
  • *v.i.* **1** бить (*impf.*); ли́ться (*impf.*) пото́ком **2** (fig., infml, make speeches) разглаго́льствовать (*impf.*)

sprain /spreɪn/ *n.* растяже́ние
  • *v.t.*: ~ **one's wrist/ankle** раст|я́гивать, -яну́ть запя́стье/лоды́жку

sprang /spræŋ/ *past of* ▶ **spring²**

sprat /spræt/ *n.* шпрот(а), ки́лька

sprawl /sprɔːl/ *n.*: **urban ~** беспоря́дочный рост го́рода
  • *v.i.* **1** (person) раст|я́гиваться, -яну́ться **2** (buildings) раски́|дываться, -нуться

⚔ ключева́я ле́ксика

spray /spreɪ/ *n.* **1** (water droplets) бры́зг|и (*pl., g. —*) **2** (liquid preparation, e.g. fly spray) жи́дкость (для пульвериза́ции) **3** (device for ~ing) спрей
  ■ ~ **can** *n.* аэрозо́ль (*m.*), спрей

⚔ **spread** /spred/ *n.* **1** (dissemination, expansion) распростране́ние **2** (span) разма́х **3** (cul.) па́ста (на хлеб)
  • *v.t.* (*past and p.p.* ~) **1** (extend) распростран|я́ть, -и́ть; (unfold) ра|скла́дывать, -зложи́ть; (cover) расст|ила́ть, -ели́ть (*or* разостла́ть); ~ **butter on bread** (*or* **bread with butter**) нама́з|ывать, -ать ма́сло на хлеб (*or* хлеб ма́слом); **the bird ~ its wings** пти́ца распра́вила кры́лья; ~ (out) **a map** ра|скла́дывать, -зложи́ть ка́рту **2** (diffuse) распростран|я́ть, -и́ть
  • *v.i.* (*past and p.p.* ~) распростран|я́ться, -и́ться; расстила́ться (*impf.*); **the news soon ~** но́вость/весть бы́стро распространи́лась; **the fire is ~ing** пожа́р разраста́ется
  ■ ~**eagle** *v.t.*: **lie ~eagled** лежа́ть (*impf.*) распласта́вшись; ~**sheet** *n.* (comput.) (электро́нная) табли́ца

spree /spriː/ *n.* (infml) весе́лье

sprig /sprɪg/ *n.* ве́точка

sprightly /'spraɪtlɪ/ *adj.* (**sprightlier, sprightliest**) живо́й, бо́йкий

⚔ **spring¹** /sprɪŋ/ *n.* (season) весна́; **in ~** весно́й; (*attr.*) весе́нний
  ■ ~**-clean** *v.t. & i.* произв|оди́ть, -ести́ генера́льную убо́рку (+ *g.*); ~ **onion** *n.* (BrE) зелёный лук; ~**time** *n.* весна́

spring² /sprɪŋ/ *n.* **1** (leap) прыжо́к, скачо́к **2** (elasticity) упру́гость, эласти́чность **3** (elastic device) пружи́на **4** (of water) исто́чник, ключ, родни́к
  • *v.t.* (*past* **sprang** *or* AmE **sprung**, *p.p.* **sprung**) (produce suddenly): ~ **a surprise on sb** заст|ига́ть, -и́чь кого́-н. враспло́х; ~ **a leak** да|ва́ть, -ть течь
  • *v.i.* (*past* **sprang** *or* AmE **sprung**, *p.p.* **sprung**) **1** (leap) пры́г|ать, -нуть; скак|а́ть, -ну́ть; ~ **out of bed** вска́к|ивать, -очи́ть с посте́ли **2** (come into being) появл|я́ться, -и́ться; возн|ика́ть, -и́кнуть; **a breeze sprang up** подня́лся лёгкий ветеро́к
  ■ ~**board** *n.* (lit., fig.) трампли́н

sprinkle /'sprɪŋk(ə)l/ *v.t.*: ~ **sth with water**, ~ **water on sth** кропи́ть, о-/обры́зг|ивать, -ать что-н. водо́й; ~ **sth with salt/sand**, ~ **salt/ sand on sth** пос|ыпа́ть, -ы́пать что-н. со́лью/ песко́м

sprinkler /'sprɪŋklə(r)/ *n.* разбры́згиватель (*m.*), пульвериза́тор; (in fire safety) спри́нклер

sprint /sprɪnt/ *n.* спринт
  • *v.i.* бежа́ть (*det.*) с максима́льной ско́ростью

sprinter /'sprɪntə(r)/ *n.* спри́нтер

sprocket /'sprɒkɪt/ *n.* **1** звёздочка (це́пи) **2** (*also* ~ **wheel**) цепно́е/зубча́тое колесо́; (in film, tape) зубча́тый бараба́н

sprout /spraʊt/ *n.* (*in pl., also* **Brussels ~s**) брюссе́льская капу́ста
  • *v.i.* (of plant) пус|ка́ть, -ти́ть ростки́; (of seed)

прораст|а́ть, -и́

spruce¹ /spru:s/ *n.* (tree) ель

spruce² /spru:s/ *adj.* опря́тный, наря́дный
- *v.t.*: ~ **up** нав|оди́ть, -ести́ красоту́/блеск на + *a.*; ~ **oneself up** прихора́шиваться (*impf.*)

sprung /sprʌŋ/ *p.p. and* AmE *past of* ▶ spring²

spun /spʌn/ *past and p.p. of* ▶ spin

spur /spə:(r)/ *n.* **1** (on rider's heel) шпо́ра **2** (fig.) побужде́ние, сти́мул; **on the ~ of the moment** в сиюмину́тном порыве
- *v.t.* (**spurred, spurring**) (fig.) побу|жда́ть, -ди́ть; под|гоня́ть, -огна́ть; ~**red on by ambition** подгоня́емый честолю́бием

spurious /ˈspjʊərɪəs/ *adj.* подде́льный

spurn /spə:n/ *v.t.* отв|ерга́ть, -е́ргнуть

spurt¹ /spə:t/ *n.* (sudden effort) порыв; (in race) рыво́к; **put on a ~** рвану́ться (*pf.*)

spurt² /spə:t/ *n.* (jet) струя́
- *v.i.* бить (*impf.*) струёй; хлы́нуть (*pf.*)

sputnik /ˈspʊtnɪk/ *n.* (иску́сственный) спу́тник

spy /spaɪ/ *n.* шпио́н
- *v.t.* (discern) разгля́д|ывать, -е́ть
- *v.i.* (engage in espionage) шпио́нить (*impf.*); ~ **on sb** подгля́дывать (*impf.*) за кем-н.

spying /ˈspaɪɪŋ/ *n.* шпиона́ж

squabble /ˈskwɒb(ə)l/ *v.i.* перека́ться (*impf.*) (*с кем*); вздо́рить, по-

squad /skwɒd/ *n.* **1** (mil.) гру́ппа, кома́нда, отделе́ние **2** (gang, group) отря́д; рабо́чая брига́да
- ■ ~ **car** *n.* полице́йская патру́льная (авто)маши́на

squadron /ˈskwɒdrən/ *n.* (aeron.) эскадри́лья; (mil.) эскадро́н; (naut.) эска́дра

squalid /ˈskwɒlɪd/ *adj.* ни́зкий, ни́зменный, гну́сный

squall /skwɔ:l/ *n.* шквал; порывистый ве́тер

squalor /ˈskwɒlə(r)/ *n.* убо́жество; (sordidness) ни́зость, гну́сность

squander /ˈskwɒndə(r)/ *v.t.* пром|а́тывать, -ота́ть; растра́|чивать, -тить

♂ **square** /skweə(r)/ *n.* **1** (shape) квадра́т **2** (on chessboard etc.) кле́тка; **we are back to ~ one** (fig.) мы верну́лись в исхо́дное положе́ние **3** (open space in town) пло́щадь
- *adj.* **1** (geom., math., shape) квадра́тный; ~ **metre** квадра́тный метр; ~ **root (of)** квадра́тный ко́рень (из + *g.*); (right-angled) прямоуго́льный **2** (even) то́чный; в поря́дке; **we are all** ~ мы кви́ты
- *adv.* **1** (at right angles) перпендикуля́рно **2** (straight) прямо **3**: **ten feet** ~ де́сять фу́тов в ширину́ и де́сять в длину́
- *v.t.* **1** (straighten) выпрямля́ть, вы́прямить; ~ **one's shoulders** распр|авля́ть, -а́вить пле́чи **2** (settle) ула́|живать, -дить **3** (math.) возв|оди́ть, -ести́ в квадра́т; **3 ~d is 9** три в квадра́те равно́ девяти́
- *v.i.* **1** (agree) согласо́в|ываться, -а́ться; ~ **with** сходи́ться (*impf.*) с + *i.*; **this statement does not ~ with the facts** э́то заявле́ние

расхо́дится с фа́ктами **2**: ~ **up** (sc. settle accounts) **with sb** поквита́ться (*pf.*) с кем-н.

squash¹ /skwɒʃ/ *n.* (crush) да́вка; (BrE, drink) фрукто́вый напи́ток; (game) сквош
- *v.t.* (crush) дави́ть, раз-; (compress) сж|има́ть, -ать; **I ~ed the fly against the wall** я раздави́л му́ху на стене́; **the tomatoes were ~ed** помидо́ры помя́лись
- *v.i.* (crowd) потесни́ться (*pf.*); **they ~ed up to make room for me** они́ потесни́лись, чтобы дать мне ме́сто

squash² /skwɒʃ/ *n.* (*pl.* ~ *or* ~**es**) (bot.) (winter ~) ты́ква; (summer ~) кабачо́к

squat /skwɒt/ *adj.* (**squatter, squattest**) призе́мистый
- *v.i.* (**squatted, squatting**) **1** (be crouching) сиде́ть (*impf.*) на ко́рточках **2** (occupy building illegally) незако́нно всел|я́ться, -и́ться в чужо́й дом

squatter /ˈskwɒtə(r)/ *n.* (illegal occupant) челове́к, незако́нно всели́вшийся в (чужо́й) дом

squawk /skwɔ:k/ *v.i.* пронзи́тельно крича́ть, за-

squeak /skwi:k/ *n.* **1** (of mouse etc.) писк **2** (of hinge etc.) скрип, визг
- *v.i.* **1** (of person or animal) пища́ть, пи́скнуть **2** (of object) скрипе́ть, скри́пнуть

squeaky /ˈskwi:kɪ/ *adj.* (**squeakier, squeakiest**) пискли́вый, визгли́вый; скрипу́чий

squeal /skwi:l/ *v.i.* визжа́ть, за-

squeamish /ˈskwi:mɪʃ/ *adj.* брезгли́вый; **feel** ~ чу́вствовать, по- тошноту́

squeeze /skwi:z/ *n.* **1** (pressure) сжа́тие, пожа́тие **2** (crush) теснота́, да́вка; **we got in, but it was a tight** ~ нам удало́сь вти́снуться, но бы́ло о́чень те́сно **3** (fin.) ограниче́ние креди́та
- *v.t.* **1** (compress) сж|има́ть, -ать; сда́в|ливать, -и́ть; (to extract moisture etc.) выжима́ть, выжать; (extort): ~ **a confession from sb** вынужда́ть, вынудить призна́ние у кого́-н. **2** (force, cram) вти́с|кивать, -нуть
- *v.i.* проти́с|киваться, -нуться

squid /skwɪd/ *n.* кальма́р

squiggle /ˈskwɪɡ(ə)l/ *n.* загогу́лина, кара́кул|я (*g. pl.* -ей)

squint /skwɪnt/ *n.* косогла́зие; **she has a ~ in her right eye** она́ коси́т на пра́вый глаз
- *v.i.* **1** коси́ть (*impf.*) **2** (half-shut one's eyes) щу́риться (*impf.*); прищу́ри|ваться, -ться **3**: ~ **at sth** смотре́ть, по- и́скоса на что-н.

squirm /skwə:m/ *n.* извива́ться (*impf.*); ко́рчиться (*impf.*); **he made me** ~ **with embarrassment** он меня́ так смути́л, что я не знал, куда́ де́ться

squirrel /ˈskwɪr(ə)l/ *n.* бе́лка

squirt /skwə:t/ *v.t.* пры́с|кать, -нуть; ~ **water in the air** пус|ка́ть, -ти́ть струю́ воды́ в во́здух; ~ **scent from an atomizer** бры́згать, по- духа́ми из пульвериза́тора
- *v.i.* бить (*impf.*) струёй; разбры́зг|иваться, -аться

Sri Lanka /ʃri: ˈlæŋkə/ *n.* Шри-Ланка́

S

St *abbr. of* (**Saint**) св., Св. (свят|о́й, -а́я)

St. *abbr. of* (**street**) ул. (у́лица)

stab /stæb/ *n.* **1** уда́р (о́стрым ору́жием); ~ **in the back** (fig.) нож/уда́р в спи́ну **2** (fig., sharp pain) внеза́пная о́страя боль; уко́л
• *v.t.* (**stabbed, stabbing**): ~ **sb in the chest with a knife** нан|оси́ть, -ести́ кому́-н. уда́р в грудь ножо́м

stability /stə'bɪlɪti/ *n.* стаби́льность, усто́йчивость

stabilize /'steɪbɪlaɪz/ *v.t. & i.* стабилизи́ровать(ся) (*impf., pf.*)

stable¹ /'steɪb(ə)l/ *n.* коню́шня

stable² /'steɪb(ə)l/ *adj.* (**stabler, stablest**) усто́йчивый, стаби́льный

staccato /stə'kɑːtəʊ/ *n.* (*pl.* ~**s**) & *adv.* стакка́то (*nt. indecl.*)
• *adj.* отры́вистый

stack /stæk/ *n.* **1** (of hay etc.) стог; скирда́ **2** (pile): ~ **of wood** поле́нница, шта́бель (*m.*) дров; ~ **of papers** ки́па/сто́пка бума́г; ~ **of plates** стопа́/сто́пка таре́лок **3** (infml) (*usu. in pl.*) (large amount) ма́сса, ку́ча, гру́да
• *v.t.*: ~ **books on the floor** скла́дывать, сложи́ть кни́ги сто́пками на полу́

stadium /'steɪdɪəm/ *n.* стадио́н

⚹ **staff** /stɑːf/ *n.* (employees) штат; **teaching** ~ преподава́тельский соста́в
• *v.t.* укомплекто́в|ывать, -а́ть (*что or штат чего*)
■ ~ **meeting** *n.* (of teachers) педагоги́ческий сове́т; ~ **room** *n.* (BrE, at school) учи́тельская

stag /stæg/ *n.* (deer) оле́нь-саме́ц (*m.*)
■ ~ **party** *n.* (infml) мальчи́шник

⚹ **stage** /steɪdʒ/ *n.* **1** (theatr.) сце́на, подмо́стки; (as profession) теа́тр, сце́на; **go on the** ~ идти́, пойти́ на сце́ну **2** (phase) ста́дия, фа́за, эта́п; **the war reached a critical** ~ война́ вступи́ла в крити́ческую фа́зу; **I shall do it in** ~**s** я сде́лаю э́то постепе́нно
• *v.t.*: ~ **a play** ста́вить, по- пье́су; (organize) устр|а́ивать, -о́ить; организова́ть (*impf., pf.*)
■ ~ **manager** *n.* постано́вщик

stagger /'stægə(r)/ *v.t.* **1** (disconcert) потряс|а́ть, -ти́; пора|жа́ть, -зи́ть; ошеломл|я́ть, -и́ть; ~**ing success** потряса́ющий успе́х **2**: ~ **working hours, holidays,** *etc.* распредел|я́ть, -и́ть часы́ рабо́ты, отпуска́ *и т. д.*
• *v.i.* шата́ться (*impf.*); пошатываться (*impf.*)

stagnant /'stægnənt/ *adj.* (water) стоя́чий; (pond) застоя́вшийся

stagnate /stæg'neɪt/ *v.i.* заст|а́иваться, -оя́ться

stagnation /stæg'neɪʃ(ə)n/ *n.* засто́й

staid /steɪd/ *adj.* степе́нный

stain /steɪn/ *n.* **1** пятно́ **2** (for colouring) краси́тель (*m.*)
• *v.t.* **1** (soil) па́чкать, за-/ис- **2** (colour) окра́|шивать, -сить; ~ **wood** мори́ть, заде́рево
■ ~**ed glass** *n.* цветно́е стекло́; ~**ed-glass window** витра́ж

⚹ ключева́я ле́ксика

stainless /'steɪnlɪs/ *adj.*: ~ **steel** нержаве́ющая сталь

stair /steə(r)/ *n.* **1** (step) ступе́нька **2** (*in pl.*) ле́стница; **he ran up the** ~**s** он взбежа́л по ле́стнице
■ ~ **case,** ~**way** *nn.* ле́стница; ле́стничная кле́тка

stake /steɪk/ *n.* **1** (post) столб, кол (ко́лья) **2** (wager) ста́вка, закла́д **3** (share in a business) до́ля; (an interest) заинтересо́ванность **4**: **his reputation was at** ~ его́ репута́ция была́ поста́влена на ка́рту
• *v.t.* **1** (support with ~) укреп|ля́ть, -и́ть коло́м **2** (wager) ста́вить, по-; (risk, gamble) рискова́ть (*impf.*) + *i.*
□ ~ **out** *v.t.*: ~ **out a boundary** отм|еча́ть, -е́тить ве́хами грани́цу; ~ **out a place** (infml, keep under surveillance) вести́ (*det.*) наблюде́ние за (+ *i.*)
■ ~**holder** *n.* посре́дник; ~**-out** *n.* (infml) полице́йский надзо́р

stalactite /'stæləktaɪt/ *n.* сталакти́т

stalagmite /'stæləgmaɪt/ *n.* сталагми́т

stale /steɪl/ *adj.* (**staler, stalest**) несве́жий; ~ **bread** чёрствый хлеб; (of air) спёртый, за́тхлый

stalemate /'steɪlmeɪt/ *n.* (chess) пат; (fig., impasse) тупи́к, безвы́ходное положе́ние

stalk¹ /stɔːk/ *n.* (stem) сте́бель (*m.*); чере́шок

stalk² /stɔːk/ **1** (pursue stealthily) выслеживать, вы́следить **2** (persecute obsessively) пресле́довать (*impf.*)

stalker /'stɔːkə(r)/ *n.* челове́к, патологи́чески пресле́дующий предме́т своего́ внима́ния; навя́зчивый пресле́дователь

stall¹ /stɔːl/ *n.* **1** (for animal) сто́йло **2** (in market etc.) прила́вок, сто́йка; **book** ~ кио́ск **3** (*in pl.*) (BrE, theatr.) парте́р, кре́сла (*nt. pl.*)
• *v.i.* (of engine) гло́хнуть, за-
■ ~**holder** *n.* (BrE) владе́лец (-ица) пала́тки (*на ры́нке*)

stall² /stɔːl/ *v.i.* (play for time) тяну́ть, затя́гивать (*both impf.*) вре́мя

stallion /'stælɪən/ *n.* жеребе́ц

stalwart /'stɔːlwət/ *adj.*: ~ **supporter** я́р|ый сторо́нни|к (-ая -ца), сто́йкий приве́рженец

stamina /'stæmɪnə/ *n.* выно́сливость

stammer /'stæmə(r)/ *n.* заика́ние
• *v.i.* заика́ться (*impf.*)

stamp /stæmp/ *n.* **1** (instrument) штамп, печа́ть, клеймо́ **2** (mark) печа́ть, клеймо́; (postage etc.) ма́рка
• *v.t.* **1** (imprint) штампова́ть, про-; ста́вить, по- штамп/печа́ть на + *a.* **2** (beat on ground): ~ **one's feet** то́пать (*impf.*) нога́ми
• *v.i.* (feet) то́п|ать, -нуть
□ ~ **out** *v.t.* (lit.): ~ **out a fire** зат|а́птывать, -опта́ть ого́нь; (fig., exterminate, destroy) уничт|ожа́ть, -о́жить; (fig., suppress) подавл|я́ть, -и́ть (*восста́ние*)
■ ~ **collecting** *n.* коллекциони́рование ма́рок; ~ **duty** *n.* ге́рбовый сбор

stampede /stæm'piːd/ *n.* бе́гство
• *v.i.* разбе|га́ться, -жа́ться врассыпну́ю

stance /stɑːns/ *n.* пози́ция

✓ **stand** /stænd/ *n.* **1** (support) подста́вка **2** (stall) сто́йка; (BrE, for display) стенд **3** (for spectators) трибу́на **4** (for taxis etc.) стоя́нка **5** (position) ме́сто; (fig.): **take a firm ~** зан|има́ть, -я́ть твёрдую пози́цию; **make a ~ against sb/sth** ока́з|ывать, -а́ть сопротивле́ние кому́-н./ чему́-н.

• *v.t.* (*past and p.p.* **stood**) **1** (place, set) ста́вить, по-; **he stood the ladder against the wall** он приста́вил ле́стницу к стене́ **2** (bear) терпе́ть, вы́-; выноси́ть, вы́нести; перен|оси́ть, -ести́; **she can't ~ him** она́ его́ не выно́сит (*or* терпе́ть не мо́жет)

• *v.i.* (*past and p.p.* **stood**) **1** (be or stay in upright position) стоя́ть (*impf.*) **2** (remain): **our house will ~ for another fifty years** наш дом просто́ит ещё пятьдеся́т лет **3** (hold good) ост|ава́ться, -а́ться в си́ле **4** (be situated) стоя́ть (*impf.*); находи́ться (*impf.*) **5** (find oneself, be): **I shall leave the text as it ~s** я оставля́ю текст, как он есть; **as matters ~** при да́нном положе́нии веще́й; **how do we ~ for money?** как у нас (обстои́т) с деньга́ми? **6** (rise to one's feet) вста|ва́ть, -ть **7** (assume or move to specified position): **I'll ~ here** я (в)ста́ну сюда́; **we had to ~ in a queue** (BrE), **in line** (AmE) нам пришло́сь постоя́ть в о́череди; **~ back!** (отступи́те) наза́д!

• *with preps.*: **we will ~ by** (*sc. support*) **you** мы вас подде́ржим; **I ~ by what I said** я не отступа́юсь от свои́х слов; **~ for office** (BrE) выставля́ть, вы́ставить свою́ кандидату́ру; **~ for Parliament** (BrE) баллоти́роваться (*impf.*) в парла́мент; **we ~ for freedom** мы стои́м за свобо́ду; **'Mg' ~s for magnesium** Mg обознача́ет ма́гний; **I will not ~ for such impudence** я не потерплю́ тако́й на́глости; **he ~s to win/lose £1,000** его́ ждёт вы́игрыш/ про́игрыш в ты́сячу фу́нтов

□ **~ about, ~ around** *vv.i.* стоя́ть (*impf.*) без де́ла

□ **~ aside** *v.i.* стоя́ть (*impf.*) в стороне́

□ **~ back** *v.i.* (also fig.) от|ходи́ть, -ойти́ в сто́рону

□ **~ by** *v.i.* (be ready) быть/стоя́ть (*impf.*) нагото́ве

□ **~ down** *v.i.*: **he stood down in favour of his brother** он снял свою́ кандидату́ру в по́льзу бра́та; (of minister etc.) под|ава́ть, -а́ть в отста́вку

□ **~ in** *v.i.* (substitute): **~ in for sb else** замен|я́ть, -и́ть кого́-н. друго́го

□ **~ out** *v.i.* (be prominent) выделя́ться (*impf.*); выдава́ться (*impf.*)

□ **~ up** *v.t.*: **he stood his bicycle up against the wall** он прислони́л свой велосипе́д к стене́; (infml): **his girlfriend stood him up** его́ подру́га не пришла́ на свида́ние

• *v.i.*: **he stood up as I entered** он встал, когда́ я вошёл; **he ~s up for his rights** он отста́ивает свои́ права́; **he stood up bravely to his opponent** он оказа́л му́жественное сопротивле́ние проти́внику

■ **~-alone** *adj.* (comput.) автоно́мный; **~by**

n. (state of readiness) гото́вность; **keep on ~by** держа́ть (*impf.*) нагото́ве; (dependable thing or person) надёжная опо́ра; испы́танное сре́дство; **~-in** *n.* замести́тель (-ница); **~-offish** *adj.* (aloof) сде́ржанный; (haughty) высокоме́рный; **~point** *n.* то́чка зре́ния; **~still** *n.*: **come to a ~still** остан|а́вливаться, -ови́ться; засто́пориться (*pf.*); **at a ~still** на мёртвой то́чке; **many factories are at a ~still** мно́го фа́брик безде́йствует/ проста́ивает

✓ **standard** /ˈstændəd/ *n.* **1** (flag) зна́мя, штанда́рт **2** (norm) станда́рт; (level) у́ровень (*m.*); **come up to ~** соотве́тствовать (*impf.*) тре́буемому у́ровню; **~ of living** жи́зненный у́ровень, у́ровень жи́зни

• *adj.* **1** станда́ртный **2** (model, basic) норм ати́вный, образцо́вый; (general) типово́й **3**: **~ lamp** (BrE) напо́льная ла́мпа, торше́р

standardize /ˈstændədaɪz/ *v.t.* стандартизи́ровать (*impf., pf.*)

standing /ˈstændɪŋ/ *n.* **1** (rank) положе́ние; (reputation) репута́ция **2** (duration) продолжи́тельность; **a custom of long ~** стари́нный обы́чай

• *adj.*: **~ army** регуля́рная/постоя́нная а́рмия; **~ invitation** приглаше́ние приходи́ть в любо́е вре́мя; **~ order** (BrE, to banker) прика́з о регуля́рных платежа́х

stank /stæŋk/ *past of* ▶ **stink**

stanza /ˈstænzə/ *n.* строфа́

staple[1] /ˈsteɪp(ə)l/ *n.* (for papers) ско́бка (*для сте́плера*)

• *v.t.*: **~ papers together** скреп|ля́ть, -и́ть бума́ги сте́плером

staple[2] /ˈsteɪp(ə)l/ *n.* **1** (principal commodity) основно́й това́р/проду́кт **2** (chief material) осно́ва

• *adj.* основно́й, гла́вный

stapler /ˈsteɪplə(r)/ *n.* (for paper) сте́плер

✓ **star** /stɑː(r)/ *n.* **1** звезда́; **five-~ hotel** пятизвёздочная гости́ница **2** (famous actor etc.) звезда́; **film ~** кинозвезда́ **3** (asterisk) звёздочка

• *v.i.* (**starred, starring**): **~ in a film** игра́ть (*impf.*) гла́вную роль в фи́льме

■ **~fish** *n.* морска́я звезда́; **~ sign** *n.* знак зодиа́ка; **~-studded** *adj.* (fig.) с уча́стием мно́жества звёзд

starboard /ˈstɑːbəd/ (naut.) *n.* пра́вый борт

• *adj.* пра́вый; **~ side** пра́вый борт; **~ wind** ве́тер с пра́вого бо́рта

starch /stɑːtʃ/ *n.* крахма́л

stardom /ˈstɑːdəm/ *n.*: **rise to ~** ста|нови́ться, -ть звездо́й

stare /steə(r)/ *n.* при́стальный взгляд

• *v.i.* глазе́ть (*impf.*); **~ at sb** при́стально смотре́ть/гляде́ть (*impf.*) на кого́-н.

stark /stɑːk/ *adj.* **1** (desolate) го́лый **2** (sharply evident) я́вный; **be in ~ contrast to** ре́зко контрасти́ровать (*impf.*) с + *i.*

• *adv.*: **~ naked** соверше́нно го́лый; в чём мать родила́ (infml)

starling /ˈstɑːlɪŋ/ *n.* скворе́ц

S

start /stɑːt/ *n.* **1** (sudden movement) вздра́гивание, содрога́ние; **he woke with a ~** он вздро́гнул и просну́лся **2** (beginning) нача́ло; (of journey) отправле́ние; (of race) старт
● *v.t.* **1** (begin) начина́ть, -а́ть; **it is ~ing to rain** начина́ется дождь; **we ~ed our journey** мы отпра́вились в путь; **she ~ed crying** она́ начала́ пла́кать/распла́каться (*with many verbs, the pf. formed with* за- *means 'to start …ing'*) **2** (set in motion): **~ (up) an engine** зав|оди́ть, -ести́ (*or* запус|ка́ть, -ти́ть) мото́р/дви́гатель **3** (initiate): **~ (up) a business** осно́в|ывать, -а́ть (*or* нач|ина́ть, -а́ть) би́знес/де́ло; **~ a family** зав|оди́ть, -ести́ семью́
● *v.i.* **1** (make sudden movement) вздр|а́гивать, -о́гнуть; содрог|а́ться, -ну́ться **2** (begin) нач|ина́ться, -а́ться; (arise) появля́ться, -и́ться; возн|ика́ть, -и́кнуть; **it ~ed raining** пошёл/начался́ дождь; **we had to ~ again from scratch** пришло́сь нача́ть всё с нача́ла; **there were 12 of us to ~ with** снача́ла/сперва́ нас бы́ло 12 (челове́к); **to ~ with, you should write to him** пре́жде всего́ (*or* для нача́ла) вы должны́ написа́ть ему́ **3** (set out) отпр|авля́ться, -а́виться **4** (of engine etc.): **the car ~ed without any trouble** маши́на завела́сь без пробле́м
□ **~ off** *v.i.* (leave) пойти́, пое́хать (*both pf.*); **she ~ed off by apologizing for being late** она́ начала́ с извине́ний за своё опозда́ние
□ **~ out** *v.i.* (leave) отпр|авля́ться, -а́виться; пойти́, пое́хать (*both pf.*)
□ **~ over** *v.i.* (AmE) нач|ина́ть, -а́ть сно́ва
□ **~ up** *v.t. see* ▶ **start** *v.t.* **2,** ▶ **start** *v.t.* **3**
■ **~ing price** *n.* нача́льная/ста́ртовая цена́

starter /ˈstɑːtə(r)/ *n.* (BrE, first course) заку́ска; **for ~s** (infml) для нача́ла

startle /ˈstɑːt(ə)l/ *v.t.* (scare) пуга́ть, ис-; вспу́г|ивать, -ну́ть

startling /ˈstɑːtlɪŋ/ *adj.* порази́тельный, потряса́ющий

starvation /stɑːˈveɪʃ(ə)n/ *n.* го́лод, голода́ние; **die of ~** ум|ира́ть, -ере́ть от го́лода (*or* с го́лоду)

starve /stɑːv/ *v.t.* мори́ть, у-/за- (го́лодом); (fig.): **the child was ~ed of affection** ребёнок страда́л от отсу́тствия любви́
● *v.i.* (go hungry) голода́ть (*impf.*); **I'm ~ing!** я ужа́сно проголода́лся!; я го́лоден как волк!

stash /stæʃ/ *n.* скры́тый запа́с
● *v.t.* (infml): **he has £1,000 ~ed away** у него́ припря́тана ты́сяча фу́нтов

ꝰ **state¹** /steɪt/ *n.* **1** (condition) состоя́ние, положе́ние **2** (country, government) госуда́рство; (*attr.*) госуда́рственный; **United S~s** Соединённые Шта́ты (Аме́рики) (*abbr.* США) **3** (pomp): **~ apartments** пара́дные поко́и (*m. pl.*); **~ visit** госуда́рственный визи́т
■ **~-aided** *adj.* получа́ющий дота́цию/субси́дию от госуда́рства; **S~ Department** *adj.* (AmE) госуда́рственный департа́мент, министе́рство иностра́нных дел; **~-of-the-**

art *adj.* ультрасовреме́нный, нове́йший

ꝰ **state²** /steɪt/ *v.t.* (declare; say clearly) заяв|ля́ть, -и́ть о + *p.*; сказа́ть (*pf.*) что; утвержда́ть (*impf.*) что; сообщ|а́ть, -и́ть о + *p.*; (indicate) ука́з|ывать, -а́ть

stateless /ˈsteɪtlɪs/ *adj.* не име́ющий гражда́нства

stately /ˈsteɪtlɪ/ *adj.* (**statelier**, **stateliest**) вели́чественный, велича́вый
■ **~ home** *n.* (BrE) дом-дворе́ц

ꝰ **statement** /ˈsteɪtmənt/ *n.* (declaration) заявле́ние; (fin.) отчёт

statesman /ˈsteɪtsmən/ *n.* госуда́рственный де́ятель

static /ˈstætɪk/ *n.* **1** (**~ electricity**) стати́ческое электри́чество **2** (as radio interference) (атмосфе́рные) поме́хи (*f. pl.*)
● *adj.* **1** (stationary) неподви́жный, стациона́рный **2** (opp. dynamic) стати́ческий, стати́чный

ꝰ **station** /ˈsteɪʃ(ə)n/ *n.* **1** (base, headquarters) ста́нция; **police ~** полице́йский уча́сток; (in Russia) отделе́ние мили́ции **2** (rail.) ста́нция; (large, mainline ~) вокза́л
● *v.t.* распол|ага́ть, -ожи́ть; **~ a guard at the gate** выставля́ть, вы́ставить карау́л у воро́т; (mil.) разме|ща́ть, -сти́ть; дислоци́ровать (*impf., pf.*)
■ **~ wagon** *n.* (AmE) универса́л (infml) (*тип кузова*)

stationary /ˈsteɪʃənərɪ/ *adj.* неподви́жный

stationery /ˈsteɪʃənərɪ/ *n.* канцеля́рские принадле́жности (*f. pl.*)/това́ры (*m. pl.*)

statistical /stəˈtɪstɪk(ə)l/ *adj.* статисти́ческий

statistician /stætɪˈstɪʃ(ə)n/ *n.* стати́стик

statistics /stəˈtɪstɪks/ *n.* статисти́ческие да́нные

statue /ˈstætjuː/ *n.* ста́туя

statuesque /stætjuˈesk/ *adj.* велича́вый, вели́чественный

statuette /stætjuˈet/ *n.* статуэ́тка

stature /ˈstætʃə(r)/ *n.* **1** (height) рост **2** (fig.) масшта́б, кали́бр

ꝰ **status** /ˈsteɪtəs/ *n.* ста́тус
■ **~ quo** *n.* ста́тус-кво (*m. & nt. indecl.*)

statute /ˈstætjuːt/ *n.* стату́т; (law) зако́н

statutory /ˈstætjʊtərɪ/ *adj.* предусмо́тренный зако́ном

staunch /stɔːntʃ/ *adj.* (loyal) лоя́льный; (devoted): **a ~ socialist** непрекло́нный/убеждённый социали́ст

stave /steɪv/ *v.t.*: **~ off** предотвра|ща́ть, -ти́ть

ꝰ **stay** /steɪ/ *n.* **1** (sojourn) пребыва́ние **2**: **~ of execution** отсро́чка исполне́ния
● *v.i.* **1** (stop, put up) (at a place) остан|а́вливаться, -ови́ться; (with sb) гости́ть (*impf.*); остан|а́вливаться, -ови́ться; **we are ~ing with friends** мы останови́лись/гости́м у друзе́й **2** (remain) ост|ава́ться, -а́ться; не уходи́ть (*impf.*); **~ at home** сиде́ть (*impf.*) до́ма; **I ~ed away from work** я не пошёл/вы́шел на рабо́ту; **can you ~ for, to tea?** вы мо́жете оста́ться на чай?; **I am ~ing in today** сего́дня я не выхожу́ (*or* я сижу́ до́ма); **he**

~ed on at the university он остáлся при университéте; she is allowed to ~ out till midnight ей разрешáют не приходи́ть домóй до 12 часóв нóчи; ~ up late не ложи́ться (*impf.*) (спать) допозднá 🛐 (endure in race etc.): he has no ~ing power у негó нет никакóй вынóсливости

STD *abbr.* (*of* **sexually transmitted disease**) заболевáние, передавáемое половы́м путём

stead /sted/ *n.*: **stand sb in good** ~ сослужи́ть (*pf.*) комý-н. хорóшую слýжбу

steadfast /'stedfɑ:st/ *adj.* (reliable) надёжный; (unwavering) непоколеби́мый

steady /'stedɪ/ *adj.* (**steadier, steadiest**) 🛐 (firmly fixed) прóчный, усто́йчивый, твёрдый; **keep the camera** ~! не дви́гайте фотоаппарáт!; (unfaltering): **a** ~ **gaze** твёрдый взгляд 🔁 (even) рóвный; (constant) постоя́нный; **he works steadily** он упóрно рабóтает; ~ **demand** постоя́нный спрос
 ● *v.t.* (strengthen): **the doctor gave him sth to** ~ **his nerves** дóктор дал емý лекáрство для укреплéния нéрвов

steak /steɪk/ *n.* (of beef) бифштéкс (натурáльный)

⚔ **steal** /sti:l/ *v.t.* (*past* **stole**, *p.p.* **stolen**) 🛐 ворова́ть (*impf.*); красть, у-; **I had my handbag stolen** у меня́ украли сýмку 🔁 (fig.): ~ **a glance at sb** взгляну́ть (*pf.*) украдкой на когó-н.
 ● *v.i.* (*past* **stole**, *p.p.* **stolen**) 🛐 (thieve) ворова́ть (*impf.*) 🔁 (move secretly or silently) красться (*impf.*); **he stole round to the back door** он прокра́лся к зáдней двéри

stealth /stelθ/ *n.*: **by** ~ тайкóм, украдкой, втихомóлку (infml)

stealthy /'stelθɪ/ *adj.* (**stealthier, stealthiest**): ~ **glance** взгляд украдкой; ~ **tread** краду́щаяся похóдка

steam /sti:m/ *n.* пар; **let off** ~ (lit.) выпускáть, вы́пустить пары́; (fig.) дава́ть, -ть вы́ход чýвствам; **run out of** ~ (fig.) выдыха́ться, вы́дохнуться
 ● *v.t.* 🛐 (cook with ~) пáрить (*impf.*); ~ed **fish** рыба, пригото́вленная на парý 🔁 (cover with ~): **the carriage windows were** ~ed **up** вагóнные óкна запотéли
 ● *v.i.* выделя́ть (*impf.*) пар/испарéния; пус|кáть, -ти́ть пар
 ■ ~ **engine** *n.* паровóз; ~roller *n.* паровóй катóк

steamer /'sti:mə(r)/ *n.* (ship) парохóд

steamy /'sti:mɪ/ *adj.* (**steamier, steamiest**) (full of steam) пóлный пáра; (infml, sexy) любóвный

steed /sti:d/ *n.* (poet.) конь (*m.*)

steel /sti:l/ *n.* сталь; (*attr.*) стальнóй
 ● *v.t.*: ~ **oneself** (pluck up courage) соб|ира́ться, -ра́ться с дýхом
 ■ ~mill, ~works *nn.* сталелитéйный завóд

steely /'sti:lɪ/ *adj.* (**steelier, steeliest**) (fig., unyielding) желéзный, непреклóнный; (stern) сурóвый

steep¹ /sti:p/ *adj.* 🛐 крутóй; (fig.): **there has been a** ~ **decline in trade** в торгóвле произошёл рéзкий спад 🔁 (infml, excessive) чрезмéрный, непомéрный; **we had to pay a** ~ **price** нам э́то влетéло в копéечку

steep² /sti:p/ *v.t.* (soak) зам|áчивать, -очи́ть

steeple /'sti:p(ə)l/ *n.* (bell tower) колокóльня; (spire) шпиль (*m.*)
 ■ ~chase *n.* стипль-чéз; скáчки (*f. pl.*) /бег с препя́тствиями

steer¹ /stɪə(r)/ *n.* (animal) вол

steer² /stɪə(r)/ *v.t.* 🛐 (ship, vehicle, etc.) управля́ть (*impf.*) + *i.* 🔁 (person, activity, etc.) вести́ (*det.*); напр|авля́ть, -áвить
 ● *v.i.* 🛐 (of steersman) управля́ть/пра́вить (*both impf.*) рулём 🔁 (of person): ~ **clear of** избегáть (*impf.*) + *g.*

steering wheel /'stɪərɪŋ wi:l/ *n.* (of car) руль (*m.*)

stem¹ /stem/ *n.* 🛐 (bot.) стéбель (*m.*) 🔁 (of wine glass) нóжка 🛐 (gram.) оснóва
 ■ ~ **cell** *n.* (biol.) стволовáя клéтка

stem² /stem/ *v.t.* (**stemmed, stemming**) (check, stop) остан|áвливать, -ови́ть

stench /stentʃ/ *n.* вонь

stencil /'stensɪl/ *n.* трафарéт
 ● *v.t.* (**stencilled, stencilling**, AmE **stenciled, stenciling**) расп|и́сывать, -áть при пóмощи трафарéта

⚔ **step** /step/ *n.* 🛐 (movement, distance, sound, manner of ~ping) шаг 🔁 (lit., action) шаг; мéра; **take** ~s **towards** предприн|имáть, -я́ть шаги́ к + *d.* 🛐 (raised surface) ступéнь; (of staircase etc.) ступéнька 🔁 (*in pl.*) (BrE) (*also* ~ladder) стремя́нка
 ● *v.i.* (**stepped, stepping**) шаг|áть, -нýть; ступ|áть, -и́ть; **someone** ~ped **on my foot** ктó-то наступи́л мне нá ногу
 □ ~ **aside** *v.i.* сторони́ться, по-; (fig.) уступ|áть, -и́ть (дорóгу) другóму
 □ ~ **back** *v.i.* отступ|áть, -и́ть
 □ ~ **down** *v.i.*: **he** ~ped **down off the ladder** он спусти́лся/сошёл с лéстницы; **he** ~ped **down in favour of a more experienced man** он уступи́л мéсто бóлее óпытному человéку
 □ ~ **in** *v.i.* (intervene) вмéш|иваться, -áться; (replace sb): **thanks for** ~ping **in** спаси́бо, что вы́ручили
 □ ~ **up** *v.t.* (increase) пов|ышáть, -ы́сить; уси́ли|вать, -ть
 ■ ~-by-~ *adj.* постепéнный ● *adv.* постепéнно; ~ping **stone** *n.* кáмень для перехóда (*через ручей и т. п.*); (fig.) трамплин; **a** ~ping **stone to success** ступéнь к успéху; ~ladder *n.* = step n. 4

step|- /step/ *comb. form*: ~brother *n.* свóдный брат; ~child *n.* (boy) пáсынок; (girl) пáдчерица; ~daughter *n.* пáдчерица; ~father *n.* óтчим; ~mother *n.* мáчеха; ~sister *n.* свóдная сестрá; ~son *n.* пáсынок

steppe /step/ *n.* степь

stereo /'sterɪəʊ/ *n.* (*pl.* ~s) (~phonic system) стереосистéма; **personal** ~ плéер

stereotype /'sterɪəʊtaɪp/ *n.* стереоти́п; (*attr.*) стереоти́пный

S

stereotypical /ˌsterɪəʊ'tɪpɪk(ə)l/ *adj.*
стереоти́пный

sterile /'steraɪl/ *adj.* **1** (of land) неплодоро́дный; (of person or animal) беспло́дный **2** (germ-free) стери́льный

sterility /stə'rɪlɪtɪ/ *n.* беспло́дие

sterilize /'sterɪlaɪz/ *v.t.* стерилизова́ть (*impf., pf.*)

sterling /'stɜːlɪŋ/ *n.* сте́рлинг; фунт сте́рлингов

stern[1] /stɜːn/ *n.* (of ship) корма́

stern[2] /stɜːn/ *adj.* (severe) суро́вый

stern|um /'stɜːnəm/ *n.* (*pl.* ~ums *or* ~a) груди́на

steroid /'steroɪd/ *n.* стеро́ид

stethoscope /'steθəskəʊp/ *n.* стетоско́п

stew /stjuː/ *n.* рагу́ (*nt. indecl.*)
● *v.t.* (meat, fish, vegetables) туши́ть, по-; (fruit) вари́ть (*impf.*); ~ed fruit компо́т

steward /'stjuːəd/ *n.* (of estate, club, etc.) управля́ющий, эконо́м, стю́ард; (of race meeting) распоряди́тель (*m.*); (on ship) стю́ард; (on train) проводни́к; (on plane) бортпроводни́к, стю́ард

stewardess /stjuːə'des/ *n.* (on plane) стюарде́сса, бортпроводни́ца

stick[1] /stɪk/ *n.* **1** (for support, punishment) па́лка; (*in full* **walking** ~) трость; (*in full* **hockey** ~) клю́шка; ~ of chalk мело́к; ~ of celery/rhubarb сте́бель (*m.*) сельдере́я/реве́ня; ~ of dynamite динами́тная ша́шка

✒ **stick**[2] /stɪk/ *v.t.* (*past and p.p.* **stuck**) **1** (insert point of) втыка́ть, воткну́ть; I stuck a pin in the map я воткну́л була́вку в ка́рту **2** (cause to adhere) прикле́и|вать, -ть (*что к чему*); накле́и|вать, -ть (*что на что*); (affix): ~ a notice on the door ве́шать, пове́сить объявле́ние на дверь **3** (infml, put): ~ that book on the shelf су́ньте э́ту кни́гу на по́лку; he stuck his head round the door он просу́нул го́лову в дверь **4** (BrE, infml, endure) терпе́ть, вы- **5** (infml uses of pass. with preps.): get stuck into sth (BrE, make serious start on) прин|има́ться, -я́ться за что-н. всерьёз; be stuck with (unable to get rid of) быть не в состоя́нии отде́латься от чего́-н.
● *v.i.* (*past and p.p.* **stuck**) **1** (be implanted): a dagger ~ing in his back кинжа́л, торча́щий у него́ в спине́ **2** (remain attached, adhere) прил|ипа́ть, -и́пнуть (*к чему*); прикле́и|ваться, -ться; these pages have stuck (together) э́ти страни́цы скле́ились; ~ing plaster (BrE) лейкопла́стырь (*m.*), ли́пкий пла́стырь **3** (cling, cleave): ~ to the point не отступа́ть (*impf.*) от те́мы; ~ to one's principles ост|ава́ться, -а́ться ве́рным свои́м при́нципам; the accused stuck to his story обвиня́емый упо́рно стоя́л на своём **4** (*also* be stuck, get stuck) (become embedded, fixed) застр|ева́ть, -я́ть; the drawer ~s я́щик застря́л; can you help with this problem? I'm stuck помоги́те мне,

пожа́луйста, с э́той зада́чей — я совсе́м запу́тался; one thing ~s in my mind одно́ у меня́ засе́ло в па́мяти
□ ~ **around** *v.i.* (infml) не уходи́ть (*impf.*)
□ ~ **down** *v.t.* (seal): have you stuck the envelope down? вы закле́или конве́рт?
□ ~ **on** *v.t.* (affix) прикле́и|вать, -ть
□ ~ **out** *v.t.*: ~ one's tongue out высо́вывать, вы́сунуть язы́к; ~ one's head out высо́вываться, вы́сунуться
● *v.i.* (project) торча́ть (*impf.*); his ears ~ out у него́ торча́т у́ши
□ ~ **together** *v.t.* (with glue) скле́и|вать, -ть
● *v.i.*: good friends ~ together настоя́щие друзья́ стоя́т друг за дру́га (горо́й)
□ ~ **up** *v.t.* (protrude upwards) торча́ть (*impf.*); ~ up for (defend) заступ|а́ться, -и́ться за (*кого/что*)

sticker /'stɪkə(r)/ *n.* накле́йка

sticky /'stɪkɪ/ *adj.* (**stickier**, **stickiest**) кле́йкий, ли́пкий

stiff /stɪf/ *adj.* **1** (not flexible or soft) жёсткий **2** (not working smoothly) туго́й; ~ hinges туги́е пе́тли **3** (of person or parts of body) онеме́лый, окостене́лый; I have a ~ neck у меня́ ше́я онеме́ла; he has a ~ leg у него́ нога́ пло́хо сгиба́ется; I feel ~ я не могу́ ни согну́ться, ни разогну́ться **4** (forceful) си́льный; a ~ drink хоро́ший глото́к спиртно́го **5** (difficult) тру́дный, тяжёлый; a ~ examination тру́дный экза́мен; (severe) суро́вый; he got a ~ sentence ему́ вы́несли суро́вый пригово́р **6** (constrained) натя́нутый, чо́порный **7** (*pred.*) (infml): he was scared ~ он перепуга́лся до́ смерти; I was bored ~ я чуть не у́мер со ску́ки

stiffen /'stɪf(ə)n/ *v.t.* прид|ава́ть, -а́ть жёсткость + *d.*
● *v.i.* (become rigid) де́латься, с- жёстким; (of body) кочене́ть, о-, костене́ть, о-

stifl|e /'staɪf(ə)l/ *v.t.* **1** (smother, suffocate) души́ть, за-; it is ~ing in here здесь ду́шно **2** (e.g. rebellion, feelings) подавл|я́ть, -и́ть

stigma /'stɪgmə/ *n.* позо́р, пятно́

stigmatize /'stɪgmətaɪz/ *v.t.* клейми́ть, за-

stile /staɪl/ *n.* (steps) перела́з (*ступеньки у забора, стены*)

stiletto /stɪ'letəʊ/ *n.* (*pl.* ~s) (*usu. in pl.*) (thin high heel) шпи́лька; (shoe) ту́фля на шпи́льке

✒ **still** /stɪl/ *adj.* **1** (quiet, calm) ти́хий **2** (motionless) неподви́жный; sit/stand ~ сиде́ть/стоя́ть (*impf.*) споко́йно **3** (BrE, not fizzy) негазиро́ванный
● *adv.* **1** (even now, then; as formerly) (всё) ещё; до сих пор; по-пре́жнему **2** (nevertheless) тем не ме́нее, всё-таки, всё равно́ **3** (*with comp.*) (even, yet) ещё
■ ~ **life** *n.* (art) натюрмо́рт

stilt /stɪlt/ *n.* **1** ходу́ля; walk on ~s ходи́ть (*indet.*) на ходу́лях **2** (supporting a building) сва́я

stilted /'stɪltɪd/ *adj.* (of style etc.) высокопа́рный

stimulant /'stɪmjʊlənt/ *n.* (med.) стимули́рующее сре́дство

✒ ключева́я ле́ксика

stimulate /'stɪmjʊleɪt/ v.t. **1** (rouse, incite) (*sb to do sth*) побу|жда́ть, -ди́ть (*кого + inf.* or *к чему*); стимули́ровать (*impf., pf.*) **2** (excite, arouse) возбу|жда́ть, -ди́ть; the story ~d my curiosity расска́з возбуди́л моё любопы́тство

stimulus /'stɪmjʊləs/ n. (*pl.* ~li /-laɪ/) (incentive) сти́мул, побужде́ние

sting /stɪŋ/ n. **1** (of insect, etc.) жа́ло **2** (by insect) уку́с
● v.t. (*past and p.p.* **stung**) **1** (of insect, etc.) жа́лить, у-; куса́ть, укуси́ть; (of plant) обж|ига́ть, -е́чь; жечь (*impf.*) **2** (of pain, smoke, etc.) обж|ига́ть, -е́чь
● v.i. (*past and p.p.* **stung**) **1** (of insect, etc.) жа́литься (*impf.*); куса́ться (*impf.*) **2** (feel pain) жечь (*impf.*); the smoke made my eyes ~ дым ел мне глаза́
■ ~ing nettle n. (жгу́чая) крапи́ва

stingy /'stɪndʒɪ/ adj. (**stingier, stingiest**) скупо́й

stink /stɪŋk/ n. вонь
● v.i. (*past* **stank** or **stunk**, *p.p.* **stunk**) воня́ть (*impf.*); the room ~s of onions в ко́мнате воня́ет лу́ком

stint /stɪnt/ n. уро́к
● v.t.: he did not ~ on his praise он не скупи́лся на похвалы́

stipend /'staɪpend/ n. (of clergyman) жа́лованье; (of student) стипе́ндия

stipulate /'stɪpjʊleɪt/ v.t. (demand) обусло́в|ливать, -ить

stir /stə(r)/ n.: the news caused a ~ э́то изве́стие наде́лало мно́го шу́ма
● v.t. (**stirred, stirring**): the wind ~s the trees ве́тер колы́шет дере́вья; ~ one's tea разме́ш|ивать, -а́ть чай; ~ the soup меша́ть, по- суп
● v.i. (**stirred, stirring**) шевели́ться, за-
□ ~ up v.t. (arouse): ~ up rebellion се́ять (*impf.*) сму́ту

stirrup /'stɪrəp/ n. стре́мя (*nt.*)

stitch /stɪtʃ/ n. **1** (sewing) стежо́к; (knitting) петля́ **2** (med.) шов **3** (pain in side) ко́лик|и (*pl., g.* —) в боку́
● v.t. (sew together) сши|ва́ть, -ть; (esp. med.) заш|ива́ть, -и́ть

stoat /stəʊt/ n. горноста́й (в ле́тнем меху́)

stock /stɒk/ n. **1** (store, supply) запа́с, инвента́рь (*m.*); in ~ в ассортиме́нте; take ~ of (fig., appraise) крити́чески оце́н|ивать, -и́ть **2** (lineage) семья́, происхожде́ние **3** (of farm) (*in full* **live**~) скот, поголо́вье скота́ **4** (cul.) (кре́пкий) бульо́н **5** (comm.) а́кции (*f. pl.*); фо́нды (*m. pl.*)
● adj. (regularly used) обы́чный, шабло́нный
● v.t. **1** (equip with) снаб|жа́ть, -ди́ть (*что чем*); обору́довать (*impf., pf.*) **2** (keep in ~) держа́ть (*impf.*); име́ть (*impf.*) в нали́чии
● v.i. (~ **up**): we ~ed up with fuel for the winter мы запасли́сь то́пливом на́ зиму
■ ~broker n. биржево́й ма́клер; ~ cube n. бульо́нный ку́бик; S~ Exchange n. фо́ндовая би́ржа; ~ market n. фо́ндовая би́ржа; ~pile v.t. запаса́ть, -ти́ + a. or g.; ~-still adv. неподви́жно; ~taking n.

инвентариза́ция

Stockholm /'stɒkhəʊm/ n. Стокго́льм

stocking /'stɒkɪŋ/ n. чуло́к

stockist /'stɒkɪst/ n. (BrE) ро́зничный продаве́ц (*определённых товаров*)

stocky /'stɒkɪ/ adj. (**stockier, stockiest**) корена́стый, призе́мистый

stodgy /'stɒdʒɪ/ adj. (**stodgier, stodgiest**) (BrE, of food) тяжёлый

stoic /'stəʊɪk/ n. (of either sex) сто́ик
● adj. стои́ческий

stoical /'stəʊɪk(ə)l/ adj. стои́ческий

stoicism /'stəʊɪsɪz(ə)m/ n. стоици́зм

stoke /stəʊk/ v.t. (*also* ~ **up**) (put more fuel on) загру|жа́ть, -зи́ть (*топку*)

stole /stəʊl/ *past of* ▶ steal

stolen /'stəʊlən/ *p.p. of* ▶ steal

stomach /'stʌmək/ n. **1** (internal organ) желу́док **2** (external part of body; belly) живо́т, брю́хо
● v.t. (fig., tolerate): I can't ~ him я его́ не переношу́; я его́ терпе́ть не могу́
■ ~ ache n. ко́лик|и (*pl., g.* —) в животе́

stomp /stɒmp/ v.i. (infml, tread heavily) то́пать, про-

stone /stəʊn/ n. (*sense 4: pl.* ~) **1** ка́мень (*m.*) **2** (rock, material): built of local ~ постро́енный из ме́стного ка́мня **3** (of plum etc.) ко́сточка **4** (BrE, weight) сто́ун (*6,35 кг*)
● v.t. **1** (pelt with ~) поб|ива́ть, -и́ть камня́ми **2**: ~ cherries оч|ища́ть, -и́стить ви́шни от ко́сточек **3**: ~d (infml) (drunk) пья́ный вдре́безги (infml); (with drugs) обдо́лбанный (sl.)
■ S~ Age n. ка́менный век; ~ circle n. кро́млех; ~ cold adj. холо́дный как лёд; ~-deaf adj. соверше́нно глухо́й; ~mason n. ка́менщик

stony /'stəʊnɪ/ adj. (**stonier, stoniest**) камени́стый; (fig., unfeeling) ка́менный

stood /stʊd/ *past and p.p. of* ▶ stand

stooge /stuːdʒ/ n. (sl.) (comedian's foil) партнёр ко́мика; (deputy of low standing) подставно́е лицо́

stool /stuːl/ n. табуре́т(ка)

stoop /stuːp/ n. суту́лость; he walks with a ~ он суту́лится при ходьбе́
● v.i. **1** (of posture) суту́литься, с-; (bend down) наг|иба́ться, -ну́ться; сгиба́ться, согну́ться **2** (lower oneself): he never ~ed to lying он никогда́ не унижа́лся до лжи

stop /stɒp/ n. **1** (halt, halting place) остано́вка; come to a ~ остан|а́вливаться, -ови́ться; put a ~ to положи́ть (*pf.*) коне́ц (+ *d.*) **2** (in telegram) (full ~) то́чка (*abbr.* тчк)
● v.t. (**stopped, stopping**) **1** (*also* ~ **up**) (close, plug) закр|ыва́ть, -ы́ть; зат|ыка́ть, -кну́ть; заде́л|ывать, -ать **2** (arrest motion of) остан|а́вливать, -ови́ть; he ~ped the car он останови́л маши́ну **3** (arrest progress of; bring to an end) остан|а́вливать, -ови́ть; заде́рж|ивать, -а́ть; прекра|ща́ть, -ти́ть; rain ~ped play дождь оста́н|овил игру́; ~ the cheque (BrE), check (AmE) я приостанови́л платёж по э́тому че́ку; (cut off, disallow, ~ provision of): my

father ∼ped my allowance отéц перестáл
выделя́ть мне дéньги **4** (prevent): ∼ sb
from удéрж|ивать, -áть когó-н. от + g.; не
да|вáть, -ть (комý) (+ inf.); I tried to ∼ him
(from) telling her я пытáлся помешáть емý
сказáть ей **5** (with gerund: discontinue, leave off)
перест|авáть, -áть (+ inf.); прекра|щáть,
-ти́ть (+ n. obj.); ∼ teasing the cat!
перестáньте дразни́ть кóшку!; they ∼ped
talking when I came in когдá я вошёл, они́
умóлкли
 • *v.i.* (**stopped, stopping**) **1** (come to
a halt) остан|áвливаться, -ови́ться **2** (in
speaking) зам|олкáть, -óлкнуть; замолчáть
(*pf.*) **3** (cease activity) перест|авáть, -áть;
кончáть, кóнчить **4** (come to an end)
прекра|щáться, -ти́ться; кончáться,
кóнчиться; перест|авáть, -áть; the rain ∼ped
дождь кóнчился/перестáл; the road ∼ped
suddenly неожи́данно дорóга кóнчилась
□ ∼ by *v.i.* за|ходи́ть, -йти́; (in a vehicle)
за|езжáть, -éхать
□ ∼ off, ∼ over *vv.i.* остан|áвливаться, -ови́ться
 ■ ∼gap *n.* (person) врéменная замéна; (thing)
затычка; врéменная мéра; ∼-off, ∼over *nn.*
останóвка (в пути́); ∼watch *n.* секундомéр
stoppage /'stɒpɪdʒ/ *n.* (strike) забастóвка;
(stopping, discontinuing) прекращéние
stopper /'stɒpə(r)/ *n.* (of bottle etc.) прóбка
storage /'stɔːrɪdʒ/ *n.* (storing) хранéние; (in
warehouse) склади́рование
 ■ ∼ heater *n.* (BrE) электрообогревáтель (*m.*),
аккумули́рующий теплó
♂ **store** /stɔː(r)/ *n.* **1** (stock, reserve) запáс, резéрв,
припáсы (*m. pl.*); he has a surprise in ∼ for
you у негó для вас припасён сюрпри́з (*in
pl.*) (supplies) припáсы (*m. pl.*), резéрвы (*m.
pl.*) **3** (AmE, shop) магази́н, лáвка; department
∼ универмáг
 • *v.t.* **1** (keep) храни́ть (*impf.*) **2**: ∼ up
запас|áть, -ти́ **3** (deposit in ∼) сда|вáть, -ть на
хранéние
 ■ ∼keeper *n.* лáвочни|к (-ца); ∼room *n.*
кладовáя
storey /'stɔːrɪ/ (AmE **story**) *n.* этáж
stork /stɔːk/ *n.* áист
storm /stɔːm/ *n.* бýря; (thunder ∼) грозá
 • *v.t.* (mil.) штурмовáть (*impf.*); брать, взять
штýрмом/при́ступом
 • *v.i.*: he ∼ed out of the room он в гнéве
выбежáл из кóмнаты
 ■ ∼ cloud *n.* грозовáя тýча
stormy /'stɔːmɪ/ *adj.* (**stormier, stormiest**)
бýрный (also fig.)
♂ **story**[1] /'stɔːrɪ/ *n.* **1** (tale, account) расскáз,
истóрия; (fairy tale) скáзка; short ∼ расскáз,
новéлла **2** (newspaper report) отчёт, статья́
 ■ ∼book *n.* сбóрник расскáзов; ∼teller *n.*
расскáзчи|к (-ца)
story[2] /'stɔːrɪ/ *n.* (AmE) = **storey**
stout /staʊt/ *n.* (beer) тёмное пи́во
 • *adj.* **1** (strong) крéпкий, прóчный
 2 (corpulent) пóлный, дорóдный

♂ ключевáя лéксика

stove /stəʊv/ *n.* печь, пéчка; (for cooking) плитá
stow /stəʊ/ *v.t.* укла́дывать, уложи́ть
 ■ ∼away *n.* безбилéтный пассажи́р, «зáяц»
St Petersburg /s(ə)nt 'piːtəzbəːg/ *n.* Санкт-
Петербýрг
straddle /'stræd(ə)l/ *v.t.* (extend across)
охвáт|ывать, -и́ть; (sit with legs on either side of):
∼ a fence сидéть, сесть верхóм на забóре
straggle /'stræg(ə)l/ *v.i.*: the children ∼ed
home from school дéти брели́/тащи́лись
из шкóлы домóй; a ∼ing line of houses
беспоря́дочный ряд домóв
straggler /'stræglə(r)/ *n.* отстáвший
straggly /'stræglɪ/ *adj.* (**stragglier,
straggliest**) (hair) всклокóченный,
растрёпанный; (plants) увя́дший
♂ **straight** /streɪt/ *n.* (of racecourse): home ∼
фи́нишная прямáя
 • *adj.* **1** прямóй; in a ∼ line прямо в ряд;
she had ∼ hair у неё бы́ли прямы́е вóлосы;
I couldn't keep a ∼ face я не мог удержáться
от улы́бки **2** (level) рóвный; (neat, in order)
ýбранный, приведённый в поря́док;
put the record ∼ (fig.) вн|оси́ть, -ести́
я́сность; let's get this ∼ давáйте внесём
определённость в э́тот вопрóс **3** (frank,
honest) прямóй, чéстный **4** (orthodox): ∼
play (theatr.) (чи́стая) дрáма; (heterosexual)
гетеросексуáльный **5** (undiluted)
неразбáвленный
 • *adv.* **1** прямо; sit (up) ∼! сиди́(те) прямо!;
keep ∼ on! иди́те прямо!; (directly): I am
going ∼ to Paris я éду прямо в Пари́ж; I told
him ∼ (out) я сказáл емý прямо **2**: ∼ away,
off срáзу, тóтчас
 ■ ∼forward *adj.* (frank) прямóй; (uncomplicated)
простóй
straighten /'streɪt(ə)n/ *v.t.* **1** выпрямля́ть,
вы́прямить; распрям|ля́ть, -и́ть; he ∼ed
his back он вы́прямился; он распрями́л
спи́ну **2** (put in order) прив|оди́ть, -ести́ в
поря́док; ула́|живать, -дить; I will try to ∼
things out я постарáюсь всё ула́дить
strain /streɪn/ *n.* **1** (tension) натяжéние;
(wearing effect): the ∼s of modern life
напряжённость/стресс совремéнной жи́зни;
(muscular ∼) растяжéние (мышц) **2** (of animals,
plants) порóда
 • *v.t.* **1** (exert) напр|ягáть, -я́чь; I ∼ed my
ears to catch his words я напря́г слух, чтóбы
улови́ть егó словá **2** (overexert): ∼ one's
eyes переутом|ля́ть, -и́ть глазá; пóртить,
ис- зрéние; ∼ oneself над|рывáться,
-орвáться **3** (overtax): ∼ sb's patience
испы́т|ывать, -áть чьё-н. терпéние **4** (filter)
(*also* ∼ off) проце́|живать, -ди́ть;
отце́|живать, -ди́ть; сце́|живать, -ди́ть
 • *v.i.* (exert oneself) напр|ягáться, -я́чься
strainer /'streɪnə(r)/ *n.* си́то; (tea ∼) си́течко
strait /streɪt/ *n.* **1** (of water) проли́в **2**: in dire
∼s в отчáянном положéнии
 ■ ∼jacket *n.* смири́тельная рубáшка; ∼-laced
adj. пуритáнский
straitened /'streɪtənd/ *adj.*: ∼ circumstances
стеснённые обстоя́тельства

strand¹ /strænd/ *v.t.* (*usu. in pass.*) сажа́ть, посади́ть на мель; **I was ~ed in Paris** я застря́л в Пари́же

strand² /strænd/ *n.* (fibre, thread) прядь, нить

ⱷ **strange** /streɪndʒ/ *adj.* **1** (unfamiliar) незнако́мый, неизве́стный **2** (remarkable) стра́нный, необыкнове́нный, необы́чный; **~ to say** (*or* **~ly enough**) **he loves her** как (э́то) ни стра́нно, он лю́бит её

strangeness /ˈstreɪndʒnɪs/ *n.* (remarkableness) стра́нность; (unfamiliarity) непривы́чность

stranger /ˈstreɪndʒə(r)/ *n.* **1** (unknown person) незнако́м|ец (-ка); посторо́нний (челове́к) **2** (foreigner): **I am a ~ here** я здесь чужо́й

strangle /ˈstræŋɡ(ə)l/ *v.t.* души́ть, за-; удави́ть (*pf.*)

■ **~hold** *n.* (lit., fig.) заси́лье

strap /stræp/ *n.* реме́нь (*m.*); (of dress) брете́лька

● *v.t.* (**strapped, strapping**) стя́|гивать, -ну́ть ремнём

strapless /ˈstræplɪs/ *adj.* без брете́лек

strapping /ˈstræpɪŋ/ *adj.* ро́слый, здоро́вый (infml)

Strasbourg /ˈstræzbɜːɡ/ *n.* Стра́сбург

strata /ˈstrɑːtə/ *pl. of* ▸ **stratum**

stratagem /ˈstrætədʒəm/ *n.* уло́вка

strategic /strəˈtiːdʒɪk/ *adj.* стратеги́ческий

strategist /ˈstrætɪdʒɪst/ *n.* страте́г

ⱷ **strategy** /ˈstrætədʒɪ/ *n.* страте́гия

stratif|y /ˈstrætɪfaɪ/ *v.t.* (arrange in strata) насла́|ивать, -о́ить; **~ied rock** сло́истый ка́мень

stratosphere /ˈstrætəsfɪə(r)/ *n.* стратосфе́ра

strat|um /ˈstrɑːtəm/ *n.* (*pl.* **~a**) слой

ⱷ **straw** /strɔː/ *n.* **1** (collect.) соло́ма; (attr.) соло́менный **2** (single ~) соло́минка; **clutch at ~s** (fig.) хвата́ться, схвати́ться за соло́минку; **that was the last ~** э́то бы́ло после́дней ка́плей

■ **~ poll, ~ vote** (AmE) *nn.* (неофициа́льный) опро́с; голосова́ние

strawberry /ˈstrɔːbərɪ/ *n.* (in pl., collect.) клубни́ка; (wild) земляни́ка

stray /streɪ/ *adj.* **1** (wandering, lost) заблуди́вшийся, бездо́мный; **~ dog** бездо́мная соба́ка **2** (off-target): **a ~ bullet** шальна́я пу́ля

● *v.i.* **1** (wander) заблуди́ться (*pf.*); сбива́ться, сби́ться с пути́; **we must not ~ too far from the path** мы не должны́ отклоня́ться сли́шком далеко́ от тропи́нки **2** (of thoughts, affections) блужда́ть (*impf.*)

streak /striːk/ *n.* **1** полоска, прожи́лка; **~ of lightning** вспы́шка мо́лнии **2** (fig, trace, tendency) черта́, накло́нность

● *v.t.*: **~ed with red** с кра́сными поло́сками

● *v.i.* (infml, move rapidly) прон|оси́ться, -ести́сь

stream /striːm/ *n.* **1** (brook) руче́й; (rivulet) ре́чка **2** (flow) пото́к, тече́ние; **~ of abuse** пото́к руга́тельств (*nt. pl.*) /бра́ни

● *v.i.* течь, струи́ться, ли́ться (*all impf.*); **tears ~ed down her cheeks** слёзы струи́лись/

лили́сь/текли́ у неё по щека́м; **light ~ed in at the window** свет струи́лся в окно́; **her eyes were ~ing** у неё из глаз лили́сь слёзы

■ **~line** *v.t.* прид|ава́ть, -а́ть обтека́емую фо́рму + *d.*; (fig.) упро́|щать, -сти́ть, рационализи́ровать (*impf., pf.*); **~lined** *adj.* стро́йный; упрощённый

streamer /ˈstriːmə(r)/ *n.* руло́н бума́жной ле́нты; (flag) вы́мпел

streaming /ˈstriːmɪŋ/ *adj.* **1** (of a cold): **he had a ~ cold** у него́ был стра́шный на́сморк **2**: (comput.): **~ video** пото́ковое ви́део

ⱷ **street** /striːt/ *n.* у́лица; **he lives in the next ~ (to us)** он живёт на сосе́дней у́лице

■ **~car** *n.* (AmE) трамва́й; **~ credibility** (infml) (also **~ cred**) *n.* и́мидж; **~ lamp** *n.* у́личный фона́рь; **~wise** *adj.* (infml) о́пытный, зна́ющий, у́шлый

ⱷ **strength** /streŋkθ/ *n.* **1** си́ла; (of structure, material, beam) про́чность; (of wine, solution) кре́пость **2** (basis): **on the ~ of** на основа́нии + *g.*

strengthen /ˈstreŋkθ(ə)n/ *v.t.* укреп|ля́ть, -и́ть; уси́ли|вать, -ть

strenuous /ˈstrenjʊəs/ *adj.* (requiring effort) напряжённый; (energetic) уси́ленный, интенси́вный

ⱷ **stress** /stres/ *n.* **1** (tension) напряже́ние; (pressure) давле́ние, нажи́м; (psych.) стресс **2** (emphasis) ударе́ние; **lay ~ on** де́лать, с- ударе́ние на + *p.*

● *v.t.* **1** (subject to ~) напр|яга́ть, -я́чь; **I'm ~ed out** я живу́ в постоя́нном стре́ссе/напряже́нии **2** (emphasize) подчёрк|ивать, -ну́ть; де́лать, с- ударе́ние на + *a.*

stressful /ˈstresfʊl/ *adj.* стре́ссовый

ⱷ **stretch** /stretʃ/ *n.* **1** (elasticity) растяжи́мость, эласти́чность **2** (expanse) простра́нство **3** (of time) отре́зок; **he works 8 hours at a ~** он рабо́тает во́семь часо́в подря́д

● *v.t.* **1** (lengthen) выт|я́гивать, вы́тянуть; (broaden) раст|я́гивать, -ну́ть **2** (pull to fullest extent): **~ a rope between two posts** натя́|гивать, -ну́ть верёвку ме́жду двумя́ столба́ми; **~ oneself** потя́|гиваться, -ну́ться; **~ one's legs** разм|ина́ть, -я́ть но́ги **3** (strain, exert): **~ the truth** преувели́чи|вать, -ть

● *v.i.* **1** (be elastic) растя́гиваться (*impf.*) **2** (extend) прост|ира́ться, -ере́ться; (of time) дли́ться, про- (**~ oneself**) потя́|гиваться, -ну́ться

■ **~ fabric** *n.* эласти́чная мате́рия

stretcher /ˈstretʃə(r)/ *n.* носи́л|ки (-ок)

strew /struː/ *v.t.* (*p.p.* **strewn** *or* **strewed**) разбр|а́сывать, -оса́ть

stricken /ˈstrɪkən/ *adj.* (lit.) ра́неный; (fig.) поражённый

strict /strɪkt/ *adj.* **1** (precise) стро́гий, то́чный **2** (stringent): **in ~ confidence** в строжа́йшей та́йне **3** (stern) стро́гий, взыска́тельный

stride /straɪd/ *n.* (long step) (большо́й) шаг; **he took the exam in his ~** он с лёгкостью сдал экза́мен; **science has made great ~s** нау́ка доби́лась больши́х успе́хов

S

● *v.i.* (*past* **strode**, *p.p.* **stridden** /'strɪd(ə)n/) шага́ть (*impf.*)

strident /'straɪd(ə)nt/ *adj.* ре́зкий, пронзи́тельный

strife /straɪf/ *n.* борьба́, вражда́

♂ **strike** /straɪk/ *n.* **1** (of workers) забасто́вка; **be on ~** бастова́ть (*impf.*); **go on ~** забастова́ть (*pf.*) **2** (attack; blow) нападе́ние; уда́р; налёт
● *v.t.* (*past* **struck**, *p.p.* **struck** *or archaic* **stricken**) **1** (hit) уд|аря́ть, -а́рить (*чем по чему; что обо что; кого чем*); **the ship struck a rock** кора́бль наскочи́л на скалу́ **2** (fig., impress) пора|жа́ть, -зи́ть; каза́ться, по- + *d.*; **he was struck by her beauty** он был поражён её красото́й; **the idea ~s me as a good one** э́та мысль ка́жется мне уда́чной **3** (fig., discover) нап|ада́ть, -а́сть на + *a.*; на|ходи́ть, -йти́; откр|ыва́ть, -ы́ть; **they struck oil** они́ откры́ли нефтяно́е месторожде́ние **4**: **~ a match** чи́рк|ать, -нуть спи́чкой **5** (of bell, clock, etc.) бить (*impf.*), проб|ива́ть, -и́ть; **the clock struck midnight** часы́ проби́ли по́лночь **6** (arrive at): **~ a bargain** заключ|а́ть, -и́ть сде́лку; **~ a balance** подв|оди́ть, -ести́ бала́нс/ито́ги; (fig.) на|ходи́ть, -йти́ компроми́сс
● *v.i.* (*past* **struck**, *p.p.* **struck** *or archaic* **stricken**) **1** (hit) уд|аря́ть, -а́рить **2** (of clock, etc.) бить, про- **3** (go on ~) бастова́ть (*impf.*) (**for:** чтобы доби́ться + *g.*)

□ **~ down** *v.t.* (fell) сби|ва́ть, -ть с ног; сра|жа́ть, -зи́ть; (of illness, etc.) сва́л|ивать, -и́ть; сра|жа́ть, -зи́ть

□ **~ off** *v.t.* (delete): **~ sb** (*or* sb's name) **off** вычёркивать, вы́черкнуть кого́-н. (*or* чьё-н. и́мя) (из спи́ска и *т. п.*)

□ **~ out** *v.t.* (delete) вычёркивать, вы́черкнуть

□ **~ up** *v.t.*: **~ up an acquaintance** завя́з|ывать, -а́ть знако́мство
● *v.i.* (begin playing/singing) заигра́ть, запе́ть (*both pf.*)

striker /'straɪkə(r)/ *n.* **1** (person on strike) забасто́вщи|к (-ца) **2** (sport) напада́ющий

striking /'straɪkɪŋ/ *adj.* порази́тельный, замеча́тельный

string /strɪŋ/ *n.* **1** верёвка, бечёвка; **pull ~s** наж|има́ть, -а́ть на все кно́пки **2** (of mus. instrument, racket) струна́; the **~s** (of orchestra) стру́нные инструме́нты (*m. pl.*) **3** (set of objects): **~ of pearls** ни́тка же́мчуга; **~ of onions/sausages** связка лу́ка/соси́сок; **~ of boats/houses** ряд ло́док/домо́в
● *v.t.* (*past and p.p.* **strung**) **1** (furnish with **~**): **~ a bow** натя́|гивать, -ну́ть тетиву́; **~ a racket** натя́|гивать, -ну́ть стру́ны **2** (thread on **~**) нани́з|ывать, -а́ть **3** (remove **~**y fibre from): **~ beans** чи́стить, по- фасо́ль

□ **~ along** *v.i.*: **~ along with sb** (infml, accompany) тащи́ться, по- за кем-н.
● *v.i.* (infml, deceive) води́ть (*impf.*) за́ нос

□ **~ out** *v.t.* (extend) раст|я́гивать, -ну́ть; **the houses were strung out along the beach** дома́ тяну́лись вдоль побере́жья

■ **~ quartet** *n.* стру́нный кварте́т

stringent /'strɪndʒ(ə)nt/ *adj.* стро́гий, то́чный

strip¹ /strɪp/ *n.* полоса́; (of cloth) поло́ска, ле́нта; **~ of land** поло́ска земли́

■ **~ cartoon** *n.* расска́з в карти́нках; **~ lighting** *n.* нео́новое освеще́ние

strip² /strɪp/ *v.t.* (**stripped**, **stripping**) **1** (tear off) сдира́ть, содра́ть **2** (denude) разд|ева́ть, -е́ть; **the room was ~ped bare** из ко́мнаты вы́несли всю ме́бель; (**down**) **a machine/weapon** раз|бира́ть, -обра́ть (*or* демонти́ровать (*impf., pf.*)) маши́ну/ору́жие
● *v.i.* (**stripped**, **stripping**): **~ (naked)**, **~ off** разд|ева́ться, -е́ться (донага́)

stripe /straɪp/ *n.* полоса́, поло́ска

striped /straɪpt/ *adj.* полоса́тый

stripling /'strɪplɪŋ/ *n.* юне́ц

stripper /'strɪpə(r)/ *n.* стриптизёр (-ка/-ша)

strive /straɪv/ *v.i.* (*past* **strove** *or* **strived**, *p.p.* **striven** /'strɪv(ə)n/ *or* **strived**) стреми́ться (*impf.*) (**after, for:** к + *d.*)

strode /strəʊd/ *past of* ▶ **stride**

stroke¹ /strəʊk/ *n.* **1** уда́р; **at a ~** (fig.) одни́м уда́ром/ма́хом **2** (paralytic attack) уда́р, инсу́льт **3** (in swimming) стиль (*m.*) **4** (single instance): **~ of genius** гениа́льная мысль; **~ of luck** (неожи́данная) уда́ча; везе́ние **5** (with pen etc.) штрих; (with brush) мазо́к

stroke² /strəʊk/ *v.t.* гла́дить, по-

stroll /strəʊl/ *n.* прогу́лка
● *v.i.* гуля́ть (*impf.*); прогу́л|иваться, -я́ться

stroller /'strəʊlə(r)/ *n.* (AmE, for child) прогу́лочная коля́ска

♂ **strong** /strɒŋ/ *adj.* (**stronger** /'strɒŋɡə(r)/, **strongest** /'strɒŋɡɪst/) **1** (powerful) си́льный, кре́пкий; **~ measures** круты́е ме́ры; **~ argument** ве́ский аргуме́нт; **~ evidence** убеди́тельное доказа́тельство **2** (tough; durable) кре́пкий; про́чный; **~ cloth** кре́пкая мате́рия; **~ walls** про́чные сте́ны **3** (robust) кре́пкий, здоро́вый **4** (of faculties): **oratory is his ~ point** его́ си́ла в красноре́чии **5** (of smell, taste, etc.): **~ flavour** о́стрый/ре́зкий при́вкус **6** (concentrated): **~ drink** кре́пкий напи́ток; **a ~ cup of tea** ча́шка кре́пкого ча́я **7** (sharply defined): **~ light** ре́зкий свет; **~ accent** си́льный акце́нт; **~ colour** я́ркий/насы́щенный цвет
● *adv.*: **going ~** в прекра́сной фо́рме

■ **~hold** *n.* кре́пость, тверды́ня; **~-willed** *adj.* реши́тельный, волево́й

♂ **strongly** /'strɒŋlɪ/ *adv.* си́льно, кре́пко; (fig.) твёрдо; **I ~ believe that** я твёрдо убеждён, что; **I feel ~ about** я твёрдо уве́рен в чём (*or* в том, что); **I am ~ opposed to** я (настро́ен) реши́тельно про́тив + *g.*

stroppy /'strɒpɪ/ *adj.* (**stroppier**, **stroppiest**) (BrE, infml) несгово́рчивый, сварли́вый, стропти́вый

strove /strəʊv/ *past of* ▶ **strive**

struck /strʌk/ *past and p.p. of* ▶ **strike**

structural /'strʌktʃər(ə)l/ *adj.*: **~ defects** дефе́кты (в) констру́кции

■ **~ engineer** *n.* инжене́р-строи́тель (*m.*)

ơ' **structure** /'strʌktʃə(r)/ *n.* **1** (abstract) структу́ра **2** (concrete) строе́ние, сооруже́ние; (building) зда́ние
● *v.t.* стро́ить, по-; организо́в|ывать, -а́ть

ơ' **struggle** /'strʌg(ə)l/ *n.* (lit., fig.) борьба́; (tussle) схва́тка, потасо́вка
● *v.i.* **1** (fight) боро́ться (*impf.*); би́ться (*impf.*) **2** (try hard) боро́ться (*impf.*); he ~d to make himself heard он из-за всех сил пыта́лся перекрича́ть други́х; he ~d for breath он хвата́л ртом во́здух; he ~d to his feet он с трудо́м подня́лся на́ ноги

strum /strʌm/ *v.t. & i.* (**strummed**, **strumming**) бренча́ть (*impf.*) (на + *p.*)

strung /strʌŋ/ *past and p.p. of* ▸ string

strut[1] /strʌt/ *v.i.* (**strutted**, **strutting**) ходи́ть (*indet.*) с ва́жным ви́дом

strut[2] /strʌt/ *n.* (support) сто́йка, распо́рка, подпо́рка

stub /stʌb/ *n.* (of pencil) огры́зок; (of cigarette) оку́рок; (of cheque etc.) корешо́к
● *v.t.* (**stubbed**, **stubbing**) **1**: ~ (out) a cigarette гаси́ть, по- папиро́су **2**: ~ one's toe on sth спот|ыка́ться, -кну́ться о(бо) что-н.

stubble /'stʌb(ə)l/ *n.* (in field) жнивьё, стерня́ (*сжатое поле с остатками соломы на корню*); (of beard) щети́на

stubborn /'stʌbən/ *adj.* упря́мый

stuck /stʌk/ *past and p.p. of* ▸ stick[2]

stuck-up /'stʌk'ʌp/ *adj.* (infml, conceited) высокоме́рный

stud[1] /stʌd/ *n.* (of horses) ко́нный заво́д

stud[2] /stʌd/ *n.* (metal decoration) кно́пка; (on boots) шип; (collar ~) за́понка

ơ' **student** /'stju:d(ə)nt/ *n.* студе́нт (-ка); (*attr.*) студе́нческий; (pupil) учени́|к (-ца), уча́щ|ийся (-аяся)
■ ~ **teacher** *n.* учи́тель-практика́нт (учи́тельница-практика́нтка)

ơ' **studio** /'stju:dɪəʊ/ *n.* (*pl.* ~s) **1** (of artist etc.) мастерска́я, сту́дия, ателье́ (*nt. indecl.*) **2** (broadcasting ~) (radio) радиосту́дия; (TV) телесту́дия **3** (cin.) киносту́дия

studious /'stju:dɪəs/ *adj.* усе́рдный

ơ' **study** /'stʌdɪ/ *n.* **1** (learning) изуче́ние, учёба, нау́ка; ~ies заня́тия (*nt. pl.*) **2** (room) кабине́т
● *v.t.* изуч|а́ть, -и́ть; иссле́довать (*impf., pf.*)
● *v.i.* учи́ться (*impf.*)

ơ' **stuff** /stʌf/ *n.* **1** (substance) материа́л, вещество́, вещь **2** (infml, things) ве́щи (*f. pl.*)
● *v.t.* **1** (fill) наб|ива́ть, -и́ть (*что чем*); (cul.) фарширова́ть, за-, начин|я́ть, -и́ть **2** (cram) запи́х|ивать, -а́ть/-ну́ть (*что во что*)

stuffing /'stʌfɪŋ/ *n.* **1** (of cushion etc.) наби́вка **2** (cul.) начи́нка, фарш

stuffy /'stʌfɪ/ *adj.* (**stuffier**, **stuffiest**) (of room) ду́шный; (of person) чо́порный

stultify /'stʌltɪfaɪ/ *v.t.* (deaden) притуп|ля́ть, -и́ть

stumble /'stʌmb(ə)l/ *v.i.* **1** (miss one's footing) оступ|а́ться, -и́ться; спот|ыка́ться, -кну́ться **2** (speak haltingly) зап|ина́ться, -ну́ться; спот|ыка́ться, -кну́ться **3**: ~e across, upon

(find by chance) нат|а́лкиваться, -олкну́ться на + *a.*
■ ~ing block *n.* ка́мень (*m.*) преткнове́ния

stump /stʌmp/ *n.* (of tree) пень (*m.*); (of limb) культя́, обру́бок; (of pencil) огры́зок
● *v.t.*: I was ~ed by the question э́тот вопро́с поста́вил меня́ в тупи́к

stun /stʌn/ *v.t.* (**stunned**, **stunning**) **1** (knock unconscious) оглуш|а́ть, -и́ть **2** (amaze) пора|жа́ть, -зи́ть; a ~ning dress потряса́ющее пла́тье

stung /stʌŋ/ *past and p.p. of* ▸ sting

stunk /stʌŋk/ *past and p.p. of* ▸ stink

stunt /stʌnt/ *n.* трюк, но́мер
● *v.t.*: ~ growth заде́рж|ивать, -а́ть рост; ~ed trees низкоро́слые дере́вья
■ ~ man *n.* (cin.) каскадёр

stupefy /'stju:pɪfaɪ/ *v.t.* ошелом|ля́ть, -и́ть

stupendous /stju:'pendəs/ *adj.* изуми́тельный; (in size) огро́мный, колосса́льный

stupid /'stju:pɪd/ *adj.* (**stupider**, **stupidest**) глу́пый

stupidity /stju:'pɪdɪtɪ/ *n.* глу́пость

stupor /'stju:pə(r)/ *n.* остолбене́ние, сту́пор

sturdy /'stɜ:dɪ/ *adj.* (**sturdier**, **sturdiest**) (person) кре́пкий; (thing) про́чный

sturgeon /'stɜ:dʒ(ə)n/ *n.* осётр; (as food) осётр, осетри́на

stutter /'stʌtə(r)/ *n.* заика́ние
● *v.i.* заика́ться (*impf.*)

sty, **stye** /staɪ/ *n.* (on eye) ячме́нь (*m.*)

ơ' **style** /staɪl/ *n.* **1** (manner) стиль (*m.*), мане́ра **2** (elegance): she has ~ у неё есть вкус; live in ~ жить (*impf.*) широко́ **3** (fashion) мо́да, фасо́н
● *v.t.*: she had her hair ~d она́ сде́лала себе́ причёску

stylish /'staɪlɪʃ/ *adj.* (fashionable) мо́дный; (smart) элега́нтный, сти́льный

stylishness /'staɪlɪʃnɪs/ *n.* элега́нтность

stylist /'staɪlɪst/ *n.* стили́ст; hair ~ парикма́хер-модельѐр

stylistic /staɪ'lɪstɪk/ *adj.* стилисти́ческий

stylize /'staɪlaɪz/ *v.t.* стилизова́ть (*impf., pf.*)

stymie /'staɪmɪ/ *v.t.* (**stymies**, **stymied**, **stymieing**) (fig.) меша́ть (*impf.*) + *d.*; препя́тствовать (*impf.*) + *d.*

suave /swɑ:v/ *adj.* обходи́тельный, учти́вый

subconscious /sʌb'kɒnʃəs/ *n.* (the ~) подсозна́ние
● *adj.* подсозна́тельный

subcontinent /sʌb'kɒntɪnənt/ *n.* субконтине́нт

subcontract /sʌbkən'trækt/ *v.t.*: the work was ~ed out рабо́ту о́тдали субподря́дчику

subcontractor /sʌbkən'træktə(r)/ *n.* субподря́дчик

subculture /'sʌbkʌltʃə(r)/ *n.* субкульту́ра

subdivide /'sʌbdɪvaɪd/ *v.t. & i.* подразде́л|я́ть(ся), -и́ть(ся)

subdivision /'sʌbdɪvɪʒ(ə)n/ *n.* подразделе́ние

subdue /səb'dju:/ *v.t.* (**subdues**, **subdued**, **subduing**) **1** (subjugate) подав|ля́ть,

S

-и́ть **2** (soften) смягч|а́ть, -и́ть; ∼d light мя́гкий свет **3** (restrain): he seems ∼d today он сего́дня что-то прити́х

subedit /'sʌbedɪt/ v.t. (**subedited, subediting**) (BrE) редакти́ровать, от- пе́ред набо́ром; гото́вить, под- к набо́ру

subeditor /'sʌbedɪtə(r)/ n. (BrE) помо́щник реда́ктора; техни́ческий реда́ктор (abbr. техре́д) (infml)

subhuman /sʌb'hjuːmən/ n. недочелове́к
• adj. нечелове́ческий

◦' **subject¹** /'sʌbdʒɪkt/ n. **1** (pol.) по́дданный **2** (gram.) подлежа́щее **3** (theme) те́ма, предме́т; change the ∼ перев|оди́ть, -ести́ разгово́р на другу́ю те́му **4** (branch of study) предме́т
• adj. **1** (subordinate) подчинённый; all citizens are ∼ to the law зако́н распространя́ется на всех гра́ждан **2** (liable): he is ∼ to changes of mood он подве́ржен (бы́стрым) сме́нам настрое́ния; trains are ∼ to delay возмо́жны опозда́ния поездо́в **3**: ∼ to (conditional upon) подлежа́щий + d.; the treaty is ∼ to ratification догово́р подлежи́т ратифика́ции
■ ∼ matter n. содержа́ние, предме́т (чего)

subject² /səb'dʒekt/ v.t. (expose) подв|ерга́ть, -е́ргнуть (кого/что чему); he was ∼ed to insult его́ подве́ргли оскорбле́нию

subjective /səb'dʒektɪv/ adj. субъекти́вный

subjectivity /sʌbdʒek'tɪvɪtɪ/ n. субъекти́вность

sub judice /sʌb 'dʒuːdɪsɪ/ adj. находя́щийся на рассмотре́нии (суда́)

subjugate /'sʌbdʒʊgeɪt/ v.t. покор|я́ть, -и́ть

subjunctive /səb'dʒʌŋktɪv/ adj. сослага́тельное наклоне́ние

sub|let /'sʌblet/ (∼letting, past and p.p. ∼let) v.t. перед|ава́ть, -а́ть в субаре́нду

sublime /sə'blaɪm/ adj. (**sublimer, sublimest**) возвы́шенный

subliminal /səb'lɪmɪn(ə)l/ adj. подсозна́тельный

submachine gun /sʌbmə'ʃiːn gʌn/ n. автома́т (оружие)

submarine /sʌbmə'riːn/ n. подво́дная ло́дка

submerge /səb'mɜːdʒ/ v.t. & i. погру|жа́ть(ся), -зи́ть(ся)

submission /səb'mɪʃ(ə)n/ n. **1** (subjection) подчине́ние **2** (presentation) представле́ние, предъявле́ние

submissive /səb'mɪsɪv/ adj. поко́рный, смире́нный

◦' **submit** /səb'mɪt/ v.t. (**submitted, submitting**) (present) предст|авля́ть, -а́вить
• v.i. (**submitted, submitting**) подчин|я́ться, -и́ться

subordinate /sə'bɔːdɪnət/ n. подчинённый
• adj. подчинённый

subpoena /sə'piːnə/ v.t. (past and p.p. **subpoenaed** or **subpoena'd**) вызыва́ть, вы́звать в суд

◦' ключевая лексика

sub-prime /sʌb'praɪm/ adj. субстанда́ртный; ∼ mortgage ипоте́чный заём, вы́данный заёмщику с плохо́й креди́тной исто́рией

subscribe /səb'skraɪb/ v.i.: ∼ to a journal подпи́с|ываться, -а́ться на журна́л; I cannot ∼ to that view я не могу́ согласи́ться с э́тим мне́нием

subscriber /səb'skraɪbə(r)/ n. подпи́счик

subscription /səb'skrɪpʃ(ə)n/ n. (fee) взнос; ∼ to a newspaper подпи́ска на газе́ту

subsequent /'sʌbsɪkwənt/ adj. после́дующий, сле́дующий; ∼ly впосле́дствии

subservience /səb'sɜːvɪəns/ n. раболе́пие, послуша́ние

subservient /səb'sɜːvɪənt/ adj. раболе́пный

subset /'sʌbset/ n. гру́ппа (в составе чего-л.)

subside /səb'saɪd/ v.i. **1** (of ground or building) ос|еда́ть, -е́сть **2** (of water) спа|да́ть, -сть **3** (of fever) па́дать, упа́сть; (of wind, storm, etc.) ут|иха́ть, -и́хнуть

subsidence /səb'saɪd(ə)ns/ n. (of ground) оседа́ние, оса́дка

subsidiary /səb'sɪdɪərɪ/ n. (comm.) филиа́л
• adj. вспомога́тельный, второстепе́нный; (of company) доче́рний

subsidize /'sʌbsɪdaɪz/ v.t. субсиди́ровать (impf., pf.)

subsidy /'sʌbsɪdɪ/ n. субси́дия

subsist /səb'sɪst/ v.i. существова́ть (impf.)

subsistence /səb'sɪst(ə)ns/ n. существова́ние

substance /'sʌbst(ə)ns/ n. **1** (essential elements) суть **2** (type of matter) вещество́ **3** (solidity): a piece of writing that lacks ∼ сочине́ние, лишённое содержа́ния; there is no ∼ in the rumour э́тот слух ниче́м не подкреплён

substandard /sʌb'stændəd/ adj. нестанда́ртный, низкока́чественный

◦' **substantial** /səb'stænʃ(ə)l/ adj. **1** (solid) кре́пкий; a ∼ building соли́дное зда́ние; a ∼ dinner сы́тный обе́д **2** (considerable): a ∼ sum поря́дочная су́мма; a ∼ improvement значи́тельное/заме́тное улучше́ние

substantiate /səb'stænʃɪeɪt/ v.t. обосно́в|ывать, -а́ть

substitute /'sʌbstɪtjuːt/ n. (person) заме́на, замести́тель (m.); (in sport) запасно́й (игрок)
• v.t. (use instead) испо́льзовать (impf., pf.) (for: вме́сто + g.)
• v.i.: ∼ for заме|ща́ть, -сти́ть; подмен|я́ть, -и́ть; (sport) замен|я́ть, -и́ть (игрока)

substitution /sʌbstɪ'tjuːʃ(ə)n/ n. заме́на, замеще́ние, подме́на

subsume /səb'sjuːm/ v.t. включ|а́ть, -и́ть в каку́ю-н. катего́рию; отн|оси́ть, -ести́ к како́й-н. катего́рии, гру́ппе и т. п.

subterfuge /'sʌbtəfjuːdʒ/ n. уло́вка

subterranean /sʌbtə'reɪnɪən/ adj. подзе́мный

subtitles /'sʌbtaɪt(ə)lz/ n. pl. (cin.) субти́тры (m. pl.)

subtle /'sʌt(ə)l/ adj. (**subtler, subtlest**) (fine, perceptive) то́нкий; (refined) утончённый

subtlety /'sʌtəlti/ *n.* тонкость; утончённость

subtotal /'sʌbtəʊt(ə)l/ *n.* промежуточный итог

subtract /səb'trækt/ *v.t.* вычитать, вычесть

subtraction /səb'trækʃ(ə)n/ *n.* вычитание

subtropical /sʌb'trɒpɪk(ə)l/ *adj.* субтропический

suburb /'sʌbɜːb/ *n.* пригород

suburban /sə'bɜːbən/ *adj.* пригородный

suburbia /sə'bɜːbɪə/ *n.* (*collect.*) пригороды *m. pl.*

subversion /səb'vɜːʃ(ə)n/ *n.* подрывная деятельность

subversive /səb'vɜːsɪv/ *adj.* подрывной

subway /'sʌbweɪ/ *n.* (BrE, passage under road) подземный переход; (AmE, railway) метро (*nt. indecl.*), подземка (infml)

sub-zero /sʌb'zɪərəʊ/ *adj.*: ∼ temperatures минусовые температуры

♂ **succeed** /sək'siːd/ *v.t.* (as heir) наследовать (*impf., pf.*) + *d.*; (as replacement) сменя́ть, -и́ть ● *v.i.* (be, become successful) преуспева́ть, -е́ть; доб|ива́ться, -и́ться успе́ха/своего́; he ∼ed in tricking us all ему́ удало́сь всех нас обману́ть

♂ **success** /sək'ses/ *n.* успе́х, уда́ча; my holidays were not a ∼ this year мой кани́кулы в э́том году́ бы́ли неуда́чными

♂ **successful** /sək'sesfʊl/ *adj.* успе́шный, уда́чный; I tried to persuade him, but was not ∼ я пыта́лся убеди́ть его́, но мне э́то не удало́сь

succession /sək'seʃ(ə)n/ *n.* **1** (sequence) после́довательность; in ∼ подря́д **2** (series) ряд, цепь **3** (succeeding to office etc.) насле́дство, насле́дование (*о поря́дке переда́чи*)

successive /sək'sesɪv/ *adj.* после́довательный; on three ∼ occasions три ра́за подря́д

successor /sək'sesə(r)/ *n.* прее́мни|к (-ца), насле́дни|к (-ца)

succinct /sək'sɪŋkt/ *adj.* сжа́тый

succulent /'sʌkjʊlənt/ *adj.* со́чный

succumb /sə'kʌm/ *v.i.* уступ|а́ть, -и́ть; подд|ава́ться, -а́ться; they ∼ed to the enemy's superior force они́ уступи́ли превосходя́щей си́ле проти́вника; she did not ∼ to temptation она́ не поддала́сь искуше́нию

♂ **such** /sʌtʃ/ *adj.* **1** (of the kind mentioned; of this, that kind) тако́й; ∼ places таки́е места́; I have never seen ∼ a sight я никогда́ не ви́дел подо́бного зре́лища; I said no ∼ thing я ничего́ подо́бного не говори́л; some ∼ thing что́-то в э́том ро́де; how could you do ∼ a thing? как вы могли́ так поступи́ть? **2** ∼ as (of a kind ...): ∼ grapes as you never saw тако́й виногра́д, како́го вы в жи́зни не ви́дели; I am not ∼ a fool as to believe him я не тако́й дура́к, что́бы пове́рить ему́; (like): a picture ∼ as that is valuable тако́го ро́да карти́ны высоко́ це́нятся
■ ∼-and-∼ *adj.* тако́й-то; ∼like *pron.* что-н. подо́бное; theatres, cinemas, and ∼like

теа́тры, кино́ и тому́ подо́бное

suck /sʌk/ *v.t.* **1** соса́ть (*impf.*); (∼ in, imbibe) вс|а́сывать, -оса́ть; тяну́ть (*impf.*) (*через соло́минку и т. п.*) **2** (squeeze or dissolve in mouth) соса́ть (*impf.*)
□ ∼ out *v.t.* (with pump etc.) выса́сывать, вы́сосать
□ ∼ up *v.t.* (dust etc.) вс|а́сывать, -оса́ть
□ ∼ up to *v.t.* (infml, behave obsequiously to) подли́зываться, -а́ться к кому́-н.

sucker /'sʌkə(r)/ *n.* **1** (organ, device) присо́ска, присо́сок **2** (bot.) отро́сток, боково́й побе́г **3** (sl., gullible person) проста́|к (-чка), лох (sl.)

suction /'sʌkʃ(ə)n/ *n.* вса́сывание

Sudan /su:'dɑːn/ *n.* Суда́н

Sudanese /su:də'niːz/ *n.* (*pl.* ∼) суда́н|ец (-ка)
● *adj.* суда́нский

sudden /'sʌd(ə)n/ *n.*: (all) of a ∼ внеза́пно, вдруг
● *adj.* (unexpected) внеза́пный, неожи́данный

♂ **suddenly** /'sʌd(ə)nlɪ/ *adv.* внеза́пно, вдруг

suddenness /'sʌd(ə)nnɪs/ *n.* внеза́пность, неожи́данность

suds /sʌdz/ *n. pl.* мы́льная пе́на

sue /sjuː/ *v.t.* (**sues, sued, suing**) возбу|жда́ть, -ди́ть иск/де́ло про́тив + *g.*; ∼ (sb) for libel/for damages возбу|жда́ть, -ди́ть иск/де́ло про́тив + *g.* за клевету́/о возмеще́нии убы́тков
● *v.i.* под|ава́ть, -а́ть в суд (на + *a.*)

suede /sweɪd/ *n.* за́мша; (*attr.*) за́мшевый

suet /'suːɪt/ *n.* нутряно́е са́ло; по́чечный жир

♂ **suffer** /'sʌfə(r)/ *v.t.* испы́т|ывать, -а́ть; претерп|ева́ть, -е́ть; (defeat) терпе́ть, по-
● *v.i.* страда́ть (*impf.*) (from: от + *g.*); he ∼s from shyness он (о́чень) засте́нчив; he is ∼ing from measles он боле́ет ко́рью; у него́ корь

sufferance /'sʌfərəns/ *n.*: on ∼ из ми́лости; с молчали́вого согла́сия

sufferer /'sʌfrə(r)/ *n.* страда́лец

suffering /'sʌfrɪŋ/ *n.* страда́ние

suffice /sə'faɪs/ *v.i.* быть доста́точным; хват|а́ть, -и́ть

sufficient /sə'fɪʃ(ə)nt/ *adj.* доста́точный

suffix /'sʌfɪks/ *n.* су́ффикс

suffocat|e /'sʌfəkeɪt/ *v.t.* души́ть, за-; he was ∼ed by poisonous fumes он задохну́лся от ядови́того ды́ма; ∼ing heat уду́шливая жара́
● *v.i.* зад|ыха́ться, -охну́ться

suffocation /sʌfə'keɪʃ(ə)n/ *n.* удуше́ние, уду́шье

suffrage /'sʌfrɪdʒ/ *n.* избира́тельное пра́во

sugar /'ʃʊɡə(r)/ *n.* са́хар
■ ∼ beet *n.* са́харная свёкла; ∼ cane *n.* са́харный тростни́к; ∼ lump *n.* кусо́(че)к са́хара

sugary /'ʃʊɡərɪ/ *adj.* **1** са́харный, са́хари́стый **2** (fig., of tone, smile, etc.) сла́дкий, слаща́вый

♂ **suggest** /sə'dʒest/ *v.t.* предл|ага́ть, -ожи́ть; сове́товать, по-; I ∼ you try again я сове́тую вам попро́бовать ещё раз(о́к)

♂ **suggestion** /sə'dʒestʃ(ə)n/ *n.* **1** (proposal) предложе́ние, сове́т **2** (implication) намёк,

S

доля; (tinge) оттенок

suggestive /sə'dʒestɪv/ *adj.*: ~ of напоминающий; (improper) непристойный

suicidal /ˌsuːɪ'saɪd(ə)l/ *adj.* (person) склонный к самоубийству; (action) самоубийственный

✓ **suicide** /'suːɪsaɪd/ *n.* **1** (also fig.) самоубийство; **commit** ~ кончать, (по)кончить с собой **2** (person) самоубийца (*c.g.*)

✓ **suit** /sjuːt/ *n.* **1** (of clothes) костюм **2** (law) иск, дело **3** (of cards) масть
• *v.t.* **1** (be convenient for) под|ходить, -ойти + *d.*; устр|аивать, -оить; **would Sunday** ~ **you?** воскресенье вам подойдёт (*or* вас устроит)? **2** (be appropriate or good for) под|ходить, -ойти + *d.*; **the role does not** ~ **him** эта роль ему не подходит; **they are** ~**ed to one another** они подходят друг другу **3** (please): **he tries to** ~ **everybody** он старается всем угодить **4** (enhance): **that hat** ~**s her** эта шляпа ей идёт
■ ~**case** *n.* чемодан

suitable /'sjuːtəb(ə)l/ *adj.* подходящий, годный

suitably /'sjuːtəblɪ/ *adv.* соответственно, правильно

suite /swiːt/ *n.* (set): ~ **of furniture** мебельный гарнитур; (in hotel) (номер) люкс

suitor /'sjuːtə(r)/ *n.* (wooer) жених, поклонник

sulfur /'sʌlfə(r)/ *n.* (AmE) = sulphur

sulfuric /sʌl'fjʊərɪk/ *adj.* (AmE) = sulphuric

sulk /sʌlk/ *v.i.* быть в дурном настроении; дуться (*impf.*) (infml)

sulky /'sʌlkɪ/ *adj.* (**sulkier, sulkiest**) надутый, мрачный

sullen /'sʌlən/ *adj.* (sulky) надутый; (sombre) мрачный

sulphur /'sʌlfə(r)/ (AmE **sulfur**) *n.* сера

sulphuric /sʌl'fjʊərɪk/ (AmE **sulfuric**) *adj.*: ~ **acid** серная кислота

sultana /sʌl'tɑːnə/ *n.* изюминка; (*collect.*) кишмиш (*об изюме*)

sultry /'sʌltrɪ/ *adj.* (**sultrier, sultriest**) знойный

✓ **sum** /sʌm/ *n.* **1** (total) итог **2** (amount) сумма **3** (calculation) (арифметическая), задача
• *v.t.* (**summed, summing**) (*usu.* ~ **up**) сумми́ровать (*impf., pf.*); подв|одить, -ести итоги + *g.*
• *v.i.* (**summed, summing**): ~ **up** сумми́ровать (*impf., pf.*)

summarize /'sʌməraɪz/ *v.t.* сумми́ровать (*impf., pf.*); резюми́ровать (*impf., pf.*)

summary /'sʌmərɪ/ *n.* резюме (*nt. indecl.*), сводка

✓ **summer** /'sʌmə(r)/ *n.* лето; **in** ~ летом; (*attr.*) летний
■ ~ **house** *n.* беседка; ~ **school** *n.* летняя школа; ~**time** *n.* лето

summery /'sʌmərɪ/ *adj.*: ~ **weather** летняя/тёплая погода; ~ **clothes** лёгкая/летняя одежда

summit /'sʌmɪt/ *n.* (lit., fig.) вершина, верх; ~ (meeting) саммит, встреча в верхах

✓ ключевая лексика

summon /'sʌmən/ *v.t.* **1** (send for) приз|ывать, -вать; (also law) вызывать, вызвать **2**: ~ **up one's energy/courage** соб|ираться, -раться с силами/духом

summons /'sʌmənz/ *n.* (*pl.* ~**es**) вызов; (law) судебная повестка, вызов в суд
• *v.t.* вызывать, вызвать в суд

sumptuous /'sʌmptʊəs/ *adj.* роскошный

✓ **sun** /sʌn/ *n.* солнце; (astron.) Солнце; **lie in the** ~ лежать (*impf.*) на солнце
■ ~**bathe** *v.i.* загорать (*impf.*); ~**bed** *n.* (BrE, lounger) шезлонг; (for acquiring tan) солярий; ~**burn** *n.* (inflammation) солнечный ожог; ~**burnt** *adj.* (tanned) загорелый; (inflamed) обожжённый солнцем; ~**dial** *n.* солнечные часы (*m. pl.*); ~**flower** *n.* подсолнечник; ~**glasses** *n. pl.* солнцезащитные очки; ~ **hat** *n.* шляпа от солнца; ~**lamp** *n.* кварцевая лампа; ~**light** *n.* солнечный свет; ~**rise** *n.* восход (солнца); **at** ~**rise** на заре; ~**roof** *n.* (of car) раздвижная крыша; ~**set** *n.* заход солнца, закат; **at** ~**set** на закате; ~**shade** *n.* (солнечный) зонтик; ~**shine** *n.* солнечный свет; ~**stroke** *n.* солнечный удар; ~**tan** *n.* загар; ~**tan lotion** крем для загара

✓ **Sunday** /'sʌndeɪ/ *n.* воскресенье

sundries /'sʌndrɪz/ *n. pl.* разное

sundry /'sʌndrɪ/ *adj.* разный, различный; **all and** ~ всё и вся; все без исключения

sung /sʌŋ/ *p.p. of* ▶ sing

sunk /sʌŋk/ *past and p.p. of* ▶ sink

sunken /'sʌŋkən/ *adj.* (of cheeks etc.) впалый; (submerged) подводный

Sunni /'sʊnɪ/ *n.* суннит

sunny /'sʌnɪ/ *adj.* (**sunnier, sunniest**) солнечный; **a** ~ **disposition** жизнерадостный характер

super /'suːpə(r)/ *adj.* замечательный, превосходный

superb /suː'pəːb/ *adj.* превосходный, великолепный

supercilious /ˌsuːpə'sɪlɪəs/ *adj.* высокомерный

superficial /ˌsuːpə'fɪʃ(ə)l/ *adj.* поверхностный

superficiality /ˌsuːpəfɪʃɪ'ælɪtɪ/ *n.* поверхностность

superfluous /suː'pəːflʊəs/ *adj.* излишний

superhuman /ˌsuːpə'hjuːmən/ *adj.* сверхчеловеческий

superimpose /ˌsuːpərɪm'pəʊz/ *v.t.* на|кладывать, -ложить (*что на что*)

superinjunction /ˌsuːpərɪn'dʒʌŋkʃ(ə)n/ *n.* суперзапрет (*судебное решение, запрещающее разглашать некую информацию, а также упоминать сам факт существования запрета*)

superintendent /ˌsuːpərɪn'tend(ə)nt/ *n.* (manager) заведующий; (of police) начальник; (AmE, of a building) комендант

superior /suː'pɪərɪə(r)/ *n.* старший, начальник
• *adj.* **1** (of higher rank) старший, высший **2** (better) превосходный, превосходящий **3** (supercilious): **a** ~ **smile** презрительная улыбка; **don't look so** ~! бросьте эту вашу

высокоме́рную мане́ру!

superiority /suːˌpɪərɪˈɒrɪtɪ/ *n.* старшинство́

superlative /suːˈpɜːlətɪv/ *n.* (gram.)
превосхо́дная сте́пень
● *adj.* велича́йший, высоча́йший

superman /ˈsuːpəmæn/ *n.* (*pl.* **supermen**)
сверхчелове́к, супермéн

supermarket /ˈsuːpəmɑːkɪt/ *n.* суперма́ркет

supermodel /ˈsuːpəmɒd(ə)l/ *n.* супермодéль

supernatural /suːpəˈnætʃər(ə)l/ *n.*: **a belief in
the ~** ве́ра в сверхъесте́ственное
● *adj.* сверхъесте́ственный

superpower /ˈsuːpəpaʊə(r)/ *n.* сверхдержа́ва

supersede /suːpəˈsiːd/ *v.t.* смен|я́ть, -и́ть

supersonic /suːpəˈsɒnɪk/ *adj.* сверхзвуково́й

superstar /ˈsuːpəstɑː(r)/ *n.* суперзвезда́

superstition /suːpəˈstɪʃ(ə)n/ *n.* суевéрие

superstitious /suːpəˈstɪʃəs/ *adj.* суевéрный

superstore /ˈsuːpəstɔː(r)/ *n.* гиперма́ркет

superstructure /ˈsuːpəstrʌktʃə(r)/ *n.*
надстро́йка

supervise /ˈsuːpəvaɪz/ *v.t.* надзира́ть (*impf.*)
за + *i.*

supervision /suːpəˈvɪʒ(ə)n/ *n.* надсмо́тр/
надзо́р (**of:** за + *i.*)

supervisor /ˈsuːpəvaɪzə(r)/ *n.* надсмо́трщи|к
(-ца); (academic) (нау́чный) руководи́тель

supervisory /ˈsuːpəvaɪzərɪ/ *adj.*
контро́льный, надзира́ющий; **~ body**
контро́льный о́рган; **~ duties** обя́занности
по надзо́ру

supine /ˈsuːpaɪn/ *adj.* (face up) лежа́щий
на́взничь; (fig.) безде́ятельный, ине́ртный,
вя́лый

supper /ˈsʌpə(r)/ *n.* у́жин; **have ~** у́жинать,
по-

supplant /səˈplɑːnt/ *v.t.* (replace) вытесня́ть,
вы́теснить; (oust) выжива́ть, вы́жить

supple /ˈsʌp(ə)l/ *adj.* (**suppler**, **supplest**)
ги́бкий

supplement¹ /ˈsʌplɪmənt/ *n.* **1** (dietary)
доба́вка **2** (of book etc.) дополне́ние
3 (surcharge) допла́та

supplement² /ˈsʌplɪment/ *v.t.* доп|олня́ть,
-о́лнить

supplementary /sʌplɪˈmentərɪ/ *adj.*
дополни́тельный, доба́вочный

supplier /səˈplaɪə(r)/ *n.* поставщи́|к (-ца)

⚲ **suppl|y** /səˈplaɪ/ *n.* **1** (providing) снабже́ние
(*чем*) **2** (thing supplied, stock) запа́с; **take, lay
in a ~y of sth** запас|а́ться, -ти́сь чем-н.;
bread is in short ~y хлеб в дефици́те;
~ies (mil.) (бое)припа́сы (*m. pl.*) **3** (econ.)
предложе́ние; **~y and demand** спрос и
предложе́ние
● *v.t.* **1** (furnish, equip) снаб|жа́ть, -ди́ть;
обеспе́чи|вать, -ть (*both кого/что чем*)
пита́ть (*impf.*) **2** (give, yield) да|ва́ть, -ть;
дост|авля́ть, -а́вить (*что кому/чему*); **cows
~y milk** коро́вы даю́т молоко́
■ **~y teacher** *n.* (BrE) внешта́тн|ый учи́тель,
рабо́тающ|ий (-ая -ница, -ая) по замеще́нию

⚲ **support** /səˈpɔːt/ *n.* подде́ржка; **give, lend ~**

ока́з|ывать, -а́ть подде́ржку + *d.*; **in ~ of** в
подде́ржку + *g.*
● *v.t.* **1** (hold up) подде́рж|ивать, -а́ть;
подп|ира́ть, -ере́ть; (fig., assist): **which
party do you ~?** каку́ю па́ртию вы
подде́рживаете? **2** (provide subsistence for)
содержа́ть (*impf.*); **he cannot ~ a family** он
не в состоя́нии содержа́ть семью́ **3** (confirm)
подкреп|ля́ть, -и́ть **4** (a particular sports team)
боле́ть (*impf.*) за + *a.*
■ **~ing actor** *n.* акт|ёр (-ри́са) второ́го пла́на

⚲ **supporter** /səˈpɔːtə(r)/ *n.* (of cause, motion, etc.)
сторо́нни|к (-ца), приве́рженец; (BrE, of sports
team) боле́льщи|к (-ца)

supportive /səˈpɔːtɪv/ *adj.*
подде́рживающий, лоя́льный

⚲ **suppose** /səˈpəʊz/ *v.t.* **1** (assume) предпол|ага́ть,
-ожи́ть; допус|ка́ть, -ти́ть; **supposing he came,
what would you say?** е́сли бы он пришёл, что
бы вы сказа́ли?; **~ they find out?** а вдруг они́
узна́ют? **2** (imagine, believe): **he is ~d to be rich**
счита́ется/говоря́т, что он бога́т **3** (*pass.*)
(be expected): **this is ~d to help you sleep** э́то
должно́ помо́чь вам засну́ть; **he is ~d to wash
the dishes** ему́ поло́жено мыть посу́ду

supposedly /səˈpəʊzɪdlɪ/ *adv.*
предположи́тельно

supposition /sʌpəˈzɪʃ(ə)n/ *n.*
предположе́ние, гипо́теза, дога́дка

suppository /səˈpɒzɪtərɪ/ *n.* (med.)
суппозито́рий, све́чка

suppress /səˈpres/ *v.t.* **1** (prevent;
restrain) подав|ля́ть, -и́ть; сде́рж|ивать,
-а́ть **2** (conceal) скры|ва́ть, -ть; **they
succeeded in ~ing the truth** им удало́сь
скрыть пра́вду

suppression /səˈpreʃ(ə)n/ *n.* (restraining)
подавле́ние, сде́рживание; (banning)
запреще́ние; (silencing) зама́лчивание

supremacy /suːˈpreməsɪ/ *n.* госпо́дство,
превосхо́дство

supreme /suːˈpriːm/ *adj.* **1** (of authority)
верхо́вный **2** (greatest): **he made the ~
sacrifice** он поже́ртвовал (свое́й) жи́знью

surcharge /ˈsɜːtʃɑːdʒ/ *n.* допла́та, припла́та

⚲ **sure** /ʃɔː(r)/ *adj.* **1** (certain, confident)
уве́ренный, убеждённый; **he is very ~ of
himself** он о́чень уве́рен в себе́; **I'm ~ you
are right** я уве́рен (*or* не сомнева́юсь),
что вы пра́вы; **I'm not ~ whether to go
or not** я не зна́ю, пойти́ и́ли нет **2** (safe)
ве́рный, надёжный; **there can be no ~
proof** абсолю́тных доказа́тельств не мо́жет
быть **3** (with inf., certain, to be relied on): **he is ~
to come** он непреме́нно придёт; **it is ~ to be
wet** наверняка́ бу́дет дождли́во
4: **for ~** несомне́нно, непреме́нно; то́чно,
наверняка́ **5**: **make ~** (convince, satisfy oneself)
убе|жда́ться, -ди́ться; удостовер|я́ться,
-е́риться (*all в чём*) **6**: **I made ~** (sc.
ensured) **that he would come** я позабо́тился
о том, что́бы он (обяза́тельно) пришёл
● *adv.*: **~ enough** действи́тельно, коне́чно
■ **~-fire** *adj.* (infml) ве́рный, надёжный

⚲ **surely** /ˈʃɔːlɪ/ *adv.* **1** (without doubt)

S

несомне́нно, ве́рно, наверняка́ **2** (expr. strong hope or belief): ~ **I have met you before** я уве́рен, что мы с ва́ми встреча́лись

surf /sɜːf/ n. прибо́й
- v.i. занима́ться (impf.) сёрфингом
- v.t.: ~ **the Internet** путеше́ствовать (impf.) по Интерне́ту
- ■ ~**board** n. доска́ для сёрфинга

✍ **surface** /'sɜːfɪs/ n. пове́рхность; **his politeness is only on the** ~ его́ ве́жливость чи́сто вне́шняя/показна́я
- v.t.: ~ **a road** покр|ыва́ть, -ы́ть доро́гу асфа́льтом и т. п.
- v.i. вспл|ыва́ть, -ы́ть на пове́рхность

surfeit /'sɜːfɪt/ n. (excess of eating etc.) изли́шество, избы́ток; (repletion, satiety, also fig.) пресыще́ние
- v.t. (**surfeited, surfeiting**) (satiate) прес|ыща́ть, -ы́тить

surfer /'sɜːfə(r)/ n. сёрфинги́ст (-ка); челове́к, занима́ющийся сёрфингом

surfing /'sɜːfɪŋ/ n. сёрфинг

surge /sɜːdʒ/ n. (of waves, water) во́лны (f. pl.); вал; (of crowd, emotion, etc.) волна́, прили́в; (of elec. current) и́мпульс
- v.i. **1** (of waves, water) вздыма́ться (impf.) **2** (of crowd): **the crowd** ~**d forward** толпа́ подала́сь вперёд **3** (of emotions) нахл|ы́нуть (pf.)

surgeon /'sɜːdʒ(ə)n/ n. хиру́рг

✍ **surgery** /'sɜːdʒərɪ/ n. **1** (operation) опера́ция **2** (BrE, office) приёмная/кабине́т (врача́); **the doctor holds a** ~ **every morning** врач принима́ет ка́ждое у́тро

surgical /'sɜːdʒɪk(ə)l/ adj. хирурги́ческий
- ■ ~ **spirit** n. (BrE) медици́нский спирт

surly /'sɜːlɪ/ adj. (**surlier, surliest**) неприве́тливый

surmise /sə'maɪz/ n. (conjecture) дога́дка; (supposition) предположе́ние
- v.i. предпол|ага́ть, -ожи́ть

surmount /sə'maʊnt/ v.t. (overcome) преодол|ева́ть, -е́ть

surmountable /sə'maʊntəb(ə)l/ adj. преодоли́мый

surname /'sɜːneɪm/ n. фами́лия

surpass /sə'pɑːs/ v.t. прев|осходи́ть, -зойти́

surplice /'sɜːplɪs/ n. стиха́рь (m.) (дли́нное одея́ние с широ́кими рукава́ми, надева́емое свяще́нниками на вре́мя слу́жбы)

surplus /'sɜːpləs/ n. изли́шек
- adj. изли́шний, избы́точный

✍ **surprise** /sə'praɪz/ n. **1** (astonishment) удивле́ние **2** (unexpected news, gift, etc.) неожи́данность, сюрпри́з **3** (unexpected action): **catch, take sb by** ~ заст|ига́ть, -и́чь кого́-н. враспло́х
- v.t. **1** (astonish) удив|ля́ть, -и́ть; **I was** ~**d to hear you had been ill** я с удивле́нием узна́л, что вы бы́ли больны́ **2** (capture by ~) захва́т|ывать, -и́ть врасплох; **we** ~**d him in the act of stealing** мы пойма́ли

✍ ключева́я ле́ксика

его́ с поли́чным на воровстве́ (or при соверше́нии кра́жи)

surprising /sə'praɪzɪŋ/ adj. удиви́тельный, порази́тельный; **he eats** ~**ly little** он удиви́тельно/на удивле́ние ма́ло ест

surreal /sə'rɪəl/ adj. сюрреалисти́ческий

surrealism /sə'rɪəlɪz(ə)m/ n. сюрреали́зм

surrealist /sə'rɪəlɪst/ n. сюрреали́ст
- adj. сюрреалисти́ческий

surrender /sə'rendə(r)/ n. (handing over) сда́ча; (giving up) отка́з (**of**: от + g.); (capitulation) капитуля́ция
- v.t. **1** (yield) сда|ва́ть, -ть **2** (give up) отка́з|ываться, -а́ться от + g.
- v.i. сдава́ться, -а́ться; капитули́ровать (impf., pf.)

surreptitious /ˌsʌrəp'tɪʃəs/ adj. та́йный

surrogate /'sʌrəgət/ n. суррога́т
- ■ ~ **mother** n. суррога́тная мать

✍ **surround** /sə'raʊnd/ v.t. окруж|а́ть, -и́ть; **the** ~**ing countryside** окре́стности (f. pl.)

surroundings /sə'raʊndɪŋz/ n. pl. ме́стность, окре́стности (f. pl.); обстано́вка

surveillance /sə'veɪləns/ n. надзо́р
- ■ ~ **camera** n. ка́мера скры́того наблюде́ния

✍ **survey¹** /'sɜːveɪ/ n. **1** (inspection, investigation) иссле́дование, обсле́дование; (BrE, of building) оце́нка состоя́ния до́ма/зда́ния; (by asking questions) опро́с **2** (of land) съёмка, проме́р

survey² /sə'veɪ/ v.t. **1** (view) обозр|ева́ть, -е́ть **2** (inspect) осм|а́тривать, -отре́ть **3** (land etc.) межева́ть (impf.); произв|оди́ть, -ести́ съёмку + g.

surveyor /sə'veɪə(r)/ n. **1** (BrE, of houses) строи́тельный инспе́ктор **2** (of land etc.) землеме́р

survival /sə'vaɪv(ə)l/ n. выжива́ние

✍ **survive** /sə'vaɪv/ v.t. **1** (outlive) переж|ива́ть, -и́ть (во вре́мени) **2** (come alive through): ~ **an illness** перен|оси́ть, -ести́ боле́знь
- v.i. выжива́ть, вы́жить; (be preserved) сохрани́ться, уцеле́ть (both pf.); **the custom still** ~**s** э́тот обы́чай ещё сохрани́лся

survivor /sə'vaɪvə(r)/ n. оста́вшийся в живы́х, уцеле́вший

susceptible /sə'septɪb(ə)l/ adj.: ~ **to** восприи́мчивый к + d.; **he is** ~ **to colds** он подве́ржен простуде

suspect¹ /'sʌspekt/ n. подозрева́емый
- adj. подозри́тельный; не внуша́ющий дове́рия

✍ **suspect²** /sə'spekt/ v.t. **1** подозрева́ть (impf.); **I** ~**ed him to be lying** я подозрева́л, что он лжёт **2** (doubt) сомнева́ться, усомни́ться в + p.

suspend /sə'spend/ v.t. **1** (hang up) подве́|шивать, -сить **2** (stop for a time) приостан|а́вливать, -ови́ть; ~**ed sentence** усло́вное осужде́ние/наказа́ние **3** (from office etc.) вре́менно отстран|я́ть, -и́ть

suspender /sə'spendə(r)/ n. (AmE) (in pl.) (braces) подтя́ж|ки (-ек)
- ■ ~ **belt** n. (BrE) (же́нский) по́яс с подвя́зками

suspense /sə'spens/ *n.* напряже́ние, напряжённость; **keep sb in** ~ держа́ть (*impf.*) кого́-н. в неизве́стности

suspension /sə'spenʃ(ə)n/ *n.* **1** (stoppage) приостановле́ние **2** (from office etc.) отстране́ние

suspicion /sə'spɪʃ(ə)n/ *n.* подозре́ние; **arouse** ~ возбу|жда́ть, -ди́ть подозре́ния

suspicious /sə'spɪʃəs/ *adj.* **1** (mistrustful) подозри́тельный, недове́рчивый (**towards, of:** к + *d.*) **2** (arousing suspicion) подозри́тельный

suss /sʌs/ *v.t.* (BrE, infml): **she's got him** ~ed она́ его́ раскуси́ла; **he** ~ed **out the best route** он разузна́л лу́чший маршру́т

sustain /sə'steɪn/ *v.t.* **1** (lit., fig., support) подде́рж|ивать, -а́ть **2** (suffer) нести́, по-; **the enemy** ~ed **heavy losses** проти́вник понёс тяжёлые поте́ри; ~ **an injury** перен|оси́ть, -ести́ тра́вму; получ|а́ть, -и́ть уве́чье **3** (maintain): ~ **one's efforts** не ослабля́ть (*impf.*) уси́лий

sustainability /səsteɪnə'bɪlɪtɪ/ *n.* усто́йчивость

sustenance /'sʌstɪnəns/ *n.* пита́ние, пи́ща

suture /'su:tʃə(r)/ *n.* (med.) шов

swab /swɒb/ *n.* (med.) тампо́н

swagger /'swægə(r)/ *v.i.* расха́живать (*impf.*) с ва́жным ви́дом

Swahili /swə'hi:lɪ/ *n.* (*pl.* ~) (language, people) суахи́ли (*m. indecl.*)

swallow¹ /'swɒləʊ/ *n.* (bird) ла́сточка

swallow² /'swɒləʊ/ *n.* (gulp) глото́к
● *v.t.* прогл|а́тывать, -оти́ть; загл|а́тывать, -оти́ть; **he had to** ~ **his pride** ему́ пришло́сь поступи́ться свои́м самолю́бием
● *v.i.* глота́ть (*impf.*)

swam /swæm/ *past of* ▶ **swim**

swamp /swɒmp/ *n.* боло́то
● *v.t.* **1** (with water) зал|ива́ть, -и́ть **2** (fig., overwhelm): **we were** ~ed **with applications** мы бы́ли зава́лены заявле́ниями

swampy /'swɒmpɪ/ *adj.* (**swampier, swampiest**) боло́тистый

swan /swɒn/ *n.* ле́бедь (*m.*)

swank /swæŋk/ (infml) *n.* показу́ха
● *v.i.*: ~ **about sth** хва́стать (*impf.*) чем-н.

swanky /'swæŋkɪ/ *adj.* (**swankier, swankiest**) (infml) шика́рный

swap, swop /swɒp/ *n.* обме́н
● *v.t.* (**swapped, swapping** *or* **swopped, swopping**) (exchange for sth else) меня́ть, по- (**for:** на + *a.*); **he** ~ped **his car for a motorbike** он поменя́л маши́ну на мотоци́кл; (exchange with sb else) меня́ться, по- + *i.* (**with sb:** с + *i.*); **will you** ~ **places with me?** вы не поменя́етесь со мной места́ми?

swarm /swɔːm/ *n.*: ~ **of ants/bees** мурави́ный/пчели́ный рой
● *v.i.* **1** (of bees, ants, etc.) рои́ться (*impf.*) **2** (of people): **children** ~ed **around him** де́ти столпи́лись вокру́г него́ **3** (teem) кише́ть (*impf.*) + *i.*; **the town is** ~ing **with tourists** го́род наводнён тури́стами

swarthy /'swɔːðɪ/ *adj.* (**swarthier, swarthiest**) сму́глый

swastika /'swɒstɪkə/ *n.* сва́стика

swat /swɒt/ *v.t.* (**swatted, swatting**) (an insect) прихло́пнуть (*pf.*)

swathe /sweɪð/ *v.t.* (wrap): ~d **in bandages** обмо́танный бинта́ми; ~d **in blankets** заку́танный одея́лами

sway /sweɪ/ *n.*: **have, hold** ~ **over sb** держа́ть (*impf.*) кого́-н. в подчине́нии
● *v.t.* **1** (rock) кач|а́ть, -ну́ть **2** (influence) влия́ть, по-; колеба́ть, по-
● *v.i.* кача́ться, качну́ться

swear /sweə(r)/ *v.t. & i.* (*past* **swore**, *p.p.* **sworn**) **1** (promise) кля́сться, по-; **they swore eternal friendship** они́ покляли́сь в ве́чной дру́жбе **2** (bind by an oath) прив|оди́ть, -ести́ к прися́ге; **the jury was sworn in** прися́жных привели́ к прися́ге; **he was sworn to secrecy** с него́ взя́ли кля́тву о неразглаше́нии та́йны; **sworn enemies** закля́тые враги́
● *v.i.* (*past* **swore**, *p.p.* **sworn**) **1** (take an oath) кля́сться, по-; (fig.): **he** ~s **by aspirin** он (безграни́чно) ве́рит в по́льзу аспири́на **2** (curse) брани́ться (*impf.*); руга́ться (*impf.*)
■ ~ **word** *n.* руга́тельство

swearing /'sweərɪŋ/ *n.* брань, руга́нь

sweat /swet/ *n.* **1** пот, испа́рина **2** (state of ~ing) поте́ние, пот; **a cold** ~ холо́дный пот
● *v.i.* (*past and p.p.* **sweated** *or* AmE ~) поте́ть, вс-
■ ~**shirt** *n.* хлопчатобума́жный (спорти́вный) сви́тер, толсто́вка

sweater /'swetə(r)/ *n.* сви́тер

sweaty /'swetɪ/ *adj.* (**sweatier, sweatiest**): ~ **hands** по́тные ру́ки

Swede /swi:d/ *n.* (person) швед (-ка); (**s**~) (BrE, vegetable) брю́ква

Sweden /'swi:d(ə)n/ *n.* Шве́ция

Swedish /'swi:dɪʃ/ *n.* (language) шве́дский язы́к
● *adj.* шве́дский

sweep /swi:p/ *n.* **1** (with broom etc.): **give a room a good** ~ хороше́нько подме|та́ть, -сти́ ко́мнату **2** (~ing movement) взмах, разма́х **3** (long flowing curve) изги́б **4** (*in full* **chimney** ~) трубочи́ст
● *v.t.* (*past and p.p.* **swept**) **1** (rush over): **the waves swept the shore** во́лны набега́ли на бе́рег **2** (carry forcefully): **a wave swept him overboard** его́ смы́ло волно́й (за́ борт); **he swept her off her feet** (fig.) он вскружи́л ей го́лову **3** (clean, brush) подме|та́ть, -сти́; чи́стить, вы́-; **he swept the litter into a corner** он замё́л му́сор в у́гол; ~ **a chimney** проч|ища́ть, -и́стить трубу́; (fig.): ~ **sth under the carpet** заме|та́ть, -сти́ что-н. под ковёр
● *v.i.* (*past and p.p.* **swept**) **1** (rush, dash) прон|оси́ться, -ести́сь; **rain swept across the country** дождь прошё́л по всей стране́; **fear swept over him** страх охвати́л его́ **2** (walk majestically): **she swept into the room** она́

го́рдо вошла́ в ко́мнату **3** (brush) мести́, под-; подме|та́ть, -сти́
□ **~ aside** *v.t.*: he swept aside my protestations он не стал слу́шать мои́х возраже́ний
□ **~ away** *v.t.* сме|та́ть, -сти́; the storm swept everything away бу́ря всё смела́
□ **~ up** *v.t.*: be sure and **~** up all the dirt смотри́те, вы́метите весь му́сор как сле́дует
 • *v.i.*: I had to **~** up after them мне пришло́сь по́сле них убира́ть

sweeping /'swi:pɪŋ/ *adj.* (comprehensive) всеобъе́млющий; **~** changes радика́льные измене́ния; (too general): a **~** statement огу́льное утвержде́ние

⚹ **sweet** /swi:t/ *n.* **1** (BrE, piece of confectionary) конфе́та **2** (BrE, dessert) сла́дкое, тре́тье
 • *adj.* **1** (to taste) сла́дкий; my brother has a **~** tooth мой брат — сладкое́жка (*c.g.*)
 2 (fragrant) сла́дкий, души́стый; how **~** the roses smell! как сла́дко па́хнут ро́зы!
 3 (infml, charming, nice) ми́лый; a **~** little dog симпати́чная соба́чка
■ **~-and-sour** *adj.* ки́сло-сла́дкий; **~corn** *n.* (столо́вая) кукуру́за; **~heart** *n.* возлю́бленн|ый (-ая); (as form of address) дорого́й, ми́лый, люби́мый; **~** talk *n.* (infml) лесть; **~talk** *v.t.* (infml) загов|а́ривать, -ори́ть кому́-н. зу́бы

sweeten /'swi:t(ə)n/ *v.t.* подсла́|щивать, -сти́ть

sweetener /'swi:tənə(r)/ *n.* (sugar substitute) замени́тель (*m.*) са́хара; (BrE, bribe) взя́тка

swell /swel/ *n.* (of sea) зыбь
 • *v.t.* (*p.p.* **swollen** *or* **swelled**) **1** (increase size of) разд|ува́ть, -у́ть; my finger is swollen у меня́ па́лец опу́х/распу́х **2** (increase number of) увели́чи|вать, -ть
 • *v.i.* (*p.p.* **swollen** *or* **swelled**) **1** (expand, dilate) (*also* **~** up) над|ува́ться, -у́ться; (of part of body) оп|уха́ть, -у́хнуть **2** (increase in size or volume) выраста́ть, вы́расти; the crowd **~**ed to over six thousand толпа́ увели́чилась до шести́ с ли́шним ты́сяч (челове́к)

swelling /'swelɪŋ/ *n.* о́пухоль

sweltering /'sweltərɪŋ/ *adj.* нестерпи́мо жа́р␣кий

swept /swept/ *past and p.p. of* ▶ **sweep**

swerve /swɜːv/ *v.i.* (кру́то) пов|ора́чиваться, -ерну́ться

swift /swɪft/ *n.* (bird) стриж
 • *adj.* (rapid) бы́стрый; (prompt) ско́рый

swig /swɪɡ/ (infml) *n.* глото́к
 • *v.t.* (**swigged**, **swigging**) хлеба́ть (*impf.*)

swill /swɪl/ *n.* по́йло; (pig food) помо́|и (-ев)
 • *v.t.* **1** (BrE, wash, rinse) мыть, вы́-; полоска́ть, вы́- **2** (drink heavily) лака́ть, вы́-, хлеба́ть, вы́-, хлеста́ть, вы́- (all infml)

swim /swɪm/ *n.*: have, go for a **~** купа́ться, ис-
 • *v.t.* (**swimming**, *past* **swam**, *p.p.* **swum**) **1** (cross by **~**ming) перепл|ыва́ть, -ы́ть **2** (cover by **~**ming): **~** a mile пропл|ыва́ть, -ы́ть ми́лю

 • *v.i.* (**swimming**, *past* **swam**, *p.p.* **swum**) **1** пла́вать (*indet.*), плыть (*det.*), по- **2** (fig., swirl): everything was **~**ming before my eyes всё поплы́ло у меня́ пе́ред глаза́ми
■ **~suit** *n.* купа́льник

swimmer /'swɪmə(r)/ *n.* плов|е́ц (-чи́ха)

swimming /'swɪmɪŋ/ *n.* пла́вание
■ **~ bath** (BrE), **~ pool** *nn.* (пла́вательный) бассе́йн

swindle /'swɪnd(ə)l/ *n.* моше́нничество
 • *v.t.* обма́н|ывать, -у́ть; **~** money out of sb выма́нивать, вы́манить у кого́-н. де́ньги

swindler /'swɪndlə(r)/ *n.* моше́нник

swine /swaɪn/ *n.* (*pl.* **~**, *also* (fig.) **~s**) (lit., fig.) свинья́

swing /swɪŋ/ *n.* **1** (movement) кача́ние, колеба́ние; in full **~** (fig.) в (по́лном) разга́ре **2** (shift): the polls showed a **~** to the left вы́боры показа́ли ре́зкое увеличе́ние популя́рности «ле́вых» **3** (rhythm) ритм; I couldn't get into the **~** of things я ника́к не мог включи́ться в де́ло **4** (seat on rope) каче́л|и (-ей)
 • *v.t.* (*past and p.p.* **swung**) **1** (apply circular motion to): **~** one's arms разма́хивать (*impf.*) рука́ми **2** (cause to turn) пов|ора́чивать, -ерну́ть; разв|ора́чивать, -ерну́ть
 • *v.i.* (*past and p.p.* **swung**) **1** (sway) кача́ться (*impf.*), колеба́ться (*impf.*); (dangle) висе́ть, свиса́ть, болта́ться (all *impf.*) **2** (turn) пов|ора́чиваться, -ерну́ться; враща́ться (*impf.*); the door swung open in the wind дверь распахну́лась от ве́тра
■ **~ doors**, **~ing doors** (AmE) *nn. pl.* свобо́дно распа́хивающаяся (двуство́рчатая) дверь

swingeing /'swɪndʒɪŋ/ *adj.* (BrE): a **~** blow ошеломля́ющий уда́р; a **~** majority подавля́ющее большинство́; a **~** fine грома́дный/огро́мный; штраф

swipe /swaɪp/ *v.t.* (infml) (hit) с си́лой уд|аря́ть, -а́рить по + *d.*; (steal) стащи́ть (*pf.*)
■ **~ card** *n.* магни́тная ка́рточка

swirl /swɜːl/ *v.i.* (of water) крути́ться (*impf.*) в водоворо́те; (of snow) ви|хри́ться (*impf.*); (of leaves etc.) кружи́ться, за-

Swiss /swɪs/ *n.* (*pl.* **~**) швейца́р|ец (-ка)
 • *adj.* швейца́рский

⚹ **switch** /swɪtʃ/ *n.* **1** (elec.) выключа́тель (*m.*), переключа́тель (*m.*) **2** (change) поворо́т, переме́на
 • *v.t.* (transfer) перев|оди́ть, -ести́; переключ|а́ть, -и́ть
 • *v.i.*: he **~**ed from one extreme to the other он перешёл/бро́сился из одно́й кра́йности в другу́ю
□ **~ off** *v.t.* выключа́ть, вы́ключить; **~** off a lamp гаси́ть, по- ла́мпу
□ **~ on** *v.t.* включ|а́ть, -и́ть; (light) заж|ига́ть, -е́чь
■ **~board** *n.* коммута́тор; **~board operator** телефони́ст (-ка)

Switzerland /'swɪtsələnd/ *n.* Швейца́рия

swivel /'swɪv(ə)l/ *v.t. & i.* (**swivelled**, **swivelling**, AmE **swiveled**, **swiveling**) пов|ора́чивать(ся), -ерну́ть(ся) (на шарни́рах)

swollen /'swəʊlən/ *p.p. of* ▶ swell

swoop /swu:p/ *v.i.* (aeron.) пики́ровать, с-; the eagle ~ed (down) on its prey орёл стреми́тельно упа́л на свою́ же́ртву; the enemy ~ed on the town неприя́тель соверши́л внеза́пный налёт на го́род

swop /swɒp/ *n. & v.t.* = swap

sword /sɔ:d/ *n.* (cutting weapon) меч; (light thrust weapon) шпа́га

swore /swɔ:(r)/ *past of* ▶ swear

sworn /swɔ:n/ *p.p. of* ▶ swear

swot /swɒt/ (BrE) *n.* зубри́ла (*c.g.*)
• *v.i.* (**swotted, swotting**) зубри́ть (*impf.*)

swum /swʌm/ *p.p. of* ▶ swim

swung /swʌŋ/ *past and p.p. of* ▶ swing

sycamore /'sɪkəmɔ:(r)/ *n.* я́вор

sycophantic /sɪkə'fæntɪk/ *adj.* подхали́мский, льсти́вый

Sydney /'sɪdnɪ/ *n.* Си́дней

syllable /'sɪləb(ə)l/ *n.* слог

syllabus /'sɪləbəs/ *n.* програ́мма (*уче́бная*)

symbiosis /sɪmbaɪ'əʊsɪs/ *n.* симбио́з

symbol /'sɪmb(ə)l/ *n.* си́мвол; (sign, e.g. math.) знак

symbolic /sɪm'bɒlɪk/ *adj.* символи́ческий, символи́чный

symbolism /'sɪmbəlɪz(ə)m/ *n.* символи́зм

symbolize /'sɪmbəlaɪz/ *v.t.* символизи́ровать (*impf., pf.*)

symmetrical /sɪ'metrɪk(ə)l/ *adj.* симметри́чный

symmetry /'sɪmɪtrɪ/ *n.* симме́трия

sympathetic /sɪmpə'θetɪk/ *adj.*
1 (compassionate) сочу́вственный
2 (supportive): I am ~ towards his ideas его́ иде́и мне близки́

sympathize /'sɪmpəθaɪz/ *v.i.* сочу́вствовать (*impf.*) (with: + *d.*)

sympathizer /'sɪmpəθaɪzə(r)/ *n.* сторо́нни|к (-ца)

sympathy /'sɪmpəθɪ/ *n.* (compassion) сочу́вствие, сострада́ние; (agreement) согла́сие; the power workers came out in ~ рабо́тники электроста́нции забастова́ли в знак солида́рности

symphony /'sɪmfənɪ/ *n.* симфо́ния

■ ~ **concert** *n.* симфони́ческий конце́рт; ~ **orchestra** *n.* симфони́ческий орке́стр

symposi|um /sɪm'pəʊzɪəm/ *n.* (*pl.* ~a *or* ~ums) симпо́зиум

✍ **symptom** /'sɪmptəm/ *n.* симпто́м

symptomatic /sɪmptə'mætɪk/ *adj.* симптомати́чный, симптомати́ческий

synagogue /'sɪnəgɒg/ *n.* синаго́га

sync /sɪŋk/ *n.* (infml): out of ~ несинхро́нный

synchronize /'sɪŋkrənaɪz/ *v.t.* синхронизи́ровать (*impf., pf.*)
■ ~d **swimming** *n.* синхро́нное пла́вание

syncopation /sɪŋkə'peɪʃ(ə)n/ *n.* синко́па

syndicate /'sɪndɪkət/ *n.* синдика́т

syndrome /'sɪndrəʊm/ *n.* синдро́м

synonym /'sɪnənɪm/ *n.* сино́ним

synonymous /sɪ'nɒnɪməs/ *adj.* (fig.) равнозна́чный (with: + *d.*)

synopsis /sɪ'nɒpsɪs/ *n.* (*pl.* **synopses** /-si:z/) резюме́ (*nt. indecl.*)

syntax /'sɪntæks/ *n.* си́нтаксис

synthesis /'sɪnθɪsɪs/ *n.* (*pl.* **syntheses** /-si:z/) си́нтез

synthesize /'sɪnθɪsaɪz/ *v.t.* синтези́ровать (*impf., pf.*)

synthesizer /'sɪnθɪsaɪzə(r)/ *n.* синтеза́тор

synthetic /sɪn'θetɪk/ *adj.* синтети́ческий
• *n.* (*usu. in pl.*) синте́тика (*collect.*)

syphilis /'sɪfɪlɪs/ *n.* си́филис

Syria /'sɪrɪə/ *n.* Си́рия

Syrian /'sɪrɪən/ *n.* сири́|ец (-йка)
• *adj.* сири́йский

syringe /sɪ'rɪndʒ/ *n.* шприц

syrup /'sɪrəp/ *n.* (juice) сиро́п; (treacle) па́тока; golden ~ све́тлая па́тока

✍ **system** /'sɪstəm/ *n.* **1** (complex; method) систе́ма **2** (network) сеть **3** (body as a whole) органи́зм; get sth out of one's ~ (fig.) изба́вляться, -а́виться от чего́-н.
■ ~s **analysis** *n.* систе́мный ана́лиз; ~s **analyst** *n.* систе́мный анали́тик

systematic /sɪstə'mætɪk/ *adj.* системати́ческий

systemic /sɪ'stemɪk/ *adj.* относя́щийся ко всему́ органи́зму, соматический; ~ **poison** общеядови́тое отравля́ющее вещество́

S

Tt

tab /tæb/ *n.* **1** (projecting flap) ушко́ **2** (infml, check): **the police are keeping ∼s on him** поли́ция присма́тривает за ним

⚜ **table** /'teɪb(ə)l/ *n.* **1** стол **2** (arrangement of data) табли́ца
● *v.t.* **1** (BrE, present for discussion) ста́вить, по- на обсужде́ние **2** (AmE, postpone) от|кла́дывать, -ложи́ть
■ ∼**cloth** *n.* ска́терть; ∼ **mat** *n.* (BrE) подста́вка (*под тарелку и т. п.*); ∼**spoon** *n.* столо́вая ло́жка; ∼ **tennis** *n.* насто́льный те́ннис, пинг-по́нг

tablet /'tæblɪt/ *n.* **1** табле́тка **2** (comput.) планше́тный компью́тер, планше́т

tabloid /'tæblɔɪd/ *n.* табло́ид; **the ∼s** бульва́рная пре́сса

taboo /tə'buː/ *n.* табу́ (*nt. indecl.*)

tacit /'tæsɪt/ *adj.* молчали́вый (*согласие, одобрение*)

taciturn /'tæsɪtɜːn/ *adj.* неразгово́рчивый, молчали́вый

taciturnity /ˌtæsɪ'tɜːnɪtɪ/ *n.* неразгово́рчивость, молчали́вость

tack /tæk/ *n.* **1** (small nail) гво́здик **2** (fig.): **he is on the wrong ∼** он на ло́жном пути́
● *v.t.* **1** (fasten) прикреп|ля́ть, -и́ть гвоздя́ми **2** (stitch) намёт|ывать, -а́ть **3**: ∼ **on** (fig., add) доб|авля́ть, -а́вить

tackle /'tæk(ə)l/ *n.* **1** (football) блокиро́вка **2**: **fishing ∼** рыболо́вные сна́сти (*f. pl.*)
● *v.t.* (grapple with) бра́ться, взя́ться за + *a.*; **I ∼d him on the subject** я по́днял э́тот вопро́с в разгово́ре с ним; (football) блоки́ровать (*impf., pf.*)

tacky¹ /'tækɪ/ *adj.* (**tackier, tackiest**) (sticky) ли́пкий, кле́йкий

tacky² /'tækɪ/ *adj.* (**tackier, tackiest**) (infml, tasteless) безвку́сный (*вульгарный*)

tact /tækt/ *n.* такт

tactful /'tæktfʊl/ *adj.* такти́чный

tactic /'tæktɪk/ *n.* та́ктика; (*in pl.*) (mil.) та́ктика

tactical /'tæktɪk(ə)l/ *adj.* такти́ческий

tactician /tæk'tɪʃ(ə)n/ *n.* та́ктик

tactile /'tæktaɪl/ *adj.* осяза́тельный, такти́льный

tactless /'tæktlɪs/ *adj.* беста́ктный

tadpole /'tædpəʊl/ *n.* голова́стик

tag /tæɡ/ *n.* ярлы́к
● *v.i.* (**tagged, tagging**) (follow): **the children ∼ged along behind** де́ти тащи́лись сза́ди; **to ∼ along with sb** увя́з|ываться, -а́ться за кем-н.

⚜ ключева́я ле́ксика

Tahiti /tə'hiːtɪ/ *n.* Таи́ти (*m. indecl.*)

t'ai chi ch'uan /taɪ 'tʃiː 'tʃwɑːn/, **t'ai chi** /taɪ 'tʃiː/ *n.* тайцзицюа́нь (*f. indecl.*)

tail /teɪl/ *n.* **1** (of animal) хвост **2** (of a coin) ре́шка **3**: ∼**s** (coat) фрак
● *v.t.* (shadow) висе́ть (*impf.*) на хвосте́ у + *g.*
● *v.i.* убыва́ть, -ы́ть; **the attendance figures ∼ed off** посеща́емость упа́ла; **his voice ∼ed away into silence** его́ го́лос (постепе́нно) зати́х
■ ∼**back** *n.* (BrE) дли́нная верени́ца автомоби́лей в про́бке; многокиломе́тровая про́бка

tailor /'teɪlə(r)/ *n.* портно́й
● *v.t.* (fig.) приспос|а́бливать, -о́бить; **his speech was ∼ed to the situation** его́ речь была́ соста́влена с учётом ситуа́ции
■ ∼**-made** *adj.* (clothes) сде́ланный на зака́з; (fig.) подходя́щий

taint /teɪnt/ *v.t.* по́ртить, ис-; ∼**ed money** гря́зные де́ньги; ∼**ed reputation** подмо́ченная репута́ция

Taiwan /taɪ'wɑːn/ *n.* Тайва́нь (*m.*)

Tajik /tɑː'dʒiːk/ *n.* **1** (person) таджи́к (-чка) **2** (language) таджи́кский язы́к
● *adj.* таджи́кский

Tajikistan /tədʒiːkɪ'stɑːn/ *n.* Таджикиста́н

⚜ **take** /teɪk/ *n.* (cin.) дубль (*m.*), монта́жный кадр
● *v.t.* (*past* **took**, *p.p.* **taken** /'teɪk(ə)n/)
1 (pick up, grasp) брать, взять; **he took her by the hand** он взял её за́ руку; **she took a coin out of her purse** она́ вы́нула моне́ту из кошелька́; **the last mile took it out of me** на после́дней ми́ле я вы́дохся **2** (capture) брать, взять; **he was ∼n captive** его́ взя́ли в плен; (assume) прин|има́ть, -я́ть на себя́; **you must ∼ the initiative** вы должны́ взять на себя́ инициати́ву; **he took control** он взял управле́ние в свои́ ру́ки; (win) выи́грывать, вы́играть; **she took first prize** она́ получи́ла пе́рвый приз **3** (acquire): **these seats are ∼n** э́ти места́ за́няты; (in payment): **they took £50 in one evening** они́ вы́ручили 50 фу́нтов за оди́н ве́чер; (by enquiry or examination) определя́ть, -и́ть; **the doctor took my temperature** врач изме́рил мне температу́ру; (unlawfully): **the thieves took all her jewellery** во́ры забра́ли все её драгоце́нности **4** (avail oneself of): **please ∼ a seat** пожа́луйста, сади́тесь; (travel by): **let's ∼ a taxi** дава́йте возьмём такси́ **5** (accept) прин|има́ть, -я́ть; **will you ∼ a cheque?** вы при́мете чек?; **will you ∼ £50 for it?** вы отдади́те э́то за 50 фу́нтов?; **∼ my advice!** послу́шайте меня́!; **I ∼ responsibility** я беру́

на себя́ отве́тственность; **can't you ~ a joke?** вы что, шу́ток не понима́ете?; (receive) брать (*impf.*); **she ~s lessons in Spanish** она́ берёт уро́ки испа́нского языка́; (submit to): **when do you ~ your exams?** когда́ вы сдаёте экза́мены? **6** (use regularly) прин|има́ть, -я́ть; **he has begun to ~ drugs** он на́чал принима́ть нарко́тики; **do you ~ sugar in your tea?** вы пьёте чай с са́харом?; (of size in clothes): **I ~ a ten in shoes** у меня́ деся́тый разме́р о́буви **7** (make or obtain from original source): **may I ~ your photograph?** позво́льте мне вас сфотографи́ровать? **8** (convey) (on foot) отн|оси́ть, -ести́; (by transport) отв|ози́ть, -езти́; брать, взять; перед|ава́ть, -а́ть; **he was ~n to hospital** его́ отвезли́ в больни́цу **9** (require): **the job will ~ a long time** рабо́та займёт мно́го вре́мени; **how long does it ~ to get there?** ско́лько (вре́мени) туда́ добира́ться?; **it took us 3 hours to get there** нам потре́бовалось три часа́, что́бы добра́ться туда́; **he's got what it ~s** (infml) у него́ есть для э́того все зада́тки

● *v.t.* (*past* **took**, *p.p.* **taken** /'teɪk(ə)n/)
1 (~ effect; succeed): **the vaccination has not ~n** вакци́на не привила́сь **2** ~ **after** (resemble): **he ~s after his father** он похо́ж на (своего́) отца́ **3**: ~ **to** (resort to) приб|ега́ть, -е́гнуть к + *d.*; **she took to her bed** она́ слегла́; **he took to drink** он за́пил; **he has ~n to getting up early** он стал ра́но встава́ть; (feel well disposed towards): **I took to him from the start** он мне сра́зу понра́вился

□ ~ **apart** *v.t.* (dismantle) раз|бира́ть, -обра́ть

□ ~ **away** *v.t.* (remove) уб|ира́ть, -ра́ть; заб|ира́ть, -ра́ть; **the police took his gun away** поли́ция отобрала́ у него́ пистоле́т; **he was ~n away to prison** его́ отвезли́ в тюрьму́; (subtract) вычита́ть, вы́честь

□ ~ **back** *v.t.* (return) верну́ть (*pf.*); (retract): **I ~ back everything I said** я беру́ наза́д всё, что сказа́л

□ ~ **down** *v.t.* (remove) сн|има́ть, -я́ть; (lengthen): **she took her dress down an inch** она́ отпусти́ла пла́тье на дюйм; (dismantle) сн|оси́ть, -ести́; **the shed was ~n down** сара́й снесли́; (write down) запи́с|ывать, -а́ть

□ ~ **in** *v.t.* (lit.) вн|оси́ть, -ести́; (give shelter to): **they took him in when he was starving** они́ приюти́ли его́, когда́ он голода́л; (let accommodation to): **she ~s in lodgers** она́ берёт посто́яльцев; (make smaller): **she took in her dress** она́ уши́ла пла́тье; (comprehend) усв|а́ивать, -о́ить; (deceive) обма́н|ывать, -у́ть

□ ~ **off** *v.t.* (remove) сн|има́ть, -я́ть; (deduct from price): **I will ~ 10% off for cash** е́сли вы пла́тите нали́чными, я сбро́шу 10 проце́нтов; (BrE, infml, mimic) имити́ровать (*impf.*), копи́ровать (*impf.*)
● *v.i.* (become airborne) взлет|а́ть, -е́ть

□ ~ **on** *v.t.* (hire) брать, взять; (undertake) брать, взять на себя́; **he took on too much** он взял на себя́ сли́шком мно́го; (assume) приобре|та́ть, -сти́

□ ~ **out** *v.t.* (extract) вынима́ть, вы́нуть; **he took out his wallet** он вы́нул бума́жник; **he had**

all his teeth ~n out ему́ удали́ли все зу́бы; **he took his girlfriend out to dinner** он повёл свою́ подру́гу в рестора́н; (vent one's feelings) срыва́ть, сорва́ть; **he took it out on his wife** он сорва́л всё на свое́й жене́

□ ~ **over** *v.t.* & *i.* (assume control (of)) прин|има́ть, -я́ть руково́дство (+ *i.*)
● *v.i.* (replace sb): **let me ~ over!** я вас сменю́!

□ ~ **up** *v.t.* (lift) подн|има́ть, -я́ть; (accept) прин|има́ть, -я́ть; **will he ~ up the challenge?** он при́мет вы́зов?; (shorten): **she had to ~ up her dress** ей пришло́сь укороти́ть пла́тье; (occupy) зан|има́ть, -я́ть; (pursue): **I shall ~ the matter up with the Minister** я обращу́сь с э́тим де́лом к мини́стру; (accept challenge or offer): **I'll ~ you up on that!** (я) ловлю́ вас на сло́ве!; (interest oneself in) бра́ться, взя́ться за + *a.*
● *v.i.* (consort) свя́зываться, -а́ться (**with:** с + *i.*)

■ ~**away** *n.* (BrE) (shop) рестора́н, продаю́щий еду́ на вы́нос; (meal) еда́ на вы́нос; ~**home** *attr. adj.*: ~-home pay чи́стый за́работок; ~**off** *n.* (impersonation) подража́ние, паро́дия; (of aircraft, also fig.) взлёт; ~**out** *n.* (AmE) = takeaway; ~**over** *n.* (comm.) поглоще́ние (*како́й-н. компа́нии друго́й компа́нией*)

taking /'teɪkɪŋ/ *n.* взя́тие; овладе́ние; **the money was there for the ~** де́ньги текли́ пря́мо в ру́ки
● *adj.* привлека́тельный

takings /'teɪkɪŋz/ *n. pl.* (money taken) вы́ручка; **the ~ were lower than expected** сбор оказа́лся ме́ньше, чем рассчи́тывали

talcum /'tælkəm/ *n.*: ~ **powder** тальк

tale /teɪl/ *n.* **1** расска́з, по́весть **2** (malicious or idle report): **tell ~s** я́бедничать, на- (**about:** на + *a.*)

✎ **talent** /'tælənt/ *n.* тала́нт, дар

talented /'tæləntɪd/ *adj.* тала́нтливый

talisman /'tælɪzmən/ *n.* (*pl.* ~**s**) талисма́н

✎ **talk** /tɔːk/ *n.* **1** (speech, conversation) разгово́р, бесе́да **2** (lecture) ле́кция; докла́д; **give a ~** чита́ть, про- ле́кцию **3** (discussion) (*usu. in pl.*) перегово́ры (*m. pl.*)
● *v.t.* **1** (express) говори́ть (*impf.*); **you are ~ing nonsense** вы говори́те чепуху́ **2** (discuss) обсу|жда́ть, -ди́ть; **they were ~ing politics** они́ говори́ли о поли́тике **3** (bring or make by ~ing): **he ~ed me into it** он уговори́л меня́ сде́лать э́то; **I tried to ~ her out of it** я пыта́лся отговори́ть её от э́того
● *v.i.* говори́ть (*impf.*) (**about:** о + *p.*); **a ~ing parrot** говоря́щий попуга́й

□ ~ **over** *v.t.* (discuss) обсу|жда́ть, -ди́ть

■ ~ **show** *n.* ток-шо́у (*nt. indecl.*)

talkative /'tɔːkətɪv/ *adj.* разгово́рчивый, болтли́вый

talking-to /'tɔːkɪŋ/ *n.* (infml) вы́говор

tall /tɔːl/ *adj.* высо́кий, высо́кого ро́ста; **how ~ are you?** како́го вы ро́ста?; **six feet ~** ро́стом в шесть фу́тов

Tallinn /'tælɪn/ *n.* Та́ллин

tally /'tælɪ/ *n.* счёт
● *v.i.* соотве́тствовать (*impf.*)

talon /'tælən/ *n.* ко́готь (*m.*)

tambourine /tæmbə'riːn/ *n.* бу́бен

tame /teɪm/ *adj.* (domesticated) ручно́й, дома́шний; (submissive) послу́шный; (dull) пре́сный
● *v.t.* прируч|а́ть, -и́ть; (of savage animals) укро|ща́ть, -ти́ть

Tamil /'tæmɪl/ *n.* (person) тами́л (-ка); (language) тами́льский язы́к
● *adj.* тами́льский

tamper /'tæmpə(r)/ *v.i.*: ~ with (meddle in) вме́ш|иваться, -аться в + *a.*

tampon /'tæmpɒn/ *n.* тампо́н

tan /tæn/ *n.* (colour) (желтова́то-/рыжева́то-)кори́чневый цвет; (tint of skin) зага́р; **he went to Spain to get a** ~ он пое́хал загора́ть в Испа́нию
● *adj.* (желтова́то-/рыжева́то-)кори́чневый
● *v.t.* (**tanned, tanning**) (make brown): a ~ned face загоре́лое лицо́
● *v.i.* (**tanned, tanning**): she ~s easily она́ бы́стро загора́ет

tangent /'tændʒ(ə)nt/ *n.* (geom.) каса́тельная; (fig.): **he went off at a** ~ он отклони́лся от те́мы

tangerine /'tændʒəriːn/ *n.* мандари́н, танжери́н

tangible /'tændʒɪb(ə)l/ *adj.* осяза́емый

tangle /'tæŋg(ə)l/ *n.* сплете́ние
● *v.t.* спу́т|ывать, -ать; **the wool had got** ~d **up** ни́тки спу́тались
● *v.i.* (infml) свя́з|ываться, -а́ться

tango /'tæŋgəʊ/ *n.* (*pl.* ~**s**) та́нго (*nt. indecl.*)
● *v.i.* (**tangoes, tangoed**) танцева́ть, с- та́нго

tangy /'tæŋɪ/ *adj.* (**tangier, tangiest**) о́стрый, те́рпкий

tank /tæŋk/ *n.* **1** (container) бак, цисте́рна; **petrol** ~ бензоба́к; **water** ~ бак для воды́ **2** (armoured vehicle) танк

tankard /'tæŋkəd/ *n.* высо́кая пивна́я кру́жка

tanker /'tæŋkə(r)/ *n.* (ship) та́нкер; (vehicle) автоцисте́рна

tantalize /'tæntəlaɪz/ *v.t.* (tease) дразни́ть (*impf.*)

tantamount /'tæntəmaʊnt/ *adj.*: ~ **to** равноси́льный + *d.*

tantrum /'tæntrəm/ *n.* вспы́шка раздраже́ния; **the child is in a** ~ ребёнок капри́зничает

Tanzania /tænzə'niːə/ *n.* Танза́ния

Tanzanian /tænzə'niːən/ *n.* танзани́|ец (-йка)
● *adj.* танзани́йский

tap¹ /tæp/ *n.* кран
● *v.t.* (**tapped, tapping**) (fig.): **the line is being** ~ped разгово́р подслу́шивают

tap² /tæp/ *n.* (light blow) стук
● *v.t.* (**tapped, tapping**) легко́ уд|аря́ть, -а́рить; стуча́ть, по-
● *v.i.* (**tapped, tapping**) стуча́ться, по-; **he** ~ped **on the door** он постуча́лся в дверь
■ ~**dance,** ~**-dancing** *nn.* чечётка

tape /teɪp/ *n.* (strip of fabric etc.) тесьма́, ле́нта; **adhesive** ~ ли́пкая ле́нта; (magnetic ~)
(магнитофо́нная) ле́нта/плёнка
● *v.t.* **1** (bind with ~) свя́з|ывать, -а́ть тесьмо́й **2** (record) запи́с|ывать, -а́ть (на плёнку)
■ ~ **measure** *n.* руле́тка, (санти)ме́тр; ~ **recorder** *n.* магнитофо́н; ~**worm** *n.* ле́нточный червь

taper /'teɪpə(r)/ *v.t. & i.* сужа́ть(ся), су́зить(ся)

tapestry /'tæpɪstrɪ/ *n.* гобеле́н

tar /tɑː(r)/ *n.* дёготь (*m.*)

tarantula /tə'ræntjʊlə/ *n.* тара́нтул

tardy /'tɑːdɪ/ *adj.* (**tardier, tardiest**) (slow-moving) медли́тельный; (late in coming, belated) запозда́вший, запозда́лый

✍ **target** /'tɑːgɪt/ *n.* (for shooting etc.) мише́нь (also fig.), цель; (objective) цель
● *v.t.* (**targeted, targeting**) **1** (select as object) де́лать, с- мише́нью **2** (aim) напр|авля́ть, -а́вить

tariff /'tærɪf/ *n.* (duty) тари́ф

tarmac® /'tɑːmæk/ *n.* гудро́н, асфа́льт; (aeron.) бетони́рованная площа́дка

tarnish /'tɑːnɪʃ/ *v.t.*: ~ed **by damp** потускне́вший от вла́ги; **he has a** ~ed **reputation** он запятна́л свою́ репута́цию
● *v.i.* тускне́ть, по-

tarpaulin /tɑː'pɔːlɪn/ *n.* брезе́нт

tarragon /'tærəgən/ *n.* эстраго́н, тарху́н

tart¹ /tɑːt/ *n.* (flat pie) откры́тый пиро́г с фру́ктами/я́годами
● *v.t.*: ~ **up** (BrE, infml, embellish) приукра́ш|ивать, -сить; **she was all** ~ed **up** она́ была́ разоде́та с головы́ до ног

tart² /tɑːt/ *adj.* (of taste) ки́слый

tartan /'tɑːt(ə)n/ *n.* (fabric) шотла́ндка (*клетчатая ткань*)

Tartar /'tɑːtə(r)/ (hist.) *n.* тата́ро(-)монго́л
● *adj.* тата́ро(-)монго́льский

Tashkent /tæʃ'kent/ *n.* Ташке́нт

✍ **task** /tɑːsk/ *n.* зада́ча, зада́ние
■ ~ **force** *n.* (mil.) операти́вная гру́ппа; ~**master** *n.*: **he is a hard** ~**master** он из тебя́ все со́ки выжима́ет

Tasmania /tæz'meɪnɪə/ *n.* Тасма́ния

tassel /'tæs(ə)l/ *n.* ки́сточка (*украшение*)

✍ **taste** /teɪst/ *n.* (sense; flavour) вкус; (act of tasting; small portion for tasting): **have a** ~ **of this!** попро́буйте/отве́дайте э́того!; (fig., liking): **she has expensive** ~**s in clothes** она́ лю́бит носи́ть дороги́е ве́щи; (fig., discernment) вкус; **he is a man of** ~ он челове́к со вку́сом; **bad** ~ дурно́й вкус
● *v.t.* **1** (perceive flavour of) чу́вствовать, по-; **can you** ~ **the garlic?** вы чу́вствуете чесно́к? **2** (eat small amount of) есть, по- **3** (experience) вку|ша́ть, -си́ть; изве́д|ывать, -ать
● *v.i.*: **the meat** ~**s horrible** у мя́са отврати́тельный вкус; ~ **of** име́ть (*impf.*) привкус + *g.*

tasteful /'teɪstfʊl/ *adj.* изя́щный; со вку́сом

tasteless /'teɪstlɪs/ *adj.* (insipid; showing no taste) безвку́сный; (behaviour) беста́ктный

tasty /'teɪstɪ/ *adj.* (**tastier, tastiest**) вку́сный, ла́комый

Tatar /'tɑːtə(r)/ (inhabitant of Tatarstan etc.) тата́р|ин (-ка)
• *adj.* тата́рский

tattered /'tætəd/ *adj.* по́рванный, разо́рванный

tatters /'tætəz/ *n. pl.* клочь|я (-ев), лохмо́ть|я (-ев)

tattoo /tæ'tuː/ *n. (pl.* ∼**s**) (on skin) татуиро́вка
• *v.t.* (**tattoos, tattooed**) татуи́ровать (*impf., pf.*)

tatty /'tætɪ/ *adj.* (**tattier, tattiest**) (infml) потрёпанный

taught /tɔːt/ *past and p.p. of* ▸ **teach**

taunt /tɔːnt/ *v.t.* дразни́ть (*impf.*)

Taurus /'tɔːrəs/ *n.* (astron.) Теле́ц

taut /tɔːt/ *adj.* (tight) туго́й, ту́го натя́нутый

tautological /tɔːtə'lɒdʒɪk(ə)l/ *adj.* тавтологи́ческий

tautology /tɔː'tɒlədʒɪ/ *n.* тавтоло́гия

tavern /'tæv(ə)n/ *n.* (archaic) таве́рна

tawdry /'tɔːdrɪ/ *adj.* (**tawdrier, tawdriest**) крича́щий, безвку́сный

✎ **tax** /tæks/ *n.* нало́г
• *v.t.* обл|ага́ть, -ожи́ть нало́гом; (fig.): he ∼**es** my patience он испы́тывает моё терпе́ние
■ ∼ **collector** *n.* сбо́рщик нало́гов; ∼ **disc** *n.* (BrE) накле́йка об упла́те доро́жного нало́га; ∼**-free** *adjs.* не облага́емый нало́гом; ∼ **haven** *n.* страна́ с ни́зкими нало́гами; ∼**payer** *n.* налогоплате́льщик

taxable /'tæksəb(ə)l/ *adj.* подлежа́щий обложе́нию нало́гом

taxation /tæk'seɪʃ(ə)n/ *n.* налогообложе́ние

taxi /'tæksɪ/ *n. (pl.* ∼**s**) такси́ (*nt. indecl.*)
• *v.i.* (**taxies, taxied, taxiing**) (of aircraft) рули́ть (*impf.*)
■ ∼ **rank**, ∼ **stand** (AmE) *nn.* стоя́нка такси́

taxidermist /'tæksɪdəːmɪst/ *n.* таксидерми́ст, наби́вщик чу́чел

taxidermy /'tæksɪdəːmɪ/ *n.* таксидерми́я, наби́вка чу́чел

taxonomic /tæksə'nɒmɪk/ *adj.* таксономи́ческий

taxonomy /tæk'sɒnəmɪ/ *n.* система́тика, таксоно́мия

TB *abbr.* (*of* **tuberculosis**) туберкулёз

TBA *abbr.* (*of* **to be announced, to be arranged**) бу́дет объя́влено дополни́тельно

Tbilisi /təbɪ'liːsɪ/ *n.* Тбили́си (*m. indecl.*)

tea /tiː/ *n.* (plant, beverage) чай; (BrE, meal) по́лдник; **make (the)** ∼ зава́р|ивать, -и́ть чай; **have** ∼ пить, вы́- чай/ча́я/ча́ю
■ ∼ **bag** *n.* паке́тик ча́я, ча́йный паке́тик; ∼ **break** *n.* (BrE) переры́в на чай; ∼**cup** *n.* ча́йная ча́шка; ∼**pot** *n.* ча́йник (для зава́рки); ∼ **shop** *n.* кафе́ (*nt. indecl.*); ∼**spoon** *n.* ча́йная ло́жечка; ∼**spoonful** *n.* одна́/це́лая ча́йная ло́жка; ∼**-strainer** *n.* ча́йное си́течко; ∼**time** *n.* (BrE) ра́нний ве́чер, вре́мя (вече́рнего) чаепи́тия; ∼ **towel** *n.* (BrE) ку́хонное/посу́дное полоте́нце

✎ **teach** /tiːtʃ/ *v.t.* (*past and p.p.* **taught**)

1 (instruct) учи́ть, на-; обуч|а́ть, -и́ть; **she taught me Russian** она́ учи́ла меня́ ру́сскому языку́ **2** *v.t. & i.* (give instruction) (school etc.) учи́ть (*impf.*); (university etc.) преподава́ть (*impf.*); ∼**ing staff** преподава́тельский соста́в **3** (elliptical): **that will** ∼ **you!** э́то бу́дет вам уро́ком!; **I'll** ∼ **you (a lesson)!** я вас проучу́!

✎ **teacher** /'tiːtʃə(r)/ *n.* учи́тель (*m.*) (-ница); педаго́г
■ ∼ **training college** *n.* педагоги́ческий институ́т

✎ **teaching** /'tiːtʃɪŋ/ *n.* преподава́ние

teak /tiːk/ *n.* (wood) тик; (tree) тик, ти́ковое де́рево

✎ **team** /tiːm/ *n.* (sport) кома́нда; (of workers etc.) брига́да
■ ∼ **game** *n.* (sport) кома́ндная игра́; ∼ **spirit** *n.* коллективи́зм; (sport) кома́ндный дух; ∼**work** *n.* коллекти́вная рабо́та

✎ **tear¹** /tɪə(r)/ *n.* слеза́; **burst into** ∼**s** распла́каться (*pf.*)
■ ∼**drop** *n.* слези́нка; ∼ **gas** *n.* слезоточи́вый газ

tear² /teə(r)/ *n.* (rent) разры́в, дыра́
• *v.t.* (*past* **tore**, *p.p.* **torn**) **1** (rip) раз|рыва́ть, -орва́ть; рвать, по-; **I tore my shirt on a nail** я порва́л руба́шку о гвоздь; **he tore open the envelope** он разорва́л/вскрыл конве́рт **2** (remove by force) от|рыва́ть, -орва́ть; срыва́ть, сорва́ть
• *v.i.* (*past* **tore**, *p.p.* **torn**) **1** (become torn) рва́ться, по- **2** (rush) мча́ться, по-; нести́сь, по-
• *with advs.*: **I could not** ∼ **myself away** я не мог оторва́ться; **several pages had been torn out** не́сколько страни́ц бы́ло вы́рвано; **the letter was torn up** письмо́ разорва́ли

tearful /'tɪəfʊl/ *adj.* запла́канный

tease /tiːz/ *v.t.* дразни́ть (*impf.*)

teat /tiːt/ *n.* сосо́к

✎ **technical** /'teknɪk(ə)l/ *adj.* техни́ческий; ∼ **term** специа́льный те́рмин

technicality /teknɪ'kælɪtɪ/ *n.* техни́ческая дета́ль

technician /tek'nɪʃ(ə)n/ *n.* те́хник

✎ **technique** /tek'niːk/ *n.* (skill) те́хника; (method) приём

technocrat /'teknəkræt/ *n.* технокра́т

technological /teknə'lɒdʒɪk(ə)l/ *adj.* техни́ческий

technologist /tek'nɒlədʒɪst/ *n.* те́хник; (in particular area) техно́лог

✎ **technology** /tek'nɒlədʒɪ/ *n.* те́хника; (in particular area) техноло́гия

teddy /'tedɪ/ *n.* (*also* ∼ **bear**) (плю́шевый) ми́шка

tedious /'tiːdɪəs/ *adj.* ну́дный

teem /tiːm/ *v.i.*: **the house is** ∼**ing with ants** дом киши́т муравья́ми

teen /tiːn/ *n.*: **he is in his** ∼**s** ему́ ещё нет двадцати́ (лет); он подро́сток
■ ∼**age** *adj.* (characteristic of teenagers) подростко́вый, ю́ношеский; (girl, boy)

t

несовершеннолéтний; **~ager** n. подрóсток, юноша (m.) /дéвушка до двадцати́ лет; тинéйджер

teeter /ˈtiːtə(r)/ v.i. кача́ться (impf.)

teeth /tiːθ/ pl. of ▶ **tooth**

teeth|e /tiːð/ v.i.: baby is **~ing** у ребёнка ре́жутся зу́бы
■ **~ing troubles** n. pl. (fig.) «дéтские болéзни» (f. pl.)

teetotal /tiːˈtəʊt(ə)l/ adj. непью́щий

TEFL /ˈtef(ə)l/ abbr. (of **teaching of English as a foreign language**) преподава́ние англи́йского языка́ как иностра́нного

Tehran, Teheran /teəˈrɑːn/ n. Тегера́н

Tel Aviv /ˈtel əˈviːv/ n. Тель-Ави́в

telecommunications /ˌtelɪkəmjuːnɪˈkeɪʃ(ə)nz/ n. pl. телекоммуника́ции (f. pl.)

teleconference /ˈtelɪkɒnfərəns/ n. телеконферéнция

telegram /ˈtelɪɡræm/ n. телегра́мма

telegraph /ˈtelɪɡrɑːf/ n. телегра́ф
● v.t. & i. телеграфи́ровать (impf., pf.)
■ **~ pole** n. телегра́фный столб

telepathic /ˌtelɪˈpæθɪk/ adj. телепати́ческий

telepathy /tɪˈlepəθɪ/ n. телепа́тия

🔑 **telephone** /ˈtelɪfəʊn/ n. телефóн; **he is (talking) on the ~** (BrE) он разгова́ривает по телефóну; **someone wants you on the ~** вас прóсят к телефóну; **he picked up the ~** он поднял тру́бку; **~ public** телефóн-автома́т
● v.t. & i. звони́ть, по- (кому) по телефóну
■ **~ booth, ~ box** (BrE) nn. телефóнная бу́дка; **~ call** n. телефóнный звонóк; **~ directory** n. телефóнный спра́вочник; **~ number** n. телефóнный нóмер, (infml) телефóн; **~ operator** n. телефони́ст (-ка)

telephonist /tɪˈlefənɪst/ n. (BrE) телефони́ст (-ка)

telesales /ˈtelɪseɪlz/ n. pl. прода́жа по телефóну

telescope /ˈtelɪskəʊp/ n. телескóп

telescopic /ˌtelɪˈskɒpɪk/ adj. **1** (of or constituting a telescope) телескопи́ческий **2** (visible by telescope) ви́димый посре́дством телескóпа **3** (consisting of retracting and extending sections) складнóй, выдвижнóй
■ **~ aerial** n. выдвижна́я антéнна; **~ lens** n. телескопи́ческий объекти́в

teletext /ˈtelɪtekst/ n. телетéкст

televise /ˈtelɪvaɪz/ v.t. пока́зывать, -а́ть по телеви́дению

🔑 **television** /ˈtelɪvɪʒ(ə)n, -ˈvɪʒ(ə)n/ n. (system, process) телеви́дение; **what's on ~?** что пока́зывают по телеви́дению?; (apparatus) (also ~ **set**) телеви́зор
■ **~ camera** n. телека́мера; **~ programme** n. телевизиóнная переда́ча, телепереда́ча, телепрогра́мма; **~ studio** n. телеступди́я

🔑 **tell** /tel/ v.t. (past and p.p. **told**) **1** (relate; inform of; make known) расска́з|ывать, -а́ть, сообщ|а́ть, -и́ть; ука́з|ывать, -а́ть; **~ me all about it!** расскажи́те мне всё как есть/бы́ло! **2** (speak,

🔑 ключевая лексика

say) говори́ть, сказа́ть; **are you ~ing the truth?** вы говори́те пра́вду? **3** (decide, know) определ|я́ть, -и́ть; узн|ава́ть, -а́ть; **can she ~ the time yet?** она́ ужé умéет определя́ть врéмя?; **you never can ~** никогда́ не зна́ешь **4** (distinguish) отлич|а́ть, -и́ть; различ|а́ть, -и́ть; **I can't ~ them apart** я не могу́ их различи́ть **5** (instruct) прика́з|ывать, -а́ть; говори́ть, сказа́ть; **he was told to wait outside** ему́ сказа́ли/велéли подожда́ть за двéрью; **~ him not to wait** скажи́те ему́, чтóбы он не жда́л **6** (predict) предска́з|ывать, -а́ть; **I told you so!** я вам говори́л!
● v.i. (past and p.p. **told**) **1** (give information) расска́з|ывать, -а́ть; **he told of his adventures** он рассказа́л о свои́х приключéниях; **don't ~ on me!** (infml) не выдава́й меня́!; **he promised not to ~** (divulge secret) он обеща́л молча́ть **2** (have an effect) ска́з|ываться, -а́ться
□ **~ off** v.t. (infml, reprove) отчи́т|ывать, -а́ть
■ **~tale** n. сплéтник, я́беда (c.g.); (attr.) предáтельский

telling /ˈtelɪŋ/ adj. си́льный; **a ~ argument** убеди́тельный дóвод; **a ~ example** нагля́дный примéр; **a ~ blow** ощути́мый уда́р

telly /ˈtelɪ/ n. (BrE, infml) тéлик (infml)

temerity /tɪˈmerɪtɪ/ n. смéлость

temp /temp/ n. (infml) рабóтающ|ий (-ая) врéменно
● v.i. рабóтать (impf.) врéменно

temper /ˈtempə(r)/ n. **1** (disposition) нрав; (mood) настроéние; **he lost his ~** он вы́шел из себя́ **2** (anger) вспы́льчивость; несдéржанность; **he has a quick ~** он вспы́льчив(ый); **he flew into a ~** он вспыли́л; **he left in a ~** он разозли́лся и ушёл
● v.t. **1** (harden) зака́л|ивать, -и́ть **2** (mitigate) ум|еря́ть, -éрить

temperament /ˈtemprəmənt/ n. темперáмент

temperamental /ˌtemprəˈment(ə)l/ adj. капри́зный

temperate /ˈtempərət/ adj. умéренный

🔑 **temperature** /ˈtemprɪtʃə(r)/ n. температу́ра; (fever) жар; **he has (or is running) a ~** у негó температу́ра/жар

tempest /ˈtempɪst/ n. бу́ря

tempestuous /temˈpestjʊəs/ adj. бу́рный

tempi /ˈtempiː/ pl. of ▶ **tempo**

template /ˈtempleɪt/ n. модéль; (comput.) шаблóн

temple¹ /ˈtemp(ə)l/ n. (relig.) храм, святи́лище

temple² /ˈtemp(ə)l/ n. (anat.) висóк

temp|o /ˈtempəʊ/ n. (pl. **~os** or **~i**) темп

temporal /ˈtempər(ə)l/ adj. (of time) временнóй; (of this life; secular) мирскóй, свéтский; (anat.) височнáя

temporarily /ˈtempərərɪlɪ/ adv. врéменно

temporary /ˈtempərərɪ/ adj. врéменный

tempt /tempt/ *v.t.* соблазн|я́ть, -и́ть; иску|ша́ть, -си́ть; **I was ~ed to agree with him** я был склоне́н с ним согласи́ться; **~ing** соблазни́тельный

temptation /temp'teɪʃ(ə)n/ *n.* собла́зн, искуше́ние

temptress /'temptrɪs/ *n.* искуси́тельница, соблазни́тельница

⚡ **ten** /ten/ *n.* де́сять; (figure; thing numbered 10; group of **~**) деся́тка
 ● *adj.* де́сять + *g. pl.*
 ■ **~pin bowling** *n.* ке́гл|и (-ей); **~pins** *n. pl.* (AmE) = tenpin bowling

tenable /'tenəb(ə)l/ *adj.* 1 (defensible) разу́мный, здра́вый; **a ~ argument** разу́мный до́вод 2 (to be held): **the office is ~ for three years** срок полномо́чий — три го́да

tenacious /tɪ'neɪʃəs/ *adj.* насто́йчивый

tenacity /tɪ'næsɪtɪ/ *n.* це́пкость; насто́йчивость

tenancy /'tenənsɪ/ *n.* наём помеще́ния

tenant /'tenənt/ *n.* (one renting from landlord) (private individual) жиле́ц, квартира́нт; (company) аренда́тор

tend[1] /tend/ *v.t.* (look after) присм|а́тривать, -отре́ть за + *i.*

⚡ **tend**[2] /tend/ *v.i.* (be inclined) склоня́ться (*impf.*) (*к чему*); **he ~s to get excited** он легко́ возбужда́ется

tendency /'tend(ə)nsɪ/ *n.* скло́нность; **he has a ~ to forget** он забы́вчив(ый)

tender[1] /'tendə(r)/ *n.* (comm.) предложе́ние
 ● *v.t.* предл|ага́ть, -ожи́ть; **he ~ed his resignation** он по́дал заявле́ние об отста́вке

tender[2] /'tendə(r)/ *adj.* (**tenderer**, **tenderest**) 1 (sensitive, loving) не́жный; **my finger is still ~** мой па́лец всё ещё боли́т 2 (not tough): **a ~ steak** мя́гкий бифште́кс

tenderness /'tendənɪs/ *n.* не́жность; (of meat etc.) мя́гкость

tendon /'tend(ə)n/ *n.* сухожи́лие

tendril /'tendrɪl/ *n.* у́сик (*растения*)

tenement /'tenɪmənt/ *n.* (block of flats) многокварти́рный дом; (flat) кварти́ра

tenet /'tenɪt/ *n.* до́гмат, при́нцип

tenner /'tenə(r)/ *n.* (BrE, infml, ten pounds, tenpound note) деся́тка

tennis /'tenɪs/ *n.* те́ннис
 ■ **~ court** *n.* те́ннисный корт; **~ player** *n.* тенниси́ст (-ка)

tenor /'tenə(r)/ *n.* (mus.) те́нор

tense[1] /tens/ *n.* (gram.) вре́мя (*nt.*)

tense[2] /tens/ *adj.* натя́нутый, напряжённый
 ● *v.t.* натя́|гивать, -ну́ть; напр|яга́ть, -я́чь

tension /'tenʃ(ə)n/ *n.* (stretching; mental strain) напряже́ние; (stretched state) натяже́ние

tent /tent/ *n.* пала́тка

tentacle /'tentək(ə)l/ *n.* щу́пальце

tentative /'tentətɪv/ *adj.* осторо́жный

tenterhooks /'tentəhʊks/ *n. pl.*: **I was on ~** я сиде́л как на иго́лках

tenth /tenθ/ *n.* 1 (date) деся́тое число́ 2 (fraction) деся́тая часть; **one ~** одна́ деся́тая
 ● *adj.* деся́тый

tenuous /'tenjʊəs/ *adj.* сла́бый

tenure /'tenjə(r)/ *n.* (holding of office) пребыва́ние в до́лжности; (period of office) срок полномо́чий; (of property) усло́вия (*nt. pl.*) владе́ния иму́ществом; (security of **~**) постоя́нная шта́тная до́лжность

tepid /'tepɪd/ *adj.* теплова́тый

tera- /'terə/ *comb. form* тера…
 ■ **~byte** *n.* терабайт; **~watt** *n.* теравáтт

⚡ **term** /tɜːm/ *n.* 1 (fixed or limited period) пери́од; **~ of office** срок полномо́чий; (in school etc.) триме́стр, уче́бная че́тверть 2 (expression) те́рмин; **in ~s of** с то́чки зре́ния + *g.*; в смы́сле + *g.* 3 (*in pl.*) (conditions) усло́вия (*nt. pl.*); **they came to ~s** они́ пришли́ к соглаше́нию 4 (*in pl.*) (relations) отноше́ния (*nt. pl.*); **I kept on good ~s with him** я подде́рживал с ним хоро́шие отноше́ния
 ● *v.t.* наз|ыва́ть, -ва́ть

terminal /'tɜːmɪn(ə)l/ *n.* 1 (of transport) коне́чный пункт; (rail) вокза́л; **air ~** (in city) (городско́й) аэровокза́л 2 (at airport) термина́л 3 (elec.) кле́мма, зажи́м 4 (comput., *also*, where oil/gas are stored) термина́л
 ● *adj.* (coming to or forming the end point) коне́чный
 ■ **~ illness** *n.* смерте́льная боле́знь

terminate /'tɜːmɪneɪt/ *v.t.* заверш|а́ть, -и́ть
 ● *v.i.* зак|а́нчиваться, -о́нчиться

termination /tɜːmɪ'neɪʃ(ə)n/ *n.* заверше́ние; коне́ц, **~ of pregnancy** прекраще́ние бере́менности, або́рт

terminology /tɜːmɪ'nɒlədʒɪ/ *n.* терминоло́гия, номенклату́ра

terminus /'tɜːmɪnəs/ *n.* (BrE) коне́чный пункт

terrace /'terəs/ *n.* (raised area) терра́са; (BrE, row of houses) ряд однотипных домов, примыка́ющих друг к дру́гу

terraced /'terəst/ *adj.* (of land, a garden) терра́сный; (of house) стоя́щий в ряду́ однотипных домов

terracotta /terə'kɒtə/ *n.* терако́та (*жёлтая/ красная обожжённая гончарная глина*); (*attr.*) терако́товый (*из такой глины; цвет*)

terrain /te'reɪn/ *n.* ме́стность

terrapin /'terəpɪn/ *n.* пресново́дная черепа́ха

terrestrial /tə'restrɪəl/ *adj.* земно́й

terrible /'terɪb(ə)l/ *adj.* стра́шный

terribly /'terɪblɪ/ *adv.* ужа́сно, стра́шно

terrier /'terɪə(r)/ *n.* терье́р

terrific /tə'rɪfɪk/ *adj.* (infml, huge) колосса́льный; (infml, marvellous) потряса́ющий

terrify /'terɪfaɪ/ *v.t.* ужас|а́ть, -ну́ть

territorial /terɪ'tɔːrɪəl/ *adj.* территориа́льный

⚡ **territory** /'terɪtərɪ/ *n.* террито́рия

terror /'terə(r)/ *n.* у́жас, страх

⚡ **terrorism** /'terərɪz(ə)m/ *n.* террори́зм

⚡ **terrorist** /'terərɪst/ *n.* террори́ст (-ка)

terrorize /'terəraɪz/ *v.t.* терроризи́ровать (*impf., pf.*)

terse /tɜːs/ *adj.* (**terser**, **tersest**) кра́ткий, сжа́тый

t

terseness /'tɜːsnɪs/ *n.* кра́ткость, сжа́тость

tertiary /'tɜːʃərɪ/ *adj.* (geol., med., etc.) трети́чный; ~ **education** вы́сшее образова́ние

✿ **test** /test/ *n.* испыта́ние, прове́рка; **his promises were put to the** ~ его́ обеща́ния подве́рглись прове́рке на де́ле; (examination in school) контро́льная рабо́та; (at college) зачёт; (oral) опро́с, зачёт; **blood** ~ ана́лиз кро́ви
● *v.t.* **1** (make trial of) подв|ерга́ть, -е́ргнуть испыта́нию; пров|еря́ть, -е́рить **2** (subject to ~s) пров|еря́ть, -е́рить
■ ~ **case** *n.* показа́тельный слу́чай; (law) де́ло-прецеде́нт; **T~ match** *n.* (cricket, rugby) междунаро́дный матч; ~ **pilot** *n.* лётчик-испыта́тель (*m.*); ~ **tube** *n.* проби́рка; ~-**tube baby** ребёнок «из проби́рки» (*зача́тый вне матери́нского чре́ва*)

testament /'testəmənt/ *n.* (clear sign) свиде́тельство; (bibl.): **the Old/New T~** Ве́тхий/Но́вый Заве́т

testicle /'testɪk(ə)l/ *n.* (anat.) яи́чко

testify /'testɪfaɪ/ *v.i.* **1** (affirm) свиде́тельствовать (*impf.*) **2**: ~ **to** (be evidence of) свиде́тельствовать (*impf.*) о + *p.*

testimonial /testɪ'məʊnɪəl/ *n.* рекоменда́ция

testimony /'testɪmənɪ/ *n.* (statement) показа́ния (*nt. pl.*); (evidence) доказа́тельство

testosterone /te'stɒstərəʊn/ *n.* тестостеро́н

tetanus /'tetənəs/ *n.* (med.) столбня́к

tetchy /'tetʃɪ/ *adj.* (**tetchier, tetchiest**) раздражи́тельный; оби́дчивый

tête-à-tête /ˌtetɑː'tet/ *n.* тет-а-те́т
● *adv.* (to talk) тет-а-те́т; с гла́зу на гла́з; (to dine) вдвоём

tether /'teðə(r)/ *n.* при́вязь; (fig.): **he was at the end of his** ~ он дошёл до ру́чки (infml)
● *v.t.* привя́з|ывать, -а́ть

Teutonic /tjuː'tɒnɪk/ *adj.* тевто́нский, герма́нский

✿ **text** /tekst/ *n.* текст
● *v.t.* пос|ыла́ть, -ла́ть SMS/СМС (*pron.* эс-эм-э́с) (кому́)
■ ~**book** *n.* уче́бник; ~ **message** *n.* SMS/СМС-сообще́ние

textile /'tekstaɪl/ *n.* ткань

textual /'tekstʃʊəl/ *adj.* текстово́й; ~ **criticism** текстоло́гия

texture /'tekstʃə(r)/ *n.* (of fabric): **this cloth has a smooth** ~ э́та ткань мя́гкая на о́щупь

Thai /taɪ/ *n.* (*pl.* ~ **or** ~**s**) таила́нд|ец (-ка)
● *adj.* таила́ндский

Thailand /'taɪlænd/ *n.* Таила́нд

Thames /temz/ *n.* Те́мза

✿ **than** /ðæn/ *conj.* чем; **he's got more money** ~ **me** у него́ бо́льше де́нег, чем у меня́; **he is taller** ~ **me** он вы́ше меня́; **the visitor was none other** ~ **his father** посети́телем был не кто ино́й, как его́ оте́ц

✿ **thank** /θæŋk/ *v.t.* благодари́ть, по-; (by returning favour) отблагодари́ть (*pf.*); ~ **you (very much)** (большо́е) спаси́бо; ~ **God you are**

safe сла́ва бо́гу, вы в безопа́сности
■ ~ **you** *n.*: **he left without as much as a** ~ **you** он ушёл, да́же не сказа́в спаси́бо; (*attr.*) ~-**you letter** благода́рственное письмо́

thankful /'θæŋkfʊl/ *adj.* благода́рный

thankless /'θæŋklɪs/ *adj.* неблагода́рный

✿ **thanks** /θæŋks/ *n. pl.* благода́рность; ~ **for everything** спаси́бо за всё; ~ **to** благодаря́ + *d.*
■ ~**giving** *n.* **1** благодаре́ние **2**: T~**giving (Day)** День благодаре́ния

✿ **that** /ðæt/ *pron.* (*pl.* **those**) **1** (demonstrative) э́то; **those were the days!** вот э́то бы́ли времена́!; **what is** ~? что э́то (тако́е)?; **who is** ~? кто э́то?; ~'**s a nice hat!** кака́я краси́вая шля́пка!; ~'**s it!** (sc. the point) вот и́менно!; (sc. right) пра́вильно!; так!; ~ **is how the war began** вот как начала́сь война́; ~'**s right!** пра́вильно!; ве́рно!; ~'**s all** э́то всё; вот и всё!; **I'm going, and** ~'**s** ~ я ухожу́: всё; ~ **is (to say)** то́ есть **2** (*rel.*) кото́рый; **the book** ~ **I am talking about** кни́га, о кото́рой я говорю́; **he was the best man** ~ **I ever knew** он был са́мым лу́чшим челове́ком, како́го я когда́-л. знал
● *adj.* (*pl.* **those**) э́тот, тот; **I'll take** ~ **one** я возьму́ (вот) э́тот; **at** ~ **time** в то вре́мя
● *adv.*: **I can't walk** ~ **far** я не могу́ так мно́го ходи́ть; **it is not all** ~ **cold** не так уж (и) хо́лодно
● *conj.* что; **I think** ~ **you're wrong** я ду́маю, что вы непра́вы; (expr. wish) что́бы; **I wish** ~ **he would go away** я хочу́, что́бы он ушёл

thatch /θætʃ/ *n.* (straw) соло́ма; (reeds) тростни́к
● *v.t.* крыть, по- соло́мой/тростнико́м; **a** ~**ed roof** соло́менная/тростнико́вая кры́ша

thatched /θætʃt/ *adj.* соло́менный

thaw /θɔː/ *n.* (also fig.) о́ттепель
● *v.t.* (ground, river) отта́|ивать, -ять; (food) размор|а́живать, -о́зить
● *v.i.* (of ground, river) отта́|ивать, -ять; (of food) размор|а́живаться, -о́зиться; (fig.) смягч|а́ться, -и́ться

✿ **the** /ðə, ðiː/ *definite article* (*usu. untranslated*) (if more emphatic) э́тот, тот (са́мый); ~ **one with** ~ **blue handle** тот, что с голубо́й ру́чкой; **he is** ~ **man for** ~ **job** он са́мый подходя́щий челове́к для э́той рабо́ты
● *adv.*: ~ **more** ~ **better** чем бо́льше, тем лу́чше; **he was none** ~ **worse (for it)** он (при э́том) ниско́лько не пострада́л

✿ **theatre** /'θɪətə(r)/ (AmE **theater**) *n.* теа́тр
■ ~**goer** *n.* театра́л

theatrical /θɪ'ætrɪk(ə)l/ *adj.* театра́льный

theft /θeft/ *n.* кра́жа

✿ **their** /ðeə(r)/ *adj.* их; (referring to grammatical subject) свой; **they want a house of** ~ **own** они́ хотя́т име́ть (свой) со́бственный дом

theirs /ðeəz/ *pron.* их, свой; **the money was** ~ **by right** де́ньги принадлежа́ли им по пра́ву; **it is a habit of** ~ у них така́я привы́чка

✿ **them** /ðem/ *obj. of* ▶ **they**

thematic /θɪ'mætɪk/ *adj.* темати́ческий

✿ ключева́я ле́ксика

♂ **theme** /θiːm/ *n.* тéма

■ **~ park** *n.* темати́ческий парк; **~ song** (also **~ tune**) *n.* лейтмоти́в

♂ **themselves** /ðəm'selvz/ *pron.* **1** (refl.) себя́ (*d., p.* себé, *i.* собóй); -сь (*suff.*); **they blamed ~** они́ вини́ли себя́; **they were proud of ~** они́ горди́лись собóй; **did they hurt ~?** они́ уши́блись?; **they live by ~** они́ живýт одни́; **they did it by ~** они́ сдéлали э́то сáми; **they have only ~ to blame** они́ сáми винова́ты **2** (emph.): **they did the work ~** они́ сдéлали э́ту рабóту сáми

♂ **then** /ðen/ *n.*: **before ~** до э́того/тогó врéмени; **by ~** к э́тому/тому́ врéмени; **since ~** с тех пор

● *adv.* **1** (at that time) тогдá **2** (next) дáльше, дáлее **3** (furthermore) крóме тогó; опя́ть-таки (infml) **4** (in that case) тогдá; **~ what do you want?** чегó же вы тогдá (*or* в такóм слýчае) хоти́те?

thence /ðens/ *adv.* оттýда

theologian /θɪə'ləʊdʒ(ə)n/ *n.* богослóв, теóлог

theological /θɪə'lɒdʒɪk(ə)l/ *adj.* богослóвский, теологи́ческий

theology /θɪ'ɒlədʒɪ/ *n.* богослóвие, теоло́гия

theorem /'θɪərəm/ *n.* теорéма

theoretical /θɪə'retɪk(ə)l/ *adj.* теорети́ческий

theorist /'θɪərɪst/ *n.* теорéтик

theorize /'θɪəraɪz/ *v.i.* теоретизи́ровать (*impf.*)

♂ **theory** /'θɪərɪ/ *n.* теóрия; **in ~** в теóрии; теорети́чески

therapeutic /θerə'pjuːtɪk/ *adj.* терапевти́ческий, лечéбный

therapist /'θerəpɪst/ *n.* терапéвт

♂ **therapy** /'θerəpɪ/ *n.* терапи́я, лечéние

♂ **there** /ðeə(r)/ *adv.* **1** (in or at that place) там; вон (infml); вон тáм; **that man ~ is my uncle** (вот) тот человéк — мой дя́дя **2** (to that place) тудá **3** (at that point) тут, здесь **4** (demonstrative): **~ you go again!** опя́ть вы за своё!; **~ you are, take it!** вот вам, держи́те!; **oh, ~ you are!: I was looking for you** вот и вы! А я вас искáл **5** (with v. 'to be', expr. presence, availability, etc.): **~'s a fly in my soup** у меня́ в сýпе мýха; **is ~ a doctor here?** тут есть врач?; **~ seems to have been a mistake** тут, кáжется, произошлá оши́бка; **~ was plenty to eat** едьí бы́ло полнó

● *int.*: **~! what did I tell you?** ну вот! что з вам говори́л?

thereabouts /ˈðeərə'baʊts/ *adv.* (nearby) побли́зости; (approximately) óколо э́того; приблизи́тельно

thereby /ðeə'baɪ/ *adv.* э́тим

♂ **therefore** /'ðeəfɔː(r)/ *adv.* поэ́тому, слéдовательно

thereupon /ðeərə'pɒn/ *adv.* за э́тим

thermal /'θəːm(ə)l/ *n.* (aeron.) восходя́щий потóк тёплого вóздуха

● *adj.*: **~ capacity** теплоёмкость; **~ reactor** (я́дерный) реáктор на теплов́ых нейтрóнах, теплов́ой я́дерный реáктор; **~ springs** горя́чие истóчники; **~ underwear**

───────────────

термобельё

thermodynamics /θəːməʊdaɪ'næmɪks/ *n.* термодинáмика

thermometer /θə'mɒmɪtə(r)/ *n.* термóметр

Thermos® /'θəːməs/ *n.* (*in full* **~ flask**) тéрмос

thermostat /'θəːməstæt/ *n.* термостáт

thesaurus /θɪ'sɔːrəs/ *n.* тезáурус

these /ðiːz/ *pl. of* ▸ **this**

thesis /'θiːsɪs/ *n.* (*pl.* **theses** /-siːz/) (dissertation) диссертáция; (contention) тéзис

thespian /'θespɪən/ *n.* (joc.) актёр (-ри́са)

♂ **they** /ðeɪ/ *pers. pron.* (*obj.* **them**, *poss.* **their**, **theirs**) они́; **~ who ... те, котóрые/кто...;** **both of them** они́ óба

thick /θɪk/ *n.*: **in the ~ of the crowd** в гýще толпьí; **in the ~ of the fighting** в сáмом пéкле бóя

● *adj.* **1** (of solid substance) тóлстый; (of liquid) густóй **2** (dense) густóй **3** (infml, stupid) тупóй

● *adv.* гýсто, чáсто; **the blows came ~ and fast** удáры сы́пались оди́н за другим

■ **~set** *adj.* коренáстый; **~-skinned** *adj.* (lit., fig.) толстокóжий

thicken /'θɪkən/ *v.t.* сгу|щáть, -сти́ть; дéлать, с- бóлее густьíм

● *v.i.* (liquid) дéлаться, с- бóлее густьíм; (fog) сгу|щáться, -сти́ться

thicket /'θɪkɪt/ *n.* зáросл|и (-ей)

thickness /'θɪknɪs/ *n.* толщинá, густотá; (layer) слой

thief /θiːf/ *n.* (*pl.* **thieves**) вор

thieve /θiːv/ *v.i.* красть, у-; ворова́ть, (infml pf.) с-

thieves /θiːvz/ *pl. of* ▸ **thief**

thigh /θaɪ/ *n.* бедрó

thimble /'θɪmb(ə)l/ *n.* напёрсток

thin /θɪn/ *adj.* (**thinner**, **thinnest**) **1** (not fat; of person) худóй; (of body, parts of body) тóнкий; **she has got ~** онá похудéла **2** (not thick; of paper, blanket) тóнкий **3** (not dense; of hair) рéдкий **4** (of liquids) жи́дкий

● *adv.* тóнко

● *v.t.* (**thinned**, **thinning**) (liquid) разб|авля́ть, -áвить

● *v.i.* (**thinned**, **thinning**): **the crowd ~ned (out)** толпá поредéла; **his hair is ~ning** у негó редéют вóлосы

♂ **thing** /θɪŋ/ *n.* **1** (object) вещь, предмéт **2** (*in pl.*) (belongings) имýщество; вéщи (*f. pl.*) **3** (*in pl.*) (equipment) принадлéжности (*f. pl.*) **4** (matter) дéло; вещь; **for one ~, he's too old** начнём с тогó, что он сли́шком стар; **how are ~s?** как делá?; **all ~s considered** принимáя во внимáние всё **5** (act) дéйствие; постýпок; **that was a silly ~ to do** э́то был глýпый постýпок **6** (event): **what a terrible ~ to happen!** какóе ужáсное несчáстье! **7** (remark): **what a ~ to say!** как мóжно сказáть такóе! **8** (issue): **the ~ is, can you afford it?** хвáтит ли у вас на э́то дéнег? — вот в чём дéло **9** (a ~): (something): **it's a ~ I have never done before** я э́того никогдá рáньше не дéлал; (*with neg.*) nothing; **I can't** see a ~ я ничего не ви́жу **10** (of persons or animals) созда́ние; poor ~ бедня́га (*c.g.*)

⚜ **think** /θɪŋk/ *v.t. & i.* (*past and p.p.* **thought**) (opine) ду́мать, по-; полага́ть (*impf.*); счита́ть (*impf.*); **I** ~ (я) ду́маю; мне ка́жется; **I don't** ~ **so** не ду́маю; **yes, I** ~ **so** да, пожа́луй; **I** ~ **I'll go** я, пожа́луй, пойду́; (judge) ду́мать, счита́ть, полага́ть (all *impf.*); **do you** ~ **she's pretty?** вы ду́маете она́ хоро́шенькая?/вы счита́ете её хоро́шенькой?; (reflect) ду́мать, по-; мы́слить (*impf.*); (expect) ду́мать (*impf.*); (imagine): **I can't** ~ **how he does it** я не могу́ себе́ предста́вить, как он э́то де́лает; (*with preps. about/of*) **I have other things to** ~ **about** у меня́ мно́го други́х забо́т; **have you thought about going to the police?** вы не ду́мали пойти́ в поли́цию?; **I couldn't** ~ **of his name** я не мог вспо́мнить, как его́ зову́т; **who first thought of the idea?** кому́ пе́рвому пришла́ в го́лову э́та иде́я? ● *with advs.*: ~ **it over!** обду́майте э́то!; **he never** ~s **his answers through** он никогда́ не проду́мывает свои́ отве́ты (до конца́); ~ **up** (devise) приду́м|ывать, -ать; (invent) выду́мывать, вы́думать

■ ~ **tank** *n.* (infml) мозгово́й центр

thinker /'θɪŋkə(r)/ *n.* мысли́тель (*m.*); **he is a quick** ~ он бы́стро сообража́ет

thinking /'θɪŋkɪŋ/ *n.* **1** (process of thought) размышле́ние **2** (opinion) мне́ние; **to my way of** ~ на мой взгляд

⚜ **third** /θɜ:d/ *n.* **1** (date) тре́тье (число́); **my birthday is on the** ~ мой день рожде́ния тре́тьего (числа́) **2** (fraction) треть; **two** ~s две тре́ти ● *adj.* тре́тий; **the T**~ **World** тре́тий мир

■ ~**-class** *adj.* тре́тьего кла́сса; ~**-generation** *adj.* тре́тьего поколе́ния; ~ **party** *n.* (law etc.) тре́тья сторона́

thirdly /'θɜ:dlɪ/ *adv.* в-тре́тьих

thirst /θɜ:st/ *n.* жа́жда; ~ **for knowledge** жа́жда зна́ний

thirsty /'θɜ:stɪ/ *adj.* (**thirstier, thirstiest**) испы́тывающий жа́жду; **I am/feel** ~ мне хо́чется (*or* я хочу́) пить

thirteen /θɜ:'ti:n/ *n.* трина́дцать ● *adj.* трина́дцать + *g. pl.*

thirteenth /θɜ:'ti:nθ/ *n.* (date) трина́дцатое число́; (fraction) одна́ трина́дцатая ● *adj.* трина́дцатый

thirtieth /'θɜ:tɪɪθ/ *n.* (date) тридца́тое число́; (fraction) одна́ тридца́тая ● *adj.* тридца́тый

thirt|y /'θɜ:tɪ/ *n.* три́дцать; **in the** ~**ies** в тридца́тых года́х; **he is in his** ~**ies** ему́ за три́дцать ● *adj.* три́дцать + *g. pl.*

⚜ **this** /ðɪs/ *pron.* (*pl.* **these**) э́то; ~ **is what I think** вот, что я ду́маю; **are these your shoes?** э́то ва́ши ту́фли?; **we talked of** ~ **and that** мы (по)говори́ли о том, о сём ● *adj.* (*pl.* **these**) э́тот; да́нный; ~ **book here** вот э́та кни́га; **come here** ~ **minute!** иди́

сюда́ сию́ же мину́ту!; **these days** (nowadays) в настоя́щее вре́мя, в на́ши дни ● *adv.*: **about** ~ **high** приме́рно тако́й высоты́

thistle /'θɪs(ə)l/ *n.* чертополо́х

thong /θɒŋ/ *n.* **1** реме́нь (*m.*) **2** (garment) тру́сик|и (*pl., g.* -ов) «та́нга», та́нга (*pl. indecl.*), стри́нг|и (*pl., g.* -ов)

thorn /θɔ:n/ *n.* колю́чка, шип

thorny /'θɔ:nɪ/ *adj.* (**thornier, thorniest**) колю́чий; (fig.): **a** ~ **problem** сло́жная пробле́ма

thorough /'θʌrə/ *adj.* (search, investigation) тща́тельный, всесторо́нний; (person) скрупулёзный

■ ~**bred** *n.* чистопоро́дное живо́тное ● *adj.* чистокро́вный, чистопоро́дный; ~**fare** *n.* тра́нспортная магистра́ль; **'No** ~**fare!'** «прохо́да/прое́зда нет!»

thoroughly /'θʌrəlɪ/ *adv.* (satisfied, ashamed) соверше́нно; (study) тща́тельно

thoroughness /'θʌrənɪs/ *n.* тща́тельность; основа́тельность; скрупулёзность

those /ðəʊz/ *pl. of* ▸ that

⚜ **though** /ðəʊ/ *adv. & conj.* хотя́, хоть; несмотря́ на то, что…; **even** ~ **it's late** пусть уже́ по́здно, но…; **he said he would come; he didn't,** ~ он сказа́л, что придёт; одна́ко же не пришёл; **as** ~ как бу́дто бы; **it looks as** ~ **he will lose** похо́же на то, что он проигра́ет

⚜ **thought¹** /θɔ:t/ *n.* **1** (thinking) мысль; **modern scientific** ~ совреме́нная нау́чная мысль **2** (reflection) размышле́ние; **deep in** ~ погружённый в размышле́ния; **on second** ~s поду́мав **3** (idea, opinion) мысль, иде́я, соображе́ние

■ ~**-provoking** *adj.* заставля́ющий (серьёзно) заду́маться

thought² /θɔ:t/ *past and p.p. of* ▸ think

thoughtful /'θɔ:tfʊl/ *adj.* **1** (well considered): **a** ~ **essay** вду́мчивое/содержа́тельное эссе́ **2** (considerate) внима́тельный, чу́ткий

thoughtless /'θɔ:tlɪs/ *adj.* (careless) неосмотри́тельный; (inconsiderate) невнима́тельный

⚜ **thousand** /'θaʊz(ə)nd/ *n. & adj.* (*pl.* ~s *or* (with numeral or qualifying word) ~) ты́сяча + *g. pl.*

thousandth /'θaʊzəndθ/ *n.* ты́сячная часть ● *adj.* ты́сячный

thrash /θræʃ/ *v.t.* (beat) изб|ива́ть, -и́ть; (fig., defeat) побе|жда́ть, -ди́ть ● *v.i.*: **the swimmer** ~**ed about in the water** плове́ц изо всех сил колоти́л рука́ми и нога́ми по воде́; **he** ~**ed about in bed** он мета́лся в посте́ли □ ~ **out** *v.t.* (fig.) обстоя́тельно обсу|жда́ть, -ди́ть; **let us** ~ **out this problem** дава́йте разберём э́тот вопро́с по пу́нктам

thread /θred/ *n.* **1** (spun fibre) нить, ни́тка; **he lost the** ~ **of his argument** он потеря́л нить рассужде́ний **2** (of a screw etc.) резьба́ ● *v.t.* прод|ева́ть, -е́ть ни́тку в + *a.*; нани́з|ывать, -а́ть

■ ~**bare** *adj.* потёртый

✓ **threat** /θret/ *n.* угро́за

✓ **threaten** /'θret(ə)n/ *v.t. & i.* грози́ть, при- + *d.*; **he ~ed to leave** он угрожа́л, что уйдёт; он грози́лся уйти́

✓ **three** /θriː/ *n.* (число́/но́мер) три; (**~ people**) тро́е; (figure, thing numbered 3; group of **~**) тро́йка
● *adj.* три + *g. sg.*
■ **~-cornered** *adj.* треуго́льный; **~-dimensional** *adj.* (lit.) трёхме́рный; **~-fold** *adv.* втро́е; **~-piece** *adj.*: **~-piece suit** (костю́м-)тро́йка; **~-piece suite** дива́н с двумя́ кре́слами; **~-year-old** *adj.* трёхле́тний

threshold /'θreʃhəʊld/ *n.* поро́г

threw /θruː/ *past of* ▶ throw

thrift /θrɪft/ *n.* бережли́вость, эконо́мность

thrifty /'θrɪftɪ/ *adj.* (**thriftier, thriftiest**) бережли́вый, эконо́мный

thrill /θrɪl/ *n.* (physical sensation) дрожь, тре́пет; (excitement) восто́рг, восхище́ние
● *v.t.* восхи|ща́ть, -ти́ть; **a ~ing finish** захва́тывающий коне́ц

thriller /'θrɪlə(r)/ *n.* три́ллер

thrive /θraɪv/ *v.i.* (prosper) процвета́ть (*impf.*); (grow vigorously) разраст|а́ться, -и́сь

throat /θrəʊt/ *n.* го́рло; **I have a sore ~** у меня́ боли́т го́рло

throb /θrɒb/ *v.i.* (**throbbed, throbbing**) стуча́ть (*impf.*)

thrombosis /θrɒm'bəʊsɪs/ *n.* (*pl.* **thromboses** /-siːz/) (med.) тромбо́з

throne /θrəʊn/ *n.* трон, престо́л

throng /θrɒŋ/ *n.* толпа́
● *v.i.* ст|ека́ться, -е́чься

throttle /'θrɒt(ə)l/ *v.t.* души́ть, за-

✓ **through** /θruː/ *adj.* **1** прямо́й; сквозно́й; **'No ~ road!'** (as notice) «проезда нет!»; **a ~ train** прямо́й по́езд **2** (various pred. uses): **you must wait till I'm ~** (*finished*) **with the paper** вам придётся подожда́ть, пока́ я дочита́ю газе́ту; **she told him she was ~ with him** она́ ему́ сказа́ла, что ме́жду ни́ми всё ко́нчено
● *adv.* (from beginning to end; completely) до конца́; **have you read it ~?** вы всё прочита́ли?; **you will get wet ~** вы промо́кнете наскво́зь; **the whole night ~** всю ночь напролёт; (all the way): **the train goes ~ to Paris** по́езд идёт пря́мо до Пари́жа
● *prep.* **1** че́рез + *a.*; **he came ~ the window** он влез че́рез окно́; (esp. suggesting difficulty) сквозь + *a.*; (into, in) в + *a.*; **look ~ the window!** посмотри́(те) в окно́!; (via): **we drove ~ Germany** мы е́хали че́рез Герма́нию **2** (during) в тече́ние + *g.* **3** (from, because of) из-за + *g.*; по + *d.*; **~ laziness** из-за ле́ни; **~ stupidity** по глу́пости; (of desirable result) благодаря́ + *d.* **4** (AmE, up to and including): **from Monday ~ Saturday** с понеде́льника по суббо́ту включи́тельно **5** (over the area of): **the news quickly spread ~ the town** весть бы́стро распространи́лась по го́роду
■ **~way** *n.* (AmE) автостра́да

✓ **throughout** /θruː'aʊt/ *adv.* (in every part) везде́; повсю́ду; (in all respects) во всём
● *prep.* (from end to end of) че́рез + *a.*; **~ the**

country по всей стране́; (for the duration of): **~ the 20th century** на протяже́нии всего́ XX двадца́того ве́ка; **it rained ~ the night** всю ночь шёл дождь

✓ **throw** /θrəʊ/ *n.* **1** (act of **~**ing) броса́ние, мета́ние **2** (in wrestling) бросо́к
● *v.t.* (*past* **threw**, *p.p.* **thrown**) **1** бр|оса́ть, -о́сить; кида́ть, ки́нуть; **his horse threw him** ло́шадь сбро́сила его́; **the news threw me** (infml) изве́стие потрясло́ меня́ **2** (organize) устр|а́ивать, -о́ить; **let's ~ a party** дава́йте устро́им вечери́нку
□ **~ away** *v.t.* (discard) выбра́сывать, вы́бросить; (forgo) упус|ка́ть, -ти́ть
□ **~ back** *v.t.* отбр|а́сывать, -о́сить наза́д
□ **~ in** *v.t.* вбр|а́сывать, -о́сить; (fig., include) доб|авля́ть, -а́вить; (contribute): **may I ~ in a suggestion?** разреши́те мне внести́ предложе́ние?
□ **~ off** *v.t.* сбр|а́сывать, -о́сить; **he threw off his clothes** он сбро́сил с себя́ оде́жду
□ **~ on** *v.t.*: **he threw on a coat** он набро́сил пальто́
□ **~ out** *v.t.* выбра́сывать, вы́бросить; (reject) отклон|я́ть, -и́ть; (expel) исключ|а́ть, -и́ть; **~ the rubbish out** выбрасывайте, выбросьте
□ **~ together** *v.t.* (compile) сост|авля́ть, -а́вить; (bring into contact) соб|ира́ть, -ра́ть вме́сте
□ **~ up** *v.t.* подбр|а́сывать, -о́сить
● *v.i.* (vomit): **he threw up** его́ вы́рвало
■ **~away** *adj.* ра́зового по́льзования; **~-in** *n.* вбра́сывание (мяча́) (*в футбо́ле и ре́гби*)

thrown /θrəʊn/ *p.p. of* ▶ throw

thrush¹ /θrʌʃ/ *n.* (bird) дрозд

thrush² /θrʌʃ/ *n.* (disease) моло́чница

thrust /θrʌst/ *n.* толчо́к
● *v.t.* (*past and p.p.* **thrust**) толк|а́ть, -ну́ть; **he ~ a note into my hand** он су́нул мне в ру́ку запи́ску

thud /θʌd/ *n.* глухо́й звук; стук
● *v.i.* (**thudded, thudding**) глу́хо уд|аря́ться, -а́риться

thug /θʌg/ *n.* банди́т, головоре́з

thuggery /'θʌɡərɪ/ *n.* бандити́зм, хулига́нство

thuggish /'θʌɡɪʃ/ *adj.* хулига́нский

thumb /θʌm/ *n.* большо́й па́лец (руки́); **~s down** знак неодобре́ния; **~s up** знак одобре́ния; **he is completely under her ~** он по́лностью у неё под каблуко́м
● *v.t.* **1**: **~ through** перели́ст|ывать, -а́ть **2**: **~ a lift** (infml) голосова́ть (*impf.*)
■ **~tack** *n.* (AmE) кно́пка

thump /θʌmp/ *n.* (blow) тяжёлый уда́р; (noise) глухо́й стук/шум
● *v.t.* бить (*impf.*); колоти́ть (*impf.*)
● *v.i.* би́ться (*impf.*); колоти́ться (*impf.*)

thunder /'θʌndə(r)/ *n.* гром
● *v.i.*: **it is ~ing** гром греми́т
■ **~bolt** *n.* уда́р мо́лнии; **~clap** *n.* уда́р гро́ма; **~storm** *n.* гроза́; **~struck** *adj.* (fig.) ошеломлённый

✓ **Thursday** /'θɜːzdeɪ/ *n.* четве́рг

✓ **thus** /ðʌs/ *adv.* (in this way) таки́м о́бразом;

t

(accordingly) сле́довательно, таки́м о́бразом

thwart /θwɔːt/ *v.t.* меша́ть, по- + *d.*; **∼ sb's plans** расстра́|ивать, -о́ить чьи-н. пла́ны

thyme /taɪm/ *n.* тимья́н

thyroid /'θaɪrɔɪd/ *n.* (*in full* ∼ **gland**) щитови́дная железа́

tiara /tɪ'ɑːrə/ *n.* тиа́ра, диаде́ма

Tibet /tɪ'bet/ *n.* Тибе́т

Tibetan /tɪ'bet(ə)n/ *n.* тибе́т|ец (-ка)
• *adj.* тибе́тский

tick¹ /tɪk/ *n.* **1** (of clock etc.) ти́канье; ∼**-tock** тик-та́к **2** (checking mark) га́лочка, пти́чка
• *v.i.* ти́кать (*impf.*)
• *v.t.* отм|еча́ть, -е́тить га́лочкой
□ ∼ **off** *v.t.* (infml, reprove) отчи́т|ывать, -а́ть; (mark with ∼): **she** ∼**ed off the items** она́ отмеча́ла предме́ты га́лочками

tick² /tɪk/ *n.* (parasite) клещ

ɗ **ticket** /'tɪkɪt/ *n.* (for travel, seating, etc.) биле́т; (tag) ярлы́к; (AmE, list of election candidates) спи́сок кандида́тов на вы́борах; (printed notice of offence): **he got a** ∼ **for speeding** он получи́л штраф за превыше́ние ско́рости
■ ∼ **office** *n.* биле́тная ка́сса

tickle /'tɪk(ə)l/ *v.t.* щекота́ть, по-

ticklish /'tɪklɪʃ/ *adj.*: **she is** ∼ она́ бои́тся щеко́тки; (tricky) щекотли́вый

tidal /'taɪd(ə)l/ *adj.* прили́вный
■ ∼ **wave** *n.* прили́вная волна́

tidbit /'tɪdbɪt/ *n.* (AmE) = **titbit**

tide /taɪd/ *n.* (rise) морско́й прили́в; (fall) морско́й отли́в; (fig.) волна́, тече́ние; **the rising** ∼ **of excitement** уси́ливающееся возбужде́ние

tidiness /'taɪdɪnɪs/ *n.* аккура́тность, опря́тность

tidings /'taɪdɪŋz/ *n. pl.* (liter. and joc.) ве́сти (*f. pl.*), но́вости (*f. pl.*)

tidy /'taɪdɪ/ *adj.* (**tidier, tidiest**) (neat) опря́тный, аккура́тный; (considerable): **a** ∼ **sum** прили́чная су́мма
• *v.t.* (*also* ∼ **up**) прив|оди́ть, -ести́ в поря́док; приб|ира́ть, -ра́ть
• *v.i.* (*usu.* ∼ **up**) нав|оди́ть, -ести́ поря́док

ɗ **tie** /taɪ/ *n.* **1** (*also* **neck** ∼) га́лстук **2** (part that fastens or connects) завя́зка, связь; шнуро́к **3** (fig., bond) у́з|ы (*pl.*, *g.* —) **4** (fig., restriction) обу́за **5** (equal score) ничья́; **the match ended in a** ∼ матч зако́нчился ничье́й/вничью́
• *v.t.* (**tying**) **1** (fasten) свя́з|ывать, -а́ть; привя́з|ывать, -а́ть **2** (arrange in bow or knot) перевя́з|ывать, -а́ть; завя́з|ывать, -а́ть; шнурова́ть, за-
• *v.i.* (**tying**) **1** (fasten) завя́з|ываться, -а́ться **2** (make equal score) равня́ть, с- счёт; игра́ть, сыгра́ть вничью́
□ ∼ **back** *v.t.*: **she wore her hair** ∼**d back** она́ завя́зывала во́лосы сза́ди
□ ∼ **down** *v.t.* (lit.) привя́з|ывать, -а́ть; (fig., restrict) свя́з|ывать, -а́ть
□ ∼ **in (with)** *v.i.* соотве́тствовать (*impf.*)

ɗ ключева́я ле́ксика

(+ *d.*); согласо́в|ываться, -а́ться (с + *i.*)
□ ∼ **up** *v.t.* (lit.) привя́з|ывать, -а́ть; свя́з|ывать, -а́ть; (fig.): **I'm** ∼**d up this week** на э́той неде́ле у меня́ дел под завя́зку; **his capital is** ∼**d up** его́ капита́л инвести́рован
■ ∼**breaker** *n.* реша́ющая игра́ (*после ничьей*)

tier /tɪə(r)/ *n.* ряд; я́рус

tiff /tɪf/ *n.* (infml) размо́лвка

tiger /'taɪɡə(r)/ *n.* тигр

tight /taɪt/ *adj.* **1** (with no slack) туго́й; (close-fitting) те́сный; (of clothes) облега́ющий; **my shoes are too** ∼ мои́ ту́фли жмут **2** (strict) стро́гий **3** (under pressure): **I have a** ∼ **schedule** у меня́ жёсткое расписа́ние
• *adv.* (fitting) те́сно, пло́тно; (screwed) кре́пко; (stretched) туго́; **hold** ∼! держи́тесь кре́пко!; **shut your eyes** ∼! кре́пко зажму́рьте глаза́!
■ ∼**-fisted** *adj.* скупо́й, прижи́мистый; ∼**(ly)-fitting** *adj.* пло́тно облега́ющий; ∼**rope** *n.* натя́нутый кана́т

tighten /'taɪt(ə)n/ *v.t.* (grip) сж|има́ть, -а́ть; (bonds) закреп|ля́ть, -и́ть; (screw, belt) затя́г|ивать, -яну́ть

tights /taɪts/ *n. pl.* (BrE) колго́т|ки (-ок)

tigress /'taɪɡrɪs/ *n.* тигри́ца

tile /taɪl/ *n.* (for roof) черепи́ца; (for floor etc.) пли́тка
• *v.t.* (roof) крыть, по- черепи́цей; (walls) крыть, по- пли́ткой

till¹ /tɪl/ *n.* ка́сса

till² /tɪl/ (*see also* ▶ **until**) *prep.* до + *g.*; **he will not come** ∼ **after dinner** он придёт то́лько по́сле у́жина
• *conj.* пока́... (не); до тех пор пока́ (не); **don't go** ∼ **I come back** не уходи́те, пока́ я не верну́сь

tilt /tɪlt/ *v.t.* наклон|я́ть, -и́ть
• *v.i.* (slope) наклон|я́ться, -и́ться

timber /'tɪmbə(r)/ *n.* (wood) древеси́на; (trees) лес; (beam) ба́лка

timbre /'tæmbə(r)/ *n.* тембр

ɗ **time** /taɪm/ *n.* **1** вре́мя (*nt.*); **in** ∼, **with** ∼ с тече́нием вре́мени; ∼ **will tell** вре́мя пока́жет **2** (duration, period, opportunity): **after a** ∼ че́рез не́которое вре́мя; **all the** ∼ всё вре́мя, всегда́; **all in good** ∼ всему́ своё вре́мя; **in no** ∼ (at all) момента́льно; **I haven't seen him for a long** ∼ я его́ давно́ не ви́дел; **take your** ∼! не торопи́тесь! **3** (experience): **have a good** ∼! жела́ю вам прия́тно провести́ вре́мя; **we had the** ∼ **of our lives** мы отли́чно провели́ вре́мя **4** (∼ of day or night) час, вре́мя; **what's the** ∼? кото́рый час?, ско́лько вре́мени?; **what** ∼ **do you make it?** ско́лько на ва́ших (часа́х)?; **the** ∼ **is 8 o'clock** сейча́с 8 часо́в; **at that** ∼ (hour) в э́тот час; **what** ∼ **do you go to bed?** в кото́ром часу́ вы ложи́тесь спать? **5** (moment) вре́мя; **I was away at the** ∼ меня́ тогда́ (*or* в то вре́мя) не́ было; **at** ∼**s** иногда́, времена́ми; **at all** ∼**s** всегда́; во всех слу́чаях; **by the** ∼ **I got back he had gone** (к тому́ вре́мени,) когда́ я верну́лся, его́ уже́ не́ было; **from** ∼ **to** ∼ иногда́, вре́мя от вре́мени; **it's** ∼ **for bed** пора́ спать; **the train was on** ∼ по́езд пришёл

во́время **6** (occasion) раз; **nine ~s out of ten** в девяти́ слу́чаях из десяти́; **another ~** когда́-нибудь; в друго́й раз; **one at a ~!** по одному́; не все сра́зу!; **the first ~ I saw him** когда́ я впервы́е (*or* в пе́рвый раз) уви́дел его́ **7** (in multiplication): **6 ~s 2 is 12** 6 (умно́жить) на 2 — 12; ше́стью два — двена́дцать **8** (period) вре́мя, времена́ (*nt. pl.*), эпо́ха **9** (mus.) такт, ритм; **in ~ with the music** в такт му́зыке
• *v.t.* **1** (do at a chosen ~) выбира́ть, вы́брать вре́мя для + *g.* **2** (measure ~ of or for) зас|ека́ть, -е́чь вре́мя + *g.* **3** (schedule): **the train was ~d to leave at 6** по́езд до́лжен был отойти́ в 6 часо́в

■ **~ bomb** *n.* бо́мба заме́дленного де́йствия; **~-consuming** *adj.* тре́бующий мно́го вре́мени; **~ limit** *n.* преде́льный срок; **~ off** *n.* о́тпуск; **~share** *n.* та́ймшер, совме́стное владе́ние куро́ртным помеще́нием; **~table** *n.* расписа́ние; гра́фик; **~ zone** *n.* часово́й по́яс

timeless /ˈtaɪmlɪs/ *adj.* ве́чный

timely /ˈtaɪmli/ *adj.* (**timelier, timeliest**) своевре́менный

timer /ˈtaɪmə(r)/ *n.* та́ймер, часово́й механи́зм

timid /ˈtɪmɪd/ *adj.* (**timider, timidest**) засте́нчивый

timing /ˈtaɪmɪŋ/ *n.* (choosing of appropriate ~) вы́бор (наибо́лее подходя́щего) вре́мени

timpani, tympani /ˈtɪmpəni/ *n.* лита́вры (*f. pl.*)

timpanist, tympanist /ˈtɪmpənɪst/ *n.* литаври́ст

tin /tɪn/ *n.* **1** (metal) о́лово **2** (container) (жестяна́я) ба́нка; (*also* **tin can**) (BrE, for preserving food) консе́рвная ба́нка; (for biscuits) (металли́ческая) коро́бка **3** (for baking cakes) фо́рма; (for roasting) про́тивень (*m.*)
• *v.t.* (**tinned, tinning**) консерви́ровать, за-; **~ned goods** консерви́рованные проду́кты

■ **~foil** *n.* фольга́; **~ opener** *n.* (BrE) консе́рвный нож

tinge /tɪndʒ/ *n.* отте́нок
• *v.t.* (**tinging** *or* **tingeing**) слегка́ окра́|шивать, -сить; (fig.): **her voice was ~d with regret** в её го́лосе звуча́ло лёгкое сожале́ние

tingl|e /ˈtɪŋɡ(ə)l/, **tingling** /ˈtɪŋɡlɪŋ/ *nn.* пощи́пывание; (of pleasure etc.) тре́пет
• *v.i.*: **a ~ing sensation** ощуще́ние пощи́пывания; **they were ~ing with excitement** они́ дрожа́ли от возбужде́ния

tinker /ˈtɪŋkə(r)/ *v.i.* (meddle etc.) вози́ться (*impf.*)/ (с чем)

tinkle /ˈtɪŋk(ə)l/ *n.* (sound) звон; звя́канье
• *v.i.*: **the bell ~d** колоко́льчик зазвене́л

tinsel /ˈtɪns(ə)l/ *n.* мишура́

tint /tɪnt/ *n.* отте́нок; тон
• *v.t.*: **~ed glasses** тёмные очки́

⚒ **tiny** /ˈtaɪni/ *adj.* (**tinier, tiniest**) кро́шечный

tip¹ /tɪp/ *n.* (pointed end) ко́нчик; верху́шка; (part attached, e.g. of arrow) наконе́чник; **the ~s of my fingers are freezing** у меня́ мёрзнут ко́нчики па́льцев

■ **~toe** *n.*: **on ~toe(s)** на цы́почках • *v.i.* ходи́ть (*indet.*) на цы́почках

tip² /tɪp/ *n.* (BrE, for rubbish) сва́лка
• *v.t.* (**tipped, tipping**) **1** (tilt) наклон|я́ть, -и́ть **2** (overturn) выва́ливать, вы́валить; опорожн|я́ть, -и́ть
□ **~ over** *v.t. & i.* опроки́|дывать(ся), -нуть(ся): **the boat ~ped over** ло́дка переверну́лась

tip³ /tɪp/ *n.* **1** (piece of advice) сове́т; намёк **2** (gratuity) чаев|ы́е (-ы́х)
• *v.t.* (**tipped, tipping**) **1** (BrE, predict): **the horse was ~ped to win** предска́зывали, что победи́т э́та ло́шадь **2** (remunerate) да|ва́ть, -ть на чай + *d.*
□ **~ off** *v.t.* (infml) предупре|жда́ть, -ди́ть
■ **~-off** *n.* (infml): **the police had a ~-off** поли́цию предупреди́ли

Tipp-Ex®, Tippex /ˈtɪpeks/ *n.* (BrE) корректи́рующая жи́дкость

tipple /ˈtɪp(ə)l/ *n.* (infml) напи́ток, питьё
• *v.i.* выпива́ть (*impf.*)

tipster /ˈtɪpstə(r)/ *n.* (at races) «жучо́к» (*на ска́чках*)

tipsy /ˈtɪpsi/ *adj.* (**tipsier, tipsiest**) подвы́пивший; (*pred.*) навеселе́

tirade /taɪˈreɪd/ *n.* тира́да

tire¹ /ˈtaɪə(r)/ *n.* (AmE) = **tyre**

tire² /ˈtaɪə(r)/ *v.t.* утом|ля́ть, -и́ть
• *v.i.* утом|ля́ться, -и́ться; уст|ава́ть, -а́ть

tired /ˈtaɪəd/ *adj.* уста́лый; **she's ~** она́ уста́ла; **I'm ~ out** я соверше́нно вы́мотался (infml); **you will soon get ~ of him** вы ско́ро от него́ уста́нете

tireless /ˈtaɪəlɪs/ *adj.* неутоми́мый

tiresome /ˈtaɪəsəm/ *adj.* надое́дливый, ну́дный

tissue /ˈtɪʃuː/ *n.* (handkerchief) салфе́тка; (text., biol.) ткань
■ **~ paper** *n.* то́нкая обёрточная бума́га

tit¹ /tɪt/ *n.* (bird) сини́ца

tit² /tɪt/ *n.* (vulg., breast) си́ська (infml)

titbit /ˈtɪtbɪt/ (AmE **tidbit** /ˈtɪdbɪt/) *n.* ла́комый кусо́чек; (fig.): **a ~ of news** пика́нтная но́вость

titillate /ˈtɪtɪleɪt/ *v.t.* (tickle) щекота́ть (*impf.*); (excite) прия́тно возбу|жда́ть, -ди́ть

titivate /ˈtɪtɪveɪt/ *v.i.* прихора́шиваться (*impf.*)

⚒ **title** /ˈtaɪt(ə)l/ *n.* **1** (of book etc.) назва́ние **2** (of rank etc.) ти́тул
■ **~-holder** *n.* чемпио́н; **~ role** *n.* загла́вная роль

titter /ˈtɪtə(r)/ *n.* хихи́канье
• *v.i.* хихи́кать (*impf.*)

tiz /tɪz/, **tizzy** /ˈtɪzi/ *nn.* (infml) возбужде́ние, ажиота́ж; **she got into a ~** она́ пришла́ в стра́шное возбужде́ние

⚒ **to** /tuː/ *adv.* **1**: **pull the door ~!** закро́й дверь! **2**: **~ and fro** взад и вперёд; **he went ~ and fro in his search for a compromise** он колеба́лся в своём вы́боре, ища́ компроми́ссное реше́ние

● *prep.* **1** (expr. indirect obj., recipient) (usu. expr. by d. case): **a letter ~ my wife** письмо́ мое́й жене́; **~ me that is absurd** по-мо́ему, э́то глу́по; (expr. support): **here's ~ our victory** за на́шу побе́ду (*тост*) **2** (expr. destination, with place names, countries, etc.) в + *a.*; **~ Moscow** в Москву́; **~ Russia** в Росси́ю; **~ the theatre** в теа́тр (BrE), theater (AmE); (expr. direction): **the road ~ London** доро́га в Ло́ндон; (with islands, planets, left and right, etc.) на + *a.*; **~ Cyprus** на Кипр; **back ~ Earth** обра́тно на Зе́млю; **turn ~ the right!** поверни́те напра́во!; **~ a concert** на конце́рт; **~ war** на войну́; **~ the factory** на заво́д/фа́брику; **~ the station** на ста́нцию; (with persons) к + *d.*; **he went ~ his parents'** он пое́хал к роди́телям; (towards) к + *d.* **3** (up to, as far as) до + *g.*; на + *a.*; по + *a.*; **is it far ~ town?** до го́рода далеко́?; **~ the bottom** на са́мое дно; **from 10 ~ 4** с десяти́ до четырёх; **from morning ~ night** с утра́ до́ но́чи; **ten (minutes) ~ six** (BrE) без десяти́ (мину́т) шесть; **from April to June** с апре́ля по ию́нь **4** (expr. end state): **smash ~ pieces** разб|ива́ть, -и́ть на куски́; **from bad ~ worse** всё ху́же и ху́же **5** (expr. response) на + *a.*; к + *d.*; **an answer ~ my letter** отве́т на моё письмо́ **6** (expr. result or reaction) к + *d.*; **~ my surprise** к моему́ удивле́нию **7** (expr. attachment, suitability) к + *d.*; от + *g.*; в + *a.*; **the key ~ the door** ключ от две́ри **8** (expr. reference or relationship): **he is good ~ his employees** он хорошо́ отно́сится к свои́м сотру́дникам; **attention ~ detail** внима́ние к деталя́м **9** (expr. ratio or proportion): **ten ~ one he won't succeed** де́сять про́тив одного́, что ему́ э́то не уда́стся **10** (expr. score) на + *a.*; **we won by six goals ~ four** мы вы́играли со счётом 6:4 **11** (expr. position): **~ my right** спра́ва от меня́; **~ the south of Minsk** к ю́гу от Ми́нска

● *particle with v. forming inf.* **1** (as subj. or obj. of v.): **~ err is human** челове́ку сво́йственно ошиба́ться; **he learnt ~ swim** он научи́лся пла́вать **2** (as extension of adj.): **this book is easy ~ read** э́та кни́га легко́ чита́ется; **too hot ~ touch** тако́й горя́чий, что не дотро́нуться **3** (expr. purpose) (с тем *or* для того́), что́бы...; (with inf. only): **I came ~ help** я пришёл(, что́бы) помо́чь; (expr. request): **I asked him ~ help** я попроси́л его́ помо́чь; (expr. result, sequel): **I arrived only ~ find him gone** когда́ я прие́хал, оказа́лось, что его́ уже́ нет **4** (as substitute for complete inf.): **I was going ~ write but I forgot** я собира́лся написа́ть, но забы́л

toad /təʊd/ *n.* жа́ба

■ **~stool** *n.* пога́нка

toady /ˈtəʊdɪ/ *n.* лизоблю́д, подхали́м

● *v.i.* подли́зываться (*impf.*) (*к кому*)

toast¹ /təʊst/ *n.* (toasted bread) тост, гре́нка

● *v.t.* поджа́ри|вать, -ть

toast² /təʊst/ *n.*: **drink a ~ to sth** пить, вы́- за что-н.

───────────

⚔ ключева́я ле́ксика

● *v.t.* пить, вы́- за (*чьё-н.*) здоро́вье

toaster /ˈtəʊstə(r)/ *n.* то́стер

tobacco /təˈbækəʊ/ *n.* (*pl.* **~s**) таба́к

tobacconist /təˈbækənɪst/ *n.* (BrE) торго́вец таба́чными изде́лиями

toboggan /təˈbɒɡən/ *n.* са́н|и (-е́й); тобо́гган, тобога́н

⚔ **today** /təˈdeɪ/ *adv. & n.* сего́дня; сего́дняшний день; **what's ~?** како́й сего́дня день?; **~'s newspaper** сего́дняшняя газе́та; (fig., the present time) настоя́щее вре́мя, сего́дня; **young people of ~** совреме́нная молодёжь

toddler /ˈtɒdlə(r)/ *n.* ребёнок, начина́ющий ходи́ть

toe /təʊ/ *n.* **1** (of foot) па́лец (ноги́); **big ~** большо́й па́лец (ноги́); **little ~** мизи́нец (ноги́) **2** (of shoe or sock) носо́к

● *v.t.* (**toes, toed, toeing**): **~ the line** (fig., conform) ходи́ть (*indet.*) по стру́нке (infml)

■ **~nail** *n.* но́готь (*m.*) на па́льце ноги́

toffee /ˈtɒfɪ/ *n.* ири́ска

⚔ **together** /təˈɡeðə(r)/ *adv.* **1** (in company) вме́сте; **~ with** (in addition to) вме́сте с + *i.* **2** (simultaneously) одновреме́нно

toggle /ˈtɒɡ(ə)l/ *n.* (comput.) ту́мблер

toil /tɔɪl/ *v.i.* (work hard) труди́ться (*impf.*)

toilet /ˈtɔɪlɪt/ *n.* туале́т

■ **~ paper** *n.* туале́тная бума́га

toiletries /ˈtɔɪlɪtrɪz/ *n. pl.* туале́тные принадле́жности

token /ˈtəʊkən/ *n.* **1** (sign) знак **2** (substitute for coin) жето́н **3** (*attr.*) символи́ческий

Tokyo /ˈtəʊkjəʊ/ *n.* То́кио (*m. indecl.*)

told /təʊld/ *past and p.p. of* ▸ **tell**

tolerable /ˈtɒlərəb(ə)l/ *adj.* терпи́мый

tolerance /ˈtɒlərəns/ *n.* (forbearance) терпи́мость; (resistance to hard conditions etc.) вы́носливость

tolerant /ˈtɒlərənt/ *adj.* терпи́мый

tolerate /ˈtɒləreɪt/ *v.t.* (endure) терпе́ть (*impf.*); (permit) допус|ка́ть, -ти́ть

toll¹ /təʊl/ *n.* (tax) по́шлина, сбор

■ **~ call** *n.* (AmE) междугоро́дный разгово́р

toll² /təʊl/ *n.* (of bell) колоко́льный звон

● *v.i.* звони́ть (*impf.*)

tom /tɒm/**:**

■ **~boy** *n.* девчо́нка-сорване́ц; **~cat** *n.* кот

tomato /təˈmɑːtəʊ/ *n.* (*pl.* **~es**) помидо́р

■ **~ paste** (also **~ purée**) *n.* тома́тная па́ста; **~ juice** *n.* тома́тный сок; **~ sauce** *n.* тома́тный со́ус

tomb /tuːm/ *n.* моги́ла

■ **~stone** *n.* (standing) надгро́бный па́мятник; (laid over) надгро́бная плита́

tome /təʊm/ *n.* (liter.) том

⚔ **tomorrow** /təˈmɒrəʊ/ *adv. & n.* за́втра; **~ morning** за́втра у́тром; **the day after ~** послеза́втра; **~ week** (BrE) че́рез 8 дней

ton /tʌn/ *n.* то́нна; (fig.): **he has ~s of money** у него́ ку́ча де́нег

⚔ **tone** /təʊn/ *n.* **1** (quality of sound, colour) тон; (teleph.) гудо́к **2** (character) хара́ктер

□ **~ down** *v.t.* смягч|а́ть, -и́ть

□ **~ in** *v.i.* гармони́ровать (*impf.*)

◻ **~ up** *v.t.* укреп|ля́ть, -и́ть

■ **~-deaf** *adj.* лишённый музыка́льного слу́ха

toner /'təʊnə(r)/ *n.* (for printer) то́нер

tongs /tɒŋz/ *n. pl.* щипц|ы́ (-о́в)

tongue /tʌŋ/ *n.* **1** (lit., and as food) язы́к; **put, stick one's ~ out** высо́вывать, вы́сунуть язы́к **2** (fig., article so shaped) язы́к, язычо́к **3** (language) язы́к; **mother/native ~** родно́й язы́к

■ **~-tied** *adj.* лиши́вшийся да́ра ре́чи; **~-twister** *n.* скорогово́рка

tonic /'tɒnɪk/ *n.* **1** (medicine) тонизи́рующее сре́дство; (fig.) подде́ржка **2** (**~ water**) то́ник

◦ **tonight** /tə'naɪt/ *adv. & n.* **1** (this evening) сего́дня ве́чером; (this night) сего́дня но́чью

tonne /tʌn/ *n.* (метри́ческая) то́нна

tonsil /'tɒns(ə)l/ *n.* минда́лина

tonsillitis /tɒnsɪ'laɪtɪs/ *n.* тонзилли́т, анги́на

◦ **too** /tuː/ *adv.* **1** (also) та́кже, то́же **2** (excessively) сли́шком; **it's ~ cold for swimming** сли́шком хо́лодно, что́бы купа́ться; **that is ~ much!** э́то уж сли́шком!

took /tʊk/ *past of* ▸ **take**

◦ **tool** /tuːl/ *n.* инструме́нт, ору́дие

■ **~bar** *n.* (comput.) пане́ль инструме́нтов

tooth /tuːθ/ *n.* (*pl.* **teeth**) зуб

■ **~ache** *n.* зубна́я боль; **~brush** *n.* зубна́я щётка; **~paste** *n.* зубна́я па́ста; **~pick** *n.* зубочи́стка

toothless /'tuːθlɪs/ *adj.* беззу́бый

◦ **top¹** /tɒp/ *n.* **1** (summit; highest part) верх (-и́); верху́шка, верши́на; (of hill, tree, head) маку́шка (infml); **at the ~ of the hill** на верши́не холма́; **at the ~ of the page** в нача́ле страни́цы; **she cleaned the house from ~ to bottom** она́ тща́тельно убрала́ дом **2** (fig., highest rank, foremost place) веду́щее положе́ние; пе́рвое ме́сто; **he came ~ of the class** он стал пе́рвым в кла́ссе **3** (fig., utmost degree) верх; **at the ~ of his voice** во весь го́лос **4** (upper surface) пове́рхность; верх; **on ~** (lit.) наверху́; (fig.): **I feel on ~ of the world** я чу́вствую себя́ на седьмо́м не́бе; **on ~ of everything I caught a cold** вдоба́вок ко всему́ я ещё (и) простуди́лся **5** (lid) верх; кры́шка **6** (attr.): **~ secret** соверше́нно секре́тный; **at ~ speed** на максима́льной ско́рости

● *v.t.* (**topped**, **topping**) **1** (serve as ~ to) венча́ть, у- **2** (be higher than; exceed) превы|ша́ть, -́сить

◻ **~ up** *v.t.* должива́ть, -и́ть; **may I ~ you up?** вам доли́ть?

■ **~ hat** *n.* цили́ндр; **~-heavy** *adj.* неусто́йчивый; **~-up** *n.* (BrE): **can I give you a ~-up?** вам доли́ть?

top² /tɒp/ *n.* (toy) волчо́к

topaz /'təʊpæz/ *n.* топа́з; (attr.) топа́зовый

topiary /'təʊpɪərɪ/ *adj.*: **the ~ art** фигу́рная стри́жка кусто́в

◦ **topic** /'tɒpɪk/ *n.* те́ма

topical /'tɒpɪk(ə)l/ *adj.* актуа́льный

topicality /tɒpɪ'kælɪtɪ/ *n.* актуа́льность

topless /'tɒplɪs/ *adj.* с обнажённой гру́дью

● *adv.* то́плес(с)

topmost /'tɒpməʊst/ *adj.* (highest) са́мый ве́рхний; (most important) са́мый ва́жный

topographical /tɒpə'græfɪk(ə)l/ *adj.* топографи́ческий

topography /tə'pɒɡrəfɪ/ *n.* топогра́фия; (features) релье́ф

topping /'tɒpɪŋ/ *n.* (cul.) ве́рхний слой; (sauce) подли́вка

topple /'tɒp(ə)l/ *v.t.* вали́ть, с-

● *v.i.* вали́ться, с-

topsy-turvy /tɒpsɪ'tɜːvɪ/ *adj.* переве́рнутый вверх дном (infml)

● *adv.* вверх дном

Torah /'tɔːrɑː/ *n.* (relig.) То́ра

torch /tɔːtʃ/ *n.* (flaming) фа́кел; (BrE): **electric ~** (электри́ческий) фона́рь

tore /tɔː(r)/ *past of* ▸ **tear²**

torment¹ /'tɔːment/ *n.* муче́ние

torment² /tɔː'ment/ *v.t.* му́чить (*impf.*)

tormentor /tɔː'mentə(r)/ *n.* мучи́тель (-ница)

torn /tɔːn/ *p.p. of* ▸ **tear²**

tornado /tɔː'neɪdəʊ/ *n.* (*pl.* **~es** *or* **~s**) смерч

torpedo /tɔː'piːdəʊ/ *n.* (*pl.* **~es**) торпе́да

torpid /'tɔːpɪd/ *adj.* вя́лый, апати́чный; (in hibernation) находя́щийся в состоя́нии спя́чки

torpidity /tɔː'pɪdɪtɪ/, **torpor** /'tɔːpə(r)/ *nn.* вя́лость, апа́тия

torrent /'tɒrənt/ *n.* (lit., fig.) пото́к

torrential /tə'renʃ(ə)l/ *adj.*: **~ rain** проливно́й дождь

torrid /'tɒrɪd/ *adj.* жа́ркий; (passionate) стра́стный

torso /'tɔːsəʊ/ *n.* (*pl.* **~s**) ту́ловище, торс

tortoise /'tɔːtəs/ *n.* черепа́ха

tortuous /'tɔːtʃʊəs/ *adj.* изви́листый

torture /'tɔːtʃə(r)/ *n.* (physical) пы́тка; (mental) му́ки (*f. pl.*)

● *v.t.* пыта́ть (*impf.*); му́чить (*impf.*)

torturer /'tɔːtʃərə(r)/ *n.* мучи́тель (*m.*), пала́ч

Tory /'tɔːrɪ/ *n.* (infml) то́ри (*m. indecl.*)

toss /tɒs/ *n.* бросо́к

● *v.t.* **1** (throw) бр|оса́ть, -о́сить; **they ~ed a coin to decide** они́ подки́нули моне́ту, что́бы реши́ть исхо́д де́ла **2** (agitate) швыр|я́ть, -ну́ть

● *v.i.* мета́ться (*impf.*); **the child ~ed in its sleep** ребёнок мета́лся во сне

◻ **~ off** *v.t.* (do quickly) де́лать, с- наспех

◻ **~ up** *v.i.*: **shall we ~ up to see who goes?** дава́йте бро́сим жре́бий, кому́ идти́

tot¹ /tɒt/ *n.* (BrE, of liquor) глото́к

tot² /tɒt/ *v.t.* (**totted**, **totting**): **~ up** сост|авля́ть, -а́вить (*сумму*); сумми́ровать (*impf., pf.*); **he ~ted up the figures** он подвёл ито́г

◦ **total** /'təʊt(ə)l/ *n.* су́мма, ито́г

● *adj.* (whole) о́бщий; **the ~ figure** о́бщая ци́фра; (complete): **~ failure** по́лный прова́л

● *v.t.* (**totalled**, **totalling**, AmE **totaled**, **totaling**) (also **~ up**) подсчи́т|ывать, -а́ть

totalitarian /təʊtælɪ'teərɪən/ *adj.* тоталита́рный

t

totalitarianism /təʊtælɪ'teərɪənɪz(ə)m/ *n.* тоталитари́зм

totality /təʊ'tælɪtɪ/ *n.* (sum total) вся су́мма, о́бщее коли́чество; (the whole of sth) (по́лная) совоку́пность; ~ of sth что́-л. в по́лном объёме; **in sth's** ~ в це́лом, в совоку́пности, во всей полно́те; (astron.) вре́мя по́лного затме́ния

✧ **totally** /'təʊtəlɪ/ *adv.* соверше́нно, абсолю́тно

totter /'tɒtə(r)/ *v.i.* ковыля́ть (*impf.*)

✧ **touch** /tʌtʃ/ *n.* **1** (light pressure) прикоснове́ние **2** (sense) осяза́ние **3** (of pen or brush) штрих **4** (tinge) чу́точка, отте́нок, налёт; **a** ~ **of frost in the air** лёгкий моро́зец **5** (style) стиль (*m.*); **you must have lost your** ~ вы я́вно утра́тили (былу́ю) хва́тку **6** (communication) конта́кт, обще́ние; **we must keep in** ~ мы должны́ подде́рживать конта́кт друг с дру́гом; **how can I get in** ~ **with you?** как мо́жно с ва́ми связа́ться?; **we lost** ~ **with him** мы потеря́ли с ним конта́кт/связь **7** (football) пло́щадь за боковы́ми ли́ниями по́ля; **to kick a ball into** ~ выбива́ть, вы́бить мяч за боковую́ (ли́нию)
● *v.t.* **1** (contact physically) тро́|гать, -нуть; каса́ться, косну́ться + *g.*; **he** ~**ed her (on the) arm** он косну́лся её руки́; **it was** ~ **and go исхо́д был неизве́стен до са́мого конца́ 2** (reach) дост|ава́ть, -а́ть до + *g.*; дост|ига́ть, -и́гнуть + *g.* **3** (approach in excellence) равня́ться (*impf.*) с + *i.*; сравни́ться (*pf.*) с + *i.*; идти́ (*det.*) в сравне́ние с + *i.* **4** (affect) тро́|гать, -нуть; волнова́ть, вз- **5** (taste) прик|аса́ться, -осну́ться к + *d.*; **I never** ~ **a drop** (of alcohol) я не прикаса́юсь к спиртно́му **6** (concern) каса́ться (*impf.*) + *g.* **7** (treat lightly) (*also v.i.* **with prep. on**) затр|а́гивать, -о́нуть; каса́ться, косну́ться + *g.*
● *v.i.* соприк|аса́ться, -осну́ться
■ ~**down** *n.* (aeron.) поса́дка; (rugby) попы́тка; (American football) тачда́ун; ~**line** *n.* боковая́ ли́ния (поля); ~**-type** *v.i.* печа́тать (*impf.*) вслепу́ю/слепы́м ме́тодом

touched /tʌtʃt/ *adj.* тро́нутый

touching /'tʌtʃɪŋ/ *adj.* тро́гательный

touchy /'tʌtʃɪ/ *adj.* (**touchier, touchiest**) оби́дчивый

✧ **tough** /tʌf/ *adj.* **1** (of meat) жёсткий **2** (strong, hardy) кре́пкий; (person) выно́сливый **3** (difficult) тру́дный; (stubborn) упря́мый **4** (severe) круто́й; жёсткий

toughen /'tʌf(ə)n/ *v.t.* де́лать, с- жёстким; (body, character) де́лать, с- выно́сливым

toughness /'tʌfnɪs/ *n.* (of food, regime, etc.) жёсткость; (strength; hardiness) про́чность; выно́сливость; (uncompromising nature) несгово́рчивость; упря́мство

toupee /'tu:peɪ/ *n.* небольшо́й пари́к, накла́дка

✧ **tour** /tʊə(r)/ *n.* **1** (extended visit) путеше́ствие; (short) пое́здка; (of museum, garden) экску́рсия **2** (of performer, sports team, politician) турне́ (*nt. indecl.*), тур; (of performer) гастро́ли (*f. pl.*); **to be on** ~ быть в турне́/на гастро́лях;

✧ **ключевая лексика**

гастроли́ровать (*impf.*)
● *v.t. & i.* соверш|а́ть, -и́ть экску́рсию (по + *d.*)
■ ~ **operator** *n.* (company) турфи́рма, туропера́тор

tourism /'tʊərɪz(ə)m/ *n.* тури́зм

✧ **tourist** /'tʊərɪst/ *n.* тури́ст (-ка)

tournament /'tʊənəmənt/ *n.* турни́р

tousled /'taʊz(ə)ld/ *adj.*: ~ **hair** взъеро́шенные во́лосы

tow /təʊ/ *n.*: **can I give you a** ~? взять вас на букси́р?
● *v.t.* букси́ровать (*impf.*); **they** ~**ed the car away** маши́ну отбукси́ровали

✧ **towards** /tə'wɔːdz/, **toward** /tə'wɔːd/ *prep.* **1** (in the direction of) к + *d.*; на + *a.*; по направле́нию к + *d.* **2** (in relation to) к + *d.*; по отноше́нию к + *d.*; относи́тельно + *g.*; **they seemed friendly** ~ **us** каза́лось, что они́ бы́ли располо́жены к нам дру́жески **3** (for the purpose of) для + *g.* **4** (near) к + *d.*; о́коло + *g.*; ~ **evening** к ве́черу, под ве́чер

towel /'taʊəl/ *n.* полоте́нце

tower /'taʊə(r)/ *n.* ба́шня; (fig.): **a** ~ **of strength** опло́т; надёжная опо́ра
● *v.i.* вы́ситься, возвыша́ться (*both impf.*)
■ ~ **block** *n.* (BrE) многоэта́жный/высо́тный дом, высо́тка

✧ **town** /taʊn/ *n.* **1** го́род; **go to** ~ (infml) разверну́ться (*pf.*) вовсю́ **2** (attr.) городско́й
■ ~ **council** *n.* мэ́рия; ~ **hall** *n.* мэ́рия; ра́туша; ~ **planning** *n.* градострои́тельство

township /'taʊnʃɪp/ *n.* **1** (hist., in South Africa) негритя́нский кварта́л **2** (AmE) райо́н

toxic /'tɒksɪk/ *adj.* ядови́тый

toxicologist /tɒksɪ'kɒlədʒɪst/ *n.* токсико́лог

toxicology /tɒksɪ'kɒlədʒɪ/ *n.* токсиколо́гия

toxin /'tɒksɪn/ *n.* токси́н

toy /tɔɪ/ *n.* игру́шка
● *v.i.*: **he** ~**ed with his pencil** он верте́л в рука́х каранда́ш; **he** ~**ed with her affections** он игра́л её чу́вствами
■ ~ **boy** *n.* (infml) молодо́й любо́вник; ~**shop** *n.* магази́н игру́шек

trac|e /treɪs/ *n.* след
● *v.t.* **1** (delineate) черти́ть, на-; (with transparent paper) перев|оди́ть, -ести́; ~**ing paper** ка́лька **2** (follow the tracks of) высле́живать, вы́следить; **the thief was** ~**ed to London** следы́ во́ра вели́ в Ло́ндон **3** (discover by search) устан|а́вливать, -ови́ть

traceable /'treɪsəb(ə)l/ *adj.* просле́живаемый

trachea /trə'kiːə/ *n.* (*pl.* **tracheae** /-'kiːiː/ *or* **tracheas**) (anat.) трахе́я

tracheotomy /trækɪ'ɒtəmɪ/ *n.* трахеотоми́я

✧ **track** /træk/ *n.* **1** (mark) след; **we lost** ~ **of him** мы потеря́ли его́ след **2** (path) путь (*m.*), тра́сса **3** (for racing etc.) (бегова́я) доро́жка; (for bicycle and motor racing) трек **4** (of railway) путь **5** (of tank etc.) гу́сеница **6** (recording of one song etc.) за́пись, трек
● *v.t.* следи́ть за + *i.*; выслёживать, вы́следить
□ ~ **down** *v.t.* (person) выслёживать,

вы́следить; (object) оты́ск|ивать, -а́ть

■ ~**suit** *n.* трениро́вочный костю́м

tracker /'trækə(r)/ *n.* (hunter) охо́тник

■ ~ **dog** *n.* соба́ка-ище́йка

tract /trækt/ *n.* (region) уча́сток, райо́н

traction /'trækʃ(ə)n/ *n.* тя́га

■ ~ **engine** *n.* тя́говый дви́гатель (*m.*); тяга́ч

tractor /'træktə(r)/ *n.* тра́ктор

✧ **trade** /treɪd/ *n.* **1** (business) ремесло́; профе́ссия; **he is a builder by** ~ он по профе́ссии строи́тель **2** (commerce) торго́вля
  ● *v.t.* (exchange) меня́ть (*impf.*); **they** ~**d furs for food** они́ меня́ли меха́ на проду́кты
  ● *v.i.* торгова́ть (*impf.*); **he** ~**s in sables** он торгу́ет соболя́ми
  □ ~ **in** *v.t.*: **I** ~**d in my old car for a new one** я о́тдал ста́рую маши́ну в счёт поку́пки но́вой
■ ~**mark** *n.* това́рный знак; ~ **name** *n.* назва́ние фи́рмы; ~**off** *n.* компроми́сс; ~ **secret** *n.* профессиона́льный секре́т; ~**sman** *n.* торго́вец; ~**smen's entrance** чёрный ход; ~(**s**) **union** *n.* профсою́з

trader /'treɪdə(r)/ *n.* торго́вец

✧ **tradition** /trə'dɪʃ(ə)n/ *n.* тради́ция

✧ **traditional** /trə'dɪʃən(ə)l/ *adj.* традицио́нный

traditionalist /trə'dɪʃənəlɪst/ *n.* традиционали́ст

✧ **traffic** /'træfɪk/ *n.* **1** (movement of vehicles etc.) (доро́жное) движе́ние, тра́нспорт; **heavy** ~ большо́е движе́ние **2** (trade) торго́вля
  ● *v.i.* (**trafficked**, **trafficking**) торгова́ть (*чем*)
■ ~ **jam** *n.* про́бка; ~ **lights** *n. pl.* светофо́р; ~ **warden** *n.* (BrE) инспе́ктор, контроли́рующий соблюде́ние пра́вил парко́вки и стоя́нки (*в че́рте го́рода*)

trafficker /'træfɪkə(r)/ *n.* (pej.) деле́ц, торго́вец; **drug** ~ наркоде́лец

tragedy /'trædʒɪdɪ/ *n.* траге́дия

tragic /'trædʒɪk/ *adj.* траги́ческий

trail /treɪl/ *n.* (path) доро́жка, тропи́нка; (mark left) след; **the storm left a** ~ **of destruction** бу́ря оста́вила по́сле себя́ полосу́ разруше́ния
  ● *v.t.* **1** (draw or drag behind) тащи́ть (*impf.*); волочи́ть (*impf.*) **2** (pursue) идти́ (*det.*) по сле́ду + *g.*
  ● *v.i.* **1** (be drawn or dragged) тащи́ться (*impf.*); волочи́ться (*impf.*) **2** (straggle) плести́сь (*impf.*) **3** (grow or hang loosely) све́шиваться (*impf.*)

trailer /'treɪlə(r)/ *n.* **1** (vehicle) прице́п; (AmE, caravan) жило́й автоприце́п, тре́йлер **2** (cin., TV) ано́нс

✧ **train** /treɪn/ *n.* **1** (*also* **railway** ~) по́езд; **I came by** ~ я прие́хал по́ездом **2** (procession) проце́ссия; карава́н; (mil.) обо́з **3** (fig.) ряд, цепь; **I don't follow your** ~ **of thought** мне тру́дно улови́ть ход ва́ших мы́слей **4** (of dress etc.) шлейф
  ● *v.t.* **1** (give instruction to) учи́ть, об-/обуча́|ть, -и́ть (**in**: + *d.*); (prepare for a career) гото́вить (*impf.*); (sportsman) тренирова́ть (*impf.*); (animals) дрессирова́ть (*impf.*) **2** (direct)

нав|оди́ть, -ести́
  ● *v.i.* **1** (learn skill) учи́ться, об-/обуча́|ться, -и́ться; (undertake preparation) гото́виться (*impf.*); (of sportsman) тренирова́ться (*impf.*); **she is** ~**ing to be a teacher** она́ гото́вится стать учи́телем
■ ~ **driver** *n.* машини́ст

trainee /treɪ'niː/ *n.* стажёр; учени́|к (-ца)

trainer /'treɪnə(r)/ *n.* **1** тре́нер; (of horses etc.) дрессиро́вщи|к (-ца) **2** (BrE, sports shoe) кроссо́вка

✧ **training** /'treɪnɪŋ/ *n.* **1** (instruction) подгото́вка, обуче́ние **2** (physical preparation) трениро́вка

traipse /treɪps/ *v.i.* (infml) таска́ться (*impf.*) (*по у́лицам и т. п.*)

trait /treɪt/ *n.* осо́бенность, сво́йство

traitor /'treɪtə(r)/ *n.* преда́тель (*m.*) (-ница), изме́нни|к (-ца)

trajectory /trə'dʒektərɪ/ *n.* траекто́рия

tram /træm/ *n.* (BrE) трамва́й

tramp /træmp/ *n.* бродя́га

trample /'træmp(ə)l/ *v.t.* топта́ть, по-, раст|а́птывать, -опта́ть
  ● *v.i.* тяжело́ ступа́ть (*impf.*); (fig.): **he** ~**d on everyone's feelings** он не счита́лся ни с чьи́ми чу́вствами

trampoline /'træmpəliːn/ *n.* бату́т

trampolining /'træmpəliːnɪŋ/ *n.* прыжки́ (*m. pl.*) на бату́те

trance /trɑːns/ *n.* транс

tranquil /'træŋkwɪl/ *adj.* споко́йный, ми́рный

tranquillity /træŋ'kwɪlɪtɪ/ *n.* споко́йствие

tranquillizer /'træŋkwɪlaɪzə(r)/ (AmE **tranquilizer**) *n.* успокои́тельное сре́дство, транквилиза́тор

transaction /træn'zækʃ(ə)n/ *n.* сде́лка

transatlantic /trænzət'læntɪk/ *adj.* трансатланти́ческий

transcend /træn'send/ *v.t.* превы́ша́ть, -ы́сить

transcendental /trænsen'dent(ə)l/ *adj.* (phil.) трансцендента́льный

transcontinental /trænzkɒntɪ'nent(ə)l/ *adj.* трансконтинента́льный

transcribe /træn'skraɪb/ *v.t.* перепи́с|ывать, -а́ть

transcript /'trænskrɪpt/ *n.* ко́пия

transcription /træn'skrɪpʃ(ə)n/ *n.* перепи́сывание; ко́пия, транскри́пция; **phonetic** ~ фонети́ческая транскри́пция

✧ **transfer¹** /'trænsfə:(r)/ *n.* (of object) перенесе́ние, перено́с; (of worker, money) перево́д; (of footballer) перехо́д; (conveyance, handing over) переда́ча

✧ **transfer²** /træns'fə:(r)/ *v.t.* (**transferred**, **transferring**) **1** (object) перен|оси́ть, -ести́ **2** (hand over) перед|ава́ть, -а́ть **3** (footballer, worker, money) перев|оди́ть, -ести́
  ● *v.i.* (**transferred**, **transferring**) (of footballer, worker) пере|ходи́ть, -йти́; (to another vehicle) переса́|живаться, -́сть

transferable /træns'fə:rəb(ə)l/ *adj.* (ticket, vote) тот, кото́рый мо́жет быть пе́редан

t

другому лицу; (skills) универсáльный, пригóдный в любóй ситуáции

transference /'trænsfərəns/ n. перенесéние; перевóд; **thought** ~ передáча мы́сли на расстоя́ние

transfix /træns'fɪks/ v.t. прикóв|ывать, -áть к мéсту; **he was** ~**ed with horror** он оцепенéл от ýжаса

ɗ **transform** /træns'fɔ:m/ v.t. преобразóв|ывать, -áть

transformation /trænsfə'meɪʃ(ə)n/ n. преобразовáние

transformer /træns'fɔ:mə(r)/ n. (elec.) трансформáтор

transfusion /træns'fju:ʒ(ə)n/ n. переливáние (крóви)

transgress /trænz'gres/ v.t. & i. (infringe) пере|ходи́ть, -йти́ грани́цы + g.; нар|ушáть, -ýшить (закон и т. п.)

transgression /trænz'greʃ(ə)n/ n. (infringement) простýпок; (offence) нарушéние; (sin) грех

transience /'trænzɪəns/ n. быстротéчность; мимолётность

transient /'trænzɪənt/ adj. (impermanent) врéменный; (brief) мимолётный

transistor /træn'zɪstə(r)/ n. транзи́стор

transit /'trænzɪt/ n. транзи́т, перевóзка; **lost in** ~ потéрянный при перевóзке; **in** ~ транзи́том

■ ~ **camp** n. транзи́тный лáгерь

transition /træn'zɪʃ(ə)n/ n. перехóд

transitional /træn'zɪʃən(ə)l/ adj. перехóдный; промежýточный

transitive /'trænsɪtɪv/ adj. (gram.) перехóдный

transitory /'trænsɪtərɪ/ adj. преходя́щий, мимолётный

translate /trænz'leɪt/ v.t. & i. перев|оди́ть, -ести́; **these poems do not** ~ **well** э́ти стихи́ не поддаю́тся перевóду

translation /trænz'leɪʃ(ə)n/ n. перевóд

translator /trænz'leɪtə(r)/ n. перевóдчи|к (-ца)

transliterate /trænz'lɪtəreɪt/ v.t. транслитери́ровать (impf., pf.)

translucence /trænz'lu:s(ə)ns/ n. просвéчиваемость, полупрозрáчность

translucent /trænz'lu:s(ə)nt/ adj. просвéчивающий, полупрозрáчный

transmission /trænz'mɪʃ(ə)n/ n. передáча, трансми́ссия

transmit /trænz'mɪt/ v.t. & i. перед|авáть, -áть

transmitter /trænz'mɪtə(r)/ n. передáтчик

transparency /træn'spærənsɪ/ n. **1** прозрáчность **2** (picture) транспарáнт

transparent /træn'spærənt/ adj. прозрáчный

transpire /træn'spaɪə(r)/ v.i. (come to be known) обнарýжи|ваться, -ться; (infml, happen) случ|áться, -и́ться

transplant¹ /'trænsplɑ:nt/ n. пересáдка

transplant² /træns'plɑ:nt/ v.t. (hort., med.) перес|áживать, -ади́ть

transplantation /trænsplɑ:n'teɪʃ(ə)n/ n. пересáдка, трансплантáция; (fig.) переселéние

ɗ **transport¹** /'trænspɔ:t/ n. трáнспорт; **public** ~ общéственный трáнспорт

transport² /træn'spɔ:t/ v.t. перев|ози́ть, -езти́; транспорти́ровать (impf., pf.)

transportation /trænspɔ:'teɪʃ(ə)n/ n. (of goods etc.) перевóзка, транспортирóвка

transpose /træns'pəʊz/ v.t. перест|авля́ть, -áвить

transsexual /trænz'sekʃʊəl/ n. транссексуáл

Trans-Siberian /trænzsaɪ'bɪərɪən/ adj.: ~ **Railway** (BrE), **Railroad** (AmE) Транссиби́рская магистрáль

transvestite /trænz'vestaɪt/ n. трансвести́т

trap /træp/ n. **1** (for animals etc.) западня́ **2** (light vehicle) рессóрная двукóлка

● v.t. (**trapped, trapping**) лови́ть, пойма́ть в ловýшку/капкáн; (fig., catch): **his fingers were** ~**ped in the door** он защеми́л пáльцы двéрью

■ ~**door** n. люк

trapeze /trə'pi:z/ n. трапéция (циркова́я)

trapezi|um /trə'pi:zɪəm/ n. (pl. ~**a or** ~**ums**) (geom.) трапéция

trapper /'træpə(r)/ n. охóтник(, стáвящий капкáны) на пушнóго звéря

trappings /'træpɪŋz/ n. pl. (harness) сбрýя; (fig.): **the** ~ **of office** внéшние атрибýты (m. pl.) влáсти

trash /træʃ/ n. мýсор

■ ~ **can** n. (AmE) мýсорное ведрó; (outside) мýсорный бак

trauma /'trɔ:mə/ n. (pl. ~**s**) трáвма

traumatic /trɔ:'mætɪk/ adj. (distressing) тя́жкий; (of physical injury) травмати́ческий

traumatize /'trɔ:mətaɪz/ v.t. травми́ровать (impf., pf.)

ɗ **travel** /'træv(ə)l/ n. путешéствие, поéздка

● v.t. (**travelled, travelling**, AmE usu. **traveled, traveling**) путешéствовать (impf.) по + d.; éздить (indet.) по + d.

● v.i. (**travelled, travelling**, AmE usu. **traveled, traveling**) путешéствовать (impf.); éздить, съ-; (move) дви́гаться (impf.); перемещáться (impf.)

■ ~ **agency** n. тури́стическое агéнтство, турагéнтство; ~ **agent** n. тури́стический агéнт; ~**sickness** n. тошнотá при езде́

traveller /'trævələ(r)/ (AmE **traveler**) n. путешéственник

■ ~**'s cheque** (BrE), **traveler's check** (AmE) nn. дорóжный чек

travelling /'trævəlɪŋ/ n. путешéствие

● adj. путешéствующий

■ ~ **salesman** n. коммивояжёр

traverse /'trævəs, trə'və:s/ v.t. перес|екáть, -éчь

travesty /'trævɪstɪ/ n. пародия (of: на + a.)

trawl /trɔ:l/ n. (in full ~ **net**) трал, трáловая сеть; дóнный нéвод

ɗ ключевáя лéксика

● *v.t. & i.* тра́лить (*impf.*); лови́ть (*impf.*) рыбу тра́лом; **the fishermen ~ed their nets for herring** они́ тра́лили сельдь; (fig., search thoroughly) проч|ёсывать, -еса́ть

trawler /'trɔːlə(r)/ *n.* тра́улер

tray /treɪ/ *n.* подно́с

treacherous /'tretʃərəs/ *adj.* преда́тельский

treachery /'tretʃərɪ/ *n.* преда́тельство

treacle /'triːk(ə)l/ *n.* (BrE) па́тока

tread /tred/ *n.* **1** (manner or sound of walking) похо́дка **2** (of tyre) проте́ктор

● *v.t.* (*past* **trod**, *p.p.* **trodden** *or* **trod**) ступа́ть (*impf.*) по + *d.*; шага́ть (*impf.*) по + *d.*

● *v.i.* (*past* **trod**, *p.p.* **trodden** *or* **trod**): ~ **on that cockroach!** растопчи́те/раздави́те э́того тарака́на!; **don't ~ on the grass!** по газо́нам не ходи́ть!

■ **~mill** *n.* бегова́я доро́жка; (fig.) однообра́зная рабо́та

treason /'triːz(ə)n/ *n.* (госуда́рственная) изме́на

treasonable /'triːzənəb(ə)l/ *adj.* изме́ннический

treasure /'treʒə(r)/ *n.* сокро́вище

● *v.t.* (store up) храни́ть, co-; **~d memories** дороги́е воспомина́ния; (value highly) высоко́ цени́ть (*impf.*)

treasurer /'treʒərə(r)/ *n.* казначе́й

treasury /'treʒərɪ/ *n.* (public department) казна́

⚹ **treat** /triːt/ *n.* удово́льствие; **it's my ~!** я угоща́ю!

● *v.t.* **1** (behave towards) обраща́ться (*impf.*) c + *i.*; **he ~s me like a child** он обраща́ется со мной, как с ребёнком **2** (regard) рассма́тривать (*impf.*); отн|оси́ться, -ести́сь к + *d.* **3** (deal with; discuss) осве|ща́ть, -ти́ть; рассм|а́тривать, -отре́ть; **he ~ed the subject in detail** он подро́бно освети́л те́му **4** (give medical care to) лечи́ть (*impf.*) **5** (apply chemical process to) обраб|а́тывать, -о́тать **6** (give sb sth at one's own expense) уго|ща́ть, -сти́ть; **he ~ed me to a whisky** он угости́л меня́ ви́ски; **I shall ~ myself to a holiday** я устро́ю себе́ о́тпуск

treatise /'triːtɪs/ *n.* тракта́т; нау́чный труд

⚹ **treatment** /'triːtmənt/ *n.* **1** (handling) обраще́ние; рассмотре́ние **2** (chem. etc.) обрабо́тка **3** (med.) лече́ние; (session of therapy) процеду́ра

treaty /'triːtɪ/ *n.* догово́р

treble /'treb(ə)l/ *n.* (voice) ди́скант; **~ clef** скрипи́чный ключ

● *adj.* тройно́й

● *v.t. & i.* утр|а́ивать(ся), -о́ить(ся)

⚹ **tree** /triː/ *n.* де́рево

trek /trek/ *n.* перехо́д

● *v.i.* (**trekked**, **trekking**) соверш|а́ть, -и́ть дли́тельный похо́д

trellis /'trelɪs/ *n.* шпале́ра

tremble /'tremb(ə)l/ *v.i.* дрожа́ть (*impf.*); трясти́сь (*impf.*)

tremendous /trɪ'mendəs/ *adj.* (huge) огро́мный; (infml, splendid) замеча́тельный

tremor /'tremə(r)/ *n.* (quivering) содрога́ние, дрожь; (thrill) тре́пет; **there was a ~ in his voice** его́ го́лос дрожа́л; **earth ~** подзе́мный толчо́к

tremulous /'tremjʊləs/ *adj.* (trembling) дрожа́щий

trench /trentʃ/ *n.* ров, кана́ва; (mil.) транше́я

⚹ **trend** /trend/ *n.* направле́ние, тенде́нция; **set a ~** вв|оди́ть, -ести́ мо́ду (**for**: на + *a.*)

trendy /'trendɪ/ *adj.* (**trendier**, **trendiest**) (infml) мо́дный

trepidation /trepɪ'deɪʃ(ə)n/ *n.* тре́пет, дрожь; **in ~** трепеща́

trespass /'trespəs/ *v.i.* вт|орга́ться, -о́ргнуться в чужи́е владе́ния

trespasser /'trespəsə(r)/ *n.* лицо́, вторга́ющееся в чужи́е владе́ния; **~s will be prosecuted** наруши́тели бу́дут пресле́доваться

⚹ **trial** /'traɪəl/ *n.* **1** (test) испыта́ние, про́ба; **I discovered the truth by ~ and error** я пришёл к и́стине путём проб и оши́бок; **he took the car on a week's ~** он взял автомаши́ну на неде́льное испыта́ние **2** (*attr.*) про́бный **3** (judicial examination) суде́бный проце́сс; **he went on ~ for murder** его́ суди́ли за уби́йство

■ **~ run** *n.* испыта́тельный пробе́г

triangle /'traɪæŋg(ə)l/ *n.* треуго́льник

triangular /traɪ'æŋgjʊlə(r)/ *adj.* треуго́льный; **a ~ argument** спор ме́жду тремя́ ли́цами

triathlon /traɪ'æθlən/ *n.* троебо́рье

tribal /'traɪb(ə)l/ *adj.* племенно́й

tribe /traɪb/ *n.* пле́мя (*nt.*)

tribulation /trɪbjʊ'leɪʃ(ə)n/ *n.* страда́ние, беда́

tribunal /traɪ'bjuːn(ə)l/ *n.* трибуна́л

tributary /'trɪbjʊtərɪ/ *n.* прито́к

tribute /'trɪbjuːt/ *n.* дань; **he paid ~ to his wife's help** он вы́разил благода́рность свое́й жене́ за по́мощь

trice /traɪs/ *n.*: **in a ~** вмиг, ми́гом

trick /trɪk/ *n.* **1** (dodge) приём, хи́трость; **he knows all the ~s of the trade** он зна́ет все хо́ды и вы́ходы **2** (deception) обма́н, трюк; (prank) шу́тка; **he is always playing ~s on me** он всегда́ надо мной подшу́чивает **3** (feat) шту́ка; **that will do the ~** э́то срабо́тает наверняка́ **4** (knack) хва́тка **5** (at cards) взя́тка

● *v.t.* обма́н|ывать, -у́ть; над|ува́ть, -у́ть; **they ~ed him out of a fortune** они́ вы́манили у него́ ма́ссу де́нег

trickery /'trɪkərɪ/ *n.* обма́н, надува́тельство

trickle /'trɪk(ə)l/ *n.* стру́йка

● *v.t.* ка́пать (*impf.*)

● *v.i.* сочи́ться (*impf.*); ка́пать (*impf.*); (fig.): **the crowd began to ~ away** толпа́ ста́ла постепе́нно расходи́ться

tricky /'trɪkɪ/ *adj.* (**trickier**, **trickiest**) (awkward) сло́жный, мудрёный; (crafty) хи́трый, кова́рный

t

tricycle /'traɪsɪk(ə)l/ n. трёхколёсный велосипед

trifle /'traɪf(ə)l/ n. **1** (thing of small value) пустя́к, ме́лочь **2** (BrE, sweet dish) бискви́т со взби́тыми сли́вками
● v.i. относи́ться (impf.) несерьёзно к + d.; he ~d with her affections он игра́л её чу́вствами

trifling /'traɪflɪŋ/ adj. пустяко́вый; незначи́тельный

trigger /'trɪɡə(r)/ n. куро́к
● v.t. (usu. ~ off) вызыва́ть, вы́звать

trigonometry /trɪɡə'nɒmɪtrɪ/ n. тригономе́трия

trilby /'trɪlbɪ/ n. (BrE) мя́гкая фе́тровая шля́па

trill /trɪl/ n. трель
● v.i.: the birds were ~ing пти́цы залива́лись тре́лями

trillion /'trɪljən/ n. (pl. ~s or (with numeral or qualifying word) ~) (10¹², million million) триллио́н

trilogy /'trɪlədʒɪ/ n. трило́гия

trim /trɪm/ n. **1** (order, fitness) поря́док; состоя́ние гото́вности; we must get into ~ before the race нам ну́жно набра́ть фо́рму пе́ред соревнова́нием **2** (light cut) подре́зка, стри́жка
● adj. (**trimmer, trimmest**) аккура́тный, опря́тный
● v.t. (**trimmed, trimming**) **1** (cut to desired shape) подр|еза́ть, -е́зать; подр|а́внивать, -овня́ть **2** (decorate) отде́л|ывать, -ать; a hat ~med with fur ша́пка, отде́ланная ме́хом

trimming /'trɪmɪŋ/ n. (on dress etc.) отде́лка; (infml, accessory) гарни́р

Trinity /'trɪnɪtɪ/ n. Тро́ица
■ ~ **Sunday** n. день Свято́й Тро́ицы

trinket /'trɪŋkɪt/ n. безделу́шка

trio /'triːəʊ/ n. (pl. ~s) (group of three) тро́йка; (mus.) три́о (nt. indecl.)

trip /trɪp/ n. (excursion) пое́здка; (longer one) путеше́ствие
● v.t. (**tripped, tripping**) (cause to stumble) (also ~ up) ста́вить, по- подно́жку + d.; (fig.) запу́т|ывать, -ать, сби|ва́ть, -ть с то́лку
● v.i. (**tripped, tripping**) **1** (run lightly): she came ~ping down the stairs она́ легко́ сбежа́ла вниз по ле́стнице **2** (stumble) (also ~ up) спот|ыка́ться, -кну́ться

tripartite /traɪ'pɑːtaɪt/ adj. трёхсторо́нний

tripe /traɪp/ n. (offal) требуха́; (infml, rubbish) чепуха́, вздор

triple /'trɪp(ə)l/ adj. тройно́й, утро́енный
■ ~ **jump** n. (sport) тройно́й прыжо́к

triplet /'trɪplɪt/ n.: ~s (children) тро́йня (sg.)

triplicate /'trɪplɪkət/ n.: in ~ в трёх экземпля́рах

tripod /'traɪpɒd/ n. трено́га

trite /traɪt/ adj. бана́льный, изби́тый

triumph /'traɪʌmf/ n. (joy at success) торжество́; (success) триу́мф
● v.i. побе|жда́ть, -ди́ть; восторжествова́ть

(pf.); he ~ed over adversity он преодоле́л все невзго́ды

triumphant /traɪ'ʌmf(ə)nt/ adj. (victorious) победоно́сный; (exultant) торжеству́ющий

trivia /'trɪvɪə/ n. ме́лочи (f. pl.)

trivial /'trɪvɪəl/ adj. (trifling) ме́лкий, незначи́тельный; (everyday) обы́денный

triviality /trɪvɪ'ælɪtɪ/ n. незначи́тельность, тривиа́льность

trivialize /'trɪvɪəlaɪz/ v.t. оп|ошля́ть, -о́шлить

trod /trɒd/ past and p.p. of ▶ tread

trodden /'trɒd(ə)n/ p.p. of ▶ tread

trolley /'trɒlɪ/ n. (pl. ~s) (BrE, for luggage, purchases) теле́жка; (AmE, streetcar) трамва́й
■ ~**bus** n. тролле́йбус; ~ **car** n. (AmE) трамва́й

trombone /trɒm'bəʊn/ n. тромбо́н

trombonist /trɒm'bəʊnɪst/ n. тромбони́ст

◆ **troop** /truːp/ n. **1** (mil. unit) батаре́я **2** (in pl.) (soldiers) войска́|(pl., g. —)

trooper /'truːpə(r)/ n. **1** (soldier) (in armoured unit) танки́ст; (in cavalry) кавалери́ст **2** (AmE, policeman) полице́йский

trophy /'trəʊfɪ/ n. трофе́й

tropic /'trɒpɪk/ n. тро́пик; in the ~s в тро́пиках

tropical /'trɒpɪk(ə)l/ adj. тропи́ческий

trot /trɒt/ n. рысь; on the ~ (BrE) подря́д
● v.i. (**trotted, trotting**) (of a horse) идти́ (det.) ры́сью; (of person) семени́ть (impf.)
□ ~ **out** v.t. (infml): he ~ted out the usual excuses он, как обы́чно, привёл свои́ ста́рые отгово́рки

◆ **trouble** /'trʌb(ə)l/ n. **1** (anxiety) волне́ние, трево́га; беспоко́йство; (misfortune) го́ре, беда́, несча́стье **2** (difficulties) хло́п|оты (-о́т), тру́дности (f. pl.); (difficulty) затрудне́ние; money ~s де́нежные затрудне́ния; I am having ~ with the car у меня́ нела́дки (f. pl.) с маши́ной; what's the ~? в чём де́ло? **3** (predicament) неприя́тность; he's always getting into ~ он ве́чно попада́ет в исто́рии **4** (inconvenience): he saved me the ~ он изба́вил меня́ от э́той необходи́мости **5** (care, effort) забо́та, труд, хло́п|оты (-о́т); she took a lot of ~ over the cake она́ приложи́ла нема́ло стара́ний, чтобы пригото́вить э́тот торт **6** (unrest) волне́ния (nt. pl.)
● v.t. **1** (worry) трево́жить (impf.); волнова́ть (impf.); don't let it ~ you не принима́йте э́то бли́зко к се́рдцу **2** (afflict) беспоко́ить (impf.); му́чить (impf.); he is ~d with a cough его́ му́чит ка́шель **3** (put to inconvenience) беспоко́ить, по-, затрудн|я́ть, -и́ть; don't ~ yourself не беспоко́йтесь; sorry to ~ you! прости́те за беспоко́йство!
■ ~-**free** adj. (reliable) надёжный, безотка́зный; ~**maker** n. смутья́н (-ка); ~**shooter** n. специали́ст по разреше́нию конфли́ктных/кри́зисных ситуа́ций (в компании и т. п.); ~ **spot** n. горя́чая то́чка

troublesome /'trʌb(ə)lsəm/ adj. тру́дный; хло́потный

trough /trɒf/ n. **1** (food ∼) кормушка; (drinking ∼) поилка **2** (dip) впадина

troupe /truːp/ n. труппа

trousers /'traʊzəz/ n. pl. штан|ы́ (-о́в), брюк|и (pl., g. —); **a pair of** ∼ пара брюк

trout /traʊt/ n. форель

trowel /'traʊəl/ n. (for bricklaying etc.) мастеро́к; (for gardening) (садо́вый) сово́к, лопа́тка

truancy /'truːənsɪ/ n. прогу́л

truant /'truːənt/ n. прогу́льщик; **did you ever play** ∼? вы когда́-нибудь прогу́ливали уро́ки?

truce /truːs/ n. переми́рие

truck /trʌk/ n. (BrE, railway wagon) откры́тая грузова́я платфо́рма; (lorry) грузови́к; (barrow) теле́жка

trucker /'trʌkə(r)/ n. води́тель (m.) грузовика́

truculent /'trʌkjʊlənt/ adj. агресси́вный, драчли́вый

trudge /trʌdʒ/ v.i. тащи́ться (impf.)

⚡ **true** /truː/ adj. (**truer, truest**) **1** (in accordance with fact) ве́рный, правди́вый; **is it** ∼ **that ...?** (э́то) пра́вда, что...?; **a** ∼ **story** правди́вый расска́з; **all my dreams came** ∼ все мои́ мечты́ сбыли́сь/осуществи́лись **2** (in accordance with reason; genuine) правди́вый; настоя́щий; и́стинный **3** (conforming accurately) ве́рный, пра́вильный; ∼ **to life** правди́вый **4** (loyal; dependable) пре́данный, ве́рный; надёжный

truffle /'trʌf(ə)l/ n. (fungus, candy) трю́фель (m.)

truism /'truːɪz(ə)m/ n. избита́я и́стина, трюи́зм; **it is a** ∼ **that** общеизве́стно, что…

⚡ **truly** /'truːlɪ/ adv. **1** (truthfully) и́скренне; (accurately) правди́во **2** (sincerely) и́скренне; **yours** ∼ (at end of letter) пре́данный Вам

trump /trʌmp/ n. (in full ∼ **card**) ко́зырь (m.); **the weather turned up** ∼**s** (BrE) нам (неожи́данно) повезло́ с пого́дой

trumpet /'trʌmpɪt/ n. труба́; **blow one's own** ∼ (fig.) хвали́ться (impf.)

trumpeter /'trʌmpɪtə(r)/ n. труба́ч

truncate /trʌŋ'keɪt/ v.t. усе|ка́ть, -е́чь; **a** ∼**d cone** усечённый ко́нус; **his speech was** ∼**d** его́ речь уре́зали

truncheon /'trʌntʃ(ə)n/ n. (BrE) (полице́йская) дуби́нка

trundle /'trʌnd(ə)l/ v.t. & i. кати́ть(ся) (impf.)

trunk /trʌŋk/ n. **1** (of tree) ствол **2** (of body) ту́ловище **3** (box) сунду́к **4** (of elephant) хо́бот **5** (in pl.) (garment) пла́в|ки (-ок) **6** (AmE, boot of car) бага́жник
▪ ∼ **road** n. (BrE) магистра́ль

⚡ **trust** /trʌst/ n. **1** (confidence) дове́рие; ве́ра **2** (law) довери́тельная со́бственность
● v.t. **1** (have confidence in, rely on) дов|еря́ть, -е́рить + d. **2** (entrust) вв|еря́ть, -е́рить
● v.i. **1** (have faith, confidence) дов|еря́ться, -е́риться (in: + d.); **she** ∼**ed in God** она́ отдала́сь на во́лю Бо́жью **2** (commit oneself with confidence) дов|еря́ться, -е́риться (to: + d.); **he** ∼**ed to luck** он дове́рился уда́че
▪ ∼ **fund** n. целево́й фонд

trustee /trʌs'tiː/ n. довери́тельный со́бственник; опеку́н

trusting /'trʌstɪŋ/ adj. дове́рчивый

trustworthiness /'trʌstwɜːðɪnɪs/ n. надёжность

trustworthy /'trʌstwɜːðɪ/ adj. надёжный

trusty /'trʌstɪ/ adj. (**trustier, trustiest**) ве́рный, надёжный

⚡ **truth** /truːθ/ n. пра́вда; (verity) и́стина

truthful /'truːθfʊl/ adj. (of person) правди́вый; (of statement etc.) правди́вый, ве́рный, то́чный

truthfulness /'truːθfʊlnɪs/ n. правди́вость; ве́рность, то́чность

⚡ **try** /traɪ/ n. **1** (attempt) попы́тка **2** (test): **why not give it a** ∼? почему́ бы не попро́бовать? **3** (rugby) прохо́д с мячо́м в зачётное по́ле сопе́рника, попы́тка
● v.t. **1** (attempt) пыта́ться, по-; стара́ться, по-; **he tried his best** он стара́лся изо всех сил; **he tried hard** он о́чень стара́лся **2** (sample) про́бовать, по-; (taste) отве́д|ывать, -ать; (experiment with): **have you tried aspirin?** вы про́бовали аспири́н? **3** (law, a person) суди́ть (impf.) **4** (subject to strain): **he tries my patience** он испы́тывает моё терпе́ние; **a** ∼**ing situation** тру́дное положе́ние **5** (test) испы́т|ывать, -а́ть; пров|еря́ть, -е́рить
● v.i.: ∼ **harder next time!** в сле́дующий раз приложи́те бо́льше уси́лий!; **I tried for a prize** я добива́лся при́за, я претендова́л на приз
□ ∼ **on** v.t. прим|еря́ть, -е́рить
□ ∼ **out** v.t. испы́т|ывать, -а́ть; опро́бовать (pf.)

tsar, tzar /zɑː(r)/ n. царь (m.)

T-shirt /'tiːʃɜːt/ n. футбо́лка

tsunami /tsuː'nɑːmɪ/ n. (pl. ∼**s**) цуна́ми (nt. indecl.)

tub /tʌb/ n. **1** ка́дка; бо́чка **2** (bath) ва́нна **3** (of margarine) упако́вка; (of ice cream, yogurt) стака́нчик

tuba /'tjuːbə/ n. ту́ба

tubby /'tʌbɪ/ adj. (**tubbier, tubbiest**) (of person) коротконо́гий и то́лстый

tube /tjuːb/ n. **1** (of metal, glass, etc.) труба́, тру́бка **2** (of toothpaste, etc.) тю́бик **3** (of tyre) ка́мера (ши́ны) **4** (in the body) труба́ **5** (BrE, infml, underground railway) метро́ (nt. indecl.)

tuberculosis /tjʊbɜːkjʊ'ləʊsɪs/ n. туберкулёз

tuck¹ /tʌk/ v.t. (stow) пря́тать, с-; под|бира́ть, -обра́ть
□ ∼ **away** v.t. запря́т|ывать, -ать
□ ∼ **in** v.t. запр|авля́ть, -а́вить; ∼ **your shirt in!** запра́вьте руба́шку!
□ ∼ **up** v.t.: **he tucked up his sleeves** он засучи́л рука́ва; **they** ∼**ed the children up (in bed)** дете́й уложи́ли в крова́ть и укры́ли одея́лом

tuck² /tʌk/ v.i.: **they** ∼**ed into their supper** они́ уплета́ли у́жин за о́бе щёки; ∼ **in!** налета́й(те)! (на еду)

⚡ **Tuesday** /'tjuːzdeɪ/ n. вто́рник

tuft /tʌft/ n. (of grass, hair, etc.) пучо́к

tug /tʌɡ/ n. **1** (pull) рыво́к, дёрганье **2** (boat) букси́р
● v.t. (**tugged, tugging**) тащи́ть (impf.)

● *v.i.* (**tugged, tugging**) дёр|гать, -нуть; he ~ged at my sleeve он дёрнул меня́ за рука́в

■ ~ **of war** *n.* перетя́гивание кана́та

tuition /tjuːˈɪʃ(ə)n/ *n.* обуче́ние

tulip /ˈtjuːlɪp/ *n.* тюльпа́н

tumble /ˈtʌmb(ə)l/ *n.* **1** (fall) паде́ние; **take a ~** упа́сть (*pf.*) **2** (acrobatic feat) кувыро́к
● *v.i.* (mus.) сва́л|иваться, -и́ться
● *with adv.*: **the house seemed about to ~ down** дом, каза́лось, вот-во́т разва́лится

■ ~ **dryer** *n.* (BrE) электри́ческая суши́лка для белья́

tumbler /ˈtʌmblə(r)/ *n.* (glass) стака́н

tummy /ˈtʌmɪ/ *n.* (infml) живо́т(ик)

tumour /ˈtjuːmə(r)/ (AmE **tumor**) *n.* о́пухоль

tumult /ˈtjuːmʌlt/ *n.* сумато́ха

tumultuous /tjʊˈmʌltʃʊəs/ *adj.* шу́мный, беспоко́йный; **he received a ~ welcome** ему́ устро́или бу́рную встре́чу

tuna /ˈtjuːnə/ *n.* туне́ц

tundra /ˈtʌndrə/ *n.* ту́ндра

tune /tjuːn/ *n.* **1** (melody) мело́дия; моти́в **2** (correct pitch): **you are not singing in ~** вы фальши́вите; **he plays out of ~** он игра́ет фальши́во; **the piano is out of ~** фортепиа́но расстро́ено
● *v.t.* **1** (mus., bring to right pitch) настра́|ивать, -о́ить; **tuning fork** камерто́н **2** (adjust running of) настра́|ивать, -о́ить; регули́ровать, от-
□ ~ **in** *v.t. & i.* настра́|ивать(ся), -о́ить(ся); **he ~d in to the BBC** он настро́ил приёмник на Би-би-си́

tuneful /ˈtjuːnfʊl/ *adj.* музыка́льный, мело́дичный

tuneless /ˈtjuːnlɪs/ *adj.* немузыка́льный, немело́дичный

tuner /ˈtjuːnə(r)/ *n.* (of pianos etc.) настро́йщик; (radio component) тю́нер; (receiver) (ра́дио)приёмник

tunic /ˈtjuːnɪk/ *n.* (ancient garment) туни́ка; (part of uniform) ки́тель (*m.*)

Tunisia /tjuːˈnɪzɪə/ *n.* Туни́с

Tunisian /tjuːˈnɪzɪən/ *n.* туни́с|ец (-ка)
● *adj.* туни́сский

tunnel /ˈtʌn(ə)l/ *n.* тонне́ль (*m.*), тунне́ль (*m.*)
● *v.t.* (**tunnelled, tunnelling**, AmE **tunneled, tunneling**): **they ~led their way out** (of prison) они́ сде́лали подко́п и сбежа́ли (из тюрьмы́)
● *v.i.* (**tunnelled, tunnelling**, AmE **tunneled, tunneling**) про|кла́дывать, -ложи́ть тонне́ль

turban /ˈtɜːbən/ *n.* тюрба́н

turbine /ˈtɜːbaɪn/ *n.* турби́на

turbulence /ˈtɜːbjʊləns/ *n.* бу́рность; (aeron.) турбуле́нтность; (fig.) суета́, сумато́ха

turbulent /ˈtɜːbjʊlənt/ *adj.* бу́рный; (fig.) беспоко́йный

✐ ключева́я ле́ксика

turf /tɜːf/ *n.* (*pl.* **turfs** *or* **turves**) (grassy topsoil) дёрн; (peat) торф
● *v.t.* **1** (cover with ~) (*also* ~ **over**) покр|ыва́ть, -ы́ть дёрном **2**: ~ **out** (BrE, infml, eject) выбра́сывать, вы́бросить

turgid /ˈtɜːdʒɪd/ *adj.* (fig.) напы́щенный

Turk /tɜːk/ *n.* тур|о́к (-ча́нка)

Turkey /ˈtɜːkɪ/ *n.* **1** (country) Ту́рция **2** (**t~**, *pl.* **t~s**) (bird) инд|ю́к (-е́йка); (as food) инде́йка, индю́шка

Turkish /ˈtɜːkɪʃ/ *n.* туре́цкий язы́к
● *adj.* туре́цкий

■ ~ **delight** *n.* раха́т-луку́м

Turkmen /ˈtɜːkmən/ *n.* (*pl.* ~ *or* ~**s**) (person) туркме́н (-ка); (language) туркме́нский язы́к
● *adj.* туркме́нский

Turkmenistan /tɜːkmenɪˈstɑːn/ *n.* Туркмениста́н

turmeric /ˈtɜːmərɪk/ *n.* куркума́ (*азиатская пряность*)

turmoil /ˈtɜːmɔɪl/ *n.* беспоря́док; смяте́ние

✐ **turn** /tɜːn/ *n.* **1** (rotation) поворо́т, оборо́т **2** (change of direction) поворо́т; **I took a right ~** я поверну́л напра́во **3** (change in condition) переме́на; **his condition took a ~ for the worse** его́ состоя́ние уху́дшилось **4** (chance of doing sth in proper order) о́чередь; **it's your ~ next** вы сле́дующий; **they all spoke in ~** (*or* took ~**s to speak**) они́ говори́ли по о́череди **5** (service) услу́га; **he did me a good ~** он оказа́л мне до́брую услу́гу **6** (performance) но́мер **7** (infml, shock) потрясе́ние; **you gave me quite a ~** вы меня́ поря́дком испуга́ли
● *v.t.* **1** (cause to move round) пов|ора́чивать, -ерну́ть; **he ~ed his head** он поверну́л го́лову; он оберну́лся; **she ~ed the pages** она́ перелиста́ла страни́цы **2** (direct) напр|авля́ть, -а́вить; **he can ~ his hand to anything** он всё уме́ет; (incline): ~ **sb against sb/sth** настра́|ивать, -о́ить кого́-н. про́тив + *g.* **3** (pass round or beyond) пов|ора́чивать, -ерну́ть за + *a.*; **slow down as you ~ the corner** повора́чивая за́ у́гол, сба́вьте ско́рость; **it has ~ed two o'clock** уже́ два часа́; **he has ~ed fifty** ему́ испо́лнилось 50 лет **4** (transform) превра|ща́ть, -ти́ть; **he ~ed the water into wine** он обрати́л во́ду в вино́ **5** (cause to become): **the shock ~ed his hair white** он поседе́л от потрясе́ния **6** (send forcibly) прог|оня́ть, -на́ть; **he was ~ed out of the house** его́ вы́гнали из до́ма/из до́му
● *v.i.* **1** (move round) пов|ора́чиваться, -ерну́ться; враща́ться (*impf.*); **the key won't ~** ключ не повора́чивается; (fig.): **everything ~s on his answer** всё зави́сит от его́ отве́та; (revolve): **the discussion ~ed upon the meaning of democracy** спор враща́лся вокру́г по́длинного значе́ния демокра́тии **2** (change direction) свора́чивать, сверну́ться; направля́ться (*impf.*); **right ~!** напра́во!; **who can I ~ to?** к кому́ я могу́ обрати́ться?; **he ~ed on his attackers** он бро́сился на свои́х оби́дчиков **3** (change) превра|ща́ться,

-ти́ться; **the tadpoles** ~ed **into frogs** голова́стики преврати́лись в лягу́шек; **he** ~ed **into a miser** он стал скря́гой **4** (become) ста|нови́ться, -ть; де́латься, с-; **she** ~ed **pale** она́ побледне́ла; **it has** ~ed **warm** потепле́ло

□ ~ **away** v.t. (refuse admittance to) прог|оня́ть, -на́ть; не пус|ка́ть, -ти́ть

 • v.i.: **she** ~ed **away in disgust** она́ с отвраще́нием отверну́лась

□ ~ **back** v.t. (repel) от|сыла́ть, -осла́ть наза́д; **we were** ~ed **back at the frontier** нас верну́ли с грани́цы; (return to former position): **we cannot** ~ **the clock back** (fig.) мы не мо́жем поверну́ть вре́мя вспять

 • v.i. пов|ора́чивать, -ерну́ть наза́д; пойти́ (pf.) обра́тно

□ ~ **down** v.t. (reduce by ~ing) уб|авля́ть, -а́вить; ~ **the volume down!** (TV, etc.) уба́вьте звук!; (reject) отв|ерга́ть, -е́ргнуть; отка́з|ываться, -а́ться от + g.; **my offer was** ~ed **down** моё предложе́ние бы́ло отве́ргнуто

□ ~ **in** v.t. (hand over) сда|ва́ть, -ть; **he** ~ed **himself in to the police** он сда́лся поли́ции

□ ~ **off** v.t. (e.g. light, engine) выключа́ть, вы́ключить; гаси́ть, по-; (tap) закр|ыва́ть, -ы́ть

 • v.i. (make a diversion) св|ора́чивать, -ерну́ть

□ ~ **on** v.t. (e.g. light, engine, radio) включ|а́ть, -и́ть; (tap) откр|ыва́ть, -ы́ть; (fig.): **this music** ~s **me on** (infml) э́та му́зыка заво́дит меня́

□ ~ **out** v.t. (expel) прог|оня́ть, -на́ть; исключ|а́ть, -и́ть; (switch off) гаси́ть, по-; туши́ть, по-; (produce) выпуска́ть, вы́пустить; произв|оди́ть, -ести́; (empty) вывора́чивать, вы́вернуть

 • v.i. (prove) ока́з|ываться, -а́ться; **let us see how things** ~ **out** посмо́трим, како́й оборо́т при́мут дела́; **he** ~ed **out to be a liar** он оказа́лся лжецо́м; **it** ~ed **out that he was right** получи́лось, что он был прав; (assemble) соб|ира́ться, -ра́ться

□ ~ **over** v.t. (overturn) перев|ора́чивать, -ерну́ть; опроки́|дывать, -нуть; (reverse position of): **I** ~ed **over the page** я переверну́л страни́цу; (hand over) перед|ава́ть, -а́ть; (have as a turnover, comm.) име́ть (impf.) оборо́т + g.

 • v.i. (overturn) перев|ора́чиваться, -ерну́ться; (change position) перев|ора́чиваться, -ерну́ться; (revolve): **is the engine** ~ing **over?** дви́гатель враща́ется?

□ ~ **round** v.t. (change or reverse position of) перев|ора́чивать, -ерну́ть; **he** ~ed **his car round** он разверну́л маши́ну

 • v.i. (change position): **he** ~ed **round to look** он оберну́лся, что́бы посмотре́ть; (revolve) враща́ться (impf.)

□ ~ **up** v.t. (increase flow of) приб|авля́ть, -а́вить; уси́ли|вать, -ть

 • v.i. (arrive) появ|ля́ться, -и́ться; (be found; occur) ока́з|ываться, -а́ться; подв|ёртываться, -ерну́ться; (happen; become available) подверну́ться (pf.)

■ ~**around** n. (reversal of policy, opinion, etc.) поворо́т на 180 гра́дусов; ~**off** n. поворо́т, бокова́я доро́га; (repulsive thing) что-н. отврати́тельное; ~**out** n. (assembly): **there was a very good** ~**out** собра́лось о́чень

мно́го наро́ду; ~**over** n. (in business) оборо́т (капита́ла); (of staff) теку́честь (ка́дров); ~**pike** n. (AmE, tolled highway) пла́тная автомагистра́ль; ~**stile** n. турнике́т; ~**-up** n. (BrE, of trouser) манже́та, оборо́т

turner /'tə:nə(r)/ n. то́карь (m.)

turning /'tə:nɪŋ/ n. поворо́т

■ ~ **point** n. (fig.) кри́зис, перело́м; **it was a** ~ **point in his career** э́то был поворо́тный моме́нт в его́ карье́ре

turnip /'tə:nɪp/ n. ре́па

turquoise /'tə:kwɔɪz/ n. бирюзо́вый цвет

turret /'tʌrɪt/ n. ба́шенка; (on a tank, warship, etc.) ба́шня

turtle /'tə:t(ə)l/ n. черепа́ха

tusk /tʌsk/ n. клык, би́вень (m.)

tussle /'tʌs(ə)l/ n. дра́ка

tutor /'tju:tə(r)/ n. (private teacher) репети́тор; (university teacher) преподава́тель (-ница (infml))

tutorial /tju:'tɔ:rɪəl/ n. ≈ семина́р

tutu /'tu:tu:/ n. па́чка (балери́ны)

tuxedo /tʌk'si:dəʊ/ n. (pl. ~s or ~es) (AmE) смо́кинг

✍ **TV** abbr. (of **television**) ТВ (телеви́дение); (set) телеви́зор, (infml) те́лик, я́щик

twang /twæŋ/ n. (of plucked string) звеня́щий звук натя́нутой струны́; (nasal voice) гнуса́вый го́лос

tweak /twi:k/ v.t. **1** (pull sharply) ущипну́ть (pf.) **2** (infml, adjust) соверше́нствовать, у-

tweed /twi:d/ n. твид; **a** ~ **jacket** тви́довый пиджа́к

tweet /twi:t/ n. **1** щебет, чири́канье **2** (comput., a message posted using Twitter®) твит

 • v.i. **1** щебета́ть (impf.); чири́кать (impf.) **2** (comput., post a message using Twitter®) тви́тить (impf.)

tweezers /'twi:zəz/ n. pl. пинце́т

twelfth /twelfθ/ n. (date) двена́дцатое число́; (fraction) одна́ двена́дцатая

 • adj. двена́дцатый

twelve /twelv/ n. двена́дцать

 • adj. двена́дцать + g. pl.

twentieth /'twentɪθ/ n. (date) двадца́тое число́; (fraction) одна́ двадца́тая

 • adj. двадца́тый

twent|y /'twentɪ/ n. два́дцать; **she is still in her** ~**ies** ей ещё нет тридцати́; **the** ~**ies** (decade) двадца́тые го́ды

 • adj. два́дцать + g. pl.

✍ **twice** /twaɪs/ adv. (two times) два́жды, два ра́за; (doubly) вдво́е, в два ра́за; ~ **a day** два́жды (or два ра́за) в день; **he is** ~ **my age** он вдво́е ста́рше меня́; ~ **as much** в два ра́за (or вдво́е) бо́льше

twiddl|e /'twɪd(ə)l/ v.t. верте́ть (impf.); крути́ть (impf.); **he sat there** ~ing **his thumbs** он бил баклу́ши; он безде́льничал

twig /twɪg/ n. (on tree) ве́тка; (when cut) прут

twilight /'twaɪlaɪt/ n. су́мер|ки (-ек)

t

twin /twɪn/ *n.* близне́ц; (*in pl.*) близнецы́, дво́йня (*f. sg.*)
 ● *adj.* одина́ковый; **they are ~ brothers** они́ (бра́тья-)близнецы́
 ● *v.t.* (**twinned, twinning**) (fig.) соедин|я́ть, -и́ть
 ■ **~ beds** *n. pl.* две односпа́льные крова́ти

twine /twaɪn/ *n.* бечёвка, шнуро́к

twinge /twɪndʒ/ *n.* при́ступ о́строй бо́ли; (fig.) му́ка; **~s of conscience** угрызе́ния со́вести

twinkle /'twɪŋk(ə)l/ *v.i.* мерца́ть (*impf.*); сверка́ть (*impf.*); **his eyes ~d with amusement** его́ глаза́ ве́село блесте́ли

twirl /twɜːl/ *n.* враще́ние
 ● *v.t. & i.* верте́ть(ся) (*impf.*); крути́ть(ся) (*impf.*)

twist /twɪst/ *n.* **1** (sharp turning motion) круче́ние **2** (sharp change of direction) изги́б, поворо́т; **a ~ in the plot** круто́й поворо́т сюже́та **3** (sth ~ed or spiral in shape) петля́; у́зел
 ● *v.t.* **1** (screw round) крути́ть (*or* скру́чивать), с-; **I ~ed my ankle** я подверну́л но́гу **2** (contort) искрив|ля́ть, -и́ть; (fig.) иска|жа́ть, -зи́ть **3** (wind) обв|ива́ть, -и́ть; обм|а́тывать, -ота́ть
 ● *v.i.* **1** (wriggle) ко́рчиться (*impf.*); извива́ться (*impf.*) **2** (twine) обв|ива́ться, -и́ться; **the tendrils ~ed round their support** побе́ги расте́ния вили́сь вокру́г жёрдочки
 □ **~ off** *v.t.* откру́|чивать, -ти́ть

twisted /'twɪstɪd/ *adj.* (perverted) извращённый

twit /twɪt/ *n.* (BrE, infml) о́лух (infml)

twitch /twɪtʃ/ *n.* подёргивание, су́дорога
 ● *v.t.* **1** (jerk) дёргать (*impf.*) **2** (move spasmodically) подёргивать (*impf.*) + *i.*
 ● *v.i.* дёргаться (*impf.*), подёргиваться (*impf.*)

twitter /'twɪtə(r)/ *n.* **1** (chirping) щебет **2** (T~®) (service for micro-blogging) Тви́ттер
 ● *v.i.* (chirp) щебета́ть (*impf.*)

✱ **two** /tuː/ *n.* (число́/но́мер) два; (~ people) дво́е; **~ each, in ~s,** *or* **at a time, ~ by ~** по́ два/дво́е; (cut, divide): **in ~** на́двое/попола́м; **the plate broke in ~** таре́лка разби́лась на две ча́сти; (figure, thing numbered 2) дво́йка; **I put ~ and ~ together** я сообрази́л, что к чему́; **that makes ~ of us** вот и я то́же
 ● *adj.* два + *g. sg.*; (for masculine nouns denoting

people and pluralia tantum, also) дво́е + *g. pl.*; ~ **students** два студе́нта, дво́е студе́нтов; ~ **children** дво́е дете́й; два ребёнка; ~ **watches** дво́е часо́в
 ■ **~-dimensional** *adj.* двухме́рный; **~-faced** *adj.* (fig.) двули́чный; **~-fold** *adj.* двойно́й
 ● *adv.* вдво́е; **~-seater** *n.* двухме́стный автомоби́ль/самолёт; **~-time** *v.t.* (infml) обма́н|ывать, -у́ть; измен|я́ть, -и́ть (жене́/му́жу); **~-way** *adj.* (e.g. traffic) двусторо́нний

tycoon /taɪ'kuːn/ *n.* (business magnate) магна́т

tying /'taɪɪŋ/ *pres. part. of* ▶ **tie**

tympani /'tɪmpəni/ *n.* = timpani

tympanist /'tɪmpənɪst/ *n.* = timpanist

✱ **type** /taɪp/ *n.* **1** (class) тип, род **2** (letters for printing) шрифт
 ● *v.t.* (write with ~writer/computer) печа́тать, на- (на маши́нке/компью́тере)
 ● *v.i.* печа́тать (*impf.*) (на маши́нке/компью́тере)
 ■ **~cast** *adj.*: **he is ~cast as the butler** он всегда́ игра́ет роль дворе́цкого; **~face** *n.* шрифт; **~writer** *n.* пи́шущая маши́нка

typhoid /'taɪfɔɪd/ *n.* (*also* ~ **fever**) брюшно́й тиф

typhoon /taɪ'fuːn/ *n.* тайфу́н

✱ **typical** /'tɪpɪk(ə)l/ *adj.* типи́чный; **that is ~ of him** э́то сво́йственно ему́

typify /'tɪpɪfaɪ/ *v.t.* быть типи́чным представи́телем + *g.*

typist /'taɪpɪst/ *n.* (female) машини́стка

typographic /taɪpə'græfɪk/, **typographical** /taɪpə'græfɪk(ə)l/ *adjs.* типогра́фский

typography /taɪ'pɒgrəfɪ/ *n.* (art, process) полиграфи́я; (of books) книгопеча́тание; (appearance of printed matter) оформле́ние (*кни́ги и т. п.*)

tyrannical /tɪ'rænɪk(ə)l/ *adj.* тирани́ческий

tyrannize /'tɪrənaɪz/ *v.t. & i.* тира́нить (*impf.*)

tyranny /'tɪrənɪ/ *n.* тирани́я

tyrant /'taɪərənt/ *n.* тира́н

tyre /'taɪə(r)/ (AmE **tire**) *n.* ши́на

tzar /zɑː(r)/ *n.* = tsar

t

Uu

UAE *abbr.* (*of* **United Arab Emirates**) ОАЭ (Объединённые Ара́бские Эмира́ты)

ubiquitous /juːˈbɪkwɪtəs/ *adj.* вездесу́щий, повсеме́стный

ubiquity /juːˈbɪkwɪti/ *n.* вездесу́щность

udder /ˈʌdə(r)/ *n.* вы́мя (*nt.*)

UEFA /juːˈeɪfə/ *abbr.* (*of* **Union of European Football Associations**) УЕФА́ (*m. & f. indecl.*)

UFO /juːefˈəʊ, ˈjuːfəʊ/ *n.* (*pl.* **UFOs**) (*of* **unidentified flying object**) НЛО (*m. indecl.*) (неопо́знанный лета́ющий объе́кт)

Uganda /juːˈgændə/ *n.* Уга́нда

Ugandan /juːˈgændən/ *n.* уганди́|ец (-йка)
● *adj.* уганди́йский

ugly /ˈʌglɪ/ *adj.* (**uglier**, **ugliest**) **1** (unsightly) уро́дливый, безобра́зный **2** (threatening) опа́сный
■ ∼ **duckling** *n.* га́дкий утёнок

UK *abbr.* (*of* **United Kingdom**) Соединённое Короле́вство (*Великобрита́нии и Се́верной Ирла́ндии*)
● *adj.* (великобрита́нский

Ukraine /juːˈkreɪn/ *n.* Украи́на; **in** ∼ в Украи́не

Ukrainian /juːˈkreɪnɪən/ *n.* (person) украи́н|ец (-ка); (language) украи́нский язы́к
● *adj.* украи́нский

Ulan Bator /uːˈlɑːn ˈbɑːtə(r)/ *n.* Ула́н-Ба́тор

ulcer /ˈʌlsə(r)/ *n.* я́зва

ulcerated /ˈʌlsəreɪtɪd/ *adj.* изъязвлённый

Ulster /ˈʌlstə(r)/ *n.* О́льстер

ulterior /ʌlˈtɪərɪə(r)/ *adj.* скры́тый, невы́раженный
■ ∼ **motive** *n.* скры́тый моти́в

ultimate /ˈʌltɪmət/ *adj.* после́дний, оконча́тельный

ultimately /ˈʌltɪmətlɪ/ *adv.* в конце́ концо́в

ultimatum /ˌʌltɪˈmeɪtəm/ *n.* ультима́тум

ultrasound /ˈʌltrəsaʊnd/ *n.* ультразву́к; ∼ **scan** иссле́дование с по́мощью ультразвуково́го излуче́ния

ultraviolet /ˌʌltrəˈvaɪələt/ *adj.* ультрафиоле́товый

umbilical /ʌmˈbɪlɪk(ə)l/ *adj.*: ∼ **cord** пупови́на

umbrage /ˈʌmbrɪdʒ/ *n.* оби́да; **take** ∼ (**at**) об|ижа́ться, -и́деться (на + *a.*)

umbrella /ʌmˈbrelə/ *n.* зо́нтик, зонт

umpire /ˈʌmpaɪə(r)/ *n.* (arbitrator) посре́дник; (in games) судья́ (*m.*)

umpteenth /ʌmpˈtiːnθ/ *adj.* (infml) э́нный; **I have told you for the** ∼ **time!** ско́лько раз я тебе́ говори́л!

UN *abbr.* (*of* **United Nations (Organization)**) ООН (*f. indecl.*) (Организа́ция Объединённых На́ций)

un- /ʌn/ *neg. pref.* (*often expressed by pref.*) не… (*e.g.* ▶ **unable**), *or* без…, бес… (*e.g.* ▶ **unashamed**)

unable /ʌnˈeɪb(ə)l/ *adj.* неспосо́бный; **he is** ∼ **to swim** он не уме́ет пла́вать; **I am** ∼ **to say** я не могу́ сказа́ть

unabridged /ˌʌnəˈbrɪdʒd/ *adj.* несокращённый, по́лный

unacceptable /ˌʌnəkˈseptəb(ə)l/ *adj.* неприе́млемый

unaccompanied /ˌʌnəˈkʌmpənɪd/ *adj.* нике́м не сопровожда́емый; (mus.) без аккомпанеме́нта

unaccountable /ˌʌnəˈkaʊntəb(ə)l/ *adj.* (inexplicable) необъясни́мый; (irrational) безотчётный; (not responsible): ∼ **to** не несу́щий отве́тственности пе́ред + *i.*

unaccounted for /ˌʌnəˈkaʊntɪd/ *adj.* (missing): **two people were** ∼ не досчита́лись двух челове́к

unaccustomed /ˌʌnəˈkʌstəmd/ *adj.* непривы́кший; ∼ **as I am to public speaking** хотя́ я и не привы́к выступа́ть

unacknowledged /ˌʌnəkˈnɒlɪdʒd/ *adj.* непри́знанный

unadulterated /ˌʌnəˈdʌltəreɪtɪd/ *adj.* настоя́щий, неподде́льный; ∼ **nonsense** чисте́йший/полне́йший вздор; **the** ∼ **truth** чи́стая пра́вда

unaffected /ˌʌnəˈfektɪd/ *adj.* **1** (without affectation) непринуждённый **2** (not harmed or influenced): **our plans were** ∼ **by the weather** пого́да не измени́ла на́ших пла́нов

unaided /ʌnˈeɪdɪd/ *adj.* без посторо́нней по́мощи

unalloyed /ˌʌnəˈlɔɪd/ *adj.* нелеги́рованный, чи́стый (*о мета́лле*); (fig.): ∼ **pleasure** ниче́м не омрачённая ра́дость

unambiguous /ˌʌnæmˈbɪɡjʊəs/ *adj.* недвусмы́сленный

unanimity /ˌjuːnəˈnɪmɪti/ *n.* единоду́шие

unanimous /juːˈnænɪməs/ *adj.* единоду́шный, единогла́сный; **the resolution was passed** ∼**ly** резолю́ция была́ при́нята единогла́сно

unannounced /ˌʌnəˈnaʊnst/ *adj.* (to arrive, enter) без докла́да

unanswered /ʌnˈɑːnsəd/ *adj.* оста́вшийся без отве́та

unapologetic /ˌʌnəpɒləˈdʒetɪk/ *adj.* не прибега́ющий к оправда́ниям

unappealing /ˌʌnəˈpiːlɪŋ/ *adj.* неприя́тный

unappreciative /ˌʌnəˈpriːʃ(ɪ)ətɪv/ *adj.* неблагодáрный

unapproachable /ˌʌnəˈprəʊtʃəb(ə)l/ *adj.* недостýпный

unarmed /ʌnˈɑːmd/ *adj.* невооружённый ■ ~ **combat** *n.* самозащúта без орýжия

unashamed /ˌʌnəˈʃeɪmd/ *adj.* бессты́дный

unasked /ʌnˈɑːskt/ *adj.* непрóшеный

unassailable /ˌʌnəˈseɪləb(ə)l/ *adj.*: an ~ fortress непристýпная крéпость; an ~ argument неопровержúмый дóвод

unassuming /ˌʌnəˈsjuːmɪŋ/ *adj.* непритязáтельный

unattached /ˌʌnəˈtætʃt/ *adj.* не привя́занный/ прикреплённый (**to:** к + *d.*); she is ~ онá однóка

unattainable /ˌʌnəˈteɪnəb(ə)l/ *adj.* недосягáемый

unattractive /ˌʌnəˈtræktɪv/ *adj.* непривлекáтельный

unauthorized /ʌnˈɔːθəraɪzd/ *adj.* неразрешённый; (person) посторóнний

unavailable /ˌʌnəˈveɪləb(ə)l/ *adj.* недостýпный; he was ~ он был зáнят

unavoidabl|e /ˌʌnəˈvɔɪdəb(ə)l/ *adj.* (sure to happen) неизбéжный; I was ~y detained я не мог освободúться (рáньше)

unaware /ˌʌnəˈweə(r)/ *adj.* незнáющий; he was ~ of my presence он не подозревáл о моём присýтствии; I was ~ that he was married я не знал, что он женáт

unawares /ˌʌnəˈweəz/ *adv.* нечáянно; I was taken ~ by his question егó вопрóс застúг меня́ врасплóх

unbalanced /ʌnˈbælənst/ *adj.* (biased) односторóнний; (mentally disturbed) неуравновéшенный, неустóйчивый

unbearable /ʌnˈbeərəb(ə)l/ *adj.* невыносúмый

unbeaten /ʌnˈbiːt(ə)n/ *adj.* непревзойдённый

unbeknown /ˌʌnbɪˈnəʊn/ (infml **unbeknownst** /-ˈnəʊnst/) *adv.*: he did it ~ to me он сдéлал э́то без моегó вéдома

unbelievable /ˌʌnbɪˈliːvəb(ə)l/ *adj.* (infml, amazing) невероя́тный

unbiased, unbiassed /ʌnˈbaɪəst/ *adj.* беспристрáстный

unblemished /ʌnˈblemɪʃt/ *adj.* чúстый; (fig.) незапя́тнанный

unblock /ʌnˈblɒk/ *v.t.*: the plumber ~ed the drain водопровóдчик прочúстил водостóк

unbolt /ʌnˈbəʊlt/ *v.t.* (door) отп|ирáть, -ерéть

unborn /ʌnˈbɔːn/ *adj.*: her ~ child её ещё не родúвшийся ребёнок

unbounded /ʌnˈbaʊndɪd/ *adj.* безмéрный

unbridled /ʌnˈbraɪd(ə)ld/ *adj.* (fig.) необýзданный

unbroken /ʌnˈbrəʊkən/ *adj.*: only one plate was ~ тóлько однá тарéлка уцелéла; his spirit remained ~ егó дух нé был слóмлен;

an ~ record непревзойдённый/непобúтый рекóрд; ~ sleep непреры́вный сон

unburden /ʌnˈbɜːd(ə)n/ *v.t.*: he ~ed his soul (or himself) to me он излúл мне дýшу

unbutton /ʌnˈbʌt(ə)n/ *v.t.* расстёг|ивать, -нýть

uncalled for /ʌnˈkɔːld fɔː(r)/ *adj.* неумéстный

uncanny /ʌnˈkænɪ/ *adj.* (**uncannier, uncanniest**) стрáнный

unceasing /ʌnˈsiːsɪŋ/ *adj.* беспреры́вный

unceremonious /ˌʌnserɪˈməʊnɪəs/ *adj.* (abrupt, discourteous) бесцеремóнный

uncertain /ʌnˈsɜːt(ə)n/ *adj.* **1** (hesitant, in doubt) неувéренный; he was ~ what to do он не знал, что дéлать **2** (not clear) нея́сный; in no ~ terms весьмá недвусмы́сленно **3** (changeable, unreliable): the weather is ~ погóда измéнчива; my position is ~ (shaky) моё положéние неопределённо

uncertainty /ʌnˈsɜːtəntɪ/ *n.* **1** (hesitation) неувéренность **2** (unreliable nature) измéнчивость

unchanged /ʌnˈtʃeɪndʒd/ *adj.* неизменúвшийся; to remain ~ ост|авáться, -áться без изменéний

uncharitable /ʌnˈtʃærɪtəb(ə)l/ *adj.* жестóкий

uncharted /ʌnˈtʃɑːtɪd/ *adj.* не отмéченный на кáрте; (also fig.) неисслéдованный, неизвéданный

unchecked /ʌnˈtʃekt/ *adj.*: an ~ advance (mil.) беспрепя́тственное продвижéние

uncivilized /ʌnˈsɪvɪlaɪzd/ *adj.* нецивилизóванный

uncle /ˈʌŋk(ə)l/ *n.* дя́дя (*m.*)

unclean /ʌnˈkliːn/ *adj.* нечúстый

uncomfortable /ʌnˈkʌmftəb(ə)l/ *adj.* (lit., fig.) неудóбный; (situation) нелóвкий

uncommon /ʌnˈkɒmən/ *adj.* рéдкий

uncommunicative /ˌʌnkəˈmjuːnɪkətɪv/ *adj.* неразговóрчивый

uncomplimentary /ˌʌnkɒmplɪˈmentərɪ/ *adj.* нелéстный

uncompromising /ʌnˈkɒmprəmaɪzɪŋ/ *adj.* бескомпромúссный

unconcealed /ˌʌnkənˈsiːld/ *adj.* нескрывáемый

unconcern /ˌʌnkənˈsɜːn/ *n.* беззабóтность, беспéчность; безразлúчие, равнодýшие

unconcerned /ˌʌnkənˈsɜːnd/ *adj.* (carefree) беззабóтный; (indifferent) безразлúчный

unconditional /ˌʌnkənˈdɪʃən(ə)l/ *adj.* безуслóвный, безоговóрочный

unconfirmed /ˌʌnkənˈfɜːmd/ *adj.* неподтверждённый

unconnected /ˌʌnkəˈnektɪd/ *adj.* не свя́занный

unconscious /ʌnˈkɒnʃəs/ *n.*: the ~ (psych.) подсознáние
● *adj.* **1** (senseless) потеря́вший сознáние; he was ~ он был без сознáния/в обмóроке; he was knocked ~ он потеря́л сознáние от удáра **2** (unaware) не сознаю́щий **3** (unintentional) невóльный

u

unconsciousness /ʌnˈkɒnʃəsnɪs/ *n.* (physical) бессозна́тельное/обморочное состоя́ние; (unawareness) отсу́тствие (о)созна́ния, неосо́знанность

unconstitutional /ʌnkɒnstɪˈtjuːʃən(ə)l/ *adj.* неконституцио́нный, противоре́чащий конститу́ции

uncontested /ʌnkənˈtestɪd/ *adj.* неоспори́мый

uncontrollable /ʌnkənˈtrəʊləb(ə)l/ *adj.*: an ∼ temper неукроти́мый нрав; an ∼ child неуправля́емый ребёнок

unconventional /ʌnkənˈvenʃən(ə)l/ *adj.* нетрадицио́нный; (person, behaviour) нешабло́нный

unconvincing /ʌnkənˈvɪnsɪŋ/ *adj.* неубеди́тельный

uncooked /ʌnˈkʊkt/ *adj.* сыро́й

uncooperative /ʌnkəʊˈɒpərətɪv/ *adj.* равноду́шный

uncountable /ʌnˈkaʊntəb(ə)l/ *adj.* (gram.) неисчисля́емый

uncouth /ʌnˈkuːθ/ *adj.* гру́бый

uncover /ʌnˈkʌvə(r)/ *v.t.* (take cover off) сн|има́ть, -ять покро́в с + *g.*; (fig.) раскр|ыва́ть, -ы́ть

unctuous /ˈʌŋktʃʊəs/ *adj.* (ingratiating) еле́йный (liter.), чрезме́рно уго́дливый, слаща́во-любе́зный

uncultivated /ʌnˈkʌltɪveɪtɪd/ *adj.* (of land) необрабо́танный; (of person) некульту́рный

uncut /ʌnˈkʌt/ *adj.* (page, loop) неразре́занный; (grass) неподстри́женный; the film was shown ∼ фильм показа́ли в по́лной ве́рсии

undamaged /ʌnˈdæmɪdʒd/ *adj.* неповреждённый

undaunted /ʌnˈdɔːntɪd/ *adj.* неустраши́мый

undecided /ʌndɪˈsaɪdɪd/ *adj.* (not settled) нерешённый; (hesitating) нереши́тельный

undeniable /ʌndɪˈnaɪəb(ə)l/ *adj.* неоспори́мый, я́вный

⚬ **under** /ˈʌndə(r)/ *adv.* вниз; the ship went ∼ кора́бль затону́л
● *prep.* **1** под + *i.*; (of motion) под + *a.*; (out) from ∼ из-под + *g.* **2** (less than) ме́ньше + *g.*; ни́же + *g.*; he earns ∼ £400 a week он зараба́тывает ме́ньше четырёхсо́т фу́нтов в неде́лю; children ∼ 14 де́ти моло́же (or в во́зрасте до) четы́рнадцати лет **3** (var. uses): you are ∼ arrest вы аресто́ваны; ∼ the circumstances при сложи́вшихся обстоя́тельствах; ∼ discussion обсужда́емый; (in progress): the investigation is ∼ way ведётся рассле́дование

underarm /ˈʌndərɑːm/ *adj.*: an ∼ deodorant дезодора́нт для подмы́шек; an ∼ throw бросо́к сни́зу; serve ∼ под|ава́ть, -а́ть сни́зу

undercarriage /ˈʌndəkærɪdʒ/ *n.* (of a plane) шасси́ (*nt. indecl.*)

undercharge /ʌndəˈtʃɑːdʒ/ *v.t.* брать, взять с кого́-н. недоста́точно

underclothes /ˈʌndəkləʊðz/ *n. pl.* ни́жнее бельё

undercoat /ˈʌndəkəʊt/ *n.* (of paint) грунто́вка

undercover /ʌndəˈkʌvə(r)/ *adj.* та́йный

undercurrent /ˈʌndəkʌrənt/ *n.* подво́дное тече́ние; (fig.) скры́тая тенде́нция

undercut /ʌndəˈkʌt/ *v.t.*: he ∼ his competitor он назна́чил це́ну ни́же, чем его́ конкуре́нт

underdeveloped /ʌndədɪˈveləpt/ *adj.* недора́звитый; ∼ countries слабора́звитые стра́ны

underdog /ˈʌndədɒɡ/ *n.* (sport) побеждённая сторона́; (downtrodden person) неуда́чник

underdone /ʌndəˈdʌn/ *adj.* (of food) недожа́ренный

underestimate /ʌndərˈestɪmeɪt/ *v.t.* недооце́н|ивать, -и́ть

underfed /ʌndəˈfed/ *adj.* недоеда́ющий; (infant) недоко́рмленный

underfoot /ʌndəˈfʊt/ *adv.* под нога́ми

underfunded /ʌndəˈfʌndɪd/ *adj.*: the project was ∼ прое́кт получи́л недоста́точное финанси́рование

undergo /ʌndəˈɡəʊ/ *v.t.* испы́т|ывать, -а́ть; he has to ∼ an operation ему́ предстои́т опера́ция

undergraduate /ʌndəˈɡrædjʊət/ *n.* студе́нт (-ка)

underground /ˈʌndəɡraʊnd/ *n.* **1** (BrE, ∼ railway) метро́ (*indecl.*) **2** (∼ movement) подпо́лье
● *adj.* подзе́мный; (fig., secret, subversive) подпо́льный
● *adv.* (position) под землёй; (direction) под зе́млю; (fig.) подпо́льно

undergrowth /ˈʌndəɡrəʊθ/ *n.* подле́сок

underhand /ˈʌndəhænd/ *adj.* (secret, deceitful) закули́сный, та́йный

underlay /ˈʌndəleɪ/ *n.* (fabric) подкла́дка, подсти́лка

underl|ie /ʌndəˈlaɪ/ *v.t.* (fig.): ∼ying causes причи́ны, лежа́щие в осно́ве (*чего*)

underline /ʌndəˈlaɪn/ *v.t.* (lit., fig.) подч|ёркивать, -еркну́ть

underling /ˈʌndəlɪŋ/ *n.* ме́лкий чино́вник

undermine /ʌndəˈmaɪn/ *v.t.* подк|а́пывать, -опа́ть; (fig.) разр|уша́ть, -у́шить; his authority is ∼d его́ авторите́т подрыва́ют

underneath /ʌndəˈniːθ/ *adv.* внизу́, ни́же
● *prep.* под + *i.*; (of motion) под + *a.*

undernourished /ʌndəˈnʌrɪʃt/ *adj.* недоеда́ющий; (infant) недоко́рмленный

underpants /ˈʌndəpænts/ *n. pl.* (мужски́е) трус|ы́ (-о́в)

underpass /ˈʌndəpɑːs/ *n.* прое́зд под полотно́м желе́зной доро́ги

underpay /ʌndəˈpeɪ/ *v.t.* (worker) недопла́|чивать, -ти́ть + *d.*

underpin /ʌndəˈpɪn/ *v.t.* подв|оди́ть, -ести́ фунда́мент под + *a.*; (fig.) подде́рж|ивать, -а́ть

underprivileged /ʌndəˈprɪvɪlɪdʒd/ *adj.* неиму́щий

underrate /ʌndəˈreɪt/ *v.t.* недооце́н|ивать, -и́ть

u

underscore /ˌʌndəˈskɔː(r)/ *v.t.* подч|ёркивать, -еркну́ть

undersecretary /ˌʌndəˈsekrətəri/ *n.* замести́тель (*m.*) /помо́щник мини́стра

undersell /ˌʌndəˈsel/ *v.t.* прод|ава́ть, -а́ть деше́вле (*кого*)

undershirt /ˈʌndəʃɜːt/ *n.* (AmE) ма́йка

underside /ˈʌndəsaɪd/ *n.* низ; ни́жняя часть; (fig., less favourable aspect) непригля́дная сторона́

understaffed /ˌʌndəˈstɑːft/ *adj.* неукомплекто́ванный

ᵩ **understand** /ˌʌndəˈstænd/ *v.t.* **1** (comprehend) пон|има́ть, -я́ть; **he can make himself understood in English** он мо́жет объясни́ться по-англи́йски; **he ~s children** он уме́ет обраща́ться с детьми́ **2** (gather): **I ~ you are leaving** я слы́шал, что вы уезжа́ете

understandable /ˌʌndəˈstændəb(ə)l/ *adj.* поня́тный

ᵩ **understanding** /ˌʌndəˈstændɪŋ/ *n.* **1** (intellect) ум **2** (comprehension) понима́ние **3** (sympathy) понима́ние **4** (agreement) соглаше́ние; **on the clear ~ that …** то́лько при усло́вии, что… ● *adj.* (sympathetic) отзы́вчивый, чу́ткий

understatement /ˈʌndəsteɪtmənt/ *n.* преуменьше́ние

understudy /ˈʌndəstʌdi/ *n.* дублёр

undertake /ˌʌndəˈteɪk/ *v.t.* **1** (take on) предприн|има́ть, -я́ть **2** (promise) обя́з|ываться, -а́ться

undertaker /ˈʌndəteɪkə(r)/ *n.* заве́дующий похоро́нным бюро́

undertaking /ˌʌndəˈteɪkɪŋ/ *n.* (enterprise) предприя́тие; (pledge) обяза́тельство

undertone /ˈʌndətəʊn/ *n.* полуто́н; **in an ~** вполго́лоса; (fig.) отте́нок

undervalue /ˌʌndəˈvæljuː/ *v.t.* недооце́н|ивать, -и́ть

underwater /ˌʌndəˈwɔːtə(r)/ *adj.* подво́дный

underwear /ˈʌndəweə(r)/ *n.* (ни́жнее) бельё

underweight /ˈʌndəweɪt/ *adj.*: **she's ~** она́ сли́шком худа́я

underworld /ˈʌndəwɜːld/ *n.* (criminal society) престу́пный мир

underwriter /ˈʌndəraɪtə(r)/ *n.* (insurer) страхо́вщик; (guarantor) гара́нт

undeserved /ˌʌndɪˈzɜːvd/ *adj.* незаслу́женный

undesirable /ˌʌndɪˈzaɪərəb(ə)l/ *adj.* нежела́тельный

undetected /ˌʌndɪˈtektɪd/ *adj.* необнару́женный

undeveloped /ˌʌndɪˈveləpt/ *adj.* неразвито́й; **an ~ country** слабора́звитая страна́; **~ land** необрабо́танная земля́

undignified /ʌnˈdɪɡnɪfaɪd/ *adj.* недосто́йный

undisciplined /ʌnˈdɪsɪplɪnd/ *adj.* недисциплини́рованный

undiscovered /ˌʌndɪˈskʌvəd/ *adj.* неоткры́тый

undiscriminating /ˌʌndɪˈskrɪmɪneɪtɪŋ/ *adj.* неразбо́рчивый

undisguised /ˌʌndɪsˈɡaɪzd/ *adj.* незамаскиро́ванный

undisputed /ˌʌndɪˈspjuːtɪd/ *adj.* неоспори́мый

undisturbed /ˌʌndɪˈstɜːbd/ *adj.* (peaceful) споко́йный; (untouched) нетро́нутый; (indifferent) равноду́шный; **he was ~ by the news** но́вость (ничу́ть) не встрево́жила его́

undivided /ˌʌndɪˈvaɪdɪd/ *adj.*: **~ attention** неразде́льное внима́ние

undo /ʌnˈduː/ *v.t.* **1** (unfasten) развя́з|ывать, -а́ть **2** (annul) уничт|ожа́ть, -о́жить; (treaty, agreement) аннули́ровать (*impf., pf.*)

undoubted /ʌnˈdaʊtɪd/ *adj.* несомне́нный; **you are ~ly right** вы, несомне́нно/ безусло́вно, пра́вы

undress /ʌnˈdres/ *v.t. & i.* разд|ева́ть(ся), -е́ть(ся)

undrinkable /ʌnˈdrɪŋkəb(ə)l/ *adj.* неприго́дный для питья́

undue /ʌnˈdjuː/ *adj.* чрезме́рный

undulate /ˈʌndjʊleɪt/ *v.i.* волнова́ться (*impf.*); колыха́ться (*impf.*); **an ~ing landscape** холми́стый пейза́ж

undulating /ˈʌndjʊleɪtɪŋ/ *adj.*: холми́стый

unduly /ʌnˈdjuːli/ *adv.* чрезме́рно

undying /ʌnˈdaɪɪŋ/ *adj.* бессме́ртный

unearned /ʌnˈɜːnd/ *adj.* незарабо́танный; **~ income** ре́нтный дохо́д, дохо́д от сбереже́ний, це́нных бума́г, недви́жимости

unearth /ʌnˈɜːθ/ *v.t.* выка́пывать, вы́копать; **the body was ~ed** те́ло вы́копали; (fig., discover) раск|а́пывать, -опа́ть

unearthly /ʌnˈɜːθli/ *adj.* **1** (supernatural) неземно́й **2** (ghostly) при́зрачный **3** (infml): **at this/that/some/an ~ hour** ни свет ни заря́; **don't call me again at that/this ~ hour!** не звони́ мне бо́льше в таку́ю рань!

unease /ʌnˈiːz/ *n.* нело́вкость, стеснённость; (distress) трево́га

uneasiness /ʌnˈiːzɪnɪs/ *n.* нело́вкость (*смуще́ние*)

uneasy /ʌnˈiːzi/ *adj.* **1** (anxious) беспоко́йный **2** (ill at ease) стеснённый

uneconomic /ˌʌniːkəˈnɒmɪk/ *adj.* неэконо́мный; нерента́бельный

uneconomical /ˌʌniːkəˈnɒmɪk(ə)l/ *adj.* неэконо́мный

uneducated /ʌnˈedjʊkeɪtɪd/ *adj.* необразо́ванный

unemployable /ˌʌnɪmˈplɔɪəb(ə)l/ *adj.* нетрудоспосо́бный

unemployed /ˌʌnɪmˈplɔɪd/ *adj.* безрабо́тный; (*as n.*) **the ~** безрабо́тные (*pl.*)

unemployment /ˌʌnɪmˈplɔɪmənt/ *n.* безрабо́тица

■ **~ benefit** *n.* посо́бие по безрабо́тице

unending /ʌnˈendɪŋ/ *adj.* несконча́емый, бесконе́чный

unenthusiastic /ˌʌnɪnθjuːziˈæstɪk/ *adj.* невосто́рженный

u

unenviable /ʌnˈenvɪəb(ə)l/ *adj.* незави́дный

unequal /ʌnˈiːkw(ə)l/ *adj.* нера́вный

unequivocal /ʌnɪˈkwɪvək(ə)l/ *adj.* недвусмы́сленный; (support) определённый

unerring /ʌnˈɜːrɪŋ/ *adj.* безоши́бочный

UNESCO /juːˈneskəʊ/ *n.* (*abbr. of* **United Nations Educational, Scientific, and Cultural Organization**) ЮНЕ́СКО (*f. indecl.*) (Организа́ция Объединённых На́ций по вопро́сам образова́ния, нау́ки и культу́ры)

unethical /ʌnˈeθɪk(ə)l/ *adj.* неэти́чный

uneven /ʌnˈiːv(ə)n/ *adj.* неро́вный; неравноме́рный

uneventful /ʌnɪˈventfʊl/ *adj.* ти́хий

unexceptionable /ʌnɪkˈsepʃənəb(ə)l/ *adj.* безупре́чный

unexceptional /ʌnɪkˈsepʃən(ə)l/ *adj.* неисключи́тельный, зауря́дный

unexciting /ʌnɪkˈsaɪtɪŋ/ *adj.* ску́чный

unexpected /ʌnɪkˈspektɪd/ *adj.* неожи́данный

unfailing /ʌnˈfeɪlɪŋ/ *adj.* (friend) ве́рный; (support) неизме́нный

unfair /ʌnˈfeə(r)/ *adj.* несправедли́вый; ∼ **advantage** незако́нное преиму́щество

unfairness /ʌnˈfeənɪs/ *n.* несправедли́вость

unfaithful /ʌnˈfeɪθfʊl/ *adj.* неве́рный; **his wife was ∼ to him** жена́ ему́ измени́ла

unfaithfulness /ʌnˈfeɪθfʊlnɪs/ *n.* неве́рность (**to:** + *d.*)

unfamiliar /ʌnfəˈmɪljə(r)/ *adj.* незнако́мый; **I am ∼ with the district** я не зна́ю э́тот райо́н

unfashionable /ʌnˈfæʃənəb(ə)l/ *adj.* немо́дный

unfasten /ʌnˈfɑːs(ə)n/ *v.t.* открепля́ть, -и́ть; (untie) отвя́з|ывать, -а́ть; (unbutton, unclasp) отстёг|ивать, -ну́ть; (open) откр|ыва́ть, -ы́ть

unfavourable /ʌnˈfeɪvərəb(ə)l/ (AmE **unfavorable**) *adj.* неблагоприя́тный

unfeeling /ʌnˈfiːlɪŋ/ *adj.* бесчу́вственный; жесто́кий

unfinished /ʌnˈfɪnɪʃt/ *adj.* незако́нченный

unfit /ʌnˈfɪt/ *adj.* неподходя́щий; **food ∼ for (human) consumption** него́дная к употребле́нию пи́ща; **∼ to rule** неспосо́бный пра́вить

unflattering /ʌnˈflætərɪŋ/ *adj.* нелестный

unfold /ʌnˈfəʊld/ *v.t.* развёр|тывать, -ну́ть; (fig.) раскр|ыва́ть, -ы́ть
• *v.i.* развёр|тываться, -ну́ться; **as the story ∼s** по хо́ду повествова́ния

unforeseeable /ʌnfɔːˈsiːəb(ə)l/ *adj.* непредви́димый

unforeseen /ʌnfɔːˈsiːn/ *adj.* непредви́денный

unforgettable /ʌnfəˈgetəb(ə)l/ *adj.* незабыва́емый

unforgivable /ʌnfəˈgɪvəb(ə)l/ *adj.* непрости́тельный

unforgiving /ʌnfəˈgɪvɪŋ/ *adj.* непроща́ющий

unfortunate /ʌnˈfɔːtʃənət/ *adj.* (person) несча́стный; (remark) неуда́чный

✔ **unfortunately** /ʌnˈfɔːtʃənətlɪ/ *adv.* к сожале́нию; **∼ for him** к несча́стью для него́

unfounded /ʌnˈfaʊndɪd/ *adj.* необосно́ванный

unfriendly /ʌnˈfrendlɪ/ *adj.* недружелю́бный

unfulfilled /ʌnfʊlˈfɪld/ *adj.* неудовлетворённый

unfurnished /ʌnˈfɜːnɪʃt/ *adj.* немеблиро́ванный, необста́вленный

ungainly /ʌnˈgeɪnlɪ/ *adj.* нело́вкий, неуклю́жий

ungodly /ʌnˈgɒdlɪ/ *adj.* (infml) = **unearthly** 3

ungovernable /ʌnˈgʌvənəb(ə)l/ *adj.* неуправля́емый

ungracious /ʌnˈgreɪʃəs/ *adj.* неве́жливый

ungrammatical /ʌngrəˈmætɪk(ə)l/ *adj.* негра́мотный (*о тексте*)

ungrateful /ʌnˈgreɪtfʊl/ *adj.* неблагода́рный

unguarded /ʌnˈgɑːdɪd/ *adj.* (e.g. town) незащищённый; (e.g. prisoner) неохраня́емый; (careless) неосторо́жный

unhappily /ʌnˈhæpɪlɪ/ *adv.* **1** (without happiness) несча́стливо **2** (unfortunately) к несча́стью

unhappiness /ʌnˈhæpɪnɪs/ *n.* несча́стье, грусть

unhappy /ʌnˈhæpɪ/ *adj.* (sorrowful) несчастли́вый, несча́стный, гру́стный; (unfortunate) неуда́чный

unharmed /ʌnˈhɑːmd/ *adj.* невреди́мый; (*pred.*) цел и невреди́м

unhealthy /ʌnˈhelθɪ/ *adj.* **1** (in or indicating ill health) нездоро́вый, боле́зненный **2** (infml, dangerous) вре́дный

unheard of /ʌnˈhɜːd ɒv/ *adj.* неслы́ханный, небыва́лый

unheeded /ʌnˈhiːdɪd/ *adj.* незаме́ченный; **his advice went ∼** к его́ сове́ту не прислу́шались

unhelpful /ʌnˈhelpfʊl/ *adj.* бесполе́зный; (person) неотзы́вчивый

unhinge /ʌnˈhɪndʒ/ *v.t.* (lit.) сн|има́ть, -ять с пе́тель; (fig.) расстра́|ивать, -о́ить; **the tragedy ∼d his mind** от пережи́той траге́дии он помеша́лся

unhook /ʌnˈhʊk/ *v.t.* расстёг|ивать, -ну́ть

unhurried /ʌnˈhʌrɪd/ *adj.* неторопли́вый

unhurt /ʌnˈhɜːt/ *adj.* невреди́мый

unhygienic /ʌnhaɪˈdʒiːnɪk/ *adj.* негигиени́чный

unicorn /ˈjuːnɪkɔːn/ *n.* единоро́г

unidentified /ʌnaɪˈdentɪfaɪd/ *adj.* неопо́знанный

unification /juːnɪfɪˈkeɪʃ(ə)n/ *n.* объедине́ние

uniform /ˈjuːnɪfɔːm/ *n.* фо́рма; (esp. mil.) мунди́р
• *adj.* однообра́зный; одина́ковый; станда́ртный

uniformed /ˈjuːnɪfɔːmd/ *adj.* оде́тый в фо́рму; в мунди́ре

uniformity /juːnɪˈfɔːmɪtɪ/ *n.* единообра́зие

unify /ˈjuːnɪfaɪ/ *v.t.* объедин|я́ть, -и́ть

u

unilateral /juːˈnɪˈlætər(ə)l/ *adj.*
односторо́нний
unimaginable /ˌʌnɪˈmædʒɪnəb(ə)l/ *adj.*
невообрази́мый
unimaginative /ˌʌnɪˈmædʒɪnətɪv/ *adj.*
прозаи́чный
unimpeachable /ˌʌnɪmˈpiːtʃəb(ə)l/ *adj.*
безупре́чный, безукори́зненный
unimpeded /ˌʌnɪmˈpiːdɪd/ *adj.*
беспрепя́тственный
unimportant /ˌʌnɪmˈpɔːt(ə)nt/ *adj.*
нева́жный, незначи́тельный
unimpressed /ˌʌnɪmˈprest/ *adj.*: I was ~ by
his threats его́ угро́зы не произвели́ на меня́
никако́го впечатле́ния
uninhabitable /ˌʌnɪnˈhæbɪtəb(ə)l/ *adj.*
неприго́дный для жилья́
uninhabited /ˌʌnɪnˈhæbɪtɪd/ *adj.*
необита́емый
uninhibited /ˌʌnɪnˈhɪbɪtɪd/ *adj.* откры́тый,
нестесни́тельный
uninitiated /ˌʌnɪˈnɪʃɪeɪtɪd/ *adj.*
непосвящённый
uninjured /ˌʌnˈɪndʒəd/ *adj.* непострада́вший;
he was ~ by his fall при паде́нии он не
пострада́л
unintelligible /ˌʌnɪnˈtelɪdʒɪb(ə)l/ *adj.*
неразбо́рчивый
unintended /ˌʌnɪnˈtendɪd/ *adj.*
ненаме́ренный; (unforeseen)
непредусмо́тренный
unintentional /ˌʌnɪnˈtenʃən(ə)l/ *adj.*
ненаме́ренный
uninterested /ˌʌnˈɪntrestɪd/ *adj.*
безразли́чный (in: к + *d.*)
uninteresting /ˌʌnˈɪntrestɪŋ/ *adj.*
неинтере́сный
uninvited /ˌʌnɪnˈvaɪtɪd/ *adj.* незва́ный
uninviting /ˌʌnɪnˈvaɪtɪŋ/ *adj.*
непривлека́тельный; an ~ prospect
неприя́тная перспекти́ва
✓ **union** /ˈjuːnjən/ *n.* **1** (joining, uniting)
объедине́ние, сою́з **2** (association) сою́з;
students' ~ студе́нческий сою́з; (building)
студе́нческий клуб **3** (trade ~) профсою́з
■ U~ Jack *n.* госуда́рственный флаг
Великобрита́нии
✓ **unique** /juːˈniːk/ *adj.* уника́льный,
еди́нственный (в своём ро́де)
unisex /ˈjuːnɪseks/ *adj.*: ~ clothes оде́жда,
подходя́щая для обо́их поло́в; ~
hairdresser's парикма́херская для мужчи́н
и же́нщин
unison /ˈjuːnɪs(ə)n/ *n.* (fig.) гармо́ния; they
acted in perfect ~ они́ де́йствовали в
по́лном согла́сии
✓ **unit** /ˈjuːnɪt/ *n.* **1** (single entity) едини́ца; це́лое
2 (math., and of measurement) едини́ца; monetary
~ де́нежная едини́ца **3** (mil.) часть
4 (of furniture etc.) се́кция
■ ~ trust *n.* (BrE) дове́рительный паево́й фонд

✓ ключева́я ле́ксика

unite /juːˈnaɪt/ *v.t.* соедин|я́ть, -и́ть; the
U~d Nations (organization) Организа́ция
Объединённых На́ций; the U~d Kingdom
Соединённое Короле́вство; the U~d States
Соединённые Шта́ты
● *v.i.* соедин|я́ться, -и́ться; ~d front еди́ный
фронт
unity /ˈjuːnɪti/ *n.* **1** (oneness; coherence) еди́нство
2 (concord) согла́сие
universal /juːnɪˈvɜːs(ə)l/ *adj.* всео́бщий,
универса́льный
universe /ˈjuːnɪvɜːs/ *n.* вселе́нная
✓ **university** /juːnɪˈvɜːsɪti/ *n.* университе́т
unjust /ʌnˈdʒʌst/ *adj.* несправедли́вый
unjustified /ʌnˈdʒʌstɪfaɪd/ *adj.* неопра́вданный
unkempt /ʌnˈkempt/ *adj.* растрёпанный
unkind /ʌnˈkaɪnd/ *adj.* недо́брый, злой;
(unpleasant) нелюбе́зный; be ~ to sb пло́хо
обраща́ться (*impf.*) с кем-н.
unkindness /ʌnˈkaɪndnɪs/ *n.* злость;
нелюбе́зность
unknown /ʌnˈnəʊn/ *n.* неизве́стное
● *adj.* неизве́стный
unlace /ʌnˈleɪs/ *v.t.* расшнуро́в|ывать, -а́ть
unlawful /ʌnˈlɔːfʊl/ *adj.* незако́нный
unleaded /ʌnˈledɪd/ *adj.*: ~ petrol
неэтили́рованный бензи́н
unleash /ʌnˈliːʃ/ *v.t.* спус|ка́ть, -ти́ть с
при́вязи; (fig.) да|ва́ть, -ть во́лю + *d.*
unleavened /ʌnˈlev(ə)nd/ *adj.* пре́сный
(хлеб)
✓ **unless** /ʌnˈles/ *conj.* (if not) е́сли (то́лько) не; I
shall go ~ it rains я пойду́, е́сли (то́лько) не
бу́дет дождя́; (until) пока́ не; I won't continue
~ he apologizes я не бу́ду продолжа́ть,
пока́ он не извини́тся; (except if) ра́зве (что/
то́лько); I don't know why he is late, ~
he has lost his way не зна́ю, почему́ он
опа́здывает — ра́зве что заблуди́лся
✓ **unlike** /ʌnˈlaɪk/ *adj. & prep.* (different from)
непохо́жий, ра́зный; he is ~ his sister он
не похо́ж на свою́ сестру́; ~ the others, he
works hard в отли́чие от други́х он рабо́тает
усе́рдно
unlikelihood /ʌnˈlaɪklɪhʊd/ *n.*
неправдоподо́бие; маловероя́тность;
невероя́тность
✓ **unlikely** /ʌnˈlaɪklɪ/ *adj.* (tale)
неправдоподо́бный; (not to be expected): it
is ~ he will recover маловероя́тно, что он
попра́вится
unlimited /ʌnˈlɪmɪtɪd/ *adj.* неограни́ченный;
(expanse) безграни́чный
unlined /ʌnˈlaɪnd/ *adj.* **1**: ~ paper
нелино́ванная бума́га **2**: an ~ coat пальто́
без подкла́дки
unload /ʌnˈləʊd/ *v.t.* выгружа́ть, вы́грузить;
разгру|жа́ть, -зи́ть; (fig.): she ~ed her worries
on to him она́ облегчи́ла ду́шу, подели́вшись
с ним свои́ми забо́тами
unlock /ʌnˈlɒk/ *v.t.* отп|ира́ть, -ере́ть (ключо́м)
unluckily /ʌnˈlʌkɪlɪ/ *adv.* к несча́стью; ~ for
him к несча́стью для него́

unlucky /ʌn'lʌkɪ/ *adj.* (having bad luck): **he is** ∼ **at cards** ему́ не везёт в ка́ртах; (causing bad luck) несчастли́вый

unmanageable /ʌn'mænɪdʒəb(ə)l/ *adj.* неуправля́емый

unmarried /ʌn'mærɪd/ *adj.* (man) нежена́тый, холосто́й; (woman) незаму́жняя; **he is** ∼ он не жена́т; **she is** ∼ она́ не за́мужем

unmask /ʌn'mɑːsk/ *v.t.* (fig.) разоблача|́ть, -и́ть

unmentionable /ʌn'menʃənəb(ə)l/ *adj.* неприли́чный, запре́тный

unmistakable /ʌnmɪ'steɪkəb(ə)l/ *adj.* ве́рный, я́сный, очеви́дный

unmitigated /ʌn'mɪtɪɡeɪtɪd/ *adj.* по́лный

unmoved /ʌn'muːvd/ *adj.* бесчу́вственный

unnamed /ʌn'neɪmd/ *adj.* нена́званный; (unidentified) неизве́стный

unnatural /ʌn'nætʃər(ə)l/ *adj.* неесте́ственный

unnecessary /ʌn'nesəsərɪ/ *adj.* нену́жный; (excessive) изли́шний

unnerve /ʌn'nɜːv/ *v.t.* обесси́ли|вать, -ть

unnoticed /ʌn'nəʊtɪst/ *adj.* незаме́ченный

unobservant /ʌnəb'zɜːv(ə)nt/ *adj.* ненаблюда́тельный

unobstructed /ʌnəb'strʌktɪd/ *adj.* незагоро́женный

unobtainable /ʌnəb'teɪnəb(ə)l/ *adj.* недосту́пный

unobtrusive /ʌnəb'truːsɪv/ *adj.* скро́мный

unoccupied /ʌn'ɒkjʊpaɪd/ *adj.* неза́нятый, свобо́дный; **an** ∼ **house** пусто́й дом

unofficial /ʌnə'fɪʃ(ə)l/ *adj.* неофициа́льный

unorthodox /ʌn'ɔːθədɒks/ *adj.* неортодокса́льный, сме́лый

unpack /ʌn'pæk/ *v.t. & i.* распако́в|ывать(ся), -а́ть(ся)

unpaid /ʌn'peɪd/ *adj.* **1** неопла́ченный; (of debt, bill, etc.) неупла́ченный **2** (of person, unsalaried) не получа́ющий пла́ты/жа́лованье

unpalatable /ʌn'pælətəb(ə)l/ *adj.* невку́сный; (fig.) неприя́тный; **an** ∼ **truth** го́рькая пра́вда

unparalleled /ʌn'pærəleld/ *adj.* несравни́мый

unpatriotic /ʌnpætrɪ'ɒtɪk/ *adj.* (behaviour) непатриоти́ческий; (person) непатриоти́чный

unperturbed /ʌnpə'tɜːbd/ *adj.* невозмути́мый

unpick /ʌn'pɪk/ *v.t.* распа|́рывать, -оро́ть (*шов*)

unplanned /ʌn'plænd/ *adj.* незаплани́рованный; (unexpected) неожи́данный

unpleasant /ʌn'plez(ə)nt/ *adj.* неприя́тный

unpleasantness /ʌn'plezəntnɪs/ *n.* неприя́тность

unplug /ʌn'plʌɡ/ *v.t.* отключ|а́ть, -и́ть

unpopular /ʌn'pɒpjʊlə(r)/ *adj.* непопуля́рный

unprecedented /ʌn'presɪdentɪd/ *adj.* беспрецеде́нтный

unpredictable /ʌnprɪ'dɪktəb(ə)l/ *adj.* непредсказу́емый

unpremeditated /ʌnprɪ'medɪteɪtɪd/ *adj.* непреднаме́ренный

unprepared /ʌnprɪ'peəd/ *adj.* неподгото́вленный; **his speech was** ∼ он произнёс свою́ речь экспро́мтом

unprepossessing /ʌnpriːpə'zesɪŋ/ *adj.* нераспола́гающий

unpretentious /ʌnprɪ'tenʃəs/ *adj.* непретенцио́зный

unprincipled /ʌn'prɪnsɪp(ə)ld/ *adj.* беспринци́пный

unprintable /ʌn'prɪntəb(ə)l/ *adj.* нецензу́рный

unproductive /ʌnprə'dʌktɪv/ *adj.* непродукти́вный

unprofessional /ʌnprə'feʃ(ə)n(ə)l/ *adj.* непрофессиона́льный; ∼ **conduct** наруше́ние профессиона́льной э́тики

unprofitable /ʌn'prɒfɪtəb(ə)l/ *adj.* невы́годный

unprompted /ʌn'prɒmptɪd/ *adj.* неподска́занный, спонта́нный

unprotected /ʌnprə'tektɪd/ *adj.* незащищённый; ∼ **sex** незащищённый секс

unprovoked /ʌnprə'vəʊkt/ *adj.* неспровоци́рованный

unqualified /ʌn'kwɒlɪfaɪd/ *adj.* **1** (without reservations) безогово́рочный **2** (not competent) некомпете́нтный; **I am** ∼ **to judge this** я недоста́точно компете́нтен, что́бы суди́ть об э́том

unquestionable /ʌn'kwestʃənəb(ə)l/ *adj.* (undoubted) несомне́нный; (indisputable) неоспори́мый

unravel /ʌn'ræv(ə)l/ *v.t.* (**unravelled**, **unravelling**, AmE **unraveled**, **unraveling**) распу́т|ывать, -ать; (fig.) разга́д|ывать, -а́ть

unreal /ʌn'rɪəl/ *adj.* (imaginary) нереа́льный; (strange) фантасти́ческий

unrealistic /ʌnrɪə'lɪstɪk/ *adj.* нереа́льный

unreasonable /ʌn'riːzənəb(ə)l/ *adj.* не(благо)разу́мный; (excessive) чрезме́рный

unrecognizable /ʌn'rekəɡnaɪzəb(ə)l/ *adj.* неузнава́емый

unrelated /ʌnrɪ'leɪtɪd/ *adj.* **1** (not connected) несвя́занный (**to:** c + *i.*) **2** (not kin): **he is** ∼ **to me** он мне не ро́дственник

unrelenting /ʌnrɪ'lentɪŋ/ *adj.* (implacable) неумоли́мый; (ceaseless) неослабева́ющий

unreliable /ʌnrɪ'laɪəb(ə)l/ *adj.* (person) ненадёжный; (information) недостове́рный

unremitting /ʌnrɪ'mɪtɪŋ/ *adj.* неосла́бный; (incessant) беспреста́нный

unrequited /ʌnrɪ'kwaɪtɪd/ *adj.*: ∼ **love** неразделённая/безотве́тная любо́вь

unreserved /ʌnrɪ'zɜːvd/ *adj.* (not set aside) незаброни́рованный; (open, frank) открове́нный; (wholehearted) по́лный; **I agree with you** ∼**ly** я по́лностью с ва́ми согла́сен

unresolved /ʌnrɪ'zɒlvd/ *adj.* нереши́тельный

u

unrest /ʌn'rest/ n. (disquiet) беспокойство; (social, political) волнения (nt. pl.)

unrestricted /ʌnrɪ'strɪktɪd/ adj. неограниченный

unrewarding /ʌnrɪ'wɔ:dɪŋ/ adj. неблагодарный

unripe /ʌn'raɪp/ adj. неспелый, незрелый

unrivalled /ʌn'raɪv(ə)ld/ (AmE **unrivaled**) adj. непревзойдённый

unroll /ʌn'rəʊl/ v.t. & i. развёр|тывать(ся), -ну́ть(ся)

unruffled /ʌn'rʌf(ə)ld/ adj. (fig.) невозмутимый

unruly /ʌn'ru:lɪ/ adj. (**unrulier, unruliest**) непокорный

unsafe /ʌn'seɪf/ adj. небезопасный

unsaid /ʌn'sed/ adj.: some things are better left ~ есть вещи, о которых лучше умолчать

unsatisfactory /ʌnsætɪs'fæktərɪ/ adj. неудовлетворительный

unsatisfied /ʌn'sætɪsfaɪd/ adj. неудовлетворённый

unsavoury /ʌn'seɪvərɪ/ (AmE **unsavory**) adj. (fig.) сомнительный

unscathed /ʌn'skeɪðd/ adj. цел и невредим

unscheduled /ʌn'ʃedju:ld/ adj. незапланированный; an ~ flight рейс вне расписания

unscrew /ʌn'skru:/ v.t. & i. отви́н|чивать(ся), -ти́ть(ся)

unscrupulous /ʌn'skru:pjʊləs/ adj. беспринципный

unseasonable /ʌn'si:zənəb(ə)l/ adj. не по сезону; ~ weather погода не по сезону; (fig., untimely) ~ несвоевременный

unseemly /ʌn'si:mlɪ/ adj. непристойный

unseen /ʌn'si:n/ adj. невидимый

unselfish /ʌn'selfɪʃ/ adj. бескорыстный

unsettled /ʌn'set(ə)ld/ adj. неустойчивый

unsettling /ʌn'setlɪŋ/ adj. тревожный

unshakeable /ʌn'ʃeɪkəb(ə)l/ adj. непоколебимый

unshaken /ʌn'ʃeɪkən/ adj. (resolute) непоколебимый, непоколебленный

unshaven /ʌn'ʃeɪv(ə)n/ adj. небритый

unsightly /ʌn'saɪtlɪ/ adj. некрасивый, неприглядный

unskilled /ʌn'skɪld/ adj. неквалифицированный; ~ labourer разнорабочий

unsociable /ʌn'səʊʃəb(ə)l/ adj. необщительный

unsocial /ʌn'səʊʃ(ə)l/ adj. антиобщественный; to work ~ hours работать во время, отличающееся от общепринятого

unsolicited /ʌnsə'lɪsɪtɪd/ adj. (not asked for) непрошеный; (given, done voluntarily) добровольный

unsophisticated /ʌnsə'fɪstɪkeɪtɪd/ adj. (person, approach) простой, простодушный; (thing, work) безыскусный

unsound /ʌn'saʊnd/ adj. (bad, rotten) испорченный, гнилой; (unwholesome) нездоровый; (unstable) непрочный; ~ views необоснованные взгляды; of ~ mind душевнобольной; a man of ~ judgement человек, лишённый здравого смысла

unsparing /ʌn'speərɪŋ/ adj. (merciless) беспощадный, безжалостный; (generous) щедрый; (diligent) усердный; ~ in his efforts не щадящий сил

unspeakable /ʌn'spi:kəb(ə)l/ adj. невыразимый

unspoiled /ʌn'spɔɪld/, **unspoilt** /ʌn'spɔɪlt/ adjs. неиспорченный; (of person) неизбалованный

unspoken /ʌn'spəʊkən/ adj. невысказанный

unstable /ʌn'steɪb(ə)l/ adj. неустойчивый, нестабильный

unsteady /ʌn'stedɪ/ adj. нетвёрдый; he was ~ on his legs он нетвёрдо держался на ногах

unstinting /ʌn'stɪntɪŋ/ adj. (generous) щедрый

unstuck /ʌn'stʌk/ adj.: the stamp came ~ марка отклеилась; (fig., infml): my schemes came ~ мои планы рухнули

unsubstantiated /ʌnsəb'stænʃɪeɪtɪd/ adj. недоказанный

unsuccessful /ʌnsək'sesfʊl/ adj. безуспешный, неудачный; he was ~ in the exam он не сдал экзамен

unsuitable /ʌn'sju:təb(ə)l/ adj. неподходящий

unsung /ʌn'sʌŋ/ adj. (not celebrated) невоспетый; an ~ hero невоспетый герой

unsure /ʌn'ʃɔ:(r)/ adj. (not confident) неуверенный; he was ~ of his ground он не чувствовал себя достаточно компетентным; ~ of oneself не уверенный в себе

unsuspecting /ʌnsə'spektɪŋ/ adj. неподозревающий

unsweetened /ʌn'swi:t(ə)nd/ adj. неподслащённый

unswerving /ʌn'swɜ:vɪŋ/ adj. (fig.) непоколебимый

unsympathetic /ʌnsɪmpə'θetɪk/ adj. чёрствый, несочувствующий

untangle /ʌn'tæŋg(ə)l/ v.t. распут|ывать, -ать

untaxed /ʌn'tækst/ adj. не облагаемый налогом

untenable /ʌn'tenəb(ə)l/ adj.: ~ arguments неубедительные доводы; an ~ position (mil.) позиция, непригодная для обороны; невыгодная позиция

unthinkable /ʌn'θɪŋkəb(ə)l/ adj. немыслимый

unthinking /ʌn'θɪŋkɪŋ/ adj. (thoughtless) бездумный; (inadvertent) нечаянный; машинальный

untidiness /ʌn'taɪdɪnɪs/ n. неопрятность, неаккуратность

---

untidy /ʌnˈtaɪdɪ/ *adj.* неопря́тный, неаккура́тный

untie /ʌnˈtaɪ/ *v.t.* разва́з|ывать, -а́ть; отвя́з|ывать, -а́ть; расшнуро́в|ывать, -а́ть

⚮ **until** /ənˈtɪl/ *prep. & conj.* = till²; unless and ∼ то́лько когда́/е́сли

untimely /ʌnˈtaɪmlɪ/ *adj.* (premature) преждевре́менный; (ill-timed) неуме́стный

untiring /ʌnˈtaɪərɪŋ/ *adj.* (person) неутоми́мый; (work, efforts) неуста́нный

unto /ˈʌntʊ/ *prep.* (archaic) = to

untold /ʌnˈtəʊld/ *adj.* **1** (suffering, delight) невырази́мый **2** (damage) неисчисли́мый; ∼ wealth несме́тные бога́тства

untouchable /ʌnˈtʌtʃəb(ə)l/ *n.* (member of lowest-caste Hindu group) неприкаса́емый
 ● *adj.* (unattainable) недосяга́емый, недосту́пный; (impossible to compete with) недосяга́емый

untoward /ʌntəˈwɔːd/ *adj.*: nothing ∼ happened ничего́ плохо́го не случи́лось

untrained /ʌnˈtreɪnd/ *adj.* необу́ченный

untranslatable /ʌntrænzˈleɪtəb(ə)l/ *adj.* непереводи́мый

untroubled /ʌnˈtrʌb(ə)ld/ *adj.* невозмути́мый

untrue /ʌnˈtruː/ *adj.* (inaccurate) неве́рный, ло́жный; (unfaithful) неве́рный

untrustworthy /ʌnˈtrʌstwəːðɪ/ *adj.* ненадёжный

untruth /ʌnˈtruːθ/ *n.* непра́вда

untruthful /ʌnˈtruːθfʊl/ *adj.* (of thing) неве́рный, ло́жный; (of person or thing) лжи́вый

unused¹ /ʌnˈjuːzd/ *adj.* (not put to use) неиспо́льзованный; my ticket was ∼ я не испо́льзовал свой биле́т

unused² /ʌnˈjuːst/ *adj.* (unaccustomed) непривы́кший (to: к + d.); I am ∼ to this я к э́тому не привы́к

⚮ **unusual** /ʌnˈjuːʒʊəl/ *adj.* необыкнове́нный, необы́чный; ∼ly осо́бенно, исключи́тельно

unutterable /ʌnˈʌtərəb(ə)l/ *adj.* невырази́мый, несказа́нный

unvarnished /ʌnˈvɑːnɪʃt/ *adj.* (fig.): the ∼ truth неприкра́шенная/го́лая пра́вда

unveil /ʌnˈveɪl/ *v.t.* (statue) откры|ва́ть, -ы́ть; (plans) излага́ть, -ожи́ть

unwanted /ʌnˈwɒntɪd/ *adj.* нежела́нный; they made me feel ∼ они́ да́ли мне поня́ть, что я ли́шний среди́ них

unwarranted /ʌnˈwɒrəntɪd/ *adj.* необосно́ванный

unwary /ʌnˈweərɪ/ *adj.* неосторо́жный

unwavering /ʌnˈweɪvərɪŋ/ *adj.* непоколеби́мый

unwelcome /ʌnˈwelkəm/ *adj.* неприя́тный

unwell /ʌnˈwel/ *adj.* нездоро́вый; I felt ∼ мне нездоро́вилось; I have been ∼ я был нездоро́в

unwieldy /ʌnˈwiːldɪ/ *adj.* (**unwieldier**, **unwieldiest**) громо́здкий

unwilling /ʌnˈwɪlɪŋ/ *adj.* нежела́ющий; he was ∼ to agree он не пожела́л согласи́ться

unwillingness /ʌnˈwɪlɪŋnɪs/ *n.* нежела́ние

unwind /ʌnˈwaɪnd/ *v.t. & i.* разм|а́тывать(ся), -ота́ть(ся); (fig.): the wine helped him to ∼ вино́ помогло́ ему́ рассла́биться

unwise /ʌnˈwaɪz/ *adj.* не(благо)разу́мный

unwitting /ʌnˈwɪtɪŋ/ *adj.* неча́янный

unworthy /ʌnˈwəːðɪ/ *adj.* недосто́йный (кого/чего)

unwrap /ʌnˈræp/ *v.t.* разв|ора́чивать (or разв|ёртывать), -ерну́ть

unwritten /ʌnˈrɪt(ə)n/ *adj.*: an ∼ law непи́саный зако́н

unzip /ʌnˈzɪp/ *v.t.* (coat) расстёг|ивать, -ну́ть; (bag) раскр|ыва́ть, -ы́ть

⚮ **up** /ʌp/ *n.*: ∼s and downs (of fortune) взлёты (*m. pl.*) и паде́ния (*nt. pl.*)
 ● *adv.* **1** (in a higher position) вверху́, наверху́; high ∼ in the sky высоко́ в не́бе; 'this side ∼!' «верх!»; the notice was ∼ on the board на доске́ висе́ло объявле́ние; prices are ∼ це́ны подняли́сь; (advanced): he is 20 points ∼ on his opponent он на два́дцать очко́в впереди́ проти́вника; he is well ∼ in his subject он прекра́сно зна́ет свой предме́т; (with greater intensity): sing ∼!/speak ∼! (по́йте)/(говори́те) гро́мче! **2** (into a higher position) вверх, наве́рх; she carried the suitcases ∼ она́ отнесла́ чемода́ны наве́рх; (∼wards) вы́ше, бо́льше; children from the age of twelve ∼ де́ти от двена́дцати (лет) и ста́рше **3** (out of bed; standing; active): he was already ∼ when I called когда́ я пришёл, он уже́ встал; she was soon ∼ and about again она́ вско́ре опра́вилась; I was ∼ late last night я вчера́ о́чень по́здно лёг **4** (expr. completion or expiry): time's ∼ вре́мя истекло́; the game is ∼! ка́рта би́та! **5** (infml, happening; amiss): what's ∼? в чём де́ло?; что тут происхо́дит?; there's something ∼ with the radio (ра́дио)приёмник барахли́т **6** ∼ against (in contact with): the table was (right) ∼ against the wall стол стоя́л (пря́мо) у стены́ (or вплотну́ю к стене́); (confronted by): you are ∼ against stiff opposition вы име́ете де́ло с упо́рным сопротивле́нием **7** ∼ to (equal to): I don't feel ∼ to it я не чу́вствую себя́ в си́лах сде́лать э́то; (as far as) до + g.; ∼ to now, ∼ till now до сих пор; I am ∼ to chapter 3 я дочита́л до тре́тьей главы́; (incumbent upon): it is ∼ to us to help э́то мы должны́ помо́чь; it's ∼ to you now тепе́рь э́то/всё зави́сит от вас; (occupied with): what is he ∼ to? чем он занима́ется?; he is ∼ to no good он замы́слил что-то недо́брое
 ● *prep.*: they live ∼ the hill они́ живу́т на горе́/холме́; he ran ∼ the hill он взбежа́л на́ гору, на хо́лм; the cat was ∼ a tree кот взобра́лся на де́рево; he went ∼ the stairs он подня́лся по ле́стнице; they live ∼ the street (further along) они́ живу́т по/на э́той у́лице

up-and-coming /ʌpənˈkʌmɪŋ/ *adj.* многообеща́ющий

upbeat /ˈʌpbiːt/ *adj.* оптимисти́чный, бо́дрый

upbringing /ˈʌpbrɪŋɪŋ/ *n.* воспита́ние

ⓕ **update** /ʌp'deɪt/ v.t. (one's wardrobe) обновл|я́ть, -и́ть; (equipment) модернизи́ровать (impf., pf.); (records) испр|авля́ть, -а́вить

upgrade n. /'ʌpɡreɪd/ (modernization) модерниза́ция; (comput., of software) обновле́ние, апгре́йд (infml); (comput., of hardware) модерниза́ция, апгре́йд (infml); (of travel class) перево́д в бо́лее высо́кий класс обслу́живания
● v.t. /ʌp'ɡreɪd/ (modernize) модернизи́ровать (impf., pf.); (comput., software) обновл|я́ть, -и́ть; (comput., hardware) модернизи́ровать (impf., pf.); (raise in rank) пов|ыша́ть, -ы́сить в до́лжности; (a traveller) перев|оди́ть, -ести́ в бо́лее высо́кий класс (обслу́живания); **we were ∼d to business class** нас перевели́ в би́знес-класс

upheaval /ʌp'hi:v(ə)l/ n. (political) потрясе́ния (nt. pl.); (emotional) потрясе́ние

uphill /'ʌphɪl/ adj. иду́щий в го́ру; **an ∼ task** тяжёлая зада́ча
● adv. в го́ру

uphold /ʌp'həʊld/ v.t. (support) (lit., fig.) подде́рж|ивать, -а́ть

upholster /ʌp'həʊlstə(r)/ v.t. об|ива́ть, -и́ть; подб|ива́ть, -и́ть; **an ∼ed chair** кре́сло с мя́гкой оби́вкой

upholstery /ʌp'həʊlstəri/ n. оби́вка

upkeep /'ʌpki:p/ n. содержа́ние

uplift¹ /'ʌplɪft/ n. (act of raising) подъём; (moral elevation) духо́вный подъём

uplift² /ʌp'lɪft/ v.t. подн|има́ть, -я́ть

upload /ʌp'ləʊd/ v.t. (comput.) загру|жа́ть, -зи́ть на друго́й (удалённый) компью́тер

upmarket /ʌp'mɑ:kɪt/ adj. элита́рный, дорого́й

ⓕ **upon** /ə'pɒn/ prep. **1** see ▶ **on 2**: **once ∼ a time** одна́жды; **once ∼ a time there lived …** жи́л-бы́л… (fem. жила́-была́…); **∼ my word, soul!** (expressing surprise etc.) Го́споди!; **∼ my honour!** че́стное сло́во!; **the holidays are ∼ us** приближа́ются кани́кулы; **the enemy is ∼ us** враг уже́ бли́зок

ⓕ **upper** /'ʌpə(r)/ adj. ве́рхний; вы́сший; **he got the ∼ hand** он одержа́л верх
■ **∼ class** adj. относя́щийся к вы́сшему о́бществу; **U∼ House** n. (in UK) пала́та ло́рдов; (in USA) сена́т; **∼most** adj. са́мый ве́рхний, вы́сший; **it was ∼most in my mind** э́то бо́льше всего́ занима́ло мои́ мы́сли

upright /'ʌpraɪt/ adj. (erect) вертика́льный; (honourable) че́стный
● adv.: **stand ∼** стоя́ть (impf.) пря́мо

uprising /'ʌpraɪzɪŋ/ n. (rebellion) восста́ние

uproar /'ʌprɔ:(r)/ n. (noise) шум; (confusion) возмуще́ние

uproarious /ʌp'rɔ:rɪəs/ adj. (noisy) шу́мный, бу́рный, бу́йный; (funny) ужа́сно/ невозмо́жно смешно́й

uproot /ʌp'ru:t/ v.t. вырыва́ть, вы́рвать с ко́рнем; (fig., displace) высел|я́ть, вы́селить

ⓕ ключевая лексика

upset¹ /'ʌpset/ n. **1** (physical) недомога́ние; **stomach ∼** расстро́йство желу́дка **2** (emotional shock) огорче́ние

upset² /ʌp'set/ v.t. (knock over) опроки́|дывать, -нуть; (make unhappy) расстр|а́ивать, -о́ить; (food): **rich food ∼s my stomach** от жи́рной пи́щи у меня́ расстра́ивается желу́док

upshot /'ʌpʃɒt/ n. развя́зка

upside down /ʌpsaɪd 'daʊn/ adv. вверх дном, вверх нога́ми

upstage /ʌp'steɪdʒ/ v.t. (fig., overshadow) затм|ева́ть, -и́ть

upstairs /ʌp'steəz/ adv. (position) наверху́; (direction) наве́рх; **he ran ∼** он побежа́л наве́рх; (attr.) **the ∼ rooms** ве́рхние ко́мнаты

upstanding /ʌp'stændɪŋ/ adj. **1** (honest) че́стный, прямо́й **2** (standing up) стоя́щий; **be ∼!** вста́ньте!

upstart /'ʌpstɑ:t/ n. вы́скочка (c.g.)

upstream /'ʌpstri:m/ adv. про́тив тече́ния; **∼ of** вы́ше + g.

upsurge /'ʌpsɜ:dʒ/ n. (of unrest, in production) подъём; (of feelings) наплы́в

uptake /'ʌpteɪk/ n.: **quick on the ∼** (infml) сообрази́тельный, бы́стро сообража́ющий

uptight /ʌp'taɪt/ adj. (infml, tense, angry) напряжённый, нерво́зный

up-to-date /ʌptə'deɪt/ adj. совреме́нный, нове́йший, (са́мый) после́дний

upturn /'ʌptɜ:n/ n. (fig.) сдвиг (к лу́чшему); улучше́ние

upward /'ʌpwəd/ adj. напра́вленный вверх; **an ∼ trend in prices** тенде́нция к повыше́нию цен
● adv. (also **∼s**) вверх

Urals /'jʊər(ə)lz/ n. pl. (mountains) Ура́льские го́ры (f. pl.), Ура́л

uranium /jʊ'reɪnɪəm/ n. ура́н; (attr.) ура́новый

Uranus /'jʊərənəs/ n. Ура́н

ⓕ **urban** /'ɜ:bən/ adj. городско́й

urbane /ɜ:'beɪn/ adj. све́тский, учти́вый

urchin /'ɜ:tʃɪn/ n. беспризо́рни|к (-ца)

Urdu /'ʊədu:/ n. (язы́к) урду́ (m. indecl.)

ⓕ **urge** /ɜ:dʒ/ n. побужде́ние, стремле́ние
● v.t. **1** (impel) (also **∼ on, ∼ forward**) гнать (impf.); под|гоня́ть, -огна́ть **2** (exhort) угова́ривать (impf.)

urgency /'ɜ:dʒ(ə)nsɪ/ n. сро́чность, неотло́жность; **as a matter of ∼** в сро́чном поря́дке

urgent /'ɜ:dʒ(ə)nt/ adj. сро́чный, неотло́жный; **he is in ∼ need of money** он кра́йне нужда́ется в деньга́х

urinal /jʊə'raɪn(ə)l/ n. писсуа́р

urinary /'jʊərɪnərɪ/ adj. мочево́й

urinate /'jʊərɪneɪt/ v.i. мочи́ться, по-

urine /'jʊərɪn/ n. моча́

URL abbr. (of **uniform/universal resource locator**) (comput.) URL-а́дрес

urn /ɜ:n/ n. (vase for ashes etc.) у́рна, ва́за

Uruguay /'jʊərəɡwaɪ/ n. Уругва́й

Uruguayan /ʊərə'gwaɪən/ *n.* уругва́|ец
(-йка)
● *adj.* уругва́йский

US, USA *abbr.* (*of* **United States of
America**) США (*pl., indecl.*) (Соединённые
Шта́ты Аме́рики)
● *adj.* америка́нский

♂ **us** /ʌs/ *obj. of* ▶ **we**

usable /'juːzəb(ə)l/ *adj.* примени́мый,
(при)го́дный

usage /'juːsɪdʒ/ *n.* **1** (utilization) употребле́ние,
испо́льзование; по́льзование (of: + *i.*)
2 (habitual process) у́зус, пра́ктика,
обыкнове́ние; **in accordance with general
~** согла́сно общепри́нятой пра́ктике; **a
guide to English ~** уче́бник англи́йского
словоупотребле́ния

♂ **use¹** /juːs/ *n.* **1** (utilization) употребле́ние,
испо́льзование; по́льзование (of: + *i.*);
make good ~ of your time! испо́льзуйте
ва́ше вре́мя как сле́дует!; **he put his talents
to good ~** он пра́вильно испо́льзовал
свой спосо́бности **2** (purpose) назначе́ние;
примене́ние **3** (value) по́льза, толк; **this
machine is no longer (of) any ~** э́та маши́на
бо́льше не годи́тся; **will this be of ~ to you?**
вам э́то пригоди́тся?; **it's no ~** grumbling
что то́лку ворча́ть? **4** (power of using): **he lost
the ~ of his legs** он утра́тил спосо́бность
ходи́ть **5** (right to use): **I gave him the ~ of
my car** я разреши́л ему́ по́льзоваться мое́й
маши́ной

♂ **use²** /juːz/ *v.t.* **1** (employ) употреб|ля́ть, -и́ть;
по́льзоваться, вос- + *i.*; испо́льзовать (*impf.,
pf.*); **a ~d car** поде́ржанная маши́на **2** (~ up:
consume) расхо́довать, из-; тра́тить, по-;
испо́льзовать (*impf., pf.*); **this car ~s a lot of
fuel** э́та маши́на расхо́дует мно́го бензи́на
3 (treat) обраща́ться (*impf.*) с + *i.*; об|ходи́ться,
-ойти́сь с + *i.* **4** (exploit): **I feel as if I have been
~d** я чу́вствую, что меня́ испо́льзовали в
чьи́х-то це́лях

used¹ /juːst/ *pred. adj.* **1** (accustomed): **get ~
to** прив|ыка́ть, -ы́кнуть к + *d.*; **he is ~ to it**
он к э́тому привы́к; **he is ~ to dining late** он
привы́к обе́дать по́здно **2** (+ inf., of habitual
situation in the past): **he ~ to be a teacher** он
ра́ньше был учи́телем; **I ~ not to like him**
пре́жде он мне не нра́вился

used² /juːzd/ *attr. adj.* **1** (already having been
made use of): **a ~ envelope** ста́рый конве́рт
2 (AmE, second-hand) поде́ржанный

♂ **useful** /'juːsfʊl/ *adj.* поле́зный

useless /'juːslɪs/ *adj.* (worthless) неприго́дный;
(futile) бесполе́зный; (infml, incompetent): **he is**

~ at tennis он никуды́шный тенниси́ст

♂ **user** /'juːzə(r)/ *n.* (one who uses)
употребля́ющий; потреби́тель (*m.*); (comput.)
по́льзователь (*m.*)
■ **~-friendly** *adj.* удо́бный в употребле́нии;
(comput.) дру́жественный

usher /'ʌʃə(r)/ *v.t.* (*also* **~ in**) вв|оди́ть, -ести́

usherette /ʌʃə'ret/ *n.* биле́тёрша (infml)

USSR *abbr.* (*of* **Union of Soviet Socialist
Republics**) (hist.) СССР (*m. indecl.*) (Сою́з
Сове́тских Социалисти́ческих Респу́блик)

♂ **usual** /'juːʒʊəl/ *adj.* обы́чный, обыкнове́нный;
it is ~ to remove one's hat шля́пу при́нято
снима́ть; **he is late as ~** он, как всегда́,
опа́здывает; **the bus was fuller than ~**
авто́бус был перепо́лнен бо́льше обы́чного

♂ **usually** /'juːʒʊəlɪ/ *adv.* обы́чно

usurp /jʊ'zɜːp/ *v.t.* узурпи́ровать (*impf., pf.*)

usury /'juːʒərɪ/ *n.* ростовщи́чество

utensil /juː'tens(ə)l/ *n.* инструме́нт; (*pl.,
collect.*) у́тварь

uterus /'juːtərəs/ *n.* (anat.) ма́тка

utilitarian /jʊtɪlɪ'teərɪən/ *n.* утилитари́ст (-ка)
● *adj.* утилита́рный

utility /juː'tɪlɪtɪ/ *n.* **1** (usefulness) поле́зность,
практи́чность, вы́годность **2**: **public ~ies**
коммуна́льные услу́ги (*f. pl.*)
■ **~y room** *n.* кладова́я

utilization /juːtɪlaɪ'zeɪʃ(ə)n/ *n.*
испо́льзование; утилиза́ция

utilize /'juːtɪlaɪz/ *v.t.* испо́льзовать (*impf., pf.*)

utmost /'ʌtməʊst/ *n.*: **he did his ~ to avoid
defeat** он сде́лал всё возмо́жное, что́бы
избежа́ть пораже́ния
● *adjs.* кра́йний

Utopia /juː'təʊpɪə/ *n.* уто́пия

Utopian /juː'təʊpɪən/ *adj.* утопи́ческий

utter¹ /'ʌtə(r)/ *adj.* по́лный, абсолю́тный,
соверше́нный

utter² /'ʌtə(r)/ *v.t.* (sound, cry) изд|ава́ть, -а́ть;
(words) произн|оси́ть, -ести́

utterance /'ʌtərəns/ *n.* **1** (action)
произнесе́ние; **he gave ~ to his anger**
он вы́разил свой гнев **2** (something said,
pronouncement) выска́зывание

utterly /'ʌtəlɪ/ *adv.* соверше́нно

U-turn /'juːtɜːn/ *n.* разворо́т; (fig.) ре́зкое
измене́ние поли́тики

UV *abbr.* (*of* **ultraviolet**) ультрафиоле́товый

Uzbek /'ʊzbek/ *n.* (person) узбе́|к (-чка);
(language) узбе́кский язы́к
● *adj.* узбе́кский

Uzbekistan /ʊzbekɪ'staːn/ *n.* Узбекиста́н

u

Vv

v. *abbr.* (*of* **versus**) про́тив + g.

vacanc|y /ˈveɪkənsɪ/ *n.* (job) вака́нсия; (place on course etc.) ме́сто; (room): **no ~ies** свобо́дных ко́мнат нет, «мест нет»

vacant /ˈveɪk(ə)nt/ *adj.* **1** (unoccupied) свобо́дный; **a ~ post** вака́нтная до́лжность, вака́нсия **2** (of mind, expression, etc.) отсу́тствующий

vacate /veɪˈkeɪt/ *v.t.* освобо|жда́ть, -ди́ть; **he will ~ the post in May** он уйдёт с до́лжности в ма́е

vacation /vəˈkeɪʃ(ə)n/ *n.* **1** (at university) кани́кул|ы (*pl.*, *g.* —); **long ~** ле́тние кани́кулы **2** (holiday) о́тпуск, о́тдых; **on ~** в о́тпуске

vaccinate /ˈvæksɪneɪt/ *v.t.* де́лать, с- приви́вку (+ *d.*) (**against:** + *g.*)

vaccination /væksɪˈneɪʃ(ə)n/ *n.* приви́вка

vaccine /ˈvæksiːn/ *n.* вакци́на

vacillate /ˈvæsɪleɪt/ *v.i.* колеба́ться (*impf.*)

vacuous /ˈvækjʊəs/ *adj.* пусто́й

vacuum /ˈvækjʊəm/ *n.* **1** (empty place) ва́куум **2** (infml) (*in full* **~ cleaner**) пылесо́с
  ● *v.t. & i.* (infml) (clean with **~ cleaner**) пылесо́сить, про-
  ■ **~ flask** *n.* (BrE) те́рмос

vagabond /ˈvægəbɒnd/ *n.* (vagrant) бродя́га (*c.g.*), скита́лец

vagary /ˈveɪgərɪ/ *n.* причу́да, капри́з

vagina /vəˈdʒaɪnə/ *n.* влага́лище

vaginal /vəˈdʒaɪn(ə)l/ *adj.* влага́лищный, вагина́льный

vagrant /ˈveɪgrənt/ *n.* бродя́га (*c.g.*)

vague /veɪg/ *adj.* **1** неопределённый, сму́тный, нея́сный; **he was rather ~ about his plans** он был весьма́ укло́нчив относи́тельно свои́х пла́нов

vagueness /ˈveɪgnɪs/ *n.* неопределённость, сму́тность, нея́сность

vain /veɪn/ *adj.* **1** (unavailing; fruitless) тще́тный, напра́сный; **they tried in ~ to get a seat** они́ безуспе́шно пыта́лись найти́ ме́сто **2** (conceited) тщесла́вный

valedictory /vælɪˈdɪktərɪ/ *adj.* проща́льный; (AmE, as n.) речь на шко́льном вы́пуске

valentine /ˈvæləntaɪn/ *n.* (missive) валенти́нка, (анони́мное) любо́вное посла́ние в день свято́го Валенти́на

valet /ˈvæleɪ/ *n.* камерди́нер, слуга́ (*m.*)

valiant /ˈvæljənt/ *adj.* до́блестный; (of effort) герои́ческий

valid /ˈvælɪd/ *adj.* **1** (sound) ве́ский, обосно́ванный; **~ objections** убеди́тельные

возраже́ния **2** (law) действи́тельный; **a ticket ~ for 3 months** биле́т, действи́тельный в тече́ние трёх ме́сяцев

validate /ˈvælɪdeɪt/ *v.t.* утвер|жда́ть, -ди́ть

validation /vælɪˈdeɪʃ(ə)n/ *n.* утвержде́ние, подтвержде́ние

valley /ˈvælɪ/ *n.* (*pl.* **~s**) доли́на

valour /ˈvælə(r)/ (*AmE* **valor**) *n.* до́блесть

valuable /ˈvæljʊəb(ə)l/ *n.* (*usu. in pl.*) це́нности (*f. pl.*)
  ● *adj.* це́нный, поле́зный, ва́жный

valuation /væljʊˈeɪʃ(ə)n/ *n.* оце́нка

✍ **value** /ˈvæljuː/ *n.* **1** (worth) це́нность, ва́жность **2** (in money etc.) це́нность, сто́имость; **property is rising in ~** недви́жимое иму́щество поднима́ется в цене́; **the book is good ~ for money** (BrE) э́та кни́га — вы́годная поку́пка **3** (*in pl.*) (standards) (*духо́вные и т. п.*) це́нности (*f. pl.*)
  ● *v.t.* (**values, valued, valuing**) **1** (estimate **~ of**) оце́н|ивать, -и́ть **2** (regard highly) цени́ть (*impf.*)

valuer /ˈvæljʊə(r)/ *n.* (BrE) оце́нщик

valve /vælv/ *n.* кла́пан

vampire /ˈvæmpaɪə(r)/ *n.* вампи́р

van /væn/ *n.* фурго́н

vandal /ˈvænd(ə)l/ *n.* ванда́л

vandalism /ˈvændəlɪz(ə)m/ *n.* вандали́зм

vandalize /ˈvændəlaɪz/ *v.t.* разр|уша́ть, -у́шить

vanguard /ˈvængɑːd/ *n.* аванга́рд

vanilla /vəˈnɪlə/ *n.* вани́ль; (attr.) вани́льный

vanish /ˈvænɪʃ/ *v.i.* исч|еза́ть, -е́знуть

vanity /ˈvænɪtɪ/ *n.* тщесла́вие

vanquish /ˈvæŋkwɪʃ/ *v.t.* побе|жда́ть, -ди́ть; покор|я́ть, -и́ть

vantage /ˈvɑːntɪdʒ/ *n.*: **~ point** вы́годная пози́ция

vapour /ˈveɪpə(r)/ (*AmE* **vapor**) *n.* **1** (steam) пар **2** (gaseous manifestation): **~ trail** инверсио́нный след

variable /ˈveərɪəb(ə)l/ *n.* (math.) переме́нная (величина́)
  ● *adj.* изме́нчивый, непостоя́нный

variance /ˈveərɪəns/ *n.*: **this is at ~ with what we heard** э́то противоре́чит тому́, что мы слы́шали

variant /ˈveərɪənt/ *n.* вариа́нт

variation /veərɪˈeɪʃ(ə)n/ *n.* **1** (fluctuation) измене́ние; колеба́ние; **~s of temperature** колеба́ния (nt. pl.) температу́ры **2** (divergence) отклоне́ние

varicose /ˈværɪkəʊs/ *adj.* варико́зный
  ■ **~ veins** *n. pl.* варико́зные ве́ны

✍ ключева́я ле́ксика

varied /'veərɪd/ *adj.* разнообра́зный

variegated /'veərɪgeɪtɪd/ *adj.* разноцве́тный, пёстрый

◆ **variety** /və'raɪətɪ/ *n.* **1** (diversity) разнообра́зие **2** (number of different things) ряд; мно́жество; **for a ~ of reasons** по це́лому ря́ду соображе́ний, по ря́ду причи́н **3**: **~ show** эстра́дное представле́ние **4** (type) разнови́дность, вид, сорт

varifocals /'veərɪfəʊk(ə)lz/ *n. pl.* (spectacles) очк|и́ (-о́в) с переме́нным фо́кусным расстоя́нием

◆ **various** /'veərɪəs/ *adj.* **1** (diverse) разли́чный, ра́зный, разнообра́зный **2** (with pl.) (several) мно́гие (*pl.*); ра́зные (*pl.*)

varnish /'vɑːnɪʃ/ *n.* лак; (fig.) лоск
●*v.t.* покр|ыва́ть, -ы́ть ла́ком

◆ **var|y** /'veərɪ/ *v.t.* меня́ть (*impf.*); измен|я́ть, -и́ть; разнообра́зить (*impf.*)
●*v.i.* **1** (change) меня́ться (*impf.*); **the menu never ~ies** меню́ никогда́ не меня́ется **2** (differ) ра|сходи́ться, -зойти́сь; отлич|а́ться, -и́ться; **opinions ~y** мне́ния расхо́дятся

vase /vɑːz/ *n.* ва́за

vasectomy /və'sektəmɪ/ *n.* (med.) вазэктоми́я

Vaseline® /'væsɪliːn/ *n.* вазели́н

◆ **vast** /vɑːst/ *adj.* обши́рный; огро́мный; (grandiose) грандио́зный

vastness /'vɑːstnɪs/ *n.* ширь; огро́мность; грандио́зность

VAT /viːeɪ'tiː, væt/ *n.* (BrE) (*abbr. of* **value added tax**) НДС (нало́г на доба́вленную сто́имость)

vat /væt/ *n.* бо́чка, чан

Vatican /'vætɪkən/ *n.* Ватика́н

vault[1] /vɔːlt/ *n.* **1** (arched roof) свод **2** (underground room) подва́л, по́греб; (of a bank) храни́лище

vault[2] /vɔːlt/ *v.t. & i.* перепры́г|ивать, -нуть

VCR *abbr.* (*of* **video cassette recorder**) видеомагнитофо́н

VD *abbr.* (*of* **venereal disease**) венери́ческая боле́знь

VDU (BrE) *abbr.* (*of* **visual display unit**) диспле́й

veal /viːl/ *n.* теля́тина

veer /vɪə(r)/ *v.i.* изменя́ть, -и́ть направле́ние; пов|ора́чивать(ся), -ерну́ть(ся)

vegan /'viːgən/ *n.* стро́гий вегетариа́нец

vegetable /'vedʒtəb(ə)l/ *n.* о́вощ
●*adj.* овощно́й; **~ oils** расти́тельные масла́

vegetarian /vedʒɪ'teərɪən/ *n.* вегетариа́н|ец (-ка)
●*adj.* вегетариа́нский

vegetate /'vedʒɪteɪt/ *v.i.* (fig.) прозяба́ть (*impf.*)

vegetation /vedʒɪ'teɪʃ(ə)n/ *n.* (plant life) расти́тельность

veggie burger /'vedʒɪ bɜːgə(r)/ *n.* вегетариа́нский га́мбургер

vehemence /'viːəməns/ *n.* си́ла, я́рость

vehement /'viːəmənt/ *adj.* си́льный, я́ростный

◆ **vehicle** /'vɪək)l/ *n.* тра́нспортное сре́дство

veil /veɪl/ *n.* вуа́ль
●*v.t.*: **a ~ed threat** скры́тая угро́за

vein /veɪn/ *n.* **1** (anat.) ве́на, жи́ла **2** (fissure in rock) жи́ла **3** (style): **in the same ~** в то́м же ду́хе/то́не/сти́ле

Velcro® /'velkrəʊ/ *n.*: **~ fastener** застёжка «велкро́», липу́чка

velocity /vɪ'lɒsɪtɪ/ *n.* ско́рость; быстрота́

velvet /'velvɪt/ *n.* ба́рхат; **a ~ dress** ба́рхатное пла́тье

velvety /'velvɪtɪ/ *adj.* ба́рхатный, бархати́стый

vendetta /ven'detə/ *n.* венде́тта

vending machine /'vendɪŋ/ *n.* (торго́вый) автома́т (*по продаже сигарет, напитков и т. п.*)

vendor /'vendə(r)/ *n.* продав|е́ц (-щи́ца)

veneer /vɪ'nɪə(r)/ *n.* шпон, фане́ра; (fig.) вне́шний лоск

venerable /'venərəb(ə)l/ *adj.* **1** (revered) почте́нный; **~ ruins** дре́вние/свяще́нные разва́лины **2**: **V~** (as title) преподо́бный

venerate /'venəreɪt/ *v.t.* чтить (*impf.*); почита́ть (*impf.*); благогове́ть (*impf.*) пе́ред + *i.*

veneration /venə'reɪʃ(ə)n/ *n.* почте́ние, благогове́ние

venereal /vɪ'nɪərɪəl/ *adj.*: **~ disease** венери́ческая боле́знь

Venetian /vɪ'niːʃ(ə)n/ *n.* венециа́н|ец (-ка)
●*adj.* венециа́нский
■ **~ blind** *n.* жалюзи́ (*pl. indecl.*)

Venezuela /venɪ'zweɪlə/ *n.* Венесуэ́ла

Venezuelan /venɪ'zweɪlən/ *n.* венесуэ́л|ец (-ка)
●*adj.* венесуэ́льский

vengeance /'vendʒ(ə)ns/ *n.* **1** месть; отмще́ние (liter.) **2**: **with a ~** (infml, in a high degree) вовсю́, с лихво́й

vengeful /'vendʒfʊl/ *adj.* мсти́тельный

Venice /'venɪs/ *n.* Вене́ция

venison /'venɪs(ə)n/ *n.* олени́на

venom /'venəm/ *n.* яд; (fig.) яд, зло́ба

venomous /'venəməs/ *adj.* ядови́тый

vent /vent/ *n.* дымохо́д; **he gave ~ to his feelings** он дал во́лю свои́м чу́вствам
●*v.t.* (fig.) изл|ива́ть, -и́ть; да|ва́ть, -ть вы́ход + *d.*

ventilate /'ventɪleɪt/ *v.t.* прове́три|вать, -ть

ventilation /ventɪ'leɪʃ(ə)n/ *n.* вентиля́ция

ventilator /'ventɪleɪtə(r)/ *n.* (also med.) вентиля́тор

ventriloquist /ven'trɪləkwɪst/ *n.* чревовеща́тель (*m.*)

venture /'ventʃə(r)/ *n.* **1** (risky undertaking) риско́ванное предприя́тие **2** (business enterprise) (комме́рческое) предприя́тие
●*v.i.* (dare) осме́л|иваться, -ться; **~ to suggest** осме́люсь предложи́ть; **~ out** риск|ова́ть, -ну́ть вы́сунуть нос на у́лицу
■ **~ capital** *n.* (fin.) ве́нчурный капита́л

venue /'venjuː/ *n.* ме́сто (проведе́ния) (*конце́рта/соревнова́ний*)

veracity /vəˈræsɪti/ *n.* правди́вость; достове́рность

veranda /vəˈrændə/ *n.* вера́нда

verb /vɜːb/ *n.* глаго́л

verbal /'vɜːb(ə)l/ *adj.* **1** (of or in words) слове́сный **2** (oral) у́стный

verbalize /'vɜːbəlaɪz/ *v.t.* (put into words) выража́ть, вы́разить слова́ми

verbatim /vɜːˈbeɪtɪm/ *adv.* досло́вно

verbiage /'vɜːbɪɪdʒ/ *n.* многосло́вие; пустосло́вие

verbose /vɜːˈbəʊs/ *adj.* многосло́вный

verbosity /vɜːˈbɒsɪti/ *n.* многосло́вие

verdict /'vɜːdɪkt/ *n.* (law) верди́кт, пригово́р; **the jury brought in a ~ of guilty/not guilty** суд прися́жных вы́нес обвини́тельный/ оправда́тельный пригово́р; (fig., judgement) заключе́ние, пригово́р; **what's the ~?** како́в пригово́р?

verge /vɜːdʒ/ *n.* край; (BrE, of road) обо́чина; (fig.): **on the ~ of destruction** на краю́ ги́бели; **on the ~ of tears** на гра́ни слёз; **he was on the ~ of betraying his secret** он чуть не вы́дал свою́ та́йну
● *v.i.*: **it ~s on madness** э́то грани́чит с безу́мием

verifiable /'verɪfaɪəb(ə)l/ *adj.* поддаю́щийся прове́рке

verification /ˌverɪfɪˈkeɪʃ(ə)n/ *n.* прове́рка; подтвержде́ние

verify /'verɪfaɪ/ *v.t.* (check accuracy of) пров|еря́ть, -е́рить; (confirm) подтвер|жда́ть, -ди́ть

veritable /'verɪtəb(ə)l/ *adj.* настоя́щий, су́щий

vermicelli /ˌvɜːmɪˈtʃeli/ *n.* вермише́ль

vermin /'vɜːmɪn/ *n.* **1** (rats, foxes, etc.) вреди́тели (*m. pl.*) **2** (parasitic insects) парази́ты (*m. pl.*)

vernacular /vəˈnækjʊlə(r)/ *n.* **1** (local language) иско́нный язы́к; **Latin gave place to the ~** латы́нь уступи́ла ме́сто иско́нным языка́м **2** (dialect) диале́кт; наре́чие **3** (jargon) жарго́н, арго́ (*nt. indecl.*) **4** (colloquial speech) просторе́чие
● *adj.* иско́нный, ме́стный; просторе́чный

versatile /'vɜːsətaɪl/ *adj.* (person) разносторо́нний; (device) универса́льный

versatility /ˌvɜːsəˈtɪlɪti/ *n.* разносторо́нность; универса́льность

verse /vɜːs/ *n.* **1** (stanza of poem, song) строфа́; (in Bible) стих **2** (*sg. or pl.*) (poetry, poems) стихи́ (*m. pl.*); **he wrote in ~** он писа́л в стиха́х

◆ **version** /'vɜːʃ(ə)n/ *n.* **1** (individual account) ве́рсия, расска́з **2** (form or variant of text etc.) вариа́нт, текст

versus /'vɜːsəs/ *prep.* про́тив + g.

◆ ключева́я ле́ксика

vertebra /'vɜːtɪbrə/ *n.* (*pl.* **vertebrae** /-breɪ/) позвоно́к

vertebrate /'vɜːtɪbrət/ *n.* позвоно́чное (живо́тное)

vertical /'vɜːtɪk(ə)l/ *adj.* вертика́льный; **a ~ cliff** отве́сный утёс

vertigo /'vɜːtɪɡəʊ/ *n.* головокруже́ние

verve /vɜːv/ *n.* жи́вость, эне́ргия

◆ **very** /'veri/ *adj.* **1** (exact; identical) тот са́мый; **this ~ day** сего́дня же **2** (extreme) са́мый; **at the ~ end** в са́мом конце́ **3** (in emphasis): **the ~ idea of it** одна́ мысль об э́том
● *adv.* **1** (exceedingly) о́чень; **I don't feel ~ well** я чу́вствую себя́ нева́жно; **I can't sing ~ well** я дово́льно пло́хо пою́ **2** (emph., with superl. etc.) са́мый; **the ~ best** са́мый лу́чший; наилу́чший; **the ~ next day** на сле́дующий же день; **you may keep it for your ~ own** мо́жете э́то взять (себе́) насовсе́м

vessel /'ves(ə)l/ *n.* **1** (receptacle) сосу́д **2** (ship) су́дно, кора́бль (*m.*) **3** (anat.) сосу́д; **blood ~** кровено́сный сосу́д

vest[1] /vest/ *n.* (BrE, undergarment) ма́йка; (AmE, waistcoat) жиле́т

vest[2] /vest/ *v.t.*: **~ed interest** ли́чная заинтересо́ванность

vestibule /'vestɪbjuːl/ *n.* вестибю́ль (*m.*)

vestige /'vestɪdʒ/ *n.* след

vestment /'vestmənt/ *n.* (eccl.) облаче́ние, ри́за

vestry /'vestri/ *n.* (eccl., room) ри́зница

vet[1] /vet/ *n.* (veterinary surgeon) ветвра́ч, ветерина́р
● *v.t.* (**vetted, vetting**) (investigate) пров|еря́ть, -е́рить

vet[2] /vet/ *n.* (AmE, infml, veteran) ветера́н

veteran /'vetərən/ *n.* (lit., fig.) ветера́н
● *adj.* многоо́пытный, старе́йший

veterinarian /ˌvetərɪˈneərɪən/ *n.* (AmE) ветерина́р

veterinary /'vetərɪnəri/ *adj.*: **~ surgeon** (BrE) ветерина́рный врач

veto /'viːtəʊ/ *n.* (*pl.* **~es**) ве́то (*nt. indecl.*)
● *v.t.* (**vetoes, vetoed**) нал|ага́ть, -ожи́ть ве́то на + a.

vex /veks/ *v.t.* доса|жда́ть, -ди́ть; раздраж|а́ть, -и́ть; **a ~ed question** больно́й вопро́с

VHF *abbr.* (of **very high frequency**) ОВЧ (о́чень высо́кая частота́)

◆ **via** /'vaɪə/ *prep.* че́рез + a.

viable /'vaɪəb(ə)l/ *adj.* (able to survive) жизнеспосо́бный; (infml, feasible) осуществи́мый

viaduct /'vaɪədʌkt/ *n.* виаду́к, путепрово́д

vibes /vaɪbz/ *n. pl.* (infml) (atmosphere) флюи́ды (*m. pl.*); (mus., vibraphone) вибрафо́н

vibrancy /'vaɪbrənsi/ *n.* (liveliness) жи́вость; (of colours) я́ркость

vibrant /'vaɪbrənt/ *adj.* (lively) живо́й, по́лный жи́зни; (of colours) со́чный, я́ркий

vibraphone /'vaɪbrəfəʊn/ *n.* вибрафо́н

vibrate /vaɪˈbreɪt/ *v.i.* вибри́ровать, дрожа́ть (*both impf.*)

vibration /vaɪˈbreɪʃ(ə)n/ *n.* вибра́ция, дрожь

vibrato /vɪ'brɑːtəʊ/ n. & adv. (mus.) вибра́то (nt. indecl.)

vicar /'vɪkə(r)/ n. свяще́нник

vicarage /'vɪkərɪdʒ/ n. дом свяще́нника

vicarious /vɪ'keərɪəs/ adj. ко́свенный; **feel ~ pleasure** пережива́ть (impf.) чужу́ю ра́дость

vice¹ /vaɪs/ n. поро́к

vice² /vaɪs/ (AmE **vise**) n. (tool) тиск|и́ (-о́в)

vice³ /vaɪs/:
■ ~ **chairman** n. замести́тель (m.) председа́теля; ~ **chancellor** n. (BrE) ре́ктор; ~**-president** n. ви́це-президе́нт

vice versa /vaɪs 'vɜːsə/ adv. наоборо́т

vicinity /vɪ'sɪnɪti/ n. окру́га, окре́стность; **in the ~ of** в райо́не + g.

vicious /'vɪʃəs/ adj. **1** (spiteful) злой **2**: **a ~ circle** поро́чный круг

viciousness /'vɪʃəsnɪs/ n. зло́бность

vicissitude /vɪ'sɪsɪtjuːd/ n. превра́тность

⚬ **victim** /'vɪktɪm/ n. же́ртва; (of accident) пострада́вший

victimization /ˌvɪktɪmaɪ'zeɪʃ(ə)n/ n. пресле́дование

victimize /'vɪktɪmaɪz/ v.t. подв|ерга́ть, -е́ргнуть пресле́дованию

victor /'vɪktə(r)/ n. победи́тель (m.)

Victorian /vɪk'tɔːrɪən/ n. викториа́н|ец (-ка) ● adj. викториа́нский; (fig.) старомо́дный

victorious /vɪk'tɔːrɪəs/ adj. победоно́сный, побе́дный

⚬ **victory** /'vɪktəri/ n. побе́да (**over:** над + i.)

⚬ **video** /'vɪdɪəʊ/ n. (pl. ~**s**) (a ~ recorder (BrE), film, cassette) ви́део (indecl.)
● v.t. (**videoes**, **videoed**) запи́с|ывать, -а́ть на ви́део
■ ~ **camera** n. видеока́мера; ~ **cassette** n. видеокассе́та; ~ (**cassette**) **recorder** n. видеомагнитофо́н; ~ **clip** n. (видео)кли́п; ~ **conference** n. видеоконфере́нция; ~ **game** n. видеоигра́; ~**phone** n. видеотелефо́н; ~**tape** n. видеоле́нта; видеоплёнка

vie /vaɪ/ v.i. (**vying**) состяза́ться (impf.); сопе́рничать (impf.); **they ~d with each other for first place** они́ состяза́лись за пе́рвое ме́сто

Vienna /vɪ'enə/ n. Ве́на

Vietnam /ˌvjet'næm/ n. Вьетна́м

Vietnamese /ˌvɪetnə'miːz/ n. (pl. ~) (person) вьетна́м|ец (-ка); (language) вьетна́мский язы́к ● adj. вьетна́мский

⚬ **view** /vjuː/ n. **1** (scene, prospect) вид; пейза́ж; **you get a good ~ from here** отсю́да хоро́ший вид **2** (sight; field of vision) вид; **in full ~ of the audience** на виду́ у пу́блики **3** (fig.): **look at it from my point of ~** посмотри́те на э́то с мое́й то́чки зре́ния **4** (inspection) смотр, просмо́тр; **private ~(ing)** закры́тый просмо́тр **5** (mental attitude or opinion) взгляд, мне́ние; (in pl.) взгля́ды (m. pl.), убежде́ния (nt. pl.); **in my ~** по-мо́ему; по моему́ мне́нию **6** (intention) наме́рение; **I am saving with a ~ to buying a house** я коплю́ де́ньги, что́бы купи́ть дом **7** (consideration): **in ~ of**

ввиду́ + g.; **in ~ of recent developments** в све́те после́дних происше́ствий
● v.t. **1** (survey; gaze on) смотре́ть, по- на + a.; рассм|а́тривать, -отре́ть **2** (inspect) осм|а́тривать, -отре́ть **3** (fig., consider) рассм|а́тривать, -отре́ть; оцен|ивать, -и́ть
■ ~**finder** n. видоиска́тель (m.); ~**point** n. то́чка зре́ния

viewer /'vjuːə(r)/ n. (of TV) (теле)зри́тель (-ница)

vigil /'vɪdʒɪl/ n. бде́ние

vigilance /'vɪdʒɪləns/ n. бди́тельность

vigilant /'vɪdʒɪlənt/ adj. бди́тельный

vigilante /ˌvɪdʒɪ'lænti/ n. ≈ дружи́нник

vigorous /'vɪgərəs/ adj. энерги́чный, бо́дрый

vigour /'vɪgə(r)/ (AmE **vigor**) n. эне́ргия, бо́дрость

Viking /'vaɪkɪŋ/ n. ви́кинг

vile /vaɪl/ adj. гну́сный, ни́зкий

vilify /'vɪlɪfaɪ/ v.t. поноси́ть (impf.); черни́ть, о-

villa /'vɪlə/ n. ви́лла

⚬ **village** /'vɪlɪdʒ/ n. дере́вня; (larger) село́

villager /'vɪlɪdʒə(r)/ n. дереве́нск|ий/ се́льск|ий жи́тель (-ая -ница)

villain /'vɪlən/ n. злоде́й

Vilnius /'vɪlnɪəs/ n. Ви́льнюс

vinaigrette /ˌvɪnɪ'gret/ n. сала́тная запра́вка из у́ксуса, оли́вкового ма́сла и спе́ций

vindicate /'vɪndɪkeɪt/ v.t. опра́вд|ывать, -а́ть

vindication /ˌvɪndɪ'keɪʃ(ə)n/ n. оправда́ние

vindictive /vɪn'dɪktɪv/ adj. мсти́тельный

vindictiveness /vɪn'dɪktɪvnɪs/ n. мсти́тельность

vine /vaɪn/ n. (grape~) виногра́дная лоза́; (climbing or trailing plant) вью́щееся/ползу́чее расте́ние

vinegar /'vɪnɪgə(r)/ n. у́ксус

vineyard /'vɪnjɑːd/ n. виногра́дник

vintage /'vɪntɪdʒ/ n. **1** (year of wine production): **the 1950 ~** вино́ урожа́я ты́сяча девятьсо́т пятидеся́того го́да; **this is a good ~** э́то хоро́ший год (о вине); ~ **wine** ма́рочное вино́ **2** (fig.): **a ~ car** (BrE) автомоби́ль (m.) ста́рой ма́рки

vinyl /'vaɪnɪl/ n. вини́л; (attr.) вини́ловый

viola¹ /vɪ'əʊlə/ n. (musical instrument) альт

viola² /'vaɪələ/ n. (bot.) фиа́лка

violate /'vaɪəleɪt/ v.t. **1** (infringe, transgress) нар|уша́ть, -у́шить; преступ|а́ть, -и́ть **2** (profane) оскверн|я́ть, -и́ть

violation /ˌvaɪə'leɪʃ(ə)n/ n. наруше́ние; оскверне́ние

⚬ **violence** /'vaɪələns/ n. си́ла, наси́лие; **he resorted to ~** он прибе́г(нул) к наси́лию

⚬ **violent** /'vaɪələnt/ adj. **1** (strong, forceful) си́льный, неи́стовый, я́ростный **2** (using or involving force): **he became ~** он на́чал буйствовать

violet /'vaɪələt/ n. (bot.) фиа́лка; (colour) фиоле́товый цвет
● adj. (of colour) фиоле́товый

violin /ˌvaɪə'lɪn/ n. скри́пка

V

violinist /vaɪə'lɪnɪst/ n. скрипа́ч (-ка)

VIP abbr. (of **very important person**) высокопоста́вленное лицо́, высо́кий гость, VIP-гость

viper /'vaɪpə(r)/ n. гадю́ка

viral /'vaɪər(ə)l/ adj. ви́русный

virgin /'vɜːdʒɪn/ n. (female) де́вственница; (male) де́вственник
■ ~ **forest** n. де́вственный лес

virginal /'vɜːdʒɪn(ə)l/ adj. де́вственный; непоро́чный

virginity /və'dʒɪnɪtɪ/ n. де́вственность, неви́нность, непоро́чность; **lose one's** ~ теря́ть, по- неви́нность, лиш|а́ться, -и́ться де́вственности

Virgo /'vɜːgəʊ/ n. (pl. ~s) Де́ва

virile /'vɪraɪl/ adj. мужественный

virility /vɪ'rɪlɪtɪ/ n. (sexual potency) мужска́я си́ла, полова́я поте́нция; (manliness) мужественность

virologist /vaɪ'rɒlədʒɪst/ n. вирусо́лог

virology /vaɪ'rɒlədʒɪ/ n. вирусоло́гия

virtual /'vɜːtʃʊəl/ adj. ❶ факти́ческий; **we remained** ~ **strangers** факти́чески мы остава́лись соверше́нно незнако́мыми людьми́ ❷ (comput., phys.) виртуа́льный
■ ~ **reality** n. (comput.) виртуа́льная реа́льность

♂ **virtually** /'vɜːtʃʊəlɪ/ adv. факти́чески, практи́чески; **the dress was** ~ **new** э́то бы́ло факти́чески/практи́чески но́вое пла́тье; **it's** ~ **impossible** э́то факти́чески/практи́чески невозмо́жно

virtue /'vɜːtʃuː/ n. ❶ (moral excellence) доброде́тель ❷ (good quality, advantage) досто́инство, преиму́щество ❸ (consideration): **by** ~ **of his long service** на основа́нии его́ многоле́тней слу́жбы

virtuosity /vɜːtʃʊ'ɒsɪtɪ/ n. виртуо́зность

virtuoso /vɜːtʃʊ'əʊsəʊ/ n.: **a** ~ **performance** виртуо́зное исполне́ние

virtuous /'vɜːtʃʊəs/ adj. доброде́тельный

virulence /'vɪrʊləns/ n. (of poison) си́ла, смерте́льность; (of disease) тя́жесть; (of bacteria) вируле́нтность; (of temper, speech, etc.) зло́ба, я́рость

virulent /'vɪrʊlənt/ adj. (of poison) сильноде́йствующий; смерте́льный; (of disease) тяжёлый; (of bacteria) вируле́нтный; (of temper, words, etc.) зло́бный, я́ростный

virus /'vaɪərəs/ n. (also comput.) ви́рус

visa /'viːzə/ n. ви́за

viscount /'vaɪkaʊnt/ n. вико́нт

viscountess /'vaɪkaʊntɪs/ n. виконте́сса

viscous /'vɪskəs/ adj. вя́зкий, ли́пкий

vise /vaɪs/ n. (AmE) = vice²

visibility /vɪzɪ'bɪlɪtɪ/ n. ви́димость

visibl|e /'vɪzɪb(ə)l/ adj. ❶ (perceptible by eye) ви́димый ❷ (apparent; obvious) я́вный, очеви́дный; **she was** ~**y annoyed** она́ была́ заме́тно раздражена́

♂ ключева́я ле́ксика

♂ **vision** /'vɪʒ(ə)n/ n. ❶ (faculty of sight) зре́ние ❷ (imaginative insight) проница́тельность ❸ (apparition) при́зрак; привиде́ние ❹ (sth imagined or dreamed of) мечта́

visionary /'vɪʒənərɪ/ n. прови́д|ец (-ица)
● adj. дальнови́дный, му́дрый

♂ **visit** /'vɪzɪt/ n. (call) визи́т, посеще́ние; (trip, stay) пое́здка, пребыва́ние; **make, pay a** ~ **to sb** посе|ща́ть, -ти́ть (or наве|ща́ть, -сти́ть) кого́-н.
● v.t. (**visited, visiting**) (place) посе|ща́ть, -ти́ть; (person) наве|ща́ть, -сти́ть; **he** ~**ed Europe** он побыва́л в Евро́пе; он съе́здил в Евро́пу; **I have never** ~**ed New York** я никогда́ не быва́л в Нью-Йо́рке
● v.i. (AmE): ~ **with** (go to see) посе|ща́ть, -ти́ть (or наве|ща́ть, -сти́ть) кого́-н.
■ ~**ing card** n. (BrE) визи́тная ка́рточка; ~**ing hours** n. pl. приёмные часы́; часы́ посеще́ния

♂ **visitor** /'vɪzɪtə(r)/ n. гость (m.), посети́тель (m.)

visor /'vaɪzə(r)/ n. (of helmet) щито́к; (of windscreen) солнцезащи́тный щито́к

vista /'vɪstə/ n. перспекти́ва, вид

visual /'vɪʒʊəl/ adj. зри́тельный; визуа́льный
■ ~ **aids** n. pl. нагля́дные посо́бия; ~ **arts** n. pl. изобрази́тельные иску́сства

visualize /'vɪʒʊəlaɪz/ v.t. предст|авля́ть, -а́вить себе́

♂ **vital** /'vaɪt(ə)l/ adj. ❶ (concerned with life) жи́зненный; ~ **statistics** (joc., woman's measurements) объём груди́, та́лии и бёдер ❷ (essential) насу́щный; **it is of** ~ **importance** э́то вопро́с/де́ло первостепе́нной ва́жности ❸ (lively) живо́й

vitality /vaɪ'tælɪtɪ/ n. жи́вость

vitamin /'vɪtəmɪn/ n. витами́н
■ ~ **C** n. витами́н С (pronounced це)

viticulture /'vɪtɪkʌltʃə(r)/ n. виногра́дарство

vitriolic /vɪtrɪ'ɒlɪk/ adj. ядови́тый (коммента́рий и т. п.)

viva /'vaɪvə/ (BrE) у́стный экза́мен

vivacious /vɪ'veɪʃəs/ adj. живо́й, оживлённый

vivacity /vɪ'væsɪtɪ/ n. жи́вость, оживле́ние

vivid /'vɪvɪd/ adj. ❶ (bright) я́ркий ❷ (lively) живо́й, пы́лкий; **a** ~ **imagination** пы́лкое воображе́ние ❸ (clear and distinct) чёткий, я́сный

vividness /'vɪvɪdnɪs/ n. я́ркость, жи́вость; чёткость

vivisection /vɪvɪ'sekʃ(ə)n/ n. вивисе́кция

vixen /'vɪks(ə)n/ n. лиси́ца(-са́мка)

viz. /vɪz/ adv. то есть, т. е., а и́менно

vocabulary /və'kæbjʊlərɪ/ n. (of an individual) слова́рный запа́с; (of a language) слова́рный соста́в

vocal /'vəʊk(ə)l/ adj. ❶ (of or using the voice) голосово́й, речево́й ❷ (eloquent) красноречи́вый
● n. (usu. in pl.) вока́льная па́ртия

vocalist /'vəʊkəlɪst/ n. вокали́ст (-ка)

vocation /və'keɪʃ(ə)n/ n. призва́ние

vocational /və'keɪʃən(ə)l/ adj. профессиона́льный

vociferous /vəˈsɪfərəs/ *adj.* шумный

vodka /ˈvɒdkə/ *n.* водка

vogue /vəʊg/ *n.* мода; **in ~** в моде

♂ **voice** /vɔɪs/ *n.* голос; **he shouted at the top of his ~** он кричал во весь голос; **I lost my ~** я потерял голос
● *v.t.* выражать, выразить
■ **~ mail** *n.* голосовая почта; **~-over** *n.* (TV etc.) голос за кадром; закадровый комментарий

void /vɔɪd/ *n.* пустота
● *adj.* **1** (empty) пустой; лишённый (*чего*) **2** (invalid) недействительный

volatile /ˈvɒlətaɪl/ *adj.* (of person) непостоянный, изменчивый

volcanic /vɒlˈkænɪk/ *adj.* вулканический

volcano /vɒlˈkeɪnəʊ/ *n.* (*pl.* **~es**) вулкан

Volga /ˈvɒlgə/ *n.* Волга

volley /ˈvɒlɪ/ *n.* (*pl.* **~s**) **1** (simultaneous discharge) залп; (fig.): **a ~ of oaths** поток брани **2** (tennis etc.) удар с лёта
● *v.t.* (**volleys, volleyed**) удар|ять, -арить с лёта

volleyball /ˈvɒlɪbɔːl/ *n.* волейбол

volt /vəʊlt/ *n.* вольт

voltage /ˈvəʊltɪdʒ/ *n.* напряжение, вольтаж

♂ **volume** /ˈvɒljuːm/ *n.* **1** (tome) том **2** (of sound) громкость
■ **~ control** *n.* регулятор громкости

voluminous /vəˈluːmɪnəs/ *adj.* огромный; **~ folds** пышные складки; **a ~ work** объёмистое произведение; **a ~ writer** плодовитый писатель

voluntary /ˈvɒləntərɪ/ *adj.* добровольный
■ **~ redundancy** *n.* добровольный уход с работы; **~ work** *n.* общественная работа

volunteer /vɒlənˈtɪə(r)/ *n.* добровольный помощник; (in army) доброволец
● *v.t.* предл|агать, -ожить; делать, с-добровольно
● *v.i.* вызываться, вызваться сделать что-н.;

no one ~ed желающих не нашлось

voluptuous /vəˈlʌptʃʊəs/ *adj.* чувственный

vomit /ˈvɒmɪt/ *n.* рвота
● *v.i.* (**vomited, vomiting**): **he ~ed** его вырвало

voracious /vəˈreɪʃəs/ *adj.* прожорливый

♂ **vote** /vəʊt/ *n.* **1** (act of voting) голосование **2** (~ cast) голос **3** (affirmation) вотум; **a ~ of confidence** вотум доверия **4** (right to ~) право голоса
● *v.i.* голосовать, про-; **they are voting on the resolution** они голосуют резолюцию
● *with adv.*: **they were ~d in by a large majority** их избрали большинством голосов

♂ **voter** /ˈvəʊtə(r)/ *n.* избиратель (*m.*)

voting /ˈvəʊtɪŋ/ *n.* голосование; участие в выборах (*об избирателях*)

vouch /vaʊtʃ/ *v.i.* руча́ться, поручи́ться; **I can ~ for his honesty** я готов поручиться за его честность

voucher /ˈvaʊtʃə(r)/ *n.* талон

vow /vaʊ/ *n.* обет, клятва; **he broke his marriage ~s** он нарушил брачный обет
● *v.t.* кля́сться, по-; **he ~ed** (*sc.* resolved) **never to return** он поклялся никогда не возвращаться

vowel /ˈvaʊəl/ *n.* (ling.) гласный (*звук*)

voyage /ˈvɔɪɪdʒ/ *n.* (by sea) (морское) путешествие; плавание

voyeur /vwaːˈjɜː(r)/ *n.* вуайерист

vs *abbr.* (of **versus**) против + *g.*

V-sign /ˈviːsaɪn/ *n.* **1** (BrE, gesture of contempt) ≈ фига (*жест*) **2** (for victory) знак победы

vulgar /ˈvʌlgə(r)/ *adj.* вульгарный, пошлый, грубый

vulgarity /vʌlˈgærɪtɪ/ *n.* вульгарность, пошлость, грубость

vulnerable /ˈvʌlnərəb(ə)l/ *adj.* уязвимый

vulture /ˈvʌltʃə(r)/ *n.* гриф (*птица*)

vulva /ˈvʌlvə/ *n.* (*pl.* **~s**) (anat.) вульва

Ww

V

W

wacky /ˈwækɪ/ *adj.* (**wackier, wackiest**) (infml) сумасшедший, чокнутый

wad /wɒd/ *n.* **1** (pad) комок **2** (of papers, banknotes) пачка

waddle /ˈwɒd(ə)l/ *v.i.* ходить (*indet.*) вразвал(оч)ку (infml)

wade /weɪd/ *v.i.* проб|ираться, -раться; (fig.): **I have ~d through all his novels** я (с трудом) одолел все его романы

wafer /ˈweɪfə(r)/ *n.* (cul.) вафля

waffle[1] /ˈwɒf(ə)l/ *n.* (cul.) вафля

waffle[2] /ˈwɒf(ə)l/ (infml) *n.* (BrE, verbiage) вода (*в речи, в статье*)
● *v.i.* (*also* **~ on**) (BrE) заниматься (*impf.*) болтовнёй

waft /wɒft/ *v.t.* дон|осить, -ести
● *v.i.* дон|оситься, -естись

wag /wæg/ *v.t.* (**wagged, wagging**) (one's tail) вил|ять, -ьнуть + *i.*
● *v.i.* (**wagged, wagging**) (of dog's tail)

вил|я́ть, -ьну́ть; **this will set tongues ~ging** э́то даст по́вод к спле́тням

⚥ **wage¹** /weɪdʒ/ *n.* (*also* **wages** *pl.*)
за́работная пла́та; зарпла́та; **a living ~** прожи́точный ми́нимум

■ **~ earner** *n.* наёмный рабо́чий; (breadwinner) корми́л|ец (-ица)

wage² /weɪdʒ/ *v.t.* (war) вести́ (*impf.*); (campaign) проводи́ть, -ести́

wager /'weɪdʒə(r)/ *n.* пари́ (*nt. indecl.*); **lay a ~** держа́ть (*impf.*) пари́

waggle /'wæg(ə)l/ *v.t. & i.* (ears, toes) шевели́ть, по- + *i.*
● *v.i.* (of ears, toes) шевели́ться, по-; (shake slightly) пока́чиваться (*impf.*)

wagon /'wægən/ *n.* **1** (horse-drawn) пово́зка; (with cover) фурго́н **2** (BrE, on railway) ваго́н-платфо́рма **3**: **he is on the ~** (fig., not drinking alcohol) он бро́сил пить

wail /weɪl/ *n.* **1** (cry, howl) вопль (*m.*); (fig., of the wind, sirens) вой
● *v.i.* вопи́ть (*impf.*); выть (*impf.*)

waist /weɪst/ *n.* та́лия

■ **~coat** *n.* (BrE) жиле́т

⚥ **wait** /weɪt/ *n.* **1** (act or time of ~ing) ожида́ние; **we had a long ~ for the bus** мы до́лго жда́ли авто́буса **2** (ambush): **the robbers lay in ~ for their victim** граби́тели подстерега́ли свою́ же́ртву
● *v.t.*: **you must ~ your turn** вы должны́ дожда́ться свое́й о́череди
● *v.i.* **1** (refrain from action) ждать (*impf.*), подожда́ть (*pf.*); **we must ~ and see what happens** подождём — посмо́трим, что бу́дет да́льше; **I could hardly ~ to ...** я сгора́л от нетерпе́ния (+ *inf.*); **I ~ed for the rain to stop** я ждал, когда́ ко́нчится дождь **2** (act as servant): **she ~s on him hand and foot** она́ его́ по́лностью обслу́живает; **he ~ed at table** он прислу́живал за столо́м **3** **~ up: she ~ed up for him** она́ не ложи́лась (спать) до его́ прихо́да

■ **~ing list** *n.* спи́сок (*кандида́тов, очередникóв*); о́чередь; **~ing room** *n.* (doctor's etc.) приёмная; (on station) зал ожида́ния

waiter /'weɪtə(r)/ *n.* официа́нт

waitress /'weɪtrɪs/ *n.* официа́нтка

waive /weɪv/ *v.t.* (forgo) отка́з|ываться, -а́ться от + *g.*; (claims) возде́рж|иваться, -а́ться от + *g.*; (rules) не соблюда́ть, -сти́ + *g.*

waiver /'weɪvə(r)/ *n.* отка́з (от + *g.*)

⚥ **wake¹** /weɪk/ *v.t.* (*past* **woke**, *p.p.* **woken**) буди́ть, раз-
● *v.i.* (*past* **woke**, *p.p.* **woken**) (*also* **~ up**) прос|ыпа́ться, -ну́ться; **~ up!** (lit., fig.) просни́тесь!

wake² /weɪk/ *n.* (of vessel) кильва́тер; (fig.): **there was havoc in the ~ of the storm** бу́ря оста́вила по́сле себя́ многочи́сленные разруше́ния

wakeful /'weɪkfʊl/ *adj.* (person) бо́дрствующий; **we had a ~ night** мы провели́ бессо́нную ночь

⚥ ключева́я ле́ксика

waken /'weɪkən/ *v.t.* буди́ть, раз-; (fig.) буди́ть, про-

Wales /weɪlz/ *n.* Уэ́льс

⚥ **walk** /wɔ:k/ *n.* **1** (action of ~ing) ходьба́; **a short ~ away** в нéскольких шага́х отсю́да/оттýда **2** (excursion) (пéшая) прогу́лка; (long-distance) похо́д; **I'm going for a ~** я пойду́ прогуля́юсь/погуля́ю; **I went on a ten-mile ~** я был в десятими́льном похо́де **3** (~ing pace) шаг **4** (gait) похо́дка, по́ступь **5** (route for ~ing): **there are some pleasant ~s round here** здесь есть прия́тные места́ для прогу́лок **6** (path) тропа́ **7** (contest): **long-distance ~** (спорти́вная) ходьба́ на дли́нную диста́нцию
● *v.t.* (take for a ~) выгу́ливать, вы́гулять; гуля́ть, по- с (+ *i.*); (cause to ~): **he ~ed his horse up the hill** он пусти́л ло́шадь ша́гом в го́ру; (accompany) сопрово|жда́ть, -ди́ть; **he offered to ~ her home** он вы́звался проводи́ть её домо́й
● *v.i.* **1** (move on foot) ходи́ть (*indet.*), идти́ (*det.*); (stroll about) прогу́ливаться (*impf.*); **I ~ed ten miles** я прошёл де́сять миль; **I ~ed into a shop** я вошёл в магази́н; **they ~ed into an ambush** они́ попа́ли в заса́ду **2** (opp. ride) ходи́ть (*indet.*), идти́ (*det.*) пешко́м **3** (opp. run): **he ~ed the last 100 metres** после́дние сто ме́тров он прошёл ша́гом **4** (take exercise etc. on foot) ходи́ть (*indet.*) пешко́м; (stroll) гуля́ть (*impf.*); **I spent 2 weeks ~ing in Scotland** я броди́л две неде́ли по Шотла́ндии
□ **~ away** *v.i.* уходи́ть, уйти́; **he ~ed away with several prizes** он без труда́ завоева́л/получи́л не́сколько призо́в
□ **~ in** *v.i.* входи́ть, войти́
□ **~ off** *v.t.* (annul by ~ing): **he was ~ing off a heavy lunch** он соверша́л прогу́лку по́сле сы́тного обе́да
● *v.i.* уходи́ть, уйти́; **someone ~ed off with my hat** кто-то унёс мою́ шля́пу
□ **~ on** *v.i.* (continue ~ing) продолжа́ть (*impf.*) идти́
□ **~ out** *v.i.* выходи́ть, вы́йти; **the men are threatening to ~ out** (strike) рабо́чие грозя́т забасто́вкой
□ **~ up** *v.i.* (approach) под|ходи́ть, -ойти́; **I ~ed up to him** я подошёл к нему́
■ **~over** *n.* лёгкая побе́да; **~way** *n.* перехо́д (*сооруже́ние*)

walker /'wɔ:kə(r)/ *n.* челове́к, соверша́ющий пе́шие/пешехо́дные прогу́лки; пе́ший тури́ст; **a popular route for ~s** популя́рный пешехо́дный маршру́т

walkie-talkie /wɔ:kɪ'tɔ:kɪ/ *n.* ра́ция

walking /'wɔ:kɪŋ/ *n.* ходьба́
■ **~ shoes** *n. pl.* о́бувь для ходьбы́; **~ stick** *n.* трость

Walkman® /'wɔ:kmən/ *n.* плééр

⚥ **wall** /wɔ:l/ *n.* (lit., fig.) стена́, сте́нка; (*attr.*) насте́нный
● *v.t.*: **~ed garden** обнесённый стено́й сад
■ **~paper** *n.* обо́|и (-ев) ● *v.t.* обкле́и|вать, -ть обо́ями

wallaby /'wɒləbɪ/ *n.* кенгуру́-валла́би (*m. indecl.*)

wallet /ˈwɒlɪt/ n. бума́жник
wallop /ˈwɒləp/ v.t. (**walloped,
walloping**) (infml) дуба́сить, от-
wallow /ˈwɒləʊ/ v.i. (in mud, water) валя́ться
(*impf.*); (fig.) купа́ться (*impf.*) (*в чём*); ~ **in**
grief упива́ться (*impf.*) свои́м го́рем
walnut /ˈwɔːlnʌt/ n. гре́цкий оре́х; (wood) оре́х
walrus /ˈwɔːlrəs/ n. морж
waltz /wɔːls/ n. вальс
• v.i. танцева́ть (*impf.*) вальс
wan /wɒn/ adj. (**wanner, wannest**)
бле́дный, изнурённый; a ~ **light** сла́бый/
ту́склый свет; a ~ **smile** сла́бая улы́бка
wand /wɒnd/ n. волше́бная па́лочка
wander /ˈwɒndə(r)/ v.t. броди́ть,
стра́нствовать, скита́ться (*all impf.*) по + d.
• v.i. **1** (go aimlessly) броди́ть (*impf.*); his
mind was ~ing (absent-mindedly) его́ мы́сли
блужда́ли; (in delirium) он бре́дил **2** (stray)
заблуди́ться (*pf.*); (lit., fig.) отклон|я́ться,
-и́ться; **we** ~ed **from the track** мы сби́лись
с пути́; **don't let your attention** ~ не
отвлека́йтесь
□ ~ **about** v.i. броди́ть (*impf.*)
□ ~ **off** v.i. брести́, по- куда́-н.
wanderer /ˈwɒndərə(r)/ n. стра́нник,
скита́лец
wane /weɪn/ v.i. (of the moon) убыва́ть (*impf.*);
(fig., decline) ослабева́ть (*impf.*)
wangle /ˈwæŋg(ə)l/ v.t. заполучи́ть
(*pf.*) хи́тростью; **he** ~d **£5 out of me** он
вы́клянчил (infml) у меня́ 5 фу́нтов
wannabe /ˈwɒnəbɪ/ n. (sl.) челове́к,
мечта́ющий стать (*кем-н.*)
✓ **want** /wɒnt/ n. **1** (lack) недоста́ток,
отсу́тствие; **for** ~ **of** за неиме́нием + g.
2 (need) нужда́
• v.t. **1** (need; require) нужда́ться (*impf.*) в +
p.; **I don't** ~ **any bread today** сего́дня мне
хлеб не ну́жен; **he is** ~ed **by the police** его́
разы́скивает поли́ция; **you're** ~ed **on the
telephone** вас (про́сят) к телефо́ну **2** (desire)
хоте́ть (*impf.*) (+ g. or a. or inf.); жела́ть
(*impf.*) (+ g. or a. or inf.); **what do you** ~? что вы
хоти́те?; что вам ну́жно?; **she** ~s **to go away**
она́ хо́чет уе́хать/уйти́; **she** ~s **me to go
away** она́ хо́чет, что́бы я уе́хал/ушёл
wanting /ˈwɒntɪŋ/ adj. недоста́точный;
he was tried and found ~ он не вы́держал
испыта́ния
wanton /ˈwɒnt(ə)n/ adj. (wilful) своенра́вный;
~ **cruelty** бессмы́сленная жесто́кость
✓ **war** /wɔː(r)/ n. **1** война́; **make, wage** ~ **on**
вести́ (*det.*) войну́ с + i. **2** (*attr.*) вое́нный
■ ~ **game** n. (in pl.) (military exercises) (вое́нные)
уче́ния; (leisure activity) вое́нная игра́;
~**head** n. боеголо́вка; ~**like** adj. (martial)
вои́нственный; ~**ship** n. вое́нный кора́бль;
~**time** n. вое́нное вре́мя
ward /wɔːd/ n. **1** (person under guardianship)
подопе́чный **2** (urban division) о́круг **3** (in
hospital etc.) пала́та
• v.t.: ~ **off** (a blow) отра|жа́ть, -зи́ть; ~ **off
danger** отвра|ща́ть, -ти́ть опа́сность

warden /ˈwɔːd(ə)n/ n. **1** (BrE, of hostel)
коменда́нт **2**; (BrE) инспе́ктор,
контроли́рующий соблюде́ние пра́вил
парко́вки и стоя́нки (*в черте города*)
warder /ˈwɔːdə(r)/ n. (BrE, in prison)
надзира́тель (m.)
wardrobe /ˈwɔːdrəʊb/ n. **1** гардеро́б
2 (theatr.) костюме́рная
warehouse /ˈweəhaʊs/ n. (това́рный) склад
wares /weəz/ n. pl. това́ры (m. pl.)
warfare /ˈwɔːfeə(r)/ n. война́
✓ **warm** /wɔːm/ adj. тёплый
• v.t. греть (*impf.*); (food, water) подогр|ева́ть,
-е́ть; нагр|ева́ть, -е́ть; ~ **oneself at the fire**
гре́ться (*impf.*) у ками́на/огня́
• v.i. гре́ться (*impf.*); (of objects) нагр|ева́ться,
-е́ться; (of people, room) согр|ева́ться,
-е́ться; (fig.): **he** ~ed **to the subject as he
went on** по ме́ре расска́за он всё бо́льше
воодушевля́лся; **I** ~ed **to(wards) him as I got
to know him** чем лу́чше я его́ узнава́л, тем
бо́льше расположе́ния он вызыва́л у меня́
□ ~ **up** v.t. разогр|ева́ть, -е́ть; согр|ева́ть, -е́ть;
a fire will ~ **up the room** ками́н обогре́ет
ко́мнату
• v.i. согр|ева́ться, -е́ться; **it** (sc. the weather)
is ~ing **up** тепле́ет; **he** ~ed **up before the
race** он сде́лал разми́нку пе́ред нача́лом
соревнова́ния
■ ~-**hearted** adj. серде́чный; ~-**up** n.
разми́нка
warmth /wɔːmθ/ n. теплота́
✓ **warn** /wɔːn/ v.t. (caution) предупре|жда́ть,
-ди́ть; (of danger etc.) предостер|ега́ть, -е́чь
✓ **warning** /ˈwɔːnɪŋ/ n. предупрежде́ние,
предостереже́ние; **give** ~ **of**
предупре|жда́ть, -ди́ть о + p.
• adj. предупрежда́ющий;
предостерега́ющий
warp /wɔːp/ v.t. **1** (distort) коро́бить, по-;
искрив|ля́ть, -и́ть **2** (fig.) иска|жа́ть, -зи́ть; **a**
~ed **sense of humour** извращённое чу́вство
ю́мора
• v.i. коро́биться, по-
warrant /ˈwɒrənt/ n. о́рдер; суде́бное
распоряже́ние
• v.t. опра́вд|ывать, -а́ть
warranty /ˈwɒrəntɪ/ n. гара́нтия
warren /ˈwɒrən/ n. (rabbits') кро́личья нора́;
(fig.) лабири́нт
warrior /ˈwɒrɪə(r)/ n. во́ин
Warsaw /ˈwɔːsɔː/ n. Варша́ва
wart /wɔːt/ n. борода́вка
wary /ˈweərɪ/ adj. (**warier, wariest**)
осторо́жный; **be** ~ **of** остерега́ться (*impf.*) + g.
was /wɒz/ 1st and 3rd pers. sg. past of ▶ be
wash /wɒʃ/ n. **1** (act of ~ing) мытьё; **I must
have a** ~ мне на́до помы́ться/умы́ться; **she
gave the floor a good** ~ она́ тща́тельно
вы́мыла пол **2** (laundry) сти́рка **3** (motion of
water etc.) прибо́й
• v.t. (cleanse with water etc.) мыть, по-/вы́-;
(hands, face, child) ум|ыва́ть, -ы́ть; (clothes)
стира́ть, по-/вы́-; ~ **one's hands and face**

мыть, по-/вы- ру́ки и лицо́; ~ dishes мыть, по-/вы- посу́ду
● *v.i.* (~ oneself) мы́ться, по-/вы-
□ ~ **away** *v.t.* (carry off) см|ыва́ть, -ыть
□ ~ **out** *v.t.* (of colour): you look ~ed out у вас утомлённый вид
□ ~ **up** *v.t. & i.* (BrE, dishes) мыть, по-/вы- (посу́ду); (AmE, have a wash) мы́ться, по-/вы-; (on to shore) выбра́сывать, вы́бросить на бе́рег
■ ~basin, ~bowl *nn.* ра́ковина; ~cloth *n.* (AmE) махро́вая салфе́тка для лица́; ~out *n.* прова́л, неуда́ча

washable /'wɒʃəb(ə)l/ *adj.* мо́ющийся
washer /'wɒʃə(r)/ *n.* (tech.) прокла́дка
washing /'wɒʃɪŋ/ *n.* **1** (action) мытьё, умыва́ние, сти́рка **2** (clothes) бельё
■ ~ **machine** *n.* стира́льная маши́на; ~ **powder** *n.* (BrE) стира́льный порошо́к; ~-**up** *n.* (BrE) do the ~-up мыть, по-/вы- посу́ду; ~-up liquid *n.* (BrE) сре́дство для мытья́ посу́ды
Washington /'wɒʃɪŋt(ə)n/ *n.* Вашингто́н
wasp /wɒsp/ *n.* оса́
waspish /'wɒspɪʃ/ *adj.* язви́тельный, ко́лкий
wastage /'weɪstɪdʒ/ *n.* убы́ток, уте́чка
⚜ **waste** /weɪst/ *n.* **1** (extravagant use; failure to use) (рас)тра́та, растра́чивание; ~ of money пуста́я тра́та де́нег; go, run to ~ пропада́ть (*impf.*) да́ром **2** (refuse, superfluous material) отхо́ды (*m. pl.*), отбро́сы (*m. pl.*), му́сор
● *adj.* **1** (superfluous) ли́шний, ненужный; (rejected) брако́ванный; ~ products отхо́ды (*m. pl.*) **2** (of land): ~ ground невозде́ланная земля́; ~land пусты́рь (*m.*), пу́стошь; lay ~ опустош|а́ть, -и́ть
● *v.t.* **1** (make no use of, squander) тра́тить, ис-/по- да́ром/зря/впусту́ю; растра́|чивать, -тить; ~ one's chance тра́тить, -тить случай **2** (wear away) изнур|я́ть, -и́ть
■ ~basket *n.* (AmE) му́сорная корзи́на; ~ **paper** *n.* макулату́ра; ~-**paper basket** *n.* (BrE) корзи́на для бума́г; ~ **pipe** *n.* сливна́я/водоотво́дная труба́
wasteful /'weɪstfʊl/ *adj.* расточи́тельный
waster /'weɪstə(r)/ *n.* (wasteful person) расточи́тель (*m.*); (infml, good-for-nothing) никуды́шный/никчёмный челове́к; безде́льник
⚜ **watch¹** /wɒtʃ/ *n.* **1** (alert state) надзо́р, присмо́тр, наблюде́ние; keep ~ (guard) наблюда́ть (*impf.*) (on: за + *i.*); the dog keeps ~ on, over the house соба́ка карау́лит/сторожи́т дом
● *v.t.* **1** (look at) смотре́ть (*impf.*); he was ~ing TV он смотре́л телеви́зор; I ~ed him draw я смотре́л, как он рису́ет **2** (keep under observation) следи́ть (*impf.*) за + *i.*; смотре́ть (*impf.*) за + *i.*; (be careful of) следи́ть (*impf.*) за + *i.*; ~ your step! (fig.) (infml *also* ~ it!) бу́дьте осторо́жны! **3** (guard) сторожи́ть (*impf.*)
● *v.i.* **1** смотре́ть, наблюда́ть, следи́ть (*all impf.*); he ~ed for the postman он поджида́л почтальо́на; he ~ed over her interests

он стоя́л на стра́же её интере́сов **2** (be careful): ~ how you cross the street! бу́дьте осторо́жны (or смотри́те) при перехо́де у́лицы!
□ ~ **out** *v.i.* (beware) остерега́ться + *g.*
■ ~dog *n.* (lit.) сторожева́я соба́ка; (fig.) наблюда́тель (*m.*); ~man *n.* сто́рож; ~word *n.* деви́з
watch² /wɒtʃ/ *n.* (timepiece) час|ы́ (*pl., g.* -о́в)
■ ~band (AmE), ~ **strap** (BrE) *nn.* ремешо́к для часо́в
watchful /'wɒtʃfʊl/ *adj.* бди́тельный
⚜ **water** /'wɔːtə(r)/ *n.* **1** вода́ **2** (*attr.*): ~ sports во́дные ви́ды спо́рта
● *v.t.* **1** (plants) пол|ива́ть, -и́ть водо́й **2** (animals) пои́ть, на-
● *v.i.* **1** (of eyes) слези́ться (*impf.*); his eyes were ~ing with the wind от ве́тра у него́ слези́лись глаза́; the sight of food made my mouth ~ при ви́де еды́ у меня́ потекли́ слю́нки
□ ~ **down** *v.t.* (lit.) разб|авля́ть, -а́вить; (fig.) смягч|а́ть, -и́ть
■ ~colour (AmE ~color) *n.* (paint) акваре́ль, акваре́льные кра́ски (*f. pl.*); (painting) акваре́ль, акваре́льный рису́нок; ~course *n.* ру́сло; ~cress *n.* кресс водяно́й; ~fall *n.* водопа́д; ~ **feature** *n.* (in gardening) элеме́нт аквадиза́йна (*искусственный пруд, фонтан*); ~ **level** *n.* у́ровень (*m.*) воды́; ~ **lily** *n.* кувши́нка; ~logged *adj.* заболо́ченный; ~ **main** *n.* водопрово́дная магистра́ль; ~mark *n.* водяно́й знак; ~melon *n.* арбу́з; ~proof *adj.* непромока́емый ● *n.* (BrE) непромока́емый плащ; ~skiing *n.* воднолы́жный спорт; ~skis *n. pl.* во́дные лы́жи (*f. pl.*); ~tight *adj.* (lit.) водонепроница́емый; (fig., of argument etc.) неопровержи́мый; ~way *n.* фарва́тер; ~works *n. pl.* водопрово́дная ста́нция
watering /'wɔːtərɪŋ/ *n.* поли́вка
■ ~ **can** *n.* ле́йка
watery /'wɔːtərɪ/ *adj.* водяни́стый, жи́дкий; ~ eyes слезя́щиеся глаза́
watt /wɒt/ *n.* ватт
wattage /'wɒtɪdʒ/ *n.* мо́щность в ва́ттах
⚜ **wave** /weɪv/ *n.* **1** (ridge of water) волна́ **2** (fig., temporary increase) подъём, волна́; crime ~ ре́зкий рост престу́пности **3** (phys.) волна́; short/medium/long ~s коро́ткие/сре́дние/дли́нные во́лны **4** (undulation): her hair has a natural ~ у неё (от приро́ды) выющиеся во́лосы **5** (gesture) взмах
● *v.t.* **1** (move to and fro or up and down) маха́ть, по- + *i.*; разма́хивать (*impf.*) + *i.* **2** (express by hand-waving): ~ goodbye маха́ть, по- (руко́й) на проща́ние
● *v.i.* **1** (move to and fro or up and down) развева́ться (*impf.*); кача́ться (*impf.*) **2** (~ one's hand) маха́ть, по-; ~ at sb маха́ть, по- кому́-н.
■ ~band *n.* диапазо́н волн; ~length *n.* длина́ волны́; he and I are on the same ~length (fig.) мы с ним легко́ нахо́дим о́бщий язы́к

⚜ ключевая лексика

waver /'weɪvə(r)/ *v.i.* **1** (falter) дрожа́ть, за-; дро́гнуть (*pf.*) **2** (hesitate) колеба́ться (*impf.*)

wavy /'weɪvɪ/ *adj.* (**wavier, waviest**) волни́стый; ~ hair вью́щиеся во́лосы

wax¹ /wæks/ *n.* воск; (in the ears) се́ра
∎ ~**work** *n.* (dummy) восковáя фигу́ра; ~**works** *n.* (museum) галере́я восковы́х фигу́р

wax² /wæks/ *v.i.* (of moon) прибыва́ть (*impf.*)

waxy /'wæksɪ/ *adj.* (**waxier, waxiest**) восково́й

ᔐ **way** /weɪ/ *n.* **1** (road, path) доро́га, путь (*m.*); (track) тропá **2** (route, journey) путь (*m.*); which is the best ~ to London? как лу́чше проéхать в Ло́ндон?; we made our ~ to the dining room мы прошли́ в столо́вую; (with preps.): by ~ of London че́рез Ло́ндон; by the ~ (incidentally) кстáти; ме́жду про́чим; on the ~ по доро́ге; на/по пути́; he was on his ~ to the bank он шёл в банк; he went out of his ~ to help me он прояви́л немáлое усе́рдие, что́бы помо́чь мне; out of the ~ (remote) в стороне́; далеко́; (with adv. indicating direction): ~ back обрáтная доро́га; ~ in вход; ~ out (lit., fig.) вы́ход **3** (direction) сторонá, направле́ние; which ~ did they go? в каку́ю сто́рону они́ пошли́?; this ~ сюда́; you can't have it both ~s ли́бо одно́, ли́бо друго́е; что́-нибудь одно́ **4** (of reversible things): his hat is on the wrong ~ round он надéл шля́пу зáдом наперёд; the picture is the wrong ~ up картина пове́шена вверх ногáми; is the flag the right ~ up? флаг пове́шен прáвильно? **5** (distance, time) расстоя́ние; a long ~ off (away) далеко́; it is only a little ~ to the shop до магази́нов совсе́м недалеко́; all the ~ всю доро́гу; (fig.) по́лностью **6** (a long ~) back далеко́; ~ back (long ago) давны́м-давно́; ~ ahead of the others намно́го впереди́ остальны́х **7** (clear passage) проéзд, прохо́д; get in the ~ мешáть, по- (*кому*); get out of the ~! (прочь) с доро́ги!; make ~ for the President! доро́гу президе́нту!; you are standing in the ~ вы загорáживаете доро́гу; give ~ (fail to resist) поддавáться, -áться; (collapse) провáл|иваться, -и́ться; раз|рывáться, -орвáться; ру́хнуть (*pf.*); his legs gave ~ у него́ подкоси́лись но́ги; (make concessions) уступáть, -и́ть; (allow precedence) уступáть, -и́ть доро́гу **8** (means) сре́дство, ме́тод, приём **9** (manner) сре́дство, спо́соб, о́браз, ме́тод, приём; in this ~ таки́м о́бразом; one ~ or another так и́ли инáче; in the same ~ (то́чно) так же; I love the ~ he smiles мне о́чень нрáвится, как он улыбáется; try to see it my ~ попытáйтесь встать на моё ме́сто; let's put it this ~ скáжем так; either ~ (in either fashion) любы́м из двух спо́собов; (in either case) в обо́их слу́чаях, в любо́м слу́чае; whichever ~ you look at it с какóй стороны́ (на э́то) ни посмотре́ть; by ~ of an apology в кáчестве извине́ния; (preference): have it your own ~! будь/пусть бу́дет по-вáшему!; have, get one's own ~ доб|ивáться, -и́ться своего́ **10** (custom) обы́чай, привы́чка; ~ of life о́браз жи́зни; he has a ~ of not

paying his bills у него́ есть привы́чка не плати́ть по счетáм; that's the ~ of the world так уж заведено́/во́дится на све́те; mend one's ~s испр|авля́ться, -áвиться **11** (state) положе́ние, состоя́ние **12** (sense) смысл, отноше́ние; in a ~ в не́котором смы́сле/ отноше́нии; in some ~s в не́которых отноше́ниях; in no ~ ничу́ть, нико́им о́бразом; were you involved in any ~? бы́ли ли вы каки́м-нибудь о́бразом в э́том замéшаны? **13** (scale, degree): in a big ~ в широ́ком/большо́м масштáбе
∎ ~**lay** *v.t.* подстер|егáть, -е́чь; ~**out** *adj.* (infml) замечáтельный, бесподо́бный; ~**side** *n.* обо́чина (доро́ги); (*attr.*) придоро́жный; **fall by the** ~**side** (fig.) выбивáться, вы́быть из стро́я

wayward /'weɪwəd/ *adj.* своенрáвный

waywardness /'weɪwədnɪs/ *n.* своенрáвие

WC (BrE) *abbr.* (of **water closet**) туале́т (убо́рная)

ᔐ **we** /wiː/ *pers. pron.* (*obj.* **us**, *poss.* **our, ours**) мы; ~ lawyers мы, адвокáты

ᔐ **weak** /wiːk/ *adj.* слáбый
∎ ~**willed** *adj.* слабово́льный

weaken /'wiːkən/ *v.t.* осл|абля́ть, -áбить ● *v.i.* слабе́ть, о-

weakling /'wiːklɪŋ/ *n.* хи́лый челове́к

weakness /'wiːknɪs/ *n.* слáбость, хи́лость

wealth /welθ/ *n.* богáтство, состоя́ние; (fig., profusion) оби́лие; a ~ of detail мно́жество подро́бностей; a ~ of experience богате́йший о́пыт

wealthy /'welθɪ/ *adj.* (**wealthier, wealthiest**) богáтый, состоя́тельный

wean /wiːn/ *v.t.* отн|имáть, -я́ть от груди́; (fig.) отуч|áть, -и́ть (*от чего*)

ᔐ **weapon** /'wepən/ *n.* ору́жие; (piece of artillery) ору́дие
∎ ~**s of mass destruction** *n. pl.* ору́жие мáссового пораже́ния/уничтоже́ния

weaponry /'wepənrɪ/ *n.* ору́жие

ᔐ **wear** /weə(r)/ *n.* **1** (articles or type of clothing) оде́жда, плáтье; beach ~ пля́жная оде́жда; (~ing of clothes): a suit for everyday ~ бу́дничный/повседне́вный костю́м **2** (continued use) изно́с; this material stands up to hard ~ э́тот материáл прекрáсно но́сится
● *v.t.* (*past* **wore**, *p.p.* **worn**) **1** (garments or accessories) носи́ть (*indet.*); (put on) над|евáть, -е́ть; what shall I ~? что мне надéть?; (of hair): to ~ one's hair long носи́ть (*indet.*) дли́нные во́лосы; ~ one's hair short ко́ротко стри́чься (*impf.*); (fig.): ~ing a smile с улы́бкой (на лице́); ~ing a frown нахму́рившись **2** (damage surface of) ст|ирáть, -ере́ть; (damage by use) трепáть, ис-, изн|áшивать, -оси́ть; (clothing) прот|ирáть, -ере́ть **3** (produce by friction): you've worn a hole in your trousers вы протёрли брю́ки до дыр
● *v.i.* (*past* **wore**, *p.p.* **worn**): ~ thin изн|áшиваться, -оси́ться; (fig.): his patience wore thin его́ терпе́ние бы́ло на исхо́де
□ ~ **away** *v.t. & i.* ст|ирáть(ся), -ере́ть(ся);

w

weather had worn away the inscription ве́тры и дожди́ стёрли на́дпись; **the cliffs were worn away in places** ска́лы места́ми вы́ветрились

□ ~ **down** v.t. & i. изн|а́шивать(ся), -оси́ть(ся); (fig.): **they wore down the enemy's resistance** они́ сломи́ли сопротивле́ние проти́вника

□ ~ **off** v.t. & i. ст|ира́ть(ся), -ере́ть(ся); (fig.) (постепе́нно) проходи́ть (impf.); **the novelty soon wore off** вско́ре новизна́ прошла́

□ ~ **out** v.t. & i. изн|а́шивать(ся), -оси́ть(ся); (fig.) утом|ля́ть(ся), -и́ть(ся)

weariness /ˈwɪərɪnɪs/ n. утомле́ние; (boredom) ску́ка

wearing /ˈweərɪŋ/ adj. надое́дливый

weary /ˈwɪərɪ/ adj. (**wearier**, **weariest**) **1** (tired) уста́лый; **the journey made him** ~ путеше́ствие его́ утоми́ло **2**: ~ **of** (fed up with) уста́вший от чего
• v.t. & i. утом|ля́ть(ся), -и́ть(ся)

weasel /ˈwiːz(ə)l/ n. ла́ска (хищное животное); ~ **words** (fig.) двусмы́сленные слова́, двусмы́сленности (f. pl.)
• v.t. (**weaselled**, **weaselling**, AmE **weaseled**, **weaseling**) (insinuate): **she** ~**led her way** (or **herself**) **into my confidence** она́ вкра́лась/втёрлась (infml) ко мне в дове́рие

✍ **weather** /ˈweðə(r)/ n. пого́да; **what's the** ~ **like?** кака́я сего́дня пого́да?; **be, feel under the** ~ (fig.) нева́жно себя́ чу́вствовать (impf.)
• v.t. (survive) выде́рживать, вы́держать
■ ~**-beaten** adj. обве́тренный; ~ **forecast** n. прогно́з пого́ды; ~**proof** adj. погодоусто́йчивый

weave /wiːv/ v.t. (past **wove**, p.p. **woven** or **wove**) **1** (thread, flowers, etc.) плести́, с-; спле|та́ть, -сти́ **2** (make basket, etc. by weaving) плести́, с-; (cloth) ткать, со-
• v.i. (past **wove**, p.p. **woven** or **wove**) петля́ть (impf.), идти́ (det.) непрямы́м путём

weaver /ˈwiːvə(r)/ n. ткач (-и́ха)

✍ **web** /web/ n. **1** (also **spider's** ~) паути́на; (fig.) сеть, паути́на, сплете́ние **2** (the Web, comput.) Всеми́рная паути́на, Сеть, Интерне́т
■ ~**-footed** adj. перепо́нчатый; ~**log** n. (comput.) сетево́й журна́л, блог; ~**logger** n. (comput.) бло́ггер; ~ **page** n. (comput.) веб-страни́ца, страни́ца в Интерне́те

webbed /webd/ adj. перепо́нчатый

website /ˈwebsaɪt/ n. (comput.) сайт, веб-са́йт

wedding /ˈwedɪŋ/ n. сва́дьба, бракосочета́ние; (in church) венча́ние
■ ~ **anniversary** n. годовщи́на сва́дьбы; ~ **day** n. день (m.) сва́дьбы; ~ **dress** n. сва́дебное пла́тье; ~ **ring** n. обруча́льное кольцо́

wedge /wedʒ/ n. клин; **it's the thin end of the** ~ ≈ э́то ещё (то́лько) цвето́чки(, а я́годки (бу́дут) впереди́); **a** ~ **of cake** кусо́к то́рта
• v.t. закреп|ля́ть, -и́ть кли́ном; ~ **in** вкли́н|ивать, -ить

✍ **Wednesday** /ˈwenzdeɪ/ n. среда́

weed /wiːd/ n. сорня́к; (in water) во́доросль
• v.t. (clear of ~s) поло́ть, вы́-

□ ~ **out** v.t. устран|я́ть, -и́ть
■ ~**killer** n. гербици́д

weedy /ˈwiːdɪ/ adj. (**weedier**, **weediest**) (BrE, weak-looking) то́щий

✍ **week** /wiːk/ n. неде́ля; **the** ~ **before last** позапро́шлая неде́ля; **the** ~ **after next** че́рез одну́ неде́лю; **a** ~ **today** ро́вно че́рез неде́лю; **(on) Monday** ~ (BrE) че́рез понеде́льник; ~ **in,** ~ **out** (це́лыми) неде́лями; **three times a** ~ три ра́за в неде́лю; **working** ~ рабо́чая неде́ля
■ ~**day** n. бу́дний/рабо́чий день

weekend /wiːkˈend/ n. коне́ц неде́ли, уи́к-э́нд/уике́нд, суббо́та и воскресе́нье

weekly /ˈwiːklɪ/ n. еженеде́льник
• adj. еженеде́льный
• adv. еженеде́льно

weep /wiːp/ v.i. (past and p.p. **wept**) **1** (shed tears) пла́кать, за-; (profusely) рыда́ть (impf.) **2** (of a wound) мо́кнуть (impf.)

weigh /weɪ/ v.t. **1** (find or test weight of) взве́|шивать, -сить; ~ **oneself** взве́|шиваться, -ситься; (fig., consider; compare) взве́|шивать, -сить **2** (of ~ed object: amount to) ве́сить (impf.); **what do you** ~? ско́лько вы ве́сите?; како́й у вас вес?
• v.i.: ~ **on** (be depressing or burdensome to) тяготи́ть (impf.)

□ ~ **down** v.t. (burden) отяго|ща́ть, -ти́ть; **the branches were** ~**ed down with, by fruit** ве́тви гну́лись под тя́жестью плодо́в; (fig., burdensome to) угнета́ть (impf.)

□ ~ **in** v.i. (of sportsman) взве́|шиваться, -ситься пе́ред соревнова́нием

□ ~ **out** v.t. отве́|шивать, -сить

□ ~ **up** v.t. (lit., fig.) взве́|шивать, -сить

✍ **weight** /weɪt/ n. **1** (heaviness) вес; **3 lbs in** ~ ве́сом (в) три фу́нта; **gain, put on** ~ приб|авля́ть, -а́вить в ве́се; **lose** ~ теря́ть, по- в ве́се; **pull one's** ~ (fig.) выполня́ть, вы́полнить свою́ до́лю рабо́ты; **throw one's** ~ **about** (fig.) распоряжа́ться (impf.), ва́жничать (impf.) **2** (load) тя́жесть, груз; (fig.) бре́мя (nt.); **it was a great** ~ **off my mind** у меня́ сло́вно ка́мень с души́ свали́лся **3** (object for weighing or ~ing) ги́ря **4** (importance; influence) вес; влия́ние; авторите́т; **his opinion carries great** ~ с его́ мне́нием о́чень счита́ются
• v.t. утяжел|я́ть, -и́ть
■ ~**lifter** n. штанги́ст; ~**lifting** n. подня́тие тя́жестей

weightlessness /ˈweɪtlɪsnɪs/ n. невесо́мость

weighty /ˈweɪtɪ/ adj. (**weightier**, **weightiest**) (heavy) тяжёлый; (important) ва́жный

weir /wɪə(r)/ n. плоти́на

weird /wɪəd/ adj. **1** (unearthly) таи́нственный **2** (strange) стра́нный

weirdness /ˈwɪədnɪs/ n. таи́нственность; стра́нность

✍ **welcome** /ˈwelkəm/ n. приём; **they gave us a warm** ~ они́ нас раду́шно при́няли
• adj. **1** (gladly received) жела́нный; **this is** ~ **news** э́то прия́тное изве́стие; **make sb**

✍ ключева́я ле́ксика

(feel) ~ ока́з|ывать, -а́ть кому́-н. раду́шный приём **2** (*pred.*) (ungrudgingly permitted): **you are** ~ **to take it!** пожа́луйста, бери́те!; **you're** ~ **to try!** пожа́луйста, (по)про́буйте!; **you're** ~**!** (no thanks are required) пожа́луйста!; не́ за что!
• *v.t.* приве́тствовать (*impf.*); **a welcoming smile** приве́тливая улы́бка; **I would** ~ **the opportunity** я был бы рад (тако́му) слу́чаю
• *int.* добро́ пожа́ловать!

weld /weld/ *v.t. & i.* свар|ивать(ся), -и́ть(ся)

welder /'weldə(r)/ *n.* сва́рщик

welding /'weldɪŋ/ *n.* сва́рка

welfare /'welfeə(r)/ *n.* (well-being) благополу́чие; (organized provision for social needs) социа́льное обеспе́чение; (AmE, social security) посо́бие (по безрабо́тице *и т. n.*); **the W**~ **State** госуда́рство всео́бщего благосостоя́ния/благоде́нствия; ≈ социа́льное госуда́рство

well¹ /wel/ *n.* (for water) коло́дец; (for oil) нефтяна́я сква́жина

♂ **well²** /wel/ *adj.* (**better**, **best**) (*usu. pred.*) **1** (in good health) здоро́вый; **I haven't been** ~ мне нездоро́вилось, я был нездоро́в; **you don't look** ~ вы пло́хо вы́глядите **2** (right, satisfactory): **all's** ~ всё хорошо́/прекра́сно; всё в поря́дке **3** (*as n.*): **leave** ~ ((AmE) *also* ~ **enough**) **alone** от добра́ добра́ не и́щут **4** ((just) as) ~ (advisable): **it would be ((just) as)** ~ **to ask** не меша́ло бы спроси́ть
• *adv.* (**better**, **best**) **1** (satisfactorily) хорошо́; **I did not sleep** ~ я пло́хо спал; ~ **done!** здо́рово!; молоде́ц! **2** (very, thoroughly; properly) о́чень, весьма́; **I am** ~ **aware of it** я э́то прекра́сно зна́ю; **the picture was** ~ **worth £2,000** э́та карти́на вполне́ сто́ила двух ты́сяч фу́нтов **3** (considerably, esp. with advs. & preps.) гора́здо; далеко́; ~ **past 40** далеко́ за со́рок **4** (favourably): ~ **off** бога́тый; **I wish him** ~ я жела́ю ему́ благополу́чия **5** (successfully) уда́чно, благополу́чно; **all went** ~ всё прошло́ благополу́чно **6** (wisely) разу́мно, пра́вильно; **you would be** ~ **advised to stay** с ва́шей стороны́ бы́ло бы благоразу́мно оста́ться **7** (indeed): **it may** ~ **be true** (э́то) вполне́ возмо́жно **8**: **as** ~ (in addition) то́же; та́кже; вдоба́вок; сверх того́; **there was meat as** ~ **as fish** там была́ не то́лько ры́ба, но и мя́со
• *int.* ну; ну а; (expr. surprise) ну!; вот те ра́з!; ~, ~**!** ну и ну!; (expr. expectation): ~ **then?** ну как?; (expr. impatient interrogation): ~, **what do you want?** ну, так чего́ вы хоти́те?; (expr. agreement): **very** ~, **I'll do it** хорошо́, я сде́лаю э́то; (expr. concession): ~, **you can come if you like** что ж(е), е́сли хоти́те, приходи́те; (expr. resignation): **oh** ~, **it can't be helped** (ну) что ж, ничего́ не поде́лаешь; (in summing up) ну вот; ~ **then** (ну) так вот
▪ ~-**balanced** *adj.* уравнове́шенный; **a** ~-**balanced diet** сбаланси́рованная дие́та; ~-**behaved** *adj.* (благо)воспи́танный; ~-**being** *n.* благополу́чие; ~-**disposed** *adj.* благожела́тельный; ~-**dressed** *adj.* хорошо́ оде́тый; ~-**educated** *adj.* хорошо́

образо́ванный; ~-**fed** *adj.* сы́тый; (of animals) отко́рмленный; ~-**heeled** *adj.* (infml) состоя́тельный; ~-**informed** *adj.* зна́ющий; ~-**kept** *adj.* содержа́щийся в поря́дке; ~-**known** *adj.* (of person) изве́стный; (of facts) (обще)изве́стный; ~-**made** *adj.* хорошо́ сде́ланный; ~-**mannered** *adj.* воспи́танный; ~-**meaning** *adj.* де́йствующий из лу́чших побужде́ний; ~-**off** *adj.* состоя́тельный; ~-**paid** *adj.* хорошо́ опла́чиваемый; ~-**read** *adj.* начи́танный; ~-**thought-out** *adj.* проду́манный; ~-**timed** *adj.* то́чно/хорошо́ рассчи́танный; (words/act) ска́занный/сде́ланный кста́ти; ~-**to-do** *adj.* состоя́тельный; ~-**wisher** *n.* доброжела́тель (-ница); ~-**worn** *adj.* (lit.) поно́шенный; (fig., trite) изби́тый

wellington /'welɪŋt(ə)n/ *n.* (*also* ~ **boot**) (BrE) рези́новый сапо́г

welly /'welɪ/ *n.* (BrE, infml) **1** = wellington **2** (vigour) си́ла, эне́ргия

Welsh /welʃ/ *n.* **1**: **the** ~ (*as pl.*) (people) валли́йцы (*m. pl.*), уэ́льсцы (*m. pl.*) **2** (language) валли́йский язы́к
• *adj.* валли́йский, уэ́льский

wench /wentʃ/ *n.* (archaic or joc.) де́вка

wend /wend/ *v.t.*: ~ **one's way** держа́ть (*impf.*) путь

went /went/ *past of* ▸ go

wept /wept/ *past and p.p. of* ▸ weep

were /wə(r)/ *2nd pers. sg. past, pl. past, and past subj. of* ▸ be

weren't /wɜːnt/ *neg. of* ▸ were

♂ **west** /west/ *n.* за́пад; **to the** ~ **of** к за́паду от + *g.*; **the W**~ (pol.) За́пад
• *adv.* на за́пад; к за́паду
• *adj.* за́падный
▪ **W**~ **Germany** *n.* (hist.) За́падная Герма́ния; **W**~ **Indian** *adj.* вест-и́ндский • *n.* жи́тель (*m.*) (-ница) стран(– острово́в) Кари́бского бассе́йна; **W**~ **Indies** *n. pl.* Вест-И́ндия

westerly /'westəlɪ/ (wind) за́падный ве́тер
• *adj.* за́падный

♂ **western** /'west(ə)n/ *n.* ве́стерн
• *adj.* за́падный

westerner /'westənə(r)/ *n.* жи́тель (*m.*) (-ница) за́пада

westernize /'westənaɪz/ *v.t.* внедр|я́ть, -и́ть за́падный о́браз жи́зни в + *a.*, подв|ерга́ть, -е́ргнуть вестерниза́ции

westward /'westwəd/ *adj.* за́падный
• *adv.* (*also* **westwards**) на за́пад; к за́паду, в за́падном направле́нии

wet /wet/ *adj.* (**wetter**, **wettest**) **1** (soaked) мо́крый; ~ **through** промо́кший наскво́зь/до ни́тки; **get** ~ пром|ока́ть, -о́кнуть **2** (rainy) дождли́вый **3** (damp) сыро́й, вла́жный; ~ **paint** све́жая кра́ска **4** (BrE, infml, inept) вя́лый
• *v.t.* (**wetting**, *past and p.p.* ~ *or* **wetted**) (make ~) мочи́ть, на-; **the child** ~ **itself** ребёнок мочи́лся/описа́лся (infml); **the child** ~ **its bed** ребёнок описа́л посте́ль
▪ ~ **blanket** *n.* (fig., infml) зану́да (*c.g.*), ну́дный

w

человек; ~ **suit** n. гидрокостюм

whack /wæk/ (infml) n. (blow) удар
- v.t. (hit) бить, по-; I feel ~ed (BrE, exhausted) я чувствую себя вконец разбитым

whale /weɪl/ n. **1** кит **2**: we had a ~ of a time мы потрясающе/здорово провели время

whaler /'weɪlə(r)/ n. (man) китобой; (ship) китобоец, китобойное судно

wharf /wɔːf/ n. (pl. **wharves** or **wharfs**) пристань

⚜ **what** /wɒt/ pron. **1** (interrog.) что?; ~'s that? что это (такое)?; ~ (did you say)? что (вы сказали)?; что?; ~ is it?; ~'s the matter? в чём дело?; ~ is she like? (in appearance) как она выглядит?; (in character) какая она?; ~'s the date? какое сегодня число?; ~ is his name? как его зовут?; ~ do you think? как вы думаете?; ~ about money? а деньги?; ~ about a walk? не пройтись ли нам?; ~ for? зачем?; ~ are you talking about? о чём вы говорите?; ~ if …? а что, если…? **2** (rel.) (то), что; and, ~ is more … я к тому же…; he is sorry for ~ happened он жалеет о случившемся; tell me ~ you remember расскажите мне всё, что помните; (do) you know ~?; знаете что?; I'll tell you ~! вот что я вам скажу!; ~ with one thing and another то из-за одного, то из-за другого (whatever): I will do ~ I can я сделаю (всё), что могу
- adj. **1** (interrog.) какой; каков?; ~ colour are his eyes? какого цвета у него глаза?; ~ kind of (a) какой?; ~ time is it? который час?; ~'s the use? какой смысл? **2** (rel.): ~ little he published то немногое, что он опубликовал; I gave him ~ money I had я отдал ему все деньги, какие у меня были **3** (exclamatory): ~ a fool he is! какой дурак!; ~ a pity/shame! какая жалость/ досада!; ~ lovely soup! какой прекрасный суп!
- ~-**d'ye-call-it**, ~'**sit** nn. как его; это самое…

⚜ **whatever** /wɒt'evə(r)/ pron. **1** (anything that): do ~ you like делайте, что хотите **2** (no matter what): ~ happens что бы ни случилось **3** (in questions, expressing surprise, confusion, etc.): ~ are you doing? что вы там делаете?
- adj. **1** (any): he took ~ food he could find он забрал всю еду, какую только мог найти **2** (no matter what) какой/каков бы ни **3** (emphasizing neg. or interrog.): there is no doubt ~ of his guilt в его виновности нет ни малейшего сомнения

wheat /wiːt/ n. пшеница

wheedle /'wiːd(ə)l/ v.t.: ~ sth out of sb выпрашивать, выпросить что-н. у кого-н.

wheel /wiːl/ n. колесо; (steering ~) руль (m.); he was at the ~ (sc. driving) for 12 hours он сидел за рулём 12 часов; (potter's ~) круг
- v.t. катать, возить (both indet.); катить

(det.); везти (det.)
- v.i. кружить(ся) (impf.); he ~ed round to face me он круто повернулся ко мне
- ~**barrow** n. тачка; ~**chair** n. инвалидная коляска

wheeler-dealer /'wiːlə'diːlə(r)/ n. (infml) махинатор

wheeze /wiːz/ v.i. сопеть (impf.)

wheezy /'wiːzɪ/ adj. хриплый

whelk /welk/ n. (mollusc) брюхоногий моллюск

⚜ **when** /wen/ adv. **1** (interrog.) когда; say ~! (to sb pouring a drink) скажите, когда довольно! **2** (rel.): there have been occasions ~ были случаи, когда…; the day ~ I met you день, когда я вас встретил
- with preps.: ~ do you have to be there by? к какому часу вам нужно там быть?; ~ does it date from? к какому времени это относится?; since ~? как давно?; till, until ~? до каких пор?
- conj. когда; как (только); после того как; тогда, когда; (by the time that) пока; ~ she saw him, she … когда она увидела его, она…; (and then) и тогда; как (вдруг); да вдруг; (although) хотя; they won ~ everyone thought they would lose они выиграли, хотя все думали, что они проиграют

whence /wens/ adv. & conj. (liter.) (also from ~) откуда; ~ this confusion? отчего такое смятение?; (rel.): return it ~ it came верните это по принадлежности

whenever /wen'evə(r)/ adv. & conj. **1** (at whatever time) когда; come ~ you like приходите, когда угодно **2** (on every occasion when) каждый/всякий раз, когда

⚜ **where** /weə(r)/ adv. **1** (interrog.) где; куда; ~ did he hit you? куда он вас ударил? **2** (rel.) где; the hotel ~ we stopped гостиница, в которой мы остановились; (without antecedent) там, где; that's ~ you're wrong вот где вы ошибаетесь
- with preps.: ~ from? откуда?; ~ does he come from? откуда он (родом)?; ~ to? куда?; I've no idea ~ he can have got to понятия не имею, куда он мог деться

whereabouts /'weərəbauts/ n. pl. местонахождение
- adv. где; ~ did you find it? где вы это нашли?; (whither) куда

whereas /weər'æz/ conj. тогда как; а

whereby /weə'baɪ/ adv. (liter., by means of which) посредством которого; (according to which): there is a rule ~ … существует правило, согласно которому…

whereupon /weərə'pɒn/ adv. (and then) после чего; вследствие чего; тогда

wherever /weər'evə(r)/ adj. & conj. где; куда; sit ~ you like садитесь, куда угодно; ~ he goes he makes friends где бы он ни оказался, он приобретает друзей

whet /wet/ v.t. (**whetted**, **whetting**) (fig.) возбуждать, -дить

⚜ **whether** /'weðə(r)/ conj. **1** (introducing indirect question) ли; I asked ~ he was coming with

⚜ ключевая лексика

us я спроси́л, пойдёт ли он с на́ми; **the question is** ~ **to go or stay** вопро́с в том — идти́ и́ли остава́ться **2** (introducing alternative hypotheses): ~ **you like it or not, I shall go** нра́вится вам э́то и́ли нет, а я пойду́

⚲ **which** /wɪtʃ/ *pron.* **1** (*interrog.*) како́й, кото́рый; (of person) кто; ~ **is the right answer?** како́й отве́т пра́вильный?; ~ **of these bags is the heavier?** кака́я из э́тих су́мок тяжеле́е?; **I cannot tell** ~ **is** ~ (of persons) я ника́к не могу́ разобра́ться, кто из них кто **2** (*rel.*) кото́рый; **the book (**~**) I was reading has gone** кни́га, кото́рую я чита́л, пропа́ла
● *adj.* **1** (direct or indirect question) како́й; ~ **shoes are yours?** каки́е (тут) ту́фли ва́ши?; ~ **film do you mean?** како́й фильм вы име́ете в виду́? **2** (*rel.*) како́й; кото́рый; **ten years, during** ~ **time he spoke to nobody** де́сять лет, в тече́ние кото́рых он ни с кем не говори́л

whichever /wɪtʃˈevə(r)/ *pron. & adj.* како́й бы ни, како́й уго́дно; **take** ~ **book you like** бери́те каку́ю уго́дно кни́гу; ~ **way you go, you'll have plenty of time** како́й бы доро́гой вы ни пошли́, вы вполне́ успе́ете; ~ **way you look at it** с како́й стороны́ (на э́то) ни посмотре́ть

whiff /wɪf/ *n.* дунове́ние; (pleasant smell) лёгкий арома́т; (BrE, unpleasant smell) душо́к

⚲ **while** /waɪl/ *n.* (како́е-то) вре́мя; ~ че́рез не́которое вре́мя; **I am going away for a** ~ я уезжа́ю на не́которое вре́мя; **a long, good** ~ **ago** давны́м-давно́; **a short** ~ **ago, back** неда́вно; **it may take some** (*or* quite a) ~ возмо́жно, что э́то бу́дет не ско́ро; **once in a** ~ и́зредка; **it was well worth** ~ э́то сто́ило затра́ченного вре́мени/труда́; **I will make it worth his** ~ я постара́юсь, что́бы он не разочарова́лся
● *v.t.*: ~ **away** корота́ть, с- (*время*)
● *conj.* (*also* **whilst**) **1** (during the time that) пока́; в то вре́мя, как; **be good** ~ **I'm away!** веди́ себя́ хорошо́, пока́ меня́ нет до́ма!; ~ **asleep** во сне; ~ **in Paris I visited the Louvre** во вре́мя (моего́) пребыва́ния в Пари́же, я посети́л Лувр **2** (whereas) а; тогда́ как

whilst /waɪlst/ *conj.* = **while** *conj.*

whim /wɪm/ *n.* при́хоть, капри́з

whimper /ˈwɪmpə(r)/ *n.* (of person) хны́канье; (of dog) поску́ливание
● *v.i.* (of person) хны́кать (*impf.*); (of dog) скули́ть (*impf.*)

whimsical /ˈwɪmzɪk(ə)l/ *adj.* (fanciful) причу́дливый; (capricious) капри́зный

whine /waɪn/ *n.* скули́ть (*impf.*) (also fig.)

whinge /wɪndʒ/ *v.i.* (**whingeing**) (BrE, infml) скули́ть (*impf.*) (*жаловаться*)

whinny /ˈwɪnɪ/ *n.* (gentle) ти́хое ржа́ние; (joyful) ра́достное ржа́ние
● *v.i.* (gently) ти́хо ржать, за-; (joyfully) ра́достно ржать, за-

whip /wɪp/ *n.* **1** (short) плеть, плётка; (long) кнут **2** (party official) секрета́рь (*m.*) парла́ментской фра́кции
● *v.t.* (**whipped**, **whipping**) **1** (flog)

поро́ть, вы́-; хлеста́ть, от-; сечь, вы́- **2** (beat into froth) взби́вать, -и́ть; ~**ped cream** взби́тые сли́вки **3** (infml, move rapidly): **as I entered he** ~**ped the papers into a drawer** когда́ я вошёл, он бы́стро су́нул бума́ги в я́щик (стола́)
□ ~ **up** *v.t.* (beat into froth) взби́|ва́ть, -и́ть; (fig., stimulate): ~ **up enthusiasm** возбу́ждать, -ди́ть энтузиа́зм; (infml, improvise) де́лать, с- на ско́рую ру́ку
■ ~**lash** *n.* (injury) тра́вма ше́и в результа́те ре́зкого движе́ния (*чаще всего в автоаварии*); ~**round** *n.* (BrE, infml, collection) сбор де́нег (на благотвори́тельные це́ли)

whir /wə:(r)/ *v.i.* = **whirr**

whirl /wə:l/ *n.* **1** (revolving movement) круже́ние; (fig.) смяте́ние; **my head is in a** ~ у меня́ голова́ идёт кру́гом **2** (bustling activity) водоворо́т, вихрь (*m.*)
● *v.t. & i.* верте́ть(ся) (*impf.*); кружи́ть(ся) (*impf.*)
■ ~**pool** *n.* водоворо́т; ~**wind** *n.* вихрь (*m.*)

whirr, **whir** /wə:(r)/ *v.i.* (**whirred**, **whirring**) жужжа́ть (*impf.*)

whisk /wɪsk/ *n.* муто́вка
● *v.t.* взби|ва́ть, -и́ть
● *v.i.* (move briskly) мча́ться, по-
□ ~ **away**, ~ **off** *vv.t.* (carry off quickly) бы́стро ун|оси́ть, -ести́; (lead off quickly) бы́стро ув|оди́ть, -ести́

whisker /ˈwɪskə(r)/ *n.* (*in pl.*) (facial hair) бакенба́рд|ы (*pl., g. —*); (of animal) усы́ (*m. pl.*)

whisky /ˈwɪskɪ/ (AmE **whiskey**) *n.* ви́ски (*nt. indecl.*)

whisper /ˈwɪspə(r)/ *n.* шёпот; **he spoke in a** ~ он говори́л шёпотом
● *v.i.* шепта́ться (*impf.*)
● *v.t.* шепта́ть, про-

whistle /ˈwɪs(ə)l/ *n.* **1** (sound) свист **2** (instrument) свисто́к
● *v.t.* (tune) насви́стывать, -исте́ть
● *v.i.* свисте́ть, про-, сви́стнуть; **the train** ~**d as it entered the tunnel** при вхо́де в тунне́ль по́езд дал гудо́к
■ ~**-blower** *n.* (reporter of wrongdoing) доно́счи|к (-ца)

Whit /wɪt/ *adj.*: ~ **Monday** Ду́хов день; ~ **Sunday** = **Whitsun**

⚲ **white** /waɪt/ *n.* **1** (colour) бе́лый цвет; белизна́ **2** (of the eyes, an egg) бело́к **3** (racial type) белоко́жий, бе́лый
● *adj.* бе́лый; **grow** ~ беле́ть, по-; **the W**~ **House** Бе́лый дом; **a** ~ **lie** ложь во спасе́ние
■ ~ **coffee** *n.* (BrE) ко́фе с молоко́м; ~**-collar** *adj.*: ~**-collar worker** n. служа́щий; ~ **goods** *n. pl.* (domestic appliances) бытовы́е электроприбо́ры; ~**wash** *n.* побе́лка; (fig.) обеле́ние, оправда́ние ● *v.t.* бели́ть, по-; (fig.) обеля́ть, -и́ть; опра́вд|ывать, -а́ть; ~**-water rafting** *n.* сплав вниз по го́рному пото́ку

whiten /ˈwaɪt(ə)n/ *v.t.* бели́ть, по-

Whitsun /ˈwɪts(ə)n/ *n.* (Whit Sunday) Тро́ицын день; Тро́ица; *see also* ► **Whit**

whittle /ˈwɪt(ə)l/ *v.t.* (wood) строга́ть, вы́-

W

□ ~ **away** v.t. (fig.) ум|еньша́ть, -е́ньшить; his savings were ~d away его́ сбереже́ния постепе́нно исся́кли

whizz, whiz /wɪz/ v.i. (**whizzed, whizzing**) прон|оси́ться, -ести́сь со сви́стом

■ ~**-kid** n. (infml) ≈ восходя́щая звезда́ (о молодо́м челове́ке)

♂ **who** /huː/ pron. (obj. **whom** or informally **who**, poss. **whose**) **1** (interrog.) кто; ~ **is he?** кто он (тако́й)? **2** (rel.) кото́рый, како́й, кто; **people** ~ **live in the city** лю́ди, кото́рые живу́т в го́роде; **those** ~ те, кто/кото́рые; **anyone** ~ вся́кий, кто; **Mr X,** ~ **is my uncle** г-н Х, мой дя́дя

whoever /huːˈevə(r)/ pron. **1** (rel.) (anyone who) кто бы ни, кто уго́дно; ~ **comes will be welcome** кто бы ни пришёл, бу́дет жела́нным го́стем **2** (interrog., used for emphasis) (who) кто то́лько; ~ **would have thought it?** кто бы мог поду́мать?

♂ **whole** /həʊl/ n. (single entity) це́лое; (totality) все, всё; **taken as a** ~ в це́лом; **on the** ~ в о́бщем (и це́лом); в основно́м
● adj. **1** (intact; undamaged) це́лый, невреди́мый **2** (in one piece) целико́м **3** (complete) весь, це́лый, це́льный; **he ate a** ~ **chicken** он съел це́лого цыплёнка; **the** ~ **world** весь мир
■ ~**hearted** adj. беззаве́тный; ~**heartedly** adv. от всей души́; ~**sale** n. опто́вая торго́вля
● adj. опто́вый; (fig.) ма́ссовый ● adv. о́птом; (fig.) в ма́ссовом масшта́бе; ~**saler** n. оптови́к

wholesome /ˈhəʊlsəm/ adj. **1** (promoting health) поле́зный **2** (sound) здра́вый

wholly /ˈhəʊllɪ/ adv. по́лностью; целико́м

♂ **whom** /huːm/ obj. of ▸ **who**

whopper /ˈwɒpə(r)/ n. (infml) грома́дина

whopping /ˈwɒpɪŋ/ adj. (infml) (also ~ **great**) огро́мный

whore /hɔː(r)/ n. (pej.) шлю́ха (infml)

♂ **whose** /huːz/ pron. (interrog.) чей; ~ **partner are you?** чей вы партнёр?; (rel.) кото́рого; **the people** ~ **house we bought** лю́ди, у кото́рых мы купи́ли дом

♂ **why** /waɪ/ adv. **1** (interrog.) (for what reason?) почему́; (for what purpose?) заче́м; ~ **do you ask?** почему́ вы спра́шиваете?; ~ **hurry?** заче́м спеши́ть?; ~ **not?** а почему́ нет? **2** (rel.): **I don't know** ~ **he's late** я не зна́ю, почему́ он опа́здывает; **the reasons** ~ ... причи́ны, по кото́рым...

wick /wɪk/ n. фити́ль (m.)

wicked /ˈwɪkɪd/ adj. (depraved) гре́шный; (roguish) лука́вый

wicker /ˈwɪkə(r)/ adj.: ~ **chair** плетёное кре́сло
■ ~**work** n. плете́ние

wicket /ˈwɪkɪt/ n. **1** (also ~ **gate**) кали́тка **2** (at cricket) воро́т|ца (-ец)
■ ~**keeper** n. ловя́щий мяч за воро́тцами (в кри́кете)

♂ **wide** /waɪd/ adj. **1** широ́кий; (in measuring) ширино́й в + a.; **the table is 3 feet** ~ ширина́ стола́ 3 фу́та **2** (extensive) широ́кий, обши́рный; ~ **interests** широ́кий круг интере́сов **3** (off target): **his answer was** ~ **of the mark** он попа́л па́льцем в не́бо
● adv. **1** (to full extent): **open the door** ~! откро́йте дверь на́стежь!; **he is** ~ **awake** у него́ сна ни в одно́м глазу́; **his mouth was** ~ **open** рот его́ был широко́ раскры́т **2** (off target) ми́мо це́ли
■ ~**-angle** adj.: ~**-angle lens** широкоуго́льный объекти́в; ~**-eyed** adj. (surprised) изумлённый; (naive) наи́вный; ~ **open** adj. откры́тый; ~**-ranging** adj. (intellect etc.) разносторо́нний; ~**screen** adj.: ~**screen film** широкоэкра́нный фильм; ~**spread** adj. (широко́) распространённый

♂ **widely** /ˈwaɪdlɪ/ adv. **1** (to a large extent) широко́; ~ **differing opinions** ре́зко расходя́щиеся мне́ния **2** (over a large area) далеко́; ~ **scattered** разбро́санный; **it is** ~ **believed that** ... мно́гие счита́ют, что...

widen /ˈwaɪd(ə)n/ v.t. & i. расш|иря́ть(ся), -и́рить(ся)

widow /ˈwɪdəʊ/ n. вдова́
● v.t. де́лать, с- вдово́й

widower /ˈwɪdəʊə(r)/ n. вдове́ц

width /wɪtθ/ n. ширина́

wield /wiːld/ v.t. (hold) держа́ть (impf.) в рука́х; ~ **authority** по́льзоваться (impf.) вла́стью

♂ **wife** /waɪf/ n. (pl. **wives**) жена́

Wi-Fi® /ˈwaɪfaɪ/ n. (comput.) (техноло́гия) вайфа́й, Wi-Fi, беспроводно́й Интерне́т

wig /wɪg/ n. пари́к

wiggle /ˈwɪg(ə)l/ v.t. (ears, toes) шевели́ть, по- + i.; **she** ~**s her hips** она́ пока́чивает бёдрами

wiggly /ˈwɪglɪ/ adj. (**wigglier, wiggliest**): **a** ~ **line** волни́стая ли́ния; **a** ~ **tooth** шата́ющийся зуб

wigwam /ˈwɪgwæm/ n. вигва́м

wiki /ˈwɪkɪ/ n. (pl. ~**s**) ви́ки (f. indecl.) (веб-сайт, содержа́ние кото́рого посети́тель мо́жет редакти́ровать)

♂ **wild** /waɪld/ n. **1** (~ **state**): **this animal is not found in the** ~ э́то живо́тное не встреча́ется в ди́кой приро́де **2** (in pl.) (uncultivated tract) ди́кое ме́сто; **in the** ~**s of Africa** на ди́ких просто́рах А́фрики
● adj. **1** (not domesticated; not cultivated) ди́кий **2** (not civilized) ди́кий **3** (of scenery: desolate) ди́кий **4** (unrestrained, disorderly) необу́зданный, бу́йный; **she lets her children run** ~ она́ разреша́ет де́тям бе́гать без присмо́тра; **he let the garden run** ~ он запусти́л сад **5** (tempestuous) бу́рный, бу́йный **6** (excited, passionate) вне себя́; **they were** ~ **about him** они́ бы́ли в (ди́ком) восто́рге от него́ **7** (reckless; ill-considered) безу́мный; **a** ~ **scheme** безу́мная зате́я
■ ~ **boar** n. каба́н; ~ **card** n. (comput.) универса́льный си́мвол; ~**fire** n.: **the news spread like** ~**fire** но́вость распространи́лась с молниено́сной быстрото́й; ~ **flower** n. дикорасту́щий цвето́к; ~ **goose chase** n.

♂ ключева́я ле́ксика

бессмысленное предприятие

wilderness /'wɪldənɪs/ *n.* дикая местность; пустыня

wildlife /'waɪldlaɪf/ *n.* живая природа
■ ~ **sanctuary** *n.* заповедник

wiles /waɪlz/ *n. pl.* ухищрения (*nt. pl.*)

wilful /'wɪlfʊl/ (AmE **willful**) *adj.* **1** (of person) своенравный, своевольный **2** (intentional) умышленный

wilfulness /'wɪlfʊlnɪs/ (AmE **willfulness**) *n.* своенравие, своеволие; преднамеренность

will¹ /wɪl/ *n.* **1** (faculty; determination, desire) воля; **free** ~ свобода воли; **against my** ~ против моего желания; **the** ~ **to live** воля к жизни **2** (document of bequeathal) завещание
● *v.t.* **1** (compel) заставлять, -авить; **he** ~ed himself to stay awake (усилием воли) он заставил себя бодрствовать **2**: **God** ~ing если на то будет воля Божья
■ ~**power** *n.* сила воли

will² /wɪl/ *v.t. & i.* (*3rd pers. sg. pres.* **will**) (*see also* ▶ would) **1** (expr. future): **he** ~ **be president** он будет президентом; **he said he would be back by 3** он сказал, что вернётся к трём; **I won't do it again** я больше не буду **2** (expr. willingness): **I** ~ **come with you** я пойду с вами; **he won't help me** он не хочет мне помочь; **the window won't open** окно (никак) не открывается; **pass the salt,** ~ (*or* would) **you?** будьте любезны, передайте соль **3** (expr. inevitability): **boys** ~ **be boys** мальчики есть мальчики; **accidents** ~ **happen** всякое бывает **4** (expr. habit): **he would often come to see me** он часто заходил ко мне **5** (expr. surmise, probability): **she would have been about 60 when she died** ей было, должно быть, около шестидесяти, когда она умерла

willing /'wɪlɪŋ/ *adj.* **1** (readily disposed) склонный, расположенный; **I am** ~ **to admit … я** готов признать… **2** (readily given or shown) добровольный

willingness /'wɪlɪŋnɪs/ *n.* готовность, желание

willow /'wɪləʊ/ *n.* ива

willy /'wɪlɪ/ *n.* (BrE, infml) (мужской) член

willy-nilly /wɪlɪ'nɪlɪ/ *adv.* волей-неволей

wilt /wɪlt/ *v.i.* (lit., fig.) никнуть, по-

wily /'waɪlɪ/ *adj.* (**wilier, wiliest**) хитрый

wimp /wɪmp/ *n.* (infml) слизняк

win /wɪn/ *n.* (gain) выигрыш; (victory) победа
● *v.t.* (**winning**, *past and p.p.* **won**) **1** (be victorious in) выигрывать, выиграть; **the Allies won the war** союзники выиграли войну; **who won the election?** кто победил на выборах?; ~ **a race** побеждать, -дить в забеге **2** (gain) выигрывать, выиграть; **he won £50 from me** он выиграл у меня 50 фунтов; ~ **a medal** завоёвывать, -ать медаль; ~ **sb's confidence** заслуживать, -ить чью-н. доверие
● *v.i.* (**winning**, *past and p.p.* **won**): ~ **by 4 goals to 1** выиграть (*pf.*) со счётом 4:1
□ ~ **back** *v.t.* отыгрывать, -ать

□ ~ **over,** ~ **round** *vv.t.* уговаривать, -орить

wince /wɪns/ *v.i.* содрогаться, -нуться

winch /wɪntʃ/ *n.* лебёдка
● *v.t.* поднимать, -ять с помощью лебёдки

wind¹ /wɪnd/ *n.* **1** ветер **2** (breath) дыхание; **get back one's** ~ отдышаться (*pf.*); **knock the** ~ **out of sb** (fig.) ошеломлять, -ить кого-н. **3** (BrE, in bowels etc.) газы (*m. pl.*) (*в желудке/кишечнике*); **break** ~ портить, ис- воздух **4** (~ instruments) духовые (инструменты) (*m. pl.*)
● *v.t.* (deprive of breath): **the blow** ~ed him от удара у него дух перехватило
■ ~**fall** *n.* (of money) непредвиденный доход; ~ **farm** *n.* район обслуживания ветряных электростанций; ~**mill** *n.* ветряная мельница; ~**pipe** *n.* дыхательное горло; ~**screen,** ~**shield** (AmE) *nn.* лобовое/ветровое стекло; ~**screen wiper** стеклоочиститель (*m.*), «дворник»; ~**swept** *adj.* (of terrain) открытый ветру; (of hair etc.) растрёпанный

wind² /waɪnd/ *v.t.* (*past and p.p.* **wound**) **1** (cause to encircle, curve or curl): **she wound the wool into a ball** она смотала шерсть в клубок; **a rope was wound round the pole** на шест была намотана верёвка **2** (fold, wrap) укутывать, -ать **3** (rotate) вертеть (*impf.*) **4**: ~ **a clock** заводить, -ести часы
● *v.i.* (*past and p.p.* **wound**) (twist) виться (*impf.*); извиваться (*impf.*); **the path** ~s up the hill дорожка/тропинка змейкой поднимается в гору; ~**ing staircase** винтовая лестница
□ ~ **down** *v.t.* опускать, -тить
□ ~ **up** *v.t.*: ~ **up a clock** заводить, -ести часы; (BrE, tease) дразнить (*impf.*); (fig., settle) завершать, -ить; **I am** ~**ing up my affairs** я сворачиваю свои дела; (fig., terminate) заканчивать, -ончить

window /'wɪndəʊ/ *n.* **1** окно; (dim., also cashier's etc.) окошко; (of shop) витрина; (**in full** ~ **of opportunity**) редкая возможность **2** (comput.) окно
■ ~ **box** *n.* (наружный) ящик для цветов; ~ **cleaner** *n.* мойщик окон; ~ **ledge** *n.* (наружный) подоконник; ~**pane** *n.* оконное стекло; ~ **seat** *n.* диван у окна; ~**shopping** *n.* рассматривание/разглядывание витрин; ~ **sill** *n.* подоконник

windsurfer /'wɪndsɜː(r)/ *n.* виндсёрфингист (-ка)

windsurfing /'wɪndsɜːfɪŋ/ *n.* виндсёрфинг

windy /'wɪndɪ/ *adj.* (**windier, windiest**) **1** (characterized by wind) ветреный **2** (exposed to wind) обдуваемый ветром

wine /waɪn/ *n.* (виноградное) вино
■ ~ **bar** *n.* винный бар; ~ **glass** *n.* бокал, рюмка; ~**grower** *n.* винодел; ~**growing** *n.* виноделие ● *adj.* винодельческий; ~ **list** *n.* карта вин; ~ **tasting** *n.* дегустация вин

wing /wɪŋ/ *n.* **1** (of bird, building, organization, car) крыло **2** (in pl.) (of stage) кулисы (*f. pl.*);

w

wait in the ~s (fig.) ждать (*impf.*) своего́ ча́са

winger /'wɪŋə(r)/ *n.* (player) кра́йний напада́ющий

wink /wɪŋk/ *n.* мига́ние; (as signal, joke) подми́гивание; **I didn't sleep a ~** я всю ночь не сомкну́л глаз
● *v.i.:* **~ at sb** подми́г|ивать, -ну́ть кому́-н.; (of star, light, etc.) мига́ть (*impf.*)

⚜ **winner** /'wɪnə(r)/ *n.* победи́тель (-ница); (successful thing) ве́рное де́ло

winning /'wɪnɪŋ/ *adj.* **1** (victorious) вы́игравший **2** (bringing about a win) вы́игрышный **3** (attractive) привлека́тельный
■ **~ post** *n.* фи́нишный столб

winnings /'wɪnɪŋz/ *n. pl.* вы́игрыш (*деньги*)

⚜ **winter** /'wɪntə(r)/ *n.* зима́; **in ~** зимо́й; (*attr.*) зи́мний
● *v.i.* зимова́ть, пере-
■ **~time** *n.* зима́

wintry /'wɪntrɪ/ *adj.* (**wintrier, wintriest**) зи́мний, моро́зный; (fig.) холо́дный

wipe /waɪp/ *v.t.* **1** (rub clean or dry) вытира́ть, вы́тереть; (~ surface of) обт|ира́ть, -ере́ть; **~ sb's nose** вытира́ть, вы́тереть кому́-н. нос; **~ one's eyes** вытира́ть, вы́тереть слёзы; **~ your shoes on the mat!** вы́трите боти́нки о ко́врик! **2** (erase) ст|ира́ть, -ере́ть
□ **~ away** *v.t.* ст|ира́ть, -ере́ть; (tears) вытира́ть, вы́тереть
□ **~ down** *v.t.* прот|ира́ть, -ере́ть
□ **~ off** *v.t.* ст|ира́ть, -ере́ть
□ **~ out** *v.t.* (destroy) уничт|ожа́ть, -о́жить; **the disease ~d out the entire population** эпиде́мия по́лностью уничто́жила всё населе́ние
□ **~ up** *v.t.* подт|ира́ть, -ере́ть

wire /'waɪə(r)/ *n.* **1** про́волока **2** (elec.) про́вод **3** (infml, telegram) телегра́мма
● *v.t.* **1** (elec.): **they ~d the house** они́ сде́лали прово́дку в до́ме **2** (infml, send telegram to) телеграфи́ровать (*impf., pf.*) + *d.*

wiring /'waɪərɪŋ/ *n.* (elec.) (электро)прово́дка

wiry /'waɪərɪ/ *adj.* (**wirier, wiriest**) (of person) жи́листый; (of hair) жёсткий

wisdom /'wɪzdəm/ *n.* му́дрость; (prudence) благоразу́мие
■ **~ tooth** *n.* зуб му́дрости

wise /waɪz/ *adj.* **1** (sage) му́дрый **2** (sensible) благоразу́мный; **you were ~ not to attempt it** вы пра́вильно сде́лали, что не ста́ли про́бовать **3** (well informed) осведомлённый; **now that you've told me I am none the ~r** да́же по́сле ва́шего объясне́ния я ма́ло что понима́ю
■ **~ guy** *n.* (AmE, infml) у́мник

⚜ **wish** /wɪʃ/ *n.* **1** (desire) жела́ние; (request) про́сьба; **make a ~!** загада́йте жела́ние!; **you acted against my ~es** вы поступи́ли про́тив мое́й во́ли **2** (on another's behalf) пожела́ние; **with best ~es!** с наилу́чшими пожела́ниями!
● *v.t.* **1** (want, require) жела́ть (*impf.*); хоте́ть (*impf.*) (both + *a.* or *g.*, *inf.*, or *чтобы*) **2** (expr. unfulfilled desire): **I ~ I knew everything**

если бы (то́лько) я всё знал; как бы я хоте́л всё знать; **I ~ you'd be quiet** нельзя́ ли не шуме́ть (*or* поти́ше)?; **I ~ he hadn't left so soon** как жаль, что он ушёл так ра́но; **I ~ he were alive** е́сли бы то́лько он был жив **3** (with double object): **I ~ him well** я жела́ю ему́ добра́; **I ~ you many happy returns** поздравля́ю вас с днём рожде́ния
● *v.i.:* **~ for** мечта́ть о + *p.*

wishful /'wɪʃfʊl/ *adj.:* **~ thinking** самообольще́ние; приня́тие жела́емого за действи́тельное

wisp /wɪsp/ *n.:* **a ~ of hair** прядь воло́с; **a ~ of smoke** стру́йка ды́ма

wispy /'wɪspɪ/ *adj.* (**wispier, wispiest**): **~ hair** ре́дкие во́лосы

wistaria /wɪ'steərɪə/, **wisteria** /wɪ'stɪərɪə/ *n.* (bot.) глици́ния

wistful /'wɪstfʊl/ *adj.* тоскли́вый

wit /wɪt/ *n.* **1** (*also* **~s**) (intelligence) ум, ра́зум **2** (wittiness) остроу́мие **3** (person) остря́|к (-чка (infml))

witch /wɪtʃ/ *n.* ве́дьма
■ **~craft** *n.* чёрная ма́гия; **~ doctor** *n.* зна́харь (*m.*); **~-hunt** *n.* (fig.) охо́та на ведьм

⚜ **with** /wɪð/ *prep.* **1** (in the company of) *usu.* c + *i.*; **come ~ me!** пойдёмте со мной!; **he is ~ the manager** он у заве́дующего; **the boy was left ~ his aunt** ма́льчика оста́вили у тётки (*or* c тёткой); (denoting host) y + *g.*; **we stayed ~ our friends** мы жи́ли у друзе́й **2** (denoting means): **I am writing ~ a pen** я пишу́ ру́чкой; **he walks ~ a stick** он хо́дит с па́л(оч)кой **3** (expr. antagonism or separation): **don't argue ~ me** не спо́рьте со мной; **at war ~** в состоя́нии войны́ c + *i.* **4** (denoting cause) от + *g.*; **she was shaking ~ fright** она́ дрожа́ла от стра́ха **5** (denoting characteristic): **a girl ~ blue eyes** де́вушка с голубы́ми глаза́ми; **a suit ~ grey stripes** костю́м в се́рую поло́ску **6** (denoting manner etc.): **~ pleasure** с удово́льствием; **~ care** осторо́жно **7** (in the same direction or degree as; at the same time as): **one must move ~ the times** на́до идти́ в но́гу со вре́менем; **~ the approach of spring** с наступле́нием весны́ **8** (denoting attendant circumstance): **a holiday ~ all expenses paid** по́лностью опла́ченный о́тпуск; **~ your permission** с ва́шего разреше́ния

withdraw /wɪð'drɔ:/ *v.t.* (past **withdrew**, *p.p.* **withdrawn**) отн|има́ть, -я́ть; **~ an offer** брать, взять обра́тно/наза́д предложе́ние; **~ money from the bank** сн|има́ть, -ять де́ньги со счёта (в ба́нке); **~ troops** выводи́ть, вы́вести войска́; **a ~n character** за́мкнутый челове́к
● *v.i.* (past **withdrew**, *p.p.* **withdrawn**) удал|я́ться, -и́ться; **~ into oneself** зам|ыка́ться, -кну́ться в себе́; (mil.) уходи́ть, уйти́

withdrawal /wɪð'drɔ:əl/ *n.* (of a product from the market) изъя́тие; (of a person from an election) сня́тие; (of troops) вы́вод
■ **~ symptoms** *n. pl.* абстине́нтный синдро́м

withdrawn /wɪð'drɔ:n/ *p.p. of* ▸ **withdraw**

⚜ ключева́я ле́ксика

w

withdrew /wɪð'dru:/ *past of* ▶ **withdraw**

wither /'wɪðə(r)/ *v.i.* **1** иссуш|а́ть, -и́ть
2 (fig.) губи́ть, по-; a ∼ing glance
испепеля́ющий взгляд
• *v.i.* вя́нуть, за-

withhold /wɪð'həʊld/ *v.t.* (*past and p.p.*
withheld /-'held/) отка́з|ывать, -а́ть в чём;
∼ one's consent не да|ва́ть, -ть согла́сия; ∼
payment заде́рж|ивать, -а́ть опла́ту

within /wɪ'ðɪn/ *adv.* внутри́; from ∼ изнутри́
• *prep.* **1** (inside) в + *p.*; внутри́ + *g.*; ∼
these walls в э́тих стена́х **2** (not further than;
accessible to) в преде́лах + *g.*; the library is
∼ walking distance до библиоте́ки мо́жно
дойти́ пешко́м **3** (of time) в тече́ние + *g.*; ∼
three days в тече́ние трёх дней; I can finish
the job ∼ a week я могу́ (за)ко́нчить э́ту
рабо́ту за неде́лю **4** (∼ limits of) в преде́лах/
ра́мках + *g.*; live ∼ one's income жить (*impf.*)
по сре́дствам

without /wɪ'ðaʊt/ *prep.* без + *g.*; ∼ doubt
без сомне́ния; ∼ fail непреме́нно; it goes ∼
saying само́ собо́й разуме́ется; (with gerund):
∼ thinking не ду́мая; не поду́мав

withstand /wɪð'stænd/ *v.t.* (*past and p.p.*
withstood /-'stʊd/) устоя́ть (*pf.*) пе́ред + *i.*;
выде́рживать, вы́держать

witness /'wɪtnɪs/ *n.* свиде́тель (-ница); bear
∼ свиде́тельствовать (*impf.*)
• *v.t.* **1** (event) быть свиде́телем + *g.*; no
one ∼ed the accident никто́ не ви́дел,
как произошла́ катастро́фа **2** (signature)
зав|еря́ть, -е́рить
∎ ∼ box, (AmE) stand *nn.* ме́сто для да́чи
свиде́тельских показа́ний

witticism /'wɪtɪsɪz(ə)m/ *n.* остро́та

witty /'wɪtɪ/ *adj.* (**wittier, wittiest**)
остроу́мный

wives /waɪvz/ *pl. of* ▶ **wife**

wizard /'wɪzəd/ *n.* волше́бник

WMD *abbr.* (*of* **weapons of mass
destruction**) ОМП (ору́жие ма́ссового
пораже́ния)

wobble /'wɒb(ə)l/ *v.t. & i.* (*also* ∼ **about**)
шата́ть(ся) (*impf.*)

wobbly /'wɒblɪ/ *adj.* (**wobblier,
wobbliest**) ша́ткий, неусто́йчивый

woe /wəʊ/ *n.* **1** (grief) го́ре **2** (in pl.) (troubles)
бе́ды (*f. pl.*)

woeful /'wəʊfʊl/ *adj.* скорбный, горестный;
(deplorable) жа́лкий; a ∼ countenance
скорбное лицо́; ∼ ignorance вопию́щее
неве́жество

wok /wɒk/ *n.* сковорода́ (с вы́пуклым
дни́щем) (*в кита́йской ку́хне*)

woke /wəʊk/ *past of* ▶ **wake¹**

woken /'wəʊk(ə)n/ *p.p. of* ▶ **wake¹**

wolf /wʊlf/ *n.* (*pl.* **wolves**) (animal) волк; cry
∼ (fig.) подн|има́ть, -я́ть ло́жную трево́гу
• *v.t.* (infml) (*also* ∼ **down**) прогл|а́тывать,
-оти́ть с жа́дностью
∎ ∼ whistle *n.* (infml) свист при ви́де краси́вой
де́вушки

woman /'wʊmən/ *n.* (*pl.* **women**)

1 же́нщина **2** (*attr.*): ∼ doctor же́нщина-
врач; ∼ friend подру́га, прия́тельница

womanize /'wʊmənaɪz/ *v.i.* (infml, philander)
пу́таться (*impf.*) с ба́бами (infml); гоня́ться
(*impf.*) за ю́бками

womanizer /'wʊmənaɪzə(r)/ *n.* ба́бник (infml)

womanly /'wʊmənlɪ/ *adj.* (figure)
же́нственный; (virtues) же́нский

womb /wu:m/ *n.* ма́тка

women /'wɪmɪn/ *pl. of* ▶ **woman**

won /wʌn/ *past and p.p. of* ▶ **win**

wonder /'wʌndə(r)/ *n.* **1** (miracle, marvel) чу́до;
(surprising thing): it's a ∼ that... удиви́тельно,
что...; no ∼ he was angry! неудиви́тельно,
что он рассерди́лся! **2** (amazement)
изумле́ние, восхище́ние
• *v.i.* **1** (desire to know; deliberate) (*usu. with
clause*): I ∼ who that was интере́сно/
любопы́тно, кто бы э́то мог быть; he ∼ed
if she was coming он гада́л, придёт она́ и́ли
нет; I was ∼ing whether to invite him я не
мог реши́ть, приглаша́ть его́ и́ли нет **2** (feel
curiosity) интересова́ться (*impf.*); I was ∼ing
about that я и сам разду́мывал об э́том;
'Why do you ask?' — 'I just ∼ed' «Почему́
вы спра́шиваете?» — «Про́сто так» **3** (feel
surprised, marvel (at)) удив|ля́ться, -и́ться (чему́);
пора|жа́ться, -зи́ться (чему́)

wonderful /'wʌndəfʊl/ *adj.* (pleasing)
чуде́сный, чу́дный; what ∼ weather! кака́я
чу́дная пого́да!

wonky /'wɒŋkɪ/ *adj.* (**wonkier, wonkiest**)
(BrE, infml) (unstable) ша́ткий; (crooked) криво́й

wont /wəʊnt/ (archaic or liter.) *n.*: as is his ∼ по
своему́ обыкнове́нию
• *adj.*: as he was ∼ to say как он люби́л
говори́ть

won't /wəʊnt/ *neg. of* ▶ **will²**

woo /wu:/ *v.t.* (**woos, wooed**) (archaic)
уха́живать (*impf.*) за + *i.*

wood /wʊd/ *n.* **1** *in sing. or pl.* (forest) лес;
∼ed country леси́стая ме́стность; (fig.): we're
not out of the ∼ yet ещё не все опа́сности/
тру́дности позади́ **2** (substance) де́рево;
touch, (AmE) knock on ∼! тьфу, тьфу! чтоб не
сгла́зить! **3** (as fuel) дрова́ (*pl., g.* —)
∎ ∼land *n.* леси́стая ме́стность; ∼pecker
n. дя́тел; ∼wind *n.* (collect.) деревя́нные
духовы́е инструме́нты (*m. pl.*); ∼work
n. (BrE, carpentry) столя́рная рабо́та; (articles)
деревя́нные изде́лия; ∼worm *n.* личи́нка
древото́чца

wooden /'wʊd(ə)n/ *adj.* (also fig.) деревя́нный

woody /'wʊdɪ/ *adj.* (**woodier, woodiest**)
(wooded) леси́стый; (of or like wood)
деревя́нный

woof /wʊf/ *n.* (dog's bark) га́вканье, лай; ∼!
гав!

wool /wʊl/ *n.* шерсть; pull the ∼ over sb's
eyes (fig.) пус|ка́ть, -ти́ть пыль в глаза́
кому́-н.

woollen /'wʊlən/ (AmE **woolen**) *adj.*
шерстяно́й

woolly /'wʊlɪ/ *adj.* (**woollier,
woolliest**) **1** (bearing or covered with wool) шерстистый **2** (fig., lacking definition) неясный

word /wəːd/ *n.* **1** слово; **I couldn't get a ~ in (edgeways)** мне не удалось вставить ни слова; **he never has a good ~ for anyone** он ни о ком доброго слова не скажет; **may I have a ~ with you?** можно вас на пару слов?; **in a ~** (одним) словом; **in other ~s** иначе говоря, другими словами; **a man of few ~s** немногословный человек; **put in a good ~ for sb** замолвить (*pf.*) словечко за кого-н.; **~ for ~** слово в слово; **translate ~ for ~** перев|одить, -ести дословно/буквально **2** (*in pl.*) (quarrel): **they had ~s** они поссорились **3** (*in pl.*) (text set to music) текст, слова (*nt. pl.*) **4** (news) известие, сообщение; **he sent ~ that he was not coming** он передал, что не сможет прийти; **the ~ got round that ...** стало известно, что... **5** (promise) слово, обещание; **give one's ~** да|вать, -ть слово; обещ|ать (*impf., pf.*); **keep one's ~** держать, с- слово; **his was as good as his ~** он сдержал слово; **you must take my ~ for it** вам придётся поверить мне на слово **6** (command) слово, приказ; **just say the ~!** только скажите/прикажите!
• *v.t.* формулировать, с-
■ **~ processing** *n.* редактирование текста; **~ processor** *n.* текстовый редактор

wording /'wəːdɪŋ/ *n.* редакция (*текста, статьи*)

wore /wɔː(r)/ *past of* ▶ **wear**

work /wəːk/ *n.* **1** (labour, task) работа, труд; (official, professional) работа, служба; (school etc.) занятия (*nt. pl.*); **he is at ~** он сейчас работает; **she is at ~ on a dictionary** она работает над словарём; **get to ~ on** нач|инать, -ать работу над + *i.*; **get down to ~** прин|иматься, -яться/бр|аться, взяться за работу/дело **2** (employment) работа, служба; **it is hard to find ~** трудно найти работу; **in ~** работающий; **out of ~** без работы **3** (literary or artistic composition) произведение, сочинение; (publication) издание; **the ~s of Chopin** произведения Шопена; **a ~ of art** произведение искусства **4** (*in pl.*) (parts of machine) механизм **5** (*in pl.*) (BrE, factory) завод, фабрика, предприятие; **steel ~s** сталелитейный завод
• *v.t.* (*past and p.p.* **worked**) **1** (cause to ~): **he ~s his men hard** он заставляет людей много работать; **he ~ed himself to death** он извёл себя работой **2** (set in motion) прив|одить, -ести в движение/действие; **how do you ~ this machine?** как управлять этой машиной? **3** (effect): **~ wonders** творить (*impf.*) чудеса **4** (achieve by ~ing): **he ~ed his way through university** все годы студенчества он сам зарабатывал себе на жизнь; **he ~ed his way up to the rank of manager** он пробился в директора **5** (excite) возбу|ждать, -дить; **he ~ed the crowd into a frenzy** он довёл толпу до неистовства
• *v.i.* **1** (be employed) работать (*над чем*), трудиться, служить (*all impf.*); **he ~ed for 6 hours** он работал 6 часов; **~ with sb** сотрудничать (*impf.*) с кем-н. **2** (operate) работать (*impf.*); действовать (*impf.*); **the brakes won't ~** тормоза отказали **3** (produce desired effect): **the plan ~ed** план удался; **the medicine ~ed** лекарство помогло/подействовало **4** (exert influence) работать, действовать (*both impf.*); **~ against** мешать, по- + *d.* **5** (move gradually): **a screw ~ed loose** винт ослаб
□ **~ off** *v.t.*: **he ran round the house to ~ off some of his energy** он пробежался вокруг дома, чтобы дать выход своей энергии; **I shall never be able to ~ off this debt** я никогда не смогу отработать этот долг
□ **~ out** *v.t.* (devise) разраб|атывать, -отать; (calculate) вычисл|ять, -ислить; (solve) разреш|ать, -ить
• *v.i.* (turn out) оказ|ываться, -аться; (turn out well) об|ходиться, -ойтись; **everything ~ed out** всё обошлось; (be calculated): **the expenses ~ out at £70** расходы составляют 70 фунтов; (train, of an athlete) тренироваться (*impf.*)
□ **~ up** *v.t.* (develop): **I can't ~ up any interest in economics** я никак не могу пробудить в себе интерес к экономике; (*pred.*) **I'm ~ed up** (excited) я взволнован; (worried) я расстроен
■ **~bench** *n.* верстак; **~ experience** *n.* (BrE) производственная практика (*для школьников*); **~force** *n.* рабочая сила; **~load** *n.* нагрузка; **~man** *n.* работник; **~manship** *n.* мастерство; **~out** *n.* тренировка; **~shop** *n.* (small) мастерская; (large) цех; **~station** *n.* (comput.) станция; **~top** *n.* (BrE) верхняя панель; **~-to-rule** *n.* (BrE) ≈ итальянская забастовка (*работа строго по правилам*)

workable /'wəːkəb(ə)l/ *adj.* **1** (of mine etc.) рентабельный **2** (feasible) выполнимый

workaholic /wəːkə'hɒlɪk/ *n.* трудоголик

worker /'wəːkə(r)/ *n.* работник, трудящийся; **office ~** служащий

working /'wəːkɪŋ/ *n.* **1** (*usu. in pl.*) (operation) работа, действие **2** (*attr.*) (pert. to work) рабочий; **in ~ order** в исправности
• *adj.* рабочий
■ **~ capital** *n.* оборотный капитал; **~ class** *n.* рабочий класс; **~-class** *adj.* рабочий; **~-class families** семьи рабочих; **~ conditions** *n. pl.* условия труда

world /wəːld/ *n.* **1** (universe) мир; **out of this ~** (infml, stupendous) потрясающий; **in this ~** на этом свете **2** (fig. uses): **what in the ~ has happened?** да что же, наконец, случилось?; **why in the ~ didn't you tell me?** ну почему же вы мне не сказали?; **I wouldn't hurt him for the ~** я его ни за что (на свете) не стал бы обижать; **the boss thinks the ~ of him** он у хозяина на очень высоком счету; **I felt on top of the ~** я был на седьмом небе от счастья **3** (infinite amount) много, уйма (infml); **a ~ of difference** огромная разница;

it will do him a ~ of good это пойдёт ему на пользу **4** (geog., the earth's countries and peoples) мир, свет; **(all) over the** ~ по всему свету; **go round the** ~ объ|езжа́ть, -е́хать весь свет; a ~ **power** велика́я держа́ва **5** (human affairs) жизнь; **go up in the** ~ де́лать, с- карье́ру; **go down in the** ~ утра́|чивать, -тить было́е положе́ние **6** (domain) мир; сфе́ра; **the** ~ **of nature** ца́рство приро́ды

■ **W~ Bank** n. Всеми́рный банк; ~ **champion** n. чемпио́н ми́ра; **W~ Cup** n. Ку́бок ми́ра по футбо́лу; ~**-famous** adj. всеми́рно изве́стный; ~ **record** n. мирово́й реко́рд; ~ **view** n. мировоззре́ние; ~ **war** n. мирова́я война́; ~**wide** adj. всеми́рный, мирово́й ● adv. по всему́ све́ту/ми́ру; **W~ Wide Web** n. Всеми́рная паути́на, Интерне́т, Сеть

worldly /'wəːldlɪ/ adj. (**worldlier**, **worldliest**) **1** (material) земно́й, материа́льный **2**: a ~ **person** о́пытный челове́к

■ ~**-wise** adj. о́пытный

worm /wəːm/ n. червь (m.)
 ● v.t. (extract) вытя́гивать, вы́тянуть

worn /wɔːn/ p.p. of ▶ wear

worried /'wʌrɪd/ adj. обеспоко́енный, озабо́ченный

worrier /'wʌrɪə(r)/ n.: he's a ~ он ве́чно беспоко́ится

⚡ **worry** /'wʌrɪ/ n. **1** (anxiety) трево́га, забо́та **2** (sth causing anxiety) неприя́тность, забо́та; **he is a** ~y **to me** он доставля́ет мне мно́го беспоко́йства/забо́т/хлопо́т; **financial** ~ies фина́нсовые пробле́мы (f. pl.)
 ● v.t. **1** (cause anxiety to) беспоко́ить (impf.); **what is** ~ying **you?** что вас беспоко́ит?; **I'm** ~ied **about my son** я беспоко́юсь о сы́не **2** (bother) надоеда́ть (impf.) + d.; **the noise doesn't** ~y **me** шум не меша́ет мне
 ● v.i. беспоко́иться, волнова́ться, расстра́иваться (all impf.); **don't** ~y! не беспоко́йтесь!; **you are** ~ying **over nothing** вы напра́сно расстра́иваетесь/волну́етесь

worse /wəːs/ n. ху́дшее; **there is** ~ **to come** ху́дшее ещё впереди́; **a change for the** ~ переме́на к ху́дшему; **things went from bad to** ~ положе́ние станови́лось всё ху́же и ху́же
 ● adj. ху́дший; **you will only make matters** ~ вы то́лько уху́дшите положе́ние; ~ **luck!** к сожале́нию!; (as pred.) ху́же; **the patient is** ~ **today** больно́му сего́дня ху́же; **his work is getting** ~ его́ рабо́та стано́вится ху́же; **they are** ~ **off than we** они́ в ху́дшем положе́нии, чем мы; (financially) они́ ме́нее состоя́тельны, чем мы
 ● adv. ху́же; **we played** ~ **than ever** мы игра́ли как никогда́ пло́хо; **you might do** ~ **than accept** мо́жет быть, и сто́ит приня́ть

worsen /'wəːs(ə)n/ v.t. & i. ухудша́ть(ся), уху́дшить(ся)

worship /'wəːʃɪp/ n. поклоне́ние
 ● v.t. & i. (**worshipped**, **worshipping**, AmE

worshiped, **worshiping**) поклоня́ться (impf.) + d.; ~ **God** моли́ться (impf.) Бо́гу; (attend ~) моли́ться (impf.); (adore) боготвори́ть (impf.)

worshipper /'wəːʃɪpə(r)/ (AmE **worshiper**) n. моля́щийся

worst /wəːst/ n. наиху́дшее; са́мое плохо́е; **the** ~ **is over** ху́дшее позади́; **the** ~ **of it is that ...** ху́же всего́ то, что...; **if the** ~ **comes to the** ~ в са́мом ху́дшем слу́чае; **you saw him at his** ~ вы ви́дели его́ с наиху́дшей стороны́; **at (the)** ~ **you may have to pay a fine** в кра́йнем слу́чае вам придётся уплати́ть штраф
 ● adj. наиху́дший; са́мый плохо́й; **you came at the** ~ **possible time** вы пришли́ в са́мое неподходя́щее вре́мя
 ● adv. (of objects) ху́же всего́; (of people) ху́же всех

⚡ **worth** /wəːθ/ n. (value) це́нность; (merit) досто́инство; **of great** ~ значи́тельный; (quantity of specified value): **give me a pound's** ~ **of sweets** да́йте мне конфе́т на (оди́н) фунт
 ● pred. adj. **1** (of value equal to): **it's** ~ **about £1** э́то сто́ит о́коло (одного́) фу́нта; **what is your house** ~? во ско́лько оце́нивается ваш дом?; **it's** ~ **a lot to me** для меня́ э́то о́чень це́нно/ва́жно **2** (deserving of) сто́ящий, заслу́живающий; **it's not** ~ **the trouble of asking** не сто́ит спра́шивать; **it is** ~ **while** сто́ит; **it's hardly** ~ **mentioning** об э́том вряд ли сто́ит упомина́ть; **well** ~ **having** о́чень сто́ящий/поле́зный **3** (possessed of): **he is** ~ **3 billion** его́ ли́чное состоя́ние оце́нивается в 3 миллиа́рда; (fig.): **he ran for all he was** ~ он мча́лся во весь дух

■ ~**while** adj. це́нный, сто́ящий

worthless /'wəːθlɪs/ adj. (goods) ничего́ не сто́ящий; (person, contribution) ничто́жный

worthy /'wəːðɪ/ adj. (**worthier**, **worthiest**) **1** (deserving respect) досто́йный, почте́нный; **a** ~ **cause** досто́йное де́ло **2** (deserving) досто́йный, заслу́живающий + g.; ~ **of note** досто́йный внима́ния; ~ **of a place in the team** досто́йный быть чле́ном кома́нды **3** (appropriate) подоба́ющий + d.; ~ **of the occasion** подоба́ющий слу́чаю

⚡ **would** /wʊd/ v. aux. (see also ▶ will²) **1** (conditional): **he** ~ **be angry if he knew** он бы рассерди́лся, е́сли (бы) узна́л **2** (expr. wish): **I** ~ **like to know** я хоте́л бы знать; **I** ~ **rather** я бы предпочёл **3** (of typical action etc.): **you** ~ **do that!** с тебя́ ста́нется!; **of course he** ~ **say that** ну коне́чно, он э́то ска́жет **4** (of habitual action) see ▶ will² 4

■ ~**-be** adj.: **a** ~**-be writer** начина́ющий писа́тель

wouldn't /'wʊd(ə)nt/ neg. of ▶ would

wound¹ /wuːnd/ n. ра́на, ране́ние
 ● v.t. ра́нить (impf., pf.); **he was** ~ed **in the leg** его́ ра́нило в но́гу; **there were many** ~ed бы́ло мно́го ра́неных

wound² /waʊnd/ past and p.p. of ▶ wind²

wove /wəʊv/ past of ▶ weave

woven /'wəʊv(ə)n/ p.p. of ▶ weave

w

wow /waʊ/ *int.* здо́рово!; вот э́то да́!; ух!
• *v.t.* (sl.) прив|оди́ть, -ести́ в восто́рг

WPC (BrE) *abbr.* (*of* **woman police constable**) же́нщина-полице́йский

wrangle /ˈræŋɡ(ə)l/ *n.* ссо́ра
• *v.i.* ссо́риться (*impf.*)

wrap /ræp/ *n.* ▇ (lit., shawl) шаль, плато́к; (rug) плед ▇ (fig.): **under** ~**s** (fig.) в та́йне
• *v.t.* (**wrapped, wrapping**) ▇ (cover) зав|ора́чивать, -ерну́ть; заку́т|ывать, -ать; (parcel) об|ора́чивать, -ерну́ть; **they were** ~**ping presents** они́ завора́чивали пода́рки; ~ **oneself in a blanket** зав|ора́чиваться, -ерну́ться в одея́ло ▇ (wind as a covering) об|ора́чивать, -ерну́ть; **we** ~ **sacking round the pipes in winter** зимо́й мы обора́чиваем тру́бы мешкови́ной; **he** ~**ped his arms around her** он заключи́л её в объя́тия; он обня́л её
□ ~ **up** *v.t.* (cover up) зав|ора́чивать, -ерну́ть; (conclude) свора́чивать, сверну́ть (infml); (summarize) кра́тко сумми́ровать (*impf., pf.*); (*pass.*) (be engrossed) погру|жа́ться, -зи́ться (**in:** в + *a.*)
• *v.i.* (put on extra clothes) заку́т|ываться, -аться

wrapper /ˈræpə(r)/ *n.* обёртка

wrapping /ˈræpɪŋ/ *n.* обёртка, упако́вка
■ ~ **paper** *n.* обёрточная бума́га

wrath /rɒθ/ *n.* гнев

wrathful /ˈrɒθfʊl/ *adj.* гне́вный, я́ростный

wreak /riːk/ *v.t.*: ~ **havoc (on)** нан|оси́ть, -ести́ ущерб + *d.*

wreath /riːθ/ *n.* вено́к

wreck /rek/ *n.* ▇ (~ed ship) затону́вший кора́бль ▇ (damaged vehicle, building, person, etc.) разва́лина
• *v.t.* ▇ (ship): **the ship was** ~**ed** су́дно потерпе́ло круше́ние; **the ship was** ~**ed on the cliffs** кора́бль разби́лся о ска́лы ▇ (car) разб|ива́ть, -и́ть; (building) разр|уша́ть, -у́шить; (equipment) лома́ть, с- ▇ (hope, life) разб|ива́ть, -и́ть; (weekend) по́ртить, ис-

wreckage /ˈrekɪdʒ/ *n.* (remains) обло́мки (*m. pl.*) круше́ния *и т. п.*

wren /ren/ *n.* крапи́вник (*птица*)

wrench /rentʃ/ *n.* ▇ (fig.) тоска́, боль ▇ (tool) га́ечный ключ
• *v.t.*: **he** ~**ed the door open** он ре́зко рвану́л дверь на себя́; **he** ~**ed the paper out of my hand** он вы́рвал у меня́ бума́гу из рук

wrestle /ˈres(ə)l/ *v.i.* боро́ться (*impf.*); (fig.): ~ **with a problem** би́ться (*impf.*) над зада́чей; **he** ~**d with his conscience** он боро́лся со свое́й со́вестью

wrestler /ˈreslə(r)/ *n.* боре́ц

wrestling /ˈreslɪŋ/ *n.* борьба́

wretch /retʃ/ *n.* негодя́й

wretched /ˈretʃɪd/ *adj.* (**wretcheder, wretchedest**) (miserable) несча́стный; (unpleasant) скве́рный; (damned) прокля́тый

wriggle /ˈrɪɡ(ə)l/ *n.* изги́б, изви́в
• *v.t.* (*also* ~ **about**): ~ **one's toes** шевели́ть

(*impf.*) па́льцами ног; **he** ~**d free** он вы́вернулся/вы́скользнул
• *v.i.* (*also* ~ **about**) извива́ться (*impf.*); **the baby** ~**d out of my arms** ребёнок вы́скользнул у меня́ из рук; ~ **out of a responsibility** уви́л|ивать, -ьну́ть от отве́тственности

wring /rɪŋ/ *v.t.* (*past and p.p.* **wrung**) ▇ (sb's hand) пож|има́ть, -а́ть; **he wrung his hands in despair** он в отча́янии лома́л себе́ ру́ки; (squeeze out by twisting) выжима́ть, вы́жать; ~ **clothes dry** отж|има́ть, -а́ть бельё досуха; (chicken's neck) свора́чивать, сверну́ть ▇ (fig., extract by force) вырыва́ть, вы́рвать; **I wrung a promise from him** я вы́рвал у него́ обеща́ние
□ ~ **out** *v.t.* (clothes) отж|има́ть, -жа́ть; (water) отж|има́ть, -а́ть

wrinkle /ˈrɪŋk(ə)l/ *n.* (on skin) морщи́на
• *v.t.*: ~ **one's nose** мо́рщить, с- нос
• *v.i.* мя́ться, по-/из-

wrist /rɪst/ *n.* запя́стье
■ ~**watch** *n.* нару́чные час|ы́ (-о́в)

writ /rɪt/ *n.* (written injunction) суде́бный прика́з; (summons) пове́стка; **serve a** ~ **on sb** вруч|а́ть, -и́ть кому́-н. суде́бный прика́з

◈ **write** /raɪt/ *v.t.* (*past* **wrote,** *p.p.* **written**) ▇ писа́ть, на- ▇: ~ **a cheque** (BrE), **check** (AmE) выпи́сывать, вы́писать чек ▇ (compose) писа́ть, на-; сочин|я́ть, -и́ть
• *v.i.* (*past* **wrote,** *p.p.* **written**) ▇ (*impf.*) ▇ (compose) сочин|я́ть, -и́ть; писа́ть, на-
□ ~ **away** *v.i.*: **he wrote away, off for a catalogue** он вы́писал катало́г
□ ~ **back** *v.i.* отв|еча́ть, -е́тить (письмо́м)
□ ~ **down** *v.t.* (make a note of) запи́с|ывать, -а́ть
□ ~ **off** *v.t.* (cancel): ~ **off a debt** спи́с|ывать, -а́ть долг; (recognize loss of): ~ **off £500 for depreciation** спи́с|ывать, -а́ть 500 фу́нтов на амортиза́цию; **the car had to be written off** маши́ну пришло́сь списа́ть
• *v.i.* = **write away**
□ ~ **out** *v.t.* выпи́сывать, вы́писать
■ ~**-off** *n.*: **the car was a** ~**-off** маши́ну списа́ли; ~**-up** *n.* (account) отчёт; (review) о́тзыв, реце́нзия

◈ **writer** /ˈraɪtə(r)/ *n.* ▇ (person writing) а́втор ▇ (author) писа́тель (-ница)
■ ~**'s block** *n.* отсу́тствие вдохнове́ния

writhe /raɪð/ *v.i.* ко́рчиться (*impf.*)

◈ **writing** /ˈraɪtɪŋ/ *n.* ▇ (ability, art) письмо́, гра́мота ▇ (written words; inscription) на́дпись; **in** ~ пи́сьменно; в пи́сьменной фо́рме ▇ (handwriting) по́черк ▇ (literary composition) произведе́ние
■ ~ **pad** *n.* блокно́т; ~ **paper** *n.* пи́счая бума́га

written /ˈrɪt(ə)n/ *p.p. of* ▶ **write**

◈ **wrong** /rɒŋ/ *n.* ▇ (evil) зло; (immoral action) дурно́й посту́пок ▇ (unjust action or its result) несправедли́вость, оби́да ▇ (state of error): **you are in the** ~ вы непра́вы/винова́ты
• *adj.* ▇ (sinful) гре́шный; (reprehensible) дурно́й; **it is** ~ **to steal** ворова́ть нехорошо́ ▇ (mistaken) непра́вый; **you are** ~ вы непра́вы/ошиба́етесь; **he proved them** ~ он

доказа́л, что они́ ошиба́лись **3** (incorrect) непра́вильный, неве́рный, оши́бочный; (unsuitable) неподходя́щий; take the ∼ turning сво|ора́чивать, -ерну́ть не туда́; my food went down the ∼ way пи́ща попа́ла не в то го́рло; that's the ∼ way to go about it э́то де́лается не так; this shirt is the ∼ size/ colour э́та руба́шка не того́ разме́ра/цве́та; the clock is ∼ часы́ иду́т непра́вильно; you have the ∼ number вы не туда́ попа́ли (*по телефо́ну*) нела́дный; what's ∼? что случи́лось?; what's ∼ with you? что с тобо́й?; there's something ∼ with my car с мое́й маши́ной что́-то не в поря́дке; to go ∼ срыва́ться, сорва́ться; our plans went ∼ на́ши пла́ны спу́тались; where did we go ∼? (make a mistake) в чём мы оши́блись? **5** (of health): the doctor asked me what was ∼ врач спроси́л, на что я жа́луюсь; he found nothing ∼ with me он не нашёл у меня́ никаки́х боле́зней
● *adv.* (incorrectly) непра́вильно, не так; (reprehensibly) пло́хо; you did ∼ to shout at the child ты пло́хо сде́лал, что накрича́л на ребёнка
● *v.t.* (treat unjustly) быть несправедли́вым к + *d.*
■ ∼**doer** *n.* (sinner) гре́шни|к (-ца); (offender) правонаруши́тель (-ница); ∼**foot** *v.t.* (BrE) заст|ига́ть, -и́гнуть враспло́х

wrongful /ˈrɒŋfʊl/ *adj.* несправедли́вый

wrongly /ˈrɒŋlɪ/ *adv.* (reprehensibly) ду́рно; (incorrectly) непра́вильно; (by mistake) по оши́бке

wrote /rəʊt/ *past of* ▶ write

wrought /rɔːt/ *adj.*: ∼ iron ко́ваное/ сва́рочное желе́зо

wrung /rʌŋ/ *past and p.p. of* ▶ wring

wry /raɪ/ *adj.* криво́й

WWW *abbr.* (*of* **World Wide Web**) Всеми́рная паути́на, Интерне́т, Сеть

WYSIWYG /ˈwɪzɪwɪg/ *abbr.* (*of* **what you see is what you get**) (comput.) режи́м по́лного соотве́тствия (*печа́тного изображе́ния и изображе́ния на экра́не*)

Xx

X /eks/ *n.* (unknown quantity or person) X, икс; ∼ marks the spot where the body was found кресто́м обозна́чено ме́сто, где был на́йден труп; an ∼(-rated) film фильм катего́рии X (*то́лько для взро́слых*)
■ ∼**-ray** *n.* (*in pl.*) рентге́новские лучи́ (*m. pl.*); (single image obtained) рентге́новский сни́мок; (procedure) рентге́н

● *v.t.* просве́|чивать, -ти́ть рентге́новскими луча́ми; де́лать, с- рентге́н (*чего́-н*)

xenophobia /zenəˈfəʊbɪə/ *n.* ксенофо́бия

xenophobic /zenəˈfəʊbɪk/ *adj.* отлича́ющийся ксенофо́бией, ксенофо́бский

Xmas /ˈeksməs/ *n.* = Christmas

xylophone /ˈzaɪləfəʊn/ *n.* (mus.) ксилофо́н

Yy

yacht /jɒt/ *n.* я́хта
■ ∼**sman** *n.* яхтсме́н; ∼**swoman** *n.* яхтсме́нка

yachting /ˈjɒtɪŋ/ *n.* па́русный спорт

Yank /jæŋk/ *n.* (infml) я́нки (*m. indecl.*)

yank /jæŋk/ *n.* рыво́к
● *v.t.* дёр|гать, -нуть
□ ∼ **off** *v.t.* срыва́ть, сорва́ть

yap /jæp/ *n.* тя́вканье
● *v.i.* (**yapped**, **yapping**) тя́вк|ать, -нуть

yard¹ /jɑːd/ *n.* (unit of measure) ярд (*0,9144 м*)
■ ∼**stick** *n.* (fig.) мери́ло, крите́рий

yard² /jɑːd/ *n.* **1** (BrE, of house) (*also* **court**∼) двор **2** (AmE, garden) са́д(ик) **3** (for industrial purposes): **timber** ∼ склад пиломатериа́лов; **builder's** ∼ склад стройматериа́лов

yarn /jɑːn/ *n.* **1** (spun thread) пря́жа **2** (infml, story) расска́з

yawn /jɔːn/ *n.* зево́к

w

x

y

● *v.i.* зев|а́ть, -ну́ть; (fig., of chasm) зия́ть (*impf.*)

yay /jeɪ/ *int.* (infml, expressing triumph, approval, or encouragement) ура́!

yeah /jeə/ *adv.* (infml) да; ага́

year /jɪə(r)/ *n.* **1** год; I have known him for ten ~s я его́ зна́ю уже́ де́сять лет; ~ in, ~ out из го́да в год; all the ~ round кру́глый год; he's in the third ~ (as school pupil) он в тре́тьем кла́ссе; he is in his third ~ (as college student) он на тре́тьем ку́рсе **2** (*in pl.*) (a long time): it is ~s since I saw him я его́ це́лую ве́чность не ви́дел **3** (*in pl.*) (age) лета́; he looks young for his ~s он мо́лодо вы́глядит для свои́х лет; he is getting on in ~s он (уже́) в во́зрасте

yearly /ˈjɪəlɪ/ *adj.* (happening once a year) ежего́дный; (pert. to a year): ~ income годово́й дохо́д
● *adv.* (once a year) раз в год; (every year) ка́ждый год

yearn /jɜːn/ *v.i.* **1**: ~ for тоскова́ть (*impf.*) по + *d.*; жа́ждать (*impf.*) + *g.* **2**: ~ to жажда́ть (*impf.*) (+ *inf.*); мечта́ть (*impf.*) (+ *inf.*)

yearning /ˈjɜːnɪŋ/ *n.* тоска́ (for: по + *d.*); жа́жда (for: + *g.*)

yeast /jiːst/ *n.* дро́жж|и (-е́й)

yell /jel/ *n.* (пронзи́тельный) крик
● *v.t.* выкри́кивать, вы́крикнуть
● *v.i.* вопи́ть, за-; кр|ича́ть, -и́кнуть

yellow /ˈjeləʊ/ *n.* желтизна́; жёлтый цвет
● *adj.* жёлтый; go, turn ~ желте́ть, по-
● *v.i.* желте́ть, по-
■ Y~ Pages® *n. pl.* «Жёлтые страни́цы»

yellowish /ˈjeləʊɪʃ/ *adj.* желтова́тый

yelp /jelp/ *n.* визг
● *v.i.* визжа́ть, взви́згнуть

Yemen /ˈjemən/ *n.* Йе́мен

Yemeni /ˈjemənɪ/ *n.* йе́мен|ец (-ка)
● *adj.* йе́менский

yen /jen/ *n.* (*pl.* ~) (currency) ие́на

yes /jes/ *adv.* да; (in reply to neg. question) нет; Didn't you see him? — Yes, I did Ты не ви́дел его́? — Нет, ви́дел.; ~, please да, спаси́бо

yesterday /ˈjestədeɪ/ *n.* вчера́ (*indecl.*); вчера́шний день; ~'s paper вчера́шняя газе́та; since ~ со вчера́шнего дня; the day before ~ позавчера́
● *adv.* вчера́; ~ morning/evening вчера́ у́тром/ве́чером

yet /jet/ *adv.* **1** (so far, up to now) до сих пор; пока́ ещё; as ~ пока́; (with neg.): he has not read the book ~ он ещё не чита́л э́ту кни́гу; (with interrog.) уже́, ещё; has the post arrived ~? по́чта ещё не пришла́?; по́чта уже́ пришла́? **2** (some day; before all is over) ещё; he will win ~ он ещё победи́т **3** (still) ещё; he has ~ to learn of the disaster он ещё не зна́ет о катастро́фе **4** (so early) уже́; need you go ~? вам уже́ пора́ (идти́)?; Shall we go? — Not just ~ Пойдёмте? — Не сейча́с/Чуть по́зже **5** (with comp.) (even) да́же, ещё; this book is ~ more interesting э́та кни́га

ещё интере́снее **6** (again, in addition) ещё; there is ~ another reason есть ещё и друга́я причи́на **7** (nevertheless) тем не ме́нее; всё-таки; всё же
● *conj.* одна́ко

yew /juː/ *n.* (tree, wood) тис

Yiddish /ˈjɪdɪʃ/ *n.* и́диш, евре́йский язы́к
● *adj.*: a ~ newspaper газе́та на и́дише

yield /jiːld/ *n.* **1** (crop) урожа́й **2** (return) дохо́д **3** (quantity produced) вы́ход
● *v.t.* **1** (bring in; produce) прин|оси́ть, -ести́; произв|оди́ть, -ести́; да|ва́ть, -ть **2** (give up) уступ|а́ть, -и́ть; ~ ground сда|ва́ть, -ть террито́рию; (fig.) сда|ва́ть, -ть (свои́) пози́ции
● *v.i.* уступ|а́ть, -и́ть; подд|ава́ться, -а́ться; he would not ~ to persuasion он не поддава́лся никаки́м угово́рам; (of a door) под|дава́ться, -а́ться

yob /jɒb/ *n.* (BrE, infml) хулига́н

yobbish /ˈjɒbɪʃ/ *adj.* (BrE, infml) хулига́нский

yoga /ˈjəʊgə/ *n.* йо́га

yogurt, yoghurt /ˈjɒgət/ *n.* йо́гурт

yoke /jəʊk/ *n.* (sense 2: *pl.* ~ or ~s) **1** (fitted to oxen etc.) ярмо́, хому́т **2** (fig.) и́го, ярмо́; the Tartar ~ (hist.) тата́рское и́го; shake off the ~ сбр|а́сывать, -о́сить и́го/ярмо́ **3**: ~ oxen (pair) упряжка воло́в **4** (for carrying pails etc.) коромы́сло **5** (of dress) коке́тка (*верхняя (плечевая/набедренная) часть платья/юбки, к которой пришивается основная их часть*)
● *v.t.* (lit.) впр|яга́ть, -чь в ярмо́; (fig., link) соедин|я́ть, -и́ть; сочета́ть (*impf., pf.*)

yokel /ˈjəʊk(ə)l/ *n.* дереве́нщина (*c.g.*)

yolk /jəʊk/ *n.* желто́к

you /juː/ *pers. pron.* (*obj.* you, *poss.* your, yours) **1** (familiar sg.) ты; (*pl. and polite sg.*) вы; ~ and I ты и я; мы с тобо́й/ва́ми; ~ and he ты/вы и он; вы с ним; this is for ~ э́то для тебя́/вас, э́то тебе́/вам **2** (one, anyone): ~ never can tell никогда́ не зна́ешь; кто его́ зна́ет(?)
■ ~-know-who *n.* (infml) сам зна́ешь, кто; э́тот са́мый

young /jʌŋ/ *n.*: the ~ молодёжь; (~ animals) детёныши (*m. pl.*); (birds) птенцы́ (*m. pl.*)
● *adj.* (younger /ˈjʌŋgə(r)/, youngest /ˈjʌŋgɪst/) молодо́й, ю́ный; ~ children ма́ленькие де́ти; ~ people молодёжь; he is ~er than I он моло́же меня́

youngish /ˈjʌŋɪʃ/ *adj.* дово́льно молодо́й

youngster /ˈjʌŋstə(r)/ *n.* (boy) ма́льчик; (girl) де́вочка; (child) ребёнок

your /jɔː(r)/ *adj.* (familiar sg.) твой; (*pl. and polite sg.*) ваш; (referring to subj. of clause) свой

yours /jɔːz/ *pron.* (familiar sg.) твой; (*pl. and polite sg.*) ваш; (referring to subj. of clause) свой; a friend of ~ оди́н из ва́ших прия́телей; my teacher and ~ (2 people) на́ши с ва́ми учителя́; (1 person) наш с ва́ми учи́тель; here is my hat — have you found ~? вот моя́ шля́па, а вы свою́ нашли́!

yourself /jɔːˈself/ *pron.* **1** (refl.) себя́ (*d., p.* себе́, *i.* собо́й); -ся/-сь (*suff.*); don't

deceive ∼! не обма́нывайте себя́!; не обма́нывайтесь!; **did you hurt** ∼? ты уши́бся/уши́блась? **2** (emph.) сам; **you wrote to him** ∼ вы са́ми ему́ писа́ли; **do it** ∼! сде́лай сам! **3** (after preps.): **why are you sitting by** ∼? почему́ вы сиди́те в одино́честве?; **did you do it all by** ∼? вы э́то сде́лали са́ми? **4**: **you don't look** ∼ **today** вы нева́жно вы́глядите сего́дня

✧ **youth** /juːθ/ n. **1** (state or period) мо́лодость, ю́ность; **in my** ∼ в мо́лодости **2** (young man) ю́ноша (m.) **3** (young people) молодёжь
■ ∼ **club** n. молодёжный клуб; ∼ **hostel** n. молодёжная (тур)ба́за/гости́ница

youthful /ˈjuːθʊl/ adj. ю́ный, ю́ношеский; (of face, person, etc.) молодо́й, ю́ный
youthfulness /ˈjuːθʊlnɪs/ n. мо́лодость; (of appearance) моложа́вость
yuan /jʊˈɑːn/ n. (pl. ∼) юа́нь (m.)
yucca /ˈjʌkə/ n. ю́кка
Yugoslav /ˈjuːɡəslɑːv/, **Yugoslavian** /juːɡəˈslɑːvɪən/ adjs. (hist.) югосла́вский
Yugoslavia /juːɡəˈslɑːvɪə/ n. (hist.) Югосла́вия
Yule /juːl/ n. (archaic) Рождество́; Свя́т|ки (-ок)
yummy /ˈjʌmɪ/ adj. (**yummier, yummiest**) (infml) вку́сный
yuppie /ˈjʌpɪ/ n. (infml pej.) я́ппи (m. indecl.) (преуспева́ющий молодо́й челове́к)

Zz

Zagreb /ˈzɑːɡreb/ n. За́греб
Zambia /ˈzæmbɪə/ n. За́мбия
Zambian /ˈzæmbɪən/ n. замби́|ец (-йка)
● adj. замби́йский
zany /ˈzeɪnɪ/ adj. (**zanier, zaniest**) смешно́й
zap /zæp/ (sl.) v.t. (**zapped, zapping**) (kill, destroy) мочи́ть, за- (sl.); (comput., delete) стира́ть, стере́ть
● v.i. (**zapped, zapping**) (move quickly) мча́ться (impf.)
zeal /ziːl/ n. рве́ние
zealot /ˈzelət/ n. фана́т|ик (-и́чка)
zealous /ˈzeləs/ adj. ре́вностный
zebra /ˈzebrə/ n. зе́бра
■ ∼ **crossing** n. (BrE) «зе́бра» (пешехо́дный перехо́д)
zenith /ˈzenɪθ/ n. (lit., fig.) зени́т
zero /ˈzɪərəʊ/ n. (pl. ∼s) ноль (m.), нуль (m.); **ten degrees below** ∼ ми́нус де́сять гра́дусов
■ ∼ **hour** n. час «Ч»
● v.i. (**zeroes, zeroed**): ∼ **in on a target** пристре́л|иваться, -я́ться
zest /zest/ n. пыл; энтузиа́зм; ∼ **for life** жизнера́достность
zigzag /ˈzɪɡzæɡ/ n. зигза́г
● adj. зигзагообра́зный
● v.i. (**zigzagged, zigzagging**) де́лать (impf.) зигза́ги
Zimbabwe /zɪmˈbɑːbwɪ/ n. Зимба́бве (nt. indecl.)
Zimbabwean /zɪmˈbɑːbwɪən/ n. зимбабви́|ец (-йка)

● adj. зимбабви́йский
zinc /zɪŋk/ n. цинк
Zionism /ˈzaɪənɪz(ə)m/ n. сиони́зм
Zionist /ˈzaɪənɪst/ n. сиони́ст (-ка)
zip /zɪp/ n. **1** (also **zipper**) (застёжка-) мо́лния **2** (infml, energy) пыл, эне́ргия **3**: Z∼ **code** (AmE) (почто́вый) и́ндекс
● v.t. (**zipped, zipping**) (usu. ∼ **up**) застёг|ивать, -ну́ть (на мо́лнию)
● v.i. (**zipped, zipping**) (rush) мча́ться (impf.)
zit /zɪt/ n. (AmE, infml, pimple) прыщик
zodiac /ˈzəʊdɪæk/ n. зодиа́к
zombie /ˈzɒmbɪ/ n. (fig., infml) вя́лый/апати́чный челове́к
✧ **zone** /zəʊn/ n. зо́на, по́яс
zoo /zuː/ n. зоопа́рк
zoological /zəʊəˈlɒdʒɪk(ə)l/ adj. зоологи́ческий
■ ∼ **gardens** n. pl. зоопа́рк, зоологи́ческий сад
zoologist /zəʊˈɒlədʒɪst/ n. зоо́лог
zoology /zəʊˈɒlədʒɪ/ n. зооло́гия
zoom /zuːm/ n. (attr.): ∼ **lens** объекти́в с переме́нным фо́кусным расстоя́нием
● v.i. **1** (move quickly): **cars** ∼**ed past** маши́ны проноси́лись ми́мо **2** (phot., cin.): ∼ **in on** да|ва́ть, -ть кру́пный план + g.
zucchini /zʊˈkiːnɪ/ n. (pl. ∼ or ∼s) (AmE) кабачо́к
Zumba® /ˈzʊmbə/ n. зу́мба-фи́тнес (програ́мма фи́тнеса, осно́ванная на та́нцах под латиноамерика́нскую му́зыку)
Zurich /ˈzjʊərɪk/ n. Цю́рих

y

z

Contents

Glossary of grammatical terms

NB: Items in **bold** type refer the user to a separate entry in the glossary.

Accusative: In Russian, the **case** used to express the **direct object** of a **transitive verb**; also, the case used after certain prepositions.

Active: In an active **clause**, the **subject** of the verb performs the action, e.g. '*Sam* (subject) *identified* (verb) *the suspect*' (as opposed to the passive construction 'the suspect was identified by Sam', where *the suspect* is the subject but is not doing the identifying). Cf. **Passive**.

Adjectival noun: An adjective that functions as a noun, e.g. 'the *empties*' (= empty bottles), '*mobile*' (= mobile phone), 'the *Greens*' (= environmentalists), Russian *столо́вая* 'dining room', *моро́женое* 'ice cream'.

Adjective: A word that describes a **noun** or **pronoun**, giving information about its shape, colour, size, etc., e.g. *triangular, red, large, beautiful* in 'a *triangular* sign', 'the *red* dress', 'it is *large*', 'they are *beautiful*'.

Adverb: A word expressing the manner, frequency, time, place, or extent of an action, e.g. *slowly* and *often* in 'Sue walked *slowly*', 'He *often* stumbled'. Adverbs can also **modify** clauses, e.g. 'Sue *probably* went home', **adjectives**, e.g. 'Sue is *very* tall', and other adverbs, e.g. 'Sue left *extremely* early'.

Affirmative: An affirmative **sentence** or **clause** is a positive statement that explicitly asserts a state of affairs, e.g. *The taxi is waiting*. Cf. **Negative**.

Agree: Words are said to agree when they are put in the correct form in

relation to another word. In Standard English and in Russian, a singular noun or pronoun has to have a singular verb, e.g. '*he goes*' (Russian *он идёт*), and a plural noun or pronoun has to have a plural verb, e.g. '*they go*' (Russian *они́ иду́т*). **Demonstratives** also agree in **number** with the **nouns** they modify, e.g. '*this table*' (Russian *э́тот стол*), '*these tables*' (Russian *э́ти столы́*). In Russian, adjectives, pronouns, and most declined numerals are in the same **case** as the noun they modify, and adjectives, nouns, and verbs have the same **gender** and **number**.

Animate accusative rule: A convention in Russian, whereby in some contexts the form of the accusative is identical with that of the genitive case. This applies **(a)** to masculine singular animate nouns: *Я ви́жу ма́льчика* 'I see the boy', **(b)** to all plural animate nouns: *Я ви́жу ма́льчиков/де́вочек/живо́тных* 'I see the boys/girls/animals', **(c)** to pronouns, adjectives, and participles that agree with the nouns listed under (a) and (b): *Я зна́ю э́тих но́вых учителе́й* 'I know these new teachers', and **(d)** to the numerals *оди́н, два/две, три, четы́ре*, and to *о́ба/о́бе* (also all the collective numerals): *Она́ пригласи́ла трёх подру́г* 'She invited three friends', *Он смотре́л на обо́их бра́тьев* 'He was looking at both brothers'.

Animate noun: A noun denoting a living being, e.g. *captain, elephant* (Russian *капита́н, слон*).

Antecedent: An earlier word, phrase, or clause to which another word (especially a following **relative**

pronoun) refers back, e.g. '*The man* (whom) I know' (Russian *Челове́к, кото́рого я зна́ю*).

Article: see **Definite article, Indefinite article**.

Aspect: A grammatical category of the verb that expresses the nature of an action or process, viewing it either as continuous or habitual (imperfective aspect), or as completed (perfective aspect). Cf. **Submeanings of the aspects**.

Attributive adjective: An **adjective** placed in front of the noun it modifies, e.g. *empty* in 'the *empty* house' (Russian *пусто́й дом*). Cf. **Predicative adjective**.

Auxiliary verb: In English, a verb which functions together with another verb to form a particular **tense** of the other verb, or to form the **passive**, a question, a **negative**, or an **imperative**. In Russian, the future of the verb *быть* 'to be' combines, as an auxiliary verb, with the infinitive of imperfective verbs to form the future of those verbs, e.g. *Я бу́ду рабо́тать* 'I will work', while the past and future tenses and the conditional mood of *быть* combine with the short forms of perfective passive participles to express past, future, and conditional meanings, e.g. *он был назна́чен* 'he was appointed', *он бу́дет назна́чен* 'he will be appointed', *он был бы назна́чен* 'he would be/would have been appointed'.

Case: In Russian, the form of a noun, pronoun, adjective, or numeral that shows its function within the **clause** (e.g. whether it is the **subject** or **object**). Russian has six cases (**nominative, accusative, genitive, dative, instrumental**, and **prepositional**).

Clause: A sentence, or part of a sentence, consisting of a **subject** and a **verb**, e.g. *Mike snores*, or a structure containing **participles** or **infinitives** (with no subject), e.g. '*While waiting* for a bus, I fell asleep' or 'I asked her *to call a taxi*'.

Collective: A term applied to nouns that denote a group of beings or

objects, e.g. *herd* (Russian *ста́до*), *clientele* (Russian *клиенту́ра*), *luggage* (Russian *бага́ж*). In Russian, there are also collective numerals (for the numbers from two to ten), which denote a group of individuals, e.g. *дво́е* ('two'), *тро́е* ('three'), *де́сятеро* ('ten'), or combine with **plural-only nouns**.

Comparative: The form of an **adjective** or **adverb** used when comparing one thing with another, to express a greater degree of a quality, e.g. *cheaper, more expensive, more accurately* in 'this book is *cheaper*', 'a *more expensive* holiday ', 'he described it *more accurately*'. Cf. **Superlative**.

Compound: A word or phrase created by putting two or more existing forms together. In English and Russian, compounds are sometimes written as one word, sometimes as two, and sometimes hyphenated, e.g. *motorway* (Russian *автостра́да*), *good-humoured* (Russian *доброду́шный*), *drawing board* (Russian *чертёжная доска́*), *bow tie* (Russian *га́лстук-ба́бочка*).

Conditional: A verb form which expresses what would happen, or would have happened, if something else (had) occurred. English normally uses *if* with a form of the **auxiliary verb** *would* to express this notion: *If I won the lottery I would buy a car / If I had won... I would have bought....* Russian uses the particle *бы*: *Я пое́хал бы, е́сли бы бы́ло вре́мя* 'I *would* have gone if there had been time'.

Conjugate: To list the different forms or **inflections** of a verb as they vary according to tense, number, person, or voice, e.g. the verb 'to read' is conjugated in the present tense as follows: (I) *read*, (you) *read*, (he/she/it) *reads*, (we) *read*, (you) *read*, (they) *read*. Cf. the equivalent Russian conjugation of *чита́ть*: (я) *чита́ю*, (ты) *чита́ешь*, (он/она́/оно́) *чита́ет*, (мы) *чита́ем*, (вы) *чита́ете*, (они́) *чита́ют*.

Conjugation: In inflected languages, a class to which a verb is assigned according to how it is **conjugated**. In Russian, *чита́ть* belongs to the first (or -e-) conjugation and *говори́ть* belongs to the second (or -и-) conjugation.

Conjunction: A word whose function is to join single words, **clauses**, or **phrases**. Coordinating conjunctions (notably *and* and *or*) join words, clauses, or phrases, e.g. 'John *and* Mary', 'I'll go to the cinema *or* meet my friend for dinner'. Subordinating conjunctions (e.g. *that, because, while*) join clauses, e.g. 'I think *that* he is wrong', 'They left *because* it was late', 'I'll push *while* you lift'. Correlative conjunctions consist of words corresponding to each other and regularly used together, e.g. *both ... and, either ... or.*

Consonant: A speech sound that is produced with some restriction on the flow of air, e.g. *b, ch, r*. It can be combined with a **vowel** to form a **syllable**.

Consonant mutation: The change in a consonant when it occurs adjacent to another sound.

Continuous: A verb form indicating that an action or process is or was ongoing, e.g. 'He *is waiting*', 'She *was laughing*'. Also known as *progressive*.

Dative: In Russian, the **case** used to express the **indirect object** of a **verb**; also, the case used after certain prepositions and certain verbs.

Declension: In inflected languages, the class to which a noun is assigned according to how it is **declined**. Russian has three declensions. The first affects masculine nouns (except for those ending in *-a* or *-я*) and neuter nouns, the second feminine nouns (except for those ending in a soft sign), and the third feminine soft-sign nouns.

Decline: To list the different forms or **inflections** of a noun, adjective, pronoun, or numeral as they vary according to **case**. In English, only pronouns can really be said to decline, e.g. *he, him.*

Definite article: In English, the word *the*, which introduces a noun phrase and implies that the thing mentioned has already been mentioned or is common knowledge, e.g. '*the* book on *the* table'. Russian has no definite article, but achieves the same effect through word order (with the thing which has already been mentioned in first position in the sentence, e.g. *Кни́га* на столе́ '*The* book is on the table'), or by using words such as *э́тот* 'this'. Cf. **Indefinite article**.

Delimitation: A process by which the meaning of an adjective is limited to a particular sphere, e.g. Страна́ бога́та *ле́сом* 'The country is rich *in forest*'.

Demonstrative: A word indicating the person or thing referred to, e.g. *this, that, these, those* in '*this* book' (Russian *э́та* кни́га), '*that* house' (Russian *тот* дом), '*these* books' (Russian *э́ти* кни́ги), '*those* people' (Russian *те* лю́ди).

Direct object: A word or phrase **governed** by a verb, e.g. *dogs* in 'She loves *dogs*' (Russian Она́ лю́бит *соба́к*). In an **active** sentence, the person or thing affected by the action is the direct object. In Russian, the direct object is usually expressed by the accusative case. Cf. **Indirect object**.

Direct speech: In direct speech, the speaker's words or thoughts are presented unchanged, using quotation marks, e.g. '"*The shops are still open*," said Jill'. Russian uses « » (known as guillemets) to show direct speech. Cf. **Indirect speech**.

Emphatic pronoun: The pronouns *myself, himself, themselves*, etc., used for emphasis or to personalize, e.g. 'I did it *myself*'. Russian uses *сам*: Я *сам* сде́лал э́то.

Ending: A letter or letters added to the stem of a word when it is declined or conjugated, e.g. (in English) dog*s*, laugh*ed*, (in Russian) вод*а́* 'water', на стол*е́* 'on the table', зелён*ыми* (instrumental plural) 'green', пиш*у́* 'I write', писа́*ла* 'she was writing'.

Feminine: see **Gender**.

Finite: A verb form which has a specific **tense**, **number**, and **person**, e.g. *rings* in 'She *rings* the doctor' (Russian Она *звонит* врачу). Here, *rings/звонит* is the third-person singular present tense of the verb *to ring/звонить*. A **clause** with a finite verb is called a finite clause. Cf. **Non-finite**.

Fleeting vowel: A vowel (*e*, *ё*, or *o*) that appears in some forms of a Russian word, but not in others, e.g. *e* in *болен* (masculine short form of *больной* 'sick'), *ё* in *сестёр* (genitive plural of *сестра* 'sister'), *o* in *сон* 'sleep' (genitive singular of *сна*), *разобью* (first-person singular of *разбить* 'to smash').

Future: The future **tense** is used when the time of the event described has not yet happened. English uses the auxiliary verbs *shall* and *will*, the present continuous, and *going to*, to express this notion: '*I shall meet* you in the restaurant', '*They will be* pleased', '*We're leaving* at six', '*I'm going to buy* a new car'. To express **imperfective** future meaning, Russian uses the future tense of *быть* + imperfective infinitive, e.g. Я *буду работать*, 'I shall work' or 'I *shall be working*'. To express **perfective** future meaning, Russian uses conjugated forms of the perfective verb, e.g. Я *спрошу* 'I *shall ask*'. Cf. **Aspect**.

Gender: In some languages, nouns and pronouns are divided into grammatical classes called genders. The gender of a noun or pronoun can affect the form of words such as verbs or adjectives that accompany them and may need to **agree** with them in gender. Russian has three genders, **masculine**, **feminine**, and **neuter**. The gender of a Russian noun can usually be identified from its ending: nouns ending in a consonant or *-й* are masculine (e.g. *стул* 'chair', *край* 'edge'); most nouns ending in *-a* or *-я* are feminine (e.g. *яма* 'hole', *шея* 'neck'), and nouns ending in *-o* or *-e* are neuter (e.g. *окно* 'window', *море* 'sea'). Gender in Russian applies in the singular only. Plural nouns and pronouns do not exhibit gender.

Genitive: In Russian, the **case** used to express possession; also, the case used after most cardinal numerals and after **indefinite numerals**, certain **prepositions**, and certain verbs.

Gerund: In English, a verb form in *-ing* that functions like a noun, e.g. *running* in 'She loves *running*' (cf. the Russian use of the **infinitive** in this meaning: Она любит *бегать*). By contrast, the Russian gerund is a verbal adverb that replaces a clause. The imperfective gerund usually ends in *-я* (e.g. Он стоит, *куря* 'He stands, *smoking*'), the perfective in *-в* (e.g. *Поужинав*, он встал '*Having dined*, he got up').

Govern: A word requiring a noun or pronoun to be in a particular **case** is said to govern the noun or pronoun (e.g. the Russian verb *владеть* 'to own' governs the instrumental case, and the preposition *через* 'across' governs the accusative case).

Hard consonant: A consonant that appears at the end of a word (e.g. final *-т* in *нет* 'no'), or is followed by *a*, *ы*, *o*, *y*, or (rarely) *э* (e.g. *г* and *т* in *газета* 'newspaper', *н* in *чёрный* 'black', *л* and *в* in *слово* 'word', *д* and *м* in *дума* 'duma'). Exceptions are the consonants ч and щ which are always soft even if at the end of a word or followed by the above-listed vowels, and ж, ц, and ш which are always hard. Cf. **Soft consonant**.

Historic present: Use of the present tense in order to make the description of a past event more vivid, e.g. 'Suddenly he *breaks* into a run'.

Imperative: The form of the verb used to express a command, e.g. *come* in '*Come* here!'

Imperfective: see **Aspect**.

Impersonal construction: A construction in which an action or state does not involve a specific person or thing as the grammatical subject, e.g. *Стемнело* 'It grew dark', *Как тебя зовут?* 'What is your name?'

Inanimate noun: A noun denoting a non-living thing, e.g. *hall, happiness* (Russian *зал, счастье*).

Indeclinable: A term applied to a noun, pronoun, or adjective that has no **inflections**. In English, the pronoun *you* is indeclinable (whereas *I, he, she*, and *they* change to *me, him, her*, and *them* in the object case, e.g. the dog bit *me*/you/*him/her/them*). In Russian, many **loanwords** are indeclinable (e.g. *такси* 'taxi', *беж adj.* 'beige'), as are the possessive pronouns *его*, 'his/its', *её* 'her(s)/its', *их* 'their(s)'.

Indefinite adverb: An adverb that does not refer to any place, time, manner, etc. in particular, e.g. *somewhere, sometime, somehow* (Russian *где-то, когда-то, как-то*).

Indefinite article: In English, the word *a/an*, which introduces a noun phrase and implies that the thing mentioned is non-specific, e.g. 'she bought *a* book'. Russian has no indefinite article, but achieves the same effect through word order (with an object mentioned for the first time appearing at the end of the sentence, e.g. На столе лежит *карта* '*A* map is lying on the table'). Cf. **Definite article**.

Indefinite numeral: In Russian, a numeral that denotes an indefinite quantity, e.g. *много* 'much, many', *несколько* 'several'.

Indefinite pronoun: A pronoun that does not refer to any person or thing in particular, e.g. *someone* (Russian *кто-то*), *something* (Russian *что-то*), *anyone* (Russian *кто-нибудь*), *anything* (Russian *что-нибудь*).

Indicative: The form of a verb used to express a simple statement of fact, when an event is considered to be definitely taking place or to have taken place, e.g. 'He *is asleep*' (Russian Он *спит*), 'He *fell asleep*' (Russian Он *заснул*). Cf. **Subjunctive**.

Indirect object: A word or phrase referring to the person who receives the **direct object**, e.g. *the driver* in the sentences 'She gave the ticket to *the driver*' or 'She gave *the driver* the ticket'. In Russian, the indirect object is usually expressed by the dative case, e.g. Она подарила часы *сыну* 'She gave the watch *to her son*'. Cf. **Direct object**.

Indirect speech: In indirect speech, the speaker's words or thoughts are reported in a subordinate clause using a reporting verb. In English a change of tense and person is needed, e.g. 'He said "*I want* a drink"' (direct speech) becomes 'He said *he wanted* a drink'. In Russian, only the person changes, not the tense, e.g. Он сказал: «*Я голоден*» 'He said "I'm hungry"' becomes Он сказал, что *он голоден* 'He said that *he was* hungry'.

Infinitive: The basic form of the verb, e.g. *laugh, damage, be*. It is not bound to a particular subject or tense and in English is often preceded by *to* or by another verb, e.g. 'I want *to see* her', 'She came *to see* me', 'Let me *see*'. Russian infinitives end in *-ть, -ти*, or *-чь* (e.g. *писать* 'to write', *вести* 'to lead', *мочь* 'to be able').

Inflection: A change in the form of a word (usually the ending), to express tense, gender, number, or case, etc., e.g. the English plural ending *-s* in 'cars' or the past tense inflection *-ed* in 'I visit*ed* my uncle'. Russian is a highly-inflected language in which nouns, pronouns, adjectives, and numerals decline, and verbs conjugate. Cf. **Case**, **Conjugate**, **Conjugation**, **Declension**, and **Decline**.

Instrumental: In Russian, the **case** used to express the means by which something is done; also, the case used after certain prepositions and certain verbs.

Interrogative adverb: An adverb used to ask questions, e.g. *how* in '*How* are you?' (Russian *Как* (вы) поживаете?) or *when* in '*When* will they arrive?' (Russian *Когда* они приедут?).

Interrogative pronoun: A pronoun used to ask questions, e.g. *which* in '*Which* do you want?' (Russian *Какой* вы хотите?).

Intonation: The use of the pitch of the voice to convey meaning, e.g. *Well? Did you ask her?* (rising intonation) and *Well! I've never been so insulted!* (falling intonation). Different languages have different intonation patterns.

Intransitive verb: A verb not taking a **direct object**, e.g. slept in 'He slept soundly' (Russian Он крéпко *спал*), and read in 'He can't read' (Russian Он не умéет *читáть*). Cf. **Transitive verb**.

Invariable: another term for **indeclinable** (when referring to nouns, adjectives, and pronouns). Adverbs and gerunds are also invariable in Russian.

Irregular verb: In English, a verb such as 'sing' whose **inflections** do not follow one of the usual **conjugation** patterns of the language (past sang by contrast with the usual past tense suffix -*ed*, e.g. walk*ed*). In Russian, the only truly irregular verbs are *бежáть* 'to run', *дать* 'to give', *есть* 'to eat', and *хотéть* 'to want'. Cf. **Regular verb**.

Loanword: A word borrowed from another language, e.g. Russian *кóфе* 'coffee'.

Locative case: A term used as an alternative to the prepositional case to describe prepositional phrases that denote location and are introduced by *в* 'in' or *на* 'on': *в дóме* 'in the house', *на столé* 'on the table'. Some nouns have special locative forms in stressed *у*, *ю*, or *и*: *в лесý* 'in the forest', *на краю́* 'on the edge', *на двери́* 'on the door'.

Main clause: In a **sentence** with more than one **clause**, the clause which is not **subordinate** to any of the others is known as the main clause, e.g. 'Peter stopped' in 'When it got too dark to see where he was going, Peter stopped'. A main clause can stand alone as a sentence. Cf. **Subordinate clause**.

Masculine: see **Gender**.

Mobile stress: A feature of some Russian words whereby the stressed syllable changes in one or more forms of the word's declension or conjugation, etc. Stress may move from the stem

onto the ending, e.g. *стол* 'table', genitive singular *столá*; *слóво* 'word', nominative plural *словá*; *печь* 'stove', locative singular *печи́*; masculine short form *дóрог* 'is dear', feminine *дорогá*; *пять* 'five', genitive *пяти́*. It may also move from the ending onto the stem, e.g. *рекá* 'river', accusative singular *рéку* (also *рекý*); *окнó* 'window', nominative plural *óкна*. In conjugation, stress shift occurs only from the ending onto the stem, e.g. *пишý* 'I write', *пишет* 'he writes'.

Modify: A word or phrase modifies another word or phrase when it provides additional information about it. Modifying expressions include **adjectives**, e.g. *slow* in 'A *slow* train', and **adverbs**, e.g. *slowly* in 'The train moved *slowly*'.

Negative: A negative **sentence** or **clause** asserts that something is not the case, using a negative **particle**, e.g. '*The taxi is not waiting*'. Similarly, a negative **adverb** (*nowhere, never*) or negative **pronoun** (*nobody, nothing*). Cf. **Affirmative**.

Neuter: see **Gender**.

Nominative: In Russian, the **case** used to express the **subject** of a clause.

Non-finite: A term applied to a verb form which has no specific **tense**, **number**, or **person**, e.g. *waiting* in 'While *waiting* for a bus, Peter read the paper'. Russian uses a **gerund** in such contexts, e.g. *Ожидáя* автóбус, Пи́тер читáл газéту. Cf. **Finite**.

Noun: A word that identifies a person, e.g. *milkman, girl, uncle*, a physical object, e.g. *cup, book, building*, or an abstract notion, e.g. *beauty, health, unpleasantness*.

Noun phrase: A group of words including a noun, which functions in a sentence as subject, object, or prepositional object.

Number: A grammatical classification whereby a word is either **singular** or **plural**.

Numeral: A word expressing a number. Members of the series of numbers *one, two*, etc. are referred to as cardinal numbers or cardinal numerals. Members of the series *first, second*, etc. are referred to as ordinal numbers or ordinal numerals. Russian also has a series of collective numerals, e.g. *двóе* in *двóе* детéй 'two children', *трóе* in *трóе* сáнок 'three sledges'.

Object: see **Direct object, Indirect object**.

Oblique cases: All **cases** other than the **nominative**.

Participle: In English, a word formed from a verb and used as an adjective or as a noun, or to form compound verb forms. The English present participle ends in *-ing*, e.g. '*Thinking* I was late, I hurried' (Russian uses a **gerund** in such contexts: *Дýмая*, что я опáздываю, я торопúлся), and the past participle ends in *-ed*, e.g. 'I have *finished*' (Russian uses a **finite verb** in such contexts: Я *кóнчил*). Russian has four participles, present active, past active, present passive, and past passive, which either replace **relative clauses**, e.g. Дéвочка, *читáющая/ читáвшая/прочитáвшая* книгу 'the girl *who is reading/who was reading/who has read* the book', мотóр, *провéренный* механиками 'an engine *which has been checked* by the mechanics', or (using the short form of the past passive participle) function as **predicates**, e.g. Дом *прóдан* 'The house *has been sold*'.

Particle: In Russian, a word or a part of a word that invests other words or phrases with expressive nuances of meaning, e.g. *Не* я ошибся! 'I'm not the one who got it wrong!', *Ну* и проголодáлся же я! 'Am I hungry!'

Partitive genitive: The genitive case used to denote a part, as opposed to the whole, of a substance, e.g. мнóго *молокá* 'a lot of milk', кусóк *мяса* 'a piece of meat'. Some nouns have special partitive genitive forms in *-y* or *-ю*: тарéлка сýп*у* 'a plate of soup', Хóчешь чáю? 'Would you like some tea?'

Part of speech: Any of the classes into which words are categorized for grammatical purposes. The main ones are **Noun, Adjective, Pronoun, Verb, Adverb, Preposition**, and **Conjunction**.

Passive: The form of the **clause** used when the individual referred to by the **subject** undergoes (rather than performs) the action, e.g. '*The soldier was nominated* for an award' (Russian *Солдáт был представлен* к нагрáде). Cf. **Active**.

Past: The past **tense** is used when the time of the event described precedes the time of utterance, e.g. 'Peter *lived* in London'. Cf. **Present**.

Perfect: A verb form indicating an action or process seen as completed, e.g. 'She *has paid* the bill'. In Russian this is rendered by a perfective past form of the verb, e.g. Онá *оплатила* счёт.

Perfective: see **Aspect**.

Person: Person forms are the grammatical forms (especially **pronouns**) that refer to or agree with the speaker and other individuals addressed or mentioned, e.g. *I, we* (first-person pronouns, Russian *я, мы*), *you* (second-person pronoun, Russian *ты, вы*), *he, she, it, they* (third-person pronouns, Russian *он, онá, онó, онú*).

Personal pronoun: A **pronoun** that refers to a person or to people known to the speaker, e.g. *I, he, she, it, they* (Russian *я, он, онá, онó, онú*).

Phrase: A group of words that function together in a **clause**, e.g. *The courier* is a (noun) phrase within the clause '*The courier* will go there'.

Plural: A word or form referring to more than one person or object, e.g. *children, books, we, are*. Cf. **Singular**.

Plural-only noun: A noun that has the form of a plural but can refer to a singular object or a number of like objects, e.g. *сáнки* 'sledge, sledges'.

Possessive: A pronoun indicating possession, e.g. Russian *мой* 'my, mine', *твой* 'your, yours', *егó* 'his, its', *её* 'her, hers, its', *наш* 'our, ours', *ваш* 'your, yours', *их* 'their, theirs'. Possessives are used both adjectivally (e.g. *наш дом* 'our house') and pronominally (e.g. *Этот дом — наш* 'This house is ours').

Predicate: The part of a clause that states something about the **subject**, e.g. *closed the door softly* in 'Mary *closed the door softly*', or *went home* in 'We *went home*'. Cf. **Subject**.

Predicative adjective: An **adjective** that appears in a separate **phrase** from the noun it modifies, often following the verb 'to be', e.g. *empty* in 'The house was *empty*'. Russian often uses a short-form adjective in such contexts: Дом был *пуст*. Cf. **Attributive adjective**.

Predicative adverb: In Russian, an adverb that is used as a predicate, e.g. *Весело* 'It's fun', Ему *грустно* 'He feels sad'.

Prefix: An element that is added to the beginning of a word to change its meaning or grammatical form, e.g. *mis-* and *re-* in '*mis*understand', '*re*consider', Russian *при-* in *при*бáвить 'to add' and *от-* in *от*платúть 'to pay back'. Cf. **Suffix**.

Preposition: A word governing and usually preceding a noun or pronoun, expressing its relationship to another word in the sentence, e.g. 'She arrived *after* dinner', 'What did you do it *for*?' This relationship can be spatial, e.g. 'The book is *on* the table' (Russian Кнúга *на* столé), temporal, e.g. 'He arrived *in* March' (Russian Он приéхал *в* мáрте), causal, e.g. 'She blushed *with* shame' (Russian Онá покраснéла *от* стыдá), etc. A Russian preposition governs one of the **oblique cases**.

Prepositional: In Russian, the **case** used after certain prepositions, mainly to express location. See also **Locative case**.

Present: The present **tense** is used when the time of the event described includes the time of utterance, e.g. *lives* in 'Peter *lives* in London'. Cf. **Past**.

Progressive: another term for **Continuous**.

Pronoun: A word that substitutes for a noun or noun phrase, e.g. *them* in 'Children don't like *them*' (instead of 'Children don't like *vegetables*'). Cf. Russian Дéти не лю́бят *их* (instead of *овощéй*).

Reflexive pronoun: A pronoun that is the object of the verb, but refers back to the subject of the clause in denoting the same individual, e.g. *herself* in: 'She blamed *herself*'. Russian uses the declinable reflexive pronoun *себя́* in such contexts, e.g. Он смóтрит на *себя́* 'He looks at *himself*', Он купúл *себé* мотоцúкл, 'He bought *himself* a motorcycle', Онá довóльна *собóй* 'She is pleased with *herself*'. Cf. also **Reflexive verb**.

Reflexive verb: In Russian, a verb that ends in the reflexive particle *-ся/ -сь*, e.g. Он одевáется 'He dresses (*himself*)', Я мóюсь 'I wash (*myself*)'.

Regular verb: A verb such as *laugh* whose **inflections** follow one of the usual **conjugation** patterns. In English, this involves (among other things) forming the **past tense** by adding *-ed* to the infinitive, e.g. laugh*ed* in 'They *laughed* at me'. Cf. **Irregular verb**.

Relative clause: A clause that is introduced by a **relative pronoun**.

Relative pronoun: A pronoun (*who*, *whose*, *which*, or *that*) used to introduce a subordinate clause and referring back to a person or thing in the preceding clause, e.g. 'Peter lost the book *that/which* he bought', 'The man *who* is waiting is my brother', or 'Have you met the man *whose* sister got married?' Russian uses the relevant forms of *котóрый*.

Reported speech: another term for **Indirect speech**.

Sentence: A structure with at least one **finite** verb, and consisting of one or more **clauses**, e.g. '*John laughed*', '*John sat down and waited*', '*While waiting for the bus, John saw an accident*'.

Singular: A word or form referring to just one person or thing, e.g. *child*, *book*, *I*, *is*. Cf. **Plural**.

Soft consonant: In Russian, a consonant followed by a soft sign (e.g. *m* in *мать*), or by the vowels *я, е, и, ё*, or *ю* (e.g. *n* in *пять*, *н* in *небо*, *n* in *пиво*, *л* in *лёд*, *m* in *утюг*). The consonants *ч* and *щ* are always pronounced soft, while *ж, ц*, and *ш* are always pronounced hard. Cf. **Hard consonant**.

Spelling rules: In Russian, the following rules:

(a) *ы* is replaced by *и* after г, к, х, ж, ч, ш, and щ.
(b) unstressed *о* is replaced by *е* after ж, ч, ш, щ, and ц.
(c) *ю* and *я* are replaced by *у* and *а* after г, к, х, ж, ч, ш, and щ.
(d) the preposition *о* 'about, concerning' is spelt *об* before words beginning *а, э, и, о*, and *у*, and *обо* before *мне* and *всём/всех*: *обо мне* 'about me', *обо всём* 'about everything', *обо всех* 'about everyone'.

Stem: The base form or root of the word to which **endings**, **prefixes**, and **suffixes** may be added, e.g. *box* in *boxes*, *consider* in 're*consider*' and *understand* in '*understand*ing'. Cf. Russian *книг-* in *книга* 'book', *говор-* in *говорить* 'to speak', and *-ход* in *восход* 'rising', *студент-* in *студентка* 'female student'.

Stress: The **syllable** of a word receiving relatively greater force or emphasis than the other(s) is said to receive stress or to be the stressed syllable, e.g. *window*, *карта* 'map' (stressed on the first syllable), *deduction*, *дорога* 'road' (stressed medially), *suppose*, *страна* 'country' (stressed on the final syllable).

Subject: The part of the **clause** referring to the individual of whom or the object of which the **predicate** is asserted, e.g. *Anna* in: '*Anna* closed the door' or *The picture* in '*The picture* hangs on the wall'. In Russian, the subject usually appears in the nominative case, e.g. *Анна закрыла дверь*, *Картина висит на стене*. Cf. **Predicate**.

Subjunctive: The form of the verb used in some languages when no claim is being made that the action or event actually takes (or took) place. The subjunctive is not often used in English, but can still be seen in expressions like *if I were you*. In Russian, the subjunctive is the structure used when an action is desired. It is formed using *чтобы* + past tense, e.g. *Она хочет, чтобы я ушёл* ('She wants me *to go away*'). Cf. **Indicative**.

Submeanings of the aspects: Aspectual meanings other than those that denote continuous or habitual action or process (imperfective), and those that denote completion (perfective). Submeanings describe intermittent action or process (imperfective *побаливает* 'hurts on and off'), inception (perfective *заплакать* 'to burst into tears'), and short duration (perfective *поспать* 'to have a nap'). Cf. **Aspect**.

Subordinate clause: A clause that cannot normally stand alone without a **main clause** and is usually introduced by a **conjunction**, e.g. *when it rang* in 'She answered the phone *when it rang*', or *because he is ill* in 'He is not at work *because he is ill*'. Cf. **Main clause**.

Suffix: An element that is added to the end of a word or **stem** to change its meaning or grammatical form, e.g. *-ing* and *-ness* in 'understand*ing*', 'kind*ness*', Russian *-ка* in *студентка* 'female student', *-ина* in *глубина* 'depth'. Cf. **Prefix**.

Superlative: The form of an **adjective** or **adverb** used when comparing one thing with another to express the greatest degree of a quality, e.g. *cheapest* (Russian *самый дешёвый*), *most beautiful* (Russian *самый красивый*), *least desirable* (Russian *наименее желательный*). Cf. **Comparative**.

Syllable: A unit of pronunciation that is normally less than a word but greater than a single sound, e.g. *abracadabra* has five syllables: *ab-ra-ca-dab-ra*, as does Russian *путеводи́тель* ('guide'): *пу-те-во-ди́-тель*.

Tense: The relationship between the time of utterance and the time of an event described in the clause is expressed by verb tense forms or **inflections**, e.g. 'Anna *waits*' (present tense, Russian Áнна *ждёт*), 'Anna *waited*' (past tense, Russian Áнна *ждала́*).

Transitive verb: A verb taking a **direct object**, e.g. *read* in 'She *was reading* a book' (Russian Она́ *чита́ла* кни́гу). Cf. **Intransitive verb**.

Verb: A word that expresses an action, process, or state of affairs, e.g. 'He closed the door' (Russian Он *закры́л* дверь), 'She laughs' (Russian Она́ *смеётся*), 'They were at home' (Russian Они́ *бы́ли* до́ма).

Verbal noun: In Russian, a noun derived from a verb stem and describing the action of the verb from which it derives, e.g. *разви́тие* 'development', *приготовле́ние* 'preparation', *обрабо́тка* 'processing'.

Verbs of motion: In Russian, a series of fourteen pairs of imperfective verbs that denote various types of motion, one in each pair (the 'unidirectional') describing movement in one direction (*Он идёт домо́й* 'He is on his way home'), the other (the 'multidirectional') describing movement in general (*Она́ хо́дит бы́стро* 'She walks fast'), movement in various directions (*Он хо́дит взад и вперёд* 'He is walking up and down'), or habitual movement (*Я ча́сто хожу́ в кино́* 'I often go to the cinema').

Vocative: In Russian, the form of a noun used in addressing someone. The nominative case usually fulfils this function: *Серге́й Па́влович!* 'Sergei Pavlovich!', but some truncated forms are used in colloquial Russian, e.g. *мам!* 'Mum!', *Вань!* 'Vanya!' *Бо́же* in *Бо́же мой!* 'My God!' is a relic of the former vocative case (the nominative form being *Бог*).

Voiced and voiceless consonants: Consonants pronounced, respectively, with and without vibration of the vocal cords. In Russian, the voiceless consonants are к, п, с, т, ф, х, ц, ч, ш, and щ. The other consonants are voiced.

Vowel: A basic speech sound that is produced by the unrestricted flow of air, e.g. *a* in h*a*t, *ee* in f*ee*t, or *ow* in h*ow*. A vowel forms the nucleus of a **syllable**. Cf. **Consonant**.

Russian declensions and conjugations

The following is a comprehensive but not exhaustive guide to Russian declension and conjugation.

The vertical line | shows the division between the stem and the ending of a word.

When using these tables, the reader should bear in mind the Spelling Rules (see below), e.g. the nominative plural of книга is книги, and the Notes on the declension of nouns (after Table 17 below).

Spelling Rules

The following Spelling Rules are important because they affect the endings of many nouns, adjectives, and verbs.

1. Unstressed o does not follow ж, ц, ч, ш, or щ; instead, e is used, e.g. с му́жем, шесть, ме́сяцев, с касси́ршей, хоро́шее пальто́.

2. ю and я do not follow г, к, ж, х, ц, ч, ш, or щ; they become у and a, e.g. держа́ть; я держу́, они́ де́ржат; слы́шать: я слы́шу, они́ слы́шат.

3. ы does not follow г, к, ж, х, ч, ш, or щ; it becomes и, e.g. две кни́ги, больши́е дома́.

Nouns

Masculine Nouns

TABLE		Singular	Plural
1	Nominative	авто́бус	авто́бус|ы
	Accusative	авто́бус	авто́бус|ы
	Genitive	авто́бус|а	авто́бус|ов
	Dative	авто́бус|у	авто́бус|ам
	Instrumental	авто́бус|ом	авто́бус|ами
	Prepositional	авто́бус|е	авто́бус|ах

This declension, comprising nouns ending in a hard consonant, is the most common declension for masculine nouns in Russian.

TABLE		Singular	Plural
2	Nominative	трамва́|й	трамва́|и
	Accusative	трамва́|й	трамва́|и
	Genitive	трамва́|я	трамва́|ев
	Dative	трамва́|ю	трамва́|ям
	Instrumental	трамва́|ем	трамва́|ями
	Prepositional	трамва́|е	трамва́|ях

This declension consists of nouns ending in -ай, -ей, -ой, or -уй.

Other common Russian words belonging to this declension are май, сара́й, слу́чай, урожа́й, чай; клей, руче́й, хокке́й, юбиле́й; бой, геро́й; поцелу́й.

TABLE		Singular	Plural
3	Nominative	репортáж	репортáж|и
	Accusative	репортáж	репортáж|и
	Genitive	репортáж|а	репортáж|ей
	Dative	репортáж|у	репортáж|ам
	Instrumental	репортáж|ем	репортáж|ами
	Prepositional	репортáж|е	репортáж|ах

This declension consists of nouns ending in -ж, -ш, or -щ, which are stressed on the stem in oblique cases.

Other nouns of this declension are пейзáж, пляж, фарш, óвощ, and товáрищ.

TABLE		Singular	Plural
4	Nominative	этáж	этаж|и́
	Accusative	этáж	этаж|и́
	Genitive	этаж|á	этаж|éй
	Dative	этаж|у́	этаж|áм
	Instrumental	этаж|óм	этаж|áми
	Prepositional	этаж|é	этаж|áх

These nouns differ from those in Table 3 by being stressed on the ending rather than on the stem in oblique cases; in the instrumental singular they end in -óм instead of -ем.

Other such nouns are багáж, борщ, карандáш, нож, and плащ.

TABLE		Singular	Plural
5	Nominative	сценáри|й	сценáри|и
	Accusative	сценáри|й	сценáри|и
	Genitive	сценáри|я	сценáри|ев
	Dative	сценáри|ю	сценáри|ям
	Instrumental	сценáри|ем	сценáри|ями
	Prepositional	сценáри|и	сценáри|ях

Nouns belonging to this declension tend to be obscure or technical terms. One fairly common word is гéний, meaning 'genius'.

TABLE		Singular	Plural
6	Nominative	спектáкл|ь	спектáкл|и
	Accusative	спектáкл|ь	спектáкл|и
	Genitive	спектáкл|я	спектáкл|ей
	Dative	спектáкл|ю	спектáкл|ям
	Instrumental	спектáкл|ем	спектáкл|ями
	Prepositional	спектáкл|е	спектáкл|ях

Masculine nouns ending in a soft sign belong to this declension. Other common words belonging to this group are автомобúль, апрéль (and other names of months), Кремль, портфéль, рубль, and словáрь.

Feminine nouns

TABLE		Singular	Plural
7	Nominative	газе́т|а	газе́т|ы
	Accusative	газе́т|у	газе́т|ы
	Genitive	газе́т|ы	газе́т
	Dative	газе́т|е	газе́т|ам
	Instrumental	газе́т|ой	газе́т|ами
	Prepositional	газе́т|е	газе́т|ах

This is the most common declension for feminine nouns in Russian. A few masculine nouns, e.g. де́душка, мужчи́на, and па́па, also belong to this declension.

Remember the Spelling Rules, whereby ы and unstressed o do not follow certain letters (see p. 838), e.g. кни́ги (*books*), афи́ши (*posters*), с учени́цей (*with the pupil*).

TABLE		Singular	Plural
8	Nominative	неде́л|я	неде́л|и
	Accusative	неде́л|ю	неде́л|и
	Genitive	неде́л|и	неде́л|ь
	Dative	неде́л|е	неде́л|ям
	Instrumental	неде́л|ей	неде́л|ями
	Prepositional	неде́л|е	неде́л|ях

This declension is for feminine nouns ending in a consonant + -я. A few masculine nouns also belong to this declension, e.g. дя́дя, судья́. Other feminine nouns of this declension are ба́шня, дере́вня, пе́сня, спа́льня, and ту́фля. Some nouns of this declension have a genitive plural form ending in -ей, e.g. дя́дя, семья́, and тётя. This is indicated at the dictionary entries.

TABLE		Singular	Plural
9	Nominative	ста́нци|я	ста́нци|и
	Accusative	ста́нци|ю	ста́нци|и
	Genitive	ста́нци|и	ста́нци|й
	Dative	ста́нци|и	ста́нци|ям
	Instrumental	ста́нци|ей	ста́нци|ями
	Prepositional	ста́нци|и	ста́нци|ях

This declension consists of feminine nouns ending in -ия. Other nouns of this declension are а́рмия, исто́рия, ли́ния, организа́ция, фами́лия, and the names of most countries.

TABLE		Singular	Plural
10	Nominative	галере́|я	галере́|и
	Accusative	галере́|ю	галере́|и
	Genitive	галере́|и	галере́|й
	Dative	галере́|е	галере́|ям
	Instrumental	галере́|ей	галере́|ями
	Prepositional	галере́|е	галере́|ях

This declension consists of feminine nouns ending in -ея or -уя. Other such nouns are алле́я, батаре́я, иде́я, ше́я, and ста́туя.

TABLE		Singular	Plural
11	Nominative	бол|ь	бóл|и
	Accusative	бол|ь	бóл|и
	Genitive	бóл|и	бóл|ей
	Dative	бóл|и	бóл|ям
	Instrumental	бóл|ью	бóл|ями
	Prepositional	бóл|и	бóл|ях

This declension is for feminine nouns ending in -ь. Other such nouns are жизнь, кровáть, мéбель, плóщадь, постéль, тетрáдь, and the numbers ending in -ь.

Neuter Nouns

TABLE		Singular	Plural
12	Nominative	чýвств|о	чýвств|а
	Accusative	чýвств|о	чýвств|а
	Genitive	чýвств|а	чувств
	Dative	чýвств|у	чýвств|ам
	Instrumental	чýвств|ом	чýвств|ами
	Prepositional	чýвств|е	чýвств|ах

This declension is for neuter nouns ending in -o. Other such nouns are блюдо, мáсло, молокó, пи́во, and слóво.

TABLE		Singular	Plural
13	Nominative	учи́лищ|е	учи́лищ|а
	Accusative	учи́лищ|е	учи́лищ|а
	Genitive	учи́лищ|а	учи́лищ
	Dative	учи́лищ|у	учи́лищ|ам
	Instrumental	учи́лищ|ем	учи́лищ|ами
	Prepositional	учи́лищ|е	учи́лищ|ах

This declension is for neuter nouns ending in -ще or -це. Other nouns of this declension are клáдбище, полотéнце, and сóлнце.

TABLE		Singular	Plural
14	Nominative	здáни|е	здáни|я
	Accusative	здáни|е	здáни|я
	Genitive	здáни|я	здáни|й
	Dative	здáни|ю	здáни|ям
	Instrumental	здáни|ем	здáни|ями
	Prepositional	здáни|и	здáни|ях

This declension is for neuter nouns ending in -ие. Other such nouns are внимáние, путешéствие, and удивлéние.

TABLE		Singular	Plural
15	Nominative	воскресéн|ье	воскресéн|ья
	Accusative	воскресéн|ье	воскресéн|ья
	Genitive	воскресéн|ья	воскресéн|ий
	Dative	воскресéн|ью	воскресéн|ьям
	Instrumental	воскресéн|ьем	воскресéн|ьями
	Prepositional	воскресéн|ье	воскресéн|ьях

This declension is for neuter nouns ending in -ье or -ьё. Other such nouns are варéнье, сидéнье, and счáстье.

TABLE		Singular	Plural
16	Nominative	мо́р|е	мор|я́
	Accusative	мо́р|е	мор|я́
	Genitive	мо́р|я	мор|е́й
	Dative	мо́р|ю	мор|я́м
	Instrumental	мо́р|ем	мор|я́ми
	Prepositional	мо́р|е	мор|я́х

This declension is for neuter nouns ending in a consonant + -e, but not -ще or -це. In practice, the only other two nouns of this declension are го́ре and по́ле.

TABLE		Singular	Plural
17	Nominative	вре́м|я	врем|ена́
	Accusative	вре́м|я	врем|ена́
	Genitive	вре́м|ени	врем|ён
	Dative	вре́м|ени	врем|ена́м
	Instrumental	вре́м|енем	врем|ена́ми
	Prepositional	вре́м|ени	врем|ена́х

This declension is for a small number of neuter nouns ending in -мя. Others belonging to this group are и́мя, пла́мя, and се́мя.

Notes on the declension of nouns

The accusative ending for masculine singular animate and all plural animate nouns (those denoting living beings) coincides with the genitive ending, e.g.

он уви́дел большо́го чёрного во́лка (he saw a big black wolf)
мы попроси́ли свои́х друзе́й помо́чь (we asked our friends to help)

Some masculine nouns take the ending -у́ or -ю́ in the prepositional singular after в and на, e.g. в лесу́, на мосту́; some feminine nouns ending in -ь take -и́, e.g. в тени́. They are said to be in the locative case. Where this happens it is shown at the dictionary entry.

Some masculine nouns have the ending -a in the nominative plural, e.g. па́спорт, бе́рег. Others have the ending -ья, e.g. брат, стул. Where this happens it is shown at the dictionary entry.

Some nouns are indeclinable. They usually end in a vowel, are neuter, and have been borrowed into Russian from another language. Examples are кафе́, ра́дио, такси́.

Many nouns change their stress in declension. This is shown in the individual dictionary entries.

Verbs

The -e- conjugation

чита́\|ть:

TABLE		Singular	Plural
18	1st person	чита́|ю	чита́|ем
	2nd person	чита́|ешь	чита́|ете
	3rd person	чита́|ет	чита́|ют

сия|ть:

TABLE		Singular	Plural
19	1st person	сия|ю	сия|ем
	2nd person	сия|ешь	сия|ете
	3rd person	сия|ет	сия|ют

Verbs of this type differ from those belonging to Table 18 only by having a я at the end of the stem, instead of an a.

проб|овать:

TABLE		Singular	Plural
20	1st person	проб|ую	проб|уем
	2nd person	проб|уешь	проб|уете
	3rd person	проб|ует	проб|уют

The verbs of this conjugation are not stressed on the suffix -овать.

рис|ова́ть:

TABLE		Singular	Plural
21	1st person	рис|у́ю	рис|у́ем
	2nd person	рис|у́ешь	рис|у́ете
	3rd person	рис|у́ет	рис|у́ют

Verbs of this conjugation differ from those belonging to Table 20 only in having the stress on the suffix rather than on the stem.

Note: The conjugation of other -e- conjugation verbs (those ending in -ать, -еть, -нуть, and -ять) is given in the dictionary entries.

The -i- conjugation

говор|и́ть:

TABLE		Singular	Plural
22	1st person	говор|ю́	говор|и́м
	2nd person	говор|и́шь	говор|и́те
	3rd person	говор|и́т	говор|я́т

стро́|ить:

TABLE		Singular	Plural
23	1st person	стро́|ю	стро́|им
	2nd person	стро́|ишь	стро́|ите
	3rd person	стро́|ит	стро́|ят

Verbs of this conjugation differ from those belonging to Table 22 by ending in a vowel + -ить. Other examples are кле́ить, сто́ить.

Note: The conjugation of other -i- conjugation verbs (those ending in -ать, -еть, and -ять) is given in the dictionary entries.

In addition, where the stem of a verb ends in б, п, м, в, or ф, and an л is inserted before the ending of the first person singular, this is shown in the dictionary entries (e.g. люби́ть: я люблю́; спать: я сплю).

Also, where the consonant at the end of the stem changes in the first person singular, this is shown in the dictionary entries (e.g. ви́деть: я ви́жу; плати́ть: я плачу́; спроси́ть: я спрошу́).

Adjectives

TABLE 24a	Singular			Plural
	Masculine	Feminine	Neuter	
Nominative	краси́в|ый	краси́в|ая	краси́в|ое	краси́в|ые
Accusative	краси́в|ый	краси́в|ую	краси́в|ое	краси́в|ые
Genitive	краси́в|ого	краси́в|ой	краси́в|ого	краси́в|ых
Dative	краси́в|ому	краси́в|ой	краси́в|ому	краси́в|ым
Instrumental	краси́в|ым	краси́в|ой	краси́в|ым	краси́в|ыми
Prepositional	краси́в|ом	краси́в|ой	краси́в|ом	краси́в|ых

Note: The words кото́рый and како́й decline like краси́вый, as do the ordinal numbers пе́рвый, второ́й, etc. Note that тре́тий has 'soft' endings and inserts a soft sign (-тья, -тье, -тьи).

Soft Adjectives

TABLE 24b	Singular			Plural
	Masculine	Feminine	Neuter	
Nominative	си́н|ий	си́н|яя	си́н|ее	си́н|ие
Accusative	си́н|ий	си́н|юю	си́н|ее	си́н|ие
Genitive	си́н|его	си́н|ей	си́н|его	си́н|их
Dative	си́н|ему	си́н|ей	си́н|ему	си́н|им
Instrumental	си́н|им	си́н|ей	си́н|им	си́н|ими
Prepositional	си́н|ем	си́н|ей	си́н|ем	си́н|их

Determiners/pronouns

мой (and similarly твой, свой):

TABLE 25	Singular			Plural
	Masculine	Feminine	Neuter	
Nominative	мой	моя́	моё	мои́
Accusative	мой	мою́	моё	мои́
Genitive	моего́	мое́й	моего́	мои́х
Dative	моему́	мое́й	моему́	мои́м
Instrumental	мои́м	мое́й	мои́м	мои́ми
Prepositional	моём	мое́й	моём	мои́х

наш (and similarly ваш)

	Singular			Plural
	Masculine	Feminine	Neuter	
Nominative	наш	на́ша	на́ше	на́ши
Accusative	наш	на́шу	на́ше	на́ши
Genitive	на́шего	на́шей	на́шего	на́ших
Dative	на́шему	на́шей	на́шему	на́шим
Instrumental	на́шим	на́шей	на́шим	на́шими
Prepositional	на́шем	на́шей	на́шем	на́ших

The other possessive determiners, его́, её, and их, are indeclinable.

э́тот:

TABLE 26	Singular			Plural
	Masculine	**Feminine**	**Neuter**	
Nominative	э́тот	э́та	э́то	э́ти
Accusative	э́тот	э́ту	э́то	э́ти
Genitive	э́того	э́той	э́того	э́тих
Dative	э́тому	э́той	э́тому	э́тим
Instrumental	э́тим	э́той	э́тим	э́тими
Prepositional	э́том	э́той	э́том	э́тих

сам, the emphatic pronoun, declines like э́тот and is stressed on the final syllable.

тот:

	Singular			Plural
	Masculine	**Feminine**	**Neuter**	
Nominative	тот	та	то	те
Accusative	тот	ту	то	те
Genitive	того́	той	того́	тех
Dative	тому́	той	тому́	тем
Instrumental	тем	той	тем	те́ми
Prepositional	том	той	том	тех

весь:

TABLE 27	Singular			Plural
	Masculine	**Feminine**	**Neuter**	
Nominative	весь	вся	всё	все
Accusative	весь	всю	всё	все
Genitive	всего́	всей	всего́	всех
Dative	всему́	всей	всему́	всем
Instrumental	всем	всей	всем	все́ми
Prepositional	всём	всей	всём	всех

Numbers

28

Cardinal Numbers		Ordinal Numbers	
one	оди́н/одна́/одно́	first	пе́рвый
two	два/две	second	второ́й
three	три	third	тре́тий
four	четы́ре	fourth	четвёртый
five	пять	fifth	пя́тый
six	шесть	sixth	шесто́й
seven	семь	seventh	седьмо́й
eight	во́семь	eighth	восьмо́й
nine	де́вять	ninth	девя́тый
ten	де́сять	tenth	деся́тый
eleven	оди́ннадцать	eleventh	оди́ннадцатый
twelve	двена́дцать	twelfth	двена́дцатый
thirteen	трина́дцать	thirteenth	трина́дцатый
fourteen	четы́рнадцать	fourteenth	четы́рнадцатый
fifteen	пятна́дцать	fifteenth	пятна́дцатый
sixteen	шестна́дцать	sixteenth	шестна́дцатый
seventeen	семна́дцать	seventeenth	семна́дцатый
eighteen	восемна́дцать	eighteenth	восемна́дцатый
nineteen	девятна́дцать	nineteenth	девятна́дцатый
twenty	два́дцать	twentieth	двадца́тый
twenty-one	два́дцать оди́н/одна́/одно́	twenty-first	два́дцать пе́рвый
twenty-two	два́дцать два/две	twenty-second	два́дцать второ́й
twenty-three	два́дцать три	twenty-third	два́дцать тре́тий
thirty	три́дцать	thirtieth	тридца́тый
forty	со́рок	fortieth	сороково́й
fifty	пятьдеся́т	fiftieth	пятидеся́тый
sixty	шестьдеся́т	sixtieth	шестидеся́тый
seventy	се́мьдесят	seventieth	семидеся́тый
eighty	во́семьдесят	eightieth	восьмидеся́тый
ninety	девяно́сто	nintieth	девяно́стый
hundred	сто	hundredth	со́тый
hundred and one	сто оди́н/одна́/одно́	hundred-and-first	сто пе́рвый
two hundred	две́сти	two-hundredth	двухсо́тый
three hundred	три́ста	three-hundredth	трёхсо́тый
four hundred	четы́реста	four-hundredth	четырёхсо́тый
five hundred	пятьсо́т	five-hundredth	пятисо́тый
six hundred	шестьсо́т	six-hundredth	шестисо́тый
thousand	ты́сяча	thousandth	ты́сячный
million	миллио́н	millionth	миллио́нный

оди́н:

29

	Singular			Plural
	Masculine	Feminine	Neuter	
Nominative	оди́н	одна́	одно́	одни́
Accusative	оди́н	одну́	одно́	одни́
Genitive	одного́	одно́й	одного́	одни́х
Dative	одному́	одно́й	одному́	одни́м
Instrumental	одни́м	одно́й	одни́м	одни́ми
Prepositional	одно́м	одно́й	одно́м	одни́х

For the declension of other numbers, see the dictionary entries.

Russian verbs

(a) The verb list contains examples of:

    (i)   verbs in **-чь** (e.g. бере́чь)

    (ii)   verbs in **-ти** (e.g. вести́)

    (iii)   verbs in **-сть** (e.g. сесть)

    (iv)   verbs in **-оть** (e.g. боро́ться)

    (v)   verbs in **-ереть** (e.g. запере́ть)

    (vi)   verbs in **-овать** and **-евать** (e.g. бесе́довать, воева́ть)

    (vii) verbs (first conjugation) with consonant change (e.g. писа́ть)

    (viii) verbs (second conjugation) with consonant change (e.g. бро́сить)

    (ix)   second-conjugation verbs in **-ать/-ять** (e.g. стуча́ть, стоя́ть)

    (x)   first- and second-conjugation verbs in **-еть** (e.g. име́ть, горе́ть)

    (xi)   monosyllabic verbs (e.g. брать)

    (xii) irregular verbs (e.g. хоте́ть)

(b) Most verbs listed are non-derivative (e.g. дать). Compound verbs are not normally given when a root verb is available (дать 'to give' appears, but not прода́ть 'to sell' or зада́ть 'to ask [a question]'). Some compounds have no commonly-used root verb, in which case a hyphenated root is given (e.g. -каза́ть).

(c) Also listed are verbs that have no -л in the masculine past (e.g. везти́ 'to convey', masculine past вёз).

(d) The pattern of presentation is:

    (i)   for all verbs: present or future conjugation, and meaning; the verb's other aspect (if available)

    (ii)   for selected verbs: the past tense; the government of the verb; the imperative; short forms of the perfective passive participle.

Note: Absence of a first-person singular form indicates that none exists, or that none exists in the meaning given (see, for example, греме́ть 'to thunder').

бежа́ть/по- 'to run': бегу́ бежи́шь бежи́т бежи́м бежи́те бегу́т; беги́!

бере́чь/по- 'to take care of': берегу́ бережёт берегу́т; берёг берегла́; береги́!

бесе́довать 'to converse': бесе́дую бесе́дует бесе́дуют

бить/по- 'to strike': бью бьёт бьют; бей!

бледне́ть/по- 'to grow pale': бледне́ю бледне́ет бледне́ют

блесте́ть 'to shine': блещу́ блести́т блестя́т; *pf.* **блесну́ть**

боле́ть (+ *i.*) 'to be ill (with)': боле́ю боле́ет боле́ют

боле́ть 'to hurt' (*intrans.*): боли́т боля́т

боро́ться (за + *a.*) 'to struggle (for)': борю́сь бо́рется бо́рются; бори́сь!

боя́ться (+ *g.*) 'to fear': бою́сь бои́тся боя́тся; (не) бо́йся!

брать 'to take': беру́ берёт беру́т; брал брала́ бра́ло; бери́!; *pf.* **взять**

бри́ться/по- 'to shave' (*intrans.*): бре́юсь бре́ется бре́ются

бро́сить 'to throw': бро́шу бро́сит бро́сят; брось!; бро́шен; *impf.* **броса́ть**

буди́ть/раз- 'to awaken' (*trans.*): бужу́ бу́дит бу́дят; буди́!; разбу́жен

быть 'to be': бу́ду бу́дет бу́дут; был была́ бы́ло; будь!

везти́ 'to convey': везу́ везёт везу́т; вёз везла́

ве́сить 'to weigh' : ве́шу ве́сит ве́сят

вести́ 'to lead': веду́ ведёт веду́т; вёл вела́

взять 'to take': возьму́ возьмёт возьму́т; взял взяла́ взя́ло; возьми́!; взят взята́ взя́то; *impf.* **брать**

ви́деть/у- 'to see': ви́жу ви́дит ви́дят

висе́ть 'to hang' (*intrans.*): вишу́ виси́т вися́т

владе́ть (+ *i.*) 'to own': владе́ю владе́ет владе́ют

влечь 'to attract': влеку́ влечёт влеку́т; влёк влекла́; -влечён -влечена́ (*in compounds*)

води́ть 'to lead': вожу́ во́дит во́дят

воева́ть 'to wage war': вою́ю вою́ет вою́ют

возврати́ться 'to return' (*intrans.*): возвращу́сь возврати́тся возвратя́тся; *impf.* **возвраща́ться**

вози́ть 'to convey': вожу́ во́зит во́зят

возни́кнуть 'to arise': возни́кну возни́кнет возни́кнут; возни́к возни́кла; *impf.* **возника́ть**

волнова́ться/вз- 'to be excited': волну́юсь волну́ется волну́ются; (не) волну́йся!

врать/на- or **со-** 'to tell lies': вру врёт врут; врал врала́ вра́ло; (не) ври!

встава́ть 'to get up, stand up': встаю́ встаёт встаю́т; встава́й!; *pf.* **встать**

встать 'to get up, stand up': вста́ну вста́нет вста́нут; встань!; *impf.* **встава́ть**

встре́тить 'to meet': встре́чу встре́тит встре́тят; *impf.* **встреча́ть**

вы́глядеть (+ *i.*) 'to look, appear': вы́гляжу вы́глядит вы́глядят

вы́разить 'to express': вы́ражу вы́разит вы́разят; вы́ражен; *impf.* **выража́ть**

вяза́ть/с- 'to tie': вяжу́ вя́жет вя́жут; -вя́зан (*in compounds*)

гаси́ть/за- or **по-** 'to extinguish': гашу́ га́сит га́сят; зага́шен/пога́шен

ги́бнуть/по- 'to perish': ги́бну ги́бнет ги́бнут; гиб/ги́бнул ги́бла

гла́дить/вы́- or **по-** 'to iron': гла́жу гла́дит гла́дят; вы́глажен

гляде́ть (на + *a.*) 'to look (at)': гляжу́ гляди́т глядя́т; *pf.* **гля́нуть**

гна́ться (за + *i.*) 'to chase (after)': гоню́сь го́нится го́нятся; гна́лся гнала́сь

годи́ться (в + *a.*) 'to be fit (for)': гожу́сь годи́тся годя́тся

голосова́ть/про- (за + *a.*) 'to vote (for)': голосу́ю голосу́ет голосу́ют

горди́ться (+ *i.*) 'to be proud of': горжу́сь горди́тся гордя́тся; горди́сь!

горе́ть/с- 'to burn' (*intrans.*): гори́т горя́т

гото́вить/при- 'to prepare': гото́влю гото́вит гото́вят; гото́вь!; пригото́влен

греме́ть/про- 'to thunder': греми́т гремя́т

греть 'to heat': гре́ю гре́ет гре́ют; -грет (*in compounds*)

грози́ть/при- (+ *d.*) 'to threaten': грожу́ грози́т грозя́т

грузи́ть/по- 'to load': гружу́ гру́зит гру́зят; погру́жен

дава́ть 'to give': даю́ даёт даю́т; дава́й!; *pf.* **дать**

дави́ть (на + *a.*) 'to press (upon)': давлю́ да́вит да́вят; -давлен (*in compounds*)

дать 'to give': дам дашь даст дади́м дади́те даду́т; дал дала́ да́ло; дай!; дан дана́; *impf.* **дава́ть**

де́йствовать 'to act': де́йствую де́йствует де́йствуют; де́йствуй!

держа́ть 'to hold': держу́ де́ржит де́ржат; держи́!; -держан (*in compounds*)

доба́вить 'to add': доба́влю доба́вит доба́вят; доба́вь!; доба́влен; *impf.* **добавля́ть**

дости́гнуть (+ *g.*) 'to achieve': дости́гну дости́гнет дости́гнут; дости́г дости́гла; дости́гнут; *impf.* **достига́ть**

дрема́ть 'to doze': дремлю́ дре́млет дре́млют

дрожа́ть 'to tremble': дрожу́ дрожи́т дрожа́т; *pf.* **дро́гнуть**

дуть 'to blow': ду́ю ду́ет ду́ют; *pf.* **ду́нуть**

дыша́ть 'to breathe': дышу́ ды́шит ды́шат

е́здить 'to travel': е́зжу е́здит е́здят; е́зди!

есть/съ- 'to eat': ем ешь ест еди́м еди́те едя́т; ешь!; съе́ден

е́хать/по- 'to travel': е́ду е́дет е́дут; поезжа́й!

жале́ть/по- 'to pity': жале́ю жале́ст жале́ют

жа́ловаться/по- (на + *a.*) 'to complain (of, about)': жа́луюсь жа́луется жа́луются

жать 'to press, squeeze': жму жмёт жмут; жми!; -жат (*in compounds*)

ждать/подо- (+ *a./g.*) 'to wait (for)': жду ждёт ждут; ждал ждала́ жда́ло; жди!

жева́ть 'to chew': жую́ жуёт жую́т

же́ртвовать/по- (+ *i.*) 'to sacrifice': же́ртвую же́ртвует же́ртвуют

жечь/с- 'to burn' (*trans.*): жгу жжёт жгут; жёг жгла; жги!; -жжён -жжена́ (*in compounds*)

жить 'to live': живу́ живёт живу́т; жил жила́ жи́ло

забо́титься/по- (о + *p.*) 'to care about': забо́чусь забо́тится забо́тятся

забы́ть 'to forget': забу́ду забу́дет забу́дут; (не) забу́дь!; забы́т; *impf.* **забыва́ть**

заве́довать (+ *i.*) 'to be in charge of': заве́дую заве́дует заве́дуют

зави́довать/по- (+ *d.*) 'to envy': зави́дую зави́дует зави́дуют

зави́сеть (от + *g.*) 'to depend (on)': зави́шу зави́сит зави́сят

закры́ть 'to shut': закро́ю закро́ет закро́ют; закро́й!; закры́т; *impf.* **закрыва́ть**

замёрзнуть 'to freeze' (*intrans.*): замёрзну замёрзнет замёрзнут; замёрз замёрзла; *impf.* **замерза́ть**

заме́тить 'to notice': заме́чу заме́тит заме́тят; заме́чен; *impf.* **замеча́ть**

заня́ть 'to occupy': займу́ займёт займу́т; за́нял заняла́ за́няло; займи́!; за́нят занята́ за́нято; *impf.* **занима́ть**

запере́ть 'to lock': запру́ запрёт запру́т; за́пер заперла́ за́перло; запри́!; за́перт заперта́ за́перто; *impf.* **запира́ть**

запрети́ть 'to forbid': запрещу́ запрети́шь запретя́т; запрещён запрещена́; *impf.* **запреща́ть**

заряди́ть 'to load, charge': заряжу́ заряди́шь заря́дят; заряжён заряжена́; *impf.* **заряжа́ть**

захвати́ть 'to seize': захвачу́ захва́тит захва́тят; захва́чен; *impf.* **захва́тывать**

защити́ть (от + g.) 'to defend (from)': защищу́ защити́шь защитя́т; защищён защищена́; *impf.* **защища́ть**

заяви́ть 'to declare': заявлю́ зая́вит зая́вят; зая́влен; *impf.* **заявля́ть**

звать/по- 'to call': зову́ зовёт зову́т; звал звала́ зва́ло; зови́!; -зван (*in compounds*)

звуча́ть 'to sound': звучи́т звуча́т

знако́миться/по- (c + i.) 'to become acquainted (with)': знако́млюсь знако́мится знако́мятся; знако́мься!

идти́ 'to go': иду́ идёт иду́т; шёл шла; иди́!

изобрести́ 'to invent': изобрету́ изобретёт изобрету́т; изобрёл изобрела́; изобретён изобретена́; *impf.* **изобрета́ть**

име́ть 'to have': име́ю име́ет име́ют

интересова́ться (+ i.) 'to be interested in': интересу́юсь интересу́ется интересу́ются

иска́ть (+ a./g.) 'to look for': ищу́ и́щет и́щут; ищи́!

испо́льзовать 'to use' (*impf. and pf.*): испо́льзую испо́льзует испо́льзуют; испо́льзуй!; испо́льзован

иссле́довать 'to investigate' (*impf. and pf.*): иссле́дую иссле́дует иссле́дуют; иссле́дован

исче́знуть 'to disappear': исче́зну исче́знет исче́знут; исче́з исче́зла; *impf.* **исчеза́ть**

-каза́ть (*only in compounds*): -кажу́ -ка́жет -ка́жут; -кажи́!; -ка́зан; *impf.* **-ка́зывать**

каза́ться/по- (+ i.) 'to seem': кажу́сь ка́жется ка́жутся

кати́ть 'to roll' (*trans.*): качу́ ка́тит ка́тят

ка́шлять 'to cough': ка́шляю ка́шляет ка́шляют; *pf.* **ка́шлянуть**

кипе́ть/вс- 'to boil' (*intrans.*): киплю́ (*in figurative sense only*) кипи́т кипя́т

класть 'to place': кладу́ кладёт кладу́т; клади́!; *pf.* **положи́ть**

колеба́ться/по- 'to hesitate': коле́блюсь коле́блется коле́блются

кома́ндовать (+ i.) 'to command': кома́ндую кома́ндует кома́ндуют

корми́ть/на- 'to feed': кормлю́ ко́рмит ко́рмят; нако́рмлен

кра́сить/вы́- or **по-** 'to paint': кра́шу кра́сит кра́сят; вы́крашен

красне́ть/по- 'to blush': красне́ю красне́ет красне́ют

красть/у- 'to steal': краду́ крадёт краду́т; укра́ден

кре́пнуть/о- 'to get stronger': кре́пну кре́пнет кре́пнут; креп кре́пла

крича́ть 'to shout': кричу́ кричи́т крича́т; кричи́!; *pf.* **кри́кнуть**

купи́ть 'to buy': куплю́ ку́пит ку́пят; купи́!; ку́плен; *impf.* **покупа́ть**

ла́зить 'to climb': ла́жу ла́зит ла́зят; (не) лазь!

лгать/со- or **на-** 'to tell lies': лгу лжёт лгут; лгал, лгала́, лга́ло; (не) лги!

лежа́ть 'to lie': лежу́ лежи́т лежа́т

лезть 'to climb': ле́зу ле́зет ле́зут; лез ле́зла; лезь!

лете́ть 'to fly': лечу́ лети́т летя́т

лечь 'to lie down': ля́гу ля́жет ля́гут; лёг легла́; ляг!; *impf.* **ложи́ться**

лиза́ть 'to lick': лижу́ ли́жет ли́жут; *pf.* **лизну́ть**

лить 'to pour': лью льёт льют; лил лила́ ли́ло; лей!; -лит (*in compounds*)

лови́ть 'to catch': ловлю́ ло́вит ло́вят; *pf.* **пойма́ть**

люби́ть 'to like, love': люблю́ лю́бит лю́бят

любова́ться/по- (+ *i. or* на + *a.*) 'to admire': любу́юсь любу́ется любу́ются

маха́ть (+ *i.*) 'to wave': машу́ ма́шет ма́шут; *pf.* **махну́ть**

мести́/под- 'to sweep': мету́ метёт мету́т; мёл мела́; подметён подметена́

молча́ть 'to be silent': молчу́ молчи́т молча́т; молчи́!

мочь/с- 'to be able': могу́ мо́жет мо́гут; мог могла́

мча́ться 'to race': мчусь мчи́тся мча́тся; мчись!

мы́ться/вы́- *or* **по-** 'to wash' (*intrans.*): мо́юсь мо́ется мо́ются; мо́йся!

награди́ть (за + *a.*) 'to reward (for)': награжу́ награди́т наградя́т; награждён награждена́; *impf.* **награжда́ть**

наде́ть 'to put on': наде́ну наде́нет наде́нут; наде́нь!; *impf.* **надева́ть**

наде́яться/по- (на + *a.*) 'to hope (for)': наде́юсь наде́ется наде́ются

назва́ть 'to name': назову́ назовёт назову́т; назва́л назвала́ назва́ло; на́зван; *impf.* **называ́ть**

найти́ 'to find': найду́ найдёт найду́т; нашёл нашла́; на́йден; *impf.* **находи́ть**

напа́сть (на + *a.*) 'to attack': нападу́ нападёт нападу́т; *impf.* **напада́ть**

находи́ть 'to find': нахожу́ нахо́дит нахо́дят; *pf.* **найти́**

находи́ться 'to be situated': нахожу́сь нахо́дится нахо́дятся

нача́ть 'to begin' (*trans.*): начну́ начнёт начну́т; на́чал начала́ на́чало; начни́!; на́чат начата́ на́чато; *impf.* **начина́ть**

нача́ться 'to begin' (*intrans.*): начнётся начну́тся; начался́ начала́сь; *impf.* **начина́ться**

ненави́деть 'to hate': ненави́жу ненави́дит ненави́дят

нести́ 'to carry': несу́ несёт несу́т; нёс несла́; неси́!

носи́ть 'to carry': ношу́ но́сит но́сят

ночева́ть/пере- 'to spend the night': ночу́ю ночу́ет ночу́ют

нра́виться/по- (+ *d.*) 'to please': нра́влюсь нра́вится нра́вятся

оби́деть 'to offend': оби́жу оби́дит оби́дят; оби́жен; *impf.* **обижа́ть**

обня́ть 'to embrace': обниму́ обни́мет обни́мут; о́бнял обняла́ о́бняло; обними́!; *impf.* **обнима́ть**

обогна́ть 'to overtake, outstrip': обгоню́ обго́нит обго́нят; обогна́л обогнала́ обогна́ло; *impf.* **обгоня́ть**

образова́ть 'to form' (*impf. and pf.*): образу́ю образу́ет образу́ют; образо́ван; *impf. also* **образо́вывать**

обрати́ться (к + *d.*) 'to turn (to)': обращу́сь обрати́тся обратя́тся; обрати́сь!; *impf.* **обраща́ться**

обсуди́ть 'to discuss': обсужу́ обсу́дит обсу́дят; обсуждён обсуждена́; *impf.* **обсужда́ть**

оде́ться 'to dress' (*intrans.*): оде́нусь оде́нется оде́нутся; оде́нься! *impf.* **одева́ться**

организова́ть 'to organize' (*impf. and pf.*): организу́ю организу́ет организу́ют; организо́ван

освети́ть 'to illuminate': освещу́ освети́т осветя́т; освещён освещена́; *impf.* **освеща́ть**

освободи́ть 'to free': освобожу́ освободи́т освободя́т; освобождён освобождена́; *impf.* **освобожда́ть**

остава́ться 'to remain': остаю́сь остаётся остаю́тся; остава́йся!; *pf.* **оста́ться**

останови́ться 'to stop' (*intrans.*):
остановлю́сь остано́вится остано́вятся;
останови́сь!; *impf.* **остана́вливаться**

оста́ться 'to remain': оста́нусь
оста́нется оста́нутся; оста́нься! *impf.*
остава́ться

отве́тить (на + *a.*) 'to answer':
отве́чу отве́тит отве́тят; отве́ть!; *impf.*
отвеча́ть

откры́ть 'to open' (*trans.*): откро́ю
откро́ет откро́ют; откро́й!; откры́т;
impf. **открыва́ть**

отня́ть 'to take away': отниму́ отни́мет
отни́мут; о́тнял отняла́ о́тняло; отними́!;
impf. **отнима́ть**

отпере́ть 'to unlock': отопру́ отопрёт
отопру́т; отопри́!; о́тпер отперла́
о́тперло; о́тперт отперта́ о́тперто; *impf.*
отпира́ть

ошиби́ться 'to make a mistake':
ошибу́сь ошибётся ошибу́тся; оши́бся
оши́блась; *impf.* **ошиба́ться**

па́хнуть (+ *i.*) 'to smell (of)': па́хнет
па́хнут; пах па́хла

перестава́ть 'to stop' (*intrans.*):
перестаю́ перестаёт перестаю́т; *pf.*
переста́ть

переста́ть 'to stop' (*intrans.*):
переста́ну переста́нешь переста́нут;
переста́нь!; *impf.* **перестава́ть**

петь/с- 'to sing': пою́ поёт пою́т; пой!

печь/ис- 'to bake': пеку́ печёт пеку́т;
пёк пекла́; испечён испечена́

писа́ть/на- 'to write': пишу́ пи́шет
пи́шут; пиши́!; напи́сан

пить/вы́- 'to drink': пью пьёт пьют;
пил, пила́, пи́ло; пей!; вы́пит

пла́кать 'to weep': пла́чу пла́чет
пла́чут; (не) плачь!

плати́ть/за- (за + *a.*) 'to pay (for)':
плачу́ пла́тит пла́тят; плати́!; запла́чен

плева́ть 'to spit': плюю́ плюёт плюю́т;
pf. **плю́нуть**

плыть 'to swim': плыву́ плывёт
плыву́т; плыл плыла́ плы́ло

победи́ть 'to win': победи́т победя́т;
побеждён побеждена́; *impf.* **побежда́ть**

подве́ргнуть (+ *d.*) 'to subject (to)':
подве́ргну подве́ргнет подве́ргнут;
подве́рг подве́ргла; подве́ргнут; *impf.*
подверга́ть

пове́сить 'to hang' (*trans.*): пове́шу
пове́сит пове́сят; пове́сь!; пове́шен;
impf. **ве́шать**

подня́ть 'to lift': подниму́ подни́мет
подни́мут; по́днял подняла́ по́дняло;
подними́!; по́днят поднята́ по́днято;
impf. **поднима́ть**

подтверди́ть 'to confirm': подтвержу́
подтверди́т подтвердя́т; подтверждён
подтверждена́; *impf.* **подтвержда́ть**

поздра́вить (с + *i.*) 'to congratulate
(on)': поздра́влю поздра́вит поздра́вят;
поздра́вь!; *impf.* **поздравля́ть**

покры́ть 'to cover': покро́ю покро́ет
покро́ют; покро́й!; покры́т; *impf.*
покрыва́ть

ползти́ 'to crawl': ползу́ ползёт ползу́т;
полз ползла́

по́льзоваться/вос- (+ *i.*) 'to use':
по́льзуюсь по́льзуется по́льзуются

помо́чь (+ *d.*) 'to help': помогу́
помо́жет помо́гут; помо́г помогла́;
помоги́!; *impf.* **помога́ть**

пони́зить 'to lower': пони́жу пони́зит
пони́зят; пони́жен; *impf.* **понижа́ть**

поня́ть 'to understand': пойму́ поймёт
пойму́т; по́нял поняла́ по́няло; пойми́!;
по́нят понята́ по́нято; *impf.* **понима́ть**

по́ртить/ис- 'to spoil': по́рчу по́ртит
по́ртят; испо́рчен

посади́ть 'to plant, seat': посажу́
поса́дит поса́дят; поса́жен; *impf.*
сажа́ть

посвяти́ть (+ *d.*) 'to dedicate (to)':
посвящу́ посвяти́т посвятя́т; посвящён
посвящена́; *impf.* **посвяща́ть**

посети́ть 'to visit': посещу́ посети́т
посетя́т; посещён посещена́; *impf.*
посеща́ть

пра́вить (+ *i.*) 'to rule, govern':
пра́влю пра́вит пра́вят

пра́здновать/от- 'to celebrate':
пра́здную пра́зднует пра́зднуют

преврати́ть (в + *a.*) 'to transform
(into)': превращу́ преврати́т превратя́т;
превращён превращена́; *impf.*
превраща́ть

предупреди́ть 'to warn':
предупрежу́ предупреди́т предупредя́т;
предупреждён предупреждена́; *impf.*
предупрежда́ть

прекрати́ть 'to stop, curtail':
прекращу́ прекрати́т прекратя́т;
прекрати́!; прекращён прекращена́;
impf. **прекраща́ть**

преодоле́ть 'to overcome':
преодоле́ю преодоле́ет преодоле́ют;
преодолён преодолена́; *impf.*
преодолева́ть

прибли́зиться (к + *d.*) 'to approach':
прибли́жусь прибли́зится прибли́зятся;
impf. **приближа́ться**

привы́кнуть (к + *d.*) 'to get used
(to)': привы́кну привы́кнет привы́кнут;
привы́к привы́кла; *impf.* **привыка́ть**

пригласи́ть 'to invite': приглашу́
пригласи́т приглася́т; пригласи́!;
приглашён приглашена́; *pf.*
приглаша́ть

признава́ться (в + *p.*) 'to confess
(to)': признаю́сь признаётся
признаю́тся; *pf.* **призна́ться**

приня́ть 'to accept': приму́ при́мет
при́мут; при́нял приняла́ при́няло;
прими́!; при́нят принята́ при́нято; *impf.*
принима́ть

про́бовать/по- 'to test, try': про́бую
про́бует про́буют; про́буй!

проси́ть/по- (+ *a./g.*) 'to request':
прошу́ про́сит про́сят; проси́!

прости́ть (за + *a.*) 'to forgive (for)':
прощу́ прости́т простя́т; прости́!;
прощён прощена́; *impf.* **проща́ть**

прости́ться (с + *i.*) 'to say goodbye
(to)': прощу́сь прости́тся простя́тся;
impf. **проща́ться**

простуди́ться 'to catch cold':
простужу́сь просту́дится просту́дятся;
impf. **простужа́ться**

пря́тать/с- 'to hide': пря́чу пря́чет
пря́чут; прячь!; спря́тан

пусти́ть 'to let go': пущу́ пу́стит
пу́стят; пу́щен; *impf.* **пуска́ть**

ра́доваться/об- (+ *d.*) 'to rejoice
(at)': ра́дуюсь ра́дуется ра́дуются

разби́ть 'to smash': разобью́ разобьёт
разобью́т; разбе́й! разби́т; *impf.*
разбива́ть

разви́ться 'to develop' (*intrans.*):
разовью́сь разовьётся разовью́тся;
разви́лся развила́сь; *impf.* **развива́ться**

разде́ться 'to get undressed':
разде́нусь разде́нется разде́нутся;
разде́нься!; *impf.* **раздева́ться**

расста́ться (с + *i.*) 'to part (with)':
расста́нусь расста́нется расста́нутся;
impf. **расстава́ться**

расти́/вы- 'to grow' (*intrans.*): расту́
растёт расту́т; рос росла́

рвать 'to tear': рву рвёт рвут; рвал
рвала́ рва́ло

ре́зать/раз- 'to cut': ре́жу ре́жет
ре́жут; режь!; разре́зан

рисова́ть/на- 'to draw': рису́ю рису́ет
рису́ют; нарисо́ван

руби́ть 'to chop': рублю́ ру́бит ру́бят;
-ру́блен (*in compounds*)

руководи́ть (+ *i.*) 'to manage':
руковожу́ руководи́т руководя́т

сади́ться 'to sit down': сажу́сь
сади́тся садя́тся; сади́сь!; *pf.* **сесть**

свисте́ть 'to whistle': свищу́ свисти́т
свистя́т; *pf.* **сви́стнуть**

серди́ться/рас- 'to get angry':
сержу́сь се́рдится се́рдятся; (не)
серди́сь!

сесть 'to sit down': ся́ду ся́дет ся́дут;
сядь!; *impf.* **сади́ться**

се́ять/по- 'to sow': се́ю се́ет се́ют;
посе́ян

сиде́ть 'to sit': сижу́ сиди́т сидя́т; сиди́!

сказа́ть 'to say': скажу́ ска́жет ска́жут; скажи́!; ска́зан; *impf.* **говори́ть**

скрыть 'to conceal': скро́ю скро́ет скро́ют; скрой!; скрыт; *impf.* **скрыва́ть**

слать 'to send': шлю шлёт шлют; шли!

следи́ть (за + *i.*) 'to track': слежу́ следи́т следя́т

сле́довать/по- (за + *i.*) 'to follow': сле́дую сле́дует сле́дуют

слы́шать/у- 'to hear': слы́шу слы́шит слы́шат; услы́шан

сметь/по- 'to dare': сме́ю сме́ет сме́ют

смея́ться/по- (над + *i.*) 'to laugh (at)': смею́сь смеётся смею́тся; (не) сме́йся!

смотре́ть/по- (на + *a.*) 'to look (at)': смотрю́ смо́трит смо́трят; смотри́!

снять 'to take off': сниму́ сни́мет сни́мут; снял сняла́ сня́ло; сними́!; снят снята́ сня́то; *impf.* **снима́ть**

сове́товать/по- (+ *d.*) 'to advise': сове́тую сове́тует сове́туют

согласи́ться (на + *a.*/с + *i.*) 'to agree (to something/with someone)': соглашу́сь согласи́тся соглася́тся; *impf.* **соглаша́ться**

спасти́ 'to save': спасу́ спасёт спасу́т; спас спасла́; спасён спасена́; *impf.* **спаса́ть**

спать 'to sleep': сплю спит спят; спал спала́ спа́ло; спи!

спроси́ть 'to ask': спрошу́ спро́сит спро́сят; спроси́!; *impf.* **спра́шивать**

ста́вить/по- 'to put, stand' (*trans.*): ста́влю ста́вит ста́вят; ставь!; поста́влен

стать 'to become': ста́ну ста́нет ста́нут; стань!; *impf.* **станови́ться**

стере́ть 'to erase': сотру́ сотрёт сотру́т; стёр стёрла; сотри́!; стёрт; *impf.* **стира́ть**

стоя́ть 'to stand' (*intrans.*): стою́ стои́т стоя́т; стой!

стричь/о- 'to cut (hair or nails)': стригу́ стрижёт стригу́т; стриг стри́гла; остри́жен

ступи́ть 'to step': ступлю́ сту́пит сту́пят; *impf.* **ступа́ть**

стуча́ть/по- (в + *a.*) 'to knock (at)': стучу́ стучи́т стуча́т

суди́ть 'to judge': сужу́ су́дит су́дят

танцева́ть/с- 'to dance': танцу́ю танцу́ет танцу́ют

та́ять/рас- 'to melt' (*intrans.*): та́ет та́ют

темне́ть/по- 'to grow dark': темне́ет темне́ют

тере́ть 'to rub': тру трёт трут; тёр тёрла; три!

терпе́ть 'to bear, tolerate': терплю́ те́рпит те́рпят

течь 'to flow': течёт теку́т; тёк текла́

топи́ть 'to heat': топлю́ то́пит то́пят; -то́плен (*in compounds*)

торгова́ть (+ *i.*) 'to trade (in)': торгу́ю торгу́ет торгу́ют

торопи́ться/по- 'to hurry': тороплю́сь торо́пится торо́пятся; торопи́сь!

тра́тить/ис- (на + *a.*) 'to expend (on)': тра́чу тра́тит тра́тят; трать!; истра́чен

тре́бовать/по- (+ *g./a.*) 'to demand': тре́бую тре́бует тре́буют

труди́ться 'to labour': тружу́сь тру́дится тру́дятся; труди́сь!

трясти́ 'to shake' (*trans.*): трясу́ трясёт трясу́т; тряс трясла́; *pf.* **тряхну́ть**

убеди́ть 'to convince': убеди́т убедя́т; убеждён убеждена́; *impf.* **убежда́ть**

удиви́ться (+ *d.*) 'to be surprised (at)': удивлю́сь удиви́тся удивя́тся; *impf.* **удивля́ться**

укрепи́ть 'to strengthen': укреплю́ укрепи́т укрепя́т; укреплён укреплена́; *impf.* **укрепля́ть**

умере́ть 'to die': умру́ умрёт умру́т; у́мер умерла́ у́мерло; *impf.* **умира́ть**

уме́ть 'to know how': уме́ю уме́ет уме́ют

упа́сть 'to fall': упаду́ упадёт упаду́т; *impf.* **па́дать**

употреби́ть 'to use': употреблю́ употреби́т употребя́т; употреблён употреблена́; *impf.* **употребля́ть**

успе́ть 'to have time': успе́ю успе́ет успе́ют; *impf.* **успева́ть**

установи́ть 'to establish': установлю́ устано́вит устано́вят; устано́влен; *impf.* **устана́вливать**

уча́ствовать (в + *p.*) 'to participate in': уча́ствую уча́ствует уча́ствуют

уче́сть 'to take account of': учту́ учтёт учту́т; учёл учла́; учти!; учтён учтена́; *impf.* **учи́тывать**

ходи́ть 'to go': хожу́ хо́дит хо́дят; ходи́!

хоте́ть/за- 'to want': хочу́ хо́чешь хо́чет хоти́м хоти́те хотя́т

худе́ть/по- 'to lose weight': худе́ю худе́ет худе́ют

цвести́ 'to flower': цветёт цвету́т; цвёл цвела́

чеса́ть/по- 'to scratch': чешу́ че́шет че́шут

чи́стить/вы́- *or* **по-** 'to clean': чи́щу чи́стит чи́стят; вы́чищен/почи́щен

чу́вствовать 'to feel': чу́вствую чу́вствует чу́вствуют

шепта́ть 'to whisper': шепчу́ ше́пчет ше́пчут; *pf.* **шепну́ть**

шить/с- 'to sew': шью шьёт шьют; шей!

шуме́ть 'to make a noise': шуми́т шумя́т

шути́ть/по- 'to joke': шучу́ шу́тит шу́тят

эконо́мить/с- 'to economize': эконо́млю эконо́мит эконо́мят; сэконо́млен

яви́ться (+ *i.*) 'to be': явлю́сь я́вится я́вятся; *impf.* **явля́ться**

Заметки об английской грамматике

Существительные

Артикли

Неопределённый артикль

Неопределённый артикль **a** стоит перед словами, начинающимися на согласный или на сочетания, содержащие звук /j/:

a ball	мяч
a girl	девочка
a union	союз

Перед гласным или перед непроизносимым /h/ неопределённый артикль принимает форму **an**:

an apple	яблоко
an hour	час

Неопределённый артикль обычно употребляется с исчисляемыми существительными. Рассмотрим следующие случаи употребления:

■ с названиями профессий:

She is a doctor	Она врач
He is an engineer	Он инженер

■ после предлогов:

She works as a tour guide	Она работает гидом/экскурсоводом
Anna has gone without an umbrella	Анна ушла без зонта

■ в обобщающих высказываниях:

A whale is larger than a frog	Кит больше лягушки

Определённый артикль

Определённый артикль **the** употребляется с существительными единственного и множественного числа:

the cat	кошка
the owls	совы

Определённый артикль не употребляется с существительными, обозначающими:

■ учреждения:

I don't go to church	Я не хожу в церковь
He's starting school next week	Он пойдёт в школу на следующей неделе

Но когда определённый артикль обозначает здания, а не учреждения, он употребляется:

Turn right at the school	У школы поверните направо

- время еды:
Breakfast is at 8.30	Завтрак в 8:30
Dinner is ready	Обед готов

- время суток, после предлогов (за исключением **in** и **during**):
I am never out at night	Вечером я всегда дома
They left in the morning	Они уехали утром

- абстрактные понятия:
Hatred is a destructive force	Ненависть — разрушительная сила
The book is on English grammar	Это книга об английской грамматике

- болезни:
She's got tonsillitis	У неё ангина

- времена года:
Spring is here!	Наступила весна
It's like winter today	Сегодня совсем зима

- страны:
Russia	Россия
England	Англия

- улицы, парки и т. д.:
a concert in Hyde Park	концерт в Гайд-парке
I work on Baker Street	Я работаю на Бейкер-стрит

Определённый артикль, однако, употребляется в предложениях, в которых рассматриваются конкретные примеры:

The breakfast he served was awful	Завтрак, который он подал, был ужасным
The winter of 2011 was very mild	Зима 2011 года была очень мягкая

Следующие классы существительных всегда употребляются с определённым артиклем:

- географические названия во множественном числе:
the Netherlands	Нидерланды
the United States	Соединённые Штаты
the Alps	Альпы

- названия рек, морей и океанов:
the Thames	Темза
the Black Sea	Чёрное море
the Pacific	Тихий океан

- названия гостиниц, пабов, театров, музеев и проч.:
the Hilton	Хилтон
the Fox and Hounds	Лиса и гончие
the New Theatre	Новый театр
the British Museum	Британский музей

Множественное число

Множественное число существительных обычно образуется прибавлением к слову окончания **-s**:

dog — dogs	**tape — tapes**

К словам, оканчивающимся на **-s**, **-ss**, **-sh**, **-ch**, **-x**, **-zz**, следует добавлять окончание **-es**:

dress — dresses	**box — boxes**

Такое же окончание появляется в словах, оканчивающихся на *согласный* + **y**.

Причём конечный -**y** становится -**i**-:
baby — babies

Подобного не происходит у существительных, оканчивающихся на сочетание *гласный* + **y**:
valley — valleys

Существительные, оканчивающиеся на -**o**, получают во множественном числе или -**s**, или -**es**:
potato — potatoes   tomato — tomatoes
solo — solos   zero — zeros

У существительных, оканчивающихся на -**f(e)**, возможны три варианта окончания множественного числа:
life — lives   dwarf — dwarfs/dwarves
roof — roofs

Ниже приводится список наиболее часто встречающихся нерегулярных форм множественного числа:
child — children   foot — feet
man — men   mouse — mice
tooth — teeth   woman — women

Субстантивные словосочетания

Данные сочетания строятся по следующим образцам:

существительное + существительное:
summer dress   летнее платье
tennis shoes   теннисные туфли
record collection   коллекция пластинок

существительное + герундий:
disco dancing   танцы на дискотеке
dressmaking   швейное дело

герундий + существительное:
parking meter   паркинговый автомат
writing course   писательские курсы
boarding card   посадочный талон

Множественное число таких сочетаний образуется прибавлением окончания множественного числа только к основному в смысловом отношении слову:
a record collection — record collections
a photo album — photo albums

Женский род

Категория рода у неодушевлённых существительных отсутствует в английском языке. Так, существительные **cousin**, **friend**, **doctor** могут называть лиц и мужского, и женского пола. Поэтому, если при обозначении профессии или степени родства, требуется указать на род, то используются описательные конструкции типа **a male student**, **a woman doctor**.

Родительный (притяжательный) падеж

Родительный (притяжательный) падеж оформляется сочетанием **s** с апострофом, который стоит или перед **s** или после него (**'s/s'**).

's добавляется к существительным единственного числа:

the boy's book   книга мальчика

Апостроф без **s** добавляется к существительным, оканчивающимся во множественном числе на **-s**:

the boys' room   комната мальчиков
the boys' books   книги мальчиков

Если существительное относится к нерегулярной группе, и его множественное число не оканчивается на **-s**, то в родительном (притяжательном) падеже множественного числа употребляется **-'s**:

the children's toys   игрушки детей

В родительном (притяжательном) падеже имён собственных, оканчивающихся на **-s**, может встречаться и **'s**, и **s'** (вариант с **s'** более употребительный): **Keats's poetry** или **Keats' poetry** (**поэзия Китса**). С греческими и римскими именами, оканчивающимися на **-s**, как правило, употребляется только апостроф: **Socrates' death** (**смерть Сократа**), **Catullus' poetry** (**поэзия Катулла**).

Родительный (притяжательный) падеж употребляется с существительными, обозначающими людей, животных (в особенности домашних), а также с названиями стран:

Andrew's house   дом Эндрю
the lion's den   логово льва
America's foreign policy внешняя политика Америки

Родительный (притяжательный) падеж может выражать следующие отношения:

We are going to Anne's   Мы идём к Анне (домой)
We are going to Peter and Anne's Мы идём к Питеру и Анне (домой)
(форма **Peter's and Anne's** неупотребительна, если **Peter** и **Anne** рассматриваются как смысловая пара)

Jane Austen's and George Orwell's Романы Джейн Остин и Джорджа
novels   Оруэлла
(Джейн Остин и Джордж Оруэлл рассматриваются здесь по отдельности)

I got it at the baker's/chemist's Я купил это в булочной/аптеке
(дословно: **at the baker's shop/at the chemist's shop**)

В разговорном языке довольно часто встречается форма двойного родительного падежа:

He is a friend of my brother's Он друг моего брата
It was an idea of Anne's   Это было идеей Анны/Это была идея Анны

Прилагательные

Прилагательные в английском языке имеют только одну форму. Они не согласуются с существительным ни в роде, ни в числе, ни в падеже:

an old man   пожилой мужчина
five old women пять пожилых женщин

Положение прилагательных в предложении

Прилагательные могут стоять перед определяемым существительным: **a long story** (**длинная история**), или после него: **This story is long** (**Эта история длинная**). Однако некоторые прилагательные употребляются только после существительных: **The girl is upset** (**Девочка расстроена**). Нельзя сказать **the upset girl**.

Сравнительная и превосходительная форма

Существует три степени сравнения: положительная, сравнительная и превосходная.

Односложные прилагательные образуют сравнительную и превосходную степени добавлением **-(e)r** и **-(e)st** соответственно:

dull	скучный
duller	скучнее
dullest	скучнейший
big	большой
bigger	больше
biggest	самый большой

(Обратите внимание на удвоение конечного согласного.)

nice	хороший
nicer	лучше
nicest	самый лучший

Многосложные прилагательные образуют сравнительную и превосходную степень при помощи вспомогательных слов **more** и **most**:

generous	щедрый
more generous	более щедрый, щедрее
most generous	самый щедрый, щедрейший

По такому же образцу образуются сравнительная и превосходная степени некоторых двусложных прилагательных, например, **useful** (**полезный**).

Однако в большинстве своём двусложные прилагательные не подчиняются одному определённому правилу. С большой долей вероятности можно только утверждать, что прилагательные, оканчивающиеся на **-y, -le, -ow, -er**, образуют сравнительную и превосходную степени при помощи окончаний **-er/-est**. Например:

pretty (**-y** меняется на **-i-**)	милый
prettier	милее, более милый
prettiest	милейший, самый милый
narrow	узкий
narrower	уже, более узкий
narrowest	самый узкий
curious	любопытный
more curious	любопытнее, более любопытный
most curious	любопытнейший, самый любопытный

Сравнительная и превосходная степень прилагательных, образованных от действительных и страдательных причастий, образуется при помощи вспомогательных слов **more** и **most**:

boring	скучный
more boring	скучнее, более скучный
most boring	скучнейший, самый скучный

Most также употребляется в значении «чрезвычайно», «очень»:

| **That was a most interesting story** | Это была очень интересная/интереснейшая история |

Ниже приводится список наиболее употребительных нерегулярных прилагательных:

bad	плохой
worse	хуже, более плохой
worst	самый плохой/наихудший
good	хороший
better	лучше, более хороший
best	лучший, самый лучший
little	маленький
less	меньше, меньший
least	меньше всего
many/much	много
more	больше
most	больше всего
far	далёкий
farther	более далёкий
farthest	самый далёкий (только о расстоянии)
old	старший
elder	старше
eldest	самый старший

При этом регулярные формы (**old, older, oldest — старый, старее, самый старый**) описывают и людей, и предметы.

Отрицательная форма сравнительной степени образуется при помощи слов **less/least**:

far	далёкий
less far	менее далёкий
least far	наименее далёкий

Прилагательные могут употребляться в функции существительных, особенно, когда они обозначают группу людей:

the young	молодые, молодёжь
the old	старые, старики
the unemployed	безработные

Притяжательные прилагательные

К притяжательным прилагательным относятся:

my	мой
our	наш
your	твой
your	ваш
his, her, its	его (м. р.), её (ж. р.), его (ср. р.)
their	их

Род этих прилагательных зависит от рода обладателя предмета, а не от рода самого предмета:

his mother	его мать
her mother	её мать
their mother	их мать

Притяжательные прилагательные не согласуются с определяемым существительным в числе:

| my cat | моя кошка |
| my cats | мои кошки |

Наречия

Наречия определяют:

■ прилагательные:

| The job was extremely dangerous | Работа была чрезвычайно опасной |

■ глаголы:

| He finished quickly | Он быстро закончил |

■ другие наречия:

| very quickly | очень быстро |

Extremely, quickly, very являются наречиями.

Большинство наречий образуется прибавлением **-ly** к прилагательному:

sad — sadly	(печальный — печально)
brave — bravely	(храбрый — храбро)
beautiful — beautifully	(красивый — красиво)

При образовании наречий по такой модели возможны некоторые изменения в орфографии:

true — truly	(верный — верно)
due — duly	(должный — должно)
whole — wholly	(цельный — целиком)

Другие важные орфографические изменения:

| конечный **-y** меняется на **-i-**: | **ready — readily** |
| конечное **-le** на **-ly**: | **gentle — gently** |

Некоторые наречия совпадают по форме с соответствующими им прилагательными:

back (задний, назад), **early** (ранний, рано), **far** (далеко, далёкий), **fast** (быстрый, быстро), **left** (левый, налево), **little** (маленький, мало), **long** (длинный, длинно), **only** (единственный, только), **right** (правый, направо), **still** (спокойный, спокойно), **straight** (прямой, прямо), **well** (хороший, хорошо), **wrong** (неправильный, неправильно):

a wrong answer	неправильный ответ
He did it wrong	Он сделал это неправильно
an early summer	раннее лето
Summer arrived early	Лето наступило рано
a straight road	прямая дорога
He came straight to the point	Он перешёл прямо к делу

Местоимения

Личные местоимения

Именительный падеж		Косвенный падеж	
I	(я)	me	(меня, мне, мной)
you	(ты)	you	(тебя, тебе, тобой)
he	(он)	him	(его, ему, им)
she	(она)	her	(её, ей, ею)
it	(оно)	it	(его, ему, им)
we	(мы)	us	(нас, нам, нами)
you	(вы)	you	(вас, вам, вами)
they	(они)	them	(их, им, ими)

В английском языке глагольные формы не выражают лица. Поэтому русская глагольная форма **иду** должна переводиться на английский язык сочетанием **I go**, а не отдельной формой **go**.

Местоимения в косвенных падежах являются в предложении:

■ прямыми дополнениями:

    Mary loves him   Мэри любит его

■ косвенными дополнениями без предлога:

    John gave me a lift   Джон подвёз меня

■ косвенными дополнениями с предлогом:

    The book is from her   Книга от неё

Другие функции личных местоимений

he, she

Эти местоимения иногда обозначают животных, особенно домашних:

    Poor Whiskers, we had to take   Бедный Уискерс. Нам пришлось отнести его к
    him to the vet's   ветеринару

it употребляется:

■ в безличных конструкциях:

    It's sunny   Солнечно
    It's hard to know what to do   Трудно понять, что надо делать
    It looks as though they were right   Кажется, они были правы

в конструкциях, выражающих время и пространство:

    It's five o'clock   Сейчас 5 часов
    It's January the sixth   Сегодня 6 января
    How far is it to Edinburgh?   Как далеко до Эдинбурга?

It's является сокращённой формой конструкции **it is**. Её не следует путать с притяжательным местоимением **its**.

you

Данное местоимение не имеет вежливой формы.

You употребляется в обобщённом значении, для обозначения людей вообще.

    You never know; it might be sunny   Как знать. Может быть, на этой неделе
    this week   будет солнечно
    You can't buy cars like that any more   Таких машин уже не купить

they

- употребляется в обобщённом значении для обозначения неопределённой группы людей, особенно, если они обладают какой-либо властью, силой или умением:

They don't make cars like that any more	Таких машин уже не делают
They will have to find the murderer first	Вначале им надо будет найти убийцу
You'll have to get them to repair the car	Тебе надо будет заставить их отремонтировать машину

- употребляется вместо **he** или **she** (он, она):

The person appointed will be answerable to the director. They will be responsible for...	Человек, назначенный на эту должность, будет подчиняться директору. Он будет отвечать за...
A personal secretary will assist them (= him/her)	Им будет помогать персональный секретарь

- соотносится с неопределёнными местоимениями **somebody, someone** (кто-то); **anybody, anyone** (кто-нибудь); **everybody, everyone** (всякий, все); **nobody, no one** (никто):

If anyone has seen my pen, will they please tell me?	Если кто-нибудь видел мою ручку, пусть он мне скажет

one

One, так же, как **you**, употребляется в обобщённом значении, но является более литературным:

One needs to get a clear picture of what one wants.	Человек должен точно знать, что он хочет

Следует избегать чрезмерного употребления в речи **one**.

Возвратные местоимения

myself (себя, сам)
yourself (себя, сам, сама)
himself, herself, itself (себя, сам, сама, само)

ourselves (себя, сами)
yourselves (себя, сами)
themselves (себя, сами)

примеры употребления:

I always buy myself a Christmas present (косвенное дополнение)	Я всегда покупаю себе рождественский подарок
She talks to herself (предложное дополнение)	Она разговаривает сама с собой
Do it yourself (эмфатическая конструкция)	Сделай это сам
He burned himself badly (прямое дополнение)	Он сильно обжёгся

Притяжательные местоименные существительные

mine	мой
yours	твой
his, hers	его, её
ours	наш
yours	ваш
theirs	их

Род этих слов зависит от рода их обладателя, а не от рода самого предмета:

Whose book is it? — It's hers	Чья эта книга?—Её
Whose shoes are these? — They are hers	Чьи эти туфли?—Её
Whose car is that? — It's theirs	Чья та машина?—Их